International Dictionary of Films and Filmmakers-1

FILMS

International Dictionary of Films and Filmmakers

Volume 1
FILMS

Volume 2
DIRECTORS

Volume 3
ACTORS and ACTRESSES

Volume 4
WRITERS and PRODUCTION ARTISTS

International Dictionary of Films and Filmmakers- 1

FILMS

FOURTH EDITION

EDITORS

TOM PENDERGAST
SARA PENDERGAST

ST. JAMES PRESS

AN IMPRINT OF THE GALE GROUP

DETROIT • NEW YORK • SAN FRANCISCO
LONDON • BOSTON • WOODBRIDGE, CT

Tom Pendergast, Sara Pendergast, *Editors*

Michael J. Tyrkus, *Project Coordinator*

Michelle Banks, Erin Bealmear, Laura Standley Berger, Joann Cerrito,
Jim Craddock, Steve Cusack, Nicolet V. Elert, Miranda H. Ferrara, Kristin Hart,
Melissa Hill, Laura S. Kryhoski, Margaret Mazurkiewicz, Carol Schwartz, and Christine Tomassini,
St. James Press Staff

Peter M. Gareffa, *Managing Editor*

Maria Franklin, *Permissions Manager*
Debra J. Freitas, *Permissions Assistant*
Mary Grimes, Leitha Etheridge-Sims, *Image Catalogers*

Mary Beth Trimper, *Composition Manager*
Dorothy Maki, *Manufacturing Manager*
Rhonda Williams, *Senior Buyer*

Cynthia Baldwin, *Product Design Manager*
Michael Logusz, *Graphic Artist*

Randy Bassett, *Image Database Supervisor*
Robert Duncan, *Imaging Specialists*
Pamela A. Reed, *Imaging Coordinator*
Dean Dauphinais, *Senior Editor, Imaging and Multimedia Content*

Library of Congress Cataloging-in-Publication Data
International dictionary of films and filmmakers / editors, Tom Pendergast, Sara Pendergast.—4th ed.
p. cm.
Contents: 1. Films — 2. Directors — 3. Actors and actresses — 4. Writers and production artists.
ISBN 1-55862-449-X (set) — ISBN 1-55862-450-3 (v. 1) — ISBN 1-55862-451-1 (v. 2)
— ISBN 1-55862-452-X (v. 3) — ISBN 1-55862-453-8 (v. 4)
1. Motion pictures—Plots, themes, etc. 2. Motion picture producers and directors—Biography—Dictionaries. 3. Motion picture actors and actresses—Biography—Dictionaries. 4. Screenwriters—Biography—Dictionaries. I. Pendergast, Tom. II. Pendergast, Sara.

PN1997.8.I58 2000
791.43'03—dc2100-064024 CIP

Cover photograph—Louise Brooks in *Die Büchse der Pandora*, courtesy the Kobal Collection

Printed in the United States of America

St. James Press is an imprint of Gale Group
Gale Group and Design is a trademark used herein under license
10 9 8 7 6 5 4 3 2 1

CONTENTS

EDITORS' NOTE

This is a revised edition of the 1st volume of the *International Dictionary of Films and Filmmakers*, which also includes Volume 2, *Directors*, Volume 3, *Actors and Actresses*, and Volume 4, *Writers and Production Artists*. The book contains 683 entries, including 72 entries new to this edition. Each entry contains production information, lists of crew and cast, a selected bibliography of works about the film, and a critical essay written by a specialist in the field. Most of the entries from the previous edition have been retained here, and all have been thoroughly updated. Since film is primarily a visual medium, the majority of entries are illustrated with a still.

The selection of entries is once again based on the recommendations of the advisory board. It was not thought necessary to propose strict criteria for selection: the book is intended to represent the wide range of interests within North American, British, and West European film scholarship and criticism. The variety in both the entries and the critical stances of the writers emphasizes the diversity within the field of cinematic studies.

Thanks are due to the following: Nicolet V. Elert and Michael J. Tyrkus at St. James Press, for their efforts in preparing this collection for publication; Michael Najjar, for his tireless efforts in researching the entries; our advisers, for their wisdom and broad knowledge of international cinema; and our contributors, for their gracious participation. We have necessarily built upon the work of the editors who have preceded us, and we thank them for the strong foundation they created.

A Note on the Entries

Non-English language film titles are given in the original language or a transliteration of it, unless they are better known internationally by their English title. The country or countries where the film originated is provided along with the year it was registered and the director.

The section on production information can include such details as production company, film stock, format, running time, sound type, length, date and location of release, dates and location of filming, and cost. The list of crew members identifies the major participants in the making of the film, but is not exhaustive. Similarly, the list of cast members indicates the major players in the film, but may not account for all minor roles. Finally, the awards section lists major awards garnered by the film, its creators, and its leading actors.

BOARD OF ADVISERS

CONTRIBUTORS

Charles Affron
Mirella Jona Affron
Anthony Ambrogio
Dudley Andrew
Roy Armes
Dimitar Bardarsky
Erik Barnouw
Jeanine Basinger
John Baxter
Sandra L. Beck
Audie Bock
DeWitt Bodeen
Ronald Bowers
Stephen E. Bowles
Michael Brashinsky
Stephen Brophy
Julianne Burton
Fred Camper
Scarlet Cheng
Julie Christensen
Michel Ciment
Tom Conley
David A. Cook
Samantha Cook
R. F. Cousins
Thomas Cripps
Robert von Dassanowsky
Gertraud Steiner Daviau
Pamala S. Deane
Sara Corben De Romeo
Charles Derry
Wheeler Winston Dixon
Rashmi Doraiswamy
Mike Downey
Clyde Kelly Dunagan
Robert Dunbar
Raymond Durgnat
Rob Edelman
Jane Ehrlich
Jack C. Ellis
Gretchen Elsner-Sommer
Patricia Erens
Thomas L. Erskine
Mark W. Estrin
Tamara L. Falicov
Greg S. Faller
Rodney Farnsworth
Howard Feinstein
Susan Felleman
Annette Fern
Warren French
Barry A. Fulks
Dan Georgakas
Tina Gianoulis
Jill Gillespie
Verina Glaessner
H. M. Glancy
Val Golovskoy
Douglas Gomery
Joseph A. Gomez
Viveca Gretton
Josef Gugler
Patricia King Hanson
Stephen L. Hanson
Ann Harris
Louise Heck-Rabi
Patrick Heenan
Catherine Henry
Andrew Higson
John Hill
Kyoko Hirano
Deborah H. Holdstein
Andrew Horton
Peter Hutchings
Dina Iordanova
Nick James
Timothy Johnson
Stuart M. Kaminsky
Joel E. Kanoff
Dave Kehr
Philip Kemp
Satti Khanna
Tammy Kinsey
Katherine Singer Kovács
Audrey E. Kupferberg
Monique Lamontagne
Joseph Lanza
Daniel Leab
Sharon Lee
James L. Limbacher
Richard Lippe
Kimball Lockhart
Janet E. Lorenz
Glenn Lovell
Ed Lowry
Richard Dyer MacCann
Andrew and Gina Macdonald
G. C. Macnab
Elaine Mancini
Roger Manvell
Gina Marchetti
Gerald Mast
Donald W. McCaffrey
John McCarty
Joseph McElhaney
Vaclávv Merhaut
Russell Merritt
Lloyd Michaels
Joseph Milicia
Norman Miller
Ib Monty
Donald R. Mott
John Mraz
Robert Murphy
William T. Murphy
Ray Narducy
Dennis Nastav
Kim Newman
Dan Nissen
Linda J. Obalil
Liam O'Leary
Tom Orman
Kelly Otter
R. Barton Palmer
Sylvia Paskin
Hannah Patterson
Richard Peña
Kris Percival
Julian Petley
Duncan Petrie
Gene D. Phillips
A. Pillai
Marion Pilowsky
Leland Poague
Dana B. Polan
Richard Porton
Lauren Rabinovitz
Maria Racheva
Ashish Rajadhyaksha
Herbert Reynolds
Arthur G. Robson
Sara Corben de Romero
Jonathan Romney
Chris Routledge
Elliot Rubenstein
Marie Saeli
Barbara Salvage
Stephanie Savage
Curtis Schade
Susana Schild
Steven Schneider
H. Wayne Schuth
Michael Selig
Lee Sellars
Ella Shochat
Robert Sickels
Ulrike Sieglohr
Charles L. P. Silet
Scott Simmon
P. Adams Sitney
Josef Škvorecký
Anthony Slide
Edward S. Small
Eric Smoodin
Thomas Snyder
Cecile Starr
Philip Strick
Bob Sullivan
Susan Tavernetti
Stephen Teo
Doug Tomlinson
Lee Tsiantis
Andrew Tudor
Michael J. Tyrkus
B. Urgošíkova
Ralph Anthony Valdez
Ravi Vasudevan
Ginette Vincendeau
Iris Wakulenko
William C. Wees

Paul Wells
James Michael Welsh
Dennis West
M. B. White
Daniel Williams
Robert Winning
Robin Wood
Denise J. Youngblood

LIST OF FILMS

A bout de souffle
A nous la liberté
A propos de Nice
Accattone
Adam's Rib
The Adventures of Robin Hood
The African Queen
L'Age d'or
Aguirre, der Zorn Gottes
Ahfei zheng zhuan
Ai no corrida
Akaler sandhane
Akasen chitai
L'Albero degli zoccoli
Alexander Nevsky
All about Eve
All Quiet on the Western Front
All That Heaven Allows
All the King's Men
Alphaville
Alsino y el Condor
L'America
American Beauty
American Graffiti
An American in Paris
Der Amerikanische freund
Amor de perdic&atilda;o
And Life Goes On
Andrei Rublev
Angi Vera
Angst essen Seele auf
L'Année dernière à Marienbad
Annie Hall
Anticipation of the Night
Antônio das Mortes
The Apartment
Apocalypse Now
The Apu Trilogy
Aranyer din Ratri
L'Argent
L'Arroseur arrosé
Arsenal
The Asphalt Jungle
L'Atalante
L'Avventura
Awara

Ba wang bie ji
Bab el hadid
Babettes Gaestebud
Badlands
Balada o soldate
Le Ballet mécanique
The Band Wagon
Banshun
Baron Prasil
La Bataille du rail
La Batalla de Chile: la lucha de un pueblo sin armas
La Battaglia di Algeri
Becky Sharp
Belle de jour
La Belle et la bête
Berlin: Die Sinfonie der Grossstadt
The Best Years of Our Lives
La Bête humaine
Bharat Mata
Bhumika
The Big Heat
The Big Parade
The Big Sleep
The Birds
The Birth of a Nation
Biruma no tategoto
Black Narcissus
Black Sunday
Blackmail
Blade Runner
The Blair Witch Project
Der Blaue Engel
Die Blechtrommel
Die Bleierne Zeit
Blow-Up
The Blue Lamp
Blue Velvet
Bonnie and Clyde
Das Boot
Le Boucher
Boudu sauvé des eaux
Brazil
Breakfast at Tiffany's
Breaking the Waves
The Bride of Frankenstein
Brief Encounter
Bringing Up Baby
Broken Blossoms
Bronenosets Potemkin
Die Büchse der Pandora
Budjenje pacova
Il Buono, il brutto, il cattivo
Bye Bye Brasil

Cabaret
Cabiria
La Caduta degli dei
Camille
O Cangaceiro
Le Carrosse d'or
Casablanca
Casino Royale
Casque d'or
Cat People (1942)
Celine et Julie vont en bateau: Phantom Ladies Over Paris
Central do Brasil
C'era una volta il west
C'est arrivé près de chez vous
El Chacal de Nahueltoro
Le Chagrin et la pitié
Chapayev
Un Chapeau de paille d'Italie
Le Charme discrèt de la bourgeoisie
Charulata
Chelovek s kinoapparatom

La Grande illusion
The Grapes of Wrath
The Great Dictator
Great Expectations
Greed
Gregory's Girl
Guling jie shaonian sha ren shijian
Gun Crazy
Gycklarnas afton

Hadaka no shima
La Haine
Haizi wang
Hallelujah
Hana-Bi
A Hard Day's Night
Heavenly Creatures
Heimat; Die Zweite Heimat
He Liu
Henry V
Herr Arnes Pengar
Higanbana
High Noon
High Sierra
Der Himmel Über Berlin
Hiroshima mon amour
His Girl Friday
Hitler: Ein Film aus Deutschland
Hoop Dreams
La Hora de los hornos
Howards End
Huang tudi
The Hustler

I Am a Fugitive from a Chain Gang
Idi i smotri
Idioterne
If. . .
Igla
Ikiru
Im Lauf der Zeit
In a Lonely Place
India Song
The Informer
Intolerance
Invasion of the Body Snatchers
Istoria Asi Kliachinoi kotoraia lubila da nie vyshla zamuzh
It Happened One Night
It's a Wonderful Life
Ivan Grozny

J'accuse
Jana Aranya
Jaws
The Jazz Singer
Jeanne Dielman, 23 Quai du Commerce, 1080 Bruxelles
Jeder für sich und Gott gegen alle
Les Jeux interdits
JFK
Jigokumon
Johnny Guitar
Le Joli Mai
Jonah qui aura 25 ans en l'an 2000
Le Jour se lève
Journal d'un curé de campagne
Journey of Hope

Ju Dou
Jud Süss
Judex
Jujiro
Jules et Jim

Kaagaz ke phool
Das Kabinett des Dr. Caligari
Kameradschaft
Kanal
Kaos
La Kermesse héroique
The Kid
The Killers (1946)
Kind Hearts and Coronets
King Kong
Kino-Pravda
Kiss Me Deadly
Klute
Kommisar
Kongi's Harvest
Konyets Sankt-Peterburga
Körkalen
Korol Lir
Koshikei
Koziyat rog
Kwaidan

L.A. Confidential
Ladri di biciclette
The Lady Eve
The Lady from Shanghai
The Lady Vanishes
Lan fengzheng
The Land
Lásky jedné plavovlásky
The Last Picture Show
Last Tango in Paris
The Last Wave
Laura
The Lavender Hill Mob
Lawrence of Arabia
Letter from an Unknown Woman
Letyat zhuravli
Der Letze Mann
The Life and Death of Colonel Blimp
Life Is Sweet
Limite
Little Caesar
The Little Foxes
Lola
Lola Montès
Lolita
Lone Star
The Lost Weekend
Louisiana Story
Lucia

M
Madame de . . .
Mädchen in Uniform
The Magnificent Ambersons
Malcolm X
Malenkaya Vera
The Maltese Falcon
Man of Aran

Les Quatre cents coups

Raging Bull
Raiders of the Lost Ark
Ran
Rashomon
Rear Window
Rebel Without a Cause
Red River
The Red Shoes
Red Sorghum
Los Redes
Règle du jeu
Repulsion
Reservoir Dogs
Retrato de Teresa
Ride the High Country
Rien que les heures
Rio Bravo
The River
Rocco e i suoi fratelli
The Rocky Horror Picture Show
Roma, città aperta
La Ronde
Room at the Top
A Room with a View
Rosemary's Baby

Saikaku ichidai onna
Salaam Bombay!
Le Salaire de la peur
Salt of the Earth
Salvatore Giuliano
Samma no aji
Samo jednom se ljubi
Le Samourai
Le Sang des bêtes
Le Sang d'un poete
Sans Soleil
Sansho dayu
Saturday Night and Sunday Morning
Scarface: The Shame of a Nation
The Scarlet Empress
Schatten
Schindler's List
Sciuscia
Scorpio Rising
The Searchers
Secrets and Lies
Seppuku
The Servant
Shaft
Shakespeare in Love
Shane
She Done Him Wrong
Sherlock, Jr.
Shichinin no samurai
Shoah
Shonen
Siberiade
The Silence of the Lambs
Singin' in the Rain
Det Sjunde inseglet
Skuplijaci perja
Smoke
Smultronstället
Snow White and the Seven Dwarfs
Sodom und Gomorrha
Some Like It Hot
Sommarnattens leende
Song of Ceylon
Souffle au coeur
The Southerner
Soy Cuba
The Spanish Earth
Spoorloos
Stachka
A Star Is Born
The Star Wars Saga
Staré povesti ceské
Steamboat Willie
Sterne
La Strada
Strangers on a Train
A Streetcar Named Desire
Stromboli
Der Student von Prag
Sullivan's Travels
Sult
Suna no onna
Sunrise
Sunset Boulevard
The Sweet Smell of Success
Sweet Sweetback's Baadasssss Song

Das Tagebuch einer Verlorenen
Ta'm E Guilass
Tampopo
Taxi Driver
Teni zabytykh predkov
La terra trema
The Texas Chainsaw Massacre
Thelma and Louise
Thérèse Desqueyroux
They Live by Night
O Thiasos
The Thin Man
Things to Come
The Third Man
38 - Auch das war Wien
The 39 Steps
Tiefland
Tire dié
Tirez sur le pianiste
Titanic
Todo Sobre Mi Madre
Tokyo monogatari
Tom Jones
Top Hat
Touch of Evil
Trainspotting
The Treasure of the Sierra Madre
Tretia Meshchanskaia
Triumph des Willens
Trois Couleurs
Trouble in Paradise
Turksib
Twelve Angry Men
2001: A Space Odyssey
Tystnaden

A BOUT DE SOUFFLE

(Breathless)

France, 1959

Director: Jean-Luc Godard

Production: Impéria Films, Société Nouvelle de Cinéma; black and white, 35mm; running time: 89 minutes. Released 16 March 1960, Paris. Filmed 17 August through 15 September 1959 in Paris and Marseilles; cost: 400,000 N.F. (about $120,000).

Producer: Georges de Beauregard; **screenplay:** Jean-Luc Godard, from an original treatment by François Truffaut; **photography:** Raoul Coutard; **editors:** Cécile Decugis with Lila Herman; **sound:** Jacques Maumont; **music:** Martial Solal from Mozart's Clarinet Concerto, K.622; **artistic and technical advisor:** Claude Chabrol.

Cast: Jean Seberg (*Patricia Franchini*); Jean-Paul Belmondo (*Michel Poiccard, alias Laszlo Kovacs*); Daniel Boulanger (*Police Inspector Vital*); Henri-Jacques Huet (*Antonio Berrutti*); Roger Hanin (*Carl Zombach*); Van Doude (*Journalist Van Doude*); Liliane Robin (*Liliane*); Michel Favre (*Plainclothes inspector*); Jean-Pierre Melville (*Parvulesco*); Claude Mansard (*Used car dealer, Claudius*); Jean Domarchi (*Drunk*); Jean-Luc Godard (*Informer*); André-S. Labarthe, Jean-Louis Richard, and François Mareuil (*Journalists*); Richard Balducci (*Tolmatchoff*); Philippe de Broca; Michael Mourlet; Jean Douchet; Louiguy; Virginie Ullman; Emile Villon; José Bénazéraf; Madame Paul; Raymond Ravanbaz.

Awards: Prix Jean Vigo, 1960; Best Direction, Berlin Film Festival, 1960.

Publications

Scripts:

A bout de souffle (screenplay plus Truffaut's original scenario and quotations from reviews) in *L'Avant-Scène du Cinéma* (Paris), March 1968; also published separately, Paris, 1974.

Books:

Taylor, John Russell, ''The New Wave: Jean-Luc Godard,'' in *Cinema Eye, Cinema Ear*, New York, 1964.

Egly, Max, *Regards neufs sur le cinéma*, Paris, 1965.

Goldmann, Annie, *Cinéma et société moderne: Le Cinéma de 1958 à 1968*, Paris, 1971.

Vaugeois, Gerard, and others, *A bout de souffle*, Paris, 1974.

Monaco, James, *The New Wave*, New York, 1976.

MacCabe, Colin, *Godard: Images, Sounds, Politics*, London, 1980.

Walsh, Martin, *The Brechtian Aspect of Radical Cinema*, London, 1981.

Lefèvre, Raymond, *Jean-Luc Godard*, Paris, 1983.

Douin, Jean-Luc, *La Nouvelle Vague 25 ans après*, Paris, 1984.

Bordwell, David, *Narration in the Fiction Film*, London, 1985.

Weis, Elisabeth, and John Belton, *Film Sound: Theory and Practice*, New York, 1985.

Godard, Jean-Luc, *Godard on Godard: Critical Writings*, edited by Jean Narboni and Tom Milne, New York, 1986.

Loshitzky, Yosefa, *The Radical Faces of Godard & Bertolucci*, Detroit, 1995.

Dixon, Wheeler W., *The Films of Jean-Luc Godard*, Albany, 1997.

Sterritt, David, *Jean-Luc Godard; Interviews*, Jackson, 1998.

Sterritt, David, *The Films of Jean-Luc Godard; Seeing the Invisible*, New York, 1999.

Articles:

Truffaut, François, in *Radio-Cinéma-Télévision* (Paris), 1 October 1959.

Variety (New York), 4 February 1960.

Le Monde (Paris), 18 March 1960.

Sadoul, Georges, in *Les Lettres Françaises* (Paris), March-April 1960.

Billard, Pierre, and others, ''Petit lexique de la nouvelle vague,'' in *Cinéma* (Paris), April 1960.

Chevallier, J., in *Image et Son* (Paris), April 1960.

Mopuller, Luc, ''Jean-Luc Godard,'' in *Cahiers du Cinéma* (Paris), April 1960.

Marcorelles, Louis, ''Views of the New Wave,'' in *Sight and Sound* (London), Spring 1960.

Seguin, Louis, in *Positif* (Paris), no. 33, 1960.

Crowther, Bosley, in *New York Times*, 8 February 1961.

Kauffmann, Stanley, ''Adventures of an Anti-Hero,'' in *New Republic* (New York), 13 February 1961.

Croce, Arlene, in *Film Quarterly* (Berkeley), Spring 1961.

Gow, Gordon, in *Films and Filming* (London), August 1961.

Steen, T. M. F., ''The Sound Track,'' in *Films in Review* (New York), August-September 1961.

Pearson, Gabriel, and Eric Rhode, ''Cinema of Appearance,'' in *Sight and Sound* (London), Autumn 1961.

Collet, Jean, and others, ''Entretien avec Jean-Luc Godard,'' in *Cahiers du Cinéma* (Paris), December 1962.

Feinstein, Herbert, ''An Interview with Jean-Luc Godard,'' in *Film Quarterly* (Berkeley), Spring 1964.

Lefèvre, Raymond, and Jean-Paul Warren, in *Image et son: Revue du Cinéma* (Paris), September-October 1964.

Solokov, Raymond, ''The Truth 24 Times a Second,'' in *Newsweek* (New York), 12 February 1968.

A bout de souffle

Barr, Charles, ''*A bout de souffle*,'' in *The Films of Jean-Luc Godard*, edited by Ian Cameron, London, 1969.
Houston, Beverle, and Marsha Kinder, ''Jean-Luc Godard: *Breathless*,'' in *Close-Up*, New York, 1972.
Ropars, Marie-Claire, ''The Graphic in Filmic Writing: *A bout de souffle*, or the Erratic . . . ,'' in *Enclitic* (Minneapolis), Fall 1981-Spring 1982.
Falkenburg, Pamela, '''Hollywood' and the 'Art Cinema' as a Bipolar Modeling System: *A bout de souffle* and *Breathless*,'' in *Wide Angle* (Athens, Ohio), vol. 7, no. 3, 1985.
''Godard Issue'' of *Revue Belge du Cinéma* (Brussels), Summer 1986.
Durgnat, Raymond, in *Monthly Film Bulletin* (London), August 1988.
Pulleine, Tim, in *Films and Filming* (London), August 1988.
Jensen, G. H., ''Filmvurdering,'' in *Z Filmtidsskrift* (Oslo), no. 2, 1990.
Kulset, S., ''Teoretiker til siste andedrag?'' in *Z Filmtidsskrift* (Oslo), no. 1, 1991.
de Graaff, T., ''Jongleren met ideeen,'' in *Skrien* (Amsterdam), December-January 1992–93.
''Parigi, a bout de souffle,'' in *Castoro Cinema*, March/April 1996.

* * *

A bout de souffle was the first feature directed by Jean-Luc Godard and one of the films introducing the French New Wave in the late 1950s. Godard had made several short films before *A bout de souffle*, but this feature established the international reputation of the director who is regarded as one of the most important filmmakers of the 1960s.

The film's story is fairly simple. Michel Poiccard (Jean-Paul Belmondo), a small time hood, casually kills a policeman. He goes to Paris to collect some money in order to leave the country, and tries to convince his American girlfriend Patricia Franchini (Jean Seberg) to go with him. She is less interested in accompanying him than she is in playing the role of an American intellectual in Paris. (She hawks the New York *Herald Tribune* on the Champs-Elysées while trying to establish herself as a journalist.) When Michel finally secures the money he needs and is ready to leave the city, Patricia betrays him to the police, and he is shot as he half-heartedly attempts to escape.

This basic sequence of events is the minimal thread of continuity that holds the filmic narrative together. However, causal development and character motivation in the traditional sense are relatively loose. While the film does not reject narrative conventions as a whole, it goes a long way towards weakening the tight-knit structure and explanatory mechanisms affiliated with dominant narrative. The film's visual construction works even more aggressively against conventional film style. It systematically departs from the aesthetic guidelines and rules defined by continuity editing, relying variously on long-take sequences (often shot with hand-held camera) and jump cutting. The free-wheeling, almost casual, use of the camera is typical of the New Wave style. Within individual scenes the systematic use of jump cuts and depiction of rambling, repetitious conversations are a way of testing the limits of narrative film style. It often seems that scenes are conceived to show what can be done with cinema rather than to develop the story in a coherent fashion.

While the film seems willfully to disregard the norms of commercial, studio filmmaking, it consistently refers to and plays with aspects of the American cinema. The main character, Michel, styles himself in the image of Humphrey Bogart. Early in the film he is seen standing by a movie poster admiring his hero's picture; in comparison his own status as a modern ''tough guy'' is only a weak imitation. The police on Michel's trail are similarly pale shadows of their predecessors in American films; they are bumbling, somewhat comical figures. The character of Patricia, and her portrayal by Seberg, refers to the role Seberg played in Otto Preminger's *Bonjour Tristesse.* There are also scenes constructed to ''quote'' sequences from American films. In Patricia's bedroom, Michel looks at her through a rolled-up poster. The camera zooms through the poster tube, followed by a cut to a close-up of Michel and Patricia kissing. These shots mimic a scene from Samuel Fuller's *Forty Guns* (with a rifle barrel instead of a poster) described by Godard in a review of the film as a moment of pure cinema.

The film's playfulness extends beyond the inside jokes that refer to other films. The sometimes abrupt shifts in tone, style, and plot development within and between scenes are an investigation of (and challenge to) the medium, based on familiarity with and affection for its history. The opening of the film is instructive in this regard. Michel delivers a rambling monologue as he drives through the French countryside. He is speeding, and a policeman starts to follow him. Michel drives off the road, and when he is followed, shoots the policeman. The murder is casual in manner and lacking in clear motive. It becomes almosts a comic version of more serious crime dramas in which murders are fraught with tension and often defined as the act of ruthless or psychotic individuals. Because of his manner, the character of Michel is sometimes seen to exemplify the existentially alienated hero figure often found in New Wave films. Harsher critics condemn him as a character for his amoral, nihilistic behavior. However, this moralising attitude ignores the way in which the character derives from and parodies previous film hoodlums, and the appeal of the character as portrayed by Belmondo.

In various ways the film exemplifies the conjunction of a number of factors contributing to the French New Wave cinema. This includes the use of relatively new cameras (a lightweight Eclair, easily handheld); working with low budgets, which promoted location shooting and stories with contemporary settings; and the use of new personnel, including the star Belmondo and cameraman Raoul Coutard. In addition Godard brought a set of attitudes to filmmaking shared by his fellow New Wave directors, derived from his experience as a film critic in the 1950s. Among these was the belief that the director was the responsible creative individual behind a film, that film should be approached as a mode of personal expression, and a deep admiration for the visual style of many Hollywood films.

Beyond its status as a ''New Wave film,'' *A bout de souffle* begins to define attitudes and concerns which are more fully developed in Godard's subsequent work. A broad range of cultural imagery is an integral part of the film's signifying material. Movie posters, art reproductions, and inserts of magazines and books not only function as elements of mise-en-scène, but also construct an image of contemporary life in terms of cultural collage. In addition the strategy of narrative digression is important, incorporating lengthy scenes to explore issues which do not serve to develop the story per se. In *A bout de souffle* Patricia's taking part in an interview with an author (played by French director Jean-Pierre Melville) functions in this way. Both of these practices testify to an interest in cinema as something more than a narrative medium in the conventional sense. As attention is directed to the ways in which filmic images and sounds create meaning, the very nature of cinematic signification becomes the central question for the director and his audience.

—M. B. White

A NOUS LA LIBERTÉ

France, 1931

Director: René Clair

Production: Tobis (Paris) and Filmsonor; black and white, 35mm, musical soundtrack with sound effects; running time: 97 minutes. Released 31 December 1931. Filmed 1931 in Tobis studios and around Paris.

Producer: Frank Clifford; **screenplay:** René Clair; **photography:** Georges Périnal; **editor:** René le Hénaff; **sound:** Hermann Storr; **art director:** Lazare Meerson; **music:** Georges Auric; **musical director:** Armand Bernard; **costume designer:** René Hubert; **assistant director:** Albert Valentin.

Cast: Henri Marchand (*Emile*); Raymond Cordy (*Louis*); Rolla France (*Jeanne*); Paul Ollivier (*Paul Imaque, Jeanne's uncle*); Jacques Shelly (*Paul*); André Michaud (*Foreman*); Germaine Aussey (*Maud, Louis's mistress*); Alexandre d'Arcy (*Gigolo*); William Burke (*Leader of the gangsters*); Vincent Hyspa (*Speaker*); Léon Lorin (*Fussy official*).

Publications

Scripts:

Clair, René, *A nous la liberté* in *L'Avant-Scène du Cinéma* (Paris), November 1968.

A Nous La Liberté and Entr'Acte: Films by René Clair, New York, 1970.

Books:

Viazzi, G., *René Clair*, Milan, 1946.

Bourgeois, J., *René Clair*, Geneva, 1949.

A nous la liberté

Charensol, Georges, and Roger Régent, *Un Maître du cinéma: René Clair*, Paris, 1952.
Solmi, A., *Tre maestri del cinema*, Milan, 1956.
De La Roche, Catherine, *René Clair: An Index*, London, 1958.
Amengual, Barthélemy, *René Clair*, Paris, 1963; revised edition, 1969.
Mitry, Jean, *René Clair*, Paris, 1969.
Samuels, Charles, *Encountering Directors*, New York, 1972.
McGerr, Celia, *René Clair*, Boston, 1980.
Barrot, Olivier, *René Clair; ou, Le Temps mesuré*, Renens, Switzerland, 1985.
Greene, Naomi, *René Clair: A Guide to References and Resources*, Boston, 1985.
Dale, R. C., *The Films of René Clair*, Metuchen, New Jersey, 2 vols., 1986.

Articles:

Potamkin, Harry, "René Clair and Film Humor," in *Hound and Horn* (New York), October-December 1932.
Causton, Bernard, "A Conversation with René Clair," in *Sight and Sound* (London), Winter 1932–33.
Jacobs, Lewis, "The Films of René Clair," in *New Theatre* (New York), February 1936.
"Clair Issue" of *Bianco e Nero* (Rome), August-September 1951.
Connor, Edward, and Edward Jablonski, in *Films in Review* (New York), November 1954.
Tallmer, Jerry, in *Village Voice* (New York), 16 November 1955.
Ford, Charles, "Cinema's First Immortal," in *Films in Review* (New York), November 1960.
Berti, V., "L'arte del comico in René Clair," in *Bianco e Nero* (Rome), March-April 1968.
Baxter, John, "A Conversation with René Clair," in *Focus on Film* (London), Winter 1972.
Pym, John, in *Monthly Film Bulletin* (London), October 1977.
Kramer, S. P., "René Clair: Situation and Sensibility in *A nous la liberté*," in *Literature/Film Quarterly* (Salisbury, Maryland), vol. 12, no. 2, 1984.

* * *

The fear of a static theatrical cinema resulting from the invention of the sound film was very soon dissipated by liberators such as Ernst Lubitsch and René Clair. With a concentration on music and movement while maintaining strict control over dialogue the cinema began to move again. Clair, with his first two films, had already established a style, and the cycle of development from which this style emerged is curious in itself. The French comedian Max Linder was a direct influence on Chaplin and the whole slapstick school which in turn inspired the young René Clair. And, as if the process of interchange of ideas seemed determined to go on, Chaplin in *Modern Times* drew inspiration from the assembly line sequence in Clair's *A nous la liberté*. In this film Clair satirizes the industrial malaise which reduces man to the level of a machine. That satire may seem to weaken the human element but fun and joy take over as Clair falls so much in love with his characters that he passes that affection to the audience. One cannot even harbor a grudge against the villains because they too are ridiculously human. It is not difficult to see how the film failed to measure up to the demands of socially committed critics like Georges Sadoul.

Two companions of a jail-break are the protagonists of this musical comedy. One, played with eccentric sympathy by Raymond Cordy, is clever and successful and quickly rises in the world of industry. The other, played by Henri Marchand, wanders innocently throughout the film, willing to accept the unexpected. Even the joy of his escape from prison arises from a potentially tragic situation. His courtship is as artless as everything else he does.

Employing the talents of the brilliant art director Lazare Meerson, Clair uses the vast industrial complex to its fullest until it becomes a fun palace with plenty of room for chases and horseplay. Even the building is deflated. The joyful and carefree music of Georges Auric carries the film along, while Georges Périnal's camera exploits the large white surfaces of the super-factory and the brightness of the walls.

But it is not the technical excellence of the film which remains in one's mind. It is the puncturing of pomposity, the rejection of dehumanizing technical processes, the statement of essential human values and an appreciation of the incongruities of human existence. It is a far cry from the world of *Le Chapeau de paille d'Italie*, but the child-like delight in the demolition of the pretentious in Clair is common to both films. Not for him the sighs of high romance or the exaggerations of grand opera. His heart is always with ordinary people and their simple predicaments. He sees the world through the eyes of the characters Louis and Emile. Maybe his idea of Utopia is naive and impractical but it is an ideal which has been thought of by many people. In an age of mass regimentation and super-states it remains a recurring vision.

—Liam O'Leary

A PROPOS DE NICE

(On the Subject of Nice)

France, 1930

Director: Jean Vigo

Production: Black and white, 35mm; running time: about 25 minutes. Premiered June 1930, Paris. Filmed winter 1929 through March 1930 in Nice.

Scenario: Mr. and Mrs. Jean Vigo and Mr. and Mrs. Boris Kaufman; **photography:** Boris Kaufman; **editor:** Jean Vigo.

Publications

Script:

Vigo, Jean, *Oeuvre de cinéma: Films, scénarios, projets de films, texts sur le cinéma*, edited by Pierre Lherminier, Paris, 1985.

Books:

Feldman, Harry, and Joseph Feldman, *Jean Vigo*, London, 1951.
Smith, Jean, *Jean Vigo*, New York, 1971.
Salles-Gomes, P. E., *Jean Vigo*, Paris 1957; revised edition, Los Angeles, 1971.
Smith, John M., *Jean Vigo*, New York, 1962.
Lherminier, Pierre, *Jean Vigo*, Paris, 1967.
Barnouw, Erik, *Documentary: A History of the Non-Fiction Film*, New York, 1974.
Simon, William G., *The Films of Jean Vigo*, Ann Arbor, Michigan, 1981.
Salles-Gomes, P.E., *Jean Vigo*, New York, 1999.

Articles:

Calvalcanti, Alberto, ''Jean Vigo,'' in *Cinema Quarterly* (Edinburgh), Winter 1935.
Agee, James, ''Life and Work of Jean Vigo,'' in *Nation* (New York), 12 July 1947.
Weinberg, H. G., ''The Films of Jean Vigo,'' in *Cinema* (Beverly Hills), July 1947.
Barbarow, George, ''The Work of Jean Vigo,'' in *Politics 5*, Winter 1948.
Amengual, Barthélemy, in *Positif* (Paris), May 1953.
Chardère, Bernard, ''Jean Vigo et ses films,'' in *Cinéma* (Paris), March 1955.
Mekas, Jonas, ''An Interview with Boris Kaufman,'' in *Film Culture* (New York), Summer, 1955.
Ashton, Dudley Shaw, ''Portrait of Vigo,'' in *Film* (London), December 1955.
''Vigo Issue'' of *Etudes Cinématographiques* (Paris), nos. 51–52, 1966.
Beylie, Claude, in *Ecran* (Paris), July-August 1975.
Liebman, S., in *Millenium* (New York), Winter 1977–78.
Vigo, Jean, ''Towards a Social Cinema,'' in *Millenium* (New York), Winter 1977–78.
Travelling (Lausanne), Summer 1979.
Vinnichenko, E., ''*Po povodu Nitstsy*, Frantsiia,'' in *Iskusstvo Kino* (Moscow), no. 3, 1989.
Sidler, V.,''Traeumer des Kinos, Rimbaud des Films,'' in *Filmbulletin* (Winterthur, Switzerland), no. 4, 1992.

* * *

Jean Vigo's reputation as a prodigy of the cinema rests on less than 200 minutes of film. His first venture, a silent documentary 25 minutes long, was *A propos de Nice*, and in it one can see immediately the energy and aptitude of this great talent. But *A propos de Nice* is far more than a biographical curio; it is one of the last films to come out of the fertile era of the French avant-garde and it remains one of the best examples to illustrate the blending of formal and social impulses in that epoch.

A propos de Nice

Confined to Nice on account of the tuberculosis both he and his wife were to die of, Vigo worked for a small company as assistant cameraman. When his father-in-law presented the young couple with a gift of $250, Jean promptly bought his own Debrie camera. In Paris in the summer of 1929 he haunted the ciné-club showings at the Vieux Colombier and at the Studio des Ursulines. There he met Boris Kaufman, a Russian émigré, brother of Dziga Vertov. Kaufman, already an established cameraman in the kino-eye tradition, was enthusiastic about Vigo's plan to make a film on the city of Nice. During the autumn of 1929 Kaufman and his wife labored over a script with the Vigos. From his work Jean began to save ends of film with which to load the Debrie and by year's end the filming was underway.

Originally planned as a variant of the city symphony, broken into its three movements (sea, land, and sky) *A propos de Nice* was destined to vibrate with more political energy than did *Berlin, Rien que les heures, Manhattan*, or any of the other examples of this type. From the first, Vigo insisted that the travelogue approach be avoided. He wanted to pit the boredom of the upper classes at the shore and in the casinos against the struggle for life and death in the city's poorer backstreets.

The clarity of the script was soon abandoned. Unable to shoot ''live'' in the casinos and happy to follow the lead of their rushes, Vigo and Kaufman concentrated on the strength of particular images rather than on the continuity of a larger design. They were certain that design must emerge in the charged images themselves, which they could juxtapose in editing.

The power of the images derives from two sources, their clearcut iconographic significance as social documents, and the high quality they enjoy as photographs, carefully (though not artfully) composed. Opposition is the ruling logic behind both these sources as they appear in the finished film, so that pictures of hotels, lounging women, wealthy tourists, and fancy roulette tables are cut against images of tenements, decrepit children, garbage, and local forms of back-street gambling. In the carnival sequence which ends the film, the power bursting within the city's belly spills out onto the streets of the wealthy and dramatizes a conflict which geography can't hide.

Formally the film opposes a two-dimensional optical schema, used primarily for the wealthy parts of town, to a tactile, nearly 3-D approach. Aerial shots and the voyeurism of the ''Promenade des Anglais'' define the wealthy as indolent observers of sports, while deep in the town itself everyone, including the camera, participates in the carnal dance of life, a dance whose eroticism is made explicit toward the film's end.

Entranced by Surrealism (at the premiere of this film Vigo paid homage to Luis Buñuel), the filmmakers used shock cuts, juxtaposing symbolic images like smokestacks and Baroque cemeteries. A woman is stripped by a stop-action cut and a man becomes a lobster. Swift tilts topple a grand hotel. As he proclaimed in his address, this was to be a film with a documentary point of view. To him that meant hiding the camera to capture the look of things (Kaufman was pushed in a wheelchair along the Promenade cranking away under his blanket), and then editing what they collected to their own designs.

A propos de Nice is a messy film. Full of experimental techniques and frequently clumsy camerawork, it nevertheless exudes the energy of its creators and blares forth a message about social life. The city is built on indolence and gambling and ultimately on death, as its crazy cemetery announces. But underneath this is an erotic force that comes from the lower class, the force of seething life that one can smell in garbage and that Vigo uses to drive his film. *A propos de Nice* advanced the cinema not because it gave Vigo his start and not because it is a thoughtfully made art film. It remains one of those few examples where several powers of the medium (as recorder, organizer, clarifier of issues, and proselytizer) come together with a strength and ingenuity that are irrespressible. The critics at its premiere in June 1930 were impressed and Vigo's talent was generally recognized. But the film got little distribution; the age of silent films, even experimental ones like this, was coming to an end. This is too bad. Every director should begin his or her career as Vigo did, with commitment, independence, and a sense of enthusiastic exploration.

—Dudley Andrew

ACCATTONE

Italy, 1961

Director: Pier Paolo Pasolini

Production: Cine de Duca-Arco Film; 35mm; running time: 120 minutes. Released 1961. Filmed 1960–61 in the slums of Rome.

Producer: Alfredo Bini; **screenplay:** Pier Paolo Pasolini with dialogue collaboration by Sergio Citti, from the novel *Una vita violenta* by Pasolini; **photography:** Tonino Delli Colli; **editor:** Nino Baragli; **sound:** Luigi Puri and Manlio Magara; **art director:** Flavio Mogherini; **music director:** Carlo Rustichelli; **assistant directors:** Bernardo Bertolucci and Leopoldo Savona.

Cast: Franco Citti (*Accatone/Vittorio*); Franca Pasut (*Stella*); Silvana Corsini (*Maddalena*); Paola Guidi (*Ascenza*); Adriana Asti (*Amore*); Renato Capogna (*Renato*); Mario Cipriani (*Balilla*); Roberto Scaringella (*Cartagine*); Piero Morgia (*Pio*); Umberto Bevilacqua (*The Neapolitan*); Elsa Morante (*Prisoner*); Adele Cambria (*Nannina*); Polidor (*Beechino*); Danilo Alleva (*Iaio*); Luciano Conti (*Il Moicano*); Luciano Gonino (*Piede d'Oro*); Gabriele Baldini (*Intellectual*); Adrianno Mazelli and Mario Castiglione (*Amore's clients*); Dino Frondi and Tommaso Nuevo (*Cartagine's friends*); Romolo Orazi (*Accattone's father-in-law*); Silvio Citti (*Sabino*); Adriana Moneta (*Margheritona*).

Publications

Script:

Pasolini, Pier Paolo, *Accattone*, Rome, 1961.

Books:

Pasolini, Pier Paolo, *Pasolini on Pasolini: Interviews with Oswald Stack*, Bloomington, Indiana, 1969.
Gervais, Marc, *Pier Paolo Pasolini*, Paris, 1973.
Siciliano, Enzo, *Vita di Pasolini*, Milan, 1978; as *Pasolini: A Biography*, New York, 1982.
Bertini, Antonio, *Teoria e tecnica del film in Pasolini*, Rome, 1979.
Groppali, Enrico, *L'ossessione e il fantasma: Il teatro di Pasolini e Moravia*, Venice, 1979.
Snyder, Stephen, *Pier Paolo Pasolini*, Boston, 1980.
Bellezza, Dario, *Morte di Pasolini*, Milan, 1981.
Bergala, Alain, and Jean Narboni, editors, *Pasolini cinéaste*, Paris, 1981.
Gerard, Fabien S., *Pasolini; ou, Le Mythe de la barbarie*, Brussels, 1981.
Boarini, Vittorio, and others, *Da Accatone a Salò: 120 scritti sul cinema di Pier Paolo Pasolini*, Bologna, 1982.
Pasolini, Pier Paolo, *Poems*, New York, 1982.
De Guisti, Luciano, *I film di Pier Paolo Pasolini*, Rome, 1983.
Carotenuto, Aldo, *L'autunno della coscienza: Ricerche psicologiche su Pier Paolo Pasolini*, Turin, 1985.
Michalczyk, John J., *The Italian Political Film-makers*, Cranbury, New Jersey, 1986.
Pasolini, Pier Paolo, *Lettere 1940–1954: Con una cronologia della vita e delle opere*, edited by Nico Naldini, Turin, 1986.
Schweitzer, Otto, *Pier Paolo Pasolini: Mit Selbstzeugnissen und Bilddokumenten*, Hamburg, 1986.
Klimke, Cristoph, *Kraft der Vergangenheit: Zu Motiven der Filme von Pier Paolo Pasolini*, Frankfurt, 1988.
Van Watson, William, *Pier Paolo Pasolini & the Theatre of the Word*, Lewiston, 1989.
Rumble, Patrick, *Pier Paolo Pasolini; Contemporary Perspectives*, Toronto, 1993.
Baranski, Zymunt G., *Pasolini Old & New; Surveys & Studies*, Dublin, 1999.

Articles:

Murray, William, ''Letter from Rome,'' in *New Yorker*, 21 April 1962.
Cameron, Ian, in *Movie* (London), September 1962.
Bean, Robin, in *Films and Filming* (London), 12 September 1962.
Nowell-Smith, Geoffrey, in *Sight and Sound* (London), Autumn 1962.
Bragin, John, ''Interview with Pasolini,'' in *Film Culture* (New York), Fall 1966.
Conrad, Randall, in *Film Quarterly* (Berkeley), Winter 1966–67.
Kauffmann, Stanley, ''Poet and the Pimp,'' in *New Republic* (New York), 6 April 1968.
Sarris, Andrew, in *Village Voice* (New York), 6 June 1968.
MacDonald, Susan, ''Pasolini: Rebellion, Art, and a New Society,'' in *Screen* (London), May-June 1969.
Bragin, John, ''Pier Paolo Pasolini: Poetry as a Compensation,'' in *Film Society Review* (New York), nos. 5–7, 1969.
Purdon, Noel, ''Pasolini: The Film of Alienation,'' in *Cinema* (London), August 1970.
Armes, Roy, ''Pasolini,'' in *Films and Filming* (London), June 1971.
Séquences (Montreal), July 1973.
''Pasolini Issues'' of *Etudes Cinématographiques* (Paris), nos. 109–111, 1976, and nos. 112–114, 1976.
''Pasolini Issue'' of *Cinéma* (Zurich), no. 2, 1976.
Gervais, M., in *Wide Angle* (Athens, Ohio), no. 4, 1977.

Accattone

Téllez, T. L., in *Contracampo* (Madrid), December 1980.
La Greca, A., in *Cinema Nuovo* (Bari), January-February 1986.
Pezzotta, A., "Io sono una forza del passato," in *Filmcritica* (Rome), October-November 1988.
Thirard, P. L., "Se suicider, c'est l'idee la plus simple," in *Positif* (Paris), September 1989.
Beylot, Pierre, "Pasolini, du réalisme au mythe," in *CinémAction* (Courbevoie), January 1994.
Castoro Cinema, July/August 1994.
Orr, Christopher, "Pasolini's *Accattone*, or Naturalism and Its Discontents," in *Film Criticism* (Meadville), Spring 1995.
Campani, E.M., "Death and Narrative: an Itinerary," in *Blimp* (Graz), no. 34, Summer 1996.
Kino (Warsaw), July-August 1998.

* * *

Himself an alien in Rome, isolated by his regional Friulian upbringing, his homosexuality, and his poverty, the young Pier Paolo Pasolini had felt an instant affinity with the young street kids of the crowded, war-ruined city when he arrived there in the winter of 1949. He quickly developed his taste for sexual rough trade among the *ragazzi* of the city, the sarcastic kids dispossessed and wised-up by post-war greed and the opportunism encouraged by the Marshall Plan. In 1955 Pasolini published his first novel, *Ragazzi di vita*, a picture of life in the shantytowns and among the pimping, petty-thieving boys he now knew well. *Una vita violenta*, four years later, explored the same ground through the brief, violent life of Tommaso, smart enough to sense fitfully the ruin of his future. *Una vita violenta* became the basis of Pasolini's first film, and Tommaso the model for Vittorio, the delinquent his pals call Accattone.

Fellini was to have backed the film but pulled out after Pasolini submitted some test footage in which he had overreached himself in trying to shoot in the style of Dreyer's *Trial of Joan of Arc.* With Italian film heading away from neorealism towards a high style and elaborate production values mirroring the new wealth of the cities, Fellini was also dubious about Pasolini's chosen location, a run-down street in the heart of the Roman slums. Nor had he any reason to believe that Franco Citti could carry the leading role; inexperienced, uncommunicative, Citti was the younger brother of the man who had been Pasolini's adviser on Roman dialect for the script editing work he did on films by Fellini and Mauro Bolognini.

It was Bolognini who, seeing stills from the test footage on Pasolini's desk, understood what he was trying to do and interested producer Alfredo Bini in the project. The result was a film more characteristic of Pasolini's temperament than of Italian cinema. To the music of Bach's *St. Matthew Passion*, Citti moves around a Rome of decadent religious imagery, crumbling buildings, a city pervaded by a sun-dazed, numbed sense of mortality. Dreams show the *ragazzi* buried half-naked in rubble, an evocative image of the ruin Pasolini saw reflected in both the morality and the architecture of his adopted city. Aiming for "an absolute simplicity of expression," Pasolini in fact achieved a studied stylization that was to become typical of his films. Citti became a star, and *Accattone* established Pasolini as a star himself in yet another field, matching his eminence in poetry, fiction, and criticism. Today, with Pasolini dead at the hands of just such a boy as Vittorio, it is difficult to see the film as anything but an ironic signpost to the fate of this mercurial polymath.

—John Baxter

ADAM'S RIB

USA, 1949

Director: George Cukor

Production: Metro-Goldwyn-Mayer Pictures Corp.; black and white, 35mm; running time: 101 minutes. Released 1949. Filmed at MGM studios.

Producer: Lawrence Weingarten; **screenplay:** Ruth Gordon and Garson Kanin; **photography:** George J. Folsey; **editor:** George Boemler; **art directors:** Cedric Gibbons and William Ferrari; **music:** Miklos Rozsa.

Cast: Spencer Tracy (*Adam Bonner*); Katharine Hepburn (*Amanda Bonner*); Judy Holliday (*Doris Attinger*); Tom Ewell (*Warren Attinger*); David Wayne (*Kip Lurie*); Jean Hagen (*Beryl Caighn*); Hope Emerson (*Olympia La Pere*); Eve March (*Grace*); Clarence Kolb (*Judge Reiser*); Emerson Treacy (*Jules Frikke*); Polly Moran (*Mrs. McGrath*); Will Wright (*Judge Marcasson*); Elizabeth Flournoy (*Dr. Margaret Brodeigh*).

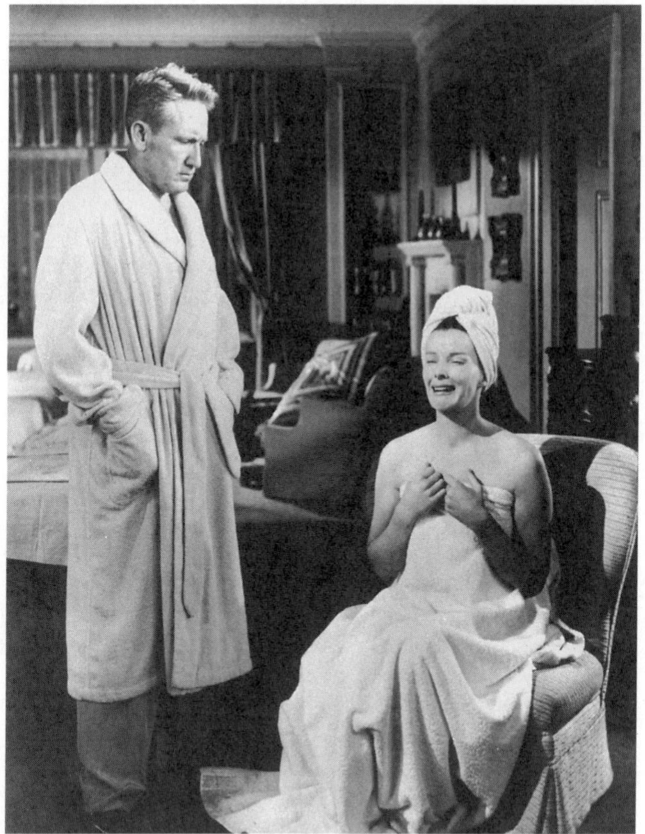

Adam's Rib

Publications

Script:

Gordon, Ruth, and Garson Kanin, *Adam's Rib*, New York, 1971.

Books:

Langlois, Henri, and others, *Hommage à George Cukor*, Paris, 1963.
Domarchi, Jean, *George Cukor*, Paris, 1965.
Deschner, Donald, *The Films of Spencer Tracy*, New York, 1968.
Carey, Gary, *Cukor and Company: The Films of George Cukor and His Collaborators*, New York, 1971.
Kanin, Garson, *Tracy and Hepburn*, New York, 1971.
Dickens, Homer, *The Films of Katharine Hepburn*, New York, 1971.
Lambert, Gavin, *On Cukor*, New York, 1972.
Tozzi, Romano, *Spencer Tracy*, New York, 1973.
Marill, Alvin H., *Katharine Hepburn*, New York, 1973.
Cavell, Stanley, *Pursuits of Happiness: The Hollywood Comedy of Remarriage*, Cambridge, Massachusetts, 1981.
Phillips, Gene D., *George Cukor*, Boston, 1982.
Carey, Gary, *Katharine Hepburn: A Biography*, London, 1983.
Britton, Andrew, *Katharine Hepburn: The Thirties and After*, Newcastle-upon-Tyne, 1984.
Freedland, Michael, *Katharine Hepburn*, London, 1984.
Morley, Sheridan, *Katharine Hepburn: A Celebration*, London, 1984.
Bernadoni, James, *George Cukor: A Critical Study and Filmography*, Jefferson, North Carolina, 1985.
Edwards, Anne, *Katharine Hepburn: A Biography*, London, 1986.
Davidson, Bill, *Spencer Tracy: Tragic Idol*, London, 1987.
Levy, Emanuel, *George Cukor, Master of Elegance; Hollywood's Legendary Director and His Stars*, New York, 1994.
McGilligan, *George Cukor: The Book*, New York, 1997.

Articles:

Crowther, Bosley, in *New York Times*, 24 December 1949.
Houston, Penelope, "Cukor and the Kanins," in *Sight and Sound* (London), Spring 1955.
Tozzi, Romano, "Katharine Hepburn," in *Films in Review* (New York), December 1957.
"Cukor Issue" of *Cahiers du Cinéma* (Paris), February 1964.
Tozzi, Romano, "Spencer Tracy," in *Films in Review* (New York), December 1966.

Gilliatt, Penelope, "The Most Amicable Combatants," in *New Yorker*, 23 September 1972.

Lynch, Anne Louise, in *Magill's Survey of Cinema 1*, Englewood Cliffs, New Jersey, 1980.

Tobin, Yann, in *Positif* (Paris), May 1985.

Aarts, A., in *Skrien* (Amsterdam), September-October 1985.

Detassis, P., "*La costola di Adamo* di George Cukor," in *Cineforum* (Bergamo, Italy), October 1989.

Shumway, D. R., "Screwball Comedies: Constructing Romance Mystifying Marriage," in *Cinema Journal* (Austin, Texas), no. 4, 1991.

Nacache, Jacqueline, "'Madame porte la culotte': maris et femmes," in *Mensuel du Cinéma*, October 1993.

* * *

Adam's Rib represents a climax in the evolution of the classic Hollywood screwball comedy. In the 1930s, screwball comedies united antagonistic couples whose clashes revolved around egos, class conflicts, and attitudes about money and values. In the 1940s, screwball comedies replaced these conflicts with ones that revolved around egos and career-marriage decisions. In such films as *His Girl Friday, Woman of the Year, Take a Letter, Darling*, and *They All Kissed the Bride*, the comic crises hinged on the heroines' decisions regarding their professional careers and domestic roles. In 1949, George Cukor's *Adam's Rib* took the familiar marriage-career crisis formula of the screwball comedy to its logical conclusion—a comic study of sex role stereotyping and the invalidity of narrowly defined sex roles.

The film reunited Katharine Hepburn and Spencer Tracy, who had previously teamed on *Woman of the Year, Keeper of the Flame, Without Love*, and *State of the Union*, and whose successful on-screen romances seemed to radiate some of the genuine love and affection of their off-screen relationship. The film also features a brilliant screenplay by the husband-wife team Garson Kanin and Ruth Gordon. All the principals—director, stars, and writers—had proven track records, and in a financially bad year for Hollywood, their combined box-office appeal led to the three-way teaming on a film project that otherwise might not have been possible.

The movie is about Adam and Amanda Bonner, husband and wife lawyers who find themselves on opposite sides of a courtroom case. The legal case in question concerns a woman (Judy Holliday) who has shot her adulterous husband (Tom Ewell). Defense attorney Amanda Bonner views her case as a woman's rights issue, and she bases her defense on the premise that the husband would have been exempt from prosecution if the roles were reversed. In front of her district attorney husband, she turns the courtroom and the trial into a hilarious forum for a public debate on the "double standard" and the narrowness of sexual stereotypes. In the meantime, the courtroom competition begins to threaten the Bonner's marriage.

Much of the film's humor arises from the many sex-role reversals. Through such reversals, the movie simultaneously comments on how traditional social roles are defined by stereotypes of masculinity and femininity. The film literally takes this notion to its extreme when it depicts what the unwitting husband, wife, and lover (Jean Hagen), who are the subjects of the trial, would be like if their sexes were reversed. Meanwhile, the Bonner's crumbling marriage, one based on mutual respect and liberation from sexual stereotypes, requires a series of further role reversals to be put back together again. Adam wins his wife's sympathies by crying; Amanda apologizes by sending her husband a new hat.

Amanda ultimately wins her case and husband without giving up her principles. Adam learns about humility without losing his masculinity. But when the reconciled Bonners finally fall into bed together behind a curtain, the on-screen veil and their final unresolved argument about sex roles, competition, and sex differences cinematically deny their absolute integration as a unified couple. Like many screwball comedies that preceded it, *Adam's Rib* ends with a marital reconciliation that establishes the couple's unity without resolving the individuals' ongoing differences.

The writing, acting, and directing team that made *Adam's Rib* a success reunited in 1952 for a screwball comedy about a manager and his professional female athlete in *Pat and Mike*. The successful story formula from *Adam's Rib* further inspired a 1973 television series with the same name.

—Lauren Rabinovitz

THE ADVENTURE

See **L'AVVENTURA**

THE ADVENTURES OF ROBIN HOOD

USA, 1938

Directors: Michael Curtiz and William Keighley

Production: Warner Bros. Pictures Inc.; Technicolor, 35mm; running time: 102 minutes. Released 1938. Filmed at Warner Bros. studios.

Producer: Hal Wallis; **screenplay:** Norman Reilly Raine and Seton I. Miller from the Robin Hood legends; **photography:** Tony Gaudio, Sol Polito, and W. Howard Green; **editor:** Ralph Dawson; **art director:** Carl Weyl; **music:** Eric Wolfgang Korngold, with orchestrations by Hugo Friedhofer and Milan Roder; **costume designer:** Milo Anderson.

Cast: Errol Flynn (*Robin Hood, or Sir Robin of Locksley*); Olivia de Havilland (*Lady Marian Fitzwalter*); Basil Rathbone (*Sir Guy of Gisbourne*); Claude Rains (*Prince John*); Alan Hale (*Little John*); Eugene Pallette (*Friar Tuck*); Ian Hunter (*King Richard the Lion-Hearted*); Melville Cooper (*High Sheriff of Nottingham*); Patric Knowles (*Will Scarlett*); Herbert Mundin (*Much the Miller's son*); Una O'Connor (*Bess*); Montagu Love (*Bishop of Black Canon*).

Awards: Oscars for Interior Decoration, Best Original Score, and Best Editing, 1938.

The Adventures of Robin Hood

Publications

Script:

Raine, Norman Reilly, and Seton I. Miller, *The Adventures of Robin Hood*, edited by Rudy Behlmer, Madison, Wisconsin, 1979.

Books:

Martin, Pete, *Hollywood Without Makeup*, New York, 1948.
Flynn, Errol, *My Wicked, Wicked Ways*, New York, 1959.
Parish, James Robert, editor, *Errol Flynn*, New York, 1969.
Thomas, Tony, Rudy Behlmer, and Clifford McCarty, *The Films of Errol Flynn*, New York, 1969.
Canham, Kingsley, *Michael Curtiz, Raoul Walsh, Henry Hathway*, London, 1973.
Thomas, Tony, *Cads and Cavaliers: The Film Adventurers*, New York, 1973.
Rosenzweig, Sidney, *Casablanca and Other Major Films of Michael Curtiz*, Ann Arbor, Michigan, 1982.
Valenti, Peter, *Errol Flynn: A Bio-Bibliography*, Westport, Connecticut, 1984.
Kinnard, Roy, and R. J. Vitone, *The American Films of Michael Curtiz*, Metuchen, New Jersey, 1986.
Behlmer, Rudy, *Inside Warner Brothers; Nineteen Thirty-Five to Nineteen Fifty-One*, New York, 1987.
Robertson, James, *The Casablanca Man; The Career of Michael Curtiz*, New York, 1993.

Articles:

Thomas, Anthony, ''Errol Flynn,'' in *Films in Review* (New York), January 1960.
Callenbach, Ernest, ''Comparative Anatomy of Folk-Myth Films: *Robin Hood* and *Antônio das Mortes*,'' in *Film Quarterly* (Berkeley), Winter 1969–70.
Nolan, Jack Edmund, ''Michael Curtiz,'' in *Films in Review* (New York), November 1970.
Gow, Gordon, ''Swashbuckling,'' in *Films and Filming* (London), January 1972.
Carcedo, J., in *Image et Son* (Paris), September 1978.
Chevasu, F., in *Image et Son* (Paris), February 1978.
Eyquem, O., ''Sherwood, USA (A propos des *Aventures de Robin des Bois*),'' in *Positif* (Paris), April 1978.
Renaud, T., in *Cinéma* (Paris), February 1978.
Morsberger, Robert, in *Magill's Survey of Cinema 1*, Englewood Cliffs, New Jersey, 1980.
Raynes, D., in *Soundtrack* (Hollywood), March 1984.
Sayre, Nora, ''Curtiz: A Man for All Genres. . . ,'' in *New York Times*, 29 November 1992.
Holt, Wesley G., ''*The Adventures of Robin Hood*,'' in *Filmfax* (Evanston), April-May 1993.
Télérama (Paris), 13 September 1995.

* * *

The Adventures of Robin Hood, a Warner Brothers studio production, reveals many facets and details of the studio system. The film was originally planned as a vehicle for James Cagney following the success of *Midsummer Night's Dream*, but contract problems with Cagney and the success of *Captain Blood* prompted the studio to cast Errol Flynn as the rogue outlaw. Once production on the film began, a directorial change occurred after the original director, William Keighley, led the production over budget and behind schedule. He was replaced by Michael Curtiz, though both men share the director's credit.

The film reflects the studio's plan to produce a more prestigious product than the musicals and gangster films of the early 1930s. Even so, the film does show the studio's frequent thematic concern with common folk banding together to achieve a goal of correcting an injustice, economic or otherwise.

The film's cast members have generally been acclaimed for matching the literary image of their characters. Even the supporting characters such as Alan Hale's Little John and Eugene Pallette's Friar Tuck seem to be perfectly suited for their roles. Under the direction of Curtiz and Keighley, the principal actors play off each other and promptly reveal much of their characters in this straight-forward narrative. Claude Rains portrays Prince John as a schemer, a man with a thirst for power; while Basil Rathbone's Sir Guy, with his good looks and his sinister bearing, makes an equal adversary for Flynn's Robin. Olivia de Havilland as Marian seems to be a pure aristocrat whether in the court or in the forest, or when facing death or confessing her love for Robin.

Errol Flynn's Robin is a man of action but also of wit. Following Douglas Fairbanks's silent film portrayal of Robin, Flynn's Robin engages in daring deeds but not on such a large scale (in part due to Warner's tight budget). The film also follows Fairbanks's lead in giving Robin a sense of humor as Robin throws verbal arrows at any villains in sight. Even in the love scenes, Robin can joke with and tease Marian.

The Adventures of Robin Hood, a very successful film when first released, has become something more than an accomplished film from the 1930s. For many, the influence of this film is immense. There is, for example, a great deal of similarity between the action of Robin's men in the forest capturing a gold shipment and the attack of the Ewoks against the Stormtroopers in *Return of the Jedi*. Not only does it remain one of the quintessential films of the swashbuckling genre but it is also the definitive Robin Hood legend for scores of film-goers and television viewers. Much like that of *The Wizard of Oz*, *Robin Hood's* audience has grown through repeated and successful television screenings. *TV Guide* once listed it as one of the top five films on television as selected by station programmers.

—Ray Narducy

THE AFRICAN QUEEN

USA, 1951

Director: John Huston

Production: Horizon Romulus Productions; Technicolor, 35mm; running time: 103 minutes. Released 1951. Filmed at various film studios in London; exteriors shot along the Ruiki River in the Belgian Congo and what was then the British protectorate of Uganda.

Producer: Sam Spiegel; **screenplay:** James Agee and John Huston with Peter Viertel, from the novel by C. S. Forester; **photography:** Jack Cardiff; **editor:** Ralph Kemplen; **sound engineer:** John Mitchell; **art director:** John Hoesli; **music:** Allan Gray, executed by the Royal Philharmonic Orchestra under the direction of Norman del Mar; **special effects:** Cliff Richardson; **costume designer:** Doris Langley Moore.

Cast: Katharine Hepburn (*Rose Sayer*); Humphrey Bogart (*Charlie Allnut*); Robert Morley (*Rev. Samuel Sayer*); Peter Bull (*Captain of the Luisa*); Theodore Bikel (*1st Officer of the Luisa*); Walter Cotell (*2nd Officer of the Luisa*); Gerald Ohn (*Officer of the Luisa*); Peter Swanwick (*1st Officer of the Shoona*); Richard Marner (*2nd Officer of the Shoond*).

Awards: Oscar, Best Actor (Bogart), 1951; American Film Institute's ''100 Years, 100 Movies,'' 1998.

Publications

Scripts:

Agee, James, *Agee on Film 2: Five Film Scripts*, foreword by John Huston, New York, 1960.

Books:

Davay, Paul, *John Huston*, Paris, 1957.
Allais, Jean-Claude, *John Huston*, Paris, 1960.
Nolan, William F., *John Huston: King Rebel*, Los Angeles, 1965.
Gehman, Richard, *Bogart*, Greenwich, Connecticut, 1965.
Michael, Paul, *Humphrey Bogart: The Man and His Films*, Indianapolis, 1965.
McCarty, Clifford, *Bogey: The Films of Humphrey Bogart*, New York, 1965.
Benayoun, Robert, *John Huston*, Paris, 1966; revised edition, 1985.
Dickens, Homer, *The Films of Katharine Hepburn*, New York, 1971.
Barbour, Alan, *Humphrey Bogart*, New York, 1973.
Marill, Alvin H., *Katharine Hepburn*, New York, 1973.
Benchley, Nathaniel, *Humphrey Bogart*, Boston, 1975.
Kaminsky, Stuart M., *John Huston, Maker of Magic*, Boston, 1978.
Madsen, Axel, *John Huston*, New York, 1978.
Huston, John, *An Open Book*, New York, 1980.
Giannetti, Louis, *Masters of the American Cinema*, Englewood Cliffs, New Jersey, 1981.
Pettigrew, Terence, *Bogart: A Definitive Study of His Film Career*, London, 1981.
Carey, Gary, *Katharine Hepburn: A Biography*, London, 1983.
Britton, Andrew, *Katharine Hepburn: The Thirties and After*, Newcastle-upon-Tyne, 1984.
Freedland, Michael, *Katharine Hepburn*, London, 1984.
Morley, Sheridan, *Katharine Hepburn: A Celebration*, London, 1984.
Hammen, Scott, *John Huston*, Boston, 1985.
Winkler, Willi, *Humphrey Bogart und Hollywoods Schwarze Serie*, Munich, 1985.
Edwards, Anne, *Katharine Hepburn: A Biography*, London, 1986.
McCarty, John, *The Films of John Huston*, Secaucus, New Jersey, 1987.
Hepburn, Katharine, *The Making of ''The African Queen''; or, How I Went to Africa with Bogart, Bacall, and Huston and Almost Lost My Life*, New York and London, 1987.
Brill, Lesley, *John Huston's Filmmaking*, New York, 1997.
Cunningham, Ernest W., *Ultimate Bogie*, Los Angeles, 1999.

Articles:

''Life Goes on Location in Africa,'' in *Life* (New York), 7 September 1951.
Reisz, Karel, ''Interview with Huston,'' in *Sight and Sound* (London), January-March 1952.
''Huston Issue'' of *Positif* (Paris), January 1952.
Hart, Henry, in *Films in Review* (New York), February 1952.
Bowen, Clarissa, in *Sight and Sound* (London), April-June 1952.
Sadoul, Georges, in *Lettres Françaises* (Paris), 10 April 1952.
Demeure, Jacques, and Michel Subiela, ''*The African Queen*, John Huston, and Humphrey Bogart,'' in *Positif* (Paris), August 1952.
''Huston Issue'' of *Positif* (Paris), January 1957.
''Special Issue'' of *Bianco e Nero* (Rome), April 1957.
Archer, Eugene, ''A Monograph on John Huston,'' in *Films and Filming* (London), September and October 1959.
Jones, DuPre, ''Beating the Devil: 30 Years of John Huston,'' in *Films and Filming* (London), January 1973.

The African Queen

de Selva, L., in *Image et Son* (Paris), 331 bis, 1978.
Snyder, Ellen J., in *Magill's Survey of Cinema 1*, Englewood Cliffs, New Jersey, 1980.
Fultz, J. R., ''A Classic Case of Collaboration . . . *The African Queen*,'' in *Literature/Film Quarterly* (Salisbury, Maryland), vol. 19, no. 1, 1982.
Eyquem, O., ''Entretien avec Peter Viertel, scenariste,'' in *Positif* (Paris), May 1990.
Rasmussen, S., ''Tykhuder,'' in *Levende Billeder* (Copenhagen), June 1990.
Brill, Lesley, ''*The African Queen* and John Huston's Filmmaking,'' in *Cinema Journal* (Austin), Winter 1995.

* * *

From the beginning, director John Huston insisted that *The African Queen* be shot on location. To find a river identical to the one in C. S. Forester's novel, he logged 25,000 flying miles criss-crossing Africa until he settled on the Ruiki in the then Belgian Congo. At a time (1951) when on-location shooting was nowhere near as common as today, traveling 1,100 miles up the Congo to make what is essentially a filmed dialogue must have seemed fanatical. And subsequent encounters with blood flukes, crocodiles, soldier ants, wild boars, stampeding elephants, malaria, and dysentery were hardly reassuring.

Yet *The African Queen* is more than a simple encounter between a man and a woman. It is a story of two very different people growing to love and respect one another after sharing and surviving severe hardships. Huston maintained that on-location shooting was the only way to make that suffering and subsequent romance believable and authentic. At Huston's insistence even the scenes shot off location were filmed under realistic conditions. For example, although Humphrey Bogart actually emerged from London rather than Ugandan waters (after pulling the *African Queen*), the leeches that covered him were the genuine article. Bogart's revulsion and shivering during that particular scene are convincing arguments for Huston's point-of-view.

Indeed, *The African Queen*'s main strength is the acting of the two principal players—Humphrey Bogart as the seedy Canadian boat captain, Charlie Allnut, and Katharine Hepburn as the ''Psalm-singing skinny old maid,'' British missionary Rose Sayer. According to Huston, although Bogart initially resisted and didn't like his character, after mimicking the director's gestures and expressions, ''all at once he got under the skin of that wretched, sleazy, absurd, brave little man.'' Hepburn, too, had trouble at the beginning; her portrayal was brittle, cold, and humorless. However, once Huston suggested that she play her part as if she were that Grand Lady Eleanor Roosevelt, she became both funny and refined, and a humor inherent in neither the novel nor the screenplay emerged between the two characters.

The humor is essential to the success of the film not because it makes the film more entertaining, but because it arises out of the equality and individuality of two eccentric and strong-willed adversaries. They may end up falling in love, but not without an often hysterical struggle. Bogart's character begins as a self-indulgent drunk who mimics the missionary's prim ways; she, on the other hand, frowns upon his drinking and cowardice, disagreeing with his lax views on human nature: ''Nature is what we were put on earth to rise above.'' But in courageously facing and solving problems together, the two head towards a middle ground. Allnut stops drinking (Rose has thrown his gin overboard) and shaves, while Rose changes her mind about human nature. After encountering her first rapids, for example, she ecstatically exclaims, ''I never dreamed any mere physical experience could be so stimulating! . . . I don't wonder you love boating, Mr. Allnut.'' Finally, after escaping both the Germans and the allegedly uncrossable rapids, the two impulsively embrace and fall in love. The humor does not stop here, however. After their first tender night together, Rose shyly asks Allnut, ''Dear, what is your first name?'' Their mutual delight in his response is completely captivating.

Our captivation with the two characters allows us to accept many of the film's more improbable moments—the quick dispatch of Brother Samuel Sayer, the sun shining in the eyes of a German sharpshooter as naively predicted by Rose, heavy rains freeing the mired *African Queen* after Rose prays to God, and the *deus ex machina* ending. In fact, the ending had been changed several times. Writer James Agee hadn't written it yet when he suffered a heart attack, so Huston tried to write one with Peter Viertel; before the fourth and final ending was conceived, three others were apparently considered: (1) a British warship rescues Rose and Charlie after a heroic battle with the *Louisa*, (2) Rose proposes marriage before the first available British consul, (3) Charlie remembers the wife he had left behind in England and hadn't thought of for 20 years. The first and second endings combined were similar to what occurred in the original novel (that is, Forester's second ending—even he had problems resolving the plot).

Huston's fourth and happy ending—which miraculously saves Rosie and Charlie from their postnuptial death by hanging—is atypical, as are other elements in the script. Many of Huston's previous films had a bleaker view of humanity and ended unhappily (e.g. *The Maltese Falcon, The Treasure of the Sierra Madre*). Both Charlie and Rose exhibit an honesty and integrity at odds with such Hustonian liars and tricksters as Sam Spade, Brigid O'Shaughnessy, Rick Leland, and Dobbs. The two survive because of an internal nobility that Huston's seedier characters outwardly lack.

Huston's new optimism/idealism struck the right note with the public. *The African Queen* became one of 1952's top moneymakers, having been nominated for Best Actor (Bogart won), Best Actress, Best Direction, and Best Screenplay. British readers of *Picturegoer* voted Bogart the year's best actor, and Hepburn experienced the greatest box office hit of her career. A film that began as a vehicle for Charles Laughton and Elsa Lanchester, and later Bette Davis and David Niven, had found the perfect couple for its improbable romance.

—Catherine Henry

AFTER LIFE

See **WANDAFURU RAIFU**

L'AGE D'OR

(The Golden Age)

France, 1930

Director: Luis Buñuel

Production: Black and white, 35mm; running time: 60 minutes (some French sources list 80 minutes). Released 28 November 1930, Paris. Filmed in Studios Billancourt-Epinay, France.

Producer: Charles Vicomte de Noailles; **screenplay:** Luis Buñuel and Salvador Dalí; **photography:** Albert Duverger; **editor:** Luis Buñuel; **production designer:** Pierre Schilzneck; **original music:** Van Parys, montage of extracts from Mozart, Beethoven, Mendelssohn, Debussy, and Wagner.

Cast: Lya Lys (*The Woman*); Gaston Modot (*The Man*); Max Ernst (*Bandit Chief*); Pierre Prévert (*Péman, a Bandit*); Caridad de Labaerdesque; Madame Noizet; Liorens Artigas; Duchange Ibanez; Lionel Salem; Pancho Cossio; Valentine Hugo; Marie Berthe Ernst; Jacques B. Brunius; Simone Cottance; Paul Eluard; Manuel Angeles Ortiz; Juan Esplandio; Pedro Flores; Juan Castañe; Joaquin Roa; Pruna; Xaume de Maravilles.

Publications

Scripts:

Buñuel, Luis, and Salvador Dali, *L'Age d'or, and Un Chien andalou*, New York, 1968.

Buñuel, Luis, and Salvador Dali, *L'Age d'or*, in *Avant-Scène du Cinéma* (Paris), November 1983.

Books:

Brunius, Jacques B., *En marge du cinéma français*, Paris, 1947.

Kyrou, Ado, *Le Surréalisme au cinéma*, Paris, 1953; revised edition, 1963.

Moullet, Luc, *Luis Buñuel*, Brussels, 1957.

L'age d'or

Kyrou, Ado, *Luis Buñuel*, Paris, 1962.

Grange, Frédéric, and Charles Rebolledo, *Luis Buñuel*, Paris, 1964.

Aranda, Francisco, *Luis Buñuel: Biografia critica*, Madrid, 1969.

Durgnat, Raymond, *Luis Buñuel*, Berkeley, 1968; revised edition, 1977.

Breton, André, *Manifestoes of Surrealism*, Ann Arbor, Michigan, 1969.

Buache, Freddy, *Luis Buñuel*, Lyons, 1970; as *The Cinema of Luis Buñuel*, New York and London, 1973.

Matthews, J. H., *Surrealism and the Film*, Ann Arbor, Michigan, 1971.

Harcourt, Peter, "Luis Buñuel: Spaniard and Surrealist," in *Six European Directors*, London, 1974.

Aranda, José Francisco, *Luis Buñuel: A Critical Biography*, London and New York, 1975.

Cesarman, Fernando, *El ojo de Buñuel*, Barcelona, 1976.

Hammond, Paul, editor, *The Shadow and Its Shadow: Surrealist Writings on Cinema*, London, 1978.

Mellen, Joan, editor, *The World of Luis Buñuel: Essays in Criticism*, New York, 1978.

Higginbotham, Virginia, *Luis Buñuel*, Boston, 1979.

Bazin, André, *The Cinema of Cruelty: From Buñuel to Hitchcock*, New York, 1982.

Edwards, Gwynne, *The Discreet Art of Luis Buñuel: A Reading of His Films*, London, 1982.

Buñuel, Luis, *My Last Breath*, London and New York, 1983.

Rees, Margaret A., editor, *Luis Buñuel: A Symposium*, Leeds, 1983.

Lefèvre, Raymond, *Luis Buñuel*, Paris, 1984.

Vidal, Agustin Sanchez, *Luis Buñuel: Obra Cinematografica*, Madrid, 1984.

Aub, Max, *Conversaciones con Buñuel: Seguidas de 45 entrevistas con familiares, amigos y colaboradores del cineasta aragones*, Madrid, 1985.

Bertelli, Pino, *Buñuel: L'arma dello scandalo: L'anarchia nel cinema di Luis Buñuel*, Turin, 1985.

Oms, Marcel, *Don Luis Buñuel*, Paris, 1985.

De la Colina, Jose, and Tomás Pérez Turrent, *Luis Buñuel: Prohibido asomarse al interior*, Mexico, 1986.

Sandro, Paul, *Diversions of Pleasure: Luis Buñuel and the Crises of Desire*, Columbus, Ohio, 1987.

Williams, Linda, *Figures of Desire; A Theory and Analysis of Surrealist Film,* Berkeley, 1992.

De La Colina, Jose, *Objects of Desire; Conversations with Luis Buñel*, New York, 1993.

Evans, Peter W., *The Films of Luis Buñuel; Subjectivity & Desire*, New York, 1995.
Hammond, Paul, *L'Age D'Or*, London, 1998.
Baxter, John, *Buñuel*, New York, 1999.

Articles:

Chavance, Louis, ''Les Influences de *L'Age d'or*,'' in *Revue du Cinéma* (Paris), 1 January 1931.
Miller, Henry, in *New Review* (Paris), 1931; reprinted in Spanish in *Contracampo* (Madrid), October-November 1980.
Aranda, Francesco, ''Surrealist and Spanish Giant,'' in *Films and Filming* (London), October 1961.
''Buñuel Issue'' of *La Méthode* (Paris), January 1962.
Durgnat, Raymond, in *Films and Filming* (London), April 1962.
''Manifeste des surréalistes à propos de *L'Age d'or*,'' in *L'Avant-Scène du Cinéma* (Paris), 15 July 1963.
Lyon, E. H., ''The Process of Dissociation in Three Films,'' in *Cinema Journal* (Evanston, Illinois), Fall 1973.
Tena, Jean, ''*L'Age d'or* à l'ombre du Teide,'' in *Cahiers de la Cinémathèque* (Perpignan), Summer-Autumn 1980.
Logette, L., ''Surréalisme et cinéma,'' in *Jeune Cinéma* (Paris), April-May 1981.
Magny, Joel, ''*L'Age d'or:* Un Manifeste de la subversion devenu pièce de musée,'' in *Cinéma* (Paris), July-August 1981.
Bonnet, Jean-Claude, in *Cinématographe* (Paris), July 1981.
Bonitzer, P., ''Un documentaire anamorphique,'' in *Cahiers du Cinéma* (Paris), September 1981.
Kral, P., ''*L'Age d'or* aujourd'hui,'' in *Positif* (Paris), October 1981.
Logette, L., ''Un Film irrécupérable: *L'Age d'or*,'' in *Jeune Cinéma* (Paris), October 1981.
Logette, L., ''Sur un film de Buñuel peu connu,'' in *Jeune Cinéma* (Paris), January-February 1991.
Fieschi, J.-A., ''L'oeil tranche,'' in *Revue Belge du Cinéma* (Brussels), no. 33–34-35, 1993.
Perry, J. W., ''*L'Age d'or* and *Un Chien andalou*,'' in *Filmfax* (Evanston, Illinois), August-September 1993.
Rabourdin, D., ''Souvenirs de *L'Age d'or*,'' in *Positif* (Paris), October 1993.
Douin, Jean-Luc, ''Mécènes du désordre,'' in *Télérama* (Paris), 20 October 1993.
Logette, Lucien, and Luis Buñuel, ''Un cachet de philosophie souriante,'' in *Jeune Cinéma* (Paris), January 1994.
Cinémathèque, Autumn 1994.

* * *

L'Age d'or represents a key moment in surrealist filmmaking, indeed in the history of the experimental cinema. It is also important because it formally initiated the long and distinguished career of its director, Luis Buñuel. Both these strands are inexorably intertwined in any history of European filmmaking.

Buñuel met the artist Salvador Dalí at the University of Madrid in the early 1920s, and after working with Fritz Lang and Jean Epstein, made his first film (with Dalí), the noted surrealist short *Un Chien andalou* (1928). After this, Buñuel threw himself completely into the surrealist movement and its guerrilla campaign against the conventional and repressive.

But he needed funds for filmmaking activities. It was thus crucial when he met a wealthy patron, the Vicomte de Noailles, who had taken to commission a film every year for his wife's birthday. (In 1930 it would be Jean Cocteau's *Blood of a Poet.*) In short order Buñuel had a million francs to make any film he wanted. Dalí and Buñuel tried to work together, but failed. (Dalí's credit as co-screenwriter for what would become *L'Age d'or* amounted to but a few suggestions.) *L'Age d'or* truly stands as Buñuel's first film.

The plot of *L'Age d'or* is remarkably simple; two lovers (Gaston Modot and Lya Lys) declare war on a bourgeois French society intent on thwarting the fulfillment of their desires. And the film did not lack for name talent. For example, the lead, Gaston Modot, was a longtime French film star, who started with Gaumont in 1909 and worked for all the great directors of the French cinema: Louis Delluc in *Fièvre* (1921), René Clair in *Sous les toits de Paris* (1930), Marcel Carné in *Les Enfants du paradis* (1945), and Jean Renoir in *La Règle du jeu* (1939) and *La Grande Illusion* (1937).

L'Age d'or features moment after moment of surrealist juxtapositions. A poor beggar is savagely beaten, a proud dowager is slapped, a father shoots his son. The themes of the film follow the concerns of *Un Chien andalou:* frustrated love, society's repression of sexuality, the constancy of physical violence, attacks on the clergy.

But *L'Age d'or*, a longer work, is far more complex. Although the actions of the frustrated lovers are central, the film goes off in all sorts of directions. Indeed it opens with documentary footage of scorpions. This leads into incidents on a rocky seashore where a gang of bandits (led by surrealist painter Max Ernst) are invaded by first a group of chanting bishops and then dignitaries who ''have come to found the Roman Empire.'' The film ends with a sequence of a cross in the snow, covered tresses blowing in the wind to the tune of a *paso doble*. Ironically for Buñuel, when *L'Age d'or* was first shown it attracted the interest of a European agent for the Hollywood studio MGM. He signed Buñuel to a six-month contract at $250 a week for what was then Hollywood's most powerful studio. Buñuel left for the United States in December 1930, just as the furore around *L'Age d'or* was about to begin.

Late in 1930 *L'Age d'or* opened to the public at Studio 28 in Paris. (Studio 28 had been founded two years earlier and was exclusively devoted to the screening of avant garde films.) At the premiere two right-wing vigilante groups, the Patriots' League and the Anti-Jewish League, stormed Studio 28, hurling ink and rotten eggs at the screen, setting off tear gas and stink bombs, and clubbing members of the audience with cries of ''Death to the Jews.''

Later the police instructed the theatre's director to cut two scenes and the conservative press initiated a campaign to have this ''pornographic'' film banned completely. *Le Figaro* decried *L'Age d'or* as ''an exercise in Bolshevism.'' By mid-December the film had been banned and all copies confiscated.

For the next 50 years the film was a tantalizing memory for only a few. Celebrations such as that by the noted film historian Georges Sadoul, present at the premier, declared that *L'Age d'or* was a ''masterpiece in its violence, its purity, its lyric frenzy, its absolute sincerity.'' Only in 1980 (in New York, a year later in Paris) was the film again re-released. By then its shock value had worn off, and the film was seen more as a precedent for Buñuel's later work than a work attacking the core values of western civilization.

—Douglas Gomery

AGUIRRE, DER ZORN GOTTES

(Aguirre, The Wrath of God)

West Germany, 1973

Director: Werner Herzog

Production: Werner Herzog Filmproduktion; Eastmancolor, 35mm; running time: 93 minutes. Released 1973. Filmed in the jungles of Peru, along the Amazon.

Producer: Werner Herzog; **screenplay:** Werner Herzog, from the journal of Gaspar De Carvajal; **photography:** Thomas Mauch; **editor:** Beate Mainka-Jellinghaus; **sound:** Herbert Prasch; **music:** Popol Vuh; **special effects:** Juvenal Herrera and Miguel Vasquez.

Cast: Klaus Kinski (*Don Lope de Aguirre*); Helena Rojo (*Inez de Atienza*); Ruy Guerra (*Pedro de Ursua*); Del Negro (*Caspar de Carvajal*); Don Fernando de Guzman (*Peter Berling*); Cecilia Rivera (*Flores de Aguirre*); Dany Ades (*Perucho*); Armando Polanah (*Armando*); Edward Roland (*Okello*); Daniel Farafan, Alejandro Chavez, Antonio Marquez, Julio Martinez, and Alejandro Repulles (*The Indians*); and 270 Indians from the Cooperative of Lauramarca.

Publications

Script:

Herzog, Werner, ''*Aguirre, The Wrath of God*,'' in *3 Screenplays*, New York, 1980.

Books:

Schutte, Wolfram, and others, *Herzog/Kluge/Straub*, Vienna, 1976.
Greenberg, Alan, *Heart of Glass*, Munich, 1976.
Sandford, John, *The New German Cinema*, Totowa, New Jersey, 1980.
Franklin, James, *New German Cinema: From Oberhausen to Hamburg*, Boston, 1983.
Phillips, Klaus, editor, *New German Filmmakers: From Oberhausen Through the 1970s*, New York, 1984.
Corrigan, Timothy, *The Films of Werner Herzog; Between Mirage and History*, New York, 1986.
Gabrea, Radu, *Werner Herzog et la mystique rhénane*, Lausanne, 1986.

Articles:

Baxter, Brian, ''Werner Herzog,'' in *Film* (London), Spring 1969.
Ghali, Noureddine, ''Werner Herzog: 'Comme un rêve puissant. . . ,''' in *Jeune Cinéma* (Paris), September-October 1974.
Ghali, Noureddine, ''Werner Herzog: Le Réel saisi par le rêve,'' in *Jeune Cinéma* (Paris), November 1974.
Combs, Richard, in *Monthly Film Bulletin* (London), January 1975.
Elley, Derek, in *Films and Filming* (London), February 1975.
Zimmer, J., in *Image et Son* (Paris), March 1975.
Gauthier, G., and Derek Elley, in *Films and Filming* (London), April 1975.
Simsolo, Noël, in *Ecran* (Paris), April 1975.
Rayns, Tony, in *Sight and Sound* (London), Winter 1974–75.
Oudart, J. P., in *Cahiers du Cinéma* (Paris), July-August 1975.
Schlepelern, P., in *Kosmorama* (Copenhagen), no. 132, 1976.
Garel, A., in *Image et Son* (Paris), September, 1976.
Clarembeaux, M., in *Revue Belge du Cinéma* (Brussels), June 1977.
McCreadie, M., in *Films in Review* (New York), June-July 1977.
Dorr, J. H., ''The Enigma of Werner Herzog,'' in *Millimeter* (New York), October 1977.
''*Aguirre* Issue'' of *Avant-Scène du Cinéma* (Paris), 15 June 1978.
Coursen, D., ''Two Films by Werner Herzog,'' in *Cinemonkey* (Portland, Oregon), no. 1, 1979.
Fritze, R., ''Werner Herzog's Adaptation of History in *Aguirre, The Wrath of God*,'' in *Film and History* (Newark, New Jersey), December 1985.
Stiles, V. M., ''Fact and Fiction: Nature's Endgame in Werner Herzog's *Aguirre, The Wrath of God*,'' in *Literature/Film Quarterly* (Salisbury, Maryland), no. 3, 1989.
Génin, Bernard, ''L'enfer vert,'' in *Télérama* (Paris), 5 April 1995.

* * *

Aguirre der Zorn Gottes is Werner Herzog's hypnotic epic of megalomania and delusional myths. The story concerns the search of Spanish conquistadors for El Dorado in the jungles of South America. The journey is made with the assistance of native slaves over mountains and down an uncharted river. Initiated under the aegis of the Spanish crown, the expedition experiences progressive disintegration. Aguirre, originally named second-in-command, usurps control in pursuit of a golden territory to rule on his own. At the same time, the very instruments and characters sustaining the journey are gradually eliminated. Food, rafts, supplies, and crew members are lost; the landscape changes until there is no land properly speaking to conquer, only river and swamps. In the face of desolation. Aguirre maintains obsessive faith in the reality of his dreams, weaving tales of his future glory.

This journey, with its imaginary goal, is presented in the guise of an historical account. An opening title explains that the events come from a journal kept by a monk during the course of the expedition. The diary provides the text of a voice-over narration which intermittently comments on events. But El Dorado—the goal of the journey, purpose of the expedition, and subject of the diary—is a known fiction, an external dream destined to failure. Moreover, the journal is described as the remaining record of an expedition which disappeared in the depths of the Amazonian jungle; it cannot, in fact, exist. Thus from the outset the film defines its subject as a doomed journey and spurious history. Indeed, history is immediately construed in terms of myth.

As the film posits this mythical history and a goal-less journey, *Aguirre* transforms its world into a realm of hallucination. Crew members are attacked by arrows and darts from invisible sources. When the monk is struck by an arrow near the end of the film he denies its very being, ''This is no arrow.'' The monk and Okello, one

Aguirre, der Zorn Gottes

of the native slaves, also deny the existence of a boat hull (''There is no boat'') which is shown suspended in a tree. In the face of an uncontrollable phenomenal world what counts above all else is the faith one sustains in fictions of one's own making. And it is this quality that defines Aguirre as a hero. The greatest and only believer in the myths of his own creation, he stands as the quintessential heroic figure of history.

With its striking images the film successfully constructs an impression of having entered an unworldly territory. The opening is particularly effective, as the expedition is seen in extreme long shots weaving its way down the mountains through the fog to the banks of the river. The audience is positioned with the expedition throughout the journey. What lies beyond the river on its overgrown banks—a source of beauty, monotony, and danger—remains a mystery throughout the film. The final shot of the film reinforces the tenacity of the journey's confining vision, as the camera circles rapidly around the raft. Littered with dead bodies, overrun with monkeys, the raft is locked into an aimless drift as the hero and self-proclaimed ''great traitor'' asserts his power for the last time: ''I am the wrath of God.''

—M. B. White

AHFEI ZHENG ZHUAN

(Days of Being Wild)

Hong Kong, 1991

Director: Wong Kai-Wai

Production: In-Gear Film; Colour, 35mm; running time: 94 minutes.

Producer: Rover Tang; **executive producer:** Alan Tang; **screenplay:** Wong Kai-Wai; **photography:** Christopher Doyle; **editor:** Kai Kit-wai; **assistant directors:** Rosanna Ng, Johnny Kong, Tung Wan-Wai, Tsui Pui-Wing, Poon Kin-Kwan; **production design:** William Chang Suk-ping; **sound:** Steve Chan Wai-hung; **music:** Chan Do-ming.

Cast: Leslie Cheung (*Yuddy*); Maggie Cheung (*Su Li-zhen*); Tony Leung Chiu-wei (*Smirk*); Karina Lau (*Leong Fung-yung*); Andy Lau (*Tide*); Jacky Cheung (*Sab*); Rebecca Pan Dihua (*Rebecca*); Carina Lau (*Mimi*).

Awards: Hong Kong Film Awards for Best Film, Best Director, Best Actor (Leslie Cheung), Best Cinematographer, and Best Art Director.

Publications

Articles:

James, Caryn, ''Days of Being Wild,'' *The New York Times*, 23 March 1991.

Variety (New York), 1 April 1991.

Ho, Sam, ''The Withering Away of the Family,'' The 15th Hong Kong International Film Festival (catalogue), May 1991.

Shu, Kei, ''Notes on Hong Kong Cinema 1990,'' The 15th Hong Kong International Film Festival (catalogue), May 1991.

Rayns, T., *Sight and Sound* (London), December 1994.

Lehtinen, L., ''Katoamatonta aikaa tekemassa,'' in *Filmihullu* (Helsinki), no. 5, 1996.

Stephens, C. ''*Wong Kar-Wai* and the Persistence of Memory,'' in *Film Comment* (New York), January/February 1996.

Jousse, T., ''Boy Meets Girl,'' in *Cahiers du Cinéma* (Paris), March 1996.

Niogret, H., ''Nos annees sauvages,'' in *Positif* (Paris), March 1996.

Morsiani, A., ''I capolavori di Hong Kong,'' in *Segnocinema* (Vicenza), July/August 1996.

* * *

A young man strolls down a corridor, stops at a refreshment stand, and takes a bottle of Coke from an ice chest. He leans over the counter and catches the attention of the sales clerk, telling her, quite casually, ''From this moment on, we can become one-minute friends.''

They turn their faces to the wall clock and watch the second hand scroll over the markers. One, two, three, four, five seconds . . . sixty seconds pass.

Soon they become lovers. They meet for an hour each day in his apartment, sharing aimless conversation, and cigarettes.

Wong Kar-wai's desultory tale of 1960s Hong Kong has a nostalgic and bittersweet lyricism. Its antihero is a callow young man, Yuddy (Leslie Cheung), around whom hapless friends and lovers

Ahfei zheng zhuan

spin. The Chinese title is ''The Story of an Ah Fei''—''ah fei'' being a Chinese version of a teddy boy.

Cocky and narcissistic, Yuddy is the pretty boy that all the young women fall for, but he never falls for them. As he says, ''In this life I will like many, many women, but to the end I won't know whom I love most.''

Failing to get any commitment from him, Su Li-zhen (Maggie Cheung), the sales clerk, threatens to leave. When she walks out, he continues slicking back his hair, gazing placidly into the medicine chest mirror. However, Li-zhen keeps coming back, lurking in corridors and outside the apartment, even after he begins an affair with a pretty dancehall girl, Mimi (Carina Lau). The young policeman who walks the beat (Andy Lau) has noticed the odd goings-on in the second-room flat. Late one night he takes pity on Li-zhen, chatting with her and loaning her cab fare to get home. Before they part he points to a nearby phone booth and remarks, ''Every night I'm here at this time.''

He waits there night after night, but he never hears from her. One day she leaves town, and eventually, so does he.

Some vague reason for Yuddy's misogyny is provided: Long ago, his real mother gave him over to a friend (played by old time chanteuse Pan Dihua) to raise. And the stepmother, an aging dowager with a penchant for young gigolos, has steadfastly refused to reveal his real mother's identity to Yuddy.

They torment each other with this game constantly. He wants to know; she refuses to tell him. He hates her. And she replies, tartly, ''I just want you to hate me, then at least you won't forget me.'' But one day she tires of the game. She's planning to emigrate, and she finally reveals what he has long wanted to know.

With the information, Yuddy takes off to find his real mother in the Philippines. He goes to her mansion but is refused entrance. He walks quickly away, not giving her the satisfaction (somehow he knows she is watching him from behind) of looking back. In town, he gets drunk and is about to be robbed in the street but a stranger, a man from Hong Kong, comes to his rescue. Unbeknown to Yuddy, this fellow is the policeman who used to walk his street, who has now fulfilled his lifelong dream to become a sailor, and is waiting to join his ship.

The outstanding cinematography is by Christopher Doyle, a frequent collaborator with the Wong Kar-wai, and one the most famous scenes in contemporary Chinese cinema is the long tracking shot towards the end of the film. We travel down a street, go through the doorway of a colonial-style building, and up a stairway into the waiting room of a train station. There we find an inebriated Yuddy posed over a jukebox. He turns away and does a jig. He finds his newfound friend slumped at a table.

Cutting away to the backroom, Yuddy is pulling a scam on a local. When caught, guns are pulled out and people are shot. Yuddy and the sailor make a run for it, over the roofs, jumping into a train headed they know not where.

At this point the sailor says in disgust, ''Not everyone's like you—nothing better to do in life!''

The dreamy, tall jungles of Philippines pass by, pass by. ''I've heard of bird, a bird without legs, that flies and flies and never lands,'' says the wounded Yuddy. ''It only lands once in his life—and that's when he dies.''

The movie ends with a non sequitur in a small, low-ceiled flat, a dapper fellow (Tony Leung Chiu-wei) finishes filing his nails, gets dressed, and tucks cigarettes and a huge wad of bills into his pockets. He turns off the lights and exits. We have never seen this character before. This is the gambler—who was supposed to feature in part two of *Days of Being Wild*, but since part one went overtime and overbudget, part two was never made.

Though *Days of Being Wild* is a pleasure to watch and carries one along its melancholic, fragmented rhythm, one feels a certain emptiness after it's over. The film is more style than substance, favouring mood and mannerisms over plot and characterization.

The work announced Wong as one of the outstanding film stylist to emerge from Hong Kong in this decade. Commercially, it proved a flop, but it won five awards at the Hong Kong Film Awards, including Best Film, Best Director, Best Actor for Leslie Cheung, Best Cinematographer for Christopher Doyle, and Best Art Direction for William Cheung. On the international film festival circuits, it has become a cult favourite.

—Scarlet Cheng

AI NO CORRIDA

(In the Realm of the Senses)

France-Japan, 1976

Director: Nagisa Oshima

Production: Argos Films (Paris), Oshima Productions (Tokyo), and Océanique Productions (some sources list Shibatu Organization as one of the production companies involved); Eastmancolor, 35mm, Vistavision; running time: 110 minutes, some versions 115 minutes. Released 1976. Filmed in Japan.

Producer: Anatole Dauman; **screenplay:** Nagisa Oshima; **photography:** Hideo Itoh; **editor:** Keiichi Uraoka; **art director:** Shigemasa Toda; **music:** Minoru Miki; **lighting:** Ken'ichi Okamoto.

Cast: Tatsuya Fuji (*Kichizo*); Eiko Matsuda (*Sada Abe*); Aoi Nakajima; Taiji Tonoyama (*Tramp*); Kanae Kobayashi; Akiko Koyama; Naomi Shiraishi; Machiko Aoki; Kyoko Okada; Yasuko Matsui; Katsue Tomiyama.

Awards: Best Director, Cannes Film Festival, 1978.

Publications

Books:

Bock, Audie, *Japanese Film Directors*, New York, 1978; revised edition, Tokyo, 1985.

Oshima, Nagisa, *Ecrits (1956–1978): Dissolution et jaillissement*, Paris, 1980.

Tessier, Max, editor, *Le cinéma Japonais au présent 1959–1979*, Paris, 1980.

Ai no corrida

Sato, Tadao, *Currents in Japanese Cinema* (in English), Tokyo, 1982.
Magrelli, Enrico, and Emanuela Martini, *Il rito, il rivolta: Il cinema di Nagisa Oshima*, Rome, 1984.
Polan, Dana B., *The Political Language of Film and the Avant-Garde*, Ann Arbor, Michigan, 1985.
Danvers, Louis, and Charles Tatum, *Nagisa Oshima*, Paris, 1986.
Turim, Maureen, *The Films of Nagisa Oshima; Images of a Japanese Iconoclast*, Berkeley, 1998.

Articles:

Bonitzer, P., in *Cahiers du Cinéma* (Paris), March-April 1976. *Positif* (Paris), May 1976.
Bernheim, N. L., ''Entretien avec Nagisa Oshima,'' in *Cinématographe* (Paris), June 1976.
Monty, Ib, in *Kosmorama* (Copenhagen), no. 132, 1976.
Zimmer, J., in *Image et Son* (Paris), September 1976.
''Special Issue'' of *Filmcritica* (Rome), September 1976.
Cinema Papers (Melbourne), September-October 1976.
Bonitzer, P., ''L'Essence du pire,'' in *Cahiers du Cinéma* (Paris), September-October 1976.
Rayns, Tony, in *Film Comment* (New York), September-October 1976.
Eder, Richard, in *New York Times*, 1 October 1976.
Interview with Nagisa Oshima in *New York Times*, 3 October 1976.
Bonnet, J. C., in *Cinématographe* (Paris), October-November 1976.
Passek, J. L., in *Cinéma* (Paris), November 1976.
McCormick, R., in *Cineaste* (New York), Winter 1976–77.
Silverman, M., in *Film Quarterly* (Berkeley), Winter 1976–77.
Bouras, J., ''In the Realm of the Censors,'' in *Film Comment* (New York), January-February 1977.
Berman, B., in *Take One* (Montreal), March 1977.
Heath, Stephen, ''The Question Oshima,'' in *Wide Angle* (Athens, Ohio), no. 1, 1978.
High, P. B., ''Oshima: A Vita Sexualis on Film,'' in *Wide Angle* (Athens, Ohio), no. 4, 1978.
Dawson, Jan, in *Monthly Film Bulletin* (London), May 1978.
Oshima, Nagisa, in *Cahiers du Cinéma* (Paris), May 1978.
Grossini, G., in *Cinema Nuovo* (Turin), June 1979.
Oshima, Nagisa, ''Le Drapeau de l'eros flotte dans les cieux,'' in *Cahiers du Cinéma* (Paris), March 1980.
Garroni, E., and A. Balzola, ''Le funzioni della critica e la critica dell' erotismo,'' in *Cinema Nuovo* (Bari), April 1980.

Oshima, Nagisa, and others, in *Contracampo* (Madrid), July—August 1980.
Frias, I. Leon, ''El ascetismo erotico de *El imperio de los sentidos*,'' in *Hablemos de Cine* (Lima), May 1982.
Polan, Dana, ''Politics as Process in Three Films by Nagisa Oshima,'' in *Film Criticism* (Meadville, Pennsylvania), Fall 1983.
Tesson, C., ''L'Image et son écho,'' in *Cahiers du Cinéma* (Paris), April 1984.
Lehman, P., ''Oshima,'' in *Filmihullu* (Helsinki), no. 5. 1989.
Novielli, R., ''L'impero dei dissensi nei film di Nagisa Oshima,'' in *Quaderni di Cinema* (Florence), May-August 1989.
Turim, Maureen, ''Wie es ist, nicht mehr jung zu sein: Sex, Tod und Leben,'' in *Frauen und Film* (Frankfurt am Main), June 1991.
Iskusstvo Kino (Moscow), July 1992.
Breillat, Catherine, ''L'empire des sens: Nagisa Oshima,'' in *Cahiers du Cinéma* (Paris), 1993.
Piazzo, Philippe, ''Le scandaleux de Tokyo,'' in *Télérama* (Paris), 2 October 1996.
Marran, Christine, ''Cinematic Sexualities: The Two Faces of Abe Sada in Japanese 'poruno' films,'' in *Asian Cinema* (Drexel Hill), vol. 8, no. 2, Winter 1996–1997.

* * *

The first film to break down the barriers between the commercial art film and hard-core pornography, the all-explicit *Ai no corrida* was for Japanese director Nagisa Oshima both a political and a psycho-cultural exploration. In keeping with his consistent treatment of sensitive issues in the guise of dramatic films, Oshima conceived this project at the suggestion of French producer Anatole Dauman to do a hard-core film. Immediately subsequent to the abolition of anti-obscenity laws in France, *Corrida* was the sensation of the 1976 Cannes International Film Festival, where an unprecedented thirteen screenings were mounted to meet the demand. Shot entirely in Japan, where police ordinarily seize in the developing laboratory films revealing so much as a pubic hair, the exposed footage was sent to France for processing. When re-imported to Japan as a French production, with every explicit scene air-brushed into white haze by the censors, it was nevertheless hailed as the first porno film for women. Oshima was therefore arrested and prosecuted for obscenity in the screenplay, which had been published in book form in Japan. After four years in court, he was found innocent by the supreme court, but he did not succeed in overturning the legal concept of obscenity.

Like all of Oshima's films, *Corrida* is based on a true story, the apprehension of Sada Abe, who strangled her lover with his consent and then cut off his genitals in 1936, months before Japan's full-scale aggression against China would open World War II. The appearance of Japanese flags and marching soldiers elucidate a background theme of sexuality as escape from political and social oppression, one of Oshima's persistent concerns.

Corrida is an exploration of the limits of sexuality. Sada (Eiko Matsuda) and Kichizo (Tatsuya Fuji) gradually reject the outside world in order to pursue the ultimate in sexual pleasure. Couched in a linear narrative with few but important stylistic deviations from a conventional exposition, the sexual exploits quickly lose any prurient quality. These lovers are too analytical; they comment too much; they allow and seek out too much intrusion upon their acts. Finally, they develop too much need for violence to stimulate themselves as over-indulgence dulls the pleasure. The desire to possess another person ends in Kichizo's death.

The major reversal of the conventions of the porno film lie in Kichizo's aim of giving pleasure to Sada. She gradually changes from addressing him as ''master'' (of the inn where she has worked as a maid) to adopting male speech and giving him orders. Some psychiatrists have seen this as a calculated role reversal, in which Kichizo takes on first a passive quality, then a maternal aspect for Sada. Indeed Sada becomes the aggressor, initiator and possessor in every sense. But Oshima characteristically ends the film without any comment but the historical facts: Sada was arrested with Kichizo's genitalia on her person, tried and jailed for murder. But she became celebrated as a folk heroine.

Aside from the universal interest of the possession urge in sexuality, Oshima layers his film with cultural references. He uses the formula of the Kabuki theater, the lovers' journey (michiyuki, as they go to the inn that will be their refuge and site of the murder) to presage a doomed alliance. He taps the rich pornographic history of feudal Japan in the voyeurism, exploitation, and sado-masochistic play of the geisha and maids at the inns, and he mocks the elaborate ritual of the Japanese wedding ceremony. Use of traditional Japanese musical instruments on the sound track, lush color photography even in the confinement of the small inn room, and superb acting from non-stars and amateurs add to the disturbing appeal of this psychological landmark of the cinema.

—Audie Bock

AKALER SANDHANE

(In Search of Famine)

India, 1981

Director: Mrinal Sen

Production: D.K Films Enterprise; colour; running time: 131 minutes (also 124 minute and 115 minute version); language: Bengali. First public screening 12 February 1982. Filmed on location in Hatui and neighboring villages, Bengal.

Producer: Dhiresh Kumar Chakraborty; **screenplay:** Mrinal Sen, from a novel by Amalendu Chakraborty; **photography:** K.K. Mahajan; **editor:** Gangadhar Naskar; **art direction:** Suresh Chandra; **music:** Salil Chowdhury.

Cast: Dhritiman Chaterjee (*Director*); Smita Patil (*Actress*); Sreela Majumdar (*Woman*); Gita Sen (*Widow*); Dipankar Dey (*Star*).

Awards: Silver Bear, Berlin 1981.

Publications

Script:

Sen, Mrinal, *In Search of Famine: a film by Mrinal Sen*, script reconstructed and translated by Bandyopadhyay, Samik: Calcutta, 1983.

Akaler Sandhane

Books:

Bandyopadhyay, Samik, editor, *In Search of Famine*, Calcutta, 1983.
Cunha, Uma da, *The New Generation: 1960–1980*, New Delhi, 1981.
Hood, John W., *Chasing the Truth*, Calcutta, 1993.
Mukhopadhyay, Deepankar, *Maverick Maestro Mrinal Sen*, Indus Publishing Company, 1995.

Articles:

Guha, Jagannath, ''Films and Famine: On Mrinal Sen's Search for Famine'' in *Maadhyam* (New Delhi), March/April 1981.
Hoberman, Jim, ''New Delhi's Film Bazaar'' in *American Film* (New York), Vol. 6 no. 7, May 1981.
Chakravarty, Sumita S., ''An Interview with Mrinal Sen'' in *Cine-Tracts* (Quebec), Summer/Autumn 1981.
Malcolm, Derek, ''Guerilla Fighter: Mrinal Sen'' in *Sight and Sound* (London), Autumn 1981.
Ciment, Michel, ''Entretien avec Mrinal Sen'' in *Positif* (Paris), January 1982.
Sen, Mrinal, ''Towards Another Moment of Truth'' interview with Swapan Mullick in *Cinema in India*, Vol. 1 no. 4, October-December 1987.

* * *

Mrinal Sen's self-critical film, and one of his best known 1980s productions, shows the experiences of a contemporary film unit going into a Bengali village to fictionally reconstruct the 1943 man-made Bengal famine. The director describes that tragedy: ''. . . in our country, in Bengal, still undivided, not a shot was fired, not a bomb burst. And yet in a year five million people starved to death. They just starved and dropped dead.''

The 1943 Bengal famine—one of pre-independent India's most horrifying human disasters—has been the subject of considerable literature and several plays and films. One of the reasons for so much literature is that, in a real sense, the event remains impossible to assimilate or even understand. An estimated five million people died through starvation (official figures in 1945 put the figure at 1.5 million). It was as a consequence of war profiteering, a complacent state administration that refused to acknowledge a crisis until the famine was a reality, and a quiescent peasantry that refused to rise up in revolt.

In 1943 the Indian Peoples' Theatre Association made its debut with the epochal production of Bijon Bhattacharya's *Nabanna*, addressing the famine. This play, staged by Sombhu Mitra, remains one of the landmarks for the modern Indian theatre. In 1960 Mrinal Sen himself made a film set in the famine, *Baishey Shravana* (*The Wedding Day*), and in 1973 Satyajit Ray adapted a Bibhutibhushan Bandyopadhyay story to make *Ashani Sanket* (*Distant Thunder*). This was not the only famine to hit the region, as *Akaler Sandhaney*'s film unit shows when they play the game of guessing from photographs which year the corpses could have come from. But the extent of the literature, theatre and cinema that address the 1943 event is an important sub-text for the film, which critiques that body of work as much as it critiques itself and its maker.

There are three sets of histories that weave into the plot: the film unit arrives in Hatui on 7 September (presumably the day Sen's own unit began filming) and quickly has problems. The unit's own professional unconcern for the issues their production seeks to address culminate in the actress Devika plucking her eyebrows and cutting her hair short, and being summarily expelled from the cast. The second history features the village itself, invaded by mass culture including a Communist Jatra (Bengal has had a Communist government in power since 1967) which has taken to ''Hitler, Lenin and Stalin'' in the words of Haren, loudspeakers advertising *The Guns of Navarone*, and the film unit which promptly buys up all the food from the village and is accused of starting a new famine. Some villagers, led by Haren (played by noted filmmaker Rajen Tarafdar), try to cooperate with the crew, but divisions erupt when Haren tries to get Chatterjee's daughter to replace the expelled Devika as an actress (because the role is that of a woman reduced to prostitution during the famine). The schoolmaster has to remind Chatterjee, and other local notables, that they were themselves descendants of 1943 war profiteers. The third, and the most poignant, is that of the dying Zamindar and his wife, in whose abandoned mansion the crew lives: this story is juxtaposed with that of Durga, who forms the only living memory of the tragedy of 1943, and whose intimations of the future—the ''flash-forward'' death of her son—making up the end of the film (as the crew returns to Calcutta, their film unfinished).

Mrinal Sen is of course best known for his late 1960s and 1970s style, of a freewheeling, politically involved and didactic cinema using numerous alienation-effects that he once described as ''playing around with tools as often as I could, as a child plays with building blocks. Partly out of sheer playfulness, partly out of necessity, also partly to shock a section of our audiences [to violate the] outrageously conformist . . . mainstream of our cinema.'' (''Towards Another Moment of Truth,'' 1987). The style changed dramatically with *Ek Din Pratidin* (1979), a relatively straightforward tale with a minimal plot—in which a middle-class woman ''disappears'' for a night—into a realist idiom usually set in Calcutta's middle-class, where a large number of characters would respond in various tell-tale ways to an event that disrupts their lives and values for the brief period (*Chaalchitra*, 1981; *Kharij*, 1982) before normalcy returns.

Akaler Sandhaney is the most ambitious of this genre. The story here too is straightforward, but the numerous disruptions on the soundtrack, the playful effects of several Bengali and Hindi (Smita Patil) actors and Sen regulars playing themselves, and the freeze-frame ending on Durga, is more reminiscent of his late 1970s Calcutta trilogy, more inclined to break out of linear dramatic idioms.

—Ashish Rajadhyaksha

AKASEN CHITAI

(Street of Shame)

Japan, 1956

Director: Kenji Mizoguchi

Production: Daiei Kyoto; black & white; running time: 94 minutes. Released 18 March 1956, Japan. Filmed at Daiei Studios in Tokyo.

Producer: Masaichi Nagata; **screenplay:** Masashige Narusawa, from the short story ''Susaki No Onna'' by Yoshiko Shibaki; **photography:** Kazuo Miyagawa; **sound:** Mitsuo Hasagawa; **art director:** Hiroshi Mizutani; **music:** Toshiro Mayuzumi.

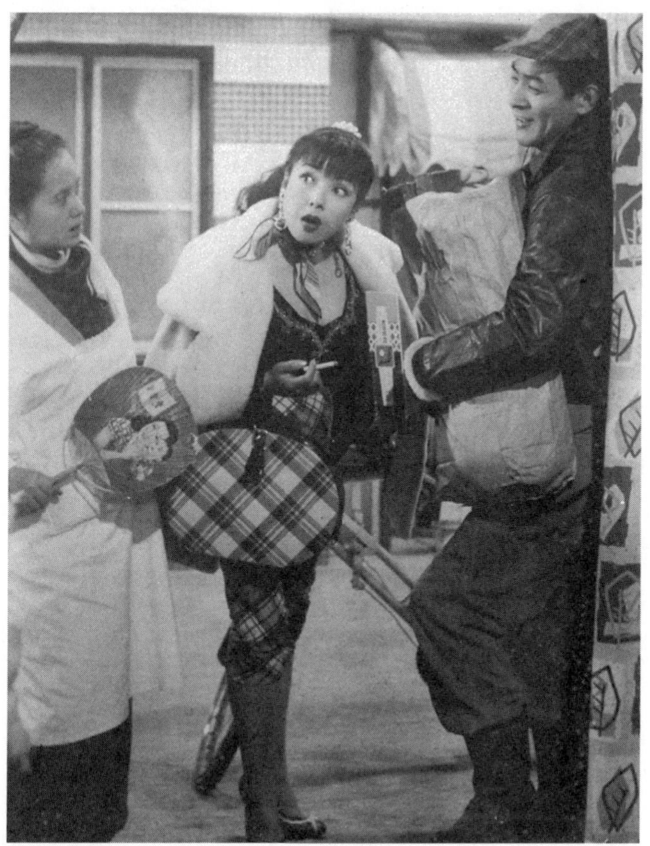

Akasen Chitai

Cast: Machiko Kyo (*Mickey*); Aiko Mimasu (*Yumeko*); Ayako Wakao (*Yasumi*); Michiyo Kogure (*Hanae*); Yasuko Kawakami (*Shizuko*); Eitoro Shindo (*Kurazo Taya*); Kenji Sugawara (*Eikoh*); Bontaro Miake (*Patrolman*); Toranosuke Ogawa (*Mickey's father*); Kumeko Urabe (*Otane*); Sadako Sawamura (*Tatsuko Taya*); Hiroko Machida (*Yorie*).

Publications

Books:

Mesnil, Michel, *Mizoguchi Kenji,* Paris, 1965.
Douchet, Jean, *Connaissance de Kenji Mizoguchi*, Paris, 1978.
McDonald, Keiko, *Kenji Mizoguchi*, Boston, 1984.
Serceau, Daniel, *Mizoguchi: de la revolte aux songes*, Paris, 1983.
Andrew, Dudley, in *Magill's Survey of Cinema - Foreign Language Films, volume 6*, edited by Magill, Frank, New Jersey, 1985.

Articles:

Yamauchi, Matsuo, ''Street of Shame and Objective Depiction'' in *Eiga Hyoron* (Tokyo), June 1956.
Variety (New York), 25 July 1956.
Takizawa, Osamu, ''Watered-down Sake: Kenji Mizoguchi's Street of Shame'' in *Eiga Geijutsu* (Tokyo), September 1956.
Izawa, Jun, in *Shinario* (Tokyo), October 1956.
Lane, John Francis, in *Films and Filming* (London), November 1956.
Rhomer, Eric, ''Rue de la Honte'' in *Arts* (Paris), no. 642, 1957.
Demonsablon, Phillipe, ''Plus de Lumiere'' in *Cahiers du Cinéma* (Paris), December 1957.
Gillett, John, in *Sight and Sound* (London), Spring 1958.
Gortori, Carlos, in *Film Ideal* (Madrid), January 1965.
Tessier, Max, ''La Rue de la Honte'' in *Image et Son* (Paris), September 1980.
Magny, Joel, ''Le Testament de Mizoguchi?'' in *Cinéma* (Paris), October 1980.
Masson, Alain, ''L'ordre du bordel'' in *Positif* (Paris), November 1980.
Burdeau, Emmanuel & others, ''Mizoguchi encore,'' in *Cahiers du Cinéma* (Paris), July-August 1996.

* * *

Everyone interested in Japanese film must be deeply indebted to Noel Burch's *To the Distant Observer: Form and Meaning in Japanese Cinema*—but indebted more for the questions his strictly formalist analyses raise than for the tendentious and problematic answers. At their root is Burch's antagonism to Hollywood and American cultural imperialism: films are valued or not according to their deviation from the shooting/editing codes of classical Hollywood cinema. As far as Mizoguchi is concerned, Burch's interest is restricted to certain films of the 30s and 40s; everything subsequent is dismissed.

Street of Shame, Mizoguchi's last film, raises interesting questions about the relation between form and meaning: it reverts to the thematics of the 30s and 40s, realized in the stylistics of the 50s. Clearly well outside Burch's range of interest, it contains not a single shot that would be out of place in a classical Hollywood movie (while retaining the dominant characteristics of Mizoguchi's late period: fairly long takes, with much use of camera movement, depth of field, and much use of foreground/background simultaneous action).

My own position is that a film should be evaluated not according to its formal devices (deviant or otherwise) but according to its totality: the richness and complexity of meaning that has been realized in the interaction of all its elements, thematic, stylistic, political. *Street of Shame* is the last in the series of impassioned feminist protests that (in forms varying sharply from period to period) traverses Mizoguchi's entire career as far as we can know it (many early films are lost). One may compare it, then, with two earlier films: *Sisters of the Gion* (1936, admired by Burch) and *My Love Has been Burning* (1949, ignored, hence presumably dismissed). The former is built upon a system of extremely long takes, mainly in long shot, mainly static, employing only one or two brief camera movements whose function is to hold us back from, rather than draw us toward, the characters. The latter also employs very long takes, often sequence-shots, but their function is entirely different: there is a great deal of camera movement, much less camera distance, and most of the scenes end with the camera leading us in toward the heroine, the scene embodying a lesson she has learned and that we share with her. The earlier film is built upon distanciation (there is no character with whom we can identify, we are to see all of them, male and female, trapped within and corrupted by a specific social system); the latter is built upon a subtle and beautifully realized form of identification, the heroine being an exemplary feminist figure whose progress toward a full awareness of the oppression of women within patriarchal culture we are invited to share.

Street of Shame, rather than restrict itself to an imposed formal system, adopts the relative freedom and flexibility (within certain limitations, certain agreed or defined rules, without which communicative art is not possible) of classical Hollywood: the camera is free to move from character to character, position to position (so long as the basic rules are not shattered), in the interests of maximum expressivity. The result (common in classical Hollywood) is the achievement of a balance between distance and identification. We follow, over a period of a few months, the lives of five women working as prostitutes in a brothel in Tokyo's Yoshiwara district. All are presented with varying degrees of sympathy, but the constant movement among the various characters and plot-threads forbids full identification, leaving us a degree of freedom of judgment. That sympathy is not (or is only barely) extended to the male characters is a logical consequence of the rigorous and unrelenting way in which every manifestation of women's oppression is exposed.

Hanae works to support her tubercular husband and their infant son; the husband (the least *un*sympathetic of the male characters) rewards her efforts to hold the family together by attempting suicide. Yumeko has resorted to prostitution to see her son through college; *her* reward is his shame and rage, and his total rejection of her when (entering middle age) she suggests they live together. Yorie leaves the brothel to marry, only to discover that her husband treats her as an unpaid servant; Mickey, outwardly tough, gum-chewing, westernized, is rebelling against a father who sees women merely as the adjuncts of ''respectability'' to aid his rise in the business world. When he visits the brothel to bring her home (he has married one of his numerous mistresses within months of his wife's death, and needs Mickey to reconstruct a family), her facade collapses and she expresses her vulnerability and rage, finally offering herself to him for money as the ultimate expression of contempt. Only Yasumi escapes the brothel, through a process of cultivating total ruthlessness, exploiting not only men but the women she works with in order to build up the capital she needs.

The last minutes of the film introduce a new character, a teenage country girl whose father has become paralyzed after a mining accident. She is at first naively delighted by the food she is given, unlike any she has eaten before. The film ends with her night of initiation (replacing Yasumi, who has bought up a bankrupt clothing business). We watch her being dressed, groomed, made up, her innocent young face vanishing behind a mask of paint and powder. The film's devastating last image, and its only single-character close-up, has her hovering, terrified, behind a pillar, trying to find the courage to signal to her first prospective customer.

—Robin Wood

L'ALBERO DEGLI ZOCCOLI

(The Tree of the Wooden Clogs)

Italy, 1978

Director: Ermanno Olmi

Production: RAI (Rete I)-Italnoleggio Cinematografico; Gevacolor, 35mm; running time: 175 minutes. Released 1978, Cannes Film Festival. Filmed on location in Lombardy, Italy; cost: lire 320,000,000.

Producer: Attilio Torricelli; **screenplay:** Ermanno Olmi; **photography:** Ermanno Olmi; **editor:** Ermanno Olmi; **sound:** Amedeo Casati; **art director:** Enrico Tovaglieri; **music:** J. S. Bach, executed on the organ by Fernando Germani; **costume designer:** Francesca Zucchelli.

Cast: Luigi Ornagli (*Batisti*); Francesca Moriggi (*Baptisti's wife*); Omar Brignoli (*Minek, the son*); Antonio Ferrari (*Toni*); Teresa Brecianini (*Widow Runc*); Giuseppe Brignoli (*Grandpa Anselmo*); Carlo Rota (*Peppino*); Pasqualina Brolis (*Teresina*); Massimo Fratus (*Pierino*); Francesca Villa (*Annetta*); Maria Grazia Caroli (*Bettina*); Battista Trevaina (*Finard*); Giuseppina Sangaletti (*Mrs. Finard*); Lorenzo Pedroni (*Grandpa Finard*); Felice Cervi (*Usti*); Pierangelo Bertoli (*Secondo*); Brunella Migliaccio (*Olga*); Franco Pilenga (*Stefano, Maddalena's husband*); Guglielmo Badoni and Laura Locatelli (*Stefano's parents*); Carmelo Silva (*Don Carlo*); Mario Brignoli (*Landowner*); Emilio Pedroni (*Farm Bailiff*); Vittorio Cappelli (*Frichi*); Francesca Bassurini (*Suor Maria*); Lina Ricci (*Woman of the ''Segno''*).

Awards: Palme d'Or, Cannes Film Festival, 1978; David of Donatello special plaque award to Olmi, Italy, 1978; New York Film Critics Award, Best Foreign Film, 1979.

Publications

Script:

''A facida faja: rezletch a forzatokonyvbol'' (script extract), in *Filmkultura* (Budapest), January-February 1979.

Books:

Olmi, Ermanno, *L'albero degli zoccoli*, Bergamo, 1979.
Dell'Acqua, Gian Piero, *L'albero degli zoccoli nell'Italia 1978*, Milan, 1979.
Dillon, Jeanne, *Ermanno Olmi*, Florence, 1986.

Articles:

Ahlander, L., ''Traskor och diktatorer Rapport fran Cannes 78,'' in *Chaplin* (Stockholm), no. 157, 1978.
Devillers, M., and others, ''Ermanno Olmi,'' in *Cinématographe* (Paris), no. 40, 1978.
Prono, F., in *Cinema Nuovo* (Bari), July-August 1978.
Masson, A., and others, in *Positif* (Paris), September 1978.
Zambetti, S., ''La realta contadina del Bergamasco nel film di Olmi e nei dati storici,'' in *Cineforum* (Bergamo), November 1978.
Borseno, C., in *Revue du Cinéma* (Paris), series 23, 1979.
McCormick, R., in *Cineaste* (New York), no. 4, 1979.
Bonneville, L., in *Séquences* (Montreal), April 1979.
Salje, G., in *Film und Ton* (Munich), May 1979.
Coleman, John, in *New Statesman* (London), 11 May 1979.
Castell, D., in *Films Illustrated* (London), June 1979.
D'Elia, G., ''Angeli e peccatori nell' *Albero degli zoccoli*,'' in *Cineforum* (Bergamo), June 1979.
Pym, John, in *Monthly Film Bulletin* (London), June 1979.
Seesslen, G., ''Das Land verliert, die Stadt gewinnt, der Bauer wird vertrieben,'' in *Film und Ton* (Munich), June 1979.
Canby, Vincent, in *New York Times*, 1 June 1979.

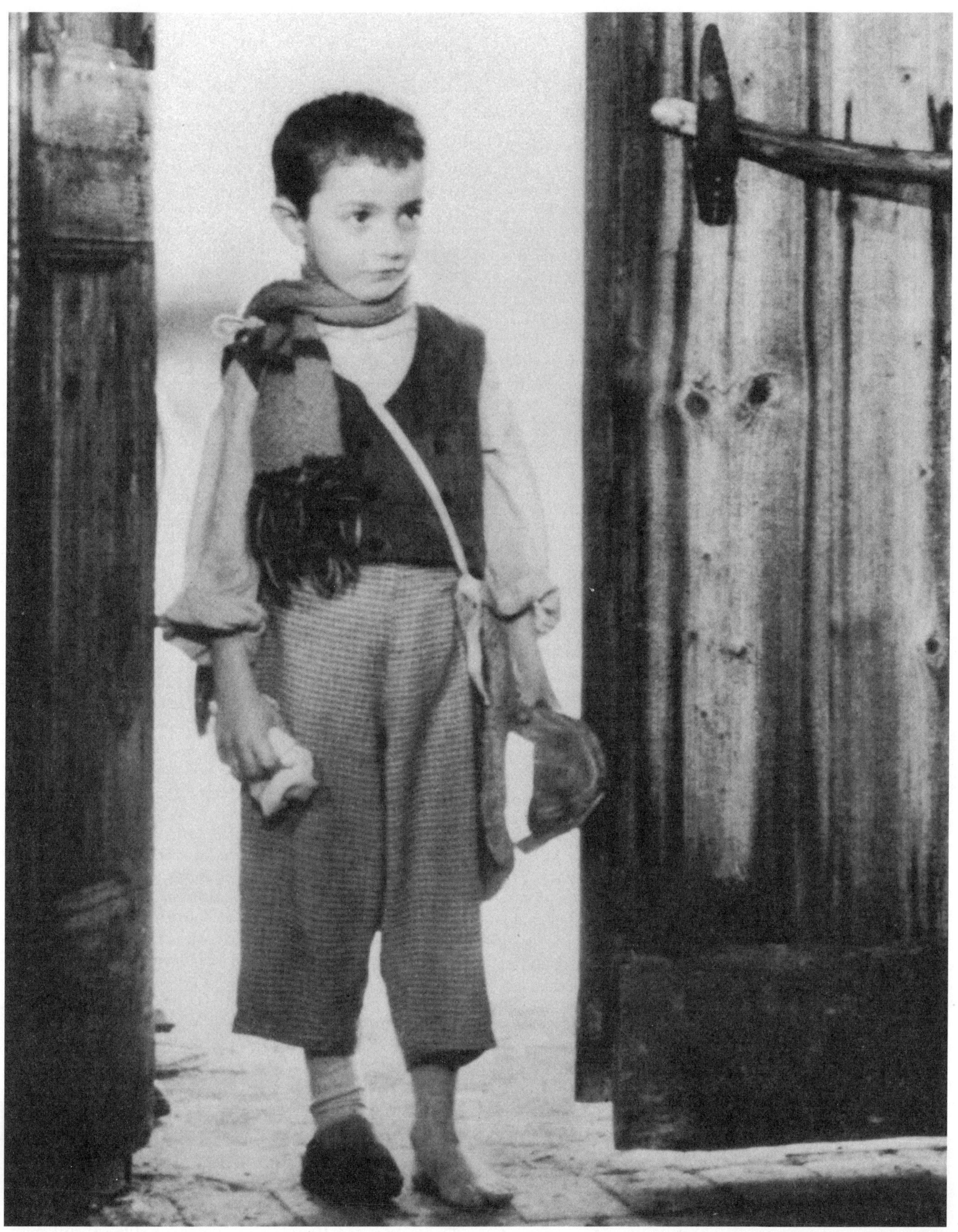

L'Albero degli zoccoli

Kauffmann, Stanley, "Curious Career," in *New Republic* (New York), 2 June 1979.
Sarris, Andrew, in *Village Voice* (New York), 4 June 1979.
Kroll, Jack, "An Italian Classic," in *Newsweek* (New York), 4 June 1979.
Gill, Brendan, in *New Yorker*, 18 June 1979.
Martin R., in *Films in Review* (New York), August-September 1979.
Simon, John, "The Soil and the Soiled," in *National Revue* (New York), 3 August 1979.
Gladych, Michael B., in *Film Quarterly* (Berkeley), Winter 1980–81.
Hirshfield, C., in *Film and History* (Newark, New Jersey), February 1981.
Leigh, Mike, "L'arbre aux sabots," in *Positif* (Paris), June 1994.

* * *

At the same time, Italy produced two films about peasant life at the turn of the century: Bertolucci's *1900* and Olmi's *Tree of the Wooden Clogs*, yet Olmi's work received more unqualified praise and caused more fierce debate than did the opus of his younger colleague. After *Tree* won the Golden Palm at Cannes, there were those who declared it a masterpiece, a supreme vision of beauty and poetry, a profoundly humanist testament. The film didn't deal directly with history; it was history. Other critics viewed it as an egocentric and myopic vision, dealing with personal nostalgia, negating historical and social issues, and taking refuge in a strict Catholicism. Everyone, no matter what their ideological bias, did agree that it was an exceedingly beautiful work of formal perfection. With this, his ninth feature, Olmi shared the limelight that had not been his since the time of *Il posto* and *I fidanzati. Tree of the Wooden Clogs* belongs to the finest works of the tradition of cinematic realism. Olmi has stated that the masters who had greatly influenced him were Robert Flaherty (especially *Louisiana Story* and *Man of Aran*) and Roberto Rossellini. One could add Georges Rouquier's study of French Catholic farmers in *Farrebique* and Luchino Visconti's epic-length film on Sicilian fishermen, *La terra trema.* In regard to this tradition, Olmi's film has both similarities and differences. Like all the above, Olmi feels a deep dedication to his work and often spends years carefully choosing his subject matter and planning each film project. Olmi had conceived the idea 20 years before he realized this film; he had based his subject on stories told to him by his grandfather. For the film, like Visconti, Olmi spent months living in villages and interviewing thousands of peasants, a score of which became the principal actors of the film. Olmi began without a definite script; the actions and dialogue came from the actors themselves. Rare to Italian cinema, Olmi insisted upon shooting with direct sound and utilizing only the Bergamesque dialect, although, like Visconti in 1948, marketing difficulties demanded that Olmi produce a version in Italian as well. In this case, however, the Italian version was dubbed by the actors themselves. Olmi obtained a completely natural performance from his characters who are all framed in centrally based compositions in the film. Although there are many close-ups, the eyes of the characters are rarely aimed directly at the camera and thus do not confront the spectator. The richly saturated colors—russets, deep greens, browns, and tans—are earth tones natural to the countryside and peasant life.

Except in a few isolated cases, the Italian cinema has rarely dealt directly with the peasantry, but Olmi has added nothing extra to what would normally occur in the pre-industrial countryside. As in the best of the realist tradition, all shooting was done on location and natural lighting prevails. Contrary to Rossellini and Visconti, and much closer to Rouquier, for example, is the fact that almost nothing happens in the film. Given its episodic nature that follows seasonal changes in the lives of five families in Lombardy, the highlights are the birth of a baby, the slaughtering of a pig, the discovery of a gold coin in the dirt, a couple's honeymoon trip on a barge to Milan, and a father who cuts down a tree in order to make a sandal for his son, from whence comes the film's title. One particular scene caused much of the divided critical opinion—the miracle of the cow. A woman's cow is ill; she prays for it and it miraculously regains its health. Olmi here stressed the primacy of religious faith; a Catholicism which offered a world of culture and learning to the peasantry as well as providing a source of magic and myth, symbols and stories.

—Elaine Mancini

ALEXANDER NEVSKY

USSR, 1938

Director: Sergei Eisenstein

Production: Mosfilm; black and white, 35mm; length: 3044 meters. Released 23 November 1938. Filmed June through November 1938 in Moscow.

Scenario: Sergei Eisenstein and Pyotr Pavlenko; **collaborating director:** D. J. Vasiliev; **photography:** Edward Tisse; **editor:** Sergei Eisenstein; **sound:** B. Volsky and V. Popov; **production design:** Isaac Shpinel, Nikolai Soloviov, and K. Yeliseyev from Eisenstein's sketches; **music:** Sergei Prokofiev; **costume designers:** Isaac Shpinel, Nikolai Soloviov, and K. Yeliseyev from Eisenstein's sketches; **consultant on work with actors:** Elena Telesheva.

Cast: Nikolai Cherkasov (*Prince Alexander Yaroslavich Nevsky*); Nikolai Okhlopkov (*Vasili Busali*); Alexander Abrikosov (*Gavrilo Oleksich*); Dmitri Orlov (*Ignat, Master Armorer*); Vasili Novikov (*Pavsha, Governor of Pskov*); Nikolai Arsky (*Domash Tverdislavich*); Vera Ivasheva (*Olga, a Novogorod girl*); Varvarra Massalitinova (*Amelfa Timofeyevna*); Anna Danilova (*Vasilisa, a girl of Pskov*); Vladimir Yershov (*Von Blak, Grand Master of the Livonian Order*); Sergei Blinnikov (*Tverdilo, traitorous Mayor of Pskov*); Ivan Lagutin (*Ananias*); Lev Fenin (*Bishop*); Naum Rogozhin (*Black-robed Monk*).

Awards: Order of Lenin award, Soviet Union, 1939.

Publications

Script:

Eisenstein: 3 Films, edited by Jay Leyda, New York, 1974.

Books:

Rotha, Paul, and others, *Eisenstein 1898–1948*, London, 1948.
Eisenstein, Sergei, *Film Form*, New York, 1949.
Eisenstein, Sergei, *Notes of a Film Director*, London, 1959.
Leyda, Jay, *Kino*, London, 1960.

Alexander Nevsky

Mitry, Jean, *S. M. Eisenstein*, Paris, 1961.
Konlecher and Kubelka, editors, *Sergei Michailowitsch Eisenstein*, Vienna, 1964.
Moussinac, Léon, *Sergei Eisenstein*, New York, 1970.
Martin, Marcel, and others, *The Complete Works of Sergei Eisenstein*, New York, 1971.
Barna, Yon, *Eisenstein*, Bloomington, Indiana, 1974.
Fernandez, Dominique, *Eisenstein*, Paris, 1975.
Sudendorf, W., and others, *Sergei M. Eisenstein: Materialien zu Leben und Werk*, Munich, 1975.
Weise, E., editor, *Sergei M. Eisenstein in Selbstzeugnissen und Bilddokumenten*, Reinbek, 1975.
Eisenstein, Sergei, *Film Sense*, New York, 1975.
Swallow, Norman, *Eisenstein: A Documentary Portrait*, New York, 1977.
Seton, Marie, *Sergei Eisenstein*, London, 1978.
Leyda, Jay, and Zina Vovnow, *Eisenstein at Work*, New York, 1982.
Eisenstein, Sergei, *Immortal Memories: An Autobiography*, Boston, 1983.
Marshall, Herbert, *Masters of the Soviet Cinema: Cripplied Creative Biographies*, London, 1983.
Polan, Dana B., *The Political Language of Film and the Avant-Garde*, Ann Arbor, Michigan, 1985.
Aumont, Jacques, *Montage Eisenstein*, London, 1987.
Eisenstein, Sergei, *Selected Works 1: Writings 1922–1934*, edited by Richard Taylor, London, 1988.
Jassenjawsky, Igor, *Von Eisenstein bis Tarkovskij; Die Malerei der Filmregisseure Russlands*, Munchen, 1990.
Goodwin, James, *Eisenstein, Cinema, & History*, Champaign, 1993.
Taylor, Richard, *S.M. Eisenstein: Writings, 1934–47,* London, 1996.
Bergan, Ronald, *Sergei Eisenstein: A Life in Conflict*, New York, 1999.

Articles:

Nugent, Frank S., in *New York Times*, 23 March 1939.
Kunitz, J., ''Eisenstein's Resurgence,'' in *New Republic* (New York), 29 March 1939.
Weinberg, Herman, in *Sight and Sound*, (London), Spring 1939.
Hoellering, F., ''Eisenstein Has Been Subordinated to the Orders of the Monolithic State,'' in *Nation* (New York), 8 April 1939.
Maddow, Ben, ''Eisenstein and the Historical Films,'' in *Hollywood Quarterly*, October 1945.
Soliski, Waclaw, ''The End of Sergei Eisenstein: Case History of an Artist under Dictatorship,'' in *Commentary* (New York), March 1949.
Kawicki, Dennis, in *Cineaste* (New York), Fall 1968.
Jurenev, R., ''Cuvstvo Rodiny,'' in *Iskusstvo Kino* (Moscow), November 1973.

Levaco, R., ''The Eisenstein-Prokofiev Correspondence,'' in *Cinema Journal* (Iowa City), Fall 1973.

Kjorup, S., in *Kosmorama* (Copenhagen), no. 136, 1977.

Roberts, P. D., ''Prokofiev's Score and Cantata for Eisenstein's *Alexander Nevsky*,'' in *Semiotica* (New York), nos. 1–2, 1977.

Gallez, Douglas W., ''The Prokofiev-Eisenstein Collaboration: *Nevsky* and *Ivan* Revisited,'' in *Cinema Journal* (Evanston, Illinois), no. 2, 1978.

Balter, L., *Film Culture* (New York), nos. 70–71, 1983.

Guilbert, Pierre, ''Ou vitrail à la scène,'' in *Cahiers de la Cinémathèque* (Perpignan), 1986.

Turner, George, ''*Alexander Nevsky* Comes Back in Style,'' in *American Cinematographer* (Los Angeles), November 1987.

Firstenberg, Jean Picker, ''*Alexander Nevsky:* A Classic Collaboration,'' in *American Film* (Washington, D.C.), November 1987.

Guneratne, A. R., ''History as Propaganda: The Portrait of Stalin as Medieval Hero and its Epic Frame,'' in *Cinefocus* (Bloomington, Indiana), no. 2, 1990.

Furie, K., ''*Nevsky* Alive and Well,'' in *New York Times*, 20 October 1991.

Merritt, Russell, ''Recharging *Alexander Nevsky:* Tracking the Eisenstein-Prokofiev War Horse,'' in *Film Quarterly* (Berkeley), Winter 1994.

Saada, N., ''Serguei Prokofiev: *Alexandre Nevski*,'' in *Cahiers du Cinéma* (Paris), nos. 127–128, 1995.

Vallerand, F., ''Musiques pour Eisenstein,'' in *Séquences* (Haute-Ville), no. 183, March/April 1996.

* * *

The cinematic works of Sergei Eisenstein demonstrate a continuous effort to explore and develop the elements of his theory of montage. Two marked phases of style and technique are evident in this development. The first phase consists of Eisenstein's silent films of the 1920s, the second is associated with his 1930s and 1940s sound films. In the first phase of his cinematic career Eisenstein introduces the formal concepts of intellectual montage, mise-en-scène, and a revolutionary new narrative concept: the portrayal of the mass as hero. With *Alexander Nevsky* Eisenstein enters a second phase in which the individual within the collective dominates the narrative, while vertical montage and pictorial composition replace intellectual montage as the primary formal devices in his films. These new techniques are not totally divorced from Eisenstein's early film methods, but have evolved from them.

The emphasis upon the individual within the collective in *Alexander Nevsky* can be seen as the maturing of the earlier concept in which the mass is portrayed as hero. Reflecting upon Soviet silent cinema, Eisenstein writes that the films are flawed in that they fail to fully represent the concept of collectivity: ''collectivism means the maximum development of the individual within the collective . . . Our first mass films missed this deeper meaning.'' In the depiction of ''the general-revolutionary slogan'' of the 1920s, the mass as hero functioned well, but to convey the more specific Communist message of the 1930s, images of leading individuals were needed.

In *Alexander Nevsky* the theme of the Russian people's patriotism is emphasized through such exemplary characters as Prince Alexander, Busali, and Gavrilo Oleksich. Even though this narrative approach resembles that of more traditional cinema, Eisenstein's characters embody patriotic ideals in such an extreme way that they become symbols rather than simple heroic personalities. The story of *Alexander Nevsky* lends itself to this larger-than-life treatment of its characters. It presents historical figures and events of such mythic proportions that, while the viewer may sympathize with the characters, he does not easily identify with them, and so the viewer is not distracted from the general theme of the film. It is intended that the ideas the characters represent will be remembered rather than their individual personalities. The characters must support, even succumb to, the dominant theme of the strength and patriotism of the Russian people.

Structuring a film so that all its individual elements are controlled by the theme is a formal concern common to both silent and sound film in Eisenstein's work. In the early silent films this formal method was referred to as overtonal montage, and dictated that all the visual images of a film, which have been developed through the use of intellectual, metric, rhythmic, and tonal montage, serve to reveal and illustrate the dominant theme. The controlling formal method in *Alexander Nevsky*, vertical montage, is much the same as overtonal, but with the additional element of sound. Vertical montage, according to Eisenstein, links different spheres of feeling—particularly the visual image with the sound image—to create a single, unified effect. The audio and visual elements are not only governed by the dominant theme of the film, but work together to convey that theme in a strongly emotional manner.

The attack of the German wedge on the Russian army in ''The Battle on the Ice'' sequence in *Alexander Nevsky* demonstrates this appeal to the emotions. The musical score contributes greatly to the pacing and emotional tone of the sequence. Changes in the pace of pictorial movement are accompanied by a corresponding rhythmic or melodic change. In addition, Eisenstein uses the combination of sound and image to suggest to the viewer things that cannot actually be seen on screen. Although this approach resembles that of intellectual montage, it functions on a more poetic or metaphorical level. For example, Eisenstein causes us to experience the leaping and pounding of horses' hooves as equivalent to the beating of an agitated heart, a heart experiencing the increasing terror of the battle on the ice.

The most obvious use of vertical montage in *Alexander Nevsky* is in the relationship throughout the film between the musical score and the pictorial composition. This relationship was developed through several different methods. For some sequences the music was written with a general theme or idea in mind. In other sequences the music was written for an already assembled visual episode. In yet other sequences, the visual images were edited to music already on the sound track. The final result of these editing methods is a connection between the visuals and the musical score that goes beyond the enhancement of the mood of a sequence. Throughout *Alexander Nevsky* Eisenstein strives for a complete correspondence between the movement of the music and the movement of the eye over the lines of the plastic composition. The same motion found within the image composition of a shot sequence can be found in the complementary musical score for that sequence. That is, the ascending or descending shape of the notes of the written musical score correspond directly to the movement of the eye over the planes of the composition within each shot of a film sequence. Although the details of this complex sound-image relationship may not be apparent while viewing *Alexander Nevsky*, what is apparent is the solidity this relationship lends to the film. The sound and visual elements combine to create a unified whole. Eisenstein states that, in comparison to the films of the 1920s, the new Soviet sound cinema appeared more traditional ''and much closer to the foreign cinema than those films that once declared war to the death against its (the foreign cinema's) very principles and methods.'' Two elements that contribute to the traditional appearance of *Alexander Nevsky* are its story and pictorial composition which are based in conventional techniques drawn from literature and painting. In the 1930s Eisenstein had become interested in the application of other art forms to film. Literature, he felt, offered ''the dramatics of subject.'' Cinema should again be concerned with story and plot—concepts Eisenstein had condemned in the 1920s—but this was not a call for a return to conventional content. Eisenstein felt that conventional forms could be utilized to present fresh content. The new story would not be centered around a traditional bourgeois hero, but would instead feature modern protagonists who represent the individual within the collective. These individuals, as we see in *Alexander Nevsky*, would embody the ideology of the proletariat.

In contrast to the photographic quality of Eisenstein's earlier films, the individual frames of *Alexander Nevsky* are reminiscent of painted battle scenes and landscapes. This is why the battle scenes may appear unrealistic: they are highly stylized, like paintings. An example of this approach is the creation of ''The Battle on the Ice.'' Not only was the composition of individual shots stylized, but the landscape itself was totally simulated. The winter battle scene was actually shot in the heat of July; the ice and snow were created with melted glass, alabaster, chalk, and salt. The appearance of the summer sky was altered with the use of a filter on the camera lens. The scene was almost literally painted on a blank canvas.

Although some critics were disappointed with Eisenstein's variations on, or departure from, his earlier methods, *Alexander Nevsky* was a success upon its release in 1938. Probably Eisenstein's most commercially popular film in his own country, it also survived the scrutiny of Joseph Stalin, earning the symbol of official government approval, the Order of Lenin, in February of 1939. Soviet and foreign critics alike applauded the film as the work which, after more than six years of unproductivity, not all of it voluntary, returned Eisenstein to his former status as one of the foremost creative talents of the Soviet cinema.

Alexander Nevsky is viewed in much the same manner today as it was upon its original release. It is not considered Eisenstein's best film but its epic qualities and cinematic achievement, and particularly the ''Battle on the Ice'' sequence, are appreciated. The concept of vertical montage, however, has come under closer scrutiny than in past years. Although critics may disagree on the extent to which the sound-image unity of vertical montage is at work in this particular film, they do seem to agree on the importance of Eisenstein's theoretical effort: he was one of the first to attempt an articulation of the relationship between sound and image in cinema.

—Marie Saeli

ALI: FEAR EATS THE SOUL

See **ANGST ESSEN SEELE AUF**

ALL ABOUT MY MOTHER

See **TODO SOBRE MI MADRE**

ALL QUIET ON THE WESTERN FRONT

USA, 1930

Director: Lewis Milestone

Production: Universal Pictures Corp.; Moviestone sound, black and white, 35mm (also silent version with synchronized music); running time: 140 minutes; length: 14 reels, 12,423 feet (with synchronized music 15 reels). Released April 1930, Los Angeles. Re-released 1939 but reduced to 10 reels; re-released 1950 in the United States; re-released 1963 in France. Filmed 1930 in Universal Studio backlots; battle scenes shot at Irvine Ranch, California.

Producer: Carl Laemmle, Jr.; **screenplay:** Dell Andrews, Maxwell Anderson, and George Abbott; **titles:** Walter Anthony, from the novel by Erich Maria Remarque; **photography:** Arthur Edeson, Karl Freund, and Tony Gaudio; **editors:** Edgar Adams and Milton Carruth; **sound technician:** William W. Hedgecock; **art directors:** Charles D. Hall and William Schmidt; **music and synchronization:** David Broekman; **recording engineer:** C. Roy Hunter; **special effects:** Frank Booth; **dialogue director:** George Cukor.

Cast: Louis Wolheim (*Katczincky*); Lew Ayres (*Paul Baumer*); John Wray (*Himmelstoss*); George (Slim) Summerville (*Tiaden*); Russell Gleason (*Muller*); Raymond Griffith (*Gerard Duval*); Ben Alexander (*Kemmerich*); Owen Davis, Jr. (*Peter*); Beryl Mercer (*Mrs. Baumer;* in silent version ZaSu Pitts is Mrs. Baumer); Joan Marsh (*Poster girl*); Yola d'Avril (*Suzanne*); Arnold Lucy (*Kantorek*); Scott Kolk (*Leer*); Walter Browne Rogers (*Behm*); Richard Alexander (*Westhus*); Renee Damonde and Poupee Andriot (*French girls*); Edwin Maxwell (*Mr. Baumer*); Harold Goodwin (*Detering*); Marion Clayton (*Miss Baumer*); G. Pat Collins (*Lieutenant Berlenck*); Bill Irving (*Ginger*); Edmund Breese (*Herr Mayer*); Heinie Conklin (*Hammacher*); Bertha Mann (*Sister Libertine*); William Bakewell (*Albert*); Bodil Rosing (*Watcher*); Tom London (*Orderly*); Vince Barnett (*Cook*); Fred Zinnemann (*Man*).

Awards: Oscars for Best Picture and Best Direction, 1929/30; American Film Institute's ''100 Years, 100 Movies,'' 1998.

Publications

Script:

Andrews, Dell, Maxwell Anderson, and George Abbott, *All Quiet on the Western Front*, in *Best American Screenplays 1*, edited by Sam Thomas, New York, 1982.

Books:

Rotha, Paul, *Celluloid: The Film Today*, London, 1931.
Higham, Charles, and Joel Greenberg, *The Celluloid Muse: Hollywood Directors Speak*, Chicago, 1969.

All Quiet on the Western Front

Tuska, John, editor, ''Lewis Milestone,'' in *Close Up: The Contract Director*, New Jersey, 1976.
Millichap, Joseph R., *Lewis Milestone*, Boston, 1981.

Articles:

Dean, Loretta K., in *American Cinematographer* (Hollywood), March 1930.
Close Up (London), March 1930.
Variety (Hollywood), 7 May 1930.
Beaton, Welford, ''Should Old Acquaintance Be Forgot?'' in *Hollywood Spectator*, 25 September 1937.
Reisz, Karel, ''Milestone and War,'' in *Sequence* (London), 1950.
Jones, Dorothy, ''War Without Glory,'' in *Quarterly of Film, Radio, and Television* (Berkeley), Spring 1954.
Cutts, John, in *Films and Filming* (London), April 1963.
Avant-Scène du Cinéma (Paris), 15 November 1963.
Spears, Jack, ''Louis Wolheim,'' in *Films in Review* (New York), March 1972.
Diehl, Digby, ''An Interview with Lewis Milestone,'' in *Action* (Los Angeles), July-August 1972.
Canham, Kingsley, ''Lewis Milestone,'' in *Henry King, Lewis Milestone, Sam Wood*, by Canham and others, London, 1974.
Schlech, Eugene P. A., ''*All Quiet on the Western Front:* A History Teacher's Reappraisal,'' in *Film and History*, December 1978.
Fox, J., in *Films and Filming* (London), April 1980.
Pym, John, in *Monthly Film Bulletin* (London), May 1980.
Weemaes, G., in *Filme en Televisie* (Brussels), May-June 1981.
Mitchell, G. J., ''Making *All Quiet on the Western Front*,'' in *American Cinematographer* (Hollywood), September 1985.
Kelly, Andrew, ''*All Quiet on the Western Front*: 'Brutal cutting, stupid censors and bigoted politicos','' in *Historical Journal of Film, Radio and Television* (Abingdon), vol. 9, no. 2, June 1989.
Whiteclay Chambers, John, III, ''*All Quiet on the Western Front* (1930): The Anti-war Film and the Image of the First World War,'' in *Historical Journal of Film, Radio and Television* (Abingdon), vol. 14, no. 4, October 1994.

* * *

All Quiet on the Western Front made Lew Ayres a star and was responsible for the start of George Cukor's screen career and the establishment of Lewis Milestone as a director of international repute. Milestone directed four further films concerned with war, notably *A Walk in the Sun*, but none measured up to *All Quiet*, and, indeed, the director never achieved the same success as this film brought. The film also boded well for the production career of Carl Laemmle, Jr., a much derided executive, who turned out a surprising number of major artistic features at his father's studio in the early through mid-1930s.

A passionate portrayal of the horror of war, the film was the first to depict the ''Hun'' as simply a scared boy. *All Quiet* can be divided into four distinct parts. The first details the enlistment of the young recruits; the second their arrival at the front; the third the various incidents of war; and, finally, the hero Paul Baumer's homecoming, his hastened return to the front, and his death. The film remains faithful to the Erich Maria Remarque novel. It was the most successful of a trio of features released at this time which take a pacifist approach to World War I, the other two being the British *Journey's End* and the German *Westfront 1918. All Quiet on the Western Front* was the first sound film to use a giant mobile crane, particularly for filming the realistically-staged battle sequences, and one of the first talkies to boast a mobility of camerawork in general. Credit for this must, of course, go to Lewis Milestone, but George Cukor's contribution to the film should not be—as it is so often—overlooked. It was Cukor who rehearsed the actors and established a neutrality to their accents which is of inestimable value in putting across the production's emotional message.

There are no real stars in *All Quiet*, with each actor giving a passionate cameo performance, be it Louis Wolheim as the brusque yet sympathetic Katczinsky, Raymond Griffith as the French soldier killed by Baumer, William Bakewell as Baumer's pal, Albert, or Beryl Mercer as Baumer's mother (a role played in the silent version by ZaSu Pitts).

Released initially in a 140-minute version. *All Quiet on the Western Front* has been successively cut through the years, until most prints today run as short as 90 or 110 minutes. These truncated versions fail to capture the film's momentum as the recruits become more and more involved in the war and its horrors. The most extraordinary edited version of the feature, however, was a 1939 reissue which included an anti-Nazi narration.

—Anthony Slide

ALL THAT HEAVEN ALLOWS

USA, 1955

Director: Douglas Sirk

Production: Universal-International; Technicolor; running time: 89 minutes; released October 1955.

Producer: Ross Hunter; **screenplay:** Peg Fenwick, from a story by Edna L. Lee and Harry Lee; **photography:** Russell Metty; **editors:** Frank Gross, Fred Baratta; **sound:** Leslie I. Carey, Joe Lapis; **art director:** Alexander Golitzen, Eric Orbom; **music supervisor:** Joseph Gershenson.

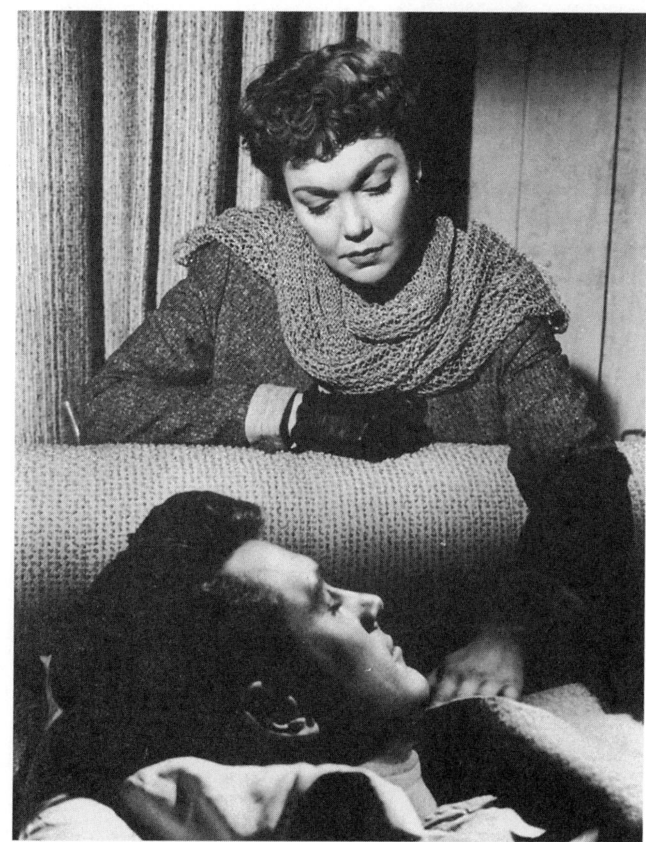

All That Heaven Allows

Cast: Jane Wyman (*Cary Scott*); Rock Hudson (*Ron Kirby*); Agnes Moorehead (*Sara Warren*); Conrad Nagel (*Harvey*); Virginia Grey (*Alida Anderson*); Gloria Talbott (*Kay Scott*); William Reynolds (*Ned Scott*); Jacqueline de Wit (*Mona Plash*); Charles Drake (*Mick Anderson*)

Publications

Books:

Halliday, Jon, *Sirk on Sirk*, London, 1971; New York, 1972.
Bourget, Jean-Loup, *Douglas Sirk*, Paris, 1984.
Althen, Michael, *Rock Hudson: Seine Filme, sein leben*, Munich, 1986.
Hudson, Rock, and Sara Davidson, *Rock Hudson: His Story*, London, 1986.
Quirk, Lawrence J., *Jane Wyman, the Actress and the Woman: An Illustrated Biography*, New York, 1986.
Gledhill, Christine, editor, *Home is Where the Heart Is: Studies in Melodrama and the Woman's Film*, London, 1987.
Läufer, Elisabeth, *Skeptiker des Lichts: Douglas Sirk und seine Filme*, Frankfurt, 1987.

Articles:

Variety (New York), 26 October 1955.
Monthly Film Bulletin (London), October 1955.
Comolli, Jean-Louis, ''L'Aveugle et le miroir; ou, L'Impossible Cinéma de Douglas Sirk,'' in *Cahiers du Cinéma* (Paris), April 1967.

Willemen, Paul, ''Distanciation and Douglas Sirk,'' in *Screen* (London), Summer 1971.

Elsaesser, Thomas, ''Tales of Sound and Fury: Observations on the Family Melodrama,'' in *Monogram* (London), no. 4, 1972.

Willemen, Paul, ''Towards an Analysis of the Sirkian System,'' in *Screen* (London), Winter 1972–73.

McCourt, J., ''Douglas Sirk: Melo Maestro,'' in *Film Comment* (New York), November-December 1975.

Fassbinder, Rainer Werner, ''Fassbinder on Sirk,'' in *Film Comment* (New York), November-December 1975.

Thousand Eyes Magazine (New York), January 1976.

Creed, Barbara, ''The Position of Women in Hollywood Melodramas,'' in *Australian Journal of Screen Theory* (Kensington, New South Wales), no. 3, 1977.

Mulvey, Laura, ''Notes on Sirk and Melodrama,'' in *Movie* (London), Winter, 1977–78.

Kleinhans, Chuck, ''Notes on Melodrama and the Family under Capitalism,'' in *Film Reader* (Evanston, Illinois), no. 3, 1978.

Film Psychology Review (New York), Summer-Fall 1980.

McNiven, R. D., ''The Middle-Class American Home of the Fifties,'' in *Cinema Journal* (Chicago), Summer 1983.

Kuiper, E., ''Douglas Sirk: Analyse op de montagetafel,'' in *Skoop* (Amsterdam), June-July 1985.

Hunter, Ross, in *American Film* (Washington, D.C.), April 1988.

Poppe, E., ''Reflexions sur le role thematique: la veuve dans *All That Heaven Allows*, de D. Sirk,'' in *Iris* (Iowa City), no. 2, 1988.

Klasen, B., ''Het voordeel van de twijfel,'' in *Versus* (Am Nijmegen), 1, 1989.

Babington, Bruce and Evans, P., ''All That Heaven Allowed,'' in *Movie*, 34–35, Winter 1990.

Metz, W.C., ''Pomp(ous) Sirk-umstance: Intertextuality, Adaptation, and *All That Heaven Allows*,'' in *Journal of Film and Video* (Atlanta), vol. 45, no. 4, Winter 1993.

Reimer, Robert C., ''Comparison of Douglas Sirk's *All That Heaven Allows* and R. W. Fassbinder's *Ali: Fear Eats the Soul;* or, How Hollywood's New England Dropouts Became Germany's Marginalized Other,'' in *Literature/Film Quarterly* (Salisbury), vol. 24, no. 3, 1996.

* * *

With the politicizing of film criticism in the early 1970s, Douglas Sirk and his films took on a major importance. Already a distinguished theatre and film director before fleeing Nazi Germany for America, Sirk, who held leftist sympathies, had been influenced by Brechtian aesthetic theory. Of his Hollywood films, Sirk's 1950s melodramas were of particular interest: on the one hand, he was under an obligation to the studio to fulfil the viewer's expectations regarding the genre's dictates; on the other, Sirk, through formal strategies (lighting, decor, colour, etc., and the foregrounding of conventions) introduced disruptive and distancing elements into his films. As he readily acknowledged in interviews, his ''excessive'' presentation of the material was intended to make the ideological assumptions and values underpinning the films' concerns more fully apparent and, therefore, open to a critical scrutiny.

Under contract to Universal-International throughout the 1950s, Sirk most often worked with the producer Ross Hunter who gravitated towards the ''woman's film'' in order to provide vehicles for more mature female stars. *All That Heaven Allows* was made in response to the highly popular *Magnificent Obsession* which teamed Jane Wyman and Rock Hudson who, because of the film, became a major star. In addition to *All That Heaven Allows, There's Always Tomorrow*, and *Imitation of Life* are particularly notable Hunter-produced Sirk films. *There's Always Tomorrow*, which is one of Sirk's finest works, has not received the amount of critical attention it deserves. This may have occurred because the film is not Sirk at his most audacious—there is, for instance, nothing in the film that approaches the famous scene in *All That Heaven Allows* in which Wyman's children, after being instrumental in breaking up her relationship with Hudson, present her with a television on Christmas Eve so that she can ''experience'' life at her finger tips. This extraordinary sequence ends with a shot of Wyman's reflection on the television's blank screen.

Sirk faced a major constraint with the *All That Heaven Allows* project in that the film had to have a happy ending in which Wyman and Hudson are reunited as they were at the conclusion of their previous film. Conceivably, the demand contributes to the awkwardness of the film's resolution. On the other hand, the film's subject matter gave Sirk a particularly strong opportunity to mount a scathing critique, which is astonishingly direct, of middle-class American society in which class and gender oppression are the structuring principles. Wyman, a 40-ish widow of prominent social position living in a small New England town, is rejected by her peers when she becomes romantically involved with Hudson who, in addition to being considerably younger, practises gardening, i.e., labouring, to help finance his plan to own a nursery. Preceding Wyman's relationship with Hudson, the film indicates what is expected of her: the devoting of her remaining years to her husband's memory and the taking care of their children who are already young adults; alternatively, if she should remarry, it would be solely for the purpose of companionship. Yet, in the first country club sequence, Wyman experiences an attempted physical seduction and is offered a clandestine affair; and, in the second sequence, in which she tries formally to introduce Hudson into her social circle, she is subjected to verbal derision. (In the latter sequence, the occasion being celebrated is a middle-aged man's engagement to a much younger woman.) Sirk uses both of these sequences to present the bourgeoisie as hypocritical, emotionally bankrupt, and vicious when it comes to maintaining their social elitism. In addition to the external pressures, Wyman is also rebuked by her children who are totally committed to their middle-class identities and fear, as she does, social ostracism.

Although Sirk takes full advantage of these aspects of the material, he has difficulty in providing an alternative to the dominant ideology, given the genre's dictates and Hollywood's ideological imperatives. Hudson, who is associated with nature, self-definition, and the rejection of social status, offers Wyman a retreat, visually represented by the abandoned mill which he converts into their ''new'' home, into a mythic vision of what America represents. Interestingly, Hudson's position prefigures the counter-culture movements of the 1960s but, like those, it doesn't have a coherent political platform and, as such, is an inadequate solution. Most likely Sirk was obliged to find an alternative *within* American culture which accounts for the Thoreau references; presumably, to signal the failure of such an endeavour, Sirk repeatedly defines the Wyman/Hudson relationship in relation to the fragile: for example, Wyman accidentally smashes the Wedgwood tea pot which Hudson has reconstructed but, more tellingly, the film concludes with Hudson being incapacitated. In the film's ambiguous final shot, the fawn, which has been previously associated with Hudson, is seen through a window which separates the couple from nature. (The Christmas Eve sequence is introduced with a shot of Wyman peering out from a window watching carol singers and children. Again, the image suggests confinement and isolation.) As a result, although Sirk clearly intends the film's happy-ending convention to be less than satisfying, the specific reason for his undercutting of the film's resolution remains inarticulated.

Wyman's screen persona is well used. Thoughout the film's initial sequences, she conveys both the character's passive identity *and* her unformulated resistance (given expression through the red dress she wears to the country club) to the life she is supposed to be content with. And, with this film, Hudson fully established his screen persona—while exerting a masculine image of inner strength, he also convincingly suggests, in the intimate sequences with Wyman in the abandoned mill, a strong emotional vulnerability which challenges traditional gender-role expectations.

Although the formal aspects of Sirk's work led to the initial critical attention, his films, as melodramas, have been equally of interest to the concerns of feminist film criticism. As an analysis of a middle-class woman's oppression, *All That Heaven Allows* is an extremely powerful statement.

—Richard Lippe

ALL THE KING'S MEN

USA, 1949

Director: Robert Rossen

Production: Columbia Pictures Corp.; black and white, 35mm; running time: 109 minutes. Released 1949. Filmed in Columbia studios.

Producer: Robert Rossen; **screenplay:** Robert Rossen from the novel by Robert Penn Warren; **photography:** Burnett Guffey; **editors:** Al Clark and Robert Parrish; **production designers:** Sturges Carne and Louis Diage; **music:** Louis Gruenberg and Morris Stoloff; costume designer; Jean Louis; **consultant:** Robert Parrish.

Cast: Broderick Crawford (*Willie Stark*); Joanne Dru (*Anne Stanton*); John Ireland (*Jack Burden*); John Derek (*Tom Stark*); Mercedes McCambridge (*Sadie Burke*); Sheppard Strudwick (*Adam Stanton*); Anne Seymour (*Lucy Stark*); Raymond Greenleaf (*Judge Stanton*); Ralph Dumke (*Tiny Duffy*); Katherine Warren (*Mrs. Burden*); Walter Burke (*Sugar Boy*); Will Wright (*Dolph Pillsbury*); Grandon Rhodes (*Floyd McEvoy*); H. C. Miller (*Pa Stark*); Richard Hale (*Hale*); William Bruce (*Commissioner*).

Awards: Oscars for Best Film, Best Actor (Crawford), and Best Supporting Actress (McCambridge), 1949; New York Film Critics' Awards for Best Film and Best Actor (Crawford), 1949.

Publications

Script:

Rossen, Robert, *All the King's Men*, edited by Steven Rossen, in *Three Screenplays*, New York, 1972.

Books:

Callenbach, Ernest, *Our Modern Art: The Movies*, Chicago, 1955.
Casty, Alan, *The Films of Robert Rossen*, New York, 1969.
Ireland, John A., *Living in Hollywood & Other Crimes of Passion; An Intimate Biography of Actor John Ireland*, Fresno, 1997.

Articles:

Hitchcock, Peggy, in *Films in Review* (New York), February 1950.
Winnington, Richard, in *Sight and Sound* (London), June 1950.
Rossen, Robert, "The Face of Independence," in *Films and Filming* (London), August 1962.
"Rossen Issue" of *Films in Review* (New York), June-July 1962.
Noames, Jean-Louis, "Lessons Learned in Combat: Interview with Robert Rossen," in *Cahiers du Cinéma in English* (New York), January 1967.
Dark, C., "Reflections of Robert Rossen," in *Cinema* (London), August 1970.
Mellen, Joan, "Fascism in the Contemporary Film," in *Film Quarterly* (Berkeley), Summer 1971.
Wald, M., "Robert Rossen," in *Films in Review* (New York), August-September 1972.
Milne, Tom, in *Monthly Film Bulletin* (London), February 1986.
Combs, Richard, in *Listener* (London), 7 July 1988.

* * *

All the King's Men is one of the best political films of all time. It is based on Robert Penn Warren's Pulitzer Prize-winning novel of the same name which became a major best-seller, and has retained its reputation as one of the great works of American fiction. The film is a riveting account of the career of Willie Stark, a character loosely based on Louisiana's notorious governor Huey Long, the "kingfish" of Southern politics in the 1920s and 1930s. Although Warren's novel also concerns the career of Stark, who rises from small-town lawyer to governor, Stark himself is a secondary character. The protagonist as well as narrator of the novel is newspaper reporter Jack Burden whose life, thoughts, and reactions to the political goings-on are related with frequent jumps back and forth in time.

In Rossen's film version, Willie Stark becomes the main character and Burden, although still the narrator, is much less important. The film also tells the story in chronological sequence, thus relying on a more traditional type of plot. Although in recent years many films have successfully used devices such as flashbacks and flashforwards without regard to traditional chronological story progression, in 1949 this would have been startling and probably unsuccessful. By shifting the emphasis to the central character and restructuring the narrative, Rossen was able to retain the spirit of the Warren novel while still making a highly dramatic and entertaining film. Unlike many adaptations, of the novels of Ernest Hemingway or F. Scott Fitzgerald, for example, which have often been unsuccessful because they were either too close to or too removed from the original, *All the King's Men* as a film is different from, but equally as effective as the novel.

Another major reason for the success of the film is the quality of the acting. As Stark, Broderick Crawford gives a dynamic performance in the only major starring role of his career. His Academy Award

All the King's Men

for Best Actor of the year was well deserved; he is equally convincing as the meek, naive country lawyer trying to help the members of his small community and as the spellbinding, power-hungry governor. The shift in his character's personality could have been a major problem with the film yet Crawford's acting makes both sides of the man believable. Mercedes McCambridge also won an Academy Award for her performance as the hard-shelled Sadie Burke. Others, including John Ireland as Jack Burden, are also very good, though they lack the opportunity afforded Crawford and McCambridge for a great performance.

While many films which make political or sociological statements tend to date badly in a few years. *All the King's Men* still seems fresh and powerful. The contradictory character of Stark, a man who wants to do good, but who succumbs to the temptation of power and the demands of his own ambition, becoming the embodiment of corrupt politics, is as relevant today as in 1949. The character of the demagogue has been known in literature for centuries, but few works have examined that figure as thoroughly and successfully as *All the King's Men.*

—Patricia King Hanson

ALPHAVILLE

France-Italy, 1965

Director: Jean-Luc Godard

Production: Chaumiane (Paris) and Filmstudio (Rome); black and white, 35mm; running time: 98 minutes (some sources list 100 minutes). Released 1965. Filmed January through February 1965 in Paris.

Producer: Andre Michelin; **screenplay:** Jean-Luc Godard, based on a character created by Peter Cheyney; **assistant directors:** Charles Bitsch, Jean-Paul Savignac, and Helene Kalouguine; **photography:** Raoul Coutard; **editor:** Agnes Guillemot; **sound:** Rene Levert; **music:** Paul Misraki.

Cast: Eddie Constantine (*Lemmy Caution*); Anna Karina (*Natasha von Braun*); Howard Vernon (*Professor von Braun*); Akim Tamiroff (*Henri Dickson*); Laszlo Szabo (*Chief Engineer*); Michel Delahaye (*von Braun's Assistant*); Jean-André Fieschi (*Professor Heckell*); Jean-Louis Comolli (*Professor Jeckell*); Alpha 60 (*Itself*).

Awards: Best Film, Berlin Film Festival, 1965.

Publications

Script:

Godard, Jean-Luc, *Alphaville*, London, 1966; New York, 1968.

Books:

Roud, Richard, *Jean-Luc Godard*, New York, 1967.
Mussman, Tony, editor, *Jean-Luc Godard: A Critical Anthology*, New York, 1968.
Cameron, Ian, editor, *The Films of Jean-Luc Godard*, London, 1969.
Collet, Jean, editor, *Jean-Luc Godard*, New York, 1970.
Brown, Royal, editor, *Focus on Godard*, Englewood Cliffs, New Jersey, 1972.
Godard, Jean-Luc, *Godard on Godard*, edited by Tom Milne, London, 1972; revised edition, New York, 1986.
Farassino, Alberto, *Jean-Luc Godard*, Florence, 1974.
Parrish, James Robert, *The Great Spy Pictures*, Metuchen, New Jersey, 1974.
Monaco, James, *The New Wave*, New York, 1976.
MacCabe, Colin, *Godard: Images, Sounds, Politics*, London, 1980.
Walsh, Martin, *The Brechtian Aspect of Radical Cinema*, London, 1981.
Lefèvre, Raymond, *Jean-Luc Godard*, Paris, 1983.
Bordwell, David, *Narration in the Fiction Film*, London, 1985.
Weis, Elisabeth, and John Belton, *Film Sound: Theory and Practice*, New York, 1985.
Loshitzky, Yosefa, *The Radical Faces of Godard and Bertolucci*, Detroit, 1995.
Dixon, Wheeler W., *The Films of Jean-Luc Godard*, Albany, New York, 1997.
Sterritt, David, *Jean-Luc Godard; Interviews*, Jackson, Mississippi, 1998.
Sterritt, David, *The Films of Jean-Luc Godard; Seeing the Invisible*, New York, 1999.

Alphaville

Articles:

New Yorker, 21 August 1965.
Roud, Richard, ''Anguish: *Alphaville*,'' in *Sight and Sound* (London), Autumn 1965.
Jacob, Gilles, and Claire Clouzot, in *Sight and Sound* (London), Autumn 1965.
Mekas, Jonas, in *Village Voice* (New York), 16 September 1965.
Coutard, Raoul, ''Light of Day,'' in *Sight and Sound* (London), Winter 1965–66.
Sarris, Andrew, in *Village Voice* (New York), 3 November 1965.
Bond, Kirk, in *Film Society Review* (New York), March 1966.
Gow, Gordon, in *Films and Filming* (London), May 1966.
Thomas, John in *Film Quarterly* (Berkeley), Fall 1966.
Federman, Raymond, ''Jean-Luc Godard and Americanism,'' in *Film Heritage* (Dayton, Ohio), Spring 1968.
Nolan, Jack Edmund, ''Eddie Constantine,'' in *Films in Review* (New York), August-September 1968.
Crofts, Stephen, ''The Films of Jean-Luc Godard,'' in *Cinema* (London), June 1969.
Kozloff, Max, in *Film Culture* (New York), Winter/Spring 1970.
Ropars-Wuilleumier, Marie-Claire, ''Loss of Language,'' in *Wide Angle* (Athens, Ohio), no. 3, 1976.
Maclean, R., ''Wittgenstein and Godard's *Alphaville*,'' in *Sight and Sound* (London), Winter 1977–78.
Blanchet, C., in *Cinéma* (Paris), May 1983.
Pinciroli, G., ''La completezza del gesto in *Alphaville*,'' in *Cineforum* (Bergamo, Italy), December 1989.
Darke, Chris, ''It All Happened In Paris,'' in *Sight & Sound* (London), vol. 4, no. 7, July 1994.
Castoro Cinema, no. 176, March-April 1996.
Brown, R.S., ''Alphaville,'' in *Cineaste* (New York), vol. 22, no. 1, 1996.
Marek, Petr, in *Film a Doba* (Prague), vol. 42, no. 4, Winter 1996.

* * *

Since the early 1950s a tendency has begun to manifest itself in the genre of the science-fiction film as an increasing number of important directors use the sci-fi form to express their views on society, mankind, the present and the future. One of these is Jean-Luc Godard, whose 1965 *Alphaville* takes place in a utopian world of the future. Godard's world is not one of joy and happiness; Alphaville is governed by a totalitarian system in which the individual counts for almost nothing, and its alienated people have no use for art, love, or even thought. People are reduced essentially to the level of robots, identified only by numbers, without a will of their own, with no ideas or feelings.

Even though it belongs in the category of science fiction, Godard's film does not closely follow the conventional patterns of the genre. As a member of the French New Wave, Godard has held, since his debut, an individual and well-defined view of the cinema. One of the most important features of his work is his emphasis on the contemporary world. All of his films deal with modern man; we do not find a return to the past in his entire work. The stamp of the present can also be seen in his sole excursion into the future. *Alphaville*, which is less about what the world will be like tomorrow than what it is like today, and what it is gradually becoming before our very eyes without our realizing it. In the present and the past Godard sees the potential seeds of a future world, and therefore the story has an admonitory subtext. From this thematic interpretation flows the film's realization, its formal execution and visual aspect. The viewer encounters on the screen nothing that appears to be unusual or extraordinary, and Godard even forgoes any futuristic mise-en-scène. His Alphaville of the future is the Paris of 1965, in which a dehumanizing atmosphere is expressed through the camera work of Raoul Coutard, who shoots buildings of concrete and glass in high contrast, alternates positive and negative images in very short takes, and makes particularly effective use of Paris by night. The most unusual aspect of the film is the sound, particularly the monotonous voice of the central brain governing Alphaville, a voice in contrast to the somewhat ingratiating music of Paul Misraki.

A characteristic feature of the entire French New Wave was a certain admiration for the American cinema—its perfect craftsmanship and its ability to entertain, move, or thrill with suspense. In *Alphaville*, Godard's affinity for popular film can be seen, for example, in the choice of Eddie Constantine for the starring role—viewers know him chiefly from gangster films—and in the dramatic structure influenced by both film serials of the 1930s and by comic strips. Another striking feature of Godard's direction is his free use of ideas and resources borrowed from other films and other art forms; Godard summons these according to his own needs. In *Alphaville* we find links with the work of Jean Cocteau in the sequence in which Lemmy converses with Alpha 60; the labyrinthine passages recall the phantasmic world of the novels of Franz Kafka; and we find a reference to the ancient myth of Eurydice and the Biblical story of Lot's wife. There are also references to the unforgotten Fascist past, as in the tattooed numbers worn by the city's inhabitants, the name of the designer of the central brain, Professor von Braun, or the use of actual rooms of the Parisian Hotel Continental, where the Gestapo was quartered during the Occupation. These references in the film are not incidental; they are utilized intentionally to broaden and deepen the picture and shift the story to another, more relevant level. However, they do not destroy the integrity and unity of the film even when the viewer is aware of them.

Godard's films of the 1960s were often received by a portion of the public and by some critics with an enthusiasm that was almost excessive. In the course of time, some of these films have lost their appeal. This has not happened in the case of *Alphaville*, which remains part of a valuable current of science fiction while holding its place in the history of cinema.

—B. Urgosíková

ALSINO Y EL CONDOR

(Alsino and the Condor)

Nicaragua, 1982

Director: Miguel Littin

Production: Nicaraguan Film Institute, Cuban Institute of Cinematographic Art and Industry, Latin American Production of Mexico, Costa Rican Cinematographic Co-Operative; colour, 35mm; running time: 89 minutes. Filmed on location in Nicaragua.

Producers: Lilia Alfaro, Jose Ramon Perez; **executive producer:** Herman Littin; **screenplay:** Miguel Littin, Isadora Aguirre, Tomas Turrent; **photography:** Jorge Herrera, Pablo Martinez; **editor:** Miriam Talavera; **sound:** Germinal Hernandez; **art director:** Elly Menz; **music:** Leo Brower.

Cast: Alan Esquivel (*Alsino*); Dean Stockwell (*Frank*); Carmen Bunster (*Mama Buela*); Alejandro Parodi (*Garin*); Delia Casanova (*Rosario*); Marta Lorena Perez (*Lucia*); Reinaldo Miravalles (*Don Nazario*); Marcelo Gaete (*Lucia's Grandfather*).

Awards: 1st Nicaraguan Fiction Feature.

Publications

Script:

Littin, Miguel, and others, *Alsino y el Condor*, Nicaragua, 1982.

Articles:

Variety (New York), 9 February 1983.
Valdes, Zoe, ''Alsino: Las Alas del Sueno'' in *Cine Cubano* (Havana), number 106, 1983.
Canby, Vincent, *New York Times,* 1 May 1983.
Fernandez, Enrique, *Village Voice* (New York), 10 May 1983.
Denby, David, *New Yorker*, 16 May 1983.
Perez, Marta, *Iskusstvo Kino* (Moscow), December 1983.
Positif (Paris), April 1984.
Bassan, Raphael, ''Alsino et le Condor—Une Allegorie pour un Pays Neuf'' in *Image et Son* (Paris), May 1984.
Jaros, J., *Film A Doba* (Prague), May 1984.
Dunnage, G., ''Nicaragua: L'enfant qui voulait voler'' in *Jeune Cinema* (Paris), June 1984.

* * *

Miguel Littin, Chilean director in exile and former head of Chile Films, flirted with magic Realism, a style increasingly popular in fiction and following on from this, cinema, in the 1970s, with *El Recurso del Metodo*, and then returned to the Chileans-in-exile theme of direct criticism and allegories of the political events in Chile with *Alsino y el Condor*. Nearly all those involved in Chile Films during Allende's brief tenure in office in the country were thrown out of Chile after Pinochet's takeover of power in 1973 (some after a period of imprisonment), and despite money difficulties, some managed to keep up a form of film production. Those who did so were mostly in Socialist regimes—the Soviet Union or Cuba—but because of his contacts in the Mexican film business, Miguel Littin was able to continue his career there. This mass exodus of filmmakers from Chile who actually managed to continue filmmaking, and provide an alternative point of view to the very small number of films produced under Pinochet at this time, lead to the peculiar situation of almost an entire country's film output being made in exile.

Alsino y el Condor made at the time of the Sandanista overthrow of the Somoza regime in Nicaragua, is an allegory of the Nicaraguan people rising up to meet their oppressor. The film is a Mexican-Cuban-Nicaraguan co-production, yet despite this, it has the distinctive Littin touch. Littin's shortest film to this point was criticized by some for its too blatant use of political allegory.

The hero of the film is 10-year-old Alsino, a dreamer. He lives with his *mamabuela*, an old lady shrouded in the mystery of her past, who bewitches Alsino with travel tales of her dead sailor-husband and shows him old postcards from Amsterdam.

There is a contrast between Alsino's dreams and the realities of his country as it heads towards revolution. Alsino likes to climb trees and to imagine himself flying. His dreams are ignited by the US Army helicopter that begins to hover over his head. Alsino wants to fly. The fact that the helicopter is fighting the very people who want to liberate his own people is lost on him. Alsino's dreams are the dreams of his people, although as he is a child he cannot realize this and it is only after he falls from the tree and becomes hunchbacked that he becomes conscious of reality. After meeting the guerilla he returns home to find his town abandoned and his *mamabuela* dead, the Dutch postcards burnt and scattered to the wind, like his dreams. Alsino becomes one of the guerillas himself. Finally understanding the war and foreign aggression he can fly on the wings of his dreams of freedom.

The very obvious allegories here are the illusion of liberty through flying, and real dictatorial oppression and North American aggression expressed by the helicopter. Cultural domination is expressed by Alsino's wanting to possess the foreign object, the helicopter—even though it represents aggression. The film is full of symbols—in fact it could be said that there is not one real character in the film, merely symbols and emblems. There are birds unable to fly because their wings have been clipped, and Alsino becomes hunchbacked because he falls from a tree and only then begins to see things in a different light.

This film was respected in the West and even nominated for an Academy Award for best foreign film, although its obvious and heavy-handed political allegory was too much for the North American critics. *Cine Cubano*, however, loved it, and praised it for the beauty of using the innocent eyes of childhood awakening to political consciousness as the medium for the message. One could say, however, that Littin's vision has never been so schematized before and presents a very simplified vision of a country's problems.

—Sara Corben de Romero

THE AMBUSH

See **ZASEDA**

L'AMERICA

Italy, 1994

Director: Gianni Amelio

Production: Alia Film/Cecchi Gori Group Tiger. Color, 35mm, Cinemascope; running time: 120 mins. Released 1994. Filmed between August and December 1993, and in June 1994, in Albania.

Producer: Mario Cecchi Gori and Vittorio Cecchi Gori; **screenplay:** Gianni Amelio, Andrea Porporati, Alessandro Sermoneta; **photography:** Luca Bigazzi; **editor:** Simona Paggi; **sound:** Alessandro Zanon; **music:** Franco Piersanti; **set designer:** Giuseppi M. Gaudino; **costumes:** Liliana Sotira, Claudia Tenaglia.

Cast: Enrico Lo Verso (*Gino*); Michele Placido (*Fiore*); Carmelo di Mazzarelli (*Spiro*); Piro Milkani (*Selimi*); Elida Janushi (*Selimi's Cousin*); Sefer Pema (*Prison Warden*); Nikolin Elezi (*Boy Who Dies*); Artan Marina (*Ismail*); Besim Kurti (*Policeman*); Esmeralda Ara (*Little Girl*).

Awards: Best Director, Venice Film Festival; Felix Award, Best European Film; Nastri D'Argento, Best Picture and Director.

Publications

Articles:

Young, Deborah, in *Variety* (New York), 12 September, 1994.
Menashe, Louis, in *Cineaste* (New York), vol. 21, no. 4, 1995.
Maslin, Janet, in *New York Times*, 4 October 1995.
Carr, Jay, in *Boston Globe*, 20 December 1995.
Wilmington, Michael, in *Chicago Tribune*, 24 December 1995.
Crowdus, Gary and Richard Porton, ''Beyond Neorealism: Preserving a Cinema of Social Conscience,'' in *Cineaste* (New York), vol. 21, no. 4, 1995.
Agovino, Michael J., ''His Mind Fixed on the Moment, Eyes on the Past,'' in *New York Times*, 17 December 1995.
James, Caryn, ''The Little Things Mean a Lot,'' in *New York Times*, 17 December 1995.

* * *

Gianni Amelio's *L'America* is a biting, profoundly moving drama that illustrates how the downtrodden of society, beneath the hoopla of political change and the redistribution of power, are fated to do little more than shift from one kind of exploitation to another.

The specifics of the scenario relate to the downfall of communism in Europe. The year is 1991, and Albania has been liberated from the iron hand of the hammer and sickle. The Albanian people are hungry and desperate; thousands of them are determined to make their way to Italy, where they hope to find employment. In the decades leading up to the events in the film, political dissidents in Albania were incarcerated in labor camps. One of them is seventy-year-old Spiro Milkami (Carmelo di Mazzarelli), a bedraggled, feeble-minded man who is ironically not Albanian but an Italian farmer who had deserted the army in the 1940s. Spiro becomes the pawn in a scheme concocted by two Italian businessmen, Gino (Enrico Lo Verso) and Fiore (Michele Placido), who plan to purchase a shoe factory, with the assistance of an unscrupulous government official, and set up a fraudulent corporation that will allow them to squeeze a fortune out of Albania's economic chaos. In order to observe the rules of privatization, an Albanian must be involved in the venture. Fiore has discovered Spiro, who seems the perfect tool and fool: a passive, mindless old man who can be fitted into a suit and paraded about whenever necessary. Confused and senile, Spiro is caught in a time warp: he thinks he is still twenty years old and is obsessed with returning to Italy, and to his wife, because it is time to harvest his olives. If she is not already dead, Spiro's wife is now an elderly woman—but in his mind she remains as young as when he last saw her.

The crux of *L'America* centers on the relationship between Spiro and Gino, the younger of the businessmen. Spiro escapes from the orphanage where he had been left by Gino and Fiore, and Gino sets out after him across the barren Albanian countryside. Along the way, this insolent young capitalist is stripped of his jeep and belongings—and even his clothing. He comes to know the feeling of poverty and statelessness and develops an affinity for the plight of the Albanian people, as well as sympathy for Spiro's hopeless quest. Gino eventually is arrested and jailed because of his alliance with the corrupt official. He has been deserted by Fiore, who has left the country. Gino's passport is impounded, and he finds himself one of the nameless, faceless masses of refugees desperate to reach Italy. At the finale, he and the ever-hopeful Spiro are reunited on a refugee ship. Gino comes to recognize the force of Spiro's confidence, and the potency of his dreams.

L'America is a film in the neorealist tradition in that Amelio's concerns are profoundly political and humanist. The scenario condemns the abuse of power by the avaricious businessmen; back in the 1940s, Gino and Fiore would have been fascists rather than capitalists. Similar to the neorealist classics of Rossellini and De Sica, in *L'America* Amelio spotlights the individual's thirst for the barest necessities amid a landscape of political, economic, and moral disorder. While he has not made a documentary, his film reflects a heightened sense of reality derived from the experience of life. The film was shot on location and mixes professional actors (Lo Verso and Placido) with non-professionals (di Massarelli, an eighty-year-old retired fisherman-laborer-janitor making his screen debut).

What distances *L'America* from the earlier neorealist films lies in the questions the film poses. Some are practical to the individual: What will the Albanian refugee who does make it to Italy find there? Is Italy truly a promised land? Or is the quality of life more reflective of the inane programs constantly broadcast on Italian television? These queries are answered by the declaration that it is better to wash dishes in Italy than to starve in Albania. In Italy, the film flatly states, young men only die in car accidents. But *L'America* poses other questions that are more elusive, and more universal: Have Albanians (or, for that matter, Romanians, East Germans, or Poles) found freedom, after decades under communist rule? Or, has a new kind of tyranny, that of capitalism and greed, replaced the old?

Finally, in *L'America* Amelio touchingly captures the feeling of what it must be like to be a refugee. His is a story of the dreams and aspirations of people who, in reality, are so downtrodden that they have no logical reason to latch onto hope. It is Amelio's contention that, in the end, all the powerless have to cling to are their dreams. Even if they are irreversibly unrealistic, as is the case with Spiro, dreams still must be grasped onto because they are all that will help sustain life.

—Rob Edelman

AMERICAN BEAUTY

USA, 1999

Director: Sam Mendes

Production: DreamWorks SKG; 35 mm, color (DeLuxe); running time: 121 minutes; DTS/Dolby Digital/SDDS. Released September 1999 USA. Filmed in 1998 and 1999 in Los Angeles and Sacramento, California, and at Warner Brothers Studios in Burbank, California; additional scenes shot at South High School, Torrance, California; cost: $15,000,000 (US).

Producers: Alan Ball, Bruce Cohen, Dan Jinks, and Stan Wlodkowski; **screenplay:** Alan Ball; **photography:** Conrad L. Hall; **assistant directors:** Tony Adler, Rosemary Cremona, Carey Dietrich, and Chris Edmonds; **editors:** Tariq Anwar and Chris Greenbury; **supervising sound editor:** Scott Martin Gershin; **art director:** David S. Lazan; **production designer:** Naomi Shohan; **costume designer:** Julie Weiss; **set designer:** Jan K. Bergstrom; **music:** Original score by Thomas Newman; additional songs by Pete Townshend; **special effects:** CFC/MVFX, Los Angeles.

Cast: Kevin Spacey (*Lester Burnham*); Annette Bening (*Carolyn Burnham*); Thora Birch (*Jane Burnham*); Wes Bentley (*Ricky Fitts*); Mena Suvari (*Angela Hayes*); Peter Gallagher (*Buddy Kane*); Chris Cooper (*Colonel Frank Fitts*); Allison Janney (*Barbara Fitts*); Scott Bakula (*Jim Olmeyer*); Sam Robards (*Jim Berkley*); Barry Del Sherman (*Brad Dupree*).

Awards: Oscars for Best Actor (Kevin Spacey), Best Director (Sam Mendes), Best Picture (Bruce Cohen and Dan Jinks), Best Original Screenplay (Alan Ball), and Best Cinematography (Conrad L. Hall), 2000; British Academy Awards for Best Film, Best Actress, Best Actor, Achievement in Film Music (Thomas Newman), Cinematography, and Editing (Tariq Anwar and Christopher Greenbury), 2000; Broadcast Film Critics Association Awards for Best Director, Best Picture, and Best Original Screenplay, 2000; Chicago Film Critics Association Awards for Best Actor, Best Director, Best Picture, and Most Promising Actor (Wes Bentley), 2000; Directors Guild of America Award for Outstanding Directorial Achievement in Motion Pictures (Sam Mendes, et al.), 2000; Golden Globes for Best Director—Motion Picture, Best Motion Picture—Drama, and Best Screenplay—Motion Picture, 2000; London Critics Circle Awards for Actor of the Year (Kevin Spacey), Actress of the Year (Annette Bening), Director of the Year, Film of the Year, and Screenwriter of the Year, 2000; Screen Actors Guild Awards for Outstanding Performance by a Cast in a Theatrical Motion Picture, Outstanding Performance by a Female Actor in a Leading Role (Annette Bening) and Outstanding Performance by a Male Actor in a Leading Role (Kevin Spacey), 2000; Los Angeles Film Critics Association Awards for Best Director, 1999; National Board of Review Award (USA) for Breakthrough Performance by an Actor (Wes Bentley), 1999; National Society of Film Critics Awards (USA) for Best Cinematography, 1999.

Publications:

Script:

Ball, Alan, *American Beauty: The Shooting Script* (introduction by director Sam Mendes), New York, 1999.

Articles:

Weinraub, Bernard, ''A Wunderkind Discovers the Wonders of Film,'' in *New York Times*, 12 September 1999.
McCarthy, Todd, '''American' Dream, Worked Over,'' in *Variety* (Los Angeles) 13 September 1999.
Maslin, Janet, ''Dad's Dead, and He's Still a Funny Guy,'' in *New York Times*, 15 September 1999.
Denby, David, ''Transcending the Suburbs: *American Beauty* Goes from Satire to a Vision of the Sublime,'' in *New Yorker*, 20 September 1999.
Marshall, Alexandra, ''What's Wrong with this Picture?,'' in *American Prospect* (Princeton, NJ), 6 December 1999.
Kemp, Philip, ''Sam Mendes' *American Beauty:* The Nice Man Cometh,'' in *Sight and Sound* (London), January 2000.
Jackson, Kevin, ''American Beauty,'' in *Sight and Sound* (London), February 2000.

* * *

Not since Mike Nichols' *Who's Afraid of Virginia Wolfe* (1966) has a theatre director made as auspicious a leap to the silver screen as Sam Mendes. Mendes came to Hollywood by way of the London stage, where he directed such hits as *The Rise and Fall of Little Voice* and *The Blue Room.* Mendes was hand picked to direct *American Beauty* by Steven Spielberg, whose DreamWorks SKG (controlled by Spielberg, Jeffrey Katzenberg, and David Geffen) owned the rights to Alan Ball's original screenplay. Although seemingly an odd choice, Mendes' beautifully crafted, superbly acted, and critically acclaimed film proves Spielberg an astute judge of directorial potential.

American Beauty tells the story of Lester Burnham, a mid-level ad man going through a mid-life melt down. Lester lives in the suburbs in a two story house surrounded by a white picket fence. But despite the exterior sheen, all is not well in the Burnham household. Lester is burned out, tired of conforming to the expectations of the American middle class. His wife Carolyn is an emasculating shrew, apparently more concerned about appearing ''normal'' than being happy. Their daughter Jane is a confused and embittered teen who is saving up for breast enhancement surgery despite already being well endowed. The neighbors on one side are the Fitts family, consisting of the Colonel, a homophobic ex-marine, his wife Barbara, a shattered person, and their son Ricky, a drug dealing video voyeur. On the other side live Jim Olmeyer and Jim Berkley, a gay couple who, ironically, are by far the most ''normal'' people in the neighborhood. Early in the film Lester meets Jane's friend Angela, on whom he develops a crush that becomes the catalyst for the remainder of the action.

The film's scathing portrayal of American suburbia is neither groundbreaking nor innovative as the suburbs have been the subject of artistic contempt dating back to at least John Cheever's short fiction of the early 1950s. In cinema the suburbs have been skewered for years in exemplary films such as *The Graduate* (Nichols, 1967), *Blue Velvet* (Lynch, 1986), and *The Ice Storm* (Lee, 1997). Furthermore, many of the narrative lines in *American Beauty* recall earlier

American Beauty

films; for example, Lester's voice over from beyond the grave is reminiscent of Joe Gillis' (William Holden) in *Sunset Boulevard* (Wilder, 1950); his infatuation with Angela has echoes of *Lolita* (Kubrick, 1962); and Ricky Fitts' video voyeurism is a contemporary version of L.B. ''Jeff'' Jefferies' (Jimmy Stewart) window watching in *Rear Window* (Hitchcock, 1954). Despite its stereotypical treatment of suburban malaise and at times derivative narrative, *American Beauty* is a riveting film; what makes it so is Conrad L. Hall's poetic cinematography, which alternates between Lester's reality and his surreal visions of life as he would like it to be, and its across-the-board phenomenal acting.

While all involved turn in stellar work, two performances in particular stand out: Annette Bening as Carolyn and Kevin Spacey as Lester. Carolyn Burnham is a problematic character for a variety of reasons, not the least of which is the script's inherent misogyny towards her. Carolyn is all shrew, an impossible-to-like screaming control freak. And yet she is in the same position as Lester; life has not at all turned out as she had hoped and the costs extracted have left her hollow on the inside. Just as Lester does, so too does Carolyn deviate from expectations in search of something that will fulfill her. She ends up in an affair with Buddy Kane, a fabulously smarmy real estate ''king,'' and takes up pistol shooting as a hobby. As written, we're set up to hate her for her transgressions, whereas when Lester deviates we can't help but root for him. Bening nevertheless manages to find in Carolyn something redeeming; her humane portrayal of this uniformly unsympathetic character is a tour de force.

Conversely, the script's sympathy is heavily weighted towards Lester. After meeting Angela, Lester says, ''I feel like I've been in a coma for the past twenty years. And I'm just now waking up.'' His ''waking up'' involves trading in his Lexus for a 1970 Pontiac Firebird, quitting his ad agency job in favor of counter work at a fast food restaurant, beginning a physical training program that will enable him to ''look good naked,'' which he hopes will make him more attractive to Angela, drinking beer at all hours of the day, a resumption of the pot smoking he loved as a teen, and, most importantly, his reasserting himself as the unquestioned authority figure in the Burnham household. Lester's reversion to a young-girl-loving, beer-swilling jerk is a rehabilitation of the American male as defined by Larry Flynt. But when at one point in the film he defiantly shoves his fist in the air and says, ''I rule,'' audience members, both male and female, cheer; this reaction is a testament to Spacey's interpretation of Lester. He goes beyond what was written and finds in

Lester a heart; Spacey's sensitive delivery of Lester's lines, accompanied by telling facial expressions and body language, renders what could have been an irredeemable character a lovable everyman. In accepting the Academy Award for Best Actor, Spacey himself summed up why the award was so richly deserved when he said, "And that's why I loved playing Lester, because we got to see all of his worst qualities and we still grew to love him."

In the end Lester is redeemed, and so too is the film, which because of the craftsmanship of the actors and crew manages to rise well above its stereotypical subject matter. In addition, *American Beauty* will likely be remembered for three reasons. First, in winning the Academy Award for Best Picture the film legitimized DreamWorks SKG as a studio to be reckoned with. Next, it marked Sam Mendes as filmmaker to watch in coming years. And finally, Kevin Spacey's performance in *American Beauty* cemented his position as one of the finest actors of his generation.

—Robert Sickels

THE AMERICAN FRIEND

See **DER AMERIKANISCHE FREUND**

AMERICAN GRAFFITI

USA, 1972

Director: George Lucas

Production: A Universal-Lucasfilm Ltd.-Coppola Production; color, 35mm; running time: 110 minutes. Released 1973. Filmed 1972 in Petaluma and San Rafael, California; cost: about $700,000.

Producers: Francis Ford Coppola and Gary Kurtz; **screenplay:** George Lucas, Gloria Katz, and Willard Huyck, from an idea by George Lucas; **photography:** Ron Eveslage and Jan D'Alquen; **editors:** Verna Fields and Marcia Lucas; **sound:** Walter Murch; musical score comprised of original versions of several rock-and-roll "classics" from early 1960s.

Cast: Richard Dreyfuss (*Curt Henderson*); Ron Howard (*Steve Bolander*); Paul Le Mat (*John Milner*); Charles Martin Smith (*Terry Fields*); Cindy Williams (*Laurie Henderson*); Candy Clark (*Debbie*); Mackenzie Phillips (*Carol*); Suzanne Sommers (*Girl in T-Bird*); Wolfman Jack (*Disc jockey*); Harrison Ford (*Drag racer*).

Awards: New York Film Critics Award, Best Screenwriting, 1973; American Film Institute's "100 Years, 100 Movies," 1998.

Publications

Script:

Lucas, George, and others, *American Graffiti: A Screenplay*, New York, 1973.

Books:

Pollock, Dale, *Skywalking: The Life and Films of George Lucas*, New York, 1983.

Mabery, D.L., *George Lucas*, Minneapolis, 1987.

Champlin, Charles, *George Lucas; The Creative Impulse: Lucasfilm's First Twenty Years*, New York, 1997.

Kline, Sally, *George Lucas; Interviews*, Jackson, 1999.

White, Dana, *George Lucas*, Minneapolis, 1999.

Articles:

Dempsey, M., in *Film Quarterly* (Berkeley), Fall 1973.

Ney, J., in *Interview* (New York), September 1973.

New York Times, 7 October 1973.

Houston, Beverle, and Marsha Kinder, in *Film Heritage* (Dayton, Ohio), Winter 1973–74.

Combs, Richard, in *Monthly Film Bulletin* (London), February 1974.

Sturhahn, Larry, "The Filming of *American Graffiti*," in *Filmmakers' Newsletter* (Ward Hill, Massachusetts), March 1974.

Dawson, Jan, in *Sight and Sound* (London), Spring 1974.

Farber, Steven, "George Lucas: The Stinky Kid Hits the Big Time," in *Film Quarterly* (Berkeley), Spring 1974.

Rosenthal, S., in *Focus on Film* (London), Spring 1974.

Warner, A., in *Films and Filming* (London), May 1974.

Segond, J., "Lettre de Londres," in *Positif* (Paris), September 1974.

Sodowsky, A., and others, "The Epic World of *American Graffiti*," in *Journal of Popular Culture* (Bowling Green, Ohio), vol. 4, no. 1, 1975.

MacCabe, Colin, "Theory of Film: Principles of Realism and Pleasure," in *Screen* (London), no. 3, 1976.

"George Lucas," in *Current Biography Yearbook*, New York, 1978.

Fairchild, Jr., B. H., "Songs of Innocence and Experience: The Blakean Vision of George Lucas," in *Literature/Film Quarterly* (Salisbury, Maryland), no. 2, 1979.

Pye, M., and L. Myles, "The Man Who Made *Star Wars*," in *Atlantic Monthly* (Boston), March 1979.

Prouty, Howard H., in *Magill's Survey of Cinema 1*, Englewood Cliffs, New Jersey, 1980.

Harmetz, Aljean, "George Lucas—Burden of Dreams," in *American Film* (Washington, D.C.), June 1983.

Douin, Jean-Luc, "À toute berzingue," in *Télérama* (Paris), 26 May 1993.

Speed, Lesley, "Tuesday's Gone: The Nostalgic Teen Film," in *Journal of Popular Film and Television* (Washington, D.C.), vol. 26, no. 1, Spring 1998.

* * *

If *Star Wars* is George Lucas's idealized dream of the future, *American Graffiti* is his idealized dream of the past, a past in which optimism and naiveté were cherished sentiments before cynicism became a national past time. What joins these two films, however, is a devotion to entertainment, to the depiction of glorious worlds in which adventure is triumphant.

American Graffiti

With the assistance of Francis Ford Coppola, Lucas's remembrance of teenage life in his home town of Modesto, California was brought to the screen, ushering in a wave of nostalgia for the music and lifestyle of an era ten years past, an era which subsequently became a staple of television situation comedies such as *Happy Days* and *Laverne and Shirley*, Ron Howard and Cindy Williams moving easily from this film to their television roles.

The central organizing device of this film is the musical score, permissions for which totalled $80,000 of the $700,000 budget. Music, which functions as the narrator of teen dreams and frustrations, as omnipresent companion, and as motivator of lifestyle, joins the various narrative threads and the three central locales: the hop where you danced to a band, the diner where you played the jukebox, and the strip where you listened to Spiritual Father Wolfman Jack on the car radio. To accentuate the overriding function of the music, Lucas strove for a visual quality which resembled the aura of a 1962 ''Hot-Rods-to-Hell'' jukebox. For many growing up is a musical experience and, along with Barry Levinson's *Diner, American Graffiti* is the best evocation of that idea.

The narrative of *American Graffiti* is that of a day in the life of four central male characters coming of age after indulging in a series of misadventures. Lucas located a mood of optimism and naiveté by setting the film in 1962, the period immediately prior to the Kennedy assassination and the resultant politicization of American youth and music. Naive optimism was so firmly entrenched that individuals refused to admit the necessity for personal development. Curt, whose avowed dream is to shake the hand of JFK, almost succumbs to the complacent notion of ''why leave home to find a new home?'' At the end of the film, after much indecisiveness, he does leave in pursuit of a future beyond the confines of family and home town. As such he is representative of those students of the sixties who overcame their innocence and ventured forth.

In Lucas's sentimental view of growing up, he lovingly portrayed the innocence and freedom of life-before-twenty and perhaps unwittingly, the seductive mythology of the teen dream. Audiences bought the dream overwhelmingly. *American Graffiti* grossed over $50 million in its first year, making it, to that point, the most successful film made for under $1 million. Its release in Japan helped foster a booming business there in American musical and fashion nostalgia.

—Doug Tomlinson

AN AMERICAN IN PARIS

USA, 1950

Director: Vincente Minnelli

Production: Metro-Goldwyn-Mayer Picture Corp.; Technicolor, 35mm; running time: 113 minutes. Released 1950. Filmed 1 August 1950 through fall 1950 at MGM studios, Culver City, California; also on location in Paris.

Producer: Arthur Freed; **screenplay:** Alan Jay Lerner; **photography:** Al Gilks and John Alton (final ballet); **editor:** Adrienne Fazan; **art directors:** Preston Ames and Cedric Gibbons; **set decorators:** Keogh Gleason and Edwin B. Willis; **music:** George Gershwin and Ira Gershwin; **music directors:** Johnny Green and Saul Chaplin; **costume designers:** Orry-Kelly, Walter Plunkett (Beaux-Arts Ball costumes), Irene Sharaff (final ballet costumes); **choreography:** Gene Kelly.

Cast: Gene Kelly (*Jerry Mulligan*); Leslie Caron (*Lise Borvier*); Oscar Levant (*Adam Cook*); Georges Guetary (*Henri Baurel*); Nina Foch (*Milo Roberts*); Eugene Borden (*Georges Mattieu*); Martha Bamattre (*Mathilde Mattieu*); Mary Young (*Old woman dancer*); Ann Codee (*Therese*); George Davis (*Francola*); Hayden Rourke (*Tommy Baldwin*); Paul Maxey (*John McDowd*); Dick Wessel (*Ben Macrow*).

Awards: Oscars for Best Picture, Story and Screenplay, Cinematography—Color, Art Direction—Color, Scoring, Costume Design—Color, 1951; American Film Institute's ''100 Years, 100 Movies,'' 1998.

Publications

Books:

de la Roche, Catherine, *Vincente Minnelli*, Wellington, New Zealand, 1959; reprinted in *Film Culture* (New York), June 1959.

Griffith, Richard, *The Cinema of Gene Kelly*, New York, 1962.

Truchaud, François, *Vincente Minnelli*, Paris, 1966.

Springer, John, *All Talking, All Singing, All Dancing*, New York, 1966.

Kobal, John, *Gotta Sing, Gotta Dance*, New York, 1970.

Burrows, Michael, *Gene Kelly: Versatility Personified*, St. Austell, Cornwall, 1971.

Thomas, Lawrence B., *The MGM Years*, New Rochelle, New York, 1972.

Knox, Donald, *The Magic Factory: How MGM Made ''An American in Paris,''* New York, 1973.

Hirschhorn, Clive, *Gene Kelly: A Biography*, London, 1974; revised edition 1984.

Stern, Lee Edward, *The Movie Musical*, New York, 1974.

Delameter, James, *Dance in the Hollywood Musical*, Ann Arbor, Michigan, 1981.

Guerif, François, *Vincente Minnelli*, Paris, 1984.

Brion, Patrick, and others, *Vincente Minnelli*, Paris, 1985.

Minnelli, Vincente, *I Remember it Well*, Hollywood, 1990.

Harvey, Stephen, *Directed by Vincente Minnelli*, New York, 1990.

Naremore, James, *The Films of Vincent Minnelli*, New York, 1993.

Yudkoff, Alvin, *Gene Kelly; A Life of Dance and Dreams*, New York, 1999.

Articles:

Jablonski, Edward, in *Films in Review* (New York), October 1951.

Harcourt-Smith, Simon, in *Sight and Sound* (London), January-March 1952.

Johnson, A., ''The Films of Vincente Minnelli,'' in *Film Quarterly* (Berkeley), Winter 1958 and Spring 1959.

Minnelli, Vincente, ''The Rise and Fall of the Film Musical,'' in *Films and Filming* (London), January 1962.

Behlmer, Rudy, ''Gene Kelly,'' in *Films in Review* (New York), January 1964.

Cutts, John, ''Dancer, Actor, Director,'' in *Films and Filming* (London), August-September 1964.

Truchaud, François, in *Télérama* (Paris), 13 December 1964.

Steinhauer, W., ''Ruekblende,'' in *Film und Ton* (Munich), March 1973.

Classic Film Collector (Indiana, Pennsylvania), Fall 1976.

Johnson, Julia, in *Magill's Survey of Cinema 1*, Englewood Cliffs, New Jersey, 1980.

Verstraten, P., in *Skrien* (Amsterdam), February-March 1984.

Medhurst, Andy, ''The Musical,'' in *The Cinema Book*, edited by Pam Cook, London, 1985.

Dalle Vacche, A., ''A Painter in Hollywood: Vincente Minnelli's *An American in Paris*,'' in *Cinema Journal* (Austin, Texas), no. 1, 1992.

Blaney, Dorothy Gulbenkian, ''Gene Kelly and the Melting Pot,'' in *USA Today* (Arlington, Virginia), 3 August 1992.

Sharaff, Irene, ''Un Américain à Paris,'' in *Positif* (Paris), July-August 1996.

Zetterberg, Anna, in *Chaplin* (Stockholm), vol. 38, no. 2, 1996.

Cohen, Clélia, ''Un Américain à Paris,'' in *Cahiers du Cinéma* (Paris), December 1997.

* * *

An American in Paris, one of the most successful and popular musicals in the history of film, is also one of the few Technicolor musicals to be taken seriously by critics during the Golden Age of Hollywood when many such films were made. Its grand finale, a 17-minute ballet, focused attention on the fact that films did not have to contain a serious message to be worthy examples of the art form. *An American in Paris* won the Academy Award for Best Picture of 1951, captured five other Academy Awards, and was placed on most lists of best films for that year. It stands as a prime example of a type of musical collaboration made during the studio system.

Difficult critical questions arise regarding the complicated assigning of credit involved in evaluating such movies. First of all, *An American in Paris* is an example of ''producer cinema,'' being one of a list of musicals made by the famous Arthur Freed unit at Metro-Goldwyn-Mayer. The Freed unit was also responsible for *The Bandwagon, Singin' in the Rain, The Pirate, Meet Me in St. Louis*, and many others. Secondly, the creative input of star Gene Kelly, who did the choreography of the ballet, is undeniable, as are the myriad contributions made by MGM's outstanding roster of technicians—costume designer Irene Sharaff, cinematographer John Alton, art director Preston Ames, musicians Johnny Green and Saul Chaplin, and many more. Finally, it is most certainly a film by director

An American in Paris

Vincente Minnelli as it contains his recurring theme of characters in pursuit of their dreams, as well as his typical use of color, costume, and decor. Minnelli's musicals are among the most elegant and polished of the MGM musicals and his flair for camera movement, elaborately constructed long takes, and richly styled backgrounds contribute much to the film.

The opening scenes of *An American in Paris*, in which its characters wake up in "this star called Paris" and go about their daily routines, constitute an homage to Rouben Mamoulian's 1932 film *Love Me Tonight.* In addition to the famous ballet, the innovative musical numbers contain a subjective characterization of Leslie Caron, presented through music, dance, and color. As she is described, images of her appear on screen, each with a different Gershwin tune, different color, costume, setting and color-coordinated background. She is portrayed as sexy, studious, demure, athletic, etc., while the style of dance interprets her inner quality. Other musical numbers include the pas de deux "Our Love Is Here to Stay," which is a beautiful blend of music, setting, costume, and dance, photographed simply with a tight frame around the two dancers as the camera follows their movements. The old-fashioned "I'll Build a Staircase to Paradise" is a tribute to an earlier tradition, the Ziegfeld Follies musical number. The musical highlight of the film is the ballet itself, which is based visually on a series of famous paintings by Dufy, Utrillo, Toulouse-Lautrec, and others. The ballet's story parallels the film's narrative in an oblique manner. An ex-G.I., who has stayed on in Paris after the war, meets a young French girl, falls in love with her, and loses her. Following the ballet, a brief scene depicts a reconciliation, allowing for the inevitable happy ending.

An American In Paris has undergone something of a critical devaluation in the past decade. Other Minnelli musicals (*Meet Me in St. Louis, The Pirate, The Bandwagon*) are considered superior works, and the Kelly/Stanley Donen *Singin' in the Rain* is more popular with general audiences. *An American in Paris* is frequently criticized as being too sentimental, too romantic and, because of the ballet, too pretentious. Nevertheless, the film undoubtedly contributed to the maturing process of the musical genre. By challenging the idea that audiences would not understand or accept a long ballet deeply linked to the narrative of the film it helped to free the dance visually and to expand the horizons of viewers as well as the creative possibilities for the artists making musical films.

—Jeanine Basinger

DER AMERIKANISCHE FREUND

(The American Friend)

West Germany-France, 1977

Director: Wim Wenders

Production: Road Movies Filmproduktion GmbH (Berlin), Les Films du Losange (Paris), Wim Wenders Produktion (Munich), and Westdeutschen Rundfunk (Cologne); Eastmancolor, 35mm; running time: 123 minutes (some sources list 127 minutes). Released 1977. Filmed in Paris.

Producer: Wim Wenders; **screenplay:** Wim Wenders, from the novel *Ripley's Game* by Patricia Highsmith; **photography:** Robby Müller; **editor:** Peter Przygodda; **art director:** Sickerts; **music:** Jürgen Knieper.

Cast: Bruno Ganz (*Jonathan Zimmerman*); Dennis Hopper (*Tom Ripley*); Lisa Kreuzer (*Marianne Zimmerman*); Gérard Blain (*Raoul Minot*); Nicholas Ray (*Derwatt*); Samuel Fuller (*The American*); Peter Lilienthal (*Marcangelo*); Daniel Schmid (*Ingraham*); Jean Eustache (*Man in restaurant*); Sandy Whitelaw (*Man in Paris*); Wim Wenders (*Mafia member*); Lou Castel (*Rodolphe*); Andreas Dedecke (*Daniel*).

Publications

Books:

Dawson, Jan, *Wim Wenders*, Toronto, 1976.
Sandford, John, *The New German Cinema*, Totowa, New Jersey, 1980.
Geist, Kathe, *The Cinema of Wim Wenders 1967–1977*, Ann Arbor, Michigan, 1981.
Johnston, Sheila, *Wim Wenders*, London, 1981.
Boujut, Michel, *Wim Wenders*, Paris, 1982; 3rd edition, 1986.
Buchka, Peter, *Augen kann man nicht Kaufen: Wim Wenders und seine Filme*, Munich, 1983.
Franklin, James, *New German Cinema: From Oberhausen to Hamburg*, Boston, 1983.
Grob, Norbert, *Die Formen des filmische Blicks: Wenders: Die fruhen Filme*, Munich, 1984.
Phillips, Klaus, editor, *New German Filmmakers: From Oberhausen Through the 1970s*, New York, 1984.
Devillers, Jean-Pierre, *Berlin, L.A., Berlin: Wim Wenders*, Paris, 1985.
Geist, Kathe, *The Cinema of Wim Wenders: From Paris, France, to Paris, Texas*, Ann Arbor, Michigan, 1988.
Wenders, Wim, *The Logic of Images: Essays and Conversations*, translated by Michael Hofmann, London, 1991.
Kolker, Robert Phillip, *The Films of Wim Wenders: Cinema as Vision and Desire*, New York, 1993.
Wenders, Wim, *Written in the West*, London, 1996.
Cook, Roger F., and Gerd Gemünden, editors, *The Cinema of Wim Wenders: Image, Narrative, and the Postmodern Condition*, Detroit, 1997.

Articles:

Dahan, L., ''Wim Wenders,'' in *Cinématographe* (Paris), June 1977.
Moskowitz, G., in *Variety* (New York), 8 June 1977.
Niogret, H., in *Positif* (Paris), July-August 1977.
Canby, Vincent, in *New York Times*, 23 September 1977.
Clarens, C., ''King of the Road: Wim Wenders Interviewed,'' in *Film Comment* (New York), September-October 1977.
Masson, A., ''Le Romanesque et le spectaculaire,'' in *Positif* (Paris), October 1977.
Masson, A., and H. Niogret, ''Entretien avec Wim Wenders,'' in *Positif* (Paris), October 1977.
Dawson, Jan, ''Filming Highsmith,'' in *Sight and Sound* (London), Winter 1977–78.
Sauvaget, D., in *Image et Son* (Paris), November 1977.
Narboni, Jean, ''Traquenards,'' in *Cahiers du Cinéma* (Paris), November 1977.
McCreadie, M., in *Films in Review* (New York), December 1977.
Jaehne, K., in *Sight and Sound* (London), Spring 1978.
Winter, L. D., ''De emotionele reizen van Wim Wenders,'' in *Skrien* (Amsterdam), April 1978.
Schlunk, J. D., ''The Image of America in German Literature and in the New German Film: Wim Wenders *Der amerikanische Freud*,'' in *Literature/Film Quarterly* (Salisbury, Maryland), no. 3, 1979.
Kinder, Marsha, in *Film Quarterly* (Berkeley), no. 2, 1979.
''Im Laden ces Bilderrahmers,'' in *Film und Ton* (Munich), December 1979.
Niogret, H., in *Positif* (Paris), May 1982.
Torres, A. R., in *Cinema Novo* (Porto), July-August 1982.
Linville, S., and K. Casper, ''Imitations, Dreams and Origins in Wim Wenders' *The American Friend*,'' in *Literature/Film Quarterly* (Salisbury, Maryland), October 1985.
Snyder, Stephen, ''Wim Wenders: The Hunger Artist in America,'' in *Post Script* (Jacksonville, Florida), Winter 1987.
Benoit, C., ''*L'Ami Americain*,'' in *Jeune Cinéma* (Paris), December 1989.
Rush, J. S., ''Who's In On the Joke: Parody as Hybridized Narrative Discourse,'' in *Quarterly Review of Film and Video* (New York), nos. 1–2, 1990.
Schreckenberg, E., ''Wenn Filme Texte sind,'' in *Filmbulletin* (Winterthur), no. 5, 1994.
Barral, M.A., in *Nosferatu* (San Sebastian), October 1994.
Medina de la Serna, R., in *Dicine*, November/December 1995.
Saada, N., in *Cahiers du Cinéma* (Paris), Hors serie no. 126, 1995.

* * *

While marketing forged paintings in Hamburg, American expatriate Tom Ripley is introduced to picture-framer Jonathan Zimmermann. Suspecting something of Ripley's shady background, Jonathan snubs him. Ripley is hurt, and when he discovers that Jonathan is suffering from leukaemia, he gives his name to Raoul Minot, a gangster who is looking to pay someone with a clean record to wipe out his rivals. Anxious that his wife Marianne and small son Daniel will have enough to live on after his death, Jonathan accepts Monot's offer. But by this time Ripley, who really wants to be friends with Jonathan, regrets what he has done. However, it is too late, and both become caught up in an increasingly nightmarish scenario involving gangsters, murder, and pornography.

Der Amerikanische Freund

The *American Friend* continues the twin themes of *Kings of the Road:* male friendship and the relationship between Germany and America, especially in the area of cinema. This is a film absolutely drenched in cinematic resonances: the animosity-turned-friendship between Ripley and Jonathan is reminiscent of a whole host of romantic Hollywood comedies; the film is based (very loosely) on a novel by Patricia Highsmith, who wrote *Strangers on a Train*, the plot of which is echoed in the Jonathan/Minot deal; not only is Ripley played by Dennis Hopper, but there are also cameo roles from Sam Fuller and Nicholas Ray, thus evoking the kind of Hollywood cinema loved by European cineastes and cinephiles (Godard's *Made in USA* was dedicated to Ray and Fuller, and the latter also appeared in it). The Nouvelle Vague connection is further strengthened by Minot being played by Gerard Blain from Truffaut's *Les Mistons* and Chabrol's *Les Cousins*, and by a curious similarity with *Pierrot le Fou* in that both films end with explosions on deserted beaches and a surviving character named Marianne. Jonathan's home contains a model of a Maltese cross (one of the inventions that made cinema possible), a zoetrope, and a lampshade which animates a picture of the locomotive made famous by Buster Keaton's *The General.* Modern cinema, meanwhile, is represented by the pornographic films (co-productions, naturally) in which the gangsters are involved. And so on.

The American Friend is perhaps best described as a contemporary Franco-German film noir in colour. Like most of its earlier American counterparts it's firmly set in the city, but here the cityscape is European (Hamburg, Paris, Munich) and only briefly American (New York), though one can't but help being reminded of the States when the Sam Fuller character is pushed downstairs in an echo of the famous murder by Richard Widmark in Henry Hathaway's *Kiss of Death.* And then again, all the cities look alike—that is, American—anyway, inhabited, or rather, passed through, by dislocated, rootless characters with an increasingly shaky sense of personal identity. Wenders himself has explained that he chose a combination of film stock and lenses to "obtain a certain strange, artificial atmosphere" and "an image close to hyperrealism," and in this he and his cameraman Robby Müller were quite strikingly successful. One is reminded both of Edward Hopper and Hitchcock, and again Wenders has said that he used Hitchcockian framing in order to achieve "archetypes of images that are at the same time realist and artificial." Indeed, part of the undoubted fascination of *The American Friend* lies in its extraordinary combination of elements that one associates with the Hollywood cinema and the European art cinema. Wenders has described it as ''really dialectical in its attitude to the American cinema: it's full of love and hatred,'' and Timothy Corrigan has elaborated on this point, noting that, on the one hand, there is a ''rigorous decomposition of shots throughout the film, a kind of dissecting and emptying . . . whereby the visual excess of so many deep-focus, Hollywood films becomes a flat Wendersian exactitude'' whilst, on the other, many shots ''recreate the textual brilliance that intentionally echoes and reproduces the texture of so many American films.'' Similarly, although the film is superficially a thriller and part of the crime genre, it is visually devoid of conventional psychological explanations, the characters are for the most part extremely ambiguous and hard to read, and the gangster plot lines convoluted to the point of absurdity.

Clearly, then, *The American Friend* is not just about the uneasy relationship between a particular German and a particular American. It also concerns the relationship between Germany and America. Fears of Americanisation in Germany go back into the nineteenth century (as indeed they do in Britain), and of course the American colonization of the German subconscious has always been a consistent Wenders theme. But this, like his other films, is no simple anti-American parable like Herzog's *Stroszek.* Jonathan, like many a Wenders hero, and indeed like the director himself, clearly likes a good deal about American culture and, as Kathe Geist has observed, ''far from being a man with no culture, Ripley possesses a rich and vibrant culture which Wenders enthusiastically shows us in Ripley's dress (blue jeans, cowboy boots, and cowboy hat) and furnishings (a jukebox, Coca-Cola machine, pool table, and neon Canada Dry sign).'' If there is American exploitation here it is, to a large extent, accepted and even welcomed. As Corrigan has put it, the relationship between Ripley and Jonathan in the film, like the relationship between the American and German film industries, is less a matter of exploitation and ''more accurately described as a series of shared twists, contradictions, and compromises in which one's responses encourage the other's actions.'' In both the film and the industry, the friendship develops around mutual need, admiration and resentment; in both the film and the industry, the friendship is inherently, to borrow Jean Varboni's phrase, ''a malady of love.'' This analogy works extremely well, especially when one considers the problems Wenders faced with *Hammett*, where he played Jonathan to Coppola's Ripley.

—Julian Petley

AMOR DE PERDICÃO

(Doomed Love)

Portugal, 1978

Director: Manoel de Oliveira

Production: Instituto Portuguese de Cinema; color, originally shot in 16mm; running time: 260 minutes. Released 1978. Filmed in Portugal.

Producer: Anabela Goncaldes; **screenplay:** Manoel de Oliveira, from the novel by Camilo Castelo Branco; **photography:** Manuel Costa e Silva; **editor:** Soldeig Nordlund; **art director:** Antonio Casmiro; **music:** João Paes and Handel.

Cast: Antonio Sequeira Lopes (*Simão Botelho*); Cristina Hauser (*Tereza*); Elsa Wallencamp (*Mariana da Cruz*); Antonio Costa (*Juao de Cruz*); Pedro Dinheiro and Manuela de Melo (*Narrators*).

Publications

Books:

Manoel de Oliveira, Lisbon, 1981.

Franca, J. A., and others, *Introdução à de M. de Oliveira*, Lisbon, 1982.

Articles:

Desclimont, B., in *Revue du Cinéma* (Paris), series 23, 1979.

Daney, S., ''Manoel de Oliveira and *Amour de perdition*,'' in *Cahiers du Cinéma* (Paris), June 1979.

Bassan, R., in *Ecran* (Paris), 15 June 1979.

Bonnet, J. C., in *Cinématographe* (Paris), July 1979.

Frenais, J., in *Cinéma* (Paris), July-August 1979.

Bachellier, E., in *Cahiers du Cinéma* (Paris), September 1979.

Lopes, João, ''O voto de Simão e Teresa,'' in *Diário de Noticias* (Lisbon), November 1979.

Ramasse, F., ''M. de Oliveira: Le Passé et le present,'' in *Positif* (Paris), March 1980.

Holloway, D., in *Variety* (New York), 15 October 1980.

Alnaee, K., ''Det stillstående kamera,'' in *Film & Kino* (Oslo), no. 4, 1981.

Zunsunegui, S., ''Artificio, enunciácion, emocion: La obra de M. de Oliveira,'' in *Contracampo* (Madrid), January 1981.

Clarens, C., ''Manoel de Oliveira and *Doomed Love*,'' in *Film Comment* (New York), May-June 1981.

Gillett, John, ''Manoel de Oliveira,'' in *Sight and Sound* (London), Summer 1981.

Tesson, C., and J. C. Biette, interview with Oliveira, in *Cahiers du Cinéma* (Paris), October 1981.

Fonseca, M. S., ''M. de Oliveira, o cinema e a crueldade,'' in *Expresso* (Lisbon), October 1981.

Bonnet, J. C., and E. Decaux, interview with Oliveira, in *Cinématographe* (Paris), November 1981.

Coelho, E. P., ''*Amor de perdicao*,'' in *Revue Belge du Cinéma* (Brussels), no. 26, 1989.

Scarpetta, Guy & Rollet, Sylvie, ''Manoel de Oliveira,'' in *Positif* (Paris), September 1998.

Avant-Scène Cinéma, January-February 1999.

* * *

At the age of 70 Manoel de Oliveira completed *Amor de perdicão*, a 260-minute version of Camilo Castelo Branco's 19th-century,

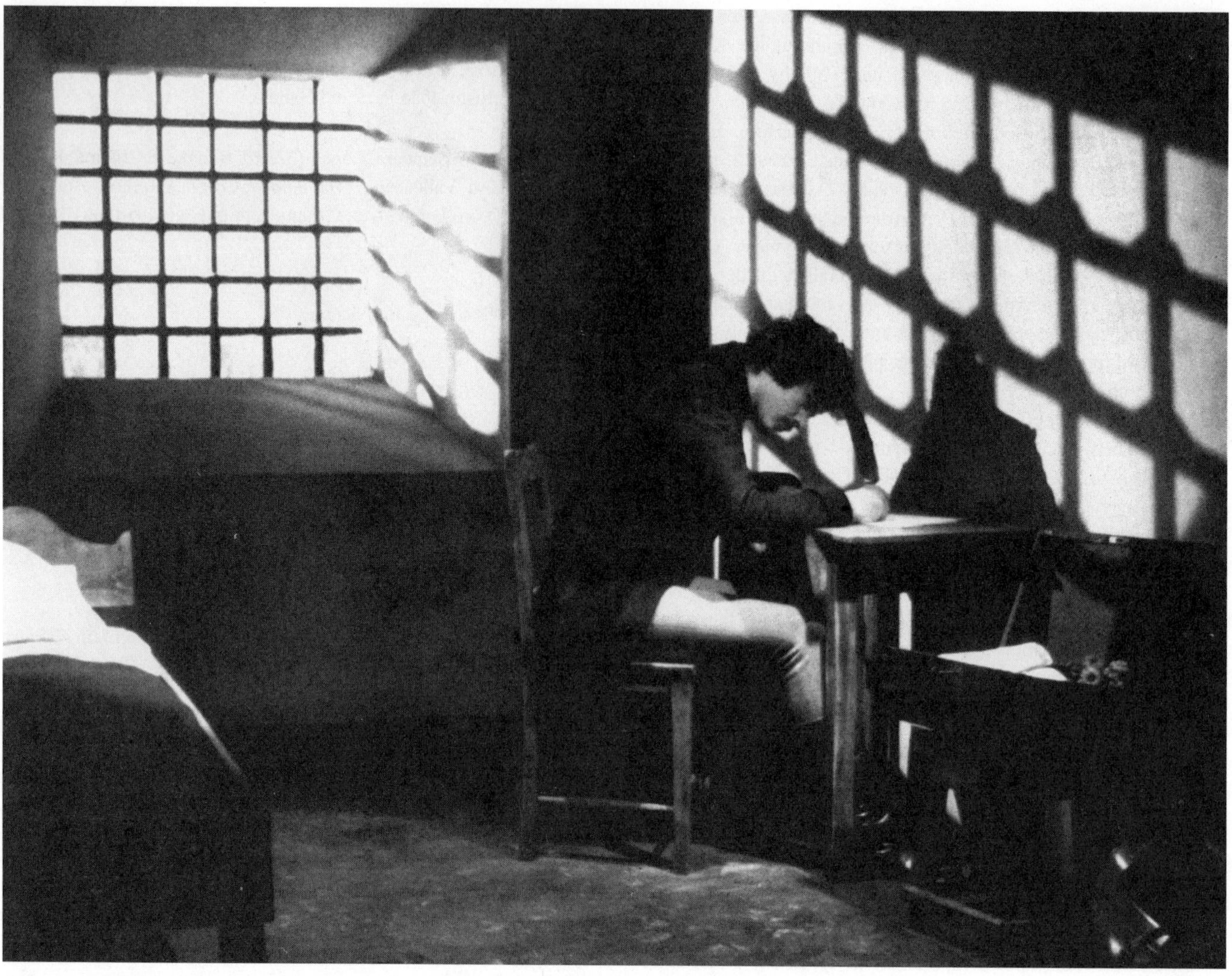

Amor de perdicão

hyper-romantic novel of the same name. It was the twelfth film in the career of Portugal's most famous filmmaker, a career which began in 1931.

As meticulously as the novel, the film renders events in a procession of extremely long sequence-shots, often between five and ten minutes each. *Amor de perdicão* consciously occupies a precarious historical position: in a style wholly characteristic of the advanced cinema of the 1970s, with a startling original use of the zoom lens, it depicts events of the late 18th and early 19th centuries, mediated by the deliberately anachronistic language of the 1861 novel. The film resonates with allusions to the Iberian pictorial tradition (Velázquez and Goya are the most obvious references), yet it calls attention to the modalities of camera position, shot duration, illusionary movement created by the zoom, and the artificiality of its museum-like sets and occasional painted backdrops. Oliveira is indebted to the major historical films of the previous decade, especially *La Prise du pouvoir de Louis XIV, Il gattopardo*, and *Barry Lyndon* in his use of the zoom and his historical distanciation, but he is far more systematic and abstract than his major predecessors. More obviously, he follows Robert Bresson in his cool resistance to imitating the histrionics of the text he adapts; but he avoids the truly radical deflation of drama typical of the later films of Straub and Huillet. Yet, perhaps he has learned something from their early work; for the breathtaking pace with which the Botelho family history is recounted, in elliptical jumps, in the first half hour of the film, recalls the most disorienting moments of *Nicht versont.* The novel and the film recount the miseries of the star-crossed lovers, Simão Botelho and his neighbor Tereza, whose father forbids their marriage because of a family feud. In an intricate plot, which would be long in summary, Simão goes to jail for killing the man Tereza's father wants her to marry. In jail he is attended by the peasant girl, Mariana da Cruz, whose devotion to him takes the form of obsessive love. Eventually Simão dies en route to the Indies, as a penal worker; Tereza, already withdrawn into a convent, dies as his boat passes; and Mariana jumps overboard to her death. Only Oliveira's genius transmutes this morbid excess into a cinema of sustained beauty and restraint.

Though he shot the film in 16mm because he couldn't afford 35mm for the first time in his career, he exploited the loss of definition and the grain brilliantly. His compositions are consistently artificial, evoking enlarged indoor spaces by posing the characters far from the camera or, following the examples of Velázquez's *Las Meninas*, using a mirror to reflect offscreen depths. The continual interlacing of the voice-overs of narrators Simão and Tereza bring a stylistic device already abstracted by Bresson and Hanoun to a new level of intensity and abstraction.

The very duration of the film, its plethora of information spread over so many nearly static compositions, the extended meditation on confinement, and the beauty of its deliberate rhythms and compositions make *Amor de perdicão* one of the most impressive films of the 1970s, and one of the very greatest historical fiction films.

—P. Adams Sitney

AND ... GOD CREATED WOMAN

See **ET ... DIEU CREA LA FEMME**

AND LIFE GOES ON

(Zendegi Edame Darad; Life and Nothing More)

Iran, 1992

Director: Abbas Kiarostami

Production: Institute for the Intellectual Development of Children and Young Adults; color, 35 mm; running time: 91 minutes (95 in Iran; 108 in Canada); sound: mono. Filmed in Koker and Poshteh, Iran.

Producer: Ali Reza Zarrin; **screenplay:** Abbas Kiarostami; **cinematographer:** Homayun Payvar; **editor:** Abbas Kiarostami; **assistant director:** Hassen Afakrimi, Alirfa Akbari, Behram Kadhemi; **production supervisor:** Nemet Allah Yahifi, Khada Dad Ahmed, Mahrem Fifi; **production manager:** Sadika Sarfrazian; **costume design:** Hassan Zahidi; **artistic supervisor:** Ferched Bachirzada, Djalil Chaabani, Saad Saidi; **sound:** Abbas Kiarostami, Djenkis Sayed.

Cast: Farhad Kheradmand (*Film Director*); Buba Bayour (*Puya*); Hocine Rifahi; Ferhendeh Feydi; Marhem Feydi; Bahrovz Aydini; Mohamed Hocinerouhi; Hocine Khadem; Maassouma Berouana; Mohamed Reda Berouana; Chahrbanov Chefahi; Youssef Branki; Chahine Ayzen; Mohamed Bezdani; and others.

Publications

Articles:

Libiot, Eric, review in *Première* (Paris), November 1992.

Ångström, Anna, ''Livet efter katastrofen,'' in *Svenska Dagbladet* (Sweden), 3 June 1994.

James, Nick, review in *Sight and Sound* (London), October 1996.

* * *

And Life Goes On is the middle film of a trilogy, preceded by *Where Is the Friend's Home?* and followed by *Through the Olive Trees.* The three films (rightly regarded as among the great achievements of contemporary world cinema) are intricately interconnected; only the first might be considered self-sufficient. Briefly, *Where Is the Friend's Home?* is a straightforward neo-realist film about the predicament of two small boys in an adult world too preoccupied with its own problems to listen to children. *And Life Goes On* is set in the same district of Iran a year or so later: the great earthquake has intervened, and the director of the first film (played by an actor, and never named within the film) journeys by car with his young son to find out whether the two children who acted the main roles in the previous film have survived. *Through the Olive Trees* carries the self-reflexiveness even further, at times into quite dizzying convolutions: Kiarostami (played this time by a different actor, though now named) returns again to the area to make a film about the filming of *And Life Goes On*, partly involving the reconstruction of scenes from that film; at one point, then, we have Kiarostami himself (off screen) directing an actor playing Kiarostami directing the actor who played him in *And Life Goes On.* With this in mind, it may seem paradoxical to add that the most obvious characteristic of Kiarostami's films is their simplicity. The complications are in the material, never in its filmic realization. If one also wishes to describe his filmmaking as virtuoso, that is again not really a contradiction: the music of Mozart (with which Kiarostami's work, in its emotional delicacy and complexity, might be felt to have an affinity) might also be described as at once simple and virtuosic. Consider, for example, the now famous last shots of both *And Life Goes On* and *Through the Olive Trees*, the moments often referred to as ''epiphanies'': what could be simpler than simply placing the camera in the necessary viewing position and refusing to move it or cut throughout a lengthy action shown in extreme long-shot? And the action itself is as simple as possible: a car trying to climb a steep hill, a young man running to catch up with the woman he loves to propose one last time. Yet the suspense is edge-of-your-seat, the end a whole new beginning, such is the emotional investment asked of the spectator.

Kiarostami's aesthetic roots are in Italian neo-realism (one notes a particular affinity with the greatest of the neo-realists, making it especially appropriate that he was given the Rossellini prize at an Italian film festival). The self-reflexivity comes perhaps from the French New Wave, especially Godard, though it seems so natural to Kiarostami, to arise so logically from his work, that one wonders whether he invented it independently. *Where Is the Friend's Home?* never calls its (fictional) reality into question. *And Life Goes On* remains faithful to the basic neo-realist principles, with everything shot on location using non-professional actors (''real people''), yet it is also the interrogation of neo-realism: the figure of the filmmaker now appears in the film, the previous film is revealed *as* a film, a fiction, and the ''real people'' were in fact acting: one of them, encountered en route, complains that Kiarostami made him dress and behave quite differently from his everyday self. We are of course free to ask whether Kiarostami *told* him to say this, especially in retrospect from *Through the Olive Trees*, in which we see the director insist (against all odds) that the recalcitrant actors speak the lines they have been given.

Yet the levels never cancel each other out. If we are aware of a dislocation between fiction and reality, we are also constantly aware

And Life Goes On

of their close relationship. As the director drives through devastated landscapes, we know that the rubble is real, that the earthquake was a fact, that the two boys could have died, even while we know that we are watching a carefully constructed film and are at liberty to reflect that Kiarostami must already have known whether they were alive or not. We care about finding the boys because we know they are ''real'' boys from that area, but also because they were the *characters* from the previous film (which is, after all, how we know them), still bearing their (fictional) emotional weight. Kiarostami demonstrates that it is possible to be completely honest about the fabricated nature of filmmaking (*all* filmmaking, even documentary) without jeopardizing the possibility of the emotional involvement we look for in fiction. The self-reflexivity functions more as counterpoint than as contradiction.

—Robin Wood

ANDALUSIAN DOG

See **UN CHIEN ANDALOU**

ANDREI RUBLEV

USSR, 1969

Director: Andrei Tarkovsky

Production: Mosfilm Studio (Moscow); black and white with a color sequence, 35mm, Cinemascope; running time: 185 minutes; length: 5180 meters. Released 1969 in France; not released in USSR until 1972 though the film had been screened in Moscow in 1965. The film was censored and re-edited (not by Tarkovsky) several times between production and release in 1969. Filmed 1965.

Screenplay: Andrei Mikhalkov-Konchalovsky and Andrei Tarkovsky; **photography:** Vadim Youssov; **editors:** N. Beliaeva and L. Lararev; **sound:** E. Zelentsova; **production designer:** Eugueni Tcheriaiev; **music:** Viatcheslac Ovtchinnikov.

Cast: Anatoli Solonitzine (*Rubliov*); Ivan Lapikov (*Dirill*); Nikolai Grinko (*Daniel the Black*); Nikolai Sergueiev (*Theophanes the Greek*);

Irma Raouch Tarkovskaya (*Deaf-mute*); Nikolai Bourliaiev (*Boriska*); Youri Nasarov (*Grand Duke*); Rolan Bykov (*Buffoon*); Youri Nikulin (*Patrikey*); Mikhail Kononov (*Fomka*); S. Krylov; Sos Sarkissyan; Bolot Eichelanev; N. Grabbe; B. Beijenaliev; B. Matisik; A. Oboukhov; Volodia Titov.

Awards: Cannes Film Festival, International Critics Award, 1969.

Publications

Script:

Tarkovsky, Andrei, *Andrei Rublev*, Paris, 1970.

Books:

Vronskaya, Jeanne, *Young Soviet Film Makers*, London, 1972.
Cohen, Louis H., *The Cultural-Political Traditions and Development of the Soviet Cinema: 1917–1972*, New York, 1974.
Stoil, Michael Jon, *Cinema Beyond the Danube: The Camera and Politics*, Metuchen, New Jersey, 1974.
Liehm, Mira and Antonin, *The Most Important Art: East European Film after 1945*, Berkeley, 1977.
Tarkovsky, Andrei, *Sculpting in Time: Reflections on the Cinema*, London, 1986.
Borin, Fabrizio, *Andrej Tarkovskij*, Venice, 1987.
Jacobsen, Wolfgang, and others, *Andrej Tarkovskij*, Munich, 1987.
Le Fanu, Mark, *The Cinema of Andrei Tarkovsky*, New York, 1987.
Johnson, Vida T., and Graham Petrie, *The Films of Andrei Tarkovsky: A Visual Fugue*, Bloomington, Indiana, 1994.
Goldenberg, Mikhail, *V Glubinakh Sudeb Lyudskikh—In the Depths of Destinies*, Baltimore, 1999.
Andrei Tarkovsky: Collected Screenplays, London, 1999.

Articles:

Gregor, U., ''Schwierigkeiten beim Filmen de Geschichte,'' *Kinemathek* (Germany), no. 41, July 1969.
Lebedewa, J.A., ''Andrej Rubljow und seine Zeit,'' *Kinemathek* (Germany), no. 41, July 1969.
Tarkovsky, A. ''Die bewahrte Zeit,'' *Kinemathek* (Germany), no. 41, July 1969.
Vronskaya, Jeanne, in *Monogram* (London), Summer 1971.
Wiersewski, W., ''Artysta na gościńcu epoki: *Andrej Rublow*,'' in *Kino* (Warsaw), November 1972.
''Andre Rubliov Issue'' of *Filmrutan* (Sweden), no. 2, 1973.
Povše, J., ''*Andrej Rublov*—film projekcije po projekciji,'' in *Ekran* (Ljubljana, Yugoslavia), no. 108–110, 1973.
Cetinjski, M., in *Ekran* (Ljubljana, Yugoslavia), no. 194–195, 1973.
Amengual, B., ''Allégori et Stalinisme dans quelques films de l'est,'' in *Positif* (Paris), January 1973.
Gerasimov, Sergei, and others, in *Filmkultura* (Budapest), March-April 1973.
Montagu, Ivor, ''Man and Experience: Tarkovsky's World,'' in *Sight and Sound* (London), Spring 1973.
Tarrat, M., in *Films and Filming* (London), November 1973.
O'Hara, J., in *Cinema Papers* (Australia), 1975.
Grande, M., in *Filmcritica* (Rome), January-February 1976.
Rineldi, G., in *Cineforum* (Bergamo), January-February 1976.
Prono, F., in *Cinema Nuovo* (Turin), March-April 1976.
Chapier, Henry, in *Cambat* (Paris), 20 November 1979, excerpt reprinted in *Avant-Scène du Cinéma* (Paris) 15 December 1979.
Ciment, Michel, ''Richesse et diversité du nouveau cinéma soviétique,'' in *Avant-Scène du Cinéma* (Paris), 15 December 1979.
Ward, M., ''The Idea that Torments and Exhausts,'' in *Stills* (London), Spring 1981.
Torp Pedersen, B., in *Filmrutan* (Stockholm), 1984.
van der Kaap, H., and G. Zuilhof, in *Skrien* (Amsterdam), Summer 1985.
Anninskii, L., ''Popytka ochishcheniia?'' in *Iskusstvo Kino* (Moscow), no. 1, 1989.
Illg, E., and L. Noiger, ''Vstat' na lut',''in *Iskusstvo Kino* (Moscow), no. 2, 1989.
''Tarkovskijs rad till blivande kolleger,'' in *Chaplin* (Stockholm), no. 4, 1989.
Vinokurova, T., ''Khozhdenie po mukam *Andreiia Rubleva*,'' in *Iskusstvo Kino* (Moscow), no. 10, 1989.
Pistoia, M., ''Elogio del piano-sequenza,'' in *Filmcritica* (Rome), January-February 1991.
Strick, P., ''Releasing the Balloon, Raising the Bell,'' in *Monthly Film Bulletin* (London), February 1991.
Giavarini, L., ''*Andrei Roublev*, un film de Russie,'' in *Cahiers du Cinéma* (Paris), December 1991.
Bleeckere, Sylvain De, ''De religiositeit van de beeldcultuur: Tarkovsky and Andrei Roeblev,'' *Film en Televisie + Video* (Brussels), February 1992.
Kovacs, A. B., ''Tarkovszkij szellimi utja,'' in *Filmvilag* (Budapest), no. 12, 1992.
Leutrat, J.-L., ''Considerations intempestives autour d'*Andrei Roublev*,'' in *Positif* (Paris), April 1992.
Meeus, M. ''De passie van Andrei,'' *Film en Televisie + Video* (Brussels), September 1994.
Elrick, Ted, ''The Prince, the Kid, and the Painter,'' *DGA Magazine* (Los Angeles), vol. 20, no. 2, April/May 1995.
Schillaci, F., ''Lo spazio il tempo nell'opera di Andrej Tarkovskij,'' *Spettacolo*, vol. 46, no. 1, 1996.
Wiese, I. ''Andrej Tarkovskij,'' *Z* (Oslo), no. 1, 1996.
''Nel giusto mezzo: *Andrej Rublev*,'' *Castoro Cinema* (Milan), no. 181, January/February 1997.

* * *

Andrei Tarkovsky's second feature film did not have an easy passage. Conceived and written in the early 1960s and completed in 1966, it finally arrived at Cannes, where it was awarded the International Critics Prize, in 1969. It did not surface in Soviet cinemas until 1972, after the authorities there had attacked it as unhistorical and narratively obscure, and had raised objections to its level of violence. To Western eyes, this attempt to muzzle and belittle what was so obviously a monumental work reeked of pre-perestroika censorship, and epitomized the typical muddle-headedness of the cultural dogma of socialist realism. However, as Ivor Montagu, erstwhile collaborator with Eisenstein, observed in the British Magazine, *Sight and Sound*, not many European or American directors are given the opportunity to make ''colour, widescreen, 3'' hour superproductions'' about the intimate life of medieval monks. Although Tarkovsky did remove 14 minutes from his original version, he professed himself

Andrei Rublev

happy with the amendments. The oft-stated notion of Tarkovsky as the prophet without honour in his own country, who had to look westward to find confirmation of his merits, must be tempered by the knowledge that he was able to make historical epics like this, science-fiction films (*Solaris* and *Stalker*), a war film (*Ivan's Childhood*), and a highly idiosyncratic personal memoir of childhood (*Mirror*): these films do not offer much evidence of artistic compromise or of kow-towing to the authorities.

Andrei Rublev was co-scripted by Tarkovsky's fellow Moscow film school graduate, Konchalovsky, and photographed by Vadim Youssov, Tarkovsky's trusted cameraman until he refused to work on *Mirror* (1974), claiming that the director's script was self-indulgent and unintelligible. *Andrei Rublev* charts seven episodes in the life of its eponymous hero, an artist and monk who, from the cocooned seclusion of a monastery, is exposed to the horrors of the 15th-century world. In a magical mystery tour, Rublev is confronted with brutality, torture, drunkenness, tartar despoliation, rape, pillage, and famine, but manages to maintain his faith in humanity. Inspired by a young waif, Boriska (played by Nikolai Bourliaiev, the protagonist in *Ivan's Childhood*, Tarkovsky's first feature, made in 1962), who assumes responsibility for the making of a huge bell, finding and moulding the clay, requisitioning the silver, supervising a veritable army of older and more experienced assistants, all the time aware that if the bell fails to chime he will be put to death by the arch-duke, Rublev learns that, in the midst of social upheaval and wholesale destruction, creativity is still possible.

Perhaps the aspect of *Andrei Rublev* that most irritated Soviet authorities was its religious iconography. Rublev, being a monk, is necessarily Christian. For Tarkovsky, who as a film director seems to have identified closely with the icon painter, Rublev's creativity and his faith are inextricable: the former is merely the embodiment of the latter. Creativity is not about character or milieu or means of production. In the film it is presented as a mystical transcendent force that must, nonetheless, take into account the exterior world. Throughout the film, counterpointing Rublev and acting as his foil, is a fellow artist, Theophanes the Greek. Theophanes witnesses the same medieval maelstrom as Rublev, but reacts to it in a very different way. Whereas Rublev overcomes his revulsion, and is able to forgive and even to love humanity, Theophanes feels nothing but disgust. He sees human kind as base and fallen, and tries to immure himself. In his isolation, he is the inferior artist.

The film is not an historical record. There are few details extant of Andrei Rublev's life. Tarkovsky and Konchalovsky offer him materiality, a psychology, and an ability to bear witness to his own epoch. And from the virtuoso opening crane-shots, showing a medieval hot-air balloonist, to the tartars' razing of the cathedral, to frenzied pagan ritual, to all the palaver of the building of an enormous bell, *Andrei Rublev* is on an epic scale. Tarkovsky shows an unerring instinct for filming landscape, for filming the elements. His vision of the middle ages does not seem to allow for the possibility of sunshine; on his grim backcloth, wind and rain are pretty well constant. There is plenty of mud and water in which characters can get stuck, and blood is forever being spilled. There is nothing coy or cosmetic about Tarkovsky's imagined world, nothing too rarefield: this is visceral and violent terrain. Horses—Tarkovsky, like Kurosawa, is an expert at photographing the beasts—gallop up and down the landscape to great effect. Anatoli Solonitzine, Tarkovsky's favourite actor, plays Rublev with quiet and stoical dignity. But Rublev is so impassive and austere a figure, and so taciturn, that it is hard to have much sympathy for him. Though Tarkovsky always claimed that Dovzhenko was the Soviet director he felt most affinity with, *Andrei Rublev* echoes Eisenstein's *Ivan the Terrible* and *Alexander Nevsky*, both in its grandiose reconstruction of a period in Russian history, and in its facility in depicting battle scenes and dealing with crowds.

The jerky jumps between episodes, often shooting us forward a matter of years in an instant, are somewhat bewildering. Tarkovsky's disdain for linear narrative, which he likens to the proof of a geometrical theorem, is well charted. He defended *Andrei Rublev* from the charge of obscurity by citing Engels, who claimed that the more sophisticated the work, the more intricate was its use of formal device. However, *Andrei Rublev* does not have the multi-layered narrative of, for example, *Mirror*, which shifts easily from generation to generation, and from place to place. Three hours of saturnine medieval gloom, even if relieved by a gallery of wonderfully grotesque Breughelian physiognomies, is hard to take. Nonetheless, as a rigorous meditation on faith, art, and creation in a time of fratricide and civil strife, as a moral fable, and as a bravura piece of filmmaking, *Andrei Rublev* is magnificent.

The film, which has been in black and white, ends with a tremendous explosion of colour as we finally see images of Rublev's celebrated icons, in particular his *Trinity*, which is to be found at the Trinity-St. Sergius monastery in Zagorsk. These paintings, beautiful and abstracted from the world in which they were created, are the film's justification. Out of degradation, murder, carnage, out of the turbulent landscape of 15th-century Russia, ungodly, riven by civil war, Rublev is able to create sublime and timeless works of art.

—G. C. Macnab

ANGEL WITH THE TRUMPET

See **DER ENGEL MIT DER POSAUNE**

ANGI VERA

Hungary, 1978

Director: Pál Gábor

Production: MAFILM Objektív Stúdió; color, 35 mm; running time: 92 minutes; language: Hungarian; distributed by Hungarofilm. Released 1978.

Screenplay: Pál Gábor and Endre Vészi; **photography:** Lajos Koltai; **editor:** Éva Kármentö; **production designer:** András Gyürki; **costumes:** Éva Z. Varga; **original music:** György Selmeczi; **sound:** György Fék; **assistant director:** Dezsö Koza.

Cast: Veronika Papp (*Vera Angi*); Erzsi Pásztor (*Anna Traján*); Éva Szabó (*Mária Muskát*); Tamás Dunai (*István André*); László Horváth (*József Neubauer*); László Halász (*Sas*); and others.

Awards: Silver Seashell/Best Director (Pál Gábor), San Sebastián (Spain) International Film Festival, 1979; Audience Award for Best Feature, São Paulo (Brazil) International Film Festival, 1979.

Angi Vera

Publications

Books:

Burns, Bryan, *World Cinema: Hungary*, Trowbridge, 1996.
Burns, Bryan, *Angi Vera*, Trowbridge, 1996.

Articles:

Gallagher, Michael, ''*Angi Vera*: A Conversation with Pál Gábor,'' in *Cineaste* (New York), vol. 10, no. 2, Spring 1980.
Quart, Leonard, ''*Angi Vera*,'' in *Film Quarterly* (Berkeley), vol. 34, no. 1, Autumn 1980.

* * *

At a compulsory political propaganda session at a hospital in communist Hungary in the fall of 1948 Vera Angi, a shy 18-year-old nursemaid, raises and courageously criticizes the hospital's corruption and its neglect of the patients. Her criticism impresses the comrades, particularly as it legitimates their plans to get rid of some politically untrustworthy doctors. The fact that Vera is an orphan of working-class background is particularly useful—she fits the template for new cadres that the Communist Party is looking to promote. The Party needs people like Vera, and soon she is sent to a six-month long political education course for party functionaries.

Vera is aware of her political ignorance, but she is willing to learn; her ''tabula rasa'' attitude is particularly welcome by the Party well-wishers. The course also enrolls other upwardly mobile workers. Amidst all of them, however, Vera is the best. She is a natural, a genius of the new political correctness. Rather than making friends with younger women, she is attracted to an older aparatchik—Anna Trajan, a sour old maid—who is preparing to enter the nomenklatura as a newspaper editor-in-chief. Anna's tutelage is crucial—she teaches Vera how to recognize and denounce political untrustworthiness, and how to report on the politically deviant.

One of Vera's classmates, a miner, develops an attraction to her, but she rebuffs him. She is interested in another man instead, the group seminar leader István Andre, a family man. During a party they come close to each other as they dance, holding a small ball between their foreheads, an erotically loaded scene that sharply contrasts with the austere surroundings. Soon thereafter Vera confesses her love to István; he admits he is also attracted to her. That same night she visits him secretly and they have sex. The following day, however, she begins persistently to avoid him. At a criticism and self-criticism party meeting which follows, Vera publicly denounces her affair with István. She claims to be ashamed and blames it all on herself. István is driven to admit his love in public, only to be rebuffed by Vera, who says she does not really love him. István is removed from the course, and a new study group leader takes over.

The others in the group ostracize Vera. During the graduation ceremony, she collapses on the stage. When she comes back to her senses, after the course is over, everyone else have left for their places of origin. She, however, does not have anywhere to go and does not want to return to the hospital. Anna Trajan informs her the Party has decided to make her a journalist as she has proven to be suitable for this responsible profession. She takes Vera away in a car. On the road they pass by one of the women, a fellow student, who does not even want to look at Vera. The concluding shot of the movie shows Vera in a close up, introvertedly looking in front of her. She is alone. She has begun her ascent to her future career.

Angi Vera is the story of an individual's doomed attempt to break free in a society which has banned individuality in principle. Rather than challenging and confronting the system, Vera Angi becomes its voluntary victim. Her crippled personality fits well the psychological profile drafted by the communists. She has rejected human warmth, friendship, and love, and she does not care very much about being alone. She is a monster, subtly indicted by the filmmakers.

The early Stalinist years—the period after the so-called ''amalgamation,'' the coercive co-optation of all liberal parties under the Communist one—provide the social context for the film. The film, however, treats party politics as an extension of personal politics. The individuals who are the center of attention are concerned about their own survival and are prepared to adjust by swiftly changing political colors. The narrative is structured around collective events, culminating in the depressing party meetings which most people seem to detest but in which Vera learns to thrive. The meetings, at which everybody undergoes harsh scrutiny and self-criticism, are regularly attended by high-placed party comrades. The meetings are designed so that the attendees maintain a constant feeling of unspecified guilt; they cultivate uncritical conformism.

With its exploration of suppressed sexuality and its numerous references to Vera's deprived childhood, *Angi Vera* is a finely crafted psychological study of an individual in a constraining social context. The exquisite cinematography of Lajos Koltai, István Szabó's regular director of photography, subtly problematizes the relationship between public and private by juxtaposing extreme close ups and scenes of mass gatherings. The gray, dull light of winter afternoons amidst a cold landscape justifies the choice of subdued colors that work greatly to enhance the message of alienation and constraint.

Pál Gábor's next film, the acclaimed but lesser known *Wasted Lives* (*Kettévált mennyezet*), (1981), was also set in the 1950s and continued the director's interest in the issues of individual fate in the context of Stalinist confines. This topic has been a defining interest for other leading Hungarian directors as well—for Károy Makk's subtle *Love* (1979) and *Another Way* (1982), for Marta Mészarós's utterly personal *Diary Trilogy* (1982–1990), for Péter Bacsó's satire *The Witness* (1969) and *Oh, Bloody Life!*, (1983), and for István Szabó's psychological study, *Father* (1966). Like *Angi Vera*, many of these films treat the period from a coming-of-age point of view and offer fine studies of personality formation in a society that demands conformism.

—Dina Iordanova

ANGST ESSEN SEELE AUF

(Ali: Fear Eats the Soul)

West Germany, 1973

Director: Rainer Werner Fassbinder

Production: Tango-Film Productions; color, 35mm; running time: 90 minutes. Released 1973. Filmed in Germany.

Producer: Rainer Werner Fassbinder; **screenplay:** Rainer Werner Fassbinder; **photography:** Jürgen Jüges; **editor:** Thea Eymes; **sound:** Fritz Müller-Scherz; **art director:** Rainer Werner Fassbinder; **costume designer:** Helga Kempke.

Cast: Brigitte Mira (*Emmi*); El Hedi ben Salem (*Ali/El Hedi ben Salem M'Barek Mohammed Mustapha*); Barbara Valantin (*Barbara*); Irm Hermann (*Krista*); Peter Gauhe (*Bruno*); Karl Scheydt (*Albert*); Rainer Werner Fassbinder (*Eugen*); Marquand Bohm (*Herr Gruber*); Walter Sedlmayer (*Herr Angermeyer*); Doris Mattes (*Frau Angermeyer*); Liselotte Eder (*Frau Munchmeyer*); Gusti Kreissel (*Paula*); Elma Karlowa; Anita Bucher; Margit Symo; Katharina Herberg; Lilo Pompeit; Hannes Gromball; Hark Bohm; Rudolf Waldemar; Peter Moland.

Awards: Cannes Film Festival, International Critics' Award (shared with Bresson's *Lancelot du Lac*), 1974.

Publications

Books:

Limmer, Wolfgang, *Fassbinder*, Munich, 1973.

Thomsen, Christian, *I Fassbinders Spejl*, Copenhagen, 1975.

Pflaum, Hans, *Das bisschen Realitat, das ich brauche: Wir Filme entstehen*, Munich, 1976.

Rayns, Tony, *Fassbinder*, London, 1976.

Peter, Jansen, and Wolfram Schütte, editors, *Reihe Film 2: Rainer Werner Fassbinder*, Munich, 1979.

Angst essen Seele auf

Sandford, John, *The New German Cinema*, Totowa, New Jersey, 1980.
Baer, Harry, *Schlafen kann ich, wenn ich tot bin: Das atemlose Leben des Rainer Werner Fassbinder*, Cologne, 1982.
Eckhardt, Bernd, *Rainer Werner Fassbinder: Im 17 Jahren 42 Filme—Stationen eines Lebens fur den Deutschen Film*, Munich, 1982.
Iden, Peter, and others, *Rainer Werner Fassbinder*, Munich, 1982.
Raab, Kurt, and Karsten Peters, *Die Sehnsucht des Rainer Werner Fassbinder*, Munich, 1982.
Foss, Paul, editor, *Fassbinder in Review*, Sydney, 1983.
Franklin, James, *New German Cinema: From Oberhausen to Hamburg*, Boston, 1983.
Fassbinder, Rainer Werner, *Film Befreien den Kopf: Essays und Arbeitsnotizen*, edited by Michael Töteburg, Frankfurt, 1984.
Hayman, Ronald, *Fassbinder: Film-maker*, London, 1984.
Phillips, Klaus, *New German Filmmakers: From Oberhausen Through the 1970s*, New York, 1984.
Fassbinder, Rainer Werner, *Die Anarchie der Phantasie: Gespräche und Interviews*, edited by Michael Töteburg, Frankfurt, 1986.
Katz, Robert, and Peter Berling, *Love Is Colder Than Death: The Life and Times of Rainer Werner Fassbinder*, London 1987.
Shattuc, Jane, *Television, Tabloids, and Tears: Fassbinder and Popular Culture*, Minneapolis, 1995.
Elsaesser, Thomas, *Fassbinder's Germany: History, Identity, Subject*, Amsterdam, 1996.
Kardish, Laurence, editor, *Rainer Werner Fassbinder*, New York, 1997.

Articles:

Thomas, Christian Braad, ''Fassbinder's Holy Whores,'' in *Take One* (Montreal), July-August 1973.
Sander, Helke, ''Die Darstellung alter Frauen in Film,'' in *Frauen und Film* (Berlin), no. 3, 1974.
Grant, J., in *Cinéma* (Paris), July-August 1974.
Rayns, Tony, in *Sight and Sound* (London), Autumn 1974.
Amengual, Barthélemy, in *Positif* (Paris), September 1974.
Hepnerova, E., in *Film a Doba* (Prague), September 1974.
Sauvaget, D., in *Image et Son* (Paris), September 1974.
Canby, Vincent, in *New York Times*, 7 October 1974.
Combs, Richard, in *Monthly Film Bulletin* (London), November 1974.

Farber, Manny, and Patricia Patterson, ''Rainer Werner Fassbinder,'' in *Film Comment* (New York), November-December 1975.

Hughes, John, and Brooks Riley, ''A New Realism: Fassbinder Interviewed,'' in *Film Comment* (New York), November-December 1975.

Thomas, Paul, ''Fassbinder—The Poetry of the Inarticulate,'' in *Film Quarterly* (Berkeley), Winter 1976–1977.

Franklin, James, ''Method and Message: Forms of Communication in Fassbinder's *Angst essen Seele auf*,'' in *Literature/Film Quarterly* (Salisbury, Maryland), no. 3, 1979.

Santamaria, J. V. G., in *Contracampo* (Madrid), 1980.

Stefanoni, L., in *Cineforum* (Bergamo), January-February 1982.

Woodward, K. S., ''European Anti-Melodrama: Godard, Truffaut, and Fassbinder,'' in *Post Script* (Jacksonville, Florida), Winter 1984.

Hartsough, D., ''Cine-feminism Renegotiated: Fassbinder's *Ali* as Interventionist Cinema,'' in *Wide Angle* (Baltimore, Maryland), no. 1, 1990.

LaValley, A., ''The Gay Liberation of Rainer Werner Fassbinder: Male Subjectivity, Male Bodies, Male Lovers,'' in *New German Critique*, no. 63, Fall 1994.

Sharma, S., ''Fassbinder's *Ali* and the Politics of Subject Formation,'' in *Post Script* (Commerce, Texas), vol. 14, no. 1–2, 1994–95.

Reimer, R.C., ''Comparison of Douglas Sirk's *All That Heaven Allows* and Rainer Werner Fassbinder's *Ali: Fear Eats the Soul*; or, how Hollywood's New England Dropouts Became Germany's Marginalized Other,'' in *Literature/Film Quarterly* (Salisbury, Maryland), vol. 24, no. 3, 1996.

Medhurst, Andy, ''The Long Take,'' in *Sight and Sound* (London), vol. 6, no. 2, February 1996.

* * *

Rainer Werner Fassbinder's fifteenth film, *Angst essen Seele auf*, represents perhaps the peak of his renowned domestic melodrama period, bracketed approximately by *The Merchant of Four Seasons* and *Angst von Angst.* The story of an improbable romance between Ali, a young black *Gastarbeiter* in Munich, and Emmi, an elderly, widowed German cleaning woman, *Angst essen Seele auf* is patterned rather explicitly on the Hollywood ''women's pictures'' of Douglas Sirk; in this case, *All That Heaven Allows*, where bourgeois widow Jane Wyman falls in love with her younger gardener, Rock Hudson, and finds herself ostracized by her children as well as the country club set. Admiring Sirk for his ability to deal with interpersonal politics in the context of melodrama (a genre animated by personal crisis in a social/familial context), Fassbinder was equally impressed by the visual stylization of Sirk's mise-en-scène.

Employing a Sirkian stylization in camera angle, framing, color, and lighting, Fassbinder takes on the conventions of melodrama in *Angst essen Seele auf*, yet exaggerates them in the direction of Bertolt Brecht, emphasizing the social typage of the characters, arranging characters in frozen tableaux at key moments, and distancing the viewer by constantly framing through doorways and in long shot. The effect is to force the contradictions of the story to reveal themselves on an intellectual level, to remove the viewer from the level of pure empathy to that of understanding the ways in which the characters' lives are determined by age, social status, and economic class. Like Sirk's characters, Ali and Emmi face social ostracism for their love—the harrassment of neighbors, co-workers, and merchants, and the horror of family and friends. After returning from a trip to get away from it all, they finally find themselves accepted; but only to the extent that returning them to their ''proper'' social roles allows them to be exploited once again by those around them.

It is a very cold world which Fassbinder depicts, a world in which emotion and love are exploited. Writing on Sirk, Fassbinder (whose first film is appropriately titled *Love is Colder Than Death*) asserted his conviction that ''love is the best, most insidious, most effective instrument of social repression''; and *Angst essen Seele auf* is an unblinking illustration of his point. Once relieved of the social pressure which brought the lonely Ali and Emmi together, they find their personal relationship determined by many of the the same prejudices and assumptions, playing out their ''types'' and becoming more like those who despised them.

What emerges is a scathing critique of social repression seen from the lowest rungs of society's ladder. The ungrammatical title, translated literally ''fear eat up soul,'' is a phrase used by Ali to describe the pain he is suffering in his relationship with Emmi, a pain which eventually manifests itself as an ulcerated stomach—a malady, a doctor tells Emmi, suffered by many foreign workers. The irony that this strange, almost grotesque couple must suffer a fate which is normal, typical, and utterly anti-romantic adds a chilling sense of truth to the film's epigraph, ''Happiness is not always fun.''

It would be incorrect to assert that the analytic aspects of the film preclude an emotional response; for if Fassbinder makes it almost impossible to empathize with Ali and Emmi in the conventional sense, it is only to provoke more deeply disturbing feelings. Fassbinder has been quoted to the effect that ''films that say the feelings you believe you have don't really exist, that they are only the sentiments which you think you ought to have as a well-functioning member of society—such films have to be cold.'' Yet the coldness of *Angst essen Seele auf* is not emotionless; far from dulling the viewer, it produces a profound shiver, marking the success of Fassbinder in constructing a film which will make audiences both think *and* feel.

—Ed Lowry

L'ANNÉE DERNIÈRE À MARIENBAD

(Last Year at Marienbad)

France-Italy, 1961

Director: Alain Resnais

Production: Terra Films, Société Nouvelle des Films Cormoran, Argos Films, Précitel, Como Films, Les Films Tamara, Cinetel, Silver Films (Paris), and Cineriz (Rome); black and white, 35mm, Dyaliscope; running time: 100 minutes; English version: 93 minutes. Released September 1961, Paris. Filmed September through November 1960 in Photosonar Studios, Paris, and on location in Munich at various chateaux including Nymphenburg and Schleissheim.

Producer: Pierre Courau and Raymond Froment; **screenplay:** Alain Robbe-Grillet; **main titles:** Jean Fouchet; **English subtitles:** Noele Gillmor; **photography:** Sacha Vierny; **editors:** Henri Colpi and Jasmine Chasney; **sound:** Guy Villette; **art director:** Jacques Saulnier; **music:** Francis Seyrig; **musical director:** André Girard; **costume**

designers: Bernard Evein and Chanel; **2nd assistant director:** Volker Schlöndorff.

Cast: Delphine Seyrig (*A*); Giorgio Albertazzi (*X*); Sacha Pitoëff (*M*); Françoise Bertin; Luce Garcia-Ville; Hélèna Kornel; Françoise Spira; Karin Toech-Mittler; Pierre Barbaud; Wilhelm Von Deek; Jean Lanier; Gérard Lorin; Davide Montemuri; Gilles Quéant; Gabriel Werner.

Awards: Lion of St. Mark, Venice Film Festival, 1961.

Publications

Scripts:

Robbe-Grillet, Alain, *L'Année dernière à Marienbad*, Paris 1961; as *Last Year at Marienbad*, London and New York, 1962.

Books:

Cordier, Stephane, *Alain Resnais; ou, La Création au cinéma*, Paris, 1961.
Pingaud, Bernard, *Alain Resnais*, Lyons, 1961.
Bounourre, Gaston, *Alain Resnais*, Paris, 1962.
Cowie, Peter, *Antonioni, Bergman, Resnais*, London, 1963.
Miesch, Jean, *Robbe-Grillet*, Paris, 1965.
Alter, J. V., *La Vision du monde d'Alain Robbe-Grillet*, Geneva, 1966.
Durgnat, Raymond, *Nouvelle Vague: The First Decade*, Loughton, Essex, 1966.
Geduld, Harry M., editor, *Film Makers on Filmmaking*, Bloomington, Indiana, 1967.
Armes, Roy, *The Cinema of Alain Resnais*, London, 1968.
Graham, Peter, *The New Wave*, New York, 1968.
Prédal, René, *Alain Resnais*, Paris, 1968.
Ward, John, *Alain Resnais; or, The Theme of Time*, New York, 1968.
Bertetto, Paolo, *Resnais, Alain Resnais*, Italy, 1976.
Kreidl, John Francis, *Alain Resnais*, Boston, 1977.
Monaco, James, *The Role of Imagination*, New York, 1978.
Van Wert, William F., *In the Theory and Practice of the Ciné-Roman*, New York, 1978.
Thiher, Allen, *The Cinematic Muse: Critical Studies in the History of French Cinema*, London, 1979.
Houston, Beverle, and Marsha Kinder, *Self and Cinema: A Transformalist Perspective*, New York, 1980.
Sweet, Freddy, *The Film Narratives of Alain Resnais*, Ann Arbor, Michigan, 1981.
Benayoun, Robert, *Alain Resnais: Arpenteur de l'imaginaire*, Paris, 1980; revised edition, 1986.
Vergerio, Flavio, *I film di Alain Resnais*, Rome, 1984.
Roob, Jean-Daniel, *Alain Resnais: Qui êtes-vous?* Lyons, 1986.
Riambau, Esteve, *La cience y la ficcion: El cine de Alain Resnais*, Barcelona, 1988.
Thomas, François, *L'atelier d'Alain Resnais*, Paris, 1989.
Alain Resnais, with Beiträgen von Wolfgang Jacobsen et al., München, 1990.
Instituto Franco-Portugûes de Lisboa, *Alain Resnais*, Lisbon, 1992.
Callev, Haim, *The Stream of Consciousness in the Films of Alain Resnais*, New York, 1997.
Núria Bou, et al, *Alain Resnais: viaje al centro de un demiurgo*, Barcelona, 1998.
Fleischer, Alain, *L'art d'Alain Resnais*, Paris, 1998.

Articles:

''Introduction à la méthode d'Alain Resnais et d'Alain Robbe-Grillet,'' in *Lettres Françaises* (Paris), 10 August 1961.
Robbe-Grillet, Alain, in *Sight and Sound* (London), Autumn 1961.
Interview with Resnais, in *Cahiers du Cinéma* (Paris), September 1961, reprinted in *Films and Filming* (London), March 1962.
Labarthe, Andre, ''Marienbad Année Zero,'' in *Cahiers du Cinéma* (Paris), September 1961.
Brunius, Jacques, and Penelope Houston in *Sight and Sound* (London), Winter 1961–62.
Houston, Penelope, in *Sight and Sound* (London), Winter 1961–62.
Colpi, Henri, in *New York Film Bulletin*, no. 2, 1962.
Labarthe, André, and Jacques Rivette, ''A Conversation with Alain Resnais and Alain Robbe-Grillet,'' in *New York Film Bulletin*, no. 2, 1962.
Resnais, Alain, ''Trying to Understand My Own Film,'' in *Films and Filming* (London), February 1962.
Crowther, Bosley, in *New York Times*, 8 March 1962.
Brunius, Jacques, ''Every Year at Marienbad; or, The Discipline of Uncertainty,'' in *Sight and Sound* (London), Summer 1962.
Oxenhandler, Neal, ''*Marienbad* Revisited,'' in *Film Quarterly* (Berkeley), Fall 1963.
Taylor, John Russell, ''Alain Resnais,'' in *Cinema Eye, Cinema Ear* (New York), 1964.
Stanbrook, Alan, ''The Time and Space of Alain Resnais,'' in *Films and Filming* (London), January 1964.
Ollier, Jean, ''Film et roman: Problèmes du récit,'' in *Cahiers du Cinéma* (Paris), December 1966.
Pingaud, Bernard, ''Nouveau roman et nouveau cinema,'' in *Cahiers du Cinéma* (Paris), December 1966.
Roud, Richard, ''Memories of Resnais,'' in *Sight and Sound* (London), Summer 1969.
Noguera, Rui, ''Interview with Delphine Seyrig,'' in *Sight and Sound* (London), Autumn 1969.
Goldmann, Annie, ''*Muriel*'' and ''*L'Année dernière à Marienbad*,'' in *Cinéma et Societé* (Paris), 1971.
Blumenberg, Richard, ''10 Years after Marienbad,'' in *Cinema Journal* (Evanston, Illinois), Spring 1971.
Skoller, D., ''Aspects of Cinematic Consciousness,'' in *Film Comment* (New York), September-October 1972.
Harcourt, Peter, ''Memory Is Kept Alive with Dreams,'' in *Film Comment* (New York), November-December 1973.
Rocher, D., ''Le Symbolisme du noir et blanc dans *L'Année dernière à Marienbad*,'' in *Etudes Cinématographiques* (Paris), nos. 100–103, 1974.
Dupont, G., ''Lieux du cinema: De Versaille à Marienbad,'' in *Cinématographe* (Paris), February 1979.
Armes, Roy, ''Ricardou and *Last Year at Marienbad*,'' in *Quarterly Review of Film Studies* (New York), Winter 1980.
Blaetz, R., ''L'impiego della retorica in due film di Resnais,'' in *Cinema Nuovo* (Turin), August-October 1982.
Jones, Elizabeth, ''Locating Truth in Film 1940–80,'' in *Post Script* (Jacksonville, Florida), Fall 1986.
Pisters, Patricia, ''Passie onder steen,'' *Skrien* (Amsterdam), no. 193, December/January 1993–94.

Alemany-Galway, M. ''Vid postmodernismens brytpunkt,'' *Filmhaftet* (Sverige, Sweden), vol. 23, no. 4, 1995.

Istomina, E. ''Granitsy *Marienbada*,'' *Iskusstvo Kino* (Moscow), no. 11, 1996.

Kirsch, Walter, Jr., ''Marienbad Revisited: A Feast for the Senses,'' *Creative Screenwriting* (Washington D.C.), vol. 3, no. 1, Summer 1996.

Mason, M., ''Dodici armadi per arredare una residenza estiva,'' *Forum*, vol. 37, 1997.

* * *

Alain Resnais's *Last Year at Marienbad* shares, with a handful of other films (notably Truffaut's *The 400 Blows* and *Jules and Jim*, Godard's *Breathless*, and Resnais's own *Hiroshima mon amour*), the distinction of being a landmark of the French New Wave, and as such, a major influence upon later film styles. Unlike those other films, it remains controversial: it is often dismissed or despised as pretentious nonsense by some while admired as a masterpiece by others. In any case, it remains, far more than the other films, distinctly avant-garde in its conception of narrative.

Co-authorship of the film must be assigned to screenwriter Alain Robbe-Grillet, whose earlier novels (notably *Jealousy*, 1959) share themes and narrative techniques with *Marienbad.* Robbe-Grillet's later works—films he directed as well as novels—have an even stronger resemblance to this first screenplay. This is not to deny major credit to Resnais, whose fascination with themes of time and memory runs through virtually all his films, and who had already displayed in an earlier feature and in a series of short subjects a mastery of montage and gliding camera movements characteristic of *Marienbad.* *Marienbad's* initial fame was based on certain surface qualities: the baroque palace setting with its eerie formal gardens (Poe's Haunted Palace brought to life), the frozen postures of the guests, the ''Marienbad'' game the guests play (a brief fad after the film's release), and the puzzling plot of a man (''X'') who attempts to convince a languid woman (''A'') to leave her sinister husband or lover as—X claims—she had already agreed to do last year at Marienbad. A, however, claims not to know X. A radical feature of the film is the frequent number of flashbacks, and possible flashforwards, which may in fact be fantasy scenes; the subjective visions of X or A or both. The film is also radical in its use of narrative voice. At times descriptions by the voice do not correspond to the actions on the screen; or the narrator's sentence is finished by the dialogue of an actor in an amateur play; or minor characters repeat earlier speeches of the narrator verbatim.

Faced with the impossibility of working out a linear, coherent narrative from this material, some have rejected the entire work as deliberately incoherent, while others have reveled in its intoxicated images and rhythms: the splendid black-and-white cinemascope compositions; the sweeping, occasionally dizzying tracking shots; the abrupt yet controlled contrasts of light and shadow. The film need not, however, be taken as an abstract or ''contentless'' work. It simply demands to be considered in terms of its significant images and rhythms, and the matters discussed by the characters and the narrator, rather than in terms of a traditional narrative and psychological analysis of the characters.

The film is clearly epistomological in its interests. It is about how one constructs ''reality'' for oneself, as X evidently so convinces A that they did meet at Marienbad that his possible fantasy becomes her reality. In his valuable preface to his film script, Robbe-Grillet suggests that whatever a film shows is ''present tense,'' unlike the novel's past and conditional tenses; hence what may be X's or A's fantasies become reality not only for them but for the viewer as well. The film can also be said to be about how people attach meanings to existence. Characters in the film discuss the possible symbolism of a mysterious, hauntingly expressive statue. This artwork surely corresponds to the film itself. The viewer must interpret the characters and their motives, must decide what among the scenes witnessed is fantasy or lies, and what, if anything, is fact. Indeed, in the first 15 minutes of the film, the viewer must figure out which of the large number of ''guests'' investigated by the roaming camera are to be the main characters: the camera teasingly eavesdrops and gives misleading hints.

The film is also about the relation of life to art and artifice. As we make an effort to remember the past, we ''freeze'' an image of it which is not reality, but a picture, an artwork, or perhaps a fantasy. This epistemological theme is developed by the film not only in its basic drama but in its constant attention to works of art and to the artificiality of the characters: statuary and people who pose like statues; a theatrical production even more stylized than the actual performances in the film; engravings and photographs; and the palace-hotel itself with its formal gardens. The baroque setting is perfect. Its curvilinear forms suggest frozen and symmetrical plant life, while the geometrical gardens are an exceedingly artificial arrangement of real plants. Ultimately the film suggests that perception itself is the creation of artifice.

Marienbad may be read on other, but necessarily incompatible, levels as well. Freudians may see it as a fantasia on an Oedipal triangle, with both veiled and explicit images of sexual violence. Or it may be taken as a drama of entrapment or self-entrapment, like Jean-Paul Sartre's *No Exit:* a spectacle of people who cannot escape the prison of their own egos or the dominance of others.

It is difficult to trace the precise influence of Marienbad on later films, except for some specific cases such as the films of Robbe-Grillet, beginning with *L'Immortelle* (1963). Also included are the structures and rhythms in the films of Nicholas Roeg from *Performance* (1970) to *Bad Timing/A Sensual Obsession* (1981); and Edward Dmytryk's *Mirage* (1965), a spy/murder-mystery in which an amnesia victim's memories, actual and false, are periodically flashed forth in *Marienbad* style. Thanks largely to *Marienbad* and other films by Resnais, the instant flashback (as opposed to the traditional slow ones signaled by dreamy music and blurred frames) and the interweaving of past and present events in a continuous flow have become a basic part of the vocabulary of contemporary filmmaking.

—Joseph Milicia

ANNIE HALL

USA, 1977

Director: Woody Allen

Production: Jack Rollins-Charles H. Joffe Productions; Deluxe color, 35mm, Panavision; running time: 93 minutes. Released 1977 by United Artists. Filmed 1976 in New York City and Los Angeles.

Annie Hall

Producers: Charles H. Joffe and Jack Rollins with Robert Greenhut and Fred T. Gallo; **screenplay:** Woody Allen and Marshall Brickman; **photography:** Gordon Willis; **editor:** Ralph Rosenblum; **sound engineer:** James Sabat; **production designers:** Robert Drumheller and Justin Scoppa Jr.; **art director:** Mel Bourne; **costume designer:** Ruth Morley.

Cast: Woody Allen (*Alvy Singer*); Diane Keaton (*Annie Hall*); Tony Roberts (*Rob*); Paul Simon (*Tony Lacey*); Carol Kane (*Allison*); Janet Margolin (*Robin*); Shelley Duvall (*Pam*); Christopher Walken (*Duane Hall*); Collen Dewhurst (*Annie's mother*); Donald Symington (*Annie's father*); Helen Ludlam (*Grammy Hall*); Joan Newman (*Alvy's mother*); Mordecai Lawner (*Alvy's father*); Jonathan Munk (*Alvy as a child*); Ruth Volner (*Alvy's aunt*); Martin Rosenblatt (*Alvy's uncle*); Hy Ansel (*Joey Nichols*); Rashel Novikoff (*Aunt Tessie*); Russell Horton (*Man in line at movies*); Marshall McLuhan (Himself); Dick Cavett (Himself); Christine Jones (*Dorrie*); Mary Boland (*Miss Reed*); Wendy Gerard (*Janet*); John Doumanian (*Man with drugs*); Bob Maroff (*1st Man in front of the movie theater*); Rick Petrucelli (*2nd Man in front of the movie theater*); Lee Callahan (*Cashier*); Chris Gampel (*Doctor*); Mark Lenard (*Marine officer*); Dan Ruskin (*Comic at the ''Rallye''*); John Glover (*Actor friend of Annie's*); Bernie Styles (*Comic's business manager*); Johnny Haymer (*Comic*); Ved Bandhu (*Maharishi*); John Dennis Johnston (*L.A. policeman*); Lauri Bird (*Tony Lacey's girl*); Jim McKrell, Jeff Goldblum, William Callawy, Roger Newman, Alan Landers, and Dean Sarah Frost (*Partygoers*); Vince O'Brien (*Hotel doctor*); Humphrey Davis (*Alvy's psychiatrist*); Veronica Radburn (*Annie's psychiatrist*); Robin Mary Paris (*Girl in Alvy's play*); Charles Levin (*Man in Alvy's play*); Wayne Carson (*Stage manager of Alvy's play*); Michael Karm (*Director of Alvy's play*); Beverly D'Angelo (*Actress in Rob's TV show*); Tracy Walter (*Actor in Rob's TV show*); Sigourney Weaver (*Alvy's friend at the movies*); Walter Bernstein (*Annie's friend at the movies*).

Awards: Oscars for Best Picture, Best Director, Best Actress (Keaton), and Best Original Screenplay, 1977; New York Film Critics' Awards for Best Film, Best Director, Best Actress (Keaton), and Best Screenplay, 1977.

Publications

Script:

Allen, Woody, and Marshall Brickman, *Annie Hall*, in *Four Films of Woody Allen*, New York, 1983.

Books:

Jacobs, Diane, *But We Need the Eggs: The Magic of Woody Allen*, New York, 1982.
Lahr, John, *Automatic Vaudeville: Essays on Star Turns*, New York, 1984.
Brode, Douglas, *Woody Allen: His Films and Career*, London, 1985.
Benayoun, Robert, *Woody Allen: Beyond Words*, London 1987.
Bendazzi, G., *The Films of Woody Allen*, Florence, 1987.
Jarvie, Ian, *Philosophy of the Film: Epistemology, Ontology, Aesthetics*, London, 1987.
Navacelle, Thierry de, *Woody Allen on Location*, London, 1987.
Poger, Nancy, *Woody Allen*, Boston, 1987.
Cowie, Peter, *Annie Hall*, London, 1996.

Articles:

McBride, J., in *Variety* (New York), 30 March 1977.
Drew, B., ''Woody Allen Is Feeling Better,'' in *American Film* (Washington, D.C.), May 1977.
Trow, G. W. S., ''A Film about a Very Funny Man,'' in *Film Comment* (New York) May-June 1977.
Malmiaer, P., ''Mig og moneterne,'' in *Kosmorama* (Copenhagen), Autumn 1977.
Brown, Geoff, in *Sight and Sound* (London), Autumn 1977.
Dawson, Jan, in *Monthly Film Bulletin* (London), October 1977.
Karman, M., ''Comedy Directors: Interviews with Woody Allen,'' in *Millimeter* (New York), October 1977.
Benayoun, Robert, ''Le Rire et la culture: Le Citoyen Allen et Spinoza (*Annie Hall*),'' in *Positif* (Paris), November 1977.
Carrere, E., ''Portrait de l'artiste en masochiste serein,'' in *Positif* (Paris), November 1977.
Daney, Serge, ''Le Cinéphile à la voix forte,'' in *Cahiers du Cinéma* (Paris), November 1977.
Garel, A., in *Image et Son* (Paris), November 1977.
Stuart, A., in *Films and Filming* (London), November 1977.
Ledgard, R., in *Hablemos de Cine* (Lima), 1977–78.

Baker, D., in *Cinema Papers* (Melbourne), August-September 1978.
Halberstadt, I., "Scenes from a Mind," in *Take One* (Montreal), November 1978.
Yacowar, Maurice, "Forms of Coherence in the Woody Allen Comedies," in *Wide Angle* (Athens, Ohio), no. 2, 1979.
Funck, J., "L'Un Dit gestion de ça, voir (sur *Annie Hall* de Woody Allen)," in *Positif* (Paris), February 1979.
Johnson, Timothy, in *Magill's Survey of Cinema 1*, Englewood Cliffs, New Jersey, 1980.
Median de la Serna, R., "El cine de Woody Allen," in *Cine* (Mexico City), March 1980.
Schatz, Thomas, "*Annie Hall* and the Issue of Modernism," in *Literature/Film Quarterly* (Salisbury, Maryland), July 1982.
Gallanfent, E., "*Moonshine:* Love and Enchantment in *Annie Hall* and *Manhattan*," in *Cineaction* (Toronto), Summer 1989.
Girlanda, E., and A. Tella, "Allen, Manhattan transfert," in *Castoro Cinema* (Florence), July-August 1990.
Deleyto, C., "The Narrator and the Narrative: The Evolution of Woody Allen's Film Comedies," in *Film Criticism* (Meadville, Pennsylvania), vol. 19, no. 2, 1994–95.
Boon, Kevin A., "Scripting Gender. Writing Difference," in *Creative Screenwriting* (Washington, D.C.), vol. 4, no. 1, Spring 1997.

* * *

In *Annie Hall* Woody Allen finally delivered a unified work, one that relied on more than his episodic one-liner format. In the film he brought together many of his past obsessions, among them his love of New York, his lack of affection for L.A., the inability to handle success; but this time, he merged them with an in-depth examination of his feelings about family and relationships. It was as if, after 21 years of Freudian analysis, he finally decided to deal with his neuroses on the screen. Occasionally speaking with a confessional directness that destroys the film's illusion of reality and separates him momentarily from the episodic ramblings of his stream-of-consciousness narrative, he situates the spectator as analyst. Throughout the film the customary Allen episodes are cleverly linked together through memory, with dialogue precipitating flashbacks.

The film opens with a monologue which pays homage to three key individuals: Groucho Marx, Sigmund Freud, and Annie Hall. He pays respects to Groucho, from whom he learned comedy; to Freud, from whom he learned how to deal with his childhood; and to Annie, from whom he learned of both love and despair. At the end of the monologue, he moves from comedy to melancholy as he states: "... Annie and I broke up . . . I keep sifting the pieces of the relationship through my mind . . . ." Searching for the answer to the breakup, he begins by sifting through the wreckage of his childhood—a Freudian analysis laced with (Groucho) Marxian wit.

With *Annie Hall*, Allen the director is absorbed with his past, as is Alvy Singer, the character Allen portrays in this film. He uses many strategies to comment on the past, from interjecting himself as Alvy into a scene aurally, to interjecting himself visually. Early on both strategies are situated. Alvy's first childhood memories concern depression and his recurring difficulty of distinguishing between fantasy and reality. These scenes use a voice-over narration by Alvy as if to dispel any notion that he is unable to distinguish between the two as an adult. Immediately, however, he begins a strategy of interjecting himself physically into the past, proving that the inability does indeed exist. In a classroom scene he moves from observing himself as a child to participating in the scene as an adult attempting to clarify his childhood actions to his classmates.

Another key aspect of the film is Allen's ability to remove himself from the on-screen reality. This he achieves in a number of ways, from voice-over commentary and/or subtitles which contradict the on-screen dialogue, to physically stepping out of the scene either to comment on the narrative action or to correct the flow of events. After Annie and Alvy meet for the first time their dialogue is heard on the soundtrack but their real thoughts are shown in subtitles at the bottom of the screen: while Alvy says "The medium enters in as a condition of the art form itself," a subtitle reads "I don't know what I'm saying—she senses I'm shallow." At other points in the film Alvy simple uses voice-over to comment on the ridiculousness of an on-screen event: when the comic who wants Alvy to write his material minces around the office, Alvy, in voice-over comments, "Look at him mincing around, like he thinks he's real cute . . . ." In other scenes he is much more assertive. Unable to bear another moment of academic pretension from a man standing behind him in a theater lobby, he directly addresses the audience: "What do you do when you get stuck in a movie line with a guy like this behind you?" After embarrassing the academic by having Marshall McLuhan step out from behind a marquee to say: "How you got to teach a course in anything is totally amazing," Alvy turns to the camera once again and states: "Boy if life were only like this!"

At the film's end Alvy is writing a play about his breakup with Annie. Where in *Manhattan* the book he is writing becomes the film we are seeing, here the play he is writing becomes, in retrospect, the film we've just seen. In this film Allen stretched the limits of his narrative technique by developing strategies for showing how the past and present interact in life and art as well as analysis. The film succeeded beyond any of Allen's earlier work, brought new life to the romantic comedy genre, gave American audiences a new leading lady, Diane Keaton, and fashion designers a new look to market.

—Doug Tomlinson

ANTICIPATION OF THE NIGHT

US, 1958

Director: Stan Brakhage

Production: Color, silent, 16mm: running time: 48 minutes.

Producer: Stan Brakhage.

Publications

Books:

Brakhage, Stan, *Metaphors on Vision*, Film Culture Inc., 1963.
Renan, Sheldon, *An Introduction to the American Underground Film*, New York, 1967.

Brakhage, Stan, *A Moving Picture Giving and Taking Book*, Frontier Press, 1971.
Sitney, P. Adams, *Visionary Film*, Oxford and New York, 1979.
James, David E., *Allegories of Cinema*, Princeton, 1989.
Peterson, James, *Dreams of Chaos, Visions of Order*, Detroit, 1994.

* * *

Arguably the central film in the Brakhage canon, *Anticipation of the Night* (1958) inaugurated a radical change in experimental filmmaking techniques and aesthetics. Prior to this film, American experimental cinema employed either a "Trance" (or "Psychodrama") model, as established by Maya Deren (*Meshes of the Afternoon*), Kenneth Anger (*Fireworks*), and Sidney Peterson and James Broughton (*The Potted Psalm*), or a "Graphic" model, as established (in different forms) by Mary Ellen Bute (*Tarantella*), Harry Smith (*Early Abstractions*), and Len Lye (*Colour Box*). The Trance/Psychodrama approach emphasized surreal, dream narratives of psychological revelation in which the filmmaker typically performed as an on-screen protagonist. This protagonist experienced a literal and metaphorical journey of self-exploration built upon representational imagery that alternated between objective and subjective perspectives. The Graphic approach featured animated, abstract images often hand-applied directly onto the film. The film itself functioned as a scroll which could be "unwound" at different projector speeds or by hand.

In *Anticipation of the Night*, Stan Brakhage abandoned both models (or perhaps more accurately *combined* both models) and rejected aesthetic norms for an intensely personal and extremely subjective expression of self that emphasized the various "visions" of the filmmaker. This "Lyrical" approach teasingly appeared in earlier Brakhage films (such as *Reflections on Black, The Way to Shadow Garden*, and *Wonder Ring*) and would reach full expression in his 1960s films (such as *Thigh Line Lyre Triangular*, *Window Water Baby Moving*, and *Dog Star Man*), but *Anticipation of the Night* stands as the first fully realized Lyrical film and a paradigm of the model. Working as a "diary" in which Brakhage recorded the events of his life and his feelings about them, *Anticipation of the Night* ushered in a new experimental model which synthesized a Romantic mythopoesis and the reflexive Modernism of Abstract Expressionism.

P. Adams Sitney, one of the central figures of experimental film criticism and author of the seminal text *Visionary Film*, explains that Lyrical cinema:

> . . . postulates the film-maker behind the camera as the first-person protagonist of the film. The images of the film are what he sees, filmed in such a way that we never forget his presence and we know how he is reacting to his vision. In the lyrical form there is no longer a hero; instead the screen is filled with movement, and that movement, both of the camera and the editing, reverberates with the idea of a man looking. As viewers we see this man's intense experience of seeing.

This boldly original technique of expressing the impression of sight via an abstracted, first-person point of view resulted in a very poor reception when *Anticipation of the Night* was first shown (reportedly causing a riot at the 1959 Brussels World Fair). Yet according to Sitney, the great achievement of *Anticipation of the Night* is exactly this emphasis; its distillation of "an intense and complex interior crisis into an orchestration of sights and associations which cohere in a new formal rhetoric of camera movement and montage."

In *Anticipation of the Night*, Brakhage created a film of self-exploration and psychological revelation that did *not* depend on a journey metaphor, a linear narrative structure, or an on-screen protagonist (although vestiges of these Trance conventions are noticeable). Brakhage strove to communicate a "totality of vision" (what he saw, perceived, felt, imagined, and dreamt) through a complete identification between himself and a "liberated camera." Using a constantly moving hand-held camera, unfocused images, under- and over-exposure, random compositions, distorting lenses and filters, flash frames, varying camera speeds, fragmented time and space, "plastic cutting," and in later films, the scratching, bleaching, and painting of the film stock, Brakhage equated the process of filmmaking and the abstraction of reality with the expression of his emotions and imagination (much like the "action painting" of Abstract Expressionism). James Peterson refers to these techniques as a type of "personification strategy" where the film's manipulation represents the filmmaker's consciousness. *Anticipation of the Night* "personifies" Brakhage's mental state in terms of a purely visual, subjective cinema.

A "difficult" and ambiguous film, *Anticipation of the Night* does not readily lend itself to an adequate description that can do justice to its poetry; its abstractions and ideas need to be experienced and pondered. Notwithstanding, Brakhage offers an excellent summary that manages to capture the emotions and themes of the film. Writing in *Filmwise* (1961) he says:

> The daylight shadow of a man in movement evokes lights in the night. A rose bowl, held in hand, reflects both sun and moon-like illumination. The opening of a doorway onto trees anticipates the twilight into the night. A child is born on the lawn, born of water, with promissory rainbow, and the wild rose. It becomes the moon and the source of all night light. Lights of the night become young children playing a circular game. The moon moves over a pillared temple to which all lights return. There is seen the sleep of innocents and their animal dreams, becoming their amusement, their circular game, becoming the morning. The trees change color and lose their leaves for the morn, becomes the complexity of branches on which the shadow man hangs himself.

Yet even Brakhage's description fails to convey the play of textures and light, the excitement of motion, the endearing innocence of children and nature, the giddiness of a carnival, and the non-narrative simultaneity caused by his fragmented "hyper-editing."

In *Metaphors on Vision* (which Brakhage began writing while developing the Lyrical mode), Brakhage discusses the psychological and artistic context of *Anticipation of the Night.* He explains how the film was to be his last about "fulfilling the myth of myself;" that it would function as a way out from the style and themes of the Psychodrama. The journey and suicide of the filmmaker/protagonist marks an end of Brakhage's early cinema and the start of a new artistic approach (much like Godard's "end of film/end of cinema" at the close of *Weekend*). More personally, Brakhage admits to a type of depression which colored the film (and provided its title): ''pit seemed as if there was nothing but night out there, and I then thought of all my life as being in anticipation of that night. That night could only cast one shadow for me, could only form itself into one black shape, and that was the hanged man.'' Brakhage tells the story of how he accidentally hung himself while shooting the final sequence and what this revealed to him. ''I was sure that I had intended for months to finish the editing of *Anticipation of the Night* up to that point, go out in the yard, climb up on a chair camera in hand, jump off the chair, and while hanging run out as much film as I could, leaving a note saying 'Attach this to the end of *Anticipation of the Night*'.''

Sitney's acclamation that *Anticipation of the Night* was the ''first American film about and structured by the nature of the seeing experience; how one encounters a sight, how it is recalled, how it affects later vision, and where it leads the visionary'' may deny the influence of Mary Ellen Bute, Jim Davis, and Marie Menken, but it does stress the importance of light and ''untutored'' or ''innocent'' vision in Brakhage's subsequent work. Brakhage explains this importance in the often quoted opening to *Metaphors on Vision*:

> Imagine an eye unruled by man-made laws of perspective, an eye unprejudiced by compositional logic, an eye which does not respond to the name of everything but which must know each objected encountered in life through an adventure of perception. . . . Imagine a world alive with incomprehensible objects and shimmering with an endless variety of movement and innumerable gradations of color.

Anticipation of the Night began the examination of this world of intense personal visions and subjective filmic expression.

—Greg S. Faller

ANTÔNIO DAS MORTES

(O dragão da maldade contra o santo querreiro)

Brazil, 1969

Director: Glauber Rocha

Production: Produções Cinematográficas Mapa; Eastmancolor, 35mm; running time: 100 minutes. Released June 1969, Rio de Janeiro. Filmed on location in Milagres in the Brazilian Northwest.

Producers: Zelito Viana (executive producer), Claude-Antoine Mapa, and Glauber Rocha; **screenplay:** Glauber Rocha, from the legends about the bounty hunter who killed the famous bandit Corisco in 1939; **photography:** Alfonso Beato; **editor:** Eduardo Escorel; **sound:** Walter Goulart; **art director:** Glauber Rocha; **music:** Marlos Nobre, Walter Queiroz, and Sérgio Ricardo.

Cast: Maurício do Valle (*Antônio das Mortes*); Odete Lara (*Laura*); Hugo Carvana (*Police Chief Mattos*); Othon Bastos (*The Professor*); Jofre Soares (*Colonel Horacio*); Lorival Pariz (*Coirana*); Rosa Maria Penna (*Sanata Bárbara*); Mário Gusmão (*Antão*); Vinivius Salvatori (*''Mata Vaca''*); Emanuel Cavalcanit (*Priest*); Sante Scaldaferri (*Batista*); the people of Milagres.

Awards: Best Director (tied with Vojtech Jasny), Cannes Film Festival, 1969.

Publications

Script:

Rocha, Glauber, *Antônio das Mortes*, in *Roteiros do terceyro mundo*, Rio de Janeiro, 1985.

Books:

Second Wave, New York, 1970.
Martinez, Augusto, and Manuel Pere Estremera, *Nuevo cine latinoamericano*, Barcelona, 1973.
Gerber, Raquel, editor, *Glauber Rocha*, Rio de Janiero, 1977.
Rocha, Glauber, *Revolução do cinema novo*, Rio de Janeiro, 1981.
Johnson, Randall, and Robert Stam, *Brazilian Cinema*, New Brunswick, New Jersey, 1982.
Rocher, Glauber, *O seculo do cinema*, Rio de Janeiro, 1983.
Bandeira, Roberto, *Pequeno dictionario critico do cinema brasileiro*, Rio de Janeiro, 1983.
Burton, Julianne, *The New Latin American Cinema: An Annotated Bibliography of Sources in English, Spanish, and Portuguese*, New York, 1983.
Sarno, Geraldo, *Glauber Rocha e o cinema latino-americano*, Rio de Janiero, 1994.

Articles:

Callenbach, Ernest, ''Comparative Anatomy of Folk-Myth Films: *Robin Hood* and *Antônio das Mortes*,'' in *Film Quarterly* (Berkeley), Winter 1969–70.
Interview with Rocha, in *Afterimage* (New York), April 1970.
Rocha, Glauber, ''The Aesthetics of Violence,'' in *Afterimage* (New York), April 1970.
McGuinness, Richard, in *Village Voice* (New York), 21 May 1970.
Interview with Rocha, in *Cineaste* (New York), Summer 1970.
Hitchens, Gordon, interview with Rocha, in *Film Quarterly* (Berkeley), Fall 1970.
Wallington, Mike, in *Sight and Sound* (London), Autumn 1970.
Fisher, Jack, ''Politics by Magic: *Antônio das Mortes*,'' in *Film Journal* (New York), Spring 1971.
Haakman, A., ''*Antônio Das Mortes*, de mooie revolutie,'' in *Skoop* (The Hague), vol. 8, no. 5, 1972.
Simsolo, Noël, ''*Antônio das Mortes*,'' in *Image et Son* (Paris), March 1972.
Proppe, Hans, and Susan Tarr, ''Cinema Novo: Pitfalls of Cultural Nationalism,'' in *Jump Cut* (Chicago), June 1976.

Antônio das Mortes

Graham, Bruce, ''Music in Glauber Rocha's Films: Brazilian Renaissance, Part 2,'' in *Jump Cut* (Chicago), May 1980.

Rocha, Glauber, ''The History of Cinema Novo,'' in *Framework* (Norwich), Summer 1980.

Mistron, Deborah, ''The Role of Myth in *Antônio das Mortes,*'' in *Enclitic* (Minneapolis), Fall 1981 and Spring 1982.

Vega, J., ''Glauber Rocha: el santo guerrero del cinema novo,'' in *Cine Cubano* (Havana), no. 134, 1992.

* * *

In his lyric-mythic epic, *Antônio das Mortes*, Glauber Rocha creatively integrates elements of Brazilian popular religious culture, politics, folklore, social history, music, literature, and dance. Because of this thoroughly Brazilian context, the film is difficult for foreign viewers. Furthermore, the emblematic characters are not simple allegories but rather complex, synthetic creations representing real or fictional persons, social types, mystical or mythic motifs, social movements, or ideas.

The complexity of these unusual characterizations is exemplified by the protagonist, Antônio das Mortes. This figure had appeared in Rocha's earlier film *Deus e o Diabo na Terra do Sol.* According to Rocha, Antônio das Mortes is based on a historical figure, the bounty-hunter who in 1939 succeeded in killing Corisco, a famous *cangaceiro* (bandit) of the Northeastern backlands. In the film Antônio first appears as a *jagunco* (hired gunman) contracted to kill *cangaceiros* and protect a powerful landowner. After mortally wounding the *cangaceiro* Coirana, Antônio undergoes a political conversion and becomes a revolutionary who uses his rifle against the forces of oppression represented by the landowner and his hired gunslingers. The ending of the film is ambiguous in terms of the possible future role of the lone revolutionary. Antônio is last seen as a solitary figure walking—rifle in hand—down a backlands highway past a Shell Oil sign; the suggestion may be that a lone gunman can provoke a revolutionary situation in an underdeveloped regional setting, but he will be unable to halt massive exploitation in the new era of the multinationals.

In *Antônio das Mortes*, Rocha reworks the Christian myth of St. George versus the dragon in terms of Brazil's mythical consciousness. The St. George and the dragon myth is announced in the film's opening triptych and alluded to in a closing sequence: in three rapid montage shots. Antão lances the landowner from horseback. Antônio das Mortes is not the only warrior saint, or St. George figure, in the film. Antão, whose name is similar to Antônio's, is a black associated with Afro-Brazilian religions. Antão's conversion from passive religious follower to armed warrior continues the tradition of black revolt in Brazil.

In order to ritually reenact the St. George and the dragon myth, Rocha theatricalizes the continuity of his film and its mise-en-scène. Many of the scenes take place in stage-like settings such as the cavern-amphitheater or the village square. The costuming, choreography, and the use of color, poetry, and music recall theater and opera. Rocha's method of shooting imitates theatrical time and space. He prefers either lengthy sequences with a few cuts or long sequence shots. Conventional shot-reverse shot or cross-cutting are generally rejected in favor of capturing the scene's significant elements within the shot and the frame.

Rocha has argued that Brazilian filmmakers should not use European and American cinematic strategies and techniques to depict Latin America's unique social problems. In *Antônio das Mortes*, Rocha seeks to contribute to the decolonization of Brazilian cinema by meshing new cinematic strategies with Brazilian reality. One such strategy is Rocha's use of a Brazilian color code: the bright colors of buildings and costumes are natural and authentic colors that convey cultural significance for Brazilian audiences. During the location filming, Rocha drew directly on the knowledge and experience of the backlanders. The music and the dancing of the Antônio-Coirana duel scene are largely a creation of the local people.

Antônio das Mortes was well received by the Brazilian film-going public. In Europe and the United States, the film was widely acclaimed by critics, and a debate erupted concerning the film's revolutionary qualities (or lack thereof). Today most critics regard the film as one of the greatest achievements—both aesthetically and culturally—of the Brazilian Cinema Novo.

—Dennis West

APARAJITO

See **THE APU TRILOGY**

THE APARTMENT

USA, 1960

Director: Billy Wilder

Production: Mirisch Company; black and white, Panavision; running time: 125 minutes. Released May 1960.

Producer: Billy Wilder; **associate producers:** Doane Harrison, I. A. L. Diamond; **screenplay:** Billy Wilder, I. A. L. Diamond; **photography:** Joseph LaShelle; **editor:** Daniel Mandell; **sound:** Fred Lau; **art director:** Alexander Trauner; **music:** Adolph Deutsch.

Cast: Jack Lemmon (*C. C. Baxter*); Shirley MacLaine (*Fran Kubelik*); Fred MacMurray (*J. D. Sheldrake*); Ray Walston (*Dobisch*); David Lewis (*Kirkeby*); Jack Kruschen (*Dr. Dreyfuss*); Joan Shawlee (*Sylvia*); Edie Adams (*Miss Olsen*); Hope Holiday (*Margie MacDougall*);

The Apartment

Johnny Seven (*Karl Matuschka*); Naomi Stevens (*Mrs. Drefuss*); Frances Weintraub Lax (*Mrs. Lieberman*); Joyce Jameson (*Blonde*); Willard Waterman (*Vanderhof*); David White (*Eichelberger*).

Awards: Oscars for Best Picture, Best Direction, Best Original Story and Screenplay, and Best Editing, 1960. British Film Academy Awards for Best Film and Best Foreign Actor (Lemmon).

Publications

Script:

Wilder, Billy, and I. A. L. Diamond, *The Apartment and The Fortune Cookie: Two Screenplays*, New York, 1970.

Books:

Madsen, Axel, *Billy Wilder*, Bloomington, Indiana, 1969.

Baltake, Joe, *The Films of Jack Lemmon*, Secaucus, New Jersey, 1977; revised edition, 1987.

Seidman, Steve, *The Film Career of Billy Wilder*, Boston, 1977.

Erens, Patricia, *The Films of Shirley MacLaine*, South Brunswick, New Jersey, 1978.

Dick, Bernard F., *Billy Wilder*, Boston, 1980.

Ciment, Michel, *Les Conquérants d'un nouveau monde: Essais sur le cinéma américain*, Paris, 1981.

Giannetti, Louis, *Masters of the American Cinema*, Englewood Cliffs, New Jersey, 1981.

Freedland, Michael, *Jack Lemmon*, London, 1985.

Jacob, Jerome, *Billy Wilder*, Paris, 1988.

Seidl, Claudius, *Billy Wilder: Seine Filme, sein Leben*, Munich, 1988.

Armstrong, Richard, *Billy Wilder, American Film Realist*, Jefferson, North Carolina, 2000.

Articles:

Variety (New York), 18 July 1960.

P. J. D., in *Monthly Film Bulletin* (London), August 1960.

Cutts, John, in *Films and Filming* (London), September 1960.

Dyer, Peter John, in *Sight and Sound* (London), Autumn 1960.

Douchet, Jean in *Cahiers du Cinéma* (Paris), November 1960.

Domarchi, Jean, and Jean Douchet, ''Entretien avec Billy Wilder,'' in *Cahiers du Cinéma* (Paris), August 1962.

Onosko, Tom, ''Billy Wilder,'' in *Velvet Light Trap* (Madison, Wisconsin), Winter 1971.

Sarris, Andrew, ''Billy Wilder, Closet Romanticist,'' in *Film Comment* (New York), July-August 1976.

Tobin, Yann, in *Positif* (Paris), September 1983.

Combs, Richard, in *Listener* (London), 29 August 1985.

Bertoni, Aline, ''Billy Wilder on 'la vulgaritá congénitale','' in *Revue du Cinéma*, no. 422, December 1986.

Koch, Gertrud, ''Alle Sinnlichkeit der Macht. Zu Billy Wilder's *The Apartment* (1960),'' in *Frauen und Film* (Frankfurt am Main), no. 43, December 1987.

Denby, D., ''Always Making Wisecrackers,'' in *Premiere* (New York), November 1990.

Onaindia, M., ''For a method of analysis of the classical cinema script,'' in *Archivos de la Filmoteca*, no. 14, June 1993.

* * *

Billy Wilder entered the late period of his career, arguably the richest, with the hugely successful *Some Like It Hot;* in addition to confirming Jack Lemmon's reputation as a gifted comedian, the film initiated what developed into a long-term professional association between the two. To a degree, *The Apartment*, a project purportedly conceived as a vehicle for Lemmon, finds Wilder returning to his early 1950s period. Like *Sunset Boulevard* and *Ace in the Hole* (*The Big Carnival*), *The Apartment* presents a very bleak vision of contemporary American society: fully under the sway of capitalist and patriarchal ideologies, it is a society that pays lip-service to the work ethic and moral integrity but, in actuality, reduces the terms of success to the prostitution of oneself and the exploitation of others. It is a society in which prostitution and exploitation exist in both the professional and personal spheres and what passes for an intimate relationship is often nothing more than a deal or arrangement that benefits the person who holds social and/or economic power.

The Apartment differs from the above-mentioned 1950s dramas in two important ways: 1) the film undercuts the abrasiveness of the earlier works by employing actors who are essentially identified as comedians and mixes the comic and the dramatic mode, although, with the introduction of the Shirley MacLaine/Fred MacMurray relationship, *The Apartment* becomes predominantly dramatic in tone; 2) Wilder displays a generous and sympathetic attitude towards those characters who are in a powerless position. (This attitude is also found in the highly underrated *Kiss Me, Stupid*, a particularly pungent piece of satirical social criticism that is, in the main, very broadly drawn. Nevertheless, the Ray Walston and Kim Novak characters, roughly in equivalent positions to those held by Lemmon and MacLaine in *The Apartment*, are humanized because of Novak's innate integrity and vulnerability and the emotional response it solicits from Walston.) In *The Apartment* both Lemmon and MacLaine, who are meant to be representative of the ''average'' young American male and female, are involved in a form of prostitution. In regard to Lemmon, he is advancing up the ladder of the corporate business world by letting higher ranking male employees use, in return for a promotion, his apartment to conduct extra-marital affairs; unlike Lemmon, MacLaine, who is genuinely in love with the married MacMurray, isn't literally practising prostitution although she's led to perceive herself as doing such—in addition to her discovering that she's merely the latest of MacMurray's mistresses, he, in taking leave of her on Christmas Eve to join his wife and family, gives her a hundred dollar bill as a present. (As in Max Ophüls's *The Reckless Moment*, a film which is also highly critical of American bourgeois society, Wilder undermines the viewer's sentimental notions about the holiday season; MacLaine's suicide attempt, which is provoked by both despair and her sense of degradation, takes place on Christmas Eve.)

While Lemmon is shown to be exploited to the extent that he's willing to be complicit, MacLaine is simply a victim of emotional and sexual exploitation. In contrast, MacMurray, an emblem of the successful male, holds and, at the film's conclusion, retains a position of power and control. The film's devastating critique of the business world is never countered—MacMurray even maintains his image as a faithful husband. (In the film, traditional marriage is shown to be corrupted through the male's practice of the ''double standard''; in contrast, the film offers the Jewish couple who are Lemmon's neighbours but these characters are primarily used as stock comic figures.) Although Lemmon regains his moral integrity by refusing MacMurray further access to his apartment when he comprehends how totally indifferent MacMurray is to MacLaine's well-being and happiness, the film doesn't offer any route he may take from there. On the other hand, Lemmon's act, in addition to extricating him from the cycle of prostitution and exploitation, restores to MacLaine the self-respect she has forfeited through her affair with MacMurray. The act also makes her understand the degree to which she values what Lemmon offers her—a relationship in which both partners are on an equal basis. The couple Wilder presents here differs considerably from the conventional heterosexual couple used to give a film its happy ending in the emphasis on companionship rather than romantic love.

Wilder's admiration for Ernst Lubitsch is well known and *The Apartment* can be seen as his homage to Lubitsch's *Shop Around the Corner*. Like the Lubitsch film, *The Apartment* is centred on two characters who are trying to survive in a competitive environment that breeds self-depreciation, loneliness, and alienation. With *The Apartment*, Wilder matches the delicacy Lubitsch displays in the handling of characterization while retaining his extremely rigorous and uncompromising vision of human existence in the contemporary world.

—Richard Lippe

APOCALYPSE NOW

USA, 1979

Director: Francis Ford Coppola

Production: United Artists; initial release in color, 70mm, Dolby sound; later releases in color, 35mm, Dolby sound with added footage of large-scale air attack which serves as backdrop for credit sequence; running time: 153 minutes, also 139 minutes. Released 1979. Filmed 1976–77, though pre-production work began mid-1975 and post-production lasted until 1979; shot on location in the Philippines; cost: about $30,000,000.

Producer: Francis Ford Coppola; **screenplay:** John Milius and Francis Ford Coppola suggested by the novella *Heart of Darkness* by Joseph Conrad; **narration:** Richard Marks; **photography:** Vittorio Storaro; **editor:** Richard Marks; **sound:** Walter Murch, Mark Berger, Richard Beggs, and Nat Boxer; **production designer:** Dean Tavoularis; **art director:** Angelo Graham; **original music:** Carmine Coppola and Francis Ford Coppola; **song:** ''This Is the End'' by the Doors; **special effects:** A. D. Flowers.

Cast: Marlon Brando (*Colonel Walter E. Kurtz*); Robert Duvall (*Lieutenant Colonel Kilgore*); Martin Sheen (*Captain Benjamin L. Willard*); Frederic Forrest (*Chef*); Albert Hall (*Chief*); Sam Bottoms (*Lance*); Larry Fishburne (*Clean*); Dennis Hooper (*Freelance photographer*); G. D. Spradlin (*General*); Harrison Ford (*Colonel*).

Awards: Oscars for Best Cinematography and Best Sound, 1979; Palme d'Or (Shared with *The Tin Drum*), Cannes Film Festival, 1979.

Publications

Script:

Milius, John, and Francis Ford Coppola, *L'apocalisse e poi*, from the collection *Cinema e Cinema*, vol. 24, Venice, 1980.

Books:

Coppola, Eleanor, *Notes*, New York, 1979.
Pye, Michael, and Lynda Myles, *The Movie Brats: How the Film Generation Took Over Hollywood*, London, 1979.
Kolker, Robert Phillip, *A Cinema of Loneliness: Penn, Kubrick, Coppola, Scorsese, Altman*, Oxford, 1980; revised edition, 1988.
Adair, Gilbert, *Vietnam on Film: From ''The Green Berets'' to ''Apocalypse Now,''* New York 1981; revised edition, as *Hollywood's Vietnam*, London, 1989.
Thomson, David, *Overexposures: The Crisis in American Filmmaking*, New York, 1981.
Chaillet, Jean-Paul, and Elizabeth Vincent, *Francis Ford Coppola*, Paris, 1984.
Zuker, Joel S., *Francis Ford Coppola: A Guide to References and Resources*, Boston, 1984.
Frundt, Bodo, and others, *Francis Ford Coppola*, Munich, 1985.
Belton, John, and Elizabeth Weis, editors, *Film Sound; Theory and Practice*, New York, 1985.
Weiss, Ulli, *Das neue Hollywood: Francis Ford Coppola, Steven Spielberg, Martin Scorsese*, Munich, 1986.
Wood, Robin, *Hollywood from Vietnam to Reagan*, New York, 1986.
Chown, Jeffrey, *Hollywood Auteur; Francis Coppola*, New York, 1987.
Palmer, William J., *The Films of the 1970s: A Social History*, Metuchen, New Jersey, 1987.
Cowie, Peter, *Coppola*, London, 1989.
Von Gunden, Kenneth, *Postmodern Auteurs: Coppola, Lucas, De Palma, Spielberg & Scorsese*, Jefferson, 1991.
Lourdeaux, Lee, *Italian & Irish Filmmakers in America: Ford, Capra, Coppola & Scorsese*, Springfield, 1993.
Lewis, Jon, *Whom God Wishes to Destroy: Francis Coppola & The New Hollywood*, Durham, 1997.
Bergan, Ronald, *Francis Ford Coppola-Close Up: The Making of His Movies*, New York, 1998.
French, Karl, *Apocalypse Now: The Ultimate A-Z*, New York, 1999.
Horsley, Jake, *Millennial Blues, from ''Apocalypse Now'' to ''The Matrix'': Vol II*, Lanham, 1999.

Articles:

Carcassone, P., ''Dossier: 1979: Francis Ford Coppola,'' in *Cinématographe* (Paris), March 1979.
''Testimonianza: La storia di *Apocalypse Now*,'' in *Filmcritica* (Rome), May 1979.
Anderson, S. H., ''*Apocalypse Now* Film Stuns Cannes,'' in *New York Times*, 21 May 1979.
Haskell, Molly, in *Village Voice* (New York), 21 May 1979.
Pollack, D., ''An Archival Detailing of UA's *Apocalypse Now* since 1967 Start,'' in *Variety* (New York), 23 May 1979.
''Entretien avec Francis Ford Coppola,'' in *Cahiers du Cinéma* (Paris), July-August 1979.
Toubiana, Serge, in *Cahiers du Cinéma* (Paris), July-August 1979.
McCormick, R., in *Cineaste* (New York), no. 4, 1979.
Honickel, T., in *Film und Ton* (Munich), August 1979.
Variety (New York), 15 August 1979.
Canby, Vincent, in *New York Times*, 15 August 1979.
''CinemaScore's 781 Interviews on *Apocalypse Now*,'' in *Variety* (New York), 22 August 1979.
Bock, Audie, ''Zoetrope and *Apocalypse Now*,'' in *American Film* (Washington, D.C.), September 1979.
Geng, V., in *New Yorker*, 3 September 1979.
Kauffmann, Stanley, in *New Republic* (New York), 15 September 1979.
Thompson, R., ''Francis Ford Coppola: Courte histoire d'un scenario: Entretien avec John Milius,'' in *Ecran* (Paris), 15 September 1979.
Riley, B., ''Heart Transplant,'' in *Film Comment* (New York), September-October 1979.
Anderson, P. and J. Wells, in *Films in Review* (New York), October 1979.
Bonitzer, P. and S. Daney, in *Cahiers du Cinéma* (Paris), October 1979.
Levin, G. R., ''Francis Ford Coppola Discusses *Apocalypse Now*,'' in *Millimeter* (New York), October 1979.
Zimmer, J., in *Revue du Cinéma* (Paris), October 1979.
Wood, Michael, in *New York Review of Books*, October 1979.
Tessitore, J., ''The Literary Roots of *Apocalypse Now*,'' in *New York Times*, 21 October 1979.

Apocalypse Now

Gow, Gordon, in *Films and Filming* (London), November 1979.

Heijs, J., in *Skrien* (Amsterdam), November 1979.

Marcus, Greil, ''Journey up the River,'' in *Rolling Stone* (New York), 1 November 1979.

Vallely, J., ''Martin Sheen: Heart of Darkness, Heart of Gold,'' in *Rolling Stone* (New York), 1 November 1979.

Bitomsky, H., in *Filmkritik* (Munich), December 1979.

Jensen, N., ''Coppolas dommedag,'' in *Kosmorama* (Copenhagen), Winter 1979.

Kinder, Marsha, ''The Power of Adaptation in *Apocalypse Now*,'' in *Film Quarterly* (Berkeley), Winter 1979–80.

Yurick, S., ''*Apocalypse Now*/Capital Flow,'' in *Cineaste* (New York), Winter 1979–80.

Broeske, Pat H., in *Magill's Survey of Cinema 1*, Englewood Cliffs, New Jersey, 1980.

Zablotny, Elaine, ''American Insanity—*Apocalypse Now*,'' in *Film Psychology Review* (New York), Winter-Spring 1980.

Sharrett, C., ''Operation Mind Control: *Apocalypse Now* and the Search for Clarity,'' in *Journal of Popular Film and Television* (Washington, D.C.), Spring 1980.

Interview with Coppola, in *Cine* (Mexico City), March 1980.

Alutto, Massimo, in *Cinema e Cinema* (Venice), July-September 1980.

Boehringer, Kathe, ''Banality Now,'' in *Australian Journal of Screen Theory* (Kensington, New South Wales), no. 8, 1980.

Franz, R. C., ''*Apocalypse Now* and *The Deer Hunter:* The Lies Aren't Over,'' in *Jump Cut* (Chicago), October 1980.

Klein, M., ''*Apocalypse Now:* The Absence of History,'' in *Jump Cut* (Chicago), October 1980.

Rich, B. Ruby, ''*Apocalypse Now:* Coppola's American Way,'' in *Jump Cut* (Chicago), October 1980.

''*Apocalypse Now* Issue'' of *Cinema e Cinema* (Venice), October-December 1980.

Vien, N. K., ''*Apocalypse Now* Viewed by a Vietnamese,'' in *Framework* (Norwich), Spring 1981.

Przylipiak, M., ''*Apokalipsa* przed prgiem wielkosci,'' in *Kino* (Warsaw), March 1981.

Jacobs, Diane, ''Coppola Films Conrad in Vietnam,'' in *The English Novel and the Movies*, edited by Michael Klein and Gillian Parker, New York, 1981.

Bourget, Jean-Loup, ''D'un opéra à l'autre,'' in *Positif* (Paris), December 1982.

De Antonio, Emile, ''Interview with Martin Sheen,'' in *American Film* (Washington, D.C.), December 1982.

Wander, P., ''The Aesthetics of Fascism,'' in *Journal of Communication* (Philadelphia), Spring 1983.

''Vietnam Issue'' of *Wide Angle* (Athens, Ohio), vol. 7, no. 4, 1985.

Viviani, Christian, ''Quelques réflexions sur Coppola, histoire de faire le point,'' in *Positif* (Paris), January 1987.

Schneider, Tassilo, "From Cynicism to Self-Pity: *Apocalypse Now* and *Platoon*," in *Cinefocus* (Bloomington, Indiana), no. 2, 1990.

Guneratne, A. R., "Coppola's Apocalyptic Vision: Something Like an Answer to Tassilo Schneider," in *Cinefocus* (Bloomington, Indiana), no. 2, 1990.

Dibble, T., "Another Response to Schneider's 'From Cynicism to Self-Pity . . . ,'" in *Cinefocus* (Bloomington, Indiana), no. 2, 1990.

Hirshey, Gerri, "The Artist as Big Fat Baby," in *GQ—Gentlemen's Quarterly* (New York), October 1991 .

Karren, H., "Bungle in the Jungle," in *Premiere* (New York), Winter 1991.

Worthy, K., "Hearts of Darkness: Making Art, Making History, Making Money, Making Vietnam," in *Cineaste* (New York), no. 2–3, 1992.

Cahir, L. C., "Narratological Parallels in Joseph Conrad's *Heart of Darkness* and Francis Ford Coppola's *Apocalypse Now*," in *Literature/Film Quarterly* (Salisbury, Maryland), no. 3, 1992.

Greiff, L. K., "Soldier, Sailor, Surfer, Chef: Conrad's Ethics and the Margins of *Apocalypse Now*," in *Literature/Film Quarterly* (Salisbury, Maryland), no. 3, 1992.

Whaley, D. M., "The Hero-Adventurer in the Land of Nam," in *Literature/Film Quarterly* (Salisbury, Maryland), no. 3, 1992.

Uszynski, J., "Poza granicami oikoumene," in *Kino* (Warsaw), April 1992.

van Tongeren, P., "The Horror, the Horror. . . ," in *Skoop* (Amsterdam), July-August 1992.

Kuchta, T.M., "Framing 'The Horror': Voice and Voice-over in *Heart of Darkness* and *Apocalypse Now*," in *Studies in the Humanities*, no. 1, 1994.

Petri, Elio, "*Apocalypse Now*," in *Positif* (Paris), no. 415, September 1995.

Worthy, K., "Emissaries of Difference: Conrad, Coppola, and *Hearts of Darkness*," in *Women's Studies*, no. 2, 1996.

Film Threat (Beverly Hills), April 1996.

Trussler, M., "Apocalypse 'Now': Does Conrad Really Sound Like Jim Morrison?" in *Arachne*, no. 1, 1997.

Film:

Coppola, Eleanor, *Hearts of Darkness: A Filmmaker's Apocalypse*, 1991.

* * *

As he set out to plan *Apocalypse Now* filmmaker Francis Ford Coppola ranked as one of the most important young talents then working in Hollywood. His two *Godfather* films (1972, 1974) had landed on the list of the most profitable in Hollywood history, while *The Conversation* (1974) had been hailed as a masterful "art film." In *Apocalypse Now* Coppola attempted to create both a personal look at America's recent tragic war in Vietnam, and a film which could compete at the box-office with *Jaws* and *The Towering Inferno*. As *Apocalypse Now* moved from the story boards into actual production, however, Coppola's attempt to become a complete popular culture mogul had begun to sour. His considerable investments (in a magazine, movies, and even a legitimate theatre) simply were draining him of his then considerable wealth. *Apocalypse Now* would have to be a true blockbuster simply to enable Coppola to recover financially and pay off mounting debts.

But Coppola has always been a risk-taker, and his diminishing portfolio hardly lessened his enthusiasm or his ambition. When first conceived the film had been planned as purely an action-adventure war film; quickly it transformed Vietnam into a metaphor for the downfall and corruption of an entire generation of Americans. The budget and screenplay pushed this $12 million potential blockbuster into a $31 million extravaganza. Coppola fully intended *Apocalypse Now* to be his magnum opus. What actually took place stands as one of the great epic journeys in movie-making history.

Much has been made of how the production of the film seemed to mirror America's involvement in the war itself. *Apocalypse Now* required four grueling months on location; the film's star Martin Sheen suffered a heart attack; vast arrays of military equipment never seemed to work just right. Coppola's movie company pumped $100,000 *per week* into production while on location in the Philippines. (In paying the Marcos government for the use of military equipment, however, Coppola was supporting a government as corrupt as the Vietnam regime of Diem.) To meet constant cost overruns (Brando demanded a million dollars for his minor part) Coppola mortgaged his dwindling assets, so if the film failed at the box-office it would be ruin for him. In the end, *Apocalypse Now* went on to earn about $200 million worldwide, but, in a way, the making of the movie offered a more gripping narrative than the actual movie itself.

The structure of *Apocalypse Now* was borrowed from Joseph Conrad's novella *Heart of Darkness:* a journey up a primitive river as a metaphor serving for an excursion into the darkest parts of the human mind. However, Coppola's formulation of this narrative never was able to grip audience interest. The greatest successes of *Apocalypse Now* can be found in moments of extraordinary visual texture, capturing the look and feel of a war of madness. Whether it is in a jungle where the vegetation dwarfs all human activity, or a PT boat racing up a river filled with black soldiers fighting for the rights of the oppressed when they know what they will find back home, or an armada of helicopters steaming in and destroying a village so primitive it could have been built 2,000 years earlier, we feel, at times, we are actually there.

For example, the scene in which Robert Duvall, as crazed Lieutenant Colonel Kilgore, leads his troops in a helicopter assault on a defenseless village brilliantly portrays the horror and passion of war. As the rockets jump from the war ships, to Wagner's operatic overtones, for a moment we are "in the battle." Yet this particular violence serves no purpose. Duvall's men are mercilessly murdering the very people they are meant to "help."

Apocalypse Now is a film of moments, with a fuzzy monologue by Colonel Kurtz (Brando) at the close never fully wrapping things up. Coppola wanted his film to mean something, and as such raced around the world interpreting for anyone who would listen. (His boldest claim: "This isn't a film about Vietnam. This film is Vietnam.") In the end, as with his best films, *Apocalypse Now* remains structurally disjointed and thematically inconsistent, yet it will always be watched and studied for its moments of cinematic grandeur.

—Douglas Gomery

THE APU TRILOGY

Director: Satyajit Ray

PATHER PANCHALI

(Father Panchali)

India, 1956

Production: Government of West Bengal; black and white, 35mm; running time: 112 minutes. Released 1956. Begun in 1950, though principal filming done in 1952 in a small village in southern India.

Screenplay: Satyajit Ray, from the novel by Bibhuti Bannerji; **photography:** Subrata Mitra; **editor:** Dulal Dutta; **art director:** Bansi Chandragupta; **music:** Ravi Shankar.

Cast: Kanu Banerji (*The Father*); Karuna Banerji (*The Mother*); Subir Banerji (*Apu*); Uma Das Gupta (*The Daughter*); Chunibali Devi (*Old woman*).

Awards: Best Human Document, Cannes Festival, 1956; Selznick Golden, Berlin Festival, 1957; Kinema Jumpo Award as Best Foreign Film, Tokyo Film Festival, 1966; Bodil Award as Best Non-European Film, Denmark, 1966.

Publications

Scripts:

Ray, Satyajit, *Pather Panchali*, in *L'Avant-Scène du Cinéma* (Paris), 1 February 1980.
Ray, Satyajit, *The Apu Trilogy* (in English), Calcutta, 1985.

Books:

Barnouw, Erik, and S. Krishnaswamy, *Indian Film*, New York 1963; revised edition, 1980.
Seton, Marie, *Portrait of a Director—Satyajit Ray*, Bloomington, Indiana, 1971.
Wood, Robin, *The Apu Trilogy*, New York, 1971.
Satyajit Ray, New Delhi, 1976.
Satyajit Ray: Study Guide, Washington, D.C., 1979.
Rangoonwalla, Firoze, *Satyajit Ray's Art*, New Delhi, 1980.
Micciollo, Henri, *Satyajit Ray*, Lausanne, 1980.
Das Gupta, Chidananda, editor, *Satyajit Ray: An Anthology*, New Delhi, 1981.
Gandhy, Behroze, and Paul Willemen, *Indian Cinema*, London, 1982.
Ramachandran, T. M., *70 Years of Indian Cinema (1913–1983)*, Bombay, 1985.
Nyce, Ben, *Satyajit Ray: A Study of His Films*, New York, 1988.
Robinson, Andrew, *Satyajit Ray: The Inner Eye*, Berkeley, 1989.
Tesson, Charles, *Satyajit Ray*, Paris, 1992.
Cooper, Darius, *The Cinema of Satyajit Ray: Between Tradition and Modernity*, New York, 1999.
Ganguly, Suranjan, *Satyajit Ray: In Search of the Modern*, Lanham, Maryland, 2000.

Articles:

Ray, Satyajit, in *Sight and Sound* (London), Spring 1957.
Seton, Marie, ''Journey Through India,'' in *Sight and Sound* (London), Spring 1957.
''Personality of the Month,'' in *Films and Filming* (London), December 1957.
Dyer, Peter, in *Films and Filming* (London), February 1958.
Hart, Henry, in *Films in Review* (New York), February 1958.
Mekas, Jonas, in *Village Voice* (New York), 12 November 1958.
Croce, Arlene, in *Film Culture* (New York), no. 19, 1959.
McVay, Douglas, ''The Ray Trilogy,'' in *Film* (London), March-April 1960.
''Talk with the Director,'' in *Newsweek* (New York), 26 September 1960.
Rhode, Eric, ''Satyajit Ray: A Study,'' in *Sight and Sound* (London), Summer 1961.
Kael, Pauline, in *I Lost It at the Movies*, New York, 1966.
Ray, Satyajit, ''From Film to Film,'' in *Cahiers du Cinéma in English* (New York), February 1966.
Ray, Satyajit, ''A Long Time on the Little Road,'' in *Film Makers on Film Making*, edited by Harry Geduld, Bloomington, Indiana, 1967.
Blue, James, ''Satyajit Ray,'' in *Film Comment* (New York), Summer 1968.
Dutta, K., ''An Interview with Satyajit Ray's Cinematographers,'' in *Filmmakers' Newsletter* (Ward Hill, Massachusetts), January 1975.
Gillett, John, ''Satyajit Ray,'' in *Film* (London), October-November 1975.
Williams, A., in *Movietone News* (Seattle), April 1976.
Hughes, John, ''A Voyage in India: Satyajit Ray Interviewed,'' in *Film Comment* (New York), September-October 1976.
Ray, Satyajit, ''Dialogue on Film,'' in *American Film* (Washington, D.C.), July-August 1978.
''Pather Panchali Issue'' of *L'Avant-Scène du Cinéma* (Paris), 1 February 1980.
Palekar, S., ''So Close to Children,'' in *Cinema in India* (Bombay), no. 4, 1992.

APARAJITO

(The Unvanquished)

India, 1957

Production: Epic Films; black and white, 35mm; running time: 108 minutes. Released 1957. Filmed 1956.

Screenplay: Satyajit Ray, from a novel by Bibhuti Bannerji; **photography:** Subrata Mitra; **editor:** Dulal Dutta; **art director:** Bansi Chandragupta; **music:** Ravi Shankar.

The Apu Trilogy: Apur Sansar

Cast: Kanu Banerji (*The Father*); Karuna Banerji (*The Mother*); Pinaki Sen Gupta (*Apu, as a boy*); Smaran Ghosal (*Apu, as an adolescent*); Ramani Sen Gupta (*1st Uncle*); Subodh Ganguly (*Headmaster*); Ramani Sen Gupta (*2nd Uncle*).

Awards: Best Film: Lion of St. Mark, Venice Festival, 1957; Bodil Award as Best Non-European Film, Denmark, 1967.

Publications

Articles:

Hart, Henry, in *Films in Review* (New York), February 1959.
Mekas, Jonas, in *Village Voice* (New York), 13 May 1959.
Johnson, Albert, in *Film Quarterly* (Berkeley), Summer 1959.
Sarka, Kobita, "Indian Family," in *Films and Filming* (London), April 1960.
Sarka, Kobita, "The Great 3-in-1," in *Films and Filming* (London), December 1964.

Also see list of publications following *Pather Panchali* credits.

APUR SANSAR

(The World of Apu)

India, 1960

Production: Satyajit Ray Productions; black and white, 35mm; running time: 103 minutes. Released 1959. Filmed 1959.

Screenplay: Satyajit Ray, from a story by Satyajit Ray, based on the novel by Bibhuti Bannerji; **photography:** Subrata Mitra; **editor:** Dulal Dutta; **art director:** Bansi Chandragupta; **music:** Ravi Shankar.

Cast: Soumitra Chatterjee (*Apu*); Sharmila Tagore (*Wife of Apu*); Alok Chakravarty (*Kajol*); Dhiresh Mazumaer (*Grandfather*).

Awards: Sutherland Award Trophy, London Film Festival, 1960.

Publications

Articles:

Hart, Henry, in *Films in Review* (New York), March 1960.
Harker, Jonathan, in *Film Quarterly* (Berkeley), Spring 1960.
Croce, Arlene, in *Film Culture* (New York), Summer 1960.
Mekas, Jonas, in *Village Voice* (New York), 6 October 1960.
Gillett, John, in *Sight and Sound* (London), Winter 1960–61.
Durgnat, Raymond, in *Films and Filming* (London), May 1961.
Hanan, D., ''Patriarchal Discourse in Some Early Films of Satyajit Ray,'' *Deep Focus* (Bangalore, India), vol. 3, no. 1, 1990.
Or, Victor, ''A Study of Asian Tradition in Satyajit Ray's *The World of Apu*,'' *Asian Cinema* (Drexel Hill, Pennsylvania), vol. 8, no. 2, Winter 1996/97.

Also see list of publications following *Pather Panchali* credits.

* * *

Satyajit Ray's *Apu Trilogy*, made over a period of eight years and not originally conceived of as a trilogy, had a profound effect on filmmaking within India and an important effect on the attention paid to Indian films outside India. Within India, the unobtrusive style of lighting, dialogue, and action employed in the *Trilogy* challenged the prevailing operatic style and led to new conventions of realism. Abroad, the *Trilogy* stirred interest in other Indian cinema, and led to a wider market for Indian films as well as to significant contact between Indian and non-Indian filmmakers.

After returning to India from a business trip to London for Keymer's advertising agency, Ray set about finding a crew and finances for a film based on the famous Bengali novel, *Pather Panchali.* In his work as a graphic artist, Ray had already illustrated a Bengali abridgement of the novel and he was able to obtain rights for a modest sum (about $1300) on the basis of his active interest. Finances proved more difficult to procure for the film itself: Ray pawned his wife's jewelry and was finally advanced money to complete the film by the government of West Bengal. For its first two weeks in Calcutta, the film played to small audiences. Then the theater filled and the film recovered its costs in Ray's native city within the first thirteen weeks. In Bombay, in 1956, the film was reviewed by Adib in the following terms: ''It is banal to compare it with any other Indian picture—for even the best of the pictures produced so far have been cluttered with clichés. *Pather Panchali* is pure cinema. There is no trace of the theater in it. It does away with plot, with grease and paint, with the slinky charmer and the sultry beauty, with the slapdash hero breaking into song on the slightest provocation or no provocation at all.'' For many critics, Ray's completion of *Aparajito*, in 1956, confirmed the novelty of his approach and the strength of his talent. Stanley Kauffmann reported that Ray was forging in the Apu films the uncreated conscience of his race.

All three films of the trilogy are organized by an open form: the progression of events is episodic and interest in the narrative derives from character and location rather than from the dynamics of plot. In *Pather Panchali*, the poor Brahmin priest and his wife have a son born to them, the father must leave home to make a living, their daughter dies, the son watches the world change around him, the family is forced to leave the village. The viewer's attention is engaged less by what is going to happen than by the way in which things do happen. The editing allows the viewer to soak in the atmosphere of a landscape or an evening. As son and daughter (Apu and Durga) run to the edge of the village to watch a steam train, the camera registers soft white tufts of flax waving in the air. When the train appears, it hurtles not only past the village, but across the viewer's inner rhythms which had been slowed by the waving flax. The episode of the train in *Pather Panchali* also indicates Ray's classicism, his practice of creating a strong response in the viewer and subsequently disciplining that response. During the course of the *Trilogy*, the viewer's empathetic experience of an event is frequently punctuated by a distancing perspective. In *Pather Panchali*, when the father breaks down in grief over his dead daughter, Ray cuts to the young Apu standing apart, watching his sorrowing father. In *Apur Sansar*, Ray cuts from the climactic reconciliation of Apu and his son Kajal to the dour father-in-law, who will add this episode to the many other curious episodes he has witnessed in his life.

The open form also allows Ray to annotate the feelings of his characters by referring to the natural world. At their simplest, these references function as analogies. When Apu's mother is happy, the water skates and dragonflies dance an insect version of happiness. But at their best, images of the natural world become surcharged with meaning: the monsoon clouds in *Pather Panchali* gather to themselves the pent-up emotions of the mother and the children; the fireflies in *Aparajito* signify the beauty and the remoteness of nature; and the river gleaming behind Apu, in *Apur Sansar*, while Apu debates whether to marry his friend's cousin, signifies both the burden of the moment and the flow of time into which individual moments run indistinguishably.

Although Ray and his cameraman, Subrata Mitra, made remarkable experiments towards recreating the effect of daylight on sets (by bouncing studio lights off of cotton sheeting stretched above the set), the *Apu Trilogy* did not constitute innovation in cinematic technique. The excellence of the *Trilogy* derived from its tact. Using long takes, reaction shots and unhurried action, Ray was able to place in suspension before the viewer multiple points of view: that of the aged aunt who must cadge food to survive and that of the young mother Sarbojaya, who will not extend herself indefinitely and who refuses to help the aged aunt pour water from a pitcher. The multiple points of view are validated by an evenness of regard: the camera attends as calmly to the ailing aunt as to the determined mother, to the grief-stricken father as fully as to the observing Apu.

Ray's cinema has developed considerably in complexity and scope since the *Apu Trilogy.* Nonetheless, his first films retain their capacity to move the viewer. Their power derives from the internal consistency of Ray's style and from the cultural importance of Ray's story. The *Apu Trilogy* epitomizes the migration of many poor, Third World families from the village to the city. In the *Apu Trilogy*, Ray leaves the outcome of the migration open: Apu has not yet made his peace with the brisk anonymous ways of the city as, later, the protagonist of *Seemabaddha* is to embrace the city's modernity. When Ray turns, in his mid-career films, to examine the opportunities the city offers to idealistic young men, the optimism of the early films is lost.

In Bengal the effect of Ray's realism (his scaling of dialogue, action and lighting closer to everyday reality) was felt immediately in the work of Mrinal Sen and Tapan Sinha, but his example took 15 years to reach the principal film production center of Bombay. Only in the late 1960s and early 1970s did new directors begin making Hindi films without melodrama, trusting the subtlety of action, atmosphere and editing to transmit their intentions. The new movement, known as "parallel cinema," did not defeat the operatic style—most Hindi films are still extravaganzas—but they enabled Hindi cinema to begin inquiry into the conditions of ordinary life in India. The way towards this inquiry was first explored by Ray in the *Apu Trilogy.*

—Satti Khanna

APUR SANSAR

See **THE APU TRILOGY**

ARABIAN NIGHTS

See **FIORE DELLE MILLE E UNA NOTTE**

ARANYER DIN RATRI

(Days and Nights in the Forest)

India, 1969

Director: Satyajit Ray

Production: Priya Films; black and white; running time: 115 minutes. Language: Bengali.

Producer: Nepal Dutta, Ashim Dutta; **cinematographer:** Soumendu Roy, Purnendu Bose; **screenplay:** Satyajit Ray, based on a novel by Sunil Ganguly; **editor:** Dulal Dutta; **music:** Satyajit Ray; **production design:** Bansi Chandragupta; **art direction:** Ashoke Bose; **sound:** Sujit Sarkar.

Cast: Soumitra Chatterjee (*Ashim*); Subhendu Chatterjee (*Sanjoy*); Samit Bhanja (*Hari*); Robi Ghosh (*Sekhar*); Pahadi Sanyal (*Sadashiv Tripathi*); Sharmila Tagore (*Aparna*); Kaberi Bose (*Jaya*); Simi Garewal (*Duli*); Aparna Sen (*Hari's former lover*).

Publications:

Books:

Seton, Marie, *Portrait of a Director: Satyajit Ray*, Bloomington, 1971.

Robinson, Andrew, *Satyajit Ray: The Inner Eye*, Berkeley, 1992.

Sarkar, Bidyut, *World of Satyajit Ray*, Columbia, 1992.

Banerjee, Tarapada, and Satayjit Ray, *Satyajit Ray: A Portrait in Black and White*, New York, 1993.

Banerjee, Surabhi, *Satyajit Ray: Beyond the Frame*, Flushing, 1996.

Das, Santi, editor, *Satyajit Ray: An Intimate Master*, Flushing, 1998.

Cooper, Darius, *The Cinema of Satyajit Ray: Between Tradition and Modernity*, Cambridge, 2000.

Articles:

Milne, Tom, in *Sight & Sound* (London), vol. 41, no. 1, Winter 1971–1972.

Interview with Satyajit Ray, in *Sight & Sound* (London), vol. 42, no. 1, Winter 1972–1973.

Paul, W., "Dim Day of a Recent Past," in *Village Voice* (New York), vol. 18, 12 April 1973.

Kauffmann, S., "Films," in *The New Republic* (Marion), vol. 168, 21 April 1973.

Schickel, Richard, "Days and Nights in the Art House," in *Film Comment* (New York), vol. 28, no. 3, May-June 1992.

Ramnarayan, Gowri, "To Western Audiences, the Filmmaker Satyajit Ray is Synonymous with Indian Cinema," in *Interview*, vol. 22, no. 6, June 1992.

Sengoopta, Chandak, "Satyajit Ray: The Plight of a Third-World Artist," in *American Scholar*, vol. 62, no. 2, Spring 1993.

Ciment, Michel, and Hubert Niogret, "Satyajit Ray," in *Positif* (Paris), no. 399, May 1994.

Sragow, Michael, "An Art Wedded to Truth," in *The Atlantic Monthly*, vol. 274, no. 4, October 1994.

Ganguly, S., "No Moksha: Arcadia Lost in Satyajit Ray's *Days and Nights in the Forest*," in *Film Criticism* (Meadville), vol. 19, no. 2, Winter 1994–1995.

Robinson, Andrew, "Works of a Master Made Whole Again," in *The New York Times*, 2 April 1995.

Sen, Amartya, "Our Culture, Their Culture: Satyajit Ray and the Art of Universalism," in *The New Republic*, vol. 214, no. 14, 1 April 1996.

Corliss, Richard, "From Asia's Film Factories: 10 Golden Greats," in *Time International*, vol. 154, no. 7/8, 23 August 1999.

* * *

Satyajit Ray always insisted that his films were made first and foremost for his own fellow-Bengalis, adding that foreign viewers, unless exceptionally well up on Bengali language and culture, would inevitably miss a lot of what was going on. Despite such claims, several of Ray's films found more appreciative (and, it could be argued, more perceptive) audiences outside India. One such was *Days and Nights in the Forest*, widely hailed by Western critics as one of the director's finest films, but received by his compatriots with puzzlement and indifference.

Indian viewers, by all accounts, were put off by the loose-limbed, seemingly random flow of the narrative. "People in India kept saying: What is it about, where is the story, the theme?" Ray observed regretfully in a *Sight & Sound* interview. "And the film is about so many things, that's the trouble. People want just one theme, which they can hold in their hands." He likened the structure of the film to a fugue, in which different elements appear and reappear developed, interwoven, transformed, and subtly balanced against each other.

The musical analogy is apt. Ray often acknowledged the influence of composers, above all Mozart, along with that of writers and other film-makers, and *Days and Nights* is his most Mozartian work: like

Aranyer din Ratri

Cosi Fan Tutte or *La Nozze di Figaro* it treats serious matters in a seemingly light-hearted way. On the surface the mode is comedy of manners. Four middle-class young men from Calcutta take a few days vacation in the forests of Bihar, to the west of Bengal, where they meet another group of city people—elderly father, daughter, and widowed daughter-in-law—as well as beautiful young woman of the local Santhal tribe. There ensues a complex pattern of social cross-currents and tentative relationships. Ashim (played by Soumitra Chatterjee), the most affluent and assured of the young men, is attracted to the poised and intelligent Aparna (Sharmila Tagore). Jaya, the young widow, tries to seduce the shy Sanjoy but humiliatingly fails. Hari, the none-too-bright sportsman, seduces the Santhali woman, Duli, and is badly beaten by one of her fellow-villagers. Sekhar (another of Ray's favourite actors, the roly-poly Robi Ghosh) gambles compulsively and plays the fool.

The heart of the film is the picnic sequence, where the six young Calcuttans sit round and play a memory game in which each player has to choose the name of a famous person and also remember, in sequence, all the previous choices. Subtle, elegantly structured, and delectably funny, the scene discloses a wealth of emotional and psychological detail: like the various members of a sextet, each character reveals him- or herself in the way he or she plays, from Aparna's graceful flute to Sekhar's galumphing bassoon. The scene shows us a process of insight getting under way. By the end of the film each of the young men—with the exception of Sekhar—has experienced a moment of epiphany, brought up short by self-realization. None of them, we can guess, will ever be quite the same again.

But there's also a political dimension to the film. *Days and Nights* can be seen as a prelude to the three films often grouped together as Ray's "City Trilogy": *The Adversary*, *Company Limited*, and *The Middleman.* In these films Ray engaged, for the first time in his career, the social and political upheavals that were then shaking Bengal, and in *Days and Nights* he hints at the kind of class- and caste-based attitudes that underlay this unrest. The four young men from the city are not unlikable, but their treatment of the local "tribal" people reveals an unthinking arrogance that at times verges on brutality. Hari, having mislaid his wallet, at once accuses the villager co-opted as their servant of stealing it, and hits him—an injustice which later rebounds on him. Even Ashim, the most intelligent and politically aware of the four, browbeats the caretaker of their bungalow into accepting a bribe, then mockingly comments (in English, significantly), ''Thank God for corruption.''

As so often in Ray's films, the women come off rather better than the men, being far more adult, sensitive, and attuned to what's going on around them. In particular, Ray uses Sharmila Tagore's cool, intelligent screen persona as the film's moral touchstone (as he would again in *Company Limited*); it is Aparna who brings home to Ashim the full extent of his thoughtlessness. Having brushed aside as excuses the caretaker's concern about his sick wife, he's taken aback when Aparna suggests he should look for himself—and appalled when he sees that the woman is close to death. It's a moment that anticipates the similar shock felt by the complacent young Brahmin (also played by Soumitra Chatterjee) in *Distant Thunder* when he registers the ravages of famine on his fellow villagers.

Days and Nights in the Forest marks a transition in Ray's filmmaking career, turning his talents for social comedy, emotional nuance, and quiet, understated irony towards more contemporary concerns. At the same time it demonstrates the subtlety of his narrative control, concealing a carefully devised dramatic shape beneath the seemingly casual flow of everyday life. Far from being shapeless or lacking a theme, as its first audiences imagined, the film is subtly orchestrated throughout: there isn't a scene or incident, barely even a gesture, that doesn't contribute to the overall purpose.

—Philip Kemp

L'ARGENT

France, 1929

Director: Marcel L'Herbier

Production: Cinemondial and Cineromans; black and white, 35mm, silent; length: 5344 meters, running time: 195 minutes. Released 10 January 1929. Filmed in Francouer studios at Joinville; exteriors shot at La Bourse, Place de l'Opera, the Paris Stock Exchange, and Le Bourget; cost: more than 3 million francs.

Producer: Simon Schiffrin; **screenplay:** Marcel L'Herbier, from the novel by Emile Zola; **photography:** Jules Kruger; **production designers:** Lazare Meerson and André Barsacq; **art director:** Jacques Manuel; **costume designer:** Jacques Manuel.

Cast: Mary Glory (*Line Hamelin*); Brigitte Helm (*Baron Sandorf*); Yvette Guilbert (*Le Méchain*); Marcelle Pradot (*Countess Alice de Beauvilliers*); Esther Kiss, Elaine Tayar, and Josette Racon (*Switchboard operators*); Mona Goya, Yvonne Dumas, Maries Costes (*Extras*); Pierre Alcover (*Nicolas Saccard*); Alfred Abel (*Alphonse Gunderman, the banker*); Henry Victor (*Jacques Hamelin*); Pierre Juvenet (*Baron Defrance*); Antonin Artaud (*Mazaud*); Jules Berry (*Huret, the reporter*); Alexandre Mihalesco (*Salomon Massias*); Raymond Rouleau (*Jantrou*); Jean Godard (*Dejoie*); Armand Bour (*Daigremont*); Roger Karl (*Banker*); Jimmy Gaillard (*The groom*); plus Les Rocky Twins, Raymond Dubreuil, Garaudet, and Tardif.

Publications

Script:

L'Herbier, Marcel, *L'Argent* (includes list of scenes, some dialogue), in *L'Avant-Scène du Cinéma* (Paris), 1 June 1978.

Books:

Jaque-Catelain présente Marcel L'Herbier, Paris, 1950.
Sadoul, Georges, *French Film*, London, 1953.
Armes, Roy, *French Cinema*, New York, 1970.
Burch, Noël, *Marcel L'Herbier*, Paris, 1973.
Brossard, Jean-Pierre, editor, *Marcel L'Herbier et son temps*, La-Chaux-de-Fonds, Switzerland, 1980.
Canosa, Michele, *Marcel L'Herbier*, Parma, 1985.

Articles:

New York Times, 23 September 1968.
Blumer, R. H., ''The Camera as Snowball: France 1918–1927,'' in *Cinema Journal* (Evanston, Illinois), Spring 1970.
Jouvet, P., in *Cinématographe* (Paris), May 1977.
''*L'Argent* Issue'' of *Avant-Scène du Cinéma* (Paris), 1 June 1978.
Trosa, S., ''Archéologie du cinéma,'' in *Cinématographe* (Paris), December 1978.
Petat, J., ''La Gratuité ce *L'Argent*,'' in *Cinéma* (Paris), March 1979.
Fieschi, J., ''Marcel L'Herbier,'' in *Cinématographe* (Paris), December 1979.
Cousins, R. F., ''Adapting Zola for the Silent Cinema: The Example of Marcel L'Herbier,'' in *Literature/Film Quarterly* (Salisbury, Maryland), January 1984.
Ciment, Michel, ''Je ne cherche pas une description mais une vision des choses,'' in *Positif* (Paris), no. 430, December 1996.
Le Clezin, J-M. G., ''A penz,'' in *Filmvilag* (Hungary), vol. 40, no. 10, 1997.

Marcel L'Herbier is a key figure of 1920s French cinema and his modernization of Emile Zola's novel, *L'Argent*, released in 1929 on the eve of the sound revolution, is his most ambitious work. The scope of the film is inspired by Abel Gance's *Napoléon*, but rather than talk

L'Argent

of heroes, L'Herbier has chosen to attack what he hated most, the power of money. Though he took Zola's novel as his starting point, he retained little beyond the title and the outline of the plot. The film's action is transferred to the 1920s and unfolds within opulent, oversized sets built by Lazare Meerson and André Barsacq. The film's largest set, however, is an actual location, the Paris Stock Exchange borrowed for three days over Easter and filmed with a complex multi-camera technique by a team led by Jules Kruger, who had earlier worked on *Napoléon.* The visual style, echoing the major spectacles of 1920s German cinema, is enhanced by the presence of Brigitte Helm and Alfred Abel, as the villains in L'Herbier's cast. Despite the enormous resources deployed—the film cost over three million francs—*L'Argent*'s plot line is remarkably straighforward: a young aviator and his wife become involved in a dubious financial scheme set up by the lecherous and unscrupulous Saccard. The latter in turn is destroyed by an even more sinister figure, the banker Gunderman, abetted by the Baroness Sandorf. Though thwarted in his attempt to seduce the wife and destroy the aviator when he is ruined, Saccard is left in prison plotting his next financial coup, while Gunderman rules untroubled.

The 1920s was a period in which directors like Gance and L'Herbier seized the opportunities for individual expression offered by the disorganization of the French film industry. This was a cinema in which the key contributions of noted set designers were set against a continuing interest in location filming. As *L'Argent* shows, a preoccupation with visual effects—decor and movement, masking and superimpositions, slow motion photography, symbolic lighting and so on—did not imply any disregard for the real social world or for nature. *L'Argent* was not particularly highly esteemed by traditional film historians, but recent critical work, especially that of Noël Burch, has pointed to the great richness of the film even if the ''modernity'' claimed for it remains a problematic concept.

L'Herbier, like other 1920s filmmakers, refused to subordinate the visual style of his filmmaking to the demands of narrative continuity, which was already dominant in the United States and elsewhere. The type of cinema of which *L'Argent* is a key example can only be understood if the claims to primacy of narrative are disregarded and film is accepted as a mode of expression which may legitimately captivate its audience by other means. In this sense a work like *L'Argent* forces upon us a widening of the conception of cinema to take in forms fundamentally alien to the Hollywood tradition. The question of what value is to be attached to this alternative approach is, however, more complex. Noël Burch and others have prized *L'Argent* very highly as an example of a vitally important modernist cinema. But in a sense this distorts history, since the conventions L'Herbier was disregarding were not as fully established in France, and the Hollywood-style production practices which would have supported them were totally lacking. Moreover the weight of 19th-century traditions of art and literature weighs heavily on L'Herbier, and a true evaluation of *L'Argent* would need to take into account also the conventional content, subject matter and ideological assumptions, as well as the visual and rhythmical audacities. But Burch's claims do make a refreshing alternative to the customary denigration of 1920s French cinema and open fascinating perspectives for future research.

—Roy Armes

L'ARROSEUR ARROSE

(The Sprayer Sprayed)

France, 1895

Director: Louis Lumière

Production: Produced by Louis Lumière to demonstrate his *cinématographe;* black and white; running time: approximately one minute. Released June 1895 in Lyons.

Cast: François Clerc (*The gardener*); Daniel Duval (*The boy*).

Publications

Books:

Kubnick, Henry, *Les Frères Lumière*, Paris, 1938.

Leroy, Paul, *Au seuil de paradis des images avec Louis Lumière*, Paris, 1948.

Bessy, Maurice, and Lo Duca, *Louis Lumière, inventeur*, Paris, 1948.

Pernot, Victor, *A Paris, il y a soixante ans, naissant le cinéma*, Paris, 1955.

Sadoul, Georges, *Louis Lumière*, Paris, 1964.

Mitry, Jean, *Filmographie Universelle 2*, Paris, 1964.

Chardère, Bernard, and others, *Les Lumière*, Lausanne, 1985.

Sauvage, Leo, *L'Affaire Lumière: Du mythe à l'histoire: Enquête sur les origines du cinema*, Paris, 1985.

Redi, Riccardo, *Lumière*, Rome, 1986.

André, Jacques, and Maria André, *Une Saison Lumière à Montpelier*, Perpignan, 1987.

Articles:

''Lumière Jubilee'' in *Time* (New York), 18 November 1935.

Sadoul, Georges, ''Lumière—The Last Interview,'' in *Sight and Sound* (London), Summer 1948.

Deutelbaum, Marshall, ''Structural Patterning in the Lumière Films,'' in *Wide Angle* (Athens, Ohio), no. 1, 1979.

Vaughan, Dai, ''Let There Be Lumière,'' in *Sight and Sound* (London), Spring 1981.

Ciné-Tracts (Montreal), Summer-Fall 1981.

''Les Pionniers du Cinéma Français Issue'' of *Avant-Scène du Cinéma* (Paris), November 1984.

Positif (Paris), January 1986.

* * *

At the Annual Meeting of the French Photographic Society held in Lyons 10–12 June 1895, Louis Lumière presented a series of short, one-minute films to demonstrate the technical qualities of his recently patented *cinématographe*, which was uniquely both a camera and a projector. In a varied programme he not only showed the potential of his invention to record everyday scenes both public (*La Sortie des Usines Lumière*) and private (*Le Goûter du Bébé*), but also, and ultimately of more momentous importance, established that no obvious distinction could be made between these observed and unrehearsed events, and an event stage-managed for the camera. With *Le Jardinier et le petit espiègle*, subsequently to become better known as *L'Arroseur arrosé*, Lumière created the first comic sequence to be recorded on film, and in so doing heralded a generation of silent slapstick movies.

The film depicts a gardener innocently watering a vegetable patch, when a mischievous boy surreptitiously cuts off the water supply by treading on the hose. The bemused gardener looks down the nozzle of the hose to determine the cause of the interruption, at which point the young prankster releases the water. It then gushes up to soak the gardener and to knock off his hat. After a short chase the boy is caught and duly spanked, and the gardener resumes his task.

The origins of the film have been disputed. According to Lumière the sequence is simply a re-enactment of an actual prank played by his younger brother Edouard on the family gardener François Clerc. However according to Georges Sadoul, the filmed sequence, if not the event itself, may have been inspired by a well-known comic strip cartoon frequently reproduced in late 19th-century children's books. He cites as an example the cartoon strip composed by the artist Herman Vogel and published in 1887 by Quantin. Here the narrative, illustrated in nine images, is titled *L'Arroseur*, and relates precisely those events depicted in the film, so that the cartoon sequence could easily be mistaken for the story-board for Lumière's production. In this respect *L'Arroseur arrosé* may be considered the first example of screen adaptation.

The sequence was filmed at the family home in Lyons in the spring of 1895. François Clerc duly played out his role as the gardener, but the part of the boy was acted not by Edouard who was considered to be too young, but by Daniel Duval, a juvenile apprentice carpenter at the Lumière factory. A single fixed camera records the carefully staged events.

In contrast to the other demonstration films which were no more than a recorded fragment of a larger event, *L'Arroseur arrosé* is complete and self-contained. The simple cause and effect narrative, presented from a single omniscient viewpoint, takes the audience through a variety of emotions, in an expressive use of space. The opening frames establish the gardener in his normal routine occupying the left-hand side of the screen. This normality is subverted by the arrival from the right of the mischievous boy who invades the gardener's space to interrupt the water supply. The audience is now privileged with information denied the gardener and can anticipate the comic outcome of the unsuspecting victim looking down the hose.

However the audience is momentarily deprived of its omiscient viewpoint when the gardener, clearly intent on retribution, chases the prankster out of camera-shot. The two characters return now closer to the fixed camera position so that the punishment of the naughty boy can be clearly seen. With the closing images showing the gardener once more watering his vegetable patch, and the guilty boy banished from the screen, normality has been restored and traditional morality upheld.

Although Lumière made other comic sequences such as *Chez le photographe* and *Charcuterie mécanique*, it was *L'Arroseur arrosé* which captured the imagination of the early cinema audiences. The sequence was quickly imitated by Georges Méliès with *L'Arroseur* in 1896, and in 1958 François Truffaut paid homage to Lumière's pioneering achievements with an affectionate pastiche of the gag in his film *Les Mistons*.

—R. F. Cousins

ARSENAL

USSR, 1928

Director: Alexander Dovzhenko

Production: VUFCO-Odessa; black and white, 35mm, silent; length: 7 reels, 1820 meters. Released 25 February 1929, Kiev. Filmed during the second half of 1928 in and around Kiev.

Scenario and editing: Alexander Dovzhenko; **photography:** Danylo Demutsky; **production designers:** Isaac Shpinel and Vladimir Mueller; **music score for performance:** Ihor Belza; **assistant directors:** Alexei Kapler, Lazar Bodyk.

Cast: Semen Svashenko (*Tymish*); Amvroziy Buchma (*German soldier*); Mykola Nademsky (*Official*); M. Kuchynsky (*Petlyura*); D. Erdman (*German officer*); O. Merlatti (*Sadovsky*); A. Yevdakov (*Nicholas II*); S. Petrov (*German soldier*); Mykhaylovsky (*Ukrainian nationalist*); H. Kharkov (*Red Army soldier*).

Publications

Script:

Dovzhenko, Alexander, *Arsenal*, in *Alexander Dovzhenko: Izbrannoe*, edited by N. S. Tikhonova, Moscow, 1957.

Arsenal, edited by Y. I. Solntseva and L. I. Pazhitnova, Moscow, 1977.

Books:

Yourenev, R., *Alexander Dovzhenko*, Moscow, 1958 (author's name transliterated as R. Jurenew in German translation, 1964).

Leyda, Jay, *Kino: A History of the Russian and Soviet Film*, London, 1960.

Rachuk, Igor, *Poetika Dovzhenko*, Moscow, 1964.

Schnitzer, Luda and Jean, *Dovzhenko*, Paris, 1966.

Mariamov, Alexandr, *Dovzhenko*, Moscow, 1968.

Oms, Marcel, *Alexandre Dovjenko*, Lyons, 1968.

Amengual, Bathélemy, *Alexandr Dovjenko*, Paris, 1970.

Carynnk, Marco, editor, *The Poet as Filmmaker*, Cambridge, Massachusetts, 1973.

Kepley, Vance, Jr., *In the Service of the State: The Cinema of Alexander Dovzhenko*, Madison, Wisconsin, 1986.

Articles:

Borisov, O., ''Film in Work,'' in *Kino* (Moscow), no. 10, 1928.

Hamilton, James Shelley, in *National Board of Review Magazine* (New York), November 1929.

Hall, Mordaunt, in *New York Times*, 11 November 1929.

Moore, John C., ''Pabst, Dovzhenko: A Comparison,'' in *Close Up* (London), September 1932.

Leyda, Jay, ''Index to the Creative Work of Alexander Dovzhenko,'' in *Sight and Sound* (London), supplement, index series November 1947.

Montagu, Ivor, ''Dovzhenko—Poet of Life Eternal,'' in *Sight and Sound* (London), Summer 1957.

''Dovzhenko Issue'' of *Film* (Venice), August 1957.

Shibuk, Charles, ''The Films of Alexander Dovzhenko,'' in *New York Film Bulletin*, nos. 11–14, 1961.

Carynnyk, Marco, ''The Dovzhenko Papers,'' in *Film Comment* (New York), Fall 1971.

Frejlih, S., ''Fin unserer Epoch'' and ''Ein Poet des Films,'' in *Film und Fernsehen* (Berlin), August-September 1974.

''Dovzhenko Issue'' of *Iskusstvo Kino* (Moscow), September 1974.

Krautz, A., ''Zu Problemen des stilistischen Einflusses der bildenden Kunst auf die Stummfilme Alexander Dowshenko,'' in *Information* (Berlin), no. 2, 1977.

Christie, Ian, in *Monthly Film Bulletin* (London), September 1977.

Pliouchtch, L., ''Dovjenko et *Arsenal*,'' in *Revue de la Cinémathèque* (Montreal), October-November 1989.

Kepley, V., Jr., ''Dovzhenko and Montage: Issues of Style and Narration in the Silent Films''; M. Smith, ''The Influence of Socialist Realism on Soviet Montage: *The End of St. Petersburg, Fragment of an Empire*, and *Arsenal*''; and W.M. Osadnik and E. Wilk, ''Toward a Formal Semiotic Analysis of Dovzhenko's *Arsenal*,'' all in *Journal of Ukrainian Studies*, vol. 19, no. 1, 1994.

* * *

In *Arsenal*, Alexander Dovzhenko, perhaps the most radical of the Soviet directors of the silent period, altered the already extended conventions of cinematic structure to a degree greater than had even the innovative Sergei Eisenstein in his bold *October*. The effect of this tinkering with the more or less accepted proprieties of motion picture construction produced a work that is actually less a film than it is a highly symbolic visual poem. For example, in a more linearly structured piece like *October*, the metaphors, allusions, and analogies that arise through the construction of the various montages replace rather than comment on essential actions within the film. In *Arsenal*, however, the symbolism is so purposely esoteric, with seemingly deliberate barriers established to block the viewer's perception, that the relationship of individual symbols or sequences to the various actions of the film is not immediately clear.

Arsenal

The film's central theme obviously revolves around the idea of the sheer horror of war and is most fundamentally incarnate in the physical symbol of an arsenal in the midst of Russia's civil war. Yet, this theme is fragmented throughout the film within three distinct visual contexts. First, Dovzhenko exploits the inherent metaphorical potential of the individual shot as it is brilliantly exemplified in an opening image of a barbed wire trench barrier suddenly and unexpectedly exploding after a prolonged period of stasis. The contrast thus established between the transfixed image and the force of the off-camera shell explosion sets the stage for an interaction of fixed and moving images that runs the course of the film and establishes a semblance of poetic meter.

Second, the area between shots which is normally used in silent films for dialogue, location, or explanation is used here by Dovzhenko for thematic purposes. In an early scene, a series of three titles reading: ''There was a mother who had three sons,'' ''There was a war,'' ''. . . and the mother had no sons,'' are interspersed between shots of a solitary woman and two camera angles of men on a moving train. This combination effected in sets of three (a recurrent image pattern throughout the film) not only establishes the concept of men going off to face the horrors of war but also ingrains in the audience a particular sentiment toward the idea.

A final thematic employment of symbolic images and one that runs through the entire course of the film in one form or another is the director's juxtaposition of stasis and movement within individual shots and between shots as well. Images of a train, of a platoon of soldiers moving almost relentlessly forward, a religious procession, and a number of other dynamic elements, are interjected around and between relatively static shots (usually grim), and effectively frame each immobile image as an individual symbolic and poetic unit with a meaningful parallel somewhere else in the film. In one sequence, a catatonic soldier is shot by an officer for not moving. The static shots of his execution are broken up by shots of a faceless platoon of soldiers moving forward. We never see the execution, only still images of each stage. The isolated shots, however, prefigures a parallel execution, again done in a sequence of three images, and that in turn foreshadows the fall of the arsenal itself. The middle shot in the execution sequence is nothing more than a symbolic pile of empty cartridges, but, as it turns out, the strikers who have taken over the arsenal are doomed by a lack of ammunition. Their plight is subsequently dramatized by three titles interjected between shots of the men. The titles read: ''The 24th hour.'' ''The 48th hour,'' and ''The 72nd hour,'' to show that not only ammunition but time is running out.

Arsenal is a difficult film that makes many demands upon the viewer and is stubbornly resistant to easy interpretation. Consequently it rewards a number of viewings and repeated analysis. Under intense scrutiny its thematic patterns emerge and the real genius of its creator becomes apparent. Although many of its images now appear dated as, in fact, do Eisenstein's, ample power remains to substantiate the relatively untutored Dovzhenko's reputation as one of the early giants of Soviet cinema, on a level with both Eisenstein and Pudovkin.

—Stephen L. Hanson

ASHES AND DIAMONDS

See **POPIOL I DIAMENT**

THE ASPHALT JUNGLE

USA, 1950

Director: John Huston

Production: M.G.M.; black and white; running time: 105 minutes; released August 1950.

Producer: Arthur Hornblow Jr.; **screenplay:** Ben Maddow and John Huston, from the novel by W. R. Burnett; **photography:** Harold Rosson; **editor:** George Boemler; **sound:** Douglas Shearer; **art directors:** Cedric Gibbons and Randall Duell; **music:** Miklos Rosza.

Cast: Sterling Hayden (*Dix Handley*); Louis Calhern (*Alonzo D. Emmerich*); Jean Hagen (*Doll Conovan*); James Whitmore (*Gus Minissi*); Sam Jaffe (*Doc Riedenschneider*); John McIntire (*Police Commissioner Hardy*); Marc Lawrence (*Cobby*); Barry Kelley (*Lt. Dietrich*); Anthony Caruso (*Louis Ciavelli*); Teresa Celli (*Maria Ciavelli*); Marilyn Monroe (*Angela Phinlay*).

Publications

Script:

Maddow, Ben, and John Huston, *The Asphalt Jungle*, Carbondale, Illinois, 1980.

Books:

Benayoun, Robert, *John Huston: La Grande Ombre de l'aventure*, Paris 1966; revised edition, 1985.
Kaminsky, Stuart M., *John Huston, Maker of Magic*, Boston, 1978.
Madsen, Axel, *John Huston*, New York, 1978.
Giannetti, Louis, *Masters of the American Cinema*, Englewood Cliffs, New Jersey, 1981.
Hammen, Scott, *John Huston*, Boston, 1985.
McCarty, John, *The Films of John Huston*, Secaucus, New Jersey, 1987.

Articles:

Variety (New York), August 1950.
Lightman, Herb A., ''Realism with a Master's Touch,'' in *American Cinematographer* (Los Angeles), August 1950.
Houston, Penelope, in *Monthly Film Bulletin* (London), September 1950.
Lambert, Gavin, in *Sight and Sound* (London), November 1950.
''Huston Issue'' of *Positif* (Paris), August 1952.
Cinéma (Paris), June 1972.
Bitomsky, H., in *Filmkritik* (Munich), January 1980.
Audibert, Louis, in *Cinématographe* (Paris), May 1981.
Combs, Richard, in *Listener* (London), 14 August 1986.

The Asphalt Jungle

Reid's Film Index (New South Wales, Australia), no. 10, 1993.
Telotte, J.P., ''Fatal Capers: Strategy and Enigma in Film Noir,'' *Journal of Popular Film and Television* (Washington, D.C.), vol. 23, no. 4, Winter 1996.

* * *

With *The Asphalt Jungle*, John Huston laid down the definitive pattern of the heist movie. A gang of criminals, each with a particular skill, is gathered together; the job (typically a robbery) is pulled with measured professionalism; but ill-chance, or internal dissension, undermines the gang's success, bringing them to diaster and death. The formula was to be taken up, and creatively reworked any number of ways, by directors as varied as Kubrick (*The Killing*), Mackendrick (*The Ladykillers*), Becker (*Touchez pas au grisbi*), Dassin (*Rififi*) and Monicelli (*I soliti ignoti*); but Huston's film still sustains comparison with any of its successors.

The Asphalt Jungle also broke new ground in presenting crime as an occupation like any other, carried out not by the preening megalomaniacs of 1930s gangster movies, nor by the disillusioned antiheroes of the 1940s, but by ordinary people motivated by everyday preoccupations and small private ambitions. The expert cracksman (Anthony Caruso) has ''mouths to feed, rent to pay''; the tough hood, Dix Handley (Sterling Hayden), dreams of buying back the Kentucky farm of his childhood. Crime, muses Louis Calhern's crooked lawyer in the script's most famous line, ''is only a left-handed form of human endeavor.''

Resisting the studio's desire for big-name stars, Huston cast his film with character actors and relative unknowns, a policy which paid off handsomely. Hayden and Calhern gave the performances of their careers, as did Sam Jaffe in the role of Doc Riedenschneider, the mastermind with a fatal weakness for nymphets, and Jean Hagen as Handley's sad-eyed moll. Around them Huston deployed a fine roster of supporting players: Caruso's safe-cracker, James Whitmore's cat-loving hunchback, and Marc Lawrence as a cringing bookie (''Money makes me sweat. That's the way I am''). And, touchingly eager and tentative in her first worthwhile screen role, Marilyn Monroe as Calhern's childlike mistress—a relationship treated with unexpected tenderness and a total lack of prurience.

The absence of stars accentuates the movie's fatalistic mood. There's no controlling boss-figure, pulling strings and calling the shots; neither Reidenschneider with his brains, nor Emmerich (Calhern) with his social status, is any less at the mercy of events than his accomplices. Rarely do we see anyone alone; Harold Rosson's camera frames tautly, holding the characters in tight complicit groupings—a closed community severally trapped by their obsessions, each one's needs involving and ensnaring the rest. ''One way or another,'' Riedenschneider observes, ''we all work for a vice.'' Huston's spare, uncluttered style conveys tension and urgency, but no sense of spurious excitement. Violence is staged without ceremony; shots are fired at close quarters in sudden, edgy confusion, and death strikes more by accident than by design.

As always, what interests Huston is relationships under pressure, how people react when the chips are down. Betrayal, recurrent theme of all his early movies, features strongly; but it's less endemic here than in the slick, cynical world of *The Maltese Falcon*. Loyalty, in *The Asphalt Jungle*, can still survive, despite greed and the fear of failure. And even the betrayers deserve sympathy: Emmerich, scrawling a hopeless, unfinished note to his wife before shooting himself, or Cobby, the bookie, abjectly weeping as he cracks under police pressure. Huston's hostility is reserved for the cops. Posing before the flashbulbs, the Commissioner makes play with a bank of police radios, and spins yellow-press clichés around the fugitive Dix Handley, ''a hardened killer . . . a man without human feeling or human mercy.''

From these melodramatic words, obsequiously noted down by the reporters, we fade to Handley, his lifeblood seeping away, sustained only by his obsession as he heads doggedly back towards his lost childhood dream. In the film's final shot he lies dead on the grass of a wide Kentucky meadow, while three horses graze around him, nuzzling his body. It's an image at once comforting and desolate; of all the downbeat, elegiac endings in Huston's films, none is more moving than this.

Unhampered by its lack of star names, *The Asphalt Jungle* scored a hit with the public; apart from *The African Queen*, it provided Huston with his only box-office hit of the decade. Most directors, having pioneered such a popular genre, would have felt tempted to return to it; but Huston, who always hated to repeat himself, never made another heist movie. Which may be cause for regret since, on the evidence of *The Asphalt Jungle*, few filmmakers were better qualified to do so.

—Philip Kemp

ASYA'S HAPPINESS

See **ISTORIA ASI KLIACHINOI KOTORAIA LUBILA DA NIE VYSHLA ZAMUZH**

L'ATALANTE

France, 1934

Director: Jean Vigo

Production: Black and white, 35mm; running time: 89 minutes (originally 82 minutes); length: 7343 feet. Released 1934 as *Le Chaland qui passe* with 7 minutes cut out. Re-released 1945 restored to its original form. Filmed in Paris.

Producer: J. L. Nounez; **screenplay:** Jean Vigo and Blaise Cendrars (some sources list Albert Riéra as a collaborator), from a scenario by Jean Guinée; **photography:** Boris Kaufman; **editor:** Louis Chavance; **production designer:** Francis Jourdain; **music:** Maurice Jaubert.

Cast: Jean Dasté (*Jean*); Dita Parlo (*Juliette*); Michel Simon (*Père Jules*); Gilles Margaritis (*Peddler*); Louis Lefèvre (*Boy*); Raya Diligent (*Bargeman*); Maurice Gilles (*Barge owner*).

Publications

Script:

Vigo, Jean, *Oeuvre de cinema: Films, scenarios, projets de films, texts sur le cinema*, edited by Pierre Lherminier, Paris, 1985.

Books:

Kyrou, Ado, *Le Surréalisme au cinéma*, Paris, 1953; revised edition, 1963.
Kyrou, Ado, *Amour, erotisme, et cinéma*, Paris, 1957.
Salles-Gomes, P. E., *Jean Vigo*, Paris, 1957; revised edition, Los Angeles, 1971.
Buache, Freddy, and others, editors, *Hommage à Jean Vigo*, Lausanne, 1962.
Lherminier, Pierre, *Jean Vigo*, Paris, 1967.
Lovell, Alan, *Anarchist Cinema*, London, 1967.
Smith, John M., *Jean Vigo*, London, 1972.
Klinowski, Jacek, and Adam Garbicz, editors, *The Magic Vehicle: A Guide to Its Achievement: Journey One: The Cinema Through 1949*, Metuchen, New Jersey, 1975.
Simon, William G., *The Films of Jean Vigo*, Ann Arbor, Michigan, 1981.
Dudley, Andrew, *Film in the Aura of Art*, Princeton, New Jersey, 1984.
Warner, Marina, *L'Atalante*, London, 1993.
Salles-Gomes, P.E., *Jean Vigo*, New York, 1999.

Articles:

Les Nouvelles Litéraires (Paris), 29 September 1934.
Cavalcanti, Alberto, ''Jean Vigo,'' in *Cinema Quarterly* (Edinburgh), Winter 1935.
Kracauer, Siegfried, ''Jean Vigo,'' in *Hollywood Quarterly*, April 1947.
Weinberg, H. G., ''The Films of Jean Vigo,'' in *Cinema* (Beverly Hills), July 1947.
Agee, James, ''Life and Work of Jean Vigo,'' in *Nation* (New York), 12 July 1947.
''Vigo Issue'' of *Ciné-Club* (Paris), February 1949.
Manvell, Roger, ''Revaluations: *L'Atalante*, 1934,'' in *Sight and Sound* (London), February 1951.
Positif (Paris), May 1953.
Mekas, Jonas, ''An Interview with Boris Kaufman,'' in *Film Culture* (New York), Summer 1955.
Chardère, Bernard, ''Jean Vigo et ses films,'' in *Cinéma* (Paris), March 1955.

Premier Plan (Lyon), no. 19, 1961.

Ellerby, John, ''The Anarchism of Jean Vigo,'' in *Anarchy* (London), August 1961.

Teush, B., ''The Playground of Jean Vigo,'' in *Film Heritage* (Dayton, Ohio), Fall 1973.

Baldwin, D., ''*L'Atalante* and the Maturing of Jean Vigo,'' in *Film Quarterly* (Berkeley), Fall 1985.

Ganteur, Claude, on André Antoine, in *Cinéma* (Paris), 8 January 1986.

Amengual, B., ''Restitution des rimes,'' in *Positif* (Paris), September 1990.

Insdorf, A., ''*L'Atalante*, a Slow Boat Bound for Lasting Fame,'' in *New York Times*, 14 October 1990.

Hoberman, J., ''Jean Vigo in Toto,'' in *Première* (Paris), January 1991.

Pellizzari, L., ''Quel barcone che passa. . . ,'' in *Cineforum* (Bergamo, Italy), October 1991.

Sidler, V., ''Traeumer des Kinos, Rimbaud des Films,'' in *Filmbulletin* (Winterthur, Switzerland), no. 4, 1992.

Conomos, John, ''Voyaging with Vigo on *L'Atalante*,'' in *Filmnews*, vol. 21, no. 4, May 1991.

Faulkner, C., ''Affective Identities: French National Cinema and the 1930s,'' in *Canadian Journal of Film Studies* (Montreal), vol. 3, no. 2, 1994.

* * *

The subject of *L'Atalante*—Vigo's only feature-length film, completed just before his death—was not of his own choosing. The interest of the film lies in his engagement with material that was partly congenial in its unconventionality (life on a barge, with its freedom from the restrictions of established society, its alternative community of unsocialized eccentrics), and partly highly conventional (problems of the heterosexual couple, mutual adjustment to marriage, break-up and reunion). The subject enabled him to develop the affectionate examination of anarchic behaviour already expressed in *Zéro de conduite*, but within the confines of an archetypal classical narrative of order (equated with marriage)/disruption of order/restoration of order.

Crucial to Vigo's personal background was his allegiance to his anarchist father, who died in prison under mysterious circumstances, and about whom Vigo wanted to make a film; crucial to his aesthetic background was the Surrealist movement. He wrote an adulatory review of *Un Chien anadalou* and, while not Surrealist in the strict sense, his films are faithful to the spirit of Surrealism, with its commitment to Freudian theories of dream and the unconscious and to the overthrow of repressive bourgeois social and moral codes. *L'Atalante* opens with a wedding procession, which Vigo presents as if it were a funeral: everyone is in black, everyone looks glum, almost everyone is coupled. The only brief outburst of spontaneous energy comes from the one single man, who tries to pinch the behind of the woman in front of him and is sternly reprimanded. This is Vigo's succinct depiction of established society. Against it, in the same sequence, he sets the characters from the barge: ''le père Jules,'' whose relationship to mainstream culture and its rituals is summed up in his quick dash back into the church to splash himself with holy water and pronounce the couple man and wife; and the (nameless) boy who, having knocked the wedding bouquet into the canal, runs off to find a substitute and returns bearing great festoons of wild creeper, looking like a juvenile pagan nature god.

The barge departs, the social order is left behind, and the film swiftly establishes the bride, Juliette, as its central character and central problem. The film's great distinction lies partly in the honesty with which that problem is confronted, its ultimate failure lies in the way it withdraws from its implications. The Surrealist movement, while dedicated to sexual liberation, failed to develop any viable feminist theory and never successfully conceptualized the position of women: its commitment to *l'amour fou* was never disengaged from an emphasis on machismo. What is especially remarkable about *L'Atalante* is not only the intense erotic charge it conveys between its central couple (it could be described as an attempt to reconcile *l'amour fou* with domesticity), but also the way if foregrounds the position of the woman, raising the question of what this liberation means for *her*. For Juliette really has no place on the barge. Its little community appears to have functioned perfectly well before her appearance, the traditionally ''feminine'' reforms she effects (such as washing Jules's underwear) seem superfluous, and she never finds a role within the male work-world.

The culmination of the first half of the film is the marvellous scene in which Jules shows Juliette the treasures of his cabin (a veritable Surrealist world of unexpected juxtapositions). It ends with the brutal intervention of Jean, his smashing of Jules's collection of momentoes, and his striking of Juliette. He is re-establishing conjugal possession, and we register his behaviour as thoroughly negative. The nature of the threat Jean feels is extremely complex, not at all the simple one of erotic rivalry; and to understand it, we must consider the character of Jules and what he represents. Presented without ambiguity as an admirably robust and healthy figure, Jules transgresses, directly or by implication, every major bourgeois rule. (1) Money-value: his souvenirs are treasured solely for the associations they evoke, not for monetary worth. (2) Cleanliness: his physical robustness is unaffected by his living among cats which produce litters in the beds, and by his total lack of interest in bourgeois standards of hygiene. (3) Physical squeamishness: to demonstrate the efficiency of a native knife, he casually slices open his own hand. (4) Patriarchal dominance: he relates to Juliette as an equal, reducing the notion of male authority to a game (the tattered puppet of an orchestral conductor). (5) Death: he keeps the fore-arms of his best friend pickled in a jar, treating the souvenir without the least morbidity, but simply as a momento to live with. (6) Monogamy: he shows Juliette a photograph of himself with two women, telling her, ''There's a story to that.'' We never get to hear it, but it is clear that Jules is unattached yet strongly sexual. (Neither does he *exploit* women: witness the later scene with the fortune-teller, where the seduction is delightfully mutual). (7) Sexual identity: the dead friend was the person he was closest to, and although bisexuality is not necessarily implied, it is perfectly in keeping with the freedom from bourgeois conditioning Jules represents. (8) Property: Jules shows great affection for his souvenirs, but is not in the least bound to them. After Jean wrecks his cabin he casually picks up an unbroken piece of bric-à-brac, remarks, ''there's one he missed,'' and smashes it. What Juliette is attracted to, and what her husband experiences as a threat, is precisely Jules's freedom—a freedom that can easily encompass loyalty, affection and loving relationship, but that quite precludes the exclusivity of marriage. Further, through Jean's behavior, the film clearly establishes marriage as characterized by the man's possession of, and assumption of absolute right over, the woman.

It is scarcely suprising that a film made within the capitalist production/distribution system for a bourgeois audience could not pursue further the implications of its own liberating perceptions. In fact, its second half is largely devoted to a retraction of those implications. Two related strategies are involved: the substitution of the peddler for ''le père Jules,'' and the partial transformation of Jules's function. The bistro sequence with the peddler is clearly a repetition of/variation on the cabin scene. Juliette is attracted to the promise of freedom, the display of wonders, and Jean intervenes to reclaim her. But the peddler is not Jules: he is a slight figure, explicitly described as the ''peddler of dreams,'' and the freedom and glamour with which he tempts Juliette are quite illusory. Jean is proved right in rejecting him. If Jules poses a substantial and formidable threat to the institution of marriage, the peddler only *seems* to, and the film can deal with him easily. Finally, Jules becomes indeed ''le père'' Jules: the father-figure who retrieves the fugitive Juliette, slings her over his shoulder, restores her to her husband, and pulls shut the hatch over them. The film is quite explicit about Juliette's imprisonment, but the narrative resolution demands that she be shown to accept it gladly. The famous last shot—the phallic symbol of the barge pushing on through the sunlit canal—represents a celebration of sexuality about which we cannot help, today, feeling deeply uneasy.

—Robin Wood

AN AUTUMN AFTERNOON

See **SAMMA NO AJI**

L'AVVENTURA

(The Adventure)

Italy, 1959

Director: Michelangelo Antonioni

Production: Produzioni Cinematografiche Europee, Cino del Duca, (Rome), and Société Cinématographique (Paris); black and white, 35mm; running time: 139 minutes, also 130 minutes. Released 25 September 1960, Bologna and Paris. Filmed September 1959 through January 1960 in Rome and Sicily (the isles of Lipari, Milazzo, Catania, and Taormina).

Producer: Amato Pennasilico; **screenplay:** Michelangelo Antonioni, Elio Bartolini, and Tonino Guerra, from an original story by Michelangelo Antonioni; **photography:** Aldo Scavarda; **editor:** Eraldo da Roma; **sound:** Claudio Maielli; **scene designer:** Piero Polletto; **music:** Giovanni Fusco; **costume designer:** Adriana Berselli.

Cast: Monica Vitti (*Claudia*); Gabriele Ferzetti (*Sandro*); Lea Massari (*Anna*); Dominique Blanchar (*Giulia*); Renzo Ricci (*Anna's Father*); James Addams (*Corrado*); Dorothy De Poliolo (*Gloria Perkins*); Lelio Luttazzi (*Raimondo*); Giovanni Petrucci (*Young Painter*); Esmeralda Ruspoli (*Patrizia*); with Enrico Bologna; Franco Cimino; Giovanni Danesi; Rita Molé; Renato Pincicoli; Angela Tommasi di Lampedusa; Vincenzo Tranchina; Joe Fisherman from Panarea (*Old man on the island*); Prof. Cucco (*Ettore*).

Awards: Special Jury Prize, Cannes Festival, 1960.

Publications

Scripts:

Screenplays of Michelangelo Antonioni, New York, 1963.
Antonioni, Michelangelo, *Sei Film*, Turin, 1964.

Books:

Cowie, Peter, *Antonioni, Bergman, Resnais*, New York, 1963.
Lephrohon, Pierre, *Michelangelo Antonioni: An Introduction*, New York, 1963.
Taylor, John Russell, *Cinema Eye, Cinema Ear*, New York, 1964.
Strick, Philip, *Antonioni*, London, 1965.
Sarris, Andrew, *Interviews with Film Directors*, New York, 1967.
Cameron, Ian, and Robin Wood, *Antonioni*, New York, 1969.
Samuels, Charles Thomas, *Encountering Directors*, New York, 1972.
Rifkin, Ned, *Antonioni's Visual Language*, Ann Arbor, Michigan, 1982.
Barthes, Roland, and others, *Michelangelo Antonioni*, Munich, 1984.
Biarese, Cesare, and Aldo Tassone, *I film di Michelangelo Antonioni*, Rome, 1985.
Dervin, Daniel, *Through a Freudian Lens Deeply: A psychoanalysis of Cinema*, Hillsdale, New Jersey, 1985.
Fonseca, M.S., *Michelangelo Antonioni*, Lisbon, 1985.
Antonioni, Michelangelo, *That Bowling Alley on the Tiber: Tales of a Director*, Oxford, 1986.
Perry, Ted, and Rene Prieto, *Michelangelo Antonioni: A Guide to References and Resources*, Boston, 1986.
Tinazzi, Giorgio di, Michelangelo Antonioni, Firenze, 1989.
Cuccu, Lorenzo, *Antonioni: il discorso dello sguardo: da Blow up a Identificazione di una donna*, Pisa, 1990.
Giaume, Joëelle Mayet, *Michelangelo Antonioni: le fil intérieur*, Crisnée, Belgium, 1990.
Ranieri, Nicola, Amor vacui: il cinema di Michelangelo Antonioni, Chieti, 1990.
Rohdie, Sam, *Antonioni*, London, 1990.
Prédal, René, *Michelangelo Antonioni, ou, La vigilance du désir*, Paris, 1991.
Kock, Bernhard, *Michelangelo Antonionis Bilderwelt: eine phänomenologische Studie*, München, 1994.
Arrowsmith, William, *Antonioni: The Poet of Images*, New York, 1995.
Cuccu, Lorenzo, *Antonioni: il discorso dello sguardo e altri saggi*, Pisa, 1997.
Brunette, Peter, *The Films of Michelangelo Antonioni*, Cambridge, 1998.
Scemama-Heard, Céline, *Antonioni: le désert figuré*, Paris, 1998.

Articles:

Houston, Penelope, in *Sight and Sound* (London), Winter 1960–61.
Manceaux, Michele, ''An Interview with Antonioni,'' in *Sight and Sound* (London), Winter 1960–61.
''Antonioni Issue'' of *Films and Filming* (London), January 1961.
Sarris, Andrew, in *Village Voice* (New York), 23 March 1961.
Fitzpatrick, Ellen, in *Films in Review* (New York), May 1961.
Sandall, Robert, in *Film Quarterly* (Berkeley), Summer 1961.

L'avventura

Durgnat, Raymond, in *Films and Filming* (London), March 1962.
Antonioni, Michelangelo, "Making a Film Is My Way of Life," in *Film Culture* (New York), Spring 1962.
Aristarco, Guido, in *Film Culture* (New York), Spring 1962.
Schleifer, Marc, in *Film Culture* (New York), Spring 1962.
"Antonioni Issue" of *Film Quarterly* (Berkeley), Fall 1962.
Lane, John Francis, "Oh, Oh Antonioni," in *Films and Filming* (London), December 1962.
Lesser, Simon O., "*L'avventura:* A Closer Look," in *Yale Review* (New Haven, Connecticut), Fall 1964.
Nowell-Smith, Geoffrey, "The Event and the Image: Michelangelo Antonioni," in *Sight and Sound* (London), Winter 1964–65.
Doniol-Valcroze, Jacques, "The R-H Factor and the New Cinema," in *Cahiers du Cinéma in English* (New York), January 1966.
Hernacki, Thomas, "Michelangelo Antonioni and the Imagery of Disintegration," in *Film Heritage* (Dayton, Ohio), Spring 1970.
Kauffmann, Stanley, in *Horizon* (Los Angeles), Autumn 1972.
Lockhart, Kimball, "Empêchement visuel et point de fruite dans *L'avventura* and *Professione: Reporter*," in *Camera/Stylo* (Paris), November 1982.
Audibert, L., in *Cinématographe* (Paris), March 1983.
Blanchet, C., in *Cinéma* (Paris), April 1983.
Domecq, J. P., in *Positif* (Paris), April 1983.
Antonioni, Michelangelo, "Vi parlo di me per raccontani un film," in *Cinema Nuovo* (Bari), August-October 1983.
Bohne, L., "The Discourse of Narcissism in *L'avventura*," in *Film Criticism* (Meadville, Pennsylvania), Fall 1984.
De Santis, Giuseppe, "L'ovvio e l'ottuso: índirezioni del senso in Antonioni," *Cineforum* (Bergamo, Italy), vol. 27, November 1987.
Tomasulo, F. P., "The Architectonics of Alienation: Antonioni's Edifice Complex," in *Wide Angle* (Baltimore, Maryland), no. 3, 1993.
Predal, R., "L'eclipse, l'ellipse," in *Avant Scène du Cinéma* (Paris), February 1993.
Schenk, I., "Natur und Anti-Natur in den Filmen von Michelangelo Antonioni," *Cinema (Switerland)* (Zurich), vol. 40, 1994.
Di Marino, B., "La citta che sente," *Filmcritica* (Rome), May/July 1995.
Nowell-Smith, G., "Antonioni," *Sight and Sound* (London), vol. 5, December 1995.
Prédal, René, "Le longue nuit d'une mort attendue," *Avant-Scène Cinéma* (Paris), November 1995.

Lubelski, T. ''(Sto) 100 lat kina: 1960,'' *Kino* (Warsaw), vol. 30, May 1996.
Nasta, D., ''De la critique de cinema a la critique de film: la modernite antonionienne, effet de critique ou demarche d'auteur?,'' *Cinemas* (Quebec), vol. 6, no. 2/3, 1996.

* * *

When *L'avventura* was screened at the 1960 Cannes Film Festival its audience whistled, stamped, and shouted. They were not expressing enthusiasm. Antonioni's film had proved incomprehensible to them, as it was to prove to many an audience all over Europe. Significantly, however, this did not prevent the film from finding admirers and achieving remarkably large audience figures in several countries. This was the beginning of the age of the art-movie, and *L'avventura* was perfectly suited to the growing number of art-houses. After the debacle at Cannes, 35 critics and filmmakers issued a statement of support for *L'avventura* and its director, a view which was echoed in film criticism around the world. Within a year *L'avventura* had secured its place in film history.

What was it about the film that encouraged such extremes of disgust and admiration? The most common charge of the dissenters was that *L'avventura* was quite meaningless and, consequently, utterly boring. Foolishly, some defenders sought to turn that argument by making a virtue out of meaninglessness itself. To them *L'avventura* was the perfect aesthetic object: beautiful to observe but devoid of any cognitive or moral import. Apart from the fact that it is patently not devoid of such features, this view (not uncommon in art-house circles) makes the peculiar assumption that the look of a film is somehow independent of meaning, that beauty and meaning are separate elements in art. Others argued more cogently that *L'avventura* worked with and developed a new language of cinema, and that to understand it was to master an alien form. Hence the anger at Cannes among those not prepared to make that effort.

This claim does have some truth to it, thought it overstates the film's innovative qualities. *L'avventura* shares much with its two immediate predecessors, *Le amiche* and *Il grido*, both in theme and style. It hardly emerged from nowhere, though it is perhaps more unremittingly austere than anything its director had previously made. But it clearly does play down conventional narrative to the point of extinction. The ''plot'' of *L'avventura* (and the term is barely applicable) can be described in a couple of sentences. A young woman, Anna, disappears while cruising near Sicily in the company of a group of rich Italians. Her lover, Sandro, and her friend, Claudia, search unsuccessfully for her, developing a tenuous relationship in the process. There is no resolution of the conventional type. Anna's disappearance is never explained, and ceases to be of any interest. At the end of the film Claudia and Sandro achieve a bleak sympathy, but hardly a consummation. Nor are we permitted any semblance of orthodox narrative involvement. The film is paced very slowly, much of its action seen in real time. Its characters communicate little in dialogue, and more often than not, are to be found looking away from each other out into the bleak and arid Sicilian landscape. We are invited to contemplate them, but not to identify. Point-of-view shots are rare, and shot-reverse shot sequences, where they exist, usually include both parties fully in the shot. In these and other ways *L'avventura* excludes us from emotional involvement in any but the most cerebral sense.

Perhaps, then, the Cannes reception is unsurprising. In the two decades since *L'avventura*'s first appearance, narrative conventions have changed, but they have still nowhere near approached Antonioni's limit. In respect of its form *L'avventura* is as striking today as it was then, its invitation to contemplate its agonized characters as demanding as ever. Its meanings, however, are less elusive than they appeared to many in 1960. Hindsight and the cultural changes of the intervening years have rendered the film more transparent, its ideas more clearly part of their period. Antonioni himself, in a statement accompanying the film at Cannes, said that *L'avventura* charted a world in which ''we make use of an aging morality, of outworn myths, of ancient conventions.'' The world had changed, yet human beings were trapped by the old standards. His characters, accordingly, can find no meaningful way to relate to each other, finally arriving, as he describes it, ''at a sort of reciprocal pity.''

Embedded in this diffuse account of modern social ills is a more specific lament at the degradation of creativity and sexuality. The love-making in *L'avventura* (except, briefly, for Claudia, the only fleetingly optimistic figure in a deeply depressing film) is without meaning or joy. Creative aspirations are stultified. As Sandro observes in a rare moment of self-perception, ''I saw myself as a genius working in a garret. Now I've got two flats and I've neglected to become a genius.'' Materialism, alienation, and neurosis are the watchwords of this world. These were not new ideas, of course, and by 1960 there was a well established tradition of such despair in European art. What was new, and remains hugely impressive, was Antonioni's facility at expressing such ideas in a cinema shorn of conventional narrative aids. A sense of the alienation of people from their environment and from each other is conveyed in every stark composition, in every studied camera movement. The meaning of the film is there in its very fabric. *L'avventura* is never meaningless; if anything it is overloaded with meaning.

In an interview with Georges Sadoul, Antonioni made this observation, ''when I finished *L'avventura* I was forced to reflect on what it meant.'' The lasting impact of the film has been to force the rest of us to take seriously the idea of a genuinely reflective cinema.

—Andrew Tudor

THE AWAKENING OF THE RATS

See **BUDJENJE PACOVA**

AWARA

(The Vagabond)

India, 1951

Director: Raj Kapoor

Production: R. K. Films; running time: 100 minutes. Released 1951.

Producer in charge: Mamaji; **producer:** Raj Kapoor; **screenplay:** Ahmad Abbas; **story:** Ahmad Abbas, V. P. Sathe; **photography:** Radhu Karmakar; **editor:** G. G. Mayekar; **sound:** Allauddin; **art director:** M. R. Achrekar; **music:** Shankar, Jaikishen; **lyrics:** Hasrat Jaipuri, Shailendra; **Dream Dance:** Madame Simkie.

Cast: Privthviraj Kapoor (*Judge Raghunath*); Nargis (*Rita*); Raj Kapoor (*Raj*); K. N. Singh (*Jagga Daku*); Leela Chitnis (*Bharati*); Shashi Kapoor (*Raj as a boy*); with: Cuckoo, B. M. Vyas, Baby Zubeida, Leela Misra, Om Parkash Rajoo, Mansaram, Rajan, Manek, Paryag, Ravi, Vinni, Bali, Royal India Ballet and Opera.

Publications

Books:

Barnouw, Erik, and S. Krishnaswamy, *Indian Film*, New York, 1965.
Sarkar, Kobita, *The Indian Cinema Today*, New Delhi, 1975.
Abbas, Ahmad, *I Am Not An Island: An Experiment in Autobiography*, New Delhi, 1977.
Burra, Rani, editor, *Looking Back 1896–1960*, New Delhi, 1981.
Ramachandran, T. M., *70 Years of Indian Cinema (1913–83)*, Bombay, 1985.
Dissanayake, W. and M. Sahay, *Raj Kapoor's Films: Harmony of Discourses*, New Delhi, 1987.

Articles:

''Special Issue'' of *Film Français* (Paris), Spring 1953.
Film India (Bombay), February 1952.
Kine Weekly (London), 24 June 1954.
Monthly Film Bulletin (London), August 1954.
Variety (New York), 11 April 1956.
Jeune cinéma (Paris), September 1965.
Hoberman, J., in *Voice* (Los Angeles), 5 August 1981.
Pym, John, in *Financial Times* (London) 17 August 1984.
Thomas, R., ''Indian Cinema: Pleasures and Popularity,'' in *Screen* (London), May-August 1985.
Ghosh, S., ''K. A. Abbas: A Man in Tune with History,'' in *Screen* (Bombay), 19 June 1987.
Slingo, Carol J., ''K. A. Abbas (1914–87),'' in *Jump Cut* (Berkeley), February 1988.

* * *

Awara is very much the first major instance of the Hindi cinema's international influence, and as such provides an important index of the peculiar fascination of the Hindi film. Raj Kapoor's work has been hugely popular not only in the traditional markets in the Middle East and Africa, but in Eastern Europe and, according to recent accounts, in China. His films implicate us in a universe both parallel to and incestuously coupled with that other world cinema, Hollywood. The popular Hindi cinema occupies a colonial and post-colonial territory of conflicting identities and philosophical irreconcilables. The East presents itself as ''other'' than the West: Hollywood is flagrantly mimicked, but in a knowing, distorting, and finally disavowing way.

Awara is a sprawling work on identity: it revolves around the loss and recovery of a respectable, upper-class social position by the protagonist, Raj (Raj Kapoor). The script-writer, Ahmad Abbas, a left-wing novelist, journalist, and filmmaker, intended *Awara* as a criticism of the inflexible notions of a social hierarchy incompatible, so he believed, with the new India. However, the expression of these ideas within the framework of a popular Hindi movie opened them to ambivalence. Abbas accepted that Kapoor did not tamper with the story but only added the song and dance conventionally used in the popular cinema. But it is precisely in this way that the popular cinema presents the spectator with the possibility of a parallel realm of pleasure which may controvert (though in a kind of co-existing, unironic way) the work done in the narrative. Thus Raj, denied his proper place in society, and struggling to feed his starving mother, is compelled to take to crime. The role is glamorized by Kapoor's star performance and by songs which indicate, even amid the concluding pathos of the story—when the hero is jailed and separated from his sweetheart—that the life of the vagabond is an attractive one.

This kind of ambivalence is not restricted to scenes of spectacle, but is embedded in the narration. Popular Hindi cinema uses a melodramatic audio-visual register, where music, sound effects, and codings of dress and facial expression serve to emphasise the moral meanings of the fiction for the audience. But this moral sign-system is invariably manipulated to introduce narrative disorders, which indicate that the moral terms of the fiction are in fact not so stable.

For example, in *Awara* the villain, Jagga (K. N. Singh), often appears to be the shadow of Raj's father (Prithviraj Kapoor), insofar as both exclude Raj from legitimacy. Rita (Nargis), the character who will ultimately come to Raj's aid, is also an ambiguous figure. She is contaminated with the same attributes of wealth and class which bar the hero from social position. In this manifestation she is regressive and therefore coded as ''Western.'' By presenting ''good'' figures (the father and the sweetheart) in this way, the narrative actually registers certain truths: the fear of the father, especially in his representation of the oppressive law of the social order, and the sexual fascination with that ''Westernness'' (actually very much part of contemporary Indian culture) reflected in the Rita figure. But in the course of the narrative, these truths are submerged in the cause of recovering and stabilizing a ''pure'' Indian identity: the father has to be established as unambiguously ''good,'' while Rita has to be divested of the pejorative ''Western'' image.

Though it represents all these general and contradictory features of the Hindi film, *Awara* is still very much an epochal work of the post-independence era. In its delineation of disinherited social types in a pathetic yet glamorous way, in its underlying scepticism about the legal-rational order, it maps out the territory which would be traversed by the rural sagas of the 1950s and 1960s (for example, Mehboob Khan's *Mother India* and Nitin Bose's *Jamuna*) and which would be built into the highly successful revenge-saga films of the 1970s featuring Amithab Bachchan.

—Ravi Vasudevan

BA WANG BIE JI

(Farewell My Concubine)

Hong Kong-China, 1993

Director: Chen Kaige

Production: Tomson (HK) Films in association with China Film Co-production Corp/Beijing Film Studio; colour, 35mm; running time: 170 minutes, original version; 157 minutes, US version. Released 2 September 1993, Beijing. Filmed in 1992 in Beijing.

Producer: Hsu Feng; **executive producers:** Hsu Bin, Jade Hsu; **screenplay:** Lilian Lee, Lu Wei, from the novel by Lilian Lee; **assistant directors:** Zhang Jinzhan, Bai Yu, Jin Ping, Zhang Jinting; **photography:** Gu Changwei; **editor:** Pei Xiaonan; **art directors:** Yang Yuhe, Yang Zhanjia; **sound:** Yang Zhanshan, Han Lin; **music:** Zhao Jiping; **music performed by:** Central Orchestra of China, Orchestra of the Peking Opera Academy; **costume design:** Chen Changmin; **subtitles:** Linda Jaivin.

Cast: Leslie Cheung (*Cheng Dieyi*); Zhang Fengyi (*Duan Xiaolou*); Gong Li (*Juxian*); Lu Qi (*Guan Jifa*); Ying Da (*Na Kun*); Ge You (*Master Yuan*); Li Chun (*Xiao Si as a teenager*); Lei Han (*Xiao Si as an adult*); Tong Di (*Old Man Zhang*); Ma Mingwei (*Douzi as a child*); Yin Zhi (*Douzi as a teenager*); Fei Yang (*Shitou as a child*); Zhao Hailong (*Shitou [teenage]*); Li Dan (*Laizi*); Jiang Wenli (*Douzi's mother*).

Awards: Palme d'Or, International Critics' Prize, Cannes 1993.

Publications

Articles:

Rayns, Tony, ''Nights at the Opera'' in *Sight and Sound* (London), December 1992.

Variety (New York), 24 May 1993.

Tessier, Max, and others, ''Art over Politics'' in *Cinemaya* (New Delhi), Summer 1993.

Cineforum (Italy), vol. 33, no. 328, October 1993.

Bertin-Maghit, J.-P., and Guy Gauthier, ''Adieu ma concubine,'' in *Mensuel du Cinéma*, no. 11, November 1993.

Alleva, Richard, *Commonweal*, 3 December 1993.

Sight and Sound (London), January 1994.

Films in Review (New York), January/February 1994.

Zha, Jianying, ''Chen Kaige and the Shadows of the Revolution'' in *Sight and Sound* (London), February 1994.

Chen, Pauline, ''History Lessons'' in *Film Comment* (New York), March 1994.

Rayns, Tony, ''The Narrow Path'' in *Projections 3*, London, 1994.

Lau, Jenny Kwok Wah, ''*Farewell My Concubine:* History, Melodrama, and Ideology in Contemporary Pan-Chinese Cinema,'' in *Film Quarterly* (Berkeley), Fall 1995.

Xu, B., ''*Farewell My Concubine* and Its Nativist Critics,'' in *Quarterly Review of Film and Video* (Reading), vol. 16, no. 2, 1997.

* * *

In 1984 Chen Kaige's *The Yellow Earth* (with cinematography by fellow Beijing Film Academy graduate Zhang Yimou) signalled the exciting emergence of the Fifth Generation of Chinese filmmakers. A decade later, in 1993, his film *Farewell My Concubine* signalled that generation's arrival on the international scene.

Although based on a novella by Hong Kong writer Lilian Li, director Chen Kaige himself reworked the story of *Farewell My Concubine* to its current, more complex form about the friendship of two Peking opera stars over 50 years of turbulent Chinese history.

The film begins in 1924 in Beijing as a young boy, Douzi (Ma Mingwei), is brought to the All Luck and Happiness Peking Opera School by his prostitute mother (Jiang Wenli). Desperate to give him a future she herself does not have, she pleads pitifully with the headmaster to admit her son. Though prettily turned, he does have one defect—an extra finger on his left hand. In order to gain admission, the mother tearfully chops off the offending digit.

At this time Peking opera was at its height of popularity. ''If you belong to the human race, you go to the opera,'' lectures one opera master. ''If you don't go to the opera, you're not a human being. . . .You are lucky to be part of it.''

Soon Douzi is brought under the protection of gruff but kindly classmate Shitou (Fei Yang), who becomes his dearest friend. The sequences of opera training—holding agonizing positions for hours, singing at the crack of dawn, withstanding the schoolmaster's cane—are intensely powerful and moving ones.

In one scene, the boys line a river bank in the falling snow and sing out the lines of the fallen king in the classic play, *The King Parts from His Concubine* (which is also the Chinese title of the film, ''Ba Wang Bie Ji''): ''I am so strong/I can uproot the mountains./My courage is renowned,/I have fallen on hard times.''

As they grow up, the effeminate Douzi (played as a teenager by Yin Zhi) is cast in female roles, specializing in the role of the self-sacrificing concubine who kills herself for loyalty to her king in this drama. Shitou (played by Zhao Hailong) is cast in masculine, heroic parts, such as the King in the same work. As adults, they rise to become stars of the Peking opera world. Dreamy Douzi, adopting the stage name of Cheng Dieyi (Leslie Cheung), remains half in love with his stage brother Shitou, now called Duan Xiaolou (Zhang Fengyi).

Ba wang bie ji

But Xiaolou has another life he wants to lead—off stage—and marries Juxian (Gong Li), a courtesan he has been seeing. Douzi, of course, gets deeply jealous.

Meanwhile, their theater troupe is subjected to the caprice of successive waves of conquerors—Japanese, Kuomingtang, Communist, then the Red Guards of the Cultural Revolution—that wash over the city. It is under the Cultural Revolution that they suffer the most. Not only is the practice of their art interrupted, they are forced to denounce one another in public, betraying friends and lovers alike.

In the film, the story of the politics of modern China is told alongside Dieyi's confusion between theater and reality. While the politics is kept deliberately vague, we are made well aware of the gap between theater and reality. In the end, human beings fail to achieve the sterling archetypes in such dramas like *The King Parts from His Concubine*, being much weaker creatures in the face of adversity.

However, some of the most marvelous scenes in *Farewell* remain at the beginning, with the boys in their early days of Peking opera training. It reflects Chen's own fascination with the art form. ''Peking opera is amazing. You have to spend your whole life training,'' the director has said. ''There is something about Chinese opera that is fundamentally Chinese.''

These early scenes have the crisp vision of early Chen Kaige films, while the story of the adults becomes muddled and at times unconvincing. For example, the character of the third person in the triangle, Juxian, is never fleshed out.

Produced by a Hong Kong film company run by former Taiwan film star Hsu Feng, *Farewell* was a Chinese film that spared no expenses. The period costuming and sets were meticulously reconstructed, and the color-saturated cinematography by Gu Changwei captures their sumptuousness.

This ambitious epic managed to turn the heads of the Cannes International Film Festival jury in May 1993, and the top prize of the Palme d'Or was awarded to two extraordinary films that year — Chen Kaige's *Farewell My Concubine* and Jane Campion's *The Piano*. The film went on to win other awards, as well, including best foreign film from both the New York Film Critics Circle and the Golden Globe, as well as a place in the New York Film Festival that fall and a nomination for the Oscar.

In Hong Kong, where the audience was jaded and impatient with a nearly three-hour piece of cultural history, the film came and went, but in the two other Chinas, in Taiwan and on the mainland, it churned up its share of controversy before finding huge audiences. In Taiwan, following current regulations, it was banned for having too many mainland actors; in China, it was banned for unspecified, though certainly political, reasons. A quick change in the regulations allowed it to be shown in Taiwan, where it made box office records. Minor edits allowed it to be shown in China.

For Chen, whose who had never had a popular success in his own country and whose previous film *Life on a String* was banned there, the showing of *Farewell* in China was especially gratifying.

Chen Kaige (b. 1952) is one of the two best known of Fifth Generation directors, along with Zhang Yimou. He is the son of veteran Chinese director Chen Huaikai, who made film versions of Chinese opera in his heyday.

—Scarlet Cheng

BAB EL HADID

(Cairo Station; Cairo: Central Station; Iron Gate)

Egypt, 1957

Director: Youssef Chahine

Production: Gabriel Talhami Productions; black and white; running time: 90 minutes.

Producer: Gibrail Abdel Hay Adib; **screenplay:** Gibrail Hay Adib; **dialogue:** Mohamed Abou Yussef; **photography:** Alvise; **editor:** Kamal Abou el-Ela; **music:** Fouad al-Zahiry.

Cast: Farid Chawky (*Abou Serih*); Hind Roustom (*Hannoumat*); Youssef Chahine (*Kenawi*); Hassan Al-Baroudi; Abdel Najdi.

Publications

Books:

Khan, M., *An Introduction to the Egyptian Cinema,* London, 1969.
Malkmus, Lizbeth, and Armes, Roy, *Arab and African Film Making,* London, 1991.

Articles:

Markus, Bert, ''Tatort . . . Hauptbahnof Kairo'' in *Filmwoche* (Denmark), 1982.
Cine-Revue (Brussels), 17 June 1982.
Hollywood Reporter (Los Angeles), 7 August 1990.

* * *

Cairo Station—as *Bab el Hadid* is most widely known in English—is perhaps especially memorable for its rich visual content. It includes frequent long shots which place the main characters against the complex and busy background of the real railroad station of the title. It has occasional and highly effective sequences of complete silence, which contrast with the usual noise and bustle and place the weight of the story on visual explication alone. It also includes such powerful single images as the sight of living human beings dwarfed by a gigantic statue of the ancient ruler Rameses II. The fact that Youssef Chahine, who both directed the film and stars in it, was initially trained as a painter before turning to filmmaking comes as no surprise.

Yet films are far more than just the moving pictures they were initially labelled and dismissed as; and a film may be memorable for its visual content because the other elements that make it up are inadequate or unsatisfying. It must be stressed that *Cairo Station* is by no means a bad film—whether that means simply boring, or implies technical shortcomings, implausible plotting, wooden acting, or other defects. It is entertaining, thought-provoking, and on the whole worth spending time watching and absorbing. Yet it does fall short of the real greatness in other departments that its sheer visual brilliance deserves. The main problem is that it attempts to do too many things at once and thus ends up doing none of them as well as it might have.

If the film is taken, for example, as being mainly a portrayal of life among those who work in and pass through the ''iron gate,'' the main railroad station in the Egyptian capital, it stands comparison with other films about great meeting places—such as *Grand Hotel* or even the *Airport* series. Just as they preserve forever the manners and interactions, down to clothes and haircuts, of particular types of people in a great public space at a particular time, so *Cairo Station* succeeds in creating, in a manner which looks effortless but must have been time-consuming and difficult, a convincing version of the sights and sounds of meeting and parting, buying and selling, eating and drinking. Even so, by 1958, for both Egyptian and non-Egyptian audiences, tugging at the heart-strings with meetings and partings between unnamed and briefly shown mothers and sons, conscripted soldiers and their families and other such clichéd figures was surely all too familiar a method for both evoking the audience's feelings and frustrating them. Thus what was presumably meant to underline the point that life goes on as usual, even as the central tragedy unfolds, continues to be valuable as a documentary record but, as a mainstay of the story, comes across as unfocused and uninvolving.

While such use of stereotypes in composing the background to the narrative is understandable—after all, an attempt at anything more complex or unpredictable might have ended up fussy and distracting—the dependence of the main story on similar stereotypes is a definite weakness. Kenawi, the disabled newspaper vendor whose unrequited love leads him to a violent mental collapse, is that stock character of both Arab and European literature, a man of peasant stock adrift in the big, frightening city. The lemonade seller, Hannoumat, who leads him on, only to repel him in the end, is the wearisomely familiar figure of the woman defined by her physique and her supposed instincts, apparently incapable of thought or initiative. The man she really loves, Abou Serih the porter, is handsome, popular, and—in a subplot which promises to deepen the complexities of the film but merely confuses them—nobly but mystifyingly committed to forming a union among his fellow-workers. But what are the motivations for their respective actions, beyond the obvious ones? A more daring, more critical, and—not an irrelevant consideration—more truly entertaining film might have depicted all three as real people, allowing Kenawi at least to try to overcome his constantly emphasized isolation, Hannoumat to have relatives and friends and a life of her own and Abou Serih to have doubts and anxieties about his personal and union affairs alike. But *Cairo Station*, for all its depth of field and breadth of vision, lacks psychological depth or social breadth. The final scene, when Kenawi is taken away in a straitjacket through the crowds, having been persuaded that he is dressing up for a wedding that will never take place, is indeed as moving and as ironic as it was no doubt meant to be, but would have been even more effective if the audience had been given more to sympathize with, to react against and to think about.

In its combination of technical brilliance with rhetorical hollowness *Cairo Station* is indeed no worse than most of the films produced by the dream factories of Hollywood or elsewhere. It may even be somewhat unfair and inappropriate to be disappointed by a film which was produced under similar conditions to the melodramas of the Hollywood golden age; which, at least for Egyptian audiences, can be compared and contrasted with others of Chahine's numerous films; and which was probably intended more as entertainment than as any kind of social commentary. But as with other melodramas of unrequited love and social fatalism, it is surely just as legitimate to regret the opportunities which were missed or frustrated as to give due praise to the ways in which other opportunities were taken and fully realized.

—Patrick Heenan

BABETTES GAESTEBUD

(Babette's Feast)

Denmark, 1987

Director: Gabriel Axel

Production: Panorama Film International; color; 35mm; running time: 102 minutes. Released in Denmark 28 August 1987; distributed in USA by Orion Classics. Filmed on location in Jutland, Denmark.

Producers: Just Betzer and Bo Christensen; **screenplay:** Gabriel Axel, from the story by Isak Dinesen (Karen Blixen); **photography:** Henning Kristiansen; **editor:** Finn Hendriksen; **sound:** Hans-Eric Ahrn; **production design:** Sven Wichmann; **costume designer:** Annelise Hauberg; **music:** Per Norgaard, with additional music by Mozart and Brahms; **gastronomic consultant:** Jan Petersen.

Cast: Stéphane Audran (*Babette*); Bodil Kjer (*Filippa*); Birgitte Federspiel (*Martine*); Jarl Kulle (*Lorenz Lowenhielm*); Jean-Philippe Lafont (*Achille Papin*); Bibi Andersson (*Swedish court lady*); Ghita Norby (*narrator*); Hanna Stensgaard (*Young Filippa*); Vibeki Hastrup (*Young Martine*); Gudmar Wivesson (*Young Lorens*); Else Petersen (*Solveig*); Pouel Kern (*the minister/father*); Erik Petersen (*Erik*).

Awards: Oscar for Best Foreign Film, 1988; Rouen Nordic Film Festival Grand Jury Prize and Audience Award, 1988; British Academy Award for Best Film Not in the English Language, 1989.

Publications

Articles:

Chevassu, F., and D. Parra, ''*La festin de Babette*/Entretien avece Gariel Axel/Entretien avec Stéphane Audran,'' in *Revue du Cinéma* (Paris), no. 437, April 1988.

''*Babette's Fest*,'' in *EPD Film* (Berlin), vol. 5, no. 12, December 1988.

Daems, P., ''De discrete charme van Stéphane Audran,'' in *Film + Televisie* (Brussels), no. 381, February 1989.

* * *

Few could have predicted that an unheralded Danish film would become one of the more esteemed European films of the late 1980s. *Babette's Feast* unexpectedly won the Oscar for Best Foreign Film as well as a number of other international awards; became one of the most popular—indeed, beloved—films on the American art-house circuit; inspired ambitious restaurants to offer a menu duplicating the titular feast (at a princely cost); and set a pathway for more recent ''great food'' movies like Ang Lee's *Eat Drink Man Woman* and Stanley Tucci's *Big Night.* Its director, whose first film appeared in 1955 and who was 68 when the film was released, was relatively unknown outside Scandinavia before the success of *Babette* and has remained so. Thus, the film's non-Danish admirers have been left to conclude, rightly or wrongly, that its success, even perfection of a sort, was due to a felicitous coming together of a classic novella faithfully adapted, an excellent cast with particularly memorable faces, and splendid photography capturing not only those faces but the somber landscapes, the spartan dwellings, and of course the sumptuous food.

Axel changed Isak Dinesen's original setting amid Norwegian fjords and mountains to a flatter Danish Jutland—possibly for budgetary reasons, but certainly with dramatic appropriateness, considering the greater austerity of the land to match the sober lives of the villagers (no competition here for the spectacle of the dinner). He also offered a village of uniform gray houses rather than the ''toy-town. . . painted gray, yellow, pink and many other colors'' of the story. Changes in the narrative are slight, but telling. For example, soon after Babette, the mysterious Parisian political refugee, is taken in as a servant by a unmarried pair of kindly but puritanical Danish sisters, she is taught how to make their dreary daily food of cod and ale-bread, a kind of porridge. In the story, ''during the demonstration the Frenchwoman's face became absolutely expressionless,'' but she soon learns the task, and eventually the food. The food, which the sisters distribute in daily charity rounds, ''acquired a new, mysterious power to stimulate and strengthen their poor and sick.'' But in Axel's film, we see Babette buy onions from the grocer and pick wild herbs for her dish, and watch the pleased faces of the indigent sampling her version (as well as their chagrin when Babette is briefly out of town and the sisters' sludgy recipe is revived).

The overall arc of the story remains the same. We are immediately introduced to the elderly sisters and the other villagers, disciples of the ascetic sect founded by the women's father, then learn of each sister's missed opportunity for a youthful love affair—Martine with a young officer army officer and Filippa with an opera singer who spots her vocal talent—and of the arrival of Babette, before we return to the present time (about 1887) for the main event of the tale. In his lengthy flashback Axel dwells more than Dinesen on smart details of

Babettes Gaestebud

the officers' barracks, and he inserts a cameo for Bibi Andersson in the parallel story of the opera singer (appropriately a Don Giovanni who fails to win over his Danish Zerlina). In both episodes the color and dash of the more elegant settings bring out the plainness of the sisters' lives all the more.

In the second half Axel adheres scrupulously to Dinesen's tale, while using Stephane Audran's elegant bearing and air of "having lived"—not to mention auburn hair—as a foil to the sweet simplicity of the sisters. (The actresses playing the latter with great poignancy, both veterans of Danish film, look like an elderly Loretta Young and Olivia de Havilland.) In story and film Babette wins a lottery, asks the sisters for permission to serve them and the other disciples a celebration dinner on the evening of their late father's centenary (though "a very plain supper with a cup of coffee was the most sumptuous meal to which they had ever asked any guest to sit down"), terrifies them with her imported ingredients (a huge live turtle is only part of what they now fear will be some kind of witch's sabbath), and ultimately serves a feast that only a great artist, once chef of one of Paris' greatest restaurants, could conceive and execute. The heart of the drama—and Axel and his crew rise to the occasion—is the breakdown of the disciples' resistance to the splendid meal, and their attainment of a joyful, life-changing state of grace that seems to go beyond the aesthetic and sensuous into the spiritual—both touching and comical to watch.

Axel's succession of images builds steadily toward the dinner itself: the procession of the foodstuffs past the houses of astonished villagers, the ironing of the white tablecloth, the close-ups of quail carcasses being plucked and carved up, as matter-of-factly as in a Dutch still life. As in the story, the surprise extra guest—the officer, now a retired general, who has lived in Paris—provides an entry to the scene for us, as the one person perfectly cognizant of how truly extraordinary the meal is. (The other guests watch him for clues on how to eat the odder fare.) Otherwise there is no one center of attention: we take in the glow of glasses of sherry and champagne and red wine against the black clothing and white hair of the diners; the General's comical astonishment over each course and beverage; the sounds of cutlery and conversation and champagne fizzing (gentle soundtrack music is intermittent and discreet); the neighbor called Solveig taking wonderful delight in her wine; the carriage man—a bit player straight out of a John Ford film (as is the diner who can't hold back an occasional "Hallelujah!")—hanging out in the kitchen and sampling the food and drink; Erik, the teenage server, soberly carrying out Babette's instructions; and Babette herself taking an occasional moment to savor the fabulous wine she has ordered. Many of these details are inventions of the filmmaker that broaden Dinesen's love feast to include all the characters, not just those at the table.

In the novella it snows the night of the feast but the sky clears momentarily when the guests leave the sisters' house, slipping in the drifts and playing like children as they hold hands. In the film there is only a misty rain before the feast, but Axel's diners too hold hands under a starry sky—here, forming a circle around the well as they sing a hymn. The snow, a cozy white blanket in Dinesen, here begins to fall only in the final moments, and is seen only through the cottage windows, as a hint of death or transience to accompany the dialogue and a guttering candle. But the overwhelming sense of joy as well as evanescence remains, and the film itself, like the dinner it dramatizes, becomes an example of great art springing from what the sophisticated world may call an obscure setting.

—Joseph Milicia

BADLANDS

USA, 1973

Director: Terrence Malick

Production: Pressman-Williams Enterprises; CFIC colour, 35mm; running time: 94 minutes.

Badlands

Producer: Terrence Malick; **executive producer:** Edward R. Pressman; **screenplay:** Terrence Malick; **assistant directors:** John Broderick, Carl Olsen; **photography:** Tak Fujimoto, Brian Probyn, Stevan Larner; **editor:** Robert Estrin; **associate editor:** William Weber; **art directors:** Jack Fisk, Ed Richardson; **sound editor:** James Nelson; **music:** George A. Tipton; **costumes:** Rosanna Norton.

Cast: Martin Sheen (*Kit Carruthers*); Sissy Spacek (*Holly*); Warren Oates (*Holly's Father*); Ramon Bieri (*Cato*); Alan Vint (*Deputy*); Gary Littlejohn (*Sheriff*); John Carter (*Rich Man*); Bryan Montgomery (*Boy*); Gail Threlkeld (*Girl*).

Publications

Books:

Thompson, D.K, in *Magill's Survey of Cinema, Second Series, vol.1* edited by Frank Magill, Englewood Cliffs, New Jersey, 1981.
Peary, Danny, *Cult Movies*, New York, 1981.
Williams, Mark, *Road Movies*, New York, 1982.

Articles:

Variety (New York), 10 October 1973.
Monaco, J., *Take One* (Montreal), January 1974.
Buckley, M., *Films in Review* (New York), April 1974.
Johnson, William, *Film Quarterly* (Berkeley), Spring 1974.
Kinder, Marsha, "The Return of the Outlaw Couple," in *Film Quarterly* (Berkeley), Summer 1974.
King, M., "Badlands; shoot first. . ." in *Jump Cut* (Chicago), May-June 1974.
Rosenbaum, J., *Monthly Film Bulletin* (London), November 1974.
Gow, G., *Films and Filming* (London), December 1974.
Combs, R., *Sight and Sound* (London), Winter 1974–75.
Walker, B., "Malick on Badlands" in *Sight and Sound* (London), Spring 1975.
Ciment, Michel, "Entretien avec Terrence Malick" in *Positif* (Paris), June 1975.
Sineux, M., "Un cauchemar de douceur" in *Positif* (Paris), June 1975.
Martin, M., *Ecran 75* (Paris), July-August 1975.
Rabourdin, D., *Cinéma* (Paris), July-August 1975.
Béhar, H., "La ballade sauvage" in *Image et Son* (Paris), September 1975.
Henderson, B., "Exploring Badlands" in *Wide Angle* (Baltimore), 1983.
Mooney, J. "Martin Sheen in *Badlands*," Movieline (Escondido, California), vol. 6, December 1994.
Stein, Michael Eric, "The New Violence or Twenty Years of Violence in Films: An Appreciation," *Films in Review* (New York), vol. 46, January/February 1995.

* * *

Twenty-eight year old Terrence Malick's sublime debut as writer/producer/director of *Badlands*, has endured through time to foster admiration from, and satisfaction for, the spectator, as it did upon its release in 1973. Perhaps Malick's career as a philosophy teacher before entering filmmaking provided a foundation to the clarity of his vision in this work.

Kit Carruthers (Martin Sheen), a garbage collector, meets Holly Sargis (Sissy Spacek) as he walks past her front lawn. She is practicing baton twirling and is charmed by his apparent worldliness. The banal cynicism of the midwest setting and the sleepy pace are disrupted as Kit murders Holly's father because he disapproves of their relationship.

This is the beginning of Kit's killing spree from South Dakota to finally, the badlands of Montana. Kit ultimately surrenders to the authorities, basking in their admiration of him and his legendary wild man status. Holly has realized that she no longer wants to be around the "hell bent type anymore," and has abandoned Kit just prior to his arrest.

Both repellent and magnetic, Malick draws us into the world of Kit, whose subsequent violent journey is intoned through the sporadic ethereal narration of Holly.

Through the brilliantly droll script we become disassociated from Kit's violence and rather, feel sympathy for the dysfunctional protagonist. This reflects Holly's own journey with Kit and her observation at one point, "The world seemed like a faraway planet." From Holly's father's attempts to keep her away from Kit—"He said if the piano didn't keep me off the streets maybe the clarinet would"—to Holly's reaction to sex—"Gosh, what was everyone talkin' about?"—Malick's writing shines throughout. On second or third viewing of this film the dialogue seems to increase in its hilarity and enunciates Kits and Holly's childlike naivety and stupidity.

Although Malick used three photographers, all with diverse filmic backgrounds, there remains visual fluidity and continuity throughout *Badlands*. The visual style achieves harmony with the emotional framework, objective, yet intensely intimate. George Tipton's score, with its fairground music quality, reinforces the innocence of the piece whilst underpinning the malevolence of Kit.

Badlands is a masterful work and fully deserves the many accolades that have been awarded to it.

—Marion Pilowsky

THE BAKER'S WIFE

See **LA FEMME DU BOULANGER**

BALADA O SOLDATE

(Ballad of a Soldier)

USSR, 1959

Director: Grigori Chukhrai

Production: Mosfilm; black and white, 35mm; running time: 89 minutes; length: 8045 feet. Released 1959. Filmed 1958.

Screenplay: Grigori Chukhrai and Valentin Yoshov; **photography:** V. Nikolaev and Era Savelieva; **editor:** M. Timofeieva; **art direction:** B. Nemechek; **music:** Mikhail Siv.

Cast: Vladimir Ivashov (*Alyosha Skvortsov*); Shanna Prokhorenko (*Shura*); Antonina Maximova (*Mother*); Nikolai Kruchkov (*General*); Evgeni Urbanski (*Crippled soldier*).

Awards: Cannes Film Festival, Special Jury Prize, 1960; honored at All-Union Film Festival of Russia and at the Czechoslovak Film Festival for Working People, 1960; Lenin Prize to Grigori Chukhrai, 1961.

Publications

Script:

Chukhrai, Grigori, and Valentin Yoshov, *Balada o soldate*, Moscow, 1967; extract in *Films and Filming* (London), July 1961.

Books:

Chang, Kuang-nien, *An Example of Modern Revisionist Art: A Critique of the Films and Statements of Grigori Chukhrai* (in English), Peking, 1965.

Shneiderman, Isaak, *Grigorii Chukhrai*, Leningrad, 1965.

Liehm, Mira, and Antonin J. Liehm, *The Most Important Art: East European Art after 1945*, Berkeley, 1977.

Veress, József, *Grigorij Cshuraj*, Budapest, Hungary, 1978.

Garbicz, Adam, and Jacek Kalinowski, editors, *Cinema, The Magic Vehicle: A Guide to Its Achievement: Journey Two: The Cinema of the Fifties*, Metuchen, New Jersey, 1979.

Articles:

Johnson, Albert, in *Film Quarterly* (Berkeley), Winter 1960.

Film a Doba (Prague), no. 11, 1960.

Crowther, Bosley, in *New York Times*, 26 December 1960.

Clark, Arthur, in *Films in Review* (New York), January 1961.

Gerasimov, Sergei, "Views of Life Compared: Chukhrai and Fellini," in *Films and Filming* (London), March 1961.

Whitehall, Richard, in *Films and Filming* (London), July, 1961.

Herlinghaus, Hermann, "A Talk with Grigori Chukhrai," in *Film Culture* (New York), no. 26, 1962.

"Discussion in Villepre," in *Iskusstvo Kino* (Moscow), no. 5, 1962.

Chukhrai, Grigori, "Keeping the Old on Their Toes," in *Films and Filming* (London), October 1962.

Badder, D. J., "Grigori Chukhrai," in *Film Dope* (London), April 1975.

De Libero, L., in *Cinema Nuovo* (Bari), January-February 1977.

Donets, L., in *Iskusstvo Kino* (Moscow), no. 1, 1989.

Iensen, T., "Četyre dnja bez vojny," in *Iskusstvo Kino* (Moscow), no. 5, May 1995.

* * *

Superficially, Grigori Chukhrai's *Ballad of a Soldier* has the naivety of a recruitment poster. At the height of the Nazi invasion, a young signalman, Vladimir Ivashov (Alyosha Skvortsov), cripples three tanks, and is given a week's leave to visit his mother. Struggling towards his home village by car and train, he sacrifices his time, little by little, to those who need it more. He helps an amputee frightened of returning to his young wife, delivers a precious gift of soap to the family of a soldier he meets on the road, saves victims of an air raid and befriends a girl, Shura, with whom he falls in love. Alyosha reaches the village on the last day, spends only a few minutes with his mother, then leaves, never to return. We know from the outset that he'll be killed in battle and buried by strangers, far from home, known to them only as "a Russian soldier."

Accustomed to think of Soviet film in terms of Eisenstein's historical epics or collectivist propaganda of *The Brave Tractor Driver* variety, Western audiences of the late 1950s welcomed Gerasimov's *And Quiet Flows the Don*, Kalatozov's *The Cranes Are Flying*, and especially Chukhrai's *The Forty First* and *Ballad of a Soldier* as assurances that the 19th-century humanism of Tolstoy and Turgenev survived under "social realism."

Critics who looked deeper recognised the films as covertly symptomatic of repression. All were set during World War II, one of the few "safe" historical periods under Stalin, and on their plots the dogmas of collectivism, national unity, suspicion of foreign entanglements, and the immersion of cultural minorities rested a heavy hand. From the first sequence of *Ballad*, where Alyosha's bereaved mother (clearly a metaphoric Mother Russia, just as Alyosha is a symbol of selfless anonymous service to the state) stands amid collectivised wheat and remembers the son of whom, until he left for war, she had known "everything there was to know," one is aware of a society where a shared accountability, not only for one's work but for one's thoughts, is ingrained from birth.

Ballad of a Soldier is not without its tentatively subversive elements. Authority figures may be revered, but Chukhrai does show a venal sentry extorting a bribe of canned beef to let Alyosha on the train (though he's later exposed and punished by a kindly officer). Free enterprise raises its head in a market at a railroad terminus, but the tone of this scene, where Alyosha buys a scarf as a gift for his mother, is absurdly furtive. The bartering peasants circling one another in cautious silence might be selling heroin rather than the family samovar.

Politically, the most significant encounter of the boy's journey is with a group of dispossessed Ukrainians, en route to factory work in the Urals. Since Ukrainian separatists sided with the Nazis early in the war and nationalism remained rampant, not only in the Ukraine but in other republics, the appearance of these refugees in national dress, advertising their despair at losing their home ("We're like birds in the autumn. We don't know where we're flying") is unexpected.

Both Chukhrai films won Cannes Festival prizes and were circulated more widely than any Soviet productions of the time. In the popular imagination, they represented Russian cinema, much as *La dolce vita* was seen to typify Italian film or *French Cancan*, the French. But *Ballad*, with its academic visual style, reminiscent of David Lean, who cast a long shadow over post-war film in Europe and Asia, and its tone of moral rectitude directed against the unpatriotic and the unfaithful, hardly bears comparison with the best European work of the time.

Nevertheless, the film carries conviction. Chukhrai shows skill with actors, extracting in particular a moving performance from Evgeni Urbanski as the one-legged soldier who considers losing himself in Russia's vastness in preference to returning home a cripple. In a scene at a railway telegraph office that, in visual style and performance, might have been extracted from *Brief Encounter*, Urbanski tries to sends a telegram explaining his defection, but is talked out of it by Alyosha and an irate clerk, who speaks for all the women waiting at home. Urbanski's later bitterness as he waits on a platform which gradually empties of passengers, and the moving reunion with the wife are handled with an agreeable lack of sentiment and rhetoric.

Such scenes lie at the heart of the film, and excuse the coy romance (in a railway car conveniently filled with hay) of Alyosha and the chaste Shura (Shanna Prokhorenko). In general, however, *Ballad of a Soldier* and other World War II dramas belong outside the stream of Soviet film. They were made as if Dziga Vertov, Dovzhenko, even Eisenstein had never existed. In retrospect, we can see that the most important film produced by this fad for wartime propaganda was Tarkovsky's *Ivan's Childhood.* Nevertheless, *Ballad of a Soldier* and Grigori Chukhrai himself deserve a niche in Soviet film history as, if nothing else, symptoms of an early opening to the West.

—John Baxter

THE BALLAD OF NARAYAMA

See **NARAYAMA BUSHI-KO**

LE BALLET MÉCANIQUE

France, 1924

Director: Fernand Léger

Production: Black and white, 35mm, silent; running time: about 14 minutes; length: 1260 meters. Released 1924. When shown in Berlin in 1925, part or all of *Ballet mécanique* was exhibited under the title *Images Mobile.* Filming probably began with the "Charlot Cubiste" (Cubist Charlie Chaplin) sequence in 1923; filming completed in November 1924, most likely in Paris; cost: about 5000 francs.

Producer: Fernand Léger; **photography:** Dudley Murphy (some sources credit Man Ray as well); sources indicate the editing was probably handled by Dudley Murphy; **music:** George Antheil; **assistant director:** Dudley Murphy.

Cast: Kiki; Dudley Murphy.

Publications

Books:

Antheil, Georges, *Bad Boys of Music*, New York, 1945.
Manvell, Roger, editor, *Experiment in the Film*, New York, 1948; revised edition, 1970.
Tyler, Parker, *Underground Cinema*, New York, 1969.
Curtis, David, *Experimental Cinema*, New York, 1971.
Lawder, Standish, *The Cubist Cinema*,New York, 1975.
Le Grice, Malcolm, *Abstract Film and Beyond*, Cambridge, Massachusetts, 1977.

Sitney, P. Adams, *Visionary Film: The American Avant-Garde 1943–1978*, New York, 1979.
Fabre, Gladys C., Barbara Rose, and Marie-Odile Odile, *Léger and the Modern Spirit: An Avant-Garde Alternative to Non-Objective Art*, Seattle, 1983.
De Francia, Peter, *Fernand Léger*, New Haven, Connecticut, 1983.
Kosinski, Dorothy M., editor, *Fernand Léger, 1911–1924: The Rhythm of Modern Life*, Munich, 1994.
Buck, Robert T., *Fernand Léger*, New York, 1995.
Faerna, Jose M., *Léger*, New York, 1996.
Lanchner, Carolyn, *Fernand Léger*, New York, 1998.

Articles:

Bond, Kirk, ''Léger, Dreyer, and Montage,'' in *Creative Art* (New York), October 1932.
Richter, Hans, ''The Avant-Garde Film Seen from Within,'' in *Hollywood Quarterly*, Fall 1949.
Jackiewicz, A., ''Epizod filmowy w dziele Fernanda Léger,'' in *Kino* (Warsaw), March 1974.
Brown, Geoff, in *Monthly Film Bulletin* (London), April 1977.
Brenden, Richard, ''Functions of Film: Léger's Cinema on Paper and on Cellulose,'' in *Cinema Journal* (Champaign, Illinois), Fall 1984.
Serenellini, M., ''I contrastie delle forme in *Ballet mécanique*,'' in *Cinema Nuovo* (Bari), December 1984.
Fuchs, H., ''Een geschiendenis van kleur en zwart-wit,'' in *Skrien* (Amsterdam), December-January 1990–91.

* * *

Contemporary film scholarship recognizes at least three major types of production. Most familiar and most popular is the fictive narrative, with roots back beyond Griffith's 1915 feature, *The Birth of a Nation.* Comparably familiar, though less popular, is the actuality film, with its documentary tradition at least as old as the 1920s work of artists like Flaherty and Grierson. Least familiar and least understood by popular audiences is the experimental film, which had its beginnings in the European avant-garde of the 1920s.

The European avant-garde was based largely upon the efforts of painters and other artists in Germany and France. Thus certain stylistics which mark the strategies of European painting during the 1920s often mark European avant-garde films: the stylistics of Futurism, Cubism, Dadaism, and Surrealism.

One of the best books on this period of experimental film is Standish Lawder's *The Cubist Cinema.* In part, Lawder's purpose was to relate classic European avant-garde films by Richter, Eggeling, Ruttman, and Léger to classic paintings of the period by Picasso, Kandinsky, Duchamp, and Léger. Indeed, it is especially interesting to find Léger's name common to both lists in light of the fact that his film *Ballet mécanique* constitutes one of the most famous and most successful examples surviving this brief-lived but highly innovative, highly influential period of experimental production.

Typically, experimental films are brief, independently-financed productions which tend toward innovative techniques and non-narrative structures. Often they are a collaborative, being the sole product of but one or two artists. *Ballet mécanique* is no exception to these characteristics. While the camerawork is attributed to the American Dudley Murphy, the 1924 French production is otherwise the work of one man, Fernand Léger.

Before he was 20, Léger had become a Cubist painter whose subject matter eventually centered on mechanical devices and urban imagery. *Ballet mécanique* is his sole film (although he did some work with Hans Richter on *Dreams that Money Can Buy* two decades later). He recalls that the film cost him some 5,000 francs, independent financing allowing him control comparable to that which he enjoyed with his paintings. *Ballet mécanique* is a difficult film to describe, though countless film scholars have embraced that very task. It is a brief, non-narrative exploration of cubist form, black and white tonalities, and various vectors through its constant, rapidly cut movements and compositions. As Lawder details in his study, many of the film's forms and compositions are reflected in—or themselves reflect—forms and compositions in Léger's famous cubist paintings from this period. Clearly the film allowed Léger cinematic extension of the formal problems he continued to explore in his single canvases.

The film flashes through over 300 shots in less than 15 silent minutes. The subjects of these fleeting images are diverse and difficult to quickly catalog: bottles, hats, triangles, a woman's smile, reflections of the camera in a swinging sphere, prismatically crafted abstractions of light and line, gears, numbers, chrome machine (or kitchen) hardware, carnival rides, shop mannequin parts, hats and shoes, etc. All interweave a complex cinematic metaphor which bonds man and machine. Further, *Ballet mécanique's* whimsical, witty, dadaist portrait seems to center on the looped repetition of a large woman repeatedly and mechanically ascending a stair (one of the first known examples of loop-printing, a technique later to become a mainstay of international experimental film after the 1960s).

Throughout its history, *Ballet mécanique* has always been a film more for other film artists or film scholars than for a general public. Still, it continues to enjoy critical attention and acclaim, and continues to influence the ongoing expression of experimental filmmakers throughout the industrialized free world.

—Edward S. Small

THE BAND WAGON

USA, 1953

Director: Vincente Minnelli

Production: Metro-Goldwyn-Mayer Picture Corp; Technicolor, 35mm; running time: 112 minutes. Released 1953. Filmed in the MGM studios.

Producer: Arthur Freed; **screenplay:** Betty Comden and Adolph Green; **photography:** Harry Jackson; **editor:** Albert Akst; **production designers:** Edwin Willis and Keogh Gleason: **set designs for musical numbers:** Oliver Smith; **art directors:** Cedric Gibbons and Preston Ames; **music:** Howard Dietz and Arthur Schwartz; **music director:** Adolph Deutsch; **costume designer:** Mary Ann Nyberg; **dance direction:** Michael Kidd.

The Band Wagon

Cast: Fred Astaire (*Tony Hunter*); Cyd Charisse (*Gabrielle Gerard*); Nanette Fabray (*Lily Marton*); Oscar Levant (*Lester Marton*); Jack Buchanan (*Jeffrey Cordova*); James Mitchell (*Paul Byrd*).

Publications

Books:

Astaire, Fred, *Steps in Time*, New York, 1959.
de la Roche, Catherine, *Vincente Minnelli*, New Zealand, 1959; reprinted in *Film Culture* (New York), June 1959.
Springer, John, *All Singing, All Dancing*, New York, 1966.
Truchaud, Francois, *Vincente Minnelli*, Paris, 1966.
Kobal, John, *Gotta Sing, Gotta Dance*, New York, 1970.
Thomas, Lawrence, B., *The MGM Years*, New Rochelle, New York, 1972.
Minnelli, Vincente, and Hector Arce, *I Remember It Well*, New York, 1974.
Delameter, James, *Dance in the Hollywood Musical*, Ann Arbor, Michigan, 1981.
Mueller, John, *Astaire Dancing: The Musical Films*, New York, 1985.
Thomas, Bob, *Astaire: The Man, the Dancer*, London, 1985.
Drouin, Fréderique, *Fred Astaire*, Paris, 1986.
Brion, Patrick, and others, *Vincente Minnelli*, Paris, 1985.
Adler, Bill, *Fred Astaire: A Wonderful Life*, New York, 1987.
Satchell, Tim, *Astaire: The Biography*, London, 1987.
Harvey, Stephen, *Directed by Vincente Minnelli*, New York, 1990.
Naremore, James, *The Films of Vincente Minnelli*, Cambridge, 1993.

Articles:

Jablonski, Edward, in *Films in Review* (New York), August-September 1953.
Lambert, Gavin, *Sight and Sound* (London), January-March 1954.
Chaumenton, Etienne, ''L'Oeuvre de Vincente Minnelli,'' in *Positif* (Paris), November-December 1954.
Pratley, Gerald, ''Fred Astaire's Film Career,'' in *Films in Review* (New York), January 1957.
Bitsch, Charles, and Jean Domarchi, ''Entretien avec Vincente Minnelli,'' in *Cahiers du Cinéma* (Paris), August-September 1957.
Tranchant, François, ''Invitation à la danse,'' in *Image et Son* (Paris), January 1958.
Johnson, Albert, ''The Films of Vincente Minnelli,'' in *Film Quarterly* (Berkeley), Winter 1958 and Spring 1959.
Conrad, Derek, ''2 Feet in the Air,'' in *Films and Filming* (London), no. 3, 1959.
Minnelli, Vincente, ''The Rise and Fall of the Musical,'' in *Films and Filming* (London), January 1962.
Domarchi, Jean, and Jean Douchet, ''Rencontre avec Vincente Minnelli,'' in *Cahiers du Cinéma* (Paris), February 1962.
Torok, Paul, and Jacques Quincey, ''Vincente Minnelli; ou, Le Peintre de la vie revée,'' in *Positif* (Paris), March 1963.
''Minnelli Issue'' of *Movie* (London), June 1963.
de la Roche, Catherine, ''Vincente Minnelli,'' in *Premier Plan* (Paris), March 1966.
Giles, D., ''Show-Making,'' in *Movie* (London), Spring 1977.
Mueller, J., in *Dance Magazine* (New York), May 1979.
Johnson, Julia, in *Magill's Survey of Cinema 1*, Englewood Cliffs, New Jersey, 1980.
Polan, Dana B., ''It Could Be Oedipus Rex: Denial and Difference in *The Band Wagon*,'' in *Ciné-Tracts* (Montreal), Summer-Fall 1981.
de Kuyper, Eric, ''Reflexions on the 'Dancing in the Dark' Sequence from Vincente Minnelli's *The Band Wagon*,'' in *Wide Angle* (Athens, Ohio), vol. 5, no. 3, 1983.
Damisch, Hubert, ''Un trouble de mémoire au cinéma,'' in *Cinémathèque*, no. 7, Spring 1995.
Saada, N., ''Howard Dietz et Arthur Schwartz: *The Bandwagon*,'' in *Cahiers du Cinéma*, Hors serie, 1995.
Mueller, J., and G. Aachen, ''*The Band Wagon*,'' in *Reid's Film Index* (New South Wales, Australia), no. 32, 1997.

* * *

The Band Wagon represents one of the most important of the MGM musicals of the 1950s, indeed in the history of this Hollywood genre. In particular, *The Band Wagon* stands as one of the masterworks to emerge from the very productive musicals unit that producer Arthur Freed controlled at MGM during the late 1940s and early 1950s.

The Band Wagon gestated in producer Freed's mind late in 1951. With recent successes of *An American in Paris* and *Singin' in the Rain*, Freed had the idea to acquire a song catalogue as the basis for this musical, in particular the songs of Howard Dietz, and his longtime partner Arthur Schwartz. Freed appreciated the creators of songs, having joined MGM as a song writer himself twenty five years earlier. By the time of *The Band Wagon* he had turned full-time to producing, winning every possible award offered in the Hollywood. Of the films he would produce in his long, distinguished career, none would be greater than *The Band Wagon.* Freed took ''I Love Louisa,'' one of Schwartz and Dietz's hit songs, as the original title of his new musical and set the vast talents of MGM in motion. This meant first screen writers Betty Comden and Adolph Green who had penned *Take Me Out to the Ball Game* (1949), and *Singin' in the Rain* (1952), among other creations, at MGM. This also meant director Vincente Minnelli, who had long been an MGM stalwart since the successes of *Meet Me in St. Louis* (1944), *The Pirate* (1948), and *An American in Paris* (1952).

Freed had hundreds of stars from which to choose. He selected the great Fred Astaire, who although more famous for his RKO films with Ginger Rogers, had been at MGM since the early 1940s. Astaire's dance partner for *The Band Wagon* would be Cyd Charisse, who had been featured in *Singin' in the Rain* the year before.

During the first week of February 1952, Comden and Green commenced writing their original story and screenplay. (Eventually their script would include ''themselves'' in the form of Oscar Levant and Nanette Fabray couple, the principle difference being that Comden and Green were never married.) The story idea centered around ''making a show,'' a classic narrative formula for the Hollywood musical.

The Band Wagon made use of the audience's particular knowledge of the career of Astaire. For example, the film's credits are superimposed on a top hat, white gloves, and a cane, probably the most famous icons of the American musical, indeed representing to all the genius of Astaire. But when the film opens we learn that the top hat is for sale and no one will buy it. Is Astaire washed up? This enigma sets ''Astaire,'' the man, the star, the legend, squarely in the middle of the story: can he (Fred Astaire/Tony Hunter) make a successful comeback?

The Band Wagon script resolves this dilemma by having Astaire/ Hunter failing to make art (''this show is a modern version of *Faust*''), but instead again creating wonderful entertainment for the masses.

More than a dozen of the Schwartz and Dietz songs were used including ''Something to Remember You By,'' ''I Guess I Have To Change My Plans,'' ''The Beggar's Waltz,'' ''High and Low,'' and most recognizable of all, ''Dancing in the Dark.'' The only original song, composed by Schwartz and Dietz in 1952, was ''That's Entertainment,'' which later became the anthem for MGM's Golden Age of the musical.

The rehearsal period for this complex dance musical began in August, 1952; and lasted six weeks. In the process the aforementioned talent created a serious of wonderful individual numbers on which the film's fame rests. For ''Shine on Your Shoes,'' Astaire was assisted by LeRoy Daniels, a non-actor, and an $8,000 ''fun machine'' which sounded like a calliope, shot out flags, rockets, and a kaleidoscope of colors. ''The Girl Hunt'' ballet, the film's climax, presented a satire on the detective film with Astaire as the flat foot narrator, in slouch hat, dark shirt, and double breasted suit, the very antithesis of his classic top hat and tails.

The Band Wagon ended shooting late in January 1953, nearly a year from the day Comden and Green sat down to create the story. The final cost of the film came to more than two million dollars. (Indeed the ''The Girl Hunt'' ballet cost more than three hundred thousand dollars alone.) The premiere, in late July, came to glowing reviews, and upon its initial release *The Band Wagon* more than made up for its considerable investment, and thereafter has generated considerable profits for MGM.

—Douglas Gomery

THE BANDIT

See **O CANGACEIRO**

BANSHUN

(Late Spring)

Japan, 1949

Director: Yasujiro Ozu

Production: Shochiku (Ofuna); black and white; running time: 107 minutes. Released in Japan in 1949, and in USA in 1972.

Screenplay: Yasujiro Ozu and Koga Noda, from an original story by Kazuo Hirotsu; **photography:** Yuhara Attuita; **music:** Senji Ito.

Banshun

Cast: Chishu Ryu (*The Father*); Setsuko Hara (*Noriko, the Daughter*); Haruko Sugimura (*The Aunt*); Yumeji Tsukioka (*Aya, the Daughter's friend*); Jun Usami (*The Young man*).

Awards: Kinema Jumpo Prize for Best Film of the Year, Japan, 1949.

Publications

Books:

Richie, Donald, *5 Pictures of Yasujiro Ozu*, Tokyo, 1962.
Sato, Tadao, *Ozu Yasujiro no Geijutsu* (The Art of Yasujiro Ozu), Tokyo, 1971.
Richie, Donald, *Japanese Cinema: Film Style and National Character*, New York, 1971.
Satomi, Jun, and others, editors, *Ozu Yasujiro—Hito to Shigoto* (Yasujiro Ozu—The Man and His Work), Tokyo, 1972.
Schrader, Paul, *Transcendental Style in Film: Ozu, Bresson, Dreyer*, Berkeley, 1972.
Burch, Noël, *Theory of Film Practice*, New York, 1973.
Tessier, Max, ''Yasujiro Ozu,'' in *Anthologie du cinéma 7*, Paris, 1973.
Richie, Donald, *Ozu*, Berkeley, 1974.
Mellen, Joan, *The Waves at Genji's Door: Japan Through Its Cinema*, New York, 1976.
Bock, Audie, *Japanese Film Directors*, New York, 1978; revised edition, Tokyo, 1985.

Burch, Noël, *To the Distant Observer*, Berkeley, 1979.
Sato, Tadao, *Currents in Japanese Cinema* (in English), Tokyo, 1982.
Bordwell, David, *Ozu and the Poetics of Cinema*, Princeton, 1988.
Hideki, Maeda, *Ozu Yasujiro no ie: jizoku to shinto*, Tokyo, 1993.
Sho, Kida, *Ozu Yasujiro no manazashi*, Tokyo, 1999.

Articles:

Milne, Tom, "Flavour of Green Tea over Rice," in *Sight and Sound* (London), Autumn 1973.
Ryu, Chishu, "Yasujiro Ozu," in *Sight and Sound* (London), Spring 1964.
Rosenbaum, Jonathan, "Ozu," in *Film Comment* (New York), Summer 1972.
Variety (New York), 12 July 1972.
Canby, Vincent, in *New York Times*, 22 July 1972.
Winsten, Archer, in *New York Post*, 22 July 1972.
Byron, Stuart, in *Village Voice* (New York), 17 August 1972.
Kauffmann, Stanley, in *New Republic* (New York), 19 August 1972.
Zeaman, Marvin, "The Zen Artistry of Yasujiro Ozu: The Serene Poet of the Japanese Cinema," in *Film Journal* (New York), Fall-Winter 1972.
Thompson, Kristin, and David Bordwell, "Space and Narrative in the Films of Ozu," in *Screen* (London), Summer 1976.
"Ozu Section" of *Cinéma* (Paris), February 1981.
Geist, K., "The Role of Marriage in the Films of Yasujiro Ozu," in *East-West Film Journal* (Honolulu), no. 1, 1989.
"Ozu, la vita e la geometria dei film," in *Castoro Cinema* (Florence), no. 151, 1991.
Wood, Robin, "The *Noriko* Trilogy," in *Cineaction* (Toronto), Winter 1992.
Losilla, C. "En el abismo de lo nunca dicho," *Nosferatu* (Donostia-San Sebastian, Spain), no. 25, December 1997.
Zunzunegui, S., "El fin de la primavera," *Nosferatu* (Donostia-San Sebastian, Spain), no. 25, December 1997.
Zunzunegui, S."Voces distantes," *Nosferatu* (Donostia-San Sebastian, Spain), no. 25, December 1997.

* * *

Late Spring is the first of six films Ozu made with Setsuko Hara, the titles of which are often motivated by the age and situation of Hara's character; in *Late Spring* she is of the age when a young woman was expected to be married, in *Early Summer* she is getting past it, and in *Late Autum* she is a middle-aged widow. The first three films, symmetrically separated by two-year gaps and alternating with films without Hara—*Late Spring* (1949), *Early Summer* (1951), *Tokyo Story* (1953)—can be argued to form a loose trilogy. In all three (and only these three) Hara's character is named Noriko, and in each a major narrative concern is the pressure exerted upon her to marry or (in the case of *Tokyo Story*) remarry.

Late Spring, along with many other Ozu films, has suffered from the unfortunate polarization in the West of two influential but inadequate critical approaches: the kind of content analysis practised by Joan Mellen in *The Waves at Genji's Door* (plot synopsis followed by the judgement that Ozu was a conservative locked into a nostalgia for the values of a threatened or collapsed traditional Japanese patriarchy) and the formalist analysis of Nöel Burch (*To the Distant Observer*) which produces Ozu as a "modernist" filmmaker because his method resists the dominance of the Hollywood codes, an approach that renders the subject-matter of the films irrelevant. (David Bordwell's recent *Ozu and the Poetics of Cinema* represents a surprising move toward rectifying this polarization, Bordwell having been previously associated with Burch's strict formalism.) The treatment of spatial relations in Ozu's work certainly differs significantly from the Hollywood norms, and this affects our relationship to the characters and the narrative, but the narrative remains clearly dominant: Ozu's meticulous concern with the minutiae of script construction on the one hand and acting on the other cannot be simply swept aside in order to fetishize his formal devices ("pillow shots," eyeline mismatches, use of 360 degree space, etc.). As for the charge of conservatism, Ozu's critical sensitivity to all aspects of social change, its gains and losses, the erosion of old values and the emergence of new, is such that the films offer themselves at least as readily to a radical as to a conservative reading. They are in fact so complex as to resist any *simple* political classification, every position dramatized in them being qualified by others. It is often difficult to define with the necessary clarity and precision exactly what the films are *about.*

It is easy, however, to state what *Late Spring* is *not* about: it is not about a young woman trying nobly to sacrifice herself and her own happiness in order dutifully to serve her widowed father in his lonely old age. If Noriko resists the social pressures that compel her into marriage (Ozu's comprehensive analysis of those pressures shows them convincingly to be *ir*resistible), it is because she is thoroughly aware that she will never be as happy as she is within her present situation. The film precisely defines the choice that contemporary society (post-war Japan, with its conflicts between traditional values and Americanization) offers her: subordination to a husband in marriage, or entrance into the "emancipated" world of alienated labour (i.e., subordination, as secretary, to a male boss). The latter option is embodied in Noriko's best friend Aya, a young woman so completely "modernized" that her legs get stiff if she has to sit on a tatami mat. Far from denouncing the breach with traditional values, Ozu presents Aya with immense sympathy and good humour, the emphasis being on the constraints of her situation. On the other hand, traditional marriage is never presented in Ozu's films as in itself fulfilling, and especially not for the woman (Norikio's father informs her that her mother wept through most of the first years of their marriage).

With her father, Noriko has a freedom that she will never regain: she can go bicycling by the sea with handsome young men, visit sake bars with casual associates, enjoy relatively unrestricted movement. And *movement* (and its suppression) is the film's key motif and structuring principle. The first half contains (for Ozu) an unusual amount of camera movement accompanying or parelleling Noriko's sense of enjoyment and exhilaration (the train journey, the bicycle ride). The last camera movement in the film occurs in the scene in the park where her father and aunt finalize plans for her marriage. The film then moves inexorably to Noriko's entrapment in an irreversible process, her immobilization (beneath the heavy traditional wedding costume) and final obliteration (the empty mirror that replaces any depiction of the wedding ceremony). The film's final shot of the sea is commonly interpreted in terms of Zen-ian resignation and acceptance

(Ozu once remarked that western critics don't understand his films, so "they always talk about Zen or something"); it can equally be read as a reminder of the bicycle ride and the lost freedom.

—Robin Wood

BARON PRASIL

(Baron Munchausen)

Czechoslovakia, 1961

Director: Karel Zeman

Production: Ceskoslovensky Statni Film; AGFA colour, 35mm; running time: 81 minutes.

Screenplay: Karel Zeman and Josef Kainar, from the original novel by Gottfried Burger; **assistant directors:** Zdenek Rozkopal and Jan Mimra; **photography:** Jiri Tarantik; **art director:** Karel Zeman; **set design:** Zdenek Rozkopal; **music:** Zdenek Liska.

Cast: Milos Kopecky (*Baron Munchausen*); Jana Brejchova (*Bianca*); Rudolf Jelinek (*Tonik*); Jan Werich (*Captain of Dutch ship*); Rudolf Hrusinsky (*Sultan*); Eduard Kohout (*Commander of the fortress*); Karel Hoger (*Cyrano de Bergerac*); Karel Effa (*Officer of the guard*); Bohus Zahorsky (*Captain of the pirate ship*); Nadezda Blazickova (*Harem dancer*); Bohus Zahorsky (*The Admiral*).

Publications

Books:

Stephenson, Ralph, *Animation in the Cinema* (London), 1967.
Halas, John, *Masters of Animation* (London), 1987.

Articles:

Konradva, Libuse, "Putting on a Style," in *Films and Filming* (London), June 1961.
Benesova, Marie, "A New Approach to Baron Munchausen," in *Czechoslovak Film* (Prague), no. 1, 1962.
Benesova, Marie, "Munchausens heitere wiedergeburt," in *Deutsche Film Kunst* (Berlin), no. 5, 1962.
Phillipe, Pierre, "Le Baron de Crac," in *Cinéma* (Paris) and *Variety* (New York), 18 July 1962.
Cinema Nuovo (Milano), July/August 1964.
Monthly Film Bulletin (London), November 1967.
Thonen, John, "The Fabulous Adventures of Baron Munchhausen," in *Filmfax* (Evanston, Illinois), no. 26, April-May 1991.

* * *

Once named National Artist of Czechoslovakia, director, designer, artist, and animator, Karel Zemen, co-founded the Gottwaldov Studio in 1943, allying the traditional puppet entertainment long enjoyed in Czechoslovakia since the seventeenth century, and new experimental approaches to film. Zemen established his reputation with films like *Inspiration* (1944), in which he animated solid and blown glass, an apparently unyielding, if plentiful material in Czechoslovakia. The *Mr. Prokouk* cartoon series (1947) followed, and established a character who became a national hero in illustrating the shortfalls of a bureaucratic system. Zemen extended his interest in combining the material world with the conditions of the animated form in longer films like *Journey into Prehistory* (1955) and *The Invention of Destruction* (1958) which foregrounded apocalyptic warnings amidst the humour and anarchy of fantastic fiction.

Zemen's *Baron Munchhausen* (1961) is a *tour de force* exercise in how film form can properly illustrate the conceit of its subject. Combining live action, animation, and numerous theatrical devices and special effects, Zemen simultaneously creates modes of "illusion" while directly illustrating the romantic "delusion" of his eponymous hero. Deliberately referencing the "magical" aspects of Melies' films and the thematic concerns of his great literary hero, Jules Verne, Zemen deconstructs the notion of a romantic flight of fancy, literally using "flight" as the central motivating force in his quasi-picaresque narrative. "Flight" here, is simultaneously the soaring ambition of freedom, the desperate need to escape, and a mode of scientific achievement.

Emerging from the credit sequence pages of an illustrated children's book, the story commences with a storm, and the creation of an uncertain and strange world where footprints in the sand lead nowhere and a frog perches on a jug in a pool of water. The next sequence anticipates the celebrated jump-cut in *2001: A Space Odyssey* (1968) where a bone is tossed in the air by prehistoric man and becomes a spacecraft thousands of years in the future. Zemen, like Kubrick, also makes comment on the passing of time and the notion of progress by treating the sky as if it were a scroll. As each part of "the scroll" is pulled down into the frame it reveals an element in the history of aviation, from a bird to a flying man to an early aircraft through to a jet and finally, a rocket. In the rocket is the astronaut, Tonik, who lands on the moon, and is surprisingly greeted by his romantic forbears of science fiction, Cyrano de Bergerac, Barbican, and Captain Nichol from Verne's novels, and eventually, Baron Munchhausen himself. The film immediately foregrounds its interest in the tension between scientific achievement and heroic aspiration, and sustains this theme by pairing Tonik and the Baron in the adventures that follow. Tonik has been mistaken by the Baron as a "moondweller," and therefore, as an alien. This serves as a convenient metaphor for the Baron's distanciation from the astronaut, and a clear indication that for him, "the moon" may only be colonised by dreamers and romantics, and not by literally travelling there. Throughout the course of the film though, it is the Baron who must come to terms with the fact that it is the astronaut who represents a contemporary romantic hero.

Tonik and the Baron, like the other characters in the film, are live action figures but they inhabit a world which becomes a mixture of highly textured artificial sets, camera tricks distorting size and scale, colour saturated film-stocks ranging from icy-blue to warm gold, and animated sequences with all manner of flying creatures, sea monsters, and visual jokes. Zemen essentially intervenes in the Baron's telling of the tale, exposing him not merely as a romantic fraud but as a man out of touch with ''modern'' reality.

Both Tonik and the Baron fall in love with Bianca, a princess sold to a Turkish sultan by pirates, but it is ultimately Tonik who wins her hand despite of the Baron's apparently heroic exploits on her behalf. Zemen is careful to use an array of effects to illustrate these exploits, but simultaneously, such spectacle and exaggeration only casts considerable doubt upon the claims of the Baron as a hero.

While apparently creating a tale composed of heroic adventures, Zemen undermines the authenticity of the heroic gesture.

Incredible set pieces, for example, where the Baron defeats 10,000 Turks amidst a montage of sparking blades, roaring lions, collapsing silhouettes of soldiers, and swirling red clouds, are undermined by the following scene of Tonik merely knocking out the palace guard and winning Bianca's favour by playing several sonorous notes on a gong. This motif re-occurs later as the couple are re-united by notes played on a spider's web and a whistle. Zemen counterpoints the comic failings of the Baron with Tonik's guile and efficiency. Consequently, Zemen can also use the ''fantastic'' environment as a vehicle for humour. One particular example involves two-dimensional collage animation, where a ship's figurehead removes a pipe and releases the smoke from all the crew smoking within the ship. This is very reminiscent of the style later adopted by Monty Python's animator, Terry Gilliam, who acknowledged the ongoing influence of Zemen's work by re-making *The Adventures of Baron Munchhausen* in 1988. This joke is extended in Zemen's film by using the crew's smoke to camouflage a ship that the Baron is escaping on. The Turkish fleet, lined up on either side of the ship, inevitably fire over the Baron's ship and destroy each other. This would be amusing enough but Zemen uses bathos to further highlight the eccentricity of the Baron, who says, undaunted, ''A few stray balls sank our ship, but that's only to be expected!''

Though the Baron is given the opportunity to impress the princess when they are left alone together travelling the world inside the body of a whale (and Zemen can show us literal versions of the Red, Yellow, and Black Seas), it is Tonik that the Princess ultimately wants. While Tonik imagines how he might escape the conflicts in Europe, the Baron seeks out the enemy, flying on a cannonball and crashing through a window, which in true cartoon fashion, exactly replicates his splayed outline. The more foolish the Baron seems, the more truly heroic Tonik becomes, as he escapes imprisonment, accused of hiding all the army's gunpowder, re-unites with Princess Bianca, and leaves with her, initially hiding in two suits of armour.

The Baron then accidentally throws his match down a well where Tonik has indeed hidden the fortress' gunpowder—the explosive ''launches'' the fortress, which looks like a rocket, and the two lovers, whose suits of armour conveniently turn into rocket-powered astronaut suits are projected back to the moon. ''Success'' it seems, is in the hands of intelligent men employing science and technology, and not with heroic daydreamers like the Baron.

This is particularly relevant because in 1959 the Soviet Union had launched the Lunik spaceprobes which had both landed on the moon and provided the first pictures from its far side, while in 1961, the year Baron Munchhausen was released, Soviet cosmonaut, Yuri Gagarin, became the first human being to orbit the earth in *Vostok 1*. Scientific fact was rapidly catching up with, and over-taking, fantastic fiction. Zemen's film is both a lament for period-style swashbuckling romance and a recognition that ''History changes its clock,'' and as Cyrano de Bergerac says while spinning his hat into space as if it were a flying saucer in the film's elegiac yet hopeful coda, ''We are journeying towards the mighty embrace called the universe.''

—Paul Wells

BARREN LIVES

See **VIDAS SECAS**

LA BATAILLE DU RAIL

(Battle of the Rails)

France, 1945

Director: René Clément

Production: Coopérative Générale du Cinéma Français; black and white, 35mm; running time: 87 minutes; length: 7800 feet. Released 1945. Filmed, for the most part, in 1945 on location in France.

Screenplay: René Clémént and Colette Audry, with Jean Daurand, based on stories told to Colette Audry by members of the Resistance; **photography:** Henri Alekan; **editor:** Jacques Desagneaux; **music:** Yves Baudrier. The film contains documentary footage shot by an unknown amateur filmmaker.

Cast: Antoine Laurent (*Camargue*); Jacques Desagneux (*Maquis Chief*); Leroy (*Station master*); Redon (*Mechanic*); Pauléon (*Station master at St. André*); Rauzena (*Shunter*); Jean Clarieux (*Lampin*); Barnault and Kronegger (*Germans*) and the French Railwaymen. Some sources list a narration by Charles Boyer.

Awards: Cannes Film Festival, voted among the Best Films, 1946.

Publications

Script:

Clement, René, *La Bataille du rail*, Paris, 1949.

Books:

Siclier, Jacques, *René Clément*, Brussels, 1956.

Farwagi, Andre, *René Clément*, Paris, 1967.

Gabricz, Adam, and Jack Klinowski, editors, *Cinema, The Magic Vehicle: A Guide to Its Achievement: Journey One: The Cinema through 1949*, Metuchen, New Jersey, 1975.

Armes, Roy, *French Cinema Since 1946: Volume One: The Great Tradition*, New York, 1976.

La bataille du rail

Articles:

Queval, Jean, in *Ecran Français* (Paris), 16 October 1946.
Regent, Roger, in *Ecran Français* (Paris), 14 October 1947.
New York Times, 27 December 1949.
Koval, Francis, "Interview with Clément," in *Sight and Sound* (London), June 1950.
Eisner, Lotte, "Style of René Clément," in *Film Culture* (New York), no. 12–13, 1957.
"Clement Issue" of *Avant-Scène du Cinéma* (Paris), 1 February 1981.
Dossier, in *Cinéma* (Paris), July-August 1982.
La Bataille du rail (special issue, includes screenplay excerpts), *Avant-Scène du Cinéma* (Paris), no. 442, May 1995.

* * *

La Bataille du rail stands out as the only seriously realist film which the French made at the Liberation in 1945. At the first Cannes Festival in 1946 it took the grand prize. For a time its director, René Clément, was called a French neorealist, and it is true that he was much interested in and influenced by the Italian school. But Clément and his associates (Colette Audry as scriptwriter and Henri Alekan as cameraman) had thought about making this film when they had organized a discussion club in Nice well before 1945. This club later became IDHEC, the French film school.

La Bataille du rail was shot out of doors with non-actors. Its script is episodic, involving separate sets of characters for each incident. The incidents include: 1) a meeting of the Resistance in the railyards and their narrow escape thanks to a timely air raid, 2) the planting of a bomb on a train despite discovery by German guards, and 3) the taking of hostages by Germans and their pitiful death by firing squad.

Midway through the film an overall dramatic direction is given when we learn that the Allies have landed and that the Germans must get their trains to Normandy. Despite heavy losses in skirmishes with armored trains and troops, the maquis, a military branch of the French underground, destroy four of the seven trains. The film concludes with the most elaborate incident, the derailing of a huge rail convoy, shot from three different angles. This spectacular destruction concludes with a closeup of an accordion slowly falling on itself, providing a musical sigh, as in Dovzhenko's *Arsenal.* Other comparisons come to mind, especially Malraux's *Expoir* which, while shot in

1935, came out only in 1945. *La Bataille du rail* remains fresh in comparison with dramatic resistance films like Henri Calef's *Jericho* because of its immediacy, speed, and detail. Despite its spectacular violence, the derailment is less memorable than the heroic close-ups of the hostages lined up to be shot. At the instant before his death, we are given an extreme close-up from the vantage point of one of these anonymous patriots. He (and we) watch the indifferent but marvellous motions of a spider on the wall inches away. As the shots ring out, every engine in the railyard lets out a jolt of steam signalling, by its smoke and whistle, the spirit of resistance within the trains themselves.

This 85 minute film was fabled; nevertheless it didn't produce any imitations. Doubtless it had an effect on its director and cameraman who in turn were to rise to the top of the industry in France.

—Dudley Andrew

LA BATALLA DE CHILE: LA LUCHA DE UN PUEBLO SIN ARMAS

(The Battle of Chile: Struggle of People Without Arms)

Chile-Cuba, 1975, 1976, 1979

Director: Patricio Guzmán

Part 1. La insurrección de la burguesia (The Insurrection of the Bourgeoisie)

Part 2. El golpe de estado (A Blow Against the State)

Part 3. El poder popular (The Power of the People)

Production: Equipo ''Tercer Año,'' in collaboration with Chris Marker and the Instituto Cubano del Arte e Industria Cinematográficos (ICAIC); Kodak black and white; 16mm (subsequently blown up to 35mm). Part 1 released 1975, Cannes Film Festival; Part 2 released 1976, Cannes Film Festival; Part 3 released 1979. Filmed 1973 in Santiago, Chile.

Producer: Federico Elton; **screenplay:** Patricio Guzmán; **photography:** Jorge Müller Silva; **editor:** Pedro Chaskel; **sound:** Bernardo Menz; **mixing:** Carlos Fernández; **sound transfer:** Jacinto Falcón and Ramón Torrado; **special effects:** Jorge Pucheux, Delia Quesada, and Alberto Valdés; **consultants:** Julio García Espinosa, Marta Harnecker, and José Pino; **other collaborators:** Saul Yellin, Beatriz Allende, Harald Edelstam, Lilian Indseth, Juan José Mendy, Roberto Matta, Chris Marker, Rodrigo Rojas, Estudio Haynowsky, and Scheumann.

Cast: Readers—Matías Rodriguez, Pedro Fernández Vila, Jacques Bonaldi, and Bruno Colombo.

Publications

Script:

Pick, Zuzana, ''The Battle of Chile: A Schematic Shooting Script,'' in *Ciné-Tracts* (Montreal), Winter 1980.

Books:

Racinante, editor, *La insurrección de la burgesia*, Caracas, 1975.
La batalla de Chile: La lucha de un pueblo sin armas, Madrid, 1977.
Guzmán, Patricio, and P. Sempere, *Chile: El cine contra el fascismo*, edited by Fernando Torres, Valencia, 1977.

Articles:

Salinas, S., and H. Soto, ''Más vale una sólida formación política que la destreza artesanal,'' in *Primer Plano* (Valparaiso), vol. 2, no. 5, 1973.
Gauthier, Guy, ''Chili: La Première Année,'' in *Image et Son* (Paris), March 1973.
''Stadion Chile,'' in *Film und Fernsehen* (Berlin), February 1974.
Ehrman, H., and others ''Chile: Le Cinéma de l'unité populaire,'' in *Ecran* (Paris), February 1974.
''Le Cinéma dans la politique de l'Unité Populaire,'' in *Jeune Cinéma* (Paris), November 1974.
Delmas, Ginette, in *Jeune Cinéma* (Paris), July-August 1975.
Cardenac, M., in *Ecran* (Paris), December 1975.
Gauthier, Guy, in *Image et Son* (Paris), January 1976.
Biskind, Peter, ''In Latin America They Shoot Filmmakers,'' in *Sight and Sound* (London), Summer 1976.
Niogret, Hubert, in *Positif* (Paris), July-August 1976.
Martin, Marcel, in *Ecran* (Paris), January 1977.
Jeune Cinéma (Paris), February 1977.
Thirard, P. L., ''De l'histoire déja (*La Bataille du Chile*),'' in *Positif* (Paris), February 1977.
Hönig, J., ''Patricio Guzmán—ein Filmschöpfer der Unidad Popular,'' in *Information* (Berlin), no. 1, 1977.
Image et Son (Paris), April 1977.
Burton, Julianne, ''Politics and the Documentary in People's Chile,'' in *Socialist Review*, October 1977.
Chaskel, Pedro, ''América Latina: Vigencia del documental politico Chile: Analista de una batalla,'' in *Cine al Dia* (Caracas), November 1977.
Galiano, Carlos, in *Cine Cubano* (Havana), no. 91–92, 1978.
Gupta, Udayan, and FLQ Staff, ''An Interview with Patricio Guzmán, Director of *The Battle of Chile*,'' in *Film Library Quarterly* (New York), no. 4, 1978.
West, Dennis, ''Documenting the End of the Chilean Road to Socialism: *La batalla de Chile*,'' in *American Hispanist*, February 1978.
''Special Section'' of *Cine Cubano* (Havana), March 1978.
Anderson, P., in *Films in Review* (New York), June-July 1978.
Ranvaud, Don, ''Introduction to Latin America I: Chile,'' in *Framework* (Norwich), Spring 1979.
Schumann, Peter, ''Chilean Cinema in Exile,'' in *Framework* (Norwich), Spring 1979.
Guzmán, Patricio, ''Chile 3: Guzmán,'' in *Framework* (Norwich), Spring 1979.

Angry Arts group, ''*Battle of Chile* in Context,'' in *Jump Cut* (Chicago), November 1979.

Wallis, V., ''*Battle of Chile:* Struggle of People Without Arms,'' in *Jump Cut* (Chicago), November 1979.

Guzmán, Patricio, ''*The Battle of Chile:* The Origins of the Project,'' in *Ciné-Tracts* (Montreal), Winter 1980.

Pick, Zuzana, ''Chile: The Cinema of Resistance, 1973–1979,'' in *Ciné-Tracts* (Montreal), Winter 1980.

Pick, Zuzana, ''Letter from Guzmán to Chris Marker'' and ''Reflections Previous to the Filming of *The Battle of Chile,*'' in *Ciné-Tracts* (Montreal), Winter 1980.

MacCarthy, T., in *Variety* (New York), 7 May 1980.

Galiano, C., ''Wirklichkeit und Dokument,'' in *Film und Fernsehen* (Berlin), November 1980.

West, Dennis, in *Cineaste* (New York), no. 2, 1981.

* * *

The Battle of Chile, which consists of three feature-length parts, uses actuality footage to record the socio-economic and political turmoil preceding the fall of Chile's Marxist-socialist president, Salvador Allende, in 1973. While the film is an outstanding example of the documentary as a *record* of history-in-the-making, it is also a carefully conceived and clearly organized *analysis* of these events. Guzmán structured the first two parts of his film around selected ''battlegrounds'' (e.g., a strike of copper miners) where class interests clashed. The major issues and strategies in these clashes are generally presented in a dialectical fashion: for instance, the film may first show the tactics of the rightist forces and then the counter-measures with which the left responds. The filmmakers infiltrated the entire political spectrum and succeeded in showing events from multiple political perspectives as they unfolded. Part three of the film is structured differently in that it focuses on a single phenomenon—a people's power movement which first arose as a response to a bosses' strike.

This monumental documentary is Guzmán's most important film. It was made by a politically committed five-person team who faced overwhelming obstacles. Available to this film collective were one Nagra tape recorder, one 16mm Eclair camera, and film stock which had been sent from abroad by a colleague. In spite of the strict semi-clandestine measures they followed, the filmmakers at times risked their lives. After the right-wing military coup toppled Allende, all the sound tape and film footage were smuggled out of Chile. The film was edited at the Cuban Institute of Cinematographic Art and Industry in Havana.

The extensive use of the sequence-shot, *The Battle of Chile*'s predominant stylistic feature, is unusual in documentary films. Pedro Chaskel's low-key editing preserves the unity of these sequence-shots and maximizes their effect.

The Battle of Chile is one of the greatest Marxist documentaries. The influence of Marx's *The Civil War in France* and Lenin's *State and Revolution* is evident in the type of political analysis applied in the first two parts of the film. These two segments illustrate the Marxist-Leninist revolutionary lesson that there can be no peaceful transition to socialism before the repressive machinery of the bourgeois state (e.g., a standing army) is broken up and replaced. In accordance with this view, the filmmakers closely follow the military's drift to the right as well as the anti-Allende activities of the opposition-dominated legislature. Marx and Engels in the *Manifesto of the Communist Party* viewed classes as the protagonists of history, and conflict as an inherent dimension of class societies. Guzmán follows this Marxist conception in that classes are the protagonists of his film and events are framed in terms of class conflict.

This film has reportedly never been seen in Chile. In countries where the documentary has been shown, both Marxist and non-Marxist critics have hailed it as a landmark in the history of the political documentary. Because of its vast scope, *The Battle of Chile* is surely the single most valuable historical document on the final months of the Via Chilena, Chile's unique experiment in building socialism peacefully and democratically. Marxist critics have praised the film for its attack on the bourgeois ideology of cinema, an ideology which represents the capitalist mode of production and the bourgeois social order as ''givens'' and discourages viewers from challenging or questioning analytically the socio-economic status quo. In *The Battle of Chile*, the individual star of bourgeois cinema has been replaced by workers who are depicted as a class struggling to alter the capitalist mode of production and to change the world the bourgeoisie created.

—Dennis West

LA BATTAGLIA DI ALGERI

(The Battle of Algiers)

Italy-Algiers, 1966

Director: Gillo Pontecorvo

Production: Igor Films (Rome) and Casbah Film Company (Algiers); black and white, 35mm; running time: 123 minutes. Released 1966. Filmed 1965 in Algiers; cost: $800,000.

Producer: Antonio Musu and Yacef Saadi; **screenplay:** Franco Solinas and Gillo Pontecorvo; **photography:** Marcello Gatti; **editors:** Mario Serandrei and Mario Morra; **art direction:** Sergio Canevari; **music:** Gillo Pontecorvo and Ennio Morricone; **special effects:** Tarcisio Diamanti and Aldo Gasparri; **Algerian assistants:** Ali Yahia, Moussa Haddad, Azzedine Ferhi, Mohamet Zinet; **Algerian ''opérateurs'':** Youssef Bouchouchi, Ali Maroc, Belkacem Bazi, Ali Bouksani.

Cast: Yacef Saadi (*Djafar*); Brahim Haggiag (*Ali La Pointe*); Jean Martin (*Colonel Mathieu*); Tommaso Neri (*Captain Dubois*); Mohamed Ben Kassen (*Le Petit Omar*); Fawzia El Kader (*Hassiba*); Michele Kerbash (*Fathia*).

Awards: Venice Film Festival, Lion of St. Mark, 1966.

Publications

Script:

Solinas, Franco, *Gillo Pontecorvo's ''The Battle of Algiers'': A Film Written by Franco Solinas*, New York, 1973.

La Battaglia di Algeri

Books:

Saadi, Yacef, *Souvenirs de la bataille d'Alger: December 1956-September 1957*, Paris, 1962.
Mellen, Joan, *Filmguide to ''The Battle of Algiers,''* Bloomington, Indiana, 1973.
Bignardi, Irene, *Memorie estorte a uno smemorato: vita di Gillo Pontecorvo*, Milan, 1999.

Articles:

Hennebelle, Guy, ''Une Si Jeune Paix,'' in *Cinéma* (Paris), December 1965.
Porin, Pierre, ''Le Cinéma algérien et *La Bataille d'Alger*,'' in *Positif* (Paris), October 1966.
Pontecorvo, Gillo, ''*The Battle of Algiers:* An Adventure in Filmmaking,'' in *American Cinematographer* (Los Angeles), April 1967.
Castelli, Luisa, in *Occhio Critico* (Rome), May-June 1967.
Crowther, Bosley, in *New York Times*, 23 September 1967.
Gill, Brendan, ''Truthtelling,'' in *New Yorker*, 23 September 1967.
Morgenstern, Joseph, ''The Terror,'' in *Newsweek* (New York), 23 October 1967.
Kozloff, Max, ''Shooting at Wars,'' in *Film Quarterly* (Berkeley), Winter 1967–68.
Mussman, Toby, ''Gillo Pontecorvo,'' in *Medium* (New York), Winter 1967–68.
Kauffmann, Stanley, ''Recent Wars,'' in *New Republic* (New York), 16 December 1967.
Covington, Francee, ''Are the Revolutionary Techniques Employed in *The Battle of Algiers* Applicable to Harlem?'' in *Black Woman* (New York), 1970.
Wilson, David, ''Politics and Pontecorvo,'' in *Sight and Sound* (London), Autumn 1970.
Sainsbury, Peter, in *Afterimage: Third World Cinema* (London), Summer 1971.
Mellen, Joan, ''An Interview with Gillo Pontecorvo,'' in *Film Quarterly* (Berkeley), Fall 1972.
Miklay, E., ''Valóság és modell: Pontecorvo: Az algiri csata és a Queimada,'' in *Filmkultura* (Budapest), September-October 1972.
Bosséno, C., in *Image et Son* (Paris), February 1981.

Downing, John, and Nyisha Mbalia Shakur, ''Selected Third World Classic Films,'' in *Film Library Quarterly* (New York), vol. 16, no. 4, 1983.
Marshall, B., ''Birth of a Nation,'' in *Stills* (London), May-June 1983.
O'Sullivan, Thaddeus, ''Images of Liberation,'' in *Sight and Sound* (London), vol. 7, no. 3, March 1997.

* * *

In 1966 the revolutionary filmmaker Gillo Pontecorvo released his stunning chronicle of one of the major clashes of the Algerian struggle for independence: *The Battle of Algiers.* The film's fictionalized account of this crucial three-year period in Algeria's history draws on actual people and events as the basis for its story, and adopts an impressively convincing documentary style in its presentation.

The film's opening credits contain a message stating that ''not one foot'' of actual newsreel footage was used in the making of the picture, yet Pontecorvo achieves a naturalistic, cinema-verité quality through his direction, conveying the events with the immediacy of a television news broadcast. Marcello Gatti's grainy, black and white photography captures the look and texture of a newsreel, as does the jarring realism of the hand-held camerawork in many of the film's explosive crowd scenes. The use of non-professional actors (with the exception of Jean Martin as the French Colonel Mathieu) also contributes to the film's overall impression of events being recorded as they occur.

This documentary-like effect has evoked both praise and condemnation for Pontecorvo, with some critics expressing admiration for the film's achievement and others questioning the ethics of filming a partly fictional scenario in such strikingly realistic terms. For Pontecorvo and his screenwriting partner, Franco Solinas, however, the question of the ''truth'' of *The Battle of Algiers* is answered by the film's political impact as an anti-imperialist statement. If isolated moments in the film, such as its central character's harassment by a group of arrogant young Frenchmen, are the products of the authors' imaginations, they are nevertheless representative of events which occurred countless times during France's 130-year occupation of Algeria. Indeed, the film's most harrowing scenes—those of captured rebels undergoing torture at the hands of the military—demand to be shown, to demonstrate the full measure of the inhuman brutality they represent.

Yet Pontecorvo's political stance regarding the Algerian struggle does not lead him to resort to the caricatures of heroism and villainy which so often mar the impact of otherwise fine political films. Even as he reviles the policies of the French government, he forces us to confront the painful fact that these are human lives that are being lost and not mere pawns in a revolutionary uprising. His camera lingers on the faces of those who will die moments later from a planted rebel bomb, bringing home with wrenching clarity the bitter price of violent conflict. This rare approach, in a genre which frequently averts its eyes from these hard truths, places *The Battle of Algiers* at the forefront of political filmmaking by allowing each viewer to re-examine his or her own position on political violence in the harsh light of the images on the screen.

In the years since its release, *The Battle of Algiers* has become a staple of film classes and revival house theatres. Its political merits have been widely discussed and debated, with the individual outlook of each critic coming very much into play in any evaluation of the film. The film's cinematic achievements, however, remain as powerful as they first appeared in 1966, and subsequent armed revolts in other Third World countries have only served to reinforce the universality of Pontecorvo's remarkable work.

—Janet E. Lorenz

THE BATTLE OF ALGIERS

See **LA BATTAGLIA DI ALGERI**

THE BATTLE OF CHILE

See **LA BATALLA DE CHILE**

BATTLE OF THE RAILS

See **LA BATAILLE DU RAIL**

BATTLESHIP POTEMKIN

See **BRONENOSETS POTEMKIN**

BEAUTY AND THE BEAST

See **LA BELLE ET LA BÊTE**

BECKY SHARP

USA, 1935

Director: Rouben Mamoulian

Production: Pioneer Films (RKO); Technicolor, 35mm; running time: 83 minutes (1943 reissue, 67 minutes). Released 13 June 1935; reissued in 1943 as *Lady of Fortune*; restored at UCLA film archive and reissued in 1985. Cost: $400,000 (estimated).

Producers: Kenneth MacGowan and Robert Edmond Jones; **screenplay:** Francis Edwards Faragoh, from the play by Landon Mitchell and the novel *Vanity Fair* (1847–48) by William Makepeace Thackeray; **photography:** Ray Rennahan; **editor:** Archie Marshek; **production designer:** Robert Edmond Jones; **musical score:** Roy Webb; **choreographer:** Russell Lewis.

Cast: Miriam Hopkins (*Becky Sharp*); Frances Dee (*Amelia Sedley*); Cedric Hardwicke (*Marquis of Steyne*); Billy Burke (*Lady Bareacres*); Alison Skipworth (*Julia Crawley*); Nigel Bruce (*Joseph Sedley*); Alan Mowbray (*Rawdon Crawley*); G.P. Huntley, Jr. (*George Osborne*); May Beatty (*Briggs*); William Stack (*Pitt Crawley*); George Hassell (*Sir Pitt Crawley*); William Faversham (*Duke of Wellington*); Charles

Becky Sharp

Richman (*General Tufts*); Doris Lloyd (*Duchess of Richmond*); Colin Tapley (*William Dobbin*).

Awards: Best Picture (Rouben Mamoulian) and Best Color Film (Rouben Mamoulian and Ray Rennahan), Venice Film Festival, 1935.

Publications

Books:

Cook, David A., *A History of Narrative Film*, New York, 1996.

Spergel, Mark J, *Reinventing Reality: The Art and Life of Rouben Mamoulian*, Metuchen, New Jersey, 1993.

Articles:

Greene, Graham, ''Review of *Becky Sharp*; *Barcarole*; and *Public Hero No.1*,'' in *The Spectator* (London), 19 July 1935.

Mamoulian, Rouben, ''Some Problems in the Direction of Color Pictures,'' in *The International Photographer*, 1935; reprinted in Richard Koszarski, editor, *Hollywood Directors 1914–1940*, New York, 1976.

Mamoulian, Rouben, ''Controlling Color for Dramatic Effect,'' in *The American Cinematographer* (Los Angeles), June 1941; reprinted in Richard Koszarski, editor, *Hollywood Directors 1914–1940*, New York, 1976.

Gitt, Robert, and Richard Dayton, ''Restoring *Becky Sharp*,'' in *American Cinematographer* (Los Angeles), vol. 65, November 1984.

* * *

The novel *Vanity Fair* had been filmed twice before, in 1923 and 1932, when director Lowell Sherman began this adaptation for Pioneer Films. When Sherman died not long after filming began in late 1934, Rouben Mamoulian took over and all of Sherman's footage was rejected. In most respects the result is an uninteresting adaptation of Thackeray's novel based around a plodding screenplay and a cast of minor-league stars. Yet the film's place in movie history is assured despite its artistic weaknesses for it was the first feature-length film to be made in full (three-color) Technicolor.

Before *Becky Sharp*, three-color Technicolor had been used only for short films, notably by Disney in the animated *Flowers and Trees* (1932), and *The Three Little Pigs* (1933). Disney tried to tie Technicolor in to a three-year exclusive contract when it became clear that the process was commercially viable for animation, but the deal collapsed after only one year. As a result, Pioneer Films could use the process to make *La Cucaracha* (1934), the first full Technicolor live-action short, that was essentially an extended production test for the new process. The success of that project, which won an Oscar for Best Comedy Short Subject, led directly to the making of *Becky Sharp*. Despite the extra cost—which is estimated to have added thirty percent to the production costs of films in the 1930s—Technicolor's three-strip system and its later refinements dominated the movie industry until the 1950s.

Although the film is dramatically flawed, Mamoulian and cinematographer Ray Rennahan make good use of the three-color process, particularly in set pieces such as the stunning ball sequence. Mamoulian began his career working in theatre, and was aware of the possibilities for using colored lighting to signify changes in mood. For this reason he was uncertain about the suitability of *Vanity Fair* as a vehicle for color adaptation since the red uniforms of the British soldiers who play a large part in the story tended to appear too aggressive on the relatively crude new color system.

Yet despite Mamoulian's doubts, the housebound story of Becky Sharp's self-centred rise through elegant society is well chosen, since the new process needed more light than two-color systems, and was all but unusable outdoors in its early form. Reviewing the film for *The Spectator* magazine, Graham Greene thought the color in *Becky Sharp* ideal for the period setting, but wondered unkindly whether Technicolor would be able to pick out the subtleties of "the battered Buick . . . the suit worn too long, the oily hat." It is worth noting that in the late 1940s makers of low-budget film noirs returned to the cheaper black-and-white film stock to explore such grubby realities.

Although *Becky Sharp* was not a huge commercial success, it made enough money to convince others that the new system was viable despite its extra cost. Mamoulian's "wondrous adventure" of directing *Becky Sharp* in color was, he thought, as significant a step as the advent of synchronized sound. With other studios using the three-color system the technology improved rapidly. Four years later, Ray Rennahan became a Technicolor pioneer for the second time when he worked on *Gone With the Wind* with Ernest Haller and the pair won an Oscar for their cinematography. The 1939 film was the first to use Technicolor's new, faster film stock, which halved the required lighting levels. A comparison of the lighting and color definition in *Becky Sharp* and *Gone With the Wind* bears this out, making the technical achievement of the earlier film seem even more remarkable.

Because of its historical significance, *Becky Sharp* was restored by the UCLA film archives in 1984, and re-issued in three-color form in 1985. None of the original prints survives, and, as film historian David Cook points out, it is ironic that until the 1985 reissue this landmark of color cinema was available only as a two-color Cinecolor version and a heavily edited black-and-white print.

—Chris Routledge

BED AND SOFA

See **TRETIA MESHCHANSKAIA**

BEIQING CHENGSHI

See **City of Sadness**

BELLE DE JOUR

France-Italy, 1967

Director: Luis Buñuel

Production: Paris Film, Five Films (Rome); Eastmancolor; running time: 100 minutes. Released 1967.

Producers: Robert Hakim, Raymond Hakim; **production manager:** Henri Baum; **screenplay:** Luis Buñuel, Jean-Claude Carrière, based on the novel by Joseph Kessel; **assistant directors:** Pierre Lary, Jacques Fraenkel; **photography:** Sacha Vierny; **editor:** Walter Spohr; **sound:** Rene Longuet; **art director:** Robert Clavel.

Cast: Catherine Deneuve (*Séverine*); Jean Sorel (*Pierre*); Michel Piccoli (*Henri Husson*); Geneviève Page (*Mme. Anaïs*); Francisco Rabal (*Hyppolite*); Pierre Clémenti (*Marcel*); Georges Marchal (*The Duke*); Françoise Fabian (*Charlotte*); Maria Latour (*Mathilde*); Francis Blanche (*Monsieur Adolphe*); Macha Méril (*Renée*); Muni (*Pallas*); François Maistre (*The Professor*); Bernard Fresson (*Le Grêle*); Dominique Dandrieux (*Catherine*); Brigitte Parmentier (*Séverine as a Child*); Michel Charrel (*Footman*); D. de Roseville (*Coachman*); Iska Khan (*Asian Client*); Marcel Charvey (*Professor Henri*); Pierre Marcay (*Intern*); Adélaide Blasquez (*Maid*); Marc Eyraud (*Barman*); Bernard Musson (*Majordomo*).

Publications

Script:

Buñuel, Luis, and Jean-Claude Carrière, *Belle de jour*, London, 1971; also published in *Avant-Scène du Cinéma* (Paris), April 1978.

Books:

Durgnat, Raymond, *Luis Buñuel*, Berkeley, 1968; revised edition, 1977.
Buache, Freddy, *Luis Buñuel*, Lyons, 1970; as *The Cinema of Luis Buñuel*, New York and London, 1973.
Aranda, José Francisco, *Luis Buñuel: A Critical Biography*, London and New York, 1975.
Cesarman, Fernando, *El ojo de Buñuel*, Barcelona, 1976.
Mellen, Joan, editor, *The World of Luis Buñuel: Essays in Criticism*, New York, 1978.
Bazin, Andre, *The Cinema of Cruelty: From Buñuel to Hitchcock*, New York, 1982.

Belle de jour

Edwards, Gwynne, *The Discreet Art of Luis Buñuel: A Reading of His Films*, London, 1982.

Buñuel, Luis, *My Last Breath*, London and New York, 1983.

Rees, Margaret A., editor, *Luis Buñuel: A Symposium*, Leeds 1983.

Eberwein, Robert T., *Film and the Dream Screen: A Sleep and a Forgetting*, Princeton, New Jersey, 1984.

Lefèvre, Raymond, *Luis Buñuel*, Paris, 1984.

Vidal, Agustin Sanchez, *Luis Buñuel: Obra Cinematografica*, Madrid, 1984.

Aub, Max, *Conversaciones con Buñuel: Seguidas de 45 entrevistas con familiares, amigos y colaboradores del cineasta aragones*, Madrid 1985.

Bertelli, Pino, *Buñuel: L'arma dello scandalo: L'anarchia nel cinema di Luis Buñuel*, Turin 1985.

Oms, Marcel, *Don Luis Buñuel*, Paris 1985.

De la Colina, Jose, and Tomás Pérez Turrent, *Luis Buñuel: Prohibido asomarse al interior*, Mexico 1986.

Sandro, Paul, *Diversions of Pleasure: Luis Buñuel and the Crises of Desire*, Columbus, Ohio, 1987.

Williams, Linda, *Figures of Desire: A Theory and Analysis of Surrealist Film*, Berkeley, 1992.

Evans, Peter W., *The Films of Luis Buñuel: Subjectivity and Desire*, New York and Oxford, 1995.

Baxter, John, *Buñuel*, New York, 1999.

Articles:

Variety (New York), 19 April 1967.

Film Français (Paris), 9 June 1967.

Fieschi, Jean-André, ''La Fin ouverte,'' in *Cahiers du Cinéma* (Paris), June 1967.

Narboni, Jean, in *Cahiers du cinéma* (Paris), July 1967.

Seguin, Luis, in *Positif* (Paris), September 1967.

Stein, Elliot, ''Buñuel's Golden Bowl,'' in *Sight and Sound* (London), December 1967.

J.A.D. in *Monthly Film Bulletin* (London), December 1967.

Durgnat, Raymond, and Robin Wood, in *Movie* (London), no. 15, 1968.

D'Lugo, Marvin, ''Glances of Desire in *Belle de jour,*'' in *Film Criticism* (Meadville, Pennsylvania), Winter-Spring 1978.

Buñuel, Luis, ''*Dnevnaia Krasavitsa*,'' in *Iskusstvo Kino* (Moscow), no. 6, 1992.

Jousse, T., ''Buñuel face a ce qui se derobe,'' in *Cahiers du Cinéma* (Paris), February 1993.

Girard, Martin, ''*Belle de Jour*,'' in *Séquences* (Quebec), no. 180, September-October 1995.

Morris, Gary, ''*Belle de Jour*,'' in *Bright Lights* (San Francisco), no. 15, 1995.

''*Belle de Jour*,'' in *Castoro Cinema* (Firenze), no. 59, 1996.

* * *

In many ways *Belle de jour* is the perfect illustration of André Breton's famous dictum that ''everything leads us to believe that there exists a certain point of the spirit at which life and death, the real and the imaginary . . . cease to be perceived as opposites. It is vain to see in the Surrealists' activity any motive other than the location of that point.''

At first sight the film, based on a novel by Joseph Kessel, seems to be a relatively straightforward story about a young woman who indulges in masochistic day dreams and works, clandestinely, in a brothel. But, as the film progresses, the line between ''fantasy'' and ''reality'' becomes increasingly blurred. The young woman in question is Séverine, the beautiful but frigid wife of a young doctor Pierre. One of her regular fantasies involves Pierre punishing her by having her dragged from his carriage by his coachmen, who then bind, gag, whip, and rape her. Husson, one of their friends, mentions the name of a brothel run by Madame Anaïs, and Séverine, under the name Belle de Jour, goes to work there secretly every day. One of her clients, a young thug named Marcel, falls in love with her and tries to persuade her to leave the brothel. When she holds back he shoots her husband, and is himself killed by the police. Pierre is now paralysed and is looked after devotedly by Séverine. One day Husson tells him about his wife having worked in a brothel. The shock appears to kill him, then, all of a sudden, he rises from his chair, seemingly miraculously cured.

Thus at the very end of the film, just as the audience are congratulating themselves on having neatly sorted out ''fantasy'' from ''reality'' throughout the course of the narrative, Buñuel throws the whole distinction into sudden confusion by presenting what seems like a wish-fulfilment in the most straightforwardly naturalistic manner. The director's method here looks back to *The Exterminating Angel* (where extraordinary, absurd events are depicted as if they were the most normal things imaginable) and forward to *The Milky Way, The Discreet Charm of the Bourgeoisie, The Phantom of Liberty*, and *That Obscure Object of Desire*, whose less conventional, more episodic narrative structures enable Buñuel to explore his surrealist vision to the full. Indeed, Buñel's remark that these last films all evoke ''the essential mystery in all things'' and ''the search for truth, as well as the necessity of abandoning it as soon as you've found it'' serves as a suitable warning to all those who would seek to produce any kind of definitive reading of *Belle de jour.* Indeed, the whole film exists in the image of the little box that an Oriental client brings with him to the brothel. When opened, this emits a strange, high-pitched buzzing sound and greatly disturbs all of the girls—except Séverine, who is fascinated by it. The camera never reveals what ''it'' is, and, according to his autobiography, Buñuel was constantly asked by people what was in the box: his answer was always ''whatever you want there to be.'' It's worth noting, incidentally, that the original novel, which Buñuel describes as ''very melodramatic, but well constructed,'' does observe the usual literary distinctions between ''outer'' and ''inner'' events, and that the English subtitled version of the film (un)helpfully italicises the dialogue in the scenes which someone has decreed are to be read as dreams or fantasies!

Belle de jour was Buñuel's most sustained treatment of another favourite theme—that of fetishism. This had already raised its head in *El* and *The Diary of a Chambermaid*, but Séverine's clients represent a veritable cornucopia of fetishism, including a gynaecologist who plays at being a valet, and a Count who enjoys masturbating under a coffin in which Séverine (whom he calls his daughter) is lying. Apparently Buñuel wanted this scene to take place after a celebration of Mass, but censorship problems intervened—not for the first time in Buñuel's anarchic oeuvre.

—Julian Petley

LA BELLE ET LA BÊTE

(Beauty and the Beast)

France, 1946

Director: Jean Cocteau

Production: Black and white, 35mm; running time: 96 minutes (90 minutes according to some sources). Released 29 October 1946, Paris. Filmed in Saint-Maurice studios; exteriors shot at Rochecorbon in Touraine.

La Belle et la bête

Producer: André Paulvé; **screenplay:** Jean Cocteau, from the fairy tale of Jean Marie Leprince de Beaumont; **photography:** Henri Alekan; **editor:** Claude Iberia; **sound engineer:** Jean Lebreton; **sound effects:** Rouzenat; **production designers:** René Moulaert and Lucien Carré; **art director:** Roger Desormière; **costume designer:** Christian Bérard, executed by Escoffier and Castillo from the House of Paquin; **technical assistant to Cocteau:** René Clément.

Cast: Jean Marais (*The Beast* and *The Prince*); Josette Day (*Beauty*); Marcel André (*The Father*); Mila Parély (*Félicie*); Nane Germon (*Adélaïde*); Michel Auclair (*Ludovic*); Raoul Marco (*The Usurer*); Gilles Watteaux and Noel Blin.

Publications

Script:

Jean Cocteau: 3 Screenplays (The Eternal Return, Beauty and the Beast and *Orpheus*), New York, 1972.
Cocteau, Jean, ''*La Belle et la bete,*'' in *Avant-Scène du Cinéma* (Paris) July-September 1973.

Books:

Cocteau, Jean, *La Belle et la bête: Journal d'un film*, Paris, 1946; as *Diary of a Film*, New York, 1950.
Crosland, Margaret, *Jean Cocteau*, London, 1956.
Kihm, Jean-Jacques, *Cocteau*, Paris, 1956.
Pillaudin, Roger, *Jean Cocteau tourne son dernier film*, Paris, 1960.
Fraigneau, André, *Cocteau*, New York, 1961.
Fowlie, Wallace, *Jean Cocteau: The History of a Poet's Age*, Bloomington, Indiana, 1968.
Sprigge, Elizabeth, and Jean-Jacques Kihm, *Jean Cocteau: The Man and the Mirror*, New York, 1968.
Lannes, Roger, *Jean Cocteau*, Paris, 1968.
Gilson, René, *Cocteau*, New York, 1969.
Cocteau, Jean, *Professional Secrets: An Autobiography*, edited by Robert Phelps, New York, 1970.
Steegmuller, Francis, *Cocteau*, Boston, 1970.
Knapp, Bettina, *Cocteau*, New York, 1970.
Anderson, Alexandra and Carol Saltus, editors, *Jean Cocteau and the French Scene*, New York, 1984.
de Miomandre, Philippe, *Moi, Jean Cocteau*, Paris, 1985.
Keller, Marjorie, *The Untutored Eye: Childhood in the Films of Cocteau, Cornell, and Brakhage*, Cranbury, New Jersey, 1986.
Peters, Arthur King, *Jean Cocteau and his World: An Illustrated Biography*, London, 1987.

Articles:

Bazin, André, in *Le Parisien Liberé*, 11 January, 1946.
Variety (New York), 24 December 1947.
Image et Son (Paris), June-July 1972.
''*La Belle et la bête:* La critique,'' in *Avant-Scène du Cinéma* (Paris), July-September 1973.
American Image (Detroit), no. 2, 1976.
Bonnet, J. C., in *Cinématographe* (Paris), April-May 1976.
Wilson Jr., R. A., in *Audience* (Hollywood), November 1976.
Gow, Gordon, ''Astonishment: Magic Films from Jean Cocteau,'' in *Films and Filming* (London), January, 1978.
Popkin, M., ''Cocteau's *Beaty and the Beast:* The Poet as Monster,'' in *Literature/Film Quarterly* (Salisbury, Maryland), vol. 10, no. 2, 1982.
Galef, D., ''A Sense of Magic: Reality and Illusion in Cocteau's *Beauty and the Beast,*'' in *Literature/Film Quarterly* (Salisbury, Maryland), April 1984.
Smith, Malcolm, in *Starburst* (London), November 1985.
Garofalo, M., ''Once Upon a Time. . . ,'' in *Segnocinema* (Vincenza, Italy), May-June 1992.
Mousselard, Oliver-Pascal, ''Le bête et sa belle changent d'air,'' in *Télérama*, no. 2353, 15 February 1995.
Erb, C., ''Another World or the World of an Other?: The Space of Romance in Recent Versions of *Beauty and the Beast*,'' in *Cinema Journal* (Austin, Texas), vol. 34, no. 4, 1995.
Lansing Smith, Evans, ''Framing the Underworld: Threshold Imagery in Murnau, Cocteau, and Bergman,'' in *Literature/Film Quarterly* (Salisbury, Maryland), vol. 24, no. 3, 1996.
Turner, George, ''Once Upon a Time There Was *Beauty and the Beast*,'' in *American Cinematographer* (Hollywood), vol. 78, no. 9, September 1997.
Greene, N., ''Jean Cocteau: A Cinema of Baroque Unease,'' and A.S. Levitt, ''The Cinematic Magic of Jean Cocteau,'' in *Bucknell Review*, vol. 41, no. 1, 1997.

* * *

La Belle et la bête, the film which marked Jean Cocteau's return to directing after an interval of 15 years, is a work which continues the vein of fantasy which had characterised his scriptwriting during the wartime years. To this extent the film is typical of its period, for the early postwar years in France saw a basic continuity with approaches established during the Vichy period (there was no resurgence of realism in France to compare with the emergence of neorealism in Italy). But in all other ways the appropriation of a fairy tale to the filmmaker's own personal mythology is a totally individual work.

The film is based on the tale as told by Madame Leprince de Beaumont, but there is little evidence in Cocteau's approach of the childlike innocence which the director demands of his audience in his brief introduction to the film. Visually, the film is one of Cocteau's most sophisticated works. The costumes designed by Christian Bérard and the lighting and framing devised by Henri Alekan are decorative rather than functional and take their inspiration from classic Dutch painting, particularly the work of Vermeer. Despite the presence of René Clément as technical supervisor, the film shows none of the reliance on complexity of scripting and use of heavy irony so characteristic of French cinema in the late 1940s. The legend is handled in a dazzingly eclectic style. The home life of Belle's family is parodied and often broadly farcial in tone, as, for instance, in the use of cackling ducks to comment on the attitudes of her sisters. By contrast, the departure of Belle for the Beast's castle and her entry there are totally stylised, with Cocteau employing slow motion photography to obtain a dreamlike effect.

La Belle et la bête is an excellent example of Cocteau's continual concern in his film work to provide a ''realism of the unreal.'' The fairytale world of Beast's castle is given great solidity, and indeed it is arguable that the setting has been given too much weight, with the result that there is a degree of ponderousness about the film which Georges Auric's music serves only to emphasise. In evoking the magical qualities of the castle, Cocteau has made surprisingly little use of the film's trick shot potentialities which form so crucial a part of so many of his other works. Here the living faces of the statuary and the disembodied human arms that act as Beast's servants are essentially theatrical devices.

One of the great difficulties facing Cocteau was that of sustaining interest for 90 minutes in the oversimplified and largely unpersonalised characters of his source material. The solution found for the minor characters is caricature and humour. For the Beast, Cocteau and Bérard use the make-up of Jean Marais to emphasise his bestial nature, a strategy which is particularly effective in such scenes as those in which he drinks or scents game. Belle is by comparison a fairly dull figure, despite Josette Day's beauty, but the ambiguities of her attitude toward the Beast do add interest and complexity to the character. The double use of Jean Marais as both the Beast and Belle's dissolute lover avoids the danger of too easy an explanation of the film's symbolism, and the transformation into a princely figure at the end shows a characteristically lyrical approach to death on the filmmaker's part. Particularly when seen in conjunction with the intimate diary of the shooting which Cocteau published in 1946 to coincide with the release of the film, *La Belle et la bête* provides an excellent introduction to the work of one of the screen's subtlest and most evocative poets.

—Roy Armes

BERLIN: DIE SINFONIE DER GROSSSTADT

(Berlin: Symphony of a City)

Germany, 1927

Director: Walter Ruttmann

Production: Fox-Europa-Film; black and white, 35mm; running time: 53 minutes; length: 1440 meters. Released September 1927. Filmed in Berlin.

Producer: Karl Freund; **screenplay:** Karl Freund and Walter Ruttmann, from an idea by Carl Meyer; **photography:** Reimar Kuntze, Robert Babereske, and Laszlo Schaffer; **editor:** Walter Ruttmann; **sets:** Erich Kettelhut; **music:** Edmund Meisel.

Publications

Books:

Rotha, Paul, *The Film Till Now*, London, 1930.

Balázs, Báela, *Der Geist des Films*, Halle, 1930.

Rotha, Paul, *Documentary Film*, London, 1936.

Arnheim, Rudolph, *Film as Art*, Berkeley, 1957.

Barsam, Richard, *Non-fiction Film: A Critical History*, New York, 1973.

Barnouw, Erik, *Documentary: A History of the Non-Fiction Film*, New York, 1974.

Kracauer, Siegfried, *A Psychological History of the German Film*, Princeton, 1974.

Sussex, Elizbeth, *The Rise and Fall of the British Documentary*, Berkeley, 1975.

Le Grice, Malcolm, *Abstract Film and Beyond*, Cambridge, Massachusetts, 1977.

Film as Film: Formal Experiment in Film 1910–1975, London, 1979.

Walter Ruttmann: Cinema, pittura, ars acustica, Trento, Italy, 1994.

Articles:

Ruttmann, Walter, ''Wie ich meinen *Berlin*—Film drehte,'' in *Lichtbild-Bühne*, no. 241, 1927.

Ruttmann, Walter, in *Illustreirter Film-Kurier*, no. 658, 1927.

Hirsch, Leo, in *Berliner Tageblatt*, 24 September 1927.

Friedlander, Paul, ''*Berlin—die Symphonie der Grossstadt,*'' in *Die Rote Fahne*, 25 September 1927.

Kahn, Henry, in *Die Weltbühne*, 4 October 1927.

Pinthus, Kurt, in *Tagebuch*, 8 October 1927.

Blakeston, Oswell, ''Interview with Carl (Karl) Freund,'' in *Close-Up* (London), January 1929.

Potamkin, Harry Alan, ''The Rise and Fall of the German Film,'' in *Cinema* (New York), April 1930.

Rotha, Paul, ''It's in the Script,'' in *World Film News* (London), September 1938.

Evans, Wick, ''Karl Freund, Candid Cinematographer,'' in *Popular Photography* (Chicago), February 1939.

Falkenberg, Paul, ''Sound Montage: A Propos de Ruttmann,'' in *Film Culture* (New York), no. 22–23, 1961.

Cowie, Peter, in *Films and Filming* (London), August 1961.

Kolaja, J., and A. W. Foster, ''*Berlin: The Symphony of a City* as a Theme of Visual Rhythm,'' in *Journal of Aesthetics and Art Criticism* (Cleveland), Spring 1965.

Kracauer, Siegfried, ''Film 1928,'' in *Das Ornament der Masse*, Frankfurt, 1974.

Chapman, Jay, ''Two Aspects of the City: Cavalcanti and Ruttmann,'' in *The Documentary Tradition*, edited by Lewis Jacobs, 2nd edition, New York, 1979.

Pulleine, Tim, in *Monthly Film Bulletin* (London), June 1979.

''Walter Ruttmann,'' in *Travelling* (Lausanne), Summer 1979.

Nieuwstadt, M. V., ''Filmliga herdrukt 1927–1931,'' in *Skrien* (Amsterdam), Winter 1982–83.

Bernstein, Matthew, ''Visual Style and Spatial Articulation in *Berlin: Symphony of a City,*'' in *Journal of Film and Video* (River Forest, Illinois), Autumn 1984.

Brandt, H.J., ''Walter Ruttmann: Von Expressionismus zum Faschismus,'' in *Filmfaust* (Frankfurt), October-November 1985.

Kvist, P., ''*Berlin, En storbysynfoni:* et forsok pa a fange det moderne,'' in *Z Filmtidsskrift* (Oslo), no. 2, 1991.

* * *

Underlying the totality of Walter Ruttmann's work in *Berlin: Die Sinfonie der Grossstadt* was the aesthetic predicated on the wish to kineticize abstract forms as well as a concern for movement, rhythm, and alluring surface appearances. Originally embodied in a series of innovative animated abstract films *Opus I-IV*, Ruttmann's eminently permutable aesthetic enabled him to emerge as one of the exemplars of the so-called New Objectivity in film during the middle years of the Weimar Republic. In *Berlin*, a rhapsodic, quasi-documentary record of a day in the life of Germany's capital, Ruttmann's fetishization of the rhythmic and visual as ends in themselves, fused with the cult of technology and urban modernity that characterized the New Objectivity, took on the aspects of an omniverous cinematic hubris seeking gratification by the manipulation of what Ruttmann termed the ''living material'' of a metropolis and the ''absolute, purely filmic visual motifs'' it yielded.

Berlin, then, is the film's true protagonist, a vibrant, pulsating, yet organic totality whose every component—animate or inanimate—is mediated and defined by the periodicity of the whole. The film portrays a day in the life of the city, beginning with panoramic shots of the sleeping metropolis as dawn breaks and concluding with a late-night fireworks display. Compressed between these diurnal poles is a brilliantly edited optical phantasmagoria of life in Berlin. The virtuosity with which cinematic tools are employed to stress certain leitmotifs—for example, the abstract beauty of modern technology—masterfully complements the film's structure, which replicates that of a symphony inasmuch as the alleged rhythms and oscillations of urban activity are organized into a series of movements. Yet consonant with Ruttman's aesthetic, within this rhythmic whole certain icons of modernity are isolated, abstracted, and transformed into purely ornamental images devoid of content and context. The recurring shots of machines, industrial facilities, and the facades of buildings, ripped out of any discernible context and deprived of any function save that of ornamentation, are typical leitmotifs in the film. Now luminous, now in shadow, now static, now in energetic but purposeless motion, they have been ruthlessly pressed into the service of Ruttmann's unrestrained formalism and thus stripped of all independent integrity and meaning.

This fetishism is accompanied by a contempt for human autonomy and subjectivity. Berlin's human inhabitants are placed on the same existential plane as its industrial and technological icons and the traffic that repeatedly criss-crosses the screen. Soulless ornaments, the people are but another source of optical titillation. Such a dehumanizing approach accounts for the gratuitous juxtaposition of shots of chattering monkeys and people conversing on the telephone, of department store mannequins or bobbing mechanical dolls with the anonymous inhabitants of the city, of the legs of workers with those of cattle being herded into a courtyard. Far from representing any rational critique of the contradictions that inhere in and have produced this particular manifestation of urban modernity, such juxtapositions are integrated into a visual rhapsody that, though brilliant in a narrow technical sense, emanates from an obsessive interest in the richness of forms and rhythm yielded by the city. Ruttmann's view of modern life is as a purely aesthetic phenomenon, constituting abstract raw material for the filmmaker and entertaining optical cuisine for the public. This view represents not a denunciation of reificiation and dehumanization but their apotheosis.

Hailed upon its release as a revolutionary work of art, one that ''flays our retinas, our nerves, our consciousness,'' *Berlin* is still venerated by film historians for its brilliant editing and imaginative structure. However, in the 1920s some perceptive critics, including Siegfried Kracauer and Paul Friedländer, lambasted its failure to establish any meaningful connections among the phenomena it portrayed. Such censure was well-founded, for *Berlin* reduced urban modernity to the spurious common denominators of dynamism, rhythm, and an aestheticized, reified technology, all of which were enveloped in a vacuous display of optical pyrotechnics. Indeed, these ideas and attitudes came to full fruition within the embrace of National Socialism. Ruttmann's world of abstract forms and stylized technology was fully integrated into the National Socialist public sphere and thereby into the latter's consummation: the mythologization and heroicization of imperialism and barbarism. Thus *Berlin*, far from being simply another ''great film,'' must also be regarded as a precursor of a genre in which Ruttmann himself later specialized—the Nazi documentary film.

—Barry Fulks

THE BEST YEARS OF OUR LIVES

USA, 1946

Director: William Wyler

Production: Goldwyn Productions; black and white, 35mm; running time: 172 minutes. Released 1946. Filmed in RKO studios.

Producer: Samuel Goldwyn; **screenplay:** Robert Sherwood, from the novel *Glory for Me* by MacKinley Kantor; **photography:** Gregg Toland; **editor:** Daniel Mandell; **sound recordist:** Gordon Sawyer; **art direction:** George Jenkins with Perry Ferguson; **music:** Hugo Friedhofer.

Cast: Myrna Loy (*Milly Stephenson*); Fredric March (*Al Stephenson*); Dana Andrews (*Fred Derry*); Teresa Wright (*Peggy Stephenson*); Virginia Mayo (*Marie Derry*); Cathy O'Donnel (*Wilma Cameron*); Harold Russell (*Homer Parrish*); Hoagy Carmichael (*Butch Engle*).

Awards: Oscars for Best Picture, Best Direction, Best Actor (March), Best Supporting Actor (Russell), Best Screenplay, Best Editing, Best Music, and a Special Award to Harold Russell for ''bringing hope and courage to his fellow veterans,'' 1946; New York Film Critics Awards for Best Motion Picture and Best Direction, 1946.

Publications

Books:

Reisz, Karel, editor, *William Wyler: An Index*, London, 1958.

Warshow, Robert, *The Immediate Experience: Movies, Comics, Theater, and Other Aspects of Popular Culture*, New York, 1962.

Kantor, Bernar, and Irwin Blacker, editors, *Director at Work*, New York, 1970.

Quirk, Lawrence, J., *The Films of Fredric March*, New York, 1971.

Marsden, Axel, *William Wyler*, New York, 1973.

Marill, Alvin, H., *Samuel Goldwyn Presents*, South Brunswick, New Jersey, 1976.

Koszarski, Richard, *Hollywood Directors 1941–1976*, New York, 1977.

Tuska, John, editor, *Close-up: The Hollywood Director*, Metuchen, New Jersey, 1978.

Anderegg, Michael, A., *William Wyler*, Boston, 1979.

O'Connor, John E., and Martin A. Jackson, editors, *American History/American Film: Interpreting the Hollywood Image*, New York, 1979.

Epstein, Lawrence, J., *Samuel Goldwyn*, Boston, 1981.

Kern, Sharon, *William Wyler: A Guide to References and Resources*, Boston, 1984.

The Best Years of Our Lives

Bowman, Barbara, *Master Space: Film Images of Capra, Lubitsch, Sternberg, and Wyler*, Wesport, Connecticut, 1992.

Herman, Jan, *A Talent for Trouble: The Life of Hollywood's Most Acclaimed Director*, New York, 1996.

Articles:

New York Times, 17 November 1946.

Rich Isaacs, Hermine, "William Wyler: Director with a Passion and a Craft," in *Theater Arts* (New York), February 1947.

Polonsky, Abraham, in *Hollywood Quarterly*, April 1947.

Warshow, Robert, "The Anatomy of a Falsehood," in *Partisan Review* (New Brunswick, New Jersey), May-June 1947.

Koenig, Lester, "Gregg Toland, Film-Maker," in *Screen Writer* (London), December 1947.

Lyon, Peter, "The Hollywood Picture," in *Hollywood Quarterly*, Summer 1948-Summer 1949.

Griffith, Richard, "Wyler, Wellman, and Huston," in *Films in Review* (New York), February 1950.

Reisz, Karel, "The Later Films of William Wyler," in *Sequence* (London), no. 13, 1951.

Tozzi, Romano, "Fredric March," in *Films in Review* (New York), December 1958.

Reid, John Howard, "A Little Larger Than Life," in *Films and Filming* (London), February 1960.

"A Comparison of Size," in *Films and Filming* (London), March 1960.

Ringgold, Gene, "Myrna Loy," in *Films in Review* (New York), February 1963.

Sarris, Andrew, in *Village Voice* (New York), 15 July 1965.

Doeckel, Ken, "William Wyler," in *Films in Review* (New York), October 1971.

Higham, Charles, interview with Wyler in *Action* (Los Angeles), September-October 1973.

"Dialogue on Film," in *American Film* (Washington, D.C.), April 1976.

Swindell, Larry, "A Life in Film," in *American Film* (Washington, D.C.), April 1976.

Cook, P., "The Sound Track," in *Films in Review* (New York), May 1979.

Cohen, Joan, in *Magill's Survey of Cinema 1*, Englewood Cliffs, New Jersey, 1980.

Chell, S. L., "Music and Emotion in the Classic Hollywood Film," in *Film Criticism* (Meadville, Pennsylvania), Winter 1984.

Reid's Film Index (New South Wales, Australia), no. 4, 1990, and no. 19, 1996.
Gerber, D.A., ''Heroes and Misfits: The Troubled Social Reintegration of Disabled Veterans in *The Best Years of Our Lives,*'' in *American Quarterly* (Baltimore, Maryland), vol. 45, no. 4, 1994.
Toles, George, ''This May Hurt a Little: The Art of Humiliation in Film,'' in *Film Quarterly* (Berkeley), Summer 1995.

* * *

Acclaimed by critics and audiences at its release and awarded eight Academy Awards, *The Best Years of Our Lives* is imbued with the personal commitment that director William Wyler brought to his first project after his experience of shooting two documentaries for the U.S. Army Air Corps during World War II. Wyler was as much of a returning serviceman as are the heroes of this film. His problems in reintegrating himself into the community were perhaps not the same as those of Homer, the amputee, Fred, the captain who can only find work as a soda jerk and Al, the banker who confuses idealism and collateral, but the director's identification with their predicaments cannot be doubted. It is expressed in the film's unconventional structure and tone.

The film is, of course, about homecoming, and emphatically so when we realize that nearly one-third of its considerable length is exclusively devoted to that subject. The unfolding of the narrative, a slim narrative, is deferred until the film has thoroughly spatialized the notion of the return. In his pre-war films, Wyler's meticulous *mise-en-scène* served psychological portraiture in the context of melodrama. In *Best Years*, what we conventionally identify as theatrical tension is replaced by the nearly plotless placement of characters in locale and in relationship to each other. Wyler's stagings make dramatic events of the performers' positions in the frame. The three male protagonists, distinct from each other in class, backgrounds, age, and profession, are emblematized as an entity in the way their faces fit together in a bombardier's bay, during their journey back to Boone City. A taxi, with its windows and rear view mirror, provides a series of variations on their unity and singularity as it deposits them at their respective homes. Homer is caught in significant isolation, standing before his front porch, between the clear eyes of his buddies and the pitying ones of his family and sweetheart. When he waves goodbye with his prosthetic hook he *places* everyone in this less than triumphant homecoming. Al's reception, in one of the film's most famous shots (in a film full of famous shots), is a happier one. He embraces his wife Milly in a hallway whose length is a function of narrative time and camera placement rather than physical dimension.

One of the elements for which the film is distinguished is the use of quite limited spatial contexts—the bedrooms, living rooms, and kitchens of the middle class. Wyler's blockings and the deep-focus photography of Gregg Toland, then, transcend the modest areas of middle-American domesticity, without betraying or distorting their shape, finding in them the coordinates that express this drama of placement. The emotional peak of the embrace of Al and Milly is followed by Al's nervousness at being a civilian and a husband. Milly sits comfortably in a wing chair, at place in the frame; Al shifts nervously from one side of the frame to the other. His homecoming, as well as that of Fred and Homer, is incomplete. It will require the duration of the whole film to achieve something like a narrative homecoming. And even that is ambiguous in this film that so disrupts the conventions of Hollywood storytelling.

The story that is told is charted in the distances our eyes traverse in the frame. Here, as in other examples of screen narrative that exploit staging in deep fields, we are required to make sense out of what is apparently a fully constituted frame, without the distraction of frequent inter-cutting. This access to the wholeness of the cinematic image is what prompted André Bazin to consider *Best Years* a model of his realist aesthetic. Bazin pays particular attention to the scene where the foreground is occupied by Homer, playing the piano with his hooks, while in the background Fred is phoning Al's daughter to break off their relationship. The mediating figure in the frame is Al, presumably looking at Homer, yet just as much aware of what is going on behind his back. We see and understand all the elements simultaneously, just as we do at the film's end, at the wedding of Homer and Wilma in one side of the frame, and the reconciliation of Fred and Peggy in the other.

The Best Years of Our Lives represents the kind of production for which Samuel Goldwyn was renowned. No expense or effort was spared; the lighting of the cramped playing spaces required enormously complicated procedures to create the deep-focus effects. Hugo Friedhofer's score is one of the most admired in the history of film music. A star actress, Myrna Loy, played Milly, essentially a supporting role. The embodiment of one kind of American wife in the ''Thin Man'' series, she is just as well remembered for the variation she brings to the type in *Best Years.* Fredric March won his second Academy Award (the first 15 years previously in *Dr. Jekyll and Mr. Hyde*) for his portrayal of Al. Harold Russell, the non-professional chosen to play Homer, gives a performance that is as much a function of the director's ability to place him in the frame and preserve his simplicity as it is a creation of the ''actor.''

While it is impossible to ignore the non-professional status of Harold Russell or to ignore the way the fiction addresses an important social problem in 1946 America, it is equally impossible to ignore the film's formal and perceptual challenges. With almost mannerist insistence, Wyler reminds us that the screen is an *image* of depth, not the real thing. He tests that quality of the image in the long and short of the fiction's expressive physical contexts—an ex-flier (Fred) wandering through a graveyard of planes slated for demolition, an amputee finally embracing his sweetheart with the stumps of his arms, a gigantic drug store that seems to sum up the crassness of postwar America, a neighborhood bar that collects the feelings of a film unsure about our ''best years.''

—Charles Affron

LA BÊTE HUMAINE

(Judas Was a Woman; The Human Beast)

France, 1938

Director: Jean Renoir

Production: Paris Film Productions; black and white; RCA High Fidelity; running time: 88 minutes; length: 7937 feet. Released 23 December 1938. Filmed at Pathé Cinema Studios (Joinville) and on location at Le Havre. Theme song: ''Valse Ninon.''

La Bête humaine

Producers: Robert Hakim and Raymond Hakim; **screenplay:** Jean Renoir, from the novel by Emile Zola; **assistant directors:** Claude Renoir, Suzanne de Troyes; **photography:** Curt Courant; **editor:** Marguerite Renoir; **sound:** Teysseire; **art director:** Eugene Lourie; **music:** Joseph Kosma.

Cast: Jean Gabin (*Jacques Lantier*); Simone Simon (*Séverine*); Fernand Ledoux (*Roubaud*); Julien Carette (*Pecqueux*); Blanchette Brunoy (*Flore*); Gerard Landry (*Lauvergne*); Berlioz (*Grand Morin*); Jean Renoir (*Cabuche*).

Publications

Books:

Davay, Paul, *Jean Renoir*, Brussels, 1957.
Cauliez, Armand-Jean, *Jean Renoir*, Paris, 1962.
Chardère, Bernard, editor, *Jean Renoir*, in *Premier Plan* (Lyon), no. 22–24, May 1962.
Institut des Hautes Etudes Cinematographiques, *Analyses des films de Jean Renoir*, Paris, 1964.
Bennett, Susan, *Jean Renoir*, London, 1967.
Poulle, François, *Renoir 1938; ou, Jean Renoir pour rien: Enquête sur un cinéaste*, Paris, 1969.
Leprohon, Pierre, *Jean Renoir*, New York, 1971.
Braudy, Leo, *Jean Renoir: The World of His Films*, New York, 1972.
Bazin, André, *Jean Renoir*, edited by François Truffaut, Paris, 1973.
Durgnat, Raymond, *Jean Renoir*, Berkeley, 1974.
Beylie, Claude, *Jean Renoir: Le Spectacle, la vie*, Paris, 1975.
Renoir, Jean, *Essays, Conversations, Reviews*, edited by Penelope Gilliatt, New York, 1975.
Armes, Roy, *French Cinema Since 1946: Volume 1: The Great Tradition*, New York, 1976.
Faulkner, Christopher, *Jean Renoir: A Guide to References and Resources*, Boston, 1979.
Sesonske, Alexander, *Jean Renoir: The French Films 1924–1939*, Cambridge, Massachusetts, 1980.
Gauteur, Claude, *Jean Renoir: Oeuvres de cinéma inédites*, Paris, 1981.
McBride, Joseph, editor, *Filmmakers on Filmmaking 2*, Los Angeles, 1983.

Serceau, Daniel, *Jean Renoir*, Paris, 1985.
Bertin, Celia, *Jean Renoir*, Paris, 1986.
Faulkner, Christopher, *The Social Cinema of Jean Renoir*, Princeton, 1986.
Vincendeau, Ginette, and Keith Reader, *La Vie est à Nous: French Cinema of the Popular Front*, London, 1986.
Viry-Babel, Roger, *Jean Renoir: Le Jeu et la regle*, Paris, 1986.
Bessy, Maurice, *Jean Renoir*, Paris, 1989.
Braudy, Leo, *Jean Renoir: The World of His Films*, New York, 1989.
Bergan, Ronald, *Jean Renoir: Projections of Paradise*, Woodstock, 1994.

Articles:

Variety (New York), 15 February 1939.
New York Times, 26 February 1939.
Kine Weekly (London), 20 April 1939.
Galway, Peter, in *New Statesman* (London), 29 April 1939.
Monthly Film Bulletin (London), May 1939.
Greene, Graham, in *Spectator* (London), 5 May 1939.
Time and Tide (London), 13 April 1946.
''Renoir Issue'' of *Cahiers du Cinéma* (Paris), January 1952.
''Renoir Issue'' of *Cahiers du Cinéma* (Paris), Christmas 1957.
Whitehall, Richard, ''Painting Life with Movement,'' in *Films and Filming* (London), July 1960.
Whitehall, Richard, ''The Screen Is His Canvas,'' in *Films and Filming* (London), July 1960.
Harcourt, Peter, ''*Jean Renoir*,'' in *London Magazine*, December 1962.
Films and Filming (London), February 1964.
Colet, Jean, in *Télérama* (Paris), 28 May 1968.
Image et Son (Paris), no. 223, 1968.
Fofi, Goffredo, ''The Cinema of the Popular Front in France,'' in *Screen* (London), Winter 1972–73.
Interview with Renoir, in *Positif* (Paris), September 1975.
Renoir, Jean, in *Image et Son* (Paris), March 1977.
Strebel, Elizabeth Grottle, ''Jean Renoir and the Popular Front,'' in *Feature Films as History*, edited by K. R. M. Short, London, 1981.
Leahy, J., in *Monthly Film Bulletin* (London), vol. 58, April 1991.
Vincendeau, G., ''The Beauty of the Beast,'' in *Sight and Sound* (London), July 1991.
Tesson, Charles, in *Cahiers du Cinéma* (Paris), no. 482, July-August 1994.
Aldarondo, R., in *Nosferatu* (San Sebastian), no. 17/18, March 1995.
Short review, in *Télérama* (Paris), no. 2364, 3 May 1995.
Faulkner, Christopher, ''Renoir, Technology and the Affect in *La bête humaine*,'' in *Persistence of Vision* (Maspeth), no. 12–13, 1996.

* * *

After the commercial failure of his politically committed film *La Marseillaise* (1937), Renoir accepted Robert Hakim's invitation to ''make a film about trains'' for Jean Gabin. Disappointed at the collapse of Grémillon's film project *Train d'enfer*, Gabin looked to Renoir who had so successfully directed him in the role of Maréchal in *La Grande Illusion* (1937). For Renoir a screen version of Zola's *La Bête humaine* represented another opportunity to adapt a greatly admired author whose fiction had previously inspired his silent film *Nana* (1926).

Reflecting the bleak tone of Zola's portrayal of a man driven by homicidal impulses, Renoir's film is untypically dark and fatalistic for his 1930s period, and with Gabin as the doomed hero, his version has considerable affinity with the deeply pessimistic contemporary Carné-Prévert films such as *Quai des Brumes* (1938) or *Le Jour se lève* (1939). The uncharacteristic mood is largely determined by low-key lighting, and, equally untypically for Renoir, music which is external to the action. His camera too, is noticeably more mobile as it constantly relates individuals to their working environment. Bright daytime locations progressively give way to dark, nocturnal interiors or shadowy industrial landscapes, as the freedom of the fated protagonists gradually diminishes.

Although fidelity to Zola is implied by a quotation from the novel and a signed portrait of the author after the credit sequence, there are several omissions or shifts of emphasis in Renoir's screen adaptation. Whereas Zola's richly textured epic novel is partly a study of atavism, partly a portrait of the railway community, it is also a satire of the judiciary and an indictment of the corrupt Second Empire. The author's multi-layered poetic narrative explores the murderous instinct thematically through a number of minor characters and situations, but Renoir concerns himself only with the protagonists, discarding several narrative elements, such as the train crash, the train trapped by snow, and the sustained satire of the judicary with its overt political dimension. For a director intimately associated with the Popular Front, Renoir surprisingly resists the political potential, and plays down Zola's social contrasts. If in *La Marseillaise* he had explored ideas, in *La Bête humaine*, Renoir is more concerned with mood and action. For André Bazin, Renoir's adaptation provided a tighter plot and was more successful in integrating the triangular relationship between Séverine, Lantier, and Roubaud into an account of railway life.

Casting against type Renoir insisted on Simone Simon for the role of the flirtatious but frigid Séverine to play against Gabin's Lantier. Excellent performances come from Julien Carette as the stoker Pecqueux and from Fernand Ledoux as the once jealous, now broken, Roubaud. In only his second screen role, a rather melodramatic Renoir plays the poacher Cabuche wrongly accused of murder.

The sense of compulsion which permeates the film is established in the opening train sequence. The journey from Paris to Le Havre, as Alexander Sesonske has shown, is brilliantly distilled in four and a quarter minutes. Speed is conveyed not so much by cutting between shots as by the rhythm of movement within the shots. From the close-up of the train's roaring fire-box, suggesting the passionate forces at work, the camera records the train hurtling through the countryside, set on a track from which it must not deviate, with Lantier and Pecqueux working in complete harmony to harness the machine's formidable power, and to ensure punctuality. The closing sequence of the film, a return run of the journey with the men now fighting, expresses the idea of men unable to break free of predetermined patterns.

The images of the men working, the informative shots of the station yards, the ubiquitous sound of trains keep the presence of the railway to the fore, thus respecting Zola's documentary intentions. Character is intimately studied in terms of a working environment, whether on the train, in the yards, in the canteen, in the showers or at the lodgings. It is in these sequences with railway men functioning as a team and taking pride in their work that Renoir remains faithful to the values of the Popular Front. Throughout he enjoyed the invaluable technical cooperation of the French railways, and with the exception of Gabin's final suicidal leap from the locomotive, all the railway sequences were shot on location with direct sound recording.

Renoir represents Lantier's inner turmoil symbolically with the wind raging through his hair, while his psychopathic self is darkly reflected in a puddle as he reaches for a murder weapon, or, after he has stabbed Séverine, in a mirror where low-key lighting gives him a particularly monstrous appearance. Perhaps the most powerful sequence comes with Séverine's murder when a demented Lantier suddenly turns on his mistress in an uncontrollable frenzy. The music of the railway ball floods the screen with its ironic song about flirtatious love and possession, linking and contrasting scenes of public enjoyment with a scene of private horror.

Acknowledging his debt to Renoir, Fritz Lang remade *La Bête humaine* as *Human Desire* in 1954. The most detailed study of *La Bête humaine* is found in *Jean Renoir* by Alexander Sesonske.

—R. F. Cousins

BHARAT MATA

(Mother India)

India, 1957

Director: Mehboob Khan

Production: A Mehboob Production; Technicolor; running time: 120 minutes; original running time: 160 minutes, running time of 1961 version: 95 minutes. Released 1957.

Executive producer: V. J. Shah; **producer:** Mehboob Khan; **screenplay:** Vajahat Mirza, S. Ali Raza; **photography:** Faradoon A. Irani; **editor:** Shamsudin Kadri; **sound:** Kaushik; **art director:** V. H. Palnitkar; **dance director:** Chiman Seth; **costumes:** Fazaldin; **music:** Naushad; **lyrics:** Shakeel Badayuni.

Cast: Nargis (*Radha*); Sunil Dutt (*Birjoo*); Rajendra Kumar (*Ramoo*); Raaj Kumar (*Shamoo*); Kumkum (*Champa*); Chanchal (*Roop*); Kanhaiyalal (*Sukhi Lala*); Jiloo Maa (*Sunder Chachi*); Azra (*Chandre*); Master Saiid (*Birjoo, the boy*); Muqri (*Shambu*); Sheela Nayak (*Kamla*); Siddiqui (*Dalita Prasad*); Geeta (*Village girl*); Master Surendra (*Ramoo, the boy*).

Bharat Mata

Publications

Books:

Barnouw, Erik, and S. Krishnaswamy, *Indian Film*, New York, 1965.
Jha, B., editor, *Indian Motion Picture Almanac*, 10th edition, Calcutta, 1975.
Rangoonwala, F., *Pictorial History of Indian Cinema*, Calcutta, 1979.
Willemen, Paul, and Behroze Ghandy, *Indian Cinema*, London, 1982.
Pfleiderer, Beatrix, and Lothar Lutze, *The Hindi Film: Agent and Re-Agent of Cultural Change*, New Delhi, 1985.
Ramachandran, T. M., *70 Years of Indian Cinema (1913–1983)*, Bombay, 1985.
Armes, Roy, *Third World Filmmaking and the West*, Berkeley, 1987.

Articles:

FilmIndia, December 1957.
Variety (New York), 27 August 1957.
Monthly Film Bulletin (London), July 1958.
Kine Weekly (London), 16 February 1961.
City Limits (London), 18 June 1982.
Ray, Satyajit, ''Under Western Eyes,'' in *Sight and Sound* (London), Autumn 1982.
Haffner, P., ''Le Cinéma indien en Afrique noire,'' in *Filméchange* (Paris), Winter 1983.
Tesson, Charles, ''Le rêve indien,'' in *Cahiers du Cinéma* (Paris), March 1985.
Thomas, R., ''Indian Cinema: Pleasures and Popularity,'' in *Screen* (London), May-August 1985.
Thomas, R., ''Sanctity and Scandal,'' in *Quarterly Review of Film and Video* (New York), no. 3, 1989.

* * *

Mother India, one of the all-time hits of the Hindi commercial cinema, has also been a noted success in the Hindi film's traditional export markets in the Middle East and Africa. It is one of the few such films to have received exposure in Western cinemas, and even won an Oscar nomination for Best Foreign Film.

The film is very much a legendary enterprise, and one conceived perhaps on such terms. It was the last major success of the director, Mehboob Khan; it is one of the best remembered works of the music director, Naushad; it represented the last major appearance of the female lead, Nargis; and it was a remake of an earlier Mehboob film, and one of the most acclaimed of the 1940s, *Aurat* (*Woman*, 1940). In this sense, it encapsulates a number of filmic and non-filmic narratives into its own, and weaves these together into a mythical shape.

Mehboob's own story is perhaps the central one underlying *Mother India:* born in a poor rural family, he rose through menial jobs and minor acting roles in the studios of the 1930s to become a director in 1934. In Hindi movie parlance he was associated with the genre of the "social" film—melodramatic narratives oriented to exposing social malaise. His better-known films emphasized a kind of populism about the "people's" travails. The "people" are presented as the true, the genuine India, remaining faithful to their traditions even as they accept a modernizing, reformist context.

Mehboob's personal history was publicized to lend authenticity to *Mother India*'s tale of rural folk punished by the elements and struggling under the burden of debt. However, the film is very much an essay in exoticising the "simple" life. Colour—a relatively recent and still uncharacteristic phenomenon at the time of the film's making—is used to make a spectacle of nature, with the narrative and song sequences splashed in dawns and sunsets. As with later sagas of the rural life (such as *Ganga Jamuna*, Nitin Bose, 1961), communal activities, whether of tilling and reaping or in a celebration at festivals such as Holi (the spring festival), are staged in a highly choreographed style. The music director, Naushad, made a conscious attempt to bring folk rhythms into the repertoire of Hindi film music. But the stylized evocation, with its ornamentalization through spectacle, places the music too in a mythicizing distance from the "folk." The real object of the myth is not the folk but the modern nation.

The original 1940 narrative dealt with the sufferings of a peasant woman, Radha, abandoned by her husband and left to fend for her sons. Drought and debt beat down on her. The focus is on the value she places on her chastity even in the face of starvation, and on the great love with which she sustains her children. These qualities carry her family, and by extension, the village community, through the crisis. However, the nurturing mother has her negative side. An excess of love causes her to turn a blind eye to her undisciplined, hedonist son, Birjoo. This indulgence leads him into bad ways; he becomes a bandit and a threat to the community. Ultimately, the mother has to kill him, and dies, broken-hearted.

In the later film, there are a number of important changes. The issue of exploitation, which was present but marginalized in *Aurat*, is now quite central. There is an induction of nationalist discourses about whether violence or faith in God (a complete distortion of Gandhi's much more active notion of passive resistance) are to be embraced in the face of injustice. These oppositions are quite deviously solved. Birjoo, the bandit son, is now clearly a social bandit, directing his activities against the oppressive money-lending classes. But his actions are tainted; he not only kills the exploiting money-lender, he also abducts his daughter. A woman's honour—the mechanism whereby the patriarchal authority of the community at large is maintained—is threatened, and so Radhu kills her son. Thus while exploitation, presented as the impediment to the progress of the rural community, is ended, the significance of Birjoo's actions is denied. Faith and honour triumph; development, in keeping with contemporary governmental designs for the rural community, is achieved in the construction of a dam. The mother, still grief-stricken over Birjoo's death, inaugurates it as mother of the community. But the film's work of ideological denial is unbalanced when, in Radha's perception, it seems to be Birjoo's blood which flows out when the dam is opened.

Mother India is then not only the re-working of an earlier film. It is a narrativization of a certain legacy (that of the national movement) with the object of presenting certain contemporary problems of inequality, justice, and development, in an ideological way. Seeking to represent the rural people, the film actually makes of them elements in a design of colour, song, and dance, an ornate spectacle conceived to reflect the populist myths of the modern state.

—Ravi Vasudevan

BHUMIKA

(The Role)

India, 1977

Director: Shyam Benegal

Production: Blaze Film Enterprises; colour, 35mm; running time: 144 minutes.

Bhumika

Producers: Lalit M. Bijlani and Freni M. Variava; **executive producers:** Silloo Fali Variava and Bisham M. Bijlani; **screenplay:** Girish Karnad, Pandit Satyadev Dubey, and Shyam Benegal, from the book *Sandtye Aika* by Hansa Wadkar; **assistant directors:** Dayal Nihalani, Manohar Ghanekar, Swadesh Pal, and Prahlad Kakar; **photography:** Govind Nihalini; **editor:** Bhanudas; **art director:** Shama Zaidi; **sound:** Hitendra Ghosh, Robin Chaterjee, Raj Trehan; **costumes:** Kalpana Lajmi; **music:** Vanraj Bahtia; **songs:** Vanraj Bahtia, Majrooh Sultanpuri, and Vasanth Dev.

Cast: Smita Patil (*Usha*); Anant Nag (*Rajan*); Amrish Puri (*Vinayak Kale*); Naseeruddin Shah (*Sunil Sharma*); Sulabha Deshpande (*Usha's Mother*); Baby Ruksana (*Usha as a child*); Amol Palekar (*Keshar Dalvi*); Kulbhushan Kharbanda (*Producer*).

Publications

Books:

Da Cunha, Uma, *The New Generation: 1960–1980*, New Delhi, 1981.
The Directorate of Film Festivals, New Delhi, 1981.
Vasudev, Aruna, *The New Indian Cinema*, Macmillan India (New Delhi), 1986.

Articles:

Variety (New York), 15 November 1978.
Milne, Tom, *Monthly Film Bulletin* (London), April 1980.
Vasudev, Aruna, and Philippe Leglet, interview with Shyam Behegal in *Indian Cinema Superbazaar*, Vikas Publishing (New Delhi), 1983.

* * *

Shyam Benegal's fourth film marks a substantial departure from his first three works. *Bhumika* is inspired by the autobiography of the 1940s Marathi and Hindi movie star Hansa Wadkar. The book, as told to journalist Arun Sadhu, used the title of her most famous film, the mega hit musical *Sangtye Aika* (1959), translating loosely as ''Listen, and I'll Tell.'' It caused a sensation and became an instant best-seller, being an extraordinarily candid tale of a young woman who came from a tradition of *kalavantins*—courtesans from the Goa coastline renowned for their musical accomplishments but considered to be of lowly status. She joined the film industry as a child actress mainly to support her mother and grandmother, acting in stage-derived musicals. She moved to Karachi to do adventure B-movies (*Modern Youth*, 1936) before receiving her major break in the Bombay Talkies studio. Wadkar went on to become the foremost Marathi star in two extremely popular but seemingly contradictory genres, the devotional Saint-film and the bawdy folk-derived *Tamasha* musical: playing the title role in the Prabhat studios' *Sant Sakhu* (1941) and the role of Baya in V. Shantaram's *Lokshahir Ramjoshi* (1947). *Ramjoshi* and *Sangtye Aika* are among the biggest hits in the history of the Marathi cinema.

Benegal's movie adapts this story into a human interest saga of a traditional courtesan coming to terms with contemporary mass-culture, and her struggle to find her own individuality in the process. The framing narrative shows Usha, the move star, leave her husband and seek shelter first with her male co-star Rajan, and eventually in the oppressive confines of the feudal landlord of Kale's estate. Her husband arrives with the police to rescue her from Kale. Free once more, she rejects the offers of support from her husband, her now grown-up and married daughter—whose modernity marks a break with the matrilineal tradition—and her former lover Rajan, presumably in favour of the independence for which she craved.

Female protagonists seeking independence through various kinds of social engagements, failing and then ''going away,'' were a common and familiar stereotype in much of the New Indian Cinema of the time. Feminist critic Susie Tharu's remarks about Usha's counterpart Sulabha (also played by Smita Patil) in Jabbar Patel's *Umbartha* (*The Threshold*, 1981) clearly apply to the stereotype in *Bhumika* as well: ''The filmic focus . . . establishes her as the central character as well as the problem (the disruption, the enigma) the film will explore and resolve . . . it is clear that to search herself is, for a woman, a tragic enterprise. An enterprise in which she is doomed to fail, but can fail bravely and heroically'' (''Third World Women's Cinema,'' *Economic and Political Weekly*, Bombay, 17 May 1986).

The film develops its enigmatic protagonist with a dense overlay of nostalgia, through a series of sepia flashbacks showing Usha's childhood in the Konkan. Undoubtedly *Bhumika*'s most attractive aspect, these flashbacks show her meetings with her future husband, Dalvi, who claims her in return for helping her impoverished family. The scene showing her entry into the Surya Movietone reconstructs Wadkar's test at the Shalini Cinetone conducted by the framed composer Govindrao Tembe, *tabla* maestro Tirakhwan, and director Baburao Painter. Showing Usha's early roles in the movies, Benegal lovingly recreates various pre-war genres like the stunt movie, the *Mahabharata* mythological, and the social reform melodrama. Other flashbacks show her husband as a manipulative opportunist who starts managing her career, and her one major extra-marital relationship, with the poetry-spewing existentialist filmmaker Sunil, who involves her in a romantic suicide pact only to abandon her.

This mode of reconstructing the past to create an idiom of tragic fiction is all the more remarkable because of its startling contrast to Benegal's previous work: political features addressing a rural peasantry in the context of the Communist Party of India (Marxist-Leninist) ''Naxalite'' movements in the late 1960s and through the 1970s. *Ankur* (*The Seedling*, 1974) and *Nishant* (*Night's End*, 1975) were set in rural Andhra Pradesh, *Manthan* (*The Churning*, 1976) addressed the struggle of Gujarati peasants to set up a milk cooperative. All three films worked with several young actors and made them major stars, including Smita Patil and Anant Nag who feature in *Bhumika*. These films' success—especially that of his debut, *Ankur*—created a commercially viable 1970s trend of a ruralist realism, using accented Hindi to simulate the language of Telugu and Gujarati-speaking villagers, and a naturalist, stage-derived acting style that for many years came to be equated in several Indian cinemas, and later in its television, with a political and cultural authenticity.

Clearly Benegal shifts ground with *Bhumika*. The film, for one, locates the whole authenticity question into melodrama proper. It was the first Hindi film from the short-lived New Indian Cinema movement designed to reach a large audience and to receive a substantial commercial release. It went a long way in creating for its maker a reputation for providing culturally refined entertainment, in contrast to that churned out by the mainstream Hindi film industry. Until Benegal, it was only his mentor, Satyajit Ray, who was committed to the aesthetic of a cinema of taste, to define an indigenous cultural élite that otherwise sought its referents mainly through seeing American and European films. Unlike the often colonial overtones of Indian upper-class nostalgia movies of the time (e.g., Aparna Sen's *36 Chowringhee Lane*, 1981), Bengal's protagonist allows him to explore the enigmas of a specifically indigenous popular culture.

It is arguable that in making the film he saw the two genres, of a frontier ruralist realism on the one side, and of creating the fictions of a collective ''past'' on the other, as being compatible modes effectively addressing the same problem: of constructing an indigenous authenticity for an audience that would not wish to be a part of the dominant mass-entertainment modes of India's film industry. Certainly this is where *Bhumika* has proved the most influential, in the way it expanded the thematic repertoire of the New Indian Cinema, and eventually allowed a more sustained engagement with the mass-cultural idiom itself.

—Ashish Rajadhyaksha

THE BICYCLE THIEF

See **LADRI DI BICICLETTE**

THE BIG HEAT

USA, 1953

Director: Fritz Lang

Production: Columbia Pictures Corp.; black and white, 35mm; running time: 89 or 90 minutes. Released 14 October 1953. Filmed from about 21 March to 18 April 1953 in Columbia studios.

Producer: Robert Arthur; **screenplay:** Sidney Boehm, from a novel by William P. MacGivern; **photography:** Charles Lang, Jr.; **editor:** Charles Nelson; **sound:** George Cooper; **art direction:** Robert Peterson; **set decoration:** William Kiernan; **music:** Daniele Amfitheatrof, Mischa Bakaleinikoff; **costumes:** Jean Louis.

Cast: Glenn Ford (*David Bannion*); Gloria Grahame (*Debby Marsh*); Jocelyn Brando (*Katie Bannion*); Alexander Scourby (*Mike Lagana*); Lee Marvin (*Vince Stone*); Jeanette Nolan (*Bertha Duncan*); Peter Whitney (*Tierney*); Willis Buchey (*Lieutenant Wilkes*); Robert Burton (*Gus Burke*); Adam Williams (*Larry Gordon*); Howard Wendall (*Higgins*); Cris Alcaide (*George Rose*); Carolyn Jones (*Doris*); Michael Granger (*Hugo*); Dorothy Green (*Lucy Chapman*); Ric Roman (*Baldy*); Dan Seymour (*Atkins*); Edith Evanson (*Selma Parker*).

Publications

Books:

Courtade, Francis, *Fritz Lang*, Paris, 1963.
Moullet, Luc, *Fritz Lang*, Paris, 1963.
Eibel, Alfred, editor, *Fritz Lang*, Paris, 1964.
Johnston, Claire, *Fritz Lang*, London, 1969.
Jensen, Paul J., *The Cinema of Fritz Lang*, New York, 1969.
Bogdanovich, Peter, *Fritz Lang in America*, London, 1969.
Alloway, Lawrence, *Violent America: The Movies Between 1946–1964*, New York, 1971.
Bazin, André, *La Politique des auteurs: Entretiens avec Jean Renoir, etc.*, Paris, 1972; revised edition, 1984.
McArthur, Colin, *Underground U.S.A.*, London, 1972.
Mast, Gerald, *The Comic Mind*, Chicago, 1974; revised edition, 1979.
Trufaut, François, *Les Films de ma vie*, Paris, 1975; as *The Films in My Life*, New York, 1978.
Grafe, Frieda, and others, *Fritz Lang*, Munich, 1976.
Eisner, Lotte, *Fritz Lang*, London, 1977.
Armour, Robert, *Fritz Lang*, Boston, 1978.
Jenkins, Stephen, editor, *Fritz Lang*, London, 1979.
Silver, Alain, and Elizabeth Wark, *Film Noir*, Woodstock, New York, 1979.
Giannetti, Louis, *Master of the American Cinema*, Englewood Cliffs, New Jersey, 1981.
Jenkins, Stephen, editor, *Fritz Lang: The Image and the Look*, London, 1981.
Kaplan, E. Ann, *Fritz Lang: A Guide to References and Resources*, Boston, 1981.
Maibohm, Ludwig, *Fritz Lang: Seine Film—sein Leben*, Munich, 1981.
Dürrenmatt, Dieter, *Fritz Lang: Leben und Werk*, Basle, 1982.
Humphries, Reynold, *Fritz Lang: Genre and Representation in His American Films*, Baltimore, 1988.
Leblanc, Gérard, and Brigitte Devismes, *Le double scénario chez Fritz Lang*, Paris, 1991.
McArthur, Colin, *The Big Heat*, London, 1992.

Articles:

Crowther, Bosley in *New York Times*, 15 October 1953.
Truffaut, François, ''Aimer Fritz Lang,'' in *Cahiers du Cinéma* (Paris), January 1954.
Anderson, Lindsay, in *Sight and Sound* (London), Summer 1954.
Lambert, Gavin, ''Fritz Lang's America,'' in *Sight and Sound* (London), Summer 1955.
Mourlet, Michel, ''Trajectoire de Fritz Lang,'' in *Cahiers du Cinéma* (Paris), September 1959.
Legrand, Gérard, ''Notes pour un éloge de Fritz Lang,'' in *Positif* (Paris), March 1963.
Patalas, Enno, ''Fritz Lang, der Unbekannte: Jahrestreffen der deutschen Filmclubs,'' in *Frankfurter Allegmein Zeitung*, 7 May 1964.
Hartman, Rainer, ''Wirklichkeit statt Menschheitsfragen,'' in *Frankfurter Neue Presse*, 26 May 1964.
Beylie, Claude, ''L'Oeuvre américain de Fritz Lang (1936–1956),'' in *Avant-Scène du Cinéma* (Paris), February 1968.
Joannides, Paul, ''Aspects of Fritz Lang,'' in *Cinema* (London), August 1970.
Flinn, Tom, ''*The Big Heat* and *The Big Combo:* Rogue Cops and Mink-Coated Girls,'' in *Velvet Light Trap* (Madison, Wisconsin), no. 11, 1974.
Hennelly, Mark, Jr., ''American Nightmare: The Underworld in Film,'' in *Journal of Popular Culture* (Bowling Green, Ohio), no. 3, 1978.
Willis, Don, ''Fritz Lang: Only Melodrama,'' in *Film Quarterly* (Berkeley), Winter 1979–80.

The Big Heat

MacGivern, William P., in *American Film* (Washington, D.C.), October 1983.

Pulleine, Tim, in *Films and Filming* (London), February 1988.

Wood, Robin, ''Creativity and Evaluation,'' in *Cineaction* (Toronto), Summer-Fall 1990.

Wager, Jans B., ''The Big Heat,'' *Bright Lights*, no. 14, 1995.

Aldarondo, R., ''Los sobornados,'' *Nosferatu* (Donostia-San Sebastian, Spain), no. 20, January 1996.

Metz, Walter, ''Keep the Coffee Hot, Hugo: Nuclear Trauma in Lang's *The Big Heat*,'' *Film Criticism* (Meadville), vol. 21, no. 3, Spring 1997.

* * *

Like Fritz Lang's western *Rancho Notorious* (1951), *The Big Heat* is a ballad of hate, murder, and revenge. In both films, the hero is driven outside the law when his love interest is killed by sadistic minions of a crime boss (who personally disapproves of such extremes) and compelled to pull down the whole corrupt system that has perverted his world. Both feature facial scars as a recurring motif, crooked politicians, iconic close-ups of guns, and a clear-eyed criminal woman who sacrifices herself for the hero. The *noir*-ish *The Big Heat* is oddly easier on its hard-boiled protagonist, cop Dave Bannion (Glenn Ford), than *Rancho Notorious* is on cowboy Vern (Arthur Kennedy). The earlier film combines the figure of Mabuse-style mastermind and redeemed bad girl in Altar Keane (Marlene Dietrich), with whom Vern falls in love, while *The Big Heat* sets up decorative-but-sharp moll Debby (Gloria Grahame) as an outsider within the gang of smooth crime czar Lagana (Alexander Scourby), with a degree of license to criticize her dangerous boyfriend Vince Stone (Lee Marvin), making her almost the equivalent of ''good badman'' Frenchy (Mel Ferrer). The possibility of a romance between Bannion and Debby is implicit but never raised—these people are too trapped in their roles of cop/family man and crook/moll to get together—while Vern's love for Altar makes his destruction of her gang yet another tragic loss of home.

Though it tackles themes Lang dealt with as early as the Dr. Mabuse movies, *The Big Heat* is one of many exposé gangster films produced in Hollywood in the 1950s: *The Enforcer* (1951), *The Captive City* (1952), *Chicago Syndicate* (1955), *The Big Combo* (1955), *The Phoenix City Story* (1955), and *Underworld USA* (1961).

Inspired by the Kefauver Commission on organized crime, the cycle adapts the psychological approach of 1940s *noirs* to analyze not a sick mind but a sick society, depicting American towns and cities under the control of ''the Syndicate.'' The flamboyant psychopaths who would have been the lead menaces of movies like *Little Caesar* (1930) or *The Public Enemy* (1931) are demoted to the supporting role taken by Vince Stone. The real hate figures are the faceless higher-ups rarely glimpsed in the earlier movies (the ''Big Boy'' of *Little Caesar*): Lagana, an immigrant made good who hypocritically regrets the need for violence but is determined not ''to end up in the same ditch with the Lucky Lucianos,'' as a 1950s gang boss, half chairman of the board and half fascist *duce*. He speaks with the reasonable, soulless tone of the Body Snatchers, while Bannion (whom he accuses of ''tracking dirt into his house'' by mentioning the murder of a bar-girl he has ordered killed) and Stone (a neanderthal whose only come-back to Debby's sniping witticisms is to throw hot coffee in her face) are monsters from the Id.

The Big Heat is a film of violence, opening with a close-up of a gun about to be used in the suicide of corrupt cop Tom Duncan, and proceeding rapidly through its plot with jolting horrors that malform the characters. Bannion turns from family man to obsessive rogue cop when his wife (Jocelyn Brando) is blown up by a car bomb meant for him. Debby is embittered by the ruining of her beauty and takes up Bannion's quest for revenge, precipitating the big heat by confronting and murdering her ''sister under the mink,'' grasping widow Bertha Duncan (Jeanette Nolan). With Bertha's death, the evidence Tom Duncan left behind, which is enough to bring down Lagana's empire, is released. In a crucial development, prefigured in both *Fury* (1936) and *Rancho Notorious*, the embittered hero is still unable to commit cold-blood murder to achieve his purpose—Bannion stops short of assaulting Bertha—and a *doppelganger* has to step in to pull the last thread that allows justice to be done. The point is underlined in the climax, which finds Debby returning Vince's favour by dashing boiling coffee in his face and being gun-shot by the villain, prompting Bannion to trounce his ugly mirror image (a witness tags Stone as about Bannion's height but flashily dressed) in a brutal fight but not to gun him down even though Stone implores him to ''shoot!''

Grounded far more in political reality than most of Lang's *noirs*, thanks to the hard-hitting detail of William P. McGivern's novel and Sydney Boehm's script, *The Big Heat* is still indebted to expressionism, with sets that reflect the characters' overriding personality traits: the cold luxury of the Duncan house, bought with dirty money; the tasteless wealth of Lagana's mansion, with its hideous portrait of the mobster's sainted mother and jiving teenage party; the penthouse *moderne* of Vince and Debby, where the police commissioner plays cards with killers; the cramped, poor-but-honest apartment of the Bannion family, underlined by too-insistent heart-warming music; and the hotel room where Bannion ends up, his life pared down to the need for vengeance (''early nothing'' Debby comments). The tabloid sensibility of Lang's late American films (*While the City Sleeps*, 1955, *Beyond a Reasonable Doubt*, 1956) informs the depiction of squadroom and barroom, and there is a transgressive charge to the various minor cruelties (an obscene phone call taken by Mrs. Bannion, Stone stubbing a cigarette on the arm of a dice-playing girl in a bar, the famous coffee-throwing attacks) that imbues the film with an unpredictable, uneasy sense of danger. Even the finale is hardly comforting: after the fall of the crime syndicate, the widowed hero is not seen embracing his daughter and picking up his home life but returning to his desk in the Homicide Department. The welcome of workmates—expressed, of course, by an offer of coffee—is curtailed and the end title appears over Bannion putting on his hat and coat to go out and deal with ''a hit and run over on South Street.''

—Kim Newman

THE BIG PARADE

USA, 1925

Director: King Vidor

Production: Metro-Goldwyn-Mayer Pictures Corp.; originally black and white with tinted sequences, 35mm, silent with music score; running time: about 125 minutes; length: originally 13 reels at 12,550 feet, later 12 reels at 11,519 feet. Released selectively November 1925, released generally 1927. Re-released 1931 with synchronized music and sound effects.

Producer: Irving G. Thalberg; **scenario:** Harry Behn; **story:** Laurence Stallings; **titles:** Joseph W. Farnham, from the play by Farnham, and the novel *Plumes* by Stallings; **photography:** John Arnold; **editor:** Hugh Wynn; **art directors:** Cedric Gibbons, James Basevi; **music:** William Axt, David Mendoza.

Cast: John Gilbert (*James Apperson*); Renée Adorée (*Mélisande*); Hobart Bosworth (*Mr. Apperson*); Claire McDowell (*Mrs. Apperson*); Claire Adams (*Justyn Reed*); Robert Ober (*Harry*); Tom O'Brien (*Bull*); Karl Dane (*Slim*); Rosita Marstini (*French Mother*).

Publications

Books:

Vidor, King, *A Tree Is a Tree*, New York, 1953; reprinted 1977.
Brownlow, Kevin, *The Parade's Gone By . . .* , London and New York, 1969.
Baxter, John, *King Vidor*, New York, 1976.
Everson, William K., *American Silent Film*, New York, 1978.
O'Connor, John E., and Martin A. Jackson, editors, *American History/American Film: Interpreting the Hollywood Image*, New York, 1979.
Comuzio, Ermanno, *King Vidor*, Florence, 1986.
Vidor, King, with contributions by Nancy Dowd and David Shepard, *King Vidor* (Directors Guild of America Oral History Series), Lanham, Maryland, 1988.
Durgnat, Raymond, and Scott Simmon, *King Vidor—American*, Berkeley, 1989.

The Big Parade

Articles:

Smith, F. J., ''Tells How *The Big Parade* Was Made,'' in *Motion Picture Classic* (New York), May 1926.

Tully, Jim, ''Interview,'' in *Vanity Fair* (New York), June 1926.

Quirk, Lawrence J., ''John Gilbert,'' in *Films in Review* (New York), March 1956.

Davis, Henry, ''A John Gilbert Index,'' in *Films in Review* (New York), October 1962.

Brownlow, Kevin, ''King Vidor,'' in *Film* (London), Winter 1962.

Higham, Charles, ''King Vidor,'' in *Film Heritage* (Dayton, Ohio), Summer 1966.

''King Vidor at NYU,'' in *Cineaste* (New York), Spring 1968.

Uselton, Roi A., ''Renée Adorée,'' in *Films in Review* (New York), June-July 1968.

Greenberg, Joel, ''War, Wheat, and Steel,'' in *Sight and Sound* (London), Autumn 1968.

Barr, Charles, ''King Vidor,'' in *Brighton* (London), March 1970.

Luft, Herbert G., ''King Vidor: A Career That Spans Half a Century,'' in *Film Journal* (Dayton, Ohio), Summer 1971.

Durgnat, Raymond, in *Film Comment* (New York), July-August 1973.

''Vidor Issue'' of *Positif* (Paris), September 1974.

Amengual, Barthélemy, ''Entre l'horizon d'un seul et l'horizon de tous,'' in *Positif* (Paris), September 1974.

Edwards, R., ''*The Big Parade*,'' in *Films of the Golden Age* (Muscatine, Iowa), no. 5, Summer 1996.

* * *

The Big Parade propelled director King Vidor to the top as MGM's wunderkind, the Steven Spielberg of his day, who could do no wrong when it came to sensing what the public would or would not embrace in film entertainment.

The end of World War I was not even a decade in the past when the Texas-born filmmaker, who had established himself as a skillful purveyor of comedies and sentimental slices of rural American life, persuaded production chief Irving Thalberg to let him make an epic film about the war—a subject conventional wisdom said audiences would prefer to forget. Vidor countered that the huge success of the Laurence Stallings-Maxwell Anderson WWI play *What Price Glory?* on Broadway the previous year suggested otherwise. MGM gave him the green light to make *The Big Parade*.

The script by Harry Behn was based upon an outline Vidor had solicited from Stallings himself. It deals with three men from an unnamed American town who are swept up in the wave of patriotic fervor following America's entrance into the war and enlist. One, Tom O'Brien, is a salty bartender; another, Karl Dane, is a gawky, tobacco chewing blue collar type; the third, played by matinee idol John Gilbert, is the lay-about son of a wealthy mill owner. Despite their disparate backgrounds, the three become fast chums when they meet at boot camp and sustain their comradeship through the ferocious battle of Belleau Wood where they undergo their baptism of fire.

Along the way, Gilbert meets and falls in love with a French farm girl, delightfully and movingly played by Renée Adorée. The scene where he introduces her to American chewing gum is one of the most famous in silent films. It is both funny and touching, and wonderfully pantomimed by the two actors under the scrutiny of Vidor's camera, which captures the moment in an uninterrupted single take. A follow-up scene where the lovers are separated is equally memorable. As Gilbert is spirited to the front in one of a long line of battle trucks, he vows to return, tossing her mementos until she is left alone in a trail of dust.

Gilbert's buddies are killed during a nighttime assault on the German trenches, and Gilbert himself suffers a severely wounded leg that subsequently must be amputated; he returns home a cripple. The glamour studio balked at the downbeat fate visited upon the film's leading man—an incident drawn from the experience of author Stallings, who had lost a leg in the war. In his quest for realism, Vidor held his ground, however, and got his way. The scene where Gilbert's mutilation is revealed to his mother and the viewer for the first time at his homecoming is arguably the most powerful in the movie.

Despite, or perhaps because of, his affliction and hellish wartime experience, the Gilbert character has now grown and matured—in contrast to his brother (Robert Oder), previously viewed as the more serious and responsible sibling, but now as the real nothing in the family. Having stayed behind to attend to the family business, he's even stolen Gilbert's hometown sweetheart (Claire Adams)! No matter. At his mother's urging, Gilbert returns to France to find the love of his life Adorée as he'd promised.

The Big Parade is really two films. The first hour and twenty minutes are standard (though at the time prototypical) service comedy stuff dealing with Gilbert's, O'Brien's, and Dane's escapades in France prior to going into action. Part two, which runs approximately the same length, is all war—and the battle scenes remain frighteningly realistic and impressive to this day. The march through Belleau Wood, timed by Vidor to the inexorable beat of a metronome, as the troops are mowed down by snipers and machine gun fire is still a stunner. The trench warfare scenes are equally vivid. Many critics have noted the influence Vidor's staging of these scenes had on Lewis Milestone's *All Quiet on the Western Front* (1930). There is even a small moment when Gilbert plucks a lone flower from atop his trench that mirrors the finale of *All Quiet* when Lew Ayres is killed reaching for a butterfly, and which may have served as the latter's inspiration.

Where *The Big Parade* departs significantly from *All Quiet* is the clarity of its anti-war theme. *All Quiet* is uncompromisingly focused in this regard. *The Big Parade*, despite the stark believability of its warfare scenes, is, in overall aim, more of an escapist entertainment. In his later years, Vidor all but disowned the film for that reason. ''At the time, I really believed it was an anti-war movie,'' he said. ''Today, I don't encourage people to see it.''

Vidor's reassessment is too harsh. *The Big Parade* is one of the great silent films—and the model for just about every war movie that has come our way since. It should be seen for those reasons alone. While the escapist boy-meets-girl, boy-loses-girl, boy-gets-girl subplot may stray the focus away from Vidor's anti-war message at times, it eloquently engages the emotions. And the theme that war is hell, while perhaps not what the film is entirely about, is nevertheless both present and potent.

—John McCarty

THE BIG SLEEP

USA, 1946

Director: Howard Hawks

Production: Warner Bros. Pictures Inc.; black and white, 35mm; running time: 114 minutes. Released 31 August 1946. Filmed in Warner Bros. studios.

Producer: Howard Hawks; **screenplay:** William Faulkner, Leigh Brackett and Jules Furthman, from the novel by Raymond Chandler; **photography:** Sidney Hickox; **editor:** Christian Nyby; **sound:** Robert B. Lee; **production design:** Fred M. MacLean; **art direction:** Carl Jules Weyl; **music:** Max Steiner; **special effects:** Roy Davidson and Warren E. Lynch.

Cast: Humphrey Bogart (*Philip Marlowe*); Lauren Bacall (*Vivian*); John Ridgely (*Eddie Mars*); Martha Vickers (*Carmen*); Dorothy Malone (*Bookshop Girl*); Peggy Knusden (*Mona Mars*); Regis Toomey (*Bernie Ohls*); Charles Waldren (*General Sternwood*); Charles D. Brown (*Norris*); Bob Steele (*Canino*); Elisha Cook, Jr. (*Jones*); Louis Jean Heydt (*Joe Brody*); Sonia Darrin (*Agnes*); Theodore von Eltz (*Geiger*); Tom Rafferty (*Carol Lundgren*); James Flavin (*Captain Cronjager*); Thomas Jackson (*Wilde*); Don Wallace (*Owen Taylor*); Joy Barlowe (*Chauffeur*); Tom Fadden (*Sidney*); Ben Weldon (*Pete*); Trevor Bardette (*Art Huck*); Marc Lawarence.

Publications

Scripts:

Faulkner, William, Leigh Brackett, and Jules Furthman, *The Big Sleep*, New York, 1971.

Books:

Bogdanovich, Peter, *The Cinema of Howard Hawks*, New York, 1962.
Gehman, Richard, *Bogart*, Greenwich, Connecticut, 1965.

McCarty, Clifford, *The Films of Humphrey Bogart*, New York, 1965.
Michael, Paul, *Humphrey Bogart: The Man and His Films*, Indianapolis, 1965.
Missiaen, Jean-Claude, *Howard Hawks*, Paris, 1966.
Wood, Robin, *Howard Hawks*, London, 1968; revised edition, 1981.
Gili, Jean A., *Howard Hawks*, Paris, 1971.
McBride, Joseph, editor, *Focus on Howard Hawks*, Englewood Cliffs, New Jersey, 1972.
Willis, Donald, *The Films of Howard Hawks*, Metuchen, New Jersey, 1972.
Bazin, André, *La Politique des auteurs: Entretiens avec Jean Renoir, etc*, Paris, 1972; revised edition, 1984.
Barbour, Alan G., *Humphrey Bogart*, New York, 1973.
Hyams, Joe, *Bogart and Bacall*, New York, 1975.
Murphy, Kathleen A., *Howard Hawks: An American Auteur in the Hemingway Tradition*, Ann Arbor, Michigan, 1978.
Ciment, Michel, *Les Conquérants d'un nouveau monde: Essais sur le cinéma Américain*, Paris, 1981.
Giannetti, Louis, *Masters of the American Cinema*, Englewood Cliffs, New Jersey, 1981.
Pettigrew, Terence, *Bogart: A Definitive Study of his Film Career*, London, 1981.
Wood, Robin, *Howard Hawks*, London, 1981.
McBride, Joseph, editor, *Hawks on Hawks*, Berkeley, 1982.
Mast, Gerald, *Howard Hawks, Storyteller*, Oxford, 1982.
Poague, Leland, *Howard Hawks*, Boston, 1982.
Belton, John, *Cinema Stylists*, Boston, 1982.
Simsolo, Noël, *Howard Hawks*, Paris, 1984.
Kuhn, Annette, *The Power of the Image: Essays on Representation and Sexuality*, London, 1985.
Winkler, Willi, *Humphrey Bogart und Hollywood Schwarze Serie*, Munich, 1985.
Branson, Clark, *Howard Hawks: A Jungian Study*, Los Angeles, 1987.
Fuchs, Wolfgang J., *Humphrey Bogart: Cult-Star: A Documentation*, Berlin, 1987.

Articles:

Houseman, John, in *Hollywood Quarterly*, January 1947.
Agel, Henri, "Howard Hawks," in *New York Film Bulletin*, no. 4, 1962.
Sarris, Andrew, "The World of Howard Hawks," in *Films and Filming* (London), July 1962.
Bogdanovich, Peter, and others, "Howard Hawks," in *Movie* (London), December 1962.
Philipe, Claude-Jean, in *Télérama* (Paris), June 1966.
Tavernier, Bertrand, in *Humphrey Bogart*, by Bernard Eisenschitz, Paris 1967.
Blades, John, in *Film Heritage* (Dayton, Ohio), Summer 1970.
Davis, Paxton, "Bogart, Hawks, and *The Big Sleep* Revisited—Frequently," in *Film Journal* (New York), Summer 1971.
Ecran (Paris), July 1972.
Haskell, Molly, "Howard Hawks—Masculine Feminine," in *Film Comment* (New York), April 1973.
Brackett, Leigh, "From *The Big Sleep* to *The Long Goodbye* and More or Less How We Got There," in *Take One* (Montreal), January 1974.
Bellour, Raymond, "The Obvious and the Code," in *Screen* (London), Winter 1974–75.
Monaco, James, "Notes on *The Big Sleep:* 30 Years After," in *Sight and Sound* (London), Winter 1974–75.
Jensen, P., "Film Noir: The Writer: The World You Live In," in *Film Comment* (New York), November-December 1974.
Pym, John, in *Monthly Film Bulletin* (London), September 1978.
Davies, G., "Teaching about Narrative," in *Screen Education* (London), Winter 1978–79.
Carcassonne, P., "En écoutant *Le Grand Sommeil*," in *Cinématographe* (Paris), December 1978.
Sauvaget, D., in *Revue du Cinéma* (Paris), January 1979.
Kuhn, Annette, "*The Big Sleep:* A Disturbance in the Sphere of Sexuality," in *Wide Angle* (Athens, Ohio), vol. 4, no. 3, 1980.
Place, Janey, in *Magill's Survey of Cinema 1*, Englewood Cliffs, New Jersey, 1980.
Thomson, David, "At the Acme Bookshop," in *Sight and Sound* (London), Spring, 1981.
Orr, Christopher, "The Trouble with Harry: On the Hawks Version of *The Big Sleep*," in *Wide Angle* (Athens, Ohio), vol. 5, no. 2, 1982.
Librach, R. S., "Adaptation and Ontology: The Impulse Towards Closure in Howard Hawks's version of *The Big Sleep*," in *Literature/Film Quarterly* (Salisbury, Maryland), no. 3, 1991.
McCullough, J., "Pedagogy in the Perverse Text," in *Cineaction* (Toronto), Winter-Spring 1990.
Cantaloube, Thomas, "Le grand retour du Sommeil," *Cahiers du Cinema* (Paris), no. 518, November 1995.
Stein, E., "*The Big Sleep*," *Village Voice* (New York), vol. 42, January 14, 1997.

* * *

An unidentified finger presses the doorbell of the Sternwood mansion. A butler answers. The guest intones: "My name is Marlowe. General Sternwood sent for me."

This introduction thrusts us into immediate alliance with private detective Philip Marlowe, and throughout the film we traverse the world of crime as he does. As the central character, he is in every scene: we know what he knows, nothing more, nothing less. We share his experience as if on a detective training course: we see the way he works, the way he choreographs his moves and orchestrates his space to provoke a desired reaction from his opponent; we share his cognitive processes by identification with his visual point of view; we adopt his attitude by osmosis.

This is the world of film noir in which the existential hero (here played by noir favourite Humphrey Bogart) moves through oppressive atmospheres and dangerous locales, encounters wicked men and women and strives to earn his salary by solving a minor-league murder while wading through a complex and confusing series of clues. Despite a blackmail premise which exposes a whodunnit plot, this Howard Hawks film concerns itself less with why or who, than with how, more with process than result. The story line is extremely complicated (even the author of the novel, Raymond Chandler, was reputedly unable to answer a certain key question about the plot) and unfolds at breakneck speed forcing the spectator to assimilate facts and assess situations quickly or succumb to confusion. Does it really matter who is blackmailing General Sternwood, or what happened to Sean Regan, or who shot Arthur Gwynne Geiger?

In adapting the Chandler novel for the screen, many details were altered and the directly political material erased, but an essential pessimism and cynicism remained. An atmosphere of corruption was pervasive and more than an investigation of a crime, this is an investigation into modern treachery. Marlowe is deceived, beat up, and threatened with extermination as he searches for the truth of a criminal situation. We are concerned not so much with what happened to others as what is happening to Marlowe.

What does happen to him is true in spirit to the novel except in the realm of romance. Marlowe's misogynistic streak replaced by a cynisicm which erodes as the developing romance with Vivian consolidates. In a typical film noir, male/female relationships are doomed, severed by the conclusion of the film—typified by Fred MacMurray's condition at the end of *Double Indemnity* or Bogart's loss of Gloria Grahame at the end of *In a Lonely Place.* In *The Big Sleep* Hollywood romance prevailed in Hawksian style; Bogart and Bacall lived out their celebrated off-screen romance on screen.

The Big Sleep was a Warner Brother's big budgeted film, not an RKO low budget ''B''; box office stars, a top notch crew, and three major writers was not the usual treatment accorded to films of this genre. This studio treatment elevated the film to ''A'' status, but ultimately the box office was fuelled by a movie-going public anxious to witness romantic reality amidst Hollywood fiction.

—Doug Tomlinson

THE BIRDS

USA, 1963

Director: Alfred Hitchcock

Production: Alfred J. Hitchcock Productions; Technicolor, 35mm; running time: 120 minutes. Released 28 March 1963, New York, through Universal Pictures. Filmed mostly on location in Bodega Bay, California.

Producer: Alfred Hitchcock; **screenplay:** Evan Hunter, from ''The Birds'' by Daphne Du Maurier; **photography:** Robert Burks; **editor:** George Tomasini; **sound:** Remi Gassman and Oskar Sala; **sound recordists:** Waldon O. Watson and William Russell; **sound supervisor:** Bernard Herrmann; **production design:** Robert Boyle; **set decoration:** George Milo; **music:** Bernard Herrmann; **special effects:** Lawrence A. Hampton; **costumes:** Edith Head; **special photography advisor:** Ub Iwerks; **bird trainer:** Ray Berwick.

Cast: Rod Taylor (*Mitch Brenner*); Tippi Hedren (*Melanie Daniels*); Jessica Tandy (*Mrs. Brenner*); Suzanne Pleshette (*Annie Hayworth*); Veronica Cartwright (*Cathy Brenner*); Ethel Griffies (*Mrs. Bundy*); Charles McGraw (*Sebastian Sholes*); Ruth McDevitt (*Mrs. MacGruder*); Joe Mantell (*Travelling Salesman*); Doreen Lang (*Hysterical woman*); Malcolm Atterbury (*Deputy Al Malone*); Karl Swenson (*Drunk*); Elizabeth Wilson (*Helen Carter*); Lonny Chapman (*Deke Carter*); Doodles Weaver (*Fisherman*); John McGovern (*Postal clerk*); Richard Deacon (*Man in elevator*); William Quinn.

Publications

Books:

Bogdanovich, Peter, *The Cinema of Alfred Hitchcock*, New York, 1962.
Perry, George, *The Films of Alfred Hitchcock*, London, 1965.
Wood, Robin, *Hitchcock's Films*, London, 1965.
Truffaut, François, *Le Cinéma selon Hitchcock*, Paris, 1966; as *Hitchcock*, New York, 1985.
Simsolo, Noël, *Alfred Hitchcock*, Paris, 1969.
Cameron, Ian, editor, *Movie Reader*, New York, 1978.
Taylor, John Russell, *Hitch*, London and New York, 1978.
Bellour, Raymond, *L'Analyse du film*, Paris, 1979.
Nichols, Bill, *Ideology and the Image: Social Representation in the Cinema and Other Media*, Bloomington, Indiana, 1981.
Hemmeter, Thomas M., *Hitchcock the Stylist*, Ann Arbor, Michigan, 1981.
Bazin, André, *The Cinema of Cruelty: From Buñuel to Hitchcock*, New York, 1982.
Narboni, Jean, editor, *Alfred Hitchcock*, Paris, 1982.
Rothman, William, *Hitchcock—The Murderous Gaze*, Cambridge, Massachusetts, 1982.
Villien, Bruno, *Hitchcock*, Paris, 1982.
Weis, Elisabeth, *The Silent Scream: Alfred Hitchcock's Sound Track*, Rutherford, New Jersey, 1982.
Belton, John, *Cinema Stylists*, Metuchen, New Jersey, 1983.
Spoto, Donald, *The Life of Alfred Hitchcock: The Dark Side of Genius*, New York, 1982; London, 1983.
Phillips, Gene D., *Alfred Hitchcock*, Boston, 1984.
Barbier, Philippe, and Jacques Moreau, *Alfred Hitchcock*, Paris, 1985.
Bruce, Graham, *Bernard Herrmann: Film Music and Narrative*, Ann Arbor, Michigan, 1985.
Douchet, Jean, *Alfred Hitchcock*, Paris, 1985.
Dentelbaum, Marshall, and Leland Poague, *A Hitchcock Reader*, Ames, Iowa, 1986.
Hogan, David J., *Dark Romance: Sexuality in the Horror Film*, Jefferson, North Carolina, 1986.
Humphries, Patrick, *The Films of Alfred Hitchcock*, Greenwich, Connecticut, 1986.
Kloppenburg, Josef, *Die dramaturgische Funktion der Musik in Filmen Alfred Hitchcocks*, Munich, 1986.
Sinyard, Neil, *The Films of Alfred Hitchcock*, London, 1986.
Modleski, Tania, *The Women Who Knew Too Much: Hitchcock and Feminist Theory*, New York, 1988.
Leitch, Thomas M., *Find the Director and Other Hitchcock Games*, Athens, Georgia, 1991.
Raubicheck, Walter, and Walter Srebnick, eds., *Hitchcock's Rereleased Films: From Rope to Vertigo*, Detroit, 1991.

The Birds

Sharff, Stefan, *Alfred Hitchcock's High Vernacular: Theory and Practice*, New York, 1991.

Finler, Joel W., *Hitchcock in Hollywood*, New York, 1992.

Kapsis, Robert E., *Hitchcock: The Making of a Reputation*, Chicago, 1992.

Spoto, Donald, *The Art of Alfred Hitchcock: Fifty Years of His Motion Pictures*, New York, 1992.

Corber, Robert J., *In the Name of National Security: Hitchcock, Homophobia, and the Political Construction of Gender in Postwar America*, Durham, North Carolina, 1993.

Hurley, Neil P., *Soul in Suspense: Hitchcock's Fright and Delight*, Metuchen, New Jersey, 1993.

Sloan, Jane, *Alfred Hitchcock: A Guide to References and Sources*, New York, 1993.

Arginteanu, Judy, *The Movies of Alfred Hitchcock*, Minneapolis, 1994.

Sloan, Jane E., *Alfred Hitchcock: A Filmography and Bibliography*, Berkeley, 1995.

Boyd, David, editor, *Perspectives on Alfred Hitchcock*, New York, 1995.

Rebello, Stephen, *Alfred Hitchcock and the Making of Psycho*, New York, 1998.

Freedman, Jonathan, and Richard Millington, editors, *Hitchcock's America*, New York, 1999.

Auiler, Dan, *Hitchcock's Notebooks: An Authorized and Illustrated Look Inside the Creative Mind of Alfred Hitchcock*, New York, 1999.

Articles:

Cameron Ian, and V. F. Perkins, interview with Hitchcock in *Movie* (London), January 1963.

Bogdanovich, Peter, in *Film Culture* (New York), Spring 1963.

Johnson, Albert, ''Echoes from *The Birds*,'' in *Sight and Sound* (London), Spring 1963.

Sarris, Andrew, in *Village Voice* (New York), 4 April 1963.

Foote, Sterling, in *Films in Review* (New York), May 1963.

''Hitchcock on Style: Interview,'' in *Cinema* (Beverly Hills), August 1963.

Baker, Peter, in *Films and Filming* (London), September 1963.

Belz, Carl, in *Film Culture* (New York), Winter 1963–64.

Thomas, John, in *Film Society Review* (New York), September 1966.

Hitchcock, Alfred, in *Take One* (Montreal), no.10, 1968.

Cumbow, R. C., "Caliban and Bodega Bay," in *Movietone News* (Seattle), May 1975.
Simper, D., "Poe, Hitchcock, and the Well-Wrought Effect," in *Literature/Film Quarterly* (Salisbury, Maryland), Summer 1975.
Rose, J., "Paranoia and the Film System," in *Screen* (London), Winter 1976–77.
Weis, Elisabeth, "The Sound of One Wing Flapping," in *Film Comment* (New York), September-October 1978.
Nichols, Bill, "*The Birds:* At the Window," in *Film Reader* (Evanston, Illinois), no. 4, 1979.
Bergstrom, J., "Enunciation and Sexual Difference," in *Cinema Obscura* (Berkeley), Summer 1979.
Bikacsy, G., "Alfred Hitchcock," in *Filmkultura* (Budapest), September-October 1979.
Counts, Kyle B., "The Making of Alfred Hitchcock's *The Birds*," in *Cinefantastique* (Oak Park, Illinois), Fall 1980.
Krohn, B., and others, in *Cahiers du Cinéma* (Paris), June 1982.
Horwitz, Margaret M., "A Mother's Love," in *Wide Angle* (Athens, Ohio), vol. 5, no. 1, 1982.
Kapsis, Robert E., "Hollywood Filmmaking and Reputation Building: Hitchcock's *The Birds*," in *Journal of Popular Film and Television* (Washington, D.C.), Spring 1987.
Girard, M., "*The Birds*," in *Séquences* (Quebec), no. 169, February 1994.
Silet, Charles L.P., "Writing for Hitch: An Interview with Evan Hunter," and Christopher Sharrett, "The Myth of Apocalypse and the Horror Film: The Primacy of *Psycho* and *The Birds*," in *Hitchcock Annual* (New London, New Hampshire), Fall 1995–96.
Allen, R., "Avian Metaphors in *The Birds*," in *Hitchcock Annual* (New London, New Hampshire), Fall 1997–98.
Vest, James M., "Echoes of Alfred Hitchcock's *Vertigo*, *The Birds*, and *Frenzy* in Francois Truffaut's *Story of Adèle H.*," in *Hitchcock Annual* (New London, New Hampshire), Fall 1997–98.

* * *

Of *The Birds*, Peter Bogdanovich has written, "If (Alfred Hitchcock) had never made another motion picture in his life, *The Birds* would place him securely among the giants of the cinema." Released in 1963, *The Birds* is one in a series of Hitchcock collaborations with composer Bernard Herrmann, cinematographer Robert Burks, and editor George Tomasini. It was also the director's first film featuring actress Tippi Hedren, who would later star in *Marnie*, perhaps the most critically controversial film of Hitchcock's career.

The Birds seems to be a film which functions as a Rorschach test, in which every critic sees something different, and of which virtually anything can be said. It has been discussed as a generic work of horror which inaugurated a whole series of apocalyptic films; as a film of special effects and state-of-the-art matte work representing the ingenuity of Hollywood; as the most sophisticated example of Hitchcock's ability to manipulate his audiences and to play upon the spectators' fears; as a profound and personal work concerning human frailty and the importance of commitment in human relationships; as a philosophical treatise—influenced by Kafka and Poe—on the existential human condition; as a structural work examining the point-of-view shot and its relationship to the gaze of the spectator; as a repository of psychoanalytic ideology and meanings; and as the American film most influenced by and celebrative of the montage theories promulgated by the Russian cinema theorists. That this film has been interpreted in so many ways, that the memory of it remains so strong for so many filmmakers and critics, and that the film continues to excite and provoke new generations of filmgoers, are the surest signs that *The Birds* is indeed a great and lasting film.

Those who see the film for the first time may be surprised by the strength of their visceral response, but those who view the film an additional time are inevitably surprised by how much of the film has actually little to do with bird attacks and takes, instead, the relationships between human beings as its subject. Certainly *The Birds* contains some of the most disturbing and almost surrealistically beautiful images Hitchcock has ever put on film; the children's party disrupted by a bird attack; the camera's treatment of Tippi Hedren as a fetish object; the surprising aerial view of Bodega Bay which shows the city from the birds' point of view; the three virtually still shots—each catching a discreet moment of time—of Tippi Hedren watching helplessly through the window of a cafe; and, especially, the final exterior scene, poetic and mysterious, aided by the extraordinary matte paintings of Al Whitlock, as the protagonists drive off into an unearthly bird-populated landscape and an uncertain future.

—Charles Derry

THE BIRTH OF A NATION

USA, 1915

Director: D. W. Griffith

Production: Epoch Producing Corporation; black and white, 35mm, silent; length: 13,058 feet, later cut to 12,000 feet. Released 8 February 1915, Los Angeles. Re-released 1930 with musical soundtrack. Filmed 4 July through 24 September 1914 in Reliance-Majestic Studios, Los Angeles, and various outdoor locations around Los Angeles; cost: $110,000.

Producer: D. W. Griffith; **scenario:** D. W. Griffith, Thomas Dixon, and Frank Woods, from the play *The Clansman* by the Rev. Thomas Dixon; **assistants to the director include:** Eric von Stroheim, Raoul Walsh, Jack Conway, and George Siegman; **photography:** G. W. (Billy) Bitzer and Karl Brown; **editor:** James Smith; **compiler of music for the sound version:** Joseph Carl Breil, assisted by D. W. Griffith; **costume supplier:** Robert Goldstein.

Cast: Henry B. Walthall (*Ben Cameron, the "Little Colonel"*); Mae Marsh (*Flora*); Miriam Cooper (*Margaret, the older sister*); Violet Wilkey (*Flora as a child*); Josephine Crowell (*Mrs. Cameron*); Spottiswoode Aitken (*Dr. Cameron*); Andre Beranger (*Wade Cameron*); Maxfield Stanley (*Duke Cameron*); Jennie Lee (*Mammy*); William De Vaull (*Jake*); Lillian Gish (*Elsie Stoneman*); Ralph Lewis

The Birth of a Nation

(*The Hon. Austin Stoneman*); Elmer Clifton (*Phil Stoneman*); Robert Harron (*Ted Stoneman*); Mary Alden (*Lydia Brown, Stoneman's housekeeper*); Tom Wilson (*Stoneman's Negro servant*); Sam De Grasse (*Senator Sumner*); George Siegman (*Silas Lynch*); Walter Long (*Gus*); Elmo Lincoln (*White Arm Joe*); Wallace Reid (*Jeff, the blacksmith*); Joseph Henaberry (*Abraham Lincoln*); Alberta Lee (*Mrs. Lincoln*); Donald Crisp (*Gen. Ulysses S. Grant*); Howard Gaye (*Gen. Robert E. Lee*); William Freeman (*Sentry*); Olga Grey (*Laura Keene*); Raoul Walsh (*John Wilkes Booth*); Eugene Palette (*Union Soldier*); Bessie Love (*Piedmont Girl*); Charles Stevens (*Volunteer*); Erich von Stroheim (*Man who falls off roof*).

Publications

Scripts:

Huff, Theodore, *A Shot Analysis of D. W. Griffith's Birth of a Nation*, New York, 1961.

Cunibert, John, *The Birth of a Nation*, a shot by shot analysis, Woodbridge, Connecticut, 1979.

Books:

Lindsay, Vachel, *The Art of the Moving Picture*, New York, 1915; revised edition, 1922.

Paine, Albert Bigelow, *Life and Lillian Gish*, New York, 1932.

Jacobs, Lewis, *The Rise of the American Film*, New York, 1939.

Agee, James, *Agee on Film I*, New York, 1948.

Noble, Peter, *The Negro in Films*, London, 1948.

Wagenknecht, Edward, *The Movies in the Age of Innocence*, Norman, Oklahoma, 1962.

Aitken, Roy, *The Birth of a Nation Story*, as told to Al P. Nelson, Middleburg, Virginia, 1965.

Barry, Iris, *D. W. Griffith: American Film Master*, New York, 1965.

Pratt, George C., *Spellbound in Darkness*, Connecticut, 1966.

Brownlow, Kevin, *The Parade's Gone By . . .*, London and New York, 1969.

Cook, Raymond Allen, *Fire from the Flint*, Winston-Salem, North Carolina, 1968.

Gish, Lillian, with Ann Pinchot, *Lillian Gish: The Movies, Mr. Griffith, and Me*, Englewood Cliffs, New Jersey, 1969.

Silva, Fred, editor, *Focus on Birth of a Nation*, New York, 1971.

Henderson, Robert M., *D. W. Griffith: His Life and Work*, New York, 1972.
Brown, Karl, *Adventures with D. W. Griffith*, edited by Kevin Brownlow, New York and London, 1973; revised edition, 1988.
Cripps, Thomas J., *Slow Fade to Black: The Negro in American Film, 1900–1942*, New York, 1977.
Campbell, Edward D. C., Jr., *The Celluloid South*, Knoxville, 1981.
Giannetti, Louis, *Masters of the American Cinema*, Englewood Cliffs, New Jersey, 1981.
Brion, Patrick, editor, *D. W. Griffith*, Paris, 1982.
Mottet, Jean, editor, *D. W. Griffith*, Paris, 1984.
Schickel, Richard, *D. W. Griffith and the Birth of Film*, London, 1984.
Graham, Cooper C., and others, *D.W. Griffith and the Biograph Company*, Metuchen, New Jersey, 1985.
Jesionowski, Joyce E., *Thinking in Pictures: Dramatic Structures in D. W. Griffith's Biograph Films*, Berkeley, 1987.
Lang, Robert, editor, *The Birth of a Nation: D. W. Griffith, Director*, New Brunswick, New Jersey, 1994.

Articles:

New York Times, 4 March 1915.
New York Tribune, 4 March 1915.
Variety (New York), 12 March 1915.
''The Civil War in Film,'' in *Literary Digest* (New York), 20 March 1915.
New Republic (New York), 4 December 1915.
Griffith, D. W., ''The Rise and Fall of Free Speech in America,'' (a pamphlet written in answer to the reaction against *The Birth of a Nation*), Los Angeles, 1916.
Gordon, Henry Stephen, ''D. W. Griffith Recalls the Making of *The Birth of a Nation*,'' in *The Photoplay Magazine* (Hollywood), October 1916.
Platt, David D., ''The Negro in Hollywood,'' in *Daily Worker* (New York), 19–28 February 1940.
Carter, Everett, ''Cultural History Written with Lightning: The Significance of *The Birth of a Nation*,'' in *American Quarterly* (University of Pennsylvania), Fall 1960.
Fulton, A. R., ''Editing in *The Birth of a Nation*,'' in *Motion Pictures: The Development of an Art from Silent Pictures to the Age of Television*, Norman, Oklahoma, 1960.
Cripps, Thomas R., ''The Reaction of the Negro to the Motion Picture, *The Birth of a Nation*,'' in *The Historian*, May 1963.
''Griffith Issue'' of *Film Culture* (New York), Spring-Summer 1965.
Sarris, Andrew, ''*Birth of a Nation* of White Power Back When,'' in *Village Voice* (New York), 17 and 24 July 1969.
Beylie, Claude, ''*Naissance d'une Nation:* La Piste du Geant,'' in *Cinéma* (Paris), March 1971.
Casty, Alan, ''The Films of D. W. Griffith: A Style for the Times,'' in *Journal of Popular Film* (Washington, D.C.), Spring 1972.
Merritt, Russell, ''Dixon, Griffith, and the Southern Legend,'' in *Cinema Journal* (Austin, Texas), Fall 1972.
Simcovitch, Maxim, ''The Impact of Griffith's *Birth of a Nation* on Modern Ku Klux Klan,'' in *Journal of Popular Film* (Washington, D.C.), Winter 1972.
Yacowar, Maurice, ''In Defense of Minority Group Stereotyping in the Popular Film,'' in *Literature/Film Quarterly* (Salisbury, Maryland), Spring 1974.
''*Birth of a Nation* Issue'' of *Kosmorama* (Copenhagen), Summer 1975.
Turconi, D., ''G. P. and D. W. G . . . in dare e l'avere,'' in *Bianco e nero* (Rome), Summer 1975.
Oms, Marcel, ''*Naissance d'une nation:* Opera maconnique,'' in *Cahiers du Cinéma* (Paris), Christmas 1975.
''Griffithiana: Material della e per la storia del cinema . . . ,'' in *Filmcritica* (Rome), January-February 1976.
''*Birth of a Nation* Case,'' in *Classic Film Collection* (Indiana, Pennsylvania), Fall 1976.
''*Birth of a Nation* Issue'' of *Cahiers du Cinéma* (Paris), 15 October 1977.
Petric, Vlada, ''Two Lincoln Assassinations by D. W. Griffith,'' in *Quarterly Review of Film Studies* (Pleasantville, New York), Summer 1978.
''In Defence of the KKK,'' reprinted in *Monthly Film Bulletin* (London), May 1979.
Combs, R., in *Monthly Film Bulletin* (London), May 1979.
Fleener, N., ''Answering Film with Film . . . ,'' in *Journal of Popular Film and Television* (Washington, D.C.), no. 4, 1980.
Stern, Seymour, in *American Classic Screen* (Shawnee Mission, Kansas), November-December 1980.
Merritt, Russell, ''Dixon, Griffith and the Southern Legend: A Cultural Analysis of *The Birth of a Nation*,'' in *Cinema Examined*, New York, 1982.
Pinsky, Mark, ''Racism, History, and Mass Media,'' in *Jump Cut* (Berkeley) no. 28, 1983.
Martin, J. B., ''Film Out of Theatre: D. W. Griffith, *Birth of a Nation* and the Melodrama *The Clansmen*,'' in *Literature/Film Quarterly* (Salisbury, Maryland), no. 2, 1990.
Leblanc, G., ''L'art de raconter et de persuader: *La naissance d'une nation*,'' in *Cinemaction* (Conde-sur-Noireau, France), January 1990.
Taylor, C., ''The Re-birth of the Aesthetic in Cinema,'' in *Wide Angle* (Baltimore), no. 3–4, 1991.
Vanoye, Francis, ''Rhétorique de la douleur,'' in *Vertigo* (Paris), no. 6–7, 1991.
Heine, Isabelle, ''L'analyse videographique: conceptualisation et formalisation,'' in *Revue Belge du Cinéma* (Brussels), September 1992.
Hoberman, J., ''Our Troubling *Birth* Rite,'' in *Village Voice* (New York), 30 November 1993.
Couvares, F.G., ''The Good Censor: Race, Sex, and Censorship in the Early Cinema,'' in *Yale Journal of Criticism* (New Haven), vol. 7, no. 2, 1994.
Cripps, Thomas, ''The Absent Presence in America Civil War Films,'' in *Historical Journal of Film, Radio, and Television* (Hants, United Kingdom), vol. 14, no. 4, October 1994.
Grimes, William, ''An Effort to Classify a Racist Classic,'' in *New York Times*, 27 April 1994.
Moore, D.C., ''Regarding 'Racism' of D. W. Griffith,'' in *Films of the Golden Age* (Muscatine, Iowa), no. 5, Summer 1996.
Rogin, M. ''The Two Declarations of American Independence,'' *Representations* (Berkeley), no. 55, Summer 1996.
Green, J.R., ''Micheaux v. Griffith,'' in *Griffithiana* (Temple, Arizona), no. 60, October 1997.
Gill, D., ''*The Birth of a Nation* Orphan or Pariah?'' in *Griffithiana* (Temple, Arizona), no. 60, October 1997.

* * *

"More than any picture before it, it made moviegoing a middle class activity," writes Joan L. Silverman of *The Birth of a Nation* (French, ed., *The South in Film*). "Soon movie palaces were built in fashionable neighborhoods all over the United States." More than that, the film remains one of the most controversial of the medium's first century. The National Association for the Advancement of Colored People (NAACP) branded it racist; riots followed in cities such as Boston; widespread picketing and lawsuits continued for years in many cities and states. Although Griffith found it difficult to raise the $110,000 that the film cost, and production was halted at times for fund-raising drives, by the end of the silent film period, it had made $18,000,000.

Griffith's much-hailed narrative techniques are relatively simple but enormously influential adaptations and expansions of the "villain still pursued her" formulaic storytelling of 19th-century theatrical melodramas. Griffith was an unknown actor when he was hired by Biograph Studios of New York to make the one-reel, 12-minute fictional films that were changed weekly at storefront nickelodeons. By the end of 1910 he had made 250, but was losing patience with the length limitation. An experimental two-reeler, however, was split by producers into two weeks' shows. Not until the summer of 1913, after he had completed another 175 or so films, was he allowed finally to expand to four reels with *Judith of Bethulia*. Dissatisfied, he left Biograph to join Harry E. Aitken's new company to make five five-to-seven reel films during the first six months of 1914. Meanwhile he was plotting—in a double sense—to match the competition from abroad, especially Italy, where since 1911, the flamboyant poet Gabrielle D'Annunzio, had developed a series of spectacular but static films based on classical motifs into the ten-reel *Cabiria*. Critics predicted this would "convince many doubtful people that high art and the motion picture are not incompatible" (Pratt, ed., *Spellbound in Darkness*, 1966).

Griffith was determined, after moving his operations from over-crowded New York City to Los Angeles, to push American films to the forefront just at the time that European production was curtailed by World War I. He opted, however, for action over art. In 1908 he had worked briefly for the self-proclaimed bigot Thomas Dixon, Jr., who had cobbled together two of his rabble-rousing novels about the South during Reconstruction into a play called *The Clansman*. The Reverend Dixon was willing to sell the rights for the then huge sum of $10,000 (£2,000).

The opening portion of the film was apparently created on the spot by Griffith, as no script exists. The scene opens in pre-Civil War Piedmont, the gracious pastoral capital of a deep Southern state, in which the Cameron family and those "faithful souls," their household slaves, are entertaining affectionately the sons of northern Congressman Austin Stoneman (based somewhat fancifully on Pennsylvania's radical Republican Senator Thaddeus Stevens). The outbreak of war disrupts this relationship—and when the boys face each other on the battlefield, the younger son of each family is killed. Griffith proclaimed in an opening subtitle that this message was that "war must be held in abhorrence."

Ben Cameron is falsely accused of spying and sentenced to death; his mother makes a precarious trip to Washington to plead for him, and the Great Heart, President Lincoln, grants a pardon. Mrs. Cameron's cause is abetted by Elsie Stoneman, who had not visited Piedmont with her brothers, but who has come to know and love Ben while nursing him back to health. Through this episodic section of the film, Griffith interrupts the heart-rending saga of the families with what he insisted were authentic reconstructions of some of the great moments of the war and its aftermath, including the assassination of President Lincoln, whom Griffith believed could have ameliorated the situation after the war.

With the assassination, Dixon takes over; and public history gives way to private myth. Congressman Stoneman becomes the fiery apostle of Reconstruction, determined to replace traitorous Southern leaders with freed slaves whom his cabal can manipulate. He appoints Silas Lynch, his mulatto cohort, the new lieutenant-governor in Piedmont to organize this. When a renegade black soldier, inflamed by Lynch's proddings and free liquor, threatens to rape Ben Cameron's "pet sister," she jumps from a cliff to her death rather than suffer dishonour. Outraged, Ben, after watching children donning sheets and playing ghosts, is portrayed by Griffith as founding the Ku Klux Klan (KKK) to restore proper law and order to the South and keep the blacks in their place. Enraged, Silas Lynch sets out to destroy the Klan and the Camerons, and also to marry Elsie Stoneman, by force if necessary. When the Congressman learns of his henchman's audacity, he sees the error of his ways. In the most famous sequence of the film, Griffith uses the stunning effect of alternating closeups and long-shots, enhanced by printing the black images on stock tinted in a variety of colours that it was theorized influenced viewers' reactions (red for battle scenes, green for pastoral romance, etc.).

Elsie is rescued from Lynch's townhouse to join the frenzied dash to the lonely cabin where the Camerons are preparing to join their dead daughter. The Klan comes to the rescue at the last moment, paving the way for a double wedding between the Camerons and the Stonemans which restores peace to the community. However, it leaves open the question of whether the "nation" whose "birth" Griffith had in mind was that of the "Invisible Empire" of the KKK or of the disunited states, at last peacefully amalgamated by this symbolic marriage.

The first audiences saw the long runs of the big city "road shows"; a live orchestra accompanied the film, playing a rousing score by Joseph Carl Breil. Griffith travelled around the country constantly editing the film; the censors insisted upon other cuts. The results of this editing toned down the racist elements that Lillian Gish had feared might make people object to the film; however, protests to the film continued.

Griffith tried to remedy the situation by making his first talking picture *Abraham Lincoln* and by releasing a cut version of *The Birth of a Nation*, which was almost an hour shorter than the original; all references to the KKK were eliminated.

The film remains a landmark in the development of motion pictures. Its length (rarely equalled since), its exploitation of technical devices (producing startlingly new effects), and its establishment of the pattern of the horse opera that dominated American film melodrama, accord it a unique place in the evolution of American and international filmmaking.

It retains its sentimental and provocative power, but its circulation is restricted to groups studying both Griffith's reasons for making the film and the damage inflicted on a new medium by a great innovator's propagandistic vision. Perhaps the most perceptive judgement was written by a reviewer for the *New York Times* in 1921: "Sometimes it is almost epic in quality. But in many scenes it is falsely romantic and as blindly partisan as the most violent sectional tradition. It may be said that, as a rule, it comes closest to historical truth when it is furthest from Thomas Dixon.''

—Warren French

BIRUMA NO TATEGOTO

(Harp of Burma)

Japan, 1956

Director: Kon Ichikawa

Production: Nikkatsu (Japan); black and white, 35mm; running time: 116 minutes. Released 1956.

Screenplay: Natto Wada, from an original story by Michio Takeyama; **photography:** Minoru Yokoyama; **editor:** Masonori Truju; **production design:** Takashi Matsuyama; **music:** Akira Ifukube.

Cast: Shoji Yasui (*Private Mizushima*); Rentaro Mikuni (*Captain Inouye*); Taniye Kita Bayashi (*Old woman*); Tatsuya Mihashi (*Defensive commander*); Yunosuke Ito (*Village head*).

Awards: San Giorgio Prize, Venice Film Festival, 1956.

Biruma no Tategoto

Publications

Books:

Anderson, Joseph, and Donald Richie, *The Japanese Film: Art and Industry*, Rutland, Vermont, 1959.
Svensson, Arne, *Japan*, New York, 1971.
Mellen, Joan, *Voices from the Japanese Cinema*, New York, 1975.
Soumi, Angelo, *Kon Ichikawa*, Florence, 1975.
Bock, Audie, *Japanese Film Directors*, New York, 1978.
Allyn, John, *Kon Ichikawa: A Guide to References and Resources*, Boston, 1985.

Articles:

Baker, Peter, in *Films and Filming* (London), April 1960.
Richie, Donald, ''The Several Sides of Kon Ichikawa,'' in *Sight and Sound* (London), Spring 1966.
Milne, Tom, ''The Skull Beneath the Skin,'' in *Sight and Sound* (London), Autumn 1966.
Ichikawa, Kon, and others, ''The Uniqueness of Kon Ichikawa,'' in *Cinema* (Beverly Hills), Fall 1970.
Johnson, W., ''Ichikawa and the Wanderers,'' in *Film Comment* (New York), September-October 1975.
Variety (New York), 12 June 1985.
Dipont, M., in *Kino* (Warsaw), June 1986.
Dissanayake, Wimal, ''Self, Agency, and Cultural Knowledge: Reflections on Three Japanese Films,'' in Wimal Dissanayake, editor, *Narratives of Agency: Self-Making in China, India, and Japan*, Minneapolis, 1996.

* * *

Biruma no tategoto, directed by Kon Ichikawa, won the San Giorgio Prize at the 1956 Venice Film Festival. Although Ichikawa had been directing since 1945, this was the first film to bring him international recognition.

The film, starring Shoji Yasui as Private Mizushima and Rentaro Mikuni as Captain Inouye, concerns the last days of World War II in Burma. Mizushima's unit is captured and they are made prisoners of war. He is reported missing, but actually he has been commissioned to convince a garrison of Japanese soldiers to surrender rather than incur further bloodshed. He is unsuccessful in his mission, and the garrison is attacked, Mizushima becoming the sole survivor. He is nursed back to health by a Buddhist priest whose robes he steals in an effort to return to his unit. Crossing the island he comes upon several abandoned corpses and feels compelled to bury them. For the Japanese, to die on foreign soil and remain unburied is the most ignoble of deaths. By the time he meets his former companions, he is committed to his new mission of burying the dead and refuses to be repatriated.

In concept the film reflects the post-World War II pacifism prevalent in Japan as well as a spirit of international humanism. Both Japanese and British are portrayed as caring individuals caught up in an inhuman war. War and death are the enemies. Mizushima's decision to remain in Burma is an act of contrition, which emerges in part from a sense of Japanese postwar shame and guilt. Throughout his wanderings, Mizushima carries a Burmese harp. This serves as a source of inspiration, a signal, and a means of communication which unites British and Japanese. The tune, ''There's No Place Like Home,'' an American melody, is sung alternatively by both groups, signifying the peaceful commitment to home and family which Mizushima will be sacrificing by remaining in Burma. Ultimately the harp becomes Mizushima's voice.

In addition to the interplay of light and shadow, evocative close-ups, and point-of-view shots, *Biruma no tategoto* is noteworthy for its fragmented narrative structure. The story unfolds through a series of flashbacks and parallel action depicting Mizushima's plight in contrast to the experiences of his unit.

Like Ichikawa's next film, *Nobi*, the film documents the human suffering, brutality, and carnage which are inevitable results of war. However, whereas *Nobi* ends on a pessimistic note with the death of the hero, *Biruma no tategoto* closes on an inspirational note, signalling the goodness of man and universal brotherhood. Ideologically the film speaks of the value of life and survival in opposition to the pre-World War II official position of allegiance to the Emperor and dishonor in surrender.

The film plays upon the traditional conflict between *giri* and *ninjo* (desire and duty). Mizushima longs to rejoin his friends and to return to Japan. But he is equally pulled by a higher duty which calls for the burial of the dead. As in all Japanese narratives, *ninjo* wins out after an emotional struggle. Mizushima's choice is especially difficult because his voluntary isolation deprives him of group support and comradery, a crucial aspect of Japanese society. Ichikawa's emphasis upon the warmth of group solidarity makes Mizushima's loss all the more heartrending. Further, Ichikawa, in an exception to the ironic attitude which pervades the majority of his works, expresses an emotionalism, especially in the scenes where the men beg Mizushima to return with them and in Mizushima's silent determination to remain.

The film ends as the ship taking the soldiers home pulls away from shore. It is a subjective shot from Mizushima's point of view. On board the men talk of the Ginza and movies. They have already turned to the future. Only Mizushima remains to remember the past. His solitary sadness reflects a traditional view of the acceptance of life's tragedies. Yet equally, *Biruma no tategoto* marks Japan's postwar conversion from one value system to another. The film's implicit critique of feudal values reflects Japan's decision to become a full member of the international democratic community.

—Patricia Erens

BLACK GOD, WHITE DEVIL

See **DEUS E O DIABO NA TERRA DO SOL**

BLACK NARCISSUS

UK, 1947

Directors: Michael Powell, Emeric Pressburger

Production: The Archers, for Independent Productions; Technicolor; running time: 100 minutes. Released April 1947.

Producers: Michael Powell, Emeric Pressburger; **assistant producer:** George R. Busby; **screenplay:** Michael Powell and Emeric Pressburger, from the novel by Rumer Godden; **assistant director:** Sydney S. Streeter; **photographer:** Jack Cardiff; **associate photographer:** Joan Bridge; **camera operators:** Ted Scaife, Stan Sayers; **process shots:** W. Percy Day; **color control:** Natalie Kalmus; **editor:** Reginald Mills; **sound recordist:** Stanley Lambourne; **sound re-recordist:** Gordon K. McCallum; **production designer:** Alfred Junge; **assistant art director:** Arthur Lawson; **costume designer:** Hein Heckroth; **music:** Brian Easdale; **music performed by:** London Symphony Orchestra.

Black Narcissus

Cast: Deborah Kerr (*Sister Clodagh*); Sabu (*The Young general*); David Farrar (*Mr. Dean*); Flora Robson (*Sister Philippa*); Esmond Knight (*The Old general*); Jean Simmons (*Kanchi*); Kathleen Byron (*Sister Ruth*); Jenny Laird (*Blanche, ''Sister Honey''*); Judith Furse (*Sister Briony*); May Hallatt (*Angu Ayah*); Eddie Whaley, Jr. (*Joseph Anthony*); Shaun Noble (*Con*); Nancy Roberts (*Mother Dorothea*); Ley On (*Phuba*).

Publications

Books:

Durgnat, Raymond, *A Mirror for England: British Movies from Austerity to Affluence*, London, 1970.

Cosandey, Roland, editor, *Retrospective: Powell and Pressburger*, Locarno, 1982.

Gottler, Fritz, and others, *Living Cinema: Powell and Pressburger*, Munich, 1982.

Christie, Ian, *Arrows of Desire: The Films of Michael Powell and Emeric Pressburger*, London, 1985.

Martini, Emanuela, editor, *Powell and Pressburger*, Bergamo, 1986.

Powell, Michael, *A Life in Movies: An Autobiography*, London, 1986.

Articles:

Kine Weekly (London), 24 April 1947.

Variety (New York), 5 May 1947.

Christie, Ian, and R. Collins, ''Michael Powell: The Expense of Naturalism,'' in *Monogram* (London), no. 3, 1972.

Walker, Michael, in *Framework* (Warwick), Winter 1978–79.

Lacourbe, R., ''Redecouvrir Michael Powell,'' in *Ecran* (Paris), 15 February 1979.

Andrews, N., and H. Kennedy, ''Peerless Powell,'' in *Film Comment* (New York), May-June 1979.

Thompson, D., ''The Films of Michael Powell: A Romantic Sensibility,'' in *American Film* (Washington, D.C.), November 1980.

Everson, William K., in *Films in Review* (New York), August-September 1980.

McVay, Douglas, in *Films and Filming* (London), January 1982.

Durgnat, Raymond, in *Monthly Film Bulletin* (London), October 1984.

Interview with Powell in *City Limits* (London), 3 January 1986.

Combs, Richard, in *Listener* (London), 9 January 1986.

Sheehan, H., in *Film Comment* (New York), May-June 1990.

Pernod, P., ''Les fantomes de soeur Clodagh,'' *Positif* (Paris), November 1991.

* * *

When Powell and Pressburger decided to film an adaptation of Rumer Godden's tale of a failed attempt by Anglican Nuns to establish a convent in the Himalayas, the prospect of shooting in Katmandu filled some of their regular collaborators with great excitement. Such hopes were quickly dashed when it was announced that the entire film would be made in Britain. However, this inspired decision resulted in the creation of one of the most visually imaginative and expressive contributions to a cinema heralded more for its naturalism than such exercises in studio-bound artifice. The palace of Mopu, the former harem turned convent where most of the action takes place, was designed by Alfred Junge and was built at Pinewood. The Himalayan backdrop was painted on sheets of glass and the mountain breeze supplied by a gigantic wind machine. Junge was rewarded with an Oscar, as was Jack Cardiff whose Technicolor cinematography gives the film visual depth and a subtlety rare in colour productions of the time. The studio setting also allowed for total control over atmosphere and mood which, in conjunction with the technical virtuosity, explains why *Black Narcissus* continues to work its magic on new generations of cineastes.

Godden's interest in the confrontation of East and West and the struggle of the nuns who, rather than living in solitude, are forced to confront the world and remain true to their vows is transcended by Powell and Pressburger's concerns with sexuality and, more specifically, the dangers of sexual repression. Indeed Michael Walker perceptively argues that *Black Narcissus* dramatises a key Freudian syndrome: the return of the repressed. This is the sense of something terrible or uncontrollable returning to haunt the helpless protagonists. Therefore Walker suggests that the failure of the nuns to establish their convent has less to do with the ''otherness'' of the locale or the people but rather that they ''carry within them the seeds of their own defeat.''

The film is undoubtedly tinged with Orientalist cliché: the local natives are depicted as simple and childlike; Eastern mysticism represented by the mute Holy man who sits under his tree in perpetual meditation; the unbridled exoticism represented by the young general (Sabu) and Kanchi (Jean Simmons). Kanchi like the Holy man never speaks, her silence underlining her cool, seductive ''otherness'' which contrasts starkly with the increasingly hysterical voices of the sisters. Moreover, the strangeness of the environment, where ''the wind never stops blowing and the air is so clear you can see too far,'' is blamed for the rising unease amongst the Europeans. Yet *Black Narcissus* also mocks exoticism and otherness, particularly at the moment when Sabu announces that his perfume—the ''Black Narcissus'' of the title—was purchased at the Army and Navy stores. We must also remember the studio setting which renders the Oriental backdrop as literally a construct, an artificial stage which functions to frame the action and define the characters. The palace is first introduced as a watercolour representation and is last seen disappearing into the mists like Brigadoon.

But as the strain begins to tell on the nuns, as repressions return to haunt them, it becomes clear that the chief catalyst, certainly in the case of both Sister Clodagh (Deborah Kerr) and Sister Ruth (Kathleen Byron) is Mr. Dean (David Farrar), the British agent working for the local ruler who has invited the nuns. Like the natives, Dean is also sexualized in terms of appearance with his brightly coloured shirts and bare arms and legs, contrasting with the ascetic off-white habits of the nuns. At one moment of crisis he arrives on the scene stripped to the waist, giving us a wonderfully potent image of raw male sexuality.

Dean's initially prickly encounters with Clodagh mask something else altogether. Clodagh's real feelings towards him are first signalled in a brief look of longing which in turn triggers her first memory of her past in Ireland—her love for childhood sweetheart Con whose departure for America led to her becoming a nun.

Ruth's desire is more overtly portrayed as pathological. Unseen, she watches Dean and Clodagh, her eyes blazing with a mixture of lust and jealously. Indeed Ruth functions as an embodiment of the danger of Clodagh's sexual repression. While being chastised for paying too much attention to Mr. Dean, she confronts Clodagh with the unspeakable—''you seem quite pleased to see him yourself.'' This tension leads to the memorable stand-off between the two when a shocked Clodagh encounters a transformed Ruth, her habit exchanged for a crimson dress. She taunts Clodagh by lasciviously applying rouge to her lips while Clodagh sits opposite, clutching a bible.

But Dean is no more able to fully accept his own feelings for Clodagh. He is consistently rude to her and when taunted by the spurned Ruth about his love for Clodagh he flies into an uncontrolled rage screaming, ''I don't love anybody.'' Ruth's failure to seduce Dean leaves her with only one choice of action left—the destruction of her rival—and so the film builds to its devastating climax. In the golden light of dawn Ruth stalks Clodagh to the chapel before erupting out of the Palace doors like an apparition from hell and attempting to push Clodagh over the precipice as she rings the morning bell. In the struggle it is Ruth who falls to her death. This sequence was an early experiment by Powell in what he termed ''composed film,'' scored first by Brian Easdale then shot according to the rhythms of the soundtrack.

The departure of the nuns underlines the ultimate victory of repression. Clodagh and Dean exchange pleasantries, she offers him her hand which he holds momentarily. Then the rains break, interpreted by at least one critic as a symbol of sexual release, but we are left with an image of Dean, fated to remain with the ''ghosts'' which Clodagh is able to leave behind. The release of *Black Narcissus* in 1947 coincided with the end of the Raj. The retreat of the nuns not only echoes the British withdrawal from India. It is the image of Dean, the English colonialist suffering the burden of his own repressed emotions, which provides an unintentional reflection on the undoing of imperial power.

—Duncan Petrie

BLACK ORPHEUS

See **ORFEU NEGRO**

BLACK SUNDAY

US, 1977

Director: John Frankenheimer

Production: Paramount Pictures; color, 35mm, Panavision; sound: mono; running time: 143 minutes. Filmed in Beirut, Lebanon, Miami, Florida, and Oregon.

Producers: Robert Evans, Alan Levine (associate), Robert L. Rosen (executive); **music:** John Williams; **cinematograper:** John A. Alonzo; **editor:** Tom Rolfe; **casting:** Lynn Stalmaster; **sound:** Howard Beals, Gene S. Cantamessa, John Wilkinson; **special effects:** Logan Frazee, Gene Warren, Jr.; **stunts:** Everett Creach, Howard Curtis; **art direction:** Walter H. Tyler; **set decoration:** Jerry Wunderlich; **costume design:** Ray Summers; **makeup:** Sugar Blymer, Bob Dawn, Brad Wilder; **production manager:** Jerry Ziesmer.

Cast: Robert Shaw (*Kabakov*); Bruce Dern (*Lander*); Marthe Keller (*Dahlia*); Fritz Weaver (*Corley*); Steven Keats (*Moshevsky*); Bekim Fehmiu (*Fasil*); Michael V. Gazzo (*Muzi*); William Daniels (*Pugh*); Walter Gotell (*Colonel Riaf*); Victor Campos (*Nageeb*); Joseph Robbie (*Himself*); Robert Wussler (*Himself*); Pat Summerall (*Himself*); Tom Brookshier (*Himself*); Walter Brooke (*Fowler*); James Jeter (*Watchman*); Clyde Kusatsu (*Freighter*); Captain Tom McFadden (*Farley*); Robert Patten (*Vickers*); Than Wyenn (*Israeli Ambassador*); Jack Rader (*Pearson*); Nick Nickolary (*Simmons*); Hunter von Leer (*T.V. Cameraman*); Sarah Fankboner (*V.A. Receptionist*); Kathy Thornton (*Head Nurse*); Frank Logan (*Lansing*); Frank Man (*Desk Clerk*); Kenneth I. Harms (*S.W.A.T. Captain*); Kim Nicholas (*Girl Hostage*); Bert Madrid (*Bellhop*); Ian Bulloch (*Secret Service Agent* [uncredited]); Michael J. Reynolds (*Jackson*).

Publications

Books:

Pratley, Gerald, *The Cinema of John Frankenheimer*, New York, 1969.

Pratley, Gerald, *The Films of Frankenheimer: Forty Years in Film*, Bethlehem, Pennsylvania, 1998.

Articles:

Drew, B., ''John Frankenheimer: His Fall and Rise,'' in *American Film* (Washington, D.C.), vol. 2, no. 5, March 1977.

Hansard, B., ''Creating Front Projection Effects for *Black Sunday*,'' in *American Cinematographer* (Hollywood), vol. 58, no. 8, August 1977.

* * *

Black Sunday was produced in the wake of the Arab-Israeli conflicts of 1967 and 1973. Within the conventional limits of Hollywood storytelling, the film treats intelligently the relationship between political turmoil in the Middle East and the advent of international terrorism on a broad scale, one of the most significant developments of the era. *Black Sunday* thus connects more meaningfully to contemporary historical events than the ordinary American commercial film. Director John Frankenheimer offers a nightmare version of what might result from the despair of radical Palestinians at the increasingly bleak prospect of any conventional military or political settlement of their claims for repatriation and statehood. Deciding to launch a campaign of terror against the American people so that the rich and politically settled can, in the words of their leader, ''share the pain of the Palestinian people,'' members of a Black September cell plan to kill everyone present at the Super Bowl football game.

In this plot they are nearly successful. Aided by a Japanese fellow traveler, who supplies the necessary explosives, and a disaffected, perhaps insane former American soldier, who acts as their pilot, the group arrange to hijack the Goodyear blimp, normally used to help broadcast the game, load it with a bomb composed of *plastique* and a quarter million steel darts, and explode it directly over the stadium in the expectation that the vast majority of the eighty thousand spectators will be cut to ribbons. Opposing them are agents of an Israeli anti-terrorist unit and the CIA. In a spectacular conclusion, the blimp is intercepted by police helicopters just before its arrival over the stadium. After the terrorists are killed, the blimp, with the fuse of the bomb burning down, is barely towed out to sea before it explodes, harmlessly.

This closing sequence features the spectacular rescue of the Israeli agent by helicopter after he was trapped on the blimp attaching the tow rope. To an important degree, *Black Sunday* in fact is structured around action of this kind, which emphasizes its similarity to the disaster film genre so popular in the early 1970s. For what could be more disastrous than the sudden advent of a death-dealing blimp, the well-known symbol of the capitalist bond between industry and

Black Sunday

entertainment, in the midst of America's most sacred secular event? And what could be more typical of the mainstream thriller than for this well-calculated plot, artfully sustained by a series of reversals, to end, *mano a mano*, with the courageous protagonist defeating his enemies by guile and strength in order to save a faceless multitude?

Though ably supervised by Frankenheimer, these requisite action sequences were not of the greatest importance to a director, who, in the manner of a social realist, was obviously more interested in examining the cultural and political forces that have shaped the main characters in the drama. In this way, *Black Sunday* is typical of Frankenheimer's films. Only when the industry changed did he abandon his work in television, a distinguished career, in fact, directing prestigious live drama (including adaptations of Hemingway's *The Fifth Column*, *The Snows of Kilimanjaro*, and *For Whom the Bell Tolls*). Frankenheimer quickly made a name for himself in Hollywood with finely detailed studies of unusual or complex characters: the would-be gigolo and his admiring brother in *All Fall Down*; the violent convict who becomes an ornithological expert in *The Birdman of Alcatraz*; the aging businessman who seizes the opportunity to abandon the identity which now wearies him and begin life anew in *Seconds*. Unlike the big budget spectaculars of the period, these ''adult'' films (normally in black and white), and those of others from the so-called ''New York School,'' depended on literate scripts, nuanced performances, careful editing, and restrained yet effective cinematography.

Frankenheimer also specialized in political thrillers. His *The Manchurian Candidate*, *The Train*, and *Seven Days in May*, the best of a consistently distinguished body of work in the genre, are acknowledged masterpieces. Political thrillers of the Hollywood variety commonly suffer from an overemphasis on action, one-dimensional characters, and a melodramatic opposition of absolute good to absolute evil that simplifies the political conflict. Frankenheimer's thrillers, in contrast, are structured around a protagonist of divided loyalties who, though he finally chooses the ''right'' side, does so only with difficulty. *The Train*'s resistance leader, a railroad man of no culture, must come to share, in order to defeat him, the views of an educated Nazi officer, a cold-blooded aesthete who thinks that the French art treasures he is stealing are worth the sacrifice of many lives. In *Seven Days in May*, an army officer who discovers a coup planned by high-ranking generals must betray them in order to remain loyal to his oath to the president and country.

Black Sunday offers similar moral complexities. The film opens with a sequence devoted to the Black Septembrist leader, a woman (Marthe Keller) whose family, we later learn, has been destroyed in the region's wars. She meets with others of her cell in Beirut to plan the attack on the United States, and the group that night is attacked and nearly wiped out by a group of armed men who are later revealed to be Israeli agents. The attack finds the woman in the shower, and the commando leader (Robert Shaw), though he sees her there, cannot bring himself to shoot. This act of reflexive humanity allows the plot to go forward. The Israeli leader, tracking the terrorists to the United States, confesses to his younger colleague that he is no longer able to kill in the hopes of changing a situation that, during his professional life, has never changed in the least. But then his young colleague is killed by the very woman that he had allowed to live. When the two antagonists again come face to face, she, ready to go up with the blast, is in the stadium-bound blimp, while he is in the pursuing helicopter. As they recognize each other, he does not hesitate this time, killing her with a burst from his submachine gun. His act, however, cannot be seen simply an act of revenge, for the woman's death does not end the threat. Only by having himself lowered to the blimp can the commando leader affix the tow rope so it may be pulled out to sea. In the end, he is motivated as much by the urge to preserve as he is by his habit of destroying.

With its richly detailed evocation of place and political context, *Black Sunday* makes convincing and affecting what might otherwise be a somewhat cartoonish central gimmick, somewhat reminiscent of similar elements in James Bond films of the 1960s and 1970s. There is, after all, little difference between the Black Septembrist plot to use a dart-loaded blimp to turn the Super Bowl into a massacre and, say, Goldfinger's attempt to vaporize the gold in Fort Knox and create a world financial crisis. Finely coached performances by Shaw and Keller dominate the film, while Bruce Dern is also effective as a disgruntled Vietnam vet eager to get his own back. The film does not endorse either Palestinian grievance or Israeli attempts, often brutal, at pre-emptive self-defense; instead, it invokes the sad inevitability of Middle Eastern conflict, now played out in the open spaces and society of a self-satisfied, smugly fun-seeking America. The terrorists' plot, once discovered, might easily be foiled by a decision to cancel the game, but this proposed course of action is quickly dismissed by the officials in charge, though the president does change his plans to attend. The spectators in the stadium are thus saved through the working out of an international drama high above them of which they are completely unaware, the final irony in Frankenheimer's masterful thriller.

—R. Barton Palmer

BLACKMAIL

UK, 1929

Director: Alfred Hitchcock

Production: British International Pictures, black and white, 35mm; running time: 96 minutes. Released 1929. Filmed in studios in London and on location in the British Museum.

Producer: John Maxwell; **screenplay:** Alfred Hitchcock, Charles Bennett, Benn W. Levy, and Garnett Weston; from the play by Charles Bennett; **photography:** Jack Cox; **editor:** Emile Ruello; **production design:** Wilfred C. Arnold and Norman Arnold; **music:** Campbell and Connely, finished and arranged by Hubert Bath and Henry Stafford, performed by the British Symphony Orchestra under the direction of John Reynders.

Cast: Anny Ondra (*Alice White*); Sara Allgood (*Mrs. White*); John Longden (*Frank Webber*); Charles Paton (*Mr. White*); Donald Calthrop (*Tracy*); Cyril Ritchard (*The artist*).

Publications

Books:

Noble, Peter, *An Index to the Creative Work of Alfred Hitchcock*, supplement to *Sight and Sound*, index series, London, 1949.
Amengual, Barthélemy, and Raymond Borde, *Alfred Hitchcock*, Paris, 1957.
Rohmer, Eric, and Claude Chabrol, *Hitchcock*, Paris, 1957.
Bogdanovich, Peter, *The Cinema of Alfred Hitchcock*, New York, 1962.
Perry, George, *The Films of Alfred Hitchcock*, London, 1965.
Wood, Robin, *Hitchcock's Films*, London, 1965.
Truffaut, François, *Le Cinéma selon Hitchcock*, Paris, 1966; as *Hitchcock*, New York, 1985.
La Valley, Albert J., editor, *Focus on Hitchcock*, Englewood Cliffs, New Jersey, 1972.
Durgnat, Raymond, *The Strange Case of Alfred Hitchcock; or, The Plain Man's Hitchcock*, Cambridge, Massachusetts, 1974.
Yacowar, Hamden, *Hitchcock's British Films*, Hamden, Connecticut, 1977.
Taylor, John Russell, *Hitch*, London and New York, 1978.
Bellour, Raymond, *L'Analyse du film*, Paris, 1979.
Hemmeter, Thomas M., *Hitchcock the Stylist*, Ann Arbor, Michigan, 1981.
Bazin, André, *The Cinema of Cruelty: From Buñuel to Hitchcock*, New York, 1982.
Narboni, Jean, editor, *Alfred Hitchcock*, Paris, 1982.
Rothman, William, *Hitchcock—The Murderous Gaze*, Cambridge, Massachusetts, 1982.
Villien, Bruno, *Hitchcock*, Paris, 1982.
Weis, Elisabeth, *The Silent Scream: Alfred Hitchcock's Sound Track*, Rutherford, New Jersey, 1982.
Spoto, Donald, *The Life of Alfred Hitchcock: The Dark Side of Genius*, New York, 1982; London, 1983.
Phillips, Gene D., *Alfred Hitchcock*, Boston, 1984.
Barbier, Philippe, and Jacques Moreau, *Alfred Hitchcock*, Paris, 1985.
Douchet, Jean, *Alfred Hitchcock*, Paris, 1985.
Dentelbaum, Marshall, and Leland Poague, *A Hitchcock Reader*, Ames, Iowa, 1986.
Hogan, David J., *Dark Romance: Sexuality in the Horror Film*, Jefferson, North Carolina, 1986.
Humphries, Patrick, *The Films of Alfred Hitchcock*, Greenwich, Connecticut, 1986.
Kloppenburg, Josef, *Die dramaturgische Funktion der Musik in Filmen Alfred Hitchcock*, Munich, 1986.
Ryall, Tom, *Alfred Hitchcock and the British Cinema*, London, 1986.

Sinyard, Neil, *The Films of Alfred Hitchcock*, London, 1986.
Modleski, Tania, *The Women Who Knew Too Much: Hitchcock and Feminist Theory*, New York, 1988.

Articles:

Variety, 10 July 1929.
Marshall, Ernest, in *New York Times*, 14 July 1929.
MacPherson, Kenneth, in *Close Up* (London), October 1929.
Variety, 9 October 1929.
''My Own Methods,'' in *Sight and Sound* (London), Summer 1937.
Maloney, Russell, ''Alfred Joseph Hitchcock,'' in *New Yorker*, 10 September 1938.
Anderson, Lindsay, ''Alfred Hitchcock,'' in *Sequence* (London), Autumn 1949.
''Hitchcock Issue'' of *Cahiers du Cinéma* (Paris), October 1953.
''Hitchcock Issue'' of *Cahiers du Cinéma* (Paris), August-September 1956.
Higham, Charles, ''Hitchcock's World,'' in *Film Quarterly* (Berkeley), Winter 1962–63.
Vernilye, Jerry, ''An Alfred Hitchcock Index,'' in *Films in Review* (New York), April 1966.
Bond, Kirk, ''The Other Alfred Hitchcock,'' in *Film Culture* (New York), Summer 1966.
Beylie, Claude, ''4 Inedits d'Alfred Hitchcock,'' in *Ecran* (Paris), November 1976.
Lefèvre, Raymond, ''Les Premiers films parlants d'Alfred Hitchcock,'' in *Cinema 76* (Paris), November 1976.
Dagneau, G., ''Sur 4 Films d'Hitchcock,'' in *Revue du Cinéma* (Paris), December 1976.
Dahan, L., ''4 films anglais d'Hitchcock,'' in *Cinématographe* (Paris), January 1977.
Linderman, Deborah, ''The Screen in Hitchcock's *Blackmail*,'' in *Wide Angle* (Athens, Ohio), vol. 4, no. 1, 1980.
Magill's Survey of Cinema 1, Englewood Cliffs, New Jersey, 1980.
Barr, Charles, ''*Blackmail:* Silent and Sound,'' in *Sight and Sound* (London), Spring 1983.
Poague, Leland, ''Criticism and/as History: Rereading *Blackmail*,'' in *A Hitchcock Reader*, edited by Marshall Deutelbaum and Leland Poague, Ames, Iowa, 1986.
Wood, Robin, ''Symmetry, Closure, Disruption,'' in *Cineaction* (Toronto), Winter 1988–89.
Eyuboglu, S., ''The Authorial Text and Postmodernism: Hitchcock's *Blackmail*,'' in *Screen* (Oxford), no. 1, 1991.
Reincke, N., ''Antidote to Dominance: Women's Laughter as Counteraction,'' in *Journal of Popular Culture* (Bowling Green, Ohio), no. 4, 1991.
Eyübŏglu, S., ''The Authorial Text and Postmodernism: Hitchcock's *Blackmail*,'' in *Screen* (Oxford), vol. 32, no. 1, Spring 1991.
Boschi, A., ''Like Raisins in a Bun: le due versioni di *Blackmail*,'' in *Cinema & Cinema* (Bologna), January-April 1992.

* * *

Hitchcock's last silent film, *Blackmail* was also his first sound effort—and one of the first British ''talkies'' as well. A resounding popular and critical success, *Blackmail* prefigures some of the director's most famous themes and demonstrates techniques for which he would be noted.

As critic Eric Rohmer points out, the entire film ''focuses on the relationships among characters.'' Victims and victimizers alternate from scene to scene (a technique Hitchock would later perfect in his 1951 film *Strangers on a Train*). Sometimes within a single shot, for example, the moral positions of the characters shift, while the placement of the characters illustrates visually the relationship that we also know from context. As many other critics have detailed, this type of shift is ''pure Hitchcock'': scenes such as those between the blackmailer and the detective parallel scenes from the director's future work, most notably the relationship between a tennis pro and his psychotic ''fan'' in *Strangers on a Train.* This visual affirmation of moral ambiguity and transfer of guilt combines with other elements—such as the use of cinematic means to direct point of view, often at the expense of a linear storyline—that would later be considered typical of Hitchcock's films. The thematic concerns of *Blackmail* also appear in Hitchcock's Hollywood period, for example, the depiction of a woman's torments, as in *Suspicion. Blackmail* demonstrates an intriguing use of sound, especially since it was originally conceived and produced as a silent film. One notable example occurs in the use of sound for scene-to-scene continuity: the protagonist's shriek becomes the basis for transition to the next scene in which a charwoman finds a dead body. (This technique, too, was incorporated into another film, *The Thirty-Nine Steps.*) Even in this very early sound venture, Hitchcock's awareness of the possibilities of sound represents a major experimental advance in his ability to ''make the inexpressible tangible.''

Hitchcock said that he used a good many trick shots in the picture. During a sequence in the British Museum, he told Francois Truffaut, ''we used the Shüfftan process because there wasn't enough light in the museum to shoot there. You set a mirror at an angle of 45 degrees and you reflect a full picture of the British Museum in it.'' Hitchcock had nine of the pictures made, showing various rooms. But the producers knew nothing of the Shüfftan process, and since they might have objected, Hitchcock performed his magic without their knowledge.

Blackmail has an important place in cinematic and Hitchcockian film history. Not only is it one of the first British talking pictures, but it is also a prototype for Hitchcock films to follow in terms of theme, the use of sound and cinematic style. *Blackmail* initiated the suspense sub-genre many call the ''Hitchcock film,'' while innovatively transforming use of the then new sound medium within an established visual style and in the service of unique thematic purposes.

—Deborah H. Holdstein

BLADE RUNNER

USA, 1982

Director: Ridley Scott

Production: Ladd Company in association with Sir Run Run Shaw; Technicolor, 35mm, Panavision, Dolby Stereo; running time: about

Blade Runner

2 hours. Released June, 1982; re-released in 1991. Filmed 1981 in Pinewood and Twickenham Studios, England, and on location in Los Angeles.

Producer: Michael Deeley; **screenplay:** Hampton Fancher and David Peoples, from the novel *Do Androids Dream of Electric Sheep* by Philip K. Dick; **photography:** Jordan Cronenweth; **editor:** Terry Rawlings; **sound mixer:** Bud Alper; **sound editor:** Peter Pennell; **dialogue editor:** Michael Hopkins; **production designer:** Lawrence G. Paull; **art director:** David Snyder; **music:** Vangelis; **special effects:** Douglas Trumbull, Richard Yuricich, and David Dryer; **costume designers:** Charles Knode and Michael Kaplan; **visual futurist:** Syd Mead.

Cast: Harrison Ford (*Deckard*); Rutger Hauer (*Batty*); Sean Young (*Rachael*); Edward James Olmos (*Gaff*); M. Emmet Walsh (*Bryant*); Darryl Hannah (*Pris*); William Sanderson (*Sebastian*); Brion James (*Leon*); Joe Turkel (*Tyrell*); Joanna Cassidy (*Zhora*); James Hong (*Chew*); Morgan Paull (*Holden*); Kevin Thompson (*Bear*); John Edward Allen (*Kaiser*); Hy Pyke (*Taffey Lewis*); Kimiro Hiroshige (*Cambodian Lady*); Robert Okazaki (*Sushi Master*); Carolyn De Mirjian (*Saleslady*); Charles Knapp (*Bartender No. 1*); Leo Gorcey, Jr. (*Bartender No. 2*); Thomas Hutchinson (*Bartender No. 3*); Kelly Hine (*Show Girl*); Sharon Hesky (*Barfly No. 1*); Rose Mascari (*Barfly No. 2*); Susan Rhee (*Geisha No. 1*); Hiroko Kimuri (*Geisha No. 2*); Kai Wong (*Chinese Man No. 1*); Kit Wong (*Chinese Man No. 2*); Hiro Okazki (*Policeman No. 1*); Steve Pope (*Policeman No. 2*); Robert Reiter (*Policeman No. 3*).

Publications

Script:

Fancher, Hampton, and David Webb Peoples, *The Illustrated Blade Runner*, San Diego 1982.

Books:

Scroggy, David, editor, *Blade Runner Sketchbook*, San Diego, 1982.
Peary, Danny, *Cult Movies 3*, New York, 1988.

McDonald, James, *Fantasy and the Cinema*, London, 1989.
Kerman, Judith B., editor, *Retrofitting Blade Runner*, Bowling Green, Ohio, 1991.
Sammon, Paul, *Future Noir: The Making of Blade Runner*, New York, 1996.
Kerman, Judith B., editor, *Retrofitting Blade Runner: Issues in Ridley Scott's Blade Runner and Philip K. Dick's Do Androids Dream of Electric Sheep?*, Bowling Green, Ohio, 1997.
Bukatman, Scott, *Blade Runner*, London, 1998.

Articles:

Mills, Bart, "The Brave New World of Production Design," in *American Film* (Washington, D.C.), January-February 1982.
Variety (New York), 16 June 1982.
Sarris, Andrew, in *Village Voice* (New York), 8 July 1982.
Corliss, Richard, in *Time* (New York), 12 July 1982.
Kael, Pauline, in *New Yorker*, 12 July 1982.
"*Blade Runner* Issue" of *Cinefex* (Riverside, California), July 1982.
Lightman, Herb A., and Richard Patterson, "*Blade Runner:* Production Design and Photography," in *American Cinematographer* (Los Angeles), July 1982.
Kennedy, Harlan, in *Film Comment* (New York), July-August 1982.
Strick, Philip, in *Sight and Sound* (London), Summer 1982.
Colpart, G., in *Image et Son* (Paris), September 1982.
Goldschmidt, D., in *Cinématographe* (Paris), September 1982.
Milne, Tom, in *Monthly Film Bulletin* (London), September 1982.
"*Blade Runner* Issues" of *Starburst* (London), September-November 1982.
Girard, M., in *Séquences* (Montreal), October 1982.
Roddick, Nick, in *Films and Filming* (London), October 1982.
Skytte, A., in *Kosmorama* (Copenhagen), October 1982.
Dumont, P., in *Cinéma* (Paris), November 1982.
Garsault, A., in *Positif* (Paris), November 1982.
Assayas, O., and S. Le Peron, interview with Ridley Scott, in *Casablanca* (Madrid), March 1983.
Piccardi, A., in *Cineforum* (Bergamo), December 1982.
Dempsey, Michael, in *Film Quarterly* (Berkeley), Winter 1982–83.
Cardenas, F., in *Hablemos de Cine* (Lima), February 1983.
Caron, A., "Les Archetypes chez Ridley Scott," in *Jeune Cinéma* (Paris), March 1983.
Pacileo, V., in *Cinema Nuovo* (Bari), April 1983.
Durgnat, Raymond, "Art for Film's Sake," in *American Film* (Washington, D.C.), May 1983.
Martin, R., "La Photographie merité bien note mefiance," in *Revue Belge du Cinéma* (Brussels), Summer 1983.
Kellner, D., and others, "*Blade Runner:* A Diagnostic Critique," in *Jump Cut* (Berkeley), February 1984.
Dresser, D., "*Blade Runner:* Science Fiction and Transcendence," in *Literature/Film Quarterly* (Salisbury, Maryland), July 1985.
Doll, Susan and Greg Faller, "*Blade Runner* and Genre: Film Noir and Science Fiction," in *Literature/Film Quarterly* (Salisbury, Maryland), April 1986.
Olive, J. Louis, "Les Structures de l'enfermement urbain," in *Cahiers de la Cinématheque* (Perpignan), no. 44, 1986.
Camera Obscura (Berkeley), Autumn 1986.
Ruppert, P., "*Blade Runner:* The Utopian Dialectics of Science Fiction Films," in *Cineaste* (New York), no. 2, 1989.
Berg, C. R., "Immigrants, Aliens, and Extraterrestrials: Science Fiction's Alien 'Other' as (Among Other Things) New Hispanic Imagery," in *Cineaction* (Toronto), Fall 1989.
Morrision, R., "*Casablanca* Meets *Stars Wars:* The Blakean Dialectics of *Blade Runner*," in *Literature/Film Quarterly* (Salisbury, Maryland), no. 1, 1990.
Slade, J. W., "Romanticizing Cybernetics in Ridley Scott's *Blade Runner*," in *Literature/Film Quarterly* (Salisbury, Maryland), no. 1, 1990.
Shumaker, C., "More Human than Humans: Society, Salvation, and the Outsider in Some Popular Films of the 1980s," in *Journal of American Culture* (Bowling Green, Ohio), no. 4, 1990.
Wilhelmsson, P., "Design tai vallankumous," in *Filmihullu* (Helsinki), no. 6, 1990.
Attolini, G., "Dagli spazi aperti all'universo urbano," in *Quaderni di Cinema* (Florence), July-September 1990.
Telotte, J. P., "The Tremulous Public Body," in *Journal of Popular Film and Television* (Washington, D.C.), no. 1, 1991.
Levy, S., "Ridley Scissorhands," in *American Film* (Washington, D.C.), August 1991.
Marder, E., "*Blade Runner's* Moving Still," in *Camera Obscura* (Bloomington, Indiana), September 1991.
Silverman, K., "Back to the Future," in *Camera Obscura* (Bloomington, Indiana), September 1991.
Instrell, Rick, "Blade Runner: The Economic Shaping of a Film," in *Cinema & Fiction*, edited by John Orr and Colin Nicholson, Edinburgh, 1992.
Wilmington, M., "The Rain People," in *Film Comment* (New York), January-February 1992.
Rynell, T., "Den morknande framtid ar var," in *Filmhaftet* (Uppsala, Sweden), May 1992.
Albrecht, D., "*Blade Runner* Cuts Deep into American Culture," in *New York Times*, 20 September 1992.
Strick, P., "*Blade Runner:* Telling the Difference," in *Sight and Sound* (London), December 1992.
Instrell, Rick, "*Blader Runner*: The Economic Shaping of the Film," in John Orr and Colin Nicholson, editors, *Cinema and Fiction: New Modes of Adapting, 1950–1990*, Edinburgh, 1992.
Bruno, Giuliano, "Ramble City: Postmodernism and Blade Runner," in *Crisis Cinema*, edited by Christopher Sharrett, Washington, D.C., 1993.
Alliez, E., and M. Feher, "Dick City," in *Filmihulu* (Helsinki), no. 1, 1993.
Bruno, M. W., "One More Kiss My Dear," in *Segnocinema* (Vincenza, Italy), January-February 1993.
McNamara, Kevin R., "*Blade Runner*'s Post-Individual Worldspace," in *Contemporary Literature* (Madison, Wisconsin), vol. 38, no. 3, Fall 1997.
Gravett, Sharon L., "The Sacred and the Profane: Examining the Religious Subtext of Ridley Scott's *Blade Runner*," and P. Lev, "Whose Future? *Star Wars, Alien*, and *Blade Runner*," in *Literature Film Quarterly* (Salisbury, Maryland), vol. 26, no. 1, 1998.

* * *

This futuristic hard-boiled detective yarn stars Harrison Ford as a world-weary *film noir* hero whose job is to smoke out and retire (i.e., destroy) ''replicants''—androids with a human instinct for survival—in an overcrowded Los Angeles circa 2019.

Complications arise when Ford falls for an android, a gorgeous experimental model played by Sean Young, dressed up as a 1940s film noir femme fatale, and comes to the conclusion that his task of mercilessly hunting and striking down these creatures whose only crime is a belief in their humanity has dulled his own humanity—although it is subsequently revealed, somewhat obscurely, that Ford comes to identify with them because he's a replicant with deep-rooted memory chips himself.

Director Ridley Scott used his clout following the success of *Alien* (1979) to create this visually striking science-fiction piece, drawn from Philip K. Dick's novella *Do Androids Dream of Electric Sheep?* Partisans consider the novella (somewhat altered in the film version) and the film modern masterpieces of the genre. Certainly the film's milestone special effects (orchestrated by *2001*'s Douglas Trumbull and an army of technicians) are stunning. As is Scott's evocation of a teeming, twenty-first century Los Angeles perpetually drenched in rain or steam. Apart from the occasional spacecraft circling the Capitol Records building, it looks remarkably like Scott's garish evocation of present day Tokyo in his subsequent neo-*noir* (minus the sci-fi element) *Black Rain* (1989).

The film's dramatic structure is much less satisfying, however, although it has been significantly improved with the studio's release of the never-before-seen ''director's cut.''

Scott suffered a great deal of studio interference in the course of making the film. The script underwent numerous rewrites before and during filming. His woes (he called the experience ''a war'') continued through post-production and several previews until the film was released in 1982, becoming a cult favorite but a box-office flop.

Audiences were knocked out by the film's images but frustrated by the ambiguities of many major plot points (Ford's being an android among them), and bored by the constant narration inserted over and obscuring the otherwise imaginatively detailed soundtrack to help clarify them. That the narration spoken by Ford in his customary expressionless monotone slowed the film's pace to almost a crawl didn't help. There is some debate as to whether Ford's narration was planned from the start or cobbled together in a panic move during post-production. Evidence suggests the former. But the unwelcome decision not to drop it for the film's initial release hints at the latter.

In any case, when the studio re-released the film in 1991 in a newly struck 70mm ''director's cut''—the print now in circulation on video—the narration was jettisoned. It's deletion improves the film's pace considerably. (Even Harrison Ford has gone on record as saying so.) Many plot ambiguities remain, but the significant revelation that Ford himself is a replicant—and all the more human because of it, who finally realizes his brotherhood with the android combatant (Hauer) he has destroyed, is much clearer now.

Ironically, although many so-called ''director's cuts'' tend to re-insert footage—typically explicitly sexual or violent scenes—trimmed from the first-round general release, *Blade Runner—The Director's Cut* actually takes the opposite route by toning this footage down a bit. For example, Darryl Hannah's gymnastic android doesn't take quite as many bullet hits as before—nor do you see Ford gouge Hauer's eyes. Enough remains to sustain the film's R rating, however.

—John McCarty

THE BLAIR WITCH PROJECT

USA, 1999

Directors: Daniel Myrick and Eduardo Sánchez

Production: Haxan Films; distributed by Artisan Entertainment (U.S.A.), Shochiku Films (Japan), Budapest Film (Hungary), Mars Films (France), Eurocine (Argentina), Arthaus Filmverleih (Germany); 16 mm black-and-white and High 8 color video; running time: 80 minutes (U.S.A.), 81 minutes (Japan), 83 minutes (Argentina); sound mix: Dolby Digital. Released July 1999 (limited). Filmed in Seneca Creek State Park, Wheaton, and Rockville, Maryland; shot in 8 days; cost: $22,000.

Producers: Robin Cowie, Bob Eick (executive), Kevin Foxe (executive), Gregg Hale, Michael Monello (co-producer); **writing credits:** Daniel Myrick, Eduardo Sánchez; **cinematography:** Neal Fredericks; **editors:** Daniel Myrick, Eduardo Sánchez; **sound:** Dana Meeks; **art director:** Ricardo Moreno; **production designer:** Ben Rock; **original music:** Tony Cora; **sound effects editor:** Elisabeth Flaum; **foley mixer:** Shawn Kennelly.

Cast: Heather Donahue (*Heather Donahue*); Michael C. Williams (*Michael Williams*); Joshua Leonard (*Josh Leonard*); Bob Griffin (*Interviewee*); Jim King (*Interviewee*); Sandra Sánchez (*Woman with Baby—Interviewee*); Ed Swanson (*Interviewee*); Patricia Decou (*Interviewee*); Mark Mason (*Interviewee in yellow hat*).

Awards: Csapnivalo Golden Slate Awards for Best Horror Movie and Best Movie, 2000; Florida Film Critics Circle Golden Orange Award ''for furthering the cause of Florida filmmakers and independent filmmaking'' (Robin Cowie, Gregg Hale, Michael Monello, Daniel Myrick, Eduardo Sánchez), 2000.

Publications

Books:

Stern, David A., *The Blair Witch Project: A Dossier*, New York, 1999.

Pelucir, Talis, *The Unofficial Blair Witch Project Internet Guide*, Port Orchard, Washington, 2000.

Articles:

Nashawaty, Chris, ''Independents' Day,'' in *Entertainment Weekly*, vol. 1, no. 476, 12 March 1999.

Kenny, Glenn, ''Love, Death, and One Mean Butcher,'' in *Premiere* (Boulder), vol. 12, no. 8, April 1999

Ebert, Roger, ''*The Blair Witch Project*,'' in *The Chicago Sun-Times*, http://www.suntimes.com/ebert/ebert_reviews/1999/07/071603.html.

Morris, Wesley, ''Pitching Tent in Audience Psyche,'' in *The San Francisco Examiner*, 16 July 1999.

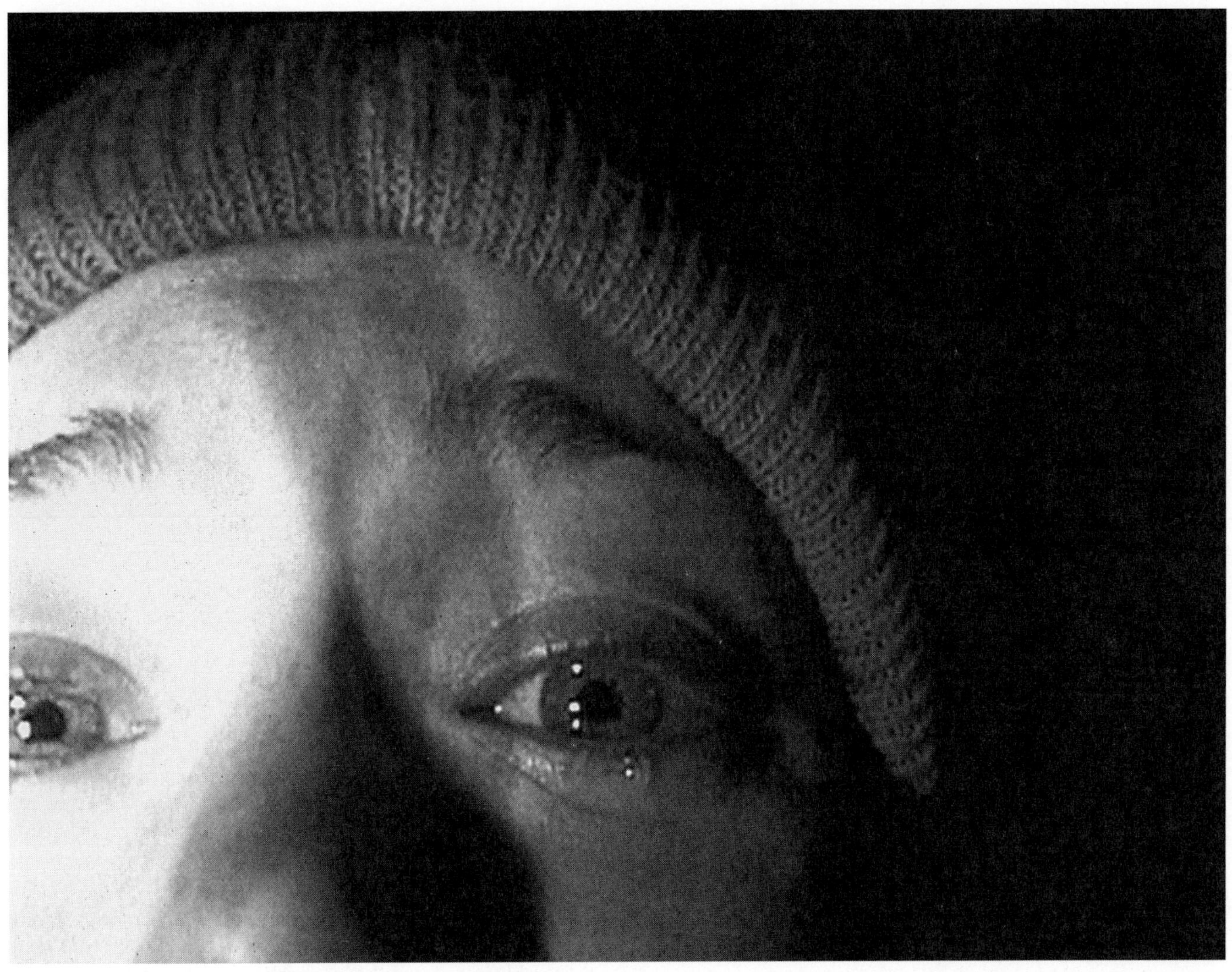

The Blair Witch Project

Ascher-Walsh, Rebecca, ''Rhymes with Rich,'' in *Entertainment Weekly* (New York), vol. 1, no. 496, 30 July 1999.

Travers, Peter, ''The Blair Witch Project,'' in *Rolling Stone* (New York), no. 818, 5 August 1999.

Corliss, Richard, ''Blair Witch Craft,'' in *Time* (New York), 16 August 1999.

Farber, Stephen, ''Mock Inspiration,'' in *Movieline* (Escondido, California), vol. 10, no. 11, August 1999.

Guthman, Edward, ''Terror Comes Alive in 'Witch': Pseudo-documentary Has Visceral Power,'' in *The San Francisco Chronicle*, 22 October 1999.

Burr, Ty, ''Video: Forest Dangers (B+),'' in *Entertainment Weekly*, vol. 1, no. 509, 29 October 1999.

Schwarzbaum, Lisa, ''Terrorvision,'' in *Entertainment Weekly*, vol. 1, no. 495, 23 July 1999.

* * *

''In October of 1994, three student filmmakers disappeared in the woods near Burkittsville, Maryland, while shooting a documentary. . . . A year later their footage was found.'' Thus begins *The Blair Witch Project*, Daniel Myrick and Eduardo Sánchez's shoestring-budgeted horror ''mockumentary,'' which parlayed an innovative marketing campaign and incredible word-of-mouth into more than $140 million in the United States alone—making it one of the most profitable independent films of all time.

Led by aspiring director Heather Donahue (the characters have the same names as the actors who play them), the three ''student filmmakers'' mentioned above make their way to Burkittsville (formerly Blair), Maryland, in order to shoot footage for a documentary they are making about a local legend, the so-called ''Blair Witch.'' Word has it that this mysterious figure has been haunting the nearby Black Hills Forest since the late 18th century, and is responsible for a number of heinous murders. After conducting interviews with some of the locals, the trio hike into the forest so as to gather additional footage. While Michael handles the sound recording, and Josh shoots in 16 mm black-and-white, Heather captures much of the action on High 8 color video. None of them experienced campers, they soon get lost, and their once-cheery demeanor deteriorates into an increasingly volatile mixture of fear, blame, frustration, and panic. To make matters worse, ominous signs begin appearing with disturbing regularity: carefully arranged piles of stones positioned outside their tent in the morning; strange and disturbing sounds at night, of whispered voices and babies crying; wooden effigies hanging in the trees. Then Josh disappears, the only clue a piece of his shirt with what looks like a piece of flesh wrapped inside it, discovered by Heather the next day. In the film's harrowing finale, Michael and Heather stumble across an apparently abandoned house. Hoping to find Jeff, they enter; what they discover is a nightmare. Through the lens of her camcorder, we see what Heather sees. And what we see is nothing much, just darkness and ruins and children's handprints on the walls, and finally, after someone or something knocks her out (Michael has already been attacked), a blank ceiling, which lasts until the tape—and the film itself—reaches an end.

The Blair Witch Project is a unique and important production insofar as it looks forward, to the future of film promotion, at the same time as it looks backward, to a time when horror movies did not rely on special effects or the concoction of gory spectacles to instill a sense of terror in audiences. Instead of the usual trailers and print ads, Myrick and Sánchez (first-time directors who met while attending the University of Central Florida) concocted an elaborate backstory—what they dubbed a ''mythology''—for *Blair Witch*, which they posted on the film's official website (http://www.blairwitch.com). The website presents the events of the film as real occurrences, and includes character bios, news clips about the disappearances, interviews with relatives, information about the police investigation (supposedly declared ''inactive and unsolved'' in 1997), excerpts from Heather's journal, and a detailed history of the Blair Witch legend. In addition, and just prior to its screening at the Cannes Film Festival in May 1999, ''MISSING'' flyers with descriptions of Heather, Michael, and Josh were put up all around town. What all of this amounts to is a symbiotic relationship between film and extratextual discourse, one in which the documentary pretensions of the former are strongly enhanced by the non-fictional cues of the latter. Of course there were various ways for people to discern that the entire story was a hoax, but a great many were simply not interested in seeing through (or all the way through) the deception. The film generated so much hype after its premiere at Sundance in January 1999 that an additional screening had to be scheduled in the 1300-seat Eccles theatre, which was filled to capacity. Soon afterwards, Artisan Entertainment picked up *The Blair Witch Project* for distribution in the United States.

Despite criticisms directed towards the film's sometimes slow pacing and non-stop, nausea-inducing handheld camerawork, it is hard to deny that *The Blair Witch Project* succeeds in its employment of *cinema verité* as a means of instilling terror in viewers. Myrick and Sánchez's unique production method has itself become the stuff of legend: not only were the actors responsible for shooting the entire film themselves (over the course of eight consecutive days and nights); they had to carry their own equipment, and improvised almost all of their lines. Three or four times a day, the directors would write notes to each cast member, sealing them in tubes for their eyes only. Explained Myrick, ''We were trying to create an environment for these actors and have this improv come to life and be as realistic as possible. That's what we think really contributed to the unseen fear that's been so very effective.'' By achieving such a high degree of realism, the directors took their product a step beyond earlier horror films with mockumentary aspirations, films such as Wes Craven's *The Last House on the Left* (1972), Tobe Hooper's *The Texas Chainsaw Massacre* (1974), and Michael and Roberta Finlay's notorious *Snuff* (1976).

By exploiting some of our most basic, inescapable fears—of the dark, of the unknown, of sounds whose source cannot be detected—Myrick and Sánchez and the film's three leads manage to elicit intense emotional responses from viewers. Some of the most terrifying moments occur when neither of the cameras are functioning, and all we are able to see is a black/blank screen (this is reminiscent of a famous scene in Robert Wise's 1963 classic, *The Haunting*). Which proves once again that what our imagination conjures up when effectively prompted is far worse than anything even the most sophisticated special effects or makeup can produce. It is to their credit that those involved in the making of *The Blair Witch Project* were well aware of this oft-forgotten fact.

—Steven Schneider

DER BLAUE ENGEL

(The Blue Angel)

Germany, 1930

Director: Josef von Sternberg

Production: Universum-Film-Aktiengesellschaft Studios (UFA), Berlin; black and white, 35mm; running time: 90 minutes; length: 2920 meters. Released 31 March 1930, Germany; American version released 3 January 1931 by Paramount. Filmed (concurrently in English and German) in late winter of 1929, UFA studios, Berlin.

Producer: Erich Pommer; **scenario:** Josef von Sternberg, Robert Liebmann, and Karl Vollmoeller; **dialogue:** Carl Zuckmayer, from the novel *Professor Unrath* by Heinrich Mann; **photography:** Günther Rittau and Hans Schneeberger; **editor:** Sam Winston; **sound effects:** Fritz Theiry; **production design:** Otto Hunte and Emil Hasler; **music:** Friedrich Holländer; **lyrics:** Robert Liebmann; **music played by:** The Weintraub Syncopators.

Cast: Emil Jannings (*Immanuel Rath*); Marlene Dietrich (*Lola Frolich*); Rosa Valetti (*Guste*); Hans Albers (*Mazeppa*); Kurt Gerron (*Kiepert*); Karl Huzar Puffy (*Proprietor*); Reinhold Bernt (*Clown*); Rolf Mueller (*Angst*); Roland Verno (*Lohmann*); Karl Bolhaus (*Ertzum*); Hans Roth (*Caretaker*); Gerhard Bienart (*Policeman*); Robert-Klein Loerk (*Goldstaub*); Wilheim Diegelmann (*Captain*); Ilsu Fuerstenbeg (*Rath's Maid*); Edward V. Winterstein (*Headmaster*).

Publications

Scripts:

Von Sternberg, Joseph and others, ''*L'Ange bleu*,'' in *L'Avant-Scène du Cinéma* (Paris), March 1966.

Von Sternberg, Joseph, and others, *The Blue Angel* (continuity script), New York, 1968.

Der Blaue Engel

Books:

Talky, Jean, *Marlène Dietrich, femme énigme*, Paris, 1932.
Kracauer, Siegfried, *From Caligari to Hitler*, New York, 1947.
Harrington, Curtis, *An Index to the Films of Josef von Sternberg*, London, 1949.
Griffith, Richard, *Marlene Dietrich—Image and Legend*, New York,1959.
Kyrou, Ado, ''Sternberg et Marlène,'' in *Le Surréalismeau au cinéma*, Paris, 1963.
von Sternberg, Josef, *Fun in a Chinese Laundry*, New York, 1965.
Sarris, Andrew, *The Films of Josef von Sternberg*, New York, 1966.
Weinberg, Herman G., *Josef von Sternberg: A Critical Study*, New York, 1967.
Brownlow, Kevin, *The Parade's Gone By . . .* , London and New York, 1969.
Eisner, Lotte, *The Haunted Screen*, Berkeley, California, 1969.
Anthologie du cinéma 6, Paris, 1971.
Baxter, John, *The Cinema of Josef von Sternberg*, New York, 1971.
Mérigeau, Pascal, *Josef von Sternberg*, Paris, 1983.
Navacelle, Thierry de, *Sublime Marlene*, London, 1984.
Seydel, Renate, *Marlene Dietrich: Eine Chronik ihres Lebens in Bilden und Dokumenten*, East Berlin, 1984.
Spoto, Donald, *Falling in Love Again: Marlene Dietrich*, Boston, 1985.
Dietrich, Marlene, *Ich bin, Gott sei dank, Berlinerin*, Frankfurt, 1987.
Spoto, Donald, *Blue Angel: The Life of Marlene Dietrich*, New York, 1992.
Wehnert, Stefanie, and Nathalie Bielfeldt, editors, *Mien Kopf und die Beine von Marlene Dietrich: Heinrich Manns, Professor Unrat, and Der Blaue Engel*, Lubeck, Germany, 1996.

Articles:

Variety (New York), 30 April 1930.
Lenauer, Jean, ''10 Days à Berlin,'' in *Revue du Cinéma* (Paris), June 1930.
Revue du Cinéma (Paris), October 1930.
Mann, Heinrich, in *Revue du Cinéma* (Paris), December 1930.
Hall, Mordaunt, in *New York Times*, 6 December 1930.
''Les Grands Rôles de Marlène Dietrich,'' in *Cinémonde* (Paris), February 1932.

Harrington, Curtis, "Arrogant Gesture," in *Theatre Arts* (New York), November 1950.
Wagner, Geoffrey, in *Quarterly Review of Film, Radio and Television* (Berkeley), Fall 1951.
Wagner, Geoffrey, "Revaluation: *The Blue Angel*," in *Sight and Sound* (London), August-September 1951.
Harrington, Curtis, "Josef von Sternberg," in *Cahiers du Cinéma* (Paris), October-November 1951.
George, Manfred, "Marlene Dietrich's Beginning," in *Films in Review* (New York), February 1952.
Audibert, Jacques, "L'Amour dans le cinéma," in *Cahiers du Cinéma* (Paris), December 1954.
Whitehall, Richard, in *Films and Filming* (London), October 1962.
"A Taste for Celluloid," in *Films and Filming* (London), July 1963.
Green, O. O., "Six Films of Josef von Sternberg," in *Movie* (London), no. 13, 1965.
Filmkritik (Frankfurt, Germany), April 1965.
Weinberg, Herman G., "Josef von Sternberg," in *Film Heritage* (Dayton, Ohio), Winter 1965–66.
"L'Oeuvre de Josef von Sternberg," in *L'Avant-Scène du Cinéma* (Paris), March 1966.
Positif (Paris), May 1966.
Cornaud, André, in *Image et Son* (Paris), no. 214, 1968.
Truscott, Harold, "Emil Jannings—A Personal View," in *Silent Picture* (London), Autumn 1970.
Martineau, Barbara, "Thoughts about the Objectification of Women," in *Take One* (Montreal), November-December 1970.
Rheuban, Joyce, "Josef von Sternberg: The Scientist and the Vamp," in *Sight and Sound* (London), Autumn 1972–73.
Weisstein, Ulrich, "Translations and Adaptations of Heinrich Mann's Novel in 2 Media," in *Film Journal* (Evanston, Illinois), Fall-Winter 1972.
Baxter, P., "On the Naked Thighs of Miss Dietrich," in *Wide Angle* (Athens, Ohio), no. 2, 1978.
Firda, R. A., "Literary Origins: Sternberg's Film *The Blue Angel*," in *Literature/Film Quarterly* (Salisbury, Maryland), no. 2, 1979.
Audibert, L., "L'Ombre du son," in *Cinématographe* (Paris), June 1979.
"Filmprotokoll: *Der Blaue Engel*," in *Film and Fernsehen* (Berlin), December 1980.
Marinero, M., in *Casablanca* (Madrid), June 1981.
Laurens, C., "L'Armature sonore de *L'Ange Bleu* de Sternberg," in *Image et Son* (Paris), December 1981.
Weemaes, G., in *Film en Televisie* (Brussels), September 1982.
Reijnhoudt, B., "Der blaue Engel: De blote dijen van miss Dietrich," in *Skoop* (The Hague), November 1985.
Koch, Gertrude, "Zwischen der Welten," in *Frauen und Film* (Berlin), December 1986.
Musatti, C., "Il Professore e l'angelo azzurro," in *Cinema Nuovo* (Rome), May-June 1990.
Grimes, William, "Dietrich Had a Fit (in Fact 3 Fits) in Screen Test," in *New York Times*, 15 October 1992.

* * *

When Josef von Sternberg arrived in Berlin in the autumn of 1929, his career was tottering. The two years since his 1927 success with *Underworld* had been spent making box-office failures in imitation of his pioneering gangster film, now out-dated by the coming of sound. A brief high-spot, the production of *The Last Command* with Emil Jannings, had led to his providential invitation from Erich Pommer of UFA to visit Germany and direct Jannings in his first sound picture.

A drama about Rasputin was suggested, partly to placate UFA backer Alfred Hugenberg's right-wing sensibilities, but von Sternberg finally chose a novel by Heinrich Mann written in 1905 as an attack on the period's reactionary politics. An upright professor is seduced by a nightclub singer, becomes a pawn of her political friends, but finally fights off their influence and re-establishes himself in the community. *Professor Unrath* was essentially a protest against the false morality and corrupt values of the German middle class, but in it von Sternberg saw the possibility of a film far closer to his personal obsessions, his sensuality, his love of decoration and photographic style.

Mann wrote a script, which von Sternberg rejected. The popular comic playwright Carl Zuckmayer wrote another, whose dialogue von Sternberg liked. UFA's resident dramaturge, Robert Liebmann, incorporated the dialogue into a story which cut the novel in half, showing only the professor's surrender to the beautiful cabaret singer and his destruction at her hands. Jannings, famous for his love of lavish emotionalism, raised no objection to the many scenes of hysteria and public humiliation—material for which he had become famous in films like *The Last Laugh.* Von Sternberg proved difficult in his choice of star to play Lola. Mann's friend Trude Hesterberg was considered. So was stage actress Greta Massine, singer Lucie Mannheim, even Brigitte Helm. Finally, with time running out, Pommer signed Kathe Haack. Then, through Karl Vollmoeller, von Sternberg met Marlene Dietrich, a minor actress in films and on stage but better known as the companion of the star Willy Forst. The meeting with the 25-year-old married woman was the beginning of a life-long sexual obsession for von Sternberg, as well as the end of his marriage and the foundation of his true career.

Der blaue Engel became, like most of von Sternberg's films, an autobiographical excursion. In the material on Rath's autocratic teaching methods, von Sternberg paid back his own early torment at the hands of his father, who had forced him to learn Hebrew with frequent physical punishment to drive home the lessons. By choosing a turn of the century setting, von Sternberg placed the story in his own childhood, and decorated it with images of adolescent eroticism. On the walls of The Blue Angel Cabaret, designed by Otto Hunte, he plastered scores of posters, and hung the cafe with nets, dangling cardboard angels, stuffed birds—a familiar von Sternberg archetype—and, everywhere, low-hung lamps that give the film an air of scented, smoky claustrophobia.

Von Sternberg poured all his energy and imagination into the role of Lola, creating a star vehicle for the young Dietrich. Borrowing from the drawings of the erotic artist Felicien Rops, he created a figure out of a teenager's sexual fantasy, a vision in black stockings and heavy make-up, wearing an arrogantly tilted top hat. Her poses and movements on stage were mapped out with choreographic care, her songs crafted for her uninspiring voice by Friedrich Holländer, who found tunes needing only two or three notes. Her feline stroll on stage, her pointed, mocking stares, her casual use of her own sexual allure to beguile the giggling, simpering Jannings became elements in a screen persona Dietrich was to exploit for the rest of her career.

By contrast Jannings is feeble and monochromatically comic. The shadings he might have hoped to receive from von Sternberg's direction did not materialize. Instead, he found himself little more than a character player to this unknown young woman. Throughout the shooting, he threw tantrums, threatening to walk off the film and doing everything he could to break down the rapport between director and star. After the film, he was to demand successfully of UFA that he have total control over the material in all his subsequent films, a decision which destroyed him as a screen star.

Shot concurrently in English and German, *Der blaue Engel* confronted von Sternberg with a technical challenge of awesome complexity. Never a skilful editor or director of action, he was committed to a style where lighting and atmosphere conveyed the story, and where each performer's ''dramatic encounter with light'' spelled out their thought. To achieve this, he added to the script a number of minor but important characters, notably the clown who morosely observes life in the cafe, and who is revealed later (when Rath is forced into the same costume) to be another of Lola's discarded lovers. When the film was remade in 1959 with Mai Britt and Curt Jurgens, von Sternberg successfully sued 20th Century-Fox for plagiarism of his interpolated scenes, not found in the original screenplay.

Even before *Der blaue Engel* was finished, its success was obvious. Von Sternberg had shown tests of Dietrich to Paramount head B.P. Schulberg when he visited Berlin, and the studio immediately signed her to a two-picture contract. The premiere, on 31 March 1930, was a sensation: that night, she and von Sternberg sailed for America, to be met at the dock at New York by von Sternberg's wife, and a process server with writs against Dietrich for libel and alienation of affections. Neither director nor star were unduly concerned. Dietrich had found a vehicle to achieve international stardom. Von Sternberg, a subject on which he could focus his contradictory but prodigious talent. *Der blaue Engel* became the foundation of perhaps the most remarkable collaboration between actress and filmmaker that the cinema has ever seen.

—John Baxter

DIE BLECHTROMMEL

(The Tin Drum)

Germany/France, 1979

Director: Volker Schlodorff

Production: Franz Seitz Filmproduktion, Bioskop Film, GGB 14 KG, Artemis Filmegesellschaft, Argos Films, Jadran Film, Film Polski; Eastmancolour, 35mm; running time: 142 minutes. Filmed in Zagreb, Munchen, and Paris, 1978.

Producer: Franz Seitz; **executive producer:** Anatole Dauman; **screenplay:** Jean-Claude Carrière, Franz Seitz, and Volker Schlondorff, with the collaboration of Günter Grass, from his original novel; **photography:** Igor Luther; **editor:** Suzanne Baron; **assistant directors:** Branko Lustig, Alexander von Richtofen, Wolfgang Kroke, Andrzej Reiter, and Richard Malbequi; **lighting:** Karl Dillitzer; **production design:** Nikos Perakis; **art director:** Bernd Lepel; **sets:** Paul Weber, Edouard Pezzoli, Marijan, and Marcijus; **music:** Maurice Jarre; **costumes:** Dagmar Niefind, Inge Heer, and Vashy Yabara; **sound recording:** Walter Grundauer, Walter Kellerhaus, and Peter Beil.

Cast: David Bennent (*Oskar Matzerath*); Mario Adorf (*Alfred Matzerath*); Angela Winkler (*Agnes Matzerath*); Daniel Olbrychski (*Jan Bronski*); Katharina Thalbach (*Maria Matzerath*); Heinz Bennent (*Greff*); Andrea Ferreol (*Lina Greff*); Fritz Hakl (*Bebra*); Mariella Oliveri (*Roswitha Raguna*); Tina Engel (*Anna Koljaiczek*); Berta Drews (*Anna Koljaiczek, as an old woman*); Roland Teubner (*Joseph Koljaiczek*); Tadeusz Kunikowski (*Uncle Vinzenz*); Ernst Jacobi (*Gauletier Lobsack*); Werner Rehm (*Scheffler*); Ilse Page (*Gretchen Scheffler*); Kate Jaenicke (*Mother Truczinski*); Helmuth Brasch (*Old Heilandt*); Wigand Witting (*Herbert Truczinski*); Marek Walczewski (*Schugger-Leo*); Charles Aznavour (*Sigismund Markus*).

Awards: Palme D'Or, Cannes Film Festival, 1979; Oscar for Best Foreign Language Film, 1980.

Publications

Script:

Sclondorff, Volker, and Günter Grass, *Die Blechtrommel als Film*, Frankfurt, 1979.

Books:

Lewandowski, Reiner, *Die Filme von Volker Schlondorff*, Hildesheim, 1981.
Franklin, James, *New German Cinema: From Oberhausen to Hamburg*, Boston, 1983.
Phillips, Klaus, editor, *New German Filmmakers: From Oberhausen through the 1970s*, New York, 1984.
Elsaesser, Thomas, *New German Cinema: A History*, London 1989.
Ginsberg, Terri, *Perspectives on German Cinema*, New York, 1996.
Elsaesser, Thomas, *The BFI Companion to German Cinema*, Bloomington, 1999.

Articles:

Bonneville, L., *Séquences* (Montreal), January 1979.
Variety (New York), 16 May 1979.
Bassan, R., *Ecran* (Courbevoie), July 1979.
Logette, L., *Jeune Cinéma* (Paris), July-August 1979.
Ramasse, F., *Positif* (Paris), July-August 1979.
Courant, G., *Cinéma* (Paris), September 1979.
Lajeunesse, J., *Image et Son* (Paris), September 1979.
Schlondorff, Volker, ''Confrence de presse,'' in *Jeune Cinéma* (Paris), September-October 1979.
Bonnet, J.-C., and F. Cuel, *Cinématographe* (Paris), October 1979.
Lardeau, Y., *Cahiers du Cinéma* (Paris), November 1979.
Jeancolas, J.-P., ''Trois Notes (Brèves),'' in *Positif* (Paris), November 1979.
Kauffmann, Stanley, ''Living through Wars,'' in *The New Republic*, 5 April 1980.
Boyum, Joy Gould, ''Günter Grass on Screen: An Allegory of Nazism,'' in *The Wall Street Journal*, 11 April 1980.
Hatch, Robert, ''The Tin Drum,'' in *The Nation*, 19 April 1980.

Die Blechtrommel

Kroll, Jack, ''Bang the Drum Loudly,'' in *Newsweek*, 21 April 1980.
Schickel, Richard, ''Dream Work,'' in *Time*, 28 April 1980.
Harvey, Stephen, ''The Beat of a Difficult Drummer,'' in *Saturday Review*, May 1980.
Blake, Richard A., ''Danzig in the Dark,'' in *America*, 3 May 1980.
O'Toole, Lawrence, ''One Oskar Tailor—Made to Win Another,'' *Maclean's*, 5 May 1980.
Simon, John, ''Interior Exiles,'' in *National Review*, 30 May 1980.
Dawason, J., *Monthly Film Bulletin* (London), June 1980.
Reed, Rex, ''The Tin Drum,'' in *Vogue*, June 1980.
Kephart, E., *Films in Review* (New York), June-July 1980.
''The Tin Drum,'' in *USA Today*, July 1980.
Beaulieu, J., *Séquences* (Montreal), July 1980.
Pachter, H., *Cineaste* (New York), autumn 1980.
Hughes, J., ''Volker Schlondorff's Dream of Childhood,'' in *Film Quarterly* (Berkeley), spring 1981.
Kaes, Anton, *Hitler to Heimat: The Return of History as Film*, Harvard University Press, Cambridge, 1989.
Hall, Conrad, ''A Different Drummer: *The Tin Drum*, Film and Novel,'' in *Literature/Film Quarterly* (Salisbury), October 1990.
Krzeminski, A., in *Kino* (Warsaw), November 1992.
Silberman, Marc, *German Cinema: Texts in Context*, Wayne State University Press, Detroit, 1995.
Feingold, M., ''A Different Drummer,'' in *Village Voice* (New York), 12 August 1997.

* * *

Volker Schlodorff's *The Tin Drum* is representative of the New German cinema, a period in the 1970s and 1980s dominated by a generation of directors who were children during and following the Third Reich. These directors have taken a retrospective look at their childhoods and their nation's history to examine the emotional wounds and sensitivities of the present. Marc Silberman in *German Cinema* states that the films of this period ''critically refigure seductive images and sounds from Germany's fascist past in order to challenge the heritage of the Nazi cinema, and for the first time since the international successes of the early Weimar cinema, German films enjoyed once again critical acclaim beyond their domestic audience.''

The movie based on Günter Grass' powerful novel about Oskar, a boy growing up in Danzig between the wars, who is so horrified by the world that he wills himself to remain little.

Like the novel, *The Tin Drum* traces the warped history of Oskar's family, beginning with his grandparents, peasants of the Polish countryside. In the first scene, a man chased by the police begs a woman to hide him. She lifts her skirts and he crawls to safe seclusion. When the police have gone he emerges, hurriedly closing the front of his pants, and in the next scene, the couple has a small child, Oskar's mother. The image of hiding under a woman's skirts for safety is repeated throughout the film, and is both a suggestion of safety and sexuality, as Oskar climbs under the skirts of his grandmother, into bed with a neighbor woman for warmth, and into bed with his housekeeper where he presumably fathers her child. The macabre notion of sexuality becomes a precarious site for comfort and safety, providing immediacy and accessibility, but is eventually spoiled by the excessive need with which it is sought. It may be a continuous reference to Oskar's wish at birth to return to the womb, but decides to stay in the world when his mother promises him a tin drum on his third birthday.

Oskar Matzerath is played by 12-year-old David Bennent, who throws himself down a flight of stairs on his third birthday, celebrated by raucous adults with drink and debauchery, to prevent himself from growing up to participate in the obscenity of adult middle-class existence. He opts for perpetual childhood before the Nazis come to power and take over Danzig, his home town. The child, a symbol of protest, recognizes that Nazism is merely an extension of the world he has already rejected. His life centers on his tin drum, and everywhere he wanders throughout the film he accompanies his steps with the stoic beat that could be the suppressed, frantic beat of his heart, his voice audible, yet untranslatable. Oskar is a perfect parody of militarism. He wanders into a Nazi rally, and the assembly soon collapses into chaos when his drumbeat sets the entire pageant off course. His other talent, piercing screams, which he discovers can shatter glass, are his willful destruction of that which inhibits or frustrates him. This voice is his defense, his weapon, screams an extradiegetic foreshadowing of Kristallnacht. When the war comes to Danzig, Oskar is there among the dead and wounded, wandering and observing. He is fifteen, but also three, and takes from the world what would please him, as though he has become that which he rejected when he decided to throw himself down the stairs to protect himself in the masquerade of childhood.

The images in *The Tin Drum* are exceedingly unpalatable on screen though they were included in Grass' novel. Oskar, whose weakness is sensed by the other children, is forced to eat soup made of boiled frogs and urine. The decomposing head of a horse is pulled from the sea and a mass of eels tumbles out of it. Later, the eeler (Oskar's father) tries to force his wife, who was sickened by the sight, to eat his catch. She flees to her bedroom where she is consoled sexually by her lover, her husband's closest friend. Later in the film she becomes obsessed with a craving for fish until her gluttony destroys her. The image of the child banging on the door behind which his mother is dying, foundering on raw fish, will be repeated in another New German film, *Deutschland, Bleiche Mutter* (*Germany, Pale Mother*) by Helma Sanders-Brahms, though Oskar's mother never opens the door to return a sense of safety or reassurance to him or to the film, as the mother in Sanders-Brahm's film eventually does. Joy Gould Boyum writes in ''Günter Grass on Screen: An Allegory of Nazism,'' in *The Wall Street Journal*, that these images, ''enlarged, intensified and made overwhelmingly graphic by the movie screen . . . disturb too much instead of calling attention to whatever point they would further, they end up calling attention only to themselves and their own jarring freakishness.''

Robert Hatch is less disturbed by the images, as his review in *The Nation* praises the film for its reconstruction of Grass' picaresque novel: ''There were more than enough scenes from which to choose: the Christ child as drummer, the ghastly harvest of eels, the storm troopers waltzing to Oskar's beat, the dwarfs' picnic atop the Normandy bunker, the siege of the Danzig post office, the seduction of Maria with fizz powder. The film is a splendid spectacle, but only a sampling of the novel's three books. It is like watching a slide show of some well-remembered land, the snapshots bringing to mind more than they can show.'' The story structure seems to be carried away as the technique of the adult Oskar's voice-over narration from an insane asylum (though this is not clear in the film), recalling the events of his childhood, is abandoned. Though this awkwardness is merely a problem of the adaptation process it does little to diminish the effectiveness of the screen presentation, which has a style rooted in Expressionism, and is powerful and original.

—Lee Sellars

DIE BLEIERNE ZEIT

(The German Sisters)

Germany, 1981

Director: Margarethe von Trotta

Production: Bioskop Film; Fujicolour, 35mm; running time: 107 minutes.

Producer: Eberhard Junkersdorf; **screenplay:** Margarethe von Trotta; **assistant director:** Helenka Hummel; **photography:** Franz Rath; **editor:** Dagmar Hirtz; **sound:** Vladimir Vizner and Hans Dieter Schwartz; **art directors:** George von Kieseritzky and Barbara Kloth; **music:** Nicolas Economou; **costumes:** Monica Hasse and Jorge Jara.

Cast: Jutta Lampe (*Juliane*); Barbara Sukowa (*Marianne*); Rudiger Volger (*Wolfgang*); Doris Schade (*Mother*); Verena Rudolph (*Sabine*); Luc Bondy (*Werner*); Franz Rudnick (*Father*); Julia Biedermann (*Marianne, age 16*); Ina Robinski (*Juliane, age 17*); Patrick Estrada-Pox (*Jan*).

Awards: Golden Lion, Venice 1981.

Publications

Script:

von Trotta, Margarethe, *Die Bleierne Zeit*, Frankfurt, 1981.

Die Bleierne Zeit

Books:

Kaplan, Ann E., *Women and Film: Both Sides of the Camera*, Methuen, 1983.

Todd, Janet, *Women and Film*, New York, 1988.

Frieden, Sandra, *Gender and German Cinema: Feminist Interventions—Volume II: German Film History/German History on Film*, Oxford, 1993.

Articles:

Variety (New York), 16 September 1981.

Nave, B., ''Les années de plomb: Margarethe von Trotta ou le refus de l'oubli,'' in *Jeune Cinéma* (Paris), November 1981.

Pellizzari, L., and others, ''Speciale anni di piombo,'' in *Cineforum* (Bergamo), March 1892.

Celemenski, M., and others, ''Margarethe von Trotta,'' in *Cinématographe* (Paris), April 1982.

Amiel, M., *Cinéma* (Paris), May 1982.

Sauvaget, D., *Image et Son* (Paris), May 1982.

Milne, Tom, *Monthly Film Bulletin* (London), June 1982.

Johnston, S., *Films and Filming* (London), July 1982.

Rabinowicz, L., ''Dark Times,'' in *Cinema Papers* (Melbourne), August 1982.

Sklar, R., and Harris, A., *Cineaste* (New York), Vol. XII, no. 3, 1983.

Alemanno, R., ''La prassi delle conoscenza in 'Anni di piombo,''' in *Cinema Nuovo* (Bari), August-October 1983.

DiCaprio, L., ''Baader-Meinhof Fictionalized,'' in *Jump Cut* (Chicago), February 1984.

Delorme, C., ''On the Film 'Marianne and Juliane' by Margarethe von Trotta,'' in *Journal of Film & Video* (Boston), Spring 1985.

Seiter, E., ''The Political Is Personal: Margarethe von Trotta's Marianne and Juliane,'' in *Journal of Film & Video* (Boston), Spring 1985.

Kaplan, E. A., ''Discourses in Terrorism, Feminism, and the Family in von Trotta's Marianne and Juliane,'' in *Persistence of Vision* (Maspeth, New York), Fall 1985.

Donougho, M., ''Margarethe von Trotta: Gynemagoguery and the Dilemmas of a Filmmaker,'' in *Literature/Film Quarterly* (Maryland), July 1989.

Toiviainen, S., in *Filmihullu* (Helsinki), no. 5, 1995.
Martin, Michel, and Maurice Elia, ''Margarethe von Trotta toujours présente,'' in *Séquences* (Haute-Ville), November-December 1996.

* * *

The German Sisters is based in part on the life of Gudrun Ensslin, one of the best known members of the Baader-Meinhof Group or Rote Armee Fraktion which carried out a campaign of terrorism in Germany in the late sixties and into the seventies. She was arrested in 1972 and sentenced to life imprisonment. In 1977 she and two other group members were found dead in their cells at Stammheim prison. The authorities claimed they had committed suicide, but this explanation has never been accepted by many, including Gudrun's sister Christiane, to whom this film is dedicated.

In *The German Sisters* Gudrun becomes Marianne and Christiane becomes Juliane, the daughters of a pastor in the German Lutheran Church. As we see through a number of flashbacks, both grow up in an atmosphere which is at one and the same time patriarchal but socially liberal and concerned. It is also strongly anti-fascist. In childhood, Marianne is dutiful and well-behaved, and Juliane is the rebel. But in the film's present, Marianne has become a terrorist, whilst Juliane has decided to try to change society peacefully by embarking on what was known at the time as ''the long march through the institutions'' and becoming a journalist on a liberal women's magazine.

As the flashback structure suggests, *The German Sisters* concerns the weight of the past on the present. Its original German title translates as ''Leaden Times,'' which could be taken as referring either to the Nazi past (which has shaped, in quite different ways, Marianne's and Juliane's oppositional attitudes to the German present), or to the dreariness of the fifties in which they had their childhood and in which they were shaped by rather more personal forces, such as sibling rivalry and patriarchal authority. The film shows us two ways of relating to these pasts—violent rejection, or reformist feminism—and is, as Ellen Seiter has claimed, ''an effective dramatisation of the feminist slogan 'the personal is political,' locating as it does the characters in their experience in the nuclear family within a specific historical, national and cultural instance.''

However, this is where the problems begin, since the film, dedicated to the real-life Christiane, and told very much from the fictional Juliane's point of view, does undoubtedly privilege reformism over terrorism. (Of course, had it done the opposite it wouldn't have got made in the first place.) Especially problematic is the fact that, since all but one of the flashbacks concern the sisters' childhoods, we have no idea why Marianne joined Baader-Meinhof in the first place, nor do we learn anything about the group's ideology and its reasons for choosing the terrorist strategy. Given this lacuna one is almost bound to look for the explanation for Marianne's actions in the carefully delineated family circumstances in which she grew up, and to fall back on the psychoanalytic suggestion that ''Marianne's blind devotion to her father, as against Juliane's resistance and identification with her mother, has made her susceptible to a new form of fanaticism.'' But, taken in association with Juliane's accusation that ''a generation ago and you would have become a member of the Bund Deutscher Madchen'' (a sort of Nazi version of the Girl Guides), this simply suggests that certain family structures produce members who are attracted to terrorist organisations and that there is thus no real fundamental difference between Left and Right wing terrorist groups (see for example Gillian Becker's *Hitler's Children*, and Helm Stierlin's *Family Terrorism and Public Terrorism*). Radical politics, Left or Right, are reduced to rebellion against the authoritarian father, Juliane is a model of responsible, social-democratic oppositional politics, and Marianne epitomises fanatical, pathological rejectionism.

Whilst there is some truth in these charges, they don't entirely do the film justice. It's true that, whilst she is alive, Marianne frequently comes across as pretty unpleasant. But this impression is mitigated by the flashback scenes, especially those in which she watches film of the concentration camps or of American atrocities in Vietnam, in which we begin to understand what might lead a socially-conscious young woman down the path from protest to terrorism. Furthermore, there is a sense in which, as Ann Kaplan has suggested, ''it is tempting to read Marianne as some kind of 'double' for Juliane—the repressed self that Juliane wanted to be.'' This is most evident in the *Persona*—like scene in prison in which, thanks to the glass screen between them and the way the scene is filmed, Juliane and Marianne seem to fuse together. But it's also there throughout the latter part of the film in which, suspecting murder, Juliane absorbs herself totally in re-enacting Marianne's death. She also thereby comes up against the real brutality of the German state, and gets an inkling of what confirmed Marianne in her hatred of and total opposition to it.

At the end of the film, Juliane takes in Marianne's son Jan, who had been fostered when she was on the run and then in prison. The fact that he has been badly burned by children who found out that he was a terrorist's son suggests a cyclical pattern, with parents' deeds being endlessly revisited on their children. On the other hand the fact that he asks to be told everything about his mother, having earlier ripped up her photograph, suggests that Jan will not reject his parents like Marianne rejected hers. However, as Kaplan notes: ''The act locates what is important firmly in the realm of the interpersonal. The vision is bleak in terms of bringing about change in the public realm.'' In this she is echoing von Trotta herself: ''Hope arises from the realisation that you have to find the way back to yourself. This is less of a rallying call than a pessimistic statement. Personally I see very few chances of exploding the power complex established by the alliance between economics and science and, above all, I see no movement on the present political horizon capable of achieving this.''

—Julian Petley

THE BLOOD OF A POET

See **LE SANG D'UN POÈTE**

BLOOD OF THE BEASTS

See **LE SANG DES BETES**

BLOOD OF THE CONDOR

See **YAWAR MALLKU**

BLOW-UP

USA, 1966

Director: Michelangelo Antonioni

Production: Metro-Goldwyn-Mayer Pictures Corp.; Metrocolor, 35mm; running time: 111 minutes; length: 9974 feet. Released December 1966, New York. Filmed during 1966 on location in London, and at MGM Studios, Boreham Wood.

Producer: Carlo Ponti; **screenplay:** Michelangelo Antonioni and Tonino Guerra, from a short story by Julio Cortazar; **photography:** Carlo di Palma; **editor:** Frank Clarke; **sound:** Robin Gregory; **art director:** Asheton Gorton; **music:** Herbie Hancock; **costumes:** Jocelyn Rickards; **photographic murals:** John Cowan.

Cast: David Hemmings (*Thomas, the photographer*); Vanessa Redgrave (*Jane*); Sarah Miles (*Patricia*); John Castle (*Bill*); Peter Bowles (*Ron*); Jane Birkin (*Blonde*); Gillian Hills (*Brunette*); Harry Hutchinson (*Old Man*); Verushka, Jill Kennington, Peggy Moffitt, Rosaleen Murray, Ann Norman, and Melanie Hampshire (*Models*); Julian Chagrin and Claude Chagrin (*The Tennis Players*).

Awards: Palme d'Or, Cannes Film Festival, 1967.

Publications

Script:

Antonioni, Michelangelo and Tonino Guerra, *Blow-Up*, Turin, 1968; New York, 1971.

Books:

Bernardini, Aldo, *Michelangelo Antonioni de Gente del Po a ''Blow-Up,''* Milan, 1967.
Sarris, Andrew, *Interviews with Film Directors*, New York, 1967.
Cameron, Ian, and Robin Wood, *Antonioni*, New York, 1969.
Boyum, Joy, and Adrienne Scott, *Film as Film: Critical Responses to Film Art*, Boston, 1971.
Huss, Roy, editor, *Focus on ''Blow-Up,''* Englewood Cliffs, New Jersey, 1971.
Bazin André, *La Politique des auteurs: Entretiens avec Jean Renoir, etc.*, Paris, 1972; revised edition, 1984.
Samuels, Charles Thomas, *Encountering Directors*, New York, 1972.
Goldman, Annie, *Cinéma et société moderne*, Paris, 1974.
Prats, A. J., *The Autonomous Image: Cinematic Narration and Humanism*, Lexington, Kentucky, 1981.
Rifkin, Ned, *Antonioni's Visual Language*, Ann Arbor, Michigan, 1982.
Barthes, Roland, and others, *Michelangelo Antonioni*, Munich, 1984.
Biarese, Cesare, and Aldo Tassone, *I film di Michelangelo Antonioni*, Rome, 1985.
Dervin, Daniel, *Through a Freudian Lens Deeply: A Psychoanalysis of Cinema*, Hillsdale, New Jersey, 1985.
Antonioni, Michelangelo, *That Bowling Alley on the Tiber: Tales of a Director*, Oxford, 1986.
Perry, Ted, and Rene Prieto, *Michelangelo Antonioni: A Guide to References and Resources*, Boston, 1986.

Articles:

Sarris, Andrew, in *Village Voice* (New York), 29 December 1966.
Cahiers du Cinéma (Paris), January 1967.
Hart, Henry, in *Films in Review* (New York), January 1967.
Knight, Arthur, in *Film Heritage* (Dayton, Ohio), Spring 1967.
Harrison, Carey, in *Sight and Sound* (London), Spring 1967.
Kozloff, Max, in *Film Quarterly* (Berkeley), Spring 1967.
Cocks, Jay, in *Take One* (Montreal), April 1967.
Bean, Robin, in *Films and Filming* (London), May 1967.
Clouzot, Claire, in *Cinéma* (Paris), May 1967.
Kinder, Marsha, ''Antonioni in Transit,'' in *Sight and Sound* (London), Summer 1967.
Samuels, Charles, ''*Blow-Up:* Sorting Things Out,'' in *American Scholar* (Washington, D.C.), Winter 1967–68.
Lefèvre, Raymond, in *Image et Son* (Paris), November 1967.
Slover, George, ''*Blow-Up:* Medium, Message and Make-Believe,'' in *Massachusetts Review*, Autumn 1968.
Fernandez, Henry, in *Film Heritage* (Dayton, Ohio), Winter 1968–69.
Corliss, Richard, ''Still Legion, Still Decent?'' in *Commonweal* (New York), 23 May 1969.
Gow, Gordon, ''Antonioni Men,'' in *Films and Filming* (London), June 1970.
Hampton, Charles, in *Film Comment* (New York), Fall 1970.
Hernacki, T., ''Michelangelo Antonioni and the Imagery of Disintergration,'' in *Film Heritage* (Dayton, Ohio), Autumn 1970.
Cohen, Hubert, ''Re-Sorting Things Out,'' in *Cinema Journal* (Evanston, Illinois), Spring 1971.
D'Lugo, Marvin, ''Signs and Meanings in *Blow-Up:* From Cortázar to Antonioni,'' in *Literature/Film Quarterly* (Salisbury, Maryland), Winter 1975.
Palmer, W. J., ''*Blow-Up:* The Game with No Balls,'' in *Literature/Film Quarterly* (Salisbury, Maryland), no. 4, 1979.
Antonioni, Michelangelo, ''Una intensa emozione che la troup interrompe,'' in *Cinema Nuovo* (Turin), June 1982.
Mátyás, G., ''Az sltünt valóság nyomában,'' in *Filmkultura* (Budapest), March-April 1983.
Martin, R., ''Quand le visible n'est plus seul visible,'' in *Revue Belge du Cinéma* (Brussels), Summer 1983.
Lee Francis, R., ''Transcending Metaphor: Antonioni's '*Blow-Up*,''' in *Literature/Film Quarterly* (Salisbury, Maryland), vol. 13, no. 1, 1985.
Pressler, M., ''Antonioni's *Blow-Up:* Myth, Order, and the Photographic Image,'' in *Post Script* (Jacksonville, Florida), Fall 1985.
Harris, Thomas, ''*Rear Window* and *Blow-Up:* Hitchcock's Straight Forwardness vs. Antonioni's Ambiguity,'' in *Literature/Film Quarterly* (Salisbury, Maryland), vol. 15, no. 1, 1987.
Hoberman, J., ''After the Orgy,'' in *Village Voice* (New York), 3 December 1991.
Wagstaff, C., ''Sexual Noise,'' in *Sight and Sound* (London), May 1992.
Tomasulo, F. P., ''The Architectonics of Alienation: Antonioni's Edifice Complex,'' in *Wide Angle* (Baltimore), no. 3, 1993.

Savage, J., ''Snapshots of the Sixties,'' in *Sight and Sound* (London), May 1993.
Bailey, E., and K. Hennessey, ''Picture Perfect,'' in *Movieline* (Escondido, California), July 1993.

* * *

The plot of Michelangelo Antonioni's *Blow-Up* is easily summarized. A photographer, Thomas (David Hemmings), chances upon a couple in a secluded park. From concealment, he photographs their apparently romantic playfulness. When the girl (Vanessa Redgrave) seeks him out and demands the negatives, he refuses. Provoked by her insistence, he later scrutinizes the photographs. As he successively enlarges selected areas of the shots (the blow-ups of the title), he discovers evidence that she has been complicit in the murder of the man with whom she was seen. Before Thomas can decide what to do with the documentation, his studio is vandalized and the photographs are taken.

A superficial mystery story, the plot is not what interests Antonioni in *Blow-Up.* His concern is directed toward the interplay among philosophical concepts of reality, illusion, and appearance that manifest themselves through metaphors of photography, painting, and pantomime. For Antonioni in *Blow-Up*, as in many of his other films (most notably *L'avventura* and *The Passenger*), the narrative is a vehicle for the director's investigation of perception and interpretation.

London in the mid-1960s was the self-proclaimed capital of pop art; it boasted trends set by the Beatles, Twiggy, and Carnaby Street. It was chic, hip, and mod, filled with clashing colors and swinging youths. A technological advance in photographic equipment complemented this environment. Equipped with compact cameras that used faster film stock, photographers could snap their subjects rapidly and spontaneously. This liberation offered the photographer the potential of capturing life in its more candid and offhand aspects. The radical new concepts of photography that prevailed in the 1960s were thus characterized by an informal and unposed factual look at odds with the more obviously artificial photographic styles that had gone before.

Although the life-styles represented in *Blow-Up* may now seem dated, they did not, of course, account for Antonioni's attraction to the situation. In fashionable London, as recorded by the candid photography of the mid-1960s Antonioni found one of his most memorable metaphors. *Blow-Up* is a film about both a society decaying from within and a photograph's ability to record an instant of truth. Both of these factors affect the young and successful photographer who is at the center of both the film and his fashionable milieu.

The photographer, only rarely identified by name in the film, is uncommitted, hostile, indifferent. He is professionally successful and an expert photographer. He is in control of himself and situations only when he is armed with his camera; without it, he is at his weakest and most vulnerable. His uncertain sexuality is especially evident in the contemptuous manner in which he treats women, dominating and humiliating them while avoiding personal involvement. (The single exception to this is his non-sexual relationship with his neighbor's lover.) He is a model of duplicity: a voyeur, a deceiver, a performer. He is, for Antonioni, the Everyman of the disaffected generation: obsessed with surfaces, but blind to the inner value of people and deeper meaning of the events he so skillfully and energetically records with his camera.

The character of the photographer is of central interest to Antonioni in *Blow-Up* because it is Thomas's transformation that provides the essential meaning of the film. The ambiguities of reality, illusion, and appearance are ever-present but ignored by the photographer and his generation, and the photographer—against his will—is forced to confront this mystery, a mystery more perplexing and shattering than the murder he believes he has documented. The process by which the insulated self-confident, self-seeking, self-indulgent, self-absorbed photographer (so typical of his time) is changed by a set of circumstances he neither comprehends nor controls is examined by Antonioni with the skill and care of a surgeon. The photographer's casual assumptions are discredited and his values are toppled. He is a different person at the end of the film than he was at the beginning.

The photographer's transformation, in this ambiguous world where it is so difficult to distinguish reality from illusion, is realized through the act of seeing. In *Blow-Up*, seeing is explored on three levels; camera sight, revealed in photographs; imaginary sight, represented by paintings and the mime troupe; and ocular sight, which moves freely but uneasily between them. The concept of seeing is emphasized through a deemphasis of verbal expression. *Blow-Up* communicates on an almost completely visual level; nothing more than implied significance is verbalized. For such an obviously searching film, it is indeed unusual that there are no metaphysical discussions, no intimate exchanges, no analytical speculations. The dialogue track, divorced from the image track, exposes the extraneous or frivolous words that are used between the interacting participants.

This attention to the visual dimensions of perception underscores the subtext represented by the mime troupe. If words are indeed superficial to the photographer, they are totally superfluous to (and consequently discarded by) the mimes. The mimes are presented to us as a framing device—they open and close the film. At the beginning, they are seen gadding about the bustling streets panhandling; at the end, the same troupe engages in a mock tennis match. At the beginning, the photographer simply finds them a momentary amusement; by the ending, however, he actually shares their experience. It is, in fact, the mime troupe that serves as the spiritual barometer by which we measure the photographer's transformation. The act of miming is crucial for Antonioni and *Blow-Up* because it is the mime who brings our attention to objects by their absence. For the mime, the imaginary tennis ball is every bit as ''real'' as the evidential photograph is ''illusory.''

It is of course, significant that the tennis match takes place at the end. It is less a conclusion than a speculation. The photographer, an outer-directed man in the beginning, would never have retrieved the tennis ball and thrown it back at the outset of the film. He is only able to perform this act of assistance to the players because of what has happened to him in the interim. However, Antonioni does not have him abandon his camera as he fetches the ball; rather, he carries it with him. What the photographer has learned is that the camera and the tennis ball can (and do) exist in the same plane of perception—reality, illusion and appearance do not fall into neat and convenient categories.

The rejection of categories is given the final placement in *Blow-Up.* The blow-ups of the murder incident are visually related by Antonioni to the abstract design of his neighbor's paintings—the grain of the photographic enlargements bear an uncanny resemblance to the color dots on the painter's canvas. Antonioni underscores this motif when, in the film's final shot, the photographer is left as isolated and indistinct as the microcosmic emulsion grains he has enlarged. Antonioni masterfully frames him in the composition of this shot to resemble a visual element in one of his own blow-ups.

As a consequence of his spiritual awakening, the photographer is a different person. His slumbering world of possessions and exploitations have been dislodged. By the film's final shot, he is awake to the dualities and complexities of life, and, ironically, that wakefulness isolates him. He can no longer return to the blind-sighted comfort of his complacent and gluttonous life; he can no longer use his camera or look at photographs in quite the same way as before.

—Stephen E. Bowles

THE BLUE ANGEL

See **DER BLAUE ENGEL**

THE BLUE EYES OF YONTA

See **Udju Azul di Yonta**

THE BLUE KITE

See **LAN FENGZHENG**

THE BLUE LAMP

UK, 1949

Director: Basil Dearden

Production: Ealing Studios, a Michael Balcon Production; black and white; running time: 84 minutes. Released January 1950.

Associate Producer: Michael Relph; **script:** T. E. B. Clarke; **additional dialogue:** Alexander Mackendrick; **original treatment:** Jan Read and Ted Willis; **photography:** Gordon Dines; **2nd unit photography:** Lionel Banes; **editor:** Peter Tanner; **art director:** Jim Morahan; **musical director:** Ernest Irving.

Cast: Jack Warner (*P.C. Dixon*); Jimmy Hanley (*P.C. Mitchell*); Meredith Edwards (*P.C. Hughes*); Robert Flemyng (*Sergeant Roberts*); Bernard Lee (*Divisional Detective Inspector Cherry*); Dirk Bogarde (*Tom Riley*); Patric Doonan (*Spud*); Peggy Evans (*Diana Lewis*); Gladys Henson (*Mrs. Dixon*); Dora Bryan (*Maisie*); Betty Ann Davies (*Mrs. Lewis*).

Awards: British Academy Award for Best Film, 1950.

Publications

Books:

Balcon, Michael, *Michael Balcon Presents: A Lifetime of Films*, London, 1969.
Clarke, T. E. B., *This Is Where I Came In*, London, 1974.
Warner, Jack, *Jack of All Trades: An Autobiography*, London, 1975.
Barr, Charles, *Ealing Studios*, London, 1977.
Perry, George, *Forever Ealing*, London, 1981.

Articles:

Kine Weekly (London), 12 January 1950.
''G.L.,'' in *Monthly Film Bulletin* (London), January-February 1950.
Sight and Sound (London), April 1950.
Motion Picture Herald (New York), 3 April 1950.
Dickinson, Thorold, ''The Work of Sir Michael Balcon at Ealing Studios,'' in *The Year's Work in the Film 1950*, edited by Roger Manvell, London, 1951.
Ellis, John, ''Made in Ealing,'' in *Screen* (London), Spring 1975.
Medhurst, Andy, ''Dirk Bogarde,'' in *All Our Yesterdays*, edited by Charles Barr, London, 1986.
Aachen, G., ''*The Blue Lamp*,'' in *Reid's Film Index* (New South Wales, Australia), no. 30, 1997.

* * *

Charles Barr, in his definitive *Ealing Studios*, locates *The Blue Lamp* at the centre of the studio's post-war work, noting the collaboration of the writer T. E. B. Clarke, who had such an enormous impact on the comedy cycle, with the director Basil Dearden, who specialised in social dramas. Like many of the most interesting Ealing films, *The Blue Lamp* revolves around the confrontation of two worlds, two models of society: the stable and steady community of ordinary people, the stuff of the nation, and the hysterical and anti-social outsiders, who threaten to destroy the community, and whose threat must therefore be contained.

In this particular case, the nation is embodied in the community of a local police station and its wider social network, which itself finds its most sublime expression in the domestic family life of one of the policemen, P.C. Dixon. Stability is established through the mundane routines of police work, and their communal social activities when off duty, the individual thoroughly subsumed into the collective. The threat comes from Riley (played by a young and gaunt Dirk Bogarde), his girlfriend, and his partner in crime, the three of them identified in a documentary-like voice-over as typical of a new post-war phenomenon, immature, improperly socialised juvenile delinquents, extreme cases, shunned by the rest of society, even by ''professional criminals!''

Barr's excellent analysis of the film sees it as a profound celebration of the values of the community: sobriety, emotional understatement, social responsibility, patrician authority, etc. But it is possible to see it also as a rather desperate attempt to restore faith in a crumbling national ideology which had found its most secure expression during the war. The film thus works to contain the emergent relatively autonomous youth culture, struggling to escape from the oppressive certainties and stifling over-protection of community life and to express the desires which it represses. Thus, where Mitchell, the young recruit to the police, comes to respect and take advice from his elders, and so becomes ''one of the family,'' Riley refuses any advice. He is situated outside the community—and unable to establish his own community, unable to work as a group with his partners, continually arguing with them in an aggressively masculine way (at one stage, as he taunts his girlfriend, he fondles his

The Blue Lamp

gun; by contrast, the police seem almost *maternal*). This particular image of youth is eventually positively valued and narratively centralised a decade later, in films like *Saturday Night and Sunday Morning*, by which time television had taken over the function of articulating the principles of the national community in soap operas like *Coronation Street* and cop series like the equally long-running *Dixon of Dock Green*, featuring the same P.C. Dixon, still played by Jack Warner (even though he had been murdered half-way through *The Blue Lamp*!).

The Blue Lamp also makes an interesting comparison with Hitchcock's crime thriller *Blackmail*, made some 20 years earlier, which also represents police work as routine, and the police force as a tight-knit community. But Hitchcock establishes this mundane picture of everyday life in order to subvert and unbalance it, and so to involve the spectator emotionally. As in *The Blue Lamp*, unconscious, repressed forces are released into the world of the everyday. But in *Blackmail*, the effect is to challenge the very premises of the everyday and its apparent securities and certainties. *The Blue Lamp*, on the other hand, establishes the ordinary in order to strengthen its moral and ideological force and the safety of routine, not to challenge it. The film thus struggles to contain disruption and reassert the ordinary: its final images neither testify to a fantastic wish-fulfilment (on the contrary, they return full-circle to the beginning, showing how the community effortlessly reproduces itself, and takes all traumas in its stride), nor leave us with *Blackmail*'s lingering, disturbing sense of guilt, and of the proximity of an underlying chaos, a turbulent world where anything can happen.

But *The Blue Lamp* cannot quite so easily contain the threats, since they are visually and narratively so much more exciting for the spectator. In effect, the film interweaves two different modes of representation. On the one hand, there is the mode of social drama, heavily influenced by the documentary-realist tradition, with a characteristically loose, relatively non-dynamic, and episodic narrative, its multiplication of dramas held in check by the limits of the community. On the other hand, embedded within and foreclosed by the former, there is the much more narratively dynamic, tightly causal, uni-linear thriller, with a very different style of lighting, framing, performance, and action reminiscent of *film noir:* a style which eroticises the body, and vicariously engages the spectator in the pleasures of suspense and uncertainty.

—Andrew Higson

BLUE VELVET

USA, 1986

Director: David Lynch

Production: De Laurentiis Entertainment Group; color; Dolby sound; running time: 120 minutes. Released September 1986.

Executive producer: Richard Roth; **screenplay:** David Lynch; **assistant directors:** Ellen Rauch, Ian Woolf; **photography:** Frederick Elmes; **assistant photographer:** Lex Dupont; **editor:** Duwayne Dunham; **sound design:** Alan Splet; **sound recordist:** Ann Kroeber; **production designer:** Patricia Norris; **music director:** Angelo Badalamenti; **special effects:** Greg Hull, George Hill; **stunt coordinator:** Richard Langdon.

Cast: Kyle MacLachlan (*Jeffrey Beaumont*); Isabella Rossellini (*Dorothy Vallens*); Dennis Hopper (*Frank Booth*); Laura Dern (*Sandy Williams*); Hope Lange (*Mrs. Williams*); Dean Stockwell (*Ben*); George Dickerson (*Detective Williams*); Priscilla Pointer (*Mrs. Beaumont*); Frances Bay (*Aunt Barbara*); Jack Harvey (*Tom Beaumont*); Ken Stovitz (*Mike*); Brad Dourif (*Raymond*); Jack Nance (*Paul*); J. Michael Hunter (*Hunter*); Dick Green (*Don Vallens*); Fred Pickler (*Yellow Man*); Philip Markert (*Dr. Gynde*); Leonard Watkins and Moses Gibson (*Double Ed*); Selden Smith (*Nurse Cindy*); Peter Carew (*Coroner*); Jon Jon Snipes (*Little Donny*).

Blue Velvet

Awards: National Society of Film Critics Award for Best Film, Best Director, Best Supporting Actor (Hopper), Best Cinematography.

Publications

Articles:

Variety (New York), 3 September 1986.

Chute, D., ''Out to Lynch,'' in *Film Comment* (New York), September-October 1986.

Magid, Ron, ''*Blue Velvet*—Small Town Horror Tale,'' in *American Cinematographer* (Los Angeles), November 1986.

Corliss, Richard, in *Film Comment* (New York), November-December 1986.

Sight and Sound (London), Winter 1986–87.

Interview with Lynch, in *Ecran Fantastique* (Paris), January 1987.

Chion, Michel, in *Cahiers du Cinéma* (Paris), January 1987.

Routt, Bill, and Diane Routt, in *Cinema Papers* (Melbourne, Australia), March 1987.

Sutton, Martin, in *Films and Filming* (London), March 1987.

Ledel, Michael, in *Filmfaust* (Frankfurt), March-April 1987.

Jenkins, Steve, in *Monthly Film Bulletin* (London), April 1987.

Borden, Lizzie, and Angela Carter, in *City Limits* (London), 9 April 1987.

Film Quarterly (Beverly Hills), Fall 1987.

Jaehne, Karen, and Laurent Bouzereau, in *Cineaste* (New York), vol. 15, no. 3, 1987.

Literature/Film Quarterly (Salisbury, Maryland), vol. 16, no. 2, 1988.

Maxfield, J. F., '''Now It's Dark': The Child's Dream in *Blue Velvet*,'' in *Post Script* (Commerce, Texas), no. 3, 1989.

Lindroth, J., ''Down the Yellow Brick Road: Two Dorothys and the Journey of Initiation in Dream and Nightmare,'' in *Literature/Film Quarterly* (Salisbury, Maryland), vol. 18, no. 3, 1990.

Pellow, C. K., ''*Blue Velvet* Once More,'' in *Literature/Film Quarterly* (Salisbury, Maryland), vol. 18, no. 3, 1990.

Preston, J. L., ''Dantean Imagery in *Blue Velvet*,'' in *Literature/Film Quarterly* (Salisbury, Maryland), vol. 18, no. 3, 1990.

Woodward, R. B., ''A Dark Lens on America,'' in *New York Times*, 14 January 1990.

Spillman, Susan, ''A Director Both Sublime and Surreal,'' in *USA Today* (Arlington, Virginia), 17 August 1990.

Breskin, David, interview with Lynch, in *Rolling Stone* (New York), 6 September 1990.

Aydemir, M., ''Nogmaals David Lynch,'' in *Skrien* (Amsterdam), April-May 1991.

Jorholt, E., ''I erotikkens vold,'' in *Kosmorama* (Copenhagen), Spring 1991.

Gyorgy, P., ''Szenvedely es eroszak,'' in *Filmvilag* (Budapest), no. 5, 1991.

Hampton, H., ''David Lynch's Secret History of the United States,'' in *Film Comment* (New York), May-June 1993.

Layton, Lynne, ''Blue Velvet: A Parable of Male Development,'' *Screen* (Oxford), vol. 35, no. 4, Winter 1994.

Younger, R., ''Song in Contemporary Film Noir,'' *Films in Review* (Denville, New Jersey), vol. 45, no. 7–8, July-August, 1994.

* * *

With *Blue Velvet*, David Lynch's career at last picked up where his stunning, unique debut feature *Eraserhead* seemed to leave off. In his Victorian gothic docu-drama *The Elephant Man* and sci-fi spectacular *Dune*—respectively a surprising critical and commercial success, and an expensive fiasco—Lynch was incorporating elements from the highly distinctive style he had established in only one feature. In *Blue Velvet*, he returns, albeit in gloriously saturated colour rather than expressionist monochrome, to the fractured vision of small-town normality of *Eraserhead.* The film's opening sequence is incredibly lush, suggestive and unsettling: As Bobby Vinton's subtly fetishist title song plays, the camera tracks from a striking red, white and blue shot of blood-roses against a pristine white picket fence against an unnaturally clear sky to a deliriously idyllic, slow-motion vision of an idyllic small town that would have done Andy Hardy or Judy Garland proud. A fire engine rolls by, the firemen waving cheerfully, a lollipop man safeguards innocent schoolchildren, an adorable dog scampers, and a proud homeowner waters his garden. But the gardener is struck with a seizure and collapses, entangled in his hose and snapped at by the dog, and Lynch takes in his camera in for a closer view and penetrates the thick grass of the garden to find a teeming, ravenous, carnivorous, cannibalistic and physically revolting horde of insects chewing away at the underside of Norman Rockwell's America.

Essentially, the rest of the film follows up this opening sequence as Jeffrey Beaumont (Kyle MacLachlan, held over from and making up for his performance in *Dune*), a college student home because of his father's heart attack, gets involved in a local mystery and is exposed to the horrors that lurk underneath the Eisenhower-style perfection—it is impossible to tell whether the film is set in the 1950s, the 1960s or the 1980s—of Lumberton, U.S.A. Jeffrey first suspects something is amiss when walking to the house where he grew up after visiting his trussed-up father in hospital, he discovers a severed human ear in a vacant lot. The ear, naturally, is crawling with ants and Lynch later, in an awe-inspiring effect, has Frederick Elmes's camera explore its interior as Alan Splet's unsettling sound effects track suggests a universe inside the head as twisted and bizarre as those of *Eraserhead* or *Dune.* With the aid of Laura Dern's Sandy Williams, the daughter of the kindly local cop, Jeffrey plumbs into the mystery which revolves around Dorothy Vallens (Isabella Rossellini), a melancholy nightclub singer known as "The Blue Lady," and Frank Booth (Dennis Hopper), a frighteningly fiend-like and primal gangster who snorts gas through an insect-like mask, speaks only in the most basic terms ("baby wants to *fuck!*") and forces Dorothy to have animalistic sex with him (Splet turns his orgasmic cries into the roar of a wild beast) by threatening to further torture her kidnapped husband, the owner of the ear.

"I don't know whether you're a detective or a pervert," Sandy tells Jeffrey when he proposes to trespass in Dorothy's apartment in search of clues, and when he finds himself in her closet as she undresses or is sexually humiliated by Frank the distinction vanishes completely. The most disturbing aspect of *Blue Velvet* is that it refuses to let its Nancy Drew and the Hardy Boys-style hero and heroine off the hook as Jeffrey becomes less an observer and more a participant in the sordid, insectile nightlife of Lumberton, overcoming his resistance to hitting Dorothy as she begs him to when they have sex, being dragged out on a wild ride with Frank, and standing around while Frank's associate Ben (Dean Stockwell), who resembles a kabuki homosexual and is referred to as "one suave fuck," mimes to Roy Orbison's "In Dreams," the song that Frank later plays as he brutally beats Jeffrey up. One of the surprises of the film is that the thriller-whodunnit plot does eventually add up, although not before the nightmarish has thoroughly invaded Jeffrey's world with the appearance of a bruised and naked Dorothy on Sandy's front lawn and a final confrontation with Frank in an apartment that contains a still-standing, still-twitching corpse. By the time of the coda, which replicates the opening sequence, in which all the proprieties are restored—Frank is dead, a mechanical robin is eating the insects, the ear probed by the camera is Jeffrey's and still attached to his head, families are united—the all-pervasive horrors have been so effectively summoned that we know they can never really be vanquished. As a character remarks early on, "It's a strange world, isn't it?"

—Kim Newman

THE BOAT

See **DAS BOOT**

BONDS THAT CHAFE

See **EROTIKON**

BONNIE AND CLYDE

USA, 1967

Director: Arthur Penn

Production: Tatira-Hiller; Technicolor, 35mm; running time: 111 minutes. Released August 1967. Filmed during 1967 on location in Texas.

Producer: Warren Beatty; **screenplay:** David Newman and Robert Benton; **photography:** Burnett Guffey; **editor:** Dede Allen; **sound:** Francis E. Stahl; **art director:** Dean Tavoularis; **set decoration:** Raymond Paul; **music:** Charles Strouse, theme "Foggy Mountain Breakdown" by Lester Flatt and Earl Scruggs; **special effects:** Danny Lee; **costumes:** Theodora Van Runkle; **consultant:** Robert Towne.

Cast: Warren Beatty (*Clyde Barrow*); Faye Dunaway (*Bonnie Parker*); Gene Hackman (*Buck Barrow*); Estelle Parsons (*Blanche*); Michael J. Pollard (*C. W. Moss*); Dub Taylor (*Ivan Moss*); Denver Pyle (*Frank Hamer*); Evans Evans (*Velma Davis*); Gene Wilder (*Eugene Grizzard*).

Awards: Oscars for Best Supporting Actress (Parsons) and Best Cinematography, 1967; New York Film Critics Award, Best Screenwriting, 1967.

Publications

Script:

Newman, David, and Robert Benton, *Bonnie and Clyde*, in *The Bonnie and Clyde Book*, edited by Sandra Wake and Nicola Hayden, New York, 1972.

Penn, Arthur, *Bonnie and Clyde*, New York, 1988.

Books:

Gelman, B., and R. Lackman, *The Bonnie and Clyde Scrapbook*, New York, 1967.
Wood, Robin, *Arthur Penn*, New York, 1969.
Rubin, Martin, and Eric Sherman, *The Director's Event*, New York, 1970.
Pechter, William S., *24 Times a Second*, New York, 1971.
Cawelti, John G., editor, *Focus on "Bonnie and Clyde,"* Englewood Cliffs, New Jersey, 1973.
Shadoin, Jack, *Dreams and Dead Ends: The American Gangster/Crime Film*, Cambridge, Massachusetts, 1977.
Murray, Edward, *10 Film Classics*, New York, 1978.
Kolker, Robert Phillip, *A Cinema of Loneliness: Penn, Kubrick, Coppola, Scorsese, Altman*, Oxford, 1980; revised edition, 1988.
Zuker, Joel A., *Arthur Penn: A Guide to References and Resources*, Boston, 1980.
Giannetti, Louis, *Masters of the American Cinema*, Englewood Cliffs, New Jersey, 1981.
Cagin, Seth, and Philip Dray, *Hollywood Films of the 1970s: Sex, Drugs, Violence, Rock 'n' Roll, and Politics*, New York, 1984.
Haustrate, Gaston, *Arthur Penn*, Paris, 1986.
Thomson, David, *Warren Beatty: A Life and a Story*, London, 1987.
Friedman, Lester D., *Bonnie and Clyde*, London, 1999.
Friedman, Lester D., editor, *Arthur Penn's Bonnie and Clyde*, Cambridge, 1999.

Articles:

Lightman, Herb, "Raw Cinematic Realism in the Photography of *Bonnie and Clyde*," in *American Cinematographer* (Los Angeles), April 1967.
Gulshanok, Paul, in *Cineaste* (New York), Fall 1967.
Alpert, Hollis, in *Saturday Review* (New York), 5 August 1967.
Crowther, Bosley, in *New York Times*, 14 August 1967.
Sarris, Andrew, in *Village Voice* (New York), 24 August 1967.
Rhode, Eric, "A Middle Western," in *Listener* (London), 14 September 1967.
Kael, Pauline, in *Saturday Review* (New York), 21 October 1967.
Ciment, Michel, "Montréal 1967, le règne de l'image," in *Positif* (Paris), November 1967.
Penn, Arthur, in *Positif* (Paris), November 1967.
Geduld, Carolyn, "*Bonnie and Clyde:* Society vs. the Clan," in *Film Heritage* (Dayton, Ohio), Winter 1967–68.
Johnson, Albert, in *Film Quarterly* (Berkeley), Winter 1967–68.
Macklin, Anthony, "*Bonnie and Clyde:* Beyond Violence to Tragedy," in *Film Heritage* (Dayton, Ohio), Winter 1967–68.
Kauffman, Stanley, in *New American Review* (Cranford, New Jersey), January 1968.
Benayoun, Robert, in *Positif* (Paris), March 1968.
Laura, Ernesto G., in *Bianco e Nero* (Rome), March-April 1968.
Chevalier, Jacques, in *Image et Son* (Paris), April 1968.
Samuels, Charles T., in *Hudson Review* (Nutley, New Jersey), Spring 1968.
Comolli, Jean-Louis, and André S. Labarthe, "*Bonnie and Clyde:* An Interview with Arthur Penn," in *Evergreen Review* (New York), June 1968.
Brode, Douglas, "Reflections on the Tradition of the Western," in *Cineaste* (New York), Fall 1968.
Farber, Stephen, in *Sight and Sound* (London), Autumn 1968.
Comuzio, Ermanno, "Gangster Story," in *Cineforum* (Bergamo), September 1968.
Penn, Arthur, in *Cineforum* (Bergamo), September 1968.
Free, William J., "Aesthetic and Moral Value in *Bonnie and Clyde*," in *Quarterly Journal of Speech* (Fall's Church, Virginia), October 1968.
Lawson, John Howard, "Our Film and Theirs: *Grapes of Wrath* and *Bonnie and Clyde*," in *American Dialogue* (New York), Winter 1968–69.
Cook, Jim, in *Screen* (London), July-August 1969.
Gould Boyum, Joy, and Adrienne Scott, in *Films as Film: Critical Responses to Film Art*, Boston, 1971.
Kinder,Marsha, and Beverle Houston, in *Close-up: A Critical Perspective on Film*, New York, 1972.
Cawelti, John, "Bonnie and Clyde Revisited," in *Focus!* (Chicago), Spring 1972 and Autumn 1972.
Childs, James "Closet Outlaws," in *Film Comment* (New York), March-April 1973.
Corliss, Richard, in *Talking Pictures: Screenwriters in the American Cinema*, New York, 1975.
Yacowar, Maurice, "Dick, Jane, Rocky and T. S. Eliot," in *Journal of Popular Film and Television* (Bowling Green, Ohio), Winter 1977.
Corliss, Richard, "The Hollywood Screenwriter, Take 2," in *Film Comment* (New York), July-August 1978.
Eorsi, I., "Veszelyes egyensuly: Penn: *Bonnie and Clyde*," in *Filmkultura* (Budapest), March-April 1979.
Leroux, A., interview with Arthur Penn, in *24 Images* (Montreal), June 1983.
Combs, Richard, in *Listener* (London), 18 July 1985.
Pym, J., "Black Hat Yellow Hat," in *Sight and Sound* (London), no. 4, 1990.
Wilmington, Michael, "Road Warriors: Outlaw Lovers on the Run," in *Chicago Tribune*, 28 August 1994.
Miller, Joyce, "From *Bonnie and Clyde* to *Thelma and Louise*: The Struggle for Justice in the Cinematic South," in *Studies in Popular Culture* (Murfreesboro, Tennessee), vol. 19, no. 2, October 1996.

* * *

To speak of Arthur Penn is to address the question of what might be termed, somewhat paradoxically, the "post-classical" American cinema. On the one hand Penn belongs with that group of post-World War II directors which came to cinema from the stage and from the early days of television—people like Nicholas Ray, Sam Peckinpah, Franklin Schaffner, Martin Ritt, and Joseph Losey. In that respect Penn is indeed an inheritor of the traditions and forms of the classical Hollywood cinema, the Western (*The Left Handed Gun*), the biography picture (*The Miracle Worker*), the gangster/detective film (*Night Moves*), etc. Perhaps Penn's loyalty to Hollywood tradition is most clearly seen in his frequent reliance upon the star system to infuse his films with certain qualities of intensity and resonance—Dustin Hoffman's performance in *Little Big Man* and Marlon Brando's and Jack Nicholson's in *The Missouri Breaks* stand out in this regard. Yet on the other hand Penn is also frequently associated with the more overtly intellectual traditions of the European art film, especially those of the French New Wave films of the early 1960s. Penn's *Mickey One*, for example, is frequently discussed in such "art film" terms. But arguably it was with *Bonnie and Clyde* that Penn's special status as a post-classical director was most forcefully asserted and confirmed.

In her classic essay on the film, Pauline Kael situates *Bonnie and Clyde*'s place in American film history by reference primarily to Fritz Lang's *You Only Live Once*, itself a version of the Bonnie and Clyde story, and to Frank Capra's *It Happened One Night*. Kael's essay was written in reply to those who saw *Bonnie and Clyde* as a glorification of violence as personified in the actions of Warren Beatty's Clyde Barrow and Faye Dunaway's Bonnie Parker, and Kael quite rightly points out that "Bonnie and Clyde are presented not as mean and sadistic, [but] as having killed only when cornered." Indeed, most of the film's explicitly graphic violence is directed *not* at society but rather at the members of the Barrow gang. This is especially clear in the film's last two ambush scenes, the first of which concludes with Buck Barrow's death throes and Blanche Barrow's agonized screams, the last of which sees Bonnie and Clyde riddled with machine gun fire. Kael's larger point, however, involves the particularly American theme of innocence at hazard and on the run, which makes Lang's melodrama and Capra's screwball comedy spiritual ancestors of Penn's alternately comic and tragic parable of the outlaw couple. The central characters in all three films long mightily, often awkwardly, to realize aspirations of spiritual and social stature. But in Lang and Penn society provides no real outlet or model for the realization of such dreams. And even in Capra it takes an act of theft (like Bonnie and Clyde, Gable and Colbert literally steal a car at one point; Ellie's father has a "getaway" car standing by during the wedding ceremony) to ensure the dream's survival.

In terms of its *story*, then, *Bonnie and Clyde* is quite properly considered a classical Hollywood film. But this story of Bonnie and Clyde is mediated by or through a very self-conscious form of visual *discourse;* hence the critical commonplace of Penn's indebtedness to the generically-derived film of Truffaut and Godard. Partly this self-consciousness is seen *within* the film's depicted world: Bonnie writes her own legend in doggerel verse throughout the film, and she and Clyde both willingly pose for Buck Barrow's Kodak. Or consider the moment after the first killing, after the scene in the movie theatre, when Bonnie dances in front of her motel room mirror while singing "We're In The Money," as if she were herself a character in a film, La Cava's *Golddiggers of 1933* perhaps. The limited self-consciousness of Penn's characters is set in thematic context by the more inclusive self-consciousness of the film's discourse. For both the characters and the director, it's a matter of images—of living up to them, of taking responsibility for them.

Perhaps the greatest irony in *Bonnie and Clyde* is the degree to which the characters drift into big-time crime, without real premeditation. Clyde's first hold-up is undertaken in response to Bonnie's sexually loaded dare. And the first bank job—from which all else follows inexorably—evolves from a similarly innocent responsiveness on Clyde's part. He and Bonnie are taking target practice when a farmer and his family pull up in their truck to take a final look at their repossessed farm. Out of sympathy Clyde puts a slug into the Midlothian State Bank's "No Trespassing" sign. Clyde offers the gun to the farmer and to his black field hand. As the farmer turns to leave, Clyde says, almost hesitantly though somewhat boastfully, as if to cement the bond between them, "we rob banks." He hasn't robbed one yet—but now he is committed to trying; though the first bank he tries is empty both of money and customers. More significantly, in wanting to live up to his "bank robber" image, Clyde unknowingly begins the progress of his own entrapment, an entrapment made chillingly clear in Penn's images. As Clyde steps through the door, gun drawn, Penn frames him through the teller's cage. Perhaps Clyde *thinks* of the holdup as an expression of his own freedom from restraint; but Penn's framing of him within the constriction of the teller's cage and through its bars shows how wrong Clyde is. This motif of freedom delimited and constrained is elaborately developed through the course of the film via a whole range of internal frames—windows, mirrors, doors, car windows, etc.

Implicit in Penn's framing is the question of responsibility—of Clyde's for stepping into the frame, of Penn's (and ours) for standing on the other side and choosing to see him framed. The film's self-awareness is most clearly evident in the way it critiques the camera, as if our need to see Bonnie and Clyde as images of a freedom we both envy and fear were very directly responsible for their deaths. "Shooting" with a gun and "shooting" with a camera are explicitly equated in the sequence with Texas Ranger Hamer, where Bonnie proposes to humiliate Hamer by taking his picture ("He'll wish he were dead," as Buck puts it). In the credit sequence, moreover, Penn's name is immediately preceded by a snapshot of three riflemen kneeling, as if he (the camera) were a gunman. And in the final ambush sequence we see Bonnie and Clyde's agonized death from a vantage point almost identical to that of Hamer and his deputies, from across the road, as if *we*, like Penn, were "shooting" the scene. No wonder the film was condemned; who wants to take that kind of responsibility? Arthur Penn, for one.

—Leland Poague

DAS BOOT

(The Boat)

Germany, 1981

Director: Wolfgang Petersen

Production: Bavaria Atelier, Radiant Film; Fuji colour, 35mm; running time: 149 minutes. Originally a television miniseries shown in 5 parts; shortened version released theatrically.

Producer: Günter Rohrbach; **co-producer:** Michael Bittins; **screenplay:** Wolfgang Petersen, from the novel by Lothar-Günther Buchheim; **photography:** Jost Vacano; **editor:** Hannes Nikel; **assistant directors:** George Borgel, Maria-Antoinette Petersen; **production design:** Rolf Zehetbauer; **art director:** Gøtz Weidner; **music:** Klaus Doldinger; **sound editing:** Mike Le Mare, Eva Claudius, Illo Endrulat; **sound recording:** Milan Bor, Trevor Pyke, Werner Bohm, Heinz Schurer, Karsten Ullrich, Stanislav Litera, Albrecht von Bethmann; **costumes:** Monika Bauert.

Cast: Jürgen Prochnow (*The Captain*); Herbert Gronemeyer (*Lieutenant Werner*); Klaus Wennemann (*Chief Engineer*); Hubertus Bengsch (*1st Lieutenant*); Martin Semmelrogge (*2nd Lieutenant*); Bernd Tauber (*Chief Quartermaster*); Erwin Leder (*Johann*); Martin May (*Ullman*); Heinz Honig (*Heinrich*); U. A. Ochsen (*Chief Bosun*);

Das Boot

Claude-Olivier Rudolph (*Ario*); Jan Fedder (*Pilgrim*); Ralph Richter (*Frenssen*); Joachim Bernhard (*Preacher*); Oliver Stritzel (*Schwalle*).

Publications

Books:

Buccheim, Lothar-Günther, *Der Film—Das Boot—Ein Journal*, Munich, 1981.

Articles:

New York, 15 February 1982.
Ciompi, Valeria, ''El último submarino,'' in *Casablanca*, no. 13, January 1982.
Grelier, R., *Image et Son* (Paris), March 1982.
Lardeau, Y., ''La Qualité allemande,'' in *Cahiers du Cinéma* (Paris), March 1982.
Gartenberg, J., *Films in Review* (New York), April 1982.
Combs, R., *Monthly Film Bulletin* (London), May 1982.
Spratt, M., *Films and Filming* (London), May 1982.
Girard, M., *Séquences* (Montreal), July 1982.
American Cinematographer (New York), December 1982.
Grab, Norbert, ''In the Line of Light: Der Fernseh-un Filmregisseur Wolfgang Petersen,'' in *EPD Film* (Frankfurt-am-Main), vol. 13, no. 6, June 1996.
Oppenheimer, J., ''Salvaging *Das Boot*,'' in *American Cinematographer* (Hollywood), vol. 78, May 1997.

* * *

Das Boot is a landmark in German cinema: it is the most expensive (at $2 million) and the most popular (at home and abroad) German film ever made; it was nominated for five Academy Awards; it has proven the most successful foreign-language film release in the United States; and it has managed to capture a certain heroism for a most unheroic period in German history.

The film closely follows a novel of the same title by Lothar-Günther Buchheim, a submariner on a U-Boat in World War II who wrote the novel more than 30 years later (1973), metamorphosizing grim and unsung war time experience into much-praised artistic prose and heroic action sequences. A shift in perspective changes our view of the sailors themselves, from sneak-attack killers in the despised service of a beaten dictatorship to a heroic brotherhood itself victimized by Nazis. The film begins with the stark announcement that 30,000 of the 40,000 German submariners in World War II failed to return home. Rather than the shadowy wolf-pack preying on unarmed civilian freighters, the sailors become victims themselves, cogs in a war machine, who retain an admirable humanity in spite of hopeless circumstances.

The film thus announces that it is time to see an important element of the German wartime experience through new eyes. This revisionism is accomplished, ironically, by revitalizing and humanizing the clichéd post-war Nuremberg defence, "I was just following orders." The crew of Unterseeboot-96 are doing just that, facing near certain death with a stalwart humanity that refutes their Allied reputation as killers and attempts to repudiate their connection with Nazism.

The creation of sympathy begins early, with an extended opening sequence in a brothel. One of the few scenes set on shore, the pre-mission officers' celebration begins with some decorum but quickly descends into revolting decadence, including officers passed out in vomit in a filthy men's room and taking drunken pistol shots into the ceiling. Jürgen Prochnow (the 30-year-old captain, "Die Alte" or "Old Man" to his men) looks on with war-wise sympathy, noting his men's fear and innocence as the British learn to sink U-boats. Prochnow's fellow captain and friend, Thomsen, mocks Hitler's leadership in a speech that temporarily quiets the room, drawing glares from the few Nazi sympathizers in attendance. The message is clear: the private selves of these submariners are racked by despair over their hopeless prospects, prospects created by an incompetent, increasingly intrusive, and completely uncaring leadership. These are truly good Germans, unlike the self-convinced, righteous robots of the new generation of Nazis.

Once set up, this message is continually repeated. Prochnow's "speech" to his men before shipping out is vintage Gary Cooper: "Well men—all set? Harbour stations!" The taciturn captain has no patience with the grandiloquent rhetoric of Nazi romanticizers of war, and runs a ship that is egalitarian and almost completely lacking in military ceremony. Though uncompromising about the need for competence and procedure in reports and duties, the captain is contemptuous of his spit-and-polish Nazi First Officer, who persists in wearing a uniform rather than the worn sweaters favoured by the other officers. Prochnow is filmed unshaven and then in dishevelled beard, asleep, slumped over controls. The ship itself is similarly domesticated, made *gemütlich* by strings of sausages hanging from the overhead pipes, loaves of bread cluttering the controls, and crates of lettuce in the torpedo room. A comic scene shows Prochnow's flexibility in the face of mortal danger and Nazi humourlessness: he leads a full-crew sing-along of "It's a Long Way to Tipperary," the British marching song, in English—an ironic challenge to his enemies, foreign and domestic.

Throughout, the film, the wolf-pack image of the U-boat crew is tamed through sympathetic touches. Some of the sailors are pathetically young; one has a pregnant French girlfriend who will suffer retribution alone since his daily letters are impossible to mail. The ultimate leaders of the enterprise are systematically undercut: as when a fly crawls over a shipboard photograph of a German admiral. After weeks at sea, the U-96 finally sinks some ships in a convoy, only to surface and see drowning British sailors, a close encounter with a suffering enemy which fills the conning tower crew with horror. When given an absurd order to pass through the enemy-held Straits of Gibraltar, the captain tries to put the First Officer and the journalist ashore, only to encounter arrogant and smug Nazi sympathizers—men totally insensitive to the frightening experiences of the submariners. The captain shares the terrors of depth charge attacks and a likely prolonged death by suffocation that outsiders don't understand and don't care to. The grimness of shipboard conditions, the nearness of death, the existential pushing on under hopeless prospects are universals that bridge nationalistic differences.

The sympathetic power of *Das Boot* and the exhilaration of its chase scenes are so great that it is easy to forget that such submariners systematically sent scores of unarmed freighters to the bottom of the sea, condemning helpless civilians to death by drowning, hypothermia, or worse: the aptly-named wolf-packs pulled down the slow, the crippled, the unwary, in acts that had more in common with execution than with warfare. *Das Boot* shows us a later period when the war was going badly for the service and Allied technology made what had previously been easy slaughter a fair fight. We see the U-boats made vulnerable, and the "cruelty and magnificence" that had initially intoxicated the journalist observer, Lt. Werner (author Buchheim), replaced by the grim reality of defeat.

The film is a splendid revision of the record to highlight an undeniable historical fact: the submariners were also victims in this period, and deserve respect for clinging to what decencies and humanity were left to them. The film is honest on this point, and though it loses the aesthetic brilliance of the novel's prose—it would take cinematography of unparalleled virtuosity to capture it, a task impossible with model submarines in a studio tank—it effectively captures the texture of life *in extremis*, the true brotherhood sustained by a common front against despair and terror, and the unutterable sadness of war.

—Andrew and Gina Macdonald

LE BOUCHER

(The Butcher)

France-Italy, 1969

Director: Claude Chabrol

Production: Films La Boétie (Paris), Euro-International (Rome); Eastmancolor; running time: 94 minutes. Released April 1970. Filmed at Le Trémolat, Périgord, France.

Producer: André Génovès; **production manager:** Fred Surin; **assistant director:** Pierre Gaucher; **screenplay:** Claude Chabrol; **photography:** Jean Rabier; **editor:** Jacques Gaillard; **sound:** Guy Chichignoud; **sound re-recordist:** Alex Prout; **art director:** Guy Littaye; **music:** Pierre Jansen; **song:** "Capri, Petite Ile" by Dominique Zardi.

Cast: Stéphane Audran (*Hélène Marcoux*); Jean Yanne (*Popaul Thomas*); Antonio Passalia (*Angelo*); Mario Beccaria (*Léon Hamel*);

Le Boucher

Pasquale Ferone (*Father Charpy*); Roger Rudel (*Police Inspector*); William Guérault (*Charles*).

Publications

Books:

Wood, Robin, and Michael Walker, *Claude Chabrol*, London, 1970.
Bracourt, Guy, *Claude Chabrol*, Paris, 1971.
Reihe 5: Claude Chabrol, Munich, 1975.
Chabrol, Claude, *Et pourtant, je tourne* . . . , Paris, 1976.
Monaco, James, *The New Wave*, New York, 1976.
Magny, Joel, *Claude Chabrol*, Paris, 1987.
Austin, Guy, *Claude Chabrol, Autoportrait*, Manchester, 1999.

Articles:

Comand, André, in *Image et Son* (Paris), March-April 1970.
Bracourt, Guy, in *Cinéma* (Paris), April 1970.
Legrand, Gérard, in *Positif* (Paris), April 1970.
Haskell, Molly, ''The Films of Chabrol: A Priest among Clowns,'' in *Village Voice* (New York), 12 November 1970.
Millar, Gavin, in *Sight and Sound* (London), Winter 1970–71.
Gow, Gordon, in *Films and Filming* (London), July 1972.
Dawson, Jan, in *Monthly Film Bulletin* (London), July 1972.
Warshow, Paul, in *Film Quarterly* (Berkeley, California), Fall 1972.
Belton, John, ''*Le Boucher:* The Limited Universe,'' in *Cinema* (Beverly Hills), Spring 1972.
''Chabrol Issue'' of *Image et Son* (Paris), December 1973.
Marty, Alain, in *Image et Son* (Paris), January 1974.
Film Psychology Review (New York), Summer-Fall 1980.
Kemp, Philip, ''Hitching Posts,'' in *Macguffin* (Victoria, Australia), no. 18, February-May 1996.
Magny, J., ''Questions de mise en scene,'' in *Cahiers du Cinéma* (Paris), Hors serie, 1997.

* * *

Set in the Périgord village of Le Trémolat, Chabrol's delicately textured film is an unconventionally chaste, and tragic, love story about two emotionally damaged characters, the village schoolmistress, Mlle. Hélène (Stéphane Audran), and the local butcher, Popaul (Jean Yanne). Both the location and the protagonists' professions are central to Chabrol's purpose.

The credit sequence, with Pierre Jansen's disquieting music distancing the viewer, rolls against images of primitive cave drawings, the work of prehistoric man attempting to relate to his world. This explicit reference to man's antecedents establishes an important theme in the film: the residual atavistic impulses in 20th-century man. Popaul incarnates the continued presence of these untamed primitive instincts and his self-knowledge renders this situation tragic. He appears gentle, considerate, rather conventional, even puritanical, and possesses an almost childlike respect for the village schoolmistress. A desperately unhappy and emotionally deprived family background, however, and 15 brutalising years in the army have left their scars: he has yet to come to terms with this past. Mlle. Hélène, liberated, self-possessed, and sophisticated, represents culture and moral authority, the epitome of the evolved, civilised human being. Yet she too has to come to terms with her own nature, and a failed relationship, which have made her wary of sentimental involvement. Her emotional needs may be satisfied with her surrogate family of pupils, and her sexual drive sublimated through Yoga, but her situation, like that of Popaul, is ultimately fragile. Each character is incomplete.

Developed from Chabrol's original conception, the two protagonists illustrate his stated commitment to films of psychological enquiry: "I am for simple plots with complicated characters." The story of their fraught relationship is evolved against positive images of a normality they cannot share. The film opens with Raoul Coutard's beautiful sweeping pan of the peaceful Dordogne countryside captured with the muted colours of early morning. These images of tranquility give way to an affectionate portrait of the sunny village busying itself for a wedding and the ensuing celebrations. The enjoyment is spontaneous, the sense of community strong in the shared happiness of the occasion. Among these genuine inhabitants the camera identifies the two protagonists, the Parisian schoolmistress now part of the village, and the butcher recently returned from war service: they are potentially another happy couple. A slow, unwinding tracking shot of their walk through the village establishes their burgeoning intimacy. Gifts are exchanged as a manageable expression of feeling: a leg of lamb from Popaul, a lighter from Hélène. Popaul reflects ominously: "If you never make love, you go crazy."

The main issues of the film are played out in two juxtaposed sequences. Mlle. Hélène rehearses her pupils for the village fete: they are dressed in Louis XIV costumes and dance elegantly, if somewhat artificially, to the music of Lully. An image of stylised sophistication is conveyed, counterpointing the spontaneity of the accordion-led dancing at the wedding reception. The zooming camera reveals, in a subjective close-up, Popaul's desire for Hélène. A dissolve switches the action to the local caves, the home of Cro-Magnon man, where Mlle. Hélène explains that were prehistoric man to re-appear in the 20th century he would have to adapt to survive. On the outcrop above the caves the thwarted sexual drive of a psychopath has expressed itself in a brutal murder. The horror is conveyed in a zoom shot, of shocking emotional force, to the victim's hand dripping blood. Hélène finds by the body a lighter which she conceals.

The viewer sharing this information becomes complicitous in Hélène's spontaneous response to protect Popaul. Tension and ambiguity are installed in the narrative framework as Hélène longs to be proved wrong even though she may be in danger herself. The mood darkens with the rain-drenched funeral contrasting the so recently sunny wedding. Chabrol leads the viewer to identify with Hélène's perceptions, to suspect the worse, to experience fear as she does when Popaul stalks her in the pitch-dark school. Her failure to respond to his obvious need for help, like Charlie's failure to respond to his wife's confession in *Tirez sur le pianiste*, leads to a self-inflicted punishment and an enduring sense of guilt in the partner found wanting at the crucial moment. The closing image of the film with Hélène at the riverside conveys emptiness and the loneliness of a personal, inadmissible sense of guilt.

Le Boucher is a subtle network of shifting emotions, of changing moods, and of psychological insights, expressed to a rare degree of perfection. The remarkable integration of form and meaning in the film is an eloquent testimony to the value of Chabrol's policy of working closely with a regular production team. His moving portrayal of the psychopath is based in a compassionate desire to understand, and must rank alongside such studies as Lang's *M* in its penetration and humanity. Although the psychologically disturbed character is the subject of later films Chabrol has yet to emulate the perfection achieved in *Le Boucher*.

—R.F. Cousins

BOUDU SAUVÉ DES EAUX

(Boudu Saved from Drowning)

France, 1932

Director: Jean Renoir

Production: Société Sirius; running time: 83 minutes. Released November 1932, Paris. Filmed summer 1932 in Epinay studios; exteriors filmed at Chennevières and in Paris.

Screenplay: Jean Renoir with Robert Valentin, from a work by René Fauchois; **assistants to the director:** Jacques Becker and Georges Darnoux; **photography:** Marcel Lucien; **editors:** Marguerite Renoir and Suzanne de Troye; **sound:** Igor B. Kalinowski; **production design:** Jean Castanier and Hugues Laurent; **music:** Raphael Strauss and Johann Strauss; **song:** "Sur les bords de la Riviera" by Leo Daniderff.

Cast: Michel Simon (*Boudu*); Charles Granval (*Edouard Lestingois*); Marcelle Hainia (*Emma Lestingois*); Séverine Lerczinska (*Anne-Marie*); Jean Dasté (*The Student*); Max Dalban (*Godin*); Jean Gehret (*Vigour*); Jacques Becker (*Poet on the river bank*); Jane Pierson (*Rose*); Régine Lutèce (*Woman walking the dog*); Georges Darnoux (*Guest at the wedding*).

Publications

Books:

Davay, Paul, *Jean Renoir*, Brussels, 1957.
Cauliez, Armand-Jean, *Jean Renoir*, Paris, 1962.
Chardère, Bernard, editor, *Jean Renoir*, in *Premier Plan* (Lyon), no. 22–24, May 1962.

Institut des Hautes Etudes Cinématographiques, *Analyses des films de Jean Renoir*, Paris, 1964.
Bennett, Susan, *Jean Renoir*, London, 1967.
Leprohon, Pierre, *Jean Renoir*, Paris, 1967; New York, 1971.
Poulle, François, *Renoir 1938; ou, Jean Renoir pour rien: Enquête sur un cinéaste*, Paris, 1969.
Braudy, Leo, *Jean Renoir: The World of His Films*, New York, 1972.
Bazin, André, *Jean Renoir*, edited by François Truffaut, Paris, 1973.
Durgnat, Raymond, *Jean Renoir*, Berkeley, 1974.
Beylie, Claude, *Jean Renoir: Le Spectacle, la vie*, Paris, 1975.
Renoir, Jean, *Essays, Conversations, Reviews*, edited by Penelope Gilliatt, New York, 1975.
Armes, Roy, *French Cinema Since 1946: Volume 1: The Great Tradition*, New York, 1976.
Faulkner, Christopher, *Jean Renoir: A Guide to References and Resources*, Boston, 1979.
Sesonske, Alexander, *Jean Renoir: The French Films 1924–1939*, Cambridge, Massachusetts, 1980.
Gauteur, Claude, editor, *Jean Renoir: Oeuvres de cinéma inédites*, Paris, 1981.
McBride, Joseph, editor, *Filmmakers on Filmmaking 2*, Los Angeles, 1983.
Serceau, Daniel, *Jean Renoir*, Paris, 1985.
Bertin, Celia, *Jean Renoir*, Paris, 1986.
Faulkner, Christopher, *The Social Cinema of Jean Renoir*, Princeton, New Jersey, 1986.
Vincendeau, Ginette, and Keith Reader, *La Vie est à Nous: French Cinema of the Popular Front*, London, 1986.
Viry-Babel, Roger, *Jean Renoir: Le Jeu et la règle*, Paris, 1986.
Cavagnac, Guy, *Jean Renoir: Le désir du monde*, Paris, 1994.
Leutrat, Jean-Louis, *Le chiene de Jean Renoir*, Crisnée, 1994.
Boston, Richard, *Boudu Saved From Drowning*, London, 1994.
O'Shaughnessy, Martin, *Jean Renoir*, New York, 2000.

Articles:

''Renoir Issue'' of *Cahiers du Cinéma* (Paris), January 1952.
''Renoir Issue'' of *Cahiers du Cinéma* (Paris), Christmas 1957.
Belanger, Jean, ''Why Renoir Favors Multiple Camera, Long Sustained Take,'' in *American Cinematographer* (Los Angeles), March 1960.
Whitehall, Richard, ''Painting Life with Movement,'' in *Films and Filming* (London), June 1960.
Whitehall, Richard, ''The Screen Is His Canvas,'' in *Films and Filming* (London), July 1960.
Harcourt, Peter, ''Jean Renoir,'' in *London Magazine*, December 1962.
Russell, Lee, ''Jean Renoir,'' in *New Left Review* (New York), May-June 1964.
Renoir, Jean, ''How I Came to Film *Boudu*,'' in *Films Society Review* (New York), February 1967.
Sarris, Andrew, in *Cahiers du Cinéma in English* (New York), March 1967.
Fofi, Goffredo, ''The Cinema of the Popular Front in France,'' in *Screen* (London), Winter 1972–73.
Abel, R., ''Collapsing Columns: Mise-en-scène in *Boudu*,'' in *Jump Cut* (Chicago), January-February 1975.
Walker, Janet, and Luli McCarroll, ''Renoir on the Bridge: A Reading of *Boudu Saved from Drowning*,'' in *Wide Angle* (Athens, Ohio), no. 4, 1981.
Strebel, Elizabeth Grottle, ''Jean Renoir and the Popular Front,'' in *Feature Films as History*, edited by K. R. M. Short, London, 1981.
O'Kane, J., ''Style, Space Ideology in *Boudu Saved from Drowning*,'' in *Enclitic* (Minneapolis), Fall 1981-Spring 1982.
Morgan, J., ''From Clochards to Cappuccinos: *Boudu* Is *Down and Out in Beverly Hills*,'' in *Cinema Journal* (Austin, Texas), no. 2, 1990.
Holmlund, C. A., ''New Cold War Sequels and Remakes,'' in *Jump Cut* (Berkeley, California), April 1990.
Andersson, L. ''*Boudu* vesien snojatti,'' *Filmihullu* (Helsinki), no. 6, 1995.
Monterde, J. E., ''Jean Renoir: anos treinta,'' *Nosferatu* (Donostia-San Sebastian), no. 17, March 1995.
Renoir, A., ''Jean Renoir conteur d'histoires,'' *Trafic*, no. 24, Winter 1997.

* * *

Boudu sauvé des eaux makes abundantly clear why Jean Renoir's work was so admired by André Bazin, and why the filmmakers of the New Wave regarded him as their supreme antecedent and father-figure. Bazin's theory of realism—especially in so far as it is concerned with the preservation of the physical realities of time and space—is repeatedly exemplified by the use in *Boudu* of long takes, camera movement, and depth-of-field, relating action to action, character to character, foreground to background and continuously suggesting the existence of a world beyond the frame. The subversive implications of the material, the use of real locations instead of studio sets, the sense of a moral freedom combining inevitably with technical freedom, the evident love of actors and performance, and the resulting effect of spontaneity—all could add up to a model for the ambitions of the New Wave.

Leo Braudy has interpreted Renoir's work in terms of a dialectic of nature and ''theatre'' (the latter to be understood both literally and metaphorically), the two concepts achieving a complex interplay. *Boudu* works very well in this light. Indeed the film opens with a *theatrical* representation of *nature* rites (Lestingois as satyr, Anne-Marie as nymph). If Renoir shows great affection for the world of nature surrounding, and epitomized by, *Boudu*—the freedom of the tramp without restrictions, the play of sunlight on water, the lush fertility of the imagery of the film's final scene—he is equally charmed by the bourgeois household of the Lestingois—by the artificial birds that Anne-Marie must dust, by Lestingois's reverence for Balzac (on whose works Boudu casually spits, not with the slightest animus but simply because it is natural to spit when you feel the need). One might add that he finds the Lestingois household charming because of the lingering traces of a subjugated, sublimated nature that continue to animate it. At the same time, he sees that it is the subjugation that makes culture possible. Windows—the barrier between nature and culture but also the means of access—are a recurrent motif throughout Renoir's work. In the films of Ophuls (with whom Renoir has many points of contact while remaining so different) windows are always being closed; in those of Renoir they are always being opened. He is centrally concerned with the possibility of free access and interchange between the two worlds, the uncertainty of being crucial.

The desire to negotiate between nature and culture encounters problems which the film can't resolve, and partially evades. On the one hand, the comic mode enables Renoir to avoid confronting the psychic misery produced by bourgeois repressiveness: Madame

Lestingois, in particular *can only* be a comic character for the film to continue to function. If her position were allowed to be explored seriously, the laughter would die immediately. The scene in which she is ''liberated'' by being raped by Boudu is saved from distastefulness solely by being played as farce. On the other hand, Renoir's equivocation in evaluating the bourgeois world results in some confusion over Boudu himself: does he or does he not represent a serious threat to it? The point gains force when one compares Michel Simon's characterization hero with his père Jules in Vigo's *L'Atalante.* Jules is at once more formidable and more consistent, and Vigo's radicalism more sharply defined. Boudu, in contrast, seems little more than a pre-socialized (and pre-sexual) child, essentially harmless. The sudden ascription to him of great sexual potency jars, considering that we are told earlier that he has never kissed anyone except his dog.

The film is typical of Renoir's work in its warmth, humanity, generosity; it also suggests the close relation between that generosity and impotence. If every way of life can be defended, then nothing need be changed.

—Robin Wood

BOY

See **SHONEN**

BRAZIL

UK, 1985

Director: Terry Gilliam

Production: Brazil Productions for 20th Century Fox; Eastmancolor; Dolby stereo; running time: 142 minutes. Released March 1985.

Producer: Arnon Milchan; **co-producer:** Patrick Cassavetti; **production coordinator:** Margaret Adams; **screenplay:** Terry Gilliam, Tom Stoppard, Charles McKeown; **2nd unit director:** Julian Doyle; **assistant directors:** Guy Travers, Chris Thompson, Richard Coleman, Christopher Newman, Terence Fitch, Kevin Westley; **photography:** Roger Pratt; **model/effects photography:** Roger Pratt, Julian Doyle, Tim Spence; **camera operator:** David Garfath; **video consultant:** Ira Curtis Coleman; **editor:** Julian Doyle; **sound editors:** Rodney Glenn, Barry McCormick; **sound recordists:** Bob Doyle, Eric Tomlinson, Andy Jackson; **sound re-recordist:** Paul Carr; **art directors:** John Beard, Keith Pain; **graphic artists:** David Scutt, Bernard Allum; **draughtsmen:** Tony Rimmington, Stephen Bream; **matte artist:** Ray Caple; **production designer:** Norman Garwood; **set dressing designer:** Maggie Gray; **costume designers:** Jams Acheson, Ray Scott, Martin Adams, Vin Burnham, Jamie Courtier, Martin Adams, Annie Hadley; **make-up:** Maggie Weston, Aaron Sherman, Elaine Carew, Sallie Evans, Sandra Shepherd, Meinir Brock; **music:** Michael Kamen; **music performed by:** National Philharmonic Orchestra; **music coordinator:** Ray Cooper; **choreographer:** Heather Seymour; **stunt arranger:** Bill Weston; **special effects supervisor:** George Gibbs; **model effects supervisor:** Richard Conway; **titles/optical effects:** Nick Dunlop, Neil Sharp, Kent Houston, Tim Ollive, Richard Morrison.

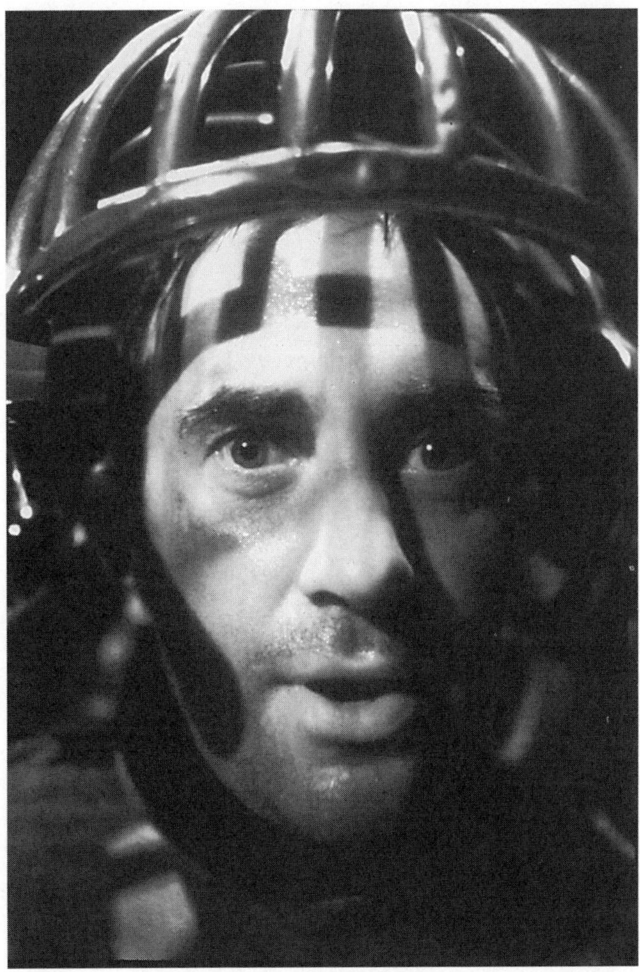

Brazil

Cast: Jonathan Pryce (*Sam Lowry*); Robert De Niro (*Archibald ''Harry'' Tuttle*); Katherine Helmond (*Mrs. Ida Lowry*); Ian Holm (*Mr. Kurtzmann*); Bob Hoskins (*Spoor*); Michael Palin (*Jack Lint*); Ian Richardson (*Mr. Warrenn*); Peter Vaughan (*Mr. Eugene Helpmann*); Kim Greist (*Jill Layton*); Jim Broadbent (*Dr. Jaffe*); Barbara Hicks (*Mrs. Terrain*); Charles McKeown (*Lime*); Derrick O'Connor (*Dowser*); Kathryn Pogson (*Shirley*); Bryan Pringle (*Spiro*); Sheila Reid (*Mrs. Buttle*); John Flanagan (*TV interviewer/salesman*); Ray Cooper (*Technician*); Brian Miller (*Mr. Buttle*); Simon Nash (*Boy Buttle*); Prudence Oliver (*Girl Buttle*); Simon Jones (*Arrest official*); Derek Deadman (*Bill, Department of Works*); Nigel Planer (*Charlie, Department of Works*); Terence Bayley (*TV commercial presenter*); Gordon Kaye (*MOI lobby porter*); Tony Portacio (*Neighbour in clerk's pool*); Bill Wallis (*Bespectacled lurker*); Winston Dennis (*Samurai warrior*); Toby Clark (*Small Sam double*); Diana Martin (*Telegram girl*); Jack Purvis (*Dr. Chapman*); Elizabeth Spender (*Alison/''Barbara'' Lint*); Antony Brown (*Porter, Information Retrieval*); Myrtle Devenish (*Typist, Jack's office*); Holly Gilliam (*Holly*); John Pierce Jones (*Basement guard*); Ann Way (*Old lady with dog*); Don Henderson (*1st Black Maria guard*); Howard Lew Lewis (*2nd Black Maria guard*); Oscar Quitak, Harold Innocent, John Grillo, Ralph Nossek, David Grant, James Coyle (*Interview officials*); Patrick Connor (*Cell guard*); Roger Ashton-Griffiths (*Priest*); Russell Keith Grant (*Young gallant at funeral*).

Publications

Script:

Gilliam, Terry, Tom Stoppard, and Charles McKeown, *Brazil*, in *The Battle of Brazil*, edited by Jack Mathews, New York, 1987.

Books:

Danvers, Louis, *Brazil de Terry Gilliam*, Brussels, 1988.
Gilliam, Terry, *Gilliam on Gilliam*, New York, 1999.
McCabe, Bob, *Dark Knights and Holy Fools: The Art and Films of Terry Gilliam*, New York, 1999.

Articles:

Rabourdin, D., ''Terry Gilliam parle de *Brazil*,'' in *Cinema* (Paris), February 1985.
Roddick, Nick, ''Just Crazy about *Brazil*,'' in *Stills* (London), February 1985.
''*Brazil* Issue'' of *Positif* (Paris), March 1985.
Chaillet, J.-P., and M. Chion, in *Cahiers du Cinéma* (Paris), March 1985.
D'Yvoire, J., in *Jeune Cinéma* (Paris), March 1985.
Pym, John, in *Monthly Film Bulletin* (London), April 1985.
Starburst (London), April 1985.
Van de Kaap, H., in *Skrien* (Amsterdam), April-May 1985.
Rushdie, Salman, ''The Location of *Brazil*,'' in *American Film* (Washington, D.C.), September 1985.
Rubenstein, Lenny, in *Cineaste* (New York), vol. 14, no. 4, 1986.
Stills (London), February 1986.
Glass, Fred, in *Film Quarterly* (Berkeley), Summer 1986.
Fohlin, J., in *Filmhaftet* (Uppsala, Sweden), December 1988.
Boyd, K. G., ''Pastiche and Postmodernism in *Brazil*,'' in *Cinefocus* (Bloomington, Indiana), no. 1, 1990.
Kremski, P., in *Filmbulletin* (Winterthur, Switzerland), no. 5–6, 1991.
Fister, Barbara, ''Mugging for the Camera: Narrative Strategies in *Brazil*,'' in *Literature/Film Quarterly* (Salisbury, Maryland), vol. 24, no. 3, 1996.
Robley, L.P., and P. Wardle, ''Terry Gilliam,'' in *Cinefantastique* (Forrest Park, Illinois), vol. 27, no. 6, 1996.

* * *

''When I started imagining things,'' says Terry Gilliam, ''I get a chemical high from it. My imagination is a cheap drug, one of my ways of dealing with reality because reality is so complex and uncontrollable.'' More than most, his career as a filmmaker seems, with its much-publicised crises of finance, production, and distribution, to have been a series of self-imposed demands for the impossible, the direct translation of a private quest into an exotic public entertainment hovering on the edge of disaster. And not surprisingly, the quartet of Gilliam adventures that began with *Jabberwocky* has one central theme: the triumph of fantasy.

In each of his films, the action revolves around a humble figure of unlikely significance—the medieval apprentice (*Jabberwocky*), the schoolboy (*Time Bandits*), the lowly clerk (*Brazil*), the derided outcast (*The Adventures of Baron Munchausen*)—who more by luck than good judgement becomes something of a hero after tackling some monstrous opponents. In each film, the ''real'' world is a cruelly chaotic environment where frantic inspiration and sheer bravado offer the only defence. And in each film, the moment of victory is precariously achieved at the cost of apparent defeat: Dennis must overwhelm the Jabberwock to win the Princess, Kevin loses home and family in the (temporary) defeat of Evil, Sam escapes from torture into placid insanity, the Baron is shot dead before riding off into the sunset where he dissolves like a ghost. It is as if the price of the whole display has been too high, an unavoidable but near-suicidal performance. ''I like the Icarus quality,'' Gilliam confirms, ''of flying too close to the sun.''

Flying high is certainly the escape route in *Brazil*, the darkest and most coherent of Gilliam's labyrinthine stories. Set ''somewhere in the 20th Century (at 8.49 p.m.),'' it parodies Orwell's *1984* to convey a less restrained but equally persuasive picture of a not-too-alternate society where nothing works as it should and nobody really cares. Gilliam's version of Winston Smith, the wild-eyed Sam Lowry, is employed in the warrens of the monolithic Ministry of Information Retrieval—where, naturally, they never tell you anything—his main function to solve the problems of his immediate superior (played by Ian Holm in a memorable portrait of vacillating bureaucracy). At night, Lowry dreams that he's devastatingly handsome in shining armour, equipped with a glorious set of white wings, and goes swooping among the clouds where a blonde goddess awaits him.

When he meets a real girl who looks just like his imaginary partner-in-flight he has little choice but to team up with her even though the ''goddess'' charges about in a huge hell-raising truck with the bright glitter of anarchy in her eyes and is marked for arrest as a trouble-maker. Sam's attempts to extract her to safe ''non-existence'' from the central computer records are in vain, and they are both doomed. But in his imagination their faraway paradise (its idyllic nature suggested by the words of the popular song ''Brazil,'' which otherwise has nothing to do with the plot) remains intact and their embrace in the sky—anticipating Gilliam's subsequent vision of ecstasy, the aerial dance between Venus and Munchausen—will last forever.

The images in *Brazil* are as outrageous as any of Gilliam's Monty Python cartoons which, with their truncated cut-outs, coils of tubes and pipes, and berserk mechanisation, the film often evokes. What gives it a special force, quite distinct from the more whimsical, fairy-tale absurdities of his other comedies, is the disturbing familiarity of the elaborately awful settings. The ugly decor of the macabre city, its walls plastered with sinister proclamations (''Don't suspect a friend—report him!''; ''Happiness—we're all in it together''), provides an enclosure of disheartening malfunction whose inhabitants are either too numb or too self-absorbed to notice. ''I'm dealing with what I think exists now,'' Gilliam says. ''There is a feeling things are out of control . . . .''

A car left briefly parked is instantly vandalised and set alight by playful kids. A guest arrives late to a party and has to be rescued by his hostess from brutish security guards who have attacked him. A terrorist bomb explodes in a restaurant but lunch continues among those diners unaffected by the blast and flames, politely screened from the writhing wounded. Such moments of ruthless humour give Gilliam's retro-future an acute satirical accuracy. Equally startling, though, are the images from nightmare, sometimes Sam's, sometimes Gilliam's, always ours. A vivid portrayal of the city-dweller's predicament comes when the pavement itself sprouts arms that hold the would-be knight back from his mission. And when another gallant rescuer, the resourceful repairman who operates stealthily outside the law, is suddenly caught up in a shroud of waste paper, a breeze blows the paper away and the human figure beneath has disintegrated and gone, a metaphor for lost hopes of reprieve.

The city under siege is a constant Gilliam battleground, vividly restaged in each of his films with ferocious bombardments and impressive crowds of scurrying extras. In *Brazil*, the war bursts in through ceilings and front doors; it even offers the opportunity for a sly reference to *Battleship Potemkin*, with a vacuum-cleaner instead of a pram on the fatal steps. The underlying contest can also be interpreted as a race against time, partly to save a crumbling world, partly—at a more personal level—to counteract physical mortality. Like the process of filmmaking itself, Gilliam's comedies are beset with giant antagonists (Sam's envisioned opponent in *Brazil*, a towering samurai, turns out to have Sam's own features), but they also bubble with resilience and humour. ''I hope people will catch themselves laughing and suddenly realise, 'I shouldn't be laughing at that, that's horrendous.' That's a nice thing to do to people. It helps us to see we're all in it together.''

—Philip Strick

BREAKFAST AT TIFFANY'S

USA, 1961

Director: Blake Edwards

Production: Jurow-Sheperd Productions and Paramount Pictures; colour, 35mm; running time: 115 minutes.

Producers: Martin Jurow and Richard Sheperd; **screenplay:** George Axelrod, from the novel by Truman Capote; **photography:** Franz Planer; **editor:** Howard Smith; **art director:** Roland Anderson; **music:** Henry Mancini; **song:** Johnny Mercer; **sound:** John Wilkinson; **assistant director:** Bill McGarry; **costumes:** Edith Head, Givenchy.

Cast: Audrey Hepburn (*Holly Golightly*); George Peppard (*Paul Varjak*); Patricia Neal (*2-E*); Mickey Rooney (*Mr. Yunioshi*); Buddy Ebsen (*Doc Golightly*); Jose Luis de Vilallonga (*Jose da Silva Perriera*); Martin Balsam (*O.J. Berman*); Dorothy Whitney (*Mag Wildwood*); Alan Reed (*Sally Tomato*).

Publications

Books:

Gilliatt, Penelope, ''A Fairytale of New York,'' in *Unholy Fools*, London 1973.

Clark, Leslie, ''Brunch on Moon River,'' in *The Modern American Novel and the Movies*, edited by Gerald Peary and Roger Schatzkin, New York 1978.

Vaccino, Roberto, *Edwards*, Florence 1979.

Brode, Douglas, *The Films of the Sixties*, New Jersey 1978.

Merbaum, Mark, *Magill's Survey of Cinema, Volume 1, First Series*, edited by Frank Magill, New Jersey 1980.

Lehman, Peter, and William Luhr, *Blake Edwards*, Ohio 1981.

Bruno, Edoardo, *Blake Edwards: l'occhio composto*, Genoa, 1997.

Articles:

Variety (New York), 11 October 1961.

Gow, Gordon, in *Films and Filming* (London), November 1961.

Monthly Film Bulletin (London), November 1961.

Breen, James, in *Sight and Sound* (London), Winter 1961/62.

Mardore, Michel, ''Le sexe d'Holly'' in *Cahiers du Cinéma* (Paris), March 1962.

Feinstein, Herbert, ''My Gorgeous Darling Sweetheart Angels: Brigitte Bardot and Audrey Hepburn'' in *Film Quarterly* (Berkeley) Spring 1962.

Bruno, Eduardo, ''I miti infranti'' in *Filmcritica* (Rome), May 1964.

Legrand, Gérard, ''Diamants sur canapé—Le rendez-vous aveugle de Blake Edwards'' in *Positif* (Paris), November 1987.

McGilligan, P., ''Irony,'' *Film Comment* (New York), vol. 31, November-December, 1995.

* * *

Although Truman Capote's popular novel served as its basis, the film version of *Breakfast at Tiffany's* is very much in debt to George Axelrod's contribution. In turn, Axelrod's screenplay owes a considerable amount to Billy Wilder's work. Axelrod and Wilder collaborated on *The Seven Year Itch*, an Axelrod play which the two adapted for the screen with Wilder directing. And, as in *The Seven Year Itch*, *Breakfast at Tiffany's* features an average man and a desirable, eccentric young woman who meet and become involved because they live in the same apartment building.

More significant, particularly in regard to the male protagonist, is the film's relationship to *Sunset Boulevard*. Paul Varjak (George Peppard), like William Holden's character in Wilder's film, is an unfulfilled writer who has taken to a form of prostitution by becoming the kept lover of a rich, older woman. Unlike Gloria Swanson, however, 2-E (Patricia Neal) isn't an actress but she displays a strong theatrical flair: on bursting into Paul's apartment and announcing that she thinks her husband may suspect the affair and has a detective trailing her, 2-E wears a vampire-like costume consisting of a black cape coat and a red turban.

But the Wilder film *Breakfast at Tiffany's* most closely resembles in tone and thematic concern is *The Apartment*, a comedy-drama in which both the male and female protagonist are involved in a sense in prostituting themselves. While Holly Golightly may not consider herself a prostitute, the film suggests the clients she has expect some sort of sexual favor in return for the ''gratuities'' they give her. And, as with the Lemmon and MacLaine characters in *The Apartment*, Paul and Holly are aligned to feelings of alienation, loneliness, and despair.

Breakfast at Tiffany's deals with characters who exploit others but the film is more concerned with how these characters are damaging themselves. For instance, Paul uses 2-E but he is also used by her; and Holly, who calls her clients ''rats,'' is cynically ''ratting'' on them. As Paul understands through observing Holly, his relationship with 2-E exists because he fears confronting himself and his future as a writer. In contrast, Holly's insecurity and identity crisis is much more severe. Holly repeatedly exhibits an inability to be fully honest with herself and others: 1) she lives as a transient yet she keeps Cat whom she refers to as ''poor slob''; 2) she claims she wants to give her brother Fred a home but she seems to be incapable of saving the necessary money to buy the ranch in Mexico; 3) she associates Paul with her brother which is a means of keeping the relationship platonic

Breakfast at Tiffany's

and non-threatening; 4) she attempts to reconstruct herself in a domestic image when she thinks a rich South American wants to marry her. Ultimately, the film's dramatic conflict resides in Holly's refusal to admit that Paul understands her and wants to make a commitment to her and the relationship.

In one of the film's most engaging sequences, Holly and Paul spend a day together doing things the other hasn't done: in their final escapade, Holly takes Paul to a five and dime store with the intention that they steal something. In addition to alluding to Holly's child-like sensibility, the action is also telling in that what they wind up stealing are Halloween masks—Holly leaves the store wearing a cat-face mask. During the course of the film, Holly is forced into shedding the various masks she uses to protect herself; the process culminates in a painful confrontation in which she attempts to dismiss Paul and disown her feelings by abandoning Cat. Although Holly's desperate gesture jars her into admitting to her need for affection, the scene carries an emotional intensity that almost undercuts the film's upbeat resolution.

Axelrod provides the film with nuanced characterizations and a skillfully constructed screenplay; he creates characters who are intelligent, witty and emotionally complex. Axelrod's contribution is matched by Blake Edwards. *Breakfast at Tiffany's* is the film that established him as a major directorial presence. Edwards is extremely assured in his handling of a wide range of modes and mood changes. The film encompasses broad farce (arguably, Mickey Rooney's characterization and performance are too silly to warrant racist objections), social satire (the New York City high society fringe element), the playful humour that Holly and Paul exhibit; it also captures the edgy mood swings that Holly displays and the emotional pain she experiences. Edwards is ably assisted by Henry Mancini, who in addition to co-writing the melancholy ''Moon River,'' provides the film with a highly evocative score.

As Paul Varjak, George Peppard gives a disciplined and highly appealing performance. In what could have easily become a secondary role, Peppard is assertive and compelling but is so in a gentle manner. As did *Home From the Hill*, *Breakfast at Tiffany's* indicates that Peppard had the potential to become a great leading man. He had a strong sexual presence and a masculine persona which wasn't dependent on swagger; instead, it is his good looks and low-keyed charm that make him seductive. While Peppard is a great asset, *Breakfast at Tiffany's* is Audrey Hepburn's film and Holly Golightly is perhaps her most endearing ''waif'' characterization. On the other hand, the film marks a turning point in her career with Hepburn moving from the child-woman to a more adult, worldly image. In *Breakfast at Tiffany's* Hepburn is less of an innocent but she manages to maintain her vulnerability and emotional expressiveness.

Given that the role has become so significant to Hepburn's career, it is interesting to note that Marilyn Monroe had been the initial choice for the project; instead, Monroe did *The Misfits*, the film which was intended to reveal her as a mature personality and actor. Ironically, *Breakfast at Tiffany's* might have better served Monroe's needs than the project which had been conceived specially to spotlight her development.

Breakfast at Tiffany's has a fairy tale quality about it but, like Wilder's *The Apartment*, the film is bittersweet and explores modern day existence with insight and compassion.

—Richard Lippe

BREAKING THE WAVES

Denmark, 1996

Director: Lars von Trier

Production: Zentropa Entertainments in collaboration with Trust Film Svenska AB, Liberator Productions S.a.r.l., Argus Film Productie, Northern Lights; color, 35mm CinemaScope; running time: 158 minutes. Released 5 July 1996, Copenhagen. Cost: DKK 52 million.

Producers: Vibeke Windeløv, Peter Aalbæk Jensen; **screenplay:** Lars von Trier in collaboration with Peter Asmussen and David Pirie; **photography:** Robby Müller; **editor:** Anders Refn; **scenography:** Karl Juliusson; **sound:** Per Streit; **chapter photos:** Per Kirkeby; digital manipulations by Søren Buus, Steen Lyders Hansen, Niels Valentin Dal.

Cast: Emily Watson (*Bess*); Stellan Skarsgård (*Jan*); Katrin Cartlidge (*Dodo*); Adrian Rawlins (*Dr. Richardson*); Jonathan Hackett (*Priest*); Sandra Voe (*Mother*); Jean-Marc Barr (*Terry*); Udo Kier (*Sadistic sailor*).

Awards: (selected) European Film of the Year, Berlin European Film Academy Award; Grand Prix, Cannes Film Festival; Best Film, Best Script, Best Leading Actress, Best Supporting Actress, Best Editor, Best Photography, Best Sound, Best Production Design, Best Make Up, and Best Light Engineer, Danish Film Academy Awards (Robert); Best Film, Best Actress, and Best Supporting Actress, Danish Film Critics Awards (Bodil); César Award for Best Foreign Film; Best Director, Best Actress, and Best Cinematographer, New York Film Critics Circle Awards; Guldbagge Award for Best Foreign Film, Swedish Film Institute; Best Film, Best Actress, Best Cinematography, and Best Director, National Society of Film Critics (U.S.A.).

Publications

Scripts:

Trier, Lars von, *Breaking the Waves*, København, 1996.

Breaking the Waves

Articles:

Björkman, Stig, ''De glasklara bildernas magi,'' in *Chaplin*, no. 263, 1996

Kindblom, Mikaela, ''Kvinnliga offerritualer,'' in *Chaplin*, no. 265, 1996.

Björkman, Stig, ''Les nouvelles expériences de Lars von Trier,'' in *Cahiers du Cinéma* (Paris), May 1996.

Guérin, Marie-Anne, interview with Lars von Trier, in *Cahiers du Cinéma* (Paris), June 1996.

Audé, Francoise, and Christian Braad Thomsen, interview with Lars von Trier, in *Positif* (Paris), October 1996.

Guérin, Marie-Anne, and Frédéric Strauss, ''Dossier,'' in *Cahiers du Cinéma* (Paris), October 1996.

Dannowski, Hans Werner, ''Theologische Motive,'' in *EPD Film* (Frankfurt), November 1996.

Oppenheimer, Jean, and David E. Williams, ''Von Triers and Müller's Ascetic Aesthetic on *Breaking the Waves*,'' in *American Cinematographer* (Hollywood), December 1996.

Sedakova, and others, ''*Breaking the Waves* and *Ordet* Are Compared by Panel of Philosophers and Sociologists Discussing Sin, Love, Faith, Evil,'' in *Iskusstvo Kino* (Moscow), June 1997.

* * *

Breaking the Waves indicates a major new direction in Lars von Trier's output. Following the Europa trilogy—with its depiction of a world in moral and political dissolution, its perverse sex, and its doom-laden atmosphere that almost makes death a relief—in *Breaking the Waves* the director shuffles the deck to create a film set in a community fighting tooth and nail against the moral dissolution represented in its eyes by anything novel or from the outside, a film which pays tribute to pure, all-consuming love, and for the first time features a female lead. It may end in death, but also in a kind of resurrection.

Emily Watson's Bess is the all-important lead, a simple woman brought up in a strictly religious Scottish small-town community. She marries Jan, a roustabout from the oil rigs, and sacrifices herself for him, so to speak, when he is paralysed in an accident on the rig and asks her to pick up other men, have sex with them, and then describe it to him. It is the only way he can have faith in his own recovery, he tells her. Her world is populated by God, Jan, and then everyone else. She has one-to-one conversations with her God, taking it upon herself to give Him a language by altering her voice and playing his part as he communicates directly with her. God is, quite literally, her counsellor, and as she has asked him to give her Jan back, she thinks she is to blame when Jan returns as a quadriplegic; for this reason, too, she is prepared to sacrifice herself in order to liberate him from the trammels of his paralysis.

One of the scoops of the film is its depiction of her love as unstinted, devouringly carnal, as pure sexual abandon that she experiences for the first time and refuses to relinquish. Her pain at Jan's departure is heartrending, and her physical reaction—hammering away at the machinery the roustabouts use every day—strikes home psychologically. When he asks her to abandon herself to other men there is no doubt that he does so in order to help a woman who seems doomed to lose her sensuality just as she discovers it, but his request develops into an obsession, revealing a demonic side to Jan, who also achieves some kind of perverted satisfaction through it.

Bess may be regarded as a simple fool, a forerunner to the people who act the idiots in Trier's next film, *The Idiots*, in their attempts to arrive at some kind of authenticity, a notion with its base in romanticism. Or she may be regarded as a parallel to the Greek chorus of Down's Syndrome dishwashers in *Riget*, or a successor to Mrs. Drusse, with her second sight the antithesis of the studied rationality of the medical world. Almost everywhere in Trier's films rationality and irrationality are contrasted, revealing areas where the common sense of civilization fails, such as in the face of the hypnosis used in the Europa trilogy to break down barriers and arrive at memory's traumatic spots, where (self) control is switched off. At the same time Bess may be regarded as a saviour, a redeemer, whose self-sacrifice redeems Jan from a hopeless life chained to the bed and oxygen mask. Not only does she submit quite literally to people (men) and their sexual desires; she also embarks on a voyage across the Styx to the dangerous vessel where her fateful death awaits her. When she returns against all expectations, and is excommunicated by her church, she is stoned by a group of children who pursue her relentlessly on her Via Dolorosa—the path to the church that has rejected her and knows not the mercy that is otherwise part of the Kingdom of Heaven.

With provocation typical of Trier, female sexual submission is thus merged with the cruel rejection by the church of she who is pure of heart. The results were only to be expected. In Denmark the film aroused opposition and argument like no other film in recent times. Priests and women in particular felt it incumbent on them to refute its perception of religion and its image of women. In this post-feminist age Bess may be seen as an anachronism, but Emily Watson defends her, acting with a vulnerability moving and convincing in every detail as regards the pain of her loss, the sincerity of her love, the pureness of her heart. Trier has created a female figure worthy of his great compatriot Carl Theodor Dreyer, a mixture of Dreyer's Joan of Arc, who goes to the stake for her faith; *Gertrud*, who desires utter devotion and not the adoration of luke-warm men; and Anna from *Day of Wrath*, who would rather die as a witch than live with a man who renounces love to save his life.

Trier emphasizes the stylization of this romantic melodrama by the use of chapter divisions in which pictures of landscapes are visually manipulated to convey the way the romantics perceived nature. The chapter titles range from the specific "Bess gets married" and "Life with Jan" to abstracts such as "Doubt," "Faith," and "Bess' Sacrifice," thus underlining the increasingly religious, allegorical character of the tale. At the same time the melodrama is acted out in the style he invented for what he called his pot-boiler, the genre-ironic television series, *The Kingdom*. The irony may be absent from *Breaking the Waves*, but Trier still uses the hand-held camera and monochrome sepia tints that in the cinema in CinemaScope made people sea-sick. The mobile camera gives us shots of the town and landscape that are clear-cut and real in almost documentary fashion, going ultra-close-up to the characters, pursuing them into the most painful nooks and crannies of the mind, and rendering them visible. Just as Bess transgresses the conventions of her community, the director transgresses those of film narrative by tossing continuity in the normal sense to the winds, along with the classical rules for angles and edits. Instead of continuity he goes for an emotional intensity that sucks the viewer into this small-minded world of pig-headed men who only understand love and ultimate sacrifice in terms of the Bible, not of real life. And when the bells finally ring out in the sky we feel the breath of Tarkovsky and his sense of visualized metaphysics, just as the miracle from *Ordet* by Carl Theodor Dreyer is an obvious source of inspiration.

—Dan Nissen

BREATHLESS

See **A BOUT DE SOUFFLE**

THE BRIDE OF FRANKENSTEIN

USA, 1935

Director: James Whale

Production: Universal; black and white, running time: 76 minutes. Released May 1935.

Producer: Carl Laemmle Jr.; **screenplay:** John L. Balderston, William Hurlbut, from the novel by Mary Shelley; **photography:** John D. Mescall; **editor:** Ted Kent; **art director:** Charles D. Hall; **music:** Franz Waxman; **special effects:** John P. Fulton; **make-up:** Jack Pierce.

Cast: Boris Karloff (*The Monster*); Colin Clive (*Henry Frankenstein*); Valerie Hobson (*Elizabeth*); Elsa Lanchester (*The Bride/Mary Shelley*); Ernest Thesiger (*Dr. Pretorius*); O. P. Heggie (*Blind Hermit*); Dwight Frye (*Karl*); E. E. Clive (*Burgomaster*); Una O'Connor (*Minnie*); Ann Darling (*Shepherdess*); Douglas Walton (*Shelley*);

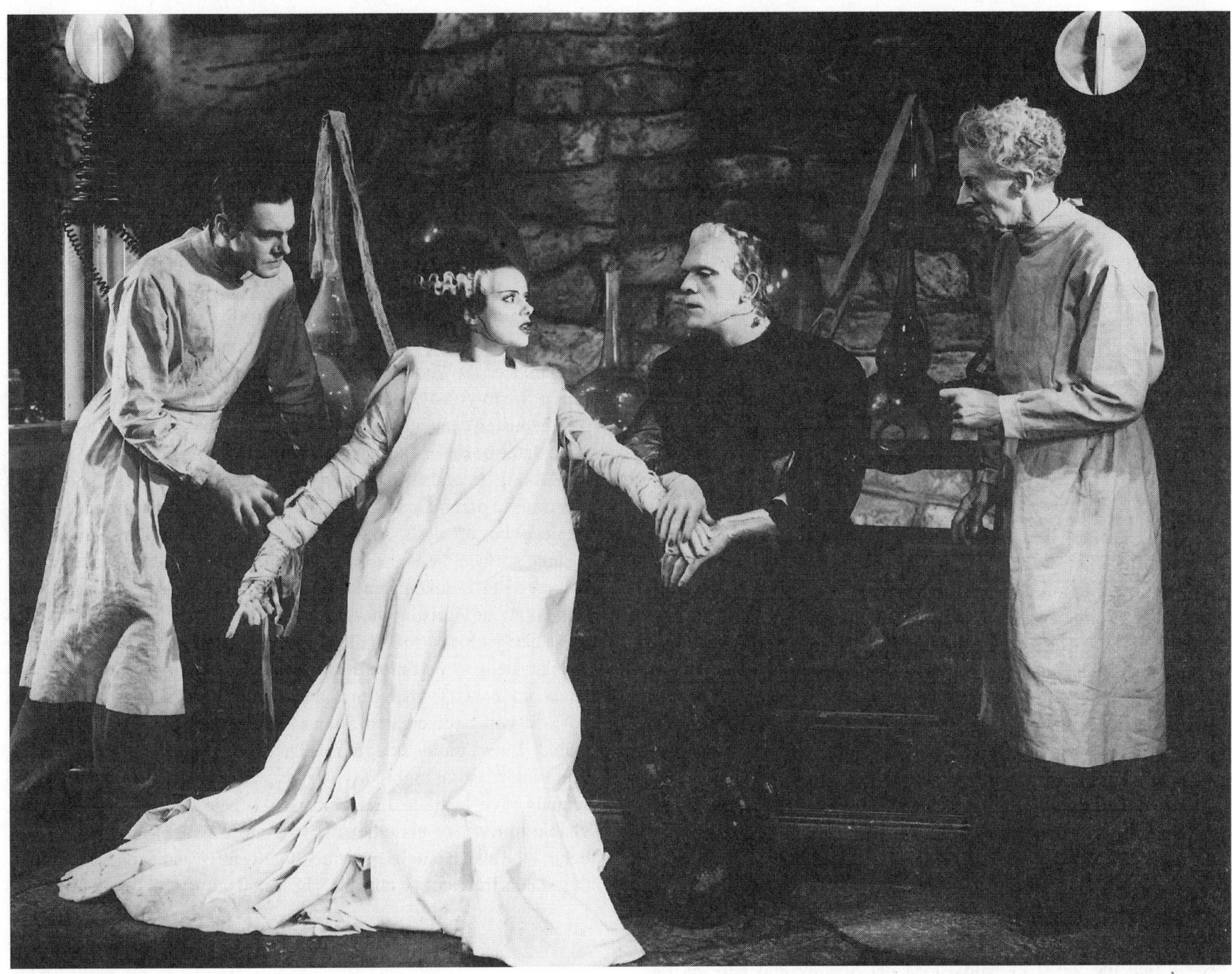

The Bride of Frankenstein

Gavin Gordon (*Lord Byron*); Ted Billings (*Ludwig*); Lucien Prival (*Butler*); John Carradine (*Woodsman*); Walter Brennan (*Neighbour*); Billy Barty (*Baby*).

Publications

Script:

Riley, Philip J., editor, *Bride of Frankenstein: The Original Shooting Script*, Absecon, New Jersey, 1989.

Books:

Butler, Ivan, *Horror in the Cinema*, revised edition, New York, 1970.
Goldblatt, Burt, and Chris Steinbrunner, *Cinema of the Fantastic*, New York, 1972.
Bojarski, Richard, and Kenneth Beale, *The Films of Boris Karloff*, Secaucus, New Jersey, 1974.
Everson, William K., *Classics of the Horror Film*, Secaucus, New Jersey, 1974.
Derry, Charles, *Dark Dreams: A Psychological History of the Modern Horror Film*, New York, 1977.
Ellis, Reed, *Journey into Darkness: The Art of James Whale's Horror Films*, New York 1980.
Curtis, James, *James Whale*, Metuchen, New Jersey, 1982.
Manguel, Alberto, *Bride of Frankenstein*, Champaign, Illinois, 1997.

Articles:

Time (New York), 29 April 1935.
New York Times, 11 May 1935.
Variety (New York), 15 May 1935.
Film Weekly (London), 28 June 1935.
Monthly Film Bulletin (London), July 1935.
Durgnat, Raymond, ''The Subconscious: From Pleasure Castle to Libido Motel,'' in *Films and Filming* (London), January 1962.
Jernsen, Paul, ''James Whale,'' in *Film Comment* (New York), Spring 1971.
Huss, Roy, ''The Creation Scene in *The Bride of Frankenstein*,'' in *Focus on the Horror Film*, edited by Huss and T. J. Ross, Englewood Cliffs, New Jersey, 1972.

Evans, Walter, "Monster Movies: A Sexual Theory," in *Journal of Popular Film* (Washington, D.C.), Fall 1973.
Milne, Tom, "One Man Crazy: James Whale," in *Sight and Sound* (London), Summer 1973.
Evans, Walter, "Monster Movies and Rites of Initiation," in *Journal of Popular Film* (Washington, D.C.), Spring 1975.
Magill's Survey of Cinema 1, Englewood Cliffs, New Jersey, 1980.
Starburst (London), no. 33, 1981.
Viviani, C., "Fausses pistes," in *Positif* (Paris), June 1983.
Senn, Bryan, "The Monster, Bride, and Son. . . ," in *Monsterscene* (Lombard, Illinois), no. 4, March 1995.
Senn, Bryan, "Elsa 'The Bride' Lanchester: A Candid Look at the Fairest Monster of Them All!" in *Filmfax* (Evanston, Illinois), no. 58, October-January 1996–97.
Henderson, J.A., and G. Turner, "A Gothic Masterpiece," in *American Cinematographer* (Hollywood), vol. 79, January 1998.

* * *

By 1935, James Whale knew the days were numbered for Universal's monster machine and offered *The Bride of Frankenstein* as the panacea to out-do any encroaching horror parodies. While the most technically proficient, lavish, and spectacular horror movie of its time, *Bride* remains the brainchild of a director grown jaded and even a bit masochistic about *Frankenstein's* unsurpassable success. Whale was so effective in making *Bride* a swansong to his genre that all subsequent scare comedies from *Abbot and Costello Meet Frankenstein* to Mel Brooks's *Young Frankenstein* are redundant.

Bride's anti-horror tone is evident from the very first scene with a literary badinage between the author Mary Shelley (Elsa Lanchester) and her cohorts Lord Byron (Gavin Gordon) and husband Percy (Douglas Walton). Despite the missing additional dialogue (excised before the film's release), this interlude is still among the most memorable and funny historical reconstructions in screen history. As Gordon's Byron commends Mary for conceiving her story, he rolls his r's like the worst of hams. Elsa (as Shelley and later as the "bride") jerks her head, contorts her eyes, and titters like a hyper-neurotic version of Brigitte Helm's robot in Fritz Lang's *Metropolis*. It is no wonder that these moments alone would inspire Ken Russell's funhouse romp in *Gothic* a half-century later.

However, once the film picks up from where the first left off, we notice how much has radically changed. Comical E. E. Clive replaces the more leaden Lionel Belmore as the town burgomaster in charge of keeping bogus order. Amidst the screaming throng, Una O'Connor (as the chambermaid Minnie) and her cacklings provide a blithe foil for Karloff's Monster. Here the Monster is reduced to a straight man when he emerges from the windmill's ruins and stands beside O'Connor—a shot that is as embarrassing as it is hilarious.

Along with the constant punch-lines and jocular atmosphere, *Bride of Frankenstein* is best distinguished by Franz Waxman's heavy-handed musical score which punctuates every gesture and leaves little room for subtlety or grace. Whale neutralizes the chills with bathos when the Monster talks (an addition to which Karloff objected). There is studied anachronism when Lucien Prival plays a butler who actually resembles a 1930s-style gangster. The film even satirizes Tod Browning's *Devil Doll* when the mad Dr. Pretorius (Ernest Thesiger) shows off his miniature life forms to induce Henry Frankenstein (Colin Clive again) to return to his electrodes and cadavers. Even the stately laboratory sequences (so creepy in the first film) are played for laughs with overly lit and distorted close-ups on the grimaces of Thesiger and Clive. Of course, there is the bride's long-awaited unveiling accompanied by wedding bells, a ceremony ruined by her shrewish hisses when the Monster arrives to claim his mate. So well does Whale slip the micky into any potential fright that he spawns a Bride of Frankenstein Syndrome which, to this day, afflicts such other morbidity moguls as George Romero and Tobe Hooper who camp up their sequels to avoid living up to their previous standards.

While demystifying the horror, Whale does, however, manage to weave more subversion into this Hays-era production than in any of his other films. The slant on sacrilege (already present in *Frankenstein*) is here augmented *ad absurdum*. Kitsch Catholicism looms over almost every scene. A maudlin church organ accompanies the prayers of thanks of the blind hermit (O. P. Heggie) when the Monster pays him a friendly visit; then the scene fades out on a glowing crucifix. The Monster is even captured by townspeople and pilloried Christ-style; later he desecrates a graveyard effigy of a bishop.

Among *Bride*'s assortment of twisted characters, Thesiger's Pretorius (a part intended for Claude Rains) is the consummate scene-stealer who, after all, sets the story's plot in motion. Beneath his Satanic surface, he is the only character rooted in his own ethics, as compared to Frankenstein (who is now even more flaky and hypocritical about Christian notions of "good" and "evil"). He is also most likely closest to Whale's own predilections. While inveigling Frankenstein to participate in the second creation, Pretorius looks coyly upon his former pupil and utters the darkly romantic line: "Alone you have created a man. Now, together we will make his mate." Like Charles Laughton's Dr. Moreau in *Island of Lost Souls*, Pretorius's sexual ambiguity suggests a counter-Eden where homosexuals give birth to heterosexuals. Whale's unabashed gayness, visible in most of his other films, is most evident in *Bride*, which, behind the cheap laughs, provides an inventive and audacious fantasy that stands the Genesis tale on its head and outwits all future imitators.

—Joseph Lanza

BRIEF ENCOUNTER

UK, 1945

Director: David Lean

Production: Cineguild; black and white, 35mm; running time: 85 minutes; length 7750 feet. Released 1945 by General Film Distributors, London, and in 1946 by Prestige Pictures. Re-released 1948 by ABFD, London. Filmed in England.

Producer: Noël Coward; **screenplay:** Noël Coward, David Lean, and Anthony Havelock-Allan, from the one-act play *Still Life* by Noël Coward; **photography:** Robert Krasker; **editor:** Jack Harris; **sound:** Stanley Lambourne and Desmond Dew; **sound editor:** Harry Miller; **production design:** L. F. Williams; **music:** from the 2nd Piano Concerto of Rachmaninoff.

Cast: Celia Johnson (*Laura Jesson*); Trevor Howard (*Dr. Alec Harvey*); Cyril Raymond (*Fred Jesson*); Joyce Carey (*Myrtle Bagot*); Stanley Holloway (*Albert Godby*); Everly Gregg (*Dolly Messiter*).

Brief Encounter

Awards: New York Film Critics' Award, Best Actress (Johnson), 1946.

Publications

Script:

Coward, Noël, David Lean, and Anthony Havelock-Allan, *Brief Encounter*, in *Three British Screenplays*, edited by Roger Manvell, London, 1950; also included in *Masterworks of the British Cinema*, London, 1974.

Books:

Gaupp, Charles John, Jr., *A Comparative Study of the Changes of 15 Stage Plays*, Doctoral Study, University of Iowa, 1950.
Levin, Milton, *Noël Coward*, New York, 1968.
Morley, Sheridan, *A Talent to Amuse: A Biography of Noël Coward*, New York, 1969.
Pratley, Gerald, *The Cinema of David Lean*, New York, 1974.
Silver, Alain, and James Ursini, *David Lean and His Films*, London, 1974.
Castelli, Louis P., and Caryn Lynn Cleeland, *David Lean: A Guide to References and Resources*, Boston, 1980.
Lahr, John, *Coward the Playwright*, London, 1982.
Anderegg, Michael A., *David Lean*, Boston, 1984.
Knight, Vivienne, *Trevor Howard: A Gentleman and a Player*, London, 1986.
Dyer, Richard, *Brief Encounter*, London, 1993.

Articles:

Variety (New York), 28 November 1945.
Lean, David, *Penguin Film Review* (London), no. 4, 1947.
Lejeune, C. A., ''The Up and Coming Team of Lean and Neame,'' in *New York Times*, 15 June 1947.
''David Lean,'' in *Current Biography Yearbook*, New York, 1953.
Holden, J., ''A Study of David Lean,'' in *Film Journal* (New York), April 1956.
Conrad, Derek, ''Living Down a Classic,'' in *Films and Filming* (London), May 1958.

Watts, Stephen, ''David Lean,'' in *Films in Review* (New York), April 1959.
Whitehall, Richard, ''Gallery of Great Artists: Trevor Howard,'' in *Films and Filming* (London), February 1961.
Burles, Kenneth T., in *Magill's Survey of Cinema 1*, Englewood Cliffs, New Jersey, 1980.
Aspinall, Sue, ''Women, Realism, and Reality in British Films 1943–53,'' in *British Cinema History*, edited by James Curran and Vincent Porter, London, 1983.
Medhurst, A., ''That Special Thrill: *Brief Encounter*, Homosexuality and Authorship,'' in *Screen* (Oxford), no. 2, Summer, 1991.
Howard, T., ''Brief Encounter,'' *Reid's Film Index* (New South Wales), no. 16, 1995.

* * *

In 1929 Leon Moussinac could, in his *Panoramique du cinéma*, declare ''L'Angleterre n'a jamais produit un vrai film anglais.'' The remarkable renaissance of the British film at the end of World War II requires a very different judgement. In 1944, David Lean made *Brief Encounter*, the most characteristic and perfect British film of all time. Its debt to Noël Coward must not be underestimated, but it is Lean's film. Lean, having worked as an editor on films by Michael Powell and Anthony Asquith, began his career as a director in association with Coward on *In Which We Serve*, *This Happy Breed*, and *Blithe Spirit*. He then directed *Brief Encounter*, about the infatuation between a housewife and a married man, with such uncanny human awareness and real creative skill that it stands out against his later more ambitious and elaborate films.

Brief Encounter is on a small scale, intimate, and probing. Everything is obvious and yet nothing is. Laura Jesson, its suburban heroine, may not reach the dramatic solution of an Anna Karenina but what she does experience is no less poignant. We share her joys and sorrows of the moment until they carry her to the edge of tragedy. It cannot be seen entirely, however, as tragedy for there is an element of values and choice. Life is not simple and the greatness of the film lies in its awareness of this complexity. An insensitive critic once described the film as, ''Two characters in search of a bed.'' French critics failed to see that there *was* a problem. But for characters like Laura and Alex, there were values that they honoured, even at the expense of pain. It is, in a way, a triumph for their common humanity. Very simply the end did not justify the means.

The happy unification of this tale of star-crossed lovers, the intense reality of their attraction and the universal nature of the experience is played against a background that is deeply and truly British. If being British is the spirit of the ''stiff upper lip,'' then it is belied by the passionate note that runs through the film. The small joys of love, the impetus towards realization and fulfillment, the sense of threatened pleasures haunts the viewer from beginning to end. The perfect performances of that most subtle of all actresses, Celia Johnson, and of Trevor Howard contribute greatly to the success of the film. It is, though, the happy fusion of all the elements that give it a perspective and unity rare in the cinema.

The setting of the suburban railway station and its vicinity sees a great human drama take place. Everything about it is authentic down to the familiars who haunt it, the funny little people with their airs and graces and their trivial jokes and quarrels. Other dramatic incidents which occur in the film include the visit to the restuarant and the cinema; the humiliation and shame when reality shatters the dream; and the unexpected friend who turns up to interrupt their one possible night together. The film thus opens with the climax which is not fully understood until the gentle pain-filled voice of Laura relives the happy but poignant days of a moment of life she will never forget.

There is one element that enhances the film in a most felicitous way. When Rachmaninoff wrote his 2nd Piano Concerto he could little have guessed that he was providing the theme music for a very beautiful and inspiring British film. Though it was not a commercial success in America, it was successful for the British cinema in terms of prestige.

—Liam O'Leary

A BRIGHTER SUMMER DAY

See **GULING JIE SHAONIAN SHA REN SHIJIAN**

BRINGING UP BABY

USA, 1938

Director: Howard Hawks

Production: RKO Radio Pictures Inc.; black and white, 35mm; running time: 102 minutes (some sources state 100 minutes). Released 1938. Filmed in RKO studios and backlots.

Producer: Cliff Reid; **screenplay:** Dudley Nichols and Hagar Wilde, from a story by Hagar Wilde; **photography:** Russell Metty; **editor:** George Hively; **music score:** Roy Webb.

Cast: Cary Grant (*David Huxley*); Katharine Hepburn (*Susan Vance*); May Robson (*Mrs. Carlton Random*); Charles Ruggles (*Major Applegate*); George Irving (*Alexander Peabody*); Virginia Walker (*Alice Swallow*); Barry Fitzgerald; Walter Catlett.

Publications

Books:

Bogdanovich, Peter, *The Cinema of Howard Hawks*, New York, 1962.
Missiaen, Jean-Claude, *Howard Hawks*, Paris, 1966.
Wood, Robin, *Howard Hawks*, London, 1968; revised edition, 1981.
Dickens, Homer, *The Films of Katharine Hepburn*, New York, 1971.
Eyles, Allen, compiler, *Cary Grant Album*, Shepperton, Surrey, 1971.
Gigli, Jean A., *Howard Hawks*, Paris, 1971.
Bazin, André, *La Politique des auteurs: Entretiens avec Jean Renoir, etc.*, Paris, 1972; revised edition, 1984.
Marill, Alvin H., *Katharine Hepburn*, New York, 1973.
Vermilye, Jerry, *Cary Grant*, New York, 1973.
Parish, James Robert, *The RKO Gals*, New Rochelle, New York, 1974.
Deschner, Donald, *The Films of Cary Grant*, Secaucus, New Jersey, 1978.
Murphy, Kathleen Q., *Howard Hawks: An American Auteur in the Hemingway Tradition*, Ann Arbor, Michigan, 1978.
Ciment, Michel, *Les Conquérants d'un nouveau monde: Essais sur le cinéma américain*, Paris, 1981.

Bringing Up Baby

Giannetti, Louis, *Masters of the American Cinema*, Englewood Cliffs, New Jersey, 1981.
McBride, Joseph, *Hawks on Hawks*, Berkeley, 1982.
Mast, Gerald, *Howard Hawks, Storyteller*, Oxford, 1982.
Poague, Leland, *Howard Hawks*, Boston, 1982.
Belton, John, *Cinema Stylists*, Metuchen, New Jersey, 1983.
Britton, Andrew, *Cary Grant: Comedy and Male Desire*, Newcastle-upon-Tyne, 1983.
Carey, Gary, *Katharine Hepburn: A Biography*, London, 1983.
McIntosh, William Currie, and William Weaver, *The Private Cary Grant*, London, 1983; revised edition, 1987.
Schickel, Richard, *Cary Grant: A Celebration*, London, 1983.
Wansell, Geoffrey, *Cary Grant: Haunted Idol*, London, 1983.
Britton, Andrew, *Katharine Hepburn: The Thirties and After*, Newcastle-upon-Tyne, 1984.
Dupuis, Jean-Jacques, *Cary Grant*, Paris, 1984.
Freedland, Michael, *Katharine Hepburn*, London, 1984.
Morley, Sheridan, *Katharine Hepburn: A Celebration*, London, 1984.
Simsolo, Noel, *Howard Hawks*, Paris, 1984.
Ashman, Chuck, and Pamela Trescott, *Cary Grant*, London, 1986.
Edwards, Anne, *Katharine Hepburn: A Biography*, London, 1986.
Branson, Clark, *Howard Hawks: A Jungian Study*, Los Angeles, 1987.
Mast, Gerald, editor, *Bringing Up Baby*, New Brunswick, 1988.
Higham, Charles, and Ray Moseley, *Cary Grant: The Lonely Heart*, New York, 1989.

Articles:

New York Times, 4 March 1938.
Tozzi, Romana T., ''Katharine Hepburn,'' in *Films in Review* (New York), December 1957.
Agel, Henri, ''Howard Hawks,'' in *New York Film Bulletin*, no. 4, 1962.
Sarris, Andrew, ''The World of Howard Hawks,'' in *Films and Filming* (London), July 1962.
Perkins, V. F., in *Movie* (London), December 1962.
''Hawks Issue'' of *Cahiers du Cinéma* (Paris), January 1963.
''Man's Favourite Director, Howard Hawks'' (interview), in *Cinema* (Beverly Hills), November-December 1963.
Wise, Naomi, ''The Hawksian Woman,'' in *Take One* (Montreal), January-February 1971.
Brackett, Leigh, ''A Comment on the Hawksian Woman,'' in *Take One* (Montreal), July-August 1971.

Murphy, K., ''Of Bones, and Butterflies,'' in *Movietone News* (Seattle), June 1977.
Johnson, Julia, in *Magill's Survey of Cinema 1*, Englewood Cliffs, New Jersey, 1980.
Trueba, F., in *Casablanca* (Madrid), July-August 1981.
Jewell, R. B., ''How Howard Hawks Brought Baby Up: An Apologia for the Studio System,'' in *Journal of Popular Film and Television* (Washington, D.C.), Winter 1984.
Keane, Marian, in *Journal of Popular Film and Television* (Washington, D.C.), Autumn 1985.
Lake, J. M., ''What Are Girls Made Of?'' *Michigan Academician* (Ann Arbor), vol. 26, no. 2, 1994.
''Bringing Up Baby,'' *Sequences* (Montreal), no. 178, May-June 1995.

* * *

Bringing Up Baby employs the successful formula of such classic films as *It Happened One Night* and *My Man Godfrey* in which madcap heiresses pit their senses of fun, irreverence, and total irresponsibility against the seriousness, logic, and dignity of working class heroes. In such screwball comedies of the 1930s the leading couple's courtships of verbal battles provide a series of humorous sexual conflicts that are overcome but unresolved in the reconciliation during the ''happy endings.'' *Bringing Up Baby* takes the antagonisms and extremes embodied in the screwball comedy a little further than any of the other films of the genre.

Starring Katharine Hepburn as the completely dotty heiress and Cary Grant as an overly stuffy, self-important paleontologist *Bringing Up Baby* exaggerates the lover-antagonist formula of the screwball comedy for a humorous battle between the sexes in which the stereotypes of sex roles are reversed. Hepburn's character is the aggressor, and her relentless pursuit of Grant engages him in a series of comic misadventures which become increasingly foolish as the movie progresses. Grant's character, who by nature is docile, submissive, and dutiful, has his dignity stripped away layer by layer in the course of Hepburn's bizarre schemes. But director Howard Hawks uses the division of his characters into masculine and feminine stereotypes in order to allow each to have a liberating effect on the other. When the two are united as a couple at the film's end, the effect is an uneasy integration of sex-role principles.

The Hawksian formula of sex-role reversals contained in comic opposites provided the underpinnings for Hawk's screwball comedies from the 1930s through the 1950s. In such movies as *Twentieth Century*, *Bringing Up Baby*, *His Girl Friday*, *Ball of Fire*, *I Was a Male War Bride*, and *Monkey Business*, Hawks relied on assertive heroines to peel away the dignity and mock seriousness of bumbling feminized heroes. As each hero's sense of identity and self-image crumbles, the ensuing confusion provides the comedy and the key to his liberation from a narrow restrictive code of behaviour. In such films as *Bringing Up Baby* and *I Was a Male War Bride*, Hawks pushes his male characters' sexual confusion to such extremes that they are forced to parade around in women's clothing.

Bringing Up Baby enjoys frequently revived popularity today due to its breakneck pace, superb comic timing, humorous swipes at sex roles, and partnering of Hepburn and Grant. But when the film was initially released in 1938, it met harsh criticism and indifferent audiences. Hepburn, who headed the Independent Theatre Owners Association list of ''box-office poison'' movie stars, grated on the critics' nerves. In addition to Hepburn's seeming unpopularity, a critical disdain for what the *New York Times* reviewer called a ''zany-ridden product of the goofy farce school'' may have contributed to the film's lack of success. However, in 1962, *Sight and Sound* critic Peter Dyer attested to the reversal in status and popularity of *Bringing Up Baby:* ''The durability of Hawks's films lies in the way that they have a mysterious life of their own going on under the familiar, facile surfaces. It is the constant cross-graining of cliché and inventive detail which produces the shock of pleasure his best work provides.''

—Lauren Rabinovitz

BROKEN BLOSSOMS

USA, 1919

Director: D. W. Griffith

Production: D. W. Griffith Inc.; black and white, 35mm, silent; running time: about 95 minutes; length: 6 reels. Released 1919 through United Artists. Filmed December 1918 and January 1919; cost: $88,000.

Producer: D. W. Griffith; **scenario:** D. W. Griffith, from the story ''The Chink and the Child'' by Thomas Burke; **photography:** G. W.

Broken Blossoms

Bitzer; **editor:** James Smith; **music:** Louis F. Gottschalk; **special effects:** Hendrick Sartov.

Cast: Lillian Gish (*Lucy, the Girl*); Richard Barthelmess (*Cheng Huan*); Donald Crisp (*Battling Burrows*); Arthur Howard (*Burrows's Manager*); Edward Peil (*Evil Eye*); George Beranger (*The Spying One*); Norman Selby or ''Kid McCoy'' (*A Prize Fighter*); George Nicholls (*London Policeman*); Moon Kwan (*Buddhist monk*).

Publications

Books:

Paine, Albert Bigelow, *Life and Lillian Gish*, New York, 1932.
Wagenknecht, Edward, *The Movies in the Age of Innocence*, Norman, Oklahoma, 1962.
Barry, Iris, *D. W. Griffith: American Film Master*, New York, 1965.
Mitry, Jean, ''Griffith,'' in *Anthologie de cinéma*, Paris, 1966.
Gish, Lillian, with Ann Pinchot, *The Movies, Mr. Griffith, and Me*, Englewood Cliffs, New Jersey, 1969.
O'Dell, Paul, *Griffith and the Rise of Hollywood*, New York, 1970.
Hart, James, editor, *The Man Who Invented Cinema: The Autobiography of D. W. Griffith*, Louisville, Kentucky, 1972.
Henderson, Robert, *D. W. Griffith: His Life and Work*, New York, 1972.
Bitzer, G. W., *Billy Bitzer: His Story*, New York, 1973.
Brown, Karl, *Adventures with D. W. Griffith*, edited by Kevin Brownlow, New York and London 1973; revised edition, 1988.
Gish, Lillian, *Dorothy and Lillian Gish*, New York, 1973.
Pratt, George C., *Spellbound in Darkness*, Connecticut, 1973.
Wagenknecht, Edward, and Anthony Slide, *The Films of D. W. Griffith*, New York, 1975.
Affron, Charles, *Star Acting: Gish, Garbo, Davis*, New York, 1977.
Williams, Martin, *Griffith: First Artist of the Movies*, New York, 1980.
Giannetti, Louis, *Masters of the American Cinema*, Englewood Cliffs, New Jersey, 1981.
Brion, Patrick, editor, *D. W. Griffith*, Paris, 1982.
Andrew, Dudley, *Film in the Aura of Art*, Princeton, New Jersey, 1984.
Mottet, Jean, editor, *D. W. Griffith*, Paris, 1984.
Schickel, Richard, *D. W. Griffith and the Birth of Film*, London, 1984.
Graham, Cooper C., and others, *D.W. Griffith and the Biograph Company*, Metuchen, New Jersey, 1985.
Jesionowski, Joyce E., *Thinking in Pictures: Dramatic Structures in D. W. Griffith's Biograph Films*, Berkeley, 1987.
Lang, Robert, *American Film Melodrama: Griffith, Vidor, Minnelli*, New Jersey, 1989.
Elsaesser, Thomas, and Adam Barker, editors, *Early Cinema: Space-Frame-Narrative*, London, 1990.
Gunning, Tom, *D.W. Griffith and the Origins of American Narrative Film: The Early Years at Biograph*, Urbana, Illinois, 1991.
Pearson, Roberta E., *Eloquent Gestures: The Transformation of Performance Style in the Griffith Biograph Films*, Berkeley, 1992.
Simmon, Scott, *The Films of D.W. Griffith*, Cambridge and New York, 1993.

Articles:

New York Times, 14 May 1919.
Variety (New York), 18 May 1919.
Mayer, A. L., ''The Origins of United Artists,'' in *Films in Review* (New York), August-September 1959.
Tozzi, Romano, ''Lillian Gish,'' in *Films in Review* (New York), December 1962.
Mitchell, George J., ''Billy Bitzer—Pioneer and Innovator,'' in *American Cinematographer* (Hollywood), December 1964 and January 1965.
Griffith issue, in *Film Culture* (New York), Spring-Summer 1965.
Meyer, Richard, ''The Films of David Wark Griffith: The Development of Themes and Techniques in 42 of His Films,'' in *Film Comment* (New York), Fall-Winter 1967.
Bowser, Eileen, and Iris Barry, in *Film Notes*, New York, 1969.
Amengual, Barthélémy, ''Quelques remarques sur *Le Lys brisé*,'' in *Cahiers du Cinéma* (Paris), Spring, 1972.
Casty, Alan, ''The Films of D. W. Griffith,'' in *Journal of Popular Culture* (Bowling Green, Ohio), Spring 1972.
Lenning, Arthur, ''D. W. Griffith and the Making of an Unconventional Masterpiece,'' in *Film Journal* (New York), Fall-Winter 1972.
Bracourt, G., in *Ecran* (Paris), February 1973.
''Griffith Issue'' of *Films in Review* (New York), October 1975.
Combs, Richard, in *Monthly Film Bulletin* (London), November 1975.
Kepley, Jr., Vance, Jr., ''Griffith's *Broken Blossoms* and the Problem of Historical Specificity,'' in *Quarterly Review of Film Studies* (Pleasantville, New York), Winter 1978.
Lesage, Julia, ''*Broken Blossoms:* Artful Racism, Artful Rape,'' in *Jump Cut* (Chicago), 1981.
Andrew, Dudley, ''*Broken Blossoms:* The Art and Eros of a Perverse Text,'' in *Quarterly Review of Film Studies* (Pleasantville, New York), Winter 1981.
Browne, Nick, ''Griffith's Family Discourse: Griffith and Freud,'' in *Quarterly Review of Film Studies* (Pleasantville, New York), Winter 1981.
Lynn, K. S., ''The Torment of D. W. Griffith,'' in *American Scholar* (Washington, D.C.), no. 2, 1990.
Vanoye, Francis, ''Rhétorique de la douleur,'' in *Vertigo*, no. 6–7, 1991.
Merritt, R., ''In and Around *Broken Blossoms*,'' in *Griffithiana* (Gemona, Italy), October 1993.
Flitterman-Lewis, S., ''The Blossom and the Bole: Narrative and Visual Spectacle in Early Film Melodrama,'' in *Cinema Journal* (Austin, Texas), vol. 33, no. 3, 1994.
DeCroix, R., and J. L. Limbacher, ''In Memory of Lillian Gish (1893–1993): First Lady of American Cinema,'' in *Journal of Popular Film and Television* (Washington, D.C.), vol. 22, no. 2, Summer 1994.

* * *

Broken Blossoms is Griffith's most intricate film, a delicate mood piece that is set within a sharply confined space and delimited amount of time. The film opened to critical acclaim in this country with reviewers responding particularly to Lillian Gish's bravura performance and Henrick Sartov's soft-focus photography. Its most profound effect, however, was felt by European filmmakers. In France, where the film premiered in 1921, it became something of a cult object. French impressionist directors like Louis Delluc, Marcel L'Herbier, and Germaine Dullac tried consciously to emulate its stylized lighting and atmospheric effects. As Vance Kepley stated, ''*Broken Blossoms* may have been to the early French experimenters what *Intolerance* was to the Soviets.'' Louis Moussinac summed up the admiration French filmmakers felt for Griffith's film: ''C'est le chef-d'oeuvre du cinema dramatique.''

Broken Blossoms came as something of a surprise to critics who knew Griffith only through *The Birth of a Nation*, *Intolerance*, or his World War I extravaganza, *Hearts of the World.* In fact, this modest film shot in 18 days on a shoe-string budget, was at first considered box office poison. When Griffith approached Paramount to distribute the film as a special, Adolph Zukor unhesitatingly turned him down. ''Everybody in it dies,'' he wrote. Mindful of the recent failure of Nazimova's *The Red Lantern* and Sessue Hayakawa's waning popularity, Zukor concluded that the brief vogue for film *chinoiserie* had passed and was eager to let Griffith distribute it himself. Griffith paid Zukor $250,000 for it, and eventually released it through the newly formed United Artists; dressed up with an elaborate live prologue, three separate orchestras and choirs, and a specially tinted screen, the film garnered a small fortune.

Today, the film's critical stock is soaring: *Broken Blossoms* is widely regarded as Griffith's masterpiece, eclipsing even his better known epics. Lillian Gish's masterful performance aside, critics have been especially impressed by the formal sophistication and narrative complexity of Griffith's film. It is, above all, a film marked by terrific compression. The concentration of time and space gives characters, objects, and decor sustained metaphorical power that is never dissipated. Just as skillful is the dramatic structure which gives the impression of simple straightforwardness while camouflaging an intricate intertwining of expository and narrative sequences.

Thematically, the film is perhaps Griffith's most adventurous work. Susan Sontag has called Griffith ''an intellect of supreme vulgarity and even inanity,'' whose work ordinarily reeks of fervid moralizing about sexuality and violence. But in *Broken Blossoms* he lowers his guard, nearly breaching his cherished Victorian convictions. Activities obviously taboo in *The Birth of a Nation* and *Intolerance*—a racially mixed love affair, auto-eroticism, opium eating, sado-masochism, revenge killing—are transformed here into sensually satisfying pastimes that resonate in dangerously nonconformist ways. For once in Griffith's work, racial bigotry is a target for reproach. The few citations to post-war 1919 American culture, far from catering to the rampant xenophobia and mood of self-congratulation, hint at the dark side of American provincialism. The glancing references to munition workers, American sailors, and First World War battles illustrate the west's penchant for self-destructiveness and violence.

—Russell Merritt

BRONENOSETS POTEMKIN

(Battleship Potemkin)

USSR, 1925

Director: Sergei Eisenstein

Production: First Goskino; black and white, 35mm, silent; running time: 86 minutes at silent speed; length 1850 meters, or 6070 feet. Released 18 January 1926. Re-released 1956 with a second musical score by Nikolai Kryukov. Filmed from July through November 1925, in Leningrad, Odessa, and aboard the *12 Apostles* (the sister ship of the *Prince Potemkin of Taurida*).

Producer: Jacob Bliokh; **scenario and screenplay:** Sergei Eisenstein, from an outline by Nina Agadzhanova-Shutko in collaboration with Sergei Eisenstein; **titles:** Nikolai Aseyev; **photography:** Edward Tisse; **editor:** Sergei Eisenstein; **art director:** Vasili Rakhals; **music (original background score):** Edmund Meisel.

Cast: Sailors of the Red Navy; Citizens of Odessa; Members of the Proletkut Theatre, Moscow; Alexander Antonov (*Vakulinchuk*); Grigori Alexandrov (*Chief Officer Gilerocsky*); Vladimir Barsky (*Captain Golikov*); Alexander Lyovshin (*Petty Officer*); Beatrice Vitoldi (*Mother with baby carriage*); I. Bobrov (*Humiliated soldier*); Andrei Fait (*Officer on piano*); Konstantin Feldman (*Student Fel'dman*); Protopopov (*Old man*); Korobei (*Legless veteran*); Yulia Eisenstein (*Lady bringing food to mutineers*); Prokopenko (*Mother of wounded Aba*); A. Glauberman (*Aba*); N. Poltautseva (*School teacher*); Brodsky (*Intellectual*); Zerenin (*Student*); Mikhail Gomarov (*Militant sailor*).

Publications

Scripts:

Eisenstein, Sergei, *The Battleship Potemkin*, London, 1968; as *Potemkin*, New York, 1968; also included in *Three Films*, edited by Jay Leyda, New York, 1974.

Books:

Ginzburg, S. S., ''Artistic Imagery in the Film *The Battleship Potemkin*,'' in *The History of Film*, Moscow, 1960.
Leyda, Jay, ''On *Potemkin*,'' in *Kino: A History of the Russian and Soviet Film*, London, 1960.
Seton, Marie, *S. M. Eisenstein*, New York, 1960.
Kleinman, N. I., and K. B. Levina, *Bronenosets Potemkin—Shedevry Sovetskogo Kino* (The Battleship Potemkin, Masterpieces of Soviet Cinema), Moscow, 1969.
Mayer, David, *Eisenstein's ''Potemkin,''* New York, 1972.
Eisenstein, S. M., *Autobiography*, translated by H. Marshall and Toby Wright, London, 1978.
Marshall, Herbert, editor, *The Battleship Potemkin*, New York, 1978.
Murray, Edward, ''*Potemkin*,'' in *10 Film Classics*, New York, 1978.
Leyda, Jay, and Zina Vignow, *Eisenstein at Work*, New York, 1982.
Eisenstein, Sergei M., *Immoral Memories: An Autobiography*, translated by Herbert Marshall, Boston, 1983.
Marshall, Herbert, *Masters of the Soviet Cinema: Crippled Creative Biographies*, London, 1983.
Polan, Dana B., *The Political Language of Film and the Avant-Garde*, Ann Arbor, Michigan, 1985.
Aumont, Jacques, *Montage Eisenstein*, London, 1987.
Eisenstein, Sergei M., *Selected Works, Volume 1: Writings 1922–1934*, edited by Richard Taylor, London, 1988.

Bronenosets Potemkin

Bordwell, David, *Cinema of Eisenstein*, Cambridge, 1993.

Goodwin, James, *Eisenstein, Cinema, and History*, Urbana, Illinois, 1993.

Lövgren, Håkan, *Eisenstein's Labyrinth: Aspects of a Cinematic Synthesis of the Arts*, Stockholm, 1996.

Termine, Liborio, *La drammaturgia del film*, Torino, 1998.

Articles:

Mendel, George Victor, in *Kinemathek* (Berlin), 5 January 1926.

Barrett, Wilton A., in *National Board of Review Magazine* (New York), November 1926.

Hall, Mordaunt, in *New York Times*, December 1926.

Grierson, John, in *New York Herald Tribune*, 5 December 1926.

Variety (New York), 8 December 1926.

Solski, ''The End of Eisenstein,'' in *Commentary* (New York), March 1949.

Evsevitsky, Vladislav, ''Soviet Films in Pre-September Poland,'' in *Kwartalnik Filmowy* (Warsaw), nos. 3–4, 1951.

Freilich, Semyon, ''A Comparison of *Potemkin* and *Ivan the Terrible:* Eisenstein Today,'' in *Soviet Literature Monthly*, 1965.

Montagu, Ivoe, ''*Potemkin* in Print,'' in *Sight and Sound* (London), Summer 1970.

Kuleshov, Lev, ''Kuleshov, Eisenstein, and the others: Part II: Kuleshov on Eisenstein,'' in *Film Journal* (New York), Fall-Winter 1972.

Kauffmann, Stanley, ''Eisenstein's *Potemkin*,'' in *Horizon* (London), Spring 1973.

''*El Acorazado Potemkin*,'' in *Cine Cubano* (Havana), no. 89–90, 1974.

''Epos Revolucii,'' in *Iskusstvo Kino* (Moscow), December 1975.

Kieiman, N., ''Tol'ko piatnadstat 'Kadrov,'' in *Iskusstvo Kino* (Moscow), no. 3, 1976.

''A for a es a tartalom egysegenek iskoklapeldaja,'' in *Filmkultura* (Budapest), May-June 1976.

Chanjutin, J., in *Film and Fernsehen* (Berlin), November 1977.

Van Wert, W. F., in *Sight and Sound* (London), Summer 1980.

Sklovski, V., ''Krizník pluje desetiletími,'' in *Film a Doba* (Prague), November 1981.

Wenden, D. J., ''Film and Reality,'' in *Feature Films as History*, edited by K.R.M. Short, London 1981.

Felden, D. L., ''Vision and Violence: The Rhetoric of *Potemkin*,'' in *Quarterly Review of Film Studies* (New York), Fall 1982.

Roth-Lindberg, O., in *Chaplin* (Stockholm), 1983.

Almendros, N., ''Fortune and Men's Eyes,'' in *Film Comment* (New York), July-August 1991.

''Yo postskriptum till unikt livsode,'' in *Chaplin* (Stockholm), no. 3, 1992.

Biorsmark, C. ''Odessa tror inte på trooper,'' *Chaplin* (Stockholm), vol. 36, no. 6, 1994/95.

De Marinis, G. ''I [love] Sergej,'' *Cineforum* (Bergamo), vol. 35, April 1995.

Eisenstein, S.M., ''Meggymag a lepcson,'' *Filmvilag* (Budapest), vol. 38, no. 8, 1995.

Seesslen, G., ''Die anderen Moeglichkeiten des Kinos,'' *EPD Film* (Frankfurt/Main), vol. 14, December 1995.

Sorenssen, B., ''Drama i sortehavet da *Panserkrysseren Potemkin* kom til Oslo,'' *Z Filmtidsskrift* (Oslo), no. 4, 1995.

Musina, M., and others, ''Boitsy vspominaiut minuvshie dni,'' *Iskusstvo Kino* (Moscow), no. 5, 1996.

Vallerand, F., ''Musiques pour Eisenstein,'' *Sequences* (Quebec), no. 183, March/April 1996.

* * *

Sergei M. Eisenstein's *Battleship Potemkin* is one of the most influential films ever made as well as one of the finest examples of film art. On its release, the film brought immediate worldwide fame to Eisenstein and the new Soviet cinema and made an important contribution to the language of the cinema—the concept of montage editing.

After the Bolshevik Revolution in 1917 the new Soviet government assumed control of the film industry, denounced the capitalist cinema of pre-Revolution Tsarist Russia, and decreed that the Soviet cinema was to be used for education and propaganda—to indoctrinate the Russian masses and to promote class consciousness throughout the world. *Battleship Potemkin* was made in order to celebrate the 20th anniversary of the unsuccessful 1905 Revolution against the Tsar. Although the film was originally supposed to chronicle the entire rebellion, Eisenstein decided to limit the story to just one representative episode—the mutiny on the Potemkin and the subsequent civilian massacre on the steps leading down to Odessa harbour.

Battleship Potemkin, like Eisenstein's earlier film, *Strike*, has several documentary-like qualities. For example, Eisenstein cast most of the characters in the film according to the notion of typage—the selection of a non-actor to play a role because he/she is the correct physical type for the part. Eisenstein preferred to use non-actors since, as he explained, ''A 30 year old actor may be called upon to play an old man of 60. He may have a few days' or a few hours' rehearsal. But an old man will have had 60 years' rehearsal.'' Eisenstein shot the film on location—on the Odessa steps and aboard the Potemkin's sister ship, The Twelve Apostles (the Potemkin had already been dismantled). The film has a collective hero; the Russian masses—the mutineers on the Potemkin, the people of Odessa, the sailors who mutiny on the other ships—who rebel against Tsarist oppression.

Despite the film's documentary look, it was very carefully constructed on every level, from the distribution of line, mass, and light in individual shots to the perfectly balanced five-act structure of the overall film. The most remarkable feature of the film's construction, however, is the montage editing.

Eisenstein's theory of montage—based on the Marxist dialectic, which involves the collision of thesis and antithesis to produce a synthesis incorporating features of both—deals with the juxtaposition of shots, and attractions (e.g. lighting, camera angle, or subject movement) within shots, to create meaning. Rather than the smooth linkage of shots favored by many of his contemporaries (e.g. V. I. Pudovkin and D. W. Griffith). Eisenstein was interested in the collision and dialectical synthesis of contradictory shots as a way to shock and agitate the audience.

Eisenstein identified five methods of montage: metric, rhythmic, tonal, overtonal, and intellectual. Metric montage concerns conflict caused by the lengths of shots. Rhythmic montage concerns conflict generated by the rhythm of movement within shots. In tonal montage, shots are arranged according to the ''tone'' or ''emotional sound'' of the dominant attraction in the shots. In overtonal montage, the basis for joining shots is not merely the dominant attraction, but the totality of stimulation provided by that dominant attraction and all of its ''overtones'' and ''undertones'': overtonal montage is, then, a synthesis of metric, rhythmic, and tonal montage, appearing not at the level of the individual frame, but only at the level of the projected film. Finally, intellectual montage involves the juxtaposition of images to create a visual metaphor.

All five types of montage may be found in *Potemkin*'s Odessa Steps sequence in which Tsarist soldiers massacre Odessa citizens who are sympathetic to the Potemkin mutineers. An example of metric montage is the increase in editing tempo to intensify audience excitement during the massacre. Rhythmic montage occurs in the conflict between the steady marching of the soldiers and the editing rhythm, which is out of synchronization with the marching, as well as the chaotic scrambling of the fleeing crowd, and the rolling movement of a runaway baby carriage. Tonal montage occurs in the many conflicts of planes, masses, light and shadow, and intersecting lines, as in the shot depicting a row of soldiers pointing their rifles down at a mother and her son, the soldiers' shadows cutting transversely across the steps and the helpless pair. Although Eisenstein claimed to have discovered overtonal montage while editing *Old and New* four years after *Battleship Potemkin*, overtonal montage can be detected in the Odessa Steps sequence in the development of the editing along simultaneous metric, rhythmic, and tonal lines—the increase in editing tempo, the conflict between editing and movement within the frame, and the juxtapositions of light and shadow, intersecting lines, etc. Finally, there is an example of intellectual montage at the end of the sequence, after the Potemkin has responded to the massacre by firing on the Tsarist headquarters in Odessa. Three shots of marble lions—the first is sleeping, the second waking, and the third rising—seen in rapid succession give the impression of a single lion rising to its feet, a metaphor for the rebellion of the Russian masses against Tsarist oppression.

When *Battleship Potemkin* was first released, it drew mixed reactions in the Soviet Union: many people praised the film, while others denounced it, charging Eisenstein with ''formalism''—a preference for aesthetic form over ideological content. However, once they realized that foreign audiences loved the film, Soviet officials began to support it, and it soon became a popular and critical success, both inside and outside the Soviet Union. Today *Battleship Potemkin* ranks with *The Birth of a Nation* and *Citizen Kane* as one of the most influential films in cinema history.

—Clyde Kelly Dunagan

DIE BÜCHSE DER PANDORA

(Pandora's Box; Lulu)

Germany, 1928

Director: George Wilhelm Pabst

Production: Nero Film A. G. (Berlin); black and white, 35mm, silent; running time: 140 minutes originally, other versions are 131 minutes and 120 minutes; length: 3254 meters originally. Released 30 January 1929. Filmed 1928 in Berlin.

Producer: George C. Horsetzky; **scenario:** Ladislaus Vajda and Joseph R. Fliesner, from 2 plays, *Erdgeist* and *Die Büchse der Pandora*, by Frank Wedekind; **photography:** Günther Krampf; **editor:** Joseph R. Fliesler; **art direction:** Andrei Andreiev and Gottlieb Hesch; **music:** Curtis Ivan Salke; **costumes:** Gottlieb Hesch.

Cast: Louise Brooks (*Lulu*); Fritz Kortner (*Dr. Peter Schön*); Franz Lederer (*Alwa Schön, the Son*); Carl Götz (*Schigolch, Papa Brommer*); Alice Roberts (*Countess Anna Geschwitz*); Daisy d'Ora (*Marie de Zarnika*); Krafft Raschig (*Rodrigo Quast*); Michael von Newlinsky (*Marquis Casti-Piani*); Siegfried Arno (*Stage manager*); Gustav Diessl (*Jack the Ripper*).

Publications

Scripts:

Vajda, Ladislaus, and Joseph R. Fliesner, *Pandora's Box (Lulu): A Film by G.W. Pabst*, New York, 1971.

Books:

Kracauer, Siegfried, *From Caligari to Hitler: A Psychological History of the German Film*, New Jersey, 1947.
Weinberg, H., and L. Boehm, *Index to the Creative Work of Pabst*, New York, 1955.
Bauche, Freddy, *G.W. Pabst*, Lyons, 1965.
Amengual, Barthélémy, *Georg Wilhelm Pabst*, Paris, 1966.
Aubry, Yves, and Jacques Pétat, ''G. W. Pabst,'' in *Anthologie du cinéma 4*, Paris, 1968.
Manvell, Roger, and Heinrich Fraenkel, *The German Cinema*, New York, 1971.
Wollenberg, H. H., *50 Years of German Film*, London, 1972.
Atwell, Lee, *G. W. Pabst*, Boston, 1977.
Brooks, Louise, *Lulu in Hollywood*, New York, 1982.

Articles:

Close Up (London), October 1928, April 1929, and May 1930.
Variety (New York), 11 December 1929.
Bouissounousse, J., in *Revue du Cinéma* (Paris), 1 May 1930.
Chiaramonte, N., in *Scenario* (Rome), no. 8, 1932.
Potamkin, Harry Alan, ''Pabst and the Social Film,'' in *Hound and Horn* (New York), January-March 1933.
Viazzi, G., in *Cinema* (Rome), no. 170, 1943.
Pandolfi, V., in *Cinema* (Rome), no. 26, 1949.
Bachmann, Gideon, editor, ''G.W. Pabst,'' in *Cinemages* (New York), May 1955.
Card, James, ''Out of Pandora's Box,'' in *Image* (Rochester, New York), September 1956.
Brooks, Louise, in *Sight and Sound* (London), Summer 1965.
Luft, Herbert, ''G. W. Pabst,'' in *Films and Filming* (London), April 1967.
Rayns, Tony, in *Monthly Film Bulletin* (London), May 1974.
Serceau, D., in *Image et Son* (Paris), March 1980.
Veillon, O. R., in *Cinématographe* (Paris), March 1980.
Petat, J., in *Cinéma* (Paris), 1 April 1980.
''*Loulou* Issue'' of *L'Avant-Scène du Cinéma* (Paris), 1 December 1980.
Ramasse, F., ''Le sexe de Pandore,'' in *Positif* (Paris), July-August 1981.
Elsaesser, Thomas, ''Lulu and the Meter Man,'' in *Screen* (London), July-October 1983.
''Pabst Issue'' of *Skrien* (Amsterdam), September 1983.
Paris, B., ''Our Wild Miss Brooks,'' in *American Film*, November 1989.
''Pabst es Lulu,'' in *Filmvilag* (Budapest), no. 4, 1991.
''*Loulou*,'' in *Séquences* (Haute-Ville), May-June 1995.
Kermabon, Jacques, ''Sous les L de *L'ange bleu*,'' in *Vertigo* (Paris), January 1996.
Hastie, Amelie, ''Louise Brooks: Star Witness,'' in *Cinema Journal* (Austin), vol. 36, no. 3, Spring 1997.

* * *

Pandora's Box brings to mind familiar questions about film-as-art—whether the art arises from the director's work, from the performances, from the editor's decisions, or from a combination of all these elements. *Pandora's Box* might well be an unremarkable film without the magnificent presence of Louise Brooks, but then again, this presence was never evoked by any director other than G. W. Pabst. The source of the magic is elusive.

Nothing about the film is obvious, least of all Pabst's technique. Pabst is known for having promoted the practice of cutting on movement as a means of minimizing the jarring effect of editing. Rather than carry the practice to a lyrical extreme, Pabst exercised restraint and made only subtle use of the technique. Yet, in his hands, cutting on even the slightest movement can communicate significantly and almost subliminally. For example, after Schigolch gives Alwa cards to put up his sleeve during the gambling ship sequence, Schigolch begins to creep away screen-right. As the scene changes, his movement is continued by Rodrigo as he creeps in the same direction towards Lulu in another part of the ship. Above and behind Rodrigo is a sculpture of a crocodile mounted high on the wall. With great economy Pabst has identified to Schigolch and Rodrigo as slimy beasts of prey. At no time do the camera work and the editing call attention to themselves. Even when watching with the express purpose of detecting technical patterns, one must constantly pull back from the hypnotic fluidity of the film. Pabst weaves the perfect storyteller's spell with his technique.

The film's style is as elusive as its technique. *Pandora's Box* seems to be composed of several segments, each with its own distinct style. Lulu's relationship with Dr. Schön is psychologically realistic. Expressionistic elements darken and distort the London coda with

Die Büchse der Pandora

Jack the Ripper. A Hollywood-style show-business revue is accompanied by a backstage sequence with a delightful play of high spirits and frantic energies crossing and colliding. It is a self-consciously comical scene, especially in the antics of the beleaguered stage manager.

This same sequence illustrates another notable quality of the film—a closeness or an inwardness which confines without being oppressive. During the revue we see the action on stage from the wings and once from the front of the stage itself, but never from the audience's perspective. Space is claustrophobic in this film. The rare outdoor scenes are hemmed in by night and/or fog, as in the London Salvation Army scenes and the escape in a rowboat from the smoke-filled gambling ship. This sense of closeness is heightened by Pabst's avoidance of any but the most sparing and economical use of camera movement.

The camera is restricted in terms of mobility, but its perspective of Lulu is privileged. Rarely is she observed from another character's point of view. The camera is a separate party in the action, a witness to all aspects of Lulu's behavior. She is watched both as a participant and as an observer, giving the viewer a rich sense of personal knowledge of the character, a familiarity which far surpasses the surface acquaintanceships secured with the other characters.

The film was not received with any enthusiasm in its debut. Perhaps its proximity to the two Frank Wedekind plays on which it was based, *Erdgeist* and *Die Büchse der Pandora*, prevented viewers from approaching the film on its own terms. The character of Lulu in the plays was characterized through her speech, while Pabst's and Brook's Lulu was presented in a manner appropriate to the film medium, in a performance which today is recognized as one of the finest, most provocative in all of film.

—Barbara Salvage

BUDJENJE PACOVA

(The Awakening of the Rats; The Rats Wake Up)

Yugoslavia, 1967

Director: Zivojin Pavlovic

Production: Filmska Radna Zajednica; running time: 86 minutes.

Screenplay: Gordan Mihic and Ljubisa Kozomara; **photography:** Milorad Jaksic-Fandjo; **editor:** Olga Skrigin; **music:** Natko Devcica.

Cast: Slobodan Perovic; Dusica Zegarac; Severin Bijelic; Nikola Milic; Snezana Lukic; Pavle Vujisic.

Publications

Articles:

Variety (New York), 12 July 1967.
Combs, Richard, *Films and Filming* (London), September 1969.

* * *

That the 1960s were a time for re-evaluation in Yugoslavia was apparent on a national level as an even more decentralized constitution was put into effect in 1963. This coincided in the cinema with a spirit of exploration, evaluation and more liberal expression that became known as New Film and later the Black Film movement.

Born in 1933, Zivojin (Zika) Pavlovic, a graduate of the Academy of Applied Arts in Belgrade, was perhaps the bleakest proponent of the Black Film wave. The bleakness of Pavlovic's vision is, however, tempered with his non-sentimental sympathy for his protagonists, who remain humane in spite of adversity. His use of ironic black humour and his carefree construction of scenes allows the viewer to perceive a complicated inner reality beyond the surface realism. He has championed manipulation of the film medium as part of his message. Yet Pavlovic tells a straightforward story in the simplest of styles.

Pavlovic is equally respected as an author, filmmaker, and professor of film direction. In his fiction writing and ten feature films to date, he has unswervingly held to an austere and brutal naturalism captured in a lean prose style and an equally non-obtrusive camera and editing style. His territory is the margin of society and his protagonists are basically simple people, good people who are overcome and betrayed by their environments. In *The Awakening of the Rats* the lover of the film's luckless male protagonist, Bamberg, tells him "I've always wanted a decent life, but one slip and it all goes to hell," just before she takes all of his borrowed money and skips town. With a script by two of Yugoslavia's best- known screenwriters and journalists, Gordan Mihíc and Ljubisa Kozomara, the film is shot as many of his early films are in darkly shadowed black and white, appropriately matching Pavlovic's dim view of human relations. The set in *The Awakening of the Rats* examines the bleak slums of the city. An equivocal and realistic record of poverty in former Yugoslavia, the film is a classic.

—Mike Downey

BUILD MY GALLOWS HIGH

See **OUT OF THE PAST**

IL BUONO, IL BRUTTO, IL CATTIVO

(The Good, the Bad, and the Ugly)

Italy, 1966

Director: Sergio Leone

Production: P.E.A.; Technicolor, 35mm, Techniscope; running time: 180 minutes, English version is 162 minutes. Released 1966 in Italy; released 1968 in US. Filmed 1965–66 in Spain.

Producer: Alberto Grimaldi; **screenplay:** Luciano Vincenzoni and Sergio Leone, from a story by Age Scarpelli, Sergio Leone, and Luciano Vincenzoni; **titles designer:** Ardani; **photography:** Tonino

Il Buono, Il Brutto, Il Cattivo

Delli Colli; **editors:** Nino Baragli and Eugenio Alabiso; **art director:** Carlo Simi; **music:** Ennio Morricone; **special effects:** Eros Bacciucchi; **costume designer:** Carlo Simi.

Cast: Clint Eastwood (*Joe*); Eli Wallach (*Tuco*); Lee Van Cleef (*Setenza*); Aldo Giuffrè; Chelo Alonso; Mario Brega; Luigi Pistilli; Rada Rassimov; Enzo Petito; Claudio Scarchilli; Al Mulock; Livio Lorenzon; Antonio Casas; Sandro Scarchilli; Angelo Novi; Benito Stefanelli; Silvana Bach; Antonio Casas; Aldo Sambrell.

Publications

Books:

Staig, Laurence, and Tony Williams, *Italian Westerns*, London, 1975.
Parish, James Robert, and Michael R. Pitts, editors, *The Great Western Pictures*, Metuchen, New Jersey, 1976.
Fornari, Oreste de, *Sergio Leone*, Milan, 1977.
Frayling, Christopher, *Spaghetti Westerns: Cowboys and Europeans: from Karl May to Sergio Leone*, London, 1981.
Johnstone, Iain, *The Man with No Name*, London, 1981.
Zwijewsky, Boris, and Lee Pfeiffer, *The Films of Clint Eastwood*, Secaucus, New Jersey, 1982.
Cole, Gerald, and Peter Williams, *Clint Eastwood*, London, 1983.
Cebe, Gilles, *Sergio Leone*, Paris, 1984.
Fornari, Oreste de, *Tutti i Film di Sergio Leone*, Milan, 1984.
Guerif, François, *Clint Eastwood*, Paris, 1984; New York, 1986.
Cumbow, Robert C., *Once Upon a Time: The Films of Sergio Leone*, Metuchen, New Jersey, 1987.
Simsolo, Noël, *Conversations avec Sergio Leone*, Paris, 1987.
Claudio, Gianni di, *Directed by Sergio Leone*, Chieti, 1990.
Ortoli, Philipe, *Une Amérique de légendes*, Paris, 1994.

Articles:

Baldelli, Pio, in *Image et Son* (Paris), May 1967.
Time (New York), 4 August 1967.
Pierre, Sylvie, in *Cahiers du Cinéma* (Paris), April-May 1968.
Durgnat, Raymond, in *Films and Filming* (London), November 1968.
Badekerl, Klaus, in *Filmkritik* (Munich), October 1969.
Frayling, Christopher, ''Sergio Leone,'' in *Cinema* (London), August 1970.
Wallington, Mike, ''Italian Westerns—A Concordance,'' in *Cinema* (London), August 1970.
Graziani, Sandro, in *Bianco e Nero* (Rome), September-October 1970.
Ferrini, Franco, ''L'anti-Western e il caso Leone,'' in *Bianco e Nero* (Rome), September-October 1971.
Baudry, Pierre, ''Idéologie du western italien,'' in *Cahiers du Cinéma* (Paris), November 1971.
Kaminsky, Stuart M., in *Take One* (Montreal), January-February 1972.
Bodeen, DeWitt, ''Clint Eastwood,'' in *Focus on Film* (London), Spring 1972.
Jameson, Richard, ''Something To Do With Death,'' in *Film Comment* (New York), March-April 1973.
Simsolo, Noël, ''Notes sur les Westerns de Sergio Leone,'' in *Image et Son* (Paris), September 1973.
Chevassu, François, ''Ennio Morricone,'' in *Image et Son* (Paris), Spring-Summer 1974.
Beale, Lewis, ''From Spaghetti Cowboys to the Jewish Gangsters of New York,'' in *Los Angeles Times Calendar*, 7 November 1982.
Mininni, F., in *Castoro Cinema* (Florence), November-December 1988.
Ovrebo, O. A., ''Makkverket, mesterverket og kulten,'' in *Z Filmtidsskrift* (Oslo), no. 4, 1992.

* * *

The western for Sergio Leone is a genre in which he can explore his own sad, comic, grotesque, and surreal vision of life. Leone is no more interested in what could or did happen in the West than he is in any conception of surface reality in his films. *The Good, the Bad, and the Ugly* is a comic nightmare more in the tradition of Kafka than that of John Ford or Howard Hawks.

Although Clint Eastwood had, with Leone, established the anti-hero in *A Fistful of Dollars* and *For a Few Dollars More*, it was here, in their third and final film together, that they set out to destroy the more simplistic image so successfully that they contributed to the decline of the western in cinema. In the film, the Eastwood character (''the Good'' of the title), called ''Blondie'' quite ironically by Tuco (''the Ugly''), is both amused by and aloof from the grotesque world. The massive destruction of the film as exemplified by the Civil War (against which the quest for buried gold is played) demonstrates an evil beyond ''the Good'' man's capacity to control it. With this totally corrupt world around him, he is more interested in living according to a certain style, showing others that he knows how to face danger with amusement and without fear. In this sense, the Eastwood/Leone hero becomes an almost mystic survivor, a new ironic Christ offering a way to face life.

"The Bad" in the film (Lee Van Cleef's "Angel Eyes," itself an ironic appellation) is in many ways similar to "the Good." Neither is defined in his goodness or badness by the traditional morality. Between the two non-extremes stands, or rather scurries, Tuco, "the Ugly"—physically coarse, bearded, a bit dirty, but vibrant and alive in contrast to the other two cold characters. Tuco is hyper-human, and can show great affection as well as great hatred and violence. He has no cunning, is open and direct with an earthy simplicity and sense of humor. Good and Bad are false moral extremes. The ugly represents the human who acts out of animal immediacy without recourse to postures or guilt. Whenever Tuco resorts to poses (as a soldier, a friend) he suffers.

In the film, Leone's use of the extreme close-up is a major device for getting to character; plot is of minimal interest. What is important is the examination of these characters. The close-up is used as ironic balance and the pan for thematic emphasis. For example, the dizzying pan which follows Tuco around the graves near the end of the film indicates the frenzy of Tuco in the midst of death as he seeks the hidden gold.

In an interview Leone said that in "*The Good, the Bad, and the Ugly*, I demystified the adjectives. What do Good, Bad or Ugly mean? What does it mean when these characters are three killers thrown into the midst of a civil war? In that film, I was pursuing the theme that Chaplin so masterfully exposed in *Monsieur Verdoux.*"

The film is filled with a number of vivid and powerful visual moments: the opening sequence ending with Tuco in freeze-frame, chicken leg in hand, flying through a window; Angel Eyes' calm murder of the man (and his family) who hired him for the job; Tuco's confrontation with his priest brother; Tuco and Blondie's trek through the desert; the battle at the river; the graveyard search for gold; and Tuco's theft of a gun from a frightened gunsmith.

The feeling of unreality is central to the film and Leone's work in general. The film is a world of bizarre coincidence and horror. The apparent joy and even comedy in the destruction and battle scenes are often followed by some personal touch that underlies the real meaning of the horror which only moments before had been amusing. The dynamiting of the bridge between the Union and Confederate troops is presented as a touch of low comedy with Blondie pushing down Tuco's rear end before the moment of explosion. Yet this scene is preceded by the death of the sympathetic Union officer and followed immediately by an encounter with the dying young man to whom Blondie gives his poncho and his cigar, the two central marks of his minimal identity. The comedy and horror of meaninglessness are thus important in the film.

The Good, the Bad, and the Ugly is a series of contradictions. It is serious and comic, moral and amoral, concerned with the meaning of history while indifferent to the facts of history, unconcerned with reality while filled with moments of tangible character and objects. Like the triumvirate it establishes in the title, the film is not about right or wrong, good or bad, just or unjust. It is a comic vision not far removed from the literature of Kafka or Celine in which we walk on the visual boundary line of comic ugliness.

That the popular press found the film amusing but meaningless upon its release is but an expected footnote in the history of works of popular culture which were unrecognized by critics who thought that a violent, comic, and highly popular work could not possibly be worthy of serious attention.

—Stuart M. Kaminsky

BURNT BY THE SUN

See **OUTOMLIONNYE SOLNTSEM**

THE BUTCHER

See **LE BOUCHER**

BYE BYE BRASIL

(Bye Bye Brazil)

Brazil, 1979

Director: Carlos Diegues

Production: Produçoes Cinematográficas L.C. Barreto; Eastmancolor, 35mm; running time: 110 minutes. Released 18 February 1980 in Rio de Janeiro/São Paulo. Filmed in north, northeast, and central Brazil in 1978–79.

Producer: L. C. Barreto; **associate producers:** Walter Clark, Carlos Braga, Luciola Villela; **screenplay:** Carlos Diegues and Leopoldo Serran; **photography:** Lauro Escorel; **editor:** Mair Tavares; **art direction:** Anisio Medeiros; **sound:** Victor Raposeiro, Jean-Claude Laurex; **music:** Chico Buarque, Roberto Menescal, and Dominguinhos.

Cast: Betty Faria (*Salomé*); José Wilker (*Lorde Cigano*); Fábio Júnior (*Ciço*); Zaira Zambelli (*Dasdô*); Príncipe Nabor (*Andorinha*); Emanoel Cavalcanti (*The Mayor*); Carlos Kroeber (*The Truck Driver*); Jofre Soares (*The Old Projectionist*); Marieta Severo (*The Social Worker*).

Publications

Books:

Oroz, Silvia, *Carlos Diegues—Os Filmes Que Nao Filmei*, Rio de Janeiro, 1984.
Johnson, Randal, *Cinema Novo X 5—Masters of Contemporary Brasilian Film*, Texas, 1984.
Mitchell, Robert, in *Magill's Survey of Cinema—Foreign Language Films—Volume 1*, edited by Frank Magill, New Jersey, 1985.
Burton, Julianne, *Cinema and Social Change in Latin America—Conversations with Filmmakers*, Texas, 1986.

Articles:

Alencar, Miriam, *Jornal do Brasil* (Rio de Janeiro), 11 January 1979.
Lima, Antônio, *Jornal da Tarde* (São Paulo), 15 September 1979.
Variety (New York), 19 December 1979.
Portinari, Maribel, *O Globo* (Rio de Janeiro), 27 December 1979.
Falcone, Maria Carolina, *Tribuna da Imprensa* (Rio de Janeiro), 7 January 1980.
Fassoni, Orlando, *Folha de São Paulo* (São Paulo), 15 February 1980.
Pereira, Edmar, *Jornal da Tarde* (São Paulo), 16 February 1980.
Perdigao, Paulo, *Veja* (São Paulo), 20 February 1980.

Bye Bye Brasil

Fassoni, Orlando, *Folha de São Paulo* (São Paulo), 22 February 1980.
Ferreira, Jairo, *Folha de São Paulo* (São Paulo), 22 February 1980.
Filho, Rubens Ewald, *A tribuna* (Santos, São Paulo), 23 February 1980.
Diegues, Carlos, *Agora* (São José dos Campos, São Paulo), 8 March 1980.
Ferreira, Fernando, *O Globo* (Rio de Janeiro), 28 March 1980.
Leite, Ricardo Gomes, *Estado de Minas* (Mines Gerais), 10 June 1980.
Grelier, R., *Image et Son* (Paris), July-August 1980.
Neves, David, *Filme Cultura*, number 35/36, July/August/September, 1980.
Schiller, Beatriz, *Jornal do Brasil* (Rio de Janeiro), 30 September 1980.
Tournes, A., ''Exploration d'un continent,'' in *Jeune Cinéma* (Paris), September-October 1980.
Schiller, Beatriz, *Jornal do Brasil* (Rio de Janeiro), 14 October 1980.
Edelman, R., ''Carlos Diegues and Cinema Novo,'' in *Films in Review* (New York), December 1980.
Cluny, C. M., *Cinéma* (Paris), December 1980.
O Globo (Rio de Janeiro), 20 December 1980.
Stam, R., *Cineaste* (New York), Winter 1980/81.
Pierre, Sylvie, ''Des douleurs des uns et du bonheur des autres,'' in *Cahiers du Cinéma* (Paris), January 1981.
Pierre, Sylvie, ''A Propos de Bye Bye Brazil,'' *Cahiers du Cinéma* (Paris), January 1981.
Maia, Reinaldo da Costa, *Filme Cultura*, number 37, January/February/March, 1981.
Pouillade, J.-L., ''Terres en transes,'' in *Positif* (Paris), May 1981.
Rollins, P. C., ''Bye Bye Brasil: An Ambivalent Allegory about Third World Development,'' in *Film and History* (New Jersey), December 1982.

* * *

''*Bye Bye Brazil* is about a country which is just finishing and making way for another one which is just beginning. I can't say exactly what is finishing, nor what is beginning. I am merely recording this unique moment, this dividing line in the story of four people, who, like any of us, seek their place in the new order, and in life.'' Carlos Diegues, one of the founders of the Cinema Novo movement, used these words to define his eighth film, in which he remained true to one of his favourite themes: ''The search for freedom and the desire for greater happiness.'' This theme had already been exploited in his fine trilogy on historical Negro figures—*Ganga Zumba, Rei dos Palmares* (his first feature, made in 1963); *Xica da Silva* (1975), and *Quilombo* (1983).

In the case of *Bye Bye Brazil*, the principal character is Brazil itself, experiencing in 1980, an incipient democracy. The country is viewed through the eyes of a troupe of circus artists whose talent for survival is greater than their ability to attract audiences to their performances, held under a patched big top in small towns in the Brazilian hinterland. In a country where so much has disappeared, the people's anxious longings for bread and circuses remain intact, although audiences of the new Brazil now favour the circus provided by the electronic media.

Fifteen thousand kilometers of the North, Northeast, and Central Brazil were covered in the filming of *Bye Bye Brazil*, following the tracks of the Caravana Rolidei (a play on the word ''holiday''). The troupe is led by Lorde Cigano (Lord Gypsy), a loquacious and charismatic wise guy, played by José Wilker. His partner in bed and on stage is the sensuous Salomé, the Queen of the Rumba (Betty Faria), while Andorinha (little sparrow) is the Muscle King (Principe Nabor). The grandiose noms de guerre of the artists are in sharp contrast to the troupe's meagre accessories—a single truck—and with the poverty stamped on the faces of whatever spectators they attract to their performances.

The Rolidei Roadshow starts its progress in a tiny town in the Northeast, on the banks of the São Francisco river. The roguish Lorde Cigano promises the audience that he will fulfill the dream of every Brazilian: he will make it ''snow'' in the dry lands of the interior. And sure enough, ''snow'' flakes start to fall on the humble and ignorant audience, to the accompaniment of ''White Christmas,'' sung by Bing Crosby—a magical moment of filmmaking. A struggling musician, Ciço (Fábio Júnior) is enchanted by the magic of the troupe; he is sick of the river and longs to see the sea. Together with his pregnant wife Dasdô, he joins the Roadshow. Their destination is rich Altamira, deep in the Amazon rainforest, symbol of the easy money obtained from illegal logging and goldmining, sustained by near-slave labour.

In a path which never runs smooth, the troupe stops to see the sea—but the waters are polluted. They come across entire towns mesmerized by a single television set, proudly occupying the town's main square. ''In the old days, politicians used to promise bridges; now they promise a television set,'' grumbles Lorde Cigano, unable to muster an audience for his show. Dominated by the fish's skeletons—as the magician refers to the television antennas—*Bye Bye Brazil* reveals a country whose regional characteristics run the risk of disappearing as a result of the massification of conduct and expectation produced by television.

In Amazônia, amongst the survivors of a ''civilized'' Indian tribe, they meet an old Indian woman who listens to her transistor radio, which seems to be glued to her ear, adores Coca Cola, and dreams of flying in an aeroplane. In Brasília, a social worker extols the wonders of the city—a city whose planners forgot to build low-income housing, relegating the workers to the outskirts of the city. Rejected and left to fend for themselves in their hereditary misery, the people co-exist with portents of progress, symbolized by televisions and the jets which take labourers to work for foreign exploiters in the Amazon. To seek redemption and happiness becomes a lottery, with few winning tickets; nor is the straight and narrow necessarily the path to success. In this confrontation between the past and the present, old traditions are nostalgically laid to rest. No audiences queue for tickets to The Rolidei Roadshow, a remnant from the time when entertainment was live and itinerant. Likewise, an old man who made his living showing classic Brazilian films on a portable screen in the town squares no longer bothers to set up his equipment.

As the members of the troupe discover a Brazil in constant transformation, they also discover each other. The art of survival requires certain concessions; thus Lorde Cigano has no qualms about abetting the prostitution of Salomé when the money runs short. Ciço falls in love with Salomé, while Lorde Cigano is taken with Dasdô, and the context of sexual liberty combined with the idea of a country which was also in search of more freedom. The couples split up in Belém, to meet years later. Each lives their own version of fulfillment. Ciço and Dasdô perform in a dance hall on the outskirts of Brasília, in a more ''modern'' way. Lorde Cigano has made money through the illegal gold market and now sports a modern truck with neon lights with Frank Sinatra singing *Aquarela do Brasil* on the sound system and a team of chorus girls. As Lorde Cigano says at the beginning of the film, ''dreams are only offensive to those who don't dream.''

With one eye on the paradoxes which permeate Brazilian society and the other on reverie, Carlos Diegues produces a bittersweet X-ray of a country undergoing change. The fluent narrative, impregnated with farce, humour, sensuality, and music broaches the varied aspects of the human, social, and geographic condition of the country. The principal characters retain their own identities, despite the highly dissimilar contexts in which they find themselves; they interact spontaneously with the host of motley secondary characters they meet along the way. Regional differences are well illustrated by the varied sound track, and the beautiful photography of Lauro Escorel's photography captures the lushness of the vegetation as well as the barren inlands, and rich regional detail, gleaned from market, river, and roadside scenes.

The key to the success, in Brazil and overseas, of *Bye Bye Brazil* lies in the solidarity of the viewer with the picaresque characters and their quest for a better life. It is dedicated to the people of the 21st Century, and does not flinch from the reality of the present nor does it discard the dream: in the final scene, Lorde Cigano and Salomé take to the road again, and drive off into the sun.

—Susana Schild

CABARET

USA, 1972

Director: Bob Fosse

Production: Allied Artists Pictures, ABC Pictures; Technicolour; 35mm; running time: 123 minutes. Filmed on location in West Berlin and at Bavaria Atelier Gesellschaft, Munchen, West Germany.

Producer: Cy Feuer; **screenplay:** Jay Allen, based on the musical play by Joe Mastertoff, from the play by John van Druten, based on the original book by Christopher Isherwood; **photography:** Geoffrey Unsworth; **editor:** David Bretherton; **choreography:** Bob Fosse; **assistant directors:** Douglas Green, Wolfgang Glattes; **production design:** Rolf Zehetbauer; **art direction:** Hans-Jurgen Kiebach; **music:** John Kander; **lyrics:** Fred Ebb; **music supervisor:** Ralph Burns; **sound:** Robert Knudson, David Hildyard; **costumes:** Charlotte Fleming.

Cast: Liza Minnelli (*Sally Bowles*); Michael York (*Brian Roberts*); Joel Grey (*Master of Ceremonies*); Helmut Griem (*Maximillian von Heune*); Fritz Wepper (*Fritz Wendel*); Marisa Berenson (*Natalia Landauer*); Elizabeth Neumann-Viertel (*Fraulein Schneider*); Helen Vita (*Fraulein Kost*); Sigrid von Richtofen (*Fraulein Mayr*).

Awards: Oscars for Best Director, Best Actress (Minnelli), Best Supporting Actor (Grey), Best Cinematography, Best Song Score, Best Editing, Best Art/Set Decoration, and Best Sound, 1972.

Publications

Books:

Altman, Rick, *The American Film Musical*, Bloomington, Indiana, 1989.

Grubb, Kevin B., *Razzle Dazzle: The Life and Work of Bob Fosse*, New York, 1989.

Gottfried, Martin, *All His Jazz: The Life and Death of Bob Fosse*, New York, 1990.

Mizejewski, Linda, *Divine Decadence: Fascism, Female Spectacle, and the Makings of Sally Bowles*, Princeton, New Jersey, 1992.

Articles:

Variety (New York), 16 February 1972.

Marill, A. H., *Films in Review* (New York), March 1972.

Filmfacts (London), number 2, 1972.

Monthly Film Bulletin (London), June 1972.

Milne, T., *Sight and Sound* (London), Summer 1972.

Vallance, T., *Focus on Film* (London), Summer 1972.

Buckley, P., *Films and Filming* (London), August 1972.

Blades, Joe, ''The Evolution of Cabaret,'' Literature/Film Quarterly (Salisbury, Maryland), vol. 1, 1973.

Chion, M., ''La comédie musicale rêve au realisme,'' in *Cahiers du Cinéma* (Paris), September 1982.

Vecchiali, P., *Image et Son* (Paris), November 1972.

Serceau, M., ''L'archetype Lola: realisme et métaphore'' in *CinémAction* (Courbevoie), April 1984.

Mizejewski, L., *Journal of Film and Video* (Boston), Fall 1987.

Clark, R., ''Bending the Genre: The Stage and the Screen,'' in *Literature/Film Quarterly* (Salisbury, Maryland), January 1991.

Rodda, Arlene, ''*Cabaret*: Utilizing the Film Medium to Create a Unique Adaptation,'' in *Literature/Film Quarterly* (Salisbury, Maryland), vol. 22, no. 1, 1994.

Campbell, V., ''Michael York in *Cabaret*,'' in *Movieline* (Escondido, California), vol. 7, July 1996.

''*Cabaret* de Bob Fosse: Découpage plan à plan aprés montage et dialogues in-extenso,'' in *Avant-Scène Cinéma* (Paris), no. 464, July 1997.

* * *

Based on the Berlin short stories by Christopher Isherwood, the play *I Am a Camera*, and the Broadway production of the same name, *Cabaret* was shot in West Germany in the early 1970s. Centered primarily around the seedy Kit Kat Klub, the film ruthlessly depicts Berlin in the last days of the decadent Weimar Republic, and the terrifying rise of Nazism in 1930s Germany.

Fosse cleverly interweaves the action taking place on the stage of the club with the political and social action occurring in the streets. The musical numbers performed for the most part impeccably by Liza Minnelli as Sally Bowles, and her entourage, a group of sleazy female musicians and dancers, mirror real life, and are directed beautifully by the manipulative Master of Ceremonies (brilliantly performed by Joel Grey).

Brian Roberts (Michael York), an aspiring author and repressed homosexual, comes to Berlin to write and to teach English. He finds himself living in the bohemian boarding house inhabited by Bowles, and is introduced to the sexually liberating atmosphere of the Kit Kat Klub. While the Master of Ceremonies reflects that: ''... life is disappointing? Forget it! In here [the club] life is beautiful,'' the seediness and obvious vulgarity of the audience and performers reinforce that this is far from the truth. In another scene, a Nazi officer is booted out of the club by the manager; later we see the same man being brutally beaten by a group of young Nazi thugs.

Although Brian makes it clear to Sally that he is not at all interested in women sexually, the pair embark on an affair. The couple find their seemingly unreal existence complicated by the rich, mercurial Baron Maximilian von Heune (Helmut Griem) who tantalizes and tempts both of them. Sally is seduced by champagne,

Cabaret

wonderful clothes, and the opulence and decadence of the baron's life—Brian, who is at first sceptical, and also a little jealous of the baron's uninhibited behaviour, is literally seduced by the man, who disappears as quickly as he enters their life. Sally discovers she is pregnant and briefly deludes herself that she and Brian have a future together. Finally she realizes that what they have experienced is completely removed from her reality, and she has an abortion. Brian leaves Germany, and Sally continues her life as a cabaret singer in Berlin.

Against this storyline, two of Brian's language students fall in love. Feckless Fritz (Fritz Wepper), a fortune hunter, seizes his chance when he meets beautiful and rich Jewish heiress, Natalia (Marisa Berenson), only to fall genuinely in love with her. Natalia believes Fritz is a Christian and recognizing the political instability of Germany, and the brutality of the Nazis she refuses to have anything to do with him. Only when Fritz confesses that he is a Jew pretending to be a Christian, does Natalia agree to marry him.

The changing political atmosphere and growth of anti-semitism in Germany is illustrated by the victimization of Natalia in her family home by a group of young boys, who eventually slaughter her dog and leave it on her doorstep. Brian also witnesses the frightening strength of the Fascists when he visits a beer garden with the baron. Arriving in the baron's limousine, the two men leave Sally sleeping in the car. While the two men are drinking, a lone very pure voice begins to sing "Tomorrow Belongs to Me," slowly and with great feeling. The camera focuses on the young man's almost perfect Aryan features, tracking the increasing fervour with which he sings. Gradually, other members of the beer garden begin to stand up and join in, the camera closing in on the glazed expressions on their faces. Finally, when almost everyone is on their feet, the camera pans down and reveals the Nazi armband of the young man who instigated the singing. This technique was used in Nazi propaganda films. Brian and the baron leave to the sound of the group's harmony, climbing into their luxurious car and driving away—indicating that because the baron is rich and Sally and Brian are foreigners they will always have the option to leave this horrendous reality behind.

Cabaret is an incredibly innovative film. Now regarded as a classic, the film's use of colour, the garishness of the costumes, the smokiness of the club, the brightness and exaggeration of the make-up emphasize the decadence of the time. The musical score and choreography are well crafted and performed, and are deliberately kept to the stage of the Kit Kat Klub ("Tomorrow Belongs to Me" is the only exception to this). Minnelli performs her songs emotively and convincingly, if anything she is too good for the small, decadent atmosphere of the Klub.

On its release in 1972, *Cabaret* was received to great acclaim—winning eight Academy Awards, and three Golden Globe Awards.

—A. Pillai

THE CABINET OF DR. CALIGARI

See **DAS KABINETT DES DR. CALIGARI**

CABIRIA

Italy, 1914

Director: Giovanni Pastrone (under the name of Piero Fosco)

Production: Itala Film (Turin); black and white, 35mm, silent; running time: originally 210 minutes; length: originally 14,746 feet, later versions cut to 8345 feet. Released 18 April 1914, Turin. Filmed 1913 in Turin on specially constructed sets; exteriors shot in Tunisia, Sicily, and the Alps; cost: 1 million lire ($100,000).

Screenplay: Giovanni Pastrone and Gabriele D'Annunzio (though D'Annunzio's contributions to the script were reportedly minimal if not non-existent); **titles:** Gabriele D'Annunzio; **photography:** Segundo de Chomon, Giovanni de Chomon, Giovanni Tomatis, Augusto Batagliotti, and Natale Chiusano; **musical score originally accompanying film:** Ildebrando Pizzetti; **literary and dramatic advisor:** Gabriele D'Annunzio.

Cast: Italia Almirante Manzini (*Sophonisba*); Vitale de Stefano (*Massinissa*); Bartolomeo Pagano (*Maciste*); Lidia Quaranta (*Cabiria*); Umberto Mozzato (*Fulvio Axilla*); Enrico Gemelli (*Archimedes*); Alex Bernard (*Siface*); Raffaele di Napoli (*Bodastoret*); Luigi Chellini (*Scipione*); Ignazio Lupi (*Arbace*).

Publications

Books:

Jarratt, Vernon, *The Italian Cinema*, London, 1951.
O'Leary, Liam, *The Silent Cinema*, London, 1965.
Museo Nazionale del Cinema Torino, *Cabiria*, Turin, 1977.
Cook, David, *A History of the Narrative Film*, New York, 1981.
Finocchiaro-Chimirri, Giovanna, *D'Annunzio e il cinema "Cabiria,"* Catania, 1986.
Gethmann, Daniel, *Daten und Fahrten: Die Geschichte der Kamerafahrt, "Cabiria" und Gabriele d'Annunzios Bilderstrategie*, Munich, 1996.

Articles:

Bioscope (London), 30 April 1914.
Kine Monthly Film Record (London), June 1914.

Cabiria

Bianco e Nero (Rome), July-August 1952.
"*Cabiria* Issue" of *Bianco e Nero* (Rome), Summer 1975.
Cugier, A., "Discours de l'idéologie, idéologie du discours," in *Cahiers de la Cinémateque* (Perpignan), no. 26–27, 1979.
Classic Images (Indiana, Pennsylvania), July 1982.
Lane, J. F., "Cabiria: And Now Pizzetti's *Fire Symphony*," in *Sight and Sound* (London), Autumn 1983.
De Vincenti, G. "Il kolossal storico-romano nell'immaginario del primo Novecento," in *Bianco e Nero* (Rome), vol. 44, no. 1, January-March, 1988.
Cherchi Usai, Paolo, "Imitation? Paraphrase? Plagiat?" in *Cinémathèque* (Paris), no. 1, May 1992.
Sequences (Montreal), no. 177, March-April 1995.
Alovisio, Silvio, "El poder de la puesta en escena: Cabiria entre la atraccion y el relato," translated by Isabel Monzo-Gandia, in *Archivos de la Filmoteca*, (Valencia), vol. 20, June 1995.
Celli, Carlo J., "*Cabiria* as a D'Annunzian Document," in *Romance Languages Annual* (West Lafayette), vol. 9, 1997.

* * *

Standing out from all the stumbling efforts toward a new expression of cinema, Giovanni Pastrone's story of the Second Punic War, *Cabiria*, demands special attention. Compared to the other colossal Italian spectacles of its time, it had an integrity and sense of purpose. From the beginning it was regarded as something special, and its premiere at the Teatro Vittorio Emmanuele, Turin, on 18 April 1914 was a great occasion. The film's accompanying score by Ildebrando

Pizzetti, performed by an orchestra of 80 and a choir of 70, added to the excitement. Viewed today, the film has lost little of its epic poetry to the zeitgeist, though the acting performances may seem dated.

This story of a young girl lost amidst the clashes of two great nations retains its human interest as well as its power to amaze and astonish. The association of Gabriele d'Annunzio's name with the film reminds us of his dictum, ''The Cinema should give spectators fantastic visions, lyric catastrophes and marvels born of the most audacious imagination,'' though, in fact, d'Annunzio's actual contribution to this film was very small. He was paid a large sum for the use of his name in promotion. What does bear his mark are the highly poeticized inter-titles which are a part of the film's continuity, as they harmonize in style and feeling with the images. The film is consistently and stylishly in the grand manner. When the servant describes Massinissa to her mistress Sophonisba she says, ''He is like a wind from the desert bringing the scent of dust and lions and the message of Astarte.'' Few film heroes have had such a build-up.

Apart from the magnificence of the sets and the pulsating action of the story, the film is important for the patient research that produced such striking results and gave conviction to the historical setting. The great Temple of Moloch must have been one of the largest structures for a film up to that time. It and the Carthaginian palaces certainly influenced Griffith's Babylon in *Intolerance.* Infinite pains were taken with details which fitted effectively into the vast canvas.

Technically the film is also remarkable for its photography by the Spaniard Segundo de Chomon. The use of the moving camera has never been so effective in its almost imperceptible transitions. Every device of camera craft is used to produce a smoothly flowing narrative.

There is so much richness in this film: the great scenes of Hannibal crossing the Alps with his army and elephants; the eruption of Etna, and the destruction of the Roman fleet at Syracuse by means of the sun-reflectors of Archimedes. Most of these effects were achieved by multiple exposure. The acting is fairly theatrical, but the performances of Italia Almirante Manzini as Sophonisba and Vitale de Stefano as Massinissa are moving and impressive, while Bartolomeo Pagano, as Maciste the strong man, adds a new figure to the mythology of the movies. *Cabiria* therefore stands as a major filmic achievement at a time when the cinema was fighting for its place among the other arts.

—Liam O'Leary

LA CADUTA DEGLI DEI

(The Damned)

Italy-Germany, 1969

Director: Luchino Visconti

Production: Pegaso Film-Italnolggio (Italy), Eichberg Film-Praesidens (West Germany); Eastmancolor, 35mm; running time: 164 minutes, English version: 155 minutes. Released December 1969.

Producers: Alfredo Levy and Ever Haggiag; **executive producer:** Pietro Notarianni; **screenplay:** Nicola Badalucco, Enrico Medioli and Luchino Visconti; **photography:** Armando Nannuzzi and Pasquale De Santis; **editor:** Ruggero Mastroianni; **sound mixer:** Renato Cadueri; **recording director:** Vittorio Trentino; **art director:** Pasquale Romano; **set designer:** Enzo Del Prato; **music:** Maurice Jarre; **special effects:** Aldo Gasparri; **costume designers:** Piero Tosi and Vera Marzot.

Cast: Dirk Bogarde (*Friedrich Bruckmann*); Ingrid Thulin (*Baroness Sophie von Essenbeck*); Helmut Griem (*Aschenbach*); Helmut Berger (*Martin von Essenbeck*); Charlotte Rampling (*Elisabeth Thallman*); Florinda Bolkan (*Olga*); Reinhard Kolldehoff (*Baron Konstantin von Essenbeck*); Umberto Orsini (*Herbert Thallman*); Albrecht Schönhals (*Baron Joachim von Essenbeck*); Renaud Verley (*Guenther von Essenbeck*); Nora Rici (*Governess*); Irina Wanka (*Lisa Keller*); Valentina Ricci (*Thilde Thallman*); Karin Mittendorf (*Erika Thallman*); Peter Dane (*Steelworks employee*); Wolfgang Hillinger (*Yanek*); Bill Vanders (*Commissar*); Howard Nelson Rubien (*Rector*); Werner Hasselmann (*Gestapo official*); Mark Salvage (*Police inspector*); Karl Otto Alberty, John Frederick, Richard Beach (*Army officers*); Claus Höhne, Ernst Kühr (*SA officers*); Wolfgang Ehrlich (*SA soldier*); Esterina Carloni and Antonietta Fiorita (*Chmbermaids*); Jessica Dublin (*Nurse*).

Publications

Script:

Badalucco, Nicola, Enrico Medioli, and Luchino Visconti, *Caduta degli dei*, Capelli, 1969.

Books:

Ferrara, Guiseppe, *Visconti*, Paris, 2nd edition, 1970.
Dickinson, Thorold, *A Discovery of Cinema*, Toronto, 1971.
Baldelli, Pio, *Luchino Visconti*, Milan, 1973.
Nowell-Smith, Geoffrey, *Visconti*, London, 1973.
Bianchi, Pietro, *Maestri del cinema*, Milan, 1977.
Ferrero, Adelio, editor, *Visconti: il cinema*, Modena, 1977.
Tornabuoni, Lietta, editor, *Album Visconti*, Milan, 1978.
Stirling, Monica, *A Screen of Time: A Study of Luchino Visconti*, New York, 1979.
Servadio, Gaia, *Luchino Visconti*, Milan, 1980; translated as *Luchino Visconti: A Biography*, London, 1981, New York, 1983.
Rondolini, Gianni, *Luchino Visconti*, Turin, 1981.
Bencivenni, Alessandro, *Luchino Visconti*, Florence, 1982.
Tonetti, Claretta, *Luchino Visconti*, Boston, 1983.
Ishaghpour, Youssef, *Luchino Visconti: Le sens et l'image*, Paris, 1984.
Sanzio, Alain, and Paul-Louis Thirard, *Luchino Visconti: Cinéaste*, Paris, 1984.
De Guisti, Luciano, *I film di Luchino Visconti*, Rome, 1985.
Geitel, Klaus, and others, *Luchino Visconti*, 4th edition, Munich, 1985.

La caduta degli dei

Mancini, Elaine, *Luchino Visconti: A Guide to References and Resources*, Boston, 1986.
Villien, Bruno, *Visconti*, Paris, 1986.
Schifano, Laurence, *Luchino Visconti: Les Feux de la passion*, Paris, 1987.
Miccichè, Lino, *Luchino Visconti: un profilo critico*, Venice, 1996.
Bacon, Henry, *Visconti: Explorations of Beauty and Decay*, Cambridge and New York, 1998.

Articles:

Hofsess, John, in *Take One* (Montreal), May-June 1969.
Wilson, David, in *Sight and Sound* (London), Winter 1969–70.
Sarris, Andrew, in *Village Voice* (New York), 18 December 1969.
Film Society Review (New York), February 1970.
Cecil, Norman, in *Films in Review* (New York), February 1970.
Crowds, Gary, in *Film Society Review* (New York), February 1970.
''Visconti Issue'' of *Cinema* (Rome), April 1970.
Davies, Brenda, in *Films and Filming* (London), May 1970.
Delmar, Rosalind, ''La Caduta degli Dei: The Damned,'' in *Monthly Film Bulletin* (London), May 1970.
Tarratt, Margaret, ''*The Damned:* Visconti, Wagner, and the Reinvention of Reality,'' in *Screen* (London), Summer 1970.
Mellen, Joan, ''Fascism in the Contemporary Film,'' in *Film Quarterly* (Berkeley), Summer 1971.
Korte, Walter F., ''Marxism and Formalism in the Films of Luchino Visconti,'' in *Cinema Journal* (Evanston, Illinois), Fall 1971.
''Ingrid Thulin Comments on Visconti,'' in *Dialogue on Film* (Washington, D.C.), no. 3, 1972.
Marx, J., ''A tragedia alkonya,'' in *Filmkultura* (Budapest), November-December 1973.
Lyons, D., ''Visconti's Magnificent Obsessions,'' in *Film Comment* (New York), March-April 1979.
Badalucco, N., ''Film architettura in tre atti,'' in *Cinema Nuovo* (Rome), July-October 1989.
Badalucco, N., ''Come si scrive una sceneggiatura,'' in *Cinema & Cinema* (Bologna), September-December 1989.
Camera/Stylo (Paris), December 1989.
Ward, E., ''The Great Films: Three Views of the Holocaust,'' in *Classic Images* (Muscatine, Iowa), September 1991.

* * *

The Damned is the story of a bitter power struggle within a family of powerful German industrialists, the von Essenbecks, set against the early years of the Third Reich. When the film opens, on the day of the burning of the Reichstag, the head of the firm, Baron Joachim von Essenbeck, is due to retire. His eventual heir is his grandson, Martin, but he has two possible immediate inheritors: his brother, Baron Konstantin, vice-president of the firm and a member of the SA, and Herbert Thallman, a liberal anti-fascist and former vice-president. Behind the scenes, however, Baroness Sophie, Martin's mother and widow of Joachim's oldest son, and her lover, Friedrich Bruckmann, the company manager, form an alliance with Joachim's nephew Aschenbach, an SS member, to gain control of the firm. They shoot Joachim, but make it look as if Herbert was the culprit, and he is forced to flee. With the aid of Martin, Friedrich becomes president, but Konstantin discovers that Martin is a paedophile and blackmails him in an attempt to gain control himself. He, however, is eliminated by the SS during the Night of the Long Knives. Sophie and Friedrich are now in complete control, but refuse to accept that they are dependent for support on SS man Aschenbach. He therefore sets out to destroy them.

Like so many of Visconti's films, *The Damned* is the story of the decline and decomposition of a family, and as in *Senso* and *The Leopard* in particular, the fortunes of individuals are linked to wider developments at a climactic moment of history. There are also, as various critics have pointed out, significant parallels with Mann's *Buddenbrooks*, which showed the decline of a German business family through the increasing paralysis of will of its various members, amounting to a kind of death wish which seemed to echo the exhaustion of the whole Imperial regime. Both film and novel open with preparations for a family dinner party, and the title of the opening chapter of the latter, "The Decadence of a Family," could easily serve as the sub-title for *The Damned* as a whole. And if Mann's family mirrors the decline of the Imperial regime, Visconti's is a microcosm of Germany's industrial elite faced with the Nazi "Machtergreifung." The film has been called "the Krupp family history as Verdi might have envisaged it," but one could just as aptly substitute the names of Kirdorf, Thyssen, Schnitzler or any of the other industrialists who supported Hitler. More specifically, the murder of Joachim could be seen as representing the liquidation of the old, conservative ruling class by the new National Socialist order; the framing of Herbert for the murder parallels the framing of the Left for the Reichstag fire (especially as his surname, Thallman, irresistibly recalls the name of Thalmann, one of the Communist leaders arrested after the fire); and the killing of Konstantin by the SS (of which Aschenbach is a member) entwines the family history in the early power struggles amongst the Nazis, which culminated in the liquidation of the more populist, "radical" elements in the famous Night of the Long Knives. It is then only a matter of time before Martin and Aschenbach are in total control, representing the fusion of party, capital, and military under a leadership which is both supreme and also pathologically unstable.

However, there are problems with relying too heavily on such a reading, which does not do justice to the film as a whole. If we go too far down this road we soon encounter a criticism made by Rosalind Delmar, among others, namely that "fascism itself remains unexplored, becoming a backdrop to the action rather than an intrinsic part of it; its relation to the family struggle remains intellectual rather than expressive." Or as Claretta Tonetti has written: "The passions of the members of the family have a separate existence from the political shaping of the country. . . . Politics remain in the background of the shocking internal struggle among the Essenbecks. The Nazi takeover has little to do with the impact of the scene in which Martin rapes his own mother." Unless, that is, one subscribes to an ultra-Reichian view of Nazism, or wants to ally *The Damned* with that curious tendency in Italian cinema, from *Germany Year Zero* to *The Conformist*, which seems worryingly keen to link support for extreme Right-wing politics with deviation from the heterosexual norm. Nor can the victory of National Socialism in Germany be explained wholly in terms of internal feuds amongst its old and new ruling interests—that way leads us straight to the by now rather stale criticism that Visconti, the one time Marxist, became increasingly over-interested in the affairs of the aristocracy and the haute bourgeoisie.

Better, then, to regard *The Damned* as one of Visconti's family melodramas, replete with his usual operatic and mythic inflections. Much of the action takes place within the sumptuous "set" of the Essenbeck mansion, and scenes between the individual characters alternate with those involving a larger "chorus." The Night of the Long Knives sequence forms a massive and spectacular central set-piece. Again like Mann, Visconti makes use of various Wagnerian leitmotifs, such as fire and play-acting, which become a key underpinning of the symbolic structure of the film. The fact that the film also carries such strong echoes of *Macbeth*, Dante's *Inferno*, Wagner's *Gotterdammerung* (the original title of the film, in fact), and the aforementioned *Buddenbrooks*, suggests strongly that Visconti sees *The Damned* not simply as a representation of history, nor simply as the working out of an intense family conflict, but also as having mythological significance (in the same way that *Vaghe Stelle Dell'Orsa* is a working out of the Oresteia myth). According to Geoffrey Nowell-Smith, "over and above what is directly stated in the film itself, myths imply a whole set of further statements about the permanence of certain driving forces in history and the trans-historical ineluctability of the tragic mechanism." The problem here, however, according to Nowell-Smith, is that "unlike in *Vaghe Stelle*, the myth element is neither unitary nor fully integrated into the structure of the narrative." As a consequence, the mythical overtones not only add nothing to the story but actually rather work against the historical and personal-dramatic elements. As Nowell-Smith concludes, "in the last analysis the Essenbecks are only the Essenbecks, more interesting to the world, perhaps, than the average family, because of the power of their capital; but their fall (only to rise again, without a doubt, in 1945) is neither the end of civilization nor its restoration."

In short, *The Damned*, without being one of Visconti's finest films, is still a remarkable work, but it is one which, for its own sake, needs to be rescued from some of the more inflated claims—political, psycho-sexual, and mythological—which have sometimes been made for it, albeit with the best of intentions.

—Julian Petley

CAIRO STATION

See **BAB EL HADID**

CAMILLE

USA, 1936

Director: George Cukor

Production: Metro-Goldwyn-Mayer Pictures Corp.; black and white, 35mm; running time: 115 minutes, some sources state 108 minutes. Released 1936. Filmed in the MGM studios.

Producer: Irving G. Thalberg, some sources list David Lewis; **screenplay:** Zoe Akins, Frances Marion, and James Hilton, from the novel and play *La Dame aux camélias* by Alexandre Dumas (fils); **photography:** William Daniels and Karl Freund; **editor:** Margaret Booth; **music:** Herbert Stothart; **costume designer:** Adrian.

Cast: Greta Garbo (*Marguerite Gautier/Camille*); Robert Taylor (*Armand Duval*); Lionel Barrymore (*Monsieur Duval*); Henry Daniell (*Baron de Varville*); Lenore Ulric (*Olympe*); Jessie Ralph (*Nanine*); Laura Hope Crews (*Prudence Duvernoy*); Elizabeth Allan (*Nichette*); Russell Hardie (*Gustave*).

Awards: New York Film Critics' Award, Best Actress (Garbo), 1937.

Camille

Publications

Books:

Bainbridge, John, *Garbo*, New York, 1955.
Conway, Michael, and others, *The Films of Greta Garbo*, New York, 1963.
Langlois, Henri, and others, *Hommage à George Cukor*, Paris, 1963.
Durgnat, Raymond, and John Kobal, *Greta Garbo*, New York, 1965.
Carey, Gary, *Cukor and Company: The Films of George Cukor and His Collaborators*, New York, 1971.
Corliss, Richard, *Greta Garbo*, London, 1976.
Phillips, Gene D., *George Cukor*, Boston, 1982.
Bernadoni, James, *George Cukor: A Critical Study and Filmography*, Jefferson, North Carolina, 1985.
McGilligan, Patrick, *George Cukor, a Double Life: A Biography of the Gentleman Director*, New York, 1991.
Levy, Emanuel, *George Cukor, Master of Elegance: Hollywood's Legendary Director and His Stars*, New York, 1994.

Articles:

New York Times, 23 January 1937.
Variety, (New York), 27 January 1937.
''How Cukor Directs Garbo,'' in *Lion's Roar* (Hollywood), November 1941.
Huff, Theodore, ''The Career of Greta Garbo,'' in *Films in Review* (New York), December 1951.
Tynan, Kenneth, ''Garbo,'' in *Sight and Sound* (London), Spring 1954.
Prouse, Derek, in *Sight and Sound* (London), Summer 1955.
Tozzi, Romano, ''George Cukor,'' in *Films in Review* (New York), February 1958.
Brooks, Louise, ''Gish and Garbo—the Executive War on Stars,'' in *Sight and Sound* (London), Winter 1958–59.
Reid, John, ''So He Became a Lady's Man,'' in *Films and Filming* (London), August 1960.
Reid, John, ''Women and Still More Women,'' in *Films and Filming* (London), September 1960.
Guez, Gilbert, ''George Cukor: de Garbo a Marilyn il a instaure le Star-System,'' in *Cinémonde* (Paris), 1 January 1963.
Bowers, Ronald, ''Robert Taylor,'' in *Films in Review* (New York), January 1963.
''Cukor Issue'' of *Cahiers du Cinéma* (Paris), February 1964.
Gillett, John, and David Robinson, ''Conversation with George Cukor,'' in *Sight and Sound* (London), Autumn 1965.
Nordberg, Carl Eric, ''Greta Garbo's Secret,'' in *Film Comment* (New York), Summer 1970.
Phillips, Gene D., ''George Cukor: An Interview,'' in *Film Comment* (New York), Spring 1972.
Grisolia, M., ''George Cukor ou comment le desir vient aux femmes,'' in *Cinéma* (Paris), February 1974.
Powers, James, editor, ''Dialogue on Film: George Cukor,'' in *American Film* (Washington, D.C.), February 1978.
Bodeen, DeWitt, in *Magill's Survey of Cinema 1*, Englewood Cliffs, New Jersey, 1980.
Bodeen, DeWitt, ''George Cukor,'' in *Films in Review* (New York), November 1981.
Palni, D., ''Le Roman de Marguerite Gautier,'' in *Cinéma* (Paris), May 1981.

Radio Times (London), 7 September 1985.
Lippe, Richard, ''Cukor and Garbo,'' in *CineAction* (Toronto), no. 35, 1994.

* * *

Garbo's *Camille* not only contains her best screen performance, but hers remains the definitive Camille. No actress in her right mind would dare do a re-make, because she would be inviting comparisons with the Garbo performance, which would not be to her advantage. In fact, some years ago, when Tallulah Bankhead was asked, along with other stars of the stage, to name what she considered the greatest of all theatrical performances, she led off instantly with ''Garbo in *Camille*,'' and no one argued her choice.

The role of Camille has always been thought of as the supreme test for the dramatic actress, just as Hamlet has become ''a consummation devoutly wished'' for the actor. As a character, she not only runs the gamut of emotion, she explores every facet of all emotion. Cukor saw *Camille* again after a long period of time, and remarked of Garbo's performance: ''I was staggered [by] her lightness of touch the wantonness, the perversity of the way she played Camille, she played it as if she was the author of her own misery.'' Even Irving Thalberg, seeing her performance, remarked that she had never been so good. It was the scene where she sits in a box in the theatre, and Cukor demurred, ''Irving, how can you tell? She's just sitting there,'' to which Thalberg remarked, ''I know, but she's *unguarded.*'' The key to her entire performance of Marguerite Gautier, the Parisian cocotte known among her coterie as ''Camille,'' can be summed up in that one word—''unguarded,'' held safe against all time. It was in the finest tradition of thoughtful restraint in acting for the camera.

In the theatre, the story of Marguerite Gautier has been acted by all the greats, including Eleonora Duse and Sarah Bernhardt. On the screen, its various versions starred such actresses as Clara Kimball Young, Theda Bara, Nazimova, and Norma Talmadge. American actresses resisted it as a talking role. Garbo alone, with Cukor's faith in her, wanted to do the part, knowing that it could be her greatest, and it was. Henry James wrote of the story that it had been written by Alexandre Dumas *fils* when he was only 25, and added: ''The play has been blown about the world at a fearful rate, but has never lost its happy juvenility, a charm that nothing can vulgarize. It is all champagne and tears, fresh perversity, fresh credulity, fresh passion, fresh pain. It carries with it an April air!''

In 1855, an American actress, Matilda Heron, was in Paris, and saw *La Dame aux camélias* played there. She made her own acting version, called it *Camille, or The Fate of a Coquette*, and played it all over the English-speaking world. She married, and gave birth to a daughter known as Bijou Heron, who married Henry Miller. Their son, Gilbert Miller, was one of the best producers Broadway and London ever knew. The stories surrounding *Camille* onstage and in films are endless, and involve nearly every important player's name. Either as *Camille* or as *The Lady of the Camellias*, it has been played by all the best actresses from Tallulah Bankhead to Ethel Barrymore, from Eva Le Gallienne to Lillian Gish, so that what they created onstage was revealed in the performance Garbo brought to the screen.

With her the part became not just about a heroine who lives well but unwisely; she became a beautiful worldly creature fated to find real love with a young man, whom she deserts because she knows that in staying with him, she is ruining his life. The lovers are reunited at her deathbed, and the audience always dissolves in tears. Seeing Garbo's death scene, an admirer remarked, ''What a pity that Garbo had to die! We shan't see her again.'' After that last fadeout, it was not easy to believe that at least two of Garbo's best roles were still ahead, with her performances as Marie Waleska, Napoleon's love, in *Conquest*, and in the title role of Lubitsch's *Ninotchka. Camille*, however, remained her triumph for all time. It was her finest hour.

—DeWitt Bodeen

CAMPANADAS A MEDIONACHE

See **CHIMES AT MIDNIGHT**

CANAL

See **KANAL**

O CANGACEIRO

(The Bandit)

Brazil, 1953

Director: Victor Lima Barreto

Production: Cia. Cinematográfica Vera Cruz; black and white; running time: 105 minutes. Released in 1953. Filmed in São Paulo.

Producer: Cid Leite da Silva; **screenplay:** Victor Lima Barreto; **dialogues:** Rachel de Queiróz, based on original by Lima Barreto; **photography:** H. E. Fowle; **editor:** Oswald Hafenrichter; **art director, production design, and costume designer:** Caribé; **sound:** Erik Rasmussen and Ernst Hack; **music:** Gabriel Migliori; **songs:** Zé do Norte, and others of public domain.

Cast: Milton Ribeiro (*Captain Galdino Ferreira*); Alberto Ruschel (*Teodoro*): Marisa Prado (*Olívia*); Vanja Orico (*Maria Clodia*); Adoniran Barbosa; Ricardo Campos; Neuza Veras; Zé do Norte; Lima Barreto; Galileu Garcia; Nieta Junqueira; Pedro Visgo; João Batista Gioto; Manoel Pinto.

Awards: Named Best Adventure Film and special mention for sound track, Cannes Film Festival, 1953.

Publications

Books:

Viany, Alex, *Introdução ao Cinema Brasileiro*, Rio de Janeiro, 1959.
Rocha, Glauber, *Revisão Crìtica do Cinema Brasileiro*, Rio de Janeiro, 1963.
Galvào, Maria Rita, *Burguesia e Cinema: O Caso Vera Cruz*, Rio de Janeiro, 1981.

O Cangaceiro

Gomes, Paulo Emìlio Salles, *Crítica de Cinema no Suplemento Literário*, São Paulo, 1982.
Xavier, Ismail, *Sertão Mar—Glauber Rocha e a Estética da Fome*, São Paulo, 1983.
Ramos, Fernão, *História do Cinema Brasileiro*, São Paulo, 1987.
Salem, Helena, *90 Anos de Cinema—Uma Aventura Brasileira*, Rio de Janeiro, 1988.

Articles:

Diário de Notícias (Rio de Janeiro), 19 April 1953.
Variety (New York), 29 April 1954.
Films in Review (New York), January 1954.
Monthly Film Bulletin (London), August 1954.
Viotti, S., *Films and Filming* (London), October 1954.
Vianna, Antônio Moniz, *Cineclube Macunaima Edition* (Rio de Janeiro), number 48, 1974.
Nardo, Silvio Di, *O Globo* (Rio de Janeiro), 8 March 1976.
Matiussi, Paulo, *Jornal do Brasil* (Rio de Janeiro), 18 March 1977.
Soares, Dirceu, *Folha de São Paulo* (São Paulo), 20 April 1977.
O Globo (Rio de Janeiro), 25 January 1978.
Nascimento, Helio, *Jornal do Comércio* (Porto Alegre), 9 May 1978.
O Globo (Rio de Janeiro), 25 November 1982.

* * *

Exhibited at Cannes in 1953, Victor Lima Barreto's *O Cangaceiro* has a place of honour on the Brazilian film scene for a number of reasons. At Cannes, it received two accolades: the prize for best adventure film and a special mention for the sound track; this recognition turned *O Cangaceiro* into the first Brazilian film to be successful overseas. (André Brazin said of the film at Cannes, ''from its earliest scenes, the film sets an explosive tone of violence and strength.'') *O Cangaceiro* became a box-office record breaker at the time of its launch, its director became a national hero, and its theme tune, *Mulher Rendeira*, became the unofficial Brazilian anthem of the 1950s.

Apart from its repercussion both at home and abroad, *O Cangaceiro* has also the merit of giving rise to the *Cangaço* genre of film. *Cangaceiro* is the name given to a particular type of bandit who used to roam the Northeast of the country in the early 20th Century, spreading terror and sacking small villages. Common to most Cangaço films are the scenario of the rustic backlands of northeastern Brazil, the disadvantaged as characters and a confrontation with police forces as the principal story line. *O Cangaceiro* was also the first in a series of ''nordestern'' or ''northeastern'' films, which ran a parallel line with the North American Western films; it was followed in this vein by a number of noteworthy films, the best known of which was *Deus e O Diabo na Terra do Sol* (*Black God, White Devil*), by Glauber Rocha.

O Cangaceiro was Victor Lima Barreto's first feature, produced after his innumerable documentaries of the 1940s. (In 1951, his documentary *Santuário*, won a prize at Venice in the ''art film'' category.) As the author of the story and the screenplay, Lima Barreto dared, at a time when Brazilian films dealt largely with urban themes, to turn the public's eyes to the poorest region of the country. Here he created images that were incontestably Brazilian, either through the exploitation of regional physiognomies or through the typically barren northeastern scenery (albeit *O Cangaceiro* was filmed in the countryside of the state of São Paulo). Notwithstanding the social concerns inherent in the plot—the right to land and the misery of the population—Lima Barreto does not address these political matters, as would later the Cinema Novo movement, which also used the Northeast of the Brazil for many of its locations.

The principal characters in the film are Captain Galdino Ferreira (Milton Ribeiro), a cruel and boorish leader of a band of *cangaceiros*, and Teodoro (Alberto Ruschel), his right hand man, who is from a good background, but has joined the gang of outlaws after killing a man. Teodoro's convictions are challenged when Galdino kidnaps a comely teacher, Olívia (Marisa Prado), provoking the jealousy of Maria (Vanja Orico)—every band of ''cangaceiro'' outlaws was, by tradition, accompanied by a woman. Teodoro falls in love with the teacher, and decides to break away with her, living a sort of ''re-deemed by love'' syndrome. At the same time, the police stalk Galdino's gang whose leader is now blind with rage at the betrayal by his henchman.

During the chase, the former outlaw becomes the protector of the pretty teacher, with whom he enjoys a series of romantic love scenes. In a violent contest, Galdino's men thwart the efforts of the police to catch them. The next battle is between Galdino and Teodoro. Teodoro resists heroically, but eventually surrenders. True to his personal code of honour, Galdino allows Teodoro one last chance to survive: the band of outlaws will all shoot at Teodoro from a distance of 500 meters at the same time. If Teodoro is not hit, he is free to go. Teodoro accepts the deal, but he is shot and dies clutching a handful of ''his'' earth. Having said ''a woman and land are the same thing—you need both to be happy,'' he dies not for an ideal, but for love. (Lima Barreto had been informed by Columbia Pictures that the authorities responsible for law and order in Europe and the United States demanded that the bad guy die at the end. Thus, a scene in which Galdino dies was also included, though not shown in Brazil.)

At the time of *O Cangaceiro*'s launch, Lima Barreto stated: ''When, years ago, I dreamed of making films in Brazil, I resolved to make films that were totally national, wholeheartedly Brazilian. The title, the story, the location, the characters and their personalities—the photography, the music, the editing—all should breathe Brazil.'' The dramatic and narrative tints of the Western and the influence of the epic Mexican school at its most grandiloquent in no way compromise the Brazilianness of *O Cangaceiro*, whose studied nationalism is emphasized by the exceptional sound track, peppered with regional songs. While Captain Galdino is almost a caricature of cruelty, Teodoro and Olívia's portrayals are altogether more reasonable and civilized. Notwithstanding the social questions inherent in the cangaço genre, Lima Barreto's plot is centred on a love story, complete with impassioned dialogues, supported by scenes of great visual impact—such as the torture of one of the men, who is dragged behind a galloping horse—and chase scenes through the countryside.

The film opens with the band of outlaws marching to the right and finishes with the same band marching off, to the sound of *Mulher Rendeira*, in the opposite direction, in a composition which is clearly reminiscent of John Ford. *O Cangaceiro* also represents one of the great disillusions of the Brazilian film industry. It was one of the final productions of the Vera Cruz Studios, an enterprise put together by a group of São Paulo businessmen to create a sort of Brazilian Hollywood, producing world class films for the first time in Brazil. To this end, foreign technicians were hired from abroad, such as H. E. Fowle, the English director of photography, the German editor, Oswald Hafenrichter or the Italian musician, Gabriel Magliori, who were all involved in *O Cangaceiro*. The artistic direction was by the famous painter Caribé, while the dialogues were written by the distinguished Rachel de Queiróz.

The Brazilian and world distribution rights were sold to Columbia Pictures; thus, Vera Cruz did not benefit from the success of *O Cangaceiro*, which was sold to 23 countries. In fact, the shutters went up on Vera Cruz not long after *O Cangaceiro*'s production. For Lima Barreto—who appears in the film as the commander of a police force—the film represented not only the pinnacle but the beginning of the end of his career. After his second fictional feature, *A Primeira Missa* (1960), he went into a long and painful decline, only to die alone and in poverty in 1982 at the age of 76. His legacy was several untouched screenplays and *O Cangaceiro*, testimony to his defense of what he considered to be the unequivocally Brazilian cinema.

—Susana Schild

CARNIVAL IN FLANDERS

See **LA KERMESSE HEROIQUE**

LE CARROSSE D'OR

(The Golden Coach)

France-Italy, 1953

Director: Jean Renoir

Production: Panaria Films and Roche Productions; Technicolor, 35mm; running time: 100 minutes, some sources list 98 minutes;

Le carrosse d'or

length: 2800 meters. Released 27 February 1953, Paris. Filming began 4 February 1952 in Cinecittà studios.

Producers: Francesco Alliata and Ray Ventura; **screenplay:** Jean Renoir, Renzo Avenzo, Giulio Macchi, Jack Kirkland, and Ginette Doynel, from the work *Le Carrosse du Saint-Sacrement* by Prosper Mérimée; **photography:** Claude Renoir and Ronald Hill; **editors:** Mario Serandrei and David Hawkins; **sound:** Joseph de Bretagne and Ovidio del Grande; **recorded by:** Mario Ronchetti; **production design:** Mario Chiari with De Gianni and Polidori; **music:** Vivaldi, Archangelo Corelli, and Olivier Metra; **arranged by:** Gino Marinuzzi; **costumes:** Mario de Matteis.

Cast: Anna Magnani (*Camilla/Colombine*); Duncan Lamont (*Ferdinand, the Viceroy*); Odoardo Spadaro (*Don Antonio, the head of the troupe*); Riccardo Rioli (*Ramon*); Paul Campbell (*Felipe Aquirre*); Nada Fiorelli (*Isabelle*); Georges Higgins (*Martinez*); Dante (*Arlequin*); Rino (*Doctor Balanzon*); Gisela Mathews (*Irène Altamirano*); Lina Marengo (*Comedienne*); Ralph Truman (*Duke of Castro*); Elena Altieri (*Duchess of Castro*); Renato Chiantoni (*Captain Fracasse*); Giulio Tedeschi (*Balthazar, the barber*); Alfredo Kolner (*Florindo*); Alfredo Medini (*Pulcinella*); John Pasetti (*Captain of the Guard*); William Tubbs (*Innkeeper*); Cecil Matthews (*Baron*); Fredo Keeling (*Viscount*); Jean Debucourt (*Bishop of Carmol*); Raf de la Torre (*Procurer*); Medini Brothers (*4 children*); Juan Perez.

Publications

Books:

Davay, Paul, *Jean Renoir*, Brussels, 1957.

Cauliez, Armand-Jean, *Jean Renoir*, Paris, 1962.

Institut des Hautes Etudes Cinématographiques, *Analyses des films de Jean Renoir*, Paris, 1966.

Bennett, Susan, *Jean Renoir*, London, 1967.

Leprohon, Pierre, *Jean Renoir*, Paris 1967, New York, 1971.

Gregor, Ulrich, editor, *Film: Eine Dokumentation de Jean Renoir*, Frankfurt, 1970.

Cuenca, Carlos, *Humanidad de Jean Renoir*, Vallodolid, 1971.

Braudy, Leo, *Jean Renoir: The World of His Films*, New York, 1972.

Bazin, André, *Jean Renoir*, edited by François Truffaut, Paris, 1973.

Durgnat, Raymond, *Jean Renoir*, Berkeley, 1974.
Beylie, Claude, *Jean Renoir: Le Spectacle, la Vie*, Paris, 1975.
Renoir, Jean, *Essays, Conversations, Reviews*, edited by Penelope Gilliatt, New York, 1975.
Faulkner, Christopher, *Jean Renoir: A Guide to References and Resources*, Boston, 1979.
Sesonske, Alexander, *Jean Renoir: The French Films 1924–1939*, Cambridge, Massachusetts, 1980.
Gauteur, Claude, editor, *Jean Renoir: Oeuvres de cinéma inédites*, Paris, 1981.
McBride, Joseph, editor, *Filmmakers on Filmmaking 2*, Los Angeles, 1983.
Renoir, Jean, *Lettres d'Amérique*, edited by Dido Renoir and Alexander Sesonske, Paris, 1984.
Serceau, Daniel, *Jean Renoir*, Paris, 1985.
Bertin, Celia, *Jean Renoir*, Paris, 1986.
Faulkner, Christopher, *The Social Cinema of Jean Renoir*, Princeton, New Jersey, 1986.
Vincendeau, Ginette, and Keith Reader, *La Vie est à Nous: French Cinema of the Popular Front*, London, 1986.
Viry-Babel, Roger, *Jean Renoir: Le Jeu et la règle*, Paris, 1986.
Braudy, Leo, *Jean Renoir: The World of His Films*, New York, 1989.
Renoir, Jean, *Renoir on Renoir*, New York, 1990.
Renoir, Jean, *My Life & My Films*, New York, 1991.
Bergan, Ronald, *Jean Renoir: Projections of Paradise*, New York, 1995.
Renoir, Jean, *Letters: Jean Renoir*, New York, 1995.
Renoir, Jean, *An Interview: Jean Renoir*, with Nicholas Frangakis, Los Angeles, 1998.

Articles:

''Renoir Issue'' of *Cahiers du Cinéma* (Paris), January 1952.
Baroncelli, Jean de, ''Commedia all'improviso,'' in *Le Monde* (Paris), 4 March 1953.
Renoir, Jean, ''Je n'ai pas tourné mon film au Pérou,'' in *Radio-Cinéma* (Paris), 15 March 1953.
Sadoul, Georges, in *Lettres Françaises* (Paris), 5 March 1953.
''Renoir Issue'' of *Cahiers du Cinéma* (Paris), Christmas 1957.
Sadoul, Georges, ''The Renaissance of French Cinema—Feyder, Renoir, Duvivier, Carné,'' in *Film: An Anthology*, edited by Daniel Talbot, New York, 1959.
Belanger, Jean, ''Why Renoir Favors Multiple Camera, Long Sustained Take Technique,'' in *American Cinematographer* (Los Angeles), March 1960.
Dyer, Peter John, ''Renoir and Realism,'' in *Sight and Sound* (London), Summer 1960.
Whitehall, Richard, in *Films and Filming* (London), June-July 1960.
Whitehall, Richard, ''Gallery of Great Artists: Anna Magnani,'' in *Films and Filming* (London), July 1961.
Petrie, G., in *Film Comment* (New York), May-June 1974.
Lindberg, I., ''Smukke Marie,'' in *Kosmorama* (Copenhagen), October 1980.
Strebel, Elizabeth Grottle, ''Jean Renoir and the Popular Front,'' in *Feature Films as History*, edited by K. R. M. Short, London, 1981.
Carbonnier, A., in *Cinéma* (Paris), January 1985.
Pellizzari, L., in *Cineforum* (Bergamo, Italy), September 1992.
Chase, D., ''Anna Magnani: Miracle Worker,'' in *Film Comment* (New York), November-December 1993.
Téchiné, André, in *Cahiers du Cinéma* (Paris), no. 482, July-August 1994.
Bagh, Peter von, in *Filmihullu* (Helsinki), no. 6, 1994.

* * *

Jean Renoir regarded *Le Carrosse d'or* as a mere *jeu d'esprit*, but in fact the film, while one of Renoir's lighter efforts, has been greatly underrated. Its *commedia dell'arte*-inspired picturesqueness encompasses one of Renoir's lifelong themes—the disaffinity between illusion and reality, life and theatre, what people really are versus the roles they play. Most important to the creative sensibility of Renoir the artist, the film concerns the artist's duty to give, not take; by doing so he experiences his greatest power and true humanity.

The film is based on Prosper Mérimée's one-act play, *Le Carrosse du Saint-Sacrement* which derived from a real-life Peruvian incident. Mérimée's play was also the inspiration for an episode in Thornton Wilder's *The Bridge of San Luis Rey*. On the surface, *Le Carrosse d'or* is a simple story of love, but Renoir gives it a Pirandellian twist with its confusion of identities while giving new meaning to Shakespeare's phrase, ''All the world's a stage.'' The plot centers around Camilla (Anna Magnani), the Columbine of a troupe of travelling theatre players in 18th century Peru, and her three loves: the Peruvian viceroy, a matador, and a young Spanish nobleman/soldier. The viceroy has just incurred the wrath and envy of his court and the church council by importing a golden coach from Europe. As Renoir stated, ''In Mérimée's play, La Périchole is an actress, and in my movie, Camilla is an actress. In the play and in the film the coach stands for worldly vanity, and in both works the conclusion is precipitated by the bishop.'' As was his practice, Renoir used his scripts as a starting point, then wove the plot around his own special view of life and human nature.

Here Renoir's point was to present a serio-comic masque, referring to the game of appearances, as a true reflection of human behavior. In a play within a play within a film, Camilla plays at love. She becomes the center of attention when the viceroy presents the coach to her as a gift, an act he hopes will dissipate the jealousies of his court. Camilla wears a variety of faces as she wavers among her three romantic choices: she can opt for the life of luxury with the viceroy; she can choose a simpler life among the Peruvian Indians with the faithful soldier; or she can elect a volatile relationship with the adored and fiery matador. But the *theatre* is her real life, her real love, and she astonishes all three lovers by presenting the coach to the Bishop of Lima so it can be used to carry the last sacraments to the dying. Renouncing desire, she stands alone at center stage as the curtain falls. When asked if she misses her three lovers, she replies, wryly, ''Just a little.''

Le Carrosse d'or is the first of Renoir's three theatre films of the 1950s—the others being *French Cancan* and *Elena et les hommes*. In each he fills the stage/screen with a spectacle of action, sets, and costumes, with a childlike glee at his powers of manipulation. In keeping with the *commedia dell'arte* flavor, he chose Vivaldi's music for its lightness of spirit, making the music an integral part of the film.

Renoir drew forth the finest performance of Anna Magnani's career with this picture and called her ''the greatest actress I have ever worked with.'' Her Camilla is a brilliant tour de force. *Le Carrosse d'or* is a charming film, and while minor Renoir, it is a testament to his warmth, good humor, and sense of whimsy.

—Ronald Bowers

CASABLANCA

USA, 1942

Director: Michael Curtiz

Production: Warner Bros. Pictures, Inc.; black and white, 35mm; running time: 102 minutes. Released November 1942. Filmed at Warner Bros. studios.

Producer: Hal B. Wallis; **screenplay:** Julius J. and Philip G. Epstein and Howard Koch, contributions by Aeneas Mackenzie and Hal Wallis among others, from an unpublished play *Everybody Comes to Rick's* by Murray Burnett and Joan Alison; **photography:** Arthur Edeson; **editor:** Owen Marks; **sound:** Francis J. Scheid; **production design:** Carl Jules Weyl; **set decoration:** George James Hopkins; **music:** Max Steiner; **songs:** Herman Hupfeld and M. K. Jerome; **special effects:** Laurence Butler and Willard Van Enger; **costumes:** Orry-Kelly (gowns); **technical advisor:** Robert Alsner; **opening montage:** Don Siegel.

Cast: Humphrey Bogart (*Rick*); Ingrid Bergman (*Ilsa Lund*); Paul Henreid (*Victor Laszlo*); Claude Rains (*Captain Louis Renault*); Conrad Veidt (*Major Strasser*); Sydney Greenstreet (*Senor Ferrari*); Peter Lorre (*Ugarte*); S. Z. Sakall (*Carl, a Waiter*); Madeleine LeBeau (*Yvonne*); Dooley Wilson (*Sam*); Joy Page (*Annina Brandel*); John Qualen (*Berger*); Leonid Kinsky (*Sascha, a Bartender*); Helmut Dantine (*Jan*); Curt Bois (*Pickpocket*); Marcel Dalio (*Croupier*); Corinna Mura (*Singer*); Ludwig Stössel (*Mr. Leuchtag*); Ilka Gruning (*Mrs. Leuchtag*); Charles La Torre (*Tonelli, the Italian officer*); Frank Puglia (*Arab vendor*); Dan Seymour (*Abdul*); Lou Marcelle (*Narrator*); Martin Garralaga (*Headwaiter*); Olaf Hytten (*Prosperous man*); Monte Blue (*American*); Paul Pracasi (*Native*); Albert Morin (*French offcer*); Creighton Hale (*Customer*); Henry Rowland (*German officer*); Richard Ryen (*Heinz*); Norma Varden (*Englishwoman*); Torben Meyer (*Banker*); Oliver Blake (*Blue Parrot waiter*); Gregory Gay (*German banker*); William Edmunds (*Contact*); George Meeker (*Friend*); George Dee (*Casselle*); Leo Mostovoy (*Fydor*); Leon Belasco (*Dealer*).

Awards: Oscars for Best Film, Best Director, and Best Screenplay, 1943.

Publications

Scripts:

Epstein, Julius J., Philip G. Epstein, and Howard Koch, *Casablanca: Script and Legend*, edited by Koch, New York, 1973; also in *Michael Curtiz's ''Casablanca,''* edited by Richard Anobile, New York 1975.

Books:

McCarty, Clifford, *Bogey: The Films of Humphrey Bogart*, New York, 1965.
Michael, Paul, *Humphrey Bogart: The Man and His Films*, Indianapolis, 1965.
Warner, Jack, *My First 100 Years in Hollywood*, New York, 1965.
McBride, Joseph, editor, *A Collection of Film Criticism*, Madison, Wisconsin, 1968.
Quirk, Lawrence J., *The Films of Ingrid Bergman*, New York, 1970.
Barbour, Alan G., *Humphrey Bogart*, New York, 1973.
Brown, Curtis F., *Ingrid Bergman*, New York, 1973.
Canham, Kingsley, *Michael Curtiz, Raoul Walsh, Henry Hathaway*, London, 1973.
Parish, James Robert, and Michael R. Pitts, editors, *The Great Spy Pictures*, Metuchen, New Jersey, 1974.
Baker, M. Joyce, *Images of Women in Film: The War Years 1941–45*, Ann Arbor, Michigan, 1980.
Francisco, Charles, *You Must Remember This: The Filming of ''Casablanca,''* Englewood Cliffs, New Jersey, 1980.
Pettigrew, Terence, *Bogart: A Definitive Study of His Film Career*, London, 1981.
Rosenzweig, Sidney, *Casablanca and Other Major Films of Michael Curtiz*, Ann Arbor, Michigan, 1982.
Taylor, John Russell, *Ingrid Bergman*, London, 1983.
Ray, Robert B., *A Certain Tendency of the Hollywood Cinema 1930–1980*, Princeton, New Jersey, 1985.
Winkler, Willi, *Humphrey Bogart und Hollywoods Schwarze Serie*, Munich, 1985.
Eco, Umberto, *Faith in Fakes*, London, 1986.
Kinnard, Roy, and R.J. Vitone, *The American Films of Michael Curtiz*, Ann Arbor, Michigan, 1986.
Leamer, Laurence, *As Time Goes By: The Life of Ingrid Bergman*, New York, 1986.
Fuchs, Wolfgang J., *Humphrey Bogart: Cult-Star: A Documentation*, Berlin, 1987.
Jarvie, Ian, *Philosophy of the Film: Epistemology, Ontology, Aesthetics*, New York, London, 1987.
Harmetz, Aljean, *Round Up the Usual Suspects: The Making of Casablanca—Bogart, Bergman, and World War Two*, New York, 1992.
Lebo, Harlan, *Casablanca: Behind the Scenes*, New York, 1992.
McArthur, Colin, *The Casablanca File*, London, 1992.
Miller, Frank, *Casablanca: As Time Goes By, 50th Anniversary Commemorative*, Atlanta, 1992.
Siegel, Jeff, *The Casablanca Companion: The Movie and More*, Dallas, 1992.
Robertson, James C., *The Casablanca Man: The Cinema of Michael Curtiz*, London, 1993.
Osborne, Richard E., *The Casablanca Companion: The Movie Classic and Its Place in History*, Indianapolis, 1997.

Articles:

New York Times, 27 November 1942.
Variety (New York), 2 December 1942.
The Times (London), 13 January 1943.
Cooke, Alistair, ''Epitaph for a Tough Guy,'' in *Atlantic Monthly* (Boston), May 1957.
Luft, Herbert, ''Peter Lorre,'' in *Films in Review* (New York), May 1960.
Sarris, Andrew, ''Likable But Elusive,'' in *Film Culture* (New York), Spring 1963.
Stein, Jeanne, ''Claude Rains,'' in *Films in Review* (New York), November 1963.
Dienstfrey, Harris, in *Film Culture* (New York), Fall 1964.

Casablanca

Nolan, Jack Edmund, ''Michael Curtiz,'' in *Films in Review* (New York), September 1970.

Sarris, Andrew, in *Village Voice* (New York), 8 January 1970.

Kinskey, Leonid, ''It Lingers Deliciously in Memory as Time Goes By,'' in *Movie Digest*, September 1972.

Vernhes, M., in *Cinéma* (Paris), March 1973.

Day, B., ''The Cult Movies: *Casablanca*,'' in *Films and Filming* (London), August 1974.

''*Casablanca* Revisited: 3 Comments,'' in *American Film* (Washington, D.C.), October 1976.

Rubinstein, L., in *Cineaste* (New York), Summer 1977.

McVay, D., in *Focus on Film* (London), 30, 1978.

Greenberg, J., ''Writing for the Movies: Casey Robinson,'' in *Focus on Film* (London), April 1979.

Hanson, Stephen L., in *Magill's Survey of Cinema 2*, Englewood Cliffs, New Jersey, 1981.

Ross, C., ''The Great Script Tease,'' in *Film Comment* (New York), November-December 1982.

Sigal, Clancy, in *Listener* (London), 12 July 1984.

Eco, Umberto, ''*Casablanca:* Cult Movie and Intertextual Collage,'' in *Substance* (Madison, Wisconsin), vol. 14, no. 2, 1985.

Altman, R., ''Dickens, Griffith, and Film Theory Today,'' in *South Atlantic Quarterly* (Durham, North Carolina), no. 2, 1989.

Parshall, P. F., ''East Meets West: *Casablanca* vs. *The Seven Samurai*,'' in *Literature/Film Quarterly* (Salisbury, Maryland), no. 4, 1989.

Jorholt, E., ''Spil den igen og igen og igen, Sam!'' in *Kosmorama* (Denmark), Fall 1989.

Wilson, Robert F., Jr., ''Romantic Propaganda: A Note on *Casablanca*'s Prefigured Ending,'' in *Film and History*, vol. 19, no. 4, December 1989.

Gabbard, K., and G. O. Gabbard, ''Play it Again,'' in *Journal of Popular Film and Television* (Washington, D.C.), no. 1, 1990.

Davis, J. H., ''Still the Same Old Story: The Refusal of Time to Go By in *Casablanca*,'' in *Literature/Film Quarterly* (Salisbury, Maryland), no. 2, 1990.

Deutelbaum, M., ''The Visual Design Program of *Casablanca*,'' in *Post Script* (Commerce, Texas), no. 3, 1990.

Helman, A., ''Dekonstruuje *Casablanke*,'' in *Kino* (Warsaw), March 1990.

Case, Brian, ''As Time Goes By,'' in *Time Out* (London), 1 July 1992.

Corliss, R., "Still Talking," in *Film Comment* (New York), November-December 1992.
Norman, Barry, in *Radio Times* (London), 12 August 1995.
Stackpole, J., "A Converted Classic," in *Audience* (Simi Valley, California), no. 188, April/May 1996.
Télérama (Paris), 6 November 1996.
Boon, Kevin A., "Scripting Gender: Writing Difference," in *Creative Screenwriting* (Washington, D.C.), Spring 1997.
Larson, R.D., in *Soundtrack!* (Mechelen), December 1997.

* * *

"I have discovered the secret of successful filmmaking," says Claude Chabrol sarcastically, "Timing!" *Casablanca* belongs in the vanguard of films created by the era they so flawlessly reflect. Assured and expert, it is not in either substance or style superior to its director Michael Curtiz's *Mildred Pierce* or *Young Man With a Horn.* Bogart, Bergman, Rains, and Henreid all gave better performances; of those by Greenstreet, Lorre, Kinsky, and Sakall, one can only remark that they seldom gave any others. Producer Robert Lord categorized the story on the first reading as "a very obvious imitation of *Grand Hotel*;" Jerry Wald saw parallels with *Algiers.* Both were right.

Hal Wallis wanted George Raft to star and William Wyler to direct. Both declined. (There is some evidence he also planned it as a vehicle for the *Kings Row* team of Ronald Reagan and Ann Sheridan, with Dennis Morgan in the Henreid role. And both Lena Horne and Ella Fitzgerald had a chance at the singing part taken eventually by Dooley Wilson.) Vincent Sherman and William Keighley likewise refused the project before it went to Curtiz.

Casablanca might have joined *Sahara* and *Istanbul* on the shelf of back-lot travelogues had an Allied landing and summit conference in the north African city not coincided with the film's November 1942 release. Topicality fed its fame. Curtiz, accepting an unexpected Academy Award in March 1944, betrayed his surprise. "So many times I have a speech ready, but no dice. Always a bridesmaid, never a mother. Now I win, I have no speech." The broken English was entirely appropriate to a film where only Bogart and Dooley Wilson were of American origin.

Beyond its timing, *Casablanca* does show the Warners' machine and Curtiz's talent at their tabloid best. The whirling globe of Don Siegel's opening montage and the portentous *March of Time* narration quickly define the city as a vision of the wartime world in microcosm. The collaborative screenplay, signed by Julius and Philip Epstein, and Howard Koch, but contributed to by, among others, Aeneas Mackenzie and Wallis himself (who came up with Bogart's final line), draws the characters in broad terms, each a compendium of national characteristics.

Bogart, chain-smoking, hard-drinking, arrogant, is the classic turned-off Hemingway American. Henreid, white-suited and courteous, is a dissident more akin to a society physician, untainted by either Communism or bad tailoring. The Scandinavian virgin, untouchable in pale linen and communicating mainly through a range of schoolgirl grins, Bergman's Ilsa succumbs to passion only when she pulls a gun on the unconcerned Rick, triggering not the weapon but a revival of their old affection.

The remaining regulars of Rick's Cafe Americain, mostly accented foreigners, dissipate their energies in Balkan bickering, petty crime, and, in the case of Claude Rains's self-satisfied Vichy policeman, some improbable lechery dictated by his role as the token, naughty Frenchman, all moues and raised eyebrows. Cliché characterization leads to a range of dubious acts, notably the fawning Peter Lorre, an arch intriguer and murderer, entrusting his treasured "letters of transit" to Bogart's moralizing ex-gunrunner, a gesture exceeded in improbability only by Bogart's acceptance of them.

As with most formula films, technique redeems *Casablanca.* Arthur Edeson's camera cranes sinuously through Carl Jules Weyl's Omar Khayyam fantasy of a set. Typical of Curtiz's work is the razor-sharp "cutting on action" by Owen Marks, a legacy of the former's Hungarian and Austrian training. He forces the pace relentlessly, even to dissolving the back projection plate in mid-scene during the Parisian flash-back, an audacious piece of visual shorthand.

Narrative economy distinguishes the film. As its original material (an unproduced play by Murray Burnett and Joan Alison) suggests, *Casablanca* in structure is a one-set play; many events take place off-stage, from the murder of the couriers to the resistance meeting attended by Henreid and Sakall that is broken up by the police. *Everybody Comes to Rick's* is an apt title, since it's the ebb and flow of people through the cafe's doors that gives the story its sole semblance of vitality. As an entity, *Casablanca* lives on the artificial respiration of ceaseless greetings, introductions, and farewells. Even the Parisian flashback does little to elucidate the characters of Rick and Ilsa. They remain at the end of the film little more than disagreeable maitre d' and troublesome patron.

In 1982, the journalist Chuck Ross circulated *Casablanca*'s script as a new work to 217 American literary agents. Of those who acknowledged reading it (most returned it unread) 32 recognized the original, while 38 did not. Clearly this betrays the profound ignorance of the agenting community. But also implicit in their ignorance is *Casablanca*'s unsure standing as a work of art. Unremarkable in 1942, it rose to fame through an accident of timing. No better written or constructed today, it exists primarily as a cultural artifact, a monument of popular culture. Woody Allen was right in his *Play It Again, Sam* to show the film as one whose morality, characters, and dialogue can be adapted to social use; icons now, they transcend their original source. It is as folklore rather than as a cinematic masterwork that *Casablanca* is likely to survive.

—John Baxter

CASINO ROYALE

(Charles K. Feldman's Casino Royale)

United Kingdom, 1967

Directors: John Huston, Ken Hughes, Val Guest, Robert Parrish, Joseph McGrath

Production: Famous Artists, Charles K. Feldman, Columbia Pictures; Panavision, Technicolor; running time: 131 minutes. Released March 1967. Location scenes filmed in England, Ireland, and France;

Casino Royale

interiors at Shepperton Studios and Pinewood/MGM Studios England; cost: $12,000,000 (approximate).

Producers: Charles K. Feldman, Jerry Bresler; **screenplay:** Wolf Mankowitz, John Law, Michael Sayers; suggested by the Ian Fleming novel; **assistant directors:** second unit, Richard Talmadge, Anthony Squire; assistants, Roy Baird, John Stoneman, Carl Mann; **photography:** Jack Hildyard; additional photography by John Wilcox and Nicholas Roeg; **editor:** Bill Lenny; **sound:** John W. Mitchell, Sash Fisher, Bob Jones, Dick Langford, Chris Greenham; **production designer:** Michael Stringer; **art directors:** John Howell, Ivor Beddoes, Lionel Couch; **costume designers:** Julie Harris; additional by Guy Laroche, Paco Rabanne, Chombert; **music:** Burt Bacharach; main title performed by Herb Alpert and The Tijuana Brass; **titles and montage effects:** Richard Williams; **special effects:** Cliff Richardson, Roy Whybrow, Les Bowie; **choreography:** Tutte Lemkow.

Cast: Peter Sellers (*Evelyn Tremble/James Bond 007*); Ursula Andress (*Vesper Lynd, 007*); David Niven (*Sir James Bond*); Orson Welles (*Le Chiffre*); Joanna Pettet (*Mata Bond*); Daliah Lavi (*The Detainer, 007*); Woody Allen (*Jimmy Bond/Dr. Noah*); Deborah Kerr (*Agent Mimi alias Lady Fiona*); William Holden (*Ransome*); Charles Boyer (*Le Grand*); John Huston (*M*); Kurt Kasznar (*Smernov*); George Raft (*Himself*); Jean-Paul Belmondo (*French Legionnaire*); Terence Cooper (*Cooper, 007*); Barbara Bouchet (*Moneypenny*); Angela Scoular (*Buttercup*); Gabriella Licudi (*Eliza*); Tracey Crisp (*Heather*); Elaine Taylor (*Peg*); Jackie Bisset (*Miss Goodthighs*); Alexandra Bastedo (*Meg*); Anna Quayle (*Frau Hoffner*); Stirling Moss (*Driver*); Derek Nimmo (*Hadley*); Ronnie Corbett (*Polo*); Colin Gordon (*Casino Director*); Bernard Cribbins (*Taxi Driver/Carlton Towers, F.O.*); Tracy Reed (*Fang Leader*); John Bluthal (*Casino Doorman/M.I.5*); Geoffrey Bayldon (*Q*); John Wells (*Q's Assistant*); Duncan Macrae (*Inspector Mathis*); Graham Stark (*Cashier*); Chic Murray (*Chic*); Jonathan Routh (*John*); Richard Wattis (*British Army Officer*); Vladek Sheybal (*Le Chiffre's Representative*); Percy Herbert (*First Piper*); Penny Riley (*Control Girl*); Jeanne Roland (*Captain of the Guard*); Peter O'Toole (*Scottish Piper*); Bert Kwouk (*Chinese General*); John Le Mesurier (*M's Driver*); Valentine Dyall (*Voice of Dr. Noah*).

Awards: Academy Award nomination for Best Music and Best Song, 1968; BAFTA nomination for Best Costume (color), 1968.

Publications

Books:

McCarty, John, *The Films of John Huston*, New York 1987.
Parrish, Robert, *Hollywood Doesn't Live Here Anymore*, New York, 1988.
Benson, Raymond, *The James Bond Bedside Companion: The Complete Guide to the World of 007*, London 1990.
Lax, Eric, *Woody Allen: A Biography*, New York, 1992.
Lewis, Roger, *The Life and Death of Peter Sellers*, New York, 1996.
Baxter, John, *Woody Allen, A Biography*, New York, 1999.

Articles:

Variety (New York), 19 April 1967.
Crowther, Bosley, in *The New York Times*, 29 April 1967.
Crist, Judith, in *New York World Journal Tribune*, 29 April 1967.
Time, 12 May 1967.
Knight, Arthur, in *Saturday Review*, 20 May 1967.
Dassanowsky, Robert, ''Casino Royale Revisited,'' in *Films in Review*, June/July 1988.

* * *

Casino Royale was a coup that Columbia Pictures had banked on: the one 007 property that got away from Broccoli and Saltzman's cash cow series. Producer Charles K. Feldman had hoped to equal or better the popularity of his Woody Allen scripted ''mod'' bedroom farce of two years earlier, *What's New Pussycat?* and trotted in a dozen stars and their star friends for the occasion. David Niven had already suggested cinematic mayhem in *Life*'s 1966 multi-page color spread by admitting that it is ''impossible to find out what we are doing,'' and the magazine claimed the film was a runaway mini-*Cleopatra* at a then outrageous twelve-million-dollar budget. Despite all the rumors and delays, the film seemed to have its finger on the pulse of psychedelia and the ''swinging London'' myth. It would beat a real James Bond entry, *You Only Live Twice*, to the box office in an early 1967 release.

In his provocative expose, *The Life and Death of Peter Sellers*, author Roger Lewis insists that the actor's career decline was first signaled by his self-indulgence in *Casino Royale.* His lack of discipline and his demands caused several more rewrites in an already *plot-du-jour* concept that had employed Wolf Mankowitz, John Law, and Michael Sayers as credited writers (with uncredited fragments by Woody Allen, Ben Hecht, Joseph Heller, John Huston, and Billy Wilder, among others) and five directors to helm the various segments of the film. The multitudinous talent here did more than mimic the Bondian shifts in plot and locale. What emerged was a kaleidoscope that utilized the original ''serious'' Ian Fleming novel, already given television treatment in 1954, as the core of a fabricated frame of plots and subplots which reduce the showdown between Bond (Sellers) and Le Chiffre (Orson Welles) at Casino Royale into the single dramatic moment of the opus.

Bond purists have always loathed the film, while others have preconceived notions of a spy parody and miss the point. The mistake has been to buy into the publicity propaganda and the original sell of the film as a new ''trippy'' Bond, a funny Bond. This was bound to cause dissension, since a parody can not be parodied, and the series was already there. The film is also an ill fit among Bond imitators like the Flint series or Matt Helm, or even Saltzman's own Harry Palmer. *Casino Royale*'s relationship to Bond is only emblematic; it is a prismatic translation of Fleming's milieu, not a linear adaptation. And it remains, even today, a wry and provocative sociopolitical satire. The often criticized inconsistencies of the film's multiple James Bonds, including the banal 007 of Terence Cooper, brought in to cover Sellers' unfinished characterization, intentionally work to confuse the issue of Bond, to overwork the paradigm until it has no value. Like Andy Warhol's canvas of multiple Marilyns, the original is mythic and its copies are but a poor stand-in fantasy.

The subversion of the modern *Übermensch* is already apparent before the credits, when Bond films customarily feature a spine tingling mini-adventure on skis or in the sky. Sellers' Bond, however, is simply picked up by a French official in a pissoir. *Casino Royale* enshrines the icon of David Niven as the retired, legendary Sir James Bond. ''Joke shop spies'' is how Sir James reacts to the technology of Cold War agents. Indeed, Vesper Lynd's (Ursula Andress) billions and Dr. Noah's (Woody Allen) confused kitchen-sink attempt to gain global control are no match for Sir James' stiff upper lip. Like a demonstration of the failed theories of limited nuclear war, the power-hungry are annihilated in attempting to make the world safe for themselves. Woody Allen's sex-hungry *schlemiel* persona may have already been a stock figure in 1967, but here, garbed in a Mao suit, he suggests the infantile psychosexual complexes behind the vengeful modern warlord.

To understand *Casino Royale* as a courtly adventure with Niven's Sir James as a poet-knight who is fated to lead the world to a new golden age, is to see the chivalric genealogy of the James Bond phenomenon. Sir James is resurrected to save a blundering world with its collective fingers on the nuclear button, but extinguishes himself in the final battle. The film has a heavy medieval, even biblical feel: the brilliance of Richard Williams' illuminated-manuscript titles; the testing of Sir James' purity at the debauched castle of M's impersonated widow (Deborah Kerr); the Faustian redemption of Vesper because she has ''loved''; the representatives from the world's Superpowers (here it is the *four* Kings) who beg for the grace and wisdom of a knight of the (black) rose. The film, with all its ideas, directions, and visions, seems to relish its own sprawling, about-to-fly-apart structure, folding over and under itself as medieval epics do and reflecting the serpentines of the *art nouveau* so present in several of the film's sets.

The mythical French casino itself provides a semiotic mapping of the film's subversion of the modern establishment. Besides the bourgeois finery of the palatial building and an art collection spanning the century, a female army garbed in Paco Rabanne's gladiator uniforms relates the modern power structure to the barbarism of ancient Rome. With their leader, Dr. Noah, acting on behalf of a vaguely Soviet SMERSH, but interested only in his own gratification, the static Cold War ideologies become reflections that turn on themselves. The film also features the music of Burt Bacharach and Debussy as well as Michael Stringer's wide catalogue of sets ranging from a Palladian estate to an East Asian temple, all linked by heraldic tones of orange/pink and blue/green, to house the goings-on. So much art, so much architecture, so many sideswipe references to high-culture. Too rich for a simple spy saga, this stylistic puzzle instead implies what is at stake in the battle between the ''immaculate priesthood'' of the individualistic and genteel Sir James and the false promise of social Darwinist technocrats.

There is a definite trajectory in the development of the sociopolitical satire of the 1960s from Billy Wilder's *One, Two, Three* (1961) to the indulgence of *Candy* (1968) to the burn-out of *The Magic Christian* (1970), which locates *Casino Royale* as the mainstream cinematic apex of the era's anarchic impulses. It is never claimed as an inspiration or influence, yet Monty Python, the subversive parodies of Mel Brooks, the manic visuals of 1960s inspired music videos and the Generation X and Y films *they* inspire ranging from *The Fifth Element* to *The Avengers*, are all heirs to *Casino Royale.* Their creators would have had to invent the film if it had not existed. *Austin Powers: International Man of Mystery* is case in point. Like *Casablanca*, *Casino Royale* is a film of momentary vision, collaboration, adaptation, pastiche, and accident. It is the anti-auteur work of all time, a film shaped by the very *Zeitgeist* it took on. As a compendium of what almost went too wrong in the twentieth century done up as a burlesque of the knightly epic, it may still frighten the modernists, but those who follow should consider it to be quite sagacious.

—Robert von Dassanowsky

CASQUE D'OR

France, 1951

Director: Jacques Becker

Production: Spéva Films and Paris-Film-Production; black and white, 35mm; running time: 96 minutes. Released 16 April 1952, Paris. Filmed fall 1951 in Paris-Studio-Cinema studios at Billancourt, and at Annet-Sur-Marne, France.

Producer: Henri Baum; **screenplay:** Jacques Becker and Jacques Companeez; **photography:** Robert Le Fèbvre; **editor:** Marguerite Renoir; **sound engineer:** Antoine Petitjean; **art direction:** Jean d'Eaubonne; **music:** Georges Van Parys; **costumes:** Mayo.

Cast: Simone Signoret (*Marie*); Serge Reggiani (*Manda*); Claude Dauphin (*Félix Leca*); William Sabatier (*Roland*); Gaston Modot (*Danard*); Loleh Bellon (*Léonie Danard*); Paul Azais (*Ponsard*); Jean Clarieux (*Paul*); Roland Lesaffre (*Anatole*); Emile Genevois (*Billy*); Claude Castaing (*Fredo*); Daniel Mendaille (*Patron Guinguette*); Dominque Davray (*Julie*); Pierre Goutas (*Guillaume*); Fernand Trignol (*Patron of l'Ange Gabriel*); Paul Barge (*Inspector Juliani*); Leon Pauleon (*Conductor*); Tony Corteggiani (*Commissioner*); Roger Vincent (*Doctor*); Marcel Melrac (*Policeman*); Marcel Rouze (*Policeman*); Odette Barencey (*Adèle*); Yvonne Yma (*Patron of l'Ange Gabriel*); Paquerette (*Grandmother*); Pomme (*Concierge*).

Publications

Script:

Becker, Jacques, and Jacques Companeez, ''*Casque d'or*'' in *Avant-Scène du Cinéma* (Paris), December 1964.

Books:

Armes, Roy, *French Cinema Since 1946, Volume 1: The Great Tradition*, New York, 1970.

Beylie, Claude, and Freddy Buache, *Jacques Becker: Études, textes, et scénarios inédits, entretiens, témoignages, florilège critique, filmographie*, Locarno, 1991.

Vey, Jean-Louis, *Jacques Becker, ou, La fausse évidence*, Lyon, 1995.

Articles:

Roche, Catherine de la, ''The Stylist,'' in *Films and Filming* (London), March 1955.

Lisbona, Joseph, ''Microscope Director,'' in *Films and Filming* (London), December 1956.

''Becker,'' in *Sight and Sound* (London), Spring 1960.

Truffaut, François, ''De vraies moustaches,'' in *Avant-Scène du Cinéma* (Paris), December 1964.

Perez Guillermo, Gilberto, ''Jacques Becker: 2 Films,'' in *Sight and Sound* (London), Summer 1969.

Amengual, Barthélemy, in *Cahiers de la Cinématheque* (Perpignan), Spring 1976.

Combs, Richard, in *Listener* (London), October 1985.

Andrew, D., ''L'identite a jamais perdue du cinéma francais,'' in *Cinemaction* (Conde-sur-Noireau, France), no. 1, 1993.

Howard, T., ''*Casque d'Or*,'' in *Reid's Film Index* (New South Wales, Australia), no. 15, 1995.

* * *

The benign influence of Jean Renoir, with whom Jacques Becker worked for eight years as assistant director, can be clearly felt in the warm humanity that suffuses *Casque d'or.* Not that the film is in the least derivative; it is unmistakably a Becker film in its central concern with love and friendship (shown here as entirely complementary affections, not as opposed loyalties), and in its richly detailed evocation of period and milieu. The world of petty criminals and prostitutes in *fin-de-siècle* Paris is presented simply and directly—not romanticized, nor rendered gratuitously squalid, but seen as a complex, living community in its own right. And although the plot (based on a true story, which Becker found in court reports of the period) recounts a tragic sequence of treachery, murder, and death by guillotine, *Casque d'or* is far from depressing; on the contrary, its lasting impression is of optimism and affirmation.

This effect derives from the strength and veracity with which Becker delineates the film's central relationship. As Marie, from whose golden hair the film takes its title, Simone Signoret gives a performance of ripe sensuality, well matched by Serge Reggiani's Manda, convincingly revealing both tenderness and tenacity beneath an appearance of taciturn frailty. Their brief, sunlit idyll together in the countryside is shot through with an erotic intensity that eschews the least trace of prurience. That the power of such love can outlast even death is suggested by the film's final image, in which, after Marie has watched Manda die on the guillotine, we see the lovers dancing slowly, endlessly down the now empty terrace of the riverside cafe at which they first met, to the ghostly strains of their first waltz.

''My characters obsess me much more than the story itself. I want them to be true.'' *Casque d'or* is notably free of caricatures or stock

Casque d'or

types; around his two protagonists, Becker assembles a vivid gallery of subsidiary characters, each one individually depicted, no matter how briefly. There is no weakness in the story, either: the narrative moves with steady, unforced momentum from the opening sunlit scene on the river (irresistibly recalling *Une Partie de campagne*), through the gathering darkness of the fatal confrontation in a drab backyard when Manda stabs Marie's former lover, to end with Marie's bleak nocturnal vigil in a room overlooking the place of execution—before the brief coda returns us to the sunshine and the riverbank. ''In my work,'' Becker wrote, ''I do not want to prove anything except that life is stronger than everything else.''

Surprisingly, *Casque d'or* was coldly received by the French critics on its initial release. In Britain, however, the film was enthusiastically acclaimed for its visual beauty, evocative period atmosphere, and fine performances. It is now generally agreed to be the outstanding masterpiece of Becker's regrettably short filmmaking career, offering the most completely realized statement of his abiding concern with, and insight into, the rich complexity of human relationships.

—Philip Kemp

CAT PEOPLE

USA, 1942

Director: Jacques Tourneur

Production: RKO Radio Pictures Inc.; black and white, 35mm; running time: 73 minutes. Released December 1942. Filmed 1942 in RKO/Radio studio in Hollywood; RKO-Pathe studio in Culver City; swimming pool scene shot at a hotel in the Alvarado district of Los Angeles; and zoo scenes shot at Central Park Zoo; cost: $134,000.

Producer: Val Lewton; **screenplay:** DeWitt Bodeen; **photography:** Nicholas Musuraca; **editor:** Mark Robson; **music:** Roy Webb.

Cast: Simone Simon (*Irena Dubrovna*); Kent Smith (*Oliver Reed*); Tom Conway (*Dr. Louis Judd*); Jane Randolph (*Alice Moore*); Jack Holt (*Commodore*); Elizabeth Russell (*Cat Woman*); Alan Napier; Elizabeth Dunne.

Cat People

Publications

Books:

Clarens, Charles, editor, *An Illustrated History of the Horror Film*, New York, 1967.
Higham, Charles, and Joel Greenberg, *The Celluloid Muse: Hollywood Directors Speak*, London, 1969.
Siegel, Joel E., *The Reality of Terror*, New York, 1973.
Everson, William K., *Classics of the Horror Film*, Secaucus, New Jersey, 1974.
Willemen, Paul, and Claire Johnston, *Jacques Tourneur*, Edinburgh, 1975.
Annan, David, *Movie Fantastic: Beyond the Dream Machine*, New York, 1975.
Telotte, J. P., *Dreams of Darkness: Fantasy and the Films of Val Lewton*, Chicago, 1985.
Fujiwara, Chris, *Jacques Tourneur*, Jefferson, North Carolina, 1998.

Articles:

Variety (New York), 18 November 1942.
Myers, Henry, ''Weird and Wonderful,'' in *Screen Writer* (London), July 1945.
Tourneur, Jacques, ''Taste Without Clichés,'' in *Films and Filming* (London), November 1956.
Sarris, Andrew, ''Esoterica,'' in *Film Culture* (New York), Spring 1963.
Ellison, Harlan, ''Three Faces of Fear,'' in *Cinema* (Beverly Hills), March 1966.
Wood, Robin, ''The Shadow Worlds of Jacques Tourneur,'' in *Film Comment* (New York), Summer 1972.
Vianni, C., in *Cahiers de la Cinémathèque* (Perpignan), Summer 1976.
Bodeen, DeWitt, in *Magill's Survey of Cinema 1*, Englewood Cliffs, New Jersey, 1980.
Combs, Richard, in *Monthly Film Bulletin* (London), July 1981.
Bertolussi, S., ''Il bacio della pantera,'' in *Cineforum* (Bergamo), April 1982.
Turner, George, ''Val Lewton's *Cat People*,'' in *Cinefantastique* (Oak Park, Illinois), May-June 1982.
Telotte, J. P., ''Dark Patches: Structures of Absence in Lewton's *Cat People*,'' in *Post Script* (Jacksonville, Florida), Autumn 1982.
Lucas, William D., ''The Two *Cat People*,'' in *Classic Images* (Muscatine, Iowa), November 1982.
Romney, Jonathan, ''New Ways to Skin a Cat,'' in *Enclitic* (Minneapolis), Spring-Fall 1984.
Barrot, O., in *Cinématographe* (Paris), December 1985.
Hollinger, K., ''The Monster as Woman: Two Generations of Cat People,'' in *Film Criticism* (Meadville, Pennsylvania), no. 2, 1989.
Bansak, E., ''Fearing the Dark: The Val Lewton Legacy, the Jacques Tourneur Films,'' in *Midnight Marquee* (Baltimore), Spring 1990.
Larson, R. D., ''The Quiet Horror Music of Roy Webb: Scoring Val Lewton,'' in *Midnight Marquee* (Baltimore), Spring 1990.
Berks, J., ''What Alice Does: Looking Otherwise at *The Cat People*,'' in *Cinema Journal* (Austin, Texas), vol. 32, no. 1, 1992.
Hollinger, Karen, ''Karen Hollinger on John Berk's 'What Alice Does: Looking Otherwise at *The Cat People*,''' in *Cinema Journal* (Austin, Texas), vol. 33, no. 1, Fall 1993.
Télérama (Paris), 24 May 1997.
Rohrer Paige, Linda, ''The Transformation of Woman: The 'Curse' of the Cat Woman in Val Lewton/Jacques Tourneur's *Cat People*, its Sequel, and Remake,'' in *Literature/Film Quarterly* (Salisbury, Maryland), Vol. 23, no. 4, October 1997.
Loban, L., ''Wise Child,'' in *Scarlet Street* (Glen Rock, New Jersey), no. 27, 1998.

* * *

While analysts of horror have long examined its psychological roots in a displacement of sexual drives and desires, few films made the link between horror and sexuality as explicit as *Cat People* (at least until the 1970s where the link becomes a central theme, as in *Carrie*, for example). The film's central conceit—that the arousal of emotion could turn a woman into a panther—is a dramatic literalization of a metaphor of sexual energy as a living force.

Yet *Cat People* represents no simple endorsement of a sexist stereotype in which feminine sexuality is connected to a notion of unbridled devouring animality (as is the case in film noir's figuration of the independent woman as a kind of spider). Quite the contrary, through a reversal of horror's usual convention where an ostensibly normal world is threatened by a monstrosity, *Cat People* puts the cat woman, Irena, in the position of a victim whose ''monstrous'' reaction to the encroachments of the world upon her is viewed by the film with a degree of pathos-filled empathy and even perhaps a positive envy.

Irena becomes a mark of difference, an exotic other, that bourgeois society cannot understand and so ignores, represses, or controls through a force of domination. As in Hitchcock's films where the villain is often more attractive than the boring good guys, so too in *Cat People* the middle-class world appears as a dull, dulling banality whose own self-confidence only partially masks an inability to recognize either its own problems or those of outsiders to its circumscribed value system. This process is most explicit in a painful scene where Oliver Reed and Alice Moore literally exile Irena from their company during a supposedly pleasant visit to a museum.

Moreover, the very force that promotes itself as a cure in such a world—that is, the force of medicine (here the psychiatrist, Dr. Judd)—reveals itself to be more of a danger than the supposed illness that it sets out to cure. Not only does Judd fail to recognize Irena's problem, but he provokes its continuation, betraying his ostensibly professional objectivity by an aggressive sexual desire. If we traditionally associate the monster with the freak, it is significant that it is Judd, not Irena, who comes off as the monstrous figure, his crippled gait a mark of deformity, an abnormality within the field of an imputed normality. Indeed, one can even suggest that the film portrays male sexuality as more dangerous than female sexuality, Irena at least tries to control rationally her own condition while the men around her advance heedlessly (for example, Oliver refuses her arguments against marriage; Judd refuses her protestations against a kiss). Thus, while *Cat People* has many of the conventional trappings of the horror film such as shadowy photography, a subtle creation of suspense (the panther's presence is often more felt than seen), and a concatenation of mysterious events, the film is finally most significant less as an efficient source of scary jolts than as a meditation on the very forces that menace us, that call into question the limits of the lives we construct for ourselves. It is also a dissection of the ways a supposedly normal world sustains itself by defining some other world as abnormal. *Cat People* is a tragedy about a world's inability to accept, or even to attempt to understand, whatever falls outside its defining frames.

—Dana B. Polan

THE CELEBRATION

See **Festen**

CELINE ET JULIE VONT EN BATEAU: PHANTOM LADIES OVER PARIS

(Celine and Julie Go Boating)

France, 1974

Director: Jacques Rivette

Production: Films du Losange, Action Films, Films Christian Fechner, Films 7, Renn Productions, Saga, Simar Films, VM Productions; colour, 35mm; running time: 192 minutes.

Producer: Barbet Schroeder; **screenplay:** Eduardo de Gregorio, Juliet Berto, Dominique Labourier, Bulle Ogier, Marie-France Pisier, Jacques Rivette, with sections based on original stories by Henry James; **assistant directors:** Luc Beraud, Pascal Lemaitre; **photography:** Jacques Renard, Michael Cenet; **editor:** Nicole Lubtchansky, Cris Tullio Altan; **sound recording:** Elvire Lerner; **sound editor:** Paul Laine, Gilbert Pereira; **music:** Jean-Marie Senia.

Cast: Juliet Berto (*Céline*); Dominique Labourier (*Julie*); Bulle Ogier (*Camille*); Marie-France Pisier (*Sophie*); Barbet Schroeder (*Olivier*); Philippe Clévenot (*Guilou*); Nathalie Asnar (*Madlyn*); Marie-Thérèse Saussure (*Poupie*); Jean Douchet (*M. Dédé*); Adéle Taffetas (*Alice*); Anne Zamire (*Lil*); Monique Clément (*Myrtille*); Jérôme Richard (*Julien*); Michael Graham (*Boris*); Jean-Marie Sénia (*Cyrille*).

Publications

Books:

Monaco, James, *The New Wave*, New York, 1976.
Carney, Raymond, *Magill's Survey of Cinema: Foreign Language Films* edited by Frank Magill, New Jersey, 1985.
Rodowick, David Norman, *The Difficulty of Difference: Psychoanalysis, Sexual Difference, and Film Theory*, New York, 1991.
Jacques Rivette: la règle du jeu, Turin, 1991.

Articles:

Delmas, J., *Jeune Cinéma* (Paris), July-August 1974.
Variety (New York), 21 August 1974.
Cornand, A., *Image et Son* (Paris), September 1974.
Frot-Coutaz, G., *Cinéma* (Paris), September-October 1974.
Tournes, A., ''Un dans trois, Rivette,'' in *Jeune Cinéma* (Paris), September-October 1974.
Rosenbaum, J., ''Work and play in the house of fiction,'' in *Sight and Sound* (London), Autumn 1974.
Jordan, I., ''Entretien avec Céline et Julie,'' in *Positif* (Paris), October 1974.
Lénne, G., ''Céline, Jacques et Julie,'' in *Ecran* (Paris), October 1974.
Legrand, J., ''Un film est un complot,'' *Positif* (Paris), October 1974.
Ashton, J., ''Reflecting consciousness: three approaches to Henry James,'' in *Literature/Film Quarterly* (Salisbury, Maryland), Summer 1976.
Milne, T., *Monthly Film Bulletin* (London), August 1976.
Gow, G., *Films and Filming* (London), November 1976.
Lesage, J., ''Subversive Fantasy,'' in *Jump Cut* (Berkeley), March 1981.
Wood, R., ''Narrative Pleasure: Two films by Jacques Rivette,'' in *Film Quarterly* (Berkeley), Fall 1981.
Levinson, J., Celine and Julie Go Story Telling,'' in *French Review*, vol. 65, no. 2, 1991.

* * *

Umberto Eco has suggested that a key factor in a work's status as a cult object is its disjointedness, which allows viewers or readers space into which they can project their own fiction-making skills. This partly explains why Rivette's loose, baggy fantasy is arguably the only genuine cult film of the *nouvelle vague*. But *Céline et Julie* further has in its favour a celebratory image of its heroines as

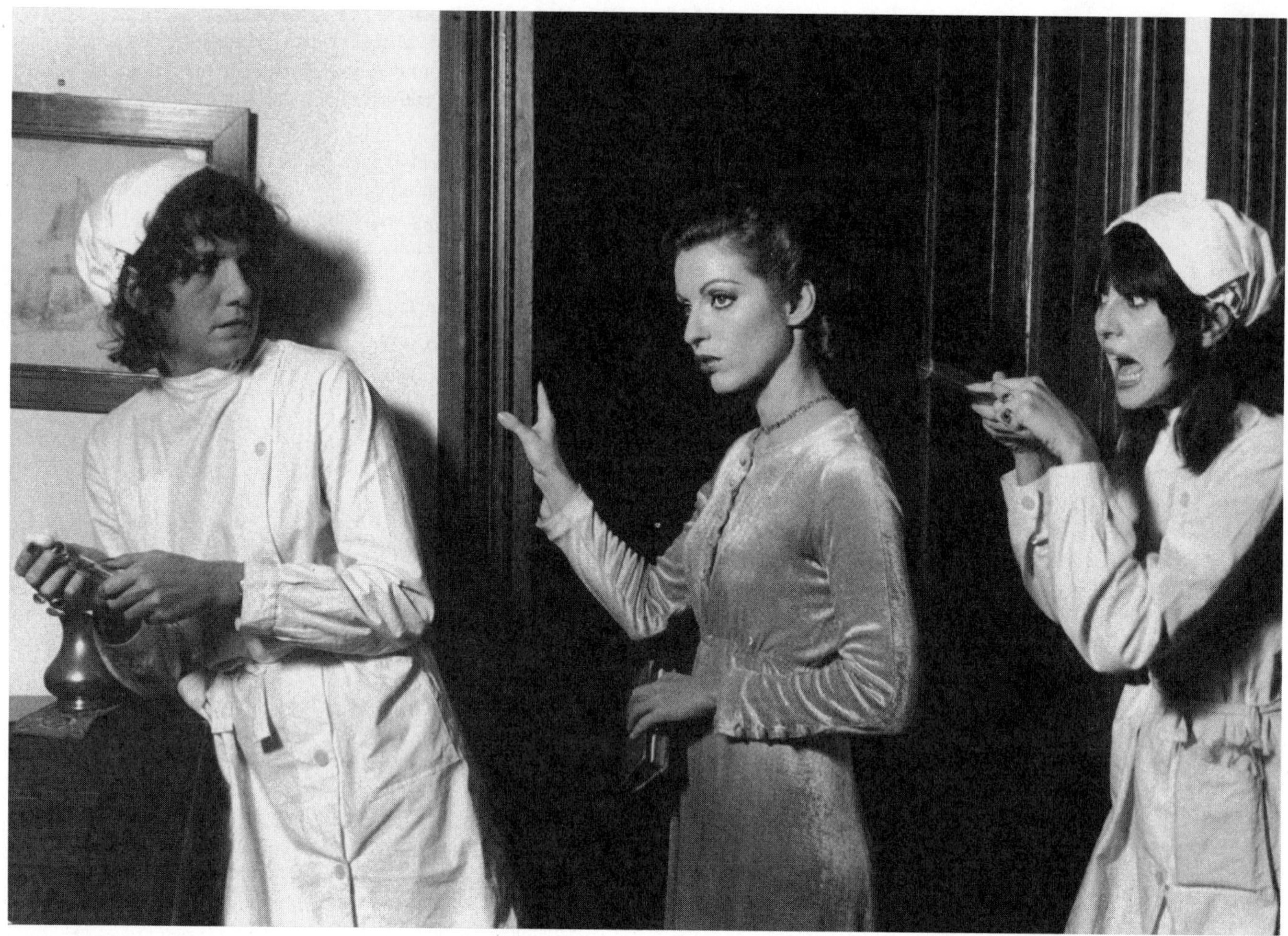

Celine et Julie vont en bateau: Phantom Ladies Over Paris

subversive fabulists in their own right, and a uniquely serious frivolity that makes the film an enormously pleasurable fictional do-it-yourself kit.

From the title onwards, the film appears to celebrate child-like leisure and gratuitousness. The heroines do, at the end, literally go boating, but ''aller en bateau'' also means to be taken for a ride, to be told a shaggy dog story; this tale is a winding river on which we, like Julie, are led into uncharted territory. The film begins with her sighting the elusive Céline, who, in one of many allusions to *Alice in Wonderland*, is the White Rabbit leading her into a narrative labyrinth. Becoming friends, counterparts and arguably lovers, they make a series of visits to a mysterious house in which a family of 'ghosts' continuously reenact a melodrama, as if trapped in their own dislocated matinee performance. This uncompleted story concerns an endangered little girl, and its heroine, an empty role to be filled by Céline and Julie, is her nurse and rescuer Miss Angèle Terre (*mystère*, but also *mise en gel*—frozen).

There are two (by no means incompatible) dominant critical views of the film. One sees it as a self-reflexive commentary on the pleasures of cinema and the spectator's active role. For the other it is an exemplary feminist narrative in which two women control the fiction-making process and challenge male orders of various kinds—including that centred around the myth of the omnipotent director. The film's authorship belongs as much to the two leads as it does to Rivette, whose role, according to Juliet Berto, was akin to ''surgery,'' cutting the material they provided into a coherent, if wilfully ragged pattern.

The main writing was undertaken by Berto and Labourier, who planned their characters and the overall narrative shape with Rivette; Eduardo de Gregorio provided the structure for the interpolated narrative, drawing on Henry James's stories ''The Other House'' and ''A Romance of Certain Old Clothes.'' With the exception of one improvised scene (Céline lets her mythomania run riot on her incredulous friends), what appears to be improvisation was in fact thoroughly scripted before shooting. In the narrative as much as in the process of making the film, ''improvisation''—an effect rather than a fact of performance—can be seen as an inventive engagement with a predetermined form, a sort of manoeuvring around a written score that constantly demands to be remade, just as the fragmentary story in the house is constantly reshaped, jigsaw-fashion.

The film provides various analogies for such inventiveness: magic (Céline's conjuring act), song-and-dance (Julie's audition as a singer) and tarot reading (inventing meanings from a limited set of cards—a traditional figure of the art of combination). Filmmaking and film watching are presented as similar and complementary processes of participation, continuous acts of mental editing: both living and watching the story of the house, Céline and Julie try to make sense of the disjointed footage that passes before their eyes.

Despite the apparently *ad hoc* nature of its conception (Rivette and Berto got the project going from scratch when another film fell through), *Céline et Julie* has a central place in Rivette's *oeuvre.* It is one of many films (from *Paris nous appartient* to his 1995 musical *Haut bas fragile*) in which young women contest patriarchal orders by throwing themselves into intrigues as fiction-makers. It is one of many in which the performers contribute to the writing, and in which the characters appear to evolve from their personalities. And, although the film could be read as being exclusively about cinema, it also concerns the relation between the real world and theatrical performance within an enclosed space. Where *L'Amour fou* and others are built around specific plays, the exorcism of the house is theatre in broader terms (as the two women play Angèle, we hear audience applause).

The film opposes two types of performance—the traditional style, in which the ghosts act out a stultifying, stylised melodrama about a nuclear family; and an anarchic improvisational style akin to the 1960s/70s notions of free theatre. Céline and Julie not only reconstruct the shattered text they perform in, but also deconstruct it, disrupting the family's stately dance by launching into a screwball tango. They are Marx Sisters, if not Marxist sisters, shattering the sexually and socially oppressive order of the house and of a certain school of classical fiction.

One other aspect of the film that has come into its own, in the two decades since it was made, is its Proustian quality, its function of preserving the past. Madlyn is a *madeleine* retrieved from lost time, and the house is obscurely linked to Julie's own childhood. The circular ending suggests a present transformed by the retrieval of memory; Céline and Julie swap places and begin the story again.

But the Proustian aspect also lies in the film's power of evoking the time and place of its making (not least through Berto's hippie-chic wardrobe). It conveys a very tangible sense of a dead Parisian summer in the early 1970s, of empty spaces and malleable time in which to indulge creative leisure (Julie abandons her librarian's post to make her own lived fiction). Characteristically charging banal locations with a sense of privileged "otherness," Rivette recreates Paris as a fictional space that paradoxically derives its magic quality from a heightened realism (the documentary style of Jacques Renard's photography). This is especially evident in the use of peripheral incident (notably, a cat's movements in a garden) in the opening chase sequence. The film is about space, both literal and imaginative—over three hours, the space for the viewer to take a holiday from adulthood, as Céline and Julie do, and rediscover the infantile but empowering pleasures of "irresponsible" fiction-making.

—Jonathan Romney

CENTRAL DO BRASIL

(Central Station)

Brazil/France, 1998

Director: Walter Salles

Production: Arthur Cohn Productions in association with Martine and Antoine de Clermont-Tonnerre (MACT Prods, France), Videofilms (Brazil), Riofilme (Brazil), and Canal Plus (France); color, 35 mm; running time: 106 minutes. Released 16 January 1998 in Switzerland; U.S. release at Sundance Film Festival, 19 January 1998, by Sony Pictures Classics. Cost: $2.9 million dollars.

Producers: Arthur Cohn and Martine Clermonte-Tonnerre; **executive producers:** Elisa Tolomelli, Lillian Birnbaum, Donald Ranvaud, Thomas Garvin; **associate producer:** Paulo Brito; **screenplay:** Joao Emanuel Carneiro and Marcos Bernstein, based on the original idea by Salles; **photography:** Walter Carvalho; **editors:** Isabelle Rathery, Felipe Lacerda; **production design:** Cassio Amarante and Carla Caffe; **set designer:** Mônica Costa; **costumes:** Cristina Camargo; **music arrangers:** Antonio Pinto and Jacques Morelembaum; **sound:** Mark A. Van Der Willigen, Jean-Claude Brisson, François Groult; **assistant director:** Kátia Lund; **casting:** Sergio Machado.

Cast: Fernanda Montenegro (*Dora*); Vinícius de Oliveira (*Josué*); Marilia Pêra (*Irene*); Soia Lira (*Ana*); Othon Bastos (*Cesar*); Otávio Augusto (*Pedrão*); Stela Frietas (*Yolanda*); Matheus Nachtergaele (*Isaías*); Caio Junqueria (*Moises*).

Awards: Berlin Film Festival Golden Bear Award for Best Film and Silver Bear Award for Best Actress (Montenegro), 1998; Golden Globe Award for Best Foreign Film, 1998; U.S. National Board of Review Award for Best Foreign Film, 1998; Sundance Film Festival Cinema 100 Script Award, 1998; Academy Award nominations for Best Foreign Film and Best Actress, 1998.

Publications

Articles:

Kaufman, Anthony, "Sentimental Journey as National Allegory: An Interview with Walter Salles," in *Cineaste* (New York), Winter 1998.

Newsweek (Latin American edition), 25 January 1998.

McCarthy, Todd, "Central Station," in *Variety* (New York), 9 February 1998.

Paxman, Andrew, "Full Salles Ahead for 'Central' Helmer," in *Variety*, 23 November 1998.

Aufderheide, Pat, "Central Station," in *Film Comment* (New York), November 1998.

Klawans, Stuart, "Central Station," in *The Nation* (New York), 7 December 1998.

"Interview: A Hot Film from Brazil," in *The New York Times*, 21 March 1999.

* * *

The film *Central Station* begins in Rio de Jainero's crowded train station, through which an estimated 300,000 people pass each day. The film focuses on Dora (Fernanda Montenegro), an older, cynical woman who earns a living there by writing letters for illiterate Brazilians. From its opening, the film depicts the faces and stories of everyday Brazilians and incorporates them into the script. A documentary style is achieved using a hidden camera to capture snapshots of real people dictating letters to Dora.

Central do Brasil

Dora befriends a young boy, Josué (Vincinus de Olivera), who is left alone after his mother is killed outside the station. Josué and his mother had previously hired Dora to write letters to Josué's father in the northeast of Brazil. Josué, now motherless, embarks on an odyessy by traversing the country in search of his father, a man he has never met. Dora, a woman without a family, and with a desire to reconcile her past troubled relationship with her own father, acts as a chaperone to Josué on this journey.

A true road movie, the film showcases Brazil's colorful landscapes, picturesque views of the rural hinterlands, and its people's rich cultural traditions. Walter Carvalho, the director of photography, captures beautifully composed panoramic scenes of the country. The director Walter Salles, whose most recent film was *Terra Estrangeira* (*Foreign Land*, 1995), teamed up with producer Arthur Cohn, who had previously worked with famed Italian neo-realist director Vittorio De Sica. The result is a film that carries on the neo-realist tradition by depicting poor and marginalized people in a way that shows their dignity despite their daily trials and tribulations of life. In addition, the majority of actors in this film are non-actors, including the boy playing the lead role of young Josué. The lead actor, Vinícius de Oliveira, was a nine-and-a-half year-old shoe shine boy at the Rio airport when Salles met him. Beating out 1,500 other applicants for the part, Oliveira in his debut performance demonstrates an extraordinary sincerity and charisma.

While Dora and Josué have a troubled relationship from the outset (due principally to Dora's moral lapses such as lying and stealing), the film shows a gradual moral transformation in Dora's character. The superb acting by the ''Grand Dame'' of the Brazilian theatre earned Montenegro numerous accolades, including a Silver Bear for Best Actress at the Berlin Film Festival, and an Oscar nomination for Best Actress.

Salles also pays homage to a 1960s Brazilian film movement called Cinema Novo. This group of politically motivated filmmakers tried to show a side of Brazil that was always ignored or made invisible by the elite. Films by these directors depicted the poor, the dispossessed, the rural peasants, and others living in the interior of Brazil, called the *sertao* (hinterlands). By shooting in the state of Bahia (the birthplace and location of many films by Cinema Novo pioneer Glauber Rocha), Salles shows that he has not forgotten the national legacy of socially conscious filmmaking in Brazil. The truck driver, Cesar, who gives a lift to Dora and Josué, is in fact the well-respected Cinema Novo actor Otton Bastos.

In contrast to Cinema Novo's mission to depict the "aesthetics of hunger," however, Salles' film has been described by film critic Fabiano Canosa as an "aesthetics of affection" or an "aesthetics of solidarity." The crux of the film lies not so much in whether Josué is able to find his father, but rather, how the unlikely paring of a dour, initially unfriendly woman with a lost, confused young boy can blossom into a strong bond of mutual caring and interdependence. Both are alone in the world, and both are struggling to survive under difficult circumstances. Walter Salles has stated that his film is about Brazilian identity, and that it is an allegory for how the nation is developing and surviving, despite its financial difficulties.

Central Station, with its sweeping landscapes of an arid Brazil replete with religious scenes (a pilgrimage scene where over 800 real pilgrims performed a ritual ceremony), colorful restaurants, and vibrantly painted dwellings, focuses on people who are often ignored by mainstream film and television. At the same time however, Dora, Josué, and others are bathed in a light that makes the story and images palatable for an international film viewership. Filmed in an area covering over 8,000 miles in a period of ten weeks, Salles' *Central Station* captures Brazil's resilient spirit in the face of adversity.

—Tamara L. Falicov

CENTRAL STATION

See **CENTRAL DO BRASIL**

C'ERA UNA VOLTA IL WEST

(Once Upon a Time in the West)

USA/Italy, 1969

Director: Sergio Leone

Production: Paramount Pictures/Rafran/San Marco; color (Techniscope), 35mm; running time: 168 minutes, some American prints are 144 minutes and various other prints of different timings are available. Released 28 May 1969, New York. Filmed on location in Almeria, Spain, at Calahorra's Station, Calahorra, Logrono, Spain, and in Arizona and Utah, USA.

Producers: Bino Cicogna (executive), Fulvio Morsella; **screenplay:** Sergio Leone, Sergio Donati, Dario Argento, Bernardo Bertollucci, Mickey Knox (dialogue); **photography:** Tonino Delli Colli; **editor:** Nino Baragli; **production design:** Carlo Simi; **music:** original score composed by Ennio Morricone.

Cast: Claudia Cardinale (*Jill McBain*); Henry Fonda (*Frank*); Jason Robards (*Cheyenne*); Charles Bronson (*The Man*, aka *Harmonica*); Gabrielle Ferzetti (*Morton*); Paolo Stoppa (*Sam*); Woody Strode (*Stony*); Jack Elam (*Knuckles*); Keenan Wynn (*Sherriff*); Frank Wolff (*Brett McBain*); Lionel Stander (*Barman*).

Publications

Books:

Cawelti, John G., *The Six-Gun Mystique*, Bowling Green, Ohio, 1971.
Staig, Laurence, and Tony Williams, *Italian Western—The Opera of Violence*, London, 1975.
Frayling, Christopher, *Spaghetti Westerns: Cowboys and Europeans from Karl May to Sergio Leone*, London, 1981.
Cèbe, Gilles, *Sergio Leone*, Paris, 1984.
De Fornari, Oreste, *Tutti i Film di Sergio Leone*, Milan, 1984.
Tuska, John, *The American West in Film*, Westport, Connecticut, 1985.
Cumbow, Robert C., *Once Upon a Time: The Films of Sergio Leone*, Metuchen, New Jersey, 1987.
Buscombe, Ed, editor, *BFI Companion to the Western*, London, 1988.
Cressard, Gilles, *Sergio Leone*, Paris, 1989.
Mininni, Francesco, *Sergio Leone*, Paris, 1989.
Belton, John, *Widescreen Cinema*, Cambridge, Massachusetts, 1992.
De Cornare, Oreste, *Sergio Leone: The Great American Dream of Legendary America*, Rome, 1997
Frayling, Christopher, *Sergio Leone: Something to Do with Death*, New York, 2000.

Articles:

Austen, David, review in *Films and Filming* (London), October 1969.
Gillett, John, review in *Monthly Film Bulletin* (London), September 1969.
Gili, Gean, "Sergio Leone," in *Cinema 69* (Paris), November 1969.
Bazin, Andre, "The Evolution of the Western," in *What is Cinema?*, translated by Hugh Grey, Berkeley, California, 1971.

* * *

Widely considered to be director Sergio Leone's masterpiece, *Once Upon a Time in the West* is his fourth Western and marks the beginning of his career in Hollywood. The preceding "Dollars" trilogy had been an unexpected success at the box office and with the critics. In attracting Leone, Paramount clearly hoped to cash in on the successful formula, using Charles Bronson in the role played by Clint Eastwood in the earlier films, and Henry Fonda as the ruthless hired gun, Frank. Fonda in particular was an inspired choice by the director, who had wanted to work with the actor for some time. Before teaming up with Leone, Fonda was best known for playing wholesome leading men, yet as Frank, we see him shoot a child in cold blood because the boy has learnt his name. Fonda had to be persuaded to go against type, but the cold-hearted killer is one of his most impressive performances. Yet despite the quality of its leading cast, *Once Upon a Time in the West* was not a success in the United States.

Once Upon a Time in the West is a long, difficult movie, the most elaborate and grotesque of Leone's "horse operas." The fact that the opening credits take over nine minutes will give an idea of its slow pace. Obscurity alone is not to blame for the failure of the film in the United States, however. In an attempt to squeeze in as many theatre performances as possible, Paramount slashed over twenty minutes from prints released in America, and one British critic claims to have seen a print shortened by as much as thirty minutes in London. Such thoughtless cutting inevitably removed important scenes, changed character motivations, and created lapses in continuity. Critics had

C'era una volta il west

difficulty understanding the film, and reviews were poor. Yet where the full-length film was shown, it was a huge success, breaking box office records in France. A new full-length print became available in 1984, and readers should take care to avoid any version much shorter than 165 minutes. The shorter prints have curiosity value only, although they do provide a lesson in what can happen when financial objectives are allowed to intrude too far into the way a film is presented.

The film is generally praised for the performances of its leading actors, and for Leone's masterful control over pace, action, and narrative tension. As with opera, music is linked to images in a direct way. Each of the four main characters has his or her own theme, from the menacing harmonica riff of Bronson's ''man with no name,'' to the romantic strings that accompany Cardinale's Jill McBain. Unusually, Ennio Morricone composed the musical score before shooting began, using the script to work out his ideas. In a reversal of the normal process, Leone fitted the action around the existing music, often playing it on set to help the actors understand particular scenes.

The basic plot of the film is standard Western fare. A wealthy railroad owner and his hired gunmen seek to evict a young woman from her land, hoping to use it as a stopping point for trains on their way to California. It is Leone's treatment of this plot, which has echoes of *Johnny Guitar* and *Shane* (both 1953), that has made it so influential. As with the ''Dollars'' trilogy, *Once Upon a Time in the West* is a brutal film, in which killing is a means to an end, and revenge is the central motivating force. Yet the society it portrays is changing. Jill McBain, a former prostitute trying to better herself, represents the need to abandon old ways of doing things and embrace the new. In this respect the film is resonant of its own time: in the late 1960s, student protests and civil unrest in Europe and the United States challenged the beliefs of an older establishment.

Once Upon a Time in the West is also a landmark in the history of the Western. Unlike Shane, whose selfless heroism saves the homesteaders from a greedy rancher, in Leone's film the man with no name (nicknamed ''Harmonica'') is driven by a desire to torture and kill his brother's murderer. Only incidentally does he protect Jill McBain and defend her land. At a deeper level, while classic Western heroes protect a society based on honesty and hard work, *Once Upon a Time in the West* reveals that such societies have their beginnings in jealousy, revenge, and murder. This is the new West, and gunfighters like Harmonica and Frank have had their day, but the optimistic town that grows up around Jill McBain's railroad station at the film's end is built on their brutality. *Once Upon a Time in the West* replaces the established Western mythology of honest struggle, endeavour, and sacrifice with a venal, perhaps more realistic, vision of how the West was won.

—Chris Routledge

CESAR

See **MARIUS TRILOGY**

C'EST ARRIVÉ PRÈS DE CHEZ VOUS

(Man Bites Dog)

Belgium, 1992

Directors: Rémy Belvaux, André Bonzel, Benoît Poelvoorde

Production: Les Artistes Anonymes; black and white, 16mm; running time: 96 minutes.

Producers: Rémy Belvaux, André Bonzel, Benoît Poelvoorde; **screenplay:** Rémy Belvaux, André Bonzel, Benoît Poelvoorde, Vincent Tavier; **assistant director:** Vincent Tavier; **photography:** André Bonzel; **editors:** Rémy Belvaux, Eric Dardill; **sound :** Alain Oppezzi, Vincent Tavier, Clotilde François, Franco Piscopo; **music:** Jean-Marc Chenut.

Cast: Benoît Poelvoorde (*Ben Patard*); Rémy Belvaux (*Reporter*); André Bonzel (*Cameraman*); Jean-Marc Chenut (*Patrick*); Alain Oppezzi (*Franco*); Vincent Tavier (*Vincent*); Jacqueline Poelvoorde-Pappaert (*Ben's grandmother*); Nelly Pappaert (*Ben's grandfather*); Jenny Drye (*Jenny*); Malou Madou (*Malou*); Willy Vandenbroeck (*Boby*); Valérie Parent (*Valérie*).

Awards: International Critic's Prize, Cannes 1992.

Publications

Book:

Kerekes, David, and David Slater, *Killing for Culture: An Illustrated History of Death Film from Mondo to Snuff*, 1993.

Articles:

Variety (New York), 25 May 1992.

Strauss, F., *Cahiers du Cinéma* (Paris), June 1992.

Andrew, G., ''Shoot to Kill'' in *Time Out* (London), 30 December 1992.

Strick, Philip, *Sight and Sound* (London), January 1993.

Variety (New York), 8 February 1993.

Mark Salisbury, ''The Man Bites Dog Men,'' in *Empire*, February 1993.

McNeil, Shane, ''Mocu(Docu)mentary'' in *Cinema Papers* (Victoria), October 1993.

Urbán, M., in *Filmkultura* (Budapest), March 1994.

Beylot, P., ''*C'est arrivé pres de chez vous*: L'imposture d'un faux cinema-verité,'' in *Cinemaction* (Conde-sur-Noireau), vol. 76, no. 3, 1995.

Roy, S., ''Dans le cadre des rendez-vous,'' in *Séquences* (Haute-Ville), March/June 1997.

* * *

Man Bites Dog was made by three film students from the INAS film school in Brussels over a period of two-and-a-half years for a mere $100,000, and yet, on its release it rapidly became the most successful Belgian film of all time, eclipsing *Toto the Hero* and beating even *Alien 3* and *Lethal Weapon 3* to the number one box office spot. Much of the financing for the film came from the Belgian province of Namur, and from the filmmakers' families and friends, many of whom appear in the film, though some were unaware of the controversial nature of its content.

Man Bites Dog is an extraordinary and daring amalgam of the serial killer film and the mock-documentary *a la Spinal Tap*. Its story of a film crew making a documentary about a serial killer and gradually becoming increasingly complicit in his crimes also has distinct links with the kind of ''Reality TV'' that now characterises so many non-fictional slots not only on American but also European (and especially Italian) television. As André Bonzel put it in an interview in *Empire:* ''in New York there's a TV programme called *Cops* and it has a camera crew following cops and going to fights. Shoplifters are arrested in front of the camera and it's really a horror film. It's the reverse of our film—you're with the good guy rather than the bad guy—but now people want it to get stronger. The camera crew are wearing bulletproof jackets and going on more criminal things with more killing because the public wants more.''

Critiques of media voyeurism and audience complicity are, of course, hardly rare in the cinema (*Ace in the Hole* and *Circle of Deceit* spring to mind at once), but what is so remarkable about *Man Bites Dog* is the way in which it uses humour to make its point. Hard though it may be to believe, the film starts out as a kind of blackly absurd Monty Pythonesque comedy and only after a particularly horrendous murder and rape, in which the film crew participate, is the spectator brought up sharply and forced to realise how complicit he or she has become with what has been portrayed up to this point. As Bonzel himself pointed out in *Killing for Culture*, the whole intention was to ''make the audience laugh, then have them think about what they've just laughed at. The whole point is to say to the viewer—look, how can you accept this?'' This is a difficult and dangerous strategy, one fraught with aesthetic and ethical pitfalls, and the fact that it is so triumphantly successful here is due in no small measure to the performance of Benoît Poelvoorde (co-director of *Man Bites Dog*) as the psychopathic Ben Patard, aptly described by Philip Strick in *Sight and Sound* as displaying ''the ingratiating brutality of Richard III as played by Robert de Niro.'' Ben may be a monster, but he is certainly no cardboard cipher or stereotype, and we actually get to know his apparently decent, ''normal,'' lower-middle-class, shop-owning background rather well.

Taking on board Robin Wood's celebrated thesis about horror film monsters representing the ''return of the repressed,'' Shane McNeil, in a particularly interesting article on the film in *Cinema Papers*, has suggested that Ben, like other movie serial killers, is ''the natural expression of the surplus sexual and political tension that bourgeois society strives so desperately to conceal. Ben, the serial killer, is simultaneously *fils loyal* and passionate son of the bourgeoisie, the logical product of a social system in crisis and the manifestation of excess in a society brimming with contradictory tensions. He is at once the quintessence of the European renaissance man and the embodiment of the Visigoth and Vandal. Little by little, parenthesised only by the shockingly explicit murders, the brilliantly structured (yet apparently random) dialogue reveals the multitudinous contradictions of his personality. Namely, how can an intellectual aesthete with a strong religious morality and a yearning for poetry, music, and ornithology be simultaneously a racist and homophobic cold-blooded assassin?''

At least one of the answers is that Ben is a fully paid-up member of what Guy Debord has called ''the society of the spectacle'' (as is one of Ben's postal carrier victims, who eagerly asks if he's on television before being murdered). That Ben appears to be acting as if starring in a movie based on his life is entirely apposite, since that is exactly what he is doing. Indeed, when the crew runs out of money, Ben subsidises the production. What we have here, then, is not simply a vicious satire on the conventional notion of documentary truth, nor merely an attack on the more lurid and sensational kinds of ''reality TV,'' but something more profound and wide-ranging, as McNeil has suggested:

> *Man Bites Dog* almost approaches a meta-analysis of the cinematic apparatus itself. The very act of filmmaking becomes a microcosmic metaphor of the entire cannibalistic enterprise, a form which feeds off and on itself. Hannibal Lecter now runs the projector. This comparison is made explicit in *Man Bites Dog* by the fact that the crew profits quite clearly and directly from Ben's criminal acts, both in terms of spectacle and capital. Film financing, and documentary filmmaking in particular, are directly linked here to the misfortunes of others. Both sides of the camera are working towards the same end: capital profit off other people's misfortunes—misfortunes the crew have, if not deliberately caused, as in the case of Ben, then certainly exacerbated by their complicity and false sense of objectivity. Literally acting as both cast and crew, Belvaux, Bonzel and Poelvoorde ruthlessly expose the mendacity of the media and its persistent tendency to obliterate, then manipulate, ''truth'' in order to make it conform respectively to the ideological and economic agendas of bias and sensationalism.

—Julian Petley

EL CHACAL DE NAHUELTORO

(The Jackal of Nahueltoro)

Chile, 1969

Director: Miguel Littin

Production: Cine Experimental de la Universidad de Chile, Cinematografia Tercer Mundo; black and white, 16mm and 35mm; running time: 88 minutes.

Screenplay: Miguel Littin; **photography:** Hector Rios; **editor:** Piedro Chaskel; **music:** Sergio Ortega.

Cast: Nelson Villagra (*José*); Shenda Roman (*Rosa*); Luis Melo (*Mayor*); Ruben Sotoconil (*Corporal Campos*); Armando Fenoglio (*Priest*); Marcelo Romo (*Reporter*); Luis Alarcon (*Judge*); Hector Noguera (*Chaplain*); Pedro Villagra (*Firing squad captain*); Roberto Navarette (*Prison Director*).

Publications

Books:

Littin, Miguel, *El Chacal de Nahueltoro—La Tierra Prometida*, Mexico, 1977.

West, Dennis, in *Magill's Survey of Cinema—Foreign language Films* edited by Frank Magill, New Jersey, 1985.

Articles:

Callenbach, E., *Film Quarterly* (Berkeley), Winter 1971–72.

Martinez, F., and others, *Hablemos de Ciné* (Lima), January-March 1972.

Weiner, B., ''Films of the Revolution'' in *Take One* (New York), April 1972.

Welsh, H., *Jeune Cinéma* (Paris), May-June 1975.

Lafond, J.D, *Image et Son* (Paris), May 1975.

Palma, E., ''El Chacal de Nahueltoro: tiempo de encuentro con su destinario'' in *Cine Cubano* (Havana), 1981.

Lopez, A., ''Parody, Underdevelopment, and the New Latin American Cinema'' in *Quarterly Review of Film & Video* (Reading), May 1990.

Thomson, F., ''Metaphors of Space: Polarization, Dualism and Third World Cinema,'' in *Screen* (Oxford), no. 1, 1993.

Vega, E. de la, ''Fichero de cineastas nacionales,'' in *Dicine*, March 1993.

Pratt, Mary Louise, ''Overwriting Pinochet: Undoing the Culture of Fear in Chile (The Places of History: Regionalism Revisited in Latin America),'' in *Modern Language Quarterly*, vol. 57, no. 2, June 1996.

* * *

Miguel Littin, born in 1942, trained in the theatre as an actor, but had a greater interest in television. He worked as a producer and

El Chacal de Nahueltoro

director, becoming increasingly interested in film. In 1969 he was one of the founding members of the Committee of Popular Unity filmmakers along with Patricio Guzman.

By 1969, when *El Chacal de Nahueltoro* was made, Chile was already several years into a land reform program which aimed to redistribute land holdings across the country. In 1970 the Marxist government of Salvador Allende took power after the first democratic elections in the country, and Littin was made director of the state production company, Chile Films, working on weekly documentary newsreels. So the background against which Littin's first full-length feature film was made was one of political upheaval and turmoil in his country, but also a more liberal one in which indirect criticism of the government had become possible.

The film *El Chacal de Nahueltoro*, made in black and white, is based on the true story of a crime that scandalized Chile in 1960. An illiterate peasant, Jose del Carmen Valenzuela, played by Nelson Villagra, murdered his wife Rosa and her five children. Jose was imprisoned, taught to read and write, and also given religious instruction whilst in jail, and then executed by firing squad. Littin's film stands as a powerful accusation of the crimes of the prevailing Chilean dictatorial regime.

The power of the film as a criticism of the government and social system in Chile comes not only from its content but also from its style. The two distinct styles—the first half a documentary-style dealing with events leading up to Jose's multiple crime, and the second half a more conventional narrative-fiction style that narrates the events after Jose's imprisonment, together form a powerful juxtaposition that unleashed Littin's criticism of the Chilean judicial system, according to A. Lopez in *Quarterly Review of Film and Video*. Instead of the usual cinematic disclaimer that no character portrayed is real by design or accident, the boundaries between fiction and fact are deliberately confused by news-style footage of actors portraying real-life events. In the first half of the film we follow the investigations of an unidentified mustached reporter who tracks down the story. We hear Rosa's voice intoning the findings of the court in Jose's case, a news announcer sensationalizing the horrors of the case and Jose himself telling us of his experience in distant tones. The soundtrack of the first half is used as the record, rather than the images. The camera work of this section is uneven, jumpy, full of short cuts and hand-held camera work—documentary-style in fact. Jose's arrest is portrayed in a manner that is direct and physical. After Jose's imprisonment the style of the film changes and becomes more conventional—as Jose's character grows and develops so does the style of filming, becoming less intrusive. By the end of Jose's time in prison he can tell a story and compose a poem, and can write enough to sign his own death certificate. We see him become a part of civilized society before he is executed.

The contrast of style serves to emphasize the message. As the film slips into conventional cinematic story-telling mode, we become less aware of our role as observer and more involved in the story-as-fiction. We are then brutally reminded that what we are seeing actually happened—and shocked as we are once again confronted with violence, when Jose is executed.

Littin's point here is the ultimate irony that Jose was educated, taught the benefits of human civilization only in order to die. As he said, Chilean society humanizes in order to destroy.

The film was well received in Chile and was awarded the Chilean Critic's Prize of 1970. It also made Miguel Littin a star in the Latin American film world. Latin American critics said that it was not a great film, (*Hablemos de Cine*, Peru, March 1984) because the meshing of the two styles of narrative did not entirely work, but it is still considered one of Littin's better pieces of cinema, and stands as a powerful critique of a brutal and inhumane regime, and a valuable historical document of a rare period of liberalization in Latin American politics of this era.

—Sara Corben de Romero

LE CHAGRIN ET LA PITIE

(The Sorrow and the Pity)

France-Germany-Switzerland, 1971

Director: Marcel Ophuls

Production: Television Rencontre (Lausanne), Nordeutscher Rundfunk (Hamburg), and Société Suisse de Radiodiffusion (Lausanne); black and white, 16mm; running time: original version—270 minutes, commercial release—256 minutes, other versions—245 minutes. Released 5 April 1971, Paris. Interview material filmed in the late 1960s in Clermont-Ferrand; film also includes newsreel footage from the 1940s.

Producers: André Harris and Alain de Sedouy; **screenplay:** Marcel Ophuls and André Harris; **photography:** André Gazut and Jurgen Thieme; **editor:** Claude Vajda; **sound:** Bernard Migy; **songs sung by:** Maurice Chevalier; **documentarists:** Eliane Filippi (France), Christoph Derschau (Germany), and Suzy Benghiat (Great Britain).

Interviews: (French witnesses) Emmanuel d'Astier de la Vigerie; Georges Bidault; Charles Braun; Pierre le Calvez; Comte Rene de Chambrun; Emile Coulaudon; MM. Danton and Dionnet; Jacques Duclos; Marcel Fouché-Degliame; Raphael Geminiani; Alexis and Louis Grave; R. du Jonchay; Marius Klein; Georges Lamirand; M. Leiris; Dr. Claude Lévy; Christian de la Mazière; Pierre Mendès-France; Commandant Menut; Monsieur Mioche; Maitre Henri Rochat; Madame Solange; Roger Tounze; Marcel Verdier; (English witnesses) The Earl of Avon (Sir Anthony Eden); General Sir Edward Spears; Maurice Buckmaster; Flight Sergeant Evans; Denis Rake; (German witnesses) Matheus Bleibinger; Dr. Elmar Michel; Dr. Paul Schmidt; Helmuth Tausend; General A. D. Walter Warlimont.

Awards: New York Film Critics' Special Citation as best documentary, 1971.

Publications

Script:

Ophuls, Marcel, and André Harris, ''*Le Chagrin et la pitié*,'' in *Avant-Scène du Cinéma* (Paris), July-September 1972; also published separately, Paris, 1980; translated as *The Sorrow and the Pity*, New York, 1972.

Books:

Barnouw, Erik, *Documentary: A History of the Non-Fiction Film*, New York, 1974.

Macbean, James Roy, *Film and Revolution*, Bloomington, Indiana, 1975.

Payán, Miguel Juan, *Max Ophuls*, Madrid, 1987.

García Riera, Emilio, *Max Ophüls*, Guadalajara, 1988.

Tassone, Aldo, *Max Ophuls: l'enchanteur*, Torino, 1994.

White, Susan M., *Cinema of Max Ophuls: Magisterial Vision and the Figure of a Woman*, New York, 1995.

Articles:

''Jean-Pierre Melville Talks to Rui Nogueira about *Le Chagrin et la pitié*,'' in *Sight and Sound* (London), Winter 1971–72.

Rubenstein, L., in *Ceneaste* (New York), Winter 1971–72.

Reilly, C. P., in *Films in Review* (New York), April 1972.

Silverman, M., in *Film Quarterly* (Berkeley), Summer 1972.

''*Le Chagrin et la pitié:* La Critique,'' in *Avant-Scène du Cinéma* (Paris), July-September 1972.

Ophuls, Marcel, ''Regardez donc dans vos greniers,'' in *Avant-Scène du Cinéma* (Paris), July-September 1972.

Gres, E., in *Kosmorama* (Copenhagen), October 1972.

Demby, B. J., ''*The Sorrow and the Pity*, A Sense of Loss, A Discussion with Marcel Ophuls,'' in *Filmmakers' Newsletter* (Ward Hill, Massachusetts), December 1972.

Busi, Frederick, ''Marcel Ophuls and *The Sorrow and the Pity*,'' in *Massachusetts Review* (Amherst), Winter 1973.

Gans, H. J., in *Film Critic* (New York), November-December 1973.

''Why Should I Give You Political Solutions. Marcel Ophuls: An Interview,'' in *Film Critic* (New York), November-December 1973.

Jutkevic, S., ''Razrusenie mifov,'' in *Iskusstvo Kino* (Moscow), June 1974.

Pehlke, Michael, ''Warte tun so leicht als wissen, was gut zu turist,'' in *Filmkritik* (Munich), October 1983.

Pehlke, Michael, in *CICIM: Revue Pour le Cinéma Francais* (Munich), March 1990.

* * *

French postwar cinema is not remarkable for its social or political analysis, and the number of films offering a critical re-examination of the Occupation during the first 25 years after the Liberation is minimal. But as part of the aftermath of the confrontations setting the authorities against students and workers in May, 1968, a move towards a more realistic approach occurs on a variety of levels. *Le Chagrin et la pitié* is a key example of this new mood, and its particular value is that it offers perhaps the first comprehensive filmic analysis of 1940–44, probing the too easily accepted myths of heroic French resistance.

The film is the work of three men who had worked together in 1967 for the current affairs programming of the French television service (ORTF): the director Marcel Ophuls (the son of the great director Max Ophüls), and the producers André Harris and Alain de Sedouy. When their programme was discontinued, the trio continued to work independently, shooting on 16mm and designing their work for television. ORTF refused *Le Chagrin et la pitié*, however, acting in a quite ingenious manner to avoid charges of censorship. Since the film had been produced independently, it would have to be viewed before it could be bought for French showing, and ORTF simply refused to set up a viewing session, even after the film had received widespread praise. *Le Chagrin et la pitié*, a work designed for an audience of millions, received its first showing in a tiny art cinema on the Left Bank, but its power and originality made it one of the most controversial films of the year.

Le Chagrin et la pitié takes as its focal point the town of Clermont-Ferrand, chosen because it was both located close to Vichy and to the center of French resistance in the Auvergne. Ophuls's method was to base his investigation on a combination of interview material shot in the late 1960s with newsreel material from the 1940s. The particular situation of Clermont-Ferrand, initially part of the ''free zone'' and not occupied by the Wehrmacht until 1942, allows the twin themes of French response to Henri Pétain's policies and reaction to German occupation to be separated out. While the central focus is Clermont-Ferrand, Ophuls has also included statements by leading political figures of the period, such as Pierre Mendès-France and Anthony Eden, who put the local developments into a wider context.

The strength of the film however, lies in its human detail, in the interviews which relate directly to the situation in Clermont-Ferrand. Those interviewed cover the whole spectrum from aristocrats to peasants, from active collaborators and German occupying troops to resistance members and ordinary people who claim to be without politics. To set against the newsreels and the proven statistics are some startling testimonies, such as the champion cyclist who does not remember ever seeing any Germans in the town, the German ex-commanding officer, wearing his wartime service medals at his daughter's wedding, who denies any army involvement in the imprisonment and deportation of Jews, and a peasant who still has as his neighbor the man who denounced him for his resistance activities. All the easy half-truths are demolished: the crowds cheering De Gaulle's entry into the town in 1944 are indistinguishable from those who had earlier saluted Marshal Pétain.

Throughout the four hours of *Le Chagrin et la pitié* Ophuls's skilful selection from some 60 hours of interview material and apposite juxtapositions make a fascinating presentation of the facts beneath the legend, the still current evasions of self-evident truth, of the sorrow and the pity of the Occupation.

—Roy Armes

CHAPAYEV

USSR, 1934

Directors: Sergei Vasiliev and Georgi Vasiliev

Production: Lenfilm (USSR); black and white, 35mm; running time: 97 minutes; length: 2600 meters or 8760 feet. Released 1934.

Screenplay: Sergei Vasiliev and Georgi Vasiliev, from a published diary by Dmitri Furmanov detailing his experiences of the Russian Civil War of 1919; **photography:** A. Sigayev and A. Xenofontov; **sound:** A. Bekker; **production designer:** I. Makhlis; **music:** Gavrill Popov.

Cast: Boris Babochkin (*Chapayev*); Boris Blinov (*Furmanov*); Varvara Myasnikova (*Anna*); Leomind Kmit (*Petka*); I. Pevtsov (*Colonel Borozdin*); Stepon Shkurat (*Potapov, a Cossack*); Nikolai Simonov (*Zhikhariev*); Boris Chirkov (*Peasant*); G. Vasiliev (*Lieutenant*); V. Volkov (*Yelan*).

Publications

Scripts:

Vasiliev Brothers, *Chapayev*, Moscow, 1936.

Vasiliev Brothers, *Tchapaiev* in *Scénarios choisis du cinéma soviétique*, Paris, 1951.

Books:

Shumyatsky, Boris, *A Cinema for the Millions*, Moscow, 1935.

Chapayev, Moscow, 1936.

Dolinski, I., *Chapayev*, USSR, 1945.

Leyda, Jay, *Kino: A History of the Russian and Soviet Film*, London, 1960.

Dickinson, Thorold, and Catherine de la Roche, *Soviet Cinema*, London, 1948, New York, 1972.

Taylor, Richard, and Ian Christie, editors, *The Film Factory: Russian and Soviet Cinema in Documents 1896–1939*, Cambridge, 1988.

Articles:

''The Whole Country is Watching *Chapaev*,'' in *Pravda* (Moscow), 21 November 1934.

Variety (New York), 22 January 1935.

New Statesman and Nation (London), 2 February 1935.

Seton, Marie, ''New Trends in Soviet Cinema,'' in *Cinema Quarterly* (London), Spring 1935 and Summer 1935.

MacDonald, Dwight, ''Soviet Cinema 1930–1940,'' in *Partisan Review* (New Brunswick, New Jersey), Summer 1938 and Winter 1939.

Montagu, Ivor, ''The Soviet Film Industry,'' in *Sight and Sound* (London), Autumn 1941.

Vas, Robert, ''Sunflowers and Commissars,'' in *Sight and Sound* (London), Summer 1962.

Chapayev

Helman, A., ''Bracia Wasiliew albo ideologiczna interpretacja rzeczywistosci,'' in *Kino* (Warsaw), June 1973.

Stábla, Z., in *Film a Doba* (Prague), January 1975.

''*Chapayev* Issue'' of *Kino* (Moscow), July 1975.

Ferro, Marc, ''L'Idéologie du régime stalinien au travers d'un film *Tchapaiev*,'' in *La Sociologie de l'Art*, (Paris), 1976.

Schmulevitch, Eric, ''Les Frères Vassiliev,'' in *Avant-Scène du Cinéma* (Paris), 1 and 15 January 1977.

Uhse, B., ''*Tschapajew*—Wir erlebten ihn wie unser eigenes Leben,'' in *Film und Fernsehen* (Berlin), July 1977.

Sklovsky, Viktor, and others, ''Chapayev—50,'' in *Iskusstvo Kino* (Moscow), November 1984.

Dobrotvorskii, S., ''Fil'm *Chapayev:* opyt strukturirovaniia total'nogo realizma,'' in *Iskusstvo Kino* (Moscow), no. 11, 1992.

Dufour, D., ''!Revolutie?'' in *Film en Televisie + Video* (Brussels), no. 448, January 1995.

''Etapy bol'shogo puti,'' in *Iskusstvo Kino* (Moscow), no. 5, 1996.

Navailh, F., ''Le drapeau rouge et les gant blancs,'' in *Cahiers de la Cinématheque* (Perpignan, France), no. 67, December 1997.

* * *

Chapayev was one of the most popular propaganda films of the Socialist Realist era, and is said to have been Joseph Stalin's favorite. As Stalin said in an address to the cinema industry in a letter in *Soviet Cinema*, ''Soviet power expects from you new successes, new films glorifying, as did the Chapayev film, the greatness of the historical struggles for power by the workers and peasants of the Soviet Union, mobilising for the carrying out of new tasks, and calling to mind the achievements as well as the difficulties of socialist construction.''

The Brothers Vasiliev was the name chosen by the unrelated filmmakers Georgi Vasiliev (1899–1946) and Sergei Vasiliev (1900–1959), contemporaries of the great creators of the Soviet silent cinema. They met and became friends in Moscow in a Sovkino laboratory where foreign films were recut and re-edited. Later they trained together at the studio of Sergei Eisenstein, the most renowned of the Russian Formalist filmmakers and theorists.

Chapayev is based upon a novel by the same name published in 1923 about communist writer and Red Army commissar Dimitry Furmanov who fought under the heroic divisional commander Chapayev against White Troops at the Eastern Front during the 1919 battles in Turkistan. The story revolves around the relationship which develops between the two when Furmanov is ''sent from the center'' to Chapayev's troops, who have preserved guerrilla tactics and follow their commander with unequivocal allegiance. Their initial confrontations grow into genuine attachment as Chapayev's attitude toward the new leader of his division changes. Furmanov, though younger than Chapayev, has a refined nature and wisdom which complements his fearless elder, who, despite the fact he only learned to read and write two years earlier, is a natural leader and strategist. At the heart of *Chapayev* is the idea of the role of the Communist Party in directing the establishment of the Red Army. As Naya Zorkaya argues in *The Illustrated History of Soviet Cinema*, ''It found expression in the Chapayev-Furmanov confrontation, in other words, a clash between spontaneous revolutionary fervor and the purposeful, organizing, and guiding will of the Party.''

A *Pravda* editorial, ''The Whole Country Is Watching *Chapayev*,'' which appeared at the time of the release of the film, celebrates its propagandistic features: ''We are indebted to the mastery of the Vasiliev brothers and the whole collective of artists employed in the film *Chapayev* for a magical return to those days when the Revolution had only just won a chance to build a new life on earth.'' The political powers in this era tolerated nothing antithetical to the goals of the Communist Party so that artists and critics alike were bound to the tenets of communism, hence the sycophantic tone of many of the reviews of *Chapayev*, which were mindful of Stalin's watchful eye. *Chapayev* is an example of a piece of art which represents the Socialist Realist style endorsed by the communist government to orient the masses and encourage compliance with the goals of the new political regime. The code of Socialist Realism included ''the ability to view the past from the height of the lofty objectives of the future,'' so the aims of the films were to enhance the Communists' prestige and to affirm the party's leading role in all spheres of Soviet life. The film was seen by the masses and Chapayev became the common person's hero.

Despite its function as propaganda, *Chapayev* is a work of quality. The artistry is evident in the honest representation of human failings, even in the Bolshevik camp, and in the performances and the oneiric beauty of the images. The pace of *Chapayev* may seem to stall due to the relatively slow cutting, few suggestive details and routinely mechanical camera angles, but these features contribute to the type of realism the Vasilievs chose to represent. The national hero, rugged and flawed, is the focus and the story which is told through dialogue and a linear narrative, a style in contrast to Formalism which collided images through montage and fast-paced editing. Eisenstein wrote that kino pravda (film truth) is achieved by allowing the camera to capture pure images of the world and that dialectical montage, the collision of images through editing, communicated ideas with the viewer as active participants rather than as passive receivers of the cinematic narrative. But the story of Chapayev is told with simplicity. Boris Shumyatsky in an extract, *A Cinema for the Millions* (1935), stated that ''This simplicity, which is a characteristic only of high art, is so organic to *Chapayev*, it constitutes such a striking contrast to every Formalist device that in the first period after the film's release a number of ''critics'' were unable to explain the reasons for its success to their own satisfaction. . . The strength of *Chapayev* lies in the profound *vital truth* of the film.''

Chapayev is truthful because it captures the spirit of the time and the struggle of the Soviet populace toward an ideal they needed to believe was worth the destruction of war. Its truthfulness is only called into question in retrospect as time revealed the transience of communist ideals.

—Kelly Otter

UN CHAPEAU DE PAILLE D'ITALIE

(An Italian Straw Hat)

France, 1927

Director: René Clair

Production: Albatros; black and white, silent, seven reels; running time: 114 minutes. Released 1927; re-released 1984.

Screenplay: René Clair, from the play by Eugene Labiche and Marc Michel; **photography:** Nicholas Roudakoff, Maurice Desfassiaux; **editor:** Henry Dobb; **design:** Lazare Meerson; **music:** (1984 version) Benedict Mason; **costume designer:** Souplet; **artistic adviser:** Alexandre Kamenka.

Cast: Albert Prejean (*Fadinard, the Bridegroom*); Marise Maia (*The Bride*); Vital Geymond (*The Officer*); Olga Tschekowa (*Anais de Beauperthuis*); Paul Olivier (*Uncle Vesinet*); Jim Gerald (*M. de Beauperthuis*); Yvonneck (*The Bride's father*); Alice Tissot (*The Aunt*); Bondi (*The Man with the necktie*); Pré fils (*The Man with the glove*); Alexandrov (*The Valet*); Valentine Tessier (*The Customer*); Volbert (*The Mayor*).

Publications

Script:

Clair, René, *Un Chapeau de paille d'italie*, in *Masterworks of the French Cinema*, New York, 1974.

Books:

Schwob, René, *Une Melodie silencieuse*, Paris, 1929.
Bardeche, Maurice, and Robert Brasillach, *Histoire du cinéma*, Paris, 1935; revised edition, 1954.
Viazzi, G., *René Clair*, Milan, 1946.
Bourgeois, J., *René Clair*, Geneva, 1949.
Charensol, Georges, and Roger Regent, *Un Maître du cinéma: René Clair*, Paris, 1952.
Manvell, Roger, *The Film and the Public*, London, 1955.
Solmi, A., *Tre maestri del cinema*, Milan, 1956.

Un Chapeau de Paille d'Italie

De La Roche, Catherine, *René Clair: An Index*, London, 1958.
Amengual, Barthélemy, *René Clair*, Paris, 1963; revised edition, 1969.
Mitry, Jean, *René Clair*, Paris, 1969.
Samuels, Charles *Encountering Directors*, New York, 1972.
McGerr, Celia, *René Clair*, Boston, 1980.
Barrot, Olivier, *René Clair; ou, Le Temps mesuré*, Renens, Switzerland, 1985.
Greene, Naomi, *René Clair: A Guide to References and Resources*, Boston, 1985.
Dale, R.C., *The Films of René Clair*, Metuchen, New Jersey, 2 vols., 1986.
Billard, Pierre, *Le mystére René Clair*, Paris, 1998.

Articles:

Close Up (London), November 1928, June 1929.
Variety (New York), 8 September 1931.
Potamkin, Harry, ''René Clair and Film Humour,'' in *Hound and Horn* (New York), October-December 1932.
Causton, Bernard, ''A Conversation with René Clair,'' in *Sight and Sound* (London), Winter 1932–33.
Jacobs, Lewis, ''The Films of René Clair,'' in *New Theatre* (New York), February 1936.
Whitebait, William, in *New Statesman* (London), 25 November 1944.
Schwab, Paul, in *Ciné-Club* (Paris), October 1947.
Sight and Sound (London), July 1950.
''Clair Issue'' of *Bianco e Nero* (Rome), August-September 1951.
Image et Son (Paris), January 1956.
Berti, V., ''L'arte del comico in René Clair,'' in *Bianco e Nero* (Rome), March-April 1968.
Baxter, John, ''A Conversation with René Clair,'' in *Focus on Film* (London), Winter 1972.
Brown, Geoff, in *The Times* (London), 28 April 1984.
Cole, Hugo, in *Guardian* (London), 30 April 1984.
Positif (Paris), February 1987.
''*The Italian Straw Hat*,'' in *The New York Times*, vol. 141, B4 and C18, 14 May 1992.
Télérama (Paris), no. 2353, 15 February 1995.
Brown, G., ''Tricks of the Trade,'' in *Village Voice* (New York), vol. 40, 4 July 1995.

* * *

If movement is the life of cinema then René Clair's delightful comedy qualifies. Taking an old boulevard farce from the end of the nineteenth century he has imbued it with life and vitality and given it a treatment that would have gladdened the heart of his acknowledged master, Mack Sennett. Apart from the early French and Italian comics, and of course Max Linder, comedy has not been a characteristically European contribution to the cinema. In this film of Clair's however there is comedy, farce and a shrewdly observed satire on bourgeois mores of the previous two centuries.

It is a drama of objects which Clair keeps up in the air with the skill of a Chinese conjurer. The hat itself, boots, bow ties, clocks all play their part in this funniest of films.

Suspense, parallel action, and mistaken identity are all used in the best of traditions. The satire is kind and gentle, and the characters are delightfully created with a disarming innocence about their follies and pretensions.

The story set in 1889 concerns a bridegroom on his way to his wedding who has the misfortune to have his horse eat a lady's straw hat which he has to replace. The lady in question is a married woman out flirting with a handsome young officer in the Bois de Vincennes. She has a jealous husband and can not arrive home without the hat. The wedding takes second place in the desperate effort of Fadinard, the groom, to get a replacement. The wedding guests grow impatient. The clandestine pair settle down in Fadinard's flat and threaten to wreck it. There is much to-ing and fro-ing before the dilemma is resolved and the wife can be found sleeping peacefully at home by her husband with the hat lying intact beside her.

In between all this Clair's inventiveness and his observation of people makes for a highly entertaining film. The mime sequence of the wedding by the pompous and wordy mayor is surely one of the great moments of cinema when the signal of the disarrangement of a man's bow tie is taken up mistakenly until the unease spreads to every man in the congregation.

Clair is well served by his actors, many of whom were to remain with him as part of the repertory in his future comedies. Albert Prejean as the distraught Fadinard, the tongue-in-cheek voluptuousness of Olga Tschekowa, poor deaf old Uncle Vesinet with his ear-trumpet getting everything wrong and being buffeted about in situations he does not understand, is beautifully played by Paul Olivier. The bossy woman with the hen-pecked husband is another dominant character in the film. Jim Gerald as the jealous husband creates another unforgettable Clair character.

The mise-en-scène is served by many talents. Lazare Meerson's feeling for the period is captured in the decors while the costumes by Souplet contribute in no small degree to the total creation.

There is another important aspect of the film. It is an Albatros Production, the head of which, Alexandre Kamenka, was artistic adviser on the film. Albatros was the production Company of the Russian Émigrés in Paris who not only produced striking films with their own units but also promoted young French directors like Clair, Jacques Feyder and Jean Epstein.

The style set in *Un Chapeau de paille d'Italie* was to be developed further with the coming of sound which Clair used with great originality but still retaining his childish delight in human foibles and eccentricities of character.

—Liam O'Leary

LE CHARME DISCRET DE LA BOURGEOISIE

(The Discreet Charm of the Bourgeoisie)

France-Italy-Spain, 1972

Director: Luis Buñuel

Production: Greenwich Film (Paris), Jet Film (Barcelona), and Dean Film (Rome); Eastmancolor, 35mm, Panavision; running time: 105 minutes. Released 15 September 1972, Paris. Filming began 23 May 1972 in France.

Producer: Serge Silberman; **screenplay:** Luis Buñuel and Jean-Claude Carrière; **photography:** Edmond Richard; **editor:** Helen Plemiannikov; **sound engineer:** Guy Villette; **sound effects:** Luis Buñuel; **production designer:** Pierre Guffroy; **music editor:** Galaxie Musique; **costume designer:** Jacqueline Guyot.

Cast: Fernando Rey (*Ambassador*); Paul Frankeur (*M. Thévenot*); Delphine Seyrig (*Mme. Thévenot*); Bulle Ogier (*Florence*); Stephane Audran (*Mme. Sénéchal*); Jean-Pierre Cassel (*M. Sénéchal*); Julien Bertheau (*Bishop*); Claude Pieplu (*Colonel*); Michel Piccoli (*Minister*); Muni (*Peasant*); Georges Douking (*The moribund gardener*); Pierre Maguelon (*Police sergeant*); François Maistre (*Commissioner*); Milena Vukotic (*Inès*); Maria Gabriella Maione (*Guerilla*); Bernard Musson (*Waiter in the tea room*); Robert Le Beal (*Tailor*).

Awards: Oscar for Best Foreign Language Film, 1972.

Publications

Script:

Buñuel, Luis, and Jean-Claude Carrière, "*Le Charme discret de la bourgeoisie*," in *L'Avant-Scène du Cinéma* (Paris), April 1973.

Books:

Durgnat, Raymond, *Luis Buñuel*, Berkeley, 1968; revised edition, 1977.
Buache, Freddy, *Luis Buñuel*, Lyons, 1970; as *The Cinema of Luis Buñuel*, New York and London, 1973.
Alcalá, Manuel, *Buñuel (Cine e ideologica)*, Madrid, 1973.
Aranda, Francisco, *Luis Buñuel: A Critical Biography*, London and New York, 1975.
Cesarman, Fernando, *El ojo de Buñuel*, Barcelona, 1976.
Drouzy, M., *Luis Buñuel, architecte du rêve*, Paris, 1978.
Mellen, Joan, editor, *The World of Luis Buñuel: Essays in Criticism*, New York, 1978.
Cameron, Ian, *Luis Buñuel*, Berkeley, 1979.
Higginbotham, Virginia, *Luis Buñuel*, Boston, 1979.
Bazin, André, *The Cinema of Cruelty: From Buñuel to Hitchcock*, New York, 1982.
Edwards, Gwynne, *The Discreet Art of Luis Buñuel: A Reading of His Films*, London, 1982.
Buñuel, Luis, *My Last Breath*, London and New York, 1983.
Rees, Margaret A., editor, *Luis Buñuel: A Symposium*, Leeds, 1983.

Eberwein, Robert T., *Film and the Dream Screen: A Sleep and a Forgetting*, Princeton, New Jersey, 1984.
Lefèvre, Raymond, *Luis Buñuel*, Paris, 1984.
Vidal, Austin Sanchez, *Luis Buñuel: Obra Cinematografica*, Madrid, 1984.
Aub, Max, *Conversaciones con Bunuel: Seguidas de 45 entrevistas con familiares, amigos, y colaboradores del cineasta aragones*, Madrid, 1985.
Bertelli, Pino, *Buñuel: L'arma dello scandalo: L'anarchia nel cinemá di Luis Buñuel*, Turin, 1985.
Oms, Marcel, *Don Luis Buñuel*, Paris, 1985.
De la Colina, Jose, and Tomás Pérez Turrent, *Luis Buñuel: Prohibido asomarse al interior*, Mexico, 1986.
Sandro, Paul, *Diversions of Pleasure: Luis Buñuel and the Crises of Desire*, Columbus, Ohio, 1987.
De La Colina, Jose, *Objects of Desire: Conversations with Luis Buñuel*, New York, 1993.
Evans, Peter W., *The Films of Luis Buñuel: Subjectivity & Desire*, New York, 1995.
Baxter, John, *Buñuel*, New York, 1999.
Kinder, Marsha, editor, *Luis Buñuel's "The Discreet Charm of the Bourgeoisie,"* New York, 1999.

Articles:

Kovacs, S., in *Film Quarterly* (Berkeley), Winter 1972–73.
Rosenbaum, Jonathan, "Interruption as Style: Bunuel's *Le Charme discret de la bourgeoisie*," in *Sight and Sound* (London), Winter 1972–73.
Fiesole, "Luis Buñuel anticapitalista romantico," in *Cinema Nuovo* (Turin), September-October 1972.
Buffa, M., "La discreta sovversione di Bunuel," in *Filmcritica* (Rome), October 1972.
Chevassu, F., in *Image et Son* (Paris), November 1972.
Oliva, L, in *Film a Doba* (Prague), December 1972.
Rice, S., in *Take One* (Montreal), December 1972.
Benayoun, Robert, in *Positif* (Paris), January 1973.
"Buñuel Issue" of *Cine Cubano* (Havana), no. 78–80, 1973.
Reilly, C. P., in *Films in Review* (New York), January 1973.
Gow, Gordon, in *Films and Filming* (London), March 1973.
Minish, G., in *Take One* (Montreal), March 1973.
Filmcritica (Rome), April 1973.
Bonneville, L., in *Séquences* (Montreal), April 1973.
Bruno, E., "*Fascino discreto della borghesia:* L'impenetrabilita di Buñuel," in *Filmcritica* (Rome), April 1973.
Delain, Michel, "Le Charme discret de Luis Buñuel," in *L'Avant-Scène du Cinéma* (Paris), April 1973.
Turroni, G., in *Filmcritica* (Rome), April 1973.
Murray, S., "Erotic Moments in the Films of Luis Buñuel," in *Cinema Papers* (Melbourne), July 1974.
Ciarletta, N., "Interpretabilita (A proposito del *Fascino descreto della borghesia*)," in *Filmcritica* (Rome), August-September 1974.
George, G. L., "The Discreet Charm of Luis Buñuel," in *Action* (Los Angeles), November-December 1974.
Durgnat, Raymond, in *Film Comment* (New York), May-June 1975.
Conrad, Randall, "A Magnificent and Dangerous Weapon: The Politics of Luis Buñuel's Later Films," in *Cineaste* (New York), no. 8, 1976.
Wertenstein, W., "Pkt z diablem albo wdziek zwat pienia," in *Kino* (Warsaw), November 1976.
"Bunuel Issue" of *Contracampo* (Madrid), October-November 1980.
Comuzio, E., "Il fascino discreto del cinema," in *Cineforum* (Bergamo), December 1981.
Listener (London), 10 December 1987.
Jousse, T., "Buñuel face a ce qui se derobe," in *Cahiers du Cinéma* (Paris), February 1993.
Peck, A., in *Positif* (Paris), October 1993.
Paulhan, J., "A Revolution Is Not a Dinner Party: The Discreet Charm of Buñuel's Bourgeoisie," in *Literature/Film Quarterly* (Salisbury), vol. 22, no. 4, October 1994.
Schmidt, N., "Montage et scenario," in *Cinémaction* (Conde-sur-Noireau), no. 72, 1994.
Irwin, G., "Luis Buñuel's Postmodern Explicador: Film, Story, and Narrative Space," in *Canadian Journal of Film Studies* (Ottawa), vol. 4, no. 1, 1995.
Chaspoul, C., in *Positif* (Paris), May 1997.
Debroux, Stefan, in *Film en Televisie + Video* (Brussels), no. 491, April 1999.

* * *

Recent critical attacks on realism have tended, at their most extreme, to collapse it with narrative itself, as if to tell a story were an act of oppression. During the 1960s and 1970s there appeared a number of important and diverse European films (Bergman's *Persona*, Pasolini's *Teorema*, Herzog's *Even Dwarfs Started Small*, Godard's *Tout va bien*, Rivette's *Céline et Julie vont en bateau* are prominent examples) whose project involved retaining narrative while calling into question its realist/illusionist tyranny. Attention was drawn to the process, and the pleasure, of narration, detaching it from the traditional support of a coherent diegetic world. *The Discreet Charm of the Bourgeoisie* belongs in this group, of which it is a particularly fascinating and delightful member.

Four levels of narrative can be distinguished within the film. (1) "Reality"—for want of a better word. Like any traditional fiction *Discreet Charm* begins by establishing characters and plausible action (a car-load of guests driving to a dinner party). This "reality-level" is never entirely undermined; the action, however, becomes increasingly implausible and absurd, a principle built mainly on the motif of meals frustrated or interrupted. (2) Dream. At four points in the film male characters wake up, and the spectator is jolted into realizing that what has preceded that moment has been a dream. The boundary between this and the "reality" of (1) is ingeniously blurred: the dreams are scarcely more fantastic than reality; their beginnings are never signalled. Retrospectively, we can work out by the use of "common sense" where each dream started; but there remains the lingering doubt as to whether common sense can validly be applied to the film at all. One of the dreams is definitely established as being contained within the dream of another character. It is not impossible to read the entire film (until the last couple of minutes) as Fernando Rey's dream. (3) Inserted narratives. During the film three stories are told (always by peripheral male characters) and rendered visually by Buñuel. Offered as truth, they are just as fantastic as the dreams or the reality; they are also the three most intense and disturbing episodes of the film. (4) The country road. Barely a "narrative," (the "story" would amount to no more than "These people went for a walk in the country"), this remains the most enigmatic aspect of the film, unrelated to reality, dreams or narrations. It seems to express the ambivalence of Buñuel's attitude to his bourgeois characters, as to whether they are redeemable or not. On the one hand, they appear to be wandering aimlessly, lost, going nowhere; on the other, they are shown otside their artificial and constricted environment, amid images of natural fertility (perhaps, after all, they could be going *somewhere?*).

The dreams and the narratives work in a dialectical relationship. The three narratives all have strong Oedipal connotations. Two are literally about parent/child relationships, the third about a symbolic father, the ''bloody sergeant'' and a rebellious son, the young revolutionary. As fantasies, they represent the reality underlying the patriarchal order, the strain and horror upon which that order is constructed. The four dreams (all dreamt by middle-aged patriarchal authority figures) are singlemindedly concerned with anxieties about the collapse of authority. This explains why no dreams are dreamt, or stories told, by the women, who have no authority to lose.

Finally, the food motif. Buñuel uses the dinner party to epitomize bourgeois rituals: its purpose is not to eat but to assert one's status. The frustration of every meal—until the last moments of the film—represents the bourgeoisie's collapse of confidence depicted in other ways in the dreams and narratives. Why can Fernando Rey eat at last, at the end of the film? He is alone; he eats because he is hungry not as part of a bourgeois ritual. He is not waited on—he serves himself out of the refrigerator—hence is acting outside the class oppression that is an essential factor in bourgeois ritual. Finally, he has just dreamed the annihilation of his entire circle, including himself. There has always been a close relationship between Buñuel and the characters Rey plays in his films: something less than identification but more than compassion.

—Robin Wood

CHARULATA

(The Lonely Wife)

India, 1964

Director: Satyajit Ray

Production: R. D. Bansal (company); black and white, 35mm; running time: 115 minutes. Released 1964. Filmed late 1963 to early 1964 in India.

Producer: R. D. Bansal; **screenplay:** Satyajit Ray, from the novel by Rabindranath Tagore; **photography:** Subrata Mitra; **editor:** Dulal Dutta; **art director:** Bansi Chandragupta; **musical score:** Satyajit Ray.

Cast: Soumitra Chatterjee (*Amal*); Madhabi Mukherjee (*Charulata*); Sailen Mukherjee (*Bhupati Dutt*); Shyamal Ghosal (*Umapeda*); Geetali Roy (*Mandakini*).

Awards: Berlin Film Festival, Best Direction, 1965.

Publications

Books:

Gelguld, Harry M., *Film Makers on Filmmaking*, Bloomington, Indiana, 1967.

Sarris, Andrew, editor, *Interviews with Film Directors*, New York, 1967.

Seton, Marie, *Portrait of a Director: Satyajit Ray*, Bloomington, Indiana, 1971.

Satyajit Ray, New Delhi, 1976.

American Film Institute, *Satyajit Ray: Study Guide*, Washington, D.C., 1979.

Micciollo, Henri, *Satyajit Ray*, Lausanne, 1980.

Rangoonwalla, Firoze, *Satyajit Ray's Art*, Shahdara, Delhi, 1980.

Ray, Satyajit, *An Anthology*, edited by Chidananda Das Gupta, New Dehli, 1981.

Willemen, Paul, and Behroze Gandhy, *Indian Cinema*, London, 1982.

Ramachandran, T. M. *70 Years of Indian Cinema (1913–1983)*, Bombay, 1985.

Nyce, Ben, *Satyajit Ray: A Study of His Films*, New York, 1988.

Robinson, Andrew, *Satyajit Ray: The Inner Eye*, Berkeley, California, 1989.

Tesson, Charles, *Satyajit Ray*, Paris, 1992.

Cooper, Darius, *The Cinema of Satyajit Ray: Between Tradition and Modernity*, New York, 1999.

Ganguly, Suranjan, *Satyajit Ray: In Search of the Modern*, Lanham, Maryland, 2000.

Articles:

''Satyajit Ray on Himself,'' in *Cinema* (Beverly Hills), July-August 1965.

Houston, Penelope, ''Ray's *Charulata*,'' in *Sight and Sound* (London), Winter 1965–66.

Stanbrook, Alan, ''The World of Ray,'' in *Films and Filming* (London), November 1965.

Gillett, John, in *Monthly Film Bulletin* (London), December 1965.

''From Film to Film,'' in *Cahiers du Cinéma in English* (New York), no. 3, 1966.

''Satyajit Ray Issue'' of *Montage*, July 1966.

Hrusa, B., ''Satyajit Ray: Genius Behind the Man,'' in *Film* (London), Winter 1966.

Pechter, William S., ''India's Chekhov,'' in *Commonweal* (New York), 16 October 1970.

Goldschmidt, Didier, in *Cinématographe* (Paris), July 1981.

Gauthier, G., in *Image et Son* (Paris), July-August 1981.

Haham, C., ''Cinema Bengali de Ray, Cinema Hindi de Bombay,'' in *Image et Son* (Paris), July-August 1981.

Magny, Joel, ''*Keerlata:* De la geometrie des sentiments dans l'espace et dans le temps,'' in *Cinéma* (Paris), July-August 1981.

Jordan, Isabelle, ''Le Bruit du vent contre la jalousie,'' in *Positif* (Paris), September 1981.

Hanan, D., ''Patriarchal Discourse in Some Early Films of Satyajit Ray,'' in *Deep Focus* (India), vol. 3, no. 1, 1990.

Ganguly, S., ''One Single Blend: A Conversation with Satyajit Ray,'' in *East-West Film Journal* (Honolulu), vol. 3, no. 2, June 1995.

Ganguly, Keya, ''Carnal Knowledge: Visuality and the Modern in *Charulata*,'' in *Camera Obscura* (Bloomington, Indiana), no. 37, January 1996.

Charulata

Giavarini, Laurence, ''L'ecriture de *Charulata*,'' in *Vertigo* (Paris), #14, 1996.

Cooper, D., ''The Indian Woman in the Bengali/Hindu Dollhouse: Satyajit Ray's *Charulata*,'' in *Women's Studies*, vol. 25, no. 2, 1996.

* * *

Charulata is the most successful film of a group Satyajit Ray made in the mid-1960s with the actress Madhabi Mukherjee. Whereas the director's first films—especially the Apu trilogy—trace the education and growth to maturity of young male heroes, these mid-1960s films treat, in a variety of periods and social contexts, the problems of women in Indian society. As in the early films, Ray's method is to use a mass of brilliantly observed and often very funny details to build a single strand of plot. *Charulata*, one of Ray's undoubted masterpieces, is adapted from a story by Rabindranath Tagore and set in a period of particular significance to the director: the last quarter of the nineteenth century. Charulata, the sensitive but bored wife of a westernized newspaper publisher finds herself drawn sexually to her husband's young cousin who comes to stay and shares her taste for literature. The film moves with beautiful precision from flirtation and almost childish competitiveness to near tragedy amid a lovingly reconstructed period setting. While Tagore's story ends in disaster, Ray is less conclusive, choosing to freeze the film's last frame as husband and wife are about to come together again. This refusal of tragedy points to the characteristic form of Ray's films. One of the creative tensions in his work is that between the often rambling narratives he adapts and the tight shaping impulse of his imagination, which produces story patterns to match the most finely wrought classical Hollywood movies. But just as villains are absent from his work, so too is narrative closure and *Charulata* is typical in its rejection of finality where the characters are concerned.

In considering Ray as a filmmaker it is important to remember that his work has no roots in the traditions of Indian cinema. His early films are resolutely independent of the devices and conventions of the Hindi movie, of which he had little if any direct knowledge at this time. Ray's is a personal synthesis of an Indian sensibility and the formal lessons of western cinema. Though he is often seen as the heir to Italian neorealism and works like Vittorio De Sica's *Bicycle Thieves* have made a profound impression on him, there are fundamental differences. In particular Ray refuses actuality—the living presence of contemporary society—which was so crucial to filmmakers like De Sica and Rossellini. Ray habitually turns to the past, and the particular significance of *Charulata*, beyond its incredibly sensitive study of personal interaction, is the period to which Ray turns. Both Ray's ancestors and the Tagore family belonged to the educated elite of the Bengali middle classes who formed the ''middle-men'' between the colonizers and the colonized. Their knowledge of English gave them key posts in education and administration under the British, and also made them a channel through which the new intellectual ideas from Europe (democracy, liberalism, nationalism, the liberation of women and social equality) flowed into Indian society. *Charulata* celebrates this moment of interaction: the husband Bhupati devotes his wealth and energy to his English-language newspaper which will disseminate the new ideas. A key moment is the party that he throws to celebrate the Liberal election victory in London. But the nineteenth-century Bengali Cultural Renaissance was not merely an assimilation of western ideas. Its participants combined this with a re-examination of traditional arts at his college—now a university—in Santineketan. Here too, Ray is faithful to his family traditions, for all his finest films are explorations of Indian society. Finally *Charulata*'s power comes from the sense of Ray's personal discovery of a key moment of fusion between India and the West.

—Roy Armes

CHELOVEK S KINOAPPARATOM

(Man with a Movie Camera)

USSR, 1929

Director: Dziga Vertov

Production: Vufku (Ukraine); black and white, 35mm, silent; running time: 67 minutes. Released 1929. Filmed 1929, mostly in Moscow.

Screenplay: Dziga Vertov; **photography:** Mikhail Kaufman; **editor:** Dziga Vertov; **assistant editor:** Yelizaveta Svilova; **special effects:** Dziga Vertov, Mikhail Kaufman.

Publications

Scripts:

Vertov, Dziga, ''*The Man with the Movie Camera*,'' in *Film Comment* (New York), Spring 1972.

Marie, Michel, ''Dziga Vertov: *L'homme à la caméra*'' (photographic continuity) in *Avant-Scène du Cinéma* (Paris), 1 December 1978.

Books:

Dickinson, Thorold, and Catherine De La Roche, *Soviet Cinema*, London, 1948.

Leyda, Jay, *Kino: A History of the Russian and Soviet Film*, London, 1960.

Abramov, Nikolai, *Dziga Vertov*, edited by Barthélemy Amengual, Lyons, 1965.

Sadoul, Georges, *Dziga Vertov*, Paris, 1971.

Barsam, Richard, *Nonfiction Film: A Critical History*, New York, 1973.

Barnouw, Erik, *Documentary: A History of the Non-Fiction Film*, New York, 1974.

Feldman, Seth, *Evolution of Style in the Early Works of Dziga Vertov*, New York, 1977.

Feldman, Seth, *Dziga Vertov: A Guide to References and Resources*, Boston, 1979.

Marshall, Herbert, *Masters of the Soviet Cinema: Crippled Creative Biographies*, London, 1983.

Vertov, Dziga, *Kino-Eye: The Writings of Dziga Vertov*, edited by Annette Michelson, Berkeley, 1984.

Waugh, Thomas, editor, *''Show us Life'': Toward a History and Aesthetics of the Committed Documentary*, Metuchen, New Jersey, 1984.

Petric, Vlada, *Constructivism in Film: The Man with the Movie Camera: A Cinematic Analysis*, Cambridge, 1987.

Articles:

Vaughn, Dai, in *Films and Filming* (London), November 1960.

Sadoul, Georges, ''Bio-Filmographie de Vertov,'' in *Cahiers du Cinéma* (Paris), August 1963.

Weinberg, Herman G., in *Film Comment* (New York), Fall 1966.

Gierke, Christopher, ''Dziga Vertov,'' in *Afterimage* (New York), April 1970.

Michelson, Annette, ''*The Man with the Movie Camera:* From Magician to Epistomologist,'' in *Art Forum* (New York), March 1972.

Bordwell, David, in *Film Comment* (New York), Spring 1972.

Helman, A., ''Dziga Wiertow albo wszechobecnosc kamery. Nasz kamery,'' in *Kino* (Warsaw), May 1973.

Vronskaya, Jean, ''The Man Without a Movie Camera,'' in *Film* (London), May 1973.

Tuch, R., ''Vertov and the Picaresque Spirit: *Man with the Movie Camera*,'' in *Film Library Quarterly* (New York), no. 1, 1975.

Cornand, J., in *Image et Son* (Paris), June-July 1975.

Crofts, S., and O. Rose, ''An Essay Towards *Man with a Movie Camera*,'' in *Screen* (London), Spring 1977.

Mayne, Judith, ''Kino-truth and Kino-praxis: Vertov's *Man with a Movie Camera*,'' in *Ciné-Tracts* (Montreal), Summer 1977.

Brejc, T., ''Slikovno polje in podoba v filmu,'' in *Ekran* (Ljubljana, Yugoslavia), no. 9–10, 1979.

Interview with Mikhail Kaufman in *October* (Cambridge, Massachusetts), Winter 1979.

Williams, A., ''The Camera Eye and the Film: Notes on Vertov's Formalism,'' in *Wide Angle* (Athens, Ohio), no. 3, 1980.

Carroll, Noel, ''Causation, the Amplification of Movement and Avant-Garde Film,'' in *Millenium Film Journal* (New York), Fall-Winter 1981–82.

Beller, J. L., ''The Circulating Eye,'' in *Communication Review* (Thousand Oaks, California), no. 2, 1993.

Crofts, S., ''Constructivism in Film: the Man with the Movie Camera: A Cinematic Analysis,'' in *Metro Magazine* (St. Kilda West), Winter 1994.

Séquences (Haute-Ville), May-June 1995.

Tsivian, Yuri, ''Dziga Vertov's Frozen Music,'' in *Griffithiana*, October 1995.

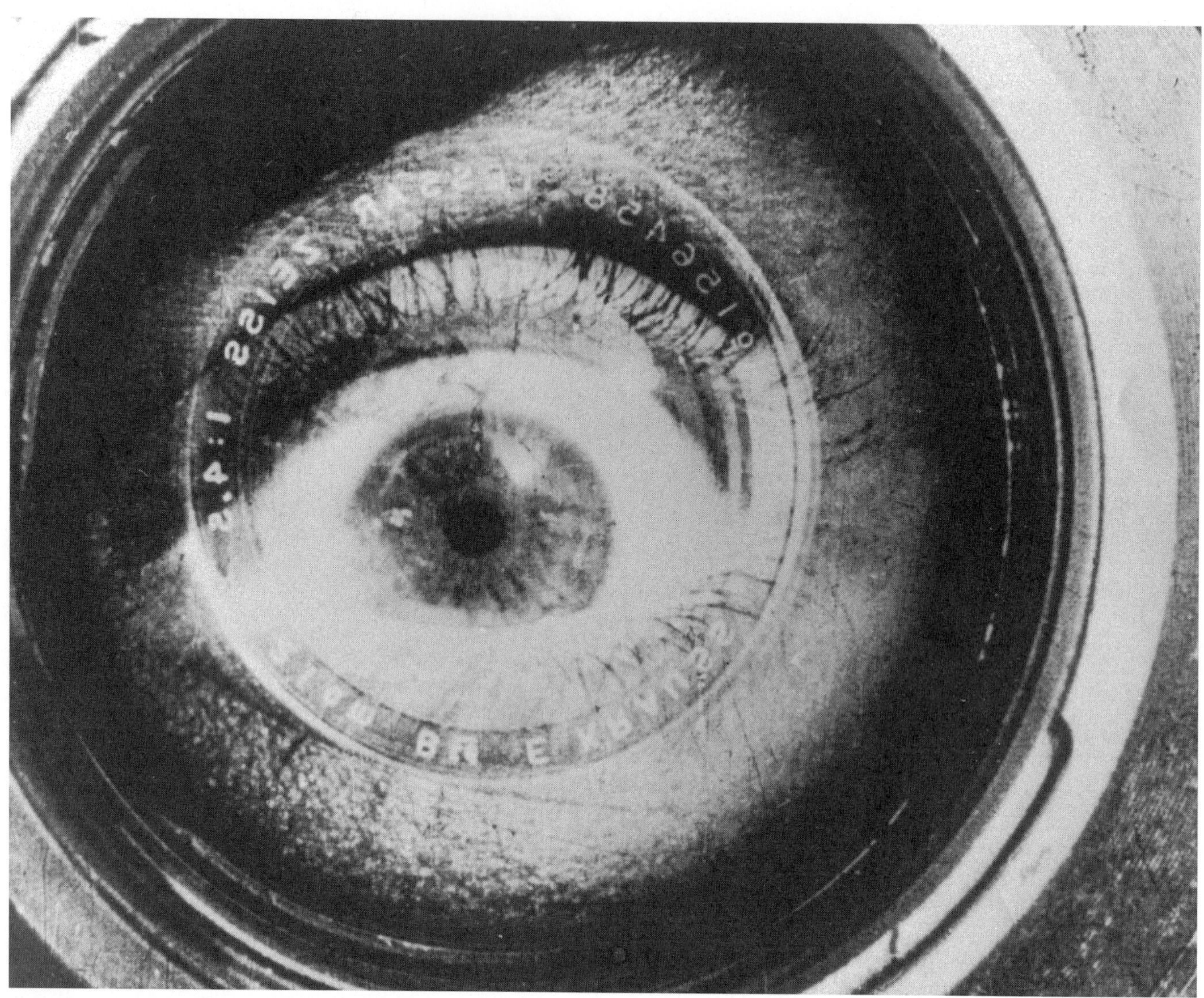

Chelovek s kinoapparatom

Segnocinema (Vicenza), November/December 1995.
Leiser, Erwin, ''Revolutionär und Poet,'' in *Film und Fernsehen* (Berlin), vol. 23, no. 5, 1995.

* * *

The product of post-revolutionary Russia, *Man with a Movie Camera* reflects that era's excitement with film and anticipates modern techniques and concern for capturing actuality. Its creator, Dziga Vertov, in the film's treatment, called *Man with a Movie Camera* an ''experiment in conveying visual phenomena without the aid of titles, scenario, or theatre (a film without actors or sets).'' The result of Vertov's experiment is a film about filmmaking and the illusions it can create.

Without the usual props of plot, titles, or sound, Vertov gives the film its structure by using the format of the city symphony films of the mid 1920s, but he brackets the scenes with references to the cinematic process. The film's protagonist is the cameraman, a picaro travelling through the city, involving himself in its daily dawn-to-dusk activities, and observing all walks of life through the eye of his camera. The camera eye takes on a persona of its own by turning frequently to the audience as though addressing it. The camera is the same apparatus Vertov personified in his early manifestos on film: ''I am a mechanical eye. I, a machine, am showing you a world, the likes of which only I can see.'' In an almost virtuoso performance of camera and editing techniques, the audience is treated to superimpositions, animation, split screens, fast motion, varying camera angles, trolleying and dollying, quick cutting, montage, and prismatic lenses, all in a rapid succession which gives the film an inherent vitality.

The scenes themselves are actualities—people working, playing, resting—but always with the constant reminder that these are *filmed* actualities. The film opens on an empty theatre; the audience arrives; the projectionist readies his film; the orchestra begins to play; and we see a film come on the screen, the film we will in fact watch. Throughout the film, we are always aware of the camera's presence; we see the camera reflected in windows and in shadows. We see the cameraman with his machine climbing a smokestack, climbing out of a beer mug, being hoisted by a crane, walking into the sea, running across roof tops, and going down a mine shaft. The self-reflexive aspects of the film become more complex as we see shots of a motorcyclist, then of the cameraman filming the motorcyclist, then the same scene being projected in the theatre. Later in the midst of an active sequence, the frame freezes; there follows a series of stills which lead us to a strip of film in an editor's hands. Now in the editing room, we see the editor hang the strip of film on a rack with other strips, some of which are shots we have already seen. At the end, we return to the theatre, the camera and tripod assemble on the screen, take a bow, and walk off. In the finale, we see a jumbling of shots from previous scenes intercut with shots of the audience watching these scenes, and finally the camera lens turned toward us with a human eye superimposed over the iris. Vertov's point is firmly established—he has shown us reality, he has expanded our vision of life, but it is a reality that only exists on film.

Greeted in 1929 as an exciting view into film's future, *Man with a Movie Camera* is still exciting to audiences because of its sophisticated approach to the art of filmmaking. The camera and editing pyrotechnics, in fact, seem quite contemporary. It is also strikingly modern in its basic concerns about the relationship between film and reality and the role the camera and cameraman play. These are also the concerns of the cinema verité filmmakers today.

—Sharon Lee

CHELSEA GIRLS

USA, 1966

Director: Andy Warhol

Production: Andy Warhol Films; black and white and Eastmancolor, 16mm; running time: 195 minutes, other versions are 210 and 205 minutes. Released 15 September 1966; uncut reels were projected side by side; in the general release version, the 1st reel appeared screen right, and a few minutes later, the second appeared screen left. Filmed 1966 in the Chelsea Hotel, New York City; other parts of New York City; and Cambridge, Massachusetts.

Producer: Andy Warhol; **photographer:** Andy Warhol; **screenplay:** Andy Warhol and Ronald Tavel; **music:** The Velvet Underground; **production assistant:** Paul Morrissey.

Cast: ''The Pope Ondine Story''—Ondine (*Pope*); Angelina Davis (*Pepper*); Ingrid Superstar; Albert René Ricard; Mary Might; International Velvet; Ronna. ''The Duchess''—Brigid Polk. ''The John''—Ed Hood (*Ed*); Patrick Flemming (*Patrick*); Mario Montez (*Transvestite*); Angelina ''Pepper'' Davis; International Velvet; Mary Might; Gerard Malanga; Albert René Ricard; Ingrid Superstar. ''Hanoi Hanna (Queen of China)''—Mary Might (*Hanoi Hanna*); International Velvet; Ingrid Superstar; Angelina ''Pepper'' Davis. ''The Gerard Malanga Story''—Marie Menken (*Mother*); Gerard Malanga (*Son*); Mary Might (*Girlfriend*). ''The Trip'' and ''Their Town (Toby Short)''—Eric Emerson. ''Afternoon''—Edie Sedgwick (*Edie*); Ondine; Arthur Loeb; Donald Lyons; Dorothy Dean. ''The Closet''—Nico; Randy Borscheidt. ''Reel 1''—Eric Emerson; Ari.

Publications

Books:

Tyler, Parker, *Underground Film: A Critical History*, New York, 1969.
Coplans, John, *Andy Warhol*, New York, 1970.
Crone, Rainer, *Andy Warhol*, New York, 1970.
Gidal, Peter, *Andy Warhol's Films and Paintings*, London, 1971, 1991.
Wilcock, John, *The Autobiography and Sex Life of Andy Warhol*, New York, 1971.
Koch, Stephen, *Andy Warhol's World and His Friends*, New York, 1973.
Koch, Stephen, *Stargazer: Andy Warhol's World and His Films*, New York, 1973; revised edition, 1985.
Smith, Patrick S., *Andy Warhol's Art and Films*, Ann Arbor, Michigan, 1986.
O'Pray, Michael, editor, *Andy Warhol: The Film Factory*, London, 1989.
Tillman, Lynne; photographs by Stephen Shore, *The Velvet Years: Warhol's Factory, 1965–67*, New York, 1995.
Suárez, Juan Antonio, *Bike Boys, Drag Queens, and Superstars: Avant-Garde, Mass Culture, and Gay Identities in the 1960s Underground Cinema*, Bloomington, Indiana, 1996.
Pratt, Alan R., editor, *The Critical Response to Andy Warhol*, Westport, Connecticut, 1997.

Articles:

Ehrenstein, David, in *Film Culture* (New York), Fall 1966.
Steller, J., ''Beyond Cinema: Notes on Some Films by Andy Warhol,'' in *Film Quarterly* (Berkeley), Fall 1966.
Sarris, Andrew, in *Village Voice* (New York), 15 December 1966.
Warhol, Andy, ''My Favourite Superstar, Notes on My Epic, *Chelsea Girls*'' in *Arts Magazine* (New York), February 1967.
Burnett, Ron, in *Take One* (Montreal), April 1967.
Tyler, Parker, ''Dragtime or Drugtime: or Film a la Warhol,'' in *Evergreen Revue* (New York), April 1967.
''*Chelsea Girls* Issue,'' of *Film Culture* (New York), Summer 1967.
Callenbach, Ernest, in *Film Quarterly* (Berkeley), Winter 1967–68.
Lugg, Andrew, ''On Andy Warhol,'' in *Cineaste* (New York), Winter 1967–68.
Price, James, in *Sight and Sound* (London), Spring 1968.
Durgnat, Raymond, in *Films and Filming* (London), August 1969.
Cipnic, D. J., ''Andy Warhol: Iconographer,'' in *Sight and Sound* (London), Summer 1972.
Bourdon, David, ''Warhol as Filmmaker,'' in *Art in America* (New York), May-June 1971.
Cowan, Bob, ''My Life and Times with the Chelsea Girls,'' in *Take One* (Montreal), September-October 1971.
Larson, R., ''A Retrospective Look at the Films of D.W. Griffith and Andy Warhol,'' in *Film Journal* (New York), Fall-Winter 1972.

* * *

A bona fide milestone of the American underground film, *Chelsea Girls* marks the apogee of the film career of pop artist Andy Warhol. Consisting of twelve 35-minute reels, each representing the activities in one room of New York's Chelsea Hotel, the film is projected two reels at a time, side by side, bringing its seven hours of footage to a running time of three hours—as fans have noted, the same length as

Gone with the Wind. The comparison is facetious, but apt, for *Chelsea Girls* not only represents one of the most significant cultural/aesthetic touchstones for the 1960s underground, but also its first "blockbuster," drawing audiences large enough for *Variety* to begin listing its grosses.

Each of the film's 12 reels consists of a single, unedited shot in which various personalities from the Warhol factory (junkies, rock singers, camp homosexuals, professional poseurs) talk and/or act out sketchy vignettes. The cinema-verité aimlessness of the recorded performances is set in contrast to the strict, though seemingly arbitrary, structure of the film. While the length and continuity of each scene are identical (with actors instructed only to remain within the frame and to occupy the allotted time), the framing and camera movement vary between them, from the perfectly static to the eternally zooming. In a similar spirit of randomness, eight of the reels are in black-and-white, while four are in colour. The dual projection, suggesting the simultaneity of action in two rooms at once, represents Warhol's final renunciation of the cinema of montage, by making cross-cutting superfluous.

Apparently, the decision to show *Chelsea Girls* two reels at a time was made only after the footage was shot; and Warhol provided no clue as to their order or as to which of the competing soundtracks should receive precedence. Thus, the projectionist took an active part in the creative process; as does the audience, which never fails to detect correspondence and contrasts between the randomly juxtaposed images. More recently, the film's projection has become conventionalized, based on the instructions of its sole distributor Ondine, star of one of the film's "climactic" scenes. The beginning of the first two reels is staggered by about five minutes, with the reel change on the first projector taking place while the second image continues, and vice versa. As currently presented, the order of the reels is structured along a line of increasingly dramatic (though basically non-narrative) scenes, and from black-and-white toward colour. The first of the film's six coupled reels features Velvet Underground cohort Nico meticulously cutting her hair on the left screen, and superstar Ondine on the right. The last two reels mirror the first, with Nico on the right (in colour) and Ondine on the left playing out the film's most emotional scene, wherein the fiction of Ondine as "Pope," taking confessions from various Factory types, flares into a genuine confrontation with one woman, followed first by a refusal to complete the scene and then by a sequence in which Ondine makes use of the camera as confessor. The episodes in between include scenes of Factory regulars Ed Hood, Mario Montez, Ingrid Superstar, and International Velvet lolling on a bed; of Brigid Polk shooting up speed through her jeans; of later exploitation queen Mary Woronov playing Hanoi Hannah, haranguing several women from a revolutionary tract; of avant-garde filmmaker Marie Mencken verbally abusing factory pretty-boy Gerard Malanga; and of young Eric Emerson doing a sort of slow striptase under psychedelic lights as he delivers an LSD-induced rap to the camera.

Seen outside the context of New York 1960s underground chic, *Chelsea Girls* still seems more than deserving of its reputation, not only as a document of a period, or even as the apotheosis of a certain influential part of the counterculture, but moreso as the epitome of Warhol's democratic notion of stardom for everyone placed in brashly contradictory juxtaposition to a passively mechanical aesthetic structured to the specifications of the culture of mass production and consumption.

—Ed Lowry

UN CHIEN ANDALOU

(Andalusian Dog)

France, 1928

Director: Luis Buñuel

Production: Black and white, 35mm, silent; running time: 17 minutes, some sources state 24 minutes; length: 430 meters. Released April 1929, Paris; re-released 1960 with musical soundtrack. Filmed March 1928 in Le Havre and Paris.

Producer and editor: Luis Buñuel; **screenplay:** Luis Buñuel and Salvador Dali; **photography:** Albert Dubergen; **production designer:** Pierre Schilzneck; **music:** Wagner with some Argentine tangos (for 1960 version).

Cast: Pierre Batcheff (*Young Man*); Simone Mareuil (*Girl*); Jaime Miravilles; Salvador Dali (*Marist priest*); Luis Buñuel (*Man with razor*).

Publications

Scripts:

Buñuel, Luis, and Salvador Dali, *Un Chien andalou*, in *L'Avant-Scène du Cinéma* (Paris), July 1963.

Buñuel, Luis, and Salvador Dali, *"L'Age d'or" and "Un Chien andalou,"* New York, 1968.

Books:

Kyrou, Ado, *Le Surréalisme au cinéma*, Paris, 1953; revised edition, 1963.

Moullet, Luc, *Luis Buñuel*, Brussels, 1957.

Kyrou, Ado, *Luis Buñuel*, Paris, 1962.

Durgnat, Raymond, *Luis Buñuel*, Berkeley, 1968; revised edition, 1977.

Breton, André, *Manifestoes of Surrealism*, Ann Arbor, Michigan, 1969.

Buache, Freddy, *Luis Buñuel*, Lyons, 1970; as *The Cinema of Luis Buñuel*, New York and London, 1973.

Matthews, J. H., *Surrealism and the Film*, Ann Arbor, Michigan, 1971.

Alcalá, Manuel, *Buñuel (Cine e ideologia)*, Madrid, 1973.

Aranda, Francisco, *Luis Buñuel: A Critical Biography*, London and New York, 1975.

Cesarman, Fernando, *El ojo de Buñuel*, Barcelona, 1976.

Hammond, Paul, editor, *The Shadow and Its Shadow: Surrealist Writings on Cinema*, London, 1978.

Mellen, Joan, editor, *The World of Luis Buñuel: Essays in Criticism*, New York, 1978.

Higginbotham, Virginia, *Luis Buñuel*, Boston, 1979.

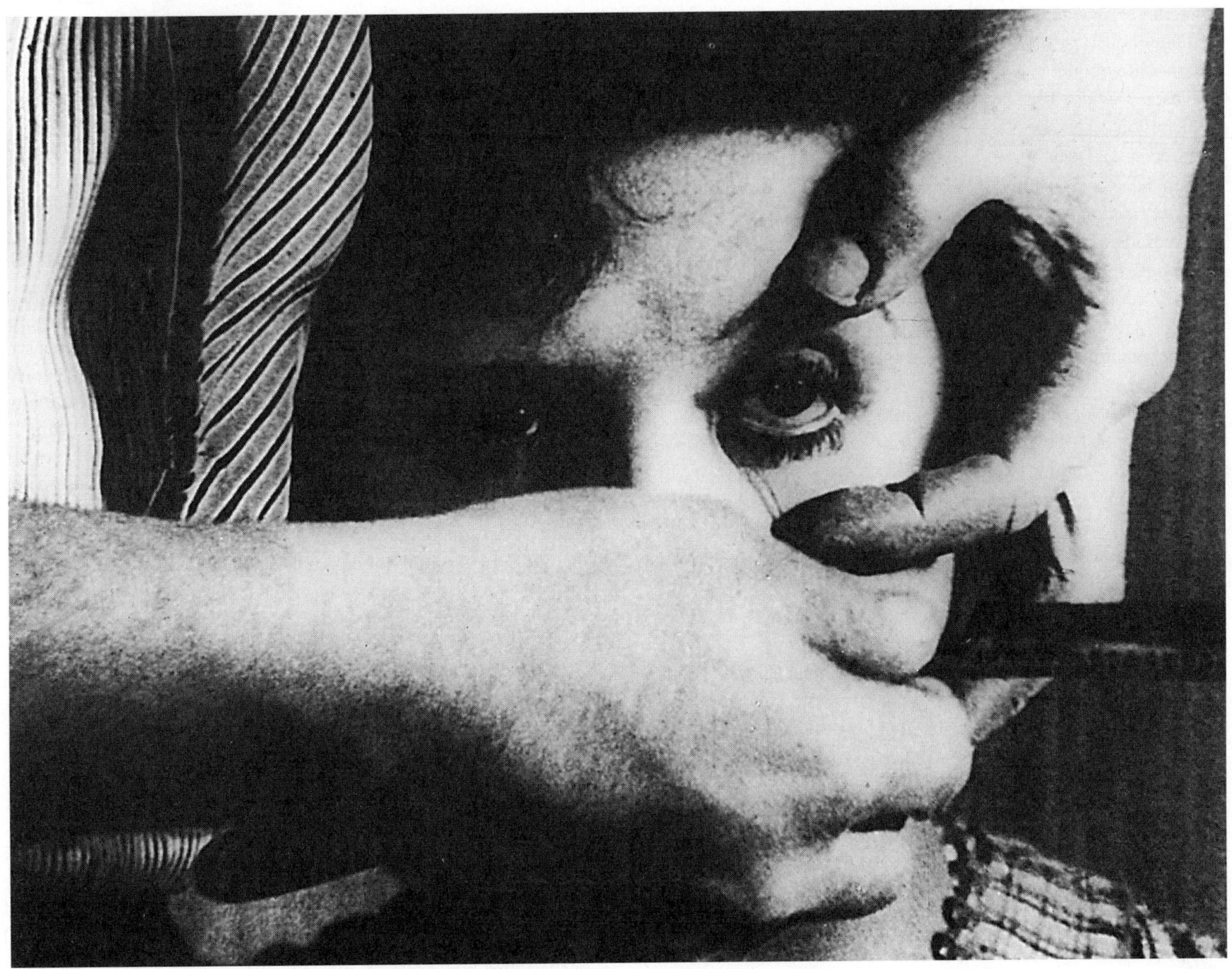

Un Chien Andalou

Thiher, Allen, *The Cinematic Muse: Critical Studies in the History of French Cinema*, Columbia, Missouri, 1979.

Williams, Linda. *Figures of Desire: A Theory and Analysis of Surrealist Film*, Urbana, Illinois, 1981.

Bazin, André, *The Cinema of Cruelty: From Buñuel to Hitchcock*, New York, 1982.

Edwards, Gwynne, *The Discreet Art of Luis Buñuel: A Reading of His Films*, London, 1982.

Buñuel, Luis, *My Last Breath*, London and New York, 1983.

Rees, Margaret A., editor, *Luis Buñuel: A Symposium*, Leeds, 1983.

Lefèvre, Raymond, *Luis Buñuel*, Paris, 1984,

Vidal, Agustin Sanchez, *Luis Buñuel: Obra Cinematografica*, Madrid, 1984.

Aub, Max, *Conversaciones con Buñuel: Seguidas de 45 entrevistas con familiares, amigos, y colaboradores del cineasta aragones*, Madrid, 1985.

Bertelli, Pino, *Buñuel: L'arma dello scandalo: L'anarchia nel cinema di Luis Buñuel*, Turin, 1985.

Oms, Marcel, *Don Luis Buñuel*, Paris, 1985.

Talens, Jenaro, *El ojo fachado: Lectura de ''Un Chien andalou'' de Luis Buñuel*, Madrid, 1986.

Sandro, Paul, *Diversions of Pleasure: Luis Buñuel and the Crises of Desire*, Columbus, Ohio, 1987.

Buñuel, Luis, *L' Age d'Or & Un Chien Andalou*, New York, 1989.

Buñuel, Luis, *Un Chien Andalou*, New York, 1994.

Evans, Peter W., *The Films of Luis Buñuel: Subjectivity & Desire*, New York, 1995.

Baxter, John, *Buñuel*, New York, 1999.

Kinder, Marsha, editor, *Luis Buñuel's ''The Discreet Charm of the Bourgeoisie,''* New York, 1999.

Articles:

Richardson, Tony, ''The Films of Luis Buñuel,'' in *Sight and Sound* (London), March 1954.

Prouse, Derek, ''Interviewing Buñuel,'' in *Sight and Sound* (London), Summer 1960.

Riera, Emilio, ''The Eternal Rebellion of Luis Buñuel,'' in *Film Culture* (New York), Summer 1960.

Aranda, Francesco, ''Surrealist and Spanish Giant,'' in *Films and Filming* (London), October 1961.

Kast, Pierre, in *Cahiers du Cinéma* (Paris), December 1961.
''Buñuel Issue'' of *La Méthode* (Paris), January 1962.
Durgnat, Raymond, in *Films and Filming* (London) April 1962.
Robinson, David, ''The Old Surrealist,'' in *London Magazine*, November 1962.
Vigo, Jean, in *Avant-Scène du Cinéma* (Paris), July 1963.
Hammond, Robert, ''Luis Alcoriza and the Films of Luis Buñuel,'' in *Film Heritage* (Dayton, Ohio), Fall 1965.
Harcourt, Peter, ''Luis Buñuel: Spanish and Surrealist,'' in *Film Quarterly* (Berkeley), Spring 1967.
Gow, Gordon, in *Films and Filming* (London), January 1969.
MacLochlainn, Alf, ''Pointed Horror: The Films of Luis Buñuel and Georges Franju,'' in *Film Journal* (New York), Summer 1971.
Lyon, E. H., ''Luis Buñuel: The Process of Dissociation in 3 Films,'' in *Cinema Journal* (Iowa City), Fall 1973.
Drummond, P., ''Textual Space in *Un Chien andalou*,'' in *Screen* (London), Autumn 1977.
Thiher, Allen, ''Surrealism's Enduring Bite: *Un Chien andalou*,'' in *Literature/Film Quarterly* (Salisbury, Maryland), Winter 1977.
Williams, Linda, ''The Prologue to *Un Chien andalou:* A Surrealist Film Metaphor,'' in *Screen* (London), Winter 1976–77.
Walker, I., ''Buñuel's Half Century, Once upon a Time,'' in *Sight and Sound* (London), Winter 1977–78.
Logette, L., ''Surréalisme et cinéma,'' in *Jeune Cinéma* (Paris), April-May 1981.
Wood, Michael, ''The Discreet Charm of Luis Buñuel,'' in *American Film* (Washington, D.C.), September 1982.
Bachelis, T., ''Slovo o Sal'vadore Dali,'' in *Iskusstvo Kino* (Moscow), no. 6, 1989.
Durgnat, R., ''Theory of Theory and Buñuel the Joker,'' in *Film Quarterly* (Berkeley), no. 1, 1990.
Jay, M., ''The Disenchantment of the Eye: Surrealism and the Crisis of Ocularcentrism,'' in *Visual Anthropology Review*, vol. 7, no. 1, 1991.
Revue Belge du Cinéma (Brussels), no. 33–34-35, 1993.
Perry, J. W., ''*L'Age d'or* and *Un Chien andalou*,'' in *Filmfax* (Evanston, Illinois), August-September 1993.
Goudet, Stéphane, in *Cinémathèque* (Paris), no. 6, Autumn 1994.
''L'esordio e il destino del testo 'insegretito','' in *Castoro Cinema* (Milan), January 1996.

* * *

Un Chien andalou is probably the most renowned surrealist film. A collaborative work by Luis Buñuel and Salvador Dali, the film, intended as ''a desperate and passionate appeal to murder,'' was immediately acclaimed for its poetry and beauty. Its enduring canonical status in film history is due not only to the reputation of its directors but also to its complex structure as a text. The film's disturbing imagery and transformation of narrative and continuity conventions help account for its appeal as a subject for critical scrutiny.

The film does present something on the order of narrative, if elusively; continuity is sustained primarily through the recurrence of the same actor-characters. However the connection between events is decidedly ambiguous. Title cards running through the film undermine any sense of coherent organization by randomly changing the temporal order and standard of reference throughout the course of the film—''Once upon a time,'' ''Eight years later,'' ''Towards 3 a.m.,'' etc. This level of narrative disorientation is supported by the film's visual construction, with its frequent use of point-of-view and continuity cutting to link ambiguously related spaces. Near the end of the film, the female character leaves an apartment which is presumably located on an upper floor of an urban building; a slight breeze blows through her hair; she smiles and waves at someone off-screen, and the next shot places her on a beach.

This kind of illogical transition and unexpected conjunction is commonly associated with Surrealism. It is also in line with Buñuel's attitudes about the potential of cinema: ''It is the best instrument to express the world of dreams, of emotions, of instinct.'' Indeed, most analyses of the film follow cures offered by dream interpretation to explain the film. In some cases this has led to reading the film as a symbolic conglomeration in which each bizarre image or event stands for something else. The deciphering process leads to an understanding of the film's ''hidden'' meanings—usually construed as an attack on bourgeois modes of behaviour, an anti-religious diatribe, and/or a study of repressed sexual impulses. One of the key images here is that of the man, after he has been rebuffed by the woman, dragging the ''baggage'' of modern society with him, including two priests and two pianos surmounted by dead donkeys.

More recently, critical attention has shifted to the film's processes of development and transformation, emphasizing the ways in which the film opens up possibilities of meaning (rather than containing it through a series of symbolic equivalents). These approaches draw on unconscious thought processes, instead of symbolization, to organize critical understanding. In this context the driving forces of the text are described in terms of condensation and displacement. In this same vein, greater consideration is devoted to the relationship between the film and its audience. By disrupting familiar patterns of spatial and narrative development. *Un Chien andalou* focuses attention on filmic processes of constructing and dismantling meaning. In fact the film opens with a brutal assault on vision, with the image of a razor blade cutting an eye. This not only throws into question the whole notion of sight as the locus of meaning, but more crucially shocks and disturbs an audience which is looking at the screen.

—M. B. White

THE CHILDREN OF PARADISE

See **LES ENFANTS DU PARADIS**

CHIMES AT MIDNIGHT

(Campanadas a medianoche)

Spain, 1966

Director: Orson Welles

Production: Internacional Films Española and Alpine Productions, presented by Harry Saltzman; black and white, 35mm; running time:

Chimes at Midnight

119 minutes, English version 115 minutes. Released May 1966. Filmed in Barcelona, Madrid, and other Spanish locations.

Producers: Emiliano Piedra and Angel Escolano; **executive producer:** Alessandro Tasca; **screenplay:** Orson Welles, from *Henry IV, Parts I and II, Henry V, Richard III, The Merry Wives of Windsor* by William Shakespeare and the *Chronicles of England* by Raphael Holinshed; **photography:** Edmond Richard; **editor:** Fritz Muller; **sound recordist:** Peter Parasheles; **art directors:** José Antonio de la Guerra and Mariano Erdorza; **music:** Angelo Francesco Lavagnino; **conductor:** Pierluigi Urbini; **music director:** Carlo Franci; **costume designer:** Orson Welles.

Cast: Orson Welles (*Sir John Falstaff*); Jeanne Moreau (*Doll Tearsheet*); Margaret Rutherford (*Hostess Quickly*); John Gielgud (*King Henry IV*); Keith Baxter (*Prince Hal, later King Henry V*); Marina Vlady (*Kate Percy*); Norman Rodway (*Henry Percy, called Hotspur*); Alan Webb (*Justice Shallow*); Walter Chiari (*Mr. Silence*); Michael Aldridge (*Pistol*); Tony Beckley (*Poins*); Fernando Rey (*Worcester*); Beatrice Welles (*Falstaff's Page*); Andrew Faulds (*Westmoreland*); José Nieto (*Northumberland*); Jeremy Rowe (*Prince John*); Paddy Bedford (*Bardolph*); Ralph Richardson (*Narrator*); Julio Peña; Fernando Hilbeck; Andrés Meguto; Keith Pyott; Charles Farrell.

Publications

Books:

Bessy, Maurice, *Orson Welles*, Paris, 1970.
Higham, Charles, *The Films of Orson Welles*, Berkeley, 1971.
Manvell, Roger, *Shakespeare and the Film*, New York, 1971.
McBride, Joseph, *Orson Welles*, London, 1972; New York, 1977.
Cowie, Peter, *A Ribbon of Dreams: The Cinema of Orson Welles*, New York, 1973.
Gottesman, Ronald, editor, *Focus on Orson Welles*, Englewood Cliffs, New Jersey, 1976.
Jorgens, Jack, *Shakespeare on Film*, Bloomington, Indiana, 1977.
Naremore, James, *The Magic World of Orson Welles*, New York, 1978.
Valentinetti, Claudio M., *Orson Welles*, Florence, 1981.

Bergala, Alain, and Jean Narboni, editors, *Orson Welles*, Paris, 1982.
Andrew, Dudley, *Film in the Aura of Art*, Princeton, 1984.
Higham, Charles, *Orson Welles: The Rise and Fall of an American Genius*, New York, 1985.
Leaming, Barbara, *Orson Welles: A Biography*, New York, 1985.
Parra, Daniele, and Jacques Zimmer, *Orson Welles*, Paris, 1985.
Weis, Elizabeth, and John Belton, editors, *Film Sound: Theory and Practice*, New York, 1985.
Taylor, John Russell, *Orson Welles: A Celebration*, London, 1986.
Lyons, Bridget G., *Chimes at Midnight*, Piscataway, 1988.
Bazin, Andre, *Orson Welles: A Critical View*, Venice, 1991.
Welles, Orson, *This Is Orson Welles*, New York, 1993.
Beja, Morris, *Perspective on Orson Welles*, New York, 1995.

Articles:

Billard, Pierre, in *Sight and Sound* (London), Spring 1965.
Cobos, Juan, and Miguel Rubio, ''A Trip to Don Quixoteland,'' in *Cahiers du Cinéma in English* (New York), no. 5, 1966.
Cobos, Juan, and Miguel Rubio, ''Welles and Falstaff,'' in *Sight and Sound* (London), Autumn 1966.
Morgenstern, J., and R. Sokolov, ''Falstaff as Orson Welles,'' in *Newsweek* (New York), 27 March 1967.
Sarris, Andrew, in *Village Voice* (New York), 30 March 1967.
Gow, Gordon, in *Films and Filming* (London), May 1967.
Price, James, in *Sight and Sound* (London), Summer 1967.
Cobos, Juan, and Miguel Rubio, ''Welles on *Falstaff*,'' in *Cahiers du Cinéma in English* (New York), September 1967.
McBride, Joseph, in *Film Quarterly* (Berkeley), Fall 1969.
Henderson, Brian, ''The Long Take,'' in *Film Comment* (New York), Summer 1971.
Bordwell, David, in *Film Comment* (New York), Summer 1971.
Rubin, Stanley, S., ''Welles/Falstaff/Shakespeare/Welles: The Narrative Structure of *Chimes at Midnight*,'' in *Film Criticism* (Edinboro, Pennsylvania), Winter-Spring 1978.
Poague, Leland, ''Reading the Prince: Shakespeare, Welles, and Some Aspects of *Chimes at Midnight*,'' in *Iowa State Journal of Research*, August 1981.
McLean, A. M., ''Orson Welles and Shakespeare: History and Consciousness in *Chimes at Midnight*,'' in *Literature/Film Quarterly* (Salisbury, Maryland), July 1983.
Chevrie, M., interview with Edmond Richard, in *Cahiers du Cinéma* (Paris), November 1985.
Anderegg, Michael, ''Every Third Word a Lie: Rhetoric and History in Orson Welles' *Chimes at Midnight*,'' in *Film Quarterly* (Berkeley), Spring 1987.
Baxter, K., ''Filming *Falstaff*,'' in *Positif* (Paris), July-August 1992.
Berthome, J.-P., and F. Thomas, ''Sept annees en noir et blanc,'' in *Positif* (Paris), July-August 1992.
Saada, Nicolas, and Joël Magny, in *Cahiers du Cinéma* (Paris), October 1995.
''Falstaff,'' in *Télérama* (Paris), 27 September 1995.

* * *

Among film scholars *Citizen Kane* is often regarded as the greatest film of all time; among Welles scholars, by contrast, *Chimes at Midnight* is often accorded pride of place as ''the fullest, most completely realized expression of everything [Welles] had been working toward since *Citizen Kane*.'' Partly such praise can be understood as admiration for the fact that Welles managed to make the film at all, coming, as it did, late in a career long plagued by financial and commercial difficulties. And certainly auteurist film critics are prone to praise films generally discounted by journalistic reviewers and contemporary audiences, as *Chimes at Midnight* was discounted if not derided at the time of its initial (somewhat haphazard, if not half-hearted) release. The evaluative paradox cannot be readily settled, nor need it be; but the comparison to *Citizen Kane* can be helpful in highlighting those aspects of *Chimes at Midnight* which urge attention.

The central paradox of the Wellesian cinema involves a conflict between energy and dissipation or constraint; Charles Foster Kane, for instance, is shown as a youth of boundless imagination, but that imaginative energy is evidenced in a narrative which begins with Kane's own death and which portrays his overall inability to put that energy to real use. In *Chimes at Midnight* there is a similar contrast of youth and age—though the contrast involves two different characters drawn from Shakespeare's Lancaster plays, Falstaff, played by Welles himself, and Prince Hal, played by Keith Baxter. Furthermore, the terms of the contrast are reversed; all in all it is Falstaff who labors to be (or seem) young, while it is Hal who most clearly appreciates the fact that his aging father (John Gielgud) will soon die, and, thus, Hal himself will soon be England's king.

In both films the energy expended in the doomed effort to outwit the facts of time finds its presentational equivalent in the remarkable wit and energy of Welles's film style. It is generally accepted that film style is more muted in *Chimes at Midnight* than in *Citizen Kane*; style does not carry the burden of mystery in the later film that it does in the earlier one. But the energy and intelligence remain evident in *Chimes at Midnight* nevertheless—not only in the justly famous Shrewsbury battle sequence (often likened, in Welles's favor, to that in Eisenstein's *Alexander Nevsky*), but also in the use Welles makes of moving camera (in the Gadshill robbery scene), of interior space (the Windsor castle sequences, as well as those at the Boar's Head tavern), and of camera angle (especially in the tavern scene where Hal plays King Henry to Falstaff's Prince). Especially moving and appropriate in this regard is the film's last shot, the intelligence of which (the camera craning slowly up to frame Falstaff's coffin against the castle in the deep background of the frame) serves to memorialize the energy lost at Falstaff's passing. Welles has long been noted for his use of such ''deep focus'' sequence shots—but the ''depth'' connoted by this shot, as by the whole of *Chimes at Midnight*, is equally as much emotional as technical.

—Leland Poague

CHINATOWN

USA, 1974

Director: Roman Polanski

Production: Paramount Pictures, Penthouse, and The Long Road Productions; Technicolor, 35mm, Panavision; running time: 131 minutes. Released 21 June 1974. Filmed on location in Los Angeles.

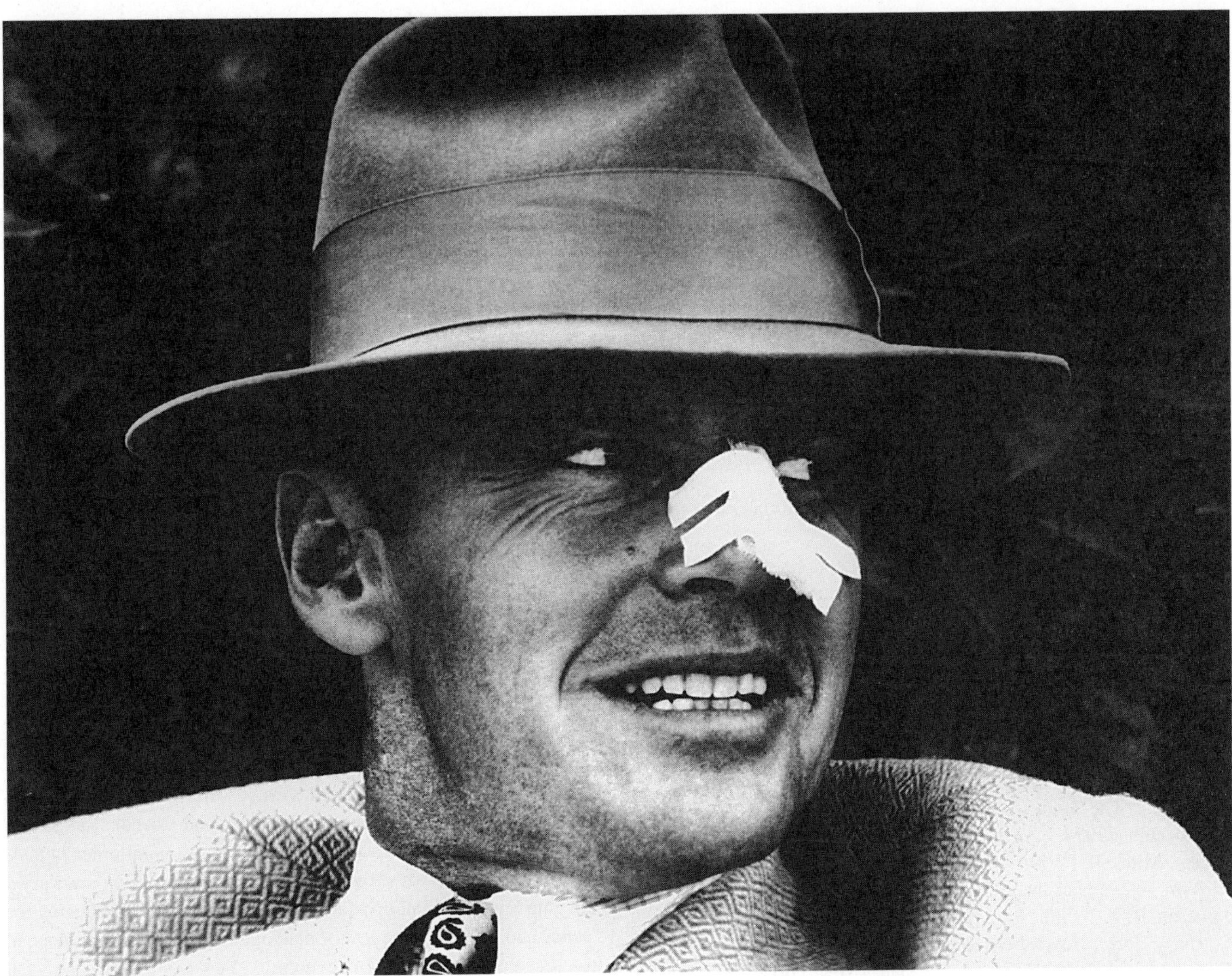

Chinatown

Producer: Robert Evans; **screenplay:** Robert Towne; **titles:** Wayne Fitzgerald; **assistant director:** Howard Koch, Jr.; **photography:** John A. Alonzo; **editor:** Sam O'Steen; **sound:** Larry Jost and Bud Grenzbach; **sound editor:** Robert Cornett; **production designer:** Richard Sylbert; **set designer:** Gabe and Robert Resh; **art director:** W. Stewart Campbell; **music score:** Jerry Goldsmith; **special effects:** Logan Frazee; **costume designer:** Anthea Sylbert.

Cast: Jack Nicholson (*J. J. Gittes*); Faye Dunaway (*Evelyn Mulwray*); John Huston (*Noah Cross*); John Hillerman (*Yelburton*); Perry Lopez (*Lieutenant Escobar*); Burt Young (*Curly*); Darrell Zwerling (*Hollis Mulwray*); Diane Ladd (*Ida Sessions*); Roy Jensen (*Mulvihill*); Roman Polanski (*Man with knife*); Dick Bakalyan (*Loach*); Joe Mantell (*Walsh*); Bruce Glover (*Duffy*); Nandu Hinds (*Sophie*); James Hong (*Evelyn's butler*); Belinda Palmer (*Katherine*); Fritzie Burr (*Mulwray's secretary*); Elizabeth Harding (*Curly's wife*).

Awards: Oscar, Best Original Screenplay, 1974; New York Film Critics' Award, Best Actor (Nicholson; award also in conjunction with his role in *The Last Detail*), 1974.

Publications

Script:

Towne, Robert, *Chinatown, The Last Detail, Shampoo: Screenplays*, New York, 1994.

Books:

Crane, Robert David, and Christopher Fryer, *Jack Nicholson—Face to Face*, New York, 1975.
Bullis, Roger Alan, *An Analysis of the Interpersonal Communication of Private Detective Characters in Selected ''Mean Street'' Motion Pictures*, Ann Arbor, Michigan, 1978.
Bisplinghoff, Gretchen, and Virginia Wexman, *Roman Polanski: A Guide to References and Resources*, Boston, 1979.
Silver, Alain, and Elizabeth Ward, editors, *Film Noir*, New York, 1979.
Kiernan, Thomas, *The Roman Polanski Story*, New York, 1980.
Leaming, Barbara, *Polanski: A Biography*, New York, 1981.
Tuska, Jon, editor, *Close-up: The Contemporary Director*, Metuchen, New Jersey, 1981.

Leaming, Barbara, *Polanski: The Filmmaker as Voyeur: A Biography*, New York, 1981; as *Polanski: His Life and Films*, London, 1982.
Downing, David, *Jack Nicholson: A Biography*, London, 1983.
Polanski, Roman, *Roman*, London, 1984.
Wexman, Virginia Wright, *Roman Polanski*, Boston, 1985.
Jacobsen, Wolfgang, and others, *Roman Polanski*, Munich, 1986.
Avron, Dominique, *Roman Polasnki*, Paris, 1987.
Parker, John, *Polanski*, London, 1995.
Eaton, Michael, *Chinatown*, London, 1997.

Articles:

Farber, Stephen, ''Violence and the Bitch Goddess,'' in *Film Comment* (New York) vol. 10, 1974.
Cohen, M. S., in *Take One* (Montreal), July 1974.
Burke, Tom, ''The Restoration of Roman Polanski,'' in *Rolling Stone* (New York), 18 July, 1974.
''Dialogue on Film: Roman Polanski,'' in *American Film* (Washington, D.C.), August 1974.
Combs, Richard, in *Monthly Film Bulletin* (London), August, 1974.
Milne, Tom, in *Sight and Sound* (London), Autumn, 1974.
Kavanagh, J., ''*Chinatown:* Other Places, Other Times,'' in *Jump Cut* (Chicago), September-October 1974.
Sperber, M., ''*Chinatown:* Do As Little as Possible: Polanski's Message and Manipulation,'' in *Jump Cut* (Chicago), September-October 1974.
Gow, Gordon, in *Films and Filming* (London), October 1974.
Stewart, Garrett, in *Film Quarterly* (Berkeley), Winter 1974.
Cook, P., ''The Sound Track,'' in *Films in Review* (New York), November 1974.
Cohen, Mitchell, ''Villains and Victims,'' in *Film Comment* (New York) November-December 1974.
Jameson, R. T., ''Film Noir: Today, Son of Noir,'' in *Film Comment* (New York), November-December 1974.
Rosenbaum, Jonathan, in *Film Comment* (New York), November-December 1974.
Andersson, W., and K. Josef, ''Amerika,'' in *Filmrutan* (Liding, Sweden) vol. 18, no. 1, 1975.
Cappabianca, A., ''L'occhio e il ragno. Note su *Chinatown* e *Il fantasma della liberta*,'' in *Filmcritica* (Rome), January-February 1975.
Mancini, M., ''Vuoto e fiction (Wyler, Polanski, Peckinpah),'' in *Filmcritica* (Rome), January-February 1975.
Kane, P., in *Cahiers du Cinéma* (Paris), February-March 1975.
Alonzo, John, ''Behind the Scenes of *Chinatown*,'' in *American Cinematographer* (Hollywood), May 1975.
McGinnis, W. D., in *Literature/Film Quarterly* (Salisbury, Maryland), Summer 1975.
Oliver, B., ''*The Long Goodbye* and *Chinatown*: Debunking the Private Eye Tradition,'' in *Literature/Film Quarterly* (Salisbury, Maryland) Summer 1975.
Palmer, R. Barton, ''*Chinatown* and the Detective Story,'' in *Literature/Film Quarterly* (Salisbury, Maryland), Spring 1977.
Beneli, D., ''Contemporary Film Noir: Questing in *Chinatown's* Maze,'' in *Cinemonkey* (Portland, Oregon), no. 4, 1978.
Albright, Charles, Jr., in *Magill's Survey of Cinema 1*, Englewood Cliffs, New Jersey, 1980.
Linderman, D., ''Oedipus in Chinatown,'' in *Enclitic* (Minneapolis), Fall 1981-Spring 1982.
Laguna, P., in *Kino* (Warsaw), July 1983.
Levy, S., ''Forget It? Never—It's *Chinatown*,'' in *Boxoffice* (Chicago), February 1990.
Horowitz, Mark, ''Fault Lines,'' in *Film Comment* (New York), November-December 1990.
Lyons, D., ''Laws in the Iris: The Private Eye in the Seventies,'' in *Film Comment* (New York), July-August 1993.
Biskind, Peter, ''The Low Road to *Chinatown*,'' in *Premiere* (New York), June 1994.
Feeney, F., ''Water and Power,'' in *Written By* (Los Angeles), vol. 1, December-January 1996–97.

* * *

The title of Polanski's film refers to the state of mind of Jack Nicholson's character, a former cop in L.A.'s Chinatown who left the force and turned private eye after getting in over his head on a case he never fully understood, bringing tragedy to a woman he'd sought to help.

History begins to repeat itself in characteristically bleak Polanskian terms when Nicholson becomes enmeshed in a case involving seeming *femme fatale* Faye Dunaway, playing the abused daughter of a local power broker (John Huston), the conniving, murderous villain behind a lucrative water rights and land grabbing scheme. Events come full circle when Nicholson again finds himself in Chinatown, this time to help Dunaway escape the clutches of her incestuous father once and for all—only to wind up getting her killed instead.

Unlike the similarly shady but virtuous white knight detectives in the fiction of Dashiell Hammett and Raymond Chandler, men who managed to restore at least some semblance of moral order to their chaotic *noir* universes at the end of each case, Nicholson's variation on Sam Spade and Phillip Marlowe succeeds only in maintaining the status quo, and, on some levels, making things worse. As his cop pal Lt. Escobar tells him at one point: ''You never learn, do you, Jake?''—no, he doesn't, because his state of mind fates him not to. ''Come on, Jake, it's Chinatown,'' Nicholson's colleague says, leading him away from this latest scene of inscrutable—and unpreventable—tragedy in the devastated detective's life. It is one of the most haunting, and memorable, closing lines in the history of *noir* cinema.

Robert Towne's Oscar-winning screenplay for this seminal Watergate-era detective thriller was written expressly for his pal Nicholson, a lifelong clothes horse who had longed to do a part where he could be a dapper dan. California native Towne had been writing a tale about a real-life incident of corruption and environmental scandal drawn from L.A.'s early history when he got the idea of turning the piece into a period detective yarn in homage to his idols Hammett and Chandler.

Nicholson quickly signed on to play the gumshoe, Jake Gittes, and suggested Polanski, another friend, as director. Paramount greenlighted the project when Polanski agreed to direct—provided Towne would subject his 180-page script to an overhaul. Towne initially resisted, then agreed to undertake the task, working closely with Polanski.

The project marked Polanski's return to mainstream Hollywood filmmaking after two back-to-back box-office failures, *Macbeth* (1971) and *What?* (1973), both made in Europe. It also marked his return to Hollywood itself, scene of the 1969 Manson murders that claimed the lives of his wife, actress Sharon Tate, and several friends. He quickly began molding Towne's period mystery into a typically dark Polanski essay on sex and violence set in the ''landscape of the mind.''

In addition to trimming and tightening Towne's screenplay in an effort to make it less convoluted and more focused, Polanski insisted on enhancing the romantic relationship between Nicholson and Dunaway, which helps to further illustrate the concept that Nicholson's character is inadvertently repeating his past. To the same end, he altered Towne's conclusion. Towne's original script not only did not conclude in Chinatown, but it ended on a very different, upbeat note with Dunaway's character (Evelyn Mulwray) surviving and her loathsome monster of a father dead; justice triumphs and Evelyn and Jake go off into the pre-smog L.A. sunset together. Towne to this day disdains Polanski's downbeat finale, which is set in Chinatown, as a too-literal and ghoulish example of ''bleak chic.'' But it is Polanski's ending that transforms the film from a polished, superbly acted evocation of the vanished pre-World War II milieu of Hammett and Chandler into a detective story of considerable and disturbing power—a seminal film of the 1970s. Indeed, it is difficult to conceive of Chinatown ending any other way than it does. Polanski's alteration gives the film its meaning (troubling though it may be); it's what the story is all about.

An ill-conceived and ill-fated 1990 sequel, *The Two Jakes*, also written by Towne and starring Nicholson, who directed as well, makes this even clearer. The sequel, set in L.A. of the 1940s and involving an oil rather than water and land scheme this time, had plot—plenty of it—but lacked a story; Polanski had already told it, superbly and definitively, 16 years earlier.

—John McCarty

CHRIST STOPPED AT EBOLI

See **CRISTO SI E FERMATO A EBOLI**

CHRONICLE OF A SUMMER

See **CHRONIQUE D'UN ÉTÉ**

CHRONICLE OF ANNA MAGDALENA BACH

See **CHRONIK DER ANNA MAGDALENA BACH**

CHRONICLE OF THE YEARS OF EMBERS

See **CHRONIQUE DES ANNÉES DE BRAISE**

CHRONIK DER ANNA MAGDALENA BACH

(Chronicle of Anna Magdalena Bach)

Germany-Italy, 1968

Director: Jean-Marie Straub

Production: (West Germany) Franz Seitz, Filmproduktion-Kuratorium Junger Deutscher Film, Hessiches Rundfunk, Radio-Televisionbessoise, Filmfonds, and Telepool; (Rome) IDI Cinematografica, PAI; black and white, 35mm; running time: 94 minutes. Released 1968, West Germany.

Producers: Gian Vittorio Baldi, with Jean-Marie Straub; **screenplay:** Jean-Marie Straub and Danièle Huillet; **photography:** Ugo Piccone, Saverio Diamanti, and Giovanni Canfarelli; **editors:** Jean-Marie Straub and Danièle Huillet; **sound:** Louis Houchet and Lucien Moreau; **music conductor:** Nikolaus Harnoncourt, Schola Cantorum Basilienses; **concert group conductor:** August Wenziner, Hanover Boys Choir; **music director:** Heinz Hennig; **costume designers:** Casa d'Arte Firenze, Vera Poggioni and Renata Morroni.

Cast: Gustav Leonhardt (*Johann Sebastian Bach*); Christiane Lang (*Anna Magdalena Bach*); Paolo Carlini (*Hölzel*); Hans-Peter Boye (*Born*); Joachim Wolf (*Rector*); Rainer Kirchner (*Superintendent*); Eckart Brüntjen (*Prefect Kittler*); Walter Peters (*Prefect Krause*); Kathrien Leonhardt (*Catherina Dorothea Bach*); Anja Fährmann (*Regine Susanna Bach*); Katja Drewanz (*Christine Sophie Henrietta Bach*); Bob van Aspern (*Johann Elias Bach*); Andrea Pangritz (*Wilhelm Friedemann Bach*); Bernd Weikl (*Singer in Cantata No. 205*); Wolfgang Schöne (*Singer in Cantata No. 82*); Karl-Heinz Lampe (*Singer in Cantata No. 42*); Nikolaus Harnoncourt (*Prince of Anthalt-Cöthen*).

Publications

Script:

Straub, Jean-Marie, and Danièle Huillet, *Chronik der Anna Magdalena Bach*, Frankfurt, 1969.

Books:

Roud, Richard, *Jean-Marie Straub*, New York, 1972.
Rossetti, Riccardo, *Straub-Huillet Film*, Rome, 1984.
Byg, Barton, *Landscapes of Resistance: The German Films of Danièle Huillet and Jean-Marie Straub*, Berkeley, 1995.

Articles:

''Frustration of Violence,'' in *Cahiers du Cinéma in English* (New York), January 1967.
Roud, Richard, in *Sight and Sound* (London), Summer 1968.
Polt, Harriet, in *Film Quarterly* (Berkeley), Winter 1968–69.
Baxter, B., ''Jean-Marie Straub,'' in *Film* (London), Spring 1969.
Engel, Andi, ''Jean-Marie Straub,'' in *Second Wave*, New York, 1970.

Chronik der Anna Magdalena Bach

Monthly Film Bulletin (London), May 1970.
Armes, Roy, ''Jean-Marie Straub,'' in *London Magazine*, September 1970.
Roth, W., and G. Pflaum, ''Gesprach mit Danièle Huillet und Jean-Marie Straub,'' in *Filmkritik* (Munich), February 1973.
''Die Filmographie—Jean-Marie Straub,'' in *Information* (Wiesbaden), January 1974.
Walsh, M., ''Political Formations in the Cinema of Jean-Marie Straub,'' in *Jump Cut* (Chicago), November-December 1974.
Seguin, L., ''La Famille, l'histoire, le roman,'' in *Cahiers du Cinéma* (Paris), October-November 1975.
Greene, N., ''Report from Vienna: Cinema and Ideology,'' in *Praxis* (Berkeley), no. 2, 1976.
''Danièle Huillet/Jean-Marie Straub's Fortini/Cani,''in *Filmkritik* (Munich), January 1977.
Dermody, S., ''Straub/Huillet: The Politics of Film Practice,'' in *Cinema Papers* (Melbourne), September-October 1976.
Simsolo, Noël, ''Jean-Marie Straub et Danièle Huillet,'' in *Cinéma* (Paris), March 1977.
Grant, J., ''Le Combat contre l'impression,'' in *Cinéma* (Paris), January 1978.
Nau, P., ''Die Kunst des Filmesehens,'' in *Filmkritik* (Munich), January 1979.
Listener (London), 27 June 1985.
Vatrican, V., ''Tout est musique,'' in *Cahiers du Cinéma* (Paris), no. 492, June 1995.

* * *

The *Chronicle of Anna Magdalena Bach* is Jean-Marie Straub and Danièle Huillet's version of film biography. The film presents biography as the rewriting and juxtaposition of prior documents; in this instance music and a chronicle are most prominent. Defined in this way, through a range of documents, Bach does not emerge as a conventional dramatic character. The importance of music in the film, which was performed and recorded during the filming rather than dubbed, stresses its centrality to the contemporary knowledge and appreciation of the historical figure Bach. In fact, Straub has said that the music was considered the basic raw material of the film, and not simply background accompaniment.

Personal aspects of the composer's life are presented, along with the musical performance, through the agency of a diary. A voice-over narration, purportedly reciting the text of Anna Magdalena's journal, provides information about financial and familial affairs in a matter-of-fact monotone. No such chronicle really exists, and the narration was constructed from various sources including letters written by and to Bach. However the actual status of the spoken text is less important than its effect in the film as a document.

Through the use of these prior texts as its basic structuring principle, the film constructs a biographical portrait while asserting its distance from its subject. In line with this approach, the film refuses to engage the viewer emotionally in its characters as psychologized individuals. To undermine any sense of realistic depiction, the actors are dressed in period costumes but do not visibly age in the course of the film. The film as a whole is visually austere and verbally reticent, and the music stands as the major mechanism of viewer involvement. The actors rarely speak and the narration is void of emotional sentiment. This ''silence'' is expressed in several visual pauses punctuating the film; two shots of the sea, one of the sky, and one of a tree intervene in the course of the film. These images serve as moments of meditation. Removed from the musical, familial, and financial concerns developed in the narrative, they offer the possibility to speculate on, among other things, the relation of these images to the filmic depiction of Bach's life; the relationship of nature to social and cultural life; and the nature of cinema. With regard to the latter, Straub is known for quoting D. W. Griffith: ''What the modern movies lack is the wind in the trees.''

The framing and lighting convey an almost academic sense of beauty, a calculatingly striking surface that denies the depth of space or character. While many of the images involve composition-in-depth, they are often so extreme and self-conscious that their status as artificial constructions—through the conjunction of set construction, lens choice, and character placement—is obvious. In addition, various camera and lens movements frequently manipulate and shift apparent depth within the course of such shots. The formal contrast and counterpoint guiding the editing are often seen as the visual counterpart of the structure of Bach's music. However, this approach to editing, insisting on the process of spatial construction, is characteristic of Straub and Huillet's films. It is a way of underscoring the artificiality of the film's visual world.

—M. B. White

CHRONIQUE DES ANNÉES DE BRAISE

(Chronicle of the Years of Embers)

Algeria, 1975

Director: Mohammed Lakhdar Hamina

Production: O.N.C.I.C. (Algeria); Eastmancolor, 70mm, Panavision; running time: 170 minutes. Filmed in Algeria.

Production manager: Mohammed (sometimes Mohamed) Lakhdar Hamina; **screenplay:** Mohammed Lakhdar Hamina and Tewfik Fares; **photography:** Marcello Gatti; **editor:** Youcef Tobni; **music:** Philippe Arthuys.

Cast: Mohammed Lakhdar Hamina (*Miloud*); Jorgo Voyagis (*Ahmed*); Leila Shenna (*Wife*); Cheik Nourredine (*Friend*); Larbi Sekkai (*Larbi*); Hassan Hassani; M. Kouiret; Francois Maistre.

Awards: Grand Prix, Cannes Film Festival, 1975.

Publications

Books:

Salmane, Hala, editor, *Algerian Cinema*, London, 1976.
Brossard, Jean-Pierre, *L'Algerie vue par son cinéma*, La Chaux-de-Fonds, Switzerland, 1981.

Articles:

Dupont, C., ''Entretien avec Lakhdar Hamina,'' in *Cahiers du Cinéma* (Paris), Spring 1975.
Moskowitz, G., in *Variety* (New York), 21 May 1975.
''Lakhdar Hamina issue'' of *Cahiers de la Cinématheque* (Perpignan), Summer 1975.
Cineforum (Bergamo), June-July 1975.
Interview with Lakhdar Hamina in *Ecran* (Paris), July-August 1975.
Cinématographe (Paris), August-September 1975.
Ecran (Paris), October 1975.
Hollywood Reporter, 29 October 1975.
Cahiers du Cinéma (Paris), May 1976.
Horvath, Z., ''Filmeposz hat tetelben,'' in *Filmkultura* (Budapest), May-June 1977.
Manoiu, A., ''De la prima incercare o lovitura de maestru,'' in *Cinema* (Bucharest), June 1977.
Manoiu, A., and V. Sava, in *Cinema* (Bucharest), August 1977.
Prochnow, C., ''Leiden und Emporung dann Alltag,'' in *Film und Fernsehen* (Berlin), April 1978.
Nassar, I., ''*The Chronicle of the Years of Embers*,'' in *American Historical Review*, vol. 99, no. 4, 1994.
Serceau, M., in *Cinemaction* (Conde-sur-Noireau), March/June 1997.

* * *

Mohammed Lakhdar Hamina is a key figure in the development of Algerian cinema, and one of the most talented and ambitious of Arab directors. Trained in Czechoslovakia, he began his career as a documentary filmmaker. His first feature, released in 1966, was one of the very first Algerian national productions. *Chronique des années de braise*, his fourth feature, made almost ten years later and designed to celebrate the outbreak of the Algerian Revolution on November 1, 1954, is without question one of the most striking of all third world films. Winning a Grand Prix at Cannes in 1975, it created a new international awareness for Algerian cinema, but for Arab critics, and for some of Lakhdar Hamina's fellow directors it has remained a controversial work. Particular attention was focused in the 1970s on its enormous cost, with critics claiming that a dozen modest features could have been made with the funds squandered on this extravagant epic.

Certainly *Chronique des années de braise* is an impressive work, with production values to match its cost. A monumental three-hour study of recent Algerian history, it gives a clear illustration of the high technical capability of the young Algerian film industry while confronting international cinema on its own terms. It is beautifully shot, with all the gloss of a Hollywood epic, but in achieving this result the director has had to sacrifice much of the specific national quality. In particular critics were hostile to the lushly orchestrated musical score by the French composer Philippe Arthuys, which owes nothing to Algerian musical traditions. It is fair to say that Lakhdar Hamina achieves something of the epic quality of the later David Lean. This is a remarkable feat in a country with a filmmaking history of barely a dozen years; but at the same time, this approach is questionable in terms of the priorities of a third world country like Algeria which in the 1970s began to take on an increasingly important international role.

In retrospect, the principal questions concerning this film derive less from its cost than from its narrative stance. Lakhdar Hamina defines his work as a personal vision and brushes aside questions of historical accuracy as mere quibbles. The film, he claims, is a poetic statement which grows directly out of his own childhood experiences (he was 20 in 1954). But the film's half-dozen or so intertitles drawing attention to the key dates in the historical development of Algeria between 1939 and 1954 deny the validity of a purely personal reading: *Chronique des années de braise* demands interpretation as an epic of the national consciousness. In this sense the film's inadequacies become clear. It offers less political insight than a purely lyrical protest; and the poverty and sufferings of the colonized are presented in lushly beautiful images which negate or, at least, defuse, the film's anger. The narrative intertwines two stories. One is that of a key Arab literary figure—the knowing madman (played with enormous gusto by Lakhdar Hamina himself)—who dies on the eve of revolution. The other concerns Ahmed, a totally mythologised figure, who is successively an uneducated peasant driven from his land, a skilled urban worker and—in a transformation all too reminiscent of western romantic melodrama—an unbelievably skilful horseman and swordsman defending his people against the savagery of the colonizers. Despite all Lakhdar Hamina's eloquence and directorial self-assurance, nothing could be more mystificatory than such a depiction of the 15-year origin of the national revolution.

—Roy Armes

CHRONIQUE D'UN ÉTÉ

(Chronicle of a Summer)

France, 1960

Directors: Jean Rouch and Edgar Morin

Production: Agros Films; black and white, 35mm; running time: 85 minutes, English version is 90 minutes. Released October 1961, Paris. Filmed summer 1960 in Paris and Saint-Tropez.

Producers: Anatole Dauman and Philippe Lifschitz; **screenplay:** Jean Rouch and Edgar Morin; **photography:** Roger Morillère, Raoul Coutard, Jean-Jacques Tarbès, and Michel Brault; **editors:** Jean Ravel, Nèna Baratier, and Françoise Colin; **sound:** Guy Rophe, Michel Fano, and Barthèlèmy.

Cast: Jean Rouch; Edgar Morin; Marceline; Angelo; Marilou; Jean-Pierre; Jean (*Factory worker*); Jacques (*Factory worker*); Régis (*Student*); Céline (*Student*); Jean-Marc (*Student*); Nadine (*Student*); Landry (*Student*); Raymond (*Student*); Jacques (*Office worker*); Simone (*Office worker*); Henri (*Artist*); Madi (*Artist*); Catherine (*Artist*); Sophie (*Model*).

Awards: International Critics Prize, Cannes Film Festival, 1961.

Publications

Script:

Rouch, Jean, and Edgar Morin, *Chronique d'un été*, Paris, 1962.

Books:

Armes, Roy, *French Cinema Since 1946, Volume 2: The Personal Style*, New York, 1966.
Ali Issari, M., *Cinema Verité*, East Lansing, Michigan, 1971.
Barnouw, Erik, *Documentary: A History of the Non-Fiction Film*, New York, 1974.
Courchay, Claude, *Chronique d'un été*, Paris, 1990.

Articles:

Sandell, Roger, ''Films by Jean Rouch,'' in *Film Quarterly* (Berkeley). Winter 1961–62.
Milne, Tom, in *Sight and Sound* (London), Summer 1962.
Gerard, David, in *Films and Filming* (London), August 1962.
Shivas, Mark, in *Movie* (London), September 1962.
Graham, Peter, ''Cinema Verité in France,'' in *Film Quarterly* (Berkeley), Summer 1964.
''Jean Rouch in Conversation with Jacqueline Veuve,'' in *Film Comment* (New York), Fall-Winter 1967.
Blue, James, ''The Films of Jean Rouch,'' in *Film Comment* (New York), Fall-Winter 1967.
Freyer, Ellen, in *The Documentary Tradition*, edited by Lewis Jacobs, New York, 1971.
Levin, G. Roy, in *Documentary Explorations: 15 Interviews with Filmmakers*, New York, 1971.
Marcorelles, L., ''Je suis mon premier spectateur,'' in *Avant-Scène du Cinéma* (Paris), March 1972.
Studies in Visual Communication, no. 1, 1985.
Ben Salama, M., M. Serceau and L. Goldmann, ''Special Section,'' in *Cinemaction* (Conde-sur-Noireau), no. 81, 1996.

* * *

Substantially distinguished as an ethnographic filmmaker, a studious if somewhat unscientific observer of rituals among the hunter-gatherers of post-Colonial Africa, Jean Rouch returned to his native

Chronique d'un été

Paris at age 40 in 1959 to encounter a new and stimulating intellectual climate. His friend, the critic and filmmaker Edgar Morin, challenged him to make a film about ''his own tribe.'' Rouch responded with *Chronique d'un été*, one of the most evocative films from the makers of that ragbag of student excess and self-aggrandizement which Françoise Giroud christened the *nouvelle vague.* Trained in the hard school of location shooting, Rouch knew the challenge of making an urban ethnographic film was largely technical. He persuaded André Coutant at Eclair to lend him the prototype of a lightweight camera under development for the military. After use by day, it was returned to the Eclair factory at night for modification and repairs. Raoul Coutard, who worked only one day on the film, disparages Rouch's search for ''cinema verité''. The effort to duplicate Alexandre Astruc's ideal of the ''*caméra stylo*,'' a camera as flexible as a pen, required as much hardware as any feature film.

Chronique betrays the constraints of technique and the causation of its makers. Set-ups are studied, montage formal, photography often imitative of the cinema of performance, while a side trip to St. Tropez for an alleged holiday to observe the beautiful at play exposes the deficiencies of Rouch's philosophy of enquiry. The film is open to the same criticism of formalism as the now-historic Drew-Leacock-Pennebaker exercises in spontaneous cinema. A delight in the exercise of technique turns the aleatory by-products of low-light wild-sound filming into elements of a new style. Grain, rambling vox pop, interviews, walking tracks are *chosen* rather than merely being tolerated in the pursuit of truth.

But *Chronique* is a brilliant pre-vision of a style and approach to actuality filming that would sweep away the standard formal Grierson documentary. To begin by asking people at random ''Are you happy?'' was a stroke of genius. Their reactions, puzzled, truculent, thoughtful, sing with spontaneity. Nor is Rouch afraid to follow a plainly disturbed girl down into the wallow of self-pity and hysteria, leaving the watcher to make a personal determination of her sincerity. The refusal to take sides is *Chronique*'s strength, and the conclusion, as Rouch and Morin pace around a museum, wondering if the experiment proved anything, aptly conveys their genuine doubts. By then, however, their work had made the question largely irrelevant. The technique they created was to be the New Wave's most powerful and durable legacy.

—John Baxter

CITIZEN KANE

USA, 1941

Director: Orson Welles

Production: RKO Radio Pictures Corp.; black and white, 35mm, running time: 120 minutes. Released 1 May 1941, New York. Filmed 30 July through 23 October 1940 in RKO studios; cost: $686,033.

Producer: Orson Welles; **original screenplay:** Herman J. Mankiewicz and Orson Welles; **photography:** Gregg Toland; **editors:** Robert Wise and Mark Robson; **sound recordists:** Bailey Fesler and James G. Stewart; **art director:** Van Nest Polglase; **music:** Bernard Herrmann; **special effects:** Vernon L. Walker; **costume designer:** Edward Stevenson.

Cast: Orson Welles (*Charles Foster Kane*); Buddy Swan (*Kane, Aged 8*); Sonny Bupp (*Kane 3rd*); Harry Shannon (*Kane's Father*); Joseph Cotten (*Jedediah Leland*); Dorothy Comingore (*Susan Alexander*); Everett Sloane (*Mr. Bernstein*); Ray Collins (*James W. Gettys*); George Coulouris (*Walter Parks Thatcher*); Agnes Moorehead (*Kane's Mother*); Paul Stewart (*Raymond*); Ruth Warrick (*Emily Norton*); Erskine Sanford (*Herbert Carter*); William Alland (*Thompson*); Georgia Backus (*Miss Anderson*); Philip van Zandt (*Mr. Rawlston*); Gus Schilling (*Head Waiter*); Fortunio Bonanova (*Signor Matiste*).

Citizen Kane

Awards: Oscar for Best Original Screenplay, 1941; New York Film Critics Award, Best Picture, 1941.

Publications

Script:

Mankiewicz, Herman J., and Orson Welles, ''The Shooting Script,'' in *The Citizen Kane Book*, by Pauline Kael, Boston, 1971.
Citizen Kane Script Book, New York, 1991.

Books:

Bazin, André, *Orson Welles*, Paris, 1950.
Noble, Peter, *The Fabulous Orson Welles*, London, 1956.
Bogdanovich, Peter, *The Cinema of Orson Welles*, New York, 1961.
Bessy, Maurice, *Orson Welles*, Paris, 1963.
Cowie, Peter, *The Citizen Kane Book*, Boston, 1971.
Higham, Charles, *The Films of Orson Welles*, Berkeley, 1971.
Bogdanovich, Peter, and Orson Welles, *This Is Orson Welles*, New York, 1972.
McBride, Joseph, *Orson Welles*, London, 1972; New York, 1977.
Cowie, Peter, *A Ribbon of Dreams: The Cinema of Orson Welles*, New York, 1973.
Gottesman, Ronald, editor, *Focus on Orson Welles*, Englewood Cliffs, New Jersey, 1976.
Naremore, James, *The Magic World of Orson Welles*, New York, 1978.
Kawin, Bruce, *Mindscreen: Bergman, Godard, and First-Person Film*, Princeton, New Jersey, 1978.
Valentinetti, Claudio M., *Orson Welles*, Florence, 1981.
Bergala, Alain, and Jean Narboni, editors, *Orson Welles*, Paris, 1982.
Wollen, Peter, *Readings and Writings: Semiotic Counter-Strategies*, London, 1982.
Andrew, Dudley, *Film in the Aura of Art*, Princeton, 1984.
Carringer, Robert L., *The Making of Citizen Kane*, Berkeley, 1985; revised, 1996.
Higham, Charles, *Orson Welles: The Rise and Fall of an American Genius*, New York, 1985.
Leaming, Barbara, *Orson Welles: A Biography*, New York, 1985.
Parra, Daniele, and Jacques Zimmer, *Orson Welles*, Paris, 1985.
Weis, Elisabeth, and John Belton, editors, *Film Sound: Theory and Practice*, New York, 1985.
Taylor, John Russell, *Orson Welles: A Celebration*, London, 1986.
Jarvie, Ian, *Philosophy of the Film: Epistemology, Ontology, Aesthetics*, London, 1987.
Joxe, Sandra, *Citizen Kane, Orson Welles*, Paris, 1990.
Lebo, Harlan, *Citizen Kane: The Fiftieth-Anniversary Album*, New York, 1990.
Berthome, Jean-Pierre, *Citizen Kane*, Paris, 1992.
Mulvey, Laura, *Citizen Kane*, London, 1992.
Cahill, Marie, *Citizen Kane*, New York, 1993.
Gottesman, Ronald, editor, *Perspectives on Citizen Kane*, New York, 1996.

Articles:

Pritt, Emile, in *New Masses* (New York), 4 February 1941.
Sage, M., in *New Republic* (New York), 24 February 1941.

Tolan, Gregg, ''Realism for *Citizen Kane*,'' in *American Cinematographer* (Los Angeles), February 1941.
Life (New York), 17 March 1941.
O'Hara, John, in *Newsweek* (New York), 17 March 1941.
Time (New York), 17 March 1941.
Crowther, Bosley, in *New York Times*, 2 May 1941.
Herrmann, Bernard, in *New York Times*, 25 May 1941.
Toland, Gregg, ''How I Broke the Rules in *Citizen Kane*,'' in *Popular Photoplay Magazine* (New York), June 1941.
The Times (London), 13 October 1941.
Leenhardt, Roger, in *Ecran Francais* (Paris), 3 July 1946.
Doniol-Valcroze, Jacques, in *Revue du Cinéma* (Paris), December 1946.
Manuel, Jacques,''Essai sur le style d'Orson Welles,'' in *Revue du Cinéma* (Paris), December 1946.
Toland, Gregg, ''L'Operateur de prises de vues,'' in *Revue du Cinéma* (Paris), January 1947.
Chartier, Jean-Pierre, in *Revue du Cinéma* (Paris), January 1947.
Viazzi, Glauco, in *Bianco e Nero* (Rome), July 1948.
Bazin, André, and Jean-Charles Tacchella, interview with Welles, in *Bianco e Nero* (Rome), 21 September 1948.
Sarris, Andrew, ''*Citizen Kane:* American Baroque,'' in *Film Culture* (New York), no. 2, 1956.
Pariante, Roberto, ''Orson Welles from *Citizen Kane* to *Othello*,'' in *Bianco e Nero* (Rome), March 1956.
''L'Oeuvre d'Orson Welles,'' in *Cahiers du Cinéma* (Paris), September 1958.
Domarchi, Jean, ''America,'' in *Cahiers du Cinéma* (Paris), July 1959.
Coursodon, Jean-Pierre, in *Cinéma* (Paris), no. 43, 1960.
Stanbrook, Alan, ''The Heroes of Orson Welles,'' in *Film* (London), no. 28, 1961.
''Welles Issue'' of *Image et Son* (Paris), no. 139, 1961.
''*Citizen Kane* Issue'' of *Avant-Scène du Cinéma* (Paris), January 1962.
''Welles Issue'' of *Cineforum* (Venice), no. 19, 1962.
Capdena, Michel, ''Citizen K,'' in *Lettres Françaises* (Paris), 27 December 1962.
Cutts, John, in *Films and Filming* (London), December 1963.
McBride, Joseph, in *Film Heritage* (Dayton, Ohio), Fall 1968.
Sarris, Andrew, in *Village Voice* (New York), 15 April 1971, 27 May 1971, and 3 June 1971.
Bordwell, David, in *Film Comment* (New York), Summer 1971.
Henderson, Brian, ''The Long Take,'' in *Film Comment* (New York), Summer 1971.
Goldfarb, Phyllis, ''Orson Welles' Use of Sound,'' in *Take One* (Montreal), July-August 1971.
Comolli, Jean-Louis, ''Technique et Idéologie: Caméra, perspective, profondeur de champ,'' in *Cahiers du Cinéma* (Paris), January-February 1972.
Cohen, H., ''The Heart of Darkness in *Citizen Kane*,'' in *Cinema Journal* (Evanston, Illinois), Fall 1972.
''*Citizen Kane* Issue'' of *Chaplin* (Stockholm), vol. 15, no. 2, 1973.
Burch, Noël, ''Propositions,'' in *Afterimage* (London), Spring 1974.
Mass, R., ''A Linking of Legends: *The Great Gatsby* and *Citizen Kane*,'' in *Literature/Film Quarterly* (Salisbury, Maryland), Summer 1974.
Smith, J., ''Orson Welles and the Great American Dummy,'' in *Literature/Film Quarterly* (Salisbury, Maryland), Summer 1974.
Ciment, Michel, ''Ouragans autour de Kane,'' in *Positif* (Paris), March 1975.
Champlin, Charles, ''More about *Citizen Kane*,'' in *American Cinematographer* (Los Angeles), April 1975.
''Semiotics and *Citizen Kane*,'' in *Film Reader* (Evanston, Illinois), no. 1, 1975.
Carringer, Robert, ''*Citizen Kane, The Great Gatsby*, and Some Conventions of American Narrative,'' in *Critical Inquiry* (Chicago), Winter 1975.
Pitiot, P., and H. Behar, in *Image et Son* (Paris), September 1976.
Firestone, B. M., ''A Rose Is a Rose Is a Columbine: *Citizen Kane* and William Styron's *Nat Turner*,'' in *Literature/Film Quarterly* (Salisbury, Maryland), Spring 1977.
Gambill, N., ''Making Up Kane,'' in *Film Comment* (New York), November-December 1978.
Jaffe, I. S., ''Film as Narration of Space: *Citizen Kane*,'' in *Literature/Film Quarterly* (Salisbury, Maryland), no. 2, 1979.
Toeplitz, J., ''Von einem, der Karriere macht: Orson Welles in Hollywood der dreissiger Jahre,'' in *Film und Fernsehen* (East Berlin), no. 2, 1979.
Westerbeck Jr., C. L., in *Commonweal* (New York), 22 June 1979.
Clipper, L. J., ''Art and nature in Welles' Xanadu,'' in *Film Criticism* (Edinboro, Pennsylvania), Spring 1981.
Haustrate, G., in *Cinéma* (Paris, July-August 1981.
Houston, Beverle, ''Power and Dis-Integration in the Films of Orson Welles,'' in *Film Quarterly* (Berkeley), Fall 1985.
Left, L. J., ''Reading Kane,'' in *Film Quarterly* (Berkeley), Fall 1985.
Beja, M., ''Orson Welles and the Attempt to Escape from Father,'' in *Literature/Film Quarterly* (Salisbury, Maryland), vol. 13, no. 1, 1985.
Maxfield, J.F., ''A Man Like Ourselves: *Citizen Kane* is Aristotelean Tragedy,'' in *Literature/Film Quarterly* (Salisbury, Maryland), vol. 14, no. 3, 1986.
Jones, Elizabeth, ''Locating Truth in Film, 1940–80,'' in *Post Script* (Jacksonville, Florida), Autumn, 1986.
Tomasulo, Frank P., ''Point-of-View and Narrative Voice in *Citizen Kane*'s Thatcher Sequence,'' in *Wide Angle* (Athens, Ohio), vol. 8, nos. 3–4, 1986.
Tarnowski, J.-F., ''Le Prologue,'' in *Revue du Cinéma* (Paris), May 1987.
Rathgeb, Douglas L., ''Fates in the Crowd: Illuminating *Citizen Kane* Through Woody Allen's *Zelig*,'' in *Post Script* (Jacksonville, Florida), Spring-Summer 1987.
Rosenbaum, Jonathan, and others, ''Dialogue: On Viewer Response to *Citizen Kane*,'' in *Cinema Journal* (Champaign, Illinois), Summer 1987.
Bates, Robin, ''Fiery Speech in a World of Shadows: Rosebud's Impact on Early Audiences,'' in *Cinema Journal* (Champaign, Illinois), Winter 1987.
Morrison, J., ''From *Citizen Kane* to *Mr. Arkadin:* The Evolution of Orson Welles's Aesthetics of Space,'' in *New Orleans Review*, no. 3, 1989.
Nielsen, N. A., ''Et allerhelvedes perspektiv,'' in *Kosmorama* (Copenhagen), Fall 1989.
Ropars-Wuilleumier, M.-C., ''Narration and Signification: A Filmic Example,'' in *Quarterly Review of Film and Video* (New York), no. 4, 1990.
Rosterman, R., ''*Citizen Kane:* 50 Years of Controversy,'' in *Hollywood: Then and Now* (Studio City, California), no. 7, 1991.
Vergne, F., ''*Citizen Kane* e *Confidential Report* di Orson Welles: la retorica dei ricordo,'' in *La Cosa Vista* (Trieste), no. 16–17, 1991.

Kyff, Robert S., "Even After 50 Years, *Citizen Kane* Resonates with a Clarity Both Technical and Allegorical," in *Chicago Tribune*, 1 May 1991.

van der Burg, J., "Toevalstreffer van de eeuw," in *Skoop* (Amsterdam), July-August 1991.

Toland, G., "Realism for *Citizen Kane*," in *American Cinematographer* (Hollywood), August 1991.

Sarris, A., "For and Against Kane," in *Sight and Sound* (London), October 1991.

Hogue, P., "The Friends of *Kane*," in *Film Comment* (New York), November-December 1991.

Maland, C., "Memories and Things Past: History and Two Biographical Flashback Films," in *East-West Film Journal* (Honolulu), no. 1, 1992.

La Polla, F., "Welles e la frequentazione delle tenebre." in *Quaderni di Cinema* (Florence), July-September 1992.

Kovacs, A. B., "Minden idok. . .," in *Filmvilag* (Budapest), no. 6, 1993.

Pipolo, T., "Screen Memories in *Citizen Kane*," in *P.O.V.* (Brussels), no. 10, 1993.

Altman, Rick, "Deep-Focus Sound: *Citizen Kane* and the Radio Aesthetic," in *Quarterly Review of Film and Video* (Reading), vol. 15, no. 3, December 1994.

Welles, Orson, "Orson Welles par Orson Welles," in *Positif* (Paris), no. 418, December 1995.

Kan, E., "Great Beginnings . . . and Endings," in *P.O.V.* (Brussels), no. 2, December 1996.

Thomson, D., "Ten Films that Showed Hollywood How to Live," in *Movieline* (Escondido, California) vol. 8, July 1997.

* * *

"Everything that matters in cinema since 1940," François Truffaut has suggested, "has been influenced by *Citizen Kane*." It is not surprising, then, that *Citizen Kane* should be one of the most written about films in cinema history; nearly every major critic since André Bazin has felt compelled to discuss it, among them Andrew Sarris, Peter Cowie, David Bordwell, Joseph McBride, and Bruce Kawin.

Of the various critical approaches taken to the film, the most trivial, though in some respects the most common, is to understand *Citizen Kane* as an only slightly disguised biography of William Randolph Hearst. Hearst certainly took it that way, and was largely responsible, through the influence of his newspaper syndicate (which refused to review RKO films for a time), for the film's box-office failure, despite the generally enthusiastic response of the critics. Pauline Kael did much to revive this line of thinking in her 1971 "Raising Kane" essay. Kael's point is essentially negative. Movies in general "are basically *kitsch*," though on occasion *kitsch* "redeemed." *Citizen Kane* is a case in point, especially given its reputation, and that of Orson Welles. Indeed, much of Kael's essay is devoted to showing that aspects of *Kane* normally attributed to Welles really represented or were indebted to the work of others—to Gregg Toland's cinematography, to the conventions of Hollywood newspaper comedy, and especially to Herman J. Mankiewicz, to whom Kael attributes the entire script. Her point even here, however, is that Mankiewicz largely retold the story of William Randolph Hearst ("What happened in Hearst's life was far more interesting" Kael argues at one point)—so that the process of making *Citizen Kane* is pictured largely as a process of disguise and oversimplification, begun by Mankiewicz and only finished by Welles. What Kael clearly fails to see is the irrelevance of her whole approach (not to mention its basic inaccuracy in regard to historical fact). As François Truffaut puts it: "It isn't San Simeon that interests me but Xanadu, not the reality but the work of art on film." To see the film as a denatured version of some past reality is simply not to see the film.

In sharp contrast to Kael's variety of historicism is the approach taken by André Bazin in his work on Welles. Rather than read the "story" of *Citizen Kane* against the background provided by the life of Hearst, Bazin focuses on film style in *Citizen Kane* especially on the degree to which style "places the very nature of the story in question." And rather than describe film style in *Citizen Kane* as being consistent with that of Hollywood generally (as Kael does in part), Bazin suggests that Welles' reliance on the sequence shot (or long take) and deep focus represents an important *break* with classical cinematic practice and with the viewing habits derived from it. Classical editing, according to Bazin, "substituted mental and abstract time" for the "ambiguity of expression" implicit in reality; whereas "depth of focus reintroduced ambiguity into the structure of the image" by transferring "to the screen the continuum of reality," in regards both to time and space. "Obliged to exercise his liberty and his intelligence, the spectator perceives the ontological ambivalence of reality directly, in the structure of its appearances."

There are problems with such an ontological approach to cinema (it focuses on sequences rather than on whole films, for instance); but Bazin's emphasis on the ambiguity of appearances in Welles is consistent with a third approach to *Citizen Kane* which sees the film as an early instance of the fragmented modernist narrative. In the words of Robert Carringer, the fact that Kane's story in the film is told from several perspectives, by several different characters, "reflects the Modernist period's general preoccupation with the relativism of points of view." Indeed, the film's "main symbolic event" is not the burning of Kane's "Rosebud" sled but rather the shattering of the little glass globe, which thus stands "for the loss of 'Kane-ness,' the unifying force behind the phenomenon of Kane." Accordingly, the effort undertaken by Thompson, the newsreel reporter, to uncover the secret of Kane's life by tracking down the meaning of "Rosebud" through interviewing Kane's friends and associates can be seen as a paradigm of the human desire to simplify the complex, though Thompson himself becomes increasingly cynical about the prospect of making sense of Charles Foster Kane.

It is arguable, however, that Thompson's cynicism—summed up when he says "I don't think any word can sum up a man's life"—is itself suspect for assuming that complexity is antithetical in intelligibility. Central to such a view of *Kane* is the premise that multiple narratives serve to cast doubt. And in a film such as Kurosawa's *Rashomon* (to which *Kane* is often compared) such is certainly the case. But the narrative of *Citizen Kane* may well work differently, at different "levels" of narration. The reporter himself comprises the first "level" of narration—in the newsreel he watches, and in the interviews he conducts. The interviews, then, constitute a second level of narration, in that they are embedded in the first. It is arguable, however, that a third level of narration exists. It can be seen in the "framing" sequences, which take us up to and then away from the gates of Xanadu; it can also be seen in the fact that the narratives of all those interviewed contain material that the person telling the tale could not have known, even at second hand (as if each such narrative were being "re-narrated"). But the third level of narration is most clearly evident in a series of visual metaphors (the recurrent visual figure of the window or door frame, for example, which repeatedly serves to cut one character off from others) which remain constant throughout the film, both in the flashbacks and in the reporter's narrative, regardless of who is ostensibly narrating the sequence. Accordingly, we can say that the entire film constitutes a single narrative with other narratives embedded; that the narratives work at different levels disallows easy assumptions that they cancel each other out, no matter how partial or biased any one narrative might be.

In terms of style and narrative, then, *Citizen Kane* is a film of remarkable complexity and depth; yet in thematic terms, *Citizen Kane* is also a hymn to failure. Kane's failure to put his remarkable energy to real use, Thompson's failure to find real meaning in Kane's life story. The shame, in Kane's case, is that his tremendous capacities and resources are wasted, used up; the closing shot of Xanadu, the smoke of Kane's burning possessions pouring from a chimney, recalls the factory smokestacks of the film's newsreel sequence, as the chainlink fence recalls the factory fences. The shame in Thompson's case is that he contributes to this waste by refusing to get to the point, refusing to see how thoroughly Kane was a product of his circumstances, as much victim as victimizer. But we need not follow Thompson's lead in this, however cinematically marvellous *Citizen Kane* might be. The sense is ours to make.

—Leland Poague

CITY LIGHTS

USA, 1931

Director: Charles Chaplin

Production: Charles Chaplin Studio; black and white, 35mm, synchronized music and sound effects; running time: 86 minutes; length: 2380 meters. Released 6 January 1931 in New York City by United Artists Corp.; re-released 8 April 1950. Filmed 1930 in Hollywood.

Producer, editor: Charles Chaplin; **screenplay:** Charles Chaplin; **assistant directors:** Harry Crocker, Henry Bergman and Albert Austin; **photography:** Rollie Totheroh, Gordon Pollack and Mark Markatt; **art director:** Charles D. Hall; **music composer:** Charles Chaplin; **arranger:** Arthur Johnston; **conductor:** Alfred Newman.

Cast: Charles Chaplin (*Little Tramp*); Virginia Cherrill (*Flower Girl*); Florence Lee (*Grandmother*); Harry Myers (*Eccentric Millionaire*); Allan Garcia (*Valet*); Hank Mann (*Boxer*); Eddie Baker (*Referee*); Henry Bergman (*Doorman*); Albert Austin (*Swindler*); Stanhope Wheatcroft (*Distinguished man at café*); John Rand (*Another tramp*); James Donnelly (*Foreman*); Robert Parrish (*Newspaper boy*); Jean Harlow (*Nightclub girl*); Stanley Sandford (*Elevator boy*).

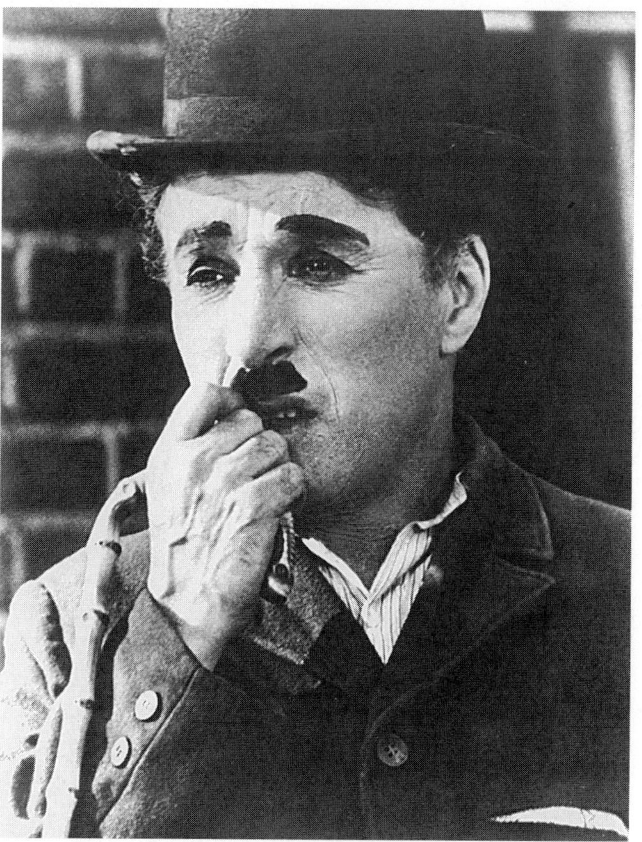

City Lights

Publications

Books:

Dodgson, William, *Charlie Chaplin: His Life and Art*, New York, 1931.
von Ulm, Gerith, *Charlie Chaplin: King of Tragedy*, Idaho, 1940.
Hardy, Forsyth, editor, *Grierson on Documentary*, New York, 1947.
Tyler, Parker, *Chaplin, Last of the Clowns*, New York, 1947.
Cotes, Peter, and Thelma Niklaus, *Charlot*, Paris, 1951.
Huff, Theodore, *Charlie Chaplin*, New York, 1951.
Bessy, Maurice, and Robert Florey, *Chaplin; ou, Le Rire dans La nuit*, Paris, 1952.
Sadoul, Georges, *Vie de Charlot*, Paris, 1952.
Franca, Jose Augusta, *Charles Chaplin: Le Self-Made Mythe*, Lisbon, 1954.
Leprohon, Pierre, *Charlot*, Paris, 1957.
Mitry, Jean, *Charlot et la fabulation chaplinesque*, Paris, 1957.
Amengual, Barthélemy, *Charles Chaplin*, Paris, 1963.
Chaplin, Charles, *My Autobiography*, London and New York, 1964.
Cotes, Peter, and Thelma Niklaus, *The Life and Work of Charles Spencer Chaplin*, New York, 1965.
McDonald, Gerald D., and others, *The Films of Charlie Chaplin*, Secaucus, New Jersey, 1965.
Martin, Marcel, *Charles Chaplin*, Paris, 1966; revised edition, 1983.
Sarris, Andrew, *Interviews with Film Directors*, New York, 1967.
Tyler, Parker, *Magic, Myth, and the Movies*, New York, 1970.
McCaffrey, Donald W., editor, *Focus on Chaplin*, Englewood Cliffs, New Jersey, 1971.
Asplund, Uno, *Chaplin's Films*, Newton Abbot, Devon, 1971.
Manvell, Roger, *Chaplin*, London and Boston, 1974.
Chaplin, Charlie, *My Life in Pictures*, London, 1974; New York, 1975.
Moss, Robert F., *Charlie Chaplin*, New York, 1975.
Lyons, Timothy J., *Charles Chaplin: A Guide to References and Resources*, Boston, 1979.
Eisenstein, Sergei, *Film Essays and a Lecture*, edited by Jay Leyda, Princeton, New Jersey, 1982.
Haining, Peter, editor, *The Legend of Charlie Chaplin*, London, 1982.

Gehring, Wes D., *Charlie Chaplin: A Bio-Bibliography*, Westport, Connecticut, 1983.
Molyneaux, Gerard, *Charlie Chaplin's "City Lights:" Its Production and Dialectic Structure*, New York, 1983.
Robinson, David, *Chaplin: The Mirror of Opinion*, London, 1983.
Kamin, Dan, *Charlie Chaplin's One-Man Show*, Metuchen, New Jersey, 1984.
Smith, Julian, *Chaplin*, Boston, 1984.
Geduld, Harry M., *Charlie Chaplin's Own Story*, Bloomington, Indiana, 1985.
Robinson, David, *Chaplin: His Life and Art*, New York and London, 1985.
Geduld, Harry M., *Chapliniana 1: The Keystone Films*, Bloomington, Indiana, 1987.
Mitry, Jean, *Tout Chaplin: L'Oeuvre complète présentée par le texte et par l'image*, Paris, 1987.
Saint-Martin, Catherine, *Charlot/Chaplin: Ou, La conscience du mythe*, Paris, 1987.
Wagenknecht, Edward, *Stars of the Silents*, Metuchen, New Jersey, 1987.
Lynn, Kenneth S., *Charlie Chaplin and His Times*, New York, 1997.
Milton, Joyce, *Tramp: The Life of Charlie Chaplin*, New York, 1998.
Turk, Ruth, *Charlie Chaplin: From Tears to Laughter*, Minneapolis, 1999.

Articles:

"Charlie Chaplin and Talking Pictures," in *Theatre Arts* (New York), November 1930.
Hall, Mordaunt, "Chaplin Hilarious in his *City Lights*," in *New York Times*, 7 February 1931.
Seldes, G., in *New Republic* (New York), 25 February 1931.
"Charlie Chaplin Defies the Talkies," in *Literary Digest* (New York), 28 February 1931.
Bakshy, Alexander, "Charlie Chaplin Falters," in *Nation* (New York), 4 March 1931.
Woolcott, Alexander, in *Collier's* (New York), 28 March 1931.
Knight, Arthur, and Theodore Huff, *Films in Review* (New York), September 1950.
Sarris, Andrew, in *Village Voice* (New York), 5 December 1963.
Lefèvre, Raymond, in *Cinéma* (Paris), March 1972.
Kauffmann, Stanley, in *Film Comment* (New York), September-October 1972.
Lyons, T. M., in *Film Culture* (New York), Spring 1972.
Benayoun, Robert, "L'Assassin de Charlot," in *Positif* (Paris), July-August 1973.
Quenin, F., in *Télécine* (Paris), December 1976.
Gorsaro, D. J., "Chaplin as satyr," in *University Film Association Journal* (Houston, Texas), no. 1, 1979.
Woods, Lynn, in *Magill's Survey of Cinema 1*, Englewood Cliffs, New Jersey, 1980.
Gerard, Molyneaux, "City Lights: Chaplin's Indictment of the 1920s," in *Mise-en-Scène* (New York), Spring 1980.
Robinson, David, "A Chaplin Mystery Solved," in *Films and Filming* (London), no. 345, June 1983.
Jespersen, A., "Chaplins tva varldar: En analys av *Stadens Ljus*," in *Filmrutan* (Stockholm), 1985.
Gross, K., "Moving Statues, Talking Statues," in *Raritan* (New Brunswick, New Jersey), no. 2, 1989.
Parrish, Robert, "Partners in Mime," in *London Evening Standard*, 30 March 1989.
McVay, Douglas, in *What's On* (London), 12 April 1989.
Robinson, David, in *The Times* (London), 12 April 1989.
Papson, S., "The IBM Tramp," in *Jump Cut* (Berkeley), April 1990.
Woal, M., and L.K. Woal, "Chaplin and the Comedy of Melodrama," in *Journal of Film and Video* (Atlanta), vol. 46, no. 3, 1994.
Séquences (Haute-Ville), May-June 1995.
Elias, J., "Sounds of the 'City'," in *Village Voice* (New York), 27 February 1996.
Hirsch, David, "Carl Davis' *City Lights*," in *Soundtrack*! (Mechelen), Vol. 15, no. 58, June 1996.
Télérama (Paris), 9 October 1996.

* * *

Early in 1931 an extraordinary event took place in New York City at the George M. Cohan Theatre. Though the talking picture had been firmly established, a new silent film premiered at the Cohan that became the talk of the town—Charles Chaplin's *City Lights*, in which he starred as the beloved Little Tramp. He was also the producer, the director, the author and scenarist, the editor, and had written the music which accompanied it. Chaplin was the solitary hold-out against the talking film, and *City Lights* was successful because it was a nine-reel comedy which revelled in its silence.

Though it had a sound track and musical accompaniment, it was, first and foremost, a tribute to the pantomimic art. Audiences loved it, and critics named it Chaplin's finest accomplishment, the perfect combination of hilarious comedy and pure pathos. One critic, Rose Pelwick, of the *New York Evening Journal*, remarked: "*City Lights* has no dialogue. And it's just as well, because if the picture had words, the laughs and applause of last evening's audience would have drowned them out."

In the first year of the Academy Awards, 1927–28, Chaplin had been nominated as Best Actor for *The Circus;* he was also nominated for Comedy Direction (a category which was discontinued after the first year of the Academy's existence); and a special statuette was awarded him "for versatility and genius in writing, acting, directing, and producing *The Circus*." Now two years later, the Academy ignored *City Lights*, although critics everywhere acknowledged that it might very well be the best of all Chaplin's films.

City Lights had an uncomfortable genesis. Chaplin had started shooting it in 1928 as a silent film; when it became obvious that talking pictures were neither a fad nor a fancy, he closed down production temporarily. When he decided to continue with it as a silent, everybody cautioned him that he was fighting a losing battle. He told Sam Goldwyn: "I've spent every penny I possess on *City Lights*. If it's a failure, I believe it will strike a deeper blow than anything else that has ever happened to me in this life."

During its production the stock market crashed, and Chaplin's situation became even more precarious, but he persisted in his distaste for talking pictures, confiding in an interview with Gladys Hall in *Motion Picture Magazine* (May, 1929): "They are spoiling the oldest art in the world—the art of pantomime. They are ruining the great beauty of silence. They are defeating the meaning of the screen, the appeal that has created the star system, the fan system, the vast popularity of the whole—the appeal of beauty. It's beauty that matters in pictures—nothing else."

In 1931, when *City Lights* was internationally premiered, Chaplin's world was younger, more innocent, ready to laugh, willing to weep, and they did both, totally succumbing to this romance of the devotion of the Little Tramp to a beautiful blind girl, charmingly played by a young divorcée, Virginia Cherrill.

The plot line is very simple. The picture opens with an introductory gag, showing a group of pompous dignitaries who have assembled for the dedication of an ugly civic statue. When it is unveiled, the Little Tramp is discovered sleeping blissfully in the lap of the central figure. He is chased away, but is attracted by the beauty of a young girl selling flowers from her sidewalk stand. He spends his last coin for a flower for his buttonhole, and only then realizes that the girl is blind.

That night he saves the life of a millionaire (Harry Myers), who is drunk and determined to throw himself in the river. The Tramp persuades him to live, and they spend the rest of the night celebrating in a night club. The millionaire invites the Tramp home, and their limousine passes the blind girl, who is setting up her flower stand on the sidewalk. The Tramp gets money from the millionaire, and buys all the flowers in the girl's basket. The limousine and driver are also lent to the Tramp, so he can take the girl home after the millionaire has been dropped off at his mansion. She thinks the Tramp must be a very rich man, and he is content to let her believe that. But when the Tramp returns to his benefactor's residence, the now sober eccentric doesn't recognize him. This is a gag which is used several times effectively. Sober, the millionaire never knows the Tramp, but when he is drunk, he always greets him like an old buddy.

The Tramp now has a purpose in life: making enough money so the girl can have an operation and regain her sight. He gets a job as a street cleaner, and even enters the ring as a prizefighter, believing that the fight is fixed in his favor; but he is in error and ends up unconscious.

He meets the millionaire again, who is happily drunk and willing to give the Tramp money for the girl's eye surgery. They go to the mansion, and as the Tramp is given the money, two thugs enter the room and try to steal it, but are vanquished when the police arrive. The millionaire, knocked unconscious briefly, is revived, but, sobered, does not recognize the Tramp, who thereupon grabs the cash, and runs away at once to the blind girl's flower stand. He puts the money in her hands, and runs away, but soon afterwards is arrested and jailed for robbery.

When he has served his term and is released, he discovers the girl working in a flower shop. She sees the Little Tramp outside, and overcome with pity, she gets some money from her cash register and goes outside to give it to him. As she puts the money in his hands, she recognizes the touch of his fingers, and realizes the truth at once. He has made everything possible for her. There follows an exchange of dialogue on inter-titles that provides for one of the most moving finales in all of Chaplin's films. ''You?'' she asks. He nods, and smiles shyly, and asks, ''You can see now?'' She nods as her smile widens, ''Yes, I can see now.'' The scene fades out with the Little Tramp smiling radiantly.

Thornton Delehanty, reviewing *City Lights* for the *New York Evening Post*, remarked: ''*City Lights* confirms the indestructibility of Chaplin's art, not only as an actor but as a director. And he has done it without making any concessions to dialogue: he remains the supreme pantomimist.''

—DeWitt Bodeen

CITY OF SADNESS

(Beiqing chengshi)

Taiwan, 1989

Director: Hou Hsiao-Hsien

Production: 3-H Films; An Era International Presentation; color; running time: 155 minutes (some copies 160 minutes); length: 14,464 feet. Filmed in Hokkien, China; dialogue in Mandarin, Hokkien, Shanghaiese, Cantonese, and Japanese.

Producer: Qiu Fusheng **executive producers:** H. T. Jan, Michael Yang; **associate producer:** Huakun; **cinematographer:** Chen Huai'en; **screenplay:** Wu Nianzhen, Zhu Tianwen; **editor:** Liao Qingsong; **production designer:** Liu Zhihua, Lin Chongwen; **music:** Tachikawa Naoki, Zhang Hongzyi; **sound:** Du Duzhi, Yang Jing'an.

Cast: Li Tianlu (*Lin Ah-Lu);* Chen Songyong (*Lin Wen-Hsung);* Gao Jie (*Lin Wen-Liang*); Tony Leung (*Lin Wen-Ching*); Wu Yifang (*Wu Hinoe*); Xin Shufen (*Wu Hinomi*); Chen Shufang (*Mio, First Brother's Wife*); Ke Suyun (*Second Brother's Wife*); and others.

Awards: Golden Lion, Venice Film Festival, 1989; Special Award, Political Film Society, 1990.

Publications

Articles:

Egger, M., ''Tournage,'' in *Positif* (Paris), no. 338, April 1989.

Young, Deborah, ''*City of Sadness* Captures Hearts, Prizes at Venice,'' in *Variety* (New York), vol. 336, no. 10, 20 September 1989.

James, C., ''Film Festival: Postwar *Sadness* in Taiwan,'' in *The New York Times*, 6 October 1989.

Wood, Robin, ''New Films by MacGillivray and Hou,'' in *CineAction* (Toronto), no. 18, Fall 1989.

Sterritt, David, ''Taiwan's Hou Hsaio-hsien Brilliantly Taps Film Medium's Affinity for Nostalgia,'' in *The Christian Science Monitor*, 16 November 1989.

Noh, D., ''Taiwanese Director's *Sadness* Recalls Island's Turbulent Past,'' in *Film Journal* (New York), vol. 93, February 1990.

Film (London), no. 33, 9 March 1990.

Rayns, Tony, ''*Beiqing chengshi (A City of Sadness)*: Not the Best Possible Face,'' in *Monthly Film Bulletin* (London), vol. 57, no. 677, June 1990.

Kauffmann, S., ''Elsewhere,'' in *New Republic*, vol. 202, 11 June 1990.

Greenland, Hall, ''Complex Pleasures,'' in *Filmnews*, vol. 20, no. 6, July 1990.

Niogret, Hubert, and others, ''Hou Hsiao-Hsien: Retrouver la mémoire,'' in *Positif* (Paris), no. 358, December 1990.

Reynaud, B., ''Three Asian Films: For a New Cinematic Language,'' in *Cinematograph* (San Francisco), vol. 4, 1991.

Cooke, D., ''A Review of Hou Hsiao-Hsien's *A City of Sadness*,'' in *Public Culture*, vol. 5, no. 2, 1993.

Liao, P.-h., ''Rewriting Taiwanese National History: The February 28 Incident as Spectacle,'' in *Public Culture*, vol. 5, no. 2, 1993.

City of Sadness

Cheshire, Godfrey, ''Time Span,'' in *Film Comment* (New York), vol. 29, no. 6, November-December 1993.

Tobin, Yann, Michel Ciment, and Pierre Eisenreich, ''Hou Hsiao-hsien,'' in *Positif* (Paris), no. 453, November 1998.

Jones, Kent, ''Cinema with a Roof Over Its Head,'' in *Film Comment* (New York), vol. 35, no. 5, September 1999.

Lopate, Phillip, ''A Master Everywhere Else is Ready to Try America,'' in *The New York Times*, 10 October 1999.

* * *

Daughter of the Nile (1987) marked a watershed in Hou's career, as his first film set entirely in the city, the ultimate stage in his transition from the ''rural'' films on which his reputation was initially built. Its successor two years later, *City of Sadness*, marks another watershed, as the first film explicitly concerned with Taiwanese history, from which viewpoint it can be seen as the first of a loose trilogy, followed by *The Puppetmaster* (1993), and completed with *Good Men, Good Women* (1995).

The film opens in 1945 on the day of the end of World War II, with the surrender of the Japanese and the release of Taiwan from Japanese occupation; it closes with a caption telling us that in 1949 the Nationalist government moved to Taiwan and made Taipei the provisional capital. The film starts, therefore, with celebration, a celebration that proves shortlived and misplaced, for ''liberation'' by mainland China proves scarcely less oppressive than Japanese rule. The five years chronicled become a history of relentlessly escalating tragedy from which the film never releases us. It can be read as a structure of concentric but overlapping circles: at its core, the love story of a Taiwanese deaf-mute (Tony Leung, one of the major stars of both Hong Kong and Taiwanese cinema) and Hinomi, the young Japanese woman who has settled in Taiwan along with her slightly older brother Hinoe; beyond that, the story of a family consisting of four brothers (of whom the deaf-mute, Wen-ching, is the youngest) and their ageing father; beyond that again, the steadily increasing persecution of dissidents by the forces of government, culminating in the death of Hinoe and the ''disappearance'' of Wen-ching, leaving Hinomi (now his wife) along with their young child within a depleted family circle. But the film also traces its disasters backward, to the war, in which one brother has vanished never to return, while the brother who *does* return (Wen-leung) comes home temporarily insane, subsequently unstable, engaging in criminal activities and given to outbreaks of uncontrollable violence. Ironically, by the film's end, he is the one apparent survivor.

Structurally and stylistically, *City of Sadness* is Hou's most audacious and uncompromising film up to that date, the first complete elaboration of the stylistics that dominant his subsequent work. One can define his style partly by reference to two great Japanese masters who may or may not be direct influences. Like Ozu, he prefers a static camera, but, like Mizoguchi, long takes. Many scenes are sequence-shots, without a cut, or sequences of at most two camera setups. As with Mizoguchi and very unlike Ozu, many scenes involve complex simultaneous foreground and background actions, using depth of field, and with actors entering and exiting the frame, giving a constant sense of lives continuing beyond the image. On the other hand, like Ozu, he is fond of using frames-within-the-frame for intimate interior scenes, replacing Ozu's shoji screens with dark walls or pillars. There are no closeups and no point-of-view shots.

Hou's treatment of violence is particularly rigorous, at the furthest possible remove from what the modern Hollywood or Hong Kong "action film" has accustomed us to. Violence in Hou is *always* in long-shot. *City of Sadness* offers a particularly striking example, in Ah-Ga's characteristically wild assault (with an accomplice) on a wagon. The sequence consists of two long takes: 1. Ah-Ga in foreground, standing in profile, medium long-shot; the wagon approaches along the track in extreme long-shot; only as Ah-Ga throws away his cigarette and turns his back to the camera, walking away toward the wagon (which has stopped), do we see the sword he is holding at his side; he begins to run, shouting (no cut, no track-in), leaving the spectator far behind, attacking the wagon and its occupants as his associate (like Ah-Ga wearing a white shirt) runs up behind it. 2. Hou cuts only when the ensuing battle splits into two, some running screen left into a field of tall grasses, others moving even further *away* from the camera down the track; even then, the cut is not a cut-in but a cut to an even more distant long-shot that can encompass the entire action and that reduces the participants to little more than specks on the screen.

Structurally, Hou makes considerable demands on the spectator, always constructed by his films as intelligent and alert. There are major ellipses in the narrative, left unexplained, where we have to "fill in" what has happened by a process of deduction (the various stages of Wen-leung's mental condition are a good example: when he is introduced he appears incurably and dangerously insane, then subsequently turns up amid the family with no intermediary account of his progress). There are also intercut sequences not initially signified as such, so that we begin by reading them as chronological then are forced to readjust when they prove to be simultaneous. Apparently disconnected scenes form a pattern which we only gradually figure out. This cannot be accounted for in terms of the duration of the film's time period: Hou omits any dramatization of major events, preferring to show us small, almost irrelevant scenes of intimacy and character-interaction that prove to have only an indirect relation to the determining historical developments offscreen. The ending carries the withholding of information to its logical extreme: we learn that Wen-ching has disappeared, certainly arrested, probably but not certainly executed for his work in printing pamphlets for the dissidents, his disability having prevented him from full engagement. The film then simply stops, and we are left in precisely the same state of uncertainty as Hinomi and the surviving relatives.

At the present time, *City of Sadness* is marginally available only on an unofficial laserdisc, in the wrong format (so that Hou's meticulous 1: 1.85 compositions are seriously mutilated, giving the impression that he doesn't know how to frame), and with subtitles that fail to translate a number of crucial explanatory intertitles (the written "dialogues" between Wen-ching and Hinomi, depriving the former of his only "voice" and undermining the film's most beautiful and touching scenes, played with great delicacy). All of Hou's films, within a healthy film culture, would by now be available on DVD.

—Robin Wood

CLEO DE CINQ A SEPT

(Cleo from 5 to 7)

France-Italy, 1962

Director: Agnès Varda

Production: Rome-Paris Films; black and white and Eastmancolor, 35mm; running time: 90 minutes. Released April 1962, Paris. Filmed in Paris.

Producers: Georges de Beauregard and Carlo Ponti; **associate producer:** Bruno Drigo; **screenplay:** Agnès Varda; **photography:** Jean Rabier; **editor:** Janine Verneau; **sound engineers:** Jean Labussière and Julien Coutellier; **sound editor:** Jacques Maumont; **art director:** Bernard Evein; **music:** Michel Legrand; **lyrics:** Agnès Varda; **costume designer:** Bernard Evein.

Cast: Corinne Marchand (*Cléo*); Antoine Bourseiller (*Antoine*); Dorothée Black (*Dorothée*); Michel Legrand (*Bob, the Pianist*); Dominique Davray (*Angèle*); José-Luis de Villalonga (*Cléo's Lover*); with: Jean-Luc Godard; Anna Karina; Eddie Constantine; Sami Frey; Danièle Delorme; Jean-Claude Brialy; Yves Robert; Alan Scott; Robert Postec; Lucienne Marchand.

Publications

Script:

Varda, Agnès, "Cleo de cinq à sept," Paris, 1962; extract as "Cleo from 5 to 7" in *Films and Filming* (London), December 1962.

Books:

Armes, Roy, *French Cinema Since 1946. Volume 2: The Personal Style,"* New York, 1966.
Betancourt, Jeanne, *Women in Focus*, Dayton, Ohio, 1974.
Barascq, Leon, *Caligari's Cabinet and Other Grand Illusions; A History of Film Design*, New York, 1976.
Smith, Alison, *Agnes Varda*, New York, 1998.

Articles:

Tailleur, Roger, "Cléo d'ici a l'éternité," in *Positif* (Paris), March 1962.
Avant-Scène du Cinéma (Paris), 15 May 1962.
Roud, Richard, in *Sight and Sound* (London), Summer 1962.

Roud, Richard, ''The Left Bank,'' in *Sight and Sound* (London), Winter 1962–63.
Shivas, M., ''*Cléo de cinq à sept* and Agnès Varda,'' in *Movie* (London), October 1962.
Manvell, Roger, in *Films and Filming* (London), December 1962.
''Pasolini-Varda-Allio-Sarris-Michelson,'' in *Film Culture* (New York), Fall 1966.
''Agnès Varda,'' in *Current Biography* (New York), 1970.
Gow, Gordon, interview with Varda, in *Films and Filming* (London), March 1970.
Confino, Barbara, interview with Varda, in *Saturday Review* (New York), 12 August 1972.
Levitin, J., ''Mother of the New Wave,'' in *Women and Film* (Santa Monica), volume 1, nos. 5–6, 1974.
Mulvey, Laura, ''Visual Pleasure and Narrative Cinema,'' in *Women and Film: A Critical Anthology*, edited by Karyn Kay and Gerald Peary, New York, 1977.
Flitterman, S., ''From 'déesse' to 'idée': Agnès Varda's *Cleo from Five to Seven*,'' in *Enclitic* (Minneapolis), Fall 1983.
Revault d'Allonnes, Fabrice, *Cinéma* (Paris), 8 January 1986.
Forbes, Jill, ''Agnès Varda: The Gaze of the Medusa?'' in *Sight and Sound* (London), Spring 1989.
Biro, Y., ''Caryatids of Time: Temporality in the Cinema of Agnès Varda,'' in *Performing Arts Journal*, vol. 19, no. 3, 1997.
Anthony, Elizabeth M., ''From Fauna to Flora in Agnès Varda's *Cléo de 5 à 7*,'' in *Literature/Film Quarterly* (Salisbury), April 1998.
Brown, Royal S., ''*Cleo from 5 to 7:* Vagabond,'' in *Cineaste* (New York), July 1998.

* * *

Agnès Varda's second feature is amongst the most rigorous and delicate films of the French New Wave. While awaiting the results of a cancer test, a pop singer, stage-name Cléo Victoire, a beautiful, dreamy, artificial creature, comes to terms with her new-found fear of death.

First, Cléo's fortune-teller predicts ''a transformation''; then her confidante, Angèle, is dismissive; the purchase of a hat only trivially lifts her morale. She daren't share her troubles with her suave lover, José (Villalonga). She is briefly reassured by rehearsals with her pianist, Bob (Michel Legrand, who also wrote the background music), until he misreads her nerviness as mere caprice. Shop-windows reflect her beauty, but also display grotesque masks and sculptures. On the jukebox of a fashionable café, her latest record serves as mere background to chatter. She is warmed by the earthy, natural nudity of her friend Dorothée, a sculptor's model, and responds to a burlesque film (featuring Godard, Karina, Eddie Constantine), with fast-motion funerals and dark-tinted spectacles. She removes her elaborate wig, and begins to notice the poignant and grotesque details of a certain street-life. In a quiet park, she meets Antoine, a gentle conscript destined for the Algerian war; he accompanies her to the hospital; and she agrees to see him off that evening. The doctor confirms her anxieties, but not her worst fears, and she feels part of life, of ''others,'' at last.

The film's running-time matches the real (or rather, possible, albeit pat) space-and-duration of Cléo's journey round Paris, between 1700–1830 hrs on 21 June 1961, and using the radio news for that day (described as a Tuesday, though actually a Wednesday). Cléo's journey can be exactly mapped, and the camera leaves her twice only, and very briefly. Thus the film adapts the classical theatre's unities (time, space, action) to a properly fluid film-equivalent. Though approximating Cléo's perceptions, Varda avoids restricting herself to 1st-person point-of-view shots, which would overly eliminate Cléo's presence, and therefore her reactions and feelings, from the screen. This near-subjectivism culminates in actual ''stream-of-consciousness,'' a volley of memory-images of earlier moments (*not* flashbacks; they include changes due to mental processes).

This ''subjectivism'' is countered by a formalism inducing, not ''alienation'' exactly, but a film-form ''concretism.'' On-screen titles announce a prologue (the fortune-teller sequence), and then 13 sections, with their exact time, and the name of a character whose personality at that moment keys the section's style. Only the prologue is in colour. Thereafter Cléo's name ''christens'' sections I (solo on a staircase), III (from hatshop to taxi), V (José), and VII (discovering the street). Angèle's name christens II (the first café) and IV (from taxi into Cléo's apartment). Bob keys VI (the rehearsal); ''Some others'' VIII (La Dôme to sculpture studio); Dorothée's IX (journey to Raoul, the projectionist); Raoul's X (the cinema). The park sequence is divided between Cléo (XI), Antoine (XII) and ''Cléo et Antoine'' (XIII). Bob's extrovert cheerfulness inspires ''swinging'' camera-movements; Angèle's style is factual and strict; Cléo progresses from an ornamental, self-centred, style (sinuous camera-calligraphy, narrow-lens close-ups of herself) to a simpler style (direct point-of-view/reaction cuts); the last section, bearing two names, suggests a *meeting* of minds, both at one with the landscape, not just ''in'' them. The cinematic styles evoke now de Sica, now Ophuls (and, of course, Démy, Varda's husband); the settings range from raw reality to a beautifully mannered rococo.

Varda describes *Cléo* as a converse to her second, uncompleted, feature, *La Mélangite*, planned as a maze of stream-of-consciousness shots. It also echoes her short *Opéra-Mouffe*, which depicted the world through the mind of a pregnant woman, though usually off-screen. Like that film, *Cléo* involves much direct cinema, and in that sense, ''objectivity.'' If details resonant to Cléo's moods abound, it's as appropriate to mental selectivity generally. The film's reconciliation of objective-casual appearances with ''expressionism'' (Varda's term; one might prefer ''impressionism'') is virtuoso work; she perfects a certain French tradition, a blending of ''camera-eye'' objectivity and Bergsonian subjectivity, which runs from Vigo to Franju, and becomes fully self-interrogating amongst the ''Left Bank'' documentarists of the New Wave (Varda acknowledges affinities with Resnais and Chris Marker). Some critics felt that *Cléo's* sensitive surface somehow lacked soul, but Varda's highly articulate interviews confirm the lucidity behind a film whose intricate symbolism, or rather, poetic suggestion (angels/Angéle/flesh/wigs) repays endless analysis, the most sensitive being Roger Tailleur's in *Positif.*

—Raymond Durgnat

A CLOCKWORK ORANGE

UK, 1971

Director: Stanley Kubrick

Production: Hawk Films; Warnercolor, 35mm; running time: 135 minutes, some sources list 137 minutes. Released 20 December 1971

A Clockwork Orange

in New York by Warner Bros. Filmed September 1970 to March 1971 in MGM British Studios, Borehamwood, England.

Producers: Stanley Kubrick with Max L. Raab and Si Litvinoff serving as executive producers; **screenplay:** Stanley Kubrick, from the novel by Anthony Burgess; **photography:** John Alcott; **editor:** Bill Butler; **sound:** John Jordan; **production designer:** John Barry; **art directors:** Russell Hagg and Peter Shields; **music:** Ludwig van Beethoven, Edward Elgar, Gioacchino Rossini, Terry Tucker, and Erika Eigen; **original electronic music:** Walter Carlos; **costume designer:** Milena Canonero; **make-up:** Fred Williamson, George Partleton, and Barbara Daly; **paintings and sculptures:** Herman Makking, Cornelius Makking, Liz Moore and Christiane Kubrick; **stunt arranger:** Roy Scammer.

Cast: Malcolm McDowell (*Alex*); Patrick Magee (*Mr. Alexander*); Michael Bates (*Chief Guard*); Warren Clark (*Dim*); John Clive (*Stage actor*); Adrienne Corri (*Mrs. Alexander*); Carl Duering (*Dr. Brodsky*); Paul Farrell (*Tramp*); Clive Francis (*Lodger*); Michael Gover (*Prison governor*); Miriam Karlin (*Cat lady*); James Marcus (*George*); Aubrey Morris (*Deltroid*); Godfrey Quigley (*Prison chaplain*); Sheila Raynor (*Mum*); Madge Ryan (*Dr. Barnom*); John Savident (*Conspirator*); Anthony Sharp (*Minister of the Interior*); Philip Stone (*Dad*); Pauline Taylor (*Psychiatrist*); Margaret Tyzack (*Conspirator*); with Steven Berkoff, Lindsay Campbell, Michael Tarn, David Prowse, Barrie Cookson, Jan Adair, Gaye Brown, Peter Burton, John J. Carney, Vivienne Chandler, Richard Connaught, Prudence Drage, Carol Drinkwater, Lee Fox, Cheryl Grunwald, Gilliam Hills, Craig Hunter, Shirley Jaffe, Virginia Wetherell, Neil Wilson, and Katya Wyeth.

Awards: New York Film Critics Awards for Best Film and Best Direction, 1971.

Publications

Script:

Stanley Kubrick's A Clockwork Orange, Based on the Novel by Anthony Burgess (shot by shot script), New York, 1972.

Books:

Kagan, Norman, *The Cinema of Stanley Kubrick*, New York, 1972.
Walker, Alexander, *Stanley Kubrick Directs*, New York, 1972.
Phillips, Gene D., *The Movie Makers: Artists in Industry*, Chicago, 1973.
Devries, Daniel, *The Films of Stanley Kubrick*, Grand Rapids, Michigan, 1973.
Bobker, Lee R., *Elements of Film*, New York, 1974.
Haskell, Molly, *From Reverence to Rape*, New York, 1974.
Phillips, Gene D., *Stanley Kubrick: A Film Odyssey*, New York, 1975.
Taylor, John Russell, *Directors and Directions: Cinema for the '70s*, New York, 1975.
Wagner, Geoffrey, *The Novel and the Cinema*, Madison, New Jersey, 1975.
Parish, James Robert, editor, *The Science Fiction Pictures*, Metuchen, New Jersey, 1977.
Ciment, Michel, *Kubrick*, Paris, 1980, revised edition, 1987; translated as *Kubrick*, London, 1983.
Kolker, Robert Phillip, *A Cinema of Loneliness: Penn, Kubrick, Coppola, Scorsese, Altman*, Oxford, 1980; revised edition, 1988.
Hummel, Christoph, editor, *Stanley Kubrick*, Munich, 1984.
Brunetta, Gian Piero, *Stanley Kubrick: Tempo, spazio, storia, e mondi possibili*, Parma, 1985.
Falsetto, Mario, *Stanley Kubrick: A Narrative and Stylistic Analysis*, Westport, Connecticut, 1994.
Corliss, Richard, *Lolita*, London, 1994.
Falsetto, Mario, editor, *Perspectives on Stanley Kubrick*, New York, 1996.
Baxter, John, *Stanley Kubrick: A Biography*, New York, 1997.
LoBrutto, Vincent, *Stanley Kubrick: A Biography*, New York, 1997.
Walker, Alexander, *Stanley Kubrick: Director*, New York, 1999.
Raphael, Frederic, *Eyes Wide Open: A Memoir of Stanley Kubrick*, New York, 1999.
Philips, Gene, editor, *Stanley Kubrick: Interviews*, Jackson, Mississippi, 2000.

Articles:

Hofsess, John, "Mind's Eye," in *Take One* (Montreal), May-June 1971.
Canby, Vincent, in *New York Times*, 20 December 1971.
Cocks, Jay, in *Time* (New York), 20 December 1971.
Alpert, Hollis, "Milk-Plus and Ultra-Violence," in *Saturday Review* (New York), 25 December 1971.
Houston, Penelope, "Kubrick Country," in *Saturday Review* (New York), 25 December 1971.
Hughes, Robert, "The Decor of Tomorrow's Hell," in *Time* (New York), 27 December 1971.
Sarris, Andrew, in *Village Voice* (New York), 30 December 1971.
Kael, Pauline, in *New Yorker*, 1 January 1972.
Canby, Vincent, "Orange, Disorienting, but Human Comedy," in *New York Times*, 9 January 1972.
Millar, Gavin, "Treatment and Ill Treatment," in *Listener* (London), 20 January 1972.
Gow, Gordon, in *Films and Filming* (London), Winter 1972.
Burgess, Anthony, "Clockwork Marmalade," in *Listener* (London), 17 February 1972.
Zimmerman, Paul, "Kubrick's Brilliant Vision," in *Newsweek* (New York), 3 January 1972.
Bourget, Jean-Loup, in *Positif* (Paris), March 1972.
Burgess, Jackson, in *Film Quarterly* (Berkeley), Spring 1972.
Houston, Penelope, and Philip Strick, "Interview with Stanley Kubrick," in *Sight and Sound* (London), Spring 1972.
Krassner, P., and others, in *Take One* (Montreal), April 1972.
Barr, Charles, "*Straw Dogs, A Clockwork Orange*, and the Critics," in *Screen* (London), Summer 1972.
Boyers, Robert, in *Film Heritage* (Dayton, Ohio), Summer 1972.
Gumenik, Arthur, "*A Clockwork Orange:* Novel into Film," in *Film Heritage* (Dayton, Ohio), Summer 1972.
Kolker, Robert Phillip, "Oranges, Dogs, and Ultraviolence," in *Journal of Popular Culture* (Bowling Green, Ohio), Summer 1972.
Benayoun, Robert, "Stanley Kubrick le libertin," *Positif* (Paris), June 1972.
Burgess, Anthony, in *Positif* (Paris), June 1972.
Ciment, Michel, "Entretien avec Stanley Kubrick," in *Positif* (Paris), June 1972.
Costello, Donald, "From Counter-Culture to Anti-Culture," in *Commonweal* (New York), 14 July 1972.
Strick, Philip, "Kubrick's Horrorshow," in *Sight and Sound* (London), Winter 1972.
McCracken, Samuel, "Novel into Film: Novelist Into Critic: *A Clockwork Orange* Again," in *Antioch Review* (Yellow Springs, Ohio), no. 3, 1973.
Isaac, Neil D., "Unstuck in Time: *Clockwork Orange* and *Slaughterhouse 5*," in *Literature/Film Quarterly* (Salisbury, Maryland), Spring 1973.
Mamber, Stephen, in *Cinema* (Los Angeles), Winter 1973.
Evans, W., "Violence and Film: The Thesis of Kubrick's *A Clockwork Orange*," in *Velvet Light Trap* (Madison, Wisconsin), Fall 1974.
Gow, Gordon, in *Films and Filming* (London), October 1975.
Feldmann, H., "Kubrick and His Discontents," in *Film Quarterly* (Berkeley), no. 1, 1976.
Elsaesser, Thomas, "Screen Violence: Emotional Structure and Ideological Function in *A Clockwork Orange*," in *Approaches to Popular Culture*, edited by C. W. E. Bigsby, London, 1976.
Moskowitz, Ken, "*A Clockwork Orange*," in *Velvet Light Trap* (Madison, Wisconsin), Fall 1976.
Moskowitz, Ken, "Clockwork Violence," *Sight and Sound* (London), Winter 1977.
Sobcharck, V. C., "Decor as Theme: *A Clockwork Orange*," in *Literature/Film Quarterly* (Salisbury, Maryland), no. 2, 1981.
Collins, F., "Implied Metaphor in the Films of Stanley Kubrick," in *New Orleans Review*, no. 3, 1989.
French, P., in *Sight and Sound* (London), no. 2, 1990.
Bourguignon, T., in *Positif* (Paris), September 1992.
Stein, M.E., "The New Violence, or Twenty Years of Violence in Films: An Appreciation," in *Films in Review* (Denville, New Jersey), vol. 46, January/February 1995.
Ng, Y., "*A Clockwork Orange*: The First 25 Years," in *Kinema* (Waterloo, Ontario), no. 5, Spring 1996.
Rouchy, Marie-Élisabeth and François Gorin, "Kubrick a des pépins," in *Télérama*, no. 2443, 6 November 1996.

* * *

Still circulating in Europe and America but withdrawn from British distribution by Kubrick in 1973, within a year of its first release, *A Clockwork Orange* currently remains a paradoxical testament to the manipulative obsessions of its director. On the one hand, Kubrick has taken to extremes his habitual attention to every detail of the shaping and presentation of his work by, in this instance, deciding not to let it be shown at all. On the other, the "suppressed" film has validated its own theme by refusing to be manipulated out of existence; instead, its notoriety has served only to enhance its creator's reputation despite his change of heart, thanks to the seductive skill and extraordinary impact with which his tale is told. That it *is* his tale, although phrased in the appealingly hybrid language devised by Anthony Burgess (who in 1962 based his brutally comical novel on a real-life incident of 20 years earlier), is obvious from the parallels in structure, emphasis and technique with all Kubrick's other dramas, from *Day of the Fight* in which arenas and split personalities find an uncanny preface, to *Full Metal Jacket* in which, once again, conditioned killers pursue the excesses of a fiercely private war.

The setting for *A Clockwork Orange* is Britain in the near future—"just as soon as you could imagine it, but not too far ahead—it's just not today, that's all"—when teenage thug Alex DeLarge (Malcolm McDowell) enjoys a daily routine of crime, sex, and Beethoven. Caught and imprisoned for murder, he volunteers for experimental shock therapy available as a government scheme to reduce prison overcrowding, which brainwashes him so effectively that he becomes in his turn a helpless victim incapable of defending himself and nauseated by all his former passions. Trapped by the deranged writer Mr. Alexander, once attacked by Alex and now intent on revenge (and author, we learn, of a book called *A Clockwork Orange*), he is driven to attempt suicide after an overdose of Beethoven's Ninth Symphony. The popular press rushes to his support, and the government hastily agrees to reverse the "rehabilitation" treatment. Like the astronaut of *2001*, Alex is reborn ("I came back to life after black, black night for what might have been a million years") and, restored to rude health, prepares to make up for lost time.

Boisterous, intimate, explicit and gaudy, Kubrick's forecast owes nothing to the high-tech elegance of *2001*, his other speculative trendsetter, except for the same scrupulous perfectionism. The costumes by Milena Canonero and the set designs by John Barry are a spectacularly lurid blend of transient fashion, stockbroker-belt kitsch, clownish irony and plundered grandeur, as if the palatial vaults of the Overlook Hotel in *The Shining* had been taken over for an acid-house boutique. The effect is more pantomime than prophecy, but it defines with hilarious clarity a society of fevered excess where the older generation clings listlessly to a dismal past while the present is ruthlessly pillaged by the young. Art has been reduced to tepid pornography, with sculpted nudes as furniture in the "milk-bars" (where drinks are automatically spiced with drugs) and erotic images as commonplace domestic wallpaper, while music has become mechanical and formulaic, even the classics (beautifully rearranged by Walter Carlos) converted to a remorseless clockwork rhythm.

In this weary, decaying environment, physicality offers the only reliable truth. With joyful energy, *Clockwork Orange* presents a torrential, dancing flow of movement, celebrating the simplicity of brute strength. A superb fight sequence quickly establishes the mood: in a derelict opera house lit by huge shafts of light across its rubbish-strewn floor, two gangs confront each other gleefully and plunge into a ballet of dazzling violence, hurling each other through furniture and windows with slapstick enthusiasm. Urged on by, and often synchronised with, Rossini's thunderous "Thieving Magpie," their exhilaration then bursts out into a headlong chase aboard the stolen Durango-95, scattering other traffic in wild panic and yelling with the sheer ecstasy of speed. Alex's night-ride recalls the toppling "Star Gate" sequence of *2001*, the rush through the hotel corridors in *The Shining*, or more subtly the long journeys of *Lolita* and *Barry Lyndon* and the flight of the nuclear bomber in *Dr. Strangelove.* These anguished, self-defeating but inescapable odysseys, shaped from Kubrick's perpetually prowling camera, continue into the final image of *Full Metal Jacket*—a defiant advance into darkness by spirits who know the worst and no longer fear it.

Repeatedly, Kubrick opens his scenes with immense tracking shots, like the low-angle spin around the record-shop just ahead of Alex on the hunt, or the triumphant sweep through the wards with the psychiatrist and her trolley of equipment. Scenes of urgency and impending disaster are filmed with a hand-held camera (held by the director himself): Alex's fight with the cat-lady, a struggle in torrential rain, a march towards retribution in muddy woodland. And more than anywhere else in his work, Kubrick uses subjective shots, identifying us with Alex so that we too are crushed to the floor, lie powerless in hospital, or, most unsettling of all, fall in despair from a window to be smashed on the pavement below. This emphasis ensures that Alex has our sympathy despite the extremes of his behaviour, that he remains the misunderstood sufferer from social injustice ready to accumulate a further load of misunderstanding as soon as the opportunity arises.

"The story can be taken on two levels," said Kubrick before the film opened: "as a sociological treatment of whether behavioural psychology will lead to evils on the part of a totalitarian government (which I think is the less important level), or as a kind of psychological fairy-tale. And I don't frankly believe that audiences in general will see *Clockwork Orange* other than as a fairy-tale, which it also resembles in its symmetry, with each character encountered again at the end. There's a lot of hypocrisy about what the human personality really is: the Id may be largely suppressed by the super-Ego but it's with us just the same—and it identifies with Alex all the time. This darker side of our subconscious finds release in Alex: he makes nothing out to be better than it is, he's completely honest. How can we *not* sympathise with him?" Soon on the defensive, his film accused of inspiring new waves of delinquency (with about as much logic as if *Full Metal Jacket* were interpreted as an army recruitment exercise), the director with characteristic discretion has temporarily retired Alex as best he can from public gaze. But he compiled a portrait too potent to be forgotten: Alex's tortured face, enfolded in straps and wires, his eyelids held open by pitiless clamps, is one of the most haunting and vital apparitions the cinema will ever have to offer.

—Philip Strick

CLOSE ENCOUNTERS OF THE THIRD KIND

USA, 1977

Director: Steven Spielberg

Production: Steven Spielberg Film Productions for Columbia Pictures; Metrocolor, 70mm, Dolby; running time: 134 minutes. Released

Close Encounters of the Third Kind

9 November 1977; re-released 1980 with additional footage under the title *Close Encounters of the Third Kind, Special Edition.* Filmed in the United States and foreign locations; cost: about $19 million.

Producers: Julia Phillips and Michael Phillips; **screenplay:** Steven Spielberg; **photography:** Vilmos Zsigmond, and Douglas Trumball, William A. Fraker, Douglas Slocombe, John Alonzo, Laszlo Kovacs, Richard Yuricich, Dave Stewart, Robert Hall, Don Jarel, and Dennis Muren; **editor:** Michael Kahn; **sound:** Buzz Knudson, Don MacDougall, Robert Glass, Gene Cantamessa, and Steve Katz; **sound editor:** Frank Warner; **production designer:** Joe Alves; **art director:** Dan Lomino; **music:** John Williams; **special effects:** Douglas Trumball; **costume designer:** Jim Linn; **consultant:** Dr. J. Allen Hynek; **stunt coordinater:** Buddy Joe Hooker; **''Extraterrestrials'' realized by:** Carlo Rambaldi.

Cast: Richard Dreyfuss (*Roy Neary*); Melinda Dillon (*Jillian Guiler*); François Truffaut (*Claude Lacombe*); Cary Guffey (*Barry Guiler*); Teri Garr (*Ronnie Neary*); Bob Balaban (*David Laughlin*).

Awards: Oscar for Cinematography (Zsigmond), 1977; Special Achievement Award from the Academy of Motion Picture Arts and Sciences to Frank Warner for Sound Effects Editing, 1977.

Publications

Script:

Spielberg, Steven, *Close Encounters of the Third Kind*, London and New York, 1977.

Books:

McConnell, *Storytelling and Mythmaking: Images from Film Literature*, New York, 1979.

Monaco, James, *American Film Now: The People, the Power, the Money, the Movies*, Oxford, 1979.

Pye, Michael, and Lynda Myles, *The Movie Brats: How the Film Generation Took Over Hollywood*, London, 1979.

Kolker, Robert Phillip, *A Cinema of Loneliness: Penn, Kubrick, Scorsese, Spielberg, Altman*, Oxford, 1980; revised edition, 1988.

Crawley, Tony, *The Steven Spielberg Story*, London, 1983.

Short, Robert, *The Gospel from Outer Space*, San Francisco, 1983.

Goldau, Antje, and Hans Helmut Prinzler, *Spielberg: Filme als Spielzeug*, Berlin, 1985.

Mott, Donald R., and Cheryl McAllister Saunders, *Steven Spielberg*, Boston, 1986.

Smith, Thomas G., *Industrial Light and Magic: The Art of Special Effects*, London, 1986.
Weiss, Ulli, *Das neue Hollywood: Francis Ford Coppola, Steven Spielberg, Martin Scorsese*, Munich, 1986.
Godard, Jean-Pierre, *Spielberg*, Paris, 1987.
Sinyard, Neil, *The Films of Steven Spielberg*, London, 1987.
McAllister, Marica, *Steven Spielberg*, Vero Beach, 1989.
Taylor, Philip M., *Steven Spielberg: The Man, His Movies & Their Meaning*, New York, 1994.
Balaban, Bob, *Close Encounters of the Third Kind Diary*, New York, 1997.
Hovanec, Erin M., *Learning About Creativity from the Life of Steven Spielberg*, New York, 1999.

Articles:

Murray, D., in *Millimeter* (New York), September 1977.
Cieslar, J., in *Film a Doba* (Prague), October 1977.
Cook, B., ''Close Encounters with Steven Spielberg,'' in *American Film* (Washington D.C.), November 1977.
Kroll, Jack, in *Newsweek* (New York), November 1977.
Kael, Pauline, in *New Yorker*, 28 November 1977.
Close Encounters section, in *Filmmakers Newsletter* (Ward Hill, Massachusetts), December 1977.
Reilly, C. P., in *Films in Review* (New York), December 1977.
Kauffmann, Stanley, in *New Republic* (New York), 10 December 1977.
Fairchild, B. H., ''An Event Sociologique: *Close Encounters*,'' in *Journal of Popular Culture* (Bowling Green, Ohio), no. 4, 1978.
''Encounter Espionage,'' in *Film Comment* (New York), January-February 1978.
Tuchman, Mitch, interview with Spielberg, in *Film Comment* (New York), January-February 1978.
''*Close Encounters* Issue'' of *American Cinematographer* (Los Angeles), January 1978.
Simon, John, in *Take One* (Montreal), January 1978.
Behar, H., ''Rencontre express avec Steven Spielberg,'' in *Image et Son* (Paris), April 1978.
Biette, J. C., in *Cahiers du Cinéma* (Paris), April 1978.
Combs, Richard, in *Monthly Film Bulletin* (London), April 1978.
Lehman, Ernest, ''Close Encounters of a Quibbling Kind,'' in *American Film* (Washington, D.C.), April 1978.
Gerrold, David, ''*Close Encounters* and *Star Wars*,'' in *Science Fantasy Film Classics*, Spring 1978.
Pym, John, ''The Middle American Sky,'' in *Sight and Sound* (London), Spring 1978.
Heathwood, G., ''Steven Spielberg,'' in *Cinema Papers* (Melbourne), April-June 1978.
Eyman, S., ''Trumball the Magician,'' in *Take One* (Montreal), May 1978.
Gow, Gordon, in *Films and Filming* (London), May 1978.
Stewart, G., ''Close Encounters of the 4th Kind,'' in *Sight and Sound* (London), Summer 1978.
Seymour, F., and R. Entman, ''*Close Encounters of the Third Kind:* Close Encounters of the Third Reich,'' in *Jump Cut* (Chicago), August 1978.
Skwara, J., ''Basn dwudziestego wieku,'' in *Kino* (Warsaw), February 1979.
Cardenaz, F., in *Hablemos de Cine* (Lima), April 1979.
Carlo, S., ''Montare, smontare, ircollare,'' in *Filmcritica* (Rome), April 1979.
Ursini, James, in *Magill's Survey of Cinema 1*, Englewood Cliffs, New Jersey, 1980.
Gordon, A., ''*Close Encounters:* The Gospel According to Steven Spielberg,'' in *Literature/Film Quarterly* (Salisbury, Maryland), no. 3, 1980.
Jameson, R. T., ''Style vs. Style,'' in *Film Comment* (New York), March-April 1980.
Munson, B., ''Greg Jein—Miniature Giant,'' in *Cinefex* (Riverside, California), August 1980.
Williams, Tony, ''Close Encounters of the Authoritarian Kind,'' in *Wide Angle* (Athens, Ohio), volume 5, no. 4, 1983.
Shay, D., ''Special Visual Effects—Robert Swarthe,'' in *Cinefex* (Riverside, California), January 1983.
Phillips, J., ''A Close Encounter of the Worst Kind,'' in *Premiere* (New York), December 1990.
Torry, R., ''Politics and Parousia in *Close Encounters of the Third Kind*,'' in *Literature/Film Quarterly* (Salisbury, Maryland), no. 3, 1991.
Sheehan, H., ''The Panning of Steven Spielberg,'' in *Film Comment* (New York), May-June 1992.
Shay, D., ''A Close Encounter with Steven Spielberg,'' in *Cinefex* (Riverside, California), February 1993.
Solman, G., ''Uncertain Glory,'' in *Film Comment* (New York), May-June 1993.
Engel, Charlene, ''Language and the Music of the Spheres: Steven Spielberg's *Close Encounters of the Third Kind*,'' in *Literature/ Film Quarterly* (Salisbury), vol. 24, no. 4, October 1996.

* * *

Following the financial success of *Jaws*, director Steven Spielberg was able to obtain funding for *Close Encounters of the Third Kind*, a large personal project about the UFO experience. Spielberg had explored this topic in a 2-hour 8mm film he had made as a youth, called *Firelight. Close Encounters* tells the story of Roy Neary, a middle-class American who becomes alienated from his family and his suburban lifestyle when he sees actual flying saucers, apparently controlled by intelligent beings from outer space. The aliens have implanted a mysterious vision in Neary's mind, the meaning of which puzzles and frustrates him. Accompanied by Jillian Guiler, a woman whose son has been kidnapped by the aliens, Neary pursues his vision to Devil's Tower, an incredible mountain formation in Wyoming. There, they witness the first physical contact between a team of UFO investigators, led by a French scientist, Claude Lacombe, and the alien visitors. With a dazzling display of special effects, the film presents a host of small space-ships led by a gigantic mother ship. According to Spielberg, the inspiration for the mother ship's design was an oil refinery in India and the city lights of the San Fernando Valley in California. At the end of the film, Jillian is reunited with her son and Neary attains his dream by flying away with the mother ship.

The ''Special Edition'' of the film added scenes of Neary inside the mother ship, but cut the sequence where Neary throws dirt into his family's home in order to re-create his vision of Devil's Tower. Both versions of the film were combined in a special presentation for network television.

Critical reaction to the film was largely favorable, although there were some strong complaints about gaps in the narrative. Critics especially noted the religious overtones in the film.

But *Close Encounters* is more than just a quasi-religious celebration of childlike innocence—it is also a celebration of communication, expressed in the film through the interplay of light and music. The film opens with a splash of light and music and closes with an intensified version of these images and sounds, as the aliens and their human counterparts use flashing lights and a specific combination of musical tones to communicate with one another. Reportedly, the composer, John Williams, actually started work for the film two years before it was finalized, and in many instances he wrote his music first while Spielberg constructed the scenes to it later.

Close Encounters combines light and music to show how communication can transcend the boundaries between the known and the unknown, the human and the alien, the real and the imagined. As Frank McConnell suggests in his *Storytelling and Mythmaking*, the film ''is not so much about aliens as about our imagination of aliens, or, rather, about the myths of film culture itself and their power to energize and ennoble our lives beyond the point of irony and dissatisfaction.''

—Tom Snyder

CLOSELY WATCHED TRAINS

See **OSTRE SLEDOVANE VLAKY**

UN COEUR EN HIVER

(A Heart in Winter)

France, 1991

Director: Claude Sautet

Production: Film Par Film, Cinea, Orly Film, Sedif, Paravision, D.A. Films, FR3 Films, with the participation of Les Soficas Sofinergie, Investimage, Creations, Canal Plus and the Centre National de la Cinematographie; colour, 35mm; running time: 104 minutes.

Cast: Daniel Auteuil (*Stéphane*); Emanuelle Béart (*Camille*); André Dussolier (*Maxime*); Elizabethe Bourgine (*Hélène*); Brigitte Catillon (*Régine*); Maurice Garrel (*Lachaume*); Myriam Boyer (*Madame Amet*); Stanislas Carre de Malberg (*Brice*); Jean-Luc Bideau (*Ostende*).

Awards: Silver Lion and International Critics' Prize, Venice 1992.

Publications

Articles:

Variety (New York), 7 September 1992.

Legrand, G., and others, *Positif* (Paris), September 1992.

Nacache, J., ''Un Coeur en hiver: attendre et vieillir'' in *Revue du Cinéma* (Paris), September 1992.

Andrew, G., ''Musical Trio'' in *Time Out* (London), 21 April 1993.

Monk, C., *Sight and Sound* (London), May 1993.

Kissin, E.H, *Films in Review* (New York), October 1993.

Lis, Renata, ''Serce Daniela Auteuil,'' in *Kino* (Warsaw), January 1995.

Zizek, S., ''There Is No Sexual Relationship,'' in *Spectator* (Los Angeles), vol. 16, no. 2, 1996.

''Special issue,'' *Avant-Scène du Cinéma* (Paris), June 1996.

* * *

Claude Sautet's subtly haunting *Un coeur en hiver* is a film about the deepest human feelings and fears, especially fear of intimacy and fear of rejection. The film is the story of three people. Maxime (André Dussolier) and Stéphane (Daniel Auteuil) are long-time professional associates who operate a small company which constructs and restores violins. The former runs the business end of the operation, and the latter is an expert craftsman who handles the repairs. One day, Maxime informs Stéphane that he has met somebody: Camille (Emmanuelle Béart), a beautiful and talented violinist. Maxim explains that he and Camille have fallen in love, and are planning to live together.

Stéphane is a loner, who is immersed in his craft. His sole confidante is Hélène, the proprietress of a bookstore, with whom he shares a platonic relationship. As Stéphane and Camille begin spending time together in their professional capacities, it becomes clear that they are attracted to each other. Stéphane admits as much to Hélène, while Camille—despite her involvement with Maxim—asks him the $64 dollar question: ''Have you ever been in love?''

Sautet communicates his characters' thoughts as much visually as verbally. Just after Camille poses this question, she is seen kissing Maxime and then turning away; next, she is shown to look forlorn. A further reason for her discomfort is that she senses a reticence on the part of Stéphane. To her, this is an enigma. Eventually, she asks him, ''Why are you hiding from me?'' Stéphane, meanwhile, can only further distance himself from her. Eventually, an elated Camille reveals to Stéphane that she wants him, and can accept the fact that he lives in an ''enclosed world.'' Stéphane replies that she misunderstands him. He cruelly tells her that he has wanted to seduce her, without loving her, and that he listens to her play her violin only because it is his ''job.'' Stéphane, of course, is covering his true feelings. At first, this seems self-destructive, as he is thwarting any chance for the involvement he desires with Camille. His remarks deeply hurt Camille, and, ultimately, she ends up settling for Maxime. At the finale, Stéphane, Camille and Maxime meet in a cafe. As the latter two depart, there is a look of sadness on Camille's face. As Stéphane is left alone, he too shares that look, but he remains unable to express his emotions and share his life with another. To his mind, his rejection of Camille is an act of self-preservation.

At the opening of *Un coeur en hiver*, it is observed that violins are the ''most precious possessions'' of violinists. This declaration has profound meaning as the scenario evolves. If the instruments are such, they are so because they are safe. They have no free will. They will never abandon their owners. If they fall apart from usage, they always can be repaired. They are dependable and reliable—unlike human

Un coeur en hiver

beings. When Maxime initially tells Stéphane of his relationship with Camille, it is noted that Maxime already is married and is planning to leave his wife. Even though the latter character is never seen, one can envision the heartache she will feel when informed by Maxime that he is in love with Camille. At another point, it is casually observed that one of Camille's fellow musicians is in love with her. While he may be a minor character, his emotions are real, and one also can imagine how he must feel as he watches Camille and Maxime.

Furthermore, even when two people connect, relations between them are inevitably less than harmonious. Caring becomes interspersed with friction; this is exactly what Stéphane observes while watching Louis, an aged music teacher, relate to his wife. And even if that relationship is one without discord, it is destined to end with the demise of one of the lovers, and the inevitable despair and loneliness of the remaining partner.

Emotions are complex, inexact, ever-changing; in human relationships, feelings are dependent upon the responses of others. Stéphane is keenly aware of all this, and it is for this reason that, despite his feelings, he distances himself from Camille. He is afraid of allowing himself to love her, because of the pain he may be forced to endure. As a result, he presents himself as passionless, which even plays itself out during an intellectual discussion in which he professes to have no opinion on the subject at hand.

The relationships in *Un coeur en hiver* are not only between lovers. Camille has for many years roomed with Régine, her manager. As Camille prepares to move in with Maxime, Régine must adjust to a new and more solitary lifestyle, a fact which she acts out by becoming angry at Camille. Later on, Stéphane tells Camille that he considers Maxime a business partner, and not a friend. Camille retorts that Stéphane's attitude is ''just a pose.'' ''It's strange how you enjoy giving yourself a bad image,'' she adds. Of course, Stéphane is not cold-hearted. He and Maxime are in fact friends, and he truly values their relationship. What Camille does not understand is that Stéphane simply is fearful of facing his emotions.

In the end, Stéphane is a lonely figure, one who is ''unconnected with life.'' His solitude shelters him, keeping him protected from the hurt feelings that are the offshoots of human connection. Is he better or worse off? To answer this question, Sautet points out that, while we all are solitary souls, if we do not choose to be brave and risk connecting emotionally with others, our lives can never be complete.

—Rob Edelman

COME AND SEE

See **IDI I SMOTRI**

THE COMMISAR

See **KOMISSAR**

COMRADESHIP

See **KAMERADSCHAFT**

UN CONDAMNÉ À MORT S'EST ÉCHAPPÉ

(Le Vent souffle ou il veut; A Man Escaped; The Spirit Breathes Where It Will)

France, 1956

Director: Robert Bresson

Production: SNE Gaumont/NEF (Paris); black and white, 35mm; running time: 102 minutes. Released 1956, France. Filmed in France.

Producers: Jean Thuillier and Alain Poiré; **screenplay:** Robert Bresson, from the account by André Devigny as published in *Le Figaro Littéraire*, 20 November 1954; **photography:** Léonce-Henry Burel; **editor:** Raymond Lamy; **sound:** Pierre-André Bertrand; **art director:** Pierre Charbonnier; **music:** Mozart; **conductor:** I. Disenhaus.

Cast: François Leterrier (*Fontaine*); Roland Monod (*Le Pasteur*); Charles Le Clainche (*Jost*); Maurice Beerblock (*Blanchet*); Jacques Ertaud (*Orsini*).

Awards: Cannes Film Festival, Best Director, 1957.

Publications

Books:

The Films of Robert Bresson, New York, 1969.
Cameron, Ian, *The Films of Robert Bresson*, London, 1970.
Armes, Roy, *French Cinema Since 1946, Volume 1: The Great Tradition*, New York, 1970.
Schrader, Paul, *Transcendantal Style on Film: Ozu, Bresson, Dreyer*, Los Angeles, 1972.
Bresson, Robert, *Notes sur le cinématographe*, Paris, 1975; as *Notes on Cinema*, New York, 1977.
Pontes Leca, C. de, *Robert Bresson o cinematografo e o sinal*, Lisbon, 1978.
Sloan, Jane, *Robert Bresson: A Guide to References and Resources*, Boston, 1983.
De Gaetano, Roberto, *Robert Bresson: Il Paradosso del Cinema*, Rome, 1998.
Amiel, Vincent, *Le Corps au Cinéma: Keaton, Bresson, Cassavetes*, Paris, 1998.
Reader, Keith, *Robert Bresson*, New York, 2000.

Articles:

Monod, Roland, ''Working with Bresson,'' in *Sight and Sound* (London), Summer 1957.
Gow, Gordon, ''The Quest for Realism,'' in *Films and Filming* (London), December 1957.
Baxter, Brian, ''Robert Bresson,'' in *Film* (London), September-October 1958.
Ford, Charles, ''Robert Bresson,'' in *Films in Review* (New York), February 1959.
Green, Marjorie, ''Robert Bresson,'' in *Film Quarterly* (Berkeley), Spring 1960.
Cameron, Ian, ''An Interview with Robert Bresson,'' in *Movie* (London), February 1963.
Sarris, Andrew, ''Robert Bresson,'' in *Interviews with Film Directors*, New York, 1967.
Sontag, Susan, ''Spiritual Style in the Films of Robert Bresson,'' in *Against Interpretation*, New York, 1969.
Skoller, Donald S., ''Praxis as a Cinematic Principle in the Films of Robert Bresson,'' in *Cinema Journal* (Evanston, Illinois), Fall 1969.
Armes, Roy, ''The Art of Robert Bresson,'' in *London Magazine*, October 1970.
''Robert Bresson,'' in *Current Biography Yearbook*, New York, 1971.
Prokosch, M., ''Bresson's Stylistics Revisited,'' in *Film Quarterly* (Berkeley), volume 15, no. 1, 1972.
Polhemusin, H. M., ''Matter and Spirit in the Films of Robert Bresson,'' in *Film Heritage* (Dayton, Ohio), Spring 1974.
Sitney, P. Adams, ''The Rhetoric of Robert Bresson,'' in *The Essential Cinema*, New York, 1975.
Petric, Vlad, ''For a Close Cinematic Analysis,'' in *Quarterly Review of Cinema Studies* (Pleasantville, New York), no. 4, 1976.
''Robert Bresson Issue'' of *Caméra/Stylo* (Paris), January 1985.
Predal, R., in *Avant Scène du Cinéma* (Paris), January-February 1992.
Elia, M., ''*Un Condamné à mort s'est échappé,*'' in *Séquences* (Haute-Ville, Quebec), no. 189, 1997.

* * *

In the words of Jesus to Nicodemus in the third chapter of St. John, ''the spirit breathes where it will.'' This alternate title for the film speaks the director's intentions with greater clarity, for here Bresson illustrates the dictum that heaven helps the man who helps himself.

Basing his screenplay on a true incident involving the successful 1943 escape of André Devigny from Fort Monluc prison in Lyons just hours before he was to have been executed, Bresson fashioned an escape film which has none of the embellishments of other films on

Un Condamné à mort s'est échappé

that subject. Disavowing grand scale action sequences and focusing on the itimate details of the process of escape, Bresson elucidates the *how* rather than the *why*, the details of the physical process rather than the psychological motivations. Beginning with fact and striving for authenticity, Bresson employed Devigny as an advisor, secured permission to film in the actual prison, and gained access to the ropes and hooks used by Devigny in his escape.

Having made two films in which performance and dialogue were central, Bresson began to develop an alternate narrative strategy with *Diary of a Country Priest.* In this and later films he disavowed all notions of theatricality, refusing to employ professional performers and insisting upon writing his screenplays in a stripped down, elliptical form. In *Un Condamné*, a voice-over monologue almost entirely replaced diegetic dialogue.

The protagonist, here named Fontaine, is the focus of the film, and yet the performance of the man who portrays him is only partially responsible for the central impact of the main character. Using first person voice-over narration and shifting the dramatic emphasis to a close examination of manual dexterity, Bresson was able to eliminate any dependence on the standard conventions of vocal and facial expression to impart dramatic emphasis. In so doing, and by avoiding a persistent use of point-of-view shots, Bresson was able to impart a spiritual dimension, making the spectator aware of the workings of fate as well as those of the individual. Fontaine's actions during the process of escape are thus transformed from a manual enterprise to a collaboration between the physical and the spiritual.

Bresson creates an ''escape'' from traditional narrative form as well by the transformation of subjects and objects, creating meaning for those performers or objects which did not previously exist; certain items are transformed into the tools of escape, prisoners are transformed into free men, non-actors are turned into credible screen characters.

Visually alternating between scenes of solitary incarceration and minimal communication, Bresson used sound to allude to the possibility of freedom. In line with his belief that the ear is more creative than the eye, sound is used sparingly, generally to conjure up, for both Fontaine and the spectator, images that refer to ideas associated with escape: the guns of execution, the rattling of the prison guards keys, and the sound of a distant train. In the final moments of the film, as indicated by the title, Fontaine does realize his quest.

Less a film about the French Resistance, *Un Condamné* is an evocation of Bresson's belief in man's existence as being governed by a combination of predestination and human will. Elucidated without embellishment, this unusually suspenseful film celebrates the mystery of fate and the power of individual will.

—Doug Tomlinson

IL CONFORMISTA

(The Conformist)

Italy-France-West Germany, 1970

Director: Bernardo Bertolucci

Production: Mars Film SPA (Rome), Marianne Productions (Paris), and Maran Film GMBH (Munich); Technicolor, 35mm; running time: 112 minutes. Released 1970. Filmed in Italy and Paris.

Producers: Maurizio Lodife with Giovanni Bertolucci as executive producer; **screenplay:** Bernardo Bertolucci, from the novel by Alberto Moravia; **photography:** Vittorio Storaro; **editor:** Franco Arcalli; **production designer:** Ferdinando Scarfiotti; **music:** Georges Delerue; **costume designer:** Gitt Margrini.

Cast: Jean-Louis Trintignant (*Marcello*); Stefania Sandrelli (*Giulia*); Dominique Sanda (*Anna Quadri*); Pierrel Clementi (*Nino Seminara*); Gastone Moschin (*Manganiello*); Enzo Tarascio (*Professor Quadri*); Jose Quaglio (*Halo*); Milly (*Marcello's mother*); Giuseppe Addobbati (*Marcello's father*); Yvonne Sanson (*Giulia's mother*); Fosco Giachetti (*The Colonel*); Benedetto Benedetti (*Minister*); Gio Vagni Luca (*Secretary*); Christian Alegny (*Raoul*); Antonio Maestri (*Priest*); Christian Belegue (*Gypsy*); Pasquale Fortunato (*Marcello as child*); Marta Lado (*Marcello's daughter*); Pierangelo Givera (*Male nurse*); Carlo Gaddi, Franco Pellerani, Claudio Cappeli, and Umberto Silvestri (*Hired killers*).

Publications

Books:

Mellen, Joan, *Women and Sexuality in the New Film*, New York, 1973.
Casetti, F., *Bertolucci*, Florence, 1975.
Horton, Andrew, and Joan Magretta, editors, *Modern European Filmmakers and the Art of Adaptation*, New York, 1981.
Kuhlbrodt, Dietrich, and others, *Bernardo Bertolucci*, Munich, 1982.
Ungari, Enzo, *Bertolucci*, Milan, 1982.
Kolker, Robert Philip, *Bernardo Bertolucci*, London, 1985.
Kline, T. Jefferson, *Bertolucci's Dream Loom: A Psychoanalytic Study of the Cinema*, Amherst, Massachusetts, 1987.
Tonetti, Claretta, *Bernardo Bertolucci*, New York, 1995.
Gerard, Fabien S., editor, *Bernardo Bertolucci: Interviews*, Jackson, Mississippi, 2000.

Articles:

Haskell, Molly, ''Jean-Louis Trintignant,'' in *Show* (Hollywood), 20 August 1970.
New York Times, 19 September 1970.
Purdon, N., ''Bernardo Bertolucci,'' in *Cinema* (London), no. 8, 1971.
Kreitzman, R., ''Bernardo Bertolucci, an Italian Young Master,'' in *Film* (London), Spring 1971.
Goldin, Marilyn, ''Bertolucci on *The Conformist*,'' in *Sight and Sound* (London), Spring 1971.
Roud, Richard, ''Fathers and Sons,'' in *Sight and Sound* (London), Spring 1971.
Vogel, Amos, ''Bernardo Bertolucci: An Interview,'' in *Film Comment* (New York), Fall 1971.
Gow, Gordon, in *Films and Filming* (London), January 1972.
Hjort, O., in *Kosmorama* (Copenhagen), February 1972.
Apon, A., ''Methoden & technieken van Brechts epies theater,'' in *Skrien* (Amsterdam), November-December 1973.
''Bernardo Bertolucci Seminar,'' in *American Film* (Washington, D.C.), April 1974.
Paenhuijsen, F., ''Le Conformiste de Bernardo Bertolucci,'' in *APEC-Revue Belge du Cinéma* (Brussels), no. 3, 1974–75.
Lopez, D., ''The Father Figure in *The Conformist* and *Last Tango in Paris*,'' in *Film Heritage* (Dayton, Ohio), Summer 1976.
Lopez, D., ''Novel into Film: Bertolucci's *The Conformist*,'' in *Literature/Film Quarterly* (Salisbury, Maryland), Fall 1976.
''Bertolucci Issue'' of *Cinema* (Zurich), December 1976.
Aitken, W., ''Bertolucci's Gay Images,'' in *Jump Cut* (Berkeley), November 1977.
Orr, C., ''Ideology and Narrative Strategy in Bertolucci's *The Conformist*,'' in *Film Criticism* (Edinboro, Pennsylvania), Spring 1980.
Italianist (Reading, Berkshire), nos. 2–3, 1982–83.
Storaro, Vittorio, ''La memoria dell'immagine,'' in *Griffithiana*, December 1989.
Elia, Maurice, ''Le conformiste de Bernardo Bertolucci,'' in *Séquences* (Haute-Ville), January-February 1996.
Pinel, Vincent, Jean-Pierre Berthomé, and Bernard Bastide, ''La restauration deo films,'' in *Positif* (Paris), March 1996.
Walker, M., ''Style and Narrative in Bertolucci's *The Conformist*,'' in *CineAction* (Toronto), no. 41, 1996.
Streitfeld, Susan, ''The Fear of Being Normal,'' in *Sight & Sound* (London), vol. 7, no. 5, May 1997.

* * *

Bernardo Bertolucci's films are often centered on the ''split'' protagonist. Sometimes (*Before the Revolution, The Conformist* and—if we take Maria Schneider as the central figure—*Last Tango in Paris*) the split is dramatized within a single individual torn between two lovers/ways of life/political allegiances; sometimes (*Partner, 1900*) it is dramatized by simultaneously paralleling and opposing two protagonists, inverted ''doubles.''

The Conformist repeats the essential structure of *Before the Revolution.* The protagonist is torn between alternatives on two levels: political—Marxism vs. conservative Fascism; and sexual—bourgeois marriage vs. a form of sexual deviancy (incest in the earlier film and homosexuality in the later, though this is touched on in the first section of the earlier film also). There are also important differences. In *The Conformist* the choice has already been made, and Marcello is presented with the quandary of whether to re-confirm or reverse it; also, because the protagonist is a (precariously) committed Fascist, Bertolucci is able to distance himself from him more successfully, achieving a degree of irony that eluded him in *Before the Revolution.* What gives the films both richness and confusion is the failure of the political and sexual levels to become coherently aligned. One expects the straightforward opposition of Marxism/sexual liberation vs. conservatism/sexual conformity, but this never quite materializes. In *Before the Revolution* the protagonist's aunt/lover (and before her, his young male friend/potential lover) is presented as apolitical and neurotic. In *The Conformist* the ''liberated'' woman with left-wing commitments and explicit lesbian tendencies is associated (via the lesbianism) with decadence and irresponsibility. The homosexual chauffeur who seduced an already sexually ambiguous Marcello in childhood is also presented as decadent and exploitive. Yet the film is quite clear in connecting Marcello's *repression* of his homosexuality with his espousal of Fascism. The tension is never resolved in the film, or elsewhere, in Bertolucci's work so far.

Fundamental to the ''Bertoluccian split'' is a tension within his cinematic allegiances. Avowedly a disciple of Godard, his stylistic affinities are with a tradition of luxuriance and excess that might be represented by Welles, Ophüls and von Sternberg—a tradition totally alien to Godard's filmic practice. When Bertolucci obtained financing from Paramount for *The Conformist*, Godard (then at his most intransigent, in the period immediately following the upheavals of May 1968) denounced him. Bertolucci took his revenge by giving Marcello's left-wing mentor, Professor Quadri, Godard's telephone number, then having the character violently assassinated. It is not surprising that the same film sees the full flowering of Bertolucci's stylistic flamboyance—elaborate camera movements, strange baroque angles, luxuriant color effects, a profusion of ornate decor, the intricate play of light and shadow. This abandonment, however, never ceases to be troubled and uneasy: baroque excess collides with Godardian distanciation. The film at once intellectually disavows ''decadence'' yet acknowledges an irresistible fascination for it. The split is not merely thematic (hence under the artist's control): it manifests itself at every level of his filmmaking.

—Robin Wood

CONTEMPT

See **LE MÉPRIS**

THE CONVERSATION

US, 1974

Director: Francis Ford Coppola

Production: American Zoetrope, Paramount Pictures, The Coppola Company, and The Directors Company; color, 35mm, Spherical; running time: 113 minutes. Filmed in Union Square, San Francisco, California.

Producers: Francis Ford Coppola, Fred Roos (co-producer), Mona Skager (associate producer); **screenplay:** Francis Ford Coppola; **cinematographer:** Bill Butler; **editors:** Walter Murch, Richard Chew; **music:** David Shire; **casting:** Jennifer Shull; **production design:** Dean Tavoularis; **set decoration:** Doug von Koss; **costume design:** Aggie Guerard Rodgers; **production manager:** Clark L. Paylow; **sound:** Walter Murch, Nathan Boxer, Art Rochester.

Cast: Gene Hackman (*Harry Caul*); John Cazale (*Stan*); Allen Garfield (*William P. ''Bernie'' Moran*); Cindy Williams (*Ann*); Frederic Forrest (*Mark*); Robert Duvall (*The Director* [uncredited]); Michael Higgins (*Paul*); Elizabeth MacRae (*Meredith*); Teri Garr (*Amy*); Harrison Ford (*Martin Stett*); Mark Wheeler (*Receptionist*); Robert Shields (*The Mime*); Phoebe Alexander (*Lurleen*); Timothy Carey (uncredited).

Awards: British Academy Awards (BAFTA) for Best Editing (Murch, Chew) and Best Soundtrack (Rochester, Boxer, Evoe, Murch), 1974; Cannes Film Festival Best Film, 1974; National Board of Review Awards for Best English-Language Film, Best Director, and Best Actor (Hackman), 1974; National Society of Film Critics Award for Best Director, 1974.

Publications:

Script:

Coppola, Francis Ford, ''*The Conversation:* Original Screenplay by Francis Ford Coppola Final Draft November 22, 1972,'' in *Film Scheduling, Film Budgeting Workbook* by Ralph S. Singleton, Beverly Hills, California, 1984; republished in *Scenario*, vol. 5, no. 1, 1999.

Books:

Johnson, Robert K., *Francis Ford Coppola*, Boston, 1977.
Pye, Michael, and Lynda Myles, *The Movie Brats: How the Film Generation Took Over Hollywood*, London, 1979.
Kolker, Robert Philip, *A Cinema of Loneliness: Penn, Kubrick, Coppola, Scorsese, Altman*, Oxford, 1980; revised edition, 1988.
Chaillet, Jean-Paul, and Elizabeth Vincent, *Francis Ford Coppola*, Paris, 1984.
Zuker, Joel S., *Francis Ford Coppola: A Guide to References and Resources*, Boston, 1984.
Frundt, Bodo, and others, *Francis Ford Coppola*, Munich, 1985.
Ray, Robert B., *A Certain Tendency of the Hollywood Cinema 1930–80*, Princeton, 1985.
Chown, Jeffrey, *Hollywood Auteur: Francis Coppola*, New York, 1987.
Cowie, Peter, *Coppola*, London, 1989.
Bergan, Ronald, *Francis Ford Coppola-Close Up: The Making of His Movies*, New York, 1998.

Articles:

De Palma, Brian, ''The Making of *The Conversation*: An Interview with Francis Ford Coppola,'' in *Filmmakers Monthly/Newsletter*, vol. 7, no. 7, May 1974.
Denby, David, ''Stolen Privacy: Coppola's *The Conversation*,'' in *Sight & Sound* (London), vol. 43, no. 3, Summer 1974.
Palmer, J.W., ''*The Conversation:* Coppola's Biography of an Unborn Man,'' in *Film Heritage*, vol. 12, no. 1, Fall 1976.

The Conversation

"'America's Culture Is Controlled by Cynical Middlemen,'' an interview with Francis Ford Coppola, in *U.S. News and World Report*, 5 April 1982.

Turner, D., ''The Subject of the Conversation,'' in *Cinema Journal* (Austin), vol. 24, no. 4, Summer 1985.

Anderson, C., ''*The Conversation* as Exemplar and Critique of Sound Technology,'' in *Post Script* (Commerce, Texas), vol. 6, no. 3, Spring-Summer 1987.

Cockburn, A., and Adam Barker, ''John and Oliver's Bogus Adventure: Cries and Whispers,'' in *Sight & Sound* (London), vol. 1, no. 10, February 1992.

Atkinson, M., ''Role Models,'' in *Movieline* (Escondido), vol. 4, July 1993.

''Classic Scene,'' in *Premiere* (Boulder, Colorado), vol. 13, no. 7, March 2000.

* * *

The early 1970s were Hollywood's era of the Cinema of Paranoia. In those edgy post-Watergate years, with the shots that killed the Kennedy brothers, Martin Luther King, and Malcolm X still echoing from the previous decade, the idea of a vast malign conspiracy behind the scenes, manipulating events and eliminating awkward witnesses, seemed all too plausible. Films such as Alan Pakula's *The Parallax View* and *All the President's Men*, Arthur Penn's *Night Moves* and Sydney Pollack's *Three Days of the Condor* fed off these anxieties—and also latched on to a growing disquiet about the threat to individual liberty from increasingly sophisticated surveillance techniques. No one and nowhere, it seemed, was safe from intrusion, and personal privacy might soon be obsolete.

Most of these paranoia films adopt the outsider viewpoint, inviting us to identify with the individual conspired against and spied on. *The Conversation* goes one better. Coppola's film takes as its protagonist one of the perpetrators of this sinister activity, and explores its corrosive effect on him as well as on the society he preys on. And in the end the machine devours its own: the bugger, punished for a momentary deviation into human feeling, becomes the bugged.

Having chosen such an unsavory figure as his hero, Coppola perversely seems to go out of his way to alienate us yet further. Harry Caul (a performance of clenched introspection by Gene Hackman) has no friends, rejects all attempts at intimacy, denies feeling any kind of personal emotion. Even his name—the result, apparently, of a typist's inspired misspelling of ''Cal''—suggests something hooded, veiled against the world; he wears a cheap grey see-through raincoat, and Coppola often shoots him through semitransparent screens. Achingly secretive, Harry can barely even bring himself to confess to a priest, even though he's a devout Catholic; as he kneels in the confessional, the words appear to be dragged in pain from his mouth. ''I don't know anything about human nature,'' he snaps at his assistant, as if the very suggestion were an insult. Regarded in his sleazy profession as ''the best bugger on the West Coast,'' his sole concern—or so he claims—is to get ''a nice fat recording'' that he can hand over to his client.

It's this recording that we see Harry securing in the film's opening sequence, a conversation between a man and woman in a busy public place (Union Square in San Francisco). This scene, a virtuoso piece of film-making in itself, will be endlessly played and replayed throughout the film, in full or in brief snatches, sometimes with pictures, sometimes just on tape or re-echoing in Harry's mind, as its various levels of meaning are gradually teased out. (This examining and re-examining, the compulsive search for hidden significance, carries resonances of two key pieces of footage from the 1960s: the Zapruder film of JFK's killing, and the park photographs from Antonioni's *Blow-Up.*) Finally, the crucial element that eludes Harry's ear until it's too late proves to be a tiny shift in emphasis: not ''He'd *kill* us if he got the chance,'' but ''He'd kill *us*. . . .''

The Conversation is a fiercely moral work. According to Coppola, what he had thought would be a film about privacy became instead one about responsibility. Once before, we learn from predatory rival snoop Bernie Moran, one of Harry's operations led to the killing of an innocent woman and child. Since then Harry has retreated into perfecting his own technical virtuosity, repeating like a mantra that he's ''not responsible'' for what his clients do with the recordings he gives them. Disused, his moral power has atrophied, and even when he finally decides to get involved he can do nothing to prevent another killing. In a dream sequence, Harry finds himself telling the supposed victim how he was paralyzed as a child (a memory drawn from Coppola's own childhood) as if to excuse his present moral paralysis. Skulking in a clinically impersonal hotel room, hands over his ears to block out the screams coming through the wall, Harry is locked into his own cold, impotent nightmare. The bathroom sequence that follows may be his dream too, but it's no less horrific for that.

In the film's final shot Harry sits amid the ruins of his devastated apartment, ripped apart in his vain search for the bug planted there. Not even a statue of the Virgin Mary has escaped destruction, and he sits playing his sole remaining intact possession, a tenor sax. In his book on Coppola, Peter Cowie finds in this shot ''a mood of tolerance and devotion. Harry is absolved . . . free.'' But the image seems equally to express utter, irretrievable desolation. With the technology he lived by turned against him, Harry's life is over; spiritually and morally he's dead already, alone in a grey featureless hell of his own making.

Coppola made *The Conversation* between *The Godfather* Parts I and II, and its sombre, melancholy tone and subdued visual palette comes as a striking contrast to the narrative and pictorial gusto of the Mafia saga. Having finished shooting, the director went straight into pre-production on *Godfather II*, leaving Walter Murch to spend nearly a year working largely unsupervised on the visual and sound editing of *The Conversation.* For the subtlety of his achievement, especially on the all-important sound mix, Murch can justifiably be credited (as Cowie suggests) as the film's co-creator.

—Philip Kemp

LA COQUILLE ET LE CLERGYMAN

(The Seashell and the Clergyman)

France, 1928

Director: Germaine Dulac

Production: Delia Film (Dulac's company) may have produced it, but there is no concrete evidence to that fact; black and white, 35mm, silent; running time: 42 minutes, some sources list 38 minutes. Released 9 February 1928. Filmed at Studio de Ursulines in Paris.

Scenario: Antonin Artaud, revised by Germaine Dulac; **photography:** Paul Guichard; **editor:** Paul Parguel; **assistant editor:** Louis Ronjat.

Cast: Alex Allin (*Priest*); Bataille (*Officer*); Gerica Athanasiou (*Woman*).

Publications

Script:

Artaud, Antonin, *La Coquille et le clergyman*, in *Nouvelle Revue Française* (Paris), November 1927.

Books:

Curtis, David, *Experimental Cinema*, London, 1971.
Matthews, J. H., *Surrealism and Film*, Ann Arbor, Michigan, 1971.
Lawder, Standish D., *The Cubist Cinema*, New York, 1975.
Le Grice, Malcolm, *Abstract Film and Beyond*, Cambridge, Massachusetts, 1977.
Heck-Rabi, Louise, *Women Filmmakers: A Critical Reception*, Metuchen, New Jersey, 1984.

Articles:

Dulac, Germaine, ''Sur le cinéma visuel,'' in *Le Rouge et le noir* (Paris), July 1928.
Dulac, Germaine, ''Jouer avec les bruits,'' in *Cinéma—Ciné pour tous* (Paris), 15 August 1929.
Ford, Charles, ''Germaine Dulac,'' in *Anthologie du Cinéma 31* (Paris), January 1968.
Cornwell, Regina, ''Maya Deren and Germaine Dulac: Activists of the Avant-Garde,'' in *Film Library Quarterly* (New York), Winter 1971–72.
Van Wert, W., ''Germaine Dulac: First Feminist Filmmaker,'' in *Women and Film* (Santa Monica, California), vol. 1, nos. 5–6, 1974.
Dozoretz, Wendy, ''Dulac vs. Artaud,'' in *Wide Angle* (Athens, Ohio), no. 1, 1979.

Travelling (Lausanne), Summer 1979.

Greene, N., ''Artaud and Film: A Reconsideration,'' in *Cinema Journal* (Champaign, Illinois), Summer 1984.

Flitterman, Sandy, ''Theorizing the Feminine: Women as the Figure of Desire in *The Seashell and the Clergyman*,'' in *Wide Angle*, (Athens, Ohio), vol. 6, no. 3, 1984.

Kolisnyk, M. H., ''Surrealism, Surreption: Artaud's Doubles,'' in *October* (Cambridge, Massachusetts), Spring 1993.

Reck, H.U., ''Dunkle Erkundungen einer verstummenden Echos,'' in *Cinema* (Switzerland), vol. 39, 1993.

Fotiade, R., ''The Untamed Eye: Surrealism and Film Theory,'' in *Screen* (Oxford), vol. 36, no. 4, 1995.

* * *

La Coquille et le clergyman may now be regarded as the first Surrealist film, released a year before Buñuel and Dali's *Un Chien andalou*, which contains the image of an eye sliced by a razor. In *Coquille*, Germaine Dulac used trick photography to create the effect of an officer's head being split in half. The films share other Surrealist devices as well.

Antonin Artaud wrote the scenario, and wanted to act the role of the priest, though he did not initially want to direct the film. He subsequently seems to have changed his mind, writing to Dulac of his annoyance that the shooting and editing of *La Coquille* were done without him. Dulac had revised his scenario, casting Alex Allin in the priest's role. The film represents the subconscious sexual cravings of the priest, and is set in dreamlike environments. In one notorious scene the priest is shown masturbating. In another, the priest encounters the frightening ghost of a woman in a ballroom. He runs away, pulling up the skirts of his cassock, which lengthens and stretches away like a tail behind him. The clergyman and the woman run through darkness, their progress marked by visions of the woman in varying forms, once with her tongue sticking out, another time with her cheek ballooning outward.

It is believed that Artaud was particularly infuriated by a scene in which the priest, wearing a frock coat, is in a wine cellar. He empties an array of glasses of red wine, then shatters all of them. With no transition, he is next seen crawling on his hands and knees in a Paris street.

Artaud criticized Dulac for softening the lean strength of his script. When Dulac premiered *La Coquille* as ''a dream of Antonin Artaud,'' he denounced the film. According to Wendy Dozoretz, in her article in *Wide Angle*, it was André Breton who yelled out, as the film's credits appeared on the screen, ''Mme. Dulac is a cow.'' Led by Artaud, critic Georges Sadoul, novelist Louis Aragon and others stopped the film projector, threw objects at the screen and walked out in protest, leaving a bewildered audience behind. In Dozoretz's words, *La Coquille* was ''the unique product of two incongruous minds.''

Certain contemporary critics contend that Artaud's scenario was superior to Dulac's interpretation. David Curtis in *Experimental Cinema* faults Dulac's pictorial conceptions as oversimplified, and her editing as too well measured, subtracting from Artaud's visions. J. H. Matthews in *Surrealism and Film* affirms that Dulac did not comprehend Artaud's artistic intentions, and did distort his script. ''She did not succeed altogether in emptying Artaud's scenario of Surrealist content. For this reason alone, her *Coquille* deserves mention among the first Surrealist films''

Dozoretz admits that the feminist Dulac's direction of the film could have resulted in misinterpretation of Artaud's misogynistic scenario. However, the optical tricks that Dulac used were those specified. As for Artaud's charge that Dulac ''feminized'' his script, Dozoretz agrees that Dulac probably did weaken the brutality of Artaud's vision.

The fact that *La Coquille* is presently well-known and often shown is owed to Henri Langlois, former head of the Cinémathèque française, who rediscovered it after decades of oblivion. *La Coquille* has aged gracefully, its potency intact, secure in its deserved niche as a classic of Surrealist cinema.

—Louise Heck-Rabi

THE CRANES ARE FLYING

See **LETYAT ZHURAVLI**

CRIA CUERVOS . . .

Spain, 1976

Director: Carlos Saura

Production: Elías Querejeta Production Company (Madrid); Eastmancolor, 35mm; running time: 112 minutes; length: 2740 meters. Released Cannes Film Festival, 1976. Filmed in Madrid.

Producer: Elías Querejeta; **screenplay:** Carlos Saura; **photography:** Teodoro Escamilla; **editor:** Pablo del Amo; **sound engineer:** Bernardo Menz; **production designer:** Rafael Palmero; **music:** Federico Mompou and Valverde Leon Y Quiroga; **costume designer:** Maiki-Marin.

Cast: Ana Torrent (*Ana*); Conchita Pérez (*Irene*); Mayte Sánchez (*Juana*); Geraldine Chaplin (*Ana, Madre-Mujer*); Mónica Randall (*Paulina*); Florinda Chico (*Rosa*); Héctor Alterio (*Anselmo*); Germán Cobos (*Nicolás*); Mirta Miller (*Amelia*); Josefina Díaz (*Abuela*).

Awards: Cannes Film Festival, Special Jury Prize, 1976.

Publications

Script:

Saura, Carlos, *Cría cuervos*, Madrid, 1976.

Books:

Brasó, Enrique, *Carlos Saura*, Madrid, 1974.

Galan, Diego, *Venturas y desventuras de la prima Angélica*, Valencia, 1974.

Gubern, Roman, *Homenaje a Carlos Saura*, Huelva, 1979.
Hopewell, John, *Out of the Past: Spanish Cinema after Franco*, London, 1987.
Borin, Fabrizio, *Carlos Saura*, Firenze, 1990.
D'Lugo, Marvin, *The Films of Carlos Saura: The Practice of Seeing*, Princeton, New Jersey, 1991.

Articles:

Maraval, P., in *Cinématographe* (Paris), Summer 1976.
Bracourt, G., and others, in *Ecran* (Paris), July 1976.
Cluny, C. M., in *Cinéma* (Paris), July 1976.
Duval, R., ''Pleurons, pleurons, c'est le plaisir des dieux,'' in *Ecran* (Paris), September 1976.
Berube, R.C., in *Séquences* (Montreal), April 1977.
Brasó, Enrique, ''Entretien avec Carlos Saura,'' in *Positif* (Paris), June 1977.
Alemanno, R., in *Cinema Nuovo* (Bari), July-August 1977.
Aitken, W., in *Take One* (Montreal), July-August 1977.
Maillet, D., ''Carlos Saura,'' in *Cinématographe* (Paris), July-August 1977.
Bodeen, DeWitt, in *Films in Review* (New York), October 1977.
Pauks, I., in *Cinema Papers* (Melbourne), October 1977.
Foll, J., in *Film a Doba* (Prague), July 1978.
Pym, John, in *Monthly Film Bulletin* (London), September 1978.
Pulleine, Tim, in *Sight and Sound* (London), Autumn 1978.
''Saura Section'' of *Avant-Scène du Cinéma* (Paris), 15 October 1978.
Interview with Carlos Saura, in *Film und Fernsehen* (East Berlin), no. 3, 1979.
Kinder, Marsha, ''Carlos Saura: The Political Development of Individual Consciousness,'' in *Film Quarterly* (Berkeley), no. 3, 1979.
Schnelle, J., in *Medien und Erziehung* (Munich), no. 2, 1979.
Frias, I.L., in *Hablemos de Cine* (Lima), no. 70, 1979.
D'Lugo, Martin, ''Carlos Saura: Constructive Imagination in Post-Franco Cinema,'' in *Quarterly Review of Film Studies* (New York), Spring 1983.
Insdorf, A., ''Sonar con tus ojos: Carlos Saura's Melodic Cinema,'' in *Quarterly Review of Film Studies* (New York), Spring 1983.
Schwartz, Ronald, ''Carlos Saura,'' in *Spanish Film Directors (1950–1985): 21 Profiles*, Metuchen, New Jersey, 1986.
''Un regista fra divieto e sogno,'' in *Castoro Cinema* (Florence), July-August 1989.
Télérama (Paris), no. 2352, 8 Feburary 1995.

* * *

Like Victor Erice's *The Spirit of the Beehive*, *Cria Cuervos* stars the remarkable Ana Torrent and can be read, on one level at least, as a none-too-veiled parable about the stifling and oppressive climate of Franco's Spain. Although it is by no means immediately apparent, the film is really one long flashback, which itself contains flashbacks and fantasy sequences, from 1995 when Ana, a young Spanish woman, looks back to her childhood, and especially to the summer of 1975 in Madrid. In particular she remembers the death of her mother, Maria, from cancer; the death of her father, Anselmo, as he is making love to Amelia, the wife of his friend and fellow army officer Nicolás, although at the time Ana believed that she had poisoned him for ill treating her mother; the arrival of Anselmo's sister-in-law Paulina at the house after his death in order to look after Ana and her two sisters; the way in which she imagined that her mother and father re-appeared to her; her crippled and mute grandmother Abuela (to whom Ana offers her ''poison'' as a means out of her predicament); and Paulina's affair with Nicolás. Ana's discovery of this results in a contretemps with Paulina, as a result of which Ana tries (unsuccessfully of course) to poison her.

The film's title refers to the Spanish saying ''raise ravens and they'll peck out your eyes.'' On the most obvious level this refers to Ana's rebellion against her upbringing, which takes its most potent form in her ''poisoning'' of her father and substitute mother. Significantly her father was a member of the División Azul, a Spanish volunteer force which fought for the Nazis in World War II, who, in the scenes with his long-suffering wife, comes across as the typical Francoist patriarch (''I am what I am'' and so on) while the household in general typifies the traditional middle classes who were the bulwark of Francoism and who were distinguished, as one commentator has put it, by their ''Catholicism, an abundance of children, sexual hypocrisies, a rigid ethic, ritualised, conventional boredom.'' At the end of the film Ana and her sisters leave the claustrophobic, somewhat febrile domestic interiors in which the bulk of the action takes place and set off for school down the noisy street; the effect is decidedly refreshing and liberating, an impression only heightened by Saura's use of a long tracking shot, and puts one in mind of the director's remark when making *Cria Cuervos* that ''Francoism was dead before Franco died.''

This being a Saura film, however, the political elements exist side by side with distinctly Freudian ones, and the parallels with Buñuel (one of the director's great heroes) are readily apparent. It is not simply the fact that the film clearly links sexual repression and political oppression, or the way in which fantasy and memory are granted the same representational status as scenes from everyday ''reality.'' But, more specifically, it is the manner in which *Cria Cuervos* relates to Freud's ideas about the ''family romance.'' In particular it works a whole series of variations on the ''substitute parents'' syndrome in which, according to Freud, ''the child's imagination becomes engaged in the task of getting free from parents of whom he now has a low opinion and of replacing them by others, who, as a rule, are of higher social standing.'' Beginning with as striking a staging of the ''primal scene'' as one could wish for (with Ana listening to Amelia and her father making love) the film then continues via Ana's relationships with various substitute mothers (Paulina obviously, but also Abuela and even Rosa the maid, from whom Ana learns something about sexuality), the sisters' games in which they act out their previous family situation (with Ana playing her mother but significantly calling herself, and being called by her sister Irene, *Amelia*), and climaxing in Paulina reworking the opening adultery scene by being discovered by Ana passionately kissing Nicolás, Amelia's husband. This process of displacement, by which one character comes to represent or stand in for another, also finds its expression in the fact that both Maria and the adult Ana are played by the same actress, Geraldine Chaplin. As Marsha Kinder has pointed out, this doubling (which has its parallel in *Peppermint Frappé*, incidentally) leaves one ''uncertain a to whether the cherished image of the mother has shaped the development of the daughter, or whether Ana's own image has been superimposed over that of the absentee.'' Seen in this light Ana's attempts at ''poisoning'' are not *actual* deeds directed at *real* people but, rather, imaginary elements in her family romance, akin to her ability to conjure up her dead parents, or to the symbolic ''death'' which awaits those who are caught in the hide-and-seek game which the sisters play.

Cria Cuervos has been much admired for its portrayal of the world of childhood, and nowhere is it more successful in this respect than in its evocation of the fluidity of the child's sense of the real and the imaginary, thanks to which death is largely devoid of the terrors which it inspires in adults.

—Sylvia Paskin

CRIES AND WHISPERS

See **VISKNINGAR OCH ROP**

LE CRIME DE MONSIEUR LANGE

(The Crime of Monsieur Lange)

France, 1936

Director: Jean Renoir

Production: Obéron; black and white, 35mm; running time: about 2 hours. Released 24 January 1936, Paris. Filmed October-November 1935 in Billancourt studios, exteriors shot in and around Paris.

Le Crime de Monsieur Lange

Screenplay: Jacques Prévert and Jean Renoir, from an idea by Jean Castanier; **photography:** Jean Bachelet; **editor:** Marguerite Renoir; **sound:** Guy Moreau, Louis Bogé, Roger Loisel, and Robert Tesseire; **production designers:** Jean Castanier and Robert Gys assisted by Roger Blin; **art director:** Marcel Blondeau; **music:** Jean Wiener; **still photography:** Dora Maar.

Cast: Jules Berry (*Paul Batala*); René Lefèvre (*Amédée Lange*); Florelle (*Valentine Cardès*); Nadia Sibirskaia (*Estelle*); Sylvia Bataille (*Edith*); Henri Guisol (*Meunier's son*); Marcel Leveseque (*Landlord*); Odette Talazac (*Landlady*); Maurice Baquet (*Landlord's son*); Jacques Brunius (*Baigneur*); Marcel Duhamel (*Foreman*); Jean Dasté (*Dick*); Paul Grimault (*Louis*); Guy Decomble, Henri Saint-Isles, and Fabien Loris (*Workers at the publishing house*); Claire Gérard (*Prostitute*); Edmond Beauchamp (*Priest on the train*); Sylvain Itkine (*Inspector Julian*); René Génin (*Client*); Janine Loris (*Worker*); with Jean Brémand, Pierre Huchet, Charbonnier and Marcel Lupovici, Michel Duran, and Dora Maar.

Publications

Books:

Davay, Paul, *Jean Renoir*, Brussels, 1957.
Cauliez, Armand-Jean, *Jean Renoir*, Paris, 1962.
Chardère, Bernard, editor, *Jean Renoir*, in *Premier Plan* (Lyons), nos. 22–24, May 1962.
Analyses des films de Jean Renoir, Paris, 1966.
Bennett, Susan, *Jean Renoir*, London, 1967.
Poulle, François, *Renoir 1938; ou, Jean Renoir pour rein: Enquête sur un cinéaste*, Paris, 1969.
Leprohon, Pierre, *Jean Renoir*, New York, 1971.
Cuenca, Carlos, *Humanidad de Jean Renoir*, Valladolid, 1971.
Braudy, Leo, *Jean Renoir: The World of His Films*, New York, 1972.
Bazin, André, *Jean Renoir*, edited by François Truffaut, Paris, 1973.
Durgnat, Raymond, *Jean Renoir*, Berkeley, 1974.
Beylie, Claude, *Jean Renoir: Le Spectacle, la vie*, Paris, 1975.
Renoir, Jean, *Essays, Conversations, Reviews*, edited by Penelope Gilliatt, New York, 1975.
Armes, Roy, *French Cinema Since 1946, Volume 1: The Great Tradition*, New York, 1976.
Faulkner, Christopher, *Jean Renoir: A Guide to References and Resources*, Boston, 1979.
Sesonske, Alexander, *Jean Renoir: The French Films 1924–1939*, Cambridge, Massachusetts, 1980.
Gauteur, Claude, *Jean Renoir: Oeuvres de cinéma inédites*, Paris, 1981.
McBride, Joseph, editor, *Filmmakers on Filmmaking 2*, Los Angeles, 1983.
Serceau, Daniel, *Jean Renoir*, Paris, 1985.
Bertin, Celia, *Jean Renoir*, Paris, 1986.
Faulkner, Christopher, *The Social Cinema of Jean Renoir*, Princeton, New Jersey, 1986.
Vincendeau, Ginette, and Keith Reader, *La Vie est à nous: French Cinema of the Popular Front 1935–1938*, London, 1986.
Viry-Babel, Roger, *Jean Renoir: Le Jeu et la règle*, Paris, 1986.

Bessy, Maurice, *Jean Renoir*, Paris, 1989.
Renoir, Jean, *My Life & My Films*, New York, 1991.
Bergan, Ronald, *Jean Renoir: Projections of Paradise*, New York, 1994.
Renoir, Jean, *Letters: Jean Renoir*, New York, 1995.
Renoir, Jean, *An Interview: Jean Renoir*, Los Angeles, 1998.

Articles:

''Renoir Issue'' of *Cahiers du Cinéma* (Paris), January 1952.
''Renoir Issue'' of *Cahiers du Cinéma* (Paris), Christmas 1957.
Sadoul, Georges, ''The Renaissance of the French Cinema—Feyder, Renoir, Duvivier, Carné,'' in *Film: An Anthology*, edited by Daniel Talbot, New York, 1959.
Belanger, Jean, ''Why Renoir Favors Multiple Camera, Long Sustained Take Technique,'' in *American Cinematographer* (Los Angeles), March 1960.
Dyer, Peter, ''Renoir and Realism'' in *Sight and Sound* (London), Summer 1960.
Whitehall, Richard, in *Films and Filming* (London), June and July 1960.
Fofi, Goffredo, ''The Cinema of the Popular Front in France,'' in *Screen* (London), Winter 1972–73.
Klinger, B., ''Renoir's *Crime de Monsieur Lange:* Visual Environments,'' in *Wide Angle* (Athens, Ohio), no. 2, 1979.
Strebel, Elizabeth Grottle, ''A Reconsideration of Renoir's Film,'' in *Sight and Sound* (London), Winter 1979–80.
Horton, A., ''Alain Tanner's *Jonah* : Echoes of Renoir's *M. Lange*,'' in *Film Criticism* (Edinboro, Pennsylvania), Spring 1980.
Pappas, P., in *Cineaste* (New York), Summer 1980.
Strebel, Elizabeth Grottle, ''Jean Renoir and the Popular Front,'' in *Feature Films as History*, edited by K. R. M. Short, London, 1981.
Beylie, Claude, ''Le Cinéma face au front populaire,'' in *Cinéma* (Paris), 4 June 1986.
Bush, L., ''Feminine Narrative and the Law in Renoir's *Le Crime de M. Lange*,'' in *Cinema Journal* (Austin, Texas), no. 1, 1989.
Poague, L., ''Figures of Narration in *Le Crime de Monsieur Lange*,'' in *New Orleans Review*, no. 2, 1990.
Simon, C., in *Cahiers du Cinéma* (Paris), no. 482, July-August 1994.
Faulkner, C., ''Affective Identities: French National Cinema and the 1930s,'' in *Canadian Journal of Film Studies* (Ottawa), no. 2, 1994.
Nosferatu (San Sebastian), no. 17, March 1995.
Tifft, Stephen, ''The Cinematic Space of the French Popular Front,'' in *Persistence of Vision* (Maspeth), no. 12–13, 1996.

* * *

For nearly three decades Jean Renoir's *Le Crime de Monsieur Lange* was a film which failed to garner the recognition it so richly deserved. At the time of its release, it was received indifferently and suffered the vicissitudes of political censorship. It was not until 1964 that the film enjoyed a U.S. release, and belatedly earned its reputation as a pivotal work in Renoir's career.

Le Crime de Monsieur Lange is the film which solidified Renoir's political reputation as the film director of the left. In sympathy with France's Popular Front, this film was Renoir's statement that the ordinary working man, through united action, can overcome the tyranny of fascism. Renoir's films were always imbued with a humanism and love for all mankind. With this film he uses a small group of Parisian workers, their families and neighbors, as a microcosm for the French common man.

Lange, played by René Lefèvre, is the author of a western pulp fiction series entitled *Arizona Jim.* When Batala (played magnificently by the great Jules Berry), the head of the nearly bankrupt publishing company, absconds with the company funds, Lange organizes a ''cooperative'' with the help of the other employees. Their venture is so successful it prompts the scoundrel publisher to return in the guise of a priest and reap the monetary rewards of the cooperative. In a brave and mandatory move, the naive and humble Lange kills the publisher to prevent the destruction of their venture. Lange and his girlfriend flee the country, are caught by border guards, but allowed to go free when the girl explains the details of Lange's crime.

The script of *Monsieur Lange* was written by Jacques Prévert from an idea by Renoir and Jean Castanier. As with all Renoir films, the script was simply a starting point around which Renoir composed his films. To emphasize the sense of community, Renoir centers all the action on the courtyard which surrounds the publishing firm as well as the homes of the workers. Thus the courtyard becomes an integral part of Renoir's mise-en-scene, as much a character in the film as any of the actors, representing a united world which in turn evokes Renoir's philosophical aspirations for all mankind. Renoir is thus able to demonstrate the importance of the interaction of his characters for the benefit of all. The beginning of the film is devoted mostly to scenes of characters one-on-one, emphasizing the lack of any central goal. When Lange begins his efforts to form the cooperative, Renoir shifts his scenes to those of group relationships. Throughout, he uses his extraordinarily fluid and cyclical camera movements to create a unity of both time and purpose.

While *Monsieur Lange* is both an intriguing story of crime and an exercise in black humor, the film encompasses much more. It is an attack on class superiority and prejudice, an attack on the church, and although Lange does commit murder, it is a crime of poetic justice exonerated by the victim's avarice and the altruism of Lange's goal. Despite its indifferent reception at its release, *Le Crime de Monsieur Lange* is today regarded as one of Renoir's best films and one which significantly captures the social consciousness of the day.

—Ronald Bowers

CRISTO SI E FERMATO A EBOLI

(Christ Stopped at Eboli)

Italy-France-Denmark, 1979

Director: Francesco Rosi

Production: Vides Cinematografica, Radiotelevisione Italiana, Action Films, Société Nouvelle des Etablissements; colour, Technoscope; running time: 155 minutes. Filmed in Matera, Craco, Rome, 1978.

Producers: Franco Cristaldi, Nicola Carraro; **associate producers:** Yves Gasser, Yves Peyrot; **screenplay:** Francesco Rosi, Tonino

Cristo si e fermato a Eboli

Guerra, Raffaele LaCapria, based on the original book by Carlo Levi; **assistant director:** Gianni Arduini; **photography:** Pasqualino DeSantis; **editor:** Ruggero Mastroianni; **art director:** Andrea Crisanti; **music:** Piero Piccioni; **sound:** Mario Bramonti, Mario Maldesi, Gianni D'Amico, Renato Marinelli.

Cast: Gian Maria Volonté (*Carlo Levi*); Paolo Bonaccelli (*Don Luigino*); Alain Cuny (*Baron Rotunno*); Lea Massari (*Luisa Levi*); Irene Papas (*Giulia Venere*); Francois Simon (*Don Trajella*); Luigi Infantino (*Chauffeur*); Accursio DeLeo (*Carpenter*); Francesco Callari (*Dr. Gibilisco*); Vincenzo Vitale (*Dr. Milillo*); Antonio Alocca (*Don Cosimino*).

Publications

Script:

Levi, Carlo, *Christ Stopped at Eboli*, translated by Frances Frenaye, Middlesex, 1982.

Books:

Tassone, Aldo, *Le cinéma italien parle*, Paris, 1982.
Michalczyk, J.J, *The Italian Political Film-makers*, London/Toronto, 1986.
Marcus, Millicent, *Italian Film in the Light of Neorealism*, Princeton, New Jersey, 1986.
Ciment, Michel, *Le dossier Rosi*, Paris 1987.

Articles:

Mitchell, T., *Sight and Sound* (London), Autumn 1978.
Ciment, M., *Positif* (Paris), February 1979.
Variety (New York), 21 March 1979.
Tournes, A., *Jeune Cinéma* (Paris), June 1979.
Peruzzi, G., *Cinema Nuovo* (Bari), June 1979.
Gili, J.A., ''Levi, Rosi, Eboli'' in *Ecran* (Paris), September 1979.
Fox, J., *Films and Filming* (London), January 1980.
Grelier, R., *Image et Son* (Paris), May 1980.
Legrand, G., and M. Sineux, ''Là-bas et maintenent autrefois et non loin'' in *Positif* (Paris), May 1980.

Magny, J., *Cinéma* (Paris), June 1980.
Berube, R.C., *Séquences* (Montreal), January 1981.
Hibbin, S., *Films and Filming* (London), June 1982.
Ranvaud, D., *Monthly Film Bulletin* (London), June 1982.
Rashish, P., *Stills* (London), Winter 1982.
Crowdus, G., ''Francesco Rosi: Italy's Postmodern Neorealist,'' in *Cineaste* (New York), vol. 20, no. 4, 1994.
Cieutat, M., ''Des Christ par centaines,'' in *Cinemaction* (Conde-sur-Noireau), no. 80, 1996.
Castoro Cinema (Milan), March 1998.

* * *

One of Francesco Rosi's finest films, *Christ Stopped at Eboli* is based on the book by Carlo Levi in which the author recalls the time when, in 1935, because of his opposition to Fascism in general and the Abyssinian War in particular, he was sent into internal exile in the village of Gagliano in Lucania, an extremely remote province of southern Italy. It's extremely easy, especially for a non-Italian audience, to misunderstand the title, whose import is that Christ *stopped short* of Gagliano. To quote Levi himself: ''Christ never came this far, nor did time, nor the individual soul, nor hope, nor the relation of cause to effect, nor reason, nor history. None of the pioneers of Western civilization brought here his sense of the passage of time, his deification of the State or that ceaseless activity which feeds upon itself. No one has come to this land except as an enemy, a conqueror, or a visitor devoid of understanding.''

Rosi had been interested in filming Levi's book since the early 1960s, and it's easy to see why, given the centrality of the ''Southern [Italy] problem'' to the entirety of his oeuvre, and to Italy's on-going crises. Rosi himself is from the South, and had also worked as Visconti's assistant on his Southern drama *La terra trema.* But whereas in the early days, he has explained, he would have filmed it ''from a perspective much closer to neo-realism, impressed by the misery, the illnesses, the backwardness of the peasants in an underdeveloped region abandoned by all, even by Christ, I think today my point of view is different. It's no longer a question of only these problems, but especially of marginalisation.'' Furthermore, he became more interested in the mutual encounter of a Northern intellectual and the Southern peasantry, and especially in the way in which Carlo's plunge into a totally alien existence enables him to ''journey into his own consciousness.''

Rosi establishes the marginalisation of Gagliano right from the start by the train, bus and car journeys which Carlo has to make in order to get there in the first place. After that, Rosi combines frequent panning shots of the bleak Lucanian landscape with much tighter shots of Gagliano's town square and of the interiors of its dwellings. The sensation is of a stifling, suffocating community lost in the vastness of an alien landscape, a feeling at once agoraphobic and claustrophobic. Rosi's alternating perspectives recall the early scene in the book in which Carlo meditates on the town's petty bourgeoisie: ''their passions, it was plain to see, were not rooted in history; they did not extend beyond the village, encircled by malaria-ridden clay; they were multiplied within the enclosure of half a dozen houses . . . . Penned up in petty souls and desolate surroundings, they seethed like the steam pressing against the lid of the widow's saucepan where a thin broth was whistling and grumbling over a low wood fire. I looked into the fire, thinking of the endless chain of days that lay ahead of me when my horizon, too, would be bounded by these dark emotions.''

Gagliano may be physically isolated and remote, but thanks to an astute use of radio broadcasts, the exploits of the fascist regime are never far from mind. On Carlo's first day he is walking through the streets when he hears a speech by the Italian aviator De Pinedo about the onward march of Italian civilization under fascism, blaring from a radio. Not only does the radio belong to a former emigrant to America who has returned home (thereby underlining peasant culture's imperviousness to ideas about progress) but Rosi makes sure that we are aware of the almost timeless nature of the primitive streets over which De Pinedo's hectorings are drifting. Another example of Gagliano's utter isolation from the rest of Mussolini's Italy is provided by the film's most famous and virtuoso sequence: the three-minute pan over the peasants tilling the fields whilst the speakers in the square blare out the dictator boasting of the conquest of Addis Ababa and the end of the war. As Don Ranvaud has put it, this scene is a ''powerful statement of the total remoteness of the villagers from any notion of the State and the identification of one savaged people with another. Rome is a meaningless voice expressing meaningless concepts; the only reality in Lucania is the landscape or the promise of New York's Little Italy.'' Or, in other words, things are no worse (or better) under Fascism than under any other sort of regime, all are remote, alien agents of oppression.

Rosi is careful, however, not to make his film an exercise in miserabilism and pauperism. What interests him most, here, is the meeting of two cultures, that of Carlo and that of the peasants. Indeed, Carlo's encounter with the peasantry is not unlike Rosi's own, for although he, unlike Carlo, is himself a Southerner, both are urban intellectuals and hence almost equally far removed from the life of the peasantry. As Rosi put it: ''travelling through the places where Levi discovered a new world, confirms a Gramsci-like optimism, a belief in a better future for men and women who are endowed with an exceptional humanity. But one aspect I want to bring out in the film is that even the best of bourgeois intellectuals and artists, like Levi, who are quite happy to live amongst these people, with whom they feel a real brotherhood, end up leaving them to it. I had the same experience with *La terra trema*. . . . . Which means that Levi in the film is a bit like me. The film is an encounter between a bourgeois intellectual representing a refined Northern culture and a completely different, distant world, the world of the peasant in one of the most neglected regions of the South. It's not only a journey into humanity, but also into nature, objects, lights, shadows, sounds, animals, inside people's houses a journey into the minds and eyes and consciousness of the people.'' Carlo's horizons, then, turn out not to be bounded, as he feared, but considerably broadened, and his inner life becomes as freed as his physical life is geographically restricted.

What we don't have here, fortunately, is a mythologisation of the peasantry in the Pasolini mode. As Millicent Marcus has put it in a particularly perceptive analysis of the film: ''It would be easy for Rosi to sensationalise the strangeness and savagery of peasant existence under the pretext of educating his protected middle-class public. But to do so would be to burst uninvited into that closed world, to profane the mystery, and to violate that otherness which Rosi, following Levi's lead, so deeply respects. When he finally does coax us into the realm of peasant thought, it is through a slow and gentle motion of understanding, and not through a shocking leap into anthropological difference.''

This process begins, strikingly, on the long journey to Gagliano, and continues with the film's gradual accommodation to the natural rhythms of the peasants' routines and of village life in general. As

Marcus notes: ''As Carlo abandons his modern, urban perspective and enters into a very different mentality, so we too are urged to abandon our conventional cinematic expectations of pacing and density of action, to embrace this slow, meditative technique that simulates, on the level of style, the very world it represents.'' By the end of this process we, like Carlo, may come to realise that, although Christ may have stopped at Eboli, Gagliano is not a godforsaken hole but simply somewhere very different from what we are accustomed to. This process involves ''a recognition of the contingency and arbitrariness of our own perceptual modes and the acceptance of equally valid alternative world views.''

Rosi's film, like Levi's book, is set in the 1930s, but its subject matter is as relevant today as ever. Gagliano's troglodytes may have been rehoused, but the South remains as poor as ever, and is increasingly the object of northern hostility, and even separationist threats. As Rosi himself has put it, the peasants now have been ''dispossessed of their culture by the arrival of a new one, via the mass media and TV which has superimposed itself on their own ancient culture. The peasants, surrounded by motorways and TV, see the evidence in the pollution and despoliation of their own culture without being able to reap any of the benefits. This land is no longer isolated physically, but there is perhaps an even more cruel marginalisation in the extent to which the South of Italy has undergone in a traumatic fashion the arrival of the consumer society without this being accompanied by a parallel evolution of other aspects of life. The South has been emptied of its workforce. In Levi's time men went to work in America, but in less great numbers than they go today to the North of Italy, to Switzerland and to Germany. Villages which numbered 3000 inhabitants ten years ago now have 1200. Young people no longer want to work the land, because they've got qualifications and they'd feel it degrading to bring in the harvest.'' And now, European recessions and cut-backs in heavy industries have made it much more difficult to find work outside the South. The problem of the two Italies is even more acute today than when the film was made.

In conclusion, it should be pointed out that *Christ Stopped at Eboli* exists in two versions, as a feature film and as a four-part series made for television lasting around four hours. Both carry Rosi's imprimatur, but the longer one is preferable, particularly given Rosi's abovementioned attention to matters of pacing.

—Julian Petley

CROSSFIRE

USA, 1947

Director: Edward Dmytryk

Production: RKO Radio Pictures Corp.; black and white, 35mm; running time: 86 minutes. Released 22 July 1947. Filming completed 28 March 1947 in RKO studios.

Crossfire

Producer: Adrian Scott; **executive producer:** Dore Schary; **screenplay:** John Paxton, from the novel *The Brick Foxhole* by Richard Brooks; **photography:** Roy Hunt; **editor:** Harry Gerstad; **sound:** John E. Tribby and Clem Portman; **art directors:** Albert D'Agostino and Alfred Herbert; **music:** Roy Webb; **music direction:** Constantin Bakaleinikoff; **special effects:** Russell A. Cully.

Cast: Robert Young (*Finlay*); Robert Mitchum (*Keeley*); Robert Ryan (*Montgomery*); Gloria Grahame (*Ginny*); Paul Kelly (*The Man*); Sam Levene (*Samuels*); Jacqueline White (*Mary Mitchell*); Steve Brodie (*Floyd*); George Cooper (*Mitchell*); Richard Benedict (*Bill*); Richard Powers (*Detective*); William Phipps (*Leroy*); Lex Barker (*Harry*); Marlo Dwyer (*Miss Lewis*).

Awards: Best Social Film, Cannes Film Festival, 1947.

Publications

Books:

McCarthy, Todd, and Charles Flynn, *Kings of the B's: Working Within the Hollywood System*, New York, 1975.

Thomas, Tony, *The Films of the Forties*, Secaucus, New Jersey, 1975.

Dmytryk, Edward, *It's a Hell of a Life But Not a Bad Living*, New York, 1978.

Silver, Alain, and Elizabeth Ward, editors, *Film Noir*, Woodstock, New York, 1979.
Dmytryk, Edward, *On Screen Directing*, London, 1984.
Dmytryk, Edward, *On Filmmaking*, Boston, 1986.
Dmytryk, Edward, *Cinema: Concept and Practice*, Stoneham, 1988.

Articles:

Variety (New York), 25 June 1947.
Crowther, Bosley, in *New York Times*, 23 July 1947.
Scott, Adrian, ''You Can't Do That,'' in *Screen Writer* (London), August 1947.
Elliott, E. Cohen, in *Commentary* (New York), August 1947 (and reply by Dore Schary, in no. 4, 1947).
Agee, James, in *Nation* (New York), 2 August 1947.
Houseman, John, in *Hollywood Quarterly*, Fall 1947.
Scott, Adrian, ''Some of My Worst Friends,'' in *Screen Writer* (London), October 1947.
Brooks, Richard, in *Films in Review* (New York), February 1952.
Ringgold, Gene, ''Robert Mitchum,'' in *Films in Review* (New York), May 1964.
Stein, Jeanne, ''Robert Ryan,'' in *Films in Review* (New York), January 1968.
Bowser, in *Film Notes*, New York, 1969.
''The Cinema of Edward Dmytryk,'' in *Films Illustrated* (London), October 1971.
Magrelli, E., in *Filmcritica* (Rome), May-June 1976.
McArthur, Colin, ''*Crossfire* and the Anglo-American Tradition,'' in *Film Form* (Newcastle-upon-Tyne), Autumn 1977.
Kelly, K., and C. Steinman, ''*Crossfire:* A Dialectical Attack,'' in *Film Reader* (Evanston, Illinois), no. 3, 1978.
Black, Louis, in *Cinema Texas Notes* (Austin), 20 February 1978.
Simmons, J. L., ''Film into Story: The Narrative Scheme of *Crossfire*,'' in *Literature/Film Quarterly* (Salisbury, Maryland), vol. 12, no. 3, 1984.
Fox, D., ''*Crossfire* and HUAC: Surviving the Slings and Arrows of the Committee,'' in *Film History*, vol. 3, no. 1, 1989.
Télérama (Paris), 10 May 1995.
Mayer, G., ''When the Film Recognizes 'You','' in *Metro Magazine* (Victoria, Australia), no. 103, 1995.
Elia, M., in *Séquences* (Haute-Ville), March/June 1997.

* * *

A fascinating and biting film noir, *Crossfire* is a good example of the message film disguised as entertainment. It is one of a series of films produced in the later 1940s when the American motion picture industry discovered that adult themes and social problems could produce good box office. The first of two films released in 1947 dealing with anti-Semitism, *Crossfire* was both a commercial smash and a critical success. It was RKO's most lucrative production, earning over $1,000,000 in profits. It also garnered outstanding reviews: film critic James Agee called it ''the best Hollywood movie in a long time'' and *Newsweek* magazine judged it ''one of the year's best films.''

The film opens on a soldier, shrouded in shadows, viciously beating a man to death. The victim was Jewish, and his killer is a pathological sadist and rabid Jew-hater (stunningly portrayed by Robert Ryan). *Crossfire* is actually concerned with why the man is beaten to death, rather than who did the killing, as less than halfway through the film the killer's identity becomes known. The setting has been described as ''that peculiar midnight-to-dawn atmosphere that ordinary surroundings acquire in those mute subdued hours,'' and includes still, almost deserted city streets, all-night movie theatres, seedy bars, and cheap apartments—as well as the disparate and somewhat shady types who inhabit this world. Before the killer is brought to justice by an avuncular but hardnosed police captain (played by Robert Young in a role against type), he also brutally strangles a fellow soldier who might have given him away. Assisting the police captain is an army sergeant (Robert Mitchum) who serves in part as a sounding board for the captain in his comments on racial prejudice.

The movie is based on *The Brick Foxhole* by Richard Brooks, who later gained a certain well-deserved fame as a screenwriter and director. The novel focused on the brutal murder of a homosexual, but as that subject was just too controversial for a Hollywood still under the domination of the Motion Picture Production Code, the filmmakers changed the victim to a Jew. The ''message'' of the film is presented by the police captain. In perhaps a too didactic sermon, he preaches the need for tolerance and an end to prejudice, and summarizes the role of bigotry in American history. The film's message and its good intentions deserve respect but, over time, have lost their forcefulness. What remains striking and powerful is the framework in which the message of the film was set. *Crossfire* is a well-crafted, carefully organized, beautifully presented melodrama which still retains its audience's interest in the story's unfolding.

—Daniel Leab

CROSSROADS

See **JUJIRO**

THE CROWD

USA, 1928

Director: King Vidor

Production: Metro-Goldwyn-Mayer Pictures Corp.; black and white, 35mm, silent with music score; running time: about 93 minutes; length: 9 reels, 8538–8548 feet. Released 3 March 1928.

Producer: King Vidor; **scenario:** King Vidor, John V.A. Weaver and Harry Behn; **titles:** Joseph Farnham; **photography:** Henry Sharp;

The Crowd

editor: Hugh Wynn; **production designers:** Cedric Gibbons and Arnold Gillespie.

Cast: Eleanor Boardman (*Mary*); James Murray (*John*); Bert Roach (*Bert*); Estelle Clark (*Jane*); Daniel G. Tomlinson (*Jim*); Dell Henderson (*Dick*); Lucy Beaumont (*Mother*); Freddie Burke Frederick (*Junior*); Alice Mildred Puter (*Daughter*).

Publications

Books:

Vidor, King, *A Tree Is a Tree*, New York, 1953; revised edition, 1977.
Brownlow, Kevin, *The Parade's Gone By*, New York, 1968.
Baxter, John, *King Vidor*, New York, 1976.
Comuzio, Ermanno, *King Vidor*, Florence, 1986.
Durgnat, Raymond, and Scott Simmon, *King Vidor—American*, Berkeley, 1988.
Vidor, King, *King Vidor*, Lanham, Maryland, 1988.

Articles:

New York Times, 20 February 1928.
Variety (New York), 22 February 1928.
Cheatham, M., interview with Vidor, in *Motion Picture Classic* (New York), June 1928.
Mulligan, W. E., ''Work of King Vidor,'' in *National Review* (New York), July 1928.
Troy, W., ''Collectivism More or Less,'' in *Nation* (New York), 24 October 1934.
Brownlow, Kevin, ''King Vidor,'' in *Film* (London), Winter 1962.
Thomas, John, in *AFFS Newsletter* (New York), November 1964.
Higham, Charles, ''King Vidor,'' in *Film Heritage* (Dayton, Ohio), Summer 1966.
''King Vidor at NYU: Discussion,'' in *Cineaste* (New York), Spring 1968.
Schonert, Vernon, ''James Murray,'' in *Films in Review* (New York), December 1968.
Luft, Herbert G., ''A Career That Spans Half a Century,'' in *Film Journal* (New York), Summer 1971.
Durgnat, Raymond, in *Film Comment* (New York), July-August 1973.

"Vidor Issue" of *Positif* (Paris), September 1974.
Vidor, King, "L'Acteur," in *Positif* (Paris), December-January 1978.
Ellis, M., "Crowd Music," in *Sight and Sound* (London), Autumn 1981.
Allen, W., "King Vidor and *The Crowd*," in *Stills* (London), Winter 1982.
Cinema e Cinema (Venice), January-April 1985.
Bush, G. W., "Like 'A Drop of Water in the Stream of Life': Moving Images of Mass Man from Griffith to Vidor," in *Journal of American Studies* (New York), no. 2, 1991.
Rhodes, C., "Filling the Void: Work and the Modern Subject in King Vidor's *The Crowd*," in *Studies in the Humanities*, vol. 20, no. 2, 1993.
Klopcic, M., "Mnozica," in *Ekran* (Ljubljana) no. 3/4, 1993.

* * *

King Vidor's career wavered between the lure of romantic, erotic melodrama and the stricter morality of his Christian Science background. After three John Gilbert vehicles, including the popular *The Big Parade*, Vidor was able to sell MGM on a bleak, expressionist urban tragedy of the sort made fashionable by the novels of Sinclair Lewis, Theodore Dreiser, and John Dos Passos. Other studios, notably Fox, already enjoyed considerable success in this area due to their importation of German and Austrian directors like Murnau and Dupont. MGM, committed to a policy of mainly Scandinavian recruitment, lacked such experts in relentless art of the "city film." Vidor persuaded Irving Thalberg to permit this single excursion into the field by offering to produce "*The Big Parade* of peace"—clearly a strategem, since *The Crowd* is as cynical and relentless as his World War I romantic drama was soft-centered and sentimental.

The Crowd is a remarkable aberration to come from the optimistic, cheerful MGM machine, mocking as it does American fictions of self-advancement and ambition. John Sims's birth on July 4th, 1900, is greeted with elation by his father. "He's a little man the world's going to hear from," he crows. But social circumstances, Vidor points out, guide our life from childhood. John's schoolboy friends already have their careers mapped out for them, especially the black boy who boasts in comic minstrel patter of the time "I detend to be a preacher man. Hallelujah!"

No less a social stereotype, John is forced by his father's early death to join the crowd who fill the streets of New York. "You've got to be good in that town if you want to beat the crowd," remarks a gaunt stranger as John watches the skyline from a ferry. As a huge office building swallows up the young Sims, we realize he has become another victim of the city, subject to its whims, threatened by its pressures.

John's early enthusiasm for city life, fuelled by visits to Coney Island, an early marriage and the unexpected windfall of a $500 slogan-writing contest prize, is crushed by the random death of his child, then unemployment and a slide to the humiliation of selling vacuum cleaners door to door, until he becomes a juggling sandwich-board man—a character seen before and mocked by Sims, but who returns like the clown in *The Blue Angel* as a *memento mori.* Interfering relatives nearly destroy Sims's marriage, but the love of his son saves him from a suicide attempt and he's finally reunited with his wife. "The crowd laughs with you always," warns a title, "but it will cry with you for only a day."

Vidor tried seven endings before shooting one incorporating this bleak moral. Sims and his family visit a vaudeville show, and are last seen howling at the antics of two clowns, swallowed in a mindless laughing crowd.

Always attracted by expressionism and stylisation, Vidor exercised his penchant for both in *The Crowd.* Characters seem swallowed by their environment; the office building where John works (actually a model) is one of thousands in the city, and the camera zooms in through a window, apparently at random, to choose him, just another wage slave in an office of identical desks reaching in forced perspective to infinity. Earlier in the film, when John hears of his father's death, Vidor creates a vision of his threatened status by placing the boy on a staircase constructed against a distorted impression of a corridor actually painted on the back wall of the set. John, sustained by a relative, seems to hover between the inquisitive crowd huddled around the doorway and a threatening, unknown future.

James Murray, a minor featured performer (and not, as Vidor claimed, an extra) superbly conveys the feckless, ukelele-plucking John Sims mindlessly letting the world carry him along. (He was never to be offered work of this standard again, and drowned in the Hudson River in 1936; used to his gagging, watchers thought he was joking and failed to attempt a rescue.) Eleanor Boardman, later Vidor's wife, is an effective support.

But, as in all "city films," the individuals are dwarfed by an unfeeling capitalist society. Vidor emphasises this isolation in the film's most striking images; trying to quiet the crowd to soothe his dying child, Sims sets himself against the hurrying mob, hands thrust out, eyes blind; clocks dictate the coming and going of the city people with a relentless Langian power; even the couple's honeymoon is dwarfed by the torrent of Niagara plunging past the ledge on which they sit. A mis-step and it will carry them away.

Thalberg was alarmed at the bleak vision Vidor presented to him. The film was delayed for a year, and released to respectful reviews but little profit. Vidor went straight on to two Marion Davies comedies for William Randolph Hearst's Cosmopolitan Pictures, then based on the MGM lot. It was not until *An American Romance* that he had a chance to deal with the larger quasi-political issues he addressed in *The Crowd*, and by then the moment had passed.

—John Baxter

CSILLAGOSOK, KATONAK

(The Red and the White)

Hungary-USSR, 1967

Director: Miklós Jancsó

Production: Mafilm Studios (Hungary) and Mosfilm (USSR); black and white, 35mm, Agascope; running time: 92 minutes, Russian version about 70 minutes; length: 2545 meters. Released November 1967, Hungary. Filmed 1967 in the Kostroma Region of central Soviet Russia.

Production managers: Jeno Götz, Yuri Rogozovskiy, Andras Nemeth, M. Shadur, Kirill Siruauev, and Istvan Daubner; **screenplay:** Georgiy Mdivani, Gyula Herńadi, and Miklós Jancsó; **assistant directors:** Zsolt Kezdi Kovacs, Ferenc Grunwalski, Vladimir Glazkov, and Liliya Kelshteyn; **photography:** Tamás Somló; **editor:** Zoltán Farkas;

Csillagosok, Katonák

sound: Zoltán Toldy; **art director:** Boris Chebotaryov; **costume designers:** Mayya Abar-Baranovskaya and Gyula Várdai.

Cast: József Madaras (*Hungarian Commander*); Tibor Molnár (*András*); András Kozák (*László*); Jácint Juhász (*István*); Anatoliy Yabbarov (*Captain Chelpanov*); Sergey Nikonenko (*Cossack officer*); Mikhail Kozakov (*Nestor*); Bolot Beyshenaliyev (*Chingiz*); Tatyana Konyukhova (*Yelizaveta, the matron*); Krystyna Mikolajewska (*Olga*); Viktor Avydyushko (*Sailor*); Gleb Strizhenov (*Colonel*); Nikita Mikhalkov (*White officer*).

Publications

Books:

Issekutz, Bela, *Id. Jancsó Miklós és Ifi, a Két Orvostudós*, Budapest, 1968.
Estève, Michel, editor, *Le Nouveau Cinema hongrois*, Paris, 1969.
Whyte, Alistair, *New Cinema in Eastern Europe*, London, 1971.
Audras, Szefku, *Fényes Szelek Fujjátok!*, Budapest, 1974.
Buttava, Giovanna, *Jancsó: Miklós Jancsó*, Florence, 1974.
Taylor, John Russell, *Directors and Directing: Cinema for the Seventies*, New York, 1975.
Armes, Roy, *The Ambiguous Image: Narrative Style in Modern European Cinema*, London, 1976.
Castaldini, Ennio, *Il Vertice Della Parabola: Cinema Bianconevo de Miklós Jancsó*, Bologna, 1976.
Liehm, Antonin, and Mira Liehm, *The Most Important Art: Eastern European Film after 1945*, Berkeley, 1977.
Bird, Yvette, *Miklós Jancsó*, Paris, 1977.
Petrie, Graham, *History Must Answer to Man: The Contemporary Hungarian Cinema*, London, 1978.
Józsa, Péter, editor, *Adalékok az Ideológia és a Jelentés Elméletéhez*, Budapest, 1979.
Marlia, Giulio, *Lo schermo liberato: il cinema di Miklós Jancsó*, Firenze, 1982.

Articles:

Variety (New York), 22 November 1967.
Green, Calvin, in *Film Society Review* (New York), 2 October 1968.
Gilliatt, Penelope, in *New Yorker*, 29 March 1969.
Strick, Philip, in *Monthly Film Bulletin* (London), May 1969.
Hatch, R., in *Nation* (New York), 9 June 1969.
Houston, Penelope, ''The Horizontal Man,'' in *Sight and Sound* (London), Summer 1969.
Price, James, ''Polarities: The Films of Miklós Jancsó,'' in *London Magazine*, August-September 1969.
Cowie, Peter, in *International Film Guide*, London, 1969.
Robinson, David, ''Quite Apart from Miklós Jancsó,'' in *Sight and Sound* (London), Spring 1970.
Czigany, Lorant, ''Jancsó Country: Miklós Jancsó and the Hungarian New Cinema,'' in *Film Quarterly* (Berkeley), Fall 1972.
Martin, Marcel, in *Ecran* (Paris), December 1972.
Mercier, M. C., in *Image et Son* (Paris), no. 269, 1973.
Amengual, Barthélemy, and Michel Estève, in *Etudes Cinématographiques* (Paris), nos. 104–08, 1975.
Alemmano, R., ''Ripensando All Violenza dei *Rossi e dei Bianchi*,'' in *Cinema Nuovo* (Turin), January-February 1975.
Losada, C., ''Miklós Jancsó,'' in *Cinema 2002* (Madrid), December 1979.
Gillett, John, ''Miklós Jancsó,'' in *Film Dope* (London), July 1983.

* * *

Mikló Jancsó's third feature was filmed in the Soviet Union as a co-production to celebrate the fiftieth anniversary of the Revolution and, fittingly, features a group of Hungarians fighting alongside the Red forces. What Hungarians made of this only 11 years after the events of 1956 one can only guess; similarly, one wonders what the Soviet authorities made of Jancsó's refusal of any Manichean perspective here, since neither side is shown as morally superior to the other. The overall impression is of watching some vast, spectacular game of chess played to mysterious rules by remote, unseen forces utterly indifferent to human suffering. As Philip Strick has evocatively described it: ''against rolling and impassive meadowland, the meaningless choreography of the huntsmen and their victims, interchangeable from one minute to the next, takes its cold and casual course. Punctuating the placid murmur of a country summer, horsemen gallop furiously with erratic purpose, men order each other repeatedly from one position to another, and snarling biplanes loom masterfully overhead. In an endless transition from idyll to nightmare, there are captures, interrogations and executions, while the obsessive, arbitrary selection of men to be shot is mercilessly pursued by both sides, indistinguishable as they are in uniform, in attitude or in action.'' What we have here is a chilling study in arbitrary authority and absolute power, in which hunter and hunted, executioner and prisoner display an equal degree of impassivity and indifference, each knowing that the tables will soon turn once more. As Penelope Houston has put it: ''All the killings are completely casual, bloodless and emotionless: the man with the gun has the power, and his victim accepts that he has it, and there is no more than that to be said. There will be no lingering shots of corpses, no mashed limbs, no emphasis on death as a violent fact rather than another move in an endlessly repeated game.'' As a meditation on the waste and senselessness of warfare, *The Red and the White* takes some beating, not least because the film makes its points implicitly, apart from the moment when one of the Hungarians refuses to massacre a group of prisoners, saying that ''it is possible to fight and still be human,'' and the scene in which a nurse at a field hospital states that ''there are no Reds and Whites here, only patients.'' The terrifying arbitrariness of war is brilliantly communicated by the narrative's extraordinarily elliptical nature, whereby little is explained and events follow one another with bewildering rapidity but seemingly little causal connection. The feeling of watching men trapped inside some mighty and complex game played out by disinterested gods is strikingly conveyed by Jancsó's famous and characteristic geometric mise-en-scene. As Graham Petrie has noted, Jancsó's films make remarkable use of the Cinemascope screen, especially *The Red and the White*, in which ''whenever groups of characters appear, they are systematically drawn into horizontal, vertical, or diagonal lines, or into patterns of circles, squares and triangles. . . . Lines of men are constantly shown extending across the width of the Cinemascope screen, or forming diagonals that intersect with the boundaries of the frame to create complex visual effects. Though many of these compositions are quite breathtaking in their own right, the effect is rarely purely gratuitous: normally, by their very formality, they accentuate the elements of coldness and inhumanity inherent in the actions taking place.'' Particularly striking here is the use of the long-shot, frequently in combination with the sequence-shot and a highly mobile camera, so that, as Petrie puts it, ''the constant uncertainty, the to-and-fro pattern of the film as a whole, is crystallised within one single camera movement.'' Furthermore, the use of long-shot denies the audience any involvement in the acion and forces it to watch it more as some kind of preordained, hermetic ritual. In this respect Michel Estève has made an interesting contrast with Jancsó's earlier *The Round-Up:* ''the 'geometry of terror' of *The Round-Up* finds here its equivalent in the evocation of a dilated space. The choice of the wide screen, the immense and bare landscapes of the Volga, the importance accorded to long-shots, to depth of field and to aerial views suggest not the fate of the prisoner suffocated by a tight, hellish circle from which he does not know how to escape, but rather the combatant lost in the immensity of space, constantly pursued by death, crushed by his destiny.''

If *The Red and the White* presents us with an almost overwhelmingly bleak picture of the world, it does so with a remarkable sense of style, as Penelope Houston has pointed out: ''the saving graces of this arid world include, as always, visual beauty: the play of light, compositions of black figures against white walls, the strong verticals of Jancsó's almost abstract patterns. Aesthetically, the paring down of content is inevitably satisfying: it has the lure of the cloister, the white habit, discipline and rigour, the Bressonian impression of spiritual geometry.'' On the other hand, however, some critics accused Jancsó of aestheticising the horrors of war—one called him ''the master of artistic atrocity,'' for example. One might also complain that *The Red and the White* offers precious little explanation of the situation which it so strikingly lays out before us. Maybe that's why, with his next film, *The Confrontation*, Jancsó began what Petrie has termed a ''systematic exploration of the morality of violence and whether good ends can ever justify the use of inhuman means to achieve them.''

—Julian Petley

CYRANO DE BERGERAC

France, 1990

Director: Jean-Paul Rappeneau

Production: Hachette Premiere et Cie/Camera One/U.G.C/D.D Productions/Films A2; colour, 35mm; running time: 138 minutes.

Producers: Michel Seydoux, Rene Cleitman; **screenplay:** Jean-Paul Rappeneau, Jean-Claude Carriere, from the play by Edmond Rostand; **subtitles:** Anthony Burgess; **photography:** Pierre Lhomme; **editor:** Noelle Boisson; **assistant directors:** Thierry Chabert, Francine Meûnier, Nathalie Bezon, Attila Monost; **art directors:** Jacques Rouxel, Tamas Banovich; **production design:** Ezio Frigerio; **music:** Jean-Claude Petit; **costumes;** Franca Squarciapino; **sound:** Jean Goudier, Pierre Gamet, Dominique Hennequin.

Cast: Gérard Dépardieu (*Cyrano de Bergerac*); Anne Brochet (*Roxane*); Vincent Perez (*Christian de Neuvillette*); Jacques Weber (*Comte de Guiche*); Roland Bertin (*Ragueneau*); Phillippe Morier-Genoud (*LeBret*); Philippe Volter (*Vicomte de Valvert*); Josiane Stoleru (*Duenna*).

Awards: Best Actor, Cannes 1990.

Publications

Script:

Rappeneau, Jean-Paul, and Jean-Claude Carrière, *Cyrano de Bergerac, d'après l'oeuvre d'Edmond Rostand*, Paris, 1990.

Articles:

Variety (New York), 4 April 1990.
Strauss, F., *Cahiers du Cinéma* (Paris), April 1990.
Merrick, H., ''Le Marivadange Héroique'' in *Revue du Cinéma* (Paris), April 1990.
Amiel, V., ''L'esprit du theatre et la beauté du cinéma'' in *Positif* (Paris), May 1990.
Manceau, J.L., *Cinéma* (Paris), May 1990.
Logett, L., ''Autour de Cyrano'' in *Jeune Cinéma* (Paris), June-July 1990.
Buruina, M., and others, *Séquences* (Montreal), September 1990.
Horguelin, T., ''Le film de Roxane'' in *24 Images* (Montreal), Autumn 1990.
''*Cyrano de Bergerac*,'' in *Reid's Film Index*, no. 6, 1991.
Strick, P., *Monthly Film Bulletin* (London), January 1991.
West, J.M., *Cineaste* (New York), February 1991.
Kermol, E., in *Le Costa Vista* (Trieste), no. 18, 1992.

Cyrano de Bergerac

Abdullaeva, Z., in *Iskusstvo Kino* (Moscow), no. 11. 1992.
Douin, Jean-Luc, in *Télérama* (Paris), 23 March 1994.

* * *

The makers of this most recent telling of the Edmond Rostand classic have accomplished a most praiseworthy feat. They have taken a century-old romance of nobility and love's sacrifice and maintained a healthy measure of the flavor of the original, while at the same time bringing it to life for audiences of the 1990s.

In 1897, Rostand first presented this self-proclaimed ''heroic comedy'' about a proud Gascoyne swordsman, poet and lover with an enormous nose. Through the first half of the 20th-century, *Cyrano* was produced on many occasions with great success. Coquelin and Walter Hampden were but two of the actors who interpreted Cyrano. In recent years, however, the lacey prose and honeyed poetry of Rostand (known to most American audiences through the traditional English translation by Brian Hooker, written in 1923) has appealed mainly to more literary audiences. The 1950 Stanley Kramer production featuring Jose Ferrer as Cyrano had been considered the definitive film adaptation, but it has been overshadowed by this more contemporary, action-packed and in some ways more relevant production.

Director Jean-Paul Rappeneau and star Gérard Dépardieu have cut through the fine embroidery of *Cyrano* to the play's solid core, and emphasize Cyrano as an individualist. He is shown as a man of principle who would rather suffer the fate of an outsider than relinquish his own brand of panache. Dépardieu offers a naturalistic performance, playing Cyrano with an earthiness and virility that permeates much of the actor's film work. With an unabashed pride and stubbornness, Cyrano scoffs at two-faced politicians and attacks mannered fops who kowtow with insincere grace in exchange for courtly favors. Dépardieu's swordsmanship is no more skillful than Jose Ferrer's was, but this production is created with a greater excitement towards the sword fight sequences. Whereas Ferrer's Cyrano parries and thrusts half-hidden amid the black and grey shadows of the back streets of Paris, Dépardieu's Cyrano duels with a greater relish in more colorful surroundings and in stronger light, to the accompaniment of a more fluid camera.

A ruggedness of atmosphere properly places Cyrano in a rough-and-tumble man's world. At the cadets' headquarters, one sees soldiers in various stages of undress. There, one can smell the musk of the leather protective gear. At the battle stations, unwashed and hungry soldiers hunt down a rat and skin it for supper. As the men suffer for lack of meat, Cyrano calls upon an elderly shepherd to sing a folk song to remind them of their proud Gascoyne heritage. These moments of unaffected custom give emphasis to the difference between Cyrano's world and the refined, phony spheres in which Cyrano's enemies, the actor Montfleury and the Compte de Guiche, travel.

The film's English subtitles, written by Anthony Burgess, present a tasteful and lively text. As one might hope, the prose pays homage to the old-fashioned, flowery recitations in the Rostand play, maintaining the original flavor of the piece. Burgess uses good judgement in occasional decisions to keep to the French language. Roxane, for example, who is cousin to Cyrano and the love of his life, is referred to as ''precieuse.'' The strength of this word and the way the lips move when it is pronounced make this the authoritative description of Cyrano's secret sweetheart. In the finale, as he dies, Cyrano's last words refer to the one laurel he will take with him to the grave: ''my panache.'' Burgess could have translated that term as Hooker did, as ''my white plume.'' But, for today's audiences, such a term seems insignificant. The French word ''panache'' holds weight.

The trio of Départdieu, Rappeneau and Burgess have assembled a *Cyrano de Bergerac* that is naturalistic in style. It is at once a respectful interpretation of its original source material and an action-packed, full-bodied production designed to appeal to contemporary audiences.

—Audrey E. Kupferberg

CZLOWIEK Z MARMURU

(Man of Marble)

Poland, 1977

Director: Andrzej Wajda

Production: Enterprise de Realization de Films: Ensembles Cinematographiques and Ensemble X; Eastmancolor, 35mm; running time: 160 minutes. Released February 1977, Warsaw. Filmed in Poland; documentary sequences were provided by the Archives des Actualites, Cinematographiques Polonaises.

Producer: Andrzej Wajda; **screenplay:** Aleksander Scibor-Rylski; **photography:** Edward Kłosinski; **editors:** Halina Pugarowa and Maria Kalinciska; **sound operator:** Piotr Zawadski; **production designers:** Allan Starski; Wojciech Majda, and Maria Osiecka-Kuminek; **music:** Andrzej Korzyński, songs performed by the group Ali Babki and the Groupe Instrumental; **costume designers:** Lidia Rzeszewska and Wieslawa Konopelska.

Cast: Jerzy Radziwilowicz (*Mateusz Birkut and his son Maciek Tomcyzyk*); Michal Tarkowski (*Wincenty Witek*); Krystyna Zachwatowicz (*Hanka Tomczyk*); Piotr Cieślak (*Michalak*); Wieslaw Wojcik (*Jodia*); Krystyna Janda (*Agnieszka*); Tadeusz Lomnicki (*Jerzy Burski*); Jacek Lomnicki (*Young Burski*); Leonard Zajaczkowski (*Leonard Frybos*); Jacek Domanski (*Sound Man*); Grzegorz Skurski (*Chauffeur/Lighting man*); Magda Teresa Wojcik (*Editor*); Boguslaw Sobczyk (*TV Writer*); Zdzislaw Kozien (*Agnieszka's father*); Irena Laskowska (*Museum employee*); Jerzy Moniak (*Moniak*); Wieslaw Drzewicz (*Manager of the restaurant*); Kazmierz Kaczor (*Security man*); Eva Zietek (*Secretary*); B. Fronczkowiak (*Official from the Ministry of the Interior*).

Awards: Prix de la Critique International, Cannes Film Festival, 1978.

Publications

Script:

Scibor-Rylski, Alexander, *Czlowiek z marmuru, Czlowiek z zelaza* (in Polish), London, 1982; also published in French (*L'Homme de marbre*) in *Avant-Scène du Cinéma* (Paris), 15 January 1980.

Books:

Douin, Jean-Luc, *Wajda*, Paris, 1981.
Paul, David W., editor, *Politics, Art, and Commitment in the Eastern European Cinema*, New York, 1983.
Wajda, Andrzej, *Un Cinéma nommé désir*, Paris, 1986.
Wajda, Andrezej, *Double Vision: My Life in Film*, New York, 1989.
Falkowska, Janina, *The Political Films of Andrzej Wajda: Dialogism in ''Man of Marble,'' ''Man of Iron,'' and ''Danton,''* New York, 1996.

Articles:

Bajer, L., in *Kino* (Warsaw), May 1977.
Holloway, D., in *Variety* (New York), 1 June 1977.
Keller, R., in *Filmfaust* (Frankfurt), no. 7, 1978.
Demeure, J., and H. Niogret, interview with Wajda, in *Positif* (Paris), October 1978.
Thirard, Paul-Louis, in *Positif* (Paris), November 1978.
Fargier, Jean-Paul, in *Cahiers du Cinéma* (Paris), December 1978.
Dawson, Jan, in *Sight and Sound* (London), no. 4, 1979.
Interview with Wajda, in *Ecran* (Paris), no. 1, 1979.
Quart, Leonard, in *Cineaste* (New York), no. 4, 1979.
Konicek, Ryszard, in *International Film Guide 1979*, edited by Peter Cowie, London, 1979.
Linehart, R., ''L'Homme de marbre et de celluloid,'' in *Cahiers du Cinéma* (Paris), March 1979.
Canby, Vincent, in *New York Times*, 17 March 1979.
Amengual, Barthélemy, ''L'Homme (de marbre) est le capital le plus precieux, pensait planov,'' in *Positif* (Paris), June 1979.
De Benedictus, in *Bianco e Nero* (Rome), September-December 1979.
Ruf, R., in *Medium* (Frankfurt), October 1979.
Pap, P., in *Filmkultura* (Budapest), November-December 1979.
Vrdlovec, Z., in *Ekran* (Ljubljana), no. 4, 1980.
''Wajda Issue'' of *Avant-Scène du Cinéma* (Paris), 15 January 1980.
Torres, Fernandez, A., in *Contracampo* (Madrid), February 1980.
Nissen, D., in *Kosmorama* (Copenhagen), October 1980.
Dossier on Wajda, in *Image et Son* (Paris), December 1980.

Czlowiek z marmuru

Bickley, D., and L. Rubinstein, ''Between the Permissible and the Impermissible: An Interview with Andrzej Wajda,'' in *Cineaste* (New York), Winter 1980–81.

Abrahamson, K. A., in *Chaplin* (Stockholm), no. 5, 1981.

New York Times, 23 January 1981.

Newsweek (New York), 9 February 1981.

Fox, G., ''Men of Wajda,'' in *Film Criticism* (Edinboro, Pennsylvania), Fall 1981.

Cohen, Joan, in *Magill's Cinema Annual*, Englewood Cliffs, New Jersey, 1982.

DiCaprio, L., ''Polish Films and Politics,'' in *Jump Cut* (Berkeley), July 1982.

Lewis, Cliff, and Carroll Britch, ''Light Out of Poland: Wajda's *Man of Marble* and *Man of Iron*,'' in *Film and History* (Newark, New Jersey), December 1982.

Janicka, Bozena, in *Film* (Poland), 18 November 1984.

Sobolewski, T., ''Cierpiacy posag,'' in *Kino* (Warsaw), August 1989.

Jankun, M., and B. Dopart, ''Barwy ochronne albo kazdemu, co mu sie nalezy,'' in *Kino* (Warsaw), December 1989.

Della Casa, S., ''Amnesia land: il cinema del dimenticare,'' in *Ikon* (Milan), October 1990.

Koltai, A., ''A versailles-i fattyu,'' in *Filmvilag* (Budapest), no. 2, 1990.

Maland, C., ''Memories and Things Past: History and Two Biographical Flashback Films,'' in *East-West Film Journal* (Honolulu), vol. 6, no. 1, 1992.

Janicka, B., in *Kino* (Warsaw), July/August 1995.

Cade, M., ''Wajda historien du present,'' in *Les Cahiers de la Cinematheque* (Perpignan), no. 67, December 1997.

* * *

After many successful and mature historical films, describing different crucial moments of the fate of the Polish, and many screen versions of famous literary pieces, Andrzej Wajda, in *Man of Marble*, succeeded in creating nearly as great and important a work as his *Ashes and Diamonds*. *Man of Marble* is a success rooted in the spirit of the actual moment when it appeared, a critical film for understanding Poland's difficult situation in the 1980s.

The film is the story of a student, Agnieszka, who wants to make her graduation film about a former ''exemplary worker'' of the late Stalin years. Being a modern, bright and courageous girl, she is astonished at the many obstacles and difficulties she has to overcome in order to learn the whole truth about the forgotten idol. Many who had previously worked with him are currently successful, but not eager to recall the past. The television managers even intervene in order to stop her. At the end, Agnieszka does manage to present the complete biography of the man.

The forgotten hero, Mateusz Birkut, was a peasant boy who went to the city, like millions of youngsters during the 1950s, in order to earn his bread. Birkut was lucky enough to catch the eye of an ambitious filmmaker, who decided to make Birkut a legend and a star. During the Stalinistic epoch, a star could only be a perfect worker; and Birkut became such through the invisible help of his fellow workers who remained anonymous. His problems occurred when he himself began to believe in his own importance. He interfered in various political activities in a way that his bosses never anticipated. He disappeared from view, and his image and memory were brutally degraded. He eventually died, though no one knew when and how.

Wajda manages in this story, masterfully written by Aleksander Scibor-Rylski, to paint a very detailed, ambivalent and strongly emotional picture of the development of his country during the last 30 years, and to portray two generations—fathers and sons—who formed the socialist system in Poland.

The structure of the film is rather sophisticated. Wajda here renounces the use of visual symbols, so typical of his usual style. He replaces the symbols with documentation—chronicles and news items—from the period; his narrative structure consists of three parallel stories, each of them taking place in a different historical time.

In spite of this complicated form, the film enjoyed an enormous audience success. One of the aims of the socialist culture is to educate people to understand an art which participates in the life and the problems of society. The artists themselves, in this case Wajda, feel themselves obliged to function as the consciousness of their compatriots, while at the same time presenting to them refined, aesthetic works.

For all the negative events shown in the film Wajda declares himself to be among the responsible. The character of Burski, the filmmaker in *Man of Marble* who gained prominence with his film on Birkut and later became a world renowned Polish artist, is a conscious allusion to Wajda himself. Wajda continues today to ask the question: Is the cinema something more than just a creator of myths?

—Maria Racheva

DAHONG DENGLONG GAOGAO GUA

(Raise the Red Lantern)

Hong Kong-China, 1991

Director: Zhang Yimou

Production: Era International, Hong Kong, in association with China Film Co-production Corporation; colour, 35mm; running time: 125 minutes.

Producers: Chiu Fu-Sheng, Hou Xiaoxian, Zhang Wenze; **screenplay:** Ni Zhen, based on a short story by Su Tong; **photography:** Zhao Fei; **editor:** Du Yuan; **assistant directors:** Zhang Haniie, Gao Jingwen; **art directors:** Cao Jiuping, Dong Huamiao; **music:** Zhao Jiping, Naoki Tachikawa; **sound:** Li Lanhua; **make-up:** Sun Wei; **costumes:** Huang Lihua.

Cast: Gong Li (*Songlian*); Ma Jingwu (*Chen Zuoqian*); He Caifei (*Meishan*); Cao Cuifeng (*Zhuoyun*); Jin Shuyuan (*Yuru*); Kong Lin (*Yan'er*); Ding Weimin (*Mother Song*); Cui Zhigang (*Doctor Gao*); Zhou Qi (*head servant*).

Publications

Articles:

Chute, David, ''Golden Hours'' in *Film Comment* (Denville, New Jersey), March/April 1991.

Reynaud, Berenice, ''China—On the Set with Zhang Yimou'' in *Sight and Sound* (London), July 1991.

Variety (New York), 7 October 1991.

Reynaud, Berenice, ''Ghosts of the Future,'' in *Sight and Sound*, (London), November 1991.

Niogret, H., ''Rouge, noir et blanc'' in *Positif* (Paris), January 1992.

Bassan, R., *Revue du Cinéma* (Paris), January 1992.

Glaessner, V., *Sight and Sound* (London), February 1992.

Garcia, M., *Films in Review* (London), May-June 1992.

Fortin, P., *Séquences* (Montreal), September 1992.

Younis, R., *Cinema Papers* (Victoria), October 1992.

Sutton, D.S., ''Ritual, History and the Films of Zhang Yimou,'' in *East-West* (Honolulu), July 1994.

Klawans, S., ''Zhang Yimou,'' in *Film Comment* (New York), vol. 31, September-October 1995.

Young-Sau Fong, Suzie, ''The Voice of Feminine Madness in Zhang Yimou's *Dahong Denglong Gaogao Gua,*'' in *Asian Cinema* (Drexel Hill), Spring 1995.

Lee, Joann, ''Zhang Yimou's *Raise the Red Lantern*: Contextual Analysis of Film through a Confucian/Feminist Matrix,'' in *Asian Cinema* (Drexel Hill), Spring 1996.

Kong, Haili, ''Symbolism through Zhang Yimou's Subversive Lens in His Early Films,'' in *Asian Cinema* (Drexel Hill), Winter 1996–1997.

Wei, Y., ''Music and Femininity in Zhang Yimou's Family Melodrama,'' in *CineAction* (Toronto), no. 42, 1997.

* * *

Raise the Red Lantern was one of the rare Chinese films successfully marketed in America and its success has been ascribed to its exotic formula of a man with five wives and the radiant beauty of the star Gong Li. The film has certainly capped the international reputation of its director Zhang Yimou and made him the most successful director among the ''Fifth Generation'' filmmakers (including Chen Kaige, Tian Zhuangzhuang, Wu Ziniu) who first made their mark in Chinese cinema in the mid-1980s.

Superficially at least, *Raise the Red Lantern* has all the hallmarks of a sizzling soap-opera melodrama featuring the beautiful Gong Li as the fourth wife of Master Chen, a wealthy, traditionalist husband of the Chinese gentry class. Master Chen's mansion is divided into four quarters or courtyards—each occupied by one of his wives, who are all enjoined to live harmoniously under one roof. It is a manor dominated by the observance of arcane rituals, family rules and regulations—a central ritual being the hanging of red lanterns in the quarters of the master's choice of sleeping partner for the night. The plot ingredients of a melodrama come into play as three of the wives—Zhuoyun (the second wife), Meishan (the third wife, an opera singer), and Songlian (the fourth and most recent wife, played by Gong Li),—become rivals for the master's affections (the first wife being too old to be a serious rival).

Zhuoyun is deceptively friendly, showing her true colours in the course of the film, as the most treacherous of the master's wives. Meishan hides her tragic vulnerability beneath a bitchy, cunning veneer, while Songlian is equally vulnerable but much less equipped to handle the politics of rivalry and jealousy. The object is not only to win the master's affections but to exert authority over the wider household of other concubines and servants. As a servant says, ''authority is where the lantern is hung.'' To complicate matters, Songlian's servant, Yan, has ambitions of her own to become one of the master's mistresses. Yan taunts Songlian by being mildly rebellious and insolent (going against regulations, she hangs up torn and patched red lanterns in her own room), and informs on her mistress' activities in Zhuoyun.

The story works as a kind of gothic melodrama when Songlian discovers a locked room on the roof of the mansion and is told that it

Dahong denglong gaogao gua

was the place where two women had died tragically by hanging themselves. It is this room that rounds off the film's climax (as third mistress Meishan, discovered for her infidelity, is dragged and locked up there) and precipitates Songlian's tragedy. The chronology of the narrative takes place over the seasons of the year; the events are confined to the settings of a single household, done in the elaborate style of a Chinese manor-house complete with multiple courtyards, rooms, antechambers, and servants' quarters, separated by walls and lanes. This architectural marvel is as much a part of the story as are the characters, who often seem minuscule against the grand setting of the building (alone in a courtyard, or standing behind a towering facade).

Indeed, the film is distinguished by Zhang Yimou's penchant for long shots which take full advantage of his marvellous location and interior sets. There are almost no close-ups in the film—the camera getting no closer to the characters than the medium shot. When closer shots are employed, Zhang almost always favours his female characters—the one overtly conscious sign of the director's story-telling sensibility motivating his series of films, beginning with *Red Sorghum*, that are all centred around women (all played by Gong Li). The master of the household is, in fact, always in long shots, with the camera deliberately avoiding showing this character in full face. The device accentuates the distance of the one significant male character, both from the perspectives of the audience as well as those of the key female characters.

The long shot is a trait shared by Zhang's Fifth Generation colleagues (Chen Kaige, in particular, for whom Zhang served as director of photography on his first two films) and is a manifestation of the objective eye. In Fifth Generation work, the objective eye functions primarily as a visual endowment of film narratives. It points up the stunning visual qualities of the director's compositions, and ''fills in'' the narrative space that is not covered by dialogue. On the other hand, the long shot tends to reinforce the structural look of a film and gains a semiotic, symbolic function as well.

In *Raise the Red Lantern*, the structural compositions and their symbolic derivatives shore up the sense of distance in time and space and the psychology of the female characters as they engage in what modern feminists would consider absurd rivalry and power-play. The strength of the Fifth Generation directors lies in the ability to exploit historical objectivity and a highly personal approach to narrative filmmaking, thus breaking with the tradition of didacticism and literary approaches in Chinese cinema. That Zhang's success in the West is attributed to exoticism is a price he must pay as his films assume more formalized and realist, down-to-earth properties (as may be seen in *The Story of Qiu Ju* and his latest, *To Live*).

—Stephen Teo

LES DAMES DU BOIS DE BOULOGNE

(Ladies of the Bois de Boulogne)

France, 1945

Director: Robert Bresson

Production: Films Raoul Ploquin; black and white, 35mm; running time: originally 96 minutes, but edited down to 84 minutes for initial release, current versions are usually 90 minutes. Released 21 September 1945. Filmed summer 1944 in France.

Producer: Robert Lavellée; **screenplay:** Robert Bresson; **dialogue:** Jean Cocteau, from a passage in ''Jacques le fataliste et son maître'' by Denis Diderot; **photography:** Philippe Agostini; **editor:** Jean Feyte; **sound:** René Louge, Robert Ivonnet, and Lucien Legrand; **production designer:** Max Douy; **music:** Jean-Jacques Grunenwald.

Cast: Paul Bernard (*Jean*); Maria Casares (*Hélène*); Elina Labourdette (*Agnès J*); Lucienne Bogaert (*Madame D*); Jean Marchat (*Jacques*); Yvette Etievant (*Chamber maid*); with Bernard Lajarrige, Nicole Regnault, Marcel Rouzé, Emma Lyonnel, Lucy Lancy, Marguerite de Morlaye, and the dog Katsou.

Awards: Louis Delluc Award, France, 1945.

Publications

Script:

Bresson, Robert, and Jean Cocteau, *Les Dames du Bois de Boulogne*, in *Avant-Scène du Cinéma* (Paris), 15 November 1977.

Books:

The Films of Robert Bresson, New York, 1969.
Armes, Roy, *French Cinema Since 1946, Volume 1: The Great Tradition*, New York, 1970.
Cameron, Ian, *The Films of Robert Bresson*, London, 1970.
Schrader, Paul, *Transcendental Style on Film: Ozu, Bresson, Dreyer*, Los Angeles, 1972.
Bresson, Robert, *Notes sur le cinématographe*, Paris, 1975; as *Notes on the Cinema*, New York, 1977.
de Pontes Leca, C., *Robert Bresson o cinematografo e o sinal*, Lisbon, 1978.
Sloan, Jane, *Robert Bresson: A Film Guide*, New York, 1983.
Hanlon, Lindley, *Fragments: Bresson's Film Style*, Cranbury, 1986.
Quandt, James, editor, *Robert Bresson*, Toronto, 1998.
Reader, Keith, *Robert Bresson*, Manchester, 2000.

Articles:

Sadoul, Georges, in *Lettres Françaises* (Paris), 29 September 1945.
Becker, Jacques, ''Hommage à Robert Bresson,'' in *Ecran Français* (Paris), 17 October 1946.
Lambert, Gavin, ''Notes on Robert Bresson,'' in *Sight and Sound* (London), Summer 1953.
Truffaut, François, in *Arts* (Paris), 22 September 1954.
Gow, Gordon, ''The Quest for Realism,'' in *Films and Filming* (London), December 1957.
Baxter, Brian, ''Robert Bresson,'' in *Film* (London), September-October 1958.
Roud, Richard, ''The Early Work of Robert Bresson,'' in *Film Culture* (New York), no. 20, 1959.
Roud, Richard, ''French Outsider with an Insider Look,'' in *Films and Filming* (London), April 1960.
New York Times, 4 April 1964.
Sarris, Andrew, ''Robert Bresson,'' in *Interviews with Film Directors*, New York, 1967.
Sontag, Susan, ''Spiritual Style in the Films of Robert Bresson,'' in *Against Interpretation*, New York, 1969.
Skoller, Donald S., ''Praxis as a Cinematic Principle in the Films of Robert Bresson,'' in *Cinema Journal* (Evanston, Illinois), Fall 1969.
''Robert Bresson,'' in *Current Biography Yearbook*, New York, 1971.
Samuels, Charles Thomas, ''Robert Bresson,'' in *Encountering Directors*, New York, 1972.
Polhemusin, H. M., ''Matter and Spirit in the Films of Robert Bresson,'' in *Film Heritage* (Dayton, Ohio), Spring 1974.
''Les Dames du Bois de Boulogne Issue'' of *Avant-Scène du Cinéma* (Paris), 15 November 1977.
''Robert Bresson Issue'' of *Caméra/Stylo* (Paris), January 1985.
Signorelli, A., ''*Les dames du Bois de Boulogne* di Robert Bresson,'' in *Cineforum*, vol. 27, no. 9, 1987.
Predal, R., in *Avant Scène du Cinéma* (Paris), January-February 1992.
Michalczyk, J.J., and Paul Guth, in *French Review*, no. 4, 1992.
Botermans, Jan, in *Film en Televisie + Video* (Brussels), October 1996.

* * *

Les Dames du Bois du Boulogne, Robert Bresson's second film, premiered just at the moment of the Liberation of France. Considered a difficult and extraordinary work, it was the first recipient of the Louis Delluc Award for the year's most important French film. What was it that made this film so difficult, and how could Bresson's severe style have attracted the attention it did?

First of all, the stifling studio look, by which Bresson was able to control every shadow, was perfectly suited to the hermetic era of the Occupation in which the film was made and to the strict moral drama of the film's literary source. The story was culled from Diderot's 18th-century classic *Jacques le fataliste*. Seemingly updated to include automobiles, electric lights, etc., Bazin once claimed that

Les Dames du Bois de Boulogne

Bresson's adaptation is in fact back-dated, that it is the aesthetic equivalent of Racine. Bresson has indeed essentialized a picaresque, ironic drama into a tragic struggle of absolutes. More accurately, he has pitted the absolute and tragic world view of Hélène, the injured, icy heroine played elegantly by Maria Casares, against the more modern and temperate world views held by the lover who has left her, and by the two women she vengefully introduces him to in the Bois du Boulogne.

Here is the crux of the film's difficulty, for 20th-century spectators are required to identify with the hardened Hélène as she spins the web of her trap, using modern, attractive characters as bait. Yet the film succeeds because Bresson has supported her with his style, if not his moral sympathy. We experience her anguish and determination within the decisive clarity of each shot and within the fatal mechanism made up by the precise concatenation of shots. No accident or spontaneous gesture is permitted to enter either Hélène's world or Bresson's mise-en-scène.

Jean Cocteau's dialogue, compressed like some dense radioactive element, continually points up the absolute stakes at play; furthermore, the lines he has written play antiphonally with the images to produce a reflective space in which every perception has already been oralized. A good example of this process is found when Jean enters Agnès's room. He takes in this closed space and then transforms it in words: ''This is her lamp, her flowers, her frame, her cushion. This is where she sits to read, this, her piano.'' And yet throughout this recitation we see only his face. The dialogue sums up and closes off sentiments, cooling passions, abstracting emotions. We observe Hélène lying wrathful on her bed for some time before she leans forward to speak her incredibly cold, ''Je me vengerai.''

Although this style insists on the overpowering strength of Hélène's response to life (in which a single errant word warrants death and damnation), the plot supports the more ordinary characters whom she has manipulated to the end. For after her plans have run their course, after she has announced to Jean at the church that he has married a loose woman, her power is spent. The grace of love, of the love born between these two humble and minor mortals, points to a life or a purpose beyond Hélène. Bresson's Jansenism mixes severity (style) and the disclosure of grace (plot).

Only the dead-time of the Occupation could have permitted such a refined and distant love story. Its timeless values, though, reflect on that period, particularly its concern with weakness, forgiveness, and the future in a world controlled by absolute political powers. More important is the full expression of a style that demands to be taken morally. Even if Bresson has since rejected this effort as too theatrical (with its music, acting, and studio lighting), the fact is that *Les Dames du Bois du Boulogne* showed the world the value of his search, a search that is at once stylistic and metaphysical, and one his later work has justified. It is a tribute to the French film community that they recognized the presence and importance of something truly different.

—Dudley Andrew

THE DAMNED

See **LA CADUTA DEGLI DEI**

DANCE, GIRL, DANCE

USA, 1940

Director: Dorothy Arzner

Production: RKO-Radio Pictures; black and white; running time: 90 minutes. Released September 1940.

Producers: Erich Pommer and Harry Edington; **screenplay:** Tess Slesinger, Frank Davis, from the novel by Vicki Baum; **assistant director:** James H. Anderson; **photography:** Russell Metty; **editor:** Robert Wise; **sound:** Hugh McDowell, Jr.; **art director:** Van Nest Polglase; **associate art director:** Al Herman; **gowns:** Edward Stevenson; **music director:** Edward Ward; **dances:** Ernst Matray.

Cast: Maureen O'Hara (*Judy*); Louis Hayward (*Jimmy Harris*); Lucille Ball (*Bubbles*); Ralph Bellamy (*Steve Adams*); Virginia Field (*Elinor Harris*); Maria Ouspenskaya (*Madame Basilova*); Mary Carlisle (*Sally*); Katherine Alexander (*Miss Olmstead*); Edward Brophie (*Dwarfie*); Walter Abel (*Judge*); Harold Huber (*Hoboken Gent*); Ernest Truex (*Bailey 1*); Chester Clute (*Bailey 2*); Vivian Fay (*Ballerina*); Lorraine Krueger (*Dolly*); Lola Jensen (*Daisy*); Emma Dunn (*Ms. Simpson*); Sidney Blackmer (*Puss in Boots*); Ludwig Stossel (*Caesar*); Erno Verebes (*Fitch*).

Publications

Books:

Johnston, Claire, *Notes on Women's Cinema*, London 1973.
Rosen, Marjorie, *Popcorn Venus: Women, Movies and the American Dream*, New York, 1973.
Haskell, Molly, *From Reverence to Rape: The Treatment of Women in the Movies*, New York, 1974.
Smith, Sharon, *Women Who Make Movies*, New York, 1975.
Johnston, Claire, editor, *The Work of Dorothy Arzner: Towards a Feminist Cinema*, London, 1975.
Kay, Karyn, and Gerald Peary, editors, *Women and the Cinema: A Critical Anthology*, New York, 1977.
Slide, Anthony, *Early Women Directors*, South Brunswick, New Jersey, 1977.
Heck-Rabi, Louise, *Women Filmmakers: A Critical Reception*, Metuchen, New Jersey, 1984.
Penley, Constance, editor, *Feminism and Film Theory*, London, 1988.
Mayne, Judith, *Directed by Dorothy Arzner*, Bloomington, 1995.

Articles:

Crowther, Bosley, in *New York Times*, 11 September 1940.
Kine Weekly (London), 12 September 1940.
Monthly Film Bulletin (London), vol. 7, no. 81, 1940.
Feldman, J., and H. Feldman, ''Women Directors,'' in *Films in Review* (New York), November 1950.
Pyros, J., ''Notes on Women Directors,'' in *Take One* (Montreal), November-December 1970.
Henshaw, Richard, ''Women Directors,'' in *Film Comment* (New York), November 1972.
Parker, F., ''Approaching the Art of Arzner,'' in *Action* (Los Angeles), July-August 1973.
Velvet Light Trap (Madison, Wisconsin), Fall 1973.
Castle, W., ''Tribute to Dorothy Arzner,'' in *Action* (Los Angeles), March-April 1975.
Kaplan, E. Ann, ''Aspects of British Feminist Film Theory,'' in *Jump Cut* (Berkeley), nos. 12–13, 1976.
Glaessner, Verina, in *Focus on Film* (London), Summer-Autumn 1976.
Laemmle, Ann, in *Cinema Texas Program Notes*, 28 February 1978.
Bergstrom, J., ''Rereading the Work of Claire Johnston,'' in *Camera Obscura* (Berkeley), Summer 1979.
Forster, A., in *Skrien* (Amsterdam), September-October 1984.
Chell, S. L., ''Dorothy Arzner's *Dance, Girl, Dance*,'' in *CineAction* (Toronto), Summer-Fall 1991.

* * *

Dance, Girl, Dance is one of the few films directed by a woman in what is known as the ''classical Hollywood'' era, when, it has been argued, the conventional narrative codes of cinema were fixed. This unique position has inevitably informed the ways in which the film has been studied. Although Dorothy Arzner herself was not a feminist, it is due to feminism that she has been reassessed. In the mid-1970s feminist critics argued that while *Dance, Girl, Dance* may appear to be just one example of the popular musical comedies and women's pictures produced by RKO in the 1930s and 1940s, Arzner's ironic point of view questions the very conventions she uses.

The film was made in the relative flexibility of RKO's production system, whereby independent directors were contracted to work under minimal supervision. It was in this context that Arzner was reputedly able to rework a confusing and scrappy script to focus on the ambivalent relationship between the two strong, but very different, main female characters, Judy, an aspiring ballerina, and Bubbles, a gold-digging showgirl. Bubbles, after finding work in burlesque, brings Judy's ''classy act'' into her show, where Judy is humiliated as her stooge. One night, Bubbles announces that she has married Jimmy Harris, a weak heavy-drinking millionaire divorcé with whom Judy has fallen in love. Consequently, in a scene that has been much discussed, Judy, overwhelmed with frustration, furiously confronts her heckling audience. The standing ovation she receives infuriates Bubbles, and they fall into a vicious fight. Judy, unrepentant, is sent to jail, but the next day, Steve Adams, a ballet director who has been pursuing her, pays her bail and summons her to his office. He intends to train her to be a professional ballerina and, it is implied, his wife.

Arzner's portrayal of the complex relationship between the two women is one of the ways in which the apparent opposition set up between art (offering ''self-expression'') and entertainment (imposing exploitation) is undermined. The ways in which each woman's dance numbers are presented subvert the stereotypes of a sexual Bubbles and an artistic Judy. For example, when Judy dances at the night-club, Fitch, Steve's associate, comments in surprise at her impressive (i.e., artistic) footwork. Steve, however, leers that ''her eyes aren't bad either.'' Arzner pinpoints with terrible clarity the tension between a woman's struggle for integrity and a male gaze that by its very nature undermines that struggle. Where, then, does this leave Bubbles? When she dances at the burlesque, the ironies of her performances are a real delight for the cinema audience. When she calls and points to her audience she is challenging them, from within the licensed confines of burlesque conventions, in a way that parallels Judy's later outburst. Both women challenge, from the stage, the men who watch them, and thereby resist their passive status. So while we are invited to gaze upon Bubbles as a non-artistic spectacle, she is also knowing, controlling, with a voice of her own. It is the sheer power of this ''voice,'' Bubbles's potent screen presence, that subverts her implied position as less worthy than Judy.

Much of the critical attention paid to Judy's furious speech has suggested that the artistic and moral criticism of the lecherous gaze of the burlesque audience also functions as a not-so-veiled attack on the cinema audience. However, the film has much invested in drawing in its audience to enjoy the display of women's bodies, and this impulse arguably triumphs over the conflicting impulse to alienate the audience, or to chastise it for its voyeurism. Judy's gesture is thus defused by being applauded, and leading into the titillating catfight. But the irony is that she has found a voice and can defiantly assert, ''I'm not ashamed,'' not within the structures of the ballet, but in those of the burlesque.

As in Arzner's earlier work, and within the conventions of the women's film, it is the scenes featuring women that are the most striking and subtle, and in contrast, the heterosexual romance appears hollow. Although a weak love-story element runs through the film, the women's desires are channelled less towards coupledom than independence. After a date with Jimmy, Judy wishes on a star that she might become a dancer too. She wants it all, romance *and* artistic integrity, and the latter is never submerged in the former. Bubbles, on the other hand, desires economic rather than artistic independence. Both her dancing and her sexual desires are grounded in a cynicism about heterosexual relationships that affords her one of the film's finest throwaway lines, describing the burlesque owner as ''a great big capitalist in the artificial limbs business.''

However, the position of strong female protagonists in a Hollywood text is a precarious one, and it is in the final scene that this is tragically realised. Steve, in a humiliating tirade, asserts that Judy has been a silly, stubborn ''girl.'' The incongruously huge hat that she wears in this scene hides her face until, as Steve embraces her and tells her to ''go ahead and laugh,'' it is revealed that she is, in fact, weeping. Arzner's final irony offers the potential for a critique of the traditional boy-gets-girl resolution, and, implicitly, of the classical Hollywood text itself.

—Samantha Cook

DAOMA ZEI

(Horse Thief)

China, 1986

Director: Tian Zhuangzhuang

Production: Xi'an Film Studio; Eastmancolour, Scope, 35mm; running time: 96 minutes. Filmed in Tibet. Distributed in the United States by China Film Import and Export.

Executive producer: Wu Tianming; **screenplay:** Zhang Rui; **photography:** Hou Yong, Zhao Fei; **assistant director:** Pan Peicheng; **production manager:** Li Changqing; **editor:** Li Jingzhong; **art director:** Huo Jianqi; **lighting:** Yao Zhuoxi; **music:** Qu Xiaosong.

Cast: Tseshang Rigzin (*Norbu*); Dan Jiji (*Dolma*); Jayang Jamco (*Tashi*); Gaoba (*Nowre*); Daiba (*Granny*); Drashi (*Grandfather*).

Publications

Book:

Berry, Chris, *Perspectives on Chinese Cinema*, London, 1991.

Articles:

Variety (New York), 2 September 1987.

Combs, R., *Monthly Film Bulletin* (London), September 1987.

Stanbrook, A., ''Sky-burial,'' in *Sight and Sound* (London), Autumn 1987.

Bourgignon, T., ''Documentaire magique,'' in *Positif* (Paris), December 1991.

Cheng, Scarlet, ''Directors: A Rebel's Cause,'' *Asiaweek*, February 16, 1994.

Sklar, Robert, ''People and Politics, Simple and Direct,'' in *Cineaste* (New York), vol. 20, no. 4, 1994.

Gladney, D.C., ''Tian Zhuangzhuang, the 5th Generation, and Minorities in Film in China,'' in *Public Culture*, vol. 8, no. 1, 1995.

Buchet, J.-M., ''Le voleur de chevaux,'' in *Les Cine-Fiches de Grand Angle*, May 1997.

* * *

It is 1923, on the remote Tibetan plains. Two horsemen dressed in sheepskin gallop over a ridge on their way to rustle a coral of horses. Half drama and half reconstructed documentary on a life long past, *Horse Thief* is director Tian Zhuangzhuang's romantic peaen to China's Noble Savage.

Norbu is the Savage in question. With his long mass of tangled hair, his well-tanned and sinuous torso, and his dark flashing eyes, he rides a horse with as much dignity and naturalness as he strides the arid plains. He may steal horses and waylay Muslim travelers in the desert, but he is, nevertheless, a devoted husband to his wife, Dolma, and doting father to his young son, Tashi. In this film we become witness to the rites and passages of traditional Tibetan life—the ritualistic offerings to the gods; a funeral wake that ends with the corpse being laid out to be pecked apart by vultures; a visit by Norbu, his wife, and son to a temple to spin a row of vertical prayer wheels mounted on columns.

In one especially stunning scene, a crowd of men gather in the valley to worship the Mountain God. They set up an endless wailing as they push the sacred sheep ahead of them. They toss wads of votive paper into air. Caught by gusts of wind, the papers swirl forward, like giant snowflakes, blanketing the valley amidst a spooky chorus of voices. In another hypnotic scene Norbu and Dolma stand, pray, and prostrate themselves across the plain against a series of superimposed religious objects and temple architecture. The sound of bells, the drone of chanting, the rhythm of a single drum—all help transport us into the primeval world of legend.

Horse thievery is one thing—but desecration is another. One day Norbu and his outlaw partner come upon a sacred ground, where offerings have been left strewn about. They begin to pick through the jewelry and ornaments. ''The big pile is for the temple, the small ones we'll split between us,'' says Norbu. Then something catches his eye. From a pile he picks out a golden medallion, which he exchanges for something of his own. Returning home, he gives it to his chortling boy: but here in the pristine, primeval world, everything is linked, and there is no crime without punishment. As the village elder says, ''Norbu has offended God. He stole the official's temple gifts.'' He continues, ''The officials demand a serious punishment, but no matter what, he's a member of my clan. According to our rules, he is to be driven out forever.''

As Noble Savage, Norbu manfully accepts his fate and leaves at once. Exile, however, is not the worst punishment. His young son soon falls ill. Norbu brings back Holy Water from the temple to dab his son's forehead; he rocks the sick child in his arms, singing, ''Go to sleep and I will give you a horse/ There's a saddle ready for you, and I have a bridle, too/ I will catch a star just for you. . . .''

But for all of Norbu's tenderness, the boy dies. Even the land itself is sick. As stock animals die off in droves, Norbu's tribe is forced to move west, and Norbu himself must steal again. In the end, he pays a desperate price for his transgressions.

Director Tian (b. 1952) entered the Beijing Film Academy in 1978, and yet he had to go elsewhere to make the two films on which his reputation is based—to the Inner Mongolia Film Studio for *On the Hunting Ground* (1985; a film about Mongolian horsemen) and to Xian Film Studio for *Horse Thief.* In *Horse Thief,* using only sparse dialogue, Tian has created a stunning poetry with visuals, editing, and sound that convey the very experience of living in an ancient tribal universe, a world of myth and immutable laws. Although the film was not well received in China, selling just seven prints, Tian himself dismissed the lack of audience. As he said in a controversial interview with Yang Ping for the magazine *Popular Cinema:* ''I shot *Horse Thief* for audiences of the next century to watch.''

—Scarlet Cheng

DAWANDEH

(The Runner)

Iran, 1984

Director: Amir Naderi

Production: Tehran Institute for the Intellectual Development of Children and Young Adults; colour, 35mm; running time: 94 minutes.

Executive producer: Fathola Dalili; **screenplay:** Amir Naderi, Behruz Gharibpur; **photography:** Firuz Malkzadeh; **editor:** Bahram Beyza'i; **assistant director:** Mohammmad Hassanzadeh; **production design:** Gholam Reza Ramezani; **sound:** Nezam-e-Din Kia'i.

Cast: Majid Nirumand (*Amiro*); Musa Torkizadeh (*Musa*); A. Gholamzadeh (*Uncle Gholam*); Reza Ramezani (*Ramezan*).

Publications

Articles:

Variety (New York), 2 October 1985.
Sabouraud, F., ''L'enfant double,'' in *Cahiers du Cinéma* (Paris), December 1986.
Glaessner, Verina, in *Monthly Film Bulletin* (London), August 1988.
Skrien (Amsterdam), April-May 1990.

* * *

Dawandeh follows the day-to-day life of 13-year-old Amiro. The boy ekes out a living amongst the underclass of an Iranian port community. Depicting the details of his life—collecting bottles discarded from ships, shining shoes, and at home on a derelict boat on the shoreline—this is a remarkable story of a boy who rises above all odds to better himself.

Amiro is charged with a will to survive: in addition to struggling to earn enough money to feed himself, he takes himself to school for literacy classes. Everything to the boy is a challenge, and the almost palpable spark within him drives him onward in his quest for triumph.

Amiro yearns for things outside his grasp: he runs along the shoreline shouting and waving at the great ships; he's fascinated by a light plane he sees at a local aerodrome and is overjoyed to see it take off, seemingly able to whisk people away from his reality of grinding poverty to a new world.

To overcome the difficulties of his life, Amiro learns to outrun his adversaries. When he joins a gang of boys collecting bottles dumped from ships and bobbing about in the shallows, he learns the quickest worker can collect the most—a lesson not without cost, he discovers, as his speed at this task leads to a fight with one of the regular collectors. Another of his attempts to earn a living is selling iced water to the dock workers. This involves buying ice some distance away from the port and running back with it. Amiro's running skills and determination are proven when he is able to wrest the melting ice away from an adult thief.

Amiro must pay for everything in his life: the inner-tube he uses to float out into the bay for the bottle collection, the ice to sell on the port, and even a burnt-out light bulb with which to decorate his makeshift home in an attempt to emulate the ''glamour'' of the outdoor cafe where he is a shoeshine boy. When one of the customers at the cafe accuses Amiro of stealing his lighter, the boy is aghast at this allegation, as he is innately honest.

This story of a poverty-ridden existence is superbly realised by director Amir Naderi, not only because it is an autobiographical account of his childhood, but also because the filmmaking is of such a high standard. Majid Nerimand as Amiro is wonderful, bringing real feeling and acting skill to his role. Naderi obviously knows his locale intimately and this shows in the film. We see life from Amiro's point of view and accept it for what it is. We have the insider's view of this world and the film gains from that—the unpretentious, yet intimate, forum is *Dawandeh*'s strongest quality.

—Lee Sellars

A DAY IN THE COUNTRY

See **UNE PARTIE DE CAMPAGNE**

DAY OF WRATH

See **VREDENS DAG**

DAYBREAK

See **LE JOUR SE LEVE**

DAYS AND NIGHTS IN THE FOREST

See **Aranyer din Ratri**

DAYS OF BEING WILD

See **AHFEI ZHENG ZHUAN**

DAYS OF HEAVEN

USA, 1978

Director: Terrence Malick

Production: O.P. Productions; Metrocolor, 35mm, Dolby sound; running time: 95 minutes. Released 13 September 1978. Filmed on location in the Midwest; cost: $2.5 million.

Producers: Bert and Harold Schneider; **executive producer:** Jacob Brickman; **screenplay:** Terrence Malick; **photography:** Nestor Almendros with additional photography by Haskell Wexler; **editor:** Billy Weber; **sound mixers:** George Ronconi, Barry Thomas; **special sound effects:** James Cox; **art director:** James Fisk; **music:** Ennio Morricone and Leo Kottke; **special effects:** John Thomas and Mel Merrells; **costume designer:** Patricia Norris.

Cast: Richard Gere (*The Brother*); Brooke Adams (*The Girl*); Sam Shepard (*The Farm owner*); Linda Manz (*The Sister*); Robert Wilke (*The Foreman*); Jackie Shultis; Stuart Margolin; Tim Scott; Gene Bell; Doug Kershaw (*Fiddle player*).

Awards: Oscar for Best Cinematography, 1978; New York Film Critics Award for Best Director, 1978; Cannes Film Festival, Best Director, 1979.

Publications

Articles:

Schreger, C., in *Variety* (New York), 13 September 1978.
Fox, T. C., in *Film Comment* (New York), September-October 1978.
Riley, B., ''Nestor Almendros Interviewed,'' in *Film Comment* (New York), September-October 1978.
Films in Review (New York), November 1978.
Insdorf, A., in *Take One* (Montreal), November 1978.
Hodenfield, Chris, ''Terrence Malick: *Days of Heaven's* Image Maker,'' in *Rolling Stone* (New York), 16 November 1978.
Films and Filming (London), December 1978.
Christian Century (Chicago), 3 January 1979.
Schlesinger, Arthur M., ''Days of High Seriousness,'' in *Saturday Review* (New York), 6 January 1979.
Corliss, Richard, in *New York Times*, 8 January 1979.
Maraval, P., ''Dossier: Hollywood 79—Terrence Malick,'' in *Cinématographe* (Paris), March 1979.
Combs, Richard, ''The Eyes of Texas: Terrence Malick's *Days of Heaven*,'' in *Sight and Sound* (London), Spring 1979.
Carcassone, P., in *Cinématographe* (Paris), June 1979.
Coleman, John, in *New Statesman* (London), 1 June 1979.
Morris, M., in *Cinema Papers* (Melbourne), September-October 1979.
Alpert, Hollis, ''The Rise of Richard Gere,'' in *American Film* (Washington, D.C.), October 1979.
Ciment, Michel, and B. Riley, ''Le Jardin de Terrence Malick,'' in *Positif* (Paris), December 1979.
Pérez Turrent, T., ''Dias de Gloria y Badlands: Terrence Malick, nueva personalidad del cine norteamericano,'' in *Cine* (Mexico City), March 1980.

Days of Heaven

Bedoya, R., in *Hablemos de Cine* (Lima), November 1980.
Donough, M., ''West of Eden: Terrence Malick's *Days of Heaven*,'' in *Post Script* (Jacksonville, Florida), Fall 1985.
Taubin, A., in *Village Voice* (New York), 8 June 1993.
Wondra, Janet, ''A Gaze Unbecoming: Schooling the Child for Femininity in *Days of Heaven*,'' in *Wide Angle* (Baltimore), vol. 16, no. 4, October 1995.
Séquences (Haute-Ville), March/June 1997.
Positif (Paris), March 1999.

* * *

Of Terrence Malick's two feature films to date, *Badlands* is perhaps the more satisfying, *Days of Heaven* the more remarkable. Malick's achievement must be seen first and foremost in terms of its opposition to the dominant Hollywood shooting and editing codes of the period. Those codes are centred on the television-derived misuse and overuse of the telephoto (plus zoom) lens, in the interests of speed and economy rather than from any *aesthetic* interest in its intrinsic properties; this is seconded by the lyrical use of shallow focus and focus-shifts as an instant signifier of ''beauty'' (flowers in focus in the foreground, out-of-focus lovers in the background, shift focus to the lovers behind a foreground of out-of-focus flowers). Bo Widerberg's use of this in *Elvira Madigan* (the decisive influence) had a certain authenticity and originality, but it quickly lapsed into automatic cliché. Within such a context the sharp-etched, crystal-clear, depth-of-field images of Malick and his magnificent cameraman, Nestor Almendros, in *Days of Heaven* assume the status of protest and manifesto. They restore the concept of ''beauty'' from its contemporary debasement.

There is a further consequence of this—what one might call the resurrection of mise-en-scène, theorized in the 1950s and 1960s as the essential art of film, and seemingly a lost art since. In place of the ''one-shot—one point'' of the flat, perfunctory images derived from television, Malick suddenly has a frame within which to compose in depth, where every segment of the image potentially signifies. The desire for precision and definition within the image here combines naturally with a most delicate feeling for nuances of emotion and interchange between the characters. Joseph Conrad's description of Henry James as ''the historian of fine consciences'' comes to mind. Aptly enough; for what is *Days of Heaven* but a re-working of the subject of James's *The Wings of the Dove*, with the sexes reversed and the protagonists transposed to the working class?

Given the film's concern with the realities of democratic capitalism—manifest inequality, poverty, class oppression—the ''beauty'' is a potential problem. Indeed it comes perilously close (especially in its opening sequences) to aestheticizing misery in the manner of, for example, Lean's *Doctor Zhivago*, where the response ''Isn't that terrible?'' is completely superseded by ''Isn't that beautifully photographed?'' The distinction of *Days of Heaven* lies partly in its careful separation of its sense of beauty from the human misery and tension depicted. The pervasive suggestion is that human existence could correspond to the natural and aesthetic beauty the film celebrates, were it not for the oppressive systems of organization that men [sic] have developed: the film's sense of tragedy is firmly grounded in an awareness of class and gender oppression. As in *Heaven's Gate*, the woman expresses her ability and freedom to love both men. It is the men who precipitate catastrophe by demanding exclusivity and ownership as their right, and as a means of bolstering their threatened egos.

Badlands explicitly acknowledged, in its final credits, the influence of Arthur Penn; in fact, its relation to *Bonnie and Clyde* is at once obvious and tenuous, restricted to its subject. Far more important seemed the influence of Godard, especially in *Les Carabiniers and Pierrot le fou.* The film's counterpointing of verbal narration and image is extremely sophisticated and, in relation to classical Hollywood narrative, audaciously unconventional. *Days of Heaven* simultaneously modifies and develops this strategy; the verbal narration of Linda Manz represents a less jarring dislocation than the use of Sissy Spacek's diary in the earlier film, but provides a continuous and subtle distancing which contributes significantly to the film's unique flavor, in which irony co-exists with intense involvement.

—Robin Wood

DE CIERTA MANERA

(One Way or Another)

Cuba, 1977

Director: Sara Gómez

Production: Instituto Cubano del Arte e Industria Cinematográficos (ICAIC); black and white, 35mm, originally shot in 16mm; running time: 79 minutes; length: 2147 meters. Released 1977.

Producer: Camilo Vives; **scenario:** Sara Gómez and Tomas González Pérez; **screenplay:** Tomas Gutíerrez Alea and Julio García Espinosa; **assistant directors:** Rigoberto López and Daniel Diaz Torres; **photography:** Luis García; **editor:** Iván Arocha; **sound:** Germinal Hernández; **production designer:** Roberto Larraburre; **music:** Sergio Vitier; **songs:** Sara González.

Cast: Mario Balmaseda (*Mario*); Yolanda Cuellar (*Yolanda*); Mario Limonta (*Humberto*).

Publications

Books:

Adelman, Alan, editor, *A Guide to Cuban Cinema*, Pittsburgh, 1981.
Chanan, Michael, *The Cuban Image: Cinema and Cultural Politics in Cuba*, London, 1985.

Articles:

Chijona, Geraldo, in *Cine Cubano* (Havana), no. 93.
López, Rigoberto, ''Hablar de Sara: *De cierta manera*,'' in *Cine Cubano* (Havana), no. 93.
''Special Sections'' of *Jump Cut* (Berkeley), December 1978 and May 1980.
Lesage, Julia, ''One Way or Another: Dialectical, Revolutionary, Feminist,'' in *Jump Cut* (Berkeley), May 1979.
Marrosu, A., in *Cine al Día* (Caracas), June 1980.
Pym, John, in *Monthly Film Bulletin* (London), July 1980.
Chanan, M., ''Otra mirada,'' in *Cine Cubano* (Havana), no. 127, 1989.
Lezcano, J. A., ''*De cierta manera* con Sara Gómez,'' in *Cine Cubano* (Havana), no. 127, 1989.
Lopez, A. M., ''Parody, Underdevelopment, and the New Latin American Cinema,'' in *Quarterly Review of Film and Video* (New York), no. 1–2, 1990.
Davies, Catherine, ''Modernity, Masculinity and Imperfect Cinema in Cuba,'' in *Screen* (Oxford), Winter 1997.

* * *

Here is a revolutionary film: dialectical in form and content, humble in the face of real human experience, proposing no final answers except the unending struggle of a people to make something out of what history has made of them. *De cierta manera* is that powerful hybrid—the fictional documentary set to a tropical beat—for which the cinema of revolutionary Cuba is justifiably famous. In this instance, the documentary deals with the destruction of slum housing and the struggle against the culture of marginality generated in such slums through the creation of a new housing project (Miraflores) and an accompanying educational program. The fictional embodiment of this historical process is seen in the clash of attitudes between Mario (a product of the slums), his lover Yolanda (a teacher who has come to Miraflores to help integrate such marginal elements into the revolution), and his friend Humberto (a fun-loving slacker). In the course of telling these stories, and others, *De cierta manera* demolishes the categories of fiction and documentary, insisting that both forms are equally mediated by the intention of the filmmaker, and that both thus require a critical stance.

This insistence on a critical attitude is conveyed, first of all, in the dialectical resonance of the film, a structure characteristic of the best of the Cuban cinema. Visually this resonance is achieved through a rich blending of fictional present and historical recreation with documentary and semi-documentary. In fact, it becomes impossible to distinguish the different forms; fictional characters are set in documentary sequences where they interact with real people and real people re-enact historical re-constructions which are not visually in accordance with their *own* telling of the stories. Further, the film repeats various sequences several times, twisting the film back on itself and requiring the audience to participate actively in analyzing the different perspectives offered on the problems posed by the film.

The sound track is as creatively textured as are the images, and is every bit as demanding of the audience. The film sets up a tension between the classical documentary and its omniscient narrator, cinema-verité interviews, and fictional cinema. The omniscient documentary provides sociological data on different facets of marginality. Although this data establishes one framework for the ''fictional'' core of the film, its deliberately pompous tone warns us that we must critically question even such ''official'' pronouncements.

This omniscient narrator is juxtaposed to the conversations which take place around different aspects of marginalism. The manifestations of the culture of marginality are seen to be manifold—work absenteeism, machismo, delinquency—and the problem is hotly debated by everyone. Humberto is criticized for taking off from work on an unauthorized four-day jaunt with a girlfriend, while lying about his ''sick mother.'' Mario is criticized for denouncing Humberto, not because his attitude was counterproductive, but because Humberto accused him of being an informer—a violation of male-bonding rules. Yolanda criticizes the mothers of children who misbehave in school, and is in turn criticized by her co-workers for her inability to empathize with women whose background is so different from hers. Although trenchant and acute, these critiques are also loving and constructive. Just as individuals in the film leave these confrontations with a clearer understanding of the revolutionary process to which they are committed, so too does the audience leave the film with a more precise notion of dialectical film.

At the end of the film, the factory workers meet where the fictional confrontation of Mario and Humberto took place and enter into a discussion of the case. They seem to rise up and incorporate themselves into the actual production of the film itself. This is as it should be, for this film demands the participation of all: real people and actors, workers and marginal elements, teachers and housewives, audience and filmmaker. The wrecking ball (in a sequence repeated several times during the film) is not only destroying the slums and (metaphorically) the slum mentality, it may also be demolishing some of the more cherished assumptions of moviegoers in bourgeois cultures.

—John Mraz

THE DEAD

UK/US/West Germany, 1987

Director: John Huston

Production: Liffey; color; running time: 83 minutes. Filmed in Dublin, Ireland, and Valencia, California.

Producer: Wieland Schulz-Keil, Chris Sievernich, William J. Quigley (executive); **screenplay:** Tony Huston, from a story by James Joyce; **cinematographer:** Fred Murphy; **editor:** Roberto Silvi; **music:** Alex North; **casting:** Nuala Moiselle; **production design:** Stephen B. Grimes, J. Dennis Washington; **set decoration:** Josie MacAvin; **costume design:** Dorothy Jeakins; **production manager:** Tom Shaw; **makeup:** Fern Buchner, Keis Maes, Anthony Cortino, Louise Dowling, Anne Dunne, Christopher Shihar.

Cast: Anjelica Huston (*Gretta Conroy*); Donal McCann (*Gabriel Conroy*); Helena Carroll (*Aunt Kate*); Cathleen Delany (*Aunt Julia*); Dan O'Herlihy (*Mr. Browne*); Donal Donnelly (*Freddy Malins*); Marie Kean (*Mrs. Malins*); Frank Patterson (*Bartell D'Arcy*); Rachael Dowling (*Lily*); Ingrid Craigie (*Mary Jane*); Maria McDernottroe (*Molly Ivors*); Sean McGlory (*Mr. Grace*); Kate O'Toole (*Miss Furlong*); Maria Hayden (*Miss O'Callaghan*); Bairbre Dowling (*Miss Higgins*); Lyda Anderson (*Miss Daly*); Colm Meaney (*Mr. Bergin*); Cormac O'Herlihy (*Mr. Kerrigan*); Paul Grant (*Mr. Duffy*); Paul Carroll (*Young Gentleman*); Patrick Gallagher (*Mr. Egan*); Dara Clarke (*Miss Power*); Brendan Dillon (*Cabman*); Redmond Gleeson (*Nightporter*); Amanda Baird (*Young Lady*).

Awards: National Society of Films Critics Award for Best Film, 1987; Special Achievement Award (John Huston), Tokyo International Film Festival, 1987; Independent Spirit Awards for Best Director and Best Actress (Angelica Huston), 1988; Best American Film Award, Bodil Festival, 1989.

Publications:

Books:

McCarty, John, *The Films of John Huston*, Secaucus, New Jersey, 1987.

Grobel, Lawrence, *The Hustons*, New York, 1989.

Studlar, Gaylyn, editor, *Reflections in a Male Eye: John Huston and the American Experience*, Washington, D.C., 1993.

Cooper, Stephen, *Perspectives on John Huston*, New York, 1994.

Brill, Lesley, *John Huston's Filmmaking*, New York, 1997.

Cohen, Allen, *John Huston: A Guide to References and Resources*, New York, 1997.

Articles:

''Zenith and Huston to Team on *The Dead*,'' in *Variety* (New York), vol. 325, 17 December 1986.

Harmetz, A., ''Patient: John Huston; Rx: Film,'' in *The New York Times*, 8 March 1987.

Huston, T., ''Family Ties,'' in *American Film*, vol. 12, September 1987.

Cart, T. McCarthy, ''Film Legend John Huston Dead at 81: Final Pic Bows at Venice,'' in *Variety* (New York), vol. 328, 2 September 1987.

Wiener, D.J., ''*The Dead*: A Study in Light and Shadow,'' in *American Cinematographer* (Hollywood), vol. 68, November 1987.

Sante, L., ''The Last Chapter: *The Dead*,'' in *Premiere* (Boulder), vol. 1, December 1987.

Cargin, P., ''Huston's Finale,'' in *Film* (London), no. 10, December 1987.

Kael, P., ''The Current Cinema: Irish Voices,'' in *New Yorker*, vol. 63, 14 December 1987.

O'Brien, T., ''Screen: Ethnic Colorings—*Emperor, The Dead*, and *Wannsee*,'' in *Commonweal*, vol. 114, 18 December 1987.

Kauffman, S., ''Stanley Kauffmann on Films: Last Rites,'' in *The New Republic*, vol. 197, 21 December 1987.

Baxter, B., in *Films and Filming* (London), no. 399, December 1987.

Pulleine, T., ''A Memory of Galway,'' in *Sight & Sound* (London), vol. 5, no. 1, 1987/1988.

The Dead

Burgess, A., ''The Task of Turning Joyce's Prose to Film Poetry,'' in *The New York Times*, vol. 137, section 2, 3 January 1988.
Denby, D., ''The Living,'' in *New York Magazine*, vol. 21, 18 January 1988.
Varjola, M., ''Elava Kuollut,'' in *Filmihullu* (Helsinki), no. 4, 1988.
James, C., ''Film View: When Film Becomes a Feast of Words,'' in *The New York Times*, vol. 138, section 2, 30 July 1989.
Cardullo, B., ''Epiphanies,'' in *Hudson Review*, vol. 41, no. 4, 1989.
Shout, J.D., ''Joyce at Twenty-Five, Huston at Eighty-One: *The Dead*,'' in *Literature/Film Quarterly* (Salisbury), vol. 17, no. 2, 1989.
Yetya, N., ''*Los Muertos*,'' in Dicine, no. 36, September 1990.
''The Angel Gabriel,'' in *New Yorker*, vol. 68, 28 December1992/4 January 1993.
Pederson, A., ''Uncovering *The Dead*: A Study of Adaptation,'' in *Literature/Film Quarterly* (Salisbury), vol. 21, no. 1, 1993.
Pilipp, F., ''Narrative Devices and Aesthetic Perception in Joyce's and Huston's *The Dead*,'' in *Literature/Film Quarterly* (Salisbury), vol. 21, no. 1, 1993.

* * *

It's hard to think of a major filmmaker who relied more on literary adaptations than John Huston. The great majority of his 36 features—and virtually all the best ones—were drawn from novels, short stories, or plays; and he was invariably, though never slavishly, faithful to the spirit of the original. This quality of loving respect for his source material shines through the culminating film of his long career, *The Dead.* A bitter-sweet meditation on transience and mortality, *The Dead* is taken from the last and longest story in James Joyce's 1914 collection *Dubliners.* The setting is Dublin in the winter of 1904 when two elderly sisters, Kate and Julia Morkan, and their niece, Mary Jane, give their annual dinner party and dance. The scenario, by Huston's son Tony, sticks closely to the original story and often uses Joyce's own dialogue. On the surface, very little happens. (''The biggest piece of action,'' Huston noted ironically, ''is trying to pass the port.'') The guests assemble; they eat, drink, dance, banter, and in one or two cases flirt mildly; the party winds to its end; and in the closing fifteen minutes we follow two of the company as they return to their hotel. We seem to be watching the casual, happening flow of life, convivial but unremarkable. No voices are raised, except now and then in song; no dramatic emphases in the acting, scoring, or camerawork urge our attention. Yet every detail, unobtrusively placed, contributes to the final effect: a rare depth of poignancy, all the more moving for being so quietly expressed.

When he made *The Dead* Huston was himself dying, and knew it. Suffering from terminal emphysema, he directed from a wheelchair, hooked up to an oxygen cylinder. He had hoped to make the film in Ireland, as a farewell to the country where he had lived for twenty years and whose citizenship he'd taken, but it proved impractical. Instead, a wintry Dublin was convincingly recreated in a warehouse in Valencia, north of Los Angeles, with a second unit sent to Ireland to pick up location shots. Much of the time, constrictions of space made it impossible for Huston to be on set with the actors, and he directed via a TV monitor. None of these limitations shows in the film, which feels effortlessly relaxed and natural.

Throughout the long party sequence that takes up the first hour of the film, Huston's camera roams around the various groupings, picking up snatches of conversation, conveying unspoken nuances in a gesture or a glance. Matters of politics and religion are touched on, sketching in a sense of the period: an assertive young woman, Molly Ivors, mocks the hostesses' nephew, Gabriel Conroy, for being a ''West Briton'' who neglects Irish culture, and Aunt Kate tactfully refers to the Protestant Mr. Browne as being ''of the other persuasion.'' The scapegrace Freddy Malins arrives tipsy, to the alarm of his mother who anxiously steers him away from further boozing. Mary Jane plays a showy piece on the piano; older guests listen politely while the younger ones escape to the drinks table in the next room. The cast, all Irish except Anjelica Huston (who, having grown up in Ireland, fits in seamlessly) and many of them from the Abbey Theatre company, give a note-perfect display of ensemble acting.

Gradually, beneath the light comedy, more sombre themes emerge. The older, frailer sister, Miss Julia, is persuaded to sing a Bellini aria; her quavery voice suggests this will be the last year she'll be there to sing it. Talk turns to lost glories of the past, to friends now dead, to monks who sleep in their coffins as a reminder of ''their last end.'' And alongside these intimations of mortality comes the idea of a love absolute and all-consuming when one of the guests recites an old Irish poem, the sole notable element in the film not drawn from Joyce's original: ''You have taken the East and the West from me, you have taken the sun and the moon from me. . . .'' During this, Gabriel casts a glance at his wife Gretta (Huston) who is listening, rapt.

This brief shot foreshadows the turning moment of the film. The party is breaking up, Gabriel and Gretta are on their way downstairs, when from above comes the voice of a tenor singing a melancholy old ballad, ''The Lass of Aughrim.'' Gretta stops on the stair, transfixed, her whole posture suggesting a sorrow long held within her like an unborn child. At the hotel she tells Gabriel how the song was once sung by a gentle boy who died—perhaps for love of her. She weeps herself to sleep, while Gabriel gloomily reflects how prosaic, by comparison, is his love for her, ''how poor a part I've played in her life.'' He muses on the dead boy, on his aunt soon to die, on others departed, and as the snow swirls outside the window, his voice-over thoughts ease into the words that end Joyce's story: ''Snow is general all over Ireland. . . falling faintly through the universe, and faintly falling, like the descent of their last end, upon all the living and the dead.'' John Huston's last film, an elegy for Ireland and for himself, closes on a grace-note at once regretful and reconciled.

—Philip Kemp

DEAD OF NIGHT

UK, 1945

Directors: Alberto Cavalcanti, Charles Crichton, Basil Dearden, Robert Hamer

Production: A Michael Balcon Production for Ealing Studios; filmed as a set of five stories, with a linking narrative directed by Dearden from a story by E. F. Benson: ''Christmas Party'' (director: Cavalcanti, from a story by Angus Macphail), ''Hearse Drivers'' (director: Dearden, from a story by E. F. Benson), ''The Haunted Mirror'' (director: Hamer, from a story by John V. Baines), ''Golfing Story'' (director: Crichton, from a story by H. G. Wells), ''The Ventriloquist Dummy'' (director: Cavalcanti, from a story by John V. Baines); black and white; running time: 102 minutes. Released September 1945.

Producer: Michael Balcon; **associate producers:** Sidney Cole, John Croydon; **screenplay:** John V. Baines, Angus Macphail; **additional dialogue:** T. E. B. Clarke; **photography:** Stan Pavey, Douglas Slocombe; **editor:** Charles Hasse; **art director:** Michael Relph; **music:** Georges Auric.

Cast: Linking narrative: Mervyn Johns (*Walter Craig*); Renee Gadd (*Mrs. Craig*); Roland Culver (*Eliot Foley*); Mary Merrall (*Mrs. Foley*); Frederick Valk (*Dr. van Straaten*); Barbara Leake (*Mrs. O'Hara*). ''Christmas Party'': Sally Ann Howes (*Sally O'Hara*);

Dead of Night

Michael Allan (*Jimmy*); Robert Wyndham (*Dr. Albury*). "Hearse Driver": Antony Baird (*Hugh*); Judy Kelly (*Joyce*); Miles Malleson (*Hearse Driver/Bus Conductor*). "The Haunted Mirror": Googie Withers (*Joan*); Ralph Michael (*Peter*); Esme Percy (*Antique Dealer*). "Golfing Story": Basil Radford (*George*); Naunton Wayne (*Larry*); Peggy Bryan (*Mary*). "The Ventriloquist's Dummy": Michael Redgrave (*Maxwell Frere*); Hartley Power (*Sylvester Kee*); Elisabeth Welch (*Beulah*); Magda Kun (*Mitzi*); Garry Marsh (*Harry Parker*).

Publications

Books:

Klaue, Wolfgang, and others, *Cavalcanti*, Berlin, 1952.
Pirie, David, *A Heritage of Horror: The English Gothic Cinema 1946–1972*, London, 1973.
Everson, William K., *Classics of the Horror Film*, New York, 1974.
Barr, Charles, *Ealing Studios*, London, 1977.
Perry, George, *Forever Ealing*, London, 1981.
Eberwein, Robert T., *Film and the Dream Screen: A Sleep and a Forgetting*, Princeton, 1984.
Brown, Geoff, *Michael Balcon: Pursuit of Britain*, New York, 1990.
Barr, Charles, *Ealing Studios*, Berkeley, 1999.

Articles:

Documentary Newsletter (London), no. 7, 1945.
Kine Weekly (London), 6 September 1945.
Variety (New York), 19 September 1945.
Monthly Film Bulletin (London), 30 September 1945.
Hollywood Reporter, 28 June 1946.
New York Times, 29 June 1946.
Variety (New York), 3 July 1946.
Motion Picture Herald (New York), 6 July 1946.
Villegas Lopez, Manuel, "Analisis de los valores, *Al morir la noche*," in *Cinema: Técnica y estatica del arte nuevo*, Madrid, 1954.
Agee, James, *Agee on Film 1*, New York, 1958.
Barr, Charles, "Projecting Britain and the British Character" (2 parts), in *Screen* (London), Spring and Summer 1974.
Brossard, Chandler, in *Film Comment* (New York), May-June 1974.
Ecran Fantastique (Paris), no. 2, 1977.
Ecran Fantastique (Paris), September 1986.
Branagh, K., in *Premiere* (Boulder), February 1993.
Aachen, G., "*Dead of Night*," in *Reid's Film Index* (Wyong), no. 30, 1997.

* * *

Dead of Night's status as the first British horror film of note (advanced most convincingly by David Pirie in his book *A Heritage of Horror*) rests largely on the Robert Hamer-directed "Haunted Mirror" episode. Certainly this masterful piece of work, with its depiction of a destructive sexuality emerging from the 19th-century setting reflected in the mirror, anticipates elements of Hammer horror in the 1950s and 1960s.

However, the film as a whole can also be seen as a response to the social dislocations caused by the end of the war, and in particular a confusion in masculine identity arising from difficulties in integrating a large part of the male population back into civilian life. On one level, *Dead of Night* reveals a male fear of domesticity, which is here equated with emasculation and the presence of strong, independent women who are seen to have usurped male authority (one thinks of Googie Withers organising her wedding while her fiancée waits passively in his flat, and of Sally Ann Howes violently rejecting the amorous advances of a fellow teenager). The film is full of weak, crippled, and/or victimised male characters: an injured racing driver, a boy murdered by his elder sister, a meek accountant dominated first by his fiancée and then by the influence of the "haunted mirror," and—in an extraordinary performance by Michael Redgrave—a neurotic ventriloquist who eventually collapses into complete insanity. It is significant in this light that the character whose dream the film turns out to be is an architect, a symbolically charged profession at a time of national reconstruction. That this architect is indecisive, frightened, and, at the end of his dream, shown as harbouring murderous desires underlines the film's lack of confidence in the future.

This can be connected with what is in effect a systematic undermining of one of the characteristic themes of British World War II cinema, namely the formation of a cohesive group out of diverse social elements. (Ealing Studios, which produced *Dead of Night*, contributed to this with, among others, *San Demetrio London* and *The Bells Go Down*.) *Dead of Night* begins with a group of characters coming together, but here this is not in the interests of establishing a national consensus. Instead this group is fragmented by the film's insistent stress on the ways in which each individual is trapped within his or her own perceptions and mental processes. Each story tells of a private experience, something that more often than not is witnessed by only one person.

The sense of alienation thereby produced further manifests itself in the many references in the film to acts of vision which are unreliable or compromised in some way. Repeatedly characters stare disbelievingly at the "impossible" events unfolding before them. Seeing is no longer believing. The faith in an objective reality central to British wartime documentaries and which also contributed to the style adopted by many fiction films has been eroded. Dreams and fantasies have taken its place, to the extent that, as one character puts it, "None of us exist at all. We're nothing but characters in Mr. Craig's dream."

The complexities of *Dead of Night* are beautifully crystallised in the moment where the psychoanalyst who throughout the film has argued for logic and reason accidentally breaks his spectacles. The clarity of vision induced by a wartime situation has been similarly shattered. All that remains is an uncertainty and fear which the film records in an obsessive and disturbing detail.

—Peter Hutchings

DEAD RINGERS

Canada, 1988

Director: David Cronenberg

Production: Mantle Clinic II Ltd., in association with Morgan Creek Productions; colour, 35mm; running time: 115 minutes.

Producers: David Cronenberg and Marc Boyman; **executive producers:** Carol Baum and Sylvio Tabet; **screenplay:** David Cronenberg

Dead Ringers

and Norman Snider, based on the book *Twins* by Bari Wood and Jack Geasland; **photography:** Peter Suschitzky; **editor:** Ronald Sanders; **music:** Howard Shore; **art director:** James McAteer; **production designer:** Carol Spier; **sound:** Bryan Day; **costumes:** Denise Cronenberg; **special effects design:** Gordon Smith.

Cast: Jeremy Irons (*Beverly Mantle/Elliot Mantle*); Geneviève Bujold (*Claire Niveau*); Stephen Lack (*Anders Wolleck*); Heidi von Palleske (*Cary*); Shirley Douglas (*Laura*); Barbara Gordon (*Danuta*); Nick Nichols (*Leo*); Lynn Cormack (*Arlene*); Damir Andrei (*Birchall*); Miriam Newhouse (*Mrs. Bookman*).

Publications

Books:

Moorman, David, *David Cronenberg: A Horror Filmer in Transformation*, Rotterdam, 1990.

Cronenberg, David, *Cronenberg on Cronenberg*, London, 1992.

Shaviro, Steven, *The Cinematic Body*, Minneapolis and London, 1993.

Parker, Andrew, ''Grafting David Cronenberg,'' in *Media Spectacles* edited by Marjorie Garber and others, New York and London, 1993.

Morris, Peter, *David Cronenberg: A Delicate Balance*, Milford, 1994.

Articles:

Jaehne, Karen, ''Double Trouble,'' in *Film Comment* (New York), September 1988.

Variety (New York), 7 September 1988.

Gleiberman, O., ''Cronenberg's Double Meanings,'' in *American Film* (Marion), October 1988.

Elia, M., *Séquences* (Paris), November 1988.

Lee, N., ''Visuals for *Dead Ringers* Inspire Belief,'' in *American Cinematographer* (New York), December 1988.

Beauchamp, M., ''Frères de sang,'' in *24 Images* (Montreal), Winter 1988–89.

Stanbrook, A., ''Cronenberg's Creative Cancers,'' in *Sight and Sound* (London), Winter 1988–89.

Baron, A.-M., *Cinéma* (Paris), January 1989.

Bunbury, S., ''David Cronenberg Doubles Up,'' in *Cinema Papers* (Melbourne), January 1989.

Cook, P., and A. Billson, *Monthly Film Bulletin* (London), January 1989.

Garcia, M., *Films in Review* (New York), January 1989.

Katsahnias, I., and others, ''La beauté intérieure,'' in *Cahiers du Cinéma* (Paris), February 1989.

Dadoun, R., ''L'épouvante intérieure ou Qu'est-ce que l'homme a dans le ventre,'' in *Positif* (Paris), March 1989.

Ramasse, F., and others, ''La chair dans l'âme,'' in *Positif* (Paris), March 1989.

Ross, P., *Revue du Cinéma* (Paris), March 1989.

Kay. S., ''Double or Nothing,'' in *Cinema Papers* (Melbourne), July 1989.

Nguyen, D. T., ''The Projectile Movie Revisited,'' in *Film Criticism* (Meadville, Pennsylvania), Spring 1990.

Creed, B., ''Phallic Panic: Male Hysteria and *Dead Ringers*,'' in *Screen* (London), Summer 1990.

Breskin, David, ''David Cronenberg: The *Rolling Stone* Interview,'' in *Rolling Stone* (New York), 6 February 1992.

Winnert, Derek, ''Doctor in Double Trouble,'' in *Radio Times* (London), 30 May 1992.

''Special Issue,'' *Post Script* (Commerce), vol. 15, no. 2, Winter-Spring 1996.

Lucas, Tim, and John Charles, in *Video Watchdog* (Cincinnati), no. 36, 1996.

* * *

Since his first commercial film *Shivers* premiered in the early seventies, David Cronenberg has been saddled with the confining stereotype best exemplified in the nickname the ''Baron of Blood.'' With subsequent films such as *Rabid*, *Scanners*, and *The Fly* Cronenberg has kept this reputation intact and his films rather foreboding to those uninitiated to the Cronenberg vision. With three films in the early 1990s (*Dead Ringers*, *Naked Lunch*, and *M. Butterfly*) however, Cronenberg departed from the conventional science-fiction/horror brand of cinema he has been known for. *Dead Ringers* is Cronenberg's first attempt at a conventional, tragic, human drama. The film functions in this respect so well that one is left emotionally drained and extremely melancholic after viewing it. In *Cronenberg on Cronenberg*, the director describes the film as follows: ''[It] has to do with that element of being human. It has to do with this ineffable sadness that is an element of human existence.''

The production saga of *Dead Ringers* began when Cronenberg first saw a headline that read something like, ''Twin Docs Found Dead in Posh Pad'' and decided that it was a story worth telling. ''It was too perfect,'' the director has since said. In 1981, the project began its gestation when Carol Baum approached Cronenberg with the vague idea of doing a film about twins. Although they initially differed on subject matter they eventually settled on the story of Stewart and Cyril Marcus, twin gynecologists who, as the above headlines stated, were found dead, the perpetrators of a joint suicide. Cronenberg next read a book loosely based on the twins called, appropriately enough, *Twins*, by Bari Wood and Jack Geasland (the name of the film would later be changed from *Twins* to *Dead Ringers* prior to release at the request of Cronenberg's old colleague Ivan Reitman so as not to clash with the Arnold Schwarzenegger comedy vehicle). Baum and Cronenberg then enlisted producer Sylvio Tabet and chose Norman Snider to write a script. The script Snider produced however was found unacceptable to Cronenberg due to Snider's attempt to fit too much of the book into the script (Cronenberg wanted as little of the book as possible) and a re-write was commissioned. Tabet's reservations about the rewritten script killed the project at this time however and, in 1982, it seemed as though the film would never be made. Two years later, Cronenberg along with producer Mark Boyman tried to raise interest in the project once again. But, the project was to be met less than enthusiastically, with the main complaint being along the lines of: ''Do they have to be gynecologists? Couldn't they be lawyers?'' This question signalled to Cronenberg the inability of the studio executives to ''get it,'' so the search for financial backing continued with Cronenberg directing *The Fly* (1986) in the interim. It was eventually Dino De Laurentiis's DEG company (the company that had produced *The Dead Zone*) that took on the project. Unfortunately, the De Laurentiis group went bankrupt shortly after agreeing to produce and Cronenberg Productions was left to produce the film independently.

Dead Ringers is the tragedy of identical twin gynecologists Beverly and Elliot Mantle (both played by Jeremy Irons). The Mantles are wunderkind doctors from Toronto who operate the famous Mantle fertility clinic where actress Claire Niveau (Geneviève Bujold) comes seeking advice on how she can become pregnant. Unfortunately, Claire is diagnosed as ''trifurcate'' (possession of three cervixes—a ''mutant'' woman) and incapable of bearing children. That evening, Elliot sleeps with Claire and then, in keeping with the twins' sharing of everything, urges Beverly to take his place the following night. Beverly, however, falls in love with Claire until, upon learning of the deception, Claire ends the ruse by refusing to see either of them. Beverly's descent begins here and he becomes addicted to both alcohol and drugs. Following a reunion with Claire, Beverly becomes insanely jealous when she leaves for a shoot and mistakenly believes she is having an affair then falls further into his drug induced depression. Elliot, who has been out of town pursuing his own career, returns to supervise his brother's detoxification but ultimately gives up when Beverly commissions the creation of gynecological instruments for operating on mutant women and uses them on actual patients, consequently destroying the clinic's reputation and the twins' practice. Elliot, in an effort to restore the perfect equilibrium they shared before they met Claire, then tries to synchronize their drug taking and keeps Beverly locked up until Claire returns and he goes to her. A week later, Claire reluctantly allows Beverly to return to his brother who has descended even further than Beverly had. The twins now lock themselves up in the clinic and gradually regress until Beverly operates on Elliot to ''separate'' them and kills him. Beverly then calls Claire but cannot speak and returns to the clinic and dies silently while lying across Elliot's body.

A major concern embedded in *Dead Ringers* is the notion of control. Cronenberg acknowledges this in the following way in *Cronenberg on Cronenberg:* ''The whole concept of free will resists the idea of anything determining destiny. Freedom of choice rests on the premise of freedom from physical and material restrictions.'' The Mantles are the device Cronenberg uses ''to investigate that, not as an aberration but as cases in point of genetic power.'' In fact, the twins have little control over their own lives until the end of the film. Cronenberg consciously constructed their world and lighted it in such a way that it resembles an enormous aquarium wherein the twins are nothing more than inhabitants who consistently run through the monotony of a fragile daily existence. The twins' synchronized world is so fragile in fact that the introduction of Claire as something the twins refuse to share completely decimates them. It is only through death that the twins assert their free will and attain the control they have lacked throughout the film. Therefore, suicide becomes the only instance in the twins' life in which they exert complete control over the outcome and sever the bizarre biological link to destiny.

Although *Dead Ringers* is a classic story of control, problems with analyzing it as such arise when categorizing that control. The determination of who is controlling who is an endless conundrum within the film. For example, the twins control Claire (who functions as a sort of symbolic representation of women) through gynecology by understanding her body in ways she cannot (Cronenberg's purely narrative construction of mutant women and instruments for operating on them is indicative of this control). At the same time, however, Claire wields control over the twins by using the same device in the guise of her sexuality. It is Claire who, through her control of Beverly, dictates the demise of the twins. The omnipresent nature of control in the film is ultimately its tragedy—you can't escape control. This tragedy erupts from the concept that biology is destiny. Cronenberg succeeds in questioning this theory while at the same time subscribing to it by suggesting that the concept of free will is the destroyer of destiny. That is, while the brothers' profession as gynecologists allows them to control biology to a certain degree, it is death that ultimately triumphs, although they still maintain a certain amount of control over that.

Beginning with *Dead Ringers*, Cronenberg has made films which seem to suggest that he has abandoned his hybrid-horror child and adopted a more cerebral and suspenseful and less sci-fi narrative style. The maturity with which these films address the Cronenbergian concerns of biological control of destiny and usurpation of that control illustrates that the new Cronenberg film is indeed grounded more in the realm of dramatic tragedy and less in either science fiction or horror.

—Michael J. Tyrkus

DEADLY IS THE FEMALE

See **GUN CRAZY**

DEATH BY HANGING

See **KOSHIKEI**

DEATH IN VENICE

See **MORTE A VENEZIA**

DEATH OF A CYCLIST

See **MUERTE DE UN CICLISTA**

DECALOGUE

See **DEKALOG**

THE DEER HUNTER

USA, 1978

Director: Michael Cimino

Production: EMI Films; Panavision, Technicolor, Dolby Stereo; running time: 183 minutes. Released November 1978.

Producers: Barry Spikings, Michael Deeley, Michael Cimino, John Peverall; **production consultant:** Joan Carelli; **screenplay:** Deric Washburn; **story:** Michael Cimino, Deric Washburn, Louis Garfinkle, Quinn K. Redeker; **assistant directors:** Charles Okun, Mike Grillo; **photography:** Vilmos Zsigmond; **editor:** Peter Zinner; **sound editors:** Teri E. Dorman, James Fritch; **art directors:** Ron Hobbs, Kim Swados; **costumes:** Eric Seelig; **special make-up:** Dick Smith, Daniel Striepeke; **music:** Stanley Myers; **main title theme performed by:** John Williams; **military adviser:** Richard Dioguardi; **Vietnamese adviser:** Eleanor Dawson.

Cast: Robert De Niro (*Michael Vronsky*); John Cazale (*Stan, ''Stosh''*); John Savage (*Steven*); Christopher Walken (*Nikanor Chevotarevich, known as Nick*); Meryl Streep (*Linda*); George Dzundza (*John*); Chuck Aspegren (*Axel*); Shirley Stoler (*Steven's Mother*); Rutanya Alda (*Angela*); Pierre Segui (*Julien*); Mady Kaplan (*Axel's Girl*); Amy Wright (*Bridesmaid*); Mary Ann Haenel (*Stan's Girl*); Richard Kuss (*Linda's Father*); Joe Grifasi (*Bandleader*); Joe Strand (*Bingo Caller*); Helen Tomko (*Helen*); Paul D'Amato (*Sergeant*); Dennis Watlington (*Cab Driver*); Charlene Darrow (*Redhead*); Jane-Colette Disko (*Girl Checker*); Michael Wollett (*Stock Boy*); Robert Beard, Joe Dzizmba (*World War Veterans*); Father Stephen Kopestonsky (*Priest*); John F. Buchmelter III (*Bar Patron*); Frank Devore (*Barman*); Tom Becker (*Doctor*); Lynn Kongkham (*Nurse*); Nongnuj Timruang (*Bar Girl*); Po Pao Pee (*Chinese Referee*); Dale Burroughs (*Embassy Guard*); Parris Hicks (*Sergeant*); Samui Muang-Intata (*Chinese Bodyguard*); Sapox Colisium (*Chinese Man*); Vitoon Winwitoon (*N.V.A. Officer*); Somsak Sengvilia (*V.C. Referee*); Charan Nusvanon (*Chinese Boss*); Hillary Brown (*Herself*), Choir of St. Theodosius Cathedral, Cleveland, Ohio.

Awards: Oscars for Best Picture, Best Director, Best Supporting Actor (Walken), Best Editing, and Best Sound, 1979. British Academy of Film and Television Award for Best Cinematography (Zsigmond), 1979.

Publications

Books:

Adair, Gilbert, *Vietnam on Film: From ''The Green Berets'' to ''Apocalypse Now,''* New York, 1981; revised edition, as *Hollywood's Vietnam*, London, 1989.

Smurthwaite, Nick, *The Meryl Streep Story*, London, 1984.

The Deer Hunter

Maychick, Diana, *Meryl Streep*, New York, 1984.
Bliss, Michael, *Martin Scorsese & Michael Cimino*, Lanham, 1985.
Cameron-Wilson, James, *The Cinema of Robert De Niro*, London, 1986.
McKay, Keith, *Robert De Niro: The Hero Behind the Masks*, New York, 1986.
Wood, Robin, *Hollywood from Vietnam to Reagan*, New York, 1986.

Articles:

Carducci, M., ''Stalking the Deer Hunter: An Interview with Michael Cimino,'' in *Millimeter* (New York), March 1978.
Henderson, Scott, ''Behind the Scenes of *The Deer Hunter*,'' in *American Cinematographer* (Los Angeles), October 1978.
Variety (New York), 29 November 1978.
Literature/Film Quarterly (Salisbury, Maryland), vol. 7, no. 4, 1979.
Combs, Richard, in *Monthly Film Bulletin* (London), March 1979.
Gow, Gordon, in *Films and Filming* (London), March 1979.
Listener (London), 8 March 1979.
Pilger, John, in *New Statesman* (London), 16 March 1979.
Fox, Terry Curtis, in *Film Comment* (New York), March-April 1979.
Pym, John, ''A Bullet in the Head: Vietnam Remembered,'' in *Sight and Sound* (London), Spring 1979.
Auster, Al, and Leonard Quart, ''Hollywood and Vietnam: The Triumph of the Will,'' in *Cineaste* (New York), Spring 1979.
Positif (Paris), April 1979.
Kinder, Marsha, and others, in *Film Quarterly* (Berkeley), Summer 1979.
Mineo, T., ''Una falsa storia Vietnamita per rimuovere la colpa americana,'' in *Cinema Nuova* (Bari), August 1979.
Journal of Popular Film and Television (Washington, D.C.), vol. 7, no. 4, 1980.
Franz, R. C., ''*Apocalypse Now* and *The Deer Hunter:* The Lies Aren't Over,'' in *Jump Cut* (Chicago), October 1980.
Krohn, B., ''Entretien avec Michael Cimino,'' in *Cahiers du Cinéma* (Paris), June 1982.
Koper, B., ''Can Movies Kill?'' in *American Film* (Washington, D.C.), July-August 1982.
Burke, F., ''In Defense of *The Deer Hunter:* The Knee Jerk Is Quicker Than the Eye,'' in *Literature/Film Quarterly* (Salisbury, Maryland), January 1983.

Francis, D., ''The Regeneration of America: Uses of Landscape in *The Deer Hunter*,'' in *Literature/Film Quarterly* (Salisbury, Maryland), January 1983.
De Marinis, G., in *Cineforum* (Bergamo), January-February 1983.
Wander, P., ''The Aesthetics of Fascism,'' in *Journal of Communication* (Philadelphia), Spring 1983.
Greene, N., ''Coppola, Cimino: The Operatics of History,'' in *Film Quarterly* (Berkeley), Winter 1984–5.
''Vietnam Issue'' of *Wide Angle* (Athens, Ohio), vol. 7, no. 4, 1985.
Salminen, K., ''Poliittenen ooppera vieraantuneesta sankarista,'' in *Filmihullu* (Helsinki), no. 7–8, 1988.
Burke, F., ''Reading Michael Cimino's *The Deer Hunter:* Interpretation as Melting Pot,'' in *Literature/Film Quarterly* (Salisbury, Maryland), no. 3, 1992.
Nery, Robert, ''How to Have Your Cake and Eat It Too,'' in *Filmnews*, December-January 1992–1993.
Morice, Jacques, in *Cahiers du Cinéma* (Paris), Hors-série, 1993.
Man, G., ''Marginality and Centrality: The Myth of Asia in 1970s Hollywood,'' in *East-West Film Journal* (Honolulu), no. 1, 1994.
Suarez, E., ''*Deliverance*: Dickey's Original Screen Play,'' in *Southern Quarterly*, vol. 33, no. 2–3, 1995.
Worsley, Wallace, ''Worsley's Year of Deliverance,'' in *DGA* (Los Angeles), vol. 12, no. 2, May-June 1997.

* * *

When it was first released, *The Deer Hunter* was widely praised as the first American film to concern itself with the aftermath, social and psychological, of the Vietnam War. Because of this film, in fact, Hollywood discovered that audiences were eager for cinematic treatments of the subject and a number of films dealing with Vietnam were produced in the early 1980s.

The Deer Hunter, however, is not a war film in the ordinary sense: although central episodes treat developments in the late stages of the Vietnam conflict, the main emphasis is on the experiences shared by a group of young men growing up in a small Pennsylvania industrial town. Like many of the so-called ''buddy films'' of the 1970s, *The Deer Hunter* is a male melodrama that treats the difficulties, discontents, and triumphs of the growth into manhood, including but not dominated by going to war. It also connects directly to the ''artistic'' trendiness of the loosely coordinated movement on the part of certain directors in the late 1960s and early 1970s (including Francis Ford Coppola, Stanley Kubrick, and Martin Scorsese) to create a ''new wave'' American film and to redefine the creative/commercial position of the director (who was to become more of an auteur in the continental sense). Like Coppola with *The Godfather* or Kubrick with *A Clockwork Orange*, Cimino dominated the production of *The Deer Hunter*, stamping it with his own developing style and thematic obsessions: it was intended to be an intensely ''personal'' film, and both commercial and artistic at the same time.

The Deer Hunter opens with a long and richly detailed examination of the young men whose lives are dominated by dangerous and grueling manual labor in the steel mills and the release of drinking and carousing. Mike (Robert De Niro), Nick (Christopher Walken), and Stevie (John Savage) are just about to depart for military training, having volunteered to go to Vietnam together. Stevie, before he leaves, is to get married to Angela, a local girl pregnant by another man, and Mike and Nick are planning to leave that same night for their annual hunting trip in the nearby mountains with three others. This slice of life is dominated by a concern with masculine styles and attitudes. Mike is cool, laconic, self-contained yet capable of self-destructive wildness. Nick is less sure of himself, competent with others and well-liked, but obviously a follower, not a leader. Stevie is the weakest of the trio, a man satisfied with a marriage of convenience to a woman considered to be a tramp and an opportunist, a man unsure of what he wants from life and who seems content to shape his life after Mike's and Nick's. In the New Hollywood style, the narrative is made to appear undirected, a random and ''realistic'' examination of working-class ethnic life, although it is in fact a careful character study. Classic Hollywood expository modes are often subverted here (withheld establishing shots or no introductions for new characters, for example), while the acting is archly naturalist in the method tradition (broken sentences, overlapping dialogue, an emphasis on inner, unspoken struggle and, inevitably, male emotion).

An excessive, ''realistic'' representation marks the difference between *The Deer Hunter* and the classic Hollywood film. But the masculine values advanced, tested, and endorsed in the film's opening sequences are thoroughly traditional. Vietnam is viewed by the trio of friends as yet another test, yet another opportunity to do the right thing and be a man. The film takes no political stand on the issue of the war. In fact, like the more recent *Platoon*, it depoliticizes the war, turning it into a morality play where positive and negative qualities of the American character act out a deadly, self-destructive drama. In both films, the real enemy is forgotten: the war becomes a struggle between different masculine styles and philosophies. Mike learns the dangers of the code he had lived by; he survives. Nick lives out the logical and psychological consequences of that code; he dies, in effect, a suicide. The treatment of maleness, however, is hopelessly compromised. Stevie lacks courage and competence; he becomes a pitiful paraplegic, married to a woman who doesn't love him. While the hero may renounce his ''right'' to assert himself, he remains a hero, at least in large part, because of his willingness to risk life and limb, to be fearless and graceful under pressure. This contradiction, at the same time, is likely what made the film's narrative so attractive to a mass audience, one willing to accept a ''softened'' maleness only as a renunciation of power, not as an alternative to it.

Historically, *The Deer Hunter* is important as the last successful realist epic produced by the artistically minded directors of the Hollywood Renaissance. Cimino's subsequent efforts in this form have met with little success. *The Deer Hunter*, however, was able to achieve an outstanding and surprising success because of its carefully calculated combination of traditional Hollywood melodrama with a style and themes borrowed, to a large degree, from the art cinema.

—R. Barton Palmer

DEKALOG

(Decalogue)

Poland, 1988

Director: Krzysztof Kieślowski

Production: Polish Television, TOR Studios; colour, 35mm; running time: 10 films 53–57 minutes each. Released 1989. *Decalogue 5* and *Decalogue 6* released theatrically in 1989 as *A Short Film About*

Killing and *A Short Film About Love*. Filmed on location in Warsaw, 1988.

Producer: Ryszard Chutkowski; **screenplay:** Krzysztof Kieślowski, Krzysztof Piesiewicz; **photography:** Wieslaw Zdort (Decalogue 1), Edward Klosinski (2), Piotr Sobocinski (3, 9), Krzysztof Pakulski (4), Slawomir Idziak (5), Witold Adamek (6), Dariusz Kuc (7), Anrzej Jaroszewicz (8), Jacek Blawut (10); **editor:** Ewa Smal; **sound:** Malgorzata Jaworska (1, 2, 4, 5), Nikodem Wolk-Laniewski (3, 6, 7, 9, 10), Wieslawa Demblinska (8); **production designer:** Halina Dobrowolska; **music:** Zbigniew Preisner.

Cast: 1: Henryk Baranowski (*Krzysztof*), Wojciech Klata (*Pawel*), Maja Komorowska (*Irena*). 2: Krystyna Janda (*Dorota*), Alexander Bardini (*Consultant*), Olgierd Lukaszewicz (*Anrzej*). 3: Daniel Olbrychski (*Janusz*), Maria Pakulnis (*Ewa*). 4: Adrianna Biedrzynska (*Anka*), Janusz Gajos (*Michal*). 5: Miroslaw Baka (*Jacek*), Krzysztof Globisz (*Piotr*). 6: Grazyna Szapolowska (*Magda*), Olaf Lubaszenko (*Tomek*). 7: Anna Polony (*Ewa*), Maja Barelkowska (*Majka*). 8: Maria Koscialkowska (*Zofia*), Teresa Marczewska (*Elzbieta*). 9: Ewa Blaszczyk (*Hanka*), Piotr Machalica (*Roman*). 10: Jerzy Stuhr (*Jerzy*), Zbigniew Zamachowski (*Arthur*).

Publications

Script:

Kieślowski, Krzysztof, and Krzysztof Piesiewicz, *The Decalogue*, London, 1991.
Kieślowski, Krzysztof, and Krzysztof Piesiewicz, *Dekalog*, in *Iskusstvo Kino* (Moscow), March-December 1993.

Books:

Michalek, Boleslaw, and Frank Turaj, *The Modern Cinema of Poland*, Bloomington, 1988.
Kieślowski, Krzysztof, *Kieślowski on Kieślowski*, London, 1993.
Garbowski, Christopher, *Krzysztof Kieślowski's Decalogue Series: The Problem of the Protagonists and Their Self-Transcendance*, Boulder, 1996.
Coates, Paul, editor, *Lucid Dreams: The Films of Krzysztof Kieślowski*, Wiltshire, 1999.
Insdorf, Annette, *Double Lives, Second Chances: The Cinema of Krzysztof Kieślowski*, New York, 1999.

Articles:

Variety (New York), 27 September 1989.
Baron, A.-M., *Cinéma* (Paris), November 1989.
Ciment, M., and others, *Positif* (Paris), December 1989.
Rigney, F.J., *Film Criticism* (Meadville, Pennsylvania), Spring 1990.
Magny, J., and A. de Baecque, ''Les régles du hasard,'' in *Cahiers du Cinéma* (Paris), March 1990.
Tobin, Y., and others, *Positif* (Paris), May 1990.
Cavendish, Phil, ''Kieślowski's Decalogue,'' in *Sight and Sound* (London), Summer 1990.
Insdorf, Annette, ''*The Decalogue*: Re-Examining God's Commands,'' in *New York Times* (New York), 28 October 1990.
Tarantino, Michael, ''The Cave,'' in *Artforum* (New York), December 1990.
Charbonneau, A., *24 Images* (Montreal), Summer 1991.
Elia, M., ''L'art du risque calculé,'' in *Séquences* (Montreal), September 1991.
Klinger, M., ''Strazce brany,'' in *Film a Doba* (Prague), Summer 1992.
Holden, Stephen, ''Chance, Fate and the Bible,'' in *New York Times* (New York), 8 March 1996.
Falkowska, J., ''Krzysztof Kieślowski's *Decalogue* Series: The Problem of Protagonists and Their Self-transcendence,'' in *Canadian Journal of Film Studies* (Ottawa), no. 2, 1997.
Perlmutter, R., ''Testament to the Father: Kieślowski's *The Decalogue*,'' in *Film Criticism* (Meadville), no. 2, 1997/1998.

* * *

Krzysztof Kieślowski, who died in Warsaw at the age of 54 while this essay was being prepared for publication, was the last great director to have emerged from Communist Poland. His *Decalogue*, made for Polish television in 1988–89, was, perhaps, the last masterpiece from what used to be ''Eastern Europe.'' A product of Kieślowski's odd preoccupation with cycles (Eric Rohmer is the only other major director, similarly obsessed, who comes to mind), *Decalogue* is not a film, but a compendium of 10 hour-long films, based, presumably, on the Ten Commandments. The premise demands moralizing. The result is far from it. The actual meaning of each film is not in how a dictum is illustrated, and not even in a twist that each story (all of them set in the present-day Poland) gives an old maxim, but in how the material transcends the dogma into a sphere of existential mystery.

There are artists who are late bloomers, who must try out various timbres before they find their own voice. It took Antonioni over ten years and a dozen films, both fiction and documentary, to make *Il Grido*, his first truly ''Antonionian'' film. It took Kieślowski over ten years and two dozen films, both fiction and documentary, to make *Decalogue*, which marks both the climax of a long search and a dramatic shift in direction and quality. That the seed was there is clear in the 1981 feature *Blind Chance*, which sketches out three possible futures for a man who, like a *tabula rasa*, is open to either one. The film shows how the filmmaker sensed what was soon to become his territory in art, but didn't yet have the formal means to make that territory his own. That *Decalogue* changed Kieślowski's life is evident in the way that all his following films—*The Double Life of Veronique*, *Blue*, *White* and *Red*—stem from *Decalogue*, developing the earlier work's motifs and sharpening its filmic finesse.

From *Decalogue* on, Kieślowski focused exclusively on the invisible and how it can be seen. He himself could show it with an incomparable grace: the mysterious links that tie us all together; the signs and omens that nature, uselessly, sends our way; the doom, materialized in things and machines; the sadness of the pond and the clouds. In this world, an ink-spill prophesies trouble, and when somebody dies, holy water freezes in the church. This kind of cinema dangerously balances between the profound and the pretentious. But if Kieślowski slipped into pretentiousness in the occasionally ponderous *Blue*, *Decalogue* has a luminosity of milk, left (in *Decalogue 1*) out in the cold overnight and turned into white ice. Its light breaks the glass of the gratuitous bottle.

Decalogue's world—the world of a grim Warsaw housing development where all the stories originate—is not a collection of entities and events, but a dense substance in which everything is connected with everything. The focus is shifted from things to what lies between them. This philosophy puts Kieślowski into a glorious chain of artists—Dreyer, Bresson, Iosseliani (the line continues with Atom Egoyan and Wong Kar-wai)—and explains why his preoccupation with cycles may not be so odd after all. As people are linked in his films, so are the films themselves. The heroine of *Blue* shows up in the courtroom of *White* and then, along with the principals of *White*, in the coda of *Red*. A fictitious Dutch Renaissance composer Van den Budelmayer from *Red* originates in *Decalogue 9*, as does *White*'s tragi-comic theme of male impotence. The brothers from *Decalogue 10* don't want to stay home; they spill into the story of *White*. A model auteur, Kieślowski in all his later years shot one film; perhaps his decision to stop, which he made in 1994 after completing the *Three Colors* trilogy, grew out of a realization that his film had come to an end. (It has been reported that Kieślowski was planning another project at the time of his death.)

Like Fassbinder's 14-part *Berlin, Alexanderplatz*, *Decalogue* brilliantly utilizes its format: from television it takes not the lack of light and cinematic quality, but the extreme intimacy between the characters and the audience. Most meaningfully, it tells chamber stories in close angles. A cast of the best Polish actors, headed by Maja Komorowska, Krystyna Janda, Grazyna Szapolowska, Daniel Olbrychski, Janusz Gajos, Jerzy Stuhr, and Zbigniew Zamachowski, the work of nine terrific cinematographers, and a touching, minimalist score by Zbigniew Preisner all make Kieślowski's vast ambition possible. From the first, heartbreaking film that puts a computer in place of the ''other God,'' that ''thou shalt not have,'' through the two highlight novellas, later expanded by the director into *A Short Film About Killing* (*Decalogue 5*) and *A Short Film About Love* (*Decalogue 6*), this is a cinema that mesmerizes you while it's showing and haunts you long after it's all over.

—Michael Brashinsky

DELIVERANCE

USA, 1972

Director: John Boorman

Production: Warner Brothers, Elmer Enterprises; Technicolor; Panavision; running time: 109 minutes. Released July 1972.

Producer: John Boorman; **production manager:** Wallace Worsley; **screenplay:** James Dickey, from his own novel; **assistant directors:** Al Jennings, Miles Middough; **photography:** Vilmos Zsigmond; **2nd unit photography:** Bill Butler; **editor:** Tom Priestley; **sound editor:** Jim Atkinson; **sound recordist:** Walter Goss; **sound re-recordist:** Doug Turner; **art director:** Fred Harpman; **music:** ''Duelling Banjos'' arranged and played by Eric Weissberg, with Steve Mandel; **creative associate:** Rospo Pallenberg; **special effects:** Marcel Vercoutere; **technical advisers:** Charles Wiggin, E. Lewis King.

Cast: Jon Voight (*Ed*); Burt Reynolds (*Lewis*); Ned Beatty (*Bobby*); Ronny Cox (*Drew*); Billy McKinney (*Mountain Man*); Herbert ''Cowboy'' Coward (*Toothless Man*) James Dickey (*Sheriff Bullard*); Ed Ramey (*Old Man*); Billy Redden (*Lonny*); Seamon Glass (*1st ''Griner''*); Randall Deal (*2nd ''Griner''*); Lewis Crone (*1st Deputy*); Ken Keener (*2nd Deputy*); Johnny Popwell (*Ambulance Driver*); John Fowler (*Doctor*); Kathy Rickman (*Nurse*); Louise Coldren (*Mrs. Biddiford*); Pete Ware (*Taxi Driver*); Hoyt T. Pollard (*Boy at Gas Station*); Belinda Beatty (*Martha Gentry*); Charlie Boorman (*Ed's Boy*).

Publications

Script:

Dickey, James, *Deliverance*, Carbondale, Illinois, 1982.

Books:

Piccardi, Adriano, *John Boorman*, Florence, 1982.
Streetbeck, Nancy, *The Films of Burt Reynolds*, Secaucus, New Jersey, 1982.
Ciment, Michel, *John Boorman*, Paris 1985; London 1986.

Articles:

Gow, Gordon, in *Films and Filming* (London), February 1972.
Variety (New York), 19 July 1972.
Strick, Philip, in *Sight and Sound* (London), Autumn 1972.
Milne, Tom, in *Monthly Film Bulletin* (London), September 1972.
Ciment, Michel, in *Positif* (Paris), October 1972.
Allombert, G., in *Image et son* (Paris), November 1972.
Grisolia, M., ''L'Amerique s'est dissociée de la nature, par un sort de névrose commune,'' interview with John Boorman in *Cinéma* (Paris), November 1972.
Dempsey, M., ''*Deliverance*/Boorman: Dickey in the Woods,'' in *Cinema* (Beverly Hills), Spring 1973.
Armour, Robert, ''*Deliverance:* Four Variations of the American Adam,'' in *Literature/Film Quarterly* (Salisbury, Maryland), Summer 1973.
Willson, Robert F. Jr., ''*Deliverance* from Novel to Film: Where Is Our Hero?'' in *Literature/Film Quarterly* (Salisbury, Maryland), Winter 1974.
''Boorman Issue'' of *Positif* (Paris), March 1974.
Dunne, Aidan, ''Labyrinth of Allusion,'' in *Film Directions* (Belfast), vol. 1 no. 4, 1978.
Combs, Richard, ''Male Myths,'' in *The Listener* (London), 4 July 1985.
Griffith, J. J., ''Damned If You Do, and Damned If You Don't: James Dickey's *Deliverance*,'' in *Post Script* (Jacksonville, Florida), Spring-Summer 1986.
Williams, Linda Ruth, ''Blood Brothers,'' in *Sight & Sound* (London), September 1994.
Suarez, E., ''*Deliverance*: Dickey's Original Screen Play,'' in *Southern Quarterly*, no. 2/3, 1995.
Atkinson, M., ''Jon Voight in *Deliverance*,'' in *Movieline* (Escondido), May 1996.
Worsley, W., ''Worsley's Year of *Deliverance*,'' in *DGA Magazine* (Los Angeles), no. 2, 1997.

* * *

Deliverance

In the early 1970s, accelerated no doubt by Watergate, the optimistic liberal tradition was in some crisis. Conspiracy and paranoia had become common currency in popular culture, a trend evident in such otherwise diverse films as Peckinpah's *Straw Dogs*, Pakula's *The Parallax View*, Coppola's *The Conversation*, and Boorman's *Deliverance.* Where ten years earlier movie protagonists routinely triumphed over adversity, the heroes of these and other 1970s films were increasingly to find themselves trapped and destroyed by the relentless logic of events.

This is the claustrophobic plight of *Deliverance's* four central characters: a group of urban men caught in an escalating series of violent confrontations with the Appalachian wilderness and its (to them) alien inhabitants. Carried along by the very linearity of the narrative's voyage structure (the four are canoeing down a wild river before it is dammed to form a lake) we directly experience the constraining force of events in the movie's unremitting emphasis on physical detail. Fat Bobby, struggling in the dirt, groped and fondled at some length before he is forcibly buggered; the close-up sight and sound of an arrow pulled from the body of his attacker; the frenzied scrabbling of the group as they dig a grave with their bare hands; the viscera hanging from the wound in Lewis's leg; Drew's body trapped against a boulder, his arm impossibly twisted behind his head. Such scenes are constant reminders of the brute materiality of this wilderness and of the quartet's inability to do anything but react to a succession of real and imagined provocations. Even after their deliverance, Ed wakes screaming, haunted by the fear and guilt embodied in his nightmare image of a hand emerging from the lake. As the credits roll, he lies in bed, unable to sleep.

At this level *Deliverance* is a pessimistic and absorbing piece of story-telling. But it is also more than that. In charting the collapse of ''civilised'' values, the film invokes larger, almost metaphysical themes. While they are never simply emblematic, *Deliverance's* four central characters do represent different aspects of the failings of civilised society, failings crystallised in their confrontation with the wilderness. ''There is something in the woods and the water that we have lost in the city'' opines Bobby, the brash salesman. ''We didn't lose it,'' Lewis replies, ''we sold it.'' Happily, any tendency to promote a mystic commitment to Nature over Civilisation (all too apparent in Boorman's later ecological parable, *The Emerald Forest*) is undercut by the fact that Lewis, the self-proclaimed survivor and man of the wilderness, is never elevated into the kind of sub-Nietzschean superman found in, say, *The Deer Hunter.* Instead, he serves as a foil to the other three, and especially to Ed, whose self-image as a decent, pipe-smoking family man is progressively eroded as the world proves more intractable than he could ever imagine. In the end, though, he does survive, forced to kill and lie to do so. Significantly, it is Drew who dies, his simple belief in the goodness of human nature (exquisitely expressed in his guitar and banjo duet with the moon-faced child and in his evident disappointment when the boy subsequently ignores him) an inadequate defence against a malevolent world.

The film's downbeat mood is sustained in its cinematography as well as its dramaturgy. Seeking to lend what he called an ''ominous quality'' to the ''pleasant and restful'' greens and blues of sky, river and trees, Boorman (in conjunction with Technicolor) developed a new color desaturation technique for *Deliverance.* The result is a film shot in threatening grey-greens, not so much washed-out as evacuated of conventionally pretty nature imagery. Although the big Panavision images of river, cliffs, and forest are impressive enough (there are some breath-taking moving compositions of the two canoes, exploiting both the format and the long lens's flattened perspective) the desaturated color always ensures that they do not become merely picturesque. As befits a story of liberal complacency confronted by brutal antagonism, it is the struggle to survive that predominates, the big screen used more to document that in close-up than to celebrate the pictorial splendours of the setting.

When the survivors emerge from the last rapids onto the lake, it is not—as it might have been—a comforting expanse of calm water that greets them and us. It is the rusting bulk of a wrecked automobile, water lapping around its fender. Bobby splashes through the shallows towards it. ''We've made it, Ed,'' he cries, grateful for this equivocal symbol of civilised society. It is an appropriately two-edged image in a film which, to the last, refuses to accept that there are simple solutions to the moral dilemmas that it poses.

—Andrew Tudor

LA DENTELLIÈRE

(The Lacemaker)

Switzerland-France-West Germany, 1977

Director: Claude Goretta

Production: Citel Films (Geneva), Actions Films (Paris), and Filmproduktion (Frankfort); Eastmancolor, 35mm; running time: 108 minutes. Released May 1977, France. Filmed in France.

Producer: Yves Peyrot with Yves Gosser; **screenplay:** Claude Goretta and Pascal Laine, from the novel by Laine; **photography:** Jean Boffety; **editor:** Joelle Van Effenterre; **sound:** Pierre Gemet and Bernard Chaumeil; **production design:** Serge Etter and Claude Chevant; **music:** Pierre Jansen; **music editor:** Georges Bacri.

Cast: Isabelle Huppert (*Béatrice*); Yves Beneyton (*François*); Florence Giorgietti (*Marylène*); Anne-Marie Duringer (*Béatrice's mother*); Jean Obe (*François' father*); Monique Chaumette (*François' mother*); Michel de Re (*The Painter*); Renata Schroeter (*Francois' friend*); Sabine Azema (*Student*).

Awards: Cannes Film Festival, Ecumenical Prize, 1977.

Publications

Script:

Goretta, Claude, and Pascal Laine, *La Dentellière*, Paris, 1981.

Articles:

Moskowitz, G., *Variety* (New York), 25 May 1977.
Roulet, C., in *Cinématographe* (Paris), June 1977.
Maillet, D., ''Claude Goretta,'' in *Cinématographe* (Paris), June 1977.
Jong, A., ''Claude Goretta en *La Dentellière*,'' in *Skoop* (Amsterdam), June-July 1977.
Chevassu, F., in *Image et Son* (Paris), September 1977.
Milne, Tom, in *Monthly Film Bulletin* (London), November 1977.
International Film Guide 1978, London, 1978.
Leroux, A., in *Séquences* (Montreal), January 1978.
Pruks, I., in *Cinema Papers* (Melbourne), April-June 1978.
Peterson-Schultz, B., in *Kosmorama* (Copenhagen), Summer 1978.
Kass, Judith, ''Claude Goretta and Isabelle Huppert,'' in *Movietone News* (Seattle), 14 August 1978.
Parker, G., in *Film Quarterly* (Berkeley), Fall 1978.
Günter, J., in *Film und Fernsehen* (Berlin), October 1978.
Brossard, Jean-Pierre, ''Trotz allem hoofe ich,'' in *Film und Fernsehen* (Berlin), October 1978.
Termino, L., in *Cinema Nuovo* (Bari), February 1980.
Cèbe, Gilles, ''Une Martyre de l'amour,'' in *Avant-Scène du Cinéma* (Paris), 15 April 1981.
Millar, Gavin, in *Listener* (London), 3 March 1983.
Télérama (Paris), 6 November 1996.

* * *

Claude Goretta's third feature film, his first made in France, tells a deceptively simple story of lost innocence against the picturesque background of the Normandy coast and the contemporary ambience of Paris. *The Lacemaker* is marked by the economy, close observations, and compassion of its director and the virtuoso performance of its star, Isabelle Huppert, who plays Béatrice, nicknamed ''Pomme,'' a shy young assistant in a Paris beauty parlor. The film depicts her first romance with a well-bred Sorbonne student named François (Yves Beneyton), who meets her while on vacation in the resort town of Cabourg and rejects her some months later, bringing on an emotional and physical collapse. Goretta has synthesized several potentially sentimental genres—*Bildungsroman*, pastoral, seduction story, poor-meets-rich romance—and managed to evoke fresh responses to his film's own particular time and place.

The Lacemaker begins by exploring the friendship between Pomme and Marylène (Florence Giorgietti), a slightly older and far more

La Dentellière

experienced beautician. Like her illustrious namesake, Marilyn Monroe, whose poster adorns a wall in her high-rise apartment, Marylène is blonde, restless, and seductive, a compulsive poseur. Pomme seems her complete opposite: small, quiet, utterly guileless. While Marylène's extroverted personality, sensuousness, and superior position in the shop clearly present her as a foil in the opening sequences, she is soon shown to be no less vulnerable to men than Pomme will become. The opening movement of *The Lacemaker* thus concludes with Marylène being jilted by her married boyfriend and deciding to forget her troubles by taking Pomme along on a vacation at the seacoast.

Marylène soon meets a new man and moves out of the hotel room she briefly shared with Pomme, who acquiesces silently. François sees her eating an ice cream at an outdoor cafe and introduces himself to the shy girl as a brilliant student of literature from Paris. Goretta departs from his customary unobtrusive cinematic style at this point with a beautiful sequence of long tracking shots and cross-cutting to depict François and Pomme looking for each other the next day. The distance between them in the panoramic vistas and the high camera placements suggest both the separate worlds they inhabit and the fate that draws them together. When they finally meet on the boardwalk, Pomme wears a white dress and François a dark t-shirt and jeans, visually underscoring their differences at the very moment their romance begins.

Goretta depicts the development of their relationship through a series of delicately woven vignettes, the most clearly symbolic of which involves a game of blindman's bluff on a steep cliff overlooking the Channel. François leads her to the very edge, but Pomme continues to follow his commands without ever opening her eyes. When she finally does, standing at the very edge of the precipice, François has to grab her to keep her from falling with fright. Soon after this strangely disturbing interlude, Pomme agrees to sleep with him, her first time with a man.

Back in Paris and now living in François's flat near the university, Pomme happily cleans and cooks after her own work at the beauty parlor is done so that he might pursue his studies. Their life together seems epitomized in a scene where she tries to eat an apple silently (her nickname, ''pomme,'' means ''apple'') without disturbing his concentration, and he becomes annoyed not so much by the sound as by her effort at self-effacement. The film's pivotal scene occurs during the couple's visit with François's parents in the country. When the dinner conversation turns to news about François's successful young friends and questions about what she does for a living, Pomme is overcome by a violent fit of choking. In moments such as these, Goretta reveals the subtle unraveling of their romance, without a single argument between them. In a high-angle long shot foreshadowing their parting, and mirroring the panoramic views of Cabourg, François rushes across a city boulevard, leaving Béatrice stranded on a traffic island. Some time after François explains how breaking up will be best for both of them and returns her to her mother's apartment, Béatrice collapses in the middle of a busy intersection.

The Lacemaker's final sequence takes place in a sanatorium where François comes to visit Béatrice, whose altered appearance is profoundly disquieting. She wears a shapeless black dress like a shroud; she moves and speaks mechanically, drained of all her former charm. As they pass the time together in a park filled with fallen yellow leaves, François asks what she has been doing since they parted. When Béatrice tonelessly describes a trip to Greece with someone she met, François seems relieved to learn she has taken other lovers. In the closing shot, however, the camera tracks in on the therapy room where Béatrice sits alone in a corner knitting in front of a bright poster of Mykonos. Her foreign travel was an illusion, both a deception and farewell gift for the guilt-ridden François. As the truth dawns, she turns to the camera with a chilling expression which Goretta then freezes. The closing title appears, with its reference to the anonymous working women—seamstresses, water-girls, lacemakers—of the paintings of the Old Masters.

Goretta's film, like his heroine's face, is deceptively simple. While seemingly inviting interpretation as a modern parable of innocence betrayed, a Marxist allegory on the plight of the working class, feminist tract against patriarchal society, or even a clinical study of mental breakdown, *The Lacemaker* remains ultimately less moralistic than Eric Rohmer's films, less political than Godard's or Tanner's, less intellectual than Resnais's. Goretta's deepest concern—and the film's ultimate ''meaning''—lies with Béatrice herself, with what she has lost and, just possibly, what she has gained.

—Lloyd Michaels

DER VAR ENGANG EN KRIG

(Once There Was a War)

Norway, 1966

Director: Palle Kjaerulff-Schmidt

Production: Nordisk Films Kompagni; black and white, 35mm, widescreen; running time: 94 minutes; length: 2565 meters, or 8460 feet. Released 16 November 1966, Copenhagen. Filmed in Denmark.

Producer: Bo Christensen; **screenplay:** Klaus Rifbjerg; **assistant director:** Tom Hedegaard; **photography:** Claus Loof; **editor:** Ole Steen; **sound:** Niels Ishsy and Hans W. Søensen; **art director:** Henning Bahs; **music:** Chopin, Beethoven, and Leo Mathisen; **costume designer:** Lotte Dandanell.

Cast: Ole Busck (*Tim*); Kjeld Jacobsen (*Father*); Astrid Villaume (*Mother*); Katja Miehe Renard (*Kate, the sister*); Birgit Bendix Madson (*Jane*); Christian Gottschalck (*Grandfather*); Yvonne Ingdal (*Lis*); Karen Marie Løwert (*Lis's mother*); Gregers Ussing (*Frank*); Jan Heinig Hansen (*Markus*); Birgit Brüel (*Markus's mother*); Jørgen Beck (*Friend*); Elsa Kourani (*Friend's wife*); Henry Skjar (*Headmaster*); Holger Perfort (*Teacher in gymnastics*).

Der var engang en krig

Publications

Script:

Rifbjerg, Klaus, and Palle Kjaerulff-Schmidt, *Der var engang en krig*, Copenhagen, 1966.

Books:

Stormgaard, Uffe, and Soren Dyssegaard, *Danish Films*, Copenhagen, 1973.

Passek, Jean-Loup, editor, *Le Cinéma danois*, Paris, 1979.

Articles:

Variety (New York), 30 November 1966.

Kosmorama (Copenhagen), December 1966.

Hollywood Reporter, 2 November 1967.

Film Quarterly (Berkeley), Winter 1967–68.

Today's Cinema, 13 June 1969.
Monthly Film Bulletin (London), August 1969.
Films and Filming (London), September 1969.
Semprun, Jorge, and Palle Kjaerulff-Schmidt, in *Chaplin* (Stockholm), no. 3, 1976.
Monty, Ib, ''Danish Film,'' in *Factsheet Denmark*, Copenhagen, 1983.
Film Dope (Nottingham), January 1985.
Schepelern, Peter, in *Kosmorama* (Copenhagen), Summer 1987.
Mitchell, G.J., ''Filmmaking History in Denmark,'' in *American Cinematographer* (Hollywood), February 1989.

* * *

Apart from Carl Th. Dreyer's *Gertrud, Der var engang en krig* is the most important Danish film of the 1960s. It is a portrait of a 15-year-old boy from middle-class Copenhagen during the German occupation. The German occupation of 1940–45 has been described in several documentaries, most notably in the unique *Your Freedom Is at Stake*, based on illegally shot material and reflecting the views of the resistance movement—a view quite critical towards the official Danish collaboration policy. Sixteen feature films were inspired by this important period in recent Danish history, most of them stressing the heroic aspects of the resistance. Contrary to this approach, *Der var engang en krig* uses the war as a background, but reflects the daily life of the Danes in a more authentic and honest manner.

The film is structured as a chain of incidents, showing the boy in relation to family, friends, teachers, and girls. The main story centers on the boy's love for one of his older sister's girlfriends. To her he is a boy, to him she is the object of his adolescent dreams. He fantasizes about her, seeing himself as a resolute hero in a number of daydream sequences, which are among the most problematic scenes in an otherwise beautifully controlled film. It is based on a meticulous care for authentic detail, and its intensity of feeling grows out of these carefully recollected views of the past. Though visually it can be considered within a realistic tradition, it is the situations, the excellently written dialogue, the characters, and the way it brings a period to life which make the film engaging and emotionally rich. The film is not without humor; but as the narrative is from the boy's point of view, he is never presented in an ironic way. The stronger feelings are condensed in the long travelling shots and pans, when the boy is cycling, expressing his feelings in physical activity.

The film was written by Klaus Rifbjerg who, like Palle Kjaerulff-Schmidt, the director, takes advantage of personal experiences to enhance his work. Rifjberg is the finest poet and author of his generation, and he and Kjaerulff-Schmidt started collaborating on films in 1959. In 1962 they made *Weekend*, a study of young adults and their emotional problems. *Weekend* was considered one of the films heralding a new, more modern era in the Danish cinema. Reality has finally returned to the Danish film after a long barren period. The collaboration between Rifbjerg and Kjaerulff-Schmidt culminated with *Der var engang en krig*, their finest achievement and one of the highlights of contemporary Danish cinema. Influenced by Truffaut (especially *The 400 Blows*) and similar to films by Ermanno Olmi and Milos Forman, *Der var engang en krig* represents the best in intimate realism. The film was received very well by Danish critics and also got very fine reviews abroad, especially in England.

—Ib Monty

LE DERNIER TANGO À PARIS

See **LAST TANGO IN PARIS**

DETOUR

US, 1945

Director: Edgar G. Ulmer

Production: Producers Releasing Corp.; black and white, 35mm, Spherical; running time: 69 minutes.

Producer: Leon Fromkess, Martin Mooney (assistant producer); **screenplay:** Martin Goldsmith, Martin Mooney (uncredited); **cinematographer:** Benjamin H. Kline; **editor:** George McGuire; **music:** Leo Erdody; **sound:** Max Hutchison; **art director:** William A. Calihan, Jr., Edward C. Jewell; **set decoration:** Glenn P. Thompson; **costume design:** Mona Barry.

Cast: Tom Neal (*Al Roberts, alias Charles Maxwell, Jr.*); Ann Savage (*Vera*); Claudia Drake (*Sue Harvey*); Edmund McDonald (*Charles Haskell Jr.*); Tim Ryan (*Diner Proprietor*); Esther Howard (*Holly*); Roger Clark (*Man*); Pat Gleason (*Man*); Don Brodie (*Used Car Salesman*).

Awards: Named to National Film Registry, National Film Preservation Board, 1992.

Publications

Books:

Sarris, Andrew, *The American Cinema: Directors and Directions 1929–1968*, Chicago, 1968.
Truffaut, Francois, *The Films in My Life*, New York, 1975.
Peary, Danny, *Cult Movies*, New York, 1981.
Hirsch, Foster, *Film Noir: The Dark Side of the Screen*, New York, 1981.
Bogdanovich, Peter, *Who the Devil Made It: Conversations with Legendary Film Directors*, New York, 1997.

Articles:

Schrader, Paul, ''Notes on Film Noir,'' in *Film Comment* (New York), vol. 8, no. 1, Spring 1972.
Combs, R., ''*Detour*,'' in *Monthly Film Bulletin* (London), vol. 49, no. 582, July 1982.
Pulleine, T., ''*Detour*,'' in *Films and Filming* (South Croydon, Surrey), no. 335, August 1982.

Detour

Belton, John, ''Edgar G. Ulmer,'' in *American Directors*, vol. 1, New York, 1983.

Miller, Ron, ''*Detour* to Immortality,'' in *San Jose Mercury News*, 16 October 1983.

Piccardi, A., ''*Detour* di Edgar G. Ulmer,'' in *Cineforum*, vol. 27, no. 261, January-February 1987.

Garsault, A., ''Un artiste,'' in *Positif* (Paris), no. 358, December 1990.

McBride, J., ''Family Drive,'' in *American Film* (Marion, Ohio), vol. 15, no. 11, August 1990.

Atkinson, Michael, ''Noir and Away. Notes on the Two Detours,'' in *Bright Lights* (Cincinnati, Ohio), no. 15, 1995.

* * *

There are more elegant and ambitious examples of classic film noir—Jacques Tourneur's *Out of the Past* and Robert Aldrich's *Kiss Me Deadly* leap to mind—but it's unlikely that you will find a more tightly plotted or single-minded example of the postwar, German Expressionist-rooted style than Edgar G. Ulmer's *Detour.* Indeed, the argument could be made that this Poverty Row gem distills noir to its basic components: suffocating fatalism, sexual paranoia, the down-on-his-luck patsy/protagonist born to come to a bad end. *Detour* also contains what for many students is the definitive noir plaint. ''It was just my luck, picking her up on the road,'' says Al Roberts (Tom Neal) in morose voice-over. ''It couldn't be Helen . . . or Mary or Evelyn or Ruth; it had to be the very last person I should ever have met. That's life. Whichever way you turn, Fate sticks out a foot to trip you.''

Of course Fate has less to do with Al's ultimate undoing than Al himself. Fate is noir's all-purpose fall guy. The real cause is Al's obsessive-compulsive personality. A frustrated pianist in a New York dive called the Break O' Dawn Club, Roberts juggles (poorly) dual obsessions: a stalled concert career (he fancies himself a budding Shoshtakovich) and a relationship with the club's pretty vocalist, Sue (Claudia Drake). Sue's decision to try her luck in Hollywood sets up her beau's fall. Eaten alive by those twin *betes noires*, jealousy and desperation, Al ''takes it on the thumb'' and follows his worst instincts west.

Half of this compact (69 minute) programmer is devoted to Al's misfortunes on the road. In Arizona he is picked up by a obnoxious bookie named Haskell (Edmund MacDonald), who rambles on about a childhood duel and some nasty scratches compliments of ''the most dangerous animal in the world—a woman.'' As Al takes his turn at the wheel, Haskell nods off, has a heart attack, and dies. In the pounding rain, Al, true to form, makes a suspicious situation worse by taking Haskell's clothes, car, and identity. His muddled reasoning: ''By that time I'd done just what the police would say I did, even if I didn't.''

Al gets himself in deeper when he picks up a sullen vixen named Vera (Ann Savage parodying the trampy, consumptive Bette Davis). Vera knows Al isn't Haskell and uses the information to blackmail him into an inheritance scam. Al, thinking only of Sue, resists both the scam and Vera's drunken advances. A fight ensues and, in an all-too-plausible accident involving a phone chord, Al finds himself fleeing another ''murder'' scene. Unable to buck Fate, he surrenders to it. ''Someday a car will stop to pick me up for a ride that I never thumbed,'' he says as a police car pulls up and a door swings open. ''Yes, Fate, or some mysterious force, can put the finger on you or me for no good reason at all.''

Adapted by Martin Goldsmith from half of his 1939 novel (which unfolds from both Al's and Sue's perspectives) and told in flashback from a Nevada diner playing, mockingly, Sue's hit song, ''I Can't Believe That You're in Love with Me,'' *Detour* was shot in six days for the notoriously cheap Producers Releasing Corp. The Czechoslovakian-born Ulmer, who had apprenticed with F.W. Murnau before emigrating to Hollywood in 1931, was, as *The Black Cat* (1934) and *Bluebeard* (1944) demonstrate, a past master at employing shadows, tight two-shots, and minimalist set design to create ambience and stretch a budget. After a brief rehearsal period, he told interviewers, he could shoot 60 to 80 setups in a day.

Forced again to economize, this time on less than $30,000, Ulmer turned *Detour* into an unrelenting journey down what he called ''that long road of Fate.'' Each element of the mise-en-scene (mirrors, fog, motel blinds, the fuming Vera in profile) serves a distinctly noir overview and sensibility. On the cross-country drive, process shots further distance the already-alienated Al from his surroundings. In the Nevada diner sequences, artificial spotlighting (of Al's twitching eyes) and exaggerated sound underscore Al's agitated mental state. As he surveys the second ''murder'' scene, Al's disorientation is suggested by a roaming camera that, as it picks out Vera's things strewn about the room, keeps going out of focus. Tracking shots down foggy roads give the impression that Al is on a conveyor belt, being dragged, inexorably, to his final destination.

Released by PRC as a routine crime ''meller'' (the tawdry poster contained the come-on ''I Used My Body for Blackmail!''), *Detour*, like many of the great noirs, was championed by France's *Cahiers du Cinéma* critics (who dubbed its director ''le plus maudit des cineaste'' or unjustly cursed) before being discovered by their American counterparts, most notably Andrew Sarris and, in his influential *Notes on Film Noir* (1972), Paul Schrader. Francois Truffaut, writing in 1956, called Ulmer ''the least-known'' of American auteurs and his *The Naked Dawn* (1955) ''a small gift from Hollywood.'' The first observation no longer applies as scholars find references to *Detour* in Hitchcock's *Psycho* and, more recently, the noir-infused works of David Lynch and Ethan and Joel Coen. The second Truffaut comment is more applicable to *Detour*, which, for too long, was an unappreciated gift from 1940s Hollywood.

Ironically, Fate wound up putting the finger on some of those connected with this film. Ulmer, confined to a wheelchair after a series of strokes, didn't live long enough to enjoy *Detour*'s critical reappraisal (he considered it his best film, along with *The Black Cat* and *Naked Dawn*). Widow Shirley Ulmer, in a 1983 interview, said he died a disappointed man. Savage went from low-budget to lowbrow, graduating to such epics as *Renegade Girl* and *Pygmy Island.* Neal fared worse. A hopeless alcoholic with a hair-trigger temper, he was imprisoned in 1965 for the murder of his third wife. Perfect tabloid-fodder, he died destitute in 1972 at age 58. An execrable, almost shot-for-shot video remake of *Detour* appeared in 1992. It was directed by Wade Williams and starred Tom Neal Jr., a dead ringer for his father.

—Glenn Lovell

DEUS E O DIABO NA TERRA DO SOL

(Black God, White Devil)

Brazil, 1964

Director: Glauber Rocha

Production: Copacabana Films (Rio de Janeiro); black and white, 35mm, running time: 125 minutes. Filmed in Monte Santo, Bahia, 1963. Released in Rio de Janeiro, 1 June 1964.

Producer: Luiz Augusto Mendez; **associate producers:** Glauber Rocha, Jarbas Barbosa; **director and screenplay assistant:** Walter Lima, Jr.; **director and dialog assistant:** Paulo Gil Soares; **screenplay:** Glauber Rocha; **photography:** Waldemar Lima; **editor:** Rafael Justo Verde: **art director:** Paulo Gil Soares; **music:** Heitor Villa-Lobos and Sergio Ricard (songs by Glauber Rocha).

Cast: Geraldo Del Rey (*Manuel*); Ioná Magalhães (*Rosa*); Othon Bastos (*Corisco*); Lídio Silva (*Sebastião*); Mauricio do Valle (*Antonio das Mortes*); Sônia dos Humildes (*Dadá*); Marrom (*Blind Julio*); João Gama (*The priest*); Antônio Pinto (*The ''Coronel''*); Milton Rosa (*''Coronel'' Moraes*).

Awards: Prize of the Mexican Critic at the International Festival of Acapulco (México), 1964; Great Prize, Festival of Free Cinema (Italy), 1964; Gold Naiade—International Festival of Porreta Terme (Italy), 1964; Great Prize Latin American, at the International Mar Del Plata Festival (Argentina), 1966.

Publications

Script:

Rocha, Glauber, *Deus e o Diabo na Terra do Sol*, Editora Civilização Brasileira, Rio de Janeiro, Brazil, 1965.

Deus e o Diabo na Terra do Sol

Books:

Rocha, Glauber, *Revisão critica do cinema brasileiro*, Rio de Janeiro, 1963.

Gardier, René, *Glauber Rocha*, Paris, 1974.

Amengual, Barthélemy, *Glauber Rocha e os caminhos da liberdade*, in *Glauber Rocha*, Rio de Janeiro, 1977.

Bernadet, Jean-Claude, *Brasil em tempo de cinema*, Rio de Janeiro, 1977.

Rocha, Glauber, *Revolução do cinema novo*, Rio de Janeiro, 1981.

Torrres, Augusto M., *Glauber Rocha*, Madrid, 1981.

Gerber, Raquel, *O mito da civilização Atlântica: Glauber Rocha, Cinema, Politica e a Estética do Inconsciente*, Rio de Janeiro, 1982.

Rocha, Glabuer, *O século do cinema*, Rio de Janeiro, 1983.

Xavier, Ismail, *Sertão Mar—Glauber Rocha e a Estética da Fome*, São Paulo, Brazil, 1983.

Hollyman, Burnes, *Glauber Rocha and the Cinema Novo in Brazil: A Study of his Critical Writings and Films*, New York, 1983.

Johnson, Randal, *Cinema Novo X5—Masters of Contemporary Brazilian Film*, (Chapter 4: Glauber Rocha: Apocalypse and Resurrection), Austin, Texas, 1984.

Nazário, Luis, *À margem do cinema*, São Paulo, Brazil, 1986.

Pierre, Sylvie, editor, *Glauber Rocha: Textes et Entretiens de Glauber Rocha, Collection ''Auteurs,''* Paris, 1987.

Passek, Jean-Loup, editor, *Le Cinéma Brésilien*, Paris, 1987.

Pierre, Sylvie, *Glauber Rocha*, Paris 1987.

Armes, Roy, *Third World Film-making and the West*, Berkeley, 1987.

Articles:

Variety (New York), 20 May 1964.

Prédal, René, *Jeune Cinéma* (Paris), October 1967.

Gardies, René, ''Terres en transes,'' in *Image et Son* (Paris), December 1967.

Rocha, Glauber, ''Memorias de Dios y el Diablo en las Tierras de Monte Santo y Coco-Robo,'' in *Cine-Cubano* (Havana), 1967.

Levy, J., ''Mythologies: un continent en trois,'' in *Cahiers du Cinéma* (Paris), January 1968.

Zele, Van, *Image et Son* (Paris), no. 233, 1969.

Francovich, Alan, *Film Quarterly* (Berkeley), Winter 1969–70.

Houston, P., *Sight and Sound* (London), Spring 1970.

Dawson, J., *Monthly Film Bulletin* (London), April 1970.

Tarrat, M., *Films and Filming* (London), May 1970.
Williams, B., ''Splintered Perspectives: Counterpoint and Subjectivity in Modernist Film Narrative,'' in *Film Criticism* (Meadville, Pennsylvania), Winter 1991.
Valdes, Zöe, ''El Desear poder Querer,'' in *Cine-Cubano* (Havana), October-November 1992.
Diegues, C., *Positif* (Paris), June 1994.

* * *

''You could say that *Deus e o Diabo na Terra do Sol (Black God, White Devil)* was a film provoked by the impossibility of doing a truly great Western, as, for instance, John Ford could. Equally, there was a trail of inspiration from Eisenstein, from *The General Line*, from *The Battleship Potemkin*, and further ideas from Visconti and Rossellini, from Kurosawa and from Buñuel. *Deus e o Diabo* arose from this tussle between Ford and Eisenstein, from the anarchy of Buñuel, and from the savage strength of the lunacy of surrealism.''

So Glauber Rocha defined the multiple influences which contributed to *Deus e o Diabo* in an April 1981 interview with João Lopes (in the book *Glauber Rocha*, by Sylvie Pierre), four months before his death at the age of 42. Shown at Cannes in 1964, *Deus e o Diabo*, together with Nelson Pereira dos Santos' *Vidas Secas (Barren Lives)*, introduced the international viewing public to the Cinema Novo, an artistic movement which strove, in the name of a political conscience, for a Brazilian identity and ethos. Enthusiastically received at Cannes—Georges Sadoul considered its style ''revolutionary''— *Deus e o Diabo* genuinely lived up to the Cinema Novo's motto: ''an idea in the head and a camera in the hand.'' Glauber Rocha, the Cinema Novo's most controversial figure, was the author of bombastic writings, such as the manifesto ''The Aesthetics of Hunger,'' (presented in Genova in January 1965 during the Reseña del Cine Latinoamericano), in which he stated that ''our originality is our hunger.'' And the concept of hunger—both literally and in reference to a hunger for social justice—is central to *Deus e o Diabo na Terra do Sol.* The film's opening is prosaic enough: Manuel (Geraldo Del Rey), a poor herdsman, married to Rosa (Yoná Magalhães) and living in the dry, barren countryside of Northeastern Brazil in the early 1940s, decides to sell his cows and buy a plot of land. Things go awry when he ends up killing the buyer of his cows. Fleeing his destiny, he embraces the first option in the gospel according to Glauber Rocha: religious fanaticism, embodied by the Negro god, Beato Sebastião (Lídio Silva), a synthesis of the messianic leaders of that time and region. Sebastião promises his flock divine salvation and foretells the day when ''the dry lands will turn into sea and the sea into dry land,'' which is the leitmotif of the film. Glauber Rocha believed that ''the people of the Northeast are truly obsessed by the desire to see the sea, a sea which signifies the broadest sort of liberty.''

As Manuel and Rosa follow the fanatic priest, Antonio das Mortes (Maurício do Valle) enters the scene; he is famous for exterminating cangaceiros, the rural and very violent bandits of the region. Hired to kill Sebastião, Antonio das Mortes is a quasi-mythological figure in his intimidating black cape. His character is further developed in a subsequent film, *O Dragão da Maldade contra o Santo Guerreiro (Antonio das Mortes).* By the time the killer reaches Sebastião, it is too late: the fanatic has already been killed by Rosa in a sacrificial ritual. On the run again, Manuel and Rosa join Corisco (Othon Bastos), the blonde devil. The physical embodiment of bitterness and cruelty, Corisco's ambition is to avenge the death of the legendary cangaceiro Lampião while proffering impassioned speeches in defense of the poor. Antonio das Mortes and Corisco face off in a stylized duel in one of the film's most effective sequences. Corisco is shot and dies screaming ''the power of the people will win out.''

Manuel and Rosa, true representatives of Corisco's ''people,'' flee headlong through the interior, leaving behind them the fanaticism and the violence until the crazy Sebastião's words become true: the dry lands become sea and the sea becomes dry land. Herein lies the utopia of Glauber Rocha. The voice of the blind man is heard explaining the reasons for so much suffering: ''divided up the way it is, the world is wrong. The land belongs to man, not to God nor to the devil.''

In *Deus e o Diabo*, Glauber Rocha's second feature, launched after *Barravento* in 1961, the director created a tragic and convulsive northeastern opera; it is strongly allegorical, with symbols for ''good'' and ''evil'' in constant interaction. Some true-to-life portrayals, such as Manuel and Rosa, contrast with others of a classically theatrical tone, notably Corisco, inspired, according to Rocha, by Brecht. Linking aspects of popular culture with elements of the western, the film is narrated and sung by a blind man, a simplification of the Greek chorus. The outstanding sound track alternates Bach with Villa-Lobos, whose Fifth Bachiana contributes to one of the film's most striking moments: the love scene of Corisco and Rosa, choreographed and rhythmical, an unexpected outpouring of guileless poetry against a desolate backdrop marked by poverty and violence.

A true exponent of the author's cinema style, with the strong political and social concern of the 1960s, Glauber Rocha's restlessness is felt through the impatient use of the hand-held camera, the originality of his framings, and the rhythm of the editing. The use of panoramics, travellings, zooms, and close-ups produces a tense and eloquent narrative, punctuated by philosophical interjections—''fate is greater than we are;'' ''we have nothing to take but our fate,'' and ''man learns nothing in peace, he needs to fight to live and he needs to die to win.''

Thirty years after it was made, *Deus e o Diabo* retains its contesting tone and the revolutionary personality of Glauber Rocha. At the age of 25, with a camera in his hand and a whirlwind of ideas in his head, Glauber Rocha created one of the most important Brazilian films through the undeniable strength, originality, and beauty of this furious fable about good and evil.

—Susana Schild

DEUTSCHLAND IM HERBST

(Germany in Autumn)

West Germany, 1978

Directors: Alf Brustellin, Hans Peter Cloos, R. W. Fassbinder, Alexander Kluge, Maximiliana Mainka, Beate Mainka-Jellinghaus, Edgar Reitz, Katja Rupé, Volker Schlöndorff, Peter Schubert, and Bernhard Sinkel

Production: Project Filmproduktion/Filmverlag der Autoren; color/black and white, 35mm; running time: 116 minutes. Filmed October 1977. Released in West Germany, 17 March 1978.

Deutschland im Herbst

Producers: Project Filmproduktion/Filmverlag der Autoren/ Hallelujah Film/Kairos Film Munich; **screenplay:** Heinrich Böll, Alf Brustellin, Hans Peter Cloos, R. W. Fassbinder, Alexander Kluge, Maximiliane Mainka, Edgar Reitz, Katja Rupé, Volker Schlöndorff, Peter Schubert, Bernhard Sinkel, Peter F. Steinbach; **photography:** Michael Ballhaus, Günter Hörmann, Jürgen Jürges, Bodo Kessler, Dietrich Lohmann, Werner Lüring, Colin Mounier, Jörg Schmidt-Reitwein; **editors:** Alexander Kluge, Beate Mainka-Jellinghaus, Heidi Genée, Mulle Goetz-Dickopp, Juliane Lorenz, Tania Schmidbauer, Christine Warnck.

Cast: Mario Adorf (*TV committee member*); Wolfgang Bächler, Heinz Bennent, Joachim Bissmeier, Joey Buschmann, Caroline Channiolleau, Hans Peter Cloos (*"Foreigner"*); Horst Ehmke, Otto Friebel, Hildegard Friese, Vadim Glowna (*Freiermuth*); Michael Gahr, Helmut Griem (*Mahler's interviewer*); Horatius Häberle, Hannelore Hoger (*Gabi Teichert*); Petra Kiener, Dieter Laser, Lisi Mangold, Enno Patalas (*TV committee member*), Lila Pempeit, Werner Possardt, Franz Priegel, Leon Rainer, Manfred Rommel, Katja Rupé (*Franziska Busch*); Walter Schmidinger, Gerhard Schneider, Corinna Spies, Franziska Walser (*Ismene*); André Wilms, Angela Winkler (*Antigone*); Eric Vilgertshofer, Manfred Zapatka. Appearing as themselves: Wolf Biermann (radical poet/singer/songwriter exiled from DDR in 1977), Rainer Werner Fassbinder, Horst Mahler, and Armin Meier.

Awards: Film Strip in Gold for Outstanding Individual Achievement: Film Conception (for the entire film team), German Film Awards, 1978.

Publications

Books:

Elsaesser, Thomas, *New German Cinema: A History*, New Brunswick, New Jersey, 1989.

Kaes, Anton, *From Hitler to Heimat: The Return of History as Film*, Princeton, New Jersey, 1989.

Corrigan, Timothy, *New German Cinema: The Displaced Image*, Bloomington, Indiana, 1994.

Elsaesser, Thomas, *Fassbinder's Germany: History, Identity, Subject*, Amsterdam, 1996.

Articles:

Hansen, Miriam, ''Cooperative Auteur Cinema and Oppositional Public Sphere,'' in *New German Critique*, no. 24–25, Fall/Winter, 1981–82.

Silberman, Marc, ''Introduction to *Germany in Autumn*,'' in *Discourse*, no. 6, 1983.

Lacoue-Labarthe, Philippe, Rainer Werner Fassbinder, Jurgen Habermas, and Heiner Muller, ''Germany in Autumn,'' in *Documenta X: The Book: Politics Poetics*, edited by Catherine David and Jean-Francois Chevrier, Ostfildern, Germany1997.

* * *

Germany in Autumn is a politically engaged combination of documentary, media footage, and fictional and autobiographical episodes that covers the emotional gamut from concern, to irony, to despair. A landmark film for the New German Cinema, this collaborative effort between nine acclaimed directors and several prominent writers, songwriters, and poets protests the political oppression of West Germany in the late 1970s. The film's nine vignettes document the rise of urban terrorism, police militancy, and the resurgence of fascist tendencies in postwar Germany.

In the fall of 1977, Germany was almost a nation under siege by its own police, security, and military forces. The headlines told of a plane hijacking and the kidnapping and subsequent murder of German industrialist Hans-Martin Schleyer. Schleyer's kidnappers, the Baader-Meinhof group, were a left-wing terrorist offshoot of the notorious Red Army Faction (RAF). Schleyer had been kidnapped in an effort to negotiate the release of the RAF's most prominent members, Andreas Baader, Gudrun Enslin, and Karl Raspe, who had been imprisoned for terrorist acts. After the failed kidnapping effort resulted in Schleyer's murder, the leaders of the RAF were found dead in Stammheim, a maximum security federal prison. The suspicious circumstances of their deaths led many to conclude that they were murdered by the state, although officials declared and still maintain otherwise. In any case, the treatment of the Baader-Meinhof group confirmed the fears of the political left that the state was willing to use extreme violence to silence its critics.

With these events as its historical backdrop, the film takes on three urgent tasks for the postwar generation: a protest against censorship and political repression; a confrontation with the persistence of fascism reflected in current events; and facing their parents' lack of accountability for the Nazi period. The films sections address these issues from various perspectives and diverse styles, and are marked by the signature styles of their directors. One sees the overall influence of Alexander Kluge, who together with Beate Mainka-Jellinghaus edited the nine hours of material into a 134 minute film.

According to Kluge—social theorist, filmmaker, author, and one of the most prominent directors of New German Cinema—the contradictions in the film ''belong to one nation: only if the contradictions are together, can one accept this history and understand it.'' Although there is no real plot, the footage is sequenced around various themes: the role of the media and the importance of debate in the public sphere, confronting the Nazi past, and the necessity to resist police brutality. At a time of official government news blackout, this acclaimed team of filmmakers offered a counter-history, an unofficial response to the official absence of reportage. The experimental montage of short fictionalized pieces even mimics the look of television, with its collection of interviews, documentary, fiction, and autobiographical pieces.

Several of the film's sections explicitly address the theme of state and media censorship and the lack of open debate. Other sections illustrate the political power wielded by those who control the media. The section by Schlöndorf and Heinrich Böll offers an ironic sketch of a contrived meeting of TV officials who ban the dramatic production of Sophocle's *Antigone.* The classic drama's portrayal of siblings in defiance of the state is seen as advocating a pro-terrorist view too analogous to recent events. This segment's satirical yet pointed testament to the political power of the media demands a public sphere in which debate is encouraged and allowed.

On a thematic level, several sections of *Germany in Autumn* addressed Germany's difficult recent history and the burden of the historical memory of the Third Reich. Kluge based his critically acclaimed feature film *The Patriot* on his short section about Gabi Teichert, a high school teacher intent on (literally) digging up Germany's past with a hand spade; in this film, however, the past is not about the extermination of the European Jews in Europe, but about the losses and deprivation of the immediate postwar period; that is, it is about German suffering.

Fassbinder's 24 minute episode, the most personal and emotionally charged of the sections, also addresses the weight of the past but from a different perspective: he confronts the effects of the generational conflict between parents and children. In a staged but highly convincing and seemingly realistic interview with his mother, he elicits the statement from her that what Germany needs today is another ''benevolent dictator.'' Interspersed with this interview, spectators witness the historical transmission of violence on a domestic, private level. Fassbinder alternately abuses, rejects, caresses, and rants with his lover in a dark claustrophobic apartment filled with booze, drugs, and misery. The message seems to be that history is accountable for interpersonal problems as well as political and governmental ones.

Germany in Autumn is also about collective mourning. Funeral scenes frame the various episodes; indeed, the opening and closing of the film documents the funeral of Hans Martin Schleyer as well as the burial of the Red Army leaders. Lastly, the film explores the fine line between patriotism and nationalism. The film uses the national anthem as an ironic leitmotif, underlining the filmmaker's distrust of the government as a result of police brutality directed at so-called leftist sympathizers. The rich texture of the images and the densely layered scenes of *Germany in Autumn* skillfully merge the terrorism of the present with the fascist totalitarianism of the past. The film remains both an artistic achievement and a statement of the political efficacy of film-making.

—Jill Gillespie

DEVIL IN THE FLESH

See **LE DIABLE AU CORPS**

THE DEVIL IS A WOMAN

USA, 1935

Director: Josef von Sternberg

Production: Paramount Pictures; black and white, 35mm; running time: 80 minutes, some sources list 82 minutes. Released 1935. Filmed in Paramount studios.

Screenplay: Josef von Sternberg, adapted by John Dos Passos and S. K. Winston, from the novel *The Woman and the Puppet* by Pierre Louys; **photography:** Josef von Sternberg and Lucien Ballard; **production designer:** Hans Dreier; **music and lyrics:** Ralph Rainger and Leo Robin.

Cast: Marlene Dietrich (*Concha Perez*); Cesar Romero (*Antonio Galvan*); Lionel Atwill (*Don Pasqual*); Edward Everett Horton (*Don Paquito*); Alison Skipworth (*Señora Perez*); Don Alvarado (*Morenito*); Morgan Wallace (*Dr. Mendez*); Tempe Pigott (*Tuerta*); Jil Dennett (*Maria*); Lawrence Grant (*Conductor*).

Publications

Books:

Harrington, Curtis, *An Index to the Films of Josef von Sternberg*, London, 1949.

Griffith, Richard, *Marlene Dietrich—Image and Legend*, New York, 1959.

Von Sternberg, Josef, *Fun in a Chinese Laundry*, New York, 1965.

Sarris, Andrew, *The Films of Josef von Sternberg*, New York, 1966.

Josef von Sternberg: Dokumentation: Eine Darstellung, Mannheim, 1966.

Weinberg, Herman G., *Josef von Sternberg*, Paris, 1966; as *Josef von Sternberg: A Critical Study*, New York, 1967.

Kobal, John, *Marlene Dietrich*, New York, 1968.

Dickens, Homer, *The Films of Marlene Dietrich*, New York, 1968.

Baxter, John, *The Cinema of Josef von Sternberg*, New York, 1971.

Silver, Charles, *Marlene Dietrich*, New York, 1974.

Morley, Sheridan, *Marlene Dietrich*, London, 1976.

Higham, Charles, *Marlene: The Life of Marlene Dietrich*, New York, 1977.

Mérigeau, Pascal, *Josef von Sternberg*, Paris, 1983.

Navacelle, Thierry de, *Sublime Marlene*, London, 1984.

Seydel, Renate, *Marlene Dietrich: Eine Chronik ihres Lebens in Bilden und Dokumenten*, East Berlin, 1984.

Walker, Alexander, *Dietrich*, London, 1984.

Spoto, Donald, *Falling in Love Again: Marlene Dietrich*, Boston, 1985.

Wilson, George M., *''Narration in Light'': Studies in Cinematic Point-of-View*, Baltimore, 1986.

Zucker, Carole, *The Idea of the Image: Josef von Sternberg's Dietrich Films*, Rutherford, 1988.

Dietrich, Marlene, *Ich bin, Gott sei dank, Berlinerin*, Frankfurt, 1987; as *My Life*, London, 1989.

Bowman, Barbara, *Master Space: Film Images of Capra, Lubitsch, Sternberg, and Wyler*, New York, 1992.

Baxter, Peter, *Just Watch!: Sternberg, Paramount and America*, London, 1993.

Bogdanovich, Peter, *Who the Devil Made It*, New York, 1997.

Articles:

New York Times, 4 May 1935.

Variety (New York), 8 May 1935.

''Creative Film Director,'' in *Cue* (New York), 14 December 1935.

Dekobra, Maurice, ''Comment Marlene Dietrich est devenue star,'' in *Cinémonde* (Paris), 16 April 1939.

Knight, Arthur, ''Marlene Dietrich,'' in *Films in Review* (New York), December 1954.

Weinberg, Herman G., ''The Lost Films: Part 1,'' in *Sight and Sound* (London), August 1962.

Weinberg, Herman G., ''Josef von Sternberg,'' in *Film Heritage* (Dayton, Ohio), Winter 1965.

Green, O. O., ''Six Films of Josef von Sternberg,'' in *Movie* (London), Summer 1965.

Higham, Charles, ''Dietrich in Sydney,'' in *Sight and Sound* (London), Winter 1965–66.

Eisenschitz, Bernard, ''L'Oeuvre de Josef von Sternberg,'' in *Avant-Scène du Cinéma* (Paris), March 1966.

Positif (Paris), May 1966.

Bowser, Ellen, and Richard Griffith, in *Film Notes*, edited by Bowser, New York, 1969.

Martineau, Barbara, ''Thoughts on the Objectification of Women,'' in *Take One* (Montreal), November-December 1970.

Flinn, Tom, ''Joe, Where Are You?'' in *Velvet Light Trap* (Madison, Wisconsin), Fall 1972.

Rheuban, Joyce, ''Josef von Sternberg: The Scientist and the Vamp,'' in *Sight and Sound* (London), Autumn 1973.

Magny, Joel, in *Téléciné* (Paris), November 1976.

Baxter, P., ''On the Naked Thighs of Miss Dietrich,'' in *Wide Angle* (Baltimore), vol. 2, no. 2, 1978.

Combs, Richard, in *Monthly Film Bulletin* (London), May 1978.

Tessier, Max, in *Revue du Cinéma* (Paris), July-August 1985.

Thomas, François, in *Positif* (Paris), January 1986.

Listener (London), 7 January 1988.

Jenkinson, P., ''Sternberg's Last Interview,'' in *Film Culture* (New York), June 1992.

Koch, Gertrude, and M. Gerber, ''Dietrich's Destiny: Strike a Pose,'' in *Sight & Sound* (London), September 1992.

Morgan, M., ''Sternberg & Dietrich Revisited,'' in *Bright Lights* (Cincinnati), July 1993.

* * *

The Devil Is a Woman is the final film starring Marlene Dietrich made by director Josef von Sternberg. The identifying characteristics of the von Sternberg/Dietrich collaboration, including the ambiguity, often difficult for viewers to accept, are evident here. *The Devil Is a Woman* is a perfect culmination to an enigmatic relationship and a breathtaking series of visually stunning films.

Based on Pierre Louys's novel, *The Woman and the Puppet*, the film is a quintessential example of the von Sternberg filmed universe. To follow the story is to travel through a narrative labyrinth, following the many changes of mood, mind, character and costume of the central character, Concha (Dietrich), the devilish woman of the title.

The Devil Is a Woman

The contradictory Concha is all surface and no depth, a beautiful, fickle, unpredictable woman, or at least that is how she is presented as Don Pasqual (Lionel Atwill) tells Antonio (Cesar Romero) about her. Concha exists at the center of the film, and von Sternberg favors the audience with as few fulfilled expectations and explanations as she has favored her lovers. At the end, Concha (through von Sternberg) has demonstrated the same cruel control over viewers as she has over her lovers, leaving an audience with nothing to grasp, much less to embrace or understand.

The Devil Is a Woman defines the von Sternberg approach to cinema, which is unique. As a film artist, he defies the conceptions most have about what film is or what it can or should do. He seldom develops a logical narrative pattern, with ordinary character motivations. On the contrary, a von Sternberg character frequently makes an abrupt shift that, in literary terms, is unexpected and unjustified. ''I changed my mind,'' Concha offers as an explanation when she turns back across the border to rejoin her rejected former lover. This arbitrary change of mind is the essence of the von Sternberg film, which forces viewers to realize that the act of seeing is itself the truest meaning of the film. By removing conventional forms of dramatic tension, character development and plot motivation, he asks viewers to accept the things that usually supplement a film story as if they were the story themselves. In never fully explaining Concha, he seduces viewers into observing her more and more closely.

The Devil Is a Woman presents an illusionary world, filled with irony, mockery, androgyny, and a certain amount of implied decadence. As is true of all his films with Dietrich, it is somewhat of a von Sternberg autobiography, with Atwill, a von Sternberg look-alike, playing the character who is toyed with by Concha. The relationship of these two characters is a complicated interplay of master and victim, puppet and manipulator, with no clear indication of which is truly the master and which the puppet.

With *The Devil Is a Woman*, von Sternberg worked against the tradition of Hollywood in the 1930s, in that he reduced narrative tension to a state in which very little seemed to be happening. ''The best source for a story,'' he said, ''is an anecdote.'' Although *The Devil Is a Woman* is based on a famous novel, von Sternberg liked trivial plots, and never took up great social or political themes. This led to an inevitable rejection of von Sternberg by both critics and audiences, and *The Devil Is a Woman* was a failure. Seen today, it is a stunning example of pictorial beauty. The use of light and shadow in intricate interplay, the long takes connected by luxuriously slow dissolves, the ironic music, the elegant compositions, and the complicated, layered images make it the work of a major visual artist.

—Jeanine Basinger

LE DIABLE AU CORPS

(Devil in the Flesh)

France, 1947

Director: Claude Autant-Lara

Production: Transcontinental Films; black and white, 35mm; running time: 110 minutes. Released 1947.

Screenplay: Jean Aurenche and Pierre Bost, from a novel by Raymond Radiguet; **photography:** Michel Kelber; **editor:** Madeleine Gug; **production designer:** Max Douy; **music:** René Cloërec.

Cast: Gérard Philipe (*François*); Micheline Presle (*Marthe*); Denise Grey; Jean Debucourt.

Le diable au corps

Publications

Script:

Autant-Lara, Claude, *Le diable au corps*, Paris, 1984.

Books:

Philipe, Anne, and Claude Roy, *Gérard Philipe: Souvenirs et temoignages*, Paris, 1960; revised edition, 1977.
Sadoul, Georges, *Gérard Philipe*, Paris, 1967; revised edition, 1979.
Perisset, Maurice, *Gérard Philipe*, Paris, 1975.
Armes, Roy, *French Cinema Since 1946, Volume 1: The Great Tradition*, New York, 1976.
Cadars, Pierre, *Gérard Philipe*, Paris, 1984.
Autant-Lara, Claude, *Le bateau coule: discours de réception à l'Académie des beaux-arts*, Paris, 1989.

Articles:

Jeanne, Rene, and Charles Ford, ''Styles du cinéma français,'' in *La Livre d'or du cinéma français 1947–48*, Paris, 1948.
Philipe, Gérard, ''In the Margin,'' in *Sequence* (London), Spring 1949.
Billard, Ginette, ''Gérard Philipe,'' in *Films and Filming* (London), October 1955.
Durgnat, Raymond, ''The Rebel with Kid Gloves,'' in *Films and Filming* (London), October and November 1960.
Autant-Lara, Claude, ''Comment j'ai pu realiser *Le diable au corps*,'' in *Ikon* (Milan), January-March 1972.
Autant-Lara, Claude, ''La Chasse aux escargots,'' in *Cahiers de la Cinémathèque* (Perpignan), Spring 1973.
Oms, Marcel, ''La Parole est à Claude Autant-Lara'' (interview), in *Cahiers de la Cinémathèque* (Perpignan), Summer 1973.
Dazat, O., ''Lecons de morale,'' in *Cinematographe* (Paris), June 1986.
Oms, M., in *Nosferatu* (San Sebastian), no. 10, October 1992.
Jeune Cinéma (Paris), January/February 1997.

* * *

Le diable au corps was certainly *the* French film of 1947. Winner of several European awards, the film was also banned in communities across the Continent. While a proud tribute to the French literary tradition, it posed as the most avant-garde example of postwar cinema in that country.

There is no paradox here, for the aesthetic ideology of the ''cinema of quality,'' of which this film serves as an outstanding example, openly mixes an interest in iconoclastic subject matter, high art tradition, and a refined studio treatment. Aurenche and Bost's careful reworking of a youthful and rebellious novel points up its key social and psychological oppositions. Claude Autant-Lara was then able to put these oppositions into play through the psychological realism of his handling of actors, and through the narrational commentary wrung out of decor, music, and cinematic figures.

Their grim intelligence and determined passion made Gérard Philipe and Micheline Presle an instantly legendary couple; he as a precocious teenage malcontent, son of an upright bourgeois, she the older woman whose husband is off at the front in World War I. Autant-Lara evinces sympathy for their questionable moral position by rendering the action through a series of flashbacks from the boy's point of view. The war is over and the town celebrates the return of its veterans, but he must hide in the room of their forbidden love and go through the anguish of recalling that love. This flashback structure, together with the doomed love of the couple, reminded critics of *Le jour se lève*, and made the public see Gérard Philipe as the heir of Jean Gabin. But the limpid expressiveness of the prewar realism had been complicated after the war. Philipe's gestures were calculated to display his passion and anguish, whereas Gabin had moved and spoken instinctively, without the hesitation of either good taste or intelligence, hallmarks of the postwar style. The same holds true for the direction. While Carné and Prévert had devised a number of highly charged objects, Autant-Lara multiplies effects wherever he can. The incessant play of reflections in mirrors and by the ferry insists on the significance of the drama, but does so from the outside. Similarly the famous 360-degree camera movement that circles the bed of the couple's lovemaking demands to be noticed as a figure supplied by an external narrator, especially since it begins on a crackling fire and ends on dying embers. This is more than a metaphor for passion, it is a poetic display that lifts an ordinary drama into telling significance.

Altogether *Le diable au corps* stuns its audience with the cockiness of its presentation as well as with the audacity of its subject matter. This is its conquest as well as its loss; for in only a few years the New Wave critics, led by Truffaut, would clamor for the downfall of psychological realism and of the paternalistic, elitist narration that preaches a liberal morality. If Radiguet, the novelist, likewise condemned a suffocating society, he did so from within, from the perceptions and language of his hero. Autant-Lara has used Radiguet's rebelliousness, has packaged it approvingly, but has made of it a mature, stylish film. Radiguet, legend has it, put everything of himself into this novel and then died. The movie pays tribute to his effort and his views, but is just another very good movie.

—Dudley Andrew

LES DIABOLIQUES

France, 1954

Director: Henri-Georges Clouzot

Production: Filmsonor (Paris); black and white, 35mm; running time: 110 minutes. Released 1954. Filmed in France.

Producer: Louis de Masure; **screenplay:** Henri-Georges Clouzot, Jérôme Géronimi, René Masson, and Frédéric Grendel, from the novel *Celle qui n'était plus* by Boileau and Narcejac; **photography:** Armand Thirard; **editor:** Madeleine Gug; **sound:** William-Robert Sivel; **production designer:** Léon Barsacq; **music:** Georges van Parys.

Cast: Simone Signoret (*Nicole*); Véra Clouzot (*Christina*); Paul Meurisse (*Michel*); Charles Vanel (*Fichet*); Jean Brochard (*Plantiveau*); Noël Roquevert (*M. Herboux*); Georges Chamarat (*Dr. Loisy*); Jacques Varennes (*Professor Bridoux*); Michel Serrault (*M. Raymond*).

Awards: Prix Louis Delluc (France), 1955; New York Film Critics Award for Best Foreign Film (shared with *Umberto D*), 1955.

Publications

Books:

Lacassin, Francis, and others, *Le Procès Clouzot*, Paris, 1964.
Pilard, Philippe, *H. G. Clouzot*, Paris, 1969.
Armes, Roy, *French Cinema Since 1946, Volume 1: The Great Tradition*, New York, 1976.
Sandre, Didier, *Simone Signoret*, Paris, 1981.
Bocquet, José-Louis, *Henri-Georges Clouzot cinéaste*, with Marc Godin, Sèvres, 1993.
David, Catherine, *Simone Signoret*, New York, 1995.

Articles:

Brunelin, Andre G., in *Cinéma* (Paris), November 1954.
Brulé, Claude, "Clouzot est-il vraiment diable?" in *Ciné-Revue* (Paris), 1955.
New York Times, 22 November 1955.
"Frenchman's Horror," in *Newsweek* (New York), 28 November 1955.
Goulder, Stanley, "The Necrophilist," in *Films and Filming* (London), December 1955.
Tennant, Sylvia, "Henri-Georges Clouzot," in *Film* (London), March-April 1956.
Forestier, J., and G. P. Richer, "H. G. Clouzot, L'homme diabolique du cinéma français," in *Lettres Françaises* (Paris), July 1960.
Schrader, Paul, "An Interview with Henri-Georges Clouzot," in *Cinema* (Beverly Hills), no. 4, 1969.
Lacourbe, Roland, "Henri-Georges Clouzot," in *Anthologie du cinéma 10*, Paris, 1979.
Devillers, M., in *Cinématographe* (Paris), March 1984.
Pulleine, Tim, in *Films and Filming* (London), December 1985.
Brown, G., "Suspicion," in *Village Voice* (New York), 25 October 1994.
Herpe, Noël, "Les films criminels de Clouzot," in *Positif* (Paris), January 1996.
Hottell, Ruth A., "The Diabolic Dialogic," in *Literature/Film Quarterly* (Salisbury), vol. 24, no. 3, 1996.
"Special Issue," *Avant-Scène du Cinéma* (Paris), June 1997.

* * *

Henri-Georges Clouzot is a key member of the generation of filmmakers who emerged during the Occupation and dominated

French cinema for a dozen years or so after the war. *Les diaboliques* is not a masterpiece to rank with such earlier Clouzot films as *Le corbeau* or *Le salaire de la peur*, but its particular contradictions allow the principal aspects of what was later to be dubbed the ''tradition of quality'' to be clearly observed.

The political events of these years—the war in Indo-China leading to the fall of Dien Bien Phu, and the beginning of the Algerian revolution which was to lead to eight years of savage fighting and eventually bring down the Fourth Republic—are ignored, and Clouzot, like so many of his contemporaries, offers a studio reconstruction of the world which is meticulously realist in detail, but essentially timeless. *Les diaboliques* is set in one of Clouzot's favorite locations—a shabby, rundown provincial school—and the tensions here between a bullying headmaster, his ailing wife and forceful mistress are methodically set up. The craftsmanship involved in the creation of this world is enormous, and nothing is allowed to stand between the director and his conception of his film. Before 1939 actors had been the *monstres sacrés* of French cinema and every aspect of a film was subordinate to their will. But Clouzot was from the first renowned for the harsh treatment he meted out to his actors. If the story that he served bad fish to the actors in *Les diaboliques* and made them eat it so as to capture an authentic sense of disgust is probably apocryphal, it certainly conveys perfectly his essential attitude.

The 1940s and early 1950s was also a time of the totally scripted film in which the diversity and contradictions of life were reduced to a single narrative line relentlessly followed. Though there might be a rich counterpoint of incident as well as the creation of multiple ironies, there was no space for gaps within the plot which would unfold with all the precision of a watch mechanism. In works like *Le corbeau* and *Quai des Orfèvres*, Clouzot had shown himself to be a master of the thriller structure, with all the subtle manipulation of audience responses which that implies. But as so often in other aspects of his work, Clouzot seems to have been driven by a desire to take the creation of suspense to extreme limits. For him, as for his contemporary, Alfred Hitchcock, whom he much admired, there could be no half measures. In *Les diaboliques* Clouzot is tempted into a display of his own narrative skills, and the logic of the film, which has plotted its first murder with brutal precision, is slowly taken apart. Inexplicable things start to happen, and the spectator's confidence in his own perceptions, in the truth of what he has seen and heard, is undermined. The contradictions are resolved in a virtuoso passage of plot twisting in the final reel, but this very ingenuity destroys the psychological realism on which the film's opening is constructed. *Les diaboliques* is exhilarating at first viewing, and proved to be both commercially successful and controversial on its first release. For most critics, however, the contrivance of the ending renders a second viewing meaningless, since it underlines the film's remoteness from a livid reality and even makes Clouzot's deeply felt black vision seem trite and superficial.

—Roy Armes

DIARY OF A COUNTRY PRIEST

See **JOURNAL D'UN CURE DE CAMPAGNE**

DIARY OF A LOST GIRL

See **TAGEBUCH EINER VERELORENEN**

DIE LEGENDE VON SÜNDE UND STRAFE

See **SODOM UND GOMORRHA**

DIRTY HARRY

USA, 1971

Director: Don Siegel

Production: Warner Bros., Malpaso; Technicolor, Panavision; running time: 101 minutes. Released December 1971.

Executive producer: Robert Daley; **producer:** Don Siegel; **screenplay:** Harry Julian Fink, Rita M. Fink, Dean Riesner; **assistant director:** Robert Rubin; **photography:** Bruce Surtees; **editor:** Carl Pingitore; **sound:** William Randall; **art director:** Dale Hennesy; **music:** Lalo Schifrin.

Cast: Clint Eastwood (*Harry Callahan*); Harry Guardino (*Lt. Bressler*); Reni Santoni (*Chico*); John Vernon (*The Mayor*); Andy Robinson (*Killer*); John Larch (*Chief*); John Mitchum (*De Georgio*); Mae Mercer (*Mrs. Russell*); Lyn Edgington (*Norma*); Ruth Kobart (*Bus Driver*); Woodrow Parfey (*Mr. Jaffe*); Josef Sommer (*Rothko*); William Paterson (*Bannerman*); James Nolan (*Liquor Proprietor*); Maurice S.; Argent (*Sid Kleinman*); Jo de Winter (*Miss Willis*); Craig G. Kelly (*Sgt. Reineke).*

Publications

Books:

Kaminsky, Stuart M., *Don Siegel: Director*, New York, 1974.
Douglas, Peter, *Clint Eastwood: Movin' On*, Chicago, 1974.
Kaminsky, Stuart M., *Clint Eastwood*, New York, 1974.
Agan, Patrick, *Clint Eastwood: The Man behind the Mask*, New York, 1975.
Downing, David, *Clint Eastwood, All-American Anti-Hero: A Critical Appraisal of the World's Top Box-Office Star and His Films*, London, 1977.
Lovell, Alan, *Don Siegel: American Cinema*, New York, 1977.
Ferrari, Philippe, *Clint Eastwood*, Paris, 1980.
Smijewsky, Boris, *The Films of Clint Eastwood*, Secaucus, New Jersey, 1982.

Dirty Harry

Kapsis, Robert E., *Clint Eastwood: Interviews*, Jackson, 1999.
Schickel, Richard, *Clint Eastwood: A Biography*, New York, 1999.

Articles:

Variety (New York), 22 December 1971.
Milne, Tom, in *Sight and Sound* (London), Spring 1972.
Velvet Light Trap (Madison, Wisconsin), Spring 1972.
Combs, Richard, in *Monthly Film Bulletin* (London), May 1972.
Films and Filming (London), June 1972.
Shadoian, J., ''Dirty Harry: A Defense,'' in *Western Humanities Review* (Salt Lake City), Spring 1974.
Friedman, Bruce Jay, ''Could Dirty Harry Take Rooster Cogburn?'' in *Esquire* (New York), September 1976.
Velvet Light Trap (Madison, Wisconsin), Fall 1976.
Bell, Philip, in *Australian Journal of Screen Theory* (Kensington, New South Wales), no. 5–6, 1979.
Alpert, Robert, ''Clint Eastwood Plays Dumb Cop,'' in *Jump Cut* (Berkeley), May 1979.
Listener (London), 14 February 1985.
Fenwick, H., ''Dirty Harry Comes Clean,'' in *Radio Times* (London), 26 November 1988.
Sarris, Andrew, ''Don Siegel: the Pro,'' in *Film Comment* (New York), vol. 27, no. 5, September-October 1991.
Hampton, H., ''Sympathy for the Devil: In the Cinematic Sniper's Nest,'' in *Film Comment* (New York), November-December 1993.
Grenier, Richard, ''Clint Eastwood Goes PC (Politically Correct) Movies,'' in *Commentary*, vol. 97, no. 3, March 1994.
Duncan, Andrew, '''If People Really Found Out About Me They'd Be Disappointed',' in *Radio Times* (London), 9 September 1995.
Persellin, K., ''Ariadne's Thread,'' in *Spectator* (Los Angeles), no. 2, 1995.
Rabinowitz, Paula, ''Screen Memories,'' in *Wide Angle* (Baltimore), October 1996.

* * *

''I know what you're thinking,'' says Harry Callahan, Inspector 71 of the San Francisco police, to the bank robber he's just shot. ''Did he fire six shots or only five? Well, to tell the truth, in all this excitement I kinda lost track myself. But being this is a .44 magnum, the most powerful handgun in the world, and would blow your head clean off, you've got to ask yourself one question. 'Do I feel lucky?''' The humourless smile widens. ''Well, do you, punk?''

For many, this speech is the most memorable thing about *Dirty Harry*. But while the film seems destined to be Siegel's masterpiece, it would be an error to confuse Callahan's challenge with the director's own ethic. A gibe in *The Line Up* (1958) is closer to his concerns. ''Ordinary people of your class,'' says the killer Dancer, ''you don't understand the criminal's need for violence.''

What Siegel illustrates in his work is the implicit contract that exists between criminals and society. We need criminals to act out our own fantasies of violence. Siegel finds proof of this symbiosis in our legal system, an imperfect tool which we ourselves sabotage. His films mock its structures. The police force of *Madigan* is corrupt. *Riot in Cell Block 11* and *Escape from Alcatraz* attack the prison system. *Coogan's Bluff*, like *Dirty Harry*, parodies sociology, legal procedure, and especially the concept of rehabilitation.

Siegel's special subject is killers, whichever side of the law they may work on. But his murderers and vigilantes are creatures of the imagination. In them, he encourages us to see mirrored our own urges for violence and anarchy. When they die, it is, in effect, for our sins.

By contrast with most real-life murderers, who usually kill loved ones in the heat of passion, Siegel's murderers are loners, conscienceless and mad. They kill for profit, as a profession, or for fun. Andy Robinson's Scorpio in *Dirty Harry* is his most malevolent creation, leering, anonymous, malign. We'd assume his weaponry had its genesis in Vietnam were it not for his twisted peace symbol belt buckle: evil has no pedigree, just as Scorpio has no biography.

Scorpio preys on innocence; a girl swimming in a penthouse pool, a 10-year-old boy, a teenager he rapes and buries alive. Other targets are a priest, an exaggeratedly effeminate homosexual, a much-robbed liquor store owner, and finally a bus filled with schoolchildren. All that stands between Scorpio and these, the helpless, is Harry Callahan—''Dirty'' Harry, because he draws every dirty job, but equally dirty because he does not flinch from violence in doing them.

Harry's methods are endorsed when he tracks the wounded killer to a football stadium. Ignoring gibbering appeals for a lawyer and a doctor, he grinds a heel into the bleeding leg until Scorpio reveals the location of the buried girl. Bruce Surtees's camera pulls back in a vertiginous helicopter shot, losing hunter and prey in night-time mist and the glare of the floodlights. This nightmare image dissolves into a blue dawn above the Golden Gate bridge as a nude corpse is hauled out of her grave and carried away. Birdsong shows nature indifferent to her death, as is the sleeping city. Only Callahan cares.

Harry has flouted every legal procedure, so the murderer goes free, and hijacks a school bus. Taking justice into his own hands, Callahan kills Scorpio, and, as the body sinks into a sump like a slaughtered horror movie monster, flings his police badge after it.

Thus *Dirty Harry's* first and last images are of this badge. The film opens on a marble honour roll of dead cops. A gold inspector's star, superimposed over a list of the dead, dissolves into the silenced barrel of Scorpio's rifle, fair warning of a significant visual subtext.

Neutral behind dark glasses, Callahan initially appears almost disdainful of his duty. Over the credits, he climbs a building to find the place where Scorpio shot from, the first of many ascents in the film. From that moment, he appears in charge of the city, its avenging angel—a role for which the satanic Scorpio challenges him. (The first word heard in the film is Callahan's expletive when he finds Scorpio's extortion note—''Jesus.'') The film thereafter is filled with Christian imagery. The square where Scorpio sets up his second killing is dominated by a church, and Callahan stakes it out from a rooftop where a revolving neon sign announces ''Jesus Saves.'' For the payoff of the ransom, Scorpio chooses a hilltop park dominated by a gigantic cross.

Critics, especially *The New Yorker*'s Pauline Kael, thought *Dirty Harry* fascistic. Others blamed it for the *Death Wish/Walking Tall* vigilante films which followed, ignoring the fact that, without exception, they lacked *Dirty Harry's* moral and psychological dimensions. To classify Harry Callahan as just another right-wing hard-hat was to miss the point of the film as surely as those who call him ''Dirty'' Harry miss the irony of his nickname. Given the spread of urban violence and the resulting change in public opinion in favour of law and order, vigilantes, gun control, and the death penalty, it must be acknowledged that, while they did not create the New York, Washington and Los Angeles of the 1980s, Siegel and his writers anticipated them with a special prescience.

—John Baxter

THE DISCREET CHARM OF THE BOURGEOISIE

See **LE CHARME DISCRET DE LA BOURGEOISIE**

DISTANT VOICES, STILL LIVES

UK, 1988

Director: Terence Davies

Production: British Film Institute, in association with Channel 4/ZDF; Metrocolor; running time: 84 minutes. Released 1988.

Producer: Jennifer Howarth; **screenplay:** Terence Davies; **assistant directors:** Andy Powell, Glyn Purcell, Marc Munden, Matthew Evans; **photography:** William Diver, Patrick Duval; **camera operator:** Harriet Cox; **editor:** William Diver; **collaborative editors:** Geraldine Creed, Toby Benton; **sound editor:** Alex Mackie; **sound recordists:** Moya Burns, Colin Nicolson; **sound re-recordists:** Aad Wirtz, Ian Turner; **art directors:** Miki van Zwanenberg, Jocelyn James; **stunt coordinator:** Alf Joint.

Cast: Freda Dowie (*Mother*); Pete Postlethwaite (*Father*); Angela Walsh (*Eileen*); Dean Williams (*Tony*); Lorraine Ashbourne (*Maisie*); Sally Davies (*Eileen as a child*); Nathan Walsh (*Tony as a child*); Susan Flanagan (*Maisie as a child*); Michael Starke (*Dave*); Vincent Maguire (*George*); Antonia Mallen (*Rose*); Debi Jones (*Micky*); Chris Darwin (*Red*); Marie Jelliman (*Jingles*); Andrew Schofield (*Les*); Anny Dyson (*Granny*); Jean Boht (*Aunty Nell*); Alan Bird (*Baptismal Priest*); Pauline Quirke (*Doreen*); Matthew Long (*Mr. Spaull*); Frances Dell (*Margie*); Carl Chase (*Uncle Ted*); Roy Ford (*Wedding Priest*).

Distant Voices, Still Lives

Awards: International Critics Prize, Cannes Film Festival, 1988.

Publications

Books:

Friedman, Lester, editor, *Fires Were Started: British Cinema and Thatcherism*, Minneapolis, 1993.

Winston, Wheeler, editor, *Re-viewing British Cinema, 1900–1902: Essays and Interviews*, Albany, 1994.

Articles:

Stills (London), November 1985.

Wyeth, P., ''Voices from the Past,'' in *Stills* (London), March 1986.

Wilson, David, in *Sight and Sound* (London), Autumn 1988.

Film Comment (New York), September-October 1988.

Barker, Adam, in *Monthly Film Bulletin* (London), October 1988.

Floyd, Nigel, ''A Pebble in the Pool and Ships like Magic,'' in *Monthly Film Bulletin* (London), October 1988.

Interview with Terence Davies in *Time Out* (London), 5 October 1988.

Interview with Terence Davies in *City Limits* (London), 13 October 1988.

Listener (London), 13 October 1988.

''Valladolid,'' in *Film* (London), December 1988.

In *Film & Kino* (Oslo), no. 4A, 1989.

Lochen, K., ''Stemmer fra fortiden,'' in *Film & Kino* (Oslo), no. 5, 1989.

Cargin, P., ''Diver on *Distant Voices*,'' in *Film* (London), January 1989.

Carr, Jay, ''Davies' Dark Pool of Memories,'' in *Boston Globe*, 13 August 1989.

Billson, A., ''The Long and Short of It,'' in *Village Voice* (New York), 15 August 1989.

Kerr, P., ''Sound Movie,'' in *Village Voice* (New York), 15 August 1989.

Turroni, G., ''Cuginanze, ovvero territori contigui,'' in *Filmcritica* (Rome), November 1989.

Lavery, D., ''Functional and Dysfunctional Autobiography: *Hope and Glory* and *Distant Voices, Still Lives*,'' in *Film Criticism* (Meadville, Pennsylvania), no. 1, 1990.

Iversen, J., ''Man kan ikke forklare magi, kan man vel?'' in *Z Filmtidsskrift* (Oslo), no. 4, 1990.

Wahlstedt, T., ''Minnets rorelse mot centrum,'' in *Chaplin* (Stockholm), no. 4, 1990.

Quart, Leonard, in *Cineaste* (New York), vol. 28, no. 3, 1990.

Keighron, P., ''Condition Critical,'' in *Screen* (Oxford), no. 2, 1991.
Lochen, K., ''I minnenes rike,'' in *Film & Kino* (Oslo), no. 5, 1992.
Joris, L., ''Terence Davies: Rode schoenen, Hitchcock and een spion,'' in *Film en Televisie + Video* (Brussels), November 1992.
White, A., ''Remembrance of Songs Past,'' in *Film Comment* (New York), May-June 1993.
Coe, Jonathan, ''Jolly and Grim (Terence Davies),'' in *Sight & Sound* (London), vol. 5, no. 10, October 1995.
Davies, Terence, ''Twilight Time,'' in *New Statesman*, vol. 126, no. 4344, 25 July 1997.

* * *

It is not often that British films win prizes at international film festivals. Truffaut, despite his penchant for Hitchcock, and Satyajit Ray have both remarked that the British are more or less temperamentally incapable of holding movie cameras. A low-budget, BFI-financed account of a working-class childhood in post-war Liverpool hardly seems likely to set the continental critics alight. Nonetheless, *Distant Voices, Still Lives* received the International Critics Prize at the Cannes Festival, and also shared the Golden Leopard at the Locarno Festival. Perhaps as a result of its European reception, the film was apotheosized by British critics, who, while lavishing extravagant praise, insisted on writing about it as if it were a remake of *A Room with a View*, as if it were yet another piece of cosy, Edwardian nostalgia: Terence Davies, the ''proletarian Proust,'' had, we were told, ''wrenched high art from the lower depths of his deprived Liverpool childhood.'' His film was like ''*Coronation Street* by Bresson.'' (It is ironic that a film which recreates an era largely through its popular culture should be treated as a piece of ''art house'' cinema.)

The film is a diptych. *Distant Voices* was shot in the autumn of 1985. At that time *Still Lives*, which was shot in 1987, had not even been written. However, the narrative is elliptical. Depicting various key moments—wedding, christening, illness, war—in the life of a Liverpool family, it jumps from tableau to tableau: there is no jarring disjunction between the two halves. If anything, the gap between them helps to give a real sense of time passing and enables characters to age convincingly.

There is an absolute refusal to see the past through rose or sepia tinted glasses. Visually, the film does not so much evoke 1950s working-class Liverpool as excoriate it, presenting the period in a self-consciously sombre fashion. Through a ''Bleach-By-Pass printing process'' (also used in Michael Radford's *1984*) all colours are desaturated; there are no primary colours, and the emphasis is always on the brown, the grey, on giving a dull clarity.

Lurking ominously at the core of the film, a morose and tacitum presence, is the father, played by Pete Postlethwaite. A splenetic, bitter man, given to arbitrary fits of violence, he beats his wife (Freda Dowie) and daughters, and terrorizes the household in a constant attempt to stifle the ''feminine'' culture—a culture embodied in radio, cinema, and song—that it represents. As much as he is demonized, the wife and mother is idealized: patient, quietly suffering, holding the family together, hers are the values with which Davies identifies. In the book and film of *The Last of England*, Derek Jarman reveals a similar split in his familial loyalty. He also reacted against a patriarchal father, allying himself with his mother. Bullying dads seem to have had a strong and positive influence on 1980s British filmmakers.

It is not only the father, with whose death the first half of the film is concerned, but men in general that Davies regards with alarm: a curious belching, farting breed who lock away their wives, on the one hand demanding respect and obedience from them, and on the other, depending on them for food and clothing, and guidance home from the pub when they are too drunk to make their own way.

The spectre of the father pervades the film, making it a peculiarly anguished and lugubrious rekindling of childhood. However, in comparison to Terence Davies's earlier *Trilogy*, filmed in penumbral monochrome and steeped in sexual and religious guilt, isolation, and fear of death, *Distant Voices, Still Lives* is a positive romp. At least it has music.

Davies has spoken of the importance of music in the film's construction. The film is full of songs: British songs, American songs, songs to be born to, songs to die to, songs to sing in the pub, songs on the radio, songs in the cinema. (Davies elicited the help of broadcasters Denis Norden, Steve Race, and Roy Hudd, among others, in tracing many of these, of which he could often remember only a phrase or a line.) Visual bleakness is counterpointed with an extraordinary aural extravagance: song cements both family and community together, enabling the women and children to endure the brutal vagaries of the men, overcoming the noise of German bombs, diffusing the horror of death.

The music is almost too positive. The central characters, detested father, adored mother, are one dimensional, and the locations, home, pub, street, are all too familiar. Even if Davies is trying not to sentimentalize the period, the constant singalongs in the pub and the community spirit which so easily transcends the brutal men's attempt to dampen it lend the proceedings an air strangely familiar to that of David Lean's *This Happy Breed.* Davies risks rejoicing in the good old days of rationing and bad housing.

What enables the film to avoid falling into either Noel Cowardly cooing arms or the kitchen sink is its structure. It discards linear narrative, instead progressing from snapshot to snapshot. There is a constant freezing of images—literally making ''still lives.'' The use of overlapping sound to link discrete scenes; the constant tension between image and sound; the way that sound motivates, humanizes, lends colour to the film's visually drab backcloth: these all combine to fracture narrative unity. One is conscious of the camera from the opening shot, a slow track through the door of the house, approaching the staircase opposite and then revolving to confront the door: before we see anyone, we hear the voice, off screen, of the mother: the voices create character, not vice versa. The film, we are told, is autobiographical, but there is no character portrayed with whom we can immediately identify the filmmaker. It is as if he has removed himself from the family: he is detached, and is looking in at his own life. His character is the camera, recording, remembering.

Arthur Miller professed surprise when *Death of a Salesman*, to him a quintessentially American play, was successfully produced in China. *Distant Voices, Still Lives*, despite being located in so specific a time and place, has a similar universality of appeal. It taps into British and American cultural memory; in the way it recreates an era through its media habits, its cinema-going and wireless listening, it is akin to Woody Allen's *Radio Days.* But its themes, marriage, birth, death, memories of the anguishes and pleasures of family life, make it accessible to almost anyone, even to xenophobic continental critics who still find it impossible to link the idea of ''cinema'' with that of ''Britain.''

—G. C. Macnab

DIVA

France, 1981

Director: Jean-Jacques Beineix

Production: Les Films Galaxie/Greenwich Film Production/Antenne 2; color, 35mm; running time: 117 minutes; some prints are 123 minutes. Filmed on location in Paris and Normandy (Gatteville Lighthouse).

Producer: Irene Silberman; **screenplay:** Beineix and Jean Van Hamme, from the novel by Delacorta; **photography:** Philippe Rousselot; **editors:** Monique Prim, Marie-Josephe Yoyotte; **sound:** Jean-Pierre Ruh; **art director:** Hilton McConnico; **production designer:** Ully Pickard; **costume design:** Claire Fraisse; **music:** Vladimir Cosma, with arias by Alfredo Catalini (''Ebben? . . . Ne andrò lontanno'' from *La Wally*) and Charles Gounod (''Ave Maria'').

Cast: Wilhelminia Wiggins Fernandez (*Cynthia Hawkins*); Frédéric Andréi (*Jules*); Richard Bohringer (*Gorodish*); An Luu Thuy (*Alba*); Jacques Fabbri (*Jean Saporta*); Anny Romand (*Paula*); Patrick Floersheim (*Zatopek*); Gerard Darmon (*L'Antillais*); Dominique Pinon (*Le curé*)

Awards: César Awards for Best Cinematography, Best Music, Best New Director and Best Sound, 1982; National Society of Film Critics (USA) Award for Best Cinematography, 1982.

Publications

Script:

Beineix, Jean-Jacques, *Diva* (scenario), in *Avant-Scène Cinéma* (Paris), December 1991.

Books:

Parent, Denis, et al., *Jean-Jacques Beineix, version originale*, Paris, 1989.

Powrie, Phil, *French Cinema in the 1980s: Nostalgia and the Crisis of Masculinity*, Oxford, 1997.

Articles:

Kelly, Ernece B., ''*Diva*: High Tech Sexual Politics,'' in *Jump Cut* (Berkeley), 1984.

Interview in *Film Comment* (New York), February 1987.

Hagen, W.M., ''Performance Space in Diva,'' in *Literature/Film Quarterly* (Salisbury), 1988.

Peary, ''A Tough Act to Follow,'' in *American Film* (Hollywood), January 1990.

Jameson, Frederick, ''*Diva* and French Socialism,'' in *Signatures of the Visible*, New York, 1992.

Yervasi, Carina L., ''Capturing the Elusive Representations in Beineix's *Diva*,'' in *Literature/Film Quarterly* (Salisbury, Maryland), 1993.

Olivier, Bert, ''No Recording Please! This Is Art. Or: What Do Cynthia Hawkins and Walter Benjamin Have in Common (Not)?'' in *South African Journal of Philosophy*, February 1996.

* * *

Diva was welcomed internationally as an early crest of a French Newer Wave and a major work by a first-time director. Though not truly radical either politically or stylistically—say, in the manner of such ''old'' New Wavers as Godard or Rivette—it had a hip 1980s sensibility that overlay its indebtedness to the lighter sort of Alfred Hitchcock thriller, in which an innocent but not quite guiltless person becomes the target of an international conspiracy. In contrast to the equally Hitchcockian murder-among-the-haute-bourgeoisie thrillers of Claude Chabrol, *Diva* was more of a pop entertainment, its hero a moped-riding postal worker who lives in a really cool industrial space, and one of the villains is a punk of the shaven-head-and-sunglasses variety. Moreover, the film featured multiracial casting and a savvy mix of very different kinds of music, from Italian opera to technopop and New Age. Director Jean-Jacques Beineix was not exactly a prodigy—he was 35 and a veteran assistant director when it was released—but *Diva*, if somewhat of a period piece today, remains brimful of youthful energy.

Beineix's script asks the viewer to accept an exceedingly unlikely premise. It is not so much that a world-class operatic soprano believes so strongly in the power and integrity of live performance that she refuses to make recordings and has never even heard her own voice—but that no one besides the film's young hero has ever smuggled a high-quality tape recorder into a concert hall to make an illicit tape of her. The whole plot hinges upon this presumption, beginning with the sinister attempts of two Taiwanese record pirates sitting behind Jules at the concert to get the tape by any means possible. To be sure, if one goes beyond the literal and the expedient (to set the plot in motion), there is much that is fascinating about this situation: for example, the spectacle of a man trying to capture the ''essence'' of a woman by robbing her, even ''violating'' her as the diva later claims; or the paradox that the sacred act of live performance, the aura of the glorious moment, can be represented by the endlessly reproducible medium of cinema.

The other moment that sets the plot in motion is the sort of coincidence common among thrillers: a woman about to be stabbed by a member of an international drug and prostitution ring slips an incriminating tape into Jules' moped bag. The presence of two tapes and two sets of criminals leads to the sort of massive confusion that can only be resolved by a final shootout. But several factors make *Diva* fresher than most conventional thrillers, and more complex than other hits of its era.

One such factor is the casting. Frédéric Andréi as Jules (an old-fashioned name according to the diva—one which ''fits you so badly that it fits you very well'') is the type of slight-of-build, intense young Frenchman embodied most famously perhaps by Jean-Pierre Léaud around the time of *Baisers Volées (Stolen Kisses)*. Wilhelminia Wiggins Fernandez, recruited from the opera stage, may not be a true diva, but as Cynthia Hawkins she is lovely enough of voice and regal

Diva

enough in demeanor to play one very well. And An Luu Thuy as Alba, the street kid alert to all things ''cool'' (her word in French), brings into play a very different cultural world from Cynthia's, while Jules appears to straddle both worlds. (Perhaps the film's initial success was due in some measure to the ''exotic'' casting of an African American and a Vietnamese women as the French hero's potential love interests.) Alba and Jules, becoming pals rather than lovers, parallel each other in interesting ways. Both are shown stealing music—he Cynthia's voice (and incidentally her gown); she recordings from a store—and both are involved with an older person, though actual sexual relations in either case are unspecified. Jules manages to talk his way into Cynthia's hotel suite and becomes increasingly intimate with her; Alba evidently lives with Gorodish, a sort of New Age guru whose loft apartment is as vast as Jules' but more serenely spare. Gorodish, played with unflappable calm by Richard Bohringer, has a curious function in the plot: seemingly detached from all the goings-on, he takes charge during the last third of the film, rescuing Jules and thwarting the villains pretty much single-handedly by doing little more than operating a few gadgets.

Diva is quite deftly edited, and photographed with great flair by Philippe Rousselot, who went on to works as diverse as *Henry and June* and *A River Runs Through It.* The crew's panache is amply in evidence in the film's most famous action sequence, a chase through the Métro with Jules on his moped and a cop (rather improbably) keeping up on foot; but there are less showy scenes that are superbly accomplished, like the opening sequence at the concert hall. Few sopranos on film can have had made a more portentous appearance onstage, with Beineix's camera alert to every detail of the stripped-down (half-renovated?) gray auditorium—so perfect a foil to the glamorous gown and voice of the diva—plus the mirrorshaded Taiwanese, the wheels of Jules' tape recorder turning and the tear running down his cheek, all set to music which begins serenely, yet suspensefully, and expands to Italianate passion.

The sets and locations often seem to be the actual stars of the film. The Parisian exteriors are gritty or blatantly romantic (Jules' and Cynthia's misty dawn walk), as the occasion demands. A Normandy lighthouse-hideaway is austerely monumental and not the least picturesque. Jules' garage/loft is a cross between an automobile graveyard and a chic art gallery, with surrealistic murals of floating cars with real headlights beyond the wrecks of actual vehicles and his elaborate sound system. Gorodish may have a conventional kitchen for teaching the Zen of baguette-buttering, but most of his loft is empty dark blue space, suitable for Alba to roller-skate around in, with just a few free-standing objects: a wave sculpture, a functioning bathtub, a jigsaw puzzle of a wave.

One other truly distinctive feature of *Diva* is its juxtapositions of very different kinds of music. The film elevated Catalini's Act I aria from *La Wally* from a number known mainly to connoisseurs to Puccinian popularity; its several repetitions along with other vocal music—as when Cynthia rehearses at the piano with a damp-from-the-bath Jules at her side—provide moments of great calm amidst the frantic goings-on of the thriller plot. In other scenes, Gorodish plays the sort of New Age music one expects to hear while buying crystals; Jules rides his moped around to stormy operatic interludes we could take for soundtrack music until he abruptly cuts off his motor; and Vladimir Cosma's actual soundtrack has an appropriate Europop beat. One satisfying auditory joke comes near the end when we discover that the icepick-wielding punk villain has been listening to Parisian cafe music, concertina and all, on his headset.

The pastiche of musical styles was one of a great many features which made *Diva* seem a perfect example of postmodernism to its early critics, including both those who loved it and those who reviled it for the same thing: being all glittering surface and attitude. In any case, Beineix's much anticipated second feature, *The Moon in the Gutter* (1983), received little but scorn upon its appearance (partly for the artifice of its sets, as in Francis Coppola's 1982 *One From the Heart*). Since then he has completed only a handful of other films, notably the erotic drama *Betty Blue* (1986). But *Diva*, whether analyzed for its representations (perhaps objectification) of women or its postmodern sensibility or celebrated for its perspectives on young love and love of music and Paris—passionate and ''cool'' at once—remains an important document of its era.

—Joseph Milicia

DO BIGHA ZAMIN

(Two Acres of Land)

India, 1953

Director: Bimal Roy

Production: Black and white, 35mm; running time: 138 minutes. Released 1953. Filmed in India.

Producer: Bimal Roy; **screenplay:** Hrishikesh Mukerjee, from a story by Salil Chaudhury; **photography:** Kamal Bose; **editor:** Hrishikesh Mukerjee; **music:** Salil Chaudhury.

Cast: Balraj Sahni (*Sambhu*); Nirum Roy; Rattan Kumar.

Awards: Prize for Social Progress, Karlovy Vary Film Festival, 1954; received one of the 10 international awards at the Cannes Film Festival, 1954.

Publications

Books:

Barnouw, Erik, and S. Krishnaswamy, *Indian Film*, New York, 1963; revised edition, 1980.

Willemen, Paul, and Behroze Gandhy, *Indian Cinema*, London, 1982.

Ramachandran, T. M., *70 Years of Indian Cinema (1913–1983)*, Bombay, 1985.

Bhattacharya, R., *Bimal Roy: A Man of Silence*, Indus Publishing, 1994.

Articles:

Ray, S. K., ''New Indian Directors,'' in *Film Quarterly* (Berkeley), Fall 1960.

Sarha, Kolita, ''Discovering India,'' in *Films and Filming* (London), December 1960.

Roy, Manobina, ''The Bimal Roy Only I Knew,'' in *Illustrated Weekly of India*, 3 August 1980.

''Film India: Indian Film Festival, Part 2: Historical Perspective,'' in *Museum of Modern Art Department of Film* (New York), Summer 1981.

Tesson, Charles, ''Le rêve indien,'' in *Cahiers du Cinéma* (Paris), March 1985.

Seton, Marie, ''The Indian Film,'' in *Film* (London), March 1985.

Binford, Mira Reym, and others, ''Indian Cinema,'' in *Quarterly Review of Film and Video* (Reading), October 1989.

Garda, B.D., ''The Great Romantics,'' in *Cinema in India* (Bombay), no. 10, 1991.

* * *

Into a cinema devoted chiefly to gaiety and adventure, Bimal Roy's *Do bigha zamin* introduced an element of seriousness and naturalism. Roy did not break with tradition in his film: *Do bigha zamin* includes songs and dances and the usual patterned dialogue. But Roy enlarged the operatic scope of popular films to include location shots of an ordinary, undramatic character (e.g., the look of trees and fields as the peasant leaves the country for Calcutta); well-observed natural actions (e.g., the habitual manner in which the peasant's wife puts out a pan to catch fresh rainwater); and grave subject matter (e.g., the stacking of legal justice against those unskilled in legalities). Roy's use of the familiar musical and melodramatic style enabled audiences to comprehend his films; at the same time the new naturalistic elements prepared the ground for the more uncompromising and formally innovative political cinema of the 1970s.

Do bigha zamin tells the story of a peasant whose meager two acres come in the way of the landlord's scheme to sell a large parcel of the village land to speculators. The landlord fabricates evidence of an unpaid debt and the peasant must leave for the city to earn the cash the landlord requires. The acting in the film veers between the rapid responsiveness of performers in a melodrama and the slow surfacing of responses characteristic of naturalism. At the landlord's, the peasant (played by the deeply intelligent actor Balraj Sahni) acts by formula, but his leave-taking from his wife is simple; his fears for her emerge into natural, unemphatic expression on his face and in his bearing. The lighting, too, varies between the full lighting characteristic of Bombay sets and the chiaroscuro of available light cinematography. The landlord's house is amply lit, but the rickshaw-puller's quarters in Calcutta retain a natural look of charcoal dilapidation.

In sum, an important, earnest, transitional film, which bespeaks the influence of Italian neorealism on Hindi cinema. It won the Prix Internationale at the 1954 Cannes film festival and the Prize for Social Progress at the Karlovy Vary film festival.

—Satti Khanna

DO THE RIGHT THING

USA, 1989

Director: Spike Lee

Production: 40 Acres and a Mule Filmworks; distributed by Universal Pictures; color (DuArt); running time: 118 minutes; Dolby SR; length: 3,292 meters (approx. 10,598 feet). Released 30 June 1989; filmed in Brooklyn, New York; cost: $6,500,000.

Producers: Jon Kilik, Spike Lee, and Monty Ross; **screenplay:** Spike Lee; **photography:** Ernest R. Dickerson; **editor:** Barry Alexander Brown; **sound:** Tom Fleischman and Skip Lievsay; **production designer:** Wynn Thomas; **costume designer:** Ruth E. Carter; **music:** Bill Lee.

Cast: Danny Aiello (*Sal*); Ossie Davis (*Da Mayor*); Ruby Dee (*Mother Sister*); Richard Edson (*Vito*); Giancarlo Esposito (*Buggin' Out*); Spike Lee (*Mookie*); Bill Nunn (*Radio Raheem*); John Turturro (*Pino*); Samuel L. Jackson (*Mister Se-or Love Daddy*); Rosie Perez (*Tina*).

Awards: Los Angeles Film Critics Association Awards for Best Picture, Best Director (Spike Lee), Best Music (Bill Lee), and Best Supporting Actor (Danny Aiello), 1989; New York Film Critics Circle Award for Best Cinematography (Ernest R. Dickerson), 1989; National Film Preservation Board (USA) selection for the National Film Registry, 1999.

Publications

Script:

Lee, Spike, *Do the Right Thing: A Spike Lee Joint*, New York, 1989.

Books:

Reid, Mark A., *Spike Lee's Do the Right Thing*, New York, 1997.

Articles:

Sanoff, Alvin P., ''Doing the Controversial Thing. (Director Spike Lee's Movie *Do the Right Thing*),'' in *U.S. News & World Report*, 10 July 1989.

Johnson, Victoria E., ''Polyphony and Cultural Expression: Interpreting Musical Traditions in *Do the Right Thing*,'' in *Film Quarterly* (Berkeley), Winter 1993.

Lindroth, Colette, ''Spike Lee and the American Tradition,'' in *Literature/Film Quarterly* (Salisbury, Maryland), January 1996.

McKelly, James C., '''The Double Truth, Ruth': *Do the Right Thing* and the Culture of Ambiguity,'' in *African American Review* (Bloomington), Summer 1998.

Radtke, Jennifer, ''Do The Right Thing in Black and White: Spike Lee's Bi-Cultural Method,'' in *The Midwest Quarterly* (Pittsburgh), Winter 2000.

* * *

Before the release of *Do the Right Thing*, Spike Lee had made a name for himself as an independent filmmaker who helped to spearhead the rise of film festivals as a market place for independent cinema in the late 1980s. His first two features, *She's Gotta Have It* (1986) and *School Daze* (1988), were unique not only because they were made outside of a studio on shoestring budgets and featured primarily black actors, but also because they managed to get mainstream distribution and turn a modest profit as well. The industry cachet these two films earned Lee enabled him to make *Do the Right Thing*, which was inspired by an actual incident in Howard Beach, New York, in which a group of white kids chased down and killed a young black man. The result is a brilliant film about racism in America that many consider Lee's best to date.

The story takes place on the hottest day of the summer and revolves around Sal's Famous Pizzeria, apparently the only white-owned business in the Brooklyn neighborhood in which the film is set. Sal and his two sons, Nino and Vito, are not without their racist tendencies (especially Nino), but they nevertheless manage to coexist with their black customers. Rather than being a film about clear rights and wrongs, *Do the Right Thing* is instead a cultural melange that is cumulatively an intricately detailed portrait of an ethnically diverse contemporary urban American neighborhood. In the first three quarters of the film Lee masterfully establishes the tone and texture of the neighborhood by introducing us to a series of interesting characters whose lives intermittently intersect. Among the most important are Mookie, who works as a pizza delivery man for Sal's; Da Mayor and Mother Sister, the neighborhood's elder statespeople; Radio Raheem, whose always booming box is a source of constant irritation for Sal; and Buggin' Out, who in his anger over Sal's wall of fame featuring exclusively Italian Americans will eventually urge his fellow African

Do the Right Thing

American Brooklynites to boycott Sal's Famous, which in part leads to the film's electrifying climax.

The catalyst to the film's rising racial tensions is the heat. Accordingly, Lee's mise en scene is carefully constructed so as to visually convey the oppressiveness of Brooklyn's dreadful heat and humidity in the dead of summer. The film as a whole was shot in saturated color, thus rendering the summer heat almost palpable. In addition to close ups of his characters' faces drenched in sweat, Lee time and again features the color red as dominant in the various frames. The characters constantly lament the heat as they all the while move slowly so as not to exert any more effort than absolutely necessary. Further contributing to his audience feeling as ill at ease as his characters is Lee's repeated use of discomforting Dutch angle shots. As the heat slowly rises, so too does his characters' volatility.

The tensions that build throughout the film eventually explode in what is among the most controversial endings in cinematic history. The differences between the Italians and the blacks in the neighborhood are accentuated by Lee's skillful use of music to compliment his characters' ethnicities. While the Italians favor Sinatraesque ballads, the African American characters frequently listen to rap, most notably by Public Enemy. This all comes to a head when Radio Raheem refuses to turn down his radio while in Sal's. Sal and Radio get in a fight and the police are called. An ugly situation turns worse when the police arrive and kill Radio in their efforts to subdue him. The crowd outside of Sal's, gathered by Buggin' Out to protest Sal's ethnically singular wall of fame, quickly turns into a mob. Mookie starts a full scale riot by throwing a garbage can through Sal's front window. Bedlam ensues as Sal's is first looted and then burned to the ground.

This scene forces viewers to take sides. The film's deceptive title becomes not so much an exhortation as a question: What is the right thing to do and what factors should people consider when determining what's right for them? This question has colored the wide and passionate range of critical responses to the film's climax. Its critics are angered by what they feel is Lee's slanted point of view, a frequently cited example of which is the pointed graffiti—''DUMP KOCH''—in the background of many scenes (at the time of filming, New York Mayor Ed Koch, who many blacks felt was ineffectual in his dealings with racial issues, was running for re-election; Lee was openly opposed to his re-election). Conversely, the film's champions claim that *Do the Right Thing* is remarkably evenhanded in its treatment of race, thus leaving it up to viewers to decide just what the right thing is. As Alvin Sanoff writes, in discussing his film Lee has said, ''It wasn't made to incite riots but to provoke discussion about racism, something people do not want to talk about.''

Ultimately, whether one sides with the film's defenders or its detractors is beside the point; in arriving at their own conclusions, viewers can't help but consider the state of race relations in America, which in the end is what Lee most hoped to accomplish by making *Do the Right Thing*, the amazing film that, along with *Malcom X*, will likely be his cinematic legacy.

—Robert C. Sickels

DR. JEKYLL AND MR. HYDE

USA, 1931

Director: Rouben Mamoulian

Production: Paramount Pictures; black and white, 35mm; running time: 82 minutes, some sources list 90 minutes. Released 1931. Filmed in Paramount studios.

Producer: Rouben Mamoulian; **screenplay:** Samuel Hoffenstein and Percy Heath, from the novel by Robert Louis Stevenson; **photography:** Karl Struss; **editor:** William Shea; **sound:** the Paramount sound department; **production designer:** Hans Dreier.

Cast: Frederic March (*Dr. Henry Jekyll/Mr. Hyde*); Miriam Hopkins (*Ivy Pearson*); Rose Hobart (*Muriel Carew*); Halliwell Hobbes (*Brigadier General Carew*); Holmes Herbert (*Dr. Lanyan*); Edgar Norton (*Poole*).

Awards: Venice Film Festival citations for Most Original Film and Favourite Actor (March), 1932, note: there were not official awards that year, but acknowledgements were by public referendum; Oscar for Best Actor (March), 1932.

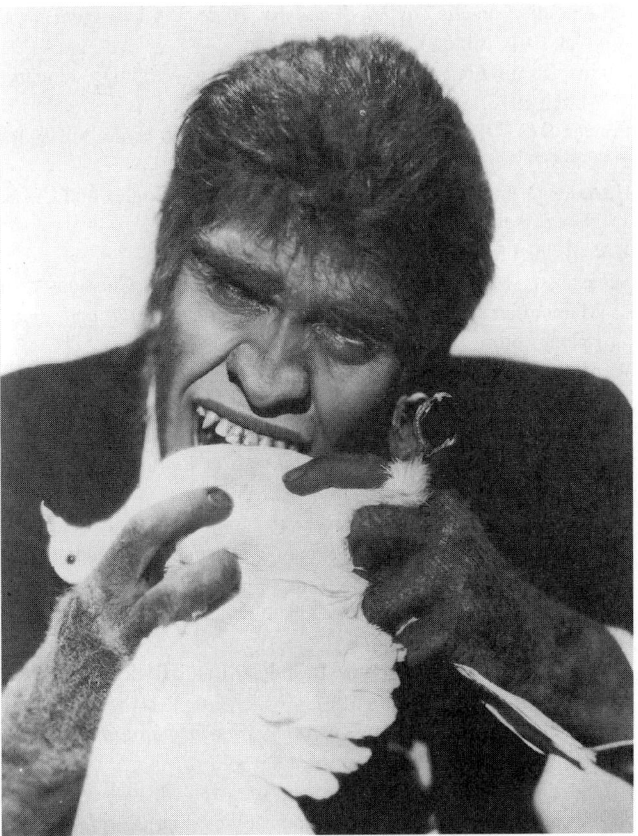

Dr. Jekyll and Mr. Hyde

Publications

Script:

Hoffenstein, Samuel, and Percy Heath, *Dr. Jekyll and Mr. Hyde*, edited by Richard Anobile, New York, 1976.

Books:

Sarris, Andrew, *Interviews with Film Directors*, New York, 1967.
Milne, Tom, *Rouben Mamoulian*, London, 1969.
Burrows, Michael, *Charles Laughton and Frederic March*, New York, 1970.
Silke, James, editor, *Rouben Mamoulian: Style Is the Man*, Washington, D.C., 1971.
Quick, Lawrence J., *The Films of Frederic March*, New York, 1971.
Everson, William K., *Classics of the Horror Film*, Secaucus, New Jersey, 1974.
Aylesworth, Thomas G., *Movie Monsters*, Philadelphia, 1975.
Luhr, William, and Peter Lehman, *Authorship and Narrative in the Cinema*, New York, 1977.
Prawer, S. S., *Caligari's Children: The Film as Tale of Terror*, New York, 1980.
Klein, Michael, and Gillian Parker, *The English Novel and the Movies*, New York, 1981.
McCarty, John, *Psychos: Eighty Years of Mad Movies, Maniacs, and Murderous Deeds*, New York, 1986.
Prinzler, Hans Helmut, and Antje Goldau, *Rouben Mamoulian: Eine Dokumentation*, Berlin, 1987.

Articles:

New York Times, 2 January 1932.
Variety (New York), 5 January 1932.
Tozzi, Romano, ''Frederic March,'' in *Films in Review* (New York), December 1958.
Robinson, David, ''Painting the Leaves Black,'' in *Sight and Sound* (London), Summer 1961.
Sarris, Andrew, ''Fallen Idols,'' in *Film Culture* (New York), Spring 1963.

''Mamoulian on His *Dr. Jekyll and Mr. Hyde*,'' in *Cinefantastique* (Oak Park, Illinois), Summer 1971.

Atkins, T., in *Film Journal* (Hollins College, Virginia), January-March 1973.

Prawer, S. S., ''Book into Films: Dr. Jekyll and Mr. Hyde,'' in *Times Literary Supplement* (London), 21 December 1979.

Huskins, D. Gail, in *Magill's Survey of Cinema 1*, Englewood Cliffs, New Jersey, 1980.

Wide Angle (Athens, Ohio), vol. 5, no. 3, 1983.

Sevastakis, Michael, ''The Stylistic Coding of Characters in Mamoulian's Jekyll and Hyde,'' in *Journal of Film and Video* (River Forest, Illinois), Autumn 1985.

Weaver, T., ''Rose Hobart,'' in *Filmfax* (Evanston, Illinois), October-November 1991.

Fyne, Robert, ''Reinventing Reality: The Life and Art of Rouben Mamoulian,'' in *Historical Journal of Film, Radio and Television* (Abingdon), vol. 15, no. 1, March 1995.

Newitz, Annalee, ''A Lower-class Sexy Monster: American Liberalism in Mamoulian's *Dr. Jekyll & Mr. Hyde*,'' in *Bright Lights* (Cincinnati), no. 15, 1995.

O'Neill, Eithne, and others, ''Stephen Frears,'' in *Positif* (Paris), May 1996.

Norman, Barry, ''Which is the Best Jekyll and Hyde?'' in *Radio Times* (London), 19 April 1997.

Turner, George, ''Wrap Shot,'' in *American Cinematographer* (Hollywood), August 1997.

Arnold, Gary, ''Overlooked American Achievements (Directors Left Out of the '100 Greatest American Movies' List),'' in *Insight on the News*, vol. 14, no. 43, 23 November 1998.

* * *

Rouben Mamoulian's *Dr. Jekyll and Mr. Hyde* is perhaps the most stylish and technically innovative of any of the several versions of Robert Louis Stevenson's classic novel, for Mamoulian integrated both the new and established film technologies into his individual filmmaking style. Dissolves, superimpositions, camera movements, and expressionistic lighting are synthesized into his vision of the struggle within man, which is the heart of Stevenson's tale.

While other directors seemed shackled by the then infant sound technology, Mamoulian freely moved the camera within the frame. *Dr. Jekyll and Mr. Hyde* in fact opens with an extensive tracking shot that the viewer quickly realizes represents the subjective point of view of Dr. Jekyll. The effect of characters directly addressing the camera (as Dr. Jekyll) is disarming. Not only is such a shot a masterful technical innovation, in light of the obstacle posed by sound recording, but it is a striking narrative device as well. Mamoulian's subjective camera foreshadows the use, some 50 years later, of the same device to similar ends by John Carpenter in *Halloween.* Since *Halloween*, it has become a characteristic element of those kinds of films which indeed bear resemblance to *Dr. Jekyll and Mr. Hyde.* No less striking is the 360-degree pan which accompanies Dr. Jekyll's initial transformation to Hyde. The shot underscores the duration of the transformation, solidly placing it in time and space. Mamoulian claims that the pan was the first of its kind in Hollywood film. The shot not only presented the obvious challenge of lighting, but also posed unique problems for recording sound. Mamoulian overcame this by mixing a sound effects track. The track is dominated rhythmically by a heartbeat (Mamoulian's own) and serves as an early example of a complex sound mix in a Hollywood film. In addition, as he had done earlier in *City Streets* and particularly in *Applause*, Mamoulian utilized multiple microphones for recording live sound. He even pioneered a mobile microphone used in situations such as the opening shot of *Dr. Jekyll and Mr. Hyde.*

This version of *Dr. Jekyll and Mr. Hyde* is ahead of its time in Mamoulian's exploitation of the potential eroticism of Stevenson's novel. Miriam Hopkin's streetwalker, Ivy, is at once sympathetic and highly sensual. Unlike Stevenson's gnarled, diminutive Hyde, Mamoulian's representation of Hyde is that of an enlarged, powerful, bestial man. Both characterizations heighten the intensity of their moments together on screen. Jekyll first meets Ivy in her room where he has gone to return a discarded garter. He finds her nearly undressed as she slips beneath the bedcovers and taunts him coquettishly. The scene closes with Ivy's legs dangling from beneath the covers deliciously—superimposed on the image of Jekyll and his friend Lanyon departing below.

Superimpositions and dissolves were not new to the cinema in 1932. However, Mamoulian's use of them to heighten aesthetically the impact of various scenes was not characteristic of Hollywood in the 1930s. For example, the superimpositions used in the scene where Jekyll meets Ivy suggest that the image of Ivy's leg lingers in Jekyll's mind. Mamoulian's use of dissolves may be somewhat more traditional in that they are the primary means for showing Jekyll's transformations into Hyde.

Dr. Jekyll and Mr. Hyde represents the strengths of Mamoulian's style. Perhaps as an extension of his experience directing theater and opera, where the proscenium limits space, Mamoulian's style emphasizes lighting and framing. In the film, when Hyde's passion for Ivy becomes rage, he begins to strangle her. The two figures fall, struggling below the frame. Only when Hyde returns to frame does the viewer understand Ivy's fate. Similarly, when Jekyll undergoes his first transformation, he falls, writhing out of frame. Mamoulian combines this technique with lighting in a later scene to create an enormous shadow—Hyde. The shadow is formed as Hyde runs from the frame, his departure signalled by his ever increasing shadow on the wall. This shot echoes a similar shot in F. W. Murnau's *Nosferatu* where Count Dracula's shadow gradually engulfs the cowering figure of Jonathan Harker.

Several nuances of Mamoulian's style are also reinforced with this film. Split-screen is used, for example, to suggest a symbolic proximity between otherwise distant spaces and events. Another characteristic is the use of counterpoint to heighten dramatic effect. When Jekyll arrives to tell his fiancée, Muriel, that they must separate it is accompanied not by a dirge, but by the waltz to which they had danced earlier. Counterpoints such as this create a dynamism between the visuals and the sound. The waltz serves as a powerful reminder of Jekyll's price for tampering with nature. Perhaps the strongest example of Mamoulian's individuality as a filmmaker is the final shot, where Lanyon and the authorities stand over the body of the fallen Jekyll. Shot from inside and behind the flames of the fireplace, it is a complete synthesis of the medium's potential for narrative discourse.

—Robert Winning

DR. MABUSE THE GAMBLER

See **DOKTOR MABUSE DER SPIELER**

DR. STRANGELOVE; OR, HOW I LEARNED TO STOP WORRYING AND LOVE THE BOMB

UK, 1964

Director: Stanley Kubrick

Production: Hawk Films, a Stanley Kubrick Production; black and white, 35mm; running time: originally 102 minutes, edited down to 93 minutes. Released 30 January 1964. Cost: $1,500,000.

Producer: Stanley Kubrick; **associate producer:** Victor Lyndon; **screenplay:** Stanley Kubrick, Terry Southern, and Peter George, originally conceived as a serious adaptation of *Red Alert* by Peter George, main titles by Pablo Ferro; **photography:** Gilbert Taylor; **editor:** Anthony Harvey; **sound supervisor:** John Cox; **sound recordist:** Richard Bird; **dub mixer:** John Aldred; **sound editor:** Leslie Hodgson; **production designer:** Ken Adam; **art director:** Peter Murton; **music:** Laurie Johnson, song ''We'll Meet Again,'' is the original recording by Vera Lynn; **special effects:** Wally Veevers; **travelling matte:** Vic Margutti; **costume designer:** Pamela Carlton; **aviation advisor:** Capt. John Crewdson.

Cast: Peter Sellers (*Group Capt. Lionel Mandrake/President Muffley/ Dr. Strangelove*); George C. Scott (*Gen. Buck Turgidson*); Sterling Hayden (*Gen. Jack D. Ripper*); Keenan Wynn (*Col. Bat Guano*); Slim Pickens (*Maj. T. J. ''King'' Kong*); Peter Bull (*Ambassador de Sadesky*); Tracy Reed (*Miss Scott*); James Earl Jones (*Lieut. Lothar Zagg*); Jack Creley (*Mr. Staines*); Frank Berry (*Lieut. H. R. Dietrich*); Glenn Beck (*Lieut. W. D. Kivel*); Shane Rimmer (*Capt. G. A. ''Ace'' Owens*); Paul Tamarin (*Lieut. B. Goldberg*); Gordon Tanner (*General Faceman*); Robert O'Neil (*Admiral Randolph*); Roy Stephens (*Frank*); Laurence Herder, John McCarthy, Hal Galili (*Burpelson defense team members*).

Award: New York Film Critics' Award, Best Direction, 1964.

Publications

Books:

Austen, David, *The Cinema of Stanley Kubrick*, London, 1969.

Walker, Alexander, *Stanley Kubrick Directs*, New York, 1972.

Kagan, Norman, *The Cinema of Stanley Kubrick*, New York, 1972.

Devries, Daniel, *The Films of Stanley Kubrick*, Grand Rapids, Michigan, 1973.

Bobker, Lee R., *Elements of Film*, New York, 1974.

Phillips, Gene D., *Stanley Kubrick: A Film Odyssey*, New York, 1975.

Leyda, Jay, editor, *Voices of Film Experience*, New York, 1977.

Monaco, James, *How to Read a Film*, New York, 1977.

O'Connor, John E., and Martin A. Jackson, editors, *American History/American Film: Interpreting the Hollywood Image*, New York, 1979.

Ciment, Michel, *Kubrick*, Paris, 1980; revised edition, 1987; translated as *Kubrick*, 1983.

Kolker, Robert Phillip, *A Cinema of Loneliness: Penn, Kubrick, Coppola, Scorsese, Altman*, Oxford, 1980; revised edition, 1988.

Hummel, Christoph, editor, *Stanley Kubrick*, Munich, 1984.

Brunetta, Gian Piero, *Stanley Kubrick: Tempo, spazia, storia, e mondi possibili*, Parma, 1985.

Articles:

Hart, Henry, in *Films in Review* (New York), February 1962.

Kubrick, Stanley, ''How I Learned to Stop Worrying and Love the Cinema,'' in *Films and Filming* (London), June 1963.

Prideaux, T., ''Take Aim: Fire at the Agonies of War,'' in *Life* (New York), 20 December 1963.

Tornabene, Lyn, ''Contradicting the Hollywood Image,'' in *Saturday Review* (New York), 28 December 1963.

Milne, Tom, in *Sight and Sound* (London), Winter 1963–64.

Taylor, Stephen, in *Film Comment* (New York), Winter 1964.

Crowther, Bosley, in *New York Times*, 31 January 1964.

Forbes, Bryan, in *Films and Filming* (London), February 1964.

Sarris, Andrew, in *Village Voice* (New York), 13 February and 11 June 1964.

Burgess, Jackson, in *Film Quarterly* (Berkeley), Spring 1964.

Milne, Tom, ''How I Learned to Stop Worrying and Love Stanley Kubrick,'' in *Sight and Sound* (London), Spring 1964.

Goldberg, Joe, ''Dr. Kubrick,'' in *Seventh Art* (New York), Spring 1964.

Price, James, ''Stanley Kubrick's Divided World,'' in *London Magazine*, May 1964.

Russell, Lee, ''Stanley Kubrick,'' in *New Left Review* (New York), Summer 1964.

Macklin, F. A., ''Sex and Dr. Strangelove,'' in *Film Comment* (New York), Summer 1965.

MacFadden, Patrick, in *Film Society Review* (New York), January 1967.

Manchel, Frank, in *Media and Methods* (Philadelphia), December 1967.

Edelman, Rob, in *Magill's Survey of Cinema 1*, Englewood Cliffs, New Jersey, 1980.

Verstappen, W., ''*Dr. Strangelove:* Analyse op de montagetafel,'' in *Skoop* (Amsterdam), October 1980.

Hoberman, J., ''When Dr. No Met Dr. Strangelove,'' in *Sight and Sound* (London), December 1993.

Lefcowitz, Eric, ''*Dr. Strangelove* Turns 30. Can it Still be Trusted?'' in *New York Times*, 30 January 1994.

Southern, T., ''*Strangelove* Outtake: Notes from the War Room,'' in *Grand Street*, no. 49, Summer 1994.

Tweg, S., ''Reading *Dr. Strangelove*,'' in *Metro Education* (Melbourne), no. 6, 1995.

Séquences (Haute-Ville), September-October 1995.

Kubrick, Stanley, ''Une comédie cauchemardesque,'' in *Positif* (Paris), September 1997.

Bourguignon, Thomas, in *Positif* (Paris), September 1997.

Macnab, Geoffrey, ''Will it Dress?'', an interview with set designer Ken Adams, in *Sight & Sound* (London), September 1999.

* * *

Stanley Kubrick's *Dr. Strangelove*, which has won wide and continued acceptance from the time of its release, has come to be considered one of the screen's great masterpieces of black comedy. Yet Kubrick had originally planned the film as a serious adaptation of Peter George's *Red Alert*, a novel concerned with the demented General Jack D. Ripper (Sterling Hayden) and his decision to order

Dr. Strangelove

a group of B-52 bombers to launch an attack inside Russia. Gradually Kubrick's attitude toward his material changed: "My idea of doing it as a nightmare comedy came in the early weeks of working on the screenplay. I found that in trying to put meat on the bones and to imagine the scenes fully, one had to keep leaving out of it things which were either absurd or paradoxical, in order to keep it from being funny; and these things seemed to be close to the heart of the scenes in question."

Kubrick remembers that he kept revising the script right through the production period. "During shooting many substantial changes were made in the script, sometimes together with the cast during improvisations. Some of the best dialogue was created by Peter Sellers himself." Sellers played not only the title role of the eccentric scientist, but also the president of the United States and Captain Mandrake, a British officer who fails to dissuade General Ripper from his set purpose.

General Ripper's mad motivation for initiating a nuclear attack is his paranoid conviction that the explanation of his diminishing sexual potency can be traced to an international Communist conspiracy to taint the drinking water. Kubrick subtly reminds us of the general's obsession by a series of suggestive metaphors that occur in the course of the film. The very opening image of the film shows a nuclear bomber being refueled in mid-flight by another aircraft, with "Try a Little Tenderness" appropriately playing on the sound track to accompany their symbolic coupling. As Ripper describes to Mandrake his concern about preserving his potency, which he refers to as his "precious bodily essence," Kubrick photographs him in close-up from below, with a huge phallic cigar jutting from between his lips while he is talking. Later, when the skipper of a B-52 bomber (Slim Pickens) manages to dislodge a bomb that has been stuck in its chamber and unleash it on its Russian target, he sits astride this mighty symbol of potency clamped between his flanks, as it hurtles toward the earth.

Black ironies abound throughout the picture. During an emergency conference called by President Muffley, a disagreement between General Buck Turgidson (George C. Scott) and the Russian ambassador (Peter Bull) threatens to turn into a brawl, and the president intervenes by reminding them, "Please, gentlemen, you can't fight here; this is the War Room!" Later, when Mandrake tries to reach the president in order to warn him about the imminent attack on Russia, he finds that he lacks the correct change for the pay telephone he is using, and that the White House will not accept a collect call. He then demands that Colonel Bat Guano (Keenan Wynn) fire into a Coca-Cola machine in order to obtain the necessary coins. Guano reluctantly agrees, ruefully reminding Mandrake that it is he who will have to answer to the Coca-Cola Company. Guano blasts the machine, bends down to scoop up the silver—and is squirted full in the face with Coca-Cola by the vindictive machine.

Kubrick had originally included a scene in which the Russians and the Americans in the War Room engage in a free-for-all with custard pies, but deleted it from the final print of the film when he decided that "it was too farcical, and not consistent with the satiric tone of the rest of the film." Very much in keeping with the satiric, dark humor of the picture is the figure of Dr. Strangelove himself, Kubrick's grim vision of man's final capitulation to the machine: he is more a robot than a human being, with his mechanical arm spontaneously saluting Hitler, his former employer, and his mechanical hand, gloved in black, at one point trying to strangle the flesh and blood still left in him.

In the end a single U.S. plane reaches its Russian target, setting off the Russian's retaliatory Doomsday machine. There follows a series of blinding explosions, while on the sound track we hear a popular song which Kubrick resurrected from World War II: "We'll meet again, don't know where, don't know when." (Kubrick used the original World War II recording by Vera Lynn, which brought popularity back not only to the song but to Ms. Lynn as well.)

One critic summed up the film by saying that the black comedy which Kubrick had originally thought to exclude from *Dr. Strangelove* provides some of its most meaningful moments. "They are made up of the incongruities, the banalities, and misunderstandings that we are constantly aware of in our lives. On the brink of annihilation, they become irresistibly absurd."

The theme that emerges from *Dr. Strangelove* is the plight of fallible man putting himself at the mercy of his "infallible" machines and thus bringing about his own destruction. Kubrick, who is always on the side of humanity in his films, indicates here, as in *2001: A Space Odyssey*, that human fallibility is less likely to destroy man than the relinquishing of his moral responsibilities to his supposedly faultless machinery. Summing up his personal vision as it is reflected in *Dr. Strangelove*, the director has said: "The destruction of this planet would have no significance on a cosmic scale. Our extinction would be little more than a match flaring for a second in the heavens. And if that match does blaze in the darkness, there will be none to mourn a race that used a power that could have lit a beacon in the stars to light its funeral pyre."

—Gene D. Phillips

DOG STAR MAN

USA, 1964

Director: Stan Brakhage

Production: Color and black and white, 16mm; silent; running time: 75 minutes (24 f.p.s.); released 1964. The film is composed of five parts which appeared separately before being brought together in the complete *Dog Star Man*; the parts are: *Prelude* (26–1/2 minutes, 1961), *Part 1* (31 minutes, 1962), *Part 2* (6–1/2 minutes, 1963), *Part 3* (8 minutes, 1964), and *Part 4* (7 minutes, 1964). Distributors continue to make the sections available for rent individually or together as a single, complete work; released in complete form on video by Mystic Fire Video, 1987.

Producer, photography, and editing: Stan Brakhage, assisted by Jane Brakhage.

Cast: Stan Brakhage and Jane Brakhage

Publications:

Books:

Clark, Dan, *Brakhage*, New York, 1966.

Brakhage, Stan, *Metaphors on Vision*, New York, 1976.

Sitney, P. Adams, *Visionary Film: The American Avant-Garde, 1943–1978*, 2nd ed, New York, 1979.

James, David, *Allegories of Cinema: American Film in the Sixties*, Princeton, New Jersey, 1989.

Wees, William C., *Light Moving in Time: Studies in the Visual Aesthetics of Avant-Garde Film*, Berkeley, California 1992.

Articles:

McClure, Michael, "*Dog Star Man*: The First 16mm Epic," *Film Culture* (New York), no. 29, Summer 1963.

Wees, William C., "Visual Renewal in Stan Brakhage's *Dog Star Man*," in *Atropos* (Montreal), vol. 1, no. 2, Spring 1979.

* * *

Widely recognized as one of the monuments of experimental/avant-garde/personal film, *Dog Star Man* is a compendium of unorthodox filmmaking techniques applied to a deceptively simple narrative: a man (played by Brakhage) carrying an axe and accompanied by a dog, struggles up a steep mountainside and chops down a dead tree. Originally, Brakhage has said, "I thought it would be a little, simple film on a woodsman, myself as the woodsman, the wood-gatherer," but "it ended up as . . . an exploration of the whole history of man. I mean, as I climb this hill the images suggest in many ways, metaphorically and in other ways, the history of man himself and his endeavor, and the meaning of whatever it is he does and makes." While that claim may sound excessively grand, it is in keeping with the formal and thematic complexity of the work, not to mention the unusually heavy demands it places on viewers' patience, visual literacy, and interpretive skills. If *Dog Star Man* is a "difficult" work, it nevertheless repays close study and repeated viewing.

Moving from complete darkness, to intermittent flares and flickers of light, and then to quick glimpses of seemingly unrelated images, *Prelude*, the first of the film's five parts, introduces the principal images and formal techniques that will recur as the film progresses. Most shots are brief and combined with other shots through superimposition and intricate, highly kinetic montage. Dynamic camera movement—usually hand-held—adds to the intense, compelling rhythm of the work. The surge and flow of light, color, texture, and rapidly changing images propel the film forward and engage the viewer in ''an adventure of perception,'' as Brakhage has called it, but the significance of the images is, at first, hard to determine—immediate perceptual impact prevails over conceptual understanding. But through repetition and associations built up among groups of related images, graspable meanings and the rudiments of a narrative begin to emerge. Like the leitmotifs in Richard Wagner's *Ring* cycle, key images—the axe-bearing woodsman, a full moon, a birth, a lactating breast, a naked woman, mountains and trees that appear to stretch and writhe, a weathered, grey, dead tree, to mention just a few—return numerous times but nearly always modified in some way: in color or texture (including being painted over or scratched on), in length and clarity, in combination with other images. The images thus accumulate multiple meanings—literal, metaphoric, symbolic—as the work progresses.

''The images,'' Jonas Mekas has suggested, ''become like words: they come back again, in little bursts, and disappear, and come back again—like in sentences—creating visual and mental impressions, experiences.'' P. Adams Sitney finds the images related to ''four basic visual themes,'' which he summarizes as, ''(1) the four elements, air, earth, fire and water; (2) the cosmos represented in stock footage of the sun, the moon, and the stars; (3) Brakhage's household—himself, his dog and cat, his baby, and particularly his wife's nude body; and (4) artificial, yet purely filmic devices such as painting or scratching on film, distorting lenses, double exposure and clear leader.'' A fifth important theme involves microscopic footage of blood vessels, close-ups of a beating heart, and other images of viscera and bodily fluids.

Part 1 offers a change of pace from *Prelude*'s ''pyrotechnic, split-second montage with as much varied material as [Brakhage] could force into a half hour'' (Sitney). Many of its shots are longer and there is only one layer of images. Its principal subject is the woodsman, with his axe and dog, working his way up a snowy mountainside, slipping and stumbling in a kind of two-steps-forward-one-step-back progression (echoed in microscopic images of the advance and retreat of blood in a vein or artery at the end of *Part 1*). *Part 2*, in which two layers of images are superimposed, features extreme close-ups of a new-born child and a technique that is new to the film: bits of images inserted into holes punched in successive frames of the film to produce a kind of animated mosaic or collage-like effect suggesting the infant's initial, disjointed engagement with the world outside the womb. Among the superimposed images are more shots of the woodsman working his way upwards as *Part 2* begins, and falling backwards as it ends.

Adding a third layer of superimposition, Brakhage devotes *Part 3* to the erotic body. Bare flesh, breasts and buttocks, vagina and penis, caressing hands and undulating bodies meet, overlap, merge, dissolve, and metamorphose. Distinctions between male and female and markers of separate individualities become increasingly blurred, and near the end the camera ''penetrates'' the fleshy, erotic surface of the body to display a beating heart and other more ambiguous images connoting the body's interior fluids, tissues, cavities, and organs. Finally, within the density of four layers of superimposition, images of the woodsman chopping the dead tree dominate *Part 4*, until the final moments when, as at the beginning of *Prelude*, the screen returns, by way of abstract flashes of light, to total darkness.

As even a brief and inadequate summary of the complete *Dog Star Man* indicates, particular images and themes introduced in *Prelude* predominate in different parts of the film, but never to the complete exclusion of the others. The result is an organic unity between the parts and the whole, reflecting, in formal terms, the work's theme of the interrelatedness of all things—animal, vegetable and mineral; microcosmic and macrocosmic; male and female; natural and artificial; external and internal (dreams, desires, the imagination, and what Brakhage has called ''closed-eye vision'' and ''patterns that move straight out from the inside of the mind through the optic nerves'').

In an interview conducted while he was in the midst of editing *Dog Star Man*, Brakhage summed up this urge to bring everything together—to ''bring forth children and films and inspire concerns with plants and rocks and all sights seen.'' While deeply personal in inspiration, *Dog Star Man* is also the preeminent example of an avant-garde film with epic scope and a hero of mythic proportions, comparable to other twentieth century, modernist classics like Ezra Pound's *Cantos* or James Joyce's *Ulysses.*

—William C. Wees

DOKTOR MABUSE DER SPIELER; DAS TESTAMENT DES DR. MABUSE

Director: Fritz Lang

DOKTOR MABUSE DER SPIELER

(Dr. Mabuse the Gambler)

Germany, 1922

Production: Uco-Film Studios; black and white, 35mm; silent; length: Part I (*Der grosse Spieler—Ein Bild der Zeit*) originally 3496 meters, Part II (*Inferno—Ein Spiel von Menschen unserer Zeit*) 2560 meters. Released 17 April 1922 (Part I) and 26 May 1922 (Part II). Filmed 1921–22. Part I in 8 weeks and Part II in 9 weeks; in Uco-Film studios in Berlin.

Screenplay: Fritz Lang and Thea von Harbou, from a novel by Norbert Jacques published in *Berliner Illustrierte Zeitung;* **photography:** Carl Hoffman; **art directors:** Carl Stahl Urach (died during production), Otto Hunte, Erich Kettelhut, and Karl Vollbrecht; **costume designer:** Vally Reinecke.

Cast: Rudolph Klein-Rogge (*Dr. Mabuse*); Aud Egede Nissen (*Cara Carezza, the dancer*); Gertrude Welcker (*Countess Told*); Alfred Abel (*Count Told*); Bernhard Goetzke (*Detective von Wenck*); Paul Richter (*Edgar Hull*); Robert Forster-Larringa (*Dr. Mabuse's servant*); Hans Adalbert Schlettow (*Georg, the chauffeur*); Georg John (*Pesche*); Karl Huszar (*Hawasch, manager of the counterfeiting factory*); Grete Berger (*Fine, Mabuse's servant*); Julius Falkenstein

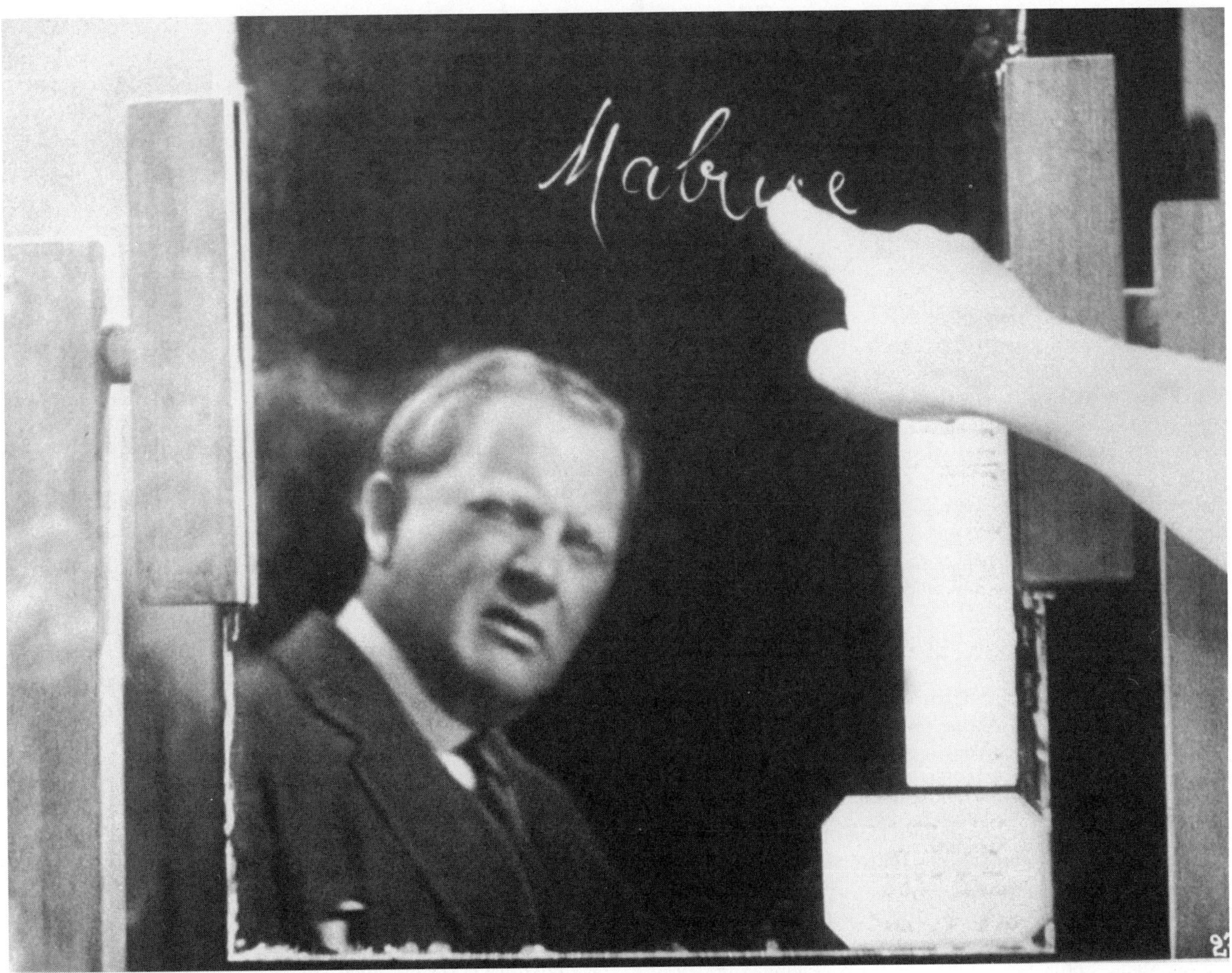

Das Testament des Dr. Mabuse

(*Karsten, Wenck's friend*); Lydia Potechina (*Russian woman*); Julius E. Herrman (*Schramm, the proprietor*); Karl Platen (*Told's servant*); Anita Berber (*Dancer*); Paul Biensfeldt (*Man with the pistol*); Edgar Pauly (*Fat Man*); Lil Dagover.

Publications

Books:

Rotha, Paul, *The Film Till Now*, London, 1930.
Weinberg, Herman G., *An Index to the Creative Work of Fritz Lang*, London, 1946.
Kracauer, Siegfried, *From Caligari to Hitler: A Psychological History of the German Film*, Princeton, 1947.
Eisenstein, Sergei, *Film Form*, New York, 1949.
Courtade, Francis, *Fritz Lang*, Paris, 1963.
Moullet, Luc, *Fritz Lang*, Paris, 1963.
Eibel, Alfred, editor, *Fritz Lang*, Paris, 1964.
Jensen, Paul M., *The Cinema of Fritz Lang*, New York, 1969.
Eisner, Lotte, *The Haunted Screen*, Berkeley, 1969.
Johnston, Claire, *Fritz Lang*, London, 1969.
Manvell, Roger, and Heinrich Fraenkel, *The German Cinema*, New York, 1971.
Henry, Michael, *Le Cinéma expressioniste allemand*, Paris, 1971.
Grafe, Frieda, Enno Patalas, and Hans Helmut Prinzler, *Fritz Lang*, Munich, 1976.
Eisner, Lotte, *Fritz Lang*, London, 1977.
Armour, Robert, *Fritz Lang*, Boston, 1978.
Ott, Frederick W., *The Films of Fritz Lang*, Secaucus, New Jersey, 1979.
Jenkins, Stephen, editor, *Fritz Lang: The Image and the Look*, London, 1979.
Kaplan, E. Ann, *Fritz Lang: A Guide to References and Resources*, Boston, 1981.
Maibohm, Ludwig, *Fritz Lang: Seine Filme—Sein Leben*, Munich, 1981.
Dürrenmatt, Dieter, *Fritz Lang: Leben und Werk*, Basel, 1982.
Bronner, S. E., and D. Kellner, *Passion and Rebellion: The Expressionist Heritage*, London, 1983.
Schnauber, Cornelius, *Fritz Lang in Hollywood*, Wein, 1986.

Jacques, Norbert, *Dr. Mabuse, der Spieler: Roman, Film, Dokumente*, St. Ingbert, 1987.
Humphries, Reynold, *Fritz Lang: Genre and Representation in His American Films*, Baltimore, 1989.
McGilligan, Patrick, *Fritz Lang: The Nature of the Beast*, New York, 1997.
Phillips, Gene D., *Exiles in Hollywood: Major European Film Directors in America*, London, 1998.

Articles:

Berliner Tageblatt, 30 April 1922.
Variety (New York), 2 June 1922.
Ihering, Herbert, in *Berliner Börsen-Courier*, 11 June 1922; reprinted in *Von Reinharft bis Brecht*, East Berlin, 1958.
Lang, Fritz, ''Kitsch: Sensation-Kultur und Film,'' in *Das Kulturfilmbuch*, edited by E. Beyfuss and P. Kossowsky, Berlin, 1924.
New York Times, 10 August 1927.
Hooper, Trask C., in *New York Times*, 20 May 1928.
Goetz, Fritz, in *New York Times*, 9 August 1928.
Eisner, Lotte, ''Notes sur le style de Fritz Lang,'' in *Revue de Cinéma* (Paris), 1 February 1947.
Wilson, Harry, ''The Genius of Fritz Lang,'' in *Film Quarterly* (London), Summer 1947.
Gesek, Ludwig, ''Fritz Lang: Suggestion und Stimmung,'' in *Gestalter der Filmkunst von Asta Nielsen bis Walt Disney*, Vienna, 1948.
Lang, Fritz, in *Penguin Film Review* (London), vol. 5, 1948.
Franju, Georges, ''Le Style de Fritz Lang,'' in *Cahiers du Cinéma* (Paris), November 1959.
Everschor, Franz, in *Film-Dienst* (Dusseldorf), 5 April 1961.
Taylor, John Russell, ''The Nine Lives of Dr. Mabuse,'' in *Sight and Sound* (London), Winter 1961.
Gregor, Ulrich, and Enno Patalas, ''Deutschland: Expressionismus und neue Sachlichkeit,'' in *Geschichte des Films*, Gütersloh, 1962.
Shivas, Mark, ''Fritz Lang Talks about Dr. Mabuse,'' in *Movie* (London), November 1962.
Berg, Gretchen, editor, ''La Nuit viennoise: Une Confession de Fritz Lang,'' in *Cahiers du Cinéma* (Paris), August 1965.
Freund, Rudolf, ''Zwischen Kunst und Kolportage,'' in *Filmspiegel* (East Berlin), 1 December 1965.
Legrand, Gérard, ''Nouvelles notes pour un éloge de Fritz Lang,'' in *Positif* (Paris), April 1968.
Toeplitz, J., in *Kino* (Warsaw), March 1972.
Burch, Noël, ''De Mabuse a M: Le Travail de Fritz Lang,'' in *Revue d'Esthétique* (Paris), 1973.
Sayre, Nora, in *New York Times*, 15 October 1973.
Milne, Tom, in *Monthly Film Bulletin* (London), May 1974.
Boost, C., ''Fritz Lang,'' in *Skoop* (Amsterdam), February 1975.
Blumenberg, Hans, ''Kino der Angst,'' in *Die Zeit* (Hamburg), 13 September 1976.
Jubak, J., ''Lang and Parole: Character and Narrative in Doktor Mabuse, der Spieler,'' in *Film Criticism* (Edinboro, Pennsylvania), no. 1, 1979.
Fischer, Lucy, ''Dr. Mabuse and Mr. Lang,'' in *Wide Angle* (Athens, Ohio), Winter 1980.
Kane, P., ''Revoir Mabuse,'' in *Cahiers du Cinéma* (Paris), March 1980.
Burch, Noël, ''Notes on Fritz Lang's First Mabuse,'' in *Ciné-Tracts* (Montreal), Spring 1981.
Johnston, S., in *Films and Filming* (London), July 1982.
Bergstrom, J., ''Expressionism and Mabuse,'' in *Iris* (Iowa City), Autumn 1992.
Brandlmeier, T., ''Mabuse komplett,'' in *EPD Film* (Frankfurt), April 1995.
Elsaesser, Thomas, ''Fritz Lang: The Illusion of Mastery (German Film Director),'' in *Sight and Sound* (London), vol. 10, no. 1, January 2000.

DAS TESTAMENT DES DR. MABUSE

(The Last Will of Dr. Mabuse)

Germany, 1933

Production: Nero-Film A.G. Studios; black and white, 35mm; running time: about 122 minutes; length 3334 meters. Released 5 December 1933 in Vienna, a French version (95 minutes) was shot simultaneously with the same technical crew and released April 1933 in Paris. Filmed in 10 weeks in 1932 in Nero-Film A.G. studios in Berlin.

Producer: Seymour Nebenzal; **screenplay:** Thea von Harbou and Fritz Lang, from the characters in a novel by Norbert Jacques; **photography:** Fritz Arno Wagner and Karl Vass; **art directors:** Karl Vollbrecht and Emil Hasler; **music:** Hans Erdmann.

Cast: Rudolph Klein-Rogge (*Dr. Mabuse*); Oskar Beregi (*Dr. Baum*); Karl Meixner (*Landlord*); Theodor Loos (*Dr. Kramm, assistant to Baum*); Otto Wernicke (*Detective Lohmann*); Klaus Pohl (*Müller, Lohmann's assistant*); Wera Liessem (*Lilli*); Gustav Diessl (*Thomas Kent*); Camilla Spira (*Jewel-Anna*); Rudolf Schündler (*Hardy*); Theo Lingen (*Hardy's friend*); Paul Oskar Höcker (*Bredow*); Paul Henckels (*Lithographer*); Georg John (*Baum's servant*); Ludwig Stössel (*Worker*); Hadrian M. Netto (*Nicolai Grigoriew*); Paul Bernd (*Blackmailer*); Henry Pless (*Dunce*); A. E. Licho (*Dr. Hauser*); Karl Platen, Anna Goltz, and Heinrich Gretler (*Sanitarium Assistants*); Gerhard Bienart, Paul Bernd, Ernst Ludwig, Klaus Pohl, and Paul Rehkopf (*Detectives*).

Publications

Articles:

Variety (New York), 9 May 1933.
Rotha, Paul, in *Cinema Quarterly* (London), Autumn 1934.
Crowther, Bosley, in *New York Times*, 20 March 1943.
Romano, Sergio, in *Cinema* (Rome), 10 November 1948.
''One Facet of Lang's Art Prophetic of Hitlerism,'' in *Herald Tribune* (New York), 21 March 1949.
Ruppert, Martin, in *Frankfurter Allgemeine Zeitung*, 13 September 1951.
G.J., in *Monthly Film Bulletin* (London), January 1954.
Kipfmuller, Erwin, ''Gespräch mit Fritz Lang,'' in *Film* (Munich), December 1956.

Mardore, Michel, ''Le Diabolique Docteur Mabuse,'' in *Cinéma* (Paris), August-September 1961.

Rhode, Eric, ''Fritz Lang (The German Period, 1919–1933),'' in *Tower of Babel*, London, 1966.

New York Times, 6 December 1973.

Greenspun, Roger, in *Film Comment* (New York), March-April 1973.

William, Paul, in *Village Voice* (New York), 12 September 1974.

Phillips, Gene D., ''Fritz Lang Gives His Last Interview,'' in *Village Voice* (New York), 16 August 1976.

Lang, Fritz, ''On Dr. Mabuse,'' in *Monthly Film Bulletin* (London), April 1978.

Audibert, L., in *Cinématographe* (Paris), December 1979.

Cluny, C. M., in *Cinéma* (Paris), January 1980.

Legrand, Gérard, ''Le Nom de l'innommable,'' in *Positif* (Paris), March 1980.

Werner, G., ''Fritz Lang and Goebbels: Myth and Facts,'' in *Film Quarterly* (Berkeley), no. 3, 1990.

Lenne, Gérard, ''Le testament du Dr Mabuse: les inventions de Lang,'' in *Mensuel du Cinéma*, no. 10, October 1993.

Brandlmeier, T., ''Mabuse komplett,'' in *EPD Film* (Frankfurt), April 1995.

Also see list of publications following the *Doktor Mabuse, Der Spieler* credits.

* * *

The popular novelist Thea von Harbou began her unbroken 12-year scripting association with Fritz Lang in 1920. Divorcing the actor Rudolf Klein-Rogge, she married Lang in 1924, working with him until 1932 when they separated and subsequently divorced after Lang's hasty departure from Germany. Lang had already gained considerable success as the writer-director of *Die Spinnen.* In Thea von Harbou, he found an ideal writing partner to develop the psychological potentiality of a psychotic genius and master-criminal, Dr. Mabuse. Mabuse became the protagonist in Lang's two celebrated films of 1922 and 1933.

Dr. Mabuse the Gambler, Part I, began by showing Mabuse making a fortune on the stock market and using hypnotism to win $50,000 from Edgar Hull, whom Mabuse finally murders after inducing his own exotic mistress, the dancer Cara Carezza, to seduce him. He induces Cara to commit suicide when she is faced with arrest. Opposed to Mabuse is von Wenck, the public prosecutor; in Part II Wenck manages to resist Mabuse's attempts to hypnotise him and traces the criminal to his head-quarters, a building placed under siege by the police. When arrested Mabuse goes insane. Reviving the character of Mabuse 10 years later in *The Last Will of Dr. Mabuse* Lang and Harbou show how the insane Mabuse uses his hypnotic powers to induce Dr. Baum, director of the asylum where he is being held, to maintain his criminal activities outside and, indeed, on Mabuse's death to accept that he is the reincarnation of the mad doctor. Commissioner Lehmann (the dedicated police superintendent Lang had introduced in *M*), exposes Baum, who finally goes mad after the model of Mabuse and inhabits the criminal's original cell. Mabuse was revived, according to Lang, as a projection of Hitler: ''I put all the Nazi slogans into the mouth of the ghost of the criminal,'' he has stated. In 1933 Goebbels banned both Mabuse films. ''Out of the Mabuses,'' Lang wrote later when *The Last Will of Dr. Mabuse* was salvaged and released in America in 1943, ''came the Heydrichs, the Himmlers and the Hitlers.'' He added, ''This film was made as an allegory to show Hitler's processes of terrorism.''

Lang always insisted that the original character of Mabuse had contemporary significance even in 1922. He seems to represent an arch criminal of that period of galloping inflation that destroyed the German currency, and with it German social morale. According to Lotte Eisner, Lang's friend and biographer, the Berlin critics accepted his reference to the times without demur. Writing of the period, Lang himself said, ''The First World War brought changes. In Europe, an entire generation of intellectuals embraced despair; young people, myself among them, made a fetish of tragedy.'' This helps to account for the fact that insanity in various forms became a recurrent theme in German cinema of the 1920s. Lang regarded his film not merely as a box-office thriller but as a document of the time, and Siegfried Kracauer terms Mabuse, ''a contemporary tyrant,'' a symbol of mad, anti-social domination, combining a lust for absolute tyranny with the desire to effect social chaos. Like Caligari before him, he is insane and makes continual use of hypnosis to overcome his victims: an attempt is even made to hypnotise the audience. Lang indeed was concerned to give his film a contemporary psychological touch; Mabuse's thirst for power and his Protean manifestations in a ceaseless flow of disguises make him seem ever-present and ever-active in society. Eric Rhode, writing in *Tower of Babel* (1966), sees the original film and the character of Mabuse as a myth of its time reflecting ''not only the confusion and anxieties of the Weimar Republic,'' but also Oswald Spengler's romantic, fatalistic thesis in his bestseller, *The Decline of the West* (1918), in which he claimed that city-bound man is doomed through his power-lust for money. This was relevant not only to Lang's *Mabuse* but to his most spectacular work of the 1920s, *Metropolis.* In *Mabuse* his primary settings are gambling dens, depraved nightclubs, and the Stock Exchange. Mabuse is a vampire gambler and cheat extraordinary, operating against society on a universal scale, typified here by such characters as the wealthy, degenerate Count and Countess Told. As played by Rudolf Klein-Rogge, Mabuse has all the appearance of an actor-like, romantic genius—the penetrating eyes and the flowing mane of hair swept back from a towering brow.

Lang, whose father was a Viennese architect and whose training had been in art, had a strongly developed visual and structural eye. Paul Rotha, himself trained as an artist, admits that Mabuse ''was far ahead of its time in décor.'' He writes of ''the perfection of camera work and lighting effects'' in Lang's films. Lang employed the irising device to dramatic effect, double, triple and quadruple exposures, and chiaroscuro lighting: for visual effect, Eric Rhode suggests the scene when the ''mad count wanders with a candelabrum through his twilit mansion.'' Lang, he points out, ''favours middle or long distance shots, and a rim lighting that gives his characters both dimension and solidity. In *Dr. Mabuse* rooms tend to be ample, while streets are so narrow that cars jam and bump into each other.'' Sergei Eisenstein, who had assisted Esther Shub in re-editing *Dr. Mabuse* for Russian audiences, commented on ''the mystic criminal reaching out towards us from our screens showing us a future as an unrelieved night crowded with sinister shadows.''

Lang was to make one further film featuring Mabuse in 1960, working again in Germany. Though adroitly made, *The Thousand Eyes of Dr. Mabuse*, a somewhat pale revival of Mabuse in the form of a madman who believes himself the reincarnation of the dead criminal but turns out to be Mabuse's son, seemed out of place by the 1960s.

—Roger Manvell

LA DOLCE VITA

(The Sweet Life)

Italy-France, 1960

Director: Federico Fellini

Production: Riama Film (Rome) and Pathé Consortium Cinéma (Paris); black and white, 35mm. Totalscope; running time: 180 minutes. Released February 1960. Rome. Filmed 16 March-27 August 1959 in Rome, the Odescalchi Palace, Fregene, and in the studios of Cinecittà.

Producers: Giuseppe Amato with Angelo Rizzoli, and Franco Magli as executive producer; **screenplay:** Federico Fellini, Tullio Pinelli, Brunello Rondi, and Ennio Flaiano, from an original story by Federico Fellini, Tullio Pinelli and Ennio Flaiano; **photography:** Otello Martelli; **editor:** Leo Cattozzo; **sound:** Agostino Moretti; **art director:** Piero Gherardi; **music:** Nino Rota; **costume designer:** Piero Gherardi; **artisic collaborator:** Brunello Rondi.

Cast: Marcello Mastroianni (*Marcello Rubini*); Walter Santesso (*Paparazzo, the photographer*); Anouk Aimée (*Maddalena*); Adriana Moneta (*Prostitute*); Yvonne Furneaux (*Emma, Marcello's mistress*); Anita Ekberg (*Sylvia, a Hollywood star*); Lex Barker (*Robert, Sylvia's fiancée*); Alan Dijon (*Frankie Stout*); Alain Cuny (*Steiner*); Valeria Ciangottini (*Paola*); Annibale Ninchi (*Marcello's father*); Magali Noel (*Fanny, a chorus girl*); Nadia Gray (*Nadia*); Jacques Sernas (*Matinee idol*); Polidor (*Clown*).

La dolce vita

Awards: Cannes Film Festival, Gold Palm, 1960; Oscar for Best Foreign Picture, 1961; New York Film Critics Award, Best Foreign Film, 1961.

Publications

Script:

Fellini, Federico, and others, *La dolce vita*, edited by Tullio Kezich, Bologna, 1960; translated as *La Dolce Vita*, New York, 1961; also included in *Quattro film*, Turin, 1974.

Books:

Renzi, Renzo, *Federico Fellini*, Lyons, 1960.
Agel, Henri, *Le Cinéma et le sacré*, Paris, 1961.
Lo Duca, Giuseppe, editor, *La Dolce Vita*, Paris, 1961.
Borde, Raymond, and André Bouissy, *Nouveau cinéma italien*, Lyons, 1963.
Budgen, Suzanne, *Fellini*, London, 1966.
Huss, Roy, and Norman Silverstein, *The Film Experience*, New York, 1968.
Richardson, Robert, *Literature and Film*, Bloomington, Indiana, 1969.
Ketcham, Charles, *Federico Fellini: The Search for a New Mythology*, New York, 1976.
Rosenthal, Stuart, *The Cinema of Federico Fellini*, London, 1976.
Strich, Christian, editor, *Fellini on Fellini*, New York, 1976.
Stubbs, John, *Federico Fellini: A Guide to References and Resources*, Boston, 1978.
Alpert, Hollis, *Fellini: A Life*, New York, 1981.
Fruttero, Carlo, and Franco Lucentini, *Je te trouve un peu pâle: Récit d'été avec trente fantasmes féminins de Federico Fellini*, Paris, 1982.
Costello, Donald, P., *Fellini's Road*, Notre Dame, Indiana, 1983.
Grazzini, Giovanni, editor, *Federico Fellini, Intervista sul cinema*, Rome, 1983.
Burke, Frank, *Federico Fellini: Variety Lights to La Dolce Vita*, Boston, 1984.
Chandler, Charlotte, *The Ultimate Seduction*, New York, 1984.
Fava, Claudio F., and Aldo Vigano, *The Films of Federico Fellini*, Secaucus, New Jersey, 1985.
Murray, Edward, *Fellini the Artist*, New York, 1985.
Kezich, Tullio, *Fellini*, Milan, 1987.
Bondanella, Peter, *The Cinema of Federico Fellini*, Princeton, 1992.
Secchiaroli, Tazio, *Tutto Fellini*, New York, 1994.
Costantini, Costanzo, *Conversations with Fellini*, San Diego, 1996.
Chandler, Charlotte, *I, Fellini*, Collingdale, 1998.

Articles:

"Su *La dolce vita* la parola a Fellini," in *Bianco e Nero* (Rome), January-February 1960.
Aristarco, Guido, in *Cinema Nuovo* (Turin), January-February 1960.
Bruno, Edoardo, in *Filmcritica* (Rome), February 1960.
Pasolino, Pier Paolo, "L'irrazionalismo cattolico di Fellini," in *Filmcritica* (Rome), February 1960.

Rondi, Brunello, ''Dialettica de *La dolce vita*,'' in *Filmcritica* (Rome), February 1960.
Laura, Ernesto, ''La stagione delle mele d'oro,'' in *Bianco e Nero* (Rome), March-April 1960.
Delouche, Dominique, ''Un Fellini baroque,'' in *Etudes Cinématographiques* (Paris), Spring 1960.
Grandi, Libero, ''Filming *La Dolce Vita* in Black-and-White and Wide-Screen,'' in *American Cinematographer* (Los Angeles), April 1960.
Lane, John Francis, ''Fellini Tells Why,'' in *Films and Filming* (London), June 1960.
Agel, Henri, in *Etudes Cinématographiques* (Paris), Summer 1960.
Laugier, Jean-Louis, ''Il dolce Fellini,'' in *Cahiers du Cinéma* (Paris), July 1960.
Mardore, Michel, in *Positif* (Paris), July-August 1960.
Lefèvre, Raymond, in *Image et Son* (Paris), October 1960.
Rhode, Eric, in *Sight and Sound* (London), Winter 1960.
Durgnat, Raymond, in *Films and Filming* (London), January 1961.
''Quattro domande sul cinema italiano,'' in *Cinema Nuovo* (Turin), January-February 1961.
Mekas, Jonas, in *Village Voice* (New York), April 1961.
Alpert, Hollis, in *Saturday Review* (New York), 15 April 1961.
Crowther, Bosley, in *New York Times*, 20 April 1961.
Kauffmann, Stanley, in *New Republic* (New York), 1 May 1961.
Lane, John Francis, in *Films and Filming* (London), June 1961.
Hart, Henry, in *Films in Review* (New York), June-July 1961.
Franchi, R. L., in *Film Quarterly* (Berkeley), Summer 1961.
Holland, Norman, ''The Follies Fellini,'' in *Hudson Review* (New York), Autumn 1961.
Peri, Enzo, ''Federico Fellini: An Interview,'' in *Film Quarterly* (Berkeley), Fall 1961.
Duprey, Richard, ''Bergman and Fellini, Explorers of the Modern Spirit,'' in *Catholic World* (Paramus, New Jersey), October 1961.
Bergtal, Eric, ''The Lonely Crowd in *La Dolce Vita*,'' in *America* (New York), 7 October 1961.
Flaus, John, in *Film Journal* (Evanston, Illinois), April 1962.
Kael, Pauline, ''The Come-Dressed-As-the-Sick-Soul-of-Europe Parties,'' in *Massachusetts Review* (Amherst), Winter 1963.
Harcourt, Peter, ''The Secret Life of Federico Fellini,'' in *Film Quarterly* (Berkeley), Spring 1966.
Levine, Irving R., ''I Was Born for the Cinema,'' in *Film Comment* (New York), Fall 1966.
Wood, Robin, ''The Question of Fellini Continues,'' in *December* (London), nos. 2–3, 1967.
Baldelli, P., ''Dilatazione visionaria del documento e nostalgia della madre chiesa in Fellini,'' in *Cinema dell'ambiguità: Rossellini, De Sica e Zavattini, Fellini*, Rome, 1971.
Lefèvre, Raymond, ''Fellini,'' in *Image et Son* (Paris), January 1971.
Julia, Jacques, ''Psychanalyse de Fellini,'' in *Cinéma* (Paris), May 1971.
Martin, Marcel, ''Un Artiste sous le chapiteau,'' in *Cinema* (Paris), May 1971.
Torres Fernández, A., in *Contracampo* (Madrid), June-July 1981.
Villien, Bruno, in *Cinématographe* (Paris), September 1981.
Film Criticism (Meadville, Pennsylvania), Autumn 1984.
Pulleine, Tim, in *Films and Filming* (London), September 1987.
Nowell-Smith, Geoffrey, in *Monthly Film Bulletin* (London), October 1987.
Rhodie, S., ''How Sweet It Is: *La Dolce Vita*,'' in *Cinema Papers* (Fitzroy), March 1989.
Kiarostami, Abbas, ''De Sophia Loren à *La dolce vita*,'' in *Positif* (Paris), June 1994.
Childebert, T., and André Moreau, ''Dolce vita dolorosa: *La dolce vita*,'' in *Télérama* (Paris), 26 October 1994.
Amengual, Barthélemy, ''Propositions pour un portrait du jeune Fellini en néo-réaliste,'' in *Positif* (Paris), July-August 1995.
Hutera, Donald, interview with David Glass, in *Time Out* (London), 3 April 1996.
Castiel, E., in *Séquences* (Haute-Ville), no. 189, March/June 1997.
Statta, Gloria, ''The Buzz About Paparazzi: Marcello Mastroianni Remembers Working with Federico Fellini and Tazio Secchiaroli, the First Paparazzo,'' in *Aperture*, no. 150, Winter 1998.
Gundle, Stephen, *La Dolce Vita*, in *History Today*, vol. 50, no. 1, January 2000.

* * *

Fellini's epic study of the loss of values at the climax of the Italian ''economic miracle,'' delineates the daily activities of a writer, turned reporter for a sensationalist journal, who is too deeply compromised by the degeneracy around him to see it, never mind report on it. The opening and closing scenes of the film are cleverly matched allusions to Dante which underscore the moral loss and its consequences for Italy, at the very moment when the revival of Fascism was beginning to make a difference in the balance of political powers.

Marcello follows a helicopter delivering a monumental statue of Christ, on a tow line, to the Vatican. From his own helicopter, he flirts with women sunbathing on a roof. The noise of the machine drowns out his voice as he tries to shout for their telephone numbers. In a parallel scene of shot-countershot the film ends with Marcello accosted by a charming and innocent girl who had once waited on his table. A stretch of water separates them and the noise of the sea makes her words inaudible to him. An Italian audience might recognize the allusion to the Medusa of the *Inferno* in the grotesquely reified image of Christ soaring through the Roman sky; even more evident would be the figure of Matilda at the top of *Purgatorio* who represents the summit of earthly beauty, irradiated by divine grace. Marcello has lost the ability to react to the grossness of the former and the saving promise of the latter. The world he inhabits is as lost as he is: Marcello moves from prostitutes to aristocratic women while, at the same time, deceiving his girlfriend; his intellectual friend, Steiner, who had urged him to find more fulfilling work, kills himself and his children; he covers for his newspaper the scene of a false miracle where someone is trampled by the enthusiastic crowd; he follows an American movie star as she utters banalities and poses for the press. In the center of the film Marcello accompanies his father on his first night in Rome since he was one of Mussolini's blackshirts (this is subtly suggested by the old man's references, never bluntly stated). The father's physical collapse and profound embarrassment when he fails to perform with a prostitute predicts the hero's eventual confrontation with the limitation of his values, just as its suggests that the playboy figure of 1959, brilliantly represented by Marcello Mastroianni, is a modern version of the Fascist ideal.

The moral atmosphere of *La dolce vita* reflects that in all of Fellini's films, but the grandeur of its scale, the refusal to resort to a pitiful or lovable protagonist, and the accuracy of its caricatures make it one of his most enduring achievements. Its initial success was, however, due in great part to the supposedly daring and sensational manner with which it dealt with sexual themes. Actually, it was one of three films to emerge from Italy at the end of the 1950s which heralded a powerful renewal of that national cinema. The others were Michelangelo Antonioni's *L'avventura* and Luchino Visconti's *Rocco e i suoi fratelli*, both released in 1960.

—P. Adams Sitney

DOM ZA VESANJE

(Time of the Gypsies)

Yugoslavia-USA, 1989

Director: Emir Kusturica

Production: Forum Film, Sarajevo TV and Columbia Pictures; colour, 35mm; running time: 142 minutes.

Producer: Mirza Pasic; **executive producer:** Milan Martinovic; **co-producer:** Harry Saltzman; **screenplay:** Emir Kusturica, Gordan Mihic; **photography:** Vilko Filac; **editor:** Andrija Zafranovic; **assistant directors:** Maja Gardinovacki, Dragan Kresoja; **production design:** Miljen Kljakovic; **music:** Goran Bregovic; **sound:** Gordana Petakovic, Ivan Zakic, Srdan Popovic, Theodore Mitchel Yannie, Mladen Prebil.

Cast: Davor Dujmovic (*Perhan*); Bora Todorovic (*Ahmed Dzida*); Ljubica Adzovic (*Baba*); Husnija Hasmovic (*Uncle Merdzan*); Sinolicka Trpkova (*Azra*); Zabit Memedov (*Zabit*); Elvira Sali (*Daca*); Suada Karisik (*Dzamila*); Ajnur Redzepi (*Perhan's son*).

Awards: Best Director, Cannes 1989.

Publications

Books:

Horton, Andrew, *''Time of the Gypsies,'' Writing the Character Centered Screenplay*, Berkeley, 1994.
Horton, Andrew, ''Ethnic Godfathers and Grandmothers: Emir Kusturica & *Time of the Gypsies*'s Balkan Makeover of Coppola's Godfathers'' in *Play It Again, Sam: Retakes on Remakes*, edited by Andrew Horton & Stuart McDougal, Berkeley, 1996.
Bertellini, Giorgio, *Emir Kusturica*, Milano, 1996.

Articles:

Variety (New York), 17 May 1989.
Brisset, S., and G. Ptillat, *Cinéma* (Paris), October 1989.
Grugeau, G., ''Entre ciel et terre'' in *24 Images* (Montreal), Fall 1989.
Gauthier, G., *Revue du Cinéma* (Paris), November 1989.
Gili, G.A., and others, ''Emir Kusturica'' in *Positif* (Paris), November 1989.
Katsahnias, I., ''Freaks, freaks. . .'' in *Cahiers du Cinéma* (Paris), November 1989.
Insadorf, Annette, ''Gypsy Life Beguiles a Film Maker'' in *The New York Times*, February 4, 1990.
Brown, G., *Monthly Film Bulletin* (London), April 1990.
Beauchamp, M., and G. Grugeau, ''La quête du pays'' in *24 Images* (Montreal), Summer 1990.
Schupp, P., *Séquences* (Montreal), June 1990.
Feldvoss, Marli, in *EPD Film* (Frankfurt), September 1991.
Binder, David, ''A Bosnian Movie Maker Laments the Death of the Yugoslav Nation'' in *The New York Times*, October 25, 1992.
Iskusstvo Kino (Moscow), December 1992.
Dakovic, Nevena, ''Mother, Myth, and Cinema: Recent Yugoslav Cinema,'' in *Film Criticism* (Meadville), vol. 21, no. 2, Winter 1996–1997.
Wrathall, John, ''Gypsy Time,'' in *Sight & Sound* (London), December 1997.
Rouyer, Philippe, and Michel Ciment, ''Emir Kusturica,'' in *Positif* (Paris), October 1998.
''Misdirected Pride (Bosnian Filmmaker Emir Kusturica),'' in *Economist*, vol. 351, no. 8115, 17 April 1999.
Horton, Andrew, '''But to Have Dreamed It All': The Balkans' Healing Irony (Balkan Cinema),'' in *Chronicle of Higher Education*, vol. 45, no. 43, 2 July 1999.

* * *

It is one of the ironies of contemporary cinema that one of the most celebrated filmmakers anywhere is Emir Kusturica, a Bosnian Muslim from Sarajevo, who has been able to draw upon his rich yet troubled former country to weave memorable tales of humor, horror and pathos, all under the banner word he calls ''joy.'' *When Father Was Away On Business* won the Palm D'Or at the Cannes Film Festival in 1985 as a powerful tale about the survival of a Muslim family under the anti-Stalinist terrorism in Yugoslavia in the 1950s, and he won the Palm D'Or a second time in 1995 for *Underground*, a darkly carnivalesque vision of the breakup of Yugoslavia mixing equal doses of realism and Balkan surrealism. And *Time of the Gypsies* won the Cannes Best Director Award in 1989 for this exuberant yet pessimistic narrative based on a true story of Yugoslav gypsies selling their own children into a form of slavery in Italy.

An appreciation of Kusturica's film today, of course, comes with the uneasy awareness of how strangely cinematic narratives can sometimes foreshadow history. For while Kusturica's tale which echoes Coppola's Godfather trilogy in a number of ways does not speak of ethnic cleansing and religious intolerance, the forces of chaos suggested in the film do seem to provide some insight into the horrors of the current Bosnian and Balkan conflicts.

Kusturica manages a difficult balancing act in this film as he was able to use American financing (Columbia Pictures produced and released the film) to shoot a film almost entirely in the gypsy language which meant it would need subtitles in every country, including the

Dom za vesanje

soon-to-collapse Yugoslavia. He also took a chance on a number of gypsy actors and actresses including the wonderful Hasnija Hasmovic who plays an almost mythical Earth Mother-Grandmother figure at the center of everything in the film.

At its core, *Time of the Gypsies* is a coming-of-age story in line with Kusturica's previous work including *Do You Remember Dolly Bell?* (1981), his first feature, which tracks a teenage Bosnian Muslim would-be rock star through his first love and sexual experience in 1970s Sarajevo. Similarly *When Father Was Away on Business* follows an eight-year-old son who is trying both to grow up and hold onto a childhood in a world fragmented by political, religious and ethnic hatreds.

Writing with one of Yugoslavia's most talented screenwriters, Goran Mihic, Kusturica fashioned in *Time of the Gypsies* a tale of young Pehan who passes through the joy and heartbreak of first love onto his rites of passage as a gypsy gangster protégé of a flamboyant gypsy Godfather played with memorable brio by Yugoslavia's John Wayne-like icon, Bora Todorovic.

Kusturica and Mihic draw strict tensions between the orphaned Pehan's love for his grandmother who is raising him and her centered life in Yugoslavia, and his desire to help his ailing sister by working as a pickpocket and common thief in Northern Italy under Todorovic's exploitive gaze. Completely caught in the middle is Azra, the girl next door, whom he marries at last, but cannot trust.

At turns tragic and comic, realistic and touching on magic realism (Pehan, for instance, has telekinetic powers that come into play for the unusual revenge scene at the end), *Time of the Gypsies* is also a vibrant hymn to the ''time of cinema'' on the big screen with big sound and big themes—the homeless, the downtrodden, the importance of love, self worth, loyalty and friendship.

It almost seems not an accident that this film came out the same year as *Cinema Paradiso* which also celebrates the power of cinema through a male coming-of-age tale. Kusturica's film is the more tragic simply because the Balkans themselves are more troubled than the sun drenched lands of Southern Italy seen in *Cinema Paradiso*.

But, rather than depressed, the viewer comes away with an admiration of a simple tale told with such elaborate gusto as well as with appreciation for what a filmmaker working at the peak of his powers can do with the craft and art of cinema. For while this film is firmly rooted in the Balkans, it is also a tribute to world cinema. Kusturica has made it abundantly clear that he is strongly influenced by John Ford, Luis Bunuel, Coppola, various Russian and Czech directors (he was educated like many Yugoslav directors of his generation in Prague at the well-known FAMU Academy) and Chaplin.

For all the heartbreak and humor, the final image of this troubled epic is of the Uncle figure, back to the camera, jacket clutched around him, doing a funny little walk, going away from us, looking amazingly like Chaplin going down the road of life as he did in the final shot of almost all of his films. For Chaplin too played the Outsider, the Homeless One, the Unlucky in Love fellow who survives and hopes and travels.

—Andrew Horton

DONA FLOR E SEUS DOIS MARIDOS

(Dona Flor and Her Two Husbands)

Brazil, 1976

Director: Bruno Barreto

Production: Produções cinematográficas L.C. Barreto; Eastmancolor, 35mm; running time: 110 minutes. Released in 1976. Filmed in Salvador and Rio de Janeiro.

Producers: Luis Carlos Barreto, Newton Rique, Cia Serrador, Paula Cezar Sesso, Nelson Potro; **screenplay:** Bruno Barreto; **adapters:** Eduardo Coutinho, Leopoldo Serran; **photography:** Maurilo Salles; **editor:** Raimundo Higino; **assistant director:** Jorge Duran, Emiliano Ribeiro; **art director:** Anisio Medeiros; **music:** Chico Buarque de Holanda; **songs:** Simone; **sound:** Walter Gulart, Antonio Cezar.

Cast: Sonia Braga (*Dona Flor*); José Wilker (*Vadinho*); Mauro Mendonça (*Teodoro*); Dinorah Brillanti (*Rozilda*); Nelson Xavier (*Mirandão*); Arthur Costa Filho (*Carlinhos*); Rui Rezende (*Cazuza*); Mario Gusmão (*Arigof*); Nelson Dantas (*Clodoaldo*); Haydil Linhares (*Norma*); Nilda Spencer (*Dinorá*); Silvia Cadaval (*Jacy*); Helio Ary (*Venceslau Diniz*); Mara Rúbia (*Claudete*); Manfredo Colassanti (*Pelanchi*).

Publications

Books:

Mitchell, Robert, in *Magill's Survey of Cinema: Foreign Language Films, Volume 2*, edited by Frank Magill, Englewood, New Jersey, 1985.

Aycock, Wendell, and Michael Schoenecke, editors, *Film and Literature: A Comparative Approach to Adaptation*, Lubbock, Texas, 1988.

Articles:

Ribeiro, Leo Gilson, *Jornal da Tarde* (São Paulo), 23 November 1976.

Veja, ''Dona Flor e o cinema brasileiro,'' *Editora Abril* (São Paulo), 1 December 1976.

Vartuck, Pola, *O Estado de São Paulo* (São Paulo), 2 December 1976.

Ferreira, Fernando, *O Globo* (Rio de Janeiro), 16 December 1976.

Queiroz, Dinah Silveira, *O Imparcial* (São Luís), 7 January 1977.

Amado, Jorge, ''A minha Dona Flor,'' *Estado de Minas* (Belo Horizonte), 29 January 1977.

Stigger, Ivo Egon, *Correio do Povo* (Porto Alegre), 17 April 1977.

Nascimento, Helio, *Jornal do Comércio* (Porto Alegre), 20 April 1977.

Branco, Heloísa Castello, *Jornal do Brasil* (Rio de Janeiro), 10 August 1977.

Variety (New York), 14 September 1977.

Lefévre, R., *Cinéma* (Paris), October 1977.

Pilla, M. R., and P. A. Paranagua, ''Deux éléphants ça trompe énormément,'' in *Postif* (Paris), November 1977.

Haun, Harry, *Daily News* (New York), 2 February 1978.

Schiller, Beatriz, *Jornal do Brasil* (Rio de Janeiro), 23 February 1978.

Maslin, Janet, *New York Times*, 27 February 1978.

Ferreira, Sonia Nolasco, *O Globo* (Rio de Janeiro), 1 March 1978.

Jornal da Tarde (São Paulo), 20 March 1978.

Francis, Paulo, *Folha de São Paulo* (São Paulo), 10 June 1978.

Webb, Michael, *Jornal do Brasil*, 25 July 1978.

Revista Filme e Cultura, number 33, May 1979.

Auty, M., *Monthly Film Bulletin* (London), June 1979.

Critical Dossiers. Embrafilme, Rio de Janeiro, Brazil.

Stjerne, H., *Chaplin* (Stockholm), vol. 22, no. 5, 1980.

Santos Moray, Mercedes, *Cine Cubano* (Habana), no. 119, 1987.

Horton, Andrew, ''Bakhtin, Carnival Triumph, and Cinema: Bruno Barreto's *Doña Flor and Her Two Husbands* and Dusan Makavejev's *Innocence Unprotected* Reconsidered,'' *Quarterly Review of Film and Video* (Reading), May 1990.

Edinger, C., ''Doña Flor in Two Cultures,'' *Literature/Film Quarterly* (Salisbury), October 1991.

* * *

Irrespective of its other qualities, *Dona Flor e seus dois maridos* is noteworthy for having attracted an audience larger than any other Brazilian film. Due to the serious crisis curtailing the output of the Brazilian film industry over the last few years, the film's public of 12 million spectators is unlikely to be surpassed before the end of the century. Bruno Barreto was aged 21 when *Dona Flor* was launched in November 1976, but, despite his youth, was not a newcomer on the film scene. He is the son of Luiz Carlos Barreto, one of the most important Brazilian producers, responsible for several significant films during the Cinema Novo period. Bruno Barreto grew up in the film world; at the age of 11 he started to film in 16 mm, and at the age of 17 concluded his first feature film, *Tati, a Garota*, establishing not only his precocity, but also a propensity for easy communication with the masses.

What, then, is the secret of the incredible success of *Dona Flor*, whose impact in Brazil is unparalleled and whose repercussion

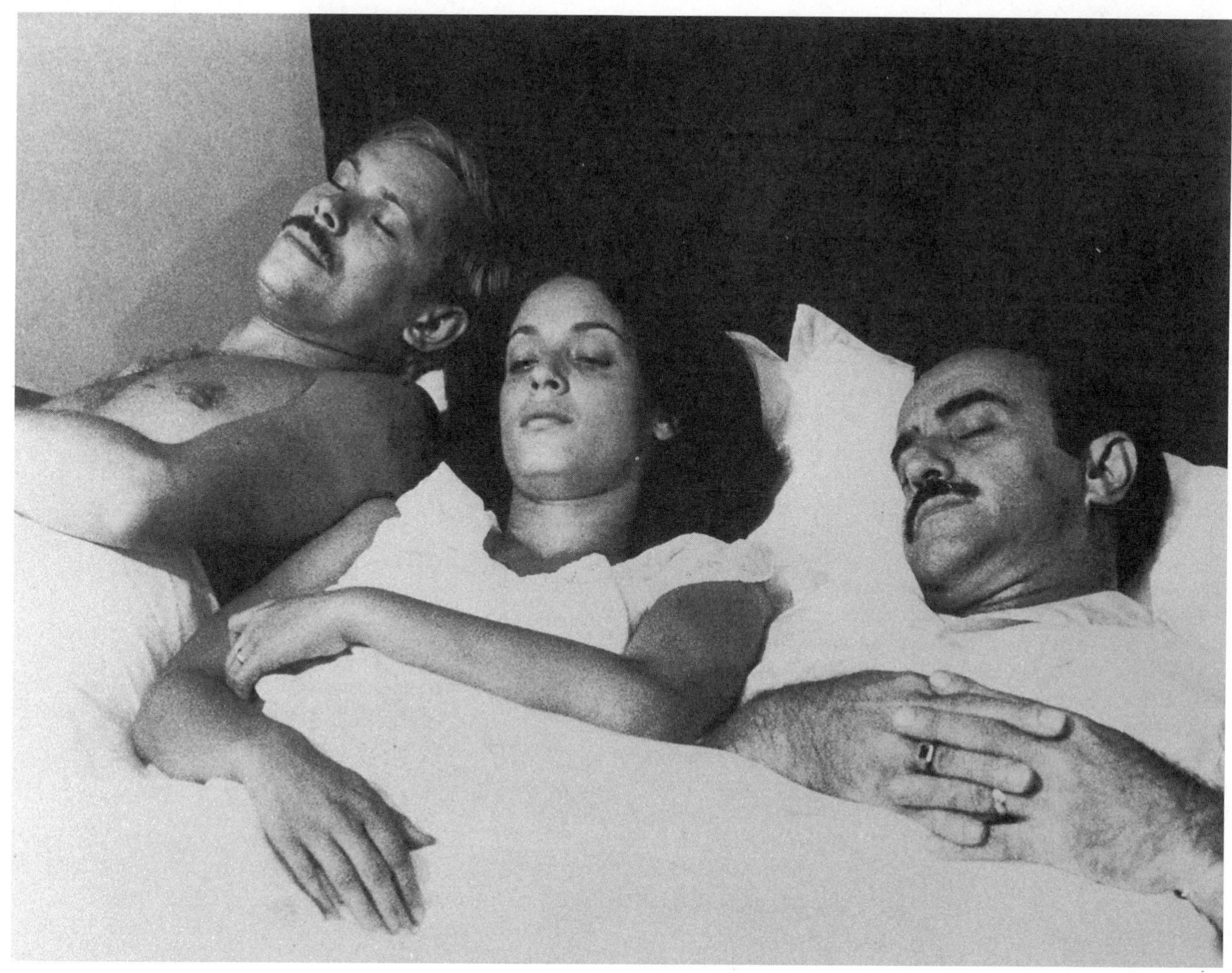

Dona Flor e seus dois maridos

abroad was such as to provoke a lackluster remake (*Kiss Me Goodbye*, directed by Robert Mulligan, with Sally Field and James Caan in the leading roles)?

In one sequence, Dona Flor (Sonia Braga) shows pupils at her tiny cookery school how to prepare a typically Bahian dish, spicy and exotic. Bruno Barreto used a variety of related ingredients in teasing the palate of the public: he took to the screen the best-selling novel of Brazil's premier popular author, Jorge Amado; he gave the title role to Sonia Braga, then a star of daily television series, whose greatest success to date had been the lead in *Gabriela Clove and Cinnamon*, also by Jorge Amado. To these, Barreto added other piquant—for their times—ingredients: the nudity of Sonia Braga and the bed scenes, which took on a forbidden flavour in a country traumatized, both culturally and politically, by the repression of the military regime.

A contemporary evaluation of *Dona Flor*, abstracted from the impact caused by its launch, reveals the keeping qualities of a delicious comedy of good and bad manners. It is set in the provincial city of Salvador, Bahia, in the early 1940s. The lightheartedness and folklore of Brazilian carnival are shared early on; beautiful girls dance for the camera and the men in drag so typical of street carnival are seen on their scandalous progress. The most outrageous of these revellers is Vadinho (José Wilker), who dies as he lived: partying. His lovely but much-abused young widow, Dona Flor, joins his grieving friends. In a vivid and sensual flash-back, she recalls with the viewer not only his gambling, drinking and womanizing, but also his talents in bed.

Dona Flor, whose dichotomous existence comprised not only the circumspect behaviour of the 1940s but also the liberated sexuality expected by moviegoers of the late 1970s, enters into a period of traditional mourning. When she finally emerges she is courted by the pharmacist Teodoro (Mauro Mendonça), a timid, hardworking and methodical man—the exact antithesis of the late Vadinho. Pressed by her mother and friends, she agrees to remarry, after a platonic courtship. Her second honeymoon is a far cry from her first, with Teodoro dressed in yellow pajamas talking about the stars and promising fidelity until death. They make love in the dark under cover of the sheets, which would have been sacrilege to Dona Flor's first husband. Vadinho, the eternal rake, had not hesitated in abandoning his new wife after some lively lovemaking on their wedding night to go gambling in the casino.

Dona Flor accepts the rules of her new marriage, at least overtly. Her sleep, however, is tortured by the ghost of her late husband, which emerges from The Hereafter to remind her of more exciting times, especially in bed. Vadinho's ghost can be interpreted either as a crystallization of Dona Flor's fantasy or as the return of a spirit which refuses to die, as in the Bahian religion, candomblé. The ghost is as irreverent as Vadinho was in life, and before long is making up a threesome with Dona Flor and Teodoro in the marriage bed. This unorthodox three-way relationship is the high point of the film. The scene in which Vadinho's ghost sits shaking with laughter on top of the wardrobe observing Dona Flor and Teodoro making love is priceless. Before long, Dona Flor and Vadinho are reunited in bed in a stormy outpouring of sexuality. Thus Dona Flor solves all her problems by acquiescing in the "presence" of Vadinho and welcomes him into her married life; in the fantasy world of Dona Flor all are free and all are equal—the living and the dead.

Freed of the pressure for narrative innovation which marked the previous decade and especially the Cinema Novo period, *Dona Flor* has won its place through its technical qualities and its outstanding popular appeal. Its success is also due to its easy consumption by the international market, captivated by the exuberance of the Bahian atmosphere, the postcard scenery and the intensity of its regional characters. The sound track is greatly enhanced by Chico Buarque de Holanda's "O Que será," a ballad laden with lyricism and sensuality.

Dona Flor turned Sonia Braga into a box-office phenomenon who was seen, for a time, as the epitome of Brazilian female sexuality. Bruno Barreto attempted, in 1983, to repeat the successful recipe with *Gabriela*, an international co-production, starring Sonia Braga in the role she had made famous on television and Marcello Mastroianni. Despite having some of the same ingredients, the production came nowhere near the spice of the delicious *Dona Flor. Gabriela* is to *Dona Flor* approximately what the dull Teodoro is to vital Vadinho.

—Susana Schild

DOOMED

See **IKIRU**

DOOMED LOVE

See **AMOR DE PERDICAO**

DOUBLE INDEMNITY

USA, 1944

Director: Billy Wilder

Production: Paramount Pictures; 1944; black and white, 355mm; running time: 107 minutes. Released 7 September 1944. Filmed 27 September-24 November 1943 in Paramount studios, and on location in Jerry's Market in Los Angeles.

Producer: Joseph Sistrom; **screenplay:** Billy Wilder and Raymond Chandler, from the novel *3 of a Kind* by James M. Cain; **photography:** John F. Sitz; **editor:** Doane Harrison; **sound:** Stanley Cooley; **art director:** Hal Pereira; **supervisor:** Hans Dreier; **set decoration:** Bertram Granger; **music:** Miklos Rozsa; **costume designer:** Edith Head.

Cast: Fred MacMurray (*Walter Neff*); Barbara Stanwyck (*Phyllis Dietrichson*); Edward G. Robinson (*Barton Keyes*); Porter Hall (*Mr. Jackson*); Jean Heather (*Lola Dietrichson*); Tom Powers (*Mr. Dietrichson*); Byron Barr (*Nino Zachette*); Richard Gaines (*Mr. Norton*); Fortunio Bonanova (*Sam Gorlopis*); John Philliber (*Joe Pete*); Clarence Muse (*Black man*).

Publications

Script:

Chandler, Raymond, and Billy Wilder, *Double Indemnity*, in *Best Film Plays 1945*, edited by John Gassner and Dudley Nichols, New York, 1946.

Books:

Del Buono, Oreste, *Billy Wilder*, Parma, 1958.
Madsen, Axel, *Billy Wilder*, Bloomington, Indiana, 1969.
Wood, Tom, *The Bright Side of Billy Wilder, Primarily*, New York, 1970.
Smith, Ella, *Starring Miss Barbara Stanwyck*, New York, 1973.
Vermilye, Jerry, *Barbara Stanwyck*, New York, 1975.
Zolotow, Maurice, *Billy Wilder in Hollywood*, New York, 1977.
Seidman, Steve, *The Film Career of Billy Wilder*, Boston, 1977.
Silver, Alain, and Elizabeth Ward, editors, *Film Noir*, Woodstock, New York, 1979.
Sinyard, Neil, and Adrian Turner, *Journey Down Sunset Boulevard: The Films of Billy Wilder*, Ryde, Isle of Wight, 1979.
Kaplan, E. Ann, editor, *Women in Film Noir*, London, 1980.
Dick, Bernard F., *Billy Wilder*, Boston, 1980.
Ciment, Michel, *Les Conquérants d'un nouveau monde: Essais sur le cinéma américain*, Paris, 1981.
Giannetti, Louis, *Masters of the American Cinema*, Englewood Cliffs, New Jersey, 1981.
Jacob, Jerome, *Billy Wilder*, Paris, 1988.
Seidl, Claudius, *Billy Wilder: Seine Filme, sein Leben*, Munich, 1988.
Schickel, Richard, *Double Indemnity*, London, 1992.
Phillips, Gene D., *Exiles in Hollywood: Major European Film Directors in America*, Bethlehem, 1998.
Sikov, Ed., *On Sunset Boulevard: The Life and Times of Billy Wilder*, New York, 1998.
Wilder, Billy, *Conversations with Wilder*, with Cameron Crowe, New York, 1999.

Double Indemnity

Articles:

Variety (New York), 26 April 1944.

New York Times, 7 September 1944.

Pryor, Thomas, ''End of a Journey,'' in *New York Times*, 23 September 1945.

Luft, Herbert, and Charles Brackett, ''Two Views of a Director: Billy Wilder,'' in *Quarterly of Radio, Television, and Film* (Berkeley), Fall 1952.

McVay, Douglas, ''The Eye of a Cynic,'' in *Films and Filming* (London), January 1960.

Domarchi, Jean, and Jean Douchet, ''Entretien avec Billy Wilder,'' in *Cahiers du Cinéma* (Paris), August 1962.

Higham, Charles, ''Cast a Cold Eye: The Films of Billy Wilder,'' in *Sight and Sound* (London), Spring 1963.

Ringgold, Gene, ''Barbara Stanwyck,'' in *Films in Review* (New York), December 1963.

Ciment, Michel, ''Sept réflexions sur Billy Wilder,'' in *Positif* (Paris), May 1971.

Farber, Stephen, ''The Films of Billy Wilder,'' in *Film Comment* (New York), Winter 1971.

Ecran (Paris), July 1972.

Bourget, Jean-Loup, ''Le Dernier Carré,'' in *Positif* (Paris), April 1973.

Jensen, Paul, ''Raymond Chandler and the World You Live In,'' in *Film Comment* (New York), November-December 1974.

Corliss, Richard, ''The Author-Auteurs,'' in *Talking Pictures: Screenwriters in the American Cinema*, New York, 1975.

Borde, Raymond, and E. Chaumeton, in *Avant-Scène du Cinéma* (Paris), 1 October 1979.

Leese, Elizabeth, in *Magill's Survey of Cinema 1*, Englewood Cliffs, New Jersey, 1980.

Bernts, T., ''Film noir: Fiktie in de fiktie,'' in *Skrien* (Amsterdam), November-December 1984.

Alsted, C., ''Kvinder uden samvittighed—en arketypisk film noir,'' in *Kosmorama* (Copenhagen), July 1985.

Buchsbaum, J., ''Tame Wolves and Phony Claims: Paranoia and Film Noir,'' in *Persistence of Vision* (Maspeth, New York), Summer 1986.

Gallagher, B., ''Sexual Warfare and Homoeroticism in Billy Wilder's *Double Indemnity*,'' in *Literature/Film Quarterly* (Salisbury, Maryland), vol. 15, no. 4, 1987.

Combs, Richard, in *Listener* (London), 4 June 1987.

Rozgonyi, J., ''The Making of *Double Indemnity*,'' in *Films in Review* (New York), June-July 1990.

Pichler, O. H., ''Some Like It Black,'' in *Blimp* (Graz, Austria), Fall 1991.

Marling, W., ''On the Relation Between American Roman Noir and Film Noir,'' in *Literature/Film Quarterly* (Salisbury, Maryland), no. 3, 1993.

Biesen, S.C., ''Censorship, Film Noir, and *Double Indemnity*,'' in *Film & History*, no. 25, 1995.

Ross, Tony, ''Updated Noir,'' in *Creative Screenwriting* (Washington, D.C.), Spring 1995.

Naremore, James, ''Making and Remaking *Double Indemnity*,'' in *Film Comment* (New York), January-February 1996.

Arthur, P., ''Los Angeles as Scene of the Crime,'' in *Film Comment* (New York), July/August 1996.

Armstrong, R., ''*Double Indemnity*: An American Tragedy,'' in *Audience* (Simi Valley), February/March 1997.

* * *

Although James M. Cain's memorable novel of crime and passion, *The Postman Always Rings Twice*, predated his equally potent, similarly themed *Double Indemnity* by almost a decade, it is *Indemnity* that has proven the more influential, due largely to the uncompromising and suspenseful film writer-director Billy Wilder made from it. Wilder's film remains the model for just about every film noir of this type (*Born to Kill*, *The Prowler*, *The Pushover*, *Body Heat*, et al.) to come our way since.

Cain's novel was translated to the screen with the full force of the author's ugly tale of lust, greed, and murder intact. In fact, the film version is in many ways tougher than its source. Wilder's intention to make it so prompted his longtime partner, writer-producer Charles Brackett, to back away from the project even though he and Wilder were one of Hollywood's most successful teams. Brackett found Cain's book distasteful and felt the film would be little more than a ''dirty movie.'' He told Wilder to get another collaborator. Wilder tried to get Cain himself, but the author was busy on another project, and Wilder opted for Raymond Chandler instead.

Chandler detested working with Wilder and disliked the final film. Cain on the other hand totally approved of what Wilder had done to his book, even considered it an improvement. The two works are certainly different. In addition to changing the names of Cain's main characters (in the book they are Walter Huff and Phyllis Nirdlinger), Wilder changed the ending and altered other aspects of the story as well. Whereas Cain unfolded his tale in a linear manner, Wilder revealed the fate of his protagonist in the opening scene. Insurance investigator MacMurray arrives at his office mortally wounded and confesses into the dictaphone of his colleague, Robinson, the murder plot and insurance scam gone awry that led to MacMurray's downfall. Wilder cuts back to the dying MacMurray several times, but for the most part the film unfolds as a series of flashbacks showing how MacMurray got embroiled with femme fatale Stanwyck in a scheme to murder her oilman husband, make it look like an accident, collect a bundle on the husband's double indemnity claim, and run away together. But when their scheme began to unravel, their relationship fell apart, and they wound up shooting each other. (In the book, the lovers get away with the crime because the Robinson character who is hot on their trail has no proof, but are doomed anyway due to their growing mistrust of one another.)

Cain loosely based his novel on the real-life Roaring Twenties case of Ruth Snyder and Judd Gray who conspired to murder Snyder's husband for $100,000 in insurance money. Snyder and Gray were caught and went to the chair. An enterprising newspaper reporter smuggled a camera into the execution chamber and snapped a shot of Snyder moments before the juice was turned on. The ghoulish shot caused a furor when it was published in the paper. Wilder wanted to end his film with a similar scene showing MacMurray's execution in California's gas chamber. The scene was shot, but Wilder decided against using it; he felt it to be too strong and anticlimactic as well. He replaced it with the trenchantly written and beautifully performed final confrontation scene between the self-destructive MacMurray and the fatherly Robinson that movingly concludes this exceptionally fine and biting film noir. As MacMurray slumps to the floor, he tells Robinson how he'd been able to elude the dogged investigator. ''Because the guy you were looking for was too close, Keyes. Right across the desk from you.'' ''Closer than that,'' Robinson responds emotionally as the film fades to black.

—John McCarty

DOUGLAS TRILOGY

Director: Bill Douglas

MY CHILDHOOD

UK, 1972

Production: British Film Institute Production Board; black and white, 16mm and 35mm; running time: 48 minutes.

Producer: Geoffrey Evans; **screenplay:** Bill Douglas; **photography:** Mick Campbell; **additional photography:** Gale Tattersall, Bahram Manocheri; **editor:** Brand Thumin; **assistant director:** Nick Moes; **sound editor:** Tony Lewis; **sound recording:** Bob Withey; **sound mixer:** Mike Billings.

Cast: Stephen Archibald (*Jamie*); Hughie Restorick (*Tommy*); Jean Taylor Smith (*Grandmother*); Karl Fiesler (*Helmut*); Bernard Mckenna (*Tommy's father*); Paul Kermack (*Jamie's father*); Helena Gloag (*Tommy's mother*); Ann Smith (*Nurse*); Helen Crummy (*Schoolteacher*).

Awards: Silver Lion and Critic's prize, Venice 1972.

MY AIN FOLK

UK, 1973

Production: British Film Institute Production Board; black and white, 16mm; running time: 55 minutes.

Douglas Trilogy: My Childhood

Producer: Nick Nascht; **screenplay:** Bill Douglas; **photography:** Gale Tattersall; **editor:** Peter West, Brand Thumin; **sound editor:** Michael Ellis, Peter West; **sound recording:** Peter Harvey.

Cast: Stephen Archibald (*Jamie*); Hughie Restorick (*Tommy*); Jean Taylor Smith (*Grandmother*); Bernard Mckenna (*Tommy's father*); Munro (*Jamie's grandfather*); Paul Kermack (*Jamie's father*); Helena Gloag (*Father's mother*).

MY WAY HOME

UK, 1978

Production: British Film Institute Production Board; black and white, 35mm; running time: 72 minutes.

Production supervisor: Judy Cottam; **screenplay:** Bill Douglas; **photography:** Ray Orton; **editor:** Mick Audsley; **art director:** Olivier Boucher, Elsie Restorick; **assistant director**: Martin Turner; **sound editor:** Peter Harvey; **sound recording:** Digby Rumsey.

Cast: Stephen Archibald (*Jamie*); Paul Kermack (*Jamie's father*); Jessie Combe (*father's wife*); William Carrol (*Archie*).

Awards: Firesci Prize, Berlin 1979. Trilogy: Interfilm Jury Special Prize, Berlin 1979.

Publications

Script:

Dick, Eddie, and others, *Bill Douglas—A Lanternist's Account*, London 1993.

Books:

Dick, Eddie, *From Limelight to Satellite: A Scottish Film Book*, London, 1990.

Dick, Eddie, and Andrew Noble, and Duncan Petrie, editors, *Bill Douglas: A Lanternist's Account*, London, 1993.

Articles:

Variety (New York), 13 September 1972.
Wilson, D., *Sight and Sound* (London), Spring 1973.
Torok, J.-P., ''Village of the Damned'' in *Positif* (Paris), December 1975.
Wilson, D., ''Images of Britain'' in *Sight and Sound* (London), Spring 1974.
Variety (New York), 20 November 1974.
Sussex, E., *Monthly Film Bulletin* (London), December 1974.
Hardwick, C., *Jeune Cinema* (Paris), September/October 1973.
Cannière, P., ''Portrait d'enfance'' in *Cinéma* (Paris), Summer 1978.
Pym, J., *Sight and Sound* (London), November 1978.
Pulleine, T., *Monthly Film Bulletin* (London), November 1978.
Variety (New York), 15 November 1978.
Elley, Derek, ''*My Way Home*,'' *Films & Filming*, December 1979.
Malmberg, C.-J., ''Hem till natten,'' *Chaplin* (Stockholm), vol. 24, no. 2, 1982.
Hassan, Mamoun, and J. Caughie, ''His ain man: *The Way Home*,'' *Sight & Sound* (London), November 1991.
Hodgson, P. and, B. Douglas, ''*My Childhood*,'' *Trafic* (Paris), no. 23, Fall 1997.
Bénoliel, Bernard, ''Ma vie de chien,'' *Cahiers du Cinéma* (Paris), June 1997.

* * *

The three intimate autobiographical films written and directed by Bill Douglas under the auspices of the BFI production board in the 1970s collectively represent one of the most original and visceral contributions to British cinema during a decade remembered more for its mediocrity than its inspiration. Yet the *Trilogy* remains as a testament to the power of the image to fundamentally move the viewer, even when rendered with a quiet and deceptive simplicity. The films chart the harrowing and poverty-stricken childhood and adolescence of a boy in a Scottish mining village in the aftermath of World War II. Jamie's path towards adulthood and the acquisition of understanding of self and others is relentless in its brutality. Yet this is ultimately a tale of redemption, of the triumph of the human spirit over material suffering, which avoids the usual sentimental and melodramatic impulses of such narratives.

The force of the *Trilogy* is rooted in Douglas's idiosyncratic approach to the medium. Eschewing the visual pyrotechnics which became popular in the 1960s and 1970s, Douglas pares his aesthetic to the very bone. The black-and-white images are marked by a profound stillness in both space and time. Not only is there minimal camera movement in the three films but individual shots are frequently left to dwell, slowly absorbing the subject matter. The only exception is the 360-degree pan around the room at the very end of *My Way Home*, a shot which signifies a subjective return to the house where Jamie spent much of his childhood. The soundtrack is also largely subordinated to the image. The dialogue is minimal and non-diegetic music entirely absent from the *Trilogy*, evoking an affinity with silent cinema.

This desire for stillness is related to Douglas's humanistic belief in the power of the camera to reveal certain ontological truths. This also explains his casting of non-actors in many of the key roles, including those of the two young boys in the film, Jamie and his cousin Tommy—the idea being that real rather than imagined experience would be rendered on screen through the faces of the performers. The pained expression of Stephen Archibald, aged beyond his years, which haunts the *Trilogy* bears witness to the success of this strategy. But Douglas is also well served by the professionals in his cast, particularly Jean Taylor Smith as the wraith-like maternal grandmother, fighting both the rigours of poverty and extreme emotional distress in the struggle to raise her two grandsons.

Yet while the images of Bill Douglas invoke poets like Dreyer or Bresson, these images are contained within highly formalized montage structures derived from Soviet stylists such as Donskoi and Dozvhenko. The *Trilogy* is constructed out of filmic blocks which progress in a relationship of dialectical tension described by John Caughie in terms of ''aesthetic distance and intense intimacy,'' serving to both objectively analyze the material poverty of Jamie's childhood while providing insights into his own limited understanding. The films also resound with narrative ellipses and echoes, providing an almost organic coherence to the meticulously crafted structures.

My Childhood centres around the triangular relationship between Jamie, Tommy, and their grandmother. The narrative is one of a groping on the part of the child towards a self knowledge. The confusion over his parentage—his mother is confined to an asylum, his father as yet unknown to him—leads him to seek companionship in Helmut, a German POW, who works in the local fields. Helmut cannot speak English, yet communication between the two is achieved through emotional warmth rather than language. There are also powerful juxtapositions of almost casual brutality with fleeting moments of tenderness which tragically capture the tenacity of humanity in the most inhumane of circumstances.

My Childhood concludes with Granny's death. *My Ain Folk* leads Jamie to the house of his paternal grandmother, an embittered old woman whose intense jealousy fires her hatred towards Jamie's mother and by extension to the young boy himself. He spends much of the film cowering in corners or hiding under the table. Yet he can never escape her malevolence. There are enough glimmers of pathos to cast her as yet another victim, a product of a brutal uncaring existence. *My Ain Folk* also extends the narrative to take in the wider community. The film begins with the image of a Technicolor sequence from a ''Lassie'' film. We see Tommy's engrossed face watching the movie in wonderment. The next cut is to a view of the mine workings, an image framed as if by a cinema screen. The camera then descends into the earth as we realize that this is the point of view of the miners starting their shift. In a later sequence which begins with Jamie fleeing his grandmother, the individual suffering of the child opens out into the context of the classroom where he sits in a puddle of his own urine. This then cuts to a shot of the miners going to work signifying an inevitable progression, a grim future for the children already mapped out. By the end of *My Ain Folk* Jamie is taken into care, echoing Tommy at the beginning.

My Way Home shifts the attention away from childhood onto the problems of adolescence. Jamie, at last, has found some comfort in the children's home yet the world of work beckons. He returns to the village but quickly realizes it has nothing to offer but a life down the mine. He lodges with a foster mother in Edinburgh and starts a job but rejects both and ends up in a dosshouse. After a final desperate return to his village the film cuts to the bright sunlight of the Egyptian desert. James has been called up and is serving in the canal zone. This journey away from home is to inadvertently provide the means whereby Jamie finds himself (the way home proving to be a rather different kind of journey) through his friendship with Robert, a young

Englishman passionately interested in the arts who opens up undreamt-of horizons. The seeds of hope and redemption have been sown enabling Jamie finally to grow and realize his own humanity.

—Duncan Petrie

DRACULA

USA, 1931

Director: Tod Browning

Production: Universal Pictures; black and white, 35mm; running time: 84 minutes, some sources list 76 minutes; length: 6978 feet. Released Valentine's Day, 1931. Re-released 1938. Filmed in Universal studios.

Producer: Carl Laemmle Jr.; **screenplay:** Garrett Fort, dialogue by Dudley Murphy, from Hamilton Deane's and John L. Balderston's stage adaptation of the novel by Bram Stoker; **photography:** Karl Freund; **editor:** Milton Carruth; **editing supervisor:** Maurice Pivar; **sound:** C. Roy Hunter; **production designer:** Charles Hall; **music director:** David Broekman; **makeup:** Jack P. Pierce.

Cast: Bela Lugosi (*Count Dracula*); Helen Chandler (*Mina*); David Manners (*Jonathan Harker*); Dwight Frye (*Renfield*); Edward Van Sloan (*Professor Van Helsing*); Herbert Bunston (*Dr. Seward*); Frances Dade (*Lucy Weston*); Joan Standing (*Briggs*); Charles Gerrard (*Martin*); Moon Carroll (*Maid*); Josephine Velez (*Nurse*); Donald Murphy (*Man in coach*); Michael Visaroff (*Innkeeper*).

Publications

Script:

Fort, Garrett, and others, *Dracula: The Original 1931 Shooting Script*, Absecon, New Jersey, 1990.

Books:

Butler, Ivan, *The Horror Film*, New York, 1967.
McBride, Joseph, editor, *Persistence of Vision: A Collection of Film Criticism*, Madison, Wisconsin, 1968.
Huss, Roy, and T. J. Ross, *Focus on the Horror Film*, Englewood Cliffs, New Jersey, 1972.
Edelson, Edward, *Great Monsters of the Movies*, New York, 1973.
Everson, William K., *Classics of the Horror Film*, Secaucus, New Jersey, 1974.
Frank, Alan G., *Horror Movies*, Secaucus, New Jersey, 1974.
Lamberti, Mark, *Transylvanian Catalogue*, Mount Vernon, New York, 1974.
Lenning, Arthur, *The Count—The Life and Films of Bela ''Dracula'' Lugosi*, New York, 1974.
Annan, David, *Beyond the Dream Machine*, New York, 1975.
Pattison, Barrie, *The Seal of Dracula*, New York, 1975.
Gifford, Denis, *Monsters of the Movies*, London, 1977.
Halliwell, Leslie, *The Dead That Walk: Dracula, Frankenstein, the Mummy, and Other Favorite Movie Monsters*, New York, 1988.
Marrero, Robert, *Dracula: The Vampire Legend on Film*, Key West, Florida, 1992.
Prüssmann, Karsten, *Die Dracula-Filme von Friedrich Wilhelm Murnau bis Francis Ford Coppola*, Munich, 1993.
Skal, David J., *Dark Carnival: The Secret World of Tod Browning, Hollywood's Master of the Macabre*, New York, 1995.

Articles:

New York Times, 13 February 1931.
Variety (New York), 18 February 1931.
Addams, Charles, ''Movie Monster Rally,'' in *New York Times Magazine*, 9 August 1953.
Geltzer, George, ''Tod Browning,'' in *Films in Review* (New York), October 1953.
Everson, William K., ''A Family Tree of Monsters,'' in *Film Culture* (New York), no. 1, 1955.
Gur, Roy, ''The Browning Version,'' in *Cinema* (Beverly Hills), June-July 1963.
Halliwell, Leslie, ''The Baron, the Count, and Their Ghoul Friends,'' in *Films and Filming* (London), June 1969.
Evans, W., ''Monster Movies: A Sexual Theory,'' in *Journal of Popular Film* (Washington, D.C.), Fall 1973.
Rosenthal, Stuart, ''Tod Browning,'' in *The Hollywood Professionals 4*, London, 1975.
Garsault, A., ''Tod Browning: A la recherche de la réalité,'' in *Positif* (Paris), July-August 1978.
Huxner, V. I., in *Magill's Survey of Cinema 1*, Englewood Cliffs, New Jersey, 1980.
Turner, George, ''The Two Faces of Dracula,'' in *American Cinematographer* (Los Angeles), May 1988.
McBride, W. T., ''Dracula and Mephistopheles: Shyster Vampires,'' in *Literature/Film Quarterly* (Salisbury, Maryland), no. 2, 1990.
Thomson, David, ''Really a Part of Me,'' in *Film Comment* (New York), January-February 1995.
Haas, R., ''The Monster Boomer: An Interview with David J. Skal,'' in *Post Script* (Commerce), no. 3, 1996.
Holt, Wesley G., ''*Dracula*,'' in *Filmfax* (Evanston), August-September 1996.
Ford, J.E., ''*Dracula*,'' in *Films of the Golden Age* (Muscatine), Fall 1997.
''Dracula Revived (Restoration that Features a New Score Composed by Philip Glass),'' in *Stereo Review's Sound & Vision*, vol. 64, no. 8, October 1999.

* * *

Like other horror films of the period (e.g., *Frankenstein*, 1931, *Dr. Jekyll and Mr. Hyde*, 1932, *Island of Lost Souls*, 1933), *Dracula* is about sex—perverse and passionate—and, like those other pictures, it has a short running time for an ''A'' film because it suffers from self- and outside censorship; material was excised from the screenplay or

Dracula (1931)

the finished film because of its ''questionable'' aspects. This and other deficiencies dilute the movie's effectiveness for contemporary audiences.

For example, the heroine, Mina, tells Professor Van Helsing that she's seen her dead friend Lucy walking about ''alive.'' The Professor promises that he will put Lucy to rest forever. In the novel, this leads to a harrowing scene wherein Van Helsing and Lucy's fiancé stake and behead the recently undead woman. Arthur Lennig says that Lucy ''actually was dispatched by Van Helsing, but this episode, along with the others, was not in the release prints.''

Later, after Mina's tearful confession, almost thrown away on the soundtrack, that Dracula opened a vein in his arm (a phallic metaphor) and made her drink, the count again visits her in her bedroom. (There's a discreet fade-out as he bends over to bite her neck; actual penetration is never shown in *Dracula.*) Then everybody converges upon Carfax Abbey for the finale. How they get there (and why they go there) is not shown.

After a half-dozen remakes of *Dracula* (none of which completely captures the excitement of the book or gets the plot right), and hundreds of other vampire films, where the sexual nature of vampirism is more explicit, it's difficult for contemporary viewers to understand the filmmakers' reticence or to feel the impact the movie had when it first opened. Universal advertised the film (released, appropriately perversely, on Valentine's Day, 1931) as ''the strangest love story ever told'' (partly because there was no established horror genre to exploit), and it certainly was that.

The attraction of the foreign lover is present in the vampire Count's power over women, but the sexual liberation (wantonness) vampirism inspires in his female victims is absent. His three ''brides'' are not the quick, alluring, dangerous creatures of the novel but staid, staring zombies. So is Lucy, in the one shot we see of her as a vampire. Only Mina is allowed a brief glimmer of desire when she eyes her fiancé's neck, but her—off-screen—coitus is interrupted by ever-vigilant Van Helsing.

The lack of a score hampers the film. It has to work harder to create mood, and often images alone aren't enough to accomplish this. The filmmakers, still laboring under the delusion that all onscreen music must spring from a ''realistic'' physical source, dispensed with it altogether, except over the opening and closing credits and during the famous scene in the theatre, where the lights go down as the music comes up, and Dracula makes his tragi-romantic assertion, ''To die, to be *really* dead—that must be glorious.''

Frankenstein suffers from the same deficiencies as *Dracula* (censorship, scorelessness) but it remains a more thrilling, fluid film. That's because *Frankenstein* was directed by the eccentric James Whale, whereas *Dracula* was directed by Tod Browning, a pedestrian director with a taste for the grotesque (no doubt because of his circus background) but no feeling for the supernatural. Except for *Dracula*, his films are all solidly, stolidly grounded in reality.

Given Browning's limitations and his particular cinematic bent, he really couldn't bring much to a subject like *Dracula*. The beginning at the Count's castle and the ending on the seemingly endless stairs of Carfax Abbey are impressive because Browning and the cinematographer Karl Freund had good sets to shoot, but neither knew what to do with the long, stagey middle section of *Dracula*, taken from the Balderston-Dean play. (Significantly, the effective Transylvanian opening and the theatre scene were written by the uncredited scenarist Louis Bromfield). So all that the viewer is left with is a lot of static shots, almost a series of still photos instead of a moving picture, animated only by some mellow performances and ripe language. For, despite its lack of background music, *Dracula* is very much a *sound* movie, full of memorable dialogue memorably delivered, especially by Bela Lugosi with his mellifluous accent, Edward Van Sloan with his pompous pronouncements, and Dwight Frye with his maniacal cackling. In contemporary jargon, it's a film about competing discourses, and on that rests its continuing appeal.

—Anthony Ambrogio

DRACULA

(Horror of Dracula)

UK, 1958

Director: Terence Fisher

Production: Hammer; Eastmancolor; running time: 82 minutes. Released May 1958.

Producer: Anthony Hinds; **screenplay:** Jimmy Sangster, from the novel by Bram Stoker; **photography:** Jack Asher; **camera operator:** Len Harris; **editors:** James Needs, Bill Lenny; **sound:** Jock May; **art director:** Bernard Robinson; **music:** James Bernard.

Cast: Peter Cushing (*Dr. Van Helsing*); Christopher Lee (*Count Dracula*); Michael Gough (*Arthur*); Melissa Stribling (*Mina*); Carol Marsh (*Lucy*); Olga Dickie (*Gerda*); John Van Eyssen (*Jonathan*); Valerie Gaunt (*Vampire Woman*).

Publications

Script:

Sangster, Jimmy, *Dracula*, in *Avant-Scène du Cinéma* (Paris), July-September 1975.

Books:

Pirie, David, *Heritage of Horror: The English Gothic Cinema 1946–1972*, London, 1973.
Eyles, Allen, Robert Adkinson, and Nicholas Fry, *The House of Horror: The Story of Hammer Films*, London, 1973; revised edition, 1981.
Glut, Donald F., *The Dracula Book*, Metuchen, New Jersey, 1975.
Rohle, Jr., Robert W., and Douglas C. Hart, *The Films of Christopher Lee*, Metuchen, New Jersey, 1983.

Articles:

Variety (New York), 7 May 1958.
Motion Picture Herald (New York), 10 May 1958.
Today's Cinema (London), 19 May 1958.
Kine Weekly (London), 22 May 1958.
Monthly Film Bulletin (London), July 1958.
Huss, Roy, "Vampire's Progress: Dracula from Novel to Film via Broadway," in *Focus on the Horror Film*, edited by Huss and T. J. Ross, Englewood Cliffs, New Jersey, 1972.
Photon, no. 27, 1976.
Schneider, M., "Hammer Horrors: The Dracula Films of Christopher Lee," in *Monsterscene* (Lombard), no. 3, Fall 1994.
Ray, F.O., "The Hammer Factory," in *Midnight Marquee* (Baltimore), no. 47, Summer 1994.
Brunas, M., in *Midnight Marquee* (Baltimore), no. 49, Summer 1995.
Fischer, D., "*Colossus/Silent Running*," in *Cinefantastique* (Forest Park), no. 8, 1997.
Thornton, S., "Barbara Shelley," in *Midnight Marquee* (Baltimore), no. 54, Summer 1997.

* * *

Many consider Terence Fisher's *Dracula* to be the director's finest film. It is certainly Fisher's most visible work, but it is unfortunate that its fame obscures the many other excellent films which he created in his lifetime. It does seem that in reviving the Gothic tradition in Britain, Fisher found a comfortable niche for himself with both the public and Hammer. *Dracula* (1958) is just one of a series of excellent Gothic romances Fisher made during Hammer's "Golden Age" (roughly 1957–65). As late as 1967, Fisher showed that he was capable of first-rate work with *The Devil Rides Out*. There is no question that he was the finest director working for Hammer during this period, but there is also no question that his current high critical reputation has been long in coming. The reason for this is simple: horror films have always been considered on the fringe of respectable cinematic discourse, because they push the limits of graphic representation.

When *Dracula* first appeared, the reviews in the popular press were almost uniformly negative, despite the great popular acclaim the film received. Hammer, for their part, did little to discourage any sort of publicity, and took the bad reviews in stride. As long as the film made money, Hammer was satisfied. Fisher's earlier films for Rank were simply ignored, and he was considered by most to be simply a commercial director with no personal investment in the films he created. Nothing could be further from the truth.

Dracula is more than a stylish, rapidly paced redaction of Bram Stoker's novel; it is a film which explores and explodes the surface of Victorian society, using Dracula as a metaphor for the release of sexual urges which had long been repressed or sublimated. *Dracula* is also seen by Fisher as a parable of righteousness against the attraction of evil; although Dracula enslaves his victims, Fisher shows that there is considerable allure in the life of the undead. Those who fall under Dracula's spell are addicted to vampirism, as one is addicted to drugs; the power of free will alone cannot save the newly recruited vampires. If Dracula is ''evil incarnate,'' as Fisher insisted he was on several occasions, the scholar/scientist represented by Cushing's Van Helsing is at once a redemptive figure who combines in equal parts faith and knowledge, with respect for the separate powers inherent in each. Lee's Dracula is a radical departure from the role as interpreted by Bela Lugosi; for the first time, Dracula is seen as a figure of sexual magnetism, rather than a rapacious animal slavering for blood alone. Fisher's Dracula is an aristocrat first, who hides his rupture with society beneath precisely clipped speech and elegant manners. It is only the night which liberates Dracula's other personality, based entirely on need, addiction, and the use and abandonment of others as mere vessels of momentary satisfaction.

What makes *Dracula* all the more remarkable is the precise assurance with which Fisher handles his camera. The opening of the film, detailing Jonathan Harker's abortive trip to rid the world of Dracula, is framed within the confines of a diary narrative. Yet the device of the diary notebook is never allowed to slow down the film; rather, Harker comes face to face with castle Dracula in the first seven shots of the film, placing him in immediate jeopardy. Fisher stages Harker's entry into the castle in smooth, contemplative tracking shots, mirroring the ease with which Dracula moves about his domain. When Dracula himself does appear, in a shot which has become justly famous, he is framed in silhouette at the top of a long staircase, which he noiselessly descends. Demonstrating his characteristic economy, Fisher holds on the shot until Dracula walks directly to the camera and addresses it in the first person (the shot is from Harker's point-of-view), dominating the frame. One must remember that, after early work as a clapper boy, magazine loader, and third assistant director, Fisher spent most of his time in the cutting room, working on many of the most important British films of the early 1940s. This precision in editorial construction thus comes from a thorough understanding of the uses and abuses of camera coverage, and it comes as no surprise to learn that Fisher shot very little more than he needed, although he never story-boarded a film in the Hitchcock manner. Jack Asher's cinematography creates a world of blues, reds, and greens, which punctuate rather than dominate Fisher's compositions.

In addition, Asher's lighting locates the actors within the confines of the set as figures fixed in stygian gloom, illuminated by shafts of light from above or from the side, but never bathed in light. This makes the final sequence in the library all the more effective, as Van Hesling runs down the refectory table, rips the curtains from the window, grabs two candlesticks to form a hastily improvised cross, and, with a combination of light and faith, sends Dracula to his doom. We realize during this climactic scene that we have been living in a world of night, or twilight, a world entirely under the control of Dracula, for most of the film. It is the light we all share, and the light of faith: these forces alone will account for our salvation. Asher's gloomy, moody lighting during the main body of the film reinforces this, and works in perfect harmony with the over-dressed, claustrophobic sets of Bernard Robinson.

The role of Dracula made Christopher Lee a star, and Peter Cushing made an indelible mark as Van Helsing, but both continued to work outside the horror genre. Fisher, however, was typecast as a horror director, and a Hammer director, and made few attempts to break away from this public perception of his work. In part this was because Fisher enjoyed making Gothics; he believed in the films he made, and spent a great deal of time and care with them, within the confines of the time and budgetary constraints imposed by Hammer.

Nevertheless, Fisher's work there, using the services of Hammer's excellent technical staff and superlative stable of character and lead actors, revitalized, transformed, and re-created the horror film for an entire new generation of viewers, who enthusiastically enjoyed Fisher's work while their elders denigrated it in favor of the Universal expressionist Gothics of the 1930s and 1940s. It is now clear that Fisher was simply ahead of his time, and the degree of graphic violence which pervades his horror films was simply a response to the needs of the viewing audience for greater generic realism. Fisher's work stands as one of the signal achievements of the British cinema, and paved the way for the next cycle of horror films, which would start with George Romero's *Night of the Living Dead*, a film shot through with a pessimistic spirit Fisher would never have allowed to inhabit his films. Though the battle may be vigorous and hazardous in Fisher's films, good, being infinite, will inevitably triumph over the finite evil of Dracula and his minions. Some see this as a structural weakness in Fisher's vision; if so, it is a weakness shared by Britain's two greatest Gothic writers, Mary Shelley and Bram Stoker.

—Wheeler Winston Dixon

O DRAGAO DA MALDADE CONTRA O SANTO QUERREIRO

See **ANTONIO DAS MORTES**

THE DRAUGHTSMAN'S CONTRACT

UK, 1982

Director: Peter Greenaway

Production: British Film Institute Production Board, in association with Channel 4; colour; 16mm; running time: 108 minutes. Released 1982.

Executive producer: Peter Sainsbury; **producer:** David Payne; **screenplay:** Peter Greenaway; **assistant director:** Andy Powell; **photography:** Curtis Clark; **rostrum camera:** Hugh Gordon; **assistant photographer:** Luke Cardiff; **editor:** John Wilson; **assistant editor:** John Taylor; **sound editor:** Doctor Lion; **sound recordists:** Godfrey Kirby, Martin Rex; **sound re-recordist:** Tony Anscombe; **art director:** Bob Ringwood; **assistant designers:** Jane Hamilton, Digby Howard; **costumes:** Sue Blane; **music:** Michael Nyman; **music producer:** David Cunningham.

Cast: Anthony Higgins (*Mr. Neville*); Janet Suzman (*Mrs. Herbert*); Anne Louise Lambert (*Sarah Talmann*); Neil Cunningham (*Thomas Noyes*); Hugh Fraser (*Louis Talmann*); Dave Hill (*Mr. Herbert*); David Gant (*Mr. Seymour*); David Meyer and Tony Meyer (*The Poulencs*); Nicolas Amer (*Mr. Parkes*); Suzan Crowley (*Mrs. Pierpoint*); Lynda Marchal (*Mrs. Clement*); Michael Feast (*The

The Draughtsman's Contract

Statue); Alistair Cummings (*Philip*); Steve Ubels (*Mr. van Hoyten*); Ben Kirby (*Augusta*); Sylvia Rotter (*Governess*); Kate Doherty (*Maid*); Joss Buckley (*Mr. Porringer*); Mike Carter (*Mr. Clarke*); Vivienne Chandler (*Laundress*); Geoffrey Larder (*Mr. Hammond*); Harry van Engel and George Miller (*Servants*).

Publications

Script:

Greenaway, Peter, ''*Meurtre dans un jardin anglais*,'' in *Avant-Scène du Cinéma* (Paris), no. 333, 1984.

Articles:

Brown, Robert, in *Sight and Sound* (London), Winter 1981–82.
Variety (New York), 8 September 1982.
Forbes, Jill, ''Marienbad Revisited,'' in *Sight and Sound* (London), Autumn 1982.
Brown, Robert, ''From a View to Death,'' in *Monthly Film Bulletin* (London), November 1982.
McVay, D., in *Films and Filming* (London), November 1982.
Malmberg, C.-J., and D. Joyeux, in *Chaplin* (Stockholm), vol. 25, no. 5., 1983.
Stills (London), May-June 1983.
Newman, B., and B. Evans, ''Super 16 for *The Draughtsman's Contract:* An Interview with Curtis Clark,'' in *American Cinematographer* (Los Angeles), September 1983.
Zocaro, E., ''Conversando con Peter Greenaway,'' in *Filmcritica* (Florence), October 1983.
Vecchi, P., in *Cineforum* (Bergamo), December 1983.
Malcomson, S., in *Film Quarterly* (Berkeley), Winter 1983–84.
Jaehne, K., ''*The Draughtsman's Contract:* An Interview with Peter Greenaway,'' in *Cineaste* (New York), vol. 13, no. 2, 1984.
Ciment, Michel, and others, in *Positif* (Paris), February 1984.
Blanchet, C., and others, in *Cinéma* (Paris), March 1984.
Tessier, Max, in *Revue du Cinéma* (Paris), March 1984.
Villien, Bruno, and others, in *Cinématographe* (Paris), March 1984.
Welsh, H., in *Jeune Cinéma* (Paris), April 1984.
''Special Issue'' of *Avant-Scène du Cinéma* (Paris), October 1984.

Frauen und Film (Berlin), August 1986.
Goerling, R., "Barocke Peruecken and postmoderne spielregein," in *Filmwaerts* (Hannover), Winter 1992.
In *Avant-Scène du Cinéma* (Paris), December-January 1992–93.
Andrew, Geoff, "Contract Chiller," in *Time Out* (London), 18 May 1994.
Gras, V., "Dramatizing the Failure to Jump the Culture/Nature Gap: The Films of Peter Greenaway," in *New Literary History*, no. 1, 1995.
Castoro Cinema (Milan), May/June 1995.
Dicine, January/February 1996.
Aldersey-Williams, Hugh, "Framing the Future (Filmmaker Peter Greenaway)," in *New Statesman*, vol. 128, no. 4466, 13 December 1999.

* * *

The Draughtsman's Contract marks something of a caesura in the Greenaway oeuvre. For one thing it cost a great deal more than any of his previous films. His earlier British Film Institute projects, *A Walk Through H* and *The Falls*, came in at £7500 and £35,000 respectively. The production of *The Draughtsman's Contract* coincided with the BFI's decision to finance fewer but larger projects, and was budgeted at £120,000. However, the final budget was around £300,000, of which half came from Channel 4, here making one of its most spectacularly successful early investments in feature film production. Secondly, the film was the nearest that Greenaway had then come to a conventional feature. This is not to say that *The Draughtsman's Contract is* a conventional feature—far from it—but simply to note certain structural traits. For example, it is the first film in which Greenaway uses actors playing characters who speak to each other and are involved in various sets of relationships. It is also his first film to be set in a specific location in the known world. The film also develops a linear narrative, in which music plays the same kind of punctuating and expressive roles as in other, more straightforward, cinematic fictions. And thirdly, *The Draughtsman's Contract* marks the point at which Greenaway moved from being the maker of quirky, obsessive conceits to a major figure in international art house cinema with films such as *A Zed and Two Noughts* and *The Belly of an Architect. The Draughtsman's Contract* has been described as "an elaborate conspiracy thriller about class, sex and landscape, set at the feverish close of the 17th century." It tells the story of Mr. Neville, an ambitious young draughtsman, who, in 1694, is contracted by Mrs. Herbert for 12 drawings of her husband's country property at Compton Anstey. On arrival he soon becomes involved in the household's complex affairs, and is also perturbed to find that every time he begins a new drawing an item of the absent Mr. Herbert's clothing is stubbornly in view. Then Mr. Herbert is discovered dead, floating in the moat.

Greenaway's films, in which a formal concern with structures rubs shoulders with something decidedly more Romantic and even absurdist, have been described as revolving around the contradiction between "the encyclopaedic minutiae of a constructed world-in-microcosm and the aleatory perception of a contingent Nature," and *The Draughtsman's Contract* is no exception to this schema. In particular, the way in which the businesslike, dispassionate Mr. Neville is constantly intruded upon by human passions and their visible traces on the landscape testifies to the impossibility of purely abstract systems of any kind—systems of representation included. Indeed, even the landscape in which Compton Anstey is set, and which forms the background to the drawings, is far from being simply natural or neutral. As both Nikolaus Pevsner and W. G. Hoskins have repeatedly pointed out, the English landscape in particular always carries the traces of human activity upon it, and can thus be read as a kind of social and political map, as well as a simply geographical one. Neville's mistake is to fail to "read" the landscape in which he finds himself: narrowly limiting himself to what he can see in his viewing frame, to formal composition and to the formal terms of his contract, he fails to understand the relations of patronage and inheritance that are inscribed upon the landscape, or to see the signs of passion and intrigue which keep breaking through onto the otherwise orderly surface. This notion of landscape as something to be "read" becomes abundantly clear after Mr. Herbert's death, when the various members of the household scrutinise Neville's drawings for clues to the identity of the murderer.

It is its concern with landscape that, above all else, marks out *The Draughtsman's Contract* as a Peter Greenaway film. However, there is much else besides—the deliberately literary dialogue shot through with puns and conceits, the concern with visual symmetry (which results in a stylised, stilted mise-en-scène which is sometimes reminiscent of *Last Year at Marienbad*), and Michael Nyman's not-quite-pastiche score, with its echoes of Purcell. It is less hermetic than his earlier films, less obsessed with purely structural matters and more concerned with telling a story. As usual the range of reference—cinematic and otherwise—is enormously wide (with Restoration comedy to the fore), but perhaps two of the strongest (and most unexpected) reference points are the costume drama and the country-house murder mystery, both of which add their curious resonances to this playful, idiosyncratic charade about the interconnections between representation, property, and sex in the England of William of Orange.

—Sylvia Paskin

DIE DREIGROSCHENOPER

(The Threepenny Opera)

USA-Germany, 1931

Director: G. W. Pabst

Production: Warner Bros. First National (USA), Tobis Klang-Film, and Nero-Film (Germany); black and white, 35mm; running time: 111 minutes (German version) and 104 minutes (French version); length 3097 meters (German version). Released 19 February 1931, Berlin. Filmed in Berlin.

Producer: Seymour Nebenzahl; **screenplay:** Leo Lania, Bela Balàsz and Ladislaus Vajda, from the play by Berthold Brecht; **adaptation for the French version:** Solange Bussi, André Mauprey, and Ninon Steinhoff; **photography:** Fritz Arno Wagner; **editors:** Hans Oser (German version), Henri Rust (French version); **sound:** Adolf Jansen; **production designer:** Andrei Andreiev; **music:** Kurt Weill; **orchestration:** Theo Mackeben.

Cast: *German:* Rudolph Forster (*Mackie Messer*); Carola Neher (*Polly*); Reinhold Schünzel (*Tiger Brown*); Fritz Rasp (*Peachum*);

Die Dreigroschenoper

Valeska Gert (*Mrs. Peachum*); Lotte Lenya (*Jenny*); Hermann Thimig (*Vicar*); Ernst Busch (*Street-singer*); Vladimir Sokolov (*Smith*); Paul Kemp, Gustav Puttjer, Oskar Höcker, and Kraft Raschig (*Mackie's Gang*); Herbert Grünbaum (*Filch*); *French:* Albert Préjean (*Mackie Messer*); Florelle (*Polly*); Jack Henley (*Tiger Brown*); Gaston Modot (*Peachum*); Jane Markem (*Mrs. Peachum*); Margo Lion (*Jenny*); Antonin Artaud, Vladimir Sokolov, and Merminod (*Mackie's Gang*).

Publications

Scripts:

Lania, Leo, Bela Balasz, and Ladislaus Vajda, *Die Dreigroschenoper*, in *Masterworks of the German Cinema*, edited by Roger Manvell, London, 1973; also published separately, Berlin, 1978.

Books:

Rotha, Paul, *Celluloid: The Film Today*, London, 1931.
Kracauer, Siegfried, *From Caligari to Hitler: A Psychological History of the German Film*, Princeton, 1947.
Joseph, Rudolph, editor, *Der Regisseur: G. W. Pabst*, Munich, 1963.
Buache, Freddy, *G.W. Pabst*, Lyons, 1965.
Amengual, Barthélemy, *Georg Wilhelm Pabst*, Paris, 1966.
Aubry, Yves, and Jacques Pétat, ''G. W. Pabst,'' in *Anthologie du cinéma 4*, Paris, 1968.
Eisner, Lotte, *The Haunted Screen*, Berkeley, 1969.
Masterworks of the German Cinema: Nosferatu, M, the Threepenny Opera, introduction by Roger Manvell, New York, 1973.
Barsacq, Leon, *Caligari's Cabinet and Other Grand Illusions: A History of Film Design*, New York, 1976.
Atwell, Lee, *G. W. Pabst*, Boston, 1977.

Articles:

Chavance, Louis, ''Un Mystérieux Musée de figures de cire,'' in *La Revue du Cinéma* (Paris), 1 May 1931.
New York Times, 18 May 1931.
Variety (New York), 20 May 1931.
Close Up (London), June 1931.
Potamkin, Harry, ''Pabst and the Social Film,'' in *Hound and Horn* (New York), January-March 1933.
Bachmann, Gideon, editor, ''Six Talks on G. W. Pabst,'' in *Cinemages* (New York), no. 3, 1955.
''Special Issue'' of *Filmkunst* (Vienna), no. 18, 1955.
Seitling, Mark, in *Films in Review* (New York), August-September 1960.
Croce, Arlene, in *Film Quarterly* (Berkeley), Fall 1960.
Stanbrook, Alan, in *Films and Filming* (London), April 1961.
Tyler, Parker, in *Classics of the Foreign Film*, New York, 1962.
Luft, Herbert, ''G. W. Pabst,'' in *Films and Filming* (London), April 1967.
Brecht, Bertolt, and V. Gerhage, ''Het Driestuiversproces—een sociologies experiment,'' in *Skrien* (Amsterdam), November-December 1973.
Rayns, Tony, in *Monthly Film Bulletin* (London), July 1974.
Pitera, Z., in *Kino* (Warsaw), August 1976.
''Special Issue'' of *Avant-Scène du Cinéma* (Paris), 1 December 1976.
Horak, J. C., ''Three Penny Opera: Brecht vs. Pabst,'' in *Jump Cut* (Chicago), no. 15, 1977.
Virmaux, Alain, and Odette Virmaux, ''L'Affaire: Quat sous de dommages et intérêts,'' in *Cinématographe* (Paris), December 1986.
''Cinema and Opera Issue'' of *Avant-Scène du Cinéma* (Paris), May 1987.
Film Dope (Nottingham), April 1994.
Löser, Claus, ''Ein ehrenvolles Schicksal,'' in *Film-Dienst* (Cologne), 7 November 1995.
Mahrenholz, S., in *EPD Film* (Frankfurt), November 1995.
Kemp, Philip, ''Mud in Your Eye,'' in *Sight & Sound* (London), October 1998.

* * *

G.W. Pabst's film version of Bertolt Brecht and Kurt Weill's *The Threepenny Opera* is a fascinating though flawed curio. The property, initially presented on the stage in 1928, is an adaptation of John Gay's *The Beggar's Opera*, a parody of Italian musical dramas first performed 200 years earlier.

While Brecht retained the basic plot of *The Beggar's Opera*, he updated it and related the satirical elements to his own era. At the same time, he was concerned more with ideas than coherent storyline or character development. In cinematizing the play, Pabst treated the plot and characters far more realistically, with greater emphasis on the feelings and motivation of the principal roles; in this regard, the film bears more the mark of Pabst than Brecht or Weill.

The sets, lighting and props are very stylized (except for the sequence detailing a beggar's demonstration) resulting in an odd conglomeration of surrealism and reality. Brecht originally collaborated on the film, but the script was rewritten when his ideas clashed with those of Pabst. Brecht and Weill were displeased with the filmmaker's interpretation, and took out a lawsuit over the material's copyright.

Brecht's social satire is still preserved though, along with this unaffected lyricism. The theme is as relevant to the present as to 1928 or 1728: the government and the underworld are as equally amoral in terms of self-interest. A once orderly world—which may only exist in the fantasies of those nostalgic for the ''good old days'' that in reality were never really so good—has been polluted by economic and political chaos. The setting is a dreary Victorian London of pimps and prostitutes, thieves and killers, and crooked politicians. (*The Threepenny Opera* was banned in London after a single showing). Polly Peachum, with the members of Mackie Messer's gang, opens a bank, in the belief that ''honest'' thievery is more profitable than larceny outside the law. In the end Polly's father (who is king of the beggars), Tiger Brown (the corrupt police commissioner), and Mackie become partners in the bank—and mainstays of society.

Weill's songs, so important in the stage production, seem less so here: some—''Ballad of Sexual Dependency,'' ''The Tango Ballad,'' and ''The Ballad for the Hangman''—were omitted by Pabst. On one level the film is difficult to evaluate because current prints are faded; and the soundtrack seems archaic because of the technology then available for recording dialogue and music. But the disunity of style (a fault) and the keenly realized satire (an asset) are both lucidly apparent.

The Threepenny Opera is one of a trio of films Pabst directed in the 1930s that were anti-capitalist, stressing the importance of friendship and the moral obligation to oppose the forces of evil. The others were *Westfront 1918 and Kameradschaft.* Though *The Threepenny Opera* is far more romantic and stylized than the first two, all are united thematically.

The film was released on the eve of Hitler's seizure of power in Germany. Pabst captured the essence of the atmosphere which allowed the existence of the Nazi state, and all original German prints were destroyed by the Third Reich. The film was shot simultaneously in both German and French, with different casts; the French *Threepenny Opera* became a success in Paris, and was hailed as a masterpiece, but the German version is more well-known in America. A complete negative of the latter was reconstructed by film distributor Thomas J. Brandon in 1960, after a decade-long search through Europe for sections and scenes.

—Rob Edelman

DRIFTERS

UK, 1929

Director: John Grierson

Production: New Era Studios for the Empire Marketing Board; black and white, 35mm; running time: about 40 minutes. Released 10 November 1929, premiered at the London Film Society. Filmed 1929 in a small fishing village in Northern England, and on board a herring boat at sea. Cost: Grierson declares cost to have been about £2500, while Rotha remembers it as being less than £2000.

Produced, scripted, directed, and edited by John Grierson; photographed by John Grierson and Basil Emmott.

Publications

Books:

Rotha, Paul, *Documentary Film*, London, 1952.

Grierson, John, *Grierson on Documentary*, edited by Forsyth Hardy, London, 1966.

Jacobs, Lewis, editor, *The Documentary Tradition: From Nanook to Woodstock*, New York, 1971.

Barsam, Richard, *Nonfiction Film: A Critical History*, New York, 1973.

Barnouw, Erik, *Documentary: A History of the Non-Fiction Film*, New York, 1974.

Sussex, Elizabeth, *The Rise and Fall of the British Documentary: The Story of the Film Movement Founded by John Grierson*, Berkeley, 1975.

Barsam, Richard, *Nonfiction Film: Theory and Criticism*, New York, 1976.

Beveridge, James, *John Grierson, Film Master*, New York, 1978.

Hardy, Forsyth, *John Grierson: A Documentary Biography*, London, 1979.

Ellis, Jack C., *John Grierson: A Guide to References and Resources*, Boston, 1986.

Ellis, Jack C., *The Documentary Idea*, Englewood Cliffs, New Jersey, 1989.

Articles:

Close Up (London), November 1929.

Bioscope (London), 27 November 1929.

Grierson, John, ''E.M.B. Film Unit,'' in *Cinema Quarterly* (London), Summer 1933.

Blumer, Ronald, ''I Derive My Authority from Moses,'' in *Take One* (Montreal), no. 9, 1970.

Sussex, Elizabeth, ''John Grierson,'' in *Sight and Sound* (London), Spring 1972.

Sight and Sound (London), Summer 1972.

''Grierson's Hammer,'' in *Films and Filming* (London), July 1972.

Sussex, Elizabeth, ''Grierson on Documentary: Last Interview,'' in *Film Quarterly* (Berkeley), Fall 1972.

Travelling (Lausanne), Summer 1979.

Forsyth, Scott, ''The Failures of Nationalism and Documentary: Grierson and Gouzenko,'' in *Canadian Journal of Film Studies* (Ottawa), vol. 1, no. 1, 1990.

Bernstein, Matthew, ''Film and Reform: John Grierson and the Documentary Film Movement,'' in *Film Quarterly* (Berkeley), vol. 47, no. 2, Winter 1993.

Acland, Charles R., ''National Dreams, International Encounters: The Formation of Canadian Film Culture in the 1930s,'' in *Canadian Journal of Film Studies* (Ottawa), Spring 1994.

Crothall, Geoffrey, ''Images of Regeneration: Film Propaganda and the British Slum Clearance Campaign, 1933–1938,'' in *Historical*

Drifters

Journal of Film, Radio and Television (Abingdon), vol. 19, no. 3, August 1999.

* * *

Drifters was John Grierson's first film, and the only one of thousands of films for which he was responsible that he completely controlled creatively. Not only did he write the script, produce, direct and edit, but, according to Forsyth Hardy in his biography of Grierson, he shot much of the film himself. In its editing he was assisted by Margaret Taylor, who became his wife.

About the work of herring fishermen in the North Sea, *Drifters* has a simple narrative structure. The men board their ships in harbor, sail to the banks, lay the nets, haul in the catch in the midst of a storm, race homeward to the auction of the catch at quayside. It includes images of Scotland and the sea, both important in Grierson's life and recurring in the films he produced. Herring fishing was a canny choice since the Financial Secretary to the Treasury was an authority on the subject.

Drifters marked the beginning of the British documentary film and served as a prototype for many of the films that followed. But, rather than evidence of an innovative genius, it represents the work of a brilliant analyst and synthesist who had absorbed what was at hand for the making of the kind of films he wanted to see made. In it are reflections of Flaherty's *Nanook of the North*, with brave men eking out their existence in the face of the elements. Eisenstein's *Potemkin* is even more heavily called upon. In *Drifters* the loving long takes of a Flaherty are cut up and banged together in Eisensteinian montage to provide a modern energy and rhythm, and the individual accomplishments of Nanook are replaced by the collective efforts of a crew, as in *Potemkin*. It is unlike both models, however, in eschewing the exotics of Flaherty and the heroics of the Soviets. In *Drifters* the drama is in the everyday workaday. By ending on the fish being sold at market, Grierson sets the fishermen's work within the context of the economic actualities of contemporary Britain.

Its premiere at the Film Society in London was as the first half of a double bill on which the British premiere of *Potemkin* was the main attraction, with Eisenstein in attendance. Though risking the comparison must have taken considerable nerve on Grierson's part, he knew that the audience for that event would comprise the intellectual elite and correspondents for the national press. *Drifters* was very well received and went on to modest commercial distribution. It was the first instance in English cinema in which work had been given this sort of importance and members of the working class were presented with dignity rather than as comic relief. As a silent film it was severely handicapped, however; at the time of its release the transition from silence to sound was becoming complete.

Rather than continuing as a personal filmmaker, as he might have done, Grierson used the success of *Drifters* as the basis for establishing the Empire Marketing Board Film Unit, for hiring others who would make more films and develop the British documentary film movement.

—Jack C. Ellis

DU RIFIFI CHEZ LES HOMMES

(Rififi)

France, 1955

Director: Jules Dassin

Production: Miracle Productions for Indus, Pathé, and Prima (France); black and white, 35mm; running time: 113 minutes, some sources list 116 minutes. Released 1955 in France.

Screenplay: René Wheeler, Jules Dassin, and Auguste le Breton, from the novel by Auguste le Breton; **photography:** Philippe Agostini; **editor:** Roger Dwyre; **sound:** J. Lebreton; art director Auguste Capelier; **music:** Georges Auric.

Cast: Jean Servais (*Tony le Stephanois*); Carl Mohner (*Jo le Suedois*); Robert Manuel (*Mario*); Perlo Vita (*Cesar*); Magali Noe (*Viviane*); Marie Subouret (*Mado*); Janine Darcy (*Louise*); Pierre Grasset (*Louise*); Robert Hossein (*Remi*); Marcel Lupovici (*Pierre*); Dominique Maurin (*Tonio*); Claude Sylvain (*Ida*).

Awards: Cannes Film Festival, Best Director (shared with Serge Vasilierv), 1955.

Publications

Books:

Ferrero, Adelio, *Jules Dassin*, Parma, 1961.
McArthur, Colin, *Underworld USA*, London, 1972.
Parish, James R., and Michael R. Pitts, *The Great Gangster Pictures*, Metuchen, New Jersey, 1976.
Siclier, Fabien, and Jacques Levy, *Jules Dassin*, Paris, 1986.

Articles:

Chabrol, Claude, and François Truffaut, interview with Dassin, in *Cahiers du Cinéma* (Paris), April-May 1955.
Wilcox, John, in *Sight and Sound* (London), Autumn 1955.
Raper, Michael, in *Films and Filming* (London), September 1955.
Hart, Henry, in *Films in Review* (New York), June-July 1956.
Crowther, Bosley, in *New York Times*, 6 June 1956.
Bourjaily, Vance, in *Village Voice* (New York), 4 July 1956.
Mayer, Andrew, in *Quarterly of Film, Radio, and Television* (Berkeley), Winter 1956.
Grenier, Cynthia, ''Jules Dassin,'' in *Sight and Sound* (London), Winter 1957–58.
Bluestone, George, ''An Interview with Jules Dassin,'' in *Film Culture* (New York), no. 17, 1958.
Johnson, Ian, in *Films and Filming* (London), April 1963.
Dassin, Jules, ''Style and Instinct,'' in *Films and Filming* (London), February 1970.
Carcassonne, P., ''Trois hommes du milieu,'' in *Cinématographe* (Paris), December 1980.
Carril, M., ''Los vaivenes de Jules Dassin,'' in *Cinemateca Revista* (Montevideo), July 1981.
Verdone, M., ''*Rififi*,'' in *Rivista del Cinematografo*, April Supplement, 1993.
Lewis, Kevin, ''Love and Noir with Jules Dassin,'' in *DGA Magazine* (Los Angeles), April-May 1995.
McGilligan, Patrick, ''I'll Always Be an American,'' in *Film Comment* (New York), November-December 1996.
Hanisch, Michael, ''Fremder in Hollywood,'' in *Film-Dienst* (Cologne), 17 December 1996.

* * *

Despite his Gallic-seeming name, *Du Rififi chez les hommes* was Jules Dassin's first French film. In the late 1940s he had pioneered a vivid new style of urban thriller, bringing an incisive, documentary-influenced realism to the mean streets of New York (*The Naked City*) and San Francisco (*Thieves' Highway*). Forced into exile by McCarthyism, he discovered an equally stark vision of London (*Night and the City*) before crossing the Channel to make (in the opinion of most critics) the finest film of his career. The richly textured evocation of Paris which Dassin created for *Rififi* perhaps betrays, in the sheer profusion of its detail, the eye of a fascinated visitor rather than the intimate glance of a native. But the film is convincingly authentic in its exact sense of milieu, its close attention to the tawdry glitter and stoic conventions of the small-time underworld it describes. Along with Jean-Pierre Melville's *Bob le flambeur* and Jacques Becker's *Touchez pas au Grisbi, Rififi* stands as one of the most accomplished French thrillers of the 1950s, all three films acknowledging, while never slavishly imitating, their American sources.

Like *Grisbi, Rififi* derives from a novel by Auguste le Breton, and shares the same downbeat, doom-laden atmosphere. The characters of *Rififi* inhabit a small, hermetic world, bounded by rigid precepts, in which even the police scarcely seem to figure. Danger threatens, not from the forces of law and order, but from rival gangs: the final shoot-out takes place in a half-built villa on the outskirts of Paris, a setting as ramshackle, bleak and devoid of bystanders as any Main Street in a western. From the first reel, the final outcome of events is never in doubt. With his racking cough and air of aging, existential gloom, Tony le Stephanois is marked down for destruction. The best he can hope for is a good death, according to his own strict code of honor.

The plot follows the accepted caper format, as laid down by John Huston's *The Asphalt Jungle:* a robbery is meticulously planned,

Du Rififi chez les hommes

flawlessly executed—but the gang is subsequently betrayed by its own weaknesses or internal dissensions, and all is lost. *Rififi's* most notable innovation, for which the film is still best remembered, is the classic half-hour sequence covering the robbery, executed in unprecedented detail and total silence, mesmerizing in its coolly sustained suspense. The gang members are depicted as conscientious craftsmen, carrying out their task steadily and skillfully, to a predetermined system. This sequence has since been much imitated (not least by Dassin himself, in *Topkapi*), but never yet surpassed.

Dassin portrays his doomed criminals with warmth and sympathy, aided by fine performances from a cast which includes (under the stage name of Perlo Vita) the director himself, as the dapper Italian cracksman whose susceptibility to women brings about the gang's downfall. *Rififi* marks the high point—and, regrettably, the conclusion—of Dassin's urban thriller cycle. Soon afterwards came the meeting with Melina Mercouri, and his descent into the pretensions of *Phaedra* and the cheerful hokum of *Never on Sunday.* Nothing in his subsequent career recaptured a fraction of the atmosphere and control of *Rififi.*

—Philip Kemp

DUCK SOUP

USA, 1933

Director: Leo McCarey

Production: Paramount Pictures; 17 November 1933; black and white, 35mm; running time: 72 minutes, some sources list 68 minutes. Released 22 November 1933.

Screenplay: Bert Kalmar and Harry Ruby, dialogue by Nat Perrin and Arthur Sheekman; **photography:** Henry Sharp; **editors:** Hans Dreier and Arthur Johnston; **music director:** Arthur Johnston.

Cast: Groucho Marx (*Rufus T. Firefly*); Harpo Marx (*Brownie*); Chico Marx (*Chicolini*); Zeppo Marx (*Bob Rolland*); Raquel Torres (*Vera Marcal*); Louis Calhern (*Ambassador Trentino*); Margaret Dumont (*Mrs. Teasdale*); Edgar Kennedy (*Lemonade Seller*); Edmund Breese (*Zander*); Edwin Maxwell (*Minister of War*); William Worthington (*Minister of Finance*); Leonid Kinsky (*Agitator*); Vera

Duck Soup

Hillie (*Secretary*); George MacQuarrie (*Judge*); Fred Sullivan (*Judge*); Davison Clark (*Minister*); Charles B. Middleton (*Prosecutor*); Eric Mayne (*Judge*).

Publications

Script:

Kalmar, Bert, and others, *Monkey Business and Duck Soup*, London, 1972.

Books:

Crichton, Kyle, *The Marx Brothers*, New York, 1951.
Marx, Harpo, *Harpo Speaks*, New York, 1961.
Eyles, Allen, *The Marx Brothers: Their World of Comedy*, London, 1966.
Zimmerman, Paul, and Burt Goldblatt, *The Marx Brothers and the Movies*, New York, 1968.
Anobile, Richard, *Why a Duck? Visual and Verbal Gems from the Marx Brothers Movies*, New York, 1971.
Matthews, J.H., *Surrealism and American Feature Film*, Boston, 1971.
Anthologie du Cinéma 7, Paris, 1973.
Gehring, Wes, *Leo McCarey and the Comic Anti-Hero in American Film*, New York, 1980.

Articles:

M.H., in *New York Times*, 23 November 1933.
Rowland, Richard, in *Hollywood Quarterly*, April 1947.
Kurnitz, Harry, "Return of the Marx Brothers," in *Holiday* (New York), January 1957.
Davey, S., and J. L. Noames, "Taking Chances: Interview with Leo McCarey," in *Cahiers du Cinéma in English* (New York), February 1965.
Carey, Gary, in *Film Notes*, edited by Eileen Bowser, New York, 1969.
Adamson, Joseph, "Duck Soup for the Rest of Your Life," in *Take One* (Montreal), September-October 1970.
Silver, C., "Leo McCarey: From Marx to McCarthy," in *Film Comment* (New York), September-October 1973.
Rosenblatt, R., "Taking Stock of Duck Soup," in *New Republic* (New York), 20 November 1976.
"Marx Brothers Issue" of *Avant-Scène du Cinéma* (Paris), 1 April 1985.
Winokur, M., "Smile, Stranger: Aspects of Immigrant Humor in the Marx Brothers Humor," in *Literature/Film Quarterly* (Salisbury, Maryland), July 1985.

Smith, M., ''Laughter, Redemption, Subversion in Eight Films by Leo McCarey,'' in *Cineaction* (Toronto), Summer-Fall 1990.
Groch, J.R., ''What Is a Marx Brother?: Critical Practice, Industrial Practice, and the Notion of an Auteur,'' in *Velvet Light Trap* (Austin), Fall 1990.
Haas, S., ''The Marx Brothers, Jews & My Four-Year-Old Daughter,'' in *Cineaste* (New York), vol. 19, no. 2–3, 1992.
Amengual, Barthélemy, in *Positif* (Paris), June 1998.
Arnold, Gary, ''Overlooked Achievements (Directors Left Out of '100 Greatest American Movies' List),'' in *Insight on the News*, vol. 14, no. 43, 23 November 1998.

* * *

Duck Soup was the fifth movie made under the Marx Brothers' five-picture contract with Paramount, and circumstances surrounding its production were not especially promising. The Paramount company was internally turbulent at the time, and in the early part of 1933 the Marx Brothers became involved in a dispute with the studio about the proceeds of some of their earlier films. Leo McCarey, whom they had selected as their director, was not enthusiastic about the project, and there were difficulties in completing the script. However, eventually all disagreements were resolved, and, amid the usual confusion surrounding Marx Brothers movies, the film was made. McCarey, often described as the only ''real'' director the Marx Brothers ever had, has said that he did not consider it one of his best pictures; later critics do not agree with him.

The virtue of *Duck Soup* is its simplicity. The unembellished plot, involving the rivalry of the Ruritanian principalities of Freedonia and Sylvania, is both a parody of the ''mythical kingdom'' genre and an ideal environment for Marx Brothers material; the setting is, in Gerald Weales's phrase, congenial rather than antagonistic to their style. There are no interpolated harp or piano solos for Harpo or Chico; in fact, there are only three musical numbers in all: a song for Groucho, and two enormous, impeccably staged and filmed production numbers, perfectly integrated into the action. There is no love interest for Zeppo, and no attempt to provide a conventional social framework for the zany personae of the stars.

Within this setting, the story is carried forward almost operatically by a remarkable profusion of gags and comedy routines. A great deal has been written about the sources of these routines; some, particularly those involving Edgar Kennedy, have been traced to the Laurel and Hardy films on which Leo McCarey had worked earlier. Many gags were recycled from other Marx Brothers material; as many as 15 routines were identified in the rediscovered scripts of *Flywheel, Shyster & Flywheel*, the 1932–33 radio program starring Groucho and Chico. Even the superlative mirror scene has it antecedents elsewhere; it is a traditional vaudeville and music hall number, described by *Variety* in its 1933 review of the film as ''the old Schwartz Bros. mirror routine,'' and used by others previously on film. But all these apparent borrowings might be viewed as no more than the use of material from a common pool of comedic material going back much further than any of these sources. What is significant in *Duck Soup* is the aptness of the material selected, and the elegance of its presentation.

McCarey, whose relaxed personality and improvisational methods seem to have combined well with those of his stars, had an unerring sense of what was best about the Marx Brothers style, and a remarkably fresh approach to its use. Harpo is still a satyr in *Duck Soup*, rather than the pixie he later became, and McCarey is not afraid to let us watch him perform his mayhem. Chico, as the spy Chicolini, perfectly logically chooses to be an Italian peanut vendor as ''cover,'' thereby setting up encounters with Edgar Kennedy's lemonade vendor in routines which combine the rhythms of Laurel and Hardy with Marx Brothers gags. And Groucho, the consummate verbal comedian, has some of his most famous dialogue scenes but also, astoundingly, performs the totally silent, completely physical, and justly renowned mirror scene with Harpo. The film contains the only musical number to feature all four of the Marx Brothers together; it marks the welcome return of Margaret Dumont as Groucho's foil; and it displays wonderful supporting performances by Louis Calhern as a sleek and impeccably tailored diplomat and Raquel Torres as a sinuous secret agent, simultaneously spoofing all Mata Hari movies and providing something for the baldheads to look at. McCarey's timing and that of the Marx Brothers work perfectly together in the overall pacing of the film; despite his insistence that he was most comfortable with physical comedy, McCarey was sensitive to the internal logic of Marx Brothers humor, which takes place at the level of the word or sentence, rather than the concept or situation.

Comparatively few critics liked the film when it was first released. *Variety* was almost alone in giving it an unreservedly favorable review, and the picture did not do well at the box office. However, later writers on film have had a great deal to say about it, and it has become a favorite with revival audiences. French critics have considered it, with the rest of the Marx Brothers *oeuvre*, as a work of surrealism. Other writers have treated it as a deliberate satire on government diplomacy, and war, or as an overtly pacifist statement. Most of the people involved with the making of *Duck Soup* have denied that they were consciously attempting anything other than entertainment, but it is certainly the case that the war in *Duck Soup* has a very silly cause, and is fought as a very silly war. If depicting a silly war can be construed as making the statement that war is silly, then *Duck Soup* is a pacifist film.

Duck Soup was the last film the Marx Brothers made for Paramount. When it was completed, Zeppo retired from show business, and Groucho, Chico, and Harpo moved to MGM where, under the guidance of Irving Thalberg, they began *A Night at the Opera*—an entirely different kind of film, and one perceived at the time as a comeback for the team. Despite its initial lack of success, *Duck Soup* has come to be considered one of the best and perhaps the most characteristic of the Marx Brothers films. Critical literature about the Marx Brothers and their work now probably exceeds the work itself in volume; indicative of the status of *Duck Soup* in the Marx Brothers canon is the fact that the periodical devoted in its entirety to Marx Brothers research is called *The Freedonia Gazette.*

—Annette Fern

DUVIDHA

(Two Roads)

India, 1973

Director: Mani Kaul

Production: Mani Kaul Productions; colour, 35mm; running time: 81 minutes. Filmed on location in Rajasthan.

Producer: Mani Kaul; **screenplay:** Mani Kaul, based on a short story by Vijaydan Detha; **photography:** Navroze Contractor; **editor:** Ravi Shankar Patnaik; **music:** Ramzan Khan, Hammu Khan, Latif, and Ski Khan.

Cast: Ravi Menon (*The Husband*); Raisa Padamsee (*The Wife*); Hardan (*The Father*); Shambudan (*The Shepherd*).

Publications

Articles:

Variety (New York), 19 November 1976.

Singh, Madan Gopal, "The Cinematic Exploration," in *Filmikon*, volume 5, number 1, December 1976.

Ray, Satyajit, "Four and a Quarter," in *Our Films, Their Films*, Orient Longman, Calcutta, 1976.

Kaul, Mani, "Towards a Cinematic Object," in *Indian Cinema Superbazaar*, Vikas Publishing, 1983.

Kaul, Mani, "Seen from Nowhere," in *Concepts of Space: Ancient and Modern*, Indira Gandhi National Centre for Art/Abhinav Publications, New Delhi, 1991.

"Mani Kaul (Interview with Indian Film Director)," in *UNESCO Courier*, July-August 1995.

Roy, L. Somi, "Mani Kaul at Flaherty," in *Wide Angle* (Baltimore), vol. 17, no. 1–4, 1995.

Roy, I.Y., P. Chatterjee, and M.G. Singh, and U. Vajpeyi, "Mani Kaul," in *Cinemaya* (New Delhi), Winter 1995/1996.

* * *

Mani Kaul's third feature, his first in colour, continued his path-breaking experimentation with what he called the "cinematic object." The film is very much a part of the director's early work (which has changed remarkably over the decades, e.g. his latest, the big budget multi-cast *Idiot*, 1919). His first two, *Uski Roti* (1969) and *Ashad Ka Ek Din* (1971), and then *Duvidha*, posed the question with great rigour—and for the first time in the long history of Indian cinema—of what the cinematic form itself was, and what it could do.

For him, at the time he made these films, cinema was explicitly *not* a composite of disciplines arriving at a specificity. He argued that whereas most forms preceding the cinema attempt transformations into specific modes, in film in sharp contrast, the extreme particularization of image/sound denotation *inhibits* any finite cinematic linguistic, and furthermore, that it is only when the specificity of the image/sound formation is treated as substantial and unique that a *violation* of this specificity becomes disciplined and positive: open to development (1983).

Towards that end he attempted a process of self-conscious specificity, emphasizing the particular, in order to be able to bracket it and eventually open it out. In *Duvidha* the location of the film's plot itself is significant to the formalist effort: it tells a Rajasthani folk story of a merchant's son who returns to his village with his new bride. He has to leave the village on business, leaving her alone. A ghost, hiding in a tree, witnesses his arrival and departure, and impersonating the husband, starts living with the wife. In time, a child is born to the woman and her ghost-husband. When the real husband returns, this causes a major dilemma, solved when the ghost is trapped by a shepherd in a leather bag. The socializing of the crisis and its neat solution, as the real husband is reinstated, of course, takes place without anyone taking the wife's feelings into account. Her silent desolation, at the end, leads the film itself to conclude with a strongly stated feminist position, one usually ignored by critics in favour of its more obviously stated formalist experiments.

Kaul himself presents in his cinematic object essay a hypothetical example that evidently relates to *Duvidha*:

> In feudal social formations it was adequate to respond to oppression as an internal phenomenon, since the external social structure was absolutely fixed. An internalized violence totalized the imagined and lived world of mythos. With the disappearance of the feudal order a violent reality externalized solidly, upon the social landscape. The course of the individual in society suddenly appeared hazardous. The older, subtler myths now appear meaningless with the collapse of an outmoded world . . . the solid mass is not able to will: nothing moves. A new abstraction.

It can be reasonably argued that in the film, the totalized internalized violence of the woman is "solidly externalized" by the ghost's physical presence. The trapping of the ghost into a bag in the end, like the trapping of the world of "mythos" by a new social system appears to be a solution, but its utter inability to solve the hazardous journey of the wife's attempt at individuation eventually means that it is no solution at all.

The film intervenes into the process of looking, of taking in that process, but instead of replicating its specificity, tries instead to seek for that abstraction which may allow for a frozen historical situation to find its mobility again.

The frozen nature of the film is of course its most critical aspect: attacked, above all by Satyajit Ray ("Four and a Quarter" in *Our Films Their Films*) for its unrealism, its exotica and its sparse visual and sound, contrasted as it was especially by the full-throated songs by Ramzan and Hammu on the title track. Into that historical freeze, however, Kaul brings in a variety of historically contradictory, till then considered hierarchical languages. The woman—especially as she enters the village in a palanquin—clearly evokes the Basohli and Kangra miniature forms, extended into the framing, editing and the colour schemes used. Contrasted by the folk nature of the tale itself, and the music that represents the form in which it is traditionally told, Kaul also orchestrates with extraordinary skill the way that classical and folk forms apparently contradict, eroticize and freeze each other, both refusing to let the other go beyond apparent specificities and into a form that can develop and adapt to historical change.

Duvidha was made with the informal support of a multi-arts co-op led by the noted painter Akbar Padamsee. Although this film was extensively screened and telecast in Europe (to a point where Kaul, nearly a dozen films later is still associated with this relatively early work), it may be added that the apparent commercial failure of this film forced the director to make only non-fiction for over 15 years, a genre to which he has returned only in the 1990s, with his explorations of Dostoevsky (*Nazar*, 1989 and *Idiot*, 1991).

—Ashish Rajadhyaksha

THE EARRINGS OF MADAME DE . . .

See **MADAME DE . .**

EARTH

See **ZEMLYA**

EAST OF EDEN

USA, 1955

Director: Elia Kazan

Production: Warner Bros. Pictures, Inc. and First National; Technicolor (Warnercolor), 35mm, CinemaScope; running time: 115 minutes; length: 3415 meters. Released 9 April 1955, New York.

Producer: Elia Kazan; **screenplay:** Paul Osborn; **dialogue:** Guy Tomajean, from the novel by John Steinbeck; **photography:** Ted McCord; **editor:** Owen Marks; **sound engineer:** Stanley Jones; **art directors:** James Basevi and Malcolm Bert; **music:** Leonard Rosenman; **costume designer:** Anna Hill Johnstone.

Cast: James Dean (*Cal Trask*); Julie Harris (*Abra*); Raymond Massey (*Adam Trask*); Richard Davalos (*Aron Trask*); Jo Van Fleet (*Kate*); Burl Ives (*Sam Cooper, the Sheriff*); Albert Dekker (*Will Hamilton*); Lois Smith (*Ann*); Harold Gordon (*Mr. Albrecht*); Timothy Carey (*Joe*); Mario Siletti (*Piscora*); Roy Turner (*Lonny Chapman*); Nick Dennis (*Rantany*).

Awards: Cannes Film Festival, Prix du Film Dramatique, 1955; Oscar, Best Supporting Actress (Van Fleet), 1955.

Publications

Script:

Osborn, Paul, in *Avant-Scène du Cinéma* (Paris), November 1975.

Books:

Bast, William, *James Dean: A Biography*, New York, 1956.
Thomas, T. T., *I, James Dean*, New York, 1957.
Tailleur, Roger, *Elia Kazan*, revised edition, Paris, 1971.
Basinger, Jeanine, John Frazer, and Joseph W. Reed, Jr., *Working with Kazan*, Middletown, Connecticut, 1973.
Ciment, Michel, *Kazan on Kazan*, New York, 1974.
Dalton, David, *James Dean—The Mutant King*, San Francisco, 1974.
Herndon, Venable, *James Dean—A Short Life*, New York, 1974.
Whittman, Mark, *The Films of James Dean*, London, 1974.
Giannetti, Louis, *Masters of the American Cinema*, Englewood Cliffs, New Jersey, 1981.
Bourget, Jean-Loup, *James Dean*, Paris, 1983.
Morrissey, Steven, *James Dean Is Not Dead*, Manchester, 1983.
Pauly, Thomas H., *An American Odyssey: Elia Kazan and American Culture*, Philadelphia, 1983.
Dalton, David, and Ron Cayen, *James Dean: American Icon*, London, 1984.
Devillers, Marcel, *James Dean*, London, 1985.
Michaels, Lloyd, *Elia Kazan: A Guide to References and Resources*, Boston, 1985.
Beath, Warren Newton, *The Death of James Dean*, London, 1986.
Jones, David Richard, *Great Directors at Work: Stanislavsky, Brecht, Kazan, Brook*, Berkeley, 1986.
Kazan, Elia, *Elia Kazan: A Life*, New York, 1988.
Ciment, Michel, *An American Odyssey: Elia Kazan*, London, 1989.

Articles:

Gavin, Arthur, ''The Photography of *East of Eden*,'' in *American Cinematographer* (Los Angeles), March 1955.
Gerstle, Ralph, in *Films in Review* (New York), March 1955.
Cole, Clayton, in *Films and Filming* (London), April 1955.
Sarris, Andrew, in *Film Culture* (New York), May-June 1955.
Prouse, Derek, in *Sight and Sound* (London), Summer 1955.
Bazin, André, ''L'Indéniable Puissance lyrique de Kazan,'' in *France-Observateur* (Paris), 3 November 1955.
Archer, Eugene, ''The Genesis of a Style,'' in *Film Culture* (New York), no. 8, 1956.
Truffaut, François, ''*Les Haricots du Mal*,'' in *Cahiers du Cinéma* (Paris), February 1956.
Archer, Eugene, ''Genesis of a Genius,'' in *Films and Filming* (London), January 1957.
Connolly, Ray, ''Eden Revisited,'' in *Motion* (London), Winter 1961–62.
Bean, Robin, ''The Young Agony,'' in *Films and Filming* (London), March 1962.
Stein, Jeanne, ''Raymond Massey,'' in *Films in Review* (New York), August-September 1963.
Bean, Robin, in *Films and Filming* (London), May 1964.
Bean, Robin, ''Dean—10 Years After,'' in *Films and Filming* (London), October 1965.
Delahare, Michel, ''Preface to an Interview,'' in *Cahiers du Cinéma in English* (New York), October 1966.

East of Eden

''A Natural Phenomenon: Interview with Elia Kazan,'' in *Cahiers du Cinéma in English* (New York), November 1966.

Benayoun, Robert, ''Cain, Abel et le dollar,'' in *Positif* (Paris), May 1967.

Byron, Stuart, and Martin L. Rubin, ''Elia Kazan Interview,'' in *Movie* (London), Winter 1971–72.

Hillier, Jim, in *Movie* (London), Winter 1971–72.

Kitses, Jim, ''Elia Kazan: A Structuralist Analysis,'' in *Cinema* (Los Angeles), Winter 1972–73.

Truffaut, François, ''James Dean est mort,'' in *Avant-Scène du Cinéma* (Paris), November 1975.

Small, Edward S., in *Magill's Survey of Cinema 1*, Englewood Cliffs, New Jersey, 1980.

Comuzio, Ermanno, in *Cineforum* (Bergamo), August 1984.

Rathgeb, D.L., ''Kazan as Auteur: The Undiscovered *East of Eden*,'' in *Literature/Film Quarterly* (Salisbury), January 1988.

Dancyger, K., ''The Bigger Picture: A Consideration of the Influence of Journalism and Theatre on the Feature Length Screenplay,'' in *Journal of Film and Video* (Los Angeles), no. 3, 1990.

Simmons, Jerrold, ''The Production Code & Precedent,'' in *Journal of Popular Film and Television* (Washington, D.C.), Fall 1992.

Larue, Johanne, in *Séquences* (Haute-Ville), September 1992.

Kino (Warsaw), June 1993.

Séquences (Haute-Ville), July-August 1995.

''A Tune Is Worth 1,000 Pictures: The Neglected Craft of Film Music,'' in *Economist*, vol. 343, no. 8018, 24 May 1997.

* * *

If *East of Eden* were remembered only for introducing to the screen its legendary star, James Dean, its place in film history would be assured. As it is, however, the techniques developed by the director to capture and translate the actor's performance most effectively within a widescreen format also lend the film the artistic distinction of being one of the first serious attempts at a creative use of CinemaScope. Elia Kazan's bag of stylistic tricks, regarded by many critics as technical abnormalities, consisted of such devices as canting the camera to distort angles, use of swinging pans to sustain a sense of movement in stagy scenes, unusually moody lighting effects, horizontal pans, and experiments with soft focus lenses. Through these techniques, the director used his camera to accompany his actors' performances, effectively and imaginatively enhancing their work. At the same time, he effected a visual impression of continuous movement while constantly redirecting the viewer's attention to the appropriate area of the screen, maximizing the dramatic advantages of its vast expanse. The resulting effect is an amplification of the film's symbolic motifs through their placement in shifting but visually highlighted contexts.

In a sense, the effective translation of *East of Eden* to the large screen required a visual equivalent to the acting method pioneered by the Actors Studio, of which Kazan was a co-founder. Drawing on his own "emotional memory," the actor recalls feelings comparable to those experienced by a fictional character. A number of Kazan's actors, particularly Dean and Marlon Brando (in *A Streetcar Named Desire*), were practitioners of "the Method," which required a considerable degree of adaptation in terms of the cinematography. Through Kazan's visual style in *East of Eden*, the camera, in a manner similar to that used in the German Expressionist films of the 1920s, reflects the psychological aspects of the characters under its scrutiny. For example, the story, a modern version of the Biblical tale of Cain and Abel, centers on the relationship between a father and his two sons. Its point of view is that of the youngest son Cal who, like his Biblical counterpart Cain, performs certain acts that are subject to at least two interpretations. Viewed simplistically, they can, in the case of both characters, be seen as the vile deeds of an inherently evil son. Yet, through Dean's eccentric interpretation, the modern boy can also be recognized as a psychologically complex, insecure child who is starved for parental love. In scenes in which Cal appears with his father Adam (Raymond Massey), Kazan tilts the camera to dramatically characterize both figures as being in an essentially aberrant, distorted relationship. Both actor and camera combine to place the character's actions within an abnormal family context and reveal Cal's actions to be those of a boy consumed by an overwhelming need to win his father's approval. It is significant that the angle of vision is most distorted in the scene in which Adam refuses his son's heartfelt but slightly tainted gift of money. Adam cannot look beneth the surface of the act to assess its meaning in terms of their relationship.

Interspersed throughout the film are long, almost theatrical scenes, indicative of the director's stage experience, which provide the film with its thematic unity as ideas are raised which will later result in violent confrontations. Even in these scenes, there is a constant sense of movement expressed through the use of settings such as a Ferris wheel or swing. Additional coherence is provided by the film's glimpse of the plight of California's immigrant population, a subject close to Kazan's heart. Some scholarship makes a case for *East of Eden* as the first in a series of Kazan films which examine various psychological and sociological aspects of the immigrant experience, a series continued by *Wild River, America, America* and *The Arrangement.*

—Stephen L. Hanson

EASY RIDER

USA, 1969

Director: Dennis Hopper

Production: Raybert Productions and Pando Company; Technicolor, 35mm (LSD sequence shot in 16mm); running time: 94 minutes; length: 2561 meters. Released 14 July 1969, New York. Filmed 1968–69 on location between California and New Orleans. Cost: about $375,000.

Producers: Peter Fonda with Bert Schneider and William L. Hayward; **screenplay:** Peter Fonda, Dennis Hopper, and Terry Southern; **photography:** Laszlo Kovacs; **editor:** Donn Cambern; **sound:** Ryder Sound Service; **sound mixer:** Leroy Robbins; **art director:** Jerry Kay; **music:** Steppenwolf, The Byrds, The Band, The Holy Modal Rounders, Fraternity of Man, The Jimi Hendrix Experience, Little Eva, The Electric Prunes, The Electric Flag, and Roger McGuinn; **special effects:** Steve Karkus; **stunt gaffer:** Tex Hall.

Cast: Peter Fonda (*Wyatt*); Dennis Hopper (*Billy*); Antonio Mendoza (*Jesus*); Phil Spector (*Connection*); Mac Mashourian (*Bodyguard*); Warren Finnerty (*Rancher*); Tita Colorado (*Rancher's Wife*); Luke Askew (*Stranger on Highway*); Luana Anders (*Lisa*); Sabrina Scharf (*Sarah*); Sandy Wyeth (*Joanne*); Robert Walker, Jr. (*Jack*); Robert Ball, Carmen Phillips, Ellie Walker, and Michael Pataki (*Mimes*); Jack Nicholson (*George Hanson*); George Fowler, Jr. (*Guard*); Keith Green (*Sheriff*); Hayward Robillard (*Cat Man*); Arnold Hess, Jr. (*Deputy*); Buddy Causey Jr., Duffy Lamont, Blase M. Dawson, and Paul Guedry (*Customers in the Café*); Toni Basil (*Mary*); Karen Black (*Karen*); Lea Marmer (*Madame*); Cathi Cozzi (*Dancing Girl*); Thea Salerno, Anne McClain, Beatriz Monteil, and Marcia Bowman (*Hookers*); David C Billodeau and Johnny David (*Men in pickup truck*).

Awards: New York Film Critics' Award, Best Supporting Actor (Nicholson), 1969; Cannes Film Festival, Best First Film, 1969.

Publications

Script:

Easy Rider: Original Screenplay by Peter Fonda, Dennis Hopper, Terry Southern plus Stills, Interviews, and Articles, edited by Nancy Hardin and Marylin Schlossberg, New York, 1969.

Books:

Springer, John, *The Fondas: The Film and Careers of Henry, Jane, and Peter Fonda*, New York, 1970.
Mast, Gerald, *A Short History of the Movies*, New York, 1971.
Downing, David, *Jack Nicholson: A Biography*, London, 1983.
Cagin, Seth, and Philip Dray, *Hollywood Films of the Seventies: Sex, Drugs, Violence, Rock'n'Roll, and Politics*, New York, 1984.
Rodriguez, Elean, *Dennis Hopper: A Madness to His Method*, New York, 1988.
Stayton, Richard, *Dennis Hopper*, New York, 1997.

Articles:

Tuten, Frederick, in *Film Society Review* (New York), May 1969.
Sarris, Andrew, in *Village Voice* (New York), 3 July and 14 August 1969.
Reif, Tony, and Iain Ewing, "Fonda," in *Take One* (Montreal), no. 3, 1969.

Easy Rider

Fonda, Peter, and Leslie Reyner, ''Thoughts and Attitudes about *Easy Rider*,'' in *Film* (London), Autumn 1969.

Macklin, F. A., ''*Easy Rider*: The Initiation of Dennis Hopper,'' in *Film Heritage* (Dayton, Ohio), Fall 1969.

Milne, Tom, in *Sight and Sound* (London), Autumn 1969.

Polt, Harriet, in *Film Quarterly* (Berkeley), Fall 1969.

''What Directors Are Saying,'' in *Action* (Los Angeles), September-October 1969.

Farber, Stephen, in *Film Quarterly* (Berkeley), Winter 1969–70.

Warshow, Paul, in *Sight and Sound* (London), Winter 1969–70.

Sullivan, Tom R., ''*Easy Rider*: Comic Epic Poem in Film,'' in *Journal of Popular Culture* (Bowling Green, Ohio), Spring 1970.

Sullivan, Mary Rose, ''*Easy Rider*: Critique of the New Hedonism,'' in *Western Humanities Review*, no. 24, 1970.

Hampton, Charles, in *Film Comment* (New York), Fall 1970.

Kael, Pauline, in *New Yorker*, 3 October 1970.

''*Easy Rider* Issue'' of *Avant-Scène du Cinéma* (Paris), September 1971.

Cohen, M. S., ''The Corporate Style of BBS,'' in *Take One* (Montreal), November 1973.

Herring, H. D., ''Out of the Dream and into the Nightmare: Dennis Hopper's Apocalyptic Vision of America,'' in *Journal of Popular Film and Television* (Washington, D.C.), Winter 1983.

Hugo, Chris, ''*Easy Rider* and Hollywood in the 1970s,'' in *Movie* (London), Winter 1986.

McGilligan, Patrick, ''The Ballad of *Easy Rider* (Or, How to Make a Drug Classic),'' in *Los Angeles Magazine*, March 1994.

MacGregor, Jeff, ''The Hot Day Terry Southern, Cool and Fatalistic, Strode In. . . ,'' in *New York Times*, 12 November 1995.

Hirschman, E.C., ''A Cinematic Depiction of Drug Addiction: A Semiotic Account,'' in *Semiotica*, no. 104, 1995.

Laderman, D., ''What a Trip: The Road Film in American Culture,'' in *Journal of Film and Video* (Los Angeles), no. 48, 1996.

Redman, Nick, in *DGA Magazine* (Los Angeles), July-August 1996.

Hampton, Howard, ''Scorpio Descending: In Search of Rock Cinema,'' in *Film Comment* (New York), March-April 1997.

Singer, Mark, ''Whose Movie is This (How Much of *Easy Rider* Belongs to Novelist Terry Southern),'' in *New Yorker*, vol. 74, no. 17, 22 June 1998.

* * *

Easy Rider remains a cinematic hallmark primarily for negative reasons; the preeminent film dealing with the subject and style typifying the late 1960s, it remains an interesting cultural and historical document of the industry's response to ''youth culture.'' Unfortunately, the film seemed trite even two years after its initial critical and public triumph. Produced for $375,000, it made over $50,000,000 and spawned a number of less-effective imitators; the film's profits convinced even the most reticent backers in Hollywood that the youth market was ready to be tapped. In fact, it may have been its imitators that made the original date so quickly; many of the films produced after *Easy Rider* were of such inferior quality that they couldn't be sold to television after their initial release in regular theaters.

The film is not without value. Film historian Gerald Mast sees *Easy Rider* as a landmark of the ''New Hollywood'' as well as the culmination of films representing our experience of the American West through the narrative device of the journey, the film being a sort of New Wave cowboy epic. It reflects the sexual and social values of the American counter-culture of the period: the protagonists are social misfits and outlaws. Unlike filmic outlaws of the past—Little Caesar, Scarface—these heros can be charming, good-humored, warm and often compassionate. Their humorless and finally deadly pursuers, predictably, represent the ''older generation.'' In Mast's words, ''Given the outlaw protagonists, the new obligatory ending was the unhappy rather than happy one. The protagonists die; law triumphs over lawlessness. However, good did not triumph over evil, for law and good were antithetical.''

Easy Rider dealt openly with violence and paranoia, appropriate themes given the ideological divisions of the United States in the late 1960s. As David Cook notes, the film ''was praised for its radical social perspective far beyond its value as a film.'' For him as well it is the western/quest film revisited: two ''hippies,'' their journey made on motorcycles rather than horses, go ''in search of America.'' The film concerns freedom, or the illusion of freedom—for ultimately the bikers ''can't find it anywhere,'' as the promotional copy read.

Easy Rider merges the American past and present, city and country, gangsters and cowboy through the main characters played by Dennis Hopper and Peter Fonda. Civilization is personified by small-town bigots and the county sheriff, and characterized by institutionalized love (a whorehouse), and even institutionalized death (a very large cemetery). The romantic journey seems less than it should be; a commune of hip kids from the city acts with as much hostility towards the easy riders as the ''straights'' in the towns. Freedom is represented by the road, but as the ending of the film illustrates, even that cannot last.

Andrew Sarris stressed the ''assortment of excellences . . . lift *Easy Rider* above the run and ruck of its genre. The first and foremost is the sterling performance of Jack Nicholson as George Hanson, a refreshingly civilized creature from Southern comfort and interplanetary fantasies.'' Among the film's other strengths are its traveling shots on the road accompanied by the rock music of Jimi Hendrix, The Byrds, Steppenwolf, The Band, Bob Dylan, Roger McGuinn, and others. But Sarris's main point is that ''with all the rousingly rhythmic revelry and splendiferously scenic motorcycling, *Easy Rider* comes to resemble a perceptual precredit sequence, but reasonably pleasant withal.'' However, ''there is something depressingly *deja vu* about the moralistic view of America from a motorcycle.'' And this from a critic who essentially *likes* the film.

Critical opprobrium of its time not withstanding, *Easy Rider*'s jury still hasn't returned a less than contradictory verdict. For all its apparent triteness, for all of its ''Man-cool mumbles,'' even mainstream critics like Sarris warn, ''beware of all generalizations, including this one; the *nouvelle vague* tricks and Bergman-Fellini-Antonioni mannerisms are no more voguish today than the UFA German Expressionist and Soviet montage tricks were in the late twenties.'' The film has dated badly, yet its value lies in capturing one of the United States' most divisive times, illustrating where the frontier legacy begun with *Stagecoach* seems to have led. It's often impossible to tell the heros from the villains in *Easy Rider*, as now.

—Deborah H. Holdstein

L'ECLISSE

(The Eclipse)

Italy-France, 1962

Director: Michelangelo Antonioni

Production: Interopa Film and Cineriz (Rome) and Paris Film Production (Paris); black and white, 35mm; running time: 125 minutes. Released 1962. Filmed in Italy.

Producers: Robert and Raymond Hakim; **screenplay:** Michelangelo Antonioni and Tonino Guerra, with Elio Bartolini and Ottiero Ottieri; **photography:** Gianni Di Venanzo; **editor:** Eraldo Da Roma; **sound:** Claudio Maielli and Mario Bramonti; **production design:** Piero Poletto; **music:** Giovanni Fusco.

Cast: Alain Delon (*Riccardo*); Monica Vitti (*Vittoria*); Francisco Rabal; Lilla Brignone; Rosanna Rory; Mirella Ricciardi; Louis Seignier.

Awards: Cannes Film Festival, Special Jury Prize and Catholic Film Office Award, 1962.

Publications

Scripts:

Antonioni, Michelangelo, and Tonino Guerra, *L'eclisse*, 1962; translated in *Screenplays of Michelangelo Antonioni*, New York, 1963.

Books:

Leprohon, Pierre, *Michelangelo Antonioni: An Introduction*, New York, 1963.

Cowie, Peter, *Antonioni, Bergman, Resnais*, New York, 1963.

Strick, Philip, *Antonioni*, London, 1965.

Cameron, Ian, and Robin Wood, *Antonioni*, London and New York, 1969.

Samuels, Charles Thomas, *Encountering Directors*, New York, 1972.

Poague, Leland, and William Cadbury, *Film Criticism: A Counter Theory*, Ames, Iowa, 1982.

Rifkin, Ned, *Antonioni's Visual Language*, Ann Arbor, Michigan, 1982.

Barthes, Roland, and others, *Michelangelo Antonioni*, Munich, 1984.

Biarese, Cesare, and Aldo Tassone, *I film di Michelangelo Antonioni*, Rome, 1985.

Dervin, Daniel, *Through a Freudian Lens Deeply: A Psychoanalysis of Cinema*, Hillsdale, New Jersey, 1985.

Antonioni, Michelangelo, *That Bowling Alley on the Tiber: Tales of a Director*, Oxford, 1986.

L'Eclisse

Perry, Ted, and Rene Prieto, *Michelangelo Antonioni: A Guide to References and Resources*, Boston, 1986.

Tinazzi, Giorgio di, *Michelangelo Antonioni*, Firenze, 1989.

Giaume, Joëlle Mayet, *Michelangelo Antonioni: le fil intérieur*, Crisnée, Belgium, 1990.

Rohdie, Sam, *Antonioni*, London, 1990.

Prédal, René, *Michelangelo Antonioni, ou, La vigilance du désir*, Paris, 1991.

Arrowsmith, William, *Antonioni: The Poet of Images*, New York, 1995.

Brunette, Peter, *The Films of Michelangelo Antonioni*, Cambridge, 1998.

Scemama-Heard, Céline, *Antonioni: le désert figuré*, Paris, 1998.

Articles:

Lane, John Francis, ''Antonioni Diary,'' in *Films and Filming* (London), March 1962.

''Antonioni Issue'' of *Film Quarterly* (Berkeley), Fall 1962.

Barthelme, Donald, in *New Yorker*, 2 March 1963.

Gerard, L. N., ''Antonioni,'' in *Films in Review* (New York), April 1963.

''Antonioni Issue'' of *7th Art* (New York), Spring 1963.

''Antonioni Issue'' of *Motion*, no. 5, 1963.

Nowell-Smith, Geoffrey, ''Shape Around the Black Point,'' in *Sight and Sound* (London), Winter 1963–64.

Houston, Penelope, ''Keeping Up with the Antonionis,'' in *Sight and Sound* (London), Autumn 1964.

Nowell-Smith, Geoffrey, ''The Event and the Image,'' in *Sight and Sound* (London), Winter 1964–65.

Godard, Jean-Luc, ''Night, Eclipse, and Dawn: An Interview with Michelangelo Antonioni,'' in *Cahiers du Cinéma in English* (New York), January 1966.

Andrew, J. Dudley, ''The Stature of Objects in Antonioni's Films,'' in *Triquarterly* (Evanston, Illinois), Winter 1968.

Gow, Gordon, ''Antonioni Men,'' in *Films and Filming* (London), June 1970.

Perry, Ted, ''A Contextual Analysis of Antonioni's *L'eclisse*,'' in *Speech Monographs*, June 1970.

Tudor, Andrew, ''Antonioni: The Road to Death,'' in *Cinema* (London), August 1970.

Hernacki, T., ''Michelangelo Antonioni and the Imagery of Disintegration,'' in *Film Heritage* (Dayton, Ohio), Autumn 1970.

Decaux, E., ''Une Musique: *L'eclisse*,'' in *Cinématographe* (Paris), November 1980.

Affron, Mirella Joan, ''Text and Memory in *Eclipse*,'' in *Literature/Film Quarterly* (Salisbury, Maryland), vol. 9, no. 3, 1981.

Tarnowski, J. F., ''Identification d'une oeuvre,'' in *Positif* (Paris), January 1983.

Esposito, J., ''Antonioni and Benjamin: Dialectical Imagery in *Eclipse*,'' in *Film Criticism* (Meadville, Pennsylvania), Fall 1984.

Perez, G., ''The Point of View of a Stranger: An Essay on Antonioni's *Eclipse*,'' in *Hudson Review* (New York), no. 2, 1991.

Tomasulo, F. P., ''The Architectonics of Alienation: Antonioni's Edifice Complex,'' in *Wide Angle* (Baltimore), no. 3, 1993.

Predal, R., ''L'eclisse, l'ellipse,'' in *Avant Scène du Cinéma* (Paris), February 1993.

Peck, Ron, ''Chance Encounters,'' in *Sight & Sound* (London), December 1994.

Landrot, Marine, ''Identification d'un cinéaste,'' in *Télérama* (Paris), 6 September 1995.

Moore, K.Z., ''Eclipsing the Commonplace: The Logic of Alienation in Antonioni's Cinema,'' in *Film Quarterly* (Berkeley), vol. 48, no. 4, Summer 1995.

Nowell-Smith, G., ''Antonioni,'' in *Sight & Sound* (London), December 1995.

Chatman, Seymour, ''The Films of Michaelangelo Antonioni,'' in *Film Quarterly* (Berkeley), vol. 53, no. 1, Fall 1999.

* * *

Michelangelo Antonioni's *L'eclisse* is the most succinct expression of moral ambiguities of the Italian ''economic miracle'' of the late 1950s and early 1960s to come from the national cinema. It is the complement of Federico Fellini's *La dolce vita.* Whereas Fellini dwells upon the hellish and grotesque dimensions of Roman life during that period, Antonioni focuses upon its inauthenticity and its impermanence. The ''eclisse'' of the title refers primarily to the brief affair of the protagonists Vittoria, a translator, and Piero, a stock jobber; and secondarily to a brief tailspin in the stockmarket which forms the backdrop of their liaison. In an even wider sense, it alludes to the brief span of human life on earth, literalized in a scene in a natural history museum which the filmmaker had to cut perhaps under pressure from the producers. The sole vestige of this dimension is a fossil Vittoria hangs as a decoration on her wall.

From the opening scene of Vittoria arranging objects in a frame to the final, magnificent montage of the nearly empty, vespertinal streets of Rome's fashionable and modernistic E.U.R. district, Antonioni's typical love of composition and attention to significant detail is in evidence. In this film, things overwhelm people. Even the accidental meeting of Piero and Vittoria for the first time occurs during an ominous pause—a literal ''minute of silence'' in the stock exchange honoring a dead broker—and they whisper to each other around a monumental pillar (the Roman stock market is built in the ruins of an ancient temple).

The rootlessness of this couple is emphasized in the scenes of their mutual seduction which take place, not in their modern apartments, but in their parents' stuffier dwellings in the center of the city. By locating their amours in the vacant parental apartments, Antonioni underlines the dimensions of compulsion and regression in their relationship. Without pain, almost cheerfully, they exploit each other, playing at seriousness and constancy.

The ironic counterpoint to their homelessness is Vittoria's neighbor, Marta, who longs for her family plantation in Kenya. Her home is decorated with African trophies and giant enlargements of photographs of East Africa. A nostalgist and a racist, who refers to the natives as ''apes,'' she had reified her environment. Antonioni underscores the illusory status of her feeling for Africa by depicting her hysterical attitude to her effeminately mannered poodle amid the vestiges of safaris.

The final minutes of the film sustain a remarkable suspense as the viewer is lead to expect either Vittoria or Piero to appear at the corner of their assignations. Instead, the camera focuses upon the objects and people that had been backdrops and tangents of their actions. As we come to realize that neither will appear, we get a glimpse of a man reading a newspaper (one of the many false identifications of the protagonists) with the headline about the threat of atomic war. The final, sustained close-up of a street light suggests a nuclear explosion which can eclipse human time.

—P. Adams Sitney

DIE EHE DER MARIA BRAUN

(The Marriage of Maria Braun)

West Germany, 1978

Director: Rainer Werner Fassbinder

Production: Albatros Film (M. Fengler), Trio Film, WDR, and Filmerlog Der Autoren (all of West Germany); Fujicolor, 35mm; running time: 120 minutes; length: 10,764 feet. Released 1978, Germany, and 28 February 1979, United States. Filmed in Germany.

Producer: Michael Fengler; **screenplay:** Peter Märthesheimer and Pea Fröhlich; **dialogue:** Rainer Werner Fassbinder; from an idea by Fassbinder; **photography:** Michael Ballhaus; **editors:** Juliane Lorenz and Franz Walsch (*Fassbinder*); **sound recordists:** Jim Willis and Milan Bor; **art directors:** Norbert Scherer, Helga Ballhaus, Claus Kottmann, and Georg Borgel; **music:** Peer Raben; **costume designers:** Barbara Baum, Susi Reichel, George Kuhn, and Ingeborg Pröller.

Cast: Hanna Schygulla (*Maria Braun*); Klaus Löwitsch (*Hermann Braun*); Ivan Desny (*Karl Oswald*); Gottfried John (*Willi Klenze*); Gisela Uhlen (*Mother*); George Byrd (*Bill*); Elisabeth Trissenaar (*Betty Klenze*); Rainer Werner Fassbinder (*Dealer*); Isolde Barth (*Vevi*); Peter Berling (*Bronski*); Sonja Neudorfer (*Red Cross Nurse*); Lieselotte Eder (*Frau Ehmke*); Volker Spengler (*Train Conductor*); Michael Ballhaus (*Counsel, Anwalf*); Günther Kaufmann (*American on train*); Karl-Heinz von Hassel (*Prosecuting counsel*).

Awards: Berlin Film Festival, Best Actress (Schygulla) and Best Technical Team, 1979.

Die Ehe der Maria Braun

Publications

Script:

Fassbinder, Rainer Werner, Peter Märthesheimer, and Pea Fröhlich, *The Marriage of Maria Braun*, in *Rutgers Films in Print 4*, Rutgers, New Jersey, 1984.

Books:

Sandford, John, *The New German Cinema*, Totowa, New Jersey, 1980.
Baer, Harry, *Schlafen kann ich, wenn ich tot bin: Das atemlose Leben des Rainer Werner Fassbinder*, Cologne, 1982.
Eckhardt, Bernd, *Rainer Werner Fassbinder: Im 17 Jahren 42 Filme—Stationen eines Lebens für den deutschen Film*, Munich, 1982.
Iden, Peter, and others, *Rainer Werner Fassbinder*, Munich, 1982.
Raab, Kurt, and Karsten Peters, *Die Sehnsucht des Rainer Werner Fassbinder*, Munich, 1982.
Foss, Paul, editor, *Fassbinder in Review*, Sydney, 1983.
Franklin, James, *New German Cinema: From Oberhausen to Hamburg*, Boston, 1983.
Bauschinger, Sigrid, Susan Cocalis, and Henry A. Lea, editors, *Film und Literatur: Literarische texte und der neue deutsche film*, Munich, 1984.
Fassbinder, Rainer Werner, *Film Befreien den Kopf: Essays und Arbeitsnotizen*, edited by Michael Töteburg, Frankfurt, 1984.
Hayman, Ronald, *Fassbinder: Film-maker*, London, 1984.
Phillips, Klaus, *New German Filmmakers: From Oberhausen through the 1970s*, New York, 1984.
Fassbinder, Rainer Werner, *Die Anarchie der Phantasie: Gespräche und Interviews*, edited by Michael Töteburg, Frankfurt, 1986.
Katz, Robert, and Peter Berling, *Love Is Colder Than Death: The Life and Times of Rainer Werner Fassbinder*, London, 1987.
Elsaesser, Thomas, *The New German Cinema*, London, 1989.
Lardeau, Yann, *Rainer Werner Fassbinder*, Paris, 1992.
Shattuc, Jane, *Television, Tabloids, and Tears: Fassbinder and Popular Culture*, Minneapolis, 1995.
Elsaesser, Thomas, *Fassbinder's Germany: History, Identity, Subject*, Amsterdam, 1996.
Kardish, Lawrence, editor, with Juliane Lorenz, *Rainer Werner Fassbinder*, New York, 1997.

Articles:

Dawson, Jan, ''Den kvinnohatande feministen: Om Fassbinder's kvinnosyn och *Die Ehe der Maria Braun*,'' in *Chaplin* (Stockholm), no. 2, 1979.
Moskowitz, G., in *Variety* (New York), 28 February 1979.
Hosman, H., ''Interview with Fassbinder,'' in *Skoop* (Amsterdam), August 1979.
Kauffmann, Stanley, in *New Republic* (New York), 29 September 1979.
Canby, Vincent, in *New York Times*, 14 October 1979.
Sarris, Andrew, in *Village Voice* (New York), 15 October 1979.
Rich, F., in *Time* (New York), 22 October 1979.
Hatch, R., in *Nation* (New York), 27 October 1979.
Adler, Renata, in *New Yorker*, 29 October 1979.
Kroll, Jack, in *Newsweek* (New York), 29 October 1979.
Curran, T., in *Films in Review* (New York), November 1979.
Lardeau, Y., in *Cahiers du Cinéma* (Paris), February 1980.
Sauvaget, D., in *Image et Son* (Paris), February 1980.
Bonnet, J.-C., in *Cinématographe* (Paris), March 1980.
Domecq, J.-P., ''Comment désire la femme au temps du miracle allemand,'' in *Positif* (Paris), March 1980.
McCormick, R., in *Cineaste* (New York), Spring 1980.
Noonan, T., in *Film Quarterly* (Berkeley), Spring 1980.
Orto, N., in *Cinema Nuovo* (Bari), June 1980.
Combs, Richard, in *Monthly Film Bulletin* (London), August 1980.
Elley, Derek, in *Films* (London), December 1980.
Reimer, R. C., ''Memories of the Past: A Study of *The Marriage of Maria Braun*,'' in *Journal of Popular Film and Television* (Washington, D.C.), Fall 1981.
Koskinen, M., ''Fassbinders kvinnotrilogo—en allegori över det tyska undret,'' in *Chaplin* (Stockholm), vol. 25, no. 1, 1983.
Ledgard, R., in *Hablemos de Cine* (Lima), February 1983.
Feinstein, Howard, ''BRD 1–2-3: Fassbinder's Postwar Trilogy and the Spectacle,'' in *Cinema Journal* (Champaign, Illinois), Fall 1983.
Kaes, A., ''History, Fiction, Memory: Fassbinder's *The Marriage of Maria Braun*,'' in *Persistence of Vision* (Maspeth, New York), Fall 1985.
Haralovich, M. B., ''The Sexual Politics of *The Marriage of Maria Braun*,'' in *Wide Angle* (Baltimore), no. 1, 1990.
Moeller, H.-B., ''Fassbinder's Use of Brechtian Aesthetics,'' in *Jump Cut* (Berkeley), April 1990.

New German Critique, no. 63, Fall 1994.
Télérama (Paris), 15 February 1995.
Séquences (Haute-Ville), September-October 1995.
Medhurst, A., ''The Long Take,'' in *Sight & Sound* (London), February 1996.
Hogan, D.J., ''The Music from Rainer Werner Fassbinder Films,'' in *Filmfax* (Evanston), no. 65, February/March 1998.
Dixon, Wheeler Winston, ''Rainer Werner Fassbinder,'' in *Film Quarterly* (Berkeley), vol. 51, no. 4, Summer 1998.

* * *

The importance of *The Marriage of Maria Braun*, released in Germany in 1978, can be seen on a number of levels. It is the first of Rainer Werner Fassbinder's works to win him popularity not only in his own country but also abroad. Prior to this film, Fassbinder's foreign success was limited to art-house audiences. *The Marriage of Maria Braun* belongs to the trilogy of films in which Fassbinder examines post-World War II Germany. These films unfold through the stories of three women whose names provide the titles—*The Marriage of Maria Braun, Veronika Voss*, and *Lola*—and whose stories present a glimpse into the history of the Federal Republic.

Maria Braun also belongs to a special group of Fassbinder films which are indebted in structure to the melodramas of Douglas Sirk. Fassbinder gave the conventional melodrama, of which Sirk's films are a prime example, new life by infusing it with the social and political concerns of modern Germany. At the same time he foregrounded and laid bare the structures of film melodrama itself. The structure of *Maria Braun* is so deeply embedded in the content that a study of one inevitably illuminates the other. The fusing of these two elements may account for the popular and also critical success of the film; audiences could easily relate to the emotionally charged story of a woman struggling to survive, while simultaneously, through the same actress in the same film, understand the options faced by a Germany struggling to survive.

Born in 1945, Fassbinder grew up in a country rebuilding itself with American aid during the ''economic miracle'' of the 1950s. Germany was surfeited with American films during this period, including the melodramas of Sirk. Fassbinder, familiar with these, attempted to discover what made them so successful, and to duplicate that success with his own work.

The intensity of the emotional scenes in Maria's story (for example, her marriage, her search for her husband, her realization that he is dead) is emphasized by lighting, music, and expressive camera angles. All of these elements stretch the limits of the conventional style of film melodrama. Yet they are undercut by the deadpan acting of Hanna Schygulla in the title role, and by the sheer profusion of heartrending situations in which Maria finds herself. The audience is drawn into the emotionally charged moment, then distanced from it and forced to look elsewhere for content. It looks instead to the social and political background to Germany's economic miracle. That history and Maria's story are so closely intertwined that the viewer may hardly notice the shift in attention. The scene, for example, in which Maria announces to her American G.I. lover that her husband is dead, implying that she is now free to go with him, ought to be feverish with emotion, but it is completely cooled by Schygulla's unemotional delivery of the line ''Mein Mann ist tot.'' The scene is heavy with the symbolism of a despondent Germany which, after the war, turned to America. Maria comes to her G.I. lover not out of love but out of need to be cared for and because he is there and willing to give. All the trappings of great emotion are present, but there is no emotion on her face or in her voice. Likewise, Germany follows America out of the same need down the capitalistic road but with no thought or emotion that would imply that it is a true alliance.

Schygulla, with a great deal of class, moves through scene after scene of a devastated Germany. Surrounded by bombed-out buildings and broken walls, she moves through the debris with courage and skill, but no integrity. The camera follows her in long sweeping movements which reflect the aplomb of her transactions; the same way, the rigid frequently off-centered cinematography reflects the starkness of the world around her. Vincent Canby sums up the essence of Schygulla's character when he refers to Maria as a Mother Courage type who wouldn't be caught dead pulling a cart.

The most important characteristic of *The Marriage of Maria Braun* is its ability to successfully blend the elements of classical melodrama with aspects of modernist theory and contemporary social-political themes. Fassbinder has not only prolonged the life of the melodramatic mode, but has also embedded the sometimes confusing characteristics of an alienating modernism into the romance of the melodrama.

—Gretchen Elsner-Sommer

8½ (EIGHT AND A HALF)

See **8½ (OTTO E MEZZO)**

ELIPPATHAYAM

(The Rat Trap)

India, 1981

Director: Adoor Gopalakrishnan

Production: General Films; Eastmancolour, 35mm; running time: 121 minutes.

Producer: Ravi; **screenplay:** Adoor Gopalakrishnan; **photography:** Ravi Varma; **editor:** M. Mani; **assistant directors:** Meera, Mohan, Babu; **art director:** Sivan; **music:** M. B. Srinivasan; **sound recording:** Deva Das, Chandran, Suresh; **costumes:** Ganeshan.

Cast: Karamani (*Unni*); Sarada (*Rajamma*); Jalaja (*Sridevi*); Rajam K. Nair (*Janamma*); Prakash (*Janamma's son*); Sonan (*Estate Manager*).

Elippathayam

Publications

Articles:

Variety (New York), 10 February 1982.
Daney, Serge, in *Cahiers du Cinéma* (Paris), March 1982.
Pulleine, T., *Monthly Film Bulletin* (London), November 1984.
Dissanayake, W., "Self and Modernization in Malayalam Cinema," in *East-West* (Honolulu), June 1987.
Film a Doba (Prague), October 1989.
"Not So Servile: Indian Films (Film Industry in India)," in *Economist*, vol. 331, no. 7863, 14 May 1994.
Ganguly, S., "Mapping Interiors: An Interview with Adoor Gopalakrishnan," in *Asian Cinema* (Drexel Hill), no. 1, 1997.
Tournès, Andrée, and Lucien Logette, "Pesaro 1997," in *Jeune Cinéma* (Paris), May-June 1998.

* * *

Gopalakrishnan's melodrama hinges around the paranoic central character of Unni. Utterly dependent for the running of his home, and for his personal needs on his unmarried sister Rajamma, Unni demonstrates his pathological insecurities with, for example, a horror of getting mud on his spotless clothing, of cows entering his ancestral yard, and through his utter inability to intervene into—or even address—the growing difficulties posed to his family by a decaying feudal system.

His elder sister arrives asking for a division of the family property; his coconut grove is invaded by thieves; his youngest sister Sridevi elopes with a flashy youth working in the Middle East. Eventually, when Rajamma collapses under the strain, Unni withdraws, literally like a rat into a hole.

The motif of the rat trap is written large into the film. It begins with a whimpering Unni, calling for assistance when a rat enters his room, and replicates the early chase for the rat with the villagers chasing Unni himself in the film's end.

This is Adoor Gopalakrishnan's third feature, his first in colour, and the film that established him as one of India's foremost independent directors. His first two, *Swayamvaram* (1972) and *Kodiyettam* (1977), were both melodramas, in which he worked with a specific, relatively unchanging style: with a few characters, an episodic narrative, and a style of quite literally shooting close to his central characters. He tries a larger expanse here, with a circular, slow pattern of shooting: typically through close-ups, tracking cutaways onto the different characters of his plot, thereby creating a series of narrative bridges from person to person, space to space. The spaces are patches of light and dark, and the soundtrack often consists of isolated units of realist effects and long silences. The result is a numbing, obsessive style, which is the only way his drama—which actually features something as abstract as a decaying feudal system—can focus on specific characters, and from them onto a loaded, obvious, repeatedly mentioned, metaphoric image of the rat caught in a trap.

Crucial to the understanding of the film is the fact that Unni comes from Kerala's Nair community: the community that, together with the Namboodiris (Brahmins) formed the land-owning class of the state. Historically a military caste, later moving towards administrative service with the formation of a modern state in Travancore (now Southern Kerala), the Nairs are most distinctive for their matrilineal family structure "so loosely arranged as to raise doubts as to whether 'marriage' existed at all" (Nossiter, 1982). It was, as Nossiter shows, the end of a long era: "the ending of the warrior role, the abolition of agrestic slavery, the growth of a money economy, and the impact of Western education that combined to undermine the relevance of Nair traditions. The young men of the *tarawad* (joint family) were condemned to idleness; the management of the estates was more difficult; the expenses of customary practices more burdensome; and the competition of rival communities, notably the Syrian Christians and Ezhavas, more challenging."

Most of these issues are directly illustrated by Gopalakrishnan's plotting: Unni's undefined marital status, his effort to keep Rajamma under his control when the three sisters—notably the eldest, Janamma—have clear rights to the family property, the thief Meenakshi's barely concealed effort to seduce the vacillating hero, Janamma's son Ravikuttan smoking idly behind the barn. In this, to some extent, the film adheres to an established literary genre pioneered by the noted novelist M. T. Vasudevan Nair, featuring the Nair community's decline in several existentialist stories (some of which he later adapted to film).

The film, however, differs from that established genre in significant ways: particularly in consonance with Gopalakrishnan's controversial next movie, *Mukha Mukham* (1984). The Nair community, it is known, were among the strongest supporters of Congress, Congress socialist, and Communist parties during the turbulent 1940s that effectively saw Travancore catapult directly from a regressive, authoritarian feudal state into one ruled by a communist agenda. Gopalakrishnan, it is arguable, attempts in both these films, *Elippathayam* and *Mukha Mukham*, to create something like a back-dated social reform for a people who saw no measured historical transition into modernity. It is as though he critiques feudalism in his state, but from a perspective that sees Kerala's emergence into modernity as a process that it had no means to comprehend. It is as though he now wishes to provide his people with that perspective through using his cinema, his slow visuals and soundtrack, so that the tragedy of Unni could itself be bracketed through a metaphor, for defining—but also evacuating—that tragic, existential, history of noncomprehension.

—Ashish Rajadhyaksha

THE EMPIRE STRIKES BACK

See **STAR WARS SAGA**

THE END OF ST. PETERSBURG

See **KONYETS SANKTA-PETERBURGA**

LES ENFANTS DU PARADIS

(The Children of Paradise)

France, 1945

Director: Marcel Carné

Production: S. N. Pathé Cinema; black and white, 35mm; running time: originally 195 minutes for both parts, current version—Part I is 100 minutes, Part II is 86–88 minutes; length: current versions—Part I is 9066 feet, Part II is 7762 feet. Released 9 March 1945, Paris. Filming began August 1943, but was interrupted by WWII, resuming 9 November 1943; filmed in Joinville studios, Paris, La Victorine studios in Nice, and on an outdoor set constructed by Carné's crew in Nice.

Screenplay: Jacques Prévert; **scenario structure:** Marcel Carné, from an original idea by Marcel Carné and Jacques Prévert; **photography:** Marc Fossard and Roger Hubert; **editors:** Henri Rust and Madeleine Bonin; **sound engineer:** Robert Teisseire; **production designers:** Léon Barsacq, Raymond Gabutti, and Alexandre Trauner; **music:** Joseph Kosma, Maurice Thierte and Georges Mouque; **music director:** Charles Munch; **costume designer:** Antoine Mayo.

Cast: Jean Louis Barrault (*Baptiste Debureau*); Arletty (*Garance*); Pierre Brasseur (*Frederick Lamaître*); Marcel Herrand (*Lacenaire*); Pierre Renoir (*Jericho*); Fabien Loris (*Avril*); Louis Salou (*Count de Montray*); Maria Cassares (*Nathalie*); Etienne Decroux (*Anselm Debureau*); Jeanne Marken (*Madame Hermine*); Gaston Modot (*Blind Man*); Pierre Palau (*Director*); Albert Remy (*Scarpia Barigni*); Paul Frankeur (*Inspector of Police*).

Award: Venice Film Festival, Special Mention, 1946.

Publications

Scripts:

Prévert, Jacques, and Marcel Carné, *Les enfants du paradis*, in *Avant-Scène du Cinéma* (Paris), July-September 1967; also as *Children of Paradise*, New York, 1968.
Carné, Marcel, *Children of Paradise*, New York, 1988.

Books:

Beranger, Jean-Louis, *Marcel Carné*, Paris, 1945.
Sadoul, Georges, *French Film*, Paris, 1947.
Quéval, Jean, *Marcel Carné*, Paris, 1952.
Landry, Bernard, *Marcel Carné: Sa vie, ses films*, Paris, n.d.
Garbicz, Adam, and Jacek Klinowski, editors, *Cinema, The Magic Vehicle: A Guide to Its Achievements: Journey 1, the Cinema Through 1949*, Metuchen, New Jersey, 1975.
Armes, Roy, *French Cinema Since 1946: The Great Tradition*, New York, 1976.
Barsacq, Leon, *Caligari's Cabinet and Other Grand Illusions: A History of Film Design*, New York, 1976.
Perez, Michel, *Les films de Carné*, Paris, 1986.
Turk, Edward B., *Child of Paradise: Marcel Carné and the Golden Age of French Cinema*, Cambridge, Massachusetts, 1989.
Forbes, Jill, *Les enfants du paradis*, London, 1997.

Articles:

Sadoul, Georges, in *Lettres Françaises* (Paris), 17 March 1945.
Manvell, Roger, in *Sight and Sound* (London), Spring 1946.
Phillips, James, in *Hollywood Quarterly*, July 1946.
New York Times, 20 February 1947.
Variety (New York), 26 February 1947.
Lambert, Gavin, "Marcel Carné," in *Sequence* (London), Spring, 1948.
Bodian, Alan, in *Village Voice* (New York), 23 November 1955.
Agee, James, in *Agee on Film 1*, New York, 1958.
Hedges, William, in *Film Quarterly* (Berkeley), Summer 1959.
Stanbrook, Alan, "The Carné Bubble," in *Film* (London), November-December 1959.
Durgnat, Raymond, in *Films and Filming* (London), October 1965.
"*Les enfants du paradis* Issue" of *Avant-Scène du Cinéma* (Paris), July-September 1967.
Chaumeton, E., in *Cahiers du Cinéma* (Paris), Winter 1973.

Les enfants du paradis

Lefèvre, Raymond, in *Cinéma* (Paris), February 1974.

Turk, E. B., ''The Birth of *Children of Paradise*,'' in *American Film* (Washington D.C.), July-August 1979.

Oms, Marcel, ''*Les enfants du paradis*: La Mutation cinématographique du mélodrame,'' in *Cahiers de la Cinématheque* (Perpignan), no. 28, 1979.

Chion, M., ''Le Dernier mot du muet,'' in *Cahiers du Cinéma* (Paris), December 1981.

Freadman, A., ''Reading the Visual,'' in *Framework* (London), nos. 30–31, 1986.

Szots, I., ''Komamasszony, hol az ollo?,'' in *Filmkultura* (Budapest), no. 1, 1990.

Zagari, P., ''Carné e Resnais echi dal boulevard,'' in *Cinema Nuovo* (Rome), March-April 1990.

Stonehill, Brian, ''Forbidden Games,'' in *Film Comment* (New York), November-December 1991.

Turan, Kenneth, ''*Children of Paradise* Regained,'' in *Los Angeles Times*, 16 January 1992.

Sellier, Genevieve, ''*Les enfants du Paradis* dans le cinema de l'occupation,'' in *1895*, no. 22, July 1997.

Vincendeau, G., ''Paradise Regained,'' in *Sight and Sound* (London), vol. 7, 1997.

* * *

Marcel Carné described his greatest work, *Les enfants du paradis*, as a ''tribute to the theatre,'' and the story breathes with the very life and soul of French theatrical tradition. Three of its characters are based on historical personages famous during the reign of Louis-Phillippe (two actors, the pantomimist, Debureau and the ambitious romantic actor, Frederick Lemaître, and a debonair but ruthless criminal known as Lacenaire). Their meeting ground is Paris in the vicinity of the Théâtre des Funambules, in the Boulevard du Temple, sometimes called the Boulevard du Crime because it was the scene for many unsolved thefts and murders. A quarter of a mile of street fronts, as well as the complete theater, were constructed at great cost.

The film, made during the Nazi occupation of Paris, took over two years to complete. Production was often deliberately sabotaged, or halted because actors had disappeared and had either to be found again or their roles re-cast. Some performers active in the Resistance arranged to have their scenes shot secretly.

The Nazis, anxious to keep film production active in France, were more than willing to cooperate. German films were not patronized by the French people, and the Nazis decided that making films in the French language was essential to the Occupation. Over 350 feature films were shot in occupied France, and the most ambitious of these was *Les enfants du paradis*, yet Carné contrived to slow up production, sometimes deliberately hiding key reels already shot from Nazi supervisors, waiting hopefully for the Germans to be forced to evacuate Paris before the film was premiered.

On March 9, 1945, *Les enfants du paradis* was finally presented in Paris, the first important movie premiere after the end of the Occupation. It was received with adoration by the public. Comprised of two parts, each of which is feature-length, the film's running time was originally 195 minutes. This shortened by 45 minutes when the picture was first shown in New York. Most of the edited film was later restored, and prints of *Les enfants du paradis* now run 188 minutes.

The genesis for the story occurred in Cannes during the second year of the Occupation when actor Jean-Louis Barrault met over lunch with director Carné and screenwriter Jacques Prévert. When Barrault learned that they were seeking a subject for filming, he suggested a story be written about Debureau, who had been France's greatest pantomimist. (In 1950, Sacha Guitry, forced into inactivity during the immediate postwar years, would create a play on this subject in verse.)

Carné and Prévert's fame was established by three fatalistic, romantic melodramas, *Quai des brumes, Hôtel du nord* and *Le jour se lève*, generally considered to exemplify ''poetic realism.'' Under the Occupation such films were banned, and they turned to a radically different style of period spectacle, first seen in the medieval fable *Les visiteurs du soir*. The scope of the movie envisioned by Carné, Prévert and Barrault was very wide. Its message—that the drama could only flourish where men are free—required a subtlety of interpretation that eluded the Nazi mind; otherwise they would never have authorized production of the film. The script is one of Prévert's finest, full of wit and aphorism; farce and tragedy are effortlessly combined. Carné's handling of both his all-star cast and the complex crowd scenes is masterly.

In French, ''paradis'' is the colloquial name for the gallery or second balcony in a theater, where common people sat and viewed a play, responding to it honestly and boisterously. The actors played to these gallery gods, hoping to win their favor, the actor himself thus being elevated to an Olympian status.

The French theatre at the time was as Dumas knew it, and as Balzac subsequently wrote about it. It was a theatre for the people, catering to their romantic and extravagant tastes. Mountebanks, clowns, and courtesans quickened its rich blood. Debureau, whose father was an actor, became the idol of his time, touching the emotions of his public with a few well-timed gestures. He rose to fame at the same time as Lemaître captured the fancy of the nation. Their fates mingled with that of the daring criminal, Lacenaire. All three loved and were loved, however briefly, by Garance, the beautiful adventuress idolized as an actress. In the film she is presented as a woman who rejects those men who try to possess her. However, only when she learns that Debureau is the father of a young son does she abandon her hold on him, relinquishing him to his wife and child while she pursues a new chapter in her life, praying that it will lead her to ultimate freedom. Garance becomes a forerunner of this century's emancipated woman, a sophisticate knowing everything about living, and resisting all attempts to control her.

Had the Germans even guessed that in authorizing production of *Les enfants du paradis*, they were condoning the exploits of a woman like Garance, they would have withdrawn their approval of the film immediately. She symbolized the activating spirit of the Free French, a spirit of revolt and independence, a spirit that can never be broken or subjugated, as Hitler's generals soon learned.

Beautifully cast, with the triumphant Arletty as Garance, the picture also boasts the presence of Jean-Louis Barrault as Debureau. He was the finest pantomimist of his generation in the French theatre, and he simply transferred his special gifts to the role he was playing. Handsome Pierre Brasseur is an immaculate Lemaître, and Marcel Herrand offered a stunning portrayal of the criminal. Lovely Maria Casarès is very appealing as the wife of Debureau.

All in all, *Les enfants du paradis*, in spite of its large canvas, remains a very intimate study of the French theatre, inviting its audience not only to know and appreciate its people, but also acquainting them with the Free French spirit.

—DeWitt Bodeen

DER ENGEL MIT DER POSAUNE

(The Angel with the Trumpet)

Austria, 1948

Director: Karl Hartl

Production: Vindobona Film; black and white, 35mm; length: 3370 meters. Released 19 August 1948 in Salzburg, Austria.

Producer: Karl Ehrlich; **screenplay:** Karl Hartl, Franz Tassié, from the novel by Ernst Lothar; **photography:** Günther Anders; **art directors:** Otto Niedermoser, Walter Schmiedl; **music arranger:** Willy Schmidt-Gentner.

Cast: Paula Wessely (*Henriette Alt*); Attila Hörbiger (*Franz Alt*); Oskar Werner (*Hermann Alt*); Hans Holt (*Hans Alt*); Maria Schell (*Selma Rosner*); Paul Hörbiger (*Otto Eberhard Alt*); Helene Thimig (*Gretel Paskiewicz*); Carl Günther (*Oberst Paskiewiecz*); Hedwig Bleibtreu (*Sophie Alt*); Fred Liewehr (*Kronprinz Rudolf*); Curd Jürgens (*Count Poldo Traun*); Gustav Waldau (*Simmerl*); Karlheinz Böhm (*son of Hans*); Hermann Erhardt (*Drauffen, painter*); Adrienne Gessner (*Countess Pauline Metternich*); Karl Paryla (*Czerny, worker*); Erni Mangold (*Martha Monica Alt*).

Der Engel mit der Posaune

Awards: Sascha-Pokal, Vienna, 1948; Venice Festival, 1948.

Publications

Books:

Lothar, Ernst, *Angel with the Trumpet*, New York, 1944.
Lothar, Ernst, *Das Wunder des Überlebens*, Vienna and Hamburg, 1961.

* * *

On August 19, 1948, people in the American occupation zone in Salzburg, Austria, could witness the premiere of a film which claimed to be an Austrian national epos, spanning the time from the suicide of Crown Prince Rudolf in Mayerling in 1889 to the present. The film was based on a novel of the same name by Ernst Lothar (1890–1974), a successful Austrian writer, theater director, and friend of Max Reinhardt. Like so many others, Lothar had to flee into exile in the United States in 1938. He joined the American army to return to Austria as soon as possible, and in June 1946 he arrived in Vienna charged with reviving the theaters, operas, and the Salzburg festival. He also took part in the de-Nazification of actors and musicians.

Lothar had published his book in English during his American emigration; the German edition also met with success. He wanted to expose the scandals hidden behind the attractive baroque facade of the Viennese home of the wealthy Alt family, decorated by the angel with the trumpet. This house symbolizes Austria: The piano manufacturer Franz Alt and his brother Otto Eberhard imitate the Emperor Franz Joseph's dedication to the status quo and suffocation of progressive ideas; Franz's wife Henriette lives a life of outward submission and deception; their son Hans, well-meaning but without orientation, represents the typical Austrian, in Lothar's view.

Lothar entrusted the filming to the experienced director Karl Hartl, the production head of Wien-Film during the Nazi era from 1938 to 1945, although he himself was no Nazi. Hartl gathered prominent actors of divergent ideological positions: returned exiles like Helene Thimig, Max Reinhardt's widow who also directed the Salzburg Festival, and Adrienne Gessner, Lothar's wife, as well as Paula Wessely and Attila Hörbiger, who had starred in the notorious anti-Semitic Nazi film *Heimkehr* (1940). It is at least surprising, if not tactless and inappropriate, that Wessely would play Henriette, this half-Jewish woman who ultimately fell victim to the Nazis. But Lothar himself reports in his autobiography, *Das Wunder des Überlebens*, that the Americans wanted Wessely for this role as a means of restoring her acting career: they considered the film a vehicle for helping Austrians to overcome the past. The filming promoted reconciliation over the settling of accounts.

The Austrian past is mirrored in the family history of the Alts and their four-story villa in the first district of Vienna. When Franz Alt, neither young nor good-looking, marries Henriette, the worldly daughter of a Jewish university professor, he knows that she had been close to Crown Prince Rudolf. However, as a patriarchal male, he never suspects that Rudolf had been his wife's great love and that she only married him when she recognized that there would be no life with Rudolf. The wedding is interrupted by the news of the Crown Prince's sudden death at Mayerling. Henriette knows that the prince committed suicide because of his father's mistreatment, but at her audience with the emperor she consoles him with the lie that he did not cause his son's death.

Several years later, the bored Henriette begins an affair—portrayed as platonic in the film, in contrast to the book—with Rudolf's friend Count Poldo Traun. The wordly count makes her all the more conscious of the restricted life in which she is trapped. When by chance her husband discovers the relationship, he challenges Count Traun to a duel, kills him, and then calmly returns to his business as usual.

The end of World War I brings not only the collapse of the monarchy and with it the value system of the Alts, but also claims other sacrifices: Franz has become paralyzed; Hans, a prisoner of war, does not return for six years but at any rate healthy; Hermann becomes a weapons dealer and Hitler follower.

Hans takes control of the family piano factory, marries an aspiring pianist, and has a family with her. In 1938, when three Nazi storm troopers try to arrest Henriette, the old woman throws herself out of the window. Lothar's book is more brutal: she is strangled by the Nazis. In 1945 Vienna lies in ruins from the bombing attacks. Only the angel with the trumpet projecting out of the rubble marks the Alt House. Hans, who now has a grown family, expresses modest optimism for the future to his workers and his children, speaking for Austria as well as for his business. He personifies the self-righteous Austria that is not conscious of any guilt.

The film offers a tame version of Ernst Lothar's angry, unsparing book. The splendid performance of Paula Wessely also leads the film in the direction of the usual lighthearted Viennese film; Henriette appears as a positive heroine, which she definitely is not in Lothar's novel. Most viewers therefore accept the film as a generational love story set in Old Vienna rather than as a mirror of the darker side of the Austrian soul and of Austrian history.

Numerous compromises were made to ensure the film's commercial success. Since film had become prudish in the late 1940s and the 1950s, care was taken to avoid offensive or controversial topics. In the book Henriette had sexual relationships with the Crown Prince and Count Traun, but the film pretends that these relationships stayed platonic. Neither is Hans the wholesome character portrayed in the film. In the book his wife Selma continues her career as an actress at the Burgtheater, while in the film she sacrifices her career as a pianist to devote herself solely to her family. Her representation as the virtuous German *hausfrau* reflects involuntarily that, perhaps unconsciously, the female role model of the Third Reich was still present in the fifties.

The Aryanization of the Alts' piano factory is never mentioned in the film. Clearly, one did not want to stir up such matters. Hermann's attraction to Nazism is glossed over by explaining that his character was damaged in the First World War. His preference for modern American dances instead of classical music proves he has a criminal character, the same naive suggestion made in some 1950s *Heimatfilme* which equate bad character with modern music or art. The film tries to serve the purpose of reconciliation by explaining the difficult political ordeal which Austria had to undergo in a relatively short time span.

The success of the film induced Sir Alexander Korda, who knew Hartl from the time they worked together for the Austrian film pioneer Count Sascha Kolowrat, to produce a British version, *The Angel with the Trumpet* (1950). Only the actors of minor roles were retained, including Maria Schell and Oskar Werner, for whom this film signified the beginning of their international career.

—Gertraud Steiner Daviau

THE ENIGMA OF KASPAR HAUSER

See **JEDER FUR SICH UND GOTT GEGEN ALLE**

ENTOTSU NO MIERU BASHO

(Where Chimneys Are Seen; The Four Chimneys)

Japan, 1953

Director: Heinosuke Gosho

Production: Studio 8 Productions and Shin Toho Co.; black and white, 35mm; running time: 108 minutes; length: 9678 feet. Released 5 March 1953, Japan. Filmed in Japan.

Producer: Yoshishige Uchiyama; **screenplay:** Hideo Ogunil, from the novel *Mujaki na Hitobito* by Rinzo Shiina; **assistant director:** Akira Miwa; **photography:** Mitsuo Miura; **editor:** Nobu Nagata; **sound:** Yuji Dogen; **art director:** Tomoo Shimogahara; **music:** Yasushi Akutagawa.

Cast: Ken Uehara (*Ryukichi Ogata*); Kinuyo Tonaka (*Hiroko Oyata*); Hiroshi Akutagawa (*Kengo Kubo*); Hideko Takamine (*Senko Azuma*); Cheiko Seki (*Yukiko Ikeda*); Haruo Tanaka (*Chujiro Tsukahara*); Ranko Hanai (*Katsuko Ishibashi*).

Awards: Kinema Jumpo, Tokyo Citizen Film Concours Prize, 1953; Berlin Film Festival, International Peace Prize, 1954.

Publications

Books:

Mellen, Joan, *The Waves at Genji's Door*, New York, 1976.

Bock, Audie, *Japanese Film Directors*, New York, 1978; revised edition, Tokyo, 1985.

Garbicz, Adam, and Jack Klinowski, editors, *Cinema, The Magic Vehicle: A Guide to Its Achievements: Journey 2*, Metuchen, New Jersey, 1979.

Anderson, Joseph, and Donald Richie, *The Japanese Film: Art and Industry*, revised edition, Princeton, 1982.

Articles:

Anderson, Joseph, and Donald Richie, "The Films of Heinosuke Gosho," in *Sight and Sound* (London), Autumn 1956.

Gillett, John, "Coca-Cola and the Golden Pavilion," in *Sight and Sound* (London), Summer 1970.

Gillett, John, "Heinosuke Gosho," in *Film Dope* (London), April 1980.

Tessier, Max, "Heinosuke Gosho," in *Image et Son* (Paris), June 1981.

Chevrie, Marc, "1. Gosho, cinéaste de la réconciliation," in *Cahiers du Cinéma* (Paris), March 1984.

Le Fanu, Mark, "To Love Is to Suffer," in *Sight & Sound* (London), Summer 1986.

Calderale, Mario, "Sette giorni di nome Gosho," in *Segnocinema* (Vicenza), September 1989.

Johnson, William, "The Splitting Image," in *Film Comment* (New York), January-February 1991.

* * *

The film's title *Where Chimneys are Seen*, refers to an industrial-residential area in Tokyo's downtown, where a set of huge chimneys is a familiar sight to its lower-middle-class inhabitants. The protagonist discovers that, according to where you are, the number of these chimneys varies from one to four. This observation typifies the philosophy of Rinzo Shiina (who wrote the original story) that nothing is absolutely true or false; everybody has to believe something or pretend to. Director Heinosuke Gosho takes splendid advantage of his most familiar subject, the life of ordinary people, and elegantly portrays their humor and pathos.

The story develops around the four main characters; Ryukichi, an honest salesman at a wholesale socks store; his diligent wife Hiroko whose previous marriage was unofficially terminated by her husband's disappearance during the war; their young upstairs lodgers, Kengo, a serious and good natured tax officer, and Senko, a pretty and vivacious bargain announcer on a commercial street. As Gosho seems to be more interested in depicting each character's personality and emotional situation and their interrelationships than in detailing a completed plot, he successfully makes the viewer feel intimate with these likable and good-willed people.

The film's light and humorous tone is first manifested in the opening narration by Ryukichi. In an aerial shot, the camera shows us downtown Tokyo, focusing on Ryukichi's busy neighborhood with its small houses packed together; his usual neighbors are presented as a constant yet unwitting source of humor (e.g., the weird, loud morning chanting of a religious leader and the radio repairman with seven children). Finally his modest household is shown, and the habitual peace is broken by the sudden appearance of the baby left by Hiroko's previous husband to Hiroko and Ryukichi. Though it obviously creates tension between the couple, ultimately the baby becomes a symbol of unification: the childless couple confirm their love through their care for the sick baby; Kengo's (the young man upstairs) voluntary efforts to locate the baby's parents make Senko aware of his character, thus drawing the couple closer together; and the baby's mother finally realizes her responsibility to reclaim the baby.

The film's narrative structure involves numerous episodes which look simplistic, but cumulatively show the charms of everyday life. A memorable example is the scene in which Senko plays with pencils on Kengo's desk during their conversation on his daily, frustrating search for the baby's parents. This scene is noteworthy not only for its intimate humor, but also for its meditative effect, for the pencils, like the chimney, make Senko realize the relativity of life. Another good example is the scene in which Senko's modern girlfriend follows an older woman on the river bank—after the older one's sandal gets broken, the other also takes off one of her shoes. This lame pair create a wryly humorous image through their leisurely walking in the airy, bright morning light.

Gosho here, as in his other films, makes use of many close ups to indicate the subtle expressions of its characters. He also uses occasional long shots and long takes. Particularly effective is a long-shot sequence from a bus window where Kengo, after an exhausting search, notices the mystery of the chimneys. The fluidly vibrating image of the chimneys as the scenery swiftly passes is visually refreshing.

This film distinctively reflects the Japanese film's *shomin-geki* genre (films about the lives of ordinary people), with its superb characterizations, successful portrayal of everyday life and emotions, rich depiction of details and the particular bittersweet atmosphere created by skillful timing, comfortable pace and excellent acting. Overall, the film displays Gosho's belief that the sincere efforts of good people are understood and rewarded. This film not only has won the highest critical acclaim, but has also remained one of the most beloved of Gosho's films in Japan.

—Kyoko Hirano

ENTR'ACTE

France, 1924

Director: René Clair

Production: Black and white, 35mm, silent; running time: 22 minutes. Released 1924, at the Theatre des Champs Elysées between acts of the ballet "Relâche" by Francis Picabia as performed by the Ballets Suédois, Paris. Re-released 1968 with musical soundtrack directed by Henri Sauguet. Filmed 1924 in and around Paris.

Producer: Rolf de Maré; **scenario:** from an outline by Francis Picabia, adapted by René Clair; **photography:** Jimmy Berliet; **editor:** René Clair; **music composed specially for the film:** Erik Satie.

Cast: Jean Borlin; Francis Picabia; Man Ray; Marcel Duchamp; Erik Satie; Marcel Achard; Pierre Scize; Louis Touchagues; Rolf de Maré; Roger Lebon; Mamy; Georges Charensol; Mlle. Friis.

Publications

Scripts:

A Nous la liberté, and Entr'acte: Films by René Clair, New York, 1970.
Clair: Four Screenplays, New York, 1970.

Books:

Viazzi, G., *René Clair*, Milan, 1946.
Bourgeois, J., *René Clair*, Geneva, 1949.
Charensol, Georges, and Roger Regent, *Un Maître du cinéma: René Clair*, Paris, 1952.
Solmi, A., *Tre maestri del cinema*, Milan, 1956.
De la Roche, Catherine, *René Clair: An Index*, London, 1958.
Amengual, Barthélemy, *René Clair*, Paris, 1963; revised edition, 1969.
Mitry, Jean, *René Clair*, Paris, 1969.
Samuels, Charles Thomas, *Encountering Directors*, New York, 1972.
McGerr, Celia, *René Clair*, Boston, 1980.
Barrot, Olivier, *René Clair; ou, Le Temps mesuré*, Renens, Switzerland, 1985.
Greene, Naomi, *René Clair: A Guide to References and Resources*, Boston, 1985.
Dale, R.C., *The Films of René Clair*, Metuchen, New Jersey, 2 vols., 1986.

Articles:

New Republic (New York), 15 September 1926.
Potamkin, Harry, ''René Clair and Film Humor,'' in *Hound and Horn* (New York), October-December 1932.
Causton, Bernard, ''A Conversation with René Clair,'' in *Sight and Sound* (London), Winter 1932–33.
Jacobs, Lewis, ''The Films of René Clair,'' in *New Theatre* (New York), February 1936.
Lambert, Gavin, ''René Clair,'' in *Sequence* (London), Winter 1948–49.
''Clair Issue'' of *Bianco e Nero* (Rome), August-September 1951.
Ford, Charles, ''Cinema's First Immortal,'' in *Films in Review* (New York), November 1960.
''Picabia, Satie, et la première d'*Entr'acte*,'' in *Avant-Scène du Cinéma* (Paris), November 1968.
Beylie, Claude, ''*Entr'acte*, le film sans maître,'' in *Cinéma* (Paris), February 1969.
Gallez, D. W., ''Satie's *Entr'acte*: A Model of Film Music,'' in *Cinema Journal* (Evanston, Illinois), no. 1, 1976.
Carroll, Noël, ''*Entr'acte*, Paris, and Dada,'' in *Millenium* (New York), Winter 1977–78.
Dale, R. C., ''René Clair's *Entr'acte*, or Motion Victorious,'' in *Wide Angle* (Athens, Ohio), no. 2, 1978.
Brunius, Jacques, in *Travelling* (Lausanne), Summer 1979.
Sandro, P., ''Parodic Narration in *Entr'acte*,'' in *Film Criticism* (Meadville, Pennsylvania), no. 1, 1979.
Magill's Survey of Cinema: Silent Films, Englewood Cliffs, New Jersey, 1982.
Amengual, Barthélemy, ''*Entr'acte* et ses mystères,'' in *Avant-Scène du Cinéma* (Paris), 1 February 1982.
Herpe, Noël, ''René Clair ou l'or du silence,'' in *Positif* (Paris), February 1993.
Trémois, Claude-Marie, ''La belle époque de René Clair,'' in *Télérama* (Paris), 8 September 1993.
Faulkner, Christopher, ''René Clair, Marcel Pagnol and the Social Dimension of Speech,'' in *Screen* (Oxford), Summer 1994.
Clair, R., ''De Stroheim a Chaplin,'' in *Positif* (Paris), January 1998.

* * *

In November of 1924, Paris anticipated another performance by The Swedish Ballet, a company which had outraged its audience since its residency began in 1920. The centerpiece of one particular evening was to be a new work created by Francis Picabia, the Dadaist artist. When Picabia learned that the opening night might be obstructed by censors, he ruefully entitled the work *Relâche*, or *Theatre Closed* or *Performance Suspended*. When the event did not take place on the announced night (due to an illness rather than censorship), patrons surmised this to be simply another Dadaist prank. Opening night finally did occur, and the events became firmly inscribed in French cultural history.

That infamous evening included a screening of the film *Entr'acte*. Shown between the two acts of *Relâche*, it was greeted with as much hissing and booing as it was with applause; the Dadaist philosophy, based in part on offending its audience, was once again triumphantly realized.

While *Relâche* remained mostly unknown until the Joffrey Ballet revived it in New York City during its 1980 season, *Entr'acte* has long since become a staple of film classes as an example of the French avant-garde cinema of the 1920s and as the prime exemplification of the Dada spirit in the film.

In his search for ''pure'' cinema, René Clair followed the Dadaist approaches of photomontage (as advocated by John Heartfield—a technique which involved ''the meeting place of a thousand spaces''), and the random (as advocated by Tristan Tzara). True to those premises, Clair juxtaposed images and events as disparate as a chess game played by Marcel Duchamp and Man Ray, a cannon ignited by Erik Satie and Francis Picabia, a funeral where the coat of arms bearing the initials of Satie and Picabia was displayed, a ballerina, a sniper, inflatable balloon heads, the Luna Park rollercoaster, etc. These events were shot from a number of angles (including the ballerina from below through a plate of glass), and at varying speeds (from Satie and Picabia jumping toward the cannon in slow motion to the funeral procession racing off at the speed of the Keystone cops). While the images stressed the content as play, the director stressed the style as playfulness.

Through his film Clair invoked the entire catalogue of available cinematic techniques, abandoned the notion of narrative causality, and in true Dadaist style, espoused the overthrow of the bourgeois norm. The audience was assaulted with a series of non-related and often provocative images—from a ''legless'' man rising from his wagon and running away at full tilt, to a ballerina transformed into a bearded man—within a work which stressed the pleasure of inventing new spatial and temporal relations while provoking random laughter. While Clair often referred to this film as ''visual babblings,'' audiences of today can see the film as a serious attempt to subvert traditional values, both cinematic and social.

—Doug Tomlinson

EQUINOX FLOWER

See **HIGANBANA**

ERASERHEAD

USA, 1976

Director: David Lynch

Production: David Lynch, AFI Centre for Advanced Film Studies; black and white, 16mm; running time: 89 minutes. Filmed in Los Angeles, 1971–76.

Producer: David Lynch; **screenplay:** David Lynch; **photography:** Frederick Elmes, Herbert Cardwell; **editor:** David Lynch; **production designer:** David Lynch; **sound:** Alan Splet; **special effects:** David Lynch; **special photographic effects:** Frederick Elmes; **art director:** Jack Fisk.

Cast: Jack Nance (*Henry Spencer*); Charlotte Stewart (*Mary*); Allan Joseph (*Bill*); Jeanne Bates (*Mary's mother*).

Publications

Books:

Peary, Danny, *Cult Movies*, New York, 1983.

Hoberman, J., and Jonathan Rosenbaum, *Midnight Movies*, New York, 1983.

Samuels, Stuart, *Midnight Movies*, New York, 1983.

Kaleta, Kenneth, *David Lynch*, New York, 1992.

Alexander, John, *The Films of David Lynch*, London, 1993.

Lynch, David, *Images*, New York, 1994.

Chion, Michel, *David Lynch*, Bloomington, 1995.

Nochimson, Martha P., *The Passion of David Lynch*, Austin, 1997.

Woods, Paul A., *Weirdsville U.S.A.*, London, 1997.

Rodley, Chris, *Lynch on Lynch*, New York, 1999.

Articles:

Variety (New York), 23 March 1977.

Taylor, D., *Monthly Film Bulletin* (London), March 1979.

Braun, E., *Films and Filming* (London), April 1979.

Island, Russ, *Cinemonkey* (Portland, Oregon), Spring 1979.

Rosenbaum, J., ''Eraserhead à New York,'' in *Cahiers du Cinéma* (Paris), April 1981.

Godwin, K. George, ''Eraserhead: The Story behind the Strangest Film Ever Made and the Cinematic Genius Who Directed It,'' in *Cinefantastique* (New York), September 1984.

Angst, W., ''David Lynch,'' in *Dark Movies*, no. 6, 1989.

Breskin, David, ''The Rolling Stone Interview with David Lynch,'' in *Rolling Stone*, no. 586, 6 September 1990.

Thomas, J.D., ''A Divide Erased,'' in *Village Voice* (New York), 7 June 1994.

Ostria, V., in *Cahiers du Cinéma* (Paris), July/August 1994.

Satuloff, Bob, ''Movie Memories,'' in *Christopher Street*, no. 225, May 1995.

Landrot, Marine, ''Le maître d'immonde: *Eraserhead*,'' in *Télérama* (Paris), 18 October 1995.

Poussu, Tarmo, in *Filmihullu* (Helsinki), no. 4–5, 1997.

* * *

In *Midnight Movies*, which devotes an entire chapter to *Eraserhead*, Jonathan Rosenbaum and J. Hoberman describe David Lynch's first feature as ''an intellectual splatter film-cum-thirty-five-millimetre nightmare sitcom of the urban soul.'' Significantly, mainly through footnotes, Rosenbaum and Hoberman qualify their account of the film as art work and cult case history with hints that neither of them *like* it all that much. In a ''Personal View'' accompanying a retrospective piece in *Cinefantastique*, K. George Godwin compares *Eraserhead* with the archetypal midnight cult movie, Jim Sharman's *The Rocky Horror Picture Show* (1975):

> They [the audience] come to laugh, to talk back at the screen, to *participate.* As the film begins, they are loud, jeering, laughing at any and everything . . . but as it progresses, the laughter thins, becomes more nervous and defensive. The film, for all of its weird humour, is not *funny;* it is strange, and its strangeness is of an unfamiliar kind. There is something uniquely disturbing about it, something which works even on those who have not come to take it seriously. Unlike Sharman's film, *Eraserhead* steadfastly refuses to provide a communal experience . . . somehow it instead isolates the individual viewer, absorbs him into a nightmare of personal experience. Seeing *Eraserhead* is an *unshared* experience: it is as if the film plays not on the screen but inside one's own head.

Lynch is an American original, committed enough to his own vision to wagon-master *Eraserhead* through nearly seven years of low-budget production, persuading collaborators to endure severe hardships (actor Jack Nance sported his character's *Bride of Frankenstein* quiff year after year as shooting continued) in the service of the end product. *Eraserhead* seems a free-form nightmare, but it has a tight narrative and strains for extreme technical sophistication. Asked what inspired the film, Lynch, in typically reductive fashion, has cited Philadelphia, where he lived in a bad neighbourhood for a while. The urban nightmare, weighed down by alienation and physical disgust, is played out in dingy apartments whose windows afford views of brick walls, with few ventures out onto grimy industrial streets and occasional fantastic plunges into a vaudeville dreamland behind a hissing radiator. Henry Spencer (Nance), who adopts Lynch's trademark blank stare, is on vacation from his job and finds himself drawn back into a relationship with Mary X (Charlotte Stewart), who invites him to her family apartment for a hideous

Eraserhead

dinner where he is presented with a tiny living cooked chicken to carve and is also shown a rabbit-like skinless mutant Mary claims is his own baby. Mary and Henry move in together with the eternally-mewling creature, but Mary leaves and Henry has a strange tryst with the Beautiful Girl Across the Hall (Judith Anna Roberts) which segues into a dream in which Henry is decapitated from within by the parasitical baby and his head is mined for rubber to put on the ends of pencils. One of the film's wryer ideas is the redundancy of featuring a "nightmare sequence" which is no more nor less realistic or fantastical than the surrounding scenes. In the climax, Henry tentatively dissects the baby, which disgorges a tide of excrement and a giant plant creature who could be the humourless twin of Audrey Jr. frm *The Little Shop of Horrors* (1960). Henry is sucked into the light where, in an almost upbeat touch repeated in *Twin Peaks: Fire Walk with Me* (1992), he is embraced by an angel, the fungus-cheeked *Lady in the Radiator* (Laurel Near). The whole story is bracketed by an observer, the Man in the Planet (art director Jack Fisk), who guides the audience into and out of Lynch's private horror show.

Of all the underground artist-turned-filmmakers, Lynch is the one who can also function as a Hollywood (or even television) professional: *Eraserhead* was "written, produced, and directed" by its *auteur*. The film probes unhealthy spots and nightmare extremes but does so with a steady, professional fascination that refuses to be classed as trash: no Warholian letting the camera run on and on without caring what's in front of it, no Kuchar Brothers home movie melodrama, no John Waters-ish community panto production values and strident amateur performances, no George Romero reliance on the conventions and concerns of low-rent horror films. These directors and their collaborators, let alone other painter-cum-filmmakers like Derek Jarman, Michael Snow, or Peter Greenaway, have never risked Academy Award nominations while Lynch (a Best Director nominee for *The Elephant Man*) and several of his crew—art director Fisk, sound designer Alan Splet (who won an Oscar for his work on *The Black Stallion*, 1979), even set decorator Sissy Spacek—have secured resident alien status in Hollywood.

Eraserhead is remarkably concentrated and consumed with disgust for the physical, free-associating weirdness as it plays out the grimy anecdote of Henry's entrapment, destruction, and (perhaps) redemption. In subsequent work, from *The Elephant Man* (1980), through *Dune* (1984), *Blue Velvet* (1986), *Wild at Heart* (1990), and the *Twin Peaks* TV series and movie, Lynch would adopt a more mainstream disguise for his concerns, adding character (especially in

The Elephant Man), colour (especially in *Blue Velvet*), and almost-warm wit (especially in *Twin Peaks*), increasingly embracing the trappings of popular culture (music, B movies, soap opera, horror films, pretty stars). Here, working in isolation from commercial cinema, he was either less compromizing or more recalcitrant, creating a work of slick strangeness which remains the dark heart of his developing *oeuvre* and whose almost subliminal artistic (and political) conservatism perhaps explains its lasting cult success. Withal, it remains—unlike much of Lynch's later films—a work of genius it is impossible to love, so personal for its makers and its individual audience members that its many admirable or astonishing features still don't make it a film whose world one cares to revisit at all often.

—Kim Newman

EROICA

Poland, 1958

Director: Andrzej Munk

Production: Film Polski, ZAF ''Kadr,'' and WFD (Warsaw); black and white, 35mm; running time: 87 minutes; length: 7787 feet. Filmed in Poland. Released January 1958.

Producer: Stanisław Adler; **screenplay:** Jerzy Stefan Stawiński, from the collection of Stawiński's short stories, *Wegrzy* and *Ucieczka*; **photography:** Jerzy Wójcik; **editors:** Jadwiga Zajiczek and Mirosława Garlicka; **sound:** Bohdan Jankowski; **art director:** Jan Grandys; **music:** Jan Krenz.

Cast: *Scherzo alla polacca*: Edward Dziewoński (*Dzidziuś Górkiewicz*); Barbara Polomska (*Zosia Górkiewicz*); Ignacy Machowski (*Major Grzmet*); Leon Niemszyk (*Hungarian officer*); Kazimierz Opaliński (*Commander of Mokotów*); *Ostinato lugubre*: Kazimierz Rudzki (*Turek*); Henryk Bak (*Krygier*); Mariusz Dmochowski (*Korwin Makowski*); Roman Kłosowski (*Szpakowski*); Bogumil Kobiela (*Lieutenant Dabecki*); Józef Kostecki (*Zak*); Tadeusz Lomnicki (*Lieutenant Zawistowski*); Józef Nowak (*Kurzawa*); Wojciech Siemion (*Marianek*).

Award: Prize of the International Film Press, the ''Fipresci,'' 1959.

Publications

Books:

Haudiquet, Philippe, *Nouveaux cinéastes polonais*, Lyons, 1963.
Andrzej Munk, Warsaw, 1964.
Liehm, Antonin, and Mira Liehm, *The Most Important Art: East European Film after 1945*, Berkeley, 1977.
Garbicz, Adam, and Jacek Klinowski, editors, *Cinema, The Magic Vehicle: A Guide to Its Achievements: Journey 2*, Metuchen, New Jersey, 1979.
Historia filmu polskiego 4, Warsaw, 1981.

Articles:

Thirard, P.-L., ''Experience du Cinéma polonais,'' in *Lettres Françaises* (Paris), no. 790, 1959.
Variety (New York), 20 May 1959.
Sadoul, Georges, ''Andrzej Munk,'' in *Lettres Françaises* (Paris), no. 894, 1961.
Sight and Sound (London), Autumn 1961.
Monthly Film Bulletin (London), September 1961.
Film (West Germany), August-September 1964.
''Andrzej Munk Issue'' of *Etudes Cinématographiques* (Paris), no. 45, 1965.
Moullet, Luc, ''Andrzej Munk,'' in *Cahiers du Cinema* (Paris), February 1965.
Brighton Film Review, April 1970.
Gyula, K., in *Filmkultura* (Budapest), July-August 1975.
Cieslar, J., ''Andrzej Munk (1921–1961),'' in *Film a Doba* (Prague), October 1981.
Modrzejewska, E., in *Iluzjion*, no. 3, 1986.
Film Dope (Nottingham), 1991.
Kino (Warsaw), May and June, 1994.
Litka, P., in *Rezyser* (Warsaw), no. 59, 1996.

* * *

Eroica, Andrzej Munk's third film, is based on the contemporary drama *Czlowiek na torze*. As in his debut *Blekitny krzyz*, he returns again to World War II for subject matter. The film consists of two parts, both of which deal with the theme of heroism which in a certain historical situation becomes myth.

The initial episode, centered on the tragic Warsaw uprising of 1944, sounds a new note in Munk's artistic method as well as for Polish cinema. It is the presentation of an ironic, sarcastic anti-hero and his deeds, a view that is quite exceptional within the body of Polish film that treated either the uprising or the war in general. The protagonist is a Warsaw good-for-nothing who is calculating and forever oscillating between cowardice and a utilitarian world view. Suddenly, and against his will, he becomes a hero. In drawing his character Munk does not obscure a single negative feature; in certain sections of the story Munk consistently emphasizes aspects of character and plot that lead the protagonist to greedy calculations of profit and loss. However, the hero is not a schematic one-dimensional character. At the moments when he sets aside his own principles to defend the uprising, Munk lends him a certain grandeur, which flows from the tragedy of the solitary deed that is ultimately useless and unnecessary. The director's ability to find elements of the comic and the grotesque even in tragic events has enabled him to catch some of the paradoxes of the Warsaw uprising. However, the film is not a satire, as has been charged by some Polish critics. Munk does not mock his hero but shows how the atmosphere of the time can influence a totally unheroic individual and impel him to act.

The second episode unfolds on a tragic plane. It takes place in a POW camp, where a significant moment in the joyless lives of the

Eroica

Polish officers occurs when the rumor that one of their comrades has managed to escape is heard. The story is false—the fugitive hides until his death inside the camp. Here Munk contemplates the meaning of an artificially sustained myth and, in this connection, examines and traces its influence on the entire camp. In this case, too, he is not demeaning the importance of the rumor; from the outset he even ascribes to it a certain power that should help the captives in their struggle for survival. Analysis of the mechanics of the story, however, gradually reveals its destructive nature, for it paralyzes activity and displaces courage and the will to act.

The structure of *Eroica* is loosely built according to the rules of musical composition using contrastive means. The tragi-comic hero of the first novella, who belongs nowhere and to nobody, is placed in the boundless space of a large city in ruins, among streets that no longer have names; the viewer does not learn where these streets lead, where they end or where they begin. The officers of the second novella, on the other hand, move within a strictly limited geometric space tightly compressed into a tense order accented by non-dynamic compositions. These images not only convey hopelessness but also show the sophistication of the enemy, who suppress their opponents through psychological stress. They understand quite well that the worst punishment for prisoners is having to live with each other.

One further note of interest: *Eroica* was supposed to have had three parts. The third section had a rather intricate and elusive story that unfolded in a mountain setting and involved a spurious nun. This novella, however, did not come up to the level of the first two, and Munk himself eliminated it from the film.

—B. Urgosíkova

EROTIKON

(Bonds That Chafe)

Sweden, 1920

Director: Mauritz Stiller

Production: Svensk Filmindustri; black and white, 35mm, silent; length: 5998 feet. Released 8 November 1920, Sweden. Filmed in Sweden, theater scenes shot in Royal Opera House, Stockholm.

Screenplay: Mauritz Stiller and Arthur Norden, from the play *A Kék Róka* by Ferenc Herczeg; **photography:** Henrik Jaenzon; **production designers:** Mauritz Stiller and Axel Esbensen; **musical score which accompanies film:** Kurt Atterburg.

Erotikon

Cast: Tora Teje (*Irene Charpentier*); Lars Hanson (*Preben*); Karin Molander (*Marthe, the niece*); Anders de Wahl (*Prof. Leo Charpentier*); Wilhelm Bryde (*Baron Felix*); Elin Lagergren (*Irene's mother*); Torsten Hammaren (*Prof. Sedonius*); Stina Berg (*Servant*); Gucken Cederborg (*Cook*); Vilhelm Berntsson (*Butler*); Bell Hedqvist (*Friend of Baron Felix*); John Lindlof (*Friend of Preben's*); Greta Lindgren (*Model*); Carl Wallin (*Furrier*); Carina Ari and Martin Oscar (*Ballet dancers*).

Publications

Books:

Idestam-Almquist, Bengt, *Den Svenska Filmens Drama: Sjöström och Stiller*, Stockholm, 1938.
Hardy, Forsyth, *Scandinavian Film*, London, 1951.
Waldenkranz, Rune, *Swedish Cinema*, Stockholm, 1959.
Beranger, Jean, *La Grande Aventure du cinéma suedois*, Paris, 1960.
Lauritzen, Einar, *Swedish Film*, New York, 1962.
Cowie, Peter, *Swedish Cinema*, London, 1966.
Werner, Gosta, *Mauritz Stiller och hans filmer*, Stockholm, 1969.
Klinowski, Jacek, and Adam Garbicz, editors, *Cinema, The Magic Vehicle: A Guide to Its Achievement: Journey 1, The Cinema Through 1949*, Metuchen, New Jersey, 1975.

Articles:

Potamkin, M. C., ''The Golden Age of Scandinavian Film,'' in *Cinema* (London), September 1930.
Idestam-Almquist, Bengt, ''The Man Who Found Garbo,'' in *Films and Filming* (London), August 1956.
''Mauritz Stiller,'' in *Anthologie du Cinéma*, vol. 3, Paris, 1968.
Combs, Richard, in *Monthly Film Bulletin* (London), November 1977.
Robertson, Jo Anne, ''Mauritz Stiller,'' in *Monthly Film Bulletin* (London), December 1977.

* * *

By 1920 the artistic achievements of the Swedish cinema, under the inspired leadership of Victor Sjöström and Mauritz Stiller, were universally recognized. Most of these films reflected the life of rural Sweden. Stiller, a cultured man, decided to make a film set in a sophisticated urban milieu. His scriptwriter, Arthur Norden, brought to his attention Ferenc Herczeg's play, *A KéK Róka*, which he and Norden adapted to their purpose, dropping any acknowledgement to the author. From its premiere at the Roda Kvarn Cinema in Stockholm on the 8 November 1920, its success was assured.

Stiller lavished attention on this film, building elaborate sets and commissioning a special exotic ballet for the theatre scenes which were shot in the Royal Opera House of Stockholm, with a host of society extras for an audience. The film reflected the fashionable life of the city and a modernity indicated by the inclusion of scenes with airplanes.

The story about a professor of entomology who is sustained in his work by his devoted niece while his neglected wife seeks consolation elsewhere seems more like the work of Noel Coward than Selma Lagerlöf, who contributed so much to the Swedish cinema. It is handled with the lightest of touches; the irony of the scene where the man who tries to reconcile the married pair becomes the wife's lover is reminiscent of Ernst Lubitsch. Stiller's stylish direction works well with his talented players. Tore Teje's delightful portrayal of the wife is witty, wise and worldly. It is in striking contrast with the peasant role she had played the previous year in Sjöström's *Karin Ingmarsdotter*. Karin Molander's charming performance as the young niece is equally effective; Torsten Hammaren's caricature of a dry old stick is inspiring; and Lars Hanson and Anders de Wahl maintains the elegant style of the film.

Erotikon helped create a new genre of social comedy, and attracted considerable attention in the movie world. Jean Renoir admired it very much; Lubitsch mentioned it as one of the best films he had ever seen and it may well have influenced his work from *The Marriage Circle* onwards; Chaplin would have seen it during his European tour and the style of *A Woman of Paris* may have been influenced by it. On the other hand, while admiring its freshness of approach, the socially conscious critic Georges Sadoul regretted that the social satire had not gone further, ''There is no satiric intention in *Erotikon*; the humor is gentle and pleasant, defensive rather than attacking . . . . we are far from Beaumarchais or even Marivaux.''

Stiller never made another film like *Erotikon*, which is curious, for it represented his own outlook on life. His next great success was the monumental *Gösta Berlings Saga*, which introduced Greta Garbo to the world. The delicacy and subtlety of the acting and the gentle observation of human foibles make *Erotikon* a film that transcends its time and fashion.

—Liam O'Leary

EL ESPIRITU DE LA COLMENA

(Spirit of the Beehive)

Spain, 1973

Director: Victor Erice

Production: Eastmancolor, 35mm; running time: 98 minutes; length 8785 feet. Released 1973. Filmed in Spain.

Producer: Elias Querejeta; **screenplay:** Francisco J. Querejeta, from an idea by Victor Erice and Angel Fernandéz Santos; **assistant director:** José Ruis Marcos; **photography:** Luis Cuadrado; **editor:** Pablo G. del Amo; **sound:** Luis Rodriguez; **sound effects:** Luis Castro and Sire Castro; **art director:** Adolfo Cofiño; **music:** Luis de Pablo.

Cast: Fernando Fernan Gomez (*Fernando*); Terésa Gimpera (*Teresa*); Ana Torrent (*Ana*); Isabel Telleria (*Isabel*); Lady Soldevilla (*Don Lucia*); Miguel Picazo (*Doctor*); José Villasante (*Frankenstein*); Juan Margallo (*Outlaw*).

Publications

Books:

Ellis, Jack C., *A History of Film*, Englewood Cliffs, New Jersey, 1979.

Schwartz, Ronald, *Spanish Film Directors (1950–1985): 21 Profiles*, Metuchen, New Jersey, 1986.

Articles:

Gillett, John, in *Sight and Sound* (London), Winter 1973–74.

Rabago, J., ''Film Spanje,'' in *Skoop* (Amsterdam), February 1974.

Mortimore, R., ''Spain: Out of the Past,'' in *Sight and Sound* (London), Autumn 1974.

Gow, Gordon, in *Films and Filming* (London), Autumn 1974.

Monthly Film Bulletin (London), November 1974.

McGuinness, R., in *Thousand Eyes Magazine* (New York), October 1976.

Simon, John, ''From Ineptitude to Incompetence,'' in *New York*, 4 October 1976.

Canby, Vincent, in *New York Times*, 10 October 1976.

Bodeen, DeWitt, in *Films in Review* (New York), November 1976.

Abet, A., in *Cinéma* (Paris), December 1976.

Jordan, I., ''La Couleur du rêve,'' in *Positif* (Paris), February 1977.

Chevalier, J., in *Image et Son* (Paris), March 1977.

Dubroux, D., ''*La Lumière et l'ombre*,'' in *Cahiers du Cinéma* (Paris), March 1977.

Predal, R., in *Jeune Cinéma* (Paris), March 1977.

Benelli, D., ''Mysteries of the Organism: Character Consciousness and Film Form in *Kasper Hauser* and *Spirit of the Beehive*,'' in *Movietone News* (Seattle), June 1977.

Troeslen, A., in *Kosmorama* (Copenhagen), Winter 1977.

Rotker, S., in *Cine al Dia* (Caracas, Venezuela), November 1977.

Vrdlovec, Z., ''Duh panja,'' in *Ekran* (Ljublana), no. 9–10, 1979.

Duarte, R., and J. Matos-Cruz in *Celuloide* (Rio Major, Portugal), May 1980.

Pellizzari, L., in *Cineforum* (Bergamo), December 1982.

Arata, L. O., ''I Ana: The Plat of the Imagination in *The Spirit of the Beehive*,'' in *Quarterly Review of Film Studies* (New York), Spring 1983.

Paranagua, P. A., ''La Solitude de Victor Erice,'' in *Positif* (Paris), April 1984.

Cobos, J., and M. Rubio, ''Tunteiden heijastumia,'' in *Filmihullu* (Helsinki), no. 8, 1989.

Castro, A., Interview with Victor Erice, in *Revue Belge du Cinéma* (Brussels), Winter 1989.

El espiritu de la colmena

Ehrlich, L. C., ''The Name of the Child: Cinema as Social Critique,'' in *Film Criticism* (Meadville, Pennsylvania), no. 2, 1990.

Kovacs, K. S., ''The Plain in Spain: Geography and National Identity in Spanish Cinema,'' in *Quarterly Review of Film and Video* (New York), no. 4, 1991.

Martin-Marquez, S. L., ''Monstrous Identity: Female Socialization in *El espíritu de la colmena*,'' in *New Orleans Review*, no. 2, 1992.

Toles, G., ''Being Well-Lost in Film,'' in *Raritan* (New Brunswick, New Jersey), no. 2, 1993.

Morgan, R., ''Victor Erice: Painting the Sun,'' in *Sight and Sound* (London), April 1993.

Hellman, M., in *Positif* (Paris), June 1994.

Bagh, Peter von, in *Filmihullu* (Helsinki), no. 4, 1995.

Poulet, Jacques, ''Espace mental et filmique dans le cinéma espagnol,'' in *Cinemaction* (Conde-sur-Noireau), April 1995.

Ehrlich, Linda C., ''Interior Gardens: Victor Erice's *Dream of Light* and the Bodegón Tradition,'' in *Cinema Journal* (Austin), Winter 1995.

* * *

Most critical attention paid to *El espiritu de la colmena* has focused on its elliptical relationship with precise moments in Spanish history, both the immediately post-Civil War (1940) of its setting and the tail-end of Franco's regime (1973) in which it was made. Whether its tactful reticence in political matters was due to artistic intent or a desire to skirt censorship, this is actually a film whose significance is as universal as it is specific. The static images and haunted faces suggest situations that have endured for centuries and which will persist no matter who rules the country. The wounded refugee from the war who turns up late in the film as a reminder of the unseen conflict stands less for adult concerns than he does an answer to the yearning fantasies of Ana, the pre-teenage heroine. To Ana, the soldier is just as real and just as magical as the Frankenstein Monster, another lost soul whom she encounters in the vicinity of her parents' desolate Castillian home.

In 1940, Ana and her slightly older sister, Isabel, attend a travelling film show and are hugely impressed by James Whale's 1931 *Frankenstein*, a work which even penetrates their bee-keeping father's veil of obsession as he is distracted from his books by snatches of Colin Clive's ranting visionary dialogue dubbed into Spanish. Discussing the film, Isabel tells Ana that the monster is a spirit who can never die, whereupon many tiny details come to convince the girl that the spirit is close: a primitive anatomy lesson in which pupils slot wooden organs into the torso of an artificial man is a reminder of the creation of the monster, a large bootprint in which Ana's tiny foot is dwarfed suggest Karloff's asphalt-spreader's boots, and the fleeing soldier—whom she unwittingly betrays to a quiet mob as dangerous as the torch-bearing peasantry of Universal's horror films—is another kindred spirit to the gentle, pained big baby of film and folklore.

The snippet from *Frankenstein* which we see is the still-powerful lakeside vignette between the monster and the little girl, which ends with his accidental drowning of her. This is the scene which is recreated in the eerily delicate finale as Ana's reflection in a pool ripples and is replaced by that of the monster, who gently joins her for a communion that ends not in death but an awakening. Choosing to inhabit entirely Ana's world, and never explaining any of the mundane or marvelous elements, Victor Erice only hints at what has passed between Ana and the monster and how it will affect her relationship with family and community, but young Ana Torrent's quite remarkable performance shows quite clearly how at odds this child is with her world. At the time of the film's release, Erice—who has not subsequently been a prolific director—said that he would like to return to Ana's story in 30 years, to see what manner of adult she became, suggesting that he too was mystified by the qualities Torrent brought to the role.

The rest of the cast seem locked into a slightly over-Bergmanesque rut—the father toiling amid his hives, the mother writing to an adopted child in France, the sister playing malevolent games with the cat and faking her own death. Ana, whose personality is as unformed as that of Karloff's creature, is far freer than these sad souls, and is the only person in the film who actually seems to be in motion. While they focus on their obsessions Ana is forever examining and being intrigued by things, allowing Erice to isolate the traces of life in his mostly poised still images. Ana resists being interpreted as a stand-in for all Spain, simply because her huge-eyed stare, which ranges across cinema from Karloff's heavy-lidded monster to Kubrick's star child, betokens too much unsettling individuality.

—Kim Newman

ET . . . DIEU CREA LA FEMME

(And . . . God Created Woman)

France, 1956

Director: Roger Vadim

Production: Iena-Films-U.C.I.L.-Cocinor; Eastmancolor, 35mm, CinemaScope; running time: 95 minutes. Released 28 November 1956, Paris. Filmed in St. Tropez.

Producer: Raoul-J. Levy; **screenplay:** Roger Vadim and Raoul-J. Levy; **photography:** Armand Thirard; **editor:** Victoria Mercanton; **sound engineer:** Pierre-Louis Calvet; **production designers:** Jean Andre with Jean Forestier and Georges Petitot; **music:** Paul Misraki

Cast: Brigitte Bardot (*Juliette Hardy*); Curt Jurgens (*Eric Carradine*); Jean-Louis Trintignant (*Michel Tardieu*); Christian Marquand (*Antoine Tardieu*); Georges Poujouly (*Christian Tardieu*); Jeanne Marken (*Mme. Morin*); Isabelle Corey (*Lucienne*); Jean Lefebvre (*René*); Philippe Grenier (*Perri*); Jacqueline Ventura (*Mme. Vigier-Lefranc*); Jean Tissier (*M. Vigier-Lefranc*); Jany Mourey (*Young Girl*); Mary Glory (*Mme. Tardieu*); Jacques Giron (*Roger*); Paul Faivre (*M. Morin*); Leopoldo Frances (*Dancer*); Toscano (*René*).

Publications

Script:

Vadim, Roger, and Raoul-J. Levy, ''*Et Dieu créa la Femme*'' (excerpts), in *Avant-Scène du Cinéma* (Paris), 15 November 1962.

Books:

Carpozi, George, *The Brigitte Bardot Story*, New York, 1961.
De Beauvoir, Simone, *Brigitte Bardot and the Lolita Syndrome*, London, 1961.
Alpert, Hollis, *The Dreams and the Dreamers*, New York, 1962.
Frydland, Maurice, *Roger Vadim*, Paris, 1963.
Armes, Roy, *French Cinema Since 1946: The Personal Style*, New York, 1966.
Durgnat, Raymond, *Films and Feelings*, Cambridge, Massachusetts, 1973.
Evans, Peter, *Bardot: Eternal Sex Goddess*, New York, 1973.
Vadim, Roger, *Memoirs of the Devil*, New York, 1977.
Crawley, Tony, *Bebe: The Films of Brigitte Bardot*, London, 1975.
Frischauer, Willi, *Bardot: An Intimate Biography*, London, 1978.
Vadim, Roger, *Bardot, Deneuve, Fonda*, New York, 1986.

Articles:

Truffaut, François, in *Arts* (Paris), November 1956.
Rivette, Jacques, in *Cahiers du Cinéma* (Paris), May 1957.
Godard, Jean-Luc, in *Cahiers du Cinéma* (Paris), July 1957.
Mardore, Michel, ''Roger Vadim,'' in *Premier Plan* (Lyons), October 1959.
Billard, G., ''Ban on Vadim,'' in *Films and Filming* (London), November 1959.
Burch, Noël, ''Qu'est-ce que la Nouvelle Vague?'' in *Film Quarterly* (Berkeley), Winter 1959.
''Two Actors,'' in *Films and Filming* (London), October 1960.
''Nouvelle Vague Issue'' of *Cahiers du Cinéma* (Paris), December 1962.
Durgnat, Raymond, ''B.B.,'' in *Films and Filming* (London), January 1963.
Haskell, Molly, ''Jean-Louis Trintignant,'' in *Show* (Hollywood), 20 August 1970.
''Conversation with Roger Vadim,'' in *Oui* (Chicago), October 1975.
Copie Zero (Montreal), no. 3, 1979.
Mancini, M., ''A Moved Feast: French Filmmakers in America,'' in *Film Criticism* (Meadville), no. 2, January 1983.
Maslin, J., in *New York Times*, no. 137, 4 March 1988.
McCarthy, T., in *Variety* (New York), no. 330, 9 March 1988.

Et ... Dieu créa la femme

Allen, M., in *Film Journal* (New York), no. 91, April 1988.
Chase, D., ''Close-ups: Roger Vadim,'' in *Millimeter* (Cleveland), no. 16, April 1988.
Harvey, S., in *Premiere* (Boulder), no. 1, April 1988.
Kauffmann, S., ''Stanley Kauffmann on Films: Stale Roles,'' in *New Republic*, no. 198, 4 April 1988.
Matthews, T., in *Boxoffice* (Chicago), no. 124, May 1988.
Williamson, B., ''Movies,'' in *Playboy*, no. 35, May 1988.
Beauchamp, M., in *24 Images* (Montreal), no. 39, Fall 1988.
Vincendeau, Ginette, ''L'ancien et le nouveau: Brigitte Bardot dans les années,'' in *Cinémaction* (Courbevoie), no. 67, March 1993.
Review, in *Séquences* (Haute-Ville), no. 179, July-August 1995.

* * *

Conventional accounts of the *nouvelle vague* commence with the *annus mirabilis* of 1959, when the new directors Truffaut, Camus and Resnais swept the Cannes Film Festival. But the true beginning took place three years earlier, when ex-*Paris Match* journalist Roger Vadim, then 28, released his debut feature *Et . . . Dieu créa la femme*. Its initial *succès de scandale* was reflected at the box office, and for the first time independent producers opened their purses to the frustrated generation of the new French filmmakers.

In 1952 Vadim had married 19-year-old Brigitte Bardot. After working as assistant to Marc Allegret, he felt confident enough to direct a vehicle for her sullen, bitchy beauty. Producer Raoul Levy helped raise funds via ex-band leader Ray Ventura. German actor Curt Jurgens agreed to take a role and guarantee the obligatory international appeal. Jean-Louis Trintignant, then unknown, played opposite the provocative Bardot, and would soon have a well-publicized affair with her.

Vadim wrote the story, based on fact, of two fisherman brothers feuding over a girl in the remote town of St. Tropez. Bardot, nude, pouting, deceitful, embodied the popular public stereotype of dissident youth. Christian Marquand and Trintignant were the brothers, Jurgens the rich man fascinated by a woman he can't buy. Pursuing his theories about the dramatic and erotic impact of color, Vadim set the tanned Bardot against white—sand, linen—to spectacular effect. Her appearance sun-bathing behind sun-dried bed sheets, and later at her own wedding breakfast wrapped in a sheet, were spectacular proof of Vadim's skill.

Shrewdly shot in Eastmancolor and CinemaScope, *Et . . . Dieu créa la femme* sold speedily to international markets, its notoriety feeding Bardot's fame and announcing to audiences everywhere that a new spirit was stirring in French cinema. Vadim's career did not flourish, but Bardot's did: in creating a character who followed her instincts in her contempt for money and for the sensibility of others, Vadim produced an emblem for the ''Me Decade.''

Jeanne Moreau is unequivocal about the significance of *Et . . . Dieu créa la femme* and Bardot's potency as a symbol. ''Brigitte was the real modern revolutionary character for women. And Vadim, as a man and a lover and a director, felt that. What was true in the New Wave is that suddenly what was important was vitality, eroticism, energy, love and passion. One has to remember it was Vadim who started everything, with Bardot.'' In 1987, Vadim re-made the film in a New Mexico setting with Rebecca de Mornay and Frank Langella. It was not a success.

—John Baxter

E.T.—THE EXTRATERRESTRIAL

USA, 1982

Director: Steven Spielberg

Production: Universal Pictures; DeLuxe color, 70mm, Dolby sound; running time: 115 minutes. Released June 1982.

Producers: Steven Spielberg and Kathleen Kennedy; **associate producer:** Melissa Mathison; **production supervisor:** Frank Marshall; **screenplay:** Melissa Mathison; **photography:** Allen Daviau; **editor:** Carol Littlestone; **production designer:** James D. Bissell; **music:** John Williams; **special effects:** Industrial Light and Magic; **supervisor:** Dennis Muren; **E.T. created by:** Carlo Rimbaldi.

Cast: Dee Wallace (*Mary*); Henry Thomas (*Elliott*); Peter Coyote (*Keys*); Robert MacNaughton (*Michael*); Drew Barrymore (*Gertie*); K.C. Martel.

Publications

Books:

Kolker, Robert Phillip, *A Cinema of Loneliness: Penn, Kubrick, Scorsese, Spielberg, Altman*, Oxford, 1980; revised edition, 1988.
Crawley, Tony, *The Steven Spielberg Story*, London, 1983.
Short, Robert, *The Gospel from Outer Space*, San Francisco, 1983.
Goldau, Antje, and Hans Helmut Prinzler, *Spielberg: Filme als Spielberg*, Berlin, 1985.
Mott, Donald R., and Cheryl McAllister Saunders, *Steven Spielberg*, Boston, 1986.
Smith, Thomas G., *Industrial Light and Magic: The Art of Special Effects*, London, 1986.
Weiss, Ulli, *Das Neue Hollywood: Francis Ford Coppola, Steven Spielberg, Martin Scorsese*, Munich, 1986.
Godard, Jean-Pierre, *Spielberg*, Paris, 1987.
Sinyard, Neil, *The Films of Steven Spielberg*, London, 1987.
Ebert, Roger, and Gene Siskel, *The Future of the Movies*, Kansas City, 1991.
Von Gunden, Kenneth, *Postmodern Auteurs: Coppola, Lucas, De Palma, Spielberg & Scorsese*, Jefferson, 1991.
Sanello, Frank, *Spielberg: The Man, the Movies, the Mythology*, Dallas, 1996.
Brode, Douglas, *The Films of Steven Spielberg*, Secaucus, New Jersey, 1997.
Perry, George, *Steven Spielberg—Close Up*, New York, 1998.
Gish, Melissa, *Steven Spielberg*, Mankato, 1999.
McBride, Joseph, *Steven Spielberg*, Cambridge, 1999.

E.T.—The Extraterrestrial

Articles:

Variety (New York), 26 May 1982.
McCarthy, Todd, ''Sand Castles: An Interview with Steven Spielberg,'' in *Film Comment* (New York), May-June 1982.
Interview with Spielberg in *Casablanca* (Madrid), September 1982.
Gartenberg, J., in *Films in Review* (New York), October 1982.
Schupp, P., in *Séquences* (Montreal), October 1982.
''The Making of *E.T.*,'' in *Cinefantastique* (Chicago), November-December 1982.
Marsh, J., in *Stills* (London), November-December 1982.
Amiel, M., in *Cinema* (Paris), December 1982.
Combs, Richard, in *Monthly Film Bulletin* (London), December 1982.
Conn, R., in *Cinema Papers* (Melbourne), December 1982.
Iversen, E., in *Kosmorama* (Copenhagen), December 1982.
Pede, R., in *Film en Televisie* (Brussels), December 1982.
Strick, Philip., in *Films and Filming* (London), December 1982.
Tessier, Max, in *Image et Son* (Paris), December 1982.
Den Uyl, B., in *Skoop* (Amsterdam), December 1982-January 1983.
Adair, Gilbert, in *Sight and Sound* (London), Winter 1982–83.
Bartolone, A., Interview with Spielberg, in *Filmcritica* (Florence), June 1982.
Lannes-Lacroutz, M., and B. Philbert, in *Cinématographe* (Paris), January 1983.
Marias, M., in *Casablanca* (Madrid), January 1983.
Sammon, P. M., ''Turn On Your Heartlight: Inside *E.T.*,'' in *Cinefex* (Riverside, California), January 1983.
Tarnowski, J. F., in *Positif* (Paris), January 1983.
Turner, George, and others, in *American Cinematographer* (Los Angeles), January 1983.
Vallerand, F., ''Accords parfaits et dissonances,'' in *Séquences* (Montreal), January 1983.
Zapiola, G., in *Cinemateca Revista* (Montevideo), January 1983.
Martini, E., and others, in *Cineforum* (Bergamo), January-February 1983.
Jameson, R. T., in *Film Comment* (New York), February 1983.
Lewis, B., in *Films and Filming* (London), February 1983.
''*E.T.* Section'' of *Filmcritica* (Montepulciano), April 1983.
Balzola, A., in *Cinema Nuovo* (Bari), April 1983.
Michalek, B., in *Kino* (Warsaw), April 1983.
Richardson, M. A., ''A Dream in the Making,'' in *Cinefex* (Riverside, California), April 1983.
Deutsch, P., in *Jump Cut* (Berkeley), April 1983.
Heung, M., ''Why E.T. Must Go Home: The New Family in American Cinema,'' in *Journal of Popular Film and Television* (Washington, D.C.), Summer 1983.
Benabou, R., ''L'Erotisme anal dans le film *E.T.*,'' in *Positif* (Paris), November 1983.

Horgas, B., in *Filmkultura* (Budapest), November-December 1983.
Dassone, M. Marcone, in *Cinema Nuovo* (Bari), December 1983.
''*E.T.* Section'' in *Movie* (London), Winter 1983.
Ledgard, M., in *Hablemos de Cine* (Lima), March 1984.
Shumaker, C., ''More Human than Humans: Society, Salvation, and the Outsider in Some Popular Films of the 1980s,'' in *Journal of American Culture* (Bowling Green, Ohio), no. 4, 1990.
Bick, Ilsa J., ''The Look Back in *E.T.*,'' in *Cinema Journal* (Austin), vol. 31, no. 4, Summer 1992.
Review, in *Séquences* (Haute-Ville), no. 181, November-December 1995.
Cole, James, ''*E.T.*: The Scenes Left Behind,'' in *Video Watchdog* (Cincinnati), no. 38, 1997.
Dursin, A., and J.H. Lee, in *Film Score Monthly* (Los Angeles), no. 2, 1997.
Redman, Nick, ''*E.T.: The Extraterrestrial*—The Signature Collection,'' in *DGA Magazine* (Los Angeles), vol. 22, no. 2, May-June 1997.

* * *

In itself, *E.T.* would hardly concern us; if not entirely negligible (it manifests certain skills, and contains a few memorable turns of dialogue, such as the question of how one explains ''school'' to a ''higher intelligence''), it has no greater claim on the attention than countless other minor Hollywood movies. It does demand consideration as a cultural phenomenon: not merely the film itself and what it signifies, but the commercial hype, the American critics' reviews, the public response, the T-shirts, the children's games, the candy advertisements. It represents a moment in American cultural history. The film is distinguishable from the Disney live action movies it otherwise so closely resembles only by virtue of Steven Spielberg's evident commitment to his own infantile fantasy. Where the Disney films seemed more or less shrewd commercial exploitations of the child-audience, we have the sense here of a filmmaker infatuated with what he is doing. Just what difference that makes is open to argument: bourgeois society sets a high value on ''sincerity,'' regardless of what the possessor of that virtue is being ''sincere'' about. Suffice it to comment that the precise *quality* of Spielberg's sincerity remains open to question. I am not convinced that it is entirely innocent and uncompromised.

E.T. belongs to the Reagan era as surely as the genuinely distinguished works of the period (the films of Martin Scorsese and Michael Cimino, or even of a minor figure like Brian De Palma) do not. It is an era profoundly inimical to serious art, especially within the field of popular culture. ''Serious art'' is, by definition, challenging and progressive; what is wanted now—after the upheavals of the 1970s, the era of Vietnam and Watergate, the era when every American institution was called into question and radical movements suddenly flourished—is reassurance, the restoration of the symbolic Father, preferably in a form that allows one simultaneously to believe and disbelieve.

The premise of *E.T.* is essentially the appearance of the ''Other'' within the bourgeois home. Roland Barthes suggests in *Mythologies* that bourgeois ideology has two ways of coping with Otherness: it either denies it, and if possible exterminates it, or converts it into a replica of itself. American civilization was founded upon the denial/extermination of the Other (in form of the Indians); during the 1970s the Other erupted in numerous forms—women, blacks, gays—demanding recognition. Now, in the Reagan era, Spielberg presents the Other in the shape of a lovable, totally innocuous little extra-terrestrial, who just wants to go home (to his own nuclear family?). The treatment of E.T. himself is shamelessly opportunistic for he becomes whatever is convenient to the development of the narrative from scene to scene: mental defective, higher intelligence, child figure, father figure.

The film is extremely sexist. Spielberg seems unable to conceive of women as anything but wives and, in particular, mothers. Apart from almost dying, the worst thing that happens to E.T. is being dressed in female clothes, an event which is shown to deprive him of his dignity. At the end of the film, as all-purpose friend, Christ figure and patriarch, he lays his finger on Elliott's head to transmit to him his power and knowledge, but tells the boy's younger sister to ''be good.'' (I have not yet found a woman who likes the film: the fantasy about childhood that it enacts is heavily male-oriented.)

Crucially, the cultural phenomenon presented in *E.T.* signifies a choice made by the critical establishment, the public, and the Academy of Motion Picture Arts and Sciences, who nominated it for many Academy Awards even though they ultimately found in *Gandhi* an even more respectable and archetypal liberal/bourgeois recipient of honors. One must compare *E.T.* with the commercial/critical failure of the infinitely more interesting *Blade Runner* (released the same week) and its troubling and complex presentation of the Other. The most pertinent comparison remains, however, with the two *It's Alive* films of Larry Cohen, which provide numerous suggestive parallels. Critically despised, they lack *E.T.*'s aura of expensiveness, an essential component of reassurance within the context of capitalism's decline.

—Robin Wood

EVERY MAN FOR HIMSELF AND GOD AGAINST ALL

See **JEDER FUR SICH UND GOTT GEGEN ALLE**

DER EWIGE JUDE

Germany, 1940

Director: Fritz Hippler

Production: Deutsche Film Gesellschaft; black and white, 35mm, documentary; running time: 78 minutes, other versions include a 67-minute print; length: 1753 feet, other versions include a 1830-foot

Der ewige Jude

print. Released 4 November 1940 in Uraufführung, Germany. Filmed in Poland and Germany, with library footage from many sources, including the United States.

Scenario: Eberhard Taubert; **photography:** A. Endrejat, A. Hafner, A. Hartman, F. C. Heere, H. Kluth, E. Stoll, and H. Winterfield; **editors:** Hans Dieter Schiller and Albert Baumeister; **music:** Franz R. Friedl.

Publications

Books:

Albrecht, G., *Nationalsozialistische Filmpolitik: Eine Soziologische Untersuchung uber die Spielfilme des Dritten Reichs*, Stuttgart, 1969.
Hull, David Stewart, *Film in the Third Reich*, Berkeley, 1969.
Baird, J. W., *The Mythical World of Nazi War Propaganda*, Minneapolis, 1974.
Leiser, Erwin, *Nazi Cinema*, New York, 1974.
Welch, David, *Propaganda and the German Cinema 1933–1945*, Oxford, 1983; revised edition, 1987.
Ahren, Yizhak, *Der Ewige Jude: Wie Goebbels Hetzte, Untersuchungen zum Nationalsozialistischen Propagandafilm*, Aachen, 1990.

Articles:

Doob, L. W., ''Goebbels' Principles of Propaganda,'' in *Public Opinion and Propaganda*, edited by D. Katz, New York, 1954.
Hoffman, Hilmar, ''Manipulation of the Masses through the Nazi Film,'' in *Film Comment* (New York), Fall 1965.
Filmstudio, January 1966.
Walker, G., ''An Analysis of *Der ewige Jude*: Its Relationship to Nazi Anti-Semitic Ideas and Policies,'' in *Wide Angle* (Athens, Ohio), no. 4, 1980.
Welch, David, ''Nazi Wartime News-Reel Propaganda,'' in *Film and Radio Propaganda*, edited by K. R. M. Short, London, 1983.

Kimmel, Daniel M., ''Goebbels' Work,'' in *Film Comment* (New York), November-December 1986.

Friedman, R. M., ''Juden-Ratten,'' in *Frauen und Film* (Frankfurt), September 1989.

Hornshoj-Moller, S., and D. Culbert, ''*Der ewige Jude:* Joseph Goebbels' Unequaled Monument to Anti-Semitism,'' in *Historical Journal of Film, Radio and Television* (Abingdon, United Kingdom), no. 1, 1992.

Avisar, Ilan, ''The Historical Significance of *Der ewige Jude*,'' in *Historical Journal of Film, Radio & TV* (Abingdon), August 1993.

Hornshoj-Moller, S., ''Kultfilm der Neonazis,'' in *Medium* (Frankfurt am Main), no. 3, 1994.

Kracauer, S., ''Program Notes by Siegfried Kracauer for Fritz Hippler's *The Eternal Jew*,'' in *Wide Angle* (Baltimore), vol. 19, no. 2, 1997.

* * *

Fritz Hippler's *Der ewige Jude* was an exemplary moment in the history of Nazi cinema. A dutiful Nazi Party functionary, Hippler was unrestrained by considerations of objectivity, balance, or even the sensibilities of the less fanatical members of his audience. Indeed, his virulent anti-Semitic excesses so repelled some German audiences that in a few cities the film attracted ''only the politically active'' segments of the populace.

Artistically, the film is a ''black masterpiece'' of the cinematic conventions of 1940; a German version of *The March of Time* style that included animated maps, falsely labeled stock footage, segments of feature films borrowed to make some ideological point, stills, decoupages of evocative bookjackets and headlines, and an omniscient voice-over narration.

The importance of *Der ewige Jude* lies not in its technique but in its brutal service to the cause of Nazi racism. Hippler, after reading law and sociology at Heidelberg, entered the German Propaganda Ministry, specializing in military films such as *Westwall, Feldzug in Polen*, and *Sieg im Westen*. On orders from Joseph Goebbels himself, Hippler in 1940 began an anti-Semitic film that, according to its official synopsis, would ''fill the spectator with a feeling of deep-seated gratification for belonging to a people whose leader has absolutely solved the Jewish problem.'' In fact, it has been asserted that *Der ewige Jude* helped prepare the German people to accept the eventual policy of genocide inflicted upon Jews.

The controlling metaphor—the Jew as parasite in an otherwise healthy host—is found throughout the film in several forms, all of them designed to reveal to Germans the ''true'' Jew underneath the veneer of European culture that concealed Jewish parasitism. Jews are introduced as a foreign, swarthy, hook-nosed, untidily bearded, sullen presence that clogs the teeming streets of middle Europe. They haggle, squabble over food at the table, hoard with wealth, conceal it from tax collectors, and grow sleek and fat at the expense of good Germans. Their religion and culture are seen as cabalistic sources of secret powers.

Animated maps alive with pulsing, arterial tentacles extending outward from Palestine invoke a history of Jewish expansion into Europe. Even distant America offers no immunity from the spread of Jewish power. Stock shots of Wall Street and outtakes from the American movie *The House of Rothschild* throb with new meaning given them by the voice-over. The world seems in the thrall of a network of great Jewish banking houses whose interlocking pedigrees are traced in animated diagrams. Reinforcing the image of the Jew as international parasite, Hippler punctuates the film with cutaways to rats crawling out of sewers, plundering granaries, and scurrying pellmell through the streets of Europe. So compelling was the imagery, the government reported the collective relief expressed by audiences at the appearance of Hitler at the end, comforting the nation with the news that Nazi race laws had saved the day.

The Nazi period of Hippler's life ended with his capture by the British in 1944. He escaped prosecution as a criminal when Allied tribunals failed to convict other filmmakers, notably Veit Harlan. After a process of ''de-Nazification'' Hippler served the American Army as a translator. In later life, he lived apart from cinema circles, earning a living as a travel agent.

—Thomas Cripps

EXOTICA

Canada, 1994

Director: Atom Egoyan

Production: Ego Film Arts and Miramax Films; color, 35 mm, Spherical; running time: 104 minutes; length: 2953 meters. Filmed in Toronto, Ontario; cost: $5 million (Canadian).

Producers: Atom Egoyan, Camilia Frieberg, Robert Lantos, David J. Webb (associate); **screenplay:** Atom Egoyan; **cinematographer:** Paul Sarossy; **music:** Mychael Danna, Leonard Cohen; **editor:** Susan Shipton; **production design:** Linda Del Rosario, Richard Paris; **art direction:** Linda Del Rosario, Richard Paris; **costume design:** Linda Muir.

Cast: Mia Kirshner (*Christina*); Elias Koteas (*Eric*); Bruce Greenwood (*Francis Brown*); Don McKellar (*Thomas Pinto*); Victor Garber (*Harold*); Arsinée Khanjian (*Zoe*); Sarah Polley (*Tracey*); Calvin Green (*Customs Officer*); David Hemblen (*Inspector*); Peter Krantz (*Man in Taxi*); Damon D'Oliveira (*Man at Opera*); Jack Blum (*Scalper*); Billy Merasty (*Man at Opera*); Ken McDougall (*Doorman*).

Awards: Genie Awards for Best Art Direction/Set Direction, Best Cinematography, Best Costume Design, Best Director, Best Film, Best Screenplay, Best Supporting Actor (McKellar), and Best Score, 1994; FIPRESCI Award, Cannes Film Festival, 1994; Best Canadian Feature Film, Toronto International Film Festival, 1994.

Publications:

Script:

Egoyan, Atom, *Exotica*, Toronto, 1995.

Exotica

Books:

Desbarats, Carole, *Atom Egoyan*, Paris, 1993.
Weinrichter, Antonio, *Emociones formales: el cine de Atom Egoyan*, Valencia, 1995.

Articles:

Banning, K., ''Lookin' in All the Wrong Places: The Pleasures and Dangers of *Exotica*,'' in *Take One* (Toronto), no. 6, Fall 1994.
James, Caryn, ''Innocence Beyond the Erotic Glimmer,'' in *The New York Times*, 24 September 1994.
Johnson, Brian D., ''Exotic Atom: With *Exotica*, Atom Egoyan Has Become the Most Celebrated Canadian Film-Maker of His Generation,'' in *Maclean's*, vol. 107, no. 40, 3 October 1994.
Dubeau, Alain, ''*Exotica:* l'anti-catharsis canadienne,'' in *Séquences* (Haute-Ville), no. 175, November-December 1994.
Masson, Alain, and others, ''Atom Egoyan,'' in *Positif* (Paris), no. 406, December 1994.
Calhoun, John, ''The New York Film Festival,'' in *TCI*, vol. 29, no. 1, January 1995.
Winters, Laura, ''Atom Egoyan Is Watching Us,'' in *Interview*, vol. 25, no. 3, March 1995.
Maslin, Janet, ''Bucking the System, but Still Part of the Buzz: Atom Egoyan May Have His Breakthrough in *Exotica*,'' in *The New York Times*, 5 March 1995.
Harcourt, Peter, ''Imaginary Images: An Examination of Atom Egoyan's Films,'' in *Film Quarterly* (Berkeley), vol. 48, no. 3, Spring 1995.
Kobel, Peter, ''They Like to Watch,'' in *Entertainment Weekly*, no. 267, 24 March 1995.
Edelstein, David, ''Discovering Atom,'' in *Vogue*, vol. 185, no. 3, March 1995.
Johnston, Trevor, ''Atomic Energy,'' in *Time Out* (London), no. 1288, 26 April 1995.
Romney, Jonathan, Tony Rayns, and Amanda Lipman, ''Exploitations/ Everybody Knows/ *Exotica*,'' in *Sight & Sound* (London), vol. 5, no. 5, May 1995.
Wise, Wyndham, ''The True Meaning of *Exotica*,'' in *Take One* (Toronto), no. 9, Fall 1995.
Baber, Brendan, ''Big Worlds in Small Packages,'' in *Interview*, vol. 27, no. 12, December 1997.

Jones, Kent, ''The Cinema of Atom Egoyan,'' in *Film Comment* (New York), vol. 34, no. 1, January 1998.

Johnson, Brian D., ''Atom's Journey: Canada's Celebrated Director Reveals the Rite of Passage Behind His Cinematic Obsessions,'' in *Maclean's*, 13 September 1999.

* * *

On the basis of *Exotica* alone, writer-director Atom Egoyan could rightly be called ''the un-Hitchcock.'' Where Hitchcock takes the point of view of a particular character through whom the clearly told, well-defined plot is revealed, Egoyan is the objective observer, cutting back and forth between seemingly unconnected scenes and frequently leading the audience to make incorrect assumptions until, at last, the various strands start fitting together. Egoyan does not confuse for confusion's sake; in *Exotica*, form follows function, and by allowing viewers to draw their incorrect assumptions, he is illustrating that, whenever we first meet someone, we invariably draw the wrong conclusions because people are always much more complex than any set of assumptions we might make based on mere outward appearances. Egoyan is not so much concerned with revealing plot as revealing character, while dealing with such concerns as the universal need for a feeling of family, the need for sex (which in a way is an extension of the need for family), and the psychic contortions individuals undergo in order to feel whole.

The film begins with a customs inspector training a new employee. As the two look through a one-way mirror at Thomas (Don McKellar), a young man having his bags inspected, the trainer says, ''You have to ask yourself what brought the person to this point. . . You have to convince yourself that this person has something hidden that you have to find.'' As the viewer soon discovers, every major character in the film has something hidden, including Thomas and his trainee. The film moves to the interior of Exotica, a gentlemen's club where strippers perform onstage, then do table dances for those willing to spend an extra five dollars. The beautiful young Christina (Mia Kirshner) comes onstage wearing a schoolgirl's uniform, and when she begins her table dance for the middle-aged, bearded Francis (Bruce Greenwood), most viewers make the same assumptions about the dynamic involved, assumptions that prove to be totally wrong. When Francis is seen paying another young woman while dropping her off in a seedy section of town, more assumptions can be drawn—the single discordant note being when Francis says to the girl, ''Say hi to your dad.'' Other major characters include the strip club's pregnant female owner, Zoe (Arsinée Khanjian), and the club's emcee, Eric (Elias Koteas), who was once Christina's lover. How these various plot strands weave together tells volumes about all the characters involved.

The film brings together a number of ideas Egoyan had been toying with for years. As a youth he was involved with a girl he later learned was a victim of child abuse. In the film, Christina was abused, and her dancing is a parody of her own sexual identity as she attempts to convince herself that that part of herself which has been destroyed is suitable for mockery, and therefore trivial; otherwise it would be too painful to deal with. Egoyan was also fascinated by such awkward encounters as those between a table dancer and the man watching her, or between a father and the baby sitter he is driving home—a situation Egoyan has referred to as ''the first encounter many adolescent women have with older men'' and ''fraught with sexual tension.'' In both cases there is little to be said, yet small talk seems mandatory because without it the tension, the weirdness of the situation, would become unbearable. Egoyan agrees with Andrei Tarkovsky's description of film as ''sculpting in time,'' and one of the things that makes this film so intriguing is what he has chosen *not* to show. We see Eric and Christina before and after their relationship, but never *during* their relationship. We see the bizarre ritual that Christina and Eric repeatedly play out, but never how it evolved.

According to Egoyan, all the relationships in the film are defined by the exchange of money because money ''makes tangible that which is too terrifyingly abstract otherwise.'' Asking a woman to dance at your table or to baby-sit your nonexistent child may be grotesque or pathological but, by putting a dollar amount on the act, it begins to seem as normal as anything else in a market economy. ''It's a way of saying, 'Hey! This is quite normal, because I pay for it.'' And in this and other films, Egoyan has had an interesting slant on such ''normal'' jobs as insurance adjuster (in his film *The Adjuster*) or tax auditor or customs inspector (in *Exotica*). As Egoyan told the *New York Times*, ''From the outside these may appear to be very banal, but they're jobs that are infused with all sorts of psychological needs. They involve digging into someone else's life, and they're a way of legitimizing what might otherwise be pathological behavior.'' All his characters demonstrate extraordinary impulses beneath mundane surfaces.

Egoyan's particular genius here is his ability to weave these and other interests and concerns into a coherent work of art that illuminates the human condition, while creating a film language unlike anything preceding it, perhaps helping the cinema to break further away from its written-word and theatrical-stage antecedents. *Exotica* won the International Critics' Prize at the 1994 Cannes Film Festival and top awards in Belgium and France; it swept the Genies in Canada; both Siskel and Ebert put it on their Top Ten lists; and it was also a commercial success, indicating that it may very well influence future filmmakers. *Exotica* shows how much a film's structure may be bent while remaining coherent and, more importantly, it suggests new structures for films far removed from mere storytelling—films that are fragmented and elusive, and therefore a better reflection of how we know and feel about the real people in our lives, as opposed to fictional characters. While simple structures may be optimal for relating plots, something more complex may be needed to relate character. As Egoyan himself has said, ''There's nothing simple about representing a human being.''

—Bob Sullivan

THE EXTRAORDINARY ADVENTURES OF MR. WEST IN THE LAND OF THE BOLSHEVIKS

See **NEOBYCHANYE PRIKLYUCHENIYA MITERA VESTA V STRANE BOLSHEVIKO**

EYES WITHOUT A FACE

See **LES YEUXS SANS VISAGE**

FACES

USA, 1968

Director: John Cassavetes

Production: Maurice McEndree; colour, 16mm; running time: 130 minutes.

Producer: Maurice McEndree; **screenplay:** John Cassavetes; **photography:** Al Ruban; **editor:** Al Ruban, Maurice McEndree; **assistant director:** George O'Halloran; **art director:** Phedon Papamichael; **music:** Jack Ackerman; **sound:** Don Pike.

Cast: John Marley (*Richard Forst*); Gena Rowlands (*Jeannie Rapp*); Lynn Carlin (*Maria Forst*); Fred Draper (*Freddie*); Seymour Cassel (*Chet*); Val Avery (*McCarthy*); Dorothy Gulliver (*Florence*); Joanne Moore Jordan (*Louise*); Darlene Conley (*Billy Mae*); Gene Darfler (*Jackson*); Elizabeth Deering (*Stella*).

Publications

Script:

Cassavetes, John, *Faces*, New York, 1970.

Books:

Adler, Renata, *A Year in the Dark: Journal of a Film Critic 1968–69*, New York, 1969.

Kael, Pauline, *Going Steady*, New York, 1970.

Sarris, Andrew, *Confessions of a Cultist: On the Cinema 1955–1969*, New York, 1970.

Kauffman, Stanley, *Figures of Light: Film Criticism and Comment*, New York, 1971.

Simon, John, *Movies into Film: Film Criticism 1967–70*, New York, 1971.

Kinder, Marsha, *Close-up: A Critical Perspective on Film*, New York, 1972.

Bowers, Ronald, in *Magill's Survey of Cinema: Volume 2*, edited by Frank Magill, Englewood, New Jersey, 1981.

Alexander, George, *John Cassavetes*, Munich, 1983.

Carney, Raymond, *American Dreaming: The Films of John Cassavetes and the American Experience*, Berkeley, 1985.

Gavron, Laurence, and Denis Lenoir, *John Cassavetes*, Paris, 1985.

Carney, Raymond, *The Films of John Cassavetes: Pragmatism, Modernism and the Movies*, Cambridge, 1994.

Amiel, Vincent, *Corps au cinèma: Keaton, Bresson, Cassavetes*, Paris, 1998.

Articles:

Variety (New York), 26 June 1968.

Austen, David, ''Masks and Faces,'' in *Films and Filming* (London), September 1968.

Madsen, Axel, *Sight and Sound* (London), Autumn 1968.

Dawson, J., *Monthly Film Bulletin* (London), December 1968.

Gow, G., *Films and Filming* (London), December 1968.

Clouzot, C., *Film Quaterly* (Berkeley), Spring 1969.

Benoliel, B., ''L'idéal du collectivisme,'' in *Revue du Cinéma* (Paris), March 1992.

Nevers, C., *Cahiers du Cinéma* (Paris), March 1992.

De Bruyn, O., *Positif* (Paris), June 1992.

Carney, Ray, ''Seven Program Notes from the American Tour of the Complete Films: *Faces, Husbands, Minnie and Moskowitz, A Woman Under the Influence, The Killing of a Chinese Bookie, Opening Night, Love Streams*,'' in *Post Script* (Commerce), vol. 11, no. 2, Winter 1992.

Levich, Jacob, ''John Cassavetes: An American Maverick,'' in *Cineaste* (New York), vol. 20, no. 2, 1993.

Hejll, A., ''Nargangen Kamera,'' in *Filmrutan* (Sundsvall), vol. 36, no. 1, 1993.

Review, in *Télérama* (Paris), no. 2365, 10 May 1995.

* * *

An admirer of the stark cinema verite style of documentarians Lionel Rogosin and Shirley Clarke, actor-director John Cassavetes strived to achieve the same sense of in-your-face realism in his fiction films.

Cassavetes's *modus operandi* was to bring together a group of his committed actor-artist friends, hand them a script that served mainly as a blueprint, then let them cut loose before his camera, capturing their improvisational investigations of character like a roving newsreel photographer, shooting on nights and weekends over several months, even years, until he had a feature length film in the can.

The end product, typically, was a somehat ragged, even amateurish, type of moviemaking in the technical sense—but a blow-out demonstration of the actor's art. Cassavetes' style of moviemaking, which he termed ''actor's cinema'' rather than ''director's cinema,'' was to foster a creative environment that enabled his actors to do their own thing—and thereby surprise him, even though he'd written the script—with the behavioral tics, twists, and turns they revealed about his characters. In a sense, his actors were left free to unmask themselves through their characters, unleashing an emotional intensity rare in the Hollywood-style American films in which Cassavetes and his chums regularly made their living. As often as not, Cassavetes's actors, many of whom (Peter Falk, Ben Gazzara) were big name stars,

Faces

gave the performances of their lives in his films—performances that often went unnoticed by most moviegoers as Cassavetes's low-budget, independent features seldom received widespread circulation.

Faces, a tale of suburban angst and adultery, was an exception. It was a major hit. *Faces* wound up on many important film critics' Ten Best lists and scored three Oscar nominations, two in the Best Supporting Actor and Actress categories (for Seymour Cassel and Lynn Carlin, respectively) and one for Cassavetes's original screenplay. None of them won, but their accomplishment was no mean feat in the face of the competition Cassavetes's $50,000 black-and-white film had that year from such films as *Oliver!, 2001: A Space Osyssey, The Lion in Winter*, and *Rosemary's Baby* (in which Cassavetes had co-starred).

Faces was Cassavetes's fourth feature as a director. He had previously helmed two films for the major studios, *Too Late Blues* (with Stella Stevens and Bobby Darin) and *A Child is Waiting* (with Judy Garland and Burt Lancaster). Finding the studio system too restrictive for his semi-improvisational style, he opted to work outside that system, bankrolling his own films from his fees as an actor in big-budget Hollywood movies and using his friends as players (they were paid a percentage of the profits, if there were any, rather than a salary), as he had done with his debut feature, *Shadows* (1960).

Cassavetes financed *Faces* from his earnings in two Hollywood blockbusters, *The Dirty Dozen* and *Rosemary's Baby.* He shot the picture over a four-year period with a hand-held 16mm camera, using his own home, the houses of his cast members and other readily accessible (i.e. inexpensive) locales. The first cut was six hours long, but Cassavetes and his editor reduced this to a releasable 129 minutes. He then had the film blown up to 35mm, the standard gauge for theatrical distribution, and launched a tireless campaign single-handedly to get the film noticed and acquired. Traveling the film festival circuit with the cans of film under his arm, and using his status as a popular movie star to trumpet his movie on talk shows from coast to coast, Cassavetes marketed *Faces* into a small but lucrative hit.

In addition to those already mentioned, the standout cast includes John Marley portraying the TV producer husband of Carlin who seeks solace from his stale marriage in the arms of a prostitute (played by Gena Rowlands, Cassavetes's real-life wife and a ubiquitous presence in most of the actor-director's handmade productions). Seymour Cassel's sympathetic hippie, who picks up Carlin when she visits a discotheque with some girlfriends, then saves her from a suicide attempt brought on by her guilt over their affair, serves as the film's conscience.

There aren't a lot of laughs in *Faces*, but there is a lot of laughter—most of it on the verge of hysteria—as Cassavetes's eavesdropping camera relentlessly exposes, with power and precision, the layers and layers of supturating emotional wounds and longstanding despair ripping apart the lives of his desperate middle-aged suburbanites.

—John McCarty

FANNY

See **MARIUS TRILOGY**

FANNY OCH ALEXANDER

(Fanny and Alexander)

Sweden, 1982

Director: Ingmar Bergman

Production: Cinematograph, for the Swedish Film Institute/Swedish Television STV 1/Gaumont/Personafilm/Tobis Filmkunst; Eastmancolor. Released for the cinema in a 189 minute version, 1982; also released as a 300 minute version in four parts.

Executive producer: Jörn Donner; **screenplay:** Ingmar Bergman; **assistant director:** Peter Schildt; **photography:** Sven Nykvist; **assistant photographers:** Lars Karlsson, Dan Myhrman; **editor:** Sylvia Ingemarsson; **sound recordists:** Owe Svensson, Bo Persson, Björn Gunnarsson, Lars Liljeholm; **art director:** Anna Asp, costume design: Marki Vos; **music:** Daniel Bell; **special effects:** Bengt Lundgren; **laterna magica:** Christian Wirsén; **puppets:** Arne Hogsander.

Cast: *The Ekdahl Residence*: Kristina Adolphson (*Siri, Housemaid*); Börje Ahlstedt (*Carl Ekdahl*); Pernilla Allwin (*Fanny Ekdahl*); Kristian Almgren (*Putte*); Carl Billquist (*Police Superintendent*); Axel Düberg (*Witness*); Allan Edwall (*Oscar Ekdahl*); Siv Ericks (*Alida, Emilie's Cook*); Ewa Fröling (*Emilie Ekdahl*); Patricia Gelin (*Statue*); Majlis Granlund (*Vega, Helena's Cook*); Maria Granlund (*Petra Ekdahl*); Bertil Guve (*Alexander Ekdahl*); Eva von Hanno (*Berta, Helena's Housemaid*); Sonya Hedenbratt (*Aunt Emma*); Olle Hilding (*Old Clergyman*); Svea Holst (*Ester, Helena's Parlour Maid*); Jarl Kulle (*Gustav Adolf Ekdahl*); Käbi Laretei (*Aunt Anna*); Mona Malm (*Alma Ekdahl*); Lena Olin (*Rosa, New Nursemaid*); Gösta Prüzelius (*Dr. Fürstenberg*); Christina Schollin (*Lydia Ekdahl*); Hans Strååt (*Clergyman at the Wedding*); Pernilla Wallgren (*Maj, Emilie's Nursemaid*); Emilie Werkö (*Jenny Ekdahl*); Gunn Wållgren (*Helena Ekdahl*); Inga Alenius (*Lisen, Emilie's Housemaid*); *The Bishop's Palace*: Marianne Aminoff (*Blenda Vergérus, the Bishop's Mother*); Harriet Andersson (*Justina, Kitchen Maid*); Mona Andersson (*Karna, Housemaid*); Hans Henrik Lerfeldt (*Elsa Bergius, the Bishop's Aunt*); Jan Malmsjö (*Bishop Edward Vergérus*); Marianne Nielsen (*Selma, Housemaid*); Marrit Olsson (*Malla Tander, Cook*); Kerstin Tidelius (*Henrietta Vergérus, the Bishop's Sister*); *Theatre*: Anna Bergman (*Miss Hanna Schwartz*); Gunnar Björnstrand (*Filip Landahl*); Nils Brandt (*Mr. Morsing*); Lars-Owe Carlberg, Hugo Hasslo, and Sven Erik Jakobsen (*Glee Singers*); Gus Dahlström (*Props Man*); Heinz Hopf (*Tomas Graal*); Maud Hyttenberg-Bartoletti (*Miss Sinclair*); Marianne Karlbeck (*Miss Palmgren*); Kerstin Karte (*Prompter*); Tore Karte (*Office Manager*); Ake Lagergren (*Johan Armfeldt*); Sune Mangs (*Mr. Salenius*); Per Mattson (*Mikael Bergman*); Lickå Sjöman (*Grete Holm*); *Jacobi's House*: Erland Josephson (*Isak Jacobi*); Stina Ekblad (*Ismael*); Mats Bergman (*Aron*); Viola Aberlé, Gerd Andersson, and Anne-Louise Bergström (*Japanese Ladies*).

Awards: Oscars for Best Foreign Language Film, Best Art Direction, Best Cinematography, and Best Costume Design, 1983.

Publications

Books:

Jones, G. William, editor, *Talking with Ingmar Bergman*, Dallas, Texas, 1983.

Lefèvre, Raymond, *Ingmar Bergman*, Paris, 1983.

Dervin, Daniel, *Through a Freudian Lens Deeply: A Psychoanalysis of Cinema*, Hillsdale, New Jersey, 1985.

Gado, Frank, *The Passion of Ingmar Bergman*, Durham, North Carolina, 1986.

Bergman, Ingmar, *Laterna Magica*, Stockholm, 1987; as *The Magic Lantern: An Autobiography*, London, 1988.

Steene, Birgitta, *Ingmar Bergman: A Guide to References and Resources*, Boston, 1987.

Cohen, James, *Through a Lens Darkly*, New York, 1991.

Bjorkman, Stig, and Torsten Maans, and Jonas Sima, *Bergman on Bergman: Interviews with Ingmar Bergman*, Cambridge, 1993.

Cohen, Hubert I., *Ingmar Bergman: The Art of Confession*, New York, 1993.

Long, Robert Emmet, *Ingmar Bergman: Film & Stage*, New York, 1994.

Tornqvist, Egil, *Between Stage and Screen: Ingmar Bergman Directs*, Amsterdam, 1995.

Blackwell, Marilyn J., *Gender and Representation in the Films of Ingmar Bergman*, Rochester, 1997.

Lloyd, Michaels, editor, *Ingmar Bergman's Persona*, New York, 1999.

Articles:

Marker, L., and F. J., "The Making of *Fanny and Alexander*," interview with Ingmar Bergman, in *Films and Filming* (London), February 1983.

Chaplin (Stockholm), February 1983.

Jensen, N., "*Fanny og Alexander* og alle de andre i Bergmans univers," in *Kosmorama* (Copenhagen), March 1983.

Pym, John, in *Sight and Sound* (London), Spring 1983.

Milne, Tom, in *Monthly Film Bulletin* (London), April 1983.

Fanny och Alexander

Bonizto, P., and M. Chion, ''Portrait de l'artiste en jeune mythomane: Bergman et Alexandre,'' in *Cahiers du Cinéma* (Paris), April 1983.

Bonnet, J.-C., and M. Lannes Lacroutz, in *Cinématographe* (Paris), April 1983.

Lefèvre, Raymond, in *Revue du Cinéma* (Paris), April 1983.

Benayoun, Robert, and others, in *Positif* (Paris), May 1983.

Corliss, Richard, and W. Wolf, ''God, Sex, and Ingmar Bergman,'' in *Film Comment* (New York), May-June 1983.

Strick, Philip, in *Stills* (London), May-June 1983.

McLean, T., ''Knocking on Heaven's Door,'' in *American Film* (Washington, D.C.), June 1983.

Solman, G., in *Films in Review* (New York), August-September 1983.

Quart, B., and L. Quart, in *Film Quarterly* (Berkeley), Fall 1983.

Giguère, A., in *Séquences* (Montreal), October 1983.

Timm, M., in *Chaplin* (Stockholm), December 1983.

Comuzio, E., and G. De Santi, in *Cineforum* (Bergamo), January-February 1984.

Fagiani, E., in *Filmcritica* (Florence), January-February 1984.

Pintus, P., in *Bianco e Nero* (Rome), January-March 1984.

Block, B. A., ''Sven Nykvist, ASC, and *Fanny and Alexander*,'' in *American Cinematographer* (Los Angeles), April 1984.

Aghed, J., in *Positif* (Paris), March 1985.

Bergman, Ingmar, ''Propos,'' in *Positif* (Paris), March 1985.

Literature/Film Quarterly (Salisbury), vol.16, no.3, 1988.

Werner, A., ''Nocy dnia,'' in *Kino* (Warsaw), May 1991.

Salinger, E., ''*Fanny et Alexandre:* Ingmar Bergman,'' in *Cahiers du Cinéma* (Paris), Hors-série, 1993.

Hayes, J., ''The Seduction of Alexander Behind the Postmodern Door: Ingmar Bergman and Baudrillard's *De la seduction*,'' in *Literature/Film Quarterly* (Salisbury), no. 1, 1997.

Jablonski, Witold, ''W poszukiwaniu utraconej familii,'' in *Kino* (Warsaw), vol. 31, no. 359, May 1997.

* * *

Ingmar Bergman has said that he made *Fanny and Alexander* as his final film. It is an ingratiating and expansive film, ultimately a festive comedy, with its bleakest moments embedded between two extended family celebrations, the Christmas during which the father of Fanny and Alexander dies, and the christenings of the sister their mother had from her second husband and the cousin a maid conceived from their married uncle. In its scope, its concatenation of realism and fantasy, and its emotional reversals, the film owes something to Charles Dickens—perhaps to *Our Mutual Friend*, in particular, for a fire that rids the story of its villains and the intercessions of a benevolent stage Jew. More overtly, Bergman pays homage to Shakespeare and Strindberg, for the children of the title are part of the third generation of a theatrical family; their father collapses during a rehearsal of *Hamlet* in which he played the ghost, and dies shortly afterwards. (Throughout the film, he haunts Alexander.) The film ends with their grandmother reading the then-fresh script of Strindberg's *A Dream Play*.

Despite the title, Alexander is the unmistakable center of the film. Bergman's autobiography, *The Magic Lantern*, indicates that much of the film is based on his life; he has given Alexander a number of autobiographical traits, including a fascination with a magic lantern, and found an actor to portray him who looks remarkably like the pre-adolescent Bergman. Yet the film projects an idealized version of that childhood, as Dickens often did; it is, in fact, Bergman's richest instance of what Freud called "the family romance." Set in turn-of-the-century Uppsala, it chronicles the Ekdahl family, their friends, servants and lovers.

Plot is secondary to characterization. After the death of Oscar Ekdahl, his widow, Emilie, marries the severe and brutal Bishop Vergérus, taking Fanny and Alexander to live with her in the Bishop's house with his two sisters. The children suffer prolonged isolation in the attic of the house, and Alexander is severely beaten for lies and defiance. Eventually Isak Jacobi, a Jewish cabalist who had been the lover of Helena, the Ekdahl matriarch, spirits away the children in a magical chest. He hides them in his shop of puppets and occult wonders until a fire destroys the Vergérus household except for Emilie, who gives birth to a daughter and rejoins her children and the Ekdahls.

The universe of *Fanny and Alexander* is "the little world" (Oscar's phrase) of the theater, an affectionate environment that reflects the greater exterior world while defending itself against it. Thus Alexander's active imagination includes an intricate meshing of fantasies, visions, lies, theatricalizations, and magical violence. At the climax of the film Bergman ambiguously intercuts parallel scenes of the Vergérus home and its inhabitants consumed by flames with an encounter between Alexander and Isak's nephew, Ismael, himself ambiguously played by a woman, so that we can read the montage as merely simultaneous or sinisterly causal. As Ismael—whom Alexander visits in his locked room against Isak's warning—caresses him in a manner suggestive of anal intercourse, he encourages the frightened and pained boy to imagine the cruel death of his antagonist.

The film is 189 minutes long; a version in four parts ran as a television serial for a total of 300 minutes. It did not alter substantially the plot of the film; rather it showed more of the Ekdahl theater and enlarged the portraits of Alexander's uncles, the morose professor Carl, and the high spirited adulterer Gustav Adolf. It also included a parable, invented by Bergman but presented as a translation from the Hebrew by Isak, into which Alexander imaginatively projects himself. The published script of the film gives Fanny and Alexander a sister, Amanda, two years older. Its "Prologue" informs us that all three of Emilie's children from her marriage to Oscar were from different fathers, implying Oscar's impotence.

—P. Adams Sitney

FANTASIA

USA, 1940

Story Directors: Joe Grant and Ben Sharpsteen

Production: Walt Disney Productions; Technicolor, 35mm, animation, Fantasound; running time: 126 minutes, British version cut to 105 minutes, later versions cut to 81 minutes; length: originally 11,361 feet, cut to 9405 feet for British version. Released 13 November 1940 by RKO/Radio. Re-released every 5–7 years, beginning in 1946. Re-released in 1982 with soundtrack in digital audio. Filmed in Walt Disney Studios. Cost: $2,280,000.

Producer: Walt Disney; **story developers:** Lee Blair, Elmer Plummer, and Phil Dike ("Toccata and Fugue in D Minor" episode); Sylvia Moberly-Holland, Norman Wright, Albert Heath, Bianca Majolie, and Grahm Heid ("The Nutcracker Suite" segment); Perce Pearce and Carl Fallberg ("The Sorcerer's Apprentice" segment); William Martin, Leo Thiele, Robert Sterner, and John Fraser McLeish ("The Rite of Spring" segment); Otto Englander, Webb Smith, Erdman Penner, Joseph Sabo, Bill Peet, and George Stallings ("Pastoral Symphony"); Martin Provensen, James Bodrero, Duke Russell, and Earl Hurd ("Dance of the Hours"); Campbell Grant, Arthur Heinemann, and Phil Dike ("Night on Bald Mountain/Ave Maria" segment); **directors:** Samuel Armstrong ("Toccata and Fugue in D Minor" and "The Nutcracker Suite" segments); James Algar ("The Sorcerer's Apprentice" segment); Bill Roberts and Paul Satterfield ("The Rite of Spring" segment); Hamilton Luske, Jim Hangley, and Ford Beebe ("Pastoral Symphony"); T. Hee and Norman Ferguson ("Dance of the Hours" segment); Wilfred Jackson ("Night on Bald Mountain/Ave Maria" segment); **animation directors:** Samuel Armstrong ("Toccata and Fugue in D Minor" and "The Nutcracker Suite"); Bill Roberts ("The Rite of Spring"); James Algar ("The Sorcerer's Apprentice"); Hamilton Luske, Jim Handley and Ford Beebe ("Pastoral Symphony"); T. Hee and Norman Ferguson ("Dance of the Hours"); and Wilfred Jackson ("Night on Bald Mountain/Ave Maria"); **musical film editor:** Stephen Csillag; **sound and music recordists:** William E. Garity, C. O. Slyfield, and J. N. A. Hawkins; sound system, called Fantasound, designed especially for the film; **art directors:** Robert Cormack ("Toccata and Fugue in D Minor" segment); Robert Cormack, Al Zinnen, Curtiss D. Perkins, Arthur Byram, and Bruce Bushman ("The Nutcracker Suite" segment); Tom Codrick, Charles Phillippi, and Zack Schwartz ("The Sorcerer's Apprentice" segment); McLaren Stewart, Dick Kelsey, and John Hubley ("The Rite of Spring" segment); Hugh Hennesy, Kenneth Anderson, J. Gordon Legg, Herbert Ryman, Yale Gracey, and Lance Nolley ("Pastoral Symphony" segment); Kendall O'Connor, Harold Doughty, and Ernest Nordli ("Dance of the Hours" segment); Kay Nielson, Terrell Stapp, Charles Payzant and Thor Putnam ("Night on Bald Mountain/Ave Maria" segment); **music director:** Edward H. Plumb; **music conductor:** Leopold Tokowski (Irwin Kostal for 1982 release); **music:** selections include Bach's "Toccata and Fugue in D Minor"; Tchaikovsky's "The Nutcracker Suite"; Dukas' "The Sorcerer's Apprentice"; Stravinsky's "The Rite of Spring"; Beethoven's "Pastoral Symphony"; Ponchielli's "Dance of the Hours"; Mussorgsky's "Night on Bald Mountain"; and Schubert's "Ave Maria"; **special animation effects:** Joshua Meador, Miles E. Pike, John F. Reed, and Daniel Leonard Pickely; **animation**

Fantasia

supervisors: Fred Moore and Vladamir Tytla (''The Sorcerer's Apprentice'' segment); Wolfgang Reitherman and Joshua Meador (''The Rite of Spring''); Fred Moore, Ward Kimball, Eric Larsen, Arthur Babbitt, Oliver Johnson Jr., and Don Townsley (''Pastoral Symphony'' segment); Norman Ferguson (''Dance of the Hours'' segment); Vladamir Tytla (''Night on Bald Mountain/Ave Maria'' segment); **animators:** Cy Young, Art Palmer, Daniel MacManus, George Rowley, Edwin Aardal, Joshua Meador, and Cornett Wood (''Toccata and Fugue in D Minor'' segment); Arthur Babbitt, Les Clark, Don Lusk, Cy Young, and Robert Stokes (''The Nutcracker Suite'' segment); Les Clark, Riley Thompson, Marvin Woodward, Preston Blair, Edward Love, Ugo D'Orsi, George Rowley, and Cornett Wood (''The Sorcerer's Apprentice'' segment); B. Wolf, J. Campbell, J. Bradbury, J. Moore, M. Neil, B. Justice, J. Elliotte, W. Kelly, D. Lusk, L. Karp, M. McLennan, R. Youngquist and H. Mamsel (''Pastoral Symphony'' segment); J. Lounsbery, H. Swift, P. Blair, H. Fraser, H. Toombs, N. Tate, H. Lokey, A. Elliott, G. Simmons, R. Patterson, and F. Grundeen (''Dance of the Hours'' segment); John McManus, W. N. Shull, Robert Carlson Jr., Lester Novros, and Don Patterson (''Night on Bald Mountain/Ave Maria'' segment).

Cast: Deems Taylor (*Narrative Introductions*).

Awards: New York Film Critics' Special Award, 1940; Oscars, Special Awards (certificates), to Walt Disney, William Garity, John N. A. Hawkins, and RCA for Contributions to the Advancement of Sound in Motion Pictures, 1941; Oscar, Special Award (certificate), to Leopold Stokowski for his Achievement in the Creation of a New Form of Visualized Music, 1941.

Publications

Books:

Taylor, Deems, *Walt Disney's Fantasia*, New York, 1940.

Field, Robert D., *The Art of Walt Disney*, New York, 1942.

Manvell, Robert, and J. Huntley, *The Technique of Film Music*, New York, 1957.

Stevenson, Ralph, *Animation in the Cinema*, New York, 1967.

Schickel, Richard, *The Disney Version: The Life, Times, Art, and Commerce of Walt Disney*, New York, 1968; revised edition, 1986.

Bessy, Maurice, *Walt Disney*, Paris, 1970.

Finch, Christopher, *The Art of Walt Disney: From Mickey Mouse to the Magic Kingdoms*, New York, 1973; revised edition, 1999.

Maltin, Leonard, *The Disney Films*, New York, 1973; revised edition, 1984, 2000.

Thomas, Bob, *Walt Disney: An American Original*, New York, 1976.

Edera, Bruno, *Full-length Animated Features*, edited by John Halas, New York, 1977.

Leebron, Elizabeth, and Lynn Gartley, *Walt Disney: A Guide to References and Resources*, Boston, 1979.

Thomas, Frank, and Ollie Johnston, *Disney Animation: The Illusion of Life*, New York, 1982.

Culhane, John, *Walt Disney's Fantasia*, New York, 1983.

Bruno, Eduardo, and Enrico Ghezzi, *Walt Disney*, Venice, 1985.

Mosley, Leonard, *Disney's World: A Biography*, New York, 1985; as *The Real Walt Disney*, London, 1986.

Culhane, Seamus, *Talking Animals and Other People*, New York, 1986.

Thomas, Frank, and Ollie Johnston, *Too Funny for Words: Disney's Greatest Sight Gags*, New York, 1987; revised edition 1999.

Grant, John, *Encyclopedia of Walt Disney's Animated Characters: From Mickey Mouse to Hercules*, New York, 1998.

Thomas, Bob, *Building a Company: Roy O. Disney and the Creation of an Entertainment Empire*, New York, 1998.

Smith, Dave, *Disney A to Z: The Updated Official Encyclopedia*, New York, 1999.

Solomon, Charles, *The Art of Disney*, New York, 2000.

Articles:

Variety (New York), 21 August 1940.

Robins, S., ''Disney Again Tries Trailblazing,'' in *New York Times Magazine*, 3 November 1940.

Variety (New York), 13 November 1940.

New York Times, 14 November 1940.

Time (New York), 18 November 1940.

Hollering, F., in *Nation* (New York), 23 November 1940.

Ferguson, O., in *New Republic* (New York), 25 November 1940.

Hartung, P. T., in *Commonweal* (New York), 29 November 1940.

Gessner, Robert, ''Class in *Fantasia*,'' in *Nation* (New York), 30 November 1940.

Hollister, P., ''Walt Disney, Genius at Work,'' in *Atlantic* (Boston), December 1940.

Isaacs, H. R., in *Theatre Arts* (New York), January 1941.

Peck, A. P., ''What Makes *Fantasia* Click?,'' in *Scientific American* (New York), January 1941.

Boone, Andrew R., ''Mickey Mouse Goes Classical,'' in *Popular Science Monthly* (New York), January 1941.

Haggin, B. H., in *Nation* (New York), 11 January 1941.

Iwerks, Ub, in *Popular Mechanics* (New York), January 1942.

Ericsson, Peter, ''Walt Disney,'' in *Sequence* (London), no. 10, 1950.

Fallberg, Carl, ''Animated Film Technique'' (series of nine articles), in *American Cinematographer* (Los Angeles), July 1958 through March 1959.

Hicks, Jimmie, in *Films in Review* (New York), November 1965.

Zinsser, W., ''Walt Disney's Psychedelic *Fantasia*,'' in *Life* (New York), 3 April 1970.

''Disney Issue'' of *Kosmorama* (Copenhagen), November 1973.

Moritz, W., ''Fischiner at Disney; or, Oscar in the Mousetrap,'' in *Millimeter* (New York), February 1977.

Paul, William, ''Art, Music, Nature, and Walt Disney,'' in *Movie* (London), Spring 1977.

Canemaker, J., ''Disney Animation: History and Technique,'' in *Film News* (New York), January-February 1979.

Canemaker, J., in *Millimeter* (New York), February 1979.

Coleman, John, in *New Statesman* (London), 30 March 1979.

Stuart, A., in *Films and Filming* (London), April 1979.

Andrault, J. M., in *Revue du Cinéma* (Paris), November 1979.

Prouty, Howard H., in *Magill's Survey of Cinema 2*, Englewood Cliffs, New Jersey, 1980.

Starburst (London), vol. 3, no. 2, 1980.

Mallow, S., ''Lens Cap: Finding *Fantasia*,'' in *Filmmakers Newsletter* (Ward Hill, Massachusetts), March 1980.

Braun, E., in *Films* (London), August 1982.

Soundtrack! (Los Angeles), September 1982.

Adler, Dick, ''Hippo's Revenge: A Behind-the-Cels Look at *Fantasia* on the 50th Anniversary of What They Called Walt's Folly,'' in *Los Angeles Magazine*, September 1990.

Adler, Dick, ''The Fantasy of Disney's *Fantasia*,'' in *Chicago Tribune*, 23 September 1990.

Alexander, M., ''Disney Sweeps the Dust off *Fantasia* at 50,'' in *New York Times*, 30 September 1990.

Solomon, Charles, ''It Wasn't Always Magic,'' in *Los Angeles Times*, 7 October 1990.

Phinney, K., ''Shot by Shot,'' in *Premiere* (New York), November 1990.

Review, in *Listener*, vol. 125, no. 3197, 3 January 1991.

Heuring, D., and G. Turner, ''Disney's *Fantasia:* Yesterday and Today,'' in *American Cinematographer* (Hollywood), February 1991.

Magid, Ron, ''Fantasia-stein,'' in *American Cinematographer* (Hollywood), vol. 71, no. 10, October 1991.

Barron, J., ''Who Owns the Rights to 'Rites'?'' in *New York Times*, no. 142, 22 January 1993.

Review, in *Séquences* (Haute-Ville), no. 178, May-June 1995.

Evans, G., ''Disney Dishes New Look for *Fantasia* in 1998,'' in *Variety* (New York), no. 358, 6/12 February 1995.

Lyons, M., ''*Fantasia 2000*,'' in *Cinefantastique* (Forest Park), no. 9, 1998.

* * *

According to Deems Taylor, writing in 1940 (although the story was later denied by Disney sources), *Fantasia* first began as a comeback vehicle for Mickey Mouse after the Disney Studio had turned from modest cartoon production to large-scale animation features. Certainly Disney had used the Silly Symphony format to introduce additional cartoon figures—Pluto in 1930, the Three Pigs in 1933, and then Donald Duck in 1934, who went on to challenge Mickey's top billing. Also in 1934 Disney began work on *Snow White and the Seven Dwarfs*, a considerable gamble that came to be regarded as ''Disney's Folly,'' but went on to turn a profit of $8 million in its first release in 1937 and earned a special Oscar from the Motion Picture Academy. *Pinocchio* followed the success of *Snow White*, introducing Jiminy Cricket as an ingenuous narrator. At this point, then, in 1938, Disney began thinking about a new role for Mickey.

Disney's solution was to make Mickey the lead figure of a special cartoon rendering of ''The Sorcerer's Apprentice'', a fairy tale that had been set to music by the French composer Paul Dukas. Needing musical advice, Disney broached the project to the conductor of the

Philadelphia Orchestra, Leopold Stokowski, who was interested not only in the Dukas/Mickey idea but also in extending the project to an animated concert feature. Disney then began thinking in terms of ''The Concert Feature'' that was to become *Fantasia*. Whether the idea to expand was Disney's or Stokowski's has also been disputed.

At any rate, Deems Taylor, the radio voice of the Metropolitan Opera, was brought in to provide further advice and to handle the narrative transitions among the concert film's various ''movements,'' involving eight different musical compositions. Disney presumably saw the project as a challenging experiment in animated technique rather than an opportunity to use animation merely as a means of popularizing classical music for the masses. In the Bach *Toccata and Fugue* portion, for example, Disney artists were encouraged to experiment visually and boldly, in ways never before imagined. This sequence, early in the film, signals its experimentalism, departing from the usual Disney style and moving in abstract directions, imitating the techniques of Oscar Fischinger, who was originally to direct that sequence but left the project before completing it, after discovering the studio had altered his original designs. Other experiments are elsewhere in evidence, as when the sound track is visualized through animation midway through the film, recalling the abstract experiments of Len Lye and anticipating those of Norman McLaren. More conventional Disney whimsy is elsewhere in evidence, however, and there is perhaps the danger of vulgarizing the music through the imposed visual patterns. In fact, the sequences are diverse and uneven.

The film has been criticized for its ''ponderous didacticism'' (the visualization of the ''paleontological cataclysm'' in the Stravinsky *Rite of Spring* sequence, for example, and the simplistic contrasts of the final sequences—Moussorgsky's *Night on Bald Mountain* against Schubert's *Ave Maria*, with Good triumphing over Evil in a finale of Christian tranquility) and praised for those sequences in which Disney contented himself with being Disney and avoided self-conscious attempts at being ''artistic.''

Fantasia came to Disney at a time when risks were being taken. After the demonstrated success of ''Disney's Folly,'' animation began on *Fantasia* early in 1938. The production cost $2,280,000, including $400,000 for the music alone. Disney began thinking in terms of wide-screen production, multiplane Technicolor, and ''Fantasound,'' representing a major technical innovation involving the use of stereophonic sound and employing a new four-track optical stereophonic system. The achievement of ''Fantasound'' was something of a compromise: according to Peter Finch, Disney ''developed a sound system utilizing seven tracks and thirty speakers,'' but the system was ''prohibitively expensive'' and only installed in a few theatres. The score was recorded at the acoustically splendid Academy of Music in Philadelphia.

For the first time, moreover, Disney became his own distributor with *Fantasia*, since, as *Variety* reported, the film was so different as to require a different sales approach. It premiered on 13 November 1940, at the Broadway Theatre in New York, and was not an immediate success. Its original running time, with an intermission, was about 130 minutes, later cut to 81 minutes. It was reissued in 1946, but it would only build its audience strength over time. By 1968, for example, it had earned $4.8 million in North American markets, more than doubling its original investment, and finally taking its place among the top 200 grossing films.

In musical terminology, a fantasia is ''a free development of a given theme.'' Disney's achievement, though often impressive and no doubt ahead of its time, has nonetheless had its detractors. Stravinsky was not pleased that his music had been restructured and that the instrumentation had been changed. ''I will say nothing about the visual complement,'' Stravinsky remarked, ''as I do not wish to criticize an unresisting imbecility . . . ''The film succeeds best when it is at its most playful—the hippopotamus ballerinas in the ''Dance of the Hours'' sequence, for example, which Richard Schickel has described as ''a broad satirical comment on the absurdities of high culture.'' The visuals for Beethoven's Pastoral Symphony strain contrivedly for a mythic charm in an Arcadian setting populated by fabulous creatures. Far more interesting are the animated dances from Tchaikovsky's Nutcracker Suite, and the whimsical treatment of Ponchielli's ''Dance of the Hours'' or Mickey's struggle with the dancing brooms in ''The Sorcerer's Apprentice,'' the conceptual core of the picture. John Tibbetts has written that the results of Mickey's ''union with high art were questionable for some, just as Walt's collision with the likes of Stravinsky, Beethoven, and Moussorgsky raised (or lowered) many a brow.''

Disney's undertaking *Fantasia* brings to mind an artisan who has only a superficial knowledge of religion undertaking to sculpt a monumental pieta out of sand as the tide moves in, threatening to erode it. Some passers-by will no doubt pause to watch out of curiosity, but the spectacle will not for most of them constitute a conversion. If anything, *Fantasia* does not teach a musical lesson, but it often fascinates and delights the eye.

Reviewing *Fantasia* in 1940, Otis Ferguson called it ''a film for everybody to see and enjoy,'' despite its ''main weakness—an absence of story, of motion, of interest.'' Bosley Crowther was less harsh, remarking that the images often tended to overwhelm the music, but praising the film for its ''imaginative excursion'' and concluding that it was a milestone in motion picture history. Despite its sometimes elaborate pretensions and its many innovations, the boldness of its concept quite overrides the ''disturbing jumble'' of its achievement. It is, indeed, a ''milestone'' in the history of animated film.

—James Michael Welsh

FAREWELL

See **PROSHCHANIE**

FAREWELL MY CONCUBINE

See **BA WANG BIE JI**

FARGO

US, 1996

Director: Joel Coen

Production: Gramercy Pictures, PolyGram Filmed Entertainment, Working Title Films; color, 35mm; running time: 98 minutes; length:

Fargo

2732 meters. Filmed in Minnesota and North Dakota; cost: $7 million.

Producers: Ethan Coen, Tim Bevan (executive), Eric Fellner (executive); **screenplay:** Joel Coen, Ethan Coen; **cinematographer:** Roger Deakins; **music:** Carter Burwell; **editors:** Ethan Coen (as Roderick Jaynes), Joel Coen (as Roderick Jaynes); **casting:** John Lyons; **production design:** Rick Heinrichs; **art direction:** Thomas P. Wilkins; **set decoration:** Lauri Gaffin; **costume design:** Mary Zophres; **makeup:** John Blake, Daniel Curet.

Cast: William H. Macy (*Jerry Lundegaard*); Steve Buscemi (*Carl Showalter*); Frances McDormand (*Marge Gunderson*); Peter Stormare (*Gaear Grimsrud*); Kristin Rudrüd (*Jean Lundegaard*); Harve Presnell (*Wade Gustafson*); Tony Denman (*Scotty Lundegaard*); Gary Houston (*Irate Customer*); Sally Wingert (*Irate Customer's Wife*); Kurt Schweickhardt (*Car Salesman*); Larissa Kokernot (*Hooker #1*); Melissa Peterman (*Hooker #2*); Steve Reevis (*Shep Proudfoot*); Warren Keith (*Reilly Diefenbach*); Steve Edelman (*Morning Show Host*); Sharon Anderson (*Morning Show Hostess*); Larry Brandenburg (*Stan Grossman*); James Gaulke (*State Trooper*); and others.

Awards: Cannes Film Festival Best Director Award (Coen), 1996; National Board of Review Awards for Best Actress (McDormand) and Best Director (Coen), 1996; Australian Film Institute Best Foreign Film Award, 1996; Casting Society of America Artios Award (John S. Lyons), 1996; Academy Award for Best Actress (Frances McDormand) and Best Writing, Screenplay Written Directly for the Screen (Ethan Coen and Joel Coen), 1997; American Cinema Editors Eddie Award for Best Edited Feature Film, 1997; Bodil Festival Award for Best American Film, 1997; British Academy Awards David Lean Award for Direction (Joel Coen), 1997; Writers Guild of America Screen Award for Best Screenplay Written Directly for the Screen (Coen and Coen), 1997; Screen Actors Guild Award for Outstanding Performance by a Female Actor in a Leading Role (McDormand), 1997; and many other awards.

Publications:

Script:

Coen, Joel, and Ethan Coen, *Fargo*, London, 1996.

Books:

Wood, Paul A., *Blood Siblings: The Cinema of Joel and Ethan Coen*, Austin, 1999.

Ashbrook, John M., and Ellen Cheshire, *Joel and Ethan Coen*, Harpenden, 2000.

Korte, *Joel and Ethan Coen*, Cambridge, 2000.

Articles:

Sante, Luc, ''The Rise of the Baroque Directors,'' in *Vogue*, vol. 182, no. 9, September 1992.

Friend, Tad, ''Inside the Coen Heads,'' in *Vogue*, vol. 184, no. 4, April 1994.

Robertson, William Preston, ''The Coen Brothers Made Easy,'' in *Playboy*, vol. 41, no. 4, April 1994.

Lally, K., ''Up North with the Coen Brothers,'' in *Film Journal* (New York), vol. 99, February 1996.

Dafoe, W., ''Frances McDormand,'' in *Bomb*, no. 55, Spring 1996.

Probst, Christopher, ''Cold-Blooded Scheming,'' in *American Cinematographer* (Hollywood), vol. 77, no. 3, March 1996.

Biskind, Peter, ''Joel and Ethan Coen,'' in *Premiere* (Boulder), vol. 9, no. 7, March 1996.

Fuller, Graham, ''Do Not Miss *Fargo*,'' in *Interview*, vol. 26, no. 3, March 1996.

McCarthy, Todd, and Derek Elley, ''Global Helmers Fill Croisette Coffers,'' in *Variety* (New York), vol. 362, no. 11, 15 April 1996.

Blake, R.A., ''Whiteout,'' in *America*, vol. 174, 20 April 1996.

Simon, J., ''Forgo *Fargo*,'' in *National Review*, vol. 48, 22 April 1996.

Francke, Lizzie, ''Hell Freezes Over,'' in *Sight & Sound* (London), vol. 6, no. 5, May 1996.

Andrew, Geoff, ''Pros and Coens,'' in *Time Out* (London), no. 1343, 15 May 1996.

''Special Issue on *Fargo*,'' in *Avant-Scène du Cinéma* (Paris), no. 456, November 1996.

Roman, Monica, ''New York Crix Circle Takes Trip to *Fargo*,'' in *Variety* (New York), vol. 365, no. 7, 16 December 1996.

Probst, Christopher, ''Exemplary Images,'' in *American Cinematographer* (Hollywood), vol. 78, no. 6, June 1997.

Norman, Barry, ''A Case of Knowing When to Go to *Fargo*,'' in *Radio Times* (London), vol. 294, no. 3839, 30 August 1997.

* * *

''This is a true story,'' reads the on-screen caption at the beginning of *Fargo*. Ethan Coen's introduction to the published script tells it rather differently: ''The story . . . aims to be both homey and exotic, and pretends to be true.'' Either way, this teasing, typically Coenesque ambiguity is something of a red herring (since fiction, in the classic definition, is a lie that tells the truth) but it makes an apt introduction to a film where the only people who win out are those who make no pretense to being anything other than they are.

Fargo marks a significant tonal shift in the Coens' work. It shares several favorite black-comedy elements with their earlier films—the solemnly off-the-wall dialogue, the laughably inept yet lethal heavies, the snowball effect of a relatively minor act of deception spiraling disastrously out of control—but also for the first time sets up a center of normality to counterpoint the off-kilter eccentricities on display elsewhere. Some previous Coen films do provide a focus for our sympathies, such as the childless Hi and Ed (Nicolas Cage and Holly Hunter) in *Raising Arizona*, but that pair are themselves fairly advanced-state deranged. *Fargo*'s Marge Gunderson (Frances McDormand), the heavily pregnant police chief, and her aptly-named husband Norm (John Carroll Lynch) present a picture of married life that's conventional to the point of stodginess, but sustained by a mutually supportive love.

Though Marge serves as the film's moral center, it's a full thirty minutes before she appears on screen. By then, the picture's been all but stolen by William H. Macy in his breakthrough role as Jerry Lundegaard, the hapless car salesman so desperate for money that he arranges to have his own wife kidnapped. With his wide, unhappy grin and paper-thin bonhomie (''You're darn tootin'!''), Jerry is visibly flailing on the edge of the abyss—and as so often happens in the Coens' tortuous world, the people he turns to for help are just as inept, and far less scrupulous, than he is.

Even in the rich gallery of Coen villains, the mismatched pair of Carl Showalter and Gaear Grimsrud stand out as relishably vivid. (A running gag is that none of the witnesses can ever describe this highly distinctive duo beyond saying they were ''kinda funny-lookin'.'') Right from the start it is clear that the teaming of the small, twitchy, voluble Carl (Steve Buscemi at his most weaselly) and the huge, menacingly taciturn Gaear (Peter Stormare) is headed for a particularly vicious meltdown. Gaear, whose name and demeanor suggest one of the less savory denizens of the Icelandic sagas, is another of those monstrous figures-from-the-id who recur in the Coens' films, close kin to the Lone Biker of the Apocalypse in *Raising Arizona* or Charlie Meadows in *Barton Fink*. He also seems to be blood-brother to Paul Bunyan, whose mad-eyed effigy we glimpse by the highway outside Brainard, carrying an axe much like the one Gaear eventually buries in Carl's neck. (Following through on these forestry impulses, he proceeds to feed his ex-partner into a wood-chipper.)

Embodiments of the destructive instinct at its most self-defeating, Carl and Gaear casually bump off anybody who irritates them or even momentarily incommodes them. The death of the luckless Jean Lundegaard, Jerry's kidnapped wife, rates just two lines—Carl: ''The fuck happen to her?'' Gaear: ''She started shrieking, y'know.'' Against these lethal clowns Marge Gunderson initially seems a hopelessly inadequate opponent, with her waddling, pregnant walk and slow speech. (The Coens, themselves Minnesota-born, have fun with local Scandinavian speech-patterns; most exchanges consist largely of ''Oh, yah?'' ''Yah.'') But Marge, compassionate but not sentimental, combines her nurturing role with the tenacity of the tough cop whose accepted image she so little resembles. Carl, Gaear, and Jerry violate everything her down-to-earth common sense believes in, summed up in her remarks to the captured Gaear: ''And for what? For a little bit of money. There's more to life than a little money, y'know. . . . And it's a beautiful day. I just don't understand it.''

Marge's innate decency, and her comfortably affectionate relationship with Norm, provide *Fargo* with the core of warmth that was often lacking from the Coens' earlier films. The filmmakers also, for the first time, admit the intrusion of genuine grief in the reaction of Jerry's son Scotty to his mother's kidnaping.

Their next film, *The Big Lebowski*, features ''Dude'' Lebowski (Jeff Bridges) a character whose instinctive (if dope-hazed) humanity stands in contrast to the cheats, double-dealers, and thugs around him. Such elements seem set to add a deeper emotional investment to the

Coens' work, without in the least detracting from their wit, inventiveness, and stylistic bravura.

—Philip Kemp

FARREBIQUE

France, 1947

Director: Georges Rouquier

Production: L'Ecran Français and Les Films Etienne Lallier; black and white, 35mm; running time: 100 minutes; some versions are 85 minutes. Released 11 February 1947. Filmed from about 1944 to 1946 on location at the farm Farrebique.

Producer: Jacques Girard; **screenplay:** Georges Rouquier, from an idea by C. Blanchard; **photography:** André Danton; editor; Madeleine Gug; **sound:** Lecuyer; **music:** Henri Sauguet; **special effects:** Jean Painleve, Daniel Senade, and Jean-Jacques Rebuffet.

Cast: The Owners of the farm of Farrebique and some of their neighbors as themselves.

Publications

Script:

Rouquier: Album de Farrebique, Paris, 1947.

Books:

Barnouw, Erik, *Documentary: A History of Non-Fiction Film*, New York, 1974.
Armes, Roy, *French Film Since 1946: The Great Tradition*, New York, 1976.
Auzel, Dominique, *Georges Rouquier: cinéaste, poète & paysan*, Rodez, 1993.

Articles:

Sight and Sound (London), Winter 1946–47.
Revue du Cinéma (Paris), January 1947.
Cinéma Français (Paris), 15 February 1947.
New York Times, 24 February 1948.
New Republic (New York), 1 March 1948.
Time (New York), 15 March 1948.
Monthly Film Bulletin (London), 30 April 1948.
Agee, James, in *Agee on Film 1*, New York, 1958.
Bowser, Eileen, ''New Acquisitions: *Le Tempestaire* and *Farrebique*,'' in *Museum of Modern Art. Film Notes*, (New York), 2 and 4 April 1978.
Weiss, J. H., ''An Innocent Eye? The Career and Documentary Vision of Georges Rouquier,'' in *Cinema Journal* (Evanston, Illinois), Spring 1981.
Jeune Cinéma (Paris), January 1984.
Olive, Jean-Louis, ''*Farrebique*, Biquefare ou les morçeaux de la memoire,'' in *Cahiers de la Cinématheque*, no. 41, Winter 1984.
Berelowitch, Iréne, and Jacques Siclier, ''Le printemps revient toujours. *Farrebique* ou les quatre saisons: Biquefarre,'' in *Télérama* (Paris), no. 2252, 10 March 1993.
Auzel, Dominique, ''Georges Rouquier, cinéaste, poète et paysan,'' in *Séquences* (Haute-Ville), no. 170, March 1994.
Sorlin, Pierre, '''Stop the Rural Exodus': Images of the Country in French Films of the 1950s,'' in *Historical Journal of Film, Radio and Television*, vol. 18, no. 2, June 1998.

*   *   *

The roots of the style which George Rouquier brought to full maturity with his first feature-length film, *Farrebique*, released in 1946, lie in a number of short documentary studies of rural crafts, such as *Le tonnelier* and *Le charron*, which the director had made during the Occupation years. In the immediate post-war years, *Farrebique*'s picture of French farming life was hailed as a break with the past, its deeply-felt concern to present realist detail being contrasted with the escapist fantasy that was felt to characterize the cinema of the Pétain years. Certainly this aspect of the film remains impressive. The everyday activity of the farming family is precisely observed—the breadmaking, ploughing and harvesting, evening prayers, and trips to church or bistro—and forms the context for the film's fictionalized sequence of events. They include the grandfather's account of the family history, his death and the birth of a baby, the younger son's injury and engagement, and they are staged in a slightly clumsy fashion which is in perfect keeping with the film's strategy of presenting its story as a ''real'' document. The understatement of joys and sorrows and the unemphatic playing reinforce this tone. But the film as a whole does not have any of the coldness or objectivity that such a stance might lead one to expect, for these family events are not presented neutrally but are fitted into what can be aptly characterised as a pageant of the seasons. The director views nature with true poetic intensity, stressing always its dynamic aspect, particularly in the long lyrical passage celebrating the coming of the spring. This vision allows the film to remain optimistic and affirmative despite the inclusion of such events as the grandfather's death, which can be seen as part of a rhythm of change and development. Though moving in itself, this death is merely part of the process of seasonal renewal and can be supplanted by the son's engagement and the promise of spring.

In the mid- and late-1940s, *Farrebique* was generally seen as belonging alongside René Clément's documentary drama *La bataille du rail*, about the French railway workers' efforts to resist the German occupiers, as an example of the postwar French realism which failed to develop on the lines of that emerging during these years in Italy. Comparisons with Italian neorealism are fruitful, for it is immediately apparent that Rouquier has not attempted to integrate rural life into a wider social framework. In *Farrebique* virtually the only contact with the outside world concerns the installation of electricity, and even this is treated as a comparatively minor incident and incorporated in the film's conception of change as part of a natural rhythm.

Certainly Rouquier offers none of the social analysis which characterises Luchino Visconti's *La terra trema*, a study of an equally isolated fishing community made some two years later. But while such an approach to *Farrebique* has great relevance and considerable

Farrebique

value, relating closely to André Bazin's 1940s advocacy of realist styles, it can be seen in retrospect as somewhat limited. Bazin's formulation of the problematics of realism leaves out of account any consideration of political issues. Yet from today's perspective one of the most fascinating aspects of *Farrebique* is the way it questions the neat separation of Occupation years from the postwar renewal that underpins so many accounts of France in the 1940s. Planned during the Occupation, *Farrebique* reflects the all-pervasive influence of the Pétainist ideology of ''work, family and fatherland'' at least as strongly as it affirms a new postwar realist approach. Far from lessening the value and significance of *Farrebique*, this essenial ambiguity makes it a key document for the re-examination of French culture that looks beneath the comfortable myths of Occupation and Resistance.

—Roy Armes

FATHER PANCHALI

See **THE APU TRILOGY**

LA FEMME DU BOULANGER

(The Baker's Wife)

France, 1938

Director: Marcel Pagnol

Production: Les Films Marcel Pagnol; black and white, 35mm; running time: 120 minutes, some sources list 110 minutes. Released 1938.

Screenplay: Marcel Pagnol, from *Jean le Bleu* by Jean Giono; **photography:** G. Benoît, R. Lendruz, and N. Daries; **editors:** Suzanne de Troye, Marguerite Houllé, and Suzanne Cabon; **music:** Vincent Scotto.

Cast: Raimu (*Aimable Castenet*); Ginette Leclerc (*Aurélie Castenet*); Charpin (*M. de Monelles*); Robert Vattier (*Priest*); Basac (*Teacher*); Charles Moulin (*Dominique*); Delmont (*Mailleterre*); Alida Rouffe

(*Marie*); Maximilliene (*Angèle*); Maupi, Dullac, Blavette, Odette Roger, Castan, Maffre, and Charblay.

Publications

Books:

Sadoul, Georges, *French Film*, London, 1953.
Armes, Roy, *French Film*, New York, 1970.
Domeyne, P., *Marcel Pagnol*, Paris, 1971.
Beylie, Claude, *Marcel Pagnol*, Paris, 1972.
Castans, Raymond, *Marcel Pagnol's m'a raconte . . .* , Paris, 1975.
Leprohon, Pierre, *Marcel Pagnol*, Paris, 1976.
Castans, R., *Il etait une fois Marcel Pagnol*, Paris, 1978.
Pagnol, Marcel, *Confidences*, Paris, 1981.
Castans, Raymond, and Andre Bernard, *Les Films du Marcel Pagnol*, Paris, 1982.
Beylie, Claude, *Marcel Pagnol: Ou, Le Cinéma en liberté*, Paris, 1986, 1995.
Pompa, Dany, *Marcel Pagnol*, Paris, 1986.
Bens, Jacques, *Pagnol*, Paris, 1994.

Articles:

Variety (New York), 12 October 1938.
Greene, Graham, in *Spectator* (London), 24 February 1939.
Whitebait, William, in *New Statesman* (London), 25 February 1939.
New York Times, 2 March 1940.
''Adieu à Raimu,'' in *L'Ecran Française* (Paris), 3 October 1951.
''Marcel Pagnol,'' in *Current Biography Yearbook 1956*, New York, 1957.
''Souvenirs sur Raimu,'' in *Figaro Litteraire* (Paris), 7 September 1963.
''Guiltry-Pagnol Issue,'' of *Cahiers du Cinéma* (Paris), 1 December 1965.
Ford, Charles, ''Marcel Pagnol,'' in *Films in Review* (New York), April 1970.
''L'Adieu de Marcel Pagnol à Raimu,'' in *Avant-Scène du Cinéma* (Paris), July-September 1970.

La femme du boulanger

Gevaudin, F., ''Marcel Pagnol: Un Cinéaste mineur?'' in *Cinéma* (Paris), June 1974.
Harvey, S., ''Pagnol, From the Source,'' in *New York Times*, 21 February 1988.
Brisset, S., ''Pagnol, cineaste de la Mediterranee,'' in *Cinema 90*, no. 470, October 1990.
La Breteque, F. de, ''Le gout pour la pedagogie et la didactique de Marcel Pagnol,'' in *Les Cahiers de la Cinematheque* (Perpignan), no. 54, December 1990.
Faulkner, C., ''Rene Clair, Marcel Pagnol and the Social Dimension of Speech,'' in *Screen* (Oxford), no. 2, 1994.
Review, in *Télérama* (Paris), no. 2377, 2 August 1995.
Bazin, A., ''The Case of Marcel Pagnol,'' in *Literature/Film Quarterly* (Salisbury), no. 3, 1995.

* * *

La femme du boulanger is a film which can stand as a summation of Marcel Pagnol's work in the cinema and of a certain style of 1930s filmmaking. It was a period in which the star and his or her attendant dialogue writer reigned supreme in French cinema. Despite the film's title, the sultry Ginette Leclerc has only a small role as the errant wife, but in compensation we are given Raimu at the height of his powers in a part shaped by Pagnol so as to give the maximum relief and humanity to the figure of a village baker deceived by his faithless wife, who runs off with a stranger. The plot could hardly be simpler: the husband now refuses to bake bread; the villagers have to join forces to ''engineer'' the wayward wife's return and acceptance by the baker.

In terms of Marcel Pagnol's work, *La femme du boulanger*, though it holds together remarkably well, is in many ways a hybrid, combining two divergent tendencies. The source of the film is a novel by Jean Giono, who had earlier provided the stimuli for the rural epics, *Angèle* and *Regain*. As with those films, *La femme du boulanger* breathes an authentic country atmosphere, with its open air meetings and sense of real village community. But here the epic qualities of Giono's vision are scaled down, and the village, though remote, is a microcosm of the city, with its social stratifications and religious differences. The performance of Raimu calls to mind the atmosphere of Pagnol's marvellous Marseilles trilogy—*Marius*, *Fanny*, and *César*—which the director and the star had completed just two years previously. This trilogy had its roots in Pagnol's writing for the stage, and it was essentially a studio work, in which the atmosphere of the Mediterranean port was summoned up through vivid dialogue and accent. Raimu's role in *La femme du boulanger* has the same verbal richness. These are speeches written to be performed—as in the theatre—and since Raimu was unhappy acting in the open air, many of them were restaged in the studio, giving the film its sometimes awkward combination of location and studio work. As always, the themes of Pagnol's work are simple, bordering on the melodramatic, but they are captured in dialogue of such verbal felicity, and shaped so cunningly as drama, that they hold the attention effortlessly, especially when—as here—they are set against a vividly drawn background.

The controversy which surrounded Marcel Pagnol's work in the late 1930s, the result of his enthusiastic welcoming of sound cinema as no more than a perfected means of recording and distributing theatrical works, has now subsided. His own work proved richer than the polemical positions which he adopted at the time. Despite his advocacy of the studio, he was in fact one of the first to record sound on location and take his players into the countryside around Marseilles. Formerly regarded as a marginal provincial figure, cut off from the mainstream of Parisian cinema, Pagnol was in fact consistently able to produce two or three films a year. That made him a major figure at a time when the major production companies had long since vanished and most films were made by ephemeral companies set to organise just a single production. Owning his own production and distribution companies, his own laboratories and cinemas, Pagnol created his films *en famille* in a uniquely personal atmosphere. *La femme du boulanger*, his last film of the 1930s, conveys perfectly the strengths of this spontaneous, uninhibited approach to production.

—Roy Armes

LA FEMME INFIDÈLE

(The Unfaithful Wife)

France, 1969

Director: Claude Chabrol

Production: Les Films La Boétie and Cinégay; Eastmancolor (print by Deluxe), 35mm; running time: 105 minutes, English version: 98 minutes; length: 2900 meters. Released January 1969, Paris. Filmed 1968 in and around Paris.

Producer: André Génovès and Georges Casati; **screenplay:** Claude Chabrol; **photography:** Jean Rabier; **editor:** Jacques Gaillard; **sound:** Guy Chichignoud; **art director:** Guy Littaye; **music:** Pierre Jansen; **music conductors:** André Girard and Dominique Zardi; **costume designer:** Maurice Albray.

Cast: Stéphane Audran (*Hélène Desvallées*); Michel Bouquet (*Charles Desvallées*); Maurice Ronet (*Victor Pegala*); Serge Bento (*Bignon*); Michel Duchaussoy (*Police officer*); Guy Marly (*Police Officer Gobert*); Stéphane Di Napoli (*Michel Desvallées*); Louise Chevalier (*Maid*); Louise Rioton (*Mother-in-Law*); Henri Mateau (*Paul*); François Moro-Giafferi (*Frédéric*); Dominque Zardi (*Truck driver*); Michel Charrel (*Policeman*); Henri Attal (*Man in cafe*); Jean-Marie Arnoux (*False witness*); Donatella Turri (*Brigitte*).

Publications

Script:

Chabrol, Claude, ''*La femme infidèle*,'' in *Avant-Scène du Cinéma* (Paris), May 1969.

Books:

Wood, Robin, and Michael Walker, *Claude Chabrol*, New York, 1970.
Fassbinder, Rainer Werner, and others, *Reihe Film 5: Claude Chabrol*, Munich, 1975.

La femme infidèle

Taylor, John, *Directors and Directions*, New York, 1975.
Armes, Roy, *French Cinema Since 1946: The Personal Style*, New York, 1976.
Monaco, James, *The New Wave*, New York, 1976.
Magny, Joel, *Claude Chabrol*, Paris, 1987.
Blanchet, Christian, *Claude Chabrol*, Paris, 1989.
Austin, Guy, *Claude Chabrol: Autoportrait,* Manchester, 1999.

Articles:

Comolli, Jean-Louis, in *Cahiers du Cinéma* (Paris), February 1969.
Baxter, Brian, ''Claude Chabrol,'' in *Film* (London), Spring 1969.
''Chabrol Issue,'' of *Avant-Scène du Cinéma* (Paris), May 1969.
Dewey, Langdon, ''Chabrol Rides the Waves,'' in *Film* (London), Summer 1969.
Millar, Gavin, in *Sight and Sound* (London), Autumn 1969.
Gow, Gordon, in *Films and Filming* (London), October 1969.
Sarris, Andrew, in *Village Voice* (New York), 13 November 1969.
Wood, Robin, in *Movie* (London), Winter 1969–70.
Allen, Don, ''Claude Chabrol,'' in *Screen* (London), February 1970.
Milne, Tom, ''Chabrol's Schizophrenic Spider,'' in *Sight and Sound* (London), Spring 1970.
Kernan, Margot, in *Film Quarterly* (Berkeley), Summer 1970.
''An Interview with Claude Chabrol,'' in *Take One* (Montreal), September-October 1970.
Legrand, Gérard, Michel Ciment, and J. Torok, ''Interview with Chabrol,'' in *Movie* (London), Winter 1970–71.
Nogueira, R., and N. Zalaffi, ''Conversation with Claude Chabrol,'' in *Sight and Sound* (London), Winter 1970–71.
Haskell, Molly, ''The Films of Chabrol—A Priest among Clowns,'' in *Village Voice* (New York), 12 November 1970.
Ebert, Roger, ''This Man Must Commit Murder,'' in *New York Times Biography Edition*, 29 November 1970.
Harcourt, P., in *Film Comment* (New York), November-December 1976.
Anderson, S., ''True Love and the Bourgeoisie,'' in *Filament* (Dayton), no. 2, 1982.
Dennis, J., ''Hitchcockian Influences on Claude Chabrol,'' in *Filament* (Dayton), no. 2, 1982.
Jousse, T., and others, ''Entretien avec Claude Chabrol,'' in *Cahiers du Cinéma* (Paris), no. 437, November 1990.

Berthomieu, P., and others, ''Entretien avec Claude Chabrol,'' in *Positif* (Paris), September 1995.
Feinstein, H., ''Killer Instincts,'' in *Village Voice* (New York), 24 December 1996.
Magny, J., ''Questions de mise en scene,'' in *Cahiers du Cinéma* (Paris), Hors-serie, 1997.

* * *

Claude Chabrol's *La femme infidèle* is perhaps the director's most characteristic film: an extraordinarily spare thriller emphasizing the subtle psychologies of its few major characters. Although the film presents Chabrol's typical triangle—Charles and his wife, Hélène, who has taken a lover—the members of the triangle never all come together; and the film is organized very formally; one scene between Hélène and her lover, one scene between Charles and her lover, and many scenes between Hélène and Charles. The film is almost completely subtext; although the film's primary subject is the relationship between Charles and Hélène (and the sociopolitical implications of its failings), not one word ever passes between Charles and Hélène about her love affair or the problems of their marriage.

The indirectness of the film seems apposite, since Chabrol indicates that the violence which erupts so suddenly in the film is repressed beneath the apparently civilized surface of bourgeois society. Chabrol emphasizes those surfaces: the beautiful greens of the couple's landscaped garden, the shine on the silverware, the bouquets of flowers, the informal family grouping outdoors which is masked by a cheery blue canopy. True to his manner, Chabrol entirely eschews sentiment, and yet—although apparently cold and distant—condemns no one. If this witty, ironic film holds neither Hélène nor Charles completely responsible for her affair, it credits the act of violence the affair precipitates for the rekindling of the couple's passions for each other, as each suddenly sees the other in a new light. By the end of the film, Hélène is all too willing to cover up her husband's crime and lovingly accept the kind of transference of guilt typical of the Hitchcock films Chabrol so obviously admires.

There are very few emotional outbursts or expressions of feeling in the film; the murder of Hélène's lover, which comes unexpectedly; three choked sobs that Hélène gives when she discovers her lover has been killed; and one truly heartfelt embrace between husband and wife. Rather, the emotion, as repressed as the natural instincts of the characters, is displaced instead onto the decor; indeed, there are flashes of red throughout—Hélène's earrings, a bedroom wall, a beauty shop awning, a bright dress, a lampshade, a cabinet, and so forth. As usual for Chabrol, objects are consistently used as symbols; a white, aloof statue that Charles tries to cleanse of red blood and which stands, perhaps, for Hélène; a huge cigarette lighter, which represents the passion Hélène has transferred from her husband to her lover; and the jigsaw puzzle, put together by the couple's son, which seems to represent their marriage and/or the narrative.

The cinematography by Jean Rabier and the score by Pierre Jansen are impeccable and provocative. So too are the performances, especially by Chabrol's wife, Stéphane Audran, as Hélène (note the cool expressiveness of her beauty as she descends the stairs at the end of the film), and Michel Bouquet as Charles. A small but perfect film, *La femme infidèle* represents only one variation on the theme in a series of films directed by Chabrol in the late 1960s and 1970s in collaboration with Audran, Rabier, and Jansen.

—Charles Derry

FESTEN

(The Celebration)

Denmark, 1998

Director: Thomas Vinterberg

Production: Nimbus Film in collaboration with DR/TV and Swedish TV; color, 35mm; running time: 106 min. Released 19 June 1998, in Copenhagen. Cost: DKK 8 mio.

Producer: Birgitte Hald; **Screenplay:** Thomas Vinterberg and Mogens Rukow, from an idea by Thomas Vinterberg based on an authentic case made public on Danish Radio. **Photography:** Anthony Dod Mantle; **Editor:** Valdis Oskarsdottir.

Cast: Ulrich Thomsen (*Christian*); Thomas Bo Larsen (*Michael*); Henning Moritzen (*Father*); Paprika Steen (*Helene*); Birthe Neumann (*Mother*); Trine Dyrholm (*Pia*); Helle Dolleriis (*Mette*); Klaus Bondam (*Toastmaster*).

Awards: (Major awards only) Prix de jury, Cannes Film Festival; Danish Film Academy Award (Robert) for Best Director, Best Actor, Best Actress, Best Supporting Actress, Best Editor, Best Cinematographer, and Best Scriptwriter; Danish Film Critics Award (Bodil) for Best Director and Best Leading Actor; Fassbinder Award as European Discovery, European Film Academy Awards, 1998; Los Angeles Film Critics Award for Best Foreign Language Film; New York Film Critics Award for Best Foreign Language Film; Swedish Film Institute Award (Guldbagge) for Best Foreign Language Film.

Publications

Script:

Vinterberg, Thomas, and Mogens Rukow, *Festen*, København, 1998.

Articles:

Interview and review, in *Positif* (Paris), no. 455, January 1999.
Macnab, Geoffrey, ''The Big Tease,'' in *Sight and Sound* (London), February 1999.
Matthews, Peter, review in *Sight and Sound* (London), March 1999.

* * *

When Lars von Trier, Thomas Vinterberg, Søren Kragh-Jacobsen, and Christian Levring signed the Dogma manifesto in 1995 their intention was to counter certain tendencies in contemporary cinema: cosmetic technical perfection, predictable dramaturgy, and superficial action. The various commandments of the Dogma manifesto, which might appear to be a straitjacket, were in fact conceived as a chance to concentrate the art of film on what matters most: the plot and the characters.

The Celebration, by Thomas Vinterberg, was the first Dogma film and from the very outset it was obvious that something extraordinary was afoot. *The Celebration* is a film born out of the happy moments when a director unites the combination of a good story and superb acting by every member of the cast into a film narrative which makes a tremendous impact with its palpitating editing, sensitively mobile camera, and striking sense of framing and composition.

The film is the story of a family party to celebrate a 60th birthday. It is attended by the birthday boy's three children, grandchildren, and sundry friends and relatives. When Christian, one of the three sons, starts his speech by thanking his father for raping him and his twin sister, who went on to commit suicide, the black comedy commences, with baroque farce alternating with excruciatingly painful revelations of stunted family relationships. Christian then tries to depart from the paralyzed company, who don't know whether it is a sickly inappropriate joke, but is persuaded by an old friend to stay and see his showdown to its conclusion. He returns to the dinner three times to maintain and elucidate his accusations, finally raising his glass to his father, "the man who murdered my sister."

Vinterberg moulds his story around the Aristotelian unities of time, place, and action, and composes it in blocks: arrival, before the party, the party, and the next day, with the conflicts of the night as a climactic epilogue. The night is an hour of truth for the doubting brother Michael, who now denies his father, beats him up in impotent fury, and refuses to let him see his grandchildren. It is a story and a form which might have called for an almost classical stage performance or been made as a theatrically played-through film the way Fassbinder made some of his best films. But Thomas Vinterberg uses the Dogma hand-held camera rule—and lightweight video equipment—and in his pursuit of his characters learned more from Cassavetes than Fassbinder. Thus the camera pursues the characters beyond the limits of modesty, does not stop when things get painful, but pinpoints and penetrates to the very core of the pain threshold. At the same time it seems omnipresent, capable of capturing the most revealing reactions of the characters and their most secret expressions. Using extremes of motion from room to room it either follows the characters or proceeds in choreographed movements towards or across their moves, thereby generating dynamic rhythm and furious intensity.

Vinterberg, whose graduation in 1993 at the age of twenty-four made him the youngest student to emerge from the National Film School of Denmark, demonstrated in his graduation film a unique talent for the film medium, for moving narrative in moving images, a talent he also demonstrated in his short fiction masterpiece, *Drengen der gik baglæns (The Boy who Walked Backwards)*, about a boy who loses his brother and tries to come to terms with the pain. But in *The Celebration*, his second feature, he shows sharper teeth and a more mature bite in the tradition of realism in which Danish film is so rich.

At the same time the film is broad enough to avoid absolute villains and absolute victims, possessing the energy and humanity to form multifaceted characters, showing if not all, then at least a large number of their facets. Christian, who makes the speech, is not only a victim, but also a stunted, introverted man and cowed son, who tries to flee but then decides to stay and assume his role of embittered avenger, choosing with suicidal stubbornness to maintain his charges until it is no longer possible to reject them as a bad joke. When his dead sister's letter, read by his other sister, proves the ultimate trump card, we glimpse Christian's wan but triumphant smile of revenge. His brother, Michael, who has tried to stop Christian with all his might, and who is portrayed throughout the film as a lout, vicious in his racial prejudice towards his surviving sister's boyfriend—a racial prejudice which he gets the company to sing along to with disturbing ease—ends with the most bitter night of reckoning with his father.

The father, played by one of the most beloved personalities in Danish theatre, starts as the celebrated, successful patriarch, but ends as a rotten, worm-riddled apple nobody wants anything to do with. But his brief, dignified speech in which he acknowledges his guilt and asks for forgiveness allows him to assume some dignity in the moment of defeat. The film is an ensemble performance at the highest level, orchestrated with a virtuosity that means that the day of reckoning between father and son is reflected and faceted by the entire company, many of whom have their own little personal vignettes.

For good reason this film has aroused enthusiasm all over the world. The otherwise ominously well-worn incest theme is given a new lease on life by a film that casts its richly faceted light on a gallery of characters so human that we feel for and suffer with them.

—Dan Nissen

FEU MATHIAS PASCAL

(The Late Matthew Pascal)

France, 1925

Director: Marcel L'Herbier

Production: Cinégraphic Albatross/Films L'Herbier; black and white, 35mm, silent; running time: English version is 192 minutes; length: 4617 feet. Filmed in Paris.

Producer: Alexandre Kamenka; **screenplay:** Marcel L'Herbier, from the novel *Il fu Mattia Pascal* by Luigi Pirandello; **photography:** René Guichard, Jean Letort, Bourgassof, and Berliet; **art directors:** Alberto Cavalcanti and Lazare Meerson.

Cast: Ivan Mosjoukine (*Mathias Pascal*); Marthe Belot (*Maria Pascal, Mathias's mother*); Pauline Carton (*Scolastique Pascal, Mathias's aunt*); Michel Simon (*Jérôme Pomino*); Marcelle Pradot (*Romilde Pescatore*); M. Barsac (*Mariana Dondi Pescatore*); Isaure Douvane (*Batta Maldagna*); Georges Terof (*Gambler*); Lois Moran (*Adrienne Paleari*); Philippe Hériat (*Anselmo Paleari*); Irma Perrot (*Saldia Caporale*); Jean Hervé (*Térence Papiano*); Pierre Batcheff (*Scipion Papiano*).

Publications

Books:

Arroy, Jean, *Ivan Mosjoukine*, Paris, 1927.
Jaque-Catelain présente Marcel L'Herbier, Paris, 1950.
Klaue, Wolfgang, and others, *Cavalcanti*, Berlin, 1952.
Sadoul, Georges, *French Film*, London, 1953.

Feu Mathias Pascal

Armes, Roy, *French Film*, New York, 1970.
Burch, Noël, *Marcel L'Herbier*, Paris, 1973.
Barsacq, Leon, *Caligari's Cabinet and Other Grand Illusions: A History of Film Design*, New York, 1976.
Brossard, Jean-Pierre, editor, *Marcel L'Herbier et son temps*, La-Chaux-de-Fonds, Switzerland, 1980.
Canosa, Michele, *Marcel L'Herbier*, Parma, 1985.

Articles:

Theatre Arts (New York), April 1927.
O'Leary, Liam, "Ivan Mosjoukine," in *Silent Picture* (London), Summer 1969.
Blumer, R. H., "The Camera as Snowball: France 1918–1927," in *Cinema Journal* (Evanston, Illinois), Spring 1970.
Burch, Noël, "Marcel L'Herbier," in *Cinema d'Aujourd'hui* (Paris), 1973.
Ecran (Paris), January 1976.
Monthly Film Bulletin (London), February 1976.
"L'Herbier Issue," of *Avant Scène du Cinéma* (Paris), 1 June 1978.
Fieschi, J., in *Cinématographe* (Paris), December 1979.
Milani, R., "Il cinema di Marcel L'Herbier: le forme evanescenti della realta," in *Filmcritica* (Siena), vol. 37, no. 364, May 1986.
"Marcel L'Herbier," in *Film Dope* (Nottingham), no. 35, September 1986.
Review, in *Variety* (New York), 2 May 1990.

* * *

Marcel L'Herbier's *Feu Mathias Pascal* is a key work of French cinema of the 1920s, valuable both for its intrinsic merits and its representative qualities. It was a period of some uncertainty in the French film industry, but the very lack of any organized studio structure on the lines similar to those which had emerged in Hollywood offered filmmakers a rare degree of freedom. This freedom was exploited to the full by filmmakers such as L'Herbier, Abel Gance and Jean Epstein, all of whom produced highly personal works the experimental and innovative visual style of which continues to astonish even today.

Feu Mathias Pascal was made in conditions that the director has described as completely ideal, produced by his own Cinégraphic company in collaboration with the Société Albatros, founded three years before by the Russian émigré producer, Alexandre Kamenka. The highly talented group around Kamenka had considerable influence on the work of French-born filmmakers, and for this film L'Herbier had the advantage of the collaboration of two of the most gifted of the exiles: his star, the great silent actor Ivan Mosjoukine, and his designer, Lazare Meerson, who had arrived in Paris just one year before and was to have a crucial shaping impact on the development of French cinema over the next dozen years through his work with Clair and Feyder. The choice of subject matter points to the literary origins of filmmakers of this generation. Like Gance and Clair, L'Herbier had envisaged a career as a writer before turning to the cinema under the influence of the American films which began to be widely shown in France after World War I. *Feu Mathias Pascal* was the first work by Luigi Pirandello to be adapted for the screen, and it is clear from later accounts that the author's literary prestige was one of the motivating impulses behind L'Herbier's decision to undertake a production which was never likely to be more than a *succès d'estime*.

In terms of L'Herbier's own artistic development, *Feu Mathias Pascal* is remarkable for its unity and balance. The director was attracted by the challenge of creating a complex narrative structure, and for once the story is not simply a pretext for that play with the whole panoply of visual effects—superimpositions, masking, dream sequences and so on—so beloved of French filmmakers of the period. L'Herbier has not pushed his film towards psychological realism, however; he was evidently fascinated, rather, by the fantastic aspects of his picaresque hero's adventures. Mosjoukine's masterly performance and magnetic personality hold the film together, and the shifts and changes of Mathias's life offer full scope for the actor's virtuoso talents. In other ways—in the mixture of studio work and location shooting and the resultant combination of play with shadows and at times almost documentary-style realism—the film shows characteristic eclecticism of the kind which had reached its extreme point in L'Herbier's previous film, *L'inhumaine*.

The qualities of the story and performance made *Feu Mathias Pascal* one of L'Herbier's most accessible works and gave it its high reputation among traditional historians. Ironically it is precisely these factors that have to some extent worked against the film in current critical evaluations. The pioneering studies by Noël Burch, which have done so much to re-establish the director's status as a major silent film maker, prize L'Herbier's work for the alternative he offers, in a film like *L'argent*, to the dominant codes of Hollywood cinema, while *Feu Mathias Pascal* is in this sense one of the director's more conventional pieces of film narrative.

—Roy Armes

FIÈVRE

France, 1921

Director: Louis Delluc

Production: Société Alhambra-Film; black and white. Released 1921.

Screenplay: Louis Delluc; **photography:** A. Gibory and Lucas; **decor:** Becan.

Cast: Eve Francis (*Sarah*); Edmond Van Daele (*Militis*); Elena Sagrary (*Orientale*); Gaston Modot (*Topinelli*); Foottit (*Man in the Grey Hat*); L. V. de Malte (*The Drunk*); Yvonne Aurel (*The Woman with the Pipe*); A. F. Brunelle (*The Little Clerk*); Solange Rugiens (*Patience*); Barral (*Card-Player*); Gastao Roxo (*Colis*); Lili Samuel (*The Dwarf*); Marcel Delville (*Pompon*); Noemi Scize (*La Rafigue*); Waroquet (*Grimail*); Leon Moussinac (*Cesar*); Bayle (*Piquignon*); Line Chaumont (*Peche verte*); Siska (*Prunelle*); Jeanne Cadix (*Flora*); Vintiane (*Javette*); Bole (*Tonneau*); W. Bouchgard (*Alvar*).

Publications

Script:

Delluc, Louis, *Fièvre*, in *Drames de cinema*, Paris, 1923.

Books:

Delluc, Louis, *La Jungle du cinéma*, Paris, 1921.
Amiguet, Philippe, *Cinéma! Cinéma!*, Lausanne, 1923.
Gance, Abel, *Prisme*, Paris, 1930.
Francis, Eve, *Temps héroïque*, Paris, 1949.
Tariol, Marcel, *Louis Delluc*, Paris, 1965.
Delluc, Louis, *Ecrits cinématographiques*, edited by Pierre Lherminier, Paris, 2 vols., 1985–86.

Articles:

''Delluc Issue'' of *Ciné-Club* (Paris), March 1949.
Bianco e Nero (Rome), no. 8–9, 1953.
Image et Son (Paris), July 1957.
Francis, Eve, and others, in *Lettres Françaises* (Paris), 19 March 1964.
McCreary, E. C., ''Louis Delluc, Film Theorist, Critic, and Prophet,'' in *Cinema Journal* (Evanston, Illinois), Fall 1976.
Régent, R., ''Le Delluc: Un Prix de copains,'' in *Avant-Scene du Cinéma* (Paris), 15 April 1981.
Abel, Richard, ''On the Threshold of French Film Theory and Criticism, 1915–1919,'' in *Cinema Journal* (Austin), vol. 25, no. 1, Fall 1985.
Cahiers de la Cinémathèque (Perpignan), Autumn 1987.
Darrigol, J., ''Un homme lumiere, Louis Delluc,'' in *Mensuel du Cinéma*, no. 14, January 1994.

* * *

It was Thoreau who said that the masses of men lead lives of quiet desperation. It is in the spirit of this pessimistic observation that Delluc assembles his motley collection of the world's misfits in a sleazy Marseilles bar. The original title of the film was *La boue* (The Mire) which didn't please, for some peculiar reason, the French film censor. Indeed, the film itself was subjected to his scissors. Such a film was at the time an innovation and was to inspire a whole new genre in French cinema, typical of which were the films of Marcel Carné.

The action, apart from some shots of the harbour and bar exteriors, takes place within the barroom, giving it a unity and intensity. Its drama occurs within a short space of time. It draws heavily on its atmosphere, and the dramatic structure is spare and economic. The interaction of the characters is subtle and significant. Topinelli, the bar owner, is jealous of his wife Sarah, who is in love with the sailor Militis. There is also the sad introspective little oriental girl who seems to represent the ideal of beauty.

As the film opens we are informed that Sarah's lover, the sailor, has deserted her and she is now married to the brute Topinelli. There is an expectancy among the women. A ship has come into port from the Orient. The sailors arrive at the bar, including Militis, the former lover of Sarah. Exotic presents are displayed. Card playing and dancing are going on. There are rough play and scuffles. Sarah dances with Militis, who has brought with him a little oriental girl whom he bought in the Far East. Drunken tensions mount. Sarah and Militis awaken their former love for each other. A fight takes place between Militis and a customer who is attacking the little girl. In the melee Militis is killed by Topinelli who departs with the sailors leaving Sarah beside the dead body of her lover. The police arrive and arrest her. A tulip in a vase attracts the little girl. The film ends with the girl seated on the ground, the flower between her fingers, smiling with a sad frozen smile.

In the hands of Delluc *Fièvre* is more than a mere slice of life. He moulds his scene and characters to fit into a sustained mood throughout. He evokes their psychological reactions to events and by suitable lighting expresses their personalities.

As Sarah, Delluc's wife Eve Francis gives a beautiful performance, as she always does in the films of her husband and those of Marcel l'Herbier. There is an air of fatality about her which holds the centre of the action. The ubiquitous Gaston Modot as Topinelli is appropriately unsympathetic and brutal. Modot has been almost a trademark of French films from Gance to Buñuel. All the other characters are equally impressive.

It is not a very long film but within its frame Delluc has evoked an intense experience of life illuminated by his poetic vision.

—Liam O'Leary

FILM D'AMORE E D'ANARCHIA

(Film of Love and Anarchy)

Italy, 1973

Director: Lina Wertmüller

Production: Europ International (Italy); Technicolor, 35mm; running time: 108 minutes, some versions are 125 minutes. Released 1973. Filmed in Italy.

Producer: Romano Cardarelli; **screenplay:** Lina Wertmüller; **photography:** Giuseppe Rotunno; **editor:** Franco Fraticelli; **sound:** Mario Bramonti; **production designer:** Enrico Job; **music:** Carlo Savina; **songs:** Nino Rota; **costume designer:** Enrico Job.

Cast: Giancarlo Giannini (*Tunin*); Mariangela Melato (*Salomé*); Lina Polito (*Tripolina*); Eros Pagni (*Spatoletti*); Pina Cei (*Madame Aida*); Elena Fiore (*Donna Carmela*); Isa Bellini; Giuliana Calandra; Isa Danieli; Anna Bonaiuto; Mario Scaccia.

Award: Cannes Film Festival, Best Actor (Giannini), 1973.

Publications

Script:

The Screenplays of Lina Wertmüller, translated by Steven Wagner, New York, 1977.

Books:

Michalczyk, John J., *The Italian Political Filmmakers*, New Jersey, 1986.

Dokumentation: Lina Wertmüller/Martin Scorsese, edited by Filmstelle Vseth/Vsu, Zurich, 1986.

Jacobsen, Wolfgang, and others, *Lina Wertmüller*, Munich, 1988.

Articles:

Delmas, J., in *Jeune Cinéma* (Paris), July-August 1973.

Rubinstein, L., in *Cineaste* (New York), no. 3, 1974.

Erens, Patricia, "*Love and Anarchy*: Passion and Pity," in *Jump Cut* (Chicago), July-August 1974.

Van Wert, W., "Love, Anarchy, and the Whole Damned Thing," in *Jump Cut* (Chicago), November-December 1974.

Gorbman, C., in *Movietone News* (Seattle), April 1975.

Jacobs, Diane, "Lina Wertmüller," in *International Film Guide* (London), 1977.

Sternborn, B., in *Filmfaust* (Frankfurt), April-May 1985.

* * *

Film d'amore e d'anarchia is Lina Wertmüller's fourth feature and the first work to bring her critical attention in the United States. The film reveals the influence of Federico Fellini for whom Wertmüller worked as an assistant director on *8½*, and it incorporates most of the elements that were to become trademarks of the Wertmüller canon. From Fellini she inherited a tendency towards comic exaggeration, both in creating types and in producing broad performances. Typical to her own concerns are the thematic interest in sexual politics, frequently set against a political backdrop; commanding heroines, and flawed, vulnerable heroes.

D'amore e d'anarchia is framed by two scenes: the first depicts the childhood trauma of the peasant Tunin (Giancarlo Giannini). When Tunin's father, a rural anarchist, is shot by the police, the young boy assumes his father's mission to assassinate Mussolini. The

Film d'amore e d'anarchia

second framing scene is his death in a Roman prison some decades later. The remainder of the film takes place in a Roman bordello where the adult Tunin meets Salomé (Mariangela Melato), an anarchist sympathizer, and Tripolino (Lina Polito), a young prostitute.

As protector and lover, Salomé provides Tunin with information that she extracts from a self-important client, Spatoletti, the head of Mussolini's secret police. Yet, gradually, Tunin falls in love with Tripolino. The climax of the film takes place on the day appointed for Mussolini's assassination. Tripolino hides the key to Tunin's bedroom; she hopes that by allowing him to oversleep, she will prevent both the deed and the punishment. She and Salomé fight over the "key" to Tunin's fate: a struggle between love and anarchy. Finally Tripolino succeeds in convincing Salomé that she should opt for personal happiness. But that is not to be; once Tunin discovers their collusion, he goes berserk, shooting widely at some policemen who have come to check the prostitute for venereal disease. The film ends with Tunin's execution, as the police repeatedly strike Tunin's head against the stone walls of his cell.

D'amore e d'anarchia is part of that outpouring of Italian films, released between 1969 and 1972, that examines the relations of individuals and institutions of authority, particularly during the Fascist period. Included in this group are Bertolucci's *Il conformista* and *Strategia del ragno*, Bellocchio's *Nel nome del padre*, and Visconti's *La caduta degli dei*. In contrast to her compatriots or the Greek Costa-Gavras (*Z* and *The Confession*, also released at this time), Wertmüller provides only minimal insight into the workings of political tyranny. Further, it is difficult to decipher her position from the evidence of the film. At the film's conclusion, a quotation from the 19th-century anarchist Malatesta cautions against assassination as a political expedient; it refers to assassins as saints as well as heroes. Yet the one clear message of the film remains the certain failure of political naiveté and the ineffectuality of individual action.

The film's most original moments are three lyrical interludes which crystalize mood rather than further plot; they demonstrate Wertmüller's ability to expose humor in the midst of dark circumstances. The interludes include a break-neck motorcycle ride through the Italian countryside; a series of seduction scenes as the prostitutes begin their day's business; and a filmic and poetic chronicle of a holiday that Tunin and Tripolino take before the final tragedy.

D'amore e d'anarchia is most memorable for its spirited performances; the lusty Salomé, the freckled and wide-eyed Tunin, the angelic Tripolino, and the bombastic Spatoletti. In addition, Giuseppe

Rotunno's fluid camerawork, Nino Rota's music, and Wertmüller's exuberant scenario combine to create an overall impression of a fine Italian opera.

—Patricia Erens

FILM-TRUTH

See **KINO-PRAVDA**

IL FIORE DELLE MILLE E UNA NOTTE

(Arabian Nights)

Italy-France, 1974

Director: Pier Paolo Pasolini

Production: PEA (Rome), Les Productions Artistes Associés (Paris); Technicolor; running time: 155 minutes. (GB version: 128 minutes.)

Producer: Alberto Grimaldi; **screenplay:** Pier Paolo Pasolini; **photography:** Giuseppe Ruzzolini; **editor:** Enzo Ocone, Nino Baragli, Tatiana Casini Morigi; **assistant directors:** Umberto Angelucci, Peter Sheperd; **art director:** Dante Ferretti; **music:** Ennio Moriccone; **sound:** Luciano Welisch; **costumes:** Danilo Donati.

Cast: Ninetto Davoli (*Aziz*); Ines Pellegrini (*Zumurrud*); Franco Citti (*Demon*); Tessa Bouche; Margaret Clementi; Franco Merli; Francesila Noel; Ali Abdulla; Christian Alegni.

Publications

Books:

Bertini, Antonio, *Teoria e tecnica del film in Pasolini*, Rome, 1979.
Snyder, Stephen, *Pier Paolo Pasolini*, Boston, 1980.
Bergala, Alain, and Jean Narboni, editors, *Pasolini Cinéaste*, Paris, 1981.
Gerard, Fabien S., *Da Accattone a Salo: 120 scritti sul cinema di Pier Paolo Pasolini*, Bologna, 1982.
Siciliano, Enzo, *Pasolini: A Biography*, New York, 1982.
DeGiusti, Luciano, *I film di Pier Paolo Pasolini*, Rome, 1983.
Greene, Naomi, *Pier Paolo Pasolini: Cinema as Heresy*, Princeton, New Jersey, 1990.
Schwartz, Barth D., *Pasolini Requiem*, New York, 1995.
Gordon, Robert S., *Pasolini: Forms of Subjectivity*, New York, 1996.
Rohdie, Sam, *The Passion of Pier Paolo Pasolini*, Bloomington, 1996.
Rumble, Patrick Allen, *Allegories of Contamination: Pier Paolo Pasolini's Trilogy of Life*, Toronto, 1996.
Baranski, Zymunt G., editor, *Pasolini: Old & New: Surveys & Studies*, Dublin, 1999.

Articles:

Bachmann, G., ''Pasolini in Persia: The Shooting of 1001 Nights'' in *Film Quarterly* (Berkeley), Winter 1973–74.
Variety (New York), 29 May 1974.
Delmas, G., *Jeune Cinéma* (Paris), July-August 1974.
Amiel, M., *Cinéma* (Paris), September-October 1974.
Allombert, G., *Image et Son* (Paris), September-October 1974.
Martin, M., *Ecran* (Paris), October 1974.
Rayns, T., *Monthly Film Bulletin* (London), April 1975.
Tellez, J. L., ''La voluntad de narrar,'' in *Contracampo*, no. 15, September 1980.
Beaulieu, J., ''Arabian Nights,'' in *Séquences* (Haute-Ville), no. 106, October 1981.
Loshitzky, Y., ''The Tourist/Traveler Gaze: Bertolucci and Bowles's 'The Sheltering Sky','' in *East-West* (Honolulu), no. 2, 1993.
Taviani, P., and V. Taviani, ''Souvenir de Pasolini,'' in *Positif* (Paris), no. 400, June 1994.
''La 'Trilogia della vita': 'Il Decameron,' 'I racconti di Canterbury,' 'Il fiore delle mille e una notte','' in *Castoro Cinema* (Milan), no. 166, July-August 1994.
Rohdie, S., ''Pasolini's Third World,'' in *Metro Magazine* (St. Kilda West), no. 107, 1996.

* * *

Pasolini was one of the most idiosyncratic of all filmmakers, the strangeness and difficulty of his work arising from his commitment to contradiction: *Arabian Nights* (the crowning achievement of the trilogy begun with *The Decameron* and continued with *The Canterbury Tales*) opens with the quotation ''The complete truth lies not in one dream but in several.'' The basis of this commitment was his refusal to abandon any of the diverse and partly irreconcilable influences that determined the nature of his art: Catholicism, Marxism, homosexuality, the urban slums (settings of his early novels), the peasantry (he wrote poetry in the Friulan dialect), neo-realism, an attachment to the fantastic and miraculous. While *Arabian Nights* seems as far removed as one can imagine from the subject-matter one associates with neo-realism (the attempt to capture both the external and internal realities of the contemporary moment), it remains remarkably faithful to the neo-realist aesthetic: the use of non-professionals, location shooting, spontaneity valued above polish or deliberation. The corollary of this is that when artifice is demanded by the subject-matter (the flight of the genie, Nureddin's encounter with the lion in the desert), the special effects are always patently visible, as primitive and naive as possible (cf. Jesus walking on the water in *The Gospel According to St. Matthew*).

It is the commitment to dramatizing (rather than attempting to reconcile or eradicate) contradiction that led Pasolini toward the experimentations with narrative that characterize his best work (*Teorema, Medea, Salo*). Nowhere is this more evident than in *Arabian Nights*, where the intricate interlocking of diverse tales seems motivated by the desire to juxtapose the several dreams that (taken in conjunction) might, if they cannot reveal, at least point toward, the complete truth.

Using the story of Nureddin and Zumurrud as a unifying thread, Pasolini contains six other stories (organized in two groups of three) within a five-part structure as follows:

Number one: Zumurrud (the ''slave'' who is allowed to choose her new ''master'') chooses the young boy Nureddin because (a) he has beautiful eyes, (b) she senses his sexual energy, (c) he is not at all an authority figure, and (d) with him she can fully express, on equal terms, *her* sexuality.

Number two: The first trio of tales (read to Nureddin by Zumurrud): the beautiful woman seen bathing (scarcely even an anecdote); the three young men chosen by the older man to enjoy mutual pleasure; the wager between the elder couple about the relative strength of sexual attraction between a young man and a young woman.

Number three: Development of the Nureddin/Zumurrud story (Zumurrud drugged and kidnapped, subsequently mistaken for a man and made king of a city; Nureddin's frantic search for her, and first two ''diversions'' with other women).

Number four: The second trio of tales: the princess's dream; the story of Aziz and the mad Badur; the story of the two artisans. Unlike the first trio, these (a) are fully developed tales with a beginning, a middle and a resolution, (b) involve the fantastic and the supernatural, and (c) are not consecutive but intertwined: we reach a point where we are watching a story within a story within a story, from which Chinese box Pasolini works his way out to return us to. . . .

Number five: The conclusion of the Nureddin/Zumurrud story.

Each trio of stories has its own internal themes. The first three (brief anecdotes) are concerned with free sexuality and equalization: the wager of the third (and most developed) ends in a tie, the demonstration that female desire and male desire are equally potent. The interwoven tales of the second trio are all concerned with notions of Fate: two stories in which fate is shown to be inescapable are enclosed within a story in which fate is overcome. Further, the story of Aziz, Aziza and Badur stands in contradiction to the framework story of Nureddin and Zumurrud. They are linked by the dictum (itself a contradiction) that ''fidelity is beautiful, but no more than infidelity.'' In the Aziz tale the conflict leads to death and castration, but in the framework story fidelity and infidelity are reconciled: Nureddin, in his search for his beloved, can be led into countless delightful sexual diversions, but his fidelity to Zumurrud is always triumphant over them, and finally rewarded in a happy ending that plays on (in order to repudiate) sexual power-relations.

The acknowledgement and celebration of diversity is an aspect of one of the central drives of Pasolini's work: the effort to rediscover a sense of the wonderful, the magical. In *Teorema*, the sense of wonder has been destroyed by the bourgeoisie and can be regained (very problematically) only through the liberation of sexuality; in *Medea*, the magical world of the opening is eroded by the growth of patriarchy and capitalism, until ''Nothing is possible any more.'' Of all Pasolini's films, *Arabian Nights* comes closest to realizing the sense of wonder, through an eroticism purged of all contamination by the pornographic.

—Robin Wood

FIRES WERE STARTED

(I Was a Fireman)

UK, 1943

Director: Humphrey Jennings

Production: Crown Film Unit, with the co-operation of the Home Office, Ministry of Home Security, and National Fire Service; black and white, 35mm; running time: 63 minutes, some sources state 60 minutes. Released 1943. Filmed in London.

Producer: Ian Dalrymple; **screenplay:** Humphrey Jennings; **photography:** C. Pennington-Richards; **editor:** Stewart McAllister; **sound recordists:** Ken Cameron and Jock May; **production designer:** Edward Carrick; **music:** William Alwyn; **musical direction:** Muir Mathieson.

Cast: Officer George Gravett (*Sub-Officer Dykes*); Lt. Fireman Philip Dickson (*Fireman Walters*); Lt. Fireman Fred Griffiths (*Johnny Daniels*); Lt. Fireman Loris Rey (*J. Rumbold*); Fireman Johnny Houghton (*S. H. Jackson*); Fireman T. P. Smith (*B. A. Brown*); Fireman John Barker (*J. Vallance*); Fireman W. Sansom (*Barrett*); Asst. Group Officer Green (*Mrs Townsend*); Firewoman Betty Martin (*Betty*); Firewoman Eileen White (*Eileen*).

Publications

Books:

Grierson, John, *Humphrey Jennings: A Tribute*, London, 1951.

Hardy, Forsyth, *Grierson on Documentary*, revised edition, London, 1966.

Lovell, Alan, and Jim Hillier, *Studies in Documentary*, New York, 1972.

Barsam, Richard, *Nonfiction Film: A Critical History*, New York, 1973.

Barnouw, Erik, *Documentary: A History of the Non-Fiction Film*, New York, 1974.

Sussex, Elizabeth, *The Rise and Fall of British Documentary: The Story of the Film Movement Founded by John Grierson*, Berkeley, 1975.

Hodkinson, Anthony, and Rodney Sheratsky, *Humphrey Jennings: More Than a Maker of Films*, Hanover, 1982.

Jennings, Mary-Lou, editor, *Humphrey Jennings: Film-Maker/Painter/Poet*, London, 1982.

Fires Were Started

Vaughan, Dai, *Portrait of an Invisible Man: The Working Life of Stewart McAllister, Film Editor*, London, 1983.

Aldgate, Anthony, and Jeffrey Richards, *Britain Can Take It: The British Cinema in the Second World War*, Oxford, 1986.

Ellis, Jack C., *The Documentary Idea*, Englewood Cliffs, 1989.

Jennings, Humphrey, *The Humphrey Jennings Film Reader*, New York, 1995.

Articles:

Wright, Basil, ''Humphrey Jennings,'' in *Sight and Sound* (London), December 1950.

Lambert, Gavin, ''Jennings' Britain,'' in *Sight and Sound* (London), May 1951.

Vedres, Nicole, ''Humphrey Jennings—A Memoir,'' in *Sight and Sound* (London), May 1951.

Mekas, Jonas, ''Index to the Creative Work of Humphrey Jennings,'' in *Film Forum* (Mesdetten), 8 July 1954.

Dand, Charles, ''Britain's Screen Poet,'' in *Films in Review* (New York), February 1955.

Strick, Philip, in *Films and Filming* (London), May 1961.

''Jennings Issue,'' of *Film Quarterly* (London), Winter 1961–62.

Millar, Gavin, in *Sight and Sound* (London), Spring 1969.

Belmans, Jacques, ''Humphrey Jennings, 1907–1950,'' in *Anthologie du Cinéma 6*, Paris, 1971.

Bitomsky, H., ''Uber Humphrey Jennings und einige seiner Filme,'' in *Filmkritik* (Munich), November 1975.

Sharatsky, R. E., ''Humphrey Jennings: Artist of the British Documentary,'' in *Film Library Quarterly* (New York), vol. 8, no. 3–4, 1975.

Anderson, Lindsay, ''Only Connect: Some Aspects of the Work of Humphrey Jennings,'' in *Non-Fiction Film Theory and Criticism*, edited by Richard Barsam, New York, 1976.

Barrot, O., in *Cinéma d'Aujourd'hui* (Paris), February-March 1977.

Colls, R., and P. Dodd, ''Representing the Nation: British Documentary Film 1930–45,'' in *Screen* (London), January-February 1985.

Nowell-Smith, Geoffrey, ''Humphrey Jennings: Surrealist Observer,'' in *All Our Yesterdays*, edited by Charles Barr, London, 1986.

Britton, A., ''Their Finest Hour: Humphrey Jennings and the British Imperial Myth of World War II,'' in *CineAction* (Toronto), Fall 1989.

Stewart, S., and Lester D. Friedman, ''An Interview with Lindsay Anderson,'' in *Film Criticism* (Meadville), vol. 16, no. 1–2, Fall-Winter 1991–92.
Thomson, D., ''A Sight for Sore Eyes,'' in *Film Comment* (New York), no. 29, March/April 1993.
Williams, D., ''Humphrey Jennings: a Sense of Conciousness,'' in *Metro Magazine* (St. Kilda West), no. 103, 1995.

* * *

Fires Were Started was one of the semi-documentary features produced in Britain during World War II by both the government Crown Film Unit and the commercial studios following the success of such prototypes as *Target for Tonight* (1941) and *In Which We Serve* (1942). This film combined the actuality of documentary (a recreated or composite and representative event portrayed by people who had actually been involved in such an event) with the narrative line and dramatic heighting of fiction.

Fires Were Started is about the work of the Auxiliary Fire Service during the dreadful German fire-bomb raids on London. It follows a new recruit through a 24-hour shift with one unit. During the day the men train and perform menial chores. Following dinner they briefly relax and their camaraderie and understated humor become fully evident. As the raid begins, they proceed to their perilous and exhausting work, on this occasion putting out a fire raging near a munitions ship docked along the Thames. Though one of their number falls from a burning building to his death, the fire is finally extinguished. The film ends with the burial of the dead fireman intercut with the munitions ship moving out to sea.

As was usual with the British wartime films, the emphasis is given to the togetherness of the British people (with the cast a cross-section of classes). The propaganda function of this particular film seems to have been to show the quality and courage of the brave men and women who were working to insure that Britain would withstand the enemy assault. The enemy remains offscreen, and none of the hatred is portrayed which might have seemed an appropriate response to the bombing; instead, the destruction is treated almost as if it were a natural disaster.

By using the device of the new recruit, Jennings can let us see and learn not only about the functioning of this fire-fighting service but also about the diverse and likable personalities it brings together. When the raid begins, we are able to follow, without aid of commentary, the tactics of the fire-fighters through their actions and conversations; the phone calls from headquarters; the maps with pins stuck in them; the chalked lists of equipment. Among other things, *Fires Were Started* is a model of teaching without didacticism.

But where its true greatness lies is in the way it simultaneously informs, persuades, and moves us. In this film Jennings goes beyond other of the semi-documentaries in differentiating and developing the characters of his non-actor firemen. Besides being very skillful at narrative, Jennings was a visual-aural poet who captured the precise image for a feeling, which also contained symbolic reverberations of English tradition and wartime exigencies—a poet who offered the exact words men might have spoken and even the songs they might have sung in the circumstances. The mood of this film may have well matched the mood of its wartime audience. It has lasted as a supplement to the national memory of what wartime England felt like.

—Jack C. Ellis

FIREWORKS

See **HANA-BI**

THE FIRST CHARGE OF THE MACHETE

See **LA PRIMERA CARGA AL MACHETE**

FISTS IN THE POCKET

See **I PUGNI IN TASCA**

FIVE EASY PIECES

USA, 1970

Director: Bob Rafelson

Production: B.B.S.; Technicolor; running time: 98 minutes; length: 8,828 feet. Released September 1970.

Executive producer: Bert Schneider; **producers:** Bob Rafelson, Richard Wechsler; **screenplay:** Adrien Joyce, from a story by Joyce, and Bob Rafelson; **assistant director:** Sheldon Schrager; **photography:** Laszlo Kovaks; **editors:** Christopher Holmes, Gerald Sheppard; **sound recordist:** Charles Knight; **art director:** Toby Rafelson.

Cast: Jack Nicholson (*Robert Eroica Dupea*); Karen Black (*Rayette Dipesto*); Lois Smith (*Partita Dupea*); Susan Anspach (*Catherine Van Ost*); Billy ''Green'' Bush (*Elton*); Fannie Flagg (*Stoney*); Ralph Waite (*Carl Fidelio Dupea*); Helena Kallianiotes (*Palm Apodaca*); Toni Basil (*Terry Grouse*); Sally Ann Struthers (*Betty*); Marlena Macguire (*Twinky*); John Ryan (*Spicer*); Irene Dailey (*Samia Glavia*); Lorna Thayer (*Waitress*); Richard Stahl (*Recording Engineer*); William Challee (*Nicholas Dupea*).

Publications

Books:

Crane, Robert David, and Christopher Fryer, *Jack Nicholson—Face to Face*, New York, 1975.
Braithwaite, Bruce, *The Films of Jack Nicholson*, Farncombe, 1977.
Downing, David, *Jack Nicholson*, London, 1983; New York, 1984.
Boyer, Jay, *Bob Rafelson: Film Director*, Bristol, 1996.

Articles:

Variety (New York), 16 September 1970.
Motion Picture Herald (New York), 23 September 1970.
Film Heritage (Dayton, Ohio), Winter 1970–71.
Mundy, Robert, in *Cinema* (Beverly Hills), Spring 1971.
Pirie, David, in *Monthly Film Bulletin* (London), April 1971.
Snoding, Clifton, in *Films and Filming* (London), May 1971.

Five Easy Pieces

Martin, Marcel, in *Cinéma* (Paris), June 1971.

Farber, Stephen, in *Sight and Sound* (London), Summer 1971.

Campbell, Gregg M., ''Beethoven, Chopin, and Tammy Wynette: Heroines and Archetypes in *Five Easy Pieces*,'' in *Literature/Film Quarterly* (Salisbury), Summer 1974.

Cohen, Mitchell, ''The Corporate Style of BBS: Seven Intricate Pieces,'' in *Take One* (Montreal), Winter 1974–75.

Thousand Eyes Magazine, June 1976.

Carcassone, P., ''Bob Rafelson,'' in *Cinématographe* (Paris), November 1979.

Combs, Richard, and John Pym, ''Prodigal's Progress: An Interview with Bob Rafelson,'' in *Sight and Sound* (London), Autumn 1981.

King, Norman, ''Mersault Goes West: *Five Easy Pieces* and Art Cinema,'' in *Framework* (Norwich), no. 20, 1983.

Grimes, Teresa, ''BBS: Auspicious Beginnings, Open Endings,'' in *Movie* (London), Winter 1986.

Combs, Richard, in *Listener* (London), 1 October 1987.

Mongin, O., ''Le crepuscule des emotions,'' in *Esprit*, no. 10, October 1989.

Seven, M., ''Letters: Toast the Screenwriter, Not the Actor,'' in *New York Times*, 20 October 1989.

Norman, Barry, in *Radio Times* (London), 17 September 1994.

Premiere (Boulder), no. 9, November 1995.

Laderman, D., ''What a Trip: The Road Film and American Culture,'' in *Journal of Film and Video*, no. 1/2, 1996.

Floyd, Nigel, ''Blood Brothers,'' in *Time Out* (London), no. 1385, 5 March 1997.

* * *

In many ways *Five Easy Pieces* marks the end of the 1960s, a decade captured best in *Easy Rider*, another film in which Jack Nicholson appeared. The youthful drugged dropouts of the earlier film are succeeded in *Five Easy Pieces* by an older dropout, one who has abandoned the world of classical music to find himself in the southern California oil fields. Bobby Dupea's new, assumed identity, evidence that he is not ''really'' an oil rigger, consists of a phoney southern accent and Rayette (Karen Black), a ''country woman'' he has impregnated. Fleeing again from responsibility, Bobby journeys to Los Angeles—his travels mirror his psychological journey—and learns from his concert-pianist sister that their father has suffered a stroke and is incapacitated at the family home in Washington. When

Bobby and Rayette, whom he cannot escape, return to his home, the trip is literal and symbolic, for here he must confront his past.

The ''homecoming'' is a disaster, for his past is his present: Carl Fidelio Dupea, his brother, is an uptight classical musician; his invalid father is still an autocrat; and his sister subscribes unthinkingly to the family's bourgeois cultural values. In effect, the family remains the society Bobby has rejected. Attracted to his brother's fiancée, Catherine Van Ost (Susan Anspach), Bobby seduces her, partly through his accomplished playing of a Chopin prelude. Catherine, however, will not leave with him when he again flees from his past, and after he successfully evades Rayette, a solitary Bobby continues his self-destructive northward journey.

Because of Nicholson's charisma, audiences overlooked Bobby's entertaining but indulgent tantrums and his ranting invectives against rigidity and conformity (behaviors Nicholson is particularly adept at portraying). The most memorable scene from the film is Bobby's manic verbal attack on the waitress, a scene at once amusing and cruel. Audiences identify and empathize with the male protagonist, who expresses the anger they share and who does not alienate them because his irresponsibility and selfishness (later expressed by Nicholson in *One Flew over the Cuckoo's Nest*) is so engagingly expressed. Bobby's treatment of Rayette is similarly ignored by an audience which regards country culture and country folk with amused contempt; the cultivated, talented pianist is simply too good for the likes of Rayette.

Fortunately, the film also provides another reading, one which questions easy assumptions about the male chauvinism of the film. The title *Five Easy Pieces* refers to a book of music which piano students must master before going on to more complex compositions, and it also suggests, through the Chopin seduction linking music and sex, Bobby's sexual conquests. If he must similarly know himself before he can confront life, then Bobby is only an accomplished pianist and womanizer, not a master of his life in pursuit of the truth. He is a drifter whose northern journey, without the coat he has given away, will culminate in death.

Five Easy Pieces concerns cultural clashes, which are reflected in the classical music associated with the Dupeas, which Bobby has mastered, and the country sound track sung by Tammy Wynette (as in Rayette), but Adrien Joyce's screenplay (based on a story she and director Rafelson wrote) does not insist on the superiority of either class. There are real people who do know themselves and conduct themselves with dignity in both classes: Bobby's friend Elton, Rayette and Catherine. Like Bobby, Catherine recognizes hypocrisy and corruption; unlike Bobby, she realizes that she cannot save herself through sex, flight, or power. She will remain true to her values and her work, rather than retreat through alienation and nihilism.

Five Easy Pieces has been compared to Truffaut's *Shoot the Piano Player*, for both concern dropouts from the world of classical music; but unlike Bobby, who plays on a moving van in a traffic jam or as a foreplay to sex, Charlie Kohler continues to play the piano. Robert Eroica Dupea (the *Eroica* is the Beethoven work dedicated to Napoleon, whose promise also lapsed into ego) becomes another contemporary American male protagonist whose life is characterized by lack of identity, impotence, and despair. When he resumes his journey at the end of the film, Bobby resembles Huck Finn ''lighting out for the territory,'' but Bobby is hardly an uneducated adolescent. Though he behaves like Huck, who comes to know himself, Bobby is an adult whose actions spring from frustrations, cruelty, and despair—he is a charming but destructive loser.

—Thomas L. Erskine

FLAMING CREATURES

USA, 1963

Director: Jack Smith

Production: Distributed by Film-Makers Cooperative; black and white, 16mm; running time: 45 minutes. Released 7 December, 1963, New York City. Filmed on a rooftop in New York City.

Screenplay: Jack Smith; **photography:** Jack Smith.

Cast: Francis Francine, Delores Flores (a.k.a. Mario Montez), Joel Markman, Shirley.

Publications

Books:

Tyler, Parker, *Underground Film: A Critical History*, New York, 1969.

Suarez, Juan Antonio, *Bike Boys, Drag Queens, Superstars: Avant-Garde, Mass Culture, and Gay Identities in the 1960s Underground Cinema*, Bloomington, 1996.

Leffingwell, Edward, Carole Kismaric, and Marvin Heiferman, editors, *Jack Smith, Flaming Creature: His Amazing Life and Times*, New York, 1997.

Articles:

''Avant-garde Movie Seized as Obscene,'' in *New York Times*, 4 March 1964.

Levy, Alan, ''Voices of the Underground Cinema,'' in *New York Times*, 19 September 1965.

Lester, Elenore, ''Mr. Godard, Fire That Cameraman!,'' in *New York Times*, 29 January 1967.

Regelson, Rosalyn, ''Where Are 'The Chelsea Girls' Taking Us?'' in *New York Times*, 24 September 1967.

Hoberman, J., ''Treasures of the Mummy's Tomb,'' in *Film Comment* (New York), vol. 33, November-December 1997.

Jerome, Judith, ''Creating a World Waiting to Be Created: Karen Finley and Jack Smith,'' in *Women & Performance* (New York), no. 1–2, 1999.

* * *

Though it was produced in the early 1960s, *Flaming Creatures*—a seminal work of the American underground cinema movement of the mid-twentieth century—is a cinematic poem born of an earlier beat generation. In the 1950s, this generation of poets—unfairly enshrined *en masse* in popular memory garbed in stereotypical black turtleneck shirts and mohair sweaters—shunned the plasticized, sterilized, march-in-step order of the decade in favor of a more shaggy, offbeat lifestyle. In keeping with the beat aesthetic, the technical values of *Flaming Creatures* are more primitive than they need have been, the camera movements purposefully herky-jerky. Actors appear in costumes and trinkets gathered from the finery of their home closets or perhaps from a Washington Square or East Village five-and-dime store. As a result, *Flaming Creatures* comes off as a homemade concoction—certainly not from the kitchen of Betty Crocker, but from the New York Greenwich Village rooftop where filmmaker Jack Smith and his friends converged to produce the film.

For decades, *Flaming Creatures* has rarely been seen and, for this reason, it has frequently been misinterpreted, misunderstood, and analyzed in generalities. Thus it is worthwhile to examine its content in greater detail. As the film unfolds, the viewer sees the faces of women from a harem and learns that Ali Baba "comes today." Then the small, handwritten credits become visible. Already difficult to read, the credits are further obscured by characters—a masked, helmeted man and a woman who sticks out her tongue—who walk left-to-right and right-to-left in front of the information. Then, with the effect of a needle hitting a phonograph turntable, the sounds of an old-fashioned, operatic rendition of "Amapola-Pretty Little Poppy" commence. A vamping woman and a drag queen wiggle, wave, and converse near a large vase of flowers. This pair and others, including more drag queens, put on lipstick to the soundtrack for a lipstick commercial. The group lies about, intermingling, and the camera wanders about the intertwined bodies at odd angles. As the soundtrack announces that this indelible lipstick does not come off "when you suck cocks," viewers see a close-up of a penis at the face of a man wearing a large false nose. Soon we hear animal noises, as if from an out-of-control kennel.

Is this a languid recovery from a sex orgy, or a drugged-out group who simply are enjoying slow-paced genital contact? Just as thoughts begin to arise of illicit lillied pipes in Limehouse opium dens, a lively, campy oriental-style song starts to play, and the action accelerates in pace. People in the group run left-to-right, right-to-left across the screen. A drag queen wrestles down a woman, who is then ravaged by several people as she screams. The camera moves to a close-up of her large, round, jiggling breast, as she gyrates and screeches. This rape sequence, to which the film returns, is a disturbing, cruel segment that seems out of place amid the otherwise offbeat but mellow exoticism.

The action continues, with cutaways to a swaying ceiling lamp, a flash of lightning and, again, the vase of flowers. The group members have their orgy, including kissing and organ caressing and stimulation, and the camera shakes wildly as it explores the scene. The orgy continues amidst shrieks and wild animal sounds. Only the ravaged woman, her single breast still hanging exposed from her dress, appears to be touched against her will. She is standing, and is dragged to a spot by a blonde woman, who peacefully caresses her. The orgy continues, and is recorded in pieces—arms, legs, faces—by the lens of the curious camera. Flower petals fall on the ravaged woman, while veils blow in front of the vase of flowers.

In the next section, a fly has landed on a piece of cloth. The top of a wooden coffin opens, and the music changes again. The soundtrack changes to the nasal strains of a country-western song, the lyrics of which declare "It Wasn't God Who Made Honky Tonk Angels," as a blonde, high-heeled drag queen arises from the coffin. She is a vampire; first she begins sucking blood from the neck of another drag queen, and then she masturbates. This sequence is chronicled in side shots, close-ups, and overhead shots. The two drag queens dance to a slow, torrid, campy South American-style song. At first, a new group of people watches them. They include a Spanish dancer with a rose between her teeth, a sailor, a drag queen carrying a lily, an African-American drag queen, and the muscular masked man in a loin cloth who was first seen in front of the credits. They all begin dancing; as they swirl about, the camera remains close, alternating frontal shots with overhead positions.

Once more the camera notices the ravaged woman with her single exposed breast. She lies on the floor, and a disengaged finger touches near her nipple. The following shots show her and her partner, and others of the group who lie near them as if in a tableau. The camera explores the group through intimate shots, including a series of close-ups of faces and a kiss between two drag queens. The cool, deliberate beat of "Bebop a Lula, She's My Baby" begins as the camera shows more close-up detail of the scene. "The End" finally appears on a piece of cloth, followed by one last glimpse of the jiggling, exposed breast of the ravaged woman.

The individuals who appear in *Flaming Creatures* constitute a sexual subculture—and, surely, back in the 1950s and early 1960s, their antics never would have been depicted on *The Dinah Shore Chevy Show* or *The Many Loves of Dobie Gillis*! Indeed, whenever a "beat" character would appear in mainstream entertainment—Maynard G. Krebs, the beatnik pal of Dobie Gillis, is a perfect case in point—that character would be stereotyped and lampooned. Beat generation types were also demonized. In countless "B" teen pot-boilers, the villain—the character who attempts to seduce the virginal heroine, or turn her on to drugs—was the goateed hipster. Yet even the most broadly cliched subculture type depicted in mainstream popular culture is orthodox when compared to the eccentric personalities portrayed in *Flaming Creatures*. Drag characters and spoofs would not be accepted by mainstream audiences for decades, until the popularity of *Tootsie* and *The Crying Game* and the eventual, above-ground fame of Divine and RuPaul. And to this day, the explicit views and fondling of genitalia in *Flaming Creatures* would label it in many quarters as a homosexual stag film.

However, the film cannot be written off as low-budget sexploitation. What seems so ragged and homespun in *Flaming Creatures*—resulting from Jack Smith's use of hand-held camera, primitive lighting, and awkward, untrained actors—is a triumph of beat art structure and content. Unsurprisingly, the film was the subject of much legal controversy. In December 1963, it was banned from the Experimental Film Festival in Belgium. The following March, filmmaker/journalist/underground film distributor Jonas Mekas and three others were arrested and, according to a report in the *New York Times*, "charged with showing an obscene motion picture" at the New Bowery Theater on Manhattan's Lower East Side. The film in question was *Flaming Creatures*. "The police seized reels of film, a projection machine and a portable screen," continued the report.

Within the underground artist communities throughout the United States, *Flaming Creatures* was considered a bold visual-poetic record of a subculture that most of America wanted to keep hidden. Smith's film gained a reputation among underground artists, including Andy Warhol, who was influenced by Smith to make films in a similar crude style. Both artists played with the mix of eccentric characters and symbols of the drag queen culture with popular culture icons to create the fundamental language of an alternative cinema.

—Audrey E. Kupferberg

FOOLISH WIVES

USA, 1922

Director: Erich von Stroheim

Production: Universal Super Jewel; black and white; originally shot in 35mm, original length: 14,210 feet; released in a version of 2,765 feet (at 24 f.p.s), running time: 77 minutes.

Producer: Carl Laemmle; **screenplay:** Erich von Stroheim; **titles:** Erich von Stroheim, Marian Ainslee; **assistant directors:** Edward Sowders, Jack R. Proctor, Louis Germonprez; **special assistant to von Stroheim:** Gustav Machaty; **photography:** Ben Reynolds, William Daniels; **illumination and lighting effects:** Harry J. Brown; **editor:** Erich von Stroheim; **editor for release version:** Arthur D. Ripley; **art directors:** E. E. Sheeley, Richard Day; **scenic artist:** Van Alstein; **technical directors:** William Meyers, James Sullivan, George Williams; **music:** Sigmund Romberg.

Cast: Rudolph Christians/Robert Edenson (*Andrew J. Hughes*); Miss Du Pont/Patsy Hannen (*Helen Hughes*); Maude George (*''Princess'' Olga Petschnikoff*); Mae Busch (*''Princess'' Vera Petschnikoff*); Erich von Stroheim (*''Count'' Sergius Karamzin*); Dale Fuller (*Maruschka*); Al Edmundsen (*Pavel Pavlich, the Butler*); Cesare Gravina (*Signor Gaston*); Malvina Polo (*Marietta, Gaston's Daughter*); Louis K. Webb (*Dr. Judd*); Mrs. Kent (*Mrs. Judd*); C. J. Allen (*Albert I, Prince of Monaco*); Edward Reinach (*Secretary of State of Monaco*).

Publications

Books:

Fronval, Georges, *Erich von Stroheim: Sa vie, ses films*, Paris, 1939.
Noble, Peter, *Hollywood Scapegoat: The Biography of Erich von Stroheim*, London, 1951.
Bergut, Bob, *Erich von Stroheim*, Paris, 1960.
Barna, Jan, *Erich von Stroheim*, Vienna, 1966.
Gobeil, Charlotte, editor, *Hommage à Erich von Stroheim*, Ottawa, 1966.
Ciment, Michel, *Erich von Stroheim*, Paris, 1967.
Finler, Joel, *Stroheim*, Berkeley, 1968.
Brownlow, Kevin, *The Parade's Gone By . . .*, London and New York, 1969.
Curtiss, Thomas Quinn, *Erich von Stroheim*, Paris, 1969.
Buache, Freddy, *Erich von Stroheim*, Paris, 1972.
Pratt, George C., *Spellbound in Darkness*, Greenwich, 1973.
Weinberg, Herman G., *Stroheim: A Pictorial Record of His Nine Films*, New York, 1975.
Bazin, André, *The Cinema of Cruelty: From Buñuel to Hitchcock*, New York, 1982.
Koszarski, Richard, *The Man You Loved to Hate: Erich von Stroheim and Hollywood*, Oxford, 1983.
Bessy, Maurice, *Erich von Stroheim*, Paris, 1984.
Lenning, Arthur, *Stroheim*, Lexington, 2000.

Articles:

New York Times, 12 January 1922.
Variety (New York), 20 January 1922.
Motion Picture Classic, April 1922.
Kine Weekly (London), 28 September and 5 October 1922.
Picturegoer, November 1922.
''Stroheim Issue,'' of *Ciné-Club* (Paris), April 1949.
Cinema (Beverly Hills), 15 March 1954.
Everson, William K., ''The Career of Erich von Stroheim,'' in *Films in Review* (New York), August-September 1957.
''Stroheim Issue'' of *Film Culture* (New York), April 1958.
''Stroheim Issue'' of *Bianco e Nero* (Rome), February-March 1959.
''Stroheim Issue'' of *Premier Plan* (Lyons), August 1963.
''Stroheim Issue'' of *Etudes Cinématographiques* (Paris), no. 48–50, 1966.
''Stroheim Issue'' of *Cinema* (Zurich), December 1973.
Rosenbaum, Jonathan, in *Monthly Film Bulletin* (London), November 1976.
Magill's Survey of Cinema, Silent Films, Englewood Cliffs, 1982.
Blanchet, C., in *Cinéma* (Paris), March 1985.
Tesson, C., in *Cahiers du Cinéma* (Paris), March 1985.
Dazat, O., in *Cinématographe* (Paris), March 1985.
Amengual, Barthélemy, ''Quelques notes sur *Folies de femmes* de Stroheim,'' in *Jeune Cinéma* (Paris), June 1985.
Legrand, Gérard, in *Positif* (Paris), June 1985.
Wide Angle (Athens, Ohio), vol. 8, no. 1, 1986.
Donovan, F., in *Cinema 89*, no. 459, 5 September 1989.
Paavolainen, Olavi, ''Kaksi mestaria - kaksi vastakohtaa,'' in *Filmihullu* (Helsinki), no. 5, 1992.
Mensuel du Cinéma, no. 10, October 1993.
Fisher, L., ''Enemies, a Love Story: von Stroheim, Women and World War I,'' in *Film History* (London), vol. 6, no. 4, Winter 1994.
Cahiers du Cinéma (Paris), no. 486, December 1994.
Cinegrafie, no. 8, 1995.
Clair, René, ''De Stroheim à Chaplin,'' in *Positif* (Paris), no. 443, January 1998.

* * *

Foolish Wives, von Stroheim's third feature as a director, presents close analogies with his first two as the last part of a triptych on the ''innocent abroad,'' a new triangle comedy with the blind husband (this time an American ambassador), his foolish wife, and the devil with his passkey (von Stroheim himself playing a pseudo-Russian Count). Far superior to *Blind Husbands* (1919), and probably to *The Devil's Passkey* (a lost film, 1920), its action is again set in Europe, Monte Carlo succeeding the Austrian Dolomites of the first film and the Paris of the second.

To measure up its originality and boldness it has to be compared to the sophisticated comedies of the time whose greatest exponent was Cecil B. De Mille with films like *Why Change Your Wife?* or *The Affairs of Anatol*. De Mille as early as 1919 brought to the American screens a mixture of spice and sex but within strict moral limits. Von Stroheim, however, through his unsparing vision of human psychology, his probing of hidden motives, and his harsh realism made the American cinema (particularly with *Foolish Wives*) enter the 20th

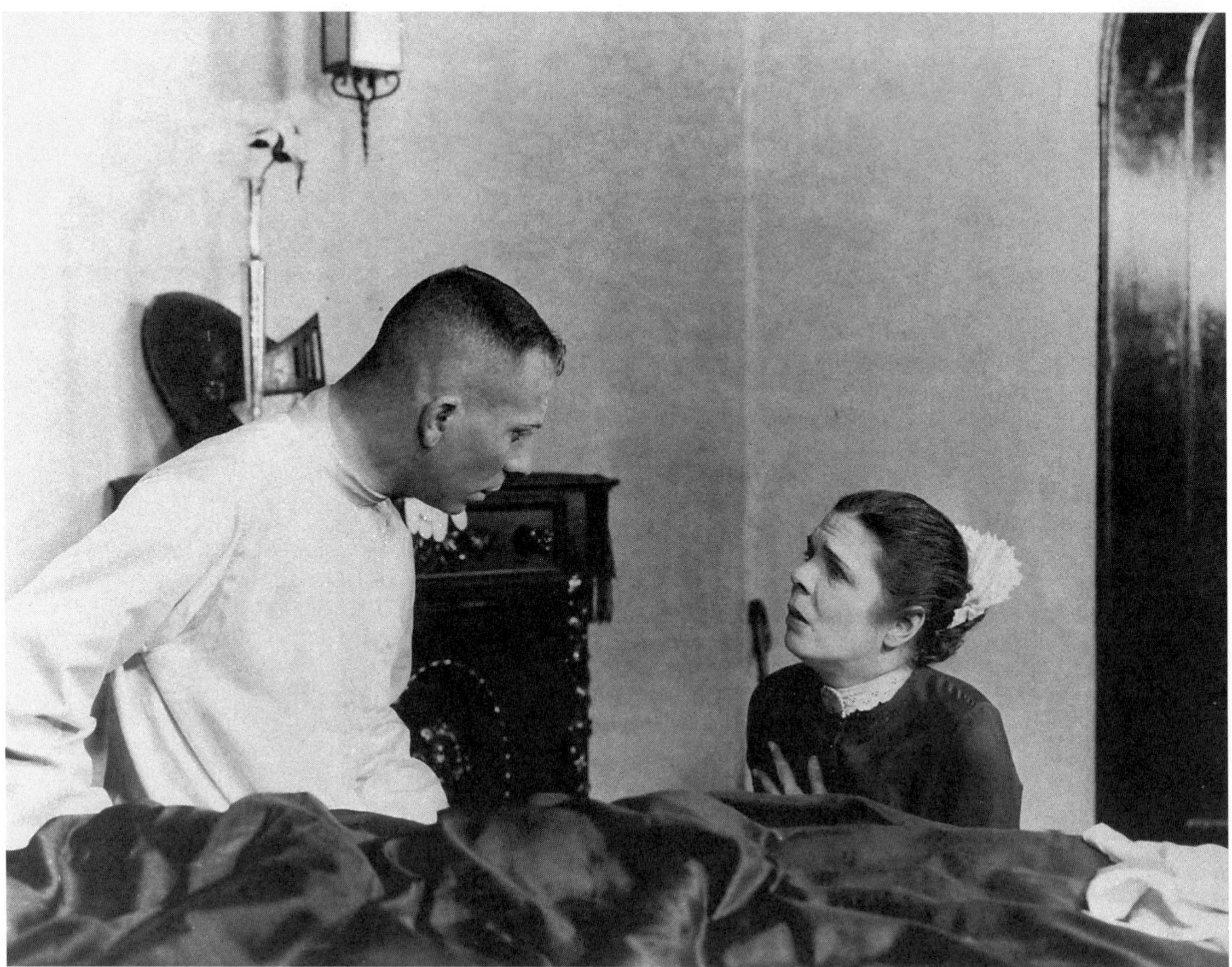

Foolish Wives

century, away from the Victorian and romantic sensibility of Griffith and Tourneur. Chaplin would soon follow with *A Woman of Paris* (1923) and Lubitsch with *The Marriage Circle* (1924).

While confirming his image of "the man you love to hate," established in the war years when he played the role of the wicked German in several films, *Foolish Wives*, his third feature for Carl Laemmle's Universal, created his reputation as a money-spender and an intractable director. Started on 12 July 1920, the shooting ended almost one year later on 15 June 1921. The costs were soaring as von Stroheim with his manic perfectionism insisted on the veracity of every detail. The main facades of the casino, the Hotel de France, and the Cafe de Paris were built by Richard Day (his first assignment) on the backlot of Universal. The initial budget of $250,000 ended up at $750,000 according to von Stroheim and $1,225,000 in the studio's estimate. In the middle of production Laemmle had appointed his 20-year-old secretary Irving Thalberg as the head of Universal, and he started to oppose von Stroheim as he would do on his next films, *Merry Go Round* and *Greed*.

Before release there were both censorship and length problems. In the wake of Fatty Arbuckle's scandal the company decided to delete the most provocative shots; after screening a rough cut of six and half hours, it took the film from von Stroheim's hands and asked Arthur Ripley to reduce it from 30 reels to 14. Ultimately it ran only ten reels.

Even in its present shape, however, the film is one of the most stunning of the silent era. It also exercised a major influence on future directors, including Renoir, Buñuel, and Vigo. Von Stroheim shows a world that lies to itself, where swindlers and rich people mix, and where the heroine reads a book called *Foolish Wives*. The writer-director deals with false appearances: the titles of Count Wladislas Sergius Karamzin and his two princess cousins are fake (von Stroheim himself was not an Austrian aristocrat as he would have us believe during his lifetime, but the son of a Jewish hat-maker), the money is counterfeit, and the sentiments are fraudulent; Karamzin playing at love to seduce his maid, the ambassador's wife, and an idiotic 14-year-old girl. This hypocrisy of the social game is set in the context of World War I, which had just ended: an armless veteran, a nurse pushing a soldier in a wheelchair, a little girl on crutches, a boy playing with a military helmet.

In *Foolish Wives* von Stroheim also gives the final—and most brilliant—touch to his portrait of the cynical seducer, equally eager for money and sex. His physical appearance is as recognisable as Chaplin's, with his military cap, his whip, and his monocle. Unlike

Don Juan who seeks his own downfall or Casanova who is constantly in love and taken in by his own illusions, von Stroheim embodies here an energy and sensuality in their purest form and seeks to destroy the world around him until his final death, not unlike a de Sade character.

But one should not forget the comic side of the film, its scathing irony, even its farcical moments. In many respects, *Foolish Wives* anticipates two subversive works that open and close the 1930s: Buñuel's *L'age d'or* and Renoir's *La règle du jeu*.

—Michel Ciment

FORBIDDEN GAMES

See **LES JEUX INTERDITS**

42nd STREET

42nd Street

USA, 1933

Director: Lloyd Bacon

Production: Warner Bros. Pictures, Inc.; black and white, 35mm; running time: 85 minutes, some sources list 89 minutes. Released 4 March 1933 (premiere). Filmed in Warner Bros. studios in Hollywood, cost: budgeted at £400,000.

Producer: Hal B. Wallis; **screenplay:** James Seymour and Rian James, from the novel by Bradford Ropes; **photography:** Sol Polito; **editor:** Thomas Pratt; **art director:** Jack Okey; **music numbers:** Al Dubin and Harry Warren; **costume designer:** Orry Kelly; **choreography:** Busby Berkeley.

Cast: Warner Baxter (*Julian Marsh*); Bebe Daniels (*Dorothy Brock*); George Brent (*Pat Denning*); Una Merkel (*Lorraine Fleming*); Ruby Keeler (*Peggy Sawyer*); Guy Kibbee (*Abner Dillon*); Ned Sparks (*Barry*); Dick Powell (*Billy Lawler*); Ginger Rogers (*Anytime Annie*); George E. Stone (*Andy Lee*); Eddie Nugent (*Terry*); Allen Jenkins (*MacElroy*); Robert McWade (*Jones*); Harry Axt (*Jerry*); Clarence Nordstrum (*Leading man*); Henry B. Whitehall (*The actor*).

Awards: National Film Registry, National Film Preservation Board, 1998.

Publications

Script:

Seymour, James, and Rian James, *42nd Street*, edited by Rocco Fuments, Madison, Wisconsin, 1980.

Books:

Springer, John, *All Talking, All Dancing*, New York, 1966.
Bergman, Andrew, *We're In The Money: Depression America and Its Films*, New York, 1971.
Pike, Bob, and Dave Martin, *The Genius of Busby Berkeley*, Resada, California, 1973.
Thomas, Tony, Jim Terry, and Busby Berkeley, *The Busby Berkeley Book*, New York, 1973.
Stern, Lee Edward, *The Movie Musical*, New York, 1974.
Kreuger, Miles, editor, *The Movie Musical from Vitaphone to 42nd Street*, New York, 1975.
Meyer, William, *Warner Brothers Directors*, New York, 1978.
Hirschhorn, Clive, *The Warner Bros. Story*, New York, 1979.
Delameter, James, *Dance in the Hollywood Musical*, Ann Arbor, Michigan, 1981.
Attman, Rick, editor, *Genre: The Musical*, London, 1981.
Feuer, Jane, *The Hollywood Musical*, London, 1982.
Roddick, Nick, *A New Deal in Entertainment: Warner Brothers in the 1930s*, London, 1983.
Morsiani, Alberto, *Il Grande Busby: Il Cinema di Busby Berkeley*, Modena, 1983.
Hoberman, J., *42nd Street*, London, 1993.

Articles:

Hall, Mordaunt, in *New York Times*, 10 March 1933.
Variety (New York), 14 March 1933.
''Lloyd Bacon . . . Warner Brothers' Ace,'' in *Cue* (New York), 6 April 1935.
''Obituary: Lloyd Bacon,'' in *New York Times*, 16 November 1955.
Thomas, Anthony, ''Dick Powell,'' in *Films in Review* (New York), May 1961.

Durgnat, Raymond, in *Films and Filming* (London), January 1962.
Brion, P., and R. Gilson, "A Style of Spectacle," and Comoll, J.-L. "Dancing Images," in *Cahiers du Cinéma in English* (New York), no. 2, 1966.
Jenkinson, Philip, "The Great Busby," in *Film* (London), Spring 1966.
Gruen, John, "Interview with Berkeley," in *Close-Up* (New York), 1968.
Sidney, George, "The Three Ages of the Musical," in *Films and Filming* (London), June 1968.
Gorton, D., "Busby and Ruby," in *Newsweek* (New York), 3 August 1970.
Bengtsson, Y., in *Filmrutan* (Stockholm), no. 1, 1973.
Knight, Arthur, "Busby Berkeley," in *Action* (Los Angeles), May-June 1974.
Hodgkinson, A. W., "*Forty-Second Street* New Deal: Some Thoughts About Early Film Musicals," in *Journal of Popular Film* (Washington, D.C.), no. 1, 1975.
Turroni, G., in *Filmcritica* (Rome), March 1975.
Fischer, Lucy, "The Image of Women: The Optical Politics of Dames," in *Film Quarterly* (Berkeley), Fall 1976.
Dyer, Richard, "Entertainment and Utopia," in *Movie* (London), no. 24, 1977.
Belton, John, "The Backstage Musical," in *Movie* (London), Spring 1977.
Roth, Mark, "Some Warners Musicals and the Spirit of the New Deal," in *Velvet Light Trap* (Madison, Wisconsin), Winter 1977.
Delameter, James, in *Wide Angle* (Athens, Ohio), volume 1, no. 1, 1979.
Johnson, Julia, in *Magill's Survey of Cinema*, Englewood Cliffs, New Jersey, 1980.
Clark, D., "Acting in Hollywood's Best Interest; Representations of Actors' Labor During the National Recovery Administration," in *Journal of Film and Video* (Los Angeles), no. 4, 1990.

* * *

42nd Street was the first of three films released in quick succession by Warner Brothers in 1933 (the other two were *Gold Diggers of 1933* and *Footlight Parade*) that are generally regarded as having revitalized the musical as a genre. *42nd Street* gave Busby Berkeley (known for his unique overhead camera shots in Eddie Cantor films) full rein to develop his ideas of choreography. The Depression-weary public was obviously fascinated: *Variety* listed *42nd Street* as one of the top six money-making films of 1933, and it was nominated for an Oscar as best picture. Based to some extent on *The Broadway Melody* (MGM, 1929), *42nd Street* continued the sub-genre of the "backstage musical" but added new dimensions with its hard-hitting references to the Depression and with Berkeley's opulent staging of the musical numbers.

The film refuses to be completely escapist: the main thrust of the narrative is the need to get a job, create a viable product (the show *Pretty Lady*) and to make money. The structural tension results from the separation of the production numbers (glimpses of *Pretty Lady*) from the narrative; those numbers are indeed escapist in nature. Richard Dyer, in "Entertainment and Utopia," regards this separation as an ideological method of suggesting that the musical numbers are the Utopia we all seek from the hard work of the narrative reality—that the "ills" of capitalism (the Depression) can be resolved through the "means" of capitalism (putting on a successful show). Mark Roth puts forward a similar theory; he notes a social connection between *42nd Street* and newly-elected President Roosevelt's New Deal: by working together under a strong leader (the director), the United States (the cast and crew) can lift itself out of the Depression and towards prosperity. (*42nd Street* opened in Washington, D.C. on March 4, 1933, the day on which Roosevelt was inaugurated).

Regardless of these factors, *42nd Street* is usually labelled a "Busby Berkeley musical." Backstage musicals had existed since the beginning of sound, but they were always shot straight-on, as if on stage. Berkeley freed the camera and took advantage of its mobility. He was not a trained dancer, and consequently his "dancers" did not dance so much as move about; the camera did the dancing. By disrupting spatial integrity (the production numbers would begin and end on a theatrical stage but would inevitably move into a realm of limitless dimension), Berkeley created a surrealistic world that thrilled movie audiences. His predilection for beautiful women resulted in some of the most voyeuristic fantasies ever put on film. Recent feminist film critics, particularly Lucy Fischer, have justifiably attacked Berkeley's objectification of the female body.

42nd Street also introduced Ruby Keeler and Dick Powell to movie audiences and contains that immortal line, ". . . You're going out a youngster, but you've got to come back a star!"

—Greg S. Faller

THE FOUR CHIMNEYS

See **ENTOTSU NO MIERU BASHO**

THE FOUR HORSEMEN OF THE APOCALYPSE

USA, 1921

Director: Rex Ingram

Production: Metro Pictures Corp.; black and white, 35mm, silent; running time: about 150 minutes; length: 11 reels. Released 6 March 1921 at the Lyric Theatre, New York.

Producer: Rex Ingram; **scenario:** June Mathis, from the novel *Los cuatros jinetes del Apocalipsis* by Vicente Blasco-Ibáñez; **art titles:** Jack W. Robson; **photography:** John F. Seitz; **editors:** Grant Whytock and June Mathis; **art directors:** Walter Mayo and Curt Rehfeld; **music for accompanying film:** Louis F. Gottschalk; **technical assistants:** Amos Myers and Joseph Calder; **makeup:** Jean Hersholt.

Cast: Rudolph Valentino (*Julio Desnoyers*); Alice Terry (*Marguerite Laurier*); Pomeroy Cannon (*Madariaga, the Centaur*); Josef Swickard (*Marcelo Desnoyers*); Brinsley Shaw (*Celendonio*); Alan Hale (*Karl von Hartrott*); Bridgetta Clark (*Doña Luisa*); Mabel Van Buren (*Elena*); Nigel De Brulier (*Tchernoff*); Bowditch Turner (*Argensola*); John Sainpolis (*Laurier*); Mark Fenton (*Senator Lacour*); Virginia Warwick (*Chichi*); Derek Ghent (*René Lacour*); Stuart Holmes (*Captain von Hartrott*); Jean Hersholt (*Professor von Hartrott*); Henry Klaus (*Heinrich von Hartrott*); Edward Connolly (*Lodgekeeper*);

The Four Horsemen of the Apocalypse

Georgia Woodthorpe (*Lodgekeeper's wife*); Kathleen Key (*Georgette*); Wallace Beery (*Lieutenant-Colonel von Richthoffen*); Jacques D'Auray (*Captain d'Aubrey*); Curt Rehfeld (*Major Blumhardt*); Harry Northrup (*The Count*); Claire De Lorez (*Mademoiselle Lucette, the model*); Bull Montana (*French butler*); Isabelle Keith (*German woman*); Jacques Lanoe (*Her husband*); Noble Johnson (*Conquest*); Minnehaha (*Old nurse*); Arthur Hoyt (*Lieutenant Schnitz*); Beatrice Dominquez (*Dancer*); also featuring Ramon Samaniegos (later Novarro) in small role.

Publications

Books:

Milne, Peter, *Motion Picture Directing: The Facts and Theories of the Newest Art*, New York, 1922.

Shulman, Irving, *Valentino*, New York, 1967.

Jacobs, Lewis, *The Rise of the American Film: A Critical History*, revised edition, New York, 1968.

Predal, René, *Rex Ingram*, Paris, 1970.

Lahue, Kalton C., *Gentlemen to the Rescue: The Heroes of the Silent Screen*, New York, 1972.

Everson, William K., *American Silent Film*, New York, 1978.

O'Leary, Liam, *Rex Ingram, Master of the Silent Cinema*, Dublin, 1980; updated revision 1994.

Articles:

Variety (New York), 18 February 1921.

New York Times, 7 March 1921.

Robinson, J., interview with Ingram in *Photoplay* (New York), August 1921.

Lambert, Gavin, "Fairbanks and Valentino: The Last Heroes," in *Sequence* (London), Summer 1949.

Huff, Theodore, "The Career of Rudolph Valentino," in *Films in Review* (New York), April 1952.

Geltzer, George, "Hollywood's Handsomest Director," in *Films in Review* (New York), May 1952.

McPherson, Mervyn, in *Films and Filming* (London), May 1956.

O'Leary, Liam, "Rex Ingram and the Nice Studios," in *Cinema Studies* (England), December 1961.

Bodeen, DeWitt, ''Rex Ingram and Alice Terry,'' in *Films in Review* (New York), February and March 1975.
Graham, Ian, ''Rex Ingram: A Seminal Influence, Unfairly Obscured,'' in *American Cinematographer* (Hollywood), vol. 74, no. 4, April 1993.
Cherchi Usai, P., ''Elogio dell'istinto,'' in *Segnocinema* (Vicenza), no. 61, May/June 1993.
Bourget, J.-L., ''Entre Stroheim et David Lean: le roi Ingram,'' in *Positif* (Paris), no. 404, October 1994.
''*Les quatre cavaliers de l'apocalypse*,'' in *Séquences* (Haute-Ville), no. 177, March-April 1995.

* * *

When screenwriter June Mathis campaigned among the executives of the then none-too-sound Metro Film Company to have Blasco Ibáñez's best-selling novel *The Four Horsemen of the Apocalypse* transferred to the screen, she was on shaky ground. The war had been over for two years, there had been a surfeit of war films, and people wanted to forget. She succeeded, however, and she also had the intelligence to recognize the talents of two young men—the director, Rex Ingram, and the actor, Rudolph Valentino. In production the film gathered momentum; there was an air of expectation. Ingram, who had hitherto produced distinguished work without achieving full recognition, had a talent for moulding actors, and the young and largely inexperienced Valentino, lithe and graceful as a dancer, with style and charm and a touch of the devil, proved ideal material for the screen. Ingram, who had come from an Irish rectory and an artistic training at the Yale School of Fine Arts, had inherited his father's capacity for study and research. He had never been to France, knew nothing of European culture, and yet he succeeded in creating in Hollywood the atmosphere of Paris in wartime and the tragedy of the destruction that had ravaged Europe.

The Four Horsemen was an immediate sensation, comparable in its success only to the major films of D. W. Griffith some years earlier. In all the large cities it was sumptuously presented with large orchestras and backstage sound effects for the battle scenes. Its story had all the ingredients for success: a dazzling gigolo hero and a tragic story of frustrated illicit love. It ranged from the pampas of South America and the glittering world of Paris, to the horrors of war and the invasion of a French village by the Germans. Pervading everything was the anti-war theme and the mystical element of the four terrible horsemen. It was also anti-German to the point of caricature: it was banned in Germany and indeed withdrawn from circulation many years later when a campaign was launched to suppress films promoting hatred between nations.

But for years it was the major box-office attraction, and was revived on the death of Valentino. Indeed, it is now remembered more for its star than for the genuine achievement of Ingram himself. Yet today's viewers, even those whose main interest is in nostalgia for Valentino, will be struck by the excellence of the film itself. With the help of his constant collaborator, the cameraman John Seitz, Ingram infused the film with great visual beauty, a sensitivity to light and shade, and an unusual feeling for composition.

The effect of the film was to shore up the finances of the shaky Metro company, recently taken over by Marcus Loew. It established Valentino as a star, and it established Ingram as a major director who henceforth had carte blanche and full control of his films. A ''Rex Ingram Production'' thereafter carried as much weight as the star's billing, and indeed Ingram can be said to have set an aesthetic standard for the screen image.

—Liam O'Leary

THE 400 BLOWS

See **LES QUATRES CENTS COUPS**

FRANKENSTEIN

USA, 1931

Director: James Whale

Production: Universal Pictures; black and white, 35mm; running time: 71 minutes. Released 1931. Filmed in Universal studios. Cost: $250,000.

Producer: Carl Laemmle Jr.; **screenplay:** Garrett Fort, Francis Faragoh, and John L. Balderston, uncredited first draft by Robert Florey, from John Balderston's adaptation of Mary Shelley's novel adapted from the play by Peggy Webling; **photography:** Arthur Edeson; **editor:** Clarence Kolster; **sound recording supervisor:** C. Roy Hunter; **art director:** Charles Hall; **music:** David Broekman; **makeup:** Jack Pierce; **laboratory equipment:** Ken Strickfadden.

Cast: Colin Clive (*Dr. Henry Frankenstein*); Boris Karloff (*The Monster*); Mae Clarke (*Elizabeth*); John Boles (*Victor*); Edward Van Sloan (*Dr. Waldman*); Dwight Frye (*Fritz*); Frederick Kerr.

Publications

Script:

Fort, Garrett, Francis Faragoh, and John L. Balderston, *James Whale's Frankenstein*, edited by Richard Anobile, New York, 1974.

Books:

Laclos, Michel, *Le Fantastique au Cinéma*, Paris, 1958.
Clarens, Carlos, *An Illustrated History of the Horror Film*, New York, 1968.
Gifford, Denis, *Movie Monsters*, New York, 1969.
Baxter, John, *Science Fiction in the Cinema*, New York, 1970.
Butler, Ivan, *Horror in the Cinema*, revised edition, New York, 1970.
Huss, Roy, and T. J. Ross, editors, *Focus on the Horror Film*, Englewood Cliffs, New Jersey, 1972.
Underwood, Peter, *Karloff: The Life of Boris Karloff*, New York, 1972.
Gifford, Denis, *Karloff: The Man, The Monster, The Movies*, New York, 1973.
Glut, Donald, *The Frankenstein Legend: A Tribute to Mary Shelley and Boris Karloff*, Metuchen, New Jersey, 1973.
Bojarski, Richard, and Kenneth Beale, *The Films of Boris Karloff*, Secaucus, New Jersey, 1974.

Frankenstein

Everson, William, *Classics of the Horror Film*, Secaucus, New Jersey, 1974.
Jensen, Paul, *Boris Karloff and His Films*, New York, 1974.
Barsacq, Leon, *Caligari's Cabinet and Other Grand Illusions: A History of Film Design*, revised and edited by Elliott Stein, Boston, 1976.
Tropp, Martin, *Mary Shelley's Monster: The Story of Frankenstein*, Boston, 1976.
Derry, Charles, *Dark Dreams: A Psychological History of the Modern Horror Film*, New York, 1977.
Ellis, Reed, *Journey Into Darkness: The Art of James Whale's Horror Films*, New York, 1980.
Klein, Michael, and Gillian Parker, editors, *The English Novel and the Movies*, New York, 1981.
Curtis, James, *James Whale*, Metuchen, New Jersey, 1982.

Articles:

New York Times, 5 December 1931.
Variety (New York), 8 December 1931.
New York Times, 20 December 1931.
Edwards, Roy, ''Movie Gothic: A Tribute to James Whale,'' in *Sight and Sound*, Autumn 1957.
Karloff, Boris, ''My Life as a Monster,'' in *Films and Filming* (London), November 1957.
Fink, Robert, and William Thomaier, ''James Whale,'' in *Films in Review* (New York), May 1962.
''Memories of a Monster,'' in *Saturday Evening Post* (New York), 3 November 1962.
Bloom, Harold, in *Partisan Review* (New Brunswick, New Jersey), Fall 1965.
Roman, Robert C., ''Boris Karloff,'' in *Films in Review* (New York), August-September 1969.
Gerard, Lillian, ''Boris Karloff: The Man Behind the Myth,'' in *Film Comment* (New York), Spring 1970.
Hitchens, Gordon, ''Some Historical Notes on Dr. Frankenstein and his Monster,'' in *Film Comment* (New York), Spring 1970.
Jensen, Paul, in *Film Comment* (New York), Fall 1970.
Jensen, Paul, ''James Whale,'' in *Film Comment* (New York), Spring 1971.
Verstappen, H., ''Schept vreugde met mij, horror freaks,'' in *Skoop* (Amsterdam), no. 2, 1972.

Dillard, R. H. W., ''Drawing the Circle: A Devolution of Values in 3 Horror Films,'' in *Film Journal* (Hollins College, Virginia), January-March 1973.
Schepelern, P., in *Kosmorama* (Copenhagen), March 1973.
Evans, Walter, ''Monster Movies: A Sexual Theory,'' in *Journal of Popular Film* (Washington, D.C.), Fall 1973.
Evans, Walter, ''Monster Movies and Rites of Initiation,'' in *Journal of Popular Film* (Washington, D.C.), Spring 1975.
Huskins, D. Gail, in *Magill's Survey of Cinema 1*, Englewood Cliffs, New Jersey, 1980.
Starburst (London), no. 32, 1981.
Viviani, C., ''Fauses pistes,'' in *Positif* (Paris), June 1983.
American Cinematographer (Los Angeles), April 1987.
Mank, G., ''Robert Florey, James Whale, and Universal's *Frankenstein*,'' in *Midnight Marquee* (Baltimore), Fall 1988.
Mank, Gregory, ''*Frankenstein* Restored,'' in *Films in Review* (New York), vol. 40, no. 6–7, June-July 1989.
Mank, Gregory, ''Little Maria Remembers,'' in *Films in Review* (New York), vol. 43, no. 9–10, September-October 1992.
Holt, Wesley G., in *Filmfax* (Evanston), no. 35, October-November 1992.
Thompson, David, ''Really a Part of Me,'' in *Film Comment* (New York), vol. 31, no. 1, January-February 1995.
Senn, B., ''The Monster, Bride, and Sonp'' in *Monsterscene* (Lombard), no. 4, March 1995.
Pizzato, M., ''The Real Edges of the Screen: Cinema's Theatrical and Communal Ghosts,'' in *Spectator* (Los Angeles), vol. 16, no. 2, 1996.
Sarver, Stephanie, ''Homer Simpson Meets Frankenstein: Cinematic Influence in Nathanael West's *The Day of the Locust*,'' in *Literature/Film Quarterly* (Salisbury), vol. 24, no. 2, April 1996.
Mitchell, C.P., ''Marilyn and the Monster,'' in *Films of the Golden Age* (Muscatine), no. 11, Winter 1997–1998.
Mitchell, C.P., ''The Unkindest Cut,'' in *Films of the Golden Age* (Muscatine), no. 11, Winter 1997–1998.

* * *

James Whale's 1931 version of *Frankenstein* remains a cinema miracle that defies time. Some 50 years since its premiere, its sensitive craftsmanship and relentlessly macabre tone still set horror movie standards, even after decades of noisome parodies and splatter-film overkill.

Whale treats his protagonist's obsession with galvanizing life from sewn corpses as a stark and shadowy moral tale, more in keeping with the German Expressionist influence of Robert Wiene's *Caligari* than Mary Shelley's Gothic overtones. Though heavy on dialogue in the beginning, *Frankenstein* unfolds as an intensely visual nightmare, a sleepwalker's journey along hideous graveyards, gibbets, and gnarly corridors—leading up to the meticulous penultimate climax when Dr. Frankenstein's creation slowly turns his face towards the camera.

Ironically, *Frankenstein* profits from the very qualities other critics have claimed drag it down. Its leaden mood, stagey acting and lack of a musical score make it all the more somber and bleak. Whale's camera is quite active throughout these funereal settings and suffers very little from the manacles inherent in other early talkies. In fact, practically all of the cinematic innovations credited to Whale's sequel *Bride of Frankenstein* are already here: the tracking camera, the sudden jumps from long-shot to close-up, the extreme high and low angles during the creation sequence, and the lurid sets with their demented religious icons.

At the same time, Whale flaunts his theatrical origins with a reverence for the stage. The very first frames when Edward Van Sloan (who plays Frankenstein's mentor, Dr. Waldman) confronts the footlights for his teasing introduction, and the later tracking shots along the opulent rooms of Baron Frankenstein's castle, remind us that this is, after all, nothing but artifice, a world where scenery is a *trompe l'oeil* projection of Dr. Frankenstein's subconscious fears.

Frankenstein still scares viewers because it works as both a horror film and a psychological study. As Frankenstein, Colin Clive, with his harsh enunciations and jittery motions, is perfect in his portrayal of a man beleaguered by twisted dreams and ambiguous morals. Is this really, as Shelley claimed, a story about the perils of hubris, or is it more concerned with a man apprehensive about falling into a connubial quagmire? By suggesting more of the latter, Whale may have directly borrowed from Thomas Edison's long lost silent version, which reportedly ends with a dissolve between the mirrored faces of Dr. Frankenstein and his Monster just before Elizabeth is about to be murdered. Edison allowed the creature to die so that the doctor could face up to marital obligations, but Whale suggests that Frankenstein's darker passions surpass the tedium Elizabeth (an appropriately bland role for Mae Clarke) has to offer him. In this regard, the Monster is less a sub-human fiend and more like the third party in a lover's triangle or quadrangle when we consider that Frankenstein's friend Victor Moritz (John Boles) has eyes on the future bride.

Whale's delight in lampooning ''normal'' sexual mores (a penchant culminating in his 1938 film *Wives under Suspicion*) is buttressed by Garrett Fort and Francis E. Farragoh's ambivalent script which questions how the characters *really* feel about one another. Elizabeth has countless anxieties about her nuptial partner and even seems coy when Victor vies for her affections. On the wedding day, when news hits that the Monster is loose, Whale inserts a curious close-up of Frankenstein's hands locking Elizabeth in her bridal chamber, suggesting perhaps that the doctor is unconsciously making her more vulnerable since the would-be killer will soon enter her room through the window. Off to reunite with his nemesis in a vigilante search, Frankenstein looks firmly into Victor's eyes while surrendering Elizabeth into his care. The scene ends with Victor creeping towards Elizabeth's room.

As a homewrecker, Frankenstein's Monster merits the humanity and dignity of Boris Karloff's performance, despite the grease paint, wire clamps, wax eyelids, and a 48-pound steel spine designed by Jack Pierce. Karloff's empathy is unfortunately diminished by the subplot in which Frankenstein's hunchback assistant Fritz (Dwight Frye as comic relief) unwittingly acquires a ''criminal'' brain from his boss, thereby ruining the notion that the Monster's brutality is a learned response.

Whale's film leaves us with the unsettling conclusion that the real monsters are the diurnal world's dim-witted denizens, a fact made more apparent when Baron Frankenstein (Frederick Kerr) predicts that the townspeople revelling over his son's wedding will soon be fighting again. Hours later, the news of little Maria's murder turns the jocular crowd into a bloodthirsty mob. The recently restored footage (missing since its screen debut) of the Monster throwing Maria (Marilyn Harris) into a lake transpires so quickly and nonchalantly that the pedophile scenarios left to our imaginations all these years are debunked. Now we have proof that the child murder was an innocent error. Not content simply to cast his Monster as a pariah, Whale promotes him to a Christ figure in the final scene when the creation throws his creator from the abandoned windmill into the vengeful crowd. An extreme long-shot of the burning mill resembles the cross on Calvary. Though he disapproved of the tacked-on happy ending when Frankenstein survives his fall, Whale still achieved that supreme inversion of "good" and "evil" that makes the best horror films survive.

—Joseph Lanza

FREAKS

USA, 1932

Director: Tod Browning

Production: Metro-Goldwyn-Mayer Pictures Corp.; black and white, 35mm; running time: 90 minutes originally, later 64 minutes, some sources state that existing copies are 53 minutes. Released February 1932, New York and San Francisco. Filmed in Hollywood.

Producer: Irving Thalberg with Harry Sharock (some filmographies state Dwain Esper as producer, but he was responsible for the 1940s re-issue, other sources list Browning as producer); **screenplay:** Willis Goldbeck, Leon Gordon, Al Boasberg, and Edgar Allen Woolf, from the book *Spurs* by Clarence Tod Robbins; **photography:** Merritt B. Gerstad; **editor:** Basil Wrangell; **sound engineer:** Gavin Barns; **art directors:** Cedric Gibbons with Merrill Pye; **music:** Gavin Barns.

Cast: Olga Baclanova (*Cleopatra*); Henry Victor (*Hercules*); Wallace Ford (*Phroso*); Harry Earles (*Hans*); Leila Hyams (*Venus*); Roscoe Ates (*Roscoe*); Rose Dione (*Mme. Tetralini*); Daisy and Violet Hilton (*Siamese Twins*); Schlitze (*Herself*); Peter Robinson (*Human Skeleton*); Elisabeth Green (*Bird Woman*); Randion (*Larva Man*, or *Living Torso*); Joseph-Josephine (*Androgyne*); Johnny Eck (*Trunk Man*); Frances O'Connor and Martha Morris (*Women without arms*); Olga Roderich (*Bearded Woman*); Koo-Koo (*Herself*); Edward Brophy and Mat-Mac Huch (*The Rollo Brothers*); Angelo Rossitto (*Angeleno*); Daisy Earles (*Frieda*); Zip and Flip (*Pinheads*).

Award: Honored at the Venice Film Festival, 1962.

Publications

Script:

Goldbeck, Willis, and others, *Freaks*, in *Avant-Scène du Cinéma* (Paris), 15 March 1981.

Books:

Thomas, John, *Focus on the Horror Film*, New Jersey, 1972.
Everson, William K., *Classics of the Horror Film*, Secaucus, New Jersey, 1974.
Skal, David J., *Dark Carnival: The Secret World of Tod Browning, Hollywood's Master of the Macabre*, New York, 1995.

Articles:

New York Times, 9 July 1932.
Variety (New York), 12 July 1932.
Geltzer, George, "Tod Browning," in *Films in Review* (New York), October 1953.
Romer, Jean-Claude, "Tod Browning," in *Bizarre* (Paris), no. 3, 1962.
Guy, Rory, "Horror: The Browning Version," in *Cinema* (Beverly Hills), June-July 1963.
Kael, Pauline, in *Kiss Kiss Bang Bang*, Boston, 1968.
Schmidt, K., in *Kosmorama* (Copenhagen), September 1972.
Savada, Eli, "Tod Browning," in *Photon* (New York), no. 23, 1973.
Beylie, Claude, in *Ecran* (Paris), July-August 1973.
Rosenthal, Stuart, "Tod Browning," in *The Hollywood Professionals 4*, London, 1975.
"*Freaks* et la critique," in *Avant-Scène du Cinéma* (Paris), July-September 1975.
Léger, Jean-Marie, "Ni Fantastique ni 'normal'," in *Avant Scène du Cinéma* (Paris), July-September 1975.
James, N., in *Classic Film Collector* (Indiana, Pennsylvania), Fall 1976.
Carcassonne, P., in *Cinématographe* (Paris), April 1978.
Biette, J.-C., and F. Ziolkowski, "Tod Browning and *Freaks*," in *Cahiers du Cinéma* (Paris), May 1978.
Cluny, C. M., "*Freaks* dans l'oeuvre de Tod Browning," in *Cinéma* (Paris), May 1978.
Sauvaget, D., in *Image et Son* (Paris), May 1978.
Hoberman, James, in *Village Voice* (New York), 17 September 1979.
Film Psychology Review (New York), Summer-Fall 1980.
"*Freaks* Issue," of *Avant-Scène du Cinéma* (Paris), 15 March 1981.
Cinématographe (Paris), May 1982.
Starburst (London), no. 59, 1983.
Moorman, M., in *Skoop* (Amsterdam), September-October 1985.
Hodges, Albert, "Remembering Johnny Eck," in *Filmfax* (Evanston), no. 26, April-May 1991.
Douin, Jean-Luc, "L'horreur est humaine," in *Télérama* (Paris), no. 2265, 9 June 1993.
Vieira, Mark A., and Gary Morris, "*Freaks:* Production and Analysis," in *Bright Lights* (Cincinnati), no. 1, Fall 1993.
Holt, Wesley G., in *Filmfax* (Evanston), no. 52, September-October 1995.
Skal, David J., and Elias Savada, "'Offend One and You Offend Them All'," in *Filmfax* (Evanston), no. 52, September-October 1995.
Skal, David J., and Elias Savada, "'One of Us'," in *Filmfax* (Evanston), no. 53, November-December 1995.
Wood, Bret, "Hollywood's Sequined Lie: The Gutter Roses of Tod Browning," in *Video Watchdog*, no. 32, 1996.

* * *

Although it has been seldom shown in the fifty years since its introduction in 1932 as a "masterpiece of horror," Tod Browning's *Freaks* has achieved near-legendary cult status and continues to exert a major influence on modern attempts at the baroque film. Certainly the powers of its wedding feast sequence was not lost on Luis Buñuel when he staged the tramp's "last supper" in his 1961 *Viridiana*. And the works of such diverse filmmakers as Max Ophüls, Federico Fellini, and Ingmar Bergman have shown traces of the film's influence.

Freaks

Today it is difficult to believe that the film was produced at MGM. It more closely resembles the kind of horror films being released during the 1930s by Universal Studios, which had in fact made a fortune with Browning's earlier *Dracula*, as well as James Whale's *Frankenstein*. However, Irving Thalberg, MGM's president, noting the success of these two efforts, purchased Clarence Robbins's grisly tale *Spurs*, hired Browning and, over considerable objections within the studio, adapted it for the screen as *Freaks*. Yet in the transition to film, the story deviated from the traditional horror format and evolved into gothic social commentary that closely resembled the kind of sociological treatments being attempted by Warner Bros. in their great gangster films of the period.

If *Freaks* is not totally satisfactory to audiences of today, that is perhaps due, for the most part, to the fundamental conflicts inherent in merging horror and social criticism. Although Browning was successful in portraying his deformed subjects sympathetically and causing his viewer to re-evaluate their concepts of what is normal, he succumbs to the obvious temptation to ''scare the pants'' off his viewers in the film's final scene. For most of the film, he portrays the freaks as human beings going about their daily rituals. (Significantly, we never see them on stage as sideshow performers.) At the wedding feast, however, when one of their number marries a ''normal'' person, we sense their solidarity as they go through an elaborate ritual to admit Cleo to their circle. This triggers a course of events in which the innate humanity of the freaks is juxtaposed with the inherent ugliness, evil and abnormality of the so-called normal people.

But in the film's final sequences, Browning emphasizes the physical grotesqueness of the freaks as they slither and crawl through the mud to exact their revenge on Cleo and the strong man Hercules after she has betrayed them. At the end of the film, we find that Cleo has turned into a freak herself at the hands of the little people. The scene, contrived as it is, clouds the image of the humanity of the deformed creatures by emphasizing the enormity of their vengeance, and because the costuming of Cleo as a freak is technically crude, it erodes the worthwhile themes of the film and makes its subjects objects of scorn.

Still, individual scenes, in their power and construction, provide unforgettable images and truly extend the boundaries of baroque filmmaking. The film is still today a virtual textbook on the horror film, and enough of its nobler aspirations come through to allow it to remain as undoubtedly the ultimate challenge to the old fiction that beauty is necessarily synonymous with truth. Although it was banned in many countries for its graphic depiction of this theme, it was honored in 1962 at the Venice Film Festival and has been shown periodically thereafter.

—Stephen L. Hanson

FRESA Y CHOCOLATE

(Strawberry and Chocolate)

Cuba, 1993

Director: Tomás Gutiérrez Alea and Juan Carlos Tabio

Production: El Instituto Cubano del Arte e Industria Cinematograficos, with the support of Instituto Mexicano de Cinematografic, TeleMadrid, La Sociedad General de Autores y Editores de España, and Tabasco Films; color, 35 mm; running time: 110 minutes. Released in the United States in 1994 by Miramax Films; Spanish with English subtitles.

Producer: Georgina Balzaretti (executive), Frank Cabrera (executive), Camilo Vives (executive), Nacho Cobo (associate), Juan Muñoz (associate); **screenplay:** Senel Paz (based on the story, *The Wolf, the Woods and the New Man*) **photography:** Mario García Joya; **editor:** Miriam Talavera, Rolando Martínez, Osvaldo Donatién; **production manager:** Miguel Mendoza; **sound editor:** Germinal Hernandez; **makeup:** Graciela Grossas, María Elena del Toro; **music:** José; María Vitier; **production designer:** Fernando O'Reilly; **costumes:** Miriam Dueñas.

Cast: Jorge Perugorria (*Diego*); Vladimir Cruz (*David*); Jorge Angelino (*Germán*); Francisco Gattorno (*Miguel*); Mirta Ibarra (*Nancy*); Marilyn Solaya (*Vivian*); Antonio Carmona (*Artist*); Diana Iris del Puerto (*Neighbor*); Andrés Cortina (*Santeria Priest*); Ricardo Ávila (*Taxi Driver*); María Elena del Toro (*Passenger*); Zolanda Oña (*Passenger*).

Awards: ARCI-NOVA Award, Audience Award, Best Actor (Jorge Perugorría), Best Actress (Luisina Brando), Best Director, Best Supporting Actress (Mirta Ibarra), FIPRESCI Award, Grand Coral First Prize, and OCIC Award, Havana Film Festival, 1993; Special Jury Prize, Silver Bear Award, and Teddy Award for Best Feature Film, Berlin International Film Festival, 1994; Golden Kikito for Best Latin Film, Gramado Latin Film Festival, 1994; Goya Award for Best Spanish Language Foreign Film, 1995; Special Jury Award, Sundance Film Festival, 1995.

Publications

Books:

Burton, Julianne, editor, *Cinema and Social Change in Latin America: Conversations with Filmmakers*, Austin, Texas, 1986.

Pick, Zuzana M., *The New Latin American Cinema: A Continental Project*, Austin, Texas, 1993.

Cook, David. A., *A History of Narrative Film*, 3rd Ed. New York, 1996.

Channan, Michael. ''New Cinemas in Latin America'' and ''Tomás Gutierrez Alea,'' in *The Oxford History of World Cinema: The Definitive History of Cinema Worldwide*, edited by Geoffrey Nowell-Smith, Oxford, 1997.

Articles:

Burton, Julianne, ''Film and Revolution in Cuba: The First Twenty-Five Years,'' in *Jump Cut: Hollywood, Politics and Counter-Cinema*, edited by Peter Steven, New York, 1985.

Alea, Tomás Gutierrez, ''I Wasn't Always a Filmmaker,'' in *Cineaste* (Berkeley), vol. 14, no. 1, 1985.

Smith, Paul, Teresa Toledo, and Philip Kemp, ''The Language of Strawberry/Intolerance/*Fresa y Chocolate*,'' in *Sight and Sound* (London), vol. 4, no. 12, December 1994.

Wise, Michael, ''In Totalitarian Cuba, Ice Cream and Understanding,'' in *New York Times*, 22 January 1995.

Ebert, Roger, '''Strawberry' Defies Notions of Cuba's Politics and Passions,'' in *Chicago Sun-Times*, 10 February 1995.

Ebert, Roger, ''Cuban Filmmaker Counts His Blessing; 'Strawberry' Harvest Tastes Better Than Making a Mint,'' in *Chicago Sun-Times*, 10 February 1995.

West, Dennis, ''Strawberry and Chocolate, Ice Cream and Tolerance: Interviews with Tomas Gutierrez Alea and Juan Carlos Tabio,'' in *Cineaste* (Berkeley), Winter-Spring 1995.

Marsolais, Gilles, ''Un humour décapant: coup d'oeil sur quelques films de Tomás Gutiérrez Alea,'' in *24 Images* (Montreal), no. 77, Summer 1995.

Hess, John, ''Melodrama, Sex, and the Cuban Revolution,'' in *Jump Cut* (Berkeley), no. 41, May 1997.

* * *

The film *Fresa y Chocolate* opened in Cuba in the year 1993 and within the space of a few months became one of the biggest box-office successes for Tomás Gutiérrez Alea, one of Latin America's celebrated and Cuba's most revered filmmakers. The story is set in 1979, a year before the upheaval of the Mariel boatlift. We meet Diego, a flamboyant, gay man who spots the beautiful young David at an ice cream shop and sets out to woo him. ''I knew he was a homosexual,'' Diego later reveals to his roommate Miguel, ''there was chocolate and he chose strawberry.''

Diego manages to lure the supremely heterosexual and devoutly Marxist David to his apartment with the promise of books, music, and other accouterments not readily available in Cuba. Diego is immediately smitten by David, who ''has a face of an angel.'' But David's only reason for befriending the non-conformist Diego is to do his duty for the Party by exposing him as a counter-revolutionary, a charge that could bring a penalty of a decade or more in prison. Here is where the real fun begins, for with their subsequent visits the issues become cloudy. David is fascinated by the quirky, educated, and cultured Diego. Moreover, there is more to Diego than meets the eye. At one point, Diego toasts their new friendship with contraband liquor from America, dubbing it ''the enemy's whiskey.'' Is Diego a counter-revolutionary or isn't he?

Some have criticized the inclusion of obvious gay clichés: Diego's apartment is cluttered with a dazzling array of eclectic antiques, he serves Indian tea on exquisite china, he revels in opera, and struts his

Fresa y Chocolate

stuff in a black tank top and blue Japanese kimono. Yet this is not a ''gay'' film. There is sexual tension, but no sex. Notes film critic Robert Ebert, the film is not ''about the seduction of a body, but about the seduction of a mind.'' Nor is the film to be dismissed as simply a light comedy about manners and morality. There are many issues cleanly woven into this unique tapestry.

Probably most striking to non-Cuban viewers is the film's serious and sensitive treatment of gay characters in a Cuban film set during a period in the country's history when anti-gay sentiment and discrimination ran especially high. For Alea however, it is more a film about tolerance than it is a call for gay rights. ''The gay subtheme,'' notes Alea in *Cineaste*, ''is merely a convenient illustration. . . .'' *Fresa y Chocolate* examines freedom of expression, surveillance, revolutionary watchfulness, the black market, and the flaws of revolutionary Cuban society.

This may seem radical, arising as it does from the camera of one of Cuba's most devoted revolutionaries. But not so if one is familiar with the firebrand tone of Alea's work. The Cuban director has never shied away from the contradictions in his country's policies. His submerged criticism of the exigencies of life in communist Cuba has resonated throughout his films. ''It's seen as a communist hell or a communist paradise,'' he was quoted as saying by the *Associated Press.* In one scene the two men escape to Diego's rooftop to take in the beauty of their city. A wide shot pans a beautiful dock with clear waters, shore birds, and small sea vessels. Diego warns David to enjoy it now ''before it collapses.'' Clearly, Diego loves Cuba but is tortured by the fact that its beauty is crumbling before his own eyes.

Fresa y Chocolate is a splendid piece of filmmaking by one of Latin America's most celebrated film artists. Alea made his mark in filmmaking with the production of *El mégano* in 1955. This documentary explored the exploitation of peasant labor in the charcoal swamps and caused Alea to be arrested by the secret police of the Batista regime. It was during this turbulent period in postwar film history that Latin American countries began to loose the stranglehold of the Hollywood machine to allow the voices of native film artists to be heard. A number of film movements emerged, including ''Cinema Novo,'' when young Latin filmmakers took on the tenants of Italian Neo-Realism and French New Wave to explore issues of colonization, slavery, economic limitation, misery, and protest, and in the process created a new Latin American cinema. It was the 1964 dark comedy *Muerta de un burócrata* (*Death of a Bureaucrat*) that helped established Alea as an international film artist.

Fresa y Chocolate is richly photographed and filled with charming portrayals and very good acting. And it makes for delightful comedy. David is a University student studying political science but is quite naive and unsophisticated. During one of many heated discussions with Diego, David confuses Truman Capote with Harry Truman for dropping the atomic bomb. He tells Diego that being gay is ''in the glands.'' Then there is Nancy, Diego's middle-aged and sexually appealing neighbor, a part-time hooker with mental baggage who supports herself by selling contraband pantyhose and cosmetics and who becomes intensely physically drawn to David—especially when she finds out he is still a virgin.

Alea, who was 69 years old at the time of the shooting of *Fresa Y Chocolate*, became ill and called upon his long-time colleague, filmmaker Juan Carlos Tabio, to complete the film. In 1996, after the release of his final film, *Guantanamera*, Alea died of cancer.

—Pamala S. Deane

FRÖKEN JULIE

(Miss Julie)

Sweden, 1950

Director: Alf Sjöberg

Production: Sandrew Bauman Produktion; black and white, 35mm; running time: 87 minutes, some sources list 90 minutes. Released 1950. Filmed in Sweden.

Producer: Rune Waldekranz; **screenplay:** Alf Sjöberg, from the play by August Strindberg; **photography:** Göran Strindberg; **editor:** Lennart Wallén; **art director:** Bibi Lindström; **music:** Dag Wirén.

Cast: Anita Björk (*Miss Julie*); Ulf Palme (*Jean*); Anders Henrikson (*The Count*); Marta Dorff (*Christine*); Lissi Alandh (*Berta, the Countess*); Inga Gill (*Viola*); Kurt-Olof Sundstrom (*The fiancé*); Ake Claessens (*Doctor*); Jan Hagerman (*Jean, as a child*); Inger Norberg (*Julie as a child*); Ake Fridell (*Robert*); Max von Sydow (*Groom*).

Award: Cannes Film Festival, Best Film (shared with *Miracolo a Milano*), 1951; Honored at Venice Film Festival, as part of a retrospective program, 1964.

Publications

Books:

Cowie, Peter, *Swedish Cinema*, New York, 1966.
Cowie, Peter, and Arne Svensson, *Sweden*, New York, 2 vols., 1970.
Barsacq, Leon, *Caligari's Cabinet and Other Grand Illusions: A History of Film Design*, New York, 1976.
Klinowski, Jacek, and Adam Garbicz, *Cinema, the Magic Vehicle: A Guide to Its Achievement: Journey Two*, Metuchen, New Jersey, 1979.
Lundin, G., *Filmregi Alf Sjöberg*, Lund, 1979.
Ek, Sverker R., *Spelplatsens magi: Alf Sjöberg regikonst 1930–1957*, Gidlund, 1988.
Esposito, Vincenzo, *Alf Sjöberg: un maestro del cinema svedese*, Rome, 1998.

Articles:

Variety (New York), 16 May 1951.
Cinématographe Français (Paris), 28 July 1951.
Cahiers du Cinéma (Paris), July-August 1951.
Sight and Sound (London), Autumn 1951.
Monthly Film Bulletin (London), no. 216, 1952.
Sight and Sound (London), January-March 1952.
Films in Review (New York), May 1952.
Variety (New York), 4 September 1952.
De La Roche, Catherine, ''Swedish Films,'' in *Films in Review* (New York), November 1953.
Morrisett, ''The Swedish Paradox,'' in *Sight and Sound* (London), Autumn 1961.
Cinema Nuovo (Turin), August 1965.
Coiner, M., ''Myth, Style and Strindberg in Sjöberg's *Miss Julie*,'' in *Literature/Film Quarterly* (Salisbury, Maryland), no. 1, 1991.
Bjorkin, M., ''*Fröken Julies* rakkniv,'' in *Filmhäftet* (Stockholm), vol. 23, no. 1/2, 1995.

* * *

In *Miss Julie*, there is a prolific use of ''flashbacks,'' one flash forward and two dream sequences, all of which serve to articulate the opposing but also disintegrating class values of Miss Julie, who represents the feudal aristocracy, and of her father's valet, Jean, who is of lower class, servant background. The difference in director Alf Sjöberg's use of the flashback device in *Miss Julie* from its standard employment in strictly conventional, (i.e. ''Hollywood'') films, is that there is not the usual cinematic punctuation demarcating exactly when the narrative is speaking about the present and when it is referring to the past.

In the play, the past is evoked through the use of dialogue, which characteristically involves an exchange among two or more people seeking mutual understanding. However, the key to the success of dialogue, insofar as its communicative status is predicated upon the arrival of this understanding, is one of intentionality. The speakers must be able to make one another recognize the meaning intended in what they are trying to express. In *Miss Julie* the dialogue—as a means of describing for example, the conflicts Miss Julie harbors about morality, class distinction, and sexual roles—has been translated cinematically into the flashback. That the flashbacks in the film are not marked off in the traditional manner indicates that they are not to be understood in the usual sense—not as simply retrogressive delineations of time. Instead they are intended by the filmmaker to illustrate, in formal terms, the indecisive and confused nature of Miss Julie's conception of herself, of her conception of how others see her, and of what she should do or be in the world.

The rules of verbal communication must be followed by the speakers involved. If they are not, of course, an incorrect meaning or set of meanings will be derived from the exchange. Specifically, flashbacks in *Miss Julie* are constructed so that there is no spatial and thus temporal differentiation made between the people, objects and places of the present and those of the past. Miss Julie's mother, who is

Fröken Julie

dead in the present time of her daughter's affair with Jean, walks into the "frame" of this time from the midst of one from the past. The camera moves with her across these two temporal dimensions passing on its way people of the present who are speaking about her in the past. This overlapping occurs as a rule of the flashback structure in the film. Its meaningful effect is one of instability, of alternating balances and contrasts of moods. The viewer understands ultimately that *Miss Julie* will remain an illusionary and impenetrable fiction.

To further create a sense of the basic unreality and illusion of imagination in the diegesis, landscapes, objects, and the natural elements (wind, etc.) are not represented or portrayed as things existing merely in themselves. Rather, Sjöberg manipulates them in such a way that they take on a symbolic life of their own. They become anthropomorphized conveyors of the character's emotions as well as expressive means of the larger and more pervasive moods of the film. This anthropomorphization process, which affords significance to objects usually represented statically, as devoid of meaning, does not in the overall perception of the film simply consign the narrative and its means of presentation to the realm of the melodramatic.

—Sandra L. Beck

FROM HERE TO ETERNITY

USA, 1953

Director: Fred Zinnemann

Production: Columbia Pictures Corp.; 1953; black and white, 35mm; running time: 118 minutes. Released 1953. Filmed in Hawaii at the Schofield Barracks.

Producer: Buddy Adler; **executive producer:** Harry Cohn; **screenplay:** Daniel Taradash, from the novel by James Jones; **photography:** Burnett Guffey; **editor:** William A. Lyon; **sound:** John P. Livadary and Columbia Studio Sound Department; **art director:** Cary Odell; **music:** George Dunning.

Cast: Burt Lancaster (*Sergeant Milton Warden*); Montgomery Clift (*Robert E. Lee "Prew" Prewitt*); Deborah Kerr (*Karen Holmes*); Frank Sinatra (*Angelo Maggio*); Donna Reed (*Alma "Lorene"*); Philip Ober (*Captain Dana Holmes*); Ernest Borgnine (*Sergeant "Fatso" Judson*).

Awards: Oscars for Best Picture, Best Supporting Actor (Sinatra), Best Supporting Actress (Reed), Best Director, Best Screenplay, Best Cinematography—Black and White, Best Sound Recording, and Best Editing, 1953; New York Film Critics' Awards for Best Motion Picture, Best Actor (Lancaster), and Best Direction, 1953; Cannes Film Festival, Out of Competition Prize, 1954.

Publications

Books:

Griffith, Richard, *Fred Zinnemann*, New York, 1958.
Thomas, Bob, *King Cohn*, New York, 1967.
Ringgold, Gene, and Clifford McCarty, *The Films of Frank Sinatra*, New York, 1971.
Phillips, Gene D., *The Movie Makers: Artists in an Industry*, Chicago, 1973.
Thomas, Tony, *Burt Lancaster*, New York, 1975.
Giannetti, Louis, *Masters of the American Cinema*, Englewood Cliffs, New Jersey, 1981.
Rausa, Guiseppe, *Fred Zinnemann*, Florence, 1985.
Goldau, Antje, and others, *Zinnemann*, Munich, 1986.
Zinnemann, Fred, *My Life in the Movies*, New York, 1992.
Nolletti, Arthur, Jr., *The Films of Fred Zinnemann*, Albany, 1999.

Articles:

Look (New York), 25 August 1953.
Kass, Robert, in *Films in Review* (New York), October 1953.
Reisz, Karel, in *Sight and Sound* (London), January-March 1954.
Wald, Jerry, ''Screen Adaptation,'' in *Films in Review* (New York), February 1954.
Taradash, Daniel, ''Into Another World,'' in *Films and Filming* (London), May 1959.
Zinnemann, Fred, ''A Conflict of Conscience,'' in *Films and Filming* (London), December 1959.
Zinnemann, Fred, ''*From Here To Eternity*,'' in *Films and Filming* (London), November 1961.
Zinnemann, Fred, ''Montgomery Clift,'' in *Sight and Sound* (London), Autumn 1966.

From Here to Eternity

Reid, John Howard, "A Man For All Movies: The Films of Fred Zinnemann," in *Films and Filming* (London), May and June 1967.
Schuster, Mel, "Burt Lancaster," in *Films in Review* (New York), August-September 1969.
Braun, Eric, "From Here to Esteem," in *Films and Filming* (London), May 1970. Also April and June 1970.
Colpart, G., in *Cinema* (Paris), November 1978.
Jensen, Jeffry Michael, in *Magill's Survey of Cinema 2*, Englewood Cliffs, New Jersey, 1980.
Lippe, R., "Montgomery Clift: A Critical Disturbance," in *Cineaction* (Toronto), Summer 1989.
Simmons, Jerrold, "The Production Code & Precedent," in *Journal of Popular Film and Television* (Washington, D.C.), vol. 20, no. 3, Fall 1992.
Hall, P., and N. Sivulich, "Letters: Military Movies," in *New York Times*, section 2, 25 April 1993.
Vineberg, S., "Fred Zinnemann's Actors," in *Film Criticism* (Meadville), vol. 18/19, no. 3/1, 1994.
Sternberg, D., "Real-life References in Four Fred Zinnemann Films," in *Film Criticism* (Meadville), vol. 18–19, Spring 1994.
Zinnemann, F., "Letter from Fred Zinnemann," in *Film Criticism* (Meadville), vol. 19, no. 2, 1994/1995.
Reid, J.H., in *Reid's Film Index*, no. 32, 1997.
Horton, R., "Fred Zinnemann," in *Film Comment* (New York), September/October 1997.
MacCabe, Colin, and Geoffrey Macnab, "Bayonets in Paradise: Soldier Stories," in *Sight & Sound* (London), vol. 9, no. 2, February 1999.

* * *

James Jones's novel *From Here to Eternity* was a bestseller. Portraying Army life immediately before Pearl Harbor, its racy sex scenes, lively and rough language, and vivid characterizations of men under stress made it one of the most widely read books to come out of World War II. Hollywood was interested but felt that the book would be a difficult project. Obviously the realistic and explicit sex scenes were the basis for much of the book's appeal. The book was also very lengthy and somewhat rambling. If one could conquer the problems of translating the language and sex to the screen, could a film be made that captured the spirit of the book? Hollywood wanted to try because the loss of its audience to television and divestiture of the studios' theater chains were forcing Hollywood to provide forms of entertainment that could not be found elsewhere.

Columbia's chief executive Harry Cohn bought the rights and worked on the project directly with producer Buddy Adler, director Fred Zinnemann, and writer Dan Taradash. Cohn appeared on the set to make suggestions and felt that he really contributed to the project. For the first and only time in his career, his name was included in the ads for the film. But Cohn and his director did not have a smooth relationship. Zinnemann had his own ideas how to handle the film.

Zinnemann was an excellent choice as a director. He was known for his respect of actors, and the film was one that for success would depend on the performance of the cast. Zinnemann had also worked on short subjects earlier in his career and had developed a technique of cutting away everything but the necessities—important in bringing *From Here To Eternity* down to a workable but effective size. Already evident in his work (*High Noon*, 1952), the thematic concern of *From Here To Eternity*, how an individual fights for what he believes to be right, was important to Zinnemann and a theme he would return to in later films (*A Nun's Story*, 1959; *A Man for All Seasons*, 1966).

Surprisingly, considering the Cold War temperament of the times, the film is not a glorification of military life. Although the problems of bad leadership and abuse of authority are solved by the army in the film (unlike the book), officers are shown to be pompous, arrogant and ignorant. Only some of the enlisted men are shown heroically. No glorious battles are depicted, and the climax is the Japanese sneak attack on Pearl Harbor. With love affairs involving an officer's wife and an enlisted man, a military outcast and a prostitute, the melodrama of military life is the focus of the film. The beach love scene of Burt Lancaster and Deborah Kerr has become a cliché, although at the time it was considered very risqué and erotic.

The film was a very big moneymaker for Columbia, and the production won eight Academy Awards. One of those, for Best Supporting Actor, marked the comeback of Frank Sinatra. Probably most important of all, Hollywood learned that the American audience would support films that attempted to deal with adult situations and problems. The next year Columbia verified this theory with another successful adult drama, *On the Waterfront*.

—Ray Narducy

FUKUSHU SURU WA WARE NI ARI

(Vengeance Is Mine)

Japan, 1979

Director: Shohei Imamura

Production: Schochiku Co. Ltd.; color, 35mm; running time: 128 minutes. Released 1979. Filmed in Japan.

Producer: Kazuo Inoue; **screenplay:** Masaru Baba, from a book by Ryuzo Saki; **photography:** Shinsaku Himeda; **editor:** Keiichi Uraoka; **music:** Shinichiro Ikebe.

Cast: Ken Ogata (*Iwao Enokizu*); Rentaro Mikuni (*Shizuo Enokizu*); Chocho Mikayo (*Kayo Enokizu*); Mitsuko Baisho (*Kazuko Enokizu*); Mayumi Ogawa (*Haru Asano*); Nijiko Kiyokawa (*Hisano Asano*).

Award: Kinema Jumpo Award, Best Film, 1979–80.

Publications

Books:

Bock, Audie, *Japanese Film Directors*, New York, 1978, revised edition, Tokyo, 1985.
Tessier, Max, editor, *Le cinéma Japonais au present: 1959–1979*, Paris, 1980.
Richie, Donald, with Audie Bock, *Notes for a Study on Shohei Imamura*, Sydney, 1983.
Piccardi, Adriano, and Angelo Signorelli, *Shohei Imamura*, Bergamo, 1987.
Quandt, James, *Shohei Imamura*, Bloomington, 1999.

Articles:

Variety (New York), 26 March 1980.
''New Directors/New Films,'' in *The Museum of Modern Art Film Notes*, 11–23 April 1980.
Sartor, F., in *Film en Televisie* (Brussels), May-June 1980.
Hoaas, S., ''Interview with Imamura,'' in *Cinema Papers* (Melbourne), September-October 1981.
Niogret, B., in *Positif* (Paris), January 1982.
Magny, Joel, in *Cinéma* (Paris), November 1982.
Tessier, Max, in *Image et Son* (Paris), November 1982.
Carrere, E., in *Positif* (Paris), December 1982.
Lardeau, Yann, ''Je tue donc je suis,'' in *Cahiers du Cinéma* (Paris), December 1982.
Gillett, John, ''Shohei Imamura,'' in *Film Dope* (London), January 1983.
Thibert, X., in *Cinématographe* (Paris), January 1983.
Welsh, H., in *Jeune Cinéma* (Paris), February 1983.
Baecque, Antoine de, ''Historie de douleur,'' in *Cahiers du Cinéma* (Paris), no. 425, November 1989.
Bouquet, Stéphane, ''Imamura: le porc et son homme,'' in *Cahiers du Cinéma* (Paris), no. 512, April 1997.
Tobin, Yann, and Hubert Niogret, ''Shohei Imamura,'' in *Positif* (Paris), no. 440, October 1997.
Eisenreich, Pierre, and Hubert Niogret, ''Shohei Imamura,'' in *Positif* (Paris), no. 454, December 1998.

* * *

After a long search, in *Vengeance Is Mine*, the Japanese police finally capture Iwao Enokizu, an almost legendary criminal who's left a trail of corpses to mark the last year of his murderous rampage across Japan. As the police drive him to prison, a flashback recounts the key moments in Enokizu's life: the humiliation of his father, a Japanese Catholic, by the military during the war; Enokizu's brutal murders; and his relationship with the proprietress of a small inn at Hamamatsu, where he has avoided the police dragnet by passing himself off as a professor from Kyoto University. After finally being brought to justice, Enokizu confronts his wife and father—who have entered into an incestuous relationship—and declares that he finally understands the reason behind his rage.

Considered by many critics to be his masterpiece, *Vengeance Is Mine* marked a return to feature filmmaking for director Shohei Imamura after an eight year ''retirement'' during which time he worked exclusively on documentaries for Japanese television. The film was extremely successful with both Japanese audiences and critics, who voted it ''Best Japanese Film of the Year'' in the prestigious film journal *Kinema Jumpo*. Its box office success allowed Imamura to enter into an advantageous financial relationship with Shochiku Studios, which gave him the possibility of a better level of production while creating new national and international outlets for his work.

Imamura's work up until 1970 can be characterized as highly textured, almost baroque narratives which freely intertwined the sociological, the sexual, and the political; this was followed by a period in which he explored the outer limits of the documentary and the possibility of attaining a kind of ''truth'' on film. *Vengeance Is Mine* introduced a new stage in Imamura's development. He returns to the narratological complexity of the pre-1970 work, but dispenses with the strong central character (usually female in the earlier films) whose odyssey structures the film. Instead, *Vengeance Is Mine* introduced a new series of films built on patterns of continuous disorientation, which causes each spectator to question the relation of each image to the next. Often, just the beginnings and ends of actions are shown; it is only later that we discover what actually happened. In *Vengeance Is Mine* the focus of the action glides between Enokizu, his father, the proprietress at Hamamatsu, and the police investigation, deliberately undercutting any concentration on a single main character. Imamura instead creates a portrait of a world, of which Enokizu is perhaps the ugliest, yet most revealing, manifestation. Brilliantly photographed by Shinsaku Himeda, one of the greatest of all Japanese cinematographers and a frequent collaborator of Imamura's, *Vengeance Is Mine* also features a superb performance by Ken Ogata as Enokizu.

—Richard Peña

FUNNY GAMES

Austria, 1997

Director: Michael Haneke

Production: Wega-Film, Vienna; distributed by Metro Tartan Distributors; first released 14 May 1997; color; sound: Dolby Digital; running time: 108 minutes, 59 seconds; length: 9,808 feet.

Producer: Veit Heiduschka; **screenplay:** Michael Haneke; **photography:** Jürgen Jürges; **assistant director:** Hanus Polak, Jr.; **editor:** Andreas Prochaska; **art director:** Christoph Kanter; **sound:** Walter Amann; **sound editor:** Bernhard Bamberger; **special effects/make-up:** Waldemar Poktomski; Simone Bachl; **special effects/stunts:** Mac Steinmeier; Danny Bellens; Willy Neuner; **costumes:** Lisy Christl; **wardrobe:** Katharina Nikl; **mixer:** Hannes Eder; **production manager:** Werner Reitmeier; **united production managers:** Alfred Strobl; Phillip Kaiser; **post-production:** Michael Katz; Ulrike Lasser; **script supervisors:** Katharina Biro; Jessica Hausner; **animals:** Animal Action; **dog trainer:** April Morley.

Cast: Susanne Lother (*Anna Schober*); Ulrich Mühe (*Georg Schober*); Arno Frisch (*Paul*); Frank Giering (*Peter*); Stefan Clapczynski (*Georg ''Schorschi'' Schober*); Doris Kunstmann (*Gerda*); Christoph Bantzer (*Fred Berlinger*); Wolfgang Glück (*Robert*); Susanne Meneghel (*Gerda's sister*); Monika Zallinger (*Eva Berlinger*).

Awards: Silver Hugo award for Best Director, Chicago International Film Festival, 1997; International Fantasy Film Special Jury Award (for Michael Haneke), Fantasporto (Portugal), 1998.

Funny Games

Publications:

Articles:

Romney, Jonathon, ''A Trial by Cinema,'' in *The Guardian* (London), 15 May 1997.

Haneke, Michael, ''Believing Not Seeing,'' in *Sight and Sound, LFF Supplement* (London), November 1997.

Hoberman, J, ''Head Trips,'' in *Village Voice* (New York), 17 March 1998.

Falcon, Richard, ''The Discreet Harm of the Bourgeoisie,'' in *Sight and Sound* (London), May 1998.

Film Ireland (Dublin), August/September 1998.

Cinema Papers (Victoria) October 1998.

Andrew, Geoff, ''Hurt of the Matter,'' in *Time Out* (London), 21–28 October 1998.

Time Out (London) 28 October-4 November 1998.

Sight and Sound (London), December 1998.

Engleberg, Achim, ''Nine Fragments about the Films of Michael Haneke,'' in *Filmwaves* (London), Winter 1999.

* * *

A celebrated writer and director of television and theatre in Austria, Michael Haneke first grabbed the attention of the international film community with his trilogy of films reporting on ''the progressive emotional glaciation'' of his country. Manifesting his hatred for the kind of sensationalized violence that, he believes, induces audience passivity, each film was designed to show how desensitization leads to societal alienation and dehumanization. The first, *The Seventh Continent* (1989), focused on a family's collective suicide; the second, *Benny's Video* (1992), examined a boy's fatal relationship with a girl and his video-camera; the third and most accessible, *71 Fragments of a Chronology of Chance* (1994), foregrounded the senselessness of motiveless murder and suicide.

With *Funny Games* Haneke went one step further to provoke his audience into considering their relationship to, and consumption of, screen violence. Challenging the conventions of the thriller genre itself, the film confounds expectation and keeps the majority of the violence off-screen, heard but not seen, witnessed only by us through the reactions of the other characters. It is this manner of stylization that most divided critics upon its release. While some were eager to praise the film for its daring originality, others accused it of being both manipulative and patronizing in its tone and approach.

The narrative of the film is simple and centers on a middle-class couple and their son whose idyllic holiday in their lakeside retreat is interrupted by the arrival of two anonymous, well-spoken youths.

Wearing clinical white gloves and calling themselves Peter and Paul (or, with referential irony, Tom and Jerry, Beavis and Butthead), the youths proceed to subject the family to a night of mental and physical torture, referring to each act as a game.

Sign-posting some classic horror/thriller conventions, the film opens upon the tranquillity of an ordered world that is soon to be disrupted by the threat of the unknown. Listening to classical music as they travel by car through the country lanes, the family is coded as safe and bourgeois. At this stage they remain blissfully unaware that, as a portent of the sudden and alarmingly vicious acts to follow, their music is being drowned out by screamingly chaotic heavy metal. Yet despite these early warning notes the film is otherwise relentlessly measured in its slow build up of tension and execution of events.

Although the situation itself seems bizarre, emphasis is placed on the realism of the family's reactions. When the son, Schorschi, is shot (his blood splashed symbolically over the television set) and the youths apparently leave, the camera fixes in excruciatingly long takes—first of the mother, Anna, and then of the father, George. Rather than attempting an immediate escape they sit motionless, caught up in their own personal humiliation and despair, too wounded to move.

To further test the viewers' perceptions of reality, Haneke seeks to increase awareness of the film's fiction. Paul, the more dominant of the psychotic pair, occasionally makes post-modern asides to the camera, psychologically taunting us as much as he taunts the family. ''What do you think?'' he asks, having told his victims that they will be dead within twelve hours, ''Do you think they have a chance of winning?'' When Anna manages to grab the shotgun and shoot Peter, he picks up the remote and rewinds the film, bringing his partner back to life again, thereby changing the course of the narrative. At one point he winks towards the screen as if to include the spectators in his game—a hint from the filmmaker that by continuing to watch they make themselves responsible for the perpetration of screen violence.

Upon the release of *Funny Games* Haneke contentiously declared that ''anyone who leaves the cinema doesn't need the film, and anyone who stays does.'' Bearing in mind the director's desire to educate, the problem with this film is its effectiveness. Although very different from most other horror/thrillers it is a worthy addition to the genre, ranking alongside other experimental works such as *The Texas Chainsaw Massacre*, *Man Bites Dog* and *Henry, Portrait of a Serial Killer*. Shockingly frightening and nihilistic, the spare visual style and subtle insinuation mesmerizes and intrigues rather than discourages. The manner of the two youths is extremely disquieting. These are not the archetypal villains whose behavior is a result of a terrible childhood or trauma—they play merely because they can, because they are bored of their middle-class existence and can no longer maintain any normal human connection. There is also a great sense of loss when the final member of the family to be killed, Anna (played by with devastating sincerity by Susanne Lothar), is pushed into her watery grave. The act finally makes real what has been a suspicion for the last third of the film, that the captors will get away with their crime and, contrary to any hopes and expectations, none of their victims will manage to survive.

Whether or not the central message of *Funny Games* will make any practical difference to the way in which violence is either presented on the screen or received by its viewers remains to be seen. One suspects not, for as an arthouse rather than a mainstream hit it clearly has a limited audience. The wider audience it seems keen to preach to will therefore remain unconverted while the rest, contrary to Haneke's wishes, will stay in the cinema, continuing to view both this and other violent films out of an ''academic'' interest.

—Hannah Patterson

FURY

USA, 1936

Director: Fritz Lang

Production: Metro-Goldwyn-Mayer; black and white; running time: 92 minutes, length: 8292 feet. Released June 1936.

Producer: Joseph L. Mankiewicz; **screenplay:** Fritz Lang and Bartlett Cormack, from the novel *Mob Rule* by Norman Krasna; **photography:** Joseph Ruttenberg; **editor:** Frank Sullivan; **art directors:** Cedric Gibbons, William A. Horning; **music:** Franz Waxman.

Cast: Spencer Tracy (*Joe Wheeler*); Sylvia Sidney (*Katherine Grant*); Walter Abel (*District Attorney*); Bruce Cabot (*Kirby Dawson*); Edward Ellis (*Sheriff*); Walter Brennan (*Bugs Meyers*); Frank Albertson (*Charlie*); George Walcott (*Tom*); Arthur Stone (*Durkin*); Morgan Wallace (*Fred Garrett*); George Chandler (*Milton Jackson*); Roger Gray (*The Stranger*); Edwin Maxwell (*Vickery*); Howard Hickman (*Governor*); Jonathan Hale (*The Defence Counsel*).

Publications

Script:

Lang, Fritz, and Bartlett Cormack, *Fury*, in *Twenty Best Screenplays*, edited by John Gassner and Dudley Nichols, New York, 1943.

Books:

Courtade, Francis, *Fritz Lang*, Paris, 1963.
Moullet, Luc, *Fritz Lang*, Paris, 1963.
Eibel, Alfred, editor, *Fritz Lang*, Paris, 1964.
Bogdanovich, Peter, *Fritz Lang in America*, New York, 1967.
Deschner, Donald, *The Films of Spencer Tracy*, New York, 1968.
Swindell, Larry, *Spencer Tracy: A Biography*, New York, 1969.
Jensen, Paul, *The Cinema of Fritz Lang*, New York, 1969.
Johnston, Claire, *Fritz Lang*, London, 1969.
Tozzi, Romano, *Spencer Tracy*, New York, 1973.
Grafe, Frieda, Enno Patalas, and Hans Prinzler, *Fritz Lang*, Munich, 1976.
Eisner, Lotte, *Fritz Lang*, edited by David Robinson, New York, 1977.
Armour, Robert, *Fritz Lang*, Boston, 1978.
Ott, Frederick, *The Films of Fritz Lang*, Secaucus, New Jersey, 1979.
Jenkins, Stephen, editor, *Fritz Lang: The Image and the Look*, London, 1981.

Giannetti, Louis, *Masters of the American Cinema*, Englewood Cliffs, New Jersey, 1981.
Kaplan, E. Ann, *Fritz Lang: A Guide to References and Resources*, Boston, 1981.
Maibohm, Ludwig, *Fritz Lang: Seine Filme, sein Leben*, Munich, 1981.
Dürrenmatt, Dieter, *Fritz Lang: Leben und Werk*, Basel, 1982.
Humphries, Reynold, *Fritz Lang: Cinéaste américain*, Paris, 1982; as *Fritz Lang: Genre and Representation in His American Films*, Baltimore, 1988.
Davidson, Bill, *Spencer Tracy, Tragic Idol*, London, 1987.
Humphries, Reynold, *Fritz Lang: Genre & Representation in His American Films*, Ann Arbor, 1989.
Levin, David J., *Richard Wagner, Fritz Lang, and the Nibelungen: The Dramaturgy of Disavowal*, Princeton, 1998.
McGilligan, Patrick, *Fritz Lang: The Nature of the Beast*, New York, 1999.

Articles:

New York Times, 6 June 1936.
Variety (New York), 10 June 1936.
Times (London), 24 June 1936.
Kine Weekly (London), 25 June 1936.
Sight and Sound (London), Summer and Autumn 1936.
Spectator (London), 3 July 1936.
Lambert, Gavin, in *Sight and Sound* (London), Summer and Autumn 1955.
Cohn, Bernard, in *Positif* (Paris), February 1964.
Springer, John, ''Sylvia Sidney,'' in *Films in Review* (New York), January 1966.
Thousand Eyes Magazine (New York), January 1977.
Listener (London), 13 August, 1987.
Kurowski, U., ''Fritz Lang,'' in *EPD Film* (Frankfurt), vol. 7, no. 12, December 1990.
Smedley, N., ''Fritz Lang's Trilogy: The Rise and Fall of a European Social Commentator,'' in *Film History* (London), vol. 5, no. 1, March 1993.
Greene, Graham, ''Deux critiques,'' in *Positif* (Paris), no. 441, November 1997.

* * *

Like many of Fritz Lang's post-Hitler films, *Fury* almost didn't get made; according to Lotte Eisner, the project was a ''last chance'' effort before Lang's one-year MGM contract lapsed. But as Lang's inaugural Hollywood effort, *Fury* was certainly worth the wait, and in retrospect can be taken as emblematic of the way Lang would be treated by successive generations of reviewers and critics.

A significant number of *Fury*'s contemporary reviewers, for example, divided the film into two halves, the first, in the words of Otis Ferguson, ''a powerful and documented piece of fiction about a lynching,'' the second ''a desperate attempt to make love, lynching, and the Hays office come out even.'' In certain respects the ''two parts'' description is accurate. Part One: En route to meet his fiancée, Katherine Grant (Sylvia Sidney), Joe Wilson (Spencer Tracy) is arrested for kidnapping on the basis of circumstantial evidence (peanuts, a five dollar bill). An anxious Katherine arrives on the scene just in time to see a mob of locals setting fire to the jailhouse while Joe watches the crowd through the bars of his second story cell. Part Two: After Joe's ''death,'' his tormentors are put on trial for murder and the only witness who will attest to Joe's presence in the jail is Katherine, who slowly comes to suspect (on the basis of a coat she once mended for Joe and a characteristically misspelled note) that Joe is not dead, a fact confirmed when conscience prompts Joe to halt the trial by ''presenting'' himself in court.

Add to this picture of *Fury*'s sharply bifurcated and allegedly ill-balanced structure related complaints about the story's overall ideological trajectory (shifting the guilt from the mob to Joe) and the film's ending (specifically the courtroom kiss of Joe and Katherine), however, and it is easy to take *Fury* as two films, its first *M*-like half the last of Lang's expressionist/social realist masterpieces, its second half the first instance of Lang's debilitating accommodation to the stylistic demands of the Hollywood system. Indeed, there is a substantial body of Lang criticism which contends that Lang never recovered from the Judas kiss of Hollywood after he bowed to MGM's dictate on the matter of Joe and Katherine's courtroom clinch.

There is considerable Langian irony in the fact that defenders of Lang's Hollywood films often derive the terms of their defense from critics, like Noel Burch, who condemn those movies as ''a silence lasting some thirty films.'' Burch, that is, praises Lang for perfecting the transparency of the ''continuity'' system early in his career, with *Dr. Mabuse, der Spieler*, after which, on Burch's reading, Lang proceeded to deconstruct continuity conventions by systematic variations, often in the form of editing and narrative ellipses (as in *Spione*) which finally become, with *M*, an ''auto-nomous'' textual system, an ''(abstract) function, but in symbiosis with the plot which they both support and challenge.'' Of the many (mostly French) critics who have written about Lang's American films in similar terms, the most important in regards to *Fury* is Reynold Humphries, whose central claim is that Lang, contra Burch, *never* stopped experimenting with the technology and epistemology of cinema.

The central figure of this epistemological concern in *Fury* is the repeated auto-reference in (of) the film to the fact of movie-going which culminates in the use of newsreel footage at the climax of the trial to prove that various defendants, despite their testimony to the contrary, were indeed at the scene of the riot. According to Humphries, the effect of the newsreel sequence, like the effect of Hollywood films generally, is to confirm the truth of the (film) world, just as Hollywood confirms the truth of our world, even though the truth confirmed is, in fact, a ''fiction,'' authored, in this case, by Joe Wilson, the fiction of Joe's death. And the irony here, in Humphries' view, is that the newsreel footage bears not at all on the question of the alleged crime. The result is that *Fury*, the frames of which exactly correspond at times to those of the newsreel image, thus undercuts its ostensible (fictive) claim to ''objective'' photographic truth.

We can go Humphries one better in this analysis by noting, as it were, the ''production history'' of the newsreel footage. It is quite clear that only a single newsreel camera was at work in the film world; we see the four-man camera/sound crew en route to Strand; we see their fixed tripod camera position in a hotel room overlooking the County Jail square; the prosecuting attorney introduces the footage as the work of a single photographer. Moreover, we saw what they were ostensibly recording (though often from positions the newsreel camera couldn't have occupied); the jail fire is lit from within the building, the crowd gathers in a now quiet square to watch the conflagration (here Katherine arrives), a kid announces the arrival of soldiers, and the crowd scatters while two men dynamite the jail.

Some of the resulting footage is quickly processed and shown in movie houses; Joe sees it some 20 times, he tells his brothers, before he shows up at his gas station, seemingly convinced, almost on its basis, that he was, in fact, ''murdered.''

And yet the footage shown in court comes as a complete shock, as if none of the defendants had ever heard of or bothered to see the newsreel. And the shock is justified; what the ''newsreel'' shows it could not have seen, or have seen that way. We get closeups of Dawson helping to wield the battering ram, though we saw that action and saw no camera crew anywhere near; we see Dawson help construct and Sally Humphrey help ignite a bonfire outside the jail, from camera positions which would have come between the two participants singled out, though both seem amazed when the footage is screened in court; we see Fred Garrett gleefully cutting firehoses with an axe while others wrestle with firemen, yet no fire trucks are evident during the jail-burning sequence, and the square is cleared of bystanders by the time authorities arrive.

All of which can be taken to ''reverse'' the Reynold Humphries scenario of *Fury*'s ''subject effect''; rather than encouraging us to take a (true) newsreel as confirming a (false) fiction, Lang encourages us to see a (false) newsreel as confirming a (true) fiction, the fiction that, among other things, human beings are capable of grotesque violence, even to their own memories (Mrs. Garrett faints in the courtroom, as if genuinely surprised by her husband's guilt). At least part of the film's desire is to recall to mind a national history of forgetfulness on the matter of racial and social violence. And that desire is finally well served by the epistemological hesitancy which Lang's narrational strategies introduce into our ''reading'' of *Fury*. You never know when it might happen to you.

—Leland Poague

OS FUZIS

(The Guns)

Brazil, 1964

Director: Ruy Guerra

Production: Copacabana Films, Embracine, and Daga Filmes (Brazil); black and white, 35mm; running time: 110 minutes; length: 3300 meters. Released 1964. Filmed in Milagres.

Producer: Jarbas Barbosa; **screenplay:** Miguel Torres and Ruy Guerra, from an adaptation by Pierre Pelegri, Demosthenes Theokary, and Philippe Dumarçay from an original story by Ruy Guerra; **photography:** Ricardo Aronovich; **editor:** Ruy Guerra; **music:** Moacyr Santos.

Cast: Atila Lorio (*Gaúcho, the truck driver*); Nelson Xavier (*Mario*); Maria Gladys (*Luisa*); Leonides Bayer (*Sergeant*); Paulo Cesar (*Soldier*); Mauricio Loyola (*Bearded prophet*); Rui Polanah (*Civilian*); Hugo Carvana (*Soldier*); Joel Bacelos (*Father of the dead baby*); Ivan Candido.

Publications

Book:

Johnson, Randall, and Robert Stam, editors, *Brazilian Cinema*, New Brunswick, New Jersey, 1982.

Articles:

Fieschi, J. A., and J. Narboni, *Cahiers du Cinéma* (Paris), April 1967.
Leduc, F., ''Interview with Guerra,'' in *Jeune Cinéma* (Paris), April 1967.
Langlois, G., ''Interview with Guerra,'' in *Cinéma* (Paris), June 1967.
Pelegri, P., in *Positif* (Paris), July 1967.
Zele, Van, in *Image et Son* (Paris), November 1969.
Ciment, Michel, ''Ruy Guerra,'' in *Second Wave* (New York), 1970.
Tarratt, Margaret, in *Films and Filming* (London), December 1972.
Elsaesser, Thomas, ''Interview with Ruy Guerra,'' in *Monogram* (London), April 1974.
Burns, Bradford E., and others, ''History in the Brazilian Cinema,'' in *Luso-Brazilian Review* (Madison, Wisconsin), Summer 1977.
''The Fall: Formal Innovation and Radical Critique,'' in *Jump Cut* (Berkeley), May 1979.
Castillo, L., ''Ruy Guerra: sonar con los pies sobre la tierra,'' in *Cine Cubano* (Habana), no. 134, 1992.

* * *

Os fuzis (The Guns) is, arguably, Ruy Guerra's greatest political film. This landmark work is unusual in that it relies primarily on a tradition of mainstream commercial cinema—the linear narrative—to convey profoundly political themes. Guerra imaginatively and effectively blends this tradition with features typical of documentary filmmaking.

The action is set in Brazil's semi-arid, underdeveloped Northeastern backlands (the *sertão*), and Guerra uses numerous devices, in addition to location shooting, to give his film the look of a documentary. Early in the film, a subtitle appears that specifies the time and place of the action. The sub-plot of the holy man and his bull is, according to Guerra, based on a historical incident. Local customs (a procession of people praying for rain) and types (the leather-clad *vaqueiros*) are observed. In interview-like sequences, elderly inhabitants recall past events and personages in the region's history, such as religious zealot Antônio Conselheiro and the government he established and defended at Canudos.

The film's plot and sub-plot weave together the political problems of the oppression of the villagers by the military and by the forces of fanatic religious mysticism. Gaúcho's solution, to battle the soldiers, fails because it springs from emotional impulses rather that from any revolutionary consciousness. Gaúcho—himself an outsider—is not a revolutionary leader; his response is personal, and it is not supported by the masses. The butchering of the sacred bull, however, is a collective revolutionary action reflecting a change of consciousness on the part of the villagers. The followers of the holy man had been seeking a fantastic solution (worshipping an animal) instead of a political and/or economic solution to the problem of hunger. The crowd's cry, ''It's meat!,'' heralds the downfall of the holy man: his bull has been discarded as a religious symbol; it is now perceived as a source of food.

Unlike many Latin American political films, *Os fuzis* not only avoids facile political solutions, but it also features complex characters and interpersonal relations. Gaúcho initially acts like a typically exploitative truck driver, but his moral behavior evolves when he sinks as low as the starving villagers. The tortuous mise-en-scène of the love scene between Mario and his girlfriend brilliantly reflects the complex approach-avoidance conflict the girl faces; she loves Mario, but she is restrained in expressing this love by her identification with the villagers and by her revulsion over Mario's complicity in the cover-up. At the end of the film, the villagers have derived no political profit from Gaúcho's suicidal act, and they will continue to be subject to military oppression. The soldiers themselves remain the corrupt victims of the system.

Many Brazilians see *Os fuzis* as a forceful condemnation of the needless killing, the corruption, and the ties to powerful landowning and entrepreneurial interests that have characterized their country's military. The references in the film to Antônio Conselheiro's rebellion (1896–97) remind viewers that the Brazilian military in the 1960s still operated much as it did during the infamous Canudos campaign—a totalitarian crime perpetrated against a backlands community.

When first shown in Brazil in 1963, *Os fuzis* did poorly because many viewers considered the film's narrative needlessly obscure and complex. Today, however, critics recognize the film as a great, typical work of the first phase of Brazil's highly regarded Cinema Novo. Guerra, like other filmmakers of this period, opposed the ideology and aesthetics of Hollywood and Brazilian commercial cinema by favoring low-budget, independently produced films shot on location. For Guerra and his colleagues, filmmaking was a key political-cultural activity in the battle against Brazil's neo-colonialism.

—Dennis West

GARAM HAWA

(Hot Winds)

India, 1973

Director: M.S. Sathyu

Production: Unit 3MM; color, 35mm; running time: 136 minutes (some prints are 144 minutes). Released 1973.

Producer: Ishan Arya, M.S. Sathyu, Abu Siwani; **screenplay:** Kaifi Azmi, Shama Zaidi, from the unpublished story by Ismat Chugtai; **photography:** Ishan Arya; **editor:** S. Chakrabort; **music:** Ustad Bahadur Khan.

Cast: Balraj Sahni (*Salim Mirza*); Gita Shauhat Kaifi (*Amina Mirza*); Jalal Agha (*Shamshad*); Dinanath Zutski (*Halim*); Badar Begum (*Salim's mother*); Abu Siwani (*Baqar Mirza*); Faroukh Shaikh (*Sikander Mizra*); Jamal Hashmi (*Kazim*).

Awards: National Award for Best Film on Integration and Best Screenplay, India, 1974; Filmfare Award for Best Screenplay and Best Story Writer, India, 1974.

Publications:

Script:

Azmi, Kafi and Shama Zaidi, *Three Hindi Film Scripts*, 1974.

Books:

Barnouw, Erik, and S. Krishnaswamy, *Indian Film*, New York and London, 1963.
Chakravarty, Sumita S., *National Identity in Indian Popular Cinema, 1947–1987*, Austin, Texas, 1993.

* * *

Garam Hawa (Hot Winds) was the first feature from director M.S. (Mysore Shrivinas) Sathyu of India. The film was controversial from its inception, as it was the first film to deal with the human consequences resulting from the 1947 partition of India. This action, ordered by British Lord Mountbatten, split India into religious coalitions, with India remaining Hindi and the new country of Pakistan serving as a refuge for Muslims.

Despite its controversial subject matter the film was initially accepted by a commercial producer, but then pressure and fear of the critical and governmental reception of such a work led to a rapid withdrawal of the offer. Sathyu turned to the government sponsored Film Financing Corporation (FFC) for support. This agency was created as an alternative for filmmakers seeking financing for work which was not commercially embraced by institutional distributors. Its aim was to free these artists from the dominance of loan agencies and their control of film content. Sathyu secured FFC financing and his film, based on an unpublished story by Marxist activist Ismat Chughtai, was completed in the city of Agra. The production of the film was plagued by a smattering of public protests; ultimately, Sathyu had to divert attention from his actual locations by using a fake second unit crew and sending them out with an unloaded camera.

Once finished, *Garam Hawa* was again the subject of controversy; it was banned as an ''instigation to communal dissension.'' Sathyu was strong in his conviction, however, and he showed the film to many government leaders and journalists. The influence of these people on the censorship board led to a reversal of the ban. The film went on to win a national award for its contribution to ''national integration.'' More recognition followed, including accolades that praised the film's efforts to create ''a language of common identity'' and to humanize the situation endured by Muslims in North India who did not wish to move from their homes after the partition.

The screenplay for *Garam Hawa* was written by Kaifi Azmi (an Indian poet and lyricist) and Shama Zaidi, Sathyu's wife. The tale is a complex narrative assembled with loving attention to detail. The story's main focal point is Salim Mirza, played by veteran actor Balraj Sahani in his final film before his death. Salim is a Muslim shoemaker and patriarch who does not want to relocate to Pakistan. There is the added element of a love story woven into this political narrative, however, and it is this element which adds greater meaning to the story. The filmmaker's adept use of light and framing adds dimension to the characters and their struggles.

Salim's daughter, Amina (Gita Shauhat Kaifi), is betrothed to Kazim (Jamal Hashmi); they are shown to be deeply in love and very happy together. Kazim goes across the border to Pakistan to find work (as there is none for Muslims in Agra as the story progresses). When he returns to marry Amina, he is arrested. She pines for her lost lover, but has the attentions of Shamshad (Jalal Agha), whom she does not love and does not wish to marry. Her agony is a reflection of her father's; these people are trapped between two worlds.

Salim is powerless against the shift in attitudes and political climate; he finds himself unable to secure bank loans, unable to keep

Garam Hawa

possession of his family home, and losing his means of survival as once-loyal customers take their business elsewhere. He has done nothing wrong, yet he is punished by the post-partition environment in Agra. As Salim's situation becomes more grave, the camera frames him in smaller spaces, implying his imprisonment in his own hometown. He says, "They have taken everything. Only our faith will survive." He is strong, but he is discouraged by the exodus of family members into Pakistan. In the end, he too makes the journey to the train. On the way, Salim and his son Sikander (Faroukh Shaikh) encounter a massive protest rally which seeks to unite the dispossessed of the nation. First Sikander, and then Salim, join the flag-waving mob. The train is forgotten, and the final scene brings a sense of hope as we see Salim accept his situation in a new way and begin to take charge of his life.

—Tammy Kinsey

GATE OF HELL

See **JIGOKUMON**

IL GATTOPARDO

(The Leopard)

Italy-France, 1962

Director: Luchino Visconti

Production: Titanus (Rome)/SN Pathe-Cinema (Paris)/SGC (Paris); DeLuxe color (original version: Technicolor); CinemaScope (original version: Technirama); running time: 184 minutes (British version 161 minutes), original running time: 205 minutes. Dubbed. Released 1962.

Producer: Goffredo Lombardo; **executive producer:** Pietro Notarianna; **screenplay:** Suso Cecchi D'Amico, Pasquale Festa Campanile, Massimo Franciosa, Enrico Medioli, Luchino Visconti, from the novel by Giuseppe Tomasi di Lampedusa; **assistant directors:** Rinaldo Ricci, Albino Cocco, Francesco Massaro, Brad Fuller; **dialogue director:** Archibald Colquhoun; **photography:** Giuseppe

Rotunno; **editor:** Mario Serandrei; **sound:** Mario Messina; **art director:** Mario Garbuglia; **costumes:** Piero Tosi; **music:** Nino Rota.

Cast: Burt Lancaster (*Don Fabrizio, Prince of Salina*); Alain Delon (*Tancredi*); Claudia Cardinale (*Angelica Sedara*); Paolo Stoppa (*Don Calogera Sedara*); Rina Morelli (*Maria Stella*); Serge Reggiana (*Don Ciccio Tumeo*); Romolo Valli (*Father Pirrone*); Leslie French (*Chevally*); Ivo Garrani (*Colonel Pallavicino*); Mario Girotti (*Count Cavriaghi*); Pierre Clementi (*Francesco Paolo*); Lucilla Morlacchi (*Concetta*); Giuliano Gemma (*The Garibaldino General*); Ida Galli (*Carolina*); Ottavia Piccolo (*Caterina*); Carlo Valenzano (*Paolo*); Anna Maria Bottini (*Mlle. Dombreuil*); Marino Mase (*Tutor*); Lola Braccini (*Donna Margherita*); Howard N. Rubien (*Don Diego*).

Publications

Script:

Visconti, Luchino, and others, *Il gattopardo*, Bologna, 1963.

Books:

Baldelli, Pio, *I film di Luchino Visconti*, Manduria, 1965.
Guillaume, Yves, *Visconti*, Paris, 1966.
Nowell-Smith, Geoffrey, *Luchino Visconti*, New York, 1968.
Baldelli, Pio, *Luchino Visconti*, Milan, 1973.
Thomas, Tony, *Burt Lancaster*, New York, 1975.
Ferrero, Adelio, editor, *Visconti: Il cinema*, Modena, 1977.
Rode, Henri, *Alain Delon*, Paris, 1977.
Tornabuoni, Lietta, editor, *Album Visconti*, Milan, 1978.
Stirling, Monica, *A Screen of Time: A Study of Luchino Visconti*, New York, 1979.
Rondolini, Gianni, *Luchino Visconti*, Turin, 1981.
Servadio, Gaia, *Luchino Visconti: A Biography*, London, 1981.
Zana, Jean-Claude, *Alain Delon*, Paris, 1981.
Bencivenni, Alessandro, *Luchino Visconti*, Florence, 1982.
Barbier, Philippe, *Alain Delon*, Paris, 1983.
Tonetti, Claretta, *Luchino Visconti*, Boston, 1983; revised edition, 1998.
Clinch, Minty, *Burt Lancaster*, London, 1984.
Hunter, Allan, *Burt Lancaster: The Man and His Movies*, New York, 1984.

Il Gattopardo

Ishaghpour, Youssef, *Luchino Visconti: Le Sens et l'image*, Paris, 1984.
Sanzio, Alain, and Paul-Louis Thirard, *Luchino Visconti: Cinéaste*, Paris, 1984.
Windeler, Robert, *Burt Lancaster*, London, 1984.
De Guisti, Luciano, *I film di Luchino Visconti*, Rome, 1985.
Geitel, Klaus, and others, *Luchino Visconti*, Munich, 1985.
Mancini, Elaine, *Luchino Visconti: A Guide to References and Resources*, Boston, 1986.
Villien, Bruno, *Visconti*, Paris, 1986.
Lacourbe, Roland, *Burt Lancaster*, Paris, 1987.
Schifano, Laurence, *Luchino Visconti: Les Feux de la passion*, Paris, 1987.
Lagny, Michèle, *Senso, Luchino Visconti: étude critique*, Paris, 1992.
Renzi, Renzo, *Visconti segreto*, Rome, 1994.
Bacon, Henry, *Visconti: His Life, His Films*, New York, 1998.
Bacon, Henry, *Visconti: Explorations of Beauty and Decay*, Cambridge, 1998.

Articles:

Cinema Nuovo (Bergamo), 1962.
Sadoul, Georges, in *Filmstudio*, no. 41, 1963.
''Visconti Issue'' of *Etudes Cinématographes* (Paris), no. 26–27, 1963.
Variety (New York), 17 April 1963.
''Visconti, the Leopard Man,'' in *Vogue* (New York), July 1963.
Motion Picture Herald (New York), 21 August 1963.
Cahiers du Cinéma (Paris), August 1963.
Martin, Marcel, ''Visconti et l'histoire,'' in *Cinéma* (Paris), September-October 1963.
Sight and Sound (London), Winter 1963–64.
Mendes Sargo, Tino, in *Film Quarterly* (Berkeley), Winter 1963–64.
Monthly Film Bulletin (London), January 1964.
Davies, Brenda, ''Can the Leopard?,'' in *Sight and Sound* (London), Spring 1964.
''Visconti Issue'' of *Cinema* (Rome), April 1970.
Bogemski, G., in *Film und Fernsehen* (Berlin), October and December 1979 and January, April, and June 1980.
Turroni, G., ''Le citazioni del gusto,'' in *Filmcritica* (Florence), January 1982.
Ehrenstein, D., ''Leopard Redux,'' in *Film Comment* (New York), September-October 1983.
Nowell-Smith, Geoffrey, in ''Lampedusa Revisited,'' in *Sight and Sound* (London), Autumn 1983.
Gordon, A., ''Has the Leopard Got Its Spots Back,'' in *Stills* (London), November-December 1983.
Ranvaud, Ron, ''Remounting the Leopard,'' in *Monthly Film Bulletin* (London), December 1983.
Lehti, S., in *Soundtrack* (Los Angeles), June 1984.
Villier, Bruno, ''Tancredi,'' in *Cinématographe* (Paris), September-October 1984.
Frauen und Film (Berlin), August 1986.
Bouvier, M., ''Entre-temps,'' in *Camera/Stylo* (Paris), December 1989.
Roberti, B., ''Ombre allo specchio,'' in *Filmcritica* (Rome), November 1991.
Piersanti, A., ''Il gattopardo e morto viva il gattopardo,'' in *Revue de la Cinémathèque* (Montreal), May 1992.
Rotunno, Giuseppe, ''Recupero dei film *Il gattopardo* e *Le notti bianche*,'' in *Cinema Nuovo* (Bari), vol. 42, no. 346, November-December 1993.
Cieslar, Jirí, ''Concettino ohlédnutí,'' in *Film a Doba* (Prague), vol. 40, no. 4, Winter 1994.
Liempt, J. Van, in *Film en Televisie + Video* (Brussels), no. 455, October 1995.
Mandolini, C., ''*Le guepard*,'' in *Séquences* (Haute-Ville), no. 189/190, March/June 1997.
Rohdie, S., ''Time and Consciousness in Luchino Visconti,'' in *Metro Magazine* (St. Kilda West), no. 113/114, 1998.

* * *

Only in recent years has it been at all possible to appreciate *Il gattopardo* in Britain and the United States, where the film was originally released in a hideously mutilated version rightly disowned by Visconti. Twentieth Century-Fox, who had co-financed the film with the Italian company Titanus, cut it from 206 to 161 minutes, printed it on DeLuxe as opposed to the original Technicolor stock (resulting in a look both muddy and garish), and substituted a crudely dubbed American soundtrack for the carefully prepared Italian original. The version now in circulation respects all of Visconti's original intentions, the running time of 186 minutes being the length to which Visconti finally cut his film.

Il gattopardo is based on the novel of the same name written by the Sicilian Prince Giuseppe Tomasi di Lampedusa and published in 1958. Like Visconti's earlier *Senso* it is set at the time of the Risorgimento, only here the setting is Sicily and the action takes place against the background of Garibaldi's expedition to Sicily to depose the Bourbon kingdom of Francis II and to unite the island with Italy. The film focuses on the Salina family, at the head of which stands Prince Fabrizio, who stands aloof from the whole Garibaldi affair, seeing it as little more than a change of dramatis personae in the same old play. However, his nephew Tancredi Falconeri joins Garibaldi's army and becomes an officer in the army of Victor Emmanuel, the first king of a unified Italy. He also falls in love with Angelica, the daughter of Don Calogero Sedara, a former peasant who has risen to the rank of mayor of Donnafugata, where Prince Salina has his summer residence. Not only is she beautiful but also very rich, and Tancredi needs her money if he is to fulfil his political ambitions, since his family, though aristocratic, are relatively impecunious. Conscious of the decline of his class, Prince Salina asks Don Calogero for the hand of his daughter on Tancredi's behalf and the film climaxes in a sumptuous ball for the noble society of Palermo at which the young couple are officially ''introduced'' to the social world.

The central, overriding theme of *Il gattopardo*, like *Senso*, is ''*trasformismo*,'' neatly encapsulated by the opportunistic Tancredi in the words ''if we want things to stay as they are, things will have to change.'' What the film presents is the gradual submergence and transformation of a noble Italian family; as Geoffrey Nowell-Smith puts it, ''the bourgeoisie marry into the aristocracy and the Byronic aristocrat sinks gently into *bien-pensant* mediocrity as the revolutionary storm subsides.'' The truly remarkable ball scene, which takes up about one-third of the film's length and involves some 200 people in 14 interconnected rooms, is not simply an incredible directorial tour-de-force; rather it decisively marks the transition from the tired, old nobility represented by Prince Salina to the thrusting ambition of the new ruling class represented by Don Calogero. Burt Lancaster's performance during this extended climax to the film is nothing short of remarkable, as is Visconti's consummate skill in blending the various intimate, personal dramas within the wider mise-en-scène. As in the rest of the film only Prince Salina seems fully aware of what is happening to his class, and as the sumptuous festivities continue he assumes an expression of increasing disgust and melancholy, at one moment pointedly studying a painting entitled *The Death of the Just*. However, his nobility and dignity never desert him, and, when Angelica invites him to waltz with her, his awareness of her youth and beauty eclipses his sadness for a moment and, in an extraordinarily moving scene, he symbolically hands over power with grace and pride.

Il gattopardo is dominated almost equally by the presence of Prince Salina and the Sicilian landscape. At one point, in conversation with a member of the Piedmontese aristocracy, Prince Salina argues that in Sicily "the environment, the climate, the landscape" all militate against change, and Visconti perfectly captures the feeling of the long, oppressively hot, sleep-inducing Sicilian summers that the original novel describes so evocatively.

—Julian Petley

THE GENERAL

USA, 1926

Directors: Buster Keaton and Clyde Bruckman

Production: Buster Keaton Productions and United Artists; black and white, 35mm, silent; running time: about 74 minutes; length: 8 reels, 7500 feet. Released 18 December 1926, New York. Re-released after 1928 with musical soundtrack and sound effects. Filmed during 1926 in Oregon. Cost: $250,000 (estimated).

Producers: Joseph Schenck and Buster Keaton; **scenario:** Al Boasberg and Charles Smith after a storyline by Buster Keaton and Clyde Bruckman, adapted by Al Boasberg and Charles Smith from *The Great Locomotive Chase* by William Pittinger; **photography:** Dev Jennings and Bert Haines; **editors:** Sherman Kell with Harry Barnes; **production designer:** Fred Gabourie; **technical director:** Fred Gabourie.

Cast: Buster Keaton (*Johnnie Gray*); Marion Mack (*Annabelle Lee*); Glen Cavender (*Capt. Anderson*); Jim Farley (*General Thatcher*); Frederick Vroom (*Southern general*); Charles Smith (*Annabelle's father*); Frank Barnes (*Annabelle's brother*); Joe Keaton, Mike Denlin, Tom Nawm (*Union generals*).

Publications

Script:

Keaton, Buster, and others, "Le Mécano de la *General*," in *Avant-Scène du Cinéma* (Paris), February 1975.

Books:

Keaton, Buster, with Charles Samuels, *My Wonderful World of Slapstick*, New York, 1960; London, 1967.
Turconi, Davide, and Francesco Savio, *Buster Keaton*, Venice, 1963.
Lebel, Jean-Patrick, *Buster Keaton*, Paris, 1964.
Oms, Marcel, *Buster Keaton*, Lyons, 1964.
Blesh, Rudi, *Keaton*, New York, 1966.
McCaffrey, Donald, *Four Great Comedians*, New York, 1968.
Robinson, David, *Hollywood in the Twenties*, New York, 1968.
Robinson, David, *Buster Keaton*, London, 1968.
Brownlow, Kevin, *The Parade's Gone By*, London and New York, 1969.
Rubinstein, E., *Filmguide to The General*, Bloomington, Indiana, 1973.
Coursodon, Jean-Pierre, *Buster Keaton*, Paris, 1973; revised edition, 1986.
Mast, Gerald, *The Comic Mind: Comedy and the Movies*, Chicago, 1974; revised edition, 1979.
Kerr, Walter, *The Silent Clowns*, New York, 1975.
Anobile, Richard, editor, *The Best of Buster*, New York, 1976.
Wead, George, *Buster Keaton and the Dynamics of Visual Wit*, New York, 1976.
Moews, Daniel, *Keaton: The Silent Features Close Up*, Berkeley, 1977.
Wead, George, and George Ellis, *The Film Career of Buster Keaton*, Boston, 1977.
Dardis, Tom, *Keaton: The Man Who Wouldn't Lie Down*, New York, 1979.
Benayoun, Robert, *The Look of Buster Keaton*, Paris, 1982; London, 1984.
Brunovska Karnick, Kristine, and Henry Jenkins, editors, *Classical Hollywood Comedy*, New York, 1995.
Mead, Marion, *Buster Keaton: Cut to the Chase*, New York, 1995.
Oldham, Gabriella, *Keaton's Silent Shorts: Beyond the Laughter*, Carbondale, 1996.
Amiel, Vincent, *Corps au cinèma: Keaton, Bresson, Cassavetes*, Paris, 1998.
Knopf, Robert, *The Theater and Cinema of Buster Keaton*, Princeton, 1999.

Articles:

Variety (New York), 9 February 1927.
Keaton, Joseph, in *Photoplay* (New York), May 1927.
Penelope Houston, in *Sight and Sound* (London), April-June 1953.
Agee, James, *Agee on Film 1*, New York, 1958.
"Keaton Issue" of *Cahiers du Cinéma* (Paris), August 1958.
Bishop, Christopher, "The Great Stone Face," in *Film Quarterly* (Berkeley), Fall 1958.
Baxter, Brian, "Buster Keaton," in *Film* (London), November-December 1958.
Strick, Philip, in *Films and Filming* (London), September 1961.
"Rétrospective Buster Keaton," in *Cahiers du Cinéma* (Paris), April 1962.
Sadoul, Georges, "Le Mécano de la *General*," in *Lettres Françaises* (Paris), 28 June 1962.

The General

Eyles, Allen, in *Films and Filming* (London), October 1963.

Gillett, John, and James Blue, ''Keaton at Venice,'' in *Sight and Sound* (London), Winter 1965–66.

Sadoul, Georges, ''Le Génie de Buster Keaton,'' in *Lettres Françaises* (Paris), 10 February 1966.

Mast, Gerald, ''*The Gold Rush* and *The General*,'' in *Cinema Journal* (Evanston, Illinois), Spring 1970.

Villelaur, Anne, ''Buster Keaton,'' in *Dossiers du cinéma: Cinéastes 1*, Paris, 1971.

Sarris, Andrew, ''Buster Keaton,'' in *The Primal Screen*, New York, 1973.

Cott, Jeremy, ''The Limits of Silent Comedy,'' in *Literature/Film Quarterly* (Salisbury, Maryland), Spring 1975.

Wead, George, ''The Great Locomotive Chase,'' in *American Film* (Washington, D.C.), July-August 1977.

Warshow, Paul, ''More Is Less, Comedy and Sound,'' in *Film Quarterly* (Berkeley), Fall 1977.

Kirby, Lynne, ''Temporality, Sexuality, and Narrative in *The General*,'' in *Wide Angle* (Athens, Ohio), vol. 9, no. 1, 1987.

Yperen, Paul van, ''Het affiche: *The General*,'' in *Skrien* (Amsterdam), no. 166, June-July 1989.

Sanders, J., ''Dreaming in Pictures,'' in *Film Quarterly* (Berkeley), vol. 47, no. 4, 1994.

Rohmer, Éric, in *Positif* (Paris), no. 400, June 1994.

Horvath, G., ''Almomban Keaton,'' in *Filmvilag* (Budapest), vol. 38, no. 12, 1995.

Review, in *Séquences* (Haute-Ville), no. 178, May-June 1995.

* * *

The General is by far the most famous of the comedy features in which Buster Keaton starred, and in several cases directed or co-directed, between 1923 and 1928. It is also one of the finest, and has appeared on many 10-best-films lists. All of his silent features followed a basic story formula (a popular one in silent comedy): a young ''failure'' finally displays prowess and wins the girl. In addition, his films demonstrated, in part or in whole, a striking cinematic imagination as well as superb comic acting. While *The General* may not be a greater artistic achievement than *The Navigator* or *Sherlock, Jr.*, it has a number of features that have made it a special favorite of silent film fans.

The film is distinctive for its Civil War setting and location shooting. It was shot mostly in Oregon, where the necessary narrow-gauge railroad tracks were still to be found. (Compare, for contrast, the studio look of Chaplin's *The Gold Rush*, made at about the same time.) The unusually fine photography (Matthew Brady comparisons are inevitable), the extensive action involving the trains, the ambitious subject based on history (the theft and recovery of the locomotive, ''The General''), and the serious element of the drama combined to give this film an epic sweep that is surely unique in silent comedy.

In the typical Buster Keaton comedy the hero is at first anything but heroic: he is callow, bumbling, and even in some films effete. Through perseverance, self-teaching, and luck he becomes a success and—sometimes as a bonus but usually as the original goal—he is united with the woman of his dreams. *The General* is distinctive in that Johnnie Gray is an expert in at least one field, railroad engineering. In fact his competence at his job is what prevents him from being accepted into the Confederate army, setting the rest of the plot in motion. Of course, he must still demonstrate bravery to win the heart of Annabelle Lee; and, to satisfy himself, must succeed as a soldier as well. To be sure, even in railroading he makes some spectacularly comic mistakes in pursuing the Yankee train-nappers. He does, however, demonstrate early on the kind of hilariously smooth efficiency that other Keaton characters learn only with time (as in *The Navigator*) or achieve in fantasy (*Sherlock, Jr.*): e.g., his clambering aboard The General and pressing the starter lever in one swift movement; or his deft way of knocking out a Yankee guard face-to face. The unself-conscious heroism and expertise of Johnnie Gray are simultaneously touching and amusing—though much of his success is also due to good fortune (as with the flyaway blade of his sword in the battle scene).

The heroine of the film, delightfully played by Marion Mack, has a larger and more unusual role than in the other Keaton features (excepting *The Navigator*). Usually a Keaton heroine is either haughty or sweet, but in each case little more than the goal to be attained; Annabelle is forced by circumstances to become skilled in railroading while fleeing southward with The General. There is some stereotyping of the foolish female in some of Annabelle's earlier efforts to block the pursuers and feed the engine, but the evolving of her role from the ''unattainable goal'' to a partner in action is still refreshing. The moment in which the exasperated Johnnie feigns strangling his dream girl and then swiftly kisses her is one of the more memorable romantic gestures in silent film.

The General is filled with surprising moments: brilliant comic gags or fine touches of sentiment that never go on long enough to become maudlin. Perhaps the comedy is especially striking because it grows out of a serious melodramatic pursuit—but it is particularly satisfying because it stems from the characters of the hero and heroine or from the ironic perspective of the camera. The point has often been made that the camera in Chaplin's films was used mainly to record the body or facial movements of its pantomime hero, while in Keaton's film the comedy often depends on special placement of the camera, or on special visual effects. A classic example in *The General* occurs when Johnnie has accidentally caused the cannon attachment to be aimed directly at his own train. However, he and his train are spared, and better yet, the Yankees are convinced of the powers of their pursuer(s), when the forepart of Johnnie's train curves left and the cannon fires directly ahead—nearly blasting the back car of the train on the track ahead. The elegance of the gag centers on the placement of the camera behind and above the cannon car, grandly recording the beautifully timed action in one shot. Another famous moment in the film—this one visually simple and emotionally complex—occurs when Johnnie, rejected by Annabelle, sits disconsolately on the crossbar of the engine's wheels as the train starts up. The crossbar carries him up and down twice before he realizes what is going on. His forlorn, unmoving body posture is at once astonishingly sad and funny; any drift into sentimentality is avoided by Johnnie's suddenly aware look as he passes into the train shed. The overall wit and irony of the shot are dependent on the camera being placed at a sufficient distance to show the small size of Johnnie's body against the sublimely indifferent machine.

Much more could be said about this shot, and has been said by analysts of the film: e.g., the way it stresses a ''togetherness'' between Johnnie and his beloved engine, which is a major subject of the film; and the way that the final shot of the film is a counterpart to it, with both Johnnie and Annabelle sitting on the crossbar. This correspondence of shots is a reminder that the construction of the film is unusually tight and balanced in its overall arc of chase and return. The more one attempts to analyze the comedy, or merely describe certain brilliant shots—such as the one of Johnnie on the cowcatcher removing logs from the tracks—the more one admires the classic assurance and economy of the film.

—Joseph Milicia

THE GERMAN SISTERS

See **DIE BLEIERNE ZEIT**

GERMANY IN AUTUMN

See **DEUTSCHLAND IM HERBST**

GERTIE THE DINOSAUR

USA, 1914

Director: Winsor McCay

Production: Black and white, 35mm, animation, silent; running time: about 7 minutes (length varies). Released as one-reel film in 1914, though the character was created and seen in a short cartoon in McCay's vaudeville act circa 1909.

Script, animation, photography, and editing: Winsor McCay; **assisted by:** John Fitzsimmons.

Gertie the Dinosaur

Publications

Books:

Madsen, Roy, *Animated Film: Concepts, Methods, Uses*, New York, 1969.

Everson, William, K., *American Silent Film*, New York, 1978.

Canemaker, John, *Winsor McCay: His Life and Art*, New York, 1987.

Articles:

Phester, Montgomery, ''People of the Stage: Winsor McCay,'' in *Cincinnati Commercial Tribune*, 28 November 1909.

''The History of the Animated Cartoon,'' in *Journal of Motion Pictures Inventors*, 24 September 1933.

McCay, Winsor, ''Movie Cartoons,'' in *New York Evening Journal*, 27 July 1934.

Wilson, H., ''McCay Before Disney,'' in *Time* (New York), 10 January 1938.

Schwerin, Jules, ''Drawings That Are Alive,'' in *Films in Review* (New York), September 1950.

O'Sullivan, Judith, ''In Search of Winsor McCay,'' in *American Film Institute Report* (Washington, D.C.), Summer 1974.

Canemaker, J., ''Winsor McCay,'' in *Film Comment* (New York), January-February 1975.

Canemaker, J., ''The Birth of Animation,'' in *Millimeter* (New York), April 1975.

Hearn, Michael Patrick, ''The Animated Art of Winsor McCay,'' in *American Artist* (New York), May 1975.

Cornand, A., ''Le Festival d'Annecy et les rencontres internationales du cinéma d'animation,'' in *Image et Son* (Paris), January 1977.

Blonder, R., ''Mosquitoes, Dinosaurs, and the Image-ination,'' in *Animatrix* (Los Angeles), no. 8, 1994/1995.

* * *

Gertie the Dinosaur is the masterpiece of early animation. It employed 10,000 animated drawings inked on rice paper and mounted on cardboard. Artist Winsor McCay used *full animation*—a new drawing for each individual frame of film—and while he himself did all the drawings of Gertie, he hired his young neighbor John Fitzsimmons to assist him in tracing the stationary background of trees, rocks and water. *Gertie* is the improvement and development of McCay's animation experiments in his first two films, *Little Nemo* and *The Story of a Mosquito*.

McCay originally made *Gertie* for his vaudeville act as a lightning-sketch artist. In the routine, McCay announced that he could make a drawing come to life; then a projected film depicting an animated dinosaur walking from the background into the foreground appeared. McCay talked to the cartoon Gertie and gave her commands to which she would respond. Gertie raised her left leg, devoured a tree stump, became distracted by a sea serpent, lay down and rolled over, tossed a passing elephant into the lake, cried like a child when scolded, and caught a pumpkin supposedly tossed to her by McCay. As the first cartoon star, she displayed the charm, personality, and mischievousness of a playful puppy. For the finale, Gertie bent down and as she got up and walked away, carried an animated man on her back, thus appearing to take McCay into the screen with her.

For wider distribution, McCay turned his *Gertie the Dinosaur* into a one-reel film which frames the animated sequence with a live-action story. In the live-action portion, McCay accepts a bet from fellow cartoonist George McManus that he can make the dinosaur come to life. McCay is then shown with his stacks of cards demonstrating the laborious process by which he made *Gertie*. At a dinner of cartoonists, he unveils his masterpiece, and the animated sequence incorporates a series of title cards for McCay's dialogue with Gertie. After the animation ends, the dinner party toasts McCay's achievement, and McManus winds up losing the bet as well as footing the bill for dinner.

In its own time, *Gertie the Dinosaur* overshadowed all prior animated films, and it inspired a generation of animators who would begin their careers over the next decade. Audiences today still marvel at the fluidity of the movement and the amount of animated detail—Gertie's sides expanding and contracting as she breathes, particles of dirt falling from the tree trunk she devours, Gertie swaying back and forth. The shimmering or vibrating lines in the background (due to a primitive retracing process) hardly matter and do not detract from the captivating dinosaur in the foreground.

McCay also used for the first time an animation method known as the *split system*. Instead of drawing an ''action'' in sequential order, he split it up into poses, drawing the first pose, the last pose, the halfway pose, and then continuing to draw the poses in between the last two drawn. In this manner, he was able to simplify timing and placement with a method that underwent further refinement only after the advent of sound cartoons in 1928, when Walt Disney insisted upon its use. McCay also discovered another labor saving device in *Gertie* by re-using drawings for repeated cycles of action. He drew Gertie making a gesture—breathing or swaying—and rephotographed the same series of drawings several times.

While it was neither the first animated cartoon nor McCay's first animated cartoon, *Gertie the Dinosaur* is generally regarded as the first *important* cartoon in film history.

—Lauren Rabinovitz

GERTRUD

Denmark, 1964

Director: Carl Theodor Dreyer

Production: Palladium (Denmark); black and white, 35mm; running time: 115 minutes; length: 3440 meters. Released 8 December 1964, Paris.

Producers: Jørgen Nielsen with John Hilbard as executive producer; **screenplay:** Carl Theodor Dreyer, from the play by Hjalmar Söderberg; **photography:** Henning Bendtsen with Arne Abrahamsen; **editor:** Edith Schlüssel; **sound:** Knud Kristensen; **art director:** Kai Rasch; **music and solo numbers:** Jørgen Jersild; **songs:** Grethe Risbjerg Thomsen; **costume designer:** Berit Nykjaer.

Cast: Nina Pens Rode (*Gertrud Kanning*); Bendt Rothe (*Gustav Kanning*); Ebbe Rode (*Gabriel Lidman*); Baard Owe (*Erland Jansson*); Axel Strøbye (*Axel Nygren*); Anna Malberg (*Kanning's Mother*); Edouard Mielche (*The Rector Magnificus*); Vera Gebuhr (*Kanning's Maid*); Karl Gustav Ahlefeldt; Lars Knutzon; William Knoblauch; Valsø Holm; Ole Sarvig.

Gertrud

Publications

Script:

Dreyer, Carl Theodor, *Gertrud*, in *Cinque Film*, Turin, 1967.

Books:

Bowser, Eileen, *The Films of Carl Dreyer*, New York, 1964.
Dreyer, Carl Theodor, *Om filmen*, Copenhagen, 1964.
Monty, Ib, *Portrait of Carl Th. Dreyer*, Copenhagen, 1965.
Dyssegaard, Soren, editor, *Carl Th. Dreyer, Danish Film Director*, Copenhagen, 1968.
Perrin, Claude, *Carl Th. Dreyer*, Paris, 1969.
Carl Theodor Dreyer, Amsterdam, 1970.
Milne, Tom, *The Cinema of Carl Dreyer*, New York, 1970.
Sémolué, Jean, *Carl Th. Dreyer*, Paris, 1970.
Schrader, Paul, *Transcendental Style in Film: Ozu, Bresson, Dreyer*, Berkeley, 1972.
Skoller, Donald, editor, *Dreyer in Double Reflection*, New York, 1973; revised edition, 1991.
Nash, Mark, editor, *Dreyer*, London, 1977.
Tone, Pier Giorgio, *Carl Theodor Dreyer*, Florence, 1978.
Bordwell, David, *The Films of Carl Theodor Dreyer*, Berkeley, 1981.
Drouzy, Maurice, *Carl Theodor Dreyer ně Nilsson*, Paris, 1982.
Carney, Raymond, *Speaking the Language of Desire: The Films of Carl Dreyer*, Cambridge, 1989.
Jensen, Jytte, editor, *Carl Dreyer: Films*, New York, 1990.
Houe, Poul, *Carl Theodor Dreyer's Cinematic Humanism*, Minneapolis, 1992.

Articles:

Kelman, Ken, "Dreyer," in *Film Culture* (New York), no. 35, 1964–65.
Téchiné, André, "La Parole de la fin," in *Cahiers du Cinéma* (Paris), no. 164, 1965.
Tournés, Andrée, in *Jeune Cinéma* (Paris), no. 5, 1965.
Trolle, Børge, "Ett spel om en dröm: En analys av Carl Th. Dreyers film *Gertrud*," in *Filmrutan* (Stockholm), no. 1, 1965.
Delahaye, Michel, "Between Heaven and Hell: Interview with Carl Dreyer," in *Cahiers du Cinema in English* (New York), no. 4, 1966.
Wright, Elsa Gress, in *Film Quarterly* (Berkeley), Spring 1966.
Trolle, Børge, "An interview with Carl Dreyer," in *Film Culture* (New York), Summer 1966.
Bond, Kirk, "The Basic Demand of Life for Love," in *Film Comment* (New York), Fall 1966.
Lerner, Carl, "My Working Is in Relation to the Future: A Conversation with Carl Dreyer," in *Film Comment* (New York), Fall 1966.
Skoller, Donald, "To Rescue *Gertrud*," in *Film Comment* (New York), Fall 1966.
Perruzzi, Giuseppe, "Corenza e modernità di *Gertrud*," in *Cinema Nuovo* (Turin), no. 190, 1967.
Jones, Chris, in *Films and Filming* (London), January 1969.
Burch, Noël, "Propositions," in *Afterimage* (Rochester, New York), no. 5, 1974.
El Geudj, F., and E. Decaux, in *Cinématographe* (Paris), October 1983.
Magny, Joel, in *Cinéma* (Paris), October 1983.
Tesson, Charles, in *Cahiers du Cinéma* (Paris), October 1983.
Sainderichin, Guy-Patrick, "*Gertrud*: Amer omnia," in *Cahiers du Cinéma* (Paris), December 1983.
"Gertrud Section" of *Avant-Scène du Cinéma* (Paris), December 1984.
Rosenbaum, Jonathan, "Gertrud: The Desire for the Image," in *Sight and Sound* (London), Winter 1985–86.
Cowie, E., "Zvijace identifikacije," in *Ekran*, vol. 16, no. 3, 1991.
Miguez, M., and J.M. Minguet Batllori, and S. Torres, in *Nosferatu* (San Sebastian), no. 5, January 1991.
Grob, Norbert, "*Gertrud*," in *EPD Film* (Frankfurt), vol. 11, no. 6, June 1994.
De La Fuente, Flavia, "El amor lo es todo," in *El Amante Cinema*, no. 52, June 1996.
Idström, Annika, "Kuolematon äiti," in *Filmihullu* (Helsinki), no. 1, 1997.

* * *

For the last 20 years of his career, Dreyer worked on a film about Jesus Christ. It was never realized, though his script was published posthumously in 1968. Near the end of his life, Dreyer was also planning a film of *Medea*. He was aiming at tragedy, reflected again in *Gertrud*, which was to be his last film.

Dreyer's last four films were based on plays. *Gertrud* is a 1906 play by Hjalmar Söderberg. It is a problem-drama in the manner of Ibsen, but while the play is naturalistic, the film is not. Dreyer considered the film an experiment; he wanted to co-ordinate the word and the image, to create harmony between what is seen and what is heard. The function of the images is to open up a perspective on the characters, who manifest themselves in the way they speak and move. *Gertrud* contains almost no close-ups; it is a film of travelling shots and long, uncut scenes. The film has only 89 shots, with very few sets and only one exterior scene. The film's depiction of life/reality is antinaturalistic and stylized, and Dreyer treats the story as a tragedy. He called the film "a portrait of time from the beginning of the century," and he has stressed typical features of that period and milieu. As in *La passion de Jeanne d'Arc* he has tried to transform the whole of "the past reality into camera-reality," to quote Siegfried Kracauer.

Gertrud is the last of Dreyer's many portraits of women. Gertrud, however, is not a suffering woman, submissive to men; she is superior to them. A free intellectual woman with strong willpower, she rejects the men in her life. While these men prefer their careers and pleasures, for Gertrud love is all. Gertrud knows she will always come second, and prefers to abandon men and withdraw into solitude. She knows that her demands on life cannot be fulfilled, so she chooses to live in accordance with her inner demands. In Gertrud, Dreyer finds a greatness which had also fascinated him about Jeanne d'Arc. This is not a naturalistic portrayal, but a tragic one—Gertrud is bound for defeat. Both she and the men are presented in a disquieting double light.

In many ways the 75-year-old Dreyer was in harmony with the modern, younger directors. In films by Antonioni, Godard and Truffaut the women characters often demand a love which should be placed above everything else, a love which was more than most men could or would grant. *Gertrud* is also amazingly in harmony with the stylistic trends of the films of the 1960s. Because Dreyer never consciously tried to keep up with his time, but kept his integrity, he was more modern in his last film than many of the directors were who tried to adjust to their time.

Gertrud, premiering in Paris, was badly received by most of the Danish and French reviewers. However, in the film magazines *Gertrud* did find more understanding critics. With his last film, Dreyer once again caused great controversy, even if he did not ask for it. *Gertrud* is still a film which divides its audience.

—Ib Monty

GIANT

USA, 1956

Director: George Stevens

Production: Warner Bros. Pictures Inc.; Warnercolor, 35mm; running time: 198 minutes. Released 1956. Filmed in Texas.

Producers: George Stevens and Henry Ginsberg; **screenplay:** Fred Guiol and Ivan Moffat, from the novel by Edna Ferber; **photography:** William C. Mellor and Edwin DuPar; **editors:** William Hornbeck, Philip W. Anderson, and Fred Bohanen; **art director:** Ralph S. Hurst; **music:** Dmitri Tiomkin; **costume designers:** Moss Mabry and Marjorie Best.

Cast: Elizabeth Taylor (*Leslie Lynnton Benedict*); Rock Hudson (*Bick Benedict*); James Dean (*Jett Rink*); Mercedes McCambridge (*Luz Benedict, the older*); Jane Withers (*Vashti Snythe*); Chill Wills (*Uncle Bawley Benedict*); Carroll Baker (*Luz Benedict, the younger*); Dennis Hopper (*Jordan Benedict III*); Elsa Cardenas (*Juana Benedict*); Fran Bennett (*Judy Benedict*).

Award: Oscar for Best Direction, 1956.

Publications

Books:

Bast, William, *James Dean: A Biography*, New York, 1956.
Richie, Donald, *George Stevens: An American Romantic*, New York, 1970, 1985.
Hirsch, Foster, *Elizabeth Taylor*, New York, 1973.
Phillips, Gene D., *The Movie Makers: Artists in the Industry*, Chicago, 1973.
d'Arcy, Susan, *The Films of Elizabeth Taylor*, London, 1974.
Dalton, David, *James Dean, The Mutant King*, San Francisco, 1974.
Whittman, Mark, *The Films of James Dean*, London, 1974.
Kelly, Kitty, *Elizabeth Taylor, The Last Star*, New York and London, 1981.
Bourget, Jean-Loup, *James Dean*, Paris, 1983.
Morrissey, Steven, *James Dean Is Not Dead*, Manchester, 1983.
Dalton, David, and Ron Cayen, *James Dean, American Icon*, London, 1984.
Wickens, Christopher, *Elizabeth Taylor: A Biography in Photographs*, New York and London, 1984.
Devillers, Marcel, *James Dean*, London, 1985.
Beath, Warren Newton, *The Death of James Dean*, London, 1986.
Petri, Bruce, *A Theory of American Film: The Films & Techniques of George Stevens*, New York, 1987.
Parker, John, *Five For Hollywood: Their Friendship, Their Fame, Their Tragedies*, Secaucus, 1991.
Tanitch, R., *James Dean the Actor*, London, 1999.

Articles:

Sarris, Andrew, in *Film Culture* (New York), no. 10, 1956.
Rowan, Arthur, ''*Giant* Enhanced by Bold, Offbeat Photography,'' in *American Cinematographer* (Los Angeles), March 1956.
Whitcomb, Jon, ''Liz Taylor as Edna Ferber's Heroine,'' in *Cosmopolitan* (New York), August 1956.
Time (New York), 22 October 1956.
Phipps, Courtland, in *Films in Review* (New York), November 1956.
Houston, Penelope, in *Sight and Sound* (London), Winter 1956–57.
Archer, E., ''George Stevens and the American Dream,'' in *Film Culture* (New York), no. 1, 1957.
Rotha, Paul, in *Films and Filming* (London), February 1957.
Luft, Herbert H., ''George Stevens,'' in *Films in Review* (New York), November 1958.
Stang, J., ''Hollywood Romantic,'' in *Films and Filming* (London), July 1959.
Whitehall, Richard, in *Films and Filming* (London), August 1962.
Mayersburg, Paul, and V. F. Perkins, in *Movie* (London), November 1962.
Bartlett, N., ''Sentiment and Humanism,'' in *Film* (London), Spring 1964.
Silke, James R., and interview with George Stevens, in *Cinema* (Beverly Hills), December 1964-January 1965.
McVay, Douglas, ''Greatest—Stevens,'' in *Films and Filming* (London), April and May 1965.
Beresford, B., ''George Stevens,'' in *Film* (London), Summer 1970.
Essoe, Gabe, ''Elizabeth Taylor,'' in *Films in Review* (New York), August-September 1970.
''Stevens Issue'' of *American Film* (Washington, D.C.), no. 1, 1972.
''Stevens Issue,'' of *American Film* (Washington, D.C.), May-June 1975.
Soule, Maria, in *Magill's Survey of Cinema 2*, Englewood Cliffs, New Jersey, 1980.
Solman, G., in *Films in Review* (New York), May 1983.
Leibman, Nina C., ''Leave Mother Out: The Fifties Family in American Film and Television,'' in *Wide Angle* (Baltimore), vol. 10, no. 4, 1988.
Larue, Johanne, ''À la défense de James Dean,'' in *Séquences* (Haute-Ville), no. 159–160, September 1992.
Reid's Film Index, no. 11, 1993.
Villaneuva, T., ''Scenes from the Movie *Giant*,'' in *Jump Cut* (Berkeley), no. 39, June 1994.

Giant

Meisel, M., ''*Giant* Reawakens,'' in *Film Journal* (New York), September 1996.

Stevens, George Jr., ''A Giant Step in Film Restoration,'' in *DGA Magazine* (Los Angeles), vol. 21, no. 4, September-October 1996.

Turner, George, ''*Giant* Still Towers: Resurrecting a Giant,'' in *American Cinematographer* (Hollywood), vol. 77, no. 10, October 1996.

''Resurrecting a *Giant*,'' in *American Cinematographer* (Hollywood), October 1996.

Score (Lelystad), no. 101, December 1996.

* * *

Giant, directed by George Stevens, is based on the novel of the same name by Edna Ferber. Stevens won an Academy Award as best director for the film. *Giant* is a saga about change: change in Texas, change in the lives of Bick and Leslie Benedict and their children and grandchildren, and, ultimately, change in America. It is a giant of a movie, running three hours and eighteen minutes, and covering over 25 years in the characters' lives. It is shot in color, with a tremendously moving musical score by Dimitri Tiomkin.

Giant is a serious picture about accepting the differences of others, be they outsiders, members of one's own culture, or even members of one's own family. It reflects social concerns in America at the time as well as predicting, in a way, the challenges of the civil rights movement to come. The film also contains the idea that people who have prejudices must change to accept and respect others, regardless of their race, background, and circumstances. This is not a new subject for Stevens. After World War II, his films took on a more serious nature, and the theme of acceptance can be clearly seen in *I Remember Mama*, where a Norwegian family has settled in San Francisco; in *Shane*, where farmers and cattlemen are at odds; and in *The Diary of Anne Frank*, where the Nazis are persecuting Jews.

The theme of acceptance is the framework for *Giant*, upon which all of the parts are attached to form the structure. Stevens believed that a film should be guided by one vision, and in this way, a sense of appropriate structure could be achieved. He said at a symposium on the arts at The Ohio State University in the early 1970s, ''I think structure in film, particularly in film of any length, is almost as important as structure in upright architecture.'' For example, it is not good if a building is leaning, or has elements out of place, or is even falling apart. The same could be said of a film. *Giant* has a coherent, solid structure which allows Stevens to tell his story and create his meaning in the mind of the viewers.

At the beginning of the film, Jordan Benedict II, known as Bick (Rock Hudson) visits the family of Leslie Lynnton (Elizabeth Taylor) on the East coast to purchase a stud horse named Warwinds to take back to his cattle ranch in Texas. As he emerges from the train, he almost blocks out the image of the land, and looms large over it. The Lynnton family members are cordial to Bick, but he is clearly from a different culture than they are. Bick and Leslie fall in love, and he takes her to Texas as his bride. The scene where Bick almost blocks out the image of the land in the East is echoed, but differently, as Bick and Leslie, on either side of the train window, provide a frame for the image of the land in the West. Together they will help alter it. So the first element of change is that Bick did not marry a Texan but a person from the East, and this integration of cultures will have a positive effect.

Bick's sister Luz (Mercedes McCambridge) cannot accept the change marriage brings to the Benedict family. She cannot control Leslie, and is killed when she is thrown from the horse Warwinds, which she symbolically cannot master.

Leslie treats the Mexican-American workers with respect, and even has the Benedict family doctor treat the sick child of a worker in the nearby town. Also, after dinner parties in her home, she doesn't want to sit with the women, but instead wants to talk politics with the men. There is tension, as Bick is not tolerant of people with Mexican heritage and has his own ideas of a woman's role in the home.

Jett Rink (James Dean), a poor worker for the Benedicts who is constantly at odds with Bick, inherits a piece of land from Luz after her death. He discovers oil on it after Leslie, with whom he is secretly in love, visits him. Her footprint symbolically fills with the black liquid. Jett becomes rich, and eventually convinces Bick to invest in oil wells in addition to cattle at the start of World War II.

The Benedicts have three children, and the theme of acceptance is stated by Leslie, who says, "All you can do is raise them. You can't live their lives for them." Bick wants son Jordan Benedict, III (Dennis Hopper) to become a cattle rancher like he is, but instead Jordan becomes a doctor and even marries a Mexican-American, Juana (Elsa Cardenas). They have a child, Jordan Benedict IV. Daughter Judy Benedict (Fran Bennett) wants to be a rancher. She even marries a rancher, but she and her husband want to have a small place of their own, thereby leaving the Benedict ranch, Reata. They also have a child, Judy Benedict II. Daughter Luz Benedict II is a rebel as well and even dates the person her father hates, the oil millionaire Jett Rink. Although Judy's husband and Jordan both serve in World War II, it is Angel Obregon III (Sal Mineo), the son of a Mexican-American worker, who is killed in battle.

In the present-day 1950s, Jett invites many rich Texans, including the Benedicts, to the opening of his new airport/hotel. Jett has always disliked those of Mexican heritage and does not allow them services in the hotel. When Juana Benedict is refused an appointment in the hotel's beauty salon, Jordan attacks Jett but loses the fight. Bick now wants to fight Jett to avenge his son's honor, and in a famous scene in the hotel's wine cellar, tells the drunk Jett, "You ain't even worth hitting." Bick knocks over ranks of liquor. Jett goes to make a speech to the assembled guests and passes out from too much drink.

Jett is a pathetic figure, for despite his money, he is unable to change his past attitudes. Luz II leaves him and goes with her family, and later goes to Hollywood to try to become an actress.

Driving home from the hotel, Bick, Leslie and Luz II go into a diner (Sarge's Place) with Juana and their grandson, Jordan Benedict IV, who resembles his Mexican-American mother. The owner, Sarge (Mickey Simpson), alludes unkindly to the child's Mexican heritage, but will serve the Benedicts. A Mexican-American family enters and Sarge asks them to leave. Bick intervenes on their behalf and finally fights with Sarge. Bick loses the fight and almost passes out on the floor among dirty dishes.

Back home, Leslie and Bick sit and watch their two grandchildren, who are in a playpen. A white sheep and a black calf are behind the playpen. One grandchild has light skin and one has dark skin. During this visual image of the importance of acceptance, Leslie, having commented on how proud she was of Bick in the restaurant, says one of the last lines of the film, which ties all of the vast elements of the structure together. She says, "After one hundred years, the Benedict family is finally a real big success."

By accepting change, from the East, from the children, and from the culture, Bick Benedict and his family are indeed a success, and in fact, have become the embodiment of the romantic American dream. They are rich and accepting. Jett Rink, on the other hand, could be considered the embodiment of the American nightmare. He is rich and unaccepting, and therefore is last seen alone in the vast empty ballroom where he was to make his speech, passing out not from fighting for what is right, but from drinking too much.

George Stevens has, within this huge story of a Texas family, provided the viewer with a structure that has universal meaning about change and acceptance, and about hope for freedom and justice for all of us. In the final shots of the film, there are dissolves to close ups of the grandchildren's eyes as the song "The Eyes of Texas are Upon You" plays on the soundtrack. The eyes of the children are the next generation looking at the viewers to see if they can live in harmony together.

—H. Wayne Schuth

GILDA

USA, 1946

Director: Charles Vidor

Production: Columbia; black and white; running time: 109 minutes; length: 9,852 feet. Released March 1946.

Producer: Virginia Van Upp; **screenplay:** Marion Parsonnet, from Jo Eisinger's adaptation of the story by E. A. Ellington; **photography:** Rudolph Maté; **editor:** Charles Nelson; **sound recordist:** Lambert Day; **art directors:** Stephen Goosson and Van Nest Polglase; **set decoration:** Robert Priestley; **gowns:** Jean Louis; **musical director:** Morris Stoloff; **arranger:** Marlin Skiles.

Cast: Rita Hayworth (*Gilda*); Glenn Ford (*Johnny Farrell*); George Macready (*Ballin Mundsen*); Joseph Calleia (*Obregon*); Steven Geray (*Uncle Pio*); Joseph Sawyer (*Casey*); Gerald Mohr (*Captain Delgado*); Robert Scott (*Gabe Evans*); Ludwig Donath (*German*); Don Douglas (*Thomas Langford*); S. Z. Martel (*Little man*); George Lewis (*Huerta*); Rosa Rey (*Maria*); Eduardo Ciannelli (*Bendolin*).

Gilda

Publications

Books:

Ringgold, Gene, *The Films of Rita Hayworth*, Secaucus, New Jersey, 1974, 1984.

Kobal, John, *Rita Hayworth: The Time, the Place, and the Woman*, New York, 1978.

Silver, Alain, and Elisabeth Ward, editors, *Film Noir*, New York, 1979.

Hill, James, *Rita Hayworth: A Memoir*, New York, 1983.

Morella, Joe, and Edward Z. Epstein, *Rita: The Life of Rita Hayworth*, New York, 1983.

Dick, Bernard F., *Columbia Pictures: Portrait of a Studio*, Lexington, 1992.

Kaplan, Ann, editor, *Women in Film Noir*, London, 1998.

Articles:

Hollywood Reporter, 13 March 1946.

New York Times, 15 March 1946.

Variety (New York), 20 March 1946.

Monthly Film Bulletin (London), April 1946.

Magill's Survey of Cinema 2, Englewood Cliffs, New Jersey, 1980.

Filme (Paris), no. 13, 1982.

Martin, Marcel, in *Revue du Cinéma* (Paris), January 1983.

Ménil, A., in *Cinématographe* (Paris), February 1983.

Petat, J., in *Cinéma* (Paris), February 1983.

Legrand, Gérard, in *Positif* (Paris), March 1983.

Doane, M. A., ''*Gilda:* Epistemology as Striptease,'' in *Camera Obscura* (Berkeley), Fall 1983.

Janssen, C., ''Film Noir: Darling, are you decent?'' in *Skoop* (Amsterdam), November 1984.

Aachen, G., and J.H. Reid, in *Reid's Film Index* (Wyong), no. 1, 1987.

Dittmar, Linda, ''From Fascism to the Cold War: *Gilda*'s 'Fantastic' Politics,'' in *Wide Angle* (Baltimore), vol. 10, no. 3, 1988.

Doane, M. A., and B. Reynaud, ''*Gilda:* Strip-tease epistemologique,'' in *Cinemaction* (Conde-sur-Noireau, France), no. 2, 1993.

McLean, A. L., '''It's Only That I Do What I Love and Love What I Do': Film Noir and the Musical Woman,'' in *Cinema Journal* (Austin), vol. 33, no. 1, 1993.

Parsi, Novid, ''Projecting Heterosexuality, Or What Do You Mean by 'It'?'' in *Camera Obscura* (Bloomington), no. 38, May 1996.

* * *

''Statistics show there are more women in the world than anything else,'' snaps the cynical hero, Johnny Farrell (Ford), adding, with peculiar loathing, ''except *insects!*'' And yet this misogyny co-exists in the film with Gilda (Hayworth), a character who is at once a total blank and a masterful ironist whose signature tune ''Put the Blame on Mame,'' to which she performs a supremely erotic striptease involving only the removal of her elbow-length velvet gloves, is a pointed exposure of the way women are made to seem responsible for the havoc wreaked by the men who become obsessed with them.

Gilda exists at the crossroads between the hardboiled neo-*noir* adventure of the 1940s and the contemporary craze for ''women's pictures.'' The former genre, epitomized in classic style by *Casablanca* and *To Have and Have Not* but perhaps better represented by such fringe-B quickies as *Calcutta*, *Macao* or *World for Ransom*, is characterized by a studio-bound ''exotic'' location, preferably centering on a shady nightclub in a Third World country under whose propellor fans can be found an array of slimy, threatening characters, almost always including a slinky *femme fatale*, who are pitted against a hardboiled American he-man hero who emerges, emotionally bruised but morally untainted, from the twisted plot. The latter, typified by the various vehicles found for strong female stars like Joan Crawford, Bette Davis and Barbara Stanwyck, deal with the romantic, social and professional struggles of independent women who usually win through, after plentiful suffering, at the end. Both genres came to prominence at a time when, thanks to the war, cinema audiences really could be sexually polarised, and so the macho adventurers could apeal to the man in the services while the determined and enterprising women were aimed at the sweethearts and fiancées left to their own devices on the home front.

Released just after the end of the war, *Gilda* draws much of its peculiar power from its jumble of genres, and the unexpected way its characters grind at each other. Johnny, a hardboiled gambler who looks suavely uncomfortable in his dinner jacket, becomes manager of a casino in Buenos Aires, working for Ballin Mundsen (Macready), a frozen-faced mastermind who wields a swordcane, enjoys spying on his customers and associates from a control room in the gambling joint, and forms the apex of a three-way love triangle that triggers the plot. Mundsen turns out to be fronting for a group of ex-Nazis, and Macready's scarred intensity serves him well as a stereotypical movie Nazi, but the trouble in the film actually comes from his marriage to the beautiful young Gilda (Hayworth), who crucially acts throughout with an un-*fatale* honesty and finally reveals herself as far stronger than either of her paramours. Johnny and Gilda were once lovers, but the hero's neurotic hatred of her comes because she has alienated the affections of Mundsen, his "best friend," and when the casino owner appears dead, he plans to marry her as a way of punishing her for her treatment of the casino owner. Mundsen returns from the grave to be killed again in a coda that strains hard to get a conventional happy ending out of a situation whose implications skirt the Hays Code's idea of the objectionable.

Photographed by Rudolph Maté with a marvellously oneiric style, making full use of the central casino sets—which are almost as evocative as those of von Sternberg's *Shanghai Gesture*—and benefiting from all the class a shaky major studio like Columbia could trot out for a prestige production, *Gilda* is, in many ways, an absolute triumph of the *cinema-bis.* Ford and Hayworth, usually limited but engaging and photogenic performers, have definitive performances drawn out of them like teeth, and Macready—elsewhere a great heavy in the likes of *My Name is Julia Ross*, *The Bandit of Sherwood Forest* and *The Big Clock*—has the time of his life as the complex villain, prevented from taking top billing for his lead role simply by the dictates of the star system. Charles Vidor was a journeyman otherwise noted—if at all—for his musicals—including a different take on Hayworth in *Cover Girl* and a replay of the obsessive triangle of *Gilda* with James Cagney taking over the Macready role as he tangles with Doris Day and Cameron Mitchell in *Love Me or Leave Me*—was here handed a studio assignment that turned out miraculously right, and has a resonance beyond its immediate exotic charm. As the posters claimed, "there *never* was a woman like *Gilda!*"

—Kim Newman

GIRLS IN UNIFORM

See **MÄDCHEN IN UNIFORM**

THE GOAT HORN

See **KOZIYAT ROG**

THE GODFATHER TRILOGY

Director: Francis Ford Coppola

THE GODFATHER

USA, 1972

Production: Paramount Pictures; Technicolor, 35mm; running time: 176 minutes. Released 11 March 1972. Filmed in New York City and in Sicily. Cost: over $5 million. Oscars for Best Picture, Best Actor (Brando), Best Screenplay, 1972; New York Film Critics' Award, Best Supporting Actor (Duvall), 1972; Directors Guild of America, Director Award (Coppola), 1972.

Producer: Albert S. Ruddy; **screenplay:** Francis Ford Coppola and Mario Puzo, from the novel by Mario Puzo; **photography:** Gordon Willis; **editors:** William Reynolds, Peter Zinner, Marc Lamb, and Murray Solomon; **sound:** Bud Granzbach, Richard Portman, Christopher Newman, and Les Lazarowitz; **production designer:** Philip Smith; **art director:** Warren Clymer; **music:** Nino Rota; **costume designer:** Anna Hill Johnstone.

Cast: Marlon Brando (*Don Vito Corleone*); Al Pacino (*Michael Corleone*); James Caan (*Sonny Corleone*); Richard Castellano (*Clemenza*); Robert Duvall (*Tom Hagen*); Diane Keaton (*Kay Adams*); Sterling Hayden (*McCluskey*); Talia Shire (*Connie Rizzi*); John Cazale (*Fredo Corleone*).

Publications

Books:

Zuckerman, Ira, *The Godfather Journal*, New York, 1972.

Carey, Gary, *Brando*, New York, 1973.

Jordan, René, *Marlon Brando*, New York, 1973.

Puzo, Mario, *The Making of The Godfather*, Greenwich, Connecticut, 1973.

Thomas, Tony, *The Films of Marlon Brando*, Secaucus, New Jersey, 1973.

Shipman, David, *Brando*, London, 1974.

Johnson, Robert K., *Francis Ford Coppola*, Boston, 1977.

Pye, Michael, and Lynda Myles, *The Movie Brats: How the Film Generation Took Over Hollywood*, London, 1979.

Kolker, Robert Philip, *A Cinema of Loneliness: Penn, Kubrick, Coppola, Scorsese, Altman*, Oxford, 1980; revised edition, 1988.

Thomson, David, *Overexposures: The Crisis in American Filmmaking*, New York, 1981.

Chaillet, Jean-Paul, and Elizabeth Vincent, *Francis Ford Coppola*, Paris, 1984.

Downing, David, *Marlon Brando*, London, 1984.

Zuker, Joel S., *Francis Ford Coppola: A Guide to References and Resources*, Boston, 1984.

Carey, Gary, *Marlon Brando, The Only Contender*, London, 1985.

Frundt, Bodo, and others, *Francis Ford Coppola*, Munich, 1985.

Ray, Robert B., *A Certain Tendency of the Hollywood Cinema 1930–80*, Princeton, 1985.

Slawson, Judith, *Robert Duvall, Hollywood Maverick*, New York, 1985.

Weiss, Ulli, *Das neue Hollywood: Francis Ford Coppola, Steven Spielberg, Martin Scorsese*, Munich, 1986.

Chown, Jeffrey, *Hollywood Auteur: Francis Coppola*, New York, 1987.

Higham, Charles, *Brando: The Unauthorized Biography*, London, 1987.

Cowie, Peter, *Coppola*, London, 1989.

Biskind, Peter, *The Godfather Companion: Everything You Ever Wanted to Know about All Three Godfather Films*, New York, 1990.

The Godfather

Gardner, Gerald C. and Harriet Modell Gardner, *The Godfather Movies: A Pictorial History*, New York, 1993.

Lebo, Harlan, *The Godfather Legacy*, New York, 1997.

Bergan, Ronald, *Francis Ford Coppola-Close Up: The Making of His Movies*, New York, 1998.

Ciongoli, A. Kenneth, editor, *Beyond 'The Godfather': Italian American Writers on the Real Italian Experience*, Hanover, 1998.

Browne, Nick, editor, *Francis Ford Coppola's 'The Godfather' Trilogy*, New York, 1999.

Cowie, Peter, *The Godfather Book*, Boulder, 1999.

Articles:

Kane, John, and Bruce Rubenstein, in *Take One* (Montreal), March-April 1971.

Arnold, Gary, in *Filmfacts* (New York), no. 15, 1972.

Berglund, P., in *Chaplin* (Stockholm), no. 116, 1972.

Rosengren, G., ''Två filmer om Maffian,'' in *Filmrutan* (Stockholm), vol. 15, no. 3, 1972.

Reilly, C. P., in *Films in Review* (New York), April 1972.

Faltysova, H., in *Film a Doba* (Prague), May 1972.

Kane, John, and Bruce Rubenstein, in *Take One* (Montreal), June 1972.

Chappetta, R., in *Film Quarterly* (Berkeley), Summer 1972.

Cowie, Peter, in *Focus on Film* (London), Autumn 1972.

Farber, Stephen, ''Coppola and *The Godfather*,'' in *Sight and Sound* (London), Autumn 1972.

Schober, S., in *Filmkritik* (Munich), October 1972.

Amiel, M., in *Cinéma* (Paris), November 1972.

Kael, Pauline, ''Alchemy,'' in *Deeper into Movies*, Boston, 1973.

''How Brando Brought Don Corleone to Life,'' and ''Keeping Up with the Corleones,'' in *Films 72–73*, edited by David Denby, Indianapolis, 1973.

Vitoux, F., ''Une Gigantesque Metaphore,'' in *Positif* (Paris), January 1973.

Latimer, J. P., ''*The Godfather*: Metaphor and Microcosm,'' in *Journal of Popular Culture* (Bowling Green, Ohio), Spring 1973.

Vogelsan, J., ''Motifs of Image and Sound in *The Godfather*,'' in *Journal of Popular Culture* (Bowling Green, Ohio), Spring 1973.

Higham, Charles, in *Action* (Los Angeles), May-June 1973.

''Francis Ford Coppola,'' in *Film Comment* (New York), July-August 1974.

Kauffmann, Stanley, *Living Images*, New York, 1975.
Yates, John, ''Godfather Saga: The Death of the Family,'' in *Journal of Popular Culture* (Bowling Green, Ohio), no. 4, 1975.
Solomon, Stanley, ''*The Godfather*,'' in *Beyond Formula*, New York, 1976.
Clarens, Carlos, ''The Godfather Saga,'' in *Film Comment* (New York), January-February 1978.
Thomson, David, ''The Discreet Charm of *The Godfather*,'' in *Sight and Sound* (London), Spring 1978.
Thomson, David, ''Two Gentlemen of Corleone,'' in *Take One* (Montreal), May 1978.
''Dialogue on Film: Mario Puzo,'' in *American Film* (Washington, D.C.), May 1979.
Cebe, G., ''Francis Ford Coppola: La Mafia, l'orare, et l'Amérique,'' in *Ecran* (Paris), 15 September 1979.
Taubman, Leslie, in *Magill's Survey of Cinema 2*, Englewood Cliffs, New Jersey, 1980.
Wisinger, I., ''Amerikai törtenet,'' in *Filmkultura* (Budapest), May-June 1982.
Greene, N., ''Coppola, Cimino: The Operatics of History,'' in *Film Quarterly* (Berkeley), Winter 1984–85.
Ciment, Michel, in *Positif* (Paris), February 1985.
Alexander, M., and H. Homsan, ''The Godfather-saga op tv,'' in *Skoop* (Amsterdam), June-July 1985.
Film Comment (New York), July-August 1987.
Hirsch, T., ''San Francisco szultanja,'' in *Filmvilag* (Budapest), no. 1, 1991.
Alm, R., ''Michael Corleones tapte illusjoner,'' in *Z Filmtidsskrift* (Oslo), no. 2, 1991.
Nordstrom, U., ''Sag du gudfadern eller gudfadern—eller var det gudfadern?,'' in *Chaplin* (Stockholm), no. 5, 1991.
Caron, A., ''Le tryptique des *Godfather*,'' in *Sequences* (Montreal), March 1991.
Ciment, M., ''Lear et l'opera: entretien avec Francis Ford Coppola,'' in *Positif* (Paris), April 1991.
Grob, N., ''The Empire Strikes Back,'' in *EPD Film* (Frankfurt), April 1991.
Morgan, D., ''Death and Aging: A Corleone Chronicle,'' in *Cinefex* (Riverside, California), May 1991.
Tsyrkun, N., ''Sud'ba Korleone v Amerike,'' in *Iskusstvo Kino* (Moscow), no. 3, 1992.
Russo, J. P., ''Tra i tre *Padrini* quale il migliore?,'' in *Cinema Nuovo* (Rome), May-June 1992.
Solman, G., ''Uncertain Glory,'' in *Film Comment* (New York), May-June 1993.
Thomson, David, ''Death and its Details,'' in *Film Comment* (New York), September-October 1993.
Steele, G., ''On Location with *The Godfather*,'' in *Mensuel du Cinéma*, no. 16, April 1994.
Rose, P. W., ''The Politics of the Trilogy Form: *Lucia*, the *Orestia*, and *The Godfather*,'' in *Film-Historia* (Barcelona), vol. 5, no. 2/3, 1995.
''I Film (1963–1979),'' in *Castoro Cinema* (Milan), no. 81, 2nd ed., July 1995.
''*The Godfather*,'' in *Premiere* (Boulder), vol. 9, March 1996.
Dargis, M., ''Dark Side of the Dream,'' in *Sight & Sound* (London), vol. 6, August 1996.
Perez, G., ''Film in Review,'' in *Yale Review*, vol. 85, no. 3, 1996.
Sragow, M., ''Godfatherhood,'' in *New Yorker*, vol. 73, 24 March 1997.
Thomson, D., ''Ten Films That Showed Hollywood How to Live,'' in *Movieline* (Escondido), vol. 8, July 1997.

THE GODFATHER, PART II

USA, 1974

Production: Paramount Pictures; Technicolor, 35mm; running time: 200 minutes. Released 12 December 1974, New York. Filmed in 9 months, 1973–74, on location in New York City, Lake Tahoe and Las Vegas, Nevada, Washington, Sicily, and the Dominican Republic. Oscars for Best Picture, Best Director, Best Supporting Actor (De Niro), Best Screenplay, Best Art Decoration, Best Original Dramatic Score, 1974; Directors Guild of America, Director Award (Coppola), 1974.

Producers: Francis Ford Coppola, Gary Frederickson, and Fred Roos; **screenplay:** Francis Ford Coppola and Mario Puzo, from the novel by Mario Puzo; **photography:** Gordon Willis; **editors:** Peter Zinner, Barry Malkin, and Richard Marks; **production designer:** Dean Tavoularis; **art director:** Angelo Graham; **music:** Nino Rota; **additional music:** Carmine Coppola; **costume designer:** Theodora Van Runkle.

Cast: Al Pacino (*Michael Corleone*); Robert Duvall (*Tom Hagen*); Diane Keaton (*Kay Adams*); Robert DeNiro (*Vito Corleone*); John Cazale (*Fredo Corleone*); Talia Shire (*Connie Corleone*); Lee Strasberg (*Hyman Roth*); Michael V. Gazzo (*Frankie Pentangeli*); Troy Donahue (*Connie's boyfriend*).

Publications

Articles:

Bachmann, Gideon, ''*Godfather II*: Zelfkritiek van Coppola,'' in *Skoop* (Amsterdam), December 1974.
Cocks, T., ''Outs,'' in *Take One* (Montreal), December 1974.
Time (New York), 16 December 1974.
Kael, Pauline, in *New Yorker*, 23 December 1974.
Quart, L., and A. Auster, in *Cineaste* (New York), vol. 6, no. 4, 1975.
Reilly, C. P., in *Films in Review* (New York), February 1975.
Hess, John, ''*Godfather II*: A Deal Coppola Couldn't Refuse,'' in *Jump Cut* (Chicago), May-July 1975.
Milne, Tom, in *Monthly Film Bulletin* (London), June 1975.
Rosenbaum, Jonathan, in *Sight and Sound* (London), Summer 1975.
Gow, Gordon, in *Films and Filming* (London), July 1975.
Behar, H., in *Image et Son* (Paris), September 1975.
Rabourdin, D., in *Cinéma* (Paris), September-October 1975.
Calum, P., in *Kosmorama* (Copenhagen), Autumn 1975.
Farber, Stephen, in *Take One* (Montreal), December 1975.

Konjar, V., in *Ekran* (Ljubljana), no. 1, 1976.

Allombert, G., in *Revue du Cinéma* (Paris), October 1976.

Bueren, P., and W. Verstappen, in *Skoop* (Amsterdam), January 1977.

Rule, P., "The Italian Connection in American Film: Coppola, Cimino, Scorsese," in *America* (New York), 17 November 1979.

Taubman, Leslie, in *Magill's Survey of Cinema 2*, Englewood Cliffs, New Jersey, 1980.

Review, in *Casablanca*, no. 34, October 1983.

See also publications for *The Godfather*.

THE GODFATHER, PART III

USA, 1990

Production: Zoetrope, Paramount Pictures; Technicolor, 35mm; running time: 161 minutes.

Producers: Francis Ford Coppola, Gray Frederickson, Fred Roos, and Charles Mulvehill; **screenplay:** Francis Ford Coppola and Mario Puzo, from the novel by Puzo; **photography:** Gordon Willis; **editors:** Barry Malkin, Lisa Fruchtman, and Walter Murch; **production designer:** Dean Tavoularis; **art director:** Alex Tavoularis; **music:** Nino Rota and Carmine Coppola; **music director:** Carmine Coppola; **costume designer:** Milena Canonero.

Cast: Al Pacino (*Michael Corleone*); Diane Keaton (*Kay Adams*); Talia Shire (*Connie Corleone*); Andy Garcia (*Vincent Mancini*); Eli Wallach (*Don Altobello*); Joe Mantegna (*Joey Zasa*); George Hamilton (*B. J. Harrison*); Bridget Fonda (*Grace Hamilton*); Sofia Coppola (*Mary Corleone*); Raf Vallone (*Cardinal Lamberto*); Franc D'Ambrosio (*Tony Corleone*); Donal Donnelly (*Archbishop Gilday*); Richard Bright (*Al Neri*); Helmut Berger (*Frederick Keinszig*); Don Novello (*Dominic Abbandando*); John Savage (*Andrew Hagen*).

Publications

Articles:

Cowie, P., "Coppola Remarried to the Mob," in *Variety* (New York), 3 January 1990.

Kroll, J., "The Offer He Didn't Refuse," in *Newsweek* (New York), 28 May 1990.

Moss, M., "*The Godfather Part III:* Recapturing the Myth," in *Boxoffice* (Chicago), October 1990.

Harrison, Barbara Grizzuti, in *Life Magazine* (New York), November 1990.

Coppola, Eleanor, "The *Godfather* Diary," in *Vogue* (New York), December 1990.

Davis, Ivor, and Sally Ogle Davis, "It Ain't Over till the Fat Man Directs: Francis Ford Coppola and the Making of *The Godfather Part III*," in *Los Angeles Magazine*, December 1990.

Garcia, G., "The Next Don?" in *American Film* (Washington, DC), December 1990.

Rohter, L., "Coppola: It Was an Offer He Couldn't Refuse," in *New York Times*, 23 December 1990.

Kroll, J., "The Corleones Return," in *Newsweek* (New York), 24 December 1990.

Cowie, P., "Gudfader med starka familjeband," in *Chaplin* (Stockholm), no. 1, 1991.

Stivers, C., "Family Reunion," in *Premiere* (New York), January 1991.

Nissen, D., "Mafia," in *Kosmorama* (Copenhagen), Spring 1991.

Hansen, H. J., "Papa Coppola," in *Levende Billeder* (Copenhagen), March 1991.

Clark, J., "*Godfather* Shoots Blanks at Palermo Premiere," in *Variety* (New York), 18 March 1991.

Grant, E., in *Films in Review* (New York), March-April 1991.

Grob, N., "The Empire Strikes Back," in *EPD Film* (Frankfurt), April 1991.

Katsahnias, I., and N. Saada, "Entretien avec Francis Ford Coppola," in *Cahiers du Cinéma* (Paris), April 1991.

Causo, M., "La catarsi del cronotopo," in *Filmcritica* (Rome), April-May 1991.

"Il cinema di Coppola (parte III)," in *Castoro Cinema* (Milan), no. 81, 2nd ed., July 1995.

See also publications for *The Godfather*.

* * *

Mario Puzo has said that one of the reasons he wrote his novel, *The Godfather*, was to get out of debt. He was aiming for a best-seller, and he achieved his goal. Published in 1969, the novel sold 500,000 copies in hardcover and more than ten million copies in paperback by the time the film version was released.

Paramount Studios bought the film rights to Puzo's sprawling *roman à clef*, which concerned the history and structure of organized crime in America, in manuscript form. The studio proposed to make the film modestly and update it to the present day to avoid costly period sets and costumes. But when the book became a runaway best-seller, it was decided to make *The Godfather* an "event movie" with widespread release and higher-than-usual ticket prices. At the insistence of producer Al Ruddy and director Francis Ford Coppola, who got the assignment because of his Italian background and low asking price, the studio was also persuaded to return the script to its period milieu (the late 1940s).

With *The Godfather*, Coppola took a tired cinematic genre, the gangster film, in which all had seemingly been done, and pushed it in an epic new direction. Brutal, bloody, shocking, scary, funny, socially and politically observant, and meticulously performed by everyone from the leads to the bit players, the film offered a panoramic glimpse into the closed society of organized crime—a society ruled by vendetta, where the most sought-after currency, respect, is acquired through fear and intimidation. It's a society where murder is "nothing personal, just business" and casts a shadow over many other levels of American life, as well. Not for nothing has the film been dubbed "the *Gone with the Wind* of gangster movies."

The film was a financial blockbuster. Paramount demanded a sequel, and Coppola demanded and got complete creative autonomy for *The Godfather, Part II.* The main criticism leveled at *The Godfather* was that Coppola had made his Mafia characters sympathetic by giving them too-human a face. Coppola's point about the banality of evil, that members of the underworld are not all eye-rolling, saliva-dripping goons, was apparently lost on them. Still, he took the criticism to heart and in the sequel determined to make the point that Michael Corleone, an antihero who kills to hold his family together through the Mafia wars of the 1940s in the first film, is a Machiavellian figure whose soul is clearly lost by the final reel of the second film.

Coppola saw the sequel not as a way of simply cashing in on the success of the first film but of expanding its elements into a much broader and richer tapestry. The film chronicles the business of organized crime in the United States from 1900 to the 1960s, weaving facts with fiction in the manner of its predecessor. Drawing upon previously unused material in Puzo's book, it flashes back and forth in time to contrast the characters of Michael Corleone and his father, Vito, to reveal that what drives Michael is not what drove his father—that Michael is a more bitter and ruthless character, whereas Vito was a product of his old country ways and viewed the world as a place where only the strong survive.

The Godfather, Part II was a rarity—a sequel that not only deepened our understanding of the first film but bettered it artistically. It was also a huge financial success, but, at twice the budget of its predecessor, not quite the blockbuster the original had been. But since the film ended in the 1960s with Michael Corleone very much alive, Paramount was savvy enough to realize the mine had not yet been fully exploited. It wanted another sequel. Coppola wasn't interested, however, and shelved the idea for almost twenty years.

The Godfather, Part III takes up the saga of Michael Corleone in 1979, as the now guilt-ridden sixty-year-old don is receiving the order of San Sebastian, the highest honor the Catholic Church can bestow upon a layman. In between coping with Mafia plotters, crooked Vatican officials, and cutthroat European businessmen, Michael faces trouble on the homefront, as well. His son has rejected the family business to become an opera singer, while his daughter is carrying on a tempestuous affair with her first cousin (the illegitimate son of Michael's dead brother, Sonny). All these intrigues come to a head during the film's vigorous final thirty minutes, when Michael bloodily settles many scores—this time, he hopes, for good. But his beloved daughter takes an assassin's bullet meant for him and the aging gangster collapses with grief, his daughter and dreams of redemption gone. He dies of a heart attack years later, a white-haired Lear-like figure, alone in his palazzo.

The Godfather, Part III is not without its virtues. Its rich, warm photography, sumptuous production design and operatic style are all remarkably consistent with the first two films in the series. But its flaws are not insignificant. Considering its whopping $55 million budget (more than four times that of *Part II*), its failure to provide a conclusion to the Corleone saga in keeping with the epic vision of the first two films is a big disappointment. Coppola intended the film to be contemplative, but the effect it produces is *ennui.* Compared to the first two films, *Part III* is dull—and its similarly intricate plot is not as gripping as those of the earlier films. In fact, it is downright hard to follow at times.

But the film's biggest flaw is the change undergone by the lead characters, especially Michael, who is simply not the same man we saw at the close of *The Godfather, Part II*—a fact that becomes strikingly apparent if the two films are viewed consecutively. Monsters may get old and tired, but the outlook that made them monsters does not vanish. Guilt and the need for redemption are simply not a part of the emotionally dead, cold-eyed character Michael had become at the close of *The Godfather, Part II.*

—John McCarty

GODZILLA, KING OF THE MONSTERS!

See **GOJIRA**

GOJIRA

(Godzilla, King of the Monsters!)

Japan, 1954

Director: Ishirô Honda; U.S. additions, Terrell O. Morse

Production: Toho, Jewell Enterprises, Embassy Pictures, Transworld Corp.; black and white, 35mm; running time: 98 minutes (Japan), 79 minutes (U.S.). Released 3 November 1954 in Japan; released 27 April 1956 in United States with English dubbing; filmed in Tokyo, Japan. Cost: $1 million.

Producer: Tomoyuki Tanaka; **screenplay:** Ishirô Honda, Takeo Murata, from a story by Shigeru Kayama; **cinematographer:** Masao Tamai; **editor:** Yasunobu Taira; **music:** Akira Ifukube; **production design:** Satoshi Chuko, Takeo Kita; **sound:** Hisashi Shimonaga; **special effects:** Eiji Tsuburaya, Kuichiro Kishida, Hiroshi Mukoyama, Akira Watanabe, Teisho Arikawa (uncredited), Fuminori Ohashi (uncredited); **stunts:** Haruo Nakajima.

Cast: Akira Takarada (*Naval Salvage Officer Hideto Ogata*); Momoko Kouchi (*Emiko Yamane*); Akihiko Hirata (*Dr. Daisuke Serizawa*); Raymond Burr (*Steve Martin* [U.S. version only]); Takashi Shimura (*Dr. Kyohei Yamane*); Fuyuki Murakami (*Dr. Tabata*); Sachio Sakai (*Reporter Hagiwara*); Toranosuke Ogawa (*President of Nankai Shipping Company*); Ren Yamamoto (*Masaji Sieji*); Miki Hayashi (*Chairman of Diet Committee*); Takeo Oikawa (*Chief of Emergency Headquarters*); Seijiro Onda (*Mr. Oyama, member of Parliament*); Toyoaki Suzuki (*Shinkichi Sieji*); Kokuten Kodo (*Gisaku, Oto Island Patriarch*); Kin Sugai (*Miss Ozawa, member of Parliament*); Tadashi Okabe (*Reporter Killed in Tower*); Ren Imaizumi (*Radio Operator*); Junpei Natsuki (*Power Substation Engineer*); Ishirô Honda (*The Hand that Throws the Switch*); Kenji Sahara (*Man aboard Ship*); Ryosaku Takasugi (*Gojira*); Katsumi Tezuka (*Hagiwara's*

Editor [Japanese version only]; *Gojira*); Haruo Nakajima (*Gojira/Newspaperman*).

Publications

Books:

Mellen, Joan, *Voices from the Japanese Cinema*, New York, Liveright, 1975.
Bock, Audie, *Japanese Film Directors*, Tokyo, New York, and San Francisco, 1978.
Glut, Donald, *Classic Movie Monsters*, Metuchen, New Jersey, 1978.
Waldecki, Michael E., *Godzilla Goes to Hollywood*, M. E. Waldecki, 1985.
Harmon, Jim, *The Godzilla Book*, San Bernardino, California, 1986.
Bueher, Beverly Bare, *Japanese Films: A Filmography and Commentary, 1921–1989*, Jefferson, North Carolina, 1990.
Lent, John A, *The Asian Film Industry*, London, 1990.
Galbraith, Stuart, IV, *Japanese Science Fiction, Fantasy, and Horror Films: A Critical Analysis of 103 Features Released in the United States, 1950–1992*, Jefferson, North Carolina, 1994.
Tucker, Guy Mariner, *Age of the Gods: A History of the Japanese Fantasy Film*, New York, 1996.
Kalat, David, *A Critical History and Filmography of Toho's Godzilla Series*, Jefferson, North Carolina, 1997.
Aberly, Rachel, *The Making of Godzilla*, New York, 1998.
Alfonsi, *The Official Godzilla Compendium*, New York, 1998.
Lees, J. D., and Marc Cerasini, compiled and edited by Alice Lovece, Frank, *Godzilla: The Complete Guide to Moviedom's Mightiest Monster*, New York, 1998.

* * *

Gojira (better known in the English-speaking world as *Godzilla*), though based on American models, is a thoroughly Japanese production. Though it achieved world-wide success, becoming perhaps the most popular science fiction film in cinema history, *Godzilla* is a significant construction of Japanese popular culture that resonates with themes specific to that country's postwar experience. In fact, it seems to confirm what sociologists such as Siegfried Kracauer have said of mainstream cinema, that, especially in times of profound social crisis, its offerings often screen the fears of disaster and hopes for deliverance that are deep in the unconsciousness of its eager spectators.

Released with great popularity into a Japan just unwillingly liberated from secular and religious authoritarianism, the film traces the depredations of an angry sea monster, a sort of fire-breathing Tyrannosaurus Rex, whom all civilian and military efforts, except the *in extremis* plan of a brilliant scientist, cannot defeat. Godzilla's sudden, inexplicable appearance, or so one of the film's scientist heroes opines, reflects the disturbance of the natural order effected by the Hiroshima and Nagasaki bombs. It was these inconceivable weapons—Emperor Hirohito had less than a decade before emphasized in his public proclamation of surrender—that forced him to think the unthinkable and bear the unbearable. This unanticipated and total capitulation brought about an irreversible turn of fortunes in the nation's political life that is recalled by the sudden advent of the monster. The radiation produced by the bombs, moreover, continued to exact a toll of deformity and disease that many Japanese felt shameful, often shunning its victims. This violation of the national body is figured by Godzilla's assault, which fills hospitals with the mutilated and dying, many of whom are beyond the power of medical science to treat. Furthermore, like the bombing campaign directed with fearful results at the Japanese homeland, Godzilla vents his destructive urges on the nation's capital, leveling the same Tokyo that had been devastated only nine years earlier by a massive firebombing that incinerated more than a hundred thousand of its citizens.

Moreover, a culturalist reading of the film might see in the army's inability to halt this monstrous threat a post-militarist fear of being overcome by a foreign invader. This nightmare had already come true, of course, in the ongoing American military occupation, one of whose results was the transformation of the once powerful Imperial army into a lightly armed defense force. However, invasion was once again threatened at the time of the film's release in 1954 by Communist expansionism in Southeast Asia—just barely and inconclusively halted the year before in Korea—which was a traditional sphere of Japanese influence and occupation. Finally, the resigned helplessness of Tokyo's populace in the face of Godzilla's assaults expresses, perhaps, a collective dread at having violated, through the failure of the war effort, the submissive spirit of traditional culture, which had been largely abandoned in a society now devoted to capitalist self-aggrandizement. Denied the opportunity to die honorably in an apocalyptic defense of the home islands, the Japanese people of the postwar era had survived in the face of an ethical imperative demanding self-annihilation before any acceptance of national dishonor. Godzilla comes, perhaps, to expiate this failure, threatening an apocalypse that is finally averted but only after unspeakable death and destruction.

In any event, the angry giant reptile, who rises from his pelagic home to attack those who have unwittingly aroused him yet is accorded something like religious awe, is unlike the monsters brought to destructive life by nuclear testing in American science fiction films of the same period, the international series to which *Godzilla* otherwise belongs. The giant aggressive ants in *Them* (1954) and the huge carnivorous grasshoppers in *The Beginning of the End* (1957), among other similar threats, find their origin in radiation-caused genetic changes. In these extinction scenarios may be glimpsed a profound terror at the uncontrolled destructiveness that this new weapon has visited upon American culture. Godzilla, in contrast, is no product of a new and terrifying scientific age. Instead, he is an ancient creature come to destroy those who have brought this new age into being. Significantly, however, the guilty party is not the American invaders and occupiers, the bomb droppers who, in an antirealistic gesture, are not to be glimpsed or even mentioned in the world of the film. Instead, the monster's target is the Japanese people themselves and their national, religious capital.

Though its contemporary cultural symbolism is both rich and undeniable, *Godzilla* actually owes its origin to the long-held desire of special effects man Eiji Tsuburaya to make not a new and potent myth, but rather his own version of *King Kong*, Hollywood's most impressive monster film to date. In addition, an obvious intertextual influence was the outpouring from Hollywood's ''B'' producers of similar science fiction films in the American market. This trend was well established when Tsuburaya received the go-ahead from the executives at Toho Studio to make something quite similar. Many of these Hollywood films had been produced on very low budgets, yet had earned proportionally large profits from exhibition to, largely, youthful American audiences, most notably the customers of the thriving drive-in outlets. Tsuburaya read this contemporary popularity accurately, but modeled his production carefully on *King Kong*, made some two decades earlier. On a very tight budget, however, he did use a man dressed in a rubber suit instead of miniatures for Godzilla. Haru Nakajima, who played Godzilla with talent and subtlety in this and many subsequent productions, became one of the country's best known actors. Tsuburaya's monster film not only did well in the domestic Japanese market, but Embassy Pictures picked up the American rights at a time when few Japanese films, outside the art cinema of Kurosawa and others, enjoyed a release in the United States.

The Hollywood version of the film, released in 1956, was every bit as effective as the original even though it was partly re-produced. Director Terrell Morse shot English language sequences that matched the photographic and compositional style of the Japanese version incredibly well. Raymond Burr, playing an American newspaperman, became the main character and narrator, replacing the Japanese reporter; the other sequences were dubbed, and a new music track added. Significantly, the casting of Burr (a familiar heavy in crime melodramas) as well as an artful use of chiaroscuro effects and voice-over flashback narration connected Godzilla to native *film noir* in the manner of several other sci-fi films of the period, most notably Don Siegel's *Invasion of the Body Snatchers* (1956). Interestingly, these noir stylizations effectively matched the tone of helpless resignation in the Japanese original.

Godzilla proved an outstanding success in the United States and, indeed, in its world-wide release. Significantly, the advertising campaign in the United States featured comparisons with *King Kong*, which, until the time of *Godzilla*'s release, had been the most successful film of this kind ever exhibited in America. Though King Kong is gunned down by attacking airplanes, Godzilla is ultimately destroyed by the invention of a reclusive scientist, reflecting the film's connection to the contemporary Hollywood monster film.

Played by Takashi Shimura (a familiar presence in the samurai films of Akira Kurosawa), the esteemed Dr. Yamano is a kind of Japanese Einstein whose theoretical work has enabled him to perfect a process that fundamentally alters water. His weapon removes its dissolved oxygen, thereby depriving the monster of what he needs to live. Like other sea creatures, Godzilla requires gills to breathe (though, like an amphibian, he seems also to have lungs and thus can survive on land as well). Dropped into Tokyo Bay, where he has retreated from the ineffective attacks of the Japanese army, this oxygen destroyer reduces Godzilla to a stripped skeleton. This ending proved unfortunate when the film's popularity made a sequel an attractive possibility. Even so, a sequel was soon produced by Toho: *Gojira no Gyakushyu*, literally ''Godzilla's Counterattack'' but, strangely, given *Godzilla*'s popularity, released in the United States as *Gigantis the Fire Monster*. In this rather uninspired imitation, Godzilla is found alive and returns to the mainland (his target this time is Osaka), where he meets with another reawakened denizen of the Jurassic period named Angurus. After winning a titanic battle of monstrous reptiles, Godzilla flees the mainland and is destroyed once again. Short on plot and with somewhat inept special effects, *Gigantis* did not receive the same enthusiastic reception from the world's filmgoers as the original *Godzilla*. As a result, the series of Godzilla remakes that was to prove popular in Japan and abroad for more than two decades did not derive directly from the original film and its tepid remake. It was the 1962 release *King Kong vs. Godzilla* that soon became a kind of mini-genre, in which the originally terrifying monster became ever more sympathetic, eventually evolving into the protector of the home islands against the attacks of resurrected pterodactyls, giant wasps, and flying turtles as big and fast as jetliners.

—R. Barton Palmer

THE GOLD RUSH

USA, 1925

Director: Charles Chaplin

Production: Charles Chaplin Studio; black and white, 35mm, silent with musical score; running time: 74 minutes; length: 2720 meters. Released 16 August 1925, New York, by United Artists. Re-released 18 April 1942 in edited version of 2150 meters with music by Chaplin, and re-released again April 1956. Filmed January 1924-May 1925 in various studios, and on location in the Sierra Nevadas.

Producer: Charles Chaplin; **screenplay:** Charles Chaplin; **photography:** R. H. Totheroh and Jack Wilson; **art director:** Charles D. Hall; **artistic consultant:** Harry d'Abbadie d'Arrast, Chaplin also assisted by Charles Reisner.

Cast: Charles Chaplin (*The Lone Prospector*); Mack Swain (*Big Jim McKay*); Tom Murray (*Black Larsen*); Georgia Hale (*The Girl*); Betty Morissey (*Chum of the Girl*); Malcolm White (*Jack Cameron*); Henry Bergman (*Hank Curtis*); John Rand, Albert Austin, Heine Conklin, Allan Garcia and Tom Wood (*Prospectors*).

Publications

Script:

Shot record by Timothy Lyons, in *Cinema* (Beverly Hills), Summer 1968.

Books:

Frank, Waldo, *Charles Chaplin: A Portrait*, New York, 1929.
Bowman, William Dodgson, *Charlie Chaplin: His Life and Art*, New York, 1931.

The Gold Rush

Cotes, Peter, and Thelma Niklaus, *Charlot*, Paris, 1951.
Huff, Theodore, *Charlie Chaplin*, New York, 1951.
Bessy, Maurice, and Robert Florey, *Chaplin et le rire dans la nuit*, Paris, 1952.
Sadoul, Georges, *Vie de Charlot*, Paris, 1953.
Tyler, Parker, *Chaplin, Last of the Clowns*, London, 1954.
Leprohon, Pierre, *Charlot*, Paris, 1957.
Mitry, Jean, *Charlot et la fabulation chaplinesque*, Paris, 1957.
Amengual, Barthélemy, *Charles Chaplin*, Paris, 1963.
Chaplin, Charles, *My Autobiography*, New York and London, 1964.
McDonald, Gerald D., Michael Conway, and Mark Ricci, editors, *The Films of Charlie Chaplin*, New York, 1965.
Martin, Marcel, *Charles Chaplin*, Paris, 1966; third edition, 1983.
McCaffrey, Donald W., editor, *Focus on Chaplin*, Englewood Cliffs, New Jersey, 1971.
Mitry, Jean, *Tout Chaplin*, Paris, 1972.
Manvell, Roger, *Chaplin*, London, 1974.
Chaplin, Charlie, *My Life in Pictures*, London, 1974; New York, 1975.
Moss, Robert F., *Charlie Chaplin*, New York, 1975.
Lyons, Timothy J., *Charles Chaplin: A Guide to References and Resources*, Boston, 1979.
Eisenstein, Sergei, *Film Essays and a Lecture*, edited by Jay Leyda, Princeton, 1982.
Haining, Peter, editor, *The Legend of Charlie Chaplin*, London, 1982.
Gehring, Wes D., *Charlie Chaplin: A Bio-Bibliography*, Westport, Connecticut, 1983.
Robinson, David, *Chaplin: The Mirror of Opinion*, London, 1983.
Kamin, Dan, *Charlie Chaplin's One-Man Show*, Metuchen, New Jersey, 1984.
Smith, Julian, *Chaplin*, Boston, 1984.
Robinson, David, *Chaplin: His Life and Art*, London, 1985.
Saint-Martin, Catherine, *Charlot/Chaplin; ou, La Conscience du mythe*, Paris, 1987.
Silver, Charles, *Charles Chaplin: An Appreciation*, New York, 1990.
Lynn, Kenneth S., *Charlie Chaplin and His Times*, New York, 1997.
Mitchell, Glenn, *The Chaplin Encyclopedia*, Phoenix, 1997.
Milton, Joyce, *Tramp: The Life of Charlie Chaplin*, New York, 1998.
Kimber, John, *The Art of Charles Chaplin*, Sheffield, 2000.

Articles:

New York Times, 17 August 1925.
Variety (New York), 19 August 1925.
Wilson, Edmund, in *New Republic* (New York), 2 September 1925.
Huff, Theodore, ''Chaplin as Composer,'' in *Films in Review* (New York), September 1950.
Dyer, Peter John, ''The True Face of the Man,'' in *Films and Filming* (London), September 1958.
Callenbach, Ernest, in *Film Quarterly* (Berkeley), Fall 1959.
Mast, Gerald, ''The Gold Rush and The General,'' in *Cinema Journal* (Evanston, Illinois), Spring 1970.
Paul, William, in *Film Comment* (New York), September-October 1972.
Mersand, J., ''The Preparation and Use of Study Guides for the Mass Media, with a Study Guide to *The Gold Rush*,'' in *Literature/Film Quarterly* (Salisbury, Maryland), Spring 1975.
Giuricin, in *Cinema Nuovo* (Turin), May-August 1975.
Carroll, Noel, in *Wide Angle* (Athens, Ohio), no. 2, 1979.
Shot analysis, in *Avant-Scène du Cinéma* (Paris), 1 January 1979.
Michaels, J. E., ''Chaplin and Brecht: *The Gold Rush* and *The Rise and Fall of the City of Mahagonny*,'' in *Literature/Film Quarterly* (Salisbury, Maryland), no. 3, 1980.
Randisi, S., ''The Flirting Angel and the Tramp,'' in *Filmfax* (Evanston, Illinois), June-July 1993.
Frumkes, R., ''More Chaplin on Laserdisc,'' in *Films in Review* (New York), vol. 45, July/August 1994.
Gill, David, ''*The Gold Rush* 1925–1942–1993,'' in *Griffithiana*, no. 54, October 1995.
''*The Gold Rush*,'' in *Score* (Lelystad), no. 101, December 1996.
Ekbom, T., ''En hemlig bild av var och en,'' *Chaplin* (Stockholm), vol. 37, no. 5/6, 1995/1996.

* * *

The Gold Rush was Chaplin's favorite among his own films, so much a favorite that he deliberately did not copyright it, allowing it to pass into the public domain as a gift to his future public. As a result, the film has been seen more frequently than any other Chaplin feature, especially between 1952 and 1972, the two decades of Chaplin's disenchantment with America, when he withdrew all his other feature films from public circulation. Inspired by stories of the Donner Party, trapped in a desert of ice, and perhaps by the icy landscapes of Robert Flaherty's popular documentary feature, *Nanook of the North*, Chaplin took his Tramp character to the frozen gold fields where human beings endure great hardships so that they might strike it rich. As usual in a Chaplin film, the Tramp is very much an outsider in the world of *The Gold Rush*, even in this society of outsiders and outcasts. The Tramp is too kind, too sensitive to human needs, and too spiritual for that isolated, materialistic world. The Tramp's kindness in befriending Georgia, an abused dance-hall girl, contrasts with other human actions in the film—with those of Jack, Georgia's handsome boyfriend who treats her as his sex object; or with those of Black Larsen, a man so hungry for gold that he robs and kills others.

Despite the serious moral issues which the film raises in its contrast of material and spiritual human pursuits, its popularity derives from the power of its comedy sequences. In one of the most famous of Chaplin's transpositions of objects—his conversion of one kind of physical object into another—the Tramp cooks a dinner for himself and his starving friend, Big Jim McKay. Lacking anything else to eat, the Tramp sacrifices one of his own symbols, his floppy shoe, which he boils carefully in a pot, testing it with a fork for tenderness. He then carves it like a roast beef, twirls the shoestrings around his fork like spaghetti and sucks on the nails like chicken bones. In a later sequence, lacking even a shoe to eat, Charlie converts himself into a mammoth chicken—or so Big Jim imagines. The contrast of Charlie's chickenish actions with the cannibalistic dreams of his sometime friend reveals the typical Chaplin method of making comedy out of the most basic and elemental human needs—love, shelter, hunger.

Balancing the comedic scenes is one of the most effective and powerful sequences of pathos and poignancy in the entire Chaplin canon. Charlie has invited Georgia, whose picture he preserves under his pillow next to a rose, and several of her friends at the dance hall to supper on New Year's Eve. They, making fun of the pathetic little Tramp, have teasingly promised to attend the supper. As he waits for them, Charlie falls asleep and dreams of the delightful dinner that will never be. He entertains the girls by sticking two rolls on the ends of two forks and using them to dance the ''Oceana Roll.'' The sight of Charlie's playful face, coyly peering over the tops of these two tiny, dancing legs is one of the most memorable single images in Chaplin's work. But Charlie awakens to find that his social success has only been a dream—like his many dreams of love and success in earlier films. The pathos of his loneliness is emphasized by the communal society of revelers singing ''Auld Lang Syne,'' while Charlie, shown isolated within the frame, stands outside the circle of their friendship and observes.

However, almost miraculously, the Tramp eventually finds both love and wealth in this film. Charlie, now rich from his gold strike, discovers Georgia on board the same ship on which he is travelling home. She has had enough of the frozen wasteland (Chaplin typically uses the hired dance-hall girl as a metaphor for prostitution, the conversion of female sexuality into a commodity to be bought and sold). Georgia reveals her kindness when she protects Charlie from the ship's captain, believing him to be a stowaway. And Charlie, in turn, returns the girl's kindness by embracing her, now that he can offer her money as well as love. In what seems Chaplin's own conscious comment on the film's happy ending, a group of shipboard photographers, taking pictures of the former Tramp now a millionaire, criticize a photograph of the Tramp's kissing Georgia: ''You've spoiled the picture.'' Chaplin seemed to have been anticipating the film's critics whom he expected to attack this last scene.

The issue that the ending raises is whether the Tramp can ever find happiness with a romantic-sexual mate. Must the Tramp, as outcast and outsider, also be disqualified from the consummation of love, which in our society is formalized by marriage? The previous Chaplin films to end with a happy, affirmative answer to this question (*The Vagabond, A Dog's Life, The Kid*) also suggest something dreamlike and impossible about such a solution. This dreamlike suggestion about the Tramp's attainment of marital happiness becomes explicit in films like *The Bank* or *Shoulder Arms*, in which his attainment of the lady of his dreams literally turns out to be a dream. His next three films, *The Circus*, *City Lights*, and *Modern Times*, will return to the marriage theme with far more ambiguity and uncertainty. *The Gold Rush*, which lies at the crossroads of Chaplin's lighter early work and his more mature and darker features, is probably his most successful film at producing a completely happy ending without ''spoiling the picture.''

—Gerald Mast

THE GOLDEN AGE

See **L'AGED'OR**

THE GOLDEN COACH

See **LE CARROSSE D'OR**

GONE WITH THE WIND

USA, 1939

Director: Victor Fleming

Production: Selznick International Pictures; Technicolor, 35mm; running time: 220 minutes; length: 20,300 feet. Released 15 December 1939 in Atlanta by MGM, some sources list the premiere date as 18 November 1939. Re-released 1947, 1954, 1967, 1969. Filmed 10 December 1938-August 1939 in RKO backlots and studios (rented to Selznick International for the film), and on location at Old Laskey Mesa, California. Cost: $4,250,000.

Producer: David O. Selznick; **screenplay:** Sidney Howard, with structural innovations by Jo Swerling and some dialogue by Ben Hecht and John van Druten, from the novel by Margaret Mitchell; **uncredited directors:** George Cukor and Sam Wood; **photography:** Ernest Haller; **cameramen:** Lee Garmes, Joseph Ruttenberg, Ray Rennahan, and Wilfred Cline; **editors:** Hal C. Kern and James E. Newcom; **sound recordist:** Frank Maher; **production designer:** William Cameron Menzies; **art director:** Lyle Wheeler; **musical score:** Max Steiner; **special effects:** Jack Cosgrove and Lee Zavitz; **costume designer:** Walter Plunkett, Scarlett's hats by John Frederics; **consulting historian:** Wilbur G. Kurtz; **dance direction:** Frank Floyd and Eddie Prinz.

Cast: Vivien Leigh (*Scarlett O'Hara*); Clark Gable (*Rhett Butler*); Leslie Howard (*Ashley Wilkes*); Olivia De Havilland (*Melanie Hamilton*); Hattie McDaniel (*Mammy*); Thomas Mitchell (*Gerald O'Hara*); Barbara O'Neil (*Ellen O'Hara*); Caroll Nye (*Frank Kennedy*); Laura Hope Crews (*Aunt Pittypat*); Harry Davenport (*Dr. Meade*); Rand Brooks (*Charles Hamilton*); Ona Munson (*Belle Watling*); Ann Rutherford (*Careen O'Hara*); George Reeves (*Stuart Tarleton*), wrongly credited on screen as Brent Tarleton; Fred Crane (*Brent Tarleton*); Oscar Polk (*Pork*); Butterfly McQueen (*Prissy*); Evelyn Keyes (*Suellen O'Hara*); Jane Darwell (*Mrs. Merriweather*); Leona Roberts (*Mrs. Meade*); Everett Brown (*Big Sam*); Eddie Anderson (*Uncle Peter*); Ward Bond (*Tom, a Yankee Captain*); Cammie King (*Bonnie Blue Butler*); J. M. Kerrigan (*Johnny Gallagher*); Isabel Jewell (*Emmy Slattery*); Alicia Rhett (*India Wilkes*); Victor Jory (*Jonas Wilkerson*); Howard Hickman (*John Wilkes*); Mary Anderson (*Maybelle Merriweather*); Paul Hurst (*Yankee Looter*); Marcella Martin (*Cathleen Calvert*); Mickey Kuhn (*Beau Wilkes*); Zack Williams (*Elijah*).

Awards: Oscars for Best Picture, Best Director, Best Actress (Leigh), Best Supporting Actress (McDaniel), Best Screenplay, Best Cinematography-Color, Best Editing, Interior Decoration, 1939; Academy of Motion Pictures Arts and Sciences Special Awards to William Cameron Menzies for Color Achievement and to Don Musgrave and Selznick International Pictures for pioneering use of coordinated equipment, 1939; New York Film Critics' Award, Best Actress (Leigh), 1939.

Gone with the Wind

Publications

Script:

Howard, Sidney, *Gone with the Wind*, edited by Richard Harwell, New York, 1980.

Books:

Thomas, Bob, *Selznick*, New York, 1950.
Howard, Leslie Ruth, *A Quite Remarkable Father*, New York, 1959.
De Havilland, Olivia, *Every Frenchman Has One*, New York, 1962.
Samuels, Charles, *The King: A Biography of Clark Gable*, New York, 1963.
Farr, Finis, *Margaret Mitchell of Atlanta: The Author of Gone with the Wind*, New York, 1965.
Essoe, Gabe, and Ray Lee, *Gable: A Complete Gallery of His Screen Portraits*, Los Angeles, 1967.
Dent, Alan, *Vivien Leigh: A Bouquet*, London, 1969.
Essoe, Gabe, *The Films of Clark Gable*, New York, 1970.
Robyns, Gwen, *Vivien Leigh*, New York, 1971.
Selznick, David O., *Memo from David O. Selznick*, edited by Rudy Behlmer, New York, 1972, 1981, 1989, 2000.
Lambert, Gavin, *GWTW*, Boston, 1973.
Flamini, Roland, *Scarlett, Rhett, and a Cast of Thousands: The Filming of Gone with the Wind*, New York, 1975.
Mitchell, Margaret, *''Gone with the Wind'' Letters*, edited by Richard Harwell, New York, 1976.
Tornabene, Lyn, *Long Live the King: A Biography of Clark Gable*, New York, 1976.
Edwards, Anne, *Vivien Leigh: A Biography*, New York, 1977.
Pratt, William, *Scarlett Fever*, New York, 1977.
Have, Ronald, *David O. Selznick's Hollywood*, New York, 1980.
Fearfar, R., *Clark Gable*, Paris, 1981.
Harwell, Richard, editor, *Gone with the Wind, As Book and Film*, Columbia, South Carolina, 1983.
Bridges, Herb, *Frankly My Dear: Gone with the Wind Memorabilia*, Macon, Georgia, 1986.
Howard, Sidney, *Gone with the Wind: The Illustrated Screenplay*, New York, 1986.

Bridges, Herb, *The Filming of Gone with the Wind*, Macon, Georgia, 1989.
Molt, Cynthia Marylee, *Gone with the Wind on Film: A Complete Reference*, Jefferson, North Carolina, 1990.
Harmetz, Aljean, *On the Road to Tara: The Making of Gone with the Wind*, New York, 1996.
Vertrees, Alan D., *Selznick's Vision: Gone with the Wind & Hollywood Filmmaking*, Austin, 1997.
Bridges, Herb, *Gone with the Wind: The Three-Day Premiere in Atlanta*, Macon, 1999.

Articles:

Variety (New York), 20 December 1939.
Nugent, Frank S., in *New York Times*, 20 December 1939.
''Directed by Victor Fleming,'' in *Lion's Roar* (Los Angeles), September 1941.
Curtis, David, and Richard Goldhurst, in *Film Culture* (New York), May-June 1955.
Dyer, Tom, in *Films in Review* (New York), May 1957.
Dickens, Homer, ''Leslie Howard,'' in *Films in Review* (New York), April 1959.
Clarens, Carlos, ''Clark Gable,'' in *Films in Review* (New York), December 1960.
Hart, Henry, in *Films in Review* (New York), May 1961.
Doyle, Neil, ''Olivia De Havilland,'' in *Films in Review* (New York), February 1962.
Bowers, Ronald, ''Vivien Leigh,'' in *Films in Review* (New York), August-September 1965.
Sarris, Andrew, in *Village Voice* (New York), 26 October 1967.
Lightman, Herb A., ''Creating the New 70mm Stereophonic Sound Version of *Gone with the Wind*,'' in *American Cinematographer* (Los Angeles), November 1967.
Reid, John Howard, ''The Man Who Made *Gone with the Wind*,'' in *Films and Filming* (London), December 1967.
De Havilland, Olivia, ''Dream That Never Died,'' in *Look* (New York), 12 December 1967.
Gow, Gordon, in *Sight and Sound* (London), November 1968.
Stevens, J. D., ''The Black Reaction to *Gone with the Wind*,'' in *Journal of Popular Film* (Washington, D.C.), Fall 1973.
Pauly, T. H., ''*Gone with the Wind* and *The Grapes of Wrath* as Hollywood Histories of the Depression,'' in *Journal of Popular Culture* (Bowling Green, Ohio), Summer 1974.
Finney, E., ''Now Hollywood Stars Achieve Success in Spite of Themselves,'' in *Classic Film Collector* (Indiana, Pennsylvania), Fall 1976.
Sarris, Andrew, ''Frankly My Dear, We Do Give a Damn,'' in *Village Voice* (New York), 29 November 1976.
Gelé, C., in *Ecran* (Paris), March 1978.
De Benedictis, M., ''Scarlett e altro: Le stagioni di un nostro amore,'' in *Bianco e Nero* (Rome), January-February 1979.
''GWTW Quiz,'' in *Films in Review* (New York), December 1979.
Lindsey, R., in *New York Times*, 31 December 1979.
Behlmer, Rudy, in *Magill's Survey of Cinema 2*, Englewood Cliffs, New Jersey, 1980.
Slifer, C.W.D., ''Creating Visual Effects for G.W.T.W.,'' in *American Cinematographer* (Los Angeles), August 1982.
Taylor, John Russell, in *Films and Filming* (London), June 1984.
Janssen, C., in *Skoop* (Amsterdam), December 1984-January 1985.
Valkay, S., and P. Szentmihalyi Szabo, in *Filmkultura* (Budapest), January 1985.
Weinberger, M., in *Cinéma* (Paris), May 1985.
Mancini, M., ''Replantation,'' in *American Film* (Washington, D.C.), January-February 1986.
Ven de Ven, L., in *Soundtrack!* (Los Angeles), June 1986.
Oney, Steve, ''A Second Wind,'' in *American Film* (Washington D.C.), December 1986.
Haun, H., in *Films in Review* (New York), vol. 42, no. 11–12, November-December 1991.
Pierpont, C. R., ''A Study in Scarlett,'' in *New Yorker*, 31 August 1992.
Beken, Ludo, ''The Making of a Legend,'' in *Film en Televisie + Video* (Brussels), no. 426, November 1992.
McCarver, Pat, ''*Gone With the Wind*: The Best Movie I've Ever Seen,'' in *Classic Images* (Muscatine), no. 218, August 1993.
Lippert, R., '''You Make Me Feel Like a Natural Woman,'' in *Frauen und Film*, no. 54–55, April 1994.
Dagle, J., and Kathryn Kalinak, ''The Representation of Race and Sexuality: Visual and Musical Reconstruction in *Gone With the Wind*,'' in *Post Script* (Commerce), vol. 8, no. 2, Winter-Spring 1994.
French, Tony, ''Has *Gone With the Wind* Gone With the Wind? or, Can we be Intelligent About the Past?'' in *CineAction* (Toronto), no. 40, May 1996.
Kaufman, D., ''LaserPacific Restores Luster to *Gone With the Wind*,'' in *American Cinematographer* (Hollywood), vol. 78, September 1997.
Tonkens, S., in *Film Score Monthly* (Los Angeles), vol. 2, no. 3, 1997.
Lovell, Glenn, ''Frankly, My Dear, This Is No Improvement,'' in *Variety* (New York), vol. 371, no. 7, 22 June 1998.

* * *

Gone with the Wind, based on Margaret Mitchell's best-selling novel about the South during the Civil War and Reconstruction, made producer David O. Selznick's name a box-office draw, made the relatively unknown Vivien Leigh an international star, and became the most popular motion picture of all time.

Soon after Selznick bought the movie rights to Mitchell's novel in July 1936, thousands of fan letters began to arrive at Selznick International Pictures, most of them demanding that Clark Gable play the role of Rhett Butler. In order to get Gable, Selznick had to make a deal with MGM and Louis B. Mayer, who held Gable's contract. In exchange for Gable's services and $1,125,000 of the film's budget, MGM would receive the distribution rights and half the profits of *GWTW*.

Since Selznick had a contract with United Artists to distribute all his films until the end of 1938, principal shooting on *GWTW* could not start before 1939. In order to maintain public interest in the film before shooting could begin, Selznick launched a nationwide talent search to find an unknown actress to play Scarlett O'Hara. In the course of the two-year search, 1400 candidates were interviewed and 90 were tested, at a total cost of $92,000. Among those considered for the part were Katharine Hepburn and Paulette Goddard. The role eventually went to Vivien Leigh, a British actress who was largely unknown to American audiences.

The production phase of *GWTW* began auspiciously in December 1938, with the Atlanta fire scene—the largest fire ever staged in a film up to that time. Principal shooting, which started six weeks later, was plagued by numerous problems and required seven months to complete. The main problem was the script, which despite the efforts of more than a dozen writers, remained a confusing mass of revisions, and revisions of revisions, until after shooting was completed. The disorganized condition of the script made shooting difficult and created tension among the production personnel. After only three weeks of principal shooting, Selznick replaced director George Cukor with Victor Fleming. Two months later, Fleming, upset by Selznick's handling of the script, went home and refused to work. Selznick quickly hired Sam Wood to direct and when Fleming decided to return to the film two weeks later, Selznick let the two men split the directorial chores.

When *GWTW* was finally completed, it turned out to be a monumental film in almost every respect. Its technical achievements included the Atlanta fire sequence, the use of matte paintings to provide distant backgrounds and to complete partially constructed sets (*GWTW* marked the second use in Technicolor film of the matte process in which painted backgrounds are blended with filmed scenes of live actors), and the railroad depot crane shot, in which the camera pulls back and up to reveal Scarlett O'Hara walking among thousands of wounded Confederate soldiers—about 2000 live extras and dummies. Its total cost was $4.25 million—equivalent to $50 million today. It had the longest running time (3 hours 40 minutes) of its day and the largest titles in cinema history—each word of the film's title fills the screen itself. It was also the first major film to successfully challenge the Production Code's prohibition of profanity—with Rhett Butler's final line, ''Frankly, my dear, I don't give a damn.''

When *GWTW* premiered in Atlanta on December 15, 1939, over one million people poured into the city of 300,000, hoping to see Clark Gable, Vivien Leigh, and the other stars who attended the premiere. After three days of parades, celebrations, and Confederate flag-waving, a select audience of 2500 people saw the film, and they loved it. *GWTW* quickly became a worldwide critical and box-office success and won ten Academy Awards, a record that stood until 1959, when *Ben Hur* won eleven.

As of 1983, *GWTW* has earned $76.7 million in domestic rentals. In 1976 NBC paid $5 million for the film's television premiere. The program, aired over two nights in November, 1976, received a 47.6 Neilsen rating—the highest rating ever received by a movie on television. CBS subsequently paid $35 million for 20 airings of *GWTW* over a 20-year period. When appropriate adjustments for inflation are made, *GWTW* is the biggest box-office success in cinema history. The current critical consensus is that *GWTW* is the quintessential Hollywood studio system product.

—Clyde Kelly Dunagan

THE GOOD, THE BAD, AND THE UGLY

See **IL BUONO, IL BRUTO, IL CATTIVO**

GOODFELLAS

USA, 1990

Director: Martin Scorsese

Production: Warner Bros.; Technicolour; 35mm; running time: 145 minutes. Filmed in New York City, 1989. Released September 1990, USA.

Producer: Irwin Winkler; **executive producer:** Barbara de Fina; **screenplay:** Martin Scorsese, Nicholas Pileggi, based on the book *Wiseguy* by Nicholas Pileggi; **photography:** Michael Balhaus; **editor:** Thelma Schoonmaker, James Kwei; **assistant directors:** Joseph Reidy, Vebe Borge, Deborah Lupard; **production designer:** Kristi Zea; **art director:** Maher Ahmad; **music editor:** Christopher Brooks; **sound editors:** Skip Lievsay, Philip Stockton, Marissa Littlefield, Fred Rosenberg, Jeff Stern, Bruce Kitzmeyer; **title design:** Saul Bass and Elaine Bass.

Cast: Ray Liotta (*Henry Hill*); Lorraine Bracco (*Karen Hill*); Robert De Niro (*Jimmy Conway*); Joe Pesci (*Tommy DeVito*); Paul Sorvino (*Paulie Cicero*); Frank Sivero (*Frankie Carbone*); Tony Darrow (*Sonny Bunz*); Chuck Low (*Morrie Kessler*); Frank Vincent (*Billy Batts*); Gina Mastrogiacomo (*Janice Rossi*); Debi Mazar (*Sandy*); Frank DiLeo (*Tuddy Cicero*); Christopher Serrone (*Young Henry*).

GoodFellas

Awards: Venice Film Festival Award for Best Director, 1990; Oscar for Best Supporting Actor (Pesci), 1990; British Academy Award for Best Director and Best Film, 1990.

Publications

Script:

Scorsese, Martin, and Nicholas Pileggi, *GoodFellas*, London, 1990.

Books:

Kelly, Mary Pat, *Martin Scorsese: A Journey*, New York, 1991.
Ehrenstein, David, *The Scorsese Picture: The Art and Life of Martin Scorsese*, New York, 1992.
Keyser, Les, *Martin Scorsese*, New York, 1992.
Connelly, Mary K., *Martin Scorsese: An Analysis of His Feature Films*, Jefferson, North Carolina, 1993.
Stern, Lesley, *Scorsese Connection*, London, 1995.
Bliss, Michael, *The Word Made Flesh: Catholicism and Conflict in the Films of Martin Scorsese,* Lanham, 1998.
Dougan, Andy, *Martin Scorsese—Close Up: The Making of His Movies*, New York, 1998.
Friedman, Lawrence S., *The Cinema of Martin Scorsese*, New York, 1998.
Brunette, Peter, editor, *Martin Scorsese: Interviews*, Jackson, 1999.

Articles:

Variety (New York), 10 September 1990.
Kael, Pauline, *New Yorker*, 24 September 1990.
Jousse, T., and B. Reynaud, *Cahiers du Cinéma* (Paris), September 1990.
Lenne, G., ''De grands enfants,'' in *Revue du Cinéma* (Paris), September 1990.
Murphy, K., ''Made Men,'' in *Film Comment* (New York), September-October 1990.
Donovan, F., *Cinéma* (Paris), October 1990.
Rollet, P., and others, ''Scorsese sur Scorsese,'' in *Cahiers du Cinéma* (Paris), October 1990.
Tobin, Y., and others, *Positif* (Paris), October 1990.
Beauchamp, M., ''Ce que filmer veut dire,'' in *24 Images* (Montreal), November-December 1990.
Bahiana, A. M., and others, *Cinema Papers* (Melbourne), December 1990.
Milne, Tom, *Monthly Film Bulletin* (London), December 1990.
Caron, A., *Séquences* (Montreal), January 1991.
Viano, M., *Film Quarterly* (Berkeley), Spring 1991.
Quart, L., *Cineaste* (New York), 1991.
''Film as Literature: Two Screenplays,'' in *Literature/Film Quarterly* (Salisbury), vol. 23, no. 1, January 1995.
Scorsese, M., ''De Niro & moi,'' in *Cahiers du Cinéma* (Paris), no. 500, March 1996.
Lippe, R., ''Style as Attitude: Two Films by Martin Scorsese,'' in *CineAction* (Toronto), no. 41, 1996.
Perez, G., ''Film in Review,'' in *Yale Review*, vol. 84, no. 3, 1996.
Bauer, Erik, ''Stephen King's Other Half: Interview with Frank Darabont,'' in *Creative Screenwriting* (Washington, D.C.), vol. 4, no. 2, Summer 1997.
Amis, M., in *Premiere* (Boulder), vol. 11, October 1997.
Murphy, Kathleen, ''Made Men,'' in *Film Comment* (New York), vol. 34, no. 3, May-June 1998.
Smith, Gavin, ''Street Smart,'' in *Film Comment* (New York), vol. 34, no. 3, May-June 1998.

* * *

Scorsese's ''GoodFellas'' are the ironically glamorized criminal underclass who occupy an ambivalent textual position somewhere between a criminal rap sheet and the pages of *Modern Screen.* With *GoodFellas*, Scorsese extends and refines his examination of those shadowy figures at the edge of collective media consciousness who seem both to shun exposure and to covet a dubious celebrity. A product of the urban working-class environment, they are ''movie stars with muscle,'' familiar with the back alleys and circuitous underground routes which seem to lead to the front rows of the urban high life.

Scorsese's wise guys are the ''real,'' marginalized characters of criminal biography but also parodic figures who espouse the centralized values of an American business ethos which prizes individualism, ruthless self-interest, and bold opportunism. The display of wealth and power is an essential feature of the guerilla economics practised in the criminal underworld, and as a boy, Henry Hill is attracted to the aura of success, literally to the impression his criminal heroes make upon the world: the self-conscious figures they cut, the garrulous social habits they establish, and the weight and aura of presence that accompany their proceedings. Scorsese records Henry's recollections in loving detail as the boy detaches himself from normative family allegiances to participate in what seems an emancipatory communal self-fashioning. Henry's childhood is the ''glorious time'' of economic expansion, of imaginative criminal subversion and empire-building.

Yet it is a world in which display and concealment must be held in delicate equilibrium, where an incomprehensible chaos simmers beneath the surface textures of ''normal'' behaviours. Criminal camaraderie co-exists uneasily with virulent self-promotion; Joe Pesci's unnerving performance as Tommy DeVito provides the central figure for an explosive and unpredictable brutality, a barbarity which is ironically both ethos and threatening ''other'' to the self-regulating world of corporate criminality. Tommy is the dangerous and disruptive ''arch-criminal'' whose pathological machismo violates a more-or-less stable corporate hierarchy. His execution is less a visitation of poetic justice than a reminder of the arbitrary stratification which excludes Henry and Jimmy Conway from true success, from the ''legitimacy'' of more comfortable criminal associations.

By occupation, and by carefully educating himself in a life of crime, Henry seems to choose social over familial connections. Yet the glamorized freedoms of criminal marginality seem to inevitably segue into the restrictive enclosures of traditional domesticity. When

Henry moves in with his mistress, Jimmy and Paulie Cicero order him to ''do the right thing,'' to return to his wife. Appearances, at least, must be kept up, and deviation from normality frequently exacts the harshest of penalties. Economic freedom itself, the marginal ''extras'' wise guys struggle after, becomes a form of imprisonment, and criminal conspiracy inevitably demands the social exclusivity of the traditional suburban enclave. As Karen Hill explains, no ''outsiders'' are admitted into their social circle: ''Being together all the time made everything seem all the more normal.''

With the combined pressure of constant police harassment and a radically unpredictable business environment, domestic behaviours are grotesquely exaggerated while at the same time boundaries between private and ''public'' life are eroded: Karen casually sits in front of the television as detectives execute yet another search warrant; the morning after Henry witnesses another of Tommy's violent depravities, Karen threatens Henry for his sexual infidelities with a loaded pistol.

Karen's perception of surface normality is ironically echoed by Henry's commentary on the acceleration of mob violence throughout the 1970's. Shooting people simply becomes a ''normal thing.'' During a lengthy though luxurious prison stay, Henry begins to deal cocaine even though on the outside dealing is an unacceptable form of enterprise because it exposes his superiors to harsh federal penalties. The romanticized illusion of a cohesive criminal community, of conspiratorial confidence, is dissipated with Tommy's execution and, ironically, with the final big score engineered by Morrie and Jimmy. Calculation and self-interest can no longer be glossed over by social familiarity, and the bodies of Jimmy's former associates garishly accumulate for months after the Lufthansa robbery.

In the final act, Henry has become the rogue individualist, dealing cocaine through a lucrative out-of-town connection. In a brilliantly adrenalized sequence during which he juggles the mounting pressures of state surveillance, banal domestic appointments, drug-intensified paranoia, professional treachery, and careless babysitters, Henry is finally outmanoeuvred by federal narcotics investigators. His arrest, of course, simultaneously exposes his treachery to his mob superiors, yet Henry remains adept in reading the duplicitous surface of a criminal society in which he has suddenly become a dangerous liability. After his final meeting with Jimmy, Henry opts into the witness protection program which, ironically, subjects him to an inescapable suburban normality. For Henry the hardest thing is not betraying lifelong associates but ''leaving the life,'' becoming the ''average nobody'' who has to ''wait around like everybody else.''

In *GoodFellas*, organized crime seems to grow out of and perpetuate class division; it is the shortcut whereby the ambitious working class achieves only a tenuous facsimile of capitalist success. Scorsese's obvious message is that the American dream feeds upon those it enthralls, that even the criminal ''success'' story, however perilous, replicates the image of mainstream cultural beliefs.

—Tom Orman

THE GOSPEL ACCORDING TO ST. MATTHEW

See **IL VANGELO SECONDO MATTEO**

GÖSTA BERLINGS SAGA

(The Story of Gösta Berling)

Sweden, 1923

Director: Mauritz Stiller

Production: Svensk Filmindustri; black and white, 35mm, silent, shown in two parts; running time: 137 minutes; length: first part-2346 meters, second part-2189 meters, eventually edited by Stiller down to about current length. Released 10 and 17 March, 1924. Re-released 1933–1934 in a re-edited version by Ragner Hylten-Cavallius, with sound. Filmed fall 1923 in Sweden.

Scenario: Mauritz Stiller and Ragner Hyltén-Cavillius, from the novel by Selma Lagerlöf; **photography:** Julius Jaenzon; **art director:** Wilhelm Bryde.

Cast: Lars Hanson (*Gösta Berling*); Gerda Lundequist-Dahlstrom (*Majorskan Samzelius*); Otto Elg-Lundgren (*Major Semzelius*); Sixten Melmerfelt (*Melchior Sinclaire*); Karin Swanstrom (*Gustafva Sinclaire*); Jenny Hasselqvist (*Marianne Sinclaire*); Ellen Cedarstrom (*Countess Martha Dohna*); Mona Martenson (*Countess Ebba Dohna*); Torsten Hammeren (*Count Hendrick Dohna*); Greta Garbo (*Countess Elizabeth Dohna*).

Gösta Berlings Saga

Publications

Books:

Idestam-Almquist, Bengt, *Den Svenska Filmens Drama: Sjöstrom och Stiller*, Stockholm, 1938.
Hardy, Forsyth, *Scandinavian Film*, London, 1951.
Idestam-Almquist, Bengt, *Classics of the Swedish Cinema*, Stockholm, 1952.
Bainbridge, John, *Garbo*, New York, 1955.
Waldenkranz, Rune, *Swedish Cinema*, Stockholm, 1959.
Beranger, Jean, *La Grande Aventure du Cinema Suédois*, Paris, 1960.
Conway, Michael, *The Films of Greta Garbo*, New York, 1963.
Cowie, Peter, *Swedish Cinema*, London, 1966.
Pensel, Hans, *Seastrom and Stiller in Hollywood*, New York, 1969.

Articles:

Potamkin, M. C., ''The Golden Age of Scandinavian Film,'' in *Cinema* (London), September 1930.
Verdone, Mario, ''Stiller,'' in *Cinema* (Milan), no. 126, 1954.
Idestam-Almquist, Bengt, ''The Man Who Found Garbo,'' in *Films and Filming* (London), August 1956.
Gronowicz, A., ''Greta Garbo and My Book,'' in *Contemporary Review* (London), December 1960.
Robertson, Jo Anne, ''Mauritz Stiller,'' in *Monthly Film Bulletin* (London), December 1977.
Werner, G., ''Svenska giganter,'' in *Filmrutan* (Stockholm), no. 3, 1981.
Paavolainen, Olavi, ''Kaski mestaria - kaski vastakohtaa,'' in *Filmihullu* (Helsinki), no. 5, 1992.
Cristalli, P., ''How Little You Know About Love,'' in *Cinegrafie* (Ancona), vol. 6, no. 10, 1997.

* * *

Gösta Berlings Saga is regarded by many as Sweden's *Gone With the Wind.* With an epic sweep, episodic structure, and numerous characters, it evokes 19th-century Swedish life and is imbued with a lyricism and vibrancy which places its director Mauritz Stiller among the masters of silent film. The film represents both the pinnacle and the swan song of the ''golden age'' of Swedish cinema—1913–24. With its plot centering on the search for redemption by Gösta Berling, the defrocked priest, and the several women who disastrously fall in love with him, it numbers, along with Griffith's *Intolerance*, among the earliest important films of social protest and one of the masterpieces of silent cinema.

Stiller was a flamboyant dandy whose early reputation was built on sophisticated comedies exhibiting visual dexterity and artful editing. In 1919, he directed what is generally regarded as his foremost masterpiece—*Sir Arne's Treasure* (*The Three Who Were Doomed*), based on a novel by the popular Nobel Prize-winning Selma Lagerlöf. He directed the De Mille-like sex comedy *Erotikon* and then returned to adapting Lagerlöf's novels with *Gunnar Hede's Saga* and finally *Gösta Berlings Saga.*

Gösta Berlings Saga was a formidable undertaking which encompassed many characters and themes, required elaborate sets and costumes and resulted in a four-hour production shown in two parts on consecutive evenings. Stiller eventually conceded this impracticality and edited the film to 137 minutes. His editing, while judiciously shortening many scenes rather than eliminating them, nonetheless imposed a disjunction which ultimately mars the continuity. Despite this shortcoming, *Gösta Berlings Saga* remains a remarkable evocation of life among the Swedish aristocracy and mirrors its repression and hypocrisy. The first half of the film is devoted to exposition and the introduction of the many characters while the second half is highlighted by the dramatic fire in Ekeby Hall, a flight from wolves by sleigh across a frozen lake, and the brilliant acting of the venerable Gerda Lundequist-Dahlstrom as the shamed mistress of the manor.

Stiller's directorial technique was displayed through an expressive visual lyricism, an artistic use of light contrasted with shadowy darker hues and a picturesque depiction of the beauty and variety of the Swedish landscape. These elements are particularly evident in his photographing (with the masterful cinematographer Julius Jaenzon) of the then unknown Greta Garbo, who played Elizabeth. Stiller's scenes of Garbo picking flowers in the garden, carrying a lamp through the mansion hallways at night, and her first close-up in the sleigh scene capture the luminescence and radiance that made her the most unique female screen image of all time.

The success of *Gösta Berlings Saga* resulted in both Stiller and Garbo being hired by MGM in 1925. His three years in Hollywood destroyed Stiller and he returned to Sweden to die at the age of 45 in 1928. That same year *Gösta Berlings Saga* was released in the United States where a number of religious groups denounced it as ''a glorified Elmer Gantry.''

Lagerlöf disdained Stiller's interpretation of her novel, claiming he had seen ''too many poor serials.'' For the most part *Gösta Berlings Saga* is remembered today as the film which introduced Garbo to the screen. However, it is a major work of the silent screen and as French critic Jean Beranger wrote: ''If all but one Swedish silent film were to perish, this, probably, would be the one to save as the best witness of its period. All the charm, intelligence, profound human resonance and technical dexterity, here blend into an indissoluble bloc.''

—Ronald Bowers

THE GRADUATE

USA, 1967

Director: Mike Nichols

Production: Embassy/Lawrence Turman; Technicolor; Panavision; running time: 108 minutes; length: 9,720 feet. Released December 1967.

Producer: Lawrence Turman; **screenplay:** Calder Willingham, Buck Henry, from the novel by Charles Webb; **assistant director:** Don

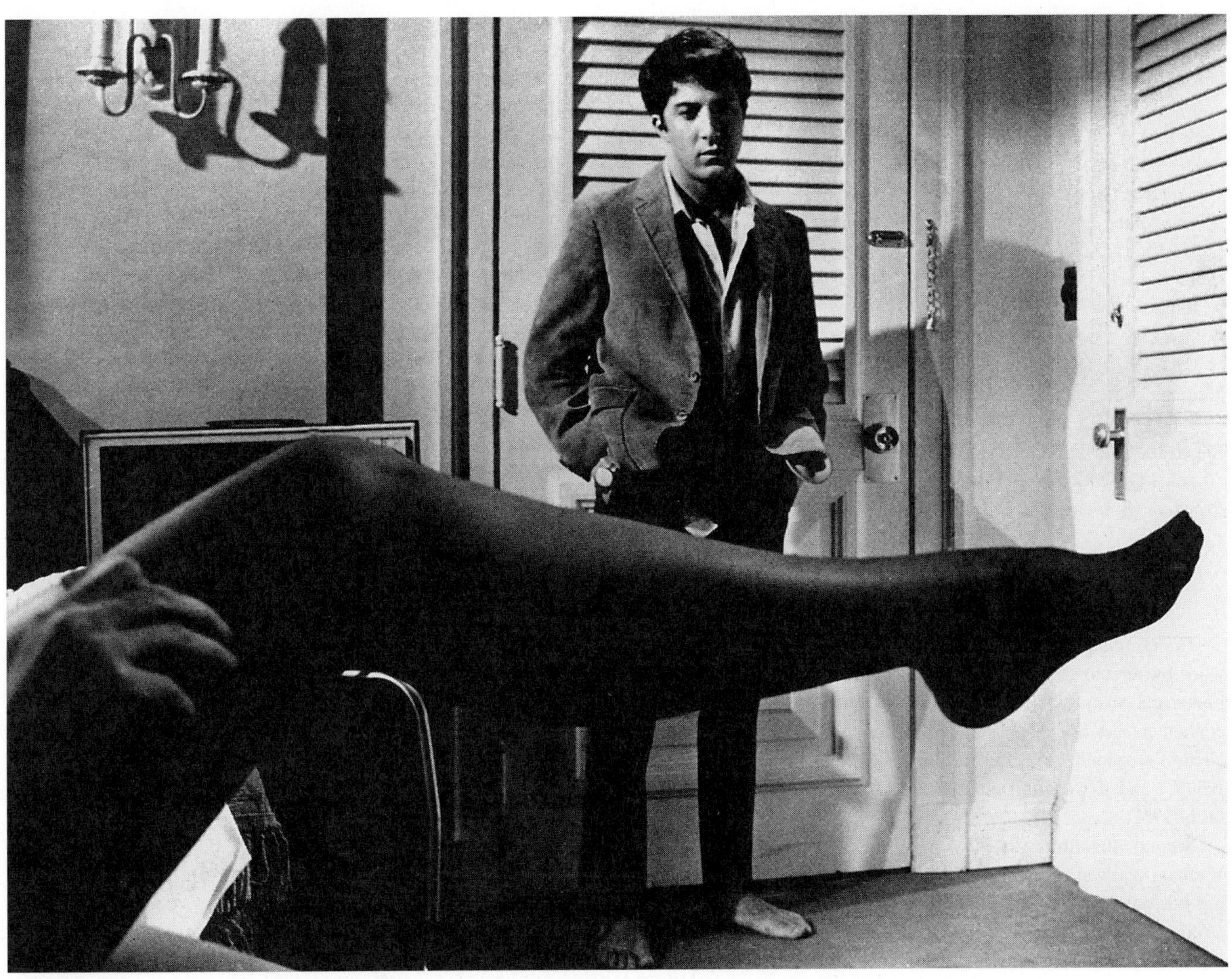

The Graduate

Kranze; **photography:** Robert Surtees; **editor:** Sam O'Steen; **sound:** Jack Solomon; **production designer:** Richard Sylbert; **music:** David Grusin; **songs:** Paul Simon; **performed by:** Simon and Garfunkel.

Cast: Anne Bancroft (*Mrs. Robinson*); Dustin Hoffman (*Ben Braddock*); Katharine Ross (*Elaine Robinson*); William Daniels (*Mr. Braddock*); Murray Hamilton (*Mr. Robinson*); Elizabeth Wilson (*Mrs. Braddock*); Brian Avery (*Carl Smith*); Walter Brooke (*Mr. Maguire*); Norman Fell (*Mr. McCleery*); Alice Ghostley (*Mrs. Singleman*); Buck Henry (*Room Clerk*); Marion Lorne (*Miss de Witt*).

Award: Oscar for Best Director, 1967.

Publications

Books:

Schuth, H. Wayne, *Mike Nichols*, Boston, 1978.

Holtzman, Will, *Seesaw: A Dual Biography of Anne Bancroft and Mel Brooks*, New York, 1979.

Dagneau, Gilles, *Dustin Hoffman*, Paris, 1981.

Sandre, Didier, *Dustin Hoffman*, Paris, 1981.

Brode, Douglas, *The Films of Dustin Hoffman*, Secaucus, New Jersey, 1983; revised edition, 1988.

Lenburg, Jeff, *Dustin Hoffman: Hollywood's Anti-Hero*, New York, 1983.

Agan, Patrick, *Hoffman vs. Hoffman: The Actor and the Man*, London, 1986.

Articles:

Variety (New York), 20 December 1967.

Hollywood Reporter, 5 January 1968.

Films in Review (New York), February 1968.

Farber, Stephen, and Estelle Changas, in *Film Quarterly* (Berkeley), Spring 1968.

Hudson, Chris, in *Monthly Film Bulletin* (London), September 1968.

Film Heritage (Dayton, Ohio), Fall 1968.

Austen, David, in *Films and Filming* (London), October 1968.

Davy, Barry, interview with Mike Nichols, in *Films and Filming* (London), November 1968.

Dawson, Jan, ''The Acid Test,'' in *Sight and Sound* (London), Winter 1968–69.

Sarris, Andrew, ''After *The Graduate*,'' in *American Film* (Washington, D.C.), July-August 1978.

Nielson, J.A., in *Filmrutan* (Stockholm), vol. 25, no. 1, 1982.

Auster, A., and L. Quart, ''American Cinema of the Sixties,'' in *Cineaste* (New York), vol. 13, no. 2, 1984.

''Simon Sues Embassy Over *Graduate* Music,'' in *Variety* (New York), no. 324, 20 August 1986.

Hendrykowski, Marek, ''Absolwent,'' in *Iluzjion*, no. 3, July-September 1989.

Denby, D., ''Coo Coo Cachoo, Mrs. Robinson,'' in *Premiere* (Boulder), vol. 4, December 1990.

Medich, R., ''Post-'Graduate' Studies,'' in *Premiere* (Boulder), June 1992.

Engel, J., ''Call This One 'The Post-Graduate','' in *New York Times*, vol. 142, section 2, 20 December 1992.

Premiere (Boulder), vol. 9, June 1996.

* * *

The Graduate is significant for three reasons. First, it is a major work by director Mike Nichols, who is characteristic of what the French call an *auteur.* (He is in complete control of his films and they contain consistent themes and elements of style.) *The Graduate* was Nichols's second film after he directed *Who's Afraid of Virginia Woolf?*, and it won him an Academy Award for best film director of 1967.

Second, the film was very popular with young people. The Vietnam War was escalating, and many young people were questioning not only the war but certain values of their society. But *The Graduate* was not a heavy protest film as *Getting Straight* or *The Strawberry Statement* were. The film's concern was not with destroying a materialistic, ''plastic'' society where people use each other as objects, but with a young man who questions this value system, decides what is important to him, and acts upon it honestly.

Third, the film stands the test of time. It possesses qualities of universality and brilliance because Nichols uses the filmic symbol system to generate laughter and cheers from his viewers.

The story concerns Benjamin (Dustin Hoffman in his screen debut) who returns to California from his eastern college and reacts zombie-like to his parents, their friends, and the values they live by. He is seduced by Mrs. Robinson (Anne Bancroft), the wife of his father's business partner, but he acquiesces to this relationship only to save himself from symbolically drowning in the values and objects of the materialistic sub-culture he is in. In fact, Mrs. Robinson uses Benjamin as an object to satisfy her desire. Benjamin and Mrs. Robinson carry on their affair until he is forced by his parents to have a date with her daughter Elaine (Katharine Ross), currently home from college. One kiss from Elaine changes Benjamin from passivity to action. He now pursues Elaine, and overcoming all odds, rescues her at a church just after she marries a medical student. Benjamin and Elaine (she is still in her wedding gown) leave together on a bus.

The Graduate shares with other Nichols's films the theme of a character who finds himself or herself ''drowning'' in some way, and who attempts to change. In *The Graduate*, Nichols shows this drowning visually. Early in the film, Benjamin is in his room alone during his graduation party staring into an aquarium which has a model of a diver at the bottom of the tank. Mrs. Robinson comes in and asks him to drive her home, throwing the car keys into the aquarium. She symbolically has the ''key'' to his survival. At her home, she makes it clear that she is available to him. He later calls her to begin the affair after he has been humiliated by his father who has given him a diving suit for a birthday present. His father has Benjamin wear the suit to ''show off'' in front of friends. In this suit, which relates to the diver in the aquarium, Benjamin enters the backyard pool and then just sinks to the bottom. He stays underwater as the camera pulls back, making him almost disappear. His voice, calling Mrs. Robinson, is heard at the end of this shot before we see him making the call from a hotel. Thus, the affair begins his emergence into life and helps him question what is really important to him.

The Graduate also shares with other Nichols films the tentative ending, where the viewer is left to ponder if enough really has changed. In the ending of *The Graduate*, Benjamin has rescued Elaine and they escape on a bus. They don't speak. Simon and Garfunkel's ''Sound of Silence'' is sung, as it was at the beginning of the film. The point Nichols is making is that perhaps not enough has changed, and that Benjamin cannot free himself from his society completely; he can only try, by seeing clearly and being true to himself and his own values.

This ending is consistent with the endings in other Nichols films. In *Working Girl*, 21 years later, which can be compared to *The Graduate*, the heroine has saved herself from ''drowning'' (she has crossed the water to Manhattan on the Staten Island ferry, for example) and has become a boss, not a secretary. The last shot has her looking out the window of a huge building with many floors above her in the hierarchy of the business world, suggesting she has made a change but that there is a long way to go.

Elements of style that Nichols uses so well in *The Graduate* that can also be found in his other films are the use of the environment to comment on the states of his characters (cool colors and white walls in *The Graduate* emphasize a sterile environment), heads that fill the screen while the background is often out of focus (Benjamin moving through the guests at his graduation party as the camera, concentrating on him, shows his isolation), and the use of filmic technique to comment on the situation (Benjamin runs to the church to rescue Elaine but appears to be running in place without getting anywhere, since Nichols had this action shot through a very long lens that flattens perspective).

The Graduate remains today as funny and profound as it was when first released. It articulates concerns about values. And for Benjamin, Elaine, and the viewer, there is a tentative note of hope.

—H. Wayne Schuth

LA GRANDE ILLUSION

France, 1937

Director: Jean Renoir

Production: Réalisations d'Art Cinématographique (R.A.C.); black and white, 35mm; running time: 117 minutes; length: 10,530 feet.

La grande illusion

Released 4 June 1937, Paris. Re-released 1946 with much footage deleted, re-released in 1959 with most original footage restored, and again in 1972. Filmed from about 30 January-2 April 1937 in Billancourt Studios, Tobis Studios, and Eclair Studios, Epinay; and on location near Neuf-Brisach, the Colmar barracks, and Haut-Koenigsbourg, Alsace.

Producers: Frank Rollmer and Albert Pinkovitch; **screenplay:** Charles Spaak and Jean Renoir; **assistant director:** Jacques Becker; **photography:** Christian Matras (1st operator) and Claude Renoir (2nd operator); **editor:** Marguerite Marthe-Huguet; **sound engineer:** Joseph de Bretagne; **production designer:** Eugène Lourié; **music:** Joseph Kosma; **lyrics:** Vincent Tully and A. Valsien; **costume designer:** Decrais; **technical advisor:** Carl Koch.

Cast: Erich von Stroheim (*von Rauffenstein*); Jean Gabin (*Maréchal*); Pierre Fresnay (*de Bœildieu*); Marcel Dalio (*Rosenthal*); Julien Carette (*Actor*); Gaston Modot (*Engineer*); Jean Daste (*Teacher*); Georges Peclet (*French soldier*); Jacques Becker (*English officer*); Sylvain Itkine (*Demolder*); Dita Parlo (*Elsa*); Werner Florian; Michel Salina; Carl Koch.

Awards: Venice Film Festival, Best Artistic Ensemble, 1937; New York Film Critics' Award, Best Foreign Film, 1938.

Publications

Script:

Spaak, Charles, and Jean Renoir, *La grande illusion*, London, 1968; Paris, 1971.

Spaak, Charles, and Jean Renoir, *Velikaja illjuzija*, in *Iskusstvo Kino* (Moscow), no. 3, March 1996.

Books:

Cauliez, Armand-Jean, *Jean Renoir*, Paris, 1962.

Chardère, Bernard, *Jean Renoir*, Lyons, 1962.

Analyses des films de Jean Renoir, Paris, 1966.

Bennett, Susan, *Study Unit 8: Jean Renoir*, London, 1967.

Leprohon, Pierre, *Jean Renoir*, New York, 1971.
Braudy, Leo, *Jean Renoir: The World of His Films*, New York, 1972.
Daniel, Joseph, *Guerre et cinéma: Grandes illusions et petits soldats 1895–1971*, Paris, 1972.
Predal, René, editor, *La Société français (1914–45)*, Paris, 1972.
Bazin, André, *Jean Renoir*, edited by Francois Truffaut, Paris, 1973; updated edition, 1992.
Durgnat, Raymond, *Jean Renoir*, Berkeley, 1974.
Renoir, Jean, *My Life and Films*, New York, 1974.
DeNitto, Dennis, and William Herman, *Film and the Critical Eye*, New York, 1975.
Giannetti, Louis D., *Godard and Others: Essays on Film Form*, Rutherford, New Jersey, 1975.
Truffaut, Francois, *Les Films de ma vie*, Paris, 1975; as *The Films in My Life*, New York, 1978.
Faulkner, Christopher, *Jean Renoir: A Guide to References and Resources*, Boston, 1979.
Sesonske, Alexander, *Jean Renoir: The French Films 1924–1939*, Cambridge, Massachusetts, 1980.
Gauteur, Claude, *Jean Renoir: Oeuvres de cinéma inédites*, Paris, 1981.
McBride, Joseph, editor, *Filmmakers on Filmmaking 2*, Los Angeles, 1983.
Serceau, Daniel, *Jean Renoir*, Paris, 1985.
Bertin, Celia, *Jean Renoir*, Paris, 1986.
Faulkner, Christopher, *The Social Cinema of Jean Renoir*, Princeton, 1986.
Vincendeau, Ginette, and Keith Reader, *La Vie est à nous: French Cinema of the Popular Front 1935–1938*, London, 1986.
Viry-Babel, Roger, *Jean Renoir: Le Jeu et la règle*, Paris, 1986.
Brunelin, André, *Gabin*, Paris, 1987.
Renoir, Jean, *Renoir on Renoir*, New York, translated by Carol Volk, 1990.
Bergan, Ronald, *Jean Renoir: Projections of Paradise*, New York, 1994.
Schneider, Bruno F., *Renoir*, New York, 1995.
Renoir, Jean, *An Interview: Jean Renoir*, with Nicholas Frangakis, Los Angeles, 1998.

Articles:

Fainsilber, Benjamin, ''Jean Renoir fait son examen de conscience,'' in *Cinémonde* (Paris), 20 May 1937.
Bianco e Nero (Rome), September 1937.
New York Times, 13 September 1938.
Variety (New York), 14 September 1938.
Hochheimer, Rita, editor, ''A Guide to the Discussion and Appreciation of the French Photoplay *Grand Illusion*,'' in *Photoplay Studies* (New York), no. 1, 1939.
''Renoir Issue'' of *Cahiers du Cinéma* (Paris), January 1952.
Hift, Fred, ''American Commentary: Says M. Renoir,'' in *Today's Cinema* (London), 9 August 1956.
''Renoir Issue'' of *Cahiers du Cinéma* (Paris), Christmas 1957.
''Un Film—*La Grande Illusion*—restauré comme un tableau,'' in *Lettres Française* (Paris), 6 March 1958.
Beylie, Claude, ''Ou est la liberté?,'' in *Cahiers du Cinéma* (Paris), November 1958.
Beylie, Claude, in *Cinéma* (Paris), November 1958.
Sadoul, Georges, ''The Renaissance of the French Cinema—Feyder, Renoir, Duvivier, Carné,'' in *Film: An Anthology*, edited by Daniel Talbot, New York, 1959.
Dyer, Peter John, ''Renoir and Realism,'' in *Sight and Sound* (London), Summer 1960.
Brunelin, André, ''Jacques Becker; ou, La Trace de l'homme,'' in *Cinéma* (Paris), July 1960.
Whitehall, Richard, ''The Screen in His Canvas,'' in *Films and Filming* (London), July 1960.
Kauffmann, Stanley, ''The Elusive Corporal and *Grand Illusion*,'' in *A World on Film*, New York, 1966.
Beylie, Claude, in *Cinéma* (Paris), November 1969.
Winsten, Archer, ''*Grand Illusion*,'' in *American Film Criticism*, edited by Stanley Kauffmann, New York, 1972.
Diehl, Digby, ''Directors Go to Their Movies: Jean Renoir,'' in *Action* (Los Angeles), May-June 1972.
Kauffmann, Stanley, in *Horizon* (Los Angeles), Summer 1972.
Fofi, Goffredo, ''The Cinema of the Popular Front in France (1934–38),'' in *Screen* (London), Winter 1972–73.
Sesonske, Alexander, in *Georgia Review* (Athens), Spring 1975.
Gauteur, Claude, ''Jean Renoir de *Nana* à *La Grande Illusion*,'' in *Image et Son* (Paris), May 1975.
Viry-Babel, Roger, in *Cahiers de la Cinémathèque* (Perpignan), Spring 1976.
Perebinossoff, P. R., ''Theatricals in Jean Renoir's *Rules of the Game* and *Grand Illusion*,'' in *Literature/Film Quarterly* (Salisbury, Maryland), Winter 1977.
Strebel, Elizabeth Grottle, ''Jean Renoir and the Popular Front,'' in *Feature Films as History*, edited by K. R. M. Short, London, 1981.
Toles, G., ''Being Well-Lost in Film,'' in *Raritan* (New Brunswick, New Jersey), no. 2, 1993.
Masson, Alain, in *Positif* (Paris), no. 395, January 1994.
Lelouch, C., ''A nagy abrand,'' in *Filmvilag* (Budapest), vol 37, no. 10, 1994.
Lelouch, C., ''La grande illusion,'' in *Cahiers du Cinéma* (Paris), no. 482, July/August 1994.
Casas, Q., J. E. Monterde, and S. Zunzunegui, in *Nosferatu* (San Sebastian), no. 17/18, March 1995.
Review, in *Séquences* (Haute-Ville), no. 178, May-June 1995.
Special Issue of *Archives: Institut Jean Vigo* (Perpignan), no. 70, February 1997.

* * *

The critical estimate of *La grande illusion* has fluctuated with the vicissitudes of critical theory. In the days when film's importance was attributed to the importance of its subject, it was widely regarded as Renoir's masterpiece, a noble humanist antiwar statement. With the development of the *auteur* theory in the late 1950s, its reputation dwindled. It came to be perceived as a less personal, less intimate and less complex work than *La règle du jeu*, which superseded it as marking the summit of Renoir's achievement. Though opposed, these views are based on the same misconception. *La grande illusion* is much too complex to be reduced to a thesis film, and although an antiwar statement can certainly be read from it (Renoir's detestation of war is not in doubt), that is incidental rather than essential to the film's meaning. In fact, it has a great deal in common with *La règle du jeu*: Renoir's own account of the thematic premise of the later film applies equally to the earlier (''My preoccupation is with the meeting; how to belong, how to meet''); both have similar four-part structures, moving to a big climactic scene at the end of part two, placing the major climax at the end of part three, with a quieter, more intimate fourth part in which the action moves out of doors or into the countryside.

''How to belong, how to meet''—another way of putting it is to say that Renoir's perennial concern is with the boundaries; that keep people apart and the possibility of transcending them. The four-part structure enables him to develop this theme through a network of shifting, interlocking relationships presented consistently in terms of difference and the overcoming of difference.

The first part consists of a prologue that introduces three of the four main characters and two of the main boundaries, class and nationality. Bœildieu and Maréchal are connected because both are French and involved in a war against Germany; Bœildieu and von Rauffenstein are connected because both are aristocrats and share a particular code that excludes the proletariat Maréchal. The film's basic assumption—that ''difference'' is socially constructed but so thoroughly internalized and so strongly institutionalized as to be very difficult to overcome—is dramatized in the parallels between the two headquarters (French/German) which are identical in structure but different in every detail, the details insisting upon ''Frenchness'' and ''German-ness'' respectively.

The second part occurs in the Prison Camp. Another main character, Rosenthal, is introduced, along with a host of minor ones who illustrate diverse aspects of the theme in the particularities of social position, profession, outlook, etc. With Rosenthal a third main boundary is established, that of race and religion. The pattern of alignments/separation becomes more complex: Maréchal/Bœildieu are linked by race and religion (Aryan, Christian) but separated by class position; Bœildieu/Rosenthal are linked by privilege but separated by class tradition (aristocrat/*nouveau riche*); Rosenthal/Maréchal are linked as non-aristocratic but separated by race/religion and social status. This section of the film makes frequent and expressive use of a favorite Renoir motif, the window, which stresses separation (outside/inside), but is also a boundary that can be crossed or communicated across. The second part culminates in the first big climax, the celebrated scene of the prisoners' camp show and defiant singing of the ''Marseillaise.'' Most important here, however, is the film's raising of the last main issue of boundary, that of gender/sexuality, especially in the extraordinary moment when the young prisoner is seen in women's clothes (for the show) and all activity and conversation abruptly cease. Its intensity exceeds anything explainable in terms of nostalgia for absent women: the androgynous figure becomes the center of the men's fascination and attraction.

The third section reintroduces von Rauffenstein (now with broken vertebrae, in a sense as much a prisoner as the men he is in charge of) and the development and culmination of the Bœildieu/von Rauffenstein alignment/separation. A leading concern here again connects the film to *Règle du jeu*: the notion that the aristocratic order the two men represent will not survive the war. The aristocracy of *Règle du jeu* is significantly different; they no longer are informed and guided by a clearly defined code of nobility. *Règle du jeu*'s Marquis is connected, not to Bœildieu, but to Rosenthal (not only are the two characters played by the same actor, but we are told that ''Rosenthal'' was the name of the Marquis's grandfather). Renoir views this inevitable destruction of a way of life with marked ambivalence. The aristocratic code is seen at once as based upon an untenable privilege and as embodying a fineness without which civilization will be poorer. This part of the film moves to the second major climax, in which Renoir magnificently ties all the major thematic and dramatic threads together: the escape of Maréchal and Rosenthal, secured by Bœildieu who sacrifices his life by compelling von Rauffenstein to shoot him. The scene echoes the climax of the second section by centering on a ''theatrical'' performance (Bœildieu playing his penny whistle on the battlements, the searchlights trained on him as ''star''). Together with the ensuing scene of Bœildieu's death and his class friend/national enemy's grief, the scene enacts the theme of the end of the aristocratic order (the proletarian Maréchal and the *nouveau riche* Rosenthal are the embryonic future). It achieves the film's supreme irony in its play on the intimate understanding and affection between two men, one of whom must kill the other.

The last section involves the escape/the farm/the border. The relation of *La grande illusion* to classical narrative (with its traditional pattern of order-disturbance of order-restoration of order) is complex and idiosyncratic. The narrative actually takes place in the hiatus between two orders: the order the war has destroyed and the new order that will be built when it is over. Between the two, Renoir manages at once to suggest the social order that was left behind and the possibility of a different order no longer based on artificial divisions. In the camps, the boundaries of class, race, and nationality are repeatedly crossed and eroded as new alignments (based on human need and sympathy) are formed. The last section restores what was crucially absent earlier: the presence of a woman. A series of three immediately consecutive scenes can be read as ''answering'' and containing the eruption of possible bisexuality in part two: Maréchal and Rosenthal sleep in each other's arms (the motive is warmth, not sexuality, but nonetheless they are in close bodily proximity); awakening, they quarrel violently, Maréchal calls Rosenthal a ''dirty Jew,'' they separate, then tentatively come together again; hiding in a barn, they hear someone coming and spring to either side of the door; the door opens and, exactly between them, the woman appears. The ensuing scenes restore the heterosexuality that, at the outset, was present only as a song (''Frou-Frou'') and a memory (Maréchal's Joséphine, the woman recalled by both Bœildieu and von Rauffenstein). This leads to the ultimate expression of togetherness/division: the Christmas celebration in which Rosenthal assists, only to be excluded as the lovers leave to go to bed. If the film celebrates the possibility of demolishing boundaries, it also acknowledges, within the existing social system, their inevitability.

—Robin Wood

THE GRAPES OF WRATH

USA, 1940

Director: John Ford

Production: Twentieth Century-Fox; black and white, 35mm; running time: 128 minutes, some prints are 115 minutes. Released 24 January 1940, New York. Filmed late Summer-early Fall 1939 in Twentieth Century-Fox studios and lots; with some footage shot on

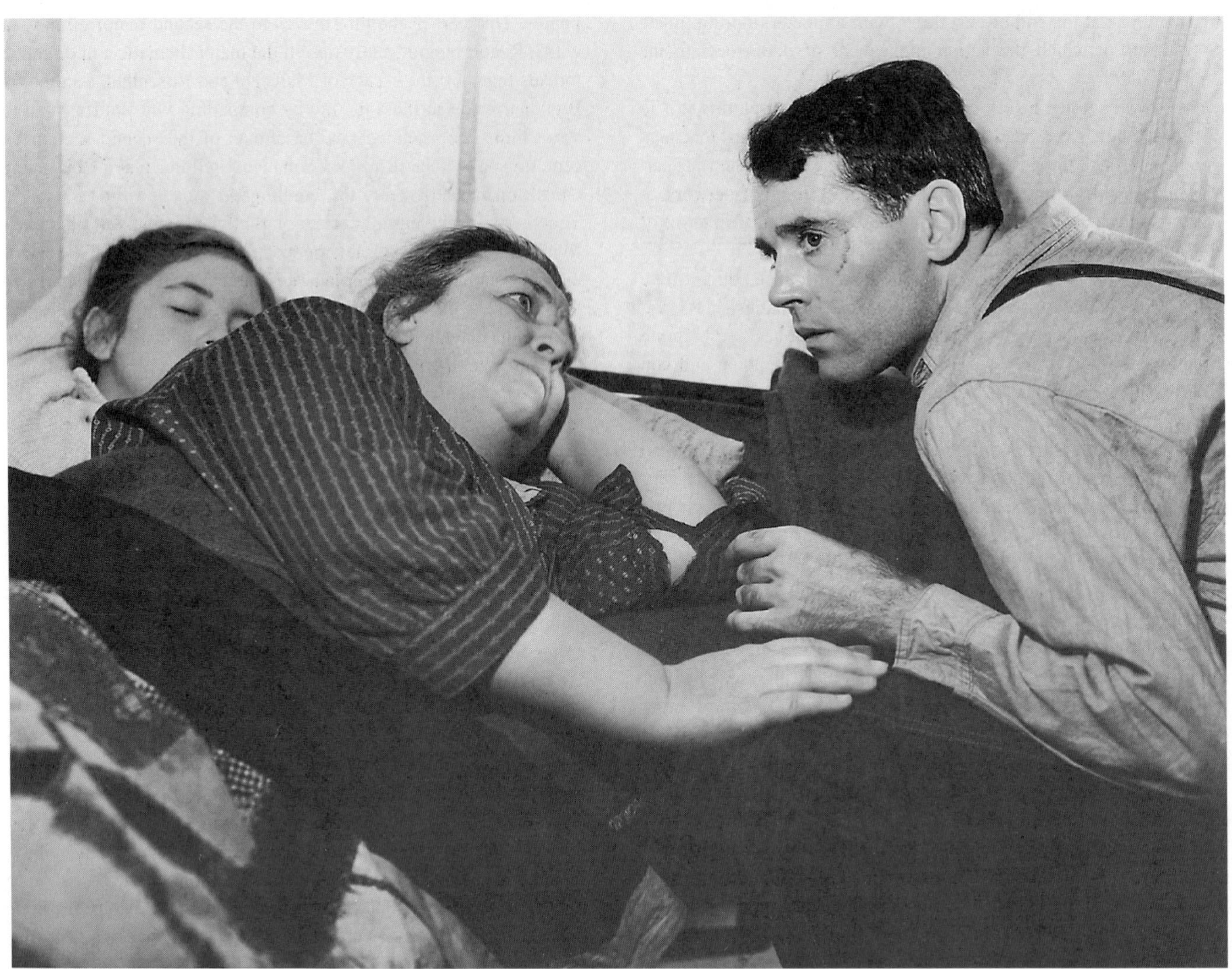

The Grapes of Wrath

location on Highway 66 between Oklahoma and California. Cost: $750,000 (estimated).

Producer: Darryl F. Zanuck; **screenplay:** Nunnally Johnson, from the novel by John Steinbeck; **photography:** Gregg Toland; **editor:** Robert Simpson; **art directors:** Richard Day and Mark Lee Kirk; **music arranger:** Alfred Newman; **special sound effects:** Robert Parrish.

Cast: *The Joad Party*: Henry Fonda (*Tom*); Jane Darwell (*Ma*); Russell Simpson (*Pa*); Charley Grapewin (*Grampa*); Zeffie Tilbury (*Granma*); Frank Darien (*Uncle John*); Frank Sully (*Noah*); O. Z. Whitehead (*Al*); Dorris Bowdon (*Rosasharn*); Eddie Quillan (*Connie Rivers*); Shirley Mills (*Ruthie*); Darryl Hickman (*Winfield*); *Others:* John Carradine (*Casey*); John Qualen (*Muley Graves*); Ward Bond (*Policeman*); Paul Guilfoyle (*Floyd*); Charles D. Brown (*Wilkie*).

Awards: Oscars for Best Director and Best Supporting Actress (Darwell), 1940; New York Film Critics' Awards for Best Picture and Best Direction, 1940.

Publications

Script:

Johnson, Nunnally, *The Grapes of Wrath*, in *Twenty Best Film Plays*, edited by John Gassner and Dudley Nichols, New York, 1943.

Books:

Mitry, Jean, *John Ford*, Paris, 1954.
Kracauer, Siegfried, *Theory of Film: The Redemption of Physical Reality*, New York, 1960.
Haudiquet, Philippe, *John Ford*, Paris, 1966.
Bogdanovich, Peter, *John Ford*, Berkeley, 1968; revised edition, 1978.
Burrows, Michael, *John Steinbeck and His Films*, 1970.
Springer, John, *The Fondas: The Films and Careers of Henry, Jane, and Peter Fonda*, New York, 1970.
Baxter, John, *The Cinema of John Ford*, New York, 1971.
French, Warren, *Filmguide to ''The Grapes of Wrath,''* Bloomington, Indiana, 1973.
McBride, Joseph, and Michael Wilmington, *John Ford*, London, 1975.

Sarris, Andrew, *The John Ford Movie Mystery*, London, 1976.
Ford, Dan, *Pappy: The Life of John Ford*, Englewood Cliffs, New Jersey, 1979.
Sinclair, Andrew, *John Ford: A Biography*, London and New York, 1979.
Stempel, Tom, *Screenwriter: The Life and Times of Nunnally Johnson*, San Diego, 1980.
Anderson, Lindsay, *About John Ford*, London, 1981.
Caughie, John, editor, *Theories of Authorship: A Reader*, London, 1981.
Fonda, Henry, and Howard Teichmann, *Fonda: My Life*, New York, 1981.
Schatz, Thomas, *Hollywood Genres: Formulas, Filmmaking, and the Studio System*, New York, 1981.
Goldstein, Norm, *Henry Fonda: His Life and Work*, London, 1982.
Thomas, Tony, *The Films of Henry Fonda*, Secaucus, New Jersey, 1983.
Cole, Gerald, and Wes Farrell, *The Fondas*, London, 1984.
Reed, Joseph W., *Three American Originals: John Ford, William Faulkner, Charles Ives*, Middletown, Connecticut, 1984.
Roberts, Allen, and Max Goldstein, *Henry Fonda: A Biography*, Jefferson, North Carolina, 1984.
Norman, Barry, *The Film Greats*, London, 1985.
Conger, Sydney Syndy M., and Janice R. Welsch, *Narrative Strategies: Original Essays in Film and Prose Fiction*, Urbana, Illinois, 1986.
Gallagher, Tag, *John Ford: The Man and His Films*, Berkeley, 1986.
Stowell, Peter, *John Ford*, Boston, 1986.
Lourdeaux, Lee, *Italian and Irish Filmmakers in America: Ford, Capra, Coppola & Scorsese*, Springfield, 1990; revised, 1993.
Davis, Ronald L., *John Ford: Hollywood's Old Master*, Norman, 1997.
Levy, Bill, *John Ford: A Bio-Bibliography*, Westport, 1998.
Eyman, Scott, *Print the Legend: The Life and Times of John Ford*, New York, 1999.

Articles:

Benton, Thomas, in *Life* (New York), 22 January 1940.
Collier's (New York), 23 January 1940.
New York Times, 25 January 1940.
Mok, M., ''Slumming with Zanuck,'' in *Nation* (New York), 3 February 1940.
Ferguson, Otis, in *New Republic* (New York), 12 February 1940.
Griffith, Richard, ''The Film Since Then,'' in *The Film Till Now* by Paul Rotha, revised edition, New York, 1949.
Bluestone, George, *Novels into Films*, Baltimore, 1957.
Hill, Derek, in *Sight and Sound* (London), Summer 1957.
Springer, John, ''Henry Fonda,'' in *Films in Review* (New York), November 1960.
Cowie, Peter, ''Fonda,'' in *Films and Filming* (London), April 1962.
McVay, Douglas, ''The Five Worlds of John Ford,'' in *Films and Filming* (London), June 1962.
Fonda, Henry, ''Fonda on Fonda,'' in *Films and Filming* (London), February 1963.
''Ford Issue'' of *Focus on Film* (London), Spring 1971.
''Ford Issue'' of *Filmkritik* (Munich), January 1972.
Pauly, T. H., ''*Gone with the Wind* and *The Grapes of Wrath* as Hollywood Histories of the Depression,'' in *Journal of Popular Culture* (Bowling Green, Ohio), Summer 1974.
Place, J., ''A Family in a Ford: *The Grapes of Wrath*,'' in *Film Comment* (New York), September-October 1976.
Campbell, R., ''The Ideology of the Social Consciousness Movie: Three Films of Darryl F. Zanuck,'' in *Quarterly Review of Film Studies* (Pleasantville, New York), Winter 1978.
Menides, L. J., ''John Huston's Wise Blood and the Myth of the Sacred Quest,'' in *Literature/Film Quarterly* (Salisbury, Maryland), 1981.
Boyero, C., in *Casablanca* (Madrid), January 1983.
Sanderson, J., ''American Romanticism in John Ford's *The Grapes of Wrath:* Horizontalness, Darkness, Christ, and F. D. R.,'' in *Literature/Film Quarterly* (Salisbury, Maryland), no. 4, 1989.
Reid's Film Index, no. 4, 1990.
Rothstein, M., ''Tom Joad: By the Book,'' in *New York Times*, no. 139, section 2, 18 March 1990.
Nielsen, R., ''Ray's Way: Eddie Quillan,'' in *Classic Images* (Muscatine), no. 194, August 1991.

* * *

A pet project of Darryl Zanuck's, *The Grapes of Wrath* exercised the packaging talents of Fox's studio head for a large part of 1939 as he put together a team appropriate to a book with the stature of Steinbeck's novel. John Ford was an obvious choice to direct, Dudley Nichols to write the script, and Henry Fonda to star as Tom Joad, the uneducated ex-convict ''Oakie'' who becomes the personification of flinty Midwestern integrity and moral worth. Knowing Fonda's wish to play Joad, Zanuck lured him into signing an eight-picture contract by advertising his intention to cast in the role either Don Ameche or Tyrone Power.

Ford, Nichols, Fonda and the supporting cast translated Steinbeck's novel to the screen with proper fidelity, the distortions far outweighed by the spectacular rightness of Fonda's casting and the remarkable cinematography of Gregg Toland, clearly influenced by the dust bowl photographs of Walker Evans and Margaret Bourke-White. The film's opening image of Tom Joad walking with tireless application out of the flat Midwestern landscape against a counterpoint of leaning telephone poles, suggests the themes of society confronted by an ecological and historical disaster against which it is helpless to act. Accustomed to such material from his frontier films, Ford took instinctive and instant command.

Clearly he felt an affinity with the plight of the dispossessed Kansas farmers of Steinbeck's story, which mirrored that of his Irish forebears turned off the land in the potato famine of the 19th century. And he had already established in films like *Four Men and a Prayer* the image of the family as not only unbreakable but an instrument for change, an institution that could act to improve social conditions. Throughout the film, it is the independents like John Carradine's itinerant preacher Casey and the half-mad fugitive Muley (John Qualen) who seem lost, desperate for companionship, while Jane Darwell and Russell Simpson as Ma and Pa Joad exhale a sense of calm and confidence. As Ma affirms at the end of the film, in a scene added by Zanuck to underline the moral and blunt the harsh dying fall of the novel, no force can destroy the will of people who are determined to live.

The picture Ford and Nichols draw of Depression America pulls few punches. Disinterested banks employ local strong-arm men to dispossess the share croppers and evict farmers unable to keep up mortgage payments on their own over-used, poorly maintained properties. Muley's futile stand against the bulldozers wilts when he recognizes one of his neighbors in the drivers seat. One has to eat even if it means betraying one's own kind. Deprived of his sacred kinship with the earth, sanctified by ''living on it and being born on it and dying on it,'' Muley becomes ''just an ol' graveyard ghost'' flitting about his crumbling house in the light of Tom Joad's lamp.

The Joads set out for California, their lurching truck loaded up with possessions, relatives and, in a touching gesture, the preacher Casey, invited along after a brief and hurried calculation of the vehicle's strength. Casey is a classic Fordian figure, a religious madman who acts as custodian of principles, the celebrant of rituals like Mose Harper (Hank Worden) in *The Searchers*. He says the brief funeral oration over Grandpa Joad when he succumbs to the trials of the journey. He also turns into a primitive union organiser when greedy employers exploit the itinerants desperate for work as fruit-pickers. He's no natural radical—just a man with a proper sense of right and wrong. Amused, he says of the bosses' thugs who hunt him, ''They think I'm the leader on account of I talk so much.'' When he dies, murdered by the employers, it is Tom who carries on his duty, instinctively sensing his destiny. ''Maybe it's like Casey says. A feller ain't got a soul of his own, but only a piece of a big soul.'' And he walks off again, as he entered the story, undramatically spreading the gospel of social reform.

The Grapes of Wrath abounds with examples of Ford's skill in visual language. Poor talkers, the Joads express much in a way of standing, looking, responding to the land through which they pass. Ma Joad's cleaning up of the old house is shown largely without dialogue, but her careful turning out of a box of mementoes, the discovery of a pair of earrings and her action of putting them on her ears and looking up into the dark at some half-forgotten moment of youthful pleasure could hardly be bettered with words. Jane Darwell is perhaps too plump, matriarchal, too *Irish* for her role, and Ford's first choice, Beulah Bondi, has a greater physical claim to the part with her gaunt, stringy resilience, but so effective is Ford's use of the actress that one can no longer imagine anyone else playing it.

Fonda remains the focus of the film, his clear-eyed sceptical gaze reaching out to the camera no matter where he stands in the frame. The strength of his moral convictions is all the more striking for the imperfection of the character which supports them. Just released from jail for a murder, Tom is unrepentant: ''Knocked his head plumb to squash,'' he recalls to an alarmed truck driver who gives him a lift. He has little understanding of politics (''What's these 'Reds' anyway?''), enjoys a drink and a dance, but has no time for abstract discussions. That such a man can be roused to moral wrath by injustice dramatizes the self-evident corruption of the system, and the belief in his conviction carries an audience to a conclusion startlingly radical by the standards of the time. Ford's reactionary politics, his populism and republicanism, must have stood in direct contradiction of the book's harsh message, which may explain his acceptance to the final suger-coated scene. Yet in Ford's world, to keep faith meant more than any political creed; better to believe in an error than not to believe at all. When Ma Joad at the end of *The Grapes of Wrath* professes the absolute faith of a peasant people in simple survival, one hears Ford's voice as clearly as that of writer, producer or star.

—John Baxter

THE GREAT DICTATOR

USA, 1940

Director: Charles Chaplin

Production: United Artists; black and white, 35mm; running time: 127 minutes. Released 1940.

Producer: Charles Chaplin; **screenplay:** Charles Chaplin; **photography:** Karl Struss and Rollie Totheroh; **editor:** Willard Nico; **art director:** J. Russell Spencer; **music:** Meredith Wilson.

Cast: Charles Chaplin (*Adenoid Hynkel, Dictator of Ptomania/A Jewish Barber*); Paulette Goddard (*Hannah*); Jack Oakie (*Benzini Napaloni, Dictator of Bacteria*); Reginald Gardiner (*Schultz*); Henry Daniell (*Garbitsch*); Billy Gilbert (*Herring*).

Publications

Books:

Tyler, Parker, *Chaplin, Last of the Clowns*, New York, 1947.
Huff, Theodore, *Charlie Chaplin*, New York, 1951.
Bessy, Maurice, and Robert Florey, *Monsieur Chaplin; ou, Le Rire dans la nuit*, Paris, 1952.
Sadoul, Georges, *Vie de Charlot*, Paris, 1952.
Leprohon, Pierre, *Charlot*, Paris, 1957; revised edition, 1970.
Mitry, Jean, *Charlot et la fabulation chaplinesque*, Paris, 1957.
Amengual, Barthélemy, *Charles Chaplin*, Paris, 1963.
Chaplin, Charles, *My Autobiography*, London, 1964.
McDonald, Gerald, and others, *The Films of Charlie Chaplin*, Secaucus, New Jersey, 1965.
Martin, Marcel, *Charlie Chaplin*, Paris, 1966; third edition, 1983.
McCaffrey, Donald, editor, *Focus on Chaplin*, Englewood Cliffs, New Jersey, 1971.
Mitry, Jean, *Tout Chaplin: Tous les films, par le texte, par le gag, et par l'image*, Paris, 1972.
Chaplin, Charles, *My Life in Pictures*, London, 1974.
Manvell, Roger, *Chaplin*, Boston, 1974.
Moss, Robert, *Charlie Chaplin*, New York, 1975.
Sobel, Raoul, and David Francis, *Chaplin: Genesis of a Clown*, London, 1977.
Baldelli, P., *Charlie Chaplin*, Florence, 1977.
Lyons, Timothy J., *Charles Chaplin: A Guide to References and Resources*, Boston, 1979.
Eisenstein, Sergei, *Film Essays and a Lecture*, edited by Jay Leyda, Princeton, 1982.
Haining, Peter, editor, *The Legend of Charlie Chaplin*, London, 1982.
Gehring, Wes D., *Charlie Chaplin: A Bio-Bibliography*, Westport, Connecticut, 1983.
Robinson, David, *Chaplin: The Mirror of Opinion*, London, 1983.
Kamin, Dan, *Charlie Chaplin's One-Man Show*, Metuchen, New Jersey, 1984.
Smith, Julian, *Chaplin*, Boston, 1984.
Robinson, David, *Chaplin: His Life and Art*, London, 1985.
Saint-Martin, Catherine, *Charlot/Chaplin; ou, La Conscience du mythe*, Paris, 1987.

The Great Dictator

Avisar, Ilan, *Screening the Holocaust: Cinema's Images of the Unimaginable*, Bloomington, Indiana, 1988.
Chaplin, Charlie, *Die Schlussrede aus dem Film Der grosse Diktator*, Hamburg, 1993.
Lynn, Kenneth S., *Charlie Chaplin and His Times*, New York, 1997.
Mitchell, Glenn, *The Chaplin Encyclopedia*, Phoenix, 1997.
Milton, Joyce, *Tramp: The Life of Charlie Chaplin*, New York, 1998.
Kimber, John, *The Art of Charles Chaplin*, Sheffield, 2000.

Articles:

Cooke, Alistair, ''Charlie Chaplin,'' in *Atlantic* (Boston), August 1939.
Life (New York), 2 September 1940.
Times (London), 16 October 1940.
Variety (New York), 16 October 1940.
New York Times, 16 October 1940.
Todd, Daniel, in *New Masses* (New York), 17 December 1940.
''Hitler and Chaplin at 54,'' in *New York Times Magazine*, 18 April 1943.
Warshow, Robert, ''A Feeling of Sad Dignity,'' in *Partisan Review* (New Brunswick, New Jersey), November-December 1954.
Baker, Peter, ''Clown with a Frown,'' in *Films and Filming* (London), August 1957.
Dyer, Peter John, ''The True Face of Man,'' in *Films and Filming* (London), September 1958.
Sarris, Andrew, in *Village Voice* (New York), 5 and 12 March 1964.
Goodman, Paul, ''Film Chronicle (1940): Chaplin Again, Again, and Again,'' in *Movie* (London), Winter 1964.
Lyons, Timothy J., ''Roland H. Totheroh Interviewed,'' in *Film Culture* (New York), Spring 1972.
Harvey, S., in *Film Comment* (New York), September-October 1972.
Chevassu, F., in *Image et Son* (Paris), November 1972.
Lefèvre, Raymond, ''Le Dictateur: Un Culot inoui,'' in *Cinéma* (Paris), November 1972.
Tarratt, Margaret, in *Films and Filming* (London), March 1973.
Bourget, J. L., ''L'Art des transitions dans *Le Dictateur*,'' in *Positif* (Paris), July-August 1973.
Boost, C., in *Skoop* (The Hague), August 1973.
Friedrich, J., ''Die letzte Tortenschlacht: Chaplins *Grosser Diktator* und das Ende des Slapsticks,'' in *Filmkritik* (Munich), November 1973.
Giuricin, G., ''La negazione del dittatore come fenomeno di massa,'' in *Cinema Nuovo* (Turin), January-February 1977.
Chaplin, Charles, ''Charles Chaplin (en) français,'' in *Image et Son* (Paris), January 1977.
''Chaplin Issue'' of *Film und Fernsehen* (Berlin), March 1978.
''Chaplin Issue'' of *University Film Association Journal* (Houston), no. 1, 1979.
Goldfarb, A., ''Adolf Hitler as Portrayed in Drama and Film,'' in *Journal of Popular Culture* (Bowling Green, Ohio), no. 1, 1979.
Sato, Tadao, ''The Comedy of Ozu and Chaplin: A Study in Contrast,'' in *Wide Angle* (Athens, Ohio), no. 2, 1979.
Goldstein, R. M., in *Film News* (New York), March-April 1979.
Bodeen, DeWitt, in *Magill's Survey of Cinema 1*, Englewood Cliffs, New Jersey, 1980.
Revue Belge du Cinéma (Brussels), Summer 1984.
Short, K. R. M., ''Chaplin's *The Great Dictator* and British Censorship 1939,'' in *Historical Journal of Film, Radio, and Television* (Abingdon, Oxfordshire), March 1985.
Gyurey, V., ''A Harmadik Birodalom es a Fuehrer ket nezopontbol,'' in *Filmkultura* (Budapest), no. 6, 1989.
'''Char': The Great Dictator,'' in *Variety* (New York), vol. 336, no. 3, 2 August 1989.
Reid's Film Index, no. 6, 1991.
Delage, C., ''La fiction contre l'histoire?: *Le Dictateur*,'' in *Vertigo* (Paris), no. 13, 1995.
Roth-Lindberg, O., ''En ironisk rockad,'' in *Chaplin* (Stockholm), vol. 37, no. 5/6, 1995/1996.
Seesslen, G., ''Chaplins spaete Filme,'' in *EPD Film* (Frankfurt), vol. 14, August 1997.
Rancière, Jacques, ''La fiction difficile,'' in *Cahiers du Cinéma* (Paris), no. 521, February 1998.

* * *

The Great Dictator was Chaplin's first dialogue film, the first film for which he wrote a script in advance, and the first film in two decades in which he does not star as the Tramp. Instead Chaplin plays a double role—a little Jewish barber, who closely resembles the Tramp, and the great dictator of Ptomania, Adenoid Hynkel, an obvious parody of Adolf Hitler, whom Chaplin ironically resembled.

The funniest sequences of the film are Chaplin's burlesques of Hitler's rhetoric, mannerisms, and delusions of grandeur. In one of those comic sequences, Hynkel delivers a political speech that is so scorching that the microphones melt and bend. Hynkel is so inflamed by his rhetorical passion that he not only has to cool his throat with water but also splashes water down the front of his pants—a brilliantly subtle Freudian suggestion that much of the fire of Hitler's political persuasion derives from the urgings of his genitals. In perhaps the most memorable sequence of the film, Hynkel converts the globe of the earth into his balloon-like plaything, performing a languid, romantic, dreamlike ballet with the floating globe, revealing his aspirations to possess the earth in almost sexual terms. This comic sexuality is reinforced by both the suggestions of masturbation in Hynkel's solo dance with the globe, and in the fact that the sort of actions he performs precisely mirror the twirls and gyrations of a bubble dancer, teasingly playing with the circular globe that hides her most mysterious parts from her leering audience.

In contrast to the delusions of the dictator is the earthy, pragmatic activity of the barber, a German soldier injured in World War I, suffering from amnesia, who awakens and returns to ''Ptomanian'' society only to find himself in an unfamiliar world where Jews are outcasts. In immediate response to the dictator's dance with the globe is the Jewish barber's snappy shaving of a customer to the precise rhythms of a Brahms Hungarian dance. The barber's snappy, vital, human-oriented actions contrast deliberately with the dictator's masturbatory solo. The barber also contrasts with the dictator in his relationship to language. As opposed to flaming rhetoric, the barber talks very little—another clear parallel to the Tramp. But at the end of the film, the barber, because of his physical resemblance, is mistaken for the dictator and asked to deliver the victorious speech to celebrate the invasion of ''Austerlich.'' The barber becomes very talkative, summoning his courage and feelings to deliver a direct appeal to all his viewers for hope, peace, and humanity. Although the lengthy, explicit political speech is deliberately woven into the film's action—which has contrasted the barber and the dictator in their relationship to human speech—the monologue struck many critics as overly explicit and impassioned, inadequately translated into Chaplin's tools of comedy, irony, and physical action.

Chaplin claims that he was unaware of the horrors of the Nazi death camps when he made the film. The outrageous sense of burlesque in the film implies the general American belief that Hitler was more of a clown to be laughed at than a menace to be feared. The reduction of Hitler's associates and allies to buffoons reveals the same pattern—Goering becomes Herring, Goebbels becomes Barbitsch, Mussolini becomes Benzino Napaloni, impersonated by a pasta-slinging Jack Oakie. Chaplin later stated that if he had known about the seriousness and murderousness of the Nazi threat he would have never made the film.

—Gerald Mast

GREAT EXPECTATIONS

UK, 1946

Director: David Lean

Production: Rank/Cineguild; black and white, 35mm; running time: 118 minutes. Released May 1947 by Universal-International Pictures.

Producer: David Lean; **screenplay:** David Lean and Ronald Neame with Anthony Havelock-Allan, Kay Walsh and Cecil McGivern; from the novel by Charles Dickens; **photography:** Guy Green; **editor:** Jack Harris; **art direction:** John Bryan; **music score:** Walter Goehr.

Cast: John Mills (*Mr. Pip*); Anthony Wager (*Pip as a boy*); Valerie Hobson (*Estella*); Jean Simmons (*Estella as a girl*); Bernard Miles (*Joe Gargery*); Francis L. Sullivan (*Jaggers*); Finlay Currie (*Magwitch*); Alec Guinness (*Herbert Pocket*); John Forrest (*Herbert as a boy*); Martita Hunt (*Miss Havisham*); Ivor Bernard (*Wemmick*); Freda Jackson (*Mrs. Joe*); Torin Thatcher (*Bentley Drummil*); Eileen Erskine (*Biddy*); Hay Petrie (*Uncle Pumblechook*); George Hayes (*Compeyson*); Richard George (*Sergeant*); Everley Gregg (*Sarah Pocket*); John Burch (*Mr. Wopsie*); O. B. Clarence (*Aged parent*).

Awards: Oscars for Best Cinematography—Black and White and Best Art Direction, 1947.

Publications

Books:

Tynan, Kenneth, *Alec Guinness*, New York, 1954.
Durgnat, Raymond, *A Mirror for England: British Movies from Austerity to Affluence*, New York, 1971.
Pratley, Gerald, *The Cinema of David Lean*, New York, 1974.
Silver, Alain, and James Ursini, *David Lean and His Films*, London, 1974; revised edition, 1991.
Zambrano, A. L., *Dickens and Film*, New York, 1977.
Castelli, Louis, and Caryn Lynn Cleeland, *David Lean: A Guide to References and Resources*, Boston, 1980.
Klein, Michael, and Gillian Parker, editors, *The English Novel and the Movies*, New York, 1981.
Hunter, Allan, *Alec Guinness on Screen*, London, 1982.
Anderegg, Michael A., *David Lean*, Boston, 1984.
Guinness, Alec, *Blessings in Disguise*, London, 1985.
Missler, Andreas, *Alec Guinness: Seine Filme, sein Leben*, Munich, 1987.
Von Gunden, Kenneth, *Alec Guinness: The Films*, Jefferson, North Carolina, 1987.
Silverman, Stephen M., *David Lean*, New York, 1989; updated version, 1992.
Brownlow, Kevin, *David Lean*, Gordonville, 1997.

Articles:

Variety (New York), 25 December 1947.
New York Times, 23 May 1947.
Lejeune, C.A., ''The Up and Coming Team of Lean and Neame,'' in *New York Times*, 15 June 1947.
Pichel, Irving, in *Hollywood Quarterly*, July 1947.
Ellin, Stanley, in *Hollywood Quarterly*, Fall 1947.
Thompson, Howard, ''Career Inventory from the Lean Viewpoint,'' in *New York Times*, 9 November 1952.
Holden, J., ''A Study of David Lean,'' in *Film Journal* (New York), April 1956.
Agee, James, *Agee on Film 1*, New York, 1958.
McVay, Douglas, ''David Lean—Lover of Life,'' in *Films and Filming* (London), August 1959.
Watts, Stephen, ''David Lean,'' in *Films in Review* (New York), April 1959.
McVay, Douglas, ''Alec Guinness,'' in *Films and Filming* (London), May 1961.
Johnson, Ian, ''Mills,'' in *Films and Filming* (London), June 1962.
Marill, Alvin, ''John Mills,'' in *Films in Review* (New York), August-September 1971.
Silver, A., ''The Untranquil Light: David Lean's Great Expectations,'' in *Literature/Film Quarterly* (Salisbury, Maryland), Spring 1974.
Zambrano, in *Literature/Film Quarterly* (Salisbury, Maryland), Spring 1974.
Wilson, D., ''Gag Bag,'' in *New Statesman* (London), 9 January 1976.
MacKay, C. H., ''A Novel's Journey into Film: The Case of Great Expectations,'' in *Literature/Film Quarterly* (Salisbury, Maryland), April 1985.
Hedling, E., ''Skuldens labyrint,'' in *Filmhaftet* (Uppsala, Sweden), December 1988.
''*Great Expectations* Section'' in *Literature/Film Quarterly* (Salisbury, Maryland), no. 1, 1992.
Reid's Film Index, no. 13, 1994.
O'Neill, Eithne, ''Les grandes espérances: Là-bas, dans les marais grelottants,'' in *Positif* (Paris), no. 410, April 1995.
Baston, Jane, ''Word and Image: The Articulation and Visualization of Power in *Great Expectations*,'' in *Literature/Film Quarterly* (Salisbury), vol. 24, no. 3, 1996.
Kendle, B., ''Lean Dickens and Admirable Crichton: Film Adaptations of Literature,'' in *Michigan Academician*, vol. 28, no. 1, 1996.
Boxoffice (Chicago), vol. 133, December 1997.

* * *

David Lean was the Great White Hope of postwar British cinema. *In Which We Serve*, which Lean co-directed with Noël Coward, was

Great Expectations

the most popular British film of the war years, and *Brief Encounter* was seen by the critics as a breakthrough into serious adult realism—though working-class audiences found Celia Johnson and Trevor Howard's over-delicate sensibilities hard to comprehend. *Great Expectations* had a wider appeal. Richard Winnington, one of the most perceptive 1940s film critics, claimed it as "the first *big* British film to be made, a film that confidently sweeps our cloistered virtues into the open, it casts a complete spell derived from some inner power."

The film was a commercial success in Britain and America (so successful that Lean couldn't resist following it up with *Oliver Twist*), and it still stands out as one of the finest of all film adaptations of Dickens. John Bryan's art direction avoids the trap so many designers fall into of striving so hard to recreate authentic period detail that Dickens's richly imaginative world is lost amidst too solid and realistic sets. Bryan, in cooperation with the brilliant cinematographer Guy Green, succeeds in creating an evocative atmosphere which gives the film much of its power and resonance.

Lean, a showman as well as an artist, talks about the need to gain the attention of audiences with a dramatic opening sequence. In *Great Expectations* he succeeds almost too well: the evocation of the bleak East Kent marshes and Pip's nightmarish encounter with Magwitch in the churchyard sets such a standard of excitement that what follows is almost an anti-climax. It is to his credit, then, that he succeeds in moulding Dickens's rambling novel into a satisfying dramatic shape. Minor characters are sacrificed, but Finlay Currie's Magwitch, Martita Hunt's Miss Havisham, Bernard Miles's Joe Gargery, and Francis L. Sullivan's Jaggers are splendid creations against which all subsequent incarnations have to be measured. In comparison, John Mills's Pip is disappointingly colourless, and the metamorphosis of Estella from Jean Simmons to Valerie Hobson destroys the aura which surrounds her in the first half of the film.

Lean's interpretation of Dickens, like Olivier's interpretation of Shakespeare, is inevitably timebound. There will always be alternative ways of interpreting *Great Expectations* or *Henry V*, while a reinterpretation of Noël Coward's slight play which Lean transformed into *Brief Encounter* could only be a remake of the film.

Thus, where *Brief Encounter*'s limitations—the prissiness of the lovers' attitudes to sex, the syrupy ending—seem movingly evocative of a lost age, *Great Expectations*'s weaknesses—its lapses into whimsicality, the predominance of upper-middle-class accents—seem correctable faults. That said, no other film or television adaptation of *Great Expectations* has managed to achieve anything like the dramatic intensity and visual richness of Lean's film. Magwitch appearing like a terrifying apparition in the windswept churchyard; Miss Havisham and Estella in their eerie, cobweb-strewn mansion; the journey out to the riverside inn and the disastrous rendezvous with the packet steamer—these are so memorably filmed as to haunt the imagination for years afterwards.

—Robert Murphy

GREED

USA, 1924

Director: Erich von Stroheim

Production: Begun under Goldwyn-von Stroheim Productions for Goldwyn Pictures; released by Metro-Goldwyn Corporation as a Louis B. Mayer Presentation; black and white, 35mm, silent; running time: about 150 minutes, a 109-minute version also exists; originally 7-hours, but Stroheim was forced to edit further, first into a 4 hour version, then into a 3 hour version supervised by Rex Ingram, and finally cut to 2½ hours by the studio; length: 10,212 feet (some sources list length as 10,067 feet or 10,500 feet); originally 47,000 feet, then 45,000 feet, then 42,000 feet, then 24,000 feet, then 18,000 feet, then 16,000 feet, and finally present length. Released December 1924, New York; all scenes with gold or gold-related objects were hand-tinted in original release prints. Filmed in 9 months, 1922–23 and edited in 1 year, 1923–24. Filmed in Oakland, California, and in Death Valley and the Panamint Mountains, California. Cost: over $450,000.

Producers: Erich von Stroheim and Samuel Goldwyn, some sources list Irving Thalberg as producer; **screenplay:** Erich von Stroheim and June Mathis, from the novel *McTeague* by Frank Norris; **original titles:** Erich von Stroheim and June Mathis; **released titles:** Joseph Farnham; **photography:** William H. Daniels, Ben F. Reynolds, and Ernest B. Schoedsack; **editor:** Frank Hull; **final version editors:** Joseph Farnham and reputedly June Mathis; **production designers:** Capt. Richard Day and Erich von Stroheim (no actual sets used); **art directors:** Louis Germonprez and Edward Sowders; **music:** James and Jack Brennan.

Cast: *In the Prologue:* Jack Curtis (*McTeague, Sr., Shift Boss at the Big Dipper Mine*) (role cut from film); Tempé Piggot (*Mother McTeague*); Gibson Gowland (*McTeague, the Son*); Günther von Ritzau (*Dr. ''Painless'' Potter*); Florence Gibson (*Hag*); *In the Play:* Gibson Gowland (*Doc McTeague*); Jean Hersholt (*Marcus Schouler*); Chester Conklin (*Popper Sieppe*); Sylvia Ashton (*Mommer Sieppe*); ZaSu Pitts (*Trina*); Austin Jewell (*''Owgoost'' Sieppe*); Oscar and Otto Gotell (*''Der Tervins,'' the twin brothers*); Joan Standing (*Selina*); Frank Hayes (*Old Grannis*); Fanny Midgley (*Miss Baker*); Max Tyron (*Mr. Oelbermann*); Hughie Mack (*Heise, the Harness Maker*); Tiny Jones (*Mrs. Heise*); J. Aldrich Libbey (*Mr. Ryer*); Rita Revela (*Mrs. Ryer*); Dale Fuller (*Maria Miranda Macapa, a Scrubwoman*); Cesare Gravina (*Zerkow, a Junkman*); Lon Poff (*Lottery Agent*); S. S. Simon (*Joe Frenna, the Saloon Keeper*); William Mollenheimer (*The Palmist*); Hugh J. McCauley (*The Photographer*); Jack McDonald (*Cribbens, a Prospector*); James Gibson (*Deputy Sheriff*).

Publications

Script:

Von Stroheim, Erich, and June Mathis, *Greed*, edited by Joel W. Finler, New York and London, 1972.
Weinberg, Herman G., *The Complete Greed by Erich von Stroheim*, New York, 1972.

Books:

Fronval, Georges, *Erich von Stroheim: Sa vie, ses films*, Paris, 1939.
Noble, Peter, *Hollywood Scapegoat: The Biography of Erich von Stroheim*, London, 1951.
Bergut, Bob, *Erich von Stroheim*, Paris, 1960.
Lawson, John Howard, *Film: The Creative Process*, New York, 1964.
Barna, Jon, *Stroheim*, Vienna, 1966.
Gobeil, Charlotte, editor, *Hommage à Erich von Stroheim*, Ottawa, 1966.
Bazin, André, *What is Cinema 1*, Berkeley, 1967.
Ciment, Michel, *Erich von Stroheim*, Paris, 1967.
Finler, Joel W., *Stroheim*, Berkeley, 1968.
Brownlow, Kenvin, *The Parade's Gone By*, London and New York, 1969.
Curtiss, Thomas Quinn, *Erich von Stroheim*, Paris, 1969.
Buache, Freddy, *Erich von Stroheim*, Paris, 1972.
Everson, William K., *American Silent Film*, New York, 1978.
Bazin, André, *The Cinema of Cruelty: From Buñuel to Hitchcock*, New York, 1982.
Koszarski, Richard, *The Man You Loved to Hate: Erich von Stroheim and Hollywood*, Oxford, 1983.
Bessy, Maurice, *Erich von Stroheim*, Paris, 1984.
Rosenbaum, Richard, *Greed*, London, 1993.
Lenning, Arthur, *Stroheim*, Lexington, 2000.

Articles:

New York Times, 5 December 1924.
Variety (New York), 10 December 1924.
Photoplay (New York), January 1925.
Davay, Paul, ''Notes sur les principaux films de Stroheim,'' in *Ecran des Arts* (Paris), 1947.
''Erich von Stroheim: His Work and Influence,'' in *Sight and Sound* (London), Winter 1947–48.
Schwerin, Jules, ''The Resurgence of von Stroheim,'' in *Films in Review* (New York), April 1950.
Lambert, Gavin, ''Stroheim Revisited,'' in *Sight and Sound* (London), April-June 1953.
Weinberg, Herman J., in *Cinemages* (New York), 1955.
Fulton, A. R., in *Films in Review* (New York), June-July 1955.
Eisner, Lotte, ''Notes sur le style de Stroheim,'' in *Cahiers du Cinéma* (Paris), January 1957.
Everson, William K., ''The Career of Erich von Stroheim,'' in *Films in Review* (New York), August-September 1957.
''Von Stroheim Issue'' of *Film Culture* (New York), April 1958.

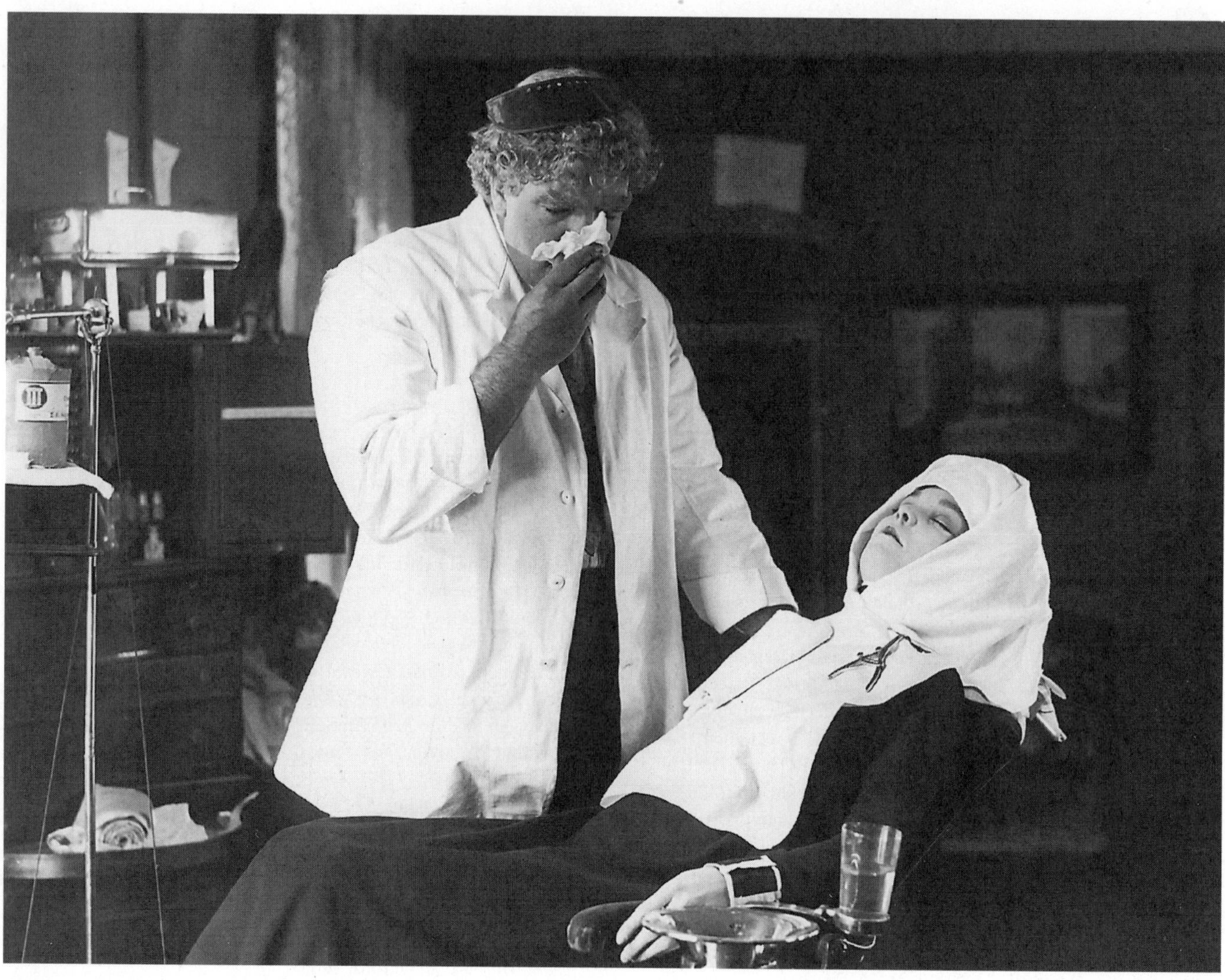

Greed

''Von Stroheim Issue'' of *Bianco e Nero* (Rome), February-March 1959.

Premier Plan (Lyons), August 1963.

Etudes Cinématographiques (Paris), no. 48–50, 1966.

Recassens, G., in *Téléciné* (Paris), January 1967.

Lee, R., ''Count von Realism,'' in *Classic Film Collector* (Indiana, Pennsylvania), Spring 1969.

Buñuel, Luis, in *Positif* (Paris), Summer 1970.

Schepelern, P., in *Kosmorama* (Copenhagen), March 1973.

Weinberg, Herman G., ''An Introduction to Greed,'' in *Focus on Films* (London), Spring 1973.

Wolfe, C., ''Resurrecting Greed,'' in *Sight and Sound* (London), Summer 1975.

Dahan, L., ''Les Rapaces d'Erich von Stroheim,'' in *Cinématographe* (Paris), April 1977.

Henley, John, in *Cinema Texas Program Notes* (Austin), 25 September 1978.

Koszarski, Richard, ''A Legend in Its Own Time,'' in *American Film* (Washington D.C.), May 1983.

Slater, Thomas, ''June Mathis,'' in *American Screenwriters, 2nd Series*, edited by Randall Clark, Detroit, 1986.

Grindon, L., ''From Word to Image: Displacement and Meaning in *Greed*,'' in *Journal of Film and Video* (Los Angeles), no. 4, 1989.

Dean, T. K., ''The Flight of McTeague's Soul-Bird: Thematic Differences Between Norris's *McTeague* and von Stroheim's *Greed*,'' in *Literature/Film Quarterly* (Salisbury, Maryland), no. 2, 1990.

Cremonini, G., in *Cineforum* (Bergamo, Italy), April 1992.

''Gold Lust,'' in *New Yorker*, vol. 69, 15 March 1993.

Séquences (Haute-Ville), no. 177, March-April 1995.

Reisz, Karel, ''Stroheim revu par Karel Reisz,'' in *Positif* (Paris), no. 411, May 1995.

Turner, George, ''Wrap Shot,'' in *American Cinematographer* (Hollywood), vol. 78, no. 9, September 1997.

McCarthy, Todd, ''Mutilated Masterpiece Gets the Loving Touch,'' in *Variety* (New York), vol. 376, no. 4, 13, September 1999.

* * *

Frank Norris' novel *McTeague* was the basis for Erich von Stroheim's film *Greed*. Though he had purchased the rights to it, he never got the production off the ground until Irving Thalberg, disgusted with von Stroheim's method of extravagant production on *Merry-Go-Round*, quarrelled with him, and von Stroheim was dismissed as Universal's most prestigious director/producer. It did not take long for von Stroheim to sign with Goldwyn studios, where it was soon announced that his first production would be a film depiction of *McTeague*.

The Norris novel is a dramatic and sordid but realistic preachment of the evils of greed. Heretofore von Stroheim had epitomized the grand scene. At Universal he had directed three big features that showed life on an extravagant scale: his characters were all venal and recklessly amoral; they were decadent, and offered to the public under such lurid titles as *Blind Husbands*, *The Devil's Passkey*, and *Foolish Wives*. His characters were the rich in an Alpine background, on the boulevards and in the boudoirs of Paris, and in the gambling casino at Monte Carlo, which was reconstructed on the Universal lot. *McTeague* took place wholly in California, specifically in San Francisco, Oakland and the Bay area, and Death Valley, in a very lower middle class, even depressed, society. The title character was a dentist from the lower classes who practiced his dentistry illegally. Both he and the girl he marries, Trina, are crass, uneducated vulgarians possessed and destroyed by a love for gold. It seemed unlike anything von Stroheim had attempted in his previous films.

Early in pre-production, the project was referred to as *Greed*, and the name soon became the accepted title. Deliberately doing a turnabout, von Stroheim saw it as a venture completely shot in its natural setting, the Bay area, as far as he could get from the studios of Hollywood. The company would even go to Death Valley to film the bitterly ironic finale of the story. He saw the project as a faithful adaptation of the Norris novel, an almost page-by-page recreation of a well-known American novel of the naturalist type. The film grew to monstrous proportions, eventually reaching an estimated nine-and-a-half hours. The studio forced von Stroheim to severely edit it. Secretly, his good friend, Rex Ingram, saw the film and helped him cut one version, but June Mathis was later called in to edit it down to under three hours. It remained, however, a hopelessly gargantuan project. Characters had to be eliminated so that the main story of McTeague, Trina, and Schouler became entirely the story of *Greed*.

Ironically, it was Irving Thalberg who ordered the drastic cuts in *Greed*. Thalberg had moved from his berth with Carl Laemmle at Universal to join the new Metro-Goldwyn. He was soon to become head of production at the amalgamated Metro-Goldwyn-Mayer Studios, where after Louis B. Mayer officially became head of production, he had his own unit. His first concern was to shape *Greed* out of the mountainous reels of footage which von Stroheim had so recklessly shot. It was at his order that *Greed* was released in 1924, but only a quarter of it contained footage shot by von Stroheim. That salvaged edition is the only one unreeled at von Stroheim retrospectives nowadays. The unused film was ordered melted down so that the silver in the negative could be salvaged. There would be no ultimate rediscovery of footage unused and fitted into subsequent re-issues of the picture. It would be another chapter in the obliteration of von Stroheim's name as a great director. Not one film he made exists as he originally envisioned it. All have been cut either maliciously or out of necessity. Only one may have escaped obliteration—Universal's *The Devil's Passkey*, but it is a lost picture. To date, no print whatsoever has survived.

The legend surrounding von Stroheim's name as a great creative director survives, however, nurtured by those who have read the original *McTeague* written by Frank Norris. There are moviegoers who can relate whole sequences of the film that are just not in the final print. Memorable, however, in the released film are such treasured moments as the wooing of Trina under sedation in a dental chair; the miserably unromantic, even comic, wedding of Trina and McTeague; the brutalization of Trina by McTeague, leading to her murder and his escape with the gold she had even slept with; McTeague's meeting with onetime friend, Marcus Schouler, and their journey across Death Valley. Schouler is slain by McTeague, but before Schouler dies, he handcuffs himself to McTeague, and the picture fades out on McTeague sitting in the murderous heat of Death Valley handcuffed to a corpse he slew.

Greed made no profit either domestic or foreign. Costing $585,000 to film (a fortune in the mid-1920s), *Greed* showed a gross of only $277,000 domestically, and the foreign receipts were even more disappointing. The world's moviegoing public simply resisted *Greed*. Von Stroheim and his few faithful cohorts could quite honestly say that the picture as he filmed it was never released. The studio also alibied that *Greed* never stood a chance of success as a product from a studio noted for creating stars. There were no box-office names in *Greed*. The cast was hand-chosen by von Stroheim himself—ZaSu Pitts, Gibson Gowland, and Jean Hersholt, who had never brought in a dime on their own. They were more often featured in comedies, as were fellow cast members Dale Fuller, Chester Conklin, and Hughie Mack, and *Greed* was certainly no comedy.

A few years later, when von Stroheim had chalked up a few more disasters, he abandoned his directorial career for a successful one as an actor. He had often played in some of his own pictures, but as an actor he is a recognizable star in Renoir's *La grande illusion* and in Hollywood's *Sunset Boulevard*.

—DeWitt Bodeen

GREGORY'S GIRL

UK, 1980

Director: Bill Forsyth

Production: Lake Film Productions, in association with the National Film Finance Corporation and Scottish Television; color; running time: 91 minutes; length: 8,182 feet. Released May 1981.

Producers: Davina Belling, Clive Parsons; **screenplay:** Bill Forsyth; **assistant directors:** Ian Madden, Terry Dalzell; **photography:** Michael Coulter; **camera operator:** Jan Pester; **editor:** John Gow; **sound recordist:** Louis Kramer; **sound re-recordist:** Tony Anscombe; **art director:** Adrienne Atkinson; **music:** Colin Tully.

Cast: John Gordon Sinclair (*Gregory*); Dee Hepburn (*Dorothy*); Jake D'Arcy (*Phil Menzies*); Clare Grogan (*Susan*); Robert Buchanan (*Andy*); William Greenlees (*Steve*); Alan Love (*Eric*); Caroline Guthrie (*Carol*); Douglas Sannachan (*Billy*); Carol Macartney (*Margo*); Allison Foster (*Madeleine*); Chic Murray (*Headmaster*); Alex Norton (*Alec*); John Bett (*Alistair*); David Anderson (*Gregory's Dad*); Billy Feeley (*Mr. Anderson*); Maeve Watt (*Miss Ford*); Muriel Romanes (*Miss Welch*); Patrick Lewsley (*Mr. Hall*); Ronald Girvan (*Alan*); Pat Harkins (*Kelvin*); Tony Whitmore (*Gordon*); Denis Criman (*Richard*); Graham Thompson (*Charlie*); Natasha Gerson (*Brenda*); Christopher Higson (*Penguin*).

Gregory's Girl

Award: Winner of British Academy Award for Best Screenplay, 1981.

Publications

Script:

Forsyth, Bill, *Gregory's Girl: The Filmscript*, edited by Paul Kelley, Cambridge, England, 1991.

Books:

Park, James, *Learning to Dream: The New British Cinema*, London, 1985.
Roddick, Nick, and Martin Auty, *British Cinema Now*, London, 1985.
Krautz, Alfred, Mille Krautz, and Joris Krautz, editors, *Encyclopedia of Film Directors in the United States & Europe: Comedy Films to 1991*, Munich, 1993.

Articles:

Continental Film Review, March 1981.
Pym, John, in *Monthly Film Bulletin* (London), June 1981.
Millar, Gavin, in *Listener* (London), 18 June 1981.
Adair, Gilbert, in *Sight and Sound* (London), Summer 1981.
Interview with Bill Forsyth, in *Sight and Sound* (London), Autumn 1981.
Hibbin, N., in *Chaplin* (Stockholm), vol. 24, no. 2, 1982.
Variety (New York), 26 May 1982.
Martineau, R., in *Séquences* (Montreal), July 1983.
Garel, A., in *Revue du Cinéma/Image et Son* (Paris), July-August 1984.
Lajeunesse, J., in *Revue du Cinéma* (Paris), Hors serie, vol. 24, 1984.
Nave, B., in *Jeune Cinéma* (Paris), October 1984.
Ardai, Z., ''Gregory baratnoje,'' in *Filmvilag* (Budapest), vol. 28, no. 11, 1985.

* * *

Forsyth was a key figure in the revival of British film production in the 1980s, and *Gregory's Girl* was both a popular and critical success. Forsyth's British work has been compared to the Ealing comedies of the late 1940s and early 1950s, with his typically light comic touch, his sense of character and detail, his quirky protagonists, and his ability to find the surreal in the most everyday people and situations.

His work—and *Gregory's Girl* is no exception—can also be seen as typical of a particular approach to the construction of a national cinema in a Britain overwhelmed by the popularity of Hollywood films: the production of low-budget films with correspondingly modest production values and low-key drama, aimed at the domestic market and the international art market rather than going for broke on the major American circuits; the casting of good character actors rather than big-name stars; the making of tasteful romances for all the family, which carefully resist indulging in the excesses of Hollywood melodrama; and the emphasis on a decidedly ordinary and specifically local or regional setting and milieu, rather than on the internationally recognizable metropolitan centre.

The film thus works within strongly enunciated British cinematic traditions, with something more than a nod to television drama in terms of the carefully limited scope of the action and the clean-cut, uncomplicated mise-en-scène, and a narrative structure (several simple stories, cleverly interwoven) reminiscent of soap opera. The film also owes something to television advertising, with its focus on suburban consumer-land, inhabited by ''ideal families'' living in modern gadget-laden houses.

The main narrative situates the film as a melodrama: gawky adolescent Gregory attempts to win the favours of the far more sophisticated Dorothy, while a conspiracy of girls effortlessly organises for him to become hitched to a far more suitable partner in Susan. But a quick look at the final four images of the film reveals a much broader filmic system, which also enables the film to articulate a network of interlocking social worlds. First there is a shot of Gregory and Susan kissing, the conventional happy ending of melodrama. In the second shot, we see Gregory and his sister, in a final incantation of the perfection and permanence of the family, in its nice, ordinary, suburban security. Thirdly, there is a reprise of the delightful running gag of Gregory's friend Andy, and his pal, this time seen hitching to Caracas in search of ''girls.'' Forsyth, like Tati, is a master of the running gag, which produces its comedy through narrative redundance and eccentric characterisation, as with Andy's search for girls, or the lost penguins, or the burly headteacher secretively playing whimsical tunes on the piano.

The final shot of the film repeats another recurrent image: Dorothy, running alone in the dark, a fleeting image of the impossible object of desire, accompanied by the now familiar, dream-like music. Dorothy's character is highly ambiguous, since she is both a sweet, innocent, asexual girl, and a version of the *femme fatale* (the most dangerous figure in the film's conspiracy of women), wherein female sexuality becomes a threateningly seductive but unattainable enigma, a mystery, both for Gregory and for the implied spectator who is equally kept apart from understanding the ways and means of the female sex. The film, in this sense, reproduces the point of view of the adolescent male.

The film thus has all the ingredients of the adult melodrama, with Gregory lured by the image of the *femme fatale*, but finally making it with the right partner. But the film is carefully tailored for the family market, offering us a sweet, innocent, adolescent romance-without-sex (or violence or horror) that has been a feature of several recent British films. This address to the family market is further secured by the very ordinariness of the people and their milieu, and by the sweet lovableness of the youthful actors, aping adult behaviour but with all the innocence and uncomplicatedness of youth. This paradox of maturity and innocence is of course a key source of the film's humour, particularly when stretched to the point of absurd incongruity (as in Gregory's kid sister's relationship with her boyfriend). But despite this veneer of innocence, the film is able to tackle profound social and psychic anxieties concerning heterosexuality and the family.

It seems significant also that a film addressed to the family should locate its drama in the perfect communities of soap powder/breakfast cereal/kitchen technology advertisements, a world that is equally uncomplicated and superficially innocent, and which is itself one of the key sites for the construction and reconstruction of the family.

And while the final shot of the film of the still unattainable Dorothy is a potentially disturbing image for patriarchy, her own apparent innocence and the innocence of the world which surrounds her diminish any such threat and restore faith in the family.

—Andrew Higson

GULING JIE SHAONIAN SHA REN SHIJIAN

(A Brighter Summer Day)

Taiwan, 1991

Director: Edward Yang

Production: Yang and His Gang Filmmakers; colour; running time: 237 minutes.

Producer: Yu Weiyan; **screenplay:** Edward Yang, Yan Hongya, Yang Shunqing, Lai Mingtang; **photography:** Zhang Huigong, Li Longyu; **editor:** Chen Bowen; **assistant directors:** Cai Guohui, Yang Shunqing; **production design:** Yu Weiyan; **sound:** Du Duzhi.

Cast: Zhang Zhen (*Xiao Si'r*); Lisa Yang (*Ming*); Zhang Guozhu (*Father*); Elaine Jin (*Mother*); Wang Juan (*Juan*); Zhang Han (*Lao Er*); Jiang Xiuqiong (*Qiong*); Lai Fanyun (*Yun*).

Publications

Articles:

City Limits (New York), 23 February 1989.

Rayns, Tony, ''Taipei Story'' in *Monthly Film Bulletin* (London), March 1989.

Variety (New York), 2 Septemer 1991.

Jousse, T., and Y. Umemoto, ''Plus de lumière'' in *Cahiers du Cinéma* (Paris), April 1992.

Bassan, R., ''Tragique jeux d'adolescents'' in *Revue du Cinéma* (Paris), May 1992.

Ciment, M., and others, ''Edward Yang'' in *Positif* (Paris), May 1992.

Guling jie shaonian sha ren shijian

Rayns, Tony, ''Lonesome Tonight'' in *Sight and Sound* (London), March 1993.
Charity, T., *Sight and Sound* (London), April 1993.

* * *

Edward Yang's *A Brighter Summer Day* comes out of a unique set of circumstances. In the late 1980s the Taiwan film industry almost ceased to exist after its most powerful producer, distributor, and exhibitor—the Nationalist Government-owned Central Motion Picture Corporation—drastically scaled down its activities. Consequently, technicians and actors sought their livelihoods elsewhere in the boom economy. Thus the New Cinema movement, in which Yang had been a leading figure with his three feature films, *That Day, On the Beach* (*Guangyin de Gushi*, 1982), *Taipei Story* (*Qingmei Zhuma*, 1985) and *The Terroriser* (*Kongbufenzi*, 1986), was left in disarray.

In these 80s films, Yang developed a multi-character narrative style of interchanging story lines that was logistically demanding. In the new circumstances, an epic on the scale of *A Brighter Summer Day*, involving more than 80 speaking parts, ought to have been unimaginable. But Yang used his position as a teacher in the drama department of the National Institute for the Arts to train most of the cast and crew himself. It is one of the immediately impressive aspects of the film that the craft skills on display are superb at every level.

Furthermore, the youth and freshness of the cast proved highly appropriate for a film set in 1960, when the director himself was 13, and built around a tentative love affair between two adolescents: Xiao Si'r, the 14-year-old son of a civil servant, and Ming, the girlfriend of a charismatic gang leader. Their tryst's tragic outcome is hinted at by the Chinese title which translates literally as ''The Boy in the Murder Incident on Guling Street.'' The story was derived from a real incident remembered from Yang's school days. In the three-hour version of the film, which won the Special Jury Prize at the 1992 Tokyo Film Festival, this relationship, with its echoes of *West Side Story* and *Rebel Without a Cause*, predominates over the carefully wrought social observation of subplot and mise-en-scène. In the released 127-minute integral version, however, the desire to explain a moment of historical crisis through the minutiae of ordinary lives is paramount.

Families who fled to Taiwan from mainland China with Chiang Kai-Shek found that much of the strict tradition of family life was also uprooted. While parents were absorbed into the militarised island's ruling elite, their children grew up under the double sway of a martial atmosphere and a promise of greater freedom inscribed in the products of the Chinese Nationalist's American backers. Many of these children became involved in gang warfare against the indigenous island youth. Yang describes this bitter period of highly conflicting values and tensions in terms of coolly-distanced melodrama, distanced not so much by a refusal to depict the expression of emotion, as in Fassbinder, but more by a determinedly stand-back camera style of deep-focus, wide-angle group shots that gives each character equal weight.

Thus Yang has Xiao Si'r drawn into the conflict between Honey's Little Park Gang and the indigenous 217 gang not only through his fascination with Ming, but also because of the pressure of academic failure which has condemned him to a less prestigious night school and to the disdain of his ultra-correct, fatally passive father Zhang Ju. Xiao Si'r himself remains a passive observer, but not as a conduit of the audience's point of view. His story provides the turning action of a kaleidoscope of quiet desperation until his inevitable emotional breakdown leads him to finally act violently against the person he idealises most.

In Nicholas Ray's *Rebel Without a Cause*, James Dean's rage and anguish is similarly set against a passive paternal figure who won't intervene in the mechanical processes of institutional authority. But Ray's film plays complicit games with the narcissism of its lead character, making it primarily about a crisis of individual conscience. Instead Yang offers a position of involved critique, forcing the viewer into an analysis of Xiao Si'r's motives even before he acts.

While the macrocosmic dilemma of an entire generation of Taiwan inhabitants unfolds, the film remains mostly within Xiao Si'r's home turf. Its nocturnal, pressure-cooker mood is circumscribed by the night school, the club house run by the Little Park gang, the bookstores of Guling Street, the pool room and garage used by the 217 gang and the homes of Xiao and his friends. We see Ming's boyfriend Honey, the charismatic leader of the Little Park Gang, return from exile only to be betrayed and murdered. A revenge raid on the 217 gang's headquarters is chaotic and indiscriminately bloody. Zhang Ju's loyalty to the state is rewarded by his arrest and interrogation on suspicion of having communist connections. Xiao Si'r discovers that Ming has been the lover of several of his acquaintances. Every move on the claustrophobic island seems to produce a self-inflicted wound.

Contrasting these apparently fatalistic results of political inevitability is the ethereal balm of Elvis Presley's ''Are You Lonesome Tonight?'' as mistranslated by Xiao Si'r's sister (the film's English title comes from Presley's delivery of the line ''does your memory stray, to a bright uh-summer day) and performed by the Little Park Gang's rock 'n' roll band. However, the semblance of transcendent hope that America represents for the protagonists is itself a chimera, presented with considerable irony by Yang.

A Brighter Summer Day shares the breadth of ambition and distanced, objective point of view of Hou Xiaoxian's 1989 allusive social panorama *A City of Sadness (Beiqing Chengshi)*, which attempted to capture the earlier moment of historical crisis of the 1949 influx. In all other respects, however, it is an utterly unique achievement, one that realises hidden resources of scale and complexity that have been untapped by filmmakers for some years.

—Nick James

GUN CRAZY

(Deadly is the Female)

USA, 1950

Director: Joseph H. Lewis

Production: King Brothers/Universal-International/Pioneer Pictures Corporation; black and white, 35mm; running time: 87 minutes. Released as *Deadly is the Female*, 26 January 1950; re-released as *Gun Crazy*, 24 August 1950.

Producers: Frank King and Maurice King; **screenplay:** MacKinlay Kantor and Dalton Trumbo (fronted by Millard Kaufman), from a *Saturday Evening Post* story by MacKinlay Kantor; **photography:** Russell Harlan; **editor:** Harry W. Gerstad; **original music:** Victor Young; **sound:** Tom Lambert.

Cast: Peggy Cummins (*Annie Laurie Starr*); John Dall (*Bart Tare*); Berry Kroeger (*Packett*); Morris Carnovsky (*Judge Willoughby*); Annabel Shaw (*Ruby Tare*); Harry Lewis (*Clyde Boston*); Nedrick Young (*Dave Allister*); Trevor Bardette (*Sheriff Boston*); Mickey Little (*Bart Tare*, age 7); Russ Tamblyn (credited as Rusty Tamblyn) (*Bart Tare*, age 14); Paul Frison (*Clyde Boston*, age 14); Dave Bair (*Dave Allister*, age 14).

Publications

Books:

Shadoian, Jack, *Dreams and Deadends: The American Gangster/Crime Film*, Cambridge, Massachusetts, 1977.

Silver, Alain, and Elizabeth Ward, *Film Noir*, New York, 1979.

Tuska, John, *Dark Cinema: American Film Noir in Perspective*, Westport, Connecticut, 1984.

Kitses, Jim, *Gun Crazy*, London, 1996.

Articles:

Anderson, Lindsay, ''*Gun Crazy*,'' in *Sequence* (London), Autumn 1950.

Mysel, Myron, ''Joseph H. Lewis: Tourist in the Asylum,'' in Todd McCarthy and Charles Flynn, editors, *Kings of the B's: Working Within the Hollywood System*, New York, 1975.

Borde, Raymond, and Etienne Chaumeton, ''A Propos du Film Noir Americain,'' in *Positif* (Paris), 1976.

Ruhmann, Lony, Steven Schwartz, and Rob Conway, ''*Gun Crazy*, 'The accomplishment of many, many minds': An Interview with Joseph H. Lewis,'' in *The Velvet Light Trap*, (Austin, Texas), Summer 1983.

Sattin, R. ''Joseph H. Lewis: Assessing an (Occasionally) Brilliant Career,'' in *American Classic Screen*, November/December 1983.

* * *

One of the highlights in the career of director Joseph H. Lewis, *Gun Crazy* is a minor classic, widely regarded as one of the best of the

"B" movies. Shot on a low budget as an independent film, it benefits from stylish photography by former stuntman Russell Harlan, who is probably best known as Howard Hawks's cinematographer on *Red River*. Lewis is known for his distinctive style as a director, and *Gun Crazy* is a showcase for his repertoire of odd camera angles, elaborate scene compositions, and the variation of long and short takes for dramatic effect. In one famous scene, a bank robbery is filmed in one take from the rear seat of the getaway car, a technique that seems to involve the viewer in the heist as it takes place.

As with many gangster and crime films, *Gun Crazy* is an adaptation of a short story, in this case written by novelist MacKinlay Kantor for the *Saturday Evening Post*. Based on the myths surrounding Bonnie and Clyde, it tells the tale of a doomed love affair between Bart and Laurie, two carnival sharpshooters who embark on a crime spree that ends in murder. Yet the ambition of the film reaches beyond its banal storyline. Bart and Laurie each have their own complex psychological reasons for acting as they do. Bart is a petty criminal lured into violence through his obsessive love for Laurie, while Laurie is a manipulative *femme fatale* of the most dangerous kind. Yet they seem to carry within themselves and their relationship a desire for self-destruction. In this respect, *Gun Crazy* is a fine example of how film noirs differ from the crime and gangster movies that preceded them. As John Tuska explains, "[t]he difference between *Gun Crazy* and the gangster film cycle in the early 'Thirties is that the protagonists, instead of behaving in a fashion which proves self-destructive, behave *according* to self-destructive impulses."

While the film itself portrays Bart and Laurie's secret life on the run, there is also an element of subterfuge in its making. Millard Kaufman, who was credited as co-writer of the film with MacKinlay Kantor, was actually "fronting" for a blacklisted writer, Dalton Trumbo. Trumbo, one of the "Hollywood Ten" filmmakers who went to prison for refusing to testify at the McCarthy hearings, wrote under various different names and was "fronted" by at least one other writer besides Kaufman. He was unable to collect an Academy Award for his work on Irving Rapper's *The Brave One* in 1956 because the screenplay had been penned by someone called "Robert Rich". He did not receive official credit for his contribution to *Gun Crazy* from the Writer's Guild until 1992.

The influence of *Gun Crazy* has spread much further than its B-movie origins might have suggested. Arthur Penn's celebrated *Bonnie and Clyde* (1967) has obvious similarities in plot, though a somewhat lighter tone, while Oliver Stone's *Natural Born Killers* (1994) repeats the story of a young couple obsessed with violence and killing and on the run from the law. *Gun Crazy* is sometimes named as one of the films that began Hollywood's postwar obsession with the connection between sex and violence, an obsession Stone's film attempts to satirize.

Joseph H. Lewis went on to make films such as *The Big Combo* (1955) and *7th Cavalry* (1956), but never again achieved the psychological insight or the overall quality of *Gun Crazy*. The film was remade unsuccessfully as *Guncrazy* in 1992 with Drew Barrymore and James LeGros in the lead roles.

—Chris Routledge

THE GUNS

See **OS FUZIS**

GYCKLARNAS AFTON

(The Naked Night; Sawdust and Tinsel)

Sweden, 1953

Director: Ingmar Bergman

Production: Sandrews for Svensk Filmindustri; black and white, 35mm; running time: 92 minutes; length: 2520 meters. Released 14 September 1953, Sweden. Filmed early summer 1953 in Sandrews studios in Stockholm; and exteriors shot in Arild, Sweden.

Producer: Rune Waldekranz; **screenplay:** Ingmar Bergman; **photography:** Hilding Bladh, Göran Strindberg, and Sven Nykvist; **editor:** Carl-Olav Skeppstedt; **art director:** Bibi Lindström; **music:** Karl-Birger Blomdahl; **costume designer:** Mago.

Cast: Harriet Andersson (*Anne*); Ake Grönberg (*Albert Johansson*); Hasse Ekman (*Frans*); Anders Ek (*Frost*); Gudrun Brost (*Alma*); Annika Tretow (*Agda, Albert's wife*); Gunnar Björnstrand (*Mr. Sjuberg*); Erik Strandmark (*Jens*); Kiki (*Dwarf*); Ake Fridell (*Officer*); Majken Torkeli (*Mrs. Ekberg*); Vanjek Hedberg (*Ekberg's son*); Curt Löwgren (*Blom*).

Publications

Books:

Béranger, Jean, *Ingmar Bergman et ses films*, Paris, 1959.
Billquist, Fritiof, *Ingmar Bergman: Teatermannen och filmskaparen*, Stockholm, 1960.
Burvenich, Jos., *Thèmes d'inspiration d'Ingmar Bergman*, Brussels, 1960.
Siclier, Jacques, *Ingmar Bergman*, Paris, 1960.
Höök, Marianne, *Ingmar Bergman*, Stockholm, 1962.
Béranger, Jean, and François Guyon, *Ingmar Bergman*, Lyons, 1964.
Donner, Jörn, *The Personal Vision of Ingmar Bergman*, Bloomington, Indiana, 1964.
Nelson, David, *Ingmar Bergman: The Search for God*, Boston, 1964.
Oldrini, Guido, *La solitudine di Ingmar Bergman*, Parma, 1965.
Steene, Birgitta, *Ingmar Bergman*, New York, 1968.
Gibson, Arthur, *The Silence of God: Creative Response to the Films of Ingmar Bergman*, New York, 1969.
Wood, Robin, *Ingmar Bergman*, New York, 1969.
Sjögren, Henrik, *Regi: Ingmar Bergman*, Stockholm, 1970.
Young, Vernon, *Cinema Borealis: Ingmar Bergman and the Swedish Ethos*, New York, 1972.
Donner, Jörn, *The Films of Ingmar Bergman*, New York, 1972.
Simon, John, *Ingmar Bergman Directs*, New York, 1972.
Björkman, Stig, and others, editors, *Bergman on Bergman*, New York, 1973.
Ranieri, Tino, *Ingmar Bergman*, Florence, 1974.
Kaminsky, Stuart M., editor, *Ingmar Bergman: Essays in Criticism*, New York, 1975.

Gycklarnas afton

Marion, Denis, *Ingmar Bergman*, Paris, 1979.

Manvell, Roger, *Ingmar Bergman: An Appreciation*, New York, 1980.

Mosley, Philip, *Ingmar Bergman: The Cinema as Mistress*, Boston and London, 1981.

Petric, Vlada, editor, *Film and Dreams: An Approach to Bergman*, New York, 1981.

Cowie, Peter, *Ingmar Bergman: A Critical Biography*, New York and London, 1982.

Livingston, Paisley, *Ingmar Bergman and the Ritual of Art*, Ithaca, New York, 1982.

Jones, G. William, editor, *Talking with Ingmar Bergman*, Dallas, 1983.

Lefèvre, Raymond, *Ingmar Bergman*, Paris, 1983.

Dervin, Daniel, *Through a Freudian Lens Deeply: A Psychoanalysis of Cinema*, Hillsdale, New Jersey, 1985.

Gado, Frank, *The Passion of Ingmar Bergman*, Durham, North Carolina, 1986.

Bergman, Ingmar, *Laterna Magica*, Stockholm, 1987; as *The Magic Lantern: An Autobiography*, London, 1988.

Steene, Birgitta, *Ingmar Bergman: A Guide to References and Resources*, Boston, 1987.

Cohen, James, *Through a Lens Darkly*, New York, 1991.

Bjorkman, Stig, and Torsten Maans, and Jonas Sima, *Bergman on Bergman: Interviews with Ingmar Bergman*, Cambridge, 1993.

Cohen, Hubert I., *Ingmar Bergman: The Art of Confession*, New York, 1993.

Long, Robert Emmet, *Ingmar Bergman: Film and Stage*, New York, 1994.

Tornqvist, Egil, *Between Stage and Screen: Ingmar Bergman Directs*, Amsterdam, 1995.

Blackwell, Marilyn J., *Gender and Representation in the Films of Ingmar Bergman*, Rochester, 1997.

Lloyd, Michaels, editor, *Ingmar Bergman's Persona*, New York, 1999.

Articles:

Austin, Paul, ''Ingmar Bergman, Magician of Swedish Cinema,'' in *Anglo-Swedish Review* (London), April 1959.

Archer, Eugene, ''The Rack of Life,'' in *Film Quarterly* (Berkeley), Summer 1959.

Alpert, Hollis, ''Style Is the Director,'' in *Saturday Review* (New York), 23 December 1961.

Nykvist, Sven, ''Photographing the Films of Ingmar Bergman,'' in *American Cinematographer* (Los Angeles), October 1962.
Lefèvre, Raymond, ''Ingmar Bergman,'' in *Image et Son* (Paris), March 1969.
Film Comment (New York), Summer 1970.
Rado, P., in *Cinema* (Budapest), March 1975.
Koustrup, A., in *Kosmorama* (Copenhagen), Spring 1978.
Listener (London), 5 March 1987.
Dahlbeck, E., ''En arbetskamrat pa vag att kanoniseras,'' in *Chaplin* (Stockholm), vol. 30, no. 2/3, 1988.
Simon, J., ''Det manskliga ansiktet,'' in *Chaplin* (Stockholm), vol. 30, no. 2/3, 1988.
Simon, John, ''The Human Face,'' in *Chaplin* (Stockholm), Special Issue, 1988.
Simon, John, ''Det manskliga ansiktet,'' in *Chaplin* (Stockholm), vol. 30, no. 2–3, 1988.
Trasatti, S., ''Bergman, il paradosso di un *Ateo cristiano*,'' in *Castoro Cinema* (Milan), no. 156, November/December 1991.

* * *

The films of Ingmar Bergman have been considered by commercial distributors as ''intellectual'' films rather than simple entertainment. The themes Bergman has chosen to present in his work—death, fate, love, loneliness—are thought to have only intellectual appeal. *The Naked Night* exhibits many typical Bergman themes and has been selected by some critics as his best film. However, this favorable acceptance of the film does not reflect the initial popular reaction.

The Naked Night was the first of Bergman's films to be given a wide release in the United States (although it was his eighteenth film as a director). A few of his early films had a limited distribution here, but they were mainly exploited for their nudity as soft-core pornography. *The Naked Night* was also publicized in this manner, as evidenced by the American title. A more literal translation of *Gycklarnas Afton* is ''twilight of the jugglers.'' France released the film as *Night of the Clowns* and England released the film as *Sawdust and Tinsel*. Only the American version was labeled with a suggestive title.

As in many of Bergman's films, the main theme of *The Naked Night* is the idea of fate. Fate dictates the kind of lives the characters must lead and they cannot escape their destinies. Their attempts to do so only make their lives more miserable. For example, Albert, the owner of a travelling circus, seeks a more secure life in the traditional family unit. When he tries to make amends with his estranged wife, she rejects him and even thanks him for having left her in the first place. Albert's visit to his wife prompts his mistress, Anne, to have an affair with a local actor. The actor later humiliates Albert in public by bragging about his new conquest. Albert's humiliation leads him to attempt suicide, but he cannot escape his fate and the attempt fails. This string of events eventually comes full circle, until Albert once again sets out on the road with Anne, following the only choice fate allows him.

The Naked Night, not surprisingly, considering the subject matter, does not have a happy ending. Obviously 1953 audiences were not ready for this kind of film as it was quite unsuccessful, not just financially but critically. The film was also unsuccessful in Sweden, as well as in most foreign markets. Critics termed the film too ''complex'' and ''depressing.'' The failure of *The Naked Night* affected Bergman deeply. He knew he would have to make changes if he was going to continue to find financial backing for his films. As a result, Bergman's next three pictures were comedies (*A Lesson in Love, Dreams*, and *Smiles of a Summer Night*). These films continued to address the issues of his earlier work (fate, love, etc.), but in a lighter vein. This new approach made his films more popular and critically recognized. The change in the reaction to his films encouraged Bergman to turn toward ''serious'' films again, such as *Persona* and *Cries and Whispers*. In the mid-1960s critics rediscovered *Gycklarnas Afton*, regarding it in a new, more positive light as one of the most significant films of his career.

—Linda J. Obalil

HADAKA NO SHIMA

(The Island)

Japan, 1961

Director: Kaneto Shindo

Production: Kindai Eiga Kyokai (Japan); black and white, 35mm; running time: 92 minutes, English version is 96 minutes. Released 1961, Japan.

Producers: Kaneto Shindo and Eisaku Matsura; **screenplay:** Kaneto Shindo; **photography:** Kiyoshi Kuroda; **editor:** Toshio Enoki; **sound:** Kunie Maruyama; **music:** Hikaru Hayashi.

Cast: Nobuko Otowa (*Toyo*); Taiji Tonoyama (*Senta*); Shinji Tanaka (*Taro*); Masanori Horimoto (*Jiro*).

Publications

Book:

Anderson, Joseph, and Donald Richie, *Japanese Cinema: Art and Industry*, New York, 1960; revised edition, Princeton, New Jersey, 1982.

Articles:

''About the Moviemaker,'' in *Newsweek* (New York), 10 September 1962.
Kuhn, Helen, in *Films in Review* (New York), October 1962.
Gow, Gordon, in *Films and Filming* (London), December 1962.
Noxor, Gerald, in *Cinema Journal* (Iowa City, Iowa), no. 3, 1963.
Fradier, George, ''Dialogue on the Film *The Island*,'' in *UNESCO Courier*, April 1963.
''Note,'' in *International Film Guide* (London), no. 2, 1965.
Potrel-Dorget, M. L., in *Image et Son* (Paris), July-August 1978.
Pasquini, C., ''Venezia 79: *Kosatsu*,'' in *Filmcritica* (Siena), vol. 30, no. 298, September 1979.

* * *

Hadaka no shima (The Island) is the thirteenth feature written and directed by Kaneto Shindo, best known for his depictions of women's lives. The film stars Nobuko Otowa who has appeared in most of his films. Released in 1961, it is Shindo's best known work outside Japan.

Constructed like a documentary drama, the film tells the story of a husband (Senta) and wife (Toyo), who live on a small island with their two sons. Their lives are consumed by the necessity of obtaining water from a nearby island twice a day. Like Robert Flaherty's *Nanook* and *Man of Aran*, the film focuses on the family's struggle against nature for survival. *Hadaka no shima* is innovative on two levels. First, the narrative is presented without dialogue. Like F. W. Murnau's silent classic, *Der letzte Mann*, which is rendered without inter-titles (save one), *Hadaka no shima* is almost purely visual. Shindo utilizes action, gesture, camera movement, rhythmic editing, close-ups, music and sound effects to make his points.

Second, Shindo experiments with elliptical editing. One scene in particular is noteworthy. On the road Senta and Toyo move towards the audience, carrying their buckets. As soon as they come close to the camera, Shindo cuts and they are once again seen in the distance in the exact position of the opening shot. This device gives the impression of a film loop, serving to emphasize the Sisyphean effort of repeating arduous chores in a never-ending cycle.

The film contains only minimal action. The main events are the accidental spilling of water, which prompts Senta to knock Toyo to the ground; the death of the oldest son after a brief illness; Toyo's reaction to this loss (she deliberately dumps water on the ground and tramples the plants); and, finally, the family's visit to the mainland where they unsuccessfully attempt to sell a fish. The remainder of the film details the twice-daily trips to the main island, the slow climb up the hill, the watering of plants, and the family's eating and bathing.

Shindo is fond of close-ups intercut between long sequence shots. He uses parallel editing, connecting the dining of the family with the eating of the animals, to provide a commentary on the simplicity and poverty of their lives. Shindo likewise includes ''pillow shots'' similar to the insertions found in Yasujiro Ozu films. Primarily these consist of the image of a small boat which the family uses to row to the main island. The shot functions as a meditative moment which possesses associational meaning like images in a *haiku* poem.

Shindo offers a portrayal of a primitive way of life, which is contrasted to the frantic mechanized life of the main island. Despite the hardships on the island, the family possesses dignity, perseverance and stamina. Their lives have purpose and meaning. There is joy at the day's end when their labors cease and they can relax with a bath and the communal meal. The couple exhibits a stoicism bred of necessity and the knowledge that life must go on. After Toyo angrily spills the water, she picks herself up and resumes work. Throughout, the family personifies a Buddhist attitude toward life: a sense of harmony with nature, resignation to man's insignificance in the universe, acceptance of the flux of life and death. *Hadaka no shima* is thus pervaded with a sense of *mono no aware*, a sad awareness of the transience of all things worldly. This attitude is expressed through the film's dominant metaphor—the island, a small sanctuary surrounded by a vast body of water. Like the famous Zen sand gardens composed of rocks surrounded by raked sand, the island represents everything from the isolated family, to the Japanese people of the island nation, to mankind itself.

Hadaka no shima was critically acclaimed in the United States. Most of the popular critics were taken with its quiet power and simplicity. Only Pauline Kael questioned whether less was really more and wondered at the adulation of such a primitive way of life. Such sentiments were also shared by several Japanese commentators who wondered at the film's foreign popularity and worried about the effect of portraying Japan as an esoteric, primitive people rather than a modern industrial nation. After *Hadaka no shima*, Shindo turned to new subject matter.

—Patricia Erens

LA HAINE

(Hate)

France, 1995

Director: Mathieu Kassovitz

Production: Les Productions Lazennec, with Studio Canal+, La Sept Cinema, Kasso Inc. Productions, and Gramercy Pictures; black and white, 35 mm; running time: 95 minutes; length: 2,731 meters. Released 31 May 1995.

Producer: Christophe Rossignon; **associate producers:** Adeline Lecallier, Alain Rocca; **screenplay:** Mathieu Kassovitz; **photography:** Pierre Aim, Georges Diane; **assistant directors:** Eric Pujol; **editors:** Mathieu Kassovitz, Scott Stevenson; **sound:** Dominique Dalmasso; **sound design:** Vincent Tulli; **production design:** Giuseppe Ponturo; **set decoration:** Sophie Quiedeville; **costume designer:** Virginie Montel.

Cast: Vincent Cassel (*Vinz*); Hubert Kounde (*Hubert*); Said Taghmaoui (*Sayid*); Francois Levantal (*Asterix*); Edouard Montoute (*Darty*); Marc Duret (*Inspector ''Notre Dame''*); Tadek Lokcinski (*Monsieur Toilettes*); Karin Viard (*Gallery Girl*); Julie Mauduech (*Gallery Girl*); Vincent Lindon (*''Really'' Drunk Man*); Karim Belkhadra (*Samir*); Abdel Ahmed Ghili (*Abdel*); Solo Dicko (*Santo*); Joseph Momo (*Ordinary Guy*); Heloise Rauth (*Sarah*); Rywka Wajsbrot (*Vinz's Grandmother*); Olga Abrego (*Vinz's Aunt*); Laurent Labasse (*Cook*); Choukri Gabteni (*Said's Brother*); Peter Kassovitz (*Gallery Patron*); Mathieu Kassovitz (*Young Skinhead*).

Awards: Best Director, Cannes Film Festival, 1995; Best Young Film, European Film Awards, 1995; Best French Film, Best Producer, and Best Editor, Cesar Awards, 1996.

Publications

Articles:

Alexander, K., and D. Styan, ''*La Haine*,'' in *Vertigo* (Paris), no. 5, 1995.

Leahy, J., ''The Children of Godard and 90s TV,'' in *Vertigo* (Paris), no. 5, 1995.

Lochen, K., ''Verden tilhorer deg,'' in *Film & Kino* (Oslo), no. 7, 1995.

Trofimenkov, M., ''O nenavisti- o nenavisti,'' in *Iskusstvo Kino* (Moscow), no. 10, 1995.

Trofimenkov, M., ''Predchuvstvie prazhdanskoi voiny,'' in *Iskusstvo Kino* (Moscow), no. 10, 1995.

Morrison, S., ''*La haine*, *Fallen Angels*, and Some Thoughts on Scorsese's Children,'' in *CineAction* (Toronto), no. 39, 1995.

Jousse, T., ''Prose combat,'' in *Cahiers du Cinéma* (Paris), June 1995.

Lebouc, G, ''*La Haine*,'' in *Grand Angle* (Mariembourg, Belgium), June 1995.

Vasse, C., ''*La Haine*,'' in *Positif* (Paris), June 1995.

Sibony, D., ''Exclusion intrinsique,'' in *Cahiers du Cinéma* (Paris), July-August 1995.

Nazzaro, G.A., ''L'odio,'' in *Cineforum* (Bergamo, Italy), October 1995.

Reader, K., ''After the Riot,'' in *Sight and Sound* (London), November 1995.

Kelly, B., ''*La Haine* Hip-Hops,'' in *Variety* (New York), 22–28 January 1996.

Schubert, G., ''Zuhanas kozben,'' in *Filmvilag* (Budapest), no. 1, 1996.

Noh, D., ''Kassovitz's Parisian *Hate*: Not *La Vie en Rose*,'' in *Film Journal* (New York), February 1996.

Swenson, K., ''Hommeboys,'' in *Premiere* (New York), February 1996.

Hammerschmidt, T., ''Filme des Monats,'' in *Medien Praktisch* (Frankfurt), February 1996.

Winters, L., ''Boyz in the Banlieu,'' in *Village Voice* (New York), 6 February 1995.

Evans, G., ''Gramercy Levels *Hate* at Young Americans,'' in *Variety* (New York), 12–18 February 1996.

Reynaud, B., ''Le Hood,'' in *Film Comment* (New York), March/April 1996.

Hollstein, M., ''Hass.,'' In *Medien Praktisch* (Frankfurt), May 1996.

Royer, G., ''*La Haine*,'' in *Sequences* (Quebec), March-June 1997.

* * *

Hate may be a French-language film, set in a specific place and time, but its depiction of alienated, dead-end teens who clash with authority is universal. As such, the film is an explosive, cutting-edge portrait of twisted, wasted lives. *Hate* is an instant classic of its genre, ranking alongside adolescent angst dramas from Nicholas Ray's 1950s breakthrough, *Rebel Without a Cause* (whose characters are misunderstood upper-class Southern Californians), to John Singleton's *Boyz N the Hood* and the Hughes Brothers' *Menace II Society.* The latter are gutsy, non-romanticized portraits of urban African-America in the 1990s, where guns, drive-by shootings, and ''gangsta'' attitude are as much a part of everyday life as flipping on a television set. In their depictions of young lives wasting away in an environment of helplessness and hopelessness, *Boyz N the Hood* and *Menace II Society* directly parallel the sensibility that permeates *Hate.* Much of the scenario of *Hate*, written and directed by 29-year-old Mathieu Kassovitz, is set in a public housing project just outside Paris. As it begins, adolescents and police have just violently clashed, with the conflict sparked by the brutal beating by the cops of a young man named Abdel, who lies near death in a hospital. The main characters are Abdel's three friends: the Arab Sayid, the Jewish Vinz, and the black Hubert.

La Haine

Of the trio, Vinz is the most sociopathic. He idolizes one of the most celebrated of all celluloid psychos: Travis Bickle, the character played by Robert De Niro in Martin Scorsese's *Taxi Driver.* As he glares into a mirror and imitates Travis, Vinz does not exude a ''you-talkin'-to-me'' cool. Rather, he contorts his face, becoming a hideous and horrifying symbol of contemporary alienated youth.

The genial Sayid is content to play tag-along, following in Vinz's shadow. Hubert, meanwhile, is the most self-aware. He is the only one who can articulate the fact that he will be unable to flourish if he cannot escape the projects. Yet Hubert, Sayid, and Vinz remain inexorably linked by their nonexistent futures. They have neither jobs nor job prospects. The concept of a ''career'' and economic independence is not in their realm. All they do is hang out and smoke marijuana, and they are constantly harassed by the police. These young men are not inherently violent or bad, yet their economic status, age, and demeanor allow the authorities to single them out as troublemakers.

Forebodingly, Vinz comes into possession of a Smith & Wesson .44. He promises that, if Abdel dies, he will get revenge by ''whacking a pig.'' It seems inevitable that Abdel will die—so watching *Hate* is like watching a firecracker waiting to explode.

Hate is loaded with perverse irony. The teens are haunted by a phrase—''The World Is Yours''—from an advertisement that is ever-present on billboards. Yet clearly, the reality is that the world is not theirs. These young men have no choices. Their lives are predetermined and, if they protest, there are plenty of police around to keep them in their places.

Another key to the film is the all-encompassing impact of American culture and consumerism on Sayid, Hubert, and Vinz, who refer to themselves as ''homeboys'' and their neighborhood as ''the hood.'' Their speech is laced with American pop cultural references, from the movies *Lethal Weapon* and *Batman* to the animated characters Sylvester and Tweetie and Mickey Mouse. A secondary character wears a Notre Dame jacket. Another dons a T-shirt which proclaims that ''Elvis Shot JFK.'' One puts down another by exclaiming, ''Your mother drinks Bud.'' Another, who is a fence, is nicknamed ''Walmart.''

Kassovitz also cannily demonstrates how poverty and hopelessness extend beyond racial barriers. Here, a Jew, an Arab, and a black are united by their common experience, and are equally alienated and anti-social. The Jew and Arab do not clash over, for example, the politics of the state of Israel, a conflict that is far removed from their daily lives. The characters are who they are as individuals, rather than being political or sociological, let alone stereotypical, mirrors of their ethnicity. They are not separated by race or religion, but rather are united by age and economic background, by drugs and wretched educations, and by the allure of the culture of violence. At one juncture, Vinz asks his younger sister why she is not in school. ''It burned down,'' is the blunt reply. All of this helps to make *Hate* seem ever more real.

Vinz, Hubert, and Sayid may live in the shadow of the Eiffel Tower and the Champs Élysées, yet the affluence and romance symbolized by these monuments to French civilization are unattainable. Because they live in a battle zone that is closer to the South Central Los Angeles depicted in *Boyz n the Hood* and *Menace II Society, Hate* has more in common with these films than with the French-language features that celebrate Paris and l'amour.

Kassovitz' choice to shoot the film in black-and-white is appropriate, as the lack of an on-screen color palette helps to stress the bleakness and sterility of his characters' surroundings. His use of a hand-held camera gives the film a gritty, cinema-verite feel, and mirrors their disorientation. Not for an instant are Vinz, Hubert, Sayid, and their cronies in any way romanticized. And that is how it should be.

—Rob Edelman

HAIZI WANG

(King of the Children)

China, 1987

Director: Chen Kaige

Production: Xi'an Film Studio; Eastmancolour, 35mm; running time: 106 minutes.

Producer: Wu Tianming; **screenplay:** Chen Kaige, Wan Zhi, based on the short story by Ah Cheng; **photography:** Gu Changwei; **editor:** Liu Miaomiao; **lighting:** Jia Tianxi; **assistant director:** Qiang Xiaolu; **art director:** Chen Shaohua; **music:** Qu Xiaosong; **sound recording:** Tao Jing, Gu Changning; **sound editor:** Liu Miaomiao.

Cast: Xie Juang (*Lao Gan*); Yang Xuewen (*Wang Fu*); Chen Shaohua (*Headmaster Chen*); Zhang Caimei (*Laidi*); Xu Guoqin (*Lao Hei*); Le Gang (*Cowherd*); Tan Tuo (*Village Team Leader*); Gu Changwei (*Secretary Wu*); Wu Xiao (*Class Monitor*); Liu Haichen (*Father*).

Haizi Wang

Publications

Books:

Chen Kaige and Rayns, Tony, *King of the Children and the New Chinese Cinema*, London, 1989.

Articles:

Aubert, J.P., ''La cinquième génération'' in *Cahiers du Cinéma* (Paris), April 1988.

Variety (New York), 18 May 1988.

Cahiers du Cinéma (Paris), June 1988.

Stanbrook, A., *Films and Filming* (London), August 1988.

Glaessner, V., and Rayns, Tony, ''Tearing Down the Temple of Culture'' in *Monthly Film Bulletin* (London), September 1988.

Tessier, M., *Revue du Cinéma* (Paris), April 1989.

Baecque, A. de, ''L'école en feu'' in *Cahiers du Cinéma* (Paris), June 1989.

Niel, P., ''Traitement de texte'' in *Positif* (Paris), July-August 1989.

Cinemaya (New Delhi), Winter 1989–90.

Chen Kaige, ''Breaking the Circle: The Cinema and Cultural Change in China'' in *Cineaste* (New York), no.3, 1990.

Chow, R., ''Male Narcissism and National Culture: Subjectivity in Chen Kaige's *King of the Children*,'' in *Camera Obscura*, January-May 1991.

CinémAction (Courbevoie), March 1993.

Brochu, D., ''Marques d'un cinéma moderne: *Le roi des enfants*,'' in *Cinémas* (Montreal), vol. 3, no. 2–3, Spring 1993.

Rayns, Tony, ''The Narrow Path: Chen Kaige'' in *Projections 3*, edited by John Boorman and Walter Donoghue, London, 1994.

Lu, A., ''Chen Kaige,'' in *Film Comment* (New York), vol. 33, September/October 1997.

* * *

King of the Children is a deceptively simple film. It tells the story of a young man who becomes a teacher of junior high school students in the Yunnan countryside and realizes, in a heart-wrenching way, the extent of his task. He discovers that his students are not given any textbooks and that they are used to learning by rote. The time is the Cultural Revolution. Lan Gan, the young man, was part of a brigade made up of city youths sent to the remote countryside for re-education by working alongside illiterate peasants. He gains a transfer from his brigade to a softer job as a teacher even though he is not qualified, having hardly graduated from high school himself.

The young man's experiences mirror director Chen Kaige's own experiences during the Cultural Revolution as a *zhishi qingnian*, or ''intellectual youth.'' Sent to Yunnan to work in a production brigade in the late 1960s, early 1970s, Chen was attracted to the story by novelist A. Cheng (a fellow production brigade member in Yunnan) because of its simplicity. But the director has invested his own aesthetic references in the adaptation. These references are entirely visual—their meanings and significance are implicit and open to interpretation. What cannot be denied is the film's emotive power conveyed entirely through its images and an interesting montage-mixture of sound effects which illustrate certain scenes (sounds of tree felling, a voice chanting folk melodies, and so on).

To begin with, Chen films his protagonist Lan Gan mostly in distant long shots, locating him in an environment of harsh, primitive beauty (by the by recalling the stunning compositions in Chen's first film, *The Yellow Earth*, where earth seems to engulf a man). As well as reinforcing the effect of rural stupor, lethargy and boredom felt by the lead character, these long shots reveal the immensity of space and the concrete, objective world in which the character finds himself. He can no more hope to transcend this space than the problems of humanity within that space. Similarly, we first see the central setting of the school in a very long shot (which in point of fact, opens the film), in a photographic time-lapse sequence from mist to clear sky to sunset. The school, where the central drama unfolds, is seen in open air, flanked by mountains—it appears as a minor, unchanging spot in a flurry of changing time.

The narrative is punctuated with elliptical cuts, deliberate omissions, and long-held shots which impart information on a subliminal level but which in fact hold the key to Chen's mode of visual storytelling. A direct, linear mode is avoided. Instead, we look to visual detail and the behaviour of the characters to draw narrative (and emotional) sustenance. Thus, the film's spare use of medium to close shots, as in the scenes of Lan Gan reacting to his students in class (particularly the sensitive Wang Fu with whom he strikes an uneasy rapport), gain even more impact. Time and space are wondrously controlled. A second viewing of the film shows how tightly edited and temporally well-sustained the narrative actually is (the film even feels shorter than its nearly two hours running time) and also reveals more clearly the rich metaphorical layers which Chen creates to underline the simple story.

The metaphor of objective space to illustrate man's smallness is obvious while it also points out the results of the more complex, and destructive urges, of man, small as he is. The protagonist is shown at crucial points in still shots standing in a wilderness of burned tree stumps. The final scenes of these tree stumps manifested as wooden statues of strawmen and other grotesque figures, the burning of the forest (for swidden agriculture), and the intriguing sub-plot of the young cowherd urinating on the ground to disconcert cows too stubborn to move along (which gives rise to Lao San's explanation of his use of a compound word made of the characters of ''cow'' and ''water'' in his valedictory lesson to his students) are all a manifestation of man making a mark on earth.

The last message of Lan Gan to Wang Fu as he leaves the school (having been dismissed for his unorthodox teaching methods) may be summed up in one word: creativity—he implores Wang Fu not to learn by rote and to start thinking for himself. However, man's creativity is compromized, Chen seems to say, by man's failure to understand and come to terms with his environment. On the other hand, even as Chen underscores the effects of human alienation, poverty and neglect, there is no simplistic explanation offered for the obviously disastrous effect that human foolishness has waged on human affairs (the devastation wrought by the Cultural Revolution on a generation of students, for example).

Chen has succeeded in bringing out the abstract core of his story without diminishing its effective simplicity. In fact, the film comes across as a moving indictment of China's education policy, its politics, and the country's backwardness and endemic poverty. *King of the Children* is also the first film in which Chen deals with the disaster of the Cultural Revolution in personal terms. It is a subject that Chen and other Fifth Generation directors have a great deal to say about having experienced it at first hand. It offers great human drama, ranging from the tragic to the absurd. In *King of the Children*, Chen depicts the Cultural Revolution as a national tragedy but he does not condemn it outright. In that sense, Chen is less interested in the political implications of the Cultural Revolution. A philosophical-minded director, Chen has shown that his real subject is man and the ambiguities and implications of his behaviour.

—Stephen Teo

HALLELUJAH

USA, 1929

Director: King Vidor

Production: Metro-Goldwyn-Mayer Pictures Corp.; black and white, 35mm, sound and silent versions; running time: about 100 minutes, some sources list 107 minutes; length: 6579 feet (silent), 9711 feet (sound). Released 20 August 1929. Filmed 1929 in MGM Studios in Culver City, California and on location in and around Memphis, Tennessee.

Producer: King Vidor; **scenario:** Wanda Tuchock; **treatment:** Richard Schayer; **dialogue:** Ranson Rideout, from an original story by King Vidor; **titles for silent version:** Marian Ainslee; **photography:** Gordon Avil; **editors:** Anson Stephenson (silent), Hugh Wynn (sound); **sound recordist:** Douglas Shearer; **art director:** Cedric Gibbons; **music:** traditional with 2 songs by Irving Berlin; **costume designer:** Henrietta Frazer.

Cast: Daniel Haynes (*Zeke*); Nina Mae McKinney (*Chick*); William Fountaine (*Hot Shot*); Harry Gray (*Parson*); Fannie B. DeKnight (*Mammy*); Everett McGarrity (*Spunk*); Victoria Spivey (*Missy Rose*); Milton Dickerson (*One of the Johnson kids*); Robert Couch (*One of the Johnson kids*); Walter Tait (*One of the Johnson kids*); Dixie Jubilee Singers.

Hallelujah

Publications

Books:

Noble, Peter, *The Negro in Films*, London, 1950.
Vidor, King, *A Tree Is a Tree*, New York, 1953.
Rotha, Paul, and Richard Griffith, *The Film Till Now*, New York, 1960.
Jacobs, Lewis, *The Rise of the American Film: A Critical History*, New York, 1968.
Bogle, Donald, *Toms, Coons, Mulattoes, Mammies, and Bucks: An Interpretative History of Blacks in American Films*, New York, 1973.
Murray, James, *To Find an Image*, Indianapolis, 1973.
Maynard, Richard A., *The Black Man on Film: Racial Stereotyping*, Rochelle Park, New Jersey, 1974.
Leab, Daniel J., *From Sambo to Superspade: The Black Experience in Motion Pictures*, Boston, 1975.
Patterson, Lindsay, *Black Films and Film-Making: A Comprehensive Anthology from Stereotype to Superhero*, New York, 1975.
Pines, Jim, *Blacks in Film: A Survey of Racial Themes and Images in the American Film*, London, 1975.
Baxter, John, *King Vidor*, New York, 1976.
Cripps, Thomas, *Slow Fade to Black: The Negro in American Film 1900–1942*, New York, 1977.
Sampson, Henry T., *Blacks in Black and White: A Source Book on Black Films*, Metuchen, New Jersey, 1977.
Comuzio, Ermanno, *King Vidor*, Florence, 1986.
Dowd, Nancy, and David Shepard, *King Vidor*, Metuchen, New Jersey, 1988.
Vidor, King, *King Vidor*, Lanham, 1988.
Durgnat, Raymond, and Scott Simmon, *King Vidor—American*, Berkeley, 1989.

Articles:

Hall, Mordaunt, in *New York Times*, 21 August 1929.
Variety (New York), 28 August 1929.
Braver-Mann, B. G., ''Vidor and Evasion,'' in *Experimental Cinema*, vol. 1, no. 3, 1931.
Harrington, Curtis, ''The Later Years: King Vidor's Hollywood Progress,'' in *Sight and Sound* (London), April-June 1953.
Vidor, King, ''Hollywood Hallelujah,'' in *Films and Filming* (London), May 1955.

Higham, Charles, ''King Vidor,'' in *Film Heritage* (Dayton, Ohio), Summer 1966.
''King Vidor at NYU: Discussion,'' in *Cineaste* (New York), Spring 1968.
Luft, Herbert G., ''A Career That Spans Half a Century,'' in *Film Journal* (New York), Summer 1971.
Durgnat, Raymond, in *Film Comment* (New York), July-August 1973.
''Vidor Issue'' of *Positif* (Paris), September 1974.
Combs, Richard, in *Monthly Film Bulletin* (London), September 1974.
Leiris, M., in *Positif* (Paris), November 1974.
Baumgarten, Marjorie, in *Cinema Texas Program Notes* (Austin), 11 October 1977.
Cocchi, John, in *Magill's Survey of Cinema 2*, Englewood Cliffs, New Jersey, 1980.
Brody, S., and P. Bates, ''Film and Photo League,'' in *Jump Cut* (Berkeley), no. 33, February 1988.
Ribemont-Dessaignes, G., in *October,* no. 60, Spring 1992.
Hoberman, J., ''Race to Race,'' in *Village Voice* (New York), vol. 39, 22 February 1994.
Lindvall, T.R., and others, ''Spectacular Transcendence: Abundant Means in the Cinematic Representation of African American Christianity,'' in *The Howard Journal of Communications*, vol. 7, no. 3, 1996.
Vidor, K., ''Transcript of Tape Recording Made by King Vidor,'' in *Wide Angle* (Baltimore), vol. 19, no. 2, 1997.

* * *

Hallelujah has fair claim to being the first masterpiece of the sound era. Certainly King Vidor could have realized his frequently-proposed all-black film only at a moment when the Broadway success of Rouben Mamoulian's *Porgy*, rumors of a similar project at Fox (*Hearts of Dixie*), and Vidor's own willingness to gamble his salary all combined with corporate confusion at MGM—the last major studio to equip for sound. Ultimately, however, *Hallelujah*'s accompanying music couldn't quite make it a musical, nor defuse its savagery; and it had as much trouble with bookings in the North as in the South.

The film tends to be remembered now under a *Birth of a Nation* stigma common to ''Southerns''—admired technically while damned for its racism. It is true that the contented matriarchal family of cotton-pickin' blacks, singing while they work their patch of land, can seem an image of slave-based Southern prosperity, and the violence of the melodramatic plot can seem straight out of Mrs. Stowe. But the characters are Uncle Tom-ish only outside the context of Vidor's other work: the same documentary of an agrarian lifestyle is at the root of his idealized white cooperative in *Our Daily Bread*; emotional intensity is everywhere a Vidorian trademark; and an identical ferocity characterizes *Northwest Passage* and *Duel in the Sun*. *Ruby Gentry*, with another murder-in-the-swampwater finale, comes closest to being his whitefolks version of *Hallelujah*. One needs to recall that Vidor was working at a time when respectable British critic James Agate could dismiss the film with: ''Personally, I don't care if it took Mr. Vidor ten years to train these niggers; all I know is that ten minutes is all I can stand of nigger ecstasy.'' If the film is flawed from the standpoint of social morality, it's for the complete exclusion of whites, which renders imprecise the family's relationship to the land they apparently sharecrop. Additionally, the four brief shots which make an ellipsis of Zeke's prison term for murdering his rival ''Hot Shot'' deny the experience of punishment—he's soon strummin' on the ol' banjo riding home to Mammy.

Whatever Vidor may have said in interviews about the film's ''good vs. evil'' structure, its tension comes from pitting against each other two mutually exclusive ''goods'': family-as-religion vs. passionate sexuality. And the temptress Chick, whose dance-hall sensuality elevates easily into religious fervor, isn't inauthentic in either incarnation. She tempts Zeke from his revivalist preaching, but considering Vidor's very consistent repudiation of narrow religion, from *The Sky Pilot* (1921) right through *Solomon and Sheba* (1959), that too might be for the best. The surrealist Ado Kyrou is close to the mark in reading *Hallelujah* as a celebration of desire.

Early sound equipment limits the musical numbers to relatively static takes, but by any criterion *Hallelujah* is technically remarkable—the ironic result of Vidor's having had to shoot location sequences silent and post-synch the often expressionistic sound effects of ecstatic wails or physical violence (a procedure which, so Vidor claims, drove his sound editor to a nervous breakdown). The aural expressionism might be written off as circumstantially unavoidable if it hadn't its visual equivalent in such shots as the featureless black half-screen into which Zeke futilely shouts for aid for his dying brother. But to stress expressionism is to ignore the ways *Hallelujah* anticipates the early-Visconti variety of neorealism, with its authentic dialects, its quirky, slack dialogue, its inexperienced actors, its documentary tracing of rural life, and its relentless analysis of the *crime passionel*.

—Scott Simmon

HANA-BI

(Fireworks)

Japan, 1997

Director: Takeshi Kitano

Production: Television Tokyo Channel, Tokyo FM Broadcasting Company, Office Kitano, Bandai Visual; color, 35mm; running time: 101 minutes. Released 3 September 1997 (Venice Film Festival), 11 November 1997 in Germany (theatrical premiere), 24 January 1998 in Japan, and 20 March 1998 in the United States.

Producers: Masayuki Mori, Yasushi Tsuge, Takio Yoshida; **screenplay:** Takeshi Kitano; **photography:** Hideo Yamamoto; **editors:** Takeshi Kitano, Yoshinori Oota; **art director:** Norishiro Isoda; **set decorator:** Tatsuo Ozeki; **original music:** Jo Hisaishi; **costume designer:** Masami Saito; **sound:** Senji Horiuchi.

Cast: Takeshi Kitano (billed as ''Beat'' Takeshi) (*Yoshitaka Nishi*); Kayoko Kishimoto (*Miyuki, Nishi's wife*); Ren Osugi (*Horibe*); Susumu Terajima (*Nakamura*); Tetsu Watanabe (*Tesuka*); Hakuryu

Hana-Bi

(*Yakuza Hitman*); Yasuei Yakushiji (*Criminal*); Taro Istumi (*Kudo*); Kenichi Yajima (*Doctor*); Makoto Ashikawa (*Tanaka*); Yuko Daike (*Tanaka's Widow*).

Awards: European Film Awards Five Continents Award, Venice Film Festival Golden Lion, Sao Paolo International Film Festival Critics Award, Camerimage Golden Frog (Hideo Yamamoto), 1997.

Publications

Articles:

Rooney, D., in *Variety* (New York), 8–14 September 1997.

Burdeau, E. and others, interview in *Cahiers du Cinéma* (Paris), November 1997.

Saada, N., ''Mirage de la vie,'' in *Cahiers du Cinéma* (Paris), November 1997.

Ciment, Michel, interview in *Positif* (Paris), November 1997.

Goudet, S., in *Positif* (Paris), November 1997.

Vasse, C., in *Positif* (Paris), November 1997.

Buccheri, V., in *Segnocinema* (Vicenza, Italy), November/December 1997.

Rayns, Tony, ''Silent Running,'' interview in *Sight & Sound* (London), December 1997.

Rayns, Tony, ''Flower and Fire,'' in *Sight & Sound* (London), December 1997.

Kehr, Dave, in *Film Comment* (New York), March/April 1998.

* * *

Superficially, the main character in Takeshi Kitano's *Hana-Bi* might be the hero of a generic Hollywood cops-and-robbers thriller. He is Yoshitaka Nishi, a tough veteran police detective who is the picture of cookie-cutter cool. Nishi rarely is without his trademark sunglasses, and he hardly ever displays emotion while going about his professional duties. In this regard, he parallels Clint Eastwood's *Dirty Harry* and Charles Bronson's character in *Death Wish.* Yet effortlessly, if not breathlessly, the character and the film transcend these cosmetic trappings, with Nishi becoming a tragic hero of Shakespearean proportion. There are dents in his armor and, as his world crashes in around him, this cop is no indestructible Superman. Nishi (who is played by the filmmaker, billed as ''Beat'' Takeshi) starts out with a couple of strikes against him, as his young daughter has recently died and his wife is fatally ill. A third strike directly relates to the hazards of his business; over the image of two men tossing a baseball, it is noted that Nishi's ''daughter dies, [his] wife gets sick, and he's a damn cop.'' The reality of police work is that it is a brutal, high-pressure profession. A cop may die in the line of duty, or he may be crippled, or a blunder may result in incalculable tragedy. All of these catastrophes befall Nishi. Once upon a time, he and his longtime partner and friend, Detective Horibe, were ''a great team.'' Yet at the outset, Horibe is shot and crippled. Additionally, Nishi is involved in a bloody confrontation with a criminal, resulting in the death of one colleague and the maiming of another. Nishi's sense of responsibility towards his wife and the deceased cop's widow leads him to borrow money from the yakuza, whose emissaries now are calling for a payback.

In *Hana-Bi*, the characters of Nishi and Horibe are laden with obstacles. But are there solutions? In a standard Hollywood entertainment, a happy ending would be *de rigeur*; it would transcend whatever anguish is experienced by the hero during the course of the scenario. Suffice to say, *Hana-Bi* is no Hollywood escapist product, no cotton-candy amusement. The wheelchair-bound Horibe, who has been abandoned by his family, commences contemplating nature and painting what he observes. Whatever pleasure he derives from this pastime is transitory and meaningless. ''I paint pictures to kill time,'' he says, matter-of-factly. Meanwhile, Nishi responds to his stresses by becoming prone to increasing outbursts of violence. Not all of his victims are the thugs who harass him for money; Nishi will arbitrarily smack an unsuspecting stranger who has the temerity to mix with him. For instance, he beats up a man who innocently chides Nishi's wife for watering dead flowers on a beach.

Conversely, when in the company of his wife, Nishi is gentle and loving: a model of compassion in a cruel contemporary world. In this regard, *Hana-Bi* offers a stinging portrait of an icy-cold society in which cityscapes and bright lights and all the modern conveniences are poor substitutes for warmth, caring, and basic humanity. Society, as depicted by Kitano, is defined by violence and gangsterism—and Nishi, the officer of the law, is reduced to the level of the street thug as he is impacted by his work, his surroundings, and his personal hell. Throughout the film, characters suffer ill luck. When they or their loved ones are afflicted with disease or paralysis, they are left to their own inner resources, their own inner demons, their own solitude.

Hana-Bi is a soulful film, with Kitano often employing the soft sounds of pianos or violins to create moods of melancholy. Most impressive of all, the film is loaded with visual and aural juxtapositions that infuse it with a profound sense of irony. Sometimes, the opposites are strictly in the imagery; on other occasions, an image may be contrasted to a sound, or a penetrating silence. For example, a shot of Nishi quietly, somberly lighting a cigarette while visiting his wife in her hospital room is followed by one of a gun blasting into the gut of Horibe, who grimaces and falls to the pavement. The second shot begins just as Nishi lights the cigarette. Later on, Nishi peacefully sits in a bar. Violent images pass through his mind. Kitano visualizes these thoughts, which appear in slow motion and without sound. As a result, the serenity of the moment is contrasted to the violence replaying in Nishi's head.

A shot of blood flowing out of the mouth of a thug Nishi has just smacked is followed by a long shot of waves crashing into a beach and two adults and a child walking in the sand. A medium shot of a man standing passively is accompanied by the groans and grunts of a violent confrontation. Nishi aims a gun at a man who is running from him; just as he pulls the trigger, Kitano cuts to Horibe splashing a glob of blood-red paint across his latest artistic creation.

Occasionally, Nishi's wife utters a giggle in response to something he does or says. Otherwise, she is silent throughout the entire film—until its final moments. ''Thank you. Thank you for everything,'' she tells her husband, as she tenderly rests her head on his shoulder. Here, Kitano incorporates the film's final juxtaposition. His camera lingers on a long shot of an idyllic sand-and-waves setting. Then, to emphasize the point that there will be no reprieve for Nishi and his wife, the lilting music on the soundtrack is interrupted by the sound of two gunshots.

The literal English translation of *Hana-Bi* is ''fireworks.'' Split in two, the title is made up of the words ''flower'' (''hana'') and ''fire'' (''bi''): a contrast that potently mirrors the two aspects of Nishi's character. He is a cop who knows all too well that violence is an intrinsic part of contemporary society; when stretched to his limit, he is a willing purveyor of violence. Yet concurrently, in his dealings with his wife, he is capable of extreme tenderness. All of this is most poignantly played out in Kitano's visual and aural juxtapositions, which ultimately mix devotion with outrage, beauty with anguish.

—Rob Edelman

HARAKIRI

See **SEPPUKU**

A HARD DAY'S NIGHT

UK, 1964

Director: Richard Lester

Production: Proscenium Films; black and white, 35mm; running time: 85 minutes. Released July 1964, London. Filmed 1964 in London.

Producers: Walter Shenson and Denis O'Dell; **screenplay:** Alun Owen; **title design:** Robert Freeman; **photography:** Gilbert Taylor; **editors:** John Jympson and Pamela Tomlin; **sound recordists:** H. L. Bird and Stephen Dalby; **sound editor:** Gordon Daniel; **art director:** Ray Simm; **music director:** George Martin; **songs by:** John Lennon, Paul McCartney and George Harrison; **performed by:** The Beatles; **costume designer:** Julie Harris.

Cast: John Lennon (*John*); Paul McCartney (*Paul*); George Harrison (*George*); Ringo Starr (*Ringo*); Wilfrid Brambell (*Grandfather*); Norman Rossington (*Norm*); Victor Spinetti (*Television director*);

A Hard Day's Night

John Junkin (*Shake*); Deryck Guyler (*Police inspector*); Anna Quayle (*Millie*); Kenneth Haigh (*Simon*); Richard Vernon (*Man on train*); Michael Trubshawe (*Club manager*); Eddie Malin (*Hotel waiter*); Robin Ray (*Television floor manager*); Lionel Blair (*Television choreographer*); Alison Seebohm (*Secretary*); David Jaxon (*Young boy*); Marianne Stone (*Society reporter*); David Langton (*Actor*); Clare Kelly (*Barmaid*).

Publications

Script:

Owen, Alun, *The Beatles in Richard Lester's ''A Hard Day's Night,''* edited by Philip DiFranco, New York, 1977.

Books:

Manvell, Roger, *New Cinema in Britain*, New York, 1969.
Kantor, Bernard, *Directors at Work: Interviews with American Film-Makers*, New York, 1970.
Betts, Ernest, *The Film Business: A History of the British Cinema*, New York, 1973.
Walker, Alexander, *Hollywood U.K.*, New York, 1974.
Rosenfeldt, Diane, *Richard Lester: A Guide to References and Resources*, Boston, 1978.
Sinyard, Neil, *The Films of Richard Lester*, London, 1985.
Yule, Andrew, *The Man Who ''Framed'' the Beatles*, New York, 1994.
Yule, Andrew, *Richard Lester and the Beatles: A Complete Biography of the Man Who Directed a Hard Day's Night, and Help!*, New York, 1995.

Articles:

Bean, Robin, ''Keeping Up with the Beatles,'' in *Films and Filming* (London), February 1964.
Baker, Peter, in *Films and Filming* (London), August 1964.
Sarris, Andrew, in *Village Voice* (New York), 27 August 1964.
Nowell-Smith, Geoffrey, in *Sight and Sound* (London), Autumn 1964.
Seelye, John, in *Film Quarterly* (Berkeley), Fall 1964.
Hagen, Ray, in *Films in Review* (New York), October 1964.

French, Philip, ''Richard Lester,'' in *Movie* (London), Autumn 1965.
Bluestone, George, ''Lunch with Lester,'' in *Film Quarterly* (Berkeley), Summer 1966.
Sugg, Alfred, ''The Beatles and Film Art,'' in *Film Heritage* (Dayton, Ohio), Summer 1966.
Lester, Richard, ''The Art of Comedy,'' in *Film* (London), Spring 1967.
''Richard Lester,'' in *New Yorker*, 28 October 1967.
Shivas, Mark, and Ian Cameron, ''An Interview with Richard Lester,'' in *Movie* (London), Winter 1968–69.
Corliss, Richard, ''A Hard Day's Night: 10 Years After,'' in *Film Comment* (New York), May-June 1974.
Johnson, Timothy, in *Magill's Survey of Cinema 2*, Englewood Cliffs, New Jersey, 1980.
Lefèvre, Raymond, in *Image et Son* (Paris), November 1982.
Bortolussi, S., in *Cineforum* (Bergamo), April 1983.
Hanke, K., ''The British Film Invasion of the 1960s,'' in *Films in Review* (New York), April 1989.
Hanke, K., ''The British Film Invasion of the 1960s, part II,'' in *Films in Review* (New York), May 1989.
Savage, J., ''Snapshots of the Sixties,'' in *Sight and Sound* (London), May 1993.
Clements, M., ''My Technology's in Turnaround,'' in *Premiere* (Boulder), vol. 8, November 1994.
Boxoffice (Chicago), October 1996.
Hampton, Howard, ''Scorpio Descending: In Search of Rock Cinema,'' in *Film Comment* (New York), vol. 33, no. 2, March-April 1997.

* * *

Following the runaway success of *Rock Around the Clock* in 1956, both British and North American filmmakers sought to capitalize on the box-office appeal of pop music. Although the resulting features were often commercial hits, they also rated low in critical prestige. The pop music film was characteristically a low-budget quickie, designed to cash in on a passing musical trend, and generally devoid of artistic ambitions other than to pack in as many musical numbers as possible or show off the film's stars to best advantage. The release of *A Hard Day's Night*, in this respect, represents something of a milestone in the history of the genre. Although a vehicle for the Beatles, aimed at exploiting the rising tide of ''Beatlemania,'' the film successfully challenged many of the old conventions of the pop film by introducing a new approach to both plot and visual presentation.

The film, for example, discards the hitherto standard pop film plots—both the ''let's put on a show'' formula which director Richard Lester had already made affectionate fun of in his earlier *It's Trad, Dad* (1962) and the ''rags to riches'' structure used in, among others, the early Elvis Presley films (such as *Loving You* and *Jailhouse Rock*). Scripted by the Liverpool playwright, Alun Owen, *A Hard Day's Night* opts instead for a much looser ''a day in the life of'' format which, also unlike the Elvis movies, requires that the Beatles play, not fictional characters, but themselves. Indeed, no small part of the film's fascination is its playful confusion of the boundaries between fact and fiction whereby what we see is all staged for the camera (and contains no actuality footage) but nonetheless assumes the air of a documentary presentation (so that the concluding television performance is often taken to have been a real one).

The film, in this regard, is heavily indebted to the French new wave and shares its characteristic blend of ciné-vérité (hand-held camera, location shooting, improvised performances, and a generally casual approach towards filming) and modernism (a self-conscious use of film technique, anti-realist editing, and cinematic pastiche). This mix is well illustrated by the film's lengthy train sequence. This is filmed on a real train using a hand-held camera (with wide-angle lens). The ''realism'' which this generates, however, is dramatically ruptured when the four Beatles decide to torment the stuffy commuter who has prevented them from opening the compartment window or playing their transistor. In one shot, the four Beatles are standing in the train corridor, their faces glued to the compartment window; in the shot of them which follows, John, Paul, and George are suddenly seen outside, running (and, in George's case, cycling) alongside the train and still shouting at the increasingly harassed passenger inside.

This indifference to the norms of ''realism'' is extended to the film's treatment of the musical numbers, and represents one of its most important contributions to the genre. Lester had already demonstrated a remarkable visual inventiveness in his filming of the acts in *It's Trad, Dad*, but had confined himself to realistically motivated performances (in the recording studio, in concert, on TV). *A Hard Day's Night* is no less reliant on the TV concert but also attempts to integrate plot and music more securely and present its musical numbers in ways other than the simulated performance. Two of these attempts are particularly striking. In the first, the Beatles end their train journey in the guard's van where they embark upon a game of cards. ''I Should Have Known Better'' is heard on the soundtrack and, shortly after, John produces a harmonica and begins to sing. The camera then cuts to the group, sitting in the same position, but now playing their instruments. As the song finishes, the instruments simply ''disappear'' and the boys bring their game to a conclusion. The song, in one sense, is ''performed'' but in a manner which would be impossible other than on film. In the second case, the element of performance is dispensed with entirely. In the course of the concert rehearsals, the group escapes through a fire door to a deserted playing field outside. As ''Can't Buy Me Love'' begins on the soundtrack, their sense of release is cleverly communicated through a spectacular montage of movement involving aerial photography and accelerated motion. For possibly the first time, the pop film demonstrated it was possible to present a musical number without the illusion of an actual performance.

Ironically, it is often this very element of technical ostentation which is condemned in Lester's work as superficial gimmickry. In the case of *A Hard Day's Night*, however, it is the very humbleness of the pop film genre, and its lack of social and moral earnestness, which makes such a complaint inappropriate. For while the film may lack substance, it does not pretend otherwise. Moreover, it is precisely because of its rather eclectic modishness that it evokes so successfully both the spirit of the music and the era which spawned it (the ''swinging sixties''). In this respect, the film wears rather better than most of the more ambitious and ''serious minded'' Lester films which were to follow.

—John Hill

HARP OF BURMA

See **BIRUMA NO TAGEGOTO**

HATE

See **LA HAINE**

HE LIU

(The River)

Taiwan, 1997

Director: Tsai Ming-liang

Production: Color; running time: 115 minutes. Released in France, 27 August 1997, and in England, 20 March 1998; filmed in Taipei, Taiwan.

Producer: Chiu Shun-Ching, Hsu Li-Kong, Chung Hu-pin (executive), Wang Shih-Fang (associate); **screenplay:** Tsai Ming-liang, Tsai Yi-chun, Yang Pi-ying; **cinematographer:** Liao Pen-jung; **editor:** Chen Sheng-Chang, Lei Chen-Ching; **production designer:** Tony Lan; **art direction:** Lee Pao-Lin; **set decoration:** Cheng Nien-Chiu, Kuo Mu-Shan; **costume design:** Yu Wang; **makeup:** Yen Pei-Wen.

Cast: Chen Chao-jung (*Anonymous Man*); Chen Shiang-chyi (*Girl*); Ann Hui (*Director*); Lee Kang-sheng (*Kang-Sheng, Xiao-Kang*); Lu Hsiao-Ling (*Mother*); Lu Shiao-Lin (*Mother's lover*); Miao Tien (*Father*); Yang Kuei-Mei (*Girl in Hotel*).

Publications

Articles:

Interview with Tsai, in *Sight & Sound* (London), March 1997.
Herpe, N., and M. Ciment, ''Tsai Ming-liang,'' in *Positif* (Paris), no. 439, September 1997.
Roy, André, ''Les noyés de Taipei,'' in *24 Images* (Montreal), no. 90, Winter 1998.
Kemp, Peter, ''Bodily Fluids,'' in *Sight and Sound* (London), vol. 8, no. 4, April 1998.

* * *

Tsai Ming-Liang is one of the most distinctive and idiosyncratic of the younger generation of Taiwanese directors. So far, unlike his predecessors such as Hou Hsiao-Hsien and Edward Yang, he's shown no interest in dealing directly with Taiwan's history; instead, he focuses on the outcome of that history, the youth of present-day Taipei—the disaffected heirs of a society that once set greater store by tradition, that held the spirits of the past in higher awe, than any other. Isolated, obscurely dissatisfied, unable or unwilling to form emotional connections with friends, lovers, or family, his young protagonists wander through a city that's bulldozed its past and jerry-built its future.

The River, the third in Tsai's Taipei cycle, shares cast, characters and motifs with its two predecessors, *Rebels of the Neon God* (*Qing Shaonian Nezha*, 1992) and *Vive l'Amour* (*Aiqing Wansui*, 1994). The lead is again taken by the pensive, delicate-featured Li Kangsheng, as before playing a youth called Xiaokang. He shares an apartment with an older couple, but so rarely do any of the three communicate with each other that it's a while before we realize they're his mother and father. (They're played by Miao Tian and Lu Hsiao-ling, who took the same roles in *Rebels.*) At one point when Xiaokang is sitting in a hospital corridor his parents, one after the other, walk straight past him without recognizing him. Xiaokang's sole evident emotional attachment is to his scooter; astride it he roams the Taipei streets with an air of obscure discontent, plainly looking for something but unlikely to know it when he finds it.

What he does find, unlooked-for, is pain. The agony that afflicts him, contorting his neck and reducing him to near-suicidal despair, seems on the face of it to result from his immersion in the noxiously polluted waters of the Tanshui river. But after his ducking and before the affliction strikes, Xiaokang has sex with an ex-classmate, Xiangqi; she's affectionate and gentle, but he remains blankly uninvolved throughout. His pain can be seen, not simply as the result of a viral infection, but as an index of his emotional denial; Tsai leaves us to make up our own minds. Still, Xiaokang's suffering at least attracts the concern of his parents, making them talk to him if not to each other. In a recurrent image, comic but touching, we see the father riding pillion behind Xiaokang on the scooter, holding his son's head upright.

As ever in Tsai's films, water represents an insidious and disruptive force. In *Rebels of the Neon God* a high-rise apartment is constantly and inexplicably flooded to a depth of several inches, with loose rubber flip-flops floating forlornly about the kitchen; the same watery theme recurs in Tsai's most recent film *The Hole* (*Dong*, 1998). In *The River* not only is Xiaokang possibly poisoned by his swim, but the father finds water seeping, then trickling, and finally pouring through the ceiling of his room. Rather than trying to stop it, he rigs up an intricate system of pipes and plastic sheets to deflect the flow out of the window. Since he too is an emotional amputee, estranged from his wife and seeking loveless sex in gay saunas, it's tempting to see this downpour as a symbol of the elements in his own life that he deflects but refuses to confront.

But water can also be taken as the metaphor of a society in a state of uncontrollable flux, where all fixed points have been abandoned. In this high-obsolescence city, where it seems that virtually every building is, or overlooks, a construction site, tradition can be of little help. Besides trying the regular hospital, Xiaokang's parents haul him round to a string of healers, but none of them does him the slightest good.

Tsai (who was born to Chinese expatriate parents in Sarawak) shows scant affection for his adopted city; his Taipei is a transient, comfortless place of drab apartments and hotel rooms, their walls painted in fecal browns and greens. His people occupy these spaces but scarcely seem to live in them, let alone personalize them with possessions or decor. Much of the film's action takes place in corridors—especially in the gay saunas frequented by the father, whose atmosphere offers rather less erotic excitement than the average supermarket. Even when a conjunction occurs, it's brief and joyless—no one speaks, let alone smiles, and only a muted shudder signals climax. Just once, after father and son have unwittingly coincided in an act of masturbatory incest, is there something more. When realization dawns, the father gives a groan of fury and slaps his son's face. Compared to the previous couplings (both gay and hetero), it seems almost like a caress.

All of which might sound terminally depressing. But there's a sly humor in Tsai's gaze, and a quiet, quizzical regard for his bemused wanderers, that rescues his films from misanthropy or facile pessimism. His aim in making *The River*, he says, was ''to go as deeply as possible into the minds of the characters.'' Despite the laconic action and minimal dialogue, he succeeds in revealing them to us—and also, unexpectedly, in making them sympathetic.

—Philip Kemp

A HEART IN WINTER

See **UN COEUR EN HIVER**

HEAVENLY CREATURES

New Zealand, 1994

Director: Peter Jackson

Production: Wingnut Films with Fontana Film Corporation GmbH, in association with the New Zealand Film Commission; color, Super 35 (2:35:1); running time: 99 minutes; original running time in New Zealand and Australia, 108 minutes. Released by Miramax Films; filmed in Christchurch, Victoria Park, and other New Zealand locations. Cost: $10,000,000 (estimated).

Producer: Jim Booth; **screenplay:** Peter Jackson and Frances Walsh; **photography:** Alun Bollinger; **editor:** Jamie Selkirk; **art director:** Jill Cormack; **production designer:** Grant Major; **music:** score by Peter Dasent, with additional music by Giacomo Puccini.

Cast: Melanie Lynskey (*Pauline Parker*); Kate Winslet (*Juliet Hulme*); Sara Peirse (*Honora Parker*); Diana Kent (*Hilda Hulme*); Clive Merrison (*Henry Hulme*); Simon O'Connor (*Herbert Rieper*); Jed Brophy (*John/Nicholas*); Peter Elliott (*Bill Perry*); Gilbert Goldie (*Dr. Bennett*); Geoffrey Heath (*Reverend Norris*); Kirsti Ferry (*Wendy Rieper*); Ben Skjellerup (*Jonathan Hulme*); Darien Takle (*Miss Stewart*); Elizabeth Waller (*Miss Waller*); Peter Jackson (*bum outside theatre*, uncredited).

Awards: Silver Lion Award for outstanding achievement, Venice Film festival, 1994; Critics' Prize for outstanding achievement, Toronto Film Festival, 1994; New Zealand Film Awards for Best Director, Best Actress (Melanie Lynskey), Best Supporting Actress (Sara Peirse), Best Screenplay, Best Cinematography, Best Foreign Performer (Kate Winslet), Best Film Score, Best Editing, and Best Design, 1995.

Publications

Articles:

''Peter Makes His Bid: Dustin Makes a Call,'' in *Onfilm* (Auckland), vol. 9, no. 9, 1992.

''*Heavenly Creatures* a 'Global' Creation,'' in *Onfilm* (Auckland), vol., 10, no. 1, 1993.

Wakefield, P., ''*Heavenly Creatures* to Debut at NZ Fests,'' in *Onfilm* (Auckland), vol. 11, no. 4, 1994.

Murray, S., ''Peter Jackson: *Heavenly Creatures*,'' in *Cinema Papers* (Fitzroy), no. 97–98, April 1994.

Feinstein, H., ''Death and the Maidens,'' in *Village Voice* (New York), vol. 39, 15 November 1994.

Weinraub, Bernard, ''Making a Film from the Horror of a Mother's Brutal Murder,'' in *The New York Times*, 24 November 1994.

'''Divinely Wicked' Film Wins New Yorkers,'' in *Onfilm* (Auckland), vol. 11, no. 11, 1994/1995.

Jones, A., in *Cinefantastique* (Forest Park), vol. 26, no. 2, 1995.

Ribeiro, L.F., in *Film Quarterly* (Berkeley), vol, 49, no. 1, 1995.

Charity, Tom, ''Gut Reaction,'' in *Time Out* (London), no. 1275, 25 January 1995.

Atkinson, Michael, ''Earthy Creatures,'' in *Film Comment* (New York), vol. 31, no. 3, May-June 1995.

Walsh, Frances, and Peter Jackson, and Tod Lippy, ''*Heavenly Creatures*: Writing and Directing *Heavenly Creatures*,'' in *Scenario*, vol. 1, no. 4, Fall 1995.

Murray, J.C., in *Metro Magazine* (St. Kilda West), no. 102, 1995.

Henderson, J., ''Hose Stalking: *Heavenly Creatures* as Feminist Horror,'' in *Canadian Journal of Film Studies* (Ottawa), vol. 6, no. 1, 1997.

Hardy, A., ''*Heavenly Creatures* and Transcendental Style: A Literal Reading,'' in *Illusions* (Wellington), no. 26, Winter 1997.

* * *

Heavenly Creatures is one of a handful of true crime films, a genre more noted for sensationalism than psychological insight, that strives to do more than just recount the events of the crime it dramatizes—in this case, matricide. It grapples with the larger issue of *why?* and relentlessly probes for the answer with such extraordinary cinematic verisimilitude that, like the most gripping and multi-leveled fiction, it succeeds in making us comprehend the incomprehensible.

The New Zealand case that inspired the film was one of the most sensational in that country's history. In 1954, two teenage girls, Pauline Yvonne Parker and her school chum Juliet Hulme, conspired

Heavenly Creatures

to murder Pauline's mother, Mrs. Honora Parker. Juliet's parents were divorcing and planned to ship their daughter to South Africa to stay with relatives. Mrs. Parker denied Pauline's impassioned but unrealistic request to accompany Juliet. The threat of impending separation prompted Pauline to launch a plan for removing the perceived obstacle by killing her mother—a plan Juliet willingly agreed to take part in.

During an outing with Mrs. Parker, Pauline and Juliet bludgeoned the woman to death, then claimed she had died from an accidental fall. Suspicion of murder fell on the two girls following the discovery of Pauline's diary. In it, Pauline outlined the murder scheme and chronicled the obsessively close-knit relationship and elaborate fantasy life governing the friends' behavior which sparked the crime. Charged with murdering Mrs. Parker, the girls admitted the crime, and voiced no remorse. They were found guilty and sent to prison, but paroled for good behavior in 1960 on the condition that they never meet again. Forty years later, as a result of the hoopla surrounding Jackson's film about the case, a reporter for a New Zealand newspaper looked into what happened to Pauline Parker and Juliet Hulme and found that Parker had changed her name and dropped from sight to lead a life of obscurity presumably ''somewhere'' in New Zealand. Hulme, on the other hand, had grown up to become Anne Perry, an internationally best selling author of mystery novels set in Victorian England!

Heavenly Creatures (a title derived from a notation in Pauline's diary) by no means turns a blind eye to the frightfulness of the crime the two girls committed, but it *is* sympathetic in its portrait of them and the reasons for their intense relationship as well as remarkably non-judgmental about it. The movie—which Jackson and co-writer Frances Walsh (the director's wife) based on court records, interviews with people who knew Parker and Hulme at the time, and Parker's diary—portrays the girls not as monstrous bad seeds approaching full growth but, despite their keen intelligence and precociousness, two lonely, socially immature children who found in each other a kindred spirit—and the missing piece in themselves.

The more unbearably intrusive and uncontrollable real life becomes for them, the more the girls seek refuge in their fantasy world where they exercise complete control—as long as they are together.

So that we understand the bizarre fantasy world the girls create for self-protection but which overtakes then horrifyingly engulfs them, Jackson plunges us headlong into that world, mixing reality and illusion (just as the girls do) with every cinematic technique available to explore the girls' inner lives and expose the psychic wounds that lead, with disturbing inexorability, to tragedy. *Heavenly Creatures* is a must-see for anyone interested in compelling true crime dramas and a masterpiece of its genre.

—John McCarty

HEIMAT; DIE ZWEITE HEIMAT

Director: Edgar Reitz

HEIMAT

(Homeland)

West Germany, 1984

Production: Edgar Reitz Filmproduktions/WDR/SFB; black and white, parts in color; running time: 924 minutes; length: 83,130 feet. Released September 1984. Later shown on television in 11 parts.

Producer: Edgar Reitz, co-producers: Joachim von Mengershausen, Hans Kwiet; **screenplay:** Edgar Reitz, Peter Steinbach; **assistant directors:** Elke Vogt, Martin Höner; **photography:** Gernot Roll; **assistant photographer:** Rainer Gutjahr; **editor:** Heidi Handorf; **sound recordist:** Gerhard Birkholz; **sound re-recordist:** Willi Schwadorf; **art director:** Franz Bauer; **costume designers:** Reinhild Paul, Ute Schwippert, Regine Bätz; **pyrotechnics:** Charly Baumgartner; **music:** Nikos Mamangakis.

Cast: Marita Breuer (*Maria Simon, née Wiegand*); Michael Lesch (*Young Paul Simon*); Dieter Schaad (*Paul Simon*); Karin Kienzler (*Young Pauline Kröber*); Eva Maria Bayerswaltes (*Pauline Kröber*); Rüdiger Weigang (*Eduard Simon*); Gertrud Bredel (*Katharina Simon, née Schirmer*); Willi Berger (*Mathias Simon*); Johannes Lobewein (*Alois Wiegand*); Kurt Wagner (*Glasisch-Karl*); Marliese Assmann (*Apollonia*); Eva Maria Schneider (*Marie-Goot*); Wolfram Wagner (*Mäthes-Pat*); Alexander Scholz (*Hänschen Betz*); Arno Lang (*Robert Kröber*); Otto Henn (*Glockzieh*); Manfred Kuhn (*Wirt*); Karin Rasenack (*Lucie Simon*); Helga Bender (*Martina*); Rolf Roth (*Young Anton Simon*); Markus Reiter (*Anton Simon*); Mathias Kniesbeck (*Old Anton Simon*); Ingo Hoffmann (*Young Ernst Simon*); Roland Bongard (*Ernst Simon*); Michael Kausch (*Old Ernst Simon*); Andrea Koloschinski (*Young Lotti Schirmer*); Anke Jendrychowski (*Lotti Schirmer*); Gabriel Blum (*Old Lotti Schirmer*); Virginie Moreno (*Horsewoman*); Rudolph Wessely (*Emigrant*); Gertrud Sherer (*Martha Wiegand*); Hans-Jürgen Schatz (*Wilfried Wiegand*); Kurt Wolfinger (*Gauleiter Simon*); Jörg Hube (*Otto Wohlleben*); Johannes Metzdori (*Fritz Pieritz*); Konrad Lindenkreuz, Ulrich Lindenkreuz (*Todt Workers*); Joachim Bernard (*Pollak*); Sabine Wagner (*Martha Simon*); Gerd Riegauer (*Gschrey*); Roswitha Werkheiser (*Erika 1*); Heike Macht (*Erika 2*); Hans-Günter Kylau (*Captain Zielke*); Alexander Katins (*Ursel*); Ralph Maria Beils (*Specht*); Gudrun Landgrebe (*Klarchen Sisse*); Joseph E. Jones (*Chauffeur*); Andreas Mertens (*Horstchen*); Frank Kleid (*Hermannchen*); Jörg Richter (*Young Hermann Simon*); Peter Harting (*Hermann Simon*); Ann Ruth (*Nurse*).

Award: BAFTA Special Award 1986.

Publications

Script:

Reitz, Edgar, and Peter Steinbach, *Heimat: Eine deutsche Chronik*, Nordlingen, 1985.

Book:

Elsaesser, Thomas, *New German Cinema: A History*, London, 1989.
Kaes, Anton, *From Hitler to Heimat: The Return of History As Film*, Cambridge, 1992.

Articles:

Lughi, P., in *Cinema Nuovo* (Bari), August-October 1984.
Film (West Germany), September 1984.
Variety (New York), 12 September 1984.
Nave, B., and others, in *Jeune Cinéma* (Paris), November 1984.
Pawlikowski, P., ''Home Movies,'' in *Stills* (London), November 1984.
Detassis, P., in *Positif* (Paris), December 1984.
Frodon, J. M., ''L'Allemagne se souvient,'' in *Cahiers du Cinéma* (Paris), December 1984.
Chalmer, M., in *Framework* (Norwich), no. 26–27, 1985.
''Dossier Edgar Reitz,'' in *Bianco e Nero* (Rome), January-March 1985.
Elsaesser, Thomas, ''Memory, Home, and Hollywood,'' in *Monthly Film Bulletin* (London), February 1985.
Petit, Chris, in *Time Out* (London), 14–20 February 1985.
City Limits (London), 15–21 February 1985.
Le Roux, H., in *Cahiers du Cinéma* (Paris), March 1985.
Ranvaud, Don, and John Pym, ''Heimat, Home, and the World,'' in *Sight and Sound* (London), Spring 1985.
Syberberg, H. J., ''The Abode of the Gods,'' in *Sight and Sound* (London), Spring 1985.
Elsaesser, Thomas, ''Our Germany,'' in *American Film* (Washington, D.C.), May 1985.
Koch, Gertrud, ''Kann man naiv werden?,'' in *Frauen und Film* (Berlin), May 1985.
Bachman, G., ''The Reitz Stuff,'' in *Film Comment* (New York), July-August 1985.
Baron, Saskia, ''Home Truths,'' in *Cinema Papers* (Melbourne), July 1985.
Hager, F., in *Filmkunst*, August-September 1985.
Berndts, T., in *Skrien* (Amsterdam), Winter 1985–86.
Soderbergh Widding, A., in *Chaplin* (Stockholm), vol. 28, no. 1, 1986.
Listener (London), 10, 17, and 24 April 1986.
Birgel, Franz E., interview with Edgar Reitz, in *Film Quarterly* (Berkeley), Summer 1986.
Schneider, R., ''Aux antipodes du simplisme hollywoodien: *Heimat*,'' in *Cinemaction* (Conde-sur-Noireau, France), October 1990.
Angier, C., ''Edgar Reitz,'' in *Sight and Sound* (London), no. 1, 1990–91.
Andres, A., ''The Music of *Heimat*,'' in *Film Score Monthly* (Los Angeles), no. 51, November 1994.
Papen, M. von, ''Keeping the Home Fires Burning?: Women and the German Homefront Film 1940–1943,'' in *Film History* (London), vol. 8, no. 1, 1996.
Liebman, Stuart, ''*Heimat*: A Chronicle of Germany,'' in *Cineaste* (New York), vol. 22, no. 3, December 1996.

DIE ZWEITE HEIMAT

(Leaving Home; Heimat II)

Germany, 1992

Production: An Edgar Reitz Production; colour/black and white; running time: 1,532 minutes. Premiered at London Film Festival, November 1992.

Producer: Edgar Reitz; **screenplay:** Edgar Reitz; **photography:** Gernot Roll (parts 1–5), Gerard Vanderberg (6–8), Christian Reitz (9–13); **editor:** Susanne Hartman; **assistant director:** Robert Busch; **production designer:** Franz Bauer; **music:** Nikos Mamangakis; **sound:** Heiko Hinderks, Haymo Heyder, Manfred Banach, and Reiner Wiehr; **costumes:** Bille Brassers and Nikola Hoeltz.

Cast: Henry Arnold (*Hermann*); Salome Kammer (*Clarissa*); Anke Sevenich (*Schnusschen*); Daniel Smith (*Juan*); Michael Schonborn (*Alex*); Franziska Traub (*Renate*); Hannelore Hoger (*Elisabeth Cerphal*); Hanna Kohler (*Frau Moretti*); Gisela Muller (*Evelyne*); Michael Seyfried (*Ansgar*); Armin Fuchs (*Volker*); Martin Maria Blau (*Jean-Marie*); Lena Lessing (*Olga*); Peter Weiss (*Rob*); Frank Roth (*Stefan*); Laszlo I. Kish (*Reinhard*); Susanne Lothar (*Esther*); Veronika Ferres (*Dorli*); Franziska Stommer (*Frau Ries*); Manfred Andrae (*Gerold Gattinger*).

Publications

Articles:

Angier, C., ''Edgar Reitz,'' in *Sight and Sound* (London), Winter 1990–91.

Nodolny, Sten, ''On Leaving Home and Perfecting Oneself,'' in *The Sequel to Heimat*, Jutta Muller, editor, Cologne, 1991.

Albano, L., ''Tra arte e vita,'' in *Filmcritica* (Rome), September-October 1992.

Angier, C., ''Like Life Itself,'' in *Sight and Sound* (London), November 1992.

Hansen, E., *Variety* (New York), 7 December 1992.

Kilb, A., ''Scènes de la vie parallele,'' in *Positif* (Paris), January 1993.

Holloway, R., in *Kino* (Warsaw), May 1993.

Pezzotta, A., ''Imitation of Life,'' in *Segnocinema* (Vicenza), no. 63, September/October 1993.

Holden, S., ''Critic's Notebook: a 25 1/2-hour German Epic of Discovery and Art,'' in *New York Times*, vol. 142, 17 June 1993.

Mepham, John, ''Visionary Storytelling,'' in *Vertigo*, Spring 1994.

Andres, A., ''The Music of *Heimat*,'' in *Film Score Monthly* (Los Angeles), no. 51, November 1994.

Feldvoss, M., ''Hannelore Hoger: Energie und Eigensinn,'' in *EPD Film* (Frankfurt), March 1998.

* * *

Described as a ''chronicle in 11 parts,'' *Heimat* tells the story of the (fictional) village of Schabbach in the Hunsruck, a rural area of the southern Rhineland, between the years 1919 and 1982, focusing in particular on the members of one family, the Simons. It was shown on West German television in 1984, and was also screened as a film (over two days) in cinemas there. It has been widely seen, both as a film and a television series, in other European countries and in America.

When *Heimat* was shown in Germany it was a major media event, surpassed only by the television screening of the American mini-series *Holocaust* in 1979. In fact, the genesis of *Heimat* lay in its director Edgar Reitz's reaction to *Holocaust.* Reitz accused *Holocaust* of reducing the misery caused by the Nazis to a ''welcome background spectacle for a sentimental family story,'' of trivializing German history and, indeed, of willfully expropriating it for simplistic, entertainment purposes. He argued that what Germans needed to do was to take ''narrative possession of our past'' thus ''breaking free of the world of judgments and dealing with it through art.'' The way to do this, he argued, was to tell stories: ''there are thousands of stories among our people worth filming, which are based on endless minutiae of experience. These stories individually rarely seem to contribute to the evaluation and explanation of history, but taken together they could compensate for this lack. We should no longer forbid ourselves to take our personal lives seriously.'' The source of the problem is, of course, the Nazi past: ''we Germans have a hard time with our stories. It is our own history that is in our way. The year 1945, the nation's 'zero hour,' wiped out a lot, created a gap in people's ability to remember. As Mitscherlich put it, an entire people has been made 'unable to mourn.' In our case that means 'unable to tell stories' because our memories are obstructed by the great historical events they are connected with. Even now, 40 years after the war, we are still troubled by the weight of moral judgments, we are still afraid that our little personal stories could recall our Nazi past and remind us of our mass participation in the Third Reich. . . . Our film, *Heimat*, consists of these suppresed or forgotten little stories. It is a chronicle of both a family and a village and is an attempt of sorts to revive memories. . . .We try to avoid making judgements.''

Heimat, then, is an example of what has come to be known as ''history from below,'' an interest in which has increasingly come to the fore in many European countries. It is concerned with oral history, the personal experiences of ordinary people, folklore, the local, the regional, ''popular memory'' and so on.

Heimat is not only a celebration of the ''positive human values and hopes'' of the rural community, it is also a lament for their passing. Indeed, a sense of loss and of nostalgia imbues the film's very title, which cannot be adequately translated into English. As Reitz himself has explained: ''the word is always linked to strong feeling, mostly remembrances and longing. 'Heimat' always evokes in me the feeling of something lost or very far away, something which one cannot easily find or find again.'' In a remarkable study of the film, Anton Kaes traces the concern with ''Heimat'' back to the late nineteenth century and the reaction against rapid industrialisation and urbanisation: ''Heimat was precisely that which was abandoned on the way into the cities; from then on the word 'Heimat' began to connote 'region,' 'province' and 'country'. . . . Heimat means the site of one's lost childhood, of family, of identity. It also stands for the possibility of secure human relations, unalienated, precapitalist labour, and the romantic harmony between the country dweller and nature. Heimat refers to everything that is not distant and foreign. . . . It conjured up a rural, archaic image of the German Reich and a German community rooted in ahistorical, mythic time.''

Reaction to the film in Germany, and elsewhere in Europe, was extremely positive. It was only when *Heimat* was shown in the United

States that the negative opinions which *had* been expressed in Germany gained a wider hearing. In the light of the above this should not have been surprising; as Thomas Elsaesser noted, calling a German film *Heimat* was a ''calculated provocation and was bound to be controversial.'' Likewise Anton Kaes: ''scenes of provincial life are never innocent in Germany.''

According to its critics, *Heimat's* main problems lie as much in what it does not show as what it does. The argument here is one leveled against any broadly realist text, namely, that it cannot escape from the mental horizons of its protagonists. The same criticism can be leveled at some versions of the ''history from below'' mentioned earlier. Major political events and wider economic factors, which undoubtedly have their influences on individual private lives, are ignored or glossed over because that is what the characters themselves do. This might matter rather less if that history did not include the Third Reich. Indeed, almost half of the film takes place in the years 1933–45. Writing in the *New York Review of Books*, Timothy Garten Ash stated: ''when you show the 1930s as a golden age of prosperity and excitement in the German countryside, when you are shown Germans as victims of the war, then you inevitably find yourself asking: But what about the other side? What about Auschwitz?'' Or as one of the film's sternest critics, Gertrud Koch, has it: ''in order to tell the myth of 'Heimat,' the trauma of Auschwitz had to be shut out of the story.'' The Third Reich seems almost to take place off screen, and when Nazi activities *are* presented (which is not often) it's in a curiously elliptical fashion and usually without much explanation—on the grounds, presumably, that this is how they were actually experienced by the characters. Accommodation with the Nazi regime is shown largely as comical, or merely opportunistic, or as the result of seduction of one form or another. Admittedly one or two characters—a Jew, a Communist—disappear, but no one seems to show the slightest curiosity about this. Again, all this might matter less were it not for the historical fact that the countryside was extraordinarily important to the National Socialists ideologically, politically andeconomically, and found a good deal of support amongst the peasantry. Reitz himself has said that to have taken on the Jewish question would have ''overburdened the narrative'' and that ''the story would have immediately taken a different turn.'' He has also argued that there were very few Jews in the Hunsruck and that people there were largely ignorant of Nazi genocide.

Unease about the representation of the Third Reich period is further compounded by the way in which postwar, modern Germany is shown. In short, it appears to be downhill all the way, and the main villain here is definitely America. (One begins to see why it was in America that misgivings about the film were voiced). But this is only the most extreme instance of a process throughout the film whereby no good comes from events, influences or people outside the Edenic, pastoral idyll of the Hunsruck. This comes dangerously close to a reactionary agrarian romanticism with disturbing similarities to the ''Blood and Soil'' ideology; moreover, it also seems to suggest that all of Germany's contemporary problems, whether it's the despoilation of the countryside or people's inability to connect with their past, can be laid at the door of the Americans, thereby neatly letting the past 100 years of German capitalism (in which the Third Reich and the ''Wirtschaftswunder'' were both highly significant episodes) neatly off the historical hook.

Die Zweite Heimat is a project even more epic than its predecessor, although it spans a much more limited time period. The entire film runs a remarkable 26 hours (cinema screenings are normally spread over three or four days, television over 13 episodes) and took a total of seven years to make, of which 552 days were taken up by shooting. There are 71 main roles, 310 smaller ones, and 2300 extras. The budget of DM40m was put together by television companies in Germany, Britain, Spain, Finland, Denmark, Norway and Austria, an indication of the enormous popularity of *Heimat* outside Germany. Although extremely well received both in Germany and abroad it was not a media event of the same proportions as the first film and, to date at least, has attracted rather less critical attention. This may be because the subject matter, and Reitz's handling of it, is simply less controversial, but it would be paradoxical indeed if this were to limit discussion of what is an undoubted masterpiece.

Die Zweite Heimat's central character is Hermann Simon, born in 1940 in the Hunsruck into the family at the centre of *Heimat.* At the start of the film he moves to Munich, vowing never to return home, to devote his life to music, and never to love again. Eventually all three vows are broken, and his love affair with the young musician Clarissa runs like a connecting thread throughout the length of the film.

If *Heimat* is about the country, stability, older generations, people who lived and died where they were born, *Die Zweite Heimat* is about the city, change, the young, those who pull up their roots. In the first film people are connected by blood ties and the pull of an ancient, close-knit community; in the second by friendship, love, commitment to art and ideas, rejection of the past, and a desire for a better present and future. Quite clearly the title signifies much more than that this is the second part of *Heimat;* there is a very strong sense of ''second home'' here. As Hermann puts it at the start of the film: ''I left for Munich's bright lights and mysteries I refused to look back even once. Ahead of me lay freedom. I would be born a second time, not from my mother's body but from my own mind. I would seek my own, my second home.'' And, since these are very much times remembered from a distance, times which include Reitz's own youthful experiences, the sense of loss and longing that imbues the word ''Heimat'' is as present here (if perhaps less obviously so) as in the first film.

With 26 hours at its disposal, *Die Zweite Heimet* succeeds where many films fail—it captures the feeling of life as it is actually lived. Characters appear, disappear, reappear much later, or not at all; at different moments different characters are predominant or subordinate; things are left unexplained and unresolved; pace and tone change from episode to episode, sometimes even within the same episode. Reitz has drawn the analogy with a stream which sometimes flows on the surface, then disappears below ground, only to rise again much later on and further away.

If one of the problems with *Heimat* was that its basically realist aesthetic meant that it was tied to the limited perceptions of its provincial characters, Reitz avoids this here by presenting us with a very different set of characters and, more importantly, by adopting a different aesthetic approach. Hermann and his friends are people who spend their lives thinking and analysing, they live and breathe ideas, they want their lives to connect with the wider world of history and politics, and above all they're interested in the relationship between their various forms of artistic practice and society at large. Indeed, the whole epic project of *Die Zweite Heimat* can be seen as a profound reflection on the nature and value of avant-garde artistic activity, and the fact that it eventually founders here is due not to the shortcomings of its practitioners but to the destructive influence of external, indeed global, forces. Reitz, as himself, along with Alexander Kluge, one of the most aesthetically radical of the new German filmmakers at one time with films such as *Cardillac, Geschichten vom Kubelkind* and *Das Goldene Ding*, presents us with a remarkably insightful and sympathetic portrait of the avant-garde, but ultimately he does not shy away from suggesting that whilst these artists were dreaming of creating the alternative society, the history that was being made behind their backs was preparing to render their efforts somewhat irrelevant.

However, unlike in *Heimat*, Reitz here remembers the avant-garde critique of the shortcomings of realism, and although he by no means abandons realism entirely, he subverts it to a quite remarkable degree. Perhaps the clearest example of Reitz's approach here is provided by the end of the crucial episode which includes the assassination of Kennedy and signals the beginning of the end for Hermann and his friends. On hearing the news, the group gather in Hermann's room, and the episode closes with a deliberately stagey, clearly fabricated and non-naturalistic shot as they all look up simultaneously to a mirror, on which there is a photo of Kennedy and Khruschev, and contemplate their collective image. This is one of the film's most obvious and decisive breaks with realism and, as Mepham has put it: "What this shot exemplifies is Reitz's method of moving beyond naturalistic image-making and the conventions of realist storytelling, to conjure up a polysemic image, which transcends its literal meaning and proposes a symbolic framework in terms of which we can read the entire episode."

One could also mention, in this context of breaks with realism, the remarkable number of times that the film self-reflexively foregrounds moments of performance of one kind or another, but even more striking, in this respect, is its use of colour and black-and-white. As a general (though by no means unbroken) rule, Reitz uses black-and-white for the daytime scenes, and colour for the night ones. The spectator is thus forced to take notice of colour, rather than unconsciously accepting it as part and parcel of the apparently literal representation of the fictional world. Here, colour, or black-and-white, become significant in their own right, and are clearly labelled as such. In a general sense, black-and-white signifies that, for Hermann and his friends, the days are dull, banal and anodyne, whilst the use of colour underlines the fact that it is at night that they really come alive. But it is much more complex than that; as Mepham puts it, throughout the film "the literal or naturalistic quality of the image is always in question, because there is no one style of image which we can accept as simply showing us what the fictional world is like. Therefore we become used to looking for more than literal significance. Visual poetry becomes the norm, and light and colour become radiant with meaning." Again, the Kennedy episode provides a good example. This opens with one of the most beautiful and haunting images of the entire film: a slow pan in the early morning light across bare trees in which crows are settling. The scene is accompanied by a song about crows, which contains the line: "soon it will snow. Lucky is he who still has a home." There is no question but that this scene has hugely symbolic, connotative overtones; we, the spectators, know exactly what is going to happen on this day, but the characters most certainly do not. However, there is no question of us being asked to accept their viewpoints here—and indeed, this opening is not observed by any of them, it is pure directorial inervention, a deliberate establishing of the symbolic framework which imbues the entire episode, much of whose poignancy stems from the spectator (and of course Reitz) knowing what the characters do not and cannot know. Here, as in many other striking scenes in this truly extraordinary film, Reitz manages triumphantly to pull off the extremely difficult feat of departing from conventional realist practices whilst at the same time presenting an epic fiction which is not only entirely coherent in its own right but deeply moving and thought-provoking at the same time.

—Julian Petley

THE HEIR OF GENGHIS KHAN

See **POTOMOK CHINGIS-KHANA**

HENRY V

UK, 1944

Director: Laurence Olivier

Production: Two Cities Film, presented by Eagle-Lion; Technicolor, 35mm; running time: 153 minutes, some versions are 137 minutes. Released 22 November 1944, Carlton Theatre, London. Filmed 9 June 1943–12 July 1944 in Enniskerry, Eire; and at Denham and Pinewood Studios, England. Cost: about £400,000.

Producers: Laurence Olivier with Dallas Bower; **screenplay:** Laurence Olivier and Alan Dent, from the play by William Shakespeare; **photography:** Robert Krasker; **editor:** Reginald Beck; **sound recordists:** John Dennis and Desmond Drew; **art directors:** Paul Sheriff assisted by Carmen Dillon; **scenic art:** E. Lindgaard; **music:** William Walton; **conductor:** Muir Mathieson; **played by:** London Symphony Orchestra; **special effects:** Percy Day; **costume designers:** Roger Furse assisted by Margaret Furse; the film is dedicated to the Commandos and Airborne Troops of Great Britain—"the spirits of whose ancestors it has humbly attempted to recapture"

Cast: Leslie Banks (*Chorus*); Felix Aylmer (*Archbishop of Canterbury*); Robert Helpmann (*Bishop of Ely*); Vernon Greeves (*English Herald*); Gerald Case (*Earl of Westmorland*); Griffith Jones (*Earl of Salisbury*); Morland Graham (*Sir Thomas Erpingham*); Nicholas Hannen (*Duke of Exeter*); Michael Warre (*Duke of Gloucester*); Laurence Olivier (*King Henry V*); Ralph Truman (*Montjoy, the French Herald*); Ernest Thesiger (*Duke of Berri, French Ambassador*); Frederick Cooper (*Corporal Nym*); Roy Emerton (*Lieutenant Bardolph*); Robert Newton (*Pistol*); Freda Jackson (*Mistress Quickley, the Hostess*); George Cole (*Boy*); George Robey (*Sir John Falstaff*); Harcourt Williams (*King Charles VI of France*); Leo Genn (*Constable of France*); Francis Lister (*Duke of Orleans*); Max Adrian (*Dauphin*); Jonathan Field (*French Messenger*); Esmond Knight (*Fluellen*); Michael Shepley (*Gower*); John Laurie (*Jamy*); Nial MacGinnis (*Macmorris*); Frank Tickle (*Governor of Harfleur*); Renée Asherson (*Princess Katherine*); Ivy St. Helier (*Lady Alice*); Janet Burnell (*Queen Isabel of France*); Brian Nissen (*Court, camp-boy*); Arthur Hambling (*John Bates*); Jimmy Hanley (*Michael Williams*); Ernest Hare (*Priest*); Valentine Dyall (*Duke of Burgundy*); and Infantry and Cavalry by members of the Eire Home Guard.

Awards: Special Oscar to Laurence Olivier for his Outstanding Achievement as Actor, Producer, and Director in bringing *Henry V* to the screen, 1946; New York Film Critics' Award, Best Actor, 1946; Venice Film Festival, Special Mention, 1946.

Henry V

Publications

Script:

Olivier, Laurence, and Alan Dent, *Henry V*, in *Film Scripts One*, edited by George P. Garrett, New York, 1971.

Books:

Oakley, C. A., *Where We Came In: 70 Years of the British Film Industry*, London, 1964.
Whitehead, Peter, and Robin Bean, *Olivier-Shakespeare*, London, 1966.
Darlington, W. A., *Laurence Olivier*, London, 1968.
Eckert, Charles W., editor, *Focus on Shakespearian Films*, Englewood Cliffs, New Jersey, 1972.
Geduld, Harry M., editor, *A Filmguide to Henry V*, Bloomington, Indiana, 1973.
Perry, George, *The Great British Picture Show, from the 90s to the 70s*, New York, 1974.
Barsacq, Leon, *Caligari's Cabinet and Other Grand Illusions: A History of Film Design*, New York, 1976.
Morley, Margaret, editor, *Olivier: The Films and Faces of Laurence Olivier*, Godalming, Surrey, 1978.
Hirsch, Foster, *Laurence Olivier*, Boston, 1979; revised edition, 1984.
Daniels, Robert, *Laurence Olivier: Theatre and Cinema*, London, 1980.
Olivier, Laurence, *Confessions of an Actor: An Autobiography*, New York, 1982.
Barker, Felix, *Laurence Olivier: A Critical Study*, Tunbridge Wells, Kent, 1984.
Bragg, Melvin, *Laurence Olivier*, London, 1984.
Silviria, Dale, *Laurence Olivier and the Art of Filmmaking*, Rutherford, New Jersey, 1985.
Tanitch, Robert, *Olivier: The Complete Career*, London, 1985.
Dunster, Mark, *Olivier*, Hollywood, 1993.
Spoto, Donald, *Laurence Olivier: A Biography*, New York, 1993.
Lewis, Roger, *The Real Life of Laurence Olivier*, New York, 1999.
Granger, Derek, *Laurence Olivier: The Life of an Actor: The Authorized Biography*, New York, 1999.

Articles:

Variety (New York), 24 April 1946.
New York Times, 16 June 1946.
Agee, James, *Agee on Film 1*, New York, 1958.
McVay, Douglas, ''Hamlet to Clown,'' in *Films and Filming* (London), September 1962.

Brown, Constance, in *Film Quarterly* (Berkeley), Summer 1967.
Hart, Henry, "Laurence Olivier," in *Films in Review* (New York), December 1967.
McCreadie, M., "Onstage and on Film," in *Literature/Film Quarterly* (Salisbury, Maryland), Fall 1977.
Manheim, M., "Olivier's Henry V and the Elizabethan World Picture," in *Literature/Film Quarterly* (Salisbury, Maryland), July 1983.
Reid's Film Index (Wyong), no. 4, 1990.
Martini, E., in *Cineforum* (Bergamo, Italy), July-August, 1990.
Nichols, Peter, "A Classy Tale," in *Sight & Sound* (London), vol. 1, no. 6, October 1991.
Deats, S. M., "Rabbits and Ducks: Olivier, Branagh, and *Henry V*," in *Literature/Film Quarterly* (Salisbury, Maryland), no. 4, 1992.
Manheim, M., "The Function of Battle Imagery in Kurosawa's Histories and the *Henry V* Films," in *Literature/Film Quarterly* (Salisbury), vol. 22, no. 2, April 1994.
Buhler, S.M., "Text, Eyes, and Videotape: Screening Shakespeare's Scripts," in *Shakespeare Quarterly*, vol. 46, no. 2, 1995.
Crowdus, Gary, in *Cineaste* (New York), vol. 22, no. 1, April 1996.
Bibliography, in *Shakespeare Quarterly*, vol. 47, no. 5, 1996.
Griffin, C.W., "Henry V's Decision: Interrogataive [sic] Texts," in *Literature/Film Quarterly* (Salisbury), vol. 25, no. 2, April 1997.
Royal, Derek, "Shakespeare's Kingly Mirror: Figuring the Chorus in Olivier's and Branagh's *Henry V*," in *Literature/Film Quarterly* (Salisbury), vol. 25, no. 2, April 1997.
Bibliography, in *Shakespeare Quarterly*, vol. 48, no. 5, 1997.

* * *

At the beginning of his career Laurence Olivier did not specialize in interpreting Shakespearean roles on the screen. He had played many of Shakespeare's greatest characters on stage, and was especially praised for having alternated with John Gielgud in the roles of Romeo and Mercutio in the 1935 production of *Romeo and Juliet* at London's New Theatre. He was charming in the 1936 film production of *As You Like It* as Orlando, but he really didn't take his film career seriously until 1939, when he played Heathcliff in Goldwyn's production of *Wuthering Heights*.

With the coming of war, his filmmaking was largely curtailed, but more than halfway through the conflict, when the Allied victory seemed certain, Olivier was released from his military duties to produce, direct, and star in a film to be made from Shakespeare's *Henry V*. Because the play is so patriotic, it was thought by the British government that the project would create a wonderful piece of nationalistic propaganda. Olivier had already played *Henry V* at the Old Vic, and knew what he wanted to achieve—a movie version that would restore glory to the common man's thinking about his own country.

There were some preliminary setbacks. David O. Selznick refused to allow Vivien Leigh to play the role of the French Princess Katherine; he thought it too small a role for the star of *Gone with the Wind*. Olivier chose Renée Asherson, Robert Donat's wife, for the part. He wanted William Wyler as director, because Wyler had directed him in *Wuthering Heights*. But Wyler was busy on another project, and suggested that Olivier himself direct the film. Olivier considered it, and began preproduction work, but the film might never have been made, were it not for the efforts of an Italian lawyer, Filippo del Giudice, who had been the driving force behind Nöel Coward in *In Which We Serve*. Del Giudice wanted another patriotic classic, and he eased Olivier's working budget of £300,000 upward more than another £100,000 for *Henry V*.

Olivier, preparing his own screenplay from the Shakespearean text, cut the play nearly a quarter so that he could give ample time to the staging of the Battle of Agincourt. He lifted the death of Falstaff from the last scenes of *Henry IV, Part II*, wisely casting a music hall comedian, George Robey, as Falstaff. He decided to begin his picture and end it as if it were a performance at the Globe Theatre in the time of Shakespeare, who had created the device himself when, in the lines of the Chorus in the Prologue, he instructs the audience, "On your imaginary forces work," leaving the way open for a very inventive cinematic trick: the camera pulls back, and we are out of the Globe and immediately into the conflict.

The critic for *Time* wrote: "At last there has been brought to the screen, with such sweetness, vigor, insight and beauty that it seemed to have been written yesterday, a play by the greatest dramatic poet who ever lived." *Henry V* ran for five months in London, and it played on Broadway for 46 weeks. It opened the door for Olivier to other Shakespearean films. His *Hamlet* (1948) came next; then *Richard III* (1955). Ten years later in 1965 it was *Othello*, with Olivier as the Moor of Venice.

—DeWitt Bodeen

HERR ARNES PENGAR

(Sir Arne's Treasure)

Sweden, 1919

Director: Mauritz Stiller

Production: Svenska Biografteatern; black and white; running time: 100 minutes (78 minutes at 18 f.p.s.); length: 5,226 feet. Released 1919.

Screenplay: Gustav Molander, Mauritz Stiller, from the novel by Selma Lagerlöf; **photography:** Julius Jaenson; **art directors:** Harry Dahlstrom, Alexander Bako; **costumes:** Axel Esbensen.

Cast: Mary Johnson (*Elsalill*); Richard Lund (*Sir Archy*); Hjalmar Selander (*Sir Arne*); Concordia Selander (*Arne's Wife*); Wanda Rothgardt (*Berghild*); Erik Stocklassa (*Sir Philip*); Bror Berger (*Sir Donald*); Axel Nilsson (*Torarin*); Gustaf Aronson (*Ship's Captain*); Stina Berg (*Innkeeper*); with Dagmar Ebbeson, Gösta Gustafsson.

Publications

Books:

Idestam-Almquist, Bengt, *Den Svenska Filmens Drama: Sjöström och Stiller*, Stockholm, 1938.
Hardy, Forsyth, *Scandinavian Film*, London, 1951.

Herr Arnes Pengar

Idestam-Almquist, Bengt, *Classics of the Swedish Cinema*, Stockholm, 1952.
Waldekranz, Rune, *Swedish Cinema*, Stockholm, 1959.
Beranger, Jean, *La Grande Aventure du cinéma suedois*, Paris, 1960.
Lauritzen, Einar, *Swedish Films*, New York, 1962.
Cowie, Peter, *Swedish Cinema*, London, 1966.
Anthologie du cinema 3, Paris, 1968.
Werner, Gösta, *Mauritz Stiller och hans filmer*, Stockholm, 1969.
Werner, Gösta, P. A. Norstedt, and Soners Forlag, *Herr Arnes Pengar*, Stockholm, 1969.

Articles:

Bioscope (London), 15 January 1920.
Kine Weekly (London), 15 January 1920.
Film Daily, 11 December 1921.
New York Times, 25 December 1921.
Variety (New York), 2 December 1925.
O'Leary, Liam, in *Films and Filming* (London), August 1960.
Milne, Tom, in *Monthly Film Bulletin* (London), December 1977.
Robertson, JoAnne, ''Maurice Stiller,'' in *Monthly Film Bulletin* (London), December 1977.
Brewster, B., and G. Sadoul, in *Filmviews* (Mitcham), vol. 30, no. 123, Autumn 1985.
Lefebvre, Thierry, ''Mary Johnson: *Le trésor du Trésor d'Arne*,'' in *Archives: Institut Jean Vigo* (Perpignan), no. 60, February 1995.
Short Review, in *Télérama* (Paris), no. 2354, 22 February 1995.

* * *

Nineteen-hundred and nineteen was a good year for cinema: *The Cabinet of Dr. Caligari*, Lubitsch's *Madame Dubarry*, Griffith's *Broken Blossoms* and Gance's *J'accuse*. From Sweden came what is probably Mauritz Stiller's best film, *Herr Arnes Pengar*. Based on Selma Lagerlöf's story this ''winter ballad'' won universal acclaim for its sensitive artistry and technical skill.

The sophisticated and authoritarian Stiller evoked the mood and feeling of sixteenth-century Sweden in the reign of John the Third. Set in a ravaged landscape during a severe winter, it tells of the activities of three mercenary Scottish officers who have escaped from prison after their armies have been banished by the king. Crazed by hunger and drink, they set fire to the parsonage of Solberga and murder all but one of the family, the adopted child Elsalill. Laden with the treasure they have stolen, they escape across the ice. By a quirk of fate Elsalill unknowingly falls in love with Sir Archy, one of the three murderers. On discovering his guilty secret, she is persuaded to denounce him to the town guard. Using her as a shield, he escapes his would-be captors but Elsalill diverts a spear-thrust meant for him to herself. At last a ship that will take him home is reached although it is still frozen in the bay. He sits beside Elsalill's body until the guards arrive to seize the guilty men. The people of Marstrand file across the frozen harbour and carry the body of Elsalill back to the town. With the evil-doers removed, the ice binding the ship melts and it sails into the open sea.

The dramatic structure is such that suspense is ever present and the doomed love affair moves to its tragic close in a deeply felt visual treatment. The camera is used most effectively to create a series of unforgettable images with taste and discretion. The moving camera is used sparingly while the iris ''in and out'' is used both for emphasis and smooth transition in the advancement of the story.

The snowy Swedish landscape dominates the film. The dwellings and the behaviour of the people have an air of authenticity. The texture of the costumes is a feature of the sensitive camerawork. A historical period is convincingly brought to life.

There is a dark occult motivation in the film, too, which plays a considerable part: the vision of the parson's wife before the attack: ''Why are they sharpening knives at Branehög?'' Elsalill's dream leads her to the tavern where she hears Sir Archy and his companions talking about their loot from the parsonage. The fisherman Torarin's dog, Grim, senses the evil that is near.

Visually the film is very impressive, especially in the scenes of the escape of the murderers across the ice, laden with their ill-gotten treasure chest. The great finale of the procession of the Marstranders across the frozen harbour to the ship must have influenced Eisenstein's treatment of the procession of the people of Moscow to Ivan the Terrible at Alexandrov. The film owes much to the camerawork of Julius Jaenson, a valued collaborator in the great films of Stiller and Sjöström.

Mary Johnson as Elsalill gives a memorable performance and was moulded by Stiller for the role in the same way he was later to introduce Garbo to the screen. Stiller was an autocratic director and made difficult demands on his players. The physical conditions involved in the production did much to give a painful realism to the film, and the winter hazards encountered during production became part of the mise-en-scène.

The film won critical acclaim outside its country of origin. English critics, for example, could say: ''It is notable for its very advanced and original technique as for its brilliant acting it is a credit to the art of the film.'' And again, ''It stands out clearly amongst the greatest of screen productions. It is great art.'' Certainly it is one of the greatest adornments of the Golden Age of Swedish cinema.

—Liam O'Leary

HIDDEN STAR

See **MEGHE DHAKA TARA**

HIGANBANA

(Equinox Flower)

Japan, 1958

Director: Yasujiro Ozu

Production: Schochiku; Agfacolor, 35mm; running time: 118 minutes. Released 1958.

Screenplay: Kogo Noda, Yasujiro Ozu, from a novel by Ton Satomi; **photography:** Yushun Atsuta; **editing:** Yoshiyasu Hamamura; **sound:** Yoshisaburo Seno; **art direction:** Tatsuo Hamada; **lighting:** Akira Aomatsu; **music:** Takayori Saito.

Cast: Shin Saburi (*Watara Hirayama*); Kinoyo Tanaka (*Kiyoko Hirayama*); Ineko Arima (*Setsuko Hirayama*); Miyuki Kuwano (*Hisako Hirayama*); Keiji Sada (*Masahiko Taniguchi*); Chieko Naniwa (*Hajime Sasaki*); Fujiko Yamamo (*Yukiko Sasaki*); Nobuo Nakamu (*Toshihiko Kawai*); Chishu Ryu (*Shukichi Mikami*); Yoshiko Kuga (*Fumiko Mikami*); Teiji Takahashi (*Shotaro Kondo*); Fumio Watanab (*Ichiro Naganuma*).

Publications

Books:

Anderson, Joseph, and Donald Richie, *The Japanese Film: Art and Industry*, New York, 1960.
Richie, Donald, *Five Pictures of Yasujiro Ozu*, Tokyo, 1962.
Richie, Donald, *The Japanese Movie: An Illustrated History*, Tokyo, 1966.
Richie, Donald, *Japanese Cinema: Film Style and National Character*, New York, 1971.
Sato, Tadao, *Ozu Yasujiro no Geijutsu* [The Art of Yasujiro Ozu], Tokyo, 1971.
Satomi, Jun, and others, *Ozu Yasujiro: Hito to shigoto* [Yasujiro Ozu: The Man and His Work], Tokyo, 1972.
Schrader, Paul, *Transcendental Style in Film: Ozu, Bresson, Dreyer*, Berkeley, 1972.
Burch, Noel, *Theory of Film Practice*, New York, 1973.
Tessier, Max, in *Anthologie du Cinema 7*, Paris, 1973.
Richie, Donald, *Ozu*, Berkeley, 1974.
Schrader, Leonard, and Haruji Nakamura, editors, *Masters of Japanese Film*, Tokyo, 1975.
Bock, Audie, *Japanese Film Directors*, New York, 1978; revised edition, Tokyo, 1985.
Burch, Noel, *To the Distant Observer*, Berkeley, 1979.
Tessier, Max, editor, *Le Cinéma japonais au présent 1959–1979*, Paris, 1980.
Sato, Tadao, *Currents in Japanese Cinema*, Tokyo, 1982.

Higanbana

Shindo, Kaneto, *Joyu Tanaka Kinuyo*, Tokyo, 1983.
Bordwell, David, *Ozu and the Poetics of Cinema*, Princeton, 1988.

Articles:

Uni-Japan Quarterly, January 1959.
Film Quarterly (Berkeley), Fall 1959.
Whitebait, William, in *New Statesman* (London), 31 October 1959.
''Ozu Issue'' of *Kinema Jumpo* (Tokyo), February 1964.
Philippe, Jean-Claude, ''Yasujiro Ozu,'' in *Dossiers du cinema 1*, Paris, 1971.
Branigan, Edward, ''The Space of Equinox Flower,'' in *Screen* (London), Summer 1976.
Thompson, Kristin, and David Bordwell, ''Space and Narrative in the Films of Ozu,'' in *Screen* (London), Summer 1976.
''Ozu Issue'' of *Cinéma* (Paris), February 1981.
Liola, S., and A. Iwaskak, ''Gesprek met Ozu,'' in *Skrien* (Amsterdam), Winter 1983–84.
''Ozu, la vita e la geometria dei film,'' in *Castoro Cinema* (Florence), no. 151, 1991.
Wood, R., ''The Noriko Trilogy,'' in *Cineaction* (Toronto), Winter 1992.
Casas, Q., ''*Flores de equinoccio*,'' in *Nosferatu* (San Sebastian), no. 25/26, December 1997.
Zunzunegui, S., ''Voces distantes,'' in *Nosferatu* (San Sebastian), no. 25/26, December 1997.

*   *   *

Though one can agree with Noel Burch (*To the Distant Observer*) that Ozu's work declined into academicism, it is possible to date the decline much later, restricting it to his last few films: it seems significant that two of them (*Ohayo* and *Floating Weeds*) are remakes of much earlier works and inferior to the originals, giving an impression of fatigue. It may also be significant that, when he began to work in colour, Ozu abandoned camera movement altogether, thereby relinquishing an expressive and/or formal potential the more effective for being used so sparingly. There is not a single camera movement in Ozu's last six films: his obsession with precise composition seems to have intensified, and he refused to disturb the constructed image by moving the camera. One can analyse in most of Ozu's films a tension between conservative and radical impulses; towards the end, the conservatism dominates, as one can see if one compares *Late Autumn* to *Late Spring*.

Equinox Flower, the first of the six colour films, stands quite apart from its successors, retaining a wonderful freshness of invention, a sense of energy and playfulness; it is also (and this is surely no coincidence) the closest Ozu came to making an explicitly feminist film (one might borrow a title from Mizoguchi and rename it *Victory of Women*). Here, the radical impulse triumphs, and the film's consistent vivacity comes across as a celebration of this. It can be read as a coda to what can be called Ozu's Setsuko Hara trilogy. Hara was clearly too old to play ''her'' character (resisting, here, not marriage *per se*, but *arranged* marriage); accordingly, the character is named not Noriko but Setsuko. Here, as in *Early Summer* and unlike in *Late Spring*, the young woman wins the right to decide her own destiny. This is essentially why *Late Spring* had to be a tragedy and *Equinox Flower* a comedy.

There has been very little critical discussion of the question of identification in Ozu's films. Understandably: Western critics have been preoccupied with the uniqueness of Ozu's methodology, and every component of it seems calculated to preclude the possibility of identification. ''Seems'' but isn't: identification is a complex phenomenon and the achievement of a contemplative distance does not preclude it but merely redefines its nature. Ozu totally rejects the technical apparatus of identification, most obviously the point-of-view shot. *Early Summer* actually contains what (given Ozu's well-documented knowledge of and fondness for the Hollywood cinema) we must take as a Hitchcock joke: Two characters walk down a corridor, the camera tracking back before them; cut to a forward point-of-view tracking shot. But then we realize that this is a different corridor in a different building, unconnected with the characters whose point-of-view we thought we were sharing. Ozu's camera is never judgmental: the most unsympathetic characters are filmed in exactly the same way as the most sympathetic. Our judgement of them, unprejudiced by camera angle, lighting, ''significant'' music, must therefore be truly *ours*: we are left free to assess their behaviour, actions, values, virtues, limitations. This does not so much preclude identification as set it free: the play of our sympathies can shift from character to character, or be divided between two or more characters at the same time. The films can be argued to be (often) about the complexity of point of view, though they are certainly not reducible to ''Everyone has his reasons'' or ''Tout comprendre, c'est tout pardonner.'' Ozu's judgement is always firm and clear, but it is defined in the movement of the scenario, not imposed by cinematic rhetoric.

Two conflicting levels of sympathy/identification are always present in Ozu's work, the conflict becoming central to the later, post-World War II films: identification with the figure of the threatened or displaced patriarch, identification with the female characters. *Equinox Flower* enacts this conflict most vividly. The theme of the film is the education by women of the traditional Japanese patriarch (Michael Uno's *The Wash* contains so many thematic and structural parallels that one wonders whether there was a direct connection between the two films). The strong feminist thrust of Ozu's films (which few seem to have perceived, though the last 15 minutes of *Tokyo Story* alone should be enough to make it obvious) is strengthened, not weakened, by the empathy he evidently feels for his patriarchs: he understands their position completely, he knows how they feel because a part of him feels the same way, and he knows that their position has become untenable. The logical climax of *Equinox Flower*, absolutely demanded by narrative convention, is the wedding of the patriarch's daughter to the man that *she*, not her father, has chosen. Ozu declines to show it, substituting the reunion of the father with his aging ex-fellow students, which culminates in a communal expression of nostalgia for values that they all recognize to be obsolete. After it, the ''victory of women''—to which all the female characters variously contribute (the film is magnificent on the subject of female solidarity)—can be completed, and the father is led to accept his daughter's right to her own judgement and choice. The film never sentimentalizes love matches by suggesting that they are likely to be any more successful than arranged ones, but it is quite unambiguous on the woman's right to reach her own decision.

The celebratory effect of the film's ending is underlined by Ozu's use of colour. He was fascinated by bright red, and in his first colour film he allowed this predilection free play. Especially, a red chair in the family's hallway figures prominently in shot after shot, yet it is always empty. Then, when the women's victory is confirmed by the phone-call in which the father finally agrees to visit his daughter and her husband, the wife at last sits in it in triumph, as on a throne. Ozu cuts to a line of washing on which a scarlet shirt stands out: a fireworks display could not have been more eloquent.

Finally, note the exactness of the film's title: ''Equinox Flower,'' the flower that blossoms out of a time of change.

—Robin Wood

HIGH NOON

USA, 1952

Director: Fred Zinnemann

Production: Stanley Kramer Productions; black and white, 35mm; running time: 84 minutes. Released 1952 by United Artists.

Producer: Stanley Kramer; **screenplay:** Carl Foreman, from the story ''The Tin Star'' by John W. Cunningham; **photography:** Floyd Crosby; **editors:** Elmo Williams and Harry Gerstad; **sound:** James Speak; **art director:** Rudolph Sternad; **music:** Dmitri Tiomkin; **song:** ''High Noon'' by Dmitri Tiomkin and Ned Washington, sung by Tex Ritter.

Cast: Gary Cooper (*Will Kane*); Thomas Mitchell (*Jonas Henderson*); Lloyd Bridges (*Harvey Pell*); Katy Jurado (*Helen Ramirez*); Grace Kelly (*Amy Kane*); Otto Kruger (*Percy Mettrick*); Ian MacDonald (*Frank Miller*); Lon Chaney (*Martin Howe*); Harry Morgan (*Sam Fuller*); Eve McVeagh (*Mildred Fuller*); Harry Shannon (*Cooper*); Lee Van Cleef (*Jack Colby*); Bob Wilke (*James Pierce*); Sheb Wooley (*Ben Miller*); Tom London (*Sam*); Ted Stanhope (*Station master*); Larry Blake (*Gillis*); William Phillips (*Barber*); Jeanne Blackford (*Mrs. Henderson*); James Millican (*Baker*); Jack Elam (*Charlie*).

Awards: Oscar for Best Actor (Cooper), Best Film Editing, Best Scoring of a Dramatic or Comedy Picture, and Best Song, 1952; New York Film Critics' Awards for Best Motion Picture and Best Direction, 1952.

High Noon

Publications

Script:

Foreman, Carl, *High Noon*, in *Three Major Screenplays*, edited by Malvin Ward and Michael Werner, New York, 1973.

Books:

Griffith, Richard, *Fred Zinnemann*, New York, 1958.
Fenin, George N., *The Western: From Silents to Cinerama*, New York, 1962.
Gehman, Richard, *The Tall American: The Story of Gary Cooper*, New York, 1963.
Dickens, Homer, *The Films of Gary Cooper*, New York, 1970.
Jordan, Rene, *Gary Cooper*, New York, 1974.
Nachbar, Jack, editor, *Focus on the Western*, Englewood Cliffs, New Jersey, 1974.
Wright, Will, *Sixguns and Society: A Structural Study of the Western*, Berkeley, 1975.
Parish, James Robert, and Michael Pitts, editors, *The Great Western Pictures*, Metuchen, New Jersey, 1976.
French, Philip, *Westerns*, New York, 1977.
Arle, Hecton, *Gary Cooper: An Intimate Biography*, New York, 1979.
Kaminsky, Stuart M., *Coop: The Life and Legend of Gary Cooper*, New York, 1980.
Swindell, Larry, *The Last Hero: A Biography of Gary Cooper*, New York, 1980.
Chardair, N., *Gary Cooper*, Paris, 1981.
Giannetti, Louis, *Masters of the American Cinema*, Englewood Cliffs, New Jersey, 1981.
Rausa, Giuseppe, *Fred Zinnemann*, Florence, 1985.
Goldau, Antje, and others, *Zinnemann*, Munich, 1986.
Buscombe, Ed, *BFI Companion to the Western*, London, 1988.
Zinnemann, Fred, *My Life in the Movies*, New York, 1992.
Drummond, Phillip, *High Noon*, London, 1997.
Meyers, Jeffrey, *Gary Cooper: An American Hero*, New York, 1998.
Nolletti, Arthur, Jr., *The Films of Fred Zinnemann*, Albany, 1999.

Articles:

Films in Review (New York), May 1952.
Zinnemann, Fred, ''Choreography of a Gunfight,'' in *Sight and Sound* (London), Summer 1952.
Burton, Howard, ''*High Noon*: Everyman Rides Again,'' in *Quarterly of Film, Radio, and Television* (Berkeley), Fall 1953.
Warshow, Robert, ''Movie Chronicle: The Westerner,'' in *Partisan Review* (New Brunswick, New Jersey), March 1954.
Schein, Harry, ''The Olympian Cowboy,'' in *American Scholar* (Washington, D.C.), Summer 1955.
Houston, Penelope, and Kenneth Cavender, ''Interview with Carl Foreman,'' in *Sight and Sound* (London), Summer 1958.
Clarens, Carlos, ''Gary Cooper,'' in *Films in Review* (New York), December 1959.
Zinnemann, Fred, ''A Conflict of Interest,'' in *Films and Filming* (London), December 1959.
Fenin, George, ''Son of Uncle Sam,'' in *Films and Filming* (London), October 1962.
Reid, John Howard, ''A Man for All Movies,'' in *Films and Filming* (London), May and June 1967.
Barsness, John A., ''A Question of Standard,'' in *Film Quarterly* (Berkeley), Fall 1967.
Folsom, James, ''Westerns as Social and Political Alternatives,'' in *Western American Literature* (Logan, Utah), Fall 1967.
Allombert, P., ''Le Train sifflera trois fois,'' in *Image et Son* (Paris), no. 269, 1973.
Interview with Carl Foreman, in *American Film* (Washington, D.C.), April 1974.
Giannetti, Louis, ''Fred Zinnemann's *High Noon*,'' in *Film Criticism* (Meadville, Pennsylvania), Winter 1976–77.
Bodeen, DeWitt, in *Magill's Survey of Cinema 2*, Englewood Cliffs, New Jersey, 1980.
Alfredsson, K., ''Sheriffen,'' in *Filmrutan* (Stockholm), 1983.
Palmer, R. B., ''A Masculinist Reading of Two Western Films, *High Noon* and *Rio Grande*,'' in *Journal of Popular Film and Television* (Washington, D.C.), Winter 1984–85.
Bergan, Ronald, in *Films and Filming* (London), May 1986.
Combs, Richard, in *Monthly Film Bulletin* (London), June 1986.
McReynolds, D. J., ''Taking Care of Things: Evolution in the Treatment of a Western Theme,'' in *Literature/Film Quarterly* (Salisbury, Maryland), no. 3, 1990.
Rapf, J. E., ''Myth, Ideology, and Feminism in *High Noon*,'' in *Journal of Popular Culture* (Bowling Green, Ohio), no. 4, 1990.
Ronnberg, M., ''Pliktgubbe moter rattsfajter,'' in *Filmhaftet* (Uppsala, Sweden), May 1990.
Comuzio, E., ''Tempo reale e tempo iconico allo scoccare del *Messogiornio di fuoco*,'' in *Cineforum* (Bergamo, Italy), January-February 1992.

Reid's Film Index (Wyong), no. 13, 1994.
Foster, Gwendolyn Audrey, "The Women in *High Noon*: a Metanarrative of Difference," in *Film Criticism* (Meadville), vol. 18–19, no. 3–1, Spring 1994.
Prince, Stephen, "Historical Perspectives and the Realist Aesthetic in *High Noon*," in *Film Criticism* (Meadville), vol. 18–19, no. 3–1, Spring 1994.
Zinnemann, F., "Letter from Fred Zinnemann," in *Film Criticism* (Meadville), vol. 19, no. 2, 1994/1995.
Prince, S., "Steven Prince Replies," in *Film Criticism* (Meadville), vol. 19, no. 2, 1994/1995.
Short Review, in *Séquences* (Haute-Ville), no. 179, July-August 1995.
Caparros-Lera, J.M., "Cinematic Contextual History of *High Noon*," in *Film-Historia* (Barcelona), vol. 6, no. 1, 1996.
Boon, Kevin A., "Scripting Gender: Writing Differences," in *Creative Screenwriting* (Washington, D.C.), vol. 4, no. 1, Spring 1997.
Orme, A., "The Impossibility of Inscribing Meaning: Interdeterminacy and the Interpretive Act in *High Noon* and John Cunningham's *The Tin Star*," in *Michigan Academician*, vol. 29, no. 3, 1997.
Lefebvre, J., "*High Noon*: le western devient majeur," in *Cinemaction* (Conde-sur-Noireau), no. 86, 1998.
Petit, O., "Sherif et marshal garants de l'ordre social," in *Cinemaction* (Conde-sur-Noireau), no. 86, 1998.

* * *

High Noon was responsible for setting the career of Gary Cooper moving again and is considered by many the single most important film in his career. However, no one knew or thought the film was destined for big things when it was first conceived.

Cooper was not producer Stanley Kramer's first choice to play Marshal Will Kane. In fact, he was fairly far down the list below Marlon Brando and Montgomery Clift. Charlton Heston was also offered the role. The chief financial backer of the film, however, a Salinas lettuce tycoon, wanted Cooper. The backer threatened to pull his money out and Kramer couldn't change his mind about using Cooper, so the script had been sent to Coop. Later Cooper said he took the film, even though he was ill and emotionally troubled, because it represented what his father had taught him, that law enforcement was everyone's job.

In an interview, Fred Zinnemann gave his recollections of Cooper and *High Noon*: "His recurring hip problem bothered him on one or two occasions. It made it difficult for him to do the fight with Lloyd Bridges, but it didn't stop him from working very hard and very long hours under some trying conditions. If I remember correctly, we made the entire film in 31 shooting days. Not once were we delayed or held up by him for whatever reason. For most of the time he had seemed in good health, and it was only two or three months after shooting had been completed that he became ill.

"He did in fact look quite haggard and drawn, which was exactly what I wanted for the character, even though this was in contrast to the unwritten law, then still in force, that the leading man must always look dashing and romantic. If I remember correctly, we used a minimum of makeup for Coop, which was perhaps a bit of a novelty in those days.

"Cooper seemed absolutely right for the part. It seemed completely natural for him to be superimposed on Will Kane."

According to Zinnemann, *High Noon* "is the one picture I directed which more than any other was a team effort. There was a marvelous script by Carl Foreman, a brilliant job of cutting by Elmo Williams, an inspired musical score by Dimitri Tiomkin, a solid contribution by Stanley Kramer. And Gary Cooper was the personification of the honor-bound man. He was in himself a very noble figure, very humble at the same time, and very inarticulate. And very unaware of himself." (Interestingly, in a 1979 interview in *American Film*, Carl Foreman claimed that he and Zinnemann had made the film apart from the Kramer company. According to Foreman, "neither Kramer nor anyone around him had any use for the film from the beginning.")

In the film, Coop's first line is the same as the first line he had ever uttered in a film back in 1928 in *Shopworn Angel*—"I do." Kane is marrying Amy on a Sunday morning. It is just past 10:30 when the tale begins, and it ends a few minutes after noon. The length of the story and the length of the film almost coincide. The film is filled with reminders of the passing time, time that brings Marshal Kane closer to having to face Frank Miller when he gets off the noon train in Hadleyville and seeks revenge against Kane, who sent him to prison. Clocks in the background show the time and tick ominously. People refer to meetings in five minutes. One by one the people whom Kane assumes he can count on in the battle against Miller and his gang find reasons or excuses to stay out of the coming fight. Only the town drunk comes forth, but Kane turns him down, realizing he is more of a liability than an asset.

At one point Kane, alone in his office, puts his head down on his desk, possibly to weep, and then wearily pulls himself up again. In the final confrontation with Miller and his gang, Kane does stand alone until the last moment, when Amy saves his life by shooting Frank Miller. Kane then throws down his badge in a sign of contempt for the town and rides out with his bride.

For his performance in *High Noon*, Cooper won his second Academy Award. Yet it is a performance in which he does less with the character than he had done with almost any of his major roles before. His walk is stiff and pained. His arms remain at his sides through most of the film. He hasn't a single extended speech. What audiences apparently responded to was the look that Zinnemann had captured and that Cooper, with years of experience, had played on. They also responded to the simple story of a man who is not supported by his community in a time of mortal crisis and who triumphs alone through courage and determination.

Will Kane and Gary Cooper were tired, sick men of 51. Cooper's performance is basically put together in relatively short takes and scenes. This was exactly what Zinnemann wanted and what he got, and it was interpreted by a public that loved Cooper as a supreme performance.

Cooper later said that when *High Noon* was finished, he was "acted out," and that pained weariness is exactly what is seen on the screen. Perhaps for the first time, he had truly become the character he portrayed, for Gary Cooper and Will Kane were the same persona. Kane's pain came from fear and his betrayal by others. Cooper's was a result of illness and domestic and career worries.

As he got older, Cooper tended more and more to be concerned about the West and its portrayal and tended to be disturbed by the lack of historical authenticity in western films. Since his own career as a western star had helped to reinforce the myth of the American fictional West rather than a re-creation of historical data, it is ironic that Cooper should turn to that position.

High Noon is indeed not a tale about the true West, but like so many westerns a presentation of contemporary ideas in the most durable popular genre, the western. In a sense, the myths of the West—and Cooper as an actor is one of them—are as culturally important as what actually transpired on the frontier a century ago.

Will Kane tells us more about how we view our history and myths than any real data we might find out about Wild Bill Hickok, Billy the Kid or Buffalo Bill. Cooper's career as a western figure lasted 35 years, as long, in fact as the time between the end of the Civil War and the start of the twentieth century, as long as the historical time of the real West.

—Stuart M. Kaminsky

HIGH SIERRA

USA, 1941

Director: Raoul Walsh

Production: Warner Bros.; black and white; running time: 100 minutes; length: 8,964 feet. Released January 1941.

Executive producer: Hal B. Wallis; **associate producer:** Mark Hellinger; **screenplay:** John Huston and W. R. Burnett, from a novel by Burnett; **assistant director:** Russ Saunders; **dialogue director:** Irving Rapper; **photography:** Tony Gaudio; **editor:** Jack Killifer; **sound:** Dolph Thomas; **art director:** Ted Smith; **music:** Adolph Deutsch; **special effects:** Bryon Haskin, H. F. Koenekamp.

Cast: Humphrey Bogart (*Roy Earle*); Ida Lupino (*Marie*); Alan Curtis (*Babe*); Arthur Kennedy (*Red*); Joan Leslie (*Velma*); Henry Hull (*Doc Banton*); Henry Travers (*Pa*); Jerome Cowan (*Healy*); Minna Gombell (*Mrs. Baughman*); Barton Maclane (*Jake Kranmer*); Elizabeth Risdon (*Ma*); Cornel Wilde (*Louis Mendoza*); Donald McBride (*Big Mac*); Paul Harvey (*Mr. Baughman*); Isabel Jewell (*Blonde*); Willie Best (*Algernon*); Spencer Charters (*Ed*); George Meeker (*Pfiffer*); Robert Strange (*Art*); John Eldredge (*Lon Preiser*); Zero the dog (*Pard*).

Publications

Script:

Huston, John, and W.R. Burnett, *High Sierra*, edited by Douglas Gomery, Madison, Wisconsin, 1979.

Books:

McCarty, Clifford, *Bogey: The Films of Humphrey Bogart*, New York, 1965.
Michael, Paul, *Humphrey Bogart: The Man and His Films*, Indianapolis, 1965.
Marmin, Michel, *Raoul Walsh*, Paris, 1970.
Canham, Kingsley, *The Hollywood Professionals*, New York, 1973.
Hardy, Phil, editor, *Raoul Walsh*, Colchester, Essex, 1974.
Walsh, Raoul, *Each Man in His Time*, New York, 1974.
Benchley, Nathaniel, *Humphrey Bogart*, Boston, 1975.
Eyles, Allen, *Bogart*, New York, 1975.
Shadoian, Jack, *Dreams and Dead Ends*, Cambridge, Massachusetts, 1977.
Pettigrew, Terence, *Bogart: A Definitive Study of his Film Career*, London, 1981.
Comuzio, Ermanno, *Raoul Walsh*, Florence, 1982.
Winkler, Willi, *Humphrey Bogart und Hollywoods Schwarze Serie*, Munich, 1985.
Giuliani, Pierre, *Raoul Walsh*, Paris, 1986.
Fuchs, Wolfgang J., *Humphrey Bogart: Cult-Star: A Documentation*, Berlin, 1987.
Coe, Jonathan, *Humphrey Bogart: Take It & Like It*, New York, 1991.
Bogart, Stephen H., and Gary Provost, *Bogart: In Search of My Father*, New York, 1995.
Schlesinger, Judith, *Bogie: A Life in Pictures*, New York, 1998.
Sperber, A.M., *Bogart*, New York, 1998.
Cunningham, Ernest W., *Ultimate Bogie*, Los Angeles, 1999.
Duchovnay, Gerald, *Humphrey Bogart: A Bio-Bibliography*, Westport, 1999.
Meyers, Jeffery, *Bogart: A Life in Hollywood*, New York, 1999.

Articles:

Variety (New York), 22 January 1941.
Motion Picture Herald (New York), 25 January 1941.
New York Times, 25 January 1941.
Cinema (Beverly Hills), 28 May 1941.
Monthly Film Bulletin (London), June 1941.
Times (London), 4 August 1941.
Whitebait, William, in *New Statesman* (London), 9 August 1941.
Vermilye, J., ''Ida Lupino,'' in *Films in Review* (New York), May 1959.
Dienstfrey, Harris, ''Hitch Your Genre to a Star,'' in *Film Culture* (New York), Fall 1964.
Huston, John, in *Film Quarterly* (Berkeley), Fall 1965.
Burnett, W. R., in *Toronto Film Society Notes*, 14 February 1966.
Alley, Kenneth D., ''High Sierra: Swansong for an Era,'' in *Journal of Popular Film* (Washington, D.C.), vol. 5, no. 3–4, 1976.
Simons, John L., ''Henry on Bogie: Reality and Romance in Dream Song No. 9 and *High Sierra*,'' in *Literature/Film Quarterly* (Salisbury, Maryland), Summer 1977.
Magill's Survey of Cinema 2, Englewood Cliffs, New Jersey, 1981.
Mate, Ken, and Patrick McGilligan, interview with W. R. Burnett, in *Film Comment* (New York), January-February 1983.
Marling, W., ''On the Relation Between American Roman Noir and Film Noir,'' in *Literature/Film Quarterly* (Salisbury, Maryland), no. 3, 1991.
Marling, W., ''On the Relation Between American Roman Noir and Film Noir,'' in *Literature/Film Quarterly* (Salisbury), vol. 21, no. 3, 1993.
Howard, T., in *Reid's Film Index* (Wyong), no. 15, 1995.

* * *

Jean-Luc Godard canonizes *High Sierra* at the end of *Breathless* when he mimes the orphic structure of Raoul Walsh's action melodrama. Walsh depicts an army of police chasing his hero up Mount Whitney, enlisting a sniper to shoot him in the back and send him plummeting down the slope. His body is mourned by a girlfriend, Marie (Ida Lupino), and a cynical bystander, a news reporter named Healy, amidst a chorus of troopers. Godard flattens the hubris that Walsh obtains from a mix of Shakespeare, Greek tragedy, and *film noir* by having his two adolescents ''play'' at the fear and terror evinced in *High Sierra*. If Godard's first feature figures at a threshold

High Sierra

between two eras of film, it suggests why Walsh's feature owns a central place in the history of cinema.

On the one hand, the film concretizes elements common both to Walsh as an *auteur* and to the Hollywood industry in general. Destined to die, an ordinary figure is caught in a skein of tragic forces woven in the later years of the Depression. The protagonist figures as a hero set in a world that has lost its legends, but he is ultimately a pawn in a plot of magnitude beyond his ken. Following Warner Brothers' affiliations with the New Deal, the film shows a world of humans caught in social contradiction. Fate is cast, the film implies, either by gods of nature, the failure of capitalism, or a highly corrupt government. In a montage following the credits that scroll upwards to the majestic sky over Mount Whitney, the initial dissolves suggest that an unnamed state official—ostensively a governor—has Roy Earle (Humphrey Bogart, whose name bears resemblance to "King Lear," a figure too *late* for his milieu, and to a sign of energy, or "oil," the hidden term of the film) sprung from prison in order to engineer a holdup at Palm Springs. Between the narrative and the visual design the plot is staged to show how profit can be gained when common news items are inflated into national media events. The "real" story does not entail the holdup at the Tropico hotel in Palm Springs but, as Godard intuited, at the end of *High Sierra* itself: when Earle is pursued up the mountain, a limelight is projected onto its rocky curtain. A radiocaster hypes the silence of the landscape into a drama that inculpates all viewers and listeners as agents of a crime, like the film, collectively contrived.

On the other hand, *High Sierra* makes obvious its own mechanism of illusion. The image-track effectively theorizes the tenets of the narration. When the squadron of police cars and motorcycles pursues Earle up the winding road, a panoramic shot of 720° encircles the steeplechase. Poised at the opening of the angle of a hairpin turn, the camera follows Earle's coupe, pans around and down to catch the oncoming motorcade, and continues its career. It thus spots its presence in the film as the origin of the narrative "destiny." Elsewhere it portrays the hero incriminating the spectator with his brutally frontal stare. Facing the windshield of his car, the camera registers Bogart's looking directly at the viewer, almost in defiance of the laws of obliquity that hold in films of the period. Ocularity becomes so pervasive that all illusion of narrative space and time is flattened: Earle stares *us* down as he looks ahead and into the space moving away in the rearview mirror. The depth of field contains elements that utterly flatten it. Optical stratagems kill the hero. Before he is ambushed Earle appears as a speck on a landscape that has lost all cardinal bearings. And earlier, quick dissolves superimpose characters over writing of vitrines and billboards so as to show how fate legibly casts its spell over the characters and narrative alike.

These objects locate where Walsh's signature is written into the film. Through car mirrors, headlights, monocular forms (an eight-ball, a ring, the circular marquee heralding the Circle Auto Court), and bar-like shadows cast over the frame, tragedy is rendered both deep and matte. Forms arch back to the director's own history of enucleation. In *High Sierra*, however, it is seen as symbolic castration that literally produces the viewing ''subject,'' the spectator whose vision is skewed and access to nature denied. In a sequence located in neither W.R. Burnett's novel that inspired the film nor John Huston's screenplay, a volley of shots catches a jackrabbit crossing the highway on the western mesa just as Earle overtakes a jalopy sputtering westward. The animal darts across the road, the two cars swerve and almost collide. Although the near-miss primes the fate of the narrative, inner allusion is made to an event that deprived Walsh of his right eye in 1928: when he was driving from the site of *In Old Arizona*, a hare jumped in front of his vehicle and struck its windshield, smashing the glass and lodging a splinter in his right eye. The traumatic instant of his own enucleation is tipped into *High Sierra* as if to draw attention to a simultaneous play of monocular and binocular views, or of coextensive flatness and deep focus, that Walsh uses, along with Renoir, Ford, and Welles, to theorize the visibility of cinema in general. Staged carefully in this film, the event recurs often throughout his oeuvre (in *The Cockeyed World*, *They Drive by Night*, *Colorado Territory*, a western remake of *High Sierra*, *Pursued*, *White Heat*, and so on), but in *High Sierra* it is turned toward broad questions entailing the ideology of Hollywood cinema. Out of the same visual trauma come elements of *film noir* and, of course, much of the speculations of New Wave theoreticians.

High Sierra shows that Raoul Walsh is far from the simple ''action director'' of fast-paced films of keen craft and slight content. Close viewing reveals a wealth of transfilmic themes and obsessions that mark an output of over 120 films (his longevity and productivity making him a Victor Hugo of American cinema), but also the strategies of Hollywood and their transformations from the silent period to the 1960s. The film is a complex study of visibility concealed in what it is: a timelessly captivating, fast-paced, action melodrama.

—Tom Conley

DER HIMMEL ÜBER BERLIN

(Wings of Desire)

Germany, 1987

Director: Wim Wenders

Production: Road Movies (Berlin), Argos Films (Paris), Westdeutscher Rundfunk (Köln); black-and-white and color (Kodak), 35mm; running time: 130 minutes. Released 18 May 1987. Filmed on location in Berlin. Cost: $3–3.5 million.

Producers: Wim Wenders, Anatole Dauman; **executive producer:** Ingrid Windisch; **screenplay:** Wim Wenders, Peter Handke; **photography:** Henri Alekan; **assistant director:** Claire Denis; **editor:** Peter Przygodda; **sound:** Jean-Paul Mugel, Axel Arft; **art director:** Heidi Lüdi; **costume designer:** Monika Jacobs; **music:** Jürgen Knieper, Laurent Petitgand (circus music), Nick Cave and the Bad Seeds (songs).

Cast: Bruno Ganz (*Damiel*); Solveig Dommartin (*Marion*); Otto Sander (*Cassiel*); Curt Bois (*Homer*); Peter Falk (*himself*); Nick Cave and the Bad Seeds (*themselves*); Lajos Kovacs (*Marion's acrobatics coach*).

Awards: Cannes Film Festival Award for Best Director, 1987; Bavarian Film Award for Best Director, 1988; German Film Awards for Outstanding Feature Film and Best Cinematography, 1988; European Film Awards for Best Director and Best Supporting Actor (Bois), 1988; National Society of Film Critics Award for Best Cinematography, 1988; New York Film Critics Circle Award for Best Cinematography, 1988; Los Angeles Film Critics Association Award for Best Foreign Film and Best Cinematography, 1988; Sao Paolo International Film Festival Audience Award for Best Feature, 1988; Independent Spirit Award for Best Foreign Film, 1989.

Publications

Script:

Wenders, Wim, and Peter Handke, *Der Himmel über Berlin, ein Filmbuch*, Frankfurt, 1987.

Books:

Kolker, Robert Phillip, and Peter Beicken, *Wim Wenders: Cinema as Vision and Desire*, Cambridge, 1993.

Morgues, Nicole de, *Les ailes du désir, Der Himmel über Berlin: étude du film de Wim Wenders*, Linnebonne, 1998.

Articles:

Jaehne, Karen, ''Angel Eyes: Wenders Soars,'' in *Film Comment* (New York), June 1988.

Paneth, Ira, ''Wim and His Wings,'' in *Film Quarterly* (Berkeley), Fall 1988.

Fusco, Coco, ''Angels, History and Poetic Fantasy: An Interview with Wim Wenders,'' in *Cineaste* (New York), vol. 16, no. 4, 1988.

Helmetag, Gharles H., ''Of Men and Angels: Literary Allusions in Wim Wenders' *Wings of Desire*,'' in *Film/Literature Quarterly* (Salisbury, Maryland), vol. 18, no. 4, 1990.

Hooks, Bell, ''Representing Whiteness: Seeing *Wings of Desire*,'' in *Yearning: Race, Gender, and Cultural Politics*, Boston, 1990.

Cook, Roger F., ''Angels, Fiction and History in Berlin: Wim Wenders' *Wings of Desire* (1991),'' in *The Cinema of Wim Wenders: Image, Narrative, and the Postmodern Condition*, by Cook and Gerd Gemunden, Detroit, 1997.

Ehrlich, Linda, ''Meditations on Wim Wenders' *Wings of Desire*,'' in *Literature/Film Quarterly* (Salisbury) vol. 19, no. 4, 1991.

Der Himmel Über Berlin

Caldwell, David, and Paul W. Rea, "Handke's and Wenders' *Wings of Desire*: Transcending Postmodernism," in *German Quarterly* (Philadelphia) vol. 64, no. 1, 1991.

Caltvedt, Les, "Berlin Poetry: Archaic Cultural Patterns in Wenders' *Wings of Desire*," in *Literature/Film Quarterly* (Salisbury), vol. 20, no. 2, 1992.

* * *

On one level, *Wings of Desire's* plot outline could be seen as the purest Hollywood-style claptrap: an angel falls in love with a mortal woman—a trapeze artist, no less!—and trades in his wings to be with her. On another level, it may be taken as a meditation on themes that have preoccupied German literature since before the age of Goethe: oppositions of spirit and matter, eternity and time, the abstract and the concrete. Of course, the film gloriously refuses to exist on merely one level, or address itself to one kind of culture—it prefers to have Rilke's angels from the *Duino Elegies* hobnob with TV's Columbo. The film could be called perfectly postmodern, except that its meanings are not all scattered on a glittering surface; rather, like a number of the great modernist works, starting with Joyce's *Ulysses*, *Wings of Desire* is a rich amalgam of high and low culture. Wim Wenders has pointed out that the pun in his German title (*Himmel* means both sky or heavens and Heaven) is untranslatable into English, besides the problem that "*The Sky Over Berlin* sounded like a war movie and *Heavens Over Berlin* was too romantic." On the other hand, "desire" (French *désir*) does not, according to Wenders, translate properly into German, so he sees both titles as valid.

Whichever title one uses, the film is certainly—on one level, one must keep adding—about Berlin itself as much as anything else. Indeed, the film now serves as a document of those last years before the Wall came down, when Potsdamer Platz was still a no-man's-land of the most forlorn bleakness, yet graffiti on the Western side of the Wall was making political/aesthetic statements of protest and renewal. One can imagine Wenders spinning his fantasy plot outward from the monuments of Berlin itself: the winged Victory Column inspiring the angels and their lofty perspective; the Wall suggesting every sort of division between humans (one of the characters complains that nowadays everybody needs a password or a toll payment to talk to another person); a modernistic library building—austere and yet somehow spiritual and grandly calming—serving as a suitable hangout for the angels, who love to accumulate knowledge; Potsdamer

Platz and other empty spaces representing the memory erasures and feelings of desolation of postwar German life (though even these spaces can be enlivened by a circus or a mural!); and in opposition to the Wall and the vacant lots, the ubiquitous coffee-and-sandwich stands, which bring people (and angels) casually together.

Berlin's dark Nazi past is evoked both through intercuts of newsreel footage and through the subplot of a movie being shot that uses the fall of Berlin as the backdrop for a detective story starring Peter Falk. (The set featuring a half-bombed building is truly Piranesian in its shadowy depths, though these scenes of the film, showing Nazi horrors made grist for the entertainment mill, also tell us something about the endless self-replications of the postmodern 1980s.) Wenders' Berlin is also an international city: many languages are heard briefly in the course of the film, and two of the major characters, Falk and Marion, speak (and are heard thinking) in English and French respectively. To be sure, a viewer might perceive the entire film not as about Berlin but the other way around, with the city merely providing convenient metaphors for the human condition—but this would ignore the film's rich specificity.

As for what Wenders means by ''desire,'' one must first consider what the angels lack—which means figuring out what they are. These soberly dressed but ponytailed creatures that hover over the city and lean over the shoulders of its citizens are not messengers in the biblical manner, or charioteers to the afterlife as in the ghastly sentimental remake, *City of Angels*. They are, however, recorders and comforters. They take notes and share stories with one another of lovely, quirky details of humans' lives, or of the natural world in the days before human occupation. (Evidently the angels have inhabited the local terrain since prehistory; only with humankind's arrival have they learned to speak—and laugh.) They do appear to bring moments of peace or inexplicable joy to people in unhappy straits, though they cannot prevent accidents or suicides. Children see them, and are amused, but as in Wordsworth, they lose their intimations of some kind of immortality as they age. Often the angels seem to be an allegory of a certain type of artist, whether poet or painter or filmmaker (Cassiel keeps a notebook; ex-angel Falk is a sketch artist; Wenders' camera and microphone seem endlessly curious): they feel deeply, they love the particulars of everyday life, but they don't make contact, they don't exactly *live*, they only record. Significantly, they are color blind—a ''dimension'' is missing. Thus when Damiel falls in love with Marion she is not only an actual woman but the embodiment of life in the flesh, of ''becoming'' (including changing and dying) rather than pure ''being.'' When he wakes up mortal, he does go looking for her at once, but he is also eager to ask a passerby the names of the colors he now sees decorating the Wall, and to taste his first cup of coffee.

A number of critics have argued that the film falls into a very traditional male—or male filmmaker's—perspective, regardless of whether Marion is a woman, Woman in the abstract, or ''earthly delights''; put most simply, the angels and Wenders' camera are voyeurs, most obviously when Damiel watches Marion undress in her room. However, it is important to note that Damiel wants not merely to watch—or to dominate/possess through seeing—but to make contact with Marion, to communicate. Later, when he and Marion finally meet, is it she who finds him—his back is to the camera as she approaches him—and she who does the talking in a rather remarkable and lengthy speech. Kolker and Beicken's book on Wenders claims that the director and his co-writer Peter Handke reclaim male dominance at the point when Marion tells Damiel the choice is now his (they also find her speech leaning toward fascism when she proposes conceiving what they call a ''master race'' with him). But telling someone he must act is not the same as relinquishing one's own free will, and the intense close-ups of both characters at the end of the speech suggest a relation of equality.

One must say too about Marion's speech that however serious it may look in script form, it is so extravagant (especially compared to most bar pickup lines), and its very first words—''Now it's time to get serious''—are so bold and spoken with such quiet amusement by Solveig Dommartin, that it is outrageously romantic and droll at the same time. Indeed, the entire film has an essential component of whimsy, even outright comedy, which is often overlooked by critics. One finds it in the almost goofy earnestness of Bruno Ganz's Damiel, and in the casting of Peter Falk as an ex-angel. (Falk's down-to-earth geniality—though he also has a serious awareness of Berlin's past—casts a kind of spell over much of the picture.) There is whimsy too in the very idea of an angel falling in love with—and literally looking up to—a trapeze artist who even wears little wings as part of her act. (Early in the film, when a stagehand makes a joke to Marion about ''an angel passing by,'' he is just alluding to her wings, but the invisible Damiel is comically thunderstruck.) And let us not forget that these angels who often seem on the verge of quoting Rilke are also quite serious fans of punk rocker Nick Cave and the Bad Seeds. Though far from making a joke of his whole proceedings, Wenders does undercut his own (or perhaps Handke's) tendency toward solemnity again and again. When Damiel talks with Cassiel about his frustration with his own ''spiritual existence''—as they sit in a BMW convertible in a showroom!—he speaks abstractly about wanting ''now'' instead of ''forever,'' but concludes that ''it would be quite something to come home after a long day, like Philip Marlowe, and feed the cat.'' When he actually becomes human—falling asleep and gently placed by Cassiel on the West side of the Wall, a moment echoing Wagner's *The Valkyrie*, when the newly mortal, formerly winged-helmeted Brunnhilde is laid to rest by Wotan—he is rudely awakened by his angel's armor crashing down upon him. But most purely hilarious is the inexpressibly weird jacket he trades his armor for. Finally, turning from drollery to a child's delight, one must consider the circus setting in itself. Circuses are by no means always amusing in movies, and American viewers should keep in mind that in much European art the acrobat is not a frivolous, ''flighty'' person but a richly poetic figure; but Wenders does stress the pleasure children take in the whole show, while seeming himself as fascinated by Marion's act (shown to us at great, even self-indulgent length) as they or Damiel.

For all its leanings toward abstraction and symbol, and its moods of deep seriousness, *Wings of Desire* is not only surprisingly light-hearted, and hopeful about love relationships (Wenders' previous *Paris, Texas* had shown some hesitant moves in that direction), but consistently sensuous in image and sound. Much admiration has been expressed for the cinematography of Henri Alekan, whose camera does its own swooping and calm gliding, even when not directly implying an angel's point-of-view. The film has a wonderful sense of light even in shots of the most ordinary city streets, and Wenders never sinks to the spiderwebs-glistening-with-dewdrops cliches of some other filmmakers when conveying the beauty of the everyday. The switch from black and white to color when Damiel loses his wings may be a trick Wenders learned from *The Wizard of Oz* and another angel movie, the Powell/Pressburger *A Matter of Life and*

Death, but it is not a simple gimmick, for he uses color shots earlier in the film to cue us in that there are other ways of seeing besides the angels', and he will continue to render Cassiel's scenes in black and white. As for the sound design of *Wings of Desire*, it is in many ways as brilliant as the images, and unusually complex in its weaving of voiceovers of people's thoughts with an ongoing poem of Handke that speaks of ''When the child was a child.'' and with music ranging from the somber strings of Jürgen Knieper's soundtrack to the live circus music and the hypnotic performances of Nick Cave.

Wings of Desire inspired a 1997 American remake, which has some fine images of angels on the rooftops and beaches of Los Angeles but is leaden in almost every other respect. (The profession of acrobat not deemed ''serious'' enough, Marion becomes a brain surgeon, and dies in an accident, while much of the film is occupied with debate over believing in the supernatural—an issue not of the least concern in Wenders' film.) Wenders himself made a sequel in 1993, *Faraway, So Close*, in which Cassiel too becomes mortal and a number of new characters are introduced, including an allegorical figure of Time. Though filled with moments of great interest, the relatively baroque plot and the repeating of some familiar material make the sequel seem less fresh, less beautifully clear in its outline, than the original. Sad and funny, conceptual and sensuous, densely complex and as airily simple as a child's storybook, *Wings of Desire* is a remarkably balanced achievement and a landmark in German cinema.

—Joseph Milicia

HIROSHIMA MON AMOUR

France-Japan, 1959

Director: Alain Resnais

Production: Argos Films-Como Films (Paris), Pathé Overseas, and Daiei (Tokyo); 1959; black and white, 35mm; running time: 91 minutes, some sources list 88 minutes. Released June 1959. Filmed September-December 1958 in film studios in Tokyo and Paris, and on location in Hiroshima and Nevers.

Producers: Sacha Kamenka, Shirakawa Takeo, and Samy Halfon; **screenplay:** Marguerite Duras; **photography:** Sacha Vierny and Michio Takahashi; **editors:** Henri Colpi, Jasmine Chasney, and Anne Sarraute; **sound:** Pierre Calvet and Yamamoto, and Rene Renault; **art directors:** Esaka, Mayo, and Petri; **music:** Giovanni Fusco and Georges Delerue; **costume designer:** Gérard Collery; **literary adviser:** Gerard Jarlot.

Cast: Emmanuelle Riva (*She*); Eiji Okada (*He*); Bernard Fresson (*The German*); Stella Dassas (*The Mother*); Pierre Barbaud (*The Father*).

Awards: Cannes Film Festival, International Critics' Award and Film Writers' Award, 1959; New York Film Critics' Award, Best Foreign Film, 1960.

Publications

Script:

Duras, Marguerite, *Hiroshima mon amour*, Paris, 1959; translated as *Hiroshima, Mon Amour*, New York, 1961; London, 1966.

Books:

Cordier, Stéphane, *Alain Resnais; ou, La Création au cinéma*, Paris, 1961.
Pingaud, Bernard, *Alain Resnais*, Lyons, 1961.
Bounoure, Gaston, *Alain Resnais*, Paris, 1962.
Ravar, Raymond, editor, *Tu n'as rien vu à Hiroshima*, Brussels, 1962.
Cowie, Peter, *Antonioni, Bergman, Resnais*, London, 1963.
Armes, Roy, *The Cinema of Alain Resnais*, London, 1968.
Ward, John, *Alain Resnais; or, The Theme of Time*, New York, 1968.
MacDonald, Dwight, *On Movies*, Englewood Cliffs, New Jersey, 1969.
Bertetto, Paolo, *Alain Resnais*, Italy, 1976.
Kreidl, John Francis, *Alain Resnais*, Boston, 1977.
Monaco, James, *Alain Resnais: The Role of Imagination*, New York, 1978.
Benayoun, Robert, *Alain Resnais: Arpenteur de l'imaginaire*, Paris, 1980; revised edition, 1986.
Sweet, Freddy, *The Film Narratives of Alain Resnais*, Ann Arbor, 1981.
Trastulli, Daniela, *Della parola all imagine: Viaggio nel cinema di Marguerite Duras*, Geneva, 1982.
Etzkowitz, Janice, *Toward a Concept of Cinematic Literature: An Analysis of ''Hiroshima Mon Amour,''* New York, 1983.
Vergerio, Falvio, *I film di Alain Resnais*, Rome, 1984.
Borgomano, Madeleine, *L'Ecriture filmique de Marguerite Duras*, Paris, 1985.
Brossard, Jean-Pierre, editor, *Marguerite Duras: Cinéaste, écrivain*, La Chaux-de-Fonde, 1985.
Guers-Villate, Yvonne, *Continuité/discontinuité de l'oeuvre Durassienne*, Brussels, 1985.
Fernandes, Marie-Pierre, *Travailler avec Duras: La Musica deuxième*, Paris, 1986.
Roob, Jean-Daniel, *Alain Resnais: Qui êtes-vous?*, Lyons, 1986.
Riambau, Esteve, *La ciencia y la ficción: El cine de Alain Resnais*, Barcelona, 1988.
Guillaume, Catherine, *Trahir la passion: des égarements passionnels aux égards du traitement*, Paris, 1992.
Bersani, Leo, and Ulysse Dutoit, *Arts of Impoverishment: Beckett, Rothko, Resnais*, Cambridge, 1994.

Articles:

''*Hiroshima mon amour*, film scandaleux?,'' in *Lettres Françaises* (Paris), 14 May 1959.
Sadoul, Georges, ''Un Grand Film, un grand homme,'' in *Lettres Françaises* (Paris), 14 May 1959.
Delahaye, Michel, interview with Alain Resnais, in *Cinéma* (Paris), July 1959.
Cahiers du Cinéma (Paris), July 1959.
Marcorelles, Louis, Henri Colpi, and Richard Roud, ''Alain Resnais and *Hiroshima, Mon Amour*,'' in *Sight and Sound* (London), Winter 1959–60.
Colpi, Henri, ''Editing *Hiroshima, Mon Amour*,'' in *Sight and Sound* (London), Winter 1959–60.

Hiroshima mon amour

Roud, Richard, ''Conversations with Marguerite Duras,'' in *Sight and Sound* (London), Winter 1959–60.

Colpi, Henri, ''Musique d'*Hiroshima*,'' in *Cahiers du Cinéma* (Paris), January 1960.

Egly, Max, interview with Alain Resnais, in *Image et Son* (Paris), February 1960.

Burch, Noël, ''A Conversation with Alain Resnais,'' in *Film Quarterly* (Berkeley), Spring 1960.

Weiler, A. H., in *New York Times*, 17 May 1960.

Mekas, Jonas, in *Village Voice* (New York), 25 May 1960.

Hart, Henry, in *Films in Review* (New York), June-July 1960.

Alexander, A. J., in *Film Culture* (New York), Summer 1961.

Labarther, Andre, and Jacques Rivette, interview with Alain Resnais, in *Cahiers du Cinéma* (Paris), September 1961.

Hart, Henry, in *Village Voice* (New York), 4 October 1961.

Kael, Pauline, ''Fantasies of the Art House Audience,'' in *Sight and Sound* (London), Winter 1961–62.

Durgnat, Raymond, in *Films and Filming* (London), May 1962.

Stanbrook, Alan, ''The Time and Space of Alain Resnais,'' in *Films and Filming* (London), January 1964.

Le Troquer, J., in *Télécinė* (Paris), February 1973.

Pór, P., in *Filmkultura* (Budapest), March-April 1973.

Hanet, K., ''Does the Camera Lie? Notes on *Hiroshima, Mon Amour*,'' in *Screen* (London), Autumn 1973.

Helman, A., in *Kino* (Warsaw), September 1974.

Van Wert, W. F., ''Point Counterpoint in *Hiroshima, Mon Amour*,'' in *Wide Angle* (Athens, Ohio), no. 2, 1978.

Mercken-Spaas, C., ''Destruction and Reconstruction in *Hiroshima, Mon Amour*,'' in *Literature/Film Quarterly* (Salisbury, Maryland), no. 4, 1980.

Boer, L., in *Skoop* (Amsterdam), December-January 1980–81.

Glassman, D., ''The Feminine Subject as History Writer in *Hiroshima, Mon Amour*,'' in *Enclitic* (Minneapolis), Spring 1981.

Cardullo, B., ''The Symbolism of *Hiroshima mon amour*,'' in *Film Criticism* (Meadville, Pennsylvania), Winter 1984.

Moses, John W., ''Vision Denied in *Night and Fog* and *Hiroshima, Mon Amour*,'' in *Literature/Film Quarterly* (Salisbury, Maryland), vol. 15, no. 3, 1987.

Astala, E., ''Hiroshima, rakastettumme,'' in *Filmihullu* (Helsinki), no. 1, 1990.

Della Casa, S., ''Amnesia land: il cinema del dimenticare,'' in *Ikon* (Milan), October 1990.

Lane, N., ''The Subject In/Of History: *Hiroshima, mon amour,''* in *Florida State University Conference on Literature and Film*, vol. 15, 1990.

Grange, M.-F., ''Paysage resnaisien ou variations autour de la mise en espace du temps,'' in *Cinemas*, vol. 5, no. 1/2, 1994.

Samson, P., ''Le montage comme articulation entre reel et fiction,'' in *Cinemaction* (Conde-sur-Noireau), vol. 72, no. 3, 1994.

O'Connell, Vincent, ''The Human Heart,'' in *Sight & Sound* (London), vol. 6, no. 3, March 1996.

Michiels, Dirk, ''Onuitwisbaar oorlogsstigma,'' in *Film en Televisie + Video* (Brussels), no. 462, May 1996.

* * *

Hiroshima mon amour was the first feature directed by Alain Resnais. Besides establishing the director's international reputation, the film was one of several released in 1959 signalling the emergence of a new generation of French filmmakers working in a modernist narrative vein. Indeed, the film is considered something of a landmark in the history of modernist cinema. The film is also seen as an exemplary instance of artistic collaboration. The scenario by Marguerite Duras, photography of Sacha Vierny, editing of Henri Colpi, and musical score by Giovanni Fusco and Georges Delerue contribute to its dense patterns of repetition and counterpoint.

In the film, an initially casual romantic encounter between a Japanese architect (''He''), and a French actress (''She'') working in Hiroshima on a film about peace provides the basis for exploring the nature of memory, experience, and representation. The love affair is important primarily for the chain of memory it triggers, as the woman gradually discloses the story of her first love, a story she has never told before. During World War II, in Nevers, she fell in love with a German soldier. On the day the city was liberated, he was shot and killed. She was subsequently submitted to public disgrace, followed by a period of imprisonment and near-madness in her parents' home. She finally recovered enough to leave home permanently, arriving in Paris on the day the war ended after the bombing of Hiroshima and Nagasaki.

This story is only revealed in stages, and establishes a complex of metaphoric relations between the past and present. The woman's first memory image is prompted by a direct visual comparison: the twitching hand of her sleeping Japanese lover resembles, and motivates a cut to, the twitching hand of the dying German soldier. This transition is a specific instance of a more complex network of comparisons constructed throughout the course of the film, a concise figure for the film's general pattern of development. A structure of metaphoric logic takes the place of the linear causality, clearly defined goals, and conscious motivation associated with dominant narrative.

For example, the German lover from the past and Japanese lover in the present are comparable as former mutual enemies of France. At the same time, we see the woman victimized in the past for her relations with the German. Her victimization is likened to the victims of the atom bomb seen in the film's opening sequence in a series of images—documentary and reconstructed—depicting the effects of the bomb. These images of destruction and deformity include loss of hair and burnt, distorted skin. Later, we see the woman's head shaved in the public square in Nevers to mark her illicit ''collaboration'' and her skin broken and bloody as she scrapes it on the walls of her parents' cellar. While the woman is thus ''like'' the Japanese, a victim of the war's end, she is nevertheless liberated from her private torture, allowed to go free, at the same time the bomb is dropped on Hiroshima.

Through the accumulation of images and narrative information, *Hiroshima mon amour* provides material for recognizing a complex network of comparison and contrast linking disparate events. As the film progresses, the terms of association become more abstract, a function of formal repetition, as tracking shots through the streets of Hiroshima are intercut with tracking shots through the streets of Nevers. Two places and times converge through the continuity afforded by the camera's point of view. At the same time the relationship between the man and woman in the present is infused with the potency of memory. The Japanese man asks the woman to stay in Hiroshima (not a viable option in any conventional sense, since she has a family in France and his wife is due home from a trip shortly), as she comes to emblemize the inconsolable memory of the past.

Yet her story, once told, transforms the experience and its memory into the order of history. The woman acknowledges this shift in value. She confronts herself in the mirror and addresses her dead lover, announcing her betrayal. At one point, she refers to the event as a ''two-penny romance,'' a common, even trivial affair. This change is a function of narration; having been recounted, the experience has undergone a change in nature. This is one way in which the film explores the nature of representation in relation to experience and memory.

In the course of exploring this issue, *Hiroshima mon amour* clearly suggests that the mediated account, whether verbal or visual, is qualitatively different from, and supplants, personal experience. The very opening of the film promotes this view, challenging any easy equation of representation and experience. Images of the Hiroshima museum and its repository of documents are accompanied by a woman's voice saying she saw and felt everything in Hiroshima—the heat, the suffering, and so on. Voice and image seem to confirm and validate one another. But a male voice denies her assertions, insisting, ''No, you saw nothing.'' The viewer not only wonders who is speaking, but also is forced to question the woman's certainty, and his own, about the nature of what he is watching. Seeing, in this way, may become misbelieving.

If the woman's narrative of her past displaces the event as pure experience, the initial recounting is not an easy task. Bringing the experience to the level of verbal presence involves the painful eruption of the past (''inconsolable memory'') into the present. Temporal distinctions get provisionally confused, and past and present seem to merge, as she first tells the story to her Japanese lover. Her language involves shifts in tense and pronoun use, as past events are spoken of in the present tense and the woman replaces the ''he'' of her story (referring to the past German lover) with ''you'' (an apparent address to her present Japanese lover). In this way the nature and act of narrating emerge as a further concern of the film. If the process of narrative is a personal and difficult activity, merging the speaking subject with event, the product eludes the control of the teller. The woman's deeply personal experience, once told, counts as a public story to be judged in the context of narrative history.

For all of these reasons the film is seen to exemplify practices associated with modernist aesthetics. It rejects linear, causal narrative progression, constructs its characters as figures involved in the process of representation, and problematizes the nature of this process. The implications of this investigation extend beyond the characters in the fiction to include the film and its audience, as *Hiroshima mon amour* challenges the viewer to recognize the metaphoric relations that confer its coherence, and also to question the value and meaning of its own representations.

—M. B. White

HIS GIRL FRIDAY

USA, 1940

Director: Howard Hawks

Production: Columbia Pictures Corp.; black and white, 35mm; running time: 92 minutes. Released 18 January 1940.

Producer: Howard Hawks; **screenplay:** Charles Lederer, with uncredited assistance by Ben Hecht, from the play *Front Page* by Ben Hecht and Charles MacArthur; **photography:** Joseph Walker; **editor:** Gene Havlick; **art director:** Lionel Banks; **music:** Morris W. Stoloff; **costume designer (gowns):** Kalloch.

Cast: Cary Grant (*Walter Burns*); Rosalind Russell (*Hildy Johnson*); Ralph Bellamy (*Bruce Baldwin*); Gene Lockhart (*Sheriff Hartwell*); Helen Mack (*Mollie Malloy*); Porter Hall (*Murphy*); Ernest Truex (*Benslinger*); Cliff Edwards (*Endicott*); Clarence Kolb (*Mayor*); Roscoe Karns (*McCue*); Frank Jenks (*Wilson*); Regis Toomey (*Sanders*); Abner Biberman (*Louis*); Frank Orth (*Duffy*); John Qualen (*Earl Williams*); Alma Kruger (*Mrs. Baldwin*); Billy Gilbert (*Joe Pettibone*); Pat West (*Warden Cooley*); Edwin Maxwell (*Dr. Egelhoffer*).

Publications

Script:

Lederer, Charles, and Alyssa Gallin, and Molly Haskell, ''*His Girl Friday*: From *The Front Page* to *His Girl Friday*: Woman's Work. The Proto-feminism of *His Girl Friday*,'' in *Scenario*, vol. 1, no. 4, Fall 1995.

Books:

Bogdanovich, Peter, *The Cinema of Howard Hawks*, New York, 1962.
Milliaen, Jean-Claude, *Howard Hawks*, Paris, 1966.
Wood, Robin, *Howard Hawks*, London, 1968.
Gili, Jean, *Howard Hawks*, Paris, 1971.
McBride, Joseph, editor, *Focus on Howard Hawks*, Englewood Cliffs, New Jersey, 1972.
Haskell, Molly, *From Reverence to Rape*, New York, 1973.
Johnston, Claire, *Notes on Women's Cinema*, London, 1973.
Mast, Gerald, *The Comic Mind*, New York, 1973.
Vermilye, Jerry, *Cary Grant*, New York, 1973.
Willis, Donald, *The Films of Howard Hawks*, Metuchen, New Jersey, 1975.
Yanni, Nicholas, *Rosalind Russell*, New York, 1975.
Deschner, Donald, *The Films of Cary Grant*, Secaucus, New Jersey, 1978.
Murphy, Kathleen A., *Howard Hawks: An American Auteur in the Hemingway Tradition*, Ann Arbor, 1978.
Cavell, Stanley, *Pursuits of Happiness: The Hollywood Comedy of Remarriage*, Cambridge, Massachusetts, 1981.
Ciment, Michel, *Les Conquérants d'un nouveau monde: Essais sur le cinéma américain*, Paris, 1981.
Giannetti, Louis, *Masters of the American Cinema*, Englewood Cliffs, New Jersey, 1981.
Mast, Gerald, *Howard Hawks, Storyteller*, Oxford, 1982.
McBride, Joseph, editor, *Hawks on Hawks*, Berkeley, 1982.
Poague, Leland, *Howard Hawks*, Boston, 1982.
Britton, Andrew, *Cary Grant: Comedy and Male Desire*, Newcastle-upon-Tyne, 1983.
Schickel, Richard, *Cary Grant: A Celebration*, London, 1983.
Dupuis, Jean-Jacques, *Cary Grant*, Paris, 1984.
Simsolo, Noël, *Howard Hawks*, Paris, 1984.
Branson, Clark, *Howard Hawks: A Jungian Study*, Los Angeles, 1987.
Higham, Charles, and Ray Moseley, *Cary Grant: The Lonely Heart*, New York, 1989.
Buehrer, Beverly B., *Cary Grant: A Bio-Bibliography*, Westport, 1990.
Hillier, Jim, *Howard Hawks: American Artist*, Champaign, 1997.
McCarthy, Todd, *Howard Hawks: The Grey Fox of Hollywood*, New York, 1997.
McCann, Graham, *Cary Grant: A Class Apart*, New York, 1998.

Articles:

Variety (New York), 10 January 1940.
Nugent, Frank S., in *New York Times*, 12 January 1940.
Roman, Robert, ''Cary Grant,'' in *Films in Review* (New York), December 1961.
Agel, Henri, ''Howard Hawks,'' in *New York Film Bulletin*, no. 4, 1962.
Sarris, Andrew, ''The World of Howard Hawks,'' in *Films and Filming* (London), July and August 1962.
''Hawks Issue'' of *Cahiers du Cinéma* (Paris), January 1963.
Rivette, Jacques, and François Truffaut, interview with Howard Hawks, in *Interviews with Film Directors*, edited by Andrew Sarris, New York, 1967.
Ringgold, Gene, ''Rosalind Russell,'' in *Films in Review* (New York), December 1970.
Wise, Naomi, ''The Hawksian Women,'' in *Take One* (Montreal), January-February 1971.
Brackett, Leigh, ''A Comment on the Hawksian Women,'' in *Take One* (Montreal), July-August 1971.
Cooney, K., ''Demonology,'' in *Movietone News* (Seattle), April 1975.
Powers, T., ''Screwball Liberation,'' in *Jump Cut* (Chicago), April 1978.

His Girl Friday

Yeck, Joanne L., in *Magill's Survey of Cinema 2*, Englewood Cliffs, New Jersey, 1980.

Guarner, J. L., in *Casablanca* (Madrid), July-August 1981.

Film Reader (Evanston, Illinois), no. 5, 1982.

Wide Angle (Athens, Ohio), no. 3, 1983.

American Film (Washington, D.C.), July-August 1983.

Cieutat, M., ''Spéciale première: Les Trois Versions de *The Front Page* ou le cinéma-roi,'' in *Positif* (Paris), September 1983.

Smith, J. A., ''*His Girl Friday* in the Cell: A Case Study of Theatre-to-Film Adaptation,'' in *Literature/Film Quarterly* (Salisbury, Maryland), April 1985.

Stevens, J. F. D., ''The Unfading Image from *The Front Page*,'' in *Film and History* (Newark, New Jersey), December 1985.

Review, in *EPD Film* (Frankfurt), vol. 6, no. 7, July 1989.

Masson, Alain, ''*La dame du vendredi:* De la satire à comédie,'' in *Positif* (Paris), no. 389–390, July-August 1993.

Vatrican, Vincent, ''*La dame du vendredi:* Howard Hawks,'' in *Cahiers du Cinéma* (Paris), Hors-série, 1993.

Lake, J.M., ''What Are Little Girls Made Of?'' in *Michigan Academician*, vol. 26, no. 2, 1994.

Hietala, V., ''Meidan vastaeronneiden kesken,'' in *Filmihullu* (Helsinki), no. 6, 1995.

Mulvey, Laura, ''*His Girl Friday*,'' in *Sight & Sound* (London), vol. 7, no. 3, March 1997.

* * *

Hollywood director Howard Hawks said he got the idea for *His Girl Friday* at a dinner party at which the guests were doing a reading of the Ben Hecht and Charles MacArthur play *The Front Page*. Hawks had handed the male reporter's part (Hildy Johnson) to one of the women while he took the managing editor's lines (Walter Burns). After a few pages of dialogue, Hawks grew excited and decided that the play was better with a girl playing Hildy Johnson. He called Hecht and suggested changing the reporter's sex for a future film project. Hecht liked the idea, but he had other project commitments; so Hawks hired Charles Lederer to write additional dialogue for a new script. Lederer had written the script of the 1931 movie version of *The Front Page*, directed by Lewis Milestone, and had co-written other Hollywood screenplays with Hecht. On *His Girl Friday*, he worked with

Hecht (who receives no screen credit) to revamp characters and dialogue while preserving the wit and style of the original.

His Girl Friday's pivotal plot issue is Hildy's (Rosalind Russell) decision whether to marry the tepid, dull Bruce Baldwin (Ralph Bellamy) or team up with her ex-boss and ex-husband, newspaper editor Walter Burns (Cary Grant). Although film critic Molly Haskell praised the way that the movie allows a woman to find her identity in a non-domestic sphere, Hildy still faces rather restrictive options—marriage to home, children, and pallid Bruce or marriage to career and ego with a maniacal Walter. Hildy's choice to remain with the press is less a decision to relinquish her "feminine" longings for home and family than a commitment to the continued excitement and kinetic activity of the world of journalism. Her decision to remarry Walter grows out of their mutual understanding, respect, and love for professionalism. Hildy's ultimate decision for an active, motion-filled life is her only possible choice in a "Hawksian" world. As Hawks himself suggested, her solution is the only way that she can work up enough sense of speed so that she won't have to think about how limited her options really are and how bad life really is.

When *His Girl Friday* premiered in 1940, it baffled and excited critics and public alike for just one reason—its speed. Hawks's actors overlapped their dialogue; they spoke in lower tones of voice; conversations ran almost simultaneously. Hawks reinforced the sensation of speed by keeping his characters in constant activity. For example, when he finds out that Hildy is getting married, Walter nervously reacts by rubbing his hand, touching the phone, picking up a carnation from a vase and slipping it into his buttonhole. All the while, he struggles to keep an impassive face. When he tries to convince Hildy to postpone her wedding plans so that she can write an important story, his impassioned, aggressive speech drives her around the room, first clockwise and then counter-clockwise. When Hawks cannot rely on his characters' motions, he uses such techniques as rapid cuts between the reporters talking into their telephones or a searchlight sweeping across the room to keep the pace frenetic. Hawks's comedy clocks in at 240 words-per-minute, about 100–140 words per minute faster than the average speaking rate; but his timing, camerawork and editing make it seem still faster.

The film is so mannered, especially in its pacing, that the degree of stylization calls attention to itself. When Walter Burns describes Bruce Baldwin, he says that he looks like "That actor—Ralph Bellamy." He later quips to one of the film's characters, "The last man that said that to me was Archie Leach just a week before he cut his throat." (Archie Leach is Cary Grant's real name.) Such references do not really disrupt the film but merely add to the movie's hilarious message on the absurdity of believing in the characters as real people. Coupled with the timing and acting, the parodic elements contribute to the development of an essay on the absurdity of any kind of ethical or moral commitments—any commitments to "normal values"—in the modern world.

His Girl Friday was the first screwball comedy to depart from the money-marriage-ego conflicts of *Holiday*, *My Man Godfrey*, and *The Philadelphia Story*, inserting into the same comic structure and pattern of action a conflict between career and marriage. Throughout the 1940s, career-marriage decisions for women provided the crises in several screwball comedies. *His Girl Friday* marked the transition from the subversion of women working for ends other than marriage to more explicit statements regarding money-marriage-sex roles in the genre in the 1940s.

—Lauren Rabinovitz

HITLER: EIN FILM AUS DEUTSCHLAND

(Hitler: A Film From Germany; Our Hitler)

West Germany, 1977

Director: Hans-Jürgen Syberberg

Production: TMS Film (Munich), WDR (Cologne), BBC (London), INA (Paris), in color; running time: 400 minutes. Released 1977.

Executive producer: Harry Nap; **screenplay:** Hans-Jürgen Syberberg; **photography:** Dietrich Lohmann; **editor:** Jutta Brandstaedter; **sound recordist:** Heymo H. Heyder.

Cast: Heinz Schubert; André Heller; Harry Baer; Peter Kern; Hellmuth Lange; Rainer V. Artenfels; Peter Moland; Martin Sperr; J. Buzalsky; Peter Lühr; and others.

Awards: BFI Special Award, London Film Festival, 1977.

Publications

Script:

Syberberg, Hans-Jürgen, *Hitler: Ein Film aus Deutschland*, Hamburg, 1978.

Books:

Sontag, Susan, *Under the Eye of Saturn*, New York, 1980.
Syberberg, Hans-Jürgen, *Die Freudlose Gesellschaft: Notizen aus dem letzen Jahr*, Munich, 1981.
Corrigan, Timothy, *New German Film: The Displaced Image*, Austin, Texas, 1983.
Rentschler, Eric, *West German Film in the Course of Time*, New York, 1984.
Elsaesser, Thomas, *New German Cinema: A History*, London, 1989.

Articles:

Pym, John, "Syberberg and the Tempter of Democracy," in *Sight and Sound* (London), Autumn 1977.
Syberberg, Hans-Jürgen, in *Cahiers du Cinéma* (Paris), October 1977.
Robinson, David, in *Times* (London), 25 November 1977.
Variety (New York), 30 November 1977.
Andrews, Nigel, "Hitler as Entertainer," in *American Film* (Washington, D.C.), April 1978.
Stimpson, Mansel, in *Montage* (London), Summer 1978.
Interview with Syberberg, in *Cinématographe* (Paris), June 1978.
Courant, Gérard, in *Cinéma* (Paris), July 1978.
Interview with Syberberg, in *Ecran* (Paris), July 1978.

Hilter: Ein Film aus Deutschland

Lajeunesse, Jacqueline, in *Image et Son* (Paris), August 1978.
''Special Issue'' of *Cahiers du Cinéma* (Paris), September 1978.
Oudart, Jean-Pierre, in *Cahiers du Cinéma* (Paris), November 1978.
Brandlmeier, Thomas, in *Medien und Erziehung* (Munich), no. 1, 1979.
Frey, Reiner, in *Filmfaust* (Frankfurt), April-May 1979.
Buckman, Peter, in *Listener* (London), 16 August 1979.
DiMatteo, Robert, in *Kino* (Berlin), October 1979.
Hoberman, J., in *Voice* (Los Angeles), 14 January 1980.
Pichter, Henry, in *Cineaste* (New York), Spring 1980.
Sharrett, C., ''Epiphany for Modernism: Anti-Illusionism and Theatrical Tradition in Syberberg's *Our Hitler,*'' in *Millenium* (New York), Fall 1981-Winter 1982.
Chaput, L., in *Séquences* (Montreal), January 1982.
D'Andrea, R., in *Cinema Nuovo* (Bari), August-October 1982.
Erkkila, Betsy, ''Hans-Jürgen Syberberg: An Interview,'' in *Literature/Film Quarterly* (Salisbury, Maryland), October 1982.
Piemme, J.-M., and others, in *Revue Belge du Cinéma* (Brussels), Spring 1983.
''On the Cinematic Photograph and the Possibility of Mourning in *Hitler* and *Nostalgia,*'' in *Wide Angle* (Athens, Ohio), vol. 9, no. 1, 1987.
Socci, S., ''Dal paradiso perduto all'inferno culturale (*Hitler*),'' in *Castoro Cinema* (Florence), September-October 1989.
Koshar, R., in *American Historical Review*, vol. 96, no. 4, 1991.
Santner, E.L, ''The Problem with Hitler: Postwar German Aesthetics and the Legacy of Fascism,'' in *New German Critique*, vol. 57, Fall 1992.
''Az inas monologja,'' in *Filmvilag* (Budapest), no. 1, 1992.
Elsaesser, Thomas, ''Filming Fascism,'' in *Sight & Sound* (London), vol. 2, no. 5, September 1992.
Hammond, Wally, ''Deutsch Courage,'' in *Time Out* (London), no. 1150, 2 September 1992.
Bacon, Henry, ''Hitler—elokuva Saksasta,'' in *Filmihullu* (Helsinki), no. 3, 1993.
Elsaesser, Thomas, ''Istorija—vseogo liš' staryj fil'm?'' in *Iskusstvo Kino* (Moscow), no. 10, October 1994.

* * *

Hans-Jürgen Syberberg's *Hitler: A Film from Germany* is the most controversial film produced in post-war Germany. The central thesis of the film propounds the notion that Hitler is within all of us.

Syberberg attempts to illuminate the German soul and German myth—and as such recalls romanticism's themes and preoccupations. Moreover, in his seven hour film, Nazi Germany is depicted as a gargantuan spectacle in which Hitler becomes the ultimate show-man-filmmaker; thus Syberberg does not only challenge what a film about Hitler should be like, but also raises important questions about cinematic representation in general.

Hitler and the previously published book about the film had so annoyed the German critical establishment that when a section was previewed at Cannes in 1977, the film was virtually boycotted by all the major German reviewers. In protest, Syberberg, who felt himself deliberately misunderstood, withdrew the film from the Berlin Film Festival and blocked its screening in his native land for a couple of years. The world premier was held at the London Film Festival in 1977 and *Hitler* was awarded the B.F.I.'s annual prize for "the most original and imaginative film of the year." Subsequently the film was on general release for several months in Paris and *Cahiers du Cinema* enthusiastically devoted a whole issue to Syberberg and his film. Susan Sontag acclaimed *Hitler* "one of the great works of art of the twentieth century."

Hitler, with two earlier films, *Ludwig—Requiem for a Virgin King* (1972) and *Karl May—In Search of Paradise Lost* (1974), forms a trilogy which meditates on German and European history and on the cinema itself. As in the two earlier films, a refined and innovative system of front projection is deployed. Syberberg perceives the idea of projection, in the symbolic sense, as the dominant idea governing the film: "We will show the world of Hitler in the form of projections, fantastic dreams, projections of the will that gave shape to these visions." Syberberg attempts nothing less than a counter-projection which takes the form of cinematic exorcism, to justify the necessary *Trauerarbeit* (the toil of mourning), i.e. to accept the guilt and loss, and also to register it as such and not to repress it.

Hitler is radically anti-realistic in style, relying on hyperbole, parody, stylization, and montage. Syberberg's aesthetic conception fuses such apparent oppositions as romanticism and modernism. The Wagnerian ideal of *Gesamtkunstwerk* is evoked through using his music and through the depiction of romantic yearnings and ecstasies—visions of renewal, paradise, and hell. Yet the Brechtian notion of epic theatre is also applicable in strategies of estrangement and distanciation. History is produced as a circus show where famous historical figures (e.g., Caligula and Napoleon) parade as Hitler. Against the background of huge projected slides (Hitler's chancellery and his house in Berchtesgarden), puppets (a toy-dog with Hitler's face), cut-out doubles, and dummies are used to portray the social imaginary of Nazi Germany. The film unfolds through a series of tableaux, endless monologues, direct address, and original sound-material.

Syberberg wants to draw parallels to cinema on different levels. He makes reference to Melies's A *Trip to the Moon*, Welles's *Citizen Kane*, and Lang's *M* (the final scene, where Peter Lorre defends his evil deeds because he can't help himself, is here reenacted by Peter Kern dressed as an SS officer). Cardboard figures from Caligari to Nosferatu punctuate the film, therefore linking them to the idea of Hitler being a subject for projection of the most evil desires in us. Moreover, Syberberg perceives the trend towards ever-increasing conformity in the developments of cinematic codes as a further basis for his comparison with facism. Thus *Greed* and its botching by MGM becomes an example, but he also examines Sergei Eisenstein's persecution under Stalin. The figures of Hitler and Himmler are shown to be merely *representations* and not embodiments, when delegating their roles to various actors, historical personalities, and marionettes. The condemnation of commercial cinema culminates in the polemical comparison between Auschwitz and McCarthy's Hollywood. In Syberberg's view it was not the actual physical presence of Hitler which historically mobilized the masses, but Hitler as representation and Nazism as spectacle. He is convinced of the vitality of the myth, which is why he wants to break its fascination through mechanisms of estrangement and montage.

And this is the crux of the controversial German reception of *Hitler*. It is not so much Syberberg's aesthetics *per se*, but the fear that his aestheticisation of politics might seduce the spectator since it is bordering on aestheticising Nazism. His "creative irrationality," many critics argue, leads to further mystification and connects too problematically to Nazi-mythology.

—Ulrike Sieglohr

HOMELAND

See **HEIMAT; DIE ZWEITE HEIMAT**

HONG GAO LIANG

See **RED SORGHUM**

HOOP DREAMS

USA, 1994

Director: Steve James

Production: Kartemquin Films/KCTA-TV; color, 35mm (blown-up from 16mm); running time: 169 minutes. Released 1994. Filmed in and around Chicago, Illinois, and at the University of Illinois between 1986 and 1991.

Producers: Frederick Marx, Steve James, and Peter Gilbert; **photography:** Peter Gilbert; **editors:** Frederick Marx, Steve James, and Bill Haugse; **sound:** Adam Singer and Tom Yore; **music:** Ben Sidran.

Cast: William Gates; Arthur Agee; Emma Gates; Curtis Gates; Willie Gates; Sheila Agee; Arthur "Bo" Agee; Tomika Agee; Joe "Sweetie" Agee; Earl Smith; Gene Pingatore; Isiah Thomas; Dick Vitale; Bobby Knight; Kevin O'Neill; Joey Meyer; Spike Lee; Bo Ellis.

Awards: Best Documentary, Sundance Film Festival; Best Documentary, Los Angeles Film Critics Association; Best Documentary, New York Film Critics Circle; Best Documentary, Boston Society of Film Critics; Best Documentary, Texas Film Critics Awards; Best Documentary, National Board of Review; Best Documentary, National Society of Film Critics; Golden Globe Award, Best Documentary.

Hoop Dreams

Publications

Books:

Joravsky, Ben, *Hoop Dreams: A True Story of Hardship and Triumph*, Atlanta, 1995, 1996.
Pierson, John, *Spike, Mike, Slackers & Dykes: A Guided Tour Across a Decade of American Independent Cinema*, New York, 1995.

Articles:

Seigel, Jessica, ''*Hoop Dreams* Rises to the Top at Sundance,'' in *Chicago Tribune*, 31 January 1994.
Ebert, Roger, in *Chicago Sun-Times*, 13 February 1994.
Collin, Glenn, in the *New York Times*, 21 February 1994.
Zwecker, Bill, in *Chicago Sun-Times*, 15 July 1994.
Christiansen, Richard, in *Chicago Tribune*, 17 July 1994.
Zwecker, Bill, in *Chicago Sun-Times*, 16 September 1994.
Wilmington, Michael, ''When Film Dreams Come True,'' in *Chicago Tribune*, 2 October 1994.
Poe, Janita, ''High School Calls a Foul, Sues Over Basketball Film,'' in *Chicago Tribune*, 6 October 1994.
Berkow, Ira, ''Dreaming *Hoop Dreams*,'' in the *New York Times*, 9 October 1994.
McGavin, Patrick Z., ''From the Streets and the Gyms to the Courtrooms and Beyond,'' in the *New York Times*, 9 October 1994.
Kornheiser, Tony, ''Living a Dream and Dreaming to Live,'' in the *Washington Post*, 3 November 1994.
Howe, Desson, in the *Washington Post*, 13 November 1994.
Will, George, ''Salvation Through Basketball,'' in the *Washington Post*, 24 November 1994.
Dretzka, Gary, ''*Hoop Dreams* Shooting for Best-Picture Oscar,'' in *Chicago Tribune*, 10 December 1994.
Cox, Dan, ''Fine Line Has *Dreams* of Best Pic,'' in *Variety* (New York), 2 January 1995.
''Acad Rebounds After *Hoop* Airball,'' in *Variety* (New York), 20 February, 1995.
Corliss, Richard, ''How the Winner Lost,'' in *Time* (New York), 27 February 1995.
Angell, Roger, ''Two Dreams: One Gets Oscar's Nod, One Gets Gumped,'' in *The New Yorker*, 13 March 1995.
Spillane, Margaret, ''Slam-dunked,'' in *The Nation* (New York), 13 March 1995.
Ansen, David, ''Why Did Oscar Drop the Ball on *Hoop Dreams?*'' in *Newsweek* (New York), 27 March 1995.
Diamos, Jason, ''Hoop Dream Shot Clock is Slowly Ticking Away,'' in the *New York Times*, 27 March 1995.
Diamos, Jason, ''A New Chapter in the Gates Story,'' in the *New York Times*, 29 March 1995.
''Dream of Conquest,'' in *Sight and Sound* (London), April 1995.
Marvel, M., in *Interview* (New York), April 1995.
Arthur, Paul and Janet Cutler, ''On the Rebound: *Hoop Dreams* and its Discontents,'' in *Cineaste* (New York), Summer 1995.
Short review, in *Séquences* (Haute-Ville), no. 177, March-April 1995.
Gower, Mike, ''Hoop Fantasies,'' in *Sight & Sound* (London), vol. 5, no. 7, July 1995.
Sperber, Murray, and Lee Jones, ''Hollywood Dreams: Hoop Realities,'' in *Jump Cut* (Berkeley), no. 40, March 1996.
Terry, Cliff, ''Kartemquin: a Different Kind of Dream Factory,'' in *American Cinematographer* (Hollywood), vol. 77, no. 4, April 1996.

* * *

Hoop Dreams is a richly human and profoundly American film. It is at once an allegory about striving to achieve, and the politics and pressures of achievement; and a story of the anguish of poverty in urban America and an indictment of the meat market aspect of contemporary scholastic and professional athletics. While the film is a documentary, there is as much drama and suspense as any deftly plotted fiction. The difference is that the emotions and lives unfolding on screen are real.

The film opens with the NBA All-Star game being played in Chicago. Just a few miles beyond the fanfare, two boys are coming of age in rough urban neighborhoods. Both watch the game on television, almost in awe, while nurturing aspirations for stardom as professional basketball players. Both dream of one-way tickets out of the ghetto, complete with new houses and spiffy cars.

William Gates and Arthur Agee have honed their athletic skills on the neighborhood playgrounds. William is seen practicing slam-dunks in a park, by a bare brick building: a world away from the glare of a Madison Square Garden or an Orlando Arena. Both teens are recruited to play basketball at St. Joseph, a suburban Catholic high school. Years earlier, former Detroit Pistons hoop star Isiah Thomas (who also appears in the film) graduated from St. Joseph. The film now asks the question: ''If Isiah can become not only a professional athlete but a perennial All-Star and certain Hall of Famer, why not William and Arthur?''

As William's career at St. Joseph progresses, the media compares him to Isiah, while Gene Pingatore, the school's basketball coach, sees within Arthur the potential to become a ''great player.'' Later on, the image of Arthur shooting hoops in a playground garbed in a red basketball uniform with the name ''Thomas'' stitched on the back speaks volumes about his dream. Being accepted at St. Joseph, however, is the initial step of a lengthy, arduous process. Arthur and William will have to acclimate themselves to a school outside their neighborhood, in an interracial climate. Each day, they must endure a three-hour commute to and from school. Once there, they will have to succeed academically as well as athletically.

Hoop Dreams is an up-close-and-personal look at five years in the lives of William and Arthur. It opens with their enrollment at St. Joseph, and concludes with their heading off to college. In between are the traumas and victories they experience on and off the basketball court, and the answering of questions which are posed as the boys begin attending St. Joseph: How will William and Arthur relate to the school, and how will the school and the drill sergeant-like coach relate to them? How will their athletic skills develop? How will their lives and perspectives change over the years? How will all this impact on their relatives? Arthur's dad, Bo, is a failed athlete who feels he ''could have made the pros,'' and does not want his son to experience the ''bad things'' he has known in his life. William's older brother Curtis is another ex-jock who lives through his sibling while observing that ''all my basketball dreams are gone.''

With keen insight, the film reflects on the value system of contemporary American society. Their basketball prowess certainly affords Arthur and William an opportunity for education, and self-improvement, in an academic environment far superior to their neighborhood high school. When William begins his freshman year at St. Joseph, his reading skills are at the fourth grade level but, by the time he is a sophomore, his reading level has gone up several grades. The film raises several societal questions here, including: ''What about all the ghetto kids who do not have William's physical aptitude?'' and ''How many kids will never have their ability tapped because they are unable to slam a ball through a hoop?'' Furthermore, Arthur and William are attending St. Joseph not out of altruism. Are they being exploited for their talents? Are they perceived as being little more than bodies, who will help a team win a championship? If they were to fail on the court, or suffer a potentially career-ending injury, will they be discarded? Arthur is only on a partial scholarship and is booted out of school because his parents cannot keep up tuition payments, then loses all academic credit. St. Joseph refuses to release his transcript until his family pays $1800 in back tuition. The welfare of the teenager becomes secondary to the collecting of a bill from a family where the breadwinner is a minimum wage-earner.

In telling the story of William, Arthur, and their respective families, *Hoop Dreams* serves to reaffirm the humanity of black males. Bo Agee sadly fits a negative stereotype of the African-American man as an irresponsible, violent, drug-abusing loser. At one point, he even abandons his family and is later seen pushing drugs in the playground where his son plays basketball. Bo's fall continues when he becomes a crack addict, beats his wife, is arrested for battery, and spends seven months in jail for burglary. While his behavior is not condoned in the film, it is clear that he is unable to adequately support his family on a minimum wage and is tragically weakened by his loss of self-esteem.

Despite the specifics of its setting and subject, *Hoop Dreams* is a film with universal meaning. Arthur is eventually enrolled in a Chicago high school, and leads his unranked team to the city championship. He and his teammates then travel downstate, to play for the state title. In one sequence, Arthur's parents are seen walking across the University of Illinois campus, where the game will be played. One of them notes that ''a child'' should have the experience of attending such a school. This idle observation expresses every dream that every parent has ever had for any child.

But what resonates long after seeing *Hoop Dreams* is an unavoidable fact of contemporary American life. For every Michael Jordan, Shaquille O'Neal, or Isiah Thomas, there are thousands of young men like Arthur Agee and William Gates: young hoop dreamers who are forged in the ghetto, and who never will earn all of the glory and affluence they so desperately crave.

—Rob Edelman

LA HORA DE LOS HORNOS

(The Hour of the Furnaces)

Argentina, 1968

Director: Fernando E. Solanas

Production: Grupo Cine Liberación; black and white, 16 and 35mm; running time: 260 minutes, French version: 200 minutes; the film is composed of 3 parts: ''Neocolonialismo y violencia'' - 90 minutes, ''Acto para la liberación'' - 120 minutes, and ''Violencia y liberación'' - 45 minutes. Released 1968. Filmed in Argentina.

Producer: Fernando E. Solanas; **screenplay:** Fernando E. Solanas and Octavio Getino; **photography:** Juan Carlos de Sanzo with Fernando E. Solanas; **editor:** Fernando E. Solanas; **sound:** Octavio Getino; **music:** Fernando E. Solanas.

Publications

Books:

Solanas, Fernando E., and Octavio Getino, *Cine, cultura y descolonización*, Mexico City, 1973.

Pick, Zuzana, editor, *Latin American Filmmakers and the Third Cinema*, Ottawa, 1978.

Solanas, Fernando E., *La mirada: reflexiones sobre cine y cultura*, with Horacio González, Buenos Aires, 1989.

Monteagudo, Luciano, *Fernando Solanas*, Buenos Aires, 1993.

Articles:

Marcorelles, Louis, ''Solanas: Film as a Political Essay,'' in *Evergreen* (New York), July 1969.

''Cinema as a Gun: An Interview with Fernando Solanas,'' in *Cineaste* (New York), Fall 1969.

Avant-Scène du Cinéma (Paris), October 1969.

"Fernando Solanas: An Interview," in *Film Quarterly* (Berkeley), Fall 1970.
MacBean, James Roy, in *Film Quarterly* (Berkeley), Fall 1970.
Matthews, John, "And After?: A Response to Solanas and Getino," in *Afterimage* (London), Summer 1971.
Haycock, Joel, "Notes on Solanas and Godard," in *Film Society Review* (New York), November and December 1971.
Getino, Octavio, and Fernando Solanas, "Towards a Third Cinema," in *Cineaste* (New York), Winter 1971.
"Algunas preguntas a Octavio Getino," in *Cine Cubano* (Havana), no. 73–75, 1972.
Solanas, Fernando, and Octavio Getino, "Voor een derde cinema," in *Skrien* (Amsterdam), Spring 1972.
Wilson, David, "Aspects of Latin American Political Cinema," in *Sight and Sound* (London), Summer 1972.
Films and Filming (London), November 1972.
MacBean, James Roy, "Fernando Solanas: An Interview," in *Film Quarterly* (Berkeley), Winter 1972.
Sibon-Blanc, A., in *Image et Son* (Paris), no. 269, 1973.
Carestia Greenwood, Concetta, "The New South American Cinema: From Neo-Realism to Expressive Realism," in *Latin American Library Review*, Spring 1973.
Hennebelle, G., "Le Réalisme magique et les élans du coeur," in *Ecran* (Paris), 15 March 1979.
Ranvaud, Don, "Fernando Solanas: An Interview," in *Framework* (Norwich), Spring 1979.
Solanas, Fernando, and others, "The Cinema: Art Form or Political Weapon," in *Framework* (Norwich), Autumn 1979.
Stam, Robert, "*Hour of the Furnaces* and the Two Avant-Gardes," in *Millenium* (New York), Fall-Winter 1980–81.
Medina, R., "*La Hora de los hornos*: Imagen de un pueblo vivo," in *Cine Cubano* (Havana), 1981.
Danvers, Louis, in *Visions* (Brussels), February 1986.
"Interview with Solanas," in *Cineaste* (New York), volume 16, nos. 1–2, 1987–88.
"Solanas Issue" of *Avant-Scène du Cinéma* (Paris), January-February 1989.
Pick, Z. M., "The Dialectical Wanderings of Exile," in *Screen* (Oxford), no. 4, 1989.
Thompson, F., "Metaphors of Space: Polarizations, Dualism and Third World Cinema," in *Screen* (Oxford), no. 1, 1993.
Menna, C., and V. Cervetto, "Cine militante clandestino en Argentina," in *Film-Historia* (Barcelona), vol. 6, no. 2, 1996.
Chanan, Michael, "The Changing Geography of Third Cinema," in *Screen* (Oxford), vol. 38, no. 4, Winter 1997.

* * *

The liberation struggles of the 1960s were a fertile seedbed for *La hora de los hornos*. Independence movements in the colonies and neo-colonies of the Third World, student revolts in the United States and Western Europe, and the brief protest by Czechoslovakians against the dull grey bureaucracy of the Soviet Union were the world context in which Fernando E. Solanas and Octavio Getino's film exploded. Argentina moved closer to a social revolution than it ever had before (or since), and *Hora* was an important expression of that movement, as well as a pivotal example for cineastes involved in national liberation movements throughout the world.

The film is a documentary of such length (4'' hours) that most viewers outside of Argentina have probably seen only the first part. Perhaps influenced by the work of the Cuban documentarist, Santiago Alvarez, the directors have created a film that takes the form of a didactic collage, committed to the denunciation of imperialism and its cultural influences. As is stated in the film: "Mass communications are more effective for neo-colonialism than napalm. What is real, true, and rational is to be found on the margin of the Law, just as are the people."

That which is most interesting about the film's form is its relation to the audience. Rather than the conventional finished cinematic product, ready for viewer consumption, the work is conceived as an open-ended militant act, in which the film itself is only important as a "detonator" or "pretext for dialogue." Parts 2 and 3 were structured with pauses in which the projector was to be turned off and discussion was to take place; groups using the film were encouraged to employ their own visual or sound accompaniment and to cut or add to the film as they saw fit. Of course, the very context in which the film was shown contributed to the sense of audience participation. Because the film was illegal, no one in the audience was a mere spectator: "On the contrary, from the moment he decided to attend the showing, from the moment he lined himself up on this side by taking risks and contributing his living experience to the meeting, he became an actor, a more important protagonist than those who appeared in the films. The situation turned everyone into accomplices of the act."

Argentina's climate of political repression also required a novel approach to production. Conceiving of their work as a guerrilla act, Solanas and Getino "provided a model for clandestine activity under an aggressively hostile regime which no filmmakers in Latin America or elsewhere have surpassed," noted the American critic Julianne Burton. Strict discipline and tight security were the rule, and all who participated in the film's production were required to develop interchangeable skills. One example of the measures required by the situation was that the film's footage had to be constantly disassembled and reassembled so that technicians in the processing laboratories would have no hint as to its subversive content.

The film's strident manichaeism ("*our* culture and *their* culture, *our* films and *their* films, *our* sense of beauty and *their* sense of beauty") and its puerile historical analysis seem dated today. But, the current situation in Latin America leaves little room for doubt that more such films are both needed and forthcoming. As Solanas and Getino stated in *Hora*, "At this time in Latin America there is room for neither passivity nor innocence. The intellectual's commitment is measured in terms of risks as well as words and ideas; what he does to further the cause of liberation is what counts." What Solanas and Getino did for the cause of liberation was make *La hora de los hornos*, which, as they reminded us in their first public statement about the film "is an *act* before it is a film—an act of liberation."

—John Mraz

HORROR OF DRACULA

See **DRACULA (1958)**

HORSE THIEF

See **DAOMA ZEI**

HOT WINDS

See **GARAM HAWA**

THE HOUR OF THE FURNACES

See **LA HORA DE LOS HORNOS**

HOWARDS END

UK, 1992

Director: James Ivory

Production: Merchant Ivory Productions; Technicolor, 35mm; running time: 142 minutes. Filmed in London, Oxfordshire, Shropshire, 1991.

Producer: Ismail Merchant; **screenplay:** Ruth Prawer Jhabvala, based on the novel by E. M. Forster; **photography:** Tony-Pierce Roberts; **editor:** Andrew Marcus; **assistant directors:** Chris Newman, Simon Moseley, Carol Oprey; **production designer:** Luciana Arrighi; **art director:** John Ralph; **music:** Richard Robbins; **sound editors:** Campbell Askew, Sarah Morton; **sound recordists:** Mike Shoring, Keith Grant; **costume design:** Jenny Beaven, John Bight.

Cast: Anthony Hopkins (*Henry Wilcox*); Emma Thompson (*Margaret Schlegel*); Vanessa Redgrave (*Ruth Wilcox*); Helen-Bonham Carter (*Helen Schlegel*); James Wilby (*Charles Wilcox*); Samuel West (*Leonard Bast*); Prunella Scales (*Aunt Juley*); Joseph Bennett (*Paul Wilcox*); Adrian Ross Magenty (*Tibby Schlegel*); Jo Kendall (*Annie*); Jemma Redgrave (*Evie Wilcoz*).

Awards: Oscars for Best Actress (Thompson), Best Adapted Screenplay, and Best Art Direction, 1992.

Publications

Books:

Long, Robert Emmet, *Films of Merchant Ivory*, New York, 1991.

Pym, John, and James Ivory, *Merchant Ivory's English Landscape: Rooms, Views, and Anglosaxon Attitudes*, New York, 1995.

Articles:

Bates, P., *Cineaste* (New York), 1992.

Variety (New York), 24 February 1992.

Anderson, P., *Films in Review* (New York), March-April 1992.

Francke, L., *Sight and Sound* (London), May 1992.

Guerin, M., ''Le collectioneur,'' in *Cahiers du Cinéma* (Paris), May 1992.

Roth-Bettoni, D., *Revue du Cinéma* (Paris), June 1992.

Sineux, M., *Positif* (Paris), June 1992.

McFarlane, B., ''Literature-Film Connections,'' in *Cinema Papers* (Melbourne), August 1992.

Benjamin, D., *Séquences* (Montreal), September 1992.

Grugeau, G., *24 Images* (Montreal), September 1992.

Frook, J.E., ''Sony Unit's 'Howard' Slow Rollout Pays Off,'' in *Variety* (New York), 11 January 1993.

Novelli, I., ''Casa Howard,'' in *Film* (Rome), no. 1, January-February 1993.

Jacobs, J., ''Indies Play the Smiling Game as Academy Honors Outsiders,'' in *Film Journal* (New York), vol. 96, March 1993.

Jaroš, Jan, in *Film a Doba* (Prague), vol. 39, no. 2, Summer 1993.

Hipsky, M., ''Anglophil(m)ia: Why Does America Watch Merchant-Ivory Movies?'' in *Journal of Popular Film and Television* (Washington, D.C.), vol. 22, no. 3, 1994.

* * *

Brand name producer-director teams are a rarity in the movies. Merchant-Ivory is one of the few producer-director teams. It is also the most successful.

Audiences know exactly what to expect of a Merchant-Ivory production: A literate script adapted from an esteemed (and seemingly unfilmable) literary source, sumptuous period decor and costumes, and impeccable acting of the classically trained rather than Method school—a genteel journey into the well-mannered past with not a car chase or explosion in sight nor a foul word to be heard. In other words, a fastidious cinematic equivalent of an episode of public television's long-running series ''Masterpiece Theatre''—a comparison Merchant-Ivory's detractors usually point to as the team's major weakness.

Merchant-Ivory's approach certainly flies in the face of conventional wisdom as to what constitutes marketability these days. But their films have been so successful in luring a lucrative new market, the ever-growing over-50 crowd, into theatres that Hollywood could no longer ignore them. As a result, Merchant-Ivory have now been folded into the gargantuan Disney organization and been given the financial backing to up their output, with guaranteed distribution for their elegant period pieces extending far beyond the art house theatres that were previously the team's domain. In addition, other producers have begun adopting the team's formula, turning out one Merchant-Ivory-type film after another like *Enchanted April, The Age of Innocence, Shadowlands, Tom and Viv*, and *Sense and Sensibility*, to name but a few.

Producer Ismail Merchant and director James Ivory (who had initially sought entrance into the movies as a set designer) have been making films since 1963. Their trademark combination of literariness, elegance, and well-bred sophistication did not manifest itself until 1979 with their adaptation of Henry James's novel *The Europeans*. But their fortunes turned most dramatically with the 1992 *Howards End*, the team's most popular film up to that time and third adaptation of an E. M. Forster novel following such earlier forays into Forster territory as *A Room With a View*, a modest success and multiple Academy Award winner that proved to be a harbinger of things to come, and *Maurice*, a relative flop. Like *A Room With a View*, *Howards End* scored big come Academy Award night in some of the ''lesser'' categories as Best Screenplay, Best Art Direction, and Best Costume Design. But it also captured the Best Actress prize for star Emma Thompson, adding millions of dollars to the picture's already substantial box office take.

A study of class distinction in Edwardian England, *Howards End* focuses on three families whose lives intersect with tragic and ironic results. Thompson and Bonham Carter play Margaret and Helen,

Howards End

sisters of obvious breeding but little means, who befriend working class bank clerk Leonard (West) in an effort to better his situation. They encourage him to get another job when they're tipped that his present employer may go under. They get the tip from wealthy businessman Henry Wilcox (Hopkins) whose wife, Ruth (Redgrave), has befriended Margaret for much the same purpose. Ruth learns that the sisters are faced with losing their home. When Ruth dies, she makes a last-minute bequest, leaving Howards End, her ancestral cottage in the country, to the soon-to-be-displaced Margaret. But Henry and his rotter son, Charles (James Wilby), keep the bequest a secret in order to keep the cottage in the family, even though it goes unused.

After Ruth's death, widower Henry takes up with the vibrant Margaret and eventually marries her. Meanwhile, Helen is made pregnant by Leonard—whose low-class wife had been seduced as a young girl, then tossed aside, by Henry himself. When Margaret learns of her manipulative husband's past indiscretion, she forgives him and requests that Helen be allowed to take up residence at Howards End to have her illegitimate baby. But Henry refuses, hypocritically spurning Helen for her indiscretion, even though it mirrors his own.

The perpetually down-on-his-luck Leonard, unaware that Helen is pregnant, shows up for another hand-out from his benefactors and is accidentally killed by Charles after being subjected to a thrashing. The ensuing scandal and exposed wounds of family dysfunction and class hostility boil to a head and Margaret threatens to leave Henry, a basically decent, albeit misguided man. Like the sisters and even the dead Leonard, he has always sought to do what's right, but achieved mostly wrong instead due to class difference. To hold onto Margaret, he agrees to her single demand that Howards End be turned over to her lock, stock, and barrel. Ironically, the tragic collision of classes has resulted in the property winding up in her hands just as the dying Ruth had long ago wished. And Helen, who had earlier been rejected as a suitable wife by another of Henry's sons, is free to live there and raise the offspring of her lower-class union.

The machinations of Forster's plot may strike some as a bit too reliant on coincidence. But Merchant-Ivory and their superlative crew and cast, lead by the engaging Thompson, bring the period story and characters so vividly to life that the coincidences seem not just credible, but inevitable.

Long, slow but never boring, *Howards End* trenchantly observes the foibles of its characters while creating a remarkable degree of empathy for them and concern for their respective fates. It grips the eye and the emotions like a good read—the good read, in fact, from which it sprang.

—John McCarty

HUANG TUDI

(Yellow Earth)

China, 1984

Director: Chen Kaige

Production: Youth Production Unit, Guangxi Film Studio; Eastmancolor; running time: 89 minutes; length: 8,010 feet. Released 1984. Subtitled version released 1986. Filmed in Mandarin and Shaanxi dialect.

Producer: Guo Keqi; **screenplay:** Zhang Ziliang, from the essay ''Echo in the Valley'' by Ke Lan; **photography:** Zhang Yimou; **lighting:** Zhang Shubin; **editor:** Pei Xiaonan; **sound recordist:** Lin Lin; **sound re-recordist:** Liu Quanye; **art director:** He Qun; **costumes:** Tian Geng and Chen Bona; **music:** Zhao Jiping; **music performed by:** The Orchestra and Traditional Music Ensemble of Xi'an Academy of Music; **subtitles:** Tony Rayns.

Cast: Xue Bai (*Cuiqiao*); Wang Xueqi (*Gu Qing*); Tan Tuo (*Father*); Liu Qiang (*Hanhan*); The Peasant Waistdrum Troupe of Ansai County.

Huang Tudi

Publications

Books:

Berry, Chris, editor, *Perspectives on Chinese Cinema*, Ithaca, New York, 1985.

Quiquemelle, Marie-Claire, and Jean-Loup Passek, *Le Cinéma chinois*, Paris, 1985.

Armes, Roy, *Third World Filmmaking and the West*, Berkeley, 1987.

Clark, Paul, *Chinese Cinema: Culture and Politics since 1949*, Cambridge, 1987.

Semsel, George Stephen, editor, *Chinese Film: The State of the Art in the Chinese Republic*, New York, 1987.

Kaige, Chen, and Tony Rayns, *King of the Children & the New Chinese Cinema*, New York, 1989.

McDougall, Bonnie S., *The Yellow Earth: A Film by Chen Kaige with a Complete Translation of the Filmscript*, Hong Kong, 1991.

Articles:

Interview with Chen Kaige, in *Skoop* (Amsterdam), February 1986.

Elley, Derek, in *Films and Filming* (London), August 1986.

Frodou, Jean-Michel, ''Lettre de Chine,'' in *Cahiers du Cinéma* (Paris), September 1986.

Rayns, Tony, in *Monthly Film Bulletin* (London), October 1986.

Films in Review (New York), December 1986.

Positif (Paris), January 1987.

Jaivin, Linda, in *Cinema Papers* (Melbourne), March and September 1987.

Film Quarterly (Berkeley), Winter 1987–88.

Sight and Sound (London), Winter 1987–88.

Rayns, Tony, in *Monthly Film Bulletin* (London), March 1988.

Interview with Chen Kaige, in *Time Out* (London), 17 August 1988.

Chow, R., ''Silent is the Ancient Plain: Music, Filmmaking, and the Conception of Reform in China's New Cinema,'' in *Discourse* (Bloomington, Indiana), Spring-Summer 1990.

Farquhar, M. A., ''The 'Hidden' Gender in *Yellow Earth*,'' in *Screen* (Oxford), no. 2, 1992.

Short Review, in *Film en Televisie + Video* (Brussels), no. 429, February 1993.

Sutton, D.S., ''Ritual, History, and the Films of Zhang Yimou,'' in *East-West Film Journal* (Honolulu), vol. 8, no. 2, 1994.

Donald, Stephanie, ''Women Reading Chinese Films: Between Orientalism and Silence,'' in *Screen* (Oxford), vol. 36, no. 4, Winter 1995.

Lu, A., ''Chen Kaige,'' in *Film Comment* (New York), vol. 33, September/October 1997.

* * *

Yellow Earth is a pivotal film in China artistically, from the point of view of competing notions of film practice, and explicitly for its place within the continuing debate about film in that country. Both Chen Kaige and his cinematographer Zhang Yimou are members of the ''Fifth Generation'' of Chinese film makers, the first group of students to graduate from the newly reopened Beijing Film Academy, China's only film school. It had been closed during the Cultural Revolution, and both personally experienced the dislocations inflicted by the policies of the ''revolution,'' having had their formal education curtailed during their teens and suffering exile to distant rural areas to labour alongside the peasants.

The film became a test case for ''innovative'' or art films. Temporarily withdrawn from circulation it was then re-released and a booklet of articles about it published in China. On its international success at foreign film festivals was hung the polemic of an important speech given in 1986 by the head of the Shanghai Film Studio, demanding that less importance be given to making ''salon successes'' and more to ''popular'' films for a local audience. (The debate is outlined by Tony Rayns in *Monthly Film Bulletin.*) *Yellow Earth* is a film deeply rooted in both the realities of Chinese peasant life and, more specifically, the facts of recent Chinese history. Set in 1939, its spare narrative tells of the visit of a young soldier from the Eighth Route Army to a poverty-stricken North Shaanxi village researching folk songs for adaptation by the Party for more polemical use. (One credo of Chinese Marxism was to learn from the people.) The film tells of the impact of his visit upon one family—a father, aged beyond his 45 years, his daughter, about to be sold into an arranged marriage, and her ''silly'' brother.

The dialogue is notably spare, but the film conveys its burden through Chen's monumental direction, Zhang Yimou's impressive cinematography, which refuses to isolate the characters from the bare, played-out fields of the Loess plateau which determine their mode of existence, and the spare and fierce beauty of the songs themselves, each telling its tale of women's oppression. Chen's austere and unwaveringly grave vision allows for no digression into melodrama, social comment, or the merely folkloric. He is not content to document peasant lives. By seeing his story in Shaanxi he ties it to the heart of Chinese Communism. It was there that Mao's legendary Long March terminated in 1935 and that he framed the discourse on art and literature that was to bear such equivocal fruits.

The ''timelessness'' of the feudal struggle for existence is shown in scenes unflinchingly illustrative of the direst poverty, meals consumed almost before they are served, a bridal feast that makes do with a carved wooden replica of the traditional fish course no one can afford, the simplicity of the domestic arrangements. Unlike earlier films in which soldiers or teachers carried the promise of revolution to distant parts, the result of soldier Gu's arrival is anything but a foregone conclusion. Gu respects the peasants' ways and speaks gently of the possibilities for change, specifically for change in women's conditions. Women soldiers have short hair and read and write. But the girl Ciuqiao's attempt to replace her traditional lament for her plight with Gu's campaign song ends with its promise of Communist victory choked off before she can complete it, by the waters closing over her head as she attempts to swim across the river to Gu's base. It is a scene which stands as an eloquent memorial to the struggles of a nation.

The same metaphorical force binds together the few crowd scenes—that of the dance to the Dragon King pleading for rain is shown to be not so different (it is viewed in much the same way) from the dance marking the farewell of the soldiers, for instance. Chen throughout shows a fine sense of overall structure and great delicacy in the handling of his performers. *Yellow Earth* is perhaps the boldest and most essentially Chinese of the films produced in that country during the last decade.

—Verina Glaessner

THE HUMAN BEAST

See **LA BETE HUMAINE**

THE HUMAN CONDITION

See **NINGEN NO JOKEN**

HUNGER

See **SULT**

THE HUSTLER

USA, 1961

Director: Robert Rossen

Production: 20th Century-Fox/Robert Rossen Enterprises; black and white; CinemaScope; running time: 135 minutes; length: 12,109 feet. Released September 1961.

Producer: Robert Rossen; **screenplay:** Robert Rossen, Sidney Carroll, from the novel by Walter Tevis; **assistant directors:** Charles Maguire, Don Kranz; **photography:** Gene Shufton (Eugen Schüfftan); **editor:** Deedee Allan; **sound:** James Shields; **art directors:** Harry Horner, Albert Brenner; **music:** Kenyon Hopkins; **technical advisor:** Willie Mosconi.

Cast: Paul Newman (*''Fast'' Eddie Felson*); Jackie Gleason (*Minnesota Fats*); Piper Laurie (*Sarah Packard*); George C. Scott (*Bert Gordon*); Myron McCormick (*Charlie Burns*); Murray Hamilton (*Findlay*); Michael Constantine (*Big John*); Stefan Gierasch (*Preacher*); Jake LaMotta and Vincent Gardinia (*Bartenders*); Gordon B. Clarke (*Cashier*); Alexander Rose (*Score Keeper*); Carolyn Coates (*Waitress*); Carl York (*Young Hustler*); Clifford Pellow (*Turk*).

Awards: Oscars for Best Art Direction and Best Black and White Cinematography, 1961. British Film Academy Awards for Best Film from any Source, and Best Actor (Newman), 1961.

Publications

Script:

Rossen, Robert, *The Hustler*, in *Three Screenplays*, New York, 1972, 1985.

Books:

Casty, Alan, *The Films of Robert Rossen*, New York, 1969.
Hamblett, Charles, *Paul Newman*, London, 1975.
Harbinson, Allen, *George C. Scott: The Man, The Actor, The Legend*, New York, 1977.
Godfrey, Lionel, *Paul Newman, Superstar: A Critical Biography*, New York, 1978.
Landry, J.C., *Paul Newman*, London, 1983.
Quirk, Lawrence J., *The Films of Paul Newman*, Secaucus, 1986.
Oumano, Elena, *Paul Newman*, Gordonville, 1989.
Quirk, Lawrence J., *Paul Newman: The Man Behind the Steel Blue Eyes*, Dallas, 1997.
Lax, Eric, *Newman: A Celebration*, London, 1999.

Articles:

Motion Picture Herald (New York), 27 September 1961.
Variety (New York), 27 September 1961.
Baker, Peter, in *Films and Filming* (London), December 1961.
Houston, Penelope, in *Monthly Film Bulletin* (London), December 1961.
Oakes, Philip, in *Sight and Sound* (London), Winter 1961–62.
Manchel, Frank, and Dan Ort, in *Screen Education*, March-April 1968.
Lloyd, Christopher, in *Brighton Film Review*, March 1970.
Royer, J.-P., in *Cinématographe* (Paris), May 1982.
Baxter, Bryan, in *Films and Filming* (London), November 1985.
Jenkins, Steve, in *Monthly Film Bulletin* (London), February 1986.
Legrand, Gérard, *Positif* (Paris), May 1987.
Breakwell, Ian, ''The Fat Man Within,'' in *Sight & Sound* (London), vol. 4, no. 6., June 1994.
Stévenin, Jean-François, ''Économie d'énergies (sur L'arnaqueur),'' in *Positif* (Paris), no. 400, June 1994.
Premiere (Boulder), vol. 10, October 1996.
Schaefer, R., in *Metro Magazine* (St. Kilda West), no. 113/114, 1998.

* * *

Unlike many other self-consciously ''serious'' American films of its period—the kind of movies Andrew Sarris once described as dealing ''Realistically with a Problem in Adult Terms''— *The Hustler* has aged remarkably well. So much so, in fact, as to encourage the retrospective conviction that more of the movie's long list of Oscar nominees merited the ultimate accolade. As it is, the film did receive awards for art direction and cinematography, the latter particularly well deserved by the German émigré cameraman Eugen Schüfftan, whose skilled monochrome work on *The Hustler* remains an object lesson in framing and lighting the wide CinemaScope image.

In 1961 that was no mean achievement, for commercial anamorphic cinematography was still less than a decade old. Nor was it only a question of adapting the 1:2.25 aspect ratio to existing criteria of pictorial elegance or of harnessing it to the particular requirements of *The Hustler*'s distinctively seedy milieu. Schüfftan also found ways of framing the movie's characters so as to underline and comment upon their changing relationships, but without that process seeming unduly obtrusive. In so doing he introduced a specifically visual element into the style of Robert Rossen, a director whose films, while always exhibiting the more ''literary'' values of careful writing and characterization, had hitherto not been especially distinguished by their visual flair.

Rossen was invariably a good director of actors, however, and all the principal performances in *The Hustler* are of the highest quality. Paul Newman's account of Fast Eddie Felson is still, perhaps, his most accomplished film characterization, Eddie's internal stresses finding expression in a kind of controlled physicality—used to enormous effect after the thumb-breaking sequence, when, with his hands encased in plaster, he is unable to light a cigarette or hold a cup, let alone wield a pool cue. As Eddie's Mephistopheles, the gambler Bert Gordon, George C. Scott smiles like a benevolent shark, modulating that now familiar sandpaper voice across a range from whiplash harshness to silky persuasion. Jackie Gleason and Myron McCormick are impeccable as Eddie's principal opponent and discarded partner respectively, while Piper Laurie captures Sarah's enigmatic self-destructiveness with such conviction as to make one deeply regret that, after *The Hustler*, she retired from acting until *Carrie* in 1976.

This last judgment, it should be noted, was not wholly shared by reviewers of the period, several of whom identified the Sarah sub-plot as the film's main weakness. In hindsight, however, it is clear that this is not Piper Laurie's failing. While it is true that Sarah is observed tangentially, that she is not as clearly defined as Eddie or Bert, it is that ambiguity that makes her significant. She is, after all, central to the film's resolution. Without her intervention, Eddie's character could not plausibly meet the developmental requirements of this most classical of narratives. Through her he comes to understand what is really meant by Bert's facile explanation of his failure to beat Minnesota Fats: that he lacks ''character.'' But he reaches that understanding not simply because she loves him, a narrative contrivance which, on its own, would be as banal as it is common in the movies, but because her suicide forces him to recognize the price of his own self-absorption. ''I loved her, Bert,'' he concedes at the film's end; ''I traded her in on a pool game.''

There is, then, a real difficulty about Sarah's role, but it is intrinsic to the movie's single-minded focus on Eddie's progress toward ''maturity.'' To make that work, a significant part of Sarah's motivation has to remain oblique for, if she kills herself solely because of Eddie's behaviour, he would then be beyond redemption. But if we are made to see her as already self-destructive, as in some part ''Perverted, Twisted, Crippled'' (the final message she scrawls over her own mirror image), it is then conventionally acceptable for Eddie to transcend the tragedy, defeat Minnesota Fats, and, as an appropriate expression of his new found ''character,'' sacrifice his future in big-time pool.

It is that redemption, of course, which is the whole point of the film. Eddie must overcome his and our irresponsible impulses—here given metaphorical form in the pool hustler's need for self-restraint in the cause of ultimate victory—if he is to realize humane values on behalf of us all. Our reward is the spine-tingling satisfaction of that final dignified exchange with Minnesota Fats, an exchange appropriately set in the pool hall Eddie has earlier dubbed the ''church of the good hustler.'' ''Fat man,'' he says, ''you shoot a great game of pool.'' ''So do you, Fast Eddie.'' Redemption indeed.

—Andrew Tudor

I

I AM A FUGITIVE FROM A CHAIN GANG

USA, 1932

Director: Mervyn LeRoy

Production: Warner Bros. Pictures, Inc.; black and white, 35mm; running time: 93 minutes. Released 10 November 1932. Filmed 28 July-7 September 1932 in Warner Bros. studios. Cost: $195,845.

Producer: Hal Wallis; **screenplay:** Howard J. Green and Brown Holmes, from the autobiography *I Am a Fugitive from a Georgia Chain Gang* by Robert E. Burns; **photography:** Sol Polito; **editor:** William Holmes; **art director:** Jack Okey; **music conductor:** Leo F. Forbstein; **costume designer:** Orry-Kelly; **technical advisors:** S. H. Sullivan and Jack Miller, uncredited assistance by Robert E. Burns.

I Am a Fugitive from a Chain Gang

Cast: Paul Muni (*James Allen*); Glenda Farrell (*Marie*); Helen Vinson (*Helen*); Noel Francis (*Linda*); Preston Foster (*Pete*); Allen Jenkins (*Barney Sykes*); Edward Ellis (*Bomber Wells*); John Wray (*Nordine*); Everett Brown (*Sebastian*); Hale Hamilton (*The Reverend Robert Allen*); Louise Carter (*Mother*); Sally Blane (*Alice*); Berton Churchill (*Judge*); David Landau (*Warden*); Willard Robertson (*Prison Board Chairman*); Robert McWade (*Attorney*); Robert Warwick (*Fuller*).

Publications

Script:

Green, Howard J., and Brown Holmes, *I Am a Fugitive from a Chain Gang*, edited by John E. O'Connor, Madison, Wisconsin, 1981.

Books:

LeRoy, Mervyn, *It Takes More Than Talent*, New York, 1953.
Warner, Jack L., with Dean Jennings, *My First Hundred Years in Hollywood*, New York, 1964.
Gussow, Mel, *Don't Say Yes Until I Finish Talking: A Biography of Darryl F. Zanuck*, New York, 1971.
The Warner Bros. Golden Anniversary Book, New York, 1973.
Lawrence, Jerome, *Actor: The Life and Times of Paul Muni*, New York, 1974.
LeRoy, Mervyn, with Dick Kleiner, *Take One*, New York, 1974.
Lorentz, Pare, *Lorentz on Film: Movies 1927–1941*, New York, 1975.
Roddick, Nick, *Warner Bros. in the 1930s: A New Deal in Entertainment*, London, 1983.

Articles:

"Article on Robert Burns," in *New York Herald Tribune*, 27 November 1932.
"Champion of the Underdog," in *Silver Screen* (New York), December 1932.
LeRoy, Mervyn, "The Making of Mervyn LeRoy," in *Films in Review* (New York), May 1953.
Campbell, Russell, in *Velvet Light Trap* (Madison, Wisconsin), June 1971.
Ebert, J., "Kracauers Abbildtheorie," in *Filmkritik* (Munich), April 1977.
Pulleine, Tim, in *Monthly Film Bulletin* (London), March 1979.
Siclier, J., in *Avant-Scène du Cinéma* (Paris), 1 October, 1979.
Cohen, Joan, in *Magill's Survey of Cinema 2*, Englewood Cliffs, New Jersey, 1980.

''Mervyn LeRoy 'Revisited','' in *Image et Son*, no. 378, December 1982.

Checklist and critical notes on Mervyn LeRoy, in *Film Dope* (Nottingham), no. 35, September 1986.

* * *

During the 1930s Warner Brothers earned a well-deserved reputation of being a studio with a strong social conscience. Hal Wallis, who was production chief at the studio for much of that decade, recalled that ''the general impression was that we were very liberal in our selection of material.'' Among the Warners' productions which helped to create that image was *I Am a Fugitive from a Chain Gang*, a well-made film that earned the studio's sound department and Paul Muni Oscar nominations. This production ranks, to use the words of film historian Clive Hirschhorn, as ''one of the most vehement, eloquent, and far-reaching of social protest films.''

I Am a Fugitive from a Chain Gang is based on a book by Robert E. Burns, who recounts his adventures with the prison system in Georgia and his two escapes from the chain gangs. The movie is generally faithful to its sources (although for various reasons Georgia is never mentioned), with some melodramatic flourishes added. The story is deceptively simple: a World War I veteran from a good family returns home after the war and becomes dissatisfied with his circumstances. He takes to the road and becomes innocently involved in a stick-up; found guilty he is sentenced for some years to a chain gang. The film in stark fashion depicts the sadistic brutality and dehumanizing violence with which chain gang inmates are treated. He escapes, goes North, makes something of himself, but is forced into marriage with a woman who has discovered his past; when ultimately he tries to leave her for another woman she denounces him to the authorities. Attempting to clear his record by going South voluntarily to serve a nominal term, he is doublecrossed and returned to the chain gang. He escapes once more, and comes out of hiding one night to see his sweetheart. Restless, fear-ridden, terrified of being returned to the chain gang, he is but a haunted shadow of his former self. In what film critic Pauline Kael has called ''one of the great closing scenes in the history of films,'' he retreats into the shadows at hearing a sound, and responds to his sweetheart's question of how he lives by saying ''I steal'' as the movie ends.

The film is a harsh indictment of the chain gang, and American movie audiences were made aware of the terrible conditions prevalent in the penal system of the South. Moreover, these audiences were presented with a bleak view of contemporary American life in keeping with the harsh realities of the Great Depression which was just then peaking in terms of its impact on life in the United States. Although the bulk of the film's action is set in the 1920s, the indictment and conditions depicted easily translated to the hard times of the early 1930s. *I Am a Fugitive from a Chain Gang*, thanks to a thoughtful script, taut direction, and vibrant central performance remains a powerful indictment and pungent commentary on social ills.

—Daniel Leab

I AM CUBA

See **Soy Cuba**

I EVEN MET HAPPY GYPSIES

See **SKUPLIJACI PERJA**

I WAS A FIREMAN

See **FIRES WERE STARTED**

IDI I SMOTRI

(Come and See)

USSR, 1985

Director: Elem Klimov

Production: Byelarusfilm, Mosfilm; Sovcolor; running time: 142 minutes.

Production manager: J.Tereshenko; **screenplay:** Ales Adamovich, Elem Klimov, based on works by Ales Adamovich, including *The Khatyn Story* and *A Punitive Squad*; **photography:** Alexei Rodionov; **editor:** V. Belova; **assistant director:** V. Pondchevni, Z. Rogozovskaya; **production designer:** Viktor Petrov; **music:** Oleg Yanchenko; **music editor:** M. Blank; **costumes:** E. Semenova; **sound;** V. Mors.

Cast: Alexei Kravshenko (*Florya*); Olga Mironova (*Glasha*); Liubomiras Laucevicius, Vladas Bagdonas, Victor Lorents.

Publications

Articles:

Diaz Torres, D., ''*Ven y mira*,'' in *Cine Cubano* (Habana), no. 114, 1985.

Variety (New York), 17 July 1985.

Portal, M., ''Klimov, un cinéaste visionnaire'' in *Jeune Cinéma* (Paris), November-December 1985.

Strick, P., *Monthly Film Bulletin* (London), March 1987.

LeFanu, M., ''Partisan'' in *Sight and Sound* (London), Spring 1987.

Bassan, R., and M. Martin, *Revue du Cinéma* (Paris), May 1987.

Goethals, Piet, ''*Idi I smotri*: die Leiden des jungen Florya,'' in *Film en Televisie + Video* (Brussels), no. 371, April 1988.

Makkonen, V. -P., ''Elem Klimov elokuviensa takana,'' in *Filmihullu* (Helsinki), no. 6, 1988.

Noel, J., and D. Fischer, "Viens et vois," in *Les Cine-Fiches de Grand Angle*, vol. 15, no. 105, May 1988.
Simons, Jan, "Beeld van de oorlog," in *Skrien* (Amsterdam), no. 174, October-November 1990.
Youngblood, D.J., "Post-Stalinist Cinema and the Myth of World War II: Tarkovskii's *Ivan's Childhood* (1962) and Klimov's *Come and See* (1985)," *Historical Journal of Film and Television* (Abingdon), vol. 14, no. 4, 1994.

Interviews:

Cinéma (Paris), 23 September 1987.
Donets, L., "Preodolenie," in *Iskusstvo Kino* (Moscow), no. 5, 1995.

* * *

Come and See is set in Byelorussia in 1943, and tells the story of German atrocities against the population through the eyes of a young boy, Florya, who, at the start of the film, joins the partisans. Whilst he is away his entire village, including his mother and little sisters, are butchered by the Germans. Returning with a partisan girl, Glasha, he discovers the awful truth, an event which virtually unhinges him. Roaming through the bleak Byelorussian countryside with an ever-dwindling band of displaced people, he eventually witnesses the German destruction of the village of Perekhody and the slaughter of its inhabitants—an event from which he narrowly escapes with his own life. The German unit responsible is caught and destroyed by the partisans, whom Florya, now aged almost beyond recognition by his terrible experiences, rejoins.

The events portrayed in *Come and See* have been drawn from at least three separate books by Ales Adanovich (who also worked on the screenplay), so that, as Philip Strick put it, "what has been reconstructed is a symbolic tragedy, drawing together a multiplicity of terrible episodes into one condensed nightmare." Indeed, an end credit tells us that there were 628 Perekhodys in Byelorussia, but new evidence unearthed since the fall of the Soviet Union suggests there were far more. Likewise a good deal of recent work emanating from Germany itself—and, in particular, a major exhibition in Hamburg in 1995—has cast a great deal of doubt on the conventional view that atrocities on the Eastern Front were carried out by the SS and various ill-assorted non-German Nazis, whilst the professional Wehrmacht got on with the job of being ordinary soldiers. So whilst it may indeed be the case, as some critics have complained, that *Come and See* will do little to foster good East-West relations, its representation of German soldiery in Byelorussia as glorying in the most vile and degraded behaviour imaginable, at least has the virtue of historical accuracy, and of puncturing the assiduously cultivated myth of the dutiful Wehrmacht.

Come and See has aptly been described as an "epic of derangement," and long before the horrors of Perekhody are presented in 25 almost unbearable minutes, the spectator has been submerged in a world that seems to have gone stark raving mad. Whether in the opening scene, in which two boys dig for buried guns in a bleak, Beckett-like landscape of sand dunes; Florya and Glasha's agonised struggle through a swamp to reach an encampment of lamenting women surrounding a charred, but still living, body; or the picaresque cross-country journey to find food, accompanied by a death's-head-like effigy of Hitler, in which only Florya survives just, this is a film informed with the spirit of Goya's *The Disasters of War*. Philip Strick has drawn a parallel with the "fevered expressionism" of Chukrai's *Ballad of a Soldier* and Kalatozov's *The Cranes are Flying*, and whilst it is true that there are plenty of bravura sequences involving long, mobile, hand-held shots, there is nothing particularly heroic about the vision of war on offer here. Indeed, from the moment Florya leaves home—not entirely willingly—it is presented as one long, utterly brutalising experience which leaves him looking like a wizened old man. In the early scene at the partisan camp in which the partisans are photographed in an heroic group pose, and the soundtrack fills with a patriotic song, it's as if Klimov is actually poking fun, not at the partisans themselves of course, but at the conventionalised image which they acquired in the post-war Soviet Union.

The sense of derangement is massively augmented by the film's remarkably orchestrated soundtrack. Aural distortion is present right from the start, when one of the boys looking for guns addresses the camera in a voice that seems to have come straight out of *The Exorcist*. It becomes much more pronounced, however, after the scene in which the partisan camp is bombed, which causes damage to Florya's hearing. From then on in the soundtrack is what Strick has described as a "stunning tinnitus of distorted tones," in particular making great play with variations on and treatments of the drone of the lone aircraft which reappears throughout the film like the sword of Damocles circling overhead. Not since *Raging Bull* or *The Texas Chainsaw Massacre* have the expressive possibilities of the soundtrack been exploited to such devastating effect.

—Julian Petley

IDIOTERNE

(The Idiots)

Denmark 1998

Director: Lars von Trier

Production: Zentropa Entertainments and Liberator Productions; color; running time: 117 min. Released 17 July 1998, Copenhagen. Cost: DKK 12 mio.

Producer: Vibeke Windeløv; **screenplay:** Lars von Trier; **photography:** Lars von Trier; **editor:** Molly Malene Stensgaard; **assistant director and photography:** Kristoffer Nyholm, Jesper Jargil, Casper Holm; **set designer:** Lene Nielsen.

Cast: Bodil Jørgensen (*Karen*); Jens Albinus (*Stoffer*); Louise Hassing (*Susanne*); Troels Lyby (*Henrik*); Nikolaj Lie Kaas (*Jeppe*); Henrik Prip (*Ped*); Luis Mesonero (*Miguel*); Louise Mieritz (*Josephine*); Knud Romer Jørgensen (*Axel*); Trine Michelsen (*Nana*); Anne-Grethe Bjarup Riis (*Katrine*).

Awards: FIPRESCI International Critics Award, London Film Festival, 1998.

Publications

Scripts:

Von Trier, Lars, and Mogens Rukow, *Idioterne*, Gyldendal, 1999.

Articles:

Skotte, Kim, ''Triers gruppeknald,'' in *Politiken*, 17 July 1998.

Piil, Morten, article in *Gyldendals filmguide: Danske film fra A til Z*, Gyldendal, 1998.

Brooks, Xan, ''Burn, Baby, Burn,'' in *Sight and Sound* (London), May 1999.

Schepelern, Peter, ''Filmen ifølge dogme,'' in *FILM*, no. 1, Danish Film Institute, 1999.

* * *

When the Dogma 95 manifesto was presented, the general view in Denmark was that Lars von Trier was primarily responsible for it. In all his films and projects he has worked with sets of rules, and now there were some new ones that in addition to saluting the *nouvelle vague* of French cinema in the 1960s might also have been inspired by the fact that in *Breaking the Waves* (1996) von Trier had just completed his biggest, most expensive production, and needed a change. It was all seen as rather a joke, but the presentation at Cannes 1998 of Thomas Vinterberg's *Festen* and Lars von Trier's *Idioterne* showed that they meant it seriously.

Whereas Vinterberg's film could have been a grand, polished production and even as a Dogma film is an aesthetic pleasure, von Trier's film is a radical breach with ordinary aesthetic rules for film as an idiom and narrative, and is an equally radical breach with the norms and conventions for film content. In this way, too, the film has its roots in the new wave of French film in the 1960s as well as the alternative ways of life and the showdown with middle-class conventions of the same period. In those days people freaked out; in Trier's hands the characters play a game in which they act the idiot, for the film seems to have the romantic notion that it is only via children and idiots that we can access our authenticity, our primitive character. At the same time the film is also a criticism of those who only regard the game as a playful opportunity for a few intense summer months, while the character with genuine pain in her past carries the game into her real life and is left as the only person to truly accept its radical qualities.

This person is Karen. She starts the film by meeting the ''idiots'' at a restaurant and is indignant when she finds out their behavior is just a game. But she joins the group and in a beautiful scene in the middle of the film she manages to shed her reservations and allow her ''inner idiot'' to speak out. The film has three layers, each getting darker and darker.

The first part of the film seems to be a game with reality, where a drink at a pub, a tour of a factory, and outings to a swimming pool and a woods provide opportunities to play the idiot in an open, anonymous social space. The second layer brings the characters closer to home, and the film becomes more painful and simultaneously grotesquely funny when the idiots confront specific individuals: good citizens who are forced to buy hopeless Christmas decorations, potential buyers of the house where the idiots hang out, the civil servant who wants to send them out of his wealthy municipality to one crowded with dysfunctional losers, and not least, the group of bikers who believe that the idiots are genuine, an illusion that must be preserved at all costs.

After these encounters the film becomes even darker in tone and perspective, for the third layer concentrates on the group itself. The costs of this serious game are revealed. When a father comes to get his daughter and breaks up a tender, burgeoning love affair the young couple's desperate farewell through a car windscreen becomes one of the emotional peaks and a distillation of the opposition between the efforts of the idiots and the reactions of the people around them. The moving climax is reached when it turns out that Karen, whose moral qualms have made her take longer than anyone else to accept the idiot game, proves to be the only one capable of playing the idiot among people she knows and loves. In the closing scene, when Karen is in the bosom of her family, for whom concealing problems is the abiding principle, and she begins to play the idiot, one loses all one's reservations about the film and its intent, and surrenders completely. Karen plays the idiot to reconcile herself with her traumatic pain over her dead baby and to get through to her lower-middle-class, convention-ridden family, for whom attendance at the funeral is the only conceivable way to express your grief.

With her reservations regarding the grotesque game of ''idiot,'' which she and many viewers find offensive, Karen becomes the figure the viewer identifies with and her pain, a pain we feel and understand. She comes into the group as a solitary figure and by the end is the only person left who is capable of carrying out the game in her own real life. She is a searching sister to Bess of *Breaking the Waves*, a woman who gives up everything, sheds her inhibitions, and shatters prejudices.

Von Trier tells his story using a hand-held camera and a radically anti-aesthetic idiom in which the scenes do not seem composed but resemble roughly-hewn fragments of a film not completed. This is emphasised by the meta-layer of the film in which von Trier interviews the idiots and they talk about their experiences, emotions, and attitudes to the group as if with hindsight after the group has split up. This lends the project the character of an improvised experiment that von Trier has been following, and the film assumes the character of an uncontrolled film, an anarchic experiment, or a home movie which failed. But the project has been controlled down to the tiniest detail, and is just as formally implemented as his earlier films. One might say that von Trier is playing the idiot with the language of film, and that just as the group breaches the conventions of middle-class society, he breaches the linguistic conventions of cinema in his own quest for authenticity.

—Dan Nissen

IF. . .

UK, 1968

Director: Lindsay Anderson

Production: Memorial Enterprises; color with tinted black and white sequences (EastmanColor), 35mm; running time: 112 minutes, American version 111 minutes. Released December 1968, London. Filmed beginning 8 March 1968 at Cheltenham College, England. Cost: budgeted at £250,000.

Producers: Roy Baird with Michael Medwin and Lindsay Anderson; **screenplay:** David Sherwin, from the original script ''Crusaders'' by David Sherwin and John Howlett; **photography:** Miroslav Ondricek; **editor:** David Gladwell; **sound recordist:** Christian Wangler; **production designer:** Jocelyn Herbert; **art director:** Brian Eatwell; **music:** Marc Wilkinson; **costume designer:** Shura Cohen.

Cast: Malcolm McDowell (*Mick*); David Wood (*Johnny*); Richard Warwick (*Wallace*); Christine Noonan (*Girl*); Rupert Webster (*Bobby Philips*); Robert Swann (*Rowntree*); Hugh Thomas (*Denson*); Michael Cadman (*Fortinbras*); Peter Sproule (*Barnes*); Peter Jeffrey (*Headmaster*); Arthur Lowe (*Mr. Kemp*); Mona Washbourne (*Matron*); Mary MacLeod (*Mrs. Kemp*); Geoffrey Chater (*Chaplain*); Ben Aris (*John Thomas*); Graham Crowden (*History Master*); Charles Lloyd Pack (*Classics Master*); Anthony Nicholls (*General Denson*); Tommy Godfrey (*Finchley*); Guy Ross (*Stephans*); Robin Askwith (*Keating*); Richard Everett (*Pussy Graves*); Philip Bagenal (*Peanuts*); Nicholas Page (*Cox*); Robert Yetzes (*Fisher*); David Griffen (*Willens*); Graham Sharman (*Van Eyssen*); Richard Tombleson (*Baird*); Richard Davis (*Machin*); Brian Pettifer (*Biles*); Michael Newport (*Brunning*); Charles Sturridge (*Markland*); Sean Bury (*Jute*); Martin Beaumont (*Hunter*).

Awards: Cannes Film Festival, Grand Prix, 1969.

Publications

Script:

Anderson, Lindsay, and David Sherwin, *If. . . : A Film by Lindsay Anderson*, New York, 1969.

Books:

Manvell, Roger, *New Cinema in Britain*, New York, 1969.
Sussex, Elizabeth, *Lindsay Anderson*, New York, 1969.
Gelmis, Joseph, *The Film Director as Superstar*, New York, 1970.
Walker, Alexander, *Hollywood, England: The British Film Industry in the Sixties*, London, 1974.
Silet, Charles L. P., *Lindsay Anderson: A Guide to References and Resources*, Boston, 1981.
Graham Allison, *Lindsay Anderson*, Boston, 1981.
Hedling, Erik, *Lindsay Anderson: Maverick Film Maker*, New York, 1998.
Lambert, Gavin, *Lindsay Anderson*, New York, 2000.

Articles:

Schrader, Paul, in *Cinema* (London), no. 3, 1968.
Robinson, David, ''Anderson Shooting *If. . .* ,'' in *Sight and Sound* (London), Summer 1968.
Miller, Gavin, in *Sight and Sound* (London), Winter 1968.
Shivas, Mark, in *Movie* (London), Winter 1968.
Powell, Dilys, in *Sunday Times* (London), 22 December 1968.
Gladwell, David, ''Editing Anderson's *If. . .* ,'' in *Screen* (London), January-February 1969.
Canby, Vincent, in *New York Times*, March 1969.
Kael, Pauline, in *New Yorker*, New York, March 1969.
Spiers, David, in *Screen* (London), March-April 1969.
Cocks, Jay, in *Time* (New York), 21 March 1969.
Hartung, Philip, in *Commonweal* (New York), 21 March 1969.
Baker, Russell, ''Observer: Youth Without Rose-Colored Glasses,'' in *New York Times*, 13 May 1969.
Ebert, Roger, in *Chicago Sun Times*, 1 June 1969.
Arnold, Gary, in *Washington Post*, 13 June 1969.
Corliss, Richard, ''Hollywood and the Student Revolt,'' in *National Review* (New York), 17 June 1969.
Farber, Stephen, ''Before the Revolution,'' in *Hudson Review* (New York), Autumn 1969.
Craddock, John, ''If. . . High School Unless,'' in *Film Society Review* (New York), September 1969.
Young, Vernon, ''Film Chronicle: Notes on the Compulsive Revolution,'' in *Hudson Review* (New York), Winter 1969.
Welsh, James, ''Bergman and Anderson for Sophomores,'' in *Cinema Journal* (Evanston, Illinois), Fall 1971.
Jensen, N., ''Lindsay Anderson—romantisk ironiker,'' in *Kosmorama* (Copenhagen), November 1973.
Marszalek, Rafal, ''Lindsay Anderson,'' in *Kino* (Warsaw), October 1974.
Rumalho, Jose Jorge, ''Un Filme que Evoca Jean Vigo,'' in *Celuloide* (Rio Major, Portugal), November 1974.
Lovell, Alan, ''Brecht in Britain—Lindsay Anderson,'' in *Screen* (London), Winter 1975.
Durgnat, Raymond, ''Britannia Waives the Rules,'' in *Film Comment* (New York), July-August 1976.
Hedling, E., ''Han sag sig om i vrede,'' in *Filmhaftet* (Uppsala, Sweden), May 1990.
Sen, M., ''La révolte des adolescents,'' in *Positif* (Paris), no. 400, June 1994.
Turcsanyi, S., ''A szabadsag fantomjai,'' in *Filmvilag* (Budapest), vol. 37, no. 12, 1994.

* * *

Lindsay Anderson's film *If. . .* , related to Rudyard Kipling's poem of the same name, has raised much debate politically, stylistically, and structurally, particularly concerning the director's use or misuse

If...

of Brechtian theory. Based on a script by David Sherwin and John Howlett entitled *Crusaders*, the film uses the British public-school system as a microcosm of society to demonstrate the repression of the individual by authority. In the published screenplay of *If. . .*, Anderson also credits another source of inspiration for the film, Jean Vigo: ''We especially saw *Zéro de conduite* again, before writing started, to give us courage.''

The mid-1950s marked significant changes in Britain. The New Left emerged, the Free Cinema began, John Osborne was energizing the theater, and Brecht was re-discovered. It was also the period Anderson was writing for *Sight and Sound*. Not unexpectedly, the influences of that period can be traced to *If. . . .* The film has a sense of ''documentary realism'' (Osborne), surprising surrealistic passages (Free Cinema), a drive to overthrow authority (New Left), and a use of self-reflexive devices (Brecht).

If. . . functions predominantly within a kind of realism typical of classic narrative films, but one that is undercut by Brechtian concerns and surrealistic images. Anderson himself declared that ''I think that *If. . .* is a rather Brechtian film.'' There are inherent difficulties with this statement (and regarding ''Brechtian cinema'' in general), but *If. . .* does exhibit two ostensible examples of the well-known *verfremdungseffekt*: the oft-cited black- and white- sections and the title cards. The film is constructed in a series of eight vignettes, each one introduced by a title card. The overall design conveys some idea of a chronology, but the ordering of the scenes could be altered without changing the thematic drive. This type of structural flexibility was central to Brecht's early writings. The use of black- and white- sections within a color film was entirely random, based on economic and practical considerations. Notwithstanding, both devices are meant to distance the spectator from the film, calling into question the production of the film as text and, theoretically, permitting cool observations of societal machinations. The fact that the fantasy sequences scattered throughout *If. . .* (the chaplain in a drawer, the naked woman at the cafe, the headmaster's wife wandering the empty corridors, and possibly the ending) are not delineated from the accepted diegetic reality reflects Anderson's belief that there are no rigid distinctions between what is real and what is fantasy. This use of surrealism blends nicely with the Brechtian aspects of the film in that it raises similar questions about constructed images and the supposed truth of realism.

To a lesser degree, *If. . .* also deals with sexuality, especially the repression of desires with its deleterious effects, and the covert homosexuality of an all-male school brought to the fore in certain relationships.

Anderson has said that no authority is necessary and that his sympathies are always with the revolutionaries. *If*. . . presents contradictions inherent in any authoritarian system and states that without resolution, radical action will be the only means of change—the quite literal ''if'' of the film.

—Greg S. Faller

IGLA

(The Needle)

USSR, 1989

Director: Rashid Nugmanov.

Production: Kazakhfilm; color; 35mm; running time: 81 minutes. Filmed on location in Alma-Ata and at the Aral Sea.

Producer: Rashid Nugmanov; **screenplay:** Alexander Baranov, Bakhyt Kilibayev; **photography:** Murat Nugmanov; **design:** Murat Musin; **music:** Viktor Tsoi.

Cast: Viktor Tsoi (*Moro*), Marina Smirnova (*Dina*), Pyotr Mamanov (*Doctor*), Aleksander Baschirov (*Spartak*).

Publications

Books:

Horton, Andrew, and Michael Brashinsky, *The Zero Hour: Glasnost and Soviet Cinema in Transition*, Princeton, New Jersey, 1992.

Lawton, Anna, editor, *The Red Screen: Politics, Society, Art in Soviet Cinema*, London and New York, 1992.

Horton, Andrew, editor, *Inside Soviet Film Satire: Laughter with a Lash,* 1993.

Brashinsky, Michael, and Andrew Horton, editors, *Russian Critics on the Cinema of Glasnost*, 1994.

Thompson, Kristin, and David Bordwell, *Film History: An Introduction*, New York, 1994.

Articles:

Abramovich, A., *Soviet Film* (Moscow), February 1989.

Plakhov, Andrei, ''Soviet Cinema into the 90's,'' in *Sight & Sound* (London), Spring 1989.

Ciesol, Forrest, ''Kazakhstan Wave,'' in *Sight and Sound* (London), Fall 1989.

Drozdova, M., and E. Stisova, *Isskustvo Kino* (Moscow), March 1989.

Variety (New York), 31 May 1989.

Horton, A., ''Nomad from Kazakhstan,'' in *Film Criticism* (Meadville, Pennsylvania), Winter 1989–90.

Brashinsky, Michael, ''The Ant Hill in the Year of the Dragon,'' in *New Orleans Review* (New Orleans), Spring 1990.

Horton, Andrew, ''Nomad from Kazakhstan: An Interview with Rashid Nugmanov,'' in *Film Criticism*, Summer 1990.

Hayes, N., ''Recent Soviet Film,'' in *Enclitic*, vol. 11, no. 4, 1994.

* * *

In the bleak filmscape of *glasnost*, *The Needle* stood out as a black sheep of a movie. The most playful and offbeat of the Soviet films of the period, it contrasted sharply to the mainstream, which was overwhelmed with revisionism of the Stalinist past and nihilistic social criticism.

Made in 1988 by a young Kazakh director, Rashid Nugmanov, fresh out of VGIK (the national film school), *The Needle* was a pioneering effort in several ways. Having come from a remote, stagnant republic of Kazakhstan, the picture set off a movement that has come to be known as the ''Kazakh New Wave.'' Represented by such works as Alexander Baranov's and Bakhyt Kilibayev's *The Three* (1988) and *Woman of the Day* (1990); Kilibayev's *The Tick* (1990); Baranov's *He and She* (1990); Abai Karpykov's *Little Fish in Love* (1989); and Serik Aprymov's *The Last Stop* (1989), the Kazakh New Wave was for the agonizing Soviet film of the late 1980s what the French New Wave was for the dusty French film of the late 1950s. *The Needle* was the movement's *a bout de souffle.* The film also became a model for the Russian version of postmodernism—uninhibited and uninformed, compensating for the lack of culture, skill, and resources with mischief and wit. A young man named Moro (played by Viktor Tsoi, the late rock 'n' roll legend from the St. Petersburg band ''Kino'') returns to his Asiatic hometown only to find his ex-girlfriend, Dina (Marina Smirnova), becoming a drug addict and himself becoming involved in the bizarre life of the city's underworld. In an attempt to save Dina, Moro takes her away to the Aral Sea, turned into a barren desert by the time they arrive. There Dina seems cured, but back in town everything starts anew. Almost desperate, Moro decides to fight the drug dealers, led by a hospital doctor (played by another rock 'n' roll star, eccentric leader of the ''Sound of Mu'' band and the future star of *Taxi Blues*, Pyotr Mamonov), when one of them stabs him in a deserted park.

''My film is really about friends who got together to have fun, while playing in filmmaking.'' What could have been a quote from Godard or Fassbinder is in fact a remark from Rashid Nugmanov. *The Needle* is indeed neither about drugs nor about a generation of Soviet youth, lost between the East and West, communism and capitalism, cynicism and romanticism (though its poignant tone hints on the latter). The film's essence emerges from the director's manipulation of various cultural stereotypes rather than social or psychological problems. The picture is dedicated ''to the Soviet television''—an ironic show of Nugmanov's trendy obsession with media technology (he likes filling the screen with television screens). In a nod to the Jackie Chan cult, the epilogue plays the outtakes of the action sequences. An inventive predecessor of *Pulp Fiction, The Needle* weaves its soundtrack out of the Soviet ''surfer music'' from the 1950s. Every twist of the narrative is ''forewarned'' by a syrupy voice-over in a manner suggestive of a children's program *a la* ''Sesame Street.'' On top of all this, the film, made by an ethnic Kazakh who never learned Kazakh and starring a Soviet-Korean from

St. Petersburg, speaks in various tongues—Kazakh, Russian, Italian, German, and English—which creates the image of a Tower-of-Babel-like world, maybe facing a similar future.

Yet *The Needle* works best when it plays on the popular image of its star and the genre scenarios it provides. Viktor Tsoi, who followed the tracks of James Dean and Wajda's early protagonist Zbigniew Cybulski when he drove into a tree and into untimely, mythical immortality in 1990, was cultivated in the Soviet pop scene as ''the last romantic.'' That is why and how he was cast in *The Needle.* Tsoi's romanticism was that of a generation which skipped Byron and Schiller and went straight for Clint Eastwood. It was an *ersatz* romanticism which could neither admit to nor accept its own secondariness—precisely what made it so unique and attractive in the context of the ''tired culture'' of remakes and references. In parallel with the Kazakh filmmakers, and indeed unbeknownst to them, the Hong Kong *auteurs*, especially John Woo, were exercising the same kind of romanticism—violent, stylized, extravagant. Its generic constituents—in *The Needle,* or in Woo's *Killer* and *Hard-Boiled*—are hard to miss: a trenchcoat (both in Alma-Ata and Hong Kong the weather suggests rather a t-shirt); sunglasses, reflecting a gun-wielding opponent; a cigarette, hanging in the corner of a mouth, its smoke not obstructing the view of a target; a wet sidewalk at night; a bluesy score; and a doomed romance—but where Rashid Nugmanov, educated behind the iron curtain, learned the art of cool remains a mystery. Whatever the source of his inspiration— smuggled comic strips or, more likely, Godard with his love/hate relationship with American pop culture and happy sensibility of the ''poor cinema''—*The Needle* stands proudly on its own. That its promise of a new filmic language was never quite realized makes it no less appealing.

—Michael Brashinsky

IKIRU

(To Live; Doomed)

Japan, 1952

Director: Akira Kurosawa

Production: Toho (Tokyo); black and white, 35mm; running time: 143 minutes; length: 3918 meters. Released 9 October 1952. Filmed 1952 in Tokyo.

Producer: Shojiro Motoki; **screenplay:** Shinobu Hashimoto, Hideo Oguni, and Akira Kurosawa; **photography:** Asakazu Nakai; **editor:** Koichi Iwashita; **sound:** Fumio Yanoguchi; **art director:** So Matsuyama; **music:** Fumio Hayasaka; **lighting:** Shigeru Mori.

Cast: Takashi Shimura (*Kanji Watanabe*); Nobuo Kaneko (*Mitsuo Watanabe*); Kyoko Seki (*Kazue Watanabe*); Makoto Kobori (*Kiichi Watanabe*); Kumeko Urabe (*Taysu Watanabe*); Yoshie Minami (*Maid*); Miki Odagiri (*Toyo Odagiri*); Kamatari Fugiwara (*Ono*); Minosuke Yamada (*Saito*); Haruo Tanaka (*Sakai*); Bokuzen Hidari (*Ohara*); Shinichi Himori (*Kimura*); Nobuo Nakamura (*Deputy Mayor*); Kazuo Abe (*City assemblyman*); Masao Shimizu (*Doctor*); Ko Kimura (*Intern*); Atsushi Watanabe (*Patient*); Yunosuke Ito (*Novelist*); Yatsuko Tanami (*Hostess*); Fuyuki Murakami (*Newspaperman*); Seiji Miyaguchi (*Gang-Boss*); Daisuke Kato (*Gangmember*); Kin Sugai, Eiko Miyoshi, Fumiko Homma (*Housewives*); Ichiro Chiba (*Policeman*); Minoru Chiaki (*Noguchi*); Toranosuke Ogawa (*Park Section Chief*); Tomoo Nagai and Hirayoshi Aono (*Reprters*); Akira Tani (*Old man at bar*); Toshiyuki Ichimura (*Pianist at cabaret*).

Award: The David O. Selznick ''Golden Laurel'' Award, 1961.

Publications

Script:

Hashimoto, Shinobu, Hideo Oguni, and Akira Kurosawa, *Ikiru*, New York, 1969; also in *Contemporary Japanese Cinema*, edited by Howard Hibbet, New York, 1977.

Books:

Anderson, Joseph, and Donald Richie, *The Japanese Film: Art and Industry*, New York, 1960; revised edition, Princeton, 1982.
Richie, Donald, *Japanese Movies*, Tokyo, 1961; as *Japanese Cinema: Film Style and National Character*, New York, 1971.
Ezratti, Sacha, *Kurosawa*, Paris, 1964.
Richie, Donald, *The Films of Akira Kurosawa*, Berkeley, 1965; revised edition, 1970; 1989; 1999.
Kenny, Don, editor, *The Complete Works of Akira Kurosawa*, Tokyo, 1971.
Mesnil, Michael, *Kurosawa*, Paris, 1973.
Bock, Audie, *Japanese Film Directors*, New York, 1978; revised edition, Tokyo, 1985.
Burch, Noël, *To the Distant Observer*, Berkeley, 1979.
Erens, Patricia, *Akira Kurosawa: A Guide to References and Resources*, Boston, 1979.
Anderson, Joseph, and Donald Richie, *The Japanese Film: Art and Industry*, expanded edition, Princeton, 1982.
Kurosawa, Akira, *Something Like an Autobiography*, New York, 1982.
Sato, Tadao, *Currents in Japanese Cinema*, Tokyo, 1982.
Tassone, Aldo, *Akira Kurosawa*, Paris, 1983.
Goodwin, James, *Akira Kurosawa & Intertextual Cinema*, Baltimore, 1993.
Goodwin, James, *Perspectives on Akira Kurosawa*, New York, 1994.
Prince, Stephen, *The Warrior's Camera*, Princeton, 1999.

Articles:

Anderson, Joseph, ''The History of Japanese Movies,'' in *Films in Review* (New York), June-July 1953.
Leyda, Jay, ''The Films of Akira Kurosawa,'' in *Sight and Sound* (London), Autumn 1954.
Miner, Earl Roy, ''Japanese Film in Modern Dress,'' in *Quarterly Review of Film, Radio, and Television* (Berkeley), Summer 1956.

Ikiru

Bazin, André, in *Cahiers du Cinéma* (Paris), March 1957.

Anderson, Lindsay, ''2 Inches off the Ground,'' in *Sight and Sound* (London) Winter 1957.

Dyer, Peter John, in *Films and Filming* (London), August 1959.

Crowther, Bosley, in *New York Times*, 30 January 1960.

Mekas, Jonas, in *Village Voice* (New York), 10 February 1960.

Roman, Robert, in *Films in Review* (New York), March 1960.

Bernhardt, William, in *Film Quarterly* (Berkeley), Summer 1960.

Filmfacts (New York), no. 3, 1960.

McVay, Douglas, in *Films and Filming* (London), July and August 1961.

''Kurosawa Issue'' of *Etudes Cinématographiques* (Paris), Spring 1964.

Richie, Donald, ''Kurosawa on Kurosawa,'' in *Sight and Sound* (London), Summer and Autumn 1964.

Kauffmann, Stanley, in *A World of Film: Criticism and Comment*, New York, 1966.

Passek, Jean-Loup, in *Cinéma* (Paris), December 1974.

Simone, R. Thomas, ''The Myths of 'The Sickness unto Death'. . . ,'' in *Literature/Film Quarterly* (Salisbury, Maryland), Winter 1975.

Sineaux, Michel, ''Eloge de la Folie,'' in *Positif* (Paris), January 1975.

Martin, Marcel, in *Image et Son* (Paris), February 1980.

Magny, Joel, in *Cinéma* (Paris), March 1980.

Van Beek, S., in *Skoop* (Amsterdam), August 1980.

Labre, C., ''Humilié et initié,'' in *Positif* (Paris), October 1980.

Nygren, S., ''Doubleness and Idiosyncrasy in Cross-Cultural Analysis,'' in *Quarterly Review of Film and Video* (New York), no. 1–3, 1991.

Torres, S., ''*Vivir*,'' in *Nosferatu* (San Sebastian), no. 11, January 1993.

MacKinnon, Gillies, ''Haunting Visions,'' in *Sight & Sound* (London), vol. 4, no. 11, November 1994.

Bovkis, Elen A., ''*Ikiru*: the Role of Women in a Male Narrative,'' in *CineAction* (Toronto), no. 40, May 1996.

Carr, Barbara, ''Goethe and Kurosawa: Faust and the Totality of Human Experience—West and East,'' in *Literature/Film Quarterly* (Salisbury), vol. 24, no. 3, 1996.

* * *

Akira Kurosawa's popularity in the West has been based primarily on his *jidai-geki* (period films). The *gendai-geki* (contemporary dramas), despite the championship of many critics, have been relatively neglected. *Ikiru* is the major exception to this rule. Its reputation rested initially on the seriousness of its subject (how does a man with only a few months left to live find meaning in life?), its humanism (Kurosawa's commitment to individual heroism, discovered in an apparently insignificant and undistinguished person), its social criticism (the satire on bureaucracy), and the power and directness of its emotional appeal. The film also became central to the anit-Kurosawa backlash led by certain *auteur* critics bent on attacking the notion that the importance of a film had any connection with the importance of its subject; to them, the humanism seemed naive, the social satire obvious, the emotional effects contrived, laborious and rhetorical. Neither view accounts for the particularity—in some ways the *oddity*—of Kurosawa's work.

The emphasis on a formal analysis of *Ikiru* in Noël Burch's brilliant book on Japanese cinema, *To the Distant Observer*, goes some way towards rectifying the inadequacy of previous approaches. Burch discusses the film in terms of its elaborate and rigorous formal system of symmetries and asymmetries contained within the overall ''rough-hewn geometry'' that he sees as Kurosawa's most distinctive general characteristic. The film falls into two strongly demarcated sections, the break coming about two-thirds of the way through. The first part begins and ends with the voice of an off-screen narrator, who tells us that Watanabe has only six months to live, and, later, that he has died. The intervening narrative takes us through Watanabe's discovery of his situation and his search to find a meaning for his life, culminating in his moment of decision. The second part (marked formally by the narrator's last intrusion and, in terms of narrative, by the death of the film's hero and central consciousness) shows Watanabe's funeral wake. The two parts are linked by a formal device: each contains five flashbacks the precise pattern of which is inverted in part two. At the same time, each part has its own highly organized formal structure. Part one consists of a prologue which includes the time preceding Watanabe's discovery of his fatal disease, and three sections. The prologue is clearly marked off from the rest by the only use in the film of a striking technical device: the shutting off of the soundtrack in the shot where Watanabe leaves the clinic in a state of shock, totally absorbed by his plight, and is nearly run down by a truck (the sound crashing in again at that moment). The ensuing three sections show the three phases of his search for meaning, each ending in disillusionment: his reevaluation of his relationship with the son to whom his life has been devoted; his plunge into the hedonism of Tokyo's nightlife; his relationship with the young girl who used to work in his office. The first part, then, covers a considerable extent of time and space; the second part (flashbacks and a brief epilogue apart) is contained within a single night and a single room. The three-section structure of part one is ''answered'' in part two by the three intrusions of outsiders into the wake: the reporters, the women from the district that has benefited from Watanabe's achievement, and the policeman who recounts the manner of his death. Where each of the three sections of part one marked a phase in the search for meaning, each of the intrusions marks a stage in the revelation of the truth about his achievements.

The ''rough-hewn geometry,'' the use of the narrator, the abrupt narrative break, and the frequently disruptive editing all combine to produce a strong sense of distanciation. What is remarkable about *Ikiru*, and crucial to the Kurosawa ''flavor,'' is the way in which this collides with the film's equally strong emotional rhetoric, setting up a continuous tension between involvement and distance.

—Robin Wood

IM LAUF DER ZEIT

(Kings of the Road)

West Germany, 1976

Director: Wim Wenders

Production: Wim Wenders Produktion; black and white, 35mm; running time: 165 minutes, some sources list 176 minutes; length: 15,740 feet. Released 17 March 1976. Filmed along the border regions between West and East Germany.

Producer: Wim Wenders; **executive producer:** Michael Wiedemann; **screenplay:** Wim Wenders; **photography:** Robbie Müller and Martin Schäfer; **editor:** Peter Przygodda; **sound recordists:** Martin Müller and Bruno Bollhalder; **sound re-recordist:** Paul Schöler; **art directors:** Heidi Lüdi and Bernd Hirskorn; **music:** Axel Linstädt; **performed by:** Improved Sound Limited.

Cast: Rüdier Vogeler (*Bruno Winter*); Hanns Zischler (*Robert Lander*); Lisa Kreuzer (*Cashier*); Rudolf Schündler (*Robert's father*); Marquard Böhm (*Man who has lost his wife*); Dieter Traier (*Garage owner*); Franziska Stömmer (*Cinema owner*); Patrick Kreuzer (*Little boy*).

Award: Cannes Film Festival, International Critics Award, 1976.

Publications

Script:

Wenders, Wim, ''Casem'' (script extract) in *Film a Doba* (Prague), August 1977.

Books:

Sandford, John, *The New German Cinema*, Totowa, New Jersey, 1980.

Geist, Kathe, *The Cinema of Wim Wenders 1967–1977*, Ann Arbor, Michigan, 1981.

Johnston, Sheila, *Wim Wenders*, London, 1981.

Buchka, Peter, *Augen kann man nicht Kaufen: Wim Wenders und seine Filme*, Munich, 1983.

Corrigan, Timothy, *New German Cinema: The Displaced Image*, Austin, Texas, 1983.

Franklin, James, *New German Cinema from Oberhausen to Hamburg*, Boston, 1983.

Grob, Norbert, *Die Formen des filmische Blicks: Wenders: Die fruhen Filme*, Munich, 1984.

Phillips, Klaus, editor, *New German Filmmakers: from Oberhausen through the 1970s*, New York, 1984.

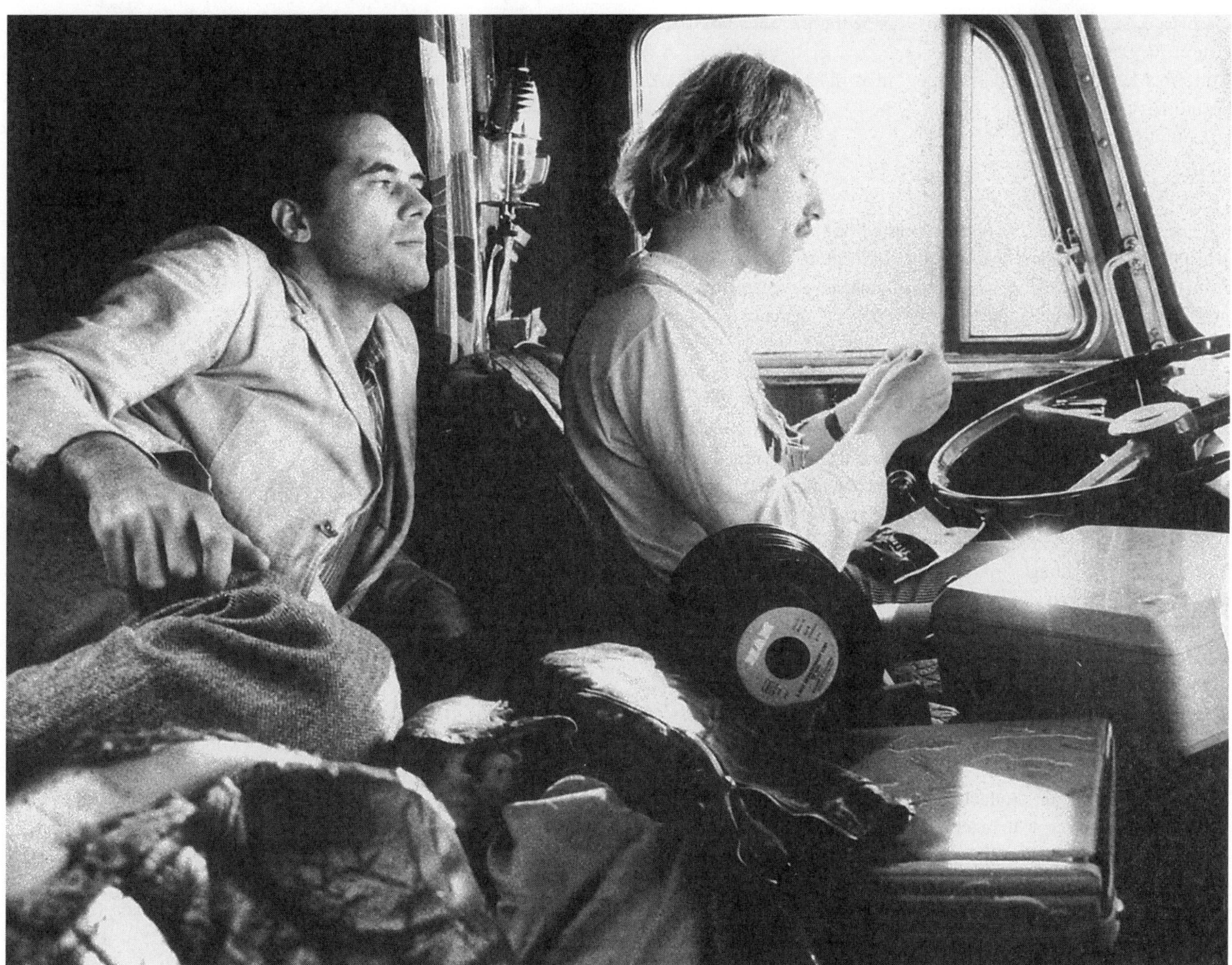

Im Lauf der Zeit

Devillers, Jean-Pierre, *Berlin, L.A., Berlin: Wim Wenders*, Paris, 1985.
Boujut, Michel, *Wim Wenders*, 3rd edition, Paris, 1986.
Geist, Kathe, *The Cinema of Wim Wenders: From Paris, France to Paris, Texas*, Ann Arbor, Michigan, 1988.
Elsaesser, Thomas, *New German Cinema: A History*, London, 1989.
Wenders, Wim, *The Logic of Images*, New York, 1992.
Kolker, Robert P., and Peter Beicken, *The Films of Wim Wenders*, New York, 1993.
Cook, Roger F., and Gerd Gemunden, *The Cinema of Wim Wenders: Image, Narrative, and the Postmodern Condition*, Detroit, 1997.
Wenders, Wim, *The Act of Seeing*, New York, 1999.

Articles:

Variety (New York), 17 March 1976.
Wiedemann, H., and F. Mueller-Scherz, Interview with Wenders in *Film und Ton Magazine* (Munich), May 1976; also in *Cinéma* (Paris), December 1976.
Skoop (Amsterdam), May 1976.
Grant, J., in *Cinéma* (Paris), June 1976.
Maraval, P., in *Cinématographe* (Paris), June 1976.
Bracourt, Guy, in *Ecran* (Paris), July 1976.
Filmkritik (Munich), July 1976.
Bonitzer, Pierre, ''Allemagne, années errantes,'' in *Cahiers du Cinéma* (Paris), July-August 1976.
Tarratt, Margaret, in *Films and Filming* (London), May 1977.
Combs, Richard, in *Monthly Film Bulletin* (London), July 1977.
''Wim Wenders on *Kings of the Road*,'' in *Monthly Film Bulletin* (London), July 1977.
Hallen, S., in *Chaplin* (Stockholm), vol. 20, no. 4, 1978.
Kass, J. M., in *Movietone News* (Seattle), 22 February 1978.
''De Emotionele reizen van Wim Wenders,'' in *Skrien* (Amsterdam), April 1978.
Alvarez, R., in *Filmcritica* (Rome), February 1979.
Bencivenni, A., in *Bianco e Nero* (Rome), May-June 1979.
Balzola, A., ''L'afasia del cinema nel silenzio di Wenders,'' in *Cinema Nuovo* (Bari), October 1980.
Huttunen, T., ''Hidas kotiinpaluu,'' in *Filmihullu* (Helsinki), no. 2, 1989.
Gemuenden, G., ''On the Way to Language: Wenders' *Kings of the Road*,'' in *Film Criticism* (Meadville, Pennsylvania), no. 2, 1991.

Hurtado, J.A., ''*Da viajes y nomadas*,'' in *Nosferatu* (San Sebastian), no. 16, October 1994.
Torreiro, M., ''En el curso del tiempo,'' in *Nosferatu* (San Sebastian), no. 16, October 1994.

* * *

The first image of *Im Lauf der Zeit* is a title specifying where and when the film was shot. The importance of location becomes obvious from the length of screen time devoted to images of the land, the road, and the small towns along the itinerary which, rather than a script, was the organizing structure of the film.

The choice of subject was made early in the production. The preeminence of the itinerary insured that the spatial dimension would structure the narrative. The choice of route allowed the filmmakers to photograph the east/west borderline guard towers, providing a visual metaphor that functions on several levels. Wenders claims to have chosen the area because it was seldom photographed, an underpopulated, forgotten area he wanted to record on film. He was also able to preserve images of the disappearing small town cinema houses, which served as subject matter in terms of both the condition of the German film industry in 1975 and the history of German cinema. These two facets of the same subject are introduced in a pseudo-interview conducted with an actual movie house owner by a fictional character. Just as important as location is an exactness of time. Wenders and cameraman Robbie Müller were able to make use of the natural light to evoke a precise sense of time of day.

Another significant production decision was to shoot chronologically, allowing the crew to react to what was found along the route—to react to their subject in the sense of documentary filmmaking. It allowed for the workings of chance.

The film does not attempt to reveal the characters psychologically through the editing style. While the film does to a certain extent represent the consciousnesses of its two protagonists, a distance is maintained. The acting is relatively unrevealing, there is little dialogue, and the camera pulls out to extreme long shot at intervals. Most important is an editing style that de-emphasizes point-of-view techniques. This includes the frequent absence of either the glance or reaction shot, a lack of signification registered in the reaction when it is present, and a tendency to cut just after the glance has turned away, rather than on the look.

A primary characteristic of the film is its length, or more exactly the length of time between ''events,'' resulting in its slowness, or sense of duration. The film covers six and a half days in three hours. It is the time between events that shifts the emphasis from story to setting. These are the summary sequences, transition scenes punctuated by wipes and dissolves. The sense of duration also comes from the types of events portrayed on the screen. It is as if Wenders wanted to record actions which usually are excluded from films—the time it takes to enter a room, climb a stairway or the process of an everyday task—in the same way that he wanted to film in an area that is usually ignored as a film location. Ellipses in this film tend to be between scenes, not within them.

The third part of a loosely connected trilogy (with *Alice in den Städten* and *Falsche Bewegung*), *Im Lauf der Zeit* possesses a documentary quality dependent primarily on its descriptive nature, a preoccupation with recording and preserving events and a concern for surfaces. Its ending suggests the possibility of change for its protagonists, but it is not so optimistic for the future of film in Germany. The last movie house owner has closed her theater, waiting for a change in the industry, but at least no longer complacent and willing to exhibit whatever she is given.

—Ann Harris

IN A LONELY PLACE

USA, 1950

Director: Nicholas Ray

Production: A Santana Production for Columbia; black and white; running time: 93 minutes; length: 8,375 feet. Released May 1950.

Producer: Robert Lord; **screenplay:** Andrew Solt, from a novel by Dorothy B. Hughes; **photography:** Burnett Guffey; **editor:** Viola Lawrence; **art director:** Robert Peterson; **music:** George Antheil.

Cast: Humphrey Bogart (*Dixon Steele*); Gloria Grahame (*Laurel Gray*); Frank Lovejoy (*Brub Nicolai*); Carl Benton Reid (*Captain Lochner*); Art Smith (*Mel Lippman*); Jeff Donnell (*Sylvia Nicolai*); Martha Stewart (*Mildred Atkinson*); Robert Warwick (*Charlie Waterman*); Ruth Gillette (*Martha*).

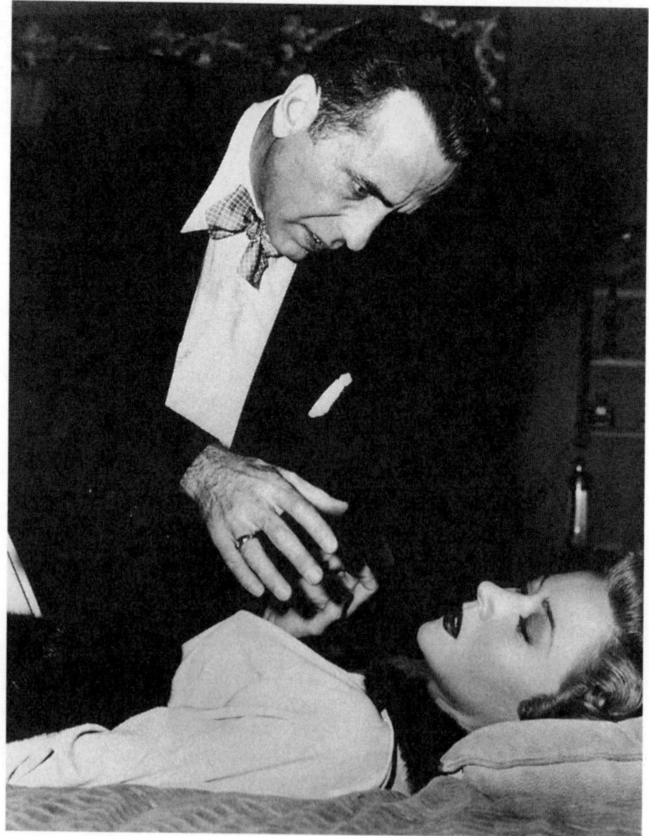

In a Lonely Place

Publications

Books:

McArthur, Colin, *Underworld U.S.A.*, London, 1972.
Eyles, Allen, *Bogart*, New York, 1975.
Kreidl, John, *Nicholas Ray*, Boston, 1977.
Pettigrew, Terence, *The Bogart File*, London, 1977.
Kaplan, E. Ann, editor, *Women in Film Noir*, London, 1978.
Silver, Alan, and Elizabeth Ward, editors, *Film Noir*, London, 1981.
Masi, Stefano, *Nicholas Ray*, Florence, 1983.
Blaine, Allan, *Nicholas Ray: A Guide to References and Resources*, Boston, 1984.
Hillier, Jim, editor, *Cahiers du cinema 1: Neo-realism, Hollywood, New Wave*, London, 1985.
Erice, Victor, and Jos Oliver, *Nicholas Ray y su tiempo*, Madrid, 1986.
Giuliani, Pierre, *Nicholas Ray*, Paris, 1987.
Wagner, Jean, *Nicholas Ray*, Paris, 1987.
Coe, Jonathan, *Humphrey Bogart: Take It and Like It*, New York, 1991.
Eisenschitz, Bernard, *Nicholas Ray*, New York, 1993, 1996.
Bogart, Stephen H., and Gary Provost, *Bogart: In Search of My Father*, New York, 1995.
Schlesinger, Judith, *Bogie: A Life in Pictures*, New York, 1998.
Sperber, A.M., *Bogart*, New York, 1998.
Cunningham, Ernest W., *Ultimate Bogie*, Los Angeles, 1999.
Duchovnay, Gerald, *Humphrey Bogart: A Bio-Bibliography*, Westport, 1999.
Meyers, Jeffery, *Bogart: A Life in Hollywood*, New York, 1999.

Articles:

Today's Cinema, 18 May 1950.
Motion Picture Herald (New York), 20 May 1950.
Monthly Film Bulletin (London), June 1950.
Place, J. A., and L. S. Peterson, ''Some Visual Motifs of Film Noir,'' in *Film Comment* (New York), January-February 1974.
McVay, Douglas, ''Outcast State: *In a Lonely Place*,'' in *Bright Lights* (Los Angeles), no. 7, 1978.
Ménil, A., ''Le Violent,'' in *Cinématographe* (Paris), July-August 1983.
Telotte, J. P., ''Film noir and the Dangers of Discourse,'' in *Quarterly Review of Film Studies* (New York), Spring 1984.
Palmer, J. W., ''*In a Lonely Place*: Paranoia in the Dream Factory,'' in *Literature/Film Quarterly* (Salisbury, Maryland), July 1985.
Williamson, Judith, in *New Statesman* (London), 22 January 1988.
Oplustil, K., in *EPD Film* (Frankfurt), vol. 6, October 1989.
Chiacchiari, F., ''*Il diritto di uccidere* di Nicholas Ray,'' in *Cineforum* (Bergamo, Italy), October 1990.
Bawden, James, ''*In a Lonely Place*,'' in *Films in Review* (New York), vol. 45, no. 7–8, July-August 1994.
King, N., ''Interview with Dana Polan,'' in *Metro Magazine* (St. Kilda West), no. 97, Autumn 1994.
Castoro Cinema (Milan), no. 105, 2nd ed., September 1995.
Chase, D., ''In Praise of the Naughty Mind: Gloria Grahame,'' in *Film Comment* (New York), vol. 33, September/October 1997.

* * *

According to Nicholas Ray, ''Bogie had seen my first film, *They Live by Night*, and had admired it greatly. He approached me to make *Knock on Any Door*, optioned me for a second film and exercised the option immediately in the form of *In a Lonely Place*.'' This second actor/director collaboration—an examination of the underside of Hollywood—was made by Humphrey Bogart's production company, Santana, with Bogart also taking the lead role of the screenwriter, Dixon Steele. In preparing this, his fourth feature, Ray immediately dismissed the 1947 novel by the successful suspense writer Dorothy B. Hughes, which was to have formed the basis of the film. He did so, claiming he was interested ''in doing a film about the violence in all of us, rather than a mass murder film or one about a psychotic.''

As with many of Ray's early films, *In a Lonely Place* involves a thoughtful examination of the nature of violence, particularly how an individual can be forced to such behavior, either by circumstances beyond his control or by the desperate need to compensate for loneliness.

Ray effectively begins the film by illustrating both the issues of loneliness and violence. As Dixon drives alone late one night down Santa Monica Boulevard, his violent nature comes to the fore as he is provoked by the insensitive comments of a fellow driver. His tendency toward violent solution erupts again later, and more dramatically, when he brutally assaults and almost kills a young college student who taunts him on the road. While the former violent outburst was encouraged by others, the latter is a result of Dixon's mounting frustration at being wrongly suspected of the murder of a young coat check girl. This situation has also taken its toll on his current relationship with Laurel Gray (Gloria Grahame), a neighbor who provided him with an alibi by telling the police that Dixon was at home when the murder was committed. While this relationship with Miss Gray has been of great importance to Dixon—personally, it has helped to heal the wounds of loneliness; professionally, it has been instrumental in his return to the typewriter—the ensuing murder investigation elicits several violent outbursts and brings about his downfall. With others encouraging her suspicions, Laurel begins to fear for her life; ultimately, in the moments before the real murderer confesses, Dixon, crazed with Laurel's doubts, attempts to strangle her.

Using this film also critically to examine Hollywood life, Ray positions Dixon Steele as a representative of what happens to many in Hollywood, as an individual whose loneliness and frustration are the direct result of a hostile artistic climate. And this is where Bogart's influence as producer (uncredited) is most felt. According to Ray, it was Bogart who insisted on the subplot of a has-been actor, Charlie Waterman (Robert Warwick), as a way of further illustrating the violence that men inflict upon each other. Dixon is the only person who defends the aging alcoholic; to everyone else he is a subject for derision.

Throughout the film, Ray effectively translates his thematic concerns of loneliness and violence into key aspects of the film's design. As J. A. Place and L. S. Peterson note in their seminal essay ''Some Visual Motifs of Film Noir,'' *In a Lonely Place* is characteristic of this cinematic style in its effective establishment of a mood of claustrophobia, paranoia, despair, and nihilism. Many of the film's key scenes occur at night, the lack of light accentuating both the loneliness of the protagonist and impending violence in the city. Early in the film, Dixon is regularly shown alone in his apartment: by day, the light harshly pierces the room through blinds which adorn the windows; by night, the light from Laurel's apartment accentuates the space that separates them. Perhaps most notably, Ray's tight compositional framings and stark lighting contrasts distinguish this as among the best of the film noir cycle.

Originally, the film was to have ended ambiguously, with the spectator never knowing whether Dixon had actually strangled Laurel or not. After shooting that ending, however, Ray cleared the set and spontaneously directed the ending which now exists, an ending in which, after almost killing Laurel, Dixon learns he has been exonerated in the murder case, only to realize that his violence has destroyed his relationship. He then exits Laurel's apartment and is seen against the criss-crossing patterns of the complex courtyard—a lonely figure in a harsh environment.

—Doug Tomlinson

IN SEARCH OF FAMINE

See **AKALER SANDANE**

IN THE REALM OF THE SENSES.

See **AI NOCORRIDA**

INDIA SONG

France, 1975

Director: Marguerite Duras

Production: Sunchild, Les Films Armorial, S. Damiani and A. Cavaglione; color, 35mm. Released 1975.

Producer: Stephane Tchalgaldjeff; **screenplay:** Marguerite Duras; **photography:** Bruno Nuytten; **editor:** Solange Leprince; **sound:** Michel Vionnet; **original music:** Carlos D'Alessio, recording at the ORTF: Gaston Sylvestre, Beethoven selection: Gerard Fremy, ''India Song Blues'' interpreted by: Raoul Verez.

Cast: Delphine Seyrig (*Anne-Marie Stretter*); Michel Lonsdale (*Vice-Counsel of France*); Matthieu Carriere (*Young attaché to the Ambassador*); Didier Flamand (*Young escort to Stretter*); Claude Mann (*Michael Richardson*); Vernon Dobtcheff (*Georges Crawn*); Claude Juan (*A guest*); Satasinh Manila (*Voice of the beggar*); Nicole Hiss, Monique Simonet, Viviane Forrester, Dionys Mascolo, and Marguerite Duras (*Voices of Time*); François Lebrun, Benoit Jacquot, Nicole-Lise Bernheim, Kevork Kutudjan, Daniel Dobbels, Jean-Claude Biette, Marie-Odile Briot, and Pascal Kane (*Voices from the reception*).

Publications

Script:

Duras, Marguerite, *India Song: Texte—theatre—filme*, Paris, 1973; translated as *India Song*, New York, 1976.

Books:

Bernheim, N.-L., *Marguerite Duras tourne un film*, Paris, 1976.

Ropars-Wuilleumier, Marie-Claire, *La Texte divisé*, Paris, 1981.

Trastulli, Daniela, *Dalla parola all imagine: Viaggio nel cinema di Marguerite Duras*, Geneva, 1982.

Borgomano, Madeleine, *L'Ecriture filmique de Marguerite Duras*, Paris, 1985.

Brossard, Jean-Pierre, editor, *Marguerite Duras: Cineaste, écrivain*, La Chaux-de-Fonde, Switzerland, 1985.

Guers-Villate, Yvonne, *Continuité/discontinuité de l'oeuvre durassienne*, Brussels, 1985.

Hofmann, Carol, *Forgetting & Marguerite Duras*, Boulder, 1991.

Hill, Leslie, *Marguerite Duras: Apocalyptic Desires*, New York, 1993.

Schuster, Marilyn R., *Marguerite Duras: Revisited*, New York, 1993.

Harvey, Robert, and Helene Volat, *Marguerite Duras: A Bio-Bibliography*, Westport, 1997.

Williams, James S., *The Erotics of Passage: Pleasure, Politics, & Form in the Later Work of Marguerite Duras*, New York, 1997.

Knapp, *Critical Essays on Marguerite Duras*, New York, 1998.

Ricouart, Janine, *Marguerite Duras Lives On*, Lanham, 1998.

Ladimer, Bethany, *Colette, Beauvoir and Duras: Age & Women Writers*, Gainesville, November 1999.

Cody, Gabrielle H., *Impossible Performances: Duras As Dramatist*, New York, 2000.

Articles:

Clouzot, C., in *Ecran* (Paris), April 1975.

Amiel, M., in *Cinéma* (Paris), June 1975.

Moskowitz, G., in *Variety* (New York), 18 June 1975.

Amengual, Barthélemy, ''Les Yeuxs fertiles,'' in *Positif* (Paris), July-August 1975.

Bonitzer, Pierre, in *Cahiers du Cinéma* (Paris), July-August 1975.

Lanol, A., in *Jeune Cinéma* (Paris), July-August 1975.

Dawson, Jan, ''*India Song*, a Chant of Love and Death: Marguerite Duras Interviewed,'' in *Film Comment* (New York), November-December 1975.

Clarens, Carlos, in *Sight and Sound* (London), Winter 1975–76.

Tarantino, M., Interview with Duras in *Take One* (Montreal), no. 4, 1976.

''Marguerite Duras,'' in *Film en Televisie* (Brussels), November 1976.

McWilliams, D., in *Wide Angle* (Athens, Ohio), no. 4, 1977.

Pym, John, in *Monthly Film Bulletin* (London), November 1977.

Straram, P., ''Tanner and Duras,'' in *Cinéma Quebec* (Montreal), no. 10, 1977.

Schepelern, P., in *Kosmorama* (Copenhagen), Summer 1978.

''*India Song* Issue'' of *Avant-Scène du Cinéma* (Paris), 1 April 1979.

Escudero, I., in *Cinema 2002* (Madrid), October 1979.

Forster, A., ''Marguerite Duras,'' in *Skrien* (Amsterdam), September 1980.

Duras, Marguerite, and E. Lyon, in *Camera Obscura* (Berkeley), Fall 1980.

De Kuyper, E., in *Skrien* (Amsterdam), May 1981.

Undercut (London), nos. 2–5, August 1981-July 1982.

Porte, M., ''The Places of Marguerite Duras,'' in *Enclitic* (Minneapolis), Fall 1983.

Loutti, M. A., ''Duras' India,'' in *Literature/Film Quarterly* (Salisbury, Maryland), vol. 14, no. 3, 1986.

India Song

Murphy, C. J., ''Duras' New Narrative Regions: The Role of Desire in the Films and Novels of Marguerite Duras,'' in *Literature/Film Quarterly* (Salisbury, Maryland), vol. 14, no. 3, 1986.

Holmlund, C. A., ''Displacing Limits of Difference: Gender, Race, and Colonialism in Edward Said and Homi Bhabha's Theoretical Models and Marguerite Duras's Experimental Films,'' in *Quarterly Review of Film and Video* (New York), no. 1–3, 1991.

Williams B., ''Splintered Perspectives: Counterpoint and Subjectivity in the Modernist Film Narrative,'' *Film Criticism* (Meadville, Pennsylvania), no. 2. 1991.

Tesson, C., ''J'ecoute *India Song*,'' in *Cahiers du Cinéma* (Paris), no. 459, September 1992.

Jutel, T., ''Marguerite Duras et le cinema de la modernite: tout [est] ce qu'il n'y a pas dans *India Song*,'' in *French Review*, vol. 66, no. 4, 1993.

Strauss, Frédéric, ''*India Song:* Marguerite Duras,'' in *Cahiers du Cinéma* (Paris), Hors-série, 1993.

Badir, S., ''*India Song* ou le temps tragique,'' in *Cinemas*, vol. 5, no. 1/2, 1994.

Vajdovich, G., ''Antiregény és antifilm,'' in *Filmkultura* (Budapest), vol. 31, no. 4, April 1995.

McMullen, K., in *Vertigo*, vol. 1, no. 6, 1996.

Everett, Wendy, ''Director as Composer: Marguerite Duras and the Musical Analogy,'' in *Literature/Film Quarterly* (Salisbury), vol. 26, no. 2, April 1998.

* * *

India Song is radical in both form and content. Like Alain Resnais's *L'année dernière à Marienbad*, Duras's film offers an ambiguity of narrative—a type of enigma which paradoxically calls for a reading and yet makes any reading tentative. The film asks, who is Anne-Marie Stretter, the protagonist? What is her relation to men? To India? Or to a beggar woman whose destiny somehow parallels her own? In answering these questions or, more precisely, in eluding any definitive answer, the film expresses some important feminist perspectives while making innovations in film narrative.

Duras, in this film, finally puts into full practice what Sergei Eisenstein posed in theory 45 years earlier—non-synchronous sound. She separates the verbal track of the film from the visual track in such a way that either the narrator or the dialogue is over-voiced with images that do not correspond on a simple story level. Both the verbal and visual tracks offer us fragmented and disparate pieces of the puzzle of Anne-Marie Stretter that the viewer must reassemble.

Duras has structured the plot in layers. Madame Stretter, wife of the French Ambassador to colonial India, has a *doppelgänger* in an insane beggar woman who haunts the embassy gardens. While we never see the woman, we hear her distant off-camera cries. Often these cries are juxtaposed with the restrained stance and expression of Madame Stretter. It is as if these cries spring from Madame Stretter's inner self, which has no outlet in the oppressive society she inhabits. The beggar woman, whom we learn has followed Madame Stretter from French Indo-China, perhaps is emblematic of India or other lands burdened by European imperialism; her cries may also be theirs.

A sense of the oppressive lends unity to the film. While we never see colonial India beyond the embassy walls, Duras conveys, through actors' movements and details in the mise-en-scène, the oppressively humid atmosphere. Colonialism is shown oppressing not only the Indians but the Europeans who seem in power. There is a double meaning in Madame Stretter's sexual enslavement of the men around her—all members of the apparent ruling-class. She and India are ineluctable forces that elude and, even to some degree, control the male hierarchy which only seems to oppress them.

Duras explores stasis in all of its forms and ramifications. The characters often remain immobile under the influence of both the sultry atmosphere and class-imposed decorum. *India Song* treats death and life at once, or more precisely, death in life; for Madame Stretter lives a death amid a mise-en-scène filled with funeral objects and flowers. Further, since sound and visuals do not match in a realistic sense, narration and dialogue seem something vaguely heard from beyond the tomb.

Interlacing the destiny of one woman with another and then comparing their situation to nations occupied by foreigners suggests that *India Song* be read as a film about political oppression on all levels—from personal to national. While some might find Duras's view—that women and, by extension, nations are able to transcend oppression—somewhat naive, the innovative techniques she uses gives this work a haunting quality beyond mere polemics.

—Rodney Farnsworth

THE INFORMER

USA, 1935

Director: John Ford

Production: RKO/Pictures Inc.; black and white, 35mm; running time: 91 minutes; length: 10 reels. Released 1935.

Producer: Cliff Reid; **screenplay:** Dudley Nichols, from the novel by Liam O'Flaherty; **photography:** Joseph H. August; **editor:** George Hively; **sound:** Hugh McDowell Jr.; **art directors:** Van Nest Polglase and Charles Kirk; **music:** Max Steiner; **costume designer:** Walter Plunkett.

Cast: Victor McLaglen (*Gypo Nolan*); Heather Angel (*Mary McPhillip*); Preston Foster (*Dan Gallagher*); Margot Grahame (*Katie Madden*); Wallace Ford (*Frankie McPhillip*); Una O'Connor (*Mrs. McPhillip*); J. M. Kerrigan (*Terry*); Joseph Sauers (*Bartly Mulholland*); Neil Fitzgerald (*Tommy Connor*); Donald Meek (*Peter Mulligan*); D'Arcy Corrigan (*Blind man*); Gaylord Pendleton (*Dennis Daly*); May Boley (*Madame Betty*); Leo McCabe (*Donahue*); Francis Ford (*Flynn*); Grizelda Harvey (*The Lady*); Dennis O'Dea.

The Informer

Awards: Oscars for Best Director, Best Actor (McLaglen), Best Screenplay, Best Score, 1935; Best Screenplay, Venice Film Festival, 1935; New York Film Critics Awards for Best Picture and Best Director, 1935.

Publications

Scripts:

Nichols, Dudley, "*The Informer*" (condensed screenplay), in *Theatre Arts* (New York), August 1951; as "*Le Mouchard*," in *Avant-Scène du Cinéma* (Paris), February 1965.

Books:

Mitry, Jean, *John Ford*, Paris, 1954.
Bluestone, George, *Novels into Films*, Berkeley, 1961.
Haudiquet, Philippe, *John Ford*, Paris, 1966.
Baxter, John, *The Cinema of John Ford*, New York, 1971.
McBride, Joseph, and Michael Wilmington, *John Ford*, London, 1975.
Bogdanovitch, Peter, *John Ford*, Berkeley, 1978.

Ford, Dan, *Pappy: The Life of John Ford*, Englewood Cliffs, New Jersey, 1979.
Sinclair, Andrew, *John Ford*, New York, 1979.
Anderson, Lindsay, *About John Ford*, London, 1981.
Caughie, John, editor, *Theories of Authorship: A Reader*, London, 1981.
Schatz, Thomas, *Hollywood Genres: Formulas, Filmmaking, and the Studio System*, New York, 1981.
Gallagher, Tag, *John Ford: The Man and His Films*, Berkeley, 1986.
Stowell, Peter, *John Ford*, Boston, 1986.
Lourdeaux, Lee, *Italian & Irish Filmmakers in America: Ford, Capra, Coppola & Scorsese*, Springfield, 1990; 1993.
Davis, Ronald L., *John Ford: Hollywood's Old Master*, Norman, 1997.
Girus, Sam B., *Hollywood Renaissance: The Cinema of Democracy in the Era of Ford, Capra, & Kazan*, New York, 1998.
Levy, Bill, *John Ford: A Bio-Bibliography*, Westport, 1998.
Eyman, Scott, *Print the Legend: The Life and Times of John Ford*, New York, 1999.

Articles:

New York Times, 10 May 1935.
Variety (New York), 15 May 1935.
Greene, Graham, in *Spectator* (London), 11 October 1935.
Mitry, Jean, ''John Ford,'' in *Films in Review* (New York), August-September 1955.
Stanbrook, Alan, in *Films and Filming* (London), July 1960.
Barkun, Michael, ''Notes on the Art of John Ford,'' in *Film Culture* (New York), no. 25, 1962.
McVay, Douglas, ''The Five Worlds of John Ford,'' in *Films and Filming* (London), June 1962.
''Special Issue'' of *Avant-Scène du Cinéma* (Paris), February 1965.
''John Ford Issue'' of *Présence du Cinéma* (Paris), March 1965.
''John Ford Issue'' of *Cahiers du Cinéma* (Paris), October 1966.
''John Ford Issue'' of *Velvet Light Trap* (Madison, Wisconsin), August 1971.
''John Ford Issue'' of *Focus on Film* (London), Spring 1971.
Anderson, Lindsay, ''John Ford,'' in *Cinema* (Beverley Hills), Spring 1971.
''Ford's Stock Company'' in *Filmkritik* (Munich), January 1972.
Scapperotti, Dan, in *Magill's Survey of Cinema 2*, Englewood Cliffs, New Jersey, 1980.
Veress, J., in *Filmkultura* (Budapest), January 1985.
Reid's Film Index (Wyong), no. 3, 1989.
Fuller, Samuel, ''Comment John Ford et Max Steiner ont fait mon film préféré,'' in *Positif* (Paris), no. 400, June 1994.

* * *

John Ford was the perfect choice to direct the film version of Liam O'Flaherty's novel about the Sinn Fein Rebellion in Dublin in 1922 as Ford's Irish heritage proved invaluable in setting the background for the film. *The Informer* was Ford's 74th film as a director and he would do 48 more before his retirement in 1966.

Flaherty's novel was first filmed as an early talkie in Great Britain in 1929 with Lars Hansen in the leading role. Six years later, Ford's version was released through RKO Radio Pictures. The mood piece surprised everyone, including the studio, by winning four Academy Awards and moving John Ford into the top echelon of Hollywood directors and Victor McLaglen into the role of one of the film industry's most trusted character actors.

Strictly observing the unities of time and space, the film traces Gypo Nolan from betrayal to death in just one 12-hour period. Whether Ford was aware he was making a *film noir* or not, he preceded the 1940s spate of ''dark'' films by having *The Informer* take place entirely at night.

The film opens with Gypo encountering a poster stating that there is a reward out for information leading to the capture of Frankie McPhillip, his rebel friend. Tearing the sign down and tossing it away, Gypo goes on his way only to discover, in one of Ford's most brilliant visual moments, that the poster takes on a life of its own and follows him down the street, eventually blowing onto his leg and clinging to it. The visual imagery continues as the viewer is introduced to Gypo's girlfriend Katie as a lovely madonna who suddenly changes into a bleach-blonde street-walker by merely removing her scarf.

Reasoning that he and Katie would be able to get a boat to the United States with the money offered to turn Frankie in, Gypo informs on the fugitive to the police. As Frankie visits clandestinely with his mother and sister, he is ambushed and killed. Gypo gets his reward, but is soon under suspicion by rebel leader Dan Gallagher. Celebrating by getting drunk, Gypo is caught and, having spent all the blood money, confesses. He hides in Katie's apartment and when she innocently reveals his whereabouts, he is shot. The wounded Gypo staggers to a church where Frankie's mother is praying. She forgives him and he dies under the altar.

Much has been said about composer Max Steiner's contribution to *The Informer*. The music suitably underscores all the action from the atmospheric beginning to the religious ending. The flawless cast, composed mainly of Irish-born actors, make the film and the plot believable, and the lighting, costuming, art direction and cinematography all contribute to the stifling and tense atmosphere. Although over 60 years old, this melodrama still holds up well in a period when another Irish rebellion has been raging in the 1990s.

—James Limbacher

INTOLERANCE

USA, 1916

Director: D. W. Griffith

Production: Wark Producing Company, some sources list studio as Epoch Releasing Corp.; black and white (with some scenes tinted in original release prints), 35mm, silent; running time: about 220 minutes, some versions are 129 minutes, original version 8 hours. Released 5 September 1916, New York. Filmed fall 1914-July 1916 in Hollywood, basically on outdoor sets constructed by Griffith and his crew. Cost: about $386,000, though figures differ in various sources. Re-released with new score by Carl Davis, London Film Festival 1988.

Producer: D. W. Griffith; **scenario:** D. W. Griffith; **photography:** G. W. (Billy) Bitzer and Karl Brown; **editors:** James and Rose Smith; **production designer (set decorator and architect):** Frank Wortman; **art directors:** Walter L. Hall and others; **music score which accompanied the film on its initial release:** Joseph Carl Breil and D. W.

Intolerance

Griffith; **assistants on film:** Eric von Stroheim, W. S. Van Dyke, Tod Browning, Joseph Henabery, Edward Dillon, George Siegman, Lloyd Ingraham, and others.

Cast: *The Modern Story*: Mae Marsh (*The Dear One*); Robert Harron (*The Boy*); Fred Turner (*The Girl's Father*); Sam de Grasse (*Jenkins*); Vera Lewis (*Miss Jenkins*); Walter Long (*Musketeer of the Slums*); Ralph Lewis (*The Governor*); Monte Blue (*Strike Leader*); Tod Browning (*Race car owner*); Miriam Cooper (*The Friendless One*). *The Babylonian Story*: Alfred Page (*Belshazzar*); Constance Talmadge (*The Mountain Girl*); Elmer Clifton (*The Rhapsode*); Seena Owen (*The Princess Beloved*); George Siegman (*Cyrus the Persian*); Tully Marshall (*High Priest of Bel*); Carl Stockdale (*King Nabonidus*); Elmo Lincoln (*Mighty Man of Valor*); Jewel Carmen, Carol Dempster, Mildred Harris, Alma Rubens, Pauline Starke, Eve Southern, Natalie Talmadge, and Anna Mae Walthall (*Slave girls and dancers*); Frank Campeau, Donald Crisp, Douglas Fairbanks, DeWolfe Hopper, Wilfred Lucas, Owen Moore, Sir Herbert Beerbohm Tre, Tammany Young, others (*Soldiers, courtiers, etc.*). *The French Story*: Margery Wilson (*Brown Eyes*); Eugene Pallette (*Prosper Latour*); Spottiswoode Aitken (*Father*); Ruth Handford (*Mother*); Josephine Crowell (*Catherine de Medici*); Frank Bennett (*Charles IX*); Maxfield Stanley (*Duc d'Anjou*); Constance Talmadge (*Marguerite de Valois*). *The Judean Story*: Howard Gaye (*The Nazarene*); Lillian Langdon (*Mary*); Olga Grey (*Mary Magdalene*); Bessie Love (*Bride of Cana*); George Walsh (*Bridegroom*); W.S. Van Dyke (*Wedding guest*); Lillian Gish (*The Woman Who Rocks the Cradle*).

Publications

Script:

Griffith, D. W., *Intolerance: Shot-by-Shot Analysis by Theodore Huff*, New York, 1966; narrative scheme also published in *Cahiers du Cinéma* (Paris), Spring 1972.

Books:

Wagenknecht, Edward, *The Movies in the Age of Innocence*, Norman, Oklahoma, 1962.

Lindgren, Ernest, *The Art of the Film*, New York, 1963.

Brownlow, Kevin, *The Parade's Gone By*, London and New York, 1969.
Gish, Lillian, *The Movies, Mr. Griffith, and Me*, New York, 1969.
O'Dell, Paul, *Griffith and the Rise of Hollywood*, New York, 1970.
Griffith, D. W., *The Man Who Invented Hollywood: The Autobiography*, edited by James Hart, Louisville, Kentucky, 1972.
Henderson, Robert, *D. W. Griffith: His Life and Work*, New York, 1972.
Bitzer, Billy, *His Story*, New York, 1973.
Brown, Karl, *Adventures with D. W. Griffith*, New York and London, 1973; revised edition, 1988.
Niver, Kemp, *D. W. Griffith: His Biograph Films in Perspective*, Los Angeles, 1974.
Wagenknecht, Edward, and Antony Slide, *The Films of D. W. Griffith*, New York, 1975.
Giannetti, Louis, *Masters of the American Cinema*, Englewood Cliffs, New Jersey, 1981.
Brion, Patrick, editor, *D. W. Griffith*, Paris, 1982.
Mottet, Jean, editor, *D. W. Griffith*, Paris, 1984.
Schickel, Richard, *D. W. Griffith and the Birth of Film*, London, 1984.
Graham, Cooper C., and others, *D. W. Griffith and the Biograph Company*, Metuchen, New Jersey, 1985.
Drew, William M., *D. W. Griffith's ''Intolerance'': Its Genesis and Its Vision*, Jefferson, North Carolina, 1986.
Jesionowski, Joyce E., *Thinking in Pictures: Dramatic Structures in D. W. Griffith's Biograph Films*, Berkeley, 1987.
Gunning, Tom, *D.W. Griffith and the Origins of American Narrative Film: The Early Years at Biograph*, Champaign, 1991.
Leondopoulos, Jordan, *Still the Moving World: Intolerance, Modernism, and Heart of Darkness*, New York, 1991.
Simmon, Scott, *The Films of D.W. Griffith*, New York, 1993.
Schickel, Richard, *D.W. Griffith: An American Life*, New York, 1996.

Articles:

New York Times, 6 September 1916.
Soule, George, in *New Republic* (New York), 30 September 1916.
Dell, Floyd, in *Masses* (New York), November 1916.
Bitzer, Billy, in *International Photographer* (Los Angeles), October 1934.
Joad, C. E. M., in *New Statesman and Nation* (London), February 1949.
Trewin, J. C., ''Rush Hour in Babylon,'' in *Sight and Sound* (London), Spring 1949.
Feldman, Joseph and Harry, ''The D. W. Griffith Influence,'' in *Films in Review* (New York), July-August 1950.
Dunham, Harold, ''Bessie Love,'' in *Films in Review* (New York), February 1959.
Esnault, Philippe, in *Cinéma* (Paris), 1960.
Tozzi, Romano, ''Lillian Gish,'' in *Films in Review* (New York), July-August 1962.
Bodeen, DeWitt, ''Blanche Sweet,'' in *Films in Review* (New York), November 1965.
Meyer, Richard J., ''The Films of David Wark Griffith,'' in *Film Comment* (New York), Fall-Winter 1967.
Casty, Alan, ''The Films of D. W. Griffith: A Style for the Times,'' in *Journal of Popular Film* (Washington, D.C.), Spring 1972.
Oms, Marcel, ''Essai de lecture thematique de *Intolérance*,'' in *Cahiers du Cinéma* (Paris), Spring 1972.
''Dossier *Intolérance*,'' in *Cahiers de la Cinémathèque* (Perpignan), Spring 1972.
Bruno, E., in *Filmcritica* (Rome), November-December 1972.
Hanson, Bernard, ''D. W. Griffith: Some Sources,'' in *Art Bulletin* (New York), December 1972.
Beylie, Claude, in *Ecran* (Paris), February 1973.
Stern, Seymour, ''D. W. Griffith's *Intolerance*: A Sun-Play of the Ages,'' in *The Essential Cinema*, New York, 1975.
Belluccio, A., ''*Cabiria e Intolerance*,'' in *Bianco e Nero* (Rome), May-August 1975.
''Griffith Issue'' of *Films in Review* (New York), October 1975.
Kepley, Vance, Jr., ''*Intolerance* and the Soviets: A Historical Investigation,'' in *Wide Angle* (Athens, Ohio), no.1, 1979.
Merritt, Russell, ''On First Looking into Griffith's Babylon: A Historical Investigation,'' in *Wide Angle* (Athens, Ohio), no.1, 1979.
Pym, John, in *Monthly Film Bulletin* (London), May 1979.
Belaygue, C., and others, ''Redecouvrir *Intolérance*,'' in *Cinéma* (Paris), 27 November 1985.
Chevrie, M., ''Le Miroir du muet,'' in *Cahiers du Cinéma* (Paris), December 1985.
Hansen, M., ''The Hieroglyph and the Whore: D. W. Griffith's *Intolerance*,'' in *South Atlantic Quarterly* (Durham, North Carolina), no. 2, 1989.
Leondopoulos, J., ''Lost in a Climate of Opinion: *Intolerance* Revisited,'' in *Literature/Film Quarterly* (Salibury, Maryland), no. 2, 1990.
Everson, W. K., in *Films in Review* (New York), January-February 1990.
Bassetti, S., ''Una questione di omogeneita,'' in *Filmcritica* (Rome), November 1990.
Toeplitz, Jerzy, ''Wspaniale widowisko: Kalendarz filmowy,'' in *Iluzjion*, no. 3–4, July-December 1991.
Werner, Gösta, ''*Intolerance* och Griffiths sax,'' in *Filmrutan* (Sundsvall), vol. 36, no. 3, 1993.
Dupre la Tour, C., ''The Written Word and Memory in Griffith's *Intolerance* and Dreyer's *La passion de Jeanne d'Arc*,'' in *Iris* (Iowa City), no. 19, Autumn 1995.
Merritt, R., '''Bloody Ludlow' auf der Leinwand,'' in *KINtop*, vol. 6, 1997.
Ent, M. van der, ''Muzikaal commentaar,'' in *Skrien* (Amsterdam), no. 212, February/March 1997.

* * *

Critical judgment remains sharply divided on *Intolerance*, D. W. Griffith's most expensive and flamboyant spectacle. Those critics who pronounce the film a failure generally point to the four stories, which, they claim, are thematically too diverse to be effectively collated. Taking their cue from Eisenstein's famous indictment, they argue that the film suffers from purposeless fragmentation and thematic incoherence. Others, notably Vachel Lindsay, Georges Sadoul, Edward Wagenknecht, and more recently Pauline Kael, list *Intolerance* among the masterworks, stressing its formal complexity, experimental daring, and thematic richness. René Clair, taking a middle position, writes, ''it combines extraordinary lyric passages, realism, and psychological detail, with nonsense, vulgarity, and painful sentimentality.''

Historians agree, however, that *Intolerance* remains Griffith's most influential film, and that among its most precocious students were the Soviet directors of the 1920s. As Vance Kepley states, ''When *Intolerance* was shown in the Soviet Union in 1919, it popularized a montage style already evolving in the hands of Soviet artists. It was reputedly studied in the Moscow Film Institute for the possibilities of montage and 'agitational' cinema (agit-film) and leading Soviet directors, including Eisenstein, Pudovkin, and Kuleshov, acknowledged a debt to Griffith in their writings.''

True to his customary practice of starting one film while finishing another, Griffith began work on *Intolerance* while editing *The Birth of a Nation* in the fall of 1914. *Intolerance* began with the modern story, originally entitled ''The Mother and the Law.'' It was intended as a companion piece to *The Escape* (released by Mutual earlier that year), a study of white slavery and the corruption of city slums.

''The Mother and the Law'' was virtually completed before *The Birth of a Nation* was released. Not until May, 1915, after *Birth*'s controversies were at their peak, did he resume work on it. Determined to surpass the Civil War movie, he decided to expand his modern story to epic proportions. He built lavish sets (notably, the Mary Jenkins ballroom and the Chicago courtroom) and—most important—expanded the story to include the famous strike sequence.

This was, in part, an effort to capitalize on the headlines surrounding John D. Rockefeller, Jr., who had been called up before the Commission on Industrial Relations to explain his role in the 1914 Ludlow massacre. *Intolerance*'s strike is loosely based on this incident, in which 23 striking employees of Rockefeller's Colorado Fuel and Iron Company were shot down by the national guard. In these new sequences, Griffith also attacked the Rockefeller Foundation, which, like its founder, came under severe public criticism as the creation of a hypocritical plutocrat, a philanthropy paid for by the exploitation of workers to enhance the reputation of their taskmaster.

Griffith continued shooting his modern story through the summer of 1915. Meanwhile, he began work on a French story, directly patterned after Meyerbeer's *Les Huguenots* which had enjoyed great popularity at the Metropolitan Opera with Caruso and Toscanini. Originally, this was to be the lustrous counterpoint to the drab modern story. In original prints, the interiors of the Louvre palace were hand-tinted, while considerable attention was paid to royal costumes and lavish Paris sets.

Not until the end of the year did he begin his most elaborate and expensive story. The Hall for Belshazzar's Feast has become perhaps the best-known set created for a silent film. Griffith had his set festooned with Egyptian bas-reliefs, Hindu elephant gods, and Assyrian bearded bulls. Practically every Near Eastern style was represented somewhere on the walls or in the costumes—except the styles of Babylon. Until Douglas Fairbanks's castle set for Robin Hood, it remained the largest backdrop ever created for a movie scene.

The result, when combined with the Passion sequence, was a conglomerate of stories and styles in search of a unifying principle. Part morality play and part three-ring circus, the movie was part of the new eclectic aesthetic that had all but buried the older ideal of organic synthesis. Along with Scott Joplin's *Treemonisha* and Charles Ives's Third Symphony, it remains one of the period's great hybrids.

As such, it won uniformly enthusiastic critical notices, but proved disappointing at the box office. Produced at a cost of $386,000 (almost four times the expense of *The Birth of a Nation*) and endowed with an extraordinary cast, it left audiences cold. Although the film cost considerably less and earned more than historians have generally reported, Griffith himself was convinced he had failed. Two years after its release, he released the modern and Babylonian episodes as two separate films. Traditionally, these productions have been dismissed as footnotes to *Intolerance*, simple attempts to relieve the producer of *Intolerance*'s burden of debt. Several recent critics, however, have argued that the modern story—released as *The Mother and the Law*—is improved when separated from the other stories and should be evaluated as a self-contained feature.

Griffith was the most eclectic of American directors, an artist whose work consistently absorbed and reflected American popular culture. Of all his films, *Intolerance* remains the one most firmly rooted in its own time, a work representing the cultural phenomena of its day. Probably no film before *Citizen Kane* touched on as many aspects of American popular taste.

Griffith's instincts cannot be called infallible. In his sweeping dragnet of the fine arts, he intuitively missed every important art movement of his time; the raw materials he gathered were an unsorted miscellany of official art treasures (like the Cluny unicorn tapestries and the Assyrian winged bulls) and parochial 19th century *kitsch*. As a muckraker, he had trouble distinguishing important social evils (like America's bloody labor wars and horrible prison conditions) from ephemeral parochial problems. The demons he fought most bitterly, like the Anti-Saloon League, the Rockefeller Foundation, and settlement workers, represented issues far more complex than he ever perceived. He had infinite charity for prodigals, but none for Pharisees, and he depicts ''uplifters'' as onesidedly in *Intolerance* as he depicted blacks in *The Birth of a Nation*.

Today, *Intolerance* is usually discussed according to memorable isolated sequences, notably Belshazzar's feast, beginning with its famous crane shot; the strike sequence; the courtship of Mae Marsh and Bobby Harron; the courtroom scene with the famous close-ups of Mae Marsh's hands; and the Babylonian battles. Although considerable attention has recently been paid to Griffith's treatment of mise-en-scène, the most durable aesthetic debate continues to center on his intercutting techniques, especially the rhythmic climax built on four intertwined catastrophes, one averted, the others not.

—Russell Merritt

INVASION OF THE BODY SNATCHERS

USA, 1956

Director: Don Siegel

Production: Allied Artists Pictures Corp.; black and white, 35mm, Superscope; running time: 80 minutes. Released 5 February1956. Filmed 1955.

Producer: Walter Wanger; **screenplay:** Daniel Mainwaring, and according to some sources uncredited scriptwriting by Sam Peckinpah, from the novel *The Body Snatchers* by Jack Finney; **photography:** Ellsworth Fredericks; **editor:** Robert S. Eisen; **sound engineer:** Ralph Butler; **sound editor:** Del Harris; **production designer:** Joseph Kish; **art director:** Edward Haworth; **music:** Carmen Dragon; **music editor:** Jerry Irvin; **special effects:** Milt Rice.

Cast: Kevin McCarthy (*Dr. Miles Bennel*); Dana Wynter (*Becky Driscoll*); Larry Gates (*Dr. Dan Kauffmann*); King Donovan (*Jack*); Carolyn Jones (*Theodora*); Jean Willes (*Sally*); Ralph Dumke (*Nick Grivett*); Virginia Christine (*Wilma Lentz*); Tom Fadden (*Uncle Ira Lentz*); Kenneth Patterson (*M. Driscoll*); Whit Bissell (*Dr. Hill*); Sam

Invasion of the Body Snatchers

Peckinpah (*Charlie Buckholtz, gas company employee*); Guy Way (*Sam Janzek*); Eileen Stevens (*Mrs. Grimaldi*); Beatrice Maude (*Grandmother Grimaldi*); Bobby Clark (*Jimmy Grimaldi*); Jean Andren (*Aunt Eleda Lentz*); Everett Glass (*Dr. Ed Percy*); Richard Deacon (*Dr. Harvey Bassett*); Dabbs Greer (*Mac*); Marie Selland (*Martha*); Pat O'Malley (*Man carrying baggage*).

Publications

Script:

Mainwaring, Daniel, ''*L'Invasion des profanateurs de sepultures*,'' in *Avant-Scène du Cinéma* (Paris), 15 July 1979.

Books:

Steinbrunner, Chris, and Burt Goldblatt, *Cinema of the Fantastic*, New York, 1972.

Johnson, William, editor, *Focus on the Science-Fiction Film*, Englewood Cliffs, New Jersey, 1972.

Kaminsky, Stuart M., *Don Siegel: Director*, New York, 1974; revised edition, Chicago, 1983.

Kaminsky, Stuart M., *American Film Genres*, Dayton, Ohio, 1974.

Lovell, Alan, *Don Siegel: American Cinema*, London, 1977.

Parish, James Robert, editor, *The Science-Fiction Pictures*, Metuchen, New Jersey, 1977.

Vaccino, Roberto, *Donald Siegel*, Florence, 1985.

Siegel, Don, *A Siegel Film*, New York, 1993.

Articles:

Sarris, Andrew, in *Film Culture* (New York), Spring 1963.

Martin, Marcel, in *Letters Françaises* (Paris), 15 November 1967.

Austen, David, in *Films and Filming* (London), May 1968.

Durgnat, Raymond, in *Films and Filming* (London), February 1969.

Farber, Manny, ''The Films of Don Siegel and Sam Fuller,'' in *December* (Los Angeles), nos. 1–2, 1970.

Mundy, Robert, ''Don Siegel: Time and Motion, Attitude and Genre,'' in *Cinema* (London), February 1970.

Bracourt, Guy, in *Image et Son* (Paris), April 1970.

Tarratt, Margaret, "Monsters from the Id," in *Films and Filming* (London), December 1970.
Gregory, Charles T., "The Pod Society vs. the Rugged Individualist," in *Journal of Popular Film and Television* (Washington, D.C.), Winter 1972.
Kaminsky, Stuart, and Peter Bogdanovitch, in *Take One* (Montreal), June 1972.
Kass, Judith M., "Don Siegel," in *The Hollywood Professionals 4* (London), 1975.
Norgaard, P., in *Kosmorama* (Copenhagen), Summer 1975.
Tarnowski, Jean-François, in *Ecran Fantastique* (Paris), no. 3, 1977.
Verstappen, W., "*Body Snatchers* op de montagetafel: Pseudo-lijken in peulen" (shot analysis), in *Skoop* (Amsterdam), December 1978-January 1979.
Johnson, G. M., "We'd Fight . . . We Had To: *The Body Snatchers*," in *Journal of Popular Film and Television* (Washington, D.C.), no. 1, 1979.
Freund, C., "Pods over San Francisco," in *Film Comment* (New York), January-February 1979.
"*Invasion of the Body Snatchers* Issue" of *Avant-Scène du Cinéma* (Paris), 15 July 1979.
Svehla, G. J., in *Midnight Marquee* (Baltimore), September 1979.
McDermott, Elizabeth, in *Magill's Survey of Cinema 2*, Englewood Cliffs, New Jersey, 1980.
Beltran, A., "El otro, el mismo," in *Contracampo* (Madrid), February 1981.
Higashi, S., in *Jump Cut* (Berkeley), March 1981.
Combs, Richard, in *Listener* (London), 13 November 1986.
Telotte, J.P., "The Doubles of Fantasy and the Space of Desire," in *Film Criticism* (Meadville), vol. 11, no. 1/2, 1987.
Kurtz, F., in *Monsterscene* (Lombard), no. 1, October 1992.
Schuman, Howard, "Gone to Pod," in *Sight & Sound* (London), vol. 2, no. 8, December 1992.
Jousse, Thierry, "*Invasion of the Body Snatchers:* Don Siegel," in *Cahiers du Cinéma* (Paris), Hors-série, 1993.
Reid's Film Index (Wyong), no. 13, 1994.
Heredero, C.F., in *Nosferatu* (San Sebastian), no. 14/15, February 1994.
Hoberman, J., "Paranoia and the Pods," in *Sight & Sound* (London), vol. 4, no. 5, May 1994.
Smith, D.G., "*Invaders from Mars* and *Invasion of the Body Snatchers*," in *Midnight Marquee* (Baltimore), no. 51, Summer 1996.
Zemnick, D.J., in *Cinefantastique* (Forest Park), vol. 28, no. 1, 1996.
Turner, George, "A Case for Insomnia," in *American Cinematographer* (Hollywood), vol. 78, no. 3, March 1997.

* * *

There are no moments of great violence in *Invasion of the Body Snatchers*. We see no one die on screen and, technically, no one dies in the film. There are no monsters and only a few special effects, which are confined totally to the construction of a few pods shown but briefly. The essence of *Invasion of the Body Snatchers* is its aura of normalcy. It is normalcy, the acceptance of the status quo, the desire to escape from the pain of the abnormal that creates the sense of horror in the film.

The thematic goals of *Invasion of the Body Snatchers* are beautifully expressed in content (the dialogue primarily) and style (the visual body). The fact that one cannot escape from the body-snatching pods is indicated by the director, Don Siegel, in the way the pods are hidden before they take over the minds of the humans. We see them in basements, automobile trunks, a greenhouse, and on a pool table. That the pods are virtually indestructible is shown by Dr. Miles Bennel's repeated attempts to destroy them. When Miles discovers the pods growing in the greenhouse, we are shown a ritual vampire killing. The camera is low in the point of view of the pod. We see Miles's anguished face as he drives the pitchfork down and leaves it like a stake through the heart. But it is not enough. Other pods appear in his trunk. He burns them in much the same way we have seen so many monsters burning in films, only to rise again in a sequel. The pods are not traditional terrors; they are indestructible modern terrors. There is no catharsis in the presentation of a monster being destroyed by love or religious ritual. Here it is the monsters who will prevail.

Siegel expects that his warning of a "pod invasion" will not be heeded. This is indicated in the film in a variety of ways. Perhaps the most striking is that of the small boy, Jimmy Grimaldi, whom we meet along with Miles at the beginning of the picture. As Jimmy runs down the road, he is stopped by Miles. Jimmy informs him that Mrs. Grimaldi (who has become a pod) is not his mother any more. Miles doesn't believe him. The world will not believe him and eventually the boy becomes a pod. Near the end of the film we also see Miles running down the road, searching for someone to tell that the people of Santa Mira (the very name of the town—"mira" in Spanish means "look"—calls attention to itself, and cries to be understood or heeded as a warning) have been consumed by pods. Like Jimmy, we know Miles will not be believed.

A sense of impending doom, or a sense of helplessness in combating the pods, is indicated by depicting Miles as constantly being driven into dark corners and forced to hide. His world is threatened by the pods, and he is reduced to constricted areas of existence. For example, he and Becky Driscoll have to hide in a closet in his office; the camera moves with them into the closet. Through a small hole in the door we see a human-turned-pod turn on a light outside. Later Miles and Becky are forced to hide in a hole in the floor of a cave which they cover with boards. We see the pod people rush over them from Miles's and Becky's point of view. In effect, the places to run have been repeatedly reduced and we suffer the confinement of choices with the protagonists.

One of the most striking and famous sequences in the film is where Miles, having finally escaped from Santa Mira, suddenly finds himself on a highway with hundreds of cars passing him, full of people who are unwilling to listen to him, and thus unwilling to save themselves. The setting is dark with Miles in a sea of machines; the people are hiding within these machines, perhaps the first step toward becoming pods. As he stands on the highway, a truck passes with the names of various cities on it. In the truck, Miles finds the pods, and he realizes they are being taken to the big cities listed on the side of the truck. We feel as hopeless in the face of the image as Miles.

Finally, an important contribution to the total power of the film lies in the performances. Kevin McCarthy (as Miles) conveys a growing frenzy combined with an unfaltering sense of determination. A less restrained actor might well have proved a disaster. The other actors have the burden of appearing normal while at the same time suggesting that they are not. It is in the performances that this ambiguity is carried. Siegel seldom relies on low key lighting, ominous shadows, radical camera angles or shock cutting to carry the terror of the situation. It is in the matter-of-fact quality of the presentation that the film holds its power; and it is Siegel's handling of actors which contributes considerably to the film which Leslie

Halliwell calls ''the most subtle film in the science-fiction cycle, with no visual horror whatever.''

—Stuart M. Kaminsky

THE ISLAND

See **HADAKA NO SHIMA**

ISTORIA ASI KLIACHINOI KOTORAIA LUBILA DA NIE VYSHLA ZAMUZH

(The Story of Asia Kliachina Who Loved but Didn't Get Married; Asya's Happiness)

USSR, 1967/1987

Director: Andrei Konchalovsky

Production: Mosfilm; black and white; running time: 99 minutes; length: 2713 meters. Finished December 1966; received censorship permit for distribution, March 1967; restored and released, 1987.

Screenplay: Yuri Klepikov; **photography:** Georgy Rerberg; **art director:** Michael Romadin; **music:** Viacheslav Ovchinnikov; **sound:** Raisa Margacheva.

Cast: Iia Savvina (*Asia*); Aleksander Surin (*Stepan*); Liubov Sokolova (*Maria*); Gennadii Jegorychev, Michail Krylov, Nickolai Nazarov, Ludmila Zaiceva, Ivan Petrov, Boris Parfenov, and others.

Award: FIPRESSI Award—Honorable Mention, Berlin International Film Festival, 1988.

Publications

Books:

Konchalovsky, Andrei, *Parabola zamysla* (*Parabola of Concept*), Moscow, 1977.

Zorkaya, Neya, *The Illustrated History of Soviet Cinema*, New York, 1989.

Fomin, Valery, *Polka* (*Shelf*), Moscow, 1992.

Articles:

''Istoria Asi Kliachinoi,'' in *Variety Film Reviews*, Vol. 15, New York, 1983.

Zorkaya, Neya, ''Ne stoit selo bez pravednicy,'' in *Iskusstvo Kino* (Moscow), no. 1, 1989.

Canby, Vincent, ''Fable of Life on Collective Farm,'' in *New York Times Film Reviews, 1987–1988*, New York, 1990.

* * *

Istoria Asi Kliachinoi kotoraia lubila da nie vyshla zamuzh (*The Story of Asia Kliachina Who Loved but Didn't Get Married*) has a long and troubled history. Production was completed in late 1966 and the film was approved by Soviet censors for release in March of 1967, but then, after numerous revisions, changes, and edits, it never was released. Movie fans had to wait twenty years, until 1987, for their first opportunity to view the film.

Even the name of the film was changed numerous times: At first, it was to be called *Istoria Asi Khromonozhki* (*Asia, the Lame One*). Then it was renamed *The Story of Asia Kliachina, Who Loved, but Didn't Get Married because She Was Too Proud.* After a number of revisions, the film was given the more optimistic title *Asia's Happiness.* When it was finally released in 1987 it bore the title *The Story of Asia Kliachina, Who Loved, but Didn't Get Married.* Yuri Klepikov's screenplay was entitled ''The Year of the Tranquil Sun.'' During the discussion phase of the script by the Committee on Cinematography (the organization which exercised total control over the movie industry in the Soviet Union), the disorder of the protagonists' lives, the crudeness of their speech, and the stark realism of many of the scenes in the movie were called into question. In preparing the director's script, Andrei Konchalovsky (also known as Andrei Mikhalkov-Konchalovsky) was compelled to make a series of corrections, change some scenes, and eliminate others.

Filming began in the summer of 1966. The entire film was shot on location in the village of Bezvodnoe in the Gorky region. It was shot using multiple cameras, almost without retakes, since the majority of the ''actors'' were non-professionals—they were real collective farm workers from the Gorky and Voronezh regions. There were only three professional actors in the film: Iia Savvina, Liubov Sokolov, and Alexander Surin. By December, the film's editing had been completed and it was shown to filmmakers.

The film astounded the professionals. It seemed at the time that the documentary style of filming and the surprisingly truthful, forthright depiction of the lives of the people, heretofore unseen in Soviet cinema, would open brand new paths for Russian filmmakers. This film, from a creative standpoint, further developed the traditions of Italian neorealism, the achievements of the ''thaw'' period (the 1960s), and the successes of Russian ''village'' prose (Rasputin, Belov, Abramov, Shukshin).

We must also remember that at this same time the tragic story of the banning of Andrei Tarkovsky's film *Andrei Rublev*, one of the screenwriters of which had been Andrei Konchalovsky, was being played out. But while Tarkovsky refused to give in to the demands of the authorities and was able to defend his prized work, Konchalovsky agreed to make extensive edits and drastic changes. As a result, *Rublev* was finally released, while *Asia* had to wait twenty years to be seen. This is understandable: Tarkovsky's historical fresco, from an ideological standpoint, was far less dangerous in the eyes of the Soviet authorities than the dismal depiction of contemporary life in the Russian villages.

Among the many criticisms of the film were its pessimism, the poverty of collective farm life, the disorderly lives of its heroes, the crassness of their language, drunkenness, and the naturalism of many of its scenes (including the rape scene, the scene of Asia's attempted suicide, and the childbirth scene.) And although the film was officially passed by the censors (#2047/67 on March 1, 1967), it was never released for viewing. The campaign mounted against the film included not only the Party leader of the Gorky region, but also the

Istoria Asi Kliachinoi kotoraia lubila da nie vyshla zamuzh

chairman of the KGB. The director submitted ''corrected'' versions of the film three times and each time more and more scenes were cut, dialogue was rewritten, songs were added, etc. For example, the director changed the reason for old man Tikhomir's eight-year absence from the village (he had been in a concentration camp), and shortened the childbirth scene and the scene of the attempted rape, among other things. The final version of the film (running approximately 90 minutes) was considerably different from the original version, but even it did not suit the Party leadership.

At the center of the film is the lame collective farm cook Asia. As played by Iia Savvina, Asia is a truly Russian character: kind, hard-working, loving, lonely, but proud. Although she is the target of endless derision from her fellow villagers (she is, after all, a cripple), Asia is optimistic and is certain of what she wants out of life. She lives in a dark hut with her great grandmother, grandmother, mother, and niece. There are no men in the house: a typical situation in Russia as the result of war. She lives according to her conscience and for love. She is in love with a shallow, stupid guy named Stepan who treats her contemptibly and has no intention of ever marrying her. A man named Chirkunov arrives from the city and offers Asia his hand in marriage and a comfortable life in a city apartment with indoor plumbing. But Asia does not love him and turns her suitor down. In desperation, Chirkunov tries to rape the pregnant Asia. The birth of her child (which in the first version of the film is a very intense and naturalistic scene) transforms Asia. From a slave to Stepan, she becomes a proud, independent woman and mother: she now has a child, a purpose in life. The talented acting of Iia Savvina made her indistinguishable from the non-professionals in the film.

In addition to the main story line of Asia's life, the film also contains a number of mass scenes (collecting the harvest, the making of the first bread, seeing a gypsy off to the army, and others), and also three dramatic monologues about life filmed in *cinema verite* style with a practically still camera, and total naturalness, simplicity, and sincerity on the part of the storyteller. The first story is told by a crippled war veteran, the second by the hunch-backed chairman of a collective farm, and the third by the old man, Tikhomir, who spent eight years in a Stalinist labor camp. These people lived through very hard times, but had not lost their dignity and optimism. Here, contemporary life was closely intertwined with the themes of war, Stalinist repressions, death, and love.

Official Soviet songs are played, but no one listens to them. Yet when the women begin singing a folk song, everyone enthusiastically joins in. The film's rich soundtrack includes the news being constantly broadcast on the radio, the roar of jet fighters flying overhead, shooting exercises, and tanks rolling by.

In *Parabola of Concept*, Konchalovsky reveals some of the principles that guided his work on this film. At its core was the use of improvisation. Other integral components were black-and-white images; the use of non-professional actors; the use of two or three cameras at once to shoot the film; the simultaneous recording of the sound; the filming of entire episodes without any cutaway shots and subsequent montage; and the predominance of wide angles, rather than close-ups. The entire film was shot in natural interiors or on location.

All of these factors ''created the feeling of authenticity, spontaneity, the sense of getting a glimpse of a true slice of life'' that the director sought to achieve. The revisions which Konchalovsky was forced to make were undoubtedly a detriment to the film. Elements were introduced that were typical of Soviet propaganda cinematography at the time (the scene of the first bread, the optimistic Soviet songs, the soldiers who help get Asia to the hospital where she gave birth, and others). As a result of the edits, it became difficult to understand what was going on in the suicide scene and old man Tikhomir's story about the Stalinist camps was abridged to the bare minimum.

In 1987, the decision was made to restore the original version of the film and release it for viewing. However, the director was unable to completely reconstruct the original version. *The Story of Asia Kliachina* has joined the ranks of a number of important films of world cinema which became legendary before they were ever seen by the public.

—Val Golovskoy

IT HAPPENED ONE NIGHT

USA, 1934

Director: Frank Capra

Production: Columbia Pictures Corp.; black and white, 35mm; running time: 105 minutes. Released 23 February 1934. Filmed between Thanksgiving and Christmas 1933.

Producer: Harry Cohn; **screenplay:** Robert Riskin, from the story ''Night Bus'' by Samuel Hopkins Adams; **photography:** Joseph Walker; **editor:** Gene Havlick; **sound recordist:** E. E. Bernds; **art director:** Stephen Gooson; **music director:** Louis Silvers; **costume designer:** Robert Kalloch.

Cast: Clark Gable (*Peter Warne*); Claudette Colbert (*Ellie Andrews*); Walter Connolly (*Alexander Andrews*); Roscoe Karns (*Mr. Shapely*); Jameson Thomas (*King Westley*); Alan Hale (*Danker*); Wallis Clark (*Lovington*); Harry Bradley (*Henderson*); Arthur Hoyt (*Zeke*); Blanche Frederic (*Zeke's wife*); Ward Bond (*Bus driver*).

Awards: Oscars for Best Picture, Best Actor (Gable), Best Actress (Colbert), Best Directing, and Best Writing—Adaptation, 1934.

Publications

Script:

Riskin, Robert, *It Happened One Night*, in *Four-Star Scripts*, edited by Lorraine Noble, New York, 1936.

Books:

Griffith, Richard, *Frank Capra*, London, 1951.
Essoe, Gabe, *The Films of Clark Gable*, New York, 1970.
Capra, Frank, *The Name above the Title*, New York, 1971.
Silke, James, *Frank Capra: One Man—One Film*, Washington, D.C., 1971.
Willis, Donald, *The Films of Frank Capra*, Metuchen, New Jersey, 1974.
Glatzer, Richard, and John Raeburn, editors, *Frank Capra: The Man and His Films*, Ann Arbor, 1975.
Poague, Leland, *The Cinema of Frank Capra*, New York, 1975.
Scherle, Victor, and William Turner Levy, *The Films of Frank Capra*, Secaucus, New Jersey, 1977.
Garceau, Jean, and Inez Cooke, *Gable: A Pictorial Biography*, New York, 1977.
Malard, Charles J., *American Visions: The Films of Chaplin, Ford, Capra and Welles*, New York, 1977.
Bohnenkamp, Dennis, and Sam Gross, *Frank Capra Study Guide*, Washington, D.C., 1979.
Malard, Charles, *Frank Capra*, Boston, 1980.
Giannetti, Louis, *Masters of the American Cinema*, Englewood Cliffs, New Jersey, 1981.
Cavell, Stanley, *Pursuits of Happiness: The Hollywood Comedy of Remarriage*, Cambridge, Massachusetts, 1981.
Fearfar, R., *Clark Gable*, Paris, 1981.
Quirk, Lawrence, *Claudette Colbert: An Illustrated Biography*, New York, 1985.
Zagarrio, Vito, *Frank Capra*, Florence, 1985.
Carney, Raymond, *American Vision: The Films of Frank Capra*, Cambridge, 1986; 1996.
Wolfe, Charles, *Frank Capra: A Guide to References and Resources*, Boston, 1987.
McBride, Joseph, *American Madness: The Life of Frank Capra*, New York, 1989.
Lourdeaux, Lee, *Italian & Irish Filmmakers in America: Ford, Capra, Coppola and Scorsese*, Springfield, 1993.
Wayne, Jane Ellen, *Clark Gable*, New York, 1994.
Gehring, Wes D., *Populism and the Capra Legacy*, Westport, 1995.
Girus, Sam B., *Hollywood Renaissance: The Cinema of Democracy in the Era of Ford, Capra, and Kazan*, Cambridge, 1998.
Sklar, Robert, editor, *Frank Capra: Authorship and the Studio System*, Philadelphia, 1998.

Articles:

Hall, Mordaunt, in *New York Times*, 23 February 1934.
Variety (New York), 27 February 1934.
Baskette, Kirtley, in *Photoplay* (New York), December 1934.

It Happened One Night

Interview with Frank Capra, in *Motion Picture* (New York), July 1935.
Agee, James, ''Comedy's Greatest Era,'' in *Life* (New York), 4 September 1949.
Films and Filming (London), May-June 1958.
Clarens, Carlos, ''Clark Gable,'' in *Films in Review* (New York), December 1960.
Martin, Marcel, in *Lettres Françaises* (Paris), 27 December 1962.
Price, James, ''Capra and the American Dream,'' in *London Magazine*, January 1964.
Richards, Jeffrey, ''Frank Capra and the Cinema of Populism,'' in *Cinema* (London), February 1970.
Pacheco, Joseph B., Jr., ''Claudette Colbert,'' in *Films in Review* (New York), May 1970.
Thompson, Howard, ''Capra, 74, Looks Back at Film Career,'' in *New York Times*, 24 June 1971.
''Capra Issue'' of *Positif* (Paris), December 1971.
Handzo, Stephen, ''A Decade of Good Deeds and Wonderful Lives: Under Capracorn,'' in *Film Comment* (New York), November-December 1972.
Stein, Elliott, ''Capra Counts His Oscars,'' in *Sight and Sound* (London), vol. 41, no. 3, 1972.
Corliss, Richard, ''Capra and Riskin,'' in *Film Comment* (New York), November-December 1972.
Richards, Jeffrey, ''Frank Capra: The Classic Populist,'' in *Visions of Yesterday*, London, 1973.
Sklar, Robert, ''The Making of Cultural Myths: Walt Disney and Frank Capra,'' in *Movie-Made America*, New York, 1975.
Manns, T., in *Chaplin* (Stockholm), no. 4, 1976.
Poague, Leland, ''*As You Like It* and *It Happened One Night*: The Generic Pattern of Comedy,'' in *Literature/Film Quarterly* (Salisbury, Maryland), Fall 1977.
Gehring, Wes, ''McCarey vs. Capra: A Guide to American Film Comedy of the '30s,'' in *Journal of Popular Film and Television* (Washington, D.C.), vol. 7, no. 1, 1978.
Brown, G., in *Monthly Film Bulletin* (London), February 1978.
Interview with Frank Capra, in *American Film* (Washington, D.C.), October 1978.
Phelps, G.A., ''The 'Populist' Films of Frank Capra,'' in *Journal of American Studies* (London), no. 3, 1979.
Self, L., and R. Self, ''Adaptation as Rhetorical Process: *It Happened One Night* and *Mr. Deeds Goes to Town*,'' in *Film Criticism* (Edinboro, Pennsylvania), Winter 1981.

Frank, Sam, ''Robert Riskin,'' in *American Screenwriters*, edited by Robert E. Morsberger, Stephen O. Lesser, and Randall Clark, Detroit, 1984.

Journal of Popular Film and Television (Washington, D.C.), Autumn 1985.

Tobin, Yann, in *Positif* (Paris), December 1986.

Reid's Film Index (Wyong), no. 3, 1989.

Ching, B., and R. Barnard, ''From Screwballs to Cheeseballs: Comic Narrative and Ideology in Capra and Reiner,'' in *New Orleans Review*, no. 3, 1990.

Shumway, D. R., ''Screwball Comedies: Constructing Romance, Mystifying Marriage,'' in *Cinema Journal* (Austin, Texas), no. 4, 1991.

Hicks, J., ''Frank Capra,'' in *Films in Review* (New York), January-February 1993.

Sibley, Brian, ''The Wonderful Mr. Capra,'' in *Radio Times* (London), vol. 294, no. 3819, 12 April 1997.

Mistichelli, Bill, ''The State of the Union: Capra, Altruism, and the Sociobiologists,'' in *Journal of Popular Film and Television*, vol. 25, no. 3, Fall 1997.

Premiere (Boulder), vol. 10, May 1997.

* * *

It Happened One Night is the film generally credited with launching the ''screwball comedy'' genre popular in the 1930s and 1940s. A difficult genre to define, the screwball comedy revolves around the characters' contradictory desires for individual identity and complete union in heterosexual romance. The films pit the couple's erotic moments of courtship against their verbal combats, battles of wit spiced with rapid-fire, brilliant repartee. Because of the resurgence of censorship in 1934 coupled with an American reluctance to be frank about sex, screwball comedies capitalized on the necessity to mask and to express *verbally* sexual tensions and conflicts. Screwball comedies usually relied upon a final reconciliation or marriage to establish the couple's unity but undercut it as a resolution to the couple's ongoing differences. *It Happened One Night* established these generic rules and provided a model for incorporating into a comic structure attitudes, fears, and tensions about social, sexual, and economic roles.

It Happened One Night, the story of a runaway madcap heiress who is befriended by an individualistic journalist so he can ''scoop'' her story, simply adapted for a Depression-era context a popular movie formula of the 1920s. Movies such as *Dancing Mothers* or *A Woman of the World* presented man-woman, husband-wife relationships in which both parties were witty, intelligent, charming, and thoroughly at odds with each other. Unlike the screwball comedies that arose later, these films extolled aristocratic life styles and proper behavior while resolving the sexual issues on superficial terms. German-emigré director Ernst Lubitsch strengthened the structural integrity of the formula and created the prototype for the screwball comedy in *Trouble in Paradise* and *Design for Living*. Impressed and influenced by Lubitsch's films, Frank Capra borrowed the comic romantic structure that Lubitsch had evolved in order to deal with middle-class sexual and social proprieties. But Capra used the formula as a vehicle for the resolution of all economic and social differences in one vast American middle class united by the virtues of caring and sharing.

Capra's simple Depression-era philosophy, often labelled ''Capracorn,'' is conveyed in *It Happened One Night* as a modern folk tale reversal of Cinderella. Rich girl Ellie Andrews flees her father so she can marry the worthless playboy of her dreams. Penniless and thrown on her own, she runs into the out-of-work ace reporter Peter Warne. In exchange for her ''story,'' Warne helps her return to the playboy. Traveling by bus, foot, and auto across the backroads of 1930s America, they discover a mutual independence of spirit, feistiness, and resiliance. Warne gets the story, Andrews gets her playboy, but both discover that what they had really been seeking they had found in each other. The rich girl ultimately gets the poor boy proving that even the wealthy, if given a chance, will subscribe to the working class values that were deemed a prescription for fighting the Depression.

One of the most successful films of its time, *It Happened One Night* is in its making and reception a ''rags-to-riches'' story. When Capra first proposed the film based on a story serialized in *Cosmopolitan*, Columbia Pictures executives disliked the idea and thought that the fad had passed for bus movies. At least five Hollywood stars turned down the leading roles. Colbert initially hated the picture, and Gable only made the movie because angry MGM executive Louis B. Mayer had loaned him to Columbia as a punishment. When the finished film finally opened, poor reviews and indifferent moviegoers led to the movie's closing after only one week. The film resurfaced, however, and went on to win the top five Academy Awards. The film made stars of Colbert, Gable, and Capra, and Gable's bare-chested appearance in one scene has been said to be responsible for a 50 percent drop in undershirt sales within the year. Critics have since tried to explain the secret of the film's enduring popularity. They have generally credited Capra with inventing a message that audiences wanted to hear. The nutty romance, a down-to-earth courtship that maintains a spirit of crazy adventure in spite of adversities, showed audiences then as well as today, as critic Andrew Sarris said, ''the private fun a man and a woman could have in a private world of their own making.''

—Lauren Rabinovitz

AN ITALIAN STRAW HAT

See **UN CHAPEAU DE PAILLE D'ITALIE**

IT'S A WONDERFUL LIFE

USA, 1946

Director: Frank Capra

Production: Liberty Films; black and white, 35mm; running time: 129 minutes. Released 1946 by RKO/Radio.

Producer: Frank Capra; **screenplay:** Frances Goodrich, Albert Hackett, and Frank Capra with additional scenes by Jo Swerling, from the story ''The Greatest Gift'' by Philip Doren Stern; **photography:** Joseph Walker and Joseph Biroc; **editor:** William Hornbeck; **sound:** Richard Van Hessen, Clem Portman, and John Aalberg; **art director:** Jack Okey; **music:** Dmitri Tiomkin; **special effects:** Russell A. Cully; **costume designer:** Edward Stevenson.

It's a Wonderful Life

Cast: James Stewart (*George Bailey*); Donna Reed (*Mary Hatch*); Lionel Barrymore (*Mr. Potter*); Thomas Mitchell (*Uncle Billy*); Henry Travers (*Clarence*); Beulah Bondi (*Mrs. Bailey*); Gloria Grahame (*Violet Bick*); H. B. Warner (*Mr. Gower*); Ward Bond (*Bert*); Frank Faylan (*Ernie*); Samuel S. Hinds (*Pa Bailey*); Mary Treen (*Cousin Tilly*); Frank Hagney (*Bodyguard*); Sheldon Leonard (*Nick*); Alfalfa Switzer (*Freddie*).

Publications

Script:

Goodrich, Frances, and others, in *The "It's a Wonderful Life" Book*, edited by Jeanine Basinger, New York, 1986.

Books:

Griffith, Richard, *Frank Capra*, London, 1951.
Jones, Ken, D., *The Films of James Stewart*, New York, 1970.
Capra, Frank, *The Name above the Title*, New York, 1971.
Silke, James, *Frank Capra: One Man—One Film*, Washington, D.C., 1971.
Willis, Donald, *The Films of Frank Capra*, Metuchen, New Jersey, 1974.
Thompson, Howard, *James Stewart*, New York, 1974.
Glatzer, Richard, and John Raeburn, editors, *Frank Capra: The Man and His Films*, Ann Arbor, 1975.
Poague, Leland, *The Cinema of Frank Capra*, New York, 1975.
Scherle, Victor, and William Levy, *The Films of Frank Capra*, Secaucus, New Jersey, 1975.
Malard, Charles J., *American Visions: The Films of Chaplin, Ford, Capra, and Welles*, New York, 1977.
Bohnenhamp, Dennis, and Sam Grogg, *Frank Capra Study Guide*, Washington, D.C., 1979.
Malard, Charles, *Frank Capra*, Boston, 1980.
Giannetti, Louis, *Masters of the American Cinema*, Englewood Cliffs, New Jersey, 1981.
Eyles, Allen, *James Stewart*, London, 1984.
Hunter, Allan, *James Stewart*, New York, 1985.
Robbins, Jhan, *Everybody's Man: A Biography of Jimmy Stewart*, New York, 1985.
Zagarrio, Vito, *Frank Capra*, Florence, 1985.
Ray, Robert B., *A Certain Tendency of the Hollywood Cinema 1930–80*, Princeton, 1985.
Carney, Raymond, *American Vision: The Films of Frank Capra*, Cambridge, 1986.

Wolfe, Charles, *Frank Capra: A Guide to References and Resources*, Boston, 1987.
McBride, Joseph, *American Madness: The Life of Frank Capra*, New York, 1989.
Lourdeaux, Lee, *Italian & Irish Filmmakers in America: Ford, Capra, Coppola & Scorsese*, Springfield, 1993.
Gehring, Wes D., *Populism and the Capra Legacy*, Westport, Connecticut, 1995.
Hawkins, Jimmy, *It's a Wonderful Life: The Anniversary Scrapbook*, Philadelphia, 1996.
Hawkins, Jimmy, *It's a Wonderful Life Trivia*, New York, 1997.
Thomas, Tony, *A Wonderful Life: The Films and Career of James Stewart*, Secaucus, 1997.
Girus, Sam B., *Hollywood Renaissance: The Cinema of Democracy in the Era of Ford, Capra, and Kazan*, Cambridge, 1998.
Sklar, Robert, editor, *Frank Capra: Authorship and the Studio System*, Philadelphia, 1998.
Quirk, Lawrence J., *James Stewart: Behind the Scenes of a Wonderful Life*, New York, 1999.

Articles:

New York Times, 23 December 1946.
Variety (New York), 25 December 1946.
Parsons, L. Q., in *Cosmopolitan* (New York), January 1947.
Mannock, P. L., in *Films and Filming* (London), September 1956.
Price, James, ''Capra and the American Dream,'' in *London Magazine*, January 1964.
Sweigart, William R., ''James Stewart,'' in *Films in Review* (New York), December 1964.
''Capra Issue'' of *Positif* (Paris), December 1971.
Handzo, Stephen, ''A Decade of Good Deeds and Wonderful Lives: Under Capracorn,'' in *Film Comment* (New York), November-December 1972.
Richards, Jeffrey, ''Frank Capra and the Cinema of Populism,'' in *Cinema* (London), February 1970.
Bergman, Mark, ''The Telephone Company, the Nation, and Perhaps the World,'' in *Velvet Light Trap* (Madison, Wisconsin), Winter 1971–72.
Richards, Jeffrey, ''Frank Capra: The Classic Populist,'' in *Visions of Yesterday*, London, 1973.
Sklar, Robert, ''The Making of Cultural Myths: Walt Disney and Frank Capra,'' in *Movie-Made American*, New York, 1975.
Rose, B., ''It's a Wonderful Life: The Stand of the Capra Hero,'' in *Journal of Popular Culture* (Bowling Green, Ohio), vol. 6, no. 2, 1977.
Wood, Robin, ''Ideology, Genre, Auteur,'' in *Film Comment* (New York), January-February 1977.
Quart, Leonard, ''Frank Capra and the Popular Front,'' in *Cineaste* (New York), Summer 1977.
Phelps, G. A., ''The 'Populist' Films of Frank Capra,'' in *Journal of American Studies* (London), no. 3, 1979.
Scheer, R., ''Double Vision: TV Remakes Frank Capra,'' in *Journal of Popular Film* (Washington, D.C.), 1980.
Dickstein, M., ''It's a Wonderful Life, But,'' in *American Film* (Washington, D.C.), May 1980.
Silverman, K., in *Framework* (Norwich), Spring 1981.
''Capra Issue'' of *Film Criticism* (Edinboro, Pennsylvania), Winter 1981.
''Capra Issue'' of *Positif* (Paris), July-August 1982.
Rodrig, A., in *Cinématographe* (Paris), December 1983.
Ahrlich, Evelyn, ''Frances Goodrich and Albert Hackett,'' in *American Screenwriters*, edited by Robert E. Morsberger, Stephen O. Lesser, and Randall Clark, Detroit, 1984.
Weinberger, M., in *Cinéma* (Paris), January 1984.
Napoleon, D., ''Wonderful Life: Broadway Bound,'' in *American Film* (Washington, D.C.), May 1986.
Film Comment (New York), November-December 1986.
Raynes, Doug, ''*It's a Wonderful Life*,'' in *Soundtrack!*, vol. 8, no. 29, March 1989.
Rothman, William, ''Hollywood and the Rise of Suburbia,'' in *East-West Film Journal* (Honolulu), vol. 3, no. 2, June 1989.
Lamm, R., ''Can We Laugh at God? Apocalyptic Comedy in Film,'' in *Journal of Popular Film and Television* (Washington, D.C.), vol. 19, no. 2, Summer 1991.
Gordon, A., ''You'll Never Get Out of Bedford Falls! The Inescapable Family in American Science Fiction and Fantasy Films,'' in *Journal of Popular Film and Television* (Washington, D.C.), vol. 20, no. 2, Summer 1992.
Diski, Jenny, ''Curious Tears,'' in *Sight & Sound* (London), vol. 2, no. 4, August 1992.
Gysin, C., ''The Real George Bailey,'' in *Premiere* (Boulder), vol. 6, January 1993.
Magny, Joël, ''*La vie est belle*: Frank Capra,'' in *Cahiers du Cinéma* (Paris), Hors-série, 1993.
Clements, M., ''My Technology's Turnaround,'' in *Premiere* (Boulder), vol. 8, November 1994.
Nicolaï, M., ''Les anges du ciné,'' in *Télérama* (Paris), no. 2345, 21 December 1994.
Herwitz, D., ''Expectations of Mastery,'' in *Spectator* (Los Angeles), vol. 16, no. 2, 1996.
Fallows, Randall, ''George Bailey is the Vital Center: Postwar Liberal Politics and *It's a Wonderful Life*,'' in *Journal of Popular Film & Television* (Washington, D.C.), vol. 25, no. 2, Summer 1997.
Alter, J., ''It's a Wonderful Legacy,'' in *Newsweek*, vol. 130, 14 July 1997.
Deneen, P.J., ''George Bailey's Secret Life,'' in *Commonweal*, vol. 124, 19 December 1997.

* * *

When Frank Capra returned to Hollywood after coordinating the *Why We Fight* propaganda series during the war, he resumed the total artistic control over his films for which he had fought during the 1930s. *It's a Wonderful Life* was made for Liberty Films, the production company organized by Capra, George Stevens, William Wyler and Sam Briskin. The film exemplifies the concept of the independent producer-director, and Capra has called it his favorite film. In the year of its release its importance was overshadowed by Wyler's *The Best Years of Our Lives* (not made for Liberty Films), but it has since gone on to be one of the most frequently revived of Capra's works.

The impetus and structure of *It's a Wonderful Life* recall the familiar model of Capra's pre-war successes. *Mr. Deeds Goes to Town, Mr. Smith Goes to Washington* and *Meet John Doe*. In each of these films, the hero represents a civic ideal and is opposed by the forces of corruption. His identity, at some point misperceived, is finally acclaimed by the community at large. The pattern receives perhaps its darkest treatment in *It's a Wonderful Life*. The film's conventions and dramatic conceits are misleading. An idyllic representation of small-town America, a guardian angel named Clarence and a Christmas Eve apotheosis seem to justify the film's perennial screenings during the holiday season. These are the signs of the ingenuous optimism for which Capra is so often reproached. Yet they function in the same way ''happy endings'' do in Moliere, where the artifice of perfect resolution is in ironic disproportion to the realities of human nature at the core of the plays.

George Bailey is presumably living the ''wonderful life'' of the title. Having abandoned his ambition to become an architect in order to run a building- and loan- association, and facing arrest for a discrepancy in the books, George is on the verge of suicide. His guardian angel offers him the chance to find out what would have happened had he not been born. George then sees the town as a nightmarish vision of corruption. No one knows him. Even his mother, a benevolent image through the rest of the film, appears hard-bitten and cruel, and refuses to recognize him in a scene that dramatizes a primal identity crisis. George does regain his identity and is euphorically acknowledged by everyone. But this joyous finale caps a film that so often represents pain and despair—from a slap that draws blood from young George's ear, to a marriage proposal expressed in utter frustration, to the images (both inside and outside the fantasy section of the film) of George in a rage, furious with himself and with those he loves. Here, as in *Mr. Smith Goes to Washington*, James Stewart embodies the hysterical energy of Capra's quintessential American hero, thereby conveying, along with the director, the ambiguities of the American dream along with its promises.

—Charles Affron

IVAN GROZNY

(Ivan the Terrible)

USSR, 1944 (Part I: Ivan Grozny) and 1958 (Part II: Boyarskii Zagovor—The Boyars' Plot)

Director: Sergei Eisenstein

Production: Part I—Alma-Ata Studio, Part II—Mosfilm Studio; Part I—black and white, 35mm, Part II—black and white and Agfacolor, 35mm; length: Part I—2745 meters, Part II—2373 meters. Released Part I—1944, Part II—1958. Shooting for Part I was begun 1 February 1943; Part II was shot September-December 1945, though not released until 1958.

Scenario: Sergei Eisenstein; **photography:** A. Moskvine and E. Tisse; **editor:** E. Tobak; **sound:** V. Bogdankevitch and B. Volsky; **production designer:** I. Chpinel; **music:** Sergei Prokofiev; **songs:** V. Louzowsky; **costume designers:** L. Naoumova and N. Bouzina for Part I, and L. Naoumova and M. Safonova for Part II; **ballet choreographer:** R. Zakharov.

Cast: N. Tcherkassov (*Ivan*); M. Jarov (*Maluta Skouratov*); A. Boutchma (*Alexei Basmanov*); M. Kouznetzov (*Fedor Basmanov*); Kolychev (*Monk Philippe*); A. Mguebrov (*Pimen, Architect of Novgorod*); V. Balachov (*Piotr Volynetz*); S. Birman (*Efrossinia Staritzkaïa*); P. Kadotchnikov (*Vladimir Andrevitch*); M. Nazvanov (*Prince Andrei Kourbsky*) (Part II only); P. Massalsky (*Sigismond, King of Pologne*) (Part II only); Erik Pyriev (*Ivan as a child*) (Part II only); L. Tzelikovskaïa (*Czarina Anastassia Romanovna*) (Part I only); Vladimir Staritsky (*Son of Staritzkaïa*) (Part I only); M. Mikhaïlov (*Archdeacon*) (Part I only); V. Pudovkin (*Nikolai*) (Part I only); S. Timochenko (*Ambassador of the Livonien Order*) (Part I only); A. Roumnev (*The Stranger*) (Part I only).

Publications

Script:

Eisenstein, Sergei, *Ivan the Terrible: A Screenplay*, New York, 1962; script of unpublished third part published in *Avant-Scène du Cinéma* (Paris), nos. 50–51, 1965.

Books:

Eisenstein, Sergei, *Film Sense*, edited by Jay Leyda, New York, 1942.
Eisenstein, Sergei, *Film Form*, edited by Jay Leyda, New York, 1948.
Seton, Marie, *Sergei Eisenstein*, London 1952.
Eisenstein, Sergei, *Notes of a Film Director*, London, 1959.
Leyda, Jay, *Kino: A History of the Russian and Soviet Film*, London, 1960.
Moussinac, Leon, *Sergei Eisenstein: An Investigation into His Films and Philosophy*, New York, 1970.
Barna, Yon, *Eisenstein*, Bloomington, Indiana, 1973.
Fernandez, Dominique, *Eisenstein*, Paris, 1975.
Sudendorf, W., and others, *Sergei M. Eisenstein: Materialen zu Leben und Werk*, Munich, 1975.
Swallow, N., *Eisenstein: A Documentary Portrait*, London, 1976.
Mitry, Jean, *S. M. Eisenstein*, Paris, 1978.
Aumont, Jacques, *Montage Eisenstein*, Paris, 1979; translated as *Montage Eisenstein*, London, 1987.
Thompson, Kristin, *Eisenstein's Ivan the Terrible: A Neoformalist Analysis*, Princeton, 1981.
Leyda, Jay, and Zina Vignow, *Eisenstein at Work*, New York, 1982.
Eisenstein, Sergei M., *Immoral Memories: An Autobiography*, Boston, 1983.
Marshall, Herbert, *Masters of the Soviet Cinema: Crippled Creative Biographies*, London, 1983.
Polan, Dana B., *The Political Language of Film and the Avant-Garde*, Ann Arbor, 1985.
Montagu, Ivor, *With Eisenstein in Hollywood*, Merrimac, 1987.
Bordwell, David, *The Cinema of Eisenstein*, Cambridge, 1993.
Goodwin, James, *Eisenstein, Cinema, and History*, Champaign, 1993.
Taylor, Richard, editor, *The Eisenstein Reader*, Bloomington, 1998.
Bergan, Ronald, *Sergei Eisenstein: A Life in Conflict*, New York, 1999.

Articles:

Maddow, Ben, ''Eisenstein and the Historical Film,'' in *Hollywood Quarterly*, October 1945.
Chartier, Jean-Pierre, in *Revue du Cinéma* (Paris), 1 October 1946.
Garga, B. D., in *Sight and Sound* (London), Spring 1958.
Weinberg, Herman, in *Film Culture* (New York), no. 20, 1959.
O'Leary, Liam, in *Films and Filming* (London), January 1959.

Ivan Grozny

Leyda, Jay, in *Film Quarterly* (Berkeley), Spring 1959.
Films and Filming (London), November 1959.
Mekas, Jonas, in *Village Voice* (New York), 9 December 1959.
Valentin, Gregory, in *Films in Review* (New York), January 1960.
Robinson, David, in *Sight and Sound* (London), Spring 1960.
Yourenev, Rostislav, ''Eisenstein,'' in *Anthologie du Cinéma 44* (Paris), 1964.
Gerstein, Evelyn, in *Film Comment* (New York), Fall 1968.
Oudart, Jean-Pierre, in *Cahiers du Cinéma* (Paris), March 1970.
Morse, David, ''Style in *Ivan the Terrible*,'' in *Monogram*, April 1971.
Aristarco, G., in *Cinema Nuovo* (Turin), July-August 1973.
Levaco, R., ''The Eisenstein-Prokofiev Correspondence,'' in *Cinema Journal* (Evanston, Illinois), Fall 1973.
Bordwell, David, ''Eisenstein's Epistemological Shift,'' in *Screen* (London), Winter 1974–75.
Thompson, Kristin, ''*Ivan the Terrible* and Stalinist Russia: A Reexamination,'' in *Cinema Journal* (Evanston, Illinois), Fall 1977.
Gallez, Douglas W., on the Eisenstein-Prokofiev correspondence, in *Cinema Journal* (Evanston, Illinois), Spring 1978 (and addenda in Autumn 1978 issue).
Machwitz, Z., in *Kino* (Warsaw), November 1979.
Iskusstvo Kino (Moscow), May 1980.
Téllez, J. L., ''*Ivan Grozni*: El abismo y la mascara,'' in *Contrecampo* (Madrid), April-June 1981.
Kinder, Marsha, ''The Image of Patriarchal Power in *Young Mr. Lincoln* and *Ivan the Terrible, Part I*,'' in *Film Quarterly* (Berkeley), Winter 1985–86.
Guibbert, Pierre, ''Du vitrail à la scène,'' in *Cahiers de la Cinémathèque* (Perpignan), No. 45, 1986.
Christie, Ian, in *Monthly Film Bulletin* (London), December 1987.
Pescatore, G., ''La grana del cinema,'' in *Cinema & Cinema* (Bologna), January-August 1989.
Guneratne, A. R., ''History as Propaganda: The Portrait of Stalin as Medieval Hero, and its Epic Frame,'' in *Cinefocus* (Bloomington, Indiana), no. 2, 1990.
Costa, A., ''Ivan e la sua ombra (Ejzenstejn, Bazin e la 'prospettiva rovesciata'),'' *Cinema & Cinema* (Bologna), September-December 1990.
Hoberman, J., ''Cut ups,'' in *Village Voice* (New York), 23 March 1993.
Griffiths, P., ''Screening the Music,'' in *New Yorker*, 31 July 1995.
Deltcheva, R., and E. Vlasov, ''From the Wax of History: Leni's *Das Wachsfigurenkabinett* and the Cinema of German Expressionism

as a Source for Eisenstein's *Ivan Groznyi*,'' in *Studies in the Humanities*, vol. 23, no. 1, 1996.

Nesbet, Anne, ''Inanimations: Snow White and Ivan the Terrible,'' in *Film Quarterly* (Berkeley), vol. 50, no. 4, Summer 1997.

* * *

Ivan the Terrible is in structure an unfinished trilogy of three films: *Part I, Ivan the Terrible, Part II, the Boyars, Part III, Ivan's Struggles*. Recent criticism has made the mistake of viewing the two extant parts as one film. Each part presented to Eisenstein different formal and ideological problems which he solved with varying degrees of success; thus, *Parts I* and *II* will be considered separately in this essay before any generalizations will be made on the trilogy as a whole.

Part I takes up the history of Ivan when he is about to take on the trappings of the Byzantine Emperors and the title of Czar (Caesar) instead of the title of his predecessors—Grand Prince of Moscow. The first scene shows his second coronation—that as Czar. This scene also sets the style of the trilogy, in that it prepares the audience for the extremely stylized expression and gestures modeled on Wagnerian music-drama, Marinsky ballet, and Japanese Kabuki theatre. Further, the first scene acts as a sort of overture introducing the three main themes of the trilogy: the personal life of Ivan; domestic problems within Russia and foreign problems of war and trade. The interweaving of these themes into a complex tapestry makes *Part I* one of the supreme masterpieces of cinematic art.

Ivan, in the solitude of absolute power, is often shown seeking companionship; with two friends, Kolychev and Kourbsky, who eventually betray him and side with his enemies, the boyars; in Anastasia, who is poisoned by Efrossinia, the leader of the boyars; and finally, near the end of the film, with the *Oprichniki*. Problems with the boyars are crucial to the structure and ideology of the work because Ivan seeks to create a monarchy with a centralized power at the expense of the fragmented powers of the aristocracy. The film is an attempt at embodying in art a part of the Marxist theory—the step from the feudal order to the stage in which the urban merchants (that is, budding capitalists) form an alliance with the monarch to break the power of the aristocrats. Of equal importance is Ivan's desire to change Russia's foreign policy from that of a princedom to that of an empire. He seeks to break the backs of the Poles and Germans to the west, as well as the Tartars to the south and east. Important too is the idea of foreign trade; for in an essay written in 1928, Eisenstein said that if he ever made a film on *Ivan*, it would show a ''merchant-czar'' rather than a character from a horror story by Poe. In *Part I*, Ivan seeks to establish trade with the other great developing European nation-state—England; but his way is blocked by the Poles and Germans.

All three themes come together in the finale of the film: Ivan, after forming the *Oprichniki*, retreats to a monastery outside Moscow; word is brought that English trading ships have bypassed the Germans and Poles by means of a northern route through the White Sea; and, the townspeople arrive from Moscow to join with their monarch in the great alliance against the boyars. This final scene, which Ivan refers to as his true coronation by the people, formally recapitulates the coronation in the opening scene of the film. The shots of the large figure of the Czar and the tiny figures of the people beyond and below—capture the quintessential relationship between the people and their leader.

Part II remains flawed by its problematic genesis: both it and the aborted *Part III* were to form one film and were to carry forth the three main themes. Unfortunately, the decision was made to divide this original second part into two and expand the material of the boyar's plot. *Part II* unfortunately resulted in a hypertrophy of the ''cloak and dagger'' material. Since Ivan's final victory against the Poles and the Germans was now saved for the third part, only two out of the three themes were allowed to be developed in the second part.

The personal aspects of the Czar, as Eisenstein admitted himself, are developed at the expense of the public figure. At one point, this symbol of ineluctable power all but grovels before his childhood friend Kolychev. The *Oprichniki*, important figures in his war against the boyars, are shown as mere companions for an orgy. There is nothing inherently wrong with any of these aspects of Ivan's character, except that each, when developed out of proportion to the whole sacrifices any formal and psychological integrity found in *Part I*. The *Oprichniki*-orgy scene proved to be a perfect chance for Eisenstein to experiment for the first time with color film stock. At several points in this scene, the filmmaker transcends the usual naturalistic use of color in order to suggest psychological states. In keeping with its excessive emphasis on the private man, the second part makes Ivan's power struggle seem more like a palace soap-opera, and less like a political struggle of national significance. Family jealousies and murder/revenge become the motive of what in the first part had been a fully rounded historical figure, Ivan IV. Worst of all, the theme of foreign policies is awkwardly tacked onto the conclusion of the film in the form of a speech by Ivan.

Taking both parts as a unity, *Ivan the Terrible* stands as one of the most courageous experiments in film art. The two completed parts of the trilogy (particularly the first) stand as a testimony against film theorists who claim that filmmaking demands by its very nature a realistic approach. *Ivan* also demonstrates that film can draw upon the other arts and yet not lose its aesthetic integrity. In this work, the great talents of Eisenstein were supplemented by those of the important Soviet composer Sergei Prokofiev to create a work that can be termed operatic—a film in which words, image, and music achieve a perfect dramatic union. Moreover, *Part I* taken by itself stands as perhaps the only masterpiece of any art which fully embodies the aesthetics preached by Stalin—namely, Soviet Socialist Realism. The first part of *Ivan the Terrible* offers a figure who is both positive and fully rounded in human complexities, yet who does not wallow excessively in the darker side of the human psyche.

—Rodney Farnsworth

JA CUBA

See **SOY CUBA**

J'ACCUSE

France, 1919

Director: Abel Gance

Production: Charles Pathé (major investor); black and white, 35mm, silent; length: 1500 meters. Released 1919. Cost: about 456,000 francs.

Scenario (at least in part): Abel Gance; **photography:** L. H. Burel, Bujord, and Forster; **editor:** André Danis; **assistant director:** Blaise Cendrars.

Cast: Séberin Mars (*François Lauron*); Romuald Joubé (*Jean Diaz*); Maryse Dauvray (*Edith*); Desjardins; Blaise Cendrars.

Publications

Script:

Gance, Abel, *J'accuse*, Paris, 1922.

Books:

Daria, Sophie, *Abel Gance, hier et demain*, Paris, 1922.
Icart, Roger, *Abel Gance*, Toulouse, 1960.
Brownlow, Kevin, *The Parade's Gone By*, London and New York, 1969.
Sadoul, Georges, *French Film*, New York, 1972.
Monaco, Paul, *Cinema and Society: France and Germany during the 20s*, New York, 1976.
Kramer, Steven, and James Welsh, *Abel Gance*, Boston, 1978.
Icart, Roger, *Abel Gance; ou, Le Promethée foudroyé*, Lausanne, 1983.
King, Norman, *Abel Gance: A Politics of Spectacle*, London, 1984.
Groppali, Enrico, *Abel Gance*, Florence, 1986.

Articles:

Kine Weekly (London), 29 April 1920.
Bioscope (London), 29 April 1920.
New York Times, 10 October 1921.
Variety (New York), 14 October 1921.
Esnault, Philippe, ''Filmographie d'Abel Gance,'' in *Cahiers du Cinéma* (Paris), January 1955.
''Gance Issue'' of *Ecran* (Paris), April-May 1958.
Brownlow, Kevin, ''Abel Gance: Spark of Genius,'' in *Films and Filming* (London), November 1969.
Lenning, Arthur, ''The French Film—Abel Gance,'' in *The Silent Voice: A Text* (New York), 1969.
''Film as Incantation: An Interview with Abel Gance,'' in *Film Comment* (New York), March-April 1974.
Kramer, Steven, and James Welsh, ''Abel Gance's Accusation against War,'' in *Cinema Joursenal* (Evanston, Illinois), Spring 1975.
Debacker, J., ''Dossier: La Censure, Monsieur J. Brunin: *J'Accuse*,'' in *Apec-Revue Belge du Cinéma* (Brussels), no. 4, 1976.
Brownlow, Kevin, ''Abel Gance,'' in *Film Dope* (London), September 1979.
Cluny, C. M., ''Abel Gance: Trop grand pour le cinéma?,'' in *Cinéma* (Paris), December 1981.
King, Noel, ''The Sound of Silents,'' in *Screen* (Oxford), vol. 25, no. 3, May-June 1984.
Veray, L., ''*J'accuse:* un film conforme aux aspirations de Charles Pathe et a l'air de temps,'' in *1895*, no. 21, December 1996.

* * *

Abel Gance was one of the most innovative filmmakers of the silent era. Most famously, in his masterpiece *Napoleon*, he projected three images on screen at once in a process he called Polyvision. But this film is not Gance's only epic. Eight years before *Napoleon*, there was *J'accuse*.

While *Napoleon* celebrates the exploits of its title character, *J'accuse* is unabashedly anti-military. The setting is a small French town. A gentle poet, who opposes war and all hostility, loves the wife of a hunter. War is declared, and the husband goes off to fight; jealous of his rival, he dispatches his wife to the Ardennes. When she is captured by the Germans, the poet himself enlists. By the finale, the hunter has been killed in battle, the wife is raped, and the poet, driven mad by the destruction that has destroyed his life, drops dead. While he does not die in combat, his demise—and the tainting of his spirit, his zest for life, his inner peace and love of beauty—becomes the symbol of the pointlessness of war.

J'accuse is one of the earliest cinematic indictments of war. This fact alone earns the film its status in film history. But, additionally, it is one of the first French films to use montage and superimposed shots. In a stunning series of images, closeups of hands grasp each other, pray and raise glasses of wine as soldiers leave to fight. Gance communicates with his audience with visual metaphors: at the film's outset, the head of a dog is placed over the head of the hunter and, at the declaration of war, the Grim Reaper is placed over the poet's work; the filmmaker's rapid montage cutting highlights the horror of the battle sequences, shot by Gance after joining a French army unit. (He perfected this last technique in *La Roue*, a melodrama released in 1923, and in *Napoleon*.) The most famous sequence in *J'accuse*

J'accuse

occurs near the finale, when the crazed poet imagines the ghosts of his dead comrades returning from the battlefield and through the countryside to observe the results of their sacrifices. Tragically, many of the real soldiers Gance utilized as extras did not themselves survive the war. (The film was shot during the final stages of the conflict. They were hired while on leave, just prior to their slaughter at Verdun.)

J'accuse was, upon its release, condemned for its anti-war sentiment by those basking in the German defeat. Gance wanted to make two sequels, to be called *The Scars (Les cicatrices)* and *The League of Nations (La Société des Nations)*. Although these films were never completed, he did revise *J'accuse* four years after its release, most notably comparing the return of the dead soldiers sequence with a victory celebration.

Gance remade *J'accuse* with sound in 1937. He wrote that this new version was ''intended as a challenge to the countries of Europe for permitting the gradual development of a situation that made war inevitable. Before the present menace became a reality, I wrote an introduction to the film which expresses the prophetic message it conveys from the screen: 'This film is dedicated to those who will die in the new war of tomorrow, although I am sure that they will view it skeptically and will fail to recognize themselves in it. . . .'''

Unfortunately, like Renoir's *Grande illusion, J'accuse* had no effect on altering the events which resulted in the next Great War.

—Rob Edelman

THE JACKAL OF NAHUELTORO

See **CHACAL DE NAHUELTORO**

JANA ARANYA

(The Middleman)

India, 1975

Director: Satyajit Ray

Production: Indus Films; black and white, 35 mm; running time: 133 minutes. Filmed in Calcutta.

Producer: Subir Guha; **screenplay:** Satyajit Ray, adapted from the novel *Jana Aranya* by Manisankar ''Sankar'' Mukherjee (also known as Samkara and Shankar); **photography:** Soumendu Roy; **editor:** Dulal Dutta; **art director:** Asok Bose; **musical director:** Satyajit Ray; **sound:** J.D. Irani, Anal Talukdar, Adinath Nag, Sujit Ghosh.

Cast: Pradip Mukherjee (*Somnath Banerjee*); Satya Banerjee (*Somnath's Father*); Dipankar Dey (*Bhombol*); Lily Chakravarti (*Kamala*); Aparna Sen (*Somnath's girlfriend*); Gautam Chakravarti (*Sukumar*); Sudesna Das (*Kauna, known as Juthika*); Uptal Dutt (*Bisu*); Rabi Ghosh (*Mr. Mitter*) Bimal Bhattacharya (*Mrs. Ganguli*); Padma Devi (*Mrs. Biswas*); Soven Lahiri (*Goenka*); Santosh Dutta (*Hiralal*).

Publications

Books:

Samkara, *Jana Aranya*, India, 1974.

Articles:

Moskowitz, G., in *Variety*, 28 July 1976.
Houston, Penelope, in *Sight and Sound* (London), no. 2, 1977.
Coleman, J., in *New Statesman* (London), 11 February 1977
Brown, G., in *Monthly Film Bulletin* (London), March 1977.
Elley, Derek, in *Films and Filming* (London), May 1977.
Kuthna, M., in *Film* (London), 11 May 1977.
Ghosal, Sumantra, in *International Film Guide* (London), 1978.

* * *

Jana Aranya is a representative Satyajit Ray film in that it features an acutely observed, personality-driven narrative and characters who are well-defined products of their surroundings. At the same time, its concerns are distinctly political, as it offers stinging commentary on the economic plight of contemporary India and the manner in which the individual is destined to be crushed and devoured by a callous material environment.

At its core, *Jana Aranya* is a story of tainted innocence. Its hero is an unsophisticated young man who is surrounded by depravity. None of the rogues in his midst are blatantly evil. Rather, their villainy is subtle, and they justify their unsavory ethics in the name of rat-race survival.

Somnath Banerjee is a sweetly handsome young man. At the outset, he is about to graduate from Calcutta University when he is victimized by a myopic instructor who cannot read his exam answers, depriving him of a graduation with honors. And so Ray starts out by offering a biting satire of a ludicrous educational bureaucracy. Yet all of Somnath's experiences while a student, and all of his book learning, have left him ill-prepared for the cruel realities he will face while attempting to enter the job market. Harsh fact first intrudes when he is told, ''You're so young. It'll be ages before you're established.'' These words are prophetic. Long months pass, and Somnath is unable to secure employment. At this point, he can compromise his ideals by marrying a young woman he has never met, enabling him to take over her father's business. But Somnath refuses. Instead, he agrees to go into ''business'' with an acquaintance. He remains trusting, even upon being told that the young man he is replacing has been missing for two months.

Somnath's job is to act as a middleman, a go-between. He will be ''ordering supplies'' and, as such, he is to ''study the market'' and ''buy cheap.'' ''What do I sell?'' he asks. ''Anything,'' is the response. He remains oblivious to the implications of his being instructed to set up bogus companies, and flash different business cards to different clients. ''You'll be fine on your own,'' the contact tells Somnath. ''In two days you'll learn everything, and if you get into trouble . . . of course you'll have to clean up your own mess.''

Somnath's ''business'' results in his inevitable mixing with an assortment of wizened, corrupt characters. His maturation process climaxes when he is called upon to act as a pimp in a business transaction, a job requirement he finds reprehensible. Furthermore, the prostitute in question is a friend's sister, who is attempting to support her family. Somnath's integrity is irrevocably tainted when his sense of self-preservation obliterates his morality, and he agrees to go along with the scheme. In so doing, he now is trafficking in human beings as well as goods. He has become just as much of a whore as the sister.

All Somnath wants is an honest job, a not-unreasonable request in a fair and equitable world. However, within the parameters of society, the young man—in order to insure his own survival—does not have the luxury of spurning those who would taint him. ''Was anyone ever rewarded for saintliness?'' asks one of Somnath's contacts, a ''public relations'' expert. ''Name a single person—no matter how high up—whose reputation is spotless.'' *Jana Aranya* is neither the first nor the last film to offer a morality tale in which individuals, in order to guarantee their survival, immerse themselves in mire. What makes it a product of a specific time and place are the economic and political conditions existing in India. ''I felt corruption, rampant corruption all around, and I didn't think there was a solution,'' Ray declared, in reference to why he chose to make *Jana Aranya.* ''I was only waiting, perhaps subconsciously, for a story that would give me an opportunity to show this.''

In *Jana Aranya*, Ray also explores a theme that is a constant in his work: familial relations, and the psychology that exists between parent and child. Somnath's obstacles are not all job-related, in that he is influenced by his widowed father's high expectations for him. The old man, lacking in understanding of the manner of the modern world, accordingly is alienated from Somnath.

In his earliest films, the ones that cemented his reputation, Ray offered revealing, humanist portraits of the inner lives of his characters. By the time he made *Jana Aranya*, he had expanded his cinematic concerns; his films had become more overtly social and political—and the scenario of *Jana Aranya* is uncompromising as it spotlights the economic dilemmas confronting contemporary India. Its narrative is uncomplicated; primarily, it is a portrait of a young man and the manner in which he is stripped of his impeccability. The film is at its most astute when Ray offers up knowing vignettes featuring the subtly and not-so-subtly repulsive characters with whom Somnath deals. On strictly visual terms, the filmmaker cleverly lampoons bureaucratic inanity. Repeated shots of young men posting job application letters convey the mind-boggling competition Somnath will face as he sets out to secure a job. He also is seen waiting on countless lines, typing and attaching photos to endless job applications, and being asked ludicrous, rapid-fire questions by job interviewers.

In these sequences, *Jana Aranya* is amusing. Yet it primarily is a serious and sobering film, an unsentimental account of the battle between maintaining one's scruples and doing what one must in order to survive.

—Rob Edelman

LE JARDINIER ET LE PETIT ESPIEGLE

See **L'ARROSEUR ARROSE**

JAWS

USA, 1975

Director: Steven Spielberg

Production: Universal Pictures; Technicolor, 35mm; running time: 124 minutes. Released 20 June 1975. Filmed summer 1974 on location on Martha's Vineyard.

Producers: Richard D. Zanuck and David Brown with William S. Gilmore, Jr.; **screenplay:** Peter Benchley and Carl Gottlieb, from the novel by Benchley; **photography:** Bill Butler; **editor:** Verna Fields; **sound:** Robert L. Hoyt, Roger Herman, Earl Madery, and John Carter; **music:** John Williams.

Cast: Roy Scheider (*Brody*); Robert Shaw (*Quint*); Richard Dreyfuss (*Hooper*); Lorraine Gary (*Ellen Brody*); Murray Hamilton (*Vaughan*); Carl Gottlieb.

Awards: Oscars for Best Sound, Best Editing, and Best Original Score, 1975.

Publications

Books:

Gottlieb, Carl, *The Jaws Log*, New York, 1975.
Blake, Edith, *On Location on Martha's Vineyard: The Making of the Movie Jaws*, New York, 1975.
Monaco, James, *American Film Now: The People, the Power, the Money, the Movies*, Oxford and New York, 1979.
Pye, Michael, and Lynda Myles, *The Movie Brats: How the Film Generation Took Over Hollywood*, London, 1979.
Kolker, Robert Phillip, *A Cinema of Loneliness: Penn, Kubrick, Scorsese, Spielberg, Altman*, Oxford, 1980; revised edition, 1988.
Daly, David Anthony, *A Comparison of Exhibition and Distribution Patterns in Three Recent Feature Motion Pictures*, New York, 1980.
Crawley, Tony, *The Steven Spielberg Story*, London, 1983.
Goldau, Antje, and Hans Helmut Prinzler, *Spielberg: Filme als Spielzeug*, Berlin, 1985.
Mott, Donald R., and Cheryl McAllister Saunders, *Steven Spielberg*, Boston, 1986.
Smith, Thomas G., *Industrial Light and Magic: The Art of Special Effects*, London, 1986.
Weiss, Ulli, *Das neue Hollywood: Francis Ford Coppola, Steven Spielberg, Martin Scorsese*, Munich, 1986.
Godard, Jean-Pierre, *Spielberg*, Paris, 1987.
Sinyard, Neil, *The Films of Steven Spielberg*, London, 1987.
Von Gunden, Kenneth, *Postmodern Auteurs: Coppola, Lucas, De Palma, Spielberg & Scorsese*, Jefferson, 1991.
Brode, Douglas, *The Films of Steven Spielberg*, Secaucus, 1997.
Yule, Andrew, *Steven Spielberg*, New York, 1997.
Knight, Bertram, *Steven Spielberg: Master of Movie Magic*, Parsippany, 1998.
Perry, George, *Steven Spielberg-Close Up: The Making of His Movies*, New York, 1998.
Taylor, Philip M., *Steven Spielberg: The Man, His Movies and Their Meaning*, New York, 1998.

Articles:

Riger, R., ''On Location with *Jaws*—Tell the Shark We'll Do It One More Time,'' in *Action* (Los Angeles), July-August 1974.
''What Directors Are Saying,'' in *Action* (Los Angeles), September-October 1974.
Cribben, M., ''On Location with *Jaws*,'' in *American Cinematographer* (Los Angeles), March 1975.
Murphy, A. D., in *Variety* (New York), 18 June 1975.
Magill, M., in *Films in Review* (New York), August-September 1975.
Shear, D., in *Film Heritage* (Dayton, Ohio), Autumn 1975.
Milne, Tom, in *Monthly Film Bulletin* (London), December 1975.
Monaco, James, in *Sight and Sound* (London), no. 1, 1975–76.
Bonitzer, P., and S. Daney, in *Cahiers du Cinéma* (Paris), April-May 1976.
Blacher, R., ''Le Point de vue d'un psychiatre sur *Les Dents de la mer*,'' in *Cinéma* (Paris), April 1976.
Fieschi, J., ''La Religion du monstre,'' in *Cinématographe* (Paris), April-May 1976.
Paini, D., ''Toujours à propos des *Dents de la mer*,'' in *Cinéma* (Paris), May 1976.
Martin, Marcel, and others, ''Vérités et mensonges du cinéma américain,'' in *Ecran* (Paris), September 1976.
Dagneau, G., in *Revue du Cinéma* (Paris), October 1976.
Cumbow, R. C., ''The Great American Eating Machine,'' in *Movietone News* (Seattle), 11 October 1976.
Michalek, B., in *Kino* (Warsaw), December 1976.
Dworkin, M. S., ''In the Teeth of Jaws,'' in *Ikon* (Milan), January-March 1977.
Kapralov, G., in *Iskusstvo Kino* (Moscow), October 1977.
Caputi, J. E., ''Jaws as Patriarchal Myth,'' in *Journal of Popular Film and Television* (Washington, D.C.), no. 4, 1978.
Verstappen, W., in *Skoop* (Amsterdam), February 1978.
''Readers' Forum,'' in *Journal of Popular Film and Television* (Washington, D.C.), no. 2, 1979.
Erickson, Glenn, in *Magill's Survey of Cinema 2*, Englewood Cliffs, New Jersey, 1980.
Vega, F., in *Casablanca* (Madrid), July-August 1981.
Fauritte, A., ''Super Star Jaws,'' in *Revue du Cinéma* (Paris), April 1984.
Fried, B., in *Chaplin* (Stockholm), 1985.
Noel, J., ''Steven Spielberg (Suite No. 3),'' in *Grand Angle* (Mariembourg, Belgium), July 1990.
Sheehan, H., ''The Panning of Steven Spielberg,'' in *Film Comment* (New York), May-June 1992.

Jaws

Torry, R., ''Therapeutic Narrative: *The Wild Bunch, Jaws*, and Vietnam,'' in *Velvet Light Trap* (Austin, Texas), Spring 1993.

Griffin, Nancy, ''In the Grip of *Jaws*,'' in *Premiere* (New York), October 1995.

Askari, Brent, ''*Jaws*: Beyond Action,'' in *Creative Screenwriting* (Washington, D.C.), vol. 3, no. 1, Summer 1996.

Lucas, Tim, ''*Jaws*: Limited Edition Signature Collection,'' in *Video Watchdog* (Cincinnati), no. 33, 1996.

Dursin, A., ''The Laserphile,'' in *Film Score Monthly* (Los Angeles), no. 76, December 1996.

Jones, Alan, ''Just When You Thought You Knew Everything About *Jaws*,'' in *Radio Times* (London), vol. 295, no. 3849, 8 November 1997.

* * *

Jaws initiated the era of the Hollywood blockbuster. This tale of shark terror, which earned more than $100 million in six months, easily surpassed *The Godfather* as the all-time Hollywood box-office champ. Although *Star Wars, E.T.* and *Raiders of the Lost Ark* set new records, *Jaws* created marketing precedents that became Hollywood standards: it proved that one film under careful guidance from its distributor, could precipitate a national pop cultural ''event.''

Universal opened *Jaws* in 409 American houses in June 1975, establishing late May/early June as the beginning of the movie season. To milk the most from its ''national'' premiere, Universal fully utilized ''saturation advertising'' on television. The company purchased at least one 30-second ad on every prime-time network television program during the evening of the three days preceding the premiere; the cost was a million dollars. So successful was this advertising campaign that it became standard operating procedure in the American film industry (thereafter New York premieres and limited newspaper advertising were the exceptions, not the rule). *Jaws* convinced movie executives that television should be fully exploited for advertising, not avoided as in the past.

In 17 days, *Jaws* earned an extraordinary $36,000,000. House records were established in cities around the country, and record grosses continued through the summer. Indeed, Universal turned 1975 into the year of the shark. The film inspired pop songs and other films. And there were, of course, the ubiquitous spin-offs: posters, T-shirts, beach towels, shark tooth pendants. The stock of Universal's parent company, MCA, moved up 22½ points in less than a month.

Jaws proved that a single film, marketed in the right way, could make millions of dollars for everyone connected with it.

One direct beneficiary was director Steven Spielberg, who completed the film before his 30th birthday. This film school graduate learned the Hollywood system with his television work for Universal; he directed episodes of *Owen Marshall, Marcus Welby, Columbo*, and television movies such as the now cult film *Duel*. The dollars generated by *Jaws* and by his other films, *Close Encounters of the Third Kind, Raiders of the Lost Ark*, and *E.T.*, have made Spielberg the most successful box-office director of all time.

But *Jaws* won few awards, for critics did not consider it a complex artefact. Rather, *Jaws* was singled out as an example of the success of Hollywood as an entertainment machine. Social and cultural critics have ''read'' the film in two different ways. *Jaws* can be seen as a ''Watergate'' film. In it a public official (the mayor) seeks to hush up a threat to the public good (a shark attack); it takes an heroic outsider (the chief of police) to kill the shark and return things to normal. The overt message seems clear enough: the world does indeed work, if ''true heroes'' stand up to be counted. But *Jaws* also skillfully exploits the machine of modern cinema. From the opening sequences Spielberg associates the camera's point-of-view (under the water) and the major musical motif with the danger of the shark attack. *Jaws* manipulates our gaze, simultaneously providing the viewer with both enjoyment and fear. It remains a remarkable example of how well Hollywood can control a viewer's vision to produce pain and pleasure. *Jaws* is about Watergate America, but it is also about the experience of filmgoing in the 1970s.

—Douglas Gomery

THE JAZZ SINGER

USA, 1927

Director: Alan Crosland

Production: Warner Bros. Pictures, Inc.; black and white, 35mm, silent with synchronized musical numbers; running time: 89 minutes. Released October 1927, New York. Filmed June through August 1927 in Warner Bros. studios, and on location in Hollywood, and the Lower East Side and in front of Shuberts' Winter Garden theater in New York City. Cost: $500,000.

Scenario: Alfred A. Cohn, from the story and play *The Day of Atonement* by Samson Raphaelson; **titles:** Jack Jarmuth; **photography:** Hal Mohr; **editor:** Harold McCord; **sound:** George R. Groves; **music score and direction:** Louis Silvers.

Cast: Al Jolson (*Jakie Rabinowitz, later Jack Robin*); Warner Oland (*Cantor Rabinowitz*); Eugenie Besserer (*Sara Rabinowitz*); Otto Lederer (*Moisha Yudelson*); Bobby Gordon (*Jakie, age 13*); Richard Tucker (*Harry Lee*); May McAvoy (*Mary Dale*); Nat Carr (*Levi*); William Demarest (*Buster Billings*); Anders Randolf (*Dillings*); Will Walling (*Doctor*); Roscoe Karns (*Agent*); Myrna Loy, Audrey Ferris (*Chorus girls*); Cantor Josef Rosenblatt (*Himself, in concert number*); Jane Arden, Violet Bird, Ernest Clauson, Marie Stapleton, Edna Gregory, and Margaret Oliver (*Extras in Coffee Dan's sequence*).

Award: Special Oscar to Warner Bros. for producing *The Jazz Singer* ''which revolutionized the industry,'' 1927–28.

Publications

Script:

Cohn, Alfred A., *The Jazz Singer*, edited by Robert Carringer, Madison, Wisconsin, 1979.

Books:

Thrasher, Frederick, *Okay for Sound: How the Screen Found Its Voice*, New York, 1946.
Jolson, Al, *Mistah Jolson*, as told to Alban Emley, Los Angeles, 1951.
Burton, Jack, *The Blue Book of Hollywood Musicals*, Watkin's Glen, New York, 1953.
Sieben, Pearl, *The Immortal Al Jolson: His Life and Times*, New York, 1962.
Springer, John, *All Singing, All Talking, All Dancing*, New York, 1966.
Kiner, Larry F., *The Al Jolson Discography*, Westport, 1983.
Freedland, Michael, *Al Jolson*, New York, 1972; London, 1984.
Griffith, Richard, editor, *The Talkies: Articles and Illustrations from Photoplay Magazine*, New York, 1972.
Stern, Lee Edward, *The Movie Musical*, New York, 1974.
Geduld, Harry M., *Birth of the Talkies: From Edison to Jolson*, Bloomington, Indiana, 1975.
Kreuger, Miles, editor, *The Movie Musical from Vitaphone to 42nd Street*, New York, 1975.
Anderton, Barrie, *Sonny Boy! The World of Al Jolson*, London, 1975.
Everson, William K., *American Silent Film*, New York, 1978.
Ellis, Jack C., *A History of Film*, Englewood Cliffs, New Jersey, 1979.
Oberfirst, Robert, *Al Jolson: You Ain't Heard Nothin' Yet*, San Diego, 1980.
McCelland, Doug, *Blackface to Blacklist: Al Jolson, Larry Parks, & ''The Jolson Story,''* Lanham, 1987.
Goldman, Herbert G., *Jolson: The Legend Comes to Life*, New York, 1990.
Fisher, James, *Al Jolson: A Bio-Bibliography*, Westport, 1994.
Freedland, Michael, *Jolson: The Al Jolson Story*, Clearwater, 1995.
Usai, Paolo C., *Burning Passions: An Introduction the Study of Silent Cinema*, Collingdale, 1999.

Articles:

''Warner Brothers Studios,'' in *Moving Picture World*, 26 March 1927.
Schallert, Edwin, ''Vitaphone Activities in Hollywood,'' in *Moving Picture World*, 8 July 1927.
''How the Vitaphone Enters In,'' in *New York Times*, 28 August 1927.
New York Times, 7 October 1927.
Variety (New York), 12 October 1927.
Calhoun, D., ''Sketch on Alan Crosland,'' in *Motion Picture Classic* (New York), June 1928.
Close Up (London), February 1929.

The Jazz Singer

''Flicker Veteran,'' in *Cue* (New York), 20 July 1935.
Amengual, Barthélemy, in *Positif* (Paris), September 1972.
Sarris, Andrew, ''The Cultural Guilt of Musical Movies: *The Jazz Singer*, 50 Years After,'' in *Film Comment* (New York), September-October 1977.
Swindell, L., ''The Day the Silents Stopped,'' in *American Film* (Washington, D.C.), October 1977.
Beylie, Claude, in *Ecran* (Paris), January 1978.
Kupferberg, A., in *Take One* (Montreal), January 1978.
Farassino A., in *Ekran* (Ljubljana), no. 2, 1978.
Bosseno, C., in *Revue du Cinéma* (Paris), 1979.
Slide, Anthony, in *Magill's Survey of Cinema 2*, Englewood Cliffs, New Jersey, 1980.
Gomery, Douglas, ''Case Study: The Coming of Sound,'' in *Film History: Theory and Practice*, by Gomery and Robert C. Allen, New York, 1985.
Reid's Film Index (Wyong), no. 3, 1989.
Wolfe, C., ''Vitaphone Shorts and *The Jazz Singer*,'' in *Wide Angle* (Baltimore), no. 3, 1990.
Rogin, M., ''Blackface, White Noise: The Jewish Jazz Singer Finds His Voice,'' in *Critical Inquiry* (Chicago), no. 3, 1992.
Rogin, M., ''Two Declarations of American Independence,'' in *Representations*, no. 55, Summer 1996.
Mulvey, Laura, ''Now You Has Jazz,'' in *Sight & Sound* (London), vol. 9, no. 5, May 1999.

* * *

As it is generally stated, *The Jazz Singer*'s place in film history as the first talkie is an erroneous one. It was not the first sound picture—sound films are as old as the cinema itself—and it was not the first Vitaphone feature—that was *Don Juan*—nor was it the first all-talking Vitaphone feature—that was *The Lights of New York. The Jazz Singer* is important because it was the first film with sound to catch the imagination of an audience. As one contemporary critic, Welford Beaton, wrote, ''*The Jazz Singer* definitely establishes the fact that talking pictures are imminent.''

Unlike the sound films that had preceded it, *The Jazz Singer* boasted all the right components in the right mixture. It had a sentimental—silly, even by the standards of the day—story involving mother love, honor and a young man's striving for success. The film featured such songs as ''Toot, Toot, Tootsie,'' ''Mother o' Mine,''

"Mammy," and "Blue Skies," which were to become lasting successes. (Irving Berlin had written "Blue Skies" a year earlier, but it became a standard after it was featured in *The Jazz Singer*.) Above all, *The Jazz Singer* starred Al Jolson, a legendary performer, on stage from the early years of the century, whose presence somehow lent validity to the production and gave it something special. Robert Benchley, writing in the old humor magazine *Life*, jokingly summed up the power of Jolson's performance: "When Jolson enters, it is as if an electric current had been run along the wires under the seats where the hats are stuck. The house came to tumultuous attention. He speaks, rolls his eyes, compresses his lips, and it is all over. He trembles his lip, and your hearts break with a loud snap. He sings, and you totter out to send a night letter to your mother." And as if Jolson's presence was not enough, Warner Bros. wisely cast a major silent screen actress, Mae McAvoy, to play opposite him.

Supposedly based on Al Jolson's own life, *The Jazz Singer* first saw life as a magazine story, "The Day of Atonement," by Samson Raphaelson. Raphaelson—who was to become a prominent screen writer in the 1930s—adapted his story into a stageplay, which became a major success for its star George Jessel (who was initially cast in the film version, but backed out at the last minute apparently in a dispute over money). The story of *The Jazz Singer* concerns Jakie Rabinowitz who yearns to sing popular songs, but whose father, a cantor, wishes him to follow in his footsteps. Jakie leaves home, changes his name to Jack Robin (selecting a Gentile name in rejection not only of his father but also of his Jewish faith), and goes on the stage. As he is about to get his big break, opening as the star of a Broadway musical, Jakie learns that his father has been taken seriously ill. Realizing his true feelings and his place in his Jewish family, serious Jakie sings the "Kol Nidre" that night, delaying the opening of his show. The musical eventually opens, starring Jakie and his Gentile girlfriend, Mary Dale, and that night Jakie's mother realizes, "He is not my boy any more. He belongs to the world."

The plot is ludicrous, and was treated as such even by contemporary critics, many of whom complained that the story was "too Jewish." (Of course, it is worth noting that despite the awfulness of the story, *The Jazz Singer* has been twice remade.) What *is* exciting about the film is its use of sound—not only the interpolated dialogue and songs, but also the musical score and sound effects arranged by Louis Silvers (who skillfully blends elements of popular music with elements of serious music by Tchaikovsky, Debussy and others).

Jolson's first spoken words—"Wait a minute, wait a minute, you ain't heard nothing yet. Wait a minute, I tell you. You ain't heard nothing yet. Do you want to hear 'Toot, Toot, Tootsie?'"—are electrifying in their intensity even today, some 60 or more years since they were first uttered. It is as if the viewer were participating in a very personal way, in a moment of historic significance. Similarly, there is something embarrassingly private about Jolson's remarks to his mother as he sits at the piano and sings "Blue Skies" to her. Jolson's apparently improvised ramblings are perhaps a little too real and, therefore, almost a little too artificial and stilted. The impact of this last dialogue sequence is further emphasized by its abrupt ending as Warner Oland (in the role of Cantor Rabinowitz) enters the scene. He looks at his wife and son, and through a title, shouts "Stop." The dialogue, the human voice, is stilled, and *The Jazz Singer* once again becomes a silent film with musical accompaniment.

Alan Crosland brings almost a documentary quality to many of the scenes, particularly the opening sequences in which Jakie, as a child, sings at a local saloon. (It is the voice of Jakie as a child, played by Bobby Gordon, that is the voice first heard in the film.) The director is obviously a highly competent technician, and gets the best from his players, even such notorious purveyors of melodrama as Warner Oland and Eugenie Besserer.

The critics admired the film, but *loved* Al Jolson. One commented that "He is as solitary upon the heights of an art he has made peculiarly his own as Chaplin is upon his." Indeed, with *The Jazz Singer* Jolson heralded a new era which was to bring about the ultimate decline of Chaplin and his contemporaries, destroying one art form and creating another. Perhaps the one irony is that despite its place in the history of the sound film, the sound system utilized for *The Jazz Singer*—Vitaphone—was not the system that ultimately became standard in the industry. Vitaphone utilized sound on disc, and the future of the industry lay with sound on film.

—Anthony Slide

JEANNE DIELMAN, 23 QUAI DU COMMERCE, 1080 BRUXELLES

Belgium-France, 1975

Director: Chantal Akerman

Production: Paradise Films (Brussels) and Unité Trois (Paris), in association with Le Ministère de la Culture française du Belgique; color; running time: 201 minutes; length: 7,232 feet. Released 1976.

Producers: Evelyne Paul, Corinne Jenart; **screenplay:** Chantal Akerman; **assistant directors:** Marilyn Watelet, Serge Brodsky, Marianne de Muylder; **photography:** Babette Mangolte; **editor:** Patricia Canino; **assistant editors:** Catherine Huhardeaux, Martine Chicot; **sound editor:** Alain Marchall; **sound recordists:** Benie Deswarte, Françoise Van Thienen; **sound re-recordist:** Jean-Paul Loublier; **art director:** Philippe Graff; **assistant art editor:** Jean-Pol Ferbus; **music extract:** "Bagatelle for Piano," No. 27, op. 126 by Ludwig van Beethoven.

Cast: Delphine Seyrig (*Jeanne Dielman*); Jan Decorte (*Sylvain Dielman*); Henri Storck (*1st Caller*); Jacques Doniol-Valcroze (*2nd Caller*); Yves Bical (*3rd Caller*); Chantal Akerman (*Voice of Neighbor*).

Publications

Books:

Margulies, Ivone, *Nothing Happens: Chantal Akerman's Hyperrealist Everyday*, Durham, 1996.

Articles:

Rosenbaum, Jonathan, in *Sight and Sound* (London), Winter 1975–76.
Maupin, Françoise, in *Image et Son* (Paris), February 1976.
Alemann, C., and H. Hurst, interview with Akerman, in *Frauen und Film* (Berlin), March 1976.
Bertolina, G., "Chantal Akerman: Il cinema puro," in *Filmcritica* (Rome), March 1976.
Dubroux, Daniele, in *Cahiers du Cinéma* (Paris), March-April 1976.

Creveling, C., ''Women Working,'' in *Camera Obscura* (Berkeley), Fall 1976.
Villien, Bruno, and P. Carcassone, ''Chantal Akerman,'' in *Cinématographe* (Paris), June 1977.
Kinder, Marsha, in *Film Quarterly* (Berkeley), Summer 1977.
Mairesse, E., ''Apropos des films de Chantal Akerman: Un Temps atmosphere,'' in *Cahiers du Cinéma* (Paris), October 1977.
Loader, Jayne, in *Jump Cut* (Berkeley), November 1977.
Patterson, Patricia, and Manny Farber, ''Kitchen without Kitsch,'' in *Film Comment* (New York), November-December 1977.
Bergstrom, Janet, in *Camera Obscura* (Berkeley), Autumn 1978.
Martin, Angela, ''Chantal Akerman's Films,'' in *Feminist Review*, no. 3, 1979.
Pym, John, in *Monthly Film Bulletin* (London), April 1979.
Perlmutter, Ruth, ''Feminine Absence: A Political Aesthetic in Chantal Akerman's *Jeanne Dielman*,'' in *Quarterly Review of Film Studies* (New York), Spring 1979.
Lakeland, M. J., ''The Color of *Jeanne Dielman*,'' in *Camera Obscura* (Berkeley), Summer 1979.
Seni, N., in *Frauen und Film* (Berlin), September 1979.
Jayamanne, L., ''Modes of Performance in Chantal Akerman's *Jeanne Dielman*,'' in *Australian Journal of Screen Theory* (Kensington, New South Wales), no. 8, 1980.
Orellana, M., ''Notas sobre un nuevo cine: El de Chantal Akerman,'' in *Cine* (Mexico City), January-February 1980.
Perlmutter, Ruth, ''Visible Narrative, Visible Woman,'' in *Millenium* (New York), Spring 1980.
Aranda, I., and A. Pagaolatos, interview with Akerman, in *Contra campo* (Madrid), March 1981.
Singer, B., in *Millennium Film Journal* (New York), Winter-Spring 1989–90.
von Bagh, P., ''Keskusteluvuorossa: Chantal Akerman,'' in *Filmihullu* (Helsinki), no. 4, 1991.
Rabinowitz, Paula, ''Screen Memories,'' in *Wide Angle* (Baltimore), vol. 18, no. 4, October 1996.
Eslami, M., ''The Portrait of a Lady,'' in *Film International* (Tehran), vol. 5, no. 2 1997.

* * *

Chantal Akerman, a 25-year-old French-speaking Belgian from a Jewish family, made in *Jeanne Dielman*, which is perhaps the most prestigious Belgian film and an emblematic masterpiece of the feminist cinema of the 1970s. With no camera movement whatsoever, and very rarely departing from a single medium-long shot per scene, the 201-minute film scrutinizes for three days the rigorously methodical life of a woman approximately 50 years old and her teenage son. The fastidious rituals of her daily existence include prostitution with what appears to be a regulated sequence of men who come to her apartment, presumably without the son's knowledge, on weekly appointments.

Inspired by Michael Snow's cinematic investigations of space and time and the ritualized gestures of Resnais's and Duras's films, Akerman radically understated the dramatic dimension of her film even though it culminates in the unexpected murder of a client after a day in which Dielman's defensive and psychically anesthesizing rituals go awry. The filmmaker's careful compositions, abetted by Babette Mangolte's brilliantly cool cinematography, so frequently recall the features of paintings of 17th-century interiors (Vermeer, De Hooch, Metsu, Ter Borch) that she seems to be commenting on the Netherlandish art of representing women cleaning house, preparing food, reading letters, grooming children, sewing, listening to music, and entertaining men. *Jeanne Dielman* recasts that treasury of lucid images in rigorously geometrical settings from the perspective of a participating woman, interpreting them as compulsive displacements of anxiety.

Akerman so protracted and extenuated the pace of her film that the subtle shifts in Dielman's behaviour as the film progresses seem to occur at the threshold of attention. The long-held distant shots, with vivid natural sounds but no movie music, and the rhythmical editing that follows the heroine around her house and at times onto the streets, remaining for a few seconds on a location she has left, or anticipating her arrival, inure the viewer to her underplayed emotions. Furthermore, the shot changes so often mark ellipses, and the dialogue is so sparse, that the viewer may become deeply enmeshed in the film before realizing the significance of a scene that occurred much earlier. For instance, the film opens with the departure of one of Dielman's afternoon clients. But it is possible to think that he is her husband, departing for a week and giving her spending money, until the next day's client appears more than an hour later.

Two intertitles, ''End of the first day'' and ''End of the second day,'' divide the film into three parts. On the second day Dielman's polished routine begins to show some roughness: she mistimes dinner and overcooks potatoes, but it is not until the third day that minute misfunctions begin to indicate an imminent breakdown: she skips a button on her housecoat, drops a shoebrush and some silverware, washes the same dishes twice, goes too early to the post office and too late to her customary cafe, fails to untie a package. These minor lapses prepare us to see the orgasm she experiences while coolly having intercourse with her afternoon client as a massive deviation from her routine of self-control. In the next shot, she drives the scissors she had to use to get her package open into his throat.

Through most of the film we watch Dielman alone. Even when she is with her son or a neighbor, she says very little. The very sparseness of speech gives weight to the rare instances of it. In this way, the recitation of Baudelaire's poem of the ravages of time, ''L'Ennemi,'' which Jeanne helps her son to memorize, takes on importance. But most of all, it is his brief bedtime discussions of love, sex, and Oedipal rage against his dead father which suggest that the sexual maturing of her son might be the catalyst for the fatal disruption of her defensive compulsions.

—P. Adams Sitney

JEDER FÜR SICH UND GOTT GEGEN ALLE

(Every Man for Himself and God Against All; The Enigma of Kaspar Hauser)

West Germany, 1974

Director: Werner Herzog

Production: Werner Herzog Film-Product and ZDF (German television); Eastmancolor, 35mm; running time: 110 minutes. Released 1974.

Jeder für sich und Gott gegen alle

Producer: Werner Herzog; **screenplay:** Werner Herzog; **photography:** Jorg Schmidt-Reitwein; **editor:** Beate Mainka-Jellinghaus; **sound:** Haymo Henry Heyder; **production designer:** Henning V. Gierke; **music:** Pachelbel, Orlandi di Lasso, Albinoni, and Mozart; **costume designers:** Gisela Storch and Ann Poppel.

Cast: Bruno S. (*Kaspar Hauser*); Walter Ladengast (*Daumer*); Brigitte Mira (*Kate, the Governess*); Hans Musaus (*The Stranger*); Willy Semmelrogge (*Circus Master*); Michael Kroecher (*Lord Stanhope*); Henry Van Lyck (*Captain of the Cavalry*); Enno Patalas (*Pastor Führmann*); Elis Pilgrim (*Pastor*); Volker Prechtel (*Hiltel, Prison guard*); Kidlat Tahmik (*Hombrecito, the Indian*); Gloria Doer (*Madame Hiltel*); Helmut Doring (*Little King*); Andi Gottwald (*Young Mozart*); Herbert Achternbusch (*Farmboy*); Wolfgang Bauer (*Farmboy*); Walter Steiner (*Farmboy*); Florian Fricke (*Monsieur Florian*); Clemens Scheitz (*Registrar*); Johannes Buzalski (*Police officer*); Dr. Willy Meyer-Furst (*Doctor*); Wilhelm Bayer (*Captain of the Cavalry, domestic*); Franz Brumbach (*Bear trainer*); Alfred Edel (*Professor of Logic*); Heribert Fritsch (*Mayor*); Peter Gebhart (*Shoemaker who discovers Kaspar*); Reinhard Hauff (*Farmer*); Dorothea Kraft (*Little Girl*); Markus Weller (*Julius, son of Hiltel*); Dr. Heinz H. Niemoller (*Pathologist*); Dr. Walter Pflaum (*Pathologist*); Otto Heinzle (*Old Priest*); Peter-Udo Schonborn (*Swordsman*).

Awards: Cannes Film Festival, Special Jury Prize, the International Critics' Award, and the Ecumenical Prize, 1975.

Publications

Script:

Herzog, Werner, *L'Enigme de Kaspar Hauser*, in *Avant-Scène du Cinéma* (Paris), June 1976.

Books:

Schütte, Wolfram, and others, *Herzog/Kluge/Straub*, Vienna, 1976.

Ebert, Roger, *Werner Herzog: Images at the Horizon*, New York, 1980.

Sandford, John, *The New German Cinema*, Totowa, New Jersey, 1980.

Franklin, James, *New German Cinema: From Oberhausen to Hamburg*, Boston, 1983.

Phillips, Klaus, editor, *New German Filmmakers: From Oberhausen through the 1970s*, New York, 1984.

Corrigan, Timothy, *The Films of Werner Herzog: Between Mirage and History*, New York, 1986.

Gabrea, Radu, *Werner Herzog et la mystique rhénane*, Lausanne, 1986.

Elsaesser, Thomas, *New German Cinema: A History*, London, 1989.

Nagib, Lúcia, *Werner Herzog: o cinema como realidade*, São Paulo, 1991.

Articles:

Eisner, Lotte, ''Herzog in Dinkelsbühl,'' in *Sight and Sound* (London), Autumn 1974.

Haakman, A., in *Skoop* (Amsterdam), February 1975.

Overbey, D. L., ''Every Man for Himself,'' in *Sight and Sound* (London), Spring 1975.

Ciment, Michel, ''Entretien avec Werner Herzog,'' in *Positif* (Paris), May 1975.

Legrand, Gérard, in *Positif* (Paris), May 1975.

Moskowitz, G., in *Variety* (New York), 14 May 1975.

Ghali, Noureddine, in *Cinéma* (Paris), September 1975.

Farocki, H., and Noureddine Ghali, in *Filmkritik* (Munich), November 1975.

Clouzot, C., ''*L'Enigme de Kaspar Hauser*: Entretien avec Werner Herzog,'' in *Ecran* (Paris), November 1975.

Milne, Tom, in *Monthly Film Bulletin* (London), December 1975.

Schaub, M., ''Bilderarbeit,'' in *Cinema* (Zurich), no. 3, 1976.

Leirens, J., ''Ce jour la à Nuremberg,'' in *Amis du Film et de la Télévision* (Brussels), March 1976.

Garel, A., in *Revue du Cinéma* (Paris), October 1976.

Bronchain, C., in *Apec-Revue Belge du Cinéma* (Brussels), October 1976.

Benelli, D., ''Mysteries of the Organism: Character Consciousness and Film Form in *Kaspar Hauser* and *Spirit of the Beehive*,'' in *Movietone News* (Seattle), June 1977.

Dorr, John, ''The Enigma of Werner Herzog,'' in *Millimeter* (New York), October 1977.

Finger, W., ''Kaspar Hauser Doubly Portrayed,'' in *Literature/Film Quarterly* (Salisbury, Maryland), no. 3, 1979.

Horak, J. C., ''Werner Herzog's Ecran Absurde,'' in *Literature/Film Quarterly* (Salisbury, Maryland), no. 3, 1979.

Perlmutter, R., ''The Cinema of the Grotesque,'' in *Georgia Review* (Athens), no. 1, 1979.

Bloom, M., ''Woyzeck and Kaspar: The Incongruities in Drama and Film,'' in *Literature/Film Quarterly* (Salisbury, Maryland), no. 4, 1980.

Korsic, I., in *Chaplin* (Stockholm), no. 3, 1981.

Stefanoni, L., ''Fata Morgana: *L'enigma di Kaspar Hauser*,'' in *Cineforum* (Bergamo), May 1981.

Cinema Nuovo (Bari), June 1981.

Scarrone, C., ''La 'domanda scomoda,''' in *Filmcritica* (Florence), September-October 1981.

Gerulaitis, R., ''Recurring Cultural Patterns: Werner Herzog's Film *Every Man for Himself and God against All, the Enigma of Caspar Hauser*,'' in *Journal of Popular Culture* (Bowling Green, Ohio), no. 4, 1989.

Hainisch, B., and T. Pilz, ''Werner Herzog's *Jeder für sich und Gott gegen alle* - ein Film,'' in *Blimp* (Graz), no. 30, Winter 1994.

Brown, G., ''Lessons of Darkness,'' in *Village Voice* (New York), vol. 41, 2 April 1996.

* * *

In many countries *Jeder für sich und Gott gegen alle (Every Man for Himself and God Against All)* is distributed under the title *Kaspar Hauser*—the name of the hero of this film based on the history of a man who in 1828 was found by chance living in a dark cave where he had apparently grown up without any contact with other human beings. Brought to civilization, he experiences many of the events of ordinary life, all of which make him feel equally uneasy.

Werner Herzog, the director, unlike François Truffaut in *The Wild Child*, is not interested in showing the painful process of adaptation to civilized surroundings; Kaspar has a special consciousness in which the laws of nature have a central place and in which the conventions and norms of civilized behavior are as artificial and inconvenient to him as the black dinner jacket he is forced to wear. His difficulties in communication are not the result of any linguistic inadequacies; simply, he is ''different'' from other men. That is why Herzog seems to wish to persuade us that, despite being gratuitous, both the early isolation and the surprising death of his hero are somehow logical.

An examination of Herzog's earlier films suggests that he always moves within the same closed circle of his imagination. All of his heroes are in some way related. The deaf-mutes in *Land of Silence and Darkness*, the dwarfs in *Even Dwarfs Started Small* or the half-crazy conquistador in *Aguirre, the Wrath of God*—like Kaspar Hauser—are outsiders, unable to adapt, creatures who have no place in human society.

His later films, if anything, stress this similarity of characters and continuity of motifs. In *Stroszek* the main characters from Kaspar Hauser reappear but in another historical context—that of our own time. Stroszek—played by Bruno S., the same Berlin hobo who played Kaspar—and his two companions, the old man (Clemens Scheitz) and the girl (Eva Mattes), can no longer find a ''place'' in their native Germany, so they emigrate to America, where they also fail. This would be the fate of Kaspar Hauser today. Aguirre, the greedy colonist, appears again in *Fitzcarraldo*—a corrective to the pessimistic conclusion of *Aguirre*. The wisdom and integrity of the Indians have profound effect on the conqueror, and he comes to see his confrontation with the jungle and the natives as a blessing that saves him from the abyss.

This summary of plot sounds like a fairy tale—and it is. Most of Herzog's films recall fables, and that is surely one of the reasons for their success. There is a kind of magical charm in the way that Herzog composes his shots: these films contain much natural beauty and slow rhythm that evokes splendor and transcience.

When one speaks of Herzog, one speaks of ''mystical cinema, transcendent, an idealistic vision of reality.'' The film *Kaspar Hauser* is an example of a kind of narration in which realistically-realized shots are perceived as a perfect, even though unrealistic, fiction.

—Maria Racheva

LES JEUX INTERDITS

(Forbidden Games)

France, 1952

Director: René Clément

Production: Silver-Film; black and white, 35mm; running time: 102 minutes, some sources list 90 minutes, others 84 minutes. Released 9 May 1952. Filmed Fall 1951.

Producer: Robert Dorfmann; **screenplay:** François Boyer; **adaptation and dialogue:** Jean Aurenche, Pierre Bost, and René Clément, from the novel by François Boyer; **photography:** Robert Juillard; **editor:** Roger Dwyre; **sound engineer:** Jacques Lebreton; **art director:** Paul Bertrand; **music adaptation and interpretation:** Narciso Yepes; **costume designer:** Major Brandley.

Cast: Brigitte Fossey (*Paulette, age 5*); Georges Poujouly (*Michel Dolle, age 11*); Lucien Herbert (*Père Dolle*); Suzanne Courtal (*Mère Dolle*); Jacques Marin (*Georges Dolle*); Laurence Badie (*Berthe Dolle*); Andre Wasley (*Père Gouard*); Amedee (*Francis Gouard*); Denise Peronne (*Jeanne Gouard*); Louis Sainteve (*Le curé*); Madeleine Barbulee; Pierre Merovee; Violette Monnier; and Fernande Roy.

Awards: Cannes Film Festival, Grand Prix Indépendant, 1952; Venice Film Festival, Best Film—Gold Lion of St. Mark, 1952; New York Film Critics' Award, Best Foreign Film, 1952; Honorary Oscar for Best Foreign-Language Film, 1952.

Publications

Script:

Aurenche, Jean, Pierre Bost, and René Clément, *Les Jeux interdits* (excerpts), in *Avant-Scene du Cinéma* (Paris), 15 May 1962.

Books:

Siclier, Jacques, *René Clément*, Brussels, 1956.
Farwagi, Andre, *René Clément*, Paris, 1967.
Armes, Roy, *French Film*, New York, 1970.
Armes, Roy, *French Cinema since 1946: The Great Tradition*, New York, 1970.
Barsacq, Léon, *Caligari's Cabinet and Other Grand Illusions: A History of Film Design*, New York, 1976.

Articles:

Eisner, Lotte, ''Style of René Clément,'' in *Film Culture* (New York), no. 12 and no. 13, 1957.
Clément, René, ''Pourquoi j'ai tourné *Jeux interdits*,'' in *Avant-Scène du Cinéma* (Paris), 15 May 1962.
McVay, Douglas, ''The Darker Side of Life,'' in *Films and Filming* (London), December 1966.
Rejjnhoudt, B., ''Bekeken,'' in *Skoop* (Amsterdam), July-August 1982.
Comuzio, E., ''Giochi proibiti di René Clément,'' in *Cineforum* (Bergamo, Italy), November 1992.
Ghiyati, Karim, ''Le petit Parisien à la campagne,'' in *Avant-Scène du Cinéma* (Paris), no. 469, February 1998.

* * *

For English-speaking audiences, *Les jeux interdits* remains one of the two or three most important French films of the pre-New Wave era. Under Clément's direction, the two children are inestimably fresher and more engaging than almost any other child actors of the time. But beyond its immediate appeal, *Forbidden Games* remains important as an early conjunction of the realist style of director René Clément on the one side and the ''cinema of quality'' of the Aurenche/Bost script on the other. A tension is created by the film's hesitation between social allegory and anthropology and between a natural and a prettified style.

The film's allegory is transparent from the outset when German Stukas strafe a line of fleeing Parisians. In the gorgeous French countryside at the waning of spring, man's urge to destroy strews bodies around the landscape. Having set a brutal tone, Clément turns to his tender drama and to Brigitte Fossey, already irresistible at five years old. Wandering away from the bodies of her parents and into a pasture of lowing cows, she narrows the film's focus from public to private morals and mores, for her subsequent adoption by a peasant family displaces the social context from international war to domestic strife.

Now little Brigitte and her soulmate, played by Georges Poujouly, observe the stupid bickerings, rituals, and greed both within their household and between the households of the village. Particularly memorable is the death of the older brother who had been kicked by a horse. The children are amused by his ugly demise and the religious trappings of his funeral. Soon they develop rituals of their own, ''les jeux interdits.'' In an abandoned barn they construct an elaborate burial ground for every sort of creature. So fascinated are they by death that they eagerly await (even bring about) the final end of insects, dogs, etc. The religious compensation of their candles and crosses is at once a grotesque and authentic displacement of the petty comforts of adult religion.

This ridicule of peasant life, particularly of religion, distinguishes the film as a serious production, as does the obvious irony at work in comparing a Parisian girl and her rural foster parents. Much of Clément's compositional strategy reinforces supercilious sentiments as when he cuts among rural families at the cemetery from a number of low angles. Such pretty shots progressively make a mockery of the

Les jeux interdits

mourners; finally, one shot is taken literally from the bottom of the grave. Clément also riducules romance: the children discover the older sister in the hay with the boy next door, who had been recently demilitarized. Altogether the dialogue is terribly pointed, even pithy, despite coming from the mouths of peasants. This whole ''quality'' flavor is summed up in the credits which are rendered over the pages of a book, as if insisting on the literary stature of the film.

But Clément's roots in realism and his command of location shooting also pull the film in other directions, some of which might be thought to presage the New Wave. Close-ups of the children are excessively lengthy and attain a documentary interest beyond their narrative motivation. They give the viewer a rather direct emotional access to these children apart from the story we find them in. The full power of this technique is reserved for the film's final sequence in which we observe, without any artifice of editing, the little girl dissolve in tears amidst hundreds like her at the Paris orphanage to which she has been taken. In short, we trust the tears of this child.

A New Wave attitude is associated with the music as well. Not only in the employment of a simple, lyrical guitar, but also in its haunting melody, which often triggers meditation on a recent dramatic action. Frequent promenades to the accompaniment of guitar are dramatic resting places wherein the film addresses the spectator in a new and more direct way.

Altogether then the film highlights in its style(s) and subject the conflicts of purity and the grotesque, of children and adults, of nature and man, of realism and parody.

—Dudley Andrew

JFK

USA, 1991

Director: Oliver Stone

Production: Warner Bros./Le Studio Canal/Regency Enterprises/ Alcor; color, 35mm, Panavision; running time: 189 minutes; director's cut runs 205 minutes. Released 20 December 1991 (U.S.A.).

JFK

Much footage filmed on location in New Orleans, Dallas, Texas, and Washington D.C. Budget: $40 Million (approx.).

Producers: A. Kitman Ho, Oliver Stone; **screenplay:** Oliver Stone, Zachary Sklar, from the books *On the Trail of the Assassins* by Jim Garrison and *Crossfire: The Plot That Killed Kennedy* by Jim Marrs; **photography:** Robert Richardson; **editors:** Joe Hutshing, Pietro Scalia; **sound:** Bill Daly (sound mixer: Dealey Plaza), Gregg Landaker, Tod A. Maitland, Michael Minkler, Wylie Stateman, Michael D. Wilhoit; **art directors:** Derek R. Hill, Alan R. Tomkins; **original music score:** John Williams; **casting:** Risa Bramon Garcia, Billy Hopkins, Heidi Levitt.

Cast: Kevin Costner (*Jim Garrison*); Sissy Spacek (*Liz Garrison*); Joe Pesci (*David Ferrie*); Tommy Lee Jones (*Clay Shaw*); Gary Oldman (*Lee Harvey Oswald*); Jay O. Sanders (*Lou Ivon*); Michael Rooker (*Bill Broussard*); Laurie Metcalf (*Susie Cox*); Gary Grubbs (*Al Osner*); John Candy (*Dean Andrews*); Jack Lemmon (*Jack Martin*); Walter Matthau (*Senator Long*); Ed Asner (*Guy Bannister*); Donald Sutherland (*X*); Kevin Bacon (*Willie O'Keefe*); Brian Doyle-Murray (*Jack Ruby*); Sally Kirkland (*Rose Cheramie*); Jim Garrison (*Earl Warren*).

Awards: Oscars for Best Cinematography and Best Film Editing (Joe Hutshing, Pietro Scalia), 1992; American Cinema Editors Award (Eddie) (Joe Hutshing, Pietro Scalia), 1992; Golden Globe Award for Best Director—Motion Picture, 1992; British Academy Award (BAFTA) for Best Editing (Joe Hutshing, Pietro Scalia) and Best Sound (Gregg Landaker, Tod A. Maitland, Michael Minkler, Wylie Stateman, Michael D. Wilhoit), 1993.

Publications

Script:

Stone, Oliver, and Zachary Sklar, *JFK: The Book of the Film*, New York, 1994.

Books:

Garrison, Jim, *On the Trail of the Assassins: My Investigation and Prosecution of the Murder of President Kennedy*, New York, 1988.
Marrs, Jim, *Crossfire: The Plot that Killed Kennedy*, New York, 1990.
Beaver, Frank, *Oliver Stone: Wakeup Cinema*, New York, 1994.

Riordan, James, *Stone: The Controversies, Excesses, and Exploits of a Radical Filmmaker*, New York, 1994.

Kunz, Don, editor, *The Films of Oliver Stone* (Filmmakers Series, No. 55), Metuchen, New Jersey, 1997.

Articles:

Anson, Robert Sam, ''The Shooting of *JFK*,'' in *Esquire* (New York), 1 November 1991.

Stone, Oliver, interview in *Time* (New York), 23 December 1991.

Crowdus, Gary, ''Getting the Facts Straight: An Interview with Zachary Sklar,'' in *Cineaste* (New York), vol. 19, no. 1, 1992.

Crowdus, Gary, ''Clarifying the Conspiracy: An Interview with Oliver Stone,'' in *Cineaste* (New York), vol. 19, no. 1, 1992.

Medhurst, Martin J., ''The Rhetorical Structure of Oliver Stone's *JFK*,'' in *Critical Studies in Mass Communication*, June 1993.

Romanowski, William D., ''Oliver Stone's *JFK*: Commercial Filmmaking, Cultural History, and Conflict,'' in *Journal of Popular Film and Television* (Washington, D.C.), Summer 1993.

Crowdus, Gary, ''History, Dramatic License, and Larger Historical Truths: An Interview with Oliver Stone,'' in *Cineaste* (New York), vol. 22, no. 4, 1997.

Sharrett, Christopher, ''Conspiracy Theory and Political Murder in America: Oliver Stone's *JFK* and the Facts of the Matter,'' in Jon Lewis, editor, *The New American Cinema*, Durham, North Carolina, 1998.

Rosenstone, Robert A., ''*JFK*: Historical Fact/Historical Film,'' in Alan Rosenthal, editor, *Why Docudrama?: Fact-Fiction on Film and TV*, Carbondale, Illinois, 1999.

* * *

Winner of two Oscars, for cinematography and editing, and nominated for five others, *JFK* has been praised as a film but heavily criticized as an historical account of the assassination of John F. Kennedy in November 1963. By 1991, when *JFK* was released, Stone was already well known as a maker of challenging and controversial films, notably about America's involvement in Vietnam. His attacks on the American government and justice system, for their pandering to big business over the needs of the people, are all the more remarkable given that they appeared in the 1980s and early 1990s, a period of conservatism in Hollywood and elsewhere. *JFK*, arguably his most impressive work as a director, consolidated his reputation as an argumentative and politically awkward filmmaker.

The film revives New Orleans District Attorney Jim Garrison's 1967 theory that Kennedy was killed in an attempted coups d'état orchestrated by military and industrial influences within the American government. Their motivation, Garrison believed, was opposition to Kennedy's aim of withdrawing American troops from Vietnam. Even before Stone began making the film, Garrison's theory had been shown to have little real evidence to support it, and *JFK* itself has since been picked over by critics eager to show the inconsistencies in Stone's account.

In attempting to provide as much detail as possible about Garrison's theory, most of it explained in Costner's deadpan drawl, Stone ran the risk of alienating much of his audience. The extreme length of the movie, which runs for well over three hours in its ''director's cut,'' might also have discouraged filmgoers. Yet *JFK* was a commercial success, at least in part because of its subject matter, which also attracted many well-known actors and others to play minor roles. The most interesting of these cameos is the real Jim Garrison playing Earl Warren. Stone also extracts fine performances from his leading actors, particularly from Tommy Lee Jones, who projects a menacing sense of suppressed violence as Clay Shaw, the businessman with whose trial and acquittal the film ends. Kevin Costner's portrayal of Jim Garrison's single-minded determination to find the truth is compelling, and Kevin Bacon, Joe Pesci, and Sissy Spacek are also impressive.

The film is also very well made; *JFK* is a masterpiece of well-judged tension, dramatic revelation, and changes of mood. By switching between film stocks, blending documentary and ''made'' footage, and introducing a series of bizarre and sinister characters, Stone manages to drive the narrative along with vigor, despite its sometimes rather detached, obsessive feel. The repeated showing of the famous Zapruder home movie of the killing helps to lend authenticity to the action, while dramatic set-pieces, such as Garrison's timing a marksman as he attempts to fire three shots from a manual rifle, give a sense of documentary objectivity.

While the film is convincingly detailed and impressive as a detective thriller, its actual value as a documentary is negligible. Stone has rightly been criticized for presenting as true events for which there is no conclusive evidence. What is perhaps more worrying, however, is Stone's manipulation of evidence to prove his point. The blurring of the distinction between documentary and ''made'' footage is a showcase for the skills of the Oscar-winning editors, but it also obscures the point at which the real evidence begins and Stone's invention ends. Even the short Zapruder film was altered in an effort to suggest the existence of bullets entering Kennedy's body from different directions. Given the authority with which such ''evidence'' is presented, it is difficult to see any real difference between Stone's manipulation of the known facts and the deception his film identifies at the heart of the Warren Commission's investigation.

As a convincing alternative to the official account of the assassination, *JFK* has many shortcomings, and one of its more unfortunate effects has been to further mythologize the circumstances of Kennedy's death. But if Stone's intention was to challenge the American government's handling of the case, and renew public interest in finding out the truth about the assassination, *JFK* was a resounding success. Indeed, the film aroused so much debate and speculation that in an attempt to satisfy public curiosity the U.S. Congress passed the JFK Assassination Records Collection Act of 1992, demanding the early release of almost all of the government's files on the case. Taking account of the controversy the film aroused, hardcore conspiracy theorists should note that Stone himself received no Oscars for *JFK*.

—Chris Routledge

JIGOKUMON

(Gate of Hell)

Japan, 1953

Director: Teinosuke Kinugasa

Production: Daiei (Tokyo); Eastmancolor, 35mm; running time: 89 minutes. Released 1953, Japan. Filmed in Japan.

Jigokumon

Producer: Masaichi Nagata; **screenplay:** Teinosuke Kinugasa, from a 20th century play by Kan Kikuchi; **photography:** Kohei Sugiyama; **art director:** Kisaku Itoh; **music director:** Yasuchi Akutagawa; **costume designer:** Sanzo Wada; **color consultant:** Sanzo Wada.

Cast: Machiko Kyo (*Wife*); Kazuo Hasegawa (*Husband*); Koreya Senda; Isao Yamagata; Yataro Kurokawa; Kataro Bando.

Awards: Oscar for Best Costume Design-Color and Special Oscar for Best Foreign Film, 1954; New York Film Critics' Award, Best Foreign Film, 1954; Cannes Film Festival, Best Film, 1954.

Publications

Books:

Shinobu Giuglaris, Marcel de, *Le Cinéma Japonais*, Paris, 1956.

Anderson, Joseph, and Donald Richie, *The Japanese Film: Art and Industry*, New York, 1960; revised edition, New Jersey, 1982.

Articles:

Life (New York), 15 November 1954.

Knight, Arthur, ''Japan's Film Revolution,'' in *Saturday Review* (New York), 11 December 1954.

Ozaki, Koji, in *Atlantic* (Boston), January 1955.

Iwabutchi, Masayoshi, ''1954 in Japan,'' in *Sight and Sound* (London), Spring 1955.

Young, Vernon, ''Reflections on Japanese Film,'' in *Art Digest* (New York), August 1955.

Anderson, Joseph, ''Seven from the Past,'' in *Sight and Sound* (London), Autumn 1957.

Cohen, R., ''A Japanese Romantic: Teinosuke Kinugasa,'' in *Sight & Sound* (London), vol. 45, no. 3, Summer 1976.

Checklist and critical notes on Teinosuke Kinugasa, in *Film Dope* (Nottingham), no. 31, January 1985.

* * *

Although today Teinosuke Kinugasa's *Jigokumon* is seldom treated as an important film, its historical position is secure. It was one of the first post-World War II Japanese films to be accepted and honored by the international film community. Not only did it win the Grand Prize at the 1954 Cannes International Film Festival but also it received two Academy Awards in the United States.

The great commercial and critical success of Akira Kurosawa's *Rashomon* (1950), Kenji Mizoguchi's *Ugetsu* (1953), and *Jigokumon* made the Western world begin to take notice of Japanese films.

Jigokumon was especially noteworthy to Western audiences because it was the first Japanese color film released in the West. Although the Eastmancolor film stock came from the United States, Kinugasa and his cinematographer, art director, and color consultant used it with an artistry and subtlety that was seldom seen in the American films of that time. Many critics praised the filmmakers for giving the color a distinctly Japanese look that was a welcome contrast to the flamboyance of Hollywood.

Although *Jigokumon* is set in the 12th century, it is based on the 20th-century Japanese play by Kan Kikuchi. The film begins with a war between rival clans, and then, when the war is over, concentrates on only three characters in a story of love, sacrifice, and grief.

The direction of Kinugasa gives intimacy to both parts of the film, even the battle scenes. Kinugasa often highlights the large-scale sequences with small details in the foreground or at the end of a scene. In one scene, for example, the march of warriors in the background is accentuated by a number of chickens fighting in the foreground, and many scenes that involve large numbers of fighting men end with a quiet close-up of an inanimate object.

The second part of the film contrasts the emotion and brutality of the warrior Moritah with the restraint of a man and his wife who value self-sacrifice above violence and revenge. When Moritah tries to take the wife away from her husband, she sacrifices her life rather than accept the warrior; after her death, the husband refuses to take vengeance. The warrior finally realizes that he must atone for his sin by continuing to live with the knowledge of what he has done. This is not a familiar theme for Western audiences, but under Kinugasa's direction the performers who play the couple convey the depth of their feeling without much overt show of emotion. (The wife, incidentally, is played by Machiko Kyo, who also was featured in *Rashomon*.)

Jigokumon is only one of the many fine films directed by Teinosuke Kinugasa in a career that spanned five decades, but to Western audiences it was a revelation in the artistry of its color and the strength of its story. The audiences that had appreciated the black-and-white masterpieces of Kurosawa and Mizoguchi were astonished by Kinugasa's use of color film. The American Motion Picture Academy gave Sanzo Wada its award for costume design, and because at that time the Academy had no foreign film category, it gave *Jigokumon* a special award as Best Foreign Film.

—Timothy Johnson

JOHNNY GUITAR

USA, 1954

Director: Nicholas Ray

Production: Republic Pictures; Trucolor, 35mm, Cinemascope; running time: 110 minutes. Released November 1954. Filmed 1953.

Johnny Guitar

Producer: Herbert J. Yates; **screenplay:** Philip Yordan, from the novel by Roy Chanslor; **photography:** Harry Stradling, Jr.; **editor:** Richard L. Van Enger; **sound:** T. A. Carmen and Howard Wilson; **production designer:** John McCarthy, Jr. and Edward G. Boyle; **art director:** James Sullivan; **music:** Victor Young, with title song by Victor Young and Peggy Lee, sung by Peggy Lee; **special effects:** Howard and Theodore Lydecker; **costume designer:** Sheila O'Brien.

Cast: Joan Crawford (*Vienna*); Sterling Hayden (*Johnny Guitar*); Mercedes McCambridge (*Emma Small*); Scott Brady (*Dancin' Kid*); Ben Cooper (*Turkey*); Ward Bond (*John McIvers*); Ernest Borgnine (*Bart Lonergan*); John Carradine (*Tom*); Royal Dano (*Corey*); Frank Ferguson (*Sheriff*); Paul Fix (*Eddie*); Rhys Williams (*Mr. Andrews*); Ian McDonald (*Zeke*); Will Wright (*Ned*); John Maxwell (*Jake*); Robert Osterloh (*Sam*); Frank Marlowe (*Frank*); Trevor Bardette (*Jenks*); Sumner Williams, Sheb Wooley, Denver Pyle, and Clem Harvey (*Possemen*).

Publications

Script:

Yordan, Philip, *Johnny Guitar*, in *Avant-Scène du Cinéma* (Paris), March 1974.

Books:

Crawford, Joan, with Jane Kesner, *A Portrait of Joan: The Autobiography*, New York, 1962.
Fenin, George N., and William K. Everson, *The Western: From Silents to Cinerama*, New York, 1962; revised edition, 1973.
Warshow, Robert, *The Immediate Experience*, New York, 1962.
Hayden, Sterling, *Wanderer*, New York, 1965.
Quirk, Lawrence J., *The Films of Joan Crawford*, New York, 1968.
Bazin, André, *What Is Cinema*, Berkeley, 1971.
Harvey, Stephen, *Joan Crawford*, New York, 1974.
French, Philip, *Westerns*, New York, 1974.
Nachbar, Jack, editor, *Focus on the Western*, Englewood Cliffs, New Jersey, 1974.
Wright, Will, *Sixguns and Society: A Structural Study of the Western*, Berkeley, 1975.
Parish, James Robert, and Michael Pitts, editors, *The Great Western Pictures*, Metuchen, New Jersey, 1976.
Kreidl, John, *Nicholas Ray*, Boston, 1977.
Walker, Alexander, *Joan Crawford: The Ultimate Star*, London, 1983.
Masi, Stefano, *Nicholas Ray*, Florence, 1983.
Blaine, Allan, *Nicholas Ray: A Guide to References and Resources*, Boston, 1984.
Erice, Victor, and Jos Oliver, *Nicholas Ray y su tiempo*, Madrid, 1986.
Guiliani, Pierre, *Nicholas Ray*, Paris, 1987.
Wagner, Jean, *Nicholas Ray*, Paris, 1987.
Buscombe, Ed, *The BFI Companion to the Western*, London, 1988.
Eisenschitz, Bernard, *Nicholas Ray: An American Journey*, New York, 1993, 1996.
Ray, Nicholas, *I Was Interrupted: Nicholas Ray on Making Movies*, Berkeley, 1993.

Articles:

Hollywood Reporter, 5 May 1954.
Crowther, Bosley, in *New York Times*, 28 May 1954.
Truffaut, François, in *Arts* (Paris), February 1955.
Godard, Jean-Luc, in *Image et Son* (Paris), July 1956.
Quirk, Lawrence J., ''Joan Crawford,'' in *Films in Review* (New York), December 1956.
Bitsch, Charles, ''Entretien avec Nick Ray,'' in *Cahiers du Cinéma* (Paris), November 1958.
Agel, Henri, ''Nicholas Ray,'' in *New York Film Bulletin*, no. 11, 1961.
Hagen, Ray, ''Mercedes McCambridge,'' in *Films in Review* (New York), May 1965.
Perkins, Victor, ''The Cinema of Nicholas Ray,'' in *Movie Reader*, edited by Ian Cameron, New York, 1972.
Rosenbaum, Jonathan, ''Circle of Pain: The Cinema of Nicholas Ray,'' in *Sight and Sound* (London), Autumn 1973.
Barr, Charles, ''Cinemascope Before and After,'' in *Film Theory and Criticism*, edited by Gerald Mast and Mark Cohen, New York, 1974.
''*Johnny Guitar* Issue'' of *Avant-Scène du Cinéma* (Paris), March 1974.
Biskind, Peter, ''Rebel without a Cause: Nicholas Ray in the Fifties,'' in *Film Quarterly* (Berkeley), Fall 1974.
Place, Janey, in *Magill's Survey of Cinema 2*, Englewood Cliffs, New Jersey, 1980.
Fernandez Santos, A., and J. G. Requena, ''Dos miradas sobre *Johnny Guitar*,'' in *Contracampo* (Madrid), December 1980.
Boyero, C., in *Casablanca* (Madrid), May 1981.
Combs, Richard, in *Listener* (London), 7 July 1988.
Charney, Leo, ''Historical Excess: *Johnny Guitar*'s Containment,'' in *Cinema Journal* (Austin), vol. 29, no. 4, Summer 1990.
Brown, G., ''B Happy,'' in *Village Voice* (New York), vol. 38, 14 September 1993.
Wollen, Peter, ''Never at Home,'' in *Sight & Sound* (London), vol. 4, no. 5, May 1994.
Robertson, Pamela, ''Camping Under Western Stars: Joan Crawford in *Johnny Guitar*,'' in *Journal of Film and Video* (Atlanta), vol. 47, no. 1–3, Spring-Fall 1995.
Peterson, Jennifer, ''The Competing Tunes of *Johnny Guitar*: Liberalism, Sexuality, Masquerade,'' in *Cinema Journal* (Austin), vol. 35, no. 3, Spring 1996.
Voisin, N., in *Positif* (Paris), no. 435, May 1997.

* * *

Johnny Guitar certainly represents one of the most important Hollywood westerns, recognized at the time by critics throughout Europe. Critic-turned-auteur Bernardo Bertolucci called it ''the first of the baroque westerns,'' while François Truffaut suggested the admiration members of the French New Wave had for the film when in his own *Mississippi Mermaid* he had Jean Paul Belmondo say to Catherine Deneuve as they emerged from a screening of *Johnny Guitar*: ''It's not about horses and guns. It's about people and emotions.'' Jean-Luc Godard in his *Pierrot le fou* had his alienated ''hero'' (again Belmondo) recommend *Johnny Guitar* to his maid, and in *Weekend* had hippie guerrillas broadcast from their hideout: ''Johnny Guitar calling Gosta Berling.''

But the origins of *Johnny Guitar* came amidst tumultuous changes in the American film business of the 1950s, and were far more humble than any art film. *Johnny Guitar* was produced by a former maker of ''B'' westerns, Republic Pictures. The studio was long famous for its regular production of westerns starring Gene Autry and Roy Rogers. In the decade following the Second World War, the studio boss, Herbert Yates, sought to move into the big time and indeed challenge the major studios. To do this it turned out a couple of big-budget films per year. *Johnny Guitar* was one of these. Others included John Ford's *The Quiet Man* (1952) and Ford's *Rio Grande* (1950). But none helped enough, and by 1958 the forces of change (television, suburbanization, government decrees) saw Republic shut down production altogether.

In Hollywood lore *Johnny Guitar* is usually remembered for bringing together a talented group of creators. The movie was director Nicholas Ray's first after leaving RKO, the studio that brought him to Hollywood. At Republic Ray was granted absolute creative freedom, even functioning as the film's producer. Ray was in the midst of his most creative and productive period. His *Rebel without a Cause*, released the following year, allowed him to function as a mainline director for the next five or so years. But after a number of box-office failures, including *King of Kings* (1961) and *55 Days at Peking* (1963), Ray never worked in Hollywood again. Like another *enfant terrible* of a decade before, Orson Welles, Nicholas Ray did not fit into the Hollywood system.

But Ray was not the lone talent involved in the creation of this most adult of westerns. Philip Yordan, one of Hollywood's most prolific screenwriters, was at the apex of his career. Indeed the following year he penned a western nearly as complex as *Johnny Guitar*: Anthony Mann's *The Man from Laramie*. Veteran cameraman Harry Stradling's almost surreal Trucolor (Republic's own) added just the right look to this garish ''oater.''

But to movie fans of the era *Johnny Guitar* is probably most remembered as the western starring two women. Joan Crawford, one of Hollywood's longest running stars, experienced a downturn in her career after her Oscar for *Mildred Pierce* (1945) and thereafter struggled to fashion a career as ''the evil older woman'' in an industry that did not know what to do with actresses over the age of 30. In *Johnny Guitar* Crawford represented depravity incarnate, always dressed in black, willing to do anything to hold on to her small saloon. The woman who wanted to take away that bar, played by Mercedes McCambridge, initiated with *Johnny Guitar* a career in which she was at her best when playing desperate characters.

Although many have labelled the film as offbeat and baroque, *Johnny Guitar* is not excessively violent. Its settings were traditional, and the cast included such familiar figures from westerns of the 1950s as Ward Bond and Scott Brady (as ''Johnny''). The plot seemed untraditional because there was no powerful central, active male figure. Johnny Logan is a notorious ''fast draw'' with a reputation that precedes him. But throughout the film Johnny does little except save Vienna (Crawford) at one point. He spends most of his time standing around, watching and commenting on the action.

It is impossible to capture the beauty in this complex genre film in a short essay, but as *Chicago Tribune* film critic Michael Wilmington wrote at the time of the film's release: ''Never trust appearances. Beauty and profundity are not always found in the 'obvious' traditional places; a Trucolor Western from humble Republic can throb with the passion of *l'amour fou* or whisper with an evening delicacy.''

—Douglas Gomery

LE JOLI MAI

France, 1963

Director: Chris Marker

Production: Sofracima; black and white, 35mm; running time: 110 and 140 minutes, American version 124 minutes. Released May 1963, Paris. Filmed spring 1962 in Paris.

Producer: Catherine Winter; **screenplay:** Catherine Varlin and Chris Marker; **photography:** Pierre Lhomme; **editor:** Eva Zora; **music:** Michel Legrand, **title song:** B. Mokkoussov and Michel Legrand, sung by Yves Montand.

Cast: *Commentators*: Yves Montand (the French commentary); Simone Signoret (the English commentary).

Awards: Venice Film Festival, Best First Film, 1963; Cannes Film Festival, International Critics' Prize, 1963.

Publications

Script:

Varlin, Catherine, and Chris Marker, *Le joli Mai*, in *Le Cinéma et la vérité*, edited by Raymond Bellour, Lyons, 1963.

Books:

Issari, Ali, *Cinema Vérité*, East Lansing, Michigan, 1971.
Barnouw, Erik, *Documentary: A History of the Non-Fiction Film*, New York, 1974.
Armes, Roy, *French Cinema Since 1946: The Personal Style*, New York, 1976.
Horrigan, William, *Chris Marker: Silent Movie*, Columbus, 1995.

Articles:

Graham, Peter, ''The Face of '63—France,'' in *Films and Filming* (London), May 1963.
Kustow, Michael, in *Sight and Sound* (London), Spring 1964.
Gow, Gordon, in *Films and Filming* (London), May 1964.
Graham, Peter, ''Cinema Vérité in France,'' in *Film Quarterly* (Berkeley), Summer 1964.
Jacob, Gilles, ''Chris Marker and the Mutants,'' in *Sight and Sound* (London), Autumn 1966.
Thomas, John, in *Film Society Review* (New York), January 1967.
Gauthier, G., in *Image et Son* (Paris), no. 274, 1973.
Roud, Richard, ''The Left Bank Revisited,'' in *Sight and Sound* (London), Summer 1977.
Gaggi, S., ''Marker and Resnais: Myth and Reality,'' in *Literature/Film Quarterly* (Salisbury, Maryland), no. 1, 1979.
Leeuwen, T. van, ''Conjunctive Structure in Documentary Film and Television,'' in *Continuum*, vol. 5, no. 1, 1991.
Kohn, O., and H. Niogret, ''Temoignages,'' in *Positif* (Paris), no. 433, March 1997.
''Special Section,'' in *Revue Pour le Cinema Francais*, no. 45–47, September 1997.

* * *

Released in 1963, Chris Marker's *Le joli Mai* was one of the first and finest examples of cinema *vérité* to come out of France. Poetic, witty, complex, the film uses as its initial focus the spring of 1962, the first spring of peace for France since 1939. With rooftop shots of Paris on the screen, the narrator in the opening commentary tells us: ''For two centuries happiness has been a new idea in Europe, and people are not used to it.'' In the very political film which follows, Marker examines that idea of happiness on the small, private scale and on a larger, societal scale.

Divided into two parts, *Le joli Mai* first concerns itself with individual happiness in a series of interviews with people from a range of social backgrounds. We meet a nervous clothing salesman concerned about money in the till, a pompous inventor intoning his philosophy of hard work and success, a young couple speaking of eternal happiness. Marker's interviewers are adept, able to elicit revealing statements about individual hopes and beliefs without overpowering the subjects. Some segments need no such devices to

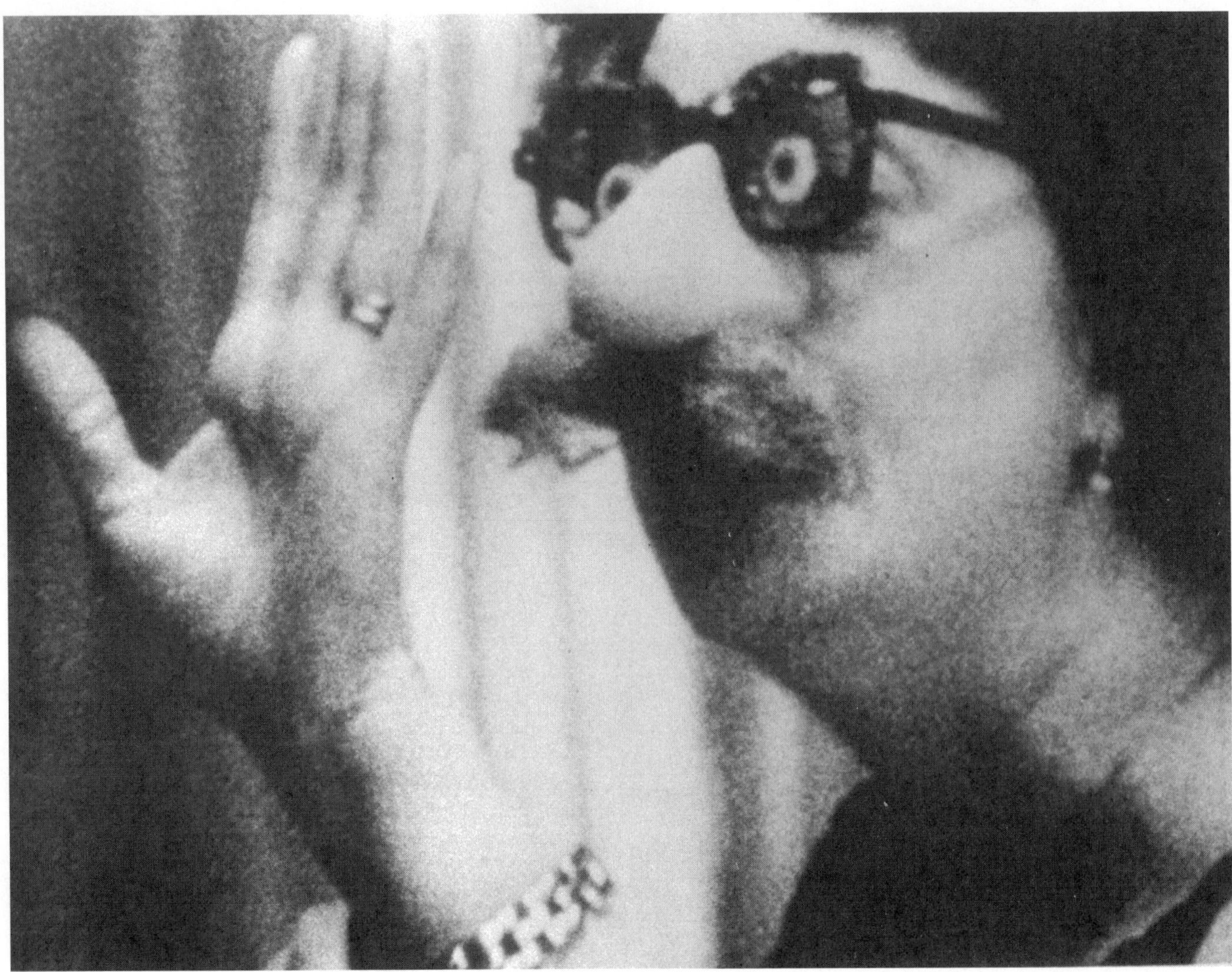

Le joli Mai

make a statement: the glum bride at the jolly wedding party, the joyous mother of eight showing her family their government flat, well-dressed literary types releasing a flock of doves to celebrate a poetry prize.

Part II places the small slices of life from the first half of the film onto a larger canvas for clearer definition. We see the shared political and social turmoil of France in 1962 in newsreel-like segments of police charges, demonstrations, and strikes. Cut against the newsreel footage are scenes from a Parisian nightclub where the dancing takes on an almost tribal quality. One of the dancers tell us: ''While scientists concentrate on microbes, I concentrate on the twist.'' The interviews in this section also contribute to the larger canvas. A black student from Dahomey reveals his first thought on seeing white people, ''So these are the people who conquered us,'' and his second, ''Some day we will conquer them.'' A communist worker-priest says he no longer has time to consider whether God exists.

Le joli Mai is distinguished by the witty artistry of its director. A poet and essayist as well as filmmaker, Marker has a wonderful flair for visual asides. When a grumbler disrupts the interview going on with two stock exchange apprentices, Marker turns the camera on the man and, complete with clapper, starts shooting as the interviewer asks the man the same question—what does money mean? When two consulting engineers in their discussion of work refer to nonworkers, Marker shows us shots of marvelously luxuriant, sleek cats. When the inventor propounds his philosophy of life, the camera watches the progress of a daddy longlegs across the man's lapel. A salesman's description of new luxury apartments is counterpointed by older people in the background washing in the street.

Throughout, the film is permeated by a bittersweet quality as it evokes the troubles of the past and present and hopes for a better future. That bittersweet tone underscores the inability of the individuals in the first part to cope with the larger reality around them. How can statements on the value of hard work, the meaning of money, the eternal quality of happiness deal with a police charge that kills eight people on the Metro? As one of the consulting engineers at the end of the film comments, ''Our dreams are too small for what already exists.'' One of the distinctions of *Le joli Mai* is that it is able to present disparate episodes from real life involving many different people and yet pull them together into a cohesive statement about the milieu in which those individuals exist.

—Sharon Lee

JONAH QUI AURA 25 ANS EN L'AN 2000

(Jonah Who Will Be 25 in the Year 2000)

France-Switzerland, 1976

Director: Alain Tanner

Production: Citel Films and SSR Télévision Suisse (Geneva), Action Films and Société Français de Production (Paris); Eastmancolor, 35mm; running time: 110 minutes, some sources list 116 minutes; length: 10,401 feet. Released 25 August 1976.

Producers: Yves Gasser and Yves Peyrot; **executive producer:** Roland Jouby; **screenplay:** John Berger and Alain Tanner; **photography:** Renato Berta; **editors:** Brigitte Sousselier and Marc Blavet; **sound recordist:** Pierre Gamet; **sound re-recordist:** Christian Londe; **music:** Jean-Marie Senia.

Cast: Jean-Luc Bideau (*Max Sitigny*); Myriam Boyer (*Mathilde Vernier*); Myriam Mzière (*Madeleine*); Rufus (*Mathieu Vernier*); Roger Jendly (*Marcel Certoux*); Jacques Denis (*Marco Perly*); Miou-Miou (*Marie*); Raymond Bussieres (*Charles*); Dominique Labourier (*Marguerite*); Jonah (*Himself*).

Publications

Script:

Berger, John, and Alain Tanner, *Jonah qui aura 25 ans en l'an 2000*, Lausanne, 1978; as *Jonah Who Will Be 25 in the Year 2000*, Berkeley, 1983.

Books:

Leach, Jim, *A Possible Cinema: The Films of Alain Tanner*, Metuchen, New Jersey, 1984.
Dimitriu, Christian, *Alain Tanner*, Paris, 1985.
Detassis, Piera, *Alain Tanner*, Firenze, 1987.

Articles:

Jaeggi, B., in *Cinema* (Zurich), no. 3, 1976.
Variety (New York), 25 August 1976.
Kael, Pauline, in *New Yorker*, 18 October 1976.
Colpart, C., in *Revue du Cinéma* (Paris), November 1976.
Image et Son (Paris), November 1976.
Haskell, Molly, in *Village Voice* (New York), 1 November 1976.
Le Pavec, J. P., in *Cinéma* (Paris), December 1976.
Rubenstein, L., ''Keeping Hope for Radical Change Alive,'' in *Cineaste* (New York), Winter 1976–77.
Stam, Robert, ''*Jonah Who Will Be 25 in the Year 2000*: The Subversive Charm of Alain Tanner,'' in *Jump Cut* (Chicago), no. 15, 1977.
Greene, L., ''*Jonah*: Subversive Charm Indeed!,'' in *Jump Cut* (Chicago), no. 15, 1977.
Positif (Paris), January 1977.
Daney, Serge, ''Les Huit 'Inside Ma,''' in *Cahiers du Cinéma* (Paris), January-February 1977.
Heinic, N., in *Cahiers du Cinéma* (Paris), January-February 1977.
Tarantino, M., in *Take One* (Montreal), March 1977.
Gitlin, T., in *Film Quarterly* (Berkeley), Spring 1977.
Séquences (Montreal), July 1977.
Brossard, J. P., ''Dialektisches Spiel mit den Ausdrucksformen,'' in *Film und Fernsehen* (Berlin), December 1977.
Dawson, Jan, in *Monthly Film Bulletin* (London), January 1978.
Listener (London), 23 February 1978.
Pulleine, Tim, in *Sight and Sound* (London), Spring 1978.
Tanner, Alain, in *Ecran* (Paris), 15 January 1979.
Monthly Film Bulletin (London), July 1979.
Harrild, A. E., in *Film Directions* (Belfast), no. 11, 1980.
Cineforum (Bergamo), January-February 1980.
Prono, F., in *Cinema Nuovo* (Bari), February 1980.
Horton, A., ''Alain Tanner's *Jonah*: Echoes of Renoir's *M. Lange*,'' in *Film Criticism* (Edinboro, Pennsylvania), Spring 1980.
Toubiana, Serge, ''*20 ans, Jonasp*,'' in *Cahiers du Cinéma* (Paris), no. 320, February 1981.
Tarantino, M., ''Going inside with Tanner,'' in *Movietone News* (Seattle), March 1981.
Cinema Journal (Evanston, Illinois), Spring 1985.
Short review, in *Listener*, vol. 118, no. 3025, 20 August 1987.
Andrew, D., ''Revolution and the Ordinary: Renoir's *La Marseillaise*,'' in *Yale Journal of Criticism*, vol. 4, no. 1, 1990.
Andrew, D., ''L'identite a jamais perdue du cinema francais,'' in *CinémAction* (Conde-sur-Noireau, France), no. 66, February 1993.

* * *

Jonah Who Will Be 25 in the Year 2000 is both a succinct commentary on the disillusionment experienced by the ''generation of 1968'' and a utopian series of vignettes that looks forward to a more egalitarian future. *Jonah* is Tanner's most successful collaboration with his frequent scenarist, the Marxist art critic John Berger, and this film follows the great promise shown by the two earlier Berger-Tanner collaborations, *La salamandre* and *The Middle of the World*.

All of Tanner's films can be viewed as critiques of the intellectual aridity of Swiss society, and *Jonah* is his buoyant rejoinder to the complacency of the Swiss bourgeoisie. *Jonah* celebrates the communitarian idealism of eight disparate individuals at a moment of alleged historical ''stasis.'' Yet the vitality of Tanner's protagonists helps to vitiate standard *Time* magazine clichés concerning the essentially ''ephemeral'' radical politics of the 1960s. For example, Max (all of the protagonists' names begin with prefix ''Ma''), the disillusioned ex-Trotskyist, and his mystically inclined girlfriend, Madeleine, would seem to represent antithetical extremes of the counter-cultural spectrum. Yet Tanner's qualified optimism enables the politicized (if temporarily sidetracked) Max and the occultish Madeleine to share the same universe of discourse.

As Robert Stam has pointed out, *Jonah*'s emphasis on the need for a radical pedagogy to replace the outmoded strictures of bourgeois discourse has deep affinities with the anarchic spirit of negation embedded in Jean Vigo's classic *Zéro de conduite*. The spirit of Rousseau's *Emile* (despite its inherent contradictions, perhaps the first primer of libertarian approaches to education) permeates *Jonah*,

Jonah qui aura 25 ans en l'an 2000

and critical potential that is always latent (but rarely appropriated) in the educational process is highlighted in one of the film's most brilliant sequences. Marco, a charmingly gauche high school teacher, demonstrates how the hallowed ''truths'' of history tend to dissolve when compared to the indisputably tangible, *material* folds of a sausage link. Subsequently, Marco teaches his class the harsh realities of economic hardship by having his girlfriend lecture on the daily annoyances of her job as a supermarket cashier. This synthesis of the personal and political is (surprisingly) never cloying, and always reiterates with pointed humor Tanner's desire for social transformation.

Jonah is ultimately one of the most astonishing examples of ''Brechtian cinema'' to have been engendered by the ongoing reexamination of the late playwright's theoretical corpus. Unlike many other contemporary directors, Tanner realizes that ''Brechtian'' does not necessarily connote humorless diatribes in the manner of ''the master's'' most sterile, didactic works. (The dreadful *The Measures Taken* comes to mind in this context.) Miou-Miou's spontaneous cabaret song, on the other hand, suggests the exuberance of Brecht and Weill, and Tanner's playful, and always unobtrusive, use of quotations from such contemporary savants as Pablo Neruda, Jean Piaget, and Walter Benjamin helps to make *Jonah* a particularly exhilarating example of 1970s *Lehrstücke*.

—Richard Porton

LE JOUR SE LÈVE

(Daybreak)

France, 1939

Director: Marcel Carné

Production: VOG Sigma (Paris); black and white, 35mm; running time: 85 minutes; length 7995 feet. Released 1939. Filmed in Paris Studios Cinema, Billancourt.

Producer: Brachet; **screenplay:** Jacques Viot; **adaptation and dialogue:** Jacques Prévert; **photography:** Curt Courant, Philippe Agostini, and André Bac; **editor:** René le Henaff; **sound recordist:** Arman Petitjean; **production designer:** Alexandre Trauner; **music:** Maurice Jaubert; **costume designer:** Boris Bilinsky.

Cast: Jean Gabin (*François*); Jacqueline Laurent (*Françoise*); Arletty (*Clara*); René Génin (*Concierge*); Mady Berry (*Concierge's wife*); Jules Berry (*M. Valentin*); Marcel Pérè (*Paulo*); Jacques Baumer (*Inspector*); René Bergeron (*Cafe proprietor*); Gabrielle Fonton (*Woman on the stairs*); Arthur Devère (*M. Gerbois*); Georges Douking (*Blind Man*); Bernard Blier (*Gaston*).

Publications

Script:

Viot, Jacques, and Jacques Prévert, *Le Jour se lève* in *Avant-Scène du Cinéma* (Paris), October 1965; translated as *Le jour se lève: A Film*, New York, 1970.

Books:

Bernager, Jean-Louis, *Marcel Carné*, Paris, 1945.
Queval, Jean, *Marcel Carné*, Paris, 1952.
Perrin, Michel, *Arletty*, Paris, 1952.
Landry, Bernard, *Marcel Carné: Sa vie, ses films*, Paris, 1952.
Chazal, Robert, *Marcel Carné*, Paris, 1965.
Amengual, Barthélemy, *Prévert, du cinéma*, Alger, 1952.
Queval, Jean, *Jacques Prévert*, Paris, 1955.
Jacob, Guy, *Jacques Prévert*, Lyons, 1960.
Bergens, Andrée, *Jacques Prévert*, Paris, 1969.
Armes, Roy, *French Film*, New York, 1970.
Sadoul, Georges, *French Film*, New York, 1972.
Gauteur, Claude, and André Bernard, *Gabin; ou, Les Avatars d'un mythe*, Paris, 1976.
Missiaen, Jean-Claude, and Jacques Siclier, *Jean Gabin*, Paris, 1977.
Betti, Jean-Michel, *Salut, Gabin!*, Paris, 1977.
Ariotti, Philippe, and Philippe de Comes, *Arletty*, Paris, 1978.
Ellis, Jack C., *A History of Film*, Englewood Cliffs, New Jersey, 1979.
Thiher, Allen, *The Cinematic Muse: Critical Studies in the History of French Cinema*, Columbia, Missouri, 1979.
Milhaud, Sylvie, *Jean Gabin*, Paris, 1981.
Rachline, Michel, *Jacques Prévert*, Paris, 1981.
Perez, Michel, *Les Films de Carné*, Paris, 1986.
Brunelin, André, *Gabin*, Paris, 1987.
Turk, Edward Baron, *Child of Paradise: Marcel Carné and the Golden Age of French Cinema*, Cambridge, Massachusetts, 1989.
Carné, Marcel, *Ma vie à belles dents: mémoires*, Paris, 1996.

Articles:

Variety (New York), 26 July 1940.
New York Times, 30 July 1940.
Lodge, J. F., "The Cinema of Marcel Carné," in *Sequence* (London), 1946.
Sadoul, Georges, and J. Boul, in *Ecrans Français* (Paris), 12 June 1946.
Manvell, Roger, in *Sight and Sound* (London), Autumn 1947.

Le jour se lève

Lambert, Gavin, "Marcel Carné," in *Sequence* (London), Spring 1948.
Duvillars, Pierre, "Jean Gabin's Instinctive Man," in *Films in Review* (New York), March 1951.
Sadoul, Georges, "Les Films de Marcel Carné: Expression de notre époch," in *Lettres Françaises* (Paris), 1 March 1956.
Stanbrook, Alan, "The Carné Bubble," in *Film* (London), November-December 1959.
Guillot, Gerard, "Les Visiteurs du soir," in *Avant-Scène du Cinéma* (Paris), February 1962.
Nolan, Jack E., "Jean Gabin," in *Films in Review* (New York), April 1963.
Cowie, Peter, "Jean Gabin," in *Films and Filming* (London), February 1964.
"Prévert Issue" of *Image et Son* (Paris), December 1965.
Helman, A., in *Kino* (Warsaw), August 1973.
Quenin, F., in *Téléciné* (Paris), December 1976.
Fieschi, J., in *Cinématographe* (Paris), January 1977.

* * *

Coming at the very end of a decade in which the French cinema reigned intellectually supreme, *Le jour se lève* was the culminating achievement of the school known as "poetic realism." Fifty years on, the realism looks uncommonly like romanticism, but there can be little doubt about the poetry. The film is suffused with a bittersweet fatalism, a soft, drifting melancholy that invests the drab settings of factory and tenement with its own sad romance. The characters, hero and villain alike, seem to move in a dream, progressing with stoic resignation towards their inescapable destiny. The parallel with prewar France, awaiting defeat with mesmerized passivity, has often been drawn, and is indeed hard to avoid.

The circularity of the film's structure mirrors its fatalistic mood—what will happen, must happen, for we have already seen it happen. In the opening seconds, a man is shot, reeling mortally wounded down the tenement stairs. As police arrive and a crowd gathers, the killer barricades himself in his attic room; and through the long night, smoking his last cigarettes, he recalls events that led him to kill. By way of a carefully structured series of flashbacks, we return full circle to the shooting, seeing it this time from inside the room. As dawn breaks, the police prepare an assault. A final shot is heard; a cloud of tear-gas creeps over a lifeless body in the early rays of the sun; and abruptly, the noise of the dead man's alarm-clock breaks the silence.

Gabin's performance, as the besieged killer, stands as the epitome of his prewar persona as doomed proletarian anti-hero, developed through Duvivier's *Pépé le Moko*, Renoir's *Labête humaine*, and his previous Carné film, *Quai des brumes.* Equally outstanding is Jules Berry's portrayal of his victim, the sadistic animal trainer so compulsively dedicated to destruction that he even brings about his own death in order to destroy others. *Le jour se lève*—like *Quai des brumes* and all Carné's other early films—was made in close collaboration with his scriptwriter, the poet Jacques Prévert, whose wit, love of language, and fatalistic poetry permeate the film to such a degree that his name should stand with the director's as co-creator.

Le jour se lève was banned under the Vichy regime, accused of having contributed to the debacle of 1940. (Carné responded that the barometer should hardly be blamed for the storm it foretells.) Widely shown and acclaimed after the war, it was then suppressed again in 1947, this time by RKO, to make way for Anatole Litvak's crass remake, *The Long Night* (with Henry Fonda in the Gabin role). Rumours that all prints had been destroyed proved mercifully unfounded. Carné's film resurfaced during the 1950s, and is now generally acknowledged, together with *Les enfants du paradis*, as the finest product of his partnership with Prévert. The film's pre-war despair has transmuted into nostalgic melancholy, closer now to Ophüls than to Renoir; its romantic appeal seems likely to survive undimmed.

—Philip Kemp

JOURNAL D'UN CURÉ DE CAMPAGNE

(Diary of a Country Priest)

France, 1950

Director: Robert Bresson

Production: Union Générale Cinématographique; black and white, 35mm; running time: 120 minutes. Released 1950.

Producer: Léon Carré; **screenplay:** Robert Bresson, from the novel by Georges Bernanos; **photography:** Léonce-Henry Burel; **editor:** Paulette Robert; **production designer:** Pierre Charbonnier; **music:** Jean Jacques Grüenwald.

Cast: Claude Laydu (*Priest of Ambricourt*); Nicole Ladmiral (*Chantal*); Nicole Maurey (*Mademoiselle Louise*); Marie-Monique Arkell (*Countess*); Armand Guibert (*Priest of Torcy*); Jean Riveyre (*Count*); Jean Danet (*Olivier*); Antoine Balpêtré (*Doctor Delbende*); Martine Lemaire (*Séraphita*); Yvette Etiévant (*Young girl*).

Awards: Prix Louis-Delluc, France, 1950; Venice Film Festival, Best Photography and International Prize, 1951.

Publications

Books:

The Films of Robert Bresson, New York, 1969.
Armes, Roy, *French Cinema Since 1946: The Great Tradition*, New York, 1970.
Cameron, Ian, *The Films of Robert Bresson*, London, 1970.
Schrader, Paul, *Transcendental Style on Film: Ozu, Bresson, Dreyer*, Los Angeles, 1972.
De Pontes Leca, C., *Robert Bresson o cinematografo e o sinal*, Lisbon, 1978.
Horton, Andrew, and Joan Magretta, editors, *Modern European Filmmakers and the Art of Adaptation*, New York, 1981.
Andrew, Dudley, *Film in the Aura of Art*, Princeton, 1984.
Arnaud, Philippe, *Robert Bresson*, Paris, 1986.
Hanlon, Lindley, *Fragments: Bresson's Film Style*, Rutherford, 1986.
Quandt, James, editor, *Robert Bresson*, Toronto, 1998.

Articles:

Douchet, Jean, ''Bresson on Location: Interview,'' in *Sequence* (London), no. 13, 1951.
Lambert, Gavin, ''Notes on Robert Bresson,'' in *Sight and Sound* (London), Summer 1953.
Gow, Gordon, ''The Quest for Realism,'' in *Films and Filming* (London), December 1957.
Baxter, Brian, ''Robert Bresson,'' in *Film* (London), September-October 1958.
Ford, Charles, ''Robert Bresson,'' in *Films in Review* (New York), February 1959.
Green, Marjorie, ''Robert Bresson,'' in *Film Quarterly* (Berkeley), Spring 1960.
Young, Colin, ''Conventional/Unconventional,'' in *Film Quarterly* (Berkeley), Spring 1960.
Roud, Richard, ''French Outsider with the Inside Look,'' in *Films and Filming* (London), April 1960.
Johnson, Ian, and Raymond Durgnat, ''Puritans Anonymous,'' in *Motion* (London), Autumn 1963.
Sontag, Susan, ''Spiritual Style in the Films of Robert Bresson,'' in *Seventh Art* (New York), Summer 1964.
Milne, Tom, ''The Two Chambermaids,'' in *Sight and Sound* (London), Autumn 1964.
Godard, Jean-Luc, and Michel Delahaye, ''The Question: Interview with Robert Bresson,'' in *Cahiers du Cinéma in English* (New York), May 1966.
Durgnat, Raymond, in *Films and Filming* (London), December 1966.
Sarris, Andrew, ''Robert Bresson,'' in *Interviews with Film Directors*, New York, 1967.

Journal d'un curé de campagne

Skoller, Ronald S., ''Praxis as a Cinematic Principle in the Films of Robert Bresson,'' in *Cinema Journal* (Evanston, Illinois), Fall 1969.

Armes, Roy, ''The Art of Robert Bresson,'' in *London Magazine*, October 1970.

Zeman, Marvin, ''The Suicide of Robert Bresson,'' in *Cinema* (London), Spring 1971.

Prokosch, M., ''Bresson's Stylistics Revisited,'' in *Film Quarterly* (Berkeley), Winter 1971–72.

Samuels, Charles Thomas, ''Robert Bresson,'' in *Encountering Directors*, New York, 1972.

Polhemusin, H. M., ''Matter and Spirit in the Films of Robert Bresson,'' in *Film Heritage* (Dayton, Ohio), Spring 1974.

Prédal, René, interview with Léonce-H. Burel, in *Cinéma* (Paris), July-August 1974.

Nogueira, Rui, ''Burel and Bresson,'' in *Sight and Sound* (London), Winter 1976–77.

Bazin, André, in *Filmkritik* (Munich), May 1979.

Estève, M., ''Bresson et Bernanos,'' in *Cinéma* (Paris), June 1983.

Brisset, S., in *Cinema89*, no. 459, September 1989.

Lopate, Phillip, ''Films as Spiritual Life,'' in *Film Comment* (New York), November-December 1991.

Predal, R., in *Avant Scène du Cinéma* (Paris), January-February 1992.

Helman, Alicja, ''Dziennik wiejskiego proboszcza Bressona,'' in *Kino* (Warsaw), vol. 47, no. 2–3, February-March 1993.

Lyons, Donald, ''Priests,'' in *Film Comment* (New York), vol. 31, no. 3, May-June 1995.

Short review, in *Film en Televisie + Video* (Brussels), no. 465, October 1996.

Amengual, Barthélemy, ''Les pouvoirs de l'abstraction,'' in *Positif* (Paris), no. 430, December 1996.

Muriac, F., ''Egy falusi plebanos naploja,'' in *Filmvilag* (Budapest), vol. 40, no. 10, 1997.

Mazierska, Ewa, ''Dziennik wiejskiego proboszcza,'' in *Kino* (Warsaw), vol. 32, no. 373, June 1998.

* * *

In the politics of adaptation, Robert Bresson's *Diary of a Country Priest* must stand out as a revolutionary event. Taking over the project of this novel after its author, Georges Bernanos, had repudiated the version offered by Aurenche and Bost, Bresson promised to get beyond the cinema in order to embody, or act out, the spiritual drama that was at its core. Initially supported by producer Pierre Gerin, Bresson found himself abandoned after Bernanos's death in 1948. Nevertheless, he obtained the rights, finished his austere and unconventional script, and appealed to Bernanos's literary executor, Albert Beguin. Not only did Beguin accept Bresson's project, but this influential editor of the journal *Esprit* also helped him secure financing through the recently established national production agency, Union Générale Cinématographique.

Bresson chose for his hero a young Swiss actor from among a great many candidates, all of them practicing Catholics. For over a year Bresson and Claude Laydu met each Sunday to discuss the role. Laydu went so far as to live for a time in a monastery to accustom himself to priestly garb and gestures. Bresson insisted that he cease acting and become a ''model,'' an instinctive presence to be sculpted by light and camera.

The French press covered the production and premiere of the film with pride. They helped guide it to a new audience, of intellectuals and of the pious, two groups that had never frequented the cinema. Cinephiles were encouraged to see the film twice. In this way *Diary of a Country Priest* opened up new options in the conception, realization, and exploitation of a film.

Using fidelity of adaptation as an issue, Bresson actually challenged the entire aesthetics of French cinema of quality. His film overturns received notions of ''the primacy of the image'' and of the ''cinematic story,'' abandoning the theatrical, public and architectural ostentation of quality for a fluid, musical, interior, and ascetic expression. Bresson spoke of his work as an ''ecriture'' (Sartre) demanding new notions of the actor, the shot, and the soundtrack. Most critics could barely digest the film, for as Bazin said, it is a film not so much to read as to directly feel. While one can analyse the subject ''christologically'' according to the Stations of the Cross (the curé's falls, the wiping of his face by Seraphita, his glorious motorcycle ride to the big city where he will die, that death occurring between two outcasts in a high attic room), Bresson's is the opposite of an allegorical film. He cut 45 minutes without hesitation because the true drama was internal and was present in the quality of each of its moments. The spirituality every critic feels emanating from the film is really an effect produced by the accumulation of details rather than by dramatic plotting. A spiritual rhythm invades the images through the repetition of scenes, gestures, sounds, lighting and decor. Dialogue, monologue, landscape shots, scenes of writing, intensely composed music and natural sounds orchestrate a meditation rather than a story.

The diary form itself becomes the true site of meditation. It is variously represented as written pages on the screen, as a voice which situates the actions we see, and as those actions themselves, when through fades, ellipses and the like we realize that what is represented is reflection upon an event, not the event itself. In the penultimate sequence at the cafe, all three diary forms are present simultaneously: we see him writing, hear him say ''I must have dozed off for a while,'' and sense that doze through a slight reframing after a dissolve. In this key moment we realize that he is recording the very episode we are watching, layering reflection on reflection as he sums up his life just before it ends.

But the diary is also treated as one physical object among others. Bresson capitalizes on the cinema's indifferent attachment to the objects of the world by filming lamps, winebottles, furniture, and prayerbooks in closeup. Bazin always claimed that style is a pattern of selection. If this is so, then Bresson gets to the interior via these objects as they interact with the hands, feet, and eyes of characters in a landscape of barren trees, narrow roads and the interiors of cold houses the doors and windows of which are at once invitations and warnings.

The gray and spongy atmosphere that lights this world is transcended by the priest in his diary. Certain scenes let us sense this transcendence in their lighting. The dialogue with Chantal in the confessional is the greatest such scene, for Bresson allows us to witness the luminosity of two faces and two hands in a dark space where only voice and intention matter. Light is the metaphor of the curé's discourse as he passes dark nights and is drawn to the warmth of lamps in windows and to the promise of dawn. At times light is not even a clarifying medium but a substance surrounded by darkness.

The curé's homelessness is seldom pictured in a single image, but exists as a rhythm of entrances and exits in which the world seems distant from him. The diary shapes a life in transit, at home only with itself and its meditation. *Diary of a Country Priest* is a landmark in subjective cinema. No establishing shots put the priest in context. Characters accelerate away from him. Bresson refuses to situate him dramatically, sociologically, or theologically. We are locked within his point of reflection. The soundtrack alone reminds him and us of the wider world. The natural sounds of feet on cobblestones, of a motorcycle, of people whispering, or of a breeze blowing constitute the true atmosphere of a search for grace. Together with the voice of the diary and the finality of the musical score (the last time Bresson would lean on a score), these natural sounds present the whole of the curé's world in each moment of the film: its pastness, its responsiveness, its fidelity, its limitation of vision, its productive loneliness and suffering.

The stakes of this film are high. Like the curé, Bresson is banking on the power of humility and discipline. Instead of achieving a life, Bresson would achieve a film. He would do so by thwarting the cinema. Many believers, especially the young *Cahiers* critics Truffaut and Godard, have had to defend their faith against those outraged by a film emanating in fragments from an obscure and obsessive mind. *Diary of a Country Priest* remains a watershed film in the history of adaptations and in the politics of style.

—Dudley Andrew

JOURNEY OF HOPE

(Reise der Hoffnung; Umud'a yolculuk)

Switzerland/Turkey, 1990

Director: Xavier Koller

Production: Catpics AG/Condor features (Switzerland), Antea, Dewe, Cinerent, SRG, RTSI, Film Four International, and Eurimages; color; running time: 111 minutes. Released in Switzerland, August 1990, and in the United States, May 1991; distributed in the United States by Miramax Films. Languages: Turkish, Kurdish, and German.

Producer: Peter-Christian Fueter and Alfi Sinniger; **screenplay:** Xavier Koller, Feride Çiçekoglu; **photography:** Elemér Ragályi;

Journey of Hope

editors: Daniel Gibal, Galip Iyitanir; **art director:** Kathrin Brunner; **costumes:** Grazia Colombini; **original music:** Manfred Eicher, with Jan Garbarek, Terje Rypdal, Arild Andersen, Egberto Gismonti.

Cast: Necmettin Çobanoglu (*Haydar Sener*); Nur Sürer (*Meryem*); Emin Sivas (*Mehmet Ali*); Yaman Okay (*Turkmen*); Erdinc Akbas (*Adama*); Mathias Gnädinger (*Truckdriver Ramser*); Dietmar Schönherr (*Massimo*); and others.

Awards: Bronze Leopard, Locarno International Film Festival, 1990; Academy Award for Best Foreign Language Film, 1991.

Publications

Articles:

Cado, Valerie, review in *Studio* (Paris), November 1991.
Neubourg, Monique, review in *Première* (Paris), November 1991.
Gentele, Jeannette, ''Prisbelönat flyktingdrama,'' in *Svenska Dagbladet* (Sweden), 6 March 1992.
Rosenthal, A., ''*Journey of Hope*: Reflections of a Documentary Screenwriter,'' in *International Documentary* (Los Angeles), vol. 16, March 1997.

* * *

Journey of Hope is the European answer to Nelson Pereira dos Santos's *Vidas Secas* (1963) and Gregory Nava's *El Norte* (1983), a story of weak and helpless people hopefully struggling to secure what they believe may be a better life. Based on a real story, it was one of the first widely seen feature films to tackle the problem of migrations from the peripheries of Europe to the rich Western societies, which have not by chance been described as ''Fortress Europe.'' The hostile and unwelcoming treatment of underprivileged newcomers has since become one of the major topics in European art and politics. Numerous cinematic works that treat these problems came into being.

A Kurdish family, pressed by economic needs, leave their native village and travel to Europe, aiming to penetrate into Switzerland and begin a new life. Leaving is particularly painful for Meryem, the wife, who has to leave behind six of her seven children. Haydar, the father, agrees that they may take along one of their boys, Mehmet Ali. The presence of the boy, however, complicates their original transfer plan, and they have to struggle to get themselves to Italy and then Switzerland as clandestines under particularly difficult conditions. They are smuggled on board a ship in a cargo container, and later on end up stranded in the hostile Alps amidst a snowstorm. The family gets separated and loses their way; Myriam is injured but eventually makes her way to safety. Heydar, however, is lost and spends the freezing night desperately wandering in the snow and looking for help. By the time he is found in the morning, his little boy is gone.

Scripted by director Koller and with impressive performances from the lead actors, the film builds on the contrasts between the self-content affluence of the West and the grim poverty of Asia Minor. It exposes exploitative individuals like the profiteers involved in human trafficking on the Swiss border, but it does not find them at fault. It rather blames the social rules designed to safeguard the rich from the poor. Most of the individual Westerners whom the clandestines encounter—an Italian sailor, a Swiss truck driver, and a Turkish émigré-interpreter—are sympathetic to them, and try to help in their limited ways. Nonetheless, the system is hostile and merciless, and there is no chance for miracles. A picture postcard from Switzerland describing the country as ''paradise'' figures as a recurring motif in the film; when the protagonists finally reach the deceptive ''paradise'' it becomes clear that for the boy it has been a journey into heaven in the literal sense.

A number of remarkable cinematic works of the past have recorded the troublesome experiences of the economic migrations of the Turks. Before *Journey of Hope*, the denigrating struggles of penetrating into ''Fortress Europe'' have been treated in films by Turkish émigré directors such as Swedish-based Tunç Okan whose film *The Bus* (1977) featured illegal Turkish immigrants left on their own in Stockholm, who do not dare to leave the vehicle and venture into the unknown territory of the Western metropolis. The unsettling experiences of life in a foreign land have been further problematized by German-based Tevfik Baser in his films *Forty Square Meters Germany* (1986) and *Farewell to False Paradise* (1989), both exploring the adaptation difficulties of Turkish protagonists in Germany.

—Dina Iordanova

JOURNEY TO ITALY

See **VIAGGIO IN ITALIA**

JU DOU

China/Japan, 1990

Directors: Zhang Yimou, Yang Fengliang (some sources list Yang as Zhang's collaborator)

Production: China Film Co-Production Corporation, China Film Export and Import Corporation, Tokuma Shoten Publishing Company Ltd., Tokuma Communications Company Ltd, Xi An Film Studio; color, 35mm.; Panavision; running time: 95 minutes. Released April 1991 in United States.

Ju Dou

Producers: Zhang Wenze, Yasuyoshi Tokuma, Hu Jian; **screenplay:** Liu Heng, based on his novella; **photography:** Gu Changwei, Yang Lun; **editor:** Du Yuan; **art directors:** Cao Juiping Cao, Xia Rujin; **original music:** Zhao Jipin; **sound:** Li Lanhua.

Cast: Gong Li (*Ju Dou*); Li Baotian (*Yang Tianqing*); Li Wei (*Yang Jinshan*); Zhang Yi (*Yang Tianbai [infant]*); Zheng Jian (*Yang Tianbai [Youth]*).

Award: Chicago Film Festival Golden Hugo Award, 1990.

Publications

Articles:

Lochen, K., in *Film & Kino* (Oslo), no. 4, 1990.
Stratton, David, in *Variety* (New York), 30 May 1990.
Grosoli, F., in *Cineforum* (Bergamo, Italy), June 1990.
Rabinovici, J., in *Cinema 90* (Paris), June 1990.
Jousse, T., in *Cahiers du Cinéma* (Paris), June 1990.
Tessier, M., in *Revue du Cinéma* (Cretail Cedex, France), July/August 1990.
Paranagua, P.A., in *Positif* (Paris), July/August 1990.

James, Caryn, ''On Oppression of Women in China,'' in *New York Times*, 22 September 1990.
Lochen, K., in *Film & Kino* (Oslo), no. 3, 1991.
Vos, J. M. de, in *Film en Televisie + Video* (Brussels), January 1991.
Kreps, K., in *Box Office* (Hollywood), January 1991.
Derobert, E. and Y. Tobin, in *Positif* (Paris), February 1991.
Bassan, R., in *Revue du Cinéma* (Cretail Cedex, France), 17 February 1991.
Koetsenruijter, B., in *Skrien* (Amsterdam), February/March 1991.
James, Caryn, ''Adultery and Aftermath in a Chinese Village,'' in *New York Times*, 17 March 1991.
Corliss, R., and J.A. Florcrus, ''Tainted Love by the Dye Vat,'' in *Time* (New York), 18 March 1991.
Hoberman, J., ''Fine China,'' in *Village Voice* (New York), 19 March 1991.
Orr, D., ''Undertones,'' in *New Statesman* (London), 22 March 1991.
Kempley, Rita, in *Washington Post*, 22 March 1991.
Denby, David, ''The Pursuit of Unhappiness,'' in *New York*, 25 March 1991.
Rayns, Tony, in *Monthly Film Bulletin* (London), April 1991.
Chua, R., ''Homeland Movies,'' in *Village Voice* (New York), 2 April 1991.
Ebert, Roger, in *Chicago Sun-Times*, 12 April 1991.
Noh, D., in *Film Journal* (New York), April/May 1991.
Worm, V., in *Levende Billeder* (Copenhagen), July 1991.
Kissin, E.H., in *Films in Review* (New York), July/August 1991.
Gansera, R., in *EPD Film* (Frankfurt), September 1991.
Skram-Jensen, U., in *Kosmorama* (Copenhagen), Fall 1991.

* * *

Ju Dou may be viewed on two levels: as a folktale of innocence and evil, a simple and powerful work of cinematic art; and as a biting and controversial political allegory. Its success helped thrust its director, Zhang Yimou, into the international spotlight. Zhang, working in collaboration with Yang Fengliang, has made a haunting film about the manner in which peoples' lives are stifled when they are ruled by rigid custom, rather than human desire.

The setting is a small village somewhere in China during the 1920s. The three primary characters, each broadly drawn, are a heroine, hero, and villain. The latter is the most conventional: Yang Jinshan, a miserly, sadistic old man who owns a dye mill. Desperate to father a male heir, Jinshan already has purchased two wives, whom he has tortured to death when they failed to bear him a child. Ju Dou is his newest spouse, his latest possession. Because she has not immediately become pregnant, he is battering her. ''I bought you, now obey me,'' he tells her. ''When I buy an animal, I treat it as I wish. And you're no better than an animal.''

Yang Tianqing is Jinshan's shy, repressed nephew. He was adopted by the old man after his parents died, and he is treated more like a slave than a relation. Each night, Tianqing silently listens to Ju Dou's screams and pleadings. He is not even introduced to her, and first sees Ju Dou while peeping at her through a hole in the wall as she removes her blouse. Inevitably, Ju Dou and Tianqing are drawn to each other—and Ju Dou becomes pregnant during their first sexual encounter. So Jinshan's own impotence is the explanation for Ju Dou's and her predecessors' inability to bear him children—and his tirades and beatings only add to his hypocrisy. Even more to the point, in feudal China, the only weapon that the poor and powerless Ju Dou and Tianqing can employ in rebellion against Jinshan is their sexual attraction.

By far the film's most intriguing character is Ju Dou, who is victimized because of her gender. While it would be unrealistic for her to openly oppose Jinshan, she defies him in a subtler—and more believable—manner. Within the boundaries of her situation, she proves to be remarkably bold and decisive. That she is able to gain a modicum of control over her life is extraordinary, given her plight. It is Ju Dou who initiates the relationship with Tianqing, and not the other way around; she is the aggressor, while he is passive. Essentially, Tianqing is weak-willed: an observer rather than participant, a peeping tom who never would defy his uncle on his own. He only resists at Ju Dou's prodding, and when overcome by his lusty urges.

After Jinshan is paralyzed from the waist down in an accident, Tianqing has the opportunity to kill him. But he does not. He and Ju Dou may now feel empowered—Ju Dou brazenly reveals to Jinshan the true identity of the father of her newborn son—but the old man has his revenge when the toddler mistakenly recognizes him as his parent. Finally, Ju Dou's and Tianqing's son grows into an angry, tyrannical devil, a pint-sized duplicate of Jinshan, with the boy manipulated by the old man into despising his real father.

And so the point is clear: in order to destroy evil, you must not allow it to fester. You must completely snuff it out. If you let it exist because you have the upper hand, it surely will regain its foothold and destroy you. Later on, after Jinshan accidentally drowns, Tianqing does not rejoice. Rather, he automatically assumes that Ju Dou murdered the old man. Tianqing insists on adhering to the customs that have made his life wretched, and have kept him from openly being with Ju Dou. ''Killing one's husband cries out for punishment,'' he pronounces. ''Didn't he deserve to die?'' Ju Dou asks. In response, Tianqing slaps her. After the town's elders deem that Ju Dou can never remarry, and that Tianqing must move out of the mill, Ju Dou wants to leave the village. But Tianqing insists on staying—and prolonging his and Ju Dou's misery.

On one level, *Ju Dou* clearly is a condemnation of the oppressiveness of feudal China and the ancient customs and ancestral heritage that resulted in a patriarchal society. Yet the film also may be interpreted as a critique of modern, communist China. The villain of the piece is a belligerent, sexually impotent old man—and the film is the product of a nation that is ruled by old men who often are perceived as contentious. *Ju Dou* might be viewed as an allegory for the manner in which a small group of elderly Maoists oversee Chinese society; meanwhile, Ju Dou and Tianqing, as they fearfully cling to one another, are representative of the beaten-down masses; and their cold, uncomprehending son symbolizes the Red Guard. The dye factory setting is not at all arbitrary. The bright pigments—and especially the reds—that dominate the coloring process are reflective of Ju Dou's and Tianqing's passion. However, unlike the colored sheets, which shine brightly in the sun, their emotions must be repressed, must remain clandestine.

Unsurprisingly, *Ju Dou*—which was partially produced with Japanese financial backing—was banned in China. Its controversy was sparked by the allegorical nature of the story, and the depiction of characters whose needs, desires, and individuality take precedence over their relation to a group. Additionally, the sexuality portrayed, while tame by Western standards, is brazen for a Chinese film.

Ju Dou could not be completely repressed. First, it was a hit on the international film festival circuit. Then it became the initial Chinese feature ever to win a Best Foreign Film Academy Award nomination.

—Rob Edelman

JUD SÜSS

Germany, 1940

Director: Harlan Veit

Production: Terra Film; black and white; running time: 85 minutes. Filmed in Berlin and Prague, March-August 1940.

Screenplay: Veit Harlan, Eberhard Wolfgang Möller, Veit Harlan, and Ludwig Metzer, from the novel by Lion Feuchtwanger; **photography:** Bruno Mondi; **music:** Wolfgang Zeller.

Cast: Ferdinand Marian (*Süss*); Werner Krauss (*Rabbi Loew, secretary Levy, and other unidentified characters*); Heinrich George (*Duke of Württemberg*); Kristina Söderbaum (*Raped girl*); Eugene Klöpfer (*Raped girl's father*); Hilde von Stolz; Malte Jäger; Albert Florath; Theodor Loos; and Wolfgang Staudte.

Publications

Script:

Knihl, Friedrich, and others, *Jud Süss: Filmprotokoli, Programmheft und Einzelanalysen*, Berlin 1983.

Books:

Feuchtwanger, Lion, *Jud Süss*, Munich, 1928.
Wulf, Joseph, *Theater und Film im Dritten Reich*, Gütersloh, 1964.
Harlan, Veit, *Im Schatten Meiner Filme*, Gütersloh, 1966.
Eisner, Lotte H., *The Haunted Screen*, Berkeley, 1973.
Hull, David Stewart, *Film in the Third Reich*, New York, 1973.
Zielinski, Siegfried, *Veit Harlan: Analysen und Materialien zur Auseinandersetzung mit einem Film-Regisseur des deutschen Faschismus*, Frankfurt/Main, 1981.
Fröhlich, Gustav, *Waren das Zeiten: Mein Film-Heldenleben*, Munich, 1983.
Friedman, Régine Mihal, *L'Image et son juif: le juif dans le cinéma nazi*, Paris, 1983.
Welch, David, *Propaganda and the German Cinema*, Oxford 1987.
Gethmann, Daniel, *Das Narvik-Projekt: Film und Krieg*, Bonn, 1998.

Articles:

Tegel, S., ''Viet Harlan and the Origins of *Jud Suess* 1938–1939: Opportunism in the Creation of Nazi Anti-Semitic Film Propoganda,'' in *Historical Journal of Film, Radio and Television* (Basingstoke), vol. 16, no. 4, 1996.

* * *

Jud Süss is very loosely based on the historical personage of Josef Süss Oppenheimer who, in the early-18th century became a financial adviser to Duke Karl Alexander of Württemberg, with the authority to collect taxes; this, naturally, did not endear him to the Duke's subjects. When Karl Alexander suddenly died, Süss was put on trial and was hanged. The eventual transmogrification of the historical Süss, and of the several previous fictions based on his fate (Wilhelm Hauff, Lion Feuchtwanger) into the Jud Süss of the movie was mainly the work of the Nazi minister of propaganda himself, Dr. Josef Goebbels.

The idea for a film about Süss had been peddled in German studios by scriptwriter Ludwig Metzger since 1921, but it wasn't until Goebbels saw the British film-adaptation of Lion Feuchtwanger's novel *Jud Süss* (1934) that he realized the anti-semitic potential the material had, if interpreted not as a human tragedy (as in the British film), but as a tale of Jewish arrogance and infiltration. The story of how the director and the actors were selected for the film is a tragic farce of coercion, extortion, and eventual capitulation to the fear endemic to cruel dictatorships.

Pieced together from sources at my disposal, it seems obvious that almost all chief actors, and the director himself, tried—by various tricks—to escape the assignment. Goebbels either outwitted them, or knew about compromising circumstances in their lives and used this knowledge for bludgeoning them into acceptance. The reluctance to participate in this politically-most-correct film shows how aware most German artists were of the fact that anti-semitism under Hitler changed from prejudice to murder. They could have, of course, refused but saying ''no'' required extraordinary courage: the dire consequences of such an act of defiance were only too easy to imagine.

One of the paradoxes of this sinister film is how many participants in the violently racist project had either Jewish spouses or relatives, were disciples of Jewish artists and known friends or Jews, or had been—before the Nazi takeover—left-leaning intellectuals, even communists (such as Heinrich George, who eventually died in a Soviet concentration camp). Thus the director Veit Harlan's first wife was Jewish, he himself had been an admirer of Max Reinhardt and Stanislavski, and, earlier in life, flirted with socialism. Werner Krauss's daughter-in-law was Jewish, and Ferdinand Marian, who played the title role, had a half-Jewish daughter from his first marriage. His second wife had been married to a Jew, whom Marian hid in his house. Another actor, Hans Meyer-Hanno, reportedly a communist, acted in Nazi films apparently to protect his Jewish wife, the pianist Irene Saager.

Harlan, who obviously did not mind making films with heavy infusions of Nazi ideology (*Der Herrscher*, 1937, and many films made after *Jud Süss*), tried very hard to avoid this particular assignment. At first he raised objections to the artistic quality of the script; when this didn't work he even volunteered for frontline military service. Goebbels proclaimed the making of *Jud Süss* a wartime duty and thus turned possible refusals into acts of desertion. Harlan's Swedish wife, Kristina Söderbaum, the leading lady of the film, who

Jud Süss

had just had a baby, attempted to use breast-feeding as an excuse; but a wet nurse was hired. Moreover, Harlan was permitted to stop all work in the studio whenever the baby became hungry. Werner Krauss tried another ruse: he knew that Goebbels disliked casting the same actor in two roles, and so he demanded that he play all the main Jewish characters arguing that the role of the rabbi was too small for an actor of his stature. Goebbels consented. Marian, on purpose, bungled his screen test but Goebbels saw through it, and all the actor could do was to get drunk, which he promptly did. After the war, Marian died in a car accident which most sources interpret as suicide. In any case, his widow committed suicide shortly after she had appeared as witness at Harlan's denazification hearings.

Some, however (for instance, Emil Jannings), succeeded in tricking their way out of the role: Jannings maintained that he was too old for the part of the Jewish Casanova, and also too fat; and since there were already two corpulent leading men in the cast (George and Klöpfer) it would be like ''an opera with three basses.''

Coerced into taking the job, Harlan tried to direct his actors in such a way that they would not sink to the level of Stürmer-like anti-semitic caricatures. He also attempted to soften the impact of the repulsive rape scene by giving Süss as motivation, revenge for having been refused the girl's hand by her father rather than ''Jewish lewdness.'' In the final scene of Süss's brutal execution Harlan wrote a defiant speech for Marian, who had biblical overtones, and condemned the German authorities. When Goebbels was shown a rough-cut copy, he flew into a rage and had the outspoken speech replaced with one in which the cowardly Jew begged for his life.

Thus, no matter how Harlan and his actors tried to dilute the vile message of the movie (Krauss, for instance, successfully argued against having to perform with an artificial crooked ''Jewish'' nose because it limited the movement of facial muscles), the outcome, in the historical context of anti-Jewish hysteria, was a film which substantially exacerbated anti-semitic feeling. For the purpose of ideology it introduced into Süss's story fictional characters (the raped ''Aryan'' girl; her husband exposed to torture on Süss's orders), and distorted the historical personage of Süss Oppenheimer to conform to the racist image of the Jew as poisoner of society.

The resulting film is a mediocre melodrama at best. Harlan's direction is, mildly speaking, uninspired. Most of the acting is bombastic, except for, on occasion, that of Krauss and Marian, whose portrayal of Jewish characters can, perhaps, be traced to Vachtangov's documentary about the Moscow Jewish theatre which, for study purposes, was screened for the cast. The camera work is a far cry from the lively photography of the best German films of the silent era. All in all, the film is not only repugnant but uninteresting as cinema.

After the Nazis came to power some of Germany's best artists, unable to compromise their artistic integrity, left the country (Fritz Lang, Marlene Dietrich, Conrad Veidt, Peter Lorre, among others). Harlan opted to compromise. The result was a number of films which are memorable only as examples of how deep art can sink if it—voluntarily or not—serves ideological lies.

—Josef Škvorecký

JUDAS WAS A WOMAN

See **LA BETE HUMAINE**

JUDEX

France, 1916

Director: Louis Feuillade

Production: Film Gaumont, Paris; serial in 12 episodes: 1. *L'ombre mysterieuse*; 2. *L'erpiation*; 3. *La meute fantastique*; 4. *La secret de la tombe*; 5. *Le moulin tragique*; 6. *Le môme reglisse*; 7. *La femme en noir*; 8. *Les souterrains du chateau rouge*; 9. *Lorsque l'enfant parut*; 10. *Le coeur de Jacqueline*; 11. *Ondine*; 12. *Le pardon d'amour*. Length: between 427 and 1262 meters per episode. Released together, 16 December 1916.

Screenplay: Arthur Bernède and Louis Feuillade; **photography:** Klausse and A. Glattli.

Cast: René Cresté (*Judex*); Musidora (*Diana Monti, Mlle. Verdier*); Yvette Andreyor (*Jacqueline*); Marcel Levesque (*Cocantin*); Bout-de-Zan (*Le Môme reglisse*); Louis Leubas (*Favraux*); Edouard Mathé (*Roger de Trémeuse*); Georges Flateau (*Vicomte de la Rochefontaine*); Gaston Michel (*Le vieux Kerjan*); Jean Devadle (*Morales*); Yvonne Dario (*Comtesse de la Trémeuse*); Olinda Mano (*Le Petit Jean*); Juliette Clarens (*Gisèle*).

Publications

Books:

Delluc, Louis, *Cinéma et compagnie*, Paris, 1919.
Védrès, Nicole, *Images du cinéma français*, Paris, 1945.
Lacassin, Francis, *Louis Feuillade*, Paris, 1964.
Anthologie du cinéma 2, Paris, 1967.
Armes, Roy, *French Film*, New York, 1970.
Barsacq, Léon, *Caligari's Cabinet and Other Grand Illusions: A History of Film Design*, New York, 1976.

Articles:

Bioscope (London), 26 July, 2 August and 23 August 1917.
Beylie, Claude, "Louis Feuillade," in *Ecran de France* (Paris), 15 May 1959.
Cinéma (Paris), no. 84, 1964.
Lacassin, Francis, "Louis Feuillade," in *Sight and Sound* (London), Winter 1964–65.
Roud, Richard, Maker of Melodrama," in *Film Comment* (New York), November-December 1976.
"Louis Feuillade," in *Film Dope* (London), September 1978.
Champreux, J., "Louis Feuillade, poète de la réalité," in *Avant-Scène du Cinéma* (Paris), 1 July 1981.
"*Judex* Issue" of *Avant-Scène du Cinéma* (Paris), April 1984.
Redi, Riccardo, in *Bianco e Nero* (Rome), January-March 1987.
Beylie, C., "*Judex* et *Les vampires*," in *Cinema 91*, no. 482, November 1991.
Masson, A., "Voila le passage secret!" in *Positif* (Paris), January 1993.
"Feuillade and the French Serial," in *Velvet Light Trap* (Austin), no. 37, Spring 1996.
Callahan, Vicki, "Detailing the Impossible," in *Sight & Sound* (London), vol. 9, no. 4, April 1999.

* * *

Unlike Feuillade's earlier *Fantômas* and *Les vampires*, *Judex* celebrates the exploits of a defender of the law and upholder of right and wrong rather than glorifying crime and ridiculing the police. Indeed, Feullade himself described it as "a spectacle for all the family, exalting the most noble sentiments." Such a change of tack can no doubt be explained partly by the censorship problems faced by *Les vampires*, which the Ministry of the Interior found too "demoralising" for wartime, and in which certain spectators found rather disturbing echoes of the activities of the anarchist Bonnot gang, which had terrorised Paris in 1912.

The twelve episodes of *Judex* are among the peaks of the French serial, which has become somewhat eclipsed by its American counterpart. In France, the serial was a development of the prewar series film which had its roots in the popular literature of the time—indigenous and imported cheap paperbacks, and the serialised stories to be found in weekly magazines and parts of the daily press. *Fantômas* was one such series (running to five separate films), and others featured heroes such as Nick Winter, Zigomar, Onésime, Rocambole, and Boute-de-Zan (The Liquorice Kid, who also crops up in *Judex*). At their height, the French serials proved a valuable counterweight to the flood of American imports and, to quote Feuillade again, showed that "French production is not definitively outclassed by the Americans and that we are not henceforward going to be reduced always to be following in others' footsteps."

Judex, the film's avenging hero, is in fact the Comte de Trémeuse, the son of a Corsican banker who killed himself after being ruined by

Judex

a former friend, Favraux. Spurred on by his mother, he swears to wreak revenge for his father's death and, disguised in black cape and broad-brimmed hat, he sets out in pursuit of Favraux. Believing that he has killed him, he falls in love with Favraux's beautiful daughter, the young widow Jacqueline, only to discover that Favraux is still alive after all. Judex imprisons him in the dungeons of a ruined castle in which he has built a laboratory, but Favraux's evil schemes are by no means at an end.

No synopsis could adequately communicate the flavour and atmosphere of *Judex*, whose basic story is simply a pretext for a seemingly endless and remarkably inventive series of incidents and striking moments. Feuillade may have reversed the moral order of *Les vampires*, but both films inhabit the same mysterious universe, underlined by the reappearance of the great comic actor Marcel Levesque as the detective Cocantin and Musidora as the vamp-ish Diana Monti. Both, along with Bout-de-Zan, were very much part of Feuillade's stock company, and Musidora herself went on to direct a number of films. Even the titles of the episodes are evocative—for example, *The Mysterious Shadow*, *The Fantastic Hounds*, *The Secret of the Tomb*, *The Tragic Mill*—and although Feuillade was dismissed by critics of the time as beneath serious consideration it should come as no surprise to discover that he was feted by the Surrealists and also now tends to be regarded as one of the precursors of "poetic realism."

What particularly attracted the Surrealists to his work was his sense of landscape and place, and in particular his entirely unforced co-mingling of the fantastic and the everyday. Like so many of the Surrealists' heroes, Feuillade had discovered the secret of revealing the surreal behind the real: by setting fantastic happenings in familiar, modern environments he succeeded in revealing the mysterious poetry of the urban and every day. Or as Breton and Aragon put it, in Feuillade's films "one discovers a real sense of our century."

With his distinctive hat, and black cape tossed over one shoulder, Judex rapidly became something of an iconic figure. Just as the early series and serials had drawn on the printed word for inspiration, so the story of Judex was serialised in *Le petit Parisien*. *Judex* was followed in 1918 by *La nouvelle mission de Judex*, and was later re-made twice—the first time by Feuillade's son-in-law Maurice Champreux in 1933, and the second by Georges Franju in 1963, from a script co-written by Feuillade's grandson Jacques Champreux.

—Sylvia Paskin

JUJIRO

(Crossroads)

Japan, 1928

Director: Teinosuke Kinugasa

Production: Kinugasa Motion Pictures Association and Shochiku; black and white, 35mm, silent; running time: about 80 minutes; length: 7 reels. Released 11 May 1928. Re-released 1976.

Producer: Teinosuke Kinugasa; **screenplay:** Teinosuke Kinugasa; **photography:** Kohei Sugiyama; **art directors:** Yozo Tomonari, some sources list Bonji Taira; **lighting:** Masao Uchida and Kinshi Tsuruta.

Cast: Junosuke Bando (*Rikiya, the brother*); Akiko Chihaya (*Older sister*); Yukiko Ogawa (*O-une, woman of Yoshiwara*); Ippei Soma (*Man with the Constable's stick*); Yoshie Nakagawa (*Woman who sells women*); Misao Seki (*Old landlord*); Myoichiro Ozawa (*Man who quarrels*); Teruko Sanjo (*Mistaken woman*).

Publications

Books:

Shinobu Giuglaris, Marcel de, *Le Cinéma Japonais*, Paris, 1956.
Anderson, Joseph, and Donald Richie, editors, *The Japanese Film: Art and Industry*, New York, 1960; revised edition, Princeton, New Jersey, 1982.
Cinémathèque Français, *Invitation au Cinéma Japonais*, Paris, 1963.
Klinowski, Jacek, and Adam Garbicz, *Cinema, The Magic Vehicle: A Guide to Its Achievement: Journey One: The Cinema Through 1949*, Metuchen, New Jersey, 1975.

Articles:

Anderson, Joseph, ''Seven from the Past,'' in *Sight and Sound* (London), Autumn 1957.
McVay, Douglas, in *Films and Filming* (London), June 1960.

* * *

After the commercial disaster of the experimental *Page of Madness* (1926), Kinugasa's independent production company made its last film, *Jujiro*, in 1928. Thus freed somewhat from the pressure of maintaining the company's image (and solvency), everybody in the staff decided to explore whatever he wanted in the company's swan song. The result was this unique avant-garde *jidaigeke* (period film): Kinugasa completely eliminated from this film swordplay, which was then the norm, and concentrated on the depiction of the characters' psychology, thus creating a new style in this genre.

Visually, the film is one of astonishing effects and powerful images. Because of financial limitations, old boxes and wood used in the previous films were collected, painted and deliberately reused to create a bizarre atmosphere of poverty. The whole set design is based on unbalanced and distorted images, which happen to be similar to those of German Expressionism. Parallel lines are carefully avoided in the shapes of roofs, at the window lines and in the interior architecture.

The strong contrast of light and shadow is also expressionistic. Particularly skillful is the highlighting of characters' dramatic emotion by exploiting a heightened effect of counterlight. Raindrops are captured dripping from the hair of the doomed sister and brother, shining in the strong counterlight. The grotesque and nasty face of the man with the constable who is trying to make advances to the helpless sister is illuminated from behind in the dark as he ascends the stairs to the attic. The chiaroscuro photography, by then the young and ambitious Kohei Sugiyama, is exquisite.

The upstairs room is symbolically presented as the only sanctuary from the lower world of evil and malice. The tragedies of the sister and the brother both originate in credulous mistakes (she believes the false identity of the man with the constable; he believes that he committed a murder which in fact never took place). This theme is conveyed by the numerous scenes of fantasy and dream, as well as by the use of the flashback and flash-forward techniques. The boundary between reality and imagination is left ambiguous in mesmerising effects created by camera movements, such as quick tracking shots, quick panning shots and numerous superimpositions.

An especially sophisticated sequence is the scene in which ashes are thrown in the brother's face dazzling him. Interrupting the fight sequence is a sequence of black- and white- designs, used to create a flickering effect: there then follows a close-up shot of the brother's agonized face within the image of a storm of falling ashes. This is followed by a shot of him staggering, frames with black- and white- lightning-like shapes, and then the shot of an object accelerating toward the camera. Finally, the camera tilts almost 90 degrees and captures the tottering brother crashing into objects. This complicated process of mixing the establishing shots and close-up shots of him staggering with images from his subjective point-of-view succeeds in conveying his despair and disorientation.

The recurrent spinning image is prevalent throughout the film. It is suggested by the image of targets at an archery shop that employs the hero's love interest. This shop is surrounded by other round and spinning images such as umbrellas and lanterns. The pattern of the woman's kimono suggests playfully those targets and arrows (relevant to the theme of stalking of a love partner). At the house of the brother and his sister, there is a big spinning wheel in the upstairs room; the downstairs is filled with round objects such as mats and straw hats.

The image of the crossroads is strikingly simple: only a few naked trees along the white roads in the dark. This set conveys artificiality, yet it also successfully suggests the helplessness and desperation of the sister finally waiting alone in vain for her brother.

Kinugasa's ambitious film was received far more appreciatively in Europe than in his home country. The re-release of *Jujiro* in Japan in 1976, however, created an excitement appropriate to the rediscovery of an avant-garde classic.

—Kyoko Hirano

Jujiro

JULES ET JIM

(Jules and Jim)

France, 1962

Director: François Truffaut

Production: Films du Carosse and SEDIF; 1962; black and white, 35mm, Franscope; running time: 105 minutes. Released 23 January 1962, Paris. Filmed 1963 Alsace, Paris, and Venice.

Producer: Marcel Berbert; **screenplay:** François Truffaut and Jean Gruault, from the novel by Henri-Pierre Roché; **photography:** Raoul Coutard; **editor:** Claudine Bouche; **sound:** Témoin; **music:** Georges Delerue, song ''Le Tourbillon'' by Bassiak; **costume designer:** Fred Capel.

Cast: Jeanne Moreau (*Katherine*); Oscar Werner (*Jules*); Henri Serre (*Jim*); Vanna Urbino (*Gilberte*); Boris Bassiak (*Albert*); Sabine Haudepin (*Sabine*); Marie Dubois (*Thérèse*); Jean-Louis Richard (*1st Customer in café*); Michel Varesano (*2nd Customer in café*); Pierre Fabre (*Drunkard in the café*); Danielle Bassiak (*Albert's friend*); Bernard Largemains (*Merlin*); Elen Bober (*Mathilde*); Michel Subor (*Narrator*).

Publications

Script:

Truffaut, François, and Jean Gruault, *Jules et Jim*, in *Avant-Scène du Cinéma* (Paris), 1962; as *Jules and Jim*, New York, 1968.

Books:

Graham, Peter, *The New Wave*, New York, 1968.
Petrie, Graham, *The Cinema of François Truffaut*, New York, 1970.
Crisp, C. G., and Michael Walker, *François Truffaut*, New York, 1971.
Boyum, Joy, and Adrienne Scott, *Film as Film: Critical Responses to Film Art*, Boston, 1971.
Crisp, C. G., *François Truffaut*, London, 1972.

Jules et Jim

Fanne, Dominique, *L'Univers de François Truffaut*, Paris, 1972.
Allen, Don, *Finally Truffaut*, London, 1973; revised edition, 1985.
Monaco, James, *The New Wave*, New York, 1976.
Collet, Jean, *Le Cinéma de François Truffaut*, Paris, 1977.
Insdorf, Annette, *François Truffaut*, Boston, 1978, 1989.
Horton, Andrew, and Joan Magretta, *Modern European Filmmakers and the Art of Adaptation*, New York, 1981.
Walz, Eugene P., *François Truffaut: A Guide to References and Resources*, Boston, 1982.
Winkler, Willi, *Die Filme von François Truffaut*, Munich, 1984.
Bergala, Alain, and others, *Le Roman de François Truffaut*, Paris, 1985.
Collet, Jean, *François Truffaut*, Paris, 1985.
Truffaut, François, *Truffaut par Truffaut*, edited by Dominique Rabourdin, Paris, 1985.
De Fornari, Oreste, *I filme di François Truffaut*, Rome, 1986.
Dalmais, Hervé, *Truffaut*, Paris, 1987.
Cahoreau, Gilles, *François Truffaut: 1932–1984*, Paris, 1989.
Brunette, Peter, editor, *Shoot the Piano Player: François Truffaut, Director*, New Brunswick, 1993.
Le Berre, Carole, *François Truffaut*, Paris, 1993.
Truffaut, François, *The Films in My Life*, Cutchogue, 1994.
Holmes, Diana, and Robert Ingram, *François Truffaut*, Manchester, 1998.
Labarthe, André S., *La nouvelle vague: Claude Chabrol, Jean-Luc Godard, Jacques Rivette, Eric Rohmer, François Truffaut/textes et entretiens parus dans les Cahiers du cinéma, réunis par Antoine de Baecque et Charles Tesson*, Paris, 1999.
Jacob, Gilles, *François Truffaut: Correspondence, 1945–1984*, Lanham, 2000.

Articles:

Marcorelles, L., ''Interview with François Truffaut,'' in *Sight and Sound* (London), Winter 1961–62.
Truffaut, François, in *Films and Filming* (London), no. 10, 1962.
''Conversation with François Truffaut,'' in *New York Film Bulletin*, no. 3, 1962.
Delahaye, Michel, ''Les Tourbillons élémentaires,'' in *Cahiers du Cinéma* (Paris), March 1962.
Sarris, Andrew, in *Village Voice* (New York), 3 May 1962.
Baker, Peter, in *Films and Filming* (London), June 1962.
Roud, Richard, in *Sight and Sound* (London), Summer 1962.

Tyler, Parker, in *Film Culture* (New York), Summer 1962.

Stanbrook, Alan, "The Stars They Couldn't Photograph," in *Films and Filming* (London), February 1963.

Graham, Peter, "The Face of '62—France," in *Films and Filming* (London), May 1963.

Greenspan, Roger, in *Sight and Sound* (London), Spring 1963.

Shatnoff, Judith, "François Truffaut: The Anarchist Imagination," in *Film Quarterly* (Berkeley), Spring 1963.

Klein, Michael, "The Literary Sophistication of François Truffaut," in *Film Comment* (New York), Summer 1965.

Solomon, Stanley, in *Film Heritage* (Dayton, Ohio), Winter 1965–66.

Rosenblatt, Daniel, in *Film Society Review* (New York), November 1968.

Houston, Beverley, and Marsha Kinder, "Truffaut's Gorgeous Killers," in *Film Quarterly* (Berkeley), Winter 1973–74.

Coffee, Barbara, "Art and Film in François Truffaut's *Jules and Jim* and *Two English Girls*," in *Film Heritage* (Dayton, Ohio), Spring 1974.

Mast, Gerald, "From *400 Blows* to *Small Change*," in *New Republic* (New York), 2 April 1977.

Thiher, A., "The Existential Play in Truffaut's Early Films," in *Literature/Film Quarterly* (Salisbury, Maryland), Summer 1977.

Davidson, D., "From Virgin to Dynamo: The 'Amoral Woman' in European Cinema," in *Cinema Journal* (Evanston, Illinois), Fall 1981.

Marinero, F., in *Casablanca* (Madrid), May 1982.

Carreno, J. M., in *Casablanca* (Madrid), February 1984.

Norman, Barry, "Barry Norman on" in *Radio Times* (London), vol. 273, no. 3572, 13 June 1992.

Murphy, K., "La belle dame sans merci," in *Film Comment* (New York), November-December 1992.

Stonehill, B., "Les auteurs terribles," in *Film Comment* (New York), November-December 1992.

Flitterman-Lewis, S., "Fascination, Friendship, and the 'Eternal Feminine' or the Discursive Production of (Cinematic) Desire," in *French Review*, vol. 66, no. 6, 1993.

Garcin, J., "*Jules et Jim*: François Truffaut," in *Cahiers du Cinéma* (Paris), Hors-série, 1993.

Lucas, Tim, "*The 400 Blows/Jules et Jim*," in *Video Watchdog* (Cincinnati), no. 19, September-October 1993.

Crowdus, Gary, "Truffaut on Laserdisc," in *Cineaste* (New York), vol. 20, no. 3, 1994.

Dalle Ore, F., "A Voice in the Dark: Feminine Figuration in Truffaut's *Jules et Jim*," in *Literature/Film Quarterly* (Salisbury), vol. 22, no. 4, October 1994.

Landrot, Marine, "La chambre ouverte," in *Télérama* (Paris), no. 2340, 16 November 1994.

Andrew, Geoff, "Rum Truffaut," in *Time Out* (London), no. 1350, 3 July 1996.

* * *

Jules and Jim is among the masterpieces of the French New Wave and may be considered the high achievement of that movement. The first films of Truffaut, Godard, Chabrol & Co. had astonished the world with a vitality that seemed evanescent, while too many of the films after 1962 are generally thought to be decadent and cloying in their search for novel effects. But with *Jules and Jim* we have a film that is at once vital, astonishing, and mature. Its solidity as well as its richness have kept it from fading even under the intense light of scholarship and criticism to which it has been continually subject.

In some respects it is not a characteristic New Wave film, for it chronicles 30 years in the lives of its characters, opening brightly in La Belle Epoche and closing in the grim era of the Depression and the rise of Hitler. Whereas most New Wave films sought to express the rhythms of their own epoch with complete freshness, Truffaut in this film retreated to the past. But in its own way *Jules and Jim* is faithful to the existentialist ethic and aesthetic of the New Wave period, for no film strives more obviously for authenticity in its quest to tap the feelings of a liberated generation whose morality must be achieved on the run.

Oddly, it was through the intermediary of a 75-year-old sensibility, that of novelist Henri-Pierre Roché, that Truffaut was able to shape this past into a pure picture of his own generation. When he read the novel upon its publication in 1955, he immediately contacted Roché, initiating a correspondence that continued until the latter's death which occurred just before the film went into production. Of course in 1955 Truffaut was but a minor critic who could only dream of the film this novel might become. Nevertheless, even at that time he mentioned it as an example of the kind of living, breathing story he claimed was missing from the moribund "Cinema of Quality" which dominated the 1950s in France.

What was it that gave this novel its vigor, and how did Truffaut succeed in letting its spirit animate his film when at length he was able to make it? One must begin with the plethora of incidents spilling out of the novel's first pages. While Truffaut has drastically reduced their number and, more certainly, the number of characters he introduces, both works dizzy their audience. La Belle Epoche is carefree and exciting as lived through Jules and Jim. It becomes more dangerous and even more exciting once they attach themselves to Katherine.

The bubbling first third of the film is a textbook in photographic and editing effects (stop frame, swish pans, stock footage, jump cuts). Only the narrator who ties together these fragments hints wistfully at the trouble to come. The film makes its inevitable descent just as Katherine accepts Jules' marriage proposal. For his dream has been attained on the eve of the outbreak of the Great War, a war so graphically documented that it brutalizes the earlier sentiments of the film, tossing its characters off their merry-go-round where they land, still and stunned. This second movement shows the reality of living with Katherine, the dream they had so hectically pursued. Her fickleness makes them prisoners of their own desires, and their imaginations, still rich with inventiveness, are tethered to one who is neither beautiful nor intelligent but for whom they would surrender their lives because she is pure woman (spontaneous, tender, cruel). The conclusion is more sombre still, as each character achieves a compensating wisdom, a sense of self. Katherine is both fire and water, the vitriol she pours down the sink. She chooses water for death, cremation for burial. Jim is romantic, a dashing Parisian novelist who travels after the war in search of the 20th century. Comfortable with his shifting feelings, he runs from Gilberte to Katherine whenever she calls him. Finally there is Jules who treasures their lives to the full. A Buddhist in sensibility, he possesses Katherine through patience. An entomologist, he would write of the loves that insects aspire to. Nothing is too small for his attention. His resignation and nostalgia place him nearest the narrator, as he looks back at a time when life was full of freedom and promise.

If the film's plot is a progressive decline, its images set off these oppositions at every turn. The film's first enthusiasts pointed to the interplay of circles and triangles. The lovers directly illustrate the triangle they are living as they welcome the morning from three separate windows at the seashore. The sharp angular pans of the camera keep us wondering in which direction love must flow. But it is the spinning circularity of the cinemascope most viewers recall, a circularity repeated in the cafe tables, the tadpoles swimming round their bowl, in Katherine's cosmology which holds the world to be an inverted bowl. Bicycles are in circles; Sabine rolls over and over to the music which culminates in Katherine's prophetic song, her ''Rondo of love.''

These two master graphic forms come together, Roger Greenspun observed, in the hourglass measuring out the final days of La Belle Epoche and the preciousness of the briefest instants of life. Art is another such measure, and *Jules and Jim* is a catalogue of the arts. Scattered through its texture are references to old films, to photography and slideshows, to statues, paintings, novels, the theater, and music. This is a story about the drive to raise life to art and art to eternity. In the abundance of its episodes, symbols, citations, and tales, and in its mixture of excitement and resignation, *Jules and Jim* never lets up in its own drive to give meaning to and express the vitality of life. This was the ambition of the New Wave, and this film is its apotheosis.

—Dudley Andrew

KAAGAZ KE PHOOL

(Paper Flowers)

India, 1959

Director: Guru Dutt

Production: Guru Dutt Films Pvt. Ltd.; colour, 35mm; CinemaScope (first Indian CinemaScope production); running time: 150 minutes.

Producer: Guru Dutt; **screenplay and dialogue:** Abrar Alvi; **photography:** V. K. Murthy; **editor:** Y. G. Chauhan; **art director:** M. R. Achrekar; **sound:** S. V. Rama; **music:** S. D. Burman; **songs:** Kaifi Azmi; **costumes:** Bhanumati.

Cast: Baby Naaz (*Pammy*); Venna (*Bina*); Mahesh Kaul (*Father-in-law*); Waheeda Rehman (*Shanti*); Guru Dutt (*Suresh Sinha*); Johnny Walker (*Bina's brother-in-law*); Minoo Mumtaz; Pratima Devi; Niloufer; Sulochana; Sheila Vaz; Bikram Kapoor; Mehmood; Mohan Choti; Haroun; Munshi Munaqqa; V. Ratra; Tony Walker; Tun Tun.

Publications

Books:

Khopkar, Arun, *Guru Dutt: A Three Act Tragedy*, Marathi, n.d.

Rangoonwala, Firoze, *Guru Dutt 1925–1965: A Monograph*, Poona, 1973.

Micciollo, Henri, *Guru Dutt*, Paris, 1978.

Burra, Rani, editor, *Looking Back, 1896–1960*, New Delhi, 1981.

Gandhy, Behroze, and Paul Willeman, *Indian Cinema*, London, 1982.

Banerjee, Shampa, *Profiles: Five Film-makers from India: V. Shantaram, Raj Kapoor, Mrinal Sen, Guru Dutt, Ritwik Ghatak*, New Delhi, 1985.

Kabir, Nasreen M., *Guru Dutt: A Life in Cinema*, New York, 1996, 1998.

Articles:

Padukone, Vasanthi, ''My Son Gurudutt,'' in *Imprint*, April 1979.

Blanchet, C., *Cinéma* (Paris), December 1984.

Bassan, R., ''Une autopsie du monde du spectacle,'' in *Revue du Cinéma* (Paris), December 1984.

Ostria, V., ''L'ombre d'un Dutt,'' in *Cahiers du Cinéma* (Paris), December 1984.

Niogret, H., ''Les moyens de l'emotion,'' in *Positif* (Paris), January 1985.

Mishra, V., ''Decentering History: Some Versions of Bombay Cinema,'' in *East-West Film Journal* (Honolulu), vol. 6, no. 1, 1992.

Rajadhyaskaha, Ashish, ''The Epic Melodrama: Themes of Nationality in Indian Cinema,'' in *Journal of Arts and Ideas*, nos. 25–26, 1993.

Khan, Pervaiz, Nasreen Munni Kabir, and Ashish Rajadhyaksha, ''The Song Picture Man,'' in *Sight & Sound* (London), vol. 4, no. 10, October 1994.

* * *

Guru Dutt's *tour de force*, *Kaagaz Ke Phool*, is a tale of a movie director who reflects on his life. Unhappily married to Bina, mainly because her elitist, colonial family cannot reconcile themselves to his career in the degraded movie industry, Suresh Sinha falls in love with a young orphaned woman, Shanti. He makes her into a famous movie star, and gossip journals suggest a romantic liaison between the two. Sinha's daughter Pammy, who believes that her parents can reconcile their differences if Shanti were to quit films, gets Shanti to promise to disappear from Sinha's life. However, her disappearance only leads to a rapid decline in Sinha's fortunes. Refusing to face Shanti in his impoverished condition, Sinha eventually dies sitting on the director's chair in a gigantic, womb-like studio interior.

The plot is often seen as Dutt's autobiography, and to some extent derives its astonishing power in the director/lead star's extraordinary impersonation of the tragic hero, rejected as it were by fate itself—as suggested in the opening musical refrain (*Waqt hai meharbaan*) and repeated throughout the film. The persona continues from Dutt's previous work, *Pyaasa*, where he plays a romantic poet exiled from the world and believed dead while his oppressors celebrate his greatness.

Such an idiom—of the romantic melodrama—was well established especially in the Hindi cinema when the film was made. Critics generally accept that the idiom, which I have elsewhere (1993) called the ''epic melodrama,'' emerged in the context of Indian nationalism, especially as the utopian dimension of the freedom struggle gave way to a coercive state, corruption, mass culture, and to the despair that Dutt, better than any other filmmaker, expresses in *Pyaasa* with his lines: ''This land of castles, thrones and crowns/ . . . /Burn this land/ Blow it away/Remove it from my sight'' (*Yeh mehlon ki duniya*). To a great extent Dutt, as actor, comes in line with the previous male stars reflecting this infantile Oedipal longing, with images built up over a body of work: Dilip Kumar (e.g. in *Deedar*, 1951, where he blinds himself), Raj Kapoor, the outcast of modern society. *Kaagaz Ke Phool* in fact refers directly to what is considered by some as the origin of this romantic stereotype: Devdas, a Saratchandra literary character filmed by P. C. Barua with K. L. Saigal in 1935, and then by Bimal Roy with Dilip Kumar in 1955. The fictional Suresh Sinha is in fact directing a *Devdas* version, and is desperately looking for an ideal Paro when he chances upon Shanti.

Kaagaz Ke Phool however, took that tradition of romantic melodrama onto a wholly new, and unprecedented plane, and to see how it did so, we need only to continue with the sequence of how Sinha discovers Shanti. He has been rejected by his wife and by his haughty father-in-law, and stands beneath a tree to shelter himself from the rain. Shanti, standing next to him and shivering in the cold, receives a gift of his overcoat, and later, arrives on his film set to return that coat. She intrudes onto Sinha's frame, and in an extraordinary follow-up, is seen in close-up in the director's editing room where he realizes that she is the star he is waiting for.

That sequence spins throughout the film a whole dimension of cinematic space, as shown by the two extraordinary and justly celebrated scenes of Sinha and Shanti standing apart in a cavernous studio, lit centrally by a straightforward metaphoric beam, as their disembodied spirits emerge and unite; and at the end when the director dies in that very space. It extends into one of the most sophisticated crane movements in what was India's first full CinemaScope film, constantly dramatizing the conflict between open and constricted spaces, spaces controlled by the director and spaces constraining him, spaces that he can enter and those from which he is excluded.

It also extends into the poet Kaifi Azmi's remarkable songs, set to music by Burman and picturized in an unprecedentedly new idiom by Dutt. The best known is of course the *Waqt hai meharbaan* which resurfaces, e.g. when the director, reduced to being an extra on a movie set, faces a giant stone eagle, and then escapes from Shanti even as nature generates a storm of protest all around him. The songs, especially, evoke something like a Sufi idiom, of the tragedy of unreachable, unattainable desire, and in the process also rescue the film from the sentimentalism that afflicts several other filmmakers working in the idiom of romantic melodrama—notably Kidar Sharma.

The film, it might be added, was a commercial failure when it was first released, prompting Dutt to not sign his future productions. Over the years it has, however, become something of a cult movie, notably for its songs and their picturization.

—Ashish Rajadhyaksha

DAS KABINETT DES DR. CALIGARI

(The Cabinet of Dr. Caligari)

Germany, 1920

Director: Robert Wiene

Production: Decla Filmgellschaft (Berlin); black and white, 35mm, silent, originally tinted in green, brown, and steely-blue; length: 4682 feet. Released February 1920, Berlin. Filmed Winter 1919 in Decla studios; cost $18,000.

Producer: Erich Pommer; **screenplay:** Carl Mayer and Hans Janowitz, from an original story by Carl Mayer and Hans Janowitz; **photography:** Willy Hameister; **production designers:** Hermann Warm, Walter Reimann, and Walter Röhrig; **costume designer:** Walter Reimann.

Cast: Werner Krauss (*Dr. Caligari*); Conrad Veidt (*Cesare*); Friedrich Feher (*Francis*); Lil Dagover (*Jane*); Hans Heinz von Twardowski (*Alan*); Rudolf Lettinger (*Dr. Olsen*); Rudolph Klein-Rogge (*Criminal*).

Publications

Script:

Mayer, Carl, and Hans Janowitz, *The Cabinet of Dr. Caligari*, edited by Robert Adkinson, New York, 1972; also included in *Masterworks of the German Cinema*, edited by Roger Manvell, London and New York, 1973.

Books:

Kracauer, Siegfried, *From Caligari to Hitler: A Psychological History of the German Cinema*, Princeton, 1947.
Wollenberg, Hans H., *50 Years of German Cinema*, London, 1948.
Huaco, George A., *The Sociology of Film Art*, New York, 1965.
Eisner, Lotte, *The Haunted Screen*, Berkeley, 1969.
Manvell, Roger, and Heinrich Fraenkel, *The German Cinema*, New York, 1971.
Everson, William K., *Classics of the Horror Film*, Secaucus, New Jersey, 1974.
Laqueur, Walter, *Weimar: A Cultural History 1918–1933*, New York, 1974.
Prawer, S. S., *Caligari's Children: The Film as Tale of Terror*, New York, and Oxford, 1980.
Barton, John D., *German Expressionist Film*, Boston, 1982.
Brunner, Stephen Eric, and Douglas Kenner, *Passion and Rebellion: The Expressionist Heritage*, London, 1983.
Budd, Mike, editor, *The Cabinet of Dr. Caligari: Texts, Contexts, Histories*, New Brunswick, New Jersey, 1990.
Hardt, Ursula, *From Caligari to California: Eric Pommer's Life in the International Film Wars*, New York, 1996.
Robinson, David, *Das Cabinet des Dr. Caligari*, London, 1998.
Jung, Uli, and Walter Schatzberg, *Beyond Caligari: The Films of Robert Wiene*, New York, 1999.

Articles:

New York Times, 4 April 1921.
Variety (New York), 8 April 1921.
Kracauer, Siegfried, in *Partisan Review* (New Brunswick, New Jersey), March-April 1947.
Melnitz, William, ''Aspects of War and Revolution in the Theater and Film of the Weimar Republic,'' in *Hollywood Quarterly*, no.3, 1948–49.
Luft, Herbert, in *Quarterly of Film, Radio, and Television* (Berkeley), Summer 1954.

Das Kabinett des Dr. Caligari

Pegge, C. Denis, ''*Caligari*: Its Innovations in Editing,'' in *Quarterly of Film, Radio, and Television* (Berkeley), Winter 1956.

Lightman, Herb A., ''From *Caligari* to *Caligari*,'' in *American Cinematographer* (Hollywood), July 1962.

Whitford, Frank, ''Expressionism in the Cinema,'' in *Studio International* (Lugano), January 1970.

Helman, A., ''Robert Wiene czyli pozory niefilmowosci,'' in *Kino* (Warsaw), April 1974.

Clement, Catherine, ''Les Charlatans et les hysteriques,'' in *Communications* (Paris), no.23, 1975.

''*Caligari* et la critique,'' in *Avant-Scène du Cinéma* (Paris), July-September 1975.

Carroll, Noël, ''The Cabinet of Dr. Kracauer,'' in *Millenium* (New York), no. 2, Spring-Summer 1978.

Budd, M., ''Retrospective Narration in Film: Re-Reading *The Cabinet of Dr. Caligari*,'' in *Film Criticism* (Edinboro, Pennsylvania), no.1, 1979.

Combs, Richard, in *Monthly Film Bulletin* (London), June 1979.

Mazowa, M., ''Sleepwalking Through Weimar,'' in *Stills* (London), Spring 1981.

Budd, M., in *Ciné-Tracts* (Montreal), Winter 1981.

Warm, Hermann, ''Naissance de Caligari: Les Trois Lumières,'' in *Cinématographe* (Paris), February 1982.

Simsolo, Noël, in *Image et Son* (Paris), October 1982.

Cardullo, B., ''Expressionism and the Real Cabinet of Dr. Caligari,'' in *Film Criticism* (Edinboro, Pennsylvania), Winter 1982.

Tomasulo, F., ''*Cabinet of Dr. Caligari*: History/Psychoanalysis/ Cinema,'' in *On Film* (Los Angeles), Summer 1983.

Budd, Michael, ''Authorship as a Commodity: The Art Cinema and *The Cabinet of Dr. Caligari*,'' in *Wide Angle* (Athens, Ohio), vol.6, no.1, 1984.

Gout, C., in *Skoop* (Amsterdam), September-October 1984.

Ahlander, L., ''Filmhistoriskt nytt: *Dr. Caligari* och *Queen Kelly*,'' in *Chaplin* (Stockholm), 1985.

Williams, D., ''*The Cabinet of Dr. Caligari:* The Remake,'' in *Film Threat* (Beverly Hills), no. 20, 1989.

Weihsmann, H., ''Die vierte dimension—architektur im film,'' in *Blimp* (Graz, Austria), Summer 1989.

Schneider, I., ''Deus ex animo, or Why a Doc?,'' in *Journal of Popular Film and Television* (Washington, D.C.), no. 1, 1990.

Cappabianca, A., ''Cine/archeologia,'' in *Filmcritica* (Rome), November 1990.

Kuleshov, L., "*Caligari, Mr. West, Aelita:* Trois conceptions du film nuet," in *Positif* (Paris), January 1991.

Pratt, D. B., "Fit Food for Madhouse Inmates: The Box Office Reception of the German Invasion of 1921," in *Griffithiana* (Gemona, Italy), October 1993.

* * *

The Cabinet of Dr. Caligari is usually identified as the first significant German Expressionist film, exemplifying the narrative and visual traits of that movement. The primary story concerns a series of murders which occur in a German town, coinciding with the arrival of Dr. Caligari who runs a side-show at the local fair. Alan and Francis, friends and rivals for the affection of the same woman, Jane, witness his show; there the somnambulist Cesare predicts the future, and forecasts Alan's impending death. That night, Alan is murdered. Francis pursues the mysterious Caligari as Cesare kidnaps Jane. In the ensuing chase, Cesare collapses and dies. The investigation then leads to a local asylum from which Cesare has reportedly escaped. Dr. Caligari is discovered to be the director of the hospital, gone mad in his obsessive efforts to re-enact an 18th century showman's murders-by-proxy. This story is presented as the narrative account of Francis. The film opens in a park; Francis sits with another man as Jane, in a trance-like state, walks by. To explain her condition, Francis recounts the bizarre events of the central story. At the end of the film, the scene returns to Francis, who is revealed to be an inmate at the asylum. His doctor is actually the Caligari figure from his tale. Upon hearing Francis's ravings in the courtyard, the doctor declares that he now understands the case.

The history of the framing device is well known, and is discussed by Siegfried Kracauer in his study of post-World War I German cinema, *From Caligari to Hitler*. It was not a part of the initial script, by Carl Mayer and Hans Janowitz, but was presumably added by the producer Erich Pommer. According to Kracauer this framing contrivance served to contain the inherent horror of the original story. A study of authoritative madness and abusive power was recast as the delusion of an insane narrator; the evil doctor was re-defined as a benign, ministering figure who can cure the lunatic. At the same time Kracauer sees the final film as a powerful expression of the inherent tensions of the collective German psyche of the period—the fear that individual freedom will lead to rampant chaos which can only be constrained by submission to tyrannical authority. If the original script depicted the potential abuses of absolute authority, the framing scenes concede to this authority and suggest it may be beneficial.

But the narrative significance of the film is not necessarily an either/or proposition as Kracauer suggests. The film does start by presenting Francis as a credible narrator. His reliability as a source is only called into question in the final scenes. In this sense the film is more equivocal and expresses a more disturbed sensibility than even Kracauer allows. Indeed, the film simultaneously presents at least two viewpoints on the depicted events: 1) Francis is in fact mad and his story totally or partially delusional; 2) Francis is a reliable source, a position assumed through most of the film. From this second perspective the director of the asylum might be considered a psychotic tyrant whose power extends to include Francis' confinement. One is not, however, led directly to this conclusion. Rather, this version of the narrative causes a disruption of any stable or conclusive perception of character status and narrational authority within the film. This in turn opens the film to a range of possible readings. The film has been seen, for example, in terms of a female fantasy, focusing on Jane as the enigmatic source of the narrative.

In other words, the film is structured in such a way that it represents contradictory ways of understanding the central sequence of events. This is supported by the consistency of the film's mise-en-scène. The artificiality and stylized exaggeration of acting, decor, and lighting are maintained throughout the film. There are no visual cues to indicate that the world of the framed tale of past events is different from the framing scenes in the asylum. The film's visual style is crucial to its exemplary status within the context of the German Expressionist film movement. In *The Haunted Screen* Lotte Eisner explains that the overall design scheme of the film creates a pervasive feeling of anxiety and terror. It is characterized by extreme contrasts in light and dark, distorted angles, exaggerated perspective and scalar relations within the decor, and painted backdrops and shadows. The basic tone of the decor extends to costume and make-up.

These qualities came to be known as the defining stylistic trait of German Expressionist film. Some critics have argued that German film producers consciously adopted this "arty" style to differentiate German film from other national cinemas (notably American) in order to compete in the international film market. Others have stressed the fact that this movement expresses the troubled state of the German national psyche after the war, or represents a retreat to Romantic despair. In addition, the film's artificiality and subversion of realistic codes of representation have led to discussion of the film as an early example of self-reflexivity and deconstructive processes in the cinema.

The film's equivocal narrative and visual stylization combine to create a disturbing fictional world. Moreover, its position in German cinema, and in German history, makes it a compelling case for examining relations between films and their social context. In these terms *The Cabinet of Dr. Caligari* provides a wealth of material to be mined by film critics and historians.

—M.B. White

KAMERADSCHAFT

(Comradeship)

France-Germany, 1931

Director: G. W. Pabst

Production: Nero-Film (Berlin) and Gaumont-Franco (Paris), the collaboration of these two companies frequently referred to as Nero-Film AG; black and white, 35mm; running time: 85 minutes, French version is 93 minutes, length: 3060 feet (German version). Released 1931.

Producer: Seymour Nebenzel; **screenplay:** Ladislaus (Laszlo) Vajda, Karl Otten, Peter Martin Lampel and Fritz Eckardt, from a story by

Kameradschaft

Karl Otten; **photography:** Fritz Arno Wagner and Robert Baberski; **editor:** Hans Oser; **sound recordist:** A. Jansen; **production designers:** Ernö Metzner and Karl Vollbrecht; **French advisor:** Robert Beaudoin.

Cast: Alexander Granach (*Kaspar*); Fritz Kampers (*Wilderer*); Daniel Mendaille (*Pierre*); Ernst Busch (*Kaplan*); Elisabeth Wendt (*Françoise*); Gustav Püttjer (*Jean*); Oskar Höcker (*Emile*); Hélèna Manson (*Albert's wife*); Andrée Ducret (*François*); Alex Bernard (*Grandfather*); Pierre Louis (*George*).

Publications

Script:

Otten, Karl, and others, *Kameradschaft*, in *Le Cinema réaliste allemande*, edited by Raymond Borde, Lyons, 1963.

Books:

Kracauer, Siegfried, *From Caligari to Hitler: A Psychological History of the German Film*, Princeton, 1947.
Joseph, Rudolpf, editor, *Der Regisseur: G. W. Pabst*, Munich, 1963.
Buache, Freddy, *G. W. Pabst*, Lyons, 1965.
Amengual, Barthélemy, *Georg Wilhelm Pabst*, Paris, 1966.
Aubry, Yves, and Jacques Pétat, ''G. W. Pabst,'' in *Anthologie du Cinéma 4*, Paris, 1968.
Eisner, Lotte, *The Haunted Screen*, Berkeley, 1969.
Manvell, Roger, and Heinrich Fraenkel, *The German Cinema*, New York, 1971.
Atwell, Lee, *G.W. Pabst*, Boston, 1977.
Barth, Hermann, *Psychagogische Strategien des Filmischen Diskurses in G. W. Pabst's Kameradschaft*, Munich, 1990.

Articles:

Metzner, Ernö, in *Close Up* (London), March 1932.
New Statesman and Nation (London), 5 March 1932.
Spectator (London), 12 March 1932.
New York Times, 9 November 1932.
Variety (New York), 15 November 1932.
Potamkin, Harry A., ''Pabst and the Social Film,'' in *Hound and Horn* (New York), January-March 1933.
Manvell, Roger, in *Sight and Sound* (London), November 1950.
''Pabst Issue'' of *Filmkunst* (Vienna), no. 18, 1955.
''Pabst Issue'' of *Cinemages* (New York), May 1955.
Image et Son (Paris), November 1960.
Cineforum (Bergamo), no. 14, 1962.
Luft, Herbert, ''G. W. Pabst,'' in *Films in Review* (New York), February 1964.
Luft, Herbert, ''G. W. Pabst,'' in *Films and Filming* (London), April 1967.
Pulleine, Tim, in *Monthly Film Bulletin* (London), March 1978.
Carroll, N., ''Lang, Pabst, and Sound,'' in *Ciné-Tracts* (Montreal), Fall 1978.
Filmkunst (Vienna), no. 86, 1980.
Cinématographe (Paris), February 1981.
Sauvaget, D., in *Image et Son* (Paris), March 1981.
''*Kameradschaft* oder Neoverismo anno 1931,'' in *Filmkunst* (Vienna), no. 124, 1990.

* * *

Kameradschaft is a noble film—in theme and execution. It reflects the proletarian idealism of its time. It smacks of Toller and Rolland, and like them it has at the back of its mind a shadow of doubt. In 1931 in Germany events were moving slowly to the rise of Hitler, which all the good will in the world could not stop, and the film does in fact end on an ironic note.

The action turns on a single event. On the borders of France and Germany a vein of coal cuts through the frontier. Above ground a frontier post separates two communities; in the mine a brick wall separates the German and French workers. From the very first shots of boys quarrelling over a game of marbles to those of three German workers who decide to spend a Saturday night in a French dance hall, the director G. W. Pabst sets the mood of the film. Action is sparked off when an explosion in the French mine is reported to the German miners as they stand naked in the great shower room with their clothes raised above the sprinklers by chains. Ernst Busch, their spokesman, decides to lead a rescue party which ultimately breaks through the frontier barrier and arrives at the gates of the French mine to the astonishment of the waiting and despairing relatives. ''Les Allemands. Ce n'est pas possible.'' The rest of the film is concerned with the rescue.

Pabst has stamped the exterior and interior of the mine with uncompromising realism. The people are the protagonists, and individual characters never leave the ambience which shapes them and to which they belong. With the brilliant cooperation of his designer, Ernö Metzner, Pabst has achieved a triumph of studio construction. Life in the mine and the terror of the disaster are translated into film terms that remain unforgettable. No music is used. The noises of the mine, the clanking of chains, metal rubbing against metal, the whirring sounds of lifts—all this brings the strange world of the miner vividly before the spectator. It is a shared and illuminated experience. Pabst's great humanity shines through the film. Its technical virtuosity is no less. Wagner's camera catches the light shining in darkness, follows the ravaged, terrified faces. It gives significance to darkness.

There is no plot as such. Human relations are hinted at. But the mine disaster leaves us in no doubt as to those relationships: Françoise and her lover; The old man and his grandson; The three German friends. All are people we know, and from the event Pabst creates a richly textured canvas of life and reality.

Faces haunt us. The hysterical miner, tap tapping a signal on metal pipe, who hears the guttural sounds of his German rescuer wearing a gasmask; he thinks he is back in the war and hurls himself on his rescuer. Anna dragging her child beside the lorry that carries her husband to the dangers of rescue work. The actors do not play in this film; they are embedded in it.

The technical problems of creating movement in a narrow space were superbly overcome, as were the problems of proportioning light in dark areas. But above all it is the great spirit of Pabst that is the real triumph of the film.

Sadly, as the miners celebrate their new found friendship—''Why must we cooperate only at times of disaster. Why not every day''—below ground the brick wall which was smashed to allow the German rescuers through is rebuilt with much official rubber-stamping and exchanging of documents. A new shadow was falling on the German people.

—Liam O'Leary

KANAL

(Canal)

Poland, 1957

Director: Andrzej Wajda

Production: Film Polski and ZAF; black and white, 35mm; running time: 95 minutes, some sources list 97 minutes; length: 8569 feet. Released April 1957. Filmed 1957 in Poland.

Producer: Stanisław Adler; **screenplay:** Jerzy Stefan Stawiński, from a short story by Jerzy Stawiński; **photography:** Jerzy Lipman; **art directors:** Roman Mann and Roman Wołzniec; **music:** Jan Krenz, ocarina theme by Adam Pawlikowski.

Cast: Wieńczysław Gliński (*Lt. Zadra*); Tadeusz Janczar (*Korab*); Teresa Izewski (*Stokrotka*); Emil Karewicz (*Madry*); Włdysła Sheybal (*Composer*); Tadeusz Gwiazdowski (*Kula*); Stanisław Mikulski (*Slim*); Teresa Berezowska (*Halinka*); Adam Pawlikowski (*German officer*).

Award: Cannes Film Festival, Special Prize, 1957.

Publications

Script:

Stawinski, Jerzy Stefan, *Kanal*, in *Three Films by Andrzej Wajda*, New York, 1973.

Books:

Rhode, Eric, *Tower of Babel: Speculations on the Cinema*, New York, 1967.

Geduld, Harry M., editor, *Film Makers on Filmmaking*, Bloomington, Indiana, 1967.

McArthur, Colin, editor, *Andrzej Wajda: Polish Cinema*, London, 1970.

Michatek, Boleslaw, *The Cinema of Andrzej Wajda*, London, 1973.

Stoil, Michael Jon, *Cinema Beyond the Danube: The Camera and Politics*, Metuchen, New Jersey, 1974.

Leihm, Mira, and Antonin Liehm, *The Most Important Art: East European Film After 1945*, Berkeley, 1977.

Douin, Jean-Luc, *Wajda*, Paris, 1981.

Paul, David W., editor, *Politics, Art, and Commitment in the Eastern European Cinema*, New York, 1983.

Wajda, Andrzej, *Un Cinéma nommé désir*, Paris, 1986.

Wajda, Andrzej, *Wajda on Film: A Master's Notes*, Los Angeles, 1989.

Wajda, Andrzej, *Double Vision: My Life in Film*, New York, 1989.

Articles:

Wajda, Andrzej, ''Destroying the Commonplace,'' in *Films and Filming* (London), November 1961.

Higham, Charles, ''Grasping the Nettle: The Films of Andrzej Wajda,'' in *Hudson Review* (New York), Autumn 1965.

''Wajda Issue'' of *Etudes Cinématographiques* (Paris), no. 69–72, 1968.

Hauru, A., ''Kanal—kirottujen tie,'' in *Filmihullu* (Helsinki), no. 2, 1979.

Holloway, Ronald, in *Variety* (New York), 5 September 1979.

''Wajda Issue'' of *Avant-Scène du Cinéma* (Paris), 1 January 1980.

''Andrzej Wajda,'' in *Village Voice* (New York), 20 December 1981.

''Andrzej Wajda,'' in *Current Biography Yearbook*, New York, 1982.

Kanal

Lewis, Clifford, and Carroll Britch, ''Andrzej Wajda's War Trilogy: A Retrospective,'' in *Film Criticism* (Meadville, Pennsylvania), Spring 1986.

Bukoski, A., ''Wajda's *Kanal* and Mrozek's *Tango*,'' in *Literature/ Film Quarterly* (Salisbury, Maryland), no. 2, 1992.

* * *

Kanal, Andrzej Wajda's second film, is based on a story by Jerzy Stefan Stawiński which appeared in the magazine *Twórczość*. The events of the story are drawn from the writer's personal experience. Stawiński had taken part in two battles for Warsaw, as an 18-year-old in 1939 and then in the Warsaw Uprising of 1944.

Wajda quite purposely renounced any possibility of producing an exhaustive chronicle of the Uprising or commemorative poem on the heroic insurgents. His approach to examining this event was different. From the outset he limited himself to the time in which the story itself is set. The Uprising lasted 63 days, and he followed his heroes from the fifty-seventh day, just a few days and nights before the Uprising was suppressed. Defeat is present in the film from the introductory commentary which presents the individual characters: ''These are the main heroic tragedies. Watch them closely; these are the last hours of their lives.'' It is from this point of view that we see the unfolding story of one group of fighters who are no longer able to hold off the enemy and must retreat through underground sewers.

The film is structured in two parts which differ from one another in their use of cinematic techniques. The first part is documentary in nature. It acquaints the viewer with the heroes and briefly conveys something of their lot before the Uprising. The camera follows them through everyday situations: they prepare their food, shave, make love, and talk about their loved ones and about their past. The effects of the war are ever present as these apparently everyday moments occur amid the ruins of the city where not a single house has been left standing. The war itself intrudes only with occasional explosions and small-scale attacks. This relative quiet is expressed through long takes, tracking shots and the use of only a minimum of detail. The actual tragedy commences only after the group has withdrawn underground. There is also a change in the style of representation, which takes on an expressive eloquence; the lighting changes, there are more contrasts of light and dark, the camera focuses on the heroes in detail, the sequences of reality alternate with scenes that have symbolic meaning. A comparison of the two parts brings out the specific use of sound, light, and darkness.

Above ground in the film's beginning, the basic component of the soundtrack is the staccato of firearms, while underground the sound component is far richer—the distorted voices of the heroes, dissonant sounds which the viewer is often unable to identify, even a solitary harmonic note of an ocarina. Here, sound has the extra function of heightening the drama, for the underground odyssey must take place in absolute stillness so that the insurgents do not betray their positions to the Germans who are lurking above. Light and shadow play a similar role. The first part is depicted in light, non-contrasting shades of grey, while darkness and sharp flashes of light are assigned to the underground sequences. Traditionally, the light/sun is a symbol of hope. For Wajda, the symbol has the opposite meaning, for the fulfilment of longing for light would mean death for the heroes. Therefore, at the conclusion both symbolic meanings—light as good, darkness as threat—flow together and empty into tragedy; both extremes of the light spectrum bring the ineluctable ending.

Kanal had its Polish premiere in the spring of 1957, the same year it was introduced at the International Festival at Cannes, where it won a prize. Its reception abroad was decidedly positive, while its appearance in Poland stirred discussions that included both positive and negative views. The country still had a tragic reminder of the Uprising; people who had been direct participants in this tragedy of modern history were still living. Their attitude towards the film was sometimes too uncompromising; they wanted it to be a literal depiction of what they had experienced. However, Wajda could not make such a film. He emphasized his personal approach as a director by presenting the experiences of a specific group of people whom he divests of heroism but does not condemn, for they chose their fate freely and fought not for glory but against bondage and enslavement, and paid the highest price.

Kanal occupies a crucial position in the Polish cinema. It ushered in a series of films noted for their sober view of the myths engendered by the war and the Uprising. From this standpoint the film is similar in function to a declaration of policy.

—B. Urgošíkova

KAOS

Italy, 1984

Directors: Paolo Taviani and Vittorio Taviani

Production: Filmtre, for RAI Channel 1; Eastmancolor; running time: 187 minutes; length: 16,816 feet. Released 1984.

Producer: Giuliani G. De Negri; **screenplay:** Paolo Taviani, Vittorio Taviani, and Tonino Guerra, from *Novelle per un anno* by Luigi Pirandello; **photography:** Giuseppe Lanci; **editor:** Roberto Perpignani; **sound recordist:** Sandro Zanon; **sound re-recordist:** Fausto Ancillai; **art director:** Francesco Bronzi; **costumes:** Lina Nerli Taviani; **music:** Nicola Piovani.

Cast: *L'Altro figlio (The Other Son):* Margarita Lozano (spoken by Fiorella Mari) (*Mother*); *Mali di luna (Moon Sickness):* Claudio Bigagli (*Bata*); Enrica Maria Modugno (*Sidora*); Massimo Bonetti (*Saro*); Anna Malvica (*Sidora's Mother*); *La giara (The Jar):* Ciccio Ingrassia (*Don Lollo*); Franco Franchi (*Zi' Diam*); *Requiem:* Biagio Barone (*Salvatore*); Salvatore Rossi (*Patriarch*); Franco Scaldati (*Father Sarso*); Pasquale Spadola (*Baron*); *Colloquio con la madre (Conversing with Mother):* Omero Antonutti (*Luigi Pirandello*); Regina Bianchi (*Mother*).

Publications

Articles:

Variety (New York), 12 September 1984.
Coleman, John, in *New Statesman* (London), 5 October 1984.
Robinson, David, in *Times* (London), 5 October 1984.
Bianco e Nero (Rome), October-December 1984.
Rayns, Tony, in *Monthly Film Bulletin* (London), November 1984.
Ranvaud, Don, ''Taking the Centre Ground,'' in *Monthly Film Bulletin* (London), November 1984.
Adair, Gilbert, ''La tragedia dell'arte,'' in *Sight and Sound* (London), Winter 1984–85.
Wahlstedt, T., in *Chaplin* (Stockholm), vol. 27, no. 3, 1985.
Amiel, M., and J. Kermabon, in *Cinéma* (Paris), January 1985.
Legrand, Gérard, in *Positif* (Paris), January 1985.
Martin, Marcel, in *Revue du Cinéma/Image et Son* (Paris), January 1985.
Philippon, A., in *Cahiers du Cinéma* (Paris), January 1985.
Delmas, G., and A. Tournes, ''Quand la terre est protagoniste: *Kaos*,'' in *Jeune Cinéma* (Paris), January-February 1985.
Orto, N., in *Cinema Nuovo* (Bari), February 1985.
Rinieri, D., in *Cinématographe* (Paris), February 1985.
Schouten, R., in *Skoop* (Amsterdam), March-April 1985.
Giguere, A., in *Séquences* (Montreal), April 1985.
Maslin, Janet, in *New York Times*, 13 October 1985.
Sarris, Andrew, in *Village Voice* (New York), 18 February 1986.
Denby, David, in *New York*, 24 February 1986.
Kael, Pauline, in *New Yorker*, 10 March 1986.
Listener (London), 27 October 1988.
Andrew, Geoff, ''Double Takes,'' in *Time Out* (London), no. 1082, 15 May 1991.
Trémois, Claude-Marie, ''*Fiorile:* Fantômes de la liberté,'' in *Télérama* (Paris), no. 2262, 19 May 1993.

* * *

While films are traditionally considered collaborative efforts, few have been so to the extent that two directors have purposefully initiated collaboration on the same film. Yet the Italian directors and

Kaos

scenarists Paolo and Vittorio Taviani, like their older English counterparts Michael Powell and Emeric Pressburger, have uniquely created through their writing and directing duality some of the most innovative films of the last decade.

Though the brothers began working as a team in the mid-1950s, their international fame was not well established until the release of *Padre padrone* in 1977. *Night of the Shooting Stars* (1983), coming after their reputations had grown, was also an international critical success.

Thus their 1984 film *Kaos*, loosely adapted by themselves and co-writer Tonino Guerra from short stories contained in Luigi Pirandello's *Novelle per un anno*, was chosen to close the 1985 New York Film Festival. Though it was not a resounding success and was not generally released in the U.S., some critics ranked it above the Taviani's previous works.

For *Kaos*, the Tavianis utilized the infrequently seen compendium format, separate short films loosely tied together by a theme or locale. *Kaos*, a title taken from the Greek word for chaos, which formed the linguistic root of the name for an area near Pirandello's birthplace in Sicily, consists of four separate stories, a prologue, and an epilogue, each illustrating aspects of Sicilian life. These cinematic folk tales, though, like Pirandello's works, contain universal elements that transcend the superficial quaintness of the stories.

Of the four tales, "The Other Son," "Moon Sickness," "The Jar," and "Requiem," the story of a lonely wife and her husband who becomes insane during the full moon, is considered the best. The brief segment before "The Other Son" sets the somber pace of the film and introduces the signature of the flying crow which is seen throughout the other segments, threading them together. The epilogue completes the cycle with Pirandello himself (played by the Taviani favorite Omero Antonutti) conversing with his mother about a pleasant experience from her childhood.

Though each segment is filmed in the aesthetic starkness typical of the Tavianis' work (which might appropriately be labelled "neo-neo Realism"), they are peppered with Pirandello's ironic fatalism: things are what they are, yet not as they seem; the lines between sanity and order and chaos and insanity cannot be distinctly drawn. His stories reflect characteristics of his region, but the psychological make-up of the characters and their sociological choices can be parallelled in any time or age.

The Tavianis have taken the currents of the Pirandello stories, if not their exact content, and elaborated them in a simple, muted style, with lingering shots and recurring images. While some critics have occasionally found their style too heavy-handed, it blends perfectly with the simple, yet unsettling nature of Pirandello's works.

—Patricia King Hanson

LA KERMESSE HÉROÏQUE

(Carnival in Flanders)

France-Germany, 1935

Director: Jacques Feyder

Production: Film Sonores Tobis, distributed through Films Sonor; black and white, 35mm; running time: 115 minutes. French version released 3 December 1935, Paris; German version released 16 January 1936, Berlin. Filmed June-July and September 1935 in Tobis d'Epinay-sur-Seine studios (France).

Screenplay: Charles Spaak, adapted by Charles Spaak and Jacques Feyder, dialogue by Bernard Zimmer (French) and A. Rabenalt (German), from a story by Charles Spaak; **photography:** Harry Stradling, Louis Page, and André Thomas; **editor:** Jacques Brillouin; **sound:** Hermann Storr; **art directors:** Lazare Meerson, Alexandre Trauner, and Georges Wakhévitch; **music:** Louis Beydte; **costume designers:** Georges K. Benda and J. Muelle; **artistic consultant:** Charles Barrois; **history consultant:** M. Sterling of the Louvre; **technical assistant:** Marcel Carné.

La Kermesse héroïque

Cast: *French version*: Louis Jouvet (*Chaplain*); Françoise Rosay (*Cornelia, the Burgomaster's wife*); Jean Murat (*Duke of Olivares*); André Alerme (*Burgomaster*); Lyne Clévers (*Fishmonger's wife*); Micheline Cheirel (*Siska*); Maryse Wendling (*Baker's wife*); Ginette Gaubert (*Innkeeper's wife*); Marguerite Ducouret (*Brewer's wife*); Bernard Lancret (*Jean Breuchel*); Alfred Adam (*Butcher*); Pierre Labry (*Innkeeper*); Arthur Devère (*Fishmonger*); Marcel Carpentier (*Baker*); Alexandre Darcy (*Captain*); Claude Sainval (*Lieutenant*); Delphin (*Midget*); *German version*: Wilhelm Holsboer (*Chaplin*); Françoise Rosay (*Burgomaster's wife*); Paul Hartmann (*Duke*); Will Dohm (*Burgomaster*); Charlott Daubert (*Siska*); Albert Lieven (*Jean Breughel*); Paul Westermeier (*Butcher*); Carsta Loegk (*Fishmonger's wife*); Trude Marlen (*Innkeeper*); Erika Helmke (*Baker's wife*); Hans Henininger (*Fishmonger*); Wilhelm Gombert (*Innkeeper*); Heintz Forster Ludwig (*Baker*); Werner Scharf (*1st Spanish Lieutenant*); Paul Wolka Walker (*Midget*).

Awards: Venice Film Festival, Best Direction, 1936; Le Grand Prix du Cinéma Français, 1936.

Publications

Script:

Spaak, Charles, and others, *La Kermesse héroïque*, in *Avant-Scène du Cinéma* (Paris), May 1963.

Books:

Buzzi, Aldo, *La kermesse eroica*, Milan, 1945.
Feyder, Jacques, and Françoise Rosay, *Le Cinéma, notre métier*, Geneva, 1946.
Jacques Feyder, ou, le Cinéma concret, Brussels, 1949.
Bachy, Victor, ''Jacques Feyder,'' in *Anthologie du Cinéma 18*, Paris, 1966.
Bachy, Victor, *Jacques Feyder, artisan du cinéma*, Louvain, 1968.
Régent, Roger, ''Louis Jouvet,'' in *Anthologie du cinéma 5*, Paris, 1969.
Sadoul, Georges, *French Film*, New York, 1972.
Ford, Charles, *Jacques Feyder*, Paris, 1973.
Barsacq, Léon, *Caligari's Cabinet and Other Grand Illusions: A History of Film Design*, New York, 1976.
Ellis, Jack, C., *A History of Film*, Englewood Cliffs, New Jersey, 1979.
Feyder; Zavattini; Trésors de cinémathèque, Perpignan, 1984.

Articles:

New York Times, 23 September 1936.
Variety (New York), 30 September 1936.

Sight and Sound (London), Autumn 1936.
Monthly Film Bulletin (London), October 1936.
Motion Picture Herald (New York), 3 October 1936.
Today's Cinema, 15 October 1936.
Greene, Graham, in *Spectator* (London), 30 October 1936.
''Hommage a Jacques Feyder,'' in *Ecran Français* (Paris), 8 June 1948.
''Feyder Issue'' of *Ciné-Club* (Paris), 2 November 1948.
Auriol, J.-G., and Mario Verdone, ''L'Art du costume dans le film,'' in *Revue du Cinéma* (Paris), Autumn 1949.
Today's Cinema, 31 December 1952.
Sadoul, Georges, ''Jouvet et le cinema,'' in *Lettres Françaises* (Paris), 25 August 1961.
Avant-Scène du Cinéma (Paris), May 1963.
Skrien (Amsterdam), December 1977.
Dossier on Jacques Feyder, in *Cahiers de la Cinémathèque* (Perpignan), no. 40, Summer 1984.
Bíró, G., in *Filmkultura* (Budapest), March 1985.
Virmaux, Alain, ''D'Alfred Machin à Jacques Feyder: Débuts du cinéma belge (années 1910–1930) (musée d'Orsay, mars-avril 1997),'' in *Jeune Cinéma* (Paris), no. 245, September-October 1997.

* * *

Jacques Feyder had already made two sound films in France; his creative skills were by no means diminished by the new dimension. His successful collaboration with Charles Spaak was to further produce one of the wittiest, most colourful and amusing comedies to reach the screen, *La kermesse héroïque*. Taking as his subject the period of the great Renaissance of Flemish painting and the less happy era of Spanish domination, Feyder made a major contribution to ''women's lib.'' The film satirizes political, religious, and moral pretentiousness, and the men come off second best when a strong-minded and realistic woman encounters a tricky diplomatic situation.

The little town of Boom's fussy Burgomaster and his officials cannot cope with the threat to their town when the news comes of the approach of the Spanish army under the command of a Duke. Cornelia, the Burgomaster's wife, has a plan. The Burgomaster will pretend to be dead, and she will receive the Duke and hope that in the sad circumstances he will be gentleman enough not to overstay his leave. The possibilities for comedy are wide open.

From this situation Feyder fashioned a film full of sly and subtle comment on human foibles, designed with lavish elegance, at all times a feast for the eye. Feyder, himself a Belgian, created a monument to the great visual artists of his country. The film was a crowning jewel in the great flowering of the French cinema of the 1930s. The designs of Lazare Meerson and the costumes of Benda come alive with the superb acting Feyder extracts from his players. The subtle and delicate humour, the gentle implications of the dialogue, are epitomized in the sly performance of Louis Jouvet as the Duke's chaplain. Needless to say, the Flemish ladies thoroughly enjoy the elegant manners of the Spaniards while their menfolk look helplessly on. There is a little sadness in the air as the Duke and his army leave. One feels life in the little town of Boom will never be the same again.

In making this film, of course Feyder trod on the toes of his fellow countrymen. The reaction was much like that of the Irish to *The Playboy of the Western World* and chauvinistic sensibilities were not easily smoothed. But the success of the film was universal, and Feyder was established as a great director.

Through an irony of history the significance of the film was soon to change. Belgium was, in fact, invaded by a less charming enemy than the Spanish Duke. Collaboration soon became a very ugly word indeed. But time was on Feyder's side, and today his masterpiece is secure in the annals of film history.

—Liam O'Leary

THE KID

USA, 1921

Director: Charles Chaplin

Production: Charles Chaplin Productions for First National; black and white, 35mm, silent; running time: about 52 minutes; length: 6 reels, 5300 feet. Released 6 February 1921.

Producer: Charles Chaplin; **screenplay:** Charles Chaplin; **photography:** Rollie Totheroh.

Cast: Jackie Coogan (*The Kid*); Edna Purviance (*The Woman*); Carl Miller (*The Man*); Charles Chaplin (*The Tramp*); Tom Wilson (*The Policeman*); Chuck Reisner (*The Bully*); Thelbert Theustin (*The Crook*); Nellie Bly Baker (*Slum Woman*); Henry Bergman (*Proprietor of lodging house*); Lita Grey (*Flirting angel*).

Publications

Books:

Tyler, Parker, *Chaplin, Last of the Clowns*, New York, 1947.
Huff, Theodore, *Charlie Chaplin*, New York, 1951.
Bessy, Maurice, and Robert Florey, *Monsieur Chaplin; ou, Le Rire dans la nuit*, Paris, 1952.
Sadoul, Georges, *Vie de Charlot*, Paris, 1952.
Leprohon, Pierre, *Charlot*, Paris, 1957; revised edition, 1970.
Mitry, Jean, *Charlot et la fabulation chaplinesque*, Paris, 1957.
Amengual, Barthélemy, *Charles Chaplin*, Paris, 1963.
Chaplin, Charles, *My Autobiography*, London, 1964.
McDonald, Gerald, and others, *The Films of Charlie Chaplin*, Secaucus, New Jersey, 1965.
Martin, Marcel, *Charlie Chaplin*, Paris, 1966; third edition, 1983.
McCaffrey, Donald, editor, *Focus on Chaplin*, Englewood Cliffs, New Jersey, 1971.
Mitry, Jean, *Tout Chaplin: Tous les films, par le texte, par le gag, et par l'image*, Paris, 1972.
Chaplin, Charles, *My Life in Pictures*, London, 1974.
Manvell, Roger, *Chaplin*, Boston, 1974.
Moss, Robert, *Charlie Chaplin*, New York, 1975.
Sobel, Raoul, and David Francis, *Chaplin: Genesis of a Clown*, London, 1977.

The Kid

Baldelli, P., *Charlie Chaplin*, Florence, 1977.
Lyons, Timothy J., *Charles Chaplin: A Guide to References and Resources*, Boston, 1979.
Eisenstein, Sergei, *Film Essays and a Lecture*, edited by Jay Leyda, Princeton, 1982.
Haining, Peter, editor, *The Legend of Charlie Chaplin*, London, 1982.
Gehring, Wes D., editor, *Charlie Chaplin: A Bio-Bibliography*, Westport, Connecticut, 1983.
Robinson, David, *Chaplin: The Mirror of Opinion*, London, 1983.
Kamin, Dan, *Charlie Chaplin's One-Man Show*, Metuchen, New Jersey, 1984.
Smith, Julian, *Chaplin*, Boston, 1984.
Robinson, David, *Chaplin: His Life and Art*, London, 1985.
Saint-Martin, Catherine, *Charlot/Chaplin; ou, La Conscience du mythe*, Paris, 1987.
Silver, Charles, *Charles Chaplin: An Appreciation*, New York, 1990.
Lynn, Kenneth S., *Charlie Chaplin and His Times*, New York, 1997.
Milton, Joyce, *Tramp: The Life of Charlie Chaplin*, New York, 1998.
Turk, Ruth, *Charlie Chaplin: From Tears to Laughter*, Minneapolis, 1999.
Kimber, John, *The Art of Charles Chaplin*, Sheffield, 2000.

Articles:

Variety (New York), 21 January 1921.
New York Times, 22 January 1921.
''Charlie Chaplin's Art Dissected,'' in *Literary Digest* (New York), 8 October 1921.
Grein, J. T., ''Chaplin as Film Producer,'' in *Illustrated London News*, 15 March 1924.
Grace, Harry A., ''Charlie Chaplin's Films and American Culture Patterns,'' in *Journal of Aesthetics and Art Criticism* (Cleveland), June 1952.
Brownlow, Kevin, ''The Early Days of Charlie Chaplin,'' in *Film* (London), Summer 1964.
Lyons, Timothy J., ''Roland H. Totheroh Interviewed: Chaplin Films,'' in *Film Culture* (New York), Spring 1972.
Schickel, Richard, ''Hail Chaplin—The Early Chaplin,'' in *New York Times Biography Edition*, 2 April 1972.
Carey, Gary, in *Film Comment* (New York), September-October 1972.
Lefèvre, Raymond, in *Cinéma* (Paris), February 1974.
Ferrari, A., in *Télécine* (Paris), March 1974.
Monthly Film Bulletin (London), March 1975.
Salko, S., in *Filmihullu* (Helsinki), no. 2, 1979.
Papson, S., ''The IBM Tramp,'' in *Jump Cut* (Berkeley), April 1990.
Randisi, S., ''The Flirting Angel and the Tramp,'' in *Filmfax* (Evanston, Illinois), June-July 1993.
Rosi, F., ''Entre *Le kid* et *La terre tremble*,'' in *Positif* (Paris), no. 400, June 1994.
Woal, M., and L.K. Woal, ''Chaplin and the Comedy of Melodrama,'' in *Journal of Film and Video* (Atlanta), vol. 46, no. 3, 1994.
Gunning, Tom, ''Buster Keaton or the Work of Comedy in the Age of Mechanical Reproduction,'' in *Cineaste* (New York), vol. 21, no. 3, 1995.
Nysenholc, A., ''Chaplin: du reve au mythe vivant,'' in *Revue Belge du Cinéma* (Brussels), no. 42, Summer 1997.

* * *

The Kid was the first feature film that Charles Chaplin devised and directed, the longest film in which he had appeared since Keystone's *Tillie's Punctured Romance* seven years earlier, three times longer than the typical two-reeler at which he had specialized for six years, and almost twice as long as his other major films produced for First National since 1918. The film's greater length reveals Chaplin's expansion of his comic focus to include more powerful and more personal social, moral, and emotional material. At the centre of the film is the Tramp's relationship to Little Jackie (Jackie Coogan), a five-year-old child who has been abandoned by his unwed mother, found and raised by the Tramp as his own surrogate son. Like the mongrel, Scraps, of *A Dog's Life* (1918), Jackie is a smaller, alternate version of the Tramp himself—a social outcast, defined as illegitimate by the laws and conventions of organized society, able to survive because he is tough though small, mentally agile though uneducated, alternately hard-headed and soft-hearted when it becomes necessary to be either.

Chaplin transferred many of the Tramp's traits, as well as many of his own comedic skills, to little Jackie. Coogan's brilliant performance, responsible for much of the success and popularity of the film, was the first by another performer that Chaplin totally dominated and controlled, in effect creating an alternative Chaplin in a different physical guise (Edna Purviance's performance in *A Woman of Paris*, Virginia Cherrill's in *City Lights*, and Paulette Goddard's in *Modern Times* would be three later such transmutations). Beneath the fictional material in the film one can strongly sense the influence of Chaplin's own personal experiences—his own life as an abandoned child of the London slums, the death of his own first child, born prematurely, and the collapse of his own first marriage, at least partially resulting from the child's death.

Framing the serio-comic study of Charlie and Jackie's domestic bliss, their poor but tranquil existence vivified by love, is material of an entirely different sort. The film begins with a sequence on the unwed mother's (Edna Purviance) difficult decision to abandon her child, depicting her relationship to the callous father (a painter who no longer thinks of the woman) and to the conventional societal definitions of morality and legitimacy (fraught with explicit Christian symbolism). Whereas the woman observes a socially ''legitimate'' marriage that pairs a young woman with an old, rich man, her own sort of affair is considered illegitimate, even if the action resulted from love and not money. The Christian symbolism returns at the end of the film when Charlie, searching for the child who has been stolen from him, falls asleep to dream of a more pleasant place where, as in so many other Chaplin dream sequences, the painful realities of earthly existence no longer exist. In this dream, considered irrelevant by some critics, Chaplin recreates a comic version of ''the Fall'' as a group of heavenly angel-people, including the Tramp and all his other neighbors in the slum, fly through the now white-washed and flower-garlanded streets of a utopian city. The dream collapses and the perfect peace turns to bitter chaos when the Satanic spirits of lechery and jealousy sneak through the gates of the heavenly city. Although the sleeping Tramp is roused from this dream to be reunited with Jackie and Edna, the dream sequence suggests Chaplin's sense of the fragility and transience of the true moments of human love and happiness, only temporary escapes from the sordid realities and painful necessities of earthly life.

—Gerald Mast

THE KILLERS

USA, 1946

Director: Robert Siodmak

Production: Mark Hellinger Productions; black and white, 35mm; running time: 105 minutes, some sources list 102 minutes. Released 28 August 1946 by Universal. Filming completed 28 June 1946 in Universal studios.

Producer: Mark Hellinger; **screenplay:** Anthony Veiller, from the short story by Ernest Hemingway; **photography:** Woody Bredell; **special photography:** David S. Horsely; **editor:** Arthur Hilton; **sound:** Bernard Brown and William Hedgecock; **art directors:** Jack Otterson and Martin Obzina; **music:** Miklos Rozsa; **costume designer:** Vera West.

Cast: Edmond O'Brien (*Riordan*); Ava Gardner (*Kitty Collins*); Albert Dekker (*Colfax*); Sam Levene (*Lubinsky*); John Miljan (*Jake*); Virginia Christine (*Lilly*); Vince Barnett (*Charleston*); Burt Lancaster (*Swede*); Charles D. Brown (*Packy*); Donald MacBride (*Kenyon*); Phil Brown (*Nick*); Charles McGraw (*Al*); William Conrad (*Max*); Queenie Smith (*Queenie*); Garry Owen (*Joe*); Harry Hayden (*George*); Bill Walker (*Sam*); Jack Lambert (*Dum Dum*); Jeff Corey (*Blinky*); Wally Scott (*Charlie*); Gabrielle Windsor (*Ginny*); Rex Dale (*Man*).

Publications

Books:

McArthur, Colin, *Underworld U.S.A.*, London, 1972.
Kaminsky, Stuart M., *American Film Genres*, Dayton, Ohio, 1974; revised edition, Chicago, 1985.
Silver, Alain, and Elizabeth Ward, editors, *Film Noir*, Woodstock, New York, 1979.
Phillips, Gene D., *Hemingway and Film*, New York, 1980.
Laurence, Frank M., *Hemingway and the Movies*, Jackson, Mississippi, 1981.
Dumont, Hervé, *Robert Siodmak: Le Maître du film noir*, Lausanne, 1981.
Alpi, Deborah Lazaroff, *Robert Siodmak: A Biography, with Critical Analyses of His Films Noirs and a Filmography of All His Works*, Jefferson, 1998.
Greco, Joseph, *The File on Robert Siodmak in Hollywood: 1941–1951*, Parkland, 1999.

Articles:

Variety (New York), 7 August 1946.
New York Times, 29 August 1946.
Marshman, D., ''Mister Siodmak,'' in *Life* (New York), 25 August 1947.
Lillich, Richard, ''Hemingway on the Screen,'' in *Films in Review* (New York), April 1959.
Taylor, John Russell, ''Encounter with Siodmak,'' in *Sight and Sound* (London), Summer-Autumn 1959.
Siodmak, Robert, and Richard Wilson, ''Hoodlums: The Myths and Their Reality,'' in *Films and Filming* (London), June 1959.
Sarris, Andrew, ''Esoterica,'' in *Film Culture* (New York), Spring 1963.
Nolan, Jack, ''Robert Siodmak,'' in *Films in Review* (New York), April 1969.
Flinn, Tom, ''Three Faces of Film Noir,'' in *Velvet Light Trap* (Madison, Wisconsin), Summer 1972.
Ecran (Paris), Summer 1972.
Eyles, Allen, ''Edmond O'Brien,'' in *Focus on Film* (London), Autumn 1974.
Kaminsky, Stuart M., ''Hemingway's *The Killers*,'' in *Take One* (Montreal), November 1974.
Jenkins, Steve, in *Monthly Film Bulletin* (London), October 1981.
Goldschmidt, D., in *Cinématographe* (Paris), July 1985.
Slater, Thomas, ''Anthony Veiller,'' in *American Screenwriters, 2nd Series*, edited by Randall Clark, Detroit, 1986.
Review, in *EPD Film* (Frankfurt), vol. 7, no. 8, August 1990.
Wald, Marvin, ''Richard Brooks and Me,'' in *Creative Screenwriting* (Washington, D.C.), vol. 1, no. 2, Summer 1994.
Aachen, G., in *Reid's Film Index* (Wyong), no. 23, 1996.
Lucas, Tim, ''*The Killers, Criss Cross, The Underneath, Brute Force, The Naked City*,'' in *Video Watchdog* (Cincinnati), no. 32, 1996.
Mumby, J., ''The 'Un-American' Film Art: Robert Siodmak and the Political Significance of Film Noir's German Connection,'' in *Iris*, no. 21, Spring 1996.
Telotte, J.P., ''Fatal Capers: Strategy and Enigma in Film Noir,'' in *Journal of Popular Film and Television* (Washington, D.C.), vol. 23, no. 4, Winter 1996.
Brierly, D., ''Robert Siodmak,'' in *Filmfax* (Evanston), no. 62, August/September 1997.

* * *

The Killers begins with literature and ends with *film noir*. The unlikely death of a filling station attendant prompts an insurance investigator to solve a puzzle of events that leads him to the cause of the murder and then envelops him in a plot ending with the murderer's death. After staging Ernest Hemingway's story in the opening sequence, the plot follows a structure that prevails in the convention of the 1940s: a man utters his last words, ''I did something wrong, once,'' to avow his fatal mistake of falling in love with a woman who doublecrosses him. His relentless passion and blindness lead the two of them and her husband to their demise.

Director Robert Siodmak makes filmic innovation from a model anticipated in Renoir's *La bête humaine* (1938) and standardized since *Double Indemnity* (1944). The opening shots afford visual splendor in deep-focus shots taken in the confines of an empty café. Hemingway's narrative is translated into a tense volley of words and images. The rest of the film ''catches up'' with the initial murder after 11 major flashbacks—and flashbacks within flashbacks—before the insurance agent (Edmond O'Brien) witnesses the dying culprit's confession inculpating his attendant spouse. Something of a proto-*nouveau roman*, the script has the narrative cross over an unnamed abyss of time—the amnesia of the Second World War—in ways that determine the absolute immobility of the present. Recent history, as if

The Killers

it were a memory too traumatic to be named, figures as a central abyss of violence gnawing at the surrounding fiction. 22 lap dissolves throw the narrative into a configuration of overlapping surfaces.

Narrative intricacy aside, the film is a masterful exercise in the creation of subjectivity that political scientists call ''interpellation,'' or the forces that determine the human being as a social subject. No other *film noir*—save Siodmak's *Phantom Lady* (1944) or *Crisscross* (1949)—makes such sustained use of voice-off as instances of interpellation. Figures on frame are continually ''marked'' by imperatives, *off*, having no discernible visual origin. They leave an eerie effect matched by back lighting that makes the characters' shadows more revealing than their persons. The resulting fragmentation and doubling of figures, along with rifts of voice and image, show where the film theorizes the conventions its narrative seems to develop so patently. The film's broken synchronies not only give evidence of what *film noir* is and how it is effected; like *Citizen Kane*, Siodmak's film anticipates future experiment in European and American cinema.

Three sequences are noteworthy. In the re-enactment of Hemingway's tale, script and deep focus are used to truncate cinematic illusion and ideation. Seated in contrapuntal relation to the two gunmen at the other end of the counter, bewildered by what he sees, Nick Adams directs his words both to the killers and the spectator. Astonished, he exclaims, ''What's the idea?'' To which the hefty thug (William Conrad) snarls (*off*) in the direction of Adams and the viewer, ''There isn't any idea.'' The riposte orients the eye away from metaphysics or invisibility of language to a richer play of prismatic form. The moment also shows how, second, the violence of history will be scripted onto the surface of the tale. In the first flashback that depicts Nick Adams's reconstruction of the victim's last days, told to the insurance investigator, the camera frames the protagonist (Burt Lancaster), standing in front of the ''Tristate Station.'' He is visibly ill at the sight of the return of his repressed, the gangster Jim Colfax, who will now set a price on his life. Standing under the marquee above him, Lancaster nods and puts his hands to his stomach. His head shifts position over the letters STATE STATIC (the O of ''station'' carefully cut in half by a pole). His head blocks and uncovers the letters ''ATE STATIC.'' The wording scripts the fate of a character as it figures a global *malaise* of narrative and political stasis in 1946. Adjacent to a sign that spells TIRES in acrostic to his left, Lancaster is a figure worn down—fatigued—by history and fate. He is not only a victim of a tri-state tryst, but also of a political atmosphere, a cold war of 1946, as "state static," determining the visible field of the narrative.

A third sequence, also crucial to the historical relation of *film noir* and *nouvelle vague*, stages a conversation between the sleuth and his boss. The latter is seen reading a newspaper clipping of 1940 recounting the story of a payroll heist from a Hackensack hat company. The present tense in the insurance office dissolves into a long crane shot that visibly depicts what is being told in words on the sound track. Seen in silence, in the style of Joseph Mankiewicz's silent flashbacks that pull an event out of time, the moving camera arches over the men staging the holdup and driving off in an exchange of mute gunfire. At one point, as it follows the vehicle exiting under the open-work metal sign over the entry to the factory (spelling the "Prentiss Hat Company"), the camera registers the reflection of the mirrored letters on the windshield, twice reversed so as to be read correctly, visibly enough to draw the spectator's attention to the reflection of the crane, the camera, and its operator. The film-in-the-film is glimpsed: invisible editing, it had for decades excluded the camera from the image-track, is broken down; omnipresence of writing makes the deep focus flat and at once visible and legible; the illusion of narrative synchrony is divided and flattened; attention is brought to deliberate camera movement that evokes a timeless oblivion of memory. The sequence heralds techniques soon exploited by Bresson, Resnais, and Godard.

Along with *Citizen Kane* and *Sullivan's Travels, The Killers* ranks as one of the more "theoretical" films of the 1940s at the same time that it concretizes the essence of *film noir*. It uses Hemingway to threshold a Baroque structure of surfaces, and its self-consciousness arches verbal and visual discourses over each other, leaving the effect of a film looking at the very forms it is unfolding. Siodmak's work occupies a central niche in the history of film theory, in *film noir*, and in the relations of cinema and literature.

—Tom Conley

KIND HEARTS AND CORONETS

UK, 1949

Director: Robert Hamer

Production: Ealing Studios; black and white, 35mm; running time: 106 minutes; length: 9529 feet. Released 1949. Filmed in England.

Producer: Michael Balcon; **screenplay:** Robert Hamer and John Dighton, from the novel *Israel Rank* by Roy Horniman; **photography:** Douglas Slocombe; **editor:** Peter Tanner; **music:** Wolfgang Mozart.

Cast: Dennis Price (*Louis Mazzini/Mazzini's father*); Joan Greenwood (*Sibella*); Valerie Hobson (*Edith*); Alec Guinness (*Ascoyne d'Ascoyne/Henry d'Ascoyne/Canon d'Ascoyne/Admiral d'Ascoyne/General d'Ascoyne/Lady Agatha d'Ascoyne/Lord d'Ascoyne/Ethelbert/the Old Duke*); Audrey Fildes (*Mrs. Mazzini*); John Penrose (*Lionel*); Miles Malleson (*Hangman*); Clive Morton (*Prison governor*).

Award: Venice Film Festival, Best Scenography, 1949.

Publications

Script:

Hamer, Robert, and John Dighton, *Kind Hearts and Coronets*, New York, 1974, revised edition, 1984.

Books:

Tynan, Kenneth, *Alec Guinness*, New York, 1955.
Balcon, Michael, *A Lifetime of Films*, London, 1969.
Butler, Ivan, *Cinema in Britain*, New York, 1973.
Betts, Ernest, *The Film Business: A History of British Cinema*, New York, 1973.
Barr, Charles, *Ealing Studios*, London, 1977, 1982, 1999.
Perry, George, *Forever Ealing*, London, 1981.
Hunter, Allan, *Alec Guinness on Screen*, London, 1982.
Kurdish, Laurence, *Michael Balcon: The Pursuit of British Cinema*, New York, 1984.
Taylor, John Russell, *Alec Guinness: A Celebration*, London, 1984, 1994.
Guinness, Alec, *Blessings in Disguise*, London, 1985.
Missler, Andreas, *Alec Guinness: Seine Filme, sein Leben*, Munich, 1987.
Von Gunden, Kenneth, *Alec Guinness: The Films*, Jefferson, North Carolina, 1987.
Brown, Geoff, *Michael Balcon: Pursuit of Britain*, New York, 1990.
Guinness, Alec, *My Name Escapes Me: The Diary of a Retiring Actor*, New York, 1998.

Articles:

Schwerin, Jules, in *Films in Review* (New York), March 1950.
Lockart, Freda Bruce, "Interview with Robert Hamer," in *Sight and Sound* (London), October-December 1951.
Hill, Derek, "Man of Many Faces," in *Films and Filming* (London), February 1955.
Tynan, Kenneth, "Ealing: The Studio in Suburbia," in *Films and Filming* (London), November and December 1955.
McVay, Douglas, "Alec Guinness," in *Films and Filming* (London), May 1961.
Houston, Penelope, "Survivor," in *Sight and Sound* (London), Winter 1962–63.
Stanbrook, Alan, in *Films and Filming* (London), April 1964.
Mazoyer, J., "Noblesse oblige," in *Image et Son* (Paris), no. 274, 1973.
Barr, Charles, "Projecting Britain and the British Character: Ealing Studios," in *Screen* (London), Summer 1974.
Hopkins, Charles, in *Magill's Survey of Cinema 2*, Englewood Cliffs, New Jersey, 1980.
Porter, Vincent, "The Context of Creativity: Ealing Studios and Hammer Films," and Ian Green, "Ealing: In the Comedy Frame," both in *British Cinema History*, edited by James Curran, and Vincent Porter, London, 1983.
Glassman, M., and J. Wolfe, "The Studio with the Team Spirit: a Look at Ealing Comedies," in *CineAction* (Toronto), no. 9, Summer 1987.
Sontag, S., "In Conclusionp" in *East-West Film Journal* (Honolulu), vol. 2, no. 1, 1987.

Kind Hearts and Coronets

Palmer, James, ''Enunciation and Comedy: *Kind Hearts and Coronets*,'' in *Screen* (Oxford), vol. 30, no. 1–2, Winter-Spring 1989.

Andrew, Geoff, ''Ealing Touch,'' in *Time Out* (London), no. 1197, 28 July 1993.

* * *

Kind Hearts and Coronets is an Ealing Comedy in name only. True, it is a comedy, and it was produced by Michael Balcon's Ealing Studios. Even so, the film has little in common with its stablemates. Ealing comedies (with the exception of Mackendrick's) were cosy. *Kind Hearts* is callous, even cruel. The humour of Ealing comedies was generally warm, cheerful, and folksy; *Kind Hearts* is cool, ironic and witty. Sex, in Ealing comedies, was kept at a safe distance, and handled (if at all) with embarrassed jocularity; *Kind Hearts* includes scenes that carry a powerful erotic charge.

Hamer stated his intentions as: ''Firstly, that of making a film not noticeably similar to any previously made in the English language. Secondly, that of using this English language, which I love, in a more varied and more interesting way. Thirdly, that of making a picture which paid no regard whatever to established, although not practised, moral convention.'' Much of the humour is indeed verbal, elegantly Wildean, carried by the hero's voice-over narration—yet always aptly counterpointed by the visual effects. The shape of the film is satisfyingly classic, a long flash-back. It opens with Louis Mazzini (Dennis Price) in prison, condemned to death for a murder of which he is innocent, composing his memoirs, in which he recounts all the murders of which he is guilty. His mother, a member of the proud d'Ascoyne clan, had married an Italian singer; for this they disowned her, condemning her to poverty and eventual death. At her grave, Louis vows vengeance, and gradually eliminates every d'Ascoyne (all played by Alec Guinness) between himself and the dukedom.

Louis's narration serves as a unifying factor, effectively sustaining the tone of cool irony throughout the film. Cool—but not cold; there is a pervasive undercurrent of passion beneath the urbane wit, motivating Louis in his systematic slaughter, and surfacing both in the erotic passages with his mistress Sibella (Joan Greenwood), and in his embittered outburst before shooting the Duke, his final victim. The Duke, most repellent of the d'Ascoynes, has been decoyed by Louis into one of his own mantraps; but Louis, too, is caught in his own trap. In revenging himself on the d'Ascoynes for their heartlessness, he has become as heartless, cold and calculating as they.

But the film can readily be enjoyed without any such consideration of its serious undertones. *Kind Hearts* is very funny, wickedly subversive, and probably the finest black comedy the British cinema has every produced. It is certainly Hamer's masterpiece, a highly successful fusion of his dominant influences: Wildean comedy, and classic French cinema (notably, in this case, Sacha Guitry and the Renoir of *La règle du jeu*). The film made Alec Guinness's international reputation, and rapidly attained the status of a classic—which it has consistently maintained. Such polished excellence makes it even more regrettable that Hamer's masterpiece was also the last major film of his sadly blighted career.

—Philip Kemp

KING KONG

USA, 1933

Directors: Merian C. Cooper and Ernest B. Schoedsack

Production: RKO Radio Pictures Inc.; black and white, 35mm; running time: 100 minutes. Released 2 March 1933, Radio City Music Hall and RKO Roxy Theatre, New York. Re-released 1938 with a few scenes censored. Filmed 1932–33 in RKO Studios and backlots, also in San Pedro Harbor and Shrine Auditorium, Los Angeles. Cost: $670,000.

Producers: Merian C. Cooper and Ernest B. Schoedsack with David O. Selznick as executive producer; **screenplay:** James Creelman and Ruth Rose, from a story by Merian C. Cooper and Edgar Wallace based on an idea conceived by Cooper; **photography:** Edward Linden, Vernon L. Walker, and J. O. Taylor; **optical photography:** Linwood C. Dunn and William Ulm; **editor:** Ted Cheesman; **sound recordist:** E. A. Wolcott; **sound effects:** Murray Spivack; **production technicians:** Mario Larrinaga and Byron L. Crabbe; **art directors:** Archie S. Marshek and Walter Daniels; **art direction supervisor:** Van Nest Polglase; **music:** Max Steiner; **chief technician:** Willis H. O'Brien; **special effects:** Harry Redmond Jr.; **Williams Matte supervision:** Frank Williams; **technical artwork:** Juan Larrinaga, Zachary Hoag, and Victor Delgado; **projection process:** Sydney Saunders; **costume designer:** Walter Plunkett; **King Kong modellist:** Marcel Delgado.

Cast: Fay Wray (*Ann Darrow*); Bruce Cabot (*Jack Driscoll*); Sam Hardy (*Weston*); James Flavin (*2nd mate*); Victor Wong (*Charley*); Paul Porcasi (*Fruit vendor*); Dick Curtis (*Crewman*); Robert Armstrong (*Carl Denham*); Frank Reicher (*Captain Englehorn*); Noble Johnson (*Native chief*); Steve Clemento (*Witch king*); Roscoe Ates (*Press photographer*); Leroy Mason (*Theater patron*).

Publications

Books:

McBride, Joseph, *Persistence of Vision*, Madison, Wisconsin, 1968.
Gifford, Denis, *Movie Monsters*, New York, 1969.
Steinbrunner, Chris, and Burt Goldblatt, *Cinema of the Fantastic*, New York, 1972.
Gubern, Roman, *Homenaje a King Kong*, Barcelona, 1974.
Goldner, Orville, and George E. Turner, *The Making of King Kong*, New York, 1973.
Gottesman, Ronald, and Harry M. Geduld, editors, *The Girl in the Hairy Paw*, New York, 1976.
Mathews, J. H., *Surrealism and American Feature Films*, Boston, 1979.
Powers, Tom J., *Movie Monsters*, Minneapolis, 1989.
Wray, Fay, *On the Other Hand: A Life Story*, New York, 1989.
Erb, Cynthia, *Tracking King Kong: A Hollywood Icon in World History*, Detroit, 1998.

Articles:

New York Times, 5 March 1933.
Variety (New York), 7 March 1933.
Troy, William, in *Nation* (New York), 22 March 1933.
Boone, Andrew R., in *Popular Science Monthly* (New York), 1933.
Kennedy, X. J., ''Who Killed King Kong,'' in *Dissent* (New York), Spring 1960.
Boullet, Jean, ''Willis O'Brien; or, The Birth of a Film from Design to Still,'' in *Midi-Minuit Fantastique* (Paris), October-November 1962.
Ollier, Claude, ''A King in New York,'' in *Cahiers du Cinéma* (Paris), May-June 1965.
Behlmer, Rudy, ''Merian C. Cooper,'' in *Films in Review* (New York), January 1966.
Peary, G., ''Orphan in the Storm: Son of Kong,'' in *Film Heritage* (Dayton, Ohio), Winter 1973–74.
Peoples, S. A., in *Films in Review* (New York), January 1974.
Osborne, A., ''Father of Kong,'' in *Cinema Papers* (Melbourne), July 1974.
Peary, G., ''A Speculation: The Historicity of King Kong,'' in *Jump Cut* (Chicago), November-December 1974.
Gow, Gordon, in *Films and Filming* (London), January 1975.
Rosen, D. N., ''Race, Sex, and Rebellion,'' in *Jump Cut* (Chicago), March-April 1975.
Mayne, Judith, ''*King Kong* and the Ideology of the Spectacle,'' in *Quarterly Review of Film Studies* (Pleasantville, New York), No. 4, 1976.
Fieschi, J., ''La Religion du monstre,'' in *Cinématographe* (Paris), April-May 1976.
Maraval, P., ''Trucages pro-filmiques et filmiques dans *King Kong*,'' in *Cinématographe* (Paris), April-May 1976.
Sabatier, J.-M., in *Image et Son* (Paris), September 1976.
Markfield, Wallace, ''The Kong and I,'' in *New York Times*, 12 December 1976.
Dunn, L. G., ''Creating Film Magic for the Original *King Kong*,'' in *American Cinematographer* (Los Angeles), January 1977.
Jackson, F., ''Doctor, I Have These Strange Dreams,'' in *Take One* (Montreal), January 1977.
''The Making of the Original *King Kong*,'' in *American Cinematographer* (Los Angeles), January 1977.
Wellman, H., ''*King Kong*—Then and Now,'' in *American Cinematographer* (Los Angeles), January 1977.
Garsault, A., and A. Marty, in *Positif* (Paris), February 1977.

King Kong

Fiedel, R., ''Sound Track: And the Beast Goes On,'' in *American Film* (Washington, D.C.), March 1977.

Broeske, Pat J., in *Magill's Survey of Cinema 2*, Englewood Cliffs, New Jersey, 1980.

''O'Brien Issue'' of *Cinefex* (Riverside, California), January 1982.

Mandrell, P. R., and George E. Turner, in *American Cinematographer* (Los Angeles), August 1983.

Strick, Philip, in *Films and Filming* (London), September 1986.

MacQueen, Scott, ''Old King Kong Gets Face Lift,'' in *American Cinematographer* (Hollywood), vol. 70, no. 1, January 1989.

Snead, J., ''Spectatorship and Capture in *King Kong*: The Guilty Look,'' in *Critical Quarterly*, vol. 33, no. 1, 1991.

''THE Marks 'Kong's' 60th Anni with Triple-whammy Release,'' in *Variety* (New York), vol. 347, 13 July 1992.

Clayton, J., ''*King Kong*: The Ultimate Fantasy,'' in *Classic Images* (Muscatine), no. 205, July 1992.

Fein, D.C., ''The Eighth Wonder,'' in *Cinefex* (Riverside), no. 51, August 1992.

''The Big Picture,'' in *Boxoffice* (Chicago), vol. 128, October 1992.

Harmetz, A., ''Kong and Wray: 60 Years of Love,'' in *New York Times*, vol. 142, sec. 2, 28 February 1993.

Girard, Martin, ''King Kong et la critique: 60 ans de relations,'' in *Séquences* (Haute-Ville), no. 164, May 1993.

Pouw, A., ''Laserdisc in opmars,'' in *Score* (Lelystad), no. 87, June 1993.

Messias, Hans, ''Kong und Ann: eine Liebesgeschichte,'' in *Film-Dienst* (Cologne), vol. 47, no. 14, 6 July 1993.

Berenstein, Rhona, ''White Heroines and Hearts of Darkness: Race, Gender, and Disguise in 1930s Jungle Films,'' in *Film History* (London), vol. 6, no. 3, Autumn 1994.

Bansak, Edmund G., ''The Children of Kong,'' in *Scarlet Street* (Glen Rock), no. 23, 1996.

Mcgurl, M., ''Making it Big: Picturing the Radio Age in *King Kong*,'' in *Critical Inquiry*, vol. 22, no. 3, 1996.

''*King Kong* Soundtrack Released,'' in *Classic Images* (Muscatine), no. 273, March 1998.

* * *

Few films can compete with the longevity of *King Kong*. The film is as popular today, on television and in revival theaters, as it first was in its initial release in 1933. Ironically, the film's contemporary setting of 1933 has now made it a period piece, though the ideas and themes have never aged.

The story was conceived by producer/director Merian C. Cooper and inspired by his trips to Africa and Southeast Asia to shoot documentary films. Cooper imagined setting a primitive giant ape against the civilization of a modern New York City. This vision was eventually realized on the screen with the aid and collaboration of special visual effects artist and innovator, Willis H. O'Brien.

The special visual techniques developed for *King Kong* were numerous. One of the more important technical advances was the development of a safe (cellulose-acetate) rear-projection screen by Sidney Saunders. Although earlier films had used a more primitive glass rear-projection screen (which, if accidently broken, could cause serious injuries to actors and crew), the cellulose-acetate screen allowed *King Kong* to be the first film to use large-scale rear projection. Another innovation was the invention and use of the optical printer by Vernon Walker and Linwood Dunn. The optical printer presented a new way of combining optical mattes that was superior to the old, and more complex, Dunning process. The enormous amount of matte work in the film (used to combine the special effects with the live action) would not have been feasible without the help of the printer.

Although stop-motion animation had been used previously in other films (such as O'Brien's *The Lost World* in 1925), *King Kong* was the first feature film to use stop-motion to create a continuous character. The model of King Kong was constructed by artist Marcel Delgado out of metal, rubber, cotton and rabbit fur, yet it was truly an "actor." He could express emotions and react logically to the situation around him.

The making of *King Kong* also presented a problem in the area of sound effects. Kong had to sound believable, yet unlike any other creature on earth. The sound department at RKO, headed by Murray Spivak, ran dozens of new and innovative experiments to create the right soundtrack. Kong's roar was a combination of lion and tiger sounds slowed down and played backwards. The music is still another example of the film's originality. Many films in the early 1930s used classical music as background accompaniment. *King Kong* was one of the first films for which an entire score was created. Composer Max Steiner carefully plotted out each scene in the film so that he could synchronize his music with the action.

The technical innovations found in *King Kong* are not the only reasons for its success; every good film must start with a good story. *King Kong* has a universal appeal, making it one of the most popular and well-known American films.

—Linda J. Obalil

KING LEAR

See **KOROL LIR**

KING OF CHILDREN

See **HAIZI WANG**

KINGS OF THE ROAD

See **IM LAUF DER ZEIT**

KINO-PRAVDA

(Film-Truth)

USSR, 1922–25

Director: Dziga Vertov

Production: Black and white, 35mm, series of 23 newsreels-documentaries, released over a period of 3 years; First issue released 21 May 1922, the 23rd and last issue released 1925. Filmed in the Soviet Union.

Photography: Mikhail Kaufman, I. Belyakov and A. Lemberg; **editor:** Dziga Vertov; **assistant editor:** Yelizaveta Svilova; **assistant director:** Ilya Kopalin.

Publications

Books:

De La Roche, Catherine, and Thorold Dickinson, *Soviet Cinema*, London, 1948; New York, 1972.

Leyda, Jay, *Kino: A History of the Russian and Soviet Film*, London, 1960.

Abramov, Nikolai, *Dziga Vertov*, Moscow, 1962; French edition, Lyons, 1965.

Vertov, Dziga, *Aufsätze, Tagebücher, Skizzen*, edited by Sergej Drobaschenko, Berlin, 1967.

Borokov, V., *Dziga Vertov*, Moscow, 1967.

Rotha, Paul, and others, *Documentary Film*, New York, 1968.

Sitney, P. Adams, editor, *Film Culture Reader*, New York, 1970.

Sadoul, Georges, *Dziga Vertov*, Paris, 1971.

Issari, M. Ali, *Cinema Vérité*, East Lansing, Michigan, 1971.

Schnitzer, Luda, Jean Schnitzer, and Marcel Martin, *Cinema in Revolution: The Heroic Era of the Soviet Film*, New York, 1973.

Rimberg, John, *The Motion Picture in the Soviet Union 1918–1952*, New York, 1973.

Cohen, Louis Harris, *The Cultural-Political Traditions and Developments of the Soviet Cinema 1917–1972*, New York, 1974.

Feldman, Seth R., *Evolution of Style in the Early Works of Dziga Vertov*, New York, 1977.

Ellis, Jack C., *A History of Film*, Englewood Cliffs, New Jersey, 1979.

Feldman, Seth R., *Dziga Vertov: A Guide to References and Resources*, Boston, 1979.

Marshall, Herbert, *Masters of the Soviet Cinema: Crippled Creative Biographies*, London, 1983.

Vertov, Dziga, *Kino-Eye: The Writings*, edited by Annette Michelson, Berkeley, 1984.

Waugh, Thomas, editor, *"Show Us Life": Toward a History and Aesthetics of the Committed Documentary*, Metuchen, New Jersey, 1984.

Petric, Vlad, *Constructivism in Film: The Man with the Movie Camera: A Cinematic Analysis*, Cambridge, 1987.

Ellis, Jack C., *The Documentary Idea*, Englewood Cliffs, New Jersey, 1989.

Devaux, Frédérique, *Homme à la camera, de Dziga Vertov*, Crisnée, 1990.

Articles:

Abramov, Nikolai, "Dziga Vertov es a dokumentufilm muveszete," in *Filmkultura* (Budapest), January 1961.

"The Writings of Dziga Vertov," in *Film Culture* (New York), Summer 1962.

Bordwell, David, "Dziga Vertov: An Introduction," in *Film Comment* (New York), Spring 1972.

Feldman, Seth R., "Cinema Weekly and Cinema Truth," in *Sight and Sound* (London), Winter 1973–74.

Mayne, Judith, "Kino-Truth and Kino-Praxis: Vertov's *Man with a Movie Camera*," in *Ciné-Tracts* (Montreal), Summer 1977.

Lebedev, A., in *Iskusstvo Kino* (Moscow), October 1977.

Dille, J., "'Konstruktivizm' and 'Kinematografiya'," in *Artforum*, vol. 16, May 1978.

* * *

The 21 May 1922 debut of the innovative newsreel *Kino-Pravda* came at a crucial time in Soviet history. The nature and reception of *Kino-Pravda* are best understood against that background. In August of the previous year, Lenin, in a desperate move to spark an economy prostrated by years of turmoil—revolution, civil war, occupation by foreign troops—had decreed a "New Economic Policy" i.e., a temporary invocation of private enterprise, including concessions to foreign interests. With striking promptness theatres began showing pre-war Russian films and imports from the major capitalist powers (e.g., *Evil Shadows*, *Daughter of Tarzan*, *The City's Temptation*). Even as their armies departed, their films flooded in, providing some of the needed economic stimulus. But the young film worker Dziga Vertov described the deluge as "living corpses of movie dramas garbed in splendid technological dressing." With the rhetorical flair for which he would become noted, he protested: "The body of cinema is numbed by the terrible poison of habit. We demand an opportunity to experiment with this dying organism, to find an antidote." For him the antidote was "reality." His apparent contempt for fiction films antagonized many in the Russian film world, but his words won support in high places. Lenin had recently declared that it hardly mattered if people were drawn to theatres by nonsense films, provided there was also a proportion dealing with world realities. The need for a "Leninist film proportion" (never clearly defined) became Soviet doctrine and seemed to be implemented with the authorized launching of *Kino-Pravda*, under the leadership of the 26-year-old Dziga Vertov.

For many Russian film-goers the monthly issues of *Kino-Pravda* released during the next two years must often have seemed the only items touching their lives. They saw such events as: the day a Moscow trolley line, long out of service in torn-up streets, resumed running; a tank levelling a field for an airport-to-be; homeless children, surviving in rubble, getting medical attention from a hospital; a hydroelectric project under construction. *Kino-Pravda* occasionally turned a camera on its own operations. One episode showed a film worker arriving in a village, setting up a screen and projector, and, when a crowd gathered, showing them a *Kino-Pravda* reel.

Kino-Pravda was the work of a compact group. Its creator, Dziga Vertov (real name, Denis Kaufman) hailed from Bialystok in the Polish part of the Tsarist domain. With the outbreak of war in 1914 his parents, both librarians, had taken their three young sons—Denis, Mikhail, Boris—to what must have seemed the comparative safety of Russia. The two older sons, Denis and Mikhail, took up university studies in St Petersburg. In 1917 both were caught up in the fever of the revolution, with Denis volunteering to the cinema committee; he was soon editing agit-prop films despatched to fighting units as well as to towns and villages. He renamed himself Dziga Vertov, names suggesting a spinning top, perhaps symbolizing a revolving film reel, or revolution itself. By 1921, as the fighting ended, he was a seasoned film worker. He foresaw a crucial role for film in the coming Soviet state and wrote manifestos to that effect. When his *Kino-Pravda* project won approval, he enlisted his brother Mikhail Kaufman, one year his junior, as chief cameraman, joined by others as needed. Vertov's wife, Yelizaveta Svilova, became *Kino-Pravda*'s editor. (Boris, youngest of the Kaufman brothers, was sent to France to be educated. He eventually pursued a notable film career there, and later in Canada and the United States).

The *Kino-Pravda* group began its work in a basement in the centre of Moscow. Vertov later described it as damp and dark with an earthen floor and holes one stumbled into at every turn. "This dampness prevented our reels of lovingly edited film from sticking together properly, rusted our scissors and our splicers." To get an issue out in time, they often worked into the night. "Before dawn—damp, cold, teeth chattering—I wrap comrade Svilova in a *third* jacket."

Vertov remained the guiding force. He outlined general strategy, then sent Mikhail and other cameramen in various directions, allowing them wide latitude. They were to shoot what seemed important. Staged action was taboo. They wished to catch life "unaware." They never asked permission. They sometimes shot from concealed positions. The epoch provided the themes. Mikhail would remember the period with nostalgia. His camera was always with him. They worked hard but never thought of it as hard work. It was "like breathing or eating." Once when Vertov ordered him to take a rest in the country, he went reluctantly. It was beautiful, "but when I could not see it with the help of my camera, it was not beauty for me."

Like the American film pioneer Robert Flaherty, a contemporary, Vertov and Mikhail considered the camera a miraculous "machine for seeing." The camera eye could help the human eye perceive things it could not otherwise see. To exploit this to the fullest, *Kino-Pravda* welcomed such devices as speeded and slowed action, and vistas from impossible angles. In one of his manifestos, Vertov lets the camera do the explaining: "I, a machine, show you a world such as only I can see. From now on and for always I cast off human immobility, I move constantly, I approach and move away from objects, I creep under them, I leap onto them, I move alongside the mouth of a galloping horse, I cut into a crowd, I turn on my back,

I take off with an airplane, I fall and rise without falling and rising bodies.'' Such words help to explain why *Kino-Pravda* was considered livelier than most newsreels. It dealt with ''the prose of life,'' but processed with any device that would convey symbolic values. Thus in issue No. 24 (1925), on the first anniversary of the death of Lenin, we see people streaming past the dead leader in his coffin. Meanwhile the living Lenin appears by superimposure in the corner of the screen as though still speaking to them.

The *Kino-Pravda* series had a considerable influence beyond its short life. Its footage and techniques were used in a number of subsequent feature-length documentaries by Vertov and his associates, notably in *Shestaya Chast Mira* (One Sixth of the World, 1926), a widely admired film.

Kino-Pravda's magazine-like newsreel seems to have contributed to *Time*'s decision to create *The March of Time*. Even more significant was the inspiration *Kino-Pravda* gave to the *cinema vérité* movement of the 1960s, which took not only its name, but some of its basic ideas, from the Vertov newsreel. Synchronized sight-and-sound shooting had by then made possible, in a fuller sense than in Vertov's time, the *Kino-Pravda* aspiration of capturing life ''on the run.''

—Erik Barnouw

KISS ME CASANOVA

See **Märchen vom Glück**

KISS ME DEADLY

USA, 1955

Director: Robert Aldrich

Production: Parklane Pictures; black and white; running time: 98 minutes, censored version 96 minutes; original length: 8,893 feet. Released April 1955.

Producer: Robert Aldrich; **screenplay:** A. I. Bezzerides, from the novel by Mickey Spillane; **photography:** Ernest Laszlo; **editor:** Mike Luciani; **art director:** William Glasgow; **music:** Frank Devol.

Cast: Ralph Meeker (*Mike Hammer*); Albert Dekker (*Dr. Soberin*); Paul Stewart (*Carl Eyello*); Juano Hernandez (*Eddie Eager*); Wesley Addy (*Pat*); Marian Carr (*Friday*); Maxine Cooper (*Velda*); Cloris Leachman (*Christina*); Nick Dennis (*Nick*).

Publications

Books:

Micha, Rene, *Robert Aldrich*, Brussels, 1957.
Higham, Charles, *The Celluloid Muse: Hollywood Directors Speak*, New York, 1969.
Combs, Richard, editor, *Robert Aldrich*, London, 1978.
Silver, Alain, and Elizabeth Ward, *Robert Aldrich: A Guide to References and Resources*, Boston, 1979.
Salizzato, Claver, *Robert Aldrich*, Florence, 1983.
Piton, Jean-Pierre, *Robert Aldrich*, Paris, 1985.
Arnold, Edwin T., and Eugene L. Miller, *The Films and Career of Robert Aldrich*, Knoxville, Tennessee, 1986.
Maheo, Michel, *Robert Aldrich*, Paris, 1987.
Silver, Alain, and James Ursini, *What Ever Happened to Robert Aldrich?: His Life and His Films*, New York, 1995.
Bogdanovich, Peter, *Who the Devil Made It: Conversations with Robert Aldrich, George Cukor, Allan Dwan, Howard Hawks, Alfred Hitchcock, Chuck Jones, Fritz Lang, Joseph H. Lewis, Sidney Lumet, Leo McCarey, Otto Preminger, Don Siegel, Josef von Sternberg, Frank Tashlin, Edgar G. Ulmer, Raoul Walsh*, New York, 1997.

Articles:

Rivette, Jacques, ''On Revolution,'' in *Cahiers du Cinéma* (Paris), no. 54, 1955.
Hollywood Reporter, 20 April 1955.
Variety (New York), 20 April 1955.
Monthly Film Bulletin (London), August 1955.
Fenin, George, interview with Aldrich, in *Film Culture* (New York), July/August 1955.
Truffaut, François, interview with Aldrich, in *Cahiers du Cinéma* (Paris), November 1956.
Jarvie, Ian, ''Hysteria and Authoritarianism in the Films of Robert Aldrich,'' in *Film Culture* (New York), Summer 1961.
Cameron, Ian, and Mark Shivas, ''Interview and Filmography,'' in *Movie* (London), April 1963.
Motion, no. 3, 1962.
Chabrol, Claude, in *Cahiers du Cinéma* (Paris), December 1964-January 1965.
Bertolucci, Bernardo, ''Dialogue,'' in *Action* (Los Angeles), March-April 1974.
Ringel, Harry, interview with Aldrich, in *Sight and Sound* (London), Summer 1974.
Silver, Alain, ''*Kiss Me Deadly:* Evidence of a Style,'' in *Film Comment* (New York), March-April 1975.
Legrand, Gérard, ''Robert Aldrich et l'incompletude du nihilism,'' in *Positif* (Paris), June 1976.
Sauvage, Pierre, ''Aldrich Interview,'' in *Movie* (London), Winter 1976–77.
''Dialogue on Film: Robert Aldrich,'' in *American Film* (Washington, D.C.), November 1978.
Combs, Richard, in *Listener* (London), 14 March 1985.
Journal of Popular Film and Television (Washington, D.C.), Summer 1985.
Wide Angle (Athens, Ohio), vol. 8, no. 3–4, 1986.
Cinema Journal (Champaign, Illinois), Spring 1988.
Telotte, J. P., ''The Big Clock of Film Noir,'' in *Film Criticism* (Meadville, Pennsylvania), no. 2, 1990.
Wood, R., ''Creativity and Evaluation,'' in *Cineaction* (Toronto), Summer-Fall 1990.
Telotte, J. P., ''The Fantastic Realism of Film Noir: *Kiss Me Deadly*,'' in *Wide Angle* (Baltimore), no. 1, 1992.

Kiss Me Deadly

Osteen, M., ''The Big Secret: Film Noir and Nuclear Fear,'' in *Journal of Popular Film*, vol. 22, no. 2, 1994.

Hill, Rodney F., ''Rememberance, Communication, and *Kiss Me Deadly*,'' in *Literature/Film Quarterly* (Salisbury), vol. 22, no. 2, April 1995.

Kohn, Olivier, and others, ''Hommage à Robert Aldrich,'' in *Positif* (Paris), no. 415, September 1995.

''What's New with the Great Whatzit?'' in *Video Watchdog* (Cincinnati), no. 40, 1997.

Lucas, Tim, ''*Kiss Me Deadly*,'' in *Video Watchdog* (Cincinnati), no. 42, 1997.

Riordan, P.M., ''Atomic Blonde,'' in *Filmfax* (Evanston), no. 63/64, October/January 1997/1998.

Thomson, David, ''Deadlily,'' in *Film Comment* (New York), vol. 33, no. 6, November-December 1997.

* * *

The end of a particular stylistic period, in film as in the other arts, is often marked by a few masterpieces whose dizzying complexity seems to carry the style as far as it can be taken. Just as the end of the Romantic symphony is marked by Mahler's last few works in that form, and the end of Hollywood silent cinema is marked by films like *Sunrise* and *Street Angel*, so at the end of the *film noir* period come the two ultimate examples of the form, *Touch of Evil* and *Kiss Me Deadly*. *Kiss Me Deadly* is also in many ways, the ultimate film of 1950s America, with its themes of speed, money, power, sex, and the atomic bomb intertwined in a tale of a detective who becomes an extortionist in an attempt to turn a chance discovery into personal gain.

The film's night-for-night opening sets the tone: A woman dressed only in a coat appears out of the darkness on a lonely highway. She forces a car driven by Mike Hammer to stop, and as they drive one is aware of the loud drone of the engine and of the disorienting darkness, in which the disembodied lights of distant cars and the white lines of the road are virtually our only co-ordinates. What is established here is worked out in detail during the whole remainder of the film, in a soundtrack which uses a variety of noises of violent intensity and intrusiveness, and in imagery which uses light/dark contrasts utterly to undermine stability.

Hammer, happening on a plot involving the theft and attempted sale of fissionable material, does not know these specifics until the film's end. He guesses only that he has lucked on to ''something big,'' and that ''a piece of something big has got to be something big.'' He follows his thread through a befuddling labyrinth of bizarre characters, common in Spillane's detective fiction, which finds its visual equivalent in the film in a panoply of foreground objects, bizarre shifts of camera perspective, and highly disjunctive editing. The camera follows Hammer down a dark street; suddenly a brightly lit newsstand comes into the foreground, utterly transforming the space. We see a beachfront fight from eye-level, and then cut to an extreme high angle. In many compositions, oblique camera angles combine with cluttered foregrounds to produce oddly asymmetrical spaces. The effect of these devices is to place the viewer in a world utterly different from that of Ford, or Walsh or Hawks. In their films, paradigms of the classical Hollywood style, the consistency of the relationship between earth and sky, or between the bodies and body-movements of the characters, serves as a kind of fixed basis against which all deviations of movement, behavior, and image may be judged. In *Kiss Me Deadly*, on the other hand, we are plunged from the opening images into a world utterly without ground, without stability, without predictability, in which the only constant is the ability of the image to suddenly transform itself into another, very different one. Space, and the objects that fill it, are presented as physically malleable; there are no absolutes. The *noir* themes of violence, paranoia, and despair, and the visual motifs that accompany them, are here carried to a visionary extreme that becomes a total world-view. This is a realm in which there can be firm basis for moral judgements, and if the film ultimately renders a negative judgment on Hammer's self-serving quest, it does so more because of the actual ugly consequences than because of any fundamental belief.

In a universe without belief, one lives for, and celebrates, the senses. Aldrich, and A. I. Bezzerides in his brilliant script, present the ethos of 1950s America quite brilliantly. Nick, Hammer's Greek auto mechanic, uses the phrase ''Va-va-voom—pow!'' to express his attraction to Hammer's fast cars and his interest in picking up ''a couple of Greek girls''—and yet, in that phrase, the film's whole plot finds epigrammatic expression. Fascinated with speed and sex, the men who pursue both often wind up endangered, injured, or dead; Nick's ''pow'' is not only the thrill of moving at maximum speed, and the thrill of orgasm, but also a forecast of the explosion that ends the film, itself only a hyperbolization of the film's earlier small explosions. The script's mythological and biblical references contrast a modern world without values and a heroic past whose heroism is now rendered, in the fragments of fables we hear, as empty actions almost devoid of meaning.

In one of the film's many small brilliant touches, a boxing promoter sees Hammer and tries to get him to bet on his latest fighter. Hammer suggests that the promoter will ultimately have the fighter throw his big fight, as he had in fact done in the past, because there's more gambling money to be made that way. The promoter replies, ''not this one.'' Later, near the film's end, Hammer, drugged with ''truth serum,'' is tied to a bed and interrogated; he soon manages to outwit and murder his captors. During this section, we hear the sound of the big fight on the radio; at the end, the fighter who had been winning suddenly loses, presumably ''throwing'' it. This is more than simply another of the venal betrayals that dot the film; it is an example of the way that the film's quest, for speed, sex, and power, must, since it is a quest without moral basis, ultimately turn back on itself, annihilating all the seekers.

—Fred Camper

KLUTE

USA, 1971

Director: Alan J. Pakula

Production: Warner Bros.; Technicolor; Panavision; running time: 114 minutes; length: 10,240 feet. Released June 1971.

Producer: Alan J. Pakula; **co-producer:** David Lange; **screenplay:** Andy K. Lewis, Dave Lewis; **assistant director:** William Gerritty; **photography:** Gordon Willis; **editor:** Carl Lerner; **sound:** Chris Newman; **art director:** George Jenkins; **music:** Michael Small.

Cast: Jane Fonda (*Bree Daniel*); Donald Sutherland (*John Klute*); Charles Cioffi (*Cable*); Roy Scheider (*Frank Ligourin*); Dorothy Tristan (*Arlyn Page*); Rita Gam (*Trina*); Vivian Nathan (*Psychiatrist*); Nathan George (*Lt. Trask*); Morris Strassberg (*Mr. Goldfarb*); Barry Snider (*Berger*); Anthony Holland (*Actor's Agent*); Richard Shull (*Sugarman*); Betty Murray (*Holly Gruneman*); Fred Burrell

Klute

(*Man in Hotel*); Jean Stapleton (*Goldfarb's Secretary*); Robert Milli (*Tom Gruneman*); Jane White (*Janie Dale*); Shirley Stoler (*Momma Reese*); Mary Louise Wilson (*Producer in Ad Agency*); Marc Malvin (*Assistant Producer in Ad Agency*); Jan Fielding (*Psychiatrist's Secretary*); Antonia Ray (*Mrs. Vasek*); Robert Ronan (*Director in Little Theatre*); Richard Ramos (*Assistant Director in Little Theatre*).

Award: Oscar for Best Actress (Fonda), 1971.

Publications

Books:

Kiernan, Thomas, *Jane: An Intimate Biography of Jane Fonda*, New York, 1977.
Kaplan, E. Ann, editor, *Women in Film Noir*, London, 1978.
Jeien, Thomas, *Jane Fonda: Ihre Filme, ihr Leben*, Munich, 1981.
Erlanger, Ellen, *Jane Fonda*, Minneapolis, 1981.
Haddad, G. G., *The Films of Jane Fonda*, Secaucus, New Jersey, 1981.
Guiles, Fred, *Jane Fonda: The Actress in Her Time*, New York, 1982.
Cole, Gerald, and Wes Farrell, *The Fondas*, London, 1984.
Robbiano, Giovanni, *Alan Pakula*, Firenze, 1985.
French, Sean, *Jane Fonda: A Biography*, London, 1998.

Articles:

Variety (New York), 30 June 1971.
Milne, Tom, in *Sight and Sound* (London), Autumn 1971.
Sirkin, Elliot, in *Film Quarterly* (Berkeley), Fall 1971.
Houston, Penelope, in *Monthly Film Bulletin* (London), November 1971.
Rignall, John, in *Monogram* (London), No. 4, 1972.
Legrand, Gérard, in *Positif* (Paris), March 1972.
Eyles, Allen, ''Donald Sutherland,'' in *Films in Review* (New York), Autumn 1973.
Cineaste (New York), vol. 11, no. 2, 1981.
Lovell, Terry, and Simon Frith, ''How Do You Get Pleasure? Another Look at *Klute*,'' in *Screen Education* (London), Summer 1981.
Kornatowska, M., ''Eros i cywilizacja,'' in *Kino* (Warsaw), August 1985.
Caputo, R., ''Film Noir: 'You Sure You Don't See What You Hear?,''' in *Continuum*, vol. 5, no. 2, 1992.
Atkinson, M., ''Jane Fonda in *Klute*,'' in *Movieline* (Escondido), vol. 6, April 1995.
Jönsson, Mats, ''Parallax Paranoia: On Alan J. Pakulas amerikanska trilogi,'' in *Filmhäftet* (Stockholm), vol. 27, no. 105, 1999.

* * *

Jane Fonda's Academy Award-winning performance as Bree Daniels, a New York prostitute with modeling aspirations, was her latest in a series of roles that paralleled the course of American society. After initially appearing as a cheerleader in *Tall Story*, Fonda had become increasingly political, prompting the ire of American conservatives by appearing in *Tout va bien*, made by Jean-Luc Godard, who in *A Letter to Jane* attacked her for the Hollywood liberalism of *Klute*. Though *Klute* did appeal to some early feminist critics who regarded it as a psychologically realistic portrait of a woman's inner conflict, later feminists have discussed it in political terms, finding a subtext which endorses patriarchy.

In an interview in *Positif* Alan Pakula stated that he regarded the film as similar to a 1940s thriller, a genre that he could use for his own purposes. In fact, *Klute* possesses several *film noir* characteristics, both in style and content, but Pakula shifts the psychological focus from Klute, the detective, to Bree, the intended victim. Klute's attempts to discover the identity of the killer pale in comparison to Bree's efforts at self-discovery, which are aided by a female psychotherapist. Thus the film is generically both *film noir* thriller and a psychological thriller, and the audience identifies with Bree, a developing character whose inner conflict torments her, not with Klute, the static and reticent male.

Bree wants to leave ''the life,'' which ironically gives her control and independence, for modeling, but the audition with its ''lineup'' and depersonalization, seems to offer only a different ''life.'' When Klute, the small-town friend of a murder victim, pursues the identity of the murderer, he seems to offer her another option, love and its accompanying dependence; for he comes to love and protect her. Ironically, his love and protection further endanger her, and as she relinquishes control to Klute, she nearly loses her life. Like Cable, the murderer, Klute poses a real threat, though it is more psychological than physical. At one point Bree attacks Klute with scissors and twice flees from him to her ex-pimp, only to find that prostitution itself involves dependency and, eventually, death. Just as Klute represents an appeal to dependency and loss of control, Cable, the murderer, represents control in the form of detachment. Neither Bree nor Cable is emotionally involved in sex, which becomes an act by which each wields power, and both wish to be emotionally numb. Even their voices, as rendered on the tape recorder, seem similar. Although the stereotypical roles of detective and criminal are antithetical, Klute and Cable actually have a great deal in common, thereby reinforcing the image of Klute as a threat to Bree. After the tape recorder is played in rural Pennsylvania, Klute appears in New York; and both men use similar methods, though for different purposes.

Just as Klute and Cable can be viewed as dramatic projections of the forces within Bree's mind, her apartment may also represent herself. She is spied on in her apartment, which is subsequently and brutally penetrated by Cable; Bree's semen-soaked underpants suggest that Cable, too, sees his action as rape. When she leaves her apartment and sleeps with Klute, she also leaves her ''self'' and becomes dependent on him. At the end of the film she and Klute leave her apartment, which is empty, except for the ringing telephone, her link with the ''johns'' and her therapist. Her furnishings, that which made the apartment ''hers,'' are gone; and she may be empty of her past, ready to acquire Klute's furnishings, his values, his life, his identity.

Though Cable's death and Bree's decision to leave dark, claustrophobic New York for the sunlight of rural Pennsylvania imply that she has opted for love and dependence, Pakula does create some ambiguity. She has told her analyst that she will probably be back next week for an appointment, but that verbal message does not carry the weight that the visual one does: standing in the empty apartment, she is wearing the same clothes she wore at the beginning of the film. Bree may have chosen love and dependency for the present, through the efforts of the female therapist who has encouraged that choice, but the choice is not without personal cost.

—Thomas L. Erskine

KNIFE IN THE WATER

See **N"Z W WODZIE**

KOMISSAR

(The Commissar)

USSR, 1967

Director: Alexander Askoldov

Production: Gorky Studios; colour, Cinemascope; running time: 108 minutes. Not released until 1988, following an unscheduled screening at the Moscow Film Festival.

Producers: V. Levin, V. Grigorev, L. Prilutzkaya; **screenplay:** Alexander Askoldov, based on the novel *In the Town of Berdichev* by Vasily Grossman; **photography:** Valery Ginsburg; **editors:** V. Isayeva, N. Loginova, S. Lyashinskaya; **assistant directors:** B. Dokuchaev, G. Balinskaya; **art director:** Sergei Serebrennikov; **music:** Alfred Shnittke; **sound:** V. Sharoy, E. Bazanov, L. Benevolskaya.

Cast: Nonna Mordyukova (*Claudia Vavilova*); Rolan Bykov (*Yefim*); Raisa Niedashkovskaya (*Maria*); Vasily Shuskin (*Commander*).

Awards: Silver Bear, Berlin 1988.

Publications

Books:

Russian Critics on the Cinema of Glasnost, Michael Brashinsky and Andrew Horton, ed., Cambridge, 1994.

Articles:

Variety (New York), 5 August 1987.

Wolf, W., and A. Williamson, ''Askoldov!,'' in *Film Comment* (New York), May-June 1988.

Carlisle, O. A., *American Film* (Washington D.C), June 1988.

Reynaud, B., and F. Strauss, in *Cahiers du Cinéma* (Paris), September 1988.

Johnson, Brian D., ''Glasnost on Screen,'' in *Maclean's* (Toronto), 26 September 1988.

Navailh, F., in *Cinéma* (Paris), October 1988.

Delmas, G., in *Jeune Cinéma* (Paris), November-December 1988.

Derobert, J., in *Positif* (Paris), December 1988.

Brub, R.-C., in *Séquences* (Montreal), January 1989.

Menashe, Louis, in *Cineaste* (New York), 1989.

Glaessner, V., in *Monthly Film Bulletin* (London), May 1989.

Sherwood, Pippa, ''The Russian Restitution,'' in *Films and Filming*, no. 415, May 1989.

Batchan, A., *Cineaste* (New York), 1989.

Stishova, E., ''Passions over Commissar'' in *Wide Angle* (Athens, Ohio), October 1990.

Navailh, F., ''Le drapeau rouge et les gants blancs,'' in *Cahiers du Cinématheque* (Perpignan, France), no. 67, December 1997.

* * *

When director Alexsandr Askoldov completed his first and only feature, *The Commissar*, in 1967, it was immediately banned and he was blacklisted as a film director. In December of 1987, in an atmosphere of *glasnost*, *The Commissar* was permitted a showing in Moscow and soon received international attention and critical praise. The film, based on the story ''In the Town of Berdichev'' by Vasily Grossman, is about love, war, maternity and betrayal, and presents a frightening foreshadowing of the Holocaust.

The pregnant commissar of a Red Army unit, Klavdia Vavilova, enters the town of Berdichev at the head of her battalion in 1922 and shoots a deserter who had escaped home to his wife. While occupying the town, this hard-edged, dedicated Bolshevik must tell her second-in-command that she must leave the Army because she is pregnant. The home of a Jewish tinsmith and his wife, mother-in-law and six children is commandeered for her confinement, and the commissar and her baby become assimilated into this family. A friendship develops between Klavdia and Raisa, the tinsmith's wife, and both begin to adopt characteristics of the other. After her baby is born, the commissar becomes nurturing, gentle, and protective of her child, while, Raisa, the tinsmith's wife, begins to assert her individuality. Realizing the fragility of new life and responsibilities of motherhood, Klavdia questions whether the consequences of war are too costly for her to return to battle. She finally decides to resume her duties as commissar and leaves her infant with the Jewish family.

The film has elements of warmth and humor as the tough commissar clashes with the gentle tinker, and as they eventually develop a strong bond. The large loving family represents a nurturing Jewish ethic, which Askoldov contrasts with the uncompromising Russian will to conquer in the name of universal justice. The Jewish family is treated sympathetically, but as William Wolf asserts in *Film Comment*, ''Paying special attention to the persecution of Jews has long conflicted with the Soviet policy of downplaying Jewish identity.''

The film was banned due to tension derived from the Soviet Union's troubled history with Jews and Askoldov's refusal to change or remove any part of the film which exposes anti-Semitism and portrays the military unfavorably. Anne Williamson stated in *Film Comment* (May/June 1988): ''In 1967, just as Israel had triumphed in the Six Day War, Askoldov was finishing the edit on *The Commissar*, which sympathetically portrays a Jewish family. Soviet censors realized that scenes like the commissar's vision of the future Holocaust and of the Magazanik family being led to the gas chambers hinted darkly at a connection between Nazism and Russian anti-Semitism and could possibly remind audiences of Stalin's appeasement of Hitler.'' In addition to the powerful flash forward of the family members trudging along to their impending terrifying demise, the film includes a disturbing child's fantasy of a pogrom. As Louis Menashe suggests in *Cineaste*, 1989, ''What appears to be Askoldov's preference for humanism over Bolshevism probably contributed to official wrath toward the film.''

The Commissar was produced at the Gorky Studio, which rejected the finished product as its ''greatest political and esthetic failure.'' Askoldov was fired for incompetence and the film was destroyed. But Gorbachev's policy of *glasnost* led to a revolution in Russia's film industry and many blacklisted films reemerged. In May, 1986, conservatives were ousted from the leadership of the Soviet Filmmakers Union and control over the movie industry shifted from the state bureaucracy to the union's new leaders—directors whose films had been shelved in the past. Askoldov was given permission to search for his film in the state archives, and he found a print in a damp cellar. The black-and-white film had been partially destroyed, but Askoldov restored it by piecing together various copies.

The Commissar is visually striking and incorporates features of Askoldov's great predecessors. Williamson identifies a brilliant metaphor in the cross-cutting of soldiers and sees Vsevolod Pudovkin's sense of realism as Klavdia struggles to push a cannon up a hill of sand and in the birth sequence. The rhythm and energy of Sergei Eisenstein are evoked in the scene of the caravan in which the commissar's revolutionary lover dies a gallant death. Brian Johnson notes in his article in *Maclean's* (26 September 1988): ''Askoldov broke the fetters of the socialist realism that prevailed at the time of the film's release with fluid camerawork and dreamlike scenes of cavalry horses galloping riderless across a battlefield.'' The clarity of the images and varying pace of editing offers moments enhanced by an excited tempo as well as those reserved for reflection and contemplation.

—Kelly Otter

KONGI'S HARVEST

Nigeria, 1970

Director: Ossie Davis

Production: Calpenny-Nigeria Films Ltd (Nigeria); color; running time: 85 minutes. Released 1970.

Producers: Francis Oladele, Arthur Dubons, and Lennart Berns; **screenplay:** Wole Soyinka, from his own play; **assistant directors:** Dandy E. Oyegunle and Tunde Adeniji; **photography:** Åke Dahlquist; **editors:** Sharon Sachs, Jerry Gränsman, and Gboyega Arulogun; **sound:** Bo Abrahamsson; **art directors:** D. Lindersay and J. K. Ogunbiyi; **costumes:** Danny Moquette, Agbo Folarin, Ayo Aderemi, and Fadeke Akinwunmi.

Cast: Wole Soyinka (*Kongi*); Rashidi Onikoyi (*Oba Danlola*); Banjo Solaru (*Sarumi*); Femi Johnson (*Organising Secretary*); Nina Baden-Semper (*Segi*); Dapo Adelugba (*Daodu*); Orlando Martins (*Dr. Gbenge*); Wale Ogunyemi (*Dende*).

Publications

Books:

Soyinka, Wole, *Kongi's Harvest*, London, 1967.

Gibbs, James, *Kongi's Harvest by Wole Soyinka* (typescript), Kenneth Library, University of Ibadan, n.d. (c. 1969).

Gibbs, James, *Study Guide to Kongi's Harvest*, London, 1973.

Gibbs, James, *Wole Soyinka*, Basingstoke, London, 1986.

Ekwuazi, Hyginus O., *Film in Nigeria*, 2d ed., Jos, Nigeria, 1991.

Articles:

Davis, Ossie, ''When Is a Camera a Weapon?'' in *New York Times*, 20 September 1970.

''People,'' in *West Africa*, no. 2821, 1971.

Soyinka, Wole, ''Class Discussion,'' in *In Person: Achebe, Awoonor, and Soyinka at the University of Washington*, edited by Karen L. Morell, Seattle, Washington, 1975.

Soyinka, Wole, ''Theatre and the Emergence of the Nigerian Film Industry,'' in *The Development and Growth of the Film Industry in Nigeria: Proceedings of a Seminar on the Film Industry and Cultural Identity in Nigeria*, edited by Alfred E. Opubor and Onuora E. Nwuneli, Lagos and New York, 1979.

Gugler, Josef, ''Wole Soyinka's *Kongi's Harvest* from Stage to Screen: Four Endings to Tyranny,'' in *Canadian Journal of African Studies*, vol. 31, 1997.

* * *

Kongi's Harvest is an important film because it is the most significant attempt to date to take a play by Wole Soyinka—Africa's preeminent playwright and winner of the Nobel Prize in 1986—to the screen. Soyinka's eponymous play was the first of several to denounce tyranny, and was perhaps the most distinguished aesthetically. *Kongi's Harvest* analyzes the degeneration of personal rule in independent Africa and satirizes the resulting tyranny in terms of the confrontation between a populist politician and a traditional ruler. When *Kongi's Harvest* was first performed in Nigeria in 1965 it was topical: just a few years after independence authoritarian one-man regimes had imposed themselves in a number of African countries. By the time the film was released in 1970, such regimes had become common throughout the region.

Kongi's Harvest is, as the playwright put it, a play ''about Power, Pomp and Ecstasy'': the power of autocratic president Kongi, the pomp of detained king Danlola, the ecstasy of Segi and Daodu who oppose the dictator. It is one of Soyinka's finest plays. The film, unfortunately, must be considered a failure. It follows the play closely in most respects but falls far short of its accomplishments and betrays it in the end. Still, it conveys Soyinka's bitter satire of the recurrent features of dictatorships—the sycophants surrounding the dictator, the dictator's megalomania, the ideological *isms* invoked to justify *absolute-ism*, the propaganda blared at the population, the repression of dissent, and the economic concomitants of such political features: mismanagement and corruption.

The film was directed by the distinguished African-American actor Ossie Davis, who appears as narrator in the early scenes. He had come to Nigeria full of enthusiasm to direct what was to be one of the very first major motion pictures produced in Africa South of the Sahara by an African film company, Francis Oladele's Calpenny-Nigeria Films. Arthur DuBow of Herald Productions had raised the funds in the U.S. and Lennart Berns of Omega Film in Sweden had furnished the crew. The film never had much exposure. In the 1970s, New Line Cinema provided limited distribution in the United States, before the film was withdrawn from distribution altogether. By now it has all but disappeared. (It may be seen at the Film Archives of the Institute of African Studies at the University of Ibadan, Nigeria.)

The film conveys the pageantry of a Yoruba royal court: the royal drums, the royal dance and chant, most strikingly the praise song to the king, in Yoruba. And it departs from the play to take advantage of the opportunities the medium offers. It presents an aerial view of

Ibadan, the largest metropolis in tropical Africa until the 1950s, including street and market scenes, preparations for the festival, a motorcade with motorcycle outriders, a street barricade, the famous Olumo rock in Abeokuta, the dictator's militia singing and drinking, Oba Danlola's large retinue, and a masquerade of the Yoruba Gelede. It adds scenes of Daodu and Segi visiting a shrine at the palace of the Alafin of Oyo, and of Kongi enacting a last supper with his twelve advisors.

The production of *Kongi's Harvest* suffered from its low budget, reported at a pitiful $300,000. The photography is amateurish, the editing poor, the sound-track bad. The stage experience of the actors in *Kongi's Harvest* turned out to be a handicap for most. Soyinka's script, while quite inspired in places, remained too beholden to the rich dialogue of his play. Endless cross-cutting and the absence of sustained dramatic sequences make the film appear disjointed. As for Ossie Davis, he had no formal training and little experience as a director. In 1969, he had been offered a role in *Cotton Comes to Harlem* and had wound up directing it. At that time he had a $1.2 million budget, but now he was operating with a much lower budget, in a foreign environment, and a very difficult one at that. In short, the film does not do justice to the magnificent play. Soyinka has gone so far as to disown the film altogether, even though he had written the script and acted, in a fine display of self irony, the role of Kongi. We are left to speculate about his reasons. He may have wanted to dissociate himself from the failed enterprise. He clearly was concerned about the political implications of the play. Probably most importantly, the film's ending drastically departed from Soyinka's script.

When the play was first performed in Nigeria in 1965 there was no doubt that Kongi stood for Kwame Nkrumah, the president of Ghana, whose regime had degenerated over the years and exhibited the very traits castigated by Soyinka. But when Nkrumah was overthrown in 1966 to popular acclaim, Soyinka, like many intellectuals, refused to join the anti-Nkrumah crowd that gathered once he was overthrown. Nkrumah had been—and Soyinka now argued should continue to work as—the foremost leader for African emancipation, socialism, and unification.

The ending of the film diverges altogether from both Soyinka's play and his film script. The tyrannicide succeeds, but in the final scene Dr. Gbenge, the leader of the opposition, is seen taking on the dictator's role, repeating the very same megalomanic slogans: ''The will of the State is supreme, destiny has entrusted in our hands the will of the State, the will of the State is supreme.'' The film thus presents a stunning reversal. This makes for a dramatic ending, and it emphasizes the point that power corrupts-a recurrent theme in Soyinka's work. However, the eclipse of the process of moral renewal that might be expected to come with a new revolutionary regime seems all too cynical. Indeed, the author has cautioned us against such a simplistic approach. He has Segi observe that, at some point in the past, ''Kongi *was* a great man.'' Likewise we should expect Dr. Gbenge to have a time of greatness before his regime deteriorates.

The change in the ending of *Kongi's Harvest* would appear not to have been acceptable to Soyinka. He has emphasized that the film does not correspond to his script, and the film, contrary to the U.S. distributor's blurb, does not credit the script to Soyinka, or anybody else for that matter. We may surmise that the film's cynical, circular view of history, or perhaps just African history, was meant to appeal to the intended U.S. audience. It is subject to charges of conservatism and racism. Ossie Davis is a most unlikely target for such charges. Soyinka has commented, with respect to anglophone African cinema, on producers' subservience to financial sponsors and the potential U.S. audience and on their dominant position vis-à-vis editors, and he has complained that *Kongi's Harvest* had been ''badly butchered'' by the overseas (i.e. U.S.) partners of Calpenny Productions. Presumably that's where the playwright, script writer, and lead actor puts the blame. It would appear that the U.S. sponsors short-changed the production of a major play by the preeminent African playwright with insufficient financing and insisted on subverting the authorial intent.

—Josef Gugler

KONYETS SANKT-PETERBURGA

(The End of St. Petersburg)

USSR, 1927

Director: Vsevolod Pudovkin

Production: Mezhrabpom-Russ; black and white, 35mm, silent; running time: about 110 minutes; length: 8202 feet. Released 1927.

Screenplay: Nathan Zarkhi, from the poem ''The Bronze Horseman'' by Pushkin and the novel *St. Petersburg* by Andrey Biely; **photography:** Anatoli Golovnya and K. Vents; **art director:** S. Kozlovsky.

Cast: A. P. Chistyakov (*Worker*); Vera Baranovskaya (*His wife*); Ivan Chuvelov (*Ivan, a peasant*); V. Chuvelov (*Friend from the village*); V. Obolensky (*Lebedev, Steel Magnate*); A. Gromov (*Revolutionary*); Vladimir Tzoppi (*Patriot*); Nikolai Khmelyov and M. Tzibulsky (*Stockbrokers*).

Publications

Books:

Korolevich, V., *Vera Baranovskaya*, Moscow, 1929.

Yezuitov, N., *Pudovkin, ''Pouti Tvortchevstva,'' Les Voies de la création*, Moscow, 1937.

De La Roche, Catherine, and Thorold Dickinson, *Soviet Cinema*, London, 1948; New York, 1972.

Mariamov, A., *Vsevolod Pudovkin*, Moscow, 1952.

Leyda, Jay, *Kino: A History of the Russian and Soviet Film*, London, 1960.

Schnitzer, Luda and Jean, *Vsevolod Poudovkine*, Paris, 1966.

Amengual, Barthélemy, *V. I. Poudovkine*, Lyons, 1968.

Schnitzer, Luda and Jean, and Marcel Martin, *Cinema in Revolution: The Heroic Era of the Soviet Film*, New York, 1973.

Rimberg, John, *The Motion Picture in the Soviet Union 1918–1952*, New York, 1973.

Dart, Peter, *Pudovkin's Films and Film Theory*, New York, 1974.

Cohen, Louis Harris, *The Cultural-Political Traditions and Developments of the Soviet Cinema 1917–1972*, New York, 1974.

Klinowski, Jacek, and Adam Garbicz, *Cinema, The Magic Vehicle: A Guide to Its Achievement: Journey One: The Cinema Through 1949*, Metuchen, New Jersey, 1975.

Taylor, Richard, *The Politics of the Soviet Cinema: Nineteen Seventeen to Nineteen Twenty-Nine*, New York, 1979.
Marshall, Herbert, *Masters of the Soviet Cinema: Crippled Creative Biographies*, London, 1983.
Masi, Stefano, *Vsevolod I. Pudovkin*, Florence, 1985.
Zorkaya, Neya, *Illustrated History of the Soviet Cinema: Nineteen Seven to Today*, New York, 1989.
Youngblood, Denise J., *Soviet Cinema in the Silent Era: 1919–1934*, Ann Arbor, 1985, 1991.
Kenez, Peter, *Cinema & Soviet Society: 1917–1953*, New York, 1992.

Articles:

Close Up (London), April 1928.
New York Times, 31 May 1928.
Variety (New York), 6 June 1928.
Potamkin, Harry A., ''Pudovkin and the Revolutionary Film,'' in *Hound and Horn* (New York), April-June 1933.
Leyda, Jay, ''Index to the Creative Work of Vsevolod Pudovkin,'' in *Sight and Sound* (London), November 1948.
''Pudovkin Issue'' of *Cahiers du Cinéma* (Paris), August-September 1953.
Weinberg, Herman, ''Vsevolod Pudovkin,'' in *Films in Review* (New York), August-September 1953.
Macdonald, Dwight, ''Eisenstein and Pudovkin in the Twenties,'' in *On Movies* (Englewood Cliffs, New Jersey), 1969; as *On Movies* (New York), 1981.
''Pudovkin Issue'' of *Iskusstvo Kino* (Moscow), February 1973.
Hudlin, E., ''Film Language: Pudovkin and Eisenstein and Russian Formalism,'' in *Journal of Aesthetic Education* (Urbano, Illinois), No. 2, 1979.
Burns, P. E., ''Linkage: Pudovkin's Classics Revisited,'' in *Journal of Popular Film and Television* (Washington, D.C.), Summer 1981.
Sasin, O., ''*Konec Sankt-Peterburga*,'' in *Iskusstvo Kino* (Moscow), no. 8, August 1987.
Sonnenberg, B., ''*Aelita, Queen of Mars*, Others from U.S.S.R.,'' in *Nation*, vol. 254, 9 March 1992.
Caruso, U.G., ''*La Madre/La fine di San Pietroburgo/Tempeste sull'Asia*,'' in *Cineforum* (Bergamo), vol. 33, no. 5(325), June 1993.
Smith, M., ''The Influence of Socialist Realism on Soviet Montage: *The End of St. Petersburg*, *Fragment of an Empire*, and *Arsenal*,'' in *Journal of Ukrainian Studies*, vol. 19, no. 1, 1994.
Kepley, V., Jr., ''Pudovkin and the Continuity Style: Problems of Space and Narration,'' in *Discourse* (Detroit), no. 17.3, Spring 1995.

* * *

Pudovkin made *The End of St. Petersburg* in 1927 for the tenth anniversary of the Soviet Revolution. From an earlier conception of the film as a 200-year history of St. Petersburg and its changing political climate, Pudovkin focused instead on the struggle for that city at the time of the Revolution. As in *Mother*, Pudovkin charted the developing awareness of the (mass) protagonist from political naiveté to Marxist consciousness. The film's distinction is in the conjunction of this personal mode of Marxist analysis with two other major points of reference: the St. Petersburg cityscape itself and its representation in the Russian literary tradition; and Pudovkin's theoretical writings (*Film Technique and Film Acting*), particularly on the role of editing.

The portrayal of a protagonist who interacts with the animated architecture of St Petersburg follows in the tradition of Pushkin's poem ''The Bronze Horseman'' and Andrey Biely's symbolist novel *St. Petersburg*, written in 1910–11 but set during the unsuccessful rebellion in 1905. Pudovkin superimposes a Marxist interpretation on Pushkin's Bronze Horseman, the ''Soul of Russia.'' Through editing, he causes the statue to cry during the bombardment of the Czar's Winter Palace. Biely's vivid city geometry becomes in the film a maze of revolutionary activity. Pudovkin shifts the major site of conflict from the homes of the workers (in Biely) to the foundries in which they work. The realism of the photographic image would serve him well, allowing him to rely on the spectator's familiarity with the architecture of the city. He vivifies the city's monumental buildings and squares (as well as its famous statues), lending credibility to his political narrative. The tradition of romanticized urbanism, from Dickens through Griffith, takes on a Marxist ideological thrust in *The End of St. Petersburg*.

Pudovkin conveys the revolutionary and urban themes through precise techniques of editing, which he had codified in *Film Technique*. His re-assemblage of filmed reality recalls Constructivism in its tight integration of form and content. The camera records real space and time; the director creates filmic space and time through editing. Pudovkin called this the ''linkage'' of the film strips, ''brick by brick.'' Kuleshov had taught him the importance of the legibility of individual shots when trying to emphasize the relationships among shots. Pudovkin would elaborate important details and eliminate others, often stressing the metaphorical nature of a particular detail. It is the editing that gives the film its strong metaphorical potential.

The various ways in which Pudovkin alternates these details in the editing gives the film its distinctive rhythm. He establishes oppositions, cutting for contrast between day and night, as well as between large open spaces and claustrophobic interiors. He inserts ironic inter-titles to contrast with visual images. Most significantly, he employs parallel editing to contrast static shots with dynamic activity. Pudovkin maintains this rhythm throughout the film, often cutting on human movement to provide fluid continuity.

Pudovkin's conception of the mass hero would unfortunately set the pattern for what would become the official aesthetic of Socialist Realism. His cinematic dynamization of St. Petersburg would remain a more enduring contribution.

—Howard Feinstein

KÖRKALEN

(The Phantom Chariot)

Sweden, 1921

Director: Victor Sjöström (Seastrom)

Production: Svensk Bio; black and white, 35mm, silent; running time: about 120 minutes; length: 5 reels, 6122 feet. Released 1 January 1921. Re-released in a re-edited version in America in 1922. Filmed 1920 in Sweden.

Screenplay: Victor Sjöström (Seastrom), from the novel by Selma Lagerlöf; **photography:** Julius Jaenzon; **art directors:** Aleksander Bako and Axel Esbensen.

Körkalen

Cast: Victor Sjöström (*David Holm*); Hilda Borgstrom (*His wife*); Astrid Holm (*Sister Edith*); Tor Weijden (*Gustafsson*); Tore Svenberg (*Georg*); Concordia Selander (*Edith's mother*); Lisa Lundholm (*Sister Maria*); Olaf Aas (*Coachman*); Nils Aréhn (*Prison chaplain*).

Publications

Books:

Charensol, Georges, *40 ans de cinéma nordique 1895–1935*, Paris, 1935.

Hardy, Forsyth, *Scandinavian Film*, London, 1951.

Idestam-Almquist, Bengt, *Den Svenska Filmens Drama: Sjöström och Stiller*, Stockholm, 1952.

Idestam-Almquist, Bengt, *Classics of the Swedish Cinema*, Stockholm, 1952.

Waldenkranz, Rune, *Swedish Cinema*, Stockholm, 1959.

Jean, Rene, and Charles Ford, *Sjöström*, Paris, 1963.

Cowie, Peter, *Swedish Cinema*, London, 1966.

''Sjöström,'' in *Anthologie du cinéma 1*, Paris, 1966.

Klinowski, Jacek, and Adam Garbicz, *Cinema, the Magic Vehicle: A Guide to Its Achievement: Journey One; The Cinema Through 1949*, Metuchen, New Jersey, 1975.

Barsacq, Léon, *Caligari's Cabinet and Other Grand Illusions: A History of Film Design*, New York, 1976.

Ellis, Jack C., *A History of Film*, Englewood Cliffs, New Jersey, 1979.

Forslund, Bengt, *Victor Sjöström*, New York, 1988.

Cowie, Peter, *Scandinavian Cinema: A Survey of the Films and Filmmakers of Denmark, Finland, Iceland, Norway and Sweden*, London, 1992.

Articles:

Potamkin, M. C., ''The Golden Age of Scandinavian Film,'' in *Cinema* (London), September 1930.

Idestam-Almquist, Bengt, ''Victor Sjöström,'' in *Biografbladet* (Stockholm), Summer 1950.

Turner, Charles L., ''Victor Sjöström,'' in *Films in Review* (New York), May and June 1960.

Bagh, Peter von, ''Seikkailu ajassa,'' in *Filmihullu* (Helsinki), no. 8, 1987.

Wiklund, K., ''Sett I medvetsloshetens ogonblick,'' in *Filmrutan* (Sundsvall), vol. 30, no. 3, 1987.

Cremonini, G., ''Il carretto fantasma di Victor Sjostrom,'' in *Cineforum* (Bergamo), vol. 34, no. 339, November 1994.

Florin, B., ''*Korkarlen*: en stilstudie,'' in *Filmhäftet* (Stockholm), vol. 23, no. 1/2, 1995.

DeBartolo, J., ''Video Tape Reviews,'' in *Classic Images* (Muscatine), no. 242, August 1995.

Florin, B., ''Camouflaged Technique: Optical Transitions in the Films of Victor Sjöström,'' in *Lahikuva*, no. 3, 1995.

''*La charrette fantôme*,'' in *Télérama* (Paris), no. 2367, 24 May 1997.

* * *

Although it was made more than 60 years ago, *The Phantom Chariot* is still considered to be a film remarkable for its sophisticated narrative structure. Though flashbacks were not unheard-of narrative devices in the cinema of that time, *The Phantom Chariot* was not understood by many audiences, and had to be re-edited to facilitate comprehension. The narrative is developed according to a mise-en-abme construction, wherein flashback issues from flashback, and stories are contained by or within other stories. Audiences of the time were sufficiently educated viewers, cinematically speaking, to grasp one temporal level of flashback description, but beyond that had some difficulty in deciphering further narrative complexities.

The articulation of the different temporal layers in the film serves to fill out its penultimate meaning (the ultimate one being concerned with repentance and redemption of the soul), which has to do with the notion that time is multi-dimensional and multi-perspectival. In *La Jetée*, Chris Marker pursues this concept, and in doing so suggests that the Western world's current perception of time is not only too restrictive but needlessly fatal as well. In *The Phantom Chariot* David Holm, the main character, is ''given another chance'' at life via a ''non-linear'' portal, the point at which the time cycle begins and also can be arrested; in this case it is New Year's Eve.

Most of the filmic narrative actually takes place or at least is generated in a cemetery where David Holm and two drinking buddies are getting ready to toast the incoming year. A shot of a nearby clock tower lets us know that it is 20 minutes to midnight. Then David Holm tells a story about how one gets to be driver of ''the phantom chariot.'' The tale has it that any man who breathes his last at the stroke of midnight before the beginning of a new year must then take over the ghastly chore of gathering up departed souls during the coming year. Another shot of the clock tower reveals that ten minutes have elapsed during the telling of this story within the diegesis of the film. A policeman comes along to ask David if he would please come and visit Edith, a salvation army nurse who had once been kind to him and is now dying of consumption. He refuses, then fights with his two companions. They knock him out and leave quickly, presuming him dead. A magnificent superimposition of David Holm's spirit leaving his body follows. At that moment the phantom chariot arrives, driven by an old drinking buddy, Georg, who has died the previous New Year's Eve at precisely midnight.

The narrative then proceeds through a series of flashbacks: we see how David Holm met Georg, and that Georg was a bad influence on him, encouraging him to drink heavily and consequently mistreat his wife and two young children; we are introduced to Edith and the Salvation Army Mission where David Holm stayed after being released from prison and finding that his wife had left him.

Returning to the cemetery once again, the film is now three fourths complete (or roughly an hour and a half into the total viewing time), and Georg has one last soul to collect—David Holm's. But, according to the time registered by the clock tower in the film it is midnight, ten minutes after David Holm had finished telling the story about the phantom chariot. Georg ties up his body with invisible yet binding rope and loads him into the carriage. David Holm's spirit rides up front with Georg as they ride to the house where Edith is about to die. Georg also ''shows'' David Holm that his wife is about to take her own life as well as the lives of their children. At the moment of Edith's death, David Holm breaks down into tears, praying desperately to God for another chance in life so that he can prevent the death of his innocent family. An abrupt cut back to the cemetery shows him waking up, his body and spirit intact. He rubs his head and eyes for an instant, then gets up—a bit shakily at first, for he is still drunk from all the liquor he has consumed this New Year's Eve. He arrives home just in time to stop his wife from going through with the fatal poisonings.

In 1920, ''zero-degree'' writing or a ''zero-degree'' narrative structure was still 40 odd years away from being invented, yet *The Phantom Chariot* is clearly an example of just such a representational construct.

—Sandra L. Beck

KOROL LIR

(King Lear)

USSR, 1971

Director: Grigori Kozintsev

Production: Lenfilm: black and white, 35mm, scope; running time: 140 minutes; length: 12,500 feet. Released 1971, USSR. Filmed 1970 in the USSR.

Producer: Grigori Kozintsev; **screenplay:** Grigori Kozintsev, from Boris Pasternak's translation of the play by William Shakespeare; **photography:** Jonas Gritsius; **sound:** Eduard Vanunts; **production designer:** Yevgeny Yenei (Jenöcek Jenei); **sets:** Vsevolod Ulitko; **music:** Dmitri Shostakovich; **costume designer:** Suliko Virsaladze.

Cast: Yuri Yarvet (*King Lear*); Elsa Radzinya (*Goneril*); Galina Volchek (*Regan*); Valentina Shendrikova (*Cordelia*); Oleg Dal (*The Fool*); Karl Sebris (*Earl of Gloucester*); Leonard Merzin (*Edgar*); Regimantas Adomaitis (*Edmund*); Vladimir Emelyanov (*Earl of Kent*); Alexander Volkach (*Duke of Cornwall*); Alexei Petrenko (*Oswald*); Yumas Budraitis (*King of France*); Donatas Banionis (*Duke of Albany*).

Publications

Books:

Kozintsev, Grigori, *Shakespeare: Time and Conscience*, New York, 1966.
Eckert, Charles, editor, *Focus on Shakespearian Film*, Englewood Cliffs, New Jersey, 1972.
Rapisarda, Guisi, editor, *La Feks: Kozintsev e Trauberg*, Rome, 1975.
Kozintsev, Grigori, *King Lear: The Space of Tragedy: The Diary of a Film Director*, Berkeley, 1977.
Liehm, Mira, and Antonin Liehm, *The Most Important Art: East European Film After 1945*, Berkeley 1977.
Leaming, Barbara, *Grigori Kozintsev*, Boston, 1980.
Buchman, Lorne Michael, *From the Globe to the Screen: An Interpretive Study of Shakespeare Through Film*, Ann Arbor, 1984.

Articles:

Barteneva, Yevgeniya, "One Day with *King Lear*," in *Soviet Film* (Moscow), no. 9, 1969.
Yutkevitch, Sergei, in *Sight and Sound* (London), Autumn 1971.
Filmfacts (New York), No. 24, 1971.
International Film Guide, London, 1972.
Tatarkiewicz, A., and Z. Pitera, in *Kino* (Warsaw), March 1972.
Koltain, T., in *Filmkultura* (Budapest), May-June 1972.
"Er widmete sein Talent der Revolution," in *Film und Fernsehen* (Berlin), September 1973.
Marienstras, R., "Deux versions du *Roi Lear*," in *Positif* (Paris), April 1974.
Welsh, James M., "To See Feelingly: *King Lear* Through Russian Eyes," in *Literature/Film Quarterly* (Salisbury, Maryland), Spring 1976.
Hodgdon, B., "Kozintsev's *King Lear*," in *Literature/Film Quarterly* (Salisbury, Maryland), Fall 1977.
Hodgdon, B., "Two King Lears: Uncovering the Filmtext," in *Literature/Film Quarterly* (Salisbury, Maryland), July 1983.
Radvliff-Umstead, "Order and Disorder in Kozintsev's *King Lear*," in *Literature/Film Quarterly* (Salisbury, Maryland), October 1983.
Schmalz, W., "Pictorial Imagery in Kozintsev's *King Lear*," in *Literature/Film Quarterly* (Salisbury, Maryland), April 1985.
Parker, R.B., "The Use of Mise-en-scene in Three Films of King Lear," in *Shakespeare Quarterly*, vol. 42, no. 1, Spring 1991.
Angulo, J., "*El rey Lear*," in *Nosferatu* (San Sebastian), no. 8, February 1992.
Daems, J., "Wijsheid in waanzin," in *Film en Televisie + Video* (Brussels), no. 441, April 1994.

* * *

Korol Lir was the last film of Kozintsev's long career, which began with the delirious experimentalism of the early 1920s and ended with two towering adaptations of Shakespeare. His version of *Hamlet* is probably the better-known of the two, but some critics have considered his *Lear* even finer. In its austere grandeur the film conveys, more effectively perhaps than any stage production could ever do, the majestic stature of the play, extending it to its utmost range without in the least distorting it. Kozintsev's *Lear* remains, with all its gritty strength, still very much Shakespeare's *Lear*.

"This is not the story of one man," Kozintsev commented; "everything occurs among many other people." His aim is to place *Lear* in context, showing that the schemes and caprices of royalty bring disaster not only to themselves, but also to the whole nation. In the opening sequence a meandering procession of ragged vagabonds (immediately recalling the line of suppliants winding through the snow in *Ivan the Terrible*) make their painful way to Lear's castle. Later, as war and destruction rage across the stark landscape, the entire populace of Britain seems to have been reduced to such scurrying wretchedness, with the king himself merely one among their number. The closing scenes take place amid the scorched and shattered ruins of Dover, whose inhabitants continue while Lear dies to forage gloomily among the rubble, indifferent to one more death after so many.

Pictorially the film is consistently superb. Kozintsev deploys his widescreen monochrome photography to impressive effect, creating panoramic compositions which echo the elemental forces unleashed by the play. In one vivid overhead shot, the camera even seems to become one with the elements as it glares down on the cowering figures of Lear and the Fool stumbling blindly across the storm-swept heath. At other times it identifies with the king in his changing moods, sweeping vertiginously upwards with him to the mad heights of the battlements, or panning slowly across a darkening horizon as if in apprehension of the coming storm.

In the title role, the Estonian actor Yuri Yarvet is imaginatively cast: a diminutive, bird-like man with quick eyes, he seems at first almost childishly unfitted for kingship, yet by the end of the film has acquired a touchingly frail nobility, transcending his own inadequacies as he gains in understanding. The other roles are equally individually characterised, drawing on a wealth of personal detail, from the gossipy fussiness of Gloucester to the Fool's crop-haired innocence. Pasternak's sinewy translation audibly recaptures, even for those with no Russian, the rhythms and inflection of Shakespeare's verse; while in its power and energy, Shostakovich's music (the last of his many outstanding film scores) perfectly complements Kozintsev's epic conception of the play.

There are no compromises in *Korol Lir*. In its visual style it is thoroughly Russian, very much Kozintsev. (The hand of the director of *New Babylon*, 40 years earlier, is clearly evident.) It conforms to a Marxist reading of the text, but without being in any way doctrinaire, nor perverting Shakespeare's intentions. Along with Kurosawa's *Throne of Blood*, and Kozintsev's own *Hamlet*, it provides a rare example of a Shakespeare film that succeeds in being at once superb cinema and superb Shakespeare.

—Philip Kemp

KOSHIKEI

(Death by Hanging)

Japan, 1968

Director: Nagisa Oshima

Production: Sozo-sha and A.T.G.; black and white, 35mm, Vistavision size; running time: 117 minutes. Released 1968, Japan. Cost: 10 million yen.

Koshikei

Producers: Masayuki Nakajima, Takuji Yamaguchi and Nagisa Oshima; **screenplay:** Tsutomu Tamura, Mamoru Sasaki, Michinori Fukao and Nagisa Oshima, from a newspaper story; **assistant director:** Kiyoshi Ogasawara; **photography:** Yasuhiro Yoshioka; **editor:** Sueko Shiraishi; **sound:** Hideo Nishizaki; **sound effects:** Akira Suzuki; **production designer:** Jusho Toda; **music:** Hikaru Hayashi.

Cast: Kei Sato (*Officer in charge of the execution*); Fumio Watanabe (*Official educator*); Yun do-Yun (*R*); Mutsuhiro Toura (*Doctor*); Hosei Komatsu (*Prosecutor*); Akiko Koyama (*Woman*); Toshiro Ishido (*Priest*); Masao Adachi (*Security officer*); Masao Matsuda (*Official witness*).

Awards: Kinema Jumpo's Best Screenplay Prize and one of Kinema Jumpo's Best Films of 1968.

Publications

Script:

Oshima, Nagisa, and others, *Koshikei*, in *Sekai no Eigasakka no. 6: Nagisa Oshima*, Tokyo, 1972.

Books:

Sato, Tadao, *Oshima Nagisa no sekai* [The World of Nagisa Oshima], Tokyo, 1973.
Mellen, Joan, *Voices from the Japanese Cinema*, New York, 1975.
Cameron, Ian, and others, *Second Wave*, New York, 1975.
Mellen, Joan, *The Waves at Genji's Door*, New York, 1976.
Bock, Audie, *Japanese Directors*, New York, 1978; revised edition, Tokyo, 1985.
Burch, Noël, *To the Distant Observer: Form and Meaning in the Japanese Cinema*, Berkeley, 1979.
Oshima, Nagisa, *Ecrits (1956–1978): Dissolution et jaillissement*, Paris, 1980.
Tessier, Max, editor, *Le Cinéma japonais au present 1959–1979*, Paris, 1980.
Sato, Tadao, *Currents in Japanese Cinema*, Tokyo, 1982.
Magrelli, Enrico, and Emanuela Martini, *Il rito, il rivolta: Il cinema di Nagisa Oshima*, Rome, 1984.
Polan, Dana B., *The Political Language of Film and the Avant-Garde*, Ann Arbor, 1985.
Danvers, Louis, and Charles Tatum, *Nagisa Oshima*, Paris, 1986.
Oshima, Nagisa, *Cinema, Censorship, and the State: The Writings of Nagisa Oshima, 1956–1978*, translated by Dawn Lawson, Cambridge, 1992.
Nagib, Lúcia, *Em torno da nouvelle vague japonesa*, Campinas, 1993.
Turim, Maureen Cheryn, *The Films of Oshima Nagisa: Images of a Japanese Iconoclast*, Berkeley, 1998.

Articles:

Tessier, Max, ''Entretien avec Oshima,'' in *Cinéma* (Paris), no. 140, 1969.
Bory, Jean-Louis, in *Nouvel Observateur* (Paris), 29 September 1969.
Niogret, Hubert, in *Positif* (Paris), October 1969.
de Baroncelli, Jean, in *Monde* (Paris), 4 October 1969.
Tournes, Andrée, in *Jeune Cinéma* (Paris), November-December 1969.
Cameron, Ian, ''Nagisa Oshima,'' in *Movie* (London), Winter 1969–70.
Gardies, René, in *Image et Son* (Paris), February 1970.
''Entretien avec Oshima,'' in *Cahiers du Cinéma* (Paris), March 1970.
International Film Guide 1971, London, 1970.
Corbucci, G., in *Cinema Nuovo* (Turin), January-February 1972.
Schepelern, P., in *Kosmorama* (Copenhagen), December 1972.
Heath, Stephen, in *Screen* (London), Winter 1976–77.
Image et Son (Paris), September 1978.
Polan, Dana, ''Politics as Process in Three Films by Nagisa Oshima,'' in *Film Criticism* (Meadville, Pennsylvania), Fall 1983.
Polan, Dana, ''Politics as Process in Three Films by Nagisa Oshima,'' in *Film Criticism* (Meadville), vol. 11, no. 1–2, Fall-Winter 1986–87.
Santos Fontenla, C., in *Nosferatu* (San Sebastian), no. 11. January 1993.

* * *

Death by Hanging is an excellent example of the marriage of Oshima's stylistic experiments to his thematic concerns. Inspired by the true story of a Korean youth condemned and hanged for raping and murdering two Japanese girls, Oshima confronts us with the problems of discrimination against Koreans in Japan, the protagonist's discovery of his own identity, nationalism and the function of the state, and the relationship of imagination and reality.

Oshima cleverly arranges a situation in which the execution of R (identified by his initial to symbolize all Koreans in Japan) fails, or, as a written title explains, ''body of R refuses to die.'' The dismayed officers try to stimulate his memory by reenacting the roles of R and the people around him, while R, in a state of amnesia, keeps asking them naive questions, thus confronting the officers and the audience with fundamental problems—for example, the meaning of the state, the definition of a ''Korean.'' Through their discussions and actions, the executioners' prejudice, their dishonorable past lives as war-criminals, their sexual frustrations, and blind faith in the authorities are revealed. The poverty and internal struggles of R's family are also illustrated, as is the historical context of Japanese importation of Koreans as forced laborers.

The intensity of the *mise-en-scène* is related to the closed and fixed space of the set of the execution ground. This set's artificiality and claustrophobic atmosphere (partly necessitated by the film's low budget) is marvellously contrasted with the open space, natural light and sound of the outdoor sequences. When the film returns to the original prison setting, it becomes more abstract and surrealistic.

One victim's body, which is visible to the audience from the beginning, is recognized by the officers one by one, and finally it comes to life as a symbolic ''sister'' of R. Her role is to agitate R politically, and awaken in him his identity as a Korean in Japan. R then refuses to be executed, condemning the nation as murderers if the execution is carried out. Finally, although he believes he is innocent, R returns to be executed, accepting it for ''all the R's in the world.'' However, the scene with the empty noose after the execution conveys the idea that the authorities are not capable of executing R.

The Japanese authorities, and Oshima's ideological position in relation to them, are represented by the director's favourite symbol, the national flag in which the rising sun appears black (because the film is black-and-white). The flag appears on the wall, frequently behind the faces of the public prosecutor and R.

Oshima also employs various experimental methods. Single actions are portrayed twice from different angles. Hand-written titles accompanied by discordant music are used to divide the film into sequences or to express the protagonist's emotions. The continuity of action between shots is intentionally broken during the first half of the film. The characters, particularly R, often talk to the camera directly. Oshima's ideological concerns require this Brechtian style.

The film's primary purpose is to provoke the audience through the visual and auditory images. It was not, despite winning the highest critical acclaim, commercially successful in Japan.

—Kyoko Hirano

KOZIYAT ROG

(The Goat Horn)

Bulgaria, 1971

Director: Métodi Andonov

Production: Studiya za igralni filmi (Sofia, Bulgaria); black and white, 35mm, wide-screen; running time: 105 minutes, some versions 95 minutes; length: 2824 meters. Released February 1972. Filmed 1971 in Bulgaria.

Screenplay: Nikolai Haitov, from the short story by Nikolai Haitov; **photography:** Dimo Kolarov; **editor:** Evgeniya Radeva; **sound:** Mithen Andreev; **production designer:** Konstantin Dzhidrov; **music:** Siméon Pironkov; **song:** Maria Neikova; **special effects pyrotechnics:** Ivan Angelov; **costume designer:** Vladislav Schmidt; **stunts:** Petar Klyavkov.

Cast: Katya Paskaléva (*Maria*); Anton Gorchev (*Karaivan*); Kliment Denchev, Stefan Manrodiev, Todor Kolev, Marin Yanev (*Turk rapists*); Milèn Pénev (*The Shepherd*); Nevena Andonova (*Maria as a girl*); Krasimira Petrova (*Turk's wife*); Ivan Obretenov (*Poor man*); Ivan Yanchev (*Man with scar*).

Awards: Bulgarian Film Festival at Varna, Prize of the Audience, 1972; Chicago Film Festival, Silver Hugo (2nd prize), 1973.

Publications

Book:

Liehm, Mira, and Antonin Leihm, *The Most Important Art: East European Film After 1945*, Berkeley, 1977.
Holloway, Ronald, *The Bulgarian Cinema*, Cranbury, 1986.

Articles:

Ignatovski, V., in *Kinoizkustvo* (Sofia), March 1972.
Variety (New York), 16 August 1972.
Ivasiuc, A., in *Cinema* (Bucharest), September 1972.
Kopanevova, G., in *Film a Doba* (Prague), October 1972.
Cowie, Peter, in *International Film Guide* (London), 1973.
Malina, Martin, in *Montreal Star*, 27 January 1973.
Greenspun, Roger, in *New York Times*, 3 April 1973.
Cinéma (Paris), May 1973.
Mruklik, B., in *Kino* (Warsaw), May 1973.
Variety (New York), 30 May 1973.
Van Gelder, Lawrence, in *New York Times*, 23 August 1973.
Gomiscek, T., in *Ekran* (Ljubljana), no. 9–10, 1979.
Grozev, Aleksandr, ''Metodi Andonov,'' in *Kinoizkustvo* (Sofia), vol. 37, no. 3, March 1982.
Young, D., ''*The Goat Horn (Kozijat rog)*,'' in *Variety* (New York), vol. 360, 7/13 August 1995.

* * *

One of the most successful Bulgarian films ever made and probably the best known abroad, *Koziyat rog* was based on a legend that was first retold and later worked into a short story by Nikolai Haitov. He emerged in the 1960s as one of the most popular of Bulgarian writers, especially famous for his descriptions of the people and traditions in the somewhat isolated and ''wild'' regions of the Rhodope mountains in the southern part of the country. The screenplay drifted yet further from the historical and psychological accuracy in search of a larger truth, that of a shattering human tragedy. An introductory title (''This bloody story happened in the XVII century. It starts with an act of violence.'') makes apparently intentional the shift from the original story of blood revenge to a more ambitious study of the devastating chain-reaction effect of violence on man's soul—which gradually becomes the film's main theme.

In parallel with the thematic evolution is a formal development: the film discards what was perhaps considered a ''more cinematic'' dramatization, with flashbacks and intriguing tension, for a straightforward narration with very sparse dialogue and a more predictable yet moving plot. Katya Paskaleva gives a memorable performance in the roles of both shepherd Karaivan's wife, raped and eventually killed by a band of Turks, and their daughter Maria, who is brought up by her father to be a man and to seek revenge, but who falls in love and commits suicide after Karaivan kills her lover. The bold treatment of sex and violence made the film a box-office record-breaker, while the critics praised its rhythm, stark black-and-white photography and its inherent Bulgarian-ness. It touched, no doubt, a very intimate chord in the collective consciousness of a country in which the last hundred years of its independence had been painfully dominated by the consequences of a fierce Ottoman oppression, threatening at times its very existence.

The song from the film, with lyrics added, became a hit, and ten years after the film's release the short story was successfully made into a ballet at the National Opera and Ballet Theatre in Sofia. *Koziyat rog* is now widely recognized by Bulgarian critics and public alike as not only the best screen adaptation of Haitov's work and the best film of director Metodi Andonov (whose untimely death in 1974 put an end to a promising career) but also as a landmark in Bulgarian cinema, one that raised its prestige for a generation of film-goers and helped to move it to the forefront of the country's contemporary culture.

—Dimitar Bardarsky

KWAIDAN

See **KAIDAN**

L.A. CONFIDENTIAL

USA, 1997

Director: Curtis Hanson

Production: Monarchy Enterprises B.V. and Regency Enterprises; distributed by Warner Brothers; 35mm, Technicolor; DTS/Dolby Digital; running time: 136 minutes; length: 3915 meters (approx. 12836 feet). Released May 14, 1997, France (Cannes Film Festival), September 5, 1997, Canada (Toronto Film Festival), September 19, 1997, U.S.A. Filmed in Hollywood, West Hollywood, and Los Angeles, California; cost: $35,000,000.

Producers: Curtis Hanson, Brian Helgeland, Dan Kolsrud, Arnon Milchan, Michael G. Nathanson, and David L. Wolper; **screenplay:** Brian Helgeland and Curtis Hanson, from the novel by James Ellroy; **photography:** Dante Spinotti; **assistant directors:** Jim Goldthwait, Heather Kritzer, Linda Montanti, and Drew Ann Rosenberg; **editor:** Peter Honess; **sound:** SoundStorm; **art director:** William Arnold; **production designer:** Jeannine Oppewall; **costume designer:** Ruth Myers; **music:** Jerry Goldsmith.

Cast: Kevin Spacey (*Jack Vincennes*); Russell Crowe (*Bud White*); Guy Pearce (*Ed Exley*); James Cromwell (*Dudley Smith*); Kim Basinger (*Lynn Bracken*); Danny DeVito (*Sid Hudgeons*); David Strathairn (*Pierce Patchett*); Ron Rifkin (*D.A. Ellis Loew*); Matt McCoy (*Brett Chase*); Graham Beckel (*Dick Stensland*); Amber Smith (*Susan Lefferts*).

Awards: Oscars for Best Supporting Actress (Kim Basinger) and Best Adapted Screenplay, 1998; Australian Film Institute Best Foreign Film Award, 1998; Golden Globe for Best Supporting Actress (Kim Basinger), 1998; London Critics Circle Awards for Director of the Year, Film of the Year, Screenwriter of the Year, and Supporting Actor of the Year (Kevin Spacey), 1998; Los Angeles Film Critics Association Awards for Best Cinematography, Best Director, Best Picture, and Best Screenplay, 1998; National Board of Review Awards (U.S.A.) for Best Director and Best Picture, 1998; National Society of Film Critics Awards (U.S.A.) for Best Director, Best Film, and Best Screenplay, 1998; New York Film Critics Circle Awards for Best Director, Best Film, and Best Screenplay, 1998.

Publications

Script:

Helgeland, Brian, and Curtis Hanson, *L.A. Confidential: The Screenplay*, New York, 1997.

Books:

Ellroy, James, *L.A. Confidential*, New York, 1997.

Articles:

Lane, Anthony, ''L.A. Confidential,'' in *The New Yorker*, 22 September 1997.

Denby, David, ''L.A. Confidential,'' in *New York*, 29 September 1997.

Ansen, David, ''The Neo-Noir '90s,'' in *Newsweek* (New York), 27 October 1997.

Taubin, Amy, ''L.A. Lurid,'' in *Sight and Sound* (London), November 1997.

Wrathall, John, ''L.A. Confidential,'' in *Sight and Sound* (London), November 1997.

Lyons, Donald, ''L.A. Confidential,'' in *Film Comment* (New York), November-December 1997.

Arthur, Paul, ''L.A. Confidential,'' in *Cineaste* (New York), Summer 1998.

* * *

Prior to the release of *L.A. Confidential*, director Curtis Hanson spent nearly 30 years learning the movie business, working as an actor, writer, producer, and director. He eventually earned a reputation as a skilled craftsman, as evidenced by lightly regarded but well made genre films such as *Bad Influence* (1990), *The Hand that Rocks the Cradle* (1992), and *The River Wild* (1994). Just as the old studio system provided filmmakers with the opportunity to hone their craft, so too did Hanson's time as a director for hire heighten his filmmaking abilities. By the time Hanson took on *L.A. Confidential*, he was poised to make the leap from workmanlike director to filmmaker par excellence; the result was a film that is widely considered the best neo-noir since *Chinatown* (1974).

Masterfully adapted from James Ellroy's novel of the same name, *L.A. Confidential* is set in Los Angeles in 1953. As the opening voice-over narration kicks in we see a montage of gorgeous Southern California shots. The stage for what follows is set by Sid Hudgeons (Danny DeVito), a sleazy tabloid reporter for *Hush-Hush* magazine: ''Life is good in Los Angeles. It's paradise on earth. That's what they tell you anyway. Because they're selling an image. They're selling it through movies, radio and television,. . . You'd think this place was the garden of Eden, but there's trouble in paradise.'' And indeed there is. The film follows the lives of three Los Angles police officers, Bud White (Russell Crowe), Jack Vincennes (Kevin Spacey), and Ed Exley (Guy Pearce), as they try to unravel the mystery of the Night Owl Cafe massacre, in which several people, including White's former partner Dick Stensland (Graham Beckel), were shot dead during what was ostensibly a robbery gone bad.

The story is a complicated, densely layered mystery that deepens at every turn. The three protagonists are all different personalities with unique motivations, but as they chase down their leads their investigations begin to cross until it becomes clear that each is after the same thing: the search for a ''truth'' that, when discovered, will also serve as a means for personal redemption. Along the way the story seamlessly blends fiction with historical fact, involving crooked cops, Los Angeles mobster Mickey Cohen, his bodyguard Johnny Stompanato (Lana Turner's real life lover, who her daughter shot and killed), hookers surgically altered to resemble movie stars (Kim Basinger's turn as Lynn Bracken, a luminous Veronica Lake look-alike, won her an Academy Award for Best Supporting Actress), and Pierce Patchett (David Strathairn), a shadowy businessman loosely based on Walt Disney. But the backdrop for it all, and in many ways the star of the picture, is Hanson's vision of Los Angeles in the 1950s. This isn't the L.A. of our dreams, but Raymond Chandler's L.A., the weary town behind the facade. Beautifully shot by Dante Spinotti, the promise of Los Angeles as a land of milk and honey is exposed as false, just another in a long line of sun drenched Hollywood fabrications. Beginning with the opening montage and including meticulously detailed period recreations such as the Night Owl Cafe, a neighborhood liquor store, and the Frolic Room bar, Hanson's Los Angeles perfectly embodies an American Eden gone awry.

The various individual investigations eventually lead to Captain Dudley Smith (James Cromwell), a L.A.P.D. institution who has all along been orchestrating a behind-the-scenes takeover of the jailed Mickey Cohen's rackets. Vincennes' discovery costs him his life, while White and Exley, who for most of the film are arch-enemies, finally join forces to face down Smith and his men in an apocalyptic gunfight at the hellish Victory Motel. Neo-noirs often try to capture the feel of Classical Hollywood Noirs, which were shot in black and white, but most fall short for either one or both of two reasons: first, the play between shadow and light normally just isn't as effective in color, and, second, most are set in the recent present, while Classical Noir narratives are inextricably rooted in the nuclear paranoia and McCarthyism of America in the late 1940s and early 1950s. *L.A. Confidential* ingeniously gets around both common shortcomings. Its taking place in 1953 neatly connects it to the Noirs of yesteryear, as does its cinematography; while the daylight scenes are awash in light, giving them a saturated look that contributes to the overall sense of decay, the nighttime scenes are shot in such a way as to highlight the contrast between light and dark. The best example of this technique is the shoot-out at the Victory Motel, during which White and Exley hole up in a dark hotel room in an attempt to fend off Smith's men. As the barrage of gunfire from the outside hits the walls of the room, each succeeding bullethole provides an opening for another shaft of ethereal blue light to pierce the darkness. Although not a movie that influenced an onslaught of neo-noirs in its wake, *L.A. Confidential* is among the best of its kind.

In addition to being an exemplary genre film, *L.A. Confidential* is one of the best critically received films ever. In fact, as of 2000, it is the only film in history to have won the best picture and the best director awards from the four major American film critics associations, the National Board of Review, the New York Film Critics Circle, the Los Angeles Association of Film Critics, and the National Society of Film Critics. It was also extremely well received internationally, both in theatrical release and on the film festival circuit. Unfortunately, although nominated for nine Academy Awards, *L.A. Confidential* had the misfortune of being released in the same year as *Titanic*, the most financially successful film ever. However, even though it was *Titanic* that walked away with the major awards at the 1998 Oscars, *Titanic* will be remembered as a well made but maudlin special effects film, while *L.A. Confidential* will be remembered as a masterpiece of its kind and the film that marked Curtis Hanson as a major Hollywood director.

—Robert C. Sickels

THE LACEMAKER

See **LA DENTELLIERE**

LADIES OF THE BOIS DE BOULOGNE

See **LES DAMES DU BOIS DE BOULOGNE**

LADRI DI BICICLETTE

(The Bicycle Thief)

Italy, 1948

Director: Vittorio De Sica

Production: Produzioni De Sica; black and white, 35mm; running time: 90 minutes. Released 1948. Filmed in Rome.

Producer: Umberto Scarpelli; **screenplay:** Cesare Zavattini with Oreste Biancoli, Suso Cecchi d'Amico, Vittorio De Sica, Adolfo Franci, Gherado Gherardi, and Gerardo Guerrier, from a novel by Luigi Bartolini; **photography:** Carlo Montuori; **editor:** Eraldo da Roma; **production designer:** Antonino Traverso; **music:** Alessandro Cicognini.

Cast: Lamberto Maggiorani (*Antonio Ricci*); Enzo Staiola (*Bruno Ricci*); Lianella Carell (*Maria Ricci*); Elena Altieri; Gino Saltamerenda; Vittorio Antonucci; Guilio Chiari; Michele Sakara; Carlo Jachino; Nando Bruno; Fausto Guerzoni; Umberto Spadaro; Massimo Randisi.

Awards: New York Film Critics Award, Best Foreign Film, 1949; Belgium World Festival of Film and Arts, Grand Prix, 1949; Festival of Film at Locarno, Social Prize, 1949; Special Oscar as Most Outstanding Foreign Film, 1949.

Publications

Script:

Zavattini, Cesare, and others, *The Bicycle Thief*, New York, 1968.

Books:

Castello, G.C., *Il cinema neorealistico italiano*, Turin, 1956.
Rondi, Brunello, *Il neorealismo italiano*, Parma, 1956.

Ladri di biciclette

Ferrara, Giuseppe, *Il nuovo cinema italiano*, Florence, 1957.

Hovald, Patrice G., *Le Néo-Realisme italien et ses créateurs*, Paris, 1959.

Bazin, André, *Qu'est-ce que le cinéma*, Paris, 1962.

Agel, Henri, *Vittorio De Sica*, Paris, 1964.

Leprohon, Pierre, *Vittorio De Sica*, Paris, 1966.

Armes, Roy, *Patterns of Realism: A Study of Italian Neo-Realist Cinema*, New York, 1971.

Samuels, Charles Thomas, *Encountering Directors*, New York, 1972.

Guaraldi-Rimini, Mario, editor, *Neorealismo e vita nazionale: Antologia di cinema nuovo*, Florence, 1975.

Mercader, Maria, *La mia vita con Vittorio De Sica*, Milan, 1978.

Anthologie du cinéma 10, Paris, 1979.

Bolzoni, Francesco, *Quando De Sica era Mister Brown*, Turin, 1984.

Darreta, John, *Vittorio De Sica: A Guide to References and Resources*, Boston, 1988.

Articles:

Jacobson, Herbert L., ''De Sica's *Bicycle Thief* and Italian Humanism,'' in *Hollywood Quarterly*, Fall 1949.

New York Times, 13 December 1949.

Variety (New York), 15 December 1949.

Zavattini, Cesare, and others, in *Ciné-Club* (Paris), January 1950.

Winnington, Richard, in *Sight and Sound* (London), March 1950.

Koval, Francis, ''Interview with De Sica,'' in *Sight and Sound* (London), April 1950.

Bazin, André, in *Cahiers du Cinéma* (Paris), March 1954.

De Sica, Vittorio, in *Films and Filming* (London), January 1956.

Chevalier, J., in *Image et Son* (Paris), December 1956.

Rhode, Eric, ''Why Neo-Realism Failed,'' in *Sight and Sound* (London), Winter 1960–61.

McVay, Douglas, ''Poet of Poverty,'' in *Films and Filming* (London), October and November 1964.

Harcourt, Peter, in *Screen Education* (London), July-August 1965.

Leprohon, Pierre, ''La Perennité du *Voleur de bicyclette*,'' in *Avant-Scène du Cinéma* (Paris), December 1967.

Passek, J.-L., ''Le Cinéma du néo-réalisme italien est en berne: Vittorio De Sica,'' in *Cinéma* (Paris), January 1975.

''De Sica Issue'' of *Bianco e Nero* (Rome), September-December 1975.

''De Sica Issue'' of *Avant-Scène du Cinéma* (Paris), 15 October 1978.

La Fuente, L., in *Cinéma* (Paris), November 1978.

Lawton, B., ''Italian Neo-Realism: A Mirror Construction of Reality,'' in *Film Criticism* (Edinboro, Pennsylvania), no. 2, 1979.
Carcassonne, P., in *Cinématographe* (Paris), January 1979.
''De Sica Issue'' of *Cahiers Lumière* (Paris), November 1980.
Tomasulo, F. P., ''Bicycle Thieves: A Rereading,'' in *Cinema Journal* (Chicago), Spring 1982.
Magny, Joel, in *Cinéma* (Paris), November 1983.
Ardanaz, S., ''Sin mi Vittorio De Sica no habría pasado a la historia del cine,'' in *Cine Cubano* (Havana), 1984.
Weemaes, G., in *Film en Televisie* (Brussels), May-June 1984.
Alix, Y., in *Positif* (Paris), February 1985.
''*Le voleur de bicyclette* de Vittorio De Sica: Decoupage plan a plan et dialogues bilingues,'' and C. Vasse, ''Qui vole une bicyclette. . . ,'' in *Avant-Scène du Cinéma* (Paris), no. 430, March 1994.
Cartier, C. Zavattini, ''*Le voleur de bicyclette* et les problemes d'ecriture: Entretien aved Suso Cecchi d'Amico,'' in *CinémAction* (Conde-sur-Noireau, France), no. 70, 1994.
Toles, George, ''This May Hurt a Little: The Art of Humiliation in Film,'' in *Film Quarterly* (Berkeley), Summer 1995.
Serceau, M., ''La ville dans le neorealisme,'' in *CinémAction* (Conde-sur-Noireau, France), no. 75, 1995

* * *

Before examining the film, it is important to point out that the oft-used English language title ''The Bicycle *Thief*'' is misleading and injurious to the meaning of the film. *Ladri di biciclette* translates as ''Bicycle Thieves,'' the plural marking an allegorical intention. Vittorio De Sica's film suggests a universe inextricably interrelated through perverse economic ties—the bicycle one man needs to work and support his family, another man steals to support his, and still another sells. Singulars will not do in this film. De Sica presents the story in terms of a man's relation to a crowd, but this crowd is more than just a picturesque background. It is the modern equivalent of a Greek chorus and represents both the higher and lower aspects of human character. It is an extension of the protagonist.

Ricci, the victimized worker, emerges from this crowd at the beginning of the film, called to work after months of unemployment, but his accession to the status of modern tragic hero is a matter of random choice and necessity, not of birth, self-determination, or desire. For a while, endowed with the promise of a steady salary and the ability to once again be the breadwinner in his family, Ricci is permitted to dream of material success. When he retrieves his bicycle from the municipal pawnshop, exchanging for it the family linen, the camera pans up, following the clerk as he climbs to deposit the sheets on what seems a pile of thousands of similar bundles. Ricci is not the exception—like the traditional tragic hero—he is the rule, one of thousands or more. Searching desperately all over the city, he will again encounter this societal chorus; as workers readying a strike; as the denizens of a black market; as a mass of poor people praying in a church; as a crowd lamenting a drowned child; as a gang of toughs in a crowded street protecting a local boy from Ricci's accusations; as a pack of football fans who thwart Ricci's feeble attempt to steal a bicycle himself in a rash, despairing decision to reject moral restraint; and finally, as an anonymous, everyday crowd, walking, going about their business peacefully, hopefully—the crowd to which Ricci is returned.

Ricci's relation to society, in general, and the political and economic situation of postwar Italian society in particular, is reflected by a series of encounters with crowds to which the protagonist's membership is cyclically articulated at the beginning and end of the film. In *Crowds and Power*, Elias Canetti offers a taxonomy of such groups: ''baiting crowds'' intent on blood; ''prohibition crowds''; ''feast crowds''; the ''lamenting pack''; and the ''hunting pack.'' Most importantly, the activities of these crowds are to be historically construed.

One significance of *Ladri di biciclette*, and to a larger extent that of neo-realism, then, lies in the predominance of the role of representation, not only of those inexhaustible details of everyday existence, but also of popular life in all its diversity. Still, *Ladri di biciclette* does not explore the area of popular, political action. Any solidarity among people in the film is a matter of personal friendship (between Ricci and the sanitation workers who help him search Rome in their truck) or that between father and son. The effectiveness of political struggle to improve the inequitable economic conditions at fault here is not considered beyond the brief glimpse of the strike preparations.

The story was brought to De Sica's attention by Cesare Zavattini, screenwriter for the film and one of the seven who adapted the novel by Luigi Bartolini; yet, no film adaptation was ever so disrespectful of its original as this one. Bartolini's protagonist is *not* a man brought forward from the crowd, a man like any other, he is a disgruntled and supercilious artist who opines the most reactionary prejudices about the poor. Moreover, in order to find his stolen bicycle, the protagonist gets about on a second one which apparently he kept around for just such emergencies.

De Sica and Zavattini use the bicycle as a ''vehicle'' to organize the narrative. The theft of a bicycle authorizes a wide search through Rome; hence, the narrative discloses itself as an odyssey structure (there are interesting parallels between Ricci and Ulysses, too). The filmmakers' immense capacity to introduce metaphor into the most everyday context and the puissance of that metaphor (we recall the white stallion in *Sciusciá*) becomes clear when we attempt to bracket the idea of the bicycle. For example, if we substitute a worker's tool box for the bicycle, the narrative loses much of its momentum, its mythical implications, and even part of its effectiveness as a tragedy.

Veteran actor De Sica's talent for molding the raw material of the non-professional actor is prominently displayed. He knew it would be difficult for the trained actor to forget his/her highly coded technique to become the man in the street. He felt that better results were to be obtained by teaching the non-actor just enough to serve the purposes of the scene being shot. Compare, for example, the lattitude of his actors with those of Visconti's in *La terra trema*. In that film, the non-professionals are stiff and gesturally inarticulate; their inexperience tends to stand in the way of a heightened dramatic communication. In the other hand, De Sica's actors signal physically a greater alertness and sensitivity to their immediate problems and awareness of the social and psychological conformations of their characters. Ricci was played by Lamberto Maggiorani, a factory worker who had brought his small son to audition for the role of Bruno; his wife Maria (Lianella Carell) was a journalist who had approached the director for an interview. Bruno (Enzo Staiola), the last cast member to be found, was watching the shooting when De Sica noticed him. The scene in which Ricci takes his son to a trattoria in order to make up for having scolded him involves some of the most subtly nuanced and believable expression of a father-son relationship in the history of cinema.

—Joel E. Kanoff

THE LADY EVE

USA, 1941

Director: Preston Sturges

Production: Paramount; black and white; running time: 94 minutes; length: 8,421 feet. Released March 1941.

Producer: Paul Jones; **screenplay:** Preston Sturges, from a story by Monckton Hoffe; **photography:** Victor Milner; **editor:** Stuart Gilmore.

Cast: Barbara Stanwyck (*Jean*); Henry Fonda (*Charles*); Charles Coburn (*''Colonel'' Harrington*); Eugene Pallette (*Mr. Pike*); William Demarest (*Muggsy*); Eric Blore (*Sir Alfred McGlennan Keith*); Melville Cooper (*Gerald*); Martha O'Driscoll (*Martha*); Janet Beecher (*Mrs. Pike*); Robert Greig (*Barrows*); Dora Clement (*Gertrude*); Luis Alberni (*Pike's Chef*).

Publications

Script:

Sturges, Preston, *The Lady Eve*, in *Five Screenplays*, edited by Brian Henderson, Berkeley, 1986.

Books:

Springer, John, *The Fondas: The Films and Careers of Henry, Jane and Peter Fonda*, New York, 1970.
Ursini, James, *The Fabulous Life and Times of Preston Sturges, An American Dreamer*, New York, 1973.
Smith, Ella, *Starring Miss Barbara Stanwyck*, New York, 1974; revised edition, 1985.
Vermilye, Jerry, *Barbara Stanwyck*, New York, 1975.
Kerbel, Michael, *Henry Fonda*, New York, 1975.
Cavell, Stanley, *Pursuits of Happiness: The Hollywood Comedy of Remarriage*, Cambridge, Massachusetts, 1981.
Cywinski, Ray, *Satires and Sideshows: The Films and Career of Preston Sturges*, Ann Arbor, Michigan, 1981.
Gordon, James R., *Comic Structure in the Films of Preston Sturges*, Ann Arbor, Michigan, 1981.
Fonda, Henry, and Howard Teichman, *Fonda: My Life*, New York, 1981.
Godl Goldstein, Norm, *Henry Fonda: His Life and Work*, London, 1982.
Curtis, James, *Between Flops: A Biography of Preston Sturges*, New York, 1982.
Thomas, Tony, *The Films of Henry Fonda*, Secaucus, New Jersey, 1983.
Di Orio, Al, *Barbara Stanwyck*, New York and London, 1983.
Cywinski, Ray, *Preston Sturges: A Guide to References and Resources*, Boston, 1984.
Dickens, Homer, *The Films of Barbara Stanwyck*, Secaucus, New Jersey, 1984.
Cole, Gerald, and Wes Farrell, *The Fondas*, London, 1984.
Roberts, Allen, and Max Goldstein, *Henry Fonda: A Biography*, Jefferson, North Carolina, 1984.
Dickos, Andrew, *Intrepid Laughter: Preston Sturges and the Movies*, Metuchen, New Jersey, 1985.
Wayne, Jane Ellen, *Stanwyck*, New York, 1985.
Spoto, Donald, *Madcap: The Life of Preston Sturges*, New York, 1990.
Jacobs, Diane, *Christmas in July: The Life & Art of Preston Sturges*, Berkeley, 1994.
Rozgonyi, Jay, *Preston Sturges's Vision of America: Critical Analyses of Fourteen Films*, Jefferson, 1995.
Harvey, James, *Romantic Comedy in Hollywood From Lubitsch to Sturges*, New York, 1998.

Articles:

New York Times, 26 February 1941.
Variety (New York), 26 February 1941.
Motion Picture Herald (New York), 1 March 1941.
Monthly Film Bulletin (London), May 1941.
Times (London), 19 May 1941.
Today's Cinema (London), 21 May 1941.
Kracauer, Seigfried, ''Preston Sturges; or, Laughter Betrayed,'' in *Films in Review* (New York), February 1950.
Farber, Manny, and W. S. Poster, ''Preston Sturges: Success in the Movies,'' in *Film Culture* (New York), no. 26, 1962.
Houston, Penelope, ''Preston Sturges,'' in *Sight and Sound* (London), Summer 1965.
Corliss, Richard, in *Cinema* (Beverly Hills), Spring 1972.
Rubinstein, Eliot, ''The End of Screwball Comedy . . . ,'' in *Post Script* (Jacksonville, Florida), Spring-Summer 1982.
Interview with William Demarest, in *Classic Images* (Indiana, Pennsylvania), February 1984.
Cavell, Stanley, in *Journal of Popular Film and Television* (Washington, D.C.), Autumn 1985.
Comuzio, Ermanno, ''L'uso della retorica in *Lady Eva* di Preston Sturges,'' in *Cineforum* (Bergamo), vol. 26, no. 259, November 1986.
Tobin, Yann, in *Positif* (Paris), December 1986.
Di Battista, M., ''*The Lady Eve* and the Comedy of Innocence,'' in *Motion*, no. 1, 1986.
Denby, D., ''Adam and Eve on a Luxury Liner,'' in *Premiere* (Boulder), vol. 5, October 1991.
Lippe, R., ''Cukor and Garbo,'' in *CineAction* (Toronto), no. 35, 1994.
Hietala, V., ''*Lady Eve/Nainen Eeva*,'' in *Filmihullu* (Helsinki), no. 6, 1995.

* * *

The Lady Eve—arguably the most completely satisfying of the brilliant but uneven series of comedies Sturges made for Paramount in the 1940s—is structured upon a thematic complex that transcends authorial and generic boundaries and is deeply rooted in the sexual politics of our culture. The most obvious parallels are with Cukor's *Two-Faced Woman* (made the same year), Hitchcock's *Vertigo*, and Minnelli's *On a Clear Day You Can See Forever*, but a serious critical inquiry into the ways in which the thematic has been treated intelligently and progressively would inevitably lead one also to the films Sternberg made with Dietrich.

The theme is that of the problem of female identity within a patriarchal culture, wherein men have the power of definition; or, more precisely, the male's attempts to construct a female identity that will flatter his ego, the woman's resistance to that construction, and

The Lady Eve

the relationship between the constructed image and the reality. In the four films cited, the woman either assumes (*The Lady Eve*, *Two-Face Woman*, *Vertigo*) or reveals (*On a Clear Day*) an alternative identity, and the man falls in love with a romantic and/or erotically fascinating image which can never be possessed in actuality (in Sturges, Cukor and Hitchcock, because it is a false and deliberate construction, in Minnelli because it existed only in the distant past, in the heroine's earlier incarnation). All these films, then, probe the relationship between romantic love and the male ego, the man's desire not for an actual woman but for a projection of his fantasy which would perfectly fulfil his desire but for the slight disadvantage that it has no real existence and must remain forever inaccessible. Sturges suggests this brilliantly in the love speech that Fonda delivers to Stanwyck in both her identities, believing her to be two different women, repeating its clauses verbatim: he is not addressing a woman so much as his own fantasy of her.

Two-Faced Woman offers the closest parallels to *The Lady Eve*, but *Vertigo* provides a particularly fascinating comparison, the relationship being that of simultaneous complement and inversion. One is a tragedy, the other a comedy; one is told almost exclusively from the male viewpoint, the other predominantly from the woman's. In *Vertigo* the woman's deceptive masquerade occupies the first part of the film, in *The Lady Eve* the second. Despite the fact that it was made sixteen years earlier (and without wishing to postulate any causal connection), one is tempted to think of *The Lady Eve* as ''Revenge of *Vertigo*.'' The generic difference is partly determined by the point of view: told from the male viewpoint, *The Lady Eve* could no longer be a comedy (Hawks's comedies of male humiliation—*Bringing Up Baby*, *I Was a Male War Bride*, *Man's Favorite Sport?*—are made possible by the fact that romantic love has no place in his imaginative universe). Most of the film's humor is dependent on the woman's control of situations, and even apparently marginal gags (Eugene Pallette's percussive response to the lateness of his breakfast) arise from the deflation of male power.

Vertigo, although narrated from the male position, is not of course an endorsement of it: from the moment at which identification is interrupted (Kim Novak's flashback), it becomes a devastating critique of the male obsession with total domination and possession known in our culture as ''romantic love.'' *Vertigo* is built upon our identification with the male gaze, its assumption of dominating/controlling the action, and the gradual recognition that it controls nothing, that the *illusion* of control is a product of the (culturally constructed) male ego. In the comic mode, the critique offered by *The Lady Eve* is scarcely less devastating. Here Jean/Stanwyck has control of the gaze from the outset, literally holding Fonda's image and actions (unbeknownst to him) in the palm of her hand—reflected in the mirror of her compact. And she is permitted to retain this control throughout most of the film, losing it temporarily only at the turning-point (her exposure as a professional cardsharp) and triumphantly regaining it in her masquerade as ''the Lady Eve.'' Cukor's original version of *Two-Faced Woman* (which should now be made generally available for reassessment—prints exist) offers very close parallels, the whole point of the bowdlerized version (after the film's condemnation by the Catholic Legion of Decency) being that it restores control to the male, thereby ruining the whole conception at a blow.

Sturges's use of star personas/personalities is masterly. Stanwyck's combination of streetwise toughness (she was often cast in proletarian roles) and a capacity for intense suffering—a combination central to her distinguished career in the woman's melodrama—adds depth to her superb comic timing. Fonda's image, developed especially by Ford in *Young Mr. Lincoln* and *Drums Along the Mohawk*, compounded of innocence, naiveté and idealism, is here subjected to astringent revision. The ''innocence'' prevents him from recognizing the sincerity of Jean's feelings, and is shown to be inseparable from an assumption of gender and class superiority, so that we register his chastisement at the hands of ''Eve'' as at once a just revenge and the necessary prerequisite for his final acceptance of the ''real'' Jean.

—Robin Wood

THE LADY FROM SHANGHAI

USA, 1948

Director: Orson Welles

Production: Columbia Pictures Corp.; black and white, 35mm; running time: 86 minutes. Released 10 June 1948. Filmed for the most part in fall 1946, in Central Park and the Maritime Union Headquarters, New York; the Aquarium and the Chinese Mandarin Theatre, San Francisco; the Walhalla Bar and Cafe, Sausalito; various locations in Acapulco; and aboard the yacht ''Zaca'' owned by Errol Flynn.

Producers: Orson Welles with Richard Wilson and William Castle; **screenplay:** Orson Welles, from the novel *Before I Die* by Sherwood King; **photography:** Charles Lawton, Jr; **editor:** Viola Lawrence; **sound:** Lodge Cunningham; **art director:** Stephen Goosson and Sturges Carne; **music:** Heinz Roemheld; **special mirror effects:** Lawrence Butler; **costume designer:** Jean Louis.

Cast: Rita Hayworth (*Elsa Bannister*); Orson Welles (*Michael O'Hara*); Everett Sloane (*Arthur Bannister*); Glenn Anders (*George Grisby*); Ted de Corsia (*Sidney Broome*); Erskine Sanford (*Judge*); Gus Schilling (*Goldie*); Carl Frank (*District attorney*); Louis Merrill (*Jake*); Evelyn Ellis (*Bessie*); Harry Shannon (*Cab driver*); Wong Show Chong (*Li*); Sam Nelson (*Yacht captain*).

Publications

Books:

Bazin, André, *Orson Welles*, Paris, 1950; revised edition, Berkeley, 1979.
Noble, Peter, *The Fabulous Orson Welles*, London, 1956.
Bogdanovich, Peter, *The Cinema of Orson Welles*, New York, 1961.
Cowie, Peter, *The Cinema of Orson Welles*, London 1965.
Higham, Charles, *The Films of Orson Welles*, London, 1965.
Bessy, Maurice, *Orson Welles*, New York, 1971.
McBride, Joseph, *Orson Welles*, London, 1972; New York, 1977.
Naremore, J., *The Magic World of Orson Welles*, New York, 1978.
Silver, Alain, and Elizabeth Ward, editors, *Film Noir*, Woodstock, New York, 1979.
Valentinetti, Claudio M., *Orson Welles*, Florence, 1981.
Bergala, Alain, and Jean Narboni, editors, *Orson Welles*, Paris, 1982.
Andrew, Dudley, *Film in the Aura of Art*, Princeton, 1984.
Higham, Charles, *Orson Welles: The Rise and Fall of an American Genius*, New York, 1985.
Leaming, Barbara, *Orson Welles: A Biography*, New York, 1985.
Parra, Daniele, and Jacques Zimmer, *Orson Welles*, Paris, 1985.
Weis, Elisabeth, and John Belton, editors, *Film Sound; Theory and Practice*, New York, 1985.
Taylor, John Russell, *Orson Welles, A Celebration*, London, 1986.
Bazin, Andre, *Orson Welles: A Critical View*, Venice, 1991.
Welles, Orson, *This Is Orson Welles*, New York, 1993.
Beja, Morris, *Perspective on Orson Welles*, New York, 1995.
Kaplan, E. Ann, *Women in Film Noir*, London, 1998.
Taylor, John Russell, *Orson Welles*, New York, 1999.

Articles:

Pariante, Roberto ''Orson Welles from *Citizen Kane* to *Othello*,'' in *Bianco e Nero* (Rome), March 1956.
''L'Oeuvre d'Orson Welles,'' in *Cahiers du Cinéma* (Paris), September 1958.
Stanbrook, Alan, ''The Heroes of Orson Welles,'' in *Film* (London), no. 28, 1962.
Cowie, Peter, ''Orson Welles,'' in *Films and Filming* (London), April 1961.
''Welles Issue'' of *Image et Son* (Paris), no. 139, 1961.
''Welles Issue'' of *Cineforum* (Venice), no. 19, 1962.
''Welles Issue'' of *Etudes Cinématographiques* (Paris), 1963.
Interview with Everett Sloane, in *Film* (London), no. 37, 1965.
Cobos, Juan, Miguel Rubio, and J. A. Pruneda, ''A Trip to Don Quixoteland: Conversations with Orson Welles,'' in *Cahiers du Cinema in English* (New York), June 1966.
Henderson, Brian, ''The Long Take,'' in *Film Comment* (New York), Summer 1971.
Goldfarb, Phyllis, ''Orson Welles' Use of Sound,'' in *Take One* (Montreal), July-August 1971.
Graham, M., ''The Inaccessibility of *The Lady from Shanghai*,'' in *Film Criticism* (Edinboro, Pennsylvania), Spring 1981.
West, A., ''A Textual Analysis of *Lady from Shanghai*,'' in *Enclitic* (Minneapolis), Fall 1981-Spring 1982.
Goldschmidt, D., in *Cinématographe* (Paris), February 1982.
Houston, Beverle, ''Power and Dis-Integration in the Films of Orson Welles,'' in *Film Quarterly* (Berkeley), Summer 1982.
Albano, L., in *Filmcritica* (Florence), February 1985.

The Lady from Shanghai

Moilanen, H., ''Aani & vimma, tasta maailmasta,'' in *Filmihullu* (Helsinki), no. 7–8, 1988.

Nielsen, N. A., ''Et allerhelvedes perspektiv,'' in *Kosmorama* (Copenhagen), Fall 1989.

Naremore, James, ''Between Works and Texts: Notes from the Welles Archive,'' in *Persistence of Vision* (Maspeth), no. 7, May 1989.

Rampazzoni, Guido, ''Cristallisation,'' in *Vertigo* (Paris), no. 6–7, 1991.

Short review, in *Revue du Cinéma* (Paris), no. 470, April 1991.

Schactman, K., in *Scarlet Street* (Glen Rock), no. 6, Spring 1992.

McLean, A. L., '''It's Only That I Do What I Love and Love What I Do': Film Noir and the Musical Woman,'' in *Cinema Journal* (Austin), vol. 33, no. 1, 1993.

Reid's Film Index (Wyong), no. 13, 1994.

Rosenbaum, Jonathan, ''The Battle Over Orson Welles,'' in *Cineaste* (New York), vol. 22, no. 3, December 1996.

Tobin, Yann, ''Près des yeux, près du coeur: Les gros plans de *La Dame de Shanghai*,'' in *Positif* (Paris), no. 449–450, July-August 1998.

*   *   *

The Lady from Shanghai can be viewed as a variation on *film noir*. Set in Orson Welles's peculiar aesthetic and autobiographical mold, it acquires its own autonomy. It makes a self-conscious and intricate use of the frame, and its lush compositions in deep focus push together the foreground and background. The script appears to be written for the purpose of coordinating glaring ruptures breaking the synchrony of image and sound tracks that had prevailed in the studio tradition. The plot develops a play of human figures confined in a closed world of cross purposes. Michael O'Hara (Welles) is victimized in a skein of machinations wrought by Elsa Bannister (Hayworth) in collusion with and against her husband (Sloane), an aging, cane-swaggering cripple who happens to be a brilliant criminal lawyer. Framed by a set of fake self-murders, Welles portrays himself as a tough, soft-hearted, anti-Fascist refugee from the Spanish Civil War, an Irish innocent who adventures through life with resolution and independence. That he is a function of the others shatters his American dream of poetic self-identity.

Simplicity and complication collapse in the mix of narrative and visual composition, the film ostensively unfolding not for its narrative but to threshold experiment in uncanny renderings of scenes that had become too standard in *film noir*. Characters are destined to meet and miss each other in what appear to be a photographer's retinal tricks. In the beginning, Welles encounters Hayworth during a carriage ride that is shot with vertical pans isolating and combining the two protagonists in two adjacent photograms. Later, they find themselves framed in backlit tableaux, notably in the sequence shot in the San Francisco aquarium. Close-ups of her sensuous profile and uncanny blonde—not red—*chevelure* are offset by lurid projections of monstrous fish, groupers swimming just behind Hayworth's face. Narrative turns into a mix of tourism, *noir*, and comedy. Obtained by the natural back lighting of the aquarium, Chiaroscuro makes Hayworth a playful figure of deceit, or a ''phallic'' female in a comic mode. Later, in the ''Crazy House'' of mirrors, the characters are multiplied prismatically as they seek to shoot their images to bits. ''If I kill you, I kill myself,'' murmurs Bannister in close-up exactly where the frame places his reflection against Elsa's. Carnival ensues, bullets shattering mirrors until they finally reach the two spouses. A cinematic potlatch, the finale celebrates and consumes the entire film exactly where it comically displaces the tensions of the protagonist's fatal attraction for the woman who charms him. Relieved, and contrary to the hero of a *noir* scenario, the narrator slips away from the destruction and into the airy cityscape of San Francisco. ''The only way to grow wise is to get old,'' he predicts, pacing off into the outdoors that eclipse him in light.

High tonal contrasts produce images with razor-sharp outlines. On the one hand, the backlit decor yields chiaroscuro and indeterminate depth of field, while on the other, in the sequences shot off the California coast, the luminosity becomes a crucial element in the story. And Welles shoots from uncanny positions, in extreme tilts and countertilts, less predictable than those used in *Citizen Kane*, to obtain a total sense of disorientation. His camera establishes intimacy between forms at once in extreme closeup and in great depth. Shots of Hayworth on the rocks off Acapulco isolate her in such extreme depth of field that her body is barely recognizable next to O'Hara's nose in the foreground. As in Renoir or in Welles's earlier work, self-conscious use of optical instruments in the film-images reflected on the convex lenses of binoculars, water tumblers, anamorphic mirrors, windshields—tend to make the objects in frame theorize the visibility of the tale that is being told. And, as usual in the director's visual style, the play within the play mirrors the diegesis in *mise-en-abyme*. Just prior to the ''Crazy House'' sequence, Hayworth, who set about to ''shanghai'' O'Hara, leads the hero into a puppet show in a Chinese playhouse near Union Square. At that moment, in a sudden frenzy, he evades the police after being framed in a kangaroo trial. Elsa and the police seek O'Hara hidden among wizened Oriental spectators in a theater in Chinatown. Gongs and cymbals deafen the ear, dancers turn in stylized motion that signals patent melodrama; Elsa's blonde beauty, seen in closeup, matches her incomprehensible whispers murmured in the ears of her underworld cronies. The sequence doubles both the story and the visual style toward which the film had directed its play of narrative and visual form.

In sum, the viewer is offered the pleasure of seeing cinema extended as neither the studio tradition nor *film noir* had yet done up to 1947. Welles works within an aesthetic matrix that had already stamped him as a foremost *auteur* in the movie industry, but his visual and narrative obsessions also inflect cinema in ways unknown up to that time. The film exceeds itself in other ways: it figures in a number of conventions but also works through Welles and Hayworth's own divorce that was taking place as they portrayed themselves in the production. Hayworth's blonde beauty emphasizes the travesty of both the narrative and visual style. *The Lady from Shanghai* cannot be easily classified. Its genre is its own and must be viewed independently of the high expectations that had been set for viewers since *Citizen Kane* or *The Magnificent Ambersons*.

—Tom Conley

LADY OF FORTUNE

See **BECKY SHARP**

THE LADY VANISHES

UK, 1938

Director: Alfred Hitchcock

Production: Gainsborough; black and white; running time: 96 minutes; length: 8,650 feet. Released 1938.

Producer: Edward Black; **screenplay:** Sidney Gilliat and Frank Launder, from the novel *The Wheel Spins* by Ethel Lina White; **additional dialogue:** Alma Reville; **photography:** Jack Cox; **editor:** R. E. Dearing; **art director:** Alec Vetchinsky; **music:** Louis Levy.

Cast: Margaret Lockwood (*Iris Henderson*); Michael Redgrave (*Gilbert*); Paul Lukas (*Dr. Hartz*); Dame May Whitty (*Miss Froy*); Googie Withers (*Blanche*); Cecil Parker (*Mr. Todhunter*); Linden Travers (*Mrs. Todhunter*); Mary Clare (*The Baroness*); Naunton Wayne (*Caldicott*); Basil Radford (*Charters*); Emile Boreo (*Hotel Manager*); Sally Stewart (*Julie*); Philip Leaver (*Signor Doppo*); Selma Vaz Dias (*Signora Doppo*); Catherine Lacey (*The Nun*).

Publications

Script:

Gilliat, Sidney, and Frank Launder, *The Lady Vanishes*, New York, 1984.

Hitchcock, Alfred, editor, *The Lady Vanishes*, New York, 1988.

Books:

Noble, Peter, *An Index to the Creative Work of Alfred Hitchcock*, London, 1949.

Findlater, Richard, *Michael Redgrave, Actor*, New York, 1956.

Amengual Barthélemy, and Raymond Borde, *Alfred Hitchcock*, Paris, 1957.

Rohmer, Eric, and Claude Chabrol, *Hitchcock*, Paris, 1957.

Bogdanovich, Peter, *The Cinema of Alfred Hitchcock*, New York, 1962.

The Lady Vanishes

Perry, Gerogr, *The Films of Alfred Hitchcock*, London, 1965.
Wood, Robin, *Hitchcock's Films*, London, 1965, updated 1989.
Truffaut, François, *Le Cinéma selon Hitchcock*, Paris, 1966; as *Hitchcock*, New York, 1985.
La Valley, Albert J., editor, *Focus on Hitchcock*, Englewood Cliffs, New Jersey, 1972.
Durgnat, Raymond, *The Strange Case of Alfred Hitchcock; or, The Plain Man's Hitchcock*, Cambridge, Massachusetts, 1974.
Brown, Geoff, *Launder and Gilliat*, London, 1977.
Yacowar, Maurice, *Hitchcock's British Films*, Hamden, Connecticut,1977.
Taylor, John Russell, *Hitch*, London and New York, 1978.
Armes, Roy, *A Critical History of British Cinema*, London, 1978.
Bellour, Raymond, *L'Analyse du film*, Paris, 1979.
Hemmeter, Thomas M., *Hitchcock, the Stylist*, Ann Arbor, Michigan, 1981.
Bazin, Andre, *The Cinema of Cruelty: From Buñuel to Hitchcock*, New York, 1982.
Narboni, Jean, editor, *Alfred Hitchcock*, Paris, 1982.
Rothman, William, *Hitchcock—The Murderous Gaze*, Cambridge, Massachusetts, 1982.
Villien, Bruno, *Hitchcock*, Paris, 1982.
Weis, Elisabeth, *The Silent Scream: Alfred Hitchcock's Sound Track*, Rutherford, New Jersey, 1982.
Spoto, Donald, *The Life of Alfred Hitchcock: The Dark Side of Genius*, New York, 1982; London, 1983.
Phillips, Gene D., *Alfred Hitchcock*, Boston, 1984.
Barbier, Philippe, and Jacques Moreau, *Alfred Hitchcock*, Paris, 1985.
Douchet, Jean, *Alfred Hitchcock*, Paris, 1985.
Deutelbaum, Marshall, and Leland Poague, *A Hitchcock Reader*, Ames, Iowa, 1986.
Humphries, Patrick, *The Films of Alfred Hitchcock*, Greenwich, Connecticut, 1986, 1994.
Hogan, David J., *Dark Romance: Sexuality in the Horror Film*, Jefferson, North Carolina, 1986.
Ryall, Tom, *Alfred Hitchcock and the British Cinema*, London, 1986.
Kloppenburg, Josef, *Die dramaturgische Funktion der Musik in Filmen Alfred Hitchcocks*, Munich, 1986.
Sinyard, Neil, *The Films of Alfred Hitchcock*, London, 1986.
Modleski, Tania, *The Women Who Knew Too Much: Hitchcock and Feminist Theory*, New York, 1988.
Sterritt, David, *The Films of Alfred Hitchcock*, New York, 1993.

Arginteanu, Judy, *The Movies of Alfred Hitchcock*, Minneapolis, 1994.
Boyd, David, editor, *Perspectives on Alfred Hitchcock*, New York, 1995.
Harris, Robert A., *Complete Films of Alfred Hitchcock*, Secaucus, 1999.

Articles:

Monthly Film Bulletin (London), no. 56, 1938.
Today's Cinema (London), 24 August 1938.
Kine Weekly (London), 25 August 1938.
Variety (New York), 31 August 1938.
Motion Picture Herald (New York), 3 September 1938.
Whitebait, William, in *New Statesman* (London), 15 October 1938.
Nugent, Frank, Jr., in *New York Times*, 26 December 1938.
''Hitchock Issue'' of *Cahiers du Cinéma* (Paris), October 1953.
Redgrave, Michael, in *Sight and Sound* (London), January-March 1955.
''Hitchcock Issue'' of *Cahiers du Cinéma* (Paris), August-September 1956.
Stanbrook, Alan, in *Films and Filming* (London), July 1963.
Kael, Pauline, in *Kiss Kiss Bang Bang*, Boston, 1968.
French, Philip, in *Observer Magazine* (London), 28 September 1980.
Ferzetti, F., in *Filmcritica* (Florence), January 1981.
Chion, M., ''Chiffre de destinée,'' in *Cahiers du Cinéma* (Paris), April 1984.
Thomas, François, ''Subtiliser: Sur trois films anglais d'Alfred Hitchcock,'' in *Positif* (Paris), July-August 1984.
Bikacsy, G., ''Londoni randevu,'' in *Filmvilag* (Budapest), vol. 29, no. 12, 1986.
Ferrara, P., ''The Discontented Bourgeoise: Bourgeois Morality and the Interplay of Light and Dark Strains in Hitchcock's Films,'' in *New Orleans Review*, vol. 14, no. 4, 1987.
Foley, J., ''*The Lady Vanishes*: Notes on Memory in Hitchcock,'' in *Bright Lights* (Cincinnati), no. 10, July 1993.
Reid's Film Index (Wyong), no. 21, 1996.
Beckman, Karen, ''Violent Vanishings: Hitchcock, Harlan, and the Disappearing Woman,'' in *Camera Obscura* (Bloomington), no. 39, September 1996.
Kock, I. de, ''De Hitchcock touch (4),'' in *Film en Televisie + Video* (Brussels), no. 473, July 1997.

* * *

The Lady Vanishes is probably Alfred Hitchcock's most popular film of the 1930s. Scripted by Sidney Gilliat and Frank Launder from a novel, *The Wheel Spins* (1936), by the best-selling novelist Ethel Lina White, the film was shot in five weeks during the late autumn of 1938. Although the project was originally offered to an American director, Roy William Neill, the film was abruptly cancelled after a Gainsborough film crew, doing some exterior shooting in Yugoslavia, created a minor political furor when the local authorities became nervous about how their native country was to be depicted in the British cinema. The film received new life, however, when Hitchcock read the script, in October 1937, and, after the director made some minor additions, Gainsborough went into almost immediate production.

In spite of the film's popular and financial success, it has fared badly at the hands of the critics. For example, John Russell Taylor described the film as the ''lightest and purist of diversions'' with little claim on logic or to any deep meaning. Donald Spoto called it a mere *divertissement*, a cinematic soufflé. Even Raymond Durgnat, after a rather lengthy analysis of the film, characterized it as one of Hitchcock's ''least substantial.'' Hitchcock himself, in his interview with François Truffaut, has added to such critical trivializing by concentrating his remarks on the technical experiment of achieving the scene in the dining car with the close-up of the drugged drinks. Yet in spite of such critical evasion there is reason to regard the film as a serious work.

Among the first substantial accounts of the film was the one written by Raymond Durgnat in his study *The Strange Case of Alfred Hitchcock*. Durgnat explores the film's contemporary political ramifications and writes about the film as a reaction to the mounting European crisis brought on by the allies' attempt to pacify Hitler at Munich. Durgnat's analysis centres on how the various British characters interact with each other in face of a ''political'' danger. At first unaware of the crisis or self-consciously avoiding it, the various members of the microcosm of British society on the train awaken to the importance of becoming involved in the effort to restrain the forces of evil represented by the German-accented doctor and his uniformed as well as un-uniformed accomplices. Such a sociological reading is not difficult to fathom given the time period of the film and given Hitchcock's preoccupation with spies and spying in his films of the 1930s, such as *Secret Agent*, *Sabotage*, and *The 39 Steps*, and although Durgnat's analysis is not particularly sophisticated as political criticism goes, it does help to refute the claim that *The Lady Vanishes* is undeserving of detailed analysis. It also opens up a wide-ranging and potentially exciting direction for further examination of Hitchcock's films of the 1930s as expressive of a variety of political issues, including a fairly critical examination of British inter-war society.

A far more complex and in many ways more difficult approach to the film has recently emerged as feminist critics, spurred on by the work of Laura Mulvey and Raymond Bellour, and as evidenced in a recent study by Tania Modleski, have come to see Hitchcock's cinema as a fruitful site for exploring the treatment of women in classical cinema. Such an approach focusses less on the *realpolitik* of the film and concentrates more forcefully on the treatment of the female characters. By shifting the critical focus back to the female protagonist, Iris Henderson (Margaret Lockwood), the analysis of the film returns the critical emphasis to questions of gender, the relationship between female characters, and women as structural agents in the narrative.

The focus of the criticism then becomes less what is happening, and its possible external meanings (Durgnat) and more on how the female character has become a cluster of values and ideologies which can be made intelligible by a careful analysis of such things as the disruptive femaleness of Miss Froy (Dame May Whitty), or the mother/daughter combination of Miss Froy and Iris Henderson and how that relationship is modified by the presence of the male protagonist, Gilbert (Michael Redgrave). This approach opens the film to depth psychology and political criticism of the most sophisticated nature.

Although it remains a popular item on film society offerings, its wit still appreciable some 50 years after it was made, *The Lady Vanishes* also now occupies, along with *The 39 Steps*, *Secret Agent*, *Sabotage*, and the early *Man Who Knew Too Much*, a central place as a formative Hitchcock film.

—Charles L. P. Silet

LAN FENGZHENG

(The Blue Kite)

Hong Kong-China, 1992

Director: Tian Zhuangzhuang

Production: Longwick Film Production, Beijing Film Studio; color; running time: 138 minutes.

Producers: Luo Guiping, Cheng Yongping; **screenplay:** Xiao Mao; **photography:** Hou Yong; **editor:** Qian Lengleng; **assistant directors:** He Jianjun, Zhang Weiyong; **art director:** Zhang Xiande; **music:** Yoshihide Otomo; **costumes:** Dong Juying.

Cast: Yi Tian (*Tietou infant*); Zhang Wenyao (*Tietou child*); Chen Xioman (*Tietou teenager*); Lu Liping (*Mother*); Pu Quanzin (*Father*); Li Xuejian (*Uncle Li*); Guo Baochang (*Stepfather*); Zhong Ping (*Chen Shusheng*).

Publications

Articles:

Variety (New York), 14 June 1993.

Lapinski, Stan, ''Woede en doortrapte mildheid,'' in *Skrien* (Amsterdam), no. 197, August-September, 1994.

Rayns, T., in *Sight and Sound* (London), February 1994.

Rayns, T., ''Flying Colours,'' in *Time Out* (London), 2 February 1994.

Sklar, Robert, ''People and Politics, Simple and Direct,'' in *Cineaste* (New York), vol. 20, no. 4, 1994.

* * *

Tian Zhuangzhuang's *The Blue Kite* is one of a number of contemporary films which charts the ever-changing face of life in post-revolutionary China. The film is most effective as an uncompromisingly humanistic examination of the impact of politics and blind revolution on the individual and family unit. In this regard, it is a sobering censure of the hypocrisy existing within China under the domain of Mao. What is the point of revolution, the film maker asks, if basic human needs (let alone common civility and compassion) end up taking a back seat to that revolution?

The Blue Kite chronicles the emotional fireworks occurring within one Chinese family during the tumultuous 1950s and 60s. The unfolding events are considered from the point of view of Tietou, a child who narrates the proceedings and is seen from infancy through adolescence. The scenario opens in 1953, upon the death of Josef Stalin. Chen Shujuan (Lu Liping), a teacher, and Lin Shaolong (Pu Quanxin), a librarian, are about to be married in Beijing, and Tietou will be their son. Not long after his birth, a movement towards nationalism begins in China and the long arm of Communist Party politics stretches into the commonplace lives of all citizens.

The point of the scenario is that all which befalls Tietou and his family does not emerge from the natural ebb and flow of life. They are not allowed to evolve with the same freedom a kite has as it sails through the sky, with only the wind determining its direction. Instead, their fates are affected by the constantly evolving political correctness. They become victims of their society, where a revolution has taken place which presumably will improve their plight. But instead, they are irrevocably thrust into chaos: during repercussions against a movement which had advocated uncensored criticism of the Party, Shaolong is thrown into a labor camp; he eventually dies, and Shujuan marries a friend who cared for her and Tietou in Shaolong's absence; after the demise of her second husband, Shujuan weds an elderly Party member. Meanwhile, Tietou (now played by Chen Xiaoman) grows into a disaffected teen. His life—and that of all others—will undergo further upheaval in 1967, at the advent of the Cultural Revolution.

The Blue Kite contrasts the rhetoric versus the reality of life in contemporary China. Under communism, all citizens are supposed to be equal, but a class system and a political hierarchy remains in place. There are haves and have-nots, Communist Party members and peasants. The sole difference from the pre-revolutionary days is the identity of those in power. Meanwhile, young people are taught that ''revolution is good,'' and politics must come first in their lives. As a result, petty adherence to Party rules takes preference over logic and humanity.

Tian vividly depicts the manner in which those who are at the political vanguard one year may find themselves chastised, beaten and scarred the next. In Communist China, yesterday's ''good politics'' just may become today's ''bad politics.'' Yesterday's comrade is today's counter-revolutionary.

Thematically speaking, *The Blue Kite* is the sister film of Chen Kaige's *Farewell, My Concubine* and Zhang Yimou's *To Live*. *Farewell, My Concubine* runs from the 1920s through the 1970s and tells the story of a trio of characters, while *To Live* follows the fortunes of one Chinese family from the 1940s on; both narratives examine the manner in which their protagonists become swept up in the events of Chinese history. Despite their larger-than-life natures, all three films are, at their core, simple, personal stories of love, devotion, loss and forgiveness. The characters are deeply human and individualistic, rather than political caricatures.

The filming of *The Blue Kite* was almost complete in 1991, when it was screened for Chinese officials. Its production was summarily halted, because of its ''political leanings.'' Postproduction was completed in Japan, using Tian's notes. Earlier, the overseas marketing of a pair of the film maker's other works, *On the Killing Ground* and *Horse Thief*, was disrupted by Chinese authorities. Similarly, the country's censors initially banned *Farewell, My Concubine* and, over the years, the Western media has reported Zhang Yimou's endless conflicts with his government, and the censuring of his films.

If *The Blue Kite*, among these other films, has been unable to directly alter the social and political fabric of China, the fact that it was completed, and made available to audiences across the world, remains a triumph in itself.

—Rob Edelman

Lan fengzheng

THE LAND

USA, 1942

Directors: Robert J. Flaherty with Frances H. Flaherty

Production: Agricultural Adjustment Agency, U.S. Department of Agriculture; black and white, 35mm; running time: 42 minutes. Though it has been shown non-theatrically, the film has never had a general release; its premiere showing was in April 1942, at the Museum of Modern Art, New York. Filmed summer 1939-March 1940 in the American South and Midwest.

Screenplay: Robert J. Flaherty; **commentary:** Russell Lord; **photography:** Irving Lerner, Douglas Baker, Floyd Crosby, and Charles Herbert; **editor:** Helen Van Dongen; **sound engineers:** A. Dillinger and Reuben Ford; **music:** Richard Arnell; **consultant:** Wayne Darrow; **research and field assistance:** W. H. Lamphere and Lamp Hart.

Cast: Robert Flaherty (*Narrator*).

Publications

Books:

Lord, Russell and Kate Lord, *Forever the Land: A Country Chronicle and Anthology*, New York, 1950.

Gromo, Mario, *Robert Flaherty*, Parma, 1952.

Rotha, Paul, *Documentary Film*, New York, 1952.

Griffith, Richard, *The World of Robert Flaherty*, New York, 1953.

Flaherty, Frances, *The Odyssey of a Film-Maker: Robert Flaherty's Story*, Urbana, Illinois, 1960.

Quintar, Fuad, *Robert Flaherty et le documentaire poétique*, Paris, 1960.

Rotha, Paul and Richard Griffith, *The Film Till Now*, New York, 1960.

Clemente, Jose L., *Robert Flaherty*, Madrid, 1963.

Cuenca, Carlos Fernandez, *Robert Flaherty*, Madrid, 1963.

Calder-Marshall, Arthur, *The Innocent Eye: The Life of Robert J. Flaherty*, London, 1963; New York, 1966.

Klaue, Wolfgang, editor, *Robert Flaherty*, East Berlin, 1964.

Agel, Henri, *Robert J. Flaherty*, Paris, 1965.

Snyder, Robert, *Pare Lorentz and the Documentary Film*, Norman, Oklahoma, 1968.

The Land

Barsam, Richard, *Nonfiction Film: A Critical History*, New York, 1973.
Barnouw, Erik, *Documentary: A History of the Non-Fiction Film*, New York, 1974.
Wright, Basil, *The Long View*, London and New York, 1974,
Napolitano, Antonio, *Robert J. Flaherty*, Florence, 1975.
Murphy, William T., *Robert Flaherty: A Guide to References and Resources*, Boston, 1979.
Weaver, Mike, *Robert Flaherty's ''The Land,''* Exeter, Devon, 1979.
Hardy, Forsyth, editor, *Grierson on the Movies*, London, 1981.
Rotha, Paul, *Robert J. Flaherty: A Biography*, Philadelphia, 1983.

Articles:

Griffith, Richard, ''Flaherty and the Future,'' in *New Movies* (New York), January 1943.
Pandolfi, Vito, ''Documentare a lotta per la vita,'' in *Cinema* (Rome), 15 December 1950.
''Gli uomini hanno fame mella terra de Flaherty,'' in *Cinema* (Rome), November 1951.
Rucon Turconi, Davide, ''Il film proibito di Flaherty,'' in *Bianco e Nero* (Rome), no. 2, 1962.
Van Dongen, Helen, ''Robert J. Flaherty,'' in *Film Quarterly* (Berkeley), Summer 1965; and in *Non-Fiction Film: Theory and Criticism*, edited by Richard Barsam, New York, 1976.
Achtenberg, Ben, ''Helen Van Dongen: An Interview,'' in *Film Quarterly* (Berkeley), Winter 1976.
Strauss, Theodore, ''The Giant Shinnies down the Beanstalk: Flaherty's *The Land*,'' in *The Documentary Tradition*, edited by Lewis Jacobs, New York, 1979.
Lee, R., ''Robert Flaherty: Free Spirit,'' in *American Cinematographer* (Hollywood), vol. 65, no. 1, January 1984.
Leacock, Richard, ''In Defense of the Flaherty Traditions,'' in *Film Culture* (New York), no. 79, Winter 1996.

* * *

The Land, the least typical, least known, and most controversial of Robert Flaherty's films, depicts a vast and vague territory across the southern and midwestern United States. Here, in the period between the Depression's end and the beginning of World War II, abandoned farmhouses lined dusty roadways, and forgotten farm people had almost ceased to hope for a better life. On the face of it, *The Land* might have become the earthly counterpart to Pare Lorentz's *The River*, easily the best known and most widely praised American documentary film. But as it turned out, *The Land* pleased few people, least of all Flaherty himself.

As head of the new U.S. Film Service, Lorentz had invited Robert Flaherty (perhaps at John Grierson's suggestion) to make a film on the New Deal's efforts to restore American farmers and farmlands to their productive fullness. Flaherty and his wife collaborator, Frances, welcomed the chance to explore their homeland as they had previously explored many distant corners of the world. Flaherty's brief experience with government sponsorship while making *Industrial Britain*, or most of it, for Grierson's E.M.B. Film Unit in 1931 had not prepared him for the frustrations and troubles that lay ahead.

To make *The Land* Robert and Frances Flaherty travelled some 100,000 miles, shooting 25,000 feet of 35mm film—all silent (narration and music were added later). ''A long and gruelling job,'' Flaherty later described it. While he was still filming, Lorentz started a new film of his own (*The Fight for Life*) and in his absence Congress abruptly dismantled the U.S. Film Service. *The Land* was shunted to Henry Wallace's Department of Agriculture. All through the summer and fall of 1941, the Department's experts tinkered with Flaherty's footage, trying to make it conform to the government's rapidly changing needs and policies. As the U.S. came closer to entering the war, unemployment gave way to a farm labor shortage, mechanization became part of the solution to the farm problems rather than a threat. It fell to Helen van Dongen (who had edited Joris Ivens' later European films, and his just finished *Power and the Land*) to find structure for Flaherty's random footage and make sense of the changing government directives.

The film's most memorable scenes are those in which Flaherty (narrating the film himself) briefly dramatizes poignant human incidents: a young couple with two small children packing their pitiful belongings on an old mule cart; an old Negro man living alone on a once-abundant plantation, wondering where everyone has gone; a boy sleeping, while his mother explains that his hands move because he thinks he's shelling peas. Flaherty conceded that the film had no specific solutions for what the camera saw; he found it amazing that so critical a film could be made at all. ''It shows that democracy can face itself in the mirror without flinching,'' he told an interviewer a short while before the film's intended release.

Within a few short weeks, however, democracy flinched. With the U.S. now at war, government officials feared that so dismal a picture would serve mainly to aid the enemies' propaganda campaigns. A prestige premiere was held at the Museum of Modern Art in early 1942, but the film's release was permanently denied. (The Museum still distributes 16mm prints for study purposes. Calder-Marshall's *The Innocent Eye*, Appendix 4, contains the final narration, written by Russell Lord based on Flaherty's comments, interspersed with critical descriptions of each sequence by Paul Rotha and Basil Wright.)

Critical opinion about *The Land* has been divided, then as now, into two more or less exclusive areas: style and content. Basil Wright has called it ''the most important film in Flaherty's development as an artist . . . a cry of protest . . . impressive because of its passionate incoherence.'' Siegfried Kracauer found its ''plot'' lacking precision and failing to get hold of the very problems it attacked; its true merits (deep honesty, the beauty of its pictures, and its avoidance of hasty conclusions) added up to ''fragments of a lost epic song.'' Frances Flaherty did not mention *The Land* in her book, *The Odyssey of Filmmaker* considering only their four ''free'' films as bearing the true Flaherty mark.

Although the first credit after the main title on *The Land* reads ''Directed by Robert J. Flaherty in collaboration with Frances H. Flaherty,'' her name often does not appear in books listing those credits. Richard Griffith, in *The World of Robert Flaherty*, details the nature of the Flahertys' ''filmmaking partnership'' in creating a film method which Frances later called ''non-preconception,'' which she championed after Flaherty's death through her writings and her talks, and through the Flaherty Seminars which she founded in 1955.

The Land was Flaherty's major effort to align himself with the social-minded documentarists. If he failed, it was no more or less a failure than his efforts to become part of the commercial movie world. Like the great Sergei Eisenstein, Flaherty was a man of mythic vision; his films were mythic too, despite earnest efforts to conform to pre-determined rules and counter-regulations. At Flaherty's death in 1951, Grierson re-assessed Flaherty's ''handful of lovely films'' with the thousands of educational and propaganda productions, made by the ''documentary people who went the other way,'' financed by the million in government services all over the world. ''I look at it all today and think with the gentler half of my head that Flaherty's path was right and the other wrong.'' Certainly Flaherty's path was right for Flaherty, if for no others.

—Cecile Starr

LÁSKY JEDNÉ PLAVOVLÁSKY

(Loves of a Blonde)

Czechoslovakia, 1965

Director: Miloš Forman

Production: Barrandov Film Studio for Ceskoslovensky Film; black and white, 35mm; length: 2915 metres. Released November 1965. Prague. Filmed 1965 in Zruč and Sázavou, Czechoslovakia.

Producer: Rudolf Hajek; **screenplay:** Jaroslav Papousěk, Ivan Passer, Miloš Forman, and Václav Sašek; **assistant director:** Ivan Passer; **photography:** Miroslav Ondříček; **editor:** Miroslav Hájek; **sound:** Adolf Böhm; **art director:** Karel Cerný; **music:** Evžen Illin.

Cast: Hana Brejchová (*Andula*); Vladimir Pucholt (*Milda*); Vladimir Menšík (*Vacovský*); Ivan Kheil (*Maňas*); Jiří Hrubý (*Burda*); Milada Ježková (*Milda's mother*); Josef Sebáek (*Milda's father*); Marie Salačová (*Marie*); Jana Nováková (*Jana*); Jana Crkalová (*Jaruška*); Zdeňka Lorencová (*Zdena*); Táňa Zelinkaová (*Girl*); Jan Vostreil (*Colonel*); Josef Kolb (*Prkorný*); Antonin Blažejovský (*Tonda*); M. Zedníčková (*Educator*).

Award: Venice Film Festival, Prize of CIDALAC, 1965.

Lásky jedné plavovlásky

Publications

Script:

Forman, Milos, and others ''*Lasky Jedne Plavovlasky,*'' in *Avant-Scène du Cinéma* (Paris), no. 60, 1966.
Forman, Milos, *Turnaround: A Memoir*, New York, 1996.
Byrge, Duane, *Private Screenings: Insiders Share a Century of Great Movie Moments*, Collingdale, 1999.

Books:

Boček, Jaroslav, *Modern Czechoslovak Film 1945–1965*, Prague, 1965.
Whyte, Alistair, *New Cinema in Eastern Europe*, New York, 1971.
Dewey, Langdon, *Outline of Czechoslovakian Cinema*, London, 1971.
Henstall, Bruce, editor, *Miloš Forman, Ingrid Thulin*, Washington, D.C., 1972.
Liehm, Antonin, *Closely Watched Films*, White Plains, New York, 1974.
Stoil, Michael Jon, *Cinema Beyond the Danube*, Metuchen, New Jersey, 1974.
Liehm, Antonin, *The Miloš Forman Stories*, White Plains, New York, 1975.
Liehm, Mira and Antonin, *The Most Important Art: East European Film after 1945*, Berkeley, 1977.
Vecchi, Paolo, *Milos Forman*, Firenze, 1981.
Poizot, Claude, *Milos Forman*, Paris, 1987.
Forman, Miloš, *Turnaround: A Memoir*, with Jan Novak, New York, 1994.

Articles:

Janouseek, J., in *Film a Doba* (Prague), no. 5, 1965.
Dyer, Peter John, ''Star-Crossed in Prague,'' in *Sight and Sound* (London), Winter 1965–66.
Gow, Gordon, in *Films and Filming* (London), February and July 1966.
''Adula's Dream,'' in *Newsweek* (New York), 19 September 1966.
Sarris, Andrew, in *Village Voice* (New York), 10 November 1966.
Kahan, Saul, in *Cinema* (Beverly Hills), December 1966.
Blue, James, and Gianfranco de Bosio, interview with Milos Forman, in *Cahiers du Cinema in English* (New York), February 1967.
Frazer, Graham, in *Take One* (Montreal), February 1967.

Clouzot, Claire, in *Film Quarterly* (Berkeley), Fall 1967.
Polt, Harriet, ''Getting the Great 10%,'' in *Film Comment* (New York), Fall 1970.
Conaway, James, ''Miloš Forman's America is Like Kafka's—Basically Comic,'' in *New York Times Magazine*, 11 July 1971.
Gow, Gordon, ''A Czech in New York: An Interview with Miloš Forman,'' in *Films and Filming* (London), September 1971.
Foldes, A., in *Filmkultura* (Budapest), September-October 1971.
Földes, A., ''Idotálló kérdések,'' in *Filmkultura* (Budapest), vol. 15, no. 5, September-October 1979.
Somen, B., ''Plavolaskine ljubezni znova,'' in *Ekran*, vol. 5, no. 2/3, 1980.
Prádná, Stanislava, ''Sila pravdivosti a hranice moznosti nehereckeho,'' in *Film a Doba* (Prague), vol. 37, no. 2, Summer 1991.
''Les amours d'une blonde,'' in *Séquences* (Haute-Ville), no. 180, September-October 1995.
Rollet, S., ''L'enigmatique present,'' in *Positif* (Paris), no. 433, March 1997.

* * *

The heroes of Miloš Forman's first films are quite ordinary young people, like most of the young people in the world. They do not stand out; they are not too good and not too bad, not particularly clever, but not particularly stupid either. In *Konkurs (The Competition)* they are girls who long to sing in the popular theater of Prague but are incapable of assessing their own abilities. In *Cerny Petr (Black Peter)* the hero is a young man who is learning to be a salesman because he has no precise goals in life. In *Loves of a Blonde* the central figures are young women who work in a shoe factory. All they want is a little happiness and a nice romantic love. Forman systematically chooses these non-heroic heroes for his films; he is interested precisely in the kind of people who will never be astronauts, outstanding scientists, actors or professional singers. In his opinion, they, too, are worthy of filmmakers' attention. This is the underlying premise of his early films, which derive their form from it, a form obviously different from traditional cinema not only in its conception of the hero but also in its distinct type of narrative. In these films Forman builds his style on the conviction that the most ordinary banalities of life contain more drama and more truth than the carefully elaborated form of a classically developed drama.

It is such everyday banalities that constitute the simple action of *Loves of a Blonde*. Its heroine, the young girl Andula, longs for love. She tries to find it with several men she happens to meet in her neighborhood. But she finds true love—or so she thinks—only after meeting a pianist from Prague. After a few beautiful moments, however, disappointment sets in, and Andula must once again content herself with her dreams. Her story, this slice of her life, is based on a linear succession of episodic situations with no gradations whatsoever. The director then develops these situations before the camera, and it is the viewer who combines them into a mosaic that has narrative value. Forman first took up filmmaking with a documentary bent; his quest for drama and truth in his films' characters in banal situations therefore has, to a certain extent, the nature of a documentary record. He follows his heroine and her comrades during their conversations at boarding school, at work in the factory, at a dance party, in talks with parents, and at meetings. The camera jumps from one face to another, fixing on them in an attempt to catch those imperceptible signs of inner feelings—boredom, longing, sadness, bitterness. The indifferent gaze of the camera could have a cruel effect, but it is softened by Forman's spontaneous sense of humor, which flows from the recognition that the most tragic occurrence, experienced and examined from without—and Forman looks at it with the same distance as the viewer—has comic and grotesque aspects. He finds and reveals the comedy in every situation involving the worker Andula, and even makes it the foundation of a love scene in which malfunctioning blinds undercut the significance Andula attaches to her feelings in her relationship with the pianist. However, Forman's humor is not malicious. He observes his heroes without ridiculing them, with kind sympathy and with the conviction that through laughter there is always a greater hope of penetratin beneath the surface of things. But he does not stop at the level of humorous portrayal. Through intimately familiar detail he brings the viewer to an understanding of the more general essence of the situations he depicts. And this essence is neither banal nor sentimental. Against the background of everyday activity, with all its comic situations, there is the weighty social problem of the isolated life of young women working in a remote Bohemian town where there are no opportunities to find acquaintances or love, resulting in the playing out of their emotional lives in cheap, demeaning short-term affairs. Ultimately, despite all the film's lighter moments, the viewer is left with a slight sense of sadness and bitterness.

Forman embarks on his subjects and themes with a thorough knowledge of the matter at hand; the life of the young women factory workers is depicted without the slightest artificiality. A contributing factor is the measured guidance of the actors, which makes one forget that, except for a few professionals, most of the actors had never been in front of a camera before. Another virtue of Forman's films of this period is the lively dialog, which becomes a vital element for enhancing the verisimilitude of the film situations.

In the history of Czechoslovak cinematography Forman's films represent a new achievement, from the standpoint of the choice of theme and content as well as techniques of expression. They have signaled a deviation from previous filmmaking and the start of a new course.

—B. Urgošiková

THE LAST LAUGH

See **DER LETZTE MANN**

THE LAST PICTURE SHOW

USA, 1971

Director: Peter Bogdanovich

Production: BBS Production and Last Picture Show Productions; black and white, 35mm; running time: 118 minutes. Released 1971 by Columbia-Warner. Filmed in Texas.

Producer: Stephen F. Friedman; **executive producer:** Burt Schneider; **screenplay:** Larry McMurtry and Peter Bogdanovich, from the novel by Larry McMurtry; **photography:** Robert Surtees; **editor:** Don Cambern; **sound:** Tom Overton; **production designer:** Polly Platt;

The Last Picture Show

art director: Walter Scott Herndon; **music:** Hank Williams, Bob Wills and the Texas Playboys, Eddy Arnold, Eddie Fisher, Phil Harris, Pee Wee King, Hank Snow, Tony Bennett, Lefty Frizzell, Frankie Laine, Johnnie Ray, Johnny Strindley, Kay Starr, Hank Thompson, Webb Pierce, and Jo Stafford.

Cast: Timothy Bottoms (*Sonny Crawford*); Jeff Bridges (*Duane Jackson*); Cybill Shepherd (*Jacy Farrow*); Ben Johnson (*Sam the Lion*); Cloris Leachman (*Ruth Popper*); Ellen Burstyn (*Lois Farrow*); Eileen Brennan (*Genevieve*); Clu Gulager (*Abilene*); Sam Bottoms (*Billy*); Sharon Taggart (*Charlene Dugs*); Randy Quaid (*Lester Marlow*); Joe Heathcock (*Sheriff*); Bill Thurman (*Coach Popper*); Barc Doyle (*Joe Bob Blanton*); Jessie Lee Fulton (*Miss Mosey*); Gary Brockette (*Bobby Sheen*); John Hillerman (*Teacher*); Helena Humann (*Jimmie Sue*); Loyd Catlett (*Leroy*); Robert Glenn (*Gene Farrow*); Janice O'Malley (*Mrs. Craig*); Floyd Mahaney (*Policeman*); Kimberley Hyde (*Annie Martin*); Noble Willingham (*Chester*); Pamela Kelier (*Jackie Lee French*); Gordon Hurst (*Monroe*); Mike Hosford (*Johnny*); Charlie Seybert (*Any Fanner*); Grover Lewis (*Mr. Crawford*); Rebecca Ulrick (*Marlene*); Merrill Shephard (*Agnes*); Buddy Wood (*Bud*); Leon Brown (*Cowboy in the cafe*).

Awards: Oscars for Best Supporting Actor (Johnson) and Best Supporting Actress (Leachman), 1971; New York Film Critics awards for Best Supporting Actor (Johnson), Best Supporting Actress (Burstyn), and Best Screenwriting (tied with *Sunday Bloody Sunday*), 1971.

Publications

Books:

Sherman, Eric, and Martin Rubin, *The Director's Event: Interviews with Five American Film-makers: Budd Boetticher, Peter Bogdanovich, Samuel Fuller, Arthur Penn, Abraham Polonsky*, New York, 1970.

Bogdanovich, Peter, *Pieces of Time*, New York, 1974.

Giacci, V., *Bogdanovich*, Florence, 1975.

Harris, Thomas J., *Bogdanovich's Picture Shows*, Metuchen, 1990.

Yule, Andrew, *Picture Shows: The Life and Times of Peter Bogdanovich*, New York, 1992.

Articles:

''*The Last Picture Show*: A Study in Black and White,'' in *American Cinematographer* (Los Angeles), January 1972.

O'Brien, G., and R. Feiden, ''Inter/View with Peter Bogdanovich,'' in *Inter/View* (New York), March 1972.

Dawson, Jan, in *Sight and Sound* (London), Spring 1972.

Pulleine, Tim, in *Film Quarterly* (Berkeley), Spring 1972.

Goodwin, M., in *Take One* (Montreal), April 1972.

Allombert, G., in *Image et Son* (Paris), May 1972.

Haustrate, G., in *Cinéma* (Paris), June 1972.

Jordan, I., in *Positif* (Paris), June 1972.

Turroni, G., in *Filmcritica* (Rome), November-December 1972.

Duprez, L., in *Filmrutan* (Tyreso, Sweden), no. 2, 1973.

Cerlich, John, ''*The Last Picture Show* and One More Adaptation,'' in *Literature/Film Quarterly* (Salisbury, Maryland), April 1973.

Piro, S., in *Cinema Nuovo* (Turin), May-June 1973.

Starr, Cecile, ''Peter Bogdanovich Remembered and Assessed,'' in *Filmmakers Newsletter* (Ward Hill, Massachusetts), September 1973.

Cohen, M. S., ''The Corporate Style of BBS,'' in *Take One* (Montreal), November 1973.

''Cybill and Peter'' (interview), in *Inter/View* (New York), June 1974.

Pietzsch, I., in *Film and Fernsehen* (Berlin), January 1977.

Bogdanovich, Peter, in *American Film* (Washington, D.C.), December 1978-January 1979.

O'Guinn, Tom, in *Cinema Texas Program Notes* (Austin), 16 January 1979.

Grimes, Teresa, ''BBS: Auspicious Beginnings, Open Endings,'' in *Movie* (London), Winter 1986.

Fleming, M., '''Picture' Return May Be Too Late for *Texasville*,'' in *Variety* (New York), 22 October 1980.

McKibbins, Adrienne, ''Bogdanovich Looks at the Past Through the Present,'' in *Filmnews*, vol. 22, no. 3, April 1992.

McReynolds, Douglas J., ''Alive and Well: Western Myth in Western Movies,'' in *Literature/Film Quarterly* (Salisbury), vol. 26, no. 1, January 1998.

* * *

The Last Picture Show is director Peter Bogdanovich's painful and moving look at life in a small Texan town. Adapted by Bogdanovich and Larry McMurtry from McMurtry's novel, the film chronicles the coming of age of two young men in an era that saw the final fadeout of the American frontier.

Underlying the film's story is its haunting theme of lost hopes and half-forgotten dreams. Bogdanovich captures the mood of desolation and boredom that grips the town of Anarene, contrasting it with the frustrated energy of the local teenagers as they struggle toward a future which holds only the emptiness they see in the lives of the adults around them. The end of their youth will bring death of their belief in a brighter life ahead, just as the passage of time has brought about the disappearance of the Old West and left a bleak, dying town in its place. Sam the Lion, the theatre and poolhall owner who had been a cowboy in his youth, is the story's link to an earlier time. His wisdom and innate dignity provide a role model for the boys, and his death marks the close of a chapter in their lives as well as the severing of the town's past and present.

The Last Picture Show is also a film about the decline of the ''Golden Age'' of Hollywood moviemaking. Set in 1951, it presents a culture on the verge of change, as the arrival of television signals the end of the studio system. The ''last picture show'' to play the local movie house before lack of business closes it down is Howard Hawks's *Red River*, one of the final epics of frontier life. Bogdanovich, a former film critic and the author of books on John Ford and Orson Welles, pays tribute in the film to the work of the legendary directors he admires. The style he adopts is reminiscent of the classic ''invisible'' approach to filmmaking favored by such directors as Ford and Hawks, whose camera remains an unobtrusive observer of the story. Like Ford, he makes use of occasional sweeping long shots, although here the shots record only the deserted, dusty streets of the town, providing a sad coda to Ford's majestic Western landscapes.

In 1970, Bogdanovich's decision to shoot his film in black and white was a somewhat radical choice. By the end of the 1960s, black and white photography had all but vanished from American feature films. Yet the powerful dramatic possibilities of the format, as well as the contrasts and shadings it offers, are ideally suited to the film's subject matter, and Robert Surtees's cinematography achieves a documentary-like realism.

This illusion is enhanced by the film's soundtrack of 1950s pop and country-western tunes and by the remarkable naturalism of its performers. From Cloris Leachman as the lonely affection-starved coach's wife to Cybill Shepherd as the beautiful, self-centred Jacy, the film is an example of ensemble playing at its finest. Particularly memorable among the strong performances is veteran character actor Ben Johnson's portrayal of Sam the Lion. Johnson, who received an Academy Award for his work, embodies the independence and strength of character which are the hallmarks of the heritage the town has lost.

The Last Picture Show is a film rich in both style and substance. Bogdanovich recaptures the atmosphere of his 1950s setting with careful attention to detail, and creates a moving portrait of a town slowly dying as America moves into a new age.

—Janet E. Lorenz

LAST TANGO IN PARIS

(Le Dernier Tango à Paris; Ultimo tango a Parigi)

Italy-France, 1972

Director: Bernardo Bertolucci

Production: P.E.A. (Rome) and Artistes Associés (Paris); Technicolor, 35mm; running time: 126 minutes. Released 15 December 1972, Paris. Filmed 1971–72 in Paris.

Producer: Alberto Grimaldi; **screenplay:** Bernardo Bertolucci and Franco Arcalli; **photography:** Vittorio Storaro; **editor:** Franco Arcalli; **sound:** Antoine Bonfanti; **production designer:** Ferdinando Scarfiotti; **music:** Gato Barbieri; **costume designer:** Gitt Magrini.

Cast: Marlon Brando (*Paul*); Maria Schneider (*Jeanne*); Jean-Pierre Léaud (*Tom*); Massimo Girotti (*Marcel*); Maria Michi (*Rosa's mother*);

Last Tango in Paris

Giovanna Galetti (*Prostitute*); Catherine Allegret (*Catherine*); Darling Legitimus (*Landlady*); Marie-Hélène Breillet (*Monique*); Catherine Breillet (*Mouchette*); Veronica Lazare (*Rosa*); Luce Marquand (*Olympia*); Gitt Magrini (*Jeanne's mother*); Rachel Kesterber (*Christine*); Armand Ablanalp (*Prostitute's client*); Mimi Pinson (*Jury president*); Ramon Mendizabal (*Orchestra leader*); Stephane Kosiak (*Small dancer*); Gérard Lepennec (*Large dancer*); Catherine Sola (*TV script girl*); Mauro Manchetti (*TV cameraman*); Dan Diament (*TV sound engineer*); Peter Schommer (*TV assistant cameraman*).

Awards: New York Film Critics Award, Best Actor (Brando), 1973.

Publications

Script:

Bertolucci, Bernardo, and Franco Arcalli, *Last Tango in Paris*, New York, 1973.

Books:

Carroll, Kent E., editor, *Close Up—Last Tango in Paris*, New York, 1973.
Mellen, Joan, *Women and Sexuality in the New Film*, New York, 1973.
Shipman, David, *Brando*, London, 1974.
Casetti, F., *Bertolucci*, Florence, 1975.
Braithwaite, Bruce, *The Films of Marlon Brando*, Secaucus, New Jersey, 1977.
Kuhlbrodt, Dietrich, and others, *Bernardo Bertolucci*, Munich, 1982.
Ungari, Enzo, *Bertolucci*, Milan, 1982.
Dowling, David, *Marlon Brando*, New York and London, 1984.
Carey, Gary, *Marlon Brando: The Only Contender*, London, 1985.
Kolker, Robert Phillip, *Bernardo Bertolucci*, London, 1985.
Higham, Charles, *Brando: The Unauthorized Biography*, London, 1987.
Kline, T. Jefferson, *Bertolucci's Dream Loom: A Psychoanalytic Study of the Cinema*, Amherst, Massachusetts, 1987.
Kline, T. Jefferson, *I film di Bernardo Bertolucci: Dialogo con Bernardo Bertolucci*, Rome, 1994.
Loshitzky, Yosefa, *The Radical Faces of Godard and Bertolucci*, Detroit, 1995.

Tonetti, Claretta Micheletti, *Bernardo Bertolucci: The Cinema of Ambiguity*, New York, 1995.
Socci, Stefano, *Bernardo Bertolucci*, Milan, 1996.
Campani, Ermelinda M., *L'anticonformista: Bernardo Bertolucci e il suo cinema*, Firenze, 1998.

Articles:

Kovacs, Steven, in *Take One* (Montreal), November-December 1971.
Roud, Richard, in *Sight and Sound* (London), Summer 1972.
Kael, Pauline, in *New Yorker*, 28 October 1972.
Benayoun, Robert, in *Point* (Paris), 11 December 1972.
Baroncelli, Jean de, in *Monde* (Paris), 16 December 1972.
Björkman, S., ''En Passion,'' in *Chaplin* (Stockholm), no. 1, 1973.
Amiel, M., ''Bernardo Bertolucci: Au cinéma le temps se glisse entre les choses et les gens . . . ,'' in *Cinéma* (Paris), January 1973.
Time (New York), 22 January 1973.
Cremonini, G., in *Cinema Nuovo* (Turin), January-February 1973.
Turroni, G., in *Filmcritica* (Rome), January-February 1973.
Avant-Scène du Cinéma (Paris), February 1973.
Cornand, A., in *Image et Son* (Paris), February 1973.
Bertolucci, Bernardo, ''Mon film n'est pas pornographique,'' in *Avant-Scène du Cinéma* (Paris), February 1973.
Martin, Michel, ''Entretien avec Bernardo Bertolucci,'' in *Ecran* (Paris), February 1973.
Kovacs, S., in *Take One* (Montreal), March 1973.
Ciment, Michel and G. Legrand, ''Entretien avec Bernardo Bertolucci,'' in *Positif* (Paris), March 1973.
Legrand, G., ''The Last Time I Saw Hollywood,'' in *Positif* (Paris), March 1973.
Jebb, Julian, ''The Unvisitable Past,'' in *Sight and Sound* (London), Spring 1973.
Bachmann, Gideon, ''Every Sexual Relationship Is Condemned: Interview,'' in *Film Quarterly* (Berkeley), Spring 1973.
Mellen, Joan, ''Sexual Politics and *Last Tango in Paris*,'' in *Film Quarterly* (Berkeley), Spring 1973.
Buffa, M., in *Filmcritica* (Rome), April 1973.
Schober, S., in *Filmkritik* (Munich), April 1973.
Robinson, H., in *Films in Review* (New York), April 1973.
Gow, Gordon, in *Films and Filming* (London), May 1973.
Weinberg, H. G., ''A Woman of Paris in 1973,'' in *Take One* (Montreal), May 1973.
Speziale-Bagliacca, R., ''Tango tra un incognita e un passato irresuperabile,'' in *Cinema Nuovo* (Turin), May-June 1973.
Phelps, G., ''Censorship and the Press,'' in *Sight and Sound* (London), Summer 1973.
Ebert, J., in *Filmkritik* (Munich), July 1973.
Bonitzer, P., ''L'Expérience en intérieur,'' in *Cahiers du Cinéma* (Paris), July-August 1973.
Kinder, Marsha and Beverle Houston, ''Bertolucci and the Dance of Danger,'' in *Sight and Sound* (London), Autumn 1973.
Rice, J. D., in *Journal of Popular Film* (Washington, D.C.), Spring 1974.
Sadkin, D., ''Theme and Structure: *Last Tango* Untangled,'' in *Literature/Film Quarterly* (Salisbury, Maryland), Spring 1974.
''Bernardo Bertolucci Seminar,'' in *American Film* (Washington, D.C.), April 1974.
Kaplan, E. Ann, ''The Importance and Ultimate Failure of *Last Tango in Paris*,'' in *Jump Cut* (Chicago), November-December 1974.
Lopez, D., ''The Father Figure in *The Conformist* and in *Last Tango in Paris*,'' in *Film Heritage* (Dayton, Ohio), Summer 1976.
Frias, I. Leon, in *Hablemos de Cine* (Lima), June 1981.
Cinema Novo (Porto), 9 October 1983.
Barr, A., ''The Better to See . . .: Improbable Vision in *Last Tango in Paris*,'' in *Film Criticism* (Meadville, Maryland), Winter 1983.
Bundtzen, L. K., ''Bertolucci's Erotic Politics and the Auteur Theory: From *Last Tango in Paris* to *The Last Emperor*,'' in *Western Humanities Review* (Salt Lake City, Utah), no. 2, 1990.
Pal'tsev, N., and A. Shemiakin, ''*Poslednee tango v Parizhe*—20 let spustia,'' in *Iskusstvo Kino* (Moscow), no. 11, 1992.

* * *

A piece of filmmaking that earned its creator a suspended two-month prison sentence in his native Italy and an X-rating in the U.S., Bernardo Bertolucci's *Last Tango in Paris* is a heartbreaking, revelatory masterpiece which has not aged one bit since its completion, a quarter of a century ago.

Although the plot concerns a private affair, the film's magnitude is that of a true tragedy, the genre that celluloid does not usually capture well. What makes it a tragedy is the intensity of its conflict that, as in *Medea* or *Hamlet*, can be solved by no means but one—death. Like any tragedy, classical or modern, *Last Tango* knows no compromise. Like any tragedy, it is inhabited by people who act according to the tragic inevitability and are led by destiny. Like any tragedy, this one has an epic dimension to it: it speaks of global changes and apocalyptic results. (That the two rare screen tragedies of recent decades—another one being Nagisa Oshima's *In the Realm of the Senses*—both tie together sex and death may say something about our times.)

Like most tragedies, *Last Tango* is about an end. Bertolucci's ambition goes further than a CAT scan of a relationship; the film depicts nothing less than the end of the modern age and character. Paul, the protagonist, who, having just lost his wife to suicide, begins a sexual relationship with a rival prospective tenant of a vacant Paris apartment, is an epitome of a modernist romantic. He is burdened by the past, rebellious against the present, and doomed for the future. That he is an American (something of a cultural virgin and an heir to Hemingway and Henry Miller) and the Marlon Brando of *Streetcar Named Desire* and *On the Waterfront* is essential. His anonymous, primal and ruthless engagement with Maria Schneider's Jeanne, who does not have a past and embodies, voluptuously, the bourgeois spirit, is juxtaposed with the cute, naive, ''French'' and Truffaut-esque romanticism of Jeanne's affair with Tom (Jean-Pierre Leaud). That affair lovingly mocks Vigo's ''L'Atalante'' and is decidedly anti-climactic. Unlike Leaud's Tom, who is an ever-filming filmmaker and a loveable impotent, Brando's Paul is virile, but cannot express himself—an Artaud without an art. Moving by the modernist trajectory, he strives to abandon culture and go back to nature; to create a world outside the real world; to reinvent the language; to start all over again. This is why *Last Tango* is rooted in sex, and this is why the sex in it is so fierce and unerotic. In its relentless deconstruction of the norm, modernist art arrives at the darkness of ''The Black Square,'' the silence of John Cage, the filmlessness of Stan Brakhage. Paul, in turn, falls in love, and thus fails his quest. Like another American in Europe, Jack Nicholson's *Passenger*, he finds it not possible to rewrite his identity or to regain the paradise lost.

Brando as Paul is a model of acting exorcism. He growls and weeps and dashes around like a caged animal; the whole world is his cage. His intensity is so high that even today, when we know what has happened with the great Marlon Brando, one fears that he will burn out there on the screen, like an overcharged fuse.

Vittorio Storaro's breathtaking camera films Brando and Schneider against the sunset spectrum of red, orange, yellow and pink—painful colors of Francis Bacon, the modernist painter who influenced Bertolucci's vision. Gato Barbieri's Latin saxophone produces swirls and crescendos that add to the desperation of the screen image.

Being one of the most intelligent films ever made, *Last Tango* is also one of the most honest. It keeps no defenses, it takes everything off—the characters, the filmmakers, and ourselves.

—Michael Brashinsky

THE LAST WAVE

Australia, 1977

Director: Peter Weir

Production: Ayer Productions Pty. Ltd., McElroy production, South Australian Film Corp., and the Australian Film Commision. Atlab color, 35mm; running time: 106 minutes; length: 9513 feet. Released 16 November 1977. Filmed in Australia.

Producers: Hal McElroy and James McElroy; **screenplay:** Tony Morphett, Petru Popescu, and Peter Weir, from an idea by Peter Weir; **photography:** Russell Boyd; **additional photography:** Ron Taylor, George Greenough and Klaus Jaritz; **editor:** Max Lemon; **sound editor:** Greg Bell; **sound recordist:** Don Connolly; **sound rerecordist:** Phil Judd; **production designer:** Goran Warff; **art director:** Neil Angwin; **music:** Charles Wain; **special effects:** Monty Fieguth and Bob Hilditch; **costume designers:** Annie Bleakley; **adviser on tribal Aboriginal matters:** Lance Bennett.

Cast: Richard Chamberlain (*David Burton*); Olivia Hammett (*Annie Burton*); Gulpilil (*Chris Lee*); Frederick Parslow (*Rev. Burton*); Nandjiwarra Amagula (*Charlie*); Vivean Gray (*Dr. Whitburn*); Walter Amagula (*Gerry Lee*); Roy Bara (*Larry*); Cedric Lalara (*Lindsey*); Morris Lalara (*Jacko*); Peter Carroll (*Michael Zeadler*); Athol Compton (*Billy Corman*); Hedley Cullen (*Judge*); Michael Duffield (*Andrew Potter*); Wallas Eaton (*Morgue doctor*); Jo England (*Babysitter*); John Frawley (*Policeman*); Jennifer de Greenlaw (*Zeadler's secretary*); Richard Henderson (*Prosecutor*); Penny Leach (*Schoolteacher*); Merv Lilley (*Publican*); John Meagher (*Morgue clerk*); Guido Rametta (*Guido*); Malcolm Robertson (*Don Fishburn*); Greg Rowe (*Carl*); Katrina Sedgwick (*Sophie Burton*); Ingrid Weir (*Grace Burton*).

Publications

Books:

Stratton, David, *The Last New Wave: The Australian Film Revival*, Sydney, 1980.

Tulloch, John, *Australian Cinema: Industry, Narrative, and Meaning*, Sydney and London, 1982.

Peeters, Theo, *Peter Weir and His Films: A Critical Biography*, Melbourne, 1983.

Hall, Sandra, *Critical Business: The New Australian Cinema in Review*, Adelaide, 1985.

Moran, Albert and Tom O'Regan, *An Australian Film Reader*, Sydney, 1985.

McFarlane, Brian, *Australian Cinema 1970–85*, London, 1987.

Mathews, Sue, *35mm Dreams: Conversations with Five Directors about the Australian Film Revival*, Ringwood, Victoria, 1987.

Haltof, Marek, *Peter Weir: When Cultures Collide*, London, 1996.

Rayner, Jonathan, *The Films of Peter Weir*, Poole, 1998.

Bliss, Michael, *Dreams Within a Dream: The Films of Peter Weir*, Carbondale, 2000.

Articles:

Cinema Papers (Melbourne), April 1977.

Murray, S., in *Cinema Papers* (Melbourne), October 1977.

Moskowitz, G., in *Variety* (New York), 16 November 1977.

Clancy, J., in *Cinema Papers* (Melbourne), January 1978.

Béhar, H., in *Image et Son* (Paris), February 1978.

Films and Filming (London), February 1978.

Garsault, A., in *Positif* (Paris), March 1978.

Tournès, A., "Naissance d'un cinéma australien," in *Jeune Cinéma* (Paris), March 1978.

Combs, Richard, in *Sight and Sound* (London), Spring 1978.

Pulleine, Tim, in *Monthly Film Bulletin* (London), April 1978.

Boyd, Russell, "Photographing *The Last Wave*," in *American Cinematographer* (Los Angeles), April 1978.

Fox, J. R., in *Cinefantastique* (Oak Park, Illinois), no. 2–3, 1979.

Buckley, T., in *New York Times*, 12 January 1979.

Jacobs, D., "His Subject—Mysteries of Different Cultures," in *New York Times*, 13 January 1979.

Canby, Vincent, in *New York Times*, 21 January 1979.

Kael, Pauline, in *New Yorker*, 22 January 1979.

Blake, R. A., in *America* (New York), 27 January 1979.

Cocchi, J., in *Boxoffice* (Kansas City), 29 January 1979.

Holthof, M., in *Film en Televisie* (Brussels), March 1979.

Childs, P., "New Wave Director Peter Weir Rides *The Last Wave* into U.S. Market," in *Millimeter* (New York), March 1979.

Kass, J. M., "It Doesn't Take Any Imagination at All to Feel Awed: Peter Weir," in *Movietone News* (Seattle), December 1979.

Vogrinc, J., in *Ekran* (Ljubljana), 1982.

Masson, A., in *Positif* (Paris), September 1982.

Poulle, F., in "Retour au fantastique: *La Dernière Vague*," in *Jeune Cinéma* (Paris), September 1982.

Piton, J.-P., and F. Schall, "Le cinema australien," in *Revue du Cinéma* (Paris), no. 386, September 1983.

Matteuzzi, F., "Peter Weir: Il mistero e il sogno," in *Cinema & Cinema* (Milan), no. 47, December 1986.

Giavarini, Laurence, "Horreurs australes," in *Cahiers du Cinéma* (Paris), no. 447, September 1991.

Routt, W. D., "Are You a Fish? Are You a Snake?: An Obvious Lecture and Some Notes on *The Last Wave*," in *Continuum* (Mt. Lawley), vol. 8, no. 2, 1994.

Coursodon, Jean-Pierre, and Michel Ciment, and Agnés Peck and Alain Garsault, "Peter Weir," in *Positif* (Paris), no. 453, November 1998.

* * *

"Hasn't the weather been strange?" muses the advertising slogan for Peter Weir's *The Last Wave*. "Could it be a warning?" This tone

The Last Wave

of covert menace, of nasty things unseen by naive protagonists, characterizes Weir's films, but none more than this atmospheric thriller. Troubled by dreams of his home city, Sydney, inundated by a vast flood, lawyer Richard Chamberlain is drawn into the underground world of Sydney's aboriginals who still live a tribal life in the slums. To them, the city is merely a transient facade obscuring ancient mysteries, the ritual objects of which remain buried in forgotten catacombs. Chamberlain's discovery of these tunnels and the resulting revelation give the film its final enigmatic scenes.

Weir conceived the film after discovering (by precognition, he feels) a piece of statuary on a Tunisian beach. Early drafts of the script represented, in a Von Daniken-like manner, ancient races dragging rafts across the Australian desert. In collaboration with various writers, Weir shaped a story of city aboriginals protecting ritual stones brought to Australia by a long dead race. As Australia is gripped by fierce storms and an unrelenting downpour, Chamberlain finds his way to the caves where ancient wall paintings foretell the world's destruction by water. He emerges on a beach to face the ultimate reality of the prophecy.

Australian backers derided the film, and a shortage of money forced many compromises—notably in the last sequence, where Weir used a clip from the surfing film *Crystal Voyager* to stand in for the tidal wave. The Aztec ruins lost something in their rough and ready construction. The use of aboriginal myths led to picketing by militant black groups who charged Weir with debasing their mythology. However, Weir acknowledged that his contact with aboriginal performers led to a widening and deepening of the script. Gulpilil's appearance in a dream, the rain streaming down, with a scored sacred stone in his out-thrust hand, is particularly striking.

Weir calls *The Last Wave* his ''roughest, most awkward'' film. But despite a certain tentativeness in the use of large resources, it is significant as the first new Australian film to reveal an interest in wider issues and a less chauvinistic sensibility.

—John Baxter

THE LAST WILL OF DR. MABUSE

See **DOKTOR MABUSE DER SPIELER; DAS TESTAMENT DES DR. MABUSE**

LAST YEAR AT MARIENBAD

See **L'ANNEE DERNIERE A MARIENBAD**

THE LATE MATTHEW PASCAL

See **FEU MATHIAS PASCAL**

LATE SPRING

See **BANSHUN**

LAURA

USA, 1944

Director: Otto Preminger

Production: Twentieth Century-Fox; black and white, 35mm; running time: 88 minutes. Released 1944. Filmed 24 April-29 June 1944 (retakes 15–20 July 1944), in Fox studios.

Producer: Otto Preminger; **screenplay:** Jay Datler, Samuel Hoffenstein and Betty Reinhardt, uncredited collaboration on screenplay by Ring Lardner, Jr., and Jerome Cady, from the play and novel by Vera Caspary; **photography:** Joseph LaShelle; **editor:** Louis R. Loeffler; **sound:** E. Clayton Ward and Harry M. Leonard; **production designers:** Thomas Little and Paul S. Fox; **art directors:** Lyle Wheeler and Leland Fuller; **music:** David Raksin; **music director:** Emil Newman; **special effect photography:** Fred Sersen; **costume designer:** Bonnie Cashin.

Cast: Gene Tierney (*Laura Hunt*); Dana Andrews (*Mark McPherson*); Clifton Webb (*Waldo Lydecker*); Vincent Price (*Shelby Carpenter*); Judith Anderson (*Anne Treadwell*); Dorothy Adams (*Bessie Clary*); James Flavin (*McAvity*); Clyde Fillmore (*Bullitt*); Tom Dillon replaced Ralph Dunn as (*Fred Callahan*); Kathleen Howard (*Louise*); Lee Tung Foo (*Waldo's Servant*); Harold Schlickenmayer, Harry Strang, and Lane Chandler (*Policemen*); *Non-Credited Roles*: Frank La Rue (*Hairdresser*); Dorothy Christie, Aileen Pringle, Terry Adams, Jean Fenwick, Kay Linaker, and Yolanda Lacca (*Women*); Cara Williams, Gloria Marlin, Beatrice Gray, Kay Connors, and Frances Gladwin (*Young girls*); Buster Miles (*Johnny*); Jane Nigh (*Secretary*); William Forrest, Alexander Sacha, Forbes Murray, Cyril Ring, and Nestor Eristoff (*Men*); John Dexter (*Jacoby*); Bess Flowers (*Girl in the hall of the theater*); Major Sam Harris (*Anne Treadwell's escort*).

Award: Oscar for Best Cinematography, 1944.

Publications

Script:

Datler, Jay, and others, *Laura*, in *Avant-Scène du Cinéma* (Paris), July-September 1978.

Books:

Lourcelles, Jacques, *Otto Preminger*, Paris, 1965.
Pratley, Gerald, *The Cinema of Otto Preminger*, New York, 1971.
Parish, James Robert, *The Fox Girls*, New Rochelle, New York, 1971.
Frischauer, Willi, *Behind the Scenes of Otto Preminger*, London, 1973.
Preminger, Otto, *An Autobiography*, New York, 1977.
McAsh, Iain, *The Films of Vincent Price*, London, 1977.
Parish, James Robert, and William T. Leonard, *The Funsters*, New Rochelle, New York, 1979.
McAsh, Iain, *Vincent Price: A Biography*, Farncombe, Surrey, 1982.
McNamara, Eugene, *Laura as Novel, Film, and Myth*, Lewiston, New York, 1992.
Bächler, Odile, *Laura: Otto Preminger*, Paris, 1995.
Williams, Lucy C., *The Complete Films of Vincent Price*, Secaucus, 1995.
Bogdanovich, Peter, *Who the Devil Made It: Conversations with Robert Aldrich, George Cukor, Allan Dwan, Howard Hawks, Alfred Hitchcock, Chuck Jones, Fritz Lang, Joseph H. Lewis, Sidney Lumet, Leo McCarey, Otto Preminger, Don Siegel, Josef von Sternberg, Frank Tashlin, Edgar G. Ulmer, Raoul Walsh*, New York, 1997.
Phillips, Gene D., *Exiles in Hollywood: Major European Film Directors in America*, Bethlehem, 1998.

Articles:

Variety (New York), 11 October 1944.
New York Times, 12 October 1944.
Times (London), 27 November 1944.
Borde, Raymond, and Etienne Chaumeton, *Panorama du film noir*, Paris, 1955.
Reid, John Howard, in *Films and Filming* (London), February and March 1961.
''Preminger Issue'' of *Présence du Cinéma* (Paris), February 1962.
''Preminger Issue'' of *Movie* (London), September 1962.
''Preminger Issue'' of *Movie* (London), no. 4, 1963.
Agel, Henri, ''*Laura*; ou, L'Epanchement de la mort dans la vie,'' in *Romance Amérique*, Paris, 1963.
''Preminger Issue'' of *Visages du Cinéma* (Paris), March 1963.
Sarris, Andrew, ''Preminger's Two Periods—Studio and Solo,'' in *Film Comment* (New York), Summer 1965.
''Clifton Webb,'' in *Films in Review* (New York), January 1970.
Caspary, Vera, ''My *Laura* and Otto's,'' in *Saturday Review* (New York), 26 June 1971.
Shields, Jonathan, ''Gene Tierney,'' in *Films in Review* (New York), November 1971.
Borok, B., ''*Laura*: The Story Behind the Picture,'' in *Thousand Eyes* (New York), November 1976.
Thompson, Kristin, ''Closure Within a Dream: Point of View in *Laura*,'' in *Film Reader* (Evanston, Illinois), no. 3, 1978.
''Laura Issue'' of *Avant-Scène du Cinéma* (Paris), July-September 1978.
McVay, Douglas, ''Faithful in His Fashion: Otto Preminger's *Laura*,'' in *Bright Lights* (Los Angeles), no. 4, 1979.
Leese, Elizabeth, in *Magill's Survey of Cinema 2*, Englewood Cliffs, New Jersey, 1980.
Film Reader (Evanston, Illinois), no. 5, 1982.
Marinero, M., in *Casablanca* (Madrid), May 1983.
Blanchet, C., in *Cinéma* (Paris), November 1983.

Laura

Legrand, G., "*Laura* et Mark Dixon, détective: Au bois dormant, une jeune Parque," in *Positif* (Paris), May 1984.
Catsos, G.J.M., "Remembering *Laura*," in *Hollywood Studio Magazine* (Studio City), vol. 20, no. 3, 1987.
Reid's Film Index (Wyong), no. 1, 1987.
Leandoer, K., "Otto Preminger's *Laura*," in *Chaplin* (Stockholm), vol. 31, no. 4, 1989.
Telotte, J. P., "The Big Clock of Film Noir," in *Film Criticism* (Meadville, Pennsylvania), no. 2, 1990.
Carluccio, G., and L. Cena, "Otto Preminger, la persistenza di uno sguardo," in *Castoro Cinema* (Florence), January-February 1990.
Ward, L.E., "The Great Films," in *Classic Images* (Muscatine), no. 177, March 1990.
Nielsen, R., "Ray's Way," in *Classic Images* (Muscatine), no. 187, January 1991.
Denby, D., "Thrillers with a Twist," in *Premiere* (Boulder), vol. 4, August 1991.
Carluccio, G., and G. Pescatore, "Dal nero. Del noir, dello schermo," in *Cinema & Cinema* (Bologna), May-August 1991.
Schactman, K., "*Laura*," in *Scarlet Street* (Glen Rock), no. 7, Summer 1992.
Raksin, David, "Music Via a Devious Root," in *Cue Sheet* (Hollywood), vol. 10, no. 1–2, Spring 1993–94.
Feigelson, Roger, "*Laura/Jane Eyre*," in *Télérama* (Paris), no. 2305, 16 March 1994.
Kock, I. de, "*Laura*," in *Film en Televisie + Video* (Brussels), no. 453, July 1995.
Care, Ross, "Forever Raksin," in *Scarlet Street* (Glen Rock), no. 22, 1996.
Loban, Lelia, "The Face in the Misty Light, *Laura*," in *Scarlet Street* (Glen Rock), no. 22, 1996.

* * *

"*Laura* is Preminger's *Citizen Kane*, at least in the sense that Otto's detractors, like Orson's [Welles] have never permitted him to live it down," comments Andrew Sarris in his essay, "Preminger's Two Periods."

The film, which is based on Vera Caspary's very popular book of the same name, was brought to Darryl F. Zanuck's attention by Otto Preminger. Although Preminger was allowed to produce it, Zanuck insisted that someone else be brought in to direct it. Rouben Mamoulian was subsequently brought into the project. However problems with the initial shooting and characterization in the film led to Mamoulian's removal as director, and subsequent replacement by Preminger.

Although Preminger claims to have reshot all of Mamoulian's earlier work, the latter states that three-quarters of the released version of *Laura* was part of his original footage—a fact that his cameraman, Lucien Ballard confirms. However, Preminger confided to Joseph La Shelle, who replaced Ballard as cameraman, that ''We're not going to leave any scene at all of Mamoulian's in this picture.''

Despite these problems and the tension that existed between cast and director when Preminger took over and characters in the script were reassessed and changed, *Laura* to everyone's surprise became a blinding success. However, the author Vera Caspary had great problems with the film's script not least of which was the use of a clock as the hiding place for the murder weapon. In Caspary's book the gun is hidden in Waldo Lydecker's cane. The author argued that this symbolized the murderer's impotence; Preminger contested that the audience would not understand this Freudian idea.

Essentially a crime story, *Laura* centers around the murder of a woman, who has been shot in the face, and the effect that it has on the people around her. The investigating detective brought in to solve the case, Mark McPherson (Dana Andrews) is a hard-boiled policeman—a far cry from the ''highly intelligent criminologist'' Andrews originally envisaged. McPherson sees a portrait of the alleged murder victim and falls in love with her. In a highly charged, very sexual scene McPherson wanders around Laura's apartment, touching her possessions, loosening his tie, and clutching a drink, as he stares moodily at the portrait. He dozes off fixating on Laura, and awakens to find the object of his passion standing before him. Lydecker (Clifton Webb) recognizes this strange fixation and says: ''You'll end up in a psycho ward. I don't think they've ever had a patient who fell in love with a corpse.''

Waldo Lydecker, the highly intellectual news columnist, tells McPherson about Laura. She approached Lydecker while he was having lunch at the Algonquin, and asked him to endorse a pen. Although he refused, he could not get Laura out of his mind and tracked her down. Taking her under his wing, Lydecker groomed her introducing her to important people. However, while Waldo fulfilled an emotional and intellectual need, Laura looked to other men for relationships. For the most part these men were meaningless until she met the debonair but spineless Shelby Carpenter (Vincent Price), and became engaged to him. Just before her murder Lydecker told Laura that her fiancé was having an affair with a young model, Diane Redfern. Laura went away to think about their relationship.

McPherson embarks on a determined quest to find the identities of the real victim and the murderer. Piecing events together he works out that the victim is Diane Redfern. Shelby reluctantly admits that he met Diane at Laura's flat. When the doorbell rang, Diane answered it and was shot in the face by her killer. Shelby panicked and left; he confesses that he thought that Laura was the murderer.

McPherson, suspicious of Lydecker goes to his flat and searches it. He finds a baroque clock identical to one in Laura's flat. Searching Laura's clock he finds the murder weapon concealed within it. He leaves to arrest Lydecker, not realizing that Lydecker is incensed that Laura is in love with McPherson, and has returned to try and kill Laura again. Luckily McPherson rescues her in time.

The male characters in *Laura* are interesting. They present different aspects of masculinity, and are all in a sense symbols of impotency. Shelby is a weak, amoral man who uses Laura for his own ends but does not really see or desire her as a woman; Lydecker is the cynical, witty friend who can never be a lover but idealizes her; and McPherson is a masculine, brawny man, who illustrates his impotency by falling in love with a dead woman. As the hero he, however, moves beyond this point into a new realm with his dream woman.

Laura does not physically enter the story until about half way through the film when her persona has already been set up. The audience is aware that she is a beautiful, intelligent, and sensual woman. Her world is one of rich, sophisticated people. She is set up on a pedestal well before she appears on screen. However in reality Gene Tierney's Laura is an ambitious woman—a woman who knows her mind, who states ''I'll never do anything that isn't of my own free will.''

The whole of the film has a dream-like feel to it. This was mostly due to La Shelle's camera work. He reportedly took hours to set up each scene, fiddling over lighting. The film contains many long shots in which the camera pans the landscape—the shot of Lydecker's apartment, which is based on an unused scene in Hitchcock's *Rebecca*, is an example of this. The end result well justified the time and deliberation that went into planning these shots as the film won an Academy Award for Best Cinematography in 1944.

—A. Pillai

THE LAVENDER HILL MOB

UK, 1951

Director: Charles Crichton

Production: A Michael Balcon Production for Ealing Studios; black and white; running time: 78 minutes; length: 7,043 feet. Released June 1951.

Producer: Michael Balcon; **associate producer:** Michael Truman; **screenplay:** T. E. B. Clarke; **photography:** Douglas Slocombe; **editor:** Seth Holt; **art director:** William Kellner; **music:** Georges Auric.

Cast: Alec Guinness (*Holland*); Stanley Holloway (*Pendlebury*); Sidney James (*Lackery*); Alfie Bass (*Shorty*); Marjorie Fielding (*Mrs. Chalk*); Edie Martin (*Miss Evesham*); Ronald Adam (*Bank Official*); Clive Morton (*Police Sergeant*); John Gregson (*Farrow*); Sidney Tafler (*Stallholder*); Patrick Barr (*Inspector*); Meredith Edwards (*P.C. Edwards*); Robert Shaw (*Police Scientist*); Michael Trubshawe (*British Ambassador*); Audrey Hepburn (*Chiquita*).

Awards: Oscar for Best Script, 1952; British Film Academy Award for Best Film, 1951.

Publications

Script:

Clarke, T. E. B., *The Lavender Hill Mob* in *The Cinema 1952*, edited by Roger Manvell and R. K. N. Baxter, London, 1952.

The Lavender Hill Mob

Books:

Tynan, Kenneth, *Alec Guinness*, New York, 1955.

Michael Balcon, *A Lifetime of Films*, London, 1969.

Butler, Ivan, *Cinema in Britain*, New York, 1973.

Betts, Ernest, *The Film Business: A History of British Cinema*, New York, 1973.

Barr, Charles, *Ealing Studios*, London, 1977.

Perry, George, *Forever Ealing*, London, 1981.

Hunter, Allan, *Alec Guinness on Screen*, London, 1982.

Kadish, Laurence, *Michael Balcon: The Pursuit of British Cinema*, New York, 1984.

Taylor, John Russell, *Alec Guinness: A Celebration*, London, 1984, 1994.

Guinness, Alec, *Blessings in Disguise*, London, 1985.

Missler, Andreas, *Alec Guinness: Seine Filme, sein Leben*, Munich, 1987.

Von Gunden, Kenneth, *Alec Guinness: The Films*, Jefferson, North Carolina, 1987.

Brown, Geoff, *Michael Balcon: Pursuit of Britain*, New York, 1990.

Guinness, Alec, *My Name Escapes Me: The Diary of a Retiring Actor*, New York, 1998.

Articles:

Today's Cinema (London), 20 June 1951.

Monthly Film Bulletin (London), July 1951.

Variety (New York), 4 July 1951.

Lambert, Gavin, in *Sight and Sound* (London), August-September 1951.

Motion Picture Herald (New York), 13 and 20 October 1951.

New York Times, 16 October 1951.

Image et Son (Paris), October 1954.

Tynan, Kenneth, ''Ealing: The Studio in Suburbia,'' in *Films and Filming* (London), November and December 1955.

McVay, Douglas, ''Alec Guinness,'' in *Films and Filming* (London), May 1961.

Barr, Charles, ''Projecting Britain and the British Character: Ealing Studios,'' in *Screen* (London), Summer 1974.

Green, Ian, ''Ealing: In the Comedy Frame,'' in *British Cinema History*, edited by James Curran and Vincent Porter, London, 1983.

* * *

In the three films which T. E. B. Clarke and Charles Crichton—respectively the most talented writer and director of the Ealing mainstream—made together at Balcon's studio, the whole trajectory of Ealing comedy can be traced. *Hue and Cry*, their first collaboration, initiated the cycle with its fresh, original approach. With their third, *The Titfield Thunderbolt*, the genre can be seen declining into self-conscious, sentimental whimsy. And between these two stands *The Lavender Hill Mob*, which in many ways qualifies as the quintessential Ealing comedy.

Mainstream Ealing comedy (as against the tougher, maverick strain of Hamer and Mackendrick) tends to act out fantasies of wish-fulfilment—in Charles Barr's words, ''the triumph of the innocent, the survival of the *un*fittest.'' *The Lavender Hill Mob* makes this explicit. Having opened on an escapist dream of tropical luxury, with Holland (Alec Guinness) dispensing largesse in a Rio bar, fawned upon by ambassadors, society hostesses, and shapely señoritas (Audrey Hepburn in a 30-second bit part), we fade back to his drab past, ''when I was merely a nonentity among all those thousands who flock every morning into the City,'' with an image that recalls *The Waste Land*:

> Under the brown fog of a winter dawn,
> A crowd flowed over London Bridge, so many,
> I had not thought death had undone so many.

And at the end of the film, in a neat ironic twist, he evades police pursuit by briefly rejoining his fellow-nonentities, one indistinguishable bowler-hatted figure among many, before taking off into his exotic dreamworld.

''Most men who long to be rich know inwardly that they will never achieve their ambition.'' Nor will we; but Holland, our meek surrogate, will achieve it for us. Hemmed in by the stuffy respectability of the Balmoral Guest House (that same Victorian world of little old ladies sardonically targeted by Mackendrick in *The Ladykillers*), and by his dismissive superiors—''He's no imagination, no initiative''—the worm turns. ''OK, you're the boss,'' says Lackery (Sidney James), as they plan the robbery. Holland leans back, a gleam of delight behind his spectacles as the idea sinks in. ''Yes. Yes, that's right. I am.''

Guinness's performance, hinting at wild insubordination lurking beneath the prissy, deferential exterior, is finely balanced by the more stolid presence of Stanley Holloway as Pendlebury, the artist manqué churning out shoddy souvenirs (''I propagate British cultural depravity''). Sex, as often with Ealing, scarcely figures as such; but the relationship between the two men takes on a tangential sexuality, as in the justly celebrated ''seduction scene'' where Holland, Eve to Pendlebury's Adam, circles slyly round his slower-witted partner dropping hints until realisation dawns: ''By Jove, Holland, it's a good job we're both honest men.'' And later, as the first of the gold-bullion Eiffel Towers emerges from the mould, Holland breathes tenderly, ''Our first-born.''

Though *Ladykillers* will also feature Guinness as gang boss, there's little otherwise in common between the two films; Mackendrick's gleeful mayhem would shatter the gentle make-believe of Clarke's comedy, where crime entails neither violence nor victim. And while Crichton's crisp editing and flair for comic pacing are everywhere in evidence, it's probably fair to consider Clarke the film's primary auteur—not only for the frequent similarities, in mood and characterisation, with other Clarke comedies such as *Passport to Pimlico* and *Hue and Cry*, but for the gusto with which the writer, himself an ex-policeman, parodies his own police chase sequence from *The Blue Lamp*.

Thoroughly characteristic of Clarke, too, is the conclusion of the film. Back in the tropical bar, the polite stranger to whom Holland has been telling his story stands up, and Holland with him. A pair of handcuffs links their wrists. The wish-fulfilment dream is over; the anti-social impulse, no matter how innocuous, how engagingly personified, must ultimately be restrained. *The Lavender Hill Mob* was hugely popular, and won an Oscar for its script. It remains lively, inventive, and a pleasure to watch. But it marks an ending; after it, the vitality drained out of Ealing comedy, save only those directed by Mackendrick. Once in place, the handcuffs proved impossible to remove.

—Philip Kemp

LAWRENCE OF ARABIA

UK, 1962

Director: David Lean

Production: Horizon Pictures; color, Super-Panavision 35mm; running time: 222 minutes. Director's cut released 1989.

Producer: Sam Spiegel; **screenplay:** Robert Bolt, Michael Wilson; **photography:** Freddie Young; **second unit photography:** Nicolas Roeg, Skeets Kelly, Peter Newbrook; **editor:** Anne V. Oates; **assistant director:** Roy Stevens; **production designer:** John Box; **art directors:** John Stoll, John Box; **music:** Maurice Jarre; **sound editor:** Winston Ryder; **sound recording:** Paddy Cunningham.

Cast: Peter O'Toole (*Lawrence*); Omar Sharif (*Sherif Ali*); Anthony Quinn (*Auda Abu Tayi*); Alec Guinness (*Prince Feisal*); Jack Hawkins (*General Allenby*); Jose Ferrer (*Turkish Bey*); Anthony Quayle (*Colonel Brighton*); Claude Rains (*Mr. Dryden*); Arthur Kennedy (*Jackson Bentley*); Donald Wolfit (*General Murray*).

Awards: Oscars for Best Picture, Best Director, Best Photography, Best Score, Best Editing, Best Art Direction, Best Sound, 1962.

Publications

Books:

Pratley, G., *The Cinema of David Lean*, New York, 1974.

Silver, Alain, and James Ursini, *David Lean and His Films*, New York, 1974.

Anderegg, M.A., *David Lean*, Boston 1984.

Wapshott, Nicholas, *Peter O'Toole: A Biography*, New York, 1984.

Silverman, S.M., *David Lean*, New York, 1989, 1992.

Morris, R.L., and Lawrence Raskin, *Lawrence of Arabia: The 30th Anniversary Pictorial History*, New York, 1992.

Hodson, Joel C., *Lawrence of Arabia & American Culture: The Making of a Transatlantic Legend*, Westport, 1995.

Brownlow, Kevin, *David Lean*, New York, 1997.

Caton, Steven C., *Lawrence of Arabia: A Film's Anthropology*, Berkeley, 1999.

Articles:

Barra, A., ''The Incredible Shrinking Epic,'' in *American Film* (Washington D.C.), March 1989.

Frumkes. R., ''The Restoration of Lawrence of Arabia,'' in *Films in Review* (New York), April and May 1989.

Solman, G., ''Uncertain Glory,'' in *Film Comment* (New York), May-June 1993.

Caron, A., in *Séquences* (Montreal), June 1989.

Combs, R., in *Monthly Film Bulletin* (London), June 1989.

Benayoun, R., ''The Long Last Cut,'' in *Positif* (Paris), July-August 1989.

Gauthier, G., in *Revue du Cinéma* (Paris), July-August 1989.

Crowdus, G., in *Cineaste* (New York), 1989.

Bohne, L., ''Leaning toward the Past,'' in *Film Criticism* (Meadville, Pennsylvania), Fall 1990.

* * *

Lawrence of Arabia has been described as a ''thinking man's epic.''

The film has all the ingredients of a classic adventure yarn. Typically in epics, these ingredients are showcased to the detriment of character and plot in order to keep the action rolling. But in David Lean's epic, the title character and the political machinations surrounding his exploits take center stage; what's more, he remains an enigma even as the final credits fade to black.

Like the vast, arid landscape that, in the words of Alec Guinness's Prince Feisel, proves such a mystical allure for this latest in a line of ''desert-loving Englishmen,'' the mystery of Lawrence's character is never quite fathomed. There is no Rosebud here. Even his rape at the hands of the Turks, which Lawrence described in his memoirs as the key assault on ''the citadel of my integrity'' and which may or may not have revealed to him a latent homosexuality, explains nothing.

The film overwhelms with its images of the desert and men at war, but the uncompromising genius of Lean's direction, Robert Bolt's screenplay and Peter O'Toole's starmaking performance as the obscure British map maker who becomes a national hero only to flee back to obscurity is that the focus always remains on the quest for

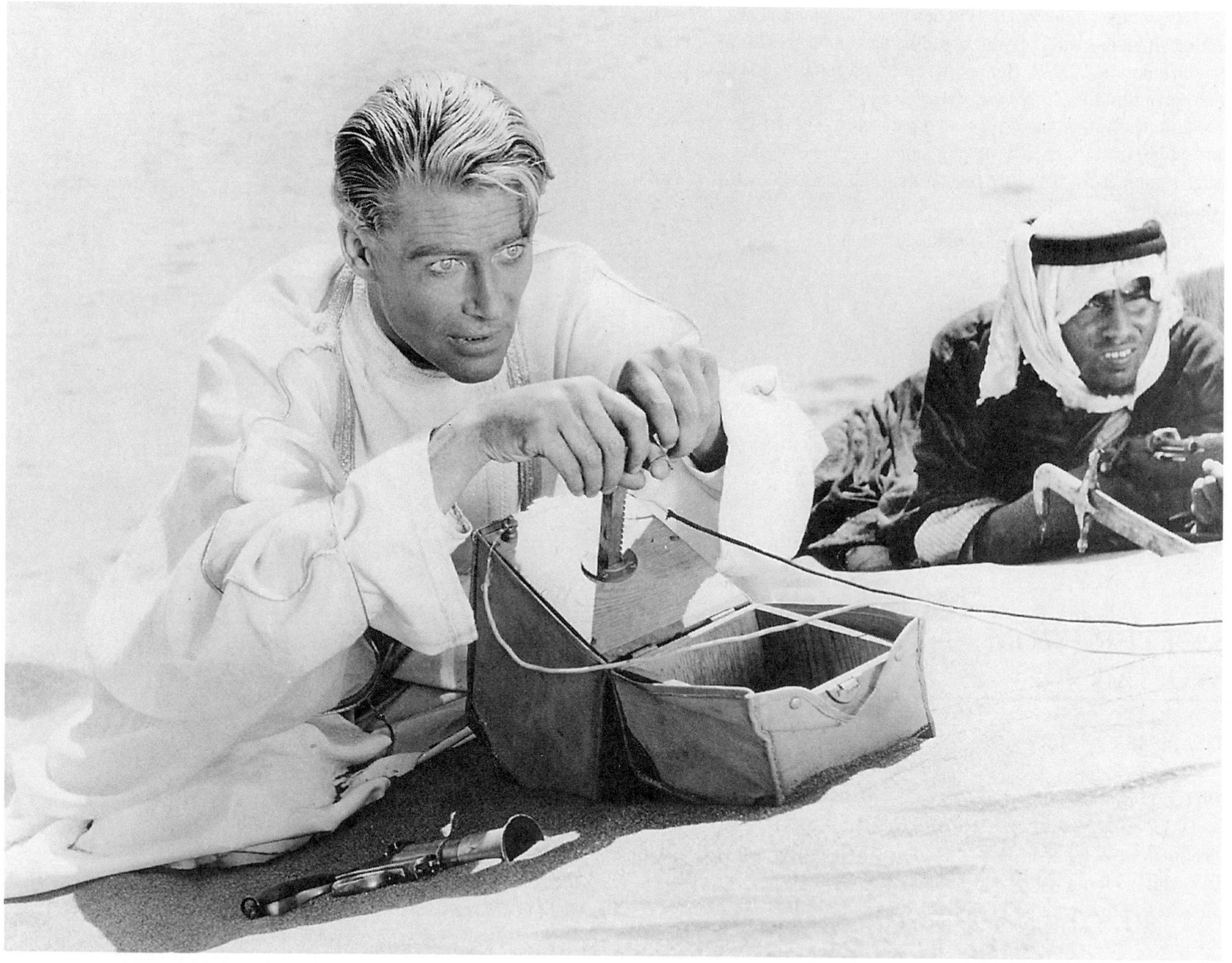

Lawrence of Arabia

Lawrence himself. You never stop thinking about and trying to understand him even though the quest ultimately proves unsuccessful, for the filmmakers and for us, just as it did for Lawrence himself. Our final image of the man as he is driven from the scene of his wartime triumphs to a yearned-for life of invisibility is through the windshield of a jeep, the dust-streaked glass obscuring his face. Even the film's initial advertising art (subsequently changed) showing Lawrence in arab head gear, his face in shadow, cued audiences to the puzzle without a solution they were in for. One can't even imagine a film—certainly not an epic one—like this being made today, where it is insisted upon that whatever we know or need to know about a given film's main character(s) is spelled out fully, usually in the first ten minutes.

Lawrence of Arabia appeared at a time when the British cinema that produced it and Lean were taking a decidedly different turn. Lean began his career as an editor then director of small, mostly black and white, dramas about English life drawn from the works of Charles Dickens and Noel Coward. He established himself a master of the epic with *The Bridge on the River Kwai* (1957), the superlative World War II adventure film that won a slew of Oscars, including one for him as Best Director.

He began preparing *Lawrence* in 1960 when the foundering British film industry was being reshaped by a younger generation of filmmakers who scorned Lean's classically trained approach to narrative moviemaking and fondness for large scale canvases and subjects. They preferred to train their cameras not on vast landscapes and enigmatic heroes but on working class anti-heroes and the dreariness of British lower class life. Their small, black and white ''kitchen sink'' dramas, not Lean's behemoth tales of romantic characters swept up in the turbulence of historical events, were the future of British films, they maintained.

After the success of *Lawrence*, which took longer to make than it took the events the film chronicled to take place, Lean continued to invite scorn by making epics. When *Lawrence* was restored for re-release in 1989, he explained why. He'd envisioned a future when the astronomical costs of making such movies would eventually become prohibitive, so he made them while he had the chance. But there was more to it. As the curtains opened on the giant 70mm screen at the London premiere of the restored *Lawrence*, the ailing director, speaking on audio tape, invited the audience to sit back and experience ''what the movies used to be''—i.e. something that could not be experienced the same way except at the movies.

His younger colleagues' "kitchen sink" dramas and even his own earlier films in a similar vein could be shown on television with no loss in emotional effect. But not the epic, and certainly not *Lawrence*. For him a film like *Lawrence of Arabia* was what cinema in the post-TV era was all about: a grand opportunity for larger than life adventure, in both the making of it and the seeing of it, that should be seized upon if for no other reason than the unlikelihood of it ever coming our way again.

—John McCarty

LEAVING HOME

See **HEIMAT; DIE ZWEITE HEIMAT**

THE LEOPARD

See **IL GATTOPARDO**

LETTER FROM AN UNKNOWN WOMAN

USA, 1948

Director: Max Ophüls

Production: A Rampart Production for Universal-International; black and white; running time: 86 minutes (re-released in 1979 in a 90 minute version); length: 7,844 feet. Released April 1948.

Producer: John Houseman; **screenplay:** Howard Koch, from the story by Stefan Zweig; **photography:** Frank Planer; **editor:** Ted J. Kent; **sound:** Leslie J. Carey, Glenn E. Anderson; **art director:** Alexander Golitzen; **music:** Daniele Amfitheatrof, David Tamkin.

Cast: Joan Fontaine (*Lisa Berndle*); Louis Jourdan (*Stefan Brand*); Mady Christians (*Frau Berndle*); Marcel Journet (*Johann Stauffer*); Art Smith (*John*); Carol Yorke (*Marie*); Howard Freeman (*Herr Kastner*); John Good (*Lt. Leopold von Kaltnegger*); Leo B. Pessin (*Stefan, Jr.*); Erskine Sandford (*Porter*); Otto Waldis (*Concierge*); Sonia Bryden (*Frau Spitzer*).

Letter from an Unknown Woman

Publications

Script:

Koch, Howard, *Letter from an Unknown Woman*, edited by Virginia Wright Wexman, New Brunswick, New Jersey, 1986.

Books:

Roud, Richard, *Index to the Work of Max Ophüls*, London, 1958.
Beylie, Claude, *Max Ophüls*, Brussels, 1958.
Annenkov, Georges, *Max Ophüls*, Paris, 1962.
Beylie, Claude, *Max Ophüls*, Paris, 1963.
Max Orphüls par Max Ophüls, edited by Robert Laffont, Paris, 1963.
Sarris, Andrew, *Interviews with Film Directors*, New York, 1967.
Wood, Robin, *Personal Views: Explorations in Films*, London, 1976.
Willeman, Paul, editor, *Ophüls*, London, 1978.
Williams, Alan Larson, *Max Ophüls and the Cinema of Desire*, New York, 1980.
Wilson, George M., *Narration in Light: Studies in Cinematic Point of View*, Baltimore, Maryland, 1986.
Payán, Miguel Juan, *Max Ophüls*, Madrid, 1987.
García Riera, Emilio, *Max Ophüls*, Guadalajara, 1988.
Guérin, William Karl, *Max Ophüls,* Paris, 1988.
Ophüls, Max, *Theater, Hörspiele, Filme*, St Ingbert, 1993.
Tassone, Aldo, *Max Ophüls: l'enchanteur*, Torino, 1994.
White, Susan M., *The Cinema of Max Ophüls: Magisterial Vision and the Figure of a Woman*, New York, 1995.
Bacher, Lutz, *Max Ophüls in the Hollywood Studios*, New Brunswick, 1996.
Berthomé, Jean-Pierre, *Le plaisir*, Paris, 1997.

Articles:

Hollywood Reporter, 8 April 1948.
New York Times, 29 April 1948.
Monthly Film Bulletin (London), August 1949.
Winnington, Richard, in *News Chronicle* (London), 7 January 1950.
Sight and Sound (London), February and March 1950.

Ray, Cyril, in *Sunday Times* (London), 16 July 1950.
Whitebait, William, in *New Statesman* (London), 22 July 1950.
Archer, Eugene, ''Ophüls and the Romantic Tradition,'' in *Yale French Studies* (New Haven), Summer 1956.
''Ophüls Issue'' of *Cahiers du Cinéma* (Paris), March 1958.
Beylie, Claude, in *Cinéma* (Paris), July-August 1969.
Williams, Forrest, ''The Mastery of Movement: An Appreciation of Max Ophüls,'' in *Film Comment* (New York), Winter 1969.
Kerbel, Michael, in *Film Comment* (New York), Summer 1971.
Sarris, Andrew, ''Max Ophüls: An Introduction,'' in *Film Comment* (New York), Summer 1971.
Velvet Light Trap (Madison, Wisconsin), Summer 1972.
Camper, Fred, in *Monogram* (London), no. 5, 1974.
Greenspun, Roger, in *Film Comment* (New York), January-February 1975.
''Ophüls Issue'' of *Filmkritik* (Munich), November 1977.
Coleman, John, in *New Statesman* (London), 23 November 1979.
Film Reader (Evanston, Illinois), no. 4, 1979.
Positif (Paris), July-August 1980.
Archibald, Lewis, in *Magill's Survey of Cinema 3*, Englewood Cliffs, New Jersey, 1981.
Perkins, V. F., in *Movie* (London), Summer 1982.
Walker, M., ''Ophüls in Hollywood,'' in *Movie* (London), Summer 1982.
Modleski, Tania, ''Time and Desire in the Woman's Film,'' in *Cinema Journal* (Champaign, Illinois), Spring 1984.
Frauen und Film (Frankfurt), December 1985.
Gallagher, Tag, in *Cinema Journal* (Champaign, Illinois), Winter 1986.
Verstraten, P., ''Raconter sa propre tragedie: *Lettre d'une inconnue*,'' in *Iris* (Iowa City), no. 8, 1988.
Cavell, S., ''Postscript (1989): To Whom it May Concern,'' in *Critical Inquiry* (Chicago), no. 2, 1990.
Fadda, M., ''Lacrime di fantasma,'' in *Cineforum* (Bergamo, Italy), September 1991.
Wood, R., ''*Letter from an Unknown Woman:* The Double Narrative,'' in *Cineaction* (Toronto), Spring/Summer 1993.

* * *

The film *Letter from an Unknown Woman* is such an icon of cinema scholarship that it is difficult to realize it was not well received when it first appeared in the spring of 1948. Described by Bosley Crowther in the *New York Times* as containing ''an hour and a half of wistfulness, of lingering love-lorn expressions and pseudo-Viennese 'schmaltz,''' the movie garnered a series of inconsequential reviews and slipped quietly into obscurity. *Letter from an Unknown Woman* was Max Ophüls's second Hollywood film after he fled the unstable political situation in Europe in the late 1930s, and although a seasoned director, he was relatively little known in America. In fact, he spent the first six years of his Hollywood exile unemployed until through the efforts of Robert Siodmak, another émigré director, Douglas Fairbanks, Jr., asked Ophüls to direct *The Exile* (1948). It was to be the first of his four American films.

His second directorial opportunity came through the screenwriter Howard Koch, already at work on the script of *Letter* from the Viennese Stefan Zweig novella *Brief einer Unbekannten*. John Houseman had been persuaded to produce the film for Joan Fontaine and her husband William Dozier who had just formed Rampart Productions. Koch knew of Ophüls's work, he was later to write, through *Liebelei* (1932) which was set in Vienna. Houseman also knew the film and approved of using Max on *Letter*. The collaboration with Koch, Houseman and Rampart Productions proved congenial, for the most part, and the shooting went smoothly with only minor disagreement about the finished musical score, which Ophüls wanted integrated carefully into the film and not just used for background atmosphere. As the critics were to discover somewhat later, Ophüls had made an exceptionally fine film.

If the movie did not attract much attention in the United States, its fate in Great Britain was quite different. Deprived of a London opening it was consigned to the provincial theatres, but due to the intervention of Gavin Lambert and Karel Reisz, then writing for the avant-garde cinema journal *Sequence*, the film was given a London run some six months after its UK release. The continued interest on the part of *Sequence* critics kept the interest in Ophüls and his work alive and eventually lead to Richard Roud's index of Ophüls's films and the Ophüls retrospectives at the National Film Theatre and Cinemathèque Française in the late 1950s. A steady series of articles and reassessments appeared during the 1960s, and in 1968 in *The American Cinema* Andrew Sarris, the influential auteurist critic, placed Ophüls in his pantheon of directors who transcended their materials with a personal vision of the world. What has followed has been an increasing fascination in Ophüls's work and in his *Letter from an Unknown Woman*.

Of the various approaches taken by critics towards Ophüls's film three stand out as clearly generative. The first was summed up most succinctly by Robin Wood in his 1974 essay ''Ewig hin der Liebe Glück'' in which he examined the formal properties of Ophüls's cinema. Extending the assessment of Sarris and other formalist critics, Wood set forth some 22 separate categories of stylistic or thematic characteristics to be found in the Ophüls oeuvre. These properties he applied especially to *Letter* as an embodiment of the romanticism to be found in formal repetition and symmetry in an attempt to elevate the film from a ''mere'' romantic woman's film to the status of a genuine work of art, albeit in the romance vein. Wood saw the film as being neither debased nor simplified for its attachment to the heroine's yearnings. The sophisticated formal properties of the film elevated its romanticism to art.

The second major critical approach to *Letter* appeared in 1978 in a publication on the director issued by the British Film Institute and edited by Paul Willemen. As Virginia Wright Wexman has observed, Willemen, as part of the editorial collective which founded *Screen*, was committed to an ideological perspective which grew out of a synthesis of ''semiotics, Althusserian Marxism, Lacanian psychoanalysis, and feminism.'' The BFI anthology followed the retrospective of Ophüls films at the Edinburgh Film Festival and reflected Willemen's ambivalence towards the auteurist critics who tended to consecrate the director as a great artist. Willemen preferred to examine the films as examples of a far ranging spectrum of political repression which were rooted, according to him, in the commercial, i.e., Hollywood, cinema. Of particular interest to him were the strategies of voyeurism and exhibitionism relating to political questions of gender difference. Ophüls's extraordinary style, under such an examination, revealed a political sub-text which supported the generic and sexual properties of the film. Such an ideological approach exposed social assumptions often obscured by aesthetic criticism. Willemen's analysis opened up Ophüls's text to new interpretations which both enriched the process of watching and of criticism.

Finally, *Letter from an Unknown Woman* has assumed a central place in the current canon of feminist film criticism. Since the film is easily subsumed into the category of ''women's films'' and since the themes of the film, such as desire, personal renunciation, and death, all fall well within the areas traditionally encompassed by the Hollywood film aimed at female audiences, feminist film critics have discovered in the film a congenial ground for exploration. Ophüls's curious position within the Hollywood system also provides an opportunity for analysis in so far as he was making movies in Hollywood but from a particularly European point of view, a position reinforced by the fact that as opposed to other émigré directors he did not stay in America but returned to Europe to finish out his career.

Within a patriarchal political and economic system, which dominated the production of the ''Hollywood Film,'' such movies as *Letter* provide a unique perspective on the place of women both within the system of texts created by the studios and within broader social contexts. If most films project women from a male point of view and determine women through the gaze of the male spectator, some films, such as *Letter*, offer a slightly different opportunity to ''see'' women as propriators of the masculine defining characteristics. The female voice-over and hence the female character in many ways ''control'' the film, limiting the freedom of the male figures in a reversal of patriarchy. Such an approach greatly problematizes the text and opens it up not only to a variety of readings but to revolutionary ones. Implicit in the text is what the text does not seem to be, and such a recognition significantly alters our experience of the film, of the director, and of the system within which the film was produced.

Max Ophüls's *Letter from an Unknown Woman* provides an exemplary instance of the interpretability of artistic texts. Each new generation of film critics has discovered in its experience with the film new perspectives and in the process reinvigorated the text with each examination. If any possibility still exists that *Letter from an Unknown Woman* is capable of eliciting only a surface wishfulfilment surely such critical resiliance should put such fears to rest.

—Charles L. P. Silet

LETYAT ZHURAVLI

(The Cranes are Flying)

USSR, 1957

Director: Mikhail Kalatozov

Production: Mosfilm; black and white, 35mm; running time: 94 minutes, some sources list 97 minutes; length: about 8,697 feet. Released October 1957.

Screenplay: Victor Rozov, from the work *Eternally Alive* by Rozov; **photography:** Sergei Urusevsky; **editor:** M. Timofeyeva; **production designer:** E. Svidetelev; **music:** Moisei Vaynberg.

Cast: Tatyana Samollova (*Veronika*); Alexeï Batalov (*Boris Borozdine*); Vassili Merkuriev (*Dr. Fedore Ivanovitch Borozdine*); A. Shvorin (*Mark*); S. Kharitonova (*Irina*); K. Nikitine (*Volodia*); Valentin Zubkov (*Stépan*); Anna Bogdanova (*Grandmother*); K. Nikitine (*Volodya*); B. Kokobkin (*Tyernov*); E. Kupriyanova (*Anna Mikhailovna*).

Award: Cannes Film Festival, Palme d'Or, 1958.

Publications

Books:

Schnitzer, Luda and Jean, *Vingt ans de cinéma soviétique*, Paris, 1964.
Rotha, Paul, and Richard Griffith, *The Film Till Now*, New York, 1967.
Liehm, Mira, and Antonin, *The Most Important Art: East European Film after 1945*, Berkeley, 1977.
Klinowski, Jacek, and Adam Garbicz, *Cinema, The Magic Vehicle: A Guide to Its Achievement: Journey Two*, Metuchen, New Jersey, 1979.
Krasnetskaya, M., *Alexei Batalov*, Moscow, 1983.

Articles:

Billard, Pierre, in *Cinéma* (Paris), June 1958.
Martin, André, in *Cahiers du Cinéma* (Paris), June 1958.
Monod, Martine, ''Un Authentique Chef-d'oeuvre,'' in *Lettres Françaises* (Paris), 19 June 1958.
Doniol-Valcroze, Jacques, ''Par la grâce du formalisme,'' in *Cahiers du Cinéma* (Paris), July 1958.
Leyda, Jay, ''Qui est Kalatozov,'' in *Cinéma* (Paris), July-August 1958.
Dyer, Peter John, in *Films and Filming* (London), November 1958.
Cros, J. Louis, in *Image et Son* (Paris), November 1958.
Image et Son (Paris), December 1959.
Lifton, Michael, in *Film Quarterly* (Berkeley), Spring 1960.
Hibbin, Nina, ''Ivan the Magnificent,'' in *Films and Filming* (London), February 1963.
Anninsky, L., in *Film a Doba* (Prague), 1971.
Yutkevich, S., in *Iskusstvo Kino* (Moscow), March 1980.
Zorkaia, N., in *Iskusstvo Kino* (Moscow), no. 5, 1995.

* * *

Along with Grigori Chukhrai's 1959 film *Ballada o soldate* (*Ballad of a Soldier*), *Letyat Zhuravli* won immediate acclaim on its release in the West, including the *Palme d'Or* at Cannes in 1958, because of its radical departure from the Socialist Realist style that had dominated Soviet cinema under Stalin. It was the product of the slight easing of constraints on Soviet film-makers at the end of the 1950s, following Khrushchev's famous denunciation of Stalin's crimes at the 20th Congress of the Soviet Communist Party in 1956. This shift is most apparent, perhaps, in the way that the film replaces the abstract entities—such as ''the people,'' ''the workers,'' or ''the nation''—that had dominated and defined the narratives of Socialist Realist cinema, with individual characters and their personal aims and desires. Predictably, this was hailed by critics in the West as a welcome return on the part of Soviet cinema to the ''universal'' themes of humanism that have ''no awareness of geographical or political bounds,'' as Bosley Crowther aptly put it in his review of the film. However, *Letyat Zhuravli* goes further than a simple focus on individuals, in its use of the conventions of classic melodrama and its relentless emphasis on the emotional vicissitudes of the romantic couple, to weave its narrative of innocent love ruined by the arbitrary events of a cruel war.

Letyat zhuravli

Veronica, a young Russian woman living in Moscow just before World War II, loves Boris, a factory worker, and they plan to marry. However, when the German army attacks the Eastern Front, Boris dutifully volunteers to fight, and triumphantly marches off to war with his fellow workers. Veronica, left homeless and alone in Moscow after a bombing raid in which her family dies and her home is obliterated, is invited to live with Boris' family by Boris' kind father Fyodor. However, during another dramatic bombing raid, she makes love to Boris' selfish, draft-dodging cousin Mark, and then marries him—even though she still loves Boris—much to the dismay of Fyodor and his family. While Veronica lives miserably with Mark, yearning for letters from Boris and spending her time nursing wounded soldiers, Boris is killed in action. Eventually, Fyodor throws Mark out of his home, having learned that he is a draft-dodger, and Veronica leaves her husband to stay with Boris' family, caring for an orphan she has adopted. Learning of Boris' death from a soldier in his regiment, she nevertheless holds out hope that he has somehow survived, until, in the final scene, she goes to welcome the troops back home from the front and is informed by Boris' closest friend that he had seen Boris die with his own eyes. Now accepting Boris' death, she hands out the flowers she had bought in the hope that Boris would return to the soldiers around her, as a flock of cranes flies over Moscow for the first time since the beginning of the war.

As this synopsis indicates, *Letyat Zhuravli* is a fairly standard melodrama. The cruel disruption of a young romance by an outside event over which the protagonists have no control: the "evil" relative waiting in the wings to exploit the heroine's loneliness and vulnerability, the "true" emotions which cannot be expressed because of circumstances, the love that persists in the face of death—all of these are familiar from countless Hollywood narratives. However, within the context of Soviet cinema, the use of a melodramatic plot in a wartime scenario is highly significant. In the cinema under Stalin, the trauma of World War II, in which one in ten Russians lost their lives, had been overwhelmingly represented in terms of the clichés of willing sacrifice and patriotic collective duty, and even the slightest hint at personal suffering had been rigorously excluded. In *Letyat Zhuravli*, however, suffering, as personified by Veronica, is both foregrounded and made into the very dynamic that drives the narrative forward. It is the pathos of Veronica's desperate hope that Boris is still alive, when we the audience know he is dead, as well as the impossibility of Veronica's own circumstances—her hapless and unhappy marriage—that sustains the central drama.

Just as crucially, Veronica's suffering is explicitly linked by the film's melodramatic structure to the war and the topsy-turvy world war produces. Once the war begins, confusion reigns and the safe, habitual social order of the opening sequences of the film is turned upside down. Veronica, for example, cannot find Boris to say good-bye to him in the mass of soldiers marching off to war, and it is in the confusion of a bombing raid, amongst darkness, breaking glass and explosions, that Veronica falls prey to Mark. Thus, *Letyat Zhuravli* boldly appropriates melodrama to articulate wartime suffering. However, it is also equally distinctive in its use of techniques reminiscent of the revolutionary Soviet cinema of the 1920s prior to the onset of official Socialist Realism. Dynamic, angular framing, extreme close-ups, and superimpositions all combine to create a highly expressionistic film, and it remains interesting today just as much for its stylistic as well as its narrative break with Stalinist Soviet cinema.

—Kris Percival

DER LETZTE MANN

(The Last Laugh)

Germany, 1924

Director: F. W. Murnau

Production: Universum-Film-Aktiengesellschaft (UFA); black and white, 35mm, silent; running time: about 73 minutes; length: 2,036 meters, 8 reels. Released 23 December 1924, Berlin. Filmed 1924 in UFA studios.

Screenplay: Carl Mayer, under the supervision of Erich Pommer; **photography:** Karl Freund; **production designers:** Robert Herlth and Walter Röhrig; **accompanying musical score:** Guiseppe Becce.

Cast: Emil Jannings (*Doorman*); Maly Delschaft (*His daughter*); Max Hiller (*Her fiancé*); Emilie Kurtz (*His aunt*); Hans Unterkircher (*Manager*); Olaf Storm (*Young hotel resident*); Hermann Valentin (*Hotel resident*); Emmy Wyda (*Thin neighbor*); Georg John (*Night watchman*).

Publications

Books:

Mitry, Jean, *Emil Jannings*, Paris, 1927.
Bie, Richard, *Emil Jannings*, Berlin, 1936.
Ihering, Herbert, *Emil Jannings*, Heidelberg, 1941.
Kurtz, Rudolph, *Emil Jannings*, Berlin, 1942.
Kracauer, Siegfried, *From Caligari to Hitler: A Psychological History of the German Film*, Princeton, 1947.
Huff, Theodore, *An Index to the Films of F. W. Murnau*, London, 1948.
Borde, Raymond, and others, *Le Cinéma réaliste allemand*, Paris, 1959.
Jameux, Charles, *Murnau*, Paris, 1965.
Domarchi, Jean, ''Murnau,'' in *Anthologie du cinema 1*, Paris, 1966.
Hempel, Rolf, *Carl Mayer: Ein Autor schreibt mit der Kamera*, Berlin, 1968.
Eisner, Lotte, *The Haunted Screen*, Berkeley, 1969.
Manvell, Roger, and Heinrich Fraenkel, *The German Cinema*, New York, 1971.
Eisner, Lotte, *Murnau*, Berkeley, 1973.
Monaco, Paul, *Cinema and Society: France and Germany During the Twenties*, New York, 1976.
Collier, Jo Leslie, *From Wagner to Murnau: The Transposition of Romanticism from Stage and Screen*, Ann Arbor, 1988.
Gehler, Fred, *Friedrich Wilhelm Murnau*, Augsburg, 1990.

Articles:

Variety (New York), 10 December 1924.
New York Times, 21 December 1924.
Josephson, Matthew, ''F. W. Murnau—The German Genius of the Films,'' in *Motion Picture Classic* (New York), October 1926.
Lane, Tamar, ''The Last Laugh is on Hollywood,'' in *Motion Picture Magazine* (New York), November 1926.
Blin, Roger, ''Murnau—ses films,'' in *Revue du Cinéma* (Paris), July 1931.
White, Kenneth, ''F. W. Murnau,'' in *Hound and Horn* (New York), July-September 1931.
Wilhelm, Wolfgang, ''Carl Mayer,'' in *Sight and Sound* (London), July 1944.
Brunius, Jacques, ''Un Hommage au scenariste de Caligari, Carl Mayer,'' in *Revue du Cinéma* (Paris), Spring 1947.
Luft, Herbert, ''Notes on the World and Work of Carl Mayer,'' in *Quarterly of Film, Radio, and Television* (Berkeley), Summer 1954.
Billard, Pierre, ''Quarante ans après,'' in *Cinéma* (Paris), November 1965.
Murnau, F. W., ''Fire and Ice,'' in *Cahiers du Cinema in English* (New York), January 1966.
Image et Son (Paris), no. 214, 1968.
''Carl Mayer e l'espressionismo Issue'' of *Bianco e Nero* (Rome), 1969.
Truscott, Harold, ''Emil Jannings—A Personal View,'' in *Silent Picture* (London), Autumn 1970.
Guillermo, Gilberto Perez, ''F. W. Murnau: An Introduction,'' in *Film Comment* (New York), Summer 1971.
Helman, A., in *Kino* (Warsaw), April 1973.
Rayns, Tony, in *Monthly Film Bulletin* (London), July 1974.
''*Der Letzte Mann* Issue'' of *Filmcritica* (Rome), July 1974.
Koch, V., in *Ekran* (Ljubljana), no. 3–4, 1977.
''Murnau Issue'' of *Avant-Scène du Cinéma* (Paris), July-September 1977.
Wynne, Cicely, in *Cinema Texas Program Notes* (Austin), 3 October 1978.
Cardullo, B., ''Der Letzte Mann Gets the Last Laugh: F. W. Murnau's Comic Vision,'' in *Post Script* (Jacksonville, Florida), Fall 1981.
Elsaesser, Thomas, ''Secret Affinities: F. W. Murnau,'' in *Sight and Sound* (London), Winter 1988–89.
Wolf, R., and others, ''De films van F. W. Murnau,'' in *Skrien* (Amsterdam), February-March 1990.

* * *

Had scenarist Carl Mayer not quarrelled with director Lupu Pick, his collaborator on two previous films, *Scherben* and *Sylvester*, *Der letzte Mann* would undoubtedly have been more like its *Kammerspeil* (literally ''chamber play'') predecessors. In these two films Mayer and Pick had abandoned the Expressionist concern for subjective vision and instead dealt with the intimate details of petit bourgeois existence. Mayer and Pick together create a *Stimmung* or ''mood'' of inevitable domestic tragedy brought on by the workings of instinct, a force so natural and all-conquering that it cannot even be expressed in language (hence, in part, the films' lack of inter-titles). This treatment of the workings of obsession, of course, suggests a *rapprochement* between the psychologism of *Caligari* and the Zolaesque determinism suitable for presenting a social critique. In fact, it is often noted that the *Kammespielfilme* as a group can be viewed as continuing the Expressionist examination of disturbed minds and emotions within settings and with characters that are essentially realistic. In the case of Pick's two efforts with Mayer, this realism even takes on socio-political overtones, developed by the contrast between the miseries of lower-middle class existence and the easy, but unattainable life of the rich.

Even with F. W. Murnau as director, *Der letzte Mann* has much in common with Mayer's two previous films, which together form a triptych. Once again, the narrative deals with the hardships suffered by the petit bourgeoisie. The central character is a hotel doorman who, as such, must serve the rich, but is still admired by his fellow tenement dwellers because of the status implied by his ornate uniform. Removed from his post because of old age, the doorman cannot adjust to his new position as lavatory attendant. His desperate struggle to retain his former standing in the neighborhood eventually fails, and he becomes an object of ridicule and shame. The doorman's decline takes on a larger socio-political significance as he seems the only mediator between life in the slums and in the luxury hotel. The film's ending, however, undercuts this sharp critique of lower-middle-classed disenchantment, symbolized, in a specifically German fashion, by the loss of the uniform. When the doorman is reduced to utter abjectness, the film's only inter-title declares that, although in the real world he would have no chance, the filmmakers will have mercy on him. What follows defies the film's carefully developed *vraisemblance*. The doorman becomes the beneficiary of an eccentric American millionaire who, having willed his fortune to the ''last man'' to serve him, had died in the hotel lavatory. The film ends with the doorman and his partner, the night watchman, enjoying a suitably vulgar and ostentatious dinner in the hotel dining room and leaving for parts unknown in a huge limousine. The carnival celebration of *Der letzte Mann's* conclusion finds no equivalent in the unrelieved grimness of the earlier *Kammerspielfilme*.

The differences between *Der letzte Mann* and its predecessors, however, are not simply those of narrative construction. *Scherbern* and *Sylvester* attained only limited critical and commercial success, while *Der letzte Mann* was hailed as a masterpiece both in Germany and abroad. It became one of the most important films to emerge from Weimar Germany and was influential in Hollywood, where it aroused an enthusiasm for German films and filmmakers that was to last for many years. Much of the acclaim centered around the cinematic techniques devised by Mayer, Murnau, and the cameraman Karl Freund to present the narrative.

Murnau often receives full credit for inventing the ''unchained camera'' that explores both the inner and outer worlds of *Der letzte Mann*, but the innovations resulted from collaborative effort. Murnau, more than Pick, was able to realize Mayer's ideas about dynamic and flexible point of view; his previous work, particularly in *Nosferatu*, reveals an expert handling of camera placement and angles. Griffith may have invented both tracking movements and point-of-view editing, but these elements of film grammar are refined and extended in *Der letzte Mann*. In the famous drunk scene, the camera records the doorman's distorted perceptions, an effect Freund achieved by strapping the camera to his chest and staggering about the set. In the dream sequence that follows, Murnau suggests an even more subjective experience, the distortions imposed by the unconscious upon conscious concerns; here the Expressionist influence is strongest and is achieved largely through special effects, not, as in *Caligari*, through set design.

This linkage between the camera and the doorman's perceptions or feelings is not sustained. Several sequences suggest the camera's independence from both narrative and character. In the opening sequence, a long travelling shot, entirely unmotivated, takes the spectator down the hotel elevator, through the lobby, and out the revolving door that serves as symbol of fate. Freund achieved this effect by mounting the camera on a bicycle. Later, at a crucial moment in the story, the camera positions itself outside a glass wall and, by means of a discreet dissolve, gradually moves into the room to record the interview between the doorman and the manager. When the doorman is later accused of slackness by an irate customer, the camera refuses to follow the manager down to the lavatory. In these sequences and others, the camera calls attention to itself rather than presenting the narrative through the doorman's experience. This reflexivity finds its culmination in the artificiality of the film's conclusion.

Der letzte Mann is noteworthy not simply because it inaugurated the use of subjective camera, but because it revealed the potentially complex relationship between camera and narrative. If its elaborate and virtuoso production exceeds the intimate atmosphere of *Kammerspielfilme*, lending the doorman's simple story a grandiosity it can hardly sustain, it is because Murnau, Mayer and Freund discovered storytelling techniques that could barely be contained by the limitations of that genre.

—R. Barton Palmer

THE LIFE AND DEATH OF COLONEL BLIMP

UK, 1943

Directors: Michael Powell and Emeric Pressburger

Production: The Archers; Technicolor; running time: 163 minutes, length: 14,701 feet. Released June 1943.

Producers: Michael Powell, Emeric Pressburger; **screenplay:** Michael Powell, Emeric Pressburger, from the cartoon character created by David Low; **photography:** Georges Périnal; **process photography:** W. Percy Day; **camera operators:** Geoffrey Unsworth, Jack Cardiff, Harold Haysom; **editor:** John Seabourne; **sound recordists:** C. C.

The Life and Death of Colonel Blimp

Stevens, Desmond Dew; **production designer:** Alfred Junge; **costume design:** Joseph Bato, Matilda Etches; **music:** Allan Gray.

Cast: Anton Walbrook (*Theo Kretschmar-Schuldorff*); Deborah Kerr (*Edith Hunter/Barbara Wynne/Angela Cannon*); Roger Livesey (*General Clive Wynne-Candy*); Roland Culver (*Colonel Betteridge*); Harry Welchman (*Major Davies*); Arthur Wontner (*Embassy Counsellor*); Albert Lieven (*von Ritter*); John Laurie (*Murdoch*); James McKechnie (*Lieutenant ''Spud'' Wilson*); David Hutcheson (*Hoppy*); Ursula Jeans (*Frau von Kalteneck*); Reginald Tate (*van Zijl*); A. E. Matthews (*President of Tribunal*); Neville Mapp (*Stuffy Graves*); Vincent Holman (*Club Porter, 1942*); Spencer Trevor (*Period Blimp*); James Knight (*Club Porter, 1942*); Dennis Arundell (*Cafe Orchestra Leader*); David Ward (*Kaunitz*); Jan van Loewen (*Indignant Citizen*); Valentine Dyall (*von Schönborn*); Carl Jaffé (*von Reumann*); Eric Maturin (*Colonel Goodhead*); Frith Banbury (*Baby-Face Fitzroy*); Robert Harris (*Embassy Secretary*); Count Zichy (*Colonel Borg*); Jane Millican (*Nurse Erna*); Phyllis Morris (*Pebble*); Muriel Aked (*Aunt Margaret*); Captain W. H. Barrett, U.S. Army (*Texan*); Corporal Thomas Palmer, U.S. Army (*Sergeant*); Yvonne Andree (*Nun*); Marjorie Gresley (*Matron*); Felix Aylmer (*Bishop*); Helen Debroy (*Mrs. Wynne*); Norman Pierce (*Mr. Wynne*); Edward Cooper (*BBC Official*); Joan Swinstead (*Secretary*).

Publications

Script:

Powell, Michael, *The Life and Death of Colonel Blimp*, London, 1994.

Books:

Robson, E. W. and M. M., *The Shame and Disgrace of Colonel Blimp*, London, 1943.

Durgnat, Raymond, *A Mirror for England: British Movies from Austerity to Affluence*, London, 1970.

Christie, Ian, editor, *Powell, Pressburger and Others*, London, 1978.

Cosandey, Roland, editor, *Retrospective: Powell and Pressburger*, Locarno, 1982.

Gottler, Fritz and others, *Living Cinema: Powell and Pressburger*, Munich, 1982.

Aldgate, Anthony, and Jeffrey Richards, *Best of British: Cinema and Society 1930–1970*, Oxford, 1983.
Christie, Ian, *Arrows of Desire: The Films of Michael Powell and Emeric Pressburger*, London, 1985, 1994.
Martini, Emanuela, editor, *Powell and Pressburger*, Bergamo, 1986.
Powell, Michael, *A Life in Movies: An Autobiography*, London, 1986, 1998.
Powell, Michael, *Million-Dollar Movie*, New York, 1995.
Howard, James, *Michael Powell*, North Pomfret, 1996.
Salwolke, Scott, *The Films of Michael Powell & the Archers*, Lanham, 1997.

Articles:

Monthly Film Bulletin (London), no. 114, 1943.
Kine Weekly (London), 10 June 1943.
Variety (New York), 23 June 1943.
Motion Picture Herald (New York), 10 July 1943.
New York Times, 30 March 1945.
Agee, James, in *Agee on Film 1*, New York, 1958.
Taylor, John Russell, ''Michael Powell: Myths and Supermen,'' in *Sight and Sound* (London), Autumn 1978.
Christie, Ian, ''The Colonel Blimp File,'' in *Sight and Sound* (London), Winter 1978–79.
Badder, David, ''Powell and Pressburger: The War Years,'' in *Sight and Sound* (London), Winter 1978–79.
Everson, William K., ''Michael Powell,'' in *Films in Review* (New York), August-September 1980.
Thompson, David, ''The Films of Michael Powell: A Romantic Sensibility,'' in *American Film* (Washington, D.C.), November 1980.
''Special Issue'' of *Avant-Scène du Cinéma* (Paris), 15 December 1980.
Bassan, Raphaël, ''Michael Powell: Un Orfèvre de l'objectif,'' in *Image et Son* (Paris), May 1981.
McVay, Douglas, ''Cinema of Enchantment: The Films of Michael Powell,'' in *Films and Filming* (London), December 1981.
Millar, Gavin, in *Listener* (London), 25 August 1983.
Scorsese, Martin, in *Time Out* (London), 18–24 July 1985.
Powell, Michael, in *City Limits* (London), 19–25 July 1985.
Combs, Richard, in *Monthly Film Bulletin* (London), August 1985.
Baxter, Brian, in *Films and Filming* (London), August 1985.
Bourget, E., ''Colonel Blimp: Le voyeur,'' in *Positif* (Paris), September 1992.
Chapman, James, ''The Life and Death of Colonel Blimp (1943) Reconsidered,'' in *Historical Journal of Film, Radio and Television* (Abingdon), vol. 15, no. 1, March 1995.
''Written, Produced and Directed by Michael Powell and Emeric Pressburger: Film Auteurs in the 1940s,'' in *Film Comment* (New York), vol. 31, no. 2, March-April 1995.
Gough-Yates, Kevin, ''Pressburger: England and Exile: Emeric Pressburger,'' in *Sight and Sound* (London), vol. 5, no. 12, December 1995.

* * *

With *The Life and Death of Colonel Blimp*, the idiosyncratic partnership of Michael Powell and Emeric Pressburger hit its stride. Though they had already made four highly individual films together, *Blimp* was the first for their newly formed independent production company, The Archers—and also their first movie in colour. Not that monochrome could be said to cramp their imaginations—witness *A Canterbury Tale* or *I Know Where I'm Going*—but colour, and especially the heightened, unreal quality of 1940s Technicolor, gave full play to the richly stylised extravagance of their vision.

If realism never counted for much in Powell-Pressburger's films, the same went for intellectual consistency, and *Blimp* thrives on ambiguity to the point of blatant self-contradiction. The original Blimp, as created by the great political cartoonist David Low, stood for all that was most crassly reactionary in the British military establishment. The film's Blimp, incarnated by Roger Livesey's General Clive Wynne-Candy, is a lovable old walrus, maybe a touch set in his ways, but altogether a spirited survivor from a more honourable age. Livesey gives the performance of a lifetime, but wholly misses the mean, vicious side of Blimp which Olivier, Powell-Pressburger's initial choice, might well have brought to the role.

Given this central characterisation, it's inevitable that the film's ostensible message (most clearly enunciated by the ''good German,'' Theo Kretschmar-Schuldorff) and its emotional drift should be at odds almost from the start. ''They are children. War is playing cricket,'' Theo reflects about his captors after World War I; and later, with the next conflict under way: ''If you let yourselves be defeated by [the Nazis], just because you are too fair to hit back the same way they hit at you, there won't *be* any methods but Nazi methods . . . This is not a gentleman's war. This time you are fighting for your very existence.'' His views are implemented by the young lieutenant in the 1943 framing episode, pulling a sneak attack ''by the authority of these guns and these men''—and we hear similar sentiments from Edith, the young woman Candy meets, loves and loses to Theo in 1902 Berlin: ''Good manners cost us . . . 6,000 men killed and 20,000 men wounded—and two years of war. When with a little common sense and *bad* manners there would have been no war at all.''

Yet this advocacy of *realpolitik* is constantly undermined, not only by Candy's own actions—far from displaying ''bad manners'' in Berlin, he accedes to a duel with scrupulous correctness—but by the affection with which the film portrays both him, and the era he represents. In a British film of this period, we might expect to see Wilhelmine Germany peopled with proto-Nazis; Powell-Pressburger view the details of ceremony and protocol with a sly delight, tinged with nostalgia, that anticipates the Ophüls of *Lola Montès* or *La Ronde*. As the duel—staged with hieratic formality in a high, white gymnasium—gets started, the camera pulls up and away through the roof in a dreamlike movement, to gaze out across a prospect of nocturnal spires swathed in drifting snow.

But again—since *Blimp* is nothing if not multi-layered—there's the covert implication that Candy preserves his ideals only through wilful ignorance, overlooking dirty tricks by others on his behalf. His mission in Berlin was to counter shameful rumours of the British herding Boer women and children into concentration camps—which of course were quite true. ''Clean fighting, honest soldiering have won,'' he muses in 1918, having left a South African major—the irony is evident—to interrogate prisoners by methods less scrupulous than his own. Throughout, the film is sustained and vitalised by these ideological tensions, which save it from slipping into the bland, celebratory mode of such Hollywood counterparts as *Forever and a Day*—and which could be seen as reflecting the disparate outlooks of its begetters, with Candy an ironic portrait of Powell, the romantic-Tory Englishman, and Theo (astringently played by Anton Walbrook, who wrote most of his own dialogue) standing in for the mid-European Pressburger.

Such ambiguity, at a time of national crisis, was scarcely calculated to appeal to the authorities. Churchill detested *Blimp* and did his best to get it banned. He failed, doing the film nothing but good at the box-office; but his curse may have had some delayed effect. For years, the only available prints were heavily truncated and rearranged, making nonsense of the subtle flashback structure. In the late 1970s, though, the National Film Archive mounted a rescue operation; and the complete version was restored to circulation, to take its place as one of the most intriguing and complex treatments of the national wartime myth.

—Philip Kemp

LIFE AND NOTHING MORE

See **AND LIFE GOES ON**

LIFE IS SWEET

UK, 1990

Director: Mike Leigh

Production: Thin Man, in association with Film Four International, British Screen; colour; 35mm; running time: 103 minutes; length: 9131 feet.

Producer: Simon Channing-Williams; **screenplay:** Mike Leigh; **photography:** Dick Pope; **editor:** Jon Gregory; **assistant directors:** Gus MacLean, Simon Moseley, David Gilchrist, Hedda Moore; **production designer:** Alison Chitty; **art director:** Sophie Becher; **music:** Rachel Portman; **sound editor:** Sue Baker; **sound recording:** Malcolm Hirst, Dick Lewzey.

Cast: Alison Steadman (*Wendy*); Jim Broadbent (*Andy*); Claire Skinner (*Natalie*); Jane Horrocks (*Nicola*); Stephen Rea (*Patsy*); Timothy Spall (*Aubrey*); David Thewlis (*Nicola's lover*); Moya Brady (*Paula*); David Neilson (*Steve*).

Publications

Books:

Clements, Paul, *The Improvised Play: The Work of Mike Leigh*, London, 1983.

Coveney, Michael, *World According to Mike Leigh*, London, 1996.

Carney, Raymond, and Leonard Quart, *The Films of Mike Leigh: Embracing the World*, New York, 2000.

Leigh, Mike, *Mike Leigh: Interviews*, edited by Howie Movshovitz, Jackson, 2000.

Articles:

Variety (New York), 24 December 1990.

Pym, J., and M.Kermode, in *Monthly Film Bulletin* (London), March 1991.

Ostria, V., ''Le sitcom idéal,'' in *Cahiers du Cinéma* (Paris), September 1991.

Kennedy, H., in *Film Comment* (New York), September-October 1991.

Cieutat, M., in *Positif* (Paris), October 1991.

Klawans, Stuart, ''*Life Is Sweet*,'' in *Nation*, vol. 253, no. 19, 2 December 1991.

Rafferty, Terrence, ''Shocks to the System (Mike Leigh Film Retrospective),'' in *New Yorker*, vol. 68, no. 1, 24 February 1992.

Bowman, James, ''*Life Is Sweet*,'' in *American Spectator*, vol. 25, no. 3, March 1992.

Quart, B., and others, in *Film Quarterly* (Berkeley), Spring 1992.

Bates, P., in *Cineaste* (New York), 1992.

Ellickson, Lee, and Richard Porton, ''I Find the Tragicomic Things in Life: An Interview with Mike Leigh,'' in *Cineaste* (New York), vol. 20, no. 3, Summer 1993.

''Leigh, Mike,'' in *Current Biography*, vol. 55, no. 6, June 1994.

Coen, Stephanie, ''More Than Words: An Interview with Mike Leigh,'' in *American Theatre* (New York), vol. 12, no. 5, May-June 1995.

Quart, Leonard, ''Raising Questions and Positing Possibilities: An Interview with Mike Leigh,'' in *Cineaste* (New York), vol. 22, no. 4, Fall 1996.

* * *

In his contributory note to the 1990 London Film Festival Programme, Director Mike Leigh mischieviously lists an alphabet of some 104 incidental items, issues, and ideas he suggests *Life Is Sweet* is about. These include accordians, Princess Margaret, and stuffed dogs, elements that figure fleetingly in the film, only part of its rich tapestry of ordinary, everyday life. But a more relevant vocabulary emerges which proves to be the underlying organising principle of the film—anorexia, catering, chocolate, chips, dieting, eatables, fatness, garlic, jam, nibbling, nutrition, pineapples, prawns, quiche, restaurants, roast lamb, sugar and spice, and tripe all detail the film's central premise of playing out the intricacies of personal relationships through scenarios involving food, an ever rich metaphor.

The story concerns Andy, a chef who buys a caravan-cum-snack bar in an attempt to liberate himself from a hum-drum job. His daughter, Nicola, is an anorexic who secretly gorges on chocolate and makes herself sick. Friend of the family Aubrey opens the ''Regret Rien'' restaurant, providing an assortment of unusual and unappealing nouveau cuisine such as ''pork cyst'' while Wendy, Andy's happy-go-lucky wife, accepts a temporary job as a waitress in Aubrey's establishment. These are merely brief summations of highly nuanced personal stories, each person seeking out some bigger purpose beyond Leigh's beautifully observed and carefully choreographed representation of social existence, an existence informed by dull routine, life-sustaining rituals and the intensity and insistence of habit.

Andy and Wendy are inspirational characters because they have not been deadened by their experience of life. Almost relentlessly cheerful, they enjoy their togetherness and share a playfulness and good humour that emerges from their complete trust in, and love for, each other. Having survived the initial difficulties of becoming pregnant with their twin daughters, Nicola and Natalie, when they were young, Andy and Wendy possess a stability and determination which enables them to engage with life in a positive way. Both take pleasure in the apparently banal, but they invest the banal with an energy and excitement that renders it rich and fulfilling. The source of

Life Is Sweet

their joy and optimism is family life, even despite the difficulties they experience with the deeply troubled, anorexic Nicola, who is perpetually anxious and antagonistic, taking solace in a hollow sounding and ill-informed commitment to feminism and political correctness. The deep-seated self-loathing that characterises Nicola is the underlying narrative tension in *Life Is Sweet*; this tension emerges in one of Leigh's customary scenes of emotional revelation—a necessary crisis in the process of healing and redemption. Rejected by her boyfriend, who refuses to satisfy her perverse sexual needs, Nicola is humiliated by her inability to articulate her feelings or experience intimacy. She does not even trust the affection of her mother, and it is this that informs one of the film's climactic scenes as Wendy addresses Nicola's joylessness and inner pain, encouraging her to fight back and not to give in, especially as she had once nearly died from starvation herself. The underlying principle here is that life is precious and must be lived positively, even in the face of great trial.

Natalie, by contrast, is stable and well adjusted. She enjoys family life, going to the pub with her friends, and anticipating her holiday to the United States. Natalie is a employed as a plumber and clearly likes the independence her job gives her—but she also harbours a longing for a family herself. Leigh is careful not to overstate these issues, as he wishes to illustrate how ordinary people merely endure their fate. Occasional scenes reveal private preoccupations in public dialogues, demonstrating different degrees of inner turmoil beneath socially conditioned modes of behaviour. Natalie discusses having a family with Nicola, but Nicola not surprisingly resists, determined as she is to distance herself from anyone else's concern for, or interest in, her life. This situation changes in the final scene of the film, after Nicola's emotional crisis with her mother, when Natalie tries to offer Nicola comfort and support. Their exchange, muted and tentative though it is, signals reconciliation and growth. The comfortable silence they share is hopeful and secure. It is in these scenes that Leigh successfully shows the inhibitions and limitations in his characters. ''Life Is Sweet'' if we accept our flaws, our self-delusions, and our inadequacies, yet still retain the capability to love.

It is perhaps Wendy who most exemplifies this principle. She supports Aubrey in his doomed enterprise of opening a restaurant and even endures the horrendous (if hilarious) opening night, when Aubrey gets drunk and makes a pass at her (he ends up semi-naked among the tables he has up-turned in his frustration). Wendy also supports Andy's snack-bar venture in the full knowledge that it more represents Andy's desire to be successful on his own terms than a genuine possibility for change. Wendy enables her daughters to accept themselves and still believes that life is worth living. She is perhaps one of Leigh's most heart-warming and moving characters in that she embodies hope in an often hopeless world.

—Paul Wells

THE LIFE OF OHARU

See **SAIKAKU ICHIDAI ONNA**

THE LIGHT

See **YEELEN**

LIMITE

Brazil, 1931

Director: Mario Peixoto

Production: Mario Peixoto; silent, black and white; running time: 120 minutes. Released 17 May 1931. Filmed in the South littoral of Rio de Janeiro.

Producer: Mario Peixoto; **screenplay:** Mario Peixoto; **photography:** Edgar Brazil; **editor:** Mario Peixoto; **musical director:** Brutus Pedreira; **director's assistant:** Rui Costa.

Cast: Olga Breno (*Womàn number 1*); Taciana Rei (*Woman number 2*); Carmen Santos (*The Whore*); Mario Peixoto (*The Man at the cemetery*); Brutus Pedreira (*Man number 2 and the pianist*); Edgar Brazil (*The Man asleep at the cinema*); Faciana Rei; Raul Schnoor.

Publications

Script:

de Mello, Sãulo Pereira, *Limite, filme de Mario Peixoto*, Ediçao Inelivro/Funarte, Rio de Janeiro, Brazil, 1979.

Books:

Andrade, R., and others, *Il Cinema Brasiliano*, Silva Editore, n.d.
Rocha, Glafuber, *Revisão critica do cinema brasileiro*, Editora Civilização Brasileira, Rio de Janeiro, 1963.
Bernadet, Jean-Claude, *Brasil em tempo de cinema*, Paz e Terra, 1977.
Ferreira, Jairo, *Cinema de invenção*, Embrafilme/Max Limonad, São Paulo, 1986.
Gomes, Paulo Emilio Salles, *Crônica de Cinema no Suplemento Literãrio*, Embrafilme/Paz e Terra, Rio de Janeiro, 1982.
Salem, Helena, *90 Anos de Cinema, Uma adentura brasileria*, Editora Nova Fronteira, Rio de Janeiro, 1988.
Peixoto, Mário, *Limite: ''Scenario Original,''* Rio de Janeiro, 1996.

Articles:

Jornal do Brasil (Rio de Janeiro), 25 July 1970.
Azeredo, Ely, *Jornal do Brasil* (Rio de Janeiro), 28 August 1977.
Ferreira, Fernando, *O Globo* (Rio de Janeiro), 26 May 1978.
Rocha, Glauber, *Folha de São Paulo*, São Paulo, 3 June 1978.
O Estado de São Paulo (São Paulo), 11 June 1978.
Schiller, Beatriz, *Jornal do Brasil* (Rio de Janeiro), 2 May 1979.
Mello, Sãulo Pereira de, *50 Anos de Limite* (pressbook), 1981.
Bassan, R., ''Le mythe Limite,'' in *Avant-Scène* (Paris), April 1983.
Chnaiderman, Miriam, ''Filmes que olham,'' *Folha de São Paulo*, 8 October 1988.
Mello, Sãulo Pereira de, *Ver Limite* (São Paulo), December/January/February, 1990.
Folha de São Paulo, 17 May 1991.
Variety (New York), 10 August 1992.

* * *

On May 17, 1931, the first public screening of *Limite*, directed by the 19 year old novice Mario Peixoto, took place in a cinema in downtown Rio de Janeiro. It is said that commotion and controversy broke out at the end of the screening. Despite the immediate enthusiasm of some intellectuals, the film failed to work any magic on the public or distributors. After a few more screenings, *Limite* was withdrawn, and remained, for the next 50 years, in the dark, surrounded by mystery and controversy. It is, without a doubt, the most legendary of all Brazilian films.

During these 50 years, everything has been said about *Limite*—even that it was never made. The career of its creator only added to the mystique. Mario Peixoto, who wrote, produced, directed, and acted in (he is the man in the cemetery) the film died in 1992, leaving two unfinished films dating from the 1930s (*Onde a Terra Acaba* and *Maré Baixa*), an autobiographical novel, poetry, and an unfilmed screenplay, *A Alma Segundo Salustre.* He spent the greater part of his life in isolation on an island off the coast of Rio de Janeiro, near to some of the *Limite* locations, surrounded by his art collection.

In 1978, 20 years of restoration work by the physicist and intellectual Plínio Sussekind Rocha and Sãulo Pereira de Mello put *Limite* back on the screen, at its original speed of 16 frames per second. The difficulties of making the film in the first place were known; its re-emergence showed that it had lasted through the laborious reconstruction process and that it continued to exercise its magic, despite an absence of 50 years. Three hundred critics and film specialists, consulted in 1989, rated *Limite* the most important Brazilian film.

Inspiration for *Limite*—the chained woman on the cover of the magazine *Vu*—came to Mario Peixoto, then a student in Paris, in 1928. To tell the story of *Limite*, however, is to over-simplify its aesthetic range, to denigrate its daring narrative and the impact of its form. The psychological depth of its characters is lost in description; its mystery becomes banal. *Limite* stands apart from everything else that was happening at that time in the embryonic Brazilian film industry for its audacity in a context that permitted no experimentation. Through flash-backs, it tells the story of three characters, a man and two women, who are adrift at sea. The film's free narrative style can be traced to the European fashion avant-garde of the 1920s, its editing to influences of the Soviet school. Its setting, however, is genuinely Brazilian, with its seascapes, luxuriant vegetation, and typical scenes of doors and window frames in poor villages.

The restorer of the film, Sãulo Pereira de Mello, defines the film: ''Limite is a cosmic tragedy, a cry of anguish, a piercing meditation on human limitations, a painful and icy acknowledgment of human defeat. It is a tragic film, a glacial tragedy.''

More than a mere vehicle for one or three stories, *Limite* expresses defeat and desolation, and the impotence of the three characters, adrift forever, at outs with the forces of nature. This defeat is shown through the careful editing, paced and rhythmical, replete with dissolving images (such as the wheel of a train which becomes the wheel of a sewing machine) or the alternating close-ups which reshape parts of the body (feet, eyes, neck, mouths, hair) and inanimate objects (the magnificent sequence of the sewing accessories—buttons, cotton reels, scissors). Another example of skillful editing which produces a highly impactful scene takes place in a cinema, during a Chaplin screening. Mario Peixoto rapidly alternates clips from the film with shots of the cackling mouths of the audience, producing a sequence of high drama.

Virtually minimalist portrayals express human despair, not through broad gestures or exalted utterings, but through inert bodies, blank and forlorn stares. Dating from the transition from silent to spoken films, *Limite* has but three titles, and imparts an eloquent silence, punctuated only by a superb sound-track, organized by Brutus Pedreira (who also acts in the film), including compositions by Eric Satie, Debussy, and Stravinsky, among others.

Mario Peixoto's castaways exhaust the limits of their strength and their hope; they live an impotent challenge to the forces of nature, perhaps the principal element in the film. The timing of the scenes, the imaginative framings and the rhythm and tension of the editing are impressive; the beauty of the images is registered by notable photographer Edgar Brasil. His camera, unlike his characters, enjoys total freedom, either to remain motionless or to spin 360 crazy degrees to capture the final storm.

A young man's only film, in no manner does *Limite* appear to be the work of a novice. At every level the high standards and confidence of a director who had fully honed the tools of his trade are evident, as are his existentialist convictions. Today, *Limite*, available in video and shown at several international festivals, is exposed to fresh scrutiny which renews its impact and mystery. But the riddle of its creator, perhaps an unwitting victim of having reached his creative limits with his first film, persists; Mario Peixoto spent the next 60 years of his life as a voluntary castaway from his time, reliving the isolation of the characters of his first and only film.

—Susana Schild

LITTLE CAESAR

USA, 1930

Director: Mervyn LeRoy

Production: Warner Bros. Pictures, Inc.; black and white, 35mm; running time: 77 minutes. Released January 1931. Filmed summer-fall 1930 in Warner Bros. studios. Cost budgeted at £700,000.

Screenplay: Frances Faragogh and Robert E. Lee, from a novel by William B. Burnett; **photography:** Tony Gaudio; **editor:** Ray Curtiss; **art director:** Anton Grot; **music director:** Erno Rapee.

Cast: Edward G. Robinson (*Cesare Bandello, alias Rico*); Douglas Fairbanks, Jr. (*Joe Massara*); Glenda Farrell (*Olga Stassoff*); Sidney Blackmer (*Big Boy*); Thomas Jackson (*Sergeant Flaherty*); Ralph Ince (*Pete Montana*); William Collier, Jr. (*Tony Passa*); Maurice Black (*Little Arnie Lorch*); Stanley Fields (*Sam Vettori*); George E. Stone (*Otero*); Armand Kaliz (*DeVoss*); Nick Bela (*Ritz Colonna*); Noel Madison (*Pepi*); Ben Hendricks, Jr. (*Kid Bean*); Lucille La Verne (*Ma Magdalena*); Landers Stevens (*Commissioner McClure*); George Daly (*Machine gunner*); Ernie Adams (*Cashier*); Larry Steers (*Cafe guest*); Louis Natheaux (*Hood*); Kerman Cripps (*Detective*).

Publications

Script:

Faragogh, Frances, and Robert E. Lee, *Little Caesar*, edited by Gerald Peary, Madison, Wisconsin, 1981.

Books:

Tyler, Parker, *The Hollywood Hallucination*, New York, 1944.

LeRoy, Mervyn, as told to Alyce Canfield, *It Takes More Than Talent*, New York, 1953.

Connell, Brian, *Knight Errant: A Biography of Douglas Fairbanks, Jr.*, New York, 1955.

Everson, William K., *The Bad Guys*, New York, 1964.

Baxter, John, *The Gangster Film*, New York, 1970.

McArthur, Colin, *Underworld U.S.A.*, London, 1971.

Lee, Raymond, and B. C. Van Hecke, *Gangsters and Hoodlums: The Underworld in Cinema*, New York, 1971.

Bergman, Andrew, *We're in the Money: Depression America and Its Films*, New York, 1971.

Parish, James Robert, and Alvin H. Marill, *The Cinema of Edward G. Robinson*, South Brunswick, New Jersey, 1972.

Canham, Kingsley, *The Hollywood Professionals*, vol. 5, 1973, London.

Robinson, Edward G., and Leonard Spigelgass, *All My Yesterdays*, New York, 1973.

Kaminsky, Stuart M., *American Film Genres*, Dayton, Ohio, 1974; revised edition, Chicago, 1985.

LeRoy, Mervyn, *Take One*, New York, 1974.

Parish, James Robert, and Michael Pitts, *The Great Gangster Pictures*, Metuchen, New Jersey, 1976.

Shadoian, Jack, *Dreams and Dead Ends: The American Gangster/Crime Film*, Cambridge, Massachusetts, 1977.

Clarens, Carlos, *Crime Movies*, New York, 1980.

Schatz, Thomas, *Hollywood Genres*, New York, 1981.

Marill, Alvin H., *The Complete Films of Edward G. Robinson*, Secaucus, 1990.

Munby, Jonathan, *Public Enemies, Public Heroes: Screening the Gangster from Little Caesar to Touch of Evil*, Chicago, 1999.

Little Caesar

Articles:

Hall, Mordaunt, in *New York Times*, 10 January 1931.
Variety (New York), 14 January 1931.
New Yorker, 17 January 1931.
LeRoy, Mervyn, "The Making of Mervyn LeRoy," in *Films in Review* (New York), May 1953.
Eyles, Allen, "Edward G. Robinson," in *Films and Filming* (London), January 1964.
Roman, Robert, "Edward G. Robinson," in *Films in Review* (New York), August-September 1966.
Warshow, Robert, "The Gangster as Tragic Hero," in *The Immediate Experience*, New York, 1970.
Velvet Light Trap (Madison, Wisconsin), June 1971.
Kaminsky, Stuart M., "*Little Caesar* and Its Role in the Gangster Film Genre," in *Journal of Popular Culture* (Bowling Green, Ohio), Summer 1972.
Kjørup, S., "Klassiske gangsterfilm og deres baggrund," in *Kosmorama* (Copenhagen), August 1973.
Peary, Gerald, "Vers une definition du film de gangster," in *Positif* (Paris), July-August 1975.
Monthly Film Bulletin (London), November 1975.
Canham, Kingsley, "Mervyn LeRoy: Star-Making, Studio Systems, and Style," in *The Hollywood Professionals 5*, London, 1976.
Perez, M., in *Avant-Scène du Cinéma* (Paris), 1 October 1979.

* * *

Little Caesar, like any of the early 1930s gangster films, provides a convenient starting point for discussing four historical (and traditional) topics: the relationship between film and society, generic evolution, censorship and self-regulation, and sound technology. I wish to stress the interdependence of these four aspects.

Many historians cite the gangster film as one of the Hollywood genres which emerged with the dissemination of sound technology. The colloquial dialogue, jazz music, and sound effects clearly help delineate the genre, but nonetheless, the gangster film began during the silent era. Sound technology merely provided the means for a secondary step in the genre's evolution. The power of this "second phase" gangster film stems from its contemporaneous setting and social commentary on violence, organized crime, Prohibition, the Depression, and the urban environment. Addressing such topical subjects invoked the threat of censorship and led to the industry's response of self-regulation. This in turn forced the genre to change once again. Since *Little Caesar* seems most readily and specifically classified as a gangster film (as opposed to a sound film or a self-regulation film) I will focus my discussion around the film as an example of the gangster genre.

Thomas Schatz, in *Hollywood Genres*, borrows from Christian Metz and Henri Focillon to analyze the evolution of genres. He proposes four stages (from Focillon): ''experimental'' which establishes visual, structural, and thematic conventions; ''classical'' which reifies the conventions and uses them to directly address cultural values; ''refined'' which adds visual and structural flourishes but maintains cultural values through reified thematic concerns; and ''baroque'' which employs self-reflexivity, intertextuality, and most importantly, deconstructs themes and cultural values. I need only address the first three stages for *Little Caesar*.

The silent gangster films like D. W. Griffith's *Musketeers of Pig Alley* (1912), Howard Hughes's *The Racket* (1927), and Josef von Sternberg's ''trilogy'' of *Underworld* (1927), *The Dragnet* (1928), and *Thunderbolt* (1929), and the early sound films like *Thunderbolt* (which began production as a silent but also released in a sound version) and Bryan Foy's *The Lights of New York* (1928) easily fit the ''experimental'' label. They developed the basic conventions of the genre, but failed to establish a strong and direct connection to the culture.

By the early 1930s, sound technology posed few problems; the ''blimped'' camera allowed exterior shooting and mobility and sound-on-film guaranteed synchronous projection. The Depression entered its worst period. Prohibition drew to a close and, as it did, gang wars escalated; the St. Valentine's Day Massacre of 1929 focussing public attention on the organized power and violence of the gangster. This combination of events provided the necessary background for the ''classical'' phase. Films of this stage, which *Little Caesar* initiated, include two other ''standards'': *Public Enemy* (1931) and *Scarface* (1932). Together these three films express the visual, structural, and thematic values most closely associated with the genre and clearly comment on the culture of the early 1930s.

Little Caesar tells the story of the rise and fall of a petty thief, Rico Bandello, with ambition to become a crime lord. He achieves his goal, but dies under the hail of machine gun fire. *Little Caesar* celebrates the gangster, establishing Rico romantically; as a ''tragic hero'' according to Robert Warshow. As a ''tragic hero'' he must die, and he dies because of a tragic flaw. Warshow sees Rico's tragic flaw, like all gangsters, as a too strong drive for success and self-assertion.

Organized crime differs from organized business only in its means and cultural stigma. Both function as rational enterprises and permit a man to become ''self-made,'' well-known, admired by his peers, and share in the wealth of America. Rico desires the same American dream Western culture assumes we all share: upward social and economic mobility and individual recognition. Denied a legitimate route to power and success, but cursed with his ''tragic flaw,'' Rico must employ means deemed ''illegal.'' His violent deeds turn the American dream of success into an American nightmare of success.

Little Caesar also depicts society's efforts to maintain social order and similarity against Rico's criminal drive for success and individuality. Rico must fall from the top of the criminal ladder and then die to emphasize what happens to those who challenge society. Exactly what constitutes the ''crime'' for which he must fall and die? His breaking of the law or his too strong drive for personal success? Both: Rico must die legally and ideologically. Rico doesn't die simply because he transgressed the law of society, he dies because he aggressively asserted himself as an individual and as a success. Gangster films, like all genres, maintain the status quo and make it ideal. *Little Caesar* shows that crime doesn't pay and that an overriding desire for wealth, power, and individuality is culturally unhealthy.

This social commentary remained part of the gangster genre since its ''classical'' stage, but never in deeper relief than during the early 1930s. The economic plight of millions of American citizens seemed to find an answer in the gangster's method. An audience, enduring the Depression and the backlash of Prohibition (organized crime greatly expanded in urban centers), could vicariously participate in a gangster's rise to wealth and power. Yet the generic demands for the gangster's legal and ideological death would re-assure an audience that those means would ultimately prove untenable. The status quo must prevail even during the double crisis of the Depression and Prohibition.

The enormous popularity of the gangster films coupled with their romantic depiction of achieving success and fame during the Depression, led to the ''classical'' stage's quick demise. By refracting so strongly the cultural climate of the day, they posed a threat to the status quo. In 1934, the Catholic Legion of Decency formed, in part to combat the popular depiction of the gangster as a folk hero, and the Hays Office created the Production Code of America essentially for the same reason. Consequently, the ''classical'' stage lasted only four years (1930–34). With the threat of censorship, boycotts, and self-regulation, the gangster film evolved into two ''diluted'' species: what Schatz labels the ''gangster-as-cop'' variation (e.g. *G-Men* [1935] and *Racket Busters* [1938]) and the ''Cain-and-Abel'' variation (e.g. *Manhattan Melodrama* [1934] and *Angels With Dirty Faces* [1938]). Both forms constitute the ''refined'' stage. They permit stylistic flourishes yet maintain, however watered-down and disguised by style, the same themes and cultural values of the ''classical'' stage.

Little Caesar stands as a perfect example of the short-lived ''classical'' period. Rico functions as the prototype of all subsequent gangsters. His career trajectory allowed audience identification and provided a warning to embrace the status quo. That the type of film *Little Caesar* initiated flourished only briefly, attests to the strength of that identification and the calling into question of American cultural values during times of crisis.

—Greg S. Faller

THE LITTLE FOXES

USA, 1941

Director: William Wyler

Production: RKO/Radio Pictures; black and white, 35mm; running time: 115 minutes. Released 1941.

Producer: Samuel Goldwyn; **screenplay:** Lillian Hellman; **additional scenes and dialogue:** Dorothy Parker, Alan Campbell, and Arthur Kober, from the play by Lillian Hellman; **photography:** Gregg Toland; **editor:** Daniel Mandell; **production designer:** Stephen Goosson; **music:** Meredith Wilson.

The Little Foxes

Cast: Bette Davis (*Regina Giddens*); Herbert Marshall (*Horace Giddens*); Teresa Wright (*Alexandra Giddens*); Richard Carlson (*David Hewitt*); Charles Dingle (*Ben Hubbard*); Carl Benton Reid (*Oscar Hubbard*); Dan Duryea (*Leo Hubbard*); Patricia Collinge (*Birdie Hubbard*).

Publications

Books:

Noble, Peter, *Bette Davis: A Biography*, London, 1948.
Griffith, Richard, *Samuel Goldwyn: The Producer and His Films*, New York, 1956.
Reisz, Karel, *William Wyler: An Index*, London, 1958.
Davis, Bette, *The Lonely Life*, New York, 1962.
Ringgold, Gene, *The Films of Bette Davis*, New York, 1965.
Bazin, André, *What Is Cinema*, Berkeley, 1971.
Madsen, Axel, *William Wyler*, New York, 1973.
Vermilye, Jerry, *Bette Davis*, New York, 1973.
Kolodiazhnaia, V., *William Wyler*, Moscow, 1975.
Marill, Alvin R., *Samuel Goldwyn Presents*, South Brunswick, New Jersey, 1976.
Tuska, Jon, editor, *Close-Up: The Hollywood Director*, Metuchen, New Jersey, 1978.
Anderegg, Michael A., *William Wyler*, Boston, 1979.
Epstein, Lawrence J., *Samuel Goldwyn*, Boston, 1981.
Higham, Charles, *Bette: A Biography of Bette Davis*, New York, 1981.
Robinson, Jeffrey, *Bette Davis: Her Film and Stage Career*, London, 1982.
Kern, Sharon, *William Wyler: A Guide to References and Resources*, Boston, 1984.
Champion, Isabelle, *Bette Davis*, Paris, 1986.
Walker, Alexander, *Bette Davis: A Celebration*, London, 1986.
Davis, Bette, with Michael Herskowitz, *This 'n' That*, New York, 1987.
Bowman, Barbara, *Master Space: Film Images of Capra, Lubitsch, Sternberg, & Wyler*, Westport, 1992.
Jacobsen, Wolfgang, and Helga Belach, and Norbert Grob, *William Wyler*, Berlin, 1996.
Herman, Jan, *A Talent for Trouble: The Life of Hollywood's Most Acclaimed Director, William Wyler*, New York, 1997.

Articles:

Times (London), 19 January 1941.
Spectator (London), 23 January 1941.
Variety (New York), 13 August 1941.
New York Times, 22 August 1941.
Monthly Film Bulletin (London), November 1941.
Isaacs, Hermine Rich, ''William Wyler: Director with a Passion and a Craft,'' in *Theatre Arts* (New York), February 1947.
Koenig, Lester, ''Gregg Toland, Film-Maker,'' in *Screen Writer* (London), December 1947.
Slocombe, Douglas, ''The Work of Gregg Toland,'' in *Sequence* (London), Summer 1949.
Griffith, Richard, ''Wyler, Wellman, and Huston,'' in *Films In Review* (New York), February 1950.
Reisz, Karel, ''The Later Films of William Wyler,'' in *Sequence* (London), no. 13, 1951.
Quirk, Lawrence J., ''Bette Davis,'' in *Films in Review* (New York), December 1955.
Mitchell, George, ''A Great Cameraman,'' in *Films in Review* (New York), December 1956.
Reid, John Howard, ''A Little Larger Than Life,'' in *Films and Filming* (London), February and March 1960.
Hanson, Curtis Lee, ''William Wyler,'' in *Cinema* (Beverly Hills), Summer 1967.
Carey, Gary, ''The Lady and the Director: Bette Davis and William Wyler,'' in *Film Comment* (New York), Fall 1970.
Doeckel, Ken, ''William Wyler,'' in *Films in Review* (New York), October 1971.
Higham, Charles, ''William Wyler,'' in *Action* (Los Angeles), September-October 1973.
American Film (Washington, D.C.), April 1976.
Von Cottom, J., ''Les Immortels du cinéma: William Wyler,'' in *Ciné Revue* (Brussels), 30 August 1979.
Karnes, Cheryl, in *Magill's Survey of Cinema 2*, Englewood Cliffs, New Jersey, 1980.

* * *

Lillian Hellman's play, a prime example of the ''well-made'' variety, is precisely the kind of successful middle-brow property that appealed to Samuel Goldwyn. He had already produced Hellman's controversial *The Children's Hour* (also directed by William Wyler, with cinematographer Gregg Toland), a play that handsomely survived a title change to *These Three* and the transformation of the issue of lesbianism into an illicit heterosexual affair. No major alterations were required for *The Little Foxes*. The film even resists the conventional ''opening up'' so often applied to theatrical texts, in the mistaken notion that fundamental cinematic values are expansively pictorial ones.

Wyler's directing energies are deployed in the concentrated focus that suits the closed-in nature of this fiction. He exploits the closure of a house, its rooms and furniture to convey the power struggles of ambitious siblings, a rotten marriage, and the coming-of-age of the daughter, in the turn-of-the-century South. The family is the scene of an action whose violence (and theatricality) is augmented by the tightness of the area in which it is enacted. The various postures of Regina Giddens provide the fulcrum for the shots of which she is the center, and of the family configuration that she dominates. She exercises her intelligence and her desire in the manipulation of the figures around her, plotting and placing them with an expertise and a tyranny that is matched by the director himself.

The expertise was recognized by André Bazin in his essay on Wyler included in the French edition of *What Is Cinema?* Bazin analyzes the properties of hard and soft focus in the scene where Regina refuses to give her husband his medicine, while he is in the throes of a heart attack. She remains rooted in her divan during his struggle from the foreground to the background of the frame. Here, the famous Wyler-Toland deep-field staging eschews hard focus on the background. Horace's death on the staircase is a function of the hard focus on Regina's face and torso. This sort of strategy is what constitutes the cinematic in *The Little Foxes*, a film that requires great attention in order to be read in its fullness. The explicit dramaturgy is contained, of course, in the dialogue and plot. But this bourgeois drama truly challenges us in the nuances of its staging, in what must be seen rather than said about family relationships—the slight camera pan on a group of four characters as Aunt Birdie confesses her drinking, the duplicitous play of the faces of the father and son in a shaving mirror, the low camera placement that captures Regina's swaying progress up her lonely staircase.

The care of the staging and the long shot durations are what make Wyler an actor's director, and no more so than in this ensemble film, where the strength of the company enhances and is enhanced by the star performance of Bette Davis. To the actress's regret, this was her last collaboration with Wyler, the director of her great successes, *Jezebel* and *The Letter*.

—Charles Affron

LITTLE VERA

See **MALENKAYA VERA**

LIUBOV V TROEM

See **TRETIA MESHCHANSKAIA**

LOLA

West Germany, 1981

Director: Rainer Werner Fassbinder

Production: Rialto Film-Preben-Philipsen and Trio Film Westdeutschen Rundfunk; color, 35mm; running time: 115 minutes; length 10,313 feet. Released 1981, West Germany.

Producers: Rainer Werner Fassbinder with Horst Wendlundt; **screenplay:** Peter Märthesheimer, Pea Frölich, and Rainer Werner Fassbinder; **photography:** Xaver Schwarzenberger; **editors:** Juliane Lorenz and Franz Walsch (Rainer Werner Fassbinder); **sound recordists:** Vladimir Vizner and Milan Bor; **art director:** Helmut Gassner; **music:** Peer Raben; **costume designers:** Barbara Baum and Egon Strasser; **artistic consultant:** Harry Baer; **choreography:** Dieter Gackstetter; **staging:** Peter Marklewitz and Uwe Ringler.

Lola

Cast: Barbara Sukowa (*Lola*); Armin Mueller-Stahl (*Von Bohm*); Mario Adorf (*Schukert*); Matthias Fuchs (*Esslin*); Helga Feddersen (*Frau Hettich*); Karin Baal (*Lola's mother*); Ivan Desny (*Wittich*); Elisabeth Volkmann (*Gigi*); Hark Böhm (*Völker*); Karl-Heinz von Hassel (*Timmerding*); Rosel Zech (*Frau Schukert*); Sonja Neudorfer (*Frau Fink*); Christine Kaufmann (*Susi*); Y Sa Lo (*Rosa*); Günther Kaufmann (*GI*); Isolde Barth (*Frau Völker*); Harry Baer (*1st demonstrator*); Rainer Will (*2nd demonstrator*); Karsten Peters (*Editor*); Herbert Steinmetz (*Concierge*); Nino Korda (*TV delivery man*); Raul Gimenez (*1st waiter*); Udo Kier (*2nd waiter*); Andrea Heuer (*Librarian*); Ulrike Vigo (*Mariechen*); Helmut Petigk (*Bouncer*); Juliane Lorenz (*Saleswoman*); Marita Pleyer (*Rahel*); Maxim Oswald (*Grandfather Berger*).

Publications

Books:

Baer, Harry, *Schlafen kann ich, wenn ich tot bin: Das atemlose Leben des Rainer Werner Fassbinder*, Cologne, 1982.

Eckhardt, Bernd, *Rainer Werner Fassbinder: Im 17 Jahren 42 Filme—Stationen eines Lebens für den deutschen Film*, Munich, 1982.

Iden, Peter, and others, *Rainer Werner Fassbinder*, Munich, 1982.

Raab, Kurt, and Karsten Peters, *Die Sehnsucht des Rainer Werner Fassbinder*, Munich, 1982.

Foss, Paul, editor, *Fassbinder in Review*, Sydney, 1983.

Franklin, James, *New German Cinema: From Oberhausen to Hamburg*, Boston, 1983.

Fassbinder, Rainer Werner, *Film befreien den Kopf: Essays und Arbeitsnotizen*, edited by Michael Töteburg, Frankfurt, 1984.

Hayman, Ronald, *Fassbinder, Film-Maker*, London, 1984.

Phillips, Klaus, *New German Filmmakers: From Oberhausen Through the 1970s*, New York, 1984.

Fassbinder, Rainer Werner, *Die Anarchie der Phantasie: Gespräche und Interviews*, edited by Michael Töteburg, Frankfurt, 1986.

Katz, Robert, and Peter Berling, *Love Is Colder Than Death: The Life and Times of Rainer Werner Fassbinder*, London, 1987.

Elsaesser, Thomas, *New German Cinema: A History*, London, 1989.

Fassbinder, Rainer Werner, *The Anarchy of the Imagination: Interviews, Essays, Notes*, Baltimore, 1992.

Elsaesser, Thomas, *Fassbinder's Germany: History, Identity, Subject*, Amsterdam, 1996.

Watson, Wallace Steadman, *Understanding Rainer Werner Fassbinder: Film as Private and Public Art*, Columbia, 1996.

Kardish, Laurence, editor, *Rainer Werner Fassbinder*, New York, 1997.

Thomsen, Christian, *Fassbinder: The Life & Work of a Provocative Genius*, New York, 1997.

Lorenz, Juliane, editor, *Chaos As Usual: Conversations About Rainer Werner Fassbinder*, New York, 1999.

Articles:

Variety (New York), 2 September 1981.

Serceau, D., in *Image et Son* (Paris), November 1981.

Audibert, L., in *Cinématographe* (Paris), November 1981.

Magny, Joel, ''*Lola, une femme allemande*: Des fantasmes de la petite-bourgeoisie liberale et des leurs consequences politiques,'' in *Cinema* (Paris), November 1981.

Bonitzer, P., in *Cahiers du Cinéma* (Paris), November 1981.

Tobin, Yann, ''Den das ist meine Welt, und sonst gar nichts . . . ,'' in *Positif* (Paris), December 1981.

Jarto, G., in *Film & Kino*, (Oslo), 1982.

Wortzelius, H., in *Filmrutan* (Stockholm), 1982.

Caron, A., in *Jeune Cinéma* (Paris), February 1982.

Auty, Chris, in *Monthly Film Bulletin* (London), April 1982.

Nelissen, I., in *Film en Televisie* (Brussels), April 1982.

Johnson, S., in *Films and Filming* (London), May 1982.

Bernts, T., and P. Janssen, in *Skrien* (Amsterdam), May-June 1982.

Boer, L. de, in *Skoop* (Amsterdam), June 1982.

Franchi, I., in *Cinema Nuovo* (Turin), August-October 1982.

Stefanoni, L., in *Cineforum* (Bergamo), September 1982.

Hoberman, J., in *American Film* (Washington, D.C.), September 1982.

Chicoine, J. F., in *Séquences* (Montreal), October 1982.

Mravcova, M., in *Film a Doba* (Prague), November 1982.

Macbean, J. R., ''The Cinema as Self Portrait: The Final Films of R. W. Fassbinder,'' in *Cineaste* (New York), 1983.

Cinema Journal (Evanston, Illinois), Fall 1983.

Turovskaya, M., in *Iskusstvo Kino* (Moscow), December 1983.

Elbert, L., in *Cinemateca Revista* (Montevideo), January 1984.

Willemse, H., in *Skoop* (Amsterdam), November 1985.

Moeller, H.-B., ''Fassbinder's Use of Brechtian Aesthetics,'' in *Jump Cut* (Berkeley), April 1990.

Levy, Shawn, ''Rainer Werner Fassbinder: When the Movies are Great, Does Their Maker's Manner Matter?'' in *American Film*, vol. 16, no. 7, July 1991.

Schlumberger, Hella, "'I've Changed Along with the Characters in My Films': An Interview with Rainer Werner Fassbinder," in *Performing Arts Journal*, no. 41, May 1992.

Seesslen, Georg, "*Lola*," in *EPD Film* (Frankfurt), vol. 9, no. 6, June 1992.

Shattuc, Jane, "R.W. Fassbinder as a Popular Auteur: The Making of an Authorial Legend," in *Journal of Film and Video* (Atlanta), vol. 45, no. 1, Spring 1993.

Niroumand, Miriam, "German as a Foreign Language: Fassbinder on Video," in *Cineaste* (New York), vol. 20, no. 1, Winter 1993.

Medhurst, Andy, "The Long Take: Films of Rainer Werner Fassbinder," in *Sight and Sound* (London), vol. 6, no. 2, February 1996.

Indiana, Gary, "All the Rage: Retrospective on Director Rainer Werner Fassbinder at the Museum of Modern Art," in *Artforum*, vol. 35, no. 6, February 1997.

* * *

Rainer Werner Fassbinder was by far the most prolific of Germany's *Neue Welle* directors, a group which includes Volker Schlöndorff, Werner Herzog, Hans-Jürgen Syberberg, and Wim Wenders. During his short life, the controversial and iconoclastic Fassbinder directed 41 feature films of which *Lola* is arguably his best, perhaps his masterpiece.

Fassbinder's prodigious cinematic *oeuvre* abounded in political statements protesting psychological and material corruption. He held a lifelong contempt for those who lived for profit. The subject matter of the majority of his films is the post-World War II Adenauer years of Fassbinder's youth when Germany underwent its economic miracle. Fassbinder's political stance was not that of a great thinker. His socio-political philosophies emanated from his personal feelings, and his dissection of Germany's materialism was saved from total misanthropy by his abrasive wit and sense of the ironic. He disavowed those who called him a cynic by explaining, "My work is not cynical; it is realistic. Pessimistic. Life is pessimistic in the end because we die, and pessimistic in between because of corruption in our daily lives . . . . It is still the fact that you win by playing by the rules, and the pure person doesn't have much of a chance."

His depiction of the corruption which permeated his homeland was never more satisfying than in his allegorical quartet: *The Marriage of Maria Braun*, *Lili Marlene*, *Lola*, and *Veronika Voss*. These films span the social history of Germany from 1938 to the late 1950s and each is told from the point of view of a strong-willed woman (the mother country).

In *Lola*, a small town in Bavaria is controlled by the power elite, birds of prey who extort the poor and underprivileged. Led by Schukert, the building contractor, these officials conspire to gain political control over von Bohm, the new building commissioner. Their *deus ex machina* is Lola, Schukert's mistress, the mother of his illegitimate daughter and the singer in his whorehouse/cabaret. Von Bohm's moral and physical seduction by Lola is Fassbinder's cinematic metaphor for German corruption.

Lola obviously is a derivation of von Sternberg's *Der blaue Engel*, but it is only a derivation and not a re-make. The film expertly employs all of Fassbinder's filmic devices—his vivid use of color, his circular moving camera and long pans, his penchant for melodrama, his expert handling of actors, and most of all the distancing of himself and his camera from the subjects on the screen. All come together to better advantage here than in his previous works, making this easily his most accessible film.

Lola is a combination of themes from *Der blaue Engel*, Lillian Hellman's *The Little Foxes*, Ibsen's *An Enemy of the People*, and the many influences of directors Fassbinder admired, such as Godard and Douglas Sirk, and stands as the best expression of his extraordinary personal cinema.

—Ronald Bowers

LOLA MONTÈS

France-West Germany, 1955

Director: Max Ophüls

Production: Gamma-Films, Florida-Films (Paris), and Oska Films (Munich); Eastmancolor, 35mm, CinemaScope; running time: original version 110 minutes, later cut to 90 minutes; length: originally 9900 feet, later cut to 8100 feet. Released 23 December 1955. Released 23 December 1955. Re-released 1968 with 30 minutes missing. Filmed 28 February-29 July 1955 in Studio Joinville, Paris, Studio Geiselgasteig, Munich, Studio Victorine, Nice, and on location in Bavaria, Côte d'Azur, and around Paris. Cost: 650 million francs.

Producer: Albert Caraco, some sources list Ralph Baum; **screenplay:** Jacques Natanson, Annette Wademant, Max Ophüls, and (for the German version) Franz Geiger, from the novel *La Vie extraordinaire de Lola Montès* by Cecil St. Laurent; **photography:** Christian Matras; **editor:** Madeleine Gug; **sound:** Antoine Petitjean with J. Neny and H. Endrulat; **production designers:** Jean d'Eaubonne, Jacques Guth, and (for the German version) William Schatz; **music:** Georges Auric; **costume designers:** Georges Annenkov, Monique Plotin, and Marcel Escoffier; **choreography:** Helge Pawlinin.

Cast: Martine Carol (*Maria Dolorès Porriz y Montèz, alias Lola Montèz*); Peter Ustinov (*Ringmaster*); Anton Walbrook (*King Louis 1st of Bavaria*); Ivan Densy (*Lt. James, 1st husband of Lola Montèz*); Lise Delamare (*Mrs. Craigie*); Henri Guisol (*Maurice, Lola's driver*); Paulette Dubost (*Josephine, servant to Lola*); Will Quadflieg (*Franz Liszt*); Oscar Werner (*The student*); Jacques Fayet (*Steward*); Daniel Mendaille (*Captain*); Jean Gallard (*Secretary to the Baron*); Claude Pinoteau (*Orchestra leader*); Béatrice Arnac (*Circus rider*); Willy Eichberger (*Carl Esmond*); Werner Finck (*Painter*); Germaine Delbat (*Stewardess*); Helena Manson (*James's sister*); Walter Kiaulehn (*Attendant in the theater*); Willy Rösner (*1st Minister*); Friedrich Domin (*Director of the circus*); Hélène Iawkoff; Gustav Waldou (*Rhino trainer*); Betty Philipsen.

Lola Montès

Publications

Script:

Natanson, Jacques, and others, ''*Lola Montès*: Scenario and Adaptation,'' edited by Claude Beylie, in *Avant-Scène du Cinéma* (Paris), January 1969.

Books:

Leprohon, Pierre, *Présences contemporaines-cinéma*, Paris, 1957.
Willans, Geoffrey, *Peter Ustinov*, London, 1957.
Golea, A., *Georges Auric*, Paris, 1958.
Roud, Richard, *Index to the Work of Max Ophüls*, London, 1958.
Beylie, Claude, *Max Ophüls*, Brussels, 1958.
Annenkov, Georges, *Max Ophüls*, Paris, 1962.
Max Ophüls par Max Ophüls, edited by Robert Laffont, Paris, 1963.
Sarris, Andrew, *Interviews with Film Directors*, New York, 1967.
Thomas, Tony, *Ustinov in Focus*, London, 1971.
Haskell, Molly, *From Reverence to Rape*, Baltimore, 1974.
Barsacq, Leon, *Caligari's Cabinet and Other Grand Illusions: A History of Film Design*, New York, 1976.
Willemen, Paul, editor, *Ophüls*, London, 1978.
Williams, Alan Larson, *Max Ophüls and the Cinema of Desire*, New York, 1980.
Tassone, Aldo, *Max Ophüls, l'enchanteur*, Torino, 1994.
White, Susan M., *The Cinema of Max Ophüls: Magisterial Vision & the Figure of a Woman*, New York, 1995.

Articles:

Truffaut, François, in *Arts* (Paris), December 1955.
Cahiers du Cinéma (Paris), January 1956.
Audibert, Jacques, in *Cahiers du Cinéma* (Paris), February 1956.
Archer, Eugene, ''Ophüls and the Romantic Tradition,'' in *Yale French Studies* (New Haven), Summer 1956.
Interview with Ophüls, in *Cahiers du Cinéma* (Paris), June 1957.
Robinson, David, in *Sight and Sound* (London), Winter 1957–58.
Cutts, John, in *Films and Filming* (London), January 1958.
''Ophüls Issue'' of *Cahiers du Cinéma* (Paris), March 1958.

Weinberg, G., in *Films In Review* (New York), Summer 1963.
Greenspun, Roger, in *Film Society Review* (New York), October 1968.
Beylie, Claude, in *Avant-Scène du Cinéma* (Paris), January 1969.
Gilliatt, Penelope, in *New Yorker*, 3 May 1969.
Williams, Forrest, ''The Mystery of Movement: An Appreciation of Max Ophüls,'' in *Film Comment* (New York), Winter 1969.
Henderson, Brian, ''The Long Take,'' in *Film Comment* (New York), Summer 1971.
Sarris, Andrew, ''Max Ophüls: An Introduction,'' in *Film Comment* (New York), Summer 1971.
Simsolo, Noel, in *Image et Son* (Paris), March 1972.
Schmidt, K., in *Kosmorama* (Copenhagen), August 1973.
Bitomsky, H., in *Filmkritik* (Munich), June 1974.
Baumgarten, Marjorie, in *Cinema Texas Program Notes* (Austin), 6 October 1977.
''Ophüls Issue'' of *Filmkritik* (Munich), November 1977.
Robinson, David, in *Sight and Sound* (London), Autumn 1978.
Milne, Tom, in *Monthly Film Bulletin* (London), October 1978.
Gow, Gordon, in *Films and Filming* (London), October 1978.
Audibert, L., and J. Tonnorred, ''La Dernière Femme de Max Ophüls,'' in *Cinématographe* (Paris), May 1980.
Le Pavec, J. P., in *Cinema* (Paris), May 1980.
Lefèvre, Raymond, in *Image et Son* (Paris), May 1980.
Tobin, Yann, ''Ich bin die Fesche Lola . . . ,'' in *Positif* (Paris), July-August 1980.
''Schein und Sein: Glanz und Grausemkeit der Repräsentation,'' in *Frauen und Film* (Berlin), February 1981.
Ophüls, Max, ''Lola Montès mat auf den Weg,'' in *Filmkritik* (Munich), February 1982.
Britton, Andrew, and others, in *Movie* (London), Summer 1982.
Lord, S., ''Fugitive Details: Readings of Image and Context in *Madame de . . .* and *Lola Montès*,'' in *Cineaction* (Toronto), Winter-Spring 1990.
Amiel, Vincent, ''Couleurs d'Ophüls,'' in *Positif* (Paris), no. 375–376, May 1992.
Belloï, Livio, ''Max Ophüls: le cristal et la tache,'' in *Cinémathèque* (Paris), no. 6, Autumn 1994.
Douin, Jean-Luc, ''La passion des femmes,'' in *Télérama* (Paris), no. 2308, 6 April 1994.
Girard, Martin, ''Le purgatoire de *Lola Montès*,'' in *Séquences* (Haute-Ville), no. 176, January-February 1995.
Burns, Mickey, ''*Lola Montès*,'' in *CineAction* (Toronto), no. 40, May 1996.
La Rochelle, R., ''Les petites révolutions,'' in *24 Images* (Montreal), no. 83/84, Autumn 1996.

* * *

From the time of its premier in Paris in December of 1955 *Lola Montès* has created controversy with the critics and the public alike. During its initial release audiences booed the film. Some grew so rowdy that the exhibitors were forced to call in the police. An open letter appeared in *Le Figaro* pleading for restraint on the part of those patrons who remained perplexed by the film. It argued that a film as technically new and audacious as *Lola* was just the breath of fresh air the cinema needed, and that to condemn the film was to do a disservice not merely to this film but to the cinema in general. The letter was signed by Jean Cocteau, Roberto Rossellini, Jacques Tati, and Jacques Becker, among others. While less impassioned, the critical response was no less polarized. On one side the film was dismissed as boring and incoherent because of its sumptuous excess of decor, mise-en-scène and narrative convolution. On the other, by reason of this same excess, it was hailed as a masterpiece of the baroque.

Much of this controversy can be attributed to the way in which the film was touted. Hoping to capitalize on the popularity of such lush costume spectacles as *Lucrece Borgia* and *Madame Du Barry*, Gamma Films advertised a super-production based on the life and loves of the most scandalous woman of all time, Lola Montès—the Spanish-Irish cabaret dancer who became the mistress of Franz Liszt and Ludwig I, King of Bavaria. The film would feature Martine Carol, France's foremost sex goddess, then at the pinnacle of her career, and would be adapted from a novel by Cecil St. Laurent, author of a series of tastefully erotic novels, including *Caroline and Cherie*. It would boast an all-star supporting cast headed by Peter Ustinov, Anton Walbrook, and the latest heart-throb from Germany, Oskar Werner. Finally, the film was to be directed by Europe's most urbane master of the ''woman's film,'' Max Ophüls, in lavish Eastmancolor and CinemaScope. All of these ingredients promised a blockbuster, a film which would provide a titillating view of tragic love among the aristocratic classes while never overstepping the boundaries of good taste and middle-class morality.

However, this was not the film that Ophüls delivered. Instead, he chose to take aim at the very mechanism that Gamma Films was using to market the film: lurid publicity. In an interview with François Truffaut, Ophüls cites the fate of Judy Garland and Diana Barrymore, which he blamed on the public's appetite for scandal and on the entrepreneurs who shamelessly exploit scandals. ''We must kill publicity . . . I find it dreadful, this vice of wanting to know everything, this irreverence in the face of mystery. It is on this theme that I have built my film: the annihilation of the personality through the cruelty and indecency of spectacles based on scandal.'' Cinema made a voyeur of everyone—producer, performer, and spectator alike. For Ophüls the true subject of *Lola Montès* became the demystification of the publicity and exhibitionism that characterizes our era. To achieve this, he turns his customary style on its head. He sets the glittering display of his previous films against itself, and transforms his formerly refined depiction of a decadent world into a virulent condemnation of itself.

All aspects of the film's technique attempt to subvert the spectator's voyeuristic gaze and turn it back on itself. The framing device of the mammoth circus serves to distance the spectator from the events of Lola's life presented in flashback. Lola, confined in a cage, is introduced by the suitably oily ringmaster as a beast more dangerous than any other found in the circus's menagerie. Lola's entrance has been preceded by a parade of clowns representing a caricature of a parade of Lola's lovers. She is displayed on a pedestal revolving in one direction, while the camera orbits about her in a 360-degree track moving in the opposite direction. A short mime show prefaces each flashback, undermining the suspense of the episodes. Even the woodenness of Martine Carol's performance, which many critics felt marred the film, is turned to advantage. Lola is treated as an object, a beautiful but hollow doll, an empty manikin, to be invested with the fantasies of the men who possess her. Like the earrings in Ophüls's earlier *Madame De . . .* , the character of Lola functions as a focal point around which the desires of the other characters (especially those of the circus spectators) are gathered and then reflected back with striking clarity.

Ophüls mustered all his expertise in mounting this, his final film. Though it marked his first use of color and CinemaScope, what he is able to accomplish is often stunning. Each flashback is set off by a dominant hue to suggest Lola's psychological state. These range from the blue of the episode of Lola as a young girl to the autumnal yellow and ochre of her sojourn at the court of Ludwig. In his encounter with the wide-screen format, Ophüls discovered solutions to compositional problems which had perplexed users of the unwieldy aspect ratio since its inception, and which look forward to effects that Anthony Mann, Nicholas Ray, and Douglas Sirk would realize in the late 1950s. Of course in his use of the moving camera Ophüls remains without peer. The circular tracking shot which opens the film, the camera's plunge which duplicates Lola's at the climax of her performance, and the final track back revealing the line of men queuing up to pay for a brush with immortality at Lola's hand, still prove capable of taking the breath away.

When *Lola Montès* failed so miserably with Parisian audiences, the producers decided to recall all prints and despite Ophüls's protests, recut the film. Their version reduced the film from 140 to 90 minutes by abandoning the flashback structure in favor of a strict chronological rendering of the story. A happy epilogue spoken by Martine Carol was also added. This mutilated version opened in Monte Carlo in February, 1957, and succeeded only in calling forth the unanimous disapprobation of both critics and the public. It was withdrawn from further distribution. By a bitter coincidence, Ophüls died in March, 1957, without completing another film. *Lola Montès* remained unseen in any version for nearly a decade. In 1966 a group of scholars purchased the prints that remained available and patched together a version which, as far as possible, corresponds to the cut Ophüls had authorized, though it still lacks 30 minutes of the original. This version premiered in 1968, and has since become a staple of film societies and re-run houses around the world. It has been justly hailed as Ophüls's masterpiece and, as Claude Beylie has written, after *Rules of the Game* and *Citizen Kane*, it is ''the third and decisive stage in the development of modern cinema.''

—Dennis Nastav

LOLITA

UK, 1962

Director: Stanley Kubrick

Production: AA Productions. An Anya Productions/Transworld Pictures production, in association with Seven Arts Productions, for MGM; black and white; running time: 153 minutes; length: 13,798 feet. Released June 1962.

Producer: James B. Harris; **screenplay:** Vladimir Nabokov, from his own novel; **additional dialogue:** Stanley Kubrick; **second unit director:** Dennis Stock; **assistant directors:** René Dupont, Roy Millichip, John Danischewsky; **photography:** Oswald Morris; **camera operator:** Denys N. Coop; **editor:** Anthony Harvey; **assistant editor:** Lois Gray; **sound editor:** Winston Ryder; **sound recordists:** Len Shilton, H. L. Bird; **art directors:** Bill Andrews, Sidney Cain; **music:** Nelson Riddle.

Cast: James Mason (*Humbert Humbert*); Sue Lyon (*Lolita Haze*); Shelley Winters (*Charlotte Haze*); Peter Sellers (*Clare Quilty*); Diana Decker (*Jean Farlow*); Jerry Stovin (*John Farlow*); Suzanne Gibbs (*Mona Farlow*); Gary Cockrell (*Richard Schiller*); Marianne Stone (*Vivian Darkbloom*); Cec Linder (*Physician*); Lois Maxwell (*Nurse Mary Lore*); William Greene (*George Swine*); C. Denier Warren (*Potts*); Isobel Lucas (*Louise*); Maxine Holden (*Receptionist*); James Dyrenforth (*Beale*); Roberta Shore (*Lorna*); Eric Lane (*Roy*); Shirley Douglas (*Mrs. Starch*); Roland Brand (*Bill*); Colin Maitland (*Charlie*); Irvine Allen (*Hospital Attendant*); Marion Mathie (*Miss Lebone*); Craig Sams (*Rex*); John Harrison (*Tom*).

Publications

Script:

Nabokov, Vladimir, *Lolita*, New York, 1974; second edition, 1983.

Books:

Austen, David, *The Cinema of Stanley Kubrick*, London, 1969.
Walker, Alexander, *Stanley Kubrick Directs*, New York, 1972.
Kagan, Norman, *The Cinema of Stanley Kubrick*, New York, 1972.
Devries, Daniel, *The Films of Stanley Kubrick*, Grand Rapids, Michigan, 1973.
Hirschhorn, Clive, *The Films of James Mason*, London, 1975.
Phillips, Gene D., *Stanley Kubrick: A Film Odyssey*, New York, 1977.
Winters, Shelley, *Shelly, Also Known as Shirley*, New York, 1980.
Ciment, Michel, *Kubrick*, Paris, 1980; revised edition, 1987; translated as *Kubrick*, London, 1983.
Kolker, Robert Philip, *A Cinema of Loneliness: Penn, Kubrick, Coppola, Scorsese, Altman*, Oxford, 1980; revised edition, 1988.
Walker, Alexander, *Peter Sellers: The Authorised Biography*, London, 1981.
Sylvester, Derek, *Peter Sellers: An Illustrated Biography*, London, 1981.
Hummel, Christoph, editor, *Stanley Kubrick*, Munich, 1984.
Brunetta, Gian Piero, *Stanley Kubrick: Tempo, spazio, storia, e mondi possibili*, Parma, 1985.
Falsetto, Mario, *Stanley Kubrick: A Narrative and Stylistic Analysis*, Westport, 1994.
Jenkins, Greg, *Stanley Kubrick and the Art of Adaptation: Three Novels, Three Films*, Jefferson, 1997.
Howard, James, *Stanley Kubrick Companion*, London, 1999.
Sweeney, Kevin, *James Mason: A Bio-Bibliography*, Westport, 1999.
Garcia Mainar, Luis M., *Narrative & Stylistic Patterns in the Films of Stanley Kubrick*, Rochester, 2000.
Nelson, Thomas Allen, *Kubrick: Inside a Film Artist's Maze*, Bloomington, 2000.

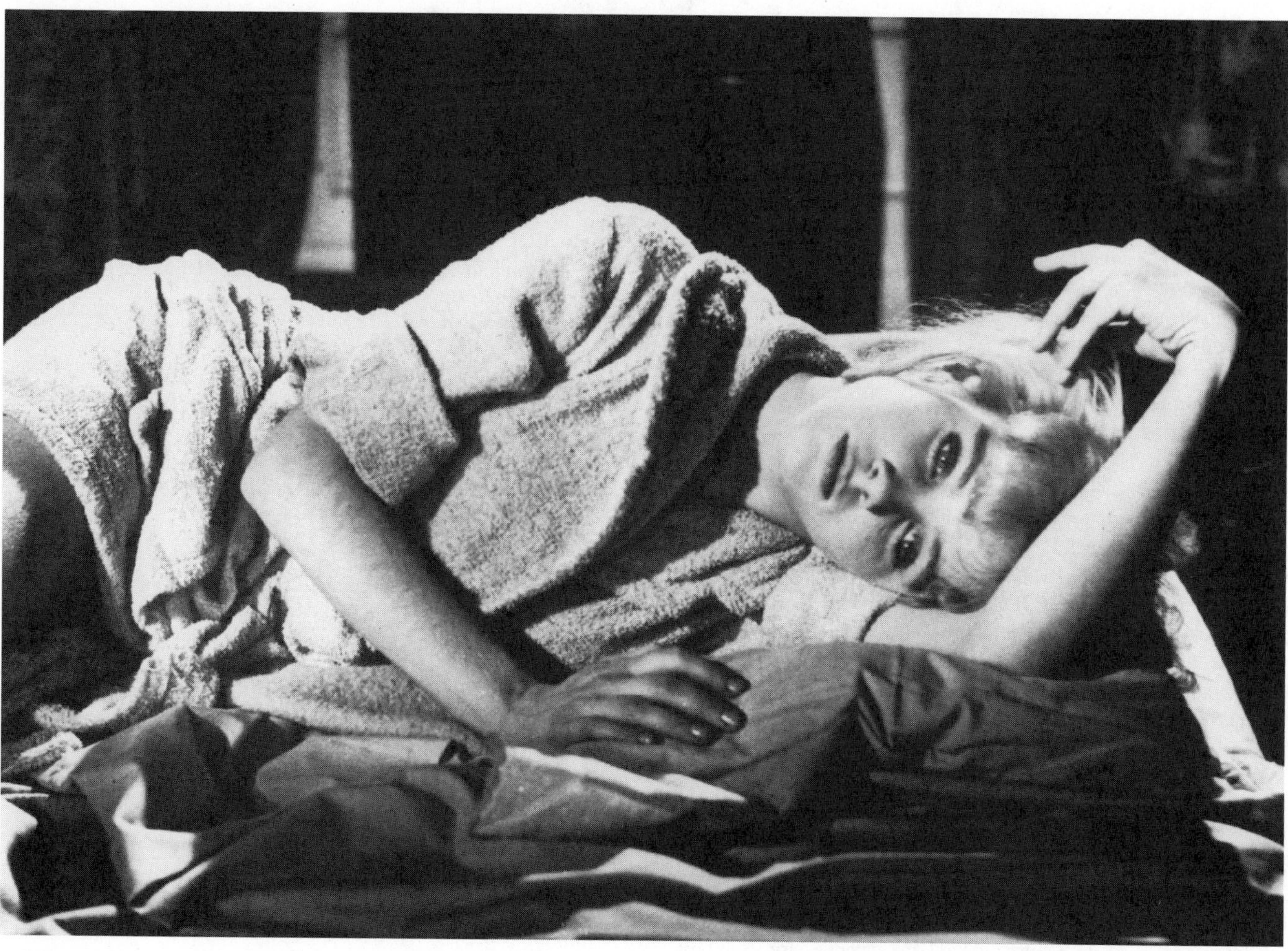

Lolita

Articles:

Hollywood Reporter, 13 June 1962.
Variety (New York), 13 June 1962.
New York Times, 14 June 1962.
Kine Weekly (London), 6 September 1962.
Croce, Arlene, in *Sight and Sound* (London), Autumn 1962.
Monthly Film Bulletin (London), October 1962.
Buckley, Michael, ''Shelley Winters,'' in *Films in Review* (New York), March 1970.
Posthumus, P., in *Skrien* (Amsterdam), February 1982.
Sineux, M., ''Lolita: De mirage en cauchemar,'' in *Positif* (Paris), March 1984.
Combs, Richard, in *Monthly Film Bulletin* (London), August 1984.
Burns, D. E., ''Pistols and Cherry Pies: Lolita from Page to Screen,'' in *Literature/Film Quarterly* (Salisbury, Maryland), October 1984.
Combs, Richard, ''Motel Passion,'' in *Listener* (London), 12 April 1985.
Schrader, Paul, ''*Lolita*,'' in *American Film*, vol. 15, no. 1, October 1989.
''Quilty by Suspicion,'' in *New Yorker*, vol. 68, 18 January 1993.
Bick, Ilsa J., and Krin Gabbard, '''That Hurts!': Humor and Sadomasochism in *Lolita*: The Circulation of Sadomasochistic Desire in the *Lolita* Texts,'' in *Journal of Film and Video* (Atlanta), vol. 46, no. 2, Summer 1994.
Gabbard, Krin, ''The Circulation of Sadomasochistic Desire in the *Lolita* Texts,'' in *Journal of Film and Video* (Atlanta), vol. 46, no. 2, 1994.
Elia, M., ''*Lolita* de Stanley Kubrick,'' in *Séquences* (Haute-Ville), no. 189/190, March/June 1997.
Taubin, A., ''Hell's Belles,'' in *Village Voice* (New York), vol. 42, 29 April 1997.
McGinn, Colin, ''The Moral Case for *Lolita*,'' in *Times Literary Supplement*, no. 4926, 29 August 1997.
Seesslen, G., ''3x *Lolita*,'' in *EPD Film* (Frankfurt), vol. 15, January 1998.

*   *   *

Undoubtedly a film by a great director benefits from being seen again in retrospect, since the films he has directed subsequently shed a new light on it. Such is the case with *Lolita* (1962), misunderstood at the time of its release when Kubrick's status as an *auteur* was not yet firmly established. The reputation of Vladimir Nabokov, author of the original and scandalous book, overshadowed the director's attempt at translating it for the screen. Two main criticisms were levelled at the film: one was its ''betrayal'' of a literary masterpiece, its failure to create an equivalent style, while the other was the disappointment of many who expected a titillating erotic experience. Seen today *Lolita* appears as a turning point in Kubrick's career.

On the most superficial level it marks his departure from America (to which he would never return). Because of the pressure of the moral leagues and also probably for financial reasons, Kubrick decided to shoot the film in London and decided to settle there. *Lolita* is the first feature where he decides to recreate a concrete world (the American province and its highways) in the artificial setting of a studio as he would with the Vietnam war of *Full Metal Jacket*. But more deeply *Lolita* is a study of madness that anticipates *Dr. Strangelove* and *The Shining*. Because of the censorship problems Kubrick displaced the focus of the story from the nymphet's relationship with an older man (Sue Lyon was too old to be a convincing nymphet anyway) to the obsessional nightmare of Humbert Humbert. From the first shot of Lolita appearing in a sunlit garden the film progressively becomes a journey to the end of the night which leads James Mason to a crisis of insanity in a dark hospital corridor and the murder of Clare Quilty (Peter Sellers) among the shadows of a baroque mansion.

The producer, James B. Harris, and Kubrick had acquired the rights of the novel in 1958 in the wake of their recent successes *The Killing* (1956) and *Paths of Glory* (1957). Asked to write an adaptation Nabokov delivered a script that would have led to a seven-hour film. He resumed work on it but eventually Kubrick changed it considerably, more than the credits suggest. In the foreword to his original screenplay, published in 1974, Nabokov writes, with wry humor and admiration, ''At a private screening I had discovered that Kubrick was a great director, that his *Lolita* was a first-rate film with magnificent actors and that only ragged odds and ends of my script had been used . . . . My first reaction to the picture was a mixture of aggravation, regret, and reluctant pleasure.''

The transformations made by Kubrick were all directed towards black humor and a sense of the grotesque. He particularly developed the character of Clare Quilty, a kind of superego for Humbert Humbert (Sellers, in anticipation of his three roles in *Dr. Strangelove*, disguises himself as a school psychiatrist, the threatening Dr. Zemph, and also a member of a Police convention, being clearly marked as an authority figure) and introduced scenes of macabre irony, like the ping-pong game before Quilty's murder.

Kubrick also emphasizes the social satire, looking at the American small town's life from the point of view of the visiting European Professor (played by the always suave and sophisticated English actor James Mason), as if he, who had just settled in England, were already a stranger in his own country. The scene in the drive-in with Lolita and her mother, the chess-game, and his listening to the mourners after Charlotte's death as he sits in the bath-tub are obvious examples of this satirical look at the vulgarity of the middle-class.

Followed as it was by the science-fiction trilogy (*Dr. Strangelove*, *2001: A Space Odyssey*, and *A Clockwork Orange*) *Lolita* may have looked at one time to be far away from Kubrick's new concerns. However, both *Barry Lyndon* and *The Shining*, two studies (among other elements) of domestic life, force us to look back on the earlier film with its intimation of the work to come. Kubrick casts the same cold eye and adopts the same pessimistic derision as he portrays the fate of his masochistic hero. But at the same time he lets the emotions come through at key moments, allowing Humbert Humbert to appear as a three-dimensional character, a rare feature in Kubrick's films, which generally tend to offer stylized heroes or abstract silhouettes.

—Michel Ciment

LONE STAR

USA, 1996

Director: John Sayles

Production: Columbia Pictures; color, 35 mm, Panavision; running time: 135 minutes; length: 3781 meters. Filmed in Eagle Pass, Texas. Cost: $5 million.

Producer: R. Paul Miller, Maggie Renzi, John Sloss (executive), Jan Foster (associate); **screenplay:** John Sayles; **cinematograper:** Stuart Dryburgh; **editor:** John Sayles; **music:** Mason Daring; **casting:** Avy Kaufman; **production design:** Dan Bishop; **art direction:** J. Kyler Black; **set decoration:** Dianna Freas; **costume design:** Shay Cunliffe.

Cast: Stephen Mendillo (*Cliff*); Stephen J. Lang (*Mikey*); Chris Cooper (*Sam Deeds*); Elizabeth Peña (*Pilar Cruz*); Oni Faida Lampley (*Celie*); Eleese Lester (*Molly*); Joe Stevens (*Deputy Travis*); Gonzalo Castillo (*Amado*); Richard Coca (*Enrique*); Clifton James (*Mayor Hollis Pogue*); Tony Frank (*Fenton*); Miriam Colon (*Mercedes Cruz*); Kris Kristofferson (*Sheriff Charlie Wade*); Jeff Monahan (*Young Hollis*); Matthew McConaughey (*Buddy Deeds*); Frances McDormand (*Bunny*); and others.

Publications

Script:

Sayles, John, *Men with Guns and Lone Star*, New York, 1998.

Books:

Sayles, John, and Gavin Smith, *Sayles on Sayles*, New York, 1998.
Ryan, Jack, *John Sayles, Filmmaker: A Critical Study of the Independent Writer-Director*, Jefferson, 1998.
Carson, Diane, *John Sayles: Interviews*, Jackson, 1999.
Molyneaux, Gerry, *John Sayles: An Unauthorized Biography of the Pioneering Indie Filmmaking*, Los Angeles, 2000.

Articles:

Ratner, M., ''Borderlines,'' in *Filmmaker: The Magazine of Independent Film* (Los Angeles), vol. 4, no. 4, 1996.
Smith, Galvin, ''John Sayles: 'I Don't Want to Blow Anything by People,''' in *Film Comment* (New York), vol. 32, no. 3, May-June 1996.
Sayles, John, and Tod Lippy, ''*Lone Star*: Writing and Directing *Lone Star*,'' in *Scenario* (Rockville), vol. 2, no. 2, Summer 1996.
Comer, Brooke, ''Sayles Concocts Authentic Tex-Mex Murder Mystery,'' in *American Cinematographer* (Hollywood), vol. 77, no. 6, June 1996.

Lone Star

Alexander, Max, ''Sayles-manship,'' in *Variety* (New York), vol. 363, no. 7, 17 June 1996.
Ungar, Sanford J., ''Immigrants' Tale, In Subtle Shades of Gray,'' in *New York Times*, 23 June 1996.
Spines, Christine, ''John Sayles,'' in *Premiere* (Boulder), vol. 9, no. 11, July 1996.
Holden, Stephen, ''Real Men: An Endangered Species on Film,'' in *New York Times*, 7 July 1996.
Simon, J., ''Small-Town Sagas,'' in *National Review*, vol. 48, 29 July 1996.
Nechak, P., ''Rapping with John Sayles,'' in *Moviemaker Magazine* (Los Angeles), no. 20, July/August 1996.
Blake, R.A., ''Texas Mosaic,'' in *America*, vol. 175, 3 August 1996.
Curtis, Gregory, ''Shooting on the Border,'' in *Texas Monthly*, vol. 24, no. 8, August 1996.
Sipe, Jeffrey R., ''Low Budget, High Art: Critically Acclaimed Independent Filmmaker John Sayles Proves That Less Equals More,'' in *Insight on the News*, vol. 12, no. 31, 19 August 1996.
Andrew, Geoff, ''Classified Sayles,'' in *Time Out* (London), no. 1363, 2 October 1996.
West, Dennis, and Joan M. West, ''Borders and Boundaries: *Lone Star*,'' in *Cineaste* (New York), vol. 22, no. 3, December 1996.
Menard, Valerie, ''Best and Worst of 1996,'' in *Hispanic*, vol. 9, no. 12, December 1996.
Philippon, A., ''A Star is Dead,'' in *Trafic* (Paris), no. 21, Spring 1997.
Linfield, Susie, ''American Graffiti: Reflections on Race, Memory and Dreams,'' in *The Nation*, vol. 268, no. 3, 5 April 1999.
Goodale, Gloria, ''Risk-Taking Director: In Life and On Screen,'' in *Christian Science Monitor*, 4 June 1999.
Stein, Harry, ''How John Sayles Learned to Stop Worrying and Love the Studio,'' in *Premiere* (Boulder), vol. 12, no. 11, July 1999.

* * *

The final words of *Lone Star* are ''Forget the Alamo.'' Along the Tex-Mex border—a region which, as local sheriff Sam Deeds remarks with laconic understatement, ''has seen a good number of disagreements over the years''—the past weighs heavy, distorting relationships between individuals, generations, and whole communities. ''All that stuff, that history—the hell with it, right?,'' says Sam's lover Pilar, aiming to break free from the trap of past guilts and enmities and start from scratch. According to John Sayles, the film is ''about history and what we do with it. Do we use it to hit each other? Is it something that drags us down?. . . At what point do you say about your parents, 'That was them, this is me?'''

Even so, the phrase, ''Forget the Alamo''—which Sayles at one point considered as a title for the film—shouldn't be taken too literally. Neither Pilar (a history teacher, after all) nor Sayles is suggesting anything so crude as simply junking the past, even if any of us could. *Lone Star* develops the theme that has underpinned all Sayles's work to date: the sense of character as a product of accumulated social and cultural influences, the way people are moulded by their backgrounds—but can surmount that conditioning if they try hard enough. ''Blood only means what you let it,'' bar-owner Otis Payne tells his grandson, even while teaching him to be proud of his mixed Afro-Seminole ancestry. ''Most people,'' says Cody, the redneck barman, ''don't want their salt and sugar in the same jar,'' but under his morose gaze two army sergeants, one black and one white, are giving him the lie as they plan their life together.

With *Lone Star* Sayles returned to the broad-canvas, multiple-character mode of *Matewan* and *City of Hope.* In many ways the film forms a companion-piece to *City of Hope*—one northern and urban, the other southern and smalltown-rural, but both tracing lines of tension and interconnection between a wide spread of individuals, charting the social cross-currents and showing how these people impinge on each other, no matter how hard they try to keep themselves separate. Several characters in *Lone Star* strive to stay aloof: Mercedes Cruz, proud of her American citizenship, rejecting her own Hispanic background; Delmore Payne, Otis's estranged son, retreating into the rigid disciplines of army life; the Anglo parents at the school, resentful at finding themselves a minority in ''their'' community. *Lone Star* is a film about connections and also, as Sayles notes, ''a film about borders'' which, however artificial, must be acknowledged—but can still be crossed. In the final scene Sam and Pilar decide to cross one of the most fundamental borders of all, the incest taboo, since it matters less than their own happiness.

In its visual style, too, the film elides borders. Flashbacks are presented, not by cuts or dissolves, but by the camera simply panning left or right, up or down into a different time-zone that nonetheless occupies part of the same space. The past, Sayles implies, *isn't* another country; it's still here and people like Sam are living in it, carrying it with them. And as the flashbacks accumulate, the line between moral absolutes also starts to blur. At first the two former sheriffs, Charlie Wade and Sam's father Buddy, are seen as polar opposites: bad guy and good guy, ''your ol' time bribe and bullets sheriff'' versus the paragon of civic integrity. But as Sam, weary of living in his dead father's shadow, digs away around the feet of the idol to expose the clay, a less clear-cut, more human figure emerges: a man less bad than Sam wants him to be, but less perfect than the legend paints him. ''It's not like there's a borderline between the good people and the bad people,'' Otis observes.

At times, the film's narrative density becomes excessive; Sayles (a fine novelist in his own right) seems to be aiming for a novel-like complexity, and several minor plot strands could be dropped without much damage. But *Lone Star*'s ambitions easily outweigh its defects; while breaking new ground in Sayles's ongoing exploration of the American myth, it retains his key qualities of intelligence, political acuteness, and narrative lucidity. An actors' director par excellence, he draws fine, naturalistic performances from his whole cast, besides giving Kris Kristofferson (as the corrupt, chuckling Charlie Wade) his first worthwhile role in years.

Sayles has always taken an inventive, oblique angle on genre, and in *Lone Star* he turns the conventions and vocabulary of the Western to his own ends. The central strand of a man gradually stripping the legend away from an admired father-figure carries echoes of Bertoluccils *Spider's Stratagem* (to say nothing of *Citizen Kane*). But, although Sayles has often said he wants his films to make people think about their own lives, not about other films, *Lone Star*'s overall structure, and especially its final revelation, come so close to the crux of *The Man Who Shot Liberty Valance* that it can only be intentional. The whole film, in fact, could be read as a covert critique of the earlier movie: where John Ford saw the passing of the old gun-law West as a matter for nostalgia and regret, Sayles celebrates the growth in tolerance and civic order it represents. And it says a lot for Sayles's achievement that, even set against Ford's elegiac classic, *Lone Star* isn't in the least diminished by the comparison.

—Philip Kemp

THE LONELY WIFE

See **CHARULATA**

THE LOST WEEKEND

USA, 1945

Director: Billy Wilder

Production: Paramount; black and white; running time: 99 minutes; length: 8,912 feet. Released August 1945.

Producer: Charles Brackett; **screenplay:** Charles Brackett and Billy Wilder, from the novel by Charles R. Jackson; **photography:** John F.

The Lost Weekend

Seitz; **process photography:** Farciot Edouart; **special effects:** Gordon Jennings; **editor:** Doane Harrison; **art directors:** Hans Dreier, Earl Hedrick; **music:** Miklos Rozsa, Guiseppe Verdi.

Cast: Ray Milland (*Don Birnam*); Jane Wyman (*Helen St. James*); Phillip Terry (*Wick Birnam*); Doris Dowling (*Gloria*); Frank Feylen (*Bim*); Mary Young (*Mrs. Deveridge*); Lillian Fontaine (*Mrs. St. James*); Anita Bolster (*Mrs. Foley*); Lewis R. Russell (*Charles St. James*); Helen Dickson (*Mrs. Frink*); David Clyde (*Dave*); Eddie Laughton (*Mr. Brophy*).

Awards: Oscars for Best Actor (Milland), Best Picture, Best Director and Best Screenplay.

Publications

Script:

Brackett, Charles, and Billy Wilder, *The Lost Weekend*, in *The Best Film Plays of 1945*, edited by John Gassner and Dudley Nichols, New York, 1946.

Books:

Madsen, Axel, *Billy Wilder*, Bloomington, Indiana, 1969.
Zolotow, Maurice, *Billy Wilder in Hollywood*, New York, 1977, 1988.
Seidman, Steve, *The Film Career of Billy Wilder*, Boston, 1977.
Cook, Jim, and Mike Lewington, editors, *Images of Alcoholism*, London, 1979.
Sinyard, Neil, and Adrian Turner, *Journey Down Sunset Boulevard: The Films of Billy Wilder*, Ryde, Isle of Wight, 1979.
Dick, Bernard F., *Billy Wilder*, Boston, 1980, 1996.
Ciment, Michel, *Les Conquérants d'un nouveau monde: Essais sur le cinéma américain*, Paris, 1981.
Giannetti, Louis, *Masters of the American Cinema*, Englewood Cliffs, New Jersey, 1981.
Morella, Joe, and Edward B. Epstein, *Jane Wyman*, New York, 1985.
Jacob, Jerome, *Billy Wilder*, Paris, 1988.
Seidl, Claudius, *Billy Wilder: Seine Filme, sein Leben*, Munich, 1988.
Lally, Kevin, *Wilder Times: The Life & Times of Billy Wilder*, New York, 1995.
Crowe, Cameron, *Conversations with Wilder*, New York, 1999.
Armstrong, Richard, *Billy Wilder: American Film Realist*, Jefferson, 2000.

Articles:

Monthly Film Bulletin (London), no. 142, 1945.
Hollywood Reporter, 14 August 1945.
Variety (New York), 15 August 1945.
Motion Picture Herald (New York), 18 August 1945.
Kine Weekly (London), 27 September 1945.
Powell, Dilys, in *Sunday Times* (London), 7 October 1945.
New York Times, 3 December 1945.
Sight and Sound (London), Winter 1945–46.
Milland, Ray, ''The Role I Liked Best,'' in *Saturday Evening Post* (Philadelphia), 8 November 1947.
Agee, James, in *Agee on Film 1*, New York, 1958.
Magill's Survey of Cinema 3, Englewood Cliffs, New Jersey, 1981.
''Le poison,'' in *Revue du Cinéma* (Paris), no. 441, 1988.
Alix, Y., ''Un, deux, trois Wilder,'' in *Positif* (Paris), no. 336, February 1989.
''*The Lost Weekend*,'' in *Reid's Film Index* (Wyong), no. 4, 1990.
Pichler, O.H., ''Some Like It Black,'' in *Blimp* (Graz), no. 18, Fall 1991.
Hirschman, E.C., ''A Cinematic Depiction of Drug Addiction: A Semiotic Account,'' in *Semiotica*, vol. 104, no. 1/2, 1995.
Linville, James, ''The Art of Screenwriting,'' in *Paris Review*, vol. 38, no. 138, Spring 1996.
Prelutsky, Burt, ''An Interview with Billy Wilder,'' in *Michigan Quarterly Review*, vol. 35, no. 1, Winter 1996.
Thomas, T., ''Rozsa noir,'' in *Film Score Monthly* (Los Angeles), vol. 2, no. 3, 1997.

* * *

This was Hollywood's first serious treatment of the problem of alcoholism and was made in spite of studio jitters, and protests from the brewers that it would *dis*courage drinking and from prohibitionists that it would *en*courage it. It also was something of a landmark in Wilder's output; as he put it, ''it was after this picture that people started noticing me.'' The film also contains the finest performance which Ray Milland had so far given in his career; however, like Gloria Swanson in *Sunset Boulevard* he was to find the role something of a mixed blessing. Bob Hope's quip on finding a hidden bottle (in *My Favorite Brunette*) ''Ray Milland's been here'' was the expression, albeit in comic form, of a certain tendency to confuse Milland with Don Birnam, the failed, alcoholic writer at the centre of *The Lost Weekend.*

The story is simple and covers five days in the life of an alcoholic who has more or less conspired to get rid of his girlfriend and brother for the weekend so that he can indulge in a massive binge. It ends with her returning and encouraging him to try to write a book about his experiences in the hope that this may keep him off the bottle. There is no such ray of hope, incidentally, at the end of Charles Jackson's original novel. Furthermore, the script also suppresses the suggestion that Birnam's drinking may be due to closet gayness, though this doesn't stop it representing the sadistic nurse in the Bellevue Hospital alcoholic ward in unmistakably gay terms.

In other respects, however, the film was undoubtedly very daring for its time, and even the ''happy ending'' is not particularly reassuring in the light of what has gone before. As Wilder himself put it ''we don't say that the man is cured. We just try to suggest that if he can lick his illness long enough to put some words down on paper, then there must be some hope.'' Certainly, for the most part, the film avoids sugar coating or preachy-ness and isn't even particularly concerned with the reasons for Birnam's state. Rather, it tries to communicate what it's like actually to be an alcoholic. But although very much a ''first person'' film, like *Double Indemnity* and *Sunset Boulevard*, it largely avoids voice-over narration and the usual ''subjective'' visual devices. This means that when they *are* used—as when Birnam falls downstairs, or in the horrific hallucination in which a bat appears to kill a mouse—they are all the more effective for being sparingly applied. Nonetheless, the whole *mise-en-scène is* the expression of Birnam's bleary, drink obsessed perspective. Everything looks drained, bleak and tawdry, the frame seems haunted by bottles, and at the opera all he can focus on in *La Traviata* are the tempting glasses in the famous ''Drinking Song.'' Rosza's Theremin-dominated score is the perfect counterpoint to this eerie, hazy vision of a world at one remove from reality. One of the film's supreme achievements in conjuring this effect is Birnam's famous walk up Third Avenue in an attempt to pawn his typewriter so that he can carry on drinking. Wilder had considerable difficulty in getting the studio to let him take his cameras out on the street, as location shooting was still relatively uncommon in those days, but the effect (which was achieved by hiding the cameras in trucks) is quite remarkable. Birnam's walk developing into a veritable Via Crucis as he discovers that all the pawn shops are closed for Yom Kippur.

Later, other movies such as *Smash Up, I'll Cry Tomorrow*, and *Days of Wine and Roses* would tackle the theme of alcoholism impressively enough. Addicts of one kind or another also crop up in other Wilder films such as *Some Like It Hot, The Private Life of Sherlock Holmes*, and *Fedora*. None of these, however, can match *The Lost Weekend*'s sheer unremitting quality, its terrifying sense of an ineluctable descent into the depths.

—Julian Petley

LOUISIANA STORY

USA, 1948

Director: Robert Flaherty

Production: Robert Flaherty Productions, Inc. (Standard Oil of New Jersey); black and white, 35mm; running time: 77 minutes. Released September 1948, New York by Lopert Pictures, premiered at Edinburgh Film Festival, August 1948. Filmed in Louisiana bayou country. Cost: $258,000.

Producers: Robert Flaherty with Richard Leacock and Helen Van Dongen; **screenplay:** Robert Flaherty and Frances Flaherty, from their original story; **photography:** Richard Leacock; **editors:** Helen Van Dongen, assisted by Ralph Rosenblum; **sound:** Benjamin Donniger; **music:** Virgil Thompson; **music performed by:** Philadelphia Orchestra under Eugene Ormandy.

Cast: Joseph Boudreaux (*Boy*); Lionel Le Blanc (*Father*); Mrs. E. Bienvenu (*Mother*); Frank Hardy (*The driller*); C. T. Guedry (*His boilerman*).

Award: Venice International Film Festival, International Award for "its lyrical beauty," 1948.

Publications

Books:

Gromo, Mario, *Robert Flaherty*, Parma, 1952.
Reisz, Karel, *The Technique of Film Editing*, New York, 1953; London, 1958.
Flaherty, Frances, *The Odyssey of a Film-Maker: Robert Flaherty's Story*, Urbana, Illinois, 1960.
Cuenca, Carlos Fernandez, *Robert Flaherty*, Madrid, 1963.
Clemente, Jose, *Robert Flaherty*, Madrid, 1963.
Calder-Marshall, Arthur, *The Innocent Eye: The Life of Robert Flaherty*, London, 1963; New York, 1966.
Klaue, Wolfgang, editor, *Robert Flaherty*, Berlin, 1964.
Agel, Henri, *Robert J. Flaherty*, Paris, 1965.
Thomson, Virgil, *Virgil Thomson*, New York, 1966; London, 1967.
Griffith, Richard, *The World of Robert Flaherty*, New York, 1970.
Barsam, Richard, *Nonfiction Film: A Critical History*, New York, 1973.
Armes, Roy, *Film and Reality: An Historical Survey*, Baltimore, 1974.
Barnouw, Erik, *Documentary: A History of the Non-Fiction Film*, New York, 1974.
Napolitano, Antonio, *Robert J. Flaherty*, Florence, 1975.
Murphy, William T., *Robert Flaherty: A Guide to References and Resources*, Boston, 1978.
Rosenblum, Ralph, and Robert Karen, *When the Shooting Stops . . . the Cutting Starts: A Film Editor's Story*, New York, 1979.
Williams, Christopher, *Realism and Cinema: A Reader*, London, 1980.
Rotha, Paul, *Robert J. Flaherty: A Biography*, Philadelphia, 1983.
Barsam, Richard M., *The Vision of Robert Flaherty: The Artist As Myth & Filmmaker*, Bloomington, 1988.
Orbanz, Eva, *Filming Robert Flaherty's Louisiana Story: The Helen Van Dongen Diary*, New York, 1998.

Articles:

Roullet, Serge, in *Revue du Cinéma* (Paris), April 1948.
Variety (New York), 22 September 1948.
New York Times, 29 September 1948.
"Old Master," in *Time* (New York), 20 September 1948.
Weinberg, Herman, in *Sight and Sound* (London), Autumn 1948.
Life (New York), 4 October 1948.
Losey, Mary, "More Seeing, Less Selling," in *Saturday Review* (New York), 9 October 1948.
Hatch, Robert, in *New Republic* (New York), 11 October 1948.
Carancini, Gaetano, in *Bianco e Nero* (Rome), April 1949.
"How He Made the *Louisiana Story* in the Bayous of Louisiana," in *Travel* (New York), May 1949.
Houston, Penelope, "Interview with Flaherty," in *Sight and Sound* (London), December 1949.
Taylor, Robert Lewis, "Flaherty—Education for Wanderlust," in *The Running Pianist*, New York, 1950.
Gray, Hugh, "Robert Flaherty and the Naturalist Documentary," in *Hollywood Quarterly*, Fall 1950.
Van Dongen, Helen, "350 Cans of Film," in *Cinema 51*, London, 1951.
Flaherty, Robert, "Films: Language of the Eye," in *Theatre Arts* (New York), May 1951.
Sammis, Edward, "Flaherty at Abbeville," in *Sight and Sound* (London), December 1951.
George, George L., "The World of Robert Flaherty," in *Film News* (New York), no. 4, 1953.
Manvell, Roger, in *The Film and the Public*, London, 1955.
Flaherty, Frances, "Explorations," and "Robert Flaherty: The Man and the Filmmaker" by Charles Siepmann, in *Film Book I: The Audience and the Filmmaker*, edited by Robert Hughes, New York, 1959.
Stanbrook, Alan, and Ralph Stephenson, in *Films and Filming* (London), December 1961.
Van Dongen, Helen, "Robert J. Flaherty," in *Film Quarterly* (Berkeley), Summer 1965.

Louisiana Story

Weinberg, Gretchen, in *Film Culture* (New York), Summer 1966.

Sadoul, Georges, ''A Flaherty Mystery,'' in *Cahiers due Cinema in English* (New York), September 1967.

Fondiller, Harvey, ''Bob Flaherty Remembered,'' in *Popular Photography* (Boulder, Colorado), March 1970.

Leacock, Richard, ''Remembering Frances Flaherty,'' in *Film Comment* (New York), November-December 1972.

Achtenberg, Ben, ''Helen Van Dongen: An Interview,'' in *Film Quarterly* (Berkeley), Winter 1976.

Skoop (Amsterdam), December 1979.

Holm, Sally V., in *Magill's Survey of Cinema 3*, Englewood Cliffs, New Jersey, 1980.

Leacock, R., ''The Making of *Louisiana Story*,'' in *Southern Quarterly*, vol. 23, no. 1, 1984.

Starr, C., ''Robert Flaherty's *Louisiana Story*,'' in *Southern Quarterly*, vol. 23, no. 1, 1984.

Lerner, Jesse, ''Flaherty in Motion: The 38th Annual Robert Flaherty Film Seminar,'' in *Afterimage* (London), vol. 20, no. 5, December 1992.

Kaneko, Ann, ''40th Annual Robert Flaherty Seminar,'' in *Afterimage* (London), vol. 22, no. 4, November 1994.

Marks, Dan, ''Ethnography and Ethnographic Film: From Flaherty to Asch and After,'' in *American Anthropologist*, vol. 97, no. 2, June 1995.

Goldstein, Yosha, ''Here's Looking at You: 41st Annual Robert Flaherty Film Seminar,'' in *Afterimage* (London), vol. 23, no. 2, September-October 1995.

Leacock, Richard, ''In Defense of the Flaherty Traditions,'' in *Film Culture* (New York), no. 79, Winter 1996.

Short review, in *Télérama* (Paris), no. 2439, 9 October 1996.

Pennebaker, D.A., ''Looking Back: Film Directors Robert Flaherty, Michael Powell and Jean-Luc Godard,'' in *Sight and Sound* (London), vol. 7, no. 4, April 1997.

* * *

Robert Flaherty's last film is a fitting culmination to a long career. It is less a documentary about the Cajun people of Louisiana's bayou country, than an autobiographical film about Flaherty himself. From the viewpoint of a Cajun boy the film reveals the mysteries of the bayou wilderness, portrayed as an enchanting world of fantasy, filled with beauty and danger. The film is a poetic reflection of Flaherty's youth, in which he explores his own life-long relationship to the wilderness and natural environment, and to the people who live there.

The opening sequence is one of the most celebrated in film history. Shots of alligators, magnificent birds, floating lily ponds, slithering snakes, and other wildlife and flora are given unity, continuity, and a sense of graceful movement. The brilliance of these sequences was the result of the troubled but highly successful collaboration between Flaherty and his talented editor, Helen Van Dongen. The outstanding night-time oil drilling sequence succeeds because of the interplay of images of the derricks accompanied by an atonal sound track. Flaherty's strength was in direction and shooting; Van Dongen's in her exceptional skill as an editor.

The film's visual beauty is so effective that it overshadows the sponsor's message. Oil drilling technology, first seen as an unknown threat to the tranquility of the bayou, in the end appears benign, leaving the impression that the unspoiled wilderness is safe.

The simple visual beauty of this film pleased most of the contemporary critics, though he film's theme or message bewildered some. Many recognized that the scenes with speaking parts were not terribly convincing. As in other Flaherty films, the cast was chosen from the locals, more for their appearance than acting ability. Making them speak their roles showed the limitation of using real people in dialogue situations that must be rehearsed. They become stilted and artificial before the camera.

Louisiana Story remains an enduring work of art for its sheer visual beauty, though some have argued its qualifications as a documentary, due to the manipulation of events depicted. Among films essentially based in reality, however, it remains one of the most successful collaborations of all time, with an impressive amalgamation of talent in direction, photography, editing, writing, and music.

—William T. Murphy

LOVES OF A BLONDE

See **LÁSKY JEDNÉ PLAVOVLÁSKY**

LUCIA

Cuba, 1968

Director: Humberto Solás

Production: Instituto Cubana del Arte e Industria Cinematograficos (ICAIC); black and white, 35mm; running time: 160 minutes. Released 1968. Filmed 1967 in Cuba.

Producer: Raúl Canosa; **screenplay:** Humberto Solás, Julio García Espinosa and Nelson Rodríguez; **photography:** Jorge Herrera; **editor:** Nelson Rodríguez; **sound engineers:** Ricardo Istueta and Carlos Fernández; **music:** Leo Brower; **costume designer:** María Elena Molinet.

Cast: Raquel Revuelta (*Lucia, Part 1*); Eslinda Núñez (*Lucia, Part 2*); Adela Legrá (*Lucia, Part 3*); Adolfo Llauradó (*Tomás*).

Award: Moscow Film Festival, Gold Medal, 1969.

Publications

Script:

Solás, Humberto, Julio García Espinosa, and Nelson Rodríguez, ''*Lucia* (Part III),'' in *Memories of Underdevelopment: The Revolutionary Films of Cuba*, edited by Michael Myerson, New York, 1973.

Books:

Nelson, L., *Cuba: The Measure of a Revolution*, Minneapolis, 1972.
Chanan, Michael, *The Cuban Image*, London, 1985.
Burton, Julianne, editor, *Cinema and Social Change in Latin America: Conversations with Filmmakers*, Austin, 1986.

Articles:

Geoffrey Minish, and M. E. Douglas, in *Take One* (Montreal), July-August 1969.
Engel, Andi, ''Solidarity and Violence,'' in *Sight and Sound* (London), Autumn 1969.
Interview with Humberto Solás, in *Atlas* (New York), April 1970.
Adler, Renata, ''Three Cuban Cultural Reports with Films Somewhere in Them,'' in *A Year in the Dark*, Berkeley, 1971.
Matthews, M., in *Films in Review* (New York), May 1974.
Biskind, P., ''*Lucia*: Struggles with History,'' in *Jump Cut* (Chicago), July-August 1974.
Blanco, Jorge Ayala, ''Cine Cubano: Revaluaciones, Devaluaciones, y Presentaciones,'' in *Movietone News* (Seattle), November 1974.
Taylor, A. M., in *Film Quarterly* (Berkeley), Winter 1974–75.
Kovacs, Steven, ''*Lucia*: Style and Meaning in Revolutionary Film,'' in *Monthly Review* (New York), June 1975.
Luxemburg, Leonardo, ''Latin American Films: Fourth Frontier,'' and ''The Role of Film in Cuban Development'' by Andres Hernandez, in *Films of a Changing World: A Critical International Guide*, edited by Jean Marie Ackerman, Washington, D.C., 1977.
''Special Issue'' of *Jump Cut* (Chicago), December 1978.
King, J., interview with Humberto Solás, in *Framework* (Norwich), Spring 1979.
Cine Cubano (Havana), no. 107, 1983.
Lopez Morales, E., ''Descubrimiento de *Lucia*,'' in *Cine Cubano* (Habana), no. 124, 1988.
Gonzalez, J.A., ''Humberto Solás o la audacia de la emocion,'' in *Cine Cubano* (Habana), no. 128, 1990.
Benamou, Catherine, ''Cuban Cinema: On the Threshold of Gender,'' in *Frontiers*, vol. 15, no. 1, Winter 1994.
Rose, P. W., ''The Politics of the Trilogy Form: *Lucia*, the *Oresteia* and *The Godfather*,'' in *Film-Historia* (Barcelona), vol. 5, no. 2/3, 1995.
Braun, Rainer, ''Kino in Kuba,'' in *EPD Film* (Frankfurt), vol. 14, no. 5, May 1997.

* * *

Lucia

Robert Phillip Kolker has called Humberto Solás's *Lucia* ''something of an encyclopedia of progressive film in the sixties,'' and this invigoratingly feminist trilogy is indeed one of the greatest examples of stylistic virtuosity to emerge from any national cinema in recent years. Solás's film depicts three women, all named Lucia, in their gradual acquisition of revolutionary consciousness, as they confront the specific historical dilemmas of their respective epochs—1895, 1932, and the post-revolutionary era of the 1960s. The film is remarkable in its ability to integrate diverse cinematic styles with an almost seamless fluidity. *Lucia* is a unique amalgam of Soviet style montage, hand-held shots in the manner of the early New Wave, and baroque stylization that recalls Antonioni and Bertolucci.

The first episode (1895) is the most ambitious in its epic grandeur, although Solás's directoral restraint prevents his mise-en-scène from becoming hopelessly florid. This segment is superficially a revenge tragedy, although the emphasis on the suffering engendered by Spanish imperialism serves as tragic counterpoint to the central, doomed love affair. The frenetic shots of impoverished black soldiers on horseback remind the viewer of the travails of war at the very point that a Hollywood film would revert to a political escapism.

After the inspired grandiosity of the 1895 segment, the second episode is conceived within the more modest requirements of Hollywood melodrama. Yet, paradoxically, this segment is perhaps the most subtly subversive of Solás's film. He has absorbed all of the mannerisms of melodramatic kitsch, but subverts them in order to make a political statement that transcends the common, soap-operaish woes of the isolated individual. The 1932 Lucia's romantic disillusion coincides with her disillusion with the regime that replaces that of the dictatorial Machado. Personal happiness and societal goals have become dialectically intertwined.

Lucia's last episode is understandably the most upbeat, although it is curiously the most dated of the trilogy. This exuberant study in ''consciousness raising'' takes place during the ambitious literacy campaign of the 1960s. This was the time when many Cuban women first grasped the ways in which sexism continued to contaminate their lives during the post-revolutionary period. Although the third episode of *Lucia* seems relatively minor when contrasted with the other two, its comic brio and good-natured didacticism make it enjoyable.

Julianne Burton has remarked that ''post-revolutionary Cuban cinema strives to unite cultural expression and political consciousness.'' *Lucia* is one of the most admirable results of his aspiration since Solás's narrative genius succeeds in explaining that much remarked-upon fusion of personal and political motivations during periods of revolutionary upheaval.

—Richard Porton

LULU

See **DIE BÜCHSE DER PANDORA**

M

(M, Mörder unter uns)

Germany, 1931

Director: Fritz Lang

Production: Nero-Film A. G. Verlag Star Film-G.m.b.H.; black and white, 35mm; running time: originally 117 minutes, according to Eisner an 89 minute version is most commonly shown now, though some sources list current version as 99 minutes. Released 11 May 1931, Berlin. Re-released 1933 in the U.S. in a dubbed version. Filmed during 6 weeks of 1931 in Nero-Film A. G. Verlag Star Film-G.m.b.H. studios in Berlin.

Producer: Seymour Nebenzal; **scenario:** Thea von Harbou and Fritz Lang, from an article by Egon Jacobson, based on the Düsseldorf child murder case; **photography:** Fritz Arno Wagner and Gustav Rathje; **editor:** Paul Falkenberg; **sound:** Adolf Jansen; **production designers:** Emil Hasler and Karl Vollbrecht; **music** (*Murderer's Theme*): Edward Grieg, based on an extract from *Peer Gynt*; **backdrop photographs:** Horst von Harbou.

Cast: Peter Lorre (*Hans Beckert, the murderer*); Gustaf Gründgens (*Schränker*); Ellen Widmann (*Mrs. Beckman*); Inge Landgut (*Elsie Beckman*); Otto Wernicke (*Inspector Lohmann*); Franz Stein (*Minister*); Theodor Loos (*Inspector Groebor*); Fritz Gnass (*Burglar*); Fritz Odemar (*Safecracker*); Paul Kemp (*Pickpocket*); Theo Lingen (*Con-Man*); Georg John (*Blind beggar*); Karl Platen (*Night Watchman*); Gerhard Bienart (*Inspector's secretary*); Rosa Valetti (*Landlady of the Crocadile Club*); Hertha von Walther (*Prostitute*); Ernst Stahl-Nachbaur (*Chief of Police*); Rudolf Blümner (*Lawyer*).

Publications

Script:

von Harbou, Thea, and Fritz Lang, *M*, edited by Gero Gandert and Ulrich Gregor, Hamburg, 1963; translated as *M*, London and New York, 1968.

M le maudit, Paris, 1990.

M, in *Iskusstvo Kino* (Moscow), no. 11, November 1994.

Books:

Kracauer, Siegfried, *From Caligari to Hitler: A Psychological History of the German Film*, Princeton, 1947.

Courtade, Francis, *Fritz Lang*, Paris, 1963.

Moullet, Luc, *Fritz Lang*, Paris, 1963.

Eibel, Alfred, editor, *Fritz Lang*, Paris, 1964.

Huaco, George, *The Sociology of Film Art*, New York, 1966.

Jensen, Paul M., *The Cinema of Fritz Lang*, New York, 1969.

Eisner, Lotte, *The Haunted Screen*, Berkeley, 1969.

Johnston, Claire, *Fritz Lang*, London, 1969.

Manvell, Roger, and Heinrich Fraenkel, *The German Cinema*, New York, 1971.

Grafe, Frieda, Enno Patalas, and Hans Helmut Prinzler, *Fritz Lang*, Munich, 1976.

Eisner, Lotte, *Fritz Lang*, London, 1977.

Armour, Robert, *Fritz Lang*, Boston, 1978.

Ott, Frederick W., *The Films of Fritz Lang*, Secaucus, New Jersey, 1979.

Jenkins, Stephen, editor, *Fritz Lang: The Image and the Look*, London, 1979.

Kaplan, E. Ann, *Fritz Lang: A Guide to References and Resources*, Boston, 1981.

Maibohm, Ludwig, *Fritz Lang: Seine Filme—Sein Leben*, Munich, 1981.

Ropars-Wuilleumier, Marie-Claire, *Le Texte divisé: Essai sur l'ecriture filmique*, Paris, 1981.

Eisner, Lotte H., *Fritz Lang*, Cambridge, 1988.

Humphries, Reynold, *Fritz Lang: Gender & Representation in His American Films*, Ann Arbor, 1989.

Levin, David, *Richard Wagner, Fritz Lang & the Nibelungen: The Dramaturgy of Disavowal*, Princeton, 1998.

McGilligan, Patrick, *Fritz Lang: The Nature of the Beast*, New York, 1998.

Gunning, Tom, *The Films of Fritz Lang: Modernity, Crime & Desire*, London, 2000.

Articles:

Lang, Fritz, ''Mein Film M: Ein Tatsachenbericht,'' in *Filmwoche* (Berlin), May 1931.

Hirsch, Leo, in *Berliner Tageblatt*, 12 May 1931.

Arnheim, Rudolf, in *Weltbühne* (Berlin), 19 May 1931.

Variety (New York), June 1931.

Hall, Mordaunt, in *New York Times*, 3 April 1933.

Troy, William, in *Nation* (New York), 19 April 1933.

Barry, Iris, in *Museum of Modern Art Bulletin* (New York), June 1933.

Eisner, Lotte, ''Notes sur le style de Fritz Lang,'' in *Revue du Cinéma* (Paris), 1 February 1947.

Wilson, Harry, ''The Genius of Fritz Lang,'' in *Film Quarterly* (London), Summer 1947.

Gesek, Ludwig, ''Fritz Lang: Suggestion und Stimmung,'' in *Gestalter der Filmkunst: Von Asta Nielsen bis Walt Disney*, Vienna, 1948.

''One Facet of Lang's Art Prophetic of Hitlerism,'' in *Herald Tribune* (New York), 21 March 1949.

M

Autera, Leonardo, ''Il parabola di Fritz Lang,'' in *Cinema* (Rome), 15 January 1954.

Mourley, Michel, ''Trajectoire de Fritz Lang,'' in *Cahiers du Cinéma* (Paris), September 1959.

Franju, Georges, ''Le Style de Fritz Lang,'' in *Cahiers du Cinéma* (Paris), November 1959.

Ramseger, Georg, ''30 Jahre alt und alterlos: In der Urania ist Fritz Langs *M* jetzt wieder greifbar,'' in *Welt* (Hamburg), 16 January 1960.

Sarris, Andrew, in *Village Voice* (New York), 1 September 1960.

Bellour, Raymond, in *Cinéma* (Paris), no. 58, 1961.

Kuhlbrodt, Dietrich, ''*M*: Wieder in Deutschland,'' in *Filmkritik* (Munich), no. 3, 1961.

Domarchi, Jean, ''Avec *M le Maudit*: Fritz Lang en 1932 annonçait la destinée de l'Allemagne,'' in *Arts* (Paris), 26 April 1961.

Gilson, René, in *Cinéma* (Paris), August-September 1961.

''Kein Mörderspiel: Fritz Lang's *M* von 1931,'' in *Frankfurter Allgemeine Zeitung*, 11 December 1961.

Lefevre, Raymond, in *Image et Son* (Paris), June 1962.

Porter, Miguel, ''La estructura profetica en *M*,'' in *M: El vampiro de Dusseldorf*, Barcelona, 1964.

Sandras, Michel, ''*M le Maudit* et l'expressionisme,'' in *Image et Son* (Paris), January 1964.

Eisner, Lotte, ''Le Style de *M le Maudit*,'' in *Avant-Scène du Cinéma* (Paris), 15 July 1964.

Jensen, Peter, in *Classics of the Film*, edited by Arthur Lennig, Madison, Wisconsin, 1965.

Jahnke, Eckart, in *Film* (East Berlin), no. 6, 1965.

Rhode, Eric, ''Fritz Lang (The German Period 1919–1933),'' in *Tower of Babel: Speculations on the Cinema*, New York, 1966.

Wiegand, Wilfried, ''Der Regisseur von *M*,'' in *Frankfurter Allgemeine Zeitung*, 5 December 1970.

Kinder, Marsha, and Beverle Houston, in *Close-Up: A Critical Perspective on Film*, New York, 1972.

Burch, Noël, ''De *Mabuse* à *M*: Le Travail de Fritz Lang,'' in *Revue d'Esthétique* (Paris), 1973.

Kuntzel, Thierry, ''The Treatment of Ideology in the Textual Analysis of Film,'' in *Screen* (London), Autumn 1973 (and reply by Nicolas Garnham in same issue).

Dadon, R., ''Le Pouvoir et sa folle,'' in *Positif* (Paris), December 1976.

Del Ministro, M., ''Una ipotesi psicoanalitica per la lettura,'' in *Cinema Nuovo* (Bari), November-December 1977.

Carroll, Noël, ''Lang, Pabst, and Sound,'' in *Ciné-Tracts* (Montreal), Fall 1978.

Chang, J. S. M. J., ''*M*: A Reconsideration,'' in *Literature/Film Quarterly* (Salisbury, Maryland), no. 4, 1979.

Audibert, L., ''Dossier: Du muet au parlant: L'Ombre du son,'' in *Cinématographe* (Paris), June 1979.

Barros, L. de, ''Uma obraprima de Fritz Lang,'' in *Celuloide* (Rio Major, Portugal), August 1979.

Petat, J., ''L'Ouverture de *M le Maudit*,'' in *Cinema* (Paris), June 1982.

Frascani, F., ''Hitler era geloso del *Morder* di Fritz Lang,'' in *Cinema Nuovo* (Rome), May-June 1989.

Garncarz, J., ''Fritz Lang's *M*: A Case of Significant Film Variation,'' in *Film History* (London), vol. 4, no. 3, 1990.

Koseluk, C., ''Comic Book Antihero,'' in *American Film*, vol. 16, no. 2, February 1991.

Rolfe, Hilda, ''The Perfectionist,'' in *Film Comment* (New York), vol. 28, no. 6, November-December 1992.

Kaes, A., ''The Cold Gaze: Notes on Mobilization and Modernity,'' in *New German Critique*, no. 59, Spring/Summer 1993.

Lattuada, A., ''Un film, un realisateur, deux comediennes,'' in *Positif* (Paris), no. 400, June 1994.

Hoberman, J., ''Stormy Weather,'' in *Village Voice* (New York), vol. 42, 17 June 1997.

Dimendberg, Edward, ''From Berlin to Bunker Hill: Urban Space, Late Modernity and Film Noir in Fritz Lang's and Joseph Losey's *M*,'' in *Wide Angle* (Baltimore), vol. 19, no. 4, October 1997.

Elsaesser, Thomas, ''Fritz Lang: The Illusion of Mastery,'' in *Sight and Sound* (London), vol. 10, no. 1, January 2000.

* * *

Fritz Lang's films are marked by an uneasy tension between moral opposites: light and dark, innocence and evil, order and chaos. No subject is too mean or sordid to be outside or beneath human experience or to be illuminated, ultimately, by the vision of the artist. According to Lang, his films are like ''the loveliest German fairy tales,'' which, despite their beauty, accumulate ''an enormous amount of brutality, of cruelty and crime.'' Lang explains why this tension works, both in children's stories and in his films:

> . . . In fairy tales the most simple and most moral law of mankind is upheld. The good are rewarded, the evil punished. The good becomes more touching through sorrow, the evil more hateful by the initial success of their wickedness. Film yields the satisfaction of the fulfilled law just as naively as does the fairy tale, only in a form which conforms with its time.

Certainly *M*, Lang's first sound film, functions in this manner. Considered by most critics to be Lang's masterwork, *M* concerns the fulfilment of moral law while amply reflecting the horrors of its time: the years following World War I in Germany, a period, according to Lang, ''of the deepest despair, hysteria, cynicism, unbridled vice.'' Rampant inflation and other chaotic elements gradually eroded the public order. By 1930, the year before Lang made *M*, Nazi paramilitary groups, with their own police and tribunals, murdered, bombed, and sabotaged while the Weimar bureaucracy slowly strangled in its own red tape.

Through a highly ordered juxtaposition of visual and aural images, and through an effective blending of expressionistic and realistic styles, Lang explores the effects of this growing chaos by depicting it on personal and social planes. On the personal plane, *M's* central character, child murderer Hans Beckert, embodies the struggle between a weakening order and an increasingly malevolent and powerful chaos. Possessed by a *doppelgänger*, Beckert is a childish, soft-bellied, petit bourgeois seized by uncontrollable homicidal passions:

> I can't help myself! I haven't any control over this evil thing that's inside me. It's there all the time, driving me out to wander through the streets. It's me, pursuing myself. I want to escape to escape from myself! But it's impossible. I have to obey.

When pursued by this *doppelgänger*, he whistles a theme from *Peer Gynt*, an appropriate leitmotif for his personal demon. A capricious and irresponsible character with no sense of self, Gynt saved his own life by allowing another man to drown. Similarly, Beckert keeps his own divided psyche intact by killing young girls, by submitting irresponsibly to his most primal urges.

Lang portrays Beckert as both *doppelgänger*, victim and victimizer, and Gynt, a self-absorbed child, in a series of images, the chief ones being mirrors and other reflective surfaces. While the police attempt to develop a psychological profile of Beckert the camera cuts to Beckert peering and making faces at himself in the mirror. In another scene the camera catches Beckert eating an apple and looking into a store window where we see him surrounded by a diamond-shaped display of knives; when the camera shifts back to Beckert's point of view, we see a mirror at the back of the window display—again surrounded by knives—where a little girl, a potential victim, suddenly appears. Beckert then begins to whistle the theme from *Peer Gynt*, indicating that his *doppelgänger* has assumed control. Finally, Beckert doesn't know that his *doppelgänger* has become visible to others as well until he sees reflected in the window the mark of Cain, the ''M,'' chalked on his shoulder.

Beckert's shadow is also a projection of the *doppelgänger*. As Elsie's ball bounces against a billboard posting a reward for the murderer, his shadow falls across the pillar—a visual echo of the ''evil man in black'' (with a chopper) portrayed in the opening children's ditty.

Such images suggest two ideas: 1) Beckert is self-absorbed and involuted, and 2) Beckert can be known only through his projections. The first point is conveyed through various visual and aural images: the target in a toy window spiralling endlessly into its own centre (recalling the circles on the policemen's map); Beckert's oral fixations (eating apples and candy, drinking brandy, smoking cigarettes, biting his hand after a foiled abduction attempt); Beckert's relative silence until the last scene when he is forced to come to his own defense (that is, he can only speak to himself or to children). His projections and oral obsessions ultimately reveal and trap him: a pack of cigarettes puts the police on his trail, and his compulsive whistling alerts the beggars to his presence. He is trapped by his own ''garbage'' as it were (another example being the red pencil shavings). Lang repeats this theme by locating Beckert's final hiding place in a small locker full of junk—a vivid metaphor both for the meaningless disorder of his mind and for his self-confinement. Other scenes reinforce this notion: Beckert is stalked by beggars who live off the refuse of others, and he is ultimately brought to trial in an abandoned brewery by society's outcasts.

Beckert's personal chaos aggravates the chaos existing on the social plane: the apparent struggle between the police (who symbolize the Weimar Republic) and the underworld (who symbolize the Nazi organization). The real struggle, however, is between the two groups, who represent control, and Beckert, who represents lack of control. The erosion of control in postwar Germany is thus reflected in the growing *similarity*, not struggle between the two organizations. Lang conveys this resemblance through skillful editing and scripting and by the use of similar settings, camera angles, and images for the two groups.

Lang's portrayal of their parallel investigations emphasizes the complementary nature of the police and the underworld. The camera cuts back and forth between police conferences and underworld meetings to show the following: a gesture and remark begun by the head of the underworld are completed by the chief of police. After a safecracker declares that the police must stop looking for Beckert in the underworld, an elderly detective concludes that the murderer must be a ''peaceful little family man who wouldn't hurt a fly.'' A burglar stands up and leans against the back of his armchair, while the scene shifts to an inspector leaning over the back of his chair. Both rooms are slowly engulfed by cigarette smoke as the meetings progress, and the people get up and wander about as the parallel discussions unfold. Identical camera angles reinforce the similarities in dialogue and settings. The ultimate exchange of identities comes near the end of the manhunt and involves the leaders of the two groups: Schränker, the head of the underworld, disguises himself as a policeman to penetrate Beckert's hiding place, and Lohmann, the chief of police, uses ''illegal'' methods (lies and blackmail) to determine where the underworld has taken Beckert to be ''tried.''

Not content to make a ''talking picture'' as such, Lang again uses the technical innovation of sound to complement the message of the camera. Film scholar Thierry Kuntzel has argued that, to connect the police and the underworld, Lang employs two separate chains of visual and aural clues. At first, the underworld's surveillance (visual) and the police interrogations (aural) yield no results. Then two important clues emerge: the letter to the press (visual) and the whistling in front of the blind man (aural). The letter ultimately yields two visual clues for the police—the cigarette pack and the pencil shavings—whereas the underworld narrows in on Beckert through two aural clues—Beckert's second whistling in front of the blind man of the *Peer Gynt* theme and the sounds he makes while trying to escape from his hiding place.

In equating the police with the underworld Lang muddies the distinction between good and evil, order and chaos, on the social plane. In *M*'s final judgment scene, the distinctions are obscured on the personal plane as well. In his eloquent plea before the kangaroo court, Beckert changes from villain to helpless victim, both of his *doppelgänger* and of the criminal element of society. How can Lang deliver his fairy tale ending of a fulfilled moral law when innocence and guilt have become so hopelessly confounded? Lang's solution is to move ''above'' the action aurally, just as in earlier scenes he moved above the action visually—employing overhead or crane shots to imply omniscience or a divine perspective. We hear off-camera, ''In the name of the law,'' and the action freezes. Because we do not see the speaker, higher law is implied—one that will stop the criminal elements of society and protect both innocent children and the murderous child within Beckert.

—Catherine Henry

MADAME DE . . .

(The Earrings of Madame de . . .)

France, 1953

Director: Max Ophüls

Production: Franco-London Films, Indus, and Rizzoli; black and white, 35mm; running time: 105 minutes. Released 1953.

Producer: Ralph Baum; **screenplay:** Max Ophüls, Marcel Achard, and Annette Wademant, from a novella by Louise de Vilmorin; **photography:** Christian Matras; **editor:** Boris Lewin; **production designer:** Jean d'Aubonne; **music:** Oscar Strauss and George Van Parys.

Cast: Danielle Darrieux (*Madame De*); Charles Boyer (*Monsieur De*); Vittorio De Sica (*Baron Donati*); Lia de Léa (*Monsieur De's mistress*); Jean Debucourt.

Publications

Script:

Ophüls, Max, Marcel Achard, and Annette Wademant, *Madame de . . .* , in *Avant-Scène du Cinéma* (Paris), June 1986.

Books:

Roud, Richard, *Max Ophüls: An Index*, London, 1958.
Annenkov, Georges, *Max Ophüls*, Paris, 1962.
Max Ophüls par Max Ophüls, Paris, 1963.
Beylie, Claude, *Max Ophüls*, Paris, 1963.
Leprohon, Pierre, *Vittorio De Sica*, Paris, 1966.
Armes, Roy, *French Film*, New York, 1970.
Armes, Roy, *French Cinema Since 1946: The Great Tradition*, New York, 1970.
Willemen, Paul, editor, *Ophüls*, London, 1978.
Williams, Alan, *Max Ophüls and the Cinema of Desire*, New York, 1980.
Swindell, Larry, *The Reluctant Lover: Charles Boyer*, New York, 1983.
Tassone, Aldo, *Max Ophüls, l'enchanteur*, Torino, 1994.
White, Susan M., *The Cinema of Max Ophüls: Magisterial Vision & the Figure of a Woman*, New York, 1995.

Articles:

Anderson, Lindsay, in *Sight and Sound* (London), April-June 1954.
New York Times, 20 July 1954.
Archer, Eugene, ''Ophüls and the Romantic Tradition,'' in *Yale French Studies* (New Haven), Summer 1956.
''Ophüls Issue'' of *Cahiers du Cinéma* (Paris), March 1958.
Whitehall, Richard, ''Danielle Darrieux,'' in *Films and Filming* (London), December 1961.
Giard, Robert, in *Seventh Art* (New York), Summer 1964.
Beylie, Claude, ''Max Ophüls,'' in *Anthologie du Cinéma*, Paris, 1965.

Madame de ...

Kael, Pauline, in *I Lost it at the Movies*, Boston, 1965.

Sarris, Andrew, ''Memory and Max Ophüls,'' in *Moviegoer*, Summer 1966.

''Ophüls Issue'' of *Film Comment* (New York), Summer 1971.

Haskell, Molly, and Peter Harcourt, in *Favourite Movies: Critics' Choice*, edited by Philip Nobile, New York, 1975.

Jouvet, P., ''Rythmes et masques,'' in *Cinématographe* (Paris), December 1977.

''Ophüls Issue'' of *Filmkritik* (Munich), November and December 1977.

Britton, Andrew, ''Metaphor and Mimesis: Madame de . . . ,'' in *Movie* (London), Summer 1982.

Amiel, V., ''Mouvements d'un couple et de la société,'' in *Positif* (Paris), August 1982.

Britton, A., ''Metaphor and Mimesis: *Madame De . . . ,*'' in *Movie* (London), no. 29/30, Summer 1982.

Lord, S., ''Fugitive Details: Readings of Image and Context in *Madame de . . .* and *Lola Montes*,'' in *Cineaction* (Toronto), Winter-Spring 1990.

Dunant, C., ''Visions of Paris,'' in *Sight and Sound* (London), no. 1, 1990–91.

Legrand, Gérard, ''*Madame de . . . :* Des effets et des feux,'' in *Positif* (Paris), no. 381, November 1992.

Murphy, K., ''Portrait of a Lady X 2,'' in *Film Comment* (New York), July-August 1993.

Belloï, Livio, ''Max Ophüls: le cristal et la tache,'' in *Cinémathèque* (Paris), no. 6, Autumn 1994.

Marty, J., ''*Madame dep* de Max Ophüls,'' in *Cahiers de la Cinémathèque* (Perpignan), no. 62, March 1995.

* * *

The Earrings of Madame de . . . is one of the four films—all made in the 1950s shortly before his death—that constitute the highest expression of Max Ophüls's personal style. Along with *La ronde, Le plaisir*, and *Lola Montès*, the film combines all the technical ingredients and thematic concerns that had preoccupied Ophüls throughout his rather ''up and down'' career. Foremost among these interests, of course, was the intricate blending of complex, dazzling camera work with the themes of mankind's obsession with material objects—and a kind of poignant romanticism usually misconstrued by critics attempting to pigeonhole him as a director of women's films much like Douglas Sirk.

In *Madame de* there is a notion of mutability: the earrings, being material, remain constant, but the changing emotional circumstances of their possessors increase their symbolic value until they become the emblems of a domestic catastrophe. To some extent, however, the characters also remain static: they are unchanging in surface demeanour, yet the rush of time alters each one's status and effects a transition in their personalities. Madame de, for example, matures from a supercilious young girl into a truly passionate woman betrayed by the depth of her emotion, while, at the same time, her husband and lover evolve correspondingly but somewhat less noticeably because they are more reluctant than Madame de to deviate from their sense of propriety.

One element in the clash between relentless time and the seeming intransigence of objects and events is Ophüls's tenacious tracking camera and its unrelenting interchange of shots and episodes. Another is the brisk unfolding of the narrative, which delicately balances a lush, rich atmosphere with lean camera technique. This interplay is particularly evident in the film's opening scene: the camera follows a woman's hand as it glides along a rack of expensive clothes in a lavishly appointed wardrobe, and then, without a pause, the camera clings to the woman as she admires her earrings in the mirror of her dressing table. In one continuous shot, Ophüls establishes a world of extravagant material possessions and then hones in on the frivolous, silly woman who seems virtually a part of them as she sits reflected in the mirror.

Later, however, in the ball sequence, the camera dazzlingly plays against the sumptuous surroundings to create a rush of time that encapsulates Madame de's progress from frivolity to tragedy without her having changed the tempo of her dance (a parallel to the changing value of the symbolic earrings as they float from hand to hand while remaining materially constant). With her lover she dances round and round from one elegant ballroom to another under the constant gaze of the encircling camera, which reveals the deepening feelings of the couple. Finally, as they slowly glide through the last dance in the sequence, the air of gaiety disappears. The camera then moves to follow a servant in one long continuous shot as he goes from light to light, extinguishing them; the sequence ends in darkness as he throws a cover over a harp.

The party is over. Frivolity has become romance, and love becomes tragedy. As in all of Ophüls's best films, every element is interconnected—technique, pacing, theme, and character—to intertwine both the light and tragic strains and to resolve the seemingly divergent tensions into a final mood of desolation.

—Stephen L. Hanson

MÄDCHEN IN UNIFORM

(Girls in Uniform)

Germany, 1931

Director: Leontine Sagan with Carl Froelich

Production: Deutsches Film Gemeinschaft; black and white, 35mm; running time: 98 minutes; length: 8799 feet. Released 1931. A new, reconstructed print was released in the 1970s.

Screenplay: Christa Winsloe and F. D. Andam, from the play *Yesterday and Today* by Christine Winsloe; **photography:** Reimar Kuntze and Franz Weihmayr; **music:** Hansom Milde-Meissner.

Cast: Dorothea Wieck (*Fraülein von Bernburg*); Hertha Thiefe (*Manuela von Meinhardis*); Emilie Unda (*Headmistress*); Ellen Schwanneke (*Ilse von Westhagen*); Hedwig Schlichter (*Fraülein von Kosten*); Gertrud de Lalsky (*Manuela's aunt*).

Publications

Books:

Kracauer, Siegfried, *From Caligari to Hitler: A Psychological History of the German Film*, Princeton, 1947.

Klinowski, Jacek, and Adam Garbicz, *Cinema, The Magic Vehicle: A Guide to Its Achievement: Journey One: The Cinema Through 1949*, Metuchen, New Jersey, 1975.

Sagan, Leontine, *Lights and Shadows: The Autobiography of Leontine Sagan*, edited and introduced by Loren Kruger, Johannesburg, 1996.

Articles:

Close Up (London), March 1932.

New York Times, 21 September 1932.

Herald Tribune (New York), 21 September 1932.

National Board of Review Magazine (New York), September-October 1932.

Hardy, Forsyth, interview with Leontine Sagan, in *Cinema Quarterly* (London), Winter 1932.

Potamkin, Harry, ''Pabst and the Social Film,'' in *Hound and Horn* (New York), January-March 1933.

Jahier, Valerio, ''42 ans de cinema,'' in *Le Role intellectuel du cinéma*, Paris, 1937.

Kael, Pauline, in *Kiss Kiss Bang Bang*, Boston, 1968.

Kjborup, S., in *Kosmorama* (Copenhagen), December 1972.

Scholar, N., in *Women in Film* (Berkeley), Summer 1975.

Rich, B. Ruby, ''From Repressive Tolerance to Erotic Liberation,'' in *Jump Cut* (Chicago), March 1981.

Schlüpmann, H., and K. Gramann, ''Vorbemerkung,'' in *Frauen und Film* (Berlin), June 1981.

Thiefe, Hertha, ''Gestern und Heute,'' an interview, in *Frauen und Film* (Berlin), June 1981.

Lefanu, Mark, in *Monthly Film Bulletin* (London), January 1982.

* * *

Mädchen in Uniform was directed by Leontine Sagan under the supervision of Carl Froelich in 1931; it was based on the play *Yesterday and Today* by Christine Winsloe. Its subversive anti-Fascist, anti-patriarchal themes seem astonishing when one realizes that the film was shot in Germany just two years before Hitler's rise to power.

Mädchen in Uniform achieved great popularity in Paris, London and Berlin, but it was later banned in Germany by Goebbels, Hitler's cultural minister, for its unhealthy moral conclusions. For the next few decades, the film was almost forgotten and received little critical attention. It seems to have been lost somewhere in film history between German expressionism and the Nazi cinema. In the early

Mädchen in Uniform

1970s interest in the film was revived by women's film festivals; it has come to be seen as the first truly radical lesbian film; and in the last decade *Mädchen in Uniform* has finally received the recognition it deserves.

The structure of the film is a mixture of montage and narrative sequences which inform each other and create an atmosphere which perhaps could not have been achieved by the use of one of these methods alone. The montage sequence at the beginning of the film—stone towers, statues, and marching soldiers—sets up a compliance and strength, a tone that introduces the audience to the life of the girls at school. From the constricting montage shots, the camera turns immediately to the girls' school. Periodically, still shots of the militaristic, patriarchal world outside the school are interspersed with the narrative. The audience is reminded that although the school is a feminine space (indeed, there are no male characters in the film), it is surrounded and even permeated by ubiquitous male authority. Yet, that authority is itself called into question by the narrative, the defiance that continues despite the prevalence of authoritarianism. By its structure, the film succeeds in creating a feminine space enclosed in the literal walls (as exemplified by the montage) of the outside world.

In her utilization of the new sound medium, Sagan was the most advanced director in pre-war Germany. Lotte Eisner said: ''With this work, the German sound film reached its highest level.'' Not only Sagan's precise use of dialogue but also her use of sound as metaphor (the sounding trumpet at the beginning and end of the film) and her creation of atmosphere, the whispers of the girls exchanging secrets, their final desperate chanting of Manuela's name—all attest to the accuracy of Eisner's statement.

Siegfried Kracauer also praised Sagan for her cinematography. He noted her ability to impart the ''symbolic power of light'' to her images. Sagan's use of shadows adds not only depth to the flat screen but also meaning and atmosphere. Sagan's cinematography is an excellent example of what Eisner calls ''*stimmung*'' (emotion), which suggests the vibrations of the soul through the use of light. The lighting and shooting of the stairway is a notable example. Its ascending shadows and its center depth create a tension in which the girls must operate, for the front, well-lighted stairs are off limits to them. The staircase is then a symbol of the girls' confinement, and its darkness literally shadows all of their activities.

Sagan also pioneered the cinematic convention of superimposition of one character's face over that of another to symbolize a deep psychological connection between them. She uses this technique in the film to convey moments of deep attraction between the teacher Fraulein von Bernburg and her student Manuela. The fusion of their images suggests the strength of their bond. It was a technique used 30 years later by Bergman in *Persona* to achieve the same effect.

Mädchen in Uniform was the first film in Germany to be cooperatively produced. The Deutsches Film Gemeinschaft was created especially for this project—a cooperative film company formed by the cast and crew in which shares rather than salaries were distributed.

—Gretchen Elsner-Sommer

THE MAGNIFICENT AMBERSONS

USA, 1942

Director: Orson Welles

Production: Mercury Productions; black and white, 35mm; running time: 88 minutes: Released 1942 by RKO Radio Pictures Inc.

Producer: Orson Welles; **screenplay:** Orson Welles, from the novel by Booth Tarkington; **photography:** Stanley Cortez; **editor:** Robert Wise; **sound:** Bailey Fesler and James G. Stewart; **art director:** Mark-Lee Kirk; **music:** Bernard Herrmann; **special effects:** Vernon L. Walker; **costume designer:** Edward Stevenson.

Cast: Joseph Cotten (*Eugene Morgan*); Dolores Costello (*Isabel Amberson Minafer*); Anne Baxter (*Lucy Morgan*); Tim Holt (*George Minafer*); Agnes Moorehead (*Fanny Amberson*); Ray Collins (*Jack Amberson*); Richard Bennett (*Major Amberson*); Don Dillaway (*Wilbur Minafer*).

Award: New York Film Critics' Award, Best Actress (Moorehead), 1942.

Publications

Books:

Bazin, André, *Orson Welles*, Paris, 1950.
Noble, Peter, *The Fabulous Orson Welles*, London, 1956.
Bogdanovich, Peter, *The Cinema of Orson Welles*, New York, 1961.
Bessy, Maurice, *Orson Welles*, Paris, 1963; as *Orson Welles*, New York, 1971.
Cowie, Peter, *The Cinema of Orson Welles*, London, 1965.
Higham, Charles, *The Films of Orson Welles*, Berkeley, 1971.
Bogdanovich, Peter, and Orson Welles, *This Is Orson Welles*, New York, 1972.
McBride, Joseph, *Orson Welles*, London, 1972, 1996.
Naremore, James, *The Magic World of Orson Welles*, New York, 1978.
Valentinetti, Claudio M., *Orson Welles*, Florence, 1981.
Bergala, Alain, and Jean Narboni, editors, *Orson Welles*, Paris, 1982.
Andrew, Dudley, *Film in the Aura of Art*, Princeton, 1984.
Higham, Charles, *Orson Welles: The Rise and Fall of an American Genius*, New York, 1985.
Leaming, Barbara, *Orson Welles: A Biography*, New York, 1985.
Parra, Daniele, and Jacques Zimmer, *Orson Welles*, Paris, 1985.
Weis, Elisabeth, and John Belton, editors, *Film Sound: Theory and Practice*, New York, 1985.
Taylor, John Russell, *Orson Welles: A Celebration*, London, 1986.
Cotten, Joseph, *Vanity Will Get You Somewhere*, New York, 1987.
Wood, Bret, *Orson Welles: A Bio-Bibliography*, Westport, 1990.
Howard, James, *The Complete Films of Orson Welles*, Secaucus, 1991.
Carringer, Robert L., *The Magnificent Ambersons: A Reconstruction*, Berkeley, 1993.
Beja, Morris, *Perspective on Orson Welles*, New York, 1995.
Callow, Simon, *Orson Welles: The Road to Xanadu*, New York, 1997.
Welles, Orson, *This Is Orson Welles*, New York, 1998.
Taylor, John Russell, *Orson Welles*, New York, 2000.

Articles:

Variety (New York), 1 July 1942.
''Controversy with RKO,'' in *Time* (New York), 20 July 1942.
Newsweek (New York), 20 July 1942.
Times (London), 5 March 1943.
Revue du Cinéma (Paris), December 1946.
Castello, G. C., ''The Magnificent Orson Welles,'' in *Bianco e Nero* (Rome), January 1949.
Prouse, Derek, ''Notes on Film Acting,'' in *Sight and Sound* (London), Spring 1955.
''Agnes Moorehead,'' in *Sight and Sound* (London), Autumn 1955.
Pariante, Roberto, ''Orson Welles from Citizen Kane to Othello,'' in *Bianco e Nero* (Rome), March 1956.
Cahiers du Cinéma (Paris), September 1958.
Stanbrook, Alan, ''The Heroes of Welles,'' in *Film* (London), no. 26, 1961.
''Welles Issue'' of *Image et Son* (Paris), no. 139, 1961.
''Welles Issue'' of *Cine Forum* (Venice), no. 19, 1962.
Bowers, Ronald, ''Agnes Moorehead,'' in *Films in Review* (New York), May 1966.
Johnson, William, ''Orson Welles: Of Time and Loss,'' in *Film Quarterly* (Berkeley), Fall 1967.
''Welles Issue'' of *Film Comment* (New York), Summer 1971.
Goldfarb, Phyllis, ''Orson Welles' Use of Sound,'' in *Take One* (Montreal), July-August 1971.
Smith, J., ''Orson Welles and the Great American Dummy; or, The Rise and Fall and Regeneration of Benjamin Franklin's Model American,'' in *Literature/Film Quarterly* (Salisbury, Maryland), Summer 1974.
Vialle, G., in *Image et Son* (Paris), no. 308 bis, 1976.
Schwartz, H., ''An American Film Institute Seminar with Stanley Cortez, ASC,'' in *American Cinematographer* (Los Angeles), November 1976.

The Magnificent Ambersons

Bawden, J., ''Anne Baxter,'' in *Films in Review* (New York), October 1977.

Passler, Susan Karnes, in *Magill's Survey of Cinema 3*, Englewood Cliffs, New Jersey, 1980.

Kalinak, Kathryn, ''The Text of Music: A Study of *The Magnificent Ambersons*,'' in *Cinema Journal* (Austin), vol. 27, no. 4, Summer 1988.

Nielsen, N. A., ''Et allerhelvedes perspekitv,'' in *Kosmorama* (Copenhagen), Fall 1989.

Rochester, D., ''Compelling Evidence,'' in *American Film*, vol. 15, no. 3, December 1989.

Doherty, Jim, ''*The Magnificent Ambersons*,'' in *Soundtrack* (Mechelen), vol. 9, no. 36, December 1990.

Cunningham, S., ''*The Magnificent Ambersons:* Deep Focus, the Long Take and Psychological Representation,'' in *Continuum*, vol. 5, no. 2, 1992.

Pernod, P., in *Positif* (Paris), July-August 1992.

La Polla, F., ''Welles e la frequentazione delle tenebre,'' in *Quaderni di Cinema* (Florence), July-September 1992.

Bogdanovich, P., ''En magnifik massaker,'' in *Chaplin* (Stockholm), no. 3, 1993.

Rosenbaum, Jonathan, ''Pages from the Endfield File,'' in *Film Comment* (New York), vol. 29, no. 6, November-December 1993.

Garcia, Maria, ''Re-inventing Orson Welles,'' in *Films in Review* (New York), vol. 45, no. 5–6, May-June 1994.

Wojahn, D., ''Beginning in Las Vegas,'' in *Michigan Quarterly Review*, vol, 35, no. 1, 1996.

''The Construction of Space and the Monstrous-Feminine in the Welles-Text,'' in *Critical Survey*, vol. 10, no. 2, May 1998.

* * *

The Magnificent Ambersons has been called Orson Welles's near-masterpiece, second to *Citizen Kane*. That qualified description derives more from the fact that the film was ''butchered'' by RKO, rather than from any intrinsic shortcoming on the part of its director.

Following the financial disaster of *Kane*, RKO executives compelled Welles to choose as his next film a subject with commercial appeal. Welles wanted to film *The Pickwick Papers* with W. C. Fields but Field's schedule would not permit it. As Booth Tarkington was a favorite novelist of Welles, he selected instead the author's 1919

Pulitzer Prize-winning novel about the decline and fall of an aristocratic family brought on by the encroaching industrial revolution at the turn of the century. Welles had already presented a radio version of the novel in 1939 starring himself and Walter Huston.

Welles wrote the script in nine days, deleting much of Tarkington's sentimentality, and with a Proustian remembrance of a life of gentility now past, concentrated on the psychological darkness which destroyed the Amberson clan. His was a literary rendering of what was essentially a second-rate novel, a lament, he says, ''not so much for an epoch as for the sense of moral values which are destroyed.'' The film centers on the ill-fated love between the gentlemanly horseless carriage manufacturer Eugene Morgan and the exquisitely beautiful Amberson matriarch, Isabel; the reaction of her spoiled son George Minafer, whose ''come-uppance'' eventually transpires; and the fate of neurotic spinster aunt Fanny Minafer.

Welles's completed version ran 148 minutes which he reduced to 131. RKO then sent him to Brazil to direct the aborted *It's All True* and proceeded to edit the film to 88 minutes, including the insertion of the hospital scene at the end. This scene had not been written by Welles and was directed by Freddie Flick and scored by Roy Webb, instead of Bernard Herrmann whose haunting score is so essential a part of the film. This truncated version, says Welles, destroyed ''the whole heart of the picture really.''

Nevertheless what remains is a luxuriant motion picture combining Welles's unique directorial flair with what Jean Cocteau called ''calm beauty.'' The beginning of the film provides a picture of a bygone era with its good humor and homey virtues, after which Welles slowly and deliberately unmasks the Ambersons' imperfections. The dramatic use of light and shadow in Stanley Cortez's deep-focus photography accentuates and enhances the characters' conflicts. Welles employed a nostalgic irising in and out to begin and end scenes, and he edited the film in the camera—scene by scene, vignette by vignette—rather than relying on the cutting room after the fact. He spoke the voice-over narration himself, a skill honed through his vast experience with radio, a narration he likened to the titles in silent films. He also incorporated overlapping dialogue and street noises as part of the sound track and used groupings of the townspeople in the film as a Greek chorus, whose chattering, gossipy observations of the vicissitudes of the Amberson-Morgans provided succinct commentary and embellished the storyline.

Paramount to the success of *Ambersons* is the excellent acting. Welles worked meticulously with his cast. Using his script as a guide, he discussed their characters with the actors, rehearsed them at length and then shot the scenes, often allowing them to improve the actual dialogue based on their understanding of their parts. The cast constituted a first-rate ensemble with Joseph Cotten a standout as the gentle, suave Eugene, though the acting honors unequivocally belong to Agnes Moorehead. Her virtuoso performance is one of the finest on the American screen and earned her the New York Film Critics Award.

Reviews of *Ambersons* were less than enthusiastic. Many seemed to expect a depiction of the typical family wrapped in sugar-spun Americana, rather than the in-depth analysis which revealed warts and all. *The New York Times* opined that Welles had wasted his abundant talents on ''a relentlessly somber drama on a barren theme.'' The picture was not the commercial success that RKO had hoped for and it was well over a decade before the film was received and appreciated for the master stroke it is.

—Ronald Bowers

MALCOLM X

USA, 1992

Director: Spike Lee

Production: Marvin Worth and Spike Lee for 40 Acres and a Mule Filmworks, in association with Largo International N.V.; 35mm; running time: 201 minutes; released 1 November 1992 by Warner Brothers. Filmed in Saudi Arabia and the USA.

Producer: Marvin Worth, Spike Lee; **screenplay:** Arnold Perl, Spike Lee, based on *The Autobiography of Malcolm X* as told to Alex Haley; **photography:** Ernest Dickerson; **editor:** Barry Alexander Brown; **assistant directors:** Randy Fletcher, H. H. Cooper, Dale Pierce, Samir Seif, Ntshavheni Wa Luruli; **production design:** Wynn Thomas; **art director:** Tom Warren; **music:** Terence Blanchard; **sound editor:** Skip Lievsay; **sound recording:** Rolf Pardula; **costumes:** Ruth E. Parker; **choreography:** Otis Sallid; **stunt coordination:** Jeff Ward.

Cast: Denzel Washington (*Malcolm X*); Angela Bassett (*Betty Shabazz*); Albert Hall (*Baines*); Al Freeman Jr. (*Elijah Muhammad*); Spike Lee (*Shorty*); Delroy Lindo (*West Indian Archie*); Theresa Randle (*Laura*); Kate Vernon (*Sophia*); Lonette McKee (*Louise Little*); Tommy Hollis (*Earl Little*); James McDaniel (*Brother Earl*); Nelson Mandella (Himself); Ossie Davis (Himself).

Publications

Script:

Lee, Spike, with Ralph Wiley, *By Any Means Necessary: The Trials and Tribulations of the Making of Malcolm X, including the Screenplay*, New York, 1992.
Hardy, James E., *Spike Lee: Filmmaker*, Broomall, 1995.
Jones, K. Maurice, *Spike Lee & the African American Filmmakers: A Choice of Colors*, Brookfield, 1996.
Haskins, Jim, *Spike Lee: By Any Means Necessary*, New York, 1997.
Chapman, Ferguson, *Spike Lee*, Mankato, 1998.
McDaniel, Melissa, *Spike Lee: On His Own Terms*, Danbury, 1999.

Articles:

Hollywood Reporter, 10 November 1992.
Variety, 10 November 1992.
Newsweek, 16 November 1992.
McCarthy, T., *Variety* (New York), 16 November 1992.
Chicago Tribune, 18 November 1992.
Christian Science Monitor, 18 November 1992.
Los Angeles Times, 18 November 1992.
New York Times, 18 November 1992.
Washington Post, 18 November 1992.
Entertainment Weekly, 20 November 1992.
Time (New York), 23 November 1992.
Harrell, Alfred D., ''*Malcolm X*: One Man's Legacy to the Letter,'' in *American Cinematographer* (Hollywood), vol. 73, no. 11, November 1992.

Malcolm X

Crowdus, Gary, and Dan Georgakas, ''Interview with Spike Lee,'' in *Cineaste* (New York), Winter 1992/1993.

Amiel, V., and others, *Positif* (Paris), February 1993.

Baecque, A. de., ''Docteur Spike et Mr. Lee,'' in *Cahiers du Cinéma* (Paris), February 1993.

Roy, A, ''La nouvelle histoire,'' in *24 Images* (Montreal), February 1993.

Alexander, K., *Sight and Sound* (London), March 1993.

Welsh, J. M., *Films in Review* (New York), March 1993.

Riley, V., *Cinema Papers* (Melbourne), May 1993.

''Malcolm Little's Big Sister,'' in *New Yorker*, vol. 70, no. 47, 30 January 1995.

Reid, M.A., ''The Brand X of Post Negritude Frontier,'' in *Film Criticism* (Meadville), vol. 20, no. 1/2, 1995/1996.

Bowman, James, ''Spike Lee: 'Artist','' in *National Review*, vol. 50, no. 14, 26 July 1999.

* * *

Malcolm X is the first film about an African American to be given a blockbuster budget by a Hollywood studio. That the film was made at all, much less as an epic, is primarily due to writer/director Spike Lee's history of producing controversial films that make money. Not surprisingly, *Malcolm X* was surrounded by racially-based tensions from the onset. Lee used racial considerations to wrest control of the project from white directors only to find himself maligned by some African American intellectuals who felt he was not qualified to take on so weighty a subject. Yet another racial nuance arose when Warner Brothers refused to approve completion funding after Lee went over budget. The director had to obtain millions in gifts from prominent African American entertainers and athletes to continue the film while Warner Brothers feuded with a bond company.

Despite this considerable pre-release sound and fury, including numerous predictions in the press that the film would surely inflame white and/or black audiences to violence, when Malcolm X finally appeared, public reaction was remarkably subdued. Rather than provoking his audiences with a film about social and racial conflict, Lee had opted for a hagiographic script stressing the theme of personal redemption. The three main sections of the film might easily have been subtitled ''Malcolm the Criminal,'' ''Malcolm the Prophet,'' and ''Malcolm the Martyr.''

After sensationalistic opening credits in which an X becomes a burning American flag and contemporary conflicts between African Americans and police are referenced, the film opens with Malcolm in his zoot suit period. An elaborate dance hall sequence has Malcolm hurrying home a respectable black woman in order to return for a tryst with Sophia, a white woman who will become his consort. He soon becomes part of Harlem's crime scene and is shown at bars handling gambling transactions but not pimping or selling drugs, other facets of his criminal years. After a fallout with West Indian Archie, the mob boss, Malcolm and his sidekick Shorty flee to Boston where they become house robbers until caught and sent to prison. The house-breaking is mainly played for laughs as are Malcolm's repeated hair straightening shampoos, painful procedures used in his autobiography to symbolize self-hatred and wanting to be white.

The prison sequences dramatize Malcolm's conversion to the Nation of Islam by a fellow inmate who will later grow jealous of his pupil's fame. This is one of many departures from the autobiography Lee vehemently insists was his final guide in shaping the script. In reality Malcolm's conversion was mainly the work of his immediate family and daily correspondence from Elijah Muhammad, the sect's leader.

Following his release from prison, Malcolm is shown having a meteoric rise through the ranks of the Nation until he is second in importance only to Elijah Muhammad. Viewers unfamiliar with the movement are likely to get the impression that it was much larger than it was (a few thousand at most), but Malcolm's pivotal role in its growth and public image is on target. His anti-white speeches and virulent attacks on civil rights leaders are mainly kept off screen while his equally strong views on personal and community self-help are spotlighted. His personal life, particularly his marriage, is projected as exemplary. In that regard, Denzel Washington who does a superb job conveying the zeal, body language, and speaking style of the public Malcolm renders a private Malcolm who is rather saccharine and humorless.

The least convincing aspects of the film chronicle Malcolm's pilgrimage to Mecca where he discovers the Nation is regarded as heretical because of its teachings that all white people are devils. Upon his return to America, Malcolm breaks with the Nation to form rival religious and secular organizations. From what is projected on the screen Malcolm's motivation appears to be disillusionment with Elijah Muhammad's spiritual authority compounded by knowledge of Elijah's sexual infidelities. What robs these crucial moments in Malcolm's life of their dynamism is the complete omission of Malcolm's subsequent trips to Africa and the Middle East.

During those journeys Malcolm met many heads of state, the majority of whom considered themselves socialists and revolutionaries. They urged him to join the civil rights movement for an integrated America and to internationalize the African American struggle by making it an issue at the United Nations. Malcolm X followed that advice by taking steps to mend the feud he had instigated with Martin Luther King and to align his new secular organization, the Organization of Afro-American Unity, with the mainstream civil rights movement. Omission of this trajectory distorts the account of his final year.

Lee takes great pains to show us CIA agents photographing Malcolm in Egypt and FBI agents bugging his phone and premises in New York. Given the context Lee has set up, this seems simple racist paranoia rather than a concern about Malcolm's international contacts and his ideological drift to the political left. Rather than probe this aspect of Malcolm's final days, the film takes the easier course of presenting the mechanics of the assassination in great detail. What amounts to an epiphany has been signalled from the start by various devices, including Malcolm's repeated visual recall of his father's persecution by klansmen. His own assassins are shown as Muslims solely motivated by religious fanaticism.

Ossie Davis's funeral oration is used to segue to a montage sequence in which Malcolm's name and image become the symbols of integrity and rebellion for black America. Black children chant, ''I am Malcolm,'' and Nelson Mandella appears as a school teacher imploring us all to study Malcolm's life. The film concludes with engaging documentary footage of the real Malcolm. These few moments offer images of a man far more vital and complex than the staid icon depicted in the fictional portions of the film.

Both the strengths and weaknesses of *Malcolm X* stem from the decision to make it an inspirational biopic. The hero's worst behavior, his most controversial ideas, and his changing political views have all been muted. What is projected is the story of how a young black man caught in the racism and crime of the big city completely remade his life and finally even shed off racism only to be gunned down by former compatriots whose vision could not grow as full as his own.

Lee's response to criticism that his film is too superficial is that he did not intend it to be the last word on Malcolm X but a stimulus for further study, particularly by young people. Using that standard as a measure, Lee more than met his goal. The baseball caps with X on them that he used to promote the film became omnipresent in black communities. The film also sent sales of books by and about Malcolm into the millions of copies. Despite a running time of 201 minutes, the film turned a modest profit while garnering its share of awards at various national and international film events.

—Dan Georgakas

MALENKAYA VERA

(Little Vera)

USSR, 1988

Director: Vasili Pichul

Production: Gorky Studios; colour, 35mm; running time: 134 minutes.

Production manager: Yuri Prober; **screenplay:** Mariya Khmelik; **photography:** Yefim Reznikov; **editor:** Yelena Zabolotskaya; **assistant director:** Valentina Pereverzeva; **art director:** Vladimir Pasternak; **music:** Vladimir Matetski; **sound editor:** Pavel Drozdov.

Cast: Natalya Negoda (*Vera*); Liudmila Zaitseva (*Mother*); Andrei Sokolov (*Sergei*); Yuri Nazarov (*Father*); Alexander Alexeyev-Negreba (*Viktor*); Alexandra Tabakova (*Christyakova*); Andrei Fomin (*Andrei*); Alexander Mironov (*Tolik*); Alexander Linkov (*Mikhail*).

Publications

Books:

Brashinsky, Michael, and Andrew Horton, *Russian Critics on the Cinema of Glasnost*, Cambridge University Press, 1994.
Beumers, Birgit, editor, *Russia on Reels: The Russian Idea in Post-Soviet Cinema*, London, 1999.

Articles:

Variety (New York), 20 July 1988.
Williamson, Anne, ''Rubles of the Game,'' in *Film Comment*, January/February 1989.
Bassan, R., in *Revue du Cinéma* (Paris), April 1989.
Legrand, J, ''Le feu aux poudres'' in *Positif* (Paris), June 1989.
Mazabrard, C., and L. Danilou, in *Cahiers du Cinéma* (Paris), June 1989.
Horton, A., in *Film Quarterly* (Berkeley), Summer 1989.
Glaessner, V., in *Monthly Film Bulletin* (London), July 1989.
Scheck, F., *in Films in Review* (New York), October 1989.
Delmas, G., in *Jeune Cinéma* (Paris), October-November 1989.
Elia, M., *in Séquences* (Montreal), November 1989.
Eagle, H., ''The Indexality of Little Vera and the End of Socialist Realism,'' in *Wide Angle* (Athens, Ohio), October 1990.
Sperling, V., ''Peeking Behind the Celluloid Curtain,'' in *Journal Of Popular Film and Television* (Berkeley), Winter 1991.
Cymbal, Evgenij, ''Into a New World,'' in *Sight and Sound* (London), vol. 2, no. 7, November 1992.
Mury, Cécile, ''La scandaleuse de Moscou,'' in *Télérama* (Paris), no. 2360, 5 April 1995.
Gessen, M., ''Sex in the Media and the Birth of the Sex Media in Russia,'' in *Genders*, no. 22, 1995.

* * *

While *Little Vera*, directed by Vasili Pichul, was the most popular film in Russia in 1988, its appearance was met with criticism and skepticism as well as excitement. As the political climate in the Soviet Republics changed once again, the country's relationship with its art transformed as well. Just as Stravinsky's *Rite of Spring* had accompanied the beginning of the 20th century with atonality and discordance in contrast to the tradition of tonality and comfortable, predictable melodic forms, *Little Vera* marked the end of Socialist Realism, which depicted reality according to the dictums of the Communist Party, in Soviet film.

This film deals with such unsavory issues as teenage sexuality, alcoholism, and criminality, suggesting the failure of the socialist experiment. As Herbert Eagle observed in *Wide Angle*, many viewers of this bold work objected to its casual portrayal of sexuality, the crass and hostile behavior of some characters, and its focus on the dismal features of modern Soviet life. ''One might therefore have the impression that *Little Vera* deals with a particularly antisocial, anarchic, uneducated or even criminal stratum of Soviet society,'' Eagle writes. ''In fact, *Little Vera*'s characters are solidly mainstream and their actions rather typical.''

Little Vera takes place in a drab, industrial Ukrainian town, Zhdanov, a standard Soviet town shown as it really is. The atmosphere is hovered with gray smoke; massive blocks of buildings, homes to thousands, are crowded together. Vera, a recent high school graduate, lives with her parents and works as a telephone operator. Her strict mother and alcoholic father are frustrated by her surly attitude and carefree lifestyle. Written by Maria Khemlik, Pichul's wife, the story addresses the hopelessness of this young woman's existence and the degree to which she is defined by the men in her life. Her brother has the elevated status of a doctor and lives in Moscow, many miles removed from his humble beginnings; her devoted boyfriend Andrei pursues Vera tirelessly and offers her secure social status through traditional marriage, which she rejects. But more importantly, as Andrew Horton argues in his review of *Little Vera* in *Film Quarterly*, ''Vera exists between the sympathetic acceptance of her quietly desperate father and the antisocial freedom represented in Sergei and their tempestuous affair. Neither wholly modern (despite her streaked hair and mod clothes) nor traditional, Vera is squarely caught in the middle with little hope of escape.''

As noted in *Soviet Cinematography, 1918–1991*, the success of *Little Vera* is incomparable with other films that became prominent in the first years of *perestroika* (thaw). Various surveys indicate this film was more popular than all the others. It can be considered a clear example of Gorbachev's *glasnost* (new openness) policy by marking a pivotal point at which the cinema defied Communist Party values and objectives, reflexively examining and criticizing the social and economic conditions arrived at in the late 20th century by communism. In these early years of *glasnost*, filmmakers treated social issues in their films with an unfiltered lens and unabashed honesty that had previously been unacceptable. This low-budget Soviet feature was the first Soviet film with a sense of sexual candor, the first to mention AIDS in a feature film, and the first to acknowledge the prevalence of non-white children of white mothers. Cinematographers considered the expansion of sexual matters in movies to be an important aspect of the struggle against official ideology; hence, the movies of 1986–1988 presented a challenge to traditional Soviet ideology by dealing with the realities of sexuality, such as the sexual activity of teenagers, which had not been addressed by official propaganda, and by presenting sexual relationships as pleasurable in and of themselves. The world in *Little Vera* is ripe with sensuality and passion—but plagued by dysfunction and brutality as well.

Glasnost allowed filmmakers to take new liberties with an audience primed for uncharted material. Pichul's film deals with working-class subject matter and was produced by Gorky Studios in Moscow, one of the smaller studios previously overshadowed by Mosfilm in Moscow and Lenfilm in Leningrad (St. Petersburg). The production quality is at times low, in contrast to the seamless, high-quality films that had established the tradition for Soviet films for decades. *Little Vera* is evidence of how contemporary Soviet cinema moved away from the idealism of Socialist Realism. As Horton observes, the film ''is an important contribution to a growing number of films that honestly capture a 'no win' mood of many Soviet young people. . . as opposed to the forced optimism of so many Socialist Realist films of the past.'' And Eagle argues that ''*Little Vera*'s stylistic raggedness seems intended as a deliberate appeal to indexicality, an assertion that this is life, not Socialist Realism.'' *Little Vera*, he believes, can be viewed as the work which marks the arrival of narrative film as an index of actual life, thus it looks and feels like a documentary filmed in a cramped environment.

Anne Williamson, writing in *Film Comment*, notes that hard-hitting features on contemporary Soviet life had been almost non-existent for nearly 50 years before the arrival of *Little Vera*: ''When Lenin declared cinema to be the most important of all the arts, he intended to harness film's energy to the ambitions of the Soviet state.

Under Stalin these aims were further refined in Socialist Realism, which promptly strangled Soviet cinema. After Stalin's passing, the effort to shape and lead the audience devolved into sentimental drivel.'' In the period of *glasnost* the cinema could explore a new, ironic beauty on the screen: images untethered by ideology and fear of political sanctions. The camera could once again function as Sergei Eisenstein's kino eye and present film truth. The cinema could capture life and project it on the screen, giving audiences a Lilliputian view of themselves. This honest, cathartic look at Russian society, one hopes, might be a move (as Vera's father toasts before swallowing a glass of vodka) ''Forward, singing.''

—Kelly Otter

THE MALTESE FALCON

USA, 1941

Director: John Huston

Production: Warner Bros. Pictures, Inc.; black and white, 35mm; running time: 100 minutes. Released 3 October 1941. Filmed June-July, 1941 in Warner Bros. studios. Cost: budgeted at $300,000.

Producers: Hal B. Wallis with Henry Blanke; **screenplay:** John Huston, from the novel by Dashiell Hammett; **photography:** Arthur Edeson; **editor:** Thomas Richards; **sound:** Oliver S. Garretson; **art director:** Robert Haas; **music:** Adolph Deutsch; **musical director:** Leo. F. Forbstein; **costume designer:** Orry-Kelly.

Cast: Humphrey Bogart (*Sam Spade*); Mary Astor (*Brigid O'Shaughnessy*); Sidney Greenstreet (*Kasper Gutman, the Fat Man*); Peter Lorre (*Joel Cairo*); Elisha Cook, Jr. (*Wilmer Cook*); Lee Patrick (*Effie Perine*); Barton MacLane (*Detective Lieutenant*); Jerome Cowan (*Miles Archer*); Gladys George (*Iva Archer*); Ward Bond (*Detective Polhaus*); James Burke (*Luke*); Murray Alper (*Frank Richman*); John Hamilton (*Bryan*); Walter Huston (*Ship's officer*).

Publications

Script:

Huston, John, *The Maltese Falcon*, New York, 1974.

Books:

Davay, Paul, *John Huston*, Paris, 1957.
Allais, Jean-Claude, *John Huston*, Paris, 1960.
Nolan, William, *John Huston, King Rebel*, New York, 1965.
Hill, Jonathan, and Jonah Ruddy, *Bogey: The Man, The Actor, The Legend*, London, 1965.
Hyams, Joe, *Bogie*, New York, 1966.
Benayoun, Robert, *John Huston*, Paris, 1966; revised edition, 1985.
Cecchini, Riccardo, *John Huston*, Viridiana, 1969.
Tozzi, Romano, *John Huston: A Picture Treasure of His Films*, New York, 1971.
McArthur, Colin, *Underworld U.S.A.*, London, 1972.
Sklar, Robert, *Movie-Made America*, New York, 1975.
Madsen, Axel, *John Huston*, New York, 1978.
Kaplan, E. Ann, editor, *Women in Film Noir*, London, 1978.
Kaminsky, Stuart M., *John Huston: Maker of Magic*, Boston, 1978.
Silver, Alain, and Elizabeth Ward, editors, *Film Noir*, Woodstock, New York, 1979.
Pettigrew, Terence, *Bogart: A Definitive Study of His Film Career*, London, 1981.
Giannetti, Louis, *Masters of the American Cinema*, Englewood Cliffs, New Jersey, 1981.
Winkler, Willi, *Humphrey Bogart und Hollywoods Schwarze Serie*, Munich, 1985.
Hammen, Scott, *John Huston*, Boston, 1985.
Fuchs, Wolfgang J., *Humphrey Bogart, Cult-Star: A Documentation*, Berlin, 1987.
McCarty, John, *The Films of John Huston*, Secaucus, New Jersey, 1987.
Studlar, Gaylyn, editor, *Reflections in a Male Eye: John Huston & the American Experience*, Washington, D.C., 1993.
Cooper, Stephen, *Perspectives on John Huston*, New York, 1994.
Luhr, William, editor, *The Maltese Falcon: John Huston, Director*, New Brunswick, New Jersey, 1996.
Brill, Lesley, *John Huston's Filmmaking*, New York, 1997.
Cohen, Allen, *John Huston: A Guide to References & Resources*, New York, 1997.
Cunningham, Ernest W., *Ultimate Bogie*, Los Angeles, 1999.

Articles:

Variety (New York), 1 October 1941.
New York Times, 4 October 1941.
Times (London), 22 June 1942.
''Huston Issue'' of *Positif* (Paris), August 1952.
''John Huston,'' in *Films and Filming* (London), October 1954.
Barnes, Peter, ''Gunman No. 1,'' in *Films and Filming* (London), September 1955.
Houston, Penelope, ''The Private Eye,'' in *Sight and Sound* (London), Summer 1956.
''Huston Issue'' of *Positif* (Paris), January 1957.
''Huston Issue'' of *Bianco e Nero* (Rome), April 1957.
Archer, Eugene, in *Film Culture* (New York), no. 19, 1959.
Archer, Eugene, in *Films and Filming* (London), September and October 1959.
Martin, Marcel, in *Cinéma* (Paris), no. 64, 1962.
Eyles, Allen, in *Films and Filming* (London), November 1964.
Mallory, David, in *Film Society Review* (New York), February 1966.
Taylor, John Russell, ''John Huston and the Figure in the Carpet,'' in *Sight and Sound* (London), Spring 1969.
Schrader, Paul, ''Notes on Film Noir,'' in *Film Comment* (New York), Spring 1972.
Naremore, James, ''John Huston and *The Maltese Falcon*,'' in *Literature/Film Quarterly* (Salisbury, Maryland), July 1973.
Gow, Gordon, ''Pursuit of the Falcon,'' in *Films and Filming* (London), March 1974.
Beal, Greg, and Peg Masterson, in *Cinema Texas Program Notes* (Austin), 16 September 1976.
Profirio, Robert, ''No Way Out,'' in *Sight and Sound* (London), Autumn 1976.

Guerif, F., in *Lumière du Cinéma* (Paris), March 1977.
McVay, Douglas, in *Focus on Film* (London), no. 30, 1978.
Journal of Popular Film (Washington, D.C), vol. 7, no. 1, 1978.
Benayoun, Robert, in *Avant-Scène du Cinéma* (Paris), 1 October 1979.
Everson, William K., in *Films in Review* (New York), March 1980.
Jenkins, Stephen, ''Dashiell Hammett and Film Noir,'' in *Monthly Film Bulletin* (London), November, 1982.
Benaquist, L., ''Function and Index in Huston's *The Maltese Falcon*,'' in *Film Criticism* (Edinboro, Pennsylvania), Winter 1982.
Johnson, W., ''Sound and Image,'' in *Film Quarterly* (Berkeley), no. 1, 1989.
Maxfield, J. F., '''La Belle Dame Sans Merci' and the Neurotic Knight: Characterization in *The Maltese Falcon*,'' in *Literature/Film Quarterly* (Salisbury, Maryland), no. 4, 1989.
Reid's Film Index (Wyong), no. 6, 1991.
Marling, W., ''On the Relation Between American Roman Noir and Film Noir,'' in *Literature/Film Quarterly* (Salisbury, Maryland), no. 3, 1993.
Edelman, Lee, ''Plasticity, Paternity, Perversity: Freud's 'Falcon,' Huston's 'Freud,''' in *American Imago*, (Highland Park, New Jersey), Spring 1994.
Thomson, D., ''Junior,'' in *Film Comment* (New York), vol. 31, September/October 1995.
Gale, Steven H., ''*The Maltese Falcon*: Melodrama or Film Noir?'' in *Literature/Film Quarterly* (Salisbury), vol. 24, no. 2, April 1996.
Marks, M., ''Music, Drama, Warner Brothers: The Cases for *Casablanca* and *The Maltese Falcon*,'' in *Michigan Quarterly Review*, vol. 35, no. 1, 1996.
Turner, George, ''*The Maltese Falcon*: A Tale Thrice Filmed,'' in *American Cinematographer* (Hollywood), vol. 78, no. 4, April 1997.
Boon, Kevin A., ''In Debt to Dashiell: John Huston's Adaptation of *The Maltese Falcon*,'' in *Creative Screenwriting* (Washington, D.C.), vol. 4, no. 2, Summer 1997.

* * *

The Maltese Falcon opens with credits appearing over the falcon statue, which casts a shadow into the depth of the frame. There follows a printed commentary, over the image, about the falcon's history. A shot of San Francisco, the Golden Gate Bridge, establishes location, and we move to the Spade and Archer sign on the window of their office. The shadow letters ''Spade and Archer'' appear on the office floor throughout the opening scene. Spade and Archer share the same office, are inextricably linked, and, we discover, even share Archer's wife, Iva (Gladys George). John Huston, in his first directing effort, quickly establishes the link between the two men so that later, when Spade (Humphrey Bogart) denounces Brigid (Mary Astor) for Archer's murder, we understand that it has nothing to do with Spade's like or dislike of his partner. The situation and atmosphere have been economically achieved.

To emphasize the construction of investigation, Huston frequently limits the space in which Spade must move. Spade's office is small; so is his apartment. In fact, in a departure from convention, Huston chose to build some of his sets with ceilings. (The more usual procedure during that period of filmmaking was not to show the ceiling so that lights could be placed above the action and the camera could be free to move upward) Huston also explored a unique style of framing with *The Maltese Falcon*. Following his own sketches, he set up shots as if they were paintings. For instance, Huston placed characters in the foreground of a shot, their faces often covering half the screen. Frequently, too, the character is not talking, but listening. His reactions thus become more important than those of the person who is speaking or moving.

The Maltese Falcon presented situations that Huston would return to again and again. Spade is the obsessed professional, a proud man who will adhere to a principle unto death. Women are a threat, temptations that can only sway the hero from his professional commitment. They may be wilfully trying to deceive, as Brigid and Iva, or (as in later Huston films), they may be the unwitting cause of the protagonist's defeat or near-defeat. Protagonists in Huston films frequently take risks, gamble with their lives. Spade constantly taunts the mad Wilmer, even using Huston's favourite personal referent—''kid''—to goad him. The taunting is potentially dangerous, but Spade enjoys it.

As Huston was to develop as a director, the image of the ill-fated group that begins with *Falcon* was to emerge more strongly. Gutman, Cairo, Wilmer, and Brigid are parts of an alliance of greed. They distrust each other but also respect each other. Spade refuses to join the group and survives. The others don't. Huston was to increasingly develop the idea that groups are doomed families, the survivors of which must learn to accept defeat with grace and dignity.

The idea of appreciating expert deception also emerges in *Falcon*. Bogart's admiration for Brigid's ability to lie is part of his love for her ''You're good, you're real good,'' he says with a smile after a particular lie. In contrast, Spade is scornful of Iva because her lies are so transparent. A Huston hero, like Huston, appreciates wit, intelligence, and a good performance even if they come from a consummate villain.

Although Huston and others have suggested that *The Maltese Falcon* is almost a line-by-line filming of the novel, there are important technical and sequential, as well as plot and character, differences between the two versions of the story. Hammett's original novel was written and set in 1928–1929; the Huston version is clearly updated to 1940. Also, the conclusions of Hammett's novel is quite different from that of Huston's film. The film ends with Sam Spade watching Brigid disappear through the prisonlike bars of the elevator of his apartment building. Hammett's novel ends with Spade back in his office, where he puts his arm around the waist of his secretary, Effie, and she pulls away from him in confusion because he has turned Brigid in. The novel's last few lines indicate that Spade will have to deal with Iva Archer, who has come to see him again.

Such alterations are, however, less important than the film's dark humor, the deceit and paranoia of its characters, and the brooding darkness and matter-of-fact presentation that made *The Maltese Falcon* the first clear step into film noir.

—Stuart M. Kaminsky

MAN BITES DOG

See **C'EST ARRIVÉ PRÈS DE CHEZ VOUS**

A MAN ESCAPED

See **UN CONDAMNE A MORT S'EST ECHAPPE**

MAN OF MARBLE

See **CZLOWIEK Z MARMURU**

MAN OF ARAN

UK, 1934

Director: Robert Flaherty

Production: Gainsborough Pictures, Ltd. for Gaumont-British Corp.; black and white, 35mm; running time: 76 minutes. Released 25 April 1934, London. Filmed approximately 1931–33 in the Aran Islands, off the coast of Ireland.

Producer: Michael Balcon; **screenplay:** Robert Flaherty with Frances Flaherty, with scenarist credit for John Goldman; **photography:** Robert Flaherty, David Flaherty, and John Taylor; **editor:** John Goldman; **sound:** H. Hand; **music:** John Greenwood.

Cast: Colman ''Tiger'' King (*A Man of Aran*); Maggie Dirrane (*His wife*); Michael Dillane (*Their son*); Pat Mullin (*Himself*); Patch Ruadh (*Red Beard*); Patcheen Flaherty and Tommy O'Roarke (*The Shark hunters*); Patcheen Conneely, Stephen Dirrane, Mac McDonough (*The Curragh men*).

Award: Venice International Film Festival, Best Foreign Film, 1934.

Publications

Books:

Griffith, Richard, *The World of Robert Flaherty*, New York, 1953.

Quintar, Fuad, *Robert Flaherty et le documentaire poetique*, Paris, 1960.

Flaherty, Frances, *The Odyssey of a Film-Maker: Robert Flaherty's Story*, Urbana, Illinois, 1960.

Clemente, Jose L., *Robert Flaherty*, Madrid, 1963.

Cuenca, Carlos Fernandez, *Robert Flaherty*, Madrid, 1963.

Calder-Marshall, Arthur, *The Innocent Eye: The Life of Robert J. Flaherty*, London, 1963; New York, 1966.

Klaue, Wolfgang, editor, *Robert Flaherty*, East Berlin, 1964.

Agel, Henri, *Robert J. Flaherty*, Paris, 1965.

Barsam, Richard, *Nonfiction Film: A Critical History*, New York, 1973.

Barnouw, Erik, *Documentary: A History of the Non-Fiction Film*, New York, 1974.

Napolitano, Antonio, *Robert J. Flaherty*, Florence, 1975.

Murphy, William T., *Robert Flaherty: A Guide to References and Resources*, Boston, 1979.

Williams, Christopher, *Realism and Cinema: A Reader*, London, 1980.

Rotha, Paul, *Robert J. Flaherty: A Biography*, Philadelphia, 1983.

Barsam, Richard, *The Vision of Robert Flaherty: The Artist as Myth and Filmmaker*, Bloomington, 1988.

Articles:

Rotha, Paul, in *Sight and Sound* (London), Summer 1934.

Sennwald, Andre, in *New York Times*, 19 October 1934.

Variety (New York), 23 October 1934.

O'Neil, Brian, in *New Masses* (New York), 30 October 1934.

Ferguson, Otis, in *New Republic* (New York), 7 November 1934.

Grenville, Vernon, in *Commonweal* (New York), 9 November 1934.

Greene, Graham, ''Subjects and Stories,'' in *Footnotes to the Film*, edited by Charles Davy, New York, 1938.

Sadoul, Georges, ''Hommage à Robert Flaherty,'' in *Lettres Françaises* (Paris), 13 September 1951.

Kempe, Fritz, ''Robert Flaherty und seine Film,'' in *Film Bild Ton* (Munich), December 1952.

Flaherty, Frances, ''How *Man of Aran* Came into Being,'' in *Film News* (New York), no. 3, 1953.

Lee, Rohama, ''Flaherty's Finest Film,'' in *Film News* (New York), no. 3, 1953.

Martin, Marcel, ''Robert Flaherty,'' in *Anthologie du cinéma 1*, Paris, 1965.

Van Dongen, Helen, ''Robert J. Flaherty,'' in *Film Quarterly* (Berkeley), Summer 1965.

Armes, Roy, ''Flaherty and the Idea of Documentary,'' in *Film and Reality: An Historical Survey*, Baltimore, 1974.

Van Dongen, Helen, ''Robert J. Flaherty,'' in *Non-Fiction Film: Theory and Criticism*, edited by Richard Barsam, New York, 1976.

Hitchens, G., ''How the Myth Was Made,'' in *Film Library Quarterly* (New York), no. 3, 1978.

Vogel, A., ''Independents,'' in *Film Comment* (New York), March-April 1979.

Lerner, Jesse, ''Flaherty in Motion: The 38th Annual Robert Flaherty Film Seminar,'' in *Afterimage* (London), vol. 20, no. 5, December 1992.

Kaneko, Ann, ''40th Annual Robert Flaherty Seminar,'' in *Afterimage* (London), vol. 22, no. 4, November 1994.

Short review, in *Télérama* (Paris), no. 2357, 15 March 1995.

Marks, Dan, ''Ethnography and Ethnographic Film: From Flaherty to Asch and After,'' in *American Anthropologist*, vol. 97, no. 2, June 1995.

Pilard, Philippe, and Richard Leacock, ''Robert Flaherty,'' in *Positif* (Paris), no. 412, June 1995.

Goldstein, Yosha, ''Here's Looking at You: 41st Annual Robert Flaherty Film Seminar,'' in *Afterimage* (London), vol. 23, no. 2, September-October 1995.

Leacock, Richard, ''In Defense of the Flaherty Traditions,'' in *Film Culture* (New York), no. 79, Winter 1996.

Pennebaker, D.A., ''Looking Back: Film Directors Robert Flaherty, Michael Powell and Jean-Luc Godard,'' in *Sight and Sound* (London), vol. 7, no. 4, April 1997.

* * *

Third in the corpus of Flaherty's four major films, *Man of Aran* is preceded by *Nanook of the North* (1922) and *Moana* (1926), followed by *Louisiana Story* (1948). It shares—in some ways makes most pronounced—the special beauties and difficulties his work presents.

Man of Aran

Its blend of idiosyncratic anthropological observation, a story constructed, for the most part, from non-fictional materials and enacted by non-actors, and the understanding it offers of the essentials of human existence are what make Flaherty's work uniquely valuable—*sui generis*.

Man of Aran has in common with the other films, as principal cast of characters, what anthropologists call the nuclear family—more appropriate to Inishmore than to Samoa. There is the strong and experienced father, the helpful and caring mother, and a boy (who moves increasingly towards the centre of the films—both as their subject and point of view—becoming dominant in *Louisiana Story*.) The mother in *Aran* is a stronger and more important figure than she is in the other films. Nature is prominent—preeminent you might even say—water and boats, hunting and fishing abound. In short it would seem the conditions in his films are much like those Flaherty grew up amidst in Northern Michigan and Canada, son of a mining engineer with Indians (as he would have called the native Americans) for companions.

These common elements may represent Flaherty's way of seeing the variegated cultures in which he set himself; they certainly become a major part of the substance of his films, organized along a simple chronological narrative line. In *Aran* he was attempting to repeat the very considerable success of *Nanook* (*Moana*, because it lacked *Nanook*'s drama it was thought, received almost no distribution) and also to move on from it.

In *Aran* the story becomes more articulated and coherent than in *Nanook*; more dramatic than in *Moana*. It still has the separate sequences dealing with various aspects of work for subsistence, but the identification is now more loosely with the son; frequently we take on his point of view. The scene in which the basking shark first appears below the cliff like a sea monster is pointed and masterful in this respect. And the drama of the storm concludes the film on a cosmic scale with the family—father, mother, son—surviving together after danger and loss in the face of the vast overwhelming sea and giant unyielding rock.

But is was exactly these elements of story and drama, the concentration on the elemental struggle that faced 20th-century Aran, that caused the film to be subjected to angry criticism—particularly from the political left in those years of deep economic depression. Rather than having the islanders recreate the capture of basking sharks, which they hadn't done for 60 years, why hadn't Flaherty dealt with the real and present economic concerns like absentee landlordism that plagued the society? The answer to that question seems to be that that was not what Flaherty saw, or what interested him anyway.

Though they had had some famous rows over these exact same issues, his old friend John Grierson, founder and leader of the British documentary movement, who had helped Flaherty set up the production of *Man of Aran*, came to his defence. Grierson singled out one of the detractors, ''whose article puts the principal objections: that Flaherty is a romantic escapist and that the film is only so much idyllic fudge. As I originally, I think, invented the word 'escapism' [in response to Flaherty's earlier work] . . . it may seem scurvy in me to double-cross a supporter. But I do not agree with his estimate either of Flaherty or *Man of Aran*.''

After praising the truths and beauties contained in *Aran*, unrivalled among films made within the commercial conditions of the theatrical film industry, Grierson returned to the central distinction between Flaherty's work and the documentary being made under his own leadership. ''Seen as the story of mankind over a period of a thousand years, the story of the Arans is very much a story of man against the sea and woman against the skyline. It is a simple story, but it is an essential story, for nothing emerges out of time except bravery. If I part company with Flaherty at that point, it is because I like my braveries to emerge otherwise than from the sea, and stand otherwise than against the sky. I imagine they shine as bravely in pursuit of Irish landlords as in the pursuit of Irish sharks.'' (''John Grierson Replies,'' *Cinema Quarterly*, Autumn 1934.)

But what ultimately seems most important in *Man of Aran*, as in all his films, is Flaherty's special use of the film medium, which grew out of his creative impulse. Stated simply, he used film to show people he loved and admired the rest of us. He was not an anthropologist; he idealized and interpreted as an artist does, a visual poet in his case. The view he offers is his view, admittedly. In some respects his films are as much about him—his pleasures, his prejudices, his convictions—as about the people he was filming. Often he set them back in time to recapture and preserve cultures that were disappearing, and he always presented them at their finest, simplest, and noblest, gaining their cooperation to achieve this presentation. But Flaherty did not invent or glamorize. *Aran* and the rest were not created from make-believe or fakery; all that he shows did happen or had happened.

To patronize Flaherty as a ''romantic,'' as Paul Rotha and others did in the 1930s, seems to me to miss the point. One can see what Rotha is thinking of if the people and settings Flaherty chose and the way he chose to present them are linked with the noble savage of Jean-Jacques Rousseau and the idealized landscapes of early 19th-century painters. But Flaherty's films have little to do with the romanticism of the romantic movement, resting as it does on individual imagination and subjective emotions. On the contrary, his work might be said to be ''classical,'' as I understand the romantic/classical dichotomy; it is spare and uninvolved with individual psychologies. He seems like a genial pagan or a prefall Adam—lacking interest in Christian notions of sin and guilt in any case.

Flaherty worked with what he understood and said what he had to say. That statement was, throughout his work, that humankind has an innate dignity, and that beauty dwells in its patterns of survival and existence. Considered in this way, *Man of Aran* takes its proper place as a master work within the Flaherty canon.

—Jack C. Ellis

THE MAN WHO SHOT LIBERTY VALANCE

USA, 1962

Director: John Ford

Production: Ford Productions-Paramount; black and white, 35mm; running time: 122 minutes. Released April 1962. Filmed September 1961 in Paramount studios. Cost: budgeted at $3.2 million, (according to Ford's grandson).

Producer: Willis Goldbeck; **screenplay:** Willis Goldbeck and James Warner Bellah, from the story by Dorothy M. Johnson; **photography:** William H. Clothier; **editor:** Otho Lovering; **sound:** Philip Mitchell; **art directors:** Hal Pereira and Eddie Imazu; **music:** Cyril Mockridge; **music director:** Irvin Talbot (theme from *Young Mr. Lincoln* by Alfred Newman); **costume designer:** Edith Head.

Cast: James Stewart (*Ransom Stoddard*); John Wayne (*Tom Doniphon*); Vera Miles (*Hallie Stoddard*); Lee Marvin (*Liberty Valance*); Edmond O'Brien (*Dutton Peabody*); Andy Devine (*Link Appleyard*); Ken Murray (*Doc Willoughby*); John Carradine (*Starbuckle*); Jeanette Nolan (*Nora Ericson*); John Qualen (*Peter Ericson*); Willis Bouchey (*Jason Tully*); Carleton Young (*Maxwell Scott*); Woody Strode (*Pompey*); Denver Pyle (*Amos Carruthers*);

The Man Who Shot Liberty Valance

Strother Martin (*Floyd*); Lee Van Cleef (*Reese*); Robert F. Simon (*Handy Strong*); O. Z. Whitehead (*Ben Carruthers*); Paul Birch (*Mayor Winder*); Joseph Hoover (*Hasbrouck*); Jack Pennick (*Barman*); Anna Lee (*Passenger*); Charles Seel (*President, Election Council*); Shug Fisher (*Drunk*); Earle Hodgins; Stuart Holmes; Dorothy Phillips; Buddy Roosevelt; Gertrude Astor; Eva Novak; Slim Talbot; Monty Montana; Bill Henry; John B. Whiteford; Helen Gibson; Major Sam Harris.

Publications

Books:

Mitchell, George J., *The Films of John Ford*, 1963.

Haudiquet, Philippe, *John Ford*, Paris, 1964.

Bogdanovich, Peter, *John Ford*, Berkeley, 1968; revised edition, 1978.

Kitses, Jim, *Horizons West*, Bloomington, Indiana, 1970.

Jones, Ken D., *The Films of James Stewart*, New York, 1970.

Ricci, Mark, and Boris and Steve Zmijewsky, *The Films of John Wayne*, New York, 1970; revised edition, as *The Complete Films of John Wayne*, Secaucus, New Jersey, 1983.

Baxter, John, *The Cinema of John Ford*, New York, 1971.

Cawelti, John, *The Six-Gun Mystique*, Bowling Green, Ohio, 1971.

Place, Janey, *The Western Films of John Ford*, Secaucus, New Jersey, 1973.

Kaminsky, Stuart M., *American Film Genres*, Dayton, Ohio, 1974; revised edition, Chicago, 1985.

Barbour, Alan, *John Wayne*, New York, 1974.

Thompson, Howard, *James Stewart*, New York, 1974.

McBride, Joseph, and Michael Wilmington, *John Ford*, New York and London, 1975.

Sarris, Andrew, *The John Ford Movie Mystery*, London, 1976.

Sinclair, Andrew, *John Ford*, London and New York, 1979.

Ford, Dan, *Pappy: The Life of John Ford*, Englewood Cliffs, New Jersey, 1979.

Eyles, Allen, *John Wayne*, South Brunswick, New Jersey, 1979.

Zec, Donald, *Marvin: The Story of Lee Marvin*, London, 1979.

Anderson, Lindsay, *About John Ford*, London, 1981; New York, 1983; 1999.

Caughie, John, editor, *Theories of Authorship: A Reader*, London, 1981.

Schatz, Thomas, *Hollywood Genres: Formulas, Filmmaking, and the Studio System*, New York, 1981.

Reed, Joseph W., *Three American Originals: John Ford, William Faulkner, Charles Ives*, Middletown, Connecticut, 1984.

Eyles, Allen, *James Stewart*, London, 1984.

Hunter, Allan, *James Stewart*, New York, 1985.

Robbins, Jhan, *Everybody's Man: A Biography of James Stewart*, New York, 1985.

Ray, Robert B., *A Certain Tendency of the Hollywood Cinema 1930–1980*, Princeton, 1985.

Kieskalt, Charles John, *The Official John Wayne Reference Book*, Secaucus, New Jersey, 1985.

Shepherd, Donald, and others, *Duke: The Life and Times of John Wayne*, London, 1985.

Gallagher, Tag, *John Ford: The Man and His Films*, Berkeley, 1986.

Stowell, Peter, *John Ford*, Boston, 1986.

Lepper, David, *John Wayne*, London, 1987.

Levy, Emanuel, *John Wayne, Prophet of the American Way of Life*, Metuchen, New Jersey, 1988.

Riggin, Judith M., *John Wayne: A Bio-Bibliography*, Westport, 1992.

Lourdeaux, Lee, *Italian & Irish Filmmakers in America: Ford, Capra, Coppola and Scorsese*, Springfield, 1993.

Davis, Ronald L., *John Ford: Hollywood's Old Master*, Norman, 1995.

Darby, William, *John Ford's Westerns: A Thematic Analysis, with a Filmography*, Jefferson, 1996.

Thomas, Tony, *A Wonderful Life: The Films & Career of James Stewart*, Secaucus, 1997.

Girgus, Sam B., *Hollywood Renaissance: The Cinema of Democracy in the Era of Ford, Capra, and Kazan*, New York, 1998.

Levy, Bill, *John Ford: A Bio-Bibliography*, Westport, 1998.

Eyman, Scott, *Print the Legend: The Life & Times of John Ford*, New York, 1999.

Articles:

Mifflin, Wilfred, in *Films in Review* (New York), May 1962.

McVay, Douglas, ''The Five Worlds of John Ford,'' in *Films and Filming* (London), June 1962.

Jones, DuPre, in *Sight and Sound* (London), Summer 1962.

Sarris, Andrew, ''Cactus Rosebud; or, *The Man Who Shot Liberty Valance*,'' in *Film Culture* (New York), Summer 1962.

Callenbach, Ernest, in *Film Quarterly* (Berkeley), Winter 1963–64.

Vöbel, F. W., in *Filmanalysen 2*, edited by Franz Everschor, Dusseldorf, 1964.

Sweigart, William, ''James Stewart,'' in *Films in Review* (New York), December 1964.

''John Ford Issue'' of *Cahiers du Cinéma* (Paris), October 1966.

Kennedy, Burt, ''Our Way West,'' in *Films and Filming* (London), October 1969.

Hall, Dennis John, ''Tall in the Saddle,'' in *Films and Filming* (London), October 1969.

Wood, Robin, ''Shall We Gather at the River: The Late Films of John Ford,'' in *Film Comment* (New York), Fall 1971.

Bordwell, David, in *Film Comment* (New York), Fall 1971.

Pechter, William, ''Persistence of Vision,'' in *24 Frames a Second*, New York, 1971.

Wollen, Peter, ''The Auteur Theory,'' in *Signs and Meaning in the Cinema*, London, 1972.

Pye, D., ''Genre and History—*Fort Apache* and *Liberty Valance*,'' in *Movie* (London), Winter 1977–78.

Coursen, D. F., ''John Ford's Wilderness—*The Man Who Shot Liberty Valance*,'' in *Sight and Sound* (London), Autumn 1978.

Lowry, Ed., in *Cinema Texas Program Notes* (Austin), 9 November 1978.

Amengual, Barthélemy, ''La Structure de l'eglantine,'' in *Positif* (Paris), June 1981.

Boyero, C., in *Casablanca* (Madrid), January 1983.

Skerry, P. J., ''The Western Film: A Sense of an Ending,'' in *New Orleans Review*, no. 3, 1990.

Braad Thomsen, C., in *Kosmorama* (Copenhagen), Summer 1990.

Della Casa, S., ''Amnesia land: il cinema del dimenticare,'' in *Ikon* (Milan), October 1990.

Darby, W., ''Musical Links in *Young Mr. Lincoln, My Darling Clementine*, and *The Man Who Shot Liberty Valance*,'' in *Cinema Journal* (Austin, Texas), no. 1, 1991.

Doyle, Kevin M., ''The L.A.P.D. and the Doniphon Syndrome (Glorification of Vigilante-style Police Tactics in Popular Movies and the Rodney King Beatings,'' in *America*, vol. 165, no. 1, 6 July 1991.

Roche, Mark W., and Vittorio Hosle, ''Vico's Age of Heroes and the Age of Men in John Ford's Film *The Man Who Shot Liberty Valance*,'' in *CLIO*, vol. 23, no. 2, Winter 1994.

Ingrassia, Catherine, '''I'm Not Kicking, I'm Talking': Discursive Economies in the Western,'' in *Film Criticism* (Meadville), vol. 20, no. 3, Spring 1996.

* * *

John Ford's *The Man Who Shot Liberty Valance* opened to mixed reviews in 1962, and played on the second half of many double bills. But two decades later critics see this film quite differently. *The Man Who Shot Liberty Valance* is now regarded as one of the greatest works of one of America's greatest filmmakers. It reaffirms John Ford's reputation as the master of the most American of the film genres, the western.

Coming late in the career of a director with a long-standing reputation as a creator of popular films, *The Man Who Shot Liberty Valance* was completely an auteur project. Ford located the property, developed a script with long-time associates Willis Goldbeck and James Warner Bellah, and raised half the proposed $3.2 million budget needed for an all-star case which included John Wayne and James Stewart in their first film together. Because Wayne had just signed a ten picture contract with Paramount (for which he was paid $6 million in advance), Ford took his package deal to that particular studio. Shooting commenced in September 1961. The completed film was released in April 1962, and quickly played out, to be resurrected a decade later in revivals and retrospectives.

The Man Who Shot Liberty Valance presents a very dark view of the western legend. Although the opening sequence is of an ''iron horse,'' confidently moving through the desert, the rest of the film is by and large confined to sequences indoors, usually taking place at night—recorded on a Hollywood sound stage. The Old West has lost the epic proportions of Monument Valley, and moved to a ramshackle town, populated by a handful of people. (An unseen range war occurs off-screen.) The West has been settled; the myth of the western hero is remembered only in flashbacks. Indeed, the western era has already past when the film begins. Senator Ransom Stoddard (James Stewart) and his wife Hallie (Vera Miles) journey to hometown Shinbone to attend the funeral of an old friend, the true western hero Tom Doniphon (John Wayne). Through a long flashback (one that comprises most of the film) we learn how progress came to the West. On his first journey to Shinbone, Stoddard, an earnest young lawyer from the East, is robbed and beaten by archetypal outlaw Liberty Valance (Lee Marvin). Stoddard seeks revenge by trying to civilize the community. But in the end Stoddard can bring the civilized values of the East only through deception and violence. He earns his fame not through the law but as a man who stood up to and killed evil incarnate, Liberty Valance.

Tom Doniphon is more tragically caught up in the conflict between civilization and chaos, order and violence. Doniphon is doomed to live in a world to which he can not adapt. Structurally, the film counterpoints the rise of Stoddard with the fall of Doniphon. Gradually Stoddard educates and draws Doniphon's ''girl'' to him through his teachings. (Stoddard literally becomes the school teacher.) Ultimately, when Stoddard does face off with Liberty Valance, the film tells the viewer that it is Doniphon, in a last heroic act, who shoots Liberty Valance. If a viewer looks closely, however, nowhere does the film actually show us who killed Liberty Valance. It is impossible to tell visually whether the bullet was from the gun of Tom Doniphon or that of Ransom Stoddard. But the myth continues. The out-of-date western hero loses his girl, and settles into a life of obscurity, while the lawyer from the East rises to heights of political power, becoming a senator in Washington, D.C.

At the nominating convention for statehood, Stoddard assumes authority. In this sequence Ford mocks the heart of the American political process. This becomes clear when the cattle-baron candidate, one Buck Langhorn, is nominated. Dressed in western dude fashion, this grotesque cowboy ''image'' is all that remains of the values and honor associated with a western hero like Tom Doniphon. Aptly, when the doors swing shut on the convention, that is the last time we see Doniphon alive. As the newspaper editor notes later about Stoddard's rise to power, ''When the legend becomes fact, print the legend.'' The desert is now a garden, full of the symbolic cactus rose. The myth is complete with ''progress'' coming to the old West. The honor and values of *Stagecoach*, the *Iron Horse*, and earlier Ford westerns will never return again.

To deconstruct the western as story, Ford finally acknowledged its role as a myth and legend in the history and development of the United States. To create a timeless world of formal artifice, Ford filmed *The Man Who Shot Liberty Valance* in black and white on a studio soundstage. Furthermore, Ford's distinction between fact and legend also involved the restructuring of the film's time by placing the act of telling between past and present, thus reinforcing the process of deconstructing mythmaking. This narrative framework, the stark stylization of mise-en-scène, and the use of lighting render the flashback (and the flashback in the flashback) into nightmare. This is a stripped down western; the colorful legend and look of Monument Valley have become a barren world of broken dreams.

In the end *The Man Who Shot Liberty Valance* is a great filmmaker's own critique of the form in which he did his best work. It probably now ranks second to *The Searchers* (1956) in Ford's oeuvre, and is part of what critics and historians now consider Ford's greatest period, the films—especially the westerns—made after World War II. Ford's career is now seen as a slow, steady parabola of change, beginning with certainties about the values of civilization and ending with abject filmmaking, always seeming to follow the rules, yet always breaking with them. *The Man Who Shot Liberty Valance* must be seen as a great achievement of a filmmaker at the height of his power and understanding.

—Douglas Gomery

THE MAN WITH THE MOVIE CAMERA

See **CHELOVEK S KINO APPARATOM**

MANHATTAN

USA, 1979

Director: Woody Allen

Production: A Jack Rollins-Charles H. Joffe Production for United Artists; black and white, 35mm, Panavision; running time: 96 minutes. Released 1979. Filmed 1978 in New York City.

Producer: Charles H. Joffe; **screenplay:** Woody Allen and Marshall Brickman; **photography:** Gordon Willis; **editor:** Susan E. Morse; **production designer:** Mel Bourne; **music:** George Gershwin; **costume designer:** Albert Wolsky.

Cast: Woody Allen (*Isaac Davis*); Diane Keaton (*Mary Wilke*); Mariel Hemingway (*Tracy*); Michael Murphy (*Yale*); Meryl Streep (*Jill*); Anne Byrne (*Emily*).

Awards: New York Film Critics Awards for Best Direction (shared with Robert Benton for *Kramer vs. Kramer*) and Best Supporting Actress (Streep, award also includes her performances in *Kramer vs. Kramer* and *Seduction of Joe Tynan*), 1979.

Publications

Script:

Allen, Woody, and Marshall Brickman, *Manhattan*, in *Four Films of Woody Allen*, New York, 1982.

Books:

Jacobs, Diane, *But We Need the Eggs: The Magic of Woody Allen*, New York, 1982.
Brode, Douglas, *Woody Allen: His Films and Career*, London, 1985, 1997.
Benayoun, Robert, *Woody Allen: Beyond Words*, London, 1987.
Bendazzi, G., *The Films of Woody Allen*, Florence, 1987.
Navacelle, Thierry de, *Woody Allen on Location*, London, 1987.
Pogel, Nancy, *Woody Allen*, Boston, 1987.
Jarvie, Ian, *Philosophy of the Film: Epistemology, Ontology, Aesthetics*, London, 1987.
McCann, Graham, *Woody Allen: New Yorker*, Malden, 1991.
Spignesi, Stephen J., *Woody Allen Companion*, Kansas City, 1992.
Champlin, Charles, *Woody Allen at Work: The Photographs of Brian Hamill*, New York, 1995.
Curry, Renee, *Perspectives on Woody Allen*, London, 1996.
Fox, Julian, *Woody: Movies from Manhattan*, New York, 1996.
Allen, Woody, *Woody Allen on Woody Allen: In Conversation with Stig Bjorkman*, Collingdale, 1998.
Lax, Eric, *Woody Allen: A Biography*, Collingdale, 1998.
Nichols, Mary P., *Reconstructing Woody: Art, Love and Life in the Films of Woody Allen*, Lanham, 1998.

Articles:

Quart, L., in *Cineaste* (New York), no. 4, 1979.
Pym, John, in *Sight and Sound* (London), no. 4, 1979.
Morris, G., ''*Manhattan*: A Cerebral Approach to Filmmaking,'' in *Take One* (Montreal), no. 6, 1979.
Maraval, P., and J. C. Bonnet, ''Images de la ville: Allen et Duras,'' in *Cinématographe* (Paris), no. 53, 1979.
Gitelson, N., ''The Maturing of Woody Allen,''; in *New York Times*, 22 April 1979.
Canby, Vincent, in *New York Times*, 25 April 1979.
Ginsberg, S., in *Variety* (New York), 25 April 1979.
Gilliatt, Penelope, in *New Yorker*, 30 April 1979.
Kroll, Jack, in *Newsweek* (New York), 30 April 1979.
Sarris, Andrew, in *Village Voice* (New York), 30 April 1979.
Denby, D., in *New York*, 7 May 1979.
New Republic (New York), 19 May 1979.
Maslin, J., ''I Share My Character's Views on Men—and Stuff Like That,'' in *New York Times*, 20 May 1979.
Corliss, Richard, in *Film Comment* (New York), May-June 1979.
Dempsey, M., ''The Autobiography of Woody Allen,'' in *Film Comment* (New York), May-June 1979.
Weidner, H., ''Woody Allen: God's Answer to Job,'' in *Christian Century* (Chicago), 6 June 1979.
Simon, John, in *Nation* (New York), 22 June 1979.
Bartholomew, D., in *Film Bulletin* (Philadelphia), June 1979.
Friend, D. M., ''Woody Allen's Jewish American Gothic,'' in *Midstream* (New York), June-July 1979.
Simon, John, ''Our Aliens and Theirs,'' in *National Review* (New York), 6 July 1979.
Grenier, R., ''Woody Allen in the Limelight,'' in *Commentary* (New York), July 1979.
Thurman, J., in *MS* (New York), July 1979.
Mallow, S., ''Lens Cap: Making Sense in Metuchen,'' in *Filmmakers Monthly* (Ward Hill, Massachusetts), July 1979.
Amiel, M., in *Cinéma* (Paris), July-August 1979.
Gow, Gordon, in *Films and Filming* (London), August 1979.
Letremble, M., in *Séquences* (Montreal), August 1979.
Alpert, Hollis, in *American Film* (Washington, D.C), September 1979.
Cebe, G., ''Woody Allen: Portrait de l'acteur en cinéaste: *Manhattan*; ou, Le Temps retrouvé,'' in *Ecran* (Paris), 15 September 1979.
McMurty, L., in *American Film* (Washington, D.C), September 1979.
Quart, L., in *USA Today* (New York), September 1979.
Kritz, J., interview with Woody Allen, in *Filmfaust* (Frankfurt), October 1979.
Baer, W., in *Film und Ton* (Munich), October 1979.
Fuksiewicz, J., in *Kino* (Warsaw), November 1979.
Wolf, W.R., in *Film en Televisie* (Brussels), December 1979.
Sarris, Andrew, ''The New Phase of Intelligence,'' in *Village Voice* (New York), 3 December 1979.
Blau, Douglas, in *Magill's Survey of Cinema 3*, Englewood Cliffs, New Jersey, 1980.
Termine, L., in *Cinema Nuovo* (Bari), February 1980.
Median de la Serna, R., ''El cine de Woody Allen,'' in *Cine* (Mexico City), March 1980.
Teitelbaum, D., ''Producing Woody: An Interview with Charles H. Joffe,'' in *Cinema Papers* (Melbourne), April-May 1980.

Manhattan

Ruiz, J., ''Dos encuentros con Woody Allen,'' in *Casablanca* (Madrid), February 1981.

Goodhill, Dan, ''*Manhattan*: Black and White Romantic Realism,'' in *American Cinematographer* (Los Angeles), November 1982.

Gallanfent, E., ''Moonshine: Love and Enchantment in *Annie Hall* and *Manhattan*,'' in *Cineaction* (Toronto), Summer 1989.

Girlanda, E., and A. Tella, ''Allen, Manhattan transfert,'' in *Castoro Cinema* (Florence), July-August 1990.

Chances, Ellen, ''Moscow Meets Manhattan: The Russian Soul of Woody Allen's Films,'' in *American Studies International*, vol. 30, no. 1, April 1992.

DeCurtis, Anthony, ''Woody Allen: The Rolling Stone Interview,'' in *Rolling Stone* (New York), no. 665, 16 September 1993.

Deleyto, C., ''The Narrator and the Narrative: The Evolution of Woody Allen's Film Comedies,'' in *Film Criticism* (Meadville), vol. 19, no. 2, 1994/1995.

Premiere (Boulder), vol. 9, January 1996.

Garbarz, F., ''*Manhattan*: une autre femme,'' in *Positif* (Paris), no. 444, February 1998.

* * *

Manhattan opens with images of New York City over which the voice of Woody Allen, as writer Isaac Davis, begins chapter one of his new book: ''He adored New York City. He idolized it out of proportion.'' The film is an homage to ''Allen-town,'' to the city that spawned him, but unlike Allen's homage to the woman of his dreams (*Annie Hall*), here he idolizes the good while systematically removing the obviously negative. In the prologue he presents us with New York City's most glorious vistas: fireworks over Central Park, the skyline at dawn, the Empire State Building, the Brooklyn Bridge, all to the lush romantic sound of George Gershwin's *Rhapsody in Blue*. Gone are the messy vistas, the untidy streets, the horrors of the subway system, people of non-white lineage. His book, an expanded version of an article he had written about his mother entitled ''The Castrating Zionist,'' is, one can assume, this movie, and Isaac Davis is its author.

With typical deprecation, Isaac decides that the best way to achieve success is to write an autobiographical novel that is neither preachy nor angry, which focuses on an explication of his desired self-image. That image, like his image of the city, is a castrated one. While dwelling on the city's physical beauty, Isaac proceeds to effect an autopsy on his social set, his ultimate desire being an exposé of the decay of contemporary culture.

That social set consists of writers. Four of the main characters belong to that occupation: Isaac Davis is a television writer who quits his job to write his book; Yale is a teacher who is working on a biography of O'Neill; Mary Wilke is a journalist who writes on art and a variety of other topics; Jill is Isaac's ex-wife who publishes a feminist tract on their marriage entitled *Marriage, Divorce and Selfhood.* Throughout the film the names of great writers are bandied about, each one cited as if he were a reference point in the psychological development of the character. Thus Isaac refers to Strindberg, Bergman, Fellini, Kafka and Groucho Marx, his strategy being both reverential and referential. As he says to Yale: ''I gotta model myself after someone!'' The blend of writers cited certifies Isaac's neurotic condition. His problems, like those of the city, are intellectual.

As with other Allen films, this one also dwells on the impossibility of lasting relationships. If Bergman and Fellini were the influences of *Interiors* and *Stardust Memories*, Orson Welles seems to be the working model here, most specifically the Welles of *The Lady from Shanghai*. A reflection of the real-life decay of Welles's marriage to Rita Hayworth, *Lady* abounds with bitter commentary on relationships. References to Hayworth, the buggy ride in Central Park, the use of the planetarium for a love scene, the romantic voice-over which begins *Manhattan*, and themes of decay all point to this film as an influence. In fact, the last line of dialogue from *Shanghai* could have been used to end *Manhattan*.

Filmed in Panavision on Technicolor stock, then printed in black and white, this film is Allen's most complex reflection on the artist as romantic—his draining of its color the most bitter-sweet stroke.

—Doug Tomlinson

MARAT/SADE

(The Persecution and Assassination of Jean-Paul Marat as Performed by the Inmates of the Asylum of Charenton under the Direction of Monsieur de Sade)

Great Britain, 1966

Director: Peter Brook

Production: United Artists; De Luxe Color; running time: 115 minutes. Released in USA February 1967.

Producer: Lord Michael Birkett with the Royal Shakespeare Company; **screenplay:** Adrian Mitchell; English translation by Geoffrey Skelton; based on a play by Peter Weiss; **assistant director:** Anthony Way; **photography:** David Watkin; **editor:** Tom Priestly; **sound:** Robert Allen; **art director:** Ted Marshall; **music:** Richard Peaslee; **choreographer:** Malcolm Goddard.

Cast: Patrick Magee (*Marquis de Sade*); Ian Richardson (*Jean-Paul Marat*); Glenda Jackson (*Charlotte Corday*); Clifford Rose (*Coulmier*); Brenda Kempner (*Mme Coulmier*); Ruth Baker (*Mlle. Coulmier*); Freddie Jones (*Cucurucu*); Robert Lloyd (*Jacques Roux*); Leon Lissek (*Lavoisier*); John Harwood (*Lavoisier*); Jack Steiner (*Dupperet*); Michael Williams (*Herald*); Hugh Sullivan (*Kokol*); Jonathan Burn (*Polpach*); Jeanette Landis (*Rossignol*); Susan Williamson (*Simone Evrard*); Mark Jones (*Abbott*); and others.

Awards: Silver Ribbon for Best Director of a Foreign Film, Italian National Syndicate of Film Journalists, 1966; Special Mention (Brook), Locarno International Film Festival, 1967.

Publications

Articles:

Brook, Peter, et. al., ''Marat/Sade Forum,'' in *Tulane Drama Review*, vol. 10, no. 4, Summer 1966.

New York Times, 23 February 1967.

White, John J., ''History and Cruelty in Peter Weiss's Marat/Sade,'' in *Modern Language Review*, vol. 63, 1968.

Roberts, David, ''Marat/Sade, or the Birth of Postmodernism from the Spirit of the Avant-Garde,'' in *Postmodern Conditions*, edited by Milner, Thompson, and Worth, New York, 1990.

Holderness, Graham, ''Weiss/Brook: *Marat/Sade*,'' in *Twentieth Century European Drama*, edited by Brian Docherty, New York, 1994.

* * *

In 1966, world-famous stage director Peter Brook adapted the visionary play by Peter Weiss, a German dramatist who lived in Sweden until his death in 1982. The full title of the film is *The Persecution and Assassination of Jean-Paul Marat as Performed by the Inmates of the Asylum at Charenton Under the Direction of the Marquis de Sade.* The complexity of the title is matched by the complicated relationship to history and politics it offers. The didactic full title of the play heralds a complex political drama rarely seen on film. This film does not aim at persuasiveness or at presenting an objective analysis of a distinct historical event. Instead, it offers a complicated unfolding of a play within a play about drama and history that simultaneously challenges the spectator to rethink political philosophy and the nature of human nature.

Brook's filmed version of Weiss's play opens in the bathhouse of the insane asylum at Charenton, France, in the year 1808. The asylum's most notorious inmate, Marquis de Sade (Patrick Magee), has been commissioned to write and direct a play for the inmates to perform ''as therapy,'' for Parisian high society. Sade stages a play about the assassination of the French revolutionary leader Jean-Paul Marat at the height of the Terror in 1793. The play itself represents four historical levels: the failed revolution in 1793, the asylum where the play was staged in 1808, the filming in 1966, and the spectator's current viewing.

The play is based on two historical truths: that the Marquis de Sade was interned in the asylum in the Paris suburb of Charenton for 13 years (from 1801 until his death in 1814); and that Marat was fatally stabbed in a bathtub by Charlotte Corday at the height of terror in the French Revolution in 1793. The sparse facts form the basis of an imagined performance by members of asylum. The play is performed by inmates of the asylum and overseen, monitored, and intermittently interrupted by the asylum's staff. The patients' white costumes and the white face worn by some of the cast provide a drab background for the opulent aristocratic audience, who have come to the asylum to watch the show. Thematically, this film is about history itself, the events of the French revolution, class conflict, and the conditions of an early nineteenth century asylum, where plays were part of the therapeutic process. But the play-within-a-play is not just a historical drama. Rather, it is clearly concerned with the problem of revolution.

Marat and Sade debate the philosophical and political impact of the French Revolution while surrounded by inmates of the asylum. Their debate circulates around certain compelling and difficult questions: are the things that are true for the masses also true for their leaders? Where, in modern times, lies the borderline of sanity? Marat advocates the need for revolution. Sade (who historically did write while an inmate of the asylum) views the world solely in individualistic terms and voices extreme pessimism about the outcome of revolution.

For Marat, the problems of existence have social and political solutions and revolution holds the potential for transformation. Sade, on the other hand, champions the depravity and perversity inherent in human nature. In addition to these two poles of belief, a chorus of other voices are present: The asylum director is present, with his wife and daughter, to interrupt the action when the revolutionary rhetoric goes too far and the historical revision not far enough. The priest strives to uphold the rules of the church, and the audience is bent on entertainment. The herald provides an ongoing ironic commentary on events, while Charlotte Corday, the narcoleptic heroine and assassin, speaks contemptuously of the slaughter in Paris, with phrases like, ''They talk of people now as gardeners talk of leaves for burning.''

The collision of existentialism with political fanaticism amid chaos provides no easy answers. Whether a parable of modern society (life is a madhouse in which we are all prisoners) or a deliberate technique designed to shock and push action and dialogue to excess, this film is not a patronizing, overwrought debate; on the contrary, it provides an intellectual, chronological, and visual challenge. In the 34 years since its premiere, the simply staged, one-room film remains unprecedented in its combination of classic Brechtian and Artaudian theory as well as Marxist political critique and experimental vision. The members of the Royal Shakespeare Company provide a compellingly disturbed rendition of the claustrophobic atmosphere of a Parisian insane asylum in the early nineteenth century.

The unusual, minimalist cinematography of Watkins creates a harsh, at times surreal, effect. His skillful camera work varies extreme, lingering close-ups with erratic camera movement to heighten the unpredictability and exacerbate the feeling of uncontrolled violence building beneath the surface. The camera work implicates the spectator in the play's unfolding, revealing that there is no safe place from which to watch the film at a distance. The use of a hand-held camera, especially, makes us feel that we too are inmates involved in the activity of the asylum.

In a similarly innovative manner, the spectator is not given a linear narrative, except in the synopsis of the entire film provided at the beginning of the play by a herald. Thus, one is forced to participate actively in the making of the meaning and message of the play (and the film). According to Graham Holderness, ''the play present[s] political violence and human extremity through a philosophical violence and a self-reflexive theatrical medium.'' The film raises such questions as, who benefits from the revolution? Do the ends justify the means? Charenton, ''an intense characterization of the wretched of the earth'' writes Holderness, was a place for the socially unacceptable (whether clinically insane or not). This institution was, acording to Weiss, a ''hiding place for the moral rejects of civilized society'' and was designed to maintain discipline, order, and social control for 'civilized' societies.

Brook's adaptation of the play reveals strong overtones of Antonin Artaud's 'Theater of Cruelty,' which touted a new dramatic language, liberated from the narrative continuity and the conventions of realist theater. The events of the play and its the setting in an asylum jar the senses of both the audience and the performers, agitating viewers at a sensory level and thus involving them emotionally as well as intellectually. One witnesses the use of Brechtian estrangement as asylum inmates constantly forget their lines, fall out of their roles, and have to be prompted. Moreover, the film is divided into episodes, all of which are continuously interrupted by formal debate, political songs, direct audience address, mime, and pageant. The characters break into song, speak in rhyme, have mental attacks (narcolepsy, seizures, itching attacks, and so forth.) This constant interruption and mixing of the different historical levels serves as a reminder of the blurry line between life and representation.

The film concludes with Marat's rising from his death to pronounce final words of faith in revolutionary collectivism: ''Others now will carry on/the fight that I Marat begun/until one day the hour shall strike/when men will share and share alike.'' Sade rejoins with pour individualism ''So for me the last word can never be spoken/I am left with a question that is always open.'' The entirely imagined encounter between Marat and Sade reflects the Marxist belief in history as a conflict between two contradictory forces, represented by the beliefs of Marat and Sade. On one level a historical drama about France in the aftermath of the 1789 revolution, and a philosophical debate between the collective and the individual, Brook's film also pushes the limits, testing whether a film should take up a political stance or maintain a dignified detachment in the interests of objectivity.

—Jill Gillespie

THE MARCH OF TIME

USA, 1935–51

Director: Louis de Rochemont

Production: Time Inc.; black and white, 35mm; running time: about 20 minutes per episode. First episode released 1 February 1935, New York, by First Division Exchanges, Inc. After 1935 *The March of Time* was distributed through RKO/Radio, and later 20th Century-Fox. The last episode was released in August, 1951. Cost: the first 3 reels cost approximately $40,000, while $150,000 was used to launch the series.

Producers: Louis de Rochemont and Roy Larsen, but during WWII Louis resigned and was replaced by his brother Richard de Rochemont; **editors:** Louis de Rochemont and Roy Larsen, Louis replaced by brother Richard during WWII; **technical management:** Jack Bradford and Lothar Wolff.

Cast: Westbrook Van Voorhis (*Narrator*).

Awards: Special oscar for the series' significance to motion pictures for having revolutionized one of the most important branches of the industry—the newsreel, 1936.

The March of Time

Publications

Books:

Bluem, A. William, *Documentary in American Television*, New York, 1965.

Elson, Robert T., *Time Inc.*, New York, 2 vols., 1968.

Fielding, Raymond, *The American Newsreel 1911–1967*, Norman Oklahoma, 1972.

Barsam, Richard, *Nonfiction Film: A Critical History*, New York, 1973.

Barnouw, Erik, *Documentary: A History of the Non-Fiction Film*, New York, 1974.

Fielding, Raymond, *The March of Time 1935–1951*, New York, 1978.

Ellis, Jack C., *The Documentary Idea*, Englewood Cliffs, New Jersey, 1989.

Articles:

Newsweek (New York), 9 February 1935.

Cooke, Alistair, in *Sight and Sound* (London) Autumn 1935.

''Celluloid Censorship,'' in *Time* (New York), 1 June 1936.

Dangerfield, George, ''Time Muddles On,'' in *New Republic* (New York), 19 August 1936.

''Freedom of Film and Press,'' in *Christian Century* (Chicago), 2 February 1938.

Galway, Peter, ''Inside Nazi Germany, 1938: *The March of Time*,'' in *New Statesman and Nation* (London), 30 April 1938.

Frakes, Margaret, ''Time Marches Back: Propaganda for Defense,'' in *Christian Century* (Chicago), 16 October 1940.

de Rochemont, Louis, in *Sight and Sound* (London), Spring 1941.

Anstey, Edgar, ''The Magazine Film,'' in *Penguin Film Review* (London), May 1949.

Fielding, Raymond, in *Quarterly of Film Radio, and Television* (Berkeley), Summer 1957.

Fielding, Raymond, ''Mirror of Discontent: *The March of Time* and Its Politically Controversial Film Issues,'' in *Wisconsin Political Quarterly* (Madison), March 1959.

Barsam, Richard, ''This Is America,'' in *Cinema Journal* (Evanston, Illinois), Spring 1973.

Lichty, L. W., and T. W. Bohn, ''*The March of Time*: News as Drama,'' in *Journal of Popular Film* (Washington, D.C), Fall 1973.

Elson, Robert T., ''Time Marches on the Screen,'' in *Non-Fiction Film: Theory and Criticism*, edited by Richard Barsam, New York, 1976.

Cook, B., ''Whatever Happened to Westbrook Van Voorhis?,'' in *American Film* (Washington, D.C), March 1977.

Rollins, P. C., ''Ideology and Film Rhetoric: Three Documentaries of the New Deal Era,'' in *Journal of Popular Film* (Washington, D.C), no. 2, 1977.

Fielding, Raymond, ''*The March of Time* 1935–51,'' in *Filmmakers Monthly* (Ward Hill, Massachusetts), February 1979.

Martin, Marcel, in *Ecran* (Paris), 20 October 1979.

Lafferty, William, ''A Reappraisal of the Semi-Documentary in Hollywood 1945–1948,'' in *Velvet Light Trap* (Madison, Wisconsin), Summer 1983.

City Limits (London), 11–17 October 1983.

Dunlap, Donald, ''*The March of Time* and *The Ramparts We Watch* (1940),'' in *Historical Journal of Film, Radio, and Television*, vol. 5, no. 2, 1985.

Hastings, M., ''Time Marches On!,'' in *Sight and Sound* (London), Autumn 1985.

Short, K. R. M., ''*The March of Time*, Time Inc., and the Berlin Blockade, 1948–1949: Selling Americans on the 'New' Democratic Germany,'' in *Historical Journal of Film, Radio and Television* (Abingdon, Oxfordshire), no. 4, 1993.

Leahy, J., ''Image, Meaning, History and the Voice of God,'' in *Vertigo* (London), vol. 1, no. 4, 1994/1995.

* * *

The March of Time had the most substantial and sustained success of any documentary-like film series prior to television; it lasted from 1935 to 1951. It offered a new and distinctive kind of screen journalism, a cross between the newsreel and the documentary. At its peak, in the late 1930s and during the years of World War II, it was seen in the United States alone by more than 20 million people a month in 9,000 theaters. It was distributed internationally as well.

The *MOT* was sponsored by the *Time-Life-Fortune* organization of Henry Luce. The monthly film series was preceded by a weekly radio series of the same title. Roy Larsen of *Time* was responsible for the initiation of both series; Louis de Rochemont became the principal creator of the film series.

Though originating from a conservative organization, the *MOT* was identified with a liberal stance, more so than *Time* magazine. This was particularly true in foreign affairs; the films tended to be more conservative or erratic on domestic issues. Still, while features in the 1930s ignored or dealt only covertly with the Depression, *MOT* acknowledged the bread lines, unemployment, and political demagoguery that it gave rise to. Internationally, while the newsreel avoided controversial political and military developments, *MOT* tackled the machinations of Hitler, Stalin, Mussolini, and Tojo. One of the most politically controversial films in the history of American cinema was *MOT*'s ''Inside Nazi Germany'' (1938). It examined in some detail (16 minutes) the regimentation of the German people, the control and consolidation of nationalistic allegiances, and the preparations being made for future military and economic expansion. This was at a time when the majority of the American public was still strongly isolationist and the government maintained a careful impartiality.

The success of *The March of Time*—fueled by the controversy it aroused by its press agentry as well as by its energetic innovations—encouraged imitations, especially after World War II began. Created along the same lines were the National Film Board of Canada's monthly *Canada Carries On* (1939–50) and *The World in Action* (1940–45). When the distribution of *The March of Time* moved from RKO to Twentieth Century-Fox in 1942, RKO replaced it with its own series, *This Is America* (1942–51). Immediately after the war, in England, the J. Arthur Rank organization produced and distributed *This Modern Age* (1946–50). The influence of *March of Time* extended into American documentaries of World War II as well, the most important being the *Why We Fight* series. *MOT* is the principal American model for what is now called the ''compilation documentary.''

A standard format for *The March of Time* was worked out early and varied little, regardless of subject. The fixed form may have been necessitated by the pressures of monthly production with modest resources; it must also have come to seem desirable given the considerable popularity of the series in the form in which it was offered. One of the most important ingredients was the voice and delivery style of its commentator, Westbrook Van Voorhis. His ''Voice of Time'' (sometimes irreverently referred to as the ''Voice of God'') was deep and commanding, ominous and reassuring at the same time. Spoken words carried the weight of the communication; the footage (largely stock), music (obvious and clichéd), and sound effects (sparse and highly selective) were cut to them. Often the pictures were given their meaning by the words, as part of ''the dramatization of the news'' that *MOT* practiced. An extreme close-up of a face and mouth at a telephone becomes ''An angry refusal''; a long shot of a city street at night with a few electric signs becomes ''That evening Shanghai is tense'' (''War in China,'' 1937). Editing was the key. The pace is fast, with a hard rhythmic impact; a great deal of information is presented dramatically to capture the attention of the popcorn-chewing Friday night audience.

Structurally, each issue had four parts, with titles announcing each part. The first established the magnitude and urgency of the problem being dealt with. The second offered a historical survey of its origins and causes. Part three presented the immediate complications, confirming its newsworthiness. The concluding part looked to the future, stressing that the problem was a matter for continuing and serious concern.

By 1951 the losses of *The March of Time* had become too heavy for even the Luce organization to sustain. It was suffering from the competition of television news and public affairs programes, which could do the same thing as *MOT* films in theaters with much greater immediacy. It was suffering even more from rising costs and inadequate rentals paid for shorts by the theaters, geared largely to the selling of feature films. And finally it was no doubt suffering from its own fixed style and approach which, through repetition of 205 issues over 16 years, had lost much of the freshness and excitement of its earlier days.

The March of Time must be acknowledged, however, as an event in the history of popular American culture. Its influence has extended down to much of the documentary and public affairs programming on television today.

—Jack C. Ellis

MÄRCHEN VOM GLÜCK

(Traum vom Glück; Kiss Me Casanova)

Austria, 1949

Director: Arthur de Glahs

Production: Belvedere Film; black and white; running time: 90 minutes. Released September 1949 by Sascha Film; reissued 1951 as *Traum vom Glück* by Panorama Film. Filmed at Belvedere Studios and Rosenhügel Studios, Vienna.

Producers: August Diglas, Emmerich Hanus, Elfi von Dassanowsky; **screenplay:** Arthur de Glahs and Franz Krpata; **photography:** Hans Nigmann; **assistant director:** Hanns Matula; **editor:** Hanns Matula; **sound:** Alfred Norkus and Hans Riedl; **production designers:** Gustav Abel and Fred Kollhanek; **music:** Franz Thurner; songs with music by Franz Thurner and lyrics by Hans Werner; music performed by Vienna Symphony Orchestra, Vienna Dance Orchestra, and Hot Club Vienna; Horst Winter; **costume designers:** Gerdago and Hedy zum Tobel, executed by Atelier Ella Bei; **production manager:** Otto Diglas; **production assistant:** Leo Höger; **choreography:** Elfi Kose; **makeup:** Hans Kres and Ludwig Langer.

Cast: O.W. Fischer (*Fernando di Castro*); Maria Holst (*Danielle*); Gretl Schörg (*Violetta Valona*); Hans Olden (*Police Chief*); Gunther Philipp (*Jean*); Erika Berghöfer (*Elvira*); Felizitas Falzari (*Marga Stella*); Edith Prager (*Tamara*); Hilde Schreiber (*Amelie*); Nadja Tiller (*Lucia*); Erich Dörner (*Minister of Police*); Richard Eybner (*Ballet Master*); Otto Fassler (*Young Cavalier*); C.W. Fernbach (*Rodrigo*); Karl Fochler (*Theater Director*); Oskar Hugelmann (*Guiseppe di Como*); Hans Kurth (*Pietro Oviedo*); Walter Ladengast (*Prof. Ferraris*); Evelyn Künneke (*Singer*); Emmerich Hanus (*Himself*).

Publications:

Articles:

Füringk, Marielies, ''Besuch in Wiens kleinstem Film-Atelier,'' in *Mein Film* (Austria), 7 March 1947.

Von Dassanowsky, Elfi, ''Märchen vom Glück am Bauernmarkt: Erinnerungen an die Belvedere-Filme und das Aufbruchstadium im österreichischen Nachkriegskino,'' in *Wiener Zeitung* (Austria), 10–11 September 1999.

* * *

Märchen vom Glück was the final and most ambitious production of Vienna's Belvedere Film company, which was created in 1946 as the first new studio in postwar Austria. During that period, all of Austria's major studio facilities were controlled by the four-power Allied occupation administration, which encouraged the birth of many short-lived independent production companies. Belvedere, however, was conceived as a traditional studio responsible for and housing all aspects of its productions. It began modestly, but soon gained wide attention and was responsible for having cultivated major talent on both sides of the camera. ''Kick-starting'' postwar German-language film, as John Walker, author of *Halliwell's Who's Who in the Movies 13th Ed.* put it, the studio also attempted to reconnect with the provocative entertainments of the interwar period and the Viennese musical-comedy genre of the Reich's semi-autonomous Wien-Film Studio. It also hoped to reinvent genres that had been tainted by Nazi cinema—the *Heimatfilm*, provincial comedies, and operetta—for a new, more sophisticated postwar audience exposed to British, French, and American film.

The studio produced only seven films, but it satisfied its goals in presenting new and important talent (on both sides of the camera), exporting its work, and attaining, if not always critical praise, then certainly popular appeal. The studio was headed by August Diglas and producers Emmerich Hanus—famed silent-film director and brother of Heinz Hanus, one of Austria's film pioneers—and Elfi von Dassanowsky. It is Von Dassanowsky, the second female film producer and studio administrator in Austrian cinema history, who has brought Belvedere's important but nearly forgotten history and legacy back to the cinematic canon in recent years. Along with many other cinema classics, all of the studio's films had been missing since the withdrawal of Soviet Occupation forces in Austria in 1955 and were deemed lost. In 1998, however, Elfi von Dassanowsky discovered a print of *Märchen vom Glück*, and an incomplete copy of another Belvedere Film, *Dr. Rosin*, in the Austrian Film Archives. As many so-called ''lost'' Austrian films, particularly from the pre-Anschluss era, have recently turned up in Russia and Eastern Europe, there is now an effort to locate the rest of this maverick studio's creations.

Märchen vom Glück may have been envisioned as a light, star-studded musical comedy destined for audiences tired of what had become a long postwar occupation trauma (see *The Third Man*), as its banal and escapist title suggests, but its risky, progressive quality makes it a stand-out in the era. The film was populated with famous character actors and provided the comeback roles for two young stars popular during the Reich: leading man O.W. Fischer, who had his only singing role in this film and went on to become one of the major figures in German cinema; and Maria Holst, an attractive musical actress who later specialized in playing elegant ladies. *Märchen vom Glück* gave German and Austrian cinema and television comedian Gunther Philipp his first film role as Jean, servant to Fischer's reticent Security Chief. The Miss Austria of 1949, Nadja Tiller, who gained international fame as a film star in the 1950s and 1960s, also had her film debut here. Additionally, singer and actress Evelyn Künneke and cinematographer Hanns Matula mark this film as the start of their long careers. The film was the most expensive one Belvedere produced and among the most expensive in postwar Austria to that date—one of the factors that contributed to the eventual shuttering of the studio.

The plot is a simple one, designed to allow a maximum of cinematic excursions into song and dance numbers, comedy set pieces, and parody. In Utopistan, a country with dictatorial overtones, shy but wealthy Fernando (Fischer), rejected by the bored socialite Danielle (Holst) for being unexciting and weak, concocts a Don Juan-like persona who kidnaps women for three days, in order to fulfill their personal romantic fantasies. The members of the government panic but fail to capture this love-bandit. Ultimately, it is Danielle's turn but Fernando reveals himself, proving he could be ''dangerous'' but also that she misunderstood what she truly wanted in a man. The swipes at an arrogant but incompetent authoritarianism are an obvious reaction to the Nazi past and the occupation of Austria, and the film

Märchen vom Glück

deals with officialdom in an iconoclastic manner reminiscent of the Marx Brother's *Duck Soup*.

Märchen vom Glück demonstrates the particular affinity Viennese comedy has for the American Screwball style with its manic language-based comedy of manners, a concept fostered in early Viennese film and exported to and developed in Hollywood by many of the exiled Austrian film talents. In overall style, the film is a precursor to such sociopolitical satires as Billy Wilder's 1961 *One, Two, Three* (itself a product of an original Austro-Hungarian text and an Austrian-American director), and the kaleidoscopic all-star international comedies of the mid-1960s, such as *Casino Royale* (1967), *Bedazzled* (1967), *The Honey Pot* (1967), and *Candy* (1968). The episodic structure, cameo appearances, and the anarchic feel of such ''experimental'' pastiches are already apparent to a large extent in *Märchen vom Glück*. Although it is unique, it is not surprising given the roots of such psychedelia in the screwball comedy, and given the shared (albeit different) ''crisis society'' which both films reflect. Von Dassanowsky maintains that the film was actually directed by Emmerich Hanus and August Diglas under the ''de Glahs'' pseudonym. Certainly the strong visuals and the brevity of dialogue in this film and in the other ''de Glahs'' opus, *Dr. Rosin*, suggests the technique of a silent-film maker (Diglas also began his career in silents) which find similarities to Chaplin's late sound work.

The film is subversive of static ''cultural tradition'' from the start: the pre-title vignette features a cameo of Hanus putting aside a copy of Goethe's *Faust*, to read the tale that is the film. Obviously deflating the cliché male-power role of the Nazi period and the lingering militarism of Cold War Europe, Fischer's Fernando is a bespectacled intellectual, a gentle-man, who is able to slip into an aggressively sexual pose at will. His character suggests that gender roles are chosen, but also that society prefers to uphold archaic ideals. He is no less a man of many costumes than the women he targets (designs by the legendary Gerdago at her best), but his alter ego, a foretaste of Jerry Lewis' Buddy Love in *The Nutty Professor* (1963), alters himself to suit the personality of the particular woman. He even rejects the amorous notions of the too-young daughter of the President, giving her instead a three-day return to the enjoyment of being a child. The ''victims,'' who appear as strong, intelligent, and independent women in comparison to their addled men, never divulge that the only thing that happened with Fernando is that he appreciated their desires and entertained them with their fantasy. The film's revision of the image of the ''leading man'' and the recognition of female sexual desire, fantasy, and self-realization are far beyond its era. *Märchen vom Glück* inspired other forays into experimentation in mainstream Austrian and West German entertainment films in its time, most notably Wolfgang Liebeneiner's futuristic satire on Austria and the Cold War, *1 April 2000* (1952). Nevertheless, its unfortunate long disappearance makes it a missing piece in Austrian cinema history that has yet to find its deserved classic status.

—Robert von Dassanowsky

THE MARIUS TRILOGY

MARIUS

France, 1931

Director: Alexander Korda

Production: French Paramount; black and white: running time: 120 minutes: length: 11,000 feet. Released 1931.

Producer: Marcel Pagnol; **screenplay:** Marcel Pagnol, from his own play; **production designer:** Vincent Korda; **art director:** Alfred Junge.

Cast: Raimu (*César*); Pierre Fresnay (*Marius*); Orane Demazis (*Fanny*); Alida Rouffe (*Honorine*); Charpin (*Panisse*).

Publications

Books:

Fronval, Georges, *Raimu: Sa vie, ses films*, Paris, 1939.
Olivier, Paul, *Raimu; ou, La Vie de César*, Paris, 1947; as *Raimu; ou, L'Epopée de César*, 1977.
Dubeux, Albert, *Pierre Fresnay*, Paris, 1950.
Tabori, Paul, *Alexander Korda*, London, 1959.
Beylie, Claude, *Marcel Pagnol*, Paris, 1972; as *Marcel Pagnol; ou, Le Cinéma en liberté*, 1986.
Kulik, Karol, *Alexander Korda: The Man Who Could Work Miracles*, London, 1975.
Fresnay, Pierre, with François Possot, *Pierre Fresnay*, Paris, 1976.
Leprohon, Pierre, *Marcel Pagnol*, Paris, 1976.
Perisset, Maurice, *Raimu*, Paris, 1976.
Ford, Charles, *Pierre Fresnay: Gentilhomme de l'ecran*, Paris, 1981.
Pagnol, Marcel, *Confidences*, Paris, 1981.
Castans, Raymond, and André Bernard, *Les Films du Marcel Pagnol*, Paris, 1982.
Pompa, Dany, *Marcel Pagnol*, Paris, 1986.
Vincendeau, Ginette, and Susan Hayward, editors, *French Film: Texts and Contexts*, London, 1989.
Stockham, Martin, *The Korda Collection: Alexander Korda's Film Classics*, London, 1992.

Articles:

New York Times, 14 April 1933.
New Yorker, 14 April 1933.
Variety (New York), 25 April 1933.
Jacobson, H. L., ''Homage to Raimu,'' in *Hollywood Quarterly*, Winter 1947–48.
Monthly Film Bulletin (London), October 1949.
Pagnol, Marcel, ''Adieu à Raimu,'' in *L'Ecran Française* (Paris), 3 October 1951.
''*Marius* Section'' of *Image et Son* (Paris), July 1958.
Fieschi, J.-A., and others, interview with Marcel Pagnol, in *Cahiers du Cinéma* (Paris), December 1965.
Leprohon, Pierre, ''Raimu,'' in *Anthologie du cinéma 2*, Paris, 1967.
Polt, Harriet, ''The Marcel Pagnol Trilogy,'' in *Film Society Review* (New York), October 1967.
Delahaye, Michel, ''La Saga Pagnol,'' in *Cahiers du Cinéma* (Paris), June 1969.
''*Pagnol* Issue'' of *Avant-Scène du Cinéma* (Paris), July/September 1970.
Turk, Edward Baron, ''Pagnol's Marseilles Trilogy,'' in *American Film* (Washington, D.C.), October 1980.

CESAR

France, 1936

Director: Marcel Pagnol

Production: Marcel Pagnol; black and white; running time: 117 minutes; length: 10,500 feet. Released 1936.

Screenplay: Marcel Pagnol; **photography:** Willy; **music:** Vincent Scotto.

Cast: Raimu (*César*); Pierre Fresnay (*Marius*); Charpin (*Panisse*); Orane Demazis (*Fanny*); André Fouche (*Cesariot*); Alida Rouffe (*Honorine*); Paul Dullac (*Escartefigue*).

Publications

Articles:

Variety (New York), 25 November 1936.
Esquire (New York), February 1938.
New York Times, 28 October 1948.
Today's Cinema (London), 15 February 1951.
Monthly Film Bulletin (London), March 1951.
Image et Son (Paris), September-October 1968–69.

Also see list of publications following *Marius*.

FANNY

France, 1932

Director: Marc Allégret

Production: Marcel Pagnol; black and white; running time: 120 minutes; length: 10,800 feet. Released 1932, not released in UK until 1950.

Producer: Marcel Pagnol; **screenplay:** Marcel Pagnol; **music:** Vincent Scotto.

Cast: Raimu (*César*); Pierre Fresnay (*Marius*); Oriane Demazis (*Fanny*); Charpin (*Panisse*); Alida Rouffe (*Honorine*); Mouries (*Escartefigue*); P. Asso (*M. Brun*).

Publications

Articles:

Variety (New York), 21 June 1948.
New Republic (New York), 2 February 1948.
New York Times, 13 February 1948.
Today's Cinema (London), 19 July 1950.
Houston, Penelope, in *Monthly Film Bulletin* (London), August 1950.

Also see list of publications following *Marius*.

* * *

When Marcel Pagnol adapted his play *Marius* for the cinema in 1931, he was a relatively well-known young playwright who had recently left behind his modest Marseillais beginnings and a teaching career. By the time *César*, the third part of the trilogy, came out in 1936 (and was the no. 1 box-office hit for that year), he had become one of the most popular filmmakers in France, was running parallel careers as novelist, journalist, and publisher, and had founded his own film production company. His ''empire'' was completed by the opening of his own cinema in Marseilles for the release of *César*. For although Pagnol had to move to Paris to ''make it,'' his roots remained in the south, and the trilogy is first of all a tribute to Marseilles and its people.

Critics at the time may have preferred the cinematically innovative work of Renoir or Grémillon, or the committed manifestos of the Popular Front, but audiences flocked to see Pagnol's films and in particular the trilogy. Constant repeats on French television show that time has done nothing to erode this tremendous popularity, and some of the trilogy's phrases have entered the national vocabulary (''tu me fends le coeur!''). Apart from a first-class cast, Pagnol's joky claim that ''I only write about clichés'' may give a clue to this lasting appeal and relevance: like all Pagnol's films, *Marius*, *Fanny*, and *César* share a direct concern with simple but basic psychological and social relations, and primarily the family. The plot is simple: in Marseilles's old harbour, Fanny (a shellfish seller) and Marius (who works in his father's bar) love each other, but Marius longs for the sea. After he sails away (at the end of *Marius)*, the pregnant Fanny has to marry the older and wealthier Panisse to save the family's honour. Marius comes back to claim his ''wife'' and son Césariot, but his father, César, sends him packing; this constitutes the plot of *Fanny. César* opens with Panisse's death (20 years later), upon which Césariot learns the truth about his paternity and seeks out his real father. Fanny and Marius are finally reunited. Although its ending seems positively to demand a sequel, *Marius* in fact was written as a single stage play. First performed in March 1929, it was an instant hit, so much so that Pagnol and Alexander Korda filmed it for Paramount in Paris, with almost the same cast. As was the practice at the time, foreign language versions were also shot (in this case German and Swedish). The film's trimph prompted Pagnol to write a follow-up, *Fanny*, also for the theatre but clearly with a film in mind. *César* was written directly as a screenplay and performed on stage only after the release of the film. The shift from stage play to film is reflected in the proportion of outdoor scenes, from the studio-bound *Marius* to *César*, where 25 minutes of the film were shot on location.

In the heated debates surrounding the coming of sound, Pagnol went against the dominant anti-sound trend, headed by people like René Clair. On the contrary, he declared that ''any sound film that can be projected silently and still remain comprehensible is a very bad film.'' True to this principle, Pagnol always considered the writer the true *auteur* of a film, and the *mise-en-scène* of the trilogy unashamedly puts the image to the service of the dialogue. Whether the films were technically directed by Korda, Marc Allégret, or Pagnol himself, they are ''Pagnol films,'' and the trilogy is, undoubtedly, theatrical, both in its overall ''classical'' structure, and in the presence of a ''chorus'' of minor characters who comment on the main action. It also draws on the tradition of stage melodrama: the illegitimate child, the overbearing father, the unexpected return of Marius in the dead of the night. Above all, it focuses on dialogue, written in Pagnol's unique blend of classical French and Marseillais idiom, spoken with the strong southern accent—its mark of local specificity and paradoxically its recipe for universal success. The trilogy was both leader and part of a new nation-wide fashion for the ''midi'' in the early 1930s, triggered off by sound cinema, although Marseilles and Provence had long boasted their own literary, theatrical, and music-hall traditions. Indeed, out of the Marseilles music-hall and theatre came most of the trilogy's actors: Raimu, Charpin, Alida Rouffe; Demazis was from Oran; Fresnay was the only non-southerner and he painstakingly—and successfully—learned the accent for *Marius.* These actors were central to the trilogy's success, cementing its unity and functioning as powerful box-office draw. But performance is also of structural importance to the films. Characters constantly perform for each other in the key spaces of French popular culture—the café, the shop, the street—while the actors act ''for'' the spectators in a manner reminiscent of the live entertainment traditions they came from, a common feature of French cinema of the 1930s. And just as the trilogy constantly mixes melodrama with comedy, they vary their register, from outrageous excess to intense sobriety (Raimu in particular excels at it). Accent, milieu, and performance lend the trilogy a naturalism which, despite its theatrical structure, makes it one of the recognised precursors of Italian Neo-Realism.

Family, patrimony, and community are at the core of *Marius*, *Fanny*, and *César.* Marius may be the archetypal romantic hero—crossed with Ulysses—but he is ultimately marginal. Whether Marius is present (in *Marius)* or absent (throughout most of the rest), the central figure is César, who is in turn father, godfather, and grandfather, the domineering and garrulous patriarch who decides or interferes with everyone's fate; the centrality of the role is given even more weight by Raimu's talent and charisma. A more benign patriarchal figure is that of Panisse, the shopkeeper who gives both name and inheritance to Fanny's son, allowing him to climb the social scale from bartender's grandson to student at the highest-ranking (Parisian, of course) university, *Polytechnique.* Meanwhile, Fanny's role is to produce a son and accept her marriage to Panisse, 30 years her senior, as atonement for her ''sin.'' To say that Pagnol's universe is oppressively patriarchal is to state the obvious. Clearly the films corresponded to dominant discourses about gender roles—either actual at the time of their release, or nostalgically desired later. However, Fanny is not, as most of her Hollywood counterparts at the time, ''punished'' by death or madness; she lives to bring up her son, happily as it turns out, accepted by the whole community, and eventually reunited with her romantic lover. *Fanny*, the central episode of the trilogy, is largely devoted to her. Interestingly, although it is rated the weakest of the three films by most critics, it was the most popular at the box-office, a success which cannot be simply ascribed to a masochistic identification on the part of women spectators. No doubt moral acceptance of Fanny's illicit pregnancy had to do with the dubious ''natalist'' ideologies of the time, but it was also a way of exposing and vindicating a woman's place in an oppressive society. In this respect, the dialogue of the trilogy gives Fanny space to vent her frustration at the patriarchs who rule her life.

Beyond individual characters, the trilogy stages a tight-knit community which vanished sociologically and geographically (if indeed it ever existed) under the bombs of World War II. In an urban setting, the films create a warm, close, pre-industrial society in which caring and nurturing are taken on by the whole group: César is a patriarch who prepares the food and sweeps the floor. Within this nostalgic structure, the melodramatic form allows the trilogy to state completely contradictory—and hence more ''realistic''—values: sexuality as both socially divisive and cohesive, escape as both condemnable (Marius) and desirable (Césariot). Reconciling opposites is the privilege of myth, a status which these crackly, stagy, old-fashioned melodramas have undoubtedly attained.

—Ginette Vincendeau

THE MARRIAGE OF MARIA BRAUN

See **DIE EHE DER MARIA BRAUN**

M*A*S*H

USA, 1970

Director: Robert Altman

Production: Twentieth Century-Fox; color, 35mm, Panavision; running time: 116 minutes. Released 1970.

Producer: Ingo Preminger; **screenplay:** Ring Lardner, Jr., from the novel by Richard Hooker; **photography:** Harold E. Stine; **editor:** Danford Greene; **art directors:** Jack Martin Smith and Arthur Lonergan; **music:** Johnny Mandel.

Cast: Donald Sutherland (*Hawkeye*); Elliott Gould (*Trapper John*); Tom Skerritt (*Duke*); Gary Burghoff (*Radar O'Reilly*); Sally Kellerman (*Major Margaret ''Hot Lips'' Houlihan*); Robert Duvall (*Major Frank Burns*); John Shuck (*Painless Pole*); Roger Bowen (*Colonel Henry Blake*); René Auberjonois (*Dago Red*); Jo Ann Pflug (*Lieutenant Dish*).

Awards: Oscar for Best Screenplay—Material from another medium, 1970; Best Film, Cannes Film Festival, 1970.

Publications

Books:

Feineman, Neil, *Persistence of Vision: The Films of Robert Altman*, New York, 1976.
Kass, Judith M., *Robert Altman: American Innovator*, New York, 1978.
Sind, Lawrence H., *Guts and Glory: Great American War Movies*, Reading, Massachusetts, 1978.
Kolker, Robert Philip, *A Cinema of Loneliness: Penn, Kubrick, Coppola, Scorsese, Altman*, Oxford, 1980; revised edition, 1988.
Bourget, Jean-Loup, *Robert Altman*, Paris, 1981.
Karp, Alan, *The Films of Robert Altman*, Metuchen, New Jersey, 1981.
Giannetti, Louis, *Masters of the American Cinema*, Englewood Cliffs, New Jersey, 1981.
Kagan, Norman, *American Sceptic: Robert Altman's Genre-Commentary Films*, Ann Arbor, Michigan, 1982.
Wexman, Virginia Wright, and Gretchen Bisplinghoff, *Robert Altman: A Guide to References and Resources*, Boston, 1984.
Plecki, Gerard, *Robert Altman*, Boston, 1985.
Wood, Robin, *Hollywood from Vietnam to Reagan*, New York, 1986.
Keyssar, Helene, *Robert Altman's America*, New York, 1991.
Cagin, Seth, *Born to Be Wild: Hollywood and the Sixties Generation*, Boca Raton, 1994.
O'Brien, Daniel, *Robert Altman: Hollywood Survivor*, New York, 1996.
Sterritt, David, editor, *Robert Altman: Interviews*, Jackson, 2000.

Articles:

Trutta, G., in *Harper's Bazaar* (New York), March 1970.
Bartlett, Louise, in *Films and Filming* (London), March 1970.
Johnson, William, in *Film Quarterly* (Berkeley), Spring 1970.
Dawson, Jan, in *Sight and Sound* (London), Summer 1970.
Time (New York), 13 July 1970.
''What Directors Are Saying,'' in *Action* (Los Angeles), July-August and November-December 1970.
Gow, Gordon, in *Films and Filming* (London), August 1970.
Tavernier, Bertrand, ''D. W. Griffith se porte bien, moi aussi, merci!,'' in *Positif* (Paris), October 1970.
Cutts, John, ''*MASH, McCloud*, and *McCabe*,'' in *Films and Filming* (London), November 1971.
Grisolia, M., ''Entretien avec Robert Altman,'' in *Cinéma* (Paris), July-August 1972.
Baker, C. A., ''The Theme of Structure in the Films of Robert Altman,'' in *Journal of Popular Film* (Washington, D.C.), Summer 1973.
Corliss, Richard, ''Outlaws, Auteurs, and Actors,'' in *Film Comment* (New York), May-July 1974.

*M*A*S*H*

''Altman Seminar'' in *Dialogue on Film* (Beverly Hills), February 1975.

Rosenbaum, Jonathan, ''Improvisations and Interactions in Altmanville,'' in *Sight and Sound* (London), Spring 1975.

Wood, Robin, ''Smart-Ass and Cutie-Pie: Notes Toward an Evaluation of Altman,'' in *Movie* (London), Autumn 1975.

''Altman Issue'' of *Film Heritage* (Dayton, Ohio), Fall 1975.

Pittman, Bruce, in *Take One* (Montreal), August 1976.

Pitiot, P., and H. Talvat, ''Robert Altman de *Mash* à *Nashville*,'' in *Jeune Cinéma* (Paris), September-October 1976.

Jacobs, Diane, ''Robert Altman,'' in *Hollywood Renaissance*, New York, 1977.

Michener, Charles, interview with Robert Altman, in *Film Comment* (New York), September-October 1978.

Desmarais, James J., in *Magill's Survey of Cinema 3*, Englewood Cliffs, New Jersey, 1980.

Yacowar, Maurice, ''Actors as Conventions in the Films of Robert Altman,'' in *Cinema Journal* (Evanston, Illinois), Fall 1980.

Olin, Joyce, ''Ring Lardner, Jr.,'' in *American Screenwriters*, edited by Robert E. Morsberger, Stephen O. Lesser, and Randall Clark, Detroit, 1984.

Freedman, C., ''History, Fiction, Film, Television, Myth: The Ideology of *M*A*S*H*,'' in *The Southern Review* (Baton Rouge, Louisiana), no. 1, 1990.

Freedman, C., ''*M*A*S*H* och anti-antikommunismen,'' in *Filmhaftet* (Uppsala, Sweden), December 1990.

Tibbetts, John C., ''Robert Altman: After 35 Years, Still the 'Action Painter' of American Cinema,'' in *Literature/Film Quarterly* (Salisbury), vol. 20, no. 1, January 1992.

Breskin, David, ''Robert Altman: The Rolling Stone Interview,'' in *Rolling Stone*, no. 628, 16 April 1992.

Norman, Barry, in *Radio Times* (London), vol. 279, no. 3649, 11 December 1993.

Buchsbaum, T., ''*M*A*S*H*,'' in *Film Score Monthly* (Los Angeles), no. 58, June 1995.

* * *

*M*A*S*H*, one of the most popular films of the early 1970s, achieved stardom for Donald Sutherland and Elliott Gould, spawned a successful television series, and gave its innovative director, Robert Altman, his first financial and critical success.

In *M*A*S*H*—and to a greater extent in his later films—Altman abandons conventional Hollywood narrative techniques in favor of a very personal style characterized by overlapping dialogue, improvisational acting, elliptical editing, wide-screen Panavision compositions, telephoto shots (specifically shots through windows and past obstructing foreground objects), and the development of a large community and of major characters within a limited time and space. These techniques alter conventions of narrative structure in two ways. First, the improvisational acting, the multiple babble of overlapping dialogue, and the frequently voyeuristic telephoto shots (particularly the shots of explicit gore in the operating scenes) generate a sense of spontaneity and authenticity usually found in documentary, rather than narrative, films. Second, the large number of characters arranged within the wide Panavision frame, the compression of space caused by the telephoto lens, and the continuous barrage of overlapping dialogue, music and P.A. announcements on the soundtrack combine to create an aural and visual denseness that demands much more of a viewer's attention and active participation than does the shallow-focus cinematography, the separation of major characters from peripheral characters, and the one-speaker-at-a-time dialogue of conventional narrative.

When *M*A*S*H* appeared in 1970, audiences—caught up in the spirit of rebellion generated by the civil rights movement, the women's movement, the drug culture, the demonstrations against the Vietnam War, etc.—revelled in the film's iconoclastic humor, its joyous deflation of patriotism, religion, heroism, and other values cherished by the establishment. The film became an immediate box office success, earning over $36 million in domestic rentals by 1983. The critics also favored *M*A*S*H*, but while they praised its innovative techniques, some critics thought that the film's humor was too smug and the scenes involving the trip to Tokyo and the football game were flaws in the film's structure. Today critics feel that *M*A*S*H* is inferior to most of Altman's later films (none of which proved as successful at the box office), though the film is still highly regarded for its innovative narrative techniques and its effective humor.

—Clyde Kelly Dunagan

THE MASQUE OF THE RED DEATH

UK, 1964

Director: Roger Corman

Production: Alta Vista/Anglo Amalgamated; Pathécolor, Panavision; running time: 84 minutes. Released August 1964.

Producer: George Willoughby; **screenplay:** Charles Beaumont and R. Wright Campbell, from the story by Edgar Allan Poe; **photography:** Nicolas Roeg; **editor:** Anne Chegwidden; **sound:** Richard Bied, Len Abbott; **art director:** Robert Jones; **music:** David Lee.

Cast: Vincent Price (*Prince Prospero*); Hazel Court (*Juliana*); Jane Asher (*Francesca*); David Weston (*Gino*); Patrick Magee (*Alfredo*); Nigel Green (*Ludovico*); Skip Martin (*Hop Toad*); John Westbrook (*Man in Red*); Gay Brown (*Senora Escobar*); Julian Burton (*Senor Veronese*); Doreen Dawn (*Anna-Marie*); Paul Whitsun-Jones (*Scarlatti*); Jean Lodge (*Scarlatti's Wife*); Verina Greenlaw (*Esmerelda*); Brian Hewlett (*Lampredi*); Harvey Hall (*Clistor*).

Publications

Script:

Beaumont, Charles, and R. Wright Campbell, *The Masque of the Red Death*, in *Avant-Scène du Cinéma* (Paris), 15 May 1980.

Books:

Will, David, and others, *Roger Corman: The Millenic Vision*, Edinburgh, 1970.
McCarthy, Todd, and Charles Flynn, *King of the Bs*, New York, 1975.
Turoni, Giuseppe, *Roger Corman*, Florence, 1976.
Marcus, Fred H., *Short Story/Short Film*, Englewood Cliffs, New Jersey, 1977.
McAsh, Iain, F., *The Films of Vincent Price*, London, 1977.
de Franco, J. Philip, *The Movie World of Roger Corman*, New York, 1979.
Hillier, Jim, and Aaron Lipstadt, *Roger Corman's New World*, London, 1981.
Naha, Ed, *The Films of Roger Corman*, New York, 1982.
McAsh, Iain F., *Vincent Price: A Biography*, Farncombe, Surrey, 1982.
Bourgoin, Stephane, *Roger Corman*, Paris, 1983.
McGee, Mark Thomas, *Fast and Furious: The Story of American International Pictures*, Jefferson, North Carolina, 1984.
Morris, Gary, *Roger Corman*, Boston, 1985.
Eisner, Joel, *The Price of Fear: The Film Career of Vincent Price*, Staunton, 1993.
Williams, Lucy C., *The Complete Films of Vincent Price*, Secaucus, 1995.
McGee, Mark Thomas, *Roger Corman: The Best of the Cheap Acts*, Jefferson, 1997.
Corman, Roger, *How I Made a Hundred Movies in Hollywood & Never Lost a Dime*, New York, 1998.
Frank, Alan, *Films of Roger Corman*, London, 1998.
Price, Victoria, *Vincent Price: A Daughter's Biography*, New York, 1999.

Articles:

Films and Filming (London), February 1964.
Hollywood Reporter, 24 June 1964.
Variety (New York), 24 June 1964.
Kine Weekly (London), 25 June 1964.
Milne, Tom, in *Monthly Film Bulletin* (London), August 1964.
New York Times, 17 September 1964.
Marill, Alvin H., ''Vincent Price,'' in *Films in Review* (New York), May 1969.
''Corman Issue'' of *Cinema Nuovo* (Turin), January-February 1984.
Del Valle, D., ''Roger Corman,'' in *Films and Filming* (London), November 1984.

The Masque of the Red Death

Newman, Kim, ''The Roger Corman Alumni Association,'' in *Monthly Film Bulletin* (London), November and December 1985.

Pearly, Gerald, ''*The Masque of Red Death*,'' in *American Film*, vol. 15, no. 9, June 1990.

Peary, Gerald, ''Roger Corman: They Call Him Cheap, Quick and 'America's Greatest Independent Film Maker',' ' in *American Film*, vol. 15, no. 9, June 1990.

Weiner, Rex, ''Thrifty Corman Healthy in 4th Decade,'' in *Variety* (New York), vol. 359, no. 10, 10 July 1995.

Farrell, Sean, ''*The Raven* & *The Masque of Red Death*,'' in *Scarlet Street* (Glen Rock), no. 20, Fall 1995.

Lucas, Tim, ''*The Raven/Masque of Red Death*,'' in *Video Watchdog* (Cincinnati), no. 29, 1995.

Lucas, Tim, ''Disque of the Red Death - Incomplete,'' in *Video Watchdog* (Cincinnati), no. 32, 1996.

* * *

The Masque of the Red Death was the seventh of Roger Corman's eight Poe adaptations, and one of two (the other being *The Tomb of Ligeia*) to be produced in Britain on slightly larger budgets than usual. Throughout the cycle Corman's distinctive *mise-en-scène*—comprising an expressive use of colour and sweeping, elegant camera movements—had represented in external form his characters' troubled psychological states. (This differentiated him sharply from the more moralistic approach adopted by contemporaneous British horror filmmakers.)

In many ways, *Masque* is the least coherent of all the Poe films. While the psychological element is still present—notably at the conclusion, where the cloaked figure which brings death to Vincent Price's Prince Prospero is played by Price himself—its development is hampered by a loss of focus within the organization of the narrative. This can be attributed to the script's rather clumsy stitching together of two of Poe's short stories, ''Hop-Frog'' and ''The Masque of the Red Death,'' and it results in Price, usually the most precise and expert of actors, seeming uncertain at times as to what tone to adopt. The banality of his ''philosophy'' of evil is a further hindrance as is the lacklustre concluding masque (which was apparently curtailed during production by budgetary restrictions).

In order then to locate the film's merits, which are considerable, one needs to look elsewhere. Firstly, to Corman's use of colour which, largely detached as it is from its usual psychologically expressive function, takes on a non-representational, kinetic force—most impressively in the various camera tracks through a series of rooms, each of which has been decorated in a different colour—which is rarely seen in mainstream commercial productions and which anticipates moments of psychedelic abstraction in Corman's later ''drug-culture'' film *The Trip*.

Secondly, all the scenes involving Juliana, played by British actress Hazel Court. Court had already appeared in several British horror films (*The Curse of Frankenstein*, *The Man Who Could Cheat Death*) in conventionally staid leading roles. In Corman's films (she also appears in *The Raven* and *The Premature Burial*) she is unexpectedly transformed into a figure of awesome sexual perversity. Her masochistic preparations for her ''marriage'' to Satan are given us in meticulous detail; first she brands herself and then has a series of hallucinations (cut from the initial British release print), all of which re-enact a brutal rape fantasy. Marriage—in a Poe-like equation—is linked to the death of the bride, and Court commits herself to this with an eagerness which is truly disturbing. The intensity of her performance has only been equalled within the horror genre in some of the films featuring Barbara Steele (another British actress who left her native country and developed her career elsewhere: she had starred in an earlier Corman production, *The Pit and the Pendulum*). It is only in these brilliantly executed scenes, in which the film's formal qualities most eloquently match its content, that Corman finds a coherent theme upon which he can exercise his formidable ability to visualise a character's perverse desires. The film's true dramatic climax is the chilling epitaph spoken by Prospero over Juliana's dead body: ''I beg you, do not mourn for Juliana. We should celebrate. She has just married a friend of mine.'' As is so often the case in Corman's work, the forces of good that eventually triumph, represented here somewhat half-heartedly by Jane Asher's Francesca, are, in comparison with this vividly drawn picture of a desire unto death, anaemic and unconvincing.

—Peter Hutchings

MAT

(Mother)

USSR, 1926

Director: Vsevolod I. Pudovkin

Production: Mezhrabpom-Russ.; black and white, 35mm, silent; running time: about 90 minutes; length: 1800 meters, or 5906 feet. Released 11 October 1926. Re-released 1935, with musical soundtrack.

Scenario: Nathan Zarkhi, from the novel by Maxim Gorky; **assistant directors:** Mikhail Doller and V. Strauss; **photography:** Anatoli Golovnya; **art director:** Sergei Kozlovsky; **music (1935):** S. Blok.

Cast: Vera Baranovskaya (*Pelageya Vlasova, the mother*); A. Tchistyakova (*Vlasov, her husband*); Nikolai Batalov (*Pavel, her son*); Alexander Savitsky (*Isaika Gorbov, the foreman*); Ivan Koval-Samborsky (*Vesovshchikiv, Pavel's friend*); Anna Zemstova (*Anna, a girl student*); Vsevolod Pudovkin (*Police officer*); N. Vidonov (*Misha*).

Publications

Script:

Zarkhi, Nathan, *Mother*, in *Mother and Earth*, New York, 1973.

Books:

Korolevich, V., *Vera Baranovskaya*, Moscow, 1929.
Yezuitov, N., *Poudouvkine, ''Pouti Tvortchestva, Les Voies de la création*,'' Moscow, 1937.
Mariamov, A., *Vsevolod Pudovkin*, Moscow, 1952.
Leyda, Jay, *Kino: A History of the Russian and Soviet Film*, London, 1960.
Schnitzer, Luda and Jean, *Vsevolod Poudouvkine*, Paris, 1966.
Amengual, Barthélemy, *V. I. Poudouvkine*, Lyons, 1968.
Dickinson, Thorold, and Catherine de la Roche, *Soviet Cinema*, New York, 1972.
Schnitzer, Luda and Jean, and Marcel Martin, editors, *Cinema in Revolution: The Heroic Era of the Soviet Film*, New York, 1973.
Dart, Peter, *Pudovkin's Films and Film Theory*, New York, 1974.
Cohen, Louis Harris, *The Cultural-Political Traditions and Developments of the Soviet Cinema*, New York, 1974.
Klinowski, Jacek, and Adam Garbicz, *Cinema, The Magic Vehicle: A Guide to Its Achievement: Journey One: The Cinema Through 1949*, Metuchen, New Jersey, 1975.
Taylor, Richard, *Film Propaganda: Soviet Russia and Nazi Germany*, London, 1979.
Leyda, Jay, *An Index to the Creative Work of V.I. Pudovkin*, New York, 1980.
Karaganov, Aleksandr Vasil'evich, *Vsevolod Pudovkin*, Moscow, 1983.
Masi, Stefano, *Vsevolod I. Pudovkin*, Florence, 1985.
Marshall, Herbert, *Masters of the Soviet Cinema: Crippled Creative Biographies*, London, 1985.

Articles:

New York Times, 8 January 1928.
Close Up (London), October-November 1928 and January 1929.
Leyda, Jay, ''Index to the Creative Work of Vsevolod Pudovkin,'' in *Sight and Sound* (London), November 1948.
Manvell, Roger, in *Sight and Sound* (London), August 1950.
''Pudovkin Issue'' of *Cahiers du Cinéma* (Paris), August-September 1953.
Weinberg, Herman, ''Vsevolod Pudovkin,'' in *Films in Review* (New York), August-September 1953.
''Pudovkin Issue'' of *Iskusstvo Kino* (Moscow), February 1973.
Stoianov-Bigor, G., in *Kinoizkustvo* (Sofia), July 1979.
Hudlin, E., ''Film Language: Pudovkin and Eisenstein and Russian Formalism,'' in *Journal of Aesthetic Education* (Urbana, Illinois), no. 2, 1979.

Burns, P. E., ''Linkage: Pudovkin's Classics Revisited,'' in *Journal of Popular Film and Television* (Washington, D.C), Summer 1981.

Rubin, S.K., ''Videotape Reviews,'' in *Classic Images* (Muscatine), no. 109, July 1984.

Dufour, Dirk, ''!Revolutie? (4): Wolken doorheen de vlag,'' in *Film en Televisie + Video* (Brussels), no. 432, May 1993.

Kepley, Vance Jr., ''Pudovkin, Socialist Realism, and the Classical Hollywood Style: Hollywood's Impact on Vsevolod Pudovkin's Film Making Style,'' in *Journal of Film and Video* (Atlanta), vol. 47, no. 4, Winter 1995.

* * *

Mother might rightfully be labelled Soviet propaganda. It is the story of a poor working-class woman at the time of the 1905 Revolution who, through her relationship with her worker son, becomes politicized. At first, she is oppressed, just another anonymous pawn of the power structure; at the finale she is exultant, a heroine and a martyr. However, the film is no boring treatise on the wonders of revolutionary spirit. *Mother* is a drama of love and conflict that can be universally understood and appreciated. In the scenario, based on a Maxim Gorky novel, a traditional theme—a mother's concern for her beloved son—may be stretched to fit into a propagandistic framework. But this fact does not obscure the heart-wrenching storyline and superior cinematic techniques of its maker, Vsevolod Illareonovitch Pudovkin.

Mother is Pudovkin's first feature produced on his own, independent of his colleagues at the State Film School. Here, under the tutelage of Lev Kuleshov, the filmmaker had defined and sharpened his cinematic grammar, and this film became his initial major achievement; he followed it a year later with *The End of St. Petersburg* and, thereafter with *The Heir to Genghis-Khan*. *Mother*, made when Pudovkin's relative inexperience prevented him from initially receiving adequate funding, is a superior example of the filmmaker's concern with camera angles, montage and editing. He and his cinematographer, Anatoli Golovnya, photographed the actors from every which angle: a military officer's self-importance would be conveyed by shooting him from below; the mother's early frustration would be emphasized by shooting her from above, and at the end, her triumph and liberation is highlighted by shooting from below. When Pudovkin places his camera in this position, the character's upper body and head seem further away, more inaccessible, reaching to the sky and towering over the viewer; when the actor is beneath the camera he becomes inferior, in that the viewer is literally looking down on him. Pudovkin does not shoot his performance straight on, as if he is recording a stage play. Mood and characterization are communicated in *Mother* not by the actor emoting before the camera; the performer is almost a passive participant in the filmmaking process.

Pudovkin believed that the manner and order in which pieces of film are spliced together can have the most powerful effect on the viewer. *Mother* is structured like a musical composition: a balance of action and reaction, seemingly disconnected shots—opposites, if you will—coming together to form a coherent whole. For example, the son receives some happy news while in prison. Instead of just editing in a simple reaction shot of his actor, Nikolai Batalov, Pudovkin combines shots of hands energetically in motion and a close-up of the bottom part of Batalov's face with scenes of a sun-lit stream, birds cavorting in a pond, and a happy child. *Mother* is a creative leap in the advancement of the editing process as an important filmmaking tool.

Pudovkin's individual images are, when contrasted to his cutting, relatively insignificant. But they are not uninteresting. One example: the mother visits the bier of her just-deceased husband. The filmmaker conveys a stark, sad mood by shooting only the dark shape of Vera Baranovskaya (who plays the role) casting an ominous shadow on the nearby grey wall, and a white sheet covering the body.

Pudovkin was also allegedly inspired by artists, painters and printmakers. The mother's characterization is modelled after the creations of Kathe Kollwitz, Picasso (especially the works of his Blue Period) and Degas. A sequence in a prison has its roots in Van Gogh's ''Prison Courtyard.'' The film's influences are also literary: the trial scenes are based more on Tolstoy's *Resurrection* than in anything from the original source material.

Mother is expertly cast, from the actors playing mother and son (Baranovskaya and Batalov were recruited from the Moscow Art Theater) to the extras on screen for a split second. Pudovkin favored using non-actors in smaller roles, people whose real-life experience would provide a heightened sense of reality. In a sequence depicting the son's arrest after a search of his home, a former tsarist officer plays the colonel supervising the interrogation. After all, who else but an authentic career military man would know how to look the part of a professional soldier?

Interestingly, *Mother* might easily have been made by another director. Yuri Zhelyabuzhsky was initially assigned to direct the film, but was unable to cast the title role and even requested that scenarist Nathan Zarkhi transform her into a father. Finally, the project came to Pudovkin, who could never have worked independently within, or outside, the Soviet cinema establishment. His films are not pure works of art: *Mother* is similar to *The End of St. Petersburg* and *The Heir to Genghis-Khan* in that its motives are unabashedly political. Every great Russian film of the era, including Eisenstein's *Battleship Potemkin*, *Strike* and *October*, are in some way linked to the Revolution. But *Mother* is the most personalized, and most poetic, of them all.

—Rob Edelman

MATKA JOANNA OD ANIOLOW

(Mother Joan of the Angels)

Poland, 1961

Director: Jerzy Kawalerowicz

Production: Kadr Film Unit for Film Polski; black and white, 35mm; running time: 125 minutes and 105 minutes, English version is 101 minutes. Released 1961, Poland.

Screenplay: Tadeusz Konwicki and Jerzy Kawalerowicz, from a novel by Jarosław Iwaszkiewicz which in turn was based on 17th century

Matka Joanna od aniolow

documents about the events at the convent in Loudon, France; **photography:** Jerzy Wójcik; **editors:** Wiesława Otocka and Felicja Ragowska; **sound recordists:** Józef Bartczak, Zygmunt Nowak, and Jozef Kensikowski; **art directors:** Roman Mann and Tadeusz Borowczyk (some sources list Tadeusz Wybult); **music:** Adam Walaciński.

Cast: Lucyna Winnicka (*Mother Joan*); Mieczysław Voit (*Father Jozef Suryn/the Rabbi*); Anna Ciepielewska (*Sister Margaret*, or *Małgorzata*); Maria Chwalibóg (*Awdosia*); Kazimierz Fabisiak (*Father Brym*); Stanisław Jasiukiewicz (*Chrzaszczewski*); Zygmunt Zintel (*Wołodkowicz*); Franciszek Pieczka (*Odryl*); Jerzy Kaczmarek (*Kaziuk*); Jarosław Kuszewski (*Juraj*); Lech Wojciechowski; Marian Nosek.

Publications

Books:

Jerzy Kawalerowicz: Filmtexte, Munich, 1963.
Grzelecki, Stanislaw, *20 Years of Polish Cinema*, Warsaw, 1969.
Wegner, Jacek, *Konwicki* (in French), Warsaw, 1973.
Liehm, Mira and Antonin, *The Most Important Art: East European Film after 1945*, Berkeley, 1977.
Kuszewski, Stanislaw, *Contemporary Polish Film*, Warsaw, 1978.

Articles:

Flacon, Michel, in *Cinéma* (Paris), no. 57, 1961.
Douchet, Jean, in *Arts* (Paris), 7 June 1961.
Siclier, Jacques, ''Paphnuce et les Chacals,'' in *Cahiers du Cinéma* (Paris), July 1961.
Thirard, Paul-Louis, ''Le Père Joseph et la Mère Jeanne,'' in *Positif* (Paris), September 1961.
Kawalerowicz, Jerzy, ''Angles on the Angels,'' in *Films and Filming* (London), November 1961.
Hitchens, Gordon, in *Vision* (New York), Spring 1962.
Durgnat, Raymond, in *Films and Filming* (London), May 1962.
Hart, Henry, in *Films in Review* (New York), May 1962.
Mekas, Jonas, in *Village Voice* (New York), 17 May 1962.
Lefèvre, Raymond, in *Image et Son* (Paris), October 1962.
Callenbach, Ernest, in *Film Quarterly* (Berkeley), Winter 1963–64.

Michalek, Boleslaw, in *Kino* (Warsaw), no. 6, 1967.
Hopfinger, Maryla, in *Kino* (Warsaw), no. 11, 1971.
Cluny, C. M., in *Cinéma* (Paris), November 1982.
Helman, Alicja., in *Kino* (Warsaw), April 1986.
Iluzjon, no. 3–4 (51–52), 1993.

* * *

''The revolt of oppressed humanity'' is how one Polish critic described *Mother Joan of the Angels* and with this definition various levels of meaning may be glimpsed. The novel of the same name by the well-known author Jarosław Iwaszkiewicz, deals with an occurrence in the eastern region of Poland in the 17th century. The young ascetic priest Suryn ventures into a cloister where, it is said, all of the nuns are in the terrible grip of Satan. Four exorcists have made every effort, but in vain, to drive out the evil.

In his first encounter with the Mother Superior Joan, the priest is somewhat disappointed—instead of a miserable creature in the Devil's grasp, he is greeted by a beautiful, dignified, and proud woman who engages him in a serious philosophical discussion. Between the two a shy, tender affection develops, a kind of halting love which they cannot resolve. The closed world of religious dogma and ritual shut out such a love. (Another nun, Małgorzata, has let herself be led astray by a nobleman who later abandons her, and she despairs of returning to the convent).

Suryn, in a tragic conflict with himself, with his feelings and his principles, decides on radical measures; to begin with he builds a screen in the attic where he meets with Joan, so that she can not come too near. Then he brings in two innocent boys with the aim of concentrating the satanic might onto them, thereby freeing Joan. In his holy foolishness, he suspects no tragic consequences; for him everything is only a game, a challenge to moral norms and customs, to the mendacity of his surroundings. For the clever woman, religion is not a calling but an opportunity to live free of the burden of a woman's fate at that time.

Even in the cloister, in the perfect, uniformed and regulated system, Joan has rebelled against a one-dimensional, determinedly average existence. She unleashes this theater of darkness, with its possession by the devil and exorcisms, in order to express her need for love and spiritual contact. That is her vengeance on the cruel world; and as is the rule in the great tragedies, she causes the sacrifice of her beloved.

Kawalerowicz has succeeded in creating a poetically stylized work full of contrasts, elevated in its sincerity. The impressive, emotionally-laden, subtle interpretations by Lucyna Winnicka (Joan) and Mieczysław Voit (Suryn), grab the viewer and awake similar feelings. Without any physical contact, only through close-ups, eyes, glimpses, hands, the film refracts a delicate, but elusive eroticism. The film is full of erotic allusions, indirect, unprovoked, transmitted through atmosphere and images. As a pure art work, *Mother Joan* embodies an almost mystic ambivalence which releases intense feelings and many-layered thoughts. It is completely wrong to view the film as a critique of the church or religion. Rather, this Polish film should be seen as a lyrical tragedy of human existence, as a striving toward spiritual freedom, toward emotion and dreams. The director's visual symbolism and his means of expression all point to this. Plagued by the contradictions of his situation, Suryn goes looking for a rabbi. Astonishingly, he discovers that the rabbi is himself (played by the same actor). He sees the situation with more wisdom and composure, realizing that there are no solutions to the existential questions of life. *Mother Joan of the Angels* is a film about the eternal quest for those answers.

—Maria Racheva

THE MATRIX

USA, 1999

Directors: Andy Wachowski and Larry Wachowski

Production: Village Roadshow Productions, Grouch II Film Partnership, and Silver Pictures; distributed by Warner Brothers; color, 35mm; running time: 136 minutes; sound mix: DTS, Dolby Digital, SDDS. Released March 1999, USA. Filmed in Sydney, Moore Park, and Waterloo, Australia, and in Istanbul, Turkey; cost: $63 million.

Producers: Bruce Berman (executive), Dan Cracchiolo (co-producer), Carol Hughes (associate), Andrew Mason (executive), Richard Mirisch (associate), Barrie Osborne (executive), Joel Silver, Erwin Stoff (executive), Andy Wachowski (executive), Larry Wachowski (executive); **screenplay:** Andy Wachowski, Larry Wachowski; **cinematography:** Bill Pope; **assistant directors:** Colin Fletcher, Bruce Hunt, James McTeigue, Toby Pease, Tom Read, Noni Roy, Jeremy Sedley, Paul Sullivan; **editor:** Zach Staenberg; **supervising sound editor:** Dane Davis; **art directors:** Hugh Bateup, Michelle McGahey; **production designer:** Owen Paterson; **costume designer:** Kym Barrett; **original music:** Don Davis; **sound effects editors:** Julia Evershade, David Grimaldi, Eric Lindemann; **casting:** Mali Finn, Shauna Wolifson; **special effects supervisors:** Steve Courtley, Brian Cox; **visual effects supervisors:** Lynne Cartwright (Animal Logic), John Gaeta; **digital effects supervisor:** Rodney Iwashina; **Bullettime composite supervisor:** John Sasaki; **stunt coordinator:** Glenn Boswell; **set designer:** Godric Cole; **music supervisor:** Jason Bentley; **kung fu choreographer:** Yuen Wo Ping.

Cast: Keanu Reeves (*Thomas A. Anderson/Neo*); Laurence Fishburne (*Morpheus*); Carrie-Anne Moss (*Trinity*); Hugo Weaving (*Agent Smith*); Gloria Foster (*Oracle*); Joe Pantoliano (*Cypher/Mr. Reagan*); Marcus Chong (*Tank*); Julian Arahanga (*Apoc*); Matt Doran (*Mouse*); Belinda McClory (*Switch*); Ray Anthony Parker (*Dozer*); Paul Goddard (*Agent Brown*); Robert Taylor (*Agent Jones*); David Aston (*Rhineheart*); Marc Gray (*Choi*); Ada Nicodemou (*DuJour*); Denni Gordon (*Priestess*); Rowan Witt (*Spoon Boy*); Fiona Johnson (*Woman in Red*); Andy Wachowski (*Window cleaner*, uncredited); Larry Wachowski (*Window cleaner*, uncredited).

Awards: Academy Awards for Best Editing (Zach Staenberg), Best Effects, Sound Effects Editing (Dane A. Davis), Best Effects, Visual Effects (Steve Courtley, John Gaeta, Janek Sirrs, Jon Thum), and Best Sound (David E. Campbell, David Lee, John T. Reitz, Gregg Rudloff), 2000; Academy of Science Fiction, Horror, and Fantasy Films Awards for Best Science Fiction Film, Best Director (Andy and Larry Wachowski), Best Actor (Keanu Reeves), Best Costume Design

The Matrix

(Kym Barrett), Best Make-Up (Nikki Gooley, Bob McCarron, Wendy Sainsbury), Best Special Effects (Courtley, Gaeta, Sirrs, Thum), Best Supporting Actor (Laurence Fishburne), and Best Writer (Andy and Larry Wachowski), 2000; American Cinema Editors Eddie Award for Best Edited Feature Film-Dramatic (Zach Staenberg), 2000; British Academy (BAFTA) Awards for Best Achievement in Special Visual Effects (Courtley, Gaeta, Sirrs, Thum), Best Sound (David E. Campbell, David Lee, John T. Reitz, Gregg Rudloff), Best Cinematography (Bill Pope), Best Editing (Staenberg), and Best Production Design (Owen Paterson), 2000; Csapnivalo Golden Slate Awards for Best Actor in a Leading Role (Keanu Reeves), Best Actress in a Leading Role (Carrie-Anne Moss), and Best Visual Effects, 2000; Hugo Award for Best Dramatic Presentation, 2000; Motion Picture Sound Editors Golden Reel Award for Best Sound Editing-Effects and Foley (crew), 2000.

Publications

Script:

Wachowski, Andy, Larry Wachowski, Geof Darrow, Phil Osterhouse, Steve Skroce, and Spencer Lamm (editor), *The Matrix: The Shooting Script and Complete Storyboards*, New York, 2000.

Articles:

Palermo, Chandra, ''Ghost in the Machine,'' in *Cinescape*, vol. 5, no. 2, March 1999.

McCarthy, Todd, ''Silly F/X, *Matrix* Are For Kids,'' in *Variety*, vol. 374, no. 6, 29 March 1999.

Schwarzbaum, Lisa, ''Techno Prisoners,'' in *Entertainment Weekly*, no. 480, 9 April 1999.

Essex, Andrew, ''Matrix Mania,'' in *Entertainment Weekly*, no. 485, 14 May 1999.

Graham, Bob, ''Reeves Lost in *The Matrix*/Skillful Effects Serve Pretentious Sci-Fi Yarn,'' in *The San Francisco Chronicle*, 24 September 1999.

Wright, Richard, ''The Matrix Rules,'' in *Film-Philosophy Internet Salon*, http://www.film-philosophy.com, vol. 5, no. 3, January 2000.

Hutchings, Peter, ''The Matrix,'' in *Scope: An Online Journal of Film Studies*, http://www. nottingham.ac.uk/film/journal/filmrev/the_matrix.htm, May 2000.

* * *

Three years after impressing critics with their Hollywood debut, *Bound*—a visually-stunning, highly suspenseful, lesbian neo-noir—Chicago-based brothers Andy and Larry Wachowski conceived of, wrote, and directed *The Matrix*, a science-fiction blockbuster that managed to effectively fuse (a là *Star Wars*) pop-philosophical themes with skillfully choreographed action sequences and state-of-the-art special effects.

The film stars Keanu Reeves (in a role that may have resuscitated his flagging career) as a dutiful company man who doubles at night as a hacker named Neo. Neo's Cartesian-esque scepticism concerning the true nature of reality is validated after a beautiful mystery woman, Trinity (Moss), introduces him to legendary zen-hacker Morpheus (Fishburne). Accepting Morpheus's invitation to take a mind/brain opening techno-drug trip, Neo discovers that the world in which he previously ''existed'' is nothing but a computer-generated Virtual Reality program controlled by the very artificial intelligence machines developed by mankind years ago. It seems that the machines, which require endless supplies of electrical current to survive, keep the entire human population (save for a smattering of rebels and one underground city) in a state of perpetual hallucination; lying unconscious in automated incubators, people are deceived into believing that they are actually living productive lives, while in reality vampiric computers are siphoning off their precious mojo. Morpheus is certain that Neo is the Messianic ''One'' who, according to legend, will show up one day to save the human race from eternal subjugation. Although initially dissuaded by a surprisingly domestic soothsayer (Foster), Neo manages to summon the inner fortitude necessary to defeat the waspy A.I. defense squad with the help of John Wooian martial arts-ballet, Sam Peckinpah-inspired slow motion gunfighting, and repeated self-affirmations.

The Matrix stands as the most successful entry in the budding sci-fi subgenre of Virtual Reality pictures. Other entries include John Carpenter's *They Live!* (1988), Paul Verhoeeven's *Total Recall* (1990), Brett Leonard's *Lawnmower Man* (1992), Katheryn Bigalow's *Strange Days* (1995), Alex Proyas's *Dark City* (1998), Josef Rysnak's *The Thirteenth Floor* (1999), and David Cronenberg's *eXistenZ* (1999). Metaphysical musings, justified paranoia, and a constant questioning of authority are staples of all these films, which find not-too-distant relatives in Peter Weir's *The Truman Show* (1998) and Gary Ross's *Pleasantville* (1998). Separating *The Matrix* from the rest of the pack are its epic pretensions, apocalyptic overtones, and breathtaking visuals. New technologies such as ''Bullettime'' super slo-mo photography, wire enhanced gymnastics, and Woo-Ping Yuen (*Black Mask, Fist of Legend*)-choreographed Kung Fu fight scenes together served to raise the bar significantly for big-budget Hollywood action sequences. At the time of its release, producer Joel Silver gushed that ''The style and the visual effects within [*The Matrix*] are something that has never been seen before, plus we have fighting styles and photographic techniques used in this movie that weren't possible even six months ago.'' Some of the fight scenes were so distinctive that spoofs turned up in the Rob Schneider vehicle, *Deuce Bigalo: Male Gigolo* (1999), as well as in one of the popular 1–800-CALL-ATT commercials starring David Arquette. Perhaps Peter Hutchings summed it up best when he wrote that *The Matrix* ''replace[s] what in Woo is possible if unlikely with what is completely impossible.''

The romanticized, even glorified depiction of violence in *The Matrix* came under attack after a pair of teenage boys, dressed in black trenchcoats not unlike the one worn by Neo, went on a shooting spree at their high school in Littleton, Colorado, a mere sixteen days after the film opened. Twelve students and one teacher were left dead; dozens more were seriously injured. Distraught parents and outraged politicians cited *The Matrix*'s numerous fight scenes—scenes in which the heroes possess a seemingly inexhausible supply of guns and ammo, move with acrobatic grace, and suffer little if any pain or negative consequences—as stimulants to the real-life massacre. (It is worth noting that the Wachowski brothers are former comic book writers, a pop literary genre in which scenes such as these are ubiquitous.) Although debate over the possible effects of cinematic violence on impressionable adolescents has raged for decades, the Littleton shootings brought the issue to the fore, and Hollywood had no choice but to respond with vague public statements and the temporary shelving of some controversial projects (the title of Kevin Williamson's *Killing Ms. Tingle*, about a nasty high school teacher who gets imprisoned by a few of her students, was changed just before its release to the far less indelicate, far less interesting, *Teaching Ms. Tingle*).

One of the most fascinating things about *The Matrix* is the manner in which the film attempts to negotiate, with only moderate success, between progressive messages of non-conformity and self-realization, and the generic imperatives imposed by Hollywood's conservative studio system. Roger Ebert put the point succintly when he wrote that ''It's cruel, really, to put tantalizing ideas on the table and then ask the audience to be satisfied with a shoot-out and a martial arts duel.'' Other critics praised the Wachowski brothers for beginning their film with an extended fight scene starring Trinity, only to note with disappointment her relegation to ''Neo's love interest'' status for the rest of the picture. *The Matrix*'s mixed messages reappear at the level of narrative. Considering that what remains of post-war planet Earth is a bleak, inhospitable ''desert of the real,'' and that the virtual world in which Neo grew up is not without its advantages, it is not entirely clear what the human resistance hopes to gain by its struggles.

In the final analysis, *The Matrix* stands as a textbook example of what has been called ''postmodern'' art, in which allusions to other texts (cinematic and otherwise) dominate, and nothing is referred to besides other representations. From the Bible to *The Wizard of Oz*, from *Sleeping Beauty* to *Alice in Wonderland*, from *The Wild Bunch* to *Hard Target*, *The Matrix* quotes from a multitude of sources, and in so doing adds an ironic twist to a film that is ostensibly concerned with exposing the limitations of simulated modes of experience.

—Steven Schneider

A MATTER OF LIFE AND DEATH

(Stairway to Heaven)

UK, 1946

Directors: Michael Powell and Emeric Pressburger

Production: The Archers; color and dye-monochrome processed in Technicolor; running time: 104 minutes; length: 9,372 feet. Released November 1946.

Producers: Michael Powell and Emeric Pressburger; **screenplay:** Michael Powell and Emeric Pressburger; **photography:** Jack Cardiff; **editor:** Reginald Mills; **sound recordist:** C. C. Stevens; **production designer:** Alfred Junge; **special effects:** Douglas Woolsey, Henry Harris, Technicolor Ltd.; **additional effects:** Percy Day; **music:** Allan Gray.

A Matter of Life and Death

Cast: David Niven (*Peter Carter*); Kim Hunter (*June*); Robert Coote (*Bob*); Kathleen Byron (*An Angel*); Richard Attenborough (*An English Pilot*); Bonar Colleano (*An American Pilot*); Joan Maude (*Chief Recorder*); Marius Goring (*Conductor 71*); Roger Livesey (*Doctor Reeves*); Robert Atkins (*The Vicar*); Bob Roberts (*Dr. Gaertler*); Edwin Max (*Dr. McEwen*); Betty Potter (*Mrs. Tucker*); Abraham Sofaer (*The Judge*); Raymond Massey (*Abraham Farlan*).

Publications

Script:

Powell, Michael, and Emeric Pressburger, *A Matter of Life and Death*, in *Avant-Scène du Cinéma* (Paris), 15 December 1980.

Books:

Durgnat, Raymond, *A Mirror for England: British Movies from Austerity to Affluence*, London, 1970.
Garrett, Gerard, *The Films of David Niven*, London, 1975.
Christie, Ian, editor, *Powell, Pressburger, and Others*, London, 1978.
Cosandey, Roland, editor, *Retrospective: Powell and Pressburger*, Locarno, 1982.
Gottler, Fritz, and others, *Living Cinema: Powell and Pressburger*, Munich, 1982.
Morley, Sheridan, *The Other Side of the Moon: A Biography of David Niven*, London, 1985.
Christie, Ian, *Arrows of Desire: The Films of Michael Powell and Emeric Pressburger*, London, 1985.
Martini, Emanuela, editor, *Powell and Pressburger*, Bergamo, 1986.
Powell, Michael, *A Life in Movies: An Autobiography*, London, 1986.
Salwolke, Scott, *The Films of Michael Powell and the Archers*, Lanham, 1997.

Articles:

Monthly Film Bulletin (London), November 1946.
Winnington, Richard, in *News Chronicle* (London), 2 November 1946.
Lejeune, C. A., in *Observer* (London), 3 November 1946.
Powell, Dilys, in *Sunday Times* (London), 3 November 1946.
Shaw, Alexander, in *Spectator* (London), 7 November 1946.

Kine Weekly (London), 7 November 1946.
Variety (New York), 13 November 1946.
Motion Picture Herald (New York), 16 November 1946.
New York Times, 26 December 1946.
Sight and Sound (London), Winter 1946–47.
Revue du Cinéma (Paris), Summer 1947.
Lightman, Herb A., "Two Worlds in Technicolor," in *American Cinematographer* (Los Angeles), July 1947.
Thomas, A., "David Niven," in *Films in Review* (New York), February 1962.
Taylor, John Russell, "Michael Powell: Myths and Supermen," in *Sight and Sound* (London), Autumn 1978.
Everson, William K., "Michael Powell," in *Films in Review* (New York), August-September 1980.
Thompson, David, "The Films of Michael Powell: A Romantic Sensibility," in *American Film* (Washington, D.C), November 1980.
Everson, William K., in *MOMA Program Notes* (New York), 7 December 1980.
McVay, Douglas, "Cinema of Enchantment: The Films of Michael Powell," in *Films and Filming* (London), December 1981.
Harper, Sue, and Vincent Porter, "*A Matter of Life and Death*: The View from Moscow," in *Historical Journal of Film, Radio and Television* (Abingdon), vol. 9, no. 2, June 1989.
Horton, Robert, "*A Matter of Life and Death*," in *Film Comment* (New York), vol. 26, no. 3, May-June 1990.
"Written, Produced and Directed by Michael Powell and Emeric Pressburger," in *Film Comment* (New York), vol. 31, no. 2, March-April, 1995.
Stein, E., in *Village Voice* (New York), vol. 40, 18 April 1995.
Tanner, Louise, "Accents and Umlauts," in *Films in Review* (New York), vol. 46, no. 5–6, July-August 1995.
Gough-Yates, Kevin, "Pressburger: England and Exile," in *Sight & Sound* (London), vol. 5, no. 12, December 1995.
Burres, S., and J. Stevenson, "*Stairway to Heaven (A Matter of Life and Death)*," in *Cinefantastique* (Forest Park), vol. 27, no. 8, 1996.

* * *

During the 1940s, Hollywood produced a number of films, mostly light comedy-dramas, which portrayed a slightly sugar-coated metaphysical world. Fantasies like *The Devil and Daniel Webster* (1941), *Here Comes Mr. Jordan* (1941), *The Ghost and Mrs. Muir* (1947), and *It's a Wonderful Life* offered stories about ordinary people who were able to change their earthly situations with the real or imagined aid of supernatural beings. Although these films each had plots that were possible only in a dream state existence, they also provided escapist, supernatural avenues for those who preferred them. Despite the popularity of this genre in Hollywood, though, the definitive example of the dream state fantasy did not come from America, but from England.

Michael Powell and Emeric Pressburger, who had solidified their co-writing, directing and producing partnership in 1943 under the composite name of "The Archers," previously produced four big-budget British films beginning with the Technicolor *The Life and Death of Colonel Blimp. A Matter of Life and Death* (released under the less metaphysical title *Stairway to Heaven* in the United States), was one of several films made by the Archers that coalesced the elements of lavish budgets, Technicolor, and fantasy, and, though an enchantingly light film on a superficial level, is one of the most metaphysically complex films ever made in the English language.

The film's narrative structure concerns a British flyer, Peter Carter (David Niven) who makes radio contact with June (Kim Hunter), an American operator stationed on the English coast just before the end of World War II. The hopelessness of Peter's situation touches June and their immediate rapport develops into an innocent kind of love. Peter bravely jumps out of his plane before it crashes into the Sea and June is certain that he has died. But, the next morning, Peter has not died. Although he at first believes he has gone to heaven, it soon becomes apparent that he has somehow lived and is near Leighwood, the village in which June is billeted. When he meets June on the road, they fall in love, marveling at their good fate.

To this point in the film, the audience and the characters are aware of the same information: Peter has somehow survived a parachuteless jump from an airplane into the English Channel. There is no obvious or plausible reason why he survived; Peter and June call it "a miracle" but don't care to explore the reason.

In a brief written prologue, the filmmakers had advised the audience that they would be seeing a story of two worlds—one that exists in reality and one that merely exists in the mind of a young flier. But the reality of Peter's survival and subsequent encounters with the metaphysical world is continually at odds with that statement.

The film develops two distinct dramatic proscenia after Peter's survival: Leighwood, an ordinary English village, and an unnamed otherworldly place, which Peter, as well as the audience, interprets as heaven. Taking a less predictable road, Powell and Pressburger decided to have Leighwood always appear in Technicolor, while the other world "up there" exists only in black-and-white.

In Leighwood, Peter and June develop their romance and Peter forms a strong friendship with Doctor Frank Reeves (Roger Livesey), a neurologist friend of June's. In the other realm, the very orderly rituals of logging and placing "new arrivals" such as Peter's dead friend, Bob Trubshaw (Robert Coote) take place according to strict schedules. This again goes against type as the supernatural world appears rigid and bureaucratic while earth seems a happier, more idealized place.

As revealed in the heavenly world, there has been an unheard of mistake—Peter was supposed to be dispatched, but his attendant, Conductor 71 (Marius Goring), got lost in the fog and Peter has inadvertently survived. To rectify this error, Conductor 71 must go to earth and bring Peter to his rightful place.

As Peter and June are picnicking, time in Leighwood stops and Peter is confronted by Conductor 71, a whimsical 17th century Frenchman. Peter is naturally sceptical, but when he starts to believe, he adamantly refuses to leave earth. He wants to stay because of June. Time starts again and Conductor 71 goes to report this new development.

The worlds begin to collide more and more frequently as the days pass. Peter, who begins to experience headaches with increasing frequency and intensity, moves into Frank's home so that Frank can observe him more closely. Though Peter relates to Frank and June all of Conductor 71's visits, his extramental reality exists only for Peter.

Frank is convinced that the "visits" are merely hallucinatory symptoms of a brain tumor. As Peter's time between headaches (the signals of the conductor's presence) decrease, he becomes desperate about his ability to hang on to life. He tells Frank that there will be a "trial" to determine the outcome of his case and that he must find someone to defend him. Convinced that Peter must have an immediate operation to relieve the pressure on his brain, Frank rushes on his motorcycle to the hospital but is killed on the road.

Even though Peter faces his operation with trepidation because Frank will not be there to perform it, he is certain that having Frank as his champion at the celestial trial will save him. While Peter is under the anaesthesia, Frank wins his case, not through the persuasive arguments that Peter thought would sway his jury, but because June (again in Peter's subconscious) has offered to exchange her life for his. As Peter comes to, he tells June that they have won.

There are several metaphorical layers in the film. Peter substitutes his fear of death from a brain tumor for fear that he will not prove the merits of his case to live in heaven. To him the ''matter of life and death'' is not medical, but metaphysical. He must prove that his survival is justified.

This is lived out in the construction of his (or the) fantasy. He secretly believes that the ''miracle'' of his survival is a mistake, so he constructs an elaborate rationale for the error. He loves an American, so his prosecutor, Abraham Farlan (Raymond Massey) is an early American patriot who hates the English. In a sense he must prove to himself that he is worthy of her love. And finally, when the man he trusts most in the world, the man who is working the hardest to save him medically, dies, he looks to him in death as his most potent defense.

Another important metaphor exists outside of Peter's subconscious self. When June visits Frank in his camera oscura over the village, they look down on Leighwood as if from heaven. Frank's vantage point makes him all seeing and all knowing. Like the scenes in which Conductor 71 appears to Peter, everything in Leighwood seems to stand still as the godlike Frank looks on.

Though most of the supernatural elements can be dismissed within the context of Peter's own dreams or fantasies, two points are never fully explained: how did Peter survive the jump from his plane and how did a book, borrowed by Conductor 71 from Frank's study, come to be in Peter's suitcase? Though logical reasons could be found for both, Powell and Pressburger do not offer them, relying instead on the audience's desire to interpret them either as aspects of escapist fantasy or additional manifestations of a medically induced trauma.

Though two later productions of ''The Archers,'' *Black Narcissus* (1946) and *The Red Shoes* (1948), have attained greater recognition among cinema historians, *A Matter of Life and Death*, remains for some their collaborative masterpiece.

—Patricia King Hanson

THE MAXIM TRILOGY

USSR, 1935–39

Directors: Grigori Kozintsev and Leonid Trauberg

PART 1: YUNOST MAXIMA (The Youth of Maxim)

PART 2: VOZVRASHCHENIYE MAXIMA (The Return of Maxim)

PART 3: VYBORGSKAYA STORONA (The Vyborg Side)

Production: Lenfilm (Leningrad); black and white, 35mm; Part 1: running time: 98 minutes, some versions 86 minutes; length: 2,678 meters; Released 27 January 1935. Part 2: running time: 112 minutes; length: 3,082 meters; released 23 May 1937. Part 3: running time: 120 minutes; length: 3,276 meters; released 2 February 1939.

Scenario and screenplay: Grigori Kozintsev and Leonid Trauberg (with Lev Slavin for Part 1); **assistant directors:** N. Kosheverova, Kh. Lokshina, and M. Nesterov; **photography:** Andrei Moskvin; **sound:** I Volk; **art directors:** Evgeny Enei (Parts 1 and 2), V. Vlasov (Part 3); **music:** Dmitri Shostakovich.

Cast: Boris Chirkov (*Maxim*); Valentina Kibardina (*Natasha*); A. Kulakov (*Andrei*); Mikhail Tarkhanov (*Polivanov*); M. Shchelkovsky (*Foreman*); S. Leontyev (*Engineer*); P. Volkov (*Worker*); Stepan Kayukov (*Dyoma*); Alexandr Zrazhevsky (*Yerofeyev*); A. Kuznetsov (*Turaev*); Mikhail Zharov (*Dymba, the Anarchist*); Vasily Vanin (*Nikolai*); A. Chistyakov (*Mishchenko*); Yuri Tolubeyev (*Bugai*); A. Bondi (*Menshevik*); Vasily Merkuriev (*Student*); N. Kriuchkov (*Soldier*); Maxim Strauch (*Lenin*); Mikhail Gelovani (*Stalin*); Natalia Uzhvi (*Yevdokia*); L. Lyubashevski (*Sverdlov*); B. Zhukovski (*Attorney*); D. Dudnikov (*Ropshin*); M. Nazarov (*Lapshin*).

Awards: Order of Lenin to Lenfilm studios for producing *Yunost Maxima*, 1935. Stalin Prize awarded to the entire trilogy, 1941.

Publications

Books:

Leyda, Jay, *Kino: A History of the Russian and Soviet Film*, London, 1960.

Verdone, Mario, and Barthélemy Amengual, *La Feks*, Paris, 1970.

Klinowski, Jacek, and Adam Garbicz, *Cinema, The Magic Vehicle: A Guide to Its Achievement: Journey One: The Cinema Through 1949*, Metuchen, New Jersey, 1975.

Rapisardi, Giusi, editor, *La Feks: Kozintsev e Trauberg*, Rome, 1975.

Learning, Barbara, *Grigori Kozintsev*, New York, 1980.

Houten, Theodore van, *Leonid Trauberg and His Films: Always the Unexpected*, 's-Hertogenbosch, 1989.

Houten, Theodore van, *'Eisenstein Was Great Eater': In Memory of Leonid Trauberg*, 's-Hertogenbosch, 1991.

Articles:

Pudovkin, V. I., in *New Theatre*, February 1935.

New York Times, 12 May 1939.

Boehnel, William, in *New York World Telegram*, 13 May 1939.

Variety (New York), 17 May 1939.

Kozintsev, Grigori, ''Over the Parisiana,'' in *Sight and Sound* (London), Winter 1962–63.

Museum of Modern Art Department of Film Program Notes (New York), 25 September-11 November 1969.

''Grigori Kozintsev,'' in *International Film Guide 1972*, London, 1971.

''A Child of the Revolution,'' in *Cinema in Revolution*, edited by Luda and Jean Schnitzer, New York, 1973.

Volochova, Sonia, ''Films from the Archive,'' in *Museum of Modern Art Department of Film Program Notes* (New York), 26–27 February 1987.

Henderson, Brian, ''Leonid Trauberg and His Films,'' in *Film Quarterly* (Berkeley), vol. 46, no. 1, Fall 1992.

Kepley, V., Jr., ''Pudovkin, Socialist Realism, and the Classic Hollywood Style,'' in *Journal of Film and Video* (Atlanta), vol. 47, no. 4, 1995/1996.

''Etpy bol'shogo puti,'' in *Iskusstvo Kino* (Moscow) no. 5, 1996.

* * *

The first episode of *The Maxim Trilogy* was released a few months after *Chapaev* and provided an alternative, equally successful, answer to that perennial but seldom soluble obsession of the Soviet arts establishment: the search for an ideal Communist hero. Whereas the Vasiliev brothers had patiently re-created Chapaev, a real-life champion, the directorial team of Grigori Kozintsev and Leonid Trauberg came up with an entirely synthetic hero, their own invention, Maxim. First envisaged as a conventional proto-Bolshevik—in an early treatment described as ''a lean lad, of intelligent appearance, with a sharp nose and a shock of straight hair, withdrawn a bookworm self-taught''—he grew in the hands of the young but highly experienced and original filmmakers into a very different, more interesting and much more believable individual, with a touch of Til Eulenspiegel perhaps, or, as Kozintsev himself observed, with his roots in the favourite characters of Russian folklore, of fairground farces, Petrushka and Ivan Durak (Ivan the Fool), the holy innocent and the dumb youngest brother who always gets the Princess in the end.

This, of course, was only Maxim's ancestry: his personality grew, as might be expected, from the workings of two creative and complementary minds. But Maxim was no test-tube baby: together with the scripts as a whole he was developed against a background of thorough research into the history and actual documents of the period and locale—pre-revolutionary St. Petersburg. Once cast in the role, Boris Chirkov joined the process and was made, for instance, to try out any number of pre-1914 songs before one was found to fit the character: it was to become a leit-motif for the whole trilogy—but the composer, Shostakovich, and the directors were well aware of the oft-neglected truth that ''music from nowhere,'' however inspired, whatever its contribution to mood, is the enemy of reality. In the first film, *The Youth of Maxim*, therefore, except for the opening prologue, there is little symphonic ''background,'' only the actual sounds of song, accordion and guitar that belonged to the environment and the era.

Sense of period is also enhanced by Andrei Moskvin's photography and Evgeny Enei's art direction; both men were regular members of K and T's team. A memorable example is the scene in which police break up a demo in front of a huge bill-board announcing ''ARA PILLS—THE BEST IN THE WORLD,'' giving us in one bold brushstroke, as it were, an uncluttered background to the action, a sharp stab of visual irony and, in the simplistic advertising message, so remote in time and space from Madison Avenue, a glimpse of a complacent and unsuspecting ''bourgeois'' society. By such juxtapositions, by a succession of apparently disparate, even ''unimportant'' images, by a series of incidents rather than a relentless plot, the whole trilogy is allowed to grow. There is, however, a stylistic unity, and the strong central character helps to hold the kaleidoscope together.

On the other hand, Maxim is not continuously shoved into the centre of things. Dovzhenko reproached K and T for this: ''Maxim is frequently out of focus!'' he complained, comparing the film, in a sense, unfavourably with *Chapaev*: that film's ''secret of success'' was said to be that ''the Commander is always to be found at the centre of things.'' But within a much freer framework, and throughout the whole trilogy, Maxim is never too far away. The *real* ''secret of success'' shared by both teams of directors (but absent from most attempts to idealize revolutionary heros) was a warm and liberating sense of humour.

Most of the belly laughs are in the first film: open and innocent, the youthful Maxim, chasing a clucking chicken or a pretty girl, singing his ''Blue Globe'' song, provides plenty of fun himself, and there are many humorous confrontations as the future revolutionary learns who his enemies are—masters, bosses, police, informers.

In Part II, *The Return of Maxim*, although he still appears to be the same naive youth, his naiveté has become a sort of disguise: for Maxim is now a revolutionary, working in the ''underground.'' In the course of this dangerous activity he has to learn who are his ''new enemies—Mensheviks and dissidents,'' says a Soviet film historian, who adds: ''Maxim shows himself unable to reconcile himself with any kind of ideological vacillation.'' But the heavy political message is made much lighter (in both senses) by a masterly evocation of the glorious summer of 1914, the last before ''the lights went out all over Europe,'' particularly poignant perhaps in Saint Petersberg.

In Part III, *The Vyborg Side* (the slummier side of St. Petersberg), although never allowed to forget, or regret, his working-class origins, and not entirely denied his sense of humour, Maxim is already a commissar somewhat sober, dignified and strict. In the final significant sequence, which is played for laughs, he confronts some definitely ''vacillating'' bank employees, who plead ''We are peaceful Russian people.'' ''What's Russian about you?'' he replies—''Messrs Schumacher, Andersen, etc. Your surnames are German: you have consorted with English spies and have thought about setting up Japanese accounting systems.'' An odd piece of dialogue, one might think, when one of the directors was called Trauberg: but, with the Nazi menace already building up, it is an early example of the shift from the ''class struggle'' towards the more chauvinistic ''patriotic'' propaganda of the following decade.

And even the immensely popular ''synthetic'' hero was not allowed to die. By popular demand the somewhat reluctant Boris Chirkov was made to re-enact Maxim (by now a member of the Central Committee) in Ermler's two-part *Great Citizen*, just before World War II and, in 1941, still singing his ''Blue Globe'' song (with appropriate new lyrics), he opened the first ''Fighting Film Album,'' under Gerasimov's direction, in *Meeting with Maxim*.

Indeed, the outstanding excellence of the *Maxim Trilogy* (and the first part, at least, is a true classic) has been almost overshadowed by the authors' successful creation of their ''Communist hero''—one of the few fictitious characters who, like Sherlock Holmes, is obstinately believed, against all the evidence, to have actually existed.

—Robert Dunbar

MEAN STREETS

USA, 1973

Director: Martin Scorsese

Production: Taplin-Perry-Scorsese; Technicolor, 35mm; running time: 110 minutes. Released 1973. Filmed in New York City.

Producer: Jonathan T. Taplin; **screenplay:** Martin Scorsese and Mardik Martin; **photography:** Norman Gerard; **editor:** Sid Levin.

Mean Streets

Cast: Harvey Keitel (*Charlie*); Robert De Niro (*Johnny Boy*); David Proval; Amy Robinson; Richard Romanus; Cesare Danova.

Publications

Books:

Jacobs, Diane, *Hollywood Renaissance*, New York, 1977.

Kolker, Robert Phillip, *A Cinema of Loneliness: Penn, Kubrick, Coppola, Scorsese, Altman*, Oxford, 1980; revised edition, 1988.

Weiss, Ulli, *Das neue Hollywood: Francis Ford Coppola, Steven Spielberg, Martin Scorsese*, Munich, 1985.

Bliss, Michael, *Martin Scorsese and Michael Cimino*, Metuchen, New Jersey, 1986.

Arnold, Frank, and others, *Martin Scorsese*, Munich, 1986.

Cietat, Michel, *Martin Scorsese*, Paris, 1986.

Domecq, Jean-Philippe, *Martin Scorsese: Un Rêve italo-américain*, Renens, Switzerland, 1986.

Wood, Robin, *Hollywood from Vietnam to Reagan*, New York, 1986.

Cameron-Wilson, James, *The Cinema of Robert De Niro*, London, 1986.

McKay, Keith, *Robert De Niro: The Hero Behind the Masks*, New York, 1986.

Weiss, Marian, *Martin Scorsese: A Guide to References and Resources*, Boston, 1987.

Lourdeaux, Lee, *Italian and Irish Filmmakers in America: Ford, Capra, Coppola, and Scorsese*, Philadelphia, 1990.

Connelly, Marie Katheryn, *Martin Scorsese: An Analysis of His Feature Films, With a Filmography of His Entire Directorial Career*, Jefferson, 1993.

Bliss, Michael, *The Word Made Flesh: Catholicism and Conflict in the Films of Martin Scorsese*, Lanham, 1995, 1998.

Friedman, Lawrence S., *The Cinema of Martin Scorsese*, New York, 1997.

Kelly, Mary P., *Martin Scorsese: A Journey*, New York, 1997.

Dougan, Andy, *Martin Scorsese - Close Up: The Making of His Movies*, New York, 1998.

Brunette, Peter, editor, *Martin Scorsese: Interviews*, Jackson, 1999.

Grist, Leighton, *The Films of Martin Scorsese, 1963–1977: Authorship and Context*, New York, 2000.

Articles:

Films in Review (New York), November 1973.
Ney, J., in *Inter/View* (New York), November 1973.
Delson, J., in *Take One* (Montreal), November 1973.
Denby, David, ''*Mean Streets*: The Sweetness of Hell,'' in *Sight and Sound* (London), Winter 1973–74.
Rubenstein, L., in *Cineaste* (New York), no. 2, 1974.
Bobrow, A. C., ''The Filming of *Mean Streets*,'' in *Filmmakers Newsletter* (Ward Hill, Massachusetts), January 1974.
Stein, J., in *Film Heritage* (Dayton, Ohio), Spring 1974.
Gow, Gordon, in *Films and Filming* (London), May 1974.
Macklin, F. A., ''It's a Personal Thing for Me,'' in *Film Heritage* (Dayton, Ohio), Spring 1975.
''Scorsese Seminar'' in *Dialogue on Film* (Beverly Hills), April 1975.
Henry, M., ''La Passion de Saint Martin Scorsese,'' in *Positif* (Paris), June 1975.
Beylie, Claude, in *Ecran* (Paris), July-August 1975.
Lindberg, I., in *Kosmorama* (Copenhagen), no. 131, 1976.
Turroni, G., in *Filmcritica* (Rome), January-February 1976.
Hosman, H., in *Skoop* (Amsterdam), February-March 1976.
Rinaldi, G., in *Cineforum* (Bergamo), March 1976.
Renaud, T., in *Cinéma* (Paris), July 1976.
Eder, K., ''Rebel Heroes der 70er Jahre: Kontaktlos und Gewalttätig: Zu zwei Filmen von Martin Scorsese,'' in *Medium* (Frankfurt), July 1976.
Cros, J. L., in *Revue du Cinéma* (Paris), October 1976.
Jansen, P. W., ''Eastside Story: *Hexenkessel* von Martin Scorsese,'' in *Film und Ton* (Munich), December 1976.
Hermann, R., in *Cinemonkey* (Portland, Oregon), no. 4, 1979.
Walsh, Michael, ''Slipping into Darkness: Figures of Waking in Cinema,'' in *Wide Angle* (Athens, Ohio), vol. 5, no. 4, 1983.
Bruce, Bryan, ''Martin Scorsese: Five Films,'' in *Movie* (London), Winter 1986.
Lane, J., ''Martin Scorsese and the Documentary Impulse,'' in *Framework* (London), no. 1, 1991.
Sitney, P. A., ''Cinematic Election and Theological Vanity,'' in *Raritan* (New Brunswick, New Jersey), no. 2, 1991.
Librach, R. S., ''The Last Temptation in *Mean Streets* and *Raging Bull*,'' in *Literature/Film Quarterly* (Salisbury, Maryland), no. 1, 1992.
Hosney, J., and others, ''The Passion of St. Charles: Martin Scorsese's *Mean Streets*,'' in *South Atlantic Quarterly* (Durham, North Carolina), no. 2, 1992.
Thompson, David, ''Harvey Keitel: Staying Power: Interview with Harvey Keitel,'' in *Sight & Sound* (London), vol. 3, no. 1, January 1993.
Penman, Ian, ''Juke-Box and Johnny Boy: Music in Martin Scorsese's Film *Mean Streets*,'' in *Sight & Sound* (London), vol. 3, no. 4, April 1993.
McGreal, Jill, ''*Mean Streets*,'' in *Sight & Sound* (London), vol. 3, no. 4, April 1993.
Clements, Marcelle, ''Martin Scorsese's Mortal Sins,'' in *Esquire*, vol. 120, no. 5, November 1993.
Chanko, Kenneth M., ''Martin Scorsese,'' in *Films in Review* (New York), vol. 44, no. 11–12, November-December 1993.
Maxfield, James F., '''The Worst Part': Martin Scorsese's *Mean Streets*,'' in *Literature/Film Quarterly* (Salisbury), vol. 23, no. 4, October 1995.
Morrison, S., ''*La haine, Fallen Angels* and Some Thoughts on Scorsese's Children,'' in *CineAction* (Toronto), vol. 39, 1995.
Scorsese, Martin, ''De Niro and moi,'' in *Cahiers du Cinéma* (Paris), no. 500, March 1996.
Blake, Richard A., ''Redeemed in Blood: The Sacramental Universe of Martin Scorsese,'' in *Journal of Popular Film and Television* (Washington, D.C.), vol. 24, no. 1, Spring 1996.
Hampton, Howard, ''Scorpio Descending: In Search of Rock Cinema,'' in *Film Comment* (New York), vol. 33, no. 2, March-April 1997.
Taubin, A., ''The Old 'Hood,'' in *Village Voice* (New York), vol. 43, 17 March 1998.
Conn, Andrew Lewis, ''The Adolescents of Martin Scorsese: The Drama of the Gifted Child,'' in *Film Comment* (New York), vol. 34, no. 3, May-June 1998.

*   *   *

Mean Streets is the film that established director Martin Scorsese's reputation, and it is often considered his most personal and emblematic work. In comparison with his later films, however, *Mean Streets* seems more like a rough sketch (both thematically and stylistically) than a fully-realized achievement, despite the film's distinction when viewed as an isolated work.

At the centre of *Mean Streets* is Charlie (Harvey Keitel). Of all of Scorsese's male protagonists he is arguably the least mentally unstable and the least prone to movement and action. Like Travis Bickle in *Taxi Driver*, Charlie's responses to his surroundings are so internalized that the film must utilize devices like voice-over monologues and subjective slow-motion shots in order to clarify those responses. But unlike Travis (or even unlike Ellen Burnstyn's Alice), there is no point in the film at which Charlie is jolted out of his inactive state. While the protagonists of Scorsese's later films almost continually create the action and upheaval that set in motion and propel forward the narrative, Charlie remains in an almost constant state of indecision and stasis, as does the movement of the narrative in *Mean Streets*.

It is the presence of Johnny Boy (Robert De Niro) that suggests Scorsese's later protagonists with their propensity towards emotional and physical violence that they are unable to fully comprehend. In Scorsese's collaborations with De Niro after *Mean Streets* the two men were able to fuse the masochistic Charlie with the violent, inarticulate Johnny Boy. But in *Mean Streets* Johnny Boy's almost total inarticulateness results in his being slightly displaced from the center of the narrative by his more ''normal'' friend Charlie, even though Johnny Boy's accumulated actions lead to the shoot-out on Charlie, Theresa and himself.

The shoot-out itself leaves the unanswered question whether Charlie will ever become active rather than (essentially) passive. In all of Scorsese's subsequent narrative films, the extremely violent and/or emotional upheavals that serve as a climax have a kind of cleansing effect, unleashing all of the psychological problems, the private demons, of the main characters. Nevertheless, the epilogues in each of these post-*Mean Streets* films tend to re-state the essential problems of the characters, giving an impression of apparent unity and order precariously on the brink of collapsing once again and thus denying any ''true'' catharsis. *Mean Streets* simply ends with the shoot-out, an act of violence perpetrated not *by* the central characters but *on* them, with Scorsese playing their would-be assassin, ending the film on a note of total disorder. Charlie, with a confused and uncertain future before him, is essentially the ''hero'' of an extraordinary work-in-progress.

—Joseph McElhaney

MEET ME IN ST. LOUIS

USA, 1944

Director: Vincente Minnelli

Production: Metro-Goldwyn-Mayer Picture Corp.; color, 35mm; running time: 113 minutes. Released 1944. Filmed in MGM studios. Cost: $1,700,000.

Producer: Arthur Freed; **screenplay:** Irving Brecher and Fred F. Finklehoffe, from the novel by Sally Benson; **photography:** George J. Folsey; **editor:** Albert Akst; **art directors:** Cedric Gibbons, Lemuel Ayers, and Jack Martin Smith; **music director:** George Stoll; **music numbers:** Ralph Blane and Hugh Martin; **costume designer:** Irene Sharaff; **choreography:** Charles Walters.

Cast: Judy Garland (*Esther Smith*); Margaret O'Brien (*Tootie Smith*); Lucille Bremer (*Rose Smith*); Mary Astor (*Mrs. Anna Smith*); Leon Ames (*Mr. Alonzo Smith*); Tom Drake (*John Truett*); Harry Davenport (*Grandpa Potter*); Marjorie Main (*Katie*); Henry H. Daniels, Jr. (*Lon Smith, Jr.*); Joan Carroll (*Agnes Smith*); Robert Sully (*Warren Sheffield*); Chill Wills (*Mr. Neely*); Hugh Marlowe (*Colonel Darly*).

Award: Oscar to Margaret O'Brien for Outstanding Child Actress, 1944.

Publications

Books:

Burton, Jack, *The Blue Book of Hollywood Musicals*, Watkins Glen, New York, 1953.
Truchaud, François, *Vincente Minnelli*, Paris, 1966.
Springer, John, *All Talking, All Singing, All Dancing*, New York, 1966.
Morella, Joe, and Edward Epstein, *Judy: The Films and Career of Judy Garland*, New York, 1969.
Astor, Mary, *A Life on Film*, New York, 1971.
Thomas, Lawrence B., *The MGM Years*, New Rochelle, New York, 1972.
Di Orio, Al, Jr., *Little Girl Lost: The Life and Hard Times of Judy Garland*, New Rochelle, New York, 1973.
Minnelli, Vincente, with Hector Arce, *I Remember It Well*, New York, 1974; 1990.
Stern, Lee Edward, *The Movie Musical*, New York, 1974.
Baxter, Brian, *The Films of Judy Garland*, London, 1974.
Juneau, James, *Judy Garland*, New York, 1974.
Edwards, Anne, *Judy Garland: A Biography*, New York, 1975.
Kepler, M., *Judy Garland*, Paris, 1981.
Guerif, Francois, *Vincente Minnelli*, Paris, 1984.
Brion, Patrick, and others, *Vincente Minnelli*, Paris, 1985.
Dyer, Richard, *Heavenly Bodies: Film Stars and Society*, London, 1987.
Harvey, Stephen, *Directed by Vincente Minnelli*, New York, 1989.
Lang, Robert, *American Film Melodrama: Griffith, Vidor, Minnelli*, Princeton, 1989.
Naremore, James, *The Films of Vincente Minnelli*, Cambridge, 1993.

Articles:

Variety (New York), 1 November 1944.
New York Times, 29 November 1944.
Times (London), 26 February 1945.
St. Johns, A. R., in *Photoplay* (New York), April 1945.
''Minnelli's Talents,'' in *Time* (New York), 14 May 1945.
Harcourt-Smith, Simon, ''Vincente Minnelli,'' in *Sight and Sound* (London), January-March 1952.
Rosterman, Robert, ''Judy Garland,'' in *Films in Review* (New York), April 1952.
Chaumeton, Etienne, ''L'Oeuvre de Vincente Minnelli,'' in *Positif* (Paris), November-December 1954.
Johnson, Albert, ''The Films of Vincente Minnelli,'' in *Film Quarterly* (Berkeley), Winter 1958 and Spring 1959.
''The Rise and Fall of the Musical,'' in *Films and Filming* (London), January 1962.
''Minnelli Issue'' of *Movie* (London), June 1963.
Galling, Dennis Lee, ''Vincente Minnelli,'' in *Films in Review* (New York), March 1964.
Galling, Dennis Lee, ''Arthur Freed,'' in *Films in Review* (New York), November 1964.
Turroni, G., ''Minnelli e l'architettura del tempo (a proposito di *Meet Me in St. Louis*),'' in *Filmcritica* (Rome), April 1976.
Britton, Andrew, ''*Meet Me in St. Louis*: Smith; or, The Ambiguities,'' in *Australian Journal of Screen Theory* (Kensington, New South Wales), no. 3, 1977.
Wood, Robin, ''The American Family Comedy: From *Meet Me in St. Louis* to *Texas Chain Saw Massacre*,'' in *Wide Angle* (Athens, Ohio), no. 2, 1979.
De Fornari, O., ''Nuove retrospettive: Due film di Judy Garland,'' in *Filmcritica* (Rome), February 1979.
Karr, Kathleen, in *Magill's Survey of Cinema 3*, Englewood Cliffs, New Jersey, 1980.
Telotte, J.P., ''Self and Society: Vincente Minnelli and Musical Formula,'' in *Journal of Popular Film and Television* (Washington, D.C.), vol. 9, no. 4, 1982.
Ward, L.E., ''The Great American Films: *Meet Me in St. Louis*,'' in *Classic Images* (Muscatine), vol. 120, June 1985.
Hoberman, J., ''Scanners: Oh, You Kid,'' in *Village Voice* (New York), vol. 30, 10 December 1985.
Aachen, G., in *Reid's Film Index* (Wyong), no. 1, 1987.
Hunsecker, J.J., ''Off Her Trolly,'' in *Sight & Sound* (London), vol. 59, no. 1, 1989/1990.
Masson, Alain, ''La douceur du foyer et le charme des soirs,'' in *Positif* (Paris), no. 374, April 1992.
Thomson, D., ''Happiness: Movies in Which Nothing Happens,'' in *Film Comment* (New York), September-October 1992.
Britton, A., ''*Meet Me in St. Louis*: Smith, or the Ambiguities,'' in *CineAction* (Toronto), no. 35, 1994.
Rimolidi, Oscar A., ''Produced by Arthur Freed,'' in *Films in Review* (New York), vol. 45, no. 7–8, July-August 1994.

Meet Me in St. Louis

Fitzpatrick, Eileen, "Tapes Offer Rare Musical Soundtracks," in *Billboard*, vol. 106, no. 34, 20 August 1994.

Care, R., "*Meet Me in St. Louis*," in *Film Score Monthly* (Los Angeles), no. 65/66/67, January/February/March 1996.

Short review, in *El Amante Cinema*, no. 53, July 1996.

Higgins, Scott, "Color at the Center: Minnelli's Technicolor Style in *Meet Me in St. Louis*," in *Style*, vol. 32, no. 3, Fall 1998.

* * *

As with many of the finest Hollywood films, the richness of *Meet Me in St. Louis* derives from the interaction of a number of sources and determinants, some of them complex in themselves, producing a filmic text to which no single, "coherent" reading can do justice. A few of these determinants include:

The dominant ideological project. Bordwell and Thompson give a clear account of this aspect in *Film Art* (unfortunately, they give the impression that there is nothing more to the film). They stress the film's release date (1944), a time when "families were often forced apart. In context *Meet Me in St. Louis* appeared as a nostalgic look back at America in 1903. It suggested an ideal of family unity for the future." The superficial level of familial celebration is the most easily perceived, and Bordwell and Thompson are doubtless correct in assuming that it was responsible for the film's contemporary popularity. Today, it is obvious that it is disrupted by numerous other factors.

Ideological contradiction. Through American art and culture the concepts "home" and "family," are central to ideological tension and conflict, perceived at once as the repositories of security and happiness where "good" values are preserved and as prisons in which energy is repressed, human beings trapped and frustrated. Beneath its level of affirmation, this tension is dramatized in *Meet Me in St. Louis* more thoroughly than in almost any other American film. To give one example only: the "happy ending" can be achieved only through the symbolic castration of the father (the "snow-people" scene), his capitulation expressing itself in the line, "We'll stay here till we rot."

Genre. The film basically crosses two genres, the musical (often regarded in terms of "celebration of vitality") and the small town domestic comedy (traditionally concerned with the *containment* of energy). Instead of concealing the potential tension here, the film consistently exploits it, making it its central principle. Even more remarkable is the eruption of a third (totally incompatible) genre: the famous Halloween sequence is built unambiguously on the iconography of the horror film and can now be seen to be the antecedent of the "demon child" movies of the 1970s (*The Exorcist*, *The Omen*, *Halloween*).

Stars. The film draws particularly on the personalities/star images of two performers: Judy Garland, with her combination of energy, neuroticism and precariously-suppressed hysteria, and Margaret O'Brien, who became famous overnight in her first film, *Journey for Margaret*, especially for her scene of prolonged hysterical breakdown.

Director. There was a time when Minnelli's musicals were critically downgraded in favour of those by Donen and Kelly: the latter certainly correspond more unproblematically to the simple "celebration of vitality" formula. Minnelli's musicals—full, like melodramas, of tension, excess, dislocation—produce continuous uneasiness. Virtually every number in *Meet Me in St. Louis* (including the famous "Trolley Song") ends not in the ultimate release of exuberance but in frustration. "Release" in Minnelli, in fact, usually takes the form of the explosion of hysteria (see, for example, the frenetic car-rides of *The Bad and the Beautiful* and *Two Weeks in Another Town*, the fairground climax of *Some Came Running*, the "goldfish" scene of *Courtship of Eddie's Father*, the "Mack the Black" fantasy of *The Pirate*). Both the major sequences of *Meet Me in St. Louis* centred on Margaret O'Brien (Halloween and the smashing of the snow people) have this function; both are also concerned with the symbolic destruction of parent-figures. Even the apparent affirmation of the end of the film is severely undercut—by its anti-climactic nature, by Tootie's dream of apocalyptic destruction, by John's casual remark that he "liked it better when it was just a swamp."

Meet Me in St. Louis, then, must be read not as a simple celebration of family life but as the point of intersection of some of the major ideological tensions in American culture. For a detailed account, the reader is referred to Andrew Britton's "Smith, or the Ambiguities" in *The Australian Journal of Screen Theory*, one of the most comprehensive and intelligent readings of a Hollywood film so far attempted.

—Robin Wood

MEG KER A NEP

(Red Psalm)

Hungary, 1971

Director: Miklos Jancso

Production: Mafilm Studio; Eastmancolor, 35mm; running time: 88 minutes; length: 7920 feet. Released 1971, Hungary. Filmed 1971.

Screenplay: Gyula Hernádi; **photography:** János Kende; **editor:** Zoltán Farkas; **art director:** Tamás Banovich; **musical arrangements:** Ferenc Sebo; **choreography:** Ferenc Pesovár.

Cast: Lajos Balázsovits (*Officer Cadet*); András Bálint (*Count*); Gyöngyi Bürös (*Young peasant woman*); Andrea Drahota (*Militant girl*); József Madoras; Tibor Molnár; Tibor Orbán; Bertalan Solti.

Award: Cannes Film Festival, Best Director, 1972.

Publications

Books:

Liehm, Mira and Antonin, *The Most Important Art: East European Film after 1945*, Berkeley, 1977.

Petrie, Graham, *History Must Answer to Man: The Contemporary Hungarian Cinema*, London, 1978.

Marlia, Giulio, *Lo schermo liberato: il cinema di Miklós Jancsó*, Firenze, 1982.

Articles:

Variety (New York), 24 May 1972.

Beylie, Claude, "Les Maelstroms de la liberté," in *Ecran* (Paris), July-August 1972.

Hollywood Reporter, 3 October 1972.

Varga, V., in *Filmkultura* (Budapest), November-December 1972.

Passek, J. L., "*Psaume rouge*: La Tactique et le rite," in *Cinéma* (Paris), December 1972.

Beylie, Claude, "L'Idéologie, la technique, et le rite," in *Ecran* (Paris), December 1972.

Langlois, G., "Miklos Jancso: 'Le Plan séquence: Le Rythme le plus près de la realité,'" in *Cinéma* (Paris), December 1972.

Desmet, P., and J. C. Guiguet, in *Image et Son* (Paris), January 1973.

Magny, Joel, in *Téléciné* (Paris), January 1973.

Cornaud, A., "Entretien avec Miklos Jancso," in *Image et Son* (Paris), January 1973.

Jeancolas, J. P., "Vers le corpus sacre de la révolution," in *Positif* (Paris), February 1973.

Cinématographe (Paris), February 1973.

Monthly Film Bulletin (London), April 1973.

Gow, Gordon, in *Films and Filming* (London), May 1973.

Andersson, W., in *Filmrutan* (Stockholm), no. 3, 1974.

Tomasino, R., "Circolarità della rivoluzione," in *Filmcritica* (Rome), August-September 1974.

Gay. B., in *Image et Son* (Paris), June-July 1975.

Film Form (Newcastle upon Tyne), Spring 1976.

Cinema Papers (Melbourne), June-July 1976.

Escobar, R., and V. Giacci, "Miklos Jancso: I riti della rivoluzione, la morte, la resurrezione, il futuro," in *Cineforum* (Bergamo), November 1976.

Baticle, Y.R., "Communication audio-visuelle et pedagogie: le message de l'affiche cinematographique," in *Revue Belge du Cinéma* (Brussels), vol. 14, no. 3, 1977.

Biro, Y., "Landscape During the Battle," in *Millennium Film Journal* (New York), no. 4/5, Summer/Fall 1979.

* * *

Of all of his films, *Meg ker a nep* perhaps best exemplifies the stylistic hallmarks with which Miklós Jancsó is most often associated: long takes (frequently 5 to 8 minutes in length), a constantly moving camera which weaves in and out of groups of moving figures, and an array of visual metaphors and exotic images rooted in Hungarian folklore and his own personal mythology.

On its most simple level, *Meg ker a nep* is set in Hungary in the 1890s and presents the emergence of agrarian socialist movements—but Jancsó isn't interested in a realistic depiction of isolated historical

Meg ker a nep

events. Through his unconventional cinematic style, Jancsó creates a "ritualistic portrayal of revolution" which takes on universal significance, and the success of the film derives from the manner in which its form *becomes* its content.

For Jancsó, "one can imagine a film other than in the form of a story. We must try to widen the limits of expression." With his reduction of the primacy of narrative, Jancsó also diminishes depth of characterization, the importance of individual action, and complex psychological explanations of behavior. In spite of these simplifications, Jancsó claims that his films are still "a means of expression with several dimensions." His undercutting of an audience's emotional identification with characters and situations creates, in his mind, "active" viewers and "makes [them] think"—and presumably take action at a later time.

If, in *Meg ker a nep*, Jancsó reduces traditional cinematic elements to a minimum, his style creates a heightened sense of the importance of movement, both in aesthetic and ideological terms. "It seems to me that life is a continual movement. In a procession, a demonstration, there's movement all the time, isn't there? It's physical and it's also philosophical: the contradiction is founded on movement, the movement of ideas, the movement of the masses. A man also is always surrounded, threatened by oppression: the camera movements I create suggest that too." In *Meg ker a nep*, the complex interweaving of the moving camera with the carefully choreographed groups of soldiers, horsemen, and villagers reflects the ideological conflicts central to the film. The long takes and the examples of nearly invisible editing allow the spectator to concentrate on non-verbal devices to understand the unfolding action. For example, foreground activity becomes background activity only to return minutes later to the foreground of the screen as a manifestation of the continual shifting nature of power. Geometric shapes (most notably vertical lines and circles) are also in constant conflict and in constant movement, and the shifting fortunes of ideological struggles are also indicated in the clash of various types of music in the film.

Music is especially important in *Meg ker a nep*; the narrative action is delineated as much by music and song as by the film's rather abstract, depersonalized dialogue. Beyond that, music universalizes the film's theme. Aside from Hungarian folk songs that tell of the events depicted in the film and the repetition of a key song in multiple contexts, Jancsó's music, which includes the Scottish ballad "Charlie Is My Darling" and the French "Marseillaise," suggests that all revolutions are part of one continuing revolution.

Miklós Jancsó, like Sergei Eisenstein and Sergei Paradzhanov, is a master of synesthesia, a director who fuses multiple art forms to create in film the perfect medium for Wagner's *Gesamtkunstwerk*. *Meg ker a nep*, which won the ''Best Director'' award at the 1972 Cannes Film Festival, is perhaps Jancsó's best example of ''fusion of the arts'' and has been justly praised as Jancsó's best film by critics John Russell Taylor and Roy Armes.

—Joseph A. Gomez

MEGHE DHAKA TARA

(Hidden Star)

India, 1959

Director: Ritwik Ghatak

Production: Chitrakalpa; colour, 35mm; running time: 126 minutes.

Screenplay: Ritwik Ghatak, from the book by Shaktipada Rajguru; **photography:** Dinen Gupta; **editor:** Ramesh Joshi; **music:** Joyotirindra Moitra; **sound:** Satyen Chattopadhyay; **art direction:** Rabi Chattopadhyay.

Cast: Supriya Chowdhury (*Nita*); Anil Chatterjee (*Shankar*); Bijon Bhattacharya (*Father*); Gita Ghatak (*Gita*); Guita De (*Mother*); Dwijen Bhowal (*Montu*); Niranjan Roy (*Sanat*); Gyanesh Mukherjee (*Bansi Dutt*); Satindra Bhattacharya (*the landlord*).

Publications

Books:

Hashmi, Safdar, *Ritwik Retrospective*, New Delhi, 1981.
Banerjee, Shampa, editor, *Ritwik Ghatak: An Attempt to Explore His Cinematic Perception*, New Delhi, 1982.
Rajakhyaksha, Ashish, *Ritwik Ghatak: A Return to the Epic*, Bombay, 1982.
Banerjee, Haimanti, *Ritwik Kumar Ghatak*, Poona, 1985.
Gangar, Amrit, and Ashish Rajadhyaksha, editors, *Ritwik Ghatak: Arguments/Stories*, Bombay, 1987.
Ghatak, Ritaban, and Satyajit Ray, editors, *Cinema and I*, Calcutta, 1987.
Joseph, Josephine, editor, *Ritwik Ghatak*, Madras, 1990.

Articles:

Shahani, K., ''Violence and Responsibility'' in *Filmfare* (Bombay), 1976.
Bhasker, I., ''Myth and Ritual in *Meghe dhaka tara*'' in *Journal of Arts and Ideas* (New Delhi), no. 3, 1982.
Kapur, G., ''Articulating the Self into History'' in *Framework* (London), 1987.
Singh, M., *Cinemaya* (New Delhi), 1989.
Amiel, V., and others, *Positif* (Paris), October 1990.
Magny, J., ''L'étoile brisée'' in *Cahiers du Cinéma* (Paris), October 1990.
Bassan, R., *Positif* (Paris), November 1990.
''Ritwik Ghatak and Some Directions for the Future,'' in *Sight & Sound* (London), vol. 1, no. 5, September 1991.
Stein, E., ''Cinema as a Weapon: Ritwik Ghatak's Unknown Masterworks,'' in *Village Voice* (New York), vol. 41, 1 October 1996.
''Ritwik Ghatak Retrospective,'' in *Cinemaya* (New Delhi), no. 35, January/February/March 1997.
Levich, Jacob, ''Subcontinental Divide: The Undiscovered Art of Ritwik Ghatak,'' in *Film Comment* (New York), vol. 33, no. 2, March-April 1997.
Kemp, Philip, ''Cloud-capped Star: *Meghe dhaka tara*,'' in *Sight & Sound* (London), vol. 7, no. 9, September 1997.

* * *

Meghe dhaka tara is a film about displacement and exile. It is about the displacement of peoples who have been uprooted in the wake of India's partition which followed her independence in 1947. It is also about the exile of the classical, creative and feminine principles which, despite their nurturing potentials, find themselves being ruthlessly edged out of the socio-cultural space.

Meghe dhaka tara is a seminal film in the history of Indian cinema for more reasons than one. First and foremost, it looks at the cultural and political formations which the topographic break in the life of the peoples of India seems to put into a major crisis. The partition of India remains one of the most traumatic divisions of peoples in recent history. In also resulted in unprecedented diaspora. In the film the crisis, however starkly lived, is viewed against the evocative simultaneity of mythic presence. Even the bare documentative inserts of buildings, offices, pavements and roads seem to invoke a poetic conscience. It is not, as has been stated by many Indian commentators, a film that ''returns to the epic.'' On the contrary, it is a work that definitively opens up a new cinema of the ''grand poetic conscience.'' The epical references are not opened up for historical enlightenment but to deepen the very grain of existence that has become increasingly vulnerable. The film, therefore, addresses the question of nationality mainly within the modes of memory and melodic excess and disavows a direct referentiality and, hence, a rhetoric of identity. In a way, it marks the beginning of Ghatak's remarkable contribution to the rich Indian melodramatic tradition. He pushes melody into the space of memory; movement-gesture into the space of myth. It is also a film that pushes the debate about nationality beyond the realm of ideological certainties. Unlike a conventional epic, it dissolves facial iconicities into sound which works through a dialectic or relay between melody and dissonance. The dissonance and distortion flow from the state of imbalance into which the image has found a fleeting sense of home almost like the uprooted refugee. Almost the entire film is shot with a 16mm lens. The film again and again *arrives at* haunting close-ups till they finally appear as the masks of light beyond the reality of socio-political space.

Meghe dhaka tara is woven around the life of a refugee family in a resettlement colony in Calcutta. Uprooted from the other Bengal during the partition, the family is pushed to the margins of middle class existence and is barely able to keep itself together. More specifically, the narrative unfolds through Nita—the eldest daughter and the sole breadwinner of the family. The basic narrative structure of the film is laid out in terms of eight movements in which Nita is

Meghe dhaka tara

seen to be returning home after a day's work outside. Through these literal and figurative movements, she is seen to become inexorably involved in the task of keeping the family afloat against severe economic uncertainties. With each new movement, the homeward journey becomes increasingly strained till, finally, she loses all sense of reality and retracts to the virtual space of myth. Getting herself cast within the paradox of the benign and narcissistic mould of the nurturing mother, she is ruthlessly exploited by her mother and her younger sister and brother. Eventually, when, one by one, all the younger members of the family leave the house for a better life outside, the bitter irony of movements towards home strikes with the ferocity of a terminal illness.

There are no more options left for Nita except that she be carried to the bills (the childhood romance having now given way to the desperation to somehow survive). As if in a ritual return to nature—the cultural gamut of life having slipped out of her hands almost fully. The reference, here, is to the goddess of Durga's immersion in the holy river after she has sojourned at her father's place for a fortnight. Nita's father and elder brother, Shankar, who have been closest to her, repeat the ritual in all its melodic/melodramatic excess and, consequently, associations of memory. This is the point in the film where, the physical spaces having completely recoiled from the terminally ill Nita, the cinema intercedes to receive her within the virtual space of the film frame, her lover having deserted her; her own young sister having usurped her place in the failed relationship; her younger brother having left the house to stay in the factory's dorm because of better food; her elder brother having left the house to protest against the injustice done to Nita by the entire family. Nita's descent into despair is thus complete. Even as she prepares to merge with an indifferent nature, cinema moves in compassionately to *save* her.

The motif of exile is also extended to the classical-romantic order to which Nita's benign and nostalgic father belongs. He seems to revel in the joyous and dramatic shifts which characterized the 19th-century Bengal renaissance where the folk articulations seemed to hold as much sway as the poetry of Keats and Wordsworth. He lapses into insignificance not being able to negotiate new forms of socio-political aggression. Yet another exile that eventually carves a niche for himself within the new world is the initially marginalized elder brother, Shankar, who is aspiring to be a classical vocalist. However, he is the one who is able to negotiate the new world in successfully asserting the dignity of the classical-romantic mode of being. Nita's anguished cry professing her desire to live even as she is facing death is to be understood within the context of this assertion of dignity. It is not possible for the feminine, creative and classical-romantic principles to survive in any other, prosaic manner. The call is, as such, extendable to the people who have been so brutally split along two zones despite belonging to the same melodic memory-resonance.

Meghe dhaka tara forms part of a larger trilogy which Ghatak made around the theme of displacement and exile. It was followed by *Komal gandhar* (*E Flat*, 1962) and *Subarnarekha* (named after the river Subarnarekha, 1964). The theme of partition and cultural split and the schism within the Indian Left and its cultural wing IPTA (the Indian People's Theatre Association) was at the core of all three films. It was taken up yet again with the traumatic birth of Bangladesh when Ghatak returned to the material energy of the Bengali culture to create *Titash eki nadir naam* (*Titash, the Name of a River*, 1972).

—Rashmi Doraiswamy

MELODY HAUNTS MY MEMORY

See **SAMO JEDNOM SE LJUBI**

MEMORIAS DEL SUBDESARROLLO

(Memories of Underdevelopment)

Cuba, 1968

Director: Tomás Gutiérrez Alea

Production: Instituto Cubano del Arte e Industria Cinematograficos (ICAIC); black and white, 35mm; running time: 104 minutes. Released 1968. Filmed in Havana.

Producer: Miguel Mendoza; **screenplay:** Tomás Gutiérrez Alea and Edmundo Desnoes, from the novel by Edmundo Desnoes; **photography:** Ramón Suárez; **editor:** Nelson Rodríguez; **sound engineers:** Eugenio Vesa, Germinal Hernández, and Carlos Fernández; **production designer:** Julio Matilla; **music:** Leo Brower, conducted by Manuel Duchezne Cuzán, recorded by Medardo Montero; **optical effects:** Jorge Pucheux; **costume designer:** Elba Perez; **animation:** Roberto Riquenes.

Cast: Sergio Corrieri (*Sergio*); Daisy Granados (*Elena*); Eslinda Núñez (*Noemi*); Omar Valdés; René de la Cruz; Yolanda Farr; Ofelia Gonzáles; José Gil Abad; Daniel Jordan; Luis López; Rafael Sosa.

Awards: Warsaw Festival, Mermaid Prize, 1970.

Publication

Script:

Gutiérrez Alea, Tomás, and Edmundo Desnoes, *Memories of Underdevelopment: The Revolutionary Films of Cuba*, edited by Michael Myerson, New York, 1973; also contained in *Memories of Underdevelopment: Tomas Gutierrez Alea, Director, Inconsolable Memories: Edmundo Desnoes, Author*, New Brunswick, New Jersey, 1990.

Books:

Nelson, L., *Cuba: The Measure of a Revolution*, Minneapolis, 1972.

Chanan, Michael, *The Cuban Image*, London, 1985.

Burton, Julianne, editor, *Cinema and Social Change in Latin America: Conversations with Filmmakers*, Austin, 1986.

Sánchez Oliva, Iraida, editor, *Viewer's Dialectic: Tomás Gutiérrez Alea*, translated by Julia Lesage, Havana, 1988.

Gutiérrez Alea, Tomás, *Tomás Gutiérrez Alea: los filmes que no filmé*, Ciudad de La Habana, 1989.

Gutiérrez Alea, and Edmundo Desnoes, *Memories of Underdevelopment/Inconsolable Memories*, introduction by Michael Chanan, New Brunswick, 1990.

Articles:

Douglas, M. E., ''The Cuban Cinema: Filmography,'' in *Take One* (Montreal), July-August 1968.

Murphy, Brian, in *Films and Filming* (London), September 1969.

Allen, Don, in *Sight and Sound* (London), Autumn 1969.

Engel, Andi, ''Solidarity and Violence,'' in *Sight and Sound* (London), Autumn 1969.

Bullita, Juan M., in *Hablemos de Cine* (Lima), no. 54, 1970.

Adler, Renata, ''Three Cuban Cultural Reports with Films Somewhere in Them,'' in *A Year in the Dark*, Berkeley, 1971.

Hamori, O., in *Filmkultura* (Budapest), January-February 1972.

Murphy, W., in *Take One* (Montreal), April 1972.

Torres Diaz, D., ''Cine Cubano en EEUU,'' in *Cine Cubano* (Havana), no. 189–90, 1974.

''The Alea Affair,'' in *Film 73/74*, edited by David Denby and Jay Cocks, Indianapolis, 1974.

Lesage, Julia, ''Images of Underdevelopment,'' in *Jump Cut* (Chicago), May-June 1974.

Martin, Marcel, in *Ecran* (Paris), December 1974.

''Three on Two: Henry Fernandez, David I. Grossvogel, and Emir Rodriguez Monegal on Desnoes and Alea,'' in *Diacritics: A Review of Contemporary Cinema*, Winter 1974.

Lieberman, S., ''Women: *The Memories of Underdevelopment*,'' in *Women and Film* (Berkeley), Summer 1975.

Burton, Julianne, in *Center for Inter-American Relations Review*, Fall 1976.

Kernan, Margot, ''Cuban Cinema: Tomás Gutiérrez Alea,'' in *Film Quarterly* (Berkeley), Winter 1976.

Burton, Julianne, ''Individual Fulfillment and Collective Achievement: An Interview with Tomás Gutiérrez Alea,'' in *Cineaste* (New York), January 1977.

Burton, Julianne, in *Cineaste* (New York), Summer 1977.

Kavanagh, Thomas M., ''Dialectics and the Textuality of Class Conflict,'' and ''Revolutionary Cinema and the Self-Reflections on a Disappearing Class'' by Albert Michales, in *Journal of Latin American Lore*, vol. 4, no. 1, 1978.

Memorias del subdesarrollo

Fernandez, Enrique, ''Witnesses Everywhere: The Rhetorical Strategies of *Memories of Underdevelopment*,'' in *Wide Angle* (Athens, Ohio), Winter 1980.

Gutiérrez Alea, Tomás, ''*Memorias del subdesarrollo*: Notas de trabajo,'' and ''Se llamaba Sergio'' by Edmundo Desnoes, in *Cine Cubano* (Havana), no. 45–46.

Burton, Julianne, ''Modernist Form in *Land in Anguish* and *Memories of Underdevelopment*,'' in *Post Script* (Jacksonville, Florida), Winter 1984.

Alexander, W., ''Class, Film Language, and Popular Cinema,'' in *Jump Cut* (Berkeley), March 1985.

Gutiérrez Alea, Tomás, ''The Viewer's Dialectic III,'' in *Jump Cut* (Berkeley), no. 32, April 1986.

Lopez, A. M., ''Parody, Underdevelopment, and the New Latin American Cinema,'' in *Quarterly Review of Film and Video* (New York), no. 1–2, 1990.

Oroz, Silvia, ''Mémoires du sous-developpement,'' an interview with Tomas Gutiérrez Alea, in *Revue de la Cinématheque* (Montreal), no. 10, February-April 1991.

Thompson, F., ''Metaphors of Space: Polarization, Dualism and Third World Cinema,'' in *Screen* (Oxford), no. 1, 1993.

''Tomas Gutiérrez Alea: Interview with Cuban Director,'' in *UNESCO Courier*, July-August 1995.

Beer, A., ''Plotting the Revolution: Identity and Territory in *Memories of Underdevelopment*,'' in *CineAction* (Toronto), no. 43, 1997.

* * *

The self and society, private life and history, individual psychology and historical situation—this is the core of *Memories*, and film has rarely (if ever) been used so effectively to portray this relationship. The dialectic of consciousness and context is presented through the character of Sergio, a wealthy but alienated member of the bourgeoisie who stays in Cuba after the triumph of the revolution and whose experiences, feelings, and thoughts in being confronted by the new reality form the basis of the film.

The formal inventiveness of the film has its origin in the dialectical resonance created through the juxtaposition of various cinematic forms, a characteristic of revolutionary Cuban cinema at its best. Here, the film begins by re-working the book which inspired it, taking the form of the novel—Sergio's subjective revolutionary Cuba, presented in documentary footage. Through this formal juxtaposition, the film ''objectifies'' the internal monologue of Sergio—criticizing and contextualizing his psychological subjectivism and confronting his attempts to retreat into his pre-revolutionary psychology and ways of seeing with the ''fact of history'' presented by the revolutionary situation.

Visually, the film's dialectic is presented through the use of three forms of cinematic structure. Documentary and semi-documentary footage is used to depict the ''collective consciousness'' of the revolutionary process, a consciousness that is pre-eminently historical. This footage presents us with the background of the revolution and establishes the historical context of the film's fictional present by placing it between the 1961 exodus in the aftermath of the failed Bay of Pigs invasion and the defensive preparations for the Missile Crisis of 1962. Fictional footage is used in two ways. The majority of the fictional sequences are presented in the traditional form of narrative cinema, in which the camera functions as omniscient narrator. However, at times the camera presents us with Sergio's point-of-view, the way in which his consciousness realizes itself in his forms of perception—what he looks at and how he sees it. Thus, the film shows and creates an identification with what it is simultaneously criticizing. Through this juxtaposition of visual forms, and through the visual contradiction of Sergio's reflections, the film insists that what we see is a function of how we believe, and that how we believe is what our history has made of us.

Sergio's way of seeing was formed in pre-revolutionary Cuba. As a member of the educated elite, he developed a disdain for Cuban reality and a scorn for those who believe that it could be changed. Critical of his bourgeois family and friends (who are, however, capable of making the commitment to leave Cuba), he is nonetheless unable to overcome his alienation and link himself to the revolution. The ''ultimate outsider,'' he attempts to content himself by colonizing and exploiting women—a metaphor for the colonization of Cuba. His personal fate is finally and paradoxically irrelevant, for as the film ends the camera moves out from his individual vision to the larger revolution beyond.

The film ''shocked'' U.S. critics when released there in 1973, and they described it variously as ''extremely rich,'' ''hugely effective,'' ''beautifully understated,'' and ''a miracle.'' No ''miracle'' at all, but simply one of the finest examples of revolutionary Cuban cinema, *Memories* has also received a warm reception from Cuban audiences, some film-goers returning to see it again and again. *Memories*' complex structure and dialectical texture merit such repeated viewings, for it transforms the now familiar themes of alienation and the ''outsider'' by placing them within a revolutionary setting. We identify with and understand Sergio, who is capable of moments of lucidity. However, we also understand that his perspective is neither universal nor timeless but a specific response to a particular situation. *Memories of Underdevelopment* insists that such situations are not permanent and that things can be changed through commitment and struggle. History is a concrete, material process which, ironically, is the salvation of the Sergios.

—John Mraz

MEMORIES OF UNDERDEVELOPMENT

See **MEMORIAS DEL SUBDESARROLLO**

MENILMONTANT

France, 1924

Director: Dimitri Kirsanoff

Production: Dimitri Kirsanoff's production company; black and white, 35mm, silent; running time: about 50 minutes; length: 1800 feet. Released 1924, France. Filmed in Paris.

Producer: Dimitri Kirsanoff; **screenplay:** Dimitri Kirsanoff; **photography:** Léonce Crouan (uncredited) and Dimitri Kirsanoff; **editor:** Dimitri Kirsanoff (uncredited).

Cast: Nadia Sibirskaia (*Younger sister*); Yolande Beaulieu (*Elder sister*); Guy Belmont (*Young man*); Jean Pasquier; Maurice Ronsard.

Publications

Articles:

Sitney, P.A., ''The Idea of Abstraction,'' in *Film Culture* (New York), no. 63/64, 1977.

Travelling (Lausanne), Summer 1979.

Brown, Geoff, in *Monthly Film Bulletin* (London), October 1981.

Prouty, Richard, ''The Well-Furnished Interior of the Masses: Kirsanoff's *Menilmontant* and the Streets of Paris,'' in *Cinema Journal* (Austin), vol. 36, no. 1, Fall 1996.

* * *

Menilmontant, the best known and the most impressive film of the Russian émigré cellist, Dimitri Kirsanoff, takes its title from the working-class district of Paris where its drama occurs. This short film is remarkable for the honesty with which it represents seduction, jealousy, and prostitution, and, even more so, for its economical and powerful use of montage to narrate a complex story completely within intertitles.

The film opens with an unexplained axe murder, brilliantly conceived in a montage of violent details. The remainder of the film describes the life of the two daughters of the murdered couple, who both fall in love with a Parisian thug; one ends up with a baby and the other becomes a prostitute. In the final moments of the film they are reconciled and return to their first job in a sweatshop, while the thug, unbeknownst to them, is murdered in an obscure brawl, the mystery and violence of which reflect the opening murders.

A series of hand-held views of Paris, together with superimpositions, simultaneously propels the story elliptically and gives us insights into the psychology of the two girls. The first such sequence marks the abrupt transition from the country to the city, and conveys in its rhythm the excitement Paris possesses for the two new arrivals. When the sister who eventually will have a baby spends her first night with her lover, another moving camera sequence, superimposed over the other sister, vividly portrays her jealousy, and her fantasy, of her sister's initiation into the excitements of the city. A gloomier version of the same dynamic camera movement is superimposed over the face of the young mother when she leaves the maternity ward, thinking (as the montage makes perfectly clear) of killing herself and her baby.

The final round of this stylistic trope introduces the idea of prostitution and culminates in the meeting of the two sisters.

They had become estranged when the first one to be seduced saw, from a distance, her sister also seduced by the thug. Kirsanoff brilliantly emphasizes her shock by cutting to a series of progressively closer shots of her face, in precisely the manner that he had earlier edited the scene in which she comes upon her slaughtered parents. By reserving this figure for those two scenes alone, he urges the viewer to connect the two traumas psychologically. The entire film is constructed around an elaborate network of such cinematic figures, making it one of the most interesting psychological narratives of its period.

—P. Adams Sitney

MEPHISTO

Hungary-West Germany, 1981

Director: István Szabó

Production: Mafilm-Objektiv Studio (Budapest) in cooperation with Manfred Durniok Productions (West Berlin); Eastmancolor, 35mm; running time: 146 minutes, some sources list 144 minutes. Released 1981. Filmed in Germany.

Producer: Manfred Durniok; **screenplay:** István Szabó and Péter Dobai, from the novel by Klaus Mann; **photography:** Lajos Koltai; **editor:** Zsuzsa Zsa Kany; **music:** Zdenkó Tamássy.

Cast: Klaus Maria Brandauer (*Hendrik Höfgen*); Krystyna Janda (*Barbara Bruckner*); Ildikó Bánsági (*Nicoletta von Niebuhr*); Karin Boyd (*Juliette Martens*); Rolf Hoppe (*The General*); Christine Harbort (*Lotte Lindenthal*); Gyögy Cserhalmi (*Hans Miklas*); Martin Hellberg (*Professor*).

Award: Oscar for Best Foreign Film.

Publications

Books:

Spangenberg, Eberhard, *Karriere eines Romans: Mephisto, Klaus Mann, und Gustav Gründgens: Ein dokumentarischer Bericht aus Deutschland und dem Exil 1925–81*, Munich, 1982.
Paech, Joachim, editor, *Literatur und Film: Mephisto*, Frankfurt, 1984.

Articles:

Szabó, István, ''Mephistopheles,'' in *Hungarofilm Bulletin* (Budapest), no. 5, 1980.
Vrdlovec, Z., in *Ekran* (Ljubljana), no. 2, 1981.
Fenyves, G., ''Leider kann man einen Film nur einmal drehen,'' in *Film und Fernsehen* (Berlin), March 1981.
Moskowitz, G., in *Variety* (New York), 18 March 1981.
New York Times, 29 September 1981.
Györffy, M., in *Filmkultura* (Budapest), September-October 1981.
Robinson, David, ''My Homeland,'' in *Sight and Sound* (London), Autumn 1981.
Auty, Martyn, in *Monthly Film Bulletin* (London), October 1981.
Frey, R., in *Filmfaust* (Frankfurt), November 1981.
Forbes, Jill, in *Films and Filming* (London), December 1981.
De Santi, G., and P. Maté, in *Cineforum* (Bergamo), December 1981.
Bader, K. L., in *Filmfaust* (Frankfurt), December 1981-January 1982.
Elley, Derek, in *International Film Guide 1982*, edited by Peter Cowie, London, 1982.
Edelman, Rob, in *Magill's Cinema Annual*, Englewood Cliffs, New Jersey, 1982.
Szabo, György, in *Filmkultura* (Budapest), no. 2, 1982.
Hagen, O., in *Film & Kino* (Oslo), 1982.
Fonda-Bonardi, C., in *Cineaste* (New York), 1982.
Engven, I., in *Filmrutan* (Stockholm), 1982.
Szabó, István, in *Cinéma* (Paris), January 1982.
Martin, Marcel, in *Image et Son* (Paris), January 1982.
Roy, J., in *Cinéma* (Paris), January 1982.
Schepelern, P., in *Kosmorama* (Copenhagen), February 1982.
Orto, N., in *Cinema Nuovo* (Turin), April 1982.
New Republic (New York), 7 April 1982.
New Yorker, 17 May 1982.
Seegers, R., in *Skrien* (Amsterdam), May-June 1982.
Szabo, G., in *Filmkultura* (Budapest), May-June 1982.
Heijer, J., in *Skoop* (Amsterdam), June 1982.
McFarlane, Brian, in *Cinema Papers* (Melbourne), June 1982.
Hughes, J. W., interview with Istvan Szabo, in *Film Quarterly* (Berkeley), Summer 1982.
Chanko, K. M., in *Films in Review* (New York), June-July 1982.
Mracová, M., in *Film a Doba* (Prague), July 1982.
Rashish, P., in *Stills* (London), Winter 1982.
Chijona, G., in *Cine Cubano* (Havana), 1983.
Bérubé, R. C. in *Séquences* (Montreal), January 1983.
Seberechts, K., in *Film en Televisie* (Brussels), January 1983.
Rutkowski, A. M., in *Filmowy Serwis Prasowy* (Warsaw), 1–15 February 1983.
Zapiola, G., in *Cinemateca Revista* (Montevideo), November 1983.
Nagy, M., in *Filmkultura* (Budapest), November-December 1983.
Somogyi, L., in *Filmkultura* (Budapest), November-December 1983.
Wanat, A., ''Höfgen i Gründgens,'' in *Kino* (Warsaw), April 1984.
Eidsvik, C., ''*Tootsie* Versus *Mephisto:* Characterization in a Cross-Cultural Context,'' in *Film Criticism* (Meadville, Pennsylvania), no. 3, 1989.
Mills, M. C., ''The Three Faces of *Mephisto:* Film, Novel, and Reality,'' in *Literature/Film Quarterly* (Salisbury, Maryland), no. 4, 1990.
Gabor, Bota, ''A Fight at the Opera: Film Director Istvan Szabo,'' an interview, in *World Press Review*, vol. 41, no. 2, February 1994.
Landrot, Marine, ''Les exorcistes,'' in *Télérama* (Paris), no. 2344, 14 December 1994.
Piette, Alain, ''The Face in The Mirror: Faust as a Self-deceived Actor,'' in *Literature/Film Quarterly* (Salisbury), vol. 26, no. 2, April 1998.

* * *

István Szabó, probably the most engagingly intelligent of the younger Hungarian filmmakers who began working after 1956,

Mephisto

earned a reputation among serious observers of the international cinema during the 1960s—most of all for the wonderfully bright and inventive *The Father* (1966). More than a decade later, his *Confidence* (1979) was nominated for an Academy Award; an exceptional film, its subtle complexities and quiet beauty did not win either the Oscar or the wider public his work deserves. Both trophies did, however, come soon thereafter with *Mephisto*, the director's first major international production.

The idea behind *Mephisto* is a promising one—to explore the psyche of a chameleon-like actor living through the rise of Nazism in Germany (the filmmakers actually choose not to specify the precise time or place) and accommodating himself to the new regime in any way necessary to maintain his position and acclaim. Most promising of all is the fact that this central character is based on the life of Gustav Gründgens (1899–1963), Germany's most commanding actor, theatrical director, and impresario of his generation. (Among his film roles, Gründgens played the wily chief of the underworld in Fritz Lang's *M* in 1931.) The screenplay, which Szabó wrote with Péter Dobai, is based on the 1936 *roman à clef*, also titled *Mephisto*, by Klaus Mann, the son of Thomas Mann and brother of Erika, to whom Gründgens was married before she fled from Hitler's Germany. (The title is an ironic reference to the actor's celebrated role, Mephistopheles in *Faust*.)

In Szabó's film, the Gründgens character is named Hendrik Höfgen. There are intimations that the fictional Höfgen shares some of Gründgen's early leftist leanings as he embarks on a propitious acting career. To keep that career afloat in the mounting tide of fascism, Höfgen ingratiates himself with a powerful leader in the new regime—a proxy for Göring, whose pretégé Gründgens became. And, like Gründgens, Höfgen chooses to remain in his position rather than avail himself of an opportunity to emigrate. *Mephisto* ends before the war, as its version of the Gründgens character begins to see himself becoming a puppet of his protectors.

The film is brilliant and enthralling, a whirlwind of color and motion that suggests its protagonist's rapid success and self-absorption. A virtuosic achievement as a succession to Szabó's finely modulated previous work, *Mephisto* is near-perfect within the scope of its ambition—to delineate the course of an opportunist whose life is nothing more or less than the sum of all the roles he plays. But its tone of moral indignation is all too easy, its moral crux so very familiar and predictable, and its rendering of the central figure a pat oversimplification of the unacknowledged character who inspired it. Klaus Maria

Brandauer's manic performance in the part of Höfgen, as is apt for this film, represents a self-illuminating style of acting that one esteems or rejects according to one's critical disposition toward work of its kind. Neither the role nor Brandauer's portrayal suggests whether Höfgen is a genuinely great actor (as Gründgens was) or simply an effectively truculent and narcissistic one. (The other performers are quite fine, although the many Hungarians in the cast have been dubbed into German for the film's distribution outside Hungary.)

Klaus Mann's aim was to condemn Gründgens. Szabó sought to universalize the character, ''a man who considers it his only possibility in life to make people accept him.'' But beyond the simple figure who appears in *Mephisto* lies the complex and ambivalent case of Gründgens himself. Despite his tacit support for Hitler, he was cleared after the war and continued his prominence in the theatres of both West and East Germany. He was even credited with upholding artistic standards during the Third Reich (Höfgen participates in plays reinterpreted to fit fascist ideology) and with helping many who were threatened by the Nazis (Höfgen does obtain an exit visa for his lover, a black actress).

In the shadow of Stalinism, many Eastern European directors have made films set around the time of World War II, with safe, anti-Nazi topics, when current issues could not be broached. Szabó understands very well the real difficulties and ambiguities of individuals who chose to continue living and working under compromising political circumstances, and in fact his own contemporary films have frequently focused on their dilemmas with sympathy and resonance. With *Mephisto* and the aspiration for wide popularity, it seems he has limited his scrutiny to an extreme case and held it at a safe distance.

—Herbert Reynolds

LE MÉPRIS

(Contempt)

France, 1963

Director: Jean-Luc Godard

Production: Rome-Paris Films, Films Concordia, Embassy; Technicolor, Franscope, 35mm; running time (restored print): 105 minutes; Italian version shortened, dubbed, with new music, against the director's wishes. Filmed on location in Cinecittà (Rome) and the Villa Curzio Malaparte, Capri. Cost: $1 million (estimated).

Producers: Georges de Beauregard, Carlo Ponti, and Joseph E. Levine; **screenplay:** Jean-Luc Godard, from the novel *Il disprezzo* by Alberto Moravia; **photography:** Raoul Coutard; **assistant director:** Charles Bitsch; **editors:** Agnes Guillemot and Lila Lakshmanan; **sound:** William Sivel; **music:** Georges Delarue.

Cast: Brigitte Bardot (*Camile Javal*); Michel Piccoli (*Paul Javal*); Jack Palance (*Jerry Prokosch*); Georgia Moll (*Francesca);* Fritz Lang (*himself*); Jean-Luc Godard (*assistant director*).

Publications

Script:

Godard, Jean-Luc, *Le Mépris* (scenario), in *Avant-Scène Cinéma* (Paris), May-June 1992.

Books:

Interview with Jean Collet, in *Jean-Luc Godard*, New York, 1968.
Mussman, Tony, ''Notes on *Contempt*,'' *Jean-Luc Godard*, New York, 1968.
Interview with Yvonne Baby, in *Focus On Godard*, Englewood Cliffs, 1972.
Lesage, Julia, *Jean-Luc Godard: A Guide to References and Resources*, Boston, 1979.
Vimenet, Pascal, *Le Mépris, Jean-Luc Godard: Un film produit par Georges de Beauregard*, Paris, 1991.
Lev, Peter, *The Euro-American Cinema*, Austin, 1993.
Marie, Michel, *Le Mépris, Jean-Luc Godard: etude critique*, Paris, 1995.
Dixon, Wheeler Winston, *The Films of Jean-Luc Godard*, New York, 1997.
Lopate, Phillip, *Totally, Tenderly, Tragically: Essays and Criticism from a Lifelong Love Affair With the Movies*, New York, 1998.
Silverman, Kaja, and Harun Frocki, *Speaking About Godard*, New York, 1998.

Articles:

MacCabe, Colin, ''*Le Mépris/Il disprezzo/Contempt*,'' in *Sight and Sound* (London), September 1996.
Kehr, Dave, ''Gods in the Details: Godard's *Contempt*,'' in *Film Comment* (New York), September-October 1997.
Rosenbaum, Jonathan, ''Critical Distance,'' in *Chicago Reader*, 5 September 1997.

* * *

Le Mépris is the closest Jean-Luc Godard has ever come to making a Hollywood-style film: international stars, relatively big budget, script based upon a ''prestige'' novel, glamorous locations shot in color and 'scope. Of course, it is subversive toward all of the above, and is, among other things, *about* the absurdities of making a Hollywood-style film. Received with a good deal of puzzlement during its initial release, it was greeted with huge critical acclaim upon its rerelease in 1997.

Freely adapting Alberto Moravia's *Il disprezzo* (Kaja Silverman and Harun Farocki's book on Godard supplies detail), Godard tells the story of a writer (Michel Piccoli) who earns the contempt of his wife (Brigitte Bardot) when he appears to pander—in more ways than one—to an American film producer (Jack Palance). Though an aspiring ''serious'' writer, Paul accepts the high-paying job of dumbing down (as we would now call it) the shooting script of a film of *The Odyssey* being directed by the venerated Fritz Lang (playing himself), and worse yet, he seems to push his beautiful wife into the philandering producer's path. To be sure, nothing is quite so simple as it seems: the rushes we see from Lang's film are so bizarrely abstract (and unlike anything the real Lang ever directed) that one may imagine the consternation of even a less crass producer than Jerry Prokosch (Palance); and Paul's "crime" against his wife is no more tangible than his urging her to go off with Jerry in the latter's two-seater to his villa while Paul takes a cab. But *Le Mépris* is among other things a semiotician's delight: Lang's footage and Paul's sendoff of his wife in the sports car are signifiers of much else, not to be taken at face value.

Much of *Le Mépris* is structured upon contrasts of the Classical and the Modern, though what Godard means by "classical" is complex and partly unorthodox. The Modern is easier to specify: it is Jerry's vulgarity and money-lust, and Paul's neurotic psychologizing over Ulysses' motives for leaving Penelope and taking so long to get back to Ithaca. Clearly Paul projects his own confused feelings about his marriage upon the ancient narrative. If *Le Mépris* were an allegory, Paul and Jerry would be modern parallels for Ulysses and the Suitors; but neither of them cuts a heroic enough figure for the analogy to be much more than a joke. When Jerry hurls a can of film in a fit of anger, inadvertently looking like a discus thrower, Lang dryly remarks, "Finally you get the feel of Greek culture."

Lang, the spokesman for the Classical (as Camille is the embodiment), insists that in *The Oyssey* there are no hidden motives, no tortured dissembling—all is starkly forthright. Lang stands for clarity, simplicity, power allied with gracefulness, as his footage with the camera revolving around Greek statues of Poseidon and Athena suggest. In another sense of the term, Godard clearly reveres Lang as a "classic"—both as a filmmaker and as a repository of culture, someone who quotes effortlessly from Dante and Hölderlin. For that matter, American movies from Griffith to Minnelli, alluded to in dialogue and posters scattered through *Le Mépris*, are classics as well.

Godard evokes the Classical in a variety of other ways as well, beginning with Georges Delarue's score for the film: stark, somber passages, seemingly tragic in mood, punctuating key moments of the drama, as hieratic as the statues in Lang's footage. Equally classical are the Mediterranean vistas so hauntingly photographed in the second half of the film—sunburnt rock, splendid blue sea, cloudless or hazy sky. (Rather more eccentrically, Godard alludes to primal matters by emphasizing the primary colors red, yellow, and blue throughout the film, most abstractly in the opening nude shot of Bardot, which uses a red and a blue filter in turn, plus a yellow cloth in the unfiltered portion.) The elegantly gliding tracking shots have their own serene beauty—though Godard also uses jump cuts and other ways of disregarding continuity rules of the classical cinema. And the face and unclad body of Bardot are equally treated as classical in their stately beauty. The most famous anecdote about the shooting of *Le Mépris* has to do with producer Joseph E. Levine demanding that Godard insert footage of a nude Bardot, and Godard complying by opening the film with a long take of his star stretched across the full length of the Franscope screen, as if to get it over with at once. But in fact her serene nudity is completely integral to the film's representation of Bardot, including one close-up as she calmly recites a list of "dirty words" and shots of her profile in the Rome villa garden. Camille is compared to one of *The Odyssey*'s Sirens as well as to Penelope, but rather than lure Paul she literally swims away from him near the end of the film. Finally, her siding with Lang against Paul and Jerry (she even reads a book on Lang in the bathtub) is one more way in which Camille/Bardot is aligned with the Classical. With all of this said, one must still be wary of schematizing a film that has so much of a feel of the improvisatory.

Le Mépris is also very much about the collapse of a marriage. The causes remain obscure, in the sense that the film does not present us with a neat set of reasons, Hollywood-style, for the breakdown. Indeed, Camille impatiently dismisses Paul's supposition of one cause of her anger, his desultory pass at Francesca, Jerry's assistant/translator/mistress. But signs of dissatisfaction, even perhaps clues to deeper problems, are scattered through the film. Most obvious is Paul's slapping Camille (after nastily knocking his hand upon a bronze female torso); more subtle is the sports-car incident (though viewers of today must make a cultural adjustment to a world in which husbands "give permission" to wives to be alone with other men). But most often we must draw conclusions from slight variations in tone of voice and body language. All these signs of distance, disagreement, distraction can be observed in the remarkable half-hour scene—practically the whole middle third of the film—in which the couple pace around their half-finished new apartment, arguing, taking baths in turn, flipping through a book of Roman erotic art which Jerry has given Paul to "inspire" him, reconciling and then renewing the quarrel, until Camille cries that Paul fills her with contempt (and Delarue's tragic music bursts out to accompany her). Godard's restless 'scope camera records all this mostly in long shot, often down corridors or through doorways, and most famously tracking back and forth between them as they sit separated by a lamp which Paul flips impatiently on and off.

In countless ways, Godard interrogates not just a marriage but the cinema itself. Here come into play his explicit homages to classic American filmmaking (most amusingly when Paul wears his hat in the bathtub to look like Dean Martin in *Some Came Running*) and at the same time his disregard of the rules of continuity editing and conventional motivation. Certain plot developments—Paul grabbing a gun but never using it, the unexpected auto crash at the end—seem more like allusions to Hollywood melodrama than integral parts of the film. *Le Mépris* begins with a shot of Raoul Coutard's camera tracking toward us and peering down at us as we peer up at it, while a voice reads not only the credits (as Orson Welles does at the end of *The Magnificent Ambersons*) but also a statement about the nature of cinema. In the last shot Lang is still shooting *The Odyssey*, with Godard himself now playing an assistant director shouting "Silence!" as the camera tracks past the shoot to gaze out at the empty horizon. Godard also plays games with the soundtrack: for example, when our characters talk to one another during a concert, the loud music does not just drop in volume, as convention dictates—it drops out entirely.

Godard surely realized that his big-star, widescreen spectacle of sex and power in a show-business milieu—his own version of *The Bad and the Beautiful* or *Two Weeks in Another Town*—would be far from what his producers were hoping for. If *Le Mépris* is an allegory in any way, it is a tale of a cinematic auteur having either to defy, pander to, or somehow trick the money-men, like Ulysses confronting not so much the Suitors as the Cyclops, while the Siren of beauty and art swims ever outward, toward the horizon.

—Joseph Milicia

MESHES OF THE AFTERNOON

USA, 1943

Director: Maya Deren

Production: Black and white, 16mm; running time: 18 minutes, some sources list 14 minutes. Released 1943.

Screenplay: Maya Deren and Alexander Hammid; **editor:** Maya Deren; **photography:** Alexander Hammid.

Cast: Maya Deren (*Woman*); Alexander Hammid (*Man*).

Publications

Books:

Deren, Maya, *An Anagram of Ideas on Art, Form, and the Film*, New York, 1946.

Jacobs, Lewis, editor, *Introduction to the Art of the Movies: An Anthology of Ideas on the Nature of Movie Art*, New York, 1960.

Tyler, Parker, *Underground Film*, New York, 1969.

A History of the American Avant-Garde Cinema, New York, 1976.

Sitney, P. Adams, *Visionary Film*, New York, 1974; revised edition, 1979.

Clark, VeVe A., and Millicent Hodson, and Catrina Neiman, and Francine B. Price, *The Legend of Maya Deren: A Documentary and Collected Works, Vol. 1, Pt. 1,* New York, 1984.

Brakhage, Stan, *Film at Wit's End: Eight Avant-garde Filmmakers*, Kingston, 1989.

Rabinovitz, Lauren, *Points of Resistance: Women, Power & Politics in the New York Avant-garde Cinema, 1943–71*, Urbana, 1991.

Sudre, Alain-Alcide, *Dialogues théoriques avec Maya Deren: du cinéma expérimental au film ethnographique*, Paris, 1996.

Sullivan, Moira, *Anagram of the Ideas of Filmmaker Maya Deren: Creative Work in Motion Pictures*, Stockholm, 1997.

Rice, Shelley, *Inverted Odysseys: Claude Cahun, Maya Deren, Cindy Sherman*, Cambridge, 1999.

Deren, Maya, *Essential Deren: Complete Film Writings*, Kingston, 2000.

Articles:

Farber, Manny, ''Maya Deren's Films,'' in *New Republic* (New York), 28 October 1946.

Tyler, Parker, ''Experimental Film: A New Growth,'' in *Kenyon Review* (Gambier, Ohio), no. 1, 1949.

''Writings of Maya Deren and Ron Rice,'' in *Film Culture* (New York), Winter 1965.

Cornwell, Regina, ''Maya Deren and Germaine Dulac: Activists of the Avant-Garde,'' in *Film Library Quarterly* (New York), vol. 5, no. 1, 1971.

Sitney, P. Adams, ''The Idea of Morphology,'' in *Film Culture* (New York), nos. 53–55, 1972.

Mayer, T., ''The Legend of Maya Deren: Champion of the American Independent Film,'' in *Film News* (New York), September-October 1979.

Bruno, Giuliana, and I. Cahn, ''Afterimage,'' in *Segnocinema* (Vicenza), vol. 4, no. 12, March 1984.

Kuhn, Annette, ''*Meshes of the Afternoon*,'' in *Monthly Film Bulletin* (London), vol. 55, no. 653, June 1988.

Carty, Brad, ''Maya Deren: Experimental Films 1943–1959,'' in *Wilson Library Bulletin*, vol. 63, no. 4, December 1988.

Ouellette, Laurie, ''Maya Deren Experimental Films,'' in *UTNE Reader*, no. 48, November-December 1991.

Fabe, Marilyn, ''Maya Deren's Fatal Attraction: A Psychoanalytic Reading of *Meshes of the Afternoon* with a Psycho-biographical Afterword,'' in *Women's Studies*, vol. 25, no. 2, January 1996.

Nekola, Charlotte, ''On Not Being Maya Deren,'' in *Wide Angle* (Baltimore), vol. 18, no. 4, October 1996.

Pramaggiore, M., ''Performance and Persona in the U.S. Avant-garde: The Case of Maya Deren,'' in *Cinema Journal* (Austin), vol. 36, no. 2, 1997.

Dilas, Vikica, ''Meshing with Lynch,'' in *Sight & Sound* (London), vol. 7, no. 10, October 1997.

* * *

Meshes of the Afternoon launched the American avant-garde film movement after World War II. Made in collaboration by Maya Deren and her husband Alexander Hammid, the film depicts a woman's imaginative dream and the way it eventually destroys the woman herself. The film established dream imagery and visual poetic devices as the chief type of cinematic language for a new generation of postwar filmmakers and their audiences.

The story of *Meshes* is this: a woman (played by Deren) enters her home and falls asleep in a chair. As she sleeps and dreams, she repeatedly encounters a mysterious hooded figure whom she chases but cannot catch. With each failure, she re-enters her house, where the household objects she employs in her waking state—a key, a knife, a flower, a phonograph, and a telephone—assume intensifying potency in an environment that becomes increasingly disoriented. Through such filmic means as creative editing, extreme camera angles, and slow motion, the movie creates a world in which it is more and more difficult for the woman to master the space and rooms around her. Finally, multiplied into three versions of herself, the woman attempts to kill her sleeping body. But she is awakened by a man (played by Hammid) only to find that physical reality, too, gives away to the dream logic of her imagination, ultimately causing her death.

Made privately in Deren's and Hammid's home over a few weeks and for a few hundred dollars, *Meshes of the Afternoon* revived a European cinematic tradition established in the 1920s a tradition in which Hammid participated in his native Czechoslovakia. *Meshes of the Afternoon* sustained and developed the cinematic style of such leading European avant-garde filmmakers of the 1920s as Germaine Dulac, Luis Buñuel, and Jean Cocteau.

Meshes is a landmark film that has provided an important model, setting the tone and style for other individual efforts over the next decade. It launched Deren's career as one of the leading avant-garde filmmakers of the 1940s and 1950s. She showed the film at colleges, museums, and film societies across Canada and the United States. Her numerous bookings encouraged many younger artists interested in a personal cinema controlled by the individual artists. The film consequently inspired poetic self-exploratory films by such other filmmakers as Kenneth Anger, Stan Brakhage, and Willard Maas.

Meshes of the Afternoon is still one of the most popular of all American experimental films. It is revered as a classic mood poem which investigates a person's psychological reality.

—Lauren Rabinovitz

METROPOLIS

Germany, 1927

Director: Fritz Lang

Production: Universum-Film-Aktiengesellschaft (Ufa) studios; black and white, 35mm, silent; running time: about 2 hours originally, no complete master copy now exists but the Staatliches Archiv in East Berlin has compiled a new copy from all remaining footage: length 4189 meters originally, current copies are now 3170 meters. Released 10 January 1927, Berlin. Filmed 1925–26, in 310 days and 60 nights, in UFA Studios, Berlin. Cost: $2,000,000. Released in a new tinted print, with musical score by Giorgis Moroder, 1985.

Screenplay: Fritz Lang and Thea von Harbou, from the novel by von Harbou (Eisner disputes this in *The Haunted Screen*, 1969, claiming the film preceded the novel); **photography:** Karl Freund and Günther Rittau; **art directors:** Otto Hunte, Erich Kettelhut, and Karl Vollbrecht; **music:** Gottfried Huppertz; **special effects:** Eugene Schüfftan; **costume designer:** Anne Willkomm; **sculptures:** Walter Schultze-Mittendorff.

Cast: Brigitte Helm (*Maria/the Mechanical Maria*); Alfred Abel (*John Fredersen*); Gustav Fröhlich (*Freder*); Rudolf Klein-Rogge (*Rotwang*); Fritz Rasp (*Slim*); Theodor Loos (*Josaphat/Joseph*); Heinrich George (*Grot, the foreman*); Olaf Storm (*Jan*); Hanns Leo Reich (*Marinus*); Heinrich Gotho (*Master of Ceremonies*); Margarete Lanner (*Woman in the car*); Max Dietze, Georg John, Walter Kühle, Arthur Reinhard, and Erwin Vater (*Workers*); Grete Berger, Olly Böheim, Ellen Frey, Lisa Gray, Rose Lichtenstein, and Helene Weigel (*Female workers*); Beatrice Garga, Anny Hintze, Margarete Lanner, Helen von Münchhofen, and Hilde Woitscheff (*Women in the Eternal Garden*); Fritz Alberti (*Robot*); 750 secondary actors; and over 30,000 extras.

Publications

Script:

Lang, Fritz, and Thea von Harbou, *Metropolis*, in *Avant-Scène du Cinéma* (Paris), 1 December 1977.

Books:

Rotha, Paul, *The Film Till Now*, London, 1930.
Kalbus, Oskar, *Vom Werden deutshcer Filmkunst, Part I: Der Stummfilm*, Altona, 1935.
Holl, W., *Gustav Frölich, Kunstler und Mensch*, Berlin, 1936.
Koch, H., *Heinrich George*, Berlin, 1940.
Kracauer, Siegfried, *From Caligari to Hitler: A Psychological History of the German Film*, Princeton, 1947.
Frews, Berta, *Heinrich George*, Hamburg, 1959.
Courtade, Francis, *Fritz Lang*, Paris, 1963.
Moullet, Luc, *Fritz Lang*, Paris, 1963.
Rhode, Eric, *Tower of Babel*, London, 1966.
Agel, Henri, *Les Grands Cinéastes que je propose*, Paris, 1967.
Durgnat, Raymond, *Films and Feelings*, London, 1967.
Jensen, Paul, *The Cinema of Fritz Lang*, New York, 1969.
Eisner, Lotte, *The Haunted Screen*, Berkeley, 1969.
Mitry, Jean, *Histoire du cinema: Art et industrie, vol. 3, 1923–30*, Paris, 1973.
Berger, Erich M., *Heinrich George in Film seiner Zeit*, Wiesbaden, 1975.
Grafe, Frieda, Enno Patalas, and Hans Helmut Prinzler, *Fritz Lang*, Munich, 1976.
Eisner, Lotte, *Fritz Lang*, London, 1977.
Armour, Robert, *Fritz Lang*, Boston, 1978.
Ott, Frederick W., *The Films of Fritz Lang*, Secaucus, New Jersey, 1979.
Jenkins, Stephen, editor, *Fritz Lang: The Image and the Look*, London, 1981.
Kaplan, E. Ann, *Fritz Lang: A Guide to References and Resources*, Boston, 1981.
Maibohm, Ludwig, *Fritz Lang: Seine Filme—Sein Leben*, Munich, 1981.
Dürrenmatt, Dieter, *Fritz Lang: Leben und Werk*, Basel, 1982.
Keiner, Weinhold, *Thea von Harbou und der deutsche Film bis 1933*, Hildesheim, 1984.
von Harbour, Horst, and Claude-Jean Philippe, *Metropolis: Un Film de Fritz Lang: Images d'un tournage*, Paris, 1985.
Gehler, Fred, *Fritz Lang, die Stimme von Metropolis*, Berlin, 1990.
Bogdanovich, Peter, *Who the Devil Made It : Conversations with Robert Aldrich, George Cukor, Allan Dwan, Howard Hawks, Alfred Hitchcock, Chuck Jones, Fritz Lang, Joseph H. Lewis, Sidney Lumet, Leo McCarey, Otto Preminger, Don Siegel, Josef von Sternberg, Frank Tashlin, Edgar G. Ulmer, Raoul Walsh*, New York, 1997.
Levin, David J., *Richard Wagner, Fritz Lang, and the Nibelungen: The Dramaturgy of Disavowal*, Princeton, 1998.
McGilligan, Patrick, *Fritz Lang: The Nature of the Beast*, New York, 1998.
Gunning, Tom, *The Films of Fritz Lang: Modernity, Crime, and Desire*, London, 2000.
Minden, Michael, and Holger Bachmann, editors, *Fritz Lang's ''Metropolis'': Cinematic Views of Technology and Fear*, Rochester, 2000.

Articles:

Lang, Fritz, ''Was ich noch zu sagen habe,'' in *Mein Film*, edited by Frederick Proges, Vienna, 1927.
''*Metropolis* Film Seen: Berlin Witnesses a Grim Portrayal of Industrial Future,'' in *New York Times*, 10 January 1927.
Hildebrandt, Fred, in *Berliner Tageblatt*, 11 January 1927.
Eggebrecht, Axel, in *Weltbühne* (Berlin), 18 January 1927.

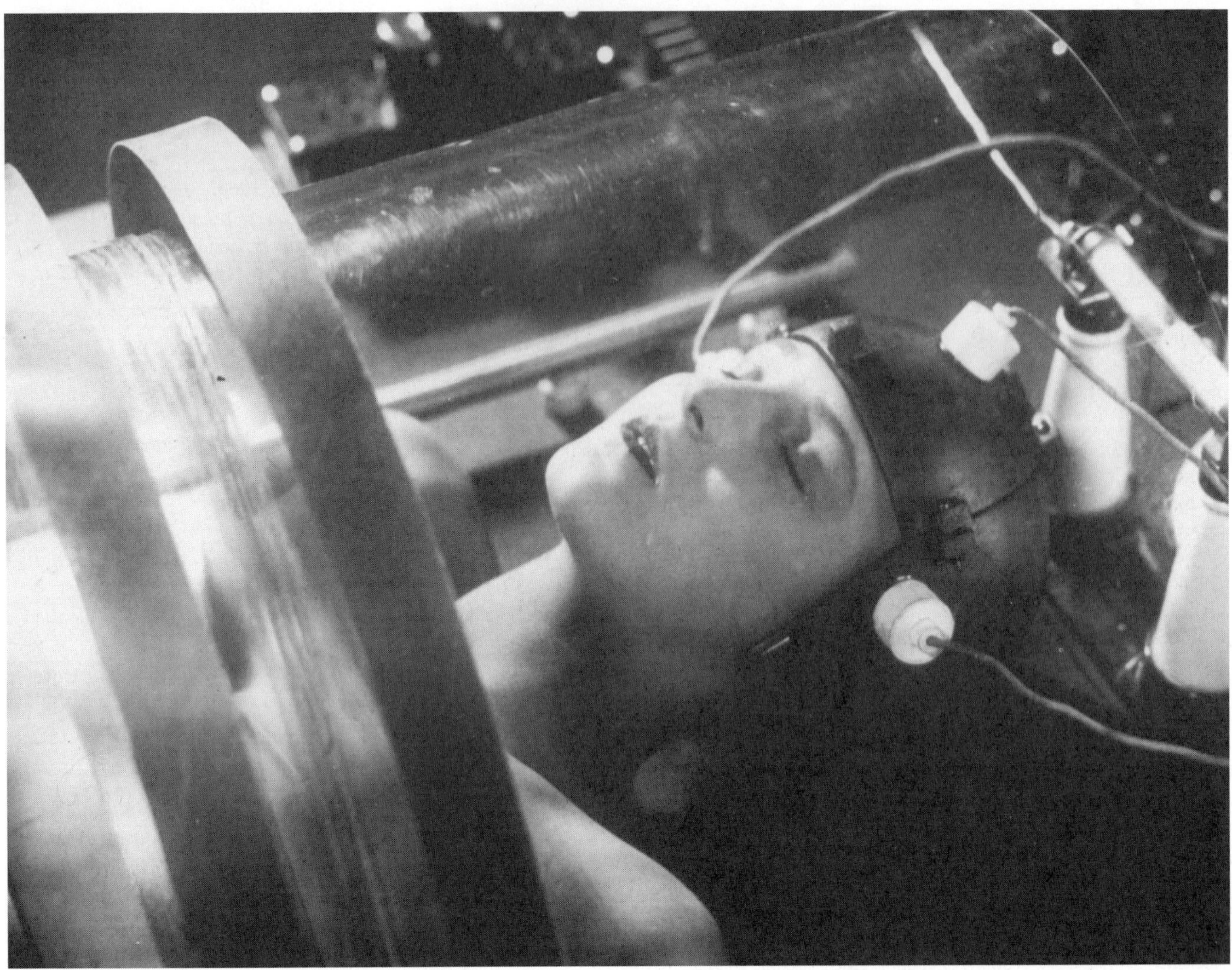

Metropolis

Arnheim, Rudolf, in *Stachelschwein*, 1 February 1927.
Gerstein, Evelyn, in *Nation* (New York), 23 March 1927.
Barry, Iris, in *Spectator* (London), 26 March 1927.
Wells, H. G., in *New York Times*, 17 April 1927.
Herring, Robert, in *London Mercury*, May 1927.
''*Metropolis* Issue'' of *Petite Illustration* (Paris), no. 372, 1928.
''*Metropolis* Issue'' of *Cinéma* (Paris), March 1928.
Eisner, Lotte, ''Notes sur le style de Fritz Lang,'' in *Revue du Cinéma* (Paris), 1 February 1947.
Gesek, Ludwig, ''Fritz Lang: Suggestion und Stimmung,'' in *Gestalter der Filmkunst, Von Asta Nielsen bis Walt Disney*, Vienna, 1948.
Douchet, Jean, ''L'Oeuvre de Fritz Lang à la cinémathèque: Le Piège consideré comme l'un des beaux-arts,'' in *Arts* (Paris), 1 July 1959.
Domarchi, Jean, and Jacques Rivette, ''Entretien avec Fritz Lang,'' in *Cahiers du Cinéma* (Paris), September 1959.
Franju, Georges, ''Le Style de Fritz Lang,'' in *Cahiers du Cinéma* (Paris), November 1959.
Luft, Herbert, ''Erich Pommer,'' in *Films in Review* (New York), November 1959.
Luft, Herbert, ''Karl Freund,'' in *Films in Review* (New York), February 1963.
Sarris, Andrew, ''Fritz Lang,'' in *Film Culture* (New York), Spring 1963.
Schütte, Wolfram, ''Kolportage, Stilisierung, Realismus: Anmerkungen zum Werk Fritz Langs,'' in *Filmstudio* (Frankfurt), September 1964.
Berg, Gretchen, ''La Nuit viennoise: Une Confession de Fritz Lang,'' in *Cahiers du Cinéma* (Paris), August 1965 and June 1966.
Pieyre de Mandiargues, André, ''L'Ecran démoniaque,'' in *Cinéma* (Paris), no. 100, 1966.
Jensen, Paul, in *Film Heritage* (Dayton, Ohio), Winter 1968.
Bunuel, Luis, in *Cahiers du Cinéma* (Paris), August-September 1971.
Williams, Alan, ''Structures of Narrativity in Fritz Lang's *Metropolis*,'' in *Film Quarterly* (Berkeley), Summer 1974.
Phillips, Gene D., ''Fritz Lang: An Interview,'' in *Focus on Film* (London), 1975.
Tulloch, John, ''Genetic Structuralism and the Cinema: A Look at Fritz Lang's *Metropolis*,'' in *Australian Journal of Screen Theory* (Kensington, New South Wales), no. 1, 1976.
Boost, C., in *Skoop* (Amsterdam), March 1976.
Basset, V., and D. Sotiaux, in *Revue Belge du Cinéma* (Brussels), June 1977.

Roth, Lane, "*Metropolis*: The Lights Fantastic: Semiotic Analysis of Lighting Codes in Relation to Character and Theme," in *Literature/Film Quarterly* (Salisbury, Maryland), Fall 1978.

Willis, Don, "Fritz Lang: Only Melodrama," in *Film Quarterly* (Berkeley), Winter 1979–80.

Mellenkamp, P., "Oedipus and the Robot in *Metropolis*," in *Enclitic* (Minneapolis), Spring 1981.

Posthumus, P., in *Skrien* (Amsterdam), Summer 1982.

Beylie, Claude, in *Cinématographe* (Paris), June 1984.

Sauvaget, D., "*Metropolis*: Rencontre Kitsch," in *Revue du Cinéma* (Paris), September 1984.

Rotondi, C. J., and E. Gerstein, in *Films in Review* (New York), October 1984.

Cieutat, B., "Fritz Lang "Morodernise"; ou, L'Art du detournement: *Metropolis*," in *Positif* (Paris), November 1984.

Elsaesser, Thomas, "Innocence Restoried," in *Monthly Film Bulletin* (London), December 1984.

Patalas, E., in *Filmkultura* (Budapest), March 1986.

Esser, M., "Rooms of Felicity," in *Filmbulletin* (Winterthur, Switzerland), no. 5, 1990.

Hogue, Peter, "Fritz Lang: Our Contemporary: 100th Anniversary of the Birth of the Noted Film Director," in *Film Comment* (New York), vol. 26, no. 6, November-December 1990.

Cieutat, B., "Le symbolisme des figures geometriques dans *Metropolis*," in *Positif* (Paris), July-August 1991.

Zagula, J.T., "Saints, Sinners and Society: Images of Women in Film and Drama from Weimar to Hitler," in *Women's Studies*, vol. 19, no. 1, 1991.

Owens, N., "Image and Object: Hegel, Madonna, *Metropolis*," in *Spectator* (Los Angeles), vol. 12, no. 2, 1992.

Rolfe, Hilda, "The Perfectionist: Film Director Fritz Lang," in *Film Comment* (New York), vol. 28, no. 6, November-December 1992.

Joselit, D., "Marcel Duchamp's 'Monte Carlo Bond' Machine," in *October*, no. 59, Winter 1992.

Rutsky, R.L., "The Mediation of Technology and Gender: *Metropolis*, Nazism, Modernism," in *New German Critique*, no. 60, Fall 1993.

Génin, Bernard, "*Metropolis*," in *Télérama* (Paris), no. 2354, 22 February 1995.

Bertellini, Giorgio, "Restoration, Genealogy and Palimpsests: On Some Historiographical Questions," in *Film History* (London), vol. 7, no. 3, Autumn 1995.

Dolgenos, Peter, "The Star on C.A. Rotwang's Door: Turning Kracauer on its Head: An Analysis of Fritz Lang's Film, the *Metropolis*," in *Journal of Popular Film and Television* (Washington, D.C.), vol. 25, no. 2, Summer 1997.

Elsaesser, Thomas, "Fritz Lang: The Illusion of Mastery," in *Sight & Sound* (London), vol. 10, no. 1, January 2000.

* * *

The year 1927 witnessed the appearance in Germany of the most significant utopian film of the silent era—*Metropolis*. In the film, director Fritz Lang achieves the realization of his ideas about the possible future organization of society. The introductory sequences present this social organization in a very attractive light. In a magnificent, gigantic city with gleaming skyscrapers, suspension bridges, and bustling street, people live in comfort and plenty, with every possibility for intellectual and physical development. However, Metropolis is not a city of freedom and equality. Below ground, working for the chosen elite, are masses of nameless workers who have no more value within the social order than a cog in a machine or a tool or production. It is for this reason that the workers revolt and almost destroy the city; only then is there a reconciliation and an equalization of rights for the two strata, the elite and the workers. Lang honestly believed in this idea of reconciliation, and his attitude to a certain extent reflected the German reality, in which there were growing indications of stabilization and attempts to resolve social problems. But Lang's views on these questions, conveyed finally in the reconciliation of the two classes under the slogan "the heart must serve as intermediary between the brain and the hands," did not sound convincingly progressive, either when the film was made or in the years that followed. Lang himself acknowledged this when, after the Nazi *Putsch*, Propaganda Minister Goebbels had him summoned: "(Goebbels) told me that years before, he and Hitler had seen my film *Metropolis* in some small town and that at that time Hitler declared that he would like me to make Nazi films." (Siegfried Kracauer: *From Caligari to Hitler: A Psychological History of the German Film*.)

In the 1920s Lang was strongly influenced by Expressionist film, particularly its artistic forms. Originally an architect, Lang was a man of unusually sensitive visual perceptions. His films of those years show an expressionistic sense for the plastic and the lighting, which emphasized architectonic lines and conveyed a sense of geometric construction that not only extends to the sets and the depicted milieu but even influenced the positioning of the actors in individual shots. In *Metropolis* the artistic techniques of expressionism were more in evidence than in Lang's previous films, which were temporally closer to the greatest blossoming of that movement in the cinema. In keeping with the conventions of expressionism, the inhabitants of the subterranean city have no individuality, and the crowd represents a compact mass from which personality projects only as a stark exception and only in a definite rhythm. Extreme stylization is used in scenes depicting the alternation of work shifts. Lang also shapes space with the help of human bodies and uses light in accordance with the principles of expressionism. Sometimes he uses light so intensively that it takes the place of sound; for example, reflectors replace a siren with light functioning as an outcry. The pictorial formulation also reflects the antagonism between the ideas in the film. A salient example is the contrast between the supermodern metropolis of the future and the house of the scientist Rotwang, the spiritual creator of Metropolis. His dwelling in the shadows of the skyscrapers belongs more to the age when alchemists attempted to discover the philosophers' stone and the elixir of life, and the clay figure of the Golem roamed the streets. Also in his appearance and behavior, Rotwang does not fit the stereotype of a modern scientist, and there are indications that he may be in league with the devil.

Metropolis inaugurated a series of utopias on film that attempted to resolve the difficulties of the contemporary state of society by projecting them into a story with a futuristic setting. The film was preceded by a large public relations campaign which stressed the grandiose nature of what was at the time a super-production by detailing and enumerating all the costs of production and the individual components (how many costumes were used in the film, how many wigs, how many extras, etc.). The premiere took place in an atmosphere of great expectation. However, the reactions of contemporary critics and reviews show that the film was, to some extent, a disappointment. There were great reservations about the plot and content, and the script by Lang's wife, Thea von Harbou, came under sharp attack. H. G. Wells, the well-known English writer of science fiction novels, criticized the film in unusually harsh terms.

Despite the reservations about the film voiced by its contemporaries and by other generations, it cannot be denied that the story of *Metropolis* is told in refined cinematic language. On this point even some critics of the 1920s agree. With the passage of time it has become possible to ascertain the film's contribution and its influence on the development of filmmaking. The film contained a number of technical innovations and influenced, for example, the narrative Hollywood films of the 1930s and 1940s. From the standpoint of film as visual art, one could cite sequences which remain to the present day examples of the potential of the film image to generate meaning. *Metropolis* particularly influenced the development of the science fiction genre. German expressionism brought new codes of artistic expression to the whole current of fantasy—uneven lines, contrasts of light and dark, half-shadows and silhouettes—which serve to suggest mysterious and menacing actions, events, and emotions. Lang applied these techniques effectively and successfully to one of the varieties of the fantasy genre—the utopian work (in modern terminology, science fiction). Some of these elements were still used in the science fiction genre when the rest of the cinema was no longer influenced by expressionism. The amorphous mass or the nameless crowd, as depicted by Lang, found its continuation in anti-utopian films of the postwar years. The wondrous atmosphere of the scene in which Rotwang brings a robot to life is encountered in a number of subsequent science fiction films, especially those that border on horror, as in *The Bride of Frankenstein*. Of course, Lang's robot, with its glittering female body, stylized breasts and inhuman mask instead of a face, is unsurpassed in its artistic beauty. The personality of the scientist Rotwang belongs to one of the most interesting antagonists of the screen. The possibility of an ambivalent interpretation of is character—he is a scientist, but also something of a sorcerer allied with satanic forces—gives him greater complexity. This character type recurs in films of the 1930s and 1940s (*Son of Frankenstein*) and continues without major changes into the most recent science fiction films, as well as into numerous horror and fantasy films.

Diverse audience response to the film's premiere influenced its fate in later years. For its time, *Metropolis* was a lengthy work. Its partial failure resulted in its release often with modifications, cuts, and abridgements. In the 1970s the film archive of the German Democratic Republic in Berlin undertook a reconstruction of the film; the work was completed in 1981 with the collaboration of several member archives of the International Federation of Film Archives (F.I.A.F.) and other film collectors. The result was an approximation of Lang's original version.

—B. Urgosíková

THE MIDDLEMAN

See **JANA ARANYA**

MIDNIGHT COWBOY

USA, 1969

Director: John Schlesinger

Production: Jerome Hellman Productions; DeLuxe colour, 35mm; running time: 113 minutes. Filmed in New York, 1968.

Producer: Jerome Hellman; **screenplay:** Waldo Salt, based on the novel by James Leo Herlihy; **photography:** Adam Holender; **editor:** Hugh A. Robertson; **assistant director:** Michael Childers; **production design:** John R. Lloyd; **music:** John Barry; **sound:** Jack Fizstephens, Vincent Connelly.

Cast: Jon Voight (*Joe Buck*); Dustin Hoffman (*Ratso Rizzo*); Sylvia Miles (*Cass*); Brenda Vaccaro (*Shirley*); John McGiver (*Mr. O'Daniel*); Barnard Hughes (*Towny*); Ruth White (*Sally Buck*); Jennifer Salt (*Annie*).

Awards: Oscars for Best Picture, Best Director, and Best Adapted Screenplay, 1969.

Midnight Cowboy

Publications

Books:

Marcus, F. H., editor, *Film and Literature: contrasts in media*, New York, 1971.

Brooker, Nancy J., editor, *John Schlesinger: A Guide to References & Resources*, London, 1978.

Phillips, Gene D., *John Schlesinger*, Boston, 1981.

Kagan, Norman, *Greenhorns: Foreign filmmakers interpret America*, Ann Arbor, Michigan, 1982.

Brode, Douglas, *The Films of Dustin Hoffman*, Secaucus, 1988.

Articles:

Variety (New York), 14 May 1969.

Dawson, J., *Sight and Sound* (London), Autumn 1969.

Gow, Gordon, *Films and Filming* (London), October 1969.

Wilson, D., *Monthly Film Bulletin* (London), January 1970.

Fiore, R.L., "The Picaresque Tradition in *Midnight Cowboy*," in *Literature/Film Quarterly* (Berkeley), Summer 1975.

Raman, N.K., "Individualism and the Pseudo-Epic Sensibility," in *Deep Focus* (Bangalor), vol. 3, no. 2, 1990.

Spotnitz, Frank, "John Schlesinger: A Director with a Blueprint and a 'Pincher' of Ideas," in *American Film*, vol. 16, no. 1, January 1991.

Moon, M., "Outlaw Sex and the 'Search for America': Representing Male Prostitution and Perverse Desire in Sixties Film (*My Hustler* and *Midnight Cowboy*)," in *Quarterly Review of Film and Video* (Reading), vol. 15, no. 1, November 1993.

Porton, Richard, and Lee Ellickson, "Reflections of an Englishman Abroad," in *Cineaste* (New York), vol. 20, no. 4, 1994.

"John Schlesinger, Joe Buck and Ratso," in *New Yorker*, vol. 70, no. 2, 28 February 1994.

Kort, Michele, "After 'Midnight,'" in *The Advocate*, no. 651, 22 March 1994.

Biskind, P., "The Other Side of 'Midnight,'" in *Premiere* (New York), vol. 7, April 1994.

Daly, Steve, "*Midnight Cowboy:* Everybody's Still Talkin' about It," *Entertainment Weekly* (New York), March 1995.

Berg, J., "*Midnight Cowboy* 25th Anniversary Edition," in *Film Threat* (Beverly Hills), no. 21, April 1995.

Nocenti, A., "My Father, Waldo Salt," "Directing *Midnight Cowboy*," and "Producing *Midnight Cowboy*," in *Scenario* (Rockville), vol. 3, no. 4, 1997.

Salt, W., in *Scenario* (Rockville), vol. 3, no. 4, 1997.

Price, Victoria, "A Life on the Edge," in *The Advocate*, 28 March 2000.

* * *

John Schlesinger wanted to make a film of James Leo Herlihy's 1965 novel *Midnight Cowboy* soon after it was published. When he suggested the project to United Artists, however, he found that a reader in their story department had already submitted an unfavourable report on the book. The reader said that the action of the novel went steadily downhill from the outset, and had recommended that the company not acquire the film rights. Schlesinger, on the other hand, saw dramatic possibilities in the story of a Texan named Joe Buck, who comes to New York with illusions that he can make easy money as a male companion to wealthy women. United Artists eventually decided to let him make *Midnight Cowboy* (1969), and the film won Academy Awards for best director, best adapted screenplay, and best film; and was a huge financial success in both America and England.

Joe (Jon Voight) is himself taken advantage of repeatedly by the assortment of tough and desperate individuals he encounters in the course of his descent into the netherworld of New York's slums, and at one point it looks as if he will become as ruthless as the rest. However, he makes a friend of Ratso Rizzo (Dustin Hoffman), a repulsive-looking bum who needs companionship as much as Joe does; and the two take refuge in each other's friendship. Their relationship is not homosexual; rather, as Schlesinger pointed out to this writer, the story shows "how two men can have a meaningful relationship without being homosexual." The film is faithful to the novel from which it is derived, but Schlesinger and screenwriter Waldo Salt exercised some degree of freedom in adapting it to the screen. The first third of the novel, dealing with Joe's lonely youth, is compressed into a few fragmented flashbacks, as he makes his way cross-country by bus. These flashbacks indicate how unsuccessful Joe's search for friendship and love has been up to this point and explain why Ratso is fulfilling a need in Joe's emotional life.

There is an interesting religious dimension that becomes apparent in the film when one examines it in-depth. While Joe travels cross-country on his way to New York, his Bible-belt religious formation is sketched for us as he listens to a faith healer preaching on the radio and notices through the bus window the words "Jesus Saves" painted on the roof of an abandoned shed. Once in New York Joe meets a Mr. O'Daniel (John McGiver), a religious fanatic who tries to force Joe to pray with him before a garish statue of Christ that flashes on and off like a neon sign. As Joe escapes from Mr. O'Daniel's shabby hotel room, Schlesinger intercuts shots of Joe's boyhood baptism in a river. Though Joe's religious experiences have not always been pleasant, there is inbred in him a need for some kind of religious belief to give meaning and purpose to his life. Significantly, the only friend that Joe makes in New York is Ratso, an Italian Catholic from the Bronx, who sleeps in the condemned tenement they share with a picture of Christ hanging over his bed. Small church candles provide illumination at night because the electric power has long since been shut off. These and other religious references in the film have a cumulative effect on the viewer. "Is God dead?" a bishop asks rhetorically in a TV sermon. One might be tempted to answer "yes"—at least in the corrupt world in which Joe finds himself among the low life of New York's slums. Yet these isolated reminders of religion, which Joe encounters throughout the film, are like so many souvenirs of a faith that he has somehow mislaid, but which he has never completely abandoned hope of finding again. It is true that Joe does not have his faith in God strengthened in any explicit way in the picture but through his friendship with Ratso, he does have his faith in mankind restored; and that in itself is significant.

As their various money-making schemes fail ludicrously, Joe and Ratso begin to care about each other's welfare—something that has never happened to either of them before. Joe literally sells his blood for money in order to buy medicine for his tubercular friend. Joe and Ratso are like two orphans in a storm, huddling together for safety. More than once they are photographed through a fence, implying that they are imprisoned together in a cruel and indifferent world and must stick together for survival. It is all the more poignant, therefore, when Joe and Ratso both begin to realize that Ratso's illness is fatal and that he is never going to recover. Frantically, Joe steals money to take Ratso to Florida before he dies, since they have both looked forward to going there as a kind of retreat to a benign earthly paradise, however Ratso dies aboard the bus just before they reach their destination. Joe, tears in his eyes, puts his arm around Ratso in the only overt gesture of affection in the film. The ending, nonetheless, is not pessimistic. Having experienced the friendship denied him in youth, Joe is ready to embark on a more mature way of life; his adolescent illusions about the easy life are now shattered.

Schlesinger says that he tried to breathe into the film ''the mixture of desperation and humour'' which he found all along Forty-second Street in New York while filming there, and in fact he does. It is noteworthy that a British director could bring such an authentic sense of realism to a film made in what for him is a foreign country. He has captured the atmosphere of New York, Miami Beach, and the Texas Pandhandle in *Midnight Cowboy* as surely as he captured the atmosphere of his native England in films like *Sunday, Bloody Sunday.*

—Gene D. Phillips

MIDNIGHT EXPRESS

UK, 1978

Director: Alan Parker

Production: Casablanca Film Works, for Columbia; Eastmancolor, 35mm; running time: 123 minutes.

Producers: David Puttnam, Alan Marshall; **screenplay:** Oliver Stone, based on the novel by Billy Hayes and William Hoffner; **photography:** Michael Seresin; **editor:** Gerry Hambling; **assistant directors:** Ray Corbett, David Wimbury, Kieron Phipps; **production design:** Geoffrey Kirkland; **art director:** Evan Hercules; **music:** Giorgio Moroder; **sound editor:** Rusty Coppleman; **sound recording:** Clive Winter; **costumes:** Milena Canonero.

Cast: Brad Davis (*Billy Hayes*); Randy Quaid (*Jimmy Booth*); John Hurt (*Max*); Irene Miracle (*Susan*); Bo Hopkins (*Tex*); Paolio Bonaccelli (*Rifki*); Paul Smith (*Hamidou*); Norbert Weisser (*Erich*); Mike Kellin (*Mr. Hayes*).

Awards: Oscars for Best Adapted Screenplay, and Best Score, 1978.

Publications

Books:

Hayes, Billy and William Hoffer, *Midnight Express*, New York, 1977.
Hacker, Jonathan, and David Price, *Take 10—Contemporary British Directors*, Oxford 1991.

Articles:

Variety (New York), 24 May 1978.
Gourdon, G., *Cinématographe* (Paris), June 1978.
Pym, J., *Monthly Film Bulletin* (London), July 1978.
Maupin, F., *Image et Son* (Paris), September 1978.
Gastellier, F., *Jeune Cinéma* (Paris), October 1978.
Ansen, David, ''Turkey Hash,'' in *Newsweek* (New York), 16 October 1978.
Schickel, Richard, ''Ugly Trips,'' in *Time* (New York), 16 October 1978.
Magny, J., *Cinéma* (Paris), November 1978.
Nordlinger, N., ''The Making of *Midnight Express*,'' in *Filmmakers Monthly* (London), November 1978.
Hodenfield, Chris and Angela Gavdioso, ''The Man Who Got Away,'' in *Rolling Stone* (New York), 30 November 1978.
Biskind, P., *Cineaste* (New York), Winter 1978–79.
Beaulieu, J., *Séquences* (Montreal), January 1979.
''Alan Parker: Director of *Midnight Express* and *Angel Heart*,'' an interview, in American *Film* (Washington, D.C.), January/February 1988.
''Michael Apted and Alan Parker,'' an interview, in *American Film*, vol. 15, no. 12, September 1990.
Basutcu, M., ''The Power and the Danger of the Image,'' in *Cinemaya* (New Delhi), no. 17/18, Autumn/Winter 1992/1993.
''Parker, Alan,'' in *Current Biography*, vol. 55, no. 3, March 1994.

* * *

British director Alan Parker told *American Film* in 1988, ''It's not my job to make you comfortable in the cinema.'' He was referring to several films in his body of work like *Shoot the Moon* and *Birdy*, but none was more uncomfortable and disturbing than *Midnight Express* (1978), a film based on the real-life story of Billy Hayes, a 23-year-old American who spent five long, agonizing years in a Turkish prison for attempting to smuggle two kilos of hashish on his way home to the USA in 1970.

Midnight Express could have been a garden variety prison picture, except for several interesting plot twists—not all factual—that place it above most films in the genre. First, there was the painful revelation that Americans, ignorant of justice systems abroad, can find themselves in trouble, with the US Government and/or its representatives often times powerless to help. As the real-life Hayes toured the college lecture circuit, according to *Rolling Stone*, he ''found the same stunning ignorance of international law among college students all over.'' He confessed, ''I was an idiot, and there are more just like me who got the brunt of it. The rich, powerful heroin dealers never got caught. Once I got through customs I thought, 'You clever son of a bitch, you really did it.''' But he didn't.

Secondly, there was the hellish nature of Sagmalcilar, the Turkish prison itself, a damp, decaying, rat-infested medieval dungeon where beatings and torture were routine for even the slightest infractions. Parker's portrayal of the turkish people and the prison system drew harsh criticism, causing the director to lament years later, ''Yes. . . there wasn't a pleasant Turk in it. Looking back, I think that I was possibly politically naïve in that respect. I was so concentrated, so determined to make a film about what I thought was an unjust, unfair prison system—which just happened to be in Turkey.'' Hayes, however, was less sympathetic to the outcries: ''If they don't like it, they should do something about the system, *not* the film. You are not seeing the Turkish people, you're seeing the lowest stratum of society, it's prisons. It's like seeing *Short Eyes* and saying it's a brutal picture of American life.''

Midnight Express

Thirdly, there was the injustice of Billy's sentence. Originally given four years, his sentence was appealed by the prosecutor to a higher court in Ankara in order to make him a political example, since President Nixon had been putting pressure on the Turkish government to curb poppy production by some 200,000 Turkish farmers. The result was that Billy's sentence was changed to life imprisonment with the possibility of parole in 30 years.

Finally, there was the revelation of Hayes' homosexual relationship with a Swedish inmate, prompting reviewer Richard Shickel of *Newsweek* to remark, ''From the first gorgeously modeled shot of Billy stripped before his captors to the hazy sequence of him and a friend doing yoga exercises behind bars (so reminiscent of the nude wrestling scene in *Women in Love*), to the final farewell kiss Billy bestows on yet another male before his escape, we are in the possession of perverse romanticism, or should one say romantic perversity?''

Much of the criticism surrounding the actual versus fictional events of *Midnight Express* can be traced to the often problematic adaptation of novels into film, as Chris Hodenfield of *Rolling Stone* noted, ''Hayes' book is about struggle. The movie focuses on decay.'' Newcomer Oliver Stone (who would go on to become one of the more controversial directors of the 1980s with such films as *Platoon*, *Born on the Fourth of July*, *JFK*, and *Natural Born Killers*) penned the adaptation of *Midnight Express*, taking a number of liberties with the novel apparently for the purpose of enhancing the film's violent assault on the senses, while at the same time turning the film into a ''statement film'' on human rights abuses abroad: (1) In real life, Billy slipped into the airport quite confidently, but the movie depicts him as sweating profusely as he passes nervously through customs and just before the two kilos of hashish taped to his body are found by the Turkish military looking for weapons or bombs carried by would-be hijackers; (2) the fictitious speech Billy delivers to the Turkish court was denounced by reviewer David Ansen of *Newsweek* when he wrote, ''Especially disturbing is the film's eagerness to arouse the worst xenophobic fantasies: scriptwriter Oliver Stone even invents an impassioned speech in which Billy denounces the Turks as pigs''; (3) Billy never murdered anyone in prison, much less his prison keeper, the brutal Hamidou, to escape to freedom; the man was actually gunned down in a café by a former Turkish inmate at Sagmalcilar prison; (4) the Billy Hayes that actor Brad Davis portrays in the film is the total opposite of the real Mr. Hayes in both looks and in his spectacularly violent actions—like ripping out the tongue of fellow inmate Rifki (a Turkih prisoner who rats on Billy's friend Max) with his own teeth; in real life this incident never happened. The downplaying of factual events, such as the relationship between Billy and the Swedish inmate, Erich, was apparently a conscious decision to make the sexual aspect of the story much more palpable and digestible for general audiences. To dismiss it completely would have been a violation of the material. To integrate it more fully might have undermined the film's hero in the eyes of the movie-going public. Even so, Hayes was quick to remark to the press: ''Columbia [Pictures] is going to hate me, but I think it's the only cop-out in the movie.'' The manufactured scenes designed to bolster the action and the violence tend to undermine the film's credibility in the long term, but obviously added to the film's overall impact. The real Mr. Hayes had the option of taking his name off the film's credits if he didn't like it, but admitted to *Rolling Stone*, ''I loved the movie. I don't want to hear about gratuitous violence. It was tokenism next to Sagmalcilar prison.'' But Hodenfield notes in his *Rolling Stone* review, Hayes' novel makes for ''a fine yarn, natural for the movies,'' giving pause to wonder if any of the invented scenes were necessary at all to enhance the story.

Despite criticisms *Midnight Express* stands out as one of the most remarkable thrillers in the 1970s, and certainly one of the more memorable prison pictures ever filmed. At the time of its release in 1978, approximately 330 Americans were still sitting in foreign prisons on drug related charges. If the film had any social impact at all, it helped to wise up an entire society—one that had become, by the late 1970s, fairly comfortable with recreational drug use—about the consequences of drug involvement abroad.

—Donald R. Mott

MILDRED PIERCE

USA, 1945

Director: Michael Curtiz

Production: Warner Bros.; black and white; running time: 110 minutes. Released October 1945.

Producer: Jerry Wald; **screenplay:** Ranald Macdougal and Catherine Turney, from the novel by James M. Cain; **photography:** Ernest Haller; **editor:** David Weisbart; **art director:** Anton Grot; **special effects:** Willard Van Enger; **music:** Max Steiner.

Cast: Joan Crawford (*Mildred Pierce*); Jack Carson (*Wally*); Zachary Scott (*Monty Beragon*); Eve Arden (*Ida*); Bruce Bennett (*Bert Pierce*); Ann Blyth (*Veda Pierce*); Jo Ann Marlowe (*Kay Pierce*); Mannart Kippen (*Dr. Gale*); Lee Patrick (*Mrs. Biederhof*); Moroni Olsen (*Inspector Peterson*); Barbara Brown (*Mrs. Forrester*); Charles Trowbridge (*Mr. Williams*); John Compton (*Ted Forrester*); Butterfly McQueen (*Lottie*); Chester Clute (*Mr. Jones*).

Award: Oscar for Best Actress (Crawford), 1945.

Publications

Script:

Macdougall, Ranald, and Catherine Turney, *Mildred Pierce*, edited by Albert J. La Valley, Madison, Wisconsin, 1980.

Books:

Tyler, Parker, *Magic and Myth of the Movies*, New York, 1947.
Quirk, Lawrence J., *The Films of Joan Crawford*, New York, 1968; Secaucus, 1988.
Canham, Kingsley, *Michael Curtiz, Raoul Walsh, Henry Hathaway*, London, 1973.
Harvey, Stephen, *Joan Crawford*, New York, 1974.
Thomas, Bob, *Joan Crawford: A Biography*, New York, 1978.
Crawford, Christina, *Mommie Dearest*, New York, 1978; London, 1979.
Kaplan, E. Ann, editor, *Women in Film Noir*, London, 1978; revised edition, 1980.
Rosenzweig, Sidney, *''Casablanca'' and Other Major Films of Michael Curtiz*, Ann Arbor, Michigan, 1982.
Walker, Alexander, *Joan Crawford: The Ultimate Star*, London and New York, 1983.
Walsh, Andrea S., *Women's Films and Female Experience*, New York, 1984.
Arden, Eve, *Three Phases of Eve: An Autobiography*, New York, 1985.
Kinnard, Roy, and R. J. Vitone, *The American Films of Michael Curtiz*, Metuchen, New Jersey, 1986.
Gledhill, Christine, editor, *Home Is Where the Heart Is: Studies in Melodrama and the Woman's Film*, London, 1987.
Robertson, James C., *The Casablanca Man: The Career of Michael Curtiz*, New York, 1993.
Guiles, Fred L., *Joan Crawford: The Last Word*, Secaucus, New Jersey, 1995.

Articles:

New York Times, 29 September 1945.
Monthly Film Bulletin (London), March 1946.
Kine Weekly (London), 14 March 1946.
Times (London), 29 April 1946.
Quirk, Lawrence J., ''Joan Crawford,'' in *Films in Review* (New York), January 1965.
Nolan, Jack Edmund, ''Michael Curtiz,'' in *Films in Review* (New York), no. 9, 1970.
David, John, ''The Tragedy of Mildred Pierce,'' in *Velvet Light Trap* (Madison, Wisconsin), Fall 1972.
Cahiers de la Cinémathèque (Perpignan), Summer 1976.
Nelson, Joyce, ''*Mildred Pierce* Reconsidered,'' in *Film Reader* (Evanston, Illinois), January 1977.
Gorbman, C., ''The Drama's Melos: Max Steiner and Mildred Pierce,'' in *Velvet Light Trap* (Madison, Wisconsin), no. 19, 1982.

Mildred Pierce

Film Reader (Evanston, Illinois), no. 5, 1982.
Krutmik, Frank, ''Desire, Transgression, and James M. Cain,'' in *Screen* (London), May-June 1982.
Literature/Film Quarterly (Salisbury, Maryland), vol. 11, no. 1, 1983.
Historical Journal of Film, Radio, and Television (Abingdon, Oxfordshire), vol. 3, no. 1, 1983.
Waymark, Peter, in *Times* (London), 11 August 1984.
Roodnat, J. ''Femme fatale: Maar niet heus,'' in *Skoop* (Amsterdam), November 1984.
Ward, L.E., ''The Great Films: *Mildred Pierce*,'' in *Classic Images* (Muscatine), no. 119, May 1985.
Telotte, J.P., ''A Consuming Passion: Food and Film Noir,'' in *Georgia Review*, vol. 39, no. 2, 1985.
Buller, R., ''James M. Cain: The Hollywood Years (1944–1946),'' in *Hollywood Studio Magazine* (Studio City), vol. 18, no. 11, 1985.
Rivera, A., ''The Ideological Function of Genres in *Mildred Pierce*,'' in *Imagenes* (Hato Rey), vol. 3, no. 1, 1987.
Scheman, N., ''Missing Mothers/Desiring Daughters: Framing the Sight of Women,'' in *Critical Inquiry*, vol. 15, no. 1, 1988.
Robertson, P., ''Structural Irony in *Mildred Pierce*, or How Mildred Lost Her Tongue,'' in *Cinema Journal* (Austin, Texas), no. 1, 1990.
Hollinger, K., ''Listening to the Female Voice in the Woman's Film,'' in *Film Criticism* (Meadville, Pennsylvania), no. 3, 1992.
Haralovich, M. B., ''Too Much Guilt Is Never Enough for Working Mothers: Joan Crawford, *Mildred Pierce*, and *Mommie Dearest*,'' in *Velvet Light Trap* (Madison, Wisconsin), Spring 1992.
Seville, J., ''The Laser's Edge: James M. Cain and Film Noir,'' in *Classic Images* (Muscatine), no. 210, December 1992.
Weiss, J., ''Feminist Film Theory and Women's History: *Mildred Pierce* and the Twentieth Century,'' in *Film & History*, vol. 22, no. 3, 1992.
Boozer, J., Jr., ''Entrepreneurs and 'Family Values' in the Postwar Film,'' in *Florida State University Conference on Literature and Film*, vol. 18, 1993.
Fox-Genovese, Elizabeth, ''Mixed Messages: Women and the Impact of World War II,'' in *Southern Humanities Review*, vol. 27, no. 3, Summer 1993.
Williams, L., and G. Vencendeau, ''*Mildred Pierce*, la Seconde Guerre mondiale et la theorie feministe du cinema,'' in *Cinemaction* (Conde-sur-Noireau, France), no. 2, 1993.
Phelps, D., ''Gros Garcon,'' in *Film Comment* (New York), September-October 1993.

Hindes, Andrew, ''Surprise Endings Highlight Actress Award Competition,'' in *Variety* (New York), vol. 357, no. 9, 2 January 1995.
Garrett, Greg, ''The Many Faces of Mildred Pierce: A Case Study of Adaptation and the Studio System,'' in *Literature/Film Quarterly* (Salisbury), vol. 23, no. 4, October 1995.
Lyons, Donald, ''Iron Mike: At Home with Michael Curtiz,'' in *Film Comment* (New York), vol. 32, no. 2, March-April 1996.

* * *

When Monty Beragon (Scott), a playboy whose worthlessness is immediately apparent from his thin moustache and quivering chin, is shot dead in a shadowy beach house—a triumphantly *noir*-ish opening sequence—restaurateur Mildred Pierce (Crawford) confesses to the crime and her complicated life story unfolds in a series of flashbacks. As in the other great James M. Cain adaption of the 1940s, *Double Indemnity*, a confessional narration ''explains'' to us the route which has taken the central character from a brightly lit, drably ordinary daytime world into a nightmare of carnality, criminality, corruption, and chaos. Mildred walks out on her marriage to dull, struggling middle-class broker Bert (Bennett) so that she can provide for her spoiled, petulant, demanding daughter Veda (Blyth). Becoming a waitress, which causes the nasty teenager to turn snobbishly against her, Mildred struggles for a living, and finally opens a restaurant, ''Mildred's,'' which becomes a successful chain. Meanwhile, she is torn between the romantic advances of the puzzled and decent Bert, the smarmily lecherous Wally (Carson), and the slickly empty Monty. She marries the playboy, and he squanders her hard-won fortune while making a play for the tramp Veda. Unlike *Double Indemnity*, which is notable for Walter Neff's unflinchingly honest confession, the film leads up to a series of revelations which cast doubt over what we have seen. Although the movie generally reveals the truths about the characters that they are trying to hide, Mildred's confessional narration is essentially a lie, designed first to throw suspicion on Wally and, then, to claim the guilt for herself, though it was actually Veda who committed the murder.

Mildred Pierce is an unusual *film noir*, in that the *amour fou* which drags the central character down into the gutter inhabited by such doomed protagonists as Edward G. Robinson in *Scarlet Street* or Robert Mitchum in *Out of the Past* is not sexual in nature. Crawford's Mildred, one of the few obsessional female protagonists in the genre, is in the line of material sacrifice that extends throughout the women's weepie genre from *Stella Dallas* to *Terms of Endearment*, while Ann Blyth's girlish monster is a less substantial *femme fatale* than is usual in *noir*, almost like the petulant teenager who will grow up into Barbara Stanwyck's Phyllis Dietrichson in *Double Indemnity*, and all the more horrifying for her lack of psychotic class. The film is rooted in the shadowy alleyways of *film noir*, and the director, Michael Curtiz, and the cinematographer, Ernest Haller, use the darkest possible compositions, while the composer, Max Steiner, overlays a driving, downbeat, relentless score to add to the oppression. A perfectly assembled Warner Brothers contract stable supporting cast—including Eve Arden as the heroine's traditional wisecracking girlfriend—are exactly right as a collection of variously feckless, selfish, flawed, and feebler-than-Joan Crawford characters.

This is a film full of night and rain, of trapped characters struggling against their situations, dragged down by their weaknesses. But *Mildred Pierce* is at least as much a woman's picture as it is a *film noir.* The versatile and visionary Curtiz, whose only pure *noir* was *The Unsuspected*, was here channelled by ex-journalist producer Jerry Wald, whose allegiance to the form resulted in such female-centered psychodramas as *Humoresque*, *Possessed*, *Flamingo Road*, *Caged*, *Miss Sadie Thompson*, and *Peyton Place.* Wald's women suffer, but generally come through in the end, and Mildred is saved despite herself, as Veda is dragged off screaming, ''I'll change, I promise I will,'' to Tehachapi while Bert reappears to take the heroine off to a possible happy ending. Whereas the male protagonists of *Scarlet Street* or *Double Indemnity* were too corrupt in their love to be free even after they have murdered their scheming mistresses, Mildred can be redeemed because her maternal love, though misguided, is untainted by sin. (Given the posthumous image of Crawford presented by *Mommie Dearest*, this aspect of the film has a heavy irony now.) Her essential strength of character, the quality which makes her movie heroine material and the quintessential Joan Crawford role, is rewarded in the understated but emotive fade-out by the implication of a bright future.

—Kim Newman

LE MILLION

France, 1931

Director: René Clair

Production: Films Sonores Tobis (France); black and white, 35mm; running time: 89 minutes. Released 1931.

Producer: Frank Clifford; **screenplay:** René Clair, from the musical comedy by Georges Berr and M. Guillemaud; **photography:** Georges Périnal and Georges Raulet; **production designer:** Lazare Meerson; **music:** Georges Van Parys, Armand Bernard and Philippe Parès.

Cast: René Lefèvre (*Michel*); Annabella (*Beatrice*); Louis Allibert (*Prosper*); Vanda Gréville (*Vanda*); Paul Olivier (*Father Tulipe, a gangster*); Odette Talazac (*Prima donna*); Constantin Stroësco (*Sopranelli, the tenor*); Raymond Cordy (*Taxi driver*).

Publications

Script:

Clair, René, *Le Million*, in *Avant-Scène Cinéma* (Paris), March 1988.

Books:

Rotha, Paul, *Celluloid; The Film Today*, London, 1931.
Viazzi, G., *René Clair*, Milan, 1946.
Bourgeois, J., *René Clair*, Geneva, 1949.
Charensol, Georges, and Roger Regent, *Un Maître du cinéma: René Clair*, Paris, 1952.
Manvell, Roger, *The Film and the Public*, London, 1955.
Solmi, A., *Tre maestri del cinema*, Milan, 1956.
De La Roche, Catherine, *René Clair: An Index*, London, 1958.
Amengual, Barthélemy, *René Clair*, Paris, 1963; revised edition, 1969.
Mitry, Jean, *René Clair*, Paris, 1969.

Le Million

Samuels, Charles Thomas, *Encountering Directors*, New York, 1972.
McGerr, Celia, *René Clair*, Boston, 1980.
Warfield, Nancy, *René Clair's Grand Maneuver*, New York, 1982.
Barrot, Oliver, *René Clair; ou, Le Temps mesuré*, Renens, Switzerland, 1985.
Greene, Naomi, *René Clair: A Guide to References and Resources*, Boston, 1985.
Dale, R. C., *The Films of René Clair*, Metuchen, New Jersey, 2 vols., 1986.
Billard, Pierre, *Le mystére René Clair*, Paris, 1998.

Articles:

New York Times, 21 May 1931.
Variety (New York), 27 May 1931.
Potamkin, Harry, ''René Clair and Film Humor,'' in *Hound and Horn* (New York), October-December 1932.
Causton, Bernard, ''A Conversation with René Clair,'' in *Sight and Sound* (London), Winter 1933.
Jacobs, Lewis, ''The Films of René Clair,'' in *New Theatre* (New York), February 1936.
Lambert, Gavin, ''The Films of René Clair,'' in *Sequence* (London), no. 6, 1949.
''Clair Issue'' of *Bianco e Nero* (Rome), August-September 1951.
Berti, V., ''L'arte del comico in René Clair,'' in *Bianco e Nero* (Rome), March-April 1968.
Helman, A., in *Kino* (Warsaw), June 1974.
Fischer, L., ''René Clair, *Le Million*, and the Coming of Sound,'' in *Cinema Journal* (Iowa City), Spring 1977.
Milne, Tom, in *Monthly Film Bulletin* (London), November 1977.
Adair, Gilbert, ''Utopia Ltd.: The Cinema of René Clair,'' in *Sight and Sound* (London), Summer 1981.
Avant-Scène du Cinéma (Paris), no. 369, March 1988.
Faulkner, C., ''René Clair, Marcel Pagnol and the Social Dimensions of Speech,'' in *Screen* (Oxford), vol. 35, no. 2, 1994.
Pappas, Ben, ''*Le Million*,'' in *Forbes*, vol. 161, no. 6, 23 March 1998.
Trumpener, Katie, ''The René Clair Moment and the Overlap Films of the Early 1930s: Detlef Sierck's *April, April!*,'' in *Film Criticism* (Meadville), Winter-Spring 1999.

* * *

Of the series of comedies that René Clair made for Tobis Films at the beginning of the sound era, *Le million* remains the most satisfying. It was preceded by the half-silent/half-musical *Under the Roofs of Paris* and followed by *A nous la liberté*, making Clair the first internationally acclaimed sound film director.

Clair had become one of the most vociferous opponents of the sound film, claiming that it could only mire down the silent film's flights of images. He had begun his career with the anarchic *Paris qui dort* (1923) and *Entr'acte* (1924), and he feared the added equipment and personnel, the excessively wordy scripts, and the close-ups of the actors speaking those scripts. It took someone as skeptical as Clair to overcome these problems in the early sound film. In *Under the Roofs of Paris* he freed the camera from street singers and let it scale an apartment house, peering in at every floor to watch the effects of their song. He joked with the medium by cutting the sound when a door was closed. In this way he made the first international talkie a success by keeping talk to a minimum.

With *Le million* his ambitions grew. Every element (sets, lighting, acting, noise, speech, and camerawork) was broken into parts capable of fitting an overriding rhythm that didn't properly belong to any of them. Characters don't walk or gesture so much as half-dance their way from scene to scene. Double chases, near misses, and parallel plots give Clair the chance to syncopate the action with his razor-edge cutting. Scenes are stopped just as one character leaves the frame, and another enters the next. Every shot offers a single dramatic or rhythmic jolt. Ultimately these tidy bits collect on stage for the delightful denouement.

The plot is as symmetrical as the decor. The lyric opera is set off against the bohemian life of two poor artists both in love with a ballerina. Their happiness depends on finding a lottery ticket which through a clever series of reversals finds its way into the jacket of the lead singer in "The Bohemians." The struggle to grab the ticket involves the police and a Robin Hood band led by the master of the underworld, the master of Paris, the master of ceremonies, Père Tulipe. At its height Clair abandons even the abstract tone of natural sound and lays the noise of a rugby crowd over the madcap actions as the jacket is passed from person to person until it appears in the hands of Père Tulipe who produces the winning ticket for our hero.

Afraid of the talkie, Clair gave cinema its purest example of what a lyrical film might be.

—Dudley Andrew

MIRACOLO A MILANO

(Miracle in Milan)

Italy, 1950

Director: Vittorio De Sica

Production: Soc. Produzioni De Sica, in cooperation with Ente Nazionale Industrie Cinematografiche (Rome); black and white, 35mm; running time: 101 minutes, some versions are 95 minutes. Released 1951. Filmed in Milan.

Screenplay: Cesare Zavattini and Vittorio De Sica with Suso Cecchi d'Amico, Mario Chiari, and Adolfo Franci, from the novel *Totò, il buono* by Cesare Zavattini; **photography:** G. R. Aldo; **editor:** Eraldo da Roma; **sound:** Bruno Brunacci; **art director:** Guido Fiorini; **music director:** Alessandro Cicognini; **special effects:** Ned Mann.

Cast: Emma Gramatica; Francesco Golisano; Paolo Stoppa; Gugliemo Barnabò; Brunella Bovo; Anna Carena; Alba Arnova; Flora Cambi; Virgilio Riento; Arturo Bragaglia; Ermino Spalla; Riccardo Bertazzolo; Francesco Rizzone; Angelo Priolil.

Awards: Cannes Film Festival, Grand Priz, 1951; New York Film Critics' Award, Best Foreign Film, 1951.

Publications

Script:

Zavattini, Cesare, and others, *Miracolo a Milano*, New York, 1968; also included in *Bianco e Nero* (Rome), April-June 1983.

Books:

Castello, G. C., *Il cinema neorealistico italiano*, Turin, 1956.
Rondi, Brunello, *Il neorealismo italiano*, Parma, 1956.
Ferrare, Giuseppe, *Il nuovo cinema italiano*, Florence, 1957.
Hovald, Patrice G., *Le Néo-Réalisme italien et ses créateurs*, Paris, 1959.
Agel, Henri, *Vittorio De Sica*, Paris, 1964.
Leprohon, Pierre, *Vittorio De Sica*, Paris, 1966.
Armes, Roy, *Patterns of Realism: A Study of Italian Neo-Realist Cinema*, New York, 1971.
Samuels, Charles Thomas, *Encountering Directors*, New York, 1972.
Guaraldi-Rimini, Mario, editor, *Neorealismo e vita nazionale: Antologia di cinema nuovo*, Florence, 1975.
Mercader, Maria, *La mia vita con Vittorio De Sica*, Milan, 1978.
Anthologie du Cinéma 10, Paris, 1979.
Bolzoni, Francesco, *Quando De Sica era Mister Brown*, Turin, 1984.
Darreta, John, *Vittorio De Sica: A Guide to References and Resources*, Boston, 1988.
Micciché, Lino, *De Sica: autore, regista, attore*, Venice, 1992.
Governi, Giancarlo, *Vittorio de Sica: Parlami d'amore Mariù*, with Anna Maria Bianchi, Rome, 1993.
Nuzzi, Paolo, and Ottavio Iemma, editors, *De Sica & Zavattini: parliamo tanto di noi*, Rome, 1997.

Articles:

Maddison, John, "The Case of De Sica," in *Sight and Sound* (London), June 1951.
New York Times, 18 December 1951.
New Yorker, 5 April 1952.
Grinstein, Alexander, "*Miracle of Milan*: Some Psychoanalytic Notes on a Movie," in *American Image* (Detroit), Fall 1953.
Sargeant, Winthrop, "Profiles: Bread, Love, and Neo-Realismo," in *New Yorker*, 29 June and 6 July 1957.
McVay, Douglas, "Poet of Poverty," in *Films and Filming* (London), October and November 1964.
"De Sica Issue" of *Bianco e Nero* (Rome), September-December 1975.
La Polla, F., "La città e lo spazio," in *Bianco e Nero*, Fall 1976.

Passalacqua, J., ''Vittorio De Sica,'' in *Films in Review* (New York), April 1978.
''De Sica Issue'' of *Avant-Scène du Cinéma* (Paris), 15 October 1978.
Bondanella, P., ''Neorealist Aesthetics and the Fantastic,'' in *Film Criticism* (Edinboro, Pennsylvania), no. 2, 1979.
''De Sica Issue'' of *Cahiers Lumière* (Paris), November 1980.
Cohn, Lawrence, ''De Sica Retro Underway in Gotham,'' in *Variety* (New York), vol. 344, no. 13, 7 October 1991.
Bonadella, Peter, ''Three Neorealist Classics by De Sica,'' in *Cineaste* (New York), vol. 23, no. 1, 1997.

* * *

Miracolo a Milano, which won the Grand Prize at the Cannes Film Festival and was named Best Foreign Film by the New York Film Critics, is one of Vittorio De Sica's lesser masterpieces, not so renowned as *Sciuscia* (1946), *The Bicycle Thief* (1948) and *Two Women* (1960). Today De Sica's reputation as a filmmaker has been diminished by a climate of film criticism which maintains that much of Italian neorealism was little more than an idealistic masquerade. Nonetheless, De Sica contributed much that was powerful and authentic in neorealism, especially with the shattering stark drama of both *Sciuscia* and *The Bicycle Thief*.

The whimsy and fairy tale atmosphere that pervade *Miracolo a Milano* were De Sica's respite from the severity of his earlier films, an exercise in satire and irony which he linked to the world of Hans Christian Anderson wherein ''virtue triumphs and evil is punished.'' He also said that he drew his inspiration from Chaplin and René Clair, an observation confirmed by the first paragraph of the *New York Times* review of the film; but he did not abandon neorealism in *Miracolo a Milano*, as so many critics have suggested. The first half of the film, (based on the novel, *Toto, il buono*, by Cesare Zavattini, de Sica's frequent collaborator) adheres to the documentary re-creation of Milan's impoverished outcasts.

Miracolo a Milano is a modern-day fable which implies that the ''pure in heart'' must seek their heaven apart from earth. Toto the Good (Francesco Golisano) is an orphan who is discovered as a baby in the cabbage patch of the kindly old Lolotta (wonderfully played by the great Emma Gramatica), who teaches him to be good and pure of heart. When she dies, he spends several years in an orphanage after which he becomes an apostle for the beggars of Milan, aided by a white dove which possesses the power of miracles—the dove being a gift from Lolotta, now his guardian angel and benefactress. As he endeavors to improve the life of the beggars he discovers seeds of caste dissent, then their sense of unity is further disrupted by the discovery of oil on their adopted encampment. When they are forced to fight the landowner's police who are armed with billy clubs and tear gas, Toto's only resource is to have his band of hobos snatch up the brooms of street cleaners and fly to a land ''where there is only peace, love, and good.''

De Sica's combination of realism and fantasy is seductive, and his use of the fanciful sometimes overshadows the social commentary about the exploitation and dispossession of the innocent when confronted by the vagaries of poverty and the industrial society. And although De Sica steadfastly refused to admit it, the film has an element of despair, of spiritual quandary, as a dominant theme.

Miracolo a Milano was greeted with sharp denunciation from critics on the Italian right, all of whom accused De Sica of Communist leanings. It was much more wholeheartedly received in the United States, although its many levels of meaning were no less discussed here than in Italy. It is a transitional film in De Sica's career, for with it he moved out of the mainstream of neorealism. It remains a charming salute to the hope and perseverance of the common man, enhanced by the consummate cinematography of G. R. Aldo, a melodious score by Alessandro Cicognini and the wholly believable and unprepossessing acting of a cast made up of professional and non-professional actors.

—Ronald Bowers

MIRROR

See **ZERKALO**

THE MISFITS

USA, 1961

Director: John Huston

Production: Seven Arts Productions; black and white, 35mm and 16mm; running time: 125 minutes.

Producer: Frank E. Taylor; **screenplay:** Arthur Miller; **photography:** Russell Metty; **editor:** George Tomasini; **assistant director:** Carl Beringer; **art directors:** Stephen Grimes, Bill Newberry; **music:** Alex North; **sound recording:** Phil Mitchell.

Cast: Clark Gable (*Gay Langland*); Marilyn Monroe (*Roslyn Taber*); Montgomery Clift (*Perce Howland*); Eli Wallach (*Guido*); Thelma Ritter (*Isabelle Steers*); Kevin McCarthy (*Raymond Taber*).

Publications

Script:

Garret, G.P., and others, *Film Scripts 3*, New York, 1972.

Books:

Kaminsky, Stuart, *John Huston: Maker of Magic*, London, 1978.
Madsen, Axel, *John Huston*, New York, 1978.
Goode, James, *The Making of The Misfits*, Indianapolis, 1986.
McCarthy, John, *The Films of John Huston*, Secaucus, New Jersey, 1987.
Studlar, Gaylyn, editor, and David Desser, *Reflections in a Male Eye: John Huston & the American Experience*, Washington, D.C., 1993.
Cooper, Stephen, editor, *Perspectives on John Huston*, New York, 1994.
Brill, Lesley, *John Huston's Filmmaking*, New York, 1997.
Cohen, Allen, *John Huston: A Guide to References and Resources*, London, 1997.

Articles:

Variety (New York), 1 February 1961.
Cieutat, M., *Positif* (Paris), October 1961.
Oms, Marcel, *Positif* (Paris), September 1961.

The Misfits

Hart, Henry, *Films in Review* (New York), February 1961.
Lejeune, C.A, *Films and Filming* (London), June 1961.
Monthly Film Bulletin (London), July 1961.
Cieutat, Michel, ''*Les Misfits*,'' in *Positif* (Paris), no. 260, October 1982.
Listener, vol. 116, no. 2967, 3 July 1986.
''Miller + Huston = *Les Misfits*,'' in *Cinéma* (Paris), no. 422, 30 December 1987.
Lippe, R., ''Montgomery Clift: A Critical Disturbance,'' in *CineAction* (Toronto), no. 17, Summer 1989.
Miller, A., ''Snips About Movies,'' in *Michigan Quarterly Review*, vol. 34, no. 4, 1995.
Shoilevska, Sanya, ''Alex North's Score for *The Misfits*,'' in *Cue Sheet* (Hollywood), vol. 7, no. 2, April 1996.
Jacobowitz, F., and R. Lippe, ''Performance and the Still Photograph: Marilyn Monroe,'' in *CineAction* (Toronto), no. 44, 1997.

* * *

Some thirty years after its release, *The Misfits* remains an impressive and affecting film but nonetheless a failure. The film, which is based on a screenplay written by Arthur Miller expressly as a homage to his wife, Marilyn Monroe, shies away from probing too deeply into its material and never manages to integrate its various thematics into an organic whole. Monroe's character, Roslyn, is the centre of the film and the character's impact on the men she meets gives the film its structure and narrative movement. In regard to Monroe/Roslyn, the film is highly reflexive and cannot but be read in part as a meditation on Monroe's star image, persona and presence.

The first time Monroe appears on-screen, she is attempting unsuccessfully to memorize the lines she needs to say in a divorce court hearing; as she rehearses, her face is seen reflected in a mirror as she puts finishing touches on her made-up face. To anyone even slightly familiar with Monroe's star image, the introductory sequence signals that the film is to be read as being about Marilyn Monroe. As the film progresses, there are other references to Monroe's public persona—like the actress, Roslyn was abandoned early on by her parents and grew up searching for love and security. Of the various references to Monroe, the strongest and most significant is the character's femininity and her almost exquisite sensitivity to human experience. Monroe/Roslyn is presented as an essence of the ''feminine.'' The image is in keeping with the direction Monroe's screen persona and presence was taking in the late 1950s—she was no longer the dumb blonde but the innocent; whereas earlier in her career, she embodied physicality, she now is presented as representing the spirit of a life-force. The film underscores this conception of Monroe/ Roslyn by having each of the principal male characters comment on her ability to feel, to intuitively respond to and empathize with human life and nature. *The Misfits* was Monroe's first dramatic film as a major star and was intended to consolidate her image as a serious person (New York and the Actor's Studio, a film with Olivier, the marriage to Arthur Miller) and actor.

With so much emphasis placed on Monroe and her femininity, it is highly fitting that her co-star in *The Misfits* is Clark Gable. Gable's star persona had been built on his masculine appeal. If Monroe was the 1950s archetypal female, Gable was the traditional archetypal male. As iconic figures the pairing of the two has a certain logic although their respective screen personas do not particularly mesh. While *The Misfits* is about Monroe, it is equally a meditation on both heterosexual relations and the conflict between the feminine and the masculine. As conceived by Miller and the film's director, John Huston, the feminine and the masculine are taken on face value. There is no consideration that an individual person may embody feminine and masculine traits or that the concepts themselves are cultural constructions. Montgomery Clift's presence and his characterization are the closest the film comes to acknowledging the possibility of a person having both a feminine and masculine identity but the character he plays is intended to be contrasted to Gable and Eli Wallach, a friend of Gable's who is gradually revealed to be irredeemably embittered, cynical and a misogynist; Gable and Wallach are ''men'' and not the man-child Clift is presented as being.

In *The Misfits* a masculine presence is interchangeable with a male's heterosexual orientation and Gable's ''manly'' image is further enhanced in that he is a cowboy. It is Gable's mature (that is, aging) cowboy which is used by the film to both place the Monroe character and provide a lament for the passing of a ''genuine'' masculine ethos which has been eroded by urbanization, women, and the death of the West and the male world of freedom, action, and mastery. In regard to Monroe and Gable's relationship, the film has two primary concerns: although Monroe is extremely attuned to other people's feelings and needs, she doesn't fully comprehend until late in the narrative that Gable is in emotional pain; and, secondly, as the mustang hunt dramatizes, while Gable is willing to acknowledge that he and the West belong to a bygone era, he needs to maintain his self-respect and not be ''broken'' ie emasculated. *The Misfits* moves to a climactic confrontation between Monroe and Gable over his sensitivity and hurt and it is Monroe who must give way if their relationship is to have a future.

The Misfits somewhat uneasily places its struggle between the female and male within the context of the crisis of the nuclear family; Roslyn had experienced an unhappy childhood, Gable's Gay has had an unsuccessful marriage and he and his children have a strained relationship, and Clift's Perce feels alienated from his mother who has chosen a second husband/lover over his affections. In the film's ''happy ending'' resolution, Monroe and Gable drive off together with her letting him know that she is now ready to have a child.

If the film's ''troubled-family'' thematic points back to the 1950s, *The Misfits* also looks forward to the 1960s and beyond. In addition to its self-conscious presentation of Monroe and, for that matter, Gable and Clift, the film is an early 1960s attempt to critically address the Western, the genre's values and its contemporary status. It is also a (post)modern film in the privileging of digression and ambience over narrative. And, in embryonic form, Monroe's identity raises issues directly relevant to feminism; she also aligns herself to what are essentially environmental and animal rights issues.

Although the film lacks a strong narrative drive, Huston's direction is taut and Russell Metty's elegantly sombre and sparse black and white images provide the feel of a spontaneous and almost documentary-like approach to the material. *The Misfits* lends itself to readings from numerous critical perspectives but it is perhaps most meaningfully a film concerned with stardom and in particular its complex relation to both the star and her or his audience. As the film illustrates, Monroe hadn't really resolved the split between her being perceived as a sex symbol (the paddle-ball sequence) and as a serious performer. And, the fact that *The Misfits* is Monroe's and Gable's final film and one of Clift's last efforts, makes it an inescapably sad film.

—Richard Lippe

MISS JULIE

See **FRÖKEN JULIE**

MR. HULOT'S HOLIDAY

See **LES VACANCES DE MONSIEUR HULOT**

MR. SMITH GOES TO WASHINGTON

USA, 1939

Director: Frank Capra

Production: Columbia Pictures Corp.; black and white, 35mm; running time: 130 minutes. Released 1939. Filmed in Columbia Pictures studios.

Producer: Frank Capra; **screenplay:** Sidney Buchman, from a story by Lewis R. Foster; **photography:** Joseph Walker; **editors:** Gene Havlick and Al Clark; **sound engineer:** Ed Bernds; **art director:** Lionel Banks; **music score:** Dimitri Tiomkin; **musical director:** M. W. Stoloff; **costume designer (gowns):** Kalloch; **montage effects:** Slavko Vorkapich.

Cast: Jean Arthur (*Saunders*); James Stewart (*Jefferson Smith*); Claude Rains (*Senator Joseph Paine*); Edward Arnold (*Jim Taylor*); Guy Kibbee (*Governor Hopper*); Thomas Mitchell (*Diz Moore*); Eugene Pallette (*Chick McGann*); Beulah Bondi (*Ma Smith*); H. B. Warner (*Senate Majority Leader*); Harry Carey (*President of the Senate*); Astrid Allwyn (*Susan Paine*); Ruth Donnelly (*Mrs. Hopper*); Grant Mitchell (*Senator MacPherson*); Porter Hall (*Senator Monroe*); Pierre Watkin (*Senate Minority Leader*); Charles Lane (*Nosey*); William Demarest (*Bill Griffith*); Dick Elliot (*Carl Cook*); Billy Watson, Delmar Watson, John Russell, Harry Watson, Gary Watson, and Baby Dumpling (*the Hopper Boys*).

Mr. Smith Goes to Washington

Awards: Oscar for Best Original Story, 1939; New York Film Critics Award, Best Actor (Stewart), 1939.

Publications

Script:

Buchman, Sidney, *Mr. Smith Goes to Washington*, in *Twenty Best Film Plays*, edited by John Gassner, and Dudley Nichols, New York, 1943.

Books:

Griffith, Richard, *Frank Capra*, London, 1951.
Jones, Ken D., *The Films of James Stewart*, New York, 1970.
Capra, Frank, *The Name above the Title*, New York, 1971.
Silke, James, *Frank Capra: One Man—One Film*, Washington, D.C., 1971.
Willis, Donald, *The Films of Frank Capra*, Metuchen, New Jersey, 1974.
Thompson, Howard, *James Stewart*, New York, 1974.
Glatzer, Richard, and John Raeburn, editors, *Frank Capra: The Man and His Films*, Ann Arbor, Michigan, 1975.
Maland, Charles, *American Visions: The Films of Chaplin, Ford, Capra, and Welles 1936–1941*, New York, 1977.
Scherle, Victor, and William Levy, *The Films of Frank Capra*, Secaucus, New Jersey, 1977, 1992.
Bohnenkamp, Dennis, and Sam Grogg, *Frank Capra Study Guide*, Washington, D.C., 1979.
Maland, Charles, *Frank Capra*, Boston, 1980.
Giannetti, Louis, *Masters of the American Cinema*, Englewood Cliffs, New Jersey, 1981.
Eyles, Allen, *James Stewart*, London, 1984.
Hunter, Allan, *James Stewart*, New York, 1985.
Robbins, Jhan, *Everybody's Man: A Biography of Jimmy Stewart*, New York, 1985.
Zagarrio, Vito, *Frank Capra*, Florence, 1985.
Carney, Raymond, *American Vision: The Films of Frank Capra*, Cambridge, 1986, 1996.
Wolfe, Charles, *Frank Capra: A Guide to References and Resources*, Boston, 1987.

McBride, Joseph, *American Madness: The Life of Frank Capra*, New York, 1990.

Lourdeaux, Lee, *Italian and Irish Filmmakers in America: Ford, Capra, Coppola and Scorsese*, Springfield, 1993.

Gehring, Wes D., *Populism and the Capra Legacy*, Westport, 1995.

Girgus, Sam B., *Hollywood Renaissance: The Cinema of Democracy in the Era of Ford, Capra, and Kazan*, New York, 1998.

Sklar, Robert, and Vito Zagarrio, *Frank Capra: Authorship and the Studio System*, Philadelphia, 1998.

McBride, Joseph, *Frank Capra: The Catastrophe of Success*, New York, 2000.

Articles:

Herzberg, Max J., editor, ''A Guide to the Appreciation of *Mr. Smith Goes to Washington*,'' in *Photoplay Studies* (New York), no. 21, 1939.

Variety (New York), 11 October 1939.

New York Times, 20 October 1939.

Ferguson, Otis, in *New Republic* (New York), 1 November 1939.

Ferguson, Otis, ''Democracy at the Box Office,'' in *New Republic* (New York), 24 March 1941.

Biberman, Herbert, ''Frank Capra's Characters,'' in *New Masses* (New York), 8 July 1941.

Capra, Frank, ''Do I Make You Laugh?,'' in *Films and Filming* (London), September 1962.

Price, James, ''Capra and the American Dream,'' in *London Magazine*, vol. 3, no. 10, 1964.

''Capra Issue'' of *Positif* (Paris), December 1971.

Handzo, Stephen, ''A Decade of Good Deeds and Wonderful Lives: Under Capracorn,'' in *Film Comment* (New York), vol. 8, no. 4, 1972.

Richards, Jeffrey, ''Frank Capra and the Cinema of Populism,'' in *Film Society Review* (New York), vol. 7, no. 6 and nos. 7–9, 1972.

Nelson, J., ''*Mr. Smith Goes to Washington*: Capra, Populism, and Comic-Strip Art,'' in *Journal of Popular Film* (Washington, D.C.), Summer 1974.

Sklar, Robert, ''The Making of Cultural Myths: Walt Disney and Frank Capra,'' in *Movie-Made America*, New York, 1975.

Rose, B., ''*It's a Wonderful Life*: The Stand of the Capra Hero,'' in *Journal of Popular Film* (Washington, D.C.), vol. 6, no. 2, 1977.

Phelps, G. A., ''The 'Populist' Films of Frank Capra,'' in *Journal of American Studies* (London), no. 3, 1979.

Browne, N., ''The Politics of Narrative Form: Capra's *Mr. Smith Goes to Washington*,'' in *Wide Angle* (Athens, Ohio), no. 3, 1980.

Dickstein, M., ''It's a Wonderful Life, But,'' in *American Film* (Washington, D.C.), May 1980.

''Capra Issue'' of *Film Criticism* (Edinboro, Pennsylvania), Winter 1981.

Edgerton, G., ''Capra and Altman: Mythmaker and Mythologist,'' in *Literature/Film Quarterly* (Salisbury, Maryland), January 1983.

Alix, Yves, ''La Machine à tuer les méchants,'' in *Positif* (Paris), November 1987.

Tomasulo, F. P., ''Colonel North Goes to Washington,'' in *Journal of Popular Film and Television* (Washington, D.C.), no. 2, 1989.

Kanjo, Judith, in *English Journal*, vol. 80, no. 2, February 1991.

Gehring, Wes D., ''The Capra Touch: *Mr. Smith Goes to Washington*,'' in *Journal of Popular Film and Television* (Washington, D.C.), vol. 19, no. 1, Spring 1991.

''Capra's America,'' in *Migration World Magazine*, vol. 20, no. 1, January-February 1992.

Alonge, A. G., ''Mr. Smith a Washington ovvero il trionfo della liberta,'' in *Quaderni di Cinema* (Florence), October-December 1992.

Hicks, J., ''Frank Capra (Part 2),'' in *Films in Review* (New York), January-February 1993.

Mortimer, L., ''The Charm of Morality: Frank Capra and His Cinema,'' in *Continuum*, vol. 7, no. 2, 1994.

Smoodin, Eric, '''Compulsory' Viewing for Every Citizen: *Mr. Smith* and the Rhetoric of Reception,'' in *Cinema Journal* (Austin), vol. 35, no. 2, Winter 1996.

Alter, Jonathan, ''It's a Wonderful Legacy: Two of Stewart's Classic Characters Helped Change How We View Our Politics - and Ourselves,'' in *Newsweek*, vol. 130, no. 2, 14 July 1997.

Ophuls, Marcel, ''Freedom and the Dream Factory: These are the Times That Try Men's Wallets In a Hollywood of Greedy Conformism,'' in *Nation*, vol. 265, no. 11, 13 October 1997.

Arnold, Gary, ''Though More Than 60 Years Old, Films of Frank Capra Stay Fresh,'' in *Insight on the News*, vol. 14, no. 5, 9 February 1998.

Hertzberg, Hendrik, ''Upset Victory: *Primary Colors* Triumphs Over the Old Politics of Hollywood,'' in *New Yorker*, vol. 74, no. 5, 23 March 1998.

Vidal, Gore, ''I Fired Capra: Recollections of the Life and Career of Frank Capra,'' in *Newsweek*, vol. 131, no. 25A, Summer 1998.

Brown, Stephen J., ''Theological Optimism in the Films of Frank Capra,'' in *Theology*, vol. 101, no. 804, November-December 1998.

* * *

The halo surrounding the accolade ''film classic'' can weigh heavily, indeed, and few films have encountered the extremes of opinion as has Frank Capra's classic, *Mr. Smith Goes to Washington*. It has been considered a most profound American tragedy. It has also been called sheer cornball on celluloid, even a veiled paean to fascism.

When an idealistic youth leader is named to the U.S. Senate to fill an unexpired term, he clashes with the party machine. Senator Paine (Claude Rains), industrial magnate Jim Taylor (Edward Arnold) and others are pushing through a bill giving the State an unneeded dam, one yielding real estate profits to the corrupt bosses. The patriotic young Jefferson Smith (James Stewart), chosen as perfect stooge for his naivete, is deflected with a bill for a boy's camp, a pet dream of his, which he wants built on the same land. Taylor attempts first to buy him off, then to break him. Framed, Smith defends himself and, in the climactic scene, challenges both the machine and the Senate itself by filibustering for 23 hours on the Senate floor, finally appealing to the now conscious-stricken Paine. He confesses all. Faith and vindication of Smith's idealism win out.

Despite the pressure to have the film withdrawn by politicians (including Joseph Kennedy), diplomats and reporters, who were either concerned that foreign powers would hold the film up as an example of corrupt Western democracy or objected to their professions being sourly painted, *Mr. Smith* became one of Capra's most successful works. Ironically, it was warmly embraced overseas, because it demonstrated the freedom America had to criticise its own system.

Made in a time when the country was still absorbing the shockwaves of the Depression and had recently seen World War II break out in Europe, knowing they would soon be involved, the illustration that America still had ideals worth fighting for struck a powerful chord. As the cynicism and seemingly moral and social disenfranchisement has grown with every decade, so has the appeal of *Mr. Smith*, Capra's commercial reminder that the spark of humanism could still flare, correct, and ultimately save.

With an everyman name, the Christ-figure allusions, and the innocent coming to a sadder-but-wiser adulthood, Smith voices a public that feels both impotent against and disconnected from a world grown cold and massive; it also illustrates the conundrum of anyone who has felt passion or imagination, and has nowhere to put it, nobody to listen to it.

Critics commenting biliously upon Capra's romanticism nevertheless have been nearly unanimous in giving credit to Capra's mastery of the film medium, from the painstaking authenticity (the Senate reconstruction, made alive as few film interiors have been, and the government ritualist procedures written into the script) to, especially, the editing, paced to both his characterisation and the dialogue's thematic importance. (The filibuster scene was shot by six cameras.) The montage expert Slavko Vorkapitch added his contribution to the mise en scene with a compilation using such U.S. monuments as the Lincoln Memorial, the Capitol Dome, the Constitution, and others. *Mr. Smith*'s ''fantasy'' is grounded in a strong physical reality.

So, too, his actors. Capra utilised a strong stable of people who consistently turned in well-crafted performances—Arnold, Stewart, Harry Carey (wonderful as the dry Senate President), Jean Arthur as the cynical secretary Saunders—even holding up production for months to gather the perfect cast. His use of faces has been a trademark, peppering his films with very American types, instinctively perceiving collective nationalistic natures. Guy Kibbee, Eugene Pallette and the others, with their years of roles ingrained on the filmgoing public, articulate before their lines are even spoken.

The dialogue is sharp and fast, segueing from verbal duets to—in Smith's speech—hoarse entreaty, to crisp and urgent explanation—in Saunders' explanation of due process—crucial to the action. Saunders' speech could be a textbook in any civics class. It serves not only as the exposition for the rest of the film, but sets the balanced tone of surface cynicism and underlying emotions, which makes James Stewart's passion completely valid.

The casting of Stewart as Jefferson Smith is inspired. Ironically, Capra had wanted Gary Cooper, but Stewart's hero is more proactive, more an articulate force for social change. Any unevenness of his character—for example, when he discovers the press has been ridiculing him, his reaction is harsh, ugly, inconsistent—is completely absorbed within his gangly sincerity. In that speech, he is by turns defensive, uncertain, defiant, wounded and inspired, all at once. It is not he who is the hero, but his beliefs; therein lies Stewart's genius: his style is organic to the character. Capra keeps this fundamental scene from being a mere photographed moral lecture. With his use of reaction shots (he reinforces what the audience already thinks, not merely creates it) and his structure of complicated relationships, such as Smith being the Senator 25 years later, with choreographed shots, makes his suicide attempt (''I'm not fit to be Senator!'') a credible outburst.

Given Capra's defining his own genre—Richard Griffith refers to it as ''the fantasy of goodwill''—his so-called moral tales, attention can be more fruitfully focused upon his technique; when tales are simple, the more important the telling, and the more glaring the faults. Those who would paint Capra as the Norman Rockwell of cinema haven't looked behind the storyline, nor have they discerned why the focus on corruption-then-restoration of ideals can come so organically from a director, an immigrant from the Italian slums who indeed made good. Hence the underlying theme of so many of his works; namely, that everything's *possible*, as well as the unavoidable frustration with and reaction to excess success. Many Capra heroes are, in addition to being unheroic, too naive, clumsy, and not on the best terms with reality. The folk artist homes in on the inherited myth of the American Past in a way that, unlike Rockwell, is neither synthetic nor saccharine, but identifiable. His happy ending in *Mr. Smith* is not sealed; less than a minute long in resolution, nothing is really changed beyond the incident; the Senate ends in turmoil and the fate of the political machine, beyond Taylor's, is unresolved.

The last quarter of the film is almost as dizzy as the best of Eisenstein's—or Vorkapitch's—montage, encapsulating numerous small vignettes and reactions, always with the central characters in focus. Yet Capra establishes the premise economically; in the film's opening, a rat-faced reporter callously spouts the news of a Senator's death into a telephone, then a swish pan sets in gear scenes leading to the stooge appointment of Smith. A series of wipes then establishes the power relationships. . . all of this in 60 seconds.

Capra's film doesn't descend into mere sentimentality due to the editing. A taut rhythm is structured, which organises chaos using surprisingly few close-ups, those being saved for reactions finely honed to audience expectation. They often act as counterpoint to cliche, as when he cuts to Saunders' cynical expression upon hearing platitudes intended to gloss over the corruption and ignorance of Taylor's crew to the naive new senator. Sour comment, too, reflecting our own jaded attitude. How that seeming immunity to moral and political optimism responds to a so-called ''fantasy'' on film is the result of somebody's skill. Must be Capra's.

—Jane Ehrlich

MRS. MINIVER

USA, 1942

Director: William Wyler

Production: Metro-Goldwyn-Mayer; black and white; running time: 133 minutes; length: 12,010 feet. Released June 1942.

Producer: Sidney Franklin; **screenplay:** Arthur Wimperis, George Froeschel, James Hilton, and Claudine West, from the novel by Jan Struther; **assistant director:** Walter Strohm; **photography:** Joseph Ruttenberg; **editor:** Harold S. Kress; **art director:** Cedric Gibbons; **associate art director:** Urie McCleary; **music:** Herbert Stothart.

Cast: Greer Garson (*Mrs. Miniver*); Walter Pidgeon (*Clem Miniver*); Teresa Wright (*Carol Beldon*); Dame May Whitty (*Lady Beldon*); Henry Travers (*Mr. Ballard*); Reginald Owen (*Foley*); Miles Mander (*German Agent's Voice*); Henry Wilcoxon (*Vicar*); Richard Ney (*Vin*); Clare Sander (*Judy*); Christopher Severn (*Toby*); Brenda Forbes (*Gladys*); Rhys Williams (*Horace*); Marie De Becker (*Ada*); Helmut Dantine (*German Flyer*); Mary Field (*Miss Spriggins*).

Mrs. Miniver

Awards: Oscars for Best Picture, Best Actress (Garson), Best Actress in a supporting Role (Teresa Wright), Best Black and White Cinematography, Best Director, Best Screenplay.

Publications

Script:

Wimperis, Arthur, and others, *Mrs. Miniver*, in *Twenty Best Film Plays*, edited by John Gassner and Dudley Nichols, New York, 1943.

Books:

Reisz, Karel, *William Wyler: An Index*, London, 1958.
Madsen, Axel, *William Wyler*, New York, 1973.
Kolodiazhnaia V., *William Wyler*, Moscow, 1975.
Tuska, Jon, editor, *Close-Up: The Hollywood Director*, Metuchen, New Jersey, 1978.
Anderegg, Michael A., *William Wyler*, Boston, 1979.
Baker, M. Joyce, *Images of Women in Film: The War Years 1941–45*, Ann Arbor, Michigan, 1980.
Kern, Sharon, *William Wyler: A Guide to References and Resources*, Boston, 1984.
Bowman, Barbara, *Master Space: Film Images of Capra, Lubitsch, Sternberg, and Wyler*, Westport, 1992.
Herman, Jan, *A Talent for Trouble: The Life of Hollywood's Most Acclaimed Director, William Wyler*, Cambridge, 1997.

Articles:

Documentary Newsletter (London), 1942.
Variety (New York), 13 May 1942.
Crowther, Bosley, in *New York Times*, 5 June 1942.
Life (New York), 8 June 1942.
Monthly Film Bulletin (London), July 1942.
Times (London), 8 July 1942.
Lejeune, C. A., in *Observer* (London), 12 July 1942.
Whitebait, William, in *New Statesman* (London), 18 July 1942.
Isaacs, Hermine Rich, ''William Wyler: Director with a Passion and a Craft,'' in *Theatre Arts* (New York), February 1947.
Griffith, Richard, ''Wyler, Wellman, and Huston,'' in *Films in Review* (New York), February 1950.
Luft, Herbert G., ''Greer Garson,'' in *Films in Review* (New York), March 1961.
Hanson, Curtis Lee, ''William Wyler,'' in *Cinema* (Beverly Hills), Summer 1967.
Marill, Alvin H., ''Walter Pidgeon,'' in *Films in Review* (New York), November 1969.
Doeckel, Ken, ''William Wyler,'' in *Films in Review* (New York), October 1971.
Higham, Charles, ''William Wyler,'' in *Action* (Los Angeles), September-October 1973.
von Cottom, J., ''Les Immortels du cinema: William Wyler,'' in *Ciné Revue* (Brussels), 30 August 1979.
Magill's Survey of Cinema 3, Englewood Cliffs, New Jersey, 1981.
Nielsen, R., ''Ray's Way,'' in *Classic Images* (Muscatine), no. 181, July 1990.
Raskin, R., ''Set-Up/Pay-Off and a Related Figure,'' in *P.O.V.*, no. 2, December 1996.
Chritensen, Jerome, ''Studio Identity and Studio Art: MGM, *Mrs. Miniver*, and Planning the Postwar Era,'' in *EHL*, vol. 67, no. 1, Spring 2000.

* * *

During the early years of World War II, when the United States was still wavering between isolationism and interventionism, Britain was facing the possibility of invasion and defeat by the Nazis. The American film industry showed marked sympathies for Britain, but had mainly used the new war as a backdrop for the usual spy stories and action/adventure films. The MGM producer Sidney Franklin, whose films often used British settings, had the idea of making a tribute to Britain at war, a feature film intended to persuade Americans to help the beleaguered British.

Mrs. Miniver was the culmination of Franklin's efforts. The sentimental yet gripping story of ''an average middle-class English family'' (as the opening titles describe them) in the midst of total war, won six Academy Awards and was the box-office hit of 1942 on both sides of the Atlantic. President Roosevelt was given a preview and urged the film's early release, and Winston Churchill referred to it as ''propaganda worth 100 battleships.''

The Miniver family, though, is anything but average. As the film opens in 1939 they are conspicuously well-off, with a large suburban home, two maids, a boat, and a new convertible car. They are a wholesome, idealized middle-class, that American audiences could respect as well as identify with. Once the identification is established, though, the Miniver's comfortable complacency is shaken by the war. The director, William Wyler, portrays the family's hardships by gradually closing their once spacious home in upon them. This process culminates during the air raid sequences, when the terrified but stoic Minivers huddle together in their tiny bomb shelter. Whistling bombs descend around them, literally destroying their home.

Despite an enthusiastic critical response in America, and the sympathetic intentions of the filmmakers, many British critics vehemently rejected this portrait of Britain at war. They found particular offence in the emphasis placed upon the heroism and sacrifice of the upper middle-class Minivers. At a time when British films were emphasizing realism and the contribution of the ordinary man to the ''people's war,'' *Mrs. Miniver* played the war for melodrama in the grand tradition of MGM. As the title suggests, this is a ''woman's film,'' with the focus of the narrative placed squarely on the shoulders of the eponymous heroine, played by Greer Garson. Garson is far too young to play a woman with a son in the RAF, but otherwise rings true in this role of dignified maturity. Teresa Wright, as the Miniver's daughter-in-law, is another sympathetic lead; and even Dame May Whitty manages to breathe life into her usual appearance as a crusty old aristocrat. The affable but vacuous male leads, Walter Pidgeon and Richard Ney, were perhaps cast so as not to detract attention from the more formidable women.

The landscape the Minivers inhabit is MGM's often used contemporary Olde England: a land of castles and quaint villages, populated by servile working-class caricatures and the landed gentry. In order to present Britain as a democracy worthy of being saved from Nazi rule, *Mrs. Miniver* attempts to alter this scenario only slightly: the middle-class Minivers are highlighted, while the marginal classes are seen to mingle harmoniously. A prolonged subplot involving the village flower show takes this idea to an absurd length. The filmmakers don't deny that an antiquated class system operates in Britain, but try to appear progressive in suggesting that class differences are differences of accent and disposition rather than economic inequalities.

Mrs. Miniver was the right film at the right time. Its blatant pro-British propaganda was somewhat alleviated in America by the U.S. entry into the war before the film was released. *Mrs. Miniver* thus came to symbolize not only the British sacrifice, but the sacrifices Americans were facing. Its enormous success encouraged MGM to embark on an entire series of films either celebrating the British at war or using their ''castles and class'' vision of England as a romantic setting. It seemed that there would indeed always be an England, so long as MGM was there to concoct it. The more memorable of these films, such as *Random Harvest*, kept the propaganda to a minimum. But the stodgy, message-filled *White Cliffs of Dover*, made just two years later, bared all of the presences of *Mrs. Miniver* without supplying the compensatory charms.

—H. M. Glancy

MODERN TIMES

USA, 1935

Director: Charles Chaplin

Production: United Artists-Charles Chaplin; black and white, 35mm, mostly synchronized musical soundtrack; running time: 85 minutes; length: 7634 feet. Released 1936.

Modern Times

Producer: Charles Chaplin; **screenplay:** Charles Chaplin; **photography:** Rollie Totheroh and Ira Morgan; **editor:** Charles Chaplin; **art directors:** Charles D. Hall and J. Russell Spencer; **music directors:** Alfred Newman; **music:** Charles Chaplin; **music arrangers:** David Raksin and Edward Powell.

Cast: Charles Chaplin (*A Worker*); Paulette Goddard (*A Gamine*); Henry Bergman (*Café proprietor*); Chester Conklin (*Mechanic*); Stanley Sandford, Louis Natheux, and Hank Mann (*Burglars*); Allan Garcia (*President of a steel corporation*).

Publications

Books:

Cooke, Alistair, editor, *Garbo and the Night Watchman*, London, 1937.
Tyler, Parker, *Chaplin, Last of the Clowns*, New York, 1947.
Cotes, Peter, and Thelma Miklaus, *The Little Fellow*, London, 1951.
Huff, Theodore, *Charlie Chaplin*, New York, 1951.
Mitry, Jean, *Charlot et la ''fabulation'' chaplinesque*, Paris, 1957.
Amengual, Barthélemy, *Charles Chaplin*, Paris, 1963.
Chaplin, Charlie, *My Autobiography*, London, 1964.
McDonald, Gerald, and others, *The Films of Charlie Chaplin*, Secaucus, New Jersey, 1965.
Martin, Marcel, *Charlie Chaplin*, Paris, 1966; 2nd edition, 1983.
Eisenstein, Sergei, *Film Essays and a Lecture*, edited by Jay Leyda, London, 1968; Princeton, 1982.

Mitry, Jean, *Tout Chaplin: Tous les films, par le texte, par le gag, et par l'image*, Paris, 1972.

Chaplin, Charlie, *My Life in Pictures*, London, 1974.

Sadoul, Georges, *Vie de Charlot*, Paris, 1978.

Lorcey, J., *Charlot*, Paris, 1978.

Lyons, T. J., *Charles Chaplin: A Guide to References and Resources*, Boston, 1979.

Haining, Peter, editor, *The Legend of Charlie Chaplin*, London, 1982.

Gehring, Wes D., *Charlie Chaplin: A Bio-Bibliography*, Westport, Connecticut, 1983.

Robinson, David, *Chaplin: The Mirror of Opinion*, London, 1983.

Smith, Julian, *Chaplin*, Boston, 1984.

Robinson, David, *Chaplin: His Life and Art*, London, 1985.

Saint-Martin, Catherine, *Charlot/Chaplin; ou, La Conscience du Mythe*, Paris, 1987.

Silver, Charles, *Charles Chaplin: An Appreciation*, New York, 1990.

Lynn, Kenneth S., *Charlie Chaplin and His Times*, New York, 1997.

Milton, Joyce, *Tramp: The Life of Charlie Chaplin*, New York, 1998.

Turk, Ruth, *Charlie Chaplin: From Tears to Laughter*, Minneapolis, 1999.

Kimber, John, *The Art of Charles Chaplin*, Sheffield, 2000.

Articles:

Shumiatski, B., in *New Masses* (New York), 24 September 1935.

New York Times, 6 February 1936.

Newsweek (New York), 8 February 1936.

Variety (New York), 12 February 1936.

Greene, Graham, in *Spectator* (London), 14 February 1936.

Van Doren, Mark, ''Charlie Chaplin,'' in *Nation* (New York), 19 February 1936.

Newhouse, Edward, ''Charlie's Critics,'' in *Partisan Review* (New Brunswick, New Jersey), April 1936.

Cooke, Alistair, ''Charlie Chaplin,'' in *Atlantic Monthly* (Boston), August 1939.

Eisenstein, Sergei, ''Charlie the Grown Up,'' in *Sight and Sound* (London), Summer 1946.

Grace, Harry A., ''Charlie Chaplin's Films and American Culture Patterns,'' in *Journal of Aesthetics and Art Criticism* (Cleveland), June 1952.

Marks, Louis, in *Films and Filming* (London), October 1954.

Whitebait, William, in *Sight and Sound* (London), January-March 1955.

Hinxman, Margaret, ''Interview with Chaplin,'' in *Sight and Sound* (London), Autumn 1957.

Sarris, Andrew, in *Village Voice* (New York), 21 May 1964.

Télécíné (Paris), January 1972.

Lefèvre, Raymond, ''Voie et revoir *Les Temps modernes*,'' in *Cinema* (Paris), January 1972.

Gow, Gordon, in *Films and Filming* (London), April 1972.

Lyons, T. J., interview with Roland H. Totheroh, in *Film Culture* (New York), Spring 1972.

Robinson, David, in *Sight and Sound* (London), Spring 1972.

Aristarco, G., ''L'uomo in pericolo nei *Tempi Moderni* di Chaplin,'' in *Cinema Nuovo* (Turin), May-June 1972.

Denby, David, in *Film Comment* (New York), September-October 1972.

Amengual, Barthélemy, ''Style et conscience de classe,'' in *Positif* (Paris), July-August 1973.

''Chaplin Issue'' of *Film und Fernsehen* (Berlin), March 1978.

''Chaplin Issue'' of *University Film Association Journal* (Houston), no. 1, 1979.

Berg, Charles, in *Magill's Survey of Cinema 3*, Englewood Cliffs, New Jersey, 1980.

Winokur, M., ''*Modern Times* and the Comedy of Transformation,'' in *Literature/Film Quarterly* (Salisbury, Maryland), vol. 15, no. 4, 1987.

Abel, ''*Modern Times*,'' in *Variety* (New York), vol. 336, no. 3, 2 August 1989.

Papson, S., ''The IBM Tramp,'' in *Jump Cut* (Berkeley), April 1990.

Troehler, M., ''Der stumme Aufstand der Bilder gegen die herrschenden Toene,'' in *Cinema (Switzerland)* (Basel), no. 36, 1990.

Robinson, D., and G. Molyneaux, ''The 'Script' of *Modern Times*,'' in *Cinefocus* (Bloomington), vol. 2, no. 1, 1991.

Marshall, C. I., ''Imitation as Imitation: The Brechtian Aspect of Chaplin's Cinema,'' in *Literature/Film Quarterly* (Salisbury, Maryland), no. 2, 1991.

Maxfield, James F., ''The Metamorphoses of the Mother: The Heroines of Chaplin's Silent Films,'' in *Midwest Quarterly*, vol. 32, no. 2, Winter 1991.

Kuriyama, Constance Brown, ''Chaplin's Impure Comedy: The Art of Survival,'' in *Film Quarterly* (Berkeley), vol. 45, no. 3, Spring 1992.

Bloom, Claire, ''Charles the Great: Remembering Charles Chaplin,'' in *Vogue*, vol. 182, no. 12, December 1992.

Lieberman, Evan A., ''Charlie the Trickster,'' in *Journal of Film and Video* (Atlanta), vol. 46, no. 3, Fall 1994.

Woal, Michael, and Linda Kowall Woal, ''Chaplin and the Comedy of Melodrama,'' in *Journal of Film and Video* (Atlanta), vol. 46, no. 3, Fall 1994.

Adorno, Theodor W., and John MacKay, ''Chaplin Times Two: Comedian Charlie Chaplin,'' in *Yale Journal of Criticism*, vol. 9, no. 1, Spring 1996.

Lemaster, David J., ''The Pathos of the Unconscious: Charlie Chaplin and Dreams,'' in *Journal of Popular Film and Television* (Washington, D.C.), vol. 25, no. 3, Fall 1997.

Faure, Elie, ''The Art of Charlie Chaplin,'' in *New England Review*, vol. 19, no. 2, Spring 1998.

Douglas, Ann, ''Charlie Chaplin: The Comedian,'' in *Time*, vol. 151, no. 22, 8 June 1998.

Doppen, Franz, ''*Modern Times*: The Industrial Revolution and the Concept of Time,'' in *Social Education*, January-February 1999.

* * *

Charles Chaplin was the last holdout in an industry that had uncritically turned its mode of production away from the visual developments of the end of the silent period to the spoken word and the theatrical trappings which that change entailed. In 1931, two years after the end of the silent period, Chaplin directed *City Lights*; five years later came *Modern Times*, his last film to extensively and specifically employ silent film strategies. A stylistic anachronism, the film was both a tribute to the glories of the silent period and a sociological perspective on industrialized society. If Chaplin considered sound likely to become an enslavingly mechanized aspect of movie making, he rendered that vision nonsensically by portraying himself as the factory worker forced to undergo a new approach to factory life—eating while working, using both mouth and body simultaneously. Not surprisingly, this experiment in modernization has disastrous consequences for our hero, the machine designed to feed the worker running disastrously amuck, serving food but rendering it inedible. Having been served by a machine, Charlie is later literally served *to* a machine. The film becomes a satire on the mechanization of thought and industry, a plea for the reinstitution of human individual values over those of industrialization and mass production.

The year of Chaplin's *City Lights*—1931—was also the year of *À nous la liberté*, René Clair's film attacking mechanized society. Both films share an assembly line scene of humorous yet socially critical implications; both directors posit a rather utopian ending in which man abandons the mechanized world for a life of individual freedom outside the urban landscape; both resist the use of dialogue as a naturalistic element of filmmaking. Although *À nous la liberté* contains some dialogue, the strength of the soundtrack is an operetta of sounds and music, occasional pieces of dialogue being part of that source. In *Modern Times*, machines, not people, are allowed voice, Chaplin using the musical soundtrack to evoke the sentimental nostalgia inherent in all of his films and ultimately to introduce us to the tramp's heretofore unheard voice, when, near the end of the film, he finds employment as a singing waiter. In this scene Chaplin defies the law of naturalism by singing a lyric totally in gibberish, preferring to detail the song's narrative through the brilliance of his pantomime. Here he recapitulates his belief that actions speak louder than words by rendering the words superfluous.

When *Modern Times* was released, Tobis, the company that controlled the rights to *À nous la liberté*, brought suit against Chaplin for his ''borrowing'' from Clair. The suit, however, was never brought to court because of Clair's refusal to sanction the action: Clair claimed that he had been greatly inspired by Chaplin, and that if that director had been inspired by him in return, he was greatly honored. Critics of the day generally noted the similarities between the two films but rarely to the detriment of either.

The staple Chaplin narrative involved a struggle, and in *Modern Times* the tramp is shown encountering the modern urban landscape with its overabundance of menacing institutions. He assumes a variety of occupations from nightwatchman to singing waiter, from worker on the assembly line to worker at a shipyard. Each time his employment is short-lived, not because Charlie is incapable but because his human qualities interfere with the system. In the factory, the monotony of his job as a bolt tightener reduces him to a machine off the job—he is unable to stop fulfilling his mechanized duties, continuing to tighten everything in sight: noses, waterplugs, buttons, etc. This problem takes him to a hospital where, after recovering, he returns to the streets. There, picking up a red warning flag which has fallen off a truck, he unwittingly becomes the front man in a parade of radicals, his carrying of the flag landing him in jail. He unwittingly thwarts a jailbreak for which he is rewarded first with more luxurious quarters, then to his dismay, with an honorable discharge. Back in the work force, he gets a job at a shipyard, only to be fired when he accidently and prematurely launches a new ship. Continuing along the path where good intentions misfire, he meets the gamine. He witnesses her act of thievery, realizes that it is provoked by hunger, and attempts to take the rap. Unfortunately, an eye witness thwarts Charlie's intentions, and the girl is taken away. Incensed, he goes about purposely committing a crime: he enters a restaurant and, after eating a large meal and smoking the best cigars, admits to having no money to pay. Gamine and tramp meet through their mutual arrests and escape together to the (dis)comfort of her waterfront shack, the location of which allows Chaplin some of his most elegant balletics, notably his dive into two feet of water in an attempt to cleanse himself.

Once again Charlie attempts to integrate himself into the modern system, this time by taking a job as a nightwatchman in a department store. Misplaced confidence in some friendly burglars ends in his being sent back to prison. When he is released, the gamine is waiting and takes him to his next job, that of a singing waiter. No sooner does he enjoy some success at this job than a juvenile court officer comes looking for the gamine. Deciding to forsake this entertainment industry job, he and the girl go arm in arm into the sunset, unemployed but happy. Optimism infuses this final image, but as always, pessimism has been firmly situated throughout: his aesthetic rejection of cinematic advances, his moral rejection of industrialization.

This last scene, the indestructible tramp walking into the sunset empty of hand but full of heart, is but one of many references in this film to Chaplin's silent comedies. In the factory he converts the moment of despair into one of humor, notably when the feeding machine goes beserk, and by so doing refers to the slapstick comedy of the teens when food was used as an arsenal rather than as goods for consumption. In the parade scene he reinterprets the meaning of an object—the flag's being transformed from a warning of danger to a symbol of freedom from incarceration; in the toy store he reinvents his roller skating scene from *The Rink* (1916); in the restaurant he recreates his *Gold Rush* dinner scene, changing the food from sustenance for the stomach to sustenance for the spirit by using the duck first as a football then a chandelier ornament rife with delight rather than calories. Throughout the film Chaplin continues to assert his belief that actions speak louder than words, that the dictum ''don't bite the hand that feeds you'' is fallacious, that optimism must prevail despite omnipresent pessimism and adversity, and that one must continue to uphold the values that have served him well in the past. The reappearance of Chester Conklin and other silent film players in this film further strengthens Chaplin's ode to the past and past values.

Initially a financial failure, *Modern Times* has since been hailed as one of Chaplin's most eloquent social statements. Accused of embodying Red propaganda, the film was banned in Germany and Italy, and in Austria it was trimmed of the flag waving scene by incensed censors. At best a flirtation with radical politics, its real message lies in the rejection of modern urban life and the need for the reinstitution of human rather than mechanical values. With *Modern Times* Chaplin retained his position as spokesman for the underprivileged.

—Doug Tomlinson

MONA LISA

UK, 1986

Director: Neil Jordan

Production: A Palace Production for Handmade Films; Technicolor; running time: 104 minutes; length: 9,368 feet. Released 1986.

Executive producers: George Harrison, Denis O'Brien; **producers:** Stephen Woolley, Patrick Cassavetti; **screenplay:** Neil Jordan, David Leland; **photography:** Roger Pratt; **camera operator:** Mike Roberts; **editor:** Lesley Walker; **sound editors:** Jonathan Bates, Chris Kelly; **sound recordists:** David John, Dave Hunt; **sound re-recordists:**

Mona Lisa

Paul Carr, Brian Paxton, Andy Jackson; **production designer:** Jamie Leonard; **art director:** Gemma Jackson; **costume designer:** Louise Frogley; **music:** Michael Kamen.

Cast: Bob Hoskins (*George*); Cathy Tyson (*Simone*); Michael Caine (*Mortwell*); Robbie Coltrane (*Thomas*); Clarke Peters (*Anderson*); Kate Hardie (*Kathy*); Zoe Nathensen (*Jeannie*); Sammi Davis (*May*); Rod Bedall (*Terry*); Joe Brown (*Dudley*); Pauline Melville (*George's Wife*); Hossein Karimbeik (*Raschid*); John Darling (*Hotel Security*); Bryan Coleman (*Gentleman in Mirror Room*); Robert Dorning (*Hotel Bedroom Man*); Raad Raawi (*Arab Servant*); David Halliwell (*Tim Devlin*); Stephen Persaud (*Black Youth in Street*); Maggie O'Neill (*Girl in Paradise Club*); Gary Cady (*Hotel Waiter*); Donna Cannon (*Young Prostitute*); Perry Fenwick (*Pimp*); Dawn Archibald (*Wig Girl in Club*); Richard Strange (*Porn Shop Man*); Alan Talbot (*Bath House Attendant*); Geoffrey Larder (*Hotel Clerk*); Helen Martin (*Peep Show Girl*); Kenny Baker, Jack Purvis, Bill Moore (*Brighton Buskers*).

Awards: Palme d'Or, Cannes Festival, 1986; BAFTA Award for Best Actor (Hoskins) 1986.

Publications

Script:

Jordan, Neil, and David Leland, *Mona Lisa*, London, 1986.

Books:

Tummolini, Stefano, and Chiara Calpini, *Neil Jordan*, Rome, 1996.

Rogers, Lori, *Feminine Nation: Performance, Gender, and Resistance in the Works of John McGahern and Neil Jordan*, Lanham, 1998.

Articles:

Stills (London), December 1985-January 1986.

Film Directions (Belfast), vol. 8, no. 31, 1986.

Variety (New York), 14 May 1986.

Hollywood Reporter, 19 June 1986.

City Limits (London), 28 August-4 September 1986.

Codelli, Lorenzo, in *Positif* (Paris), September 1986.
Combs, Richard, in *Monthly Film Bulletin* (London), September 1986.
Pym, John, in *Sight and Sound* (London), Autumn 1986.
Anderson P., in *Films in Review* (New York), October 1986.
Roddick, Nick, in *Cinema Papers* (Melbourne), January 1987.
Barra, Allen, "Here Comes Mr. Jordan: Irish Literary Man Neil Jordan Made a Splash with *Mona Lisa*: Now He Arrives in Hollywood with *We're No Angels*: Will They Let Him Stay?" in *American Film*, vol. 15, no. 4, January 1990.
Glicksman, Marlaine, "Irish Eyes: Interview with Irish Motion Picture Director Neil Jordan," in *Film Comment* (New York), vol. 26, no. 1, January-February 1990.
"Jordan, Neil," in *Current Biography*, vol. 54, no. 8, August 1993.
James, Joy, "Black Femmes Fatales and Sexual Abuse in Progressive 'White' Cinema: Neil Jordan's *Mona Lisa* and *The Crying Game*," in *Camera Obscura* (Bloomington), no. 36, September 1995.
Schruers, Fred, "Neil Jordan: Film Director," in *Rolling Stone*, no. 747, 14 November 1996.
"Borderline Case: Neil Jordan Has Gone Crazy for Things Irrational, But There Is a Power of Method in His Madness," in *Time International*, vol. 150, no. 26, 23 February 1998.

* * *

Following his characteristically ebullient and pugnacious portrayal of East End gang boss Harold Shand in *The Long Good Friday* Bob Hoskins plunges back again into the London underworld in this story of George, a small-time gangster released from a seven-year stretch for someone else's crime only to find his old world utterly changed. Eventually his former boss gives him a menial job chauffeuring Simone, a young, black, and very exclusive prostitute. George falls in love with her, but she is concerned only with finding her friend Cathy, a heroin-addicted fellow prostitute who has mysteriously disappeared. She enlists George's help and eventually they track her down. However, George then discovers, much to his chagrin, that the two women are in fact lovers.

Mona Lisa is at its best in the passages in which it comes across as a contemporary British film noir, a kind of latterday *Night and the City*. Particularly impressive in this respect are the scenes in the Kings Cross red-light district (somewhat cleaned up since the film's production) which have a genuinely infernal, *Taxi Driver*-ish feel about them, the plush hotel foyers which conceal less salubrious goings-on behind their luxurious facades, Michael Caine's briefly glimpsed but convincingly nasty gangster Mortwell (not unlike John Osborne's crime boss in *Get Carter*), the final bloodbath in Brighton, and George's seemingly endless traipse through the strip joints, peep shows, and hostess clubs of Soho. Certainly the view of human relationships which emerges from this urban nightmare is as black as anything produced by Hollywood in the 1940s: the central theme emerges clearly as the illusory nature of romantic love and, more specifically, the male habit of projecting hopelessly idealized, unrealistic images onto women to whom they are attracted. Director Neil Jordan describes it as an "anti-erotic movie" which deals with "misplaced passions and emotional devastation," whilst writer David Leland admitted that "what emerged for me working on this film is the extraordinary capacity human beings seem to have to lead double lives, and it makes me wonder if any of us can ever know who the hell it is we're living with. It must involve an incredible amount of lying to one's partner, to the other people one's close to—and to oneself." Undoubtedly the film's thoroughly unromantic view of sexual relationships of any kind owes something to the fact that Leland's previous script—*Personal Services*—also revolved around the world of prostitution.

On the other hand, *Mona Lisa*, as an urban thriller, lacks a certain necessary *élan*. The problem here (as in so much British cinema) is a tendency towards literaryness, towards spelling things out and dotting the "i's" and crossing the "t's" as opposed to embedding the themes as it were "invisibly" in the narrative. In other words what it finally lacks is the characteristic narrative economy of the Hollywood model—as the self-reflexively inserted clip from *They Live by Night* rather unfortunately emphasises. (That such a cultural transition *is* in fact possible is proved by the existence of the aforementioned *Get Carter*; typically, however, the best British thriller of recent times—Philip Saville's *Gangsters*—was made for television and now lies unseen, gathering dust in the BBC vaults.) The problem is compounded by allowing George to become something of a comic, lovable misfit—for example, in the scene (reprised from *The Long Good Friday*) in which he returns to his neighbourhood after his years inside to find it considerably changed, his rather sentimentalized relationship with his old friend Thomas, and his inability to distinguish between smart and merely flashy clothes. As Richard Combs concludes in *Monthly Film Bulletin*, "in this respect, and for all the film's toughness and violence, we are not very far from the kind of British cinema—sort of Ealing-Forsyth—which is always inclined to bury everything in eccentricity and whimsy."

—Julian Petley

MONANIEBA

See **POKAIANIE**

DIE MÖRDER SIND UNTER UNS

(The Murderers are Among Us)

East Germany, 1946

Director: Wolfgang Staudte

Production: DEFA (East Germany); black and white, 35mm; running time: 86 minutes; length: 2400 meters. Released 1946. Filmed spring 1946 in Berlin.

Producer: Herbert Uhlich; **screenplay:** Wolfgang Staudte; **photography:** Friedl Behn-Grund and Eugen Klagemann; **editor:** Lilian Seng; **sound recordist:** Dr. Klaus Jungk; **production designers:** Otto Hunte and Bruno Monden; **music:** Ernst Roters.

Cast: Hildegard Knef (sometimes Neff) (*Susanna Wallner*); Ernst Fischer (*Dr. Mertens*); Arno Paulsen (*Captain Bruckner*); Erna Sellmer (*Frau Bruckner*); Robert Forsch (*Herr Mondschein*); Albert Johann (*Herr Timm*).

Die Mörder sind unter uns

Publications

Books:

Manvell, Roger, and Heinrich Fraenkel, *The German Cinema*, New York, 1971.
Wollenberg, H. H., *50 Years of German Film*, London, 1972.
Netenjakob, Egon, *Staudte*, with Eva Orbanz, Hans Helmut Prinzler, and Heinz Ungureit, Berlin, 1991.
Ludin, Malte, *Wolfgang Staudte*, Rowohlt, 1996.

Articles:

Monthly Film Bulletin (London), no. 172, 1948.
Today's Cinema (London), 2 April 1948.
Kine Weekly (London), 15 April 1948.
Cue (New York), 21 August 1948.
Bianco e Nero (Rome), September 1948.
George, Manfred, ''Hildegard Neff,'' in *Films in Review* (New York), November 1955.
Filmkritik (Munich), no. 1, 1960.
Bachmann, J., ''Wolfgang Staudte,'' in *Film* (London), Summer 1963.
Mancia, Adrienne, ''Films from the German Democratic Republic,'' in *Museum of Modern Art Department of Film* (New York), 20 November-29 December 1975.
Information (Wiesbaden), no. 3–6, 1976.
Karkosch, K., ''Wolfgang Staudte,'' in *Film und Ton* (Munich), March 1976.
Information (Wiesbaden), January-February 1978.
Interview with Wolfgang Staudte, in *Film und Fernsehen* (Berlin), vol. 19, no. 5, May 1991.
Baker, M., '''Truemmerfilme': Postwar German Cinema, 1946–1948,'' in *Film Criticism* (Meadville), vol. 20, no. 1/2, 1995/1996.

* * *

By March 1946, nine months after the armistice, a film crew dominated by veterans of the Nazi industry was out in the streets of devastated Berlin, in front of Stettiner railway station and on flattened Alexanderplatz, shooting the first postwar German film, *Die Mörder sind unter uns*. The director, Wolfgang Staudte, worked under the auspices of DEFA, the only production company licensed in the

Soviet Zone. Founded on the remains of the old Ufa empire, DEFA had a distinct material advantage over its western counterparts: what remained of giant studios and even raw stock plants was concentrated in the eastern, Soviet Zone, of Germany. *Mörder* is both an exposé denouncing the ability of Nazi war criminals to bury their pasts and to enjoy respected positions in the new German society and a romance between a returning concentration camp survivor and a doctor whose participation in the war has left him an alcoholic with no will to rebuild his life.

The prominence of the love story and the casting of Hildegard Knef (a very unlikely looking camp victim) effectively mutes the political criticism implied by the film. Nevertheless, *Mörder* was well received by contemporary critics as a serious and realistic drama. The arrival of this film in Western Europe and America occasioned speculation that a new German film industry would soon spring to life. This prediction was, of course, premature. Today, in spite of the location shooting, it is the leftovers of an older expressionist style that seem to permeate Staudte's work. The ruins of Berlin were a ready-made horror film set, and expressionist stylization sets the tone in this film much as it did in postwar American film noir—the heavy shadows, the weird angles, the use of frames within frames. Ravaged Berlin is used as a metaphor for the broken people who live there. In one emphatic cut, the film switches from the hero's confession of his own war guilt to a long held shot of a crumbling building, dust rising from the rubble beneath it. Staudte indulges in heavy irony. The camera zooms in on a poster advertizing ''beautiful Germany'' in the midst of desolation through the rubble; he quips, ''The city is coming back to life.'' With oblique camera angles, the film also creates a subjective view of the doctor's drunken interludes.

Mörder was the first in a cycle of ''*Trümmerfilme*'' or ''rubble films,'' produced mainly by DEFA, using the streets of Berlin as backdrops for melancholy dramas concerning contemporary issues—the returning soldier, the black market, war criminals. Meanwhile, as the many competing companies licensed in the west went into action, more escapist, apolitical films began to dominate German production. Staudte, who had worked in the Nazi film industry, may have retreated from a clear coming to terms with the issue of war guilt in *Die Mörder sind unter uns*, but he did produce a serious drama securely moored in a contemporary milieu, something German filmmakers had refused to do for years. What seems lacking is a break with the past in style as well as subject matter.

—Ann Harris

MORTE A VENEZIA

(Death in Venice)

Italy, 1971

Director: Luchino Visconti

Production: Alfa Cinematografica (Rome) and P.E.C.F. (Paris); Technicolor, 35mm, Panavision; running time: 131 minutes, some versions are 128 minutes. Released 1971.

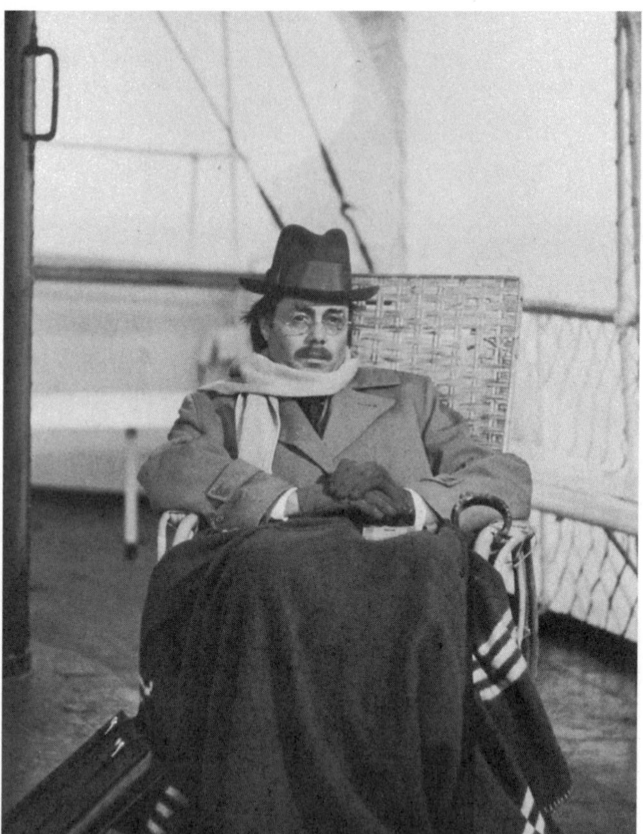

Morte a Venezia

Producers: Mario Gallo with Luchino Visconti, Nicolas Badalucco; and Robert Gordon Edwards; **screenplay:** Luchino Visconti and Nicolas Badalucco, from the novel by Thomas Mann; **photography:** Pasquale De Santis; **editor:** Ruggero Mastroianni; **sound:** Vittorio Trentino with Giuseppe Muratori; **art director:** Ferdinando Scarfiotti; **music:** Gustav Mahler; **music director:** Franco Mannino; **costume designer:** Piero Tosi.

Cast: Dirk Bogarde (*Gustav von Aschenbach*); Romolo Valli (*Director of the ''Hotel Des Bains''*); Nora Ricci (*Governess of Tadzio*); Mark Burns (*Alfried*); Marisa Berenson (*Mogol of G.V.A.*); Carole André (*Esmeralda*); Leslie French (*Cook's agent*); Sergio Garfagnoli (*Jasciu*); Franco Fabrizi (*Barber*); Dominque Darel (*English tourist*); Masha Predit (*Russian tourist*); Silvano Mangano (*Tadzio's mother*); Ciro Cristogoletti; Antonio Apicella; Bruno Boschetti; Luigi Battaglia; Mirella Pompili; Björn Andersen (*Tadzio*).

Award: Cannes Film Festival, Special Prize, 1971.

Publications

Script:

Visconti, Luchino, and Nicolas Badalucco, *Morte a Venezia*, edited by Lino Miccichè, Bologna, 1971.

Books:

Baldelli, Pio, *Luchino Visconti*, Milan, 1973.
Hinxman, Margaret, and Susan d'Arcy, *The Films of Dirk Bogarde*, London, 1974.
Ferrero, Adelio, editor, *Visconti: Il cinema*, Modena, 1977.
Bianchi, Pietro, *Maestri del cinema*, Milan, 1977.
Tornabuoni, Lietta, editor, *Album Visconti*, Milan, 1978.
Stirling, Monica, *A Screen of Time: A Study of Luchino Visconti*, New York, 1979.
Servadio, Gaia, *Luchino Visconti*, Milan, 1980; as *Luchino Visconti: A Biography*, London, 1981; New York, 1983.
Becivenni, Alessandro, *Luchino Visconti*, Florence, 1982.
Tonetti, Claretta, *Luchino Visconti*, Boston, 1983.
Ishaghpour, Youssef, *Luchino Visconti: Le Sens et l'image*, Paris, 1984.
Sanzio, Alain, and Paul-Louis Thirard, *Luchino Visconti: Cinéaste*, Paris, 1984.
De Giusti, Luciano, *I film di Luchino Visconti*, Rome, 1985.
Geitel, Klaus, and others, *Luchino Visconti*, Munich, 1985.
Mancini, Elaine, *Luchino Visconti: A Guide to References and Resources*, Boston, 1986.
Villien, Bruno, *Visconti*, Paris, 1986.
Schifano, Laurence, *Luchino Visconti: Les Feux de la passion*, Paris, 1987.
Tanitch, Robert, *Dirk Bogarde: The Complete Career Illustrated*, London, 1988.
Partridge, C.J., *Senso: Visconti's Film and Bioto's Novella: A Case Study in the Relation between Literature and Film*, Lewiston, NY, 1992.
Bacon, Henry, *Visconti: Explorations of Beauty and Decay*, Cambridge and New York, 1998.

Articles:

Elsaesser, Thomas, ''Luchino Visconti,'' in *Brighton Film Review*, February 1970.
''Visconti Issue'' of *Cinema* (Rome), April 1970.
Alpert, Hollis, in *Saturday Review* (New York), 8 August 1970.
Hinxman, Margaret, in *Sight and Sound* (London), Autumn 1970.
Radkai, K., ''Luchino Visconti,'' in *Vogue* (New York), 1 November 1970.
Tynan, Kenneth, ''*Death in Venice*: At the End of the Path of Beauty Lies Eros,'' in *Vogue* (New York), December 1970.
''*Mort à Venise* Issue'' of *Avant-Scène du Cinéma* (Paris), July 1971.
Korte, Walter, ''Marxism and Formalism in the Films of Luchino Visconti,'' in *Cinema Journal* (Evanston, Illinois), Fall 1971.
Oudart, J. P., and S. Daney, ''Le Nom-de-l'auteur,'' in *Cahiers du Cinéma* (Paris), January-February 1972.
Guiguet, J. C., in *Image et Son* (Paris), February 1972.
Hutchinson, A., in *Literature/Film Quarterly* (Salisbury, Maryland), Winter 1974.
Bogemski, G., ''Nachkomme eines alten Herrschergeschlechts,'' in *Film und Fernsehen* (Berlin), October 1979 to June 1980.
Galerstein, C., ''Images of Decadence in Visconti's *Death in Venice*,'' in *Literature/Film Quarterly* (Salisbury, Maryland), January 1985.
Amengual, Barthélemy, in *Positif* (Paris), September 1985.
Medhurst, Andy, ''Dirk Bogarde,'' in *All Our Yesterdays*, edited by Charles Barr, London, 1986.
Badalucco, N., ''Come si scrive una sceneggiatura,'' in *Cinema & Cinema* (Bologna), September-December 1989.
Bolleme, G., ''Plus beau que l'on ne saurait dire,'' in *Camera/Stylo* (Paris), December 1989.
Verdier, A., ''De l'ecrit a l'image,'' in *Camera/Stylo* (Paris), December 1989.
Málek, Petr, ''Variace na téma Viscontiho Smrti v Benátkách,'' in *Iluminace*, vol. 7, no. 1, 1995.
Hallouin, L., ''Text, Film, Memory: Note on Two Variations of Melancholy,'' in *Iris* (Iowa City), no. 19, Autumn 1995.
Bertellini, G., ''A Battle d'arrier-garde,'' in *Film Quarterly* (Berkeley), vol. 50, no. 4, 1997.
Rohdie, S., ''Time and Consciousness in Luchino Visconti,'' in *Metro* (Victoria, Australia), no. 113, 1998.

* * *

Director Luchino Visconti's screen adaption of Thomas Mann's *Death in Venice* is both a triumph of visual style and a problematic study of literature-into-film translations. In collaboration with cinematographer Pasquale De Santis, Visconti captures Mann's haunting story in images of hypnotic beauty, yet they are images which the film's verbal exposition cannot always equal.

One of the themes of Mann's brilliant novella has to do with the artist's recognition of the power and validity of physical beauty, and Visconti's cinematic approach conveys his understanding of this theme in every frame. The splendor of Venice, the elegance of Aschenbach's seaside hotel, the androgynous perfection of the boy Tadzio—all are photographed in a lush, unhurried manner that allows the viewer to linger on a detail or to simply absorb the richness of the scene as a whole. This is a story—and a film—of contemplation, and Visconti permits his audience to share in the overwhelming sensuality that will penetrate Aschenbach's emotional reserve and shatter his lifelong convictions about philosophy and art.

Yet as this is also a story of death—Aschenbach's own, as well as the destruction of his rigidly-held ideas—Visconti has permeated his film with an atmosphere of decay. Images of death are everywhere. Indeed, when Aschenbach at last allows himself to be powdered and rouged into a pathetic parody of youthfulness, his face resembles nothing so much as a death mask, streaked with black as the sun melts the paint around his eyes. This pairing of beauty and death, which lies at the heart of the story itself, lends the film an unsettling, almost oppressive air, reminiscent of flowers on the verge of wilting. Visconti himself was close to 70 when *Death in Venice* was made and would complete only three more pictures after its release. It is clear from the film's painful illumination of the gulf between youth and old age that it was a concern much on the filmmaker's own mind.

The shortcomings of *Death in Venice* are those which every film adaption must face, i.e. the nearly insurmountable difficulties inherent in transposing interior thoughts into visible images. To understand the effect that his obsession with Tadzio has on Aschenbach, one must first grasp the rejection of emotion and the physical senses that has informed Aschenbach's work as an artist. Mann conveys this information through straight-forward description of his character's meditations on art, a method not available to Visconti. Instead, the director resorts to a series of flashbacks in which Aschenbach and a friend argue bitterly over their opposing views on art and life. The resulting scenes seem static and talky when juxtaposed with Visconti's fluid—and virtually wordless—presentation of the delicate interplay between Aschenbach and the enigmatic Tadzio.

The flashbacks, however, merely lay the groundwork for most of the film's action, and in depicting Aschenbach's growing love for Tadzio and the older man's subsequent decline, Visconti's strong cinematic sense serves him well. He is aided by a finely textured performance from Dirk Bogarde, who has been made up to resemble composer Gustav Mahler, upon whom Mann is said to have based his character, and by Mahler's stirring Fifth Symphony which is the basis of the film's soundtrack. Despite its flaws, *Death in Venice* remains an absorbing and visually stunning adaption of Mann's challenging work.

—Janet E. Lorenz

MOSCOW DISTRUSTS TEARS

See **MOSKVA SLEZAM NE VERIT**

MOSCOW DOES NOT BELIEVE IN TEARS

See **MOSKVA SLEZAM NE VERIT**

MOSKVA SLEZAM NE VERIT

(Moscow Does Not Believe in Tears; Moscow Distrusts Tears)

USSR, 1979

Director: Vladimir Menshov

Production: Mosfilm; color; running time: 145 minutes.

Producer: V. Kuchinsky; **screenplay:** Valentin Yornykh; **photography:** Igor Slabnjewitsch; **editor:** Jelene Mischajora; **music:** Sergei Nikitin; **art designer:** Saïd Menyalshchikov.

Cast: Vera Alentova (*Katya*); Alexsei Batalov (*Goscha*); Irina Muravyova (*Lyuda*); Raissa Ryazanova (*Antonia*); Yuri Vasilyav (*Rudolf*).

Awards: Oscar for Best Foreign Language Film, 1980.

Publications

Articles:

Bauman, E., ''Vremia skvoz' sud'by,'' in *Iskusstvo Kino* (Moscow), no. 2, 1980.

Ishimov, V. and others, ''Pochemu tak vzolnovany zriteli,'' in *Iskusstvo Kino* (Moscow), no. 9, 1980.

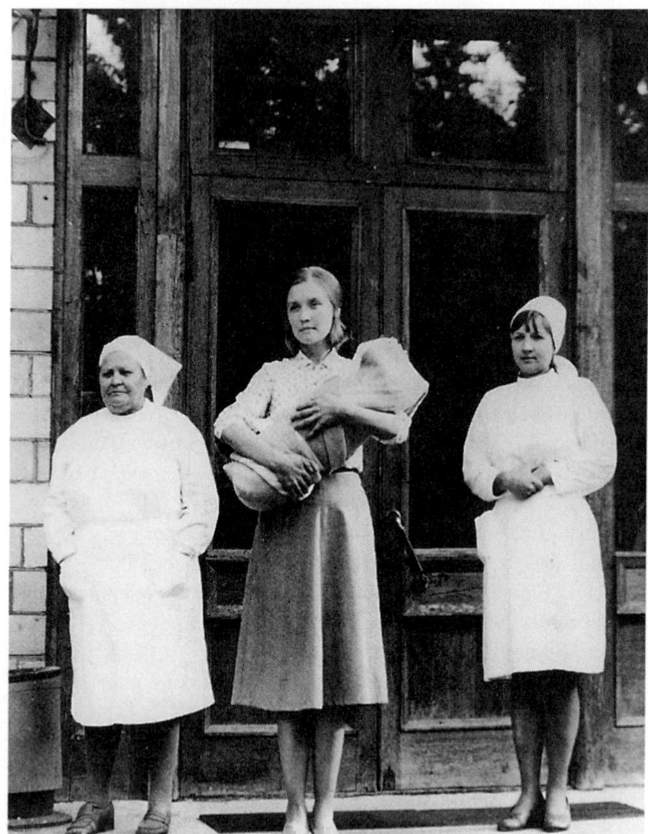

Moskva slexam ne verit

Engvan, I., ''Moskva tror inte pa tarar,'' in *Filmrutan* (Sweden), no. 4, 1981.

Fonda-Bonardi, C., in *Cineaste* (New York), vol. 11, no. 3, 1981.

Gusner, I., ''Lieber arm, aber gluecklich: der Autor des Films *Moskau glaubt den Traenen nicht*, Walentin Tschernych, ueber seine Arbeit,'' in *Film and Fernsehen* (Berlin), vol. 9, no. 1, 1981.

Tschernych, W., ''Ein phaenomenaler Erfolg,'' in *Film and Fernsehen* (Berlin), vol. 9, no. 6, 1981.

Schickel, Richard, ''Cinema: Lovers and Laziness,'' in *Time* (New York), 11 May 1981.

Kauffman, Stanley, *New Republic* (New York), 23 May 1981.

Grenier, R., ''Movies: A Soviet 'New Wave'?,'' in *Commentary* (New York), July 1981.

Stefanoni, L., ''Mosca non crede alle lacrime,'' in *Cineforum* (Bergamo), December 1981.

Poitras, H., ''Moscou est insensible aux larmes,'' in *Sequences* (London), January 1982.

Bruciamonti, A., ''Mosca non crede alle lacrime,'' in *Cinema Nuovo* (Turin), February 1982.

Portal, M., ''Moscou ne croit pas aux larmes,'' in *Jeune Cinéma* (Paris), February 1982.

Thirard, P. -L., ''Moscou ne croit pas aux larmes,'' in *Positif* (Paris), June 1982.

Schmemann, S., ''Ordinary Life Stars in Soviet Films,'' in the *New York Times*, 14 August 1983.

Skoop, vol. 22, no. 3, April-May 1986.

Galiano, C., ''Salir no quiere decir llegar,'' in *Cine Cubano* (Habana), no. 119, 1987.

Koroleva, A., ''Odnazhdy v SSSR,'' in *Iskusstvo Kino* (Moscow), no. 2, 1996.

Balynina, N., ''Moskvici i gosti stolicy,'' in *Iskusstvo Kino* (Moscow), no. 8, August 1997.

* * *

It may be true that Moscow does not believe in tears but the film by this title is at least a two-handkerchief movie. Russian sentiment is the ultimate driving force in this exploration of love, social class, success and failure, male-female roles, traditional versus modern Russian values, and the nature of family. Part I focuses on the social circle of a young working-class Russian woman, a factory worker whose ambition leads to dramatic professional and personal choices; Part II examines the consequences of these decisions 20 years later. We also see what has happened to her contemporaries over two decades, and how Soviet society has changed as well. Though romantic in its resolution, the film is also sometimes as tough-minded as its title suggests, with fairly scathing commentaries on how the new Soviet society has gone wrong.

Katerina, the heroine, played by Vera Alentova, and her more extroverted friend Ludmilla (Irina Muravyova) are non-Muscovites employed in a factory and living in a workers' dormitory in Moscow. Katerina has failed her college entrance exam by just two points, and her drive to succeed is contrasted, often amusingly, with Ludmilla's search for a quick way up. ''Life is a lottery,'' she maintains, in which women can win the right kind of socially prestigious husband and Moscow citizenship with all the privileges it brings. A third friend, Tonya is more conventional than Katerina or Ludmilla, marrying early for love and settling for a typical domestic life with a kindly man. When Ludmilla's uncle lends her a dream apartment (in fact, a real edifice built by Stalin and famed as a touchstone of unimaginable wealth), she and Katerina, claiming they are daughters of a famous professor, play host to a party for successful males (some of whom Ludmilla picks up in the Lenin library). This ploy allows Ludmilla to snare her mate, a popular athlete, and leads to the seduction of Katerina by Rudolph, a young television cameraman, who has a ready patter about the coming triumph of technology. When Katerina becomes pregnant, she refuses to press him for marriage or even help, Ludmilla's intervention notwithstanding; Rudolph proves a weak mama's boy and Katerina has the baby alone, beginning a hard life as a single mother working her way up in the male world of the factory.

Part I has some sharp defining moments which illuminate Soviet life of the late 1950s. The long nightmare of Stalin was over and young people could speak more freely than their parents ever could, but the agonizing rebuilding period after World War II, the Great Patriotic War, was not yet finished, with cramped and flimsy ''Khrushchev apartments'' unable to accommodate the flood of immigrants to the cities. Rudolph's mother says explosively that she's had enough of communal living, and won't allow Katerina and her baby into her apartment already filled with four people; crowded shots of wedding celebrations and meals accentuate her complaint, the camera angles showing ceilings and doorways framing teeming groups. The class system is alive and well, as former peasants take new roles in factories that only enforce their distance from the educated *nomenklatura*, the elite academic and managerial class. Ludmilla comments that two things give you away—incorrect speech and dumb questions—and goes on to explain that stupidities spoken with confidence become a ''point of view.'' But how she overcomes speech is never explained. There is a lusting after things urban and foreign: Rudolph the cameraman has a non-Russian name and is far more enchanted with his glitzy technology than with human or social values. A festival of French films draws groupies squealing at the sight of Russian stars in attendance, including, amusingly, Innokenty Smoktundusky, the Soviet Union's most popular star, playing himself as he was in 1958, an unknown and aging bit player. Yet in spite of these faults, Soviet society then offered hope for the future, a hope manifest in the character of Katerina and Ludmilla, both struggling in their own ways for a better life.

Part I ends with Katerina setting her alarm clock. Part II begins with the shot dissolving into an alarm ringing, but it is a newer, fancier clock, in a far nicer apartment, 20 years having passed. Katerina's daughter, Alexandra, is now a young woman, and Katerina herself is an executive running a factory, a series of shop floor promotions having provided her with a later 1970s dream lifestyle: office job, car, a nice apartment. A chance television appearance reintroduces Rudolph (now Rodion, a Russian name), who has two failed marriages behind him and is still pushing a camera around. He asks to see his daughter, but Katerina refuses. She is having an unsatisfactory affair with a married man but is still reluctant to accept the advances of Gosha, a handsome fitter she meets on a train. He pursues her charmingly, cooking meals, winning over her daughter, and generally epitomizing the idealized socialist man, a manual worker completely satisfied by the challenges of his research institute work unit, while also exhibiting literacy and amazing technical and social competence. Rudolph's crashing into the scene to see his daughter leads to Gosha walking out, not over sexual jealousy, but because Katerina has never revealed the importance and salary of her job to him; this contretemps is resolved in a very Russian way, with huge quantities of vodka. The film ends with Katerina, Gosha, and Alexandra eating at the kitchen table, a domestic tableau emblematic of the triumph of Russian family values. The passionate tangos which had dominated the background music of Katerina's earlier, superficial relationships are replaced by bitter-sweet Russian love songs indicative of her finally having found her true place.

Moscow Does Not Believe in Tears has it both ways: it is sometimes harsh in its depiction of individual frailty (alcoholism, male ego, female duplicity) while implying that the authorities provide insufficient remedies, a neat trick that surprised American audiences but not Russian ones, but it is also soft, even sentimental, in the final analysis. Katerina exclaims to Gosha, ''How long I searched for you!'' He replies, ''Eight days,'' the period of his tantrum, and she repeats her line, indicating a faith in the idea of the One True Other, the ultimate romantic concept. Gosha has complained earlier that growing cabbages is as noble a work as being an emperor. He also is offended that Katerina might think a person's social standing is more important than their personal qualities. If all Soviets had lived by these values, the Union would survive still: socialist morality and domesticity meet ambition tamed by common sense.

Unfortunately, the main characters of *Moscow* have much in common with the heroic statues of male and female workers which rise above exhibits to working-class accomplishments: they are too perfect, too idealized, simply too much to engage the long-term imagination. (Katerina and Gosha admit he is ''perfect''). As glossy exemplars of their place and time, however, they are excellent, as evidenced by the phenomenal box-office successes of this film, both in the Soviet Union (where it was the most popular film of the 1970s) and the US (Academy Award for Best Foreign Language Film of 1980). Happily, the film overcomes its hortatory roots, providing a wonderfully satisfying emotional experience: when viewed, this is *not* Soviet woman and man, but rather skillfully realized individual portraits created through fine acting and an engaging plot. Ultimately, comedy rescues *Moscow* from sentimentality—the viewer chuckles at these very human mortals struggling to get by.

—Andrew and Gina Macdonald

MOTHER

See **MAT**

MOTHER INDIA

See **BHARAT MATA**

MOTHER JOAN OF THE ANGELS

See **MATKA JOANNA OD ANIOLOW**

MUERTE DE UN CICLISTA

(Death of a Cyclist)

Spain, 1955

Director: Juan Antonio Bardem

Production: Cesareo Gonzalez (Madrid), Trionfalcine (Rome), and Guion PC (Paris); black and white, 35mm; running time: originally 91 minutes but cut by Spanish censors to 88 minutes. Released 9 September 1955, Madrid. Filmed 29 November 1954–29 March 1955.

Screenplay: Juan Antonio Bardem and Luis F. De Igoa, from the novel by De Igoa; **photography:** Alfredo Fraile; **editor:** Margarita Ochoa; **sound:** Alfonson Carvajal; **sound for French version:** Jacques Bonpaint; **art director:** Enrique Alarcon; **art director for French version:** Jacques Willemetz; **music:** Isidro B. Maztegui.

Cast: Lucia Bose (*Maria Jose de Castro*); Alberto Closas (*Juan*); Carlos Casaravilla (*Rafael Sandoval, called Rafa*); Otello Toso (*Miguel de Castro*); Bruna Corra (*Matilde*); Alicia Romay (*Cristina*); Julia Delgado Caro (*Dona Maria*); Matilde Muñoz Sampedro (*Neighbor*); Mercedes Albert (*Cristina*); Emilio Alonso (*Jorge*).

Award: Cannes Film Festival, Critics Prize, 1955.

Publications

Script:

Bardem, Juan Antonio, and Luis F. De. Ioga, *Mort d'un cycliste*, in *Avant-Scène du Cinéma* (Paris), 15 February 1964.

Books:

Oms, Marcel, *J. A. Bardem*, Lyons, n.d.

Gomez, Angel A. Perez, and Jose L. Martinez Montalban, *Cine espanol 1951–1978: Diccionario de directors*, Bilbao, 1978.

Klinowski, Jacek, and Adam Garbicz, editors, *Cinema, The Magic Vehicle: A Guide to Its Achievement: Journey Two*, Metuchen, New Jersey, 1979.

Egido, Luciano G., *J.A. Bardem*, Huelva, 1983(?).

Schwartz, Ronald, *Spanish Film Directors (1950–1985): 21 Profiles*, Metuchen, New Jersey, 1986.

Abajos de Pablos, Juan Eugenio Julio de, *Mis charlas con Juan Antonio Bardem*, Valladolid, 1996.

Articles:

''New Names: Spain,'' in *Sight and Sound* (London), Spring 1956.

Bardem, Juan, ''Spanish Highway,'' in *Films and Filming* (London), June 1957.

Aranda, J. F., ''Bardem: Une Methode de travail,'' in *Cinéma* (Paris), no. 33, 1959.

Durand, Philippe, ''Juan Antonio Bardem, homme d'Espagne,'' in *Image et Son* (Paris), October 1959.

Sadoul, Georges, ''Un Evénement important,'' in *Avant-Scène du Cinéma* (Paris), 15 February 1964.

* * *

At a meeting in Salamanca in 1955 Spain's young filmmakers declared: ''We want to struggle for a national cinema. Through our cinema we want to enter into contact with the people and the regions of Spain, with the people and the regions of the entire world.'' The spirit of Salamanca was manifested in a film released that same year, *Muerte de un ciclista*. Directed by Juan Antonio Bardem, *Muerte de un ciclista* won the critics grand prize at the Cannes Film Festival. It established contact not only with the people of Spain but also with international audiences and marked the rebirth of Spain cinema in the post-Civil War period.

The style of *Muerte de un ciclista* attests to the influence of a number of diverse filmmakers. In its dramatic use of cross-cutting it follows Eisenstein's principle of montage by collision; in its themes and subject matter it resembles such Italian neorealist works as Antonioni's *Cronaca di un amore* (1950). Indeed, some critics have criticized Bardem's style for being too eclectic and derivative. Nevertheless, *Muerte de un ciclista* is of exceptional interest as a document of the early 1950s in Spain. It reveals how privileged members of the Franco regime lived and provides a critical view of those who profited socially and financially from the dictatorship. It also offers brief glimpses of Madrid's lower classes and of university students impatient for change. Both of these groups would reject the assertion made by one of the upper class characters that they are living in a ''golden age.''

Muerte de un ciclista begins as a domestic drama. A car speeding down a windswept, deserted highway hits a man on a bicycle. After stopping and confirming that the victim is still alive, the couple in the car speed away, leaving the stricken man on the road. We subsequently learn that Juan, the man in the car, is a university professor; the woman who was driving is the wife of a wealthy businessman.

Muerte de un ciclista

Afraid that the accident will reveal their adulterous affair, they choose to let the cyclist die, thereby touching off a chain of events that leads the protagonist, a former soldier on the Falange side, to re-examine his life and to see the compromises that he has made and the ideals that he has sacrificed.

Juan is both an individual and a representative of a social class and a particular generation. He stands in sharp contrast to the university students whom he teaches. These students, like the real students in Madrid in the 1950s, hold demonstrations and denounce what they perceive to be injustices in the system. By alternating scenes between the university students and the upper class world of the lovers, Bardem expands the focus of his story and explores the social and political dimensions of the protagonists'' actions.

Although the ending of the film remains ambiguous (because of conditions imposed by the censor, some would argue), Bardem's point of view is clear. *Muerte de un ciclista* is a parable on the selfishness of the ruling classes, a meditation on the impact of Spain's past upon the present, and an expression of Bardem's fervent hope that the future will be different.

—Katherine Singer Kovács

MUI DU DU XANH

See **L'ODEUR DE LA PAPAYE VERTE**

MUJERES AL BORDE DE UN ATAQUE DE NERVIOS

(Women on the Verge of a Nervous Breakdown)

Spain, 1988

Director: Pedro Almodovar

Production: El Desoe and Lauren Films; Eastmancolor; running time: 98 minutes.

Executive producer: Agustin Almodovar; **associate producer:** Antonio Llorens; **screenplay:** Pedro Almodovar; **photography:** Jose

Luis Alcaine; **editor:** Jose Salcedo; **sound:** Guilles Ortion; **music:** Bernardo Bonezzi; **costume designer:** Jose Maria de Cossio.

Cast: Carmen Maura *(Pepa)*; Antonio Banderas *(Carlos)*; Fernando Guillén *(Ivan)*; Julieta Serrano *(Lucia)*; Maria Barranco *(Candela)*; Rossy de Palma *(Marisa)*; Kiti Manver *(Paulina)*; with Chus Lampreave, Yayo Calvo; Lotes Leon, and Angel de Andres Lopez.

Publications

Books:

Bouza Vidal, Nuria, *The Films of Pedro Almodovar*, translated by Linda Moore and Victoria Hughes, Madrid, 1988.

Smith, Paul Julian, *García Lorca/Almodóvar: Gender, Nationality, and the Limits of the Visible*, Cambridge, 1995.

Vernon, Kathleen M., and Barbara Morris, editors, *Post-Franco, Postmodern: The Films of Pedro Almodovar*, Westport, 1995.

Allinson, Mark, *A Spanish Labyrinth: The Films of Pedro Almodovar*, London, 2000.

Smith, Paul J., *Desire Unlimited: The Cinema of Pedro Almodovar*, New York, 2000.

Articles:

Bergdahl, G., ''Pedro Almodovar—en motvillig surrealist,'' in *Chaplin* (Stockholm), no. 5, 1988.

Toubiana, S., ''Femmes au bord de la crise de nerfs,'' in *Cahiers du Cinéma* (Paris), October 1988.

Interview (New York), November 1988.

Kael, Pauline, ''The Current Cinema: Unreal,'' in *New Yorker*, 14 November 1988.

Klawans, S., in *Nation* (New York), 5 December 1988.

New Republic (Washington, D.C.), 12 December 1988.

Los Angeles Times, 20 December 1988.

Razlogov, K., ''Karmen Maura na grant nervnogo sryba,'' in *Iskusstvo Kino* (Moscow), no. 4, 1989.

Robertson, R., ''Augustin Almodovar,'' in *Millimeter* (New York), January 1989.

Films in Review (New York), February 1989.

Canby, Vincent, in *New York Times Current Events Edition* (New York), 17 December 1989.

James, C., ''Film View: Sometimes Light Comes from Dark Places,'' in the *New York Times*, 24 June 1990.

D'Lugo, M., ''Almodóvar's City of Desire,'' in *Quarterly Review of Film and Video* (Reading), vol. 13, no. 4, 1991.

Warren, Michael, ''Spanish Director Samples Realism,'' in *Columbian* (Vancouver), 5 May 1996.

Neuhaus, Mel, in *Video Magazine* (New York), vol. 21, no. 8, December 1997.

Holland, Jonathan, ''Pedro Reigns in Spain: Almodovar Still Considered an Icon,'' in *Variety* (New York), vol. 370, no. 10, 20–26 April 1998.

Willem, Linda M., ''Almodóvar on the Verge of Cocteau's *La voix humaine*,'' in *Literature/Film Quarterly* (Salisbury), vol. 26, no. 2, April 1998.

Van Meter, Jonathan, ''A Man of Many Women,'' in *New York Magazine* (New York), 12 September 1999.

Cortina, Betty, ''On the Verge,'' in *Entertainment Weekly* (New York), 19 November 1999.

Terry-Azios, Diana, ''All About Almodóvar,'' in *Hispanic* (Washington, D.C.), vol. 13, no. 3, March 2000.

* * *

Pedro Almodovar's *Women on the Verge of a Nervous Breakdown*, a hilarious, offbeat and witty farce, follows the attempts of Pepa, a television actress forcefully played by Carmen Maura, to confront her estranged betrayer, an aging Lothario of a voice-over actor, who is unable to stay faithful even to his mistress. Pepa's progress can be tracked by the film's music: it begins with seductive mariachi music, a paean to love and romance, switches to mock-heroic sounds, and ends with a bitter-sweet song about broken hearts. The comedy comes from several factors: the increasing absurdity of the unravelling situation; the quasi-feminist outlook on female-male relationships; and a truly brilliant reversal of manners and expectations.

Although some action takes place at Pepa's studio, at the home of her lover's wife, in a lawyer's office, and in a wildly decorated taxi driven by a bleached blond driver, the main action, like that of a French bedroom farce, occurs in a single setting: Pepa's luxurious, but rapidly disintegrating, penthouse apartment. As she becomes more and more disturbed about her relationship to Ivan, Pepa tosses his possessions and pictures about, sets her bed on fire, throws a telephone and telephone answering machine through a window, frees chickens and ducks encaged on her balcony, and makes a dangerous, barbiturate-spiked gazpacho which guests splash on carpet and couch. At the same time, the number of people in the apartment grows rapidly as disparate actions become entangled around Pepa and her unhappy romance. Candela, who finds herself part of a Shiite terrorist conspiracy, seeks refuge from the police. Ivan's son, Carlos, and his possessive girlfriend, Marisa, come looking for an apartment to rent. Ivan's wife, crazed with jealousy, comes for a confrontation with the woman she thinks is running away with her husband. A telephone repairman and two policemen investigating an anonymous call about terrorists join the party. Downstairs, Ivan and his new girlfriend try to quietly remove his suitcase from the concierge's cubicle, only to find themselves thwarted, their car accidentally bombarded by flying objects from Pepa's apartment. What makes all this chaos doubly hilarious is the calm with which it is received: this is the way normal life works.

As in a Buñuel film, unlikely coincidences and chance encounters bring together seemingly perfect strangers—all of whom engage in intense conversations about life and love and all of whom ultimately have some interest in an evening flight to Stockholm. And as in Buñuel serious concerns are treated with a light, witty, irreverent touch. Almodovar addresses questions of insanity, parental rejection of children, marital infidelity, the breakup of marriage and family, the use and abuse of barbiturates, suicide, Shiite terrorists blowing up airplanes full of innocent passengers, lawyers who betray their clients' interest for personal gain, feminism and so on. Typical is a television advertisement for detergents: Pepa plays a typical mother, proud of her detergent which removes even the hard-to-get stains of blood and guts left on her serial-murderer son's shirts.

All of Almodovar's women are frustrated by the childish self-absorption of the men with whom they are involved. Ivan has literally driven his wife crazy. Son Carlos—a chip off the old blockhead—finds himself immediately attracted to his father's mistress, Pepa, but at the same time physically drawn to Candela, while his virginal girlfriend is passed out in a gazpacho-induced drug stupor on the patio. Candela thought her affair with a Shiite romantic, but, when he bought home his fellow terrorists, she discovered she was a safe house, not an object of affection. Pepa has had a comfortable, long-term affair with Ivan, a handsome womanizing weakling whose sexual impulses lead him to betrayal after betrayal. While continuing to mouth sweet-nothings to Pepa, he is running away with his wife's lawyer, Paulina (who helped him win his wife's case against him), and Paulina herself finds Ivan murmuring sweet nothings to Pepa at the airport on his way to Stockholm with Paulina. The initial shots of Ivan sum up the male as butterfly: he glides past beautiful woman after beautiful woman and to each murmurs words of flattery, romance and love; he wants them all and turns readily from one attraction to the next as his eyes lead him on. At the end Ivan's wife finds solace in insanity and institutionalization; Candela plunges into a new affair with Carlos—a younger Ivan; Paulina is left wondering whether she really wants this man she has betrayed her professional ethics for; Lucia has found a dream of seduction more satisfying than her real-life fiancé; and Pepa has undergone a catharsis and is ready to begin her life anew. The last scene has Pepa and Lucia exchanging female confidences, one of which is that Pepa is carrying Ivan's child; the cycle continues.

Feminist concerns, however, take a backseat to comedy. Almodovar, again like Buñuel but with his own distinctive touch, piles surreal detail on surreal detail, all presented with a completely straight face. Pepa's balcony is her "Noah's Ark," with various animals installed two by two (no one finds this odd in downtown Madrid, which itself is a fakey set). The taxi driver who continually picks her up by absurdly happy accident has shockingly bleached-blond hair and an impressive variety of dry goods for sale in the backseat; when he fails to provide eye drops for her on one trip he apologetically restocks for the next taxi ride. Pepa flirts immediately and unapologetically with her lover's grown son; he unashamedly flirts back in front of his girlfriend and a strange young woman he will almost immediately make a pass at. Pepa's apartment manager is a Jehovah's Witness who apologizes profusely for not being able to lie; she wishes she could. The climatic chase scene with an aging woman on the back of an aging Harley Davidson motorcycle potting shots at the taxi *cum* boutique is handled straight. Post-Franco Spain is a funny place, says Almodovar.

Women on the Verge is the kind of comedy that loses much in translation into critical prose, but which rewards the viewer with a hilarious experience. It is also a refreshingly sane take on male-female relations, as Almodovar's women are brought to the brink by their childishly narcissistic men, only to recover their sanity on the verge of disaster.

—Andrew and Gina Macdonald

THE MURDERERS ARE AMONGST US

See **DIE MÖRDER SIND UNTER UNS**

MURMUR OF THE HEART

See **SOUFFLE AU COUER**

THE MUSIC BOX

USA, 1932

Director: James Parrott

Production: Hal Roach; black and white; running time: 29 minutes; length: 2000 feet. Released 1932.

Screenplay: H. M. Walker; **photography:** Len Powers.

Cast: Stan Laurel, Oliver Hardy, Billy Gilbert (*Professor*).

Award: Oscar for Best Comedy Short, 1932.

Publications

Books:

Borde, Raymonde, and Charles Perrin, *Laurel et Hardy*, Paris, 1965.
Coursodon, Jean-Pierre, *Laurel et Hardy*, Paris, 1966.
Everson, William K., *The Films of Laurel and Hardy*, New York, 1967.
Barr, Charles, *Laurel and Hardy*, London, 1967.
McCaffrey, Donald, *Four Great Comedians*, New York, 1968.
Maltin, Leonard, *Movie Comedy Teams*, New York, 1970.
Maltin, Leonard, and others, *The Laurel and Hardy Book*, New York, 1973.
McCabe, John, *The Comedy World of Stan Laurel*, New York, 1974.
McCabe, John, *Laurel and Hardy*, New York, 1975; as *Mr. Laurel and Mr. Hardy*, London, 1984.
Lacourbe, Roland, *Laurel et Hardy*, Paris, 1975.
Anobile, Richard J., *A Fine Mess*, New York, 1975.
Giusti, Marco, *Laurel and Hardy*, Florence, 1978.
Guiles, Fred, *Stan*, London, 1980.
Pantieri, Jose, *I magnifico Laurel e Hardy*, Forli, 1986.
Crowther, Bruce, *Laurel and Hardy: Crown Princes of Comedy*, London, 1987.
Skretvedt, Randy, *Laurel and Hardy: The Magic Behind the Movies*, Beverly Hills, 1987, 1994.
Gehring, Wes D., *Laurel and Hardy: A Bio-Bibliography*, Westport, 1990.
Bergen, Ronald, *Laurel and Hardy*, New York, 1992.
McGarry, Annie, *Laurel and Hardy*, New York, 1992.
Grant, Neil, *Laurel and Hardy*, New York, 1995.
Mitchell, Glenn, *The Laurel and Hardy Encyclopedia*, North Pomfret, 1995.
MacGillivray, Scott, *Laurel and Hardy: From the Forties Forward*, Lanham, 1998.

Articles:

Wright, Basil, in *Cinema Quarterly* (London), Autumn 1932.
Monthly Film Bulletin (London), May 1946.

Today's Cinema (London), 8 May 1946.

Kine Weekly (London), 16 May 1946.

Robinson, David, ''The Lighter People,'' in *Sight and Sound* (London), July-September 1954.

Barnes, P., ''Cuckoo,'' in *Films and Filming* (London), August 1960.

''Laurel and Hardy Cult,'' in *Time* (New York), 14 July 1967.

Bracourt, Guy, ''Non, Loreleardi n'est pas mort!'' in *Ecran* (Paris), April and May 1972.

Allombert, G., ''V.I.P. B.I.S.,'' in *Image et Son* (Paris), no. 269, 1973.

Le Gueay, P., ''Laurel et Hardy: Une Allegorie de la catastrophe,'' in *Positif* (Paris), July-August 1978.

Classic Images (Indiana, Pennsylvania), July 1981, also September 1981, July 1982, and April 1984.

Reijnhout, B., ''Een sentimentele reis naar de wereld van Laurel & Hardy,'' in *Skoop* (Amsterdam), May-June 1984.

''*The Music Box,*'' in *Pratfall* (Universal City), vol. 2, no. 6–9, 1985.

Teleky, R., ''The Empty Box,'' in *Studies in Popular Culture*, vol. 15, no. 1, 1992.

* * *

With the combination of a superior director, James Parrott, an experienced comic writer, H. M. Walker, and a skillful photographer, Len Powers, to support the strong performances of Stan Laurel and Oliver Hardy, the 1932 Oscar winner, *The Music Box*, evolved. This three-reeler remains the quintessence of this duo of incompetence. Like many of their short works, this vehicle called for the performance of a task that baffled the meager brainpower of Stan and Ollie. While a number of misalliances concerning a domestic situation provided the basis for a string of gags and a plot for the team's films, comedy also developed from their attempt to fulfil various occupations—such as their roles as detectives, process servers, waiters, itinerant musicians, salesmen, and carpenters. In *The Music Box* they have a delivery and moving service. The task: get a piano up a hill with as many, if not more hillside steps than those employed by Sergei Eisenstein in the Odessa steps sequence of the 1925 classic, *Potemkin.*

What could have been one joke repeated over and over to the point of monotony, became, instead, a comic fugue with innovative variations. Stan and Ollie grunt and sweat to move the piano up the long flight of stairs, only to meet a nursemaid, a policeman, and a professor (played by Billy Gilbert) who interfere with their Sisyphean labors. The piano gets out of control three times because of the distractions from these onlookers and meddlers. Each time the crated piano on rollers plunges down the battery of steps, it creates increasing comic frustration for the bungling movers. At first the piano rolls by itself down the steps to the street below. Gag writer-director Parrott builds the joke with variations by having Ollie, more than Stan, become the victim of the runaway piano. Ollie tries to stop the piano the second time as it moves with a will of its own until it rolls over him; in a third plunge he catches the back of the crate and is dragged all the way down the steep steps. Yells of agony, accompanied by the jangling of the piano, punctuate the execution of this wild slapstick gag.

As in many of the team's movies, they labor with a mighty effort but obtain minimal results or a complete reversal of their goal. But with pathetic, whining determination they try again. Told by a mailman there is a back road up the hill, Stan and Ollie finally deliver the piano to the door. But, before the instrument is installed, many more mishaps occur, and they become increasingly angry with each other—to the point of exchanging effete blows. In the living room, which they have ravaged by their clumsiness and fighting, an interesting reversal develops in the humorous spirit of play. Since they have delivered a player piano, they plug it in and clean up the room as they execute a little, impromptu music-hall dance to the music. The comrades forget the recent altercations they have had over how to move the instrument. It is a light, fanciful vaudeville turn that they would later repeat in *Bonnie Scotland* (1935) when they pick up trash in a military compound.

The Music Box was considered by Stan Laurel to be the best short he and Oliver Hardy created. And, it should be realized, he often was, although he enacted the denser character of the two, the brains behind many elaborate gag variations on a situation in their features. This three-reeler ranks with some of the best short works of silent screen comedians Charles Chaplin, Harold Lloyd, and Buster Keaton. It is also testament to the fact that the silent screen tradition of innovative and cumulative gag sequences continued into the sound comedy films of the 1930s. Furthermore, *The Music Box* reveals the bond between two struggling, inferior men whose everyday lives are plagued with obstacles. Laurel and Hardy's plight promotes laughter and evokes a degree of sympathy which exceeds that accorded all other comedy teams.

—Donald W. McCaffrey

MY BEAUTIFUL LAUNDRETTE

UK, 1985

Director: Stephen Frears

Production: Working Title/SAF Productions for Channel 4; colour; 16mm; running time: 97 minutes; length: 3,507 feet. Released 1985.

Producers: Sarah Radclyffe, Tim Bevan; **screenplay:** Hanif Kureishi; **assistant directors:** Simon Hinkly, Waldo Roeg, Gary Davies; **photography:** Oliver Stapleton; **editor:** Mick Audsley; **assistant editors:** Jason Adams, Chris Cook; **sound editor:** ''Budge'' Tremlett; **sound recordist:** Albert Bailey; **sound re-recordist:** Peter Maxwell; **designer:** Hugo Luczyc Wyhowski; **music:** Ludus Tonalis.

Cast: Saeed Jaffrey (*Nasser*); Roshan Seth (*Papa*); Daniel Day-Lewis (*Johnny*); Gordon Warnecke (*Omar*); Derrick Branche (*Salim*); Shirley Anne Field (*Rachel*); Rita Wolf (*Tania*); Souad Faress (*Cherry*); Richard Graham (*Genghis*); Winston Graham (*1st Jamaican*); Dudley Thomas (*2nd Jamaican*); Garry Cooper (*Squatter*); Charu Bala Choksi (*Bilquis*); Persis Maravala (*Nasser's Elder Daughter*); Nisha Kapur (*Nasser's Younger Daughter*); Neil Cunningham (*Englishman*); Walter Donohue (*Dick O'Donnell*); Gurdial Sira (*Zaki*); Stephen Marcus (*Moose*); Dawn Archibald (*1st Gang Member*); Jonathan Moore (*2nd Gang Member*); Gerard Horan (*Telephone Man*); Ram John Holder (*Poet*); Bhasker (*Tariq*); Ayub Khan Din (*Student*); Dulice Leicier (*Girl in Disco*); Badi Uzzaman (*Dealer*);

My Beautiful Laundrette

Chris Pitt (*1st Kid*); Kerryan White (*2nd Kid*); Colin Campbell (*"Madame Butterfly" Man*); Sheila Chitnis (*Zaki's Wife*).

Publications

Script:

Kureishi, Hanif, *My Beautiful Laundrette*, London, 1986.

Books:

O'Neill, Eithne, *Stephen Frears*, Paris, 1994.

Kaleta, Kenneth C., *Hanif Kureishi: Postcolonial Storyteller*, Austin, 1998.

Articles:

Variety (New York), 21 August 1985.

Cook, Pam, in *Monthly Film Bulletin* (London), November 1985.

Lloyd, A., in *Films and Filming* (London), November 1985.

Root, Jane, "Scenes from a Marriage," in *Monthly Film Bulletin* (London), November 1985.

Walters, Margaret, in *Listener* (London), 21 November 1985.

Robinson, David, in *Sight and Sound* (London), Winter 1985–86.

Blaney, M., "The Empire Strikes Back," in *Filmfaust* (Frankfurt), February-March 1986.

Sawyer, C., in *Films in Review* (New York), June-July 1986.

Pally, M., "Kureishi like a fox," in *Film Comment* (New York), September-October 1986.

Sinyard, Neil, "Dickensian Visions in Modern British Film," in *Dickensian*, vol. 85, part 2, 1989.

Sinyard, Neil, "*Little Dorrit*," in *Cinema Papers* (Fitzroy), no. 72, March 1989.

Chari, H., "Decentered on the (A)isle of the Post-Colonial," in *Spectator* (Los Angeles), vol. 10, no. 1, 1989.

Dancyger, K., "The Bigger Picture: A Consideration of the Influence of Journalism and Theatre on the Feature Length Screenplay," in *Journal of Film and Video* (Los Angeles), no. 3, 1990.

"Frears, Stephen," in *Current Biography* (Bronx), vol. 51, no. 4, April 1990.

Gustavsson, Y., "Maktkriget i det privata," in *Filmhaftet* (Uppsala, Sweden), May 1990.

Quart, L., "The Politics of Irony: The Frears-Kureishi Films," in *Film Criticism* (Meadville, Pennsylvania), no. 1–2, 1991–92.

"Kureishi, Hanif," in *Current Biography* (Bronx), vol. 53, no. 2, February 1992.

Miller, J.B., "For His New Film, Hanif Kureishi Reaches for a *Beautiful Laundrette*," in *New York Times Current Events Edition* (New York), 2 August 1992.

Salmon, P., "Revising the Traditions: Hanif Kureishi and Contemporary British Cinema," in *Canadian Journal of Film Studies* (Ottawa), vol. 2, no. 2–3, 1993.

Séquences (Haute-Ville), no. 181, November/December 1995.

Hedling, E., "Shopkeepers, Profiteers, and Libertines," in *Lahikuva* (Turku), no. 3, 1995.

"Hanif Kureishi," in *Sight & Sound* (London), vol. 6, no. 5, May 1996.

Snyder, Trish, in *Chatelaine* (Toronto), February 1998.

* * *

In an interview, Haneif Kureishi, the writer of *My Beautiful Laundrette*, revealed that his original idea for the film was an historical epic tracing the fortunes of a Pakistani family from their emigration to Britain in 1945 until the 1970s. Yet the film was realised as a surrealistic comedy-thriller set exclusively in Thatcher-stricken south London, with the narrative drive supplied by the meteoric rise of Omar, a young Asian businessman. Commercial pressures may have insured this transformation of the *My Beautiful Laundrette* project but the end result suggests a transcendence of inevitable constraints. The film, which cost the meagre sum of £60,000, was commissioned for the "Film on Four" slot on television, but after a screening at the Edinburgh festival had received enthusiastic reviews, it succeeded on the international cinema trail, picking up prizes and helping to provoke numerous claims of a British cinema renaissance.

Critical and box-office success is unusual for a film in which the main protagonist is black and gay, a representation which until *My Beautiful Laundrette* had been virtually absent from British cinema. Kureishi has spoken of his positive prejudice against white middle-class heterosexual men within his work, a stance which is maintained by his subsequent script for *Sammie and Rosie Get Laid*. In *My Beautiful Laundrette* conventional heterosexuality is parodied in the scene which shows the opening of Omar's new laundrette. Here

Omar's uncle waltzes with his mistress Rachel among the washing machines, oblivious to both the onlooking crowd and Omar and Johnny's lusty celebrations in the back-room. One camera position during this scene is a spy's view of Nasser and Rachel from this back-room. This contributes to the ironic treatment of the heterosexual pair because it provides the audience with a vantage point on their activity. It is noteworthy, however, that this position does not coincide with the point of view of the gay lovers and that the Nasser/Rachel relationship is not representative of heterosexuality in general.

The film's politics cannot be pigeon-holed. If it was a gay separatist film we might expect it to emphasize more strongly the oppression of gay sexuality and to depart from the romantic conventions of mainstream cinema. Instead the film shows to a degree how a gay relationship may be celebrated as an old-fashioned romance. For the most part other characters are unaware of Omar and Johnny's love. The audience is asked to cherish this love as a secret rather than dwelling on the problems of a relationship barred from the public realm. When the laundrette opens Omar looks into a transparent division and sees Johnny looking back. Their reflections are shown to overlap, an effect which intimates a sublime notion of romantic union.

Equally striking is the way that *My Beautiful Laundrette* departs from the liberal view that racial minorities require positive images in order to counter-act racism and under-representation. The men within Omar's family are to an extent selfish gangsters. Omar exploits his lover Johnny; Uncle Nasser is a Rachman-style landlord; meanwhile Salim, whose status as a relation remains enigmatic and dubious, shares a store of reciprocal contempt and violence with a National Front gang. The film is out to show that the Asian minority is not automatically in opposition to the dominant ideology, while shaking the conservative assumption that British identity is a stable property.

However, Omar's male kin are not all Thatcherites. In contrast to Uncle Nasser, Omar's father has a past as a left-wing journalist in Bombay. Despite being confined to bed and the bottle he continues to advise his son that education is the only virtue. We can see here how the film retains a sense of history alongside its innovative representations of the Asian community. The opposition established between the father and Uncle Nasser alludes to a complex heritage of conflicting ideologies within the community. The development of the narrative provides us with a sense of history in which beliefs from the past become the debris of today: Omar's triumph with the washing machines makes his father's humanistic hopes seem like futile idealism and brings the father and Nasser together again as a generation which has been superseded.

The emergence of a new era is conveyed by the refurbished laundrette where the task of washing is packaged as an entertaining past-time. "Powders," as they call the building, is not just an entrepreneurial investment but also a space in which customers can play out their fantasies, as Nasser and Rachel demonstrate. The spectacular interior of "Powders" reveals the deviation of *My Beautiful Laundrette* from the strict visual code of verisimilitude, which broadly speaking has had a certain hold on ideas about what constitutes "Quality" British cinema.

The menacing atmosphere which certain scenes achieve indicates the influence of director Stephen Frears whose previous work for the cinema included the stylish gangster film *The Hit*. In particular, the encounters between Selim and the gang are nightmarish, even though this troupe of thugs are at times comically grotesque. Critics have also praised Frears's capacity to let strong performances emerge, a quality born out by his Hollywood debut, *Dangerous Liaisons*. *My Beautiful Laundrette* provided a springboard to stardom for the actor Daniel Day Lewis, while Saeed Jaffrey and Shirley Anne Field received high acclaim.

—Daniel Williams

MY BRILLIANT CAREER

Australia, 1979

Director: Gillian Armstrong

Production: New South Wales Film Corporation and Margaret Fink Films; Panavision, Eastmancolor; running time: 100 minutes; length: 9,005 feet. Released 1979.

Producer: Margaret Fink; **associate producer:** Jane Scott; **screenplay:** Eleanor Witcombe, from the novel by Miles Franklin; **assistant directors:** Mark Egerton, Mark Turnbull, Steve Andrews; **photography:** Don McAlpine; **camera operators:** Louis Irving, Peter Moss; **editor:** Nicholas Beauman; **sound editor:** Greg Bell; **sound recordist:** Don Connolly; **production designer:** Luciana Arrighi; **art director:** Neil Angwin; **costume designer:** Anna Senior; **music:** Nathan Waks.

Cast: Judy Davis (*Sybylla Melvyn*); Sam Neill (*Harry Beecham*); Wendy Hughes (*Aunt Helen*); Robert Grubb (*Frank Hawden*); Max Cullen (*Mr. McSwat*); Pat Kennedy (*Aunt Gussie*); Aileen Britton (*Grandma Bossier*); Peter Whitford (*Uncle Julius*); Carole Skinner (*Mrs. McSwat*); Alan Hopgood (*Father*); Julia Blake (*Mother*); Tony Hughes (*Peter McSwat*); Tina Robinson (*Lizer McSwat*); Aaron Corrin (*Jimmy McSwat*); Sharon Crouch (*Sarah McSwat*); Robert Austin (*Willie McSwat*); Mark Spain (*Tommy McSwat*); Simone Buchanan (*Mary Anne McSwat*); Hayley Anderson (*Rosie Jane McSwat*); Marion Shad (*Gertie*); Suzanne Roylance (*Biddy*); Zelda Smyth (*Ethel*); Amanda Pratt (*Blanche Derrick*); Bill Charlton (*Joe Archer*).

Publications

Books:

Tulloch, John, *Australian Cinema: Industry, Narrative, and Meaning*, Sydney and London, 1982.

McFarlane, Brian, *Words and Images: Australian Novels into Films*, Richmond, Victoria, 1983.

Hall, Sandra, *Critical Business: The New Australian Cinema in Review*, Adelaide, 1985.

Moran, Albert, and Tom O'Regan, editors, *An Australian Film Reader*, Sydney, 1985.

Mathews, Sue, *35mm Dreams: Conversations with Five Directors about the Australian Film Revival*, Ringwood, Victoria, 1987.

My Brilliant Career

McFarlane, Brian, *Australian Cinema 1970–85*, London, 1987.

Collins, Felicity, *The Films of Gillian Armstrong*, St. Kilda, 1999.

Articles:

Fink, Margaret, and Gillian Armstrong, in *Cinema Papers* (Melbourne) March-April 1979.

Metro, Spring 1979.

Variety (New York), 23 May 1979.

McFarlane, Brian, in *Cinema Papers* (Melbourne), September-October 1979.

Adair, Gilbert, in *Monthly Film Bulletin* (London), February 1980.

Wallace, Melanie, in *Cineaste* (New York), Spring 1980.

Image et Son (Paris), November 1980.

Oakes, Philip, in *Listener* (London), 23 February 1984.

Arnold, Gordon B., ''From Big Screen to Small Screen: *My Brilliant Career* Directed by Gillian Armstrong and Starring Judy Davis,'' in *Library Journal* (New York), vol. 114, no. 9, 15 May 1989.

Bertrand, I., ''Woman's Voice: The Autobiographical Form in Three Australian Filmed Novels,'' in *Literature/Film Quarterly* (Salisbury, Maryland), no. 2, 1993.

''Armstrong, Gillian,'' in *Current Biography* (Bronx), vol. 56, no. 8, August 1995.

Wood, Gaby, ''*My Brilliant Career* Down Under in Film and Feminism,'' in *New Statesman* (London), 27 March 1998.

* * *

Gillian Armstrong's film of Miles Franklin's novel remains remarkably true to the spirit of the original which, almost unbelievably, considering the modernity of its sentiments and the ebullient confidence of its tone, was written by a young woman of 16 and first published in 1901. That it was not reprinted until 1966 can be explained partly by the fact that it was withdrawn by its author, who was annoyed at the ''stupid literalness'' with which it was taken to be her own autobiography. However, the fact that the novel's sequel, *My Career Goes Bung*, was rejected by publishers as too outspoken and not published until 1946, also suggests that, even if it had not been withdrawn, *My Brilliant Career* would have stood little chance of establishing itself in the male-dominated pantheon of ''great'' Australian literature at the turn of the century.

The story centres on Sybylla Melvyn, a young woman living with her parents on a remote farm in the bush. She dreams of living a more intellectually and culturally rewarding life, and is writing a memoir. When she goes to stay on her grandmother's estate at Caddagat things improve somewhat, and she is also courted by Frank Hawden, a rather fatuous English immigrant, and Harry Beecham, a young landowner. She is attracted by the latter, and is faced with the choice of trying to pursue a "brilliant career" or getting married.

There are, of course, parallels with Miles Franklin's own life here—the dusty, arid Possum Gully is clearly modelled on Stillwater, the smallholding to which her family moved from a far more attractive cattle station in the mountains of New South Wales; and Caddagat is a fictional version of Talbingo, where her maternal grandmother lived and with whom she went to stay for a few years of her adolescence. But these are incidental details, and the real importance of both novel and film lies in their acute delineation of a young woman's feelings at a transitional moment in her life. As Carmen Callil has aptly noted, "Miles Franklin was decades ahead of her time, and *My Brilliant Career* was written for an audience not yet born. For in the character of Sybylla Melvyn, Miles Franklin created a character who mouths with incredible charm but deadly accuracy the fears, conflicts and torments of every girl, with an understanding usually associated with writers of the 1960s and 70s." All the qualities which Callil admires in the book have been triumphantly retained by the film which, it might be added, also manages to exclude some of the original's slightly less attractive qualities, such as its nationalism (which it shared with many of its literary contemporaries) and a certain tendency to let ebullience and exuberance overflow into gush and overly self-conscious romanticism. The dialogue, too, has been considerably updated and "de-literacised," but the *sentiments* expressed by Sybylla are very much those that animate her in the novel.

All credit must go here to Judy Davis, whose performance makes Sybylla utterly convincing and never allows her effervescence and high spirits to become wearying or trying. The only problem, perhaps, is that in her hands Sybylla comes across as so attractive, capable, and accomplished that it sometimes becomes difficult to understand the oft-mentioned fact of her "plain-ness" and the various other negative judgements passed upon her by the other characters. Gillian Armstrong's mise-en-scène is also a triumph, not simply in its loving attention to period detail but in the way in which it is used to comment on or reflect Sybylla's feelings, and in particular her growing consciousness of herself as being different from those around her and as destined for higher things. Particularly important in this respect are the contrasts between Possum Gully and Caddagat, the latter making Sybylla more aware than ever of the possibilities of life beyond the bush. Significantly, when Sybylla plays the piano at home, with no-one paying any attention, the effect is decidedly jangly, whereas at her grandmother's, with an appreciative audience, the change in style is most striking. At the same time, however, the elegance of some of the scenes at Harry Beecham's mansion suggest not simply the lifestyle which Sybylla desires but also the kinds of constraints and limitations that she fears may come with it.

Scenes such as these work extremely effectively to communicate the sense that Sybylla is still in the process of developing and maturing, that she is still trying to decide on her role in life, and is subject to all sorts of contradictory pressures, both internal and external. Important here, too, is the characterization of Harry, who is portrayed very much as a potential soul-mate and worthy partner, thus facing Sybylla with a very real and difficult choice with which the spectator can clearly emphathise. Indeed, although nothing actually "happens," some of the scenes between Sybylla and Harry contain a distinct sexual charge.

My Brilliant Career has been "rediscovered" as something of a proto-feminist text, which it undoubtedly is, but it is also very much a Bildungsroman which works remarkably well on both a particular and more general level. Like the best of all such works in the genre it is both poignant and amusing and both of these qualities have been well served by Armstrong's meticulous and occasionally sumptuous mise-en-scène, Judy Davis's splendid performance, which never goes over the top, as it so easily could, and a score which makes poignant use of (what else?) Schumann's *Scenes from Childhood.*

—Sylvia Paskin

MY DARLING CLEMENTINE

USA, 1946

Director: John Ford

Production: Twentieth Century-Fox; black and white, 35mm; running time: 97 minutes. Released November 1946. Filmed on location in Monument Valley, Utah and in New Mexico.

Producer: Samuel G. Engel; **screenplay:** Samuel G. Engel and Winston Miller based on a story by Sam Hellman, from the novel *Wyatt Earp, Frontier Marshal* by Stuart N. Lake; **photography:** Joseph P. MacDonald; **editor:** Dorothy Spencer; **art directors:** James Basevi and Lyle R. Wheeler; **music:** Cyril Mockridge and David Buttolph; **orchestrator:** Edward B. Powell; **special effects:** Fred Sersen; **costume designer:** Rene Hubert.

Cast: Henry Fonda (*Wyatt Earp*); Linda Darnell (*Chihuahua*); Victor Mature (*Doc John Holliday*); Walter Brennan (*Old Man Clanton*); Tim Holt (*Virgil Earp*); Ward Bond (*Morgan Earp*); Cathy Downs (*Clementine Carter*); Alan Mowbry (*Granville Thorndyke*); John Ireland (*Billy Clanton*); Grant Withers (*Ike Clanton*); Roy Roberts (*Mayor*); Jane Darwell (*Kate Nelson*); Russell Simpson (*John Simpson*); Francis Ford (*Dad, old soldier*); J. Farrell McDonald (*Mac the barman*); Don Garner (*James Earp*); Ben Hall (*Barber*); Arthur Walsh (*Hotel clerk*); Jack Pennick (*Coach driver*); Louis Mercier (*Francois*); Micky Simpson (*Sam Clanton*); Fred Libby (*Phin Clanton*); Harry Woods (*Luke*); Charles Stevens (*Indian Joe*); Danny Borzage (*Accordian player*); Mae Marsh.

Publications

Script:

Engel, Samuel G., and Winston Miller, in *My Darling Clementine: John Ford, Director*, edited by Robert Lyons, New Brunswick,

My Darling Clementine

New Jersey, 1984; also in *Avant-Scène Cinéma* (Paris), February 1985.

Books:

Mitry, Jean, *John Ford*, Paris, 1954.
Everson, William K., and George N. Fenin, *The Westerns: From Silents to Cinerama*, New York, 1962.
Haudiquet, Philippe, *John Ford*, Paris, 1964.
Bogdanovich, Peter, *John Ford*, Berkeley, 1968; revised edition, 1978.
Springer, John, *The Fondas: The Films and Careers of Henry, Jane and Peter Fonda*, New York, 1970.
Kitses, Jim, *Horizons West*, Bloomington, Indiana, 1970.
Baxter, John, *The Cinema of John Ford*, New York, 1971.
Place, Janey, *The Western Films of John Ford*, Secaucus, New Jersey, 1973.
McBride, Joseph, and Michael Wilmington, *John Ford*, New York and London, 1975.
Sarris, Andrew, *The John Ford Movie Mystery*, London, 1976.
Sinclair, Andrew, *John Ford*, London and New York 1979.
Ford, Dan, *Pappy: The Life of John Ford*, Englewood Cliffs, New Jersey, 1979.
Anderson, Lindsay, *About John Ford*, London, 1981; New York 1983.
Caughie, John, editor, *Theories of Authorship: A Reader*, London, 1981.
Schatz, Thomas, *Hollywood Genres: Formulas, Filmmaking, and the Studio System*, New York 1981.
Fonda, Henry, and Howard Teichmann, *Fonda: My Life*, New York, 1981.
Goldstein, Norm, *Henry Fonda: His Life and Work*, London, 1982.
Thomas, Tony, *The Films of Henry Fonda*, Secaucus, New Jersey, 1983.
Reed, Joseph W., *Three American Originals: John Ford, William Faulkner, Charles Ives*, Middletown, Connecticut, 1984.
Gallagher, Tag, *John Ford: The Man and His Films*, Berkeley, 1986.
Stowell, Peter, *John Ford*, Boston, 1986.
Lourdeaux, Lee, *Italian & Irish Filmmakers in America: Ford, Capra, Coppola and Scorsese*, Springfield, 1990; 1993.
Darby, William, *John Ford's Westerns: A Thematic Analysis, with a Filmography*, Jefferson, 1996.
Davis, Ronald L., *John Ford: Hollywood's Old Master*, Norman, 1997.

Girus, Sam B., *Hollywood Renaissance: The Cinema of Democracy in the Era of Ford, Capra, and Kazan*, New York, 1998.
Levy, Bill, *John Ford: A Bio-Bibliography*, Westport, 1998.
Eyman, Scott, *Print the Legend: The Life and Times of John Ford*, New York, 1999.

Articles:

Variety (New York), 9 October 1946.
New York Times, 4 December 1946.
New Yorker, 14 December 1946.
Auriol, Jean-Georges, ''Lettre à John Ford sur *My Darling Clementine*,'' in *Revue du Cinéma* (Paris), Spring 1947.
Rieuperout, Jean-Louis, in *Quarterly of Film, Radio and Television* (Berkeley), Winter 1952.
Springer, Henry, ''Henry Fonda,'' in *Films in Review* (New York), November 1960.
Cowie, Peter, ''Fonda,'' in *Films and Filming* (London), April 1962.
McVay, Douglas, ''The Five Worlds of John Ford,'' in *Films and Filming* (London), June 1962.
Fonda, Henry, ''Fonda on Fonda,'' in *Films and Filming* (London), February 1963.
Brode, Henry, in *Cineaste* (New York), Fall 1968.
Wood, Robin, in *Film Comment* (New York), Fall 1971.
''Ford Issue'' of *Filmkritik* (Munich), January 1972.
Buffa, M., and C. Scarrone, ''Per una rilettura del cinema classico americano,'' in *Filmcritica* (Rome), October-December 1973.
Gomery, Douglas, ''Mise-en-Scène in John Ford's *My Darling Clementine*,'' in *Wide Angle* (Athens, Ohio), vol. 2, no. 4, 1978.
Marinero, P., in *Casablanca* (Madrid), January 1983.
Darby, W., ''Musical Links in *Young Mr. Lincoln, My Darling Clementine*, and *The Man Who Shot Liberty Valance*,'' in *Cinema Journal* (Austin, Texas), no. 1, 1991.
Nielsen, R., ''Ray's Way: John Ireland in *My Darling Clementine*,'' in *Classic Images* (Muscatine), no. 191, May 1991.
Erisman, F., ''The Night Christopher Lloyd Danced with Mary Steenburgen,'' in *Jounal of Popular Film and Television*, vol. 22, no. 1, Spring 1992.
Luhr, W., ''Reception, Representation, and the OK Corral,'' in *Florida State University Conference on Literature and Film*, vol. 18, 1993.
Kermode, Mark, ''Video: *My Darling Clementine* Directed by John Ford,'' in *Sight and Sound* (London), vol. 4, no. 5, May 1994.
Combs, Richard, ''The First Cut is Still the Bleakest: *The Wild Bunch* Directed by Sam Peckinpah/*My Darling Clementine* Directed by John Ford,'' in *Times Literary Supplement* (London), no. 4832, 10 November 1995.
Romney, Jonathan, ''America's Creation Myth: *My Darling Clementine* Directed by John Ford,'' in *New Statesman & Society* (London), vol. 8, no. 381, 1 December 1995.
Simmon, Scott, ''Concerning the Weary Legs of *Wyatt Earp*: The Classic Western According to Shakespeare,'' in *Literature/Film Quarterly* (Salisbury), vol. 24, no. 2, 1996.
Yawn, M., and B. Beatty, ''John Ford's Vision of the Closing West: From Optimism to Cynicism,'' in *Film and History* (Cleveland), vol. 26, no. 1/4, 1996.
Schwengler, O., ''Exercices de style a 'OK Corral,''' in *Cinémaction* (Conde-sur-Noireau, France), vol. 86, no. 1, 1998.

* * *

My Darling Clementine is considered the archetype of the classic western. In retelling the familiar story of the Earp brothers standing up to the evil Clanton family, director John Ford proved Hollywood genre films would become great cultural artefacts. However, Ford, one of the industry's most honored directors, is usually better remembered for other masterworks. While *My Darling Clementine* is considered one of his better films, it is only one of many in a truly remarkable career.

Ford, however, did not want to direct this classic work originally. After World War II Ford, like many of Hollywood's highly rated directors, formed an independent company, in this case Argosy Pictures. But he still owed Twentieth Century-Fox one more film. (Fox's production chief Darryl F. Zanuck tried to tempt Ford to renegotiate his Fox contract for a guaranteed $600,000 per year plus limited freedom but Ford refused.) Zanuck assigned Ford to *My Darling Clementine* starring Fox stars Henry Fonda and Victor Mature. Shooting began in Monument Valley in May, 1946, and was completed within 45 days. Zanuck found Ford's version too long, and the story unclear, so he cut 30 minutes, and re-structured some of the remaining material. Released in November, 1946 the film received favorable reviews, and earned respectable, but not record-breaking revenues.

The structure of *My Darling Clementine* is straightforward, and symmetrical, opening with the ominous meeting of the Earps with the Clantons, and closing with the gun-fight at the OK Corral (and Wyatt's half-hearted promise to return). All this seems to take place in three or four days. Although the events are grounded in history (Ford claimed to have gotten this version directly from friend Wyatt Earp), the details were transformed to make a popular film. The Doc Holliday figure was transfigured the most. Like central characters in *The Searchers* and *The Man Who Shot Liberty Valance*, Holliday tragically stands between primitivism and civilization. Unlike the Earps, this character fails to find a way to reconcile his place in the changing world, and turns to alcohol and a desire for death.

Disintegration of the family was a dominant theme in Ford's work prior to World War II. In *My Darling Clementine* the contrast between the Earps and Clantons is clearly drawn, with death at the ultimate shootout predestined. The Earps are diametrically opposed to the Clantons, yet strong similarities exist. In both cases, the father holds powerful authority. ''Old Man'' Clanton beats his sons with a whip, bullying them like animals. The Earps, however, are more civilized, and continually appeal to their unseen father (''How will we tell Pa?''). In the end Wyatt and Morgan, the surviving brothers choose to return to tell Pa of recent events rather than remain to help civilize Tombstone.

My Darling Clementine seems to present a well known story, set in the familiar context of the western. Upon closer examination of the film, however, one can still see the confusion Zanuck must have sensed, such as the sequence in which the Earps come to town. Wyatt settles down for a shave when gunshots arouse him. He goes through the hotel (next to the barber shop) and emerges, in a medium long shot, alone on the sidewalk. A barber pole serves as a reference to locate him in the darkness. Wyatt goes across the street to the source of the trouble. We see him with the Oriental Saloon in the background, its doors clearly seen in deep space. Wyatt enters the Oriental saloon to capture Indian Joe, the perpetrator of the trouble. Wyatt then gathers the barber from the crowd of spectators and seeks a continuation of his shave. Later in the film we learn, through several long establishing shots, that there is *no* Oriental saloon on the other side of the street. This absence of the continual ''referential focus'' disrupts the film's visual rhythm, setting this sequence apart from the rest of the film. There are numerous other examples of visual discontinuity in this film, all violating rules of classical Hollywood style. Indeed in this seemingly simple work Ford develops a complex visual pattern of stability and disruption in the world of Tombstone. Ford seems to be foreshadowing his autocritiques of the western genre made throughout the 1950s and 1960s.

In its use of generic elements *My Darling Clementine* suggests the western myth might not be as stable as it was prior to World War II. Although in the end the film seems to promise the formation of a utopian community, the western hero does not seem to be able to reconcile his individual and social roles. He rides off in the closing sequence with only a vague suggestion he will return to Clementine and the community. To further play on the hero's ambiguous character Ford continually reminds us that he does not fit in. *My Darling Clementine*'s most cited sequence is not its elaborate gunfight, but rather a dance in which Wyatt Earp displays his lack of grace on the dance floor. This Eastern ritual is here to stay, whether the western hero fits in or not. Ford seems to have been influenced in *My Darling Clementine* by his recent military experience during World War II. Despite the fact Ford made seven films about the United States Cavalry, *My Darling Clementine* seems to be his most militarist western, both in theme and action. The Earps represent a new type of law—cold and calculating. They operate within the law, yet are always clearly able to kill in a most efficient manner. Family ties and a sense of justice seem all that is necessary to justify action. Civilization defends itself only by obliterating the other side, and then leaving when the job is done, much as the popular image of the role of the American military during World War II.

In the end, in structure, theme and style Ford seems to be undercutting the anarchic spirit of the western, so celebrated in 1939 with his *Stagecoach*. The style seems classical but upon closer inspection is not. The themes seem classical, but contradictions and loose ends abound. Even closure, the Hollywood system's point of "wrapping the package," is confused and ambiguous. *My Darling Clementine* represents the work of a filmmaker ready to break out of the studio system and go onto more complex projects, as Ford would. In an uneven path he would make his way to his masterworks, westerns of complexity and ambiguity: *The Searchers* (1956) and *The Man Who Shot Liberty Valance* (1962). *My Darling Clementine*, a masterwork in its own right, foreshadows Ford's greatest films.

—Douglas Gomery

MY LIFE TO LIVE

See **VIVRE SA VIE**

MY NAME IS JOE

Great Britain, 1998

Director: Ken Loach

Production: Parallax Pictures and Road Movies Vierte Produktion; color; running time: 103 min. Released 15 May 1998, Cannes Film Festival, France, and 6 November 1998, London. Filmed in Glasgow and Inverary, Scotland.

Producer: Rebecca O'Brien; **executive producer:** Ulrich Felsberg; **screenplay:** Paul Laverty; **photography:** Barry Ackroyd; **editor:** Jonathan Morris; **production design:** Martin Johnson; **casting:** Gillian Berrie, Steven Mochrie; **music:** George Fenton; **makeup:** Anastasia Shirley; **sound:** Ray Beckett, John Hayward.

Cast: Peter Mullan (*Joe*); Louise Goodall (*Sarah*); Edna McKay (*Liam*); Annemarie Kennedy (*Sabine*); Gary Lewis (*Shanks*); Lorraine McIntosh (*Maggie*); David Hayman (*McGowan*).

Awards: British Independent Film Awards for Best Director of an Independent British Film, Best British Independent Film, and Best Original Screenplay, 1998; Cannes Film Festival Best Actor Award (Peter Mullan), 1998; Danish Film Critics Award (Bodil) for Best Non-American Film, 1998; Danish Film Academy Award (Robert) for Best Non-American Film, 1998; London Critics Circle Award for Best British Newcomer of the Year (Peter Mullan), 1999.

Publications

Articles:

Niogret, Hubert, review in *Positif* (Paris), October 1998
Williamson, Judith, review in *Sight and Sound* (London), November 1998
Distelmeyer, Jan, review in *EPD Film* (Frankfurt), January 1999

* * *

In the 1990s Ken Loach gave us a string of powerful human dramas borne by the social commitment and humane solidarity with the weakest members of society so characteristic of the director; in his films they are not mere victims, but also strong individuals, people possessed of integrity and identity. However, the difference from his political television films of the 1960s and 1970s is pronounced. They depicted the class struggle, but in the 1990s films the focus shifted to people marginalized by the labor market who were fighting for their self-esteem in an England where industrialism was on its way out. In the 1990s, too, Loach made what is for him a rare trip beyond the shores of England to countries and periods where people could talk of revolution with hope. But *Land and Freedom* and *Carla's Song* are not Loach at his best. He is at his best when portraying the English worker.

The Joe of the title is a former alcoholic who is trying to stay on the wagon. He lives on social security and moonlighting, and works off his restless energy coaching a group of social rejects on the football field. One of his proteges is an ex-junkie, Liam, whose girlfriend Sabine is mainlining, and whose offspring is monitored by the local health department visitor, Sarah. This is how Sarah and Joe meet, and although they have both been bitten and are now twice shy, their encounter develops into a tentative, exploratory love—a rare theme for Loach, and rarer still depicted with such warmth and subtlety. Their growing love is put to the test when Joe agrees to run drugs in order to save Liam from McGowan's gangsters, to whom he owes £1500. Joe's solidarity with and human sympathy for Liam butts up against Sarah's view that he is thereby obtaining drugs to create even more Liams. The difference in perception is not only personal but also determined by class, for although they both move among the underclass, Joe is part of it and indeed grew up with McGowan, the gangster boss, while Sarah views it from without. She is a professional with a car and a regular job, and faced with the alternatives Joe lists for Liam's predicament, the natural rhetorical question is ''What would you have done?''

The film opens with a close-up of Joe telling his story to an Alcoholics Anonymous meeting, and ends on a calm long shot of Joe and Sarah leaving Liam's funeral: from the man on his own to a hint of a future together. Between the two shots we are given the story of a man who is repeatedly being forced to struggle his way out of his own and other people's problems: alcohol, drug-related jobs, debts, and old but compromising friendships. The first half of the film is related in light, comedy-colored tones, with a restless energy in the editing and movement shaped in accordance with Joe's own temperament. Everything takes place at a run as Joe keeps up his level of activity so as not to relapse into alcoholism. There is great strength and humanity in this character, a powerful warmth and charisma that Sarah falls for, too—and is afraid of. But just as Liam is the cause of their meeting, he is also the cause of their separation. The light tone fades and the story assumes gloomy hues with the assault on Liam on the football pitch cross-edited with Sabine's behavior at the social services office, which leads directly to Joe's job as a drug courier. The insoluble moral and human dilemma now becomes didactically illustrated, with Joe torn between his desire to keep his relationship and his desire to help Liam. Behind this, the other issues pile up. How and why did Liam get into this predicament? Why has Sarah been unable to do anything about a situation of which she, if anyone, is aware? However, if Liam is a loser there is a cause, and if Joe is a fighter, he is also up against impossible odds. Even if the film ends with a hint of conciliation between Sarah and Joe, any hope is not unequivocal but merely defiant.

To Joe, like other Loach characters of the 1990s, what counts is surviving with some kind of self respect, although not necessarily in accordance with the accepted definitions. In *My Name is Joe* and *Raining Stones* stealing money to pay for a dress for a first communion or stealing Brazilian football kit to boost the self-esteem of a team that has never won a match isn't depicted as breaking the law, but rather as a strength, a positive manifestation of solidarity and independent initiative. Those scenes condense the dilemma of the working class.

Ken Loach possesses a rare ability to depict a community as if it were cut straight out of real life, a reality Loach observes from a distance but with empathy and repose, devoid of sentimentality or easy answers such as those provided by feel-good films like *The Full Monty* and *Brassed Off.* Authenticity and genuineness are the key, and for viewers they endow the people and the setting with as much importance as the surrounding plot. One of the best sides of cinema has always been its inherent ability to record and capture reality. For an artist like Loach the result is a successful fusion of a human, powerful, politically and socially relevant story with images from a world that seldom appears on the silver screen, and even more rarely with the solidarity and concerned commitment characteristic of his films.

—Dan Nissen

THE NAKED CITY

USA, 1948

Director: Jules Dassin

Production: Hellinger Productions for United-International Pictures; black and white, 35mm; running time: 96 minutes. Released 4 March 1948. Filmed in Stillman's Gym, the Roxy Theater, the Whitehall Building, the City Morgue, Roosevelt Hospital, the Universal Building, and Williamsburg Bridge in New York City.

Producers: Mark Hellinger with Jules Buck; **screenplay:** Malvin Wald and Albert Maltz, from an unpublished story by Malvin Wald; **photography:** William Daniels; **editor:** Paul Weatherwax; **sound:** Leslie I. Carey and Vernon W. Kramer; **art director:** John F. DeCuir; **set decorators:** Russell Gausman and Oliver Emert; **music:** Miklos Rozsa and Frank Skinner; **music supervisor:** Milton Schwarzwald; **costume designer:** Grace Houston.

Cast: Barry Fitzgerald (*Lt. Dan Muldoon*); Howard Duff (*Frank Niles*); Dorothy Hart (*Ruth Morrison*); Don Taylor (*Jimmy Halloran*); Ted De Corsia (*Garzah*); House Jameson (*Dr. Stoneman*); Anne Sargent (*Mrs. Halloran*); Adelaide Klein (*Mrs. Batory*); Grover Burgess (*Mr. Batory*); Tom Pedi (*Detective Perelli*); Enid Markey (*Mrs. Hylton*); Frank Conroy (*Captain Donahue*).

Publications

Script:

Wald, Malvin, and Albert Maltz, *The Naked City*, edited by Matthew J. Bruccoli, Carbondale, Illinois, 1979.

Books:

Ferrero, Adelio, *Jules Dassin*, Parma, 1961.
McArthur, Colin, *Underworld USA*, London, 1972.
Silver, Alain, and Elizabeth Ward, editors, *Film Noir*, Woodstock, New York, 1979.
Siclier, Fabien, and Jacques Levy, *Jules Dassin*, Paris, 1986.

Articles:

Variety (New York), 21 January 1948.
Brooks, Richard, on Mark Hellinger, in *Screen Writer* (Los Angeles), March 1948.
New York Times, 5 March 1948.
New Yorker, 13 March 1948.
Grenier, Cynthia, ''Jules Dassin,'' in *Sight and Sound* (London), Winter 1957–58.
Lane, John Francis, ''I See Dassin Make the Law,'' in *Films and Filming* (London), September 1958.
Dassin, Jules, ''Style and Instinct,'' in *Films and Filming* (London), February and March 1970.
Martinez Carril, M., ''Los vaivenes de Jules Dassin,'' in *Cinemateca Revista* (Montevideo), July 1981.
Kozloff, S., ''Humanizing 'the Voice of God': Narration in *The Naked City*,'' in *Cinema Journal* (Champaigne, Illinois), Summer 1984.
Reid's Film Index (Wyong), no. 5, 1990.
''Classics—*The Naked City* Directed by Jules Dassin,'' in *Video Magazine* (New York), vol. 16, no. 11, February 1993.
Farrell, Sean, ''*The Naked City*,'' in *Scarlet Street* (Glen Rock), no. 21, Winter 1996.
Lucas, Tim, ''*The Killers: Criss Cross: The Underneath: Brute Force: The Naked City*,'' in *Video Watchdog* (Cincinnati), no. 32, 1996.
Patterson, Troy, ''*The Naked City*,'' in *Entertainment Weekly* (New York), vol. 470, 5 February 1999.
Atkinson, Michael, ''Shelf Life,'' in *The Village Voice* (New York), vol. 44, no. 13, 6 April 1999.

* * *

The Naked City is New York, a metropolis of playgrounds and police precincts, fire escapes and brownstones and neon lights, rush-hour subways packed like sardine cans and fire hydrants sprinkling the streets on a sweltering summer day. It is most definitely not a city constructed on a Hollywood back lot, not a set designer's stylized or otherwise exaggerated vision of Manhattan canyons. To paraphrase Mark Hellinger, the film's producer and narrator, the actors play their roles in the actual apartments, skyscrapers and city streets—107 total locations in all.

During and after World War II, several Hollywood thrillers were shot in a documentary-like manner, away from the studio in actual urban locales: *The House on 92nd Street* (the trendsetter, filmed in New York and released three years before *The Naked City*), *Panic in the Streets* and *Walk East on Beacon* (which were shot in, respectively, New Orleans and Boston). Jules Dassin's *The Naked City* may not be the first of its type, but its almost revolutionary union of actors and real people, on real streets, has inspired scores of films ever since. The camera crew worked inside a van equipped with a one-way mirror, enabling them to film the city while remaining invisible to passersby. New York, and New Yorkers, become the leading performers, the film's major attraction.

The Naked City is a series of powerful scenes, first depicting the murder of a pretty, man-hungry, larcenous young model, and then detailing the efforts of the cops to sniff out her killers. Of course, they

The Naked City

unravel the case, which culminates in a thrilling chase sequence across the Williamsburg Bridge from Manhattan's Lower East Side to Brooklyn. The homicide detectives are meticulous, but their labors are decidedly tedious and unglamorous. They are not heroically superhuman Clint Eastwoods, and they do not exchange sexy banter with voluptuous heroines whom they bed before the final reel. The major role is played by Barry Fitzgerald; he could be only May Robson's idea of a sex symbol, but his character is a sharp, 30-odd year veteran at the New York Police Department. His associate, young eager-to-please Don Taylor, might be more attractive, but he lives in an undistinguished working class neighborhood and kisses his wife goodbye each morning. Fitzgerald tells a co-worker that he hasn't had a busy day since yesterday; he and his fellow flatfoots forever "ask a question, get an answer, ask another." *The Naked City* does not contain street language or bloody corpses; it is no *Sharky's Machine* or *True Confessions* or *Prince of the City*. But it is as realistic as a major studio film could be in 1948.

The leading actors are familiar faces, but not stars. Except for, perhaps, Barry Fitzgerald, their names were unfamiliar to audiences. *The Naked City* is peopled not so much by performers as faces, everyday faces. The murder victim's parents appear in several key scenes, and the actors portraying them give heartwrenching performances. But, most importantly, they *look* like an anonymous couple from the New Jersey boondocks who have lost their only child to the glitter of the big city.

From *Brute Force* to *Rififi* to *Never on Sunday*, director Jules Dassin's career has been disconnected: *The Naked City* is more the cousin of *The House on 92nd Street* than anything else in Dassin's filmography (with the possible exception of *Night and the City*, shot in London). All have their roots more in Italian neorealism—or even the ashcan paintings of Robert Henri, George Bellows, John Sloan, George Luks and William Glackens—than in anything from Hollywood.

—Rob Edelman

THE NAKED NIGHT

See **GYCKLARNOS AFTON**

NANIWA EREJI

(Osaka Elegy)

Japan, 1936

Director: Kenji Mizoguchi

Production: Daiichi Eiga; black and white, 35mm. Released 1936.

Screenplay: Yoshikata Yoda, from the story ''Mieko'' by Saburo Okada; **photography:** Minoru Miki; **sound:** Hisashi Kase and Yasumi Mizoguchi.

Cast: Isuzu Yamada (*Ayako Murai*); Benkei Shinganoya (*Sonosuke*); Eitaro Shindo (*Yoshizo Fujino*); Kensaku Hara (*Susumu Nishimura*); Seiichi Takegawa (*Ayako's father*); Shinpachiro Asaka (*Ayako's brother*); Chiyoko Okura (*Ayako's sister*); Yoko Umemura (*Sonosuke's wife*); Shizuko Takezawa (*Mine Fukuda*); Kuneo Tamura (*Doctor Yoko*); Kiyoko Okubo (*Doctor's wife*).

Publications

Books:

Anderson, Joseph, and Donald Richie, *The Japanese Film: Art and Industry*, New York, 1960; revised edition, Princeton, 1982.
Ve-Ho, *Kenji Mizoguchi*, Paris, 1963.
Mesnil, Michel, *Kenji Mizoguchi*, Paris, 1965.
Yoda, Yoshikata, *Mizoguchi Kenji no hito to geijutsu* [Kenji Mizoguchi: The Man and His Art], Tokyo, 1970.
Tessier, Max, *Kenji Mizoguchi*, Paris, 1971.
Mellen, Joan, *Voices from the Japanese Cinema*, New York, 1975.
Mellen, Joan, *The Waves at Genji's Door: Japan Through Its Cinema*, New York, 1976.
Bock, Audie, *Japanese Film Directors*, New York, 1978; revised edition, Tokyo, 1985.
Burch, Noël, *To the Distant Observer: Form and Meaning in the Japanese Cinema*, Berkeley, 1979.
Freiberg, Freda, *Women in Mizoguchi Films*, Melbourne, 1981.
Sato, Tadao, *Currents in Japanese Cinema*, Tokyo, 1982.
Andrew, Dudley, *Kenji Mizoguchi: A Guide to References and Resources*, Boston, 1982.
Serceau, Daniel, *Mizoguchi: De la révolte aux songes*, Paris, 1983.
Andrew, Dudley, *Film in the Aura of Art*, Princeton, 1984.
McDonald, Keiko, *Mizoguchi*, Boston, 1984.
Kirihara, Donald, *Patterns of Time: Mizoguchi and the 1930s*, Madison, 1992.
O'Grady, Gerald, editor, *Mizoguchi the Master*, Ontario, 1996.
Tomasi, Dario, *Kenji Mizoguchi*, Milan, 1998.

Articles:

''Mizoguchi Issue'' of *Cinéma* (Paris), no. 6, 1955.
Richie, Donald, and Joseph Anderson, ''Kenji Mizoguchi,'' in *Sight and Sound* (London), Autumn 1955.
''Mizoguchi Issue'' of *Ecran* (Paris), February-March 1958.
''Mizoguchi Issue'' of *Cahiers du Cinéma* (Paris), March 1958.
Iwasaki, Akira, ''Mizoguchi,'' in *Anthologie du cinema 29*, Paris, 1967.
Yoda, Yoshikata, ''The Density of Mizoguchi's Scripts,'' in *Cinema* (Los Angeles), Spring 1971.
Braucourt, G., and others, ''Trois cinéastes de la femme,'' in *Ecran* (Paris), August-September 1974.
Cros, J. L., in *Image et Son* (Paris), April 1978.
Sato, Tadao, and Dudley Andrew, ''On Kenji Mizoguchi,'' in *Film Criticism* (Edinboro, Pennsylvania), Spring 1980.
McDonald, K., ''Form and Function in *Osaka Elegy*,'' in *Film Criticism* (Edinboro, Pennsylvania), Winter 1982.
Russell, Catherine, '''Overcoming Modernity': Gender and the Pathos of History in Japanese Film Melodrama,'' in *Camera Obscura* (Bloomington), no. 35, May 1995.
Burdeau, Emmanuel, and others, ''Mizoguchi Encore,'' in *Cahiers du Cinéma* (Paris), no. 504, July-August 1996.
Hoberman, J., ''Great Leaps Backward,'' in *The Village Voice* (New York), vol. 41, no. 38, 17 September 1996.

* * *

The term ''feminist'' has been applied to the films of Kenji Mizoguchi frequently and somewhat indiscriminately. The term can involve three rather different approaches: 1) films that explicitly confront and endorse the theories and values of the women's liberation movement; 2) films that analyze the ways in which women are oppressed within society; and 3) films in which the director appears to identify with, show special sympathy for, female characters. The interest in Mizoguchi's work is that it covers this entire spectrum of approaches. Only two of his films that have become accessible in the West (*Victory of Women* and *My Love Has Been Burning*) employ the first approach (both belong to the immediate aftermath of World War II and to the enforced ''democratization'' of Japan under the American occupation). The late films, especially, are examples of the third approach, and involve the constant risk of succumbing to traditional male-created myths of women, especially woman-as-redeemer, with the emphasis on female sacrifice. *Osaka Elegy* (as it is generally known in the West), like *Sisters of Gion* made later in the same year, is that of the second approach. Here the risk is that the films will become ''melodramas of defeat,'' reinforcing myths of woman-as-victim, with an emphasis on female masochism.

The importance of *Osaka Elegy* lies in its position within the series of increasingly radical feminist films that culminates in the magnificent *My Love Has Been Burning* (1949), one of Mizoguchi's greatest achievements, for which no equivalent exists within the commercial cinema of the West. *Osaka Elegy* marks, in many respects, a point of hesitation prior to the director's total (if temporary) commitment to feminist principles. Noël Burch is clearly correct (in *To the Distant Observer*) in arguing for the superiority of *Sisters of Gion*, though it is a pity the argument is conducted on purely formal grounds: the formal and stylistic rigour of the later film is paralleled in its altogether tougher and more uncompromising treatment of women's oppression, central to which is its female protagonist, whom the film credits with a rebelliousness and ideological awareness far beyond that of Ayako in *Osaka Elegy* (the two characters are played, splendidly, by

Naniwa ereji

the same actress, Isuzu Yamada, which underlines the continuity between the two films).

As Noël Burch suggests, *Osaka Elegy* is stylistically torn between a capitulation to the codes of dominant cinema—Hollywood—and the repudiation of them marked so emphatically by *Sisters of Gion*. It is also torn, thematically and dramatically, between the female masochism of earlier Mizoguchi films (such as *Taki No Shiraito*, 1933) and the feminist protest to come—marvellously anticipated in the final shot, in which Ayako walks and stares straight into camera, with a look combining defiance with denunciation of the society (i.e., the film's contemporary audience) that has condemned her to prostitution. The film also has a dimension lacking in its successors: an analysis of the oppression of women within the family, in the name of familial ''loyalty'' and ''duty''—the duty of the daughter to serve, unquestioningly, father and brother.

Where *Sisters of Gion* breaks with the codes of western cinema, *Osaka Elegy* evokes direct comparison with certain Hollywood films of the same period, especially the films of von Sternberg with Marlene Dietrich, where the resemblance is stylistic as well as thematic. It lacks the extraordinary excess and obsessiveness that give the von Sternberg films their unique distinction; on the other hand, the political rigour that was to characterize the Mizoguchi films centred on women up to 1950 is here more than embryonic.

—Robin Wood

NANOOK OF THE NORTH

Canada, 1922

Director: Robert Flaherty

Production: Révillon Frères; black and white, 35mm, silent; running time: 75 minutes; length: 1525 meters. Released 11 June 1922, New York. Re-released July 1947 with narration and music. Re-released 1976 with music track only. Filmed August 1920-August 1921 in the area around the Hudson Strait, Canada; and along the shores of the Hopewell Sound, Quebec, Canada. Cost: $55,000.

Producer: Robert Flaherty; **screenplay and photography:** Robert Flaherty; **titles:** Robert Flaherty and Carl Stearns Clancy; **editors:** Robert and Frances Flaherty.

Publications

Books:

Talbot, Frederick A., *Moving Pictures*, Philadelphia, 1923.
Flaherty, Robert, *My Eskimo Friends*, New York, 1924.
O'Dell, Scott, *Representative Photoplays Analyzed*, Los Angeles, 1924.
Canudo, Ricciotto, *L'Usine aux images*, Paris, 1927.
Stefansson, Vilhjalmur, *The Standardization of Error*, London, 1928.
Weinberg, Herman, *Two Pioneers: Robert Flaherty, Hans Richter*, London, 1946.
Grierson, John, *Grierson on Documentary*, edited by Forsyth Hardy, New York, 1947.
Gromo, Mario, *Robert Flaherty*, Parma, 1952.
Rotha, Paul, *Documentary Film*, London, 1952.
Griffith, Richard, *The World of Robert Flaherty*, New York, 1953.
Flaherty, Frances, *The Odyssey of a Film-Maker: Robert Flaherty's Story*, Urbana, Illinois, 1960.
Gobetti, Paolo, *Robert Flaherty*, Turin, 1960.
Quintar, Fuad, *Robert Flaherty et le documentaire poétique*, Paris, 1960.
De Heusch, Luc, *The Cinema and Social Science: A Survey of Ethnographic and Sociological Films*, Paris, 1962.
Clemente, Jose L., *Robert Flaherty*, Madrid, 1963.
Cuenca, Carlos Fernandez, *Robert Flaherty*, Madrid, 1963.
Calder-Marshall, Arthur, *The Innocent Eye: The Life of Robert J. Flaherty*, London, 1963; New York, 1966.
Klaue, Wolfgang, editor, *Robert Flaherty*, East Berlin, 1964.
Agel, Henri, *Robert J. Flaherty*, Paris, 1965.
Pratt, George C., *Spellbound in Darkness: A History of the Silent Film*, New York, 1966.
Barsam, Richard, *Nonfiction Film: A Critical History*, New York, 1973.
Barnouw, Erik, *Documentary: A History of the Non-Fiction Film*, New York, 1974.
Napolitano, Antonio, *Robert J. Flaherty*, Florence, 1975.

Nanook of the North

Murphy, William T., *Robert Flaherty: A Guide to References and Resources*, Boston, 1979.
Williams, Christopher, *Realism and Cinema: A Reader*, London, 1980.
Rotha, Paul, *Robert J. Flaherty: A Biography*, Philadelphia, 1983.
Barsam, Richard, *The Vision of Robert Flaherty: The Artist as Myth and Filmmaker*, Bloomington, 1988.

Articles:

Variety (New York), 16 June 1922.
Tidden, Fritz, in *Moving Picture World* (New York), 24 June 1922.
Patterson, Frances Taylor, in *New Republic* (New York), 9 August 1922.
Ramsaye, Terry, ''Flaherty, Great Adventurer,'' in *Photoplay* (New York), May 1928.
Needham, Wilbur, ''The Future of American Cinema,'' in *Close Up* (London), June 1928.
Interview with Flaherty in *Sight and Sound* (London), no. 71, 1949.
Taylor, Robert Lewis, ''Profile of Flaherty,'' in *New Yorker*, 11, 18, and 25 June 1949.
Campassi, Osvaldo, in *Cinema* (Rome), 15 July 1949.
Taylor, Robert Lewis, ''Flaherty—Education for Wanderlust,'' in *The Running Pianist*, New York, 1950.
Knight, Arthur, and Cecile Starr, in *Saturday Review* (New York), 6 January 1951.
Scherer, Maurice (i.e., Eric Rohmer), in *Cahiers du Cinéma* (Paris), June 1951.
Flaherty, Frances, ''The Flaherty Way,'' in *Saturday Review* (New York), 13 September 1951.
Sadoul, Georges, ''Hommage à Robert Flaherty,'' in *Lettres Françaises* (Paris), 13 September 1951.
''Flaherty in Review,'' in *Sight and Sound* (London), November-December 1951.
Manvell, Roger, ''Robert Flaherty, Geographer,'' in *Geographical Magazine* (New York), February 1957.
Flaherty, Frances, ''Explorations,'' and ''Robert Flaherty—The Man and the Film-Maker'' by Charles Siepmann, in *Film Book No. 1: The Audience and the Filmmaker*, edited by Robert Hughes, New York, 1959.
Flaherty, Frances, ''Flaherty's Quest for Life,'' in *Films and Filming* (London), January 1959.
Flaherty, Robert, ''How I Filmed *Nanook of the North*,'' in *Filmmakers on Filmmaking*, New York, 1967.
Flaherty, Robert, in *The Emergence of Film Art*, edited by Lewis Jacobs, New York, 1969.
Barnouw, Erik, ''Robert Flaherty,'' in *Film Culture* (New York), Spring 1972.
Helman, A., in *Kino* (Warsaw), March 1973.
Corliss, Richard, ''Robert Flaherty: The Man in the Iron Myth,'' in *Film Comment* (New York), November-December 1973.
Ruby, J., ''A Re-examination of the Early Career of Robert J. Flaherty,'' in *Quarterly Review of Film Studies* (Pleasantville, New York), Fall 1980.
Godard, Jean-Luc, ''Introduction à une véritable histoire du cinéma,'' in *Camera Obscura* (Los Angeles), Fall 1982.
Arnold, Gordon B., ''From Big Screen to Small Screen: *Nanook of the North* Directed by Robert Flaherty,'' in *Library Journal* (New York), vol. 114, no. 9, 15 May 1989.
Carpenter, E., ''Assassins and Cannibals: Or I Got Me a Small Mind and I Means to Use It,'' in *SVA Newsletter*, vol. 5, no. 1, 1989.
Everson, William K., ''Collectibles: *Nanook of the North* Directed by Robert Flaherty/*Man of Aran* Directed by Robert Flaherty/*Louisiana Story* Directed by Robert Flaherty,'' in *Video Review* (New York), vol. 12, no. 7, October 1991.
Dick, Jeff, ''North to Alaska: *Nanook of the North* Directed by Robert Flaherty,'' in *Library Journal* (New York), vol. 119, no. 9, 15 May 1994.
Wall, J.M., ''Mesmerized,'' in *Christian Century*, vol. 111, 21/28 September 1994.
Berger, Sally, ''Move Over Nanook,'' in *Wide Angle* (Baltimore), vol. 17, no. 1–4, 1995.
Shepard, David H., ''The Nanook Crisis (1960–75),'' in *Wide Angle* (Baltimore), vol. 17, no. 1–4, 1995.
Russell, Catherine, ''Jouer aux Indiens: In the Land of the Headhunters on War Canoes,'' in *Cinémas* (Montreal), vol. 6, no. 1, Fall 1995.
Grace, Sherrill, ''Exploration as Construction: Robert Flaherty and *Nanook of the North*,'' in *Essays on Canadian Writing* (Toronto), no. 59, Fall 1996.
Leacock, Richard, ''In Defense of the Flaherty Traditions,'' in *Film Culture* (New York), no. 79, Winter 1996.
Nolley, K., ''Finding Alternatives to Gossip: Reflexivity and the Paradigm of Traditional Documentary,'' in *Visual Anthropology* (Newark), vol. 9, no. 3/4, 1997.
Umland, Rebecca, and Sam Umland, ''*Nanook of the North*,'' in *Video Watchdog* (Cincinnati), no. 48, 1998.

* * *

Through the everyday life of one family, *Nanook of the North* typifies Eskimo life in the Arctic; it uses a number of sequences that demonstrate Inuit ingenuity and adaptability in one of the world's harshest climates. Flaherty filmed his documentary during the years 1920–1921 on the eastern shore of Hudson Bay's Ungava Peninsula. He brought with him a Carl Akeley gyroscope camera which required minimum lubrication in cold climates to facilitate pans and tilts; Flaherty was something of a pioneer in the camera's use. He also brought along printing equipment to process and develop the film on location and a portable theater to involve the Eskimos more intimately in the film's production, to enable them to understand its purpose.

Despite the license that Flaherty took in portraying some events and conditions, the film's most important feature was its very basis in reality. Nanook and his family were real persons who reenacted their lives before Flaherty's camera. Not to be confused with cinema verité, Flaherty carefully selected his ''cast'' and directed them to ''play'' their own roles and to carry out tasks that would demonstrate to the outside world how they conducted their lives. Through a careful selection of details, Flaherty succeeded in conveying the drama, the struggle, underlying their daily existence.

Nanook was a significant departure both from the fiction and nonfiction films that preceded it. It departs from fiction because it lacks a plot or story. The background comes to the fore. Man's struggle to survive in this bleak environment becomes an inseparable part of the film's dramatic development. Its photographic detail was also far superior to other films of actuality. The film departs from nonfiction, newsreels and other actualities, in its narrative editing (for 1922), its ability to tell a story through images, and its use of the shot as the basis of a sequence. The film provides detailed pictorial information of the environment, narrative structure, and the filmmaker's art with its implicit emotive statement.

Nanook is a reflection of Flaherty's life-long interest in the interaction of diverse cultures. To be sure, Flaherty wanted to give the outside world a glimpse of Eskimo life as he had experienced it during his years as an explorer, surveyor, and prospector in the lower Arctic region. However, he also wanted to capture on film a way of life threatened by encroaching civilization. *Nanook*, like other Flaherty films, is not depicted in a particular historical setting or context; the timeless appearance was deliberate. He also wanted to capture the Eskimos' essential nobility, to portray them as they saw themselves.

The building of the igloo sequences serves to illustrate Flaherty's technique. Detail upon detail demonstrates Nanook's amazing ingenuity. He builds a shelter out of ice and snow. The sequence is not overexplained. The audience is left to discover each new step and its significance—such as the way in which the translucent block of ice is used as a window. What perhaps has sparked the most discussion is Flaherty's shooting of the interior shots inside the igloo. Restricted to camera negative stock with relatively slow speed or slow sensitivity to light, he had an igloo constructed to twice the average size with half of it cut away to permit sunlight to brighten the scene. The Nanook family goes to sleep during the day for the benefit of Flaherty's camera. This sequence illustrates Flaherty's dictum that sometimes it is necessary to exaggerate reality in order to capture its real essence.

Professor Frances Taylor Patterson of Columbia University was one of the first to recognize the documentary value of *Nanook*. It differed from travel exotica, she wrote, because it did not wander but used one location and one hunter to present an entire culture. Later in the decade some writers criticized *Nanook* for lack of authenticity. However, most modern writers have been delighted with the film's emotive powers which have made audiences identify with the fundamental struggle to survive with all its sociological and philosophical implications.

Nanook, opening to rave reviews, almost immediately was considered one of the greatest films of all times; it quickly received worldwide distribution. Robert Sherwood, for example, called it "literally in a class by itself." No one called it a documentary, though, until as a result of the release of *Moana* (1926) and the writings of John Grierson, parallels could be seen in Flaherty's work. They became the foundation for the development of documentary film as an art form and as a new filmic sensibility. It is perhaps Edmund Carpenter, the cultural anthropologist, who best elucidated *Nanook of the North* and Flaherty's work in general by noting a relationship between this film and Eskimo art. To the Eskimo, he wrote, the creation of art is "an act of seeing and expressing life's values; it's a ritual of discovery by which patterns of nature and of human nature are revealed by man." The drama of daily existence in the North is not imposed from the outside but discovered by exploration, a process that takes into account the natural environment and a philosophy of life.

Nanook remains the most enduring of all Flaherty's films for its simplicity of purpose, structure, and design. It ennobles its subjects rather than exploits them. It relies on a few well-developed sequences. The images, sharp and uncluttered, are still memorable.

—William T. Murphy

NAPOLEON

(Napoléon vu par Abel Gance)

France, 1927

Director: Abel Gance

Production: Westi/Société générale de films, Paris; black and white, 35mm, Polyvision (some versions without Polyvision); running time: originally about 270 minutes, but the film has always existed in several versions, some up to 5 hours in length; length: originally about 32 reels. Released 7 April 1927, Paris. Released without Polyvision 1929, New York. Re-released 1934 with sound. In 1971 *Napoléon—Bonaparte et la Revolution* was re-released with sound and with some footage added and some eliminated. In 1981 *Napoléon*, the original version, was restored by Kevin Brownlow and re-released in its entirety with music by Carl Davis, also re-released in the US by Francis Coppola with some footage cut and music by Carmine Coppola. Filmed 1925–26 in France.

Producers: Wengoroff and Hugo Stinnes; **screenplay:** Abel Gance; **photography:** Jules Kruger, Léonce-Henry Burel, Jean-Paul Mundwiller, assisted by Lucas, Briquet, Emile Pierre, and Roger Hubert; **editors:** Marguerite Beaugé and Henritte Pinson; **production designers:** Alexandre Benois, Schildnecht, Jacouty, Meinhardt, and Laourie; **music:** Arthur Honegger; **consultants:** Jean Arroy, Jean Mitry, and Sacher Purnal; **assistant directors:** Henry Krauss, Alexandre Volkov, and Viatcheslaw Tourjansky.

Cast: Albert Dieudonné (*Bonaparte*); Vladimir Roudenko (*Young Bonaparte*); Edmond van Daele (*Robespierre*); Alexandre Koubitsky (*Danton*); Antonin Artaud (*Marat*); Abel Gance (*Saint-Just*); Pierre Batcheff (*Hoche*); Maxudian (*Barras*); Chakatouny (*Pozzo di Borgo*); Philippe Hériat (*Salicetti*); Nicolas Koline (*Tristan Fleuri*); Daniel Mendaille (*Fréron*); Alexandre Bernard (*Dugommier*); Philippe Rolla (*Masséna*); Robert Vidalin (*Camille Desmoulins*); Roger Blum (*Talma*); Paul Amiot (*Fouquier-Tinville*); Boudreau (*La Fayette*); Georges Lampin (*Joseph Bonaparte*); Alberty (*J.-J. Rousseau*); R. de Ansorena (*Desaix*); Jack Rye (*Louis XVI*); Armand Bernard (*Jean-Jean*); Albert Bras (*Monge*); Georges Cahuzac (*Beauharnais*); Favière (*Fouché*); Harry Krimer (*Rouget de Lisle*); Genica Missirio (*Murat*); Rauzena (*Lucien Bonaparte*); Viguier (*Couthon*); Vonelly (*André Chenier*); Jean d'Yd (*La Bussière*); Gina Manès (*Joséphine de Beauharnais*); Annabella (*Violine Fleuri*); Suzanne Blanchetti (*Marie-Antoinette*); Eugénie Buffet (*Letizia Bonaparte*); Damia (*la Marseillaise*); Yvette Dieudonné (*Elisa Bonaparte*); Marguerite Gance (*Charlotte Corday*); Simone Genevois (*Pauline Bonaparte*).

Publications

Script:

Gance, Abel, *Napoléon vu par Abel Gance*, Paris, 1927; selections in *Ecran* (Paris), April-May 1958.

Napoleon

Books:

Arroy, Jean, *En tournant ''Napoléon'' avec Abel Gance: Souvenirs et impressions d'un sans-culotte*, Paris, 1927.
Sadoul, Georges, *French Films*, London, 1953.
Icard, Roger, *Abel Gance*, Toulouse, 1960.
Brownlow, Kevin, *The Parade's Gone By*, London and New York, 1969.
Mast, Gerald, *Film/Cinema/Movie*, New York, 1977.
Kramer, Steven, and James Welsh, *Abel Gance*, Boston, 1978.
Brownlow, Kevin, *Napoléon: Abel Gance's Classic Film*, London, 1983.
Icart, Roger, *Abel Gance; ou, Le Promethée foudroyé*, Lausanne, 1983.
King, Norman, *Abel Gance: A Politics of Spectacle*, London, 1984.
Groppali, Enrico, *Abel Gance*, Florence, 1986.
Kaplan, Nelly, *Napoléon*, London, 1994.

Articles:

Graham, James, in *New York Times*, 5 June 1927.
''France Films Her Napoleon,'' in *New York Times*, 4 March 1928.
Hall, Mordaunt, in *New York Times*, 12 February 1929.
Gance, Abel, ''Les Nouveaux Chapitres de notre syntaxe,'' in *Cahiers du Cinéma* (Paris), October 1953.
Gance, Abel, in *Cahiers du Cinéma* (Paris), December 1954.
Thompson, Howard, in *New York Times*, 25 September 1967.
Lenning, Arthur, ''The French Film—Abel Gance,'' in *The Silent Voice: A Text*, New York, 1969.
Brownlow, Kevin, in *Films and Filming* (London), November 1969.
Blumer, R. H., ''The Camera as Snowball,'' in *Cinema Journal* (Evanston, Illinois), Spring 1970.
Greenspun, Roger, ''Bonaparte and the Revolution,'' in *New York Times*, 16 October 1971.
McKegney, Michael, in *Village Voice* (New York), 11 November 1971.
Brownlow, Kevin, ''Abel Gance's *Napoleon and the Revolution*,'' in *Sight and Sound* (London), Winter 1971–72.
Canby, Vincent, in *Film 71/72*, New York, 1972.
Gilliatt, Penelope, in *New Yorker*, 6 September 1976.
Brownlow, Kevin, ''*Napoléon*—A Personal Involvement,'' in *Classic Film Collector* (Indiana, Pennsylvania), 23 August 1977.
Everson, William K., in *Variety* (New York), 12 September 1979.

Grant, F., in *Broadcast* (London), 8 December 1980.
Eisenschitz, B., "The Music of Time: From *Napoleon* to *New Babylon*," in *Afterimage* (London), no. 10, 1981.
Pappas, P., "The Superimposition of Vision: *Napoleon* and the Meaning of Fascist Art," in *Cineaste* (New York), no. 2, 1981.
Brownlow, Kevin, in *American Film* (Washington, D.C), January-February 1981.
Everson, William K., "The Many Lives of Napoleon," in *Film Comment* (New York), January-February 1981.
Elley, Derek, in *Films* (London), February 1981.
Welsh, James M., in *Films in Review* (New York), March 1981.
Allen, W., interview with Kevin Brownlow, in *Stills* (London), Autumn 1981.
Assayas, O., "Mensonges et vérités," in *Cahiers du Cinéma* (Paris), December 1981.
Hogenkamp, B., in *Filmfaust* (Frankfurt), December 1981-January 1982.
French, Sean, "The Napoleon Phenomenon," in *Sight and Sound* (London), Spring 1982.
Abel, R., "Change and Counter-Change: Coherence and Incoherence in Gance's *Napoléon*," in *Film Quarterly* (Berkeley), Spring 1982.
Vallerand, F., "*Napoléon* Coppola et les autres," in *Séquences* (Montreal), April 1982.
Verstappen, W., in *Skoop* (Amsterdam), June 1982.
Tobin, Yann, "Sur *Napoléon* d'Abel Gance: La Folie du docteur Gance," in *Positif* (Paris), June 1982.
Aristarco, G., in *Cinema Nuovo* (Turin), August-October 1982.
Icart, Roger, "La Representation de Napoleon Bonaparte dans l'oeuvre d'Abel Gance," in *Cahiers de la Cinémathèque* (Perpignan), Autumn 1982.
"*Napoléon* Issue" of *Cinématographe* (Paris), November 1982.
Arnaud, C., and Jean Mitry, "Sur les ailes de l'aigle: Notes sur *Napoléon*," in *Cinématographe* (Paris), December 1982.
Philpott, R., "Whose Napoleon?," in *Framework* (Norwich), 1983.
Jeancolas, J.P., "Gance au Havre," in *Positif* (Paris), January 1983.
Lardeau, Y., "L'Empereur contre-attaque," in *Cahiers du Cinéma* (Paris), September 1983.
Bassan, R., in *Revue du Cinéma* (Paris), September 1983.
Leblanc, G., "Gance dans le regard de l'aigle," in *Cinéthique* (Paris), May 1984.
Weijel, H., in *Skoop* (Amsterdam), November 1984.
"*Napoléon* Issue" of *Skrien* (Amsterdam), November-December 1984.
Nørrested, C., in *Kosmorama* (Copenhagen), December 1984.
Deburchgrave, K., in *Film en Televisie* (Brussels), January 1985.
Filmfaust (Frankfurt), January-February 1987.
Stewart, Garrett, "Leaving History: Dickens, Gance, Blanchot," in *The Yale Journal of Criticism* (New Haven), vol. 2, no. 2, Spring 1989.
Arnold, Gordon B., "From Big Screen to Small Screen: *Napoleon* Directed by Abel Gance," in *Library Journal* (New York), vol. 114, no. 9, 15 May 1989.
Lafaye, C., "Gance et 'son' *Napoléon*," in *Cahiers de la Cinémathèque* (Perpignan, France), no. 53, 1990.
Comuzio, E., "La musica dell'Imperatore salvata dal diluvio," in *Cineforum* (Bergamo, Italy), May 1990.
Gordon, M., "Some Things I Saw," in *Salmagundi* (Saratoga Springs, New York), Fall-Winter 1990–1991.
Gerstenkorn, Jacques, "L'empire de l'analogie," in *Vertigo* (Paris), no. 6–7, 1991.
Seville, J., "The Laser's Edge: *Napoléon vu par Abel Gance*," in *Classic Images* (Muscatine), no. 194, August 1991.
Conforti, A., and M. Lori, "La metafora nel cinema: *Napoléon* di Abel Gance," in *Cineforum* (Bergamo, Italy), July-August 1992.
Fernandez, C., " *Napoléon vu par Abel Gance*: el poder de la mirada—Napoleon y el aguila," in *Film-Historia* (Barcelona), vol. 5, no. 1, 1995.

* * *

The showing of *Napoléon vu par Abel Gance* on 7 April 1927 at the Opéra in Paris was in every sense a triumphant occasion. For the invited audience it meant the culminating point of the restoration of French cinema after its virtual annihilation in 1914. For writer-director Abel Gance himself it was the climax to 18 years of work in the cinema and 10 years of rigorous and innovative exploration of the visual potential of the medium. *Napoléon* alone had taken three years of unremitting research, writing and shooting, cost several million francs, involved thousands of extras and a team of a dozen assistants and at least eight cameramen and directors of photography.

The project had been initially conceived as a massive six-part work which was to include the whole of Napoleon's life. The eventual six hours of edited footage in fact covers only a portion of the first part of this grandiose scheme, so the scale of Gance's imagination is immediately apparent. The truncation of the project means that though *Napoléon* has a greater sweep than any other Gance epic, it lacks the tragic resolution which usually completed Gance's tales of heroic endeavour, whether that of Jean Diaz in *J'accuse*, Savaronola in *Lucrèce Borgia*, or Beethoven in *Un grand amour de Beethoven*. Despite its length, the film offers only the education and shaping of its hero, leaving him at an early point of triumph—the entry of his armies into Italy.

It is the technical aspects of *Napoléon* that have always received the most attention. The context in which Gance was working was one highly receptive of visual experimentation. After the constriction of the pre-1914 system organised by Charles Pathé and Léon Gaumont, in which Gance had made his debut, the new postwar generation to which he belonged strove to give a new dignity to the cinema. Despising the underfinanced, totally commercially oriented cinema of the early 1910s, with its philistine disregard for artistic aspiration and its conception of films as products to be made as if they were canned peas, Gance and his contemporaries strove to develop the visual potential of the new medium, experimenting with mobile cameras and the new editing techniques pioneered by the emergent Hollywood narrative cinema and indulging in a profusion of optical effects—masks and superimpositions, distorting lenses and pulled focus. All of these tendencies reach their climax in *Napoléon*. To help with the massive project and the manipulation of the crowd scenes, Gance sought the assistance of fellow directors Henry Krauss, Alexandre Volkov and Viatcheslaw Tourjansky. With the aid of a team of cinematographers led by Jules Kruger, Léonce-Henry Burel and Jean-Paul Mundwiller, Gance moved his camera in every conceivable fashion—to imitate a ship tossed by a storm, the view from a galloping horse or even a snowball in flight. As if this welter of visual effects were not in itself sufficently dazzling, Gance arranged for the screen width to be tripled at the end, so that Napoleon's entry into Italy, recorded in widescreen and with triptych effects, becomes a stunningly unique visual experience.

The climate of French 1920s cinema was conducive to Gance's project, and there was nothing to restrain his exuberant imagination.

The most successful films of the decade were super-productions with an exotic, literary or historical flavour, and *Napoléon* was designed to outmatch them all. It combined breathtaking virtuosity with a totally personal conception of the subject, and not until the 1970s masterpieces of Coppola and Spielberg do we find a similar harnessing of the entire resources of an industry to an unfettered personal vision. Central to Gance's conception was a 19th-century romantic view of the artist. It has been well observed that just as *Un grand amour de Beethoven* depicts the artist as hero, *Napoléon* offers a view of the hero as artist. Though Gance himself played the role of Saint Just, he identified himself as creator of the film with Napoleon (played by Albert Dieudonné) as creator of a new France and master of the forces of history. Napoleon—man of action, politician and military genius—becomes a largely passive figure, a pensive visionary. Much stress is placed on Napoleon's childhood, and the hero's ability to crush dissent with a steely gaze is anticipated in early scenes of the schoolboy leading his side in a snowball fight. The boy is endowed with an all-too-symbolic pet eagle. But if these early scenes are often lively and well-realised, the most remarkable feature of this inevitably uneven work is the handling of action, nowhere better shown than in the celebrated scenes which intercut shots of Napoleon at sea in a tiny boat rocked by a storm with the human storm in the Convention in revolution-torn Paris.

In the 1980s *Napoléon* became probably the most celebrated of all silent masterpieces. Kevin Brownlow's 20-year self-imposed task of bringing together all extant footage of the film is a remarkable endeavour, but for film historians it raises a whole host of questions about authenticity and authorship. There are now two quite different *Napoléon* restorations, Brownlow's own English version with its music by Carl Davis and preservation of silent running speed, and the version distributed in the United States by Francis Coppola's company which is cut, run at the inappropriate speed of 24 frames a second and endowed with a questionable score by Coppola's father. Moreover, far from simply constituting a restoration of a mutilated film and a recreation of the viewing conditions of silent cinema with full orchestral accompaniment, Brownlow's five-hour version is as much a modern interpretation and distortion as Henri Langlois's seven- or eight-hour compilations of episodes from *Judex* or *Les vampires*. These versions led to the rediscovery of Louis Feuillade's work and the restoration of his reputation, but by compressing up to a dozen episodes, designed to be seen separately at fortnightly intervals, into a single massive viewing session, Langlois created a work that owed nothing to 1920s conceptions of film narrative and time-span. This new relationship of film and spectator can have an immediate ''modern'' impact, as the films of Jacques Rivette, one of the Cinémathèque Francaise's most faithful habitués, show, but it is not a recreation of the 1920s experience.

Similarly, Brownlow's ''original'' version corresponds to none that was ever shown in Paris in the 1920s, and there is nothing to indicate that audiences then would have accepted this five-hour endurance test. The actual *Napoléon*, like so many silent films, existed in several versions, and the 1927 showings were either of a shortened version with triptych effects (as at the premiere in the Opéra) or a four- or six-episode version without triple screen and shown over a period of weeks. Despite such paradoxes, the Brownlow version has many virtues, not least of which has been its revival of interest in silent cinema. Moreover, whereas Gance's own reworkings of his material—the 1934 sound version, the re-edited 1971 compilation *Bonaparte et la revolution*—like his 1960s feature *Austerlitz*, are simplifications and at times trivialisations, this 1980s version restores the work to full complexity and to its status of one of the 1920s most remarkable achievements.

—Roy Armes

NARAYAMA BUSHI-KO

(The Ballad of Narayama)

Japan, 1983

Director: Shohei Imamura

Production: Toei Company; colour, 35mm; **running time:** 130 minutes.

Producer: Jiro Tomoda, Goro Kusakabe; **screenplay:** Shohei Imamura, based on the novels *Narayama bushi-ko* and *Tohoku no zunmutachi* by Shichiro Fukazawa; **photography:** Masao Tochizawa; **editor:** Hajime Okayasu; **assistant director:** Kunio Takegishe; **music:** Shinichiro Ikebe; **sound recording:** Yoshiichi Beniya; **costumes:** Kyoto Isho.

Cast: Ken Ogata (*Tatsuhei*); Sumiko Sakamoto (*Orinyan*); Tonpei Hidari (*Risuke*); Takejo Aki (*Tama-yan*); Shoichi Ozawa (*Shozo*); Mitsuaki Fukamizu (*Tada-yan*); Seiji Kurasaki (*Kesakichi*); Junko Takada (*Matsu-yan*); Mitsuko Baisho (*Oei*).

Narayama bushi-ko

Publications

Articles:

Variety (New York), 25 May 1983.
Tesson, C., and Y. Lardeau, *Cahiers du Cinéma* (Paris), June-July 1983.
Renaud, C., *24 Images* (Montreal), Autumn 1983.
Masson, A., and others, *Positif* (Paris), September 1983.
Tessier, M., *Revue du Cinéma* (Paris), September 1983.
Magny, J., *Cinéma* (Paris), October 1983.
Beaulieu, J., *Séquences* (Montreal), January 1984.
Rayns, T., *Monthly Film Bulletin* (London), May 1984.
Stanbrook, A., ''Taking Mum to the Mountain'' in *Stills* (London), June-July 1984.
Breen, M., *Cinema Papers* (Victoria), August 1984.

* * *

The Ballad of Narayama is perhaps one of the most overrated films of recent years, an ahistorical fantasy by an urban intellectual about a rural society that never existed. Its favourable reception among some critics and audiences is more interesting than the film itself, which fails as a drama, as a commentary on Japan and as a philosophical statement.

The film is based on two novels by Fukazawa Shichiro, each of which has been adapted for the cinema before, *Narayama bushi-ko* in 1956 and *Tohoku no zunmutachi* in 1957. Imamura's decision to combine them in one allegedly realistic film, made to resemble a documentary as much as possible, is one of the sources of the film's dramatic weakness. The central plot device, the decision of Orin, an aged widow, to sacrifice herself on the mountain (Narayama) so that her family may survive, is discussed and elaborated so often that many viewers will wonder why she does not just hurry up and carry it out. It is also obscured by subplots, in which her elder son Tatsuhei enters a second marriage; her grandson Kesakichi loses his lover Matsu when her entire family is killed because her father is a thief; and her younger son Risuke, shunned by the other villagers because he smells bad, is fixed up with a woman for the first time in his life.

The narrative depends for its effect on treating legends about ancient Japan as if they were historical truths. Yet there never was a real mountain where old people abandoned themselves, or were abandoned, to the elements; there is no historical evidence that thieves were killed by their fellow-villagers, let alone their entire families; as for Risuke, perhaps people who smelled bad were indeed shunned in primitive Japan, but it is now impossible to know, nor are we told why Risuke has this particular problem—or, for that matter, how everyone else in the village manages to smell good. Imamura's refusal to specify where and when the events he depicts are taking place consigns them to an undifferentiated ''Past'' which has no plausibility, either as legend—in contrast, for example, to *Oni Baba,* or Ingmar Bergman's *The Seventh Seal*—or as a basis for trustworthy or thoughtprovoking reflection on the present.

Skillful cinematography, acting or other elements can sometimes compensate for deficiencies in the direction or writing of a film, but not in this case. The progress of the year from winter to winter is laboriously and clumsily indicated by predictable clichés: rice shoots in spring, shimmering heat in summer, leaves changing colour in the fall and snow falling and falling, with soporific effect, in winter. The actors in the film have evidently been encouraged to represent primeval drives by grunting and shouting throughout the film, and can do little with their impossible roles, ranging from the saintly Orin herself, through her sons, one laughably macho, the other irritatingly pathetic, to the monotonously hysterical Matsu.

It is particularly distressing to see Baisho Mitsuko and Ogata Ken, two highly intelligent and sophisticated actors, reduced to performing as pawns in Imamura's game, his attempt to present a shallow and unconvincing utopia as if it was once, or ever could have been, a real society. The novelist Fukazawa's intention was to recreate what he believed had been the way of life of the ancient Japanese, before the importation of, first, Chinese influences and, later, Western influences which have, in his view, corrupted the ''purity'' of Japanese culture. Imamura's intention seems to be to pass off such harmless, if threadbare, fantasies as if they were not only historically accurate but also spiritually resonant or philosophically stimulating. But there is no irony, humour or other distancing effect in the film, and Imamura excludes any character capable—as almost all real human beings have always been capable—of reflection or questioning about the customs being observed. But by demeaning the people in the film Imamura implicitly demeans the people watching it, and the gap between his grand ambitions and his shoddy achievements presents its own stark contrast with the skillfully plotted, beautifully staged and acted, historically accurate and deeply moving masterpieces of Kurosawa, Mizoguchi and other genuine masters of the Japanese cinematic tradition.

It is striking that this film, which had limited critical and commercial success in Japan, won the Grand Prize at the Cannes Film Festival in 1983 and was hailed as a masterpiece by leading Western film critics, many of whom knew little or nothing about Japan, past or present. This suggests that some Western filmgoers still cling to an outdated, misinformed and even racist notion of Japan as extremely alien and exotic, a country of people ''close to nature'' whose films can be patronised by refusing to apply normal critical standards to them; and that some Japanese, including Imamura, are all too happy to foster such attitudes, for their own nationalistic reasons.

—Patrick Heenan

NASHVILLE

USA, 1975

Director: Robert Altman

Production: Paramount Pictures; Metrocolor, 35mm, Panavision; running time: 159 minutes. Released 1975. Filmed on location in Nashville.

Producer: Robert Altman; **screenplay:** Joan Tewkesbury; **title design:** Dan Perri; **photography:** Paul Lohmann; **editors:** Sidney Levin and Dennis Hill; **sound:** Jim Webb and Chris McLaughlin; **music director:** Richard Baskin.

Cast: David Arkin (*Norman*); Barbara Baxley (*Lady Pearl*); Ned Beatty (*Delbert Reese*); Karen Black (*Connie White*); Ronee Blakley (*Barbara Jean*); Timothy Brown (*Tommy Brown*); Keith Carradine (*Tom Frank*); Geraldine Chaplin (*Opal*); Robert Doqui (*Wade*); Shelley Duvall (*L. A. Joan*); Allen Garfield (*Barnett*); Henry Gibson

Nashville

(*Haven Hamilton*); Scott Glenn (*Pfc. Glen Kelly*); Jeff Goldblum (*Tricycle man*); Barbara Harris (*Albuquerque*); David Hayward (*Kenny Fraiser*); Michael Murphy (*John Triplette*); Allan Nichols (*Bill*); Dave Peel (*Bud Hamilton*); Christina Raines (*Mary*); Bert Remsen (*Star*); Lily Tomlin (*Linnea Reese*); Gwen Welles (*Sueleen*); Keenan Wynn (*Mr. Green*).

Awards: Oscar for Best Song (''I'm Easy'' by Keith Carradine), 1975; New York Film Critics' Awards for Best Motion Picture, Best Direction, and Best Supporting Actress (Tomlin), 1975.

Publications

Script:

Tewkesbury, Joan, *Nashville*, Toronto, 1976.

Books:

Feineman, Neil, *Persistence of Vision: The Films of Robert Altman*, New York, 1976.

Kass, Judith M., *Robert Altman, American Innovator*, New York, 1978.

Kolker, Robert Phillip, *A Cinema of Loneliness: Penn, Kubrick, Coppola, Scorsese, Altman*, Oxford, 1980; revised edition, 1988.

Karp, Alan, *The Films of Robert Altman*, Metuchen, New Jersey, 1981.

Bourget, Jean-Loup, *Robert Altman*, Paris, 1981.

Giannetti, Louis, *Masters of the American Cinema*, Englewood Cliffs, New Jersey, 1981.

Tuska, Jon, editor, *Close-Up: The Contemporary Director*, Metuchen, New Jersey, 1981.

Kagan, Norman, *American Sceptic: Robert Altman's Genre-Commentary Films*, Ann Arbor, Michigan, 1982.

Wexman, Virginia Wright, and Gretchen Bisplinghoff, *Robert Altman: A Guide to References and Resources*, Boston, 1984.

Plecki, Gerard, *Robert Altman*, Boston, 1985.

Wood, Robin, *Hollywood from Vietnam to Reagan*, New York, 1986.

Keyssar, Helene, *Robert Altman's America*, New York, 1991.

McGilligan, Patrick, *Robert Altman: Jumping Off the Cliff*, New York, 1991.

Cagin, Seth, *Born to Be Wild: Hollywood and the Sixties Generation*, Boca Raton, 1994.

O'Brien, Daniel, *Robert Altman: Hollywood Survivor*, New York, 1996.

Sterritt, David, and Peter Brunette, editors, *Robert Altman: Interviews*, Jackson, 2000.

Articles:

Ciment, Michel, and M. Henry, ''Entretien avec Robert Altman,'' in *Positif* (Paris), February 1975.

''Altman Seminar'' in *Dialogue on Film* (Beverly Hills), February 1975.

Rosenbaum, Jonathan, ''Improvisations and Interactions in Altmanville,'' in *Sight and Sound* (London), Spring 1975.

Murphy, A. D., in *Variety* (New York), 11 June 1975.

Reilly, C. P., in *Films in Review* (New York), August-September 1975.

Glaessner, Verina, in *Focus on Film* (London), Autumn 1975.

Rosenbaum, Jonathan, in *Sight and Sound* (London), Autumn 1975.

Wood, Robin, ''Smart-ass and Cutie-pie: Notes Toward an Evaluation of Altman,'' in *Movie* (London), Autumn 1975.

''Altman Issue'' of *Film Heritage* (Dayton, Ohio), Fall 1975.

Gow, Gordon, in *Films and Filming* (London), October 1975.

Strick, Philip, in *Monthly Film Bulletin* (London), October 1975.

Benayoun, Robert, ''Altman, U.S.A.,'' in *Positif* (Paris), December 1975.

Interviews with Joan Tewkesbury, Ronee Blakley, and Keith Carradine, in *Positif* (Paris), December 1975.

Byrne, Connie, and William O. Lopez, in *Film Quarterly* (Berkeley), Winter 1975–76.

Blaedel, M., in *Kosmorama* (Copenhagen), no. 131, 1976.

Self, Robert, ''Invention and Death: The Commodities of Media in Robert Altman's *Nashville*,'' in *Journal of Popular Film* (Washington, D.C), no. 5, 1976.

Cardullo, R. J., ''The Space in the Distance: A Study of Altman's *Nashville*,'' in *Literature/Film Quarterly* (Salisbury, Maryland), no. 4, 1976.

Knorr, W., ''Buffalo Bill und die Indianer: *Nashville*,'' in *Medien und Padagogik* (Munich), no. 4, 1976.

Belmans, J., ''Pour bientot de Robert Altman,'' in *Amis du Film et de la Télévision* (Brussels), January 1976.

Verstappen, W., in *Skoop* (Amsterdam), March 1976.

Magrelli, E., and G. Turroni, in *Filmcritica* (Rome), April 1976.

Giuricin, G., in *Cinema Nuovo* (Turin), July-August 1976.

Colpart, G., in *Télécine* (Paris), July-August 1976.
Pitiot, P., and H. Talvat, "Robert Altman de *Mash* a *Nashville*," in *Jeune Cinéma* (Paris), September-October 1976.
Sauvaget, D., in *Revue du Cinéma* (Paris), October 1976.
Frezzato, A., in *Cineforum* (Bergamo), October 1976.
Macklin, F. A., "The Artist and the Multitude Are Natural Enemies," interview with Robert Altman, in *Film Heritage* (Dayton, Ohio), Winter 1976–77.
Binni, W., and A. Lombardo, "Poetiche ed ideologie de tre registi," in *Cinema Nuovo* (Turin), January-February 1977.
Levine, R., "R. Altman & Co.," in *Film Comment* (New York), January-February 1977.
Plazewski, J., in *Kino* (Warsaw), March 1977.
Elsaesser, Thomas, "Ou finit le spectacle?," in *Positif* (Paris), September 1977.
Sack, C., "Joan Tewkesbury on Screenwriting: An Interview," in *Literature/Film Quarterly* (Salisbury, Maryland), Winter 1978.
Cook, B., "Bob and Pauline: A Fickle Affair," in *American Film* (Washington, D.C), December 1978-January 1979.
Bowles, Stephen E., "*Cabaret* and *Nashville*," in *Journal of Popular Film* (Washington, D.C), no. 3, 1978–79.
Masbany, R., "*Saturday Night Fever* and *Nashville*: Exploring the Comic Mythos," in *Journal of Popular Film* (Washington, D.C), no. 3, 1978–79.
MacCabe, Colin, "The Discursive and the Ideological in Film: Notes on the Conditions of Political Intervention," in *Screen* (London), no. 4, 1978–79.
Tewkesbury, Joan, in *American Film* (Washington, D.C), March 1979.
Taubman, Leslie, in *Magill's Survey of Cinema 3*, Englewood Cliffs, New Jersey, 1980.
Yacowar, Maurice, "Actors as Conventions in the Films of Robert Altman," in *Cinema Journal* (Evanston, Illinois), Fall 1980.
Edgerton, G., "Capra and Altman: Mythmaker and Mythologist," in *Literature/Film Quarterly* (Salisbury, Maryland), Spring 1983.
Elsaesser, Thomas, "*Nashville*: Putting on the Show," in *Persistence of Vision* (Maspeth, New York), Summer 1984.
Listener (London), 22 August 1985.
Rush, J. S., "Who's in on the Joke; Parody as Hybridized Narrative Discourse," in *Quarterly Review of Film and Video* (New York), no. 1–2, 1990.
Comuzio, E., "Una canzone-azione in *Nashville* di Robert Altman," in *Cineforum* (Bergamo, Italy), January-February 1990.
Altman, Rick, "24-Track Narrative? Robert Altman's *Nashville*," in *Cinémas* (Montreal), vol. 1, no. 3, Spring 1991.
James, C., "Film View: *Nashville* Political Prescience," in *New York Times*, 8 November 1992.
Salamon, Julie, "On Film: Altman's in a Class by Himself," in *Wall Street Journal* (New York), 30 September 1993.
Lippy, T., "Writing *Nashville*," in *Scenario* (Rockville), vol. 1, no. 1, Winter 1995.
Tewkesbury, Joan, and Tod Lippy, "*Nashville*," in *Scenario* (Rockville), vol. 1, no. 1, Winter 1995.
Kostik, Damian, "Creation, Content and Context: Interview with Joan Tewkesbury," in *Creative Screenwriting* (Washington, D.C.), vol. 4, no. 3, Fall 1997.
Hoban, Phoebe, "The Outsider as Hollywood Favorite: Biography," in *New York Times* (New York), 15 June 1997.
Ross, B., "Neither Plot nor Hero: The Script of *Nashville*," in *Michigan Academician*, vol. 29, no. 3, 1997.
Gross, Larry, "Nothing Fails Like Success," in *Premiere* (New York), vol. 12, no. 9, May 1999.

* * *

Robert Altman's Bicentennial epic about one weekend in the lives of people in Nashville, Tennessee, conveys his personal reflection on the state of the nation and his political call to fellow Americans on the nature of the state. Altman's artistic success results from the way he shapes uniquely American materials and sensibilities into a complex ideological network.

After three prologue scenes, Altman introduces a staggering total of 24 characters in one long location sequence at the Nashville airport (only Connie White—Karen Black—is not there, but her poster image represents her). The interweaving of characters, music, sights, and sounds in the airport and freeway sequences establishes them and their lives within a modernist context, a barrage of sensory impressions which Altman choreographs into a bombardment of movement and timing. The continuously moving camera, rhythmic cuts between characters, background band music, TV announcer both on screen and as off-screen voice-over commentator, airport noises, characters talking and overlapping each other, continue to build in momentum until all characters are on the freeway on the way to town. The freeway sequence incorporates wider perspectives in aerial and high angle shots, highway noises, conversations and arguments until, as screenwriter Joan Tewkesbury said, "Everything has whirled and spun and played through your senses."

Following this barrage-like exposition, Altman departs from stylistic sensational overload and moves to a "floating narrative," much like the style of TV soap operas in which the lives and events of many characters are presented by cutting back and forth between them. Altman periodically brings together and connects his 24 characters through devices of communication: telephones and telephone conversations, radio programs, tape recorded songs, the p.a. announcements of a presidential campaign van. He presents events happening simultaneously while slowly allowing for the evolution of time. Altman then cuts between four simultaneous church scenes, offering perspectives on as many characters as possible, then moves forward by cutting events into a progressive 24-hour period. Fewer things occur simultaneously as the camera begins more and more to catch each character impressionistically rather than following them all at the same time.

Cutting back and forth between gestures, reactions, and responses, their dynamic personalities of the characters emerge. But nothing is hinted at of their internal workings. They remain the sum of their exposed surfaces as no psychological or narrative meaning is assigned to their existences. Country singing star Barbara Jean (Ronee Blakley) comes the closest to exposing an internal emotional depth, but that is because her emotions have become her raw surface, both as a star and as a person, turning her into a fragile human being. Because she is the key narrative character, her fate and its meaning is more unresolved than anyone else's at the film's end.

In the last sequence of the film, the rally at the Nashville Parthenon, Altman reunites and refocuses on all his characters in one place. Unlike the airport scene, here the characters are united by a single event on which their reactions and responses depend. The Parthenon rally and the subsequent assassination act as the narrative's culminating hub, while all the characters move like spokes of a wheel in relation to it. Altman moves from the barrage of simultaneous moments in many characters' lives to a progressively more linear pattern until he is once again able to present many perspectives simultaneously responding to one single unifying element.

By creating a mosaic of contemporary American life, *Nashville* suggests a cultural view of reality that is made up of fragmented images and their incomprehensibility. But Altman overturns a bleak finale with the optimism that learning to live with uncertainty yields an affirmation and assignment of meaning to life in and of itself.

When influential *New Yorker* critic Pauline Kael first saw the film, she applauded Altman's vision, "I've never before seen a movie I loved in quite this way." Her laudatory review, based on a screening of a pre-release version of the film, caused a minor flurry of controversy about critical responsibility and was not able to help the film out of its box-office doldrums. But despite its lack of popular success, *Nashville* has since been heralded as one of director Altman's finest films and one of the quintessential American movies of the 1970s.

—Lauren Rabinovitz

THE NEEDLE

See **IGLA**

NEOBYCHANYE PRIKLYUCHENIYA MISTERA VESTA V STRANE BOLSHEVIKOV

(The Extraordinary Adventures of Mr. West in the Land of the Bolsheviks)

USSR, 1924

Director: Lev Kuleshov

Production: Goskino; black and white, 35mm, silent; running time: 80 minutes. Released 1924.

Scenario: Nikolai Aseyev and V. I. Pudovkin; **photography:** Alexander Levitsky; **production designer:** V. I. Pudovkin; **assistants:** Alexandra Khokhlova, Leonid Obolensky, Sergei Komarov, Porfiri Podobed, and Leo Mur.

Cast: Porfiri Podobed (*Mr. J. S. West*); Boris Barnet (*Jeddy, the cowboy*); Alexandra Khokhlova (or Chochlowa) (*Countess*); V. I. Pudovkin (*Zhban, the con-man*); S. Komarov (*One-eyed man*); Leonid Obolensky (*The dandy*); V. Lopatina (*Ellie, the American girl*); G. Kharlampiev (*S'enka Svisch*); P. Galadzhev, S. Sletov, and V. Latyshevskii (*Con-men*); A. Gorjchilin (*Millionaire*); Vladimir Fogel.

Publications

Books:

Yezuitov, N., *Poudouvkine, "Pouti Tvortchestva, Les Voies de la création,"* Moscow, 1937.
Mariamov, A., *Vsevolod Pudovkin*, Moscow, 1952.
Leyda, Jay, *Kino: A History of the Russian and Soviet Film*, London, 1960.
Schnitzer, Luda and Jean, *Vsevolod Poudouvkine*, Paris, 1966.
Amengual, Barthélemy, *V. I. Poudouvkine*, Lyons, 1968.
Rimberg, John, *The Motion Picture in the Soviet Union 1918–1952: A Sociological Analysis*, New York, 1973.
Schnitzer, Luda and Jean, and Marcel Martin, editors, *Cinema in Revolution: The Heroic Era of the Soviet Film*, New York, 1973.
Levaco, Ronald, editor, *Kuleshov on Film*, Berkeley, 1974.
Dart, Peter, *Pudovkin's Films and Film Theory*, New York, 1974.
Cohen, Louis, Harris, *The Cultural-Political Traditions and Development of the Soviet Cinema*, New York, 1974.
Masi, Stefano, *Vsevolod I. Pudovkin*, Florence, 1985.
Marshall, Herbert, *Masters of the Soviet Cinema: Crippled Creative Biographies*, London, 1985.
Mariniello, Silvestra, *Lev Kulesov*, Firenze, 1990.

Articles:

Sovietski Ekran (Moscow), 12 March 1929.
Weinberg, Herman, "Vsevolod Pudovkin," in *Films in Review* (New York), August-September 1953.
Zorkaia, Neïa, "Lve Kouleshov," in *Cahiers du Cinéma* (Paris), May-June 1970.
Levaco, Ronald, "Kuleshov," in *Sight and Sound* (London), Spring 1971.
"The Classic Period of Soviet Cinema," in *Film Journal* (New York), Fall-Winter 1972.
"Soviet Silent Cinema, Part I: 1918–1925," in *Museum of Modern Art Department of Film Notes* (New York), 7 March-15 April 1974.
Duarte, F., and M.F. Feis, "Kuleshov, Kozintsev e Trauberg," in *Celuloide*, vol. 27, no. 342/343, December 1982.
Bergroth, T., and Koller M., "*The Extraordinary Adventures of Mrs. West in the Land of the Bolsheviks,*" in *Filmviews* (Mitcham), vol, 30, no. 124, Winter 1985.
Bruno, Edoardo, in *Filmcritica* (Siena), vol. 39, no. 387, September 1988.
Garroni, Emilio, in *Filmcritica* (Siena), vol, 39, no. 387, September 1988.
Montani, P., "Il viaggio interminabile e la rappresentazione dell'altro," in *Filmcritica* (Siena), vol. 39, no. 387, September 1988.
Bassan, R., "Lev Koulechov," in *Revue du Cinéma* (Paris), no. 446, February 1989.
"Lo 'scandalo' Kulesov," in *Castoro Cinema* (Florence), May-June 1989.
Kulešov, Lev, "Caligari, Mr. West, Aélita: trois conceptions du film muet," in *Positif* (Paris), no. 359, January 1991.
Sonnenberg, B., "*Aelita: Queen of Mars*, Others from the U.S.S.R.," in *Nation*, vol. 254, 9 March 1992.
Christensen, P. G., "Contextualizing Kuleshov's *Mr. West*," in *Film Criticism* (Meadville, Pennsylvania), vol. 18, no. 1, 1993.

Yampolsky, Mikhail, and Larry Joseph, ''Mask Face and Machine Face: Film Theories of Lev Kuleshov,'' in *TDR* (Cambridge), vol. 38, no. 3, Fall 1994.
Iskusstvo Kino (Moscow), no. 5, 1996.

* * *

It is doubtful whether many historians would regard a Soviet filmmaker of the 1920s as having delivered an opening salvo in what would be known as now termed the ''cold war.'' Yet Lev Kuleshov's *The Extraordinary Adventures of Mr. West in the Land of the Bolsheviks* so completely foreshadows the attitudes inherent in more modern East-West tensions that it has lost little of its satiric bite today more than 70 years after its original release. At the same time, it has grown in stature to become one of the pivotal films in the early development of cinema.

Conceived initially as a demonstration of the theory of montage developed by Kuleshov's experimental film group, the ''Kuleshov Workshop,'' which operated outside the formal curriculum of the Soviet State Film School, it advanced the art of the film on a number of fronts. Not the least of these was its employment of a number of brilliant young directors including Vsevolod Pudovkin who with Sergei Eisenstein would develop variations on the theory of montage that would produce most of the outstanding Soviet films of the 1920s. For three years preceding the production of *The Extraordinary Adventures*, the group, because of a scarcity of film stock, conducted filmless exercises in editing and reconstructing imported films such as D. W. Griffith's *Intolerance* in an effort to analyze the precise manner in which a film produces meaning.

The Extraordinary Adventures, however, provided the first lengthy, practical opportunity to put the workshop's theories into practice. Interestingly, one of the group's overriding concerns was to demonstrate that a different type of actor was needed for the screen than for the stage—still a major issue in the Soviet Union which had been relatively cut off from the films of Griffith and other innovators. Since, in Kuleshov's view, film creates meaning through a number of interacting images of which the actor constitutes only one, the acting technique must support the visual images that are intercut with it—an idea unheard of on the stage. His characters themselves, however, shared one characteristic obviously borrowed from the theater, that of personification. Mr. West, the most obvious example of this trait, is a typical American holding views representative of most of his countrymen. But his views or, more precisely, fears become personified in the symbolic characters that his entourage encounters in the Soviet Union and, though the actors deftly underplay their roles, the satiric undertones come through. For the most part the staging of West's misadventures is inspired by American Westerns and action comedies of the late teens—although probably not by the films of Charlie Chaplin or Buster Keaton, as some have suggested; few such films were exported to the Soviets during and immediately after the revolution.

The Extraordinary Adventures of Mr. West in the Land of the Bolsheviks proved that Kuleshov's theories were viable. Although he had somewhat miscalculated the degree of sophistication needed by his actors to fully carry out his goals, it was a good start. Further, it gave an emerging generation of directors the impetus that would eventually result in the great classics of theoretical montage, *Storm over Asia* (1928) and *October* (1927).

—Stephen L. Hanson

NESTO IZMEDJU

(Something in Between)

Former Yugoslavia, 1982

Director: Srdjan Karanovic

Production: Yugoslavia Centar Film, Belgrade; running time: 107 minutes. Filmed in New York, Dubrovnik, Belgrade, and Istanbul, 1982.

Executive producer: Milan Zmukic; **screenplay:** Srdjan Karanovic, Milosav Marinovic, and Andrew Horton; **photography:** Zivko Zalar; **editor:** Branko Ceperac; **art director:** Miljen Kljakovic; **music:** Zoran Simjanovic.

Cast: Caris Corfman (*Eva*); Predrag Miki-Manojlovic (*Janko*); Dragan Nikolic (*Marko*); Zorka Doknic-Manojlivic (*Mother*); Renata Ulmanski (*Aunt*); Gorica Popvic (*Dunja*); Sonja Savic (*Tvigica*); Peter Ilic-Hajne (*Son*); Nina Kirsanova (*Grandmother*).

Awards: Golden Arenas, Festival of Yugoslavian Film.

Publications

Articles:

Chion, M., in *Cahiers du Cinéma* (Paris), June-July 1983.
Coselli, L., in *Positif* (Paris), July-August 1983.
Chicoine, J. -F., in *Séquences* (Montreal), October 1983.
Chevrie, M., in *Cahiers du Cinéma* (Paris), February 1984.
Pratley, G., ''No Censorship in Yugoslavia,'' in *Cinema India International*, vol. 5, no. 4, 1988.

* * *

Srdjan Karanovic was part of a new wave of then-Yugoslav directors who trained at Prague's famous FAMU Academy, and who in their films, combined frivolous, seemingly superficial entertainment with a consideration of the current state of politics and society. According to co-screenwriter Andrew Horton, ''The Prague Group shares a concern for the ways which a degree of social realism can be juxtaposed to an expanded reality reflective of individual freedom and the free play of the imagination; none of them preaches a political dogma. The film tends to be critical of all forces that work against individual fulfilment and happiness within a social context.''

For his first film, *Drustven Igra* (*Party Games*), produced in 1972, Karanovic advertised for his cast in a newspaper, asking people to write why they would like to appear in the film, and what they would like to do. A script was constructed around the twenty ''actors'' chosen from the 4000 applications—what resulted was a playful combination of spontaneity and absurdity. *Miris Poljskog Cveca* (*The Fragrance of Wild Flowers*), his second film, continues the theme of ''film as play.'' A middle-aged actor, fed up with marriage, gives up everything to live on a barge on the Danube, just as he is about to open in Oscar Wilde's *An Ideal Husband.* His action becomes a media event, and soon the small village where he comes to rest by the Danube is transformed into a Felliniesque circus as people gather, inspired by the actor, to live out their fantasies. The film won the FIPRESCI award at Cannes in 1978.

In *Nesto Izmedju*, Eva (Caris Corfman), a journalist from New York, splits up with her boyfriend and decides to go to Turkey. She has a stopover in Belgrade, and looks up an old surgeon-friend, Janko (Predrag Miki-Manojlovic). Arriving at his mother's house she finds that he is not at home, and she is taken care of by his playboy-businessman best friend, Marko (Dragan Nikolic), a charming good-for-nothing whose English comprises mostly film titles. Eva and Marko fly to Dubrovnik for lunch (there was a time when this would not have been unusual in Yugoslavia). They meet up with Janko, who is attending a medical conference there, and Eva and Janko embark on a serious love affair.

Nesto Izmedju is a bittersweet picture typical of Karanovic. It is set in former Yugoslavia which at the time of filming was literally ''something in between''—neither East nor West, Catholic nor Muslim nor Orthodox, Balkan nor Austro-Hungarian. In the same way echoing this the characters are in limbo. Eva was on her way to Turkey and gets waylaid in former Yugoslavia; Marko wants to get to the U.S. and starts a business and is biding his time in the country; and Janko is a famous surgeon who wants a serious relationship with Eva but holds back from making a commitment.

This is Karanovic's fourth feature film. He wrote the first draft in Belgrade in 1980, and rewrote it extensively while on a Fulbright lecture visit to Harvard University in spring 1981. Shooting began in July 1982 in New York, Dubrovnik, Belgrade, and Istanbul. At the Festival of Yugoslavian Film, in Pula, it won the five top awards (Golden Arenas), as well as the jury prize in Valencia, the special jury prize in Bastia, and was screened in the ''Un Certain Regard'' section at Cannes, Montreal, and Cairo.

—Mike Downey

THE NEW BABYLON

See **NOVYI VAVILON**

NEW EARTH

See **NIEUWE GRONDEN**

DIE NIBELUNGEN

Germany, 1924

Director: Fritz Lang

PART 1: SIEGFRIED

PART 2: KRIEMHILDS RACHE

Production: Decla-Bioscop-Ufa Studios (Decla-Bioscop and Ufa merged during production); black and white, 35mm; silent; Part I: Siegfried; length: 3216 meters originally; released 14 February 1924; Part II: Kriemhilds Rache (Kriemhild's Revenge); length: 3576 meters; released 26 April 1924. Both parts were combined in a shortened version of 2743 meters, with music from Wagner's *Der Ring des Nibelungen* as arranged by Hugo Reisenfeld, released in 1925. Part I released in 1933 in a 688-meter version under the title *Siegfrieds Tod.* Parts 1 and 2 filmed simultaneously between 1922–1924 in Decla-Bioscop-Ufa Studios in Berlin.

Screenplay: Thea von Harbou and Fritz Lang, from the opera *Das Nibelungenlied* by Richard Wagner and from Norse sagas; **photography:** Carl Hoffman and Günther Rittau, with Walter Ruttman (''Dream of the Falcon'' sequence); **art directors:** Otto Hunte, Erich Kettelhut, and Karl Vollbrecht; **music:** Gottfried Huppertz; **costume designers:** Paul Gerd Guderian (who died during production) and Anne Willkomm; **armor and weapons:** Heinrich Umlauff.

Cast: Paul Richter (*Siegfried*); Margarethe Schön (*Kriemhild*); Theodor Loos (*King Gunther*); Hanna Ralph (*Brunhild*); Georg John (*Mime, the Smith*, and *Alberich*); Gertrud Arnold (*Queen Ute*); Hans Carl Müller (*Gerenot*); Erwin Biswanger (*Giselher*); Bernhard Goetske (*Volker von Alzey*); Hans Adalbert Schlettow (*Hagen Tronje*); Rudolf Rittner (*Markgraf Rüdiger von Bechlarn*); Hardy von Francois (*Dankwart*); Fritz Alberti (*Dietrich von Bern*); Georg August Koch (*Hildebrand*); Rudolph Klein-Rogge (*King Etzel*); Hubert Heinrich (*Werbel*); Grete Berger (*Hun*); Frida Richard (*Lecturer*); Georg Jurowski (*Priest*); Iris Roberts (*Page*); Rose Lichtenstein.

Publications

Books:

Von Harbou, Thea, *Das Nibelungenbuch*, Berlin, 1923.
Rotha, Paul, *The Film Till Now*, London, 1930.
Weinberg, Herman, *An Index to the Creative Work of Fritz Lang*, London, 1946.
Kracauer, Siegfried, *From Caligari to Hitler: A Psychological History of the German Film*, Princeton, 1947.
Courtade, Francis, *Fritz Lang*, Paris, 1963.
Moullet, Luc, *Fritz Lang*, Paris, 1963.
Eibel, Alfred, editor, *Fritz Lang*, Paris, 1964.
Pensen, Paul, *The Cinema of Fritz Lang*, New York, 1969.
Johnston, Claire, *Fritz Lang*, London, 1969.
Eisner, Lotte, *The Haunted Screen*, Berkeley, 1969.
Grafe, Frieda, Enno Patalas, and Hans Helmut Prinzler, *Fritz Lang*, Munich, 1976.
Eisner, Lotte, *Fritz Lang*, London, 1977.
Armour, Robert A., *Fritz Lang*, Boston, 1978.
Ott, Frederick, *The Films of Fritz Lang*, Secaucus, New Jersey, 1979.
Jenkins, Stephen, editor, *Fritz Lang: The Image and the Look*, London, 1981.
Kaplan, E. Ann, *Fritz Lang: A Guide to References and Resources*, Boston, 1981.
Maibohm, Ludwig, *Fritz Lang: Seine Filme—Sein Leben*, Munich, 1981.
Dürrenmatt, Dieter, *Fritz Lang: Leben und Werk*, Basel, 1982.
Wirwalski, Andreas, *Wie macht man einen Regenbogen?: Fritz Langs Nibelungenfilm: Fragen zur Bildhaftigkeit des Films und seiner Rezeption*, Frankfurt, 1994.

Die Nibelungen: Siegfried

Bogdanovich, Peter, *Who the Devil Made It: Conversations with Robert Aldrich, George Cukor, Allan Dwan, Howard Hawks, Alfred Hitchcock, Chuck Jones, Fritz Lang, Joseph H. Lewis, Sidney Lumet, Leo McCarey, Otto Preminger, Don Siegel, Josef von Sternberg, Frank Tashlin, Edgar G. Ulmer, Raoul Walsh*, New York, 1997.

Levin, David J., *Richard Wagner, Fritz Lang, and the Nibelungen: The Dramaturgy of Disavowal*, Princeton, 1998.

McGilligan, Patrick, *Fritz Lang: The Nature of the Beast*, New York, 1998.

Gunning, Tom, *The Films of Fritz Lang: Modernity, Crime, and Desire*, London, 2000.

Minden, Michael, and Holger Bachmann, editors, *Fritz Lang's "Metropolis": Cinematic Views of Technology and Fear*, Rochester, 2000.

Articles:

Berliner Tageblatt, 15 February 1924.

Ybarra, T. R., in *New York Times*, 29 April 1924.

Berliner Tageblatt, 2 May 1924.

Hardt, Romey, in *Kritiker* (Berlin), May-June 1924.

Barry, Iris, in *Spectator* (London), 14 June 1924.

Hall, Mordaunt, in *New York Times*, 24 August 1925.

"How Siegfried Was Produced," in *New York Times*, 6 September 1925.

Krutch, Joseph Wood, in *Nation* (New York), 16 September 1925.

Fraenkel, Heinrich, "The Story of Fritz Lang, Maker of *Siegfried*," in *Motion Picture Classic* (New York), March 1926.

New York Times, 16 October 1928.

New Republic (New York), 13 August 1930.

Eisner, Lotte, "Notes sur le style de Fritz Lang," in *Revue du Cinéma* (Paris), 1 February 1947.

Wilson, Harry, "The Genius of Fritz Lang," in *Film Quarterly* (London), Summer 1947.

Gesek, Ludwig, "Fritz Lang: Suggestion und Stimmung," in *Gestalter der Filmkunst, Von Asta Nielsen bis Walt Disney*, Vienna, 1948.

Manvell, Roger, "Siegfried 1922–1924," in *Sight and Sound* (London), April 1950.

Granich, Tom, "Fritz Lang," in *Ferrania* (Milan), August 1950.

Autera, Leonardo, "Il parabola di Fritz Lang," in *Cinema* (Rome), 15 January 1954.

Truffaut, François, ''La Cinquième victime,'' in *Arts* (Paris), 22–24 August 1956.

Luft, Herbert G., ''Erich Pommer,'' in *Films in Review* (New York), November 1959.

Berg, Gretchen, ''La Nuit viennoise: Une Confession de Fritz Lang,'' in *Cahiers du Cinéma* (Paris), August 1965 and June 1966.

Rhode, Eric, ''Fritz Lang (The German Period 1919–1933),'' in *Tower of Babel*, London, 1966.

Oudart, Jean Pierre, ''La Sature,'' in *Cahiers du Cinéma* (Paris), April and May 1969.

Barsacq, Léon, ''Toward a Film Aesthetic: Sweden and Germany 1917–1922,'' in *Le Décor de film*, Paris, 1970.

''Selbstdarstellung: Fritz Lang,'' in *Frankfurter Rundschau*, 15 May 1971.

Phillips, Gene D., ''Fritz Lang: An Interview,'' in *Focus on Film* (London), Spring 1975.

Phillips, Gene D., ''Fritz Lang Gives His Last Interview,'' in *Village Voice* (New York), 16 August 1976.

Jouvert, P., ''Les Images de Kriemhild,'' in *Cinématographe* (Paris), January 1977.

Stiles, V. M., ''The Siegfried Legend and the Silent Screens: Fritz Lang's Interpretation of a Hero Saga,'' in *Literature/Film Quarterly* (Salisbury, Maryland), no. 4, 1980.

Lorenzen, Dagmar, and Ulrike Weinitschke, in *Cahiers de la Cinémathèque* (Perpignan), Summer 1985.

Kramer, S. P., ''Fritz Lang's Definitive *Siegfried* and Its Versions,'' in *Literature/Film Quarterly* (Salisbury, Maryland), October 1985.

Hake, S., ''Architectural Hi/Stories: Fritz Lang and *The Nibelungs*,'' in *Wide Angle* (Baltimore), no. 3, 1990.

Esser, M., ''Rooms of Felicity,'' in *Filmbulletin* (Winterthur, Switzerland), no. 5, 1990.

Hauer, Stanley R., ''The Sources of Fritz Lang's *Die Nibelungen*,'' in *Literature/Film Quarterly* (Salisbury), vol. 18, no. 2, 1990; ''Additions and Corrections,'' in vol. 18, no. 4, 1990.

DeBartolo, J., ''Video Tape Reviews,'' in *Classic Images* (Muscatine), no. 235, January 1995.

* * *

The filming of a national epic was a large undertaking even for Fritz Lang. *Die Nibelungen* emerged as a masterpiece of design based on a script by the talented Thea von Harbou, Lang's wife. It was an architectural concept from beginning to end (Lang himself had been an architect), and it was a triumph of studio craftsmanship at which the Germans excelled. The castles, the forests, the brooks and caverns were all studio-made.

The story fell naturally into two parts: the love of Siegfried and Kriemhild ending in his death and the vengeance of Kriemhild wreaking destruction on her husband's murderers; to this end she gives herself to the barbarian Attila and uses her power to destroy her brothers and the sinister Hagen Tronje. The essential drama of the film lies in the contrast between the stately formal beauty of the first part and the desolate and arid lovelessness of part two. The formal patterns, magnificent though they are, exclude dynamic development, and the progress of the film is slow and static. The Soviet critic Vladimir Nilsson faults the film on these grounds. In Part 2, however, the revenge of Kriemhild hastens the pace until the final holocaust.

The version of the saga used by Lang is very different from that used by Wagner. It is concerned less with Gods and more with human beings. In their symmetrical patterned costumes Lang's people are still human; the world of magic which he evokes does not diminish them. Without any tricks of editing or visual fireworks, Lang approaches his subject with sober observation. It is nevertheless a magic world. The tall stately trees of the forest, the flower-laden banks of streams, the great steps of the cathedral, the drawbridges high in the air, the armour of the knights are all part of a world designed by Lang and his architect, Kettelhut. Scene after scene is memorably beautiful: the fight with the dragon; the flaming fortress of Brunhilde; the great cathedral of Worms.

The acting is strong and firm with a finely contrasted performance by Margarethe Schön as Kriemhild, the gentle lover who becomes the half-demented fury. In the final catastrophe, as the crazed widow of Siegfried sways in front of the blazing hostel, one thinks of the fanatical woman outside the burning jail in Lang's first American film, *Fury*. The theme of the dual nature of woman is a recurring one with Lang to which he returns in *Metropolis* in which Maria and the Robot represent the forces of love and destructiveness.

It is interesting to compare this early film with John Boorman's *Excalibur* (1981), because they have so many elements in common. But the tautness of Lang's structure gains over the looser and more diffused film by Boorman. *Die Nibelungen* is a film without offspring, a beautiful pageant by a master, to be admired and enjoyed for its own sake.

—Liam O'Leary

NIEUWE GRONDEN

(New Earth)

Netherlands, 1934

Director: Joris Ivens

Production: Capi, Amsterdam/Information Bureau, Royal Netherlands Government; black and white, 16mm; running time: 28 minutes; length: 2,050 feet. Released Amsterdam 1934.

Producer: Joris Ivens; **screenplay:** Joris Ivens; **photography:** Joris Ivens, John Fernhout, Joop Huisken, Helen van Dongen; **editor:** Helen van Dongen; **music:** Hanns Eisler.

Cast: Joris Ivens (*Narrator*).

Publications

Books:

Eisler, Hanns, and Theodore Adorno, *Composing for the Films*, New York, 1947.

Van Dongen, Helen, and others, *Joris Ivens*, edited by Wolfgang Klaue, Berlin, 1963.

Zalzman, Abraham, *Joris Ivens*, Paris, 1963.

Wegner, Hans, *Joris Ivens: Dokumentarist den Wahrheit*, Berlin, 1965.

Grelier, Robert, *Joris Ivens*, Paris, 1965.

Nieuwe Gronden

Ivens, Joris, *The Camera and I*, New York, 1969.

Kremeier, Klaus, *Joris Ivens: Ein Filmer an den Fronten der Weltrevolution*, Berlin, 1976.

Delmar, Rosalind, *Joris Ivens: 50 Years of Filmmaking*, London, 1979.

Devarrieux, Claire, *Entretiens avec Joris Ivens*, Paris, 1979.

Passek, Jean-Loup, editor, *Joris Ivens: 50 ans de cinema*, Paris, 1979.

Ivens, Joris, and Robert Destanque, *Joris Ivens; ou, La Memoire d'un regard*, Paris, 1982.

Brunel, Claude, *Joris Ivens*, Paris, 1983.

Waugh, Thomas, editor, *''Show us Life'': Towards a History and Aesthetic of the Committed Documentary*, Metuchen, New Jersey, 1984.

Bakker, Kees, *Joris Ivens and the Documentary Context*, Amsterdam, 1999.

Schoots, Hans, *Joris Ivens: Living Dangerously*, Amsterdam, 2000.

Articles:

New Republic (New York), 15 April 1936.

National Board of Review, May 1936.

Today's Cinema (London), 14 June 1944.

Monthly Film Bulletin (London), May 1945.

Variety (New York), 3 March 1947.

Cinema Nuovo (Turin), 15 February 1953.

''Ivens Issue'' of *Cine Cubano* (Havana), no. 3, 1960.

Ferguson, Otis, in *The Collected Film Criticism of Otis Ferguson*, Philadelphia, 1971.

Hogenkamp, B., ''Joris Ivens and the Problems of the Documentary Film,'' in *Framework* (Norwich), Autumn 1979.

''Ivens Issue'' of *Avant-Scène du Cinéma* (Paris), 1 January 1981.

* * *

In 1930 the Dutch Building Trades Union commissioned Joris Ivens to record Holland's reclamation from the North Sea of a half-million acres of the Zuyder Zee, her ''inland sea,'' for agriculture. The project involved 12,000 men working on a two-shift basis for ten years, and caught the international imagination, as a wonder of world engineering, although the unions had a special interest in labor's contribution. Ivens's camera-team (John Fernhout, also known as Ferno, Joop Huisken, Helen van Dongen, Eli Lotar, and Ivens himself) filmed the work over three years, alongside other industrial documentaries (some are often misdescribed as spin-offs from this project; no doubt Ivens re-used material as convenient). Scarcely was a film called *Zuyder Zee* assembled (45 minutes, 1933, silent) than the Depression hit Dutch agriculture, and the wheat grown in the laboriously reclaimed land was burned or fed to pigs. The outrageous irony provoked Ivens to shorten the existing material, overlay music by a ''leftist'' composer, and add an epilogue, combining new material, newsreel footage, a few ''staged'' shots, an accusatory voice-over, and a sarcastic song à la Brecht, to denounce the global capitalist system. The new version was banned in most countries, and most Anglophone viewers will know only a ''shorn'' version derived from it, using Eisler's music but omitting the epilogue; it's reputedly a wartime edit, devised to elicit admiration for our Dutch allies.

The Zuyder Zee sections make pictorially striking, dynamically edited, documentary narrative; they go from the initial dredging-up of sea-bed boulder-clay, and its redeposition as a sea-wall, to the closure of the last gap, through which the North Sea's violent currents flow only more fiercely as men and machines narrow it. What risked being *either* a dry record of constructional procedures, *or* a mere symphony of forms rhapsodising over man's battle against nature (or some such generality), discovers instead what can for shorthand be called *the poetics of material structuration.* The seabed becomes a barrier *against* the sea, hydraulic jets set sand *flowing* like water *against* water, the screen becomes a flux of forces involving salt water, fresh water, basalt slabs, steel claws, clay sticky or dripping, vast ''mattresses'' of woven willow, the mechanical and the manual, the hard tight shapes of machines and the formless but indefatigable sea. The spectator not only grasps this dialectic intellectually, thanks to that elementary but uncommon virtue, clear exposition, he also *feels* it, as it were in his muscles, thanks to Ivens's remarkable kinaesthetic sense. In *My Camera and I* Ivens describes how he selected the camera-angles for the stone-lifting sequence by closely analysing, and then repeatedly performing, the job himself; on discovering that the greatest strain came at the shoulder-muscles and on the chin, he used these ''organic'' work-points as visual motifs—which ''happened to be the most beautiful angle'' (exactly as the era's materialist-functionalist aesthetics, which surely influenced Ivens, would predict). Otis Ferguson brilliantly analyses the cutting's precise response to detail, to the exact interactions of operators, controls, ad machines.

Ivens structured the closure of the last, 32-km., gap (at 1302 hrs on 28/5/32) as a ''dramatic dialogue.'' ''One of our cameras was *the land-camera* and the cameraman identified himself with the land's fight against the sea. . . .Another camera was *the sea-camera,* it said: 'My current is strong, I will be here after you have given up and gone away. . . .' The third camera identified with man and machines sharing human effort.'' Though individual shots may seem as impersonal and alienating as Dziga Vertov-type ''enthusiasm,'' the structure generates an ''organic pathos'' according to Eisenstein, while the muscularity of man and machine evokes Flaherty and the ditch-digging of Vidor's *Our Daily Bread.* It's a remarkable synthesis. The first protrusion of man's submarine mountains from these angry waters is strangely poignant, providing a rare provocation to celebrate industry as something itself primeval, yet nobly creative. Eisler's music is brilliant: the expression in sound of hard energy, gutsy yet pure; thanks to its prominence, one might almost say that the film honours industry as a ''symphonic'' activity, as an expression of organising intelligence, just as ''high'' as music is.

Entirely different in style, the final section makes an extremely effective tract, but is no more the last word on ''capitalism'' than the Depression was. Though such a reading would surely distress Ivens, who became increasingly uncritical of any Communist regime, it's arguable that the usual, shorn version of the film is complete in itself, and constitutes a Social-Democratic counterpart to Leninist montage epics like *Turksib.* A *Cahiers du Cinéma* critic suggested that the shots of children happily playing would then have suggested ''our nation's future,'' and reminded contemporary spectators that the Dutch government organised the project without incurring one loan to burden its children with debt.

—Raymond Durgnat

THE NIGHT

See **LA NOTTE**

NIGHT AND FOG

See **NUIT ET BROUILLARD**

A NIGHT AT THE OPERA

USA, 1935

Director: Sam Wood

Production: Metro-Goldwyn-Mayer Picture Corp.; black and white, 35mm; running time: 96 minutes. Released 1935. Filmed in MGM studios.

Producer: Irving Thalberg; **screenplay:** George S. Kaufman and Morrie Ryskind, uncredited assistance by Bert Kalmar and Harry Ruby, with gagwriter Al Boasberg, from a screen story by James Kevin McGuiness; **photography:** Merritt B. Gerstad; **editor:** William Levanway; **sound recording director:** Douglas Shearer; **art director:** Cedric Gibbons; **music score:** Herbert Stothart; **costume designer:** Dolly Tree; **dances:** Chester Hale.

Cast: Groucho Marx (*Otis B. Driftwood*); Chico Marx (*Fiorello*); Harpo Marx (*Tomasso*); Kitty Carlisle (*Rosa Castaldi*); Allan Jones (*Ricardo Baroni*); Walter Woolf King (*Rudolfo Lassparri*); Sig Rumann (*Herman Gottlieb*); Margaret Dumont (*Mrs. Claypool*); Edward Keane (*Captain*); Robert Emmett O'Connor (*Detective Henderson*); Gino Corrado (*Steward*); Purnell Pratt (*Mayor*); Frank Yaconelli (*Engineer*); Billy Gilbert (*Engineer's assistant/peasant*); Sam Marx (*Extra on ship and at dock*); Claude Peyton (*Police captain*); Rita and Rubin (*Dancers*); Luther Hoobyar (*Ruiz*); Rodolfo Hoyos (*Count di Luna*); Olga Dane (*Azucena, Gypsy woman*); James J. Wolf (*Ferrando*); Ines Palange (*Maid*); Jonathan Hale (*Stage manager*); Otto Fries (*Elevator man*); William Gould (*Captain of police*); Leo White, Jay Eaton, and Rolfe Sedan (*Aviators*); Wilbur

A Night at the Opera

Mackand George Irving (*Committee*); George Guhl (*Policeman*); Harry Tyler (*Sign painter*); Phillip Smalley and Selmer Jackson (*Committee*); Alan Bridge (*Immigration inspector*); Harry Allen (*Doorman*); Lorraine Bridges (*Louisa*).

Publications

Script:

Kaufman, George S., and Morrie Ryskind, *A Night at the Opera*, New York, 1972.

Books:

Treadwell, Bill, *50 Years of American Comedy*, New York, 1951.
Crichton, Kyle, *The Marx Brothers*, New York, 1951.
Marx, Arthur, *Groucho*, New York, 1954.
Cahn, William, *The Laugh Makers*, New York, 1957.
Eyles, Allen, *The Marx Brothers: Their World of Comedy*, New York, 1966.
Zimmerman, Paul D., and Burt Goldblatt, *The Marx Brothers and the Movies*, New York, 1968.
Thomas, Bob, *Thalberg: Life and Legend*, New York, 1969.
Anobile, Richard, editor, *Why a Duck? Visual and Verbal Gems from the Marx Brothers Movies*, New York, 1971.
Boyum, Joy Gould, and Adrienne Scott, *Film as Film: Critical Responses to Film Art*, Boston, 1971.
Joseph Adamson, *Groucho, Harpo, Chico, and Sometimes Zeppo: A History of the Marx Brothers and a Satire on the Rest of the World*, New York, 1973.
Mast, Gerald, *The Comic Mind: Comedy and the Movies*, New York, 1973; revised edition, Chicago, 1979.
Marx, Samuel, *Mayer and Thalberg*, London, 1976.
Chandler, Charlotte, *Hello, I Must Be Going: Groucho and His Friends*, New York, 1978.
Arce, Hector, *Groucho*, New York, 1979.
Gehring, Wes D., *The Marx Brothers: A Bio-Bibliography*, Westport, 1987.
Marx, Groucho, *The Marx Brothers Scrapbook*, New York, 1989.
Bergan, Ronald, *Marx Brothers*, Edison, 1992.
Eyles, Allen, *The Complete Films of the Marx Brothers*, Secaucus, 1992.

Stables, Kate, *Marx Brothers*, New York, 1992.
Mitchell, Glenn, *The Marx Brothers Encyclopedia*, North Pomfret, 1996.

Articles:

Sennwald, Andre, in *New York Times*, 7 December 1935.
Variety (New York), 11 December 1935.
New Yorker, 14 December 1935.
''Sam Wood,'' in *Current Biography Yearbook*, New York, 1944.
Rowland, Richard, in *Hollywood Quarterly*, April 1947.
Eyles, Allen, in *Films and Filming* (London), February 1965.
Kael, Pauline, in *Kiss Kiss Bang Bang*, Boston, 1968.
Denton, Clive, ''Sam Wood,'' in *The Hollywood Professionals 2*, New York, 1974.
Prouty, Howard H., in *Magill's Survey of Cinema 3*, Englewood Cliffs, New Jersey, 1980.
Vega, J., in *Contracampo* (Madrid), October 1981.
Urban, M., in *Filmkultura* (Budapest), May 1985.
Hemming, Roy, ''LV Classics: *Singin' in the Rain/A Night at the Opera,*'' in *Video Review* (New York), vol. 9, no. 11, February 1989.
Arnold, Gordon B., ''From Big Screen to Small Screen: *A Night at the Opera* Directed by Sam Wood and Starring the Marx Brothers,'' in *Library Journal* (New York), vol. 114, no. 9, 15 May 1989.
Catsos, G. J. M., ''Allan Jones Remembers: *Night* and *Day* with the Marx Bros.,'' in *Filmfax* (Evanston, Illinois), February-March 1991.
''*A Night at the Opera*,'' in *Premiere* (New York), vol. 10, November 1996.

* * *

A Night at the Opera is the sixth Marx Brothers movie and their first with MGM Studios. *Duck Soup* (1933) had been a critical and commercial failure, and marked the end of the Marx Brothers' contract with Paramount. Zeppo Marx had left the team, and for a time it appeared that the brothers' movie career was at an end. However, producer Irving Thalberg became interested in them, and an MGM contract was negotiated. It was Thalberg's contention that the audience for Marx Brothers movies could be broadened by bringing the story line, characterizations, musical numbers, and production values up to the high standard already set by their comedy sequences; that is, by putting the Marx Brothers into a musical comedy, rather than surrounding a collection of their vaudeville-style routines with a sketch intended only to glue them together. The Marx Brothers, who had attempted something similar on Broadway without finding an appropriate property, agreed with him, and an excellent working relationship was established.

The script of *A Night at the Opera* provides sympathetic, integrated characters for all of the Marx Brothers, and the operatic and shipboard settings make an appropriate contrast to the team's anarchic comedy style and offer opportunities for good roles for regular Marx Brothers supporting players Margaret Dumont and Sig Rumann. Final credit for the screenplay went to George S. Kaufman and Morrie Ryskind, but the concept was apparently also treated earlier by Bert Kalmar and Harry Ruby, and received significant additions from gagwriter Al Boasberg. Zeppo was replaced as romantic lead by Allan Jones, a convincing actor and excellent singer who, with ingenue Kitty Carlisle, managed to supply both a believable love story and strong musical numbers.

Thalberg also suggested trying out the comedy numbers on the road for audiences, a system that the team continued to use in later productions. The Marx Brothers, with part of the rest of the cast, took a tabloid version of the show on a short tour of four western cities, accompanied by writers Ryskind and Boasberg (Kaufman, who disliked Hollywood, had returned to New York). Audience reactions were monitored and scenes rewritten for maximum effect. Filming included not only the perfected routines, but also reaction time for laughs, which had been timed by stop-watch during live performances. It appears that the completed film owes little to director Sam Wood; the concept was Thalberg's, and the execution was chiefly by the writers and the Marx Brothers themselves.

The resulting film was the Marx Brothers' most successful with both critics and the public. It contains some of the team's best comedy routines, including the famous stateroom scene; the contract scene, in which Groucho and Chico edit a legal document by simply tearing off the offending clauses; and a spectacular finale in which the three Marx Brothers demolish a full-scale production of *Il Trovatore*. However, it also has straight musical numbers which became hit songs outside the film; logical places in the plot for Harpo's and Chico's musical specialties; and an overall polish and integrity which had not been present in their earlier movies. Its success prompted the team to apply the same formula to most of their subsequent films, but only *A Day at the Races* comes close to matching its quality. Thalberg died during the making of *A Day at the Races*, and no other producer was willing to invest the same resources in a Marx Brothers comedy.

Recent critical opinion allows *A Night at the Opera* to retain status as one of the best, if not absolutely the best, of the Marx Brothers films. *Duck Soup*, despite its early failure, has become a favorite of those Marx Brothers audiences who feel that any interruption of comedy sequences is a waste of time, and of those who profess to see it as a powerful statement against war. However, *A Night at the Opera* is generally considered to equal *Duck Soup* in the perfection of its comedy routines and dialogue, and certainly to surpass it in the quality of the film as a whole.

—Annette Fern

THE NIGHT OF THE HUNTER

USA, 1955

Director: Charles Laughton

Production: United Artists; black and white, 35mm; running time: 93 minutes. Released 1955.

Producer: Paul Gregory; **screenplay:** James Agee, rewritten by Charles Laughton, from the novel by Davis Grubb; **photography:** Stanley Cortez; **editor:** Robert Golden; **art director:** Hilyard Brown; **set decorator:** Al Spencer; **music:** Walter Schumann; **special effects:** Jack Rabin and Louis De Witt.

Cast: Robert Mitchum (*''Preacher'' Harry Powell*); Shelley Winters (*Willa Harper*); Lillian Gish (*Rachel*); Billy Chapin (*John*); Sally Jane Bruce (*Pearl*); Peter Graves (*Ben Harper*); Evelyn Varden (*Icey Spoon*); Don Beddoe (*Walt Spoon*); James Gleason (*Uncle Birdie*); Gloria Castillo (*Ruby*).

The Night of the Hunter

Publications

Script:

Agee, James, *Night of the Hunter*, in *Agee on Film 2*, New York, 1960.

Books:

Brown, William, *Charles Laughton: A Pictorial Treasury of His Films*, New York, 1970.

Burrows, Michael, *Charles Laughton and Frederic March*, Cornwall, 1970.

Tomkies, Mike, *The Robert Mitchum Story*, Chicago, 1972.

Higham, Charles, *Charles Laughton: An Intimate Biography*, New York, 1976.

Matthews, J. H., *Surrealism and American Feature Films*, Boston, 1979.

Lanchester, Elsa, *Elsa Lanchester Herself*, New York, 1983.

Malcolm, Derek, *Robert Mitchum*, Tunbridge Wells, Kent, 1984.

Downing, David, *Robert Mitchum*, London, 1985.

Callow, Simon, *Charles Laughton: A Difficult Actor*, London, 1987, 1989, 1997.

Roberts, Jerry, *Robert Mitchum: A Bio-Bibliography*, Westport, 1992.

Marill, Alvin H., *The Films of Robert Mitchum*, Secaucus, New Jersey, 2000.

Articles:

Hart, Henry, in *Films in Review* (New York), August-September 1955.

Archer, Eugene, in *Film Culture* (New York), Winter 1955.

Lambert, Gavin, in *Sight and Sound* (London), Winter 1955–56.

Benayoun, Robert, ''Freud au pays de l'ogre,'' in *Demain* (Paris), 1956.

Truffaut, François, in *Arts* (Paris), 23 May 1956.

Labarthe, André S., in *Cahiers du Cinéma* (Paris), June 1956.

Tozzi, Romano, ''Lillian Gish,'' in *Films in Review* (New York), December 1962.

Vermilye, Jerry, ''Charles Laughton,'' in *Films in Review* (New York), May 1963.

Johnson, Ian, and Raymond Durgnat, editors, ''Puritans Anonymous,'' in *Motion* (London), Autumn 1963.

Ringgold, Gene, ''Robert Mitchum,'' in *Films in Review* (New York), May 1964.

Kael, Pauline, in *Kiss Kiss Bang Bang*, Boston, 1968.

Wood, Robin, ''*Night of the Hunter*: Novel into Film,'' in *On Film*, London, 1970.

Gow, Gordon, in *Films and Filming* (London), February 1975.

''*La Nuit du chasseur* Issue'' of *Avant-Scène du Cinéma* (Paris), 15 February 1978.

Hammon, P., ''Melmouth in Norman Rockwell Land: *The Night of the Hunter*,'' in *Sight and Sound* (London), no. 2, 1979.

Lucas, Blake, in *Magill's Survey of Cinema 3*, Englewood Cliffs, New Jersey, 1980.

Ferrario, D., in *Cineforum* (Bergamo), January-February 1982.

Le Pavec, J. P., in *Cinéma* (Paris), February 1982.

Tobin, Yann, in *Positif* (Paris), May 1982.

Turner, G. E., ''Creating *The Night of the Hunter*,'' in *American Cinematographer* (Los Angeles), December 1982.

Listener (London), 6 March 1986.

Ravage, Jack, ''Reviews: *The Night of the Hunter*,'' in *Film Quarterly* (Berkeley), vol. 42, no. 1, Fall 1988.

Trojan, Judith, ''Front Row Center: Lillian Gish: *The Actor's Life for Me* directed by Terry Sanders/*The Night of the Hunter* written by James Agee and directed by Charles Laughton with Lillian Gish and Robert Mitchum,'' in *Wilson Library* (Bronx), vol. 63, no. 6, February 1989.

Rainer, Peter, ''The Best Movies on Video You've Never Seen: *The Night of the Hunter* Directed by Charles Laughton,'' in *Connoisseur* (New York), vol. 221, no. 951, April 1991.

Secchi, C., ''Fiaba e sogno in *The Night of the Hunter* di Charles Laughton,'' in *Cinema & Cinema* (Bologna), May-August 1991.

Hoberman, J., ''Down by the River,'' in *Village Voice* (New York), vol. 37, 28 July 1992.

Berthome, J.-P., ''Deux voix dans la nuit,'' in *Positif* (Paris), July-August 1993.

Svehla, G.J., ''Robert Mitchum's Cinema of Evil: *Cape Fear* and *Night of the Hunter*,'' in *Midnight Marquee* (Baltimore), vol. 46, Winter 1994.

Moorhouse, Jocelyn, ''Enduring: *Night of the Hunter* Directed by Charles Laughton,'' in *Sight & Sound* (London), vol. 5, no. 4, April 1995.

Duras, Marguerite, ''*La nuit du chasseur*,'' in *Cahiers du Cinéma* (Paris), no. 501, April 1996.

Gross, Larry, ''Baby, I Don't Care,'' in *Sight & Sound* (London), vol. 7, no. 9, September 1997.

Gee, Maggie, ''Songs of the Sweet Enchanter,'' in *TLS: The Times Literary Supplement* (London), no. 5009, 2 April 1999.

Romney, Jonathan, ''Long Shadows,'' in *New Statesman* (London), vol. 12, no. 549, 2 April 1999.

Thomson, David, ''A Child's Demon,'' in *Sight & Sound* (London), vol. 9, no. 4, April 1999.

* * *

Published in 1953, Davis Grubb's Depression-era novel about a serial killer preacher in relentless pursuit of two orphans in order to get a cache of stolen loot in their possession shot to the top of the bestseller list and stayed there for months.

The book was brought to the attention of Charles Laughton by the actor's business associate, producer Paul Gregory. Though still in demand as an actor on the stage, Laughton's movie career had hit the skids; he wanted to make the transition to movie director. Gregory thought the book ideal for Laughton's debut effort. James Agee was hired to adapt the book, but his draft proved too unwieldy and unfilmable and Laughton proceeded to adapt the book himself, though he took no screen credit for his work.

To prepare for the film, which he wanted to exude an atmosphere of early rural Americana, Laughton screened a collection of silent films by the undisputed master of such atmosphere, D. W. Griffith—then, in a further nod to the master, cast Griffith's greatest leading lady, Lillian Gish, in an important role. Robert Mitchum was Laughton's first and only choice to play the killer preacher, Harry Powell, whose warring inner demons are symbolized by the words ''love'' and ''hate'' tattooed on his knuckles.

The released film was a pictorially striking but decidedly unusual combination of picaresque adventure, fairy tale, and psychological thriller that eluded the grasp of most critics, who voted ''thumbs down.'' A box-office failure, it marked not just Laughton's screen directorial debut, but swan song as well. Over the years, however, *The Night of the Hunter* has come to be viewed as a masterpiece—filmed in a kaleidoscope of styles, ranging from expressionism to film noir to avante-garde, that is breathtakingly cinematic yet boldly theatrical, employing a marvelously intricate and evocative soundtrack and extraordinary music score. Very few first-time film directors have displayed such a natural gift for the medium as Laughton did with *The Night of the Hunter*; it's a shame he never had the opportunity to direct another movie.

The performances Laughton drew from his cast are remarkable. But the standout performance is Robert Mitchum's; the actor's frequently listless performances in other films often disguise what a fine actor he can be given a guiding hand like Laughton's. His performance as Powell is one of the screen's most chilling portraits of perversity and genuine evil. He is astonishingly persuasive as he gently coaxes orphan Pearl to tell where the money is hidden, then flies into a rage scarily calling her a ''poor, silly, disgusting little wretch'' when she obeys her brother's instructions to keep silent. And his frustrated cry of sheer animal rage when the skiff carrying the fleeing children slips from his grasp as he wades into the water after them sends a cold breeze from hell up the viewer's spine to this day.

So expertly made and definitive is Laughton's memorable screen version of Grubb's novel that it would seem foolhardy for anyone to attempt to remake and improve upon it. But director David Greene tried to do so in a 1991 version made for television, starring a miscast Richard Chamberlain in the Mitchum role. Astonishingly, the remake dispensed with the final third of Grubb's novel wherein Powell is brought to justice by the orphans' savior, a Mother Courage figure named Rachel—a denouement Laughton had brought potently to life with Lillian Gish in the part.

Only Diana Scarwid's touching performance as the doomed Willa (played differently but with equal vulnerability by Shelley Winters in the original), the mother of the two children who is killed by Powell rendering them orphans, saved the remake from being worthy of total dismissal—unlike Charles Laughton's version, which remains unforgettable in every way.

—John McCarty

NIGHT ON BALD MOUNTAIN

See **UNE NUIT SUR LE MONT CHAUVE**

1900 (NINETEEN HUNDRED)

See **1900 (NOVECENTO)**

NINGEN NO JOKEN

(The Human Condition)

Japan, 1959–61

Director: Masaki Kobayashi

Production: Ningen Productions for Shochiku Co.; black and white, 35mm; Shochiku Grandscope; released in three parts: Part I: *Ningen no joken (The Human Condition)*; running time: 208 minutes; length: 5501 meters; released 1959; Part II: *Zoko ningen no joken (Road to Eternity)*; running time: 181 minutes; length: 4938 meters; released 1959; Part III: *Ningen no joken III (A Soldier's Prayer)*; running time: 190 minutes; length: 5197 meters; released 1959. All three parts rereleased in 1969.

Producers: Shigeru Wakatsuki (Parts I and III), Tatsuo Hasoya (Part II), Masaki Kobayashi (Part III); **screenplay:** Masaki Kobayashi and Zenzo Matsuyama, with Koichi Inagaki (Part III only), from the six-volume *Ningen no joken* by Jumpei Gomikawa; **photography:** Yoshio Miyajima; **editor:** Keiishi Uraoka; **sound recordist:** Hideo Nishizaki; **art director:** Kazue Hirataka; **music:** Chuji Kinoshita.

Cast: Tatsuya Nakadai (*Kaji*); Michiyo Aratama (*Michiko*); So Yamamura (*Okishima*); Eitaro Ozawa (*Okasaki*); Akira Ishihama (*Chen*); Shinji Manbara (*Kao*); Ineko Arima (*Yang Chun Lan*); Chikage Awashima (*Jin Tung Fu*); Keiji Sada (*Kageyama*); Toru Abe (*Watai*); Masao Mishima (*Kuroki*); Koji Mitsui (*Furya*); Kyu Sazanka (*Cho Meisan*); Seiji Miyaguchi (*Wang Heng Li*); Nobuo Nakamura (*Chief of Head Office*); Michio Minami (*Yoshida*); Hideo Kisho (*Kudo*); Kei Sato (*Shinjo*); Taketoshi Naito (*Tange*); Kunie Tanaka (*Obara*); Kokinjo Katsura (*Sasa*); Kaneko Iwasaki (*Nurse*); Keijiro Morozumi (*Corporal Hironaka*); Yusuke Kawazu (*Private Terada*); Kyoko Kishida (*Ryuko*); Reiko Hitomi (*Umeko*); Fijio Suga (*Captain Nagata*); Nobuo Kaneko (*Corporal Kirahara*); Tamao Nakamura (*Femle Refugee*); Hideko Takamine (*Woman in Settlers' village*); Chishu Ryu (*Village elder*).

Publications

Books:

Mellen, Joan, *Voices from the Japanese Cinema*, New York, 1975.
Bock, Audie, *Japanese Film Directors*, New York, 1978; revised edition, Tokyo, 1985.
Blouin, Claude R., *Le Chemin détourné: Essai sur Kobayashi et le cinéma japonais*, Quebec, 1982.

Articles:

Richie, Donald, ''The Youngest Talents,'' in *Sight and Sound* (London), Spring 1960.
Dyer, Peter John, in *Sight and Sound* (London), Spring 1961.
Iwabuchi, M., ''Japanese Cinema 1961'' and ''Kobayashi's Trilogy,'' in *Film Culture* (New York), Spring 1962.
Blouin, Claude R., ''Kobayashi, à l'uquam: Anarchiste ou utopiste?,'' in *Cinéma Québec* (Montreal), February-March 1974.
Tucker, Richard, ''Masaki Kobayashi,'' in *International Film Guide*, London, 1975.
Niogret, H., in *Positif* (Paris), October 1984.
Tessier, M., in *Revue du Cinéma* (Paris), October 1984.
Télérama (Paris), no. 2284, 20 October 1993.
Niogret, H., ''Entretien avec Masaki Kobayashi,'' in *Positif* (Paris), December 1993.
Gauthier, Guy, in *Mensuel du Cinéma*, no. 12, December 1993.

* * *

''It's not my fault that I'm Japanese—yet my worst fault is that I am.'' The words are those of Kaji, protagonist of Kobayashi's *Ningen no joken*; but they can also be taken, in the fierce agony of their moral paradox, as speaking for the director himself. *Ningen no joken*, nearly ten hours long, four years in the making, undertaken in the teeth of opposition from Kobayashi's studio, Shochiku, and of virulent hostility from conservative forces in Japanese society, can be seen as the most massive act of personal atonement in the history of cinema.

The film is shot through—some would say distorted—with the intensity of Kobayashi's identification with his hero, whose experiences so closely paralleled his own. (''Film'' rather than ''films,''

Ningen no joken

since though released, and often shown, in three separate parts, the work forms an aesthetic and conceptual unity.) Like Kaji, Kobayashi had been conscripted wholly against his will, had opposed the rigidly authoritarian ethos of the Imperial Army, and had been held after the war in a prisoner-of-war camp. "I am Kaji. . . . The life the hero leads is much the same life I lived as a soldier." In Jumpei Gomikawa's six-volume novel, to which Kobayashi immediately bought the film rights, the filmmaker found the ideal vehicle for his perennial theme: the struggle of the individual against a harsh and oppressive society.

Kaji, in effect, becomes the conscience of wartime Japan, a lone voice raised in protest against a system whose sole principles are blind obedience to authority and brutality to everyone else. Yet, for all his antipathy, he finds himself repeatedly implicated in the system he loathes, simply by virtue of being Japanese. Attempting to improve the appalling conditions of Chinese slave labourers in the prison camp to which he's posted, he ends up mistrusted by both sides—by the Chinese as a member of the oppressor race, and by his compatriots as an "enemy sympathiser." Transferred, by way of punishment, to the army, he tries vainly to protect younger recruits from the officially sanctioned sadism of the veterans. Their prime victim, the sensitive and delicate Obara, is driven to a wretched suicide, while Kaji—whose stubbornness, ironically, proves him potential "officer material"—survives through his initiative on the battlefield. "I am a murderer," he reflects amid the mud and corpses, "but I must go on living."

The film's bitterest irony comes in the third part. Captured by the Russians, Kaji, the idealistic socialist, expects to be treated with justice and humanity. But Russia is dominated by a system as tyrannical as that of Japan—a huge portrait of Stalin glowers down on the interrogation room—and, labelled a "fascist samurai," Kaji finds himself enslaved and degraded like the Chinese whom he once supervised. Managing to escape, he tries to trek back to his beloved wife; but the Chinese peasantry, seeing in him only the hated and despised enemy, refuse him food, and he dies in the snow.

As Kaji, Tatsuya Nakadai—Kobayashi's favourite actor, in the role which brought him to fame—dominates the action with a performance of burning conviction, off-screen for no more than a few minutes of the film's epic duration. Repeatedly, Kobayashi emphasises his moral exposure, and the hopelessness of his stance, by isolating him in a bleak, sterile terrain—the ravaged mining landscape of the first part, the battlefield of the second, the final pitiless snowscape—that exploits Yoshio Miyajima's black-and-white scope cinematography to stunning effect. Yet the film includes moments of intimacy, even tenderness—as in the scene where Kaji, allowed a brief visit from his wife and sensing they may never meet again, asks her to stand naked by the dawn-lit window, to leave him with the memory of her beauty.

Ultimately, perhaps, the film suffers from its sheer size, from its relentlessly sombre mood. Content, impelled by the uncompromising seriousness of Kobayashi's vision, has burst the bounds of form; eased of the burden of his memories, the director would proceed to a finer alignment of the two in *Seppuku* (*Harakiri*) or *Joiuchi* (*Rebellion*). But *Ningen no joken* remains an achievement of extraordinary power and emotional resonance: at once a celebration of the resilience of the individual conscience, and a purging of that forced complicity in guilt (not just of a nation but, as the title implies, of the whole human race) which Kaji expiates through his death, and Kobayashi through the making of this film.

—Philip Kemp

NINOTCHKA

USA, 1939

Director: Ernst Lubitsch

Production: Metro-Goldwyn-Mayer Pictures Corp.; black and white, 35mm; running time: 110 minutes. Released 3 November 1939. Re-released 1947. Filmed 19 May 1939–16 July 1939 in MGM studios.

Producer: Ernst Lubitsch; **screenplay:** Charles Brackett, Billy Wilder, and Walter Reisch, from the story by Melchior Lengyel; **photography:** William Daniels; **editor:** Gene Ruggiero; **sound recording director:** Douglas Shearer; **production designer:** Edwin Willis; **art director:** Cedric Gibbons; **music score:** Werner R. Heymann; **costume designer:** Adrian.

Cast: Greta Garbo (*Ninotchka*); Melvyn Douglas (*Count Léon d'Algout*); Ina Claire (*Grand Duchess Swana*); Sig Rumann (*Iranoff*); Felix Bressart (*Buljanoff*); Alexander Granach (*Kopalski*); Bela Lugosi (*Commissar Razinin*); Gregory Gayle (*Count Rakonin*); Rolfe Sedan (*Hotel Manager*); Edwin Maxwell (*Mercier*); Richard Carle (*Gaston*).

Publications

Script:

Brackett, Charles, Billy Wilder, and Walter Reisch, *Ninotchka*, New York, 1966; edited by Richard Anobile, New York, 1975.

Books:

Bainbridge, John, *Garbo*, New York, 1955.
De Acosta, Mercedes, *Here Lies the Heart*, New York, 1960.
Conway, Michael, *The Films of Greta Garbo*, New York, 1963.
Verdone, Mario, *Ernst Lubitsch*, Lyons, 1964.
Weinberg, Herman, *The Lubitsch Touch: A Critical Study*, New York, 1968, 1983.
Viertel, Salka, *The Kindness of Strangers*, New York, 1969.
Zierold, Norman, *Garbo*, New York, 1969.
Kanin, Garson, *Hollywood*, New York, 1974.
Corliss, Richard, *Talking Pictures: Screenwriters in the American Cinema 1927–1973*, Woodstock, New York, 1974.
Corliss, Richard, *Greta Garbo*, New York, 1974.
Whittemore, Don, and Philip Alan Cecchettini, editors, *Passport to Hollywood: Film Immigrants Anthology*, New York, 1976.
Poague, Leland, *The Cinema of Ernst Lubitsch: The Hollywood Films*, London, 1977.
Zolotow, Maurice, *Billy Wilder in Hollywood*, New York, 1977.
Affron, Charles, *Star Acting: Gish, Garbo, Davis*, New York, 1977.
Sands, Frederick, and Sven Broman, *The Divine Garbo*, New York, 1979.
Walker, Alexander, *Greta Garbo: A Portrait*, New York, 1980.
Linton, George, *Greta Garbo*, Paris, 1981.
Paul, William, *Ernst Lubitsch's American Comedy*, New York, 1983, 1987.
Prinzler, Hans Helmut, and Enno Patalas, editors, *Lubitsch*, Munich, 1984.
Ernst Lubitsch, Paris, 1985.
Bourget, Eithne and Jean-Loup, *Lubitsch; ou, La Satire romanesque*, Paris, 1987.
Nacache, Jacqueline, *Lubitsch*, Paris, 1987.
Bowman, Barbara, *Master Space: Film Images of Capra, Lubitsch, Sternberg, and Wyler*, Westport, 1992.
Hake, Sabine, *Passions and Deceptions: The Early Films of Ernst Lubitsch,* Princeton, 1992.
Eyman, Scott, *Ernst Lubitsch: Laughter in Paradise*, New York, 1993.
Harvey, James, *Romantic Comedy: In Hollywood, from Lubitsch to Sturges*, Cambridge, 1998.

Articles:

New York Times, 16 April and 10 and 19 November 1939.
Variety (New York), 11 October 1939.
Garbo, Greta, and Ernst Lubitsch, in *New York Times*, 22 October 1939.
Newsweek (New York), 30 October 1939.
Sight and Sound (London), Winter 1939–40.
Monthly Film Bulletin (London), 31 January 1940.
New Yorker, 29 June and 10 August 1940.
Variety (New York), 29 October and 5 and 26 November 1947.
Lengyel, Melchior (interview), in *New York Times*, 4 January 1948.
Pozzi, Gianni, "Parere su Lubitsch," in *Critica Cinematografica* (Parma), May 1948.
Weinberg, Herman, "A Tribute to Ernst Lubitsch," in *Films in Review* (New York), August-September 1951.
Paolella, Roberto, "Ernst Lubitsch, regista del tempo perduto," in *Bianco e Nero* (Rome), January 1958.
"Lubitsch Issue" of *Film Journal* (Melbourne), June 1959.
Cutts, John, in *Films and Filming* (London), March 1962.
Whiteball, Richard, "Garbo—How Good Was She?," in *Films and Filming* (London), September 1963.

Ninotchka

''Lubitsch Issue'' of *Cahiers du Cinéma* (Paris), February 1968.

Sarris, Andrew, ''Lubitsch in the 30s,'' in *Film Comment* (New York), Winter 1971–72.

Mast, Gerald, ''The 'Lubitsch Touch' and the Lubitsch Brain,'' in *The Comic Mind: Comedy and the Movies*, Indianapolis, 1973.

Trueba, F., in *Casablanca* (Madrid), May 1983.

Amiel, V., ''Paroles de Billy Wilder, 'touch' de Ernst Lubitsch,'' in *Positif* (Paris), September 1983.

Mindich, J., ''Re-reading *Ninotchka:* A Misread Commentary on Social and Economic Systems,'' in *Film & History* (Coral Gables, Florida), no. 1, 1990.

Gensler, Howard, ''Détente: *Ninotchka* Directed by Ernst Lubitsch and Starring Melvyn Douglas and Greta Garbo,'' in *Premiere* (New York), vol. 3, no. 10, June 1990.

Rosterman, R., in *Hollywood: Then and Now*, vol. 25, no. 7, 1992.

Beller, J.L., ''The Radical Imagination in American Film,'' in *Creative Screenwriting* (Washington, D.C.), vol. 1, no. 4, Winter 1994.

''*Ninotchka*,'' in *Premiere* (New York), vol. 12, no. 3, November 1998.

* * *

The advertising campaign for *Ninotchka* is proof of a publicist's faith in the collective amnesia of the American public. ''Garbo Laughs'' was treated as momentously as was ''Garbo Talks,'' the slogan that announced her first sound film, *Anna Christie*. The marketing of *Ninotchka* takes no account of Greta Garbo's frequent laughter, her smile and the lightness of her touch throughout her 1930s films. Just three years before, in *Camille*, playfulness and humor inflect her doomed ''lady of the camellias.'' *Ninotchka* is, however, her first comedy. Its principal comic ploy is a paradoxial reflection on Garbo as actress. Here she is made to play, through the first part of the film, a woman who apparently has no emotions. Audiences must read this as they would a scene that suggests that Fred Astaire is clumsy or that John Wayne is a coward. *Ninotchka* extracts much of its humor from the deadpan expression of an actress whose presence is a sign of deep emotional resonance.

The story of the rigid, businesslike commissar who awakens to luxury and love in Paris is coherent with director Ernst Lubitsch's stylistics. His major films demonstrate the connections between an elegance of decor, elegance of manner, and elegance of the heart. The film's narrative pretext is the sale of jewels; Ninotchka falls in love with an absurd hat just as she falls in love with Léon. Much humor is drawn from the contrast between a lush Parisian hotel and the austere Moscow room Ninotchka shares with a cello player and a streetcar conductor.

As is usually the case in the films of Lubitsch, the comedy reflects back upon the characters. The director uses the comedy of manners to authenticate and dramatize the feelings of the protagonists, and in this, he is at odds with the hard-edged, satirical bent that is characteristic of the writers of *Ninotchka*, Charles Brackett, Billy Wilder and Walter Reisch, a mode that becomes particularly apparent when Wilder turns to directing their scripts. The appeal of *Ninotchka* is in the mix of talents, from Garbo's emotional complexity, to Lubitsch's wry sentiment, to the writer's acerbic wit. The range of the performances includes the broadness of the three bumbling commissars and the drawing-room bitchery of the Grand Duchess Swana (to which Ina Claire brings her distinctively brittle sophistication). Melvyn Douglas provides the pratfall that inspires Garbo's celebrated laugh, and the warm charm that inspires her love.

Very successful at its release, it seemed to promise a new direction in Garbo's faltering career. Her next and final film, *Two Faced Woman*, also co-starring Melvyn Douglas, proved that considerable comic talents also require a comic script. But *Ninotchka* was reborn, first as a Cole Porter's Broadway musical, *Silk Stockings*, with film stars Hildegarde Knef and Don Ameche, and then as a musical film with Cyd Charisse and Fred Astaire.

—Charles Affron

LA NOIRE DE . . .

Senegal-France, 1966

Director: Ousmane Sembene

Production: Les films Domirev (Dakar) and Les Actualités Françaises (Paris); black and white, 35mm; running time: 70 minutes. Released March 1966, France; English version released 1969, New York.

Producer: André Zwobada; **screenplay:** Ousmane Sembene, from a short story by Sembene first published in *Voltaïque* (1961); **photography:** Christian Lacoste; **editor:** André Gaudier; **assistant director:** Ibrahima Barro; **second assistant:** Pathé Diop.

Cast: Thérèse N'Bissine Diop (*Diouana*); Robert Fontaine (*The patron*); Momar Nar Sene (*Friend*); Anne-Marie Jelinek (*The patroness*); Ibrahima Boy (*Boy with mask*); Philippe, Sophie, and Damien (*Infants*); plus the voices of Toto Bissainthe, Robert Marcy, and Sohie Leclerc; Bernard Delbaro; Nicole Donati; Raymond Lemery; Suzanne Lemery.

Awards: Prix Jean Vigo, Paris, 1966; Festival mondial des Arts nègres, Antilope d'argent, 1966; Journées cinématographiques de Carthage, Tanit d'Or, 1966.

Publications

Books:

Vieyre, Paulin Soumanou, *Ousmane Sembene, cinéaste: Première période 1962–1971*, Paris, 1972.

Vieyre, Paulin Soumanou, *Le Cinéma africain des origines à 1973*, Paris, 1975.

Martin, Angela, editor, *African Films: The Context of Production*, London, 1982.

Moore, Carrie Dailey, *Evolution of an African Artist: Social Realism in the Works of Ousmane Sembene*, Ann Arbor, Michigan, 1984.

Pfaff, Francoise, *The Cinema of Ousmane Sembene*, Westport, Connecticut, 1984.

Armes, Roy, *Third World Filmmaking and the West*, Berkeley, 1987.

Peters, Jonathan A., *Ousmane Sembene: Contemporary Griot*, Boulder, 1987.

Gadjigo, Samba, and Ralph Faulkingham, and Thomas Cassirer, and Reinhard Sander, editors, *Ousmane Sembene: Dialogues with Critics and Writers*, Amherst, 1993.

Petty, Sheila, *A Call to Action: The Films of Ousmane Sembene*, Westport, 1996.

Articles:

Morgenthau, H., ''On Films and Filmmakers,'' in *Africa Report*, May-June 1969.

Mortimer, Robert, ''Engaged Film-Making for a New Society,'' in *Africa Report*, November 1970.

Paquet, A., and G. Borremans, ''Ousmane Sembene: Les 'Franc-tireurs' senegalais,'' in *Cinéma Québec* (Montreal), March-April 1973.

Perry, G. M., interview with Ousmane Sembene, in *Film Quarterly* (Berkeley), Spring 1973.

Weaver, H. D., Jr., interview with Ousmane Sembene, in *Cineaste* (New York), vol. 6, no. 1, 1973.

Cheriaa, T., ''Ousmane Sembene, Carthage, et le cinéma africain'' and ''Problematique du cinéaste africain: L'Artiste et la révolution,'' in *Cinéma Québec* (Montreal), August 1974.

Ghali, N., ''Ousmane Sembene,'' in *Cinématographe* (Paris), April 1976.

Bonnet, J.-C., interview with Ousmane Sembene, in *Cinématographe* (Paris), June 1977.

Grelier, R., interview with Ousmane Sembene, in *Image et Son* (Paris), November 1977.

''Ousmane Sembene,'' in *Avant-Scène du Cinéma* (Paris), 1 June 1979.

Bosseno, C., interview with Ousmane Sembene, in *Image et Son* (Paris), September 1979.

Landy, M., and others, ''Ousmane Sembene's Films,'' in *Jump Cut* (Berkeley), July 1982.

Film Library Quarterly (New York), vol. 16, no. 4, 1983.

Atkinson, M., ''Ousmane Sembene,'' in *Film Comment* (New York), July-August 1993.

''Sembene, Ousmane,'' in *Current Biography* (Bronx), vol. 55, no. 4, April 1994.

Niang, Sada, ''Interview with Ousmane Sembene,'' in *Research in African Literatures* (Austin), vol. 26, no. 3, Fall 1995.

* * *

La noire de . . . , by the Senegalese filmmaker Ousmane Sembene, is the first feature-length film to come out of sub-Saharan Africa. Technically flawed, it is nevertheless a cultural and cinematographic achievement, and it marks an important date in the history of African cinema. Based on a short story of the same title, written by Sembene and published in *Voltaïque* (1961), *La noire de . . .* tells the story of a young African woman who goes to France to work for the French couple who have employed her in Dakar. Filled with joy at the prospect of the trip, she soon becomes disillusioned, and finally, feeling imprisoned and isolated from the support of her own community, kills herself.

The film is remarkable in several ways. The force of this tragic tale, itself based on a real-life incident, is developed with considerable skill, especially for a filmmaker with only two short subjects to his credit at the time. The visual impact is great—an accomplishment that is especially noteworthy when one considers that Sembene first told the story in another form, then adapted it into a film that stands completely on its own merits. Sembene's ability at adaptation distinguishes this work from unsuccessful film adaptations in general and marks his progress from the making of his second film *Niaye*, in which the original literary text is still respected to the detriment of the visual presentation. One major difference between *La noire de . . .* and the original short story is in the powerful emphasis placed on an African mask, raising it to the level of a symbol. We see the mask first in its African context, then see it given joyfully by Diouana, the African maid and central character, to the European couple after she begins to work for them. It appears again in Antibes, hung on a very white wall in the couple's apartment. When Diouana breaks into open revolt at her dismal situation, she reclaims it, and we see the two women—one white, one black—fighting over the mask. The mask is returned by the Frenchman to Diouana's family, along with her other belongings, after her death. The film closes with a wonderfully dramatic sequence in which the dead woman's younger brother, wearing the mask, pursues the Frenchman out of the African residential area, as the music in the background rises in pace and intensity.

The conditions of the making of this film are unusual, if not unique, and speak directly to Sembene's vision of cinema as both art and politics: the African actors, including the woman who plays Diouana, were all non-professionals. The film sequences—despite the extensive use of flashbacks—had to be shot in strictly chronological order because of the lack of experience and sophistication with regard to the medium, and this circumstance engendered further problems with lighting in the film. In addition, the sound was dubbed in France. Despite all of these difficulties, the film succeeds admirably in conveying, through the life of one otherwise unremarkable African woman, the brutal realities of neo-colonialism on the African continent.

Sembene's conception of his role as African artist is central to an understanding of his work. Known first as a writer of novels and short stories, he was moved to study cinema at the age of 38 by the realization that, for several reasons, his French-language writings were reaching only a minute segment of his African compatriots. Film allows him to reach many more people, and he sees it as the best way to educate the masses: he claims that he can reach more people with cinema than are likely to attend all the political rallies, all the Christian and Muslim religious gatherings. The fact that *La noire de . . .* is in French shows that the metamorphosis was incomplete at this point in his career. *Le mandat (Mandabi)*, his next film, would be in Wolof, a language spoken by some 90% of his fellow Senegalese.

—Curtis Schade

NORTH BY NORTHWEST

USA, 1959

Director: Alfred Hitchcock

Production: Metro-Goldwyn-Mayer Pictures Corp.; Technicolor, 35mm; running time: 136 minutes; length: 12,256 feet. Released 1959. Filmed in New York City, Long Island, Chicago, and at the Mount Rushmore National Memorial, South Dakota.

Producer: Alfred Hitchcock; **screenplay:** Ernest Lehman; **titles:** Saul Bass; **photography:** Robert Burks; **editor:** George Tomasini; **sound recording supervisor:** Franklin Milton; **production designer:** Robert Boyle; **set decorations:** Henry Grace and Frank McKelvey; **art directors:** William A. Horning and Merrill Pye; **music:** Bernard Herrmann; **special effects:** A. Arnold Gillespie and Lee LeBlanc.

Cast: Cary Grant (*Roger Thornhill*); Eva Marie Saint (*Eve Kendall*); James Mason (*Phillip Vandamm*); Jessie Royce Landis (*Clara Thornhill*); Leo G. Carroll (*Professor*); Philip Ober (*Lester Townsend*); Josephine Hutchinson (*Handsome woman*); Martin Landau (*Leonard*); Adam Williams (*Valerian*); Edward Platt (*Victor Larrabee*); Robert Ellenstein (*Licht*); Les Tremayne (*Auctioneer*); Philip Coolidge (*Dr. Cross*); Edward Binns (*Captain Junkett*); Pat McVey, Ken Lynch (*Chicago policemen*); John Beradino (*Sgt. Emile Klinger*); Nora Marlowe (*Housekeeper, Anna*); Doreen Lang (*Maggie*); Alexander Lockwood (*Judge Anson B. Flynn*); Stanley Adams (*Lt. Harding*); Larry Dobkin (*Cartoonist*); Madge Kennedy (*Housewife*); Tommy Farrell (*Elevator starter*); Maudie Prickett (*Maid, Elsie*); Ned Glass (*Ticket agent*); Alfred Hitchcock (*Man who misses bus*); Harvey Stephens (*Stockbroker*); Walter Coy (*Reporter*); Harry Seymour (*Captain of waiters*); Frank Wilcox (*Weltner*); Robert Shayne (*Larry Wade*); Carleton Young (*Fanning Nelson*); Paul Genge (*Lt. Hagerman*); Robert B. Williams (*Patrolman Waggoner*); James McCallion (*Valet*); Baynes Barton (*Taxi driver*); Doris Singh (*Indian girl*); Sally Fraser (*Girl attendant*); Susan Whitney (*Girl attendant*); Maura McGiveney (*Girl attendant*).

Publications

Script:

Lehman, Ernest, *North by Northwest*, New York, 1972.

Books:

Bogdanovich, Peter, *The Cinema of Alfred Hitchcock*, New York, 1962.
Manz, Hans-Peter, *Alfred Hitchcock*, Zurich, 1962.
Wood, Robin, *Hitchcock's Films*, London, 1965.
Perry, George, *The Films of Alfred Hitchcock*, London, 1965.

North by Northwest

Truffaut, François, *Le Cinéma selon Hitchcock*, Paris, 1966; as *Hitchcock*, New York, 1985.
Douchet, Jean, *Alfred Hitchcock*, Paris, 1967.
Simsolo, Noël, *Alfred Hitchcock*, Paris, 1969.
LaValley, Albert J., editor, *Focus on Hitchcock*, Englewood Cliffs, New Jersey, 1972.
Durgnat, Raymond, *The Strange Case of Alfred Hitchcock*, Cambridge, Massachusetts, 1974.
Hirschhorn, Clive, *The Films of James Mason*, London, 1975.
Taylor, John Russell, *Hitch*, London and New York, 1978.
Hemmeter, Thomas M., *Hitchcock the Stylist*, Ann Arbor, Michigan, 1981.
Narboni, Jean, editor, *Alfred Hitchcock*, Paris, 1982.
Bazin, André, *The Cinema of Cruelty: From Buñuel to Hitchcock*, New York, 1982.
Rothman, William, *Hitchcock: The Murderous Gaze*, Cambridge, Massachusetts, 1982.
Villien, Bruno, *Hitchcock*, Paris, 1982.
Weis, Elisabeth, *The Silent Scream: Alfred Hitchcock's Sound Track*, Rutherford, New Jersey, 1982.
Wollen, Peter, *Readings and Writings: Semiotic Counter-Strategies*, London, 1982.
Spoto, Donald, *The Life of Alfred Hitchcock: The Dark Side of Genius*, New York, 1982; London, 1983.
Britton, Andrew, *Cary Grant: Comedy and Male Desire*, Newcastle-upon-Tyne, 1983.
Schickel, Richard, *Cary Grant: A Celebration*, London, 1983.
Wansell, Geoffrey, *Cary Grant: Haunted Hero*, London, 1983.
Dupuis, Jean-Jacques, *Cary Grant*, Paris, 1984.
Phillips, Gene D., *Alfred Hitchcock*, Boston, 1984.
Barbier, Philippe, and Jacques Moreau, *Alfred Hitchcock*, Paris, 1985.
Douchet, Jean, *Alfred Hitchcock*, Paris, 1985.
Bruce, Graham, *Bernard Herrmann: Film Music and Narrative*, Ann Arbor, Michigan, 1985.
Wilson, George M., *Narration in Light: Studies in Cinematic Point of View*, Baltimore, 1986.
Deutelbaum, Marshall, and Leland Poague, *A Hitchcock Reader*, Ames, Iowa, 1986.
Humphries, Patrick, *The Films of Alfred Hitchcock*, Greenwich, Connecticut, 1986.
Kloppenburg, Josef, *Die dramaturgische Funktion der Musik in Filmen Alfred Hitchcock*, Munich, 1986.
Sinyard, Neil, *The Films of Alfred Hitchcock*, London, 1986.
Modleski, Tania, *The Women Who Knew Too Much: Hitchcock and Feminist Theory*, New York, 1988.
Higham, Charles, and Ray Moseley, *Cary Grant: The Lonely Heart*, New York, 1989.

Naremore, James, editor, *North by Northwest: Alfred Hitchcock, Director*, New Brunswick, New Jersey, 1993.
Sterritt, David, *The Films of Alfred Hitchcock*, New York, 1993.
Arginteanu, Judy, *The Movies of Alfred Hitchcock*, Minneapolis, 1994.
Boyd, David, editor, *Perspectives on Alfred Hitchcock*, New York, 1995.
Condon, Pauline, *Complete Hitchcock*, London, 1999.
Harris, Robert A., *Complete Films of Alfred Hitchcock*, Secaucus, 1999.
Bellour, Raymond, *The Analysis of Film*, Bloomington, 2000.
McGilligan, Patrick, *Alfred Hitchcock*, New York, 2001.

Articles:

Hitchcock, Alfred, in *Arts* (Paris), January 1959.
Houston, Penelope, in *Sight and Sound* (London), Summer-Autumn 1959.
Interview with Hitchcock, in *Films and Filming* (London), July 1959.
New York Times, 7 August 1959.
Fitzpatrick, Ellen, in *Films in Review* (New York), August-September 1959.
Baker, Peter, in *Films and Filming* (London), September 1959.
Moullet, Luc, in *Arts* (Paris), October 1959.
Douchet, Jean, ''Le Troisième Clé d'Hitchcock,'' in *Cahiers du Cinéma* (Paris), December 1959.
Richardson, A.W., in *Screen Education Yearbook* (London), 1963.
Gow, Gordon, in *Films and Filming* (London), October 1974.
''Hitchcock Issue'' of *Take One* (Montreal), 21 May 1976.
Magny, Joel, in *Cinéma* (Paris), October 1978.
Lowry, Ed., in *Cinema Texas Program Notes* (Austin), 11 November 1978.
Sator, M., in *Cahiers du Cinéma* (Paris), December 1978.
Bergstrom, Janet, ''Enunciation and Sexual Difference,'' in *Camera Obscura* (Berkeley), Summer 1979.
Keane, Marian, ''The Designs of Authorship,'' in *Wide Angle* (Athens, Ohio), vol. 4, no. 1, 1980.
Boost, C., and W. Verstappen, in *Skoop* (Amsterdam), May-June 1980.
Giacci, V., in *Filmcritica* (Florence), January 1981.
''*North by Northwest* de Bernard Herrmann,'' in *Séquences* (Montreal), April 1981.
Marinero, N., in *Casablanca* (Madrid), May 1981.
Roquena, J. G., ''En el unbral de lo in verosimil,'' in *Contracampo* (Madrid), September 1981.
Brill, L., ''*North by Northwest* and Hitchcockian Romance,'' in *Film Criticism* (Edinboro, Pennsylvania), Spring 1982.
Bourget, J. L., in *Positif* (Paris), May 1982.
Bannon, B. M., ''Double, Double, Toil and Trouble,'' in *Literature/Film Quarterly* (Salisbury, Maryland), vol. 13, no. 1, 1985.
Ven de Ven, L., ''Alfred Hitchcock's Film Music,'' in *Soundtrack* (Los Angeles), January 1985.
Dean, Peter, ''Video: *North by Northwest* Directed by Alfred Hitchcock,'' in *Sight & Sound* (London), vol. 3, no. 11, November 1993.
Burlingame, Jon, ''Scoring Hitchcock,'' in *Grand Street* (New York), vol. 13, no. 1, Summer 1994.
Petersen, George, ''Building Character Through Violence: A One-Two Punch,'' in *Creative Screenwriting* (Washington, D.C.), vol. 3, no. 1, Summer 1996.
Lehman, Ernest, ''Back Story,'' in *Fade In* (Beverly Hills), vol. 2, no. 3, 1996.
Care, Ross, ''Record Rack,'' in *Scarlet Street* (Glen Rock), no. 21, Winter 1996.
Worden, J., ''Thirty-nine Steps to Immortality,'' in Armchair Detective, vol. 29, no. 4, 1996.
Lehman, Ernest, and Joel Engel, ''*North by Northwest*/Writing North by North-West,'' in *Scenario*, vol. 3, no. 1, Spring 1997.
Morris, Christopher D., ''The Direction of *North by Northwest*,'' in *Cinema Journal* (Austin), vol. 36, no. 4, Summer 1997.
Butte, G., ''Theatricality and the Comedy of the Mutual Gaze in Hitchcock's Cary Grant Films,'' in *Hitchcock Annual* (Gambier), Fall 1997/98.
Teachout, Terry, ''The Genius of Pure Effect,'' in *Civilization* (Washington), vol. 5, no. 1, February 1998.

* * *

Screenwriter Ernest Lehman wanted to write the definitive Hitchcock movie. The assignment Hitchcock chose for him, an adaptation of Hammond Innes' novel *The Wreck of the Mary Deare*, was not it; in Lehman's opinion the novel, about a Marie Celeste-type sea mystery, began with an intriguing premise but concluded with a letdown of a denouement the writer felt was impossible to lick. He turned the master of suspense down; shortly thereafter, Hitchcock abandoned the project for the same reason. (Lehman and Hitchcock were right; the film, eventually made by Michael Anderson, failed to solve the problem.)

Still wanting to write that definitive Hitchcock movie, Lehman hastily launched into a spec script he hoped would capture the director's interest. It was a thriller Lehman initially titled *In a Northerly Direction*, then *Breathless*, about an advertising man who is mistaken by spies for a government agent on their trail. Completing it in record time, he submitted the script to Hitchcock, who was delighted with it—and the script, finally retitled *North by Northwest*, went before the cameras almost immediately.

North by Northwest is not the definitive Hitchcock movie, for while the master's metier is indeed the thriller, his thrillers are not all the same type. *Vertigo*, his previous film, is as different in style and tone from *North by Northwest* as *Psycho*, the film he made after *North*, is from both of them.

What Lehman did achieve is the definitive Hitchcock chase movie, a delightful homage to and summation of such earlier Hitchcock films in the same vein as *Saboteur, Foreign Correspondent*, and the grandaddy of them all, *The 39 Steps*, the prototypical wrong man on the lam who finds romance chase thriller that brought Hitchcock international acclaim and, ultimately, his ticket to Hollywood.

Saboteur and *Foreign Correspondent* remain noted for their memorable climactic set pieces—a fall from the Statue of Liberty in the former, a subjective eye view of a plane crash in the latter. *The 39 Steps* sparkled with charm and wit, as well as thrills, while lacking such spectacular set pieces. *North by Northwest* offers the best of all three. It is a film of spectacular set pieces linked by some of the brightest dialogue in the romantic comedy canon and performances to match.

Two of the film's set pieces are among the most famous in movie history: Grant's pursuit through a cornfield by a plane dusting crops where there aren't any crops; and the hair-raising climax on Mount Rushmore where Grant and Eva Marie Saint are chased across the faces of Presidents Washington, Jefferson, Lincoln and Roosevelt by thugs Martin Landau and Adam Williams. The crop-dusting chase was shot on location, but the Mount Rushmore sequence was not. The U.S. Department of the Interior denied its cooperation and Hitchcock was forced to shoot the scene in the studio, employing oversized sets, backdrops and photographic plates of the actual monument to remarkable effect. Next to the shower murder in *Psycho*, it's probably the most acclaimed, and frequently studied, scene in a Hitchcock movie.

North by Northwest marked the fourth and final appearance by Cary Grant, one of Hitchcock's favorite leading men, in a Hitchcock movie—in a role that was written expressly for him and suits his persona of comic urbanity to a T. As complacent ad man turned long-distance runner for his life Roger O. Thornhill (''That's me. Rot.''), Grant charms the pants off the audience and co-star Saint, the not-so-ice-cool blonde who may or may not be on his side.

James Mason makes a perfect match for Grant in the suavity department as the bad guy—and is axiomatic of Hitchcock's policy that the better the villain, the better the film. Composer Bernard Herrman's striking, and still influential, fandango score is also a high point—although, amazingly, there's only seventeen minutes of it in the entire 136-minute film!

—John McCarty

NOSFERATU

(Nosferatu, Eine Symphonie des Grauens; Nosferatu, a Symphony of Horror)

Germany, 1922

Director: F. W. Murnau

Production: Prana-Film (Berlin); black and white, 35mm, silent; running time: about 74 minutes. Released 5 March 1922, Germany. Re-released as *Die zwölfte Stunde* or *Eine Nacht des Grauens* in 1930 in a sound version, but it was re-released under mysterious circumstances as the original negative had been taken by a Dr. Waldemar Roger some time earlier. Filmed in Jofa studios, Berlin-Johannistal; exteriors shot in the Upper Tatras, Czechoslovakia, near Zakopane, Propad, and Smokovec; also at Wismar, Rostock, and Lübeck.

Scenario: Henrik Galeen, from the novel by Bram Stoker (out of copyright); **photography:** Fritz Arno Wagner and Gunther Krampf; **production designer:** Albin Grau; **original music:** Hans Erdmann; **costume designer:** Albin Grau.

Cast: Max Schreck (*Nosferatu, or Graf Orlok*); Alexander Granach (*Jonathan Knock, an estate agent*); Gustav von Wangenheim (*Hutter*); Greta Schröder (*Nina*); G. H. Schnell (*Harding, a shipbuilder*); Ruth Landshoff (*Annie Harding*); John Gottowt (*Professor*); Gustav Botz (*Town doctor*); Max Nemetz (*Captain of the ''Demeter''*); Wolfgang Heinz (*1st mate*); Albert Venohr (*2nd mate*); Hersfeld (*Innkeeper*); Hardy von François (*Hospital doctor*); Heinrich Witte.

Nosferatu

Publications

Script:

Galeen, Henrik, *Nosferatu*, in *Masterworks of the German Cinema*, edited by Roger Manvell, London, 1973; also included in *Murnau*, by Lotte Eisner, Berkeley, 1973.

Books:

Kracauer, Siegfried, *From Caligari to Hitler: A Psychological History of the German Film*, Princeton, 1947.
Huff, Theodore, *An Index to the Films of F. W. Murnau*, London, 1948, 1976.
Byrne, Richard B., *Films of Tyranny*, Madison, Wisconsin, 1966.
Anthologie du cinéma 1, Paris, 1966.
Eisner, Lotte, *The Haunted Screen*, London, 1969.
Eisner, Lotte, *Murnau*, Berkeley, 1973; revised edition, 1979.
Collier, Jo Leslie, *From Wagner to Murnau: The Transposition of Romanticism from Stage to Screen*, Ann Arbor, 1988.

Articles:

Variety (New York), 25 December 1925.
New York Times, 4 June 1929.
Blin, Roger, ''Murnau—ses film,'' in *Revue du Cinéma* (Paris), July 1931.
Mori, Phil, in *Bianco e Nero* (Rome), April 1951.
Eisner, Lotte, ''L'Enigme des deux Nosferatus,'' in *Cahiers du Cinéma* (Paris), January 1958.
Guillermo, Gilberto Perez, in *Sight and Sound* (London), Summer 1967.
Guillermo, Gilberto Perez, and Robin Wood, in *Film Comment* (New York), Summer 1971.
Kerouac, Jack, in *Focus on the Horror Film*, edited by Roy Huss and T. J. Ross, Englewood Cliffs, New Jersey, 1972.
Toeplitz, J., in *Kino* (Warsaw), February 1972.
Beylie, Claude, in *Ecran* (Paris), July-August 1973.
Milne, Tom, in *Monthly Film Bulletin* (London), February 1974.
''*Nosferatu* Issue,'' of *Avant-Scène du Cinéma* (Paris), no. 228, 1979.
Tulloch, J., ''Narrative/Structure/Ideology in Murnau's *Nosferatu*: Another Start from Propp,'' in *Australian Journal of Screen Theory* (Kensington, New South Wales), no. 5–6, 1979.
Roth, L., ''Dracula Meets the 'Zeitgeist': *Nosferatu* as Film Adaptation,'' in *Literature/Film Quarterly* (Salisbury, Maryland), no. 4, 1979.
Petat, J., and others, ''De Murnau à Herzog: L'Eternel Retour de Nosferatu le vampire,'' in *Cinéma* (Paris), March 1979.
Termine, L., in *Cinema Nuovo* (Bari), October 1979.
Exertier, S., ''La Lettre oubliée de Nosferatu,'' in *Positif* (Paris), March 1980.
Todd, Janet M., ''The Classic Vampire,'' in *The English Novel and the Movies*, edited by Michael Klein and Gillian Parker, New York, 1981.
Rognoni, L., in *Cinema Novo* (Porto), January-February 1981.
Biró, G., in *Filmkultura* (Budapest), January-February 1981.
Ishaghpour, Y., in *Cahiers du Cinéma* (Paris), September 1981.
Bouvier, M., and J. L. Leutrat, ''Pour mémoire,'' in *Cahiers du Cinéma* (Paris), March 1982.
Cherchi Usai, P., ''*Nosferatu*: Dal film all'orchestra,'' in *Segnocinema* (Vicenza), January 1985.
Elsaesser, Thomas, ''Secret Affinities: F. W. Murnau,'' in *Sight and Sound* (London), Winter 1988–89.
Wolf, R., and others, ''De films van F. W., Murnau,'' in *Skrien* (Amsterdam), February-March 1990.
Perez, G., in *Raritan* (New Brunswick, New Jersey), no. 1, 1993.
James, C., ''Critic's Notebook: *Nosferatu*, the Father of All Horror Movies,'' in *New York Times*, 2 April 1993.
Holt, Wesley G., in *Filmfax* (Evanston), no. 38, April-May 1993.
Dalle-Vacche, Angela, ''Murnau's Nosferatu: Romantic Painting as Horror and Desire in Expressionist Cinema,'' in *Post Script* (Commerce), vol. 14, no. 3, Summer 1995.
Dilivio, Lois, ''Two Reviews: Music for Silent Films in Contemporary Performance,'' in *Cue Sheet* (Hollywood), vol. 11, no. 4, October 1995.
Lansing Smith, Evans, ''Framing the Underworld: Threshold Imagery in Murnau, Cocteau, and Bergman,'' in *Literature/Film Quarterly* (Salisbury), vol. 24, no. 3, 1996.
Larson, Randall D., ''James Bernard's *Nosferatu*,'' in *Soundtrack* (Melechen), vol. 15, no. 58, June 1996.
Rhodes, Gary D., in *Filmfax* (Evanston), no. 61, June-July 1997.
Stevens, Brad, ''*Nosferatu* Rises Again,'' in *Video Watchdog* (Cincinnati), no. 44, 1998.

* * *

Nosferatu was the first film version of *Dracula*; more than 70 years later, it remains easily the most intelligent adaptation of Bram Stoker's novel (its nearest, not very close, rival being John Badham's 1978 version with Frank Langella).

Given the way in which Stoker's vampire aristocrat has haunted popular culture since the appearance of the novel in 1890, the figure's social/ideological significance can scarcely be exaggerated. Conceived at the height of Victorian sexual repression, the Count Dracula of the novel embodies, to varying degrees of explicitness, all the sexual dreads that our culture has still not exorcised or come to terms with: non-procreative sexuality, promiscuity, bisexuality, the so-called ''perversions,'' incest, even (indirectly, through the preferences of the vampirized Lucy) the sexuality of children. Much of our sexual social history can be traced through the transformations the Count has undergone from Stoker's novel to Badham's movie. With his origins in sexual repression, he transplants very logically and easily into the climate and ethos of German Expressionism.

Between Stoker's novel and Murnau's film came Freud, to whose theories of repression and the unconscious the Expressionist movement, like the Surrealist movement later, was heavily indebted. The essential difference between the two movements lies in their contrasting inflections of Freudian theory: the Surrealists were committed to liberation and the overthrow of repressive bourgeois norms whatever the costs, whereas the Expressionists consistently conceived the repressed forces as evil, their release cataclysmic. The extraordinary power, and continuing fascination, of Murnau's film are rooted in this vision.

The distinction of *Nosferatu* can be partly suggested by examining the changes Murnau and his scriptwriter Galeen made from novel to film. What novel and film have in common (and no other film version to the same degree except the Badham) is the perception that it is the woman who is the centre of the conflict, that the work is really about *her*. The uses made of this insight are, however, quite different. In Stoker's novel the battle is fought *for* the woman; in Murnau's film she becomes the vampire's active antagonist and destroyer. In Stoker the battle is fought between van Helsing and Dracula (conceived, in the terms of Victorian sexual morality, as ''good'' and ''evil''—in Freudian terms they represent superego and id); Murnau reduces van Helsing to an ineffectual old fuddy-duddy who lectures on Venus fly-traps but contributes nothing whatever to the vampire's overthrow. In the novel, the woman (Mina) must be saved from contagion and corruption: the Victorian dread of a released female sexuality is basic to the conception; in the film, the woman (now called Nina) realizes that only she can save civilization from the vampire's contagion, by offering herself to him. Murnau's Nina is a character of quite extraordinary ambivalence: emaciated, as if drained of blood, she suggests both vampire and Christian martyr; the strange abandon with which she gives herself to Dracula (first throwing open a window, then prostrating herself on the bed) suggests the close relationship between religious ecstasy and sensual fulfilment. The ambiguity is set up much earlier in the film, in the protracted and elaborate cross-cutting between Nina (ostensibly awaiting Jonathan's return) and the journeys of Jonathan and Dracula (a sequence that makes nonsense of Bazin's claim that "in neither *Nosferatu* nor *Sunrise* does editing play a decisive part"). Jonathan, who travelled by land, is returning by land; the vampire (having taken over a ship) is coming by sea. Nina sits by the shore, gazing out to sea, awaiting her "husband." Her exclamation, as she awakens from sleepwalking ("He is coming! I must go to meet him!") follows a shot, not of Jonathan, but of Dracula's ship.

Jonathan and Dracula also undergo significant alteration from their originals. Stoker's Jonathan is a conventional "noble hero" (although he doesn't actually achieve much of note). Murnau transforms him into the vampire's double, through an intricate series of "mirror" images involving arch-structures: at their first meeting, for example, Jonathan enters the castle under one arch, and this is immediately "answered" by Dracula emerging out of darkness under another. Murnau, following Freud, dramatizes the vampire quite explicitly in terms of repression: he is the repressed under-side of Jonathan, of civilization. As he falls under Dracula's influence, Jonathan is reduced to total impotence: even when he discovers the vampire asleep in his coffin, during the day, he can do nothing but cower back; when Dracula visits his bedchamber at night, to suck his blood, he can do nothing but prostrate himself. At the film's climax, when Nina reveals to him the vampire's presence at the window of the house directly opposite, across the water (another mirror-image), he once again collapses, helpless.

In the novel, Dracula himself is at first quite old, becoming progressively rejuvenated in England by fresh blood; but he is never as grotesque as Max Schreck in Murnau's version and never as romantically attractive as Frank Langella in Badham's—the two films inflect him, significantly, in precisely opposite directions. Murnau's most striking development of the original material is his elaboration of the vampire. In the novel, Dracula disappears quite early from the surface of the narrative (which is told entirely through letters, diaries, etc.) appearing only in brief glimpses; in the film he becomes the dominant figure, a redevelopment especially clear in the long central section of the voyage (for which the novel has no equivalent). Murnau greatly extends Dracula's association with animals, and with a dark, nocturnal underside of nature: he has pointed ears, is visually connected with a jackal, emerges from his castle as out of the blackness of an animal's lair. Above all, the film associates him with rats and plague: wherever he goes, rats swarm, and the precise nature of the spreading pestilence is kept carefully ambiguous.

The re-thinking of Dracula in Badham's film offers a fascinating comparison, an attempt at a "progressive" re-interpretation with a far more positive view of the repressed forces the vampire represents: the heroine becomes a "liberated" woman who freely chooses Dracula as her lover, and it is the father-figure, van Helsing, who is finally impaled on a stake. In fact, what Badham's film proves is the intractability of the material for such a purpose: Dracula becomes a kind of sexual superman, the film develops disturbing Fascist overtones, and many of the complex connotations of the vampire are eliminated. While Murnau's film—heavily determined by its Expressionist background—can depict repressed sexuality and its release only in the most negative terms, it manages to endow it with far greater force and potency, dramatizing the basic Freudian quandary—the necessity for repression, yet the appalling cost of repression—with a much more suggestive complexity.

—Robin Wood

NOT ON YOUR LIFE

See **EL VERDUGO**

NOTORIOUS

USA, 1946

Director: Alfred Hitchcock

Production: RKO; black and white; running time: 102 minutes: length: 9,136 feet. Released August 1946.

Producer: Alfred Hitchcock; **screenplay:** Ben Hecht, from a theme by Alfred Hitchcock; **assistant director:** William Dorfman; **photography:** Ted Tetzlaff; **editor:** Theron Warth; **sound:** John Tribby,

Notorious

Clem Portman; **art directors:** Albert S. D'Agostino, Carol Clark, Darrell Silvera, Claude Carpenter; **special effects:** Vernon L. Walker; **music:** Roy Webb.

Cast: Ingrid Bergman (*Alicia Huberman*); Cary Grant (*Devlin*); Claude Rains (*Alexander Sebastian*); Louis Calhern (*Paul Prescott*); Leopoldine Konstantin (*Mrs. Sebastian*); Reinhold Schunzel (*Dr. Anderson*).

Publications

Books:

Noble, Peter, *An Index to the Creative Work of Alfred Hitchcock*, London, 1949.
Amengual, Barthélemy, and Raymond Borde, *Alfred Hitchcock*, Paris, 1957.
Rohmer, Eric, and Claude Chabrol, *Hitchcock*, Paris, 1957.
Bogdanovich, Peter, *The Cinema of Alfred Hitchcock*, New York, 1962.
Perry, George, *The Films of Alfred Hitchcock*, London, 1965.
Wood, Robin, *Hitchcock's Films*, London, 1965.
Truffaut, François, *The Cinema selon Hitchcock*, Paris, 1966; as *Hitchcock*, New York, 1985.
Quirk, Lawrence J., *The Films of Ingrid Bergman*, New York, 1970.
LaValley, Albert J., editor, *Focus on Hitchcock*, Englewood Cliffs, New Jersey, 1972.
Brown, Curtis F., *Ingrid Bergman*, New York, 1973.
Vermilye, Jerry, *Cary Grant*, New York, 1973.
Durgnat, Raymond, *The Strange Case of Alfred Hitchcock; or, The Plain Man's Hitchcock*, Cambridge, Massachusetts, 1974.
Fetherling, Doug, *The Five Lives of Ben Hecht*, Toronto, 1977.
Taylor, John Russell, *Hitch*, London and New York, 1978.
Deschner, Donald, *The Films of Cary Grant*, Secaucus, New Jersey, 1978.
Hemmeter, Thomas M., *Hitchcock the Stylist*, Ann Arbor, Michigan, 1981.
Bazin, André, *The Cinema of Cruelty: From Buñuel to Hitchcock*, New York, 1982.
Narboni, Jean, editor, *Alfred Hitchcock*, Paris, 1982.
Rothman, William, *Hitchcock—The Murderous Gaze*, Cambridge, Massachusetts, 1982.
Villien, Bruno, *Hitchcock*, Paris, 1982.
Weis, Elisabeth, *The Silent Scream: Alfred Hitchcock's Sound Track*, Rutherford, New Jersey, 1982.
Spoto, Donald, *The Life of Alfred Hitchcock: The Dark Side of Genius*, New York, 1981; London, 1983.
Britton, Andrew, *Cary Grant: Comedy and Male Desire*, Newcastle-upon-Tyne, 1983.
Schickel, Richard, *Cary Grant: A Celebration*, London, 1983.
Wansell, Geoffrey, *Cary Grant: Haunted Idol*, London, 1983, New York, 1984.
Taylor, John Russell, *Ingrid Bergman*, London and New York, 1983.
Dupuis, Jean-Jacques, *Cary Grant*, Paris, 1984.
Phillips, Gene D., *Alfred Hitchcock*, Boston, 1984.
Barbier, Philippe, and Jacques Moreau, *Alfred Hitchcock*, Paris, 1985.
Martin, Jeffrey Brown, *Ben Hecht, Hollywood Screenwriter*, Ann Arbor, Michigan, 1985.
Douchet, Jean, *Alfred Hitchcock*, Paris, 1985.
Deutelbaum, Marshall, and Leland Poague, *A Hitchcock Reader*, Ames, Iowa, 1986.
Humphries, Patrick, *The Films of Alfred Hitchcock*, Greenwich, Connecticut, 1986.
Kloppenburg, Josef, *Die dramaturgische Funktion der Musik in Filmen Alfred Hitchcocks*, Munich, 1986.
Sinyard, Neil, *The Films of Alfred Hitchcock*, London, 1986.
Leamer, Laurence, *As Time Goes By: The Life of Ingrid Bergman*, New York, 1986.
Modleski, Tania, *The Women Who Knew Too Much: Hitchcock and Feminist Theory*, New York, 1988.
Higham, Charles, and Ray Moseley, *Cary Grant: The Lonely Heart*, New York, 1989.
Spoto, Donald, *Art of Alfred Hitchcock*, New York, 1991.
Kapsis, Robert E., *Hitchcock: The Making of a Reputation*, Chicago, 1993.
Sterritt, David, *The Films of Alfred Hitchcock*, New York, 1993.
Arginteanu, Judy, *The Movies of Alfred Hitchcock*, Minneapolis, 1994.
Boyd, David, editor, *Perspectives on Alfred Hitchcock*, New York, 1995.
Condon, Pauline, *Complete Hitchcock*, London, 1999.
Harris, Robert A., *Complete Films of Alfred Hitchcock*, Secaucus, 1999.
Bellour, Raymond, *The Analysis of Film*, Bloomington, 2000.
McGilligan, Patrick, *Alfred Hitchcock*, New York, 2001.

Articles:

Sight and Sound (London), no. 59, 1946.
Kine Weekly (London), 6 March 1946.
Motion Picture Herald (New York), 17 July 1946.
Variety (New York), 24 July 1946.
New York Times, 16 August 1946.
Monthly Film Bulletin (London), April 1947.
Film Heritage (Dayton, Ohio), Spring 1969.
Wide Angle (Athens, Ohio), vol. 1, no. 1, 1979, and vol. 4, no. 1, 1980.
Bonitzer, P., in *Cahiers du Cinéma* (Paris), March 1980.
Paganelli, M., in *Filmcritica* (Florence), January 1981.
Piccardi, A., ''I meccanismi del cinema di Hitchcock,'' in *Cineforum* (Bergamo), April 1982.
Clark, Randall, ''Ben Hecht,'' in *American Screenwriters*, edited by Robert E. Morsberger, Stephen O. Lesser, and Randall Clark, Detroit, 1984.
Arnold, Gordon B., ''From Big Screen to Small Screen: *Notorious* Directed by Alfred Hitchcock and Starring Cary Grant, Ingrid Bergman and Claude Rains,'' in *Library Journal* (New York), vol. 114, no. 9, 15 May 1989.
Beebe, John, ''The *Notorious* Postwar Psyche,'' in *Journal of Popular Film and Television* (Washington), vol. 18, no. 1, Spring 1990.
McGuinness, M., ''The *Notorious* Alice in Hitchcockland,'' in *Spectator* (Los Angeles), vol. 12, no. 2, 1992.
Osteen, M., ''The Big Secret: Film Noir and Nuclear Fear,'' in *Journal of Popular Film and Television* (Washington, D.C.), vol. 22, no. 2, 1994.
Byars, Jackie, and Eileen R. Meehan, ''Once in a Lifetime: Constructing 'The Working Woman' Through Cable Narrowcasting,'' in *Camera Obscura* (Bloomington), no. 33–34, May-June 1994–1995.

Howard, T., ''*Notorious*,'' in *Reid's Film Index* (Wyong), no. 16, 1995.
Suarez, J. and M. Manglis, ''Cinema, Gender, and the Topography of Enigmas: A Conversation with Laura Mulvey,'' in *Cinefocus*, vol. 3, 1995.
Kirshner, Jonathan, ''Alfred Hitchcock and the Art of Research,'' in *PS, Political Science and Politics* (Washington), vol. 29, no. 3, Washington, September 1996.
Christie, Ian, Leslie Felperin, and Nick Roddick, ''Alfred Hitchcock and the British Cinema,'' in *Sight and Sound* (London), vol. 6, no. 11, November 1996.
''Classic Scene: *Notorious*,'' in *Premiere* (New York), vol. 11, no. 3, November 1997.
Butte, G., ''Theatricality and the Comedy of the Mutual Gaze in Hitchcock's Cary Grant Films,'' in *Hitchcock Annual* (Gambier), Fall 1997/1998.
Gottlieb, S., ''Hitchcock and the Art of the Kiss: A Preliminary Survey,'' in *Hitchcock Annual* (Gambier), Fall 1997/1998.
Leff, Leonard J., ''Ingrid in the Lion's Den: Cutting *Notorious*,'' in *Film Comment* (New York), vol. 35, no. 2, March/April 1999.
Wood, Catherine, ''The Influence of Art of the Master of Suspense,'' in *The Lancet* (London), vol. 354, no. 9181, 4 September 1999.
McClain, Buzz, ''That Obscure Object of Desire,'' in *Playboy* (Chicago), vol. 47, no. 2, February 2000.

* * *

Notorious (1946) is a key film in the Hitchcock canon, one which builds upon thematic elements gradually developed in a series of British (*Blackmail*, 1929; *Sabotage*, 1936) and early American (*Rebecca*, 1940; *Suspicion*, 1941; *Shadow of a Doubt*, 1943) pictures. But *Notorious* significantly extends Hitchcock's fascination with men and women bonded in relationships, real or imagined, of an unholy nature. The film takes his portrayal of obsessive behavior in a direction that anticipates *Vertigo* (1958), *Marnie* (1964), and, notably *North by Northwest* (1959), in which, again using Cary Grant in the male lead, he replays *Notorious*'s chief romantic relationship but reshapes its brooding, uncharacteristically humorless intensity into the format of vibrant comedy.

On its surface, *Notorious* appears to exploit the period's patriotic fervor by connecting the post-World War II hunt for escaped Nazis to such narrative staples of classic Hollywood cinema as the damsel in distress and the ''bad'' woman redeemed by the love of a ''good'' man. In fact, Hitchcock and screenwriter Ben Hecht artfully interweave those plot elements to conceal *Notorious*'s true subject: sexual betrayal which poisons several sets of criss-crossing relationships within the world of the film.

Paramount among those relationships is the one between Alicia Huberman (Ingrid Bergman), the daughter of a man convicted for Nazi war crimes, and T. R. Devlin (Grant), a federal agent who convinces her to atone for her father's sins by spying on a Nazi group based in Rio de Janeiro. Alicia performs her role too well: Alex Sebastian (Claude Rains), the primary target of U.S. surveillance, proposes marriage. In one of the screenplay's dark ironies, Alicia accepts the offer because Devlin fails explicitly to dissuade her from doing so—thereby infuriating the already jealous Devlin by acquiescing to what she thought he wanted her to do in the first place. Though she clearly loves Devlin, as he loves her, she proceeds with her action largely to spite him. (''Love'' and the self-serving uses to which that word is put formulate a primary element in the *Notorious* narratology.)

The romantic relationship between Alicia and Devlin continually undermines 1940s cinema conventions. The couple is kept apart for long stretches of the film, limited to fleeting meetings in which wounded pride prevails on both sides to deny the articulation of true feeling. In Grant's against-type performance, Devlin is cynical and unyielding, a man whose cruel willingness to believe the worst of Alicia inflicts pain almost as lethal as the poison administered to her in the last section of the film. Much of the dialogue between them (within allowable limits of the period's censorship code) is as abusive as any spoken by a romantic couple in the Hitchcock canon. (Alicia: ''You can add Sebastian's name to my list of playmates.'' Devlin: ''Pretty fast work.'' Devlin: ''You almost had me believing in that little hokey-pokey miracle of yours—that a woman like you could ever change her spots'' Alicia: ''I see, some kind of love test.'' Devlin: ''You look all mashed up. Must have been quite an evening.'') Moreover, an abrupt ending fails to certify a permanent union, or even that the heroine will reach the hospital alive.

Alex Sebastian is jealous too, with justification. He functions in the narrative as another figure betrayed by the person he adores. (Devlin feels betrayed by Alicia; Alicia feels betrayed by Devlin and by her father; others in the film believe that Alicia has betrayed her Nazi father by refusing to testify on his behalf; Alex's mother feels betrayed by her son's marriage to Alicia: all are variations on the film's central preoccupation.) The presence of Alex's mother, the Nazi dragon who rules his roost and one of those oedipally inclined mother figures in the Hitchcock universe, enables Alex to become a relatively sympathetic figure, an extraordinary risk for a film released in 1946 and a major instance of Hitchcock's development of the complex villain figure. Positively exultant when she learns from him that her suspicions have been confirmed (''Mother . . . I am married to an American agent''), Madame Sebastian assumes the major burden of spectator hostility by reclaiming her authority over her son and directing the attempt on Alicia's life. The film's final shot reasserts Alex's importance to the narrative by forcing the viewer to speculate on the future of this villain manqué, another Hitchcock son who, in Norman Bates's words 14 years later, learns that ''a son is a poor substitute for a lover.''

Notorious emerges as a major film in the critical debate weighing charges against Hitchcock's alleged misogyny. Like Melanie Daniels at the end of *The Birds* (1963), Alicia Huberman is rendered virtually catatonic, near death at the film's conclusion; and it is only when she reaches this state that Devlin appears able to treat her with compassion. (See, for an illuminating and balanced reading of this issue, Tania Modleski's *The Women Who Knew Too Much: Hitchcock and Feminist Theory*, 1988.)

Camera movement and frame composition repeatedly reinforce *Notorious*'s major themes of stealth, mistrust, and betrayal. Notable among many examples of the film's visual virtuosity are distorted point-of-view shots to reflect the effects of Alicia's drinking early in the film and her poisoning toward its conclusion; pans to and closeups of keys, wine bottles, and coffee cups, props which function as instruments of violation in a film that explores the invasion of privacy on numerous levels; the frequency of intense closeups; the device of photographing Devlin with his back to the camera to deny the spectator full access to him; the justifiably famous shot in which the camera glides from a high perch downward to record the presence of a key in Alicia's hand. In a genuinely imaginative way, *Notorious* links its form tightly with its content.

—Mark W. Estrin

LA NOTTE

(The Night)

Italy-France, 1960

Director: Michelangelo Antonioni

Production: Nepi Film (Rome), Sofitedip (Paris), and Silver Films (Paris); black and white, 35mm; running time: 120 minutes. Released February 1961, Italy. Filmed 1960 in Milan.

Producer: Emanuele Cassuto; **screenplay:** Michelangelo Antonioni, Ennio Flaiano, and Tonino Guerra; **photography:** Gianni Di Venanzo; **editor:** Eraldo Da Roma; **sound:** Claudio Maielli; **art director:** Piero Zuffi; **music:** Giorgio Gaslini and his Quartette.

Cast: Jeanne Moreau (*Lidia*); Marcello Mastroianni (*Giovanni*); Monica Vitti (*Valentina Gerardini*); Bernhard Wicki (*Tommaso*); Rosi Mazzacurati (*Resy*); Maria Pia Luzi (*Nymphomaniac*); Vincenzo Corbella (*Gerardini*); Gitt Magrini (*Signora Gerardini*); Giorno Negro (*Roberto*); Guido Aimone Marsan (*Fanti*); Roberta Speroni (*Beatrice*); Vittorio Bertolini; Ugo Fortunati; Pompiani.

La notte

Award: Berlin Film Festival, Best Film, 1961.

Publications

Script:

Antonioni, Michelangelo, Ennio Flaiano, and Tonino Guerra, *La notte*, in *Screenplays*, New York, 1963.

Books:

Cowie, Peter, *Antonioni, Bergman, Resnais*, New York, 1963.
Leprohon, Pierre, *Michelangelo Antonioni: An Introduction*, New York, 1963.
Strick, Philip, *Antonioni*, London, 1965.
Cameron, Ian, and Robin Wood, *Antonioni*, New York, 1969.
Rifkin, Ned, *Antonioni's Visual Language*, Ann Arbor, Michigan, 1982.
Barthes, Roland, and others, *Michelangelo Antonioni*, Munich, 1984.
Biarese, Cesare, and Aldo Tassone, *I film di Michelangelo Antonioni*, Rome, 1985.
Dervin, Daniel, *Through a Freudian Lens Deeply: A Psychoanalysis of Cinema*, Hillsdale, New Jersey, 1985.
Antonioni, Michelangelo, *That Bowling Alley on the Tiber: Tales of a Director*, Oxford, 1986.
Perry, Ted, and Rene Prieto, *Michelangelo Antonioni: A Guide to References and Resources*, Boston, 1986.
Johnson, Charles W., *Philosophy in Literature*, San Francisco, 1992.
Arrowsmith, William, *Antonioni: The Poet of Images*, New York, 1995.
Chatman, Seymour B., *Antonioni, or, the Surface of the World*, Berkeley, 1996.
Brunette, Peter, *The Films of Michelangelo Antonioni*, New York, 1998.
Tomasulo, *Michelangelo Antonioni*, Old Tappan, 1998.
Wenders, Wim, *My Time with Antonioni*, New York, 2000.

Articles:

Fitzpatrick, Ellen, in *Films in Review* (New York), December 1961.
Nowell-Smith, Geoffrey, in *Sight and Sound* (London), Winter 1961–62.
Mekas, Jonas, in *Village Voice* (New York), 15 February 1962.
''Antonioni Issue'' of *Film Culture* (New York), Spring 1962.
Aristarco, Guido, in *Film Culture* (New York), Spring 1962.
Young, Vernon, ''Of Night, Fire, and Water,'' in *Hudson Review* (New York), Summer 1962.
''Antonioni Issue'' of *Film Quarterly* (Berkeley), Fall 1962.
Alpert, Hollis, ''Talk with Antonioni,'' in *Saturday Review* (New York), 27 October 1962.
Cinema (Beverly Hills), no. 2, 1963.
Taylor, John Russell, ''Antonioni,'' in *Cinema Eye, Cinema Ear*, New York, 1964.
Davis, Melton S., ''Most Controversial Director,'' in *New York Times Magazine*, 15 November 1964.
Godard, Jean-Luc, ''Night, Eclipse, Dawn,'' in *Cahiers du Cinema in English* (New York), January 1966.

Gow, Gordon, ''Antonioni Men,'' in *Films and Filming* (London) June 1970.
Tudor, Andrew, ''Antonioni: The Road to Death Valley,'' in *Cinema* (London), August 1970.
Hernacki, T., ''Michelangelo Antonioni and the Imagery of Disintegration,'' in *Film Heritage* (Dayton, Ohio), Autumn 1970.
Burke, F., ''The Natural Enmity of Words and Moving Images: Language, *La Notte* and the Death of the Light,'' in *Literature/Film Quarterly* (Salisbury, Maryland), no. 1, 1979.
Bonnet, J. C., Interview with Jeanne Moreau, in *Cinématographe* (Paris), December 1982.
Blanchet, C., in *Cinéma* (Paris), May 1984.
Gansera, R., in *EPD Film* (Frankfurt), April 1986.
''Antonioni, Michelangelo,'' in *Current Biography*, vol. 54, no. 5, May 1993.
Toamsulo, F. P., ''The Architectonics of Alienation: Antonioni's Edifice Complex,'' in *Wide Angle* (Baltimore), no. 3, 1993.
Perez, Gilberto, ''A Man Pointing: Antonioni and the Film Image,'' in *Yale Review*, vol. 82, no. 3, July 1994.
Rudman, Mark, ''*The Night*: On Michelangelo Antonioni,'' in *Raritan: A Quarterly Review*, vol. 14, no. 2, Fall 1994.
Moore, Kevin Z., ''Eclipsing the Commonplace: The Logic of Alienation in Antonioni's Cinema,'' in *Film Quarterly* (Berkeley), vol. 48, no. 4, Summer 1995.
''*La nuit*,'' in the Special Issue of *Avant-Scène du Cinéma* (Paris), no. 446, November 1995.
Nowell-Smith, Geoffrey, ''Antonioni: Before and After,'' in *Sight and Sound* (London), vol. 5, no. 12, December 1995.
Chatman, Seymour, ''Antonioni in 1980: An Interview,'' in *Film Quarterly* (Berkeley), vol. 51, no. 1, Fall 1997.

* * *

Michelangelo Antonioni's *La notte* is about an artist's life at the height of Italy's economic miracle; it depicts several hours, including the whole night, in the life of Giovanni Pontano, a novelist, on the day of the publication of his latest book.

The film opens with a visit by Pontano and his wife, Lidia, to the most sympathetic figure of the film, the Marxist editor Tommaso, who is in a hospital dying of cancer. Later, during a long and tedious all-night party at the home of a Milanese industrialist, who wants to buy Pontano's services to promote his business, Lidia learns that Tommaso has died.

The fascination of the film lies in its representation of boredom: a routine book party unenlivened by the actual appearance of Salvatore Quasimodo, then a recent Nobel laureate; Lidia's aimless walk at the outskirts of Milan, while Giovanni tries to nap in his study; an unsatisfying visit to a nightclub; and the endless meanderings and regroupings of the affluent guests at the party.

Within that matrix Pontano's sexual adventures become an index of his moral, and even artistic, collapse. He allows himself to be grabbed and caressed by a nymphomaniac in the hospital until two brutal nurses separate them and beat the woman; he trails the dilettante daughter of the industrialist around her mansion and ultimately fails to seduce her: and, in the film's last moments, on what appears to be the host's private golf course, he starts to make love to his wife, after she reads him an old love letter which he does not recognize as his own.

Antonioni manipulates entrances and exits and ambiguous shifts of scale, in order to shift regularly between his principal characters while maintaining the impression that their independent actions are linked together, almost as if they could see each other in their privacy. This impression is furthered by the well-ordered system of countershots which stress distance between characters even when they are behaving intimately. This is the most emphatic in the increasing lengths at which the camera is placed from the couple at the film's conclusion.

—P. Adams Sitney

1900

(Novecento)

Italy, 1976

Director: Bernardo Bertolucci

Production: TCF, PEA, Artistes Associés, and Artemis Productions; Technicolor, 35mm; running time: originally 320 minutes, US version is 245 minutes, usually shown in two parts. Released Cannes Film Festival, 1976.

Producer: Alberto Grimaldi; **screenplay:** Bernardo Bertolucci, Franco Arcalli, and Giuseppe Bertolucci; **photography:** Vittorio Stovaro; **editor:** Franco Arcalli; **art director:** Enzo Frigiero; **music:** Ennio Morricone.

Cast: Robert De Niro (*Alfredo, the grandson*); Burt Lancaster (*Alfredo, the grandfather*); Romolo Valli (*Giovanni*); Anna-Marie Gherardi (*Eleonora*); Laura Betti (*Regina*); Paolo Pavesi (*Alfredo, as a child*); Dominique Sanda (*Ada*); Sterling Hayden (*Leo Dalco*); Gérard Depardieu (*Olmo Dalco*); Roberto Maccanti (*Olmo, as a child*); Stefania Sandrelli (*Anita Foschi*); Donald Sutherland (*Attila*); Werner Bruhns (*Octavio*); Alida Valli (*Signora Pioppi*); Francesca Bertini (*Sister Desolata*).

Publications

Script:

Bertolucci, Bernardo, and others, *1900*, Turin, 1976.

Books:

Casetti, F., *Bertolucci*, Florence, 1975.
Hunter, Allan, *Burt Lancaster: The Man and His Movies*, New York, 1980; Edinburgh, 1984.
Kuhlbrodt, Dietrich, and others, *Bernardo Bertolucci*, Munich, 1982.
Ungari, Enzo, *Bertolucci*, Milan, 1982.
Kolker, Robert Phillip, *Bernardo Bertolucci*, London, 1985.
Cameron-Wilson, James, *The Cinema of Robert De Niro*, London, 1986.

1900

Lacombe, Roland, *Burt Lancaster*, Paris, 1987.
Kline, T. Jefferson, *Bertolucci's Dream Loom: A Psychoanalytic Study of the Cinema*, Amherst, Massachusetts, 1987.
Tonetti, Claretta, *Bernardo Bertolucci*, New York, 1995.

Articles:

''*1900* Issue'' of *Filmcritica* (Rome), July 1976.
Le Puyat, S., and M. Olmi, in *Téléciné* (Paris), October 1976.
Bickley, D., and others, in *Cinéaste* (Paris), Winter 1976–77.
Elbert, L., in *Cinemateca Revista* (Montevideo), 1976–77.
Gilbert, B., ''Bertolucci's *1900*: Stormy Beginnings,'' in *Cinema Papers* (Melbourne), January 1977.
Schepelern, P. in *Kosmorama* (Copenhagen), Spring 1977.
Alemanno, R., in *Cinema Nuovo* (Bari), March-April 1977.
Filmfaust (Frankfurt), April-May 1977.
Netzeband, G., in *Film und Fernsehen* (Berlin), June 1977.
di Bernardo G., interview with Bernardo Bertolucci, in *Skrien* (Amsterdam), July-August 1977.
De Vico, F., and R. Degni, ''Bertolucci: Interview 2,'' in *Skrien* (Amsterdam), September 1977.
Canby, Vincent, in *New York Times*, 8 October 1977.
Cornand, A., in *Image et Son* (Paris), November 1977.
Young, D., ''History Lessons,'' in *Film Comment* (New York), November-December 1977.
Quart, Leonard, ''*1900*: Bertolucci's Marxist Opera,'' in *Cineaste* (New York), Winter 1977–78.
Erikson, S., in *Filmavisa* (Oslo), no. 1–2, 1978.
Sevensson, A., in *Filmrutan* (Stockholm), no. 1, 1978.
Paret, R., in *Cinéma Québec* (Montreal), no. 4–5, 1978.
Dean, D., in *Films in Review* (New York), January 1978.
Forbes, Jill, in *Monthly Film Bulletin* (London), January 1978.
Aitken, W., in *Take One* (Montreal), March 1978.
Nowell-Smith, Geoffrey, in *Sight and Sound* (London), Spring 1978.
Gow, Gordon, in *Films and Filming* (London), April 1978.
Karaganov, A., ''Vom Monolog sum Epos,'' in *Film und Fernsehen* (Berlin), April 1978.
Arbasino, A., in *Cine* (Mexico City), May 1979.
Horton, A., ''History as Myth and Myth as History in Bertolucci's *1900*,'' in *Film and History* (Newark, New Jersey), February 1980.
Firas, I. Leon, in *Hablemos de Cine* (Lima), November 1980.
Filmcritica (Rome), October-November 1984.

Burgoyne, Robert, ''The Somatization of History in Bertolucci's *1900*,'' in *Film Quarterly* (Berkeley), Autumn 1986.

Burgoyne, Robert, ''Temporality as Historical Background in Bertolucci's *1900*,'' in *Cinema Journal* (Austin), Spring 1989.

Alion, Yves, ''[*Novecento*]*1900*,'' in *Mensuel du Cinéma*, July-August 1993.

Castoro Cinema, November/December 1995.

Jenkens, E., ''Charivari Rituals and the 'Revoltist Tradition,'' in *1900*,'' in *Cinefocus* (Bloomington, Indiana), vol. 4, 1996.

* * *

Bernardo Bertolucci's *1900 (Novecento)* is an attempt at a ''popular,'' accessible film presenting the complexities of the social and political history of Italy between 1901 and 1945, specifically in the region twenty miles from Parma, where the director was born and brought up. It exists in two versions—an original Italian-language epic, five and half hours long, and an abridged English and French version, 75 minutes shorter and often shown in two parts, which is what most viewers have seen. In either version the central themes of this epic film are the same: the local struggle between the peasants and the feudal landowners and, on the national and local levels alike, the rise and fall of Fascism. In taking on such an ambitious set of themes Bertolucci raises high expectations; unfortunately, he does not fulfill them.

The structure of *1900* is premised on a flashback from the opening scene—set on Liberation Day, 25 April 1945—telling the story of a friendship spanning forty years between Alfredo (Robert De Niro), from the landowning class and Olmo (Gerard Depardieu), from the peasantry, both born on 27 January 1901, the day (as we are told in the film) that the great Italian operatic composer Guiseppe Verdi died. The date presumably symbolises the end of the 19th century, but it also hints that the film is to be seen as within the tradition inaugurated by Verdi's tragic operas. The first part of the film, dealing with the relations between the two boys' families, unfolds against the background of a major peasant revolt in 1908, which includes Alfredo's grandfather, the *padrone* Berlinghieri (Burt Lancaster), among its targets; the First World War, in which Alfredo and Olmo both fight; and their witnessing of the beginnings of Fascism. Although Alfredo is shown to be sympathetic to the poor and degraded peasants, he follows the destiny of his class, while Olmo's slow development of political consciousness does not go so far as to affect their friendship. In this part Bertolucci's depiction of the peasantry, though it is said to have been largely based on memories of his own years as a middle-class child in a rural setting, is highly romanticised, with the spectacular cinematography of Vittorio Storaro, especially his long shots of the wheat fields, enhancing the picturesqueness of rural life while, ironically, cutting some of the ground from under the seriousness of the peasants' protests against their exploitation.

In the second part of the film the change in the political climate is symbolised by the wintry setting of the opening scene: the Fascist march on Rome (in 1922) has already taken place and the Berlinghieris' steward Attila (Donald Sutherland) has become head of the Black Shirts in the area. Bertolucci here uses colour and lighting effectively for atmosphere, with bright reds and yellows for the peasants and workers and darker hues for the Fascists, but the suspicion that this is simplistic and manipulative is reinforced by the presentation of the main Fascist characters, Attila and his wife Regina, as sexual sadists hungering for power. One example of this sadism is when Attlia enjoys killing a cat by smashing its head against a post. This equation of Fascism with purely individual sadism serves only to present it as a psychological manifestation, when in fact it was (and still is) a highly developed, complex and subtle ideology, and all the more dangerous because of these features. Bertolucci's caricatures, though no doubt well-meant, only undermine his attack on Fascism and what it represents.

If the peasants are portrayed as little more than figures in a landscape, and the Fascists as figures out of horror comics, what of the central figures of Alfredo and Olmo? Alfredo marries a wealthy girl while Olmo marries a politically radical school teacher and becomes involved with politicising the peasants. After the death of his father, Alfredo becomes the *padrone* and suffers a disintegrating relationship with his wife Ada (Dominique Sanda), who has become an alcoholic. Although fundamentally a liberal, Alfredo is too weak to resist the influence of Attila and thus slowly distances himself with Olmo. The story comes full circle and recounts events on Liberation Day and after, as the victims of Fascism seek revenge. In these sections we are at least presented with plausible human beings, whose emotions are mixed, whose characters develop over time and whose views cannot be reduced to slogans; yet their plausibility, well-served by the work of the principal actors, functions in a vacuum, since the external events which influence their lives are so sketchily conveyed and the other characters they deal with are so fundamentally implausible.

In short, in either of its two versions, *1900* is a fatally disjointed work. Foreground and background do not fit together; landscapes and sets threaten at times to swamp the human stories being told; epic detachment alternates with intimate narrative, psychological melodrama with broadbrush social history. It is not surprising that the Italian Communist Party, which at that time Bertolucci sympathised with, criticised the film's historical inaccuracies and ideological inconsistencies, as did many other Italian critics and groups. The party's specific criticism—that Bertolucci shows, in the scene of Alfredo's trial, an event that never happened—produced the revealing response that this scene was a fantasy. Yet nothing in the film itself indicates this—which suggests, as do the romanticisation of the peasants, the simplification of Fascism and the alternation between sympathy for Alfredo and sympathy for Olmo, that at the heart of the film is the director's own political confusion. *1900* particularly suffers by comparison with Bertolucci's earlier attempt to depict the Fascist era, *The Conformist*. Perhaps because of the discipline imposed by relying on a single literary source (Alberto Moravia's novel), perhaps because the story is small-scale and yet complex, the earlier film can make viewers ask themselves what they might have done under Fascism, while watching *1900* makes them ask what Bertolucci really thinks Fascism was about.

In *1900*, the first of Bertolucci's series of historically based epics, he evidently bit off more than he, or his audience, could chew. For all its visual beauty, its frequent scenes of convincing and moving personal drama and its occasional moments of well-composed and exciting political narrative, *1900* is ultimately disappointing, an incoherent and frustrating film unworthy of the cast and crew involved in its making.

—Monique Lamontagne

NOVYI VAVILON

(The New Babylon)

USSR, 1929

Directors: Grigori Kozintsev and Leonid Trauberg

Production: Sovkino Studies, Leningrad; black and white, silent; 6 reels, running time: 111 minutes. Released 1929. Re-screened with original score at London Film Festival, 1982.

Screenplay: Grigori Kozintsev and Leonid Trauberg, from an idea by P. Bliakin; **photography:** Andrei Moskvin and E. Mikhailov; **art director:** Yevgeni Enei; **music:** Dimitry Shostakovitch; **historical consultant:** A. Molok.

Cast: Elena Kuzmina (*Louise Poirier*); Piotr Sobolevskii (*Jean the Soldier*); David Gutman (*Grasselin*); Sophie Magarill (*An Actress*); Sergei Gerasimov (*Lutro, a journalist*); S. Gusev (*Old Poirier*); Janina Jeimo (*Therese, a needlewoman*); A. Gluchkova (*Washerwoman*); Evgeni Cherviakov (*Soldier in National Guard*); Andrei Kostrichkin (*Old shop assistant*); Anna Zarazhinskaia (*Young girl at barricades*); Vsevolod Pudovkin (*Shop assistant*).

Publications

Script:

Kozintsev, Grigori, and Leonid Trauberg, *Novyi Vavilon*, in *Avant-Scène du Cinéma* (Paris), December 1978.

Books:

Leyda, Jay, *Kino*, London, 1960.
Schnitzer, Jean and Luda, *Le Cinéma sovietique par ceux qui l'ont fait*, Paris, 1966; as *Cinema in Revolution: The Heroic Era of the Soviet Film*, London, 1973.
Verdone, Mario, and Barthélemy Amengual, *La Feks*, Paris, 1970.
Furhammer, Leif, and Folke Isaksson, *Politics and Film*, London, 1971.
Rapisarda, Giusi, editor, *La Feks: Kozintsev e Trauberg*, Rome, 1975.
Christie, Ian, and John Gillett, *Futurism, Formalism, FEKS: Eccentrism and Soviet Cinema 1918–36*, London, 1978.
Leaming, Barbara, *Grigori Kozintsev*, Boston, 1980.
Bordwell, David, *Narration in the Fiction Film*, London, 1985.
Christie, Ian, and Richard Taylor, editors, *The Film Factory: Russian and Soviet Cinema in Documents 1896–1939*, London, 1988.
Houten, Theodore van, *Leonid Trauberg and His Films: Always the Unexpected*, 's-Hertogenbosch, 1989.

Articles:

Close Up (London), June 1929.
New York Times, 2 December 1929.
Variety (New York), 4 December 1929.
Times (London), 21 November 1935.
Kozintsev, Grigori, in *Cahiers du Cinéma* (Paris), July and August-September 1971.
Positif (Paris), June 1977.
Afterimage (London), Autumn 1981.
Pulleine, Tim, in *Guardian* (London), 17 September 1982.
Brown, Geoff, in *Times* (London), 18 September 1982.
Variety (New York), 6 October 1982.
Eisenschitz, B., ''La Musique du silence,'' in *Cinématographe* (Paris), November 1982.
Elley, Derek, in *Films and Filming* (London), November 1982.
Dignam, Virginia, in *Morning Star* (London), 7 January 1983.
New York Times, 3 and 5 October 1983.
Robinson, David, interview with Leonid Trauberg, in *Times* (London), 20 November 1983.
Leyda, Jay, ''Un cinema fatto e pezzi per la musica di Sostakovic,'' in *Cinema Nuovo* (Bari), February 1984.
Listener (London), 23 January 1985.
Morrison, Richard, in *Times* (London), 13 January 1986.
Nusinova, N., ''*Novyi Vavilon:* stareiut li fil'my?'' in *Iskusstvo Kino* (Moscow), no. 4, 1990.
Tsikounas, M., ''Il était excentrique,'' in *Positif* (Paris), no. 363, May 1991.

* * *

The New Babylon is a metaphorical clash of glittering surfaces and deep social cynicism that marked the climax of Grigori Kozintsev and Leonid Trauberg's experimentations with the conventions of the Soviet silent cinema. Taking their thematic inspiration from the story of the Paris Commune of 1871, the two directors fashioned a highly conceptualized allegory of social strata under pressure that transcends its historical roots to form a sardonic comment on the human condition.

In actuality, the commune had been composed of a group of French patriots who seized power during the Franco-Prussian War after the city of Paris fell before the advance of the Germanic invaders. Though the experiment in communal government lasted but a few short weeks, it caught the attention of Marxists and Socialists alike. Yet, it was not strictly the commune's historical reality that inspired Kozintsev and Trauberg. It was the movement's symbolic re-invention of ''The City of Light''—an attempt at the creation of a universal socialistic ''Paris of the Mind'' that the two Soviet artists found most intriguing.

In 1921, Kozintsev and Trauberg had created FEKS, The Factory of the Eccentric Actor, a theatre group dedicated to the creation of avant-garde and unorthodox productions. After producing a number of controversial multi-media stage representations, the two found their true forum in the cinema, and made six highly experimental films between 1924 and 1927. *The New Babylon*, which began production in 1928, was their first project undertaken with the support of the Soviet government.

Although their desire for authenticity was extensive enough to prompt them to embark on a photographic expedition to Paris to record the sights and sounds of their subject matter, they had no intention of employing the resulting images in a conventional manner. The creation of a ''Paris of the Mind'' mandated a multi-textual approach. Thus, while Kozintsev and Trauberg embraced the paintings of Renoir and Manet and the novels of Emile Zola, they reinterpreted these cultural icons in the light of their reading of Karl Marx's *The Class Struggle in France*. The symbolic center of the film is the New Babylon, a Parisian department store which is, in effect, a crucible for the interaction of the French social classes. At the outset

Novyi Vavilon

of the film, a fast-moving camera and a collage of glittering images portrays the store as an idolatrous Babylonian temple awash with materialistic and fleshly pleasures. The mode of representation, at this point, is expressionistic in nature but not the type of dark, moody distortionism embodied by the German aesthetics of the early 1920s. Expressionism, as employed by Kozintsev and Trauberg, is much lighter, and makes calculated use of glitter and flamboyance as rhetorical devices within a visual collage. For example, the frenetic sequence of images that dominates the early department-store scenes emphasizes lavish sets strewn with such exotic objects as brocades, kimonos, fans, and parasols, and an agitated salesman (played by Vsevolod Pudovkin) hawking his wares. Such imagery dynamically conveys the psychological preoccupations of the bourgeoisie who frequent the store.

The disparate groups that comprise the film's ''class struggle'' are joined and commented upon through the interactions of Louise Poirier (Elena Kuzmina), a salesgirl at the store. Forced by the circumstances of her position to cater to the whims of the rich, it is clear that her sympathies are actually with the working-class patriots who will form the Commune. The actress Kuzmina wrote some years afterwards that the character of Louise was, ironically, not found in the literature of the time but was instead intended to be a synthetic communist girl representing the entire epoch.

The frenzy of contrasts conveyed by the opening scenes of a sale in progress at the New Babylon is sustained in the subsequent scenes of an uncomfortable Louise at the music hall. But here the filmmakers vary their mode of expression somewhat by constantly interspersing the fast-moving camera work with isolated, almost static vignettes unfolding against action filled backdrops. Prominent among these latter events is the meeting between Louise and Jean, a soldier who becomes her lover as the Prussians march into Paris.

In the film's middle and later segments, which are more conventionally sequential in nature. The early expressionism gives way to the more clearly delineated realism embodied in the battle scenes. Here, it is a combination of longer, more slowly moving sequences interspersed with short episodes that show the fall of the Paris administrative seat and the rise of the Commune.

When the Commune is ultimately betrayed by the bourgeoisie and attacked by the soldiers, Kozintsev and Trauberg create a heightened sense of irony by blending pastoral and battle images in a gross parody of reality. Through the use of repugnant close-ups of aristocrats picnicking on a hilltop at Versailles as the battle rages below, the self-serving treason of the upper classes is brought sharply into contrast with the patriotism of the workers. The film shifts dramatically between portraits of bloated faces sipping champagne and the blank faces of the dead communards on the barricades.

The New Babylon derives much of its energy and momentum from its union of narrative styles. On the visual level, the cinematography of former graphic artist Andrei Moskvin intersperses crisp black and white images reminiscent of fine engravings with the glitzy, stylized, and more softly rendered representations characteristic of Soviet expressionism. The latter visual style is also highly evident in the performances of the actors. The exaggerated facial expressions and gestures of the actors evident in such scenes as the one in the music hall are used to symbolize psychological states rather than to convey simple emotions. Finally, in a number of instances, images and motifs are structured into fast-moving collages designed to distance the viewer emotionally from the action and to elicit an intellectual awareness of how various visual components of the film interact with others to produce a particular meaning.

The music, by Dimitry Shostakovitch, is also integral to the film's narrative structure. Normally in film, the music serves to compliment or amplify the visual image. The relationship is one of conjunction. In *The New Babylon*, however, Shostakovitch creates a relationship through the opposition of sound and image. In the music hall scene, for example, the composer interfaces components of the ''can-can'' and the ''Marseillaise'' with the vulgar spectacle of the pageant to form a musical comment on the French middle class.

Although the avant-garde aspects of *The New Babylon* caused it to fall somewhat in disfavor during the regime of Josef Stalin, it is precisely those elements that cause it to remain of interest today. Although ranking somewhat below the pioneering efforts of Sergei Eisenstein and Vsevolod Pudovkin whose theories greatly influenced its creation, *The New Babylon* still represents an innovative use of the cinema and one of the highpoints of the Soviet silent cinema.

—Stephen L. Hanson

NOW VOYAGER

USA, 1942

Director: Irving Rapper

Production: Warner Bros. Pictures, Inc. black and white, 35mm; running time: 117 minutes. Released 1942.

Producer: Hal B. Wallis; **screenplay:** Casey Robinson, from the novel by Olive Higgins Prouty; **photography:** Sol Polito; **editor:** Warren Low; **art director:** Robert Haas; **music:** Max Steiner.

Cast: Bette Davis (*Charlotte Vale*); Paul Henreid (*Jerry Durrance*); Claude Rains (*Dr. Jaquith*); Gladys Cooper (*Mrs. Henry Windle Vale*); Bonita Granville (*June Vale*); Ilka Chase (*Lisa Vale*); John Loder (*Elliot Livingston*); Lee Patrick (*Deb McIntyre*); Franklin Pangborn (*Mr. Thompson*); Katherine Alexander (*Miss Trask*); James Rennie (*Frank McIntyre*); Mary Wickes (*Dora Pickford*); Janis Wilson (*Tina Durrance*); Michael Ames (*Dr. Dan Regan*); Charles Drake (*Leslie Trotter*); Frank Puglia (*Manoel*); David Clyde (*William*).

Award: Oscar for Music—Scoring of a Dramatic or Comedy Picture, 1942.

Publications

Script:

Robinson, Casey, *Now Voyager*, edited by Jeanne Thomas Allen, Madison, Wisconsin, 1984.

Books:

Davis, Bette, *The Lonely Life: An Autobiography*, New York, 1962.
Ringgold, Gene, *The Films of Bette Davis*, New York, 1966; updated edition 1990.
Mancia, Adrienne, editor, *Hal Wallis, Film Producer*, New York, 1970.
Higham, Charles, *Bette: A Biography of Bette Davis*, New York, 1981.
Robinson, Jeffrey, *Bette Davis: Her Film and Stage Career*, London, 1982.
Henreid, Paul, with Julius Fast, *Ladies Man: An Autobiography*, New York, 1984.
Champion, Isabelle, *Bette Davis*, Paris, 1986.
Walker, Alexander, *Bette Davis: A Celebration*, London, 1986.
Davis, Bette, with Michael Herskowitz, *This 'n' That*, New York, 1987.
Gledhill, Christine, editor, *Home Is Where the Heart Is: Studies in Melodrama and the Woman's Film*, London, 1987.
Leaming, Barbara, *Bette Davis: A Biography*, New York, 1993.
Riese, Randall, *All About Bette: Her Life from A to Z*, Lincolnwood, 1993.
Spada, James, *More Than a Woman*, New York, 1994.
Hadleigh, Boze, *Bette Davis Speaks*, London, 1997.

Articles:

Variety (New York), 19 August 1942.
New York Times, 23 October 1942.
Flanner, Janet, ''Bette Davis,'' in *New Yorker*, February 1943.
Times (London), 4 November 1943.
Raper, Michell, ''Mannerisms—in the Grand Manner,'' in *Films and Filming* (London), September 1955.
Quirk, Lawrence, ''Bette Davis,'' in *Films in Review* (New York), December 1955.
Stein, Jeanne, ''Claude Rains,'' in *Films in Review* (New York), November 1963.
Eyles, Allen, in *Films and Filming* (London), February 1965.
Guerin, Ann, ''Bette Davis,'' in *Show* (New York), April 1971 and May 1972.
Rhodie, Sam, ''Semiotic Constraints in *Now Voyager*,'' in *Australian Journal of Screen Theory* (Kensington, New South Wales), no. 4, 1978.
Greenberg, J., ''Writing for the Movies: Casey Robinson,'' in *Focus on Film* (London), April 1979.
Villien, Bruno, in *Cinématographe* (Paris), July 1979.
Nacache, J., in *Cinéma* (Paris), July-August 1979.
Merigeau, P., in *Revue du Cinéma* (Paris), September 1979.
Positif (Paris), October 1979.
Jacobs, L., ''*Now Voyager*: Some Problems of Enunciation and Sexual Difference,'' in *Camera Obscura* (Berkeley), Spring 1981.
m/f Journal (London), no. 9, 1984.

Now Voyager

La Place, Maria, ''Bette Davis and the Ideal of Consumption: A Look at *Now Voyager*,'' in *Wide Angle* (Athens, Ohio), vol. 6, no. 4, 1985.

Journal of Popular Film and Television (Washington, D.C.), Autumn, 1985.

Palmer, R. Barton, ''The Successful Failure of Therapy in *Now Voyager*: The Women's Picture as Unresponsive Symptom,'' in *Wide Angle* (Athens, Ohio), vol. 8, no. 1, 1986.

Cavell, S., ''Ugly Duckling, Funny Butterfly: Bette Davis and *Now Voyager*,'' in *Critical Inquiry* (Chicago), no. 2, 1990.

Reid's Film Index (Wyong), no. 4, 1990.

De Lauretis, T., ''Il fantasma del cinema: sulla funzione spettatoriale come rapporto di produzione fantasmatico-sociale,'' in *Cinema & Cinema* (Bologna), September-December 1991.

Britton, A., ''A New Servitude: Bette Davis, *Now Voyager*, and the Radicalism of the Woman's Film,'' in *CineAction* (Toronto), Winter 1992.

Wood, R., ''Letters,'' in *CineAction* (Toronto), no. 29, Fall 1992.

Greskovic, Robert, ''*Now Voyager*,'' in *The Village Voice* (New York), vol. 40, no. 42, 17 October 1995.

* * *

Now Voyager is today one of the best remembered and best loved woman's films, or ''weepies,'' of the 1930s and 1940s. Bette Davis remembers it as one of her most satisfying movies. But during its initial release in 1942, the film received a mixed critical response; the *New York Times* called the film a ''prudish fantasy.'' The low esteem in which critics held the film seems in retrospect to be due to the low regard in which critics held the ''woman's picture.'' *Now Voyager* succeeds, not because it explores any new thematic or formal areas within the genre of ''woman's pictures,'' but because it utilizes generic conventions in a highly polished manner.

The ''woman's film'' is characterized by a central female protagonist whose concerns revolve around a romantic or maternal relationship. In the case of *Now Voyager*, the film weaves both into the narrative. The first half of the film documents Charlotte Vale's (Bette Davis) growth into a sexually mature and attractive woman who must overcome the repressive influence of her mother. In the first segment, Charlotte's mother, psychiatrist, and sister-in-law discuss Charlotte before she appears, making her the center of the story without necessitating her on-screen presence. The camera introduces Charlotte with a closeup of her hands working on an ivory box, then discloses her feet walking down the stairs, finally offering a long shot of her entering the parlor. In the second segment, Dr. Jaquith (Claude Rains) and the sister-in-law discuss Charlotte before she is actually seen. The camera here introduces her with a closeup of her hands operating a loom. In the third segment, which takes place on an ocean liner, the passengers discuss Charlotte prior to the camera's introductory closeup panning from her feet up to her head. Upon Charlotte's return to New York City in the film's fourth segment, a discussion of Charlotte precedes the medium shot introducing her. Each discussion creates a sense of expectancy and interest about the character, while the introductions themselves follow a course that visually parallels Charlotte's character development from disjointed close-ups of fragmented body parts to the completely integrated portrait in one shot. It is only after an innocent shipboard romance with a married man has sexually awakened her that Charlotte achieves her sense of identity as a woman and a person. In the second half of the movie, Charlotte supplants her earlier womanly hobbies—carving ivory boxes, weaving and knitting—with socializing, mothering and philanthropy, completing her journey toward the assumption of her socially acceptabe roles.

Several motifs provide a symbolic continuity to the film. The most notable, Paul Henreid lighting Davis's cigarette, operates as a poetic visual sign that may be likened to the intricate musical dances of Fred Astaire and Ginger Rogers. Only during the shared intimacies of the couple's ''cigarette breaks'' does the camera break from the almost continuous objective viewpoint to a series of subjective shot-reverse shots of Davis and Henreid. In this way, the camera forces the audience to shift from its fixation on Davis as an object-to-be-consumed to an alternating identification with her and Henreid. The audience vicariously participates as both parties in their fleeting and harmless romantic moments. Thus, the viewer retains a distance from Charlotte Vale that makes her problems seem as though they are happening to someone else, while fully identifying with her few moments of idealized romantic pleasure.

Max Steiner's Academy Award-winning score and the references to the relationship between Charlotte's life and the art of fiction reinforce an idealized discovery of sexuality. Steiner's melodramatic lover's theme song appears not only when Henreid and Davis get together, but also as the piece the orchestra plays when the two must sit next to each other without acknowledging their love; and after Jerry (Henreid) returns to his wife and family, it comes over the radio reminding Davis and the audience of her emotional ties to him while she chats with another man. The music helps set up a world that seems to exist only to underscore the poignancy of their situation. The ludicrousness of such an idea is overcome by equating how one acts and lives with the way that novels work. Charlotte repeatedly refers to her understanding of life, and especially her life, as having come from novels, and the dissolves into and out of the flashbacks are accomplished via the turning pages of a book. Charlotte's life and world fulfill one's expectations of the romance formula, and they are believable because she believes and acts as if life is a romance formula.

The credit for making Charlotte Vale's identity and life appear so attractive should go largely to Bette Davis for suggestively giving, through gestures, movements, rhythms, timing and articulation, an assertive and independent awareness to the role. Secondly, the film preserves much of the dialogue from Olive Higgins Prouty's 1941 novel on which it is based; its rhythms, tempo and the words themselves underscore a developing assertiveness, control and mastery in Charlotte Vale's speech.

In the end, Charlotte Vale may not be able to achieve complete fulfilment of her destined womanly role through marriage to the man she loves, but she hangs on to the independence, her own identity, while she captures the semblance of a nuclear family. The resolution allows Charlotte to become adoptive mother to Jerry's unhappy daughter while he remains faithful to his legal wife. In one of the great screen romance endings of all time, Charlotte Vale's compromised balance between self-sufficient independence and romantic longings provides an impossible illusory alternative to the unmasking of romance and the loss of independence that would result in daily married life with Jerry and his daughter.

—Lauren Rabinovitz

NÓZ W WODZIE

(Knife in the Water)

Poland, 1962

Director: Roman Polanski

Production: Kamera Film Unit for Film Polski; black and white, 35mm; running time: 94 minutes. Released Poland, 1962. Filmed 1962 in Poland.

Producer: Stanisław Zyewicz; **screenplay:** Jerzy Skolimowski, Jakub Goldberg, and Roman Polanski; **photography:** Jerzy Lipman; **sound:** Halina Paszkowska; **music:** Krzysztof Komeda.

Cast: Leon Niemczyk (*Andrzej*); Jolanta Umecka (*Christine/ Krystanal*); Zygmunt Malanowicz (*Young man*).

Award: International Film Critics Award (Fipresci), Venice Film Festival, 1962.

Publications

Books:

Butler, Ivan, *The Cinema of Roman Polanski*, New York, 1970.
Kane, Pascal, *Roman Polanski*, Paris, 1970.
Belmans, Jacques, *Roman Polanski*, Paris, 1971.
Liehm, Mira and Antonin, *The Most Important Art: East European Cinema after 1945*, Berkeley, 1977.
Bisplinghoff, Gretchen, and Virginia Wexman, *Roman Polanski: A Guide to References and Resources*, Boston, 1979.
Kiernan, Thomas, *The Roman Polanski Story*, New York, 1980.
Leaming, Barbara: *Polanski: The Filmmaker as Voyeur: A Biography*, New York, 1981; as *Polanski: His Life and Films*, London, 1982.
Paul, David W., *Politics, Art, and Commitment in the Eastern European Cinema*, New York, 1983.

Polanski, Roman, *Roman*, London, 1984.
Dokumentation: Polanski und Skolimowski: Das Absurde im Film, Zurich, 1985.
Wexman, Virginia, *Roman Polanski*, Boston, 1985.
Jacobsen, Wolfgang, and others, *Roman Polanski*, Munich, 1986.
Avron, Dominique, *Roman Polanski*, Paris, 1987.
Parker, John, *Polanski*, London, 1995.

Articles:

Haudiquet, Philippe, ''Nouveaux cinéastes polonais: Roman Polanski,'' in *Premier Plan* (Lyons), no. 27, 1962.
Torok, Jean-Paul, ''Prelude à Polanski,'' in *Positif* (Paris), March 1962.
Baker, Peter, in *Films and Filming* (London), February 1963.
Sarris, Andrew, in *Village Voice* (New York), 31 October 1963.
March, Sibyl, in *Seventh Art* (New York), Winter 1963.
Weinberg, Gretchen, ''Interview with Roman Polanski,'' in *Sight and Sound* (London), Winter 1963–64.
Cinema (Beverly Hills), February-March 1964.
Delahaye, Michel, and Jean-André Fieschi, ''Landscape of the Mind: Interview with Roman Polanski,'' in *Cahiers du Cinéma in English* (New York), no. 3, 1966.
McCarty, John Alan, ''The Polanski Puzzle,'' in *Take One* (Montreal), no. 5, 1969.
Gow, Gordon, ''Satisfaction—A Most Unpopular Feeling,'' in *Films and Filming* (London), April 1969.
Nairn, Tom, ''Roman Polanski,'' in *Cinema* (London), June 1969.
Cugny, L., and H. Guibert, in *Cinématographe* (Paris), no. 40, 1978.
Lawton, A. M., ''The Double: A Dostoevskian Theme in Polanski,'' in *Literature/Film Quarterly* (Salisbury, Maryland), no. 2, 1981.
Film (Warsaw), 8 July 1984.
Kino (Warsaw), no. 8, 1987.
Andrew, Geoff, ''Stabbing Pains,'' in *Time Out* (London), no. 1177, 10 March 1993.
Thompson, David, in *Sight & Sound* (London), vol. 3, no. 3, March 1993.
Séquences (Haute-Ville), no. 180, September-October 1995.
Thompson, David, ''I Make Films for Adults,'' in *Sight and Sound* (London), vol. 5, no. 4, April 1995.
Richardson, John H., ''What I've Learned: Roman Polanski,'' in *Esquire* (New York), vol. 132, no. 6, December 1999.
Stanley, Alessandra, ''Polanski: The Once and Future Auteur,'' in *New York Times*, 16 January 2000.

* * *

Roman Polanski emerged as a highly individual artist when he made his directorial debut with a few short films—*Dwaj ludzie z szafa*; his graduation project *Gdy spadaja aniloy; Gros et le maigre*, produced in France; and the grotesque *Ssaki*. These films startled audiences and critics alike and won praise at various film festivals. They amazed viewers with their unusually innovative approach of pure experiment combined with elaborated philosophical import and elements of absurd humor. The critics anxiously awaited his first feature-length film which came in 1962 and was entitled *Nóz w wodzie (Knife in the Water)*.

What was so startling about *Nóz w wodzie*? At first glance, it seems to be a simple story with neither an attractive setting nor much external dramatic action. However, within the ordinary plot a bitter internal drama is played out in the form of a minor allegory. It is an intimate drama of three people in the enclosed space of a sailboat in the middle of a lake, and it takes place over the 24 hours of a single Sunday. A young hitchhiker steps out in front of the car of an elegant married couple, Andrzej and Christine. The hitchhiker's clumsiness appeals to the older man, who finds in it an opportunity to show off his own strength, make fun of the hitchhiker and provoke him. Andrzej invites him to go out sailing with him and his wife. Their relationship gradually comes to a critical point; more and more, Andrzej asserts his role as captain and forces the youth into an audacious reprisal. Somewhere in the relationship between the two men stands Christine. The conflict reaches a climax, when, in one of their quarrels, Andrzej throws the boy's knife into the water. The boy jumps in after it but doesn't come up. Andrzej attempts to rescue the boy, but the latter had only pretended to drown and has returned to the boat, where he again confronts Christine. With morning the drama ends. The boy goes off, and the husband and wife, having cleared up the situation, fall back into the routine of their peculiar conjugal life.

Nóz w wodzie is a cold work that exposes the general norms of human relations defined by generational conflicts and social factors. The drama is characterized by short, clipped pieces of dialogue, each of which serves to determine the character and conduct of the protagonists. Both the beginning and end of the film are wrapped in silence and the quiet, disturbing isolation of the ''heroes.'' Some critics noted, at the time of the film's release, the similarity between Polanski's development and the directorial style of Michelangelo Antonioni. Nevertheless, this work bears a uniquely individual directorial stamp. The film opens with an automobile ride; across the windshield and the faces of the husband and wife flit the shadows of branches and tree trunks. The image is cold and grey. So, too, are the world and the relationship of the central couple into which the hitchhiker intrudes. The enclosed space of the boat surrounded by water intensifies the drama of the situation and the coldness and hopelessness of the human relationships. There is an intrinsic drama hidden somewhere beneath the exterior of these people who have nothing to say to each other. The boy serves as a kind of catalyst for the development of the action, for the exposure of relationships and character. But the authors present everything as a mere game which, in the end, can start all over again despite the malicious accusations and the disclosure of egoism and cowardice; in spite of the pain and cruelty of an empty conjugal existence, everything remains as it had been. The drama is heightened by the brilliant camera work of Jerzy Lipman, which captures both the surroundings and the people in cold, grey tones; looks at them as a tangle of ropes, objects and bodies; and uses discrete images to portray the contrasts between expressions and utterances. The attention concentrated on the strangeness of human communication is emphasized further by the jazz elements in Krzysztof Komeda's music

Nóz w wodzie was the confession of a generation, the warning of dangerous trends of philistinism, thoughtlessness, and authoritarianism. It is at this general level that the film is important today as well, and it has lost nothing of its suggestiveness in the years since its first appearance. It is a masterpiece which has risen above generational conflict to confront the viewer with the universal problem of human intolerance.

—V. Merhaut

NUIT ET BROUILLARD

(Night and Fog)

France, 1955

Director: Alain Resnais

Production: Argos-Como-Cocinor (Paris); Eastmancolor, some sequences in black and white, 35mm; running time: 32 minutes. Filmed near Auschwitz. Released 1955.

Text: Jean Cayrol; **photography:** Ghislain Cloquet; **editor:** Alain Resnais; **music:** Hans Eisler; **historical consultants:** André Michel and Olga Wormser.

Cast: Michel Bouquet (*Narrator*).

Award: Prix Jean Vigo, France, 1956.

Publications

Script:

Cayrol, Jean, *Nuit et brouillard*, in *Avant-Scène du Cinéma* (Paris), February 1961; also in *Film: Book 2—Films of Peace and War*, edited by Robert Hughes, New York, 1962.

Books:

Cordier, Stéphane, editor, *Alain Resnais; ou, La Création au cinéma*, Paris, 1961.
Pinguad, Bernard, *Alain Resnais*, Lyons, 1961.
Bournoure, Gaston, *Alain Resnais*, Paris, 1962.
Cowie, Peter, *Antonioni, Bergman, Resnais*, London, 1963.
Armes, Roy, *French Cinema Since 1946: The Personal Style*, New York, 1966.
Armes, Roy, *The Cinema of Alain Resnais*, London, 1968.
Ward, John, *Alain Resnais; or, The Theme of Time*, New York, 1968.
Prédal, René, *Alain Resnais*, Paris, 1968.
Daniel, Joseph, *Guerre et Cinéma: Grandes illusions et petits soldats, 1895–1971*, Paris, 1972.
Barnouw, Erik, *Documentary: A History of the Non-Fiction Film*, New York, 1974.
Bertetto, Paolo, *Resnais, Alain Resnais*, Florence, 1976.
Kreidl, John Francis, *Alain Resnais*, Boston, 1977.
Monaco, James, *Alain Resnais: The Role of Imagination*, New York, 1978.
Benayoun, Robert, *Alain Resnais: Arpenteur de l'imaginaire*, Paris, 1980; revised edition, 1988.
Sweet, Freddy, *The Film Narratives of Alain Resnais*, Ann Arbor, Michigan, 1981.
Vergerio, Falvio, *I film di Alain Resnais*, Rome, 1984.
Roob, Jean-Daniel, *Alain Resnais: Qui êtes-vous?*, Lyons, 1986.
Riambau, Esteve, *La ciencie y la ficcion: El cine de Alain Resnais*, Barcelona, 1988.
Thomas, François, *L'atelier d'Alain Resnais*, Paris, 1989.
Bersani, Leo, and Ulysse Dutoit, *Arts of Impoverishment: Beckett, Rothko, Resnais*, Cambridge, 1994.
Callev, Haim, *Stream of Consciousness in the Films of Alain Resnais*, New York, 1997.
Fleischer, Alain, *L'art d'Alain Resnais*, Paris, 1998.

Articles:

Truffaut, François, interview with Alain Resnais, in *Arts* (Paris), 20 February 1956.
Marcorelles, Louis, in *Sight and Sound* (London), Spring 1956.
Bazin, André, ''Alain Resnais,'' in *Qu'est-ce que le cinéma* (Paris), 1959.
Sandall, Roger, in *Film Quarterly* (Berkeley), Spring 1961.
Taylor, John Russell, ''Alain Resnais,'' in *Cinema Eye, Cinema Ear* (New York), 1964.
''Resnais Issue'' of *Avant-Scène du Cinéma* (Paris), Summer 1966.
Roud, Richard, ''Memories of Resnais,'' in *Sight and Sound* (London), Summer 1969.
''Resnais Issue'' of *Cinéma* (Paris), July-August 1980.
Michael, R., in *Cineaste* (New York), 1984.
Krantz, C., ''Teaching *Night and Fog*: History and Historiography,'' in *Film and History* (Newark, New Jersey), February 1985.
Moses, John W., ''Vision Denied in *Night and Fog* and *Hiroshima mon amour*,'' in *Literature/Film Quarterly* (Salisbury, Maryland), vol. 15, no. 3, 1987.
Arnold, Gordon B., ''From Big Screen to Small Screen: *Night and Fog* (*Nuit et brouillard*) Directed by Alain Resnais,'' in *Library Journal* (New York), vol. 114, no. 9, 15 May 1989.
Donova, F., ''*Nuit et brouillard : Hiroshima mon amour,*'' in *Cinema 89* (Paris), no. 459, September 1989.
Chevallier, J., ''Le kepi de Pithiviers,'' in *Revue du Cinéma* (Paris), no. 462, July/August 1990.
Slavin, J., ''The Butterflies in the Bonfire: The Holocaust as Art,'' in *Metro Magazine* (St. Kilda West), no. 99, Summer 1994.
Rabinowitz, Paula, ''Screen Memories,'' in *Wide Angle* (Baltimore), vol. 18, no. 4, October 1996.
Jousse, Thierry, ''Trois vidéos et un CD-ROM autour de Chris Marker,'' in *Cahiers du Cinéma* (Paris), no. 515, July-August 1997.
Dümling, Albrecht, ''Eisler's Music for Resnais' *Night and Fog* (1955): A Musical Counterpoint to the Cinematic Portrayal of Terror,'' in *Historical Journal of Film, Radio and Television* (Abingdon), vol. 18, no. 4, October 1998.

* * *

Two closely related problems: How does one make a film about the concentration camps? and how does one write a reference book entry about a film about the concentration camps? The facts are too appalling to be aesthetically encompassed; any *attempt* to encompass them seems almost beyond criticism. The word that rises automatically to one's lips to describe what was done in the camps is ''inhuman''; yet it was human beings who performed those acts. For both the film-maker and the critic, it is one's own ''humanity'' that is in question.

In making *Night and Fog* director Alain Resnais and his writer Cayrol confronted a problem that is simultaneously aesthetic and moral: how does one adequately represent the enormity of the camps without so overwhelming the spectator that the only possible response

Nuit et brouillard

is a despairing impotence?—how to achieve and sustain a contemplative distance without softening or trivializing the material? Their solution, curiously *seductive* (and the strangeness of that word in such a context is deliberate), is ultimately unsatisfying. The failure lies in the fact that the kind of distance achieved is aesthetic rather than analytical; we find ourselves invited to contemplate, not the historical/material realities, but an art-object.

The film is built on a systematic pattern of related oppositions: present/past, colour/black-and-white, tranquility/horror, natural environment/buildings, footage shot for the film/archive material. Particularly stressed is the recurrent Resnais theme: importance of memory/difficulty of remembering. Nothing can mitigate the appalling impact of the newsreel material incorporated in the film, with the horrors carefully built up to, yet introduced almost casually, so that we at once expect them and are taken unawares. The problem arises from the attitude to the horror that the film, overall, constructs.

One omission—startling today, though no one seems to have commented on it at the time—is symptomatic in more than one way of the film's failure. One sequence carefully specifies the various coloured triangles that identified different groups of victims, distinguishing the Jews from other ethnic groups, political prisoners, etc. Presumably Resnais and Cayrol had very thorough documentation at their disposal, yet no reference is made to the *pink* triangle: the filmmakers surround the deaths of the (approximately) 300,000 homosexuals who died in the camps with their own "night and fog" of silence. A sinister enough comment on the "liberal" conscience in itself, this omission has implications that lead much further. The fact that the Nazis attempted to exterminate gays as well as Jews points to certain fundamental traits of Fascism that our culture generally prefers to gloss over for its own comfort. Alongside the demand for racial purity went the insistence on extreme sexual division: "masculinity" and "femininity" must be strictly differentiated, women relegated to the subordinate position of the mothers who would produce future generations of "pure" aryans. The reason why patriarchal capitalist society is so reluctant to confront this aspect of Nazism is clearly that it has its own stake in the same assumptions.

The problem, however, is not simply that Resnais and Cayrol cannot make that analysis (though it is a fundamental one); they really offer no analysis at all (with the result that they tend to repress the possibility of really understanding the camps). The final moments of the film are extremely moving: at the post-war trials, we are led through the whole hierarchy of camp authority; everyone denies responsibility; we are left with the question, "Then who is responsible?" Yet the implication is something like: "These things have always happened; they have happened again; they will always happen." Denied concrete material/historical analysis, we are thrown back on "the human condition." The answer the film (without much hope) proposes is eternal vigilance. Yet no "liberal" vigilance is going to prevent the recurrence of the camps (or related phenomena) until the fundamental premises and structures of our culture are radically transformed.

This account of *Night and Fog* is perhaps ungenerous, the problems inherent in the undertaking being so daunting. The film is intensely moving. Yet to confront the human monstrousness of the camps demands the utmost rigour from both the film-maker and the critic. Ultimately, the kind of "distance" constructed by Resnais and Cayrol seems less honourable, as a response, than the direct emotional assault of work like Schönberg's "A Survivor from Warsaw."

—Robin Wood

UNE NUIT SUR LE MONT CHAUVE

(Night on Bald Mountain)

France, 1933

Directors: Alexander Alexeieff and Claire Parker

Production: Black and white, 35mm, animation; running time: 8 minutes, some sources list 9 minutes. Released 1933, Paris.

Narrative development: Alexander Alexeieff, inspired in part by Moussorgsky's music and notes, and a short story based on a Slavic fairy tale by Gogol; **music:** Moussorgsky; **arrangement:** Rimski-Korsakov, "His Master's Voice" interpreted by: London Symphony Orchestra under the direction of Albert Coates; **animation:** Alexandre Alexeieff and Claire Parker.

Publications

Books:

Alexandre Alexeieff (catalogue), Edinburgh, 1967.
Rondolino, G., *Alexandre Alexeieff*, Este, 1971.
Starr, Cecile, *Discovering the Movies*, New York, 1972.
Bendazzi, G., editor, *Alexandre Alexeieff*, Milan, 1973.
A. Alexeieff, C. Parker: Films et eaux-fortes (catalogue), Annecy, 1975.
Russett, R., and Cecile Starr, *Experimental Animation*, New York, 1976.
Bendazzi, G., editor, *Pages d'Alexeieff*, Milan, 1983.
A. Alexeieff; ou, La Gravure animée (catalogue), Annecy, 1983.
Bisaccia, Antonio, *Alexandre Alexeieff: il cinema d'incisione*, Castel Maggiore, 1993.

Articles:

Cheronnet, L., in *Art et Décoration* (Paris), no. 63, 1934.
Priacel, S., "Gravure animée," in *Art Vivant* (Paris), no. 188, 1934.
Grierson, John, in *Cinema Quarterly* (London), Autumn 1934.
Martin, A., "Alexandre Alexeieff et les cinémas possibles," in *Cinéma* (Paris), no. 81, 1963.
Alexeieff, Alexandre, "Reflections on Motion Picture Animation," in *Film Culture* (New York), no. 32, 1964.
Alexeieff, Alexandre, "The Synthesis of Artificial Movements in Motion Picture Projection," in *Film Culture* (New York), no. 48–49, 1970.
Arnault H., editor, "Le Chant d'ombres et de lumières de 1,250,000 épingles," in *Cinéma Pratique* (Paris), no. 123, 1973.
Jouvanceau, J.P., and Gaudillière, C., "A. Alexeieff," in *Banc-Titre* (Paris), no. 25, 1982.

* * *

The power of *Night on Bald Mountain* derives from the extraordinary versatility that Alexander Alexeieff and Claire Parker brought to their unusual medium. Their "pinboard" (*l'écran d'épingles*) is an upright perforated screen, three by four feet, with 500,000 (one million in later films) headless steel pins as its physical matrix. Images created on the pinboard take their character from the depth of the pins and their oblique lighting. Pushed forward, the pins create an entirely dark surface; when fully recessed, they produce a white ground. By varying the depth of the pins, one creates between the extremes of white and black a wide variety of subtle shades the brilliance and delicacy of which exceed that of engravings. The pinboard screen yields a single picture at a time which must be photographed as part of a sequence of thousands of such shots to shape the cumulative effect.

This frame-by-frame creation during the process of filming, rather than before it, is the earliest form of direct animation. Alexeieff acknowledges the pointillism of Seurat as analogous to the character of his images. The delicacy of this process of image-building becomes apparent when one realizes that four minutes of production requires a year of work. Since the artist can see only the current frame, the procedure is akin to writing a short story sentence-by-sentence and locking away each one until completion of the narrative. During the interactive process of creating and filming, the only original of a pinboard picture that remains is its photographic negative; there are almost 12,000 for this eight-minute film.

It is important to note that *Night on Bald Mountain* has about as much affinity to Walt Disney's evocation of the same Moussorgsky work in *Fantasia* (1940) as Lotte Reininger's *Cinderella* has to Disney's version, i.e. the relationship is one of contrast more than of comparison. While Disney's *Fantasia* used cell animation in a direct and explicit way, which includes a sketching from life of Bela Lugosi as a Moussorgsky demon, Alexeieff and Parker employ indirection and impression, eminently conscious of art's power to universalize experience, of animation's power to create movement that is not "live" in the conventional ways of narrative, feature-length films. Their technique is most closely akin to the music that they visualize in their manipulation of time and space through shadowy referents. More physicists than engineers, their mobile structures reflect the changing character of thought and feeling, depict imaginary rather than static worlds. To photography and painting's laws of perspective they add the suggestive movement of implicit images. To the dance they add weightless figures whose unlimited metamorphoses invoke the license of Ovid's epic poem or the transitory, spatial and temporal fluidity of musical patterns. More than do other approaches to cinema, that of Alexeieff and Parker embodies Suzanne Langer's description of cinema as a dream mode.

Night on Bald Mountain is a nightmare, a *Walpurgisnacht*, inspired by Moussorgsky's music and written notes, by childhood recollections, by the Russian short-story writer Gogol's record of an ages-old Slavic fairytale, and by a dancing windmill in Pushkin's *Eugene Onegin*. The film's witches, demons and skeletal horses, in contrasting day and night reflection of each other, create a feverish tone poem that Moussorgsky's music "describes" as powerfully as would a verbal soundtrack. The description, however, of both sight and sound is poetic and lyric rather than narrative and prosaic. The correlative and opposing patterns of visual and musical images create unexpected harmonies whose tonalities are both elastic and balanced. The clash of old and new realities, of expected and unexpected sights and sounds that regularly, rather than continually, complement each other provides the conceptual unity that is finally as satisfying as it is initially troubling. The audience comes to realize that the animation and the music are metaphorical equivalents to one another and that in combination they tell a tragicomic story of life and death, which calls upon the vertical complexity of poetic allusion and brevity for its thrilling and very temporary resolution of basic human contradictions.

The first pinboard was built in 1932, for *Night on Bald Mountain*, and was used by Alexeieff and Parker for all their non-commercial films. Jacques Drouin's *Le paysagiste* (*Mindscape*: National Film Board of Canada, 1976) continues their tradition. Because of the difficulty of the technique, however, Alexeieff and Parker have had many more admirers than cinematic descendants.

Following the traditional path of successful experimenters, they earned well deserved critical acclaim, but the applause only gradually expanded beyond the ranks of film experts and film society aficionados. Initial success in Paris did not yield widespread distribution in spite of John Grierson's generous praise in the Autumn 1934 issue of *Cinema Quarterly*. In 1970 Norman McLaren proclaimed *Night on Bald Mountain* "first and foremost" on his list of the world's best animated films, and in 1980 it earned inclusion on a list of the eight best short animation films of all time.

—Arthur G. Robson

LES NUITS FAUVES

(Savage Nights)

France, 1992

Director: Cyril Collard

Production: Banfilm Ter, La Sept Cinéma, Erre Produzioni, SNC, Sofinergie 2, CNC, Canal Plus, Procirep; color, 35mm; running time: 126 minutes.

Producer: Nella Banfi; **screenplay:** Cyril Collard, Jacques Fieschi, from the novel by Cyril Collard; **photography:** Manuel Teran; **editor:** Lise Beaulieu; **assistant director:** Jean-Jacques Jauffret; **sound editors:** Patrice Grisolet, Frédéric Attal; **sound recording:** Michel Brethez; **costumes:** Régine Arniaud.

Cast: Cyril Collard (*Jean*); Romane Bohringer (*Laura*); Carlos Lopez (*Samy*); Corine Blue (*Laura's mother*); Claude Winter (*Jean's mother*); René Marc Bini (*Marc*); Maria Schneider (*Noria*); Clémentine Célarié (*Marianne*); Laura Favali (*Karine*).

Publications

Articles:

Toubiana, S., *Cahiers du Cinéma* (Paris), October 1992.
Strauss, F., *Cahiers du Cinéma* (Paris), November 1992.
Rooney, D., *Variety* (New York), 7 December 1992.
Roy, A., "La vie a tout prix" in *24 Images* (Montreal), February-March 1993.
Castiel, T., *Séquences* (Montreal), March 1993.
Strauss, F., and others, "Cyril Collard—un art neuf" in *Cahiers du Cinéma* (Paris), April 1993.
Lipman, A., *Sight and Sound* (London), June 1993.
Burston, P., "The Loving End" in *Time Out* (London), 9 June 1993.
Cheshire, G., "Self-Expressions" in *Film Comment* (New York), January-February 1994.
Tanner, Louise, "Who's in Town," in *Films in Review* (New York), vol. 45, no. 1–2, January-February 1994.
Travers, P., "*Savage Nights*," in *Rolling Stone*, no. 675, 10 February 1994.
Powers, J., "Anything for Love," in *New Yorker*, vol. 27, 7 March 1994.
Nash, Mark, "Chronicle(s) of a Death Foretold: Notes Apropos of *Les Nuits Fauves*," in *The Critical Quarterly* (Hull), vol. 36, no. 1, Spring 1994.
Alleva, R., "Love in the Ruins," in *Commonweal*, vol. 121, 3 June 1994.
Feinstein, Howard, "Savage Nights," in *Cineaste* (New York), vol. 20, no. 4, 1994.
Sluhovsky, M., "*Philadelphia; An Early Frost; Our Sons; Silvertake Life; The View from Here; Savage Nights*," in *American Historical Review*, vol. 99, no. 4, 1994.
Oleksiewicz, M., "Sweet Cyril?" in *Kino* (Warsaw), vol. 29, May 1995.
Worth, F.A., "Le sacre et le SIDA (AIDS): Sexuality and Its Contradictions in France 1971–1996," in *Discourse* (Detroit), vol. 19, no. 3, Spring 1997.

* * *

Oscillating abruptly between a brash, visceral dramatic style, and a quieter, more lyrical mode, Cyril Collard's *Les Nuits fauves* is distinguished precisely by its bold eclecticism. Most obviously, it is a film that strategically dispenses with generic consistency, mixing melodramatic, often violent (and occasionally turgid) emotional excess with muted art cinema introspection. This narrative heterogeneity is further extended into the film's overall stylistic design, which skillfully combines quasi-documentary, *cinema vérité* techniques and their conventional effect of energetic spontaneity, with an intricate and meticulously orchestrated *mise-en-scène*. By way of this unique narrative and stylistic quilting, the film exploits the dynamic possibilities of juxtaposition to the full, almost revelling in the power and raw exhilaration of contrasting and clashing character events, emotions and styles. Thus, it succeeds in traversing a wide range of emotions and behaviors, from the hectic and volatile dimension of the lives of the main characters, instantiated in the liberal use of *vérité* devices such as a shaky, hand-held camera and fast-paced editing, to the more subtle and often enigmatic interactions between them. For example, the erotically charged first meeting between the central protagonist Jean and his girlfriend Laura stitches together the excitement of a free-wheeling camera with a carefully organized and reflective exchange of looks and words, played out through and around the viewfinder of Jean's video camcorder.

However, this calculated patchwork of styles and modes ultimately has a more important rationale. For *Les Nuits fauves* is ostensibly a film about a young man who discovers he is HIV positive. Yet it is also, deliberately, about a lot more besides, and it is the film's above mentioned eclecticism that enables it to refuse any easy identification or comfortable ''AIDS film'' label, a difficulty that was remarked upon by a number of both hostile and sympathetic reviewers on the film's release.

The narrative centers on Jean, a professional photographer living in Paris, who discovers that he has contracted the HIV virus following his return from a job in Morocco. At first, he seemingly refuses to come to terms with the virus, becoming involved with Laura, a young actress whom he meets at an audition for a commercial he is working on. They have sex without any protection, she being unaware of his HIV status. Meanwhile, Jean also continues having clandestine gay encounters, as well as a sexual relationship with Samy, an aggressive and narcissistic young bodybuilder who becomes increasingly involved with a group of violent fascists. Laura is angry when Jean finally tells her he is HIV positive, yet her emotional attachment to him becomes more and more intense and they begin living together. She also becomes increasingly possessive of Jean and jealous of his relationship with Samy. Returning from a short vacation, Laura finds Samy and Jean living together, and she reacts furiously. Jean begins AZT treatment and goes to visit his parents. Having confided his illness in his mother who consoles him, he deliberately speeds home and crashes his car.

Jean decides to end his relationship with Laura, who is now obsessed with him to the point of self-destruction. Having gone to live with her mother, she descends further and further into hysteria, occupying her time by phoning Jean and screaming insults at him. Finally, having claimed that she herself has contracted the HIV virus, she is taken to a psychiatric hospital, where tests reveal that she does not have the virus. Meanwhile, Jean encounters Samy and his gang of fascists one night, torturing a young Arab boy in the street, and he uses his infected blood as a weapon to rescue the boy. When he sees Laura again, she has nearly fully recovered and has a new boyfriend. She now accepts that her relationship with Jean is over, and they say good-bye to each other. Refusing to settle down and wait for the gradual onset of his illness, Jean travels to the desert, where he seems to find happiness and tranquillity through a lyrical, expressionistic affirmation of his own existence and the life around him.

In spite of its use of melodrama and emotional hyperbole, *Les Nuits fauves* is refreshingly original in its rejection of the two standard narrative options—victimization and deification—typical of melodramas that use illness as their point of departure, both of which, incidentally, figure prominently in Jonathan Demme's film *Philadelphia* which also deals with HIV and AIDS. Jean, played by Collard himself, who has since died of AIDS, is neither ''victim'' nor ''saint,'' but is instead a complex creature, at once reckless with himself and with others, often cruel and calculating, having unprotected sex, for instance, with an unwitting Laura, almost killing himself in his passion for driving fast, and so on. Yet, he is also brimming full of love both for the people around him and for his world, a love that translates into a consuming, sensuous hunger for physical pleasure, companionship, and excitement, as well as an abiding moral concern for life and ''things living'' in general. In a sense, the narrative of *Les Nuits fauves* is driven by Jean's attempt to make sense of his contradictory nature, to find a common ground on which the seemingly irreconcilable elements of his identity might be unified. And it is certainly the urgency brought on by the HIV virus itself that impels this search. Yet, much more importantly, the HIV virus also functions in *Les Nuits fauves* as the catalyst for a tentative answer for Jean. Having initially refused to face his HIV status, Jean's denial turns into a conscious affirmation of life itself and the drive to experience life to the full which he exemplifies. Without a doubt, this Romantic ''answer'' to Jean's search—-his cathartic, rapturous immersion in life at the film's lyrical climax which is figured by fast, dizzying camera work and editing—-may strike many as clichéd and unsatisfactory. However, it should be recognized that Collard has effectively attempted to reinvent this well-worn Romantic cliché by appropriating it for the contemporary context of HIV and AIDS, within which it assumes a very different valence. For ultimately, it transforms *Les Nuits fauves* into a film that is not simply about HIV and the way it takes away life, but rather about what happens *to a life* when HIV enters into it.

—Kris Percival

O SLAVNOSTI A HOSTECH

(A Report on the Party and the Guests)

Czechoslovakia, 1968

Director: Jan Němec

Production: Barrendov Film Studio for Ceskoslovenský Film; black and white, 35mm; running time: 70 minutes. Released Czechoslovakia, 1968. Filmed 1966 in Czechoslovakia.

Producer: Carlo Ponti; **screenplay:** Ester Krumbachová and Jan Němec; **photography:** Jaromír Sofr; **editor:** Miroslav Hájek; **sound:** Jiři Pavlik; **art director:** Oldřich Bosák; **music:** Karel Mareś.

Cast: Ivan Vyskočil (*Host*); Jan Klusák (*Rudolf*); Jiři Němec (*Josef*); Zdena Skvorecká (*Eva*); Pavel Bosek (*František*); Helena Pejškova (*Marta*); Karel Mareš (*Karel*); Jana Pracharová (*Wife*); Evald Schorm (*Husband*).

Publications

Books:

Whyte, Alistair, *New Cinema in Eastern Europe*, New York, 1971.
Liehm, Antonín, *Closely Watched Films*, New York, 1974.
Liehm, Mira, and Antonín, *The Most Important Art*: *East European Film After 1945*, Berkeley, 1977.
Habova, Milada, and Jitka Vysekalova, editors, *Czechoslovak Cinema*, Prague, 1982.
Hames, Peter, *The Czechoslovak New Wave*, Berkeley 1985.

Articles:

Green, Calvin, in *Film Society Review* (New York), October 1968.
''Jan Němec: Filmography,'' in *International Film Guide*, London, 1968.
Gow, Gordon, in *Films and Filming* (London), March 1969.
Amengual, Barthélemy, ''Allegorie et Stalinisme dans quelques films de l'est,'' in *Positif* (Paris), January 1973.
Revue du Cinéma (Paris), no. 481, April 1992.

*　*　*

O Slavnosti a hostech is the best-known and most respected of the feature films directed by Jan Němec in Czechoslovakia. The film is his second feature and was co-scripted by Ester Krumbachová, his wife at that time.

The work is a thinly veiled critique of the Communist regime and a parable on authoritative oppression and the nature of conformity. Although the movie was completed in 1966, it was not exhibited in Czechoslovakia until 1968, following a two-year struggle supported by many of the country's leading intellectuals to have it shown. Its subsequent appearance in the 1968 New York Film Festival brought Němec to world attention.

The plot begins as a group of ordinary men and women frolic in the countryside, enjoying an afternoon picnic. Suddenly several men appear from behind the trees. Despite their smiles, the men forcefully direct the group to a clearing. A leader appears and takes up a position of authority behind a small table. He sets forth the rules by which the group will be governed and their movements confined. The women comply readily; the men make attempts to protest, but in the end acquiesce as well. Tension and incipient violence hang in the air when suddenly an older man appears, apologetic for the stridency of his hirelings, particularly the leader whom he refers to as his adopted son, Rudolph. He invites the group to a birthday celebration in the forest.

Among the trees which line the lake, banquet tables have been set with elaborate dishes and candelabras. The host speaks about the small differences in shape and design which distinguish the tables, but proudly points out how all fit together into one distinguishable whole. The host is openly paternalistic and all present toast his benevolence. The harmony is interrupted when one woman discovers she is sitting at the wrong place. Her desire to move sets a chain reaction which disturbs the entire group, much to the dismay of the host. More urgent is the discovery that one of the guests has disappeared. Finding his departure intolerable, the host instructs Rudolph to bring him back. Delighted with this opportunity, Rudolph leaves with a sharp-toothed dog and is joined in the chase by the entire party. The tables are abandoned and the film closes with the sound of the barking dog.

O Slavnosti a hostech deals with the themes common to all of Němec's films, although they are the best developed here. Most prominent are the restriction on human freedom, the reactions of human beings under stress, and the ease with which man utilizes violence. In *O Slavnosti a hostech*, however, Němec goes a step further and treats the degree to which men are complicit in their own fate. Like his other works, the film possesses a surreal quality, especially in its presentation of extraordinary occurrences in a realistic manner, such as the fairy tale-like outdoor court scene and the elaborate banquet.

The film was critically praised and Němec was considered among the front ranks of the new Czech directors. His sensibility was compared to that of Franz Kafka, his compatriot, and Feodor Dostoevski.

However, following the fall of the short-lived Dubcek government which allowed for artistic freedom in Czechoslovakia, Němec was blacklisted and unable to make films after 1968. More than his other two features, *O Slavnosti a hostech* was seen as a direct attack on

Eastern European Communism and was responsible for his being barred from directing.

—Patricia Erens

OBCHOD NA KORZE

(The Shop on Main Street)

Czechoslovakia, 1965

Directors: Ján Kadár and Elmar Klos

Production: Barrandov Film Studio for Ceskoslovenský Film; black and white, 35mm; running time: 128 minutes; length: 3428 meters. Released Czechoslovakia, 1965. Filmed 1964 Barrandov Film Studio; location scenes filmed in Sabinov, Czechoslovakia.

Producers: Marie Desmarais and Eurofilm Ltd.; **head of production:** Ladislav Hanuš; **screenplay:** Ladislav Grosman, Ján Kadár, and Elmar Klos, from the book *Obchod na korze* by Ladislav Grosman; **English sub-titles:** Lindsay Anderson; **photography:** Vladimir Novotný; **editors:** Jaromir Janáček and Diana Heringová; **sound:** Dobroslac Srámek; **art director:** Karel Skvor; **music:** Zdeněk Liška; **costume designer:** Marie Rosenfelderová.

Cast: Jozef Króner (*Tono Brtko*); Ida Kamińska (*Rozálie Lautmannová*); Hana Slivková (*Evelyna Brtková*); František Zvarík (*Markus Kolkocká*); Elena Zvaríkova (*Ružena Kolkocká*); Martin Hollý (*Imro Kuchar*); Martin Gregor (*Katz, the barber*); Adam Matejka (*Piti Báči*); Mikuláš Ladižinsky (*Marian Peter*); Eugen Senaj (*Blau, the Printer*); František Papp (*Andorić*); Gita Mišurová (*Andoričová*).

Awards: Oscar for Best Foreign Film, 1965; New York Film Critics Award, Best Foreign Film, 1966.

Publications

Books:

Boček, Jaroslav, *Modern Czechoslovak Film 1945–1965*, Prague, 1965.
Hibbin, Nina, *Eastern Europe: An Illustrated Guide*, New York, 1970.
Whyte, Alistair, *New Cinema in Eastern Europe*, New York, 1971.
Liehm, Antonín, *Closely Watched Films*, New York, 1974.
Liehm, Mira, and Antonín Liehm, *The Most Important Art: East European Film After 1945*, Berkeley, 1977.
Jan Kadar: Study Guide: The American Film Institute, Washington, D.C., 1979.
Habova, Milada, and Jitka Vysekalova, editors, *Czechoslovak Cinema*, Prague, 1982.
Hames, Peter, *The Czechoslovak New Wave*, Berkeley, 1985.

Articles:

Cowie, Peter, in *Films and Filming* (London), June and August 1965.
''Director,'' in *New Yorker*, 12 February 1966.
Wharton, Flavia, in *Films in Review* (New York), March 1966.
Sarris, Andrew, in *Village Voice* (New York), 10 March 1966.
Seelye, John, in *Film Quarterly* (Berkeley), Summer 1966.
Cohen, Jules, ''Elmar Klos and Ján Kadár,'' in *Film Comment* (New York), Fall and Winter 1967.
Livingston, Howard, in *Film Society Review* (New York), December 1967.
Bond, Kirk, ''The New Czech Film,'' in *Film Comment* (New York), Fall 1968.
''Czechs in Exile,'' in *Newsweek* (New York), 27 July 1970.
''The Czech Who Bounced Back,'' in *Films Illustrated* (London), April 1972.
Liehm, Antonín, ''En för alla . . . ,'' in *Chaplin* (Stockholm), vol. 14, no. 1, 1972.
Haller, R. A., ''Interview with Ján Kadár,'' in *Film Heritage* (Dayton, Ohio), Spring 1973.
Obituary of Kadár, in *New York Times*, 4 June 1979.
Moret, H., obituary of Kadár, in *Ecran* (Paris), 15 July 1979.
Gervais, G., obituary of Kadár, in *Jeune Cinéma* (Paris), July-August 1979.
''*The Shop on Main Street*,'' in *Reid's Film Index* (Wyong), no. 6, 1991.
Saperstein, J., '''All Men Are Jews': Tragic Transcendence in Kadár's *The Shop on Main Street*,'' in *Literature/Film Quarterly* (Salisbury, Maryland), no. 4, 1991.

* * *

In the mid-1960s, young, creative artists appeared on the Czech film scene with fresh film and projected a new conception of the present and the past in a new way. *The Shop on Main Street*, however, was made by Ján Kadár and Elmar Klos in the tradition of classical film, without any particular formal innovations such as complicated dramatic structure or impressive camera work, and even without any visible influence of the international trends of those days such as cinema verité or the French New Wave. The modernity of *The Shop on Main Street* was not based on any technical characteristics but on its content—on another way of viewing the reality of the Second World War. After a series of movies about the occupation years of 1939–1945, narrating or describing this period in a linear and uniform way, opposing heroism and cowardice, *The Shop on Main Street* concentrates instead on profoundly penetrating the thoughts and feelings of people who lived at that time and experienced a fear which broke their will to resist and led them to criminal acts. It asks the question whether a human being has the right to build his happiness and personal security on the misfortune of others, and answers that question with a story of someone who committed a crime because he did not have the strength to resist evil.

The locale of the story is a typical small town in the so-called Slovak State (established by secession of Slovakia from the Czechoslovak Republic at the beginning of the Second World War), where the citizens gradually come under the disintegrative influence of the new order organized by the government under the protection of the expanding German empire. Seemingly—at least in the beginning—this influence manifests itself in comical and provincial ways. However, behind all this funny business is a tragic reality—the Jewish residents of the town will be deported to concentration camps and face death. In this situation the moral conflict unfolds, the conflict of the main protagonist whom the viewer meets at the moment when the new society distributes power, rank and wealth. This fellow acquires a portion of the loot and although it is very negligible and almost worthless, still it signifies the first step toward a compromise which, in the end, logically leads him to crime. At the beginning of the story, he is scarcely distinguishable from his victim. Both of them—he a common little businessman, she an aging owner of a small store and a Jewess—used to accept the same moral code and honor the same rules of living. Their collision does not take place at the intellectual level but rather in the deeper layers of life. Its roots are really misunderstanding and misinterpretation of one's own actions and also of the actions of others. The old lady does not comprehend anything taking place before her eyes, anything of what looms ahead. The carpenter Brtko does not understand the senselessness and criminality of his compromise. They both pay for it by their death.

The film is made with an unusual sensitivity toward the need to alternate bearable doses of the tragicomic with fully tragic elements and situations. It has outstanding editing and music, and shows a fine sense for detail. The acting performances of the Slovak actor Jozef Kroner and the Polish actress Ida Kaminska mesh beautifully, and the picture was honored by a number of prizes.

—B. Urgošíkova

OCTOBER

See **OKTIABR**

ODD MAN OUT

UK, 1947

Director: Carol Reed

Production: Two Cities Films; black and white; running time: 116 minutes; length: 10,488 feet. Released 23 April 1947.

Producer: Carol Reed; **screenplay:** F. L. Green and R. C. Sherriff, from the novel by Green; **photography:** Robert Krasker; **editor:** Fergus McDonnell; **art director:** Ralph Brinton; **music:** William Alwyn.

Cast: James Mason (*Johnny*); Robert Newton (*Lukey*); Robert Beatty (*Dennis*); F. J. McCormick (*Shell*); Fay Compton (*Rosie*); Beryl Measor (*Maudie*); Cyril Cusack (*Pat*); Dan O'Herlihy (*Nolan*); Roy Irving (*Murphy*); Maureen Delany (*Theresa*); Kitty Kirwan (*Granny*); Min Milligan (*House-keeper*); Joseph Tomelty (*Cabby*); W. G. Fay (*Father Tom*); Arthur Hambling (*Alfie*); Kathleen Ryan (*Kathleen*); Denis O'Dea (*Head Constable*); William Hartnell (*Fencie*); Elwyn Brook-Jones (*Tober*).

Awards: BFA Award for Best Film, 1947.

Publications

Script:

Green, F. L. and R. C. Sherriff, *Odd Man Out*, in *Three British Screenplays*, edited by Roger Manvell, London, 1950.

Books:

Manvell, Roger, *The Film and the Public*, London, 1955.
Phillips, Gene D., *The Movie Makers: Artists in an Industry*, Chicago, 1973.
DeFelice, James, *Filmguide to Odd Man Out*, Bloomington, Indiana, 1975.
Hirschhorn, Clive, *The Films of James Mason*, London, 1975.
Armes, Roy, *A Critical History of the British Cinema*, London, 1978.
Mason, James, *Before I Forget*, London, 1981.
Hill, John, Kevin Rockett, and Luke Gibbons, *Cinema and Ireland*, London, 1987.
Moss, Robert, *The Films of Carol Reed*, New York, 1987.
Wapshott, Nicholas, *Carol Reed: A Biography*, New York, 1997.

Articles:

Monthly Film Bulletin (London), vol. 14, no. 160, 1947.
Polonsky, Abraham, in *Hollywood Quarterly*, January 1947.
Winnington, Richard, in *News Chronicle* (London), 1 February 1947.
Lejeune, C. A., in *Observer* (London), 2 February 1947.
Powell, Dilys, in *Sunday Times* (London), 2 February 1947.
Wright, Basil, in *Spectator* (London), 7 February 1947.
Whitebait, William, in *New Statesman* (London), 8 February 1947.
Variety (New York), 12 February 1947.
Sight and Sound (London), Spring 1947.
New York Times, 24 April 1947.
Documentary Newsletter (London), April-May 1947.
Goodman, E., ''Carol Reed'' in *Theatre Arts* (New York), May 1947.
Wright, Basil, ''The Director: Carol Reed,'' in *Sight and Sound* (London), Summer 1951.
Image et Son (Paris), October 1954.
Sarris, Andrew, ''Carol Reed in the Context of his Time,'' in *Film Culture* (New York), no. 10, 1956, and no. 11, 1957.
Sarris, Andrew, ''First of the Realists,'' in *Films and Filming* (London), September, 1957.
''Carol Reed,'' in *Encountering Directors*, by Charles Thomas Samuels, New York, 1972.
Voight, M., ''Pictures of Innocence: Sir Carol Reed,'' in *Focus on Film* (London), Spring 1974.
''James Mason,'' in *Films in Review* (New York), May 1982.
Phillips, Gene, D., ''Carol Reed,'' in *Films in Review* (New York), August-September 1982.
Interview with James Mason in *Cinéma* (Paris), September 1984.
Combs, Richard, in *Listener*, 5 June 1986.'
Polanski, Roman, ''*Odd Man Out*,'' in *Positif* (Paris), no. 400, June 1994.
Thomson, David, ''Reeds and Trees,'' in *Film Comment* (New York), vol. 30, no. 4, July 1994.
Christie, Ian, Leslie Felperin, and Nick Roddick, ''Film Criticism: *Odd Man Out* by Dai Vaughan,'' in *Sight and Sound* (London), vol. 5, no. 11, November 1995.
Howard, T., in *Reid's Film Index* (Wyong), no. 15, 1995.

* * *

Odd Man Out was Carol Reed's first postwar feature and the first of a quartet of films, including *The Fallen Idol*, *The Third Man*, and *Outcast of the Islands*, which were to mark the highpoint of a lengthy film-making career. Based on F. L. Green's novel of the same name,

Odd Man Out

the film was partly shot in Belfast with a predominantly Irish cast, including many Abbey Theatre regulars. Robert Krasker, the cameraman on *Brief Encounter*, was responsible for the film's striking photography, and William Alwyn contributed a memorable musical score, incorporating individual leitmotifs for three of the central characters. On its release, the film was met by almost unanimous praise (''the best film that has ever been made in Britain'' according to the *Daily Express*) and received the British Film Academy's award for the Best British Motion Picture of 1947.

Unlike much of the British cinema's wartime output, the film has little truck with social realism. Formally, the film is heavily indebted to both German Expressionism and French poetic realism—indeed, its ending is practically a copy of Julien Duvivier's *Pepé le Moko* (1936)—and has much in common with its similarly stylised postwar US counterpart, the film noir. This is evident in the film's approach to both plot and visual presentation. Like classical tragedy, the film's story is concerned with the irreversible consequences of an initial error. Johnny McQueen (James Mason) is shot following an ill-advised, and armed, mill robbery and is left to wander the city at night. Despite the efforts of others to save him, his fate is already sealed and, in a moving climax, Johnny meets his death in the arms of the woman he loves, while his last remaining hope of escape, the ship, is seen to sail off without him.

This aura of doom is reinforced by the film's iconography (the recurring appearance of the Albert Clock, the deteriorating weather) as well as its distinctive visual style. As in film noir, both lighting and composition are used to striking effect. Lighting is predominantly low-key, creating strong chiaroscuro contrasts and vivid patterns of light and shadow. Compositions tend to be imbalanced and claustrophobic, with characters either cramped into enclosed interiors (as at Granny's) or rendered small by their surrounding environment (as in many of the night scenes). The use of a tilted camera (almost a Reed trademark), acute angles, and wide-angle lenses adds to these effects, especially in the chase sequences involving Dennis (Robert Beatty) as he races down long and imprisoning alley-ways or clambers his way through a maze of scaffolding. While such scenes as these, with their imaginative combination of real locations and expressive visual design, have retained an air of freshness, the film's resort to full-blooded expressionism in its subjective sequences has worn less well. Although much admired at the time, the attempts to visualize Johnny's hallucinations by superimposing faces onto beer bubbles or by putting paintings into flight now seem simply belaboured (and, no doubt, represent the type of device which led Andrew Sarris to include Reed, somewhat unkindly, in his category of ''less than meets the eye'').

Debate over the merit of Reed's technique, however, has also tended to discourage too close an inspection of the meanings which the film projects (although the documentarist Edgar Anstey did attack the film at the time of its release for apparently importing French existentialism). For while the film's opening title disclaims any specific connection to the conflicts in Northern Ireland and the film itself studiously avoids referring to either Belfast or the IRA by name, it is also quite clear from the film that it is dealing with a recognisable setting and situation. Indeed, critics have, at various times, praised the film for both its distinctive Irish flavour and the enduring relevance of one of its apparent messages (the futility of violence). What the film does, in this respect, is not so much dispense with local details as deprive them of their social and political dimension. For, by employing the conventions of expressionism, and introducing an element of religious allegory, the film's interpretation of events is inevitably metaphysical rather than social. It is not history and politics which can explain the characters' motivations and actions, only an inexorable fate or destiny. In doing so, it also reinforces a view of the Northern Ireland situation as fundamentally irrational. As Tom Nairn has noted (in *The Break-up of Britain*), it has become quite common to account for the ''troubles'' in terms of what he labels ''the myth of atavism.'' It is only ''a special historical curse, a luckless and predetermined fate,'' he observes, ''which can account for the war.'' And it is this viewpoint which is effectively reinforced by *Odd Man Out*. For Johnny too is ''cursed,'' by virtue of his adoption of violence, and becomes, in his turn, the victim of an apparently ''luckless and predetermined fate.''

—John Hill

L'ODEUR DE LA PAPAYE VERTE

(Mui Du Du Xanh; The Scent of Green Papaya)

France, 1993

Director: Tran Anh Hung

Production: Les Productions Lazannec, Paris, in co-production with LA SFP Cinéma, La Sept Cinéma, Canal Plus, Centre Nationale de la Cinématographie; colour, 35mm; running time: 104 minutes. Filmed entirely on two sound stages outside Paris, at the studios of Société Francaise de Production.

Producer: Christophe Rossignon; **screenplay:** Tran Anh Hung; **photography:** Benoit Delhomme; **editor:** Nicole Dedieu, Jean-Pierre Roques; **assistant director:** Nicolas Cambois; **music:** Tiet Ton-That; **sound recording:** Michel Guiffan; **costumes:** Jean-Phillipe Abril.

Cast: Tran Nu Yên-Khê (*Mui, age 20*); Lu Man San (*Mui, age 10*); Truong Thi Loc (*Mother*); Nguyen Anh Hoa (*Old Thi*); Vuong Hoa Hoi (*Khuyen*); Ngoc Trung Tran (*Father*); Vantha Talisman (*Thu*); Keo Souvannavong (*Trung*).

Publications

Articles:

Elley, D., *Variety* (New York), 7 June 1993.

Jeancolas, J.P., ''Un vietnam mental,'' in *Positif* (Paris), July-August 1993.

Kauffman, Stanley, *The New Republic* (New York), 28 February 1994.

Corliss, Richard, *Time* (New York), 7 March 1994.

Johnson, Brian D., *Macleans*, 21 March 1994.

Romney, Jonathan, *New Statesman and Society*, 25 March 1994.

Rayns, Tony, *Sight and Sound* (London), April 1994.

Cross, A., ''Portraying the Rythm of the Vietnamese Soul,'' in *Cineaste* (New York), 1994.

Kissin, E.H., *Films in Review* (New York), 3/4, 1994.

Dinh, T., ''*The Scent of Green Papaya*: Ambiguity in the Vietnam Essence,'' in *Amerasia Journal*, vol. 20, no. 3, 1994.

L'odeur de la papaye verte

Cheng, Scarlet, *Cinemaya* (New Delhi), Summer 1994.

Dick, Jeff T., ''Fast Scans: Foreign and Indie Films,'' in *Library Journal* (New York), vol. 123, no. 7, 15 April 1998.

Winters, Laura, ''A Risk-Taking Perfectionist behind the Camera,'' in *New York Times*, 5 December 1999.

* * *

In a lushly visual and lyrical style, *L'odeur de la papaye verte (The Scent of Green Papaya)* tells the story of Mui, a 12-year-old servant girl (Lu Man San) who comes to work in a well-to-do Saigon household in the 1950s. The gentle, modest child accepts her fate and dutifully learns her tasks, even while being taunted by the younger son. But young French Vietnamese filmmaker Tran Anh Hung, who directed from his own script, makes clear that Mui is not a mere drudge. With her lively, inquisitive eyes and her sense of wonder at the limited world around her, Lu projects sensitivity and scope.

But all is not well in the seemingly tranquil household. Although the mother, played with great dignity and grace by Troung Thi Loc, tries bravely to hold the family together, earning their income by running a fabric shop adjoining the house, her profligate husband is usually absent. He returns now and then only to make off with the savings. The two sons feel the tension, with the younger one acting out his frustrations on Mui. ''I didn't want to do a documentary-style film about Vietnam,'' the director says, ''but I wanted to show a mental landscape. I wanted to create film based on the life experience of my mother. There's a certain gentleness I wanted to recreate. I wanted to show how the servitude of women transforms itself into a form of self-sacrifice.''

Ten years later, the family falls on hard times. The mistress tearfully sends Mui (now played by Tran Nu Yên-Khê) away to look after Khuyen (Vuong Hoa Hoi), a dashing young music composer recently back from his European studies. He is engaged to an equally Westernized young Vietnamese woman, but with her mercurial temper, her wild laugh, and her stiletto pumps, perhaps she is too challenging for him, too free. He finds his attention diverting more and more to the sweetly innocent and more traditionally feminine Mui.

Tran cautions against seeing the film as a mere fairy tale, where the East triumphs over the West. For him, the ending is far more ambiguous and unsettling than that. ''There's a moment that is at once the most terrible and the most beautiful in a woman's life,'' he noted.

''It's that moment when she falls in love and servitude becomes a pleasure. Love delivers woman from servitude, but at the same time reinforces servitude.''

Much of the film's power derives from its visual expressiveness. Cinematographer Benoit Delhomme captures long and loving takes of the faces of characters (all wonderfully cast), of the open architecture of the traditional-style Vietnamese domicile, of the lush green foliage and the insects abounding in the garden. There is a fascination with food and food preparation—done in a minimal outdoor kitchen, with the old housekeeper (Nguyen Anh Hoa) teaching Mui how to cook and Mui watching intently, from the time she comes to the household as a young girl to the time she begins to become a woman.

We are treated to a scene of how the famous Vietnamese green papaya salad is made—the fruit is peeled, the tender meat is hacked, then sliced off into julienned strips. The scene ends with Mui cutting the remaining fruit in half and coming upon, with wonderment and delight, the pearly black seeds nestled within the center. As she presses her small finger into the nest of seeds to touch them, to stir them, the scene becomes sensual. And indeed, the air of this film is dense with sweet sensuality, both repressed and softly expressed. While dialogue is sparse, even terse, the storytelling is nevertheless superb, with Tran, who wrote the script, showing sympathetic insight into all the characters.

Tran Ang Hung left Vietnam at age 11 with his family in 1975, just before the fall of Saigon to Communist forces. Resettling in France, he eventually went on to study film at the Ecole Louis Lumière, but he deliberately failed to get his diploma. ''If I had graduated,'' he explains, ''I would have been tempted to go into television, where I could have made a lot of money. Instead, I went to work in a bookstore for a living and ended up writing five scripts.''

While at the school, Tran made two short films, *La femme mariée de Nam Xuong* and *La Pierre de l'Attente*, which were based on Vietnamese folk tales. With the collaboration of Christophe Rossignon, who found the money, Tran was able to make *The Scent of Green Papaya*, his first feature. At first they went to Vietnam to make the film but were stopped by the rainy season. Later a co-production offer from Société Française de Production persuaded them to shoot in France, so in fact the film was shot in its entirety on two studios outside Paris.

To ensure authenticity, they gathered old photographs of Vietnamese households and village streets and carefully researched the plants and insects of the region. Tran called upon family members to help out—his mother made all the food seen in the film, his father, a tailor, made all the costumes—and, last but not least, Tran's wife played the key part of the older Mui. In fact, all the roles were filled by amateurs found in a wide-ranging talent search throughout France. The one exception was Nguyen Anh Hoa, a professional actress who played the older servant and was found in Vietnam.

In 1993 *The Scent of Green Papaya* proved another unexpected hit for Asian filmmakers. At the Cannes Film Festival, the film was selected for the Un Certain Regard program, then won the prestigious Camera d'Or for best feature by a first-time director. Later Tran picked up the French film industry's Cesar award for the same category. In 1994 the film garnered a best foreign language film nomination from the American Academy Awards, along with Chen Kaige's *Farewell My Concubine* and Ang Lee's *Wedding Banquet*. None of the Asian films took home the prize, but Tran says with great ease, ''I was happy to be nominated. I was happy to have a chance to go to the awards ceremony and meet others in the field.'' The film has been released widely in Europe, in nearly 60 U.S. cities, and in many Asian countries. In 1994 it was also featured at both the Hong Kong International Film Festival and the Singapore International Film Festival.

Having been raised in two different cultures, Tran certainly realizes that he is caught between East and West, rather like the composer in his film. ''It's complicated—I couldn't say everything in the film [*Green Papaya*]. Of course, there are certain contradictions in myself. . . But it's not disagreeable—it's rather interesting actually.''

—Scarlet Cheng

OFFRET

(The Sacrifice)

Sweden-France, 1986

Director: Andrei Tarkovsky

Production: Swedish Film Institute (Stockholm)/Argos Films (Paris), in association with Film Four International, Josephson and Nykvist, Sveriges Television/SVT 2, and Sandrew Film and Teater, with the participation of the French Ministry of Culture; Eastmancolor, part in black and white; running time: 149 minutes; length: 13,374 feet. Released 1986.

Executive producer: Anna-Lena Wilbom; **producer:** Katinka Farago; **screenplay:** Andrei Tarkovsky; **assistant directors:** Kerstin Eriksdotter, Michel Leszczylowski; **photography:** Sven Nykvist; **camera operators:** Lasse Karlsson, Dan Myhrman; **editors:** Andrei Tarkovsky, Michel Leszcyzlowski; **editorial consultant:** Henri Colpi; **sound recordists:** Owe Svensson, Bosse Persson, Lars Ulander, Christin Loman, Wikee Peterson-Berger; **art director:** Anna Asp; **music:** *The St. Matthew Passion* by J. S. Bach.

Cast: Erland Josephson (*Alexander*); Susan Fleetwood (*Adelaide*); Valérie Mairesse (*Julia*); Allan Edwall (*Otto*); Gudrún Gísladóttir (*Maria*); Sven Wollter (*Victor*); Filippa Franzen (*Marta*); Tommy Kjellqvist (*Little Man*); Per Kallman and Tommy Nordahl (*Ambulancemen*).

Award: BAFTA Award for Best Foreign Language Film, 1987.

Publications

Books:

Tarkovsky, Andrei, *Sculpting in Time: Reflections on the Cinema*, London, 1986.
Borin, Fabrizio, *Andrej Tarkovskij*, Venice, 1987.
Jacobsen, Wolfgang, and others, *Andrej Tarkovskij*, Munich, 1987.
LeFanu, Mark, *The Cinema of Andrei Tarkovsky*, London, 1987.
Gauthier, Guy, *Andrei Tarkovski*, Paris, 1988.

Borin, Fabrizio, *Cinema di Andrej Tarkovskij*, Rome, 1989.
Turovskaia, Maiia Iosifovna, *Tarkovsky: Cinema as Poetry*, translated by Natasha Ward, London, 1989.
Green, William, "Video: *The Sacrifice (Offret)* Directed by Andrei Tarkovsky," in *Sight and Sound* (London), vol. 1, no. 12, April 1992.
Johnson, Vida T., and Graham Petrie, *The Films of Andrei Tarkovsky: A Visual Fugue*, Bloomington, 1994.
Kovács, András Bálint, *Tarkovszkij: az orosz film Sztalkere*, Budapest, 1997.
Tarkovski, Larissa, *Andrei Tarkovski*, with Luba Jurgenson, Paris, 1998.

Articles:

Benayoun, Robert, and others, in *Postif* (Paris), May and June 1986.
Variety (New York), 14 May 1986.
Chaplin (Stockholm), June 1986.
Magny, Joel, in *Cahiers du Cinéma* (Paris), June 1986.
Bonitzer, P., and M. Chion, in *Cahiers du Cinéma* (Paris), July-August 1986.
LeFanu, Mark, in *Sight and Sound* (London), Autumn 1986.
Taylor, John Russell, in *Films and Filming* (London), September 1986.
Strick, Philip, in *Monthly Film Bulletin* (London), January 1987.
Filmfaust (Frankfurt), January-February 1987.
Christie, Ian, "Raising the Shroud," in *Monthly Film Bulletin* (London), February 1987.
Green, Peter, "Apocalypse and Sacrifice," in *Sight and Sound* (London), Spring 1987.
Alexander, John, "Tarkovsky's Last Vision," in *Cinema Papers* (Melbourne), May 1987.
de Brant, C.-H., "Krasota slaset mir. . . ," in *Iskusstvo Kino* (Moscow), no. 2, 1989.
Lothwall, L.-O., "Kazhdyi den' s Tarkovskim," in *Iskusstvo Kino* (Moscow), no. 2, 1989.
Lovgren, H., "Svart pa fragan ar livet sjalvt," in *Chaplin* (Stockholm), no. 3, 1990.
Iensen, T., and A. German, "Vysokaia prostota," in *Iskusstvo Kino* (Moscow), no. 6, 1990.
Iensen, T., and I. Norshtein, "Ognennoe iskushenie," in *Iskusstvo Kino* (Moscow), no. 6, 1990.
Gauthier, G., "Andrei Tarkovski et la tentation de l'Occident," in *Cinemaction* (Conde-sur-Noireau, France), July 1990.
Livingston, J., "New Rage," in *Village Voice 36*(New York), Literary Supplement, no. 99, 8 October 1991.
Levgren, K., "Leonardo da Vinchi i Zhertvoprinoshenie," in *Iskusstvo Kino* (Moscow), no. 6, 1992.
Aleksandr, L., "Tarkowski," in *Kino* (Warsaw), October 1992.
Crowdus, Gary, "Two by Tarkowski," in *Cineaste* (New York), vol. 20, no. 4, 1994.
Paquette, J. -M., "Tarkovski: Cineaste Cynique," in *Cinemas* (Montreal), vol. 4, no. 3, 1994.
"*Le Sacrifice*," in *Séquences* (Haute-Ville), no. 181, November-December 1995.
Wiese, I., "Andrej Tarkovskij," in *Z Filmtidsskrift*, no. 1, 1996.
Beasley-Murray, J., "Whatever Happened to Neorealism?: Bazin, Deleuze, and Tarkovsky's Long Take," in *Iris* (Iowa City), no. 23, Spring 1997.

* * *

There is a documentary featuring Tarkovsky at work on his last film. Made by *The Sacrifice's* editor, Michel Leszczylowski, and entitled simply *Directed by Andrei Tarkovsky*, it provides a revealing insight into the Russian's methods. One episode in particular captures Tarkovsky's attitude toward his craft. The final shot of *The Sacrifice* lasts ten minutes and depicts the protagonist of the film burning down the house round which most of the action has centred. This is a typically complex Tarkovsky "take," involving elaborate camera movement and pulling together all the discrete strands of the narrative. As Leszczylowski shows, disaster struck. Although the house burnt down to the ground in a very satisfactory manner, and although the cast followed Tarkovsky's choreography to perfection, there was no footage to record the event; Sven Nykvist's camera had jammed at the crucial moment. Tarkovsky was distraught, claiming that *The Sacrifice* would be worthless without this image. He absolutely refused to compromise. He was not going to edit or to use trick photography or to alter the script; he wanted the shot in its entirety. Somehow, despite sub-zero temperatures, despite the hiccup this would cause in the schedule and in the budget, he managed to persuade backers, cast, and crew to rebuild the house. As soon as the house was rebuilt, it was promptly burnt down again. This time Nykvist's camera did not jam. A perfectionist with a highly personal view of the film he wanted to make, Tarkovsky would let nothing stand in his way. His skill was in convincing others that his idiosyncratic vision was their own.

Given the fact that *The Sacrifice* is a meditation on death and destruction, and considering that its maker succumbed to cancer shortly after its completion, it is hard not to see the film as Tarkovsky's last testament. The mood and tempo are certainly elegaic. In over two hours, there are only 120 cuts. (Tarkovsky was opposed to "montage cinema," believing that it constrained spectators, preventing them from bringing their own personal experiences or interpretation to bear on any given set of images: montage did the spectators' work for them.) *The Sacrifice* is a difficult film to watch. If cinema for Tarkovsky is "sculpting in time"—his favourite analogy—then, to see his sculptures, spectators must commit themselves for the duration: they must sacrifice their own time. Tarkovsky is keen to let us know that cinema is no mere popular cultural form. In his hands, it is "high art." (Just so we're aware of the fact, we see the opening credits over a Leonardo painting as we listen to Bach on the soundtrack.) Why did Tarkovsky make *The Sacrifice?* As he explains in his programme notes, we are living in a spiritually impoverished era: we are slaves to materialism. We need to find our souls. (For soul finding, as Strindberg, Ibsen, and Bergman have shown us, Scandinavia is the only place. *The Sacrifice* was shot in Sweden and financed by the Swedish Film Institute.)

Something Tarkovsky's hagiographers, of whom there are many, fail to notice is that his films are made not with "spirituality" or with "devotion" or with "inscrutable poetic instinct." Like most other films—with the possible exception of some of Stan Brakhage's work—they are made with cameras. From the laudatory reviews and fawning interviews that so often accompanied Tarkovsky, one gets the impression that his films came into being already perfectly formed; that they were divinely conceived. Tarkovsky did little to disabuse us of the idea. Critics he held in some contempt, and he demanded that we react to his films intuitively, with feeling and not with intellect. Children and animals always understand his films.

The Sacrifice has a quirky narrative structure. An old actor and writer, Alexander (Erland Josephson), is celebrating his birthday with his family at his secluded country house. He has spent the morning planting a tree with his son and discussing Nietzsche with the psychic postman. Jets fly overhead. Suddenly we learn that the world is liable to be blown up. Alexander makes the vow that he will live in isolation and silence if Armageddon can be avoided. The postman tells him that he can save the world by sleeping with his Icelandic, white-witch maid. Under the cover of darkness, he borrows the postman's bicycle and pays a visit to the maid. He threatens that he will commit suicide unless he is allowed to make love to her. She accedes to his wish, and the couple literally take off, hovering several feet above her bed. The next morning, he sets fire to the family house and is taken away in an ambulance.

Tarkovsky's Swedish landscape serves him well. At the beginning of the film, before there are any intimations of nuclear disaster, it seems pastoral, idyllic, a country retreat where a foolish, fond father can play with his son, But, with the possibility of destruction, the landscape itself becomes threatening: it is transformed into bare, denuded wasteland. (Mud, water, and fire are familiar motifs in all Tarkovsky's work.) Parallels with Bergman are obvious. The Swede dealt with a similar theme in *Shame* (1968) in which two concert musicians, Max Von Sydow and Liv Ullmann, are caught up in civil war. Alexander in *The Sacrifice* is not too far removed from the old doctor of *Wild Strawberries* (1957). Both are Prospero-like figures, half estranged from their families, confronted with death, ruminating over the past. *The Sacrifice* is photographed by the celebrated "master of light," Sven Nykvist, who has also worked extensively with Bergman. (Apparently, Nykvist initially had difficulties with Tarkovsky; he felt that the Russian, who was always first to operate the camera, and who dictated exactly what he wanted within the frame, was doing his job for him.) Whatever reservations one might have about its story and about Tarkovsky's homespun homilies on life and art (this is a wordy film: the soundtrack is largely composed of monologues) there can be no doubting its visual beauty. The long, lingering pans, the slow tracking shots, the use of natural light in the interior scenes, the black and white images of the devastated city, and, above all, the mise-en-scène, make the film a pleasure to watch. A characteristic Tarkovsky conceit is to make the movement of objects, the action in the external world, correspond to human emotion. To put it simply, every event, the planting of the tree, the burning of the house, the love making, are not straightforwardly physical, but are manifstations, visual metaphors of the characters' feelings. When the planes fly overhead, all the furniture in the house begins to quake. This seems plausible. A big cabinet is rattling. Noise vibration might cause this to happen. Out of the cabinet, in a gentle slow motion, a jar of milk falls, crashes on the floor, breaks into fragments. Why one is tempted to ask, is milk kept in a cabinet anyway? Wouldn't it be better off in the kitchen? Yet the image of the fracture of the jar encapsulates the burgeoning panic of every character.

The Scandinavian country house, familial discord, and 19th-century costume lend the film a theatrical, naturalistic air. Despite this, Tarkovsky is not overly concerned with formal realism. Events are not meant to make sense. They are supposed to have a dreamlike quality. If an ambulance arrives in the middle of nowhere without anybody having telephoned it, if lovers levitate, if the family home is burnt down for a bet, all is perfectly consistent. Were it not for the film's self-important gravity, if there were a little humour to leaven proceedings, we might be watching something surrealist, something akin to a film by Buñuel (whom Tarkovsky was known to admire) or to a canvas by Chagall. Characterization is weak. There is a squabbling family, with unfilial sons and daughters, potential Gonerils and Regans, and there is Alexander's neurotic wife, Adelaide. But Tarkovsky is not interested in familial relationships. The only perspective we are offered is that of Alexander. The psychic postman, whose bicycle seems to be the film's sole comic motif, the son, who is idealized, and the white-witch maid are not embroiled in the materialistic world: they help Alexander resolve this metaphysical anxieties. In the end, *The Sacrifice* is a solipcist's film; one man's redemption seems more important than the fact that a whole world has avoided calamity. It is perhaps instructive to note that, at the time of his death, Tarkovsky was working on a *Hamlet* script.

—G. C. Macnab

OKTIABR

(October; Ten Days That Shook the World)

USSR, 1928

Director: Sergei Eisenstein

Production: Sovkino; black and white, 35mm, silent; running time: 103 minutes; length: 2000–2200 meters, originally 3800 meters and then 2800 meters in the U.S.S.R. Released 20 January 1928. Re-released with musical soundtrack by Shostakovitch, 1966, Paris. Filmed in spring 1927 in Leningrad.

Scenario: Sergei Eisenstein with Grigori Alexwithrov; from *10 Days That Shook the World* by John Reed; **associate director:** Grigori Alexwithrov; **photography:** Edward Tisse; **production designer:** Vladimir Kovrighine; **camera assistants:** Vladimir Nilsin and Vladimir Popov.

Cast: V. Nikandrov (*Lenin*); N. Popov (*Kerensky*); Boris Lianov (*Minister Tereshchenko*); Chibisov (*Minister Kishkin*); Smelsky (*Minister Verderevsky*); N. Podvoisky (*Bolshevik Podvoisky*); Edward Tisse (*A German*).

Publications

Script:

Eisenstein, Sergei, *Octobre*, edited by Jacques Charriere, Paris, 1971; also in *Eisenstein: 3 Films*, edited by Jay Leyda, New York, 1974, and *October and Alexander Nevsky*, edited by Leyda, New York, 1984.

Books:

Rotha, Paul, John Grierson, and Ivor Montagu, *Eisenstein*, London 1948.

Seton, Marie, *Eisenstein*, London, 1957.

Leyda, Jay, *Kino: A History of the Russian and Soviet Film*, New York, 1960.

Martin, Marcel, *Panorama du cinéma soviétique*, Brussels, 1960.
Sergei Eisenstein: Künstler der Revolution, Berlin, 1960.
Nizhny, Vladimir, *Lessons with Eisenstein*, London, 1962.
Konlecher and Kubelka, editors, *Serjei Michailowitsch Eisenstein*, Vienna, 1964.
Eisenstein, Sergei, *Film Form and Film Sense*, New York, 1965.
Barna, Yon, *Eisenstein*, Bloomington, Indiana, 1973.
Fernandez, Dominique, *Eisenstein*, Paris, 1975.
Klinowski, Jacek, and Adam Garbicz, editors, *Cinema, The Magic Vehicle: A Guide to its Achievement: Journey One: The Cinema Through 1949*, Metuchen, New Jersey, 1975.
Ropars-Wuilleumier, Marie-Claire, and others, *Octobre: Ecriture et idéologie*, Paris, 1976.
Swallow, Norman, *Eisenstein: A Documentary Portrait*, New York, 1977.
Aumont, Jacques, *Montage Eisenstein*, Paris, 1979; London, 1987.
Ropars-Wuilleumier, Marie-Claire, and others, *La Revolution figurée*, Paris, 1979.
Taylor, Richard, *Soviet Russia and Nazi Germany*, London, 1979.
Leyda, Jay, and Zina Vignow, *Eisenstein at Work*, New York, 1982.
Eisenstein, Sergei M., *Immoral Memories: An Autobiography*, Boston, 1983.
Marshall, Herbert, *Masters of the Soviet Cinema: Crippled Creative Biographies*, London, 1983.
Polan, Dana B., *The Political Language of Film and the Avant-Garde*, Ann Arbor, Michigan, 1985.
Eisenstein, Sergei M., *Selected Works, Volume 1: Writings 1922–1934*, edited by Richard Taylor, London, 1988.
Bordwell, David, *The Cinema of Eisenstein*, Cambridge, 1993.
Goodwin, James, *Eisenstein, Cinema, & History*, Champaign, 1993.
Lovgren, Hakan, editor, *Eisenstein's Labyrinth: Aspects of a Cinematic Synthesis of the Arts*, Philadelphia, 1996.
Taylor, Richard, editor, *The Eisenstein Reader,* Bloomington, 1998.
Bergan, Ronald, *Sergei Eisenstein: A Life in Conflict*, New York, 1999.

Articles:

Hall, Mordaunt, in *New York Times*, 3 November 1928.
Variety (New York), 7 November 1928.
Close Up (London), December 1928.
Barr, Alfred, Jr., ''Sergei Michailovitch Eisenstein,'' in *Arts* (New York), December 1928.
Grigs, Derick, and Guy Cote, in *Sight and Sound* (London), November-December, 1951.
Lachize, Samuel, ''Quand le souffle de *l'histoire passe par le baroque cinématographique*,'' in *Avant-Scène du Cinéma* (Paris), October 1967.
Macdonald, Dwight, ''Eisenstein and Pudovkin in the 20s,'' and ''Soviet Cinema, 1930–1940,'' in *On Movies*, New York, 1969.
Durgnat, Raymond, in *Films and Filming* (London), March 1970.
Brik, O. M., and V. B. Sklovskij, in *Screen* (London), Winter 1971–72.
Argan, G. C., ''Storia non come memoria ma presente a realtà in atto,'' in *Cinema Nuovo* (Turin), January-February 1972.
Simsolo, Noël, in *Image et Son* (Paris), March 1972.
Lagny, M., Marie-Claire Ropars-Wuilleumier, and Pierre Sorlin, ''*Octobre*: Quelle histoire?'' in *Image et Son* (Paris), December 1976.
Sperber, M., ''Eisenstein's *October*,'' in *Jump Cut* (Berkeley), March 1977.
Marie, M., ''La Lettre et le cinematographe,'' in *Image et Son* (Paris, April 1977.
Meisel, E., in *Filmihullu* (Helsinki), no. 5, 1977.
Eisenstein, Sergei, ''Das russische Volk filmt,'' in *Film und Fernsehen* (Berlin), January 1978.
Ropars-Wuilleumier, Marie-Claire, ''The Function of Metaphor in Eisenstein's *October*,'' in *Film Criticism* (Meadville, Pennsylvania), Winter-Spring 1978.
Berg, Charles, in *Cinema Texas Program Notes* (Austin), 14 February 1978.
Goodwin, J., ''Eisenstein: Ideology and Intellectual Cinema,'' in *Quarterly Review of Film Studies* (New York), Spring 1978.
Ropars-Wuilleumier, Marie-Claire, ''The Overture of *October*,'' in *Enclitic* (Minneapolis), Autumn 1978 and Spring 1979.
Bukatman, S., ''Battles with Songs: The Soviet Historical Film and Historical Document,'' in *Persistence of Vision* (Maspeth, New York), Summer 1986.
Mayne, J., ''Soviet Film Montage and the Woman Question,'' in *Camera Obscura* (Bloomington), no. 19, January 1989.
Kenez, Peter, ''Film Reviews: *October* (*Octiabr'*) Directed by Sergei Eisenstein,'' in *The Russian Review* (Columbus), vol. 50, no. 4, October 1991.
Dufour, Dirk, ''Revolutie? Zwierige wals tussen fictie en werkelijkheid,'' in *Film en Televisie + Video* (Brussels), no. 427, December 1992.
Sorensen, J., ''*Lef*, Eisenstein, and the Politics of Form,'' in *Film Criticism* (Meadville), vol. 19, no. 2, 1994/1995.

* * *

In 1927 Sergei Eisenstein, along with V. I. Pudovkin and Esther Shub, was commissioned to make a film to contribute to the celebration commemorating the tenth anniversary of the 1917 Revolution. Eisenstein and Edward Tisse were called away from the production of *The General Line* to begin work on the anniversary project. The film that resulted, *Oktiabr*, was not the anticipated popular successor to *Potemkin* but instead a bold experiment in intellectual montage.

Preparation for *Oktiabr* included research into newspaper reports, news photographs, newsreels, Esther Shub's footage taken in Petrograd during the revolution, and historical memoirs. An additional source was John Reed's *Ten Days That Shook The World* (the title used for the version of *Oktiabr* prepared for release abroad). The initial scenario covered the events leading up to the 1917 Revolution through post-Civil War reconstruction. Although the scope of the film was eventually narrowed, an abundance of information remains, which according to critics both in the Soviet Union and abroad was still too extensive. Much of the power of the film is lost because the viewer is faced with not only too much detail, but also with too large a vista—too large a vision to comprehend.

Portions of the film brought criticism even before *Oktiabr* was screened. As Eisenstein explains, ''the timing was accidentally unfortunate. A crisis in the Communist Party and among Government leaders coincided with the completion of a film in which both the now-divided factions were unmistakably represented on the screen.'' The two factions Eisenstein referred to were the government group headed by Joseph Stalin and the Opposition led by Leon Trotsky. As the date for the anniversary celebration approached, Stalin's offensive against Trotsky and the Opposition reached its peak. Eisenstein, as Yon Barna states, was ''expected (by Stalin) to take account of the 'new historical facts.''' As a result, only certain select reels of *Oktiabr* were ready to be screened at the jubilee on November 7, 1927. The film was re-edited and publicly released in March of 1928. Although scenes of Opposition leaders were cut from the film, Trotsky does appear in two scenes of the final version of *Oktiabr*, but not as a significant figure.

Government leaders, critics, and the general public were anticipating another *Potemkin* from Eisenstein. *Oktiabr*, however, never approached the popular appeal of that previous work. Reaction inside Russia to the completed version of the film was mixed. *Oktiabr* was praised as being the beginning of the Soviet cinema art of the future and also criticized as being too abstract for the masses—the working-class population—to comprehend, often within the same review. The elements of typage and intellectual montage, the main reasons for both the praise and the condemnation of *Oktiabr*, were first developed in *Potemkin* and are basic to Eisenstein's theory of the ''montage of attractions.''

Typage, a concept originating with Vsevolod Meyerhold, involves the use of persons whose physical appearance conveys the personality or spirit of a character as opposed to using trained actors. Through the use of typage, Eisenstein wanted to create visual impressions of models or representative figures so perfect that an audience could know the character at the first glimpse of him on the screen. The use of typage to represent Lenin on the screen in *Oktiabr* brought much criticism. The worker chosen to play Lenin, V. Nikandrov, resembled him physically but was criticized for an empty portrayal that did not convey the inner character of the man. Rather than a poor representation, however, this use of typage seems to be an attempt by Eisenstein to create a model character that embodies the mass rather than a single individual acting apart from the collective. (Eisenstein is more successful with this particular use of typage in *Alexander Nevsky.*) Eisenstein's contemporaries and critics since have argued that the symbolism was not comprehensible by the masses. Nevertheless, they did recognize Eisenstein's technique and purpose in the sequences in *Oktiabr* that are developed through intellectual montage.

Intellectual montage, the use of visual images to express abstract ideas, is the core of Eisenstein's film theory. The specific idea behind intellectual montage is that the juxtaposition of two separate images can convey an idea which is not represented by either of those images when viewed separately. Such sequences in *Oktiabr*, of which there are many, brought a wider range of responses from the film's reviewers. In one sequence, Eisenstein ridicules the concept of God through a series of symbolic deities in which a Baroque Christ figure is ultimately equated with a primitive idol. The idea of the gradual debasement of the Christ figure is conveyed through the relationships between the images of the deities and not by the individual images themselves. While acknowledging the artistic and cinematic value of this sequence and others like it (Kerensky's climb up the stairs leading to the Tsar's apartment, the association of Kerensky and Napoleon), reviewers criticized the fact that these sequences could not be interpreted by the masses. *Oktiabr* was commissioned to be part of the celebration of the proletarian revolution, but the proletariat could not understand the film.

—Marie Saeli

OLD CZECH LEGENDS

See **STARÉ POVÌSTI CISKÉ**

LOS OLVIDADOS

(The Young and the Damned)

Mexico, 1950

Director: Luis Buñuel

Production: Ultramar Films, SA for Tepeyac Studios; black and white, 35mm; running time: 88 minutes; length: 8020 feet. Released 9 November 1950, Mexico. Filmed 6 February-9 March 1950 in Mexico. Cost: budgeted at 450,000 pesos.

Producer: Oscar Dancigers; **screenplay:** Luis Buñuel, Luis Alcoriza and Oscar Dancigers; **photography:** Gabriel Figueroa; **editor:** Carlos Savage; **sound engineers:** Jesus Gonzalez and Jose B. Carles; **art director:** Edward Fitzgerald; **music:** Gustavo Pitaluga; **music arranger:** Rodolfo Halfter.

Cast: Estela Inda (*Marta, Pedro's mother*); Miguel Inclán (*Don Carmelo, the blind man*); Alfonso Mejia (*Pedro*); Roberto Cobo (*Jaibo*); Alma Delia Fuentes (*Meche*); Francisco Jambrina (*Farm school director*); Mario Ramírez (*Big-Eyes*); Efrain Arauz (*Pockface*); Javier Amezcua (*Julian*); Jesus Garcia Navarro (*Julian's father*); Jorge Perez (''*Pelón*''); Sergio Villareal.

Award: Cannes Film Festival, Best Director, 1951.

Publications

Script:

Buñuel, Luis, Luis Alcoriza, and Oscar Dancigers, *Exterminating Angel, Nazarin, and Los Olvidados: Three Films by Luis Buñuel*, London, 1972; also in *The Exterminating Angel and Los Olvidados*, London, 1984.

Books:

Kyrou, Ado, *Luis Buñuel*, Paris, 1962.
Lizalde, Eduardo, *Luis Buñuel: Odisea del demoledor*, Mexico City, 1962.
Estève, Michel, editor, *Luis Buñuel*, Paris, 1962–63.
Grange, Frédéric, and Charles Rebolledo, *Luis Buñuel*, Paris, 1964.
Goetz, Alice, and Helmut Banz, *Luis Buñuel: Eine Dokumentation*, Munich, 1965.
Buache, Freddy, *Luis Buñuel*, Lausanne, 1970.
Alcalá, Manuel, *Buñuel (cine e ideología)*, Madrid, 1973.
Buache, Freddy, *The Cinema of Luis Buñuel*, London, 1973.
Cesarman, Fernando, *El ojo de Buñuel*, Barcelona, 1976.
Drouzy, M., *Luis Buñuel, architects du rêve*, Paris, 1978.
Durgnat, Raymond, *Luis Buñuel*, Berkeley, 1978.
Mellen, Joan, editor, *The World of Luis Buñuel: Essays in Criticism*, New York, 1978.

Los olvidados

Cameron, Ian, *Luis Buñuel*, Berkeley, 1979.
Higginbottom, Virginia, *Luis Buñuel*, Boston, 1979.
Bazin, André, *The Cinema of Cruelty: From Buñuel to Hitchcock*, New York, 1982.
Edwards, Gwynne, *The Discreet Art of Luis Buñuel: A Reading of his Films*, London, 1982, 1991.
Buñuel, Luis, *My Last Breath*, London, 1983.
Rees, Margaret A., editor, *Luis Buñuel: A Symposium*, Leeds, 1983.
Lefèvre, Raymond, *Luis Buñuel*, Paris, 1984.
Vidal, Agustin Sanchez, *Luis Buñuel: Obra Cinematografica*, Madrid, 1984.
Aub, Max, *Conversaciones con Buñuel: Seguidas de 45 entrevistas con familiares, amigos y colaboradores del cineasta aragones*, Madrid, 1985.
Bertelli, Pino, *Buñuel: L' arma dello scandalo: L' anarchia nel cinema di Luis Buñuel*, Turin, 1985.
Oms, Marcel, *Don Luis Buñuel*, Paris, 1985.
De la Colina, Jose, and Tomás Pérez Turrent, *Luis Buñuel: Prohibido asomarse al interior*, Mexico City, 1986.
Sandro, Paul, *Diversions of Pleasure: Luis Buñuel and the Crises of Desire*, Columbus, Ohio, 1987.
Williams, Linda, *Figures of Desire: A Theory and Analysis of Surrealist Film*, Berkeley, 1992.
De la Colina, Jose, and Tomas P. Turrent, *Objects of Desire: Conversations with Luis Buñuel*, New York, 1994.
Evans, Peter William, *The Films of Luis Buñuel: Subjectivity and Desire*, New York, 1995.
Baxter, John, *Buñuel*, New York, 1999.
Almeida, Diane M., *The Esperpento Tradition in the Works of Ramón del Valle Inclán and Luis Buñuel*, Lewiston, 2000.

Articles:

Doniol-Valcroze, Jacques, in *Cahiers du Cinéma* (Paris), December 1951.
Kast, Pierre, ''Une fonction de constat: notes sur l'oeuvre de Buñuel,'' in *Cahiers du Cinéma* (Paris), December 1951.
Barcia, J. Rubia, ''Luis Buñuel's *Los Olvidados*,'' in *Quarterly of Film, Radio, and Television* (Berkeley), Summer 1953.
Richardson, Tony, ''The Films of Luis Buñuel,'' in *Sight and Sound* (London), January-March 1954.
Cinemages (New York), no. 1, 1955.

Garcia Riera, Emilio, ''The Eternal Rebellion of Luis Buñuel,'' in *Film Culture* (New York), no. 21, 1960.
Dale, R. C., in *Classics of the Film*, Madison, Wisconsin, 1965.
Milne, Tom, ''The Mexican Buñuel,'' in *Sight and Sound* (London), Winter 1965–66.
Hammond, Robert, ''Luis Alcoriza and the Films of Luis Buñuel,'' in *Film Heritage* (Dayton, Ohio), Fall 1965.
Harcourt, Peter, ''Luis Buñuel: Spaniard and Surrealist,'' in *Film Quarterly* (Berkeley), Spring 1967.
Cornand, André, ''Donner à voir,'' in *Avant-Scène du Cinéma* (Paris), June 1973.
Diaz, Torres, D., in *Cine Cubano* (Havana), nos. 78–80, 1973.
Lord, J., in *Lumière* (Melbourne), April-May 1974.
Dale, R. C., in *Movietone News* (Seattle), February 1975.
Fernández, Enriquè, ''A Recipe for Andalusian Chicken,'' in *Film Criticism* (Meadville, Pennsylvania), Winter-Spring 1978.
Contracampo (Madrid), October-November 1980.
Hoberman, J., ''Take Two: *Los Olvidados*,'' in *American Film* (Washington, D.C.), June 1983.
Rainer, Peter, ''*Los Olvidados/Nazarin*,'' in *American Film* (New York), vol. 14, no. 9, July 1989.
Biskind, Peter, ''New and Recommended: *Los Olvidados* Directed by Luis Buñuel, *Premiere* (New York), vol. 3, no. 1, September 1989.
Oms, M., ''Don Luis le Mexican,'' in *Cinemaction* (Conde-sur-Noireau, France), July 1990.
Schatzberg, Jerry, in *Positif* (Paris), no. 400, June 1994.
Pena, Richard, ''Que Viva Mexico: *Los Olvidados* (*The Young and the Damned*) Directed by Luis Buñuel,'' in *Film Comment* (New York), vol. 31, no. 6, November 1995.
Gaytan, F., ''*Los Olvidados* and Its Second Ending,'' in *Journal of Film Preservation* (Brussels), no. 54, April 1997.

* * *

Los olvidados was Luis Buñuel's favorite film, and the one with which he returned to mainstream motion picture directing after a 17-year hiatus. The film shocked many audiences for its pessimistic, unrelentingly realistic depiction of the futility in the lives of the abandoned children of Mexico City's slums. It is the first film of any reputation to present a realistic picture of what life was like in the Third World; its unequivocal soberness and topicality not only make it the prototype of Hector Babenco's *Pixote* and Yilmaz Guney's *Yol*, but allows it to stand on its own as a viable and searing indictment of society's ills.

Buñuel ended his exiled inactivity by signing a contract with Mexican producer Oscar Dancigers in 1947. The first film for Dancigers was *Gran casino*, ''a film with songs'' which proved unsuccessful; the second was the comedy, *El gran calavera*. The success of the latter encouraged Danciger to back Buñuel's production of *Los olvidados*, a film which Buñuel said he had to make. The budget was a meagre 450,000 pesos.

The idea for the film came from Buñuel's exploration of Mexico City where he witnessed the ''wretchedness in which many of its inhabitants lived.'' He researched the project in the files of a local reformatory and explained, ''My film is entirely based on real cases. I tried to expose the wretched condition of the poor in real terms, because I loathe films that make the poor romantic and sweet.''

Using a combination of professional and non-professional actors, Buñuel focuses his story on the bond of power and duplicity between two young Mexican boys—Jaibo (Roberto Cobo), a hardened murderer, and Pedro (Alfonso Mejia), an innocent drawn into a life of crime by the cruelty of his environment. When Pedro's father abandons him, the boy is befriended by a ruthless, miserly blind beggar. Jaibo, recently escaped from reform school, robs and stones the beggar; soon after, Pedro sees Jaibo kill another youth who had informed on him. This shared experience leads to Jaibo becoming Pedro's mentor/master as the innocent boy falls into petty thievery. Imprisoned for stealing a knife, Pedro is tested by his liberal school director and sent on the outside on an errand. He encounters Jaibo who robs and kills him; Jaibo in turn is shot down by the police. Buñuel ends his film with the devastating scene of Pedro's body thrown into the sewer by Jaibo's grandfather.

Buñuel's semi-documentary approach is mediated somewhat by the picturesque, studio-influenced cinematography of Gabriel Figueroa, but the penetrating, unsentimental surrealism of Buñuel is omnipresent. In the forward to the film, Buñuel states: ''The task of finding a solution lies with the force of progress,'' and *Los olvidados* offers no romantic answers for the social ills he records. The film is not without Buñuel's sense of symbolism, however, as evidenced by Pedro's Oedipal dream sequence and Jaibo's dying hallucinations.

Los olvidados earned Buñuel the Best Director prize at the Cannes Film Festival and was greeted with astonishment by critics internationally. André Bazin called it ''a film that lashes the mind like a red-hot iron and leaves one's conscience no opportunity for rest.'' Its pessimism and violence was too much for the *New York Times*'s conservative Bosley Crowther. Released in the U.S. under the title, *The Young and the Damned*, Crowther called the film ''brutal and unrelenting'' and added, ''Although made with meticulous realism and unquestioned fidelity to facts, its qualifications as dramatic entertainment—or even social reportage—are dim.'' Obviously Crowther missed the point of the film entirely, for while Buñuel wisely chose not to soften his interpretation by providing pat answers, the abiding message here, as in much of his work, is, as his biographer, Francisco Aranda states, ''By creating a society which is not criminal, we shall ourselves cease to be criminal.''

—Ronald Bowers

OLYMPIA

(Olympische Spiele 1936)

Germany, 1938

Director: Leni Riefenstahl

Production: Tobis Cinema (Germany); black and white, 35mm; running time: Part I. 100 minutes, and Part II, 105 minutes; length: Riefenstahl's final cut was 18,000 feet. Released 20 April 1938. Filmed 20 July-4 August 1936 in Berlin at the Olympic Games. Cost 2.2 million Reichsmarks (approximately $523,810 in 1938).

Producers: Walter Traut and Walter Grosskopf; **Screenplay:** Leni Riefenstahl; **photography:** Leni Riefenstahl, Hans Ertl, Walter Frentz, Guzzi Lantschner, Kurt Neubert, Hans Scheib, Willy Zielk; **editor:** Leni Riefenstahl; **music:** Herbert Windt.

Olympia

Awards: Biennale Film Festival, Venice, 1st Prize, 1938; State Prize (Staatspreis) of Germany, 1938; Polar Prize, Sweden, n.d.

Publications

Books:

Riefenstahl, Leni, *Schönheit im Olympischen Kampf*, Berlin, 1937.
Riefenstahl, Leni, *Notes on the Making of Olympia*, London, 1958.
Sarris, Andrew, editor, *Interviews with Film Directors*, Indianapolis, Indiana, 1967.
Mandell, Richard, D., *Nazi Olympics*, 1971.
Stewart, Hull, David, *Film in the Third Reich*, Berkeley, 1971.
Young, Vernon, *On Film: Unpopular Essays on a Popular Art*, Chicago, 1972.
Barsam, Richard, *Nonfiction Film: A Critical History*, New York, 1973.
Barnouw, Erik, *Documentary: A History of the Non-Fiction Film*, New York, 1974.
Johnson, Lincoln, F., *Film: Space, Time, Light, and Sound*, 1974.
Infield, Glenn, *Leni Riefenstahl, The Fallen Film Goddess*, New York, 1976.
Ford, Charles, *Leni Riefenstahl*, Paris, 1978.
Infield, Glenn, *Leni Riefenstahl et le 3e Reich*, Paris, 1978.
Berg-Pan, Renata, *Leni Riefenstahl*, Boston, 1980.
Welch, David, *Propaganda and the German Cinema*, Oxford, 1983; revised edition, 1987.
Graham, Cooper C., *Leni Riefenstahl and Olympia*, Metuchen, New Jersey, 1986.
Downing, Taylor, *Olympia*, London, 1992.
Kubler, Manon, *Olympia*, Caracas, 1992.
Riefenstahl, Leni, *Olympia*, New York, 1994.
Riefenstahl, Leni, *Leni Riefenstahl: A Memoir*, New York, 1995.
Salkeld, Audrey, *Portrait of Leni Riefenstahl*, London, 1996.
Hinton, David B., *The Films of Leni Riefenstahl*, Lanham, 2000.

Articles:

New York Times, 9 March 1940.
Monthly Film Bulletin (London), no. 175, 1948.

Gunston, D., ''Leni Riefenstahl,'' in *Film Quarterly* (Berkeley), Fall, 1960.

Gardner, Robert, in *Film Comment* (New York), Winter, 1965.

''Statement on Sarris-Gessner Quarrel about *Olympia*,'' in *Film Comment* (New York), Fall, 1967.

Swallow, Norman, interview with Riefenstahl on *Olympia*, in *Listener* (London), 19 September 1968.

Corliss, Richard, ''Leni Riefenstahl: A Bibliography,'' in *Film Heritage* (Dayton, Ohio), Fall 1969.

Richards, J., ''Leni Riefenstahl: Style and Structure,'' in *Silent Pictures* (London), Autumn 1970.

Barsam, Richard, ''Leni Riefenstahl: Artifice and Truth in a World Apart,'' in *Film Comment* (New York), November-December 1973.

''*Olympia* Issue'' of *Film Culture* (New York), Spring 1973.

Barkhausen, H., ''Footnote to the History of Riefenstahl's *Olympia*,'' in *Film Quarterly* (Berkeley), Fall 1974.

Riefenstahl, Leni, ''Notes on the Making of *Olympia*,'' in *Nonfiction Film: Theory and Criticism*, edited by Richard Barsam, New York, 1976.

Interview with Riefenstahl, in *Montreal Star*, 20 July 1976.

Vaughan, Dai, ''Berlin versus Tokyo,'' in *Sight and Sound* (London), Autumn 1977.

Tyler, Parker, ''Leni Riefenstahl's *Olympia*,'' in *The Documentary Tradition*, edited by Lewis Jacobs, 2nd edition, New York, 1979.

Horton, W. J., ''Capturing the Olympics,'' in *American Cinematographer* (Los Angeles), July 1984.

''American Intelligence Report on Leni Riefenstahl: May 30th, 1945,'' in *Film Culture* (New York), no. 77, 1992.

Foldenyi, F. L., ''Felhotlen almok nyomaszto vilaga,'' in *Filmvilag* (Budapest), no. 2, 1993.

Graham, C. C., ''*Olympia* in America, 1938: Leni Riefenstahl, Hollywood, and the Kristallnacht,'' in *Historical Journal of Film, Radio and Television* (Abingdon, Oxfordshire), no. 4, 1993.

Rose, Charlie, ''Film Scholars Debate Riefenstahl,'' in *Film Culture* (New York), no. 79, Winter 1996.

Hitchens, Gordon, ''Recent Riefenstahl Activities and a Commentary on Nazi Propaganda Filmmaking,'' in *Film Culture* (New York), no. 79, Winter 1996.

von Dassanowsky, Robert, ''Entertaining the Third Reich: Illusions of Wholeness in Nazi Cinema,'' in *The Germanic Review* (Washington), vol. 72, no. 4, Fall 1997.

* * *

Any film of the Olympic Games would be useless, Goebbels maintained, unless it could be shown a few days after they ended. Who could be interested after the excitement and the memory faded? Fortunately, director Leni Riefenstahl, with Hitler's approval, overrode any objections with astonishing results. While *Olympia* is a superb example of the sports documentary, it also stands on its own as an aesthetic achievement.

The fact its creator is a controversial figure whose alliance with the Nazi Party is still held up to scrutiny, and still as coolly contested by Riefenstahl, forces one to examine the boundaries of ''artistic integrity'' versus a very fundamental morality. One cannot view *Olympia* simply as film, or simply as propaganda.

There was almost as much preparation for *Olympia*'s shooting as for the Games themselves. For the best angles, uninterrupted by distracted participants, two steel towers were built in the stadium infield, and pits were dug for the sprinting and jumping events. Scaffolding platforms caught the rowing teams in their winning strokes thanks to cameras pulled along tracks by car. Hundreds of technicians and advisors were brought in, as were some of the best camera people. Several cameramen had previously worked with Riefenstahl on her earlier film, *Triumph of the Will*, a stunning record of Hitler's Nazi rallies, as well as the ''mountain'' films by Arnold Fanck that she had starred in. Despite Riefenstahl's total control, much of the look of *Olympia* was due to people such as Hans Ertl, for the celebrated diving sequences, Walter Frentz for the marathon, yachting events and the romantic opening scenes in Part II, and Gustav Lantschner for the gymnastic, equestrian and some of the diving.

Three kinds of film stock were used; one was good for half-tones, one flattering to outdoor scenes, a third for architecture. Over ten hours of film were shot each day during the 16-day games. Including training footage (incorporated into the film) and reshooting (some winning athletes were delighted to recreate their finest moments), there were 250 hours for her, alone, to edit. Logging the film took a month, viewing the rushes more than two. According to the director, editing took a year and a half: ''It was cut like a symphony . . . according to laws of aesthetics and rhythm.'' Adding the sound took another six weeks. It must be remembered that in 1936–37, there were no zoom lenses, no soundproof cameras, no computer mixing—merely what was, to us now, primitive technology.

After nearly three years, Riefenstahl was finished. Her powerful 12-minute open-sequence in Part I evokes the classical past, an analogy dear to Nazi propagandist hearts. Classical ruins—ironically to be come Nazi ones—Wagnerian strains, whirling clouds and Greek statues; together with the human body celebrated in motion via the discus throw, the shot-put and the javelin, the epic stance is firmly established. The international foundation of the games was exploited to produce a propaganda climax; in a series of shots, the torch aloft, carried from Greece, is ignited, the flame returns to life, only in Germany, only under Hitler, who pronounces the games open. With lab effects, the results are almost religious.

The high jump becomes a filmic ballet, with slow-motion, different camera angles and cross-cuts. Then follow the discus, hurdles, throwing the hammer, pole vaulting, relays. The long-jump is one of the more interesting pieces in the film, having a personal dimension. The competition between Aryan Lutz Long and American (and, gallingly for the games hosts) black star Jesse Owens. Riefenstahl, sensitive to the symbolism, accomplishes the drama effectively, incorporating the tension in the situation, the personal drive of the two contestants with honed slow-motion camera work, fast audience reaction shots (significantly, not Hitler's who rarely appears applauding any but German athletes), the sharp timing. Primarily, her camera is not aimed at documenting history-making records, but at the athletes themselves. Interestingly, more of the slow-motion effect, with the result of making the bodies almost superhuman, is aimed at the German athletes, whether or not they win, although the film's content is not, presumably, out to confirm the superiority of the ''master'' race.

The bodies seem to add another dimension, almost bursting out of the flat screen, which is seemingly barely able to contain the exuberance, the strength. And while many sports event have, by their nature, repeated actions by series of contestants, Riefenstahl films each in a slightly different manner to keep the movements fresh by her choreography.

The handling of the marathon, the antidote to any possible flagging attention, is the high point of Part I. Taylor Downing, in her book *Olympia* refers to this segment, rightly, as "a film within a film. It creates a statement about achievement and endurance, and takes the viewer right inside the race itself. Rarely has a marathon been treated with such imagination on film." Using the distorted shadows of the runners, interspersed with shots of feet pounding the pavement, leg muscles pulsing, the viewer's own body tenses, feeling the strength flowing from, then, as the runners feel the exhaustion, draining out of their bodies; each frame fairly courses with energy, and with the constant drive. The marathon is not an event, in Riefenstahl's camera eye, it is each athlete's personal trial.

One of Riefenstahl's gifts is her ability to manipulate the range of responses (within the film, within the audience) through her use of music, content, editing and tone, not only within each individual sequence but the combining/contrasting of them for the bigger effect. For example, the dramatic rowing sequence is then followed by the occasionally humorous riding event; the result is a dynamic, *filmic* flow. In Part II, she begins sensuously, with reflected pools of mist-layered water, the tiny details such as a bird's wing in flight, a drop of water trembling on a spider web, with violin music threading through shots of muscled male bodies bathing, birching one another . . . Aryan Fatherland and Mother Nature in harmony. She cuts—like a hit of ice—to the rousing ceremony march, then on to physical training, as the different nationalities get into their stride for the bustling day's events. A shot of mass gymnastics is a long pan; tens of thousands of women in endless regimented lines do push-ups. The result is oddly dehumanising; like Busby Berkeley's routines, individual grace is transformed into a pop design. Here the effect is one of uneasiness, not thrill.

Part II also ends with a crescendo. The diving sequence is justly the most celebrated in the film, even in film history. Camera people Ertl and Dorothy Poynton-Hill had to adjust for distance during the dive, change exposure the second the diver hit the water, then reverse the process when s/he resurfaced. An elevator-type device mounted by the pool insured a fluid movement. The divers become suspended, as the camera seemingly redefines the physical laws of motion, of space and of time. The divers appear in the sky from nowhere, defying gravity; in slow-motion, they become surreal. Bodies twist, twirl, arc and never descend. No commentary mars the effect. Once again, no matter how beautiful each movement, repetition with each contestant could visually numb. To avoid that, Riefenstahl matched each shot with the movement of the dive preceding it; at the end, to the dive following. Such grace shows the director at her best; one forgets the background outside the realm of pure artistry.

She has perennially maintained her political innocence, reminding us of the gold medal the Olympic Committee awarded her in 1948. To many people, her stance rings hollow. *Olympia* is a stunning, and reasonably accurate account of the games. However, she was only independent of the propaganda ministry because of Hitler's personal involvement. It partly transcends politics, but it was established for political motives for political propaganda. *Olympia* is not a product of the political naif (she would "borrow" a group of gypsies from a nearby concentration camp for a later film — then return them when she was through), but a brilliant, ambitious director who wanted her work seen. Genius can work both ways.

—Jane Ehrlich

ON THE SUBJECT OF NICE

See **A PROPOS DE NICE**

ON THE TOWN

USA, 1949

Directors: Stanley Donen and Gene Kelly

Production: Metro-Goldwyn-Mayer Picture Corp.; Technicolor, 35mm; running time: 98 minutes. Released 1949. Filmed in MGM studios and some location shots in New York City.

Producer: Arthur Freed; **screenplay:** Adolph Green and Betty Comden, from the musical play by Comden and Green based on an idea by Jerome Robbins; **photographer:** Harold Rossen; **editor:** Ralph E. Winters; **art directors:** Cedric Gibbons and Jack Martin Smith; **music director:** Lennie Hayton; **songs:** Roger Edens, Adolph Green, and Betty Comden; **additional original music:** Leonard Bernstein; **orchestrations:** Conrad Salinger; **vocal arrangements:** Saul Chaplin; **costume designer:** Helen Rose; **choreography:** Gene Kelly and Stanley Donen.

Cast: Gene Kelly (*Gabey*); Frank Sinatra (*Chip*); Betty Garrett (*Brunhilde Esterhazy*); Ann Miller (*Claire Huddesen*); Jules Munshin (*Ozzie*); Vera-Ellen (*Ivy Smith*).

Award: Oscar for Music-Scoring of a Musical Picture, 1949.

Publications

Books:

Burton, Jack, *The Blue Book of Hollywood Musicals*, New York, 1953.
Griffith, Richard, *The Cinema of Gene Kelly*, New York, 1962.
Springer, John, *All Talking, All Singing, All Dancing*, New York, 1966.
Kobal, John, *Gotta Sing, Gotta Dance: A Pictorial History of Film Musicals*, New York, 1970.
Lonstein, Albert I. and Vito R. Marino, *The Compleat Sinatra*, New York, 1970.
Ringgold, Gene, and Clifford McCarty, *The Films of Frank Sinatra*, New York, 1971.
Thomas, Lawrence B., *The MGM Years*, New York, 1972.
Stern, Lee Edward, *The Movie Musical*, New York, 1974.
Hirschhorn, Clive, *Gene Kelly*, Chicago, 1975; revised edition, London, 1984.
Charness, Casey, *Hollywood Cine-Dance: A Description of the Interrelationship of Camera Work and Choreography in the Films of Stanley Donen and Gene Kelly*, Ann Arbor, Michigan, 1978.
Altman, Rick, editor, *Genre: The Musical*, London, 1981.
Delameter, James, *Dance in the Hollywood Musical*, Ann Arbor, Michigan, 1981.

On the Town

Feuer, Jane, *The Hollywood Musical*, London, 1982.
Casper, Joseph Andrew, *Stanley Donen*, Metuchen, New Jersey, 1985.
Altman, Rick, *The American Film Musical*, London, 1989.
Silverman, Stephen M., *Dancing on the Ceiling: Stanley Donen and His Movies*, New York, 1996.
Yudkoff, Alvin, *Gene Kelly: A Life of Dance and Dreams*, New York, 1999.

Articles:

Variety (New York), 7 December 1949.
New York Times, 9 December 1949.
Time (New York, 2 January 1950.
Knight, Arthur, ''From Dance to Film Director,'' in *Dance* (New York), August 1954.
Freed, Arthur, ''Making Musicals,'' in *Films and Filming* (London), January 1956.
Johnson, Albert, ''The 10th Muse in San Francisco,'' in *Sight and Sound* (London), Summer 1956.
Knight, Arthur, ''Dance in the Movies,'' in *Dance* (New York), October 1958.
Luft, Herbert, ''Donen at Work,'' in *Films in Review* (New York), February 1961.
Behlmer, Rudy, ''Gene Kelly,'' in *Films in Review* (New York), January, 1964.
Cutts, John, ''Dancer, Actor, Director,'' in *Films and Filming* (London), August and September 1964.
Lloyd, P., ''Stanley Donen,'' in *Brighton Film Review*, March 1970.
Lucas, Blake, ''On the Town,'' in *Magill's Survey of Cinema 3*, Englewood Cliffs, New Jersey, 1980.
Telotte, J. P. ''Ideology and the Kelly-Donen Musicals,'' in *Film Criticism* (Meadville, Pennsylvania), Spring 1984.
Jousse, T., and N. Saada, ''Un Americain à Paris,'' in *Cahiers du Cinéma* (Paris), October 1989.
Parkinson, D., ''Dancing in the Streets,'' in *Sight and Sound* (London), January 1993.
Séquences (Haute-Ville), no. 179, July-August 1995.
Reid, J.H., and G. Aachen, in *Reid's Film Index* (Wyong), no. 24, 1996.

* * *

On the Town may not be the greatest Hollywood musical ever produced; *Singin' in the Rain, The Wizard of Oz, The Band Wagon*, and several others would all garner consideration with *Singin' in the Rain* probably receiving the most attention. But *On the Town*, so unconventional for its time, is separate from the rest for several very special reasons, Most significantly, the film was partially shot outdoors; it instigated the use of increased on-location shooting for films of that genre. *On the Town* is one of the few features in which the talents of two filmmakers are so happily blended; Gene Kelly and Stanley Donen, the co-directors, later went on to make *Singin' in the Rain*, and *It's Always Fair Weather*. The songs and dances—modern, as well as ballet and tap—were not necessarily by and of themselves, but were related to character development and assisted in moving along the story.

On the Town was a ground-breaking property in the theater. It was initially presented as *Fancy Free*, a modernistic ballet with music by Leonard Bernstein and choreography by James Robbins, in which a trio of sailors dance their experiences while on shore leave. From this, Betty Comden and Adolph Green fashioned a musical comedy storyline, adding a book and lyrics. The resulting Broadway musical, which opened three days after Christmas, 1944, successfully united story, song, music, comedy and dance. In this respect, it is a theatrical first.

Both Kelly and Donen made their directorial debuts with the film version, released five years later with several songs eliminated and six new ones added. Kelly pressured MGM into allowing him to film in New York, though some of the musical and dance numbers were shot on sets. Donen allegedly worked mainly with the non-dance material. Kelly, Frank Sinatra and Jules Munshin, cast as the carefree sailors who partake in various romantic escapades while on 24-hour passes, cavort outdoors on Wall Street, near Grant's Tomb and the Statue of Liberty, in Rockefeller Center, the RCA Building, Central Park and, most memorably, while singing the praises of the city—''New York, New York, it's a wonderful town''—in the Brooklyn Navy Yard. The action never halts for an elaborate production number. Characterizations are established not only by dialogue and performance but in terms of song and dance: ''Prehistoric Man,'' set in the Museum of Natural History and tap-danced by anthropology student Ann Miller, displays her character's aggressiveness in pursuing Munshin; in ''Come Up to My Place,'' shy Sinatra finally succumbs to the charms of taxi driver Betty Garrett. These two women are certainly no standard, passive heroines, and are unusually liberated for their day by the manner in which they relate to, and compete with, men.

Most of those involved in the production had worked together previously in *Take Me Out to the Ball Game*. *Ball Game*'s credits include, in similar and different capacities from *On the Town*, Kelly, Sinatra, Munshin, Donen, Comden, Green, Cedric Gibbons, Roger Edens and Arthur Freed (who produced most of Kelly's musicals from *For Me and My Gal*, 1942, through *It's Always Fair Weather*, 1955, and allowed him creative freedom here). From *Anchors Away* (also featuring Kelly and Sinatra in the navy) to *Words and Music* (in which Kelly and Vera-Ellen are superb in the ''Slaughter on Tenth Avenue'' dance sequence), various combinations of *On the Town*'s talent collaborated on other films. Yet, excluding *Singin' in the Rain*, none is as delightful or memorable. Without question, these two are the key musicals of their period rather than the then more highly regarded *An American in Paris*, which won the Best Picture Academy Award.

On the Town is an energetic, effervescent combination of reality and fantasy. *West Side Story*, *Funny Girl*, and so many other subsequent musicals owe their very existence to the creativity and vision of Gene Kelly and company.

—Rob Edelman

ON THE WATERFRONT

USA, 1954

Director: Elia Kazan

Production: Horizon Productions; black and white, 35mm, Cinemascope; running time: 108 minutes. Released 1954, by Columbia Pictures Corp. Filmed in New York and Hoboken, New Jersey.

Producer: Sam Spiegel; **screenplay:** Budd Schulberg, from his original story suggested by a series of newpaper articles by Malcolm Johnson; **photographer:** Boris Kaufman; **editor:** Gene Milford; **art director:** Richard Day; **music score:** Leonard Bernstein.

Cast: Marlon Brando (*Terry Malloy*); Eva Marie Saint (*Edie Doyle*); Karl Malden (*Father Barry*); Lee J. Cobb (*Johnny Friendly*); Rod Steiger (*Charles Malloy*); John Hamilton (''*Pop*'' *Doyle*); Pat Henning (''*Kayo*'' *Dugan*); James Westerfield (*Big Mac*); Leif Erickson (*Glover*); Martin Balsam (*Gilette*); Tony Galento (*Truck*); Tami Maurriello (*Tillio*); Abe Simon (*Barney*); John Heldabrand (*Mott*); Rudy Bond (*Moose*); Thomas Handley (*Tommy*); Anne Hegira (*Mrs. Collins*); Don Blackman (*Luke*); Arthur Keegan (*Jimmy*); Barry Macollum (J.P.); Mike O'Dowd (*Specs*); Fred Gwynn (*Slim*); Pat Hingle (*Bartender*).

Awards: Oscars for Best Picture, Best Director, Best Actor (Brando), Best Supporting Actress (Saint), Best Writing-Story and Screenplay, Best Cinematography-Black and White, Best Art Direction-Black and White, and Best Editing, 1954; New York Film Critics Awards for Best Picture, Best Direction, and Best Actor (Brando); Venice Film Festival, Silver Prize, 1954.

Publications

Script:

Schulberg, Budd, *On the Waterfront*, New York, 1955; Carbondale, Illinois, 1980.

Books:

Tailleur, Roger, *Elia Kazan*, Paris, 1966; revised edition, 1971.
Ciment, Michel, *Kazan on Kazan*, New York, 1974.
Parish, James R., and Michael Pitts, *The Great Gangster Pictures*, Metuchen, New Jersey, 1976.
Davies, Philip, and Brian Neve, *Cinema, Politics, and Society in America*, Manchester, 1981.
Giannetti, Louis, *Masters of the American Cinema*, Englewood Cliffs, New Jersey, 1981.
Pauly, Thomas H., *An American Odyssey: Elia Kazan and American Culture*, Philadelphia, 1983.
Downing, David, *Marlon Brando*, London, 1984.
Carey, Gary, *Marlon Brando: The Only Contender*, London, 1985.
Michaels, Lloyd, *Elia Kazan: A Guide to References and Resources*, Boston, 1985.
Higham, Charles, *Brando: The Unauthorized Biography*, London, 1987.
Kazan, Elia, *Elia Kazan: A Life*, New York, 1988, 1989, 1997.

On the Waterfront

Grobel, Lawrence, *Conversations with Brando*, Lanham, 1993, 1999.

Brando, Marlon, *Songs My Mother Taught Me*, with Robert Lindsey, New York, 1994.

Malden, Karl, and Carla Malden, *When Do I Start?: A Memoir*, New York, 1997.

Girgus, Sam B., *Hollywood Renaissance: The Cinema of Democracy in the Era of Ford, Capra and Kazan*, New York, 1998.

Lobrutto, *Elia Kazan*, Old Tappan, 1999.

Young, Jeff, editor, *Kazan—The Master Director Discusses His Films: Interviews with Elia Kazan*, New York, 1999.

Baer, William, editor, *Elia Kazan: Interviews*, Jackson, 2000.

Articles:

Johnson, Malcolm, ''Crime on the Waterfront,'' in *New York Sun*, 8 November-10 December 1948.

Brinson, Peter, ''Brooder,'' in *Films and Filming* (London), October 1954.

Anderson, Lindsay, ''The Last Sequence of *On the Waterfront*,'' in *Sight and Sound* (London), January-March 1955.

Hendricks, Gordon, in *Film Culture* (New York), January 1955.

Hughes, Robert, ''On the Waterfront: A Defense,'' in *Sight and Sound* (London), Spring 1955.

Laurot, Edouard De, in *Film Culture* (New York), Summer 1955.

McVay, Douglas, ''The Brando Mutiny,'' in *Films and Filming* (London), December 1962.

Tailleur, Roger, ''Elia Kazan and the House Un-American Activities Committee,'' in *Film Comment* (New York), Fall 1966.

Hall, John Dennis, ''Method Master: Rod Steiger's Career,'' in *Films and Filming* (London), December 1970 and January 1971.

Smith, J. M. ''Three Liberal Films,'' in *Movie* (London), Winter 1971–72.

Movie (London), Spring 1972.

Haskell, Molly, articles on Brando, in *Village Voice* (New York), 14 June-30 August 1973.

Biskind, Peter, ''The Politics of Power in *On the Waterfront*,'' in *Film Quarterly* (Berkeley), Fall 1975.

Borde, R., in *Filmihullu* (Helsinki), no. 5, 1976.

Theberge, Rita, in *Cinema Texas Program Notes* (Austin), 1 December 1976.

Hey, Kenneth, in *Film and History* (Newark, New Jersey), December 1979.

''Kazan Section'' of *Positif* (Paris), April 1981.
Canby, V., ''My Hero May be Your Stoolie,'' in *New York Times*, vol. 138, section 2, 27 August 1989.
Caprara, V., ''I tre 'scandali' di un capolavoro,'' in *Filmcritica* (Rome), January-February 1990.
Alion, Yves, ''Les quatre films du docteur Brando,'' in *Revue du Cinéma* (Paris), no. 479, February 1992.
Manso, P., ''Bringing Up Baby,'' in *Premiere* (New York), vol. 8, October 1994.
Catsos, Gregory J.M., ''Immediate Reward,'' in *Outré* (Evanston), vol. 1, no. 4, 1995.
Reeves, Saskia, ''Caged Birds,'' in *Sight & Sound* (London), vol. 6, no. 2, February 1996.
Braudy, L., '''No Body's Perfect': Method Acting and 50s Culture,'' in *Michigan Quarterly Review*, vol. 35, no. 1, 1996.
Schulberg, B., ''Life in Hollywood Department,'' in *New Yorker*, vol. 74, 30 March 1998.
Wheatcroft, Geoffrey, ''The Waterfront All Over Again: He Told the Truth. They Lied for Communism. And He's the Bad Guy?'' in *Wall Street Journal* (New York), 19 March 1999.
Bosworth, Patricia, ''Kazan's Choice,'' in *Vanity Fair* (New York), vol. 469, September 1999.

* * *

The genesis of *On the Waterfront* is nearly as fascinating as the film itself. In April 1948, a New York dock hiring boss was murdered; it was the second killing in a short time. Reporter Malcolm Johnson was assigned by the now-defunct *New York Sun* to cover the story. Johnson's initial inquiries developed into a full investigation of waterfront crime. His findings were revealed in a series of 24 pieces, called ''Crime on the Waterfront,'' published in the *Sun* between 8 November–10 December 1948. The exposé revealed rampant thievery, bribery, shake-downs, kickbacks, payoffs, shylocking and murder that was costing the port of New York millions of dollars in lost shipping trade. The articles earned Johnson a Pulitzer Prize.

Elia Kazan was among the most successful and influential directors on Broadway and in Hollywood at this time. Despite his considerable reputation, Kazan had fallen into disfavor with many for his cooperation with the House Un-American Activities Committee during their investigations of communist activity in the film industry. Budd Schulberg was an established author who had won esteem for his novel about motion picture business *What Makes Sammy Run*?, and his hard-hitting exposé of prize-fighting, *The Harder They Fall*, as well as the best-seller *The Disenchanted*. Like Kazan, Schulberg had also flirted with communism in the 1930s and voluntarily testified before HUAC in 1951.

Schulberg had already drafted a script based on Johnson's articles when Kazan approached him about doing a film on the east coast. Their collaboration resulted in a script based on the waterfront scandals but imbued with a message about the virtues of ''right-thinking men in a vital democracy.'' Although the project was supported by the combined expertise of Kazan/Schulberg, no Hollywood studio would finance the venture; some argued that the issues were too depressing, others that filming on actual locations would be too dangerous, but ultimately the reason for rejection seemed to be the meager commercial prospects. Just as the project seemed unrealizable, independent producer Sam Spiegel, looking for a property, accepted the challenge and financed the film.

In keeping with the documentary nature of its source material, *On the Waterfront* was to be filmed on the streets and docks of Hoboken, New Jersey, where it takes place. With a singularity of purpose, the film was to expose not only the corruption of the waterfront unions but also reflect the day-to-day struggle for work and dignity among the longshoremen. Frank Sinatra was approached for the leading role of a slow-witted dockworker who, through a strange brew of conscience and vengeance, emerges from the group to break the stranglehold maintained by the corrupt union. When terms with Sinatra could not be reached, Marlon Brando, who had won Oscar nominations in two previous Kazan films, was signed. A substantial array of acting talent was recruited for supporting roles, including Lee J. Cobb, Rod Steiger, Karl Malden and Eva Marie Saint. The production cost $820,000 and made an immediate and astonishing impression on both audiences and critics when released in 1954.

The narrative centers around Terry Malloy, a former boxer turned dockworker, who becomes the unwitting pawn in the murder of a fellow longshoreman preparing to testify against gangsters who tyrannize the docks. Through the insistent priest, Father Barry, Terry is drawn into a moral dilemma. His loyalties to the racketeers, led by Johnny Friendly and Terry's brother Charlie, have been weakened by the murder. His growing affection for Edie and the persuasive tactics of Father Barry gradually draw his allegiance away from the gangsters. Terry is served with a subpoena to testify before the Waterfront Crime Commission about the Joey Doyle murder. In love with Edie, manipulated by the priest and in disfavor with the mob, Terry's conversion is completed when his own brother is brutally murdered as a warning to him. Terry testifies against Friendly and is ostracized as a ''stoolie.'' When he confronts Friendly and his cohorts, he is brutally beaten. In a final effort of will, Terry rallies and leads the loitering longshoremen to work as an act of defiance against the racketeers.

The technique of the film is as basic and effective as the story. There are no attempts at a self-conscious aesthetics or pyrotechnics. There are no compromises in rendering the locale as anything but the urban jungle that it is. We follow the story as it takes us into the cargo holds of the ships, the slum dwelling of the workers, the shack that serves as headquarters for the union leaders, the seedy bars, the littered streets, the rooftops, the alleyways. Everything about the film is grimy and oppressive. The waterfront is presented as a harsh place where violence and betrayal have become an accepted way of life; it is a place where the strong prey upon the weak and a self-defeating code of silence prevails. We not only see and hear the sub-human malaise of the neighborhood, but we feel the suffering of the dockworkers as they mull about in a fraternal hopelessness.

At the center of *On the Waterfront* is Terry Malloy. Terry is a man in his 30s always exploited by others; Johnny Friendly callously uses him to set up Joey Doyle just as Father Barry manipulates him against his loyalties. Terry initiates nothing of his own, yet he is redeemed through love from the limitations of his background. Left to himself, it is probable that he would remain just another likable but expendable dockworker and errand boy.

At the beginning of the film, Terry is barely articulate and painfully confused about himself and his situation. Not only is he mired in the urban jungle of greed, deceit and betrayal, but he is at loss to understand it or change himself. As he tells Edie in the tavern; ''Wanna know my philosophy of life?'' Yet beneath his layered exterior of toughness, Terry possesses traits that seem contradictory to his own philosophy: his fondness for pigeons, the tender way he wears Edie's glove, the rejection he feels at being excluded from the protection and confidence of his brother.

As Brando interprets him, Terry Malloy also possesses a touch of sadness. He is a man who, at one time, had the opportunity to rise above his condition through his skill as a prizefighter. Although he could have had a personal sense of self-respect and self-worth as a contender for the title, he was prevented from it by others (including his brother). Embittered but not self-piteous, he reveals his self-awareness in a touching scene with his brother in the back seat of a cab. Although well suppressed, the seed of something better resides in him. It is Edie's love that nurtures that seed.

Reduced to its basics, *On the Waterfront* is a morality tale about how corruption *can* (indeed *must*) be fought and defeated when a man of courage and conscience emerges from the crowd to oppose the corruption. Although the narrative progresses in a linear manner without flashbacks and subplots, the power of the film is announced from the opening scene, with its assertive orchestral percussion, in which Terry is dispatched to lure Joey Doyle into a setup. In addition to dominating the Academy Awards of 1954, it garnered some additional laurels. It brought credibility to the method technique of acting taught at the Actors Studio. It certified the acting credentials of a number of talents trained for the theater. It brought acclaim and stardom to Marlon Brando, and even briefly made mumbling fashionable. It also created at least one enduring vignette (''I coulda been a contender'') which has frequently been parodied.

Even though *On the Waterfront* is universally hailed as a milestone, the film's denouement still taints its reputation as a classic. Terry informs before a congressional committee on those who have exploited him and the other longshoremen. In the context of the narrative, he is elevated to heroic proportions (even though his heroism is misunderstood by others) through a behavior that is typically classified by both the film and society as reprehensible. As a result of his informing through public testimony, Terry is considered an outcast by everyone from the police assigned to protect him to his friends who now refuse to speak to him. But after he confronts Friendly, he is the lone man of strength who wins the support of the longshoremen. In a turn-about, the act of informing is not only justified but sanitized and made admirable.

The fact that Terry moves, perhaps too conveniently, from a complex individual through the act of informing to an emblem of Christian integrity and suffering has aggravated certain viewers. Some have argued that the optimistic ending is a reversal of the film's narrative premise. In another attack, critic-filmmaker Lindsay Anderson, writing in *Sight and Sound*, considered the film's violent conclusion to be ''implicitly (if unconsciously) fascist.'' Others have cited the parallels to Kazan-Schulberg's own situation and objected to the ending as an unconvincing effort to vindicate their own informing to HUAC. Whatever interpretation one prefers, it is interesting to observe that in writing the novelization of his screenplay, Schulberg chose to end it not with Terry's heroic leadership but with his ignoble death (stabbed 27 times with an ice pick and then deposited in a barrel of lime left in a Jersey swamp).

None of these criticisms, however, has diminished the dramatic power of the film. Regardless of political considerations or implications, the film has found its way into the ranks of cinema classics.

—Stephen E. Bowles

ONCE THERE WAS A WAR

See **DER VAR ENGANG EN KRIG**

ONCE UPON A TIME IN AMERICA

USA, 1984

Director: Sergio Leone

Production: The Ladd Company, for Embassy International, Warner Bros.; Technicolour/Eastmancolour, 35 mm; running time: 229 minutes.

Producer: Arnon Milchan; **screenplay:** Leonardo Benvenuti, Piero De Bernardi, Enrico Medioli, Franco Arcalli, Franco Ferrini, and Sergio Leone, based on the novel *The Hoods* by Harry Grey (David Aaronson); **photography:** Tonino Delli Colli; **editor:** Nino Baragli; **set designer:** Giovanni Natalucci; **art directors:** Carlo Simi and James Singelis; **music:** Ennio Morricone.

Cast: Robert De Niro (*Noodles*); James Woods (*Max*); Elizabeth McGovern (*Deborah*); Treat Williams (*Jimmy O'Donnell*); Tuesday Weld (*Carol*); Burt Young (*Joe*); Joe Pesci (*Frankie*); Danny Aiello (*Police Chief Aiello*); William Forsythe (*Cockeye*); James Hayden (*Patsy*); Darlanne Fleugel (*Eve*); Larry Rapp (*Fat Moe*); Scott Tiler (*Young Noodles*); Rusty Jacobs (*Young Max*); Jennifer Connely (*Young Deborah*); James Russo (*Bugsy*); Brian Bloom (*Young Patsy*); Adrian Curran (*Young Cockeye*); Mike Monetti (*Young Fat Moe*).

Publications

Books:

Gabutti, Diego, *C'era una volta in America*, Milano, 1984.
Cumbow, Robert C., *Once Upon a Time. . . The Films of Sergio Leone*, London, 1987.
Simsolo, Nöel, *Conversations avec Sergio Leone*, Paris, 1987.
Gressard, Gilles, *Sergio Leone*, Paris, 1989.
Di Claudio, Gianni, *Directed by Sergio Leone*, Cheti, 1990.
Ortoli, Philippe, *Sergio Leone: une Amérique de légendes*, Paris, 1994.
De Cornare, Oreste, *Sergio Leone: The Great American Dream of Legendary America*, Rome, 1997.
Frayling, Christopher, *Sergio Leone: Something to Do with Death*, New York, 2000.

Articles:

Chion, M., and others, *Cahiers du Cinéma* (Paris), May 1984.
Variety (New York), 23 May 1984.

Once Upon a Time in America

Gili, J.-A., and others, ''Reflets dans un saxo d'or,'' in *Positif* (Paris), June 1984.
Hamill, P., *American Film* (Washington, D.C.), June 1984.
Simsolo, N., and others, *Revue du Cinéma* (Paris), June 1984.
Corliss, M., and E. Lomenzo, *Film Comment* (New York), July-August 1984.
Leone, Sergio, *Cahiers du Cinéma* (Paris), July-August 1984.
Nave, B., *Jeune Cinéma* (Paris), July-August 1984.
Hutchinson, C., *Films and Filming* (London), September 1984.
Martineu, R., *Séquences* (Montreal), October 1984.
Rayns, T., *Monthly Film Bulletin* (London), October 1984.
Peachment, C., ''The World Was Yours,'' in *Sight and Sound* (London), Autumn 1984.
Caputo, R., *Cinema Papers* (Victoria), December 1984.
Knee, A., *Film Criticism* (Meadville, Pennsylvania), Fall 1985.
Thomson, D., ''Leonesque,'' in *American Film*, vol. 14, September 1989.
Little, K., ''Letters: Gremlins—the In-house Batch,'' in *Film Comment* (New York), vol. 27, July/August 1991.
Weinraub, B., ''Uncut Version of 1984 Cult Film to Be Released,'' in *New York Times,* vol. 142, C19, 22 October 1992.
Norman, Barry, in *Radio Times* (London), vol. 258, no. 3760, 17 February 1996.
Lucas, Tim, ''What Are Those Strange Drops of Blood in the Scripts of Ernesto Gastaldi?'' in *Video Watchdog* (Cincinnati), no. 39, 1997.
Godden, Richard, ''Maximizing the Noodles: Class, Memory, and Capital in Sergio Leone's *Once Upon a Time in America,*'' in *Journal of American Studies* (Cambridge), vol. 31, December 1997.
Martin, A., ''Euphoria and Liberating Laughter: The Cinema of Sergio Leone,'' in *Metro Magazine* (St. Kilda West), no. 113/114, 1998.
Meyer, David N., ''Once Upon a Time, an Epic Was Shorn of Grandeur,'' in *New York Times* (New York), 14 February 1999.

* * *

Sergio Leone's *Once Upon a Time in America*—a larger-than-life title which is a variation of his earlier *Once Upon a Time in the West*—is the story of the plight and fate of a group of Jewish immigrant sons and childhood friends. They come of age on New York's Lower East Side in the early 20th century and eventually become wealthy, powerful Depression-era gangsters. The film has all the atmosphere and scope of Francis Coppola's first two *Godfather* epics, with its complex scenario crammed with corrupt public officials and gangland rivalries, references to real-life individuals and events, raw sex and bloody killings. Its narrative spans decades, all the way through the late 1960s, with past and present events blended seamlessly.

Notwithstanding all of this, *Once Upon a Time in America* is merely masquerading as a gangster movie. Primarily, it is an allegory of the experience of being a first-generation American. The principal connections in the film are between Noodles (Robert De Niro), whose real name is David Aaronson, and Max (James Woods), his closest partner-in-crime; and Noodles and Deborah (Elizabeth McGovern), his childhood sweetheart. As a teenager, Deborah reads a poem to Noodles. One of the lines—''He'll always be a two-bit punk, so he'll never be my beloved. What a shame!''—reflects the manner in which their relationship evolves.

In America, all men are supposed to be equal. But, given their roots, these immigrant sons and daughters remain eternally outside of the national fabric. They are not of the culture of their parents. ''My old man's praying and my old lady's crying,'' young Noodles observes. ''What the hell should I go home for.'' Yet their ghetto world is a universe away from Uptown New York, where families have been rooted for generations. As Jews—let alone ghetto Jews—they will not be allowed Ivy League educations and jobs in society's upper echelons. They remain separated from the mainstream of America, and so they are disaffected, and become blindly ambitious. Consequently, they crave success and acceptance. Max may store away a $1-million nest egg, but he is not satisfied. He talks of making $20 million, $50 million—friendship and loyalty be damned as he plots the betrayal of his cronies for their money. Deborah, meanwhile, aspires to become a famous actress; the entertainment industry being one of the few ''legitimate'' professions in which a ghetto child can rise in class. She tells Noodles, ''I've got to get where I'm going. . . . To the top.''

Noodles, Max and their pals start out as uncouth, unwashed youngsters whose sense of identity develops as they roll drunks, torch newsstands, and blackmail a crooked cop. Eventually, during Prohibition, they become fabulously wealthy bootleggers. However, whatever power they achieve, and whatever high circles they come to travel in, their ghetto roots (and baser instincts) remain with them throughout their lives. They may wear fancy suits and have wads of money, but they are ruthless, brutal thugs. Noodles is a man of animalistic urges, who is unable to control his sexuality. As a youngster, he has sex in a bathroom with the local tramp-in-training; as an adult, he rapes a woman during a robbery. His low point comes when he transforms a tender moment with Deborah into an ugly one as he molests her in the back of a limousine: an act which forever ends their relationship.

In order to fit in the only way they know how, the characters in *Once Upon a Time in America* go about reinventing themselves. David Aaronson might be the name of a pious rabbi, but his identity changes when he becomes ''Noodles'': a thug who might be played by James Cagney in a 1930s gangster film. As a young ghetto girl, Deborah spouts poetry; she goes on to become a renowned actress, and enjoys the glitter and fame of movie star life. As an actress, she can play roles that are as far-removed from the ghetto as Saks Fifth Avenue is from the Lower East Side. In the film's major plot twist, it is revealed that Max, whom the elderly Noodles has thought dead for over thirty years, has become the rich, powerful ''Secretary Bailey.'' Max, in fact, twice reinvents himself. He changes from ghetto kid to gangster, and from gangster to ''Secretary Bailey.'' Despite these transformations, there remains a sense of sadness to their lives, if only because they can never really escape their roots. This is especially the case with Noodles. Despite the level of power he achieves during Prohibition, he spends many of his formative years in prison. After his cronies are killed—a symbolic act which occurs in 1933, at the tail end of Prohibition—he is marked for death. He escapes from New York and fades into obscurity, passing the decades in Buffalo where, as he explains, he has been ''going to bed early'' every night. Even if, like Max, he had been able to maintain his power, his background and the coarseness of his personality would never have allowed him to mingle confidently among the elite. This, in fact, is precisely the case with Max. He may have become ''Secretary Bailey,'' and may live on a palatial Long Island estate, but he is an aged variation of a crude, crazy street kid. His wealth is not inherited, but has been earned via unsavory means. Not without irony, his past is coming to public light, as he is the focus of what has com to be known in the media as the ''Bailey scandal.''

On another level, *Once Upon a Time in America* serves as an account of the manner in which power is achieved in America. Its scenario covers the establishment of, and gangland influence in, the Teamsters Union, with Treat Williams appearing as a thinly-veiled version of James Hoffa. Leone's point is that, in America—the ''land of opportunity''—power and riches can only be achieved by corruption and thuggery.

If *Once Upon a Time in the West* is Leone's masterwork, *Once Upon a Time in America*—the last feature he completed before his death in 1989—is his most challenging film. Unfortunately, both were severely edited when released in the United States; *Once Upon a Time in America* came to theaters in a muddled, truncated 139 minutes. The complete version runs 227 minutes, and is available on video.

—Rob Edelman and Audrey E. Kupferberg

ONCE UPON A TIME IN THE WEST

See **C'ERA UNA VOLTA IL WEST**

ONE FLEW OVER THE CUCKOO'S NEST

USA, 1975

Director: Milos Forman

Production: Fantasy Films; Deluxe color, 35mm; running time: 134 minutes.

One Flew Over the Cuckoo's Nest

Producers: Saul Zaentz, Michael Douglas; **screenplay:** Lawrence Hauben, Bo Goldman, based on the novel by Ken Kesey; **photography:** Haskell Wexler; **editor:** Richard Chew, Lynzee Klingman, Sheldon Kahn; **assistant directors:** Irby Smith, William St. John; **production design:** Paul Sylbert; **art director:** Edwin O'Donovan; **music:** Jack Nitzsche; **sound editor:** Mary McGlone, Robert R. Rutledge, Veronica Selver; **sound recording:** Lawrence Jost; **costumes:** Agnes Rodgers.

Cast: Jack Nicholson (*Randall P. McMurphy*); Louise Fletcher (*Nurse Ratched*); Will Sampson (*Chief Bromden*); Brad Dourif (*Billy Bibbit*); William Redfield (*Harding*); Christopher Lloyd (*Taber*); Sydney Lassick (*Cheswick*); Danny De Vito (*Martini*); Delos V. Smith Jr. (*Scanlon*); Scatman Crothers (*Spivey*); Marya Small (*Candy*); William Duell (*Sefelt*); Louisa Moritz (*Rose*); Dean R. Brooks (*Dr. Spivey*); Michael Berryman (*Ellis*).

Awards: Oscars for Best Picture, Best Director, Best Actor (Nicholson), Best Actress (Fletcher), and Best Adapted Screenplay, 1975.

Publications

Books:

Poizot, Claude, *Milos Forman*, Paris, 1987.
Slater, Thomas J., *Milos Forman: A Bio-Bibliography*, Connecticut, 1987.
Aycock, Wendell, and Michael Schoenecke, *Film and Literature: A Comparative Approach to Adaptation*, Lubbock, Texas, 1988.
Brode, Douglas, *The Films of Jack Nicholson*, New York 1990, 1996.
Goulding, Daniel J., *Five Filmmakers*, Indianapolis, 1994.
Forman, Milos, and Jan Novak, *Turnaround: A Memoir*, London, 1994, 1996.

Articles:

Walker, B., *Sight and Sound* (London), Autumn 1975.
Variety (New York), 19 November 1975.
Cowie, P., and A. Ayles, *Focus on Film* (New York), Winter 1975–76.
MacReadie, M., *Films in Review* (New York), January 1976.
Milne, T., *Monthly Film Bulletin* (London), February 1976.
Treilhou, M.C., ''Une vielle imagerie de la follie'' in *Cinéma* (Paris), January 1976.
Maupin, F., *Image et Son* (Paris), February 1976.
Combs, R., *Sight and Sound* (London), Spring 1976.
Benoit, C., *Jeune Cinéma* (Paris), March 1976.
Ciment, M., ''Une expérience américaine'' in *Positif* (Paris), March 1976.
Martin, M., *Ecran* (Paris), March 1976.
Dawson, I., *Cinema Papers* (Melbourne), March-April 1976.
Sineux, M., ''Big Mother Is Watching you'' in *Positif* (Paris), March 1976.
Gow, G., *Films and Filming* (London), April 1976.
Daney, S., ''Réserves'' in *Cahiers du Cinéma* (Paris), May 1976.
Van Wert, W., ''An Aerial View of the Nest'' in *Jump Cut* (Berkeley), Summer 1976.
Hunter, I., *Cinema Papers* (Melbourne), June-July 1976.
McCreadie, Marsha, ''*One Flew Over the Cuckoo's Nest*: Some Reasons for One Happy Adaptation,'' in *Literature/Film Quarterly* (Salisbury), vol. 5, no. 2, Spring 1977.
Safer, E.B., '''It's the Truth Even if It Didn't Happen': Ken Kesey's *One Flew Over the Cuckoo's Nest*,'' in *Literature/Film Quarterly* (Salisbury), vol. 5, no. 2, Spring 1977.
Wexler, Haskell, and M. Douglas, in *American Film*, vol. 4, no. 10, September 1979.
Gow, G., in *Films and Filming* (London), no. 422, December 1989.
Warchol, T., ''The Rebel Figure in Milos Forman's American Films,'' in *New Orleans Review*, vol. 17, no. 1, 1990.
Sodowsky, G.R., and R.E. Sodowsky, ''Different Approaches to Psychopathology and Symbolism in the Novel and Film *One Flew Over the Cuckoo's Nest*,'' in *Literature and Psychology*, vol. 37, no. 1/2, 1991.
Zubizarreta, J., ''The Disparity of Point of View in *One Flew Over the Cuckoo's Nest*,'' in *Literature/Film Quarterly* (Salisbury), vol. 22, no. 1, January 1994.
Raskin, R., ''Set Up/Pay-Off and a Related Figure,'' in *P.O.V.*, no. 2, December 1996.

* * *

One Flew Over the Cuckoo's Nest—the first film to win Academy Awards for Best Picture, Director, Actor, Actress and Screenplay since *It Happened One Night* in 1934—is more than a superlative human drama. It is, on a broader level, one of the seminal works of its time in that it keenly reflects the systematic stifling of individuality within post-World War II American society.

The year is 1963, and Randall Patrick McMurphy (Jack Nicholson) is a new patient in a mental ward. He has been sent there from a prison work farm because he is a nonconformist, and so the authorities, having labelled him ''belligerent,'' ''resentful'' and ''lazy,'' want to evaluate him and determine if he is mentally ill.

McMurphy's ''problem'' is that he is a logic-minded individual in a society ruled by bureaucratic illogic. McMurphy dares to think for himself, and question authority. He resists taking his medication, and makes a perfectly rational declaration to Mildred Ratched (Louise Fletcher), the ward's head nurse: ''I don't like the idea of taking something if I don't know what it is.'' Her immediate response—''Don't get upset, Mr. McMurphy''—mirrors the manner in which those in power will pigeonhole the individual who questions the rules. Of course, McMurphy does not belong in a mental ward, but his objection to blind authority makes him as much a threat to society as the worst kind of sociopath. ''He's not crazy,'' one of the hospital doctors tellingly observes at one point, ''but he's dangerous.''

The situation on Nurse Ratched's ward goes directly against McMurphy's nature. His fellow patients are compliant and spiritless. They lack individuality, and are so drugged out on medication that their emotions are warped and exaggerated. The two key ones are Billy Bibbit (Brad Dourif), who incessantly stutters, and Chief Bromden (Will Sampson), a towering Indian who is presented as being deaf and dumb. McMurphy eventually learns that many of the men are self-committed, and have the freedom to leave at any time they choose. In other words, they have been so repressed by society that they have willingly accepted their fate.

McMurphy maintains his individuality by wearing jeans and colored shirts, while his fellow patients mostly are garbed in white, antiseptic hospital gowns. He promptly goes about goading the men, and showing them that it is better to try and fail than to meekly accept an unsatisfactory status quo. From the outset, he attempts to elicit a response from Chief Bromden, who eventually reveals to McMurphy that he indeed can speak and hear, but has chosen to close himself off from a society that is neck-deep in hypocrisy.

McMurphy and his irrepressible spirit are the best therapy for the men, who soon begin using their minds and expressing their feelings. The major villain of the piece is Nurse Ratched. Beneath her outwardly soothing demeanor is a neurotic, sexually repressed woman who relishes controlling the patients. She wants McMurphy kept in the hospital rather than returned to the work farm, because she is determined to break him. She knows that he will be set free once his prison sentence is completed. If he remains in the hospital, he will be under her control.

The mental ward in *One Flew Over the Cuckoo's Nest* serves as a metaphor for American society, the point being that citizens are inmates of that society. They are expected to conform, by fitting in as members of a status quo. Even more specifically, as a mirror of post-World War II America, the scenario depicts a specific point in history where conformity was encouraged and free-thinking was a perilous endeavor. During the late 1940s and 50s, the House Un-American Activities Committee was allowed to strip citizens of their constitutional rights, throw them in jail, blacklist them from their jobs. In the 1960s came the escalation of the war in Vietnam; ''good, patriotic Americans'' supported the war, while ''un-American communist dupes'' protested it. *One Flew Over the Cuckoo's Nest* takes on a political edge when McMurphy urges the patients to ''be good Americans'' and vote for changing their work detail schedule so that they may watch a World Series game on television. The analogy here is that it is the American way to think and choose for oneself, and even change a system if that system does not benefit the majority. Furthermore, what is more American than watching baseball! By coming together as a group and altering the rules, the men simply are exercising their rights as American citizens.

It is most interesting, then, that the film's director, Milos Forman, is not American-born. He is from Czechoslovakia, and was one of the leading directors of his country's ''new wave'' before Russian tanks rolled through the streets of Prague in August, 1968. As such, his background allows him insight into the manner in which freedom of expression may be stifled by authority.

One Flew Over the Cuckoo's Nest also reflects on the sexual repression of pre-1960s American society. McMurphy had been jailed for statutory rape, yet he points out that his sex partner was ''fifteen going on thirty-five. . . she told me she was eighteen, and was very willing. . . .'' His argument is that he had not committed rape, or sexually abused a child—his partner was acquiescent, and presented herself as above the age of consent, so where is his crime? Additionally, in group therapy sessions, Nurse Ratched constantly brings up topics relating to problems the men have had with wives and girlfriends. Near the finale, McMurphy smuggles two young women into the ward, and Billy Bibbit loses his virginity to one of them. Afterwards, he no longer stutters. ''No, I'm not,'' he proudly responds to Nurse Ratched's asking him if he is ''ashamed.'' But the nurse craftily exploits Billy's weaknesses. She summarily squeezes the manhood out of him by declaring, ''What worries me is how your mother's going to take this.'' Not only does Billy begin stammering again, he promptly commits suicide.

McMurphy, the autonomous rapscallion, might have escaped to freedom during all of this. But he has been transformed by his stay in the ward in that he has developed a sense of responsibility towards his new-found friends, and feels compelled to remain on the scene. He knows that Nurse Ratched—the twisted authority figure in a repressed society—is directly responsible for Billy's suicide. While McMurphy's fate is a sad one—he is lobotomized into a glassy-eyed zombie—the story ends on a positive note as Chief Bromden crashes out of the ward to freedom. The point—ever so meaningfully illustrated—is that the individual may fail in his quest for liberation, but he still may inspire those around him. His failure is no reason for the next person to remain compliant.

—Rob Edelman

ONE WAY OR ANOTHER

See **DE CIERTA MANERA**

ONLY THE HOURS

See **RIEN QUE LES HEURES**

ORDET

(The Word)

Denmark, 1955

Director: Carl Theodor Dreyer

Production: Palladium (Copenhagen); black and white, 35mm; running time: 124 minutes; length: 3440 meters. Released 10 January 1955, Denmark.

Screenplay: Carl Theodor Dreyer, from the play by Kaj Munk; **photography:** Henning Bendtsen; **editor:** Edith Schlüssel; **sound:** Knud Kristensen; **art director:** Erik Aaes; **music:** Poul Schierbeck; **costume designer:** N. Sanat Jensen; **dialogue expert:** Svend Pousen. Filmed in and near Veders, Denmark, Venice Film Festival, Leone d'Oro, 1955.

Cast: Henrik Malberg (*Morten Borgen*); Emil Hass Christensen (*Mikkel, his son*); Preben Lerdorff Rye (*Johannes, his son*); Cay Kristiansen (*Andre, his son*); Birgitte Federspiel (*Inger, Mikkel's wife*); Ann Elisabeth (*Maren*); Susanne (*Little Inger*); Ove Rud (*The priest*); Ejnar Federspiel (*Peter the tailor*); Sylvia Eckhausen (*Kirstine, the tailor's wife*); Gerda Nielsen (*Anne, the tailor's daughter*); Henry Skjaer (*The doctor*); Hanne ågesen (*Karen*); Edith Thrane (*Mette Maren*); Kirsten Andreasen and the peasants and fisherman of the district of Veders.

Publications

Script:

Dreyer, Carl Theodor, *Ordet*, in *Five Films of Carl Theodor Dreyer*, Copenhagen, 1964; also in *Four Screenplays of Carl Theodor Dreyer*, London, 1970.

Books:

Neergaard, Ebbe, *Carl Theodor Dreyer: A Film Director's Work*, London, 1950.
Trolle, Børge, *The Art of Carl Dreyer: An Analysis*, Copenhagen, 1955.
Bowser, Eileen, *The Films of Carl Dreyer*, New York, 1964.
Dreyer, Carl Theodor, *Om Filmen*, Copenhagen, 1964.
Monty, Ib, *Portrait of Carl Th. Dreyer*, Copenhagen, 1965.
Dyssegaard, Soren, editor, *Carl Th. Dreyer, Danish Film Director*, Copenhagen, 1968.
Perrin, Claude, *Carl Th. Dreyer*, Paris, 1969.
Sémolué, Jean, *Carl Th. Dreyer*, Paris, 1970.
Milne, Tom, *The Cinema of Carl Dreyer*, New York, 1971.
Skoller, Donald, editor, *Dreyer in Double Reflection*, New York, 1973.
Nash, Mark, editor, *Dreyer*, London, 1977.
Tone, Pier Giorgio, *Carl Theodor Dreyer*, Florence, 1978.
Bordwell, David, *The Films of Carl Theodor Dreyer*, Berkeley, 1981.
Carney, Raymond, *Speaking the Language of Desire: The Films of Carl Dreyer*, New York, 1989.
Jensen, Jytte, editor, *The Films of Carl Theodor Dreyer*, New York, 1989.
Dreyer, Carl Theodor, *Dreyer in Double Reflection: Carl Dreyer's Writings on Film*, Cambridge, 1991.
Drum, Jean, and Dale D. Drum, *My Only Great Passion: The Life and Films of Carl Theodor Dreyer*, Lanham, 2000.

Articles:

Ecran Français (Paris), 11 November 1947.
Wahl, Jan, ''*Ordet* og billederne,'' in *Kosmorama* (Copenhagen), no. 3, 1954.
Bianco e Nero (Rome), no. 9–10, 1955.
Fønns, Mogens, in *Films in Review* (New York), no. 1, 1955.
Neergaard, Ebbe, in *Sight and Sound* (London), no. 4, 1955.
Trolle, Børge, ''The World of Carl Dreyer,'' in *Sight and Sound* (London), Winter 1955–56.
Rohmer, Eric, ''Une Alceste chrétienne,'' in *Cahiers du Cinéma* (Paris), no. 55, 1956.
Séguin, Louis, in *Positif* (Paris), no. 16, 1956.
Schein, Harry, ''Mankind on the Border,'' in *Quarterly of Film, Radio, and Television* (Berkeley), Spring 1956.
Luft, Herbert, ''Carl Dreyer—A Master of his Craft,'' in *Quarterly of Film, Radio, and Television* (Berkeley), Winter 1956.
Mekas, Jonas, in *Film Culture* (New York), no. 1, 1958.
Montanari, Armando, ''*Ordet*, la critica, e Kierkegaard,'' in *Cinema Nuovo* (Turin), no.134, 1958.
Bruno, Eduardo, in *Filmcritica* (Rome), no. 88, 1959.
Luft, Herbert, ''Dreyer,'' in *Films and Filming* (London), June 1961.
Bond, Kirk, ''The World of Carl Dreyer,'' in *Film Quarterly* (Berkeley), Fall 1965.
Kosmorama (Copenhagen), June 1968.
Cahiers du Cinéma (Paris), December 1968.
Adams Sitney, P., editor, ''Metaphysic of *Ordet*,'' in *The Film Culture Reader*, New York, 1970.
Vaughan, Dai, ''Carl Dreyer and the Theme of Choice,'' in *Sight and Sound* (London), Summer 1974.
Petric, Vlada, ''Dreyer's Concept of Abstraction,'' in *Sight and Sound* (London), Spring 1975.
Thomsen, C.B., ''Mirakulos eller monstros,'' in *Kosmorama* (Copenhagen), vol. 35, no. 187, Spring 1989.
Minguet Batllori, J.M., ''Carl Theodore Dryer: clasicismo y cine,'' in *Nosferatu* (San Sebastian), no. 5, January 1991.
Miguez, M., in *Nosferatu* (San Sebastian), no. 5, January 1991.

* * *

By any critical standard, Carl Dreyer's *Ordet* (*The Word*) is an enormously accomplished work of film art. It combines what might be in others' hands an unwieldy mix: formal and technical mastery,

Ordet

a clean (illusive), simple style and, a qualification seen in all of his best films, enormous depth of atmosphere for powerful results.

Adapted from a play by Kaj Munk, a Lutheran pastor murdered by the Nazis for speaking out against them, Dreyer changed the ending and more than halved the dialogue, thus streamlining, ''purifying'' the play to extend it beyond a filmed moral parable that many reviewers limited it to. Indeed, there is a cinematic authenticity that is subtle but integral. The power of the play is magnified many times.

A young theology student, through overwork (or, for Munk's reason, studying Kierkegaard!), loses his grip on sanity, becoming convinced he is Christ. Now home, he lives with his father, brother Anders, and other brother Mikkel, who is married to Inger. Anders loves the tailor's daughter, Anne, but in true Romeo and Juliet tradition, both families refuse any union, because of antagonistic religious divisions. It is not until Inger suffers a miscarriage and dies that the quarrelling neighbours are united, as are the two young lovers. ''Nobody thought to ask Inger back from Death,'' says Johannes. ''She will rot because the times are rotten.'' Only Inger's daughter Maren believes in Johannes' ability to perform miracles. Because of her, or for her, he pronounces the word which brings Inger back to the living.

As with many of his films, Dreyer has sculpted a film with a life versus death theme; however, as *Jeanne d'Arc* and *Vredens Dag* (*Day of Wrath*) existed in a historical world, and *Vampyr* in a dream world, *Ordet* is very much in today's. Yet the underlying mood is spiritual, deliberate, thoughtful, conveying not only the gravity of his characters' existence, but the collective Nordic consciousness about the transience of life, of love, and, especially, of belief.

Because every image is measured—with the formal construction Dreyer is known for, each survives on its own as a beautiful still—*Ordet* withstands not only the more orthodox, critical interpretation but the viewer's own, on varying levels; the combination of Munk's text and Dreyer's visualisation creates a third ''presence'' the way the fusion of a playwright's character and an actor's portrayal does. His style—cool, stylised, austere, with sharp matte blacks and luminous whites, as opposed to the tonality of his other works—is one of elimination, simplicity for the stern Lutheran ''spiritual content.'' (The dialogue is more to be heard for its argument and exploration, less for the evocative quality as in *Vampyr.*) Even in the sequence where Ingrid gives birth, pivotal for both character and plot as is Jeanne's trial, Leone's blood transfusion in *Vampyr* and Anne's ''trial'' in *Vredens Dag*, the doctor's movements accord exactly with the beating of a pulse. And with Dreyer's long takes, some lasting 8 minutes, we are insinuated into the hearts and souls of *Ordet's* personalities.

In the Borgen household, God is fulfillment, warmth, love, *life.* The setting is cozy, the field full of ripening corn, whereas to Peter the tailor's family, God is denial, arid, mournful, *death.* The house is bare, the land flat, dry. Inger is love and life incarnate—adored by all three generations, she acts as peacemaker. (Whereas Peter's daughter Anne is meekly submissive, kept down, apart.) In an effective contrast to the black and white graphic photography and slow, deliberate camera, Dreyer builds a scene with a kind of deliberate grace. Inger attempts a ''softening up'' approach, attempting to pleade Anders' and Anne's case with her stubborn father-in-law. She rustles about, cozying the room, preparing a treat of coffee and cakes, fetching his pipe, asking him to help her wind her wool, all before gingerly raising the subject. Not fooled but amused, the older man comments drily, ''Is this why we have been having coffee?'' The gentle humour, the sense of instinctive understanding between them, reveals a deep mutual respect and affection that doesn't have to be articulated. (Later, the room is stripped almost bare for a resting place for Inger; the feeling of love being drained away from the household is palpable.) Within the Borgen house, as writer Tom Milne describes it, the incident is an example, within the austerity, of an ''expansive affection arising from the rich, warmly-observed detail of the relationship.'' We see generations entrenched, unfolding, full of potential, all deliberate. Referring to the great influence of the Swedish director extraordinaire Victor Sjöström on him, Dreyer noted, ''Rhythm and milieu go together . . . during the filming of *Ingmarssönerna* (1918), when the farmers came into the room to eat, with the heavy tread they used in the fields. They didn't enter like modern people, storming in and sitting down; they came in soberly and calmly, took their caps off and took an eternity to cross the floor . . . it was set up so that one believed it completely.''

It is not only the realms of life and death that are explored; through Dreyer's characterisation, those of the spiritual and the earthly are also evoked. Through his delusion, Johannes not only acts as a medium with the first (it is our irreconcilability with or acceptance of death as the beginning of a spiritual rebirth), but also with pure belief and dogma, a choice that the little Maren has made, even after Johannes' first unsuccessful attempt to bring Inger back. (The difference between his two approaches: the first was ''I will''—an arrogance over faith in another Being?—the second ''I will try''.) She is the bridge between structured and unstructured belief, that without question or rule, beyond quarrel.

Is Johannes ''god's fool?'' There is always one estranged character in Dreyer's major works—Jeanne, the ''witch'' Anne, Leone are but three—and the question is left unanswered with respect to his state of mind at the end. Is he now sane, therefore able to resurrect, by having to accept the reality of Inger's death? Or is he able to perform his miracle precisely because he is beyond the rigid, fighting Christian world he inhabits? The culmination centres everything; a superb example of making literary text filmic. Two more worlds come together: not only spiritual love but carnal as well. As Mikkel admits, ''I loved her body too.'' That mutuality is made clear as, upon awakening, Inger kisses him long and sensuously on his face and lips.

With his focus upon deliberate pacing, geometric setting, textural blacks and whites—visually, there are few more stunning films—Dreyer cinematically interprets the tensions between the diametrically opposed. For example, the room with the coffin, enclosing white-draped Inger, is shot in white tones with exposed light; still, serene, the ''dead'' side. In contrast, the ''living'' side, the room with the mourning family, is shot more roughly, with black tones, scattered black-robed people. The contrasting tonality of lighting, too, both reflects and creates the moods within the same space. The result is an almost hypnotic atmosphere of stillness . . . or is it one of paralysing neutrality? The possible resolution is given to Johannes who, in the final scene, makes the clearest statement of all. When Mikkel asks despairingly, ''How can one tell madness from sense?,'' the reply is ''You are coming closer.''

—Jane Ehrlich

ORFEU NEGRO

(Black Orpheus)

France-Italy-Brazil, 1958

Director: Marcel Camus

Production: Dispatfilm (Paris), Gemma Cinematografica (Rome), and Tupan; Eastmancolor, 35mm, Cinemascope; running time: 103 minutes, some sources list 106 minutes. Released 1958. Filmed in Rio de Janeiro during Carnival in both 1957 and 1958, footage with actors shot September-December 1958.

Producer: Sacha Gordine; **screenplay:** Vinicius de Moraes, adapted by Jacques Viot and Marcel Camus from the play *Orfeu da Conceição* by Vinicius de Moraes; **photography:** Jean Bourgoin; **sound:** Lenhart; **music:** Luis Bonfa and Antonio Carlos Jobim.

Cast: Brenno Melio (*Orphée*); Marapessa Dawn (*Eurídice*); Ademar da Silva (*Death*); Lourdes de Oliveria (*Mira*); Lee Garcia (*Serafina*).

Awards: Cannes Film Festival, Palme d'Or, 1959; Oscar for Best Foreign Film, 1959.

Publications

Books:

de Moraes, Vinicius, *Orfeu da Conceição*, Rio de Janeiro, 1960.
Armes, Roy, *French Film*, New York, 1970
Johnson, Randal, and Robert Stam, *Brazilian Cinema*, New Brunswick, New Jersey, 1982.

Articles:

Sadoul, Georges, ''Notes on a New Generation,'' in *Sight and Sound* (London), Summer-Autumn 1959.
Weber, Eugen, ''An Escapist Realism,'' in *Film Quarterly* (Berkeley), Winter 1959.
Alpert, Hollis, ''New Wave: Orpheus in Rio,'' in *Saturday Review* (New York), 19 December 1959.
''Orpheus Distending,'' in *Time* (New York), 19 September 1960.

Orfeu negro

Trémois, Claude-Marie, ''Comment Camus a tourné *Orfeu Negro*,'' in *Nouveaux Films Français* (Paris), no. 474, 1960.
Shipman, David, in *Films and Filming* (London), October 1983.

* * *

By transplanting the myth of Orpheus and Eurydice to the boisterous, colorful atmosphere of Brazil's Carnival, Marcel Camus rejuvenates it and infuses its universal themes with a vibrant particularity born of its interweavings with Vodoun and other Brazilian traditions.

Film anthologies routinely report that *Orfeu negro* is based on *Orfeu da Conceiçao*, a play written two years earlier by the Brazilian Vinicius de Moraes. Actually there is only a slight correspondence between the two; the play follows the original myth far more closely. Although Camus borrows two principal elements from the play—Mira as the other love interest and an avenging Maenad, and a black woman as the voice of Eurídice after death—he translates these elements as freely as those borrowed from the original myth, other Greek legends, and Brazilian customs.

The principal motif in the film is that of Orfeu as a sun god, and the film itself as a modern solar myth. In an opening scene, a boy flies a kite that looks like a sun, shouting to Serafina to ''look at the sun!'' Umbrellas (necessary only when there is no sun) are hung rapidly, one by one, by Orfeu's guitar in a pawnshop. Orfeu tells the boy, Benedetto, that he makes the sun rise, which is the principal task of a solar god; the morning after Orfeu first sleeps with Eurídice, Benedetto and a friend leave Orfeu's guitar by the door so that he'll remember to make the sun rise; the boys themselves make it rise the next day when Orfeu dies before daybreak. Orfeu's songs reflect solar themes: ''Morning when the sun rises . . . come and place tenderly your pearls of dew on nature in bloom,'' as well as ''Happiness lasts a day,'' a day being the birth-death-rebirth cycle of a sun god. At the rehearsal for the upcoming dance, Benedetto tells Eurídice that Orfeu is the sun god and his fiancée Mira is the Queen of the Day: ''Look, the sun will kiss the day.'' Orfeu's costume for Carnival is that of a golden warrior with a gold foil sun as his shield. Finally, at Carnival a number of dancers carry sun-like wands. Other motifs—Eurídice's scarf of the constellations (''houses of Heaven'') and the float of the stars, moon, and the planets that passes Orfeu after Eurídice's death—reinforce the astral themes.

The film also relates more specifically to the Orphic myth. Though he plays a more modern stringed instrument, Orfeu, like Orpheus before him, is a musician. When he discovers the name of his new-found goddess—Eurídice—he tells her, ''I have loved you a thousand years.'' Eurídice flees from Death just as Eurydice fled from Aristaeus, a shepherd intent on seducing her. While fleeing, she is electrocuted by a live wire she has seized in panic, just as Eurydice was poisoned by a viper she trod upon in her haste. After Eurídice's death, Orfeu descends to the underworld as did Orpheus. Indeed, the overhead shot of him descending a long, dark spiralling staircase, flowing red at its base, is one of the eeriest moments in the film (the final encounter with Death being the other). A dog named Cereberus guards the gate of a house where a *Vodoun* ceremony is being held, Orfeu's destination. Just as Orpheus had to sing to animate the shades of the underworld, so does Orfeu's guide urge him, once they are inside: ''Call her. She'll come. Call her, Orfeu . . . Sing to her.'' (It is here, incidentally, that Greek myth and Brazilian religion neatly coincide; in *Vodoun* the appropriate gods are expected to appear when devotees summon them by songs in their honor.) As in the original myth, Orfeu is warned not to look behind him when he is retrieving Eurídice. But when he hears her voice—''Do not turn around, Orfeu. You'll lose me forever''—he is desperate to see her and, in turning, loses her as did Orpheus before him. Finally, he is killed by a vengeful and jealous woman, just as Orpheus was killed by the Maenads.

Other elements from Greek mythology are liberally employed. The principal characters live on an Olympian mountain. A blind balloon man/guide appears at the beginning of the film to give Eurídice directions: ''I know the way without sight.'' Hermes, who functions, appropriately, as a messenger tells Eurídice the way to Serafina's and offers her sanctuary when she is threatened. He then goes to find Orfeu, tells Orfeu of Eurídice's death, and finally discovers Orfeu collapsed on the street, giving him the necessary papers to claim Eurídice's body.

It is to Camus's credit that the incorporation of all these mythic elements is rarely heavy-handed. (Only the intermittent appearance of Death seems strained, perhaps because it has no Brazilian context) This is largely due to his lively, detailed depiction of local custom—the opening scenes of women carrying cans on their heads and shopping, the commotion of the pawnshop, the rustic huts of Orfeu and Serafina, the wild and colorful dancing and music of Carnival, and the scenes of Brazilian bureaucracy. The spontaneity is enhanced by Camus's use of native Brazilian actors, many not professionals.

The vivid cinematography of Jean Bourgoin also helps to enliven the mythic themes. The day/night dichotomy is handled brilliantly—spectacular technicolor sunrises and glorious panoramas of Rio in the daylight contrast with the dimly-lit scenes of night, particularly in the encounters with Death which heighten the sense of impending doom. The scene at the tram depot is particularly frightening: we see Death, large and ominous in the foreground. Eurídice runs through the dark, and we hear more clearly than we see what is happening—Eurídice's screams of ''No!'' and ''Orfeu!,'' the creepy hum of electricity, the stacatto sound of Eurídice's high heels in flight. Such darkness is appropriate to night and it is only when Orfeu tries to turn night into day, by throwing the electric switch, that Eurídice dies.

Orfeu negro is an effective translation of an ancient Greek myth to a modern Brazilian love story. The film was an instant commercial success worldwide and won the Palme d'Or at Cannes.

—Catherine Henry

ORPHÉE

(Orpheus)

France, 1950

Director: Jean Cocteau

Production: Palais-Royal Films; black and white, 35mm; running time: 112 minutes. Released 1950. Filmed in the ruins of the Ecole de Saint-Cyr.

Producer: Andreé Paulvé; **screenplay:** Jean Cocteau, from Cocteau's play; **photography:** Nicholas Hayer; **sound:** Calvet; **production designer:** Jean d'Eaubonne; **models:** Christian Bérard; **music:** Georges Auric; **costume designer:** Marcel Escoffier.

Cast: Jean Marais (*Orphée*); Maria Casarès (*The Princess*); Marie Déa (*Eurydice*); François Périer (*Heurtebise*); Juliette Gréco (*Aglaonice*); Edouard Dermit (*Cégeste*); Henri Crémieux (*Editor*); Pierre Bertin (*Police commissioner*); Roger Blin (*Poet*); Jacques Varennes, André Carnège, René Worms (*Judges*); Renée Cosima (*A bacchant*); René Lacour (*The factor*); Maffre (*An agent*); Jean-Pierre Melville (*Hotel director*); Claude Mauriac, Jean-Pierre Mocky, Jacques Doniol-Valcroze, Claude Borelli, Philippe Bordier, Victor Tabournol, and the voice of Jean Cocteau.

Orphée

Publications

Script:

Cocteau, Jean, *Orphée*, Paris, 1961; also in *Jean Cocteau: Three Screenplays*, New York, 1972, and *Orphee: The Play and the Film*, edited by E. Freeman, Oxford, 1976.

Books:

Crosland, Margaret, *Jean Cocteau*, London, 1955.
Kihm, Jean-Jacques, *Cocteau*, Paris, 1960.
Fraigneau, André, *Cocteau*, New York, 1961.
Fowlie, Wallace, editor, *The Journals of Jean Cocteau*, Bloomington, Indiana, 1964.
Fowlie, Wallace, *Jean Cocteau: The History of a Poet's Age*, Bloomington, Indiana, 1968.
Lannes, Roger, *Jean Cocteau*, Paris, 1968.
Sprigge, Elizabeth, and Jean-Jacques Kihm, *Jean Cocteau: The Man and the Mirror*, New York, 1968.
Gilson, René, *Cocteau*, New York, 1969.
Armes, Roy, *French Cinema since 1946: The Great Tradition*, New York, 1970.
Phelps, Robert, editor, *Professional Secrets: An Autobiography of Jean Cocteau*, New York, 1970.
Steegmuller, Francis, *Cocteau*, Boston, 1970.
Evans, Arthur, *Jean Cocteau and his Films of Orphic Identity*, Philadelphia, 1977.
Anderson, Alexandra and Carol Saltus, editors, *Jean Cocteau and the French Scene*, New York, 1984.
de Miomandre, Philippe, *Moi, Jean Cocteau*, Paris, 1985.
Keller, Marjorie, *The Untutored Eye: Childhood in the Films of Cocteau, Cornell, and Brakhage*, Cranbury, New Jersey, 1986.
Cocteau, Jean, *Past Tense, Volume 1: Diaries*, London, 1987.
Peters, Arthur King, *Jean Cocteau and His World: An Illustrated Biography*, London, 1987.
Knapp, Bettina L., *Jean Cocteau*, Boston, 1989.
Philippe, Claude-Jean, *Jean Cocteau*, Courbevoie, 1989.
Mourgue, Gérard, *Cocteau*, Paris, 1990.
Tsakiridou, Cornelia A., *Reviewing Orpheus: Essays on the Cinema and Art of Jean Cocteau*, Lewisburg, 1997.

Articles:

Koval, Francis, ''Interview with Cocteau,'' in *Sight and Sound* (London), August 1950.
Lambert, Gavin, ''Cocteau and Orpheus,'' in *Sequence* (London), Autumn 1950.
Debrix, Jean R., ''Cocteau's *Orpheus* Analyzed,'' in *Films in Review* (New York), June-July 1951.
''People of Talent (1): Maria Casarès,'' in *Sight and Sound* (London), Spring 1955.
Cocteau, Jean, in *Film* (London), March 1955.
Durgnat, Raymond, in *Films and Filming* (London), October 1963.
Long, Chester Clayton, ''Cocteau's *Orphée:* From Myth to Drama to Film,'' in *Quarterly Journal of Speech*, October 1965.
Hammond, R. M., ''The Mysteries of Cocteau's *Orpheus*,'' in *Cinema Journal* (Iowa City), Spring 1972.
Gauteur, C., ''Jean Cocteau et le cinéma,'' in *Image et Son* (Paris), June-July 1972.
Avant-Scène du Cinéma (Paris), July-September 1973.
Renaud, T., ''Retrospective: Jean Cocteau: Un Cinéaste? Peut-être; Un Auteur? Certainement,'' in *Cinéma* (Paris), December 1973.
Philippon, A., ''La Magie des origines,'' in *Avant-Scène du Cinéma* (Paris), 1–15 May 1983.
Rivette, J., ''Die Malheurs des *Orphée*,'' in *CICIM: Revue Pour le Cinéma Français*, no. 24/25, January 1989.
Paech, J., ''Orpheus hinter den Spiegeln,'' in *EPD Film* (Frankfurt), July 1989.
Hogan, David J., ''Le sang du poète/*Orpheus*,'' in *Filmfax* (Evanston), no. 36, December-January 1992–1993.
Peyras, P., ''Que cache le cadre de Bazin?'' in *Focales*, no. 2, 1993.
Cieslar, Jirí, ''O soše, torzu a Orfeovi/II/Part 2,'' in *Film a Doba* (Prague), vol. 39, no. 4, Winter 1993.
Smith, E.L., ''Framing the Underworld: Threshold Imagery in Murnau, Cocteau, and Bergman,'' in *Literature/Film Quarterly* (Salisbury), vol. 24, no. 3, 1996.
Carvalho, J., ''*Orpheus*: The Absence of Myth in Cocteau,'' in *Bucknell Review*, vol. 41, no. 1, 1997.
Strauss, W.A., ''Jean Cocteau: The Difficulty of Being Orpheus,'' in *Bucknell Review*, vol. 41, no. 1, 1997.
Oxenhandler, N., ''Cocteau on Video: This Tape Could Be Hazardous to Your Health,'' in *Bucknell Review*, vol. 41, no. 1, 1997.

* * *

No discussion of modern European cinema can be complete without the inclusion of Jean Cocteau's *Orphée*. It is not only the capstone of Cocteau's artistic career but also a foremost example of poetry on film which influenced an entire generation of young filmmakers. The film represents the artistic zenith of Cocteau's lifelong pre-occupation with the myth of Orpheus. In the words of Pauline Kael, ''It was with *Orpheus* that Cocteau orchestrated the themes of the dreams and ecstasies of the poet and his obsession with the unknown.''

Orphée is Cocteau's most philosophically complete film and the second in his trilogy of *films à clef* dealing with the ''orphic identity.'' The first was the milestone *Le sang d'un poète*, an enigmatic and surreal work of art which André Bazin described as a ''documentary of the imagination.'' Cocteau completed his trilogy in 1960 with *Le testament d'Orphée*, a personalized coda to his poetic quest in which Cocteau himself played the poet.

To Cocteau ''poet'' meant the creative artist, and the Orpheus of Greek mythology—the god of the lyre, song, and poetry—was Cocteau's personal muse. For Cocteau the plight of the poet was an unending search for truth and immortality, a life of suffering and martyrdom during which the poet must experience many deaths. In his introduction to *Orphée*, Cocteau wrote: ''The poet must die several times in order to be reborn. Twenty years ago I developed this theme in *The Blood of a Poet*. But there I played it with one finger, in *Orpheus* I have orchestrated it.''

The film, derived from Cocteau's 1925 play *Orphée*, revolves around the Poet Orpheus, the conflict with his wife Eurydice, and his struggle with the unknown world of ''inspiration'' personified by the Princesses. Like the mythical Orpheus's journey to Hades, Cocteau's Orphée must journey to the unknown—herein called the ''zone''; which Cocteau, rather than building an artificial set, filmed in the bombed-out military academy of Saint-Cyr.

Cocteau's modernization of this fable is delineated much like a whodunit; Cocteau himself described it as ''a detective story, bathed on one side in myth, and on the other is the supernatural.'' To evoke the supernatural Cocteau employed a number of cinematic tricks reminiscent of Méliès, most notably the vat of mercury to depict his mirror. He was, however, no mere filmic prestidigitator. These devices were simply the technical means by which he transcended the ordinary boundaries of the narrative film to create a ''cinematograph'' (a term he invented) detailing the ''frontier incidents between one world and another.''

Orphée was greeted with indifference and ambivalence by many critics who thought Cocteau a dilettante and a visual trickster, though perhaps their animosity derived from their own homophobia. The film, however, did receive the International Critics Award at the Venice Film Festival, and through the years has achieved the deserved status of masterpiece.

—Ronald Bowers

OSAKA ELEGY

See **NANIWA EREJI**

OSSESSIONE

Italy, 1942

Director: Luchino Visconti

Production: Industrie Cinematografiche Italiane S.A.; black and white, 35mm; running time: 135 minutes originally, other versions are 110 minutes. Released 1942.

Screenplay: Antonio Pietrangeli, Luchino Visconti, Mario Alicata, Giuseppe De Santis, and Gianni Puccini, from the novel *The Postman Always Rings Twice* by James M. Cain; **photography:** Aldo Tonti and Domenico Scala; **editor:** M. Serandrei; **art directors:** Gino Franzi, and Ferrare and Ancône; **music:** Giuseppe Rosati; **music director:** Maestro Fernando Previtali; **costume designer:** Maria De Matteis.

Cast: Dhia Cristiani (*Anita, the dancer*); Elio Marcuzzo (*The Spaniard*); Vittorio Duse (*Truck driver*); Clara Calamai (*Giovanna*); Massimo Girotti (*Gino*); J. de Landa (*Giovanna's husband*); M. Sakara; Michele Riccardini.

Publications

Script:

Visconti, Luchino, and others, *Ossessione*, Bologna, 1977.

Books:

Gromo, Mario, *Cinema Italiano*, Milan, 1954.
Pellizzari, Lorenzo, *Luchino Visconti*, Milan, 1960.
Ferrara, Giuseppe, *Visconti*, Paris, 1963; 2nd edition 1970.
Baldelli, Pio, *I film di Luchino Visconti*, Manduria, 1965.
Guillaume, Yves, *Visconti*, Paris, 1966.
Nowell-Smith, Geoffrey, *Luchino Visconti*, New York, 1968.
Baldelli, Pio, *Luchino Visconti*, Milan, 1973.
Ferrero, Adelio, editor, *Visconti: Il cinema*, Modena, 1977.
Stirling, Monica, *A Screen of Time: A Study of Luchino Visconti*, New York, 1979.
Rondolini, Gianni, *Luchino Visconti*, Turin, 1981.
Servadio, Gaia, *Luchino Visconti: A Biography*, London, 1981.
Bencivenni, Alessandro, *Luchino Visconti*, Florence, 1982.
Tonetti, Clarreta, *Luchino Visconti*, Boston, 1983, 1998.
Ishaghpour, Youssef, *Luchino Visconti: Le Sens et l'image*, Paris, 1984.
Sanzio, Alain, and Paul-Louis Thirard, *Luchino Visconti: Cinéaste*, Paris, 1984.
De Guisti, Luciano, *I film di Luchino Visconti*, Rome, 1985.
Geitel, Klaus, and others, *Luchino Visconti*, 4th edition, Munich, 1985.
Mancini, Elaine, *Luchino Visconti: A Guide to References and Resources*, Boston, 1986.
Villien, Bruno, *Visconti*, Paris, 1986.
Schifano, Laurence, *Luchino Visconti: Les Feux de la passion*, Paris, 1987.
Micciché, Lino, *Visconti e il neorealismo: Ossessione, La terra trema, Bellissima*, Venice, 1990.
Renzi, Renzo, *Visconti segreto*, Rome, 1994.
Micciché, Lino, *Luchino Visconti: un profilo critico*, Venice, 1996.
Bacon, Henry, *Visconti: Explorations of Beauty and Decay*, Cambridge, 1998.

Articles:

Sight and Sound (London), Spring 1948.
Castello, Giulio Cesare, ''Luchino Visconti,'' in *Sight and Sound* (London), Spring 1956.
Poggi, Gianfranco, ''Luchino Visconti and the Italian Cinema,'' in *Film Quarterly* (Berkeley), Spring 1960.
Etudes Cinématographiques (Paris), no. 26–27, 1963.
Cinema (Rome), April 1970.
Foose, T. T., ''Authorized Cain: *Postman* Done by French, Pirated by Visconti's *Ossessione*,'' in *Variety* (New York), 10 November 1976.
Cabourg, Jean, ''Luchino Visconti, 1906–1976,'' in *Avant-Scène du Cinéma* (Paris), 1 and 15 March 1977.
Fieschi, J. ''Visconti années quarante,'' in *Cinématographe* (Paris), December 1978.

Ossessione

Cabourg, Jean, ''Luchino Visconti, 1906–1976,'' in *Anthologie du Cinéma 10* (Paris), 1979.

Lyons, D., ''Visconti's Magnificent Obsessions,'' in *Film Comment* (New York), March-April 1979.

Fieschi, J., and others, ''Huit coups de sonnette,'' in *Cinématographe* (Paris), September 1981.

Malmberg, C. J., ''Den fatala ågterkomsten,'' in *Chaplin* (Stockholm), no. 4. 1981.

''Album di *Ossessione*'' in *Cinema Nuovo* (Bari), October 1981.

Amiel, V., ''Le Paysage de ceux qui vont mourir: *Ossessione*,'' in *Positif* (Paris), September 1982.

De Santis, Giuseppe, ''E con *Ossessione* osai il primo giro di manovella,'' in *Cinema Nuovo* (Bari), June and August-October 1984.

Film Criticism (Meadville, Pennsylvania), Autumn 1984.

De Santis, Giuseppe, and L. Bohne, ''Visconti's Interpretation of Cain's Setting,'' in *Film Criticism* (Meadville, Pennsylvania), Spring 1985.

Cinema Nuovo (Bari), June 1985.

Baxter, Brian, in *Films and Filming* (London), September 1986.

Petit, Chris, in *Monthly Film Bulletin* (London), September 1986.

Gili, J. A., in *Camera/Stylo* (Paris), December 1989.

Schneider, R., ''*Ossessione*: acte de naissance du neorealisme italien,'' in *Cinemaction* (Conde-sur-Noireau), vol. 70, no. 1, 1994.

Deasy, F., ''Drenched in Longing,'' in *Sight & Sound* (London), vol. 5, no. 5, May 1995.

Piazzo, Philippe, ''Visconti, année zéro: Les amants diaboliques,'' in *Télérama* (Paris), no. 2380, 23 August 1995.

Liandrat-Guigues, S., ''Le corps a corps des images dans l'oeuvre de Visconti,'' in *Cinemas*, vol. 7, no. 1/2, 1996.

Hillman, R., ''Sites of Sound: Austrian Music and Visconti's 'Senso,''' in *Cinefocus*, vol. 4, 1996.

Lagny, M., ''*Ossessione* dans le noir,'' in *Iris* (Iowa City), no. 21, Spring 1996.

* * *

A majority of critics and theoreticians locate the first, significant instance of the neorealist aesthetic in *Ossessione*, Luchino Visconti's first directorial effort. (The term ''neorealism'' appeared initially in 1942, the same year as the film, in Umberto Barbaro's article on

French pre-war cinema.) Whether or not we choose to view *Ossessione* as elementally neorealist, it does succeed in demonstrating many of the appropriate traits of that mode.

That the film is a version of James M. Cain's thriller *The Postman Always Rings Twice* is less surprising when we realize the impact that the gritty toughness and brutal edge of Cain's prose and narrative, as well as that of the hardboiled school in general, had in Italy at that time. The idea to adapt the work probably came from Jean Renoir (whose *La bête humaine* is fraught with similarities), during the period that Visconti acted as his assistant. A legend, disputed by Geoffrey Nowell-Smith in *Visconti*, has grown up around the film to the effect that the director chose to subvert Fascist censorship and criticize the regime; however, it is believed that when Mussolini's son walked out on a preview screening, exclaiming that this was not Italy, the film was abruptly withdrawn from distribution and went unseen until the peak of neorealist interest after the war.

As would become his general practice in adapting the work of others, Visconti changes dramatic motivations and much of the story itself. He ''Italianized'' the novel's setting and characters so that the film is unique to its historical moment. *Ossessione* amalgamates operatic melodrama and realism as in later films (*Senso*, *Il gattopardo*, *La caduta degli dei*) except here it is the naturalistic, verist potential that is stressed in the mise-en-scene, not the theatrical. Instead of indulging in the palpable, material sensuality of the later works, the director does not shirk the squalid prosaicism associated with neorealism at its most ingenuous and idealized. A monochrome countryside, devoid of pictorial charge, emphasizes the dismal life of provincials. Even the sexual attraction of Gino and Giovanna, relatively unmediated by the kind of clever banter found in Wilder's *Double Indemnity* (another Cain piece with a comparable story made that year), reveals itself as a human fact, another aspect setting the film apart from the coldly sophisticated sensuality of the Fascist era films. This irrational but human passion, alluded to in the title, plays an active role in transforming these unhappy economically marginal people into murderers, and will eventually destroy them.

Characters are drawn with a deft exactitude falling just this side of stereotype or exaggeration. Giovanna has traded the uncertain and demeaning life of a casual prostitute (''I used to get men to invite me to supper'') for the vapid existence of a defeated slave. She sits in her depressing kitchen, hopelessly embattled by the boredom and servitude of a loveless marriage. On his part, Bragana adds to the claustrophobia of the relationship with his repulsive corpulence and spiteful personality. Behind him—and due in part to his association with the local priest, somewhat sinister-looking, almost Buñuelian, with his hunting rifle—we sense a whole class of greasy Braganas only too willing to impose sexual hegemony and the will of the bourgeoisie. Social signification surfaced through exacting psychological determinations and the resultant interpersonal conflict is at the root of Visconti's ''anthropomorphic cinema,'' an idea laid out around the time of this film.

Metonymic signifiers of the desires of the pair pepper the narrative in an almost Antonionian fashion: while they are making love, a wardrobe door swings open to reveal Bragana's good clothing; Bragana rushes out to shoot a troublesome cat, and as the shot rings out, we read on the lovers' faces the fear of discovering within themselves the power to do away with him in the same brutal manner.

—Joel Kanoff

OSTRE SLEDOVANÉ VLAKY

(Closely Watched Trains)

Czechoslovakia, 1966

Director: Jiří Menzel

Production: Smída-Fikar group for the Barrandov Film Studio; black and white, 35mm; running time: 92 minutes, English version is 89 minutes; length: 2509 meters. Released 1966, Czechoslovakia. Filmed 1965 in the Lodenice train station.

Presented by: Carlo Ponti; **producer:** Zdenek Oves; **screenplay:** Jiří Menzel and Bohumil Hrabal, from the novel *Ostre sledované vlaky* by Bohumil Hrabal; **photography:** Jaromír Sofr; **editor:** Jiřina Lukešová; **sound:** Jiří Pavlík; **art director:** Oldřich Bosák; **sets:** Jiří Cvrček; **music:** Jiří Sust; **costume producer:** Ružena Bulickoa; **advisers:** J. Simák and Colonel Golyšev.

Cast: Václav Neckář (*Trainee Miloš Hrma*); Jitka Bendová (*Conductor Maša*); Vladimír Valenta (*Stationmaster*); Libuše Havelková (*Stationmaster's wife*); Josef Somr (*Train Dispatcher Hubicka*); Alois Vachek (*Station assistant*); Jitka Zelenohorská (*Telegraphist*); Vlastimil Brodský (*Councilor Zedniček*); Ferdinand Kruta (*Uncle Noneman*); Kveta Fialová (*The Countess*); Nada Urbánková (*Victoria Freie*); Jiří Menzel (*Dr. Brabec*).

Awards: Grand Prize, International Film Week at Mannheim, 1966. Oscar for Best Foreign-Language Film, 1967; Grand Prix, International Film Festival at Addis Ababa, 1967.

Publications

Script:

Closely Watched Trains: A Film by Jiří Menzel and Bohumil Hrabal, New York, 1971.

Books:

Whyte, Alistair, *New Cinema in Eastern Europe*, New York, 1971.
Liehm, Antonín, *Closely Watched Films*, New York, 1974.
Liehm, Mira, and Antonín, *The Most Important Art: East European Film after 1945*, Berkeley, 1977.
Habova, Milada, and Jitka Vysekalova, editors, *Czechoslovak Cinema*, Prague, 1982.
Skvorecky, Josef, *Jiří Menzel and the History of the Closely Watched Trains*, New York, 1982.
Hames, Peter, *The Czechoslovak New Wave*, Berkeley, 1985.

Articles:

Sarris, Andrew, ''Movers,'' in *Saturday Review* (New York), 23 December 1967.
Kolodny, I., ''The Man Who Made Closely Watched Trains,'' in *Action* (Los Angeles), May-June 1968.

Ostre sledované vlaky

Morgenstern, Joseph, and John Simon, in *Film 1967–68*, edited by Richard Schickel and John Simon, New York, 1968.

Films and Filming (London), July 1968.

Levy, Alan, ''A Promised Land . . . ,'' in *New York Times Magazine*, 9 February 1969.

Szigeti, L., ''Tragizm i humor to bliznieta,'' in *Kino* (Warsaw), March 1991.

Hietala, V., ''Tarkoin vartioidut junat,'' in *Filmihullu* (Helsinki), no. 6, 1995.

* * *

In 1963, Bohumil Hrabal, almost fifty years old, made his first contribution to Czech literature with a collection of short stories entitled *Perličky na dne* (*Pearls of the Deep*). These diminutive prose pieces, remarkable for concentrating on the destinies of little people on the edges of society, the original manner of narration, and a masterly use of most varied niceties and refinements of the Czech language, immediately gained popularity with both readers and critics. The stories also captivated film people. In 1965, a group of emerging directors shot a film based on *Perličky*. One of these was Jiří Menzel who was charmed by the world of Hrabal's characters to such an extent that he has returned to it throughout his creative career. In 1966 he completed *Closely Watched Trains* from Hrabal's book of the same year. In 1980, he made *Postřižiny* and soon worked on another picture inspired by Hrabal's work, *Slavnosti sneženek* (*The Feast of the Snowdrops*).

The adaptation of Hrabal's prose, based on an uninterrupted flow of speech, monologues in which the word has an enormous significance, is not a simple matter. *Closely Watched Trains* flows in several layers: ridiculous aspects of life are permeated by cruelty, tragedy, and pathos as well as tenderness; time is treated freely, the reader being led, without obvious transitions, into various depths of the past. Menzel succeeded in transposing this multi-layered story into an art with a visual foundation. He retained almost all the conflicts of the narrative but he translated the story into a linear time sequence, arranging the succession of events according to his own needs, and gave up a multitude of *hrabalesque* details which had literally begged to be expressed. He did not allow himself to be seduced by Hrabal's magical vocabulary and he consistently pursued a visual mode of expression.

Together with Hrabal, he leads the reader to a small railroad station at a time near the end of the Second World War. Life seems to flow without great excitement. The entire story is derived from the idea that human grief, fear, and joy has its place in times of profound peace as well as in the years of a cruel war. The story of a young clerk Miloš who has problems with his love life, as well as the petty destinies of the other characters who live and work at the railroad station, are therefore linked very factually and soberly with the overwhelming events of the Second War. Menzel reminds us of the war, at the beginning, by a view of military trains, but soon it seems as if it did not exist. However, he progressively develops this theme, first in the ridiculous form in a sequence where a supervisor explains to his employees how cunningly the German army victoriously retreats, then more and more intensively through Miloš's experience of a bombardment and the dead people in the train. Together, with the increasingly frequent and terrifying reminders of war, there unfolds Miloš's erotic suffering which culminates in his liberation in love but also in his death. The film unfolds at a slow pace which accelerates only at the conclusion by paralleling and alternating the investigation of dispatcher Hubiček's ''immoral'' act and Miloš's dispassionate acts of sabotage. The comical, obscene, and tragical alternate to create a peculiar mixture of pathos and tragi-comedy which represents a new concept in Czech film. Jaromír Sofr's camera work is understated; it stresses the lyric in contrast to *hrabalesque* naturalism. The film director himself expressed accurately the poetry of his film: ''Film is too imperfect to be capable of recording everything that takes place in our fantasy when we read Hrabal's texts . . . It is necessary to compensate for the poetry of these imaginings. In my opinion, poetry of this movie s not the absurd situations themselves but in their juxtaposition, the confrontation of obscenity and tragedy.''

In the 1960s, this picture was one of the most successful Czech films, both at home and abroad. This is demonstrated by many honors at both domestic and international festivals. It remains in the repertory of Czech movie theaters and still has not lost its audience.

—B. Urgošíkova

OTAC NA SLUZBENOM PUTU

(When Father Was Away on Business)

Yugoslavia, 1985

Director: Emir Kusturica

Production: Forum/Sarajevo Film; colour, 35mm; running time: 136 minutes. Filmed in Sarajevo.

Producer: Mirza Pasic; **screenplay:** Abdulah Sidran; **photography:** Vilko Filac; **editor:** Andrija Zafranovic; **assistant director:** Zlatko Lavanic, Miroslav Mandic, Mirsad Hajdar, Zikrija Pasic, and Pero Buric; **art director:** Pedrag Lukovac; **music:** Zoran Simjanovic; **sound recording:** Ljubomir Petek and Hasan Vejzagic; **costumes:** Divna Jovanovic.

Cast: Manolo de Bartoli (*Malik*); Miki Manojlovic (*Mesac*); Mirjana Karanovic (*Senija*); Mustafa Nadarevic (*Zijo*); Mira Furlan (*Anikca*); Predrag Lakovic (*Franjo*); Pavle Vusijic (*Muzafer*); Slobodan Aligrudic (*Cekic*); Eva Ras (*Zivka*); Aleksandar Dorcev (*Dr. Ljahov*); Davor Dujmovic (*Mirza*); Amer Kapetanovic (*Joza*).

Awards: Palme d'Or, Cannes Film Festival, 1985.

Publications

Books:

Bouineau, Jean-Marc, *Mala knjiga o Emiru Kusturici*, Beograd, 1995.
Bertellini, Giorgio, *Emir Kusturica*, Milan, 1996.

Articles:

Variety (New York), 8 May 1985.
Chion, M., *Cahiers du Cinéma* (Paris), June 1985.
Nacache, J., *Cinéma* (Paris), June 1985.
Grelier, R., and D. Parra, *Revue du Cinéma* (Paris), July-August 1985.
Chevrie, M., *Cahiers du Cinéma* (Paris), October 1985.
Derobert, E., ''L'enfance et l'histoire,'' in *Positif* (Paris), October 1985.
Grelier, R., ''Le regard de l'enfance,'' in *Revue du Cinéma* (Paris), October 1985.
Manceau, J.-L., *Cinéma* (Paris), 16 October 1985.
Films and Filming (London), no. 375, December 1985.
Forbes, J., *Monthly Film Bulletin* (London), December 1985.
Anderson, Pat, in *Films in Review* (New York), vol. 37, no. 1, January 1986.
Boehringer, Kathe, in *Filmnews*, vol. 16, no. 2, May 1986.
Mitchell, H., ''Star Crossed by Stalin,'' in *Cinema Papers* (Fitzroy), no. 58, July 1986.
Horton, A., ''Oedipus Unresolved: Covert and Overt Narrative Discourse in Emir Kusturica's *When Father Was Away on Business*,'' in *Cinema Journal* (USA), Summer 1988.
Bogdanovic, D., ''Dossier historique,'' in *Avant-Scène du Cinéma* (Paris), no. 447, December 1995.
Fuller, Graham, ''The Director They Couldn't Quash,'' in *Interview* (New York), vol. 29, no. 9, September 1999.

* * *

When Father Was Away on Business achieved international success for the Yugoslav director Emir Kusturica. The story is set in the director's native Sarajevo in 1950, when Yugoslavia under Marshal Tito was beginning to distance itself from Stalin's clutches. The political and social changes of the period are seen through the eyes of six-year-old Malik (Manolo de Bartoli) who only wants to play football. Like films made in the Soviet Union or East Germany, the film may also be viewed as a historical document of a society that ceased to exist only a few years ago.

By using a child's eye view, Kusturica attempts to satirize the actions of corrupt bureaucrats in the name of the state. This is the

Otac na sluzbenom putu

central theme of the story, which tells of Malik's father, Mesac (Miki Manojlovic), sentenced to three years exile, apparently for the political crime of speaking out against a cartoon that attacked the Soviet leader, once an ally of Yugoslavia. (In the sardonic title of the film, "away on business" is the euphemism used in the former Yugoslavia for such political prisoners.) However, through Malik we see that members of his family and respected members of the community are not what they seem. Malik's father is a civil servant who uses his power to harass women until he is finally betrayed to the secret police by his former mistress Anikca (Mira Furlan), the local gym teacher; and the secret police are led by Malik's uncle Zijo, who wants Anikca for himself. The audience is invited to have much less sympathy for these characters than for Malik's mother Senija (Mirjana Karanovic), who, like many peasant women, has tolerated the infidelities of her husband but who eventually finds independence and alters her relationship with her husband. Her development mirrors the changes in the role of women in modern Yugoslavia, and the director does not fail to show us, through Malik's voice-over narrative, the antagonism between traditional peasant culture and that imposed by the modern state, in poignant scenes of circumcision and the rebuff of the state's persecution of those who follow the Orthodox Church.

Despite the suffering and betrayals within the family, a traditional wedding celebration is held for Senija's younger brother. The costumes and folk music of this event provide a memorable counterpoint to the accumulating misery and distrust among the members of the family. The young Malik accidentally sees his father violently raping Anikca in revenge for her betrayal and her attempted suicide, but once again finds his escape from brutal reality in playing with his football. Kusturica uses live football commentaries as background sounds throughout the film, presumably to reinforce the point that football is one way to escape from the lunacy of everyday life. The wedding scene can perhaps be seen as a metaphor for the political situation in Yugoslavia under Tito, which had already become past history by the time the film was made: it was a society which appeared to outsiders to be efficiently held together but which was in fact bursting at the seams with nationalistic hatred.

While this film fits within the familiar genre of the rite of passage, in which a young person acquires wisdom by observing the antics of his elders, Kusturica goes beyond the narrow concern for personal development that the genre is usually characterised by, to use the innocent child's perception in the service of a more ambitious and far-reaching exploration of the darker side of human beings, whether in their personal relationships or in their political systems. The fact that even in 1985 Kusturica could not openly criticise the regime, but had to use the story of Malik's family to make his points more covertly, in itself reinforces his criticisms. Even so the film ultimately stands or falls on the credibility of the central narrative: if the personal details were implausible the social criticism would be much less effective. It was Kusturica's good fortune, or good taste, that he managed to assemble an outstanding cast, from the extraordinary Manolo de Bartoli to the numerous extras, and to make use of locations which, only a decade after the film was completed, have been altered beyond recognition by the horrific civil war which the film can now be seen to have foreshadowed. As the society which the film convincingly portrays recedes further into the past, so its performances and locations, its evocation of childhood and its cool, detached view of human folly stand out all the more clearly as elements in a film that should not be seen merely as a record of a specific time and place. *When Father was Away on Business* is the story of Malik and his family; it is a slice of the life of Sarajevo in a period now gone forever; but it is also a thought provoking study of innocence and corruption, appearances and reality, themes which have resonance in every society.

—Monique Lamontagne

EL OTRO FRANCISCO

(The Other Francisco)

Cuba, 1975

Director: Sergio Giral

Production: Instituto Cubano del Arte e Industria Cinematográficos (ICAIC); black and white, 35mm; running time: 100 minutes. Released 1975. Filmed in Cuba.

Screenplay: Sergio Giral, from the novel *Francisco* by Anselmo Suárez y Romero written in 1838–39; **photography:** Livio Delgado; **editor:** Nelson Rodriguez; **music:** Leo Brouwer.

Cast: Miguel Benavides (*Francisco*); Ramon Veloz (*Ricardo*); Alina Sanchez (*Dorotea*); Margarita Balboa; Adolfo Llaurado.

Publications

Books:

Chanan, Michael, *The Cuban Image*, London, 1985.
Burton, Julianne, editor, *Cinema and Social Change in Latin America: Conversations with Filmmakers*, Austin, Texas, 1986.

Articles:

Werb, H., in *Variety* (New York), 6 August 1975.
Grelier, R., in *Image et Son* (Paris), March 1977.
Crowdus, Gary, and Julianne Burton, ''Cuban Cinema and the Afro-Cuban Heritage: An Interview with Sergio Giral,'' in *Black Scholar*, Summer 1977.
Hollywood Reporter, 7 July 1977.
West, Dennis, in *Cineaste* (New York), Fall 1977.
Masiello, Francine, ''*The Other Francisco:* Film Lessons on Novel Reading,'' in *Ideologies and Literature*, January-February 1978.
Lesage, Julia, ''Creating History,'' in *Jump Cut* (Berkeley), March 1985.
Forster, Imogen, ''AfroCuba: An Anthology of Cuban Writing on Race, Politics and Culture,'' in *Race and Class*, vol. 36, no. 3, January-March 1995.

* * *

Cuba's first anti-slavery novel, *Francisco*, was written in 1838–39 by Anselmo Suárez y Romero, who came from a family of slaveowners. The novel portrays an interplay of personal emotions and passions—those of masters and slaves—and contains scenes stressing the harsh lot of plantation slaves. This depiction of plantation life was submitted to Richard Madden, a British agent investigating slavery in Cuba at that time.

The film *El otro Francisco* is not a mere adaptation of the novel *Francisco*. *El otro Francisco* is a Marxist analysis of the book and its ideological framework. The film rejects the novel's liberal bourgeois idealism and uses a historical materialist perspective in an attempt to reveal the true conditions of slavery. The first half of the film may be seen as a critical ''re-reading'' of the book. The novel's melodramatic plot is followed, but two key ingredients are added: scenes illustrative of the economic situation and the class conflict, and voice-over critical commentary which underscores the novel's Romantic frame work and important social and economic facts ignored by Suárez y Romero. The second half of the film is a de-romanticized, historical materialist re-creation of the 19th century plantation where life was governed by the economics of sugar production, by class antagonism, and by Britain's overseas mercantile expansion. This section of the film also dramatizes methods of slave resistance, a subject which remained unexamined in Suárez y Romero's work. To critique history and art, Giral imaginatively drew on typical resources of the fiction film (interesting characters, plot, powerful music) and of documentary (statistics, interviews, voice-over explanation).

Giral, who is black, believes that his fellow Cubans know little about the history of slavery in their country. To fill this gap, Giral made *El otro Francisco* as well as two other features on Cuban slavery. Giral and his colleagues at the Instituto Cubano del Arte e Industria Cinematográficos have supported these projects because the film institute is committed to re-examining and reassessing the nation's history. The subject of Afro-Cuban slavery merits cinematic treatment because the Black tradition of resistance (both to slavery and to the Spanish colonial powers) represents a significant but little-known contribution to the formation of today's socialist Cuba, whose proclaimed goals include an end to all forms of domination and escape from the oppressive legacy of colonialism.

In *El otro Francisco*, Giral strived for authenticity in his depiction of the Black slave experience. Black speech patterns, chants, ceremonies, and dances were researched with the aid of the University of

Havana Folklore Group. Certain information, such as the slaves' scheduled hours of work and sleep, was drawn from Richard Madden's published documents on Cuba.

The convoluted structure and critical digressions of *El otro Francisco* appealed to critics and intellectuals but not to Cuba's general movie-going public. Because Giral proposes to reach a wide audience with his films, in his subsequent features on slavery he abandoned the structural and narrative experimentation which characterized *El otro Francisco*. Giral's cinematic experiment stands as a unique example of cinema as an instrument through which to critique literature.

—Dennis West

8½

(Otto e Mezzo)

Italy-France, 1963

Director: Federico Fellini

Production: Cineriz (Rome) and Francinex (Paris); black and white, 35mm; running time: 135 minutes. Released February 1963, released in the United States on 25 June 1963. Filmed 9 May 1962–14 October 1962, in Titanus-Appia Studios and the Cecchignola military reservation in Rome, and on location in Tivoli, Filacciano, Viterbo, and the beaches between Ostia and Fiumicino.

8½

Producer: Angelo Rizzoli; **screenplay:** Federico Fellini, Ennio Flaiano, Tullio Pinelli, and Brunello Rondi, from a story by Federico Fellini and Ennio Flaiano; **assistant directors:** Lina Wertmuller and Guidarino Guidi; **photography:** Gianni di Venanzo; **editor:** Leo Cattozzo; **sound:** Mario Faraoni and Alberto Bartolomei; **production design (scenery):** Piero Gherardi; **music:** Nino Rota; **costume designer:** Piero Gherardi; **artistic collaboration:** Brunello Rondi.

Cast: Marcello Mastroianni (*Guido Anselmi*); Anouk Aimée (*Luisa Anselmi*); Sandro Milo (*Carla*); Claudia Cardinale (*Claudia*); Rosella Falk (*Rosella*); Madeleine Lebeau (*The actress*); Caterina Boratto (*The fashionable, unknown woman*); Barbara Steele (*Gloria Moran*); Mario Pisu (*Mario Mezzabotta*); Guido Alberti (*Pace, the producer*); Mario Conocchia (*Conocchia*); Jean Rougeul (*Fabrizio Carini, Daumier*); Edra Gale (*La Saraghina*); Ian Dallas (*Maurice, the magician*); Annibale Ninchi (*Guido's father*); Giuditta Rissone (*Guido's mother*); Tito Masini (*The Cardinal*); Frazier Rippy (*The Cardinal's secretary*); Georgia Simmons (*Guido's grandmother*); Palma Mangini (*Old peasant relative*); Roberta Valli (*Little girl at the farmhouse*); Riccardo Guglielmi (*Guido at the farmhouse*); Marco Gemini (*Guido as a schoolboy*); Yvonne Casadei (*Jacqueline onbon*); Cesarino Miceli Picardi (*Cesarino, the production supervisor*); Bruno Agostino (*Bruno Agostino, the production director*); Olimpia Cavalli (*Miss Olympia, as Carla in the screen tests*); Maria Antonietta Beluzzi (*La Saraghina in some screen tests*); Comtesse Elisabetta Cini (*The Cardinal in the screen tests*); Polidor (*One of the clowns in the parade*); Mino Doro (*Claudia's agent*). The entire technical staff participated in the final circus scene.

Awards: Oscar for Best Foreign-Language Film, 1963; New York Film Critics Award, Best Foreign Film, 1963; Moscow Film Festival, Grand Prize, 1963.

Publications

Script:

Fava, Claudio G., and Aldo Viganò, *The Films of Federico Fellini*, translated by Shula Curto, Secaucus, 1985.

Fellini, Federico, and others, *8½*, edited by Camilla Cederna, Bologna, 1965; also as *8½(Otto e mezzo)*, edited by Charles Affron, New Brunswick, New Jersey, 1987.

Zaoral, Zdenek, *Federico Fellini*, Praha, 1989.

Bondanella, Peter, *The Cinema of Federico Fellini*, Princeton, 1992.

Bondanella, Peter, and Cristina Degli-Esposti, *Perspectives on Federico Fellini*, New York, 1993.

Burke, Frank, *Fellini's Films: From Postwar to Postmodern*, New York, 1996.

Books:

Borde, Raymond, and André Bouissy, *Nouveau Cinéma italien*, Lyons, 1963.

Boyer, Deena, *The 200 Days of 8½*, New York, 1964.

Budgen, Suzanne, *Fellini*, London, 1966.

Solmi, Angelo, *Fellini*, New York, 1968.

Gould Boyum, Joy, and Adrienne Scott, *Film as Film: Critical Responses to Film Art*, Boston, 1971.

Covi, Antonio, *Dibattiti di film*, Padua, 1971.

Kinder, Marsha, and Beverle Houston, *Close-Up: A Critical Perspective on Film*, New York, 1972.

Benderson, Albert Edward, *Critical Approaches to Federico Fellini's 8½*, New York, 1974.

Perry, Ted, *Filmguide to 8½*, Bloomington, Indiana, 1975.

Stubbs, John C., *Federico Fellini: A Guide to References and Resources*, Boston, 1978.

Siska, William Charles, *Modernism in the Narrative Cinema: The Art Film as a Genre*, New York, 1980.

Alpert, Hollis, *Fellini: A Life*, New York, 1981.

Fruttero, Carlo, and Franco Lucentini, *Je te trouve un peu pâle: Récit d'été avec trente fantasmes féminins de Federico Fellini*, Paris, 1982.

Costello, Donald P., *Fellini's Road*, Notre Dame, Indiana, 1983.

Grazzini, Giovanni, editor, *Federico Fellini: Intervista sul cinema*, Rome, 1983.

Burke, Frank, *Federico Fellini: Variety Lights to La Dolce Vita*, Boston, 1984.

Chandler, Charlotte, *The Ultimate Seduction*, New York, 1984.

Fava, Claudio F., and Aldo Vigano, *The Films of Federico Fellini*, Secaucus, New Jersey, 1985.

Murray, Edward, *Fellini the Artist*, 2nd edition, New York, 1985.

Kezich, Tullio, *Fellini*, Milan, 1987.

Baxter, John, *Fellini*, New York, 1994.

Costantini, Costanzo, editor, *Fellini on Fellini*, translated by Sohrab Sorooshian, London, 1995.

Gieri, Manuela, *Contemporary Italian Filmmaking: Strategies of Subversion: Pirandello, Fellini, Scola, and the Directors of the New Generation*, Toronto, 1995.

Fellini, Federico, *Fellini on Fellini*, translated by Isabel Quigley, New York, 1996.

Articles:

Comuzio, Ermanno, ''La colonna sonora di *Fellini otto e mezzo*,'' in *Cineforum* (Bergamo), March 1963.

Aristarco, Guido, ''Il gattopardo e il telepata,'' in *Cinema Nuovo* (Turin), March-April 1963.

Renzi, Renzo, ''La mezza eta del socialismo?,'' in *Cinema Nuovo* (Turin), March-April 1963.

''*8½* Issue'' of *Bianco e Nero* (Rome), April 1963.

Bachmann, Gideon, in *Film Journal* (Melbourne), April 1963.

Moravia, Alberto, in *Cinéma 63* (Paris), April 1963.

Lane, John Francis, ''A Case of Artistic Inflation,'' in *Sight and Sound* (London), Summer 1963.

Crowther, Bosley, in *New York Times*, 26 June 1963.

''Dizzy Doings on a Set: Making a Movie—*8½*,'' in *Life* (New York), 19 July 1963.

Alpert, Hollis, ''From ½ to 8½.'' in *New York Times Magazine* 21 July 1963.

Cinema (Beverly Hills), August-September 1963.

Fellini, Federico, ''Si butto in ginocchio ad abbracchiarmi,'' in *Cinema Nuovo* (Turin), September-October 1963.

Zucconi, Mario, ''La musica di otto e mezzo,'' in *Filmcritica* (Rome), October, 1963.

Hirschman, Jack, in *Film Quarterly* (Berkeley), Fall 1963.

Holland, Norman, ''Fellini's *8½:* Holland's 11,'' in *Hudson Review* (Nutley, New Jersey), Fall 1963.

Baker, Peter, in *Films and Filming* (London), October 1963.

Price, James, ''*8½:* A Quest for Ecstacy,'' in *London Magazine*, November 1963.

Cohen, Roberta, ''A Fresh Interpretation of Fellini's *8½*,'' in *Film* (London), Winter 1963.

Estève, M., ''Federico Fellini: *8½*,'' in *Etudes Cinématographiques* (Paris), Winter 1963.

Macdonald, Dwight, ''Fellini's Masterpiece,'' in *Esquire* (New York), January 1964.

Gauteur, Claude, ''Masini contre Fellini,'' in *Image et Son* (Paris), April 1966.

Robinson, W. R., editor, ''Fellini: Analyst without Portfolio,'' in *Man and the Movies*, Baton Rouge, Louisiana, 1967

Eason, Patrick, ''Notes on Double Structure and the Films of Fellini,'' in *Cinema* (Cambridge), March 1969.

Richardson, Robert, ''Wastelands: The Breakdown of Order,'' in *Literature and Film*, Bloomington, Indiana, 1969.

Linden, George, ''Film Forum: Situation, Articulation, Revelation,'' in *Reflections on the Screen*, Belmont, California, 1970.

Micha, René, ''Le Clair et l'obsur,'' in *L'Arc* (Aix-en-Provence), no. 45, 1971.

Pechter, William S., ''*8½* Times 2,'' in *24 Times a Second*, New York, 1971.

Lefèvre, Raymond, ''Fellini,'' in *Image et Son* (Paris), January 1971.

Conti, Isabelli, ''Fellini *8½* (A Jungian Analysis),'' in *Ikon* (Milan), January-March and July-December 1972.

Perry, Ted, ''Signifiers in Fellini's *8½*,'' in *Forum Italicum* (Rome), March 1972.

Metz, Christian, ''Mirror Construction in Fellini's *8½*,'' in *Film Language: A Semiotics of the Cinema*, New York, 1974.

Hyman, T., ''*8½* as an Anatomy of Melancholy,'' in *Sight and Sound* (London), Summer 1974.

Bennett, Joseph, ''Italian Film: Failure and Emergence,'' in *Kenyon Review* (New York), Fall 1974.

Greenberg, Harvey, ''*8½*—The Declensions of Silence,'' in *The Movies on Your Mind*, New York, 1975.

Stubbs, John, ''Study Guide to *8½*,'' in *Journal of Aesthetic Education* (Urbana, Illinois), April 1975.

Benderson, Albert, ''The Pinocchio Motif in Federico Fellini's *8½*,'' in *Film Studies Annual*, 1976.

Audibert, Louis, ''Le Noir et le blanc du rêve,'' in *Cinématographe* (Paris), February 1978.

Branigan, Edward, ''Subjectivity under Siege—From Fellini's *8½* to Oshima's *The Story of a Man Who Left His Will on Film*,'' in *Screen* (London), Spring 1978.

Willemen, Paul, ''Notes on Subjectivity: On Reading Edward Branigan's 'Subjectivity under Siege,''' in *Screen* (London), Spring 1978.

Telotte, J. P., "*8½* and the Evolution of the Neorealist Narrative," in *Film Criticism* (Edinboro, Pennsylvania), no. 2, 1979.

Audibert, Louis, "Le Miroir et les ombres," in *Cinématographe* (Paris), October 1979.

Burke, F., "Modes of Narration and Spiritual Development in Fellini's *8½*," in *Literature/Film Quarterly* (Salisbury, Maryland), vol. 14, no. 3, 1986.

Burke, F., "Fellini: Changing the Subject," in *Film Quarterly* (Berkeley), no. 1, 1989.

Lubelski, T., "Osiem i pol czyli potrzeba pelni," in *Kino* (Warsaw), April 1989.

Zaoralova, E., "Federico Fellini: rovnych 70," in *Film a Doba* (Prague), January 1990.

Durngat, Raymond, "*8½*," in *Monthly Film Bulletin* (London), vol. 57, no. 672, January 1990.

Canby, V., "Critic's Notebook: New Look at a Fellini Chef d'Oeuvre," in *New York Times*, vol. 142, C19, 30 October 1992.

Dean, Peter, "Video: Fellini's *8(One-Half) (Otto e mezzo)* Directed by Federico Fellini," in *Sight and Sound* (London), vol. 3, no. 5, May 1993.

James, C., "Mondo Fellini," in *New Yorker*, vol. 70, 21 March 1994.

Schickel, R., "Send in the Clowns: An Aspect of Fellini," in *Film Comment* (New York), vol. 30, September/October 1994.

Telotte, P., "Definitely-Falling-Down: *8½*, *Falling Down*, and the Death of Fantasy," in *Journal of Popular Film and Television* (Washington, D.C.), vol. 24, no. 1, Spring 1996.

Wolf, Matt, "The Other Half," in *Time Out* (London), no. 1373, 11 December 1996.

Wolf, Matt, "Nine," in *Variety* (New York), 23 December/5 January 1996/1997.

Viera, Maria, "An Homage? Not Exactly. We Just Stole the Idea Outright," in *Creative Screenwriting* (Washington, D.C.), vol. 4, no. 4, Winter 1997.

* * *

Otto e mezzo achieved its rather distinctive appellation as a result of its location within a Fellini canon which up to that point included seven films and two short pieces that the director had contributed to a pair of Italian anthology films. Given this personal linkage with its director and the film's apparent theme—one not unrelated to a case history of male menopause—as well as its numerous biographical parallels to Fellini's own life, it is tempting to regard *8½* simply as a self-indulgent though highly creative attempt to fill a void in the director's progression of films. Instead this study of a filmmaker's creative and personal crises is now recognized as a masterpiece, and one of a very small number of cinematic efforts to utter a clear statement on the intricate nature of artistic inspiration.

8½ is a film of cycles in which past, present and future are subtly intertwined in an endless continuum of meaning that exists within the mind of the artist as well as in the aesthetic itself. Utilizing a complex structure of multi-tiered symbolism common to works as diverse as Edmund Spenser's *Fairie Queene* and Herman Melville's *Moby Dick* but only rarely accomplished on the screen, the film revolves in a seemingly counter-clockwise direction pivoting on the character of Guido. It is he who imbues it with a different meaning on each level of interpretation. The various symbolic planes merge fully in the film's final scenes when all of the characters (and all that each represents) join hands to form a circle that revolves dizzily backwards until all that remains is Guido as a child, ready to begin the cycle again,

8½ is a trip backward in preparation to go forward. The end of the film is also its beginning. On every level, it is a return of the artist and the aesthetic to the formative wellsprings of the art for the inspiration that will take each into the future. On its most accessible level, the biographical one, it is the story of Guido, a motion picture director not unlike Fellini himself (although most critics are too reverential of the similarities between the two) who has lost his source of inspiration both in his art and in his life. He inevitably turns inward to examine the generative events of his development—his boyhood, the Church, his relationship with his parents, and the women in his life—as well as the nightmares accompanying each. It is only when he symbolically returns to the womb at the end of the film, by crawling under the table at the press conference where he squeezes a revolver to his temple, that he can be reborn. Stating "Clean . . . disinfect," he pulls the trigger. Like an artistic phoenix, he is reborn in his own creative ashes and rises to receive the inspiration that will enable him to create an entirely new kind of film from the experiences of the old.

At this point, a second and more abstract level of meaning begins to become apparent. The film that Guido is ultimately inspired to make is, in fact, the film that we have been watching. Thus, at the end of the biographical cycle, the beginnings of the first aesthetic level emerge. The meaning of the film, on this tier, centers on our witnessing of the creative process—the thoughts, the memories, the incidents by which a new kind of film is born. As a number of scholars, most notably Christian Metz, have suggested, "*8½* is the film of *8½* being made." This is most obvious in those scenes in which a sound-stage buzzer intrudes on the action, or those in which bright set lights are all too obviously turned on, and in the film's critical final scene where lights, cameras and crews are visible.

The final scene initiates an even more abstract cycle of meaning that becomes a commentary on the aesthetic of Italian film itself. The entire scene unfolds before an enormous monolithic structure of a rocket gantry. In front of this structure, a large crowd mills about and the entire image becomes reflective of similar scenes in the great silent epic *Quo Vadis* (1912) and *Cabiria* (1913) which represented Italy's first "golden period" of cinema. During this era, reality manifested itself in the monumental, densely populated and often frenzied forms of the epics, as well as in the grim, suffering people and dirty streets of such forerunners of neorealism as *Sperduti nel Buio* (1914). This dichotomy is reflected in *8½* in the artistic struggles Guido has with his producer who wants him to make an epic, and with himself in his expressed desire to make a film that tells the truth. Fellini merges and internalizes both concepts in *8½* to create an epic of the psyche which adequately encompasses the gritty realism of the scenes of Guido's childhood.

On this broad aesthetic level *8½* is the journey of Italian film backward to re-establish its roots in the silent period and regain the inspiration to create a new direction for the films to come. What, on the biographical level, had been a re-examination of Guido's childhood, becomes, at this extreme, a history of Italian film returning through neorealism, the white telephone comedies, and even the side show demonstrations to its beginnings. At the end of the film, as workers are dismantling the huge gantry after the press conference,

Guido sits in his car with his scriptwriter Carni who discourses on the creative artist. ''Any man,'' says the writer, ''who is really worthy to be called an artist should swear to one thing in his creative life—dedication to silence.'' With the pronunciation of the word ''silence,'' Guido's creative powers surge back and he is ready to begin the film that is *8½*.

While this scene is significant on all levels of interpretation, in the broadest sense, it is indicative that Fellini has taken film back to its golden period when experimental approaches to film forms were daring and innovative. He is clearing the stage for a new kind of film represented by *8½*, and its successor *Juliet of the Spirits*, an intertwining of reality and spectacle, but an internal one projecting the mind, imagination and emotions of its director. Although there are various other concerns in *8½* reflected in the musings and dialogues of its protagonist, they are generally supportive of the broader aesthetic levels of the film: the artist, the original work, and the tradition of the art itself. On all of these levels, Fellini has succeeded admirably in the creation of a new aesthetic from the materials of the old.

—Stephen L. Hanson

OUR HITLER

See **HITLER: EIN FILM AUS DEUTSCHLAND**

OUR TRIP TO AFRICA

See **UNSERE AFRIKAREISE**

OUT OF THE PAST

(Build My Gallows High)

USA, 1947

Director: Jacques Tourneur

Production: RKO-Radio Pictures; black and white; running time: 97 minutes; length: 8,711 feet. Released 1947.

Executive producer: Robert Sparks; **producer:** Warren Duff; **screenplay:** Geoffrey Homes (pseudonym of Daniel Mainwaring), from the novel *Build My Gallows High* by Homes; **photography:** Nicholas Musuraca; **editor:** Samuel E. Beetley; **sound:** Francis M. Sarver, Clem Portman; **art directors:** Albert S. d'Agostino, Jack Okey; **set designer:** Darrell Silvera; **music:** Roy Webb.

Cast: Robert Mitchum (*Jeff Bailey/Markham*); Jane Greer (*Kathie Moffat*); Kirk Douglas (*Whit Sterling*); Rhonda Fleming (*Meta Carson*); Richard Webb (*Jim*); Steve Brodie (*Fisher*); Virginia Huston (*Ann Miller*); Paul Valentine (*Joe Stefanos*); Dickie Moore (*The Kid*); Ken Niles (*Lloyd Eels*); Lee Elson (*Cop*); Frank Wilcox (*Sheriff Douglas*); Mary Field (*Marney*); Theresa Harris (*Eunice*); Harry Hayden (*Canby Miller*); Archie Twitchell (*Rafferty*).

Publications

Books:

McArthur, Colin, *Underworld USA*, London, 1972.
Henry, Michel, *Jacques Tourneur*, Paris, 1974.
Willemen, Paul, and Claire Johnston, *Jacques Tourneur*, Edinburgh, 1975.
Kaplan, E. Ann, editor, *Women in Film Noir*, London, 1978.
Marill, Alvin, *Robert Mitchum on the Screen*, South Brunswick, New Jersey, 1978.
Silver Alan, and Elizabeth Ward, editors, *Film Noir*, London, 1981.
Schatz, Thomas, *Hollywood Film Genres*, New York, 1981.
Eells, George, *Robert Mitchum: A Biography*, London, 1984.
Malcolm, Derek, *Robert Mitchum*, Tunbridge Wells, Kent, 1984.
Downing, David *Robert Mitchum*, New York, 1985.
Mann, Michael, *Kirk Douglas*, New York, 1985.
Douglas, Kirk, *The Ragman's Son*, New York, 1988.
Fujiwara, Chris, *Jacques Tourneur*, Jefferson, North Carolina, 1998.

Articles:

Monthly Film Bulletin (London), vol. 14, no. 168, 1947.
Variety (New York), 19 November 1947.
Crowther, Bosley, in *New York Times*, 26 November 1947.
Agee, James, in *Time* (New York), 15 December 1947.
Winnington, Richard, in *News Chronicle* (London), 20 December 1947.
Powell, Dilys, in *Sunday Times* (London), 21 December 1947.
Brion, Patrick, and Jean-Louis Comolli, interview with Tourneur, in *Cahiers du Cinéma* (Paris), August 1966.
Duboeuf, Pierre, in *Cahiers du Cinéma* (Paris), April 1967.
Tavernier, Bertrand, ''Propos de Tourneur,'' in *Positif* (Paris), November 1971.
Schrader, Paul, ''Notes on Film Noir,'' in *Film Comment* (New York), Spring 1972.
Wood, Robin, ''The Shadow Worlds of Jacques Tourneur,'' in *Film Comment* (New York), Summer 1972.
Flinn, Tom, in *Velvet Light Trap* (Madison, Wisconsin), no. 10, 1973.
Place, J. A., and L. S. Peterson, ''Some Visual Motifs of Film Noir,'' in *Film Comment* (New York), January-February 1974.
Farber, Stephen, ''The Society: Violence and the Bitch Goddess,'' in *Film Comment* (New York), November-December 1974.
''Film Noir Issue'' of *Film Reader* (Evanston, Illinois), no. 3, 1978.
Black, Louis, in *Cinema Texas Program Notes* (Austin), 15 March 1978.
Kerr, Paul, ''Out of What Past? Notes on the ''B'' Film Noir,'' in *Screen Education* (London) Autumn-Winter 1979–80.
Enclitic (Minneapolis), Fall 1981-Spring 1982.
Harvey, John, ''Out of the Light: An Analysis of Narrative in *Out of the Past*,'' in *Journal of American Studies*, no. 18, 1984.

Out of the Past

Turner, George, in *American Cinematographer* (Los Angeles), March 1984.

Camera/Stylo (Paris), May 1986.

Deutelbaum, Marshall, ''*The Birth of Venus* and the Death of Romantic Love in *Out of the Past*,'' in *Literature/Film Quarterly* (Salisbury, Maryland), vol. 15, no. 3, 1987.

Schwager, J., ''*The Past* Rewritten,'' in *Film Comment* (New York), January-February 1991.

Maxfield, J. F., ''*Out of the Past:* The Private Eye as Tragic Hero,'' in *New Orleans Review*, no. 3–4, 1992.

Gross, L., ''Baby, I Don't Care,'' in *Sight and Sound* (London), vol. 7, September 1997.

Orr, C., ''Genre Theory in the Context of the Noir and Post-Noir Film,'' in *Film Criticism* (Meadville, Pennsylvania), vol. 22, no. 1, 1997.

* * *

Though his filmmaking career spanned over 30 years and two continents, the name of Jacques Tourneur is still encountered chiefly in discussions of the Val Lewton unit at RKO, where Tourneur directed *Cat People*, *I Walked with a Zombie*, and *The Leopard Man*, the first two (at least) distinguished and distinctively poetic contributions to the horror film genre which has its roots in European folklore and the literature of English and German Romanticism. Even his auteurist partisans generally agree that Tourneur's gift for *mise-en-scène* was nourished by and flourished in the collaborative atmosphere Lewton established; Tourneur's subsequent career, apart from Lewton, exhibits a hit-or-miss pattern which seems to confirm that Tourneur was more than usually dependent upon his collaborators for inspiration.

The great exception to the ''Lewton'' rule is *Out of the Past*, produced by Warren Duff from a script by Daniel Mainwaring, adapted from his 1946 novel *Build My Gallows High*. Whether the exception proves or disproves the rule is probably beyond settlement. The film's exceptionally complicated structure, part flashback narration, part linear narrative, argues for the importance of the scriptwriter; the film's sustained pattern of self-reflexive visual metaphors argues powerfully on behalf of Tourneur as *metteur-en-scène*. In any event, there is little dispute that the particular combination of talents displayed in *Out of the Past*—significant among them the iconic screen presences of Robert Mitchum, Kirk Douglas, and Jane Greer—resulted in a distinguished contribution to another genre tradition, *film noir*, for which *Out of the Past* has become, especially since its remake as *Against All Odds*, a primary measure of excellence and source of resonance.

Latter-day (often feminist) analyses of *film noir* often assume that representational style can be taken to oppose or undermine the ''male'' vantage point typical of the genre. Many *films noir*, for example, are presented as flashback narratives of a voice-over (and sometimes on-screen) narrator; the middle sections of *Out of the Past* are often cited here. And even those films which eschew the direct representation of a point of view are presented, as it were, ''over the shoulder'' of a central male identification figure, typically the hard-bitten detective. A surprising number of *films noir* are nevertheless readable as ''female centered'' at the level of film style, the camera favoring the central woman even while the story favors male agency. Style and narrative are thus read as opposing each other at the level of interpretation in a manner analogous to the deadly conflict of male and female which tends to motivate the sex and money intrigues typical of *noir*.

The degree to which Tourneur's camera centers on and favors the Jane Greer character (Kathie Moffat) in *Out of the Past* has been elaborately and convincingly documented by Marshall Deutelbaum. Though at various times both Jeff Markham (Mitchum) and Whit Sterling (Douglas) assume Kathie is theirs to control or ''protect,'' what each discovers is that Kathie's power is the greater. Indeed, Jeff and Whit repeatedly agree on deals which seek to undo or retrieve the past—to retrieve Kathie after she shoots Whit, to retrieve incriminating tax records, to assign blame to Kathie for the death of Jeff's ex-partner—yet every attempt to undo the past only does it over again. And Kathie's importance as a figure of repetition is underlined in Tourneur's *mise-en-scène* by an elaborate series of visual allusions to Botticelli's *Birth of Venus* which serves to cast Kathie in the Venus role, god-like in her power, though perpetually (if imperfectly) ''framed'' by male views of her.

This association of Kathie with ''frames'' and ''framing'' has several important consequences. One is to call attention to Kathie's status as a screen, as something to look at. The issue is first raised when Jeff questions Sterling about his motives for wanting Kathie back after she had shot him. Surrounded by framed paintings and other art objects, Whit responds: ''I just want her back; when you see her you'll understand better.'' And Jeff's first sight of Kathie, coming after several days spent seated at a cafe table across the street from a local Acapulco cinema house, catches her walking into the darkness of the cafe through the sun-bright and screen-shaped entryway, as if she were walking off the screen and into Jeff's life. And later, when Jeff and Fisher duke it out at Jeff and Kathie's hide-out cabin, Tourneur frames the battle as a dance of shadows playing across Kathie's enigmatic, screen-like features.

The temptation to see Kathie as a receptive screen should not blind us, however, to the degree of her agency, to the sense in which she actively takes on the attributes directed at her. And the world she mirrors (frames) in her actions and gestures is the male world of financial power and masculine brutality typified by the aptly named Whit Sterling. Early on Kathie's black maid reports that Whit was in the habit of battering Kathie about; when Whit closes his last deal with Jeff (agreeing to trade Kathie to the cops in exchange for the tax documents) he again resorts to battery and death-threats to enforce his will, to erase the past by rewriting it. But Kathie deconstructs Whit's project by rewriting her own past, shooting Whit a second time, and ordering Jeff to accompany her to Mexico to pick up their romantic idyl more or less where they had left off.

And just like Whit's, Kathie's last power-gesture is fatal. Just like Kathie, who in first fleeing Whit left an unmistakable trail for Jeff to follow, and who left her incriminating bank book behind after shooting Fisher, as if signaling a desire to be caught, so too does Jeff, suddenly in the Kathie position, the female to her male, the guy with the knitting needles just like the gal with the gun (to paraphrase one of Fisher's sexist wisecracks)—so too does Jeff call down his own destruction by calling the cops. Being ''a woman'' in a world of Whit Sterlings offers a choice, really no choice at all, between the stifling domesticity of Ann Miller's Bridgeport and Kathie Moffat's suicidal power play. Like Kathie, Jeff is ''framed'' (Tourneur even frames Jeff *mise-en-abîme* against a framed portrait of Kathie at one crucial point) and the frame is deadly. The only real difference between Kathie and Jeff in this regard is that he seems more fully conscious of the frame, and wills its destruction (and his own) as a gesture of revenge. Indeed, Kathie's last act effects a like revenge in confirming Jeff's membership in the cult of suicidal ''femininity''; she shoves her gun into his crotch and pulls the trigger. From this male-brutal past there is only one way out.

—Leland Poague

OUTOMLIONNYE SOLNTSEM

(Burnt by the Sun)

Russia, 1994

Director: Nikita Mikhalkov

Production: Studio ''Tri T''/Camera One. Color, 35mm; running time: 152 mins. Released 1994. Filmed in Russia in 1992.

Producers: Nikita Mikhalkov, Michel Seydoux; **screenplay:** Nikita Mikhaklov, Roustam Ibraguimbekov, based on an original story by Mikhalkov; **photography:** Vilen Kaluta; **editor:** Enzo Meniconi; **sound:** Jean Umansky; **music:** Eduard Artemyev; **art direction and set decoration:** Vladimir Aronin, Alexandre Samulekine; **costumes:** Natalya Ivanova.

Cast: Oleg Menchikov (*Dimitri*); Nikita Mikhalkov (*Sergei Kotov*); Ingeborga Dapkounaite (*Marussya*); Nadia Mikhalkov (*Nadya*); Viatcheslav Tikhonov (*Vsevolod*); Svetlana Kriutchkova (*Mokhava*); Vladimir Ilyine (*Kirik*); Andre Oumansky (*Philippe*); Alla Kazanskaya; Nina Arkhipova; Avangard Leontiev; Inna Ulianova; Lyubov Rudnieva.

Awards: Co-winner, Jury Prize, Cannes Film Festival, 1994; Oscar for Best Foreign Film, 1994.

Outomlionnye solntsem

Publications

Books:

Borelli, Sauro, *Nikita Mikhalkov*, Firenze, 1981.
Nikita Mikhalkov: Sbornik, Moscow, 1989.

Articles:

Peigne-Giuly, A., ''Quelques jours d'un tournage de Mikhalkov,'' in *Cahiers du Cinema* (Paris), February 1994.
Maslin, Janet, ''A Dark Comedy Wins at Cannes,'' in *The New York Times*, 24 May 1994.
Murat, Pierre, ''*Soleil trompeur*/Un Russe n'a jamais connu de loi,'' in *Télérama*, #2329, 31 August 1994.
Stanley, Alessandra, ''Surviving and Disturbing in Moscow,'' in *The New York Times*, 21 March 1995.
Lipman, M., ''Russians Beam over *Sun's* Oscar,'' in *The Washington Post*, 29 March 1995.
Filipov, David, ''Post-Soviet Screen Struggle,'' in *Boston Globe*, 12 April 1995.
Thomas, Kevin, ''Welcome Rays from *Sun*,'' in *Los Angeles Times*, 22 April 1995.
Leydon, Joe, ''From Stalin to Oscar,'' in *Boston Globe*, 14 May 1995.
Neff, R., ''Mikhalkov Recalls Stalin Era with Oscar-Winning Drama,'' in *Film Journal*, vol. 98, June 1995.
Bonet, P., ''Warmed by the Oscar,'' in *World Press Review* (Marion, Ohio), July 1995.
Glaessner, Verina, ''Blind Faith,'' in *Sight and Sound* (London), vol. 6, no. 1, January 1996.

* * *

Nikita Mikhalkov's *Burnt by the Sun* is at once a heartfelt and heartbreaking drama. It is heartfelt as a depiction of a loving family, and specifically a sweet relationship between a father and daughter. It is heartbreaking because that relationship is destined to be intruded upon by the odious spectre of political hypocrisy within the confines of post-revolutionary, Stalin-ruled Russia.

In *Burnt by the Sun*, yesterday's revolutionary, whose role was so meaningful in overthrowing a ruling class, is depicted as today's undesirable: a man whose crime is having become ''middle class,'' and who is separated from his family and swiftly executed without being afforded the opportunity of self-defense.

The time is the mid-1930s, and Mikhalkov tells the story of Sergei Kotov (played by the filmmaker), one of the leaders and heroes of the Russian Revolution. Sergei is a middle-aged man who resides in the country with his family, including his wife, Marussya (Ingeborga Dapkounaite), and precocious six-year-old daughter, Nadya (played by Mikhalkov's real-life offspring). Sergei has been a confidante of Stalin, and has the well-earned respect of his fellow citizens. He is a true revolutionary, who is keenly aware of the purpose and meaning of revolution: to better the lives of the common people. He tells Nadya that the soles of his feet are ''like shoe leather'' and ''as hard and round as rocks''; they are souvenirs from his years as a young revolutionary. His hope is that his daughter will have comfortable shoes and soft socks, and will travel about in cars, trains, airplanes. What he wants for her is what he wants for all Russian children: a better future, in which all citizens can ''run, without having to flee.'' ''We're building up Soviet power for that,'' he says.

Onto the scene comes Dmitri (Oleg Menchikov), now a member of Stalin's ''political police,'' who is an old friend of the family (as well as the former lover of Marussya). His presence is welcomed, and he befriends little Nadya (who soon begins calling him ''Uncle Mitya''). But Dmitri is not paying a social visit. Symbolically, he arrives wearing a disguise, causes comical chaos in the household, and then goes about sitting in Sergei's chair. When Nadya points this out, Dmitri does not excuse himself and move. Rather, he remains in the chair, gently rocking in it with a self-satisfied look on his face.

Dmitri has come to arrest Sergei. The revolutionary's sin is that he and his family are living a ''middle-class'' life. Logically, if oppressed people are freed by revolution, shouldn't one of the benefits of that liberation be the opportunity to live in peace and comfort with one's loved ones? In Stalinist Russia, however, logic no longer exists. A new kind of oppression has replaced the old. Sergei is told by Dmitri that he soon will be signing a confession that he is a spy for the Germans and Japanese, that he is a terrorist, that he has wanted to murder Stalin. If he declines, he will be reminded that he has a wife and daughter. . . .

In the film's epilogue, we are informed that ''Comrade Kotov'' was shot on 12 April 1936, and ''rehabilitated posthumously'' twenty years later. But the fates of Marussya and Nadya are equally heartbreaking. Marussya was ''sentenced to ten years of deprivation of freedom,'' and ''died in a camp in 1940.'' Nadya was arrested with her mother, and was ''permanently rehabilitated'' in 1956. A telling, haunting question lingers during the film's final credit roll: from what have these three been rehabilitated? The sad reality is that Sergei's purpose for helping lead a revolution has been cheapened, and twisted beyond repair. Fittingly, Mikhalkov dedicates his film to ''everyone who was burnt by the sun of Revolution.''

From its opening to closing scenes, *Burnt by the Sun* is loaded with images depicting the callous disregard on the part of the Soviet power structure toward the lives of ordinary citizens. As the film begins, tanks mindlessly roll through the countryside disrupting the work of farmers. It is declared that ''the tanks are ruining the wheat,'' and the point is that the military, representing those in power, are disturbing the peasants—those who were supposed to have benefitted from the revolution—for no legitimate purpose. All that has happened is that one equally repressive ruling order has replaced another.

At the finale, as Dmitri and his fellow secret policemen drive off with Sergei, they come upon a peasant who has lost his way and run out of gas, and whose vehicle is blocking the road. This luckless fellow requests help, and ends up being shot for his trouble. His situation, and his fate, symbolize the state of post-revolutionary Russia: a nation lost and disoriented, where ordinary citizens who have committed no crime may be murdered at the whim of a secret policeman.

Mikhalkov lays the blame for the failure of the revolution squarely at the feet of Stalin. As the car drives off, an overly large banner of the ruler is set into the air. It quickly covers the sky, hovering over the corpse of the peasant and the image of Sergei speeding away to his doom.

—Rob Edelman

PAISÀ

(Paisan)

Italy, 1946

Director: Roberto Rossellini

Production: Organization Films International in collaboration with Foreign Films Productions, some sources also credit Capitani Films; black and white, 35mm; running time: 117 minutes, originally 124 minutes; length: 4195 feet. Released 1946.

Producers: Roberto Rossellini, Rod E. Geiger, and Mario Conti; **production supervisor:** Ugo Lombardi; **story:** Victor Haines, Marcello Pagiero, Sergio Amidei, Federico Fellini, Roberto Rossellini, Klaus Mann (Florence episode), and Vasco Pratolini; **screenplay:** Sergio Amidei, Federico Fellini, and Roberto Rossellini; **English dialogue:** Annelena Limentani; **English subtitles:** Herman G. Weinberg; **assistant directors:** Federico Fellini, Massimo Mida, E. Handimar, and L. Limentani; **photography:** Otello Martelli; **editor:** Eraldo da Roma; **sound:** Ovidia del Grande; **music:** Renzo Rossellini; **English narrators:** Stuart Legg and Raymond Spottiswoode.

Cast: Carmela Sazio (*Carmela*); Robert Van Loon (*Joe from Jersey*); Alfonsino Pasca (*Boy*); Maria Michi (*Francesca*); Renzo Avanzo (*Massimo*); Harriet White (*Harriet*); Dots M. Johnson (*MP*); Bill Tubbs (*Captain Bill Martin*); Benjamin Emmanuel; Raymond Campbell; Albert Heinz; Harold Wagner; Merlin Berth; Leonard Parrish; Dale Edmonds (*Dale*); Carlo Piscane (*Peasant in Sicily story*); Mats Carlson (*Soldier in Sicily story*); Gar Moore (*Fred*); Gigi Gori (*Partisan*); Cigolani (*Cigolani*); Lorena Berg (*Maddalena*); Allen Dan; M. Hugo; Anthony La Penna.

Awards: Venice Film Festival, Special Mention, 1946; New York Film Critics Award, Best Foreign Film, 1948.

Publications

Script:

Rossellini, Roberto, and others, *Paisan*, in *The War Trilogy: Open City, Paisan, Germany—Year Zero*, edited by Stefano Roncoroni, New York, 1973; also included in *Rosselliniana: Bibliografia internazionale, dossier ''Paisà''* edited by Adriano Apra, Rome, 1987.

Books:

Hovald, Patrice, *Roberto Rossellini*, Paris, 1958.

Mida, Massimo, *Roberto Rossellini*, Parma, 1961.

Verdone, Mario, *Roberto Rossellini*, Paris, 1963.

Guarner, Jose Luis, *Roberto Rossellini*, New York, 1970

Armes, Roy, *Patterns of Realism*, South Brunswick, New Jersey, 1971.

Bazin, André, *What Is Cinema?*, vol. 2, Berkely, 1971.

Leprohon, Pierre, *The Italian Cinema*, New York, 1972.

Baldelli, Pio, *Roberto Rossellini*, Rome, 1972.

Klinowski, Jacek, and Adam Garbicz, editors, *Cinema, The Magic Vehicle: A Guide to Its Achievement: Journey 1: The Cinema through 1949*, Metuchen, New Jersey, 1975.

Rondolino, Gianni, *Roberto Rossellini*, Florence, 1974.

MacBean, James Roy, *Film and Revolution*, Bloomington, Indiana, 1975.

Overby, David, editor, *Springtime in Italy: A Reader on Neo-Realism*, Hamden, Connecticut, 1978.

Ranvaud, Don, *Roberto Rossellini*, London, 1981.

Bondanella, Peter, *Italian Cinema: From Neorealism to the Present*, New York, 1983.

Rossellini, Roberto. *Le Cinéma Révélé*, edited by Alain Bergala, Paris, 1984.

Hillier, Jim, editor, *Cahiers du Cinéma 1: The 1950s: Neo-Realism, Hollywood, New Wave*, London, 1985.

Serceau, Michel, *Roberto Rossellini*, Paris, 1986.

Brunette, Peter, *Roberto Rossellini*, Oxford, 1987, 1996.

Gansera, Rainer, and others, *Roberto Rossellini*, Munich, 1987.

Rossellini, Roberto, *Il mio metodo: Scritti e intervisti*, edited by Adriano Apra, Venice, 1987.

Rossi, Patrizio, *Roberto Rossellini: A Guide to References and Resources*, Boston, 1988.

Bondanella, Peter, *Films of Roberto Rossellini*, Cambridge, 1993.

Rossellini, Roberto, *My Method: Writings and Interviews*, New York, 1995.

Gallagher, Tag, *The Adventures of Roberto Rossellini*, Cambridge, 1998.

Articles:

Barty King, Hugh, ''Seven Americans,'' in *Sight and Sound* (London), Autumn 1946.

Anderson, Lindsay, in *Sequence* (London), Winter 1947.

Crowther, Bosley, in *New York Times*, 30 March 1948.

Warshow, Robert, in *Partisan Review* (New Brunswick, New Jersey), July 1948.

Paisà

Variety (New York), 2 November 1948.

Ordway, Peter, ''Prophet with Honor: Roberto Rossellini,'' in *Theatre Arts* (New York), January 1949.

Manvell, Roger, ''*Paisan:* How It Struck Our Contemporaries,'' in *Penguin Film Review* (London), May 1949.

Koval, Francis, ''Interview with Roberto Rossellini,'' in *Sight and Sound* (London), February 1951.

Pacifici, Sergio J., ''Notes on a Definition of Neorealism,'' in *Yale French Studies* (New Haven), Summer 1956.

Rhode, Eric, ''Why Neorealism Failed,'' in *Sight and Sound* (London), Winter 1960–61.

''The Achievement of Roberto Rossellini,'' in *Film Comment* (New York), Fall 1964.

Johnson, Ian, in *Films and Filming* (London), February 1966.

Helman, A., ''Roberto Rossellini albo synteza antynomjii: Nasz Iluzjon,'' in *Kino* (Warsaw), October 1973.

Lawton, B., ''Italian Neorealism: A Mirror Construction Reality,'' in *Film Criticism* (Edinboro, Pennsylvania), no. 2, 1979.

Prédal, René, ''Roberto Rossellini, 1906–1977,'' in *Avant-Scéne du Cinéma* (Paris), 15 February 1979.

Pym, John, in *Monthly Film Bulletin* (London), November 1980.

Brunette, Peter,''Unity and Difference in *Paisan*,'' in *Studies in Literary Imagination*, vol. 16, no. 1, 1983.

Brunette, Peter, ''Rossellini and Cinematic Realism,'' in *Cinema Journal* (Evanston, Illinois), vol. 25, no. 1, 1985.

Decaux, E., in *Cinématographe* (Paris), April 1985.

Variety (New York), 24 August 1987.

Sinclair, M., ''Ellipsis in Rossellini's *Paisa*: The Privileging of the Invisible,'' in *Spectator* (Los Angeles), vol. 9, no. 1, 1988.

Pinciroli, G., ''Efficacia e completezza del gesto cinematografico a confronto in *Paisà*,'' in *Cineforum* (Bergamo, Italy), April 1990.

Roncoroni, S., and E. Bruno, ''Presentazione di due soggetti inediti di Sergio Amidei per *Paisà* di Roberto Rossellini,'' in *Filmcritica* (Rome), December 1990.

Dean, Peter, ''Video: *Paisa* Directed by Roberto Rossellini,'' in *Sight and Sound* (London), vol. 3, no. 8, August 1993.

Wagstaff, Chris, ''True Stories,'' in *Sight & Sound* (London), vol. 3, no. 8, August 1993.

Brunette, P., ''The Neo Bible,'' in *Village Voice* (New York), vol. 40, 17 October 1995.

* * *

Roberto Rossellini's *Paisà*, along with his *Roma, città aperta* (1945), introduced post-war American audiences to Italian neo-realism, which proved to be the first wave in a series of European influences that altered the shape of American cinema. Neo-realism, a movement that emerged from the shattered Italian film industry immediately after World War II, concerned itself with an almost documentary-like depiction of the hardship and suffering of the Italian people during and after World War II. Directors like Rossellini, Vittorio De Sica, and Luchino Visconti took to the streets in order to make their films. In the process they articulated an aesthetic of cinematic realism that called for the use of non-professional actors, on-location shooting, the abandonment of slick ''Hollywood'' production values, and a self-conscious rejection of commercial considerations. What emerged was a fresh and energetic film style which largely rejuvenated the pre-war stagnation of the Italian cinema. Years later Rossellini wrote that he used this new approach to attempt to understand the events of the fascist years, which had overwhelmed him personally and the Italian people generally. He chose the particular film style he did for its morally neutral approach; he simply wanted to observe reality objectively and to explore the facts that implicated his country in the fascist horror of the war. He also wanted to create a balance sheet on the experience so that Italians could begin to live life on new terms.

Paisà contains six episodes that trace the American invasion of Italy from the Allied landing in Sicily in 1934 until the Italian surrender in the spring of 1944. Rossellini does not present the war in terms of armies, strategies, and grand plans but rather as a tragedy involving the death and the suffering of human beings caught in the crush of forces beyond their control. Although some of the critics, among them Robert Warshow, found the film too sentimental in places, *Paisà* received good reviews outside of Italy, and it has retained its place as one of the classics of neo-realism, especially in the United States.

Neo-realism and Rossellini's remarks concerning *Paisà* raise some interesting questions about the mimetic nature of film and about the significance of a point of view of doctrine in shaping the final cinematic product. *Paisà* is neither a doctrinaire film nor, as Rossellini would have it, a neutral one. The film is not a long documentary, as some critics have rather simple-mindedly suggested, nor is it a film guided by a manifesto. It is a film which provides a new beginning, to borrow Rossellini's balance sheet metaphor, and does so by stripping film of the appurtenances of the pre-war studio world. Rossellini was striving for a basic sincerity in his films, and it was primarily toward that end that he made *Paisà* with a truthful simplicity which is so effective.

—Charles L. P. Silet

PANDORA'S BOX

See **DIE BUCHSE DER PANDORA**

PAPER FLOWERS

See **KAAGAZ KE PHOOL**

PARIS, TEXAS

West Germany-France, 1984

Director: Wim Wenders

Production: Road Movies Filmproduktion (West Berlin)/Argos Films (Paris), in association with Westdeutscher Rundfunk, Channel 4, and Project Film; in color; running time: 148 minutes; length: 13,320 feet. Released 1984.

Executive producer: Chris Sievernich; **producers:** Don Guest, Anatole Dauman; **screenplay:** Sam Shepard; **assistant director:** Claire Denis; **photography:** Robby Muller; **assistant photographers:** Agnes Godard, Pim Tjujerman; **editor:** Peter Pryzgodda; **assistant editor:** Anne Schnee; **sound editor:** Dominique Auvray; **sound recordist:** Jean-Paul Mugel; **sound re-recordist:** Hartmut Eichgrun; **art director:** Kate Altman; **music:** Ry Cooder.

Cast: Harry Dean Stanton (*Travis Anderson*); Dean Stockwell (*Walter R. Anderson*); Aurore Clement (*Anne Anderson*); Hunter Carson (*Hunter Anderson*); Nastassja Kinski (*Jane*); Bernhard Wicki (*Doctor Ulmer*); Sam Berry (*Gas Station Attendant*); Claresie Mobley (*Car Rental Clerk*); Viva Auder (*Woman on TV*); Socorro Valdez (*Carmelita*); Edward Fayton (*Hunter's Friend*); Justin Hogg (*Hunter, age 3*); Tom Farrell (*Screaming Man*); John Lurie (''*Slater*''); Jeni Vici (''*Stretch*''); Sally Norwell (''*Nurse Bibs*''); Sharon Menzel (*Comedienne*); The Mydolls (*Rehearsing Band*).

Awards: BAFTA Award for Best Director, 1984. Palme d'Or at Cannes, 1984.

Publications

Script:

Shepard, Sam, *Paris, Texas* (in English, French and German), edited by Chris Sievernin, Berlin, 1984.

Books:

Devillers, Jean-Pierre, *Berlin, L.A., Berlin: Wim Wenders*, Paris, 1985.

Boujut, Michel, *Wim Wenders*, third edition, Paris, 1986.

Wenders, Wim, *Written in the West: Photographien aus dem Amerikanischen Western*, Munich, 1987.

Geist, Kathe, *The Cinema of Wim Wenders: From Paris, France, to Paris, Texas*, Ann Arbor, Michigan, 1988.

Kolker, Robert P., and Peter Beicken, *The Films of Wim Wenders*, New York, 1993.

Cook, Roger F., and Gerd Gemunden, editors, *The Cinema of Wim Wenders: Image, Narrative and the Postmodern Condition*, Detroit, 1997.

Wenders, Wim, *The Act of Seeing: Essays and Conversations*, translated by Michael Hofmann, New York, 1999.

Articles:

Berthelius, M., ''Drömmen om Amerika: Historien om Wim Wenders,'' in *Chaplin* (Stockholm), vol. 26, no. 3, 1984.

Variety (New York), 23 May 1984.

Carson, Kit, in *Film Comment* (New York), May-June 1984.

Bergala, Alain, and others, in *Cahiers du Cinéma* (Paris), Summer 1984.

Welsh, H., in *Jeune Cinéma* (Paris), July-August 1984.

Johnston, Sheila, in *Monthly Film Bulletin* (London), August 1984.

''Production Diary'' in *Cinema* (West Germany), August, September, and October 1984.

Bishop, R., and T. Ryan, ''Wim Wenders: An American Saga,'' in *Cinema Papers* (Melbourne), August 1984.

Pym, John, ''The Road from Wuppertal,'' in *Sight and Sound* (London), Autumn 1984.

Ranvaud, Don, ''Paris, Texas, to Sydney, Australia,'' in *Sight and Sound* (London), Autumn 1984.

''Special Issue'' of *Positif* (Paris), September 1984.

Simsolo, Noël, and others, in *Revue du Cinéma/Image et Son* (Paris), September 1984.

Goldschmidt, D., in *Cinématographe* (Paris), September-October 1984.

Baron, Saskia, in *Stills* (London), October 1984.

Proper, R. A. F., interview with Robby Müller, in *Skoop* (Amsterdam), November 1984.

Simons, J., ''*Paris, Texas:* Wim Wenders' Wedergeboorte,'' in *Skrien* (Amsterdam), November-December 1984.

Film (West Germany), December 1984.

Kornum Larsen, J., in *Kosmorama* (Copenhagen), December 1984.

Verstappen, W., in *Skoop* (Amsterdam), December 1984-January 1985.

Dieckmann, F., in *Film Quarterly* (Berkeley), Winter 1984–85.

Wooton, Adrian, in *Film Directions* (Belfast), Winter 1984–85.

Bromet, Frans, and M. J. A. Holland, in *Skoop* (Amsterdam), February 1985.

Scharres, B., ''Robby Müller and *Paris, Texas*,'' in *American Cinematographer* (Los Angeles), February 1985.

Freitag, I., in *Filmfaust* (Frankfurt), February-March 1985.

De Gaetano, R., and P. Lughi, in *Cinema Nuovo* (Bari), June 1985.

Fantauzzi, S., ''Wenders e il suo angelo,'' in *Quaderni di Cinema* (Florence), March-April 1989.

Russell, D., ''The American Trauma: *Paris, Texas*,'' in *Movie*, no. 34–35, Winter 1990.

Saint-Ellier, A., ''L'epuisement du droit au secours des pirates?'' in *Film Exchange* (Paris), vol. 51, no. 3, 1990.

Denzin, N.K., ''*Paris, Texas* and Baudrillard on America,'' in *Theory, Culture and Society*, vol. 8, no. 2, 1991.

Van Oostrum, D., ''Wim Wender's Euro-American Construction Site: *Paris, Texas* or Texas, Paris,'' in *Florida State University Conference on Literature and Film*, vol. 16, 1991.

Luprecht, Mark, ''Freud at *Paris, Texas*: Penetrating the Oedipal Sub-Text,'' in *Literature/Film Quarterly* (Salisbury), vol. 20, no. 2, 1992.

Aldarondo, R., in *Nosferatu* (San Sebastian), no. 16, October 1994.

Edwards, C., ''Dean Stockwell,'' in *Psychotronic Video* (Narrowsburg), no. 21, 1995.

Smith, R.C., ''Open Narrative in Robbe-Grillet's *Glissements progressifs du plaisir* and Wim Wender's *Paris, Texas*,'' in *Literature/Film Quarterly* (Salisbury), vol. 23, no. 1, January 1995.

Reitinger, D.W., ''Too Long in the Wasteland: Visions of the American West in Film, 1980–1990,'' in *Film and History* (Cleveland), vol. 26, no. 1/4, 1996.

Falkowska, J., ''American and European Voices in the Films of European Filmmakers Wim Wenders, Percy Adlon and Aki Kaurismaki,'' in the *Canadian Journal of Film Studies* (Ottawa), vol. 6, no. 1, 1997.

Tunney, Tom, ''*Paris, Texas,*'' in *Sight and Sound* (London), vol. 8, no. 1, January 1998.

* * *

It is not just the title of this film which suggests a meeting between Europe and America. Production involved collaboration between the director Wim Wenders, who caught the critical eye as part of the new German cinema of the 1970s, and the scriptwriter Sam Shepard, the American author of *The Motel Chronicles*, poems and prose about highway culture in the United States. There was a deliberate policy of substantially developing the script as shooting progressed (indeed the script was completed by Kit Carson when Shepard departed for another commitment during production). Wenders has always been fascinated with Hollywood as a mode of representation. Many of his films approach the legacy of American cinema through a strategy of quotation. Yet *Paris, Texas* invests directly in an emotional folkloric tale of white America. At the same time the film opts for complexity: in particular, the present lives of the main characters are shown to be psychologically haunted by past events, and contained within the story is a special emphasis on the power of images in their own right. *Paris, Texas* knowingly reworks elements from both classical Hollywood and European art cinema. Whether it exhausts these categories or expresses a contemporary condition of nihilism is open to debate.

Road movies and family melodramas are the chief genres on which *Paris, Texas* draws. However, the way in which *mise-en-scène* establishes a sharp contrast between humanity and nature, during the opening stages in particular, is highly reminiscent of the western. The startling drama of the opening sequence depends on the way Travis, the main character, is counterposed with the desert. Yet he lacks the clear cut motivation to triumph over this wilderness. When collected by his brother Walt, Travis is incongruously dressed in a battered suit with a trucker's cap. He is silent, refusing to explain why he disappeared four years previously, and where he has been. In *Paris, Texas* the mythical conquest of nature involves recalling the hero himself from the wilderness. The latter is also a mental condition. Travis has regressed from social values, and in a sense the rest of the film is about his reintegration with American society.

Travis's first articulated memory is Paris, Texas, a plot of land which he purchased and where he claims to have been conceived. One could say that Travis's return to civilisation is marked by his recall of land ownership and the nuclear family. But Paris, Texas is a painful memory. The land remains unoccupied because Travis's own family is broken. Family reunion becomes the narrative goal.

The film renews a type of plot which theorists, notably Peter Wollen, have located within classical cinema. In this kind of plot the central protagonists search for an object of value which has disappeared in the past. The object may often be a woman. In *Paris, Texas* she is Jane, Travis's wife. Father and son quest for her after being reunited themselves, a development which tears Hunter away from the stable and caring guardianship of Walt and Annie. The quest provides a sense of purpose lacking from Wenders's previous films. Jane's discovery promises to reveal the past and save Travis. When they finally meet in a peepshow we learn that Travis's violent desire to own Jane was an initial cause of rupture.

Travis is the voyeur looking in, while Jane is confined to the sound of his voice and her reflection in a one way mirror. Somehow on a second meeting here, they achieve a degree of mutual recognition, finding catharsis through confession to one another. The narrative winds down as the film alternates between them, finally moving to her side of the partition. Slight changes of camera angle open up the oppressed space. Quick cuts between them express the return of a bond, and at the end of the scene Travis turns off his booth light so that Jane can see him. He is resigned, distant, an illuminated image, the ghostly but overwhelming memory which has returned to Jane. Thus, in a powerful fashion, through a cinematic array of devices, we are presented with an imaginary realm within the fiction.

Throughout, a form of dominance is attributed to the image itself: Paris, Texas remains a crumpled photograph; the family is only seen united, enjoying themselves in a super 8 film. Meanwhile America itself appears to be filtered through the processes of representation. Not only is the country portrayed as the endless space of the road movie, but also through such motifs as the Statue of Liberty, which pops up in the background of one shot as a mural. This detail connotes Americana, a symbolic substitute for the nation. While, the action is strictly kept to the periphery of cities, the identity of America remains mysterious, a miragelike entity viewed from the distant perspective of Travis, the outsider. Maybe one reason why a European filmmaker can deal with American mythology in the 1980s is because Hollywood's stable representations of the nation are increasingly worked through high-tech science fiction, spectacle, and more marginal discourses than in the classical era. *Paris, Texas* is surely aware of this. After all, Hunter is depicted as a *Star Wars* fan. With the older mythologies vacated by the heavyweights of Hollywood, *Paris, Texas* is left free to renew a language which is more imaginary than ever.

—Daniel Williams

UNE PARTIE DE CAMPAGNE

(A Day in the Country)

France, 1946

Director: Jean Renoir

Production: Pantheon-Production; black and white, 35mm; running time: 45 minutes; length: 1100 meters, originally 1232 meters. Released 8 May 1946, Paris. Filmed July-August 1936 near Montigny and Marlotte.

Producer: Pierre Braunberger; **executive producer:** Jacques B. Brunius, with Roger Woog; **screenplay:** Jean Renoir, from the story by Guy Maupassant; **photography:** Claude Renior; **editor:** Marguerite Houle-Renoir, final version: Marienette Cadix under Marguerite Houle-Renoir's supervision, assisted by Marcel Cravenne; **sound:** Courme de Bretagne and Joseph de Bretagne; **production designer:** Robert Gys; **music:** Joseph Kosma and Germaine Montero; **assistant to the director:** Jacques Becker and Henri Cartier-Bresson, other contributors to this film include: Claude Heymann, Luchino Visconti, and Yves Allegret.

Cast: Sylvia Bataille (*Henriette*); Georges Darnoux (*Henri*); Jeanne Marken (*Madame Dufour*); Jacques Borel (*Rodolphe*); Paul Temps (*Anatole*); Gabrielle Fontan (*Grandmother*); Jean Renoir (*Father Poulain*); Marguerite Renoir (*The servant*); Gabriello (*M. Cyprien Dufour*); Pierre Lestringuez (*Old priest*).

Publications

Script:

Renoir, Jean, *Une Partie de campagne*, in *Image et Son* (Paris), April-May 1962; excerpts in *Jean Renoir: An Investigation into His Films and Philosophy*, by Pierre Leprohon, New York, 1971.

Books:

Davay, Paul, *Jean Renoir*, Brussels, 1957.
Cauliez, Armand-Jean, *Jean Renoir*, Paris, 1962.
Renoir, Jean, *Renoir, My Father*, Boston, 1962.
Chardère, Bernard, editor, *Jean Renoir*, Lyons,1962.
Bennett, Susan, *Study Unit 8: Jean Renoir*, London, 1967.
Poulle, François, *Renoir, 1938*, Paris, 1969.
Gregor, Ulrich, editor, *Jean Renoir und seine Film: Eine Dokumentation*, Bad Ems, 1970.
Cuenca, Carlos, *Humanidad de Jean Renoir*, Valladolid, 1971.
Braudy, Leo, *Jean Renoir: The World of His Films*, New York, 1972.
Bazin, André, *Jean Renoir*, Paris, 1973.
Durgnat, Raymond, *Jean Renoir*, Berkeley, 1974.
Harcourt, Peter, *Six European Directors: Essays on the Meaning of Film Style*, Baltimore, 1974.
Beylie, Claude, *Jean Renoir: Le Spectacle, la vie*, Paris, 1975.
Gilliatt, Penelope, *Jean Renoir: Essays, Conversations, Reviews*, New York, 1975.
Faulkner, Christopher, *Jean Renoir: A Guide to References and Resources*, Boston, 1979.
Sesonske, Alexander, *Jean Renoir: The French Films 1924–1939*, Cambridge Massachusetts, 1980.
Gauteur, Claude, *Jean Renoir: Oeuvres de cinéma inédites*, Paris, 1981.
McBride, Joseph, editor, *Filmmakers on Filmmaking: The American Film Institute seminars on Motion Pictures and Television, vol. 2*, Los Angeles, 1983.
Sarceau, Daniel, *Jean Renoir*, Paris, 1985.

Une partie de campagne

Faulkner, Christopher, *The Social Cinema of Jean Renoir*, Princeton, 1986.

Vincendeau, Ginette, and Keith Reader, *La Vie est à nous: French Cinema of the Popular Front 1935–1938*, London, 1986.

Viry-Babel, Roger, *Jean Renoir: Le Jeu et la règle*, Paris, 1986.

Articles:

Crowther, Bosley, in *New York Times*, 13 December 1950.

Variety (New York), 20 December 1950.

Cahiers du Cinéma (Paris), January 1952.

Bérangert, Jean, ''The Illustrious Career of Jean Renoir,'' in *Yale French Studies*, (New Haven), Summer 1956.

Cahiers du Cinéma (Paris), Christmas 1957.

Sadoul, Georges, ''The Renaissance of the French Cinema—Feyder, Renoir, Duvivier, Carné,'' in *Film: An Anthology*, edited by Daniel Talbot, New York, 1959.

Dyer, Peter John, ''Renoir and Realism,'' in *Sight and Sound* (London), Summer 1960.

Whitehall, Richard, in *Films and Filming* (London), June and July 1960.

Durgnat, Raymond, ''Eroticism in Cinema—Part 7: Symbolism—Another Word for it,'' in *Films and Filming* (London), April 1962.

Beylie, Claude, ''Cette mâle gaité,'' in *Avant-Scène du Cinéma* (Paris), 15 December 1962.

Howard R. G., in *Film Journal* (New York), July 1964.

Kael, Pauline, in *Kiss Kiss Bang Bang*, Boston, 1968.

Nogueira, Rui, and François Truchaud, ''Interview with Jean Renoir,'' in *Sight and Sound* (London), Spring 1968.

Bodelsen, A., in *Kosmorama* (Copenhagen), October 1972.

Wiese, Epi, ''Visconti and Renoir: Shadowplay,'' in *Yale Review* (New Haven), December 1974.

Bagh, P. von, ''Kaski kertaa *Une Partie de campagne*,'' in *Filmihullu* (Helsinki), no. 7, 1976.

Magny, Joel, ''*Partie de campagne:* Les Bas-fonds,'' in *Téléciné* (Paris), April 1977.

Comolli, J. L., ''Jean Renoir: En revoyant *Une Partie de campagne. . .*,'' in *Cahiers du Cinéma* (Paris), April 1979.

Strebel, Elizabeth Grottle, ''Jean Renoir and the Popular Front,'' in *Feature Films as History*, edited by K. R. M. Short, London, 1981.

Odin, R., ''Strategia del desiderio in un' 'inquadratura di' *Une Partie de campagne*,'' in *Filmcritica* (Florence), June 1982.

Baron, R. F., ''Renoir's Neglected Masterpiece: *Une Partie de campagne*,'' in *Post Script* (Jacksonville, Florida), Fall 1983.
Pescatore, G., ''La grana del cinema,'' in *Cinema & Cinema* (Bologna), January-August 1989.
Webster, R.M., ''Renoir's *Une partie de campagne*: Film as the Art of Fishing,'' in *French Review*, vol. 64, no. 3, 1991.
Tesson, Charles, ''La robe sans couture, la danse, le patron,'' in *Cinémathèque* (Paris), no. 5, Spring 1994.
Magny, J., ''*Partie de campagne* deuxiem!'' in *Cahiers du Cinéma* (Paris), no. 479–80, May 1994.
Bénoliel, Bernard, ''Autour d'*Une partie de campagne*,'' in *Mensuel du Cinéma* (Paris), no. 18, June 1994.
Curchod, Oliver, and others, ''*Partie de campagne* de Jean Renoir,'' in *Positif* (Paris), no. 408, February 1995.

* * *

André Bazin, in his unfinished study of Jean Renoir, described *Une partie de campagne* as a ''perfectly finished work,'' one that is not only faithful in letter and spirit to the Maupassant story from which it was adapted but also actually improved by Renoir's additions and refinements to the original tale. This is high praise, indeed, when one realizes that the film's completion was highly problematic. Many of Renoir's films have had checkered careers, but none was quite so confusing as *Une partie de campagne*. Renoir originally intended to shoot a 35- or 40-minute story which he would make, he wrote later, just as if it were a full-length film. Renoir chose a gentle, 19th-century tale and planned to spend a relaxed summer filming along the banks of the Loin near Marlotte, an area he knew extremely well. The entire experience should have provided him, as Alexander Sesonske has described it, with a ''brief and pleasant respite in mid-career.'' Despite the rainiest summer in memory, an extremely volatile political climate, tensions on the set and the fact that the film sat for nearly 10 years waiting for its final editing, *Une partie de campagne* is a remarkably fine film, some say a masterpiece; Sesonske thinks that no Renoir film seems ''more unstudied, more a pure flow of life caught unaware.''

There are sound reasons for the film's critical success: it is a film of uncommon gentleness and beauty, and it forms less of a ''respite'' in Renoir's career than a concentration of his most important themes and images: the river, the countryside, the loving scrutiny of bourgeois life. *Une partie de campagne* forms a poetic centre for Renoir's French films. Rather than a sense of diversion, the film reflects a completeness. Renoir's rendering of his subject matter is incisive, his style mature, his vision complete; it is a seamless work of art. Many critics have called attention to the film's impressionistic quality, suggesting that it is a homage to the director's father, the painter Pierre Auguste Renoir. Indeed, impressionistic moments do grace the film—but for one to try to understand it as an attempt by the son to do what the father had already done with paint and canvas is to sadly underestimate the qualities of the movie. The ''painterly'' look of the films of Renoir *fils* have done much to strengthen his popular image as a director of surfaces, much to the detriment of his standing as a filmmaker of depth and perception.

The shortness of the film also has strengthened the perception of Renoir as an impressionistic filmmaker, and many critics today still respond to the film as incomplete, an interesting but unfinished experiment. The fact that Renoir left two scenes from the Maupassant story unshot has been used as evidence for regarding the film as a fragment, and considering Renoir's relative fidelity to the events of Maupassant's tale, it is an understandable, if mistaken, conclusion. Published versions of the screenplay for those ''missing'' scenes have further confused the issue. However, closer examination of the relationship between the story and the film will dispel such misconceptions. Renoir wrote in his autobiography, *My Life and My Films*, that when he was asked to increase the original footage to feature length, he refused because he felt that it would have been contrary to the intent of Maupassant's story and to his screenplay to lengthen it. Moreover, what many critics have failed to notice is that Renoir, although he adapted the events of the fiction faithfully, greatly altered the story's tone, which allowed him to drop the final scenes from the completed film without leaving the project incomplete.

Maupassant's tantalizingly brief tale is largely satiric in tone. He makes fun of the pretensions and foibles of his bourgeoisie often rather harshly; the natural setting is kept in the background; and the atmosphere of the country is diminished. Renoir not only places greater emphasis in the rural atmosphere and setting but also makes a film that by bringing such natural elements into the foreground turns Maupassant's rather strident attack on the Dufort family into a compassionate and understanding film about unrecoverable moments and the inevitable sadness of the loss of innocence and love. As André Bazin has noted, such changes do improve the original. The story is given a resonance, the characters motivation, and the ending a poignance lacking in the fictional source. As Pierre Leprohon has described it: ''there is an overflowing tenderness, and extraordinary responsiveness to the existence of things, and a transformation of the commonplace into the sublime.'' In *Une partie de campagne*, Renoir has created a poetic compression of those things that he holds dear, which is one of the reasons the film evokes such fond memories and responses from its viewers. Although unhappy and somewhat ironic, the ending is nevertheless not unhopeful. Life and the river will both flow on and be renewed.

—Charles L. P. Silet

THE PASSENGER

See **PROFESSIONE: REPORTER**

LA PASSION DE JEANNE D'ARC

(The Passion of Joan of Arc)

France, 1928

Director: Carl Theodor Dreyer

Production: Société Générale des Films (Paris); black and white, 35mm, silent; running time: originally 110 minutes, later 86–88 minutes; length: 2400 meters. Released 21 April 1928, Paladsteatret, Copenhagen. Re-released 1952 in sound version produced by Gaumont Actualité and supervised by Lo Duca, musical accompaniment from works by Scarlatti, Albinoni, Gemianani, Vivaldi, and Bach. Filmed May-October 1927 in Paris.

Screenplay: Carl Theodor Dreyer and Joseph Delteil, from a book by Joseph Delteil; **titles:** Carl Theodor Dreyer; **photography:** Rudolph

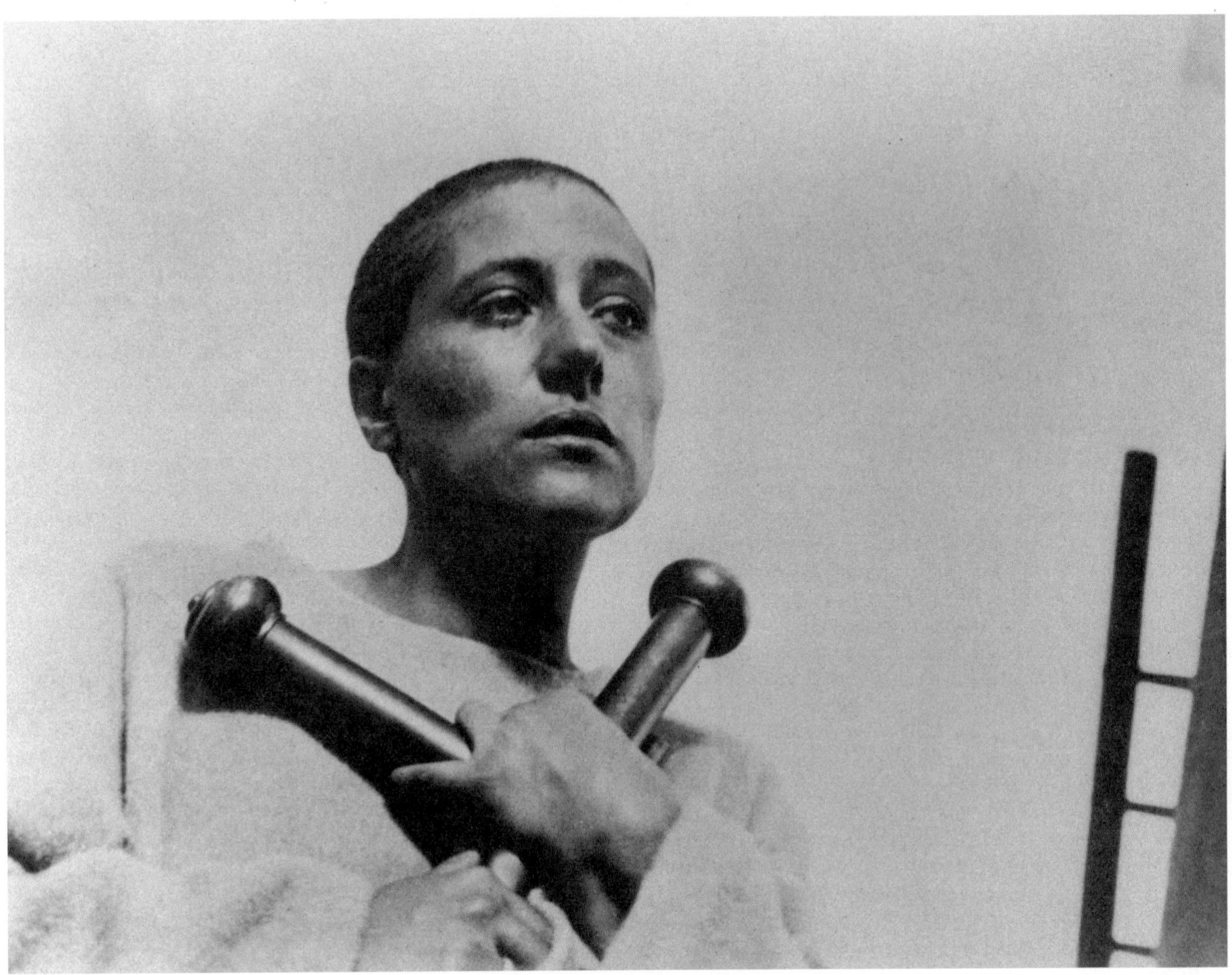

La Passion de Jeanne D'Arc

Maté; **editor:** Carl Theodor Dreyer; **art directors:** Hermann Warm and Jean Hugo; **costume designer:** Valentine Hugo; **historical consultant:** Pierre Champion; **assistants:** Paul la Cour and Ralph Holm.

Cast: Maria Falconetti (*Joan*); Eugéne Silvain (*Pierre Cauchon*); André Berley (*Jean d'Estivet*); Maurice Schutz (*Nicolas Loyseleur*); Antonin Artaud (*Jean Massieu*); Michel Simon (*Jean Lemaître*); Jean d'Yd (*Guillaume Evrard*); Ravet (*Jean Beaupére*); André Lurville; Jacques Arma; Alexandre Mihalesco; R. Narlay; Henri Gaultier; Paul Jorge.

Publications

Script:

Dreyer, Carl Theodor, ''*La passion de Jeanne d'Arc*, in *Four Screenplays*, London, 1970.

Drouzy, Maurice, and Charles Tesson, editors, *Carl Theodor Dreyer: Oeuvres cinématographiques 1926–1923*, Paris 1983.

''*La Passion de Jeanne d'Arc* Issue'' of *Avant-Scène Cinéma* (Paris), January-February 1988.

Books:

Neergaard, Ebbe, *Carl Theodor Dreyer: A Film Director's Work*, London, 1950.

Trolle, Børge, *The Art of Carl Theodor Dreyer: An Analysis*, Copenhagen, 1955.

Bowser, Eileen, *The Films of Carl Dreyer*, New York, 1964.

Dreyer, Carl Theodor, *Om Filmen*, Copenhagen, 1964.

Monty, Ib, *Portrait of Carl Th. Dreyer*, Copenhagen, 1965.

Dyssegaard, Soren, editor, *Carl Th. Dreyer, Danish Film Director*, Copenhagen, 1968.

Ayfré, Amédée, *Le Cinéma et sa vérité*, Paris, 1969.

Perrin, Claude, *Carl Th. Dreyer*, Paris, 1969.

Milne, Tom, *The Cinema of Carl Dreyer*, New York, 1971.

Ernst, Helge, *Dreyer: Carl Th. Dreyer—en dansk filmskaber*, Copenhagen, 1972.

Schrader, Paul, *Transcendental Style in Film: Ozu, Bresson, Dreyer*, Los Angeles, 1972.

Bordwell, David, editor, *Filmguide to La Passion de Jeanne d'Arc*, Bloomington, Indiana, 1973.

Skoller, Donald, editor, *Dreyer in Double Reflection*, New York, 1973.

Nash, Mark, *Dreyer*, London, 1977.
Tone, Pier Giorgio, *Carl Theodor Dreyer*, Florence, 1978.
Bordwell, David, *The Films of Carl Theodor Dreyer*, Berkeley, 1981.
Pipolo, Anthony P., *Carl Dreyer's La Passion de Jeanne d'Arc: A Comparison of Prints and Formal Analysis*, Ann Arbor, Michigan, 1981.
Bazin, André, *The Cinema of Cruelty: From Buñuel to Hitchcock*, New York, 1982.
Carney, Raymond, *Speaking the Language of Desire: The Films of Carl Dreyer*, New York, 1989.
Jensen, Jytte, editor, *The Films of Carl Theodor Dreyer*, New York, 1989.
Dreyer, Carl Theodor, *Dreyer in Double Reflection: Carl Dreyer's Writings on Film*, Cambridge, 1991.
Drum, Jean, and Dale D. Drum, *My Only Great Passion: The Life and Films of Carl Theodor Dreyer*, Lanham, 2000.

Articles:

Close Up (London), July 1928.
Variety (New York), 10 April 1929.
Theatre Arts (New York), 13 May 1929.
Ecran Français (Paris), 11 November 1947.
Winge, John, ''Interview with Dreyer,'' in *Sight and Sound* (London), January 1950
Manvell, Roger, in *Sight and Sound* (London), December 1950.
Ayfré, Amédée, in *Cahiers du Cinéma* (Paris), no. 17, 1952.
Marker, Chris, in *Regards neufs sur le cinéma*, edited by Jacques Chevallier, Paris, 1953.
Terzi, Corrado, in *Cinema Nuovo* (Turin), no. 17, 1953.
Everson, William K., ''Rudy Maté—His Work with Carl Dreyer,'' in *Films and Filming* (London), no. 2, 1955.
Dreyer, Carl, ''Thoughts on My Craft,'' in *Sight and Sound* (London), Winter 1955–56.
Trolle, Børge, ''The World of Carl Dreyer,'' in *Sight and Sound* (London), Winter 1955–56.
Luft, Herbert, ''Dreyer,'' in *Films and Filming* (London), June 1961.
Stanbrook, Alan, in *Films and Filming* (London), June 1961.
Sémolué, Jean, '''Douleur, Noblesse Unique', ou, La Passion chez Carl Dreyer,'' in *Etudes Cinématographiques* (Paris), Fall 1961.
Sémolué, Jean, ''Passion et procès (de Dreyer à Bresson),'' in *Etudes Cinématographiques* (Paris), nos. 18–19, 1962.
Luft, Herbert, ''Rudolph Maté: Photographed Dreyer's *Passion of Joan of Arc* and Became Director on His Own,'' in *Films in Review* (New York), no. 8, 1964.
Delmas, Jean, in *Jeune Cinéma* (Paris), no. 5, 1965.
Zurbuch, Werner, ''Interview med Herman Warm,'' in *Kosmorama* (Copenhagen), no. 71, 1965.
Bond, Kirk, ''The World of Carl Dreyer,'' in *Film Quarterly* (Berkeley), Fall 1965.
Milne, Tom, ''Darkness and Light: Carl Dreyer,'' in *Sight and Sound* (London), Autumn 1965.
Lerner, Carl, ''My Way of Working Is in Relation to the Future: A Conversation with Carl Dreyer,'' in *Film Comment* (New York), Fall 1966.
Amengual, Barthélemy, ''Fonctions du gros plan et du cadrage dans *La passion de Jeanne d'Arc*,'' in *Etudes Cinématographiques* (Paris), no. 53–56, 1967.
Duperly, Denis, ''Carl Dreyer: Utter Bore or Total Genius?,'' in *Films and Filming* (London), February 1968.
Kosmorama (Copenhagen), June 1968.
Cahiers du Cinéma (Paris), December 1968.
Delahaye, Michael, in *Interviews with Film Directors*, edited by Andrew Sarris, New York, 1969.
Potamkin, Harry Alan, in *The Emergence of Film Art*, by Lewis Jacobs, New York, 1969.
Avant-Scène du Cinéma (Paris), February 1970.
Buñuel, Luis, in *Positif* (Paris), February 1973.
Vaughan, Dai, ''Carl Dreyer and The Theme of Choice,'' in *Sight and Sound* (London), Summer 1974.
Wood, Robin, ''Carl Dreyer,'' in *Film Comment* (New York), March-April 1974.
Van Ness, Wilhelmina, ''Joseph Delteil: *The Passion of Joan of Arc*,'' in *Literature/Film Quarterly* (Salisbury, Maryland), no.4, 1975.
Petric, Vlada, ''Dreyer's Concept of Abstraction,'' in *Sight and Sound* (London), Spring 1975.
Bordwell, David, ''Dreyer's Joan,'' in *Sight and Sound* (London), Autumn 1975.
Hugo, V., J. de Lacretelle, and P. Morand, in *Avant-Scéne du Cinéma* (Paris), 1 December 1977.
Oudart, Jean-Pierre, ''Une Peur active,'' in *Cahiers du Cinéma* (Paris), no. 292, 1978.
Cros, J. L., in *Image et Son* (Paris), September 1978.
Linderman, Deborah, ''Uncoded Images in the Heterogeneous Text,'' in *Wide Angle* (Athens, Ohio), no. 3, 1980.
Tesson, Charles, ''Jeanne d'Arc sauvé des flammes,'' in *Cahiers du Cinéma* (Paris), December 1984.
Enberg, M., in *Kosmorama* (Copenhagen), May 1985.
Drouzy, Maurice, ''Jeanne d'Arc livrée aux borreaux,'' in *Cinématographe* (Paris), June 1985.
''Special Issue'' of *Cahiers de la Cinémathèque* (Perpignan), Summer 1985.
Nash, M., ''Joan Complete,'' in *Sight and Sound* (London), Summer 1985.
Neyt, G., in *Film en Televisie* (Brussels), October 1985.
''*Jeanne d'Arc* Section'' of *Skrien* (Amsterdam), November-December 1985.
Meyer, M.P., ''*La Passion de Jeanne d'Arc*: Muziek als hindernis,'' in *Skrien* (Amsterdam), Winter 1985–86.
''*La passion de Jeanne d'Arc*,'' in a Special Issue of *Avant-Scène du Cinéma* (Paris), no. 367–368, January-February 1988.
Willmott, G., ''Implications for a Sartrean Radical Medium: From Theatre to Cinema,'' in *Discourse* (Bloomington, Indiana), Spring-Summer 1990.
Martensen-Larsen, B., ''Inspirationen fra middelalderens miniaturer,'' in *Kosmorama* (Copenhagen), Summer 1993.
DeBartolo, J., ''Video Tape Reviews,'' in *Classic Images* (Muscatine), no. 5, May 1995.
Dupre la Tour, C., ''The Written Word and Memory in Griffith's *Intolerance* and Dreyer's *La passion de Jeanne d'Arc*,'' in *Iris* (Iowa City), no. 19, Autumn 1995.
Kauffman, S., ''French Saint: French Mortals,'' in *New Republic*, vol. 213, 20 November 1995.
Potter, Nicole, ''*The Passion of Joan of Arc/Voices of Light*,'' in *Films in Review* (New York), vol. 47, no. 3–4, March-April 1996.
O'Brien, Charles, ''Rethinking National Cinema: Dreyer's *La passion de Jeanne d'Arc* and the Academic Aesthetic,'' in *Cinema Journal* (Austin), vol. 35, no. 4, Summer 1996.

Stackpole, J., ''One Hardly Expects Language to Be a Contributing Factor,'' in *Audience* (Simi Valley), no. 192, December/January 1997.

Nichols, Peter M., ''In a Joan of Arc Season, One Telling is Timeless,'' in *New York Times*, 24 October 1999.

Smith, Gavin, ''*The Passion of Joan of Arc/Jeanne la Pucelle*,'' in *Film Comment* (New York), vol. 35, no. 6, November/December 1999.

* * *

Carl Dreyer's last silent film is one of the most famous films in the history of cinema. It is seldom missing on ''World's Ten Best Films'' lists. Few films have been studied and analyzed as thoroughly in articles and books, and one sometimes feels that the real film is buried in the theory and aesthetics. But, a true classical work of art, *La passion de Jeanne d'Arc* appeals to and moves the spectator with its beautiful simplicity. It is a pure tragedy of a young suffering woman fighting in a hostile world. The finest homage to the film is perhaps that of Jean-Luc Godard: in his film *Vivre sa vie* the prostitute (played by Anna Karina) is deeply moved by Dreyer's portrait of the legendary heroine when she sees the film in a Paris cinema in the 1960s. She can identify with the tormented young woman in this timeless film.

From the time he started his script in October 1926 until the film was finished, Dreyer worked on it for a year and a half. The historical trial of Jeanne lasted for more than a year. Dreyer concentrated the actual 29 interrogations into one long interrogation, and in the film it takes place on 30 May 1431, the last day of Jeanne's short life; Dreyer thus keeps to the unities of time, place and story.

The style of the film, which has been called a film in close-ups, is derived directly from his sources and evokes the protocol of the trial. When the film was released, the close-up technique was regarded as shocking. Dreyer defended his method by stating: ''The records give a shattering impression on the ways in which the trial was a conspiracy of the judges against the solitary Jeanne, bravely defending herself against men who displayed a devilish cunning to trap her in their net. This conspiracy could be conveyed on the screen only through the huge close-ups, that exposed, with merciless realism, the callous cynicism of the judges hidden behind hypocritical compassion—and on the other hand there had to be equally huge close-ups of Jeanne, whose pure features would reveal that she alone found strength in her faith in God.'' As in all of Dreyer's major films the style grew out of the theme of the film. In *La passion de Jeanne d'Arc* Dreyer wanted ''to move the audience so that they would themselves feel the suffering that Jeanne endured.'' It was by using close-up that Dreyer could ''lead the audience all the way into the hearts and guts of Jeanne and the judges.''

The close-up technique is the core of the film, because it lifts the drama above a given place and a given time. It is a satisfactory way of abstracting from an historically defined reality without abandoning a respect for authenticity and realism. But this striving for timelessness is reflected in all the components of the film. And there is more to the film than close-ups. Dreyer uses medium close-ups, tilts, pans, travelling shots and intricate editing. Cross-cutting is used to great effect, especially in the last part of the film, and the hectic rhythm and swiftly changing shots towards the end of the film are as masterfully controlled as the close-ups. The visual language is very complex and not in the least monotonous. The sets and the costumes were consciously created in a way that furthered the balance between the historical and the modern. The lighting, the overall whiteness of the images, contributes to the film's emphasis on the simple and the lucid.

Dramatically, *La passion de Jeanne d'Arc* is composed as one long scene. This is Jeanne's last struggle, and the battle is for her life and her soul. The film is dramatically and psychologically intensified in two scenes. The first when Jeanne breaks down mentally and, to save her life, signs a confession as a heretic. The second is the scene in which she regrets what she has done and withdraws the confession. She knows then that her death is certain, but she saves her soul, and she triumphs in her faith.

La passion de Jeanne d'Arc is an intense description of the suffering of an individual, the drama of a soul transformed into images. It is a ''cool'' look, and Dreyer called his method ''realized mysticism.'' With his sober objectivity Dreyer succeeded in making the difficult understandable and the irrational clear. The film is about the necessity of suffering for the liberation of the individual human being. As do all of Dreyer's heroines, Jeanne suffers defeat, but for Dreyer defeat or victory in this world is of no importance. The essential thing is the soul's victory over life. Dreyer's view of the historical facts is, of course, not a balanced one. Jeanne is the heroine, and Dreyer is on her side in a struggle against a cruel, official world.

In Dreyer's oeuvre *La passion de Jeanne d'Arc* brings together all the resources of the cinema at that time, and is the most pure and perfect expression of his art. Of none of his films is his own statement more fitting: ''The soul is revealed in the style, which is the artist's expression on the way he regards his material.''

The film was well received when it was released, but it was not a commercial success. Since then the film's reputation has grown, and for many years it has been continuously shown in film archives and film clubs all over the world. The original negative of *La passion de Jeanne d'Arc* was destroyed in a fire in 1928 at UFA in Berlin. Film archeologists are still working on a restoration of the film, which has survived in many slightly differing versions—but even a definitive version should not drastically change our impression of this masterpiece.

—Ib Monty

PASSPORT TO PIMLICO

UK, 1949

Director: Henry Cornelius

Production: Ealing Studios; black and white, 35mm; running time: 84 minutes. Released April 1949.

Producer: Michael Balcon; **associate producer:** E. V. H. Emmett; **screenplay:** T. E. B. Clarke; **photographer:** Lionel Banes; **art direction:** Roy Oxley; **music:** Georges Auric; **editor:** Michael Truman.

Cast: Stanley Holloway (*Arthur Pemberton*); Betty Warren (*Connie Pemberton*); Barbara Murray (*Shirley Pemberton*); Paul Dupuis

Passport to Pimlico

(*Duke of Burgundy*); Margaret Rutherford (*Professor Hatton-Jones*); Raymond Huntley (*Wix*); Hermoine Baddeley (*Eddie Randall*); Basil Radford (*Gregg*).

Publications

Books:

Balcon, Michael, *Michael Balcon Presents . . . A Lifetime of Films*, London, Hutchinson, 1969.

Durgnat, Raymond, *A Mirror For England*, London, Faber & Faber, 1970.

Clarke, T. E. B., *This Is Where I Came In*, London, Michael Joseph, 1974.

Armes, Roy, *A Critical History of British Cinema*, London, Secker & Warburg, 1978.

Barr, Charles, *Ealing Studios*, New York, Woodstock Press, 1980, 1999.

Perry, George, *Forever Ealing*, London, Pavillion/Michael Joseph, 1981.

Curran, James, and Vincent Porter, editors, *British Cinema History*, London, Weidenfield & Nicholson, 1983.

Brown, Geoff, and Laurence Kardish, *Michael Balcon: The Pursuit of British Cinema*, New York, The Museum of Modern Art, 1984; updated edition, 1990.

Murphy, Robert, *Realism and Tinsel*, London, Routledge, 1992.

Articles:

Ellis, John, ''Made in Ealing,'' from *Screen* (London), Vol 16, No. 1, Spring 1975.

Brown, Geoff, ''Ealing, Your Ealing,'' from *Sight and Sound* (London), Summer 1977.

Williams, Tony, ''The Repressed Fantastic in *Passport to Pimlico*,'' in *Film Criticism* (Meadville), vol. 16, no. 1–2, Fall-Winter 1991–1992.

* * *

Passport to Pimlico has the distinction of making pouring rain and the onset of cold weather the satisfying and suitably up-beat coda to its story. Somehow the teasingly self-conscious shots of the Mediterranean or Latin American signifiers which open the film are indeed proven to be a dupe and a distraction from the reality that is Britain in the late forties. What we see in *Passport to Pimlico*, however, is a singularly Ealingesque version of reality, informed by Producer Michael Balcon's pursuit of "Britishness" within the unique self-defining parameters of the "British Film." The film becomes a vehicle by which the British may actually experience their fantasies and dreams only to find that they do not sit easily with the much more acceptable and comfortable aspects of merely trusting and enjoying the circumstances they have inherited. Far from being a reactionary and conservative position, this is viewed within the film as progressive because it sustains particular kinds of values and behaviour which would be lost to misdirected aspirations unsuitable to a British temperament, defined it seems, by wartime consensus and a nostalgia for imagined communities and significant nationhood.

Passport to Pimlico was inspired by a news story in which it was reported that Princess Juliana had given birth to an heir to the throne during her wartime exile to Canada. It was first necessary, however, that the government make the maternity wing in which she was staying legally Dutch soil as the heir had to be born within the realm of the Netherlands. This unusual tale was adapted by screenwriter, T. E. B. Clarke into a story in which the inhabitants of Miramont Place in Pimlico suddenly discover that they are legally Burgundians when a wartime bomb accidentally explodes revealing the treasures of Burgundy and the lease that claims this piece of British soil as Burgundian. This narrative conceit produces circumstances which suggest particular scenarios about how people, and specifically, British people might behave liberated from the still operational post-war restrictions. Further, it serves as a test of the assumed power structures, value systems, and social hierarchies that constitute the cultural status quo, and thus, in turn operate as a metaphor for the flux of interests at large in the period of post-war reconstruction. This kind of narrative also becomes a model of the "What if?" scenario, so beloved of Balcon, when the Chaplinesque "little man" finds his voice and challenges the status quo at the moment of temporary social disruption. Further examples follow in *Whisky Galore* and *The Man in the White Suit.* Such films become invaluable for what they reveal and define about "Britishness."

Arthur Pemberton cherishes a plan to create a children's play area from the wartime ruins but is dismissed with the rebuff that "This borough is in no position to finance daydreams." This moment alone distills some of the film's central premises about the tensions between pragmatism and imagination, forward-thinking and backward-looking, inhibition and liberation, and the role of the individual within the community. It is also a typically "Ealing" scenario, in that important issues in Ealing movies were often explored through narratives involving children. These films include *Hue and Cry* and *Mandy.* Pemberton equates the children's play area with the future and the transition from post-war inertia into a new decade energised by the young. He sees this initiative as an opportunity to liberate a future generation into the freedoms fought for by his generation. *Passport to Pimlico* essentially examines the problems of this transition by demonstrating the possibilities inherent in having particular freedoms.

Ironically, the bomb which reveals the Burgundian treasure is accidentally set off by a group of children. The treasure is only found when Pemberton himself inadvertently falls into the bomb-sight. When Pemberton and his daughter, Shirley, research the origin of the treasure, Shirley astutely anticipates the real implications of finding the haul, by refuting her father's pride in discovering its heritage, by saying: "History, my foot. It's money!" Once it is established that "these Londoners are technically Burgundians," it becomes clear that the people of Pimlico enter a temporary Utopia which operates outside British law, and legitimises the fulfillment of individual appetites and desires. It also becomes clear that freedom from restriction reveals the deep structures of human imperatives—chiefly, the will to power and the instinct to indulge. The Burgundians celebrate by drinking, singing, and dancing, culminating their evening of liberation with the destruction of their ration books, the everyday symbol of regulation and caution. Arguably, it is also at this point when democracy and nationalism are also in flux.

The film uses the very appealing device of illustrating freedom without responsibility to demonstrate the necessity of certain social structures and institutions. These organisations preserve freedoms for everyone in the face of the inevitability of those people merely seeking to take advantage of situations for their own gain. By illustrating a possible utopia in excess, that essentially fails with the onslaught of black marketeers, criminal types, and self-interested government bureaucrats, *Passport to Pimlico* demonstrates and endorses the utopia of a civilised community with consensus politics sustaining the ideological status quo.

When the Prince of Burgundy arrives, authenticated as the true Burgundian heir by the eccentric Professor Hatton-Jones (a typically joyous and bluster-filled performance by Margaret Rutherford), he also brings a genuine "Europeaness" which authenticates the freer, more sensual aspect of the new Pimlico lifestyle. His romantic endeavours with Shirley Pemberton are constantly thwarted, however, as his role becomes further politicised, when Burgundy is forced to create its own democratic nation-state to resist the intervention of Britain. This process merely illustrates that Burgundy is a democracy modelled on Britain itself, and a microcosm of British life which best demonstrates the chief characteristics of "Britishness." These largely concur with those characteristics outlined by Sir Stephen Tallents of the Empire Marketing Board in the early thirties, which stressed the disinterestedness of Britain in international affairs (i.e. a particular kind of "inwardness"), traditions of justice, law and order, a sense of fair play and fair dealing, and a coolness in national character. *Passport to Pimlico* reinforces the inwardness of the British character, but emphasises a determination amongst the British people to see justice be done in an experiential rather than legal sense. Burgundy becomes the underdog, the disenfranchised, the mistreated, when it is estranged from the British government, but its predicament mobilises the support of the British people, who recognise their own indomitable spirit in the pursuit of a fair deal. Sympathy is further mobilised when Burgundy's food supplies (largely care parcels provided by British supporters) are lost in a flood. These moments, of course, are all signifiers of wartime trials and tribulations which contemporary audiences readily recognised, identified with, and enjoyed. Consensus on screen becomes complicit consensus amongst viewers.

When Burgundy is forced to rejoin Britain, it is the spirit of compromise and resolution which is celebrated. Pemberton succeeds in his dream to create a children's recreation area with the proceeds of the Burgundy treasure, but perhaps more importantly, he and the community have succeeded in having a democratic voice. Government has succeeded in providing a solution to a complex social problem and has been warned of its complacency. With lessons learned and victories won, the ration book, now a symbol for rationale is reinstated. *Passport to Pimlico* is a tribute to the war effort, and not merely a nostalgic longing for its terms and conditions. It is a celebration of what the British are, and what they want to be, and though it may seem conservative in its outlook to contemporary viewers, it represents a lack of cynicism which characterises the pride, dignity and hope many British people felt in the post-war period. *Passport to Pimlico* is about goodwill expressed with good humour.

—Paul Wells

PATHER PANCHALI

See **THE APU TRILOGY**

PATHS OF GLORY

USA, 1957

Director: Stanley Kubrick

Production: Harris-Kubrick Pictures Corporatoin. A Bryna Productions presentation, for United Artists; black and white; running time: 87 minutes; length: 7,783 feet. Released November 1957.

Producer: James B. Harris; **screenplay:** Stanley Kubrick, Calder Willingham, and Jim Thompson, based on the novel by Humphrey Cobb; **photography:** George Krause; **editor:** Eva Kroll; **sound:** Martin Muller; **art director:** Ludwig Reiber; **music:** Gerald Fried; **military adviser:** Baron Von Waldenfels.

Cast: Kirk Douglas (*Colonel Dax*); Ralph Meeker (*Cpl. Paris*); Adolphe Menjou (*General Broulard*); George Macready (*General Mireau*); Wayne Morris (*Lt. Roget*); Richard Anderson (*Major Saint-Auban*); Joseph Turkel (*Private Arnaud*); Timothy Carey (*Private Ferol*); Peter Capell (*Colonel Judge*); Susanne Christian (*German Girl*); Bert Freed (*Sgt. Boulanger*); Emile Meyer (*Priest*); John Stein (*Captain Rosseau*); Harold Benedict (*Captain Nichols*).

Publications

Books:

Austen, David, *The Cinema of Stanley Kubrick*, London, 1969.
Kagen, Norman, *The Cinema of Stanley Kubrick*, New York, 1972.
Walker, Alexander, *Stanley Kubrick Directs*, New York, 1972.
Devries, Daniel, *The Films of Stanley Kubrick*, Grand Rapids, Michigan, 1973.
Bobker, Lee, *Elements of Film*, New York, 1974.
Phillips, Gene D., *Stanley Kubrick: A Film Odyssey*, New York, 1975.
Ciment, Michel, *Kubrick*, Paris, 1980; revised edition, 1987; translated as *Kubrick*, London, 1983.
Kolker, Robert Phillip, *A Cinema of Loneliness: Penn, Kubrick, Coppola, Scorsese, Altman*, Oxford, 1980; revised edition, 1988.
Miller, Gabriel, *Screening the Novel: Rediscovered American Fiction in Film*, New York, 1980.
Hummel, Christoph, editor, *Stanley Kubrick*, Munich, 1984.
Brunetta, Gian Piero, *Stanley Kubrick: Tempo, spazio, storia, e mondi possibli*, Parma, 1985.
Mann, Michael, *Kirk Douglas*, New York, 1985.
Douglas, Kirk, *The Ragman's Son*, New York, 1988.
Thomas, Tony, *Films of Kirk Douglas*, Secaucus, 1991.
Falsetto, Mario, *Stanley Kubrick: A Narrative and Stylistic Analysis*, Westport, 1994.
Jenkins, Greg, *Stanley Kubrick and the Art of Adaptation: Three Novels, Three Films*, Jefferson, 1997.
Howard, James, *Stanley Kubrick Companion*, London, 1999.
Garcia Mainar, Luis M., *Narrative and Stylistic Patterns in the Films of Stanley Kubrick*, Rochester, 2000.
Nelson, Thomas Allen, *Kubrick: Inside a Film Artist's Maze*, Bloomington, 2000.

Articles:

Variety (New York), 20 November 1957.
Motion Picture Herald (New York), 23 November 1957.
Kine Weekly (London), 26 December 1957.
Lambert, Gavin, in *Sight and Sound* (London), Winter 1957–58.
Film Culture (New York), February 1958.
Houston, Penelope, in *Monthly Film Bulletin* (London), vol. 25, no. 289, 1958.
Kubrick, Stanley, ''Words and Movies,'' in *Sight and Sound* (London), Winter 1961.
Burgess, Jackson, ''The Antimilitarism of Stanley Kubrick,'' in *Film Quarterly* (Berkeley), Fall 1964.
''Stanley Kubrick'' in *Cahiers du Cinéma* (Paris), December 1964-January 1965.
Strick, Phillip, and Penelope Houston, ''Interview with Stanley Kubrick,'' in *Sight and Sound* (London), Spring 1972.
Monaco, James, ''The Films of Stanley Kubrick,'' in *New School Bulletin* (New York), Summer 1973.
Deer, Harriet and Irving, ''Kubrick and the Structures of Popular Culture,'' in *Journal of Popular Film* (Washington D.C.), Summer 1974.
Ferro, Marc, in *Jeune Cinéma* (Paris), April 1975.
Image et Son (Paris), September 1976.
Binni, W., and A. Lombardo, ''Poetiche ed ideologie di tre registi,'' in *Cinema Nuovo* (Bari), January-February 1977.
Combs, Richard, in *Monthly Film Bulletin* (London), August 1984.
Walker, Alexander, in *Radio Times* (London), 25 April, 1985.
Listener (London), 12 January 1989.
Alonge, A. G., ''Il nemico inesistente,'' in *Quaderni di Cinema* (Florence), July-September 1990.
Kelly, A., ''The Brutality of Military Incompetence: *Paths of Glory*,'' in *Historical Journal of Film, Radio and Television* (Abingdon, Oxfordshire), no. 2, 1993.
Denby, David, ''Voyage of the Damned: *Paths of Glory* Directed by Stanley Kubrick,'' in *Premiere* (New York), vol. 4, no. 11, July 1991.
Kelly, Andrew, ''The Brutality of Military Incompetence: *Paths of Glory* (1957),'' in *Historical Journal of Film, Radio and Television* (Abingdon), vol. 13, no. 2, June 1993.
Reid's Film Index (Wyong), 15 November 1995.

* * *

Humphrey Cobb's poorly written but powerful novel of the French army in World War I was published in 1935. Some people in

Paths of Glory

Hollywood wanted to film it then but to change its setting to pre-Revolutionary Russia so as not to offend any existing government. In 1957, after Stanley Kubrick, Calder Willingham, and Jim Thompson wrote the screenplay, nobody wanted to touch it until Kirk Douglas got behind the project. (Douglas claims that Kubrick then *rewrote* the story—including a happy ending with a last-minute reprieve for the condemned soldiers—in a wrong-headed effort to make it more commercial, but that he made Kubrick go back to the original script.) When it was released, the movie was not a commercial success—and it did offend the French government, which banned it for 20 years.

Paths of Glory is Kubrick's best motion picture. It lacks the discursiveness that characterizes all of his later work; true to its source, the movie is practically Aristotelian in its unity of action, time, and place. It has none of the lethargic pacing that mars parts of *Lolita*, much of *2001: A Space Odyssey*, and all of *Barry Lyndon*; unlike those films, *Paths* has a constant, driving rhythm: usually the camera or the characters are always in motion, sometimes simultaneously, as in cinematographer George Krause's celebrated tracking shots: officers move through the trenches; the army makes its abortive attack on the Anthill (delicately renamed from the Pimple of the novel); the three court-martialed soldiers are led to their deaths by the firing squad; and, all the while, the camera travels with them, inexorably leading the characters and the viewer down these "paths of glory," to the grave.

And *Paths of Glory* is happily free from Kubrick's unfortunate tendency toward misogyny. That's partly because (discounting the extras at General Broulard's soirée) there are no women *in* the movie—except for the one "enemy" captive, the only German whom we see. This young woman, coerced into singing for the rowdy troops, is the catalyst for the film's poignant ending. After all the callous disregard for human life up to this point, we see the soldiers drop their mocking bravado one by one to hum along with her. (She is played by Susanne Christian, Kubrick's third wife.)

Paths of Glory is always hailed as a great anti-war film, and—visually—it does make a statement about the horrors of war, showing the broken and wounded in the trenches (almost off-handedly, as background) and the wholesale, senseless slaughter on the battlefield. But, even more than that, it is an anti-military film (and, by extension, an indictment of all hierarchical systems which sacrifice human beings for expediency). From the opening credits, over which "La Marseillaise" is martially played, ending on a discordant note, the film expands upon the novel's themes, developing and driving home the point of the army as a corporation and its officers as ruthless businessmen, using subordinates for personal gain.

General Broulard (Adolph Menjou) of the French high command approaches ambitious General Mireau (George Macready) with an impossible task—to take a highly fortified German position within 36 hours—dangling a promotion in front of him as incentive. (Menjou played many suave villains in his career, but casting him as the manipulative Broulard is doubly appropriate, since, in his private life, he was a notorious reactionary and one of the ''friendly witnesses'' when HUAC investigated Hollywood.)

Talking himself into the success of the operation, Mireau then dumps its accomplishment on Colonel Dax (Kirk Douglas) and his battle-weary troops. (The role of Dax is fleshed out and conflated with that of Captain Etienne in the novel in order to give the film a hero, a moral center with which the audience can identify.)

Mireau even goes so far as (unsuccessfully) to command his artillery to fire on those troops when the battle doesn't go so well. He's prevented by an ordnance officer who insists on having the order in writing—illustrating the First Rule of corporate life: ''cover your ass.'' When the attack fails, Mireau wants to cover *his* ass, so looks for a scapegoat and trumps up charges of cowardice against a trio of randomly selected soldiers. Dax argues their cases eloquently at the maddening kangaroo court martial which follows, to no avail.

The novel concludes with the soldier's executions; the film goes beyond that episode, bringing the corruption around full circle: instigator Broulard is the agent of Mireau's comeuppance, giving the viewer some slight satisfaction (because the condemned men have already been killed). The ever-cynical Broulard misinterprets Dax's motives in exposing Mireau, thinking Dax has done it to gain Mireau's job (which Broulard is only too happy to give him). Dax bluntly disabuses Broulard, giving the viewer intense but fleeting satisfaction: Broulard has Dax and his men transferred back to the front. The system works—for those in charge of the system.

—Anthony Ambrogio

Peeping Tom

PEEPING TOM

UK, 1960

Director: Michael Powell

Production: Anglo Amalgamated; Eastmancolor, 35mm, running time: 109 minutes, other versions include 90 minutes and 86 minutes. Released April 1960, London.

Producers: Michael Powell with Albert Fennell; **screenplay:** Leo Marks; **photography:** Otto Heller; **editor:** Noreen Ackland; **sound:** C. C. Stevens and Gordon McCallum; **art director:** Arthur Lawson; **set decorator:** Ivor Beddows; **music:** Brian Easdale.

Cast: Karl Boehm (*Mark Lewis*); Moira Shearer (*Vivian*); Anna Massey (*Helen Stephens*); Maxine Audley (*Mrs. Stephens*); Esmond Knight (*Arthur Baden*); Bartlett Mullins (*Mr. Peters*); Shirley Ann Field (*Diane Ashley*); Michael Goodliffe (*Don Jarvis*); Brenda Bruce (*Dora*); Martin Miller (*Dr. Rosan*); Pamela Green (*Milly*); Jack Watson (*Inspector Gregg*); Nigel Davenport (*Sergeant Miller*); Brian Wallace (*Tony*); Susan Travers (*Lorraine*); Maurice Durant (*Publicity chief*); Brian Worth (*Assistant director*); Veronica Hurst (*Miss Simpson*); Miles Malleson (*Elderly gentleman*); Alan Rolfe (*Store detective*); Michael Powell (*Mr. Lewis*); John Dunbar.

Publications

Books:

Gough-Yates, Kevin, *Michael Powell*, London, 1971.
Durgnat, Raymond, *Films and Feelings*, Cambridge, Massachusetts, 1971.
Durgnat, Raymond, *A Mirror for England*, London, 1971.
Christie, Ian, editor, *Powell, Pressburger, and Others*, London, 1978.
Armes, Roy, *A Critical History of British Cinema*, New York, 1978.
Cosandey, Roland, editor, *Retrospective: Powell and Pressburger*, Locarno, 1982.
Gottler, Fritz, and others, *Living Cinema: Powell and Pressburger*, Munich, 1982.
Christie, Ian, *Arrows of Desire: The Films of Michael Powell and Emeric Pressburger*, London, 1985.
Martini, Emanuela, editor, *Powell and Pressburger*, Bergamo, 1986.
Powell, Michael, *A Life in Movies: An Autobiography*, London, 1986.
Cintra Ferreira, Manuel, *Michael Powell*, Lisbon, 1992.
Howard, James, *Michael Powell*, North Pomfret, 1996.
Salwolke, Scott, *The Films of Michael Powell and the Archers*, Lanham, 1997.

Articles:

Green, O. O., ''Michael Powell: Filmography,'' in *Movie* (London), Autumn, 1965.
Chamberlin, Phillip, in *Film Society Review* (London), January 1966.
Gough-Yates, Kevin, ''Private Madness and Public Lunacy,'' in *Films and Filming* (London), February 1972.
Collins, R., and Ian Christie, ''Interview with Michael Powell: The Expense of Naturalism,'' in *Monogram* (London), no. 3, 1972.
Romer, J. C., in *Ecran* (Paris), July-August 1973.
Renaud, Tristan, in *Cinéma*, (Paris), October 1976.
Humphries, Reynold, ''*Peeping Tom:* Voyeurism, the Camera, and the Spectator,'' in *Film Reader* (Evanston, Illinois), no. 4, 1979.
Stein, E., ''A Very Tender Film, a Very Nice One: Michael Powell's *Peeping Tom,*'' in *Film Comment* (New York), September-October 1979.
Canby, Vincent, in *New York Times*, 14 October 1979.
Sarris, Andrew, in *Village Voice*, (New York), 15 October 1979.
Sayre, N., in *Nation* (New York), 10 November 1979.
Johnson, V., ''*Peeping Tom:* A Second Look,'' in *Film Quarterly* (Berkeley), Spring 1980.
McDonough, Maitland, ''The Ambiguities of Seeing and Knowing in Michael Powell's *Peeping Tom,*'' in *Film Psychology Review* (New York), Summer-Fall 1980.
Thomson, David, ''Mark of the Red Death,'' in *Sight and Sound* (London), Autumn 1980.
Dubois, P., ''Voir, la mort, ou l'effet-Méduse de la photographie au cinéma,'' in *Review Belge du Cinéma* (Brussels), Summer 1983.
Powell, Michael, ''Leo Marks and Mark Lewis,'' in *Cinématographe* (Paris), December 1983.
Dumont, P., in *Cinéma* (Paris), January 1984.
Revault D'Allonnes, F., in *Cahiers du Cinéma* (Paris), January 1984.
Findley, J., in *Film Comment* (New York), May-June 1990.
Morris, N. A., ''Reflections on *Peeping Tom,*'' in *Movie* (London), Winter 1990.
Bourget, E., ''*Colonel Blimp*; *Le voyeur,*'' in *Positif* (Paris), no. 379, September 1992.
Bick, Ilsa J., ''The Sight of Difference,'' in *Persistence of Vision* (Maspeth), no. 10, 1993.
Redman, Nick, and Tomm Carrol, and Ted Elrick, ''They're Baaack: More Definitive Laser Versions,'' in *DGA Magazine* (Los Angeles), vol. 19, no. 5, October-November 1994.
Strick, Philip, in *Sight & Sound* (London), vol. 4, no. 11, November 1994.
Wollen, Peter, ''Dying for Art,'' in *Sight & Sound* (London), vol. 4, no. 12, December 1994.
Schundt, T., ''The Films of Nat Cohen and Stuart Levy,'' in *Delirious* (Cleveland Heights), no. 4, 1995.
Jivani, Alkarim, ''Fantastic Voyeur,'' in *Time Out* (London), no. 1422, 19 November 1997.
Massumi, B., ''To Kill is Not Enough: Gender as Cruelty,'' in *Continuum*, vol. 11, no. 2, 1997.
Singer, James, ''England's Glamour Parade,'' in *Outré* (Evanston), vol. 1, no. 7, 1997.
Maslin, Janet, ''Next to This, Norman Looks Sane,'' in *New York Times*, 29 January 1999.

* * *

Almost the most remarkable thing about *Peeping Tom* is the critical reception it provoked. This film, disingeniously described by its director Michael Powell as ''a very tender film, a very nice one,'' was uniformly abused in its own country. Derek Hill's infamous claim that ''the only really satisfactory way to dispose of *Peeping Tom* would be to shovel it up and flush it swiftly down the nearest sewer'' may have been the most violent of critical assessments, but it was all too typical. Powell's career as a feature-film director never recovered from the assault, and the road to critical re-assessment of *Peeping Tom* has been long and hard. Anyone concerned with the whys and wherefores of this process need look no further than Ian Christie (ed.) *Powell Pressburger and Others*, where the nature of the affront Powell offered to orthodox criticism is clearly analyzed. *Peeping Tom* was only the climactic case in a long series.

None of this is to suggest, however, that *Peeping Tom* is not a disturbing movie. In narrative alone it is immediately problematic: any story about a man who murders women with the sharpened leg of a tripod, filming them as they die, is likely to attract adverse attention. When the young man in question is played straight, as someone with whom we are invited to empathise, and not as some rolling eyed gothic horror, then the difficulties are redoubled. How can we empathise with such perverse pleasures? And when the film-maker involved is such a well-established talent, how can we reconcile his presumed ''seriousness'' with what is conventionally the subject for a shocker?

Today such difficulties would not be quite as pressing as they were in 1960. Ranges of acceptability have widened, and the line between Art and Exploitation is no longer so easily drawn. Yet even today *Peeping Tom* is genuinely disturbing. For all our familiarity with violent movie murder, with sexuality, with the psychology of perversion, Powell's movie can still leave a spectator profoundly uneasy. For *Peeping Tom* refuses to let us off the hook after the fashion of so many horrific movies. Its elaborate structure of films within films implicates us as spectators in the voyeurism that fuels Mark's violence. We see the murders through his viewfinder; later we see them on screen as he projects them for his pleasure. We see his father's filmed record of experiments on the young Mark, experiments which have turned him into a voyeuristic killer. We see the movie studio where he works, the setting where he will murder (of all people) Moira Shearer, star of Powell's *The Red Shoes*. As the internal cross-references multiply (and they are endless) the implication insinuates itself into our awareness. In watching film, all film, the pleasures that we take are finally no different to Mark's; the gap between his and our voyeurism is too small for comfort.

It was Powell's misfortune to make *Peeping Tom* at a time when commitment to a one-dimensional notion of realist cinema was at its height. *Peeping Tom*, like all of Powell's cinema, is founded on a highly self-conscious manipulation of film itself, and it is impossible here to do justice to the resonating visual complexity of films like *A Matter of Life and Death*, *Black Narcissus*, and, of course, *Peeping Tom.* In this cinema it is the medium that is the source of pleasure and the focus of attention, not some instantly apparent moral ingredient. *Peeping Tom* turns that cinematic awareness back on itself, offering aesthetic satisfactions along with their disturbing implications. It is a film that is paramountly about cinema, about the experience of cinema, a film which makes voyeurs of us all. That *is* genuinely disturbing.

—Andrew Tudor

PÉPÉ LE MOKO

France, 1937

Director: Julien Duvivier

Production: Paris Film Production; black and white, 35mm; running time: 93 minutes. Released 28 January 1937, Paris. Filmed in Pathe studios in Joinville, exteriors shot in Algiers, Marseille, and Sete.

Producers: Robert and Raymond Hakim; **screenplay:** Julien Duvivier and d'Henri La Barthe (under pseudonym Detective Ashelbe) with Jacques Constant and Henri Jeanson, from the novel by Detective Ashelbe; **photography:** Jules Kruger and Marc Fossard; **editor:** Marguerite Beauge; **sound:** Antoine Archaimbaud; **production designer:** Jacques Krauss; **music:** Vincent Scotto and Mohamed Yguerbouchen.

Cast: Jean Gabin (*Pépé le Moko*); Mireille Balin (*Gaby Gould*); Line Noro (*Inès*); Lucas Gridoux (*Inspector Slimane*); Gabriel Gabrio (*Carlos*); Fernand Charpin (*Régis*); Saturnin Fabre (*Grandfather*); Gilbert Gil (*Pierrot*); Roger Legris (*Max*); Gaston Modot (*Jimmy*); Marcel Dalio (*L'Arbi*); Frehel (*Tania*); Olga Lord (*Aïcha*); Renee Carl (*Mother Tarte*); Rene Bergeron (*Inspector Meunier*); Charles Granval (*Maxime Kleep*); Philippe Richard (*Inspector Janvier*); Paul Escoffier (*Commissioner Louvain*); Robert Ozanne (*Gendron*); Georges Peclet (*Barsac*); Frank Maurice (*An inspector*).

Publications

Script:

Duvivier, Julien, and Henri La Barthe, *Pépé le Moko*, in *Avant-Scéne du Cinéma* (Paris), 1 June 1981.

Books:

Gauteur, Claude, and André Bernard, *Gabin; ou, Les Avatars d'un mythe*, Paris, 1967.

Chirat, Raymond, *Julien Duvivier*, Lyons, 1968.

Anthologie du Cinéma 4, Paris, 1969.

Sadoul, Georges, *French Films*, London, 1972.

Missiaen, Jean-Claude, and Jacques Siclier, *Paris*, 1977.

Milhaud, Sylvie, *Jean Gabin*, Paris, 1981.

Brunelin, Andre, *Gabin*, Paris, 1987.

Billard, Pierre, *Julien Duvivier*, Milan, 1996.

Articles:

Variety (New York), 24 March 1937.

Greene, Graham, in *Spectator* (London), 23 April, 1937.

Sight and Sound (London), Spring 1937.

New York Times, 4 March 1941.

Duvillars, Pierre, ''Jean Gabin's Instinctual Man,'' in *Films in Review* (New York), March 1951.

Aubriant, Michel, ''Julien Duvivier,'' in *Cinémonde* (Paris), 28 November 1952.

Nolan, Jack, ''Jean Gabin,'' in *Films in Review* (New York), April 1963.

Cowie, Peter, ''Jean Gabin,'' in *Films and Filming* (London), February 1964.

Renoir, Jean, ''Duvivier, le professionel,'' in *Figaro Littéraire* (Paris), 6 November 1967.

Simsolo, Noël, in *Image et Son* (Paris), March 1972.

Vincendeau, Ginette, ''Community, Nostalgia, and the Spectacle of Masculinity,'' in *Screen* (London), November-December 1985.

Garrity, H.A., ''Narrative Space in Julien Duvivier's, *Pépé le Moko*,'' in *French Review*, vol. 65, no. 4, 1992.

* * *

Pépé le Moko had an immediate success scarcely rivalled in French film history. Its director, Julien Duvivier, was instantly hired by Hollywood, where the film itself was remade the next year, with Anatole Litvak directing Charles Boyer, as *Casbah. Pépé* ranked as the year's top film in many countries, including Japan, and it remains today a cult film of a stature similar to that which *Casablanca* enjoys in the United States.

A chronicle of the adventures of a dandy criminal hiding out in the casbah section of Algiers, *Pépé le Moko* is really a film about the bitterness of lost dreams. Pépé, as created by Jean Gabin, is in no way captive of the outlaw life he leads. Controlling his minions by dint of his authoritative personality and the notoriety of his name, he is above them all. Only Sliman, the Algiers police inspector, has an inkling of the real man and his motives. Pépé's gang is set off against the police force, while Pépé and Sliman struggle on a higher plane, respecting one another, respecting even more the fate that both believe rules them all.

The film opens with documentary footage and informational commentary about the Casbah. We learn of the mixture of races, the numbers and kinds of vices represented in the maze of alleys even the police fear to enter. Pépé's entrance is spectacular: a close-up of his hand holding a jewel, then his face tilted as he examines the jewel in the light. Soon after, while being pursued, he ducks into a secret hideaway and there encounters Gaby (Mireille Balin). Once again it is her jewels that attract both him and the camera in successive close-ups of their faces. When Sliman enters to escort Gaby back to the safety of the grand hotels, the knot is tied. Sliman even remarks, ''It is written, Pépé.''

Duvivier treats the entire intrigue as if with Sliman's magistral comprehension. Never indulging in suspense, he nevertheless inflates key moments with an abundance of stylistic flourishes. Most famous is the death of the informer Regis at the hands of Pépé and his gang. Shoved back against a wall, hysterical and pathetic, Regis bumps into a jukebox, setting off a raucous song just as his own victim, aided by pals, pumps a revolver full of bullets into his thick body. Just before this scene Pépé and Gaby express their love by reciting antiphonally the Metro stops they know, moving through a remembered Paris from opposite ends until they say together ''*La Place Blanche*.'' Sliman looks on, knowing that he has caught Pépé in the net of desire and nostalgia. The Casbah will no longer serve as a refuge now that Gaby

Pépé le Moko

and thoughts of Paris have corrupted Pépé. Later, in a moment of quiet just before the denouement, a homesick old singer, caught like Pépé in the Casbah, puts a record on the gramophone and, tears in her eyes, sings along with the record, a song about the glories of Paris. Duvivier pans along a wall from a picture of this woman when she was young and beautiful, to the record player, and then to the woman's tear-choked face. It is a magnificent summation of the film's ability to summon up unfulfilled desire and nostalgia.

The film's dynamic conclusion unrolls directly from these sentiments: Pépé's obligatory outburst against another informer (Marcel Dalio), his breaking away from his common-law wife, his descent from the Casbah—accompanied by the theme music of the film and a totally artificial rear-projection that places us inside his obsessed mind. Duvivier wrings all the pathos of the lost dream from the finale, as Pépé finds his way aboard Gaby's ship and then is arrested inches away from her, though neither of them realizes how close they are. As the ship pulls out, he sees Gaby on the deck but the whistle of the ship drowns out his call. She is looking far above him, at the Casbah he has left. He tears his stomach open with a pocketknife. Virtually a private masturbation, his suicide is the climax of his longings, represented by the mysterious and elegant Gaby and by the memory of home. Both these sentiments and their outcome are of the style and spirit of poetic realism. One can see why the film was banned as demoralizing and debilitating first by the French government at the start of the war and then by the Vichy government once the new order had come to power. After the war it returned as a classic.

—Dudley Andrew

PERSONA

Sweden, 1966

Director: Ingmar Bergman

Production: AB Svensk Filmindustri; black and white, 35mm; running time 84 minutes; length: 2320 meters. Released 18 October 1966, Stockholm. Filmed 19 July 1965–17 September 1965, with some scenes shot in February and March 1966, in Svensk Filmindustri studios, Stockholm, and on location.

Producer: Ingmar Bergman; **screenplay:** Ingmar Bergman; **photography:** Sven Nykvist; **editor:** Ulla Ryghe; **sound engineer:** P. O. Pettersson; **production designer:** Bibi Lindström; **music:** Lars-Johan Werle; **special effects:** Evald Andersson; **costume design:** Mago.

Cast: Bibi Andersson (*Alam*); Liv Ullmann (*Elisabeth Vogler*); Margaretha Krook (*Läkaren*); Gunner Björnstrand (*Herr Vogler*); Jörgen Lindström (*The boy*).

Publications

Script

Bergman, Ingmar, *Persona*, Stockholm, 1966; translated as *Persona* in *Persona and Shame*, New York, 1972.

Books:

Sjögren, Henrik, *Ingmar Bergman på teatern*, Stockhom, 1968.
Steene, Brigitte, *Ingmar Bergman*, New York, 1968.
Gibson, Arthur, *The Silence of God: Creative Response to the Films of Ingmar Bergman*, New York, 1969.
Wood, Robin, *Ingmar Bergman*, New York, 1969.
Björkman, Stig, Torsten Manns, and Jonas Sima, *Bergman on Bergman*, London, 1970.
Sjögren, Henrik, *Regi: Ingmar Bergman*, Stockholm, 1970.
Young, Vernon, *Cinema Borealis: Ingmar Bergman and the Swedish Ethos*, New York, 1971.
Simon, John, *Ingmar Bergman Directs*, New York, 1972.
Ranieri, Tino, *Ingmar Bergman*, Florence, 1974.
Kaminsky, Stuart, editor, *Ingmar Bergman: Essays in Criticism*, New York, 1975.
Ullman, Liv, *Changing*, New York, 1976.
Bergom-Larsson, Maria, *Ingmar Bergman and Society*, San Diego, 1978.
Kawin, Bruce, *Mindscreen: Bergman, Godard and the First Person Film*, Princeton, 1978.
Lange-Fuchs, Hauke, *Der frühe Ingmar Bergman*, Lübeck, 1978.
Marion, Denis, *Ingmar Bergman*, Paris, 1979.
Houston, Beverle, and Marsha Kinder, *Self and Cinema: A Transformalist Perspective*, New York, 1980.

Persona

Manvell, Roger, *Ingmar Bergman: An Appreciation*, New York, 1980.
Mosley, Philip, *Ingmar Bergman: The Cinema as Mistress*, London, 1981.
Petric, Vlada, editor, *Film and Dreams: An Approach to Bergman*, South Salem, New York, 1981.
Cowie, Peter, *Ingmar Bergman: A Critical Biography*, New York, 1982.
Livingstone, Paisley, *Ingmar Bergman and the Ritual of Art*, Ithaca, New York, 1982.
Steene, Birgitta, *A Reference Guide to Ingmar Bergman*, Boston, 1982.
Jones, G. William, editor, *Talking with Ingmar Bergman*, Dallas, 1983.
Lefèvre, Raymond, *Ingmar Bergman*, Paris, 1983.
Eberwein, Robert T., *Film and the Dream Screen: A Sleep and a Forgetting*, Princeton, 1984.
Dervin, Daniel, *Through a Freudian Lens Deeply: A Psychoanalysis of Cinema*, Hillsdale, New Jersey, 1985.
Gado, Frank, *The Passion of Ingmar Bergman*, Durham, North Carolina, 1986.
Johns, Marilyn Blackwell, *Persona: The Transcendent Image*, Chicago, 1986.
Jarvie, Ian, *Philosophy of the Film: Epistemology, Ontology, Aesthetics*, London and New York, 1987.
Bergman, Ingmar, *Laterna Magica*, Stockholm, 1987; as *The Magic Lantern: An Autobiography*, London, 1988.
Cohen, James, *Through a Lens Darkly*, New York, 1991.
Bjorkman, Stig, and Torsten Maans, and Jonas Sima, *Bergman on Bergman: Interviews with Ingmar Bergman*, Cambridge, 1993.
Cohen, Hubert I., *Ingmar Bergman: The Art of Confession*, New York, 1993.
Long, Robert Emmet, *Ingmar Bergman: Film and Stage*, New York, 1994.
Tornqvist, Egil, *Between Stage and Screen: Ingmar Bergman Directs*, Amsterdam, 1995.
Blackwell, Marilyn J., *Gender and Representation in the Films of Ingmar Bergman*, Rochester, 1997.
Michaels, Lloyd, editor, *Ingmar Bergman's Persona*, Cambridge, 1999.

Articles:

Macklin, F. A., in *Film Heritage* (Dayton, Ohio), Spring 1967.
Sarris, Andrew, in *Village Voice* (New York), 23 March 1967.
Films in Review (New York), April 1967.
Corliss, Richard, in *Film Quarterly* (Berkeley), Summer 1967.
Sadoul, Georges, in *Lettres Françaises* (Paris), 12 July 1967.
Comolli, Jean-Louis, ''The Phantom of Personality,'' in *Cahiers du Cinéma* (Paris), September 1967.
Sontag, Susan, in *Sight and Sound* (London), Autumn 1967.
Leiser, Erwin, in *Film Comment* (New York), Fall-Winter 1967.
Durgnat, Raymond, in *Films and Filming* (London), December 1967.
Harris, Michael, in *Take One* (Montreal), no. 8, 1967–68.
Wood, Robin, in *Movie* (London), Spring 1968.
Hofsess, John, in *Take One* (Montreal), August 1968.
''Ingmar Bergman: jugé par deux critiques suédois,'' in *Avant-Scène du Cinéma* (Paris), October 1968.
Bond, Kirk, in *Film Culture* (New York), Winter-Spring 1970.
Young, Vernon, ''Cinema Borealis,'' in *Hudson Review* (New York), Summer 1970.
Jones, C. J., ''Bergman's *Persona* and the Artistic Dilemma of the Modern Narrative,'' in *Literature/Film Quarterly* (Salisbury, Maryland), Winter 1977.
Iverson, E., in *Kosmorama* (Copenhagen), Spring 1978.
Campbell, P. N., ''The Reflexive Function of Bergman's *Persona*,'' in *Cinema Journal* (Evanston, Illinois), no. 1, 1979.
Scholar, N., ''Anais Nin's *House of Incest* and Ingmar Bergman's *Persona:* Two Variations on a Theme,'' in *Literature/Film Quarterly* (Salisbury, Maryland), no. 1, 1979.
Casebier, Allan, ''Reductionism Without Discontent: The Case of *Wild Strawberries* and *Persona*,'' in *Film Psychology Review* (New York), Winter-Spring 1980.
Boyd, D., ''*Persona* and the Cinema of Interpretation,'' in *Film Quarterly* (Berkeley), Winter 1983–84.
Barr, Alan P., ''The Unravelling of Characters in Bergman's *Persona*'' in *Literature/Film Quarterly* (Salisbury, Maryland), vol. 15, no. 2, 1987.
Bellour, R., ''The Film Stilled,'' in *Camera Obscura* (Bloomington, Indiana), September 1990.
Gul'chenko, V., in *Iskusstvo Kino* (Moscow), no. 8, 1991.
Kirk, Caroline, in *Premiere* (Boulder), vol. 5, no. 10, June 1991.
Sontag, S., ''Tolshcha fil'ma,'' in *Iskusstvo Kino* (Moscow), no. 8, 1991.
''Bergman, il paradosso di un 'Ateo cristiano,''' in *Castoro Cinema* (Florence), November-December 1991.
Wood, R., ''*Persona* Revisited,'' in *CineAction* (Toronto), no. 34, 1994.
Persson, Göran, ''*Persona* Psychoanalyzed: Bergman's *Persona*: Rites of Spring as Chamber Play,'' in *CineAction* (Toronto), no. 40, May 1996.
Lahr, John, ''The Demon-Lover: After Six Decades in Film and Theatre, Ingmar Bergman Talks About His Family and the Invention of Psychological Cinema,'' in *The New Yorker*, vol. 75, no. 13, 31 May 1999.

* * *

Persona may be Ingmar Bergman's most consciously crafted film; it may also be one of his most enigmatic. The plot is a tour-de-force distillation of an agon between two women, Alma (Bibi Andersson), a young nurse, and Elisabeth Vogler (Liv Ullman) her patient, a successful actress who has withdrawn into silence. The psychic tension between the two women, and the power of the silent one, reflect Strindberg's short play *The Stronger*, a source many critics of the film have noted. Yet Bergman is even more daring than Strindberg, for more is at stake in his film, and he sustains the one-sided conversation for the length of the feature film.

In many ways *Persona* is ''about'' the nature and conventions of the feature film—most obviously because Bergman begins the film by showing the ignition of an arc projector and the threading of a film, and ends it with the same projector being turned off. The greatest visual shock in all of Bergman's often startling oeuvre must be the moment near the middle of *Persona* when the film rips (or seems to rip), burns, and introduces strange material, apparently foreign to the story of the two women.

Actually, the material comes largely from a pre-title sequence. By the time *Persona* was made, the pre-title sequence had ceased to be a novelty and was on the way to becoming a tired convention. Generally, a pre-title sequence presents some bit of action preliminary to the main action of the film, but not essential to its comprehension. The pre-title sequence of *Persona*, however, is utterly unique. It is composed of material completely foreign to the imagery of the film itself (except for the eruption after the burned film), so that one truly misses ''nothing'' of the plot by starting with the titles, yet it is crucial to an understanding of what is happening in that plot.

Early in the film we see a psychiatrist who talks to Alma about her future patient, and who talks to Elisabeth, alone, about her withdrawal. Bergman uses the psychiatrist to fill us in on the background of the silent woman. Late in the film we meet Elisabeth's husband, who may be blind, when he shows up on the island where his wife is recuperating—but apparently he cannot tell Alma from Elisabeth. By this time Bergman has laid so many clues about the imaginative or psychotic perspective of the plot that we must wonder whether the husband is himself imagined or indeed whether Alma and Elisabeth are two aspects of a divided personality. This suspicion is encouraged by a repeated shot of a composite face, made up of half of each woman's face. It appears after a climactic scene in which Alma recites Elisabeth's faults to her face and ends up screaming that she is not Elisabeth Vogler herself. Interpretation of the film must depend on how one regards that scene.

Without judging the reality of any of the depicted events, however, once one sees the silent Elisabeth as a figure for the analyst and Alma as the patient, one can see that the sequence of the relationship between Alma and Elisabeth neatly corresponds to the stages of transference and counter-transference in classical psychoanalysis. Even more remarkable than the correspondence is the fact that Bergman has virtually suppressed shot-countershot in this film. This in itself is a considerable stylistic innovation for a film essentially about a single speaker and a single listener. But the few times that shot-countershot does occur, it underlines the stages of transference: first, when Alma initially makes contact with Elisabeth by reading her a letter from her husband; next, and with obsessive frequency, as Alma feels comfortable enough to describe her life and confess her excitement over an orgy and her subsequent abortion. Here shot-countershot underlines the positive transference: Alma is falling in love with Elisabeth. But when reading a private letter to Elisabeth's husband, Alma realizes that she is being coolly analyzed and her love turns to hatred (negative transference). It is when she deliberately causes harm to Elisabeth that a single instance of shot-countershot occurs and, with it, comes the ripping and burning of the film, along with all the ''repressed'' material from the pre-title scene. The climactic accusation is the final shot-countershot scene in the film. It is repeated twice as if to stress its importance and to show how a film-maker constructs shot-countershot.

As a psychoanalytic drama, *Persona* depends upon the relationship of the seemingly chaotic image of the beginning of the film to the accusations of Alma at the height of her transference anxiety. There the abortion, the rejection of Elisabeth's son, and the confusion over who sleeps with her husband are significant issues as are the frequent representations and discussions of love-making while someone looks on. The entire film actually turns on the perspective of a pre-adolescent male, seen waking up in a morgue in the pre-title scene, and reaching out, in the first initial shot-countershot structure, to touch the projected image of the faces of the two women flowing together. In the center of this labyrinthine film, there is a primal scene disturbance: a fantasy of intercourse as a violent act, yet exciting to watch, in which the child born out of it believes himself unwanted, even the victim of a willed destruction.

No film so systematically reflects the psychoanalytical encounter, although many films of lesser intensity (such as Hitchcock's *Spellbound* or Bergman's own *Face to Face*) attempt it more directly; perhaps no other film offers as many decoys to hide its psychoanalytical core. The very clues that would engage the viewer in trying to sort out what is real and what is imagined by the two (or is it one?) women are distractions from its profound concern.

—P. Adams Sitney

THE PHANTOM CHARIOT

See **KÖRKALEN**

THE PHANTOM OF THE OPERA

USA, 1925

Director: Rupert Julian

Production: Universal Pictures; black and white, (some sequences filmed in 2-strip Technicolor), 35mm. silent; running time: about 94 minutes; length: 10 reels, 8464 feet. Filmed in Hollywood. Cost:

The Phantom of the Opera

budgeted at $1 million. Released 15 November 1925, premiered 6 September 1925 in New York. Re-released 1930 with some dialogue sequences and songs added.

Presented by: Carl Laemmle; **screenplay (adaptation):** Raymond Schrock and Elliott J. Clawson, from the novel by Gaston Leroux; **titles:** Tom Reed; **additional direction:** Edward Sedgwick; **photography:** Virgil Miller, Milton Bridenbecker, and Charles Van Enger; **editor:** Maurice Pivar; **production designers:** Charles D. Hall, and Ben Carre.

Cast: Lon Chaney (*Erik*); Mary Philbin (*Christine Dace*); Norman Kerry (*Raoul de Chagny*); Snitz Edwards (*Florine Papillon*); Gibson Gowland (*Simon*); John Sainpolis (*Philippe de Chagny*); Virginia Pearson (*Carlotta*); Arthur Edmond Carew (also Carewe) (*Ledoux*); Edith Yorke (*Madame Valerius*); Anton Vaverka (*Prompter*); Bernard Siegel (*Joseph Buguet*); Olive Ann Alcorn (*La Sorelli*); Edward Cecil (*Faust*); Alexander Bevani (*Mephistopheles*); John Miljan (*Valentin*); Grace Marvin (*Martha*); George Williams (*Ricard*); Bruce Covington (*Moncharmin*); Cesare Gravina (*Manager*); Ward Crane (*Count Ruboff*); Chester Conklin (*Orderly*); William Tryoler (*Conductor*).

Publications

Books:

Clemens, Carlos, *An Illustrated History of the Horror Film*, New York, 1967.

Anderson, Robert G., *Faces, Forms, Films: The Artistry of Lon Chaney*, South Brunswick, New Jersey, 1971.

Everson, William K., *Classics of the Horror Film*, Secaucus, New Jersey, 1974.

Everson, William K., *American Silent Film*, New York, 1978.

Riley, Philip, editor, *MagicImage Filmbooks Presents the Making of the Phantom of the Opera*, Absecon, New Jersey, 1994.

Blake, Michael F., *A Thousand Faces: Lon Chaney's Unique Artistry in Motion Pictures*, Lanham, 1995.

Blake, Michael F., *The Films of Lon Chaney*, Lanham, 1998.

Articles:

Hall, Mordaunt, in *New York Times*, 7 September 1925.

Mitchell, George, "Lon Chaney," in *Films in Review* (New York), December 1953.

Behlmer, Rudy, in *Films in Review* (New York), October 1962.

Bodeen, DeWitt, "Lon Chaney: Man of a Thousand Faces," in *Focus on Film* (London), May-August 1970.

Viviani, C., "Lon Chaney; ou, La Politique de l'acteur," in *Positif* (Paris), July-August 1978.

Meth, S., "Reflections in a Cinema Eye: Lon Chaney," in *Classic Film Collector* (Indiana, Pennsylvania), July 1979.

Koszarski, R., "Career in Shadows," in *Film History* (London), vol. 3, no. 3, 1989.

MacQueen, S., "*Phantom of the Opera*—Part II," in *American Cinematographer* (Hollywood), October 1989.

Kindblom, M., "I begynnelsen var manniskan tre," in *Filmhaftet* (Uppsala, Sweden), December 1989.

Turner, George, "The Phantom's Lady Returns," in *American Cinematographer* (Hollywood), vol. 71, no. 4, April 1990.

MacQueen, S., "The 1926 *Phantom of the Opera*," in *American Cinematographer* (Hollywood), vol. 70, September 1989.

MacQueen, S., "*Phantom of the Opera*—Part II," in *American Cinematographer* (Hollywood), vol. 70, October 1989.

Pitman, J., "Chaney *Phantom of the Opera* Tinted and With Music Track, to Join the Current Craze," in *Variety* (New York), vol. 337, 25/31 October 1989.

Weaver, T., "Silent Horror Classics: The Best of the Big Screen Shockers," in *Filmfax* (Evanston), no. 25, February/March 1991.

Télérama (Paris), no. 2380, 23 August 1995.

Cahiers du Cinéma (Paris), no. 494, September 1995.

Blake, Michael F., "Lon Chaney's Phantom Turns 70," in *Filmfax* (Evanston), no. 52, September-October 1995.

Blake, Michael F., "Lon Chaney Collection (1920–25)," in *Filmfax* (Evanston), no. 52, September-October 1995.

Correspondence on the various scores for the film, by Clifford McCarty, in *Cue Sheet* (Hollywood), vol. 11, no. 4, October 1995.

Giddins, G., "The Mask," in *Village Voice* (New York), vol. 41, 23 January 1996.

* * *

There have been several versions of *The Phantom of the Opera*, but none has remained as close to the original novel by Gaston Leroux as does the Lon Chaney film. Admittedly the film stays faithful to the original work sometimes more as a result of what is not shown than what is; for example, whereas later screen versions offer fanciful explanations for the phantom's grotesque appearance, the Chaney feature makes no effort to explain why the phantom is the way he is—by default, presumably going along with Leroux's story that he was "born that way."

Encouraged by the praise and box-office rewards heaped on Chaney's previous Universal feature, *The Hunchback of Notre Dame*, Carl Laemmle budgeted one million dollars for *The Phantom of the Opera*. Rupert Julian, a long-time Universal contract director who had made a career as an actor portraying Kaiser Wilhelm in various films, was assigned to direct, but he was replaced sometime during the shooting by Edward Sedgwick, a minor comedy director. (Apparently Julian and Chaney did not get along, the result of a disagreement about the phantom's characterization.) Universal promoted the film by using the rather obvious device of permitting no advance photographs of Chaney to be shown, thus assuring an excited and enthusiastic audience for the New York premiere on September 6, 1925. Critical reaction was somewhat mixed, but the feature proved a tremendous success at the box office.

It is perhaps unfortunate that *The Hunchback of Notre Dame* and *The Phantom of the Opera* are the most frequently revived and easily accessible of Chaney's silent features, for neither film allows the actor much excuse for dramatics. His make-up, of course, is superb, but here there is no evidence of the kind of emotional range that Chaney displays, for example, in *Tell it to the Marines* (1927). Also, his supporting players, Mary Philbin and Norman Kerry, are singularly lacking in talent; Philbin, as the opera singer who unmasks the Phantom, is particularly weak.

The star of *The Phantom of the Opera* is not Chaney, but rather the magnificent sets of Charles D. Hall and Ben Carre, ranging from the awe-inspiring lobby and auditorium of the Paris Opera House to the eerie, subterranean home of the phantom. Equally impressive are the costumes, particularly the ''Death'' garment worn by Chaney in the Bal Masque sequence. This scene, together with the operatic numbers from Gounod's *Faust*, were filmed in two-strip Technicolor. The direction is weak, and the film is badly paced for a melodrama, although suspense is allowed to build, the result of Chaney's remaining masked until more than half-way through the film.

For a 1930 reissue of *The Phantom*, Universal filmed a number of dialogue sequences with Mary Philbin and Norman Kerry, and added a singing voice—not that of Philbin—to the operatic numbers. At that time some ten minutes were also cut from the film.

—Anthony Slide

PHILADELPHIA

USA, 1993

Director: Jonathan Demme

Production: TriStar Pictures; colour, 35mm; sound; running time: 120 minutes. Filmed in Philadelphia, 1993.

Producer: Edward Saxon, Jonathan Demme; **screenplay:** Ron Nyswaner; **photography:** Tak Fujimoto; **editor:** Craig McKay; **assistant director:** Ron Bozman, Drew Ann Rosenberg; **production design:** Kristi Zea; **art director:** Tim Galvin; **music:** Howard Shore; **sound editor:** Ron Bochar; **sound recording:** Chris Newman, Steve Scanlon.

Cast: Tom Hanks (*Andrew Beckett*); Denzel Washington (*Joe Miller*); Jason Robards (*Charles Wheeler*); Mary Steenburgen (*Belinda Conine*); Antonio Banderas (*Miguel Alvarez*); Ron Vawter (*Bob Seidman*); Robert Ridgley (*Walter Kenton*); Charles Napier (*Judge Garnett*); Lisa Summerour (*Lisa Miller*); Joanne Woodward (*Sarah Backett*); Roberta Maxwell (*Judge Tate*); Roger Corman (*Mr. Laird*).

Awards: Oscar for Best Actor (Hanks), 1993.

Publications

Books:

Kael, Pauline, *Pauline Kael on Jonathan Demme: A Selection of Reviews Accompanying the Retrospective Jonathan Demme, an American Director*, Minneapolis, 1988.

Bliss, Michael, and Christiana Banks, *What Goes Around Comes Around: The Films of Jonathan Demme*, Carbondale, 1996.

Falaschi, Francesco, *Jonathan Demme*, Milan, 1997.

Articles:

McCarthy, T., *Variety* (New York), 20 December 1993.

Bruzzi, S., *Sight and Sound* (London), March 1994.

Taubin, A., ''The Odd Couple,'' in *Sight and Sound* (London), March 1994.

Mueller, Matt, ''The Philadelphia Story,'' in *Empire* (London), March 1994.

Derrett, A., in *Film Score Monthly* (Los Angeles), no. 44, April 1994.

Grundman, R., and P. Sacks, *Cineaste* (New York), No. 3, 1994.

Pearson, H., *Films in Review* (New York), No. 3/4, 1994.

Harty, K.J., ''The Failures of Jonathan Demme's Philadelphia'' in *Four Quarters* (Philadelphia), Spring 1994.

Stanbrook, Alan, *Sunday Telegraph*, 9 October 1994.

Mechar, K.W., '''Every Problem Has a Solution': AIDS and the Cultural Recuperation of the American Nuclear Family in Jonathan Demme's *Philadelphia*,'' in *Spectator* (Los Angeles), vol. 15, no. 1, 1994.

Cante, R., ''A Report from *Philadelphia* and Somewhere Else,'' in *Spectator* (Los Angeles), vol. 15, no. 2, 1995.

Weis, E., ''Sync Tanks,'' in *Cineaste* (New York), vol. 21, no. 1/2 1995.

Sandler, A., ''*Philadelphia* Suit Near Accord,'' in *Variety* (New York), 12/18 February 1996.

Evans, G., ''*Philadelphia* Story Raises Muddy Issues in Filmmaking,'' in *Variety* (New York), vol. 362, 18/24 March 1996.

Evans, G., and A. Sandler, ''TriStar Settles *Philadelphia* Suit,'' in *Variety* (New York), vol. 362, 25/31 March 1996.

Van Fuqua, Joy, '''Can You Feel It, Joe?': Male Melodrama and the Family Man,'' in *Velvet Light Trap* (Austin), no. 38, Fall 1996.

Kenny, Glenn, ''Jonathan Demme,'' in *Premiere* (Boulder), vol. 12, no. 3, November 1998.

* * *

Knowing old heads around Hollywood shook with dismay when Jonathan Demme revealed his plan to follow up the surprisingly successful *The Silence of the Lambs* with another of the risky ventures he was noted for, a major production featuring homosexuality and AIDS. Films about homosexuality (since a revision in the Production Code in 1969 made the word even mentionable in films), from the camp *The Gay Deceivers* (1969) to the James Ivory/Ismail Merchant adaptation of E.M. Forster's long suppressed novel *Maurice* (1986), had never done well at the box office. Films dealing with AIDS, such as *Longtime Companion*, had played to small audiences on the small art theatre circuit. It can be argued that the cinema is developing a new, more mature audience as *Philadelphia* was a financial and critical success in a year that saw Steven Spielberg's *Schindler's List* and Ivory/Merchant's *Remains of the Day*. Nor did *Philadelphia* stir up as much controversy as nervous exhibitors had feared from protesting religious fundamentalists and other reactionary lobbies. Probably these pressure groups had given up any hope for an industry that wallowed in decadence and indecency. Surprisingly most objections to the film came from the expanding gay press that thought Demme should have taken a more militant line demanding action to conquer AIDS, the modern plague. Tom Hanks, who won the 1993 Academy Award for best actor for his extraordinarily demanding performance as AIDS victim Andrew Beckett, acknowledged this protest and explained to interviewer David Thomson:

> I think it's all very legitimate criticism . . . I'm not surprised at all that . . . anybody who is part of that aspect of the gay community that is, what? Counter-culture or whatever. What they wanted was something that was going to represent their lives. *Philadelphia* didn't do that. . . . But past that, you have to say, yes, that's true, but look what the movie is for what it is, not what it is not.

The storyline is for the most part straightforward. The *mise-en-scène* is, with one startling exception, as naturalistic as possible, especially in colour. An outstandingly promising and personable young lawyer is entrusted with a top assignment by the most prominent and respected law firm in the city. (Viewers may wonder why Philadelphia, not particularly prominent in the AIDS crisis, was chosen as the setting. The city has a traditional reputation in the United States for producing the sharpest lawyers, trained, like Beckett, at the University of Pennsylvania Law School.) The firm claims that he has been dismissed for inefficiency and failure to live up to his promise; but he claims that he was fired when they discovered he had AIDS, and he sues on the grounds that it is against the law to fire an individual for a disability that does not prevent the fulfillment of his or her duties. No other lawyer, however, is willing to oppose the powerful firm until Beckett breaks through the prejudices of a former adversary, struggling black lawyer Joe Miller, who wins the case. Justice is done in legalistic terms, but everyone loses. Beckett dies shortly after the jury decides in his favour; the old law firm loses a good deal of money and some of its long-cherished reputation; the Beckett family loses a brilliant son; and the future of Joe Miller and of Beckett's Hispanic-American lover do not appear promising despite their immediate financial rewards.

The film is not about AIDS as a social and political problem. It uses the enormous present concern over the epidemic as a means to an end in broaching a far larger, timeless problem. The issue that concerns the filmmakers is based upon a distinction that has been crucially central to the American protest movements—whether this is a nation based upon people or upon law, as Andrew Beckett makes clear when he justifies his suit by explaining, ''I love the law, to see justice done.''

The film is a very rare example of the oldest form of drama in the European tradition, classical tragedy in a medium that has been almost entirely exploited by melodrama. So far the most substantial and challenging reservations about the film have been directed at the sudden change three-quarters of the way through, from the neutral naturalism of the visual image to an unprecedented surrealistic sequence during an interview between Beckett and Joe Miller, his attorney. Miller has been trying to keep his client's mind on the testimony that he will give the next day; but Beckett becomes evasive and puts on a recording of Maria Callas singing the aria ''La Momma Morta'' from Umberto Giordano's opera *André Chénier*. The screen is suffused with a demonic red glow as a smouldering fireplace blazes forth, symbolizing the passionate fire burning in Beckett.

The producers tried to cut this episode, and many reviewers have found it irrelevant and fatuous; but Demme and Hanks fought to retain it, even though its significance has been generally misunderstood. Typical of the bewildered reaction is Alan Stanbrook's comment in *The Sunday Telegraph* that ''many will wince at the embarrassing scene where Hanks tries to explain what opera means to gays.'' As Hanks stressed in this interview, the film does not attempt to represent some collective psyche of the gay community. The episode is a strictly personal statement, as he moves from routine questions about the litigation into the vision that explains his sometimes inscrutable behaviour, when Beckett speaks for himself as an ''adventurous spirit,'' declaiming histrionically over the soaring music: ''I am divine. I am oblivious. I am the god come down from the heavens to earth to make of earth a heaven.''

This reference to divinity establishes the link between classic tragedy and the film. Whether intentionally or not, scriptwriter Roy Nyswaner echoes the myth of Philocetes, a great bowman, who is banished during the Trojan War by his fellow Greeks to a deserted island when a snakebite gives him a noxious and incurable wound; but they must bring him back as a seer decrees that Troy can only be taken with his bow and arrows. Philocetes comes to a happier end than Andrew Beckett, but their relationship is highlighted by one of the key lines in the film as the jury playing the role of the classic chorus decides that when the firm gave Beckett the big assignment, they were sending in not a disappointing employee, but their ''top gun.''

Even more pervasive as a subtext throughout the film is the myth of Icarus, the son of the ingenious Daedulus, who made the men wax wings with which to fly out of the labyrinth where they were imprisoned. Icarus flew too close to the sun and the wax melted, so that he fell to his death in the sea. Andrew Beckett is another ''adventurous spirit'' who has flown too high and taken too many risks. In the surrealist opera episode, viewers are presented a glimpse beneath the quotidian reality of the legal proceedings into the inner vision of Andrew Beckett, who is motivated by a principle that David Thomson finds at work in some of Hank's other films, that ''Fantasy soars above any hope of duty or intelligence.'' Beckett is brilliant, seeking to end injustice and make a heaven on earth; but he is also oblivious to dangerous risks in his pursuit of the ideal. This complex and still puzzling film shows the possibilities rarely realized so far of using the cinema to update classic myths as they have been used in the past in literature to probe our present condition.

—Warren French

THE PHILADELPHIA STORY

USA, 1940

Director: George Cukor

Production: Metro-Goldwyn-Mayer Pictures Corp.; black and white, 35mm; running time: 112 minutes. Released December 1940. Filmed 1940 MGM studios.

Producer: Joseph Mankiewicz; **screenplay:** Donald Ogden Stewart and Waldo Salt (uncredited), from the play by Philip Barry; **photography:** Joseph Ruttenberg; **editor:** Frank Sullivan; **sound:** Douglas Shearer; **set decorator:** Edwin Willis; **art directors:** Cedric Gibbons and Wade B. Rubottom; **music:** Franz Waxman; **costume designer:** Adrian.

The Philadelphia Story

Cast: Katharine Hepburn (*Tracy Lord*); Cary Grant (*C. K. Dexter Haven*); James Stewart (*Macauley Connor*); Ruth Hussey (*Liz Imbrie*); John Howard (*George Kittredge*); Roland Young (*Uncle Willie*); John Halliday (*Seth Lord*); Virginia Weidler (*Dinah Lord*); Mary Nash (*Margaret Lord*); Henry Daniell (*Sidney Kidd*); Lionel Pape (*Edward*); Rex Evans (*Thomas*); Russ Clark (*John*); Hilda Plowright (*Librarian*); Lita Chevret (*Manicurist*); Lee Phelps (*Bartender*); Dorothy Fay, Florine McKinney, Helene Whitney, and Hillary Brooks (*Mainliners*); Claude King (*Uncle Willie's butler*); Robert de Bruce (*Dr. Parsons*); Veda Buckland (*Elsie*).

Awards: Oscars for Best Actor (Stewart) and Best Screenplay, 1940; New York Film Critics Award, Best Actress (Hepburn), 1940.

Publications

Books:

Langlois, Henri, and others, *Hommage à George Cukor*, Paris, 1963.

Domarchi, Jean, *George Cukor*, Paris, 1965.

Cary, Grant, *Cukor and Company: The Films of George Cukor and His Collaborators*, New York, 1971.

Dickens, Homer, *The Films of Katharine Hepburn*, New York, 1971.

Lambert, Gavin, *On Cukor*, New York, 1972.

Marill, Alvin H., *Katharine Hepburn*, New York, 1973.

Clarens, Carlos, *George Cukor*, London, 1976.

Deschner, Donald, *The Films of Cary Grant*, Secaucus, New Jersey, 1978.

Pomerance, Diane Linda, *The Cinematic Style of George Cukor in the Comedy of Manners Films ''Holiday'' and ''The Philadelphia Story'': A Comparative Study*, Ann Arbor, Michigan, 1980.

Cavell, Stanley, *Pursuits of Happiness: The Hollywood Comedy of Remarriage*, Cambridge, Massachusetts, 1981.

Phillips, Gene D., *George Cukor*, Boston, 1982.

Britton, Andrew, *Cary Grant: Comedy and Male Desire*, Newcastle-upon-Tyne, 1983.

Carey, Gary, *Katharine Hepburn: A Biography*, London, 1983.

Schickel, Richard, *Cary Grant: A Celebration*, London, 1983.

Britton, Andrew, *Katharine Hepburn: The Thirties and After*, Newcastle-upon-Tyne, 1984.

Eyles, Allen, *James Stewart*, London, 1984.

Morley, Sheridan, *Katharine Hepburn: A Celebration*, London, 1984.
Bernadoni, James, *George Cukor: A Critical Study and Filmography*, Jefferson, North Carolina, 1985.
Hunter, Allan, *James Stewart*, New York, 1985.
Higham, Charles, and Ray Moseley, *Cary Grant: The Lonely Heart*, New York, 1989.
McGilligan, Patrick, *George Cukor: A Double Life: A Biography of the Gentleman Director*, New York, 1992.
Levy, Emanuel, *George Cukor: Master of Elegance: Hollywood's Legendary Director and His Stars*, New York, 1994.
Ryan, Joal, *Katherine Hepburn: A Stylish Life*, New York, 1999.
Schickel, Richard, *Cary Grant*, New York, 1999.

Articles:

Variety (New York), 27 November 1940.
Ferguson, Otis, in *New Republic* (New York), 13 December 1940.
New York Times, 27 December 1940.
The Times (London), 3 March 1941.
Tozzi, Romano V., "Katharine Hepburn," in *Films in Review* (New York), December 1957.
Tozzi, Romano V., "George Cukor: His Success Directing Women Has Obscured His Other Directional Virtues," in *Films in Review* (New York), February 1958.
Reid, John, "So He Became a Lady's Man," in *Films and Filming* (London), August 1960.
Cutts, John, in *Films and Filming* (London), July 1962.
Bureau, Patrick, "Un Etincelant Cukor," in *Lettres Françaises* (Paris), 1 November 1962.
Fieschi, Jean-André, "Ou finit le théâtre?," in *Cahiers du Cinéma* (Paris), February 1963.
Philippe, Claude Jean, "Analyse d'un grand film: *Philadelphia Story*," in *Télérama* (Paris), 8 December 1963.
"Rétrospective Cukor," in *Cahiers du Cinéma* (Paris), February 1964.
Sweigart, William, "James Stewart," in *Films in Review* (New York), December 1964.
Nightingale, B., "After Making Nine Films Together, Hepburn Can Practically Direct Cukor," in *New York Times*, 28 January 1979.
Phillips, Gene D., "Cukor and Hepburn," in *American Classic Screen* (Shawnee Mission, Kansas), Fall 1979.
Bodeen, DeWitt, "George Cukor," in *Films in Review* (New York), November 1981.
Le Pavec, J.-P., in *Cinéma* (Paris), March 1982.
Tobin, Yann, in *Positif* (Paris), May 1985.
Journal of Popular Film and Television (Washington, D.C.), Fall 1985.
Reid's Film Index (Wyong), no. 4, 1990.
Shumway, D. R., "Screwball Comedies: Constructing Romance, Mystifying Marriage," in *Cinema Journal* (Austin, Texas), no. 4, 1991.
Rosterman, R., in *Hollywood: Then and Now* (Studio City), vol. 24, no. 6, 1991.
Viviani, Christian, "Katharine Hepburn et George Cukor," in *Positif* (Paris), no. 425–426, July-August 1996.

* * *

The Philadelphia Story is one of the most successful and best loved screwball comedies of the classical Hollywood era. It is based on the 1939 Broadway production of Philip Barry's play which starred Katharine Hepburn. The film employs the 1930s screwball plot device of the idle rich whose wealth has blinded them to the simple joys of life and the worthiness of middle-class values. Tracy Lord is the arrogant Philadelphia socialite who is planning her wedding to a stuffy social climber when her ex-husband, C. K. Dexter Haven, arrives at the mansion. Haven is a charming millionaire who openly displays his love of life and his disdain of pretentiousness while he secretly longs for the reunion with his ex-wife. Jimmy Stewart and Ruth Hussey are the reporters from the scandal sheet *Spy Magazine* who have been assigned to cover the wedding. Anti-romance, verbal and witty relationships, and the tendency to poke fun at the rich are all in abundance providing humorous distractions and obstacles to Tracy's and Dexter's final reconciliation.

Director George Cukor here shows his preference for understatement in romantic comedies through his emphasis on plot and performance. Following Frank Capra's example in *It Happened One Night* and his earlier success *Holiday*, Cukor employs a screwball comic style which avoids explicit romance between two leading characters. He instead pits them against each other, creating romantic courtship through character tensions.

Because the audience knows that the characters are Hepburn and Grant, two movie stars who have been paired before in Cukor's *Sylvia Scarlett* and *Holiday* and Howard Hawks's *Bringing Up Baby*, the audience is predisposed to want them to get together. Cukor plays with this expectation throughout the film but especially in the famous opening scene: Grant is tossed out the front door; Hepburn appears at the door where she breaks one of Grant's golf clubs; she tosses the clubs after him and slams the door; Grant returns to the door and rings the bell; when Hepburn answers, he pushes her in the face.

Not a single word is spoken in this scene. Its comic success depends as much on Hepburn's star image as on the superb timing. During the latter 1930s, Hepburn headed the list by the Independent Theatre Owners Association of "box-office poison" movie stars. Critics found her grating, "mannish," or too intense. Cukor, who had directed Hepburn in five previous films, said that she was unattractive to audiences in the late 1930s because she "never was a 'love me. I'm a lovable little girl' kind of actress. She always challenged the audience, and . . . they felt something arrogant in her playing." In *The Philadelphia Story*, Hepburn and Cukor capitalized on these aspects of her image, turning them to Hepburn's advantage by establishing Tracy as a haughty, inflexible snob who becomes lovable when she exposes her underlying vulnerability and fragility.

The Philadelphia Story broke attendance records at the Radio City Music Hall in New York City. The critical and popular success of the film was especially sweet to Hepburn, who had selected the film as a vehicle for her return to movies after a two year hiatus. After *Holiday* and *Bringing Up Baby* had brought her additional negative reviews, she angrily left Hollywood. Hepburn vowed to return only if the role and circumstances were right. The Tracy Lord character in *The Philadelphia Story* not only provided the right role, but it afforded Hepburn the opportunity to create the right circumstances. During her Broadway stint in the play, she acquired the movie rights which she then sold to MGM in a deal that guaranteed her the movie role of Tracy Lord and choice of director and co-stars.

The Philadelphia Story's success led to its remake as a film musical in 1956. Though *High Society* features music and lyrics by

Cole Porter and stars Bing Crosby, Frank Sinatra, and Grace Kelly, it lacks the sparkle and comic tautness of the original.

—Lauren Rabinovitz

THE PIANO

Australia, 1993

Director: Jane Campion

Production: Jan Chapman Productions, in association with CIBY 2000; Eastmancolour, 35mm; running time: 120 minutes. Filmed in New Zealand, 1992.

Producer: Jan Chapman; **screenplay:** Jane Campion; **photography:** Stuart Dryburgh; **editor:** Veronica Jenet; **assistant director:** Mark Turnbull, Victoria Hardy, Charles Haskell, and Therese Mangos; **production design:** Andrew McAlpine; **music:** Michael Nyman; **sound editor:** Gary O'Grady and Jeanine Chialvo; **sound recording:** Tony Johnson, Gethin Creagh, and Michael J. Dutton; **costumes:** Janet Patterson.

Cast: Holly Hunter (*Ada*); Harvey Keitel (*Baines*); Sam Neill (*Stewart*); Anna Paquin (*Flora*); Kerry Walker (*Aunt Morag*); Genevieve Lemon (*Nessie*); Tungia Baker (*Hira*); Ian Mune (*Reverend*).

The Piano

Awards: Palme d'or and Best Actress, Cannes 1993; Oscars for Best Actress (Hunter), Best Supporting Actress (Paquin), and Best Original Screenplay, 1993.

Publications

Script:

Campion, Jane, *The Piano*, London, 1994.

Books:

Gatti, Ilaria, *Jane Campion,* Recco, 1998.
Wexman, Virginia W., editor, *Jane Campion: Interviews*, Jackson, 1999.
Caputo, Raffaele, and Geoff Burton, *Second Take: Australian Film-Makers Talk*, Sydney, 2000.
Margolis, Harriet, editor, *Jane Campion's The Piano*, New York, 2000.

Articles:

Stratton, D., *Variety* (New York), 10 May 1993.
Bilbrough, M., *Cinema Papers* (Melbourne), May 1993.
Bourgignon, T., and others, *Positif* (Paris), May 1993.
Strauss, F., and others, *Cahiers du Cinéma* (Paris), May 1993.
Ciment, M., and T. Bourgignon, *Positif* (Paris), June 1993.
Dumas, D., *Avant-Scène* (Montreal), July 1993.
Bruzzi, Stella, ''Bodyscape,'' in *Sight and Sound* (London), October 1993.
Younis, R., *Cinema Papers* (Melbourne), October 1993.
Francke, L., *Sight and Sound* (London), November 1993.
Eggleton, D., ''Grimm Fairytale of the South Seas,'' in *Illusions* (Wellington), Winter 1993.
Hardy, Ann, ''The Last Patriarch,'' in *Illusions* (Wellington), Winter 1993.
Greenberg, H., *Film Quarterly* (Berkeley), Spring 1994.
Pearson, H., *Films in Review* (New York), no. 3/4, 1994.
Quart, B., *Cineaste* (New York), no. 3, 1994.
Riley, V., ''Ancestor Worship: The Earthly Paradise of Jane Campion's Universe,'' in *Metro Magazine* (St. Kilda West), no. 102, 1995.
Bell, P., ''All That Patriarchy Allows: The Melodrama of *The Piano*,'' in *Metro Magazine* (St. Kilda West), no. 102, 1995.
Bruzzi, Stella, and Lynda Dyson, and Sue Gillett, ''Tempestuous Petticoats: Costume and Desire in *The Piano*/ The Return of the Repressed? Whiteness, Femininity and Colonialism in *The Piano*/ Lips and Fingers: Jane Campion's *The Piano,*'' in *Screen* (Oxford), vol. 36, no. 3, Autumn 1995.
Campbell, Russell, ''Dismembering the Kiwi Bloke: Representations of Masculinity in *Braindead, Desperate Remedies*, and *The Piano*,'' in *Illusions* (Wellington), no. 24, Spring 1995.
Cleave, Peter, ''Old New Zealand, New New Zealand,'' in *Illusions* (Wellington), no. 24, Spring 1995.
Gordon, Suzy, '''I Clipped Your Wings, That's All': Auto-Erotism and the Female Spectator in *The Piano* Debate,'' in *Screen* (Oxford), vol. 37, no. 2, Summer 1996.

Payette, P., ''*The Piano* as Maternal Melodrama,'' in *Michigan Academician* vol. 28, no. 3, 1996.
Siskel, Gene, ''Ms. Campion's Opus,'' in *TV Guide*, vol. 45, no. 13, 29 March 1997.
Chumo, Peter N., ''Keys to the Imagination: Jane Campion's *The Piano*,'' in *Literature/Film Quarterly* (Salisbury), vol. 25, no.3, July 1997.
Dapkus, Jeanne R., ''Sloughing off the Burdens: Ada's and Isabel's Parallel/Antithetical Quests for Self-Actualization in Jane Campion's *The Piano* and Henry James's Novel *The Portrait of a Lady*,'' in *Literature/Film Quarterly* (Salisbury), vol. 25, no. 3, July 1997.
Goldson, Annie, ''Piano Recital,'' in *Screen* (Oxford), vol. 38, no. 3, Autumn 1997.
Perkins, R., ''Imag(in)ing Our Colonial Past: Colonial New Zealand on Film from *The Birth of New Zealand* to *The Piano*-Part II,'' in *Illusions* (Wellington), no. 26, Winter 1997.
Hendershot, Cyndy, and Diane Long Hoeveler, ''(Re)visioning the Gothic: Jane Campion's *The Piano*/'Silence, Sex, and Feminism: An Examination of *The Piano*'s Unacknowledged Sources,''' in *Literature/Film Quarterly* (Salisbury), vol. 26, no. 2, April 1998.
Combs, R., ''Boxing Ada,'' in *Metro Magazine* (St. Kilda West), no. 113/114, 1998.

* * *

Set in the 1800s, Jane Campion's *The Piano* is a tale of repression and sensuality. Ada (Holly Hunter) is a mute, who goes to New Zealand, with her nine-year-old daughter to marry a man she has never met; essentially sold off by her father, Ada leaves Scotland for the wilderness and beauty of a new country. She comes to the country completely unprepared for her new life and armed only with her most beloved possessions: her daughter and her piano.

Music is Ada's way of communicating. She puts all of her repressed passion and sexuality into her piano playing. When her new husband Stewart (Sam Neill) refuses to bring the piano up to his house, Baines (Harvey Keitel), a man who has reportedly ''gone native,'' buys the instrument and asks Ada to teach him how to play it. He trades her the piano one key at a time in return for sexual favours. Although initially disgusted and shocked by Baines's forwardness, when he finally gives her the piano, Ada goes to him and allows him to make passionate love to her.

The film portrays the absurdity of transferring the social niceties of Western society onto a wild and unknown environment. The rigidity of the European way of life is contrasted with the freedom of the native Maori culture—and the aboriginals silent contempt and sardonic humour at the expense of Western culture.

When Stewart learns that Ada is sleeping with Baines, his response is unexpected and shocking. During Stewart's violent outburst, the audience thinks that his anger will be directed towards the piano—the symbol of Ada's hidden self—and is shocked and stunned when Stewart drags Ada out of their house and chops her finger off. This is the first expression of his feelings that Stewart has shown—illustrating that under his extremely constrained exterior he is a hotbed of seething passions.

After Stewart confronts Baines, in a scene reminiscent of the opening one in which Ada arrives on the island, Ada and her daughter leave the island with Baines—the piano strapped to the fragile boat. When the piano is thrown into the ocean to lighten the vessel's load, Ada purposely entangles her foot in a rope connected to the piano and plunges to a watery grave. Strapped to the piano Ada begins her long descent into the depths of the sea, but she struggles free and rises to the surface. Thus the piano, the symbol of her expression and repression, is no longer needed. Ada has liberated herself.

Ada is a wilful, stubborn character. Half adult, half child, she combines an iron will with a deep and passionate nature. She has been mute since the age of six, for no apparent reason other than she simply does not wish to speak—she has retreated into a world in which the piano is her only friend and only source of expression. In the end it is ironic that it is the piano, or a part of it, which betrays her. She writes a message on one of the keys and gives it to her daughter to give to Baines. Flora, her daughter, gives it to Stewart instead, beginning the chain of tragic events which result in her mother's disfigurement. Yet in a sense, Ada's choice to withdraw into herself, to keep her voice inside her head, is also about control. She is a woman existing in a patriarchal society—who has no rights, even over herself. She is sold off by her father to Stewart, and is forced to go to a completely new world because of her sex. In choosing not to speak, Ada is exercising control over one of the few things left for her to control.

Stewart and Baines are contrasting images of masculinity and of European culture. While Stewart is tied to managing his female family, and his European social customs despite the inappropriateness of his behavior, Baines is dissolute and lewd. He consorts with the natives and lives a comparatively wild and lascivious life. While Stewart and his family are buttoned-up tightly in their oppressive clothes, Baines is seen naked, or dressed in stained, sweaty clothes.

Campion's *The Piano* is a superbly filmed piece of cinema. The scope and composition of the cinematography allows the viewer to witness New Zealand through Ada's eyes. The heat and oppressiveness of the climate and landscape are mirrored in the restrictiveness of Ada's apparel. As Ada gives in to passion and frees herself from her society's rules, she loosens her ties to the piano, and to her former silent self. At the end of the film, Ada is slowly shaping words, showing that she is rebuilding her world.

—A. Pillai

PICKPOCKET

France, 1959

Director: Robert Bresson

Production: Lux Films: black and white, 35mm; running time 75 minutes. Released 1959.

Producer: Agnès Delahaie; **screenplay:** Robert Bresson; **photography:** L. H. Burel; **editor:** Raymond Lamy; **sound engineer:** Antoine Archimbault; **production designer:** Pierre Charbonnier; **music:** Lully.

Cast: Martin Lassalle (*Michel*); Marika Green (*Jeanne*); Pierre Leymarie (*Jacques*); Jean Pelegri (*Instructor*); Kassigi (*Initiator*); Pierre Etaix (*2nd accomplice*); Mme. Scal (*Mother*).

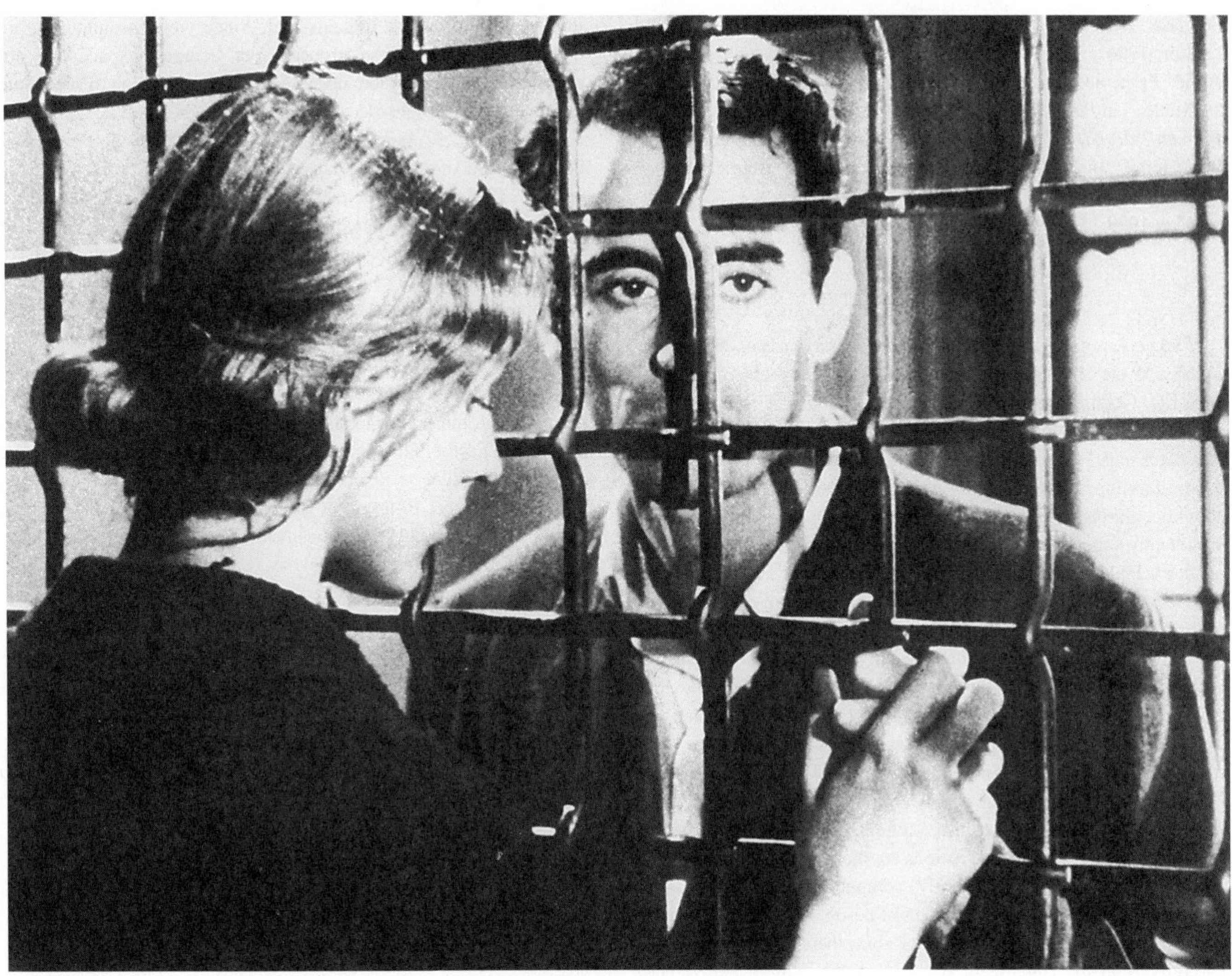

Pickpocket

Publications

Books:

5 reviewers, *The Films of Robert Bresson*, New York, 1969.
Armes, Roy, *French Cinema Since 1946*, vol. 1, New York, 1970.
Cameron, Ian, *The Films of Robert Bresson*, London, 1970.
Schrader, Paul, *Transcendental Style on Film: Ozu, Bresson, Dreyer*, Los Angeles, 1972.
Pontes Leca, C. de, *Robert Bresson o cinematografo e o sinal*, Lisbon, 1978.
Estève, Michel, *Robert Bresson: La passion du cinématographe*, Paris, 1983.
Sloan, Jane, *Robert Bresson: A Guide to References and Resources*, Boston, 1983.
Bordwell, *Narration in the Fiction Film*, London, 1985.
Arnaud, Philippe, *Robert Bresson*, Paris, 1986.
Hanlon, Lindley, *Fragments: Bresson's Film Style*, Cranbury, New Jersey, 1986.
Guerrini, Loretta, *Discorso per una lettura di L'argent di Bresson*, Rome, 1992.

Articles:

Green, Marjorie, ''Robert Bresson,'' in *Film Quarterly* (Berkeley), Spring 1960.
Sontag. Susan, ''Spiritual Style in the Films of Robert Bresson,'' in *Seventh Art* (New York), Summer 1964.
Skoller, Donald S., ''Praxis as a Cinematic Principle in the Films of Robert Bresson,'' in *Cinema Journal* (Evanston, Illinois), Fall 1969.
Armes, Roy, ''The Art of Robert Bresson,'' in *London Magazine*, October 1970.
Prokosch, M., ''Bresson's Stylistics Revisited,'' in *Film Quarterly* (Berkeley), vol. 15, no. 1, 1972.
Polhemusin, H. M., ''Matter and Spirit in the Films of Robert Bresson,'' in *Film Heritage* (Dayton, Ohio), Spring 1974.
Prédal, R., ''Léonce H. Burel'' (interview), in *Cinéma* (Paris), July-August 1974.
Westerbeck, Colin, Jr., ''Robert Bresson's Austere Vision,'' in *Artforum* (New York), November 1976.
Bensard, Patrick, ''Notes sur *Pickpocket*,'' in *Camera/Stylo* (Paris), January 1985.
Predal, R., in *Avant-Scène du Cinéma* (Paris), January-February 1992.

Schrader, Paul, ''*Pickpocket* de Bresson,'' in *Positif* (Paris), no. 400, June 1994.
Audé, Françoise, and Louis Malle, and Michel Ciment, ''Louis Malle,'' in *Positif* (Paris), no. 419, January 1996.
Film en Televisie + Video (Brussels), no. 465, October 1996.
Dick, Jeff T., in *Library Journal*, vol. 123, no. 5., 15 March 1998.
Durgnat, Raymond, in *Film Comment* (New York), vol. 35, no. 3, May 1999.

* * *

Pickpocket, made in 1959 by Robert Bresson, was not considered a ''New Wave'' film because it did not deal with the problems of what Jean-Luc Godard termed ''psychological realism.'' *Pickpocket* did not address the then burgeoning question of cinematic reality, whether this status must be assigned according to the perception of reality or in terms of its impression. In fact, contrary to the expanding discipline of semiotics during the late 1950s and early 1960s *Pickpocket* was so sufficiently depersonalized and unrealistic as to avoid being regarded as an example of a film that articulated the way in which film was a ''language system.'' The filmmakers of this genre (as it is now recognized) were concerned with the deconstruction of the ''Hollywood'' fiction film and its idiosyncratic stylization of cinematic reality. Bresson was not attempting to contribute cinematically to the ideological canons of the period. Instead, he was interested in exploring themes of redemption, a bourgeois preoccupation that did not coincide with New Wave theories of ''distancing'' and ''unrealization.'' In elucidating the ''road to redemption'' in *Pickpocket*, Bresson employs the devices of ellipsis and temporal distention. Close-ups of objects and actions are incriminating and clinical. He fragments the body frequently, compartmentalizing the parts shown into tight, claustrophobic realms of desire. One senses Michel's compulsion to ''fill up'' some kind of void; there is a relentless but carefully repressed feeling of urgency in the film to experience a wholeness. With each theft that he both approaches and moves further away from this unrecognized (until the last moment of the film) spiritual yearning. It is the action of the crime itself that interests both the character Michel and director Bresson, rather than the material gains and narative consequences it may bring.

In order that we clearly see the acts of ''adding and subtracting'' themselves, Bresson deftly shadows the movements of hands and eyes with his camera. At the moment of transference, i.e., when the money or the object ceases being owned by the ''victim,'' the shot of this precarious exchange is held for a few ''long'' seconds. The distention of this moment denies verisimilitude to the representation of the theft and serves to call it to our attention on a symbolic level. It is at this level that the viewer comes closest, through the metaphoric use of temporal distortion and fragmentation, to grasping the apostatic lengths to which Michel is blindly going, that his emptied soul might find redemption.

Pickpocket proves to be an excellent filmic discourse on the boundaries and rules of bourgeois perception. Space is repeatedly compartmentalized in the film, being marked out more and more constrictively as the main character becomes further dependent upon the illusionary efficacy of his displaced desire. Bresson reverses the denotational treatment of ''public'' and ''private'' space. The door to Michel's room has no lock or any kind of securing device, so throughout the film it remains ajar. Since western audiences are culturally attuned to the properties of bourgeois space and are accustomed to seeing them observed, it is disconcerting to accept the existence of this unguarded, undefined space.

Conversely, Bresson focuses without scruple on the scenes and bare moments of the crimes, thereby reconsolidating public space as private. The human eye can not objectively see a crime being committed. Instead, it perceives the act as it has been sedimented informationally through the media. Thus, television cameras have taken over the task. On film, the action of the crime is meta-communicated by its image. This image of the forbidden act is already motivated in terms of its signifying historicity. In *Pickpocket*, the functional status of this meta-communicated image is that of a palimpsest, allowing the viewer to see it as a diegetic trace. It shows but does not interpret or explain the main character's movements in the story. Further, this trace, insofar as it does not presuppose a narrative closure, re-posits the primordial status of pre-bourgeois, unassigned space. In terms of discovering the reason why Michel steals, Bresson intends that it be attributed anagogically, rather than accessible through scientific analysis.

—Sandra L. Beck

PICNIC AT HANGING ROCK

Australia, 1979

Director: Peter Weir

Production: South Australian Film Corporation and the Australian Film Commission; 35 mm; running time: 115 minutes. Filmed on location at Hanging Rock, Victoria, Australia.

Producers: James McElroy and Hal McElroy; **screenplay:** Cliff Green, based on the novel *Picnic at Hanging Rock* by Joan Lindsay; **photography:** Russell Boyd; **editor:** Max Lemon; **art director:** David Copping; **music:** Bruce Smeaton; **costume designer:** Judy Dorsman.

Cast: Rachel Roberts (*Mrs. Appleyard*); Dominic Guard (*Michael Fitzhubert*); Helen Morse (*Dianne de Poitiers*); Jacki Weaver (*Minnie*); Vivean Gray (*Miss MacCraw*); Kirsty Child (*Dora Lumley*); Annie Lambert (*Miranda*); Karen Robinson (*Irma*); John Jarratt (*Albert*); Margaret Nelsonn (*Sara*).

Publications

Books:

Haltof, Marek, *Peter Weir: When Cultures Collide*, New York, 1996.
Rayner, Jonathan, *The Films of Peter Weir*, London, 1998.
Bliss, Michael, *Dreams Within a Dream: The Films of Peter Weir*, Carbondale, 2000.

Picnic at Hanging Rock

Articles:

Purdon, N., ''Under Western Eyes: Notes Towards the Australian Cinema,'' in *Cinema Papers* (Melbournes), November-December 1975.

Hunter, I., ''Corsetway to Heaven: Looking Back at *Picnic at Hanging Rock,*'' in *Cinema Papers* (Melbourne), March-April 1976.

Murray, S. and A. I. Ginnane, ''Producing *Picnic,*'' in *Cinema Papers* (Melbourne), March-April 1976.

O'Donnell, V., ''Max Lemon: Out of the Woodwork,'' in *Cinema Papers* (Melbourne), June-July 1976.

Positif (Paris), July-August 1976.

Wertenstein, W., ''Niewyjasniona tajemnica,'' in *Kino* (Warsaw), May 1977.

Bonneville, L., ''Pique-nique a Hanging Rock,'' *Séquences* (Montreal), January 1978.

Cult Movies, number 2, 1979.

Nation (New York), 17 March 1979.

Time (New York), 23 April 1979.

New Australian Cinema, 1979.

McFarlane, B., ''The Films of Peter Weir,'' in *Cinema Papers* (Melbourne), April-May 1980.

Ledgard, R., in *Hablemos de Cine* (Lima), May 1982.

Jankus, M., ''Piknik pod Wiszaca Skala,'' in *Kino* (Warsaw), April 1984.

Kindblom, M., ''Stillbilden,'' in *Chaplin* (Stockholm), no. 6, 1988.

McFarlane, B., ''The Australian Literary Adaptation: An Overview,'' in *Literature/Film Quarterly* (Salisbury), vol. 21, no. 2, 1993.

Elia, Maurice, in *Séquences* (Haute-Ville), no. 181, November-December 1995.

Nichols, Peter M., ''In Peter Weir's Whodunit, an Otherworldly Force Did: The Director Has Moved On, but His Riddle of the Lost Girls in *Picnic at Hanging Rock* Endures,'' in *New York Times*, 1 November 1998.

Coursodon, Jean-Pierre, and others, ''Peter Weir,'' in *Positif* (Paris), no. 453, November 1998.

Tibbetts, John C., ''Adaptation Redux: *Hanging Rock* on Video,'' in *Literature/Film Quarterly* (Salisbury), vol. 27, no. 2, April 1999.

* * *

At a time when New Journalists such as Tom Wolfe and Truman Capote were experimenting with true stories told through fictional techniques, Australian director Peter Weir was conducting his own exploration of filmic New Journalism with *Picnic at Hanging Rock.* As with the works of the American writers, the basic elements of the Australian story are apparently historical facts; what the artist brings are fleshed-out characters, plot, dialogue, and the texture of actors and *mise-en-scene.* As a result, *Picnic* is far from documentary, but rather a rich, almost literary meditation on a mystery unresolved by conventional investigation and the passage of time. Weir's great daring in this film was to accept the tenets of the New Journalism's approach and to allow the story to end as it happened, unresolved by a neat fictional package that might satisfy critics and audiences accustomed to artistic closure. In a victory for sophistication, this courageous rejection of convention resulted in *Picnic* being considered the best film ever made in Australia up to that time and the most successful internationally.

Picnic's factual base concerns the disappearance of three girls (one eventually rediscovered) and a teacher on a school picnic at a popular Australian location for outings in 1900. The students at Appleyard College in the state of Victoria are proper Edwardian young women, being ''finished'' to take their place in Australian society. Initially, the school and its charges look more like an earlier Victorian ideal of British correctness, rather than a school in the provinces of a colony struggling to escape the English class system. In fact, we soon learn that class conflict is alive and well, with a student who is an orphan treated as a poor relative. It is sexual repression, however, that is most marked and potentially explanatory as a cause of later events. The girls are literally strait-laced: an amusing shot shows a back-to-front lineup, each pulling on the stays of the next in line. Though February 14 is in the midst of the summer season, the girls are dressed more appropriately for a cool British July, and are told they may, as a great treat, remove their white gloves because of the heat.

As the party nears Hanging Rock—a weird up-thrust of stone sacred to the Aborigines—concern about its dangers mounts. Venomous snakes are mentioned repeatedly, and the science teacher, Miss MacCraw, muses darkly on the Rock's geological origin, its lava ''forced up from deep down below,'' perhaps suggesting the suppressed emotions in this controlled society. At the picnic grounds the mood changes from girlish excitement to a languid, hot-summer-afternoon sensuality. The girls remove their sun hats and four receive permission to climb, ostensibly to find geological samples. The luminous, other-worldly Miranda, who has had a premonition of ''not being here much longer,'' hikes upward, accompanied by the dumpy complainer, Edith, and two others. Part way up the rock the girls remove their shoes and stockings after falling asleep as if in unison.

The mood is mystical, pregnant with possibility. Edith complains that the walk is ''nasty,'' and, growing steadily more fearful, turns back, seeing a ''red cloud'' and then passing Miss MacCraw on her way up, looking ''funny'' since the teacher wears no skirt, only ''pantaloons'' or ''drawers.'' George Zamphir's pan flute plays a haunting motif in the background, flocks of birds fly portentously, and the hiking girls are shot in slow motion in lazy, dance-like sequences.

Mountains violate our sense of human scale: the girls, and Weir's camera, look upward and we see nothing as familiar or as manageable as the Victorian furnishings of the school. As Miss MacCraw points out in an amusing correction of the buggy driver, Hanging Rock's time scale is inhuman as well, not ''thousands of years old,'' but ''quite young geologically speaking, a million years old.'' Appleyard College's hothouse environment has been shattered, and new, magical reality is in operation. Everyone's watch stops at twelve noon; heavenly choir and piano music accompany sweeping camera shots of flocks of birds rising. Unfamiliar fauna intrudes, including cicadas, with their weird drumming call, and strange lizards. Rumbling, thunder-like noises roll down from Hanging Rock, but there is no storm, only (apparently) the wind playing through peaks and caves. A spoken prologue has told us that ''What we see and what we seem, Are but a dream—a dream within a dream.'' This reverie is no nightmare but more like what happens during a day-time sleep on a hot day: a disturbing displacement of our conventional perceptions.

This is country Weir explored in his excellent *The Last Wave:* Western rationalism encounters the fluid, intuitive *Weltanschauung* of aboriginal Australia, an ancient mystical land full of spooky threat and indifference to European scientific certainties. There are also repeated references to Shakespearean characters and trees: the angelic Miranda, yearning upward, contrasted to chubby, ''earthbound Edith'' four young people disappearing into a forest inhabited by unseen sensual forces; ''Shall I Compare Thee to a Summer's Day'' recited by some of the girls at the picnic. While Weir is not insistent about it, the suggestion is that the disappearance of the girls is motivated by repressed sexuality, with their dream-like state an escape into another reality.

The balance of the film explores the reactions to and the consequences of the disappearances. One of the girls, Irma, is found by Michael, a young visitor entranced by Miranda at the picnic; Irma is sexually ''intact,'' as the doctor delicately puts it, although her corset is missing and she seems different, perhaps older. Irma is shunned and then abused by her fellow students when she is unable—or perhaps unwilling—to say what happened. Gardners discuss whether the girls could have fallen down a hole or whether a Jack the Ripper has struck. Parents withdraw their children; a lonely student commits suicide, leaping into a greenhouse; the picnic grounds become a media circus; the headmistress descends into alcoholism. The window into another reality has been opened, and nothing can be the same.

Weir's refusal to provide a neat explanation has a variety of artistic consequences. Besides being true to the historical record, the film has the complex resonances of real life, resonances which would be completely absent in the presence of a rational explanation. The thematic point is that it is impossible to speak about the unspeakable—in this society that denies the existence of sex, even the consequences of sex have no name (the maids call illegitimately conceived students ''you know''). The film, like Weir's *Wave* and *Witness*, thus becomes an anthropological commentary on the blindness and limits of culture when confronting events that fail to fit a frame of reference: *Picnic* may begin with fact, but ends with our most unsettling speculations.

—Andrew and Gina Macdonald

THE PICTURE OF DORIAN GRAY

USA, 1945

Director: Albert Lewin

Production: Loew's Incorporated for MGM, black and white with Technicolor inserts, 35mm, running time: 111 minutes.

Producer: Pandro S. Berman; **screenplay:** Albert Lewin from the novel by Oscar Wilde; **photography:** Harry Stradling; **editor:** Ferris Webster; **sound:** Douglas Shearer; **production designer:** Gordon Wiles; **art directors:** Cedric Gibbons, Hans Peters; **music:** Herbert Stothart; **costume designer:** Irene; **set decorator:** Edwin B. Willis; **paintings:** Henrique Medina (*before*) and Ivan Le Lorraine Albright (*after*).

Cast: George Sanders *(Lord Henry Wotton)*; Hurd Hatfield *(Dorian Gray)*; Donna Reed *(Gladys Hallward)*; Angela Lansbury *(Sibyl*

The Picture of Dorian Gray

Vane); Lowell Gilmore *(Basil Hallward)*; Peter Lawford *(David Stone)*; Richard Fraser *(James Vane)*; Miles Mander *(Sir Robert Bentley)*; Lydia Bilbrook *(Mrs. Vane)*; Morton Lowry *(Adrian Singleton)*; Douglas Walton *(Allen Campbell)*; Mary Forbes *(Lady Agatha)*; Robert Greig *(Sir Thomas)*; Moyna MacGill *(Duchess)*; Billy Bevan *(Malvolio Jones)*; Renie Carson *(Young French Woman)*; Lillian Bond *(Kate)*; Devi Dja and her Balinese Dancers, Sir Cedric Hardwicke *(narrator)*.

Awards: Best cinematography in black and white, Harry Stradling, Academy of Motion Picture Arts and Sciences, 1945.

Publications:

Books:

Thomas, Tony, *The Films of the Forties*, Seacaucus, New Jersey, 1977.

Silver, Alain, ''The Picture of Dorian Gray,'' *Magill's Survey of Cinema*, Frank N. Magill, ed., Vol. III, Englewood Cliffs, New Jersey, 1980.

Parish, James Robert and Gregory W. Mank, *The Best of MGM: The Golden Years (1928–59)*, Westport, Connecticut, 1981.

Aachen, George, ''The Picture of Dorian Gray,'' *Memorable Films of the Forties*, Sydney, Australia, 1987.

Mayne, Judith, ''Textual Analysis and Portraits of Spectatorship,'' *Cinema and Spectatorship*, London and New York, 1993.

Edelman, Rob, and Audrey Kupferberg, *Angela Lansbury: A Life on Stage and Screen*, Secaucus, 1997.

Felleman, Susan, *Botticelli in Hollywood: The Films of Albert Lewin*, New York, 1997.

Articles:

Tyler, Parker, ''Dorian Gray: Last of the Movie Draculas'' in *View* (New York), October 1946.

Arkadin [John Russell Taylor], ''Film Clips'' in *Sight and Sound* (London), Winter 1967–68.

Arnaud, Claude, ''Les statues meurent aussi,'' in *Cinématographe* (Paris), January 1982.

Combs, Richard, ''Retrospective: The Picture of Dorian Gray'' and Tom Milne, ''You Are a Professor, Of Course,'' in *Monthly Film Bulletin* (London), November 1985.

Beuselink, James, ''Albert Lewin's Dorian Gray,'' in *Films in Review* (New York), February 1986.

Reid's Film Index (Wyong), no. 1, 1987.

Nacache, Jacqueline ''Le Portrait de Dorian Gray,'' in *Cinéma* (Paris), 4–10 March 1987.

Garsault, Alain, ''Albert Lewin: un créateur à Hollywood,'' in *Positif* (Paris), July-August 1989.

Bensmaïa, Réda, ''La Figure d'inconnu ou l'inconscient épinglé: Le Portrait de Dorian Gray d'Albert Lewin,'' in *Iris* (Paris and Iowa City, Autumn 1992.

Smith, S.D., ''*The Picture of Dorian Gray*,'' in *Monsterscene* (Lombard), no. 3, Fall 1994.

Felleman, Susan, ''How high was his brow? Albert Lewin, his critics, and the problem of pretension,'' in *Film History* (New York), Winter 1995.

Piazzo, Philippe, ''Les rêves d'un amateur,'' in *Télérama* (Paris), no. 2406, 21 February 1996.

Bonesteel, Michael, ''Ivan Albright: Artist of the Living Dead,'' in *Outré* (Evanston), no. 9, 1997.

Bonesteel, Michael, ''The Man Who Was Dorian Gray,'' in *Outré* (Evanston), no. 9, 1997.

Turner, George, ''*The Picture of Dorian Gray*: Worth a Million Words,'' in *American Cinematographer* (Hollywood), vol. 78, no. 5, May 1997.

* * *

Albert Lewin, who made his directorial debut in 1942 after fifteen years as a writer and producer at MGM, directed three films during the 1940s. All featured George Sanders, *fin-de-siècle* European settings, and viewed life, art, decadence and sexual thrall through the prism of a pictorial, complex and studied *mise-en-scène. The Picture of Dorian Gray* was the most expensive and elaborate of the three productions (the other two, *The Moon and Sixpence*, 1942, and *The Private Affairs of Bel Ami*, 1947, were produced more economically by Loew-Lewin, a relatively short-lived independent production company Lewin founded with David Loew). A film of stunning self-consciousness and density, *The Picture of Dorian Gray* is a psycho-sexual horror film based on Oscar Wilde's novel about a beautiful young man who through a Faustian compact remains eternally young while his portrait registers his sins and iniquities.

Wilde and Lewin shared a profound disdain for realism, the dominant literary mode of Wilde's time and the dominant cinematic mode of Lewin's. And although a film made under the auspices of Hollywood's largest, most conservative studio in 1945 was subject to more pressure to conform to convention than a novel written by an already (in)famous aesthete in 1890, Lewin's version of Wilde's story did avoid dullness—realism's ''danger of the commonplace,'' according to its director. And, although criticized for either its literary pretensions, its Hollywood compromises, or both, it is arguably Lewin's best film, and certainly his most widely admired.

The Picture of Dorian Gray avoided the dangers of the commonplace by subjecting itself to dangers of a different order, those resulting from a kind of tightrope act: this self-described equilibrist's concerted negotiation of intellectual, artistic and commercial viability. In its realization of a not very visually detailed source, its divergences, often necessitated by Code, from Wilde's story, and its figuration of content explicitly disallowed or formally problematic, Lewin's film presents a fascinating mediation between Wilde's effete aestheticism and Hollywood's conventional realism.

The story's sexual subtext is embodied in Lewin's film visually rather than narratively. The most remarkable instance of this occurs during the all-important scene of Dorian Gray's ''seduction'' by Lord Henry's credo of youth and pleasure; it features a butterfly, a classical figurine and a bust that in one crafty dissolve momentarily reconfigure themselves into a kind of inverted image of sexual penetration, thus alluding in a flash to many ''perverse'' possibilities (see Bensmaïa). The psycho-sexual lapse configured by this dissolve is a signal instance of Lewin's wont of slipping homoerotic and other taboo content past the producers and censors, to whom even the slightest whiff of perversion was anathema.

The film employs other subtle indices of Dorian Gray's narcissistic and ambiguous sexuality, including copies of Donatello's and Verrocchio's sculptures representing the biblical David as erotically provocative youth. These Renaissance reproductions figuratively and, on one occasion, literally reflect Dorian, who, as portrayed by Hurd Hatfield, enacts his every movement, gesture, and expression with circumspect grace. Like a somnambule (as Parker Tyler put it) or a living doll, his Dorian Gray moves with choreographic precision about the film's exquisite and mannered late-Victorian interiors. Hatfield's austere, almost minimalist performance achieves a psychological uncanniness worthy of a horror film—an appropriate mood for Lewin's variation on the theme of the double. Herbert Stothart's score contributes to the film's eeriness, employing Chopin's 24th Prelude as an elegiac leitmotif.

In its first shots, of Lord Henry Wotton (Sanders) sitting in his carriage reading Baudelaire's *Les Fleurs du Mal*, the film establishes its characteristic *mise-en-scène*, focusing on frames within the film frame, creating a tension between static, manifestly ''composed'' compositions and cinematic movement. Windows, doors, mirrors, screens, signs, and paintings are among the frames that permeate the film. This propensity for conspicuous framing is reinforced by Lewin's bold foregrounding of art works as decorative and symbolic frames, particularly in the many scenes set in Dorian's house, where neo-classical bas-reliefs and Oriental figurines, often symmetrically arranged, as well as Renaissance paintings and Aubrey Beardsley illustrations are among the images that seem to delimit the characters' and the camera's movement.

The scene set at ''The Two Turtles,'' the pub where Dorian first encounters Sibyl Vane (Angela Lansbury), broadens the field of visual plenitude in which the film revels. The pub, which is as replete with props, placards, tchotchkes and other lower-class items as Dorian's home is with high art, is the site of unabashed spectacle. Its overloaded artifice is highlighted by the ''Dr. Look'' sandwich-board that follows Dorian in. The single, disembodied eye of the advertisement, with its uncanny background as Surrealist icon and apotropaic talisman, seems to watch over the scene. The strange, almost explicitly sexual performance of Mr. and Mrs. Ezekiel, a xylophone-puppet act, and any number of cinematic puns and echoes make this scene, along with that set in a den of unspecified iniquities at Blue Gate Field, one of the film's strongest and most original.

The film's preoccupation with the framing and scrutiny of visual experience and desire is brought into focus around the central image of the picture of Dorian Gray itself. While in Wilde's novel, it is the idea of such a phenomenon—a portrait that ages in lieu of its sitter—that means to horrify, in the film it is the picture itself that *moves*. Thus the fastidiously disgusting, hyper-real portrait by Ivan Albright, suspensefully withheld and then shown in Technicolor insert, casts a shadow across the cultivated visual exquisiteness of the black-and-white scenes. The idea that Beauty is Truth, the evident credo of Dorian Gray's friends and would-be lovers, is revealed as fallacy. In fact, the truth is uglier than can be imagined. In the end, *The Picture of Dorian Gray* is, if not a subversion, at least a rather disturbing contemplation, paradoxically, of the very forces that ensured its success—the seductiveness of beauty and the rapture of spectacle, and the perils that accompany succumbing to these.

—Susan Felleman

PIROSMANI

USSR, 1971

Director: Georgy Shengelaya

Production: Gruzia Films; Sovcolor, 35mm; running time: 100 minutes. Released 1971. Filming completed 1971.

Screenplay: Erlom Akhvlediani and Georgy Shengelaya; **photography:** Constantin Opryatine; **music:** V. Koukhianidzé.

Cast: Avtandil Varazi (*Niko Pirosmanichvili*); David Abachidzé; Zourad Carpianidzé; Teimouraz Beridzé; Boris Tsipouria; Chota Daouchvili; Maria Guaramadzé; Nino Setouridzé; Rosalia Mintshine.

Publications

Script:

Akhvlediana, Erlom, and Georgy Shengelaya, *Pirosmani*, in *Avant-Scene du Cinéma* (Paris), 15 December 1979.

Book:

Liehm, Mira, and Antonin Liehm, *The Most Important Art: East European Film after 1945*, Berkeley, 1977.

Articles:

Matei, G., in *Cinema* (Bucharest), April 1972.
Marazov, I., in *Kinoizkustvo* (Sofia), June 1972.
Bensch, S., in *Film a Doba* (Prague), October 1972.
Trujillo, M., in *Cine Cubano* (Havana), nos. 86–88, 1973.
Gow, Gordon, ''Unfamiliar Talents,'' in *Films and Filming* (London), February 1974.
Variety (New York), 12 June 1974.
Elley, D., in *Films and Filming* (London), September 1974.
Glaessner, Verina, in *Monthly Film Bulletin* (London), September 1974.
Capdenac, Michel, in *Ecran* (Paris), 15 November 1975.
Gauthier, G., in *Image et Son* (Paris), December 1975.
Haustrate, G., ''*Pirosmani:* Une Osmose quasi pariaite,'' in *Cinéma* (Paris), September-October 1975.
Portal, M., in *Jeune Cinéma* (Paris), September-October 1975.
Horton, A., in *Film Quarterly* (Berkeley), no. 2, 1979.
Aidan, M., ''Notes sur l'auteur de *Pirosmani:* Gueorgui Chenguelaia,'' in *Jeune Cinéma* (Paris), October-November 1989.

* * *

Pirosmani is one of the works that has contributed to the reputation of recent Georgian Soviet film. The director, Georgi Shengelaya, is a member of a prominent film family. (His father was one of the pioneers of the Georgian industry; his mother was an early star; and his brother is also a director.) The film portrays the life of Georgian primitive artist Niko Pirosmanishvili, who died in 1918. Yet if the film is considered in terms of the familiar category of the art bio-pic, it is obvious that it minimizes the dramatic and psychologizing tendencies frequently associated with this genre. The film presents events from the artist's life in episodic form: through the accretion of individual scenes, the status of the artist is gradually defined. But the film's point of view toward, and explanation of, its main character is developed almost elliptically. A distinct reticence characterizes the film as a whole and the people within it. In part this is due to the measured pauses in dialogue and silences within specific scenes. In addition, the narrative is not developed in terms of strong casual links but can only be fully understood in terms of retrospective reconstruction; each sequence does not proceed clearly and unambiguously to the next. Instead, mid-way through a particular scene, some event or line of dialogue may indicate that it is now one week, or three years, later than the previous scene.

For example, at one point Pirosmani opens a diary store. Some time later his sister and her husband unexpectedly come for a visit; their conversation indicates it has been some time since they have seen one another. His sister suggests that he should get married. The scene is immediately followed by one of a wedding. In mostly long shots one sees guests arriving, receiving flour, dancing, toasting the couple, and generally engaging in those activities associated with wedding receptions. The scene ends when Pirosmani gets up from the table and walks out. Back at his store he explains to his partner that the wedding was a trick, that the bride's relatives have stolen his flour. However, their treachery is not at all clear during the marriage scene; in context, the distribution of the flour appears as something on the order of a social custom. Moreover, whatever reticence and uneasiness Pirosmani exhibits during the wedding scene is not any different from his appearance and behaviour through most of the film. Thus, one can make sense of his departure and understand that something is wrong only after the fact; even then the extent of our comprehension is limited. Pirosmani subsequently causes his business to fall by raising prices exorbitantly on his steady paying customers and by giving his stock away to poor children. One gathers that these actions are a response to his wedding experience, an expression of general disgust and of feeling exploited. But his attitude is not fully clarified by the film.

Through such episodes the status of the artist is seen to be that of an outsider. Pirosmani never fits into any defined social group; he rejects his business and marriage. At one point some artists are interested in his work and invite him to the city. But his glory is short-lived. He is uncomfortable and out of place in the world of salon intellectuals, and his work is ridiculed by a mainstream art critic in a newspaper.

The film uses painting to structure its narrative of the artist's life. The major segments of the film are indicated by images of Pirosmani paintings, "Giraffe," "White Cow," "Easter Lamb," and others. The paintings function as titles and transitional devices. For example, the picture of the white cow precedes a shot of the main character walking through the streets among a herd of cows. Later the painting is hung outside his store, "so people will know what we sell." In fact the filmic *mise-en-scène* is modeled on the paintings. Frontal medium and long shots predominate, with simple decor and stark lighting, imitating the primitivism of the paintings we see in the film. In this way the art itself becomes the most significant structuring principle of the film and its central subject.

—M. B. White

PIXOTE A LEI DO MAS FRACO

(Pixote)

Brazil, 1981

Director: Hector Babenco

Production: H. B. Filmes Embrafilme; Eastmancolor, 35mm; running time: 127 minutes. Released 26 September 1980. Filmed in São Paulo and Rio de Janeiro.

Producers: Paolo Francini and José Pinto; **screenplay:** Hector Babenco, Jorge Duran, based on the novel *A Infacias dos Mortos* by José Louzeiro; **photography:** Rodolfo Sanchez; **editor:** Luiz Elias; **assistant director:** Maria Cecilia M. de Barros, Fatima Toledo; **art director:** Clovis Bueno; **music:** John Neschling; **sound editor:** Hugo Gama; **sound recording:** Francisco Carneiro.

Cast: Fernando Ramos da Silva (*Pixote*); Jorge Juliao (*Lilica*); Gilberto Moura (*Dito*); Edilson Lino (*Chico*); Zenildo Oliveira Santos (*Fumaca*); Claudio Bernardo (*Garotao*); Israel Feres David (*Roberto pede Iata*); José Nilson Martin Dos Santos (*Diego*); Marilia Pera (*Sueli*); Jardel Filho (*Sapatos Brancos—The Inspector*); Rubens de Falco (*Judge*); Elke Maravilha (*Debora*); Tony Tornado (*Cristal*); Beatriz Segall (*The Widow*); Joao Jose Pompeu (*Almir*); Aricle Perez (*The Teacher*); Isadora de Farias (*The Psychologist*).

Awards: New York Film Critics Award for Best Foreign Film, 1981; Los Angeles Film Critics Award for Best Foreign Film, 1981; National Society of Film Critics Award for Best Actress (Marilia Pera), 1981; Locarno Festival Silver Leopoard Award, 1981; San Sebastian Festival Special Mention Awards, 1981.

Publications

Articles:

Pereira, Edmar, *Jornal da Tarde* (Sao Paulo), 19 September 1980.
Arco e Flexa, Jairo, *Veja* (Sao Paulo), 1 October 1980.
Angelica, Joana, *O Globo* (Rio de Janeiro), 20 October 1980.
Schild, Susana, *Jornal do Brasil* (Rio de Janeiro), 24 October 1980.
Canby, Vincent, *New York Times*, 5 May 1981.
Variety (New York), 6 May 1981.
Stone, Judy, *San Francisco Chronicle*, 13 June 1981.

Pixote a lei do mais fraco

Tavares, Zulmira Ribeiro, ''A Briga de Pixote,'' in *Filme e Cultura*, number 38/39, August/November 1981.
Sullivan, James, *Films in Review* (New York), 12 September 1981.
Sullivan, J., *Films in Review* (New York), November 1981.
Kael, Pauline, *New Yorker*, 9 November 1981.
Bonneville, L., *Séquences* (Montreal), January 1982.
Corliss, Richard, *Time*, 18 January 1982.
Cuel, F., *Cinématographe* (Paris), April 1982.
Paranagua, P. A., ''Sur le fil du rasoir'' in *Positif* (Paris), April 1982.
Welsh, H., *Jeune Cinéma* (Paris), April/May 1982.
Cros, J. L., *Image et Son* (Paris), June 1982.
Csicsery, G., ''Individual Solutions'' in *Film Quarterly* (Berkeley), Fall 1982.
Imeson, J., *Monthly Film Bulletin* (London), January 1983.
LeFanu, M., *Films and Filming* (London), January 1983.
Hawken, J., and C. Htewski, ''Exploitation for Export,'' in *Screen* (London), March/April 1983.
Stam, R., *Cineaste* (New York), 1983.
Schild, Susana, *Jornal do Brasil* (Rio de Janeiro), 9 February 1986.
Schild, Susana, *Jornal do Brasil* (Rio de Janeiro), 27 February 1988.
Folha de Sao Paulo (Sao Paulo), 6 December 1989.
Azeredo, Ely, *O Globo* (Rio de Janeiro), 5 February 1993.
The New York Times, vol. 147, A34 and B29, 19 December 1997.
Purtell, Tim, in *Entertainment Weekly*, no. 414, 16 January 1998.

* * *

Pixote a lei do mais fraco directed by Hector Babenco, is one of those films whose subject matter has so escaped the darkness of the projection room as to make it impossible to comment on it merely in terms of filmmaking. Pixote's story continued, a painful and foretold tragedy, for seven years, until its dreadful epilogue.

The launch of *Pixote* (the word means ''urchin'') in 1980 hit the public like a mule's kick by addressing the shocking reality—couched in scenes of raw beauty—of one of Brazil's most serious social problems, that of abandoned children, of which there are several million in the country. The international recognition of *Pixote* (voted the third best foreign film of the 1980s by the magazine *American Film*) confirmed that Hector Babenco had conceived an outstanding film about violated youth and the painful loss of innocence, ranked with Vittorio de Sica's *Ladri di biciclette* and Luis Bunuel's *Los Olvidados.* Hector Babenco, born in Argentina, resident in Brazil since the late 1960s, found inspiration for *Pixote* in *A Infância dos Mortos (The Infancy of the Dead)* by José Lonzeiro. With *Pixote*—which followed *O Rei da Noite* (1976) and *Lucio Flávio, O Passageiro da Agonia* (1977), a huge box office success—Babenco consolidates what would become his dominant theme: people living on the fringes of society, treading the fine line between petty crime and considerable risk. The theme is resumed in his later films, *The Kiss of the Spider Woman, Ironweed*, and *At Play in the Fields of the Lord.* The underprivileged communities living on the outskirts of São Paulo provided the cast for the film: dozens of poor and ostracized youngsters, none of whom had ever acted before. Among them was Fernando Ramos da Silva, who lived with eight brothers and his widowed mother in a São Paulo shanty town. Slightly built, shy and, as Babenco put it, "with an old man's face" Fernando was 11 years old when filming began on *Pixote.* His poignant acting is a mixture of naiveté and fear, his expressions bore the cares of the world. His face became a symbol for what he was and what he represented: the drama of the abandoned child. The film was "universal in its grief," according to the author of the book on which it was based.

Following the trajectory of Pixote—first in a police station, then in a reformatory, and finally on the streets of Rio and São Paulo—the film plunges deep into the world of abandoned Brazilian youth. Pixote witnesses and is a product of the three-fold collapse which is the root cause of the tragedy of street children: the breakdowns of the family unit, the social services and the institutions. The children and adolescents have on their side one paradoxical guarantee: that of exemption from the punitive aspects of the law until they reach official adulthood at the age of 18. This impunity also makes them ideal as apprentice criminals, especially under the tutelage of fully blown adult drug runners.

The sordid environment of the reformatory is the back drop for the initial part of the film; to the insensitive attitude of those in authority is added the impotence of those who wish to help (teachers and psychologists). Only the very strong can survive the situation, where solidarity and sadism set the tone.

Hector Babenco did not recoil at revealing the atrocities of the environment—sexual abuse, police violence, early contact with drugs. However, he still manages, despite the ugliness and degradation, to produce scenes of great poetry. An example is the scene where Pixote tries to follow a football match and darts and pokes his head around the body of the woman who is cutting his hair. Later, in the classroom, he laboriously writes "the earth is round like an orange," his face is viewed close-up while he mutters the words he is writing.

The claustrophobic atmosphere of the reformatory, accentuated by cold, blue lighting, gives way to the colours of the streets of São Paulo and Rio. After fleeing the reformatory, Pixote, the youngest boy, forms a little gang with three friends, one of whom is a transvestite, Lilica (played by the excellent Jorge Julião). Having made contact with a cocaine dealer, the little gang departs for Rio to sell the drugs; increasing violence culminates in Pixote committing his first murder. His encounter with the prostitute Sueli (Marilia Pera in an outstanding performance) figures among the most significant scene in any or all Brazilian films: having killed his customer and his friend, Pixote suckles at the breast of the prostitute, who had aborted a few days previously, in a poignant allusion to the Pietá. The conclusion of the scene probes the heavy ambiguity of the prostitute in relation to motherhood.

Notwithstanding the Cinema Novo's awareness of social concerns, Hector Babenco opted for a straightforward narrative in *Pixote*, in which the camera restricts itself to depicting scenes and situations and, above all, their effect on the characters. The pace is sustained by the careers of the boys themselves and the tragedy stamped on the faces of these youthful crooks; tension is provided by the awfulness of some of the scenes and by the hopelessness of the children's lot. Babenco was remorselessly realistic in his portrayal, while remaining sympathetic in his search for lost innocence. Not wishing to produce a documentary about street children, nor attempting to identify social causes for the problem, Babenco stated that he "used the reality as a trampoline in trying to find the human being inside every juvenile offender."

Early in the film, Babenco shows hundreds of "Pixotes," slowly homing in on the group whose progress he would follow, and gradually narrowing his sights on Pixote. At the end of the film, Pixote, who carries the weight of three murders on his childish shoulders, walks alone down the railway track, a revolver his sole companion.

Fernando Ramos da Silva tried to pursue a career as an actor, following the success of *Pixote*, but his stardom was short-lived. Once again on the road to nowhere, through total lack of prospects, he ran into trouble with the authorities, and was shot dead by the police in 1987, at the age of 19. He fulfilled the destiny of the Pixote of the film; but, more tragically, that of the many Pixotes in true life, also. Fernando Ramos da Silva became Pixote—on screen and in true life—forever.

—Susana Schild

A PLACE IN THE SUN

USA, 1951

Director: George Stevens

Production: Paramount Pictures; black and white, 35mm; running time: 122 minutes. Released 1951.

Producer: George Stevens; **screenplay:** Harry Brown and Michael Wilson, from the novel *An American Tragedy* by Theodore Dreiser; **photography:** William C. Mellor; **editor:** William Hornbeck; **music:** Franz Waxman; **costume designer:** Edith Head.

Cast: Montgomery Clift (*George Eastman*); Elizabeth Taylor (*Angela Vickers*); Shelley Winters (*Alice Tripp*); Anne Revere (*Hannah Eastman*); Sheppard Strudwick (*Anthony Vickers*); Frieda Inescort (*Mrs. Vickers*); Keefe Brasselle (*Earl Eastman*); Fred Clark (*Bellows*); Raymond Burr (*Frank Marlowe*).

Awards: Oscars for Best Director, Best Screenplay, Best Cinematography—Black and White, Best Editing, Best Music—Dramatic or Comedy Picture, and Best Costume—Black and White, 1951.

A Place in the Sun

Publications

Books:

Richie, Donald, *George Stevens: An American Romantic*, New York, 1970, 1985.

Phillips, Gene D., *The Movie Makers: Artists in the Industry*, Chicago, 1973.

Hirsch, Foster, *Elizabeth Taylor*, New York, 1973.

d'Arcy, Susan, *The Films of Elizabeth Taylor*, London, 1974.

Laguaria, Robert, *Monty: A Biography of Montgomery Clift*, New York, 1977.

Bosworth, Patricia, *Montgomery Clift: A Biography*, New York, 1978.

Agte, Lloyd M., *Harry Peter McNab Brown: A Classical Stylist and Hollywood Screenwriter*, Ann Arbor, Michigan, 1980.

Petri, Bruce, *A Theory of American Film: The Films and Techniques of George Stevens*, New York, 1987.

Vermilye, Jerry, and Mark Ricci, *The Films of Elizabeth Taylor*, Secaucus, 1989.

Parker, John, *Five for Hollywood: Their Friendship, Their Fame, Their Tragedy*, Secaucus, 1991.

McCann, Graham, *Rebel Males: Clift, Brando, and Dean*, Piscataway, 1993.

Kalfatovic, Mary C., *Montgomery Clift: A Bio-Bibliography*, Westport, 1994.

Morley, Sheridan, *Elizabeth Taylor*, New York, 1999.

Articles:

Lewis, Stephen, in *Films in Review* (New York), October 1951.

Pichel, Irving, ''Revivals, Reissues, Remakes, and *A Place in the Sun*,'' in *Quarterly of Radio, Television, and Film* (Berkeley), Summer 1952.

Martin, Pete, ''The Man Who Made the Hit Called *Shane*,'' in *Saturday Evening Post* (Philadelphia), 8 August 1953.

Archer, E., ''George Stevens and The American Dream,'' in *Film Culture* (New York), no. 1, 1957.

Luft, Herbert, ''George Stevens,'' in *Films in Review* (New York), November 1958.

Stang J., ''Hollywood Romantic,'' in *Films and Filming* (London), July 1959.

''Monograph of George Stevens's Films,'' in *Cinema* (Beverly Hills), December-January 1965.

McVay, Douglas, ''George Stevens: His Work,'' in *Films and Filming* (London), April and May 1965.

Houston, Penelope, in *Sight and Sound* (London), Winter 1955–56.

Roman, Robert C., ''Montgomery Clift,'' in *Films in Review* (New York), November 1966.

Beresford, R., ''George Stevens,'' in *Film* (London), Summer 1970.

Essoe, Gabe, ''Elizabeth Taylor,'' in *Films in Review* (New York), August-September 1970.

Buckley, Michael, ''Shelley Winters,'' in *Films in Review* (New York), March 1970.

Dialogue on Film (Washington, D.C.), no. 1, 1972.

Kliman, B., ''An American Tragedy: Novel, Scenario, and Films,'' in *Literature/Film Quarterly* (Salisbury, Maryland), Summer 1977.

Kass, Judith M., in *Magill's Survey of Cinema 3*, Englewood Cliffs, New Jersey, 1980.

Kinder, M., ''The Subversive Potential of the Pseudo-Iterative,'' in *Film Quarterly* (Berkeley), no. 2, 1989–90.

Reid's Film Index (Wyong), no. 32, 1997.

* * *

When producer-director George Stevens made *A Place in the Sun*, based on the highly successful novel, *An American Tragedy* by Theodore Dreiser, in 1951, he faced the difficult job of turning a popular book into a worthwhile film.

Dreiser's book, a detailed work of 850 pages, had already been made into a film in 1931. Directed by Josef von Sternberg, the film was condemned by Dreiser as it changed the emphasis of the story, making the hero the precipitator of events rather than a victim of his society and environment. The celebrated Soviet director Sergei Eisenstein had also produced a treatment of the book when he came to Hollywood in 1930. This version emphasized the importance of society in the tragic events of the story, and was closer to Dreiser's book than any other version. However, Eisenstein's story never reached the screen.

Irving Piechl comments in his essay ''Revivals, Reissues, Remakes, and 'A Place in the Sun,''' that Stevens's film is ''not only exceptional in being more successful than the first [1931] film, it is also the first remake . . . which is made as though for the first time. It tells essentially the same story as the earlier film but with a totally different emphasis and perspective.'' *A Place in the Sun* was a success on its release, earning six Academy Awards.

Stevens's story is not an ''American tragedy'' as such. The director changed the time period of the story to the 1950s and created a hero, George Eastman (Clyde Griffith in Dreiser's book), who has a chance at achieving his dream, and misses it through a string of circumstances which combine to bring about his downfall.

George (Montgomery Clift) is a bright, handsome, but poor boy with rich connections. He visits his successful uncle and gains employment at his factory stacking swimming costumes, but he quickly shows how determined and ambitious he is by suggesting improvements to his workplace. He meets and falls in love with Angela Vickers (Elizabeth Taylor), a rich young socialite who is dating Earl, George's cousin.

Much to her parents' horror, Angela reciprocates George's love. With his uncle's support, George overcomes their opposition. However, while dreaming of Angela George makes love to Alice Tripp, a girl who works with him at the factory. When she falls pregnant and tries to blackmail him into marrying her George's whole future is put in jeopardy.

Angela and Alice are presented in opposition to each other as lightness and darkness. Angela is always dressed in pure, virginal white or conservative sober black; Alice, in contrast, wears overly tight clothes, is weary, whiny, and slovenly. Angela is the epitome of wealth and luxury; Alice represents hard work and poverty.

It is hardly surprising that George considers murdering Alice. The fact that he changes his mind at the last moment leaves the viewer ambivalent when Alice finally overturns the boat and dies. Is George responsible? Did Alice die because of George's momentary hesitation before he tries to rescue her? Is his execution just?

In the scene when the boat overturns Stevens uses a long shot and then darkness to blur the issue. We do not see what happens but we know that when Alice upsets the boat she is frightened of George: we feel her fear. We are left to make our own judgement about George's guilt.

Stevens uses montage, close-ups, and very slow scenes to create an almost dream like atmosphere. The plot moves along slowly but with great fluidity. Similarly the use of steady slow drums as George contemplates murder creates a hot, dark, and menacing atmosphere. The viewer knows that something awful is going to occur.

The famous kiss between Taylor and Clift, which is shot with a six-inch lens in close-up, conveys the intensity and passion existing between the couple—a sensuality that never exists between Alice and George. It is the last thing that George thinks of as he goes to his death, showing that no matter what has happened his love for Angela is the most important thing in his life.

A Place in the Sun is a significant film not only because of excellent performances elicited from Montgomery Clift and Elizabeth Taylor, but also because of the society it depicts. Although George has the opportunity to succeed—his upbringing, his own sense of morality bring about his downfall. In a sense George is doomed from the beginning—he is a victim.

—A. Pillai

THE PLAYER

USA, 1992

Director: Robert Altman

Production: Avenue Entertainment; DeLuxe colour, 35mm; running time: 124 minutes. Filmed in Los Angeles, 1991.

Producer: David Brown, Michael Tolkin, Nick Weschler; **screenplay:** Michael Tolkin, from his own novel; **photography:** Jean

The Player

Lepine; **editor:** Geraldine Peroni, Maysie Hoy; **assistant directors:** Allan Nichols, C. C. Barnes; **production design:** Stephen Altman; **art director:** Jerry Fleming; **music:** Thomas Newman; **sound editors:** Joseph Holsen, Ed Lachmann; **sound recording:** Rich Gooch, John Pritchet, John Vigran; **costume design:** Alexander Julian.

Cast: Tim Robbins (*Griffin Mill*); Greta Scacchi (*June Gudmundsdottir*); Fred Ward (*Walter Stuckel*); Whoopi Goldberg (*Detective Susan Avery*); Peter Gallagher (*Larry Levy*); Cynthia Stephenson (*Bonnie Sherow*); Brion James (*Joel Levison*); Vincent D'Onofrio (*David Kahane*); Dean Stockwell (*Andy Civella*); Richard E. Grant (*Tom Oakley*); Sydney Polack (*Dick Mellen*); Lyle Lovett (*Detective DeLongpre*).

Appearing as themselves: Harry Belafonte, Karen Black, Gary Busey, Robert Carradine, Cher, James Coburn, John Cusack, Brad Davis, Peter Falk, Louise Fletcher, Teri Garr, Scott Glenn, Jeff Goldblum, Elliot Gould, Joel Grey, Buck Henry, Angelica Houston, Sally Kellerman, Sally Kirkland, Jack Lemmon, Marlee Matlin, Andie McDowell, Malcolm McDowell, Nick Nolte, Burt Reynolds, Julia Roberts, Mimi Rogers, Annie Ross, Alan Rudolph, Jill St. John, Susan Sarandon, Rod Steiger, Lily Tomlin, Robert Wagner, Bruce Willis.

Awards: Best Director, Cannes Film Festival, 1992.

Publications

Books:

Kolker, Robert P., *A Cinema of Loneliness: Penn, Kubrick, Scorsese, Spielberg, Altman*, New York, 1988.

McGilligan, Patrick, *Robert Altman: Jumping Off the Cliff: A Biography of the Great American Director*, New York, 1989.

Keyssar, Helene, *Robert Altman's America*, New York, 1991.

Altman, Robert, ''Altman on Altman,'' in *Projections 2*, edited by John Boorman and Walter Donohue, London 1993.

Cagin, Seth, *Born to Be Wild: Hollywood & the Sixties Generation*, Boca Raton, 1994.

O'Brien, Daniel, *Robert Altman: Hollywood Survivor*, New York, 1996.

Sterritt, David, editor, *Robert Altman: Interviews*, Jackson, 2000.

Articles:

McCarthy, T., *Variety* (New York), 16 March 1992.
Sauvaget, D., ''Le retour du grand Bob,'' in *Revue du Cinéma* (Paris), May 1992.
Camy, G., *Jeune Cinéma* (Paris), May-June 1992.
Raymond, R., *Films in Review* (New York), May-June 1992.
Smith, G., and R. T. Jameson, *Film Comment* (New York), May-June 1992.
Henry, M., and J.-P. Coursodon, *Positif* (Paris), June 1992.
Wilmington, M., and P. Keogh, ''Laughing and Killing,'' in *Sight and Sound* (London), June 1992.
Sheehan, H., *Sight and Sound* (London), July 1992.
Blois, M. de, ''Ce que je vois de ma tour d'ivoire,'' in *24 Images* (Montreal), Summer 1992.
Quart, L., and others, *Cineaste* (New York), 1992.
Schupp, P., *Séquences* (Montreal), September 1992.
Sawhill, R., *Film Quarterly* (Berkeley), Winter 1992–93.
Travers, Peter, ''Ten Best Movies of 1992,'' in *Rolling Stone*, no. 648, 21 January 1993.
Danzinger, M., ''Basic Instinct: Grappling for Post-Modern Mind Control,'' in *Literature/Film Quarterly* (Salisbury), vol. 22, no.1, January 1994.
Sugg, R.P., ''The Role of the Writer in *The Player*: Novel and Film,'' in *Literature/Film Quarterly* (Salisbury), vol. 22, no. 1, January 1994.
La Rochelle, ''Réal: Non pas la réalité, mais celle du cinéma,'' in *24 Images* (Montreal), no. 71, February-March 1994.
Adams, D., ''Thomas Newman's *The Player*,'' in *Film Score Monthly* (Los Angeles), no. 72, August 1996.
Everett, Anna, ''The Other Pleasure: The Narrative Function of Race in the Cinema,'' in *Film Criticism* (Meadville), vol. 20, no. 1–2, Fall-Winter 1995–1996.
Elia, M., ''*The Player*,'' in *Séquences* (Haute-Ville), no. 189/190, March/June 1997.
Rush, J., and C. Baughman, ''Language as Narrative Voice: The Poetics of the Highly Inflected Screenplay,'' in *Journal of Film and Video* (Los Angeles), vol. 4, no. 3, 1997.
Nayman, Ira, ''The Adaptable Altman,'' in *Creative Screenwriting* (Washington, D.C.), vol. 4, no. 3, Fall 1997.

* * *

Movies about the movies are a staple Hollywood sub-genre that's been with us since the dawn of the movies themselves. And it's practically a formula tradition of these Hollywood behind-the-scenes pictures to cast the industry they portray in the most unsavory light possible.

Even such otherwise upbeat and exuberant glimpses into the early days of Tinseltown as the silents *Show People* and *Ella Cinders* delivered the cautionary message that stardom isn't all it's cracked up to be—a message that took even darker turns when the talkies arrived in such films as *What Price Hollywood?* and the numerous versions of *A Star is Born.* It's a stretch to imagine any other industry but Hollywood turning out a product designed by the manufacturers to trash the very industry that feeds them. But that's the salient quality of most movies about the movies.

Their consistent and self-reviling thematic thread is that Hollywood is a boulevard of broken dreams, a cutthroat business that builds careers only to destroy them, a place that eats its young and casts out its old—a wartorn landscape fueled by an ongoing blood feud between the money men and the creative artist-individual where the latter almost always comes out the loser. This portrait has been reinforced in films from *Sunset Boulevard* to *Whatever Happened to Baby Jane?* Ironically, rather then running the whistleblowers out of town, the industry as often as not has embraced them by showering their scathing exposes with Oscars!

Robert Altman's skewering of the New Hollywood, *The Player*—itself a multiple Oscar nominee—is but the latest in the long line of Hollywood on Hollywood films to follow this path. Altman even begins the film with a salute to the man who was arguably the most mistreated creative artist in Hollywood history—Orson Welles: a satiric and technically dazzling eight-minute take inspired by the opening scene of Welles's final Hollywood film, *Touch of Evil*, a movie and scene to which the numerous central characters we are introduced to in the shot make reverential reference.

Altman frameworks his acid satire on the business of Hollywood as a whodunit. Tim Robbins stars as a studio executive who receives a series of threats from an anonymous screenwriter whose career he has put in turnaround. The vengeful screenwriter vows to settle the score and the exec's hash on behalf of every scribe Robbins has shown callous disregard.

Robbins takes the threats seriously and grows progressively paranoid. As writer after writer grovels before him in his power suit pitching story ideas to make a buck, Robbins speculates if this is the one who's got him marked for death—even as he reflexively puts them and their ideas down. He finally settles on Vincent D'Onofrio, a writer whose lifeblood screenplay Robbins had treated with particular indifference, and sets up a meeting to buy the guy off. After talking at cross purposes for awhile, the two tangle physically and Robbins accidentally kills the man. To his surprise, however, the threats continue. D'Onofrio was a writer who hated him, but not *the* writer; Robbins is guilty of murdering an innocent man.

Faced with staving off a challenge from an ambitious young producer (Peter Gallagher) with an eye on Robbins's job, sidestepping the police investigation into D'Onofrio's death by starstruck detective Whoopi Goldberg, swimming with his fellow Hollywood sharks at the studio, juggling love affairs, and covering his tracks while watching his back as the threatening screenwriter closes in, Robbins finds his problems have only just begun.

It seemed inevitable that the maverick Altman, a director noted for his acerbic takes on America's socio-political scene in such films as *Nashville* and for his well known hatred of Tinseltown's power structure, would eventually make a Hollywood on Hollywood movie like *The Player.* That he chose to adapt Michael Tolkin's blackly comic assault on the wheeler-dealer ''suits'' who run the business as his comeback film, after years of being written off by those ''suits,'' was a brash act indeed. That Altman got just about every contemporary superstar in Hollywood to accept cameos for a fraction of their usual fees just to be in the movie is a measure not only of their respect for Altman's maverick status, but their own ambivalent feelings toward the system that supports them.

But that the movie itself was the most in-demand picture of the year for private screenings by the very studio executives it paints so darkly is probably most amazing of all. But that, it would seem, is show biz'.

—John McCarty

PLAYTIME

France, 1967

Director: Jacques Tati

Production: Specta Films, Eastmancolor, 70mm, stereophonic sound; running time: originally 155 minutes,versions for United States release run about 108 minutes or 93 minutes. Released 1967, France. Re-released 1972 in the United States in 35mm version. Filmed on specially constructed sets just outside Paris.

Producer: René Silvera; **screenplay:** Jacques Tati and Jacques Lagrange; **photography:** Jean Badal and Andreas Winding; **editor:** Gérald Pollicand; **production designer:** Eugene Roman; **music:** Francis Lemarque; **African themes:** James Campbell; **artistic collaboration:** Jacques Lagrange; **English dialogue:** Art Buchwald.

Cast: Jacques Tati (*M. Hulot*); Barbara Dennek (*Young tourist*); Jacqueline Lecomte (*Her friend*); Valérie Camille (*M. Luce's secretary*); France Romilly (*Woman selling eyeglasses*); France Delahalle (*Shopper in department store*); Laure Paillette and Colette Proust (*Two women at the lamp*); Erika Dentzler (*Mme. Giffard*); Yvette Ducreux (*Hat check girl*); Rita Maiden (*Mr. Schultz's companion*); Nicole Ray (*Singer*); Jack Gauthier (*The guide*); Henri Picolli (*An important gentleman*); Léon Doyen (*Doorman*); Billy Kearns (*M. Schultz*).

Publications

Books:

Armes, Roy, *French Cinema since 1946*, New York, 1970.
Gilliatt, Penelope, *Jacques Tati*, London, 1976.
Maddock, Brent, *The Films of Jacques Tati*, Metuchen, New Jersey, 1977.
Fischer, Lucy, *''Homo Ludens'': An Analysis of Four Films by Jacques Tati*, Ann Arbor, Michigan, 1978.
Fischer, Lucy, *Jacques Tati: A Guide to References and Resources*, Boston, 1983.
Harding, James, *Jacques Tati: Frame by Frame*, London, 1984.
Chion, Michael, *Jacques Tati*, Paris, 1987.
Dondey, Marc, *Tati*, with Sophie Tatischeff, Paris, 1989.
Haberer, Peter, *Aspekte der Komik in den Filmen von Jacques Tati*, Coppi, 1996.
Bellos, David, *Jacques Tati: His Life and Art*, London, 2000.

Articles:

Armes, Roy, ''The Comic Art of Jacques Tati,'' in *Screen* (London), February 1970.
Rosenbaum, Jonathan, ''Paris Journal,'' in *Film Comment* (Paris), Winter 1971–72.
Dale, R. C., in *Film Quarterly* (Berkeley), Winter 1972–73.
Gilliatt, Penelope, ''Profiles: Playing,'' in *New Yorker*, 27 January 1973.
Rosenbaum, Jonathan, ''Tati's Democracy,'' in *Film Comment* (New York), May-June 1973.
Leach, D., in *Films in Review* (New York), September 1973.
Monaco, James, in *Take One* (Montreal), September 1973.
Siegel, J. E., in *Film Heritage* (Dayton, Ohio), Spring 1974.
Fischer, Lucy, ''Beyond Freedom and Dignity: An Analysis of Jacques Tati's *Playtime*,'' in *Sight and Sound* (London), no. 4, 1976.
Rosenbaum, Jonathan, ''Afterword,'' in *Sight and Sound* (London), no. 4, 1976.
Thompson, K., ''*Playtime:* Comedy on the Edge of Perception,'' in *Wide Angle* (Athens, Ohio), no. 2, 1979.
Selig, Michael, in *Cinema Texas Program Notes* (Austin), 17 April, 1979.
Bezombes, R., ''De Hulot à Mick Jagger: *Playtime*,'' in *Cinématographe* (Paris), July 1979.
Boland, B., ''Jacques Tati: L'Autre Monde de Hulot,'' in *Cahiers du Cinéma* (Paris), September 1979.
Daney, S., ''Eloge de Tati,'' in *Cahiers du Cinéma* (Paris), September 1979.
Daney, S., *et al.*, ''Entretiens avec Jacques Tati: Propos rompus,'' in *Cahiers du Cinéma* (Paris), September 1979.
Schefer, J. L., ''Jacques Tati: La Vitrine,'' in *Cahiers du Cinéma* (Paris), September 1979.
Johnston, Sheila, in *Films and Filming* (London), August 1982.
Willmott, G., ''Implications for a Sartrean Radical Medium: From Theatre to Cinema,'' in *Discourse* (Bloomington, Indiana), Spring-Summer 1990.
Rimbau, E., and others, in *Nosferatu* (San Sebastian), no. 10, October 1992.
Génin, Bernard, in *Télérama* (Paris), no. 2244, 13 January 1993.
Chevassu, François, ''*Play Time:* les règles du jeu,'' in *Mensuel du Cinéma*, no. 3, February 1993.
''*Playtime* Section'' of *Positif* (Paris), May 1993.
Rémond, Alain, ''Tati, les toons et nous,'' in *Télérama* (Paris), no. 2294, 29 December 1993.

* * *

Jacques Tati's *Playtime* is perhaps the only epic achievement of the modernist cinema, a film that not only accomplishes the standard modernist goals of breaking away from closed classical narration and discovering a new, open form of story-telling, but also uses that form to produce an image of an entire society. After building a solid international audience through the 1950s with his comedies *Jour de fête*, *Mr. Hulot's Holiday*, and *Mon oncle*, Tati spent ten years on the planning and execution of what was to be his masterpiece, selling the rights to all his old films to raise the money he needed to construct the immense glass and steel set—nicknamed ''Tativille''—that was his vision of modern Paris. The film—two hours and 35 minutes long, in 70mm and stereophonic sound—opened in France in 1967, and was an instant failure. It was quickly reduced, under Tati's supervision, to a 108-minute version, and further reduced, to 93 minutes and 35 monaural, when it was released in the United States in 1972. Even in its truncated form, it remains a film of tremendous scope, density, and inventiveness.

Playtime is what its title suggests—an idyll for the audience, in which Tati asks us to relax and enjoy ourselves in the open space his film creates, a space cleared of the plot-line tyranny of ''what happens next?,'' of enforced audience identification with star performers, and of the rhetorical tricks of *mise-en-scène* and montage meant to keep the audience in the grip of pre-ordained emotions. Tati leaves us free to invent our own movie from the multitude of material he offers.

One of the ways in which Tati creates the free space of *Playtime* is by completely disregarding conventional notions of comic timing and cutting. There is no emphasis in the montage to tell us when to laugh, no separation in the *mise-en-scène* of the gag from the world around it. Instead of using his camera to break down a comic situation—to analyze it into individual shots and isolated movement—he uses deep-focus images to preserve the physical wholeness of the event and long takes to preserve its temporal integrity. Other gags and bits of business are placed in the foreground and background; small patterns, of gestures echoed and shapes reduplicated, ripple across the surface of the image. We can't look at *Playtime* as we look at an ordinary film, which is to say, passively, through the eyes of the director. We have to roam the image—search it, work it, play with it.

With its universe of Mies van der Rohe boxes, *Playtime* is often described as a satire on the horrors of modern architecture. But the glass and steel of *Playtime* is also a metaphor for all rigid structures, from the sterile environments that divide city dwellers to the inflexible patterns of thought that divide and compartmentalize experience, separating comedy from drama, work from play. The architecture of *Playtime* is also an image for the rhetorical structures of classical filmmaking: the hard, straight lines are the lines of plot, and the plate glass windows are the shots that divide the world into digested, inert fragments. At one point in *Playtime*, M. Hulot stands on a balcony looking down on a network of office cubicles, seeing and hearing a beehive of human activity. As an escalator slowly carries him to the ground floor, the camera maintains his point of view, and the change in perspective gradually eclipses the human figures and turns the sound to silence. It is one of the most profound images of death ever seen in a film, yet it is a death caused by nothing more than a change in camera placement. Tati's implication is that life can be restored to the empty urban desert simply by putting the camera in the right position, by finding the philosophical overview that integrates all of life's contradictory emotions, events, and movements into a seamless whole. His film is proof that such a point of view is possible.

—Dave Kehr

POKAIANIE

(Monanieba; Repentance)

USSR, 1986

Director: Tengiz Abuladze

Production: Gruziafilm; Georgian language; color, 35 mm; running time: 151 minutes. Released November 1986. Filmed in 1984 on location in Georgia, USSR.

Producer: Gruziafilm Studio; **screenplay:** Nana Djanelidze, Tengiz Abuladze, Rezo Kveselava; **photography:** Mikhail Agranovich; **art director:** Georgii Mikeladze; **music coordinator:** Nana Djanelidze.

Cast: Avtandil Makharadze (*Varlam Aravidze* and *Abel Aravidze*); Zeinab Botsvadze (*Keti Barateli*); Ia Ninidze (*Guliko Aravidze*); Merab Ninidze (*Tornike Aravidze*); Ketevan Abuladze (*Nino Barateli*); Edisher Giorgiobani (*Sandro Barateli*); Kakhi Kavsadze (*Mikhail Korisheli*); Nino Zakariadze (*Elena Korisheli*); Nato Otzhivaga (*Keti as a child*); Dato Kemkhadze (*Abel as a child*); Veriko Andzhaparidze (*old woman*).

Awards: Cannes Special Jury Prize, 1987; Lenin Prize, 1988.

Publications

Books:

Bozhovich, Viktor, editor, *Pokaianie* [Repentance], Moscow, 1988.

Woll, Josephine, and Denise J. Youngblood, *Repentance: A Companion Guide*, London, 2000.

Articles:

Batchan, Alexander, ''Mad Russian,'' in *Film Comment* (New York), May-June 1987.

Maslin, Janet, ''*Repentance*: A Satire from Soviet [sic],'' in *The New York Times*, 4 December 1987.

Pokaianie

Woll, Josephine, ''Soviet Cinema: A Day of Repentance,'' in *Dissent*, Spring 1988.

Hinson, Hal, ''*Repentance*,'' in *The Washington Post*, 14 July 1988.

Rosenberg, Karen, ''The Movies in the Soviet Union,'' in *The Nation*, 21 November 1988.

Christensen, Peter G., ''Tengiz Abuladze's *Repentance*: Despair in the Age of Perestroika,'' in *Soviet and East European Drama, Theatre, and Film*, December 1988.

Youngblood, Denise J., ''*Repentance*,'' in *American Historical Review*, October 1990.

Christensen, Julie, ''Tengiz Abuladze's *Repentance* and the Georgian Nationalist Cause,'' in *Slavic Review*, Spring 1991.

Youngblood, Denise J. ''*Repentance*: Stalinist Terror and the Realism of Surrealism,'' in Robert Rosenstone, editor, *Revisioning History: Film and the Construction of a New Past*, Princeton, New Jersey, 1995.

* * *

For most Soviet intellectuals, the heady early years of the Gorbachev era are symbolized by a novel, *Children of the Arbat* (*Deti arbata*, by Anatolii Rybakov) and a film, *Repentance*, better known in the USSR by its Russian title, *Pokaianie*, than by its native language title, *Monanieba.* Made by one of Georgia's best known directors, Tengiz Abuladze (1924–1994), *Repentance* was the third film in the Georgian historical trilogy Abuladze began in 1968 with *The Prayer* (*Vedreba* [Georgian]/*Molba* [Russian]). *The Prayer* was followed in 1977 by *The Tree of Desire* (*Natvris xe*/*Drevo zhelanie*).

Because of *Repentance*'s politically sensitive subject—the rise of Varlam Aravidze, whose surname means ''every man'' or ''no man'' in Georgian, to a position of power and terror in the 1930s—the film was bound to stir controversy. Abuladze sought to circumvent Soviet censorship by making the film for Georgian television, which had three-hour time slots for national productions that Gostelradio, the state television and radio commission, usually did not scrutinize too closely. Despite the protection afforded by Abuladze's powerful patron Eduard Shevardnadze, then Georgia's Communist Party secretary and now president of the independent Georgian republic, it took two years to complete the picture (1982–84). And it could not be released until after Mikhail Gorbachev came to power and launched *glasnost.* In May 1986, the Soviet Union of Cinematographers purged itself of its most conservative members and elected a reformer, the respected director Elem Klimov, as first secretary. Two days after his election, Klimov announced a commission to review and release previously ''shelved'' films. In November 1986, *Repentance* received its first quasi-public screening at the Dom Kino (House of Cinema), the union's headquarters. By the beginning of 1987, the film was in general distribution in the USSR and quickly exported to the West to the film festival circuit.

Repentance is an ambitious film that makes no concessions to the audience, whether Soviet or Western. Long and difficult, the film's complex, plot-within-a-plot-within-a-plot structure and abstract style, which combines flamboyant surrealism with often tendentious symbolism, requires a level of audience dedication that few contemporary directors are audacious enough to demand. Indeed, all reports from Soviet screenings indicate that while the theaters were invariably packed when the film began, they never were when the film ended.

Repentance is a landmark historical film, a challenging ''revisioning'' of the Stalin Terror and a psychological exploration of the mentality of the authoritarian state. The narrative heart of the movie lies in its protracted flashback, but it takes Abuladze some time to get there. The story does not so much *unfold* as *deconstruct*, like breaking down a *matreshka*, the Russian wooden nested doll. Western critics, unaccustomed to the narrative style of Georgian folklore, generally found the film's plot extremely difficult to follow.

Repentance begins in an apartment kitchen, with a woman putting the finishing touches on an elaborately decorated wedding cake. Her male companion is reading a newspaper obituary about the death of the ''great man'' Varlam Aravidze. Although the viewer does not realize it until later, this brief scene marks the end of the first part of the first framing story.

The second framing story opens at Varlam's funeral. The event is obviously as much a political ritual as a personal acknowledgment of the deceased. Expressions of grief are highly stylized, even from the dead man's immediate survivors, his son Abel, Abel's wife Guliko, and the couple's teenaged son Tornike. That night, a horrified Guliko discovers that Varlam's corpse has been unearthed from its grave; he stands propped against a tree in their garden. Varlam's corpse is reburied and unburied two more times, prompting increasingly frenzied (and comical) activity from both the police and the Aravidze family. Finally, after a night on vigil at the cemetery, the grave robber is captured. To everyone's surprise, it is Keti Barateli, the middle-aged baker from the opening scene.

At her trial, Keti refuses to cooperate with the proceedings. Instead, she defiantly announces that as long as she lives, ''Varlam will not rest. The sentence is final.'' She then launches into her story: ''Who was Varlam Aravidze? I was eight years old when he became mayor of this city. . . ''

As we quickly learn in Keti's flashback, she was the daughter of Sandro Barateli, a well-known artist of ancient and aristocratic lineage. Her mother was the beautiful, madonna-like Nino, named after the patron saint of Georgian Christianity. The traditionalist Sandro quickly comes into conflict with the town's ''progressive'' new mayor Varlam Aravidze over the fate of its historic church. By arguing for the preservation of the church as a monument to culture, Sandro has immediately signified himself as one who will side with faith and emotion over reason and progress. Sandro's and Varlam's conflict over values builds, culminating in the mayor's unannounced nocturnal visit to the Barateli apartment, accompanied by his young son Abel and his two henchmen Doksopoulo and Riktofelov. Varlam and Sandro discuss Sandro's art; Varlam sings Italian arias and recites Shakespeare; Varlam admires the lovely Nino. Meanwhile, the children Abel and Keti discuss heaven, and Keti assures Abel that is where his dead mother is. Shortly after the unwelcome guests leave the Baratelis', Varlam returns, to give Nino the crucifix that young Abel has taken. While Nino prophetically dreams of her family's doom, Sandro pensively plays the piano. The doorbell rings. Doksopoulo and Riktofelov have returned, clad in medieval armor, to arrest him.

The roundup has begun. Next to be arrested is Mikhail Korisheli, Sandro's longtime friend. Although he is the local Party secretary, Mikhail is nonetheless powerless to defend Sandro from tyranny, nor indeed can Mikhail ultimately save himself. In several heartbreaking scenes, we see the swift deterioration of Nino's and Keti's lives as relatives of an ''enemy of the people,'' culminating in Nino's pitiful attempt to offer herself to Varlam in exchange for her husband. In the meantime, Mikhail Korisheli, now deranged from torture, tries to persuade Sandro to confess: ''We must sign everything and reduce it all to complete absurdity. . . . We'll sign a thousand stupid statements.'' Sandro is executed (crucified) at the same moment that the medieval church is blown-up to make way for ''progress.'' Nino's arrest quickly follows.

We return now to the second part of the second flashback, as the adult Keti says to the shocked court, ''And that was the end of Nino Barateli.'' Those present erupt; ''She's insane!'' they shout. The only person who believes Keti's tale is Varlam's grandson Tornike, who receives only evasive answers when he questions his father Abel: ''Those were complicated times. . . It's difficult to explain now. . . The situation was different then.'' Despite Abel's fervent desire not to remember (which is different from ''forgetting''), he is clearly troubled. So it is left to his hardbitten wife Guliko to manage the family affairs. She decides it would be best to have Keti declared insane and committed to an asylum. As Guliko schemes, it is her own husband's sanity that is in doubt. Hamlet-like, Abel converses with his father's ghost.

The next day, as the trial continues, Guliko triumphs. But her victory over truth and memory is short-lived. As Guliko and the Aravidze clique celebrate, young Tornike takes the burden of his family's guilt and atonement on himself. He commits suicide with a rifle that was a gift from his beloved grandfather. Afterward, the grief-stricken Abel himself digs up Varlam's corpse and throws it off a cliff to the ravens. A satisfying ending: Abel at last understands that the past cannot be buried.

Except that this is not the end. In his most maddening challenge to the spectators, who have after all patiently watched to this point, Abuladze now returns to the opening scene of Keti in her kitchen, with the man reading the newspaper. Was all this no more than her revenge fantasy? An elderly woman taps at the window to ask Keti if this street leads to a church. Keti responds sadly, ''This is Varlam Street. It will not take you to a church.'' The old woman retorts, ''Then what's the use of it? What good is a road if it does not lead to a church?'' Shaking her head in dismay, she walks haltingly away.

Obviously it is impossible to do more than scratch the surface of such a rich and complicated film in a brief synopsis, even in terms of explicating its content, not to mention its form. *Repentance* is a political allegory about the rise of authoritarian culture and its persistence over generations that spoke directly to the Soviet people in the final years of the experiment that was the USSR. Despite its surrealism (the lunatic dialogue, the medieval knights and inquisitorial courts, the reveries and fantasy)—indeed *because* of it—*Repentance* also succeeds as a serious work of history on film. How better to represent an evil that is so abstract that to make it ''realistic'' is to trivialize it? Like its predecessors in Abuladze's trilogy, *Repentance* also seeks to celebrate, for better and ill, the storied culture of Georgia's ancient civilization—and rescue it from 150 years of Russian and Soviet subjugation.

Repentance, which turned out to be Abuladze's final film (like many other Soviet filmmakers, he turned to politics), is his undisputed masterpiece. The movie was quickly acknowledged as a major artistic achievement in the European and American press at the time of its release, for its political audacity, stunning cinematography, and a tour-de-force performance by the well-known Georgian theater actor Avtandil Makharadze in the dual roles of Varlam and Abel Aravidze. Indulgent nods were given to its overwrought symbolism, especially the Christian motifs which Soviet spectators also found incomprehensible, as well as to challenges presented by its unfamiliar structure.

In the USSR, the reactions were more complicated, and of course, more personal, since *Repentance* was about *their* lives, not somebody's else's troubled past. Its merits as a work of art aside, *Repentance* launched a painful national debate about history and memory, collective guilt and individual responsibility. Few films can claim to have had such sweeping social influence.

—Denise J. Youngblood

POPIOL I DIAMENT

(Ashes and Diamonds)

Poland, 1958

Director: Andrzej Wajda

Production: Film Polski; black and white, 35mm; running time: 105 minutes; length: 2938 meters. Released October 1958. Filmed 1958. Cost 5,000,000 zlotys.

Producer: Stanislaw Adler; **screenplay:** Jerzy Andrzejewski and Andrzej Wajda, from the novel by Jerzy Andrzejewski; **photography:** Jerzy Wójcik; **editor:** Halina Nawrocka; **sound engineer:** Bogdan Bienkowski; **production designer:** Roman Mann; **music:** Rhythm Quintet of the Polish Radio of Warsaw; **costume designer:** Katarzyna Chodorowicz.

Cast: Zbigniew Cybulski (*Maciek Chelmicki*); Ewa Kryzjewska (*Krystyna*); Waclaw Zastrzezynski (*Szczuka*); Adam Pawlikowski (*Andrzej*); Jan Ciecierski (*The porter*); Bogumil Kobiela (*Drewnowski*); Stanislaw Milski (*Pieniazjek*); Arthur Mlodnicki (*Kotowicz*); Halina Kwiatkowska (*Mme. Staniewicz*); Ignacy Machowski (*Waga*); Zbigniew Skowroński (*Slomka*); Barbara Krafft (*Stefka*); Aleksander Sewruk (*Swiecki*).

Award: Award from the International Cinema Press, Venice Film Festival, 1959.

Publications

Script:

Andrzejewski, Jerzy, and Andrzej Wajda, *Ashes and Diamonds*, in *Three Films by Andrzej Wajda*, London, 1973.

Books:

McArthur, Colin, editor, *Andrzej Wajda: Polish cinema*, London, 1970.
Michatek, Boleslaw, *The Cinema of Andrzej Wajda*, London, 1973.
Liehm, Mira, and Antonín Liehm, *The Most Important Art: East European Film after 1945*, Berkeley, 1977.
Ellis, Jack C., *A History of Film*, Englewood Cliffs, New Jersey, 1979.
Eder, Klaus, and others, *Andrzej Wajda*, Munich 1980; Nantes, 1982.
Historia Filmu Polskiega, vol. 4, Warsaw, 1981.
Douin, Jean-Luc, *Wajda*, Paris, 1981.
Paul, David W., *Politics, Art, and Commitment in the Eastern European Cinema*, New York, 1983.
Wajda, Andrzej, *Un Cinema nommé désir*, Paris, 1986.

Articles:

Michatek, Boleslaw, ''Polish Notes,'' in *Sight and Sound* (London), Winter 1958–59.
Jakubowski, Jan Zygmunt, ''*Ashes* Falsified,'' and Zbigniew Zaluski, ''*Ashes* Simplified,'' in *Ekran* (Ljubljana), no. 42, 1965.
Higham, C., ''Grasping the Nettle: The Films of Andrzej Wajda,'' in *Hudson Review* (New York), Autumn 1965.
Minchinton, John, ''Zbigniew Cybulski,'' in *Film* (London), Spring 1967.
Etudes Cinématographiques (Paris), no. 69–72, 1968.
Hendrykowski, M., ''Realizm i symbolizm *Popiolu i diamentu* Andrzeja Wajda,'' in *Kino* (Warsaw), January 1972.
Sirbu, E., in *Cinema* (Bucharest), May 1975.
Gow, Gordon, in *Films and Filming* (London), March 1977.
Dipont, M., ''Andrzej Wajda,'' in *Polish Film Polonaise* (Warsaw), no. 4, 1979.

Popiol i diament

Brill, E., and L. Rubenstein, ''The Best Are Dead or Numb: A Second Look at Andrzej Wajda's *Ashes and Diamonds*,'' in *Cineaste* (New York), no. 3, 1981.

Czesejko-Sochacka, E., in *Kino* (Warsaw), September 1981.

Film Criticism (Meadville, Pennsylvania), Spring 1986.

Koltai, A., ''A versailles-i fattyu,'' in *Filmvilag* (Budapest), no. 2, 1990.

Kino (Warsaw), May 1990.

Lubelski, T., in *Kino* (Warsaw), September 1992.

Paul, D., ''Andrzej Wadja's War Trilogy,'' *Cineaste* (New York), vol. 20, no. 4, 1994.

Przylipiak, Mirosław, ''Jubileusz Andrzeja Wadjy,'' *Kino* (Warsaw), vol. 30, March 1996.

Marszatek, Rafał, ''Popioł; diament: watek odnaleziony,'' *Kino* (Warsaw), vol. 32, no. 379, December 1998.

Macnab, Geoffrey, *Sight and Sound* (London), vol. 8, no. 2, February 1998.

* * *

The best work of Wajda begins in 1958, and his epic *Popiol i diament* represents the climax of the entire Polish school. The literary source for this film is the novel of the same name by Jerzy Andrzejewski published in 1948. The book, which openly speaks of the complicated Polish society at the end of the war and in the first days of peace, was initially criticized, but was eventually accepted as the best work of prose published in the postwar years. Filmmakers soon became interested, but several attempts at adapting it in the early 1950s fell through. In 1957, when a promising scenario appeared, its author was the young director Andrzej Wajda, and the novel was somewhat changed. The novel differs from the film in that it takes place in one day and one night. The setting of the story, with the exception of a few short scenes, is the hotel in town. The principal character in the novel is young Maciek Chelmicki, a member of the guerilla group ''Armii krajowej,'' which fought against the Germans during the war, jointly with communists. The deep political differences between the two groups led to the communists engaging in acts of terrorism, aimed toward the forming of a new society for the people of Poland. Maciek is a bold young man, prepared to give up his life for higher ideals, After the end of the war, he is given orders to kill a man, and so is faced with the tragic choice between a growing awareness of the absurdity of the command and his loyalty to duty. The decision to kill or not creates a conflict of conscience. To kill is to violate the law of peace; if he does not go through with it, he creates discord in a situation of war.

Maciek's counterpart is the communist, Szczuka, an ex-soldier of the Spanish revolution. Only a short time before they fought on the same side against their mutual foe. At the time when the film begins, they are confronting one another, foes in life and death, cruelly tied together by the past. Their conflict is obviously not a personal matter, but a conflict of two different conceptions of the future. It reflects a disorganized society at the boundary between war and peace. Wajda presents it with dramatic conciseness at a banquet held on the occasion of the signing of the German capitulation. At one table are gathered the former allies, and also the bourgeois politicians and an assortment of careerists and opportunists who are prepared for defeat while (at the same time) seeking the largest share of the spoils. Against the background of this gathering the fate of both heroes is being decided. These two have a divided ideological orientation, differing experiences in life and in politics, and belong to different generations. Nevertheless, they have much more in common than is seen at first glance. First of all they share an allegiance to the ideal for which they fight and work, allegiance to those with whom they together fought, and a determination to strive for the best in the positions they have been entrusted with. Their relationship becomes an image of self-contradiction or paradox; for instance, Maciek has the order to kill; that he has mistakenly killed someone else instead of Szczuka means he has done his job badly. Szczuka and his friend realize that they are incapable of the art of governing, that they do not have the necessary experience; that depresses them, exhausts them, but they know they must work for their ideal until the end of their lives. The most obvious similarities between the two are seen in consecutive sequences, Maciek, at the bar, is lighting glasses filled with alcohol as a memorial to his fallen comrades and is remembering with enthusiasm the years of fighting, which were so difficlt and at the same time so simple, where everything was clearly understood because all activities were directed to one purpose—to annihilate the foe in war. So too, Szczuka reminisces with his friend about times past, and comrades that fell in Spain. Their reminiscing is marked with sadness and nostalgia, and they also realize how, after the victorious war, everything about their nationalistic ideals was uncomplicated. Maciek and Szczuka are kept distinct from the other guests that are gathered in the hotel, and from the closing sequence, when both rebels are dying and the drunken group at the banquet is mostly asleep, emerges the main idea of the work. By validating the character and deeds of both protagonists. Wajda avoided the infertile narrative conventions which place the hero in one system. The result of understanding the complications of the story is comprehension of how difficult it was for an honest person to find his way in that mixed up situation. Maciek and Szczuka are honest people, and beyond everything that pitted them against each other, they belonged to the best that existed in the land. That is why their death, unthinkable and absurd, is a tragedy of Poland.

A new look at reality characterized Wajda's unprecedented style which sprang out of two previous films, but here reaches the epitome of art. Immersing the film in actuality and concreteness, in contrast with *Kanal*, he returns to classic dramatic construction, the unity of place and time, and gradually uncovers the heroes' character and motives. The picture is saturated with symbols and metaphors, which are capable of expressing the tension between objective actuality and the subjective aspect of expression. The use of narration and picturesque symbolic metaphors sharpens Wajda's drama and broadens the gamut of associations evoked by the conflict depicted. This may be illustrated by two important sequences. The first takes place in a cemetery and in a half-demolished church. Maciek falls in love with the girl Krystyna, he spends a night with her, and before he departs, they walk to a church. Krystyna reads an inscription on a grave stone, verse of the Polish poet Cyprian Norwida, which explains Maciek's situation and also provides the title of the film. "Here nothing but ashes will remain, the storm in an instant to oblivion will sweep them, from the ashes perhaps a diamond will emerge, shining victoriously for centuries, it will have blossomed for you." Dominating the church's interior is a picture of a statue of Jesus Christ, hung head down as a symbol of the overthrown values. It is a scene of extraordinary visual impact, but at the same time is very meaningful, because here end Maciek's doubts, his loyalty to a lost cause and his yearning for a normal life, his thoughts conform to reality. With the same intensity, symbols also inform the ending of the film, depicting the death of both protagonists. Dying Szczuka, felled by Maciek's shots, falls into Maciek's arms, and his death is accompanied by the clanging fire engines celebrating victory. Maciek is killed by a drunk from the banquet. In agony Maciek stumbles to the huge rubbish heap, like the rubbish heap of history.

In the accomplished cast, it is impossible not to mention the significance of the main character. Wajda chose the unknown actor Zbigniew Cybulski who made his debut in the film *Pokolenie* in a cameo role. This choice proved to be a happy one. Cybulski, with his capability of making an effortless transition from a state of maximum concentration to being relaxed, managed to embody in his character the zeal of exultation, emotion, strength, and gentleness. Maciek in his characterization is a boy who becomes involved with insignificant people and causes, but he is also a warrior, who is constantly in the line of fire, one who loves weapons because they give him a feeling of freedom. In that he is a man of the generation of 1945. But Cybulski, in realizing the director's intentions, communicates more. His hesitation in searching for meaning shields him from reality. The soft, thoughtful charm, underlined by black glasses and a costume which does not represent that time, makes him representative of the young people of the 1950s. With that he became a hero of two generations. This "double character," as Cybulski grasps it, added markedly to the clamorous acceptance of the film by young people. Even Andrzejewski was satisfied. "The measure of my satisfaction is that during the writing of the book, I pictured Maciek Chelmicki entirely differently. Now when I see the film, I see him only this way, as Cybulski played him."

In the postwar history of Polish film the premiere of *Popiol i diament* was the most extraordinary event in terms of opening up consideration of problems which up to that time were schematically or falsely pictured, leading to open criticism by the newer generation. Added to Wajda's success was the fact that he spoke with a new artistic tongue, without arrogance and declamation, and that he found a voice in harmony with the warmer political climate of the second half of the 1950s.

—B. Urgošíkova

PORTRAIT OF TERESA

See **RETRATO DE TERESA**

POTOMOK CHINGIS-KHAN

(The Heir of Ghenghis Khan; Storm over Asia)

USSR, 1928

Director: Vsevolod I. Pudovkin

Production: Mezhrabpomfilm (USSR); black and white, 35mm, silent; running time: 93 minutes, some sources list 102 minutes; length: 10,144 feet. Released 1928. Re-released 1949 with sound, music by Nicholas Krioukov and text and dialogue by Slavine and V. Koutchoukov.

Screenplay: Osip Brik, from a story by I. Novokshenov; **photography:** A. N. Golovnya; **art directors:** Sergei Koslovsky and N. Aaronson.

Cast: Valeri Inkishinov (*Bair, A Mongol huntsman*); I. Inkishinov (*Bair's father*); A. Chistyakov (*Commander of a partisan detachment*); A. Dedintsev (*Commander of the occupation forces*); Anna Sudakevich (*His daughter*); K. Gurnyak (*British soldier with leggings*); Boris Barnet (*British soldier with cat*); V. Tzoppi (*Mr. Smith, agent of the British fur company*); V. Ivanov (*Lama*); Vladimir Pro (*Missionary*); Paulina Belinskaya (*Wife of the commander of the occupation forces*).

Publications

Books:

Yezuitov, N., *Poudovkine, ''Pouti Tvortchestva, Les Voies de la création,''* Moscow, 1937.

Mariamov, A., *Vsevolod Pudovkin*, Moscow, 1952.

Pudovkin, Vsevolod I., *Film Techniques and Film Acting*, London, 1958.

Leyda, Jay, *Kino: A History of the Russian and Soviet Film*, London, 1960.

Schnitzer, Luda and Jean, *Vsevolod Poudovkine*, Paris, 1966.

Rotha, Paul, and Richard Griffith, *The Film Till Now*, London, 1967.

Amengual, Barthélemy, *V. I. Poudovkine*, Lyons, 1968.

Schnitzer, Luda and Jean, and Marcel Martin, editors, *Cinema in Revolution: The Heroic Age of the Soviet Film*, New York, 1973.

Dart, Peter, *Pudovkin's Films and Film Theory*, New York, 1974.

Klinowski, Jacek, and Adam Garbicz, editors, *Cinema, The Magic Vehicle: A Guide to its Achievement: Journey One, Cinema through 1949*, Methuchen, New Jersey, 1975.

Sapasnik, Tatiana, and Adi Petrowitsch, *Wsewolod Pudovkin; Die Zeit in Grossaufnahme*, East Berlin, 1983.

Marshall, Herbert, *Masters of the Soviet Cinema: Crippled Creative Biographies*, London, 1985.

Masi, Stefano, *Vsevolod I. Pudovkin*, Florence, 1985.

Articles:

Close Up (London), January and February 1929.

New Statesman and Nation (London), March 22 1930.

New York Times, 8 September 1930.

Variety (New York), 10 September 1930.

New Yorker, 13 September 1930.

Potamkin, Harry, ''Pudovkin and the Revolutionary Film,'' in *Hound and Horn* (New York), April-June 1933.

Leyda, Jay, ''Index to the Creative Work of Vsevolod Pudovkin,'' in *Sight and Sound* (London), November 1948.

Cahiers du Cinéma (Paris), August-September 1953.

Weinberg, Herman, ''Vsevolod Pudovkin,'' in *Films in Review* (New York), August-September 1953.

Wright, Basil, ''V. I. Pudovkin: 1893–1953,'' in *Sight and Sound* (London), October-December 1953.

Image et Son (Paris), Summer 1961.

Sadoul, Georges, ''Des Steppes aux rizières,'' in *Lettres Françaises* (Paris), 10 March 1966.

Martin, Marcel, in *Cinema* (Paris), April 1966.

Dupuich, J. J., in *Image et Son* (Paris), June-July 1972.

Iskusstvo Kino (Moscow), February 1973.

Mairal, J. C., in *Image et Son* (Paris), June-July 1975.

Marks, Geoffrey, in *Cinema Texas Program Notes* (Austin), 27 September 1977.

Burns, P. E., ''Linkage: Pudovkin's Classics Revisited,'' in *Journal of Popular Film and Television* (Washington, D.C.), Summer 1981.

Mihalkovic, V., '''*Potomok Cingiz-hana*', SSSR (1928),'' in *Iskusstvo Kino* (Moscow), no. 5, May 1988.

Caruso, U.G., ''*La Madre/La fine di San Pietroburgo/Tempeste sull'Asia*,'' in *Cineforum* (Bergamo), vol. 33, no. 5, June 1993.

Dufour, D., ''!Revolutie? (9),'' in *Film en Televisie + Video* (Brussels), no. 440, March 1994.

* * *

Potomok Chingis-Khan, Vsevolod Pudovkin's last great silent film, remains a significant cinematic achievement today due largely to the majestic visual sweep of its allegorical conclusion. Through a montage of linked images, the Soviet filmmaker has created a brilliantly symbolic metaphor in which shots of an onrushing horde of mongol horsemen are interspersed with shots of a blowing sandstorm to suggest a gale of righteousness sweeping tyranny from the land.

Like many of its Soviet predecessors, *Potomok Chingis-Khan* is revolutionary in theme, tracing the increasing political awareness of Bair, a young Mongol huntsman who survives a series of indignities at the hands of the Imperialistic White Army to lead his people in revolt. But Pudovkin's film is also revolutionary in its mode of realization.

Like his contemporary, Sergei Eisenstein, Pudovkin was a product of the radical ''Kuleshov Workshop'' which operated on the fringes of the V.G.I.K., the Soviet State Film School. Lev Kuleshov and his followers were early experimenters with a number of techniques of cinematic expression, particularly that of montage. According to Kuleshov, each shot in a filmed sequence possessed two intrinsic values. The first was obviously whatever meaning the shot conveyed as an accurate representation of its subject. However, the second property was the emotional or intellectual significance it acquired as a result of various juxtapositions with other images in a series. Kuleshov and his students felt that it was possible to manipulate the overall meaning of an entire sequence simply by altering the order of occurrence of specific images in relationship to the actors.

Pudovkin uses this technique in *Potomok Chingis-Khan's* concluding sequence to create an extraordinary tension between standard movement in the frame and a series of rapidly moving but conceptually related shots. In fact, fully 25 percent of the more than 2000 shots that comprise the film went into the gallop of the horsemen across the Mongolian landscape. In this sequence, the forward charge of the riders becomes so interspersed with the rapidly moving shots of blowing wind and sand that the actuality of human conflict quickly becomes an abstraction symbolically applicable to all oppressed people throughout history.

The impact of the ending is heightened by the fact that Pudovkin deliberately paces the unfolding of the narrative. At the beginning, Bair (Valeri Inkishinov) is a naive youth who takes his family's most valuable possession, the pelt of a silver fox, to sell at the annual fur market. After he is defrauded by a British fur agent, Inkishinov, under Pudovkin's direction, allows his character to become increasingly sullen as he seemingly becomes more and more aware of the exploitative nature of the foreigners occupying his homeland. Yet when he is captured and taken to be shot by a White Army corporal after an abortive attempt to retrieve the pelt, he follows his executioner like a trusting puppy who cannot believe that any harm will befall him. The poignant scene ends with a rifle shot.

In the interim, the Colonel has discovered an amulet among the boy's possessions that indicates that he might be a descendant of Ghengis Khan and orders the corporal to retrieve the gravely injured victim and provide him with medical care. The objective is to establish him as a puppet ruler of Buryat Mongolia.

Pudovkin, through a series of minor but finely tuned episodes, further darkens the young trapper's character while in captivity. One of these, in which Bair sees the silver fox fur being worn by the Colonel's daughter, starts Bair on the road to revolution. He single-handedly wrecks the White Army headquarters, steals a horse, and rides to gather a rebel band who race across the screen in wave after wave against their oppressors. Ultimately, they evolve into an abstract raging windstorm that blows the foreigners from the land.

Potomok Chingis-Khan was savaged by Soviet and American critics alike on its opening in 1927 for lacking realism and over-reliance on symbolic devices. Yet today it is recognized as a dynamic narrative, an epic visual poem that effectively demonstrates the power of linked montage to create allegory.

Although he made a number of films after *Potomok Chingis-Khan*, Pudovkin was not able to make the transition to talking pictures. He was at his best as an epic poet employing a purely visual means of expression, and remains of utmost importance to the history of cinema more as a theoretician than as a filmmaker. Yet the films which illustrate his theories (*Mother*, *The End of St. Petersburg* and *Potomok Chingis-Khan*) rank with any of the masterpieces of the silent cinema.

—Stephen L. Hanson

LA PRIMERA CARGA AL MACHETE

(The First Charge of the Machete)

Cuba, 1969

Director: Manuel Octavio Gómez

Production: Instituto Cubano del Arte e Industria Cinematográficos (ICAIC); black and white, 35mm, Panoramic; running time: 84 minutes. Released 1969. Filmed in Cuba.

Screenplay: Manuel Octavio Gómez, Alfredo L. Del Cueto, Jorge Herrera, and Julio García Espinosa; **editor:** Nelson Rodríguez; **sound:** Raúl Garcia; **music:** Leo Brouwer; **songs:** Pablo Milanés; **costume designer:** Maria Elena Molinet.

Cast: Adolfo Llauradó; Idalia Anreus; Eslinda Nuñez; Ana Viñas.

Publications

Books:

Nelson, L., *Cuba: The Measure of a Revolution*, Minneapolis, 1972.
Chanan, Michael, *The Cuban Image*, London, 1985.
Burton, Julianne, editor, *Cinema and Social Change in Latin America: Conversation with Filmmakers*, Austin, Texas, 1986.

La primera carga al machete

Articles:

Hablemos de Cine (Lima), no. 54, 1970.
Mikko, Pyhala, ''Cuba,'' in *International Film Guide*, London, 1971.
Díaz Torres, Daniel, in *Cine y revolución en Cuba*, edited by Santiago Alvarez and others, Barcelona, 1975.
Burton, Julianne, ''Popular Culture and Perpetual Quest: An Interview with Manuel Octavio Gómez,'' in *Jump Cut* (Berkeley), May 1979.
Colina, Enrique I., in *Cine Cubano* (Havana), nos. 56–57.
Lopez Morales, E., ''*La primera cargap*A la luz del tiempo,'' in *Cine Cubano* (Habana), no. 122, 1988.
Quiros, O., ''Critical Mass of Cuban Cinema: Art as the Vanguard of Society,'' in *Screen* (Oxford), vol. 37, no. 3, 1996.

* * *

Even within the context of revolutionary Cuban cinema—distinguished for its innovations in bringing history to the screen—*First Charge* is a whole new kind of historical film. Produced as a part of a cycle dedicated to the celebration of ''One Hundred Years of Struggle,'' the film fuses the political and the poetic into a reconstruction of the 1868 uprising against Spanish colonials and in so doing redefines historical cinema.

The experimental nature of *First Charge* is immediately apparent in the richness of its formal structure. The film is designed to appear as if the technological capabilities (and resulting aesthetic) of *cinema verité* had been available in 1868. Light hand-held cameras and portable sound equipment produce ''on-the-spot'' interviews and follow the Cuban rebels into the very center of the battle. This eminently modern ''TV documentary'' style is complimented, however, by a high-contrast film that resembles ancient newsreel footage and by a manner of posing individuals at the beginning of sequences as if they were in old historical photos. The clash of aesthetics at once so up-to-the-minute and so archaic results in the formal ''dialectical resonance'' for which Cuban cinema has attained such renown.

This formal juxtaposition, and the various techniques contained within it, has a meaning beyond mere experimentation for its own sake. Manuel Octavio Gómez uses this confrontation of past and present to insistently remind viewers that they are seeing an interpretation of the historical event, not the event itself. The high-contrast film also functions metaphorically, for it connotes the extremes of the struggle and the reality of sharply opposed interests, in which compromise was impossible. The use of contrast is set up against the grey tones employed in the official pronouncements of the Spanish, which are intended to convey a false impression of tranquility. The hand-held camera and the provocative interviewing style also have connotative functions, for they take on the form of participating in and helping to precipitate the struggle. Gómez's rejection of the narrative structure traditional in historical cinema is important as well, for, in place of characters with whom one identifies, the film's central protagonist is the machete—the work tool which became a weapon in 1868 and the weapon of 1868 which is today the tool of Cuba's economic struggle.

Gómez combined extensive historical research with his use of such deliberately anachronistic devices. Cuban and Spanish archives were mined for materials dealing with the struggle, and historical photographs, etchings, and documentary footage were studied in depth. The film's dialogues are constructed entirely from documents, books, speeches, reports, letters, and anecdotes from the period, and, although it was not possible to reconstruct the language patterns of 1868, the actors were required to immerse themselves in this historical material.

Audiences inside and outside of Cuba responded favorably to the film, although some people were put off by the exaggerated expressionism of the visual style. At times—most notably in the final battle—the combination of extreme high-contrast film and the widely careening hand-held camera of Jorge Herrera reduce the screen image to a swirling mass of abstract patterns. One critic saw the technique as ''obsessive and vampire-like'' in detracting from the story-line; Gómez himself acknowledged that the ''brusque and violent'' camera movements ''molest'' viewers. However, Gómez defends his film's style as part of the struggle against the ''routinization'' of audience and filmmaker. If *First Charge* does not quite attain the goals set for it by Gómez, that is because he has aimed so high.

—John Mraz

THE PRIVATE LIFE OF HENRY VIII

UK, 1933

Director: Alexander Korda

Production: London Film Productions; black and white, 35mm; running time: 97 minutes; length: 8664 feet. Released 12 October 1933, Radio City Music Hall, released 24 October 1933 in London by United Artists. Filmed in about 5 weeks in London. Cost: about 60,000 pounds.

Producer: Alexander Korda; **screenplay:** Lajos Biro and Arthur Wimperis; **photography:** Georges Périnal; **editors:** Stephen Harrison and Harold Young; **art director:** Vincent Korda; **music:** Kurt Schroeder; **costume designer:** John Armstrong; **historical adviser:** Peter Lindsey; **dance direction:** Espinosa; **falconry expert:** Captain Knight.

Cast: Charles Laughton (*Henry VIII*); Robert Donat (*Thomas Culpepper*); Franklin Dyall (*Thomas Cromwell*); Miles Mander (*Worthesly*); Lawrence Hanray (*Archbishop Cranmer*); William Austin (*Duke of Cleves*); John Loder (*Peynell*); Claude Allister (*Cornell*); Gibb McLaughlin (*French executioner*); Sam Livesy (*English executioner*); William Heughan (*Kingston*); Merle Oberon (*Anne Boleyn*); Wendy Barrie (*Jane Seymour*); Elsa Lanchester (*Anne of Cleves*); Binnie Barnes (*Katherine Howard*); Everley Gregg (*Katherine Parr*); Lady Tree (*Nurse*).

Award: Oscar for Best Actor (Laughton), 1932–33.

Publications

Script:

Biro, Lajos, and Arthur Wimperis, *The Private Life of Henry VIII*, London, 1934.

Books:

Balcon, Michael, and others, *20 Years of British Films, 1925–45*, London, 1947.
Brunel, Adrian, *Nice Work: The Story of 30 Years in British Film Production*, London, 1949.
Tabori, Paul, *Alexander Korda*, London, 1966.
Burrows, Michael, *Charles Laughton and Fredric March*, London, 1970.
Richards, Jeffrey, *Visions of Yesterday*, London, 1973.
Kulik, Karol, *Alexander Korda: The Man Who Could Work Miracles*, London, 1975.
Korda, Michael, *Charmed Lives: A Family Romance*, New York, 1979.
Lanchester, Elsa, *Charles Laughton and I*, New York, 1983.
Callow, Simon, *Charles Laughton: A Difficult Actor*, London, 1987.
Stockham, Martin, *The Korda Collection: Alexander Korda's Film Classics*, Secaucus, 1993.

Articles:

New York Times, 13 October 1933.
Variety (New York), 17 October 1933.
Spectator (London), 27 October 1933.
Watts, Stephen, ''Alexander Korda and the International Film,'' in *Cinema Quarterly* (London), Autumn 1933.
Beard, Charles, in *Sight and Sound* (London), Winter 1934.
Laver, James, in *Sight and Sound* (London), Summer 1939.
Campbell, Colin, ''The Producer: Sir Alexander Korda,'' in *Sight and Sound* (London), Summer 1951.
Gilliat, Sidney, and others, ''Sir Alexander Korda,'' in *Sight and Sound* (London), Spring 1956.
Dalrymple, Ian, and others, ''Alexander Korda,'' in *Quarterly Review of Film, Radio, and Television* (Berkeley), Spring 1957.
McVay, Douglas, ''The Intolerant Giant,'' in *Films and Filming* (London), March 1963.
Vermilye, Jerry, ''Charles Laughton,'' in *Films in Review* (New York), May 1963.

The Private Life of Henry VIII

Cowie, Peter, "Alexander Korda," in *Anthologie du cinéma 6*, Paris, 1965.
Archibald, Lewis, in *Magill's Survey of Cinema 3*, Englewood Cliffs, New Jersey, 1980.
Reid's Film Index (Wyong), no. 3, 1989.
Crafton, D., "The Portrait as Protagonist: *The Private Life of Henry VIII*," in *Iris* (Iowa City), Autumn 1992.
Tashiro, C.S., "Fear and Loathing of British Cinema," in *Spectator* (Los Angeles), vol. 14, no. 2, 1994.
Korda, Michael, "Anglisjskaja avantjura Aleksandra Kordy," in *Iskusstvo Kino* (Moscow), no. 4, April 1995.
Bagh, P. von, "Kuninkaankuvia," in *Filmihullu* (Helsinki), no. 1, 1998.

* * *

"An ace and certainly the finest picture which has come out of England to date," is the way that *Variety* hailed *The Private Life of Henry VIII*, a feature generally considered to be the first British film to have had an international impact (although certainly not the first British film to be screened in the United States, where English features had been seen from the early 'teens). *The Private Life of Henry VIII* was very much an international production: it starred Charles Laughton, a major stage and screen actor from England, and was produced by Hungarian-born Alexander Korda and photographed by the French Georges Périnal. Wisely, to emphasize that his film was no mere British feature, Alexander Korda gave *The Private Life of Henry VIII* its world premiere at New York's Radio Music Hall on October 12, 1933, two weeks prior to the London premiere.

A jovial film which equates the joy of sex with the pleasure of food, *The Private Life of Henry VIII* depicts the British Monarch's personal relationship with five of his six wives. The film does not bother with Henry's first wife, Catherine of Aragon: an opening title explains that she was too respectable. The actresses portraying three of the remaining wives—Merle Oberon, Binnie Barnes and Elsa Lanchester—were later to become familiar players in Hollywood films, as was Robert Donat (as Thomas Culpepper). Charles Laughton received an Academy Award for Best Actor for his performance, making *The Private Life of Henry VIII* the first British feature to be so honored.

Alexander Korda always maintained that the idea for the film came to him when he heard a London cab driver singing the popular Music Hall song, "I'm 'Enery the Eighth I Am." Another, more sensible, explanation for Korda's decision to make the film is that he was seeking a suitable vehicle for Charles Laughton and his wife, Elsa Lanchester, and a statue of Henry VIII made the producer aware of the resemblance between the Monarch and the actor. The film was shot in a mere five weeks at a reported cost of £60,000.

What contemporary audiences particularly enjoyed and what makes *The Private Life of Henry VIII* still entertaining is the film's comedy, particularly the dialogue between Henry and Anne of Cleves, with the former's oft-quoted line as he enters the bedchamber, "The things I've done for England!" The film has an elegance and a charm created in part by Vincent Korda's set and Périnal's photography. Alexander Korda's direction is little more than adequate and relies heavily on the quality performances delivered by his players.

—Anthony Slide

LE PROCES

(The Trial)

France-West Germany-Italy, 1962

Director: Orson Welles

Production: Paris Europa Productions, Hisa-Film (West Germany), and FI.C.IT (Italy); black and white, 35mm; running time: 120 minutes. English and German versions: 118 minutes. Italian version: 100 minutes. Released December 1962, Paris. Filmed 26 March 1962-June 1962 in the Studio de Boulogne; and on location in Paris and Zagreb.

Producers: Yves Laplanche, Miguel Salkind and Alexander Salkind with Robert Florat; **screenplay:** Orson Welles, from the novel by Franz Kafka; **photography:** Edmond Richard; **editor:** Yvonne Martin; **sound engineer:** Guy Vilette; **sound mixer:** Jacques Lebreton; **art director:** Jean Mandaroux; **set dressers:** Jean Charpentier and Francine Coureau; **scenic artist:** André Labussière; **music:** Jean Ledrut; **special effects editor:** Denise Baby; **costume designers:** Helene Thibault with Mme. Brunet and Claudie Thary.

Cast: Anthony Perkins (*Joseph K*); Jean Moreau (*Miss Burstner*); Romy Schneider (*Leni*); Elsa Martinelli (*Hilda*); Suzanne Flon (*Pittle*); Orson Welles (*Hastler*); Akin Tamiroff (*Bloch*); Madeleine Robinson (*Mrs. Grubach*); Arnoldo Foà (*Inspector A*); Fernand Ledoux (*Chief clerk*); Michel Lonsdale (*Priest*); Max Buchsbaum (*Examining magistrate*); Max Haufler (*Uncle Max*); Maurice Teynac (*Deputy manager*); Wolfgang Reichmann (*Courtroom guard*); Thomas Holtzmann (*Bert*); Billy Kearns and Jess Hahn (*Assistant inspectors*); Maydra Shore (*Irmie*); Carl Studer (*Man in leather*); Jean-Claude Remoleux and Raoul Delfosse (*Policemen*); Titorelli (*X*).

Publications

Script:

Welles, Orson, *The Trial*, New York, 1970.

Books:

Cowie, Peter, *The Cinema of Orson Welles*, London, 1965.
Wollen, Peter, *Orson Welles*, London, 1969.
Bessy, Maurice, *Orson Welles: An Investigation into His Films and Philosophy*, New York, 1971.
Higham, Charles, *The Films of Orson Welles*, Berkeley, 1971.
Bogdanovich, Peter, and Orson Welles, *This Is Orson Welles*, New York, 1972.
McBride, Joseph, *Orson Welles*, London, 1972.
Cowie, Peter, *A Ribbon of Dreams*, New York, 1973.
Wagner, Geoffrey, *The Novel and the Cinema*, Cranbury, New Jersey, 1975.
Gottesman, Ronald, editor, *Focus on Orson Welles*, Englewood Cliffs, New Jersey, 1976.
McBride, Joseph, *Orson Welles: Actor and Director*, New York, 1977.
Bazin, André, *Orson Welles: A Critical View*, New York, 1978.
Naremore, J., *The Magic World of Orson Welles*, New York, 1978.
Valentinetti, Claudio M., *Orson Welles*, Florence, 1981.
Bergala, Alain, and Jean Narboni, editors, *Orson Welles*, Paris, 1982.
Andrew, Dudley, *Film in the Aura of Art*, Princeton, 1984.
Higham, Charles, *Orson Welles: The Rise and Fall of an American Genius*, New York, 1985.
Leaming, Barbara, *Orson Welles: A Biography*, New York, 1985.
Parra, Daniele, and Jacques Zimmer, *Orson Welles*, Paris, 1985.
Weis, Elisabeth, and John Belton, editors, *Film Sound: Theory and Practice*, New York, 1985.
Taylor, John Russell, *Orson Welles: A Celebration*, London, 1986.
Cotten, Joseph, *Vanity Will Get You Somewhere*, New York, 1987.
Wood, Bret, *Orson Welles: A Bio-Bibliography*, Westport, 1990.
Howard, James, *The Complete Films of Orson Welles*, Secaucus, 1991.
Beja, Morris, *Perspective on Orson Welles*, New York, 1995.
Thomson, David, *Rosebud: The Story of Orson Welles*, New York, 1996.
Callow, Simon, *Orson Welles: The Road to Xanadu*, New York, 1997.
Welles, Orson, *This Is Orson Welles*, New York, 1998.

Articles:

Stanbrook, Alan, "The Heroes of Welles," in *Film* (London), March-April 1961.
"Prodigal Revived," in *Time* (New York), 29 June 1962.
"Orson Welles," in *Film* (London), Autumn 1962.
Fleischer, Richard, "Case for the Defense," in *Films and Filming* (London), October 1962.
Martinez, Enrique, "The Trial of Orson Welles," in *Films and Filming* (London), October 1962.
Gretchen, F., and Herman Weinberg, in *Film Culture* (New York), Spring 1963.
Crowther, Bosley, in *New York Times*, February 1963.
Pechter, William, "Trials," in *Sight and Sound* (London), Winter 1963–64.
Labarthe, André S., "Pour introduire au procès d'Orson Welles," in *Avant-Scène du Cinéma* (Paris), 15 February 1963.
Mekas, Jonas, in *Village Voice* (New York), 21 February 1963.
Shivas, Mark, in *Movie* (London), February-March 1963.
Hart, Henry, in *Films in Review* (New York), March 1963.
Lane, John Francis, in *Films and Filming* (London), March 1963.
Callenbach, Ernest, in *Film Quarterly* (Berkeley), Summer 1963.
Cutts, John, in *Films and Filming* (London), December 1963.

Le Procès

Cobos, Juan, Miguel Rubio, and J. A. Pruneda, ''A Trip to Quixoteland: Conversations with Orson Welles,'' in *Cahiers du Cinema in English* (New York), June 1966.
Nevitt, Brian, in *Take One* (Montreal), September-October 1966.
Daney, Serge, ''Welles in Power,'' in *Cahiers du Cinema in English* (New York), September 1967.
Bosseno, C., in *Image et Son* (Paris), May 1973.
Carroll, N., ''Welles and Kafka,'' in *Film Reader* (Evanston, Illinois), no. 3, 1978.
Goodwin, J., ''Orson Welles' *The Trial:* Cinema and Dream,'' in *Dreamworks*, Fall 1981.
''L'Image des mots,'' in *Amis du Film et de la Télévision* (Paris), March 1982.
Lev, P., ''Three Adaptations of *The Trial*,'' in *Literature/Film Quarterly* (Salisbury, Maryland), July 1984.
Beja, M., ''Where You Can't Get at Him: Orson Welles and the Attempt to Escape from Father,'' in *Literature/Film Quarterly* (Salisbury, Maryland), January 1985.
Edelman, P., ''Sans laisser d'addresse,'' in *Cahiers du Cinéma* (Paris), November 1985.
Berthome, J.-P., and F. Thomas, ''Sept anneen noir et blanc,'' in *Positif* (Paris), July-August 1992.
Thomas, F., ''Michael Lonsdale et *Le Proces*,'' in *Positif* (Paris), no. 378, July/August 1992.
Nielsen, N.-A., ''Magten: et sporgsmal om tid,'' in *Kosmorama* (Copenhagen), Spring 1993.
Friedman, R. -M., ''La specularite diffractee: mise en abyme et debut de film,'' in *Semiotica*, vol. 112, no. 1/2, 1996.
Dottorini, D., ''Il cinema come ri-narrazione,'' in *Filmcritica* (Siena), vol. 46, no. 466, July 1996.
Lucas, Tim, ''*The Trial*,'' in *Video Watchdog* (Cincinnati), no. 47, 1998.

* * *

Orson Welles would seem to be the perfect director to bring the tortured fiction of Franz Kafka to the screen. The deep chiaroscuro, mordant humor, and labyrinthian qualities of his films are sufficiently Kafkaesque to suggest a sympathetic match between novelist and filmmaker. Yet the filmed version of *The Trial* brought forth a chorus of negative reviews, especially from the Anglo-American press. Plagued by its own set of problems (and what recent Welles film has not been), *The Trial* elicited as violent and negative notices on its initial release as any garnered by a major director within recent memory. It was a critical lashing that has been salved only recently by those film commentators who have had the luxury of a broader perspective with which to consider *The Trial* within the context of the development of Welles's cinema.

The initial problems Welles encountered were due to his having adapted a modern literary classic, provoking a spate of reviews comparing Welles's adaptation to the original story, and since Welles had had the audacity to tamper with the novel's plot line, such as it is, he fell afoul of the critics. The largest discrepancy between the film and the fiction, however, was in Welles's making of Joseph K into a more active character. Welles later admitted in an interview that the passivity of Kafka's anti-hero just did not fit with his own world view. After the death camps and advent of the atomic age, Welles felt that Kafka's morality tale needed updating, and in typical Wellesian style he did so.

The major problems the critics pounced on had less to do with the film's faithfulness, however, than with the film's opacity. A number of critics claimed that the film was even less understandable than the book; furthermore, they found the movie boring. The attacks against *The Trial* remained fairly uniform in British and American papers and weekly magazines. In more recent assessments of Welles's career—James Naremore's *The Magic World of Orson Welles*, for example—the film has received much more careful and appreciative treatment. Naremore finds the movie a fascinating study of repressed sexuality, and he is at pains to place the film within the Welles canon, especially by making comparisons with *The Lady from Shanghai* and *Touch of Evil.* If the film remains little shown today, at least it has assumed a respectful place for students of Welles's cinema.

The Trial may not be much liked, but at least it is now dealt with. Even one of the movie's most severe critics, William Pechter, admitted that in spite of its overall failure, Welles had pushed *mise-en-scène* beyond any concern for narrative or dramatic necessity into a realm of purely visual effects, into the realm of pure cinema. At least Pechter found the experiment an interesting one. The use of the abandoned railway station as the central office set, which caused one critic to remark that the film seemed dominated by its decor, produced a brilliantly evocative visual representation of the post-war world. Moreover for Peter Cowie, *The Trial* is Welles's finest film since *Citizen Kane*, partly because it conveys so perfectly ''the terrifying vision of the modern world'' that is characteristic of Kafka's novel and partly because the film so clearly bears the stamp of Welles's personality, to rival only *Citizen Kane* and *Touch of Evil* in this respect. Cowie wrote that Welles had succeeded in not only translating the book into film but also in creating a cinematic environment that revealed the complexity of Kafka's world and reflected the inability of the human mind to grasp complexity which is ''the tragic moral of the novel and of this extraordinary, hallucinatory film.''

—Charles L. P. Silet

PROFESSIONE: REPORTER

(The Passenger)

Italy-France-Spain, 1975

Director: Michelangelo Antonioni

Production: Compagnia Cinematografica Champion (Rome), Les Films Concordia (Paris), and C.I.P.I. Cinematografica (Madrid); Metrocolor, 35mm; running time: 126 minutes. Released March 1975, Italy. Filmed on location in England, Spain, and Germany.

Producer: Carlo Ponti; **screenplay:** Mark Peploe, Peter Wollen and Michelangelo Antonioni, from an original idea by Mark Peploe;

Professione: Reporter

photography: Luciano Tovoli; **editors:** Franco Arcalli and Michelangelo Antonioni; **sound:** Cyril Collik; **sound editors:** Sandro Peticca and Franca Silvi; **sound mixer:** Franco Ancillai; **production designer:** Osvaldo Desideri; **art director:** Piero Poletto; **costume designer:** Louise St. Jensward.

Cast: Jack Nicholson (*Locke*); Maria Schneider (*The Girl*); Jenny Runacre (*Rachel*); Ian Hendry (*Knight*); Stephen Berkoff (*Stephen*); Ambroise Bea (*Achebe*); Jose Maria Cafarel (*Hotel manager*); James Campbell (*Stregone*); Manfred Spies (*Tedesco*); Jean Baptiste Tiemele (*The African*); Chuch McVehill or Mulvehill (*Robertson*); Angel del Pozo (*Police inspector*); Narcisse Pula (*African's accomplice*).

Publications

Script:

Antonioni, Michelangelo, Mark Peploe, and Peter Wollen, *Professione: Reporter*, Bologna and New York 1975.

Books:

Rifkin, Ned, *Antonioni's Visual Language*, Ann Arbor, Michigan, 1982.
Downing, David, *Jack Nicholson: A Biography*, London, 1983.
Barthes, Roland, and others, *Michelangelo Antonioni*, Munich, 1984.
Biarese, Cesare, and Aldo Tassone, *I film di Michelangelo Antonioni*, Rome, 1985.
Dervin, Daniel, *Through a Freudian Lens Deeply: A Psychoanalysis of Cinema*, Hillsdale, New Jersey, 1985.
Antonioni, Michelangelo, *That Bowling Alley on the Tiber: Tales of a Director*, Oxford and New York, 1986.
Perry, Ted, and Rene Prieto, *Michelangelo Antonioni: A Guide to References and Resources*, Boston, 1986.
Johnson, Charles W., *Philosophy in Literature*, San Francisco, 1992.
Arrowsmith, William, *Antonioni: The Poet of Images*, New York, 1995.
Chatman, Seymour B., *Antonioni, or, the Surface of the World*, Berkeley, 1996.
Brunette, Peter, *The Films of Michelangelo Antonioni*, New York, 1998.
Tomasulo, *Michelangelo Antonioni*, Old Tappan, 1998.
Wenders, Wim, *My Time with Antonioni*, New York, 2000.

Articles:

Filmcritica (Rome), March 1975.
Plumb, C., in *Take One* (Montreal), May 1975.
Reilly, C. P., in *Films in Review* (New York), May 1975.
Atwell, L., in *Film Quarterly* (Berkeley), Summer 1975.
Cowie, Peter, in *Focus on Film* (London), Summer 1975.
Roud, Richard, in *Sight and Sound* (London) Summer 1975.
Rosebaum, Jonathan, in *Monthly Film Bulletin* (London), June 1975.
Demby, B. J., ''Michelangelo Antonioni Discusses *The Passenger*,'' in *Filmmakers Newsletter* (Ward Hill, Massachusetts), July 1975.
Epstein, R., ''Antonioni Speaks . . . and Listens,'' in *Film Comment* (New York), July-August 1975.
Perry, T., ''Men and Landscapes: Antonioni's *The Passenger*,'' in *Film Comment* (New York), July-August 1975.
Gow, Gordon, in *Films and Filming* (London), August 1975.
Giroux, H. A., in *Cineaste* (New York), Fall 1975.
Gliserman, M., ''*The Passenger:* An Individual in History,'' in *Jump Cut* (Chicago), August-September 1975.
Offroy, D., in *Cinématographe* (Paris), August-September 1975.
Walsh, M., ''*The Passenger:* Antonioni's Narrative Design,'' in *Jump Cut* (Chicago), August-September 1975.
Benoit, C., in *Jeune Cinéma* (Paris), September-October 1975.
''*Profession: Reporter:* Un Film de Michelangelo Antonioni,'' in *Avant-Scène du Cinéma* (Paris), October 1975.
Stewart, G., ''Exhumed Identity: Antonioni's Passenger to Nowhere,'' in *Sight and Sound* (London), Winter 1975–76.
Tuominen, T., ''Fuuga Antonionin tapaan, Michaelangelo Antonioni: *Ammatti: Reportteri*,'' in *Filmihullu* (Helsinki), no. 1, 1976.
Bonitzer, P., ''Désir désert (*Profession reporter*),'' in *Cahiers du Cinéma* (Paris), January 1976.
Bachmann, Gideon, ''Maria Schneider: 'ik houd niet echt van acteren',,'' in *Skoop* (Wagenengen), March 1976.
Bojtar, E., ''A riportut vege: Antonioni: *Figlalkozasa: Riporter*,'' in *Filmcultura* (Budapest), July-August 1976.
Dick, P., ''*The Passenger* and Literary Existentialism,'' in *Literature/Film Quarterly* (Salisbury, Maryland), Winter 1977.
Colombo, Furio, ''Visual Structures in a Film by Antonioni,'' in *Quarterly Review of Film Studies* (New York), November 1977.
MacLean, R., ''*The Passenger* and Reporting: Photographic Memory,'' in *Film Reader* (Evanston, Illinois), no. 3, 1978.
Price, T., ''Film Maudit: The Political and Religious Meaning of Antonioni's *The Passenger*,'' in *Cinemonkey* (Portland, Oregan), vol. 5, no. 2, 1979.
Lockhart, Kimball, ''Empêchement visuel et point de fuite dans *L'avventura* et *Profession: Reporter*,'' in *Camera/Stylo* (Paris), November 1982.
Tovoli, L., ''Tecnicamente dolce il mio incontro con Antonioni,'' in *Cinema Nuovo* (Rome), November-December 1989.
Turner, J., ''*The Passenger*, Lacan, and the Real,'' in *Post Script* (Commerce, Texas), no. 1–2, 1989–90.
Eldh, M., ''Roman son filmkritik,'' in *Chaplin* (Stockholm), vol. 33, no. 4, 1991.
Tomasulo, F. P., ''The Architectonics of Alienation: Antonioni's Edifice Complex,'' in *Wide Angle* (Baltimore), no. 3, 1993.
Atkinson, M., ''Jack Nicholson in *The Passenger*,'' in *Movieline* (Escondido), vol. 8, July 1997.
Pellizzari, L., ''Sbarre,'' in *Cineforum* (Bergamo), vol. 37, no. 366, July/August 1997.

* * *

After the general confusion prompted by *Zabriskie Point*, Michelangelo Antonioni's previous feature, *Professione: Reporter* (distributed in the United States as *The Passenger*) met with critical and popular acclaim. This success may have been due as much to the cast as to either a new ''transparency'' in Antonioni's direction or a suddenly acquired sophistication of the filmgoer. Though *Professione: Reporter*, like *Zabriskie Point* and for that matter any of Antonioni's previous films, de-emphasizes classic cinematic narrative in favor of the presentation of an essentially static/dramatic situation through experimentation with expressive elements specific to film—thereby remaining what the general public would see as a ''difficult'' film: ''nothing happens'' with which one can ''identify''—*Professione: Reporter*'s stars, Jack Nicholson and Maria Schneider, were two of 1975's biggest box-office draws. Their appearance guaranteed the film a degree of financial success (necessary after *Zabriskie Point*), but also introduced a marked artificiality into the fabric of the film's fiction—Jack Nicholson virtually plays himself, all the more emphasized by the implausible turning point of the film's plot: the Nicholson character gives up his own identity to assume the identity of a man who happens to die and happens to resemble him. The presumption that such an arbitrary exchange of identities might be either workable or desirable seems to comment on the nature of acting; and later in the film when Maria Schneider finds a gun in Nicholson's luggage, he takes it away from her with an ironic monotone ''no'' which cannot fail to recall, intertextually, yet another gun, the one Schneider used to kill an even bigger box-office draw, Marlon Brando, in the film that made her famous and which is no doubt responsible for her appearance in this film, namely, Bertolucci's *Last Tango in Paris* (1972).

But the real interest in *Professione: Reporter* lies in its groundbreaking technique, one that explicitly works in opposition to the film's narrative continuity and impression of reality, effects that both mainstream critics and the general public expect of any feature film. The most discussed technical innovation concerns the film's next-to-the-last seven minute-long continuous traveling shot which moves foward into the frame at an almost imperceptible rate and which impossibly passes through the narrow iron bars of a window and into a courtyard only to come back to the same window to look through the same bars to view the same Nicholson the shot first framed but which upon return finds him dead. This shot is emblematic of a radical strategy Antonioni has since pursued in an even more global fashion in *Il mistero di Oberwald* (1979) and *Identificazione di una donna* (1982), whereby elements taken to belong exclusively to filmic technique, elements such as camera movement, framing, point of view, sound, and image tone, which are normally considered to be neutral vehicles for the transparent expression of a narrative—find themselves emphatically motivated, bearing the principal burden of signification in the face of an increasingly banal ''story.'' Such is the case in *Professione: Reporter.* Preparing the ground for these later films, and perpetuating a research Antonioni has engaged since the films of the early 1950s, the innovative technique of *Professione:*

Reporter proposes nothing short of the fictionalization of technique itself.

—Kimball Lockhart

PROSHCHANIE

(Farewell)

USSR, 1981

Director: Elem Klimov

Production: Mosfilm; in color; running time: 126 minutes; length: 11,359 feet. Released 1981. Released in USA in 1983.

Producers: A. Rasskazov, G. Sokolova; **screenplay:** Larissa Shepitko, Rudolf Tyurin, and Herman Klimov, from the novel *Farewell to Matyora* by Valentin Rasputin; **photography:** Alexei Rodionov, Yuri Skhirtladze, Sergei Taraskin; **editor:** V. Byelova; **sound recordist:** B. Vengerovsky; **art director:** V. Petrov; **music:** Artyomov, A. Shnitke.

Cast: Stefaniya Stayuta (*Darya*); Lev Durov (*Pavel*); Alexei Petrenko (*Vorontsov*); Leonid Kryuk (*Petrukha*); Vadim Yakovenko (*Andrei*); Yuri Katin-Yartsev (*Bogodul*); Denis Luppov (*Kolyanya*); Maiya Bulgakova, Naidan Gendunova, Galina Demina, Anna Kustova, Lyubov Malinovskaya, Nadezhda Pogorishnaya, Liudmila Polyakova (*Darya's Friends*); I. Bezyaev, M. Bichkov, Yu. Puchkov, V. Klap (*Fire Brigade*).

Publications

Books:

Romanenko, Aelita Romanovna, *Elem Klimov and Larisa Shepitko*, translated by Natalia Shevyrina, Moscow, 1990.

Articles:

Interview with Elem Klimov, in *Filmfaust* (Frankfurt), June-September 1983.

Variety (New York), 3 August 1983.

Martin, Marcel, and C. Zander, "Cinéastes soviétiques à la recherche de leurs racines: Entretien avec Elem Klimov," in *Jeune Cinéma* (Paris), December 1983-January 1984.

Revue du Cinéma (Paris), January 1987.

Films and Filming (London), April 1987.

Listener (London), 30 April 1987, and 12 May 1988.

Petit, Chris, in *Monthly Film Bulletin* (London), May 1987.

Filmfaust (Frankfurt), May-June 1987.

Makkonen, V., "Elem Klimov elokuviensa takana," in *Filmihullu* (Helsinki), no. 6, 1988.

Hollywood Reporter, 23 February 1988.

Lafontaine, Y., "Les adieux a matiora," in *24 Images* (Montreal), no. 43, Summer 1989.

* * *

As the white-raincoated officials from the mainland emerge from the mist we get the feeling of the doom that is to overtake the little island of Matyora and its people. It is to be flooded to become part of a vast Siberian hydro-electric project. We switch immediately to the people of the island and their way of life, which is depicted with great understanding of their essentially happy existence rooted in a love of nature and of traditions which go back to pagan origins. In a film with such tragic implications there is, however, much gaiety which makes more poignant the inevitable ending. The island is sacrificed to progress. Engineers come and go. Arrangements are made for the evacuation which must take place. There are those, however, who prefer to remain in their homes and face death in the shadow of their ancestors.

Klimov made the film in 1981, having taken it over from his wife Larissa Shepitko who was killed in a car accident. She had also written the script in collaboration with Klimov's brother Herman. It was based on a novel by the Siberian writer Valentin Rasputin. As with so many of Klimov's films it did not meet with official approval and was shelved for many years until his spectacular assignment to the powerful position of head of Soviet cinema under the glasnost policies of Gorbachov.

Klimov, hitherto noted for his satirical and critical qualities, proves himself very sympathetic and understanding to the village life he depicts in this film. It is visually rich in its gallery of peasant faces, and the village life is portrayed with warmth and liveliness. Music plays a part in the lives of the people and there is a joyous village festival in which outside influences impinge on the supposedly isolated ambience of the peasants. Television is not unknown, of course, and the exploration of other planets, as well as boogie-woogie, are part of their knowledge. But to them the mainland across the vast expanse of water is hostile to their community life together. The brutal demands of progress will not respect their feelings.

The destruction of their graveyard arouses them to action. Soon the first departures take place. Little details build up. The old lady searches frantically for her cat. Another, after locking up her house, looks back anxiously as a pile of logs collapses. The houses are closed up, and small domestic objects are rescued. Some of the houses are burnt. One house is washed and cleaned as if it was going to last for ever. All these things take us into the mind of the tragedy.

The invocation of the spirit of the earth by old Darya is central to the film, and emphasises the pantheistic beliefs of the people. It may not be a paradise they are leaving but the anguish of the heart is just as great. Following hard upon Darya's wanderings through the wood, three men appear on their way to fell an ancient tree.

The peasants are ordered to burn their houses before leaving. They depart in groups but Darya and some others prefer to remain and perish in the flood waters.

Watching the film one recalls the great traditions of the earlier Russian film-makers like Eisenstein and Dovzhenko whose spirit informs the film at so many points (the rough peasant faces and the toilworn hands who draw their strength from the land). The beauty of nature and its seasons, the poetry of rain and shine are photographed with loving care and given extra meaning to the sadness of the film. Matyora, deserted, faces the vast expanse of water which will in due course engulf it and something of value on this earth will disappear.

—Liam O'Leary

PSYCHO

USA, 1960

Director: Alfred Hitchcock

Production: Universal Pictures; black and white, 35mm; running time: 109 minutes. Released June 1960, originally by Paramount. Filmed on Universal backlots, interiors filmed at Revue Studios, locations shot on Route 99 of the Fresno-Bakersfield Highway and in the San Fernando Valley. Cost: $800,000.

Producer: Alfred Hitchcock; **screenplay:** Joseph Stefano, from a novel by Robert Bloch; **photography:** John L. Russell; **editor:** George Tomasini; **sound engineer:** Walden O. Watson and William Russell; **production designers:** Joseph Hurley, Robert Claworthy, and George Milo; **music:** Bernard Herrmann; **special effects:** Clarence Champagne; **costume designer:** Helen Colvig; **pictorial consultant:** Saul Bass.

Cast: Anthony Perkins (*Norman Bates*); Janet Leigh (*Marion Crane*); Vera Miles (*Lila Crane*); John Gavin (*Sam Loomis*); Martin Balsam (*Milton Arbogast*); John McIntyre (*Sheriff Chambers*); Lurene Tuttle (*Mrs. Chambers*); Simon Oakland (*Dr. Richmond*); Frank Albertson (*Tom Cassidy*); Pat Hitchcock (*Caroline*); Vaughn Taylor (*George Lowery*); John Anderson (*Car salesman*); Mort Mills (*Policeman*); Sam Flint, Francis De Sales, George Eldredge (*Officials*); Alfred Hitchcock (*Man outside real estate office*).

Publications

Script:

Stefano, Joseph, *Alfred Hitchcock's Psycho*, edited by Richard J. Anobile, New York, 1974.

Books:

Bogdanovitch, Peter, *The Cinema of Alfred Hitchcock*, New York, 1962.
Manz, Hans-Peter, *Alfred Hitchcock*, Zurich, 1962.
Perry, George, *The Films of Alfred Hitchcock*, London, 1965.
Wood, Robin, *Hitchcock's Films*, London, 1965.
Truffaut, Francois, *Le Cinema selon Hitchcock*, Paris, 1966; as *Hitchcock*, New York, 1985.
Simsolo, Noël, *Alfred Hitchcock*, Paris, 1969.
La Valley, Albert J., editor, *Focus on Hitchcock*, Englewood Cliffs, New Jersey, 1972.
Naremore, James, *A Filmguide to Pyscho*, Bloomington, Indiana, 1973.
Durgnat, Raymond, *The Strange Case of Alfred Hitchcock*, Cambridge, Massachusetts, 1974.
Spoto, Donald, *The Art of Alfred Hitchcock*, New York, 1976.
Derry, Charles, *Dark Dreams: A Psychological History of the Modern Horror Film*, New York, 1977.
Hemmeter, Thomas M., *Hitchcock the Stylist*, Ann Arbor, Michigan, 1981.
Thomson, David, *Overexposures: The Crisis in American Filmmaking*, New York, 1981.
Bazin, André, *The Cinema of Cruelty: From Buñuel to Hitchcock*, New York, 1982.
Narboni, Jean, editor, *Alfred Hitchcock*, Paris, 1982.
Rothman, William, *Hitchcock—The Murderous Gaze*, Cambridge, Massachusetts, 1982.
Villien, Bruno, *Hitchcock*, Paris, 1982.
Weis, Elisabeth, *The Silent Scream: Alfred Hitchcock's Sound Track*, Rutherford, New Jersey, 1982.
Wollen, Peter, *Readings and Writings: Semiotic Counter-Strategies*, London, 1982.
Spoto, Donald, *The Life of Alfred Hitchcock: The Dark Side of Genius*, New York, 1982; London, 1983.
Phillips, Gene D., *Alfred Hitchcock*, Boston, 1984.
Barbier, Philippe, and Jacques Moreau, *Alfred Hitchcock*, Paris, 1985.
Bruce, Graham, *Bernard Herrmann: Film Music and Narrative*, Ann Arbor, Michigan, 1985.
Douchet, Jean, *Alfred Hitchcock*, Paris, 1985.
Deutelbaum, Marshall, and Leland Poague, *A Hitchcock Reader*, Ames, Iowa, 1986.
Hogan, David J., *Dark Romance: Sexuality in the Horror Film*, Jefferson, North Carolina, 1986.
Humphries, Patrick, *The Films of Alfred Hitchcock*, Greenwich, Connecticut, 1986.
Kloppenburg, Josef, *Die Dramaturgische Funktion der Musik in Filmen Alfred Hitchcocks*, Munich, 1986.
Sinyard, Neil, *The Films of Alfred Hitchcock*, London, 1986.
Modleski, Tania, *The Women Who Knew Too Much: Hitchcock and Feminist Theory*, New York, 1986.
Rebello, Stephen, *Alfred Hitchcock and the Making of Psycho*, New York, 1990, 1998.
Leigh, Janet, *Psycho: Behind the Scenes of the Classic Thriller*, New York, 1995.
Boyd, David, editor, *Perspectives on Alfred Hitchcock*, New York, 1995.
Condon, Pauline, *Complete Hitchcock*, London, 1999.
Harris, Robert A., *Complete Films of Alfred Hitchcock*, Secaucus, 1999.
Bellour, Raymond, *The Analysis of Film*, Bloomington, 2000.
McGilligan, Patrick, *Alfred Hitchcock*, New York, 2001.

Articles:

Domarchi, Jean, and Jean Douchet, interview with Hitchcock, in *Cahiers du Cinéma* (Paris), December 1959.
Hitchcock, Alfred, ''Pourquoi j'ai peur la nuit,'' in *Arts* (Paris), June 1960.

Psycho

Crowther, Bosley, in *New York Times*, 17 June 1960.

Sarris, Andrew, in *Village Voice* (New York), 11 August 1960.

Callenbach, Ernest, in *Film Quarterly* (Berkeley), Fall 1960.

Dyer, Peter, in *Sight and Sound* (London), Autumn 1960.

Baker, Peter, in *Films and Filming* (London), September 1960.

Demonsablon, Philippe, "Lettre de New York," in *Cahiers du Cinéma* (Paris), September 1960.

Kaplan, Nelly, "Je suis une légende," in *Lettres Françaises* (Paris), October 1960.

Allombert, Guillaume, "Alfred Hitchcock," in *Image et Son* (Paris), November 1960.

Douchet, Jean, "Hitchcock et son public," in *Cahiers du Cinéma* (Paris), November 1960.

Wood, Robin, "Psychanalyse de Pyscho," in *Cahiers du Cinéma* (Paris), November 1960.

Boisset, Yves, interview with Hitchcock, in *Cinéma* (Paris), January 1961.

Ian, Cameron, and V. F. Perkins, interview with Hitchcock, in *Movie* (London), 6 January 1963.

Bean, Robin, "Pinning Down the Quicksilver," in *Films and Filming* (London), July 1965.

Hardison, O. B. "The Rhetoric of Hitchcock's Thrillers," in *Man at the Movies*, Baton Rouge, Louisiana, 1967.

Braudy, Leo, in *Film Quarterly* (Berkeley), Summer 1968.

Nogueira, Rui, "*Pyscho*, Rosie and a Touch of Orson: Janet Leigh Talks," in *Sight and Sound* (London), Spring 1970.

Gough-Yates, Kevin, "Private Madness and Public Lunacy," in *Films and Filming* (London), February 1972.

Corliss, Richard, "*Psycho* Therapy," in *Favorite Movies: Critics' Choice* New York, 1973.

Tarnowski, J. F., "De quelques points de théorie du cinéma," in *Positif* (Paris), September 1975.

Almendarez, Valentin, in *Cinema Texas Program Notes* (Austin), 21 September 1978.

Bellour, Raymond, "Psychosis, Neurosis, Perversion," in *Camera Obscura* (Berkeley), nos. 3–4, 1979.

Thomson, David, "The Big Hitch," in *Film Comment* (New York), March-April 1979.

Bikácsy, G., "Alfred Hitchcock," in *Filmkultura* (Budapest), September-October 1979.

Telotte, J. P., "Faith and Idolatry in the Horror Film," in *Literature/ Film Quarterly* (Salisbury, Maryland), no. 3, 1980.

Verstappen, W., "De eenvoud van Hitchcock," in *Skoop* (Amsterdam), April 1981.

Crawford, L., "Segmenting the Filmic Text," in *Enclitic* (Minneapolis), Fall 1981-Spring 1982.

Klinger, Barbara, "*Psycho:* The Institutionalization of Female Sexuality," in *Wide Angle* (Athens, Ohio), vol. 5 no. 3, 1983.

Anderson, Paul, in *Starburst* (London), January 1985.
Thomson, David, in *Film Comment* (New York), January-February 1985.
Matthew-Walker, R., ''Hitchcock's Little Joke,'' in *Films and Filming* (London), July 1986.
Tanner, L., interview with Anthony Perkins, in *Films in Review* (New York), August-September 1986.
Palmer, R. Barton, ''The Metafictional Hitchcock: The Experience of Viewing and the Viewing of Experience in *Rear Window* and *Psycho*,'' in *Cinema Journal* (Champaign, Illinois), Winter 1986.
Cardullo, B., ''Some Notes on Classic Films,'' in *New Orleans Review*, no. 2, 1990.
Iskusstvo Kino (Moscow), no. 11, 1990.
Rebello, S., ''Alfred Hitchcock Goes *Psycho*,'' in *American Film* (Washington, D.C.), April 1990.
Bruno, M. W., ''Bates Motel,'' in *Segnocinema* (Vincenza, Italy), September-October 1990.
Recchia, E., ''Through a Shower Curtain Darkly: Reflexitivity as a Dramatic Component of *Psycho*,'' in *Literature/Film Quarterly* (Salisbury, Maryland), no. 4, 1991.
Sterritt, D., ''The Diabolic Imagination: Hitchcock, Bakhtin, and the Carnivalization of Cinema,'' in *Hitchcock Annual* (Gambier, Ohio), no. 1, 1992.
Janisch, A., in *Filmvilag* (Budapest), no. 10, 1993.
Heijer, J., ''Hitchcock's *Psycho* in Stephen Frears' *The Grifters*,'' in *Canadian Journal of Film Studies* (Ottawa), vol. 3, no. 1, Spring 1994.
Williams, Linda, ''Learning to Scream,'' in *Sight & Sound* (London), vol. 4, no. 12, December 1994.
Fischer, Dennis K., ''*Psycho* with Limits,'' in *Outré* (Evanston), vol. 1, no. 2, Spring 1995.
Hall, John W., ''Touch of *Psycho*? Hitchcock's Debt to Welles,'' in *Bright Lights* (Cincinnati), no. 14, 1995.
Morrison, K., ''The Technology of Homicide: Constructions of Evidence and Truth in American Murder Films,'' in *CineAction* (Toronto), no. 38, September 1995.
Ankerich, Michael, ''Psyched-Up for *Psycho:* Janet Leigh Remembers the Classic Thriller on the Eve of its 35th Anniversary,'' in *Classic Images* (Muscatine), no. 243, September 1995.
Morris, Christopher D., ''*Psycho*'s Allegory of Seeing,'' in *Literature/Film Quarterly* (Salisbury), vol. 24, no. 1, January 1996.
Caminer, Sylvia, and John Andrew Gallagher, ''Joseph Stefano,'' in *Films in Review* (New York), vol. 47, no. 1–2, January-February 1996.
Negra, Diane, ''Coveting the Feminine: Victor Frankenstein, Norman Bates, and Buffalo Bill,'' in *Literature/Film Quarterly* (Salisbury), vol. 24, no. 2, April 1996.
Griffith, James, ''*Psycho:* Not Guilty as Charged,'' in *Film Comment* (New York), vol. 32, no. 4, July-August 1996.
Fischer, D., ''A Conversation with Janet Leigh: 'Not Just a Screamer!''' in *Filmfax* (Evanston), no. 58, October/January 1996/1997.
Thomas, D., ''On Being Norman: Performance and Inner Life in Hitchcock's *Psycho*,'' in *CineAction* (Toronto), no. 44, 1997.
Thomson, D., ''Ten Films that Showed Hollywood How to Live,'' in *Movieline* (Escondido), vol. 8, July 1997.
Lucas, Tim, in *Video Watchdog* (Cincinnati), no. 47, 1998.

* * *

There are those for whom Alfred Hitchcock is a ''master of suspense'' the premier technician of the classical narrative cinema; there are those for whom Hitchcock's mastery of film technique, of ''pure cinema'' as he liked to call it, amount to a species of pandering, or even of an audience-directed cruelty; there are others for whom Hitchcock's fables of emotions trapped and betrayed are seen as self-reflexive, enticing the viewer to participate in the drama of suspense only to call that participation into moral question; and, finally, there are those who find in Hitchcock's films submerged allegories of grace, of mistakes acknowledged, redeemed, and transcended. Despite such general differences of opinion, however, it *is* commonly agreed among Hitchcock scholars that *Psycho* raised the issue of Hitchcock's artistic status and intentions (or lack thereof) in its purest form, as if it were his most essential, most essentially Hitchcockian, film.

Indeed, the shower murder sequence in *Psycho*—wherein Janet Leigh's almost confessional cleansing is cut short by the knife wielding ''Mrs. Bates''—is frequently cited as a textbook instance of cinematic suspense and formal (montage) perfection. Moreover, it is this murder of the film's ostensible heroine, roughly a third of the way through the narrative, that most critics focus on when discussing the significance of the entire film, as if it *were* the film writ small, as if the film were itself an act of murder that we are commanded, via Hitchcock's expert use of subjective camera, to take part and pleasure in.

Two kinds of evidence are typically invoked to support such a reading of *Psycho* and of Hitchcock generally. One of these is Hitchcock's lifelong commitment to popular cinematic genres, mainly the thriller. The underlying premise here is that Hitchcock had ample opportunity to break out of the thriller format, to become an ''artist'' in the way that Fellini and Antonioni are (it is often pointed out that *Psycho* and *L'avventura* were released within a year of each other), so that his apparent decision *not* to do so can be read as a matter either of obsession (as if he feared to) or satisfaction (as if he aspired no higher). And underlying *this* premise is the conviction that popular genres, of their very nature, are inimical to serious art, are too much the product of popular tastes and box-office calculation to allow for humane insights or serious artistic self-expression—hence O. B. Hardison's argument that Hitchcock is less an artist than a ''rhetorician.''

A second sort of evidence is also cited to support the claim that neither Hitchcock nor *Psycho* need be taken seriously—his comments to interviewers, especially regarding his working methods and intentions. Hitchcock's description of *Psycho* as ''a *fun* picture,'' one that takes its audience through an emotional process ''like taking them through the haunted house at the fairground'' (in *Movie* 6), is a notorious instance of this apparent dissociation between the seriousness of his ostensible subjects (crime, murder, sexuality) and the triviality of Hitchcock's approach. As David Thomson puts it, ''*Psycho* is just the cocky leer of evil genius flaunting tragic material but never brave enough to explore it.''

The case against *Psycho* is grounded in a reading of intention and effect, the charge being that Hitchcock's intentions are mercenary and that the effect of the film is a kind of brutality, directed equally at the film's characters *and* its audience. The accepted case *for* the film follows a similar line of reasoning, though to different conclusions. Thus critics like Robin Wood and Leo Braudy would agree that in *Psycho* Hitchcock ''forces the audience . . . to face the most sinister connotations of our audience role'' by playing with, yet disturbing, our normal expectation ''that our moral sympathies and our aesthetic sympathies [will] remain fixed throughout the movie.'' Our desire to ''identify'' with sympathetic characters is thus called increasingly into question as our ''identification'' shifts from the reasonably normal Marion Crane to the seemingly normal Norman Bates—who finally becomes ''Mrs. Bates'' in an epiphany of confused identity. Indeed, it is this voyeuristic tendency to identify with others, or to identify them *as* the views we take of them, often without their knowledge, that the film calls into ethical doubt, forcing viewers ''to see the dark potentialities within all of us.''

Such arguments for and against *Psycho* are problematic, however, on several counts—not the least of which is the common assumption that the film, of its very essence, is ''naturally voyeuristic.'' Is it more or less voyeuristic than still photography, or painting, or sight generally? Also a problem is the clear implication in both arguments that audience response is so thoroughly under Hitchcock's control that ''the spectator becomes the chief protagonist.'' Upon what grounds can we claim to know how all members of a given audience, much less all members of all possible audiences, will respond to a particular film? Furthermore, what warrants our generalizing from predicted audience response to authorial intention? And of what relevance is intention to our evaluation of *Psycho* in any event? Much discussion of *Psycho* assumes that our decision to take *Psycho* seriously as a work of art *depends* upon our reading of Hitchcock's intentions regarding it; but one can more reasonably argue that the very decision to treat the film as an aesthetic object renders intention *ir*relevant. As Stanley Cavell puts it, all that matters for our *experience* of any film is ''in front of your eyes.''

A final reason for doubting the wisdom of the accepted approaches to *Psycho* is the focus they place on individual psychology, of the characters, of the viewer, at the expense of other facts of the text. One such fact, often read as an Hitchcockian irrelevancy (a ''MacGuffin''), is money—as personified by the oil-rich Mr. Cassidy and as an implicit factor in the attitudes and actions of nearly every major character. It is Sam's lack of money that prompts Marion in the first place to steal Cassidy's $40,000. Sam and Lila assume that money is behind Norman's silence regarding Marion (Norman himself hints that money played a part in the relationship of his widowed mother to her lover); the Sheriff assumes that money is behind Arbogast's disappearance. Indeed, *Psycho* can be read as a meditation on money and its effects—negative effects as far as the film's characters are concerned, but also positive effects in regard to the audience, or at least in regard to those members of the audience who take *Psycho* seriously as a warning of the deadly effects that money can have. It is in such terms that the audience *can* become an implicit ''character'' in the film—the character who *does* benefit from the past mistakes and who is therefore capable of transcending them.

—Leland Poague

THE PUBLIC ENEMY

USA, 1931

Director: William Wellman

Production: Warner Bros. Pictures Inc.; black and white, 35mm; running time: 96 minutes. Released May 1931. Filmed February-March 1931 in Warner Bros. studios. Cost: $151,000.

Producer: Darryl Zanuck; **screenplay:** Kubec Glasmon and John Bright; **adaptation and dialogue:** Harvey Thew, from a story ''Beer and Blood'' by Kubec Glasmon and John Bright; **photography:** Dev Jennings; **editor:** Ed McCormick; **art director:** Max Parker; **music conductor:** David Mendoza; **costume designer:** Earl Luick.

Cast: James Cagney (*Tom Powers*); Jean Harlow (*Gwen Allen*); Edward Woods (*Matt Doyle*); Joan Blondell (*Mamie*); Beryl Mercer (*Ma Powers*); Donald Cook (*Mike Powers*); Mae Clark (*Kitty*); Leslie Fenton (*Nails Nathan*); Robert Emmett O'Connor (*Paddy Ryan*); Murray Kinnell (*Putty Nose*); Ben Hendricks, Jr. (*Bugs Moran*); Rita Flynn (*Molly Doyle*); Clark Burroughs (*Dutch*); Snitz Edwards (*Hack Miller*); Adele Watson (*Mrs. Doyle*); Frank Coghlan, Jr. (*Tom as a boy*); Frankie Darro (*Matt as a boy*); Purnell Pratt (*Officer Powers*); Mia Marvin (*Jane*); Robert E. Homans (*Pat Burke*); Dorothy Gee (*Nail's girl*); Lee Phelps (*Steve the bartender*); Ben Hendricks III (*Bugs as a boy*); Landers Stevens (*Doctor*); Eddie Kane (*Joe, the headwaiter*); Douglas Gerrard (*Assistant tailor*); Sam McDaniel (*Black headwaiter*); William H. Strass (*Pawnbroker*); Russ Powell (*Bartender*).

Publications

Script:

Glasmon, Kubec, John Bright, and Harvey Thew, *The Public Enemy*, edited by Henry Cohen, Madison, Wisconsin, 1981.

Books:

Shulman, Irving, *Harlow: An Intimate Biography*, New York, 1964.
Conway, Michael, and Mark Ricci, *The Films of Jean Harlow*, New York, 1965.
Gussow, Mel, *Don't Say Yes Until I'm Finished Talking: A Biography of Darryl F. Zanuck*, New York, 1971.
McArthur, Colin, *Underworld USA*, London, 1972.
Bergman, Andrew, *Cagney*, New York, 1973.
Wellman, William, *A Short Time for Insanity: An Autobiography*, New York, 1974.
Freedland, Michael, *James Cagney*, London, 1974.
Higham, Charles, *Warner Brothers*, New York, 1975.
Cagney, James, *Cagney by Cagney*, New York, 1976.
Clark, Norman H., *Deliver Us from Evil: An Interpretation of American Prohibition*, New York, 1976.
Parish, James R., and Michael Pitts, *The Great Gangster Pictures*, Metuchen, New Jersey, 1976.
Shadoian, Jack, *Dreams and Dead Ends: The American Gangster/Crime Film*, Cambridge, Massachusetts, 1977.
Meyer, William R., *Warner Brothers Directors*, New York, 1978.
O'Connor, John E., and Martin A. Jackson, editors, *American History/American Film: Interpreting the Hollywood Image*, New York, 1979.
Schatz, Thomas, *Hollywood Genres*, New York, 1981.
Clinch, Minty, *Cagney: The Story of His Film Career*, London, 1982.
Jenkins, Steve, *The Death of a Gangster*, London, 1982.
McGilligan, Patrick, *Cagney: The Actor as Auteur*, San Diego, 1982.
Roddick, Nick, *A New Deal in Entertainment: Warner Bros in the 1930s*, London, 1983.

Thompson, Frank T., *William A. Wellman*, Metuchen, New Jersey, 1983, 1993.
Schickel, Richard, *James Cagney: A Celebration*, London, 1985.
Warren, Doug, *James Cagney: The Authorised Biography*, London, 1983; revised edition, 1986.
Golden, Eve, *Platinum Girl: The Life and Legends of Jean Harlow*, New York, 1991.
Stenn, David, *Bombshell: The Life and Death of Jean Harlow*, New York, 1993.
McCabe, John, *Cagney*, New York, 1997.

Articles:

New York Times, 24 April 1931.
Variety (New York), 29 April 1931.
Kirstein, Lincoln, ''Cagney and the American Hero,'' in *Hound and Horn* (New York), April 1932.
Tynan, Kenneth, ''Cagney and the Mob,'' in *Sight and Sound* (London), May 1951.
Miller, Don, ''James Cagney,'' in *Films in Review* (New York), August-September 1958.
Whitehall, Richard, in *Films and Filming* (London), January 1964.
Hanson, Curtis Lee, ''A Memorable Visit with an Elder Statesman,'' in *Cinema* (Beverly Hills), July 1966.
Warshow, Robert, ''The Gangster as Tragic hero,'' in *The Immediate Experience*, New York, 1970.
Wellman, William, Jr., ''William Wellman: Director Rebel,'' in *Action* (Los Angeles), March-April 1970.
Campbell, Russell, ''Warner Brothers in the Thirties,'' in *Velvet Light Trap* (Madison, Wisconsin), June 1971.
Fox, Julian, ''A Man's World: An Analysis of the Films of William Wellman,'' in *Films and Filming* (London), March-April 1973.
Kjørup, S., ''3 klassiska Gangsterfilm og deres Baggrund,'' in *Kosmorama* (Copenhagen), August 1973.
Peary, Gerald, ''More Than Meets the Eye,'' in *American Film* (Washington, D.C.), March 1976.
Linnéll, S.,''*Public Enemy*—Samhäallets fiende nr. 1,'' in *Chaplin* (Stockholm), no. 4, 1977.
Mank, G., ''Jean Harlow,'' in *Films in Review* (New York), December 1978.
Guérif, F., in *Revue du Cinéma* (Paris), April 1979.
Prouty, Howard H., in *Magill's Survey of Cinema 3*, Englewood Cliffs, New Jersey, 1980.
Marling, W., ''On the Relation Between American Roman Noir and Film Noir,'' in *Literature/Film Quarterly* (Salisbury, Maryland), no. 3, 1993.
Tracey, G., ''James Cagney as Immigrant Icon: Norm and Periphery in *Public Enemy* (1931), *The Mayor of Hell* (1933) and *Angels With Dirty Faces* (1938),'' in *Michigan Academician*, vol. 25, no. 3, 1993.
Desilets, E. Michael, ''Heartless Tom: Scripting Irish Myth,'' in *Creative Screenwriting* (Washington, D.C.), vol. 4, no. 1, Spring 1997.

* * *

Although *The Public Enemy* is now most remembered for the famous scene in which James Cagney smashes half a grapefruit into the face of actress Mae Clark—an act that more than one critic has termed the most vicious in all of motion picture history—the film is, in fact, one of the first of the gangster genre to examine the sociological roots of crime in a serious way. Because of some unforgettable images and a charismatic performance by Cagney in the role that made him famous, the film achieved the rare distinction of being both a major box office success and a public-spirited statement.

The film's overall treatment of violence is implied rather than graphic. Most of the violence occurs off camera, but through an innovative use of sound—for example, in the chilling scene in which Cagney murders the horse that killed his friend—the effects of the savagery are actually heightened. Similarly, the scenes in which Cagney's gift-wrapped corpse is delivered to his brother or the bizarre scene in the rain after he is wounded (which prefigures the famous Gene Kelly ''Singin' in the Rain'' number from that 1952 film) stunned audiences and justified the film's social statement. When Cagney, riddled with bullets, falls face down in a rain gutter, his blood entering the torrent, and mutters ''I ain't so tough,'' that is a restatement of the film's prologue that it is within the public's power to stamp out criminals.

Between the picture's framing prologue and epilogue, director William Wellman created powerful sequences that still retain much of their impact. Through the introduction of his characters as children and an elaborate opening pan that delineates their environment, Wellman establishes a relationship between sordid surroundings and the natural inclinations of children, that they sometimes interact to begin the evolution of the criminal. Yet much of the commentary surrounding these scenes seems simplistic to modern viewers. That the film retains much of its impact today is due largely to the performances, particularly those of Jean Harlow as Cagney's seductive mistress and Cagney himself as the gangster Tom Powers. Although the fortuitous pairing of the star with a role ideally suited to his talents was the result of one of Wellman's ''gut'' instincts, Cagney's magnetic performance made the film a smash hit and achieved some political repercussions as well: the picture unintentionally glamorized the criminal and indirectly hastened Hollywood's implementation of a self-imposed Production Code to prevent such undesirable social figures from being depicted in future in a sympathetic way. Although *The Public Enemy* may seem tame in comparison with some of the post-Code films of the last two decades, enough of its power survives to sustain it both as a film and as a creditable social document.

—Steve Hanson

I PUGNI IN TASCA

(Fists in the Pocket)

Italy, 1965

Director: Marco Bellocchio

Production: Doria Cinematografica; black and white, 35mm; running time: 105 minutes. Filmed in 9 weeks. Cost 50,000,000 lire. Released 1965.

Production director: Ugo Novello; **screenplay:** Marco Bellocchio; **assistant director:** Giuseppe Lanci; **photography:** Alberto Marrama;

editor: Aurelio Mangiarotti (pseudonym of Silvano Agosti); **production designer:** Gisella Longo; **music:** Ennio Morricone; **artistic collaboration for dubbing and montage:** Elda Tattoli.

Cast: Lou Castel (*Alessandro*); Paola Pitagora (*Giulia*); Marino Masé (*Augusto*); Liliana Gerace (*Mother*); Pier Luigi Troglio (*Leone*); Jennie MacNeil (*Lucia*); Maura Martini (*Child*); Giani Schicchi (*Tonino*); Alfredo Filippazzi (*Doctor*); Gianfranco Cella and Celestina Bellocchio (*Youths at the party*); Stefania Troglio (*Waitress*); Irene Agnelli (*Bruna*).

Awards: Locarno Film Festival, Vela d'argento; Venice Film Festival, Prize Outside of Competition, 1965.

Publications

Script:

Bellocchio, Marco, *I pugni in tasca* (scenario), Milan, 1967.

Books:

Wlaschin, Ken, *Italian Cinema since the War*, Cranbury, New Jersey, 1971.
Leprohon, Pierre, *The Italian Cinema*, New York, 1972.
Bernardi, Sandro, *Bellocchio: Marco Bellocchio*, Firenze, 1978.
Malanga, Paola, *Marco Bellocchio*, Milan, 1998.

Articles:

Interview with Marco Bellocchio, in *Cahiers du Cinéma* (Paris), September 1965.
Bontemps, Jacques, in *Cahiers du Cinéma* (Paris), September 1965.
Jacob, Gilles, ''Le Cercle de famille,'' in *Cinéma* (Paris), June 1966.
Bellocchio, Marco, ''The Sterility of Provocation,'' in *Cahiers du Cinéma in English* (New York), January 1967.
Delmas, Jean, ''Les Poings dans les poches à travers les controverses,'' in *Jeune Cinéma* (Paris), nos. 27–28, 1968.
Lisor, A., in *Image et Son* (Paris), March 1972.
Zalaffi, N., ''Entretien avec Marco Bellocchio,'' in *Image et Son* (Paris), April 1973.
Salvi, Demetrio, in *Cineforum* (Bergamo), vol. 33, no. 327, September 1993.
Masoni, T., ''I trent'anni de *I pugni in tasca*,'' in *Cineforum* (Bergamo), vol. 35, no. 335, June 1995.
Lasagna, R., ''Gli spettri l'epilessia a trent'anni da *I pugni in tasca*,'' in *Cinema Nuovo* (Bari), vol. 44, no. 356/357, July/October 1995.

* * *

After attending the Centro Sperimentale film school in Rome and then studying (on a grant) at the Slade School of Fine Arts in London, Marco Bellocchio returned to his native town of Piacenza and set out to make a feature film. Because he couldn't find a producer willing to underwrite the project, he borrowed money from one of his brothers and created a set in his family's country house near Bóbbio. He filmed for nine weeks on a shoestring budget of 50,000,000 lire (28,000 pounds sterling). The result, *Fists in the Pocket*, hit Italy like a bomb. The film was unanimously acclaimed for the skill of its direction and expressive camera work, and it received numerous awards at film festivals, thus ensuring international distribution. French critics compared the film favorably to *Zero for Conduct* by Jean Vigo and *L'age d'or* by Luis Buñuel, and Italian critics announced that they had not seen such a powerful debut since Visconti's *Ossessione*. For the next ten years Bellocchio was regarded as one of Italy's leading political filmmakers whose films also performed respectably at the box office.

Fists in the Pocket is about a family living in the provinces, and is a bitter denunciation of bourgeois values from an angry young member of the bourgeoisie. Situations are shown at their most extreme: two of the five family members are epileptics, the youngest son is an idiot, and the mother is blind—all abnormal states working as commentaries upon what Bellocchio sees as normal conditions in family life. The sister's epilepsy, for example, is a metaphor for the agonizing emotions of jealousy, incestual desire, and the fear that she always feels. The mother is blind because, as Bellocchio explained, ''When a son becomes 18, his mother no longer sees him, no longer understands him, and is no longer of use to him.'' The only family member who has normal contacts with the outside world is Augusto, but he is also clearly representative of the hypocrisy and emptiness of so-called ''normalcy.''

Alessandro, the main character, acts as catalyst in the film. He respects Augusto so much that, in order to relieve Augusto of the burden of being the patriarchal protector of the sick family, he decides to kill everyone else in the house. The tiny push he gives the mother in the cemetery (which sends her literally to her grave) is an allegorical act testifying that within the bourgeois system a minor action is sufficient enough to make the whole structure fall. Alessandro kills his younger brother in the bathtub, which, with its warm water and Freudian connotations, represents the womb from which Alessandro never wanted Leone to emerge. Alessandro also attempts to kill his sister, with whom he has had an incestuous relationship. Meanwhile Augusto, acting out his role as true patriarch, allows his underling brother to commit crimes the result of which will be advantageous to himself.

The characters are depraved, fanatical, and morbid. As well, the film's rough style makes no concession to the traditional rapport among artist/character/spectator; here the spectator must remain active and question the director's objectivity in presenting gruesome events and bizarre psychological states. Bellocchio said in an interview (in *Positif*) that, although his work had exorcised demons from his own past, he wished to present that past in the most objective and critical way so that it might then be of use to others.

—Elaine Mancini

PULP FICTION

USA, 1994

Director: Quentin Tarantino

Production: Jersey Films, in association with Miramax; color, 35mm; running time: 149.

Pulp Fiction

Producer: Lawrence Bender; **executive producers:** Danny DeVito, Michael Shamberg, and Stacey Sher; **screenplay:** Quentin Tarantino and Roger Avary, based on stories by Quentin Tarantino and Roger Avary; **photography:** Andrzej Sekula; **editor:** Sally Menke; **production designer:** David Wasco; **art designer:** Charles Collum; **casting:** Ronnie Yeskell and Gary M. Zuckerbrod; **sound:** Ken King; **special effects:** Larry Fioritto; **set designer:** Sandy Reynolds-Wasco; **costume designer:** Betsy Heimann.

Cast: John Travolta (*Vincent Vega*); Samuel L. Jackson (*Jules Winnfield*); Uma Thurman (*Mia Wallace*); Harvey Kietel (*The Wolf*); Tim Roth (*Pumpkin*); Amanda Plummer (*Honey Bunny*); Maria de Medeiros (*Fabienne*); Ving Rhames (*Marsellus Wallace*); Eric Stoltz (*Lance*); Rosanna Arquette (*Jody*); Christopher Walken (*Captain Koons*); Bruce Willis (*Butch Coolidge*); Quentin Tarantino (*Jimmie*); Steve Buscemi (*Surly Buddy Holly Waiter*); Frank Whaley (*Brett*); Duane Whitaker (*Maynard*); Peter Greene (*Zed*).

Awards: Palme d'Or, Cannes International Film Festival, 1994; New York Film Critics Circle Award, for direction and screenwriting, 1994; Oscar for Best Original Screenplay, 1995.

Publications

Script:

Tarantino, Quentin, *Pulp Fiction: A Quentin Tarantino Screenplay*, New York, 1994.

Books:

Dawson, Jeff, *Quentin Tarantino: The Cinema of Cool*, New York, 1995.

Barnes, Alan, and Marcus Hearn, *Tarantino: A to Z*, North Pomfret, 1996; revised edition, 1999.

Woods, Paul A., *King Pulp: The Wild World of Quentin Tarantino*, London, 1996, 1998.

Peary, Gerald, *Quentin Tarantino: Interviews*, Jackson, 1998.

Woods, Paul A., *Quentin Tarantino: The Film Creek Files*, Austin, 1999.

Articles:

Corliss, Richard, *Time* (New York), 10 October 1994.
Lane, Anthony Lane, *The New Yorker*, 10 October 1994.
Hirschberg, Lynn, "Tarantino Bravo," in *Vanity Fair* (New York), July 1994.
Gordinier, Jeff, "The Man in the Plastic Bubble," in *Entertainment Weekly* (New York), 21 October 1994.
Wild, David, "Quentin Tarantino," in *Rolling Stone* (New York), 3 November 1994.
Smith, Gavin, "When You Know You're in Good Hands," in *Film Comment* (New York), July-August 1994.
Siskel, Gene, "Brilliant Dialogue Makes Violent *Pulp Fiction* Special," in *Chicago Tribune*, 14 October 1994.
Hinson, Hal, "Killer Instinct: This Time, Director Tarantino's Thugs Slay You With Humor," in the *Washington Post*, 9 October 1994.
de Vries, Hilary, "Tarantino: The In-Your-Face Auteur," in *Chicago Tribune*, 9 October 1994.
Pawelczak, Andy, in *Films in Review* (New York), vol. 46, no. 1–2, January-February 1995.
Dowell, Pat, and John Fried, "Pulp Friction: Two Shots at Quentin Tarantino's *Pulp Fiction*," in *Cineaste* (New York), vol. 21, no. 3, 1995.
Petersen, George, "Building Character Through Violence: A One-Two Punch," in *Creative Screenwriting* (Washington, D.C.), vol. 3, no. 1, Summer 1996.
Chumo, Peter N., II, "The Next Best Thing to a Time Machine: Quentin Tarantino's *Pulp Fiction*," in *Post Script* (Commerce), vol. 15, no. 3, Summer 1996.
Lucas, Tim, in *Video Watchdog* (Cincinnati), vol. 32, 1996.
Stenger, J., "Power, Penetration, and Punishment: Masculinity and Male Control in *Pulp Fiction*," in *Michigan Academician*, vol. 28, no. 3, 1996.
Leitch, Thomas M., and David Lavery, "Know-Nothing Entertaintment: What to Say to Your Friends on the Right, and Why It Won't Do Any Good/'No Box of Chocolates': The Adaptation of *Forrest Gump*," in *Literature/Film Quarterly* (Salisbury), vol. 25, no. 1, January 1997.
Kimball, A. Samuel, "'Bad-Ass Dudes' in *Pulp Fiction*: Homophobia and the Counterphobic Idealization of Women," in *Quarterly Review of Film and Video* (Reading), vol. 16, no. 2, September 1997.
Zigelstein, J., "Staying Alive in the 90s: Travolta as Star and the Performance of Masculinity," in *CineAction* (Toronto), no. 44, 1997.
Davis, Todd F., and Kenneth Womack, "Shepherding the Weak: The Ethics of Redemption in Quentin Tarantino's *Pulp Fiction*," in *Literature/Film Quarterly* (Salisbury), vol. 26, no. 1, January 1998.
Wolcott, James, "Live Fast, Die Young, and Leave a Big Stain," in *Vanity Fair* (New York), no. 452, April 1998.

* * *

Newcomer Quentin Tarantino injected some Scorsesian adrenalin and an overdose of Scorsesian banter among his low-life characters into his feature film debut *Reservoir Dogs* (1992), a contemporary heist film that owed its plot to Raoul Walsh's classic gangster movie *White Heat* and its oddball narrative structure to Stanley Kubrick's heist film *The Killing.* Critically acclaimed—and controversial—because of its gritty gutter language, back-and-forth in time method of storytelling, and mixture of humor and extremely graphic violence, *Reservoir Dogs* brought Tarantino to the attention of Hollywood. But his follow-up, *Pulp Fiction*, made him the inspiration of film school graduates everywhere—even though Tarantino himself never went to film school. The director studied his craft by clerking at a video store where he watched everything on the shelves, from the classics to the wild and bloody Hong Kong action movies of Jackie Chan and John Woo, all the while writing scripts in his spare time.

Like *Reservoir Dogs*, *Pulp Fiction* deals with a disparate group of low-life gangland characters, each of whom shares one thing in common: a gift for gab and gunplay. The milieu, storylines, and characters of the drama are straight out of the pages of those tawdry dime magazines from which the film derives its wonderfully apt title. It tells several stories concurrently, some of which intersect as the film unfolds. Characters are introduced, dropped, or killed off and later returned as the film's narrative structure jumps back and forth in the non-linear way of *Reservoir Dogs* and its Kubrick model.

The film starts out with a hold-up in a restaurant by a pair of hot-headed neophytes (Tim Roth and Amanda Plummer), then picks up the story of two mob hitmen played by John Travolta and Samuel L. Jackson. Travolta's duties also include chaperoning his boss's drug addict girlfriend (Uma Thurman) around town and keeping her out of trouble while the boss is away. Yet another story involves a prizefighter (Bruce Willis) who takes it on the lam to get out from under the crooked clutches of the mob. This story, like so many of the bits and pieces of *Pulp Fiction*, owes its inspiration to Tarantino's years of movie watching; it's his take on the classic Robert Siodmack film noir *The Killers.* References to everything from Alfred Hitchcock's *Psycho* to Robert Aldrich's *Kiss Me Deadly* abound throughout *Pulp Fiction*, making it a film buff's movie. The film ends where it began, in the restaurant, where Jackson and Travolta stop for a bite to eat after their labors; Jackson not only foils the hold-up, but sets the robbers on a straight path, turning the film into a shaggy morality tale.

Like his characters, Tarantino has a gift for gunplay. *Pulp Fiction*'s graphically violent setpieces are not for the faint of heart; the blood flows as freely and as spectacularly as it does in the Hong Kong action movies Tarantino loves so much. But the scene where the desperate Travolta must jump-start Thurman's heart with a hypo after she suffers a drug overdose is arguably the film's grisliest and most potent—and there's not a gun in sight.

Tarantino also shares his characters' gift of gab. Dialogue is not typically a high point of action films. But it is in a Tarantino action movie. In fact, dialogue is Tarantino's most distinctive trademark—as well as his most individual. He thinks nothing of having his characters consume minutes of screen time spouting pages and pages of dialogue, ranging from the innocuous, to the hilarious, to the eloquent and even poignant—and all of it revealing of their characters. Travolta and Jackson's constantly bantering hitmen do most of the film's best and brightest talking. And their exchanges, wherein among other things Travolta comments on the French translation of "quarter pounder with cheese" while Jackson waxes philosophically on the possibilities of redemption, are priceless. The two actors earned Oscar nominations for their performances—Travolta as Best Actor, Jackson as Best Supporting Actor, although their parts in the film are of equal weight. Neither won. The film, however won the Palme d'Or at Cannes and an Oscar for Best Original Screenplay, transforming Tarantino into Hollywood's hottest wunderkind since Steven Spielberg.

—John McCarty

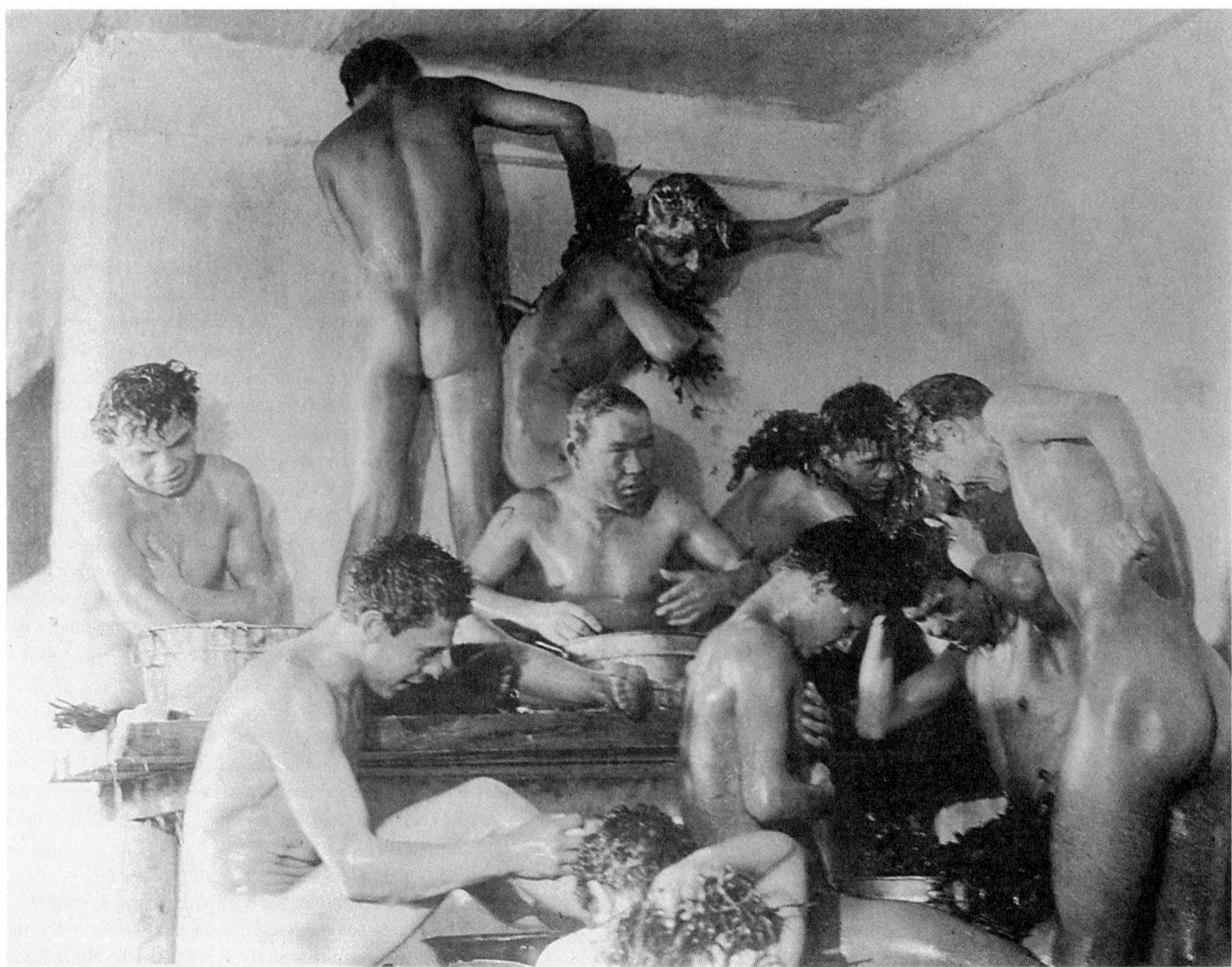

Putyovka v zhizn

PUTYOVKA V ZHIZN

(The Road to Life)

USSR, 1931

Director: Nikolai Ekk

Production: Mezhrabpomfilm (USSR); black and white, 35mm; running time: about 100 minutes; length: 3330 meters. Released June 1931. Re-released May 1957, re-edited and re-dubbed by Nikolai Ekk and Yakov Stollyar (2617 meters).

Screenplay: Nikolai Ekk, Alexander Stolper, and R. Yanushkevich; **photography:** Vasili Pronin; **sound:** E. Nesterov; **art directors:** I. Stepanov and A. Evmenko; **music:** Yakov Stollyar.

Cast: Mikhail Zharov (*Zhigan*); Nikolai Batalov (*Sergeev*); Ivan Kyrlya (*Mustafa*); A. Antropova (*Inspector*); M. Dzhagofavov (*Kolka*); V. Vesnovski (*His father*); R. Yanukevich (*Mother*); Maria Gonka (*Lolka*); Alexander Nowikov (*Saschka*).

Publications

Script:

Ekk, Nikolai, Alexander Stolper, and R. Yanushkevich, *Putyovka v Zhizn*, in *Kniga Stzenariev*, edited by K. Yukov, Moscow, 1935.

Books:

Leyda, Jay, *Kino: A History of the Russian and Soviet Film*, London, 1960.

Dickinson, Thorold, and Catherine De La Roche, *Soviet Cinema*, revised edition, New York, 1972.

Rimberg, John, *The Motion Picture in the Soviet Union 1918–1952: A Sociological Analysis*, New York, 1973.

Articles:

''Film in Moscow,'' in *Spectator* (London), 31 October 1931.

Kraszna-Krausz, A., ''The First Russian Sound Films,'' in *Close-Up* (London), December 1931.

Holba, H., ''Der Weg ins Leben: hin und zurück über Gubenkos Film *Mit gebrochenen Schwingen*,'' in *Film und Fernsehen* (Berlin), no. 9, 1979.

Stoianov-Bigor, G., in *Kinoizkustvo* (Sofia), August 1979.

Isimetov, Mikhail, ''Mustafa's Smile,'' in *Soviet Film* (Moscow), no. 9, 1981.

* * *

One of the first Soviet sound films—with an imaginative sound track far ahead of its time—Nikolai Ekk's *Road to Life* was a smash hit both in Russia and in the West, where its impact generated some dozen spin-offs on its theme of ''difficult'' children. A Soviet critic, legitimising its official function, wrote that ''the film's success depended on the social problems involved, problems of responsibility towards a new generation.'' But he added, more acutely, that the film broke new ground because ''it did not merely manipulate the life stories of the people involved in order to illustrate social problems but let the problems grow out of these life stories and their dramatic development.''

The film's theme is the reformation—or rescue—of one of the bands of *besprizorni* (homeless children) who roamed, and terrorised, city streets in the difficult post-civil war years. The gang loyalties are torn between Zhigan, a sort of Fagin character played by Mikhail Zharov, who urges them to carry on thieving, and Sergeev, the head of a ''work-commune,'' played by Nikolai Batalov, who tries to lead them into the paths of righteousness. The children themselves were not from a stage school but were inmates, or pupils, of work-communes (reform schools or rehabilitation centres in which students were expected to work on real projects—in the film, the building of a railroad). Despite their superb performances, not one of these kids later became a professional actor, not even Ivan Kyrlya, who plays the gang leader Mustafa, whose Asian features, far from inscrutable, vividly expressed every emotion. Kyrlya grew up to become a famous poet, writing in Mari, his native language.

Highly professional, the actors who played hero and villain gave performances that seem equally natural and true to life. Zharov was no Dickensian villain, but used his powerful physical presence to portray a man governed by instinct, a man able to attract as well as intimidate his teenage thieves. His moments of melancholy rapture, whenever he picks up his guitar, made the songs he sings top of the contemporary pops. Although accused therefore of romanticising thieves and their slang, Ekk had no Brechtian intention of updating the *Beggar's Opera* by introducing underworld folksongs as ''production numbers'': as he intended, they come across as spontaneous expressions of the character and are an integral part of the film.

If Zharov portrayed instinct, Batalov, the hero, portrayed thought. As, with imaginative accuracy, his dialogue is limited to the repetition of a few dozen pithy phrases, he has to convey much of his thinking with his eyes and facial expressions. But Batalov arrived at this impressive performance only after spending much time at a work-commune, getting to know its Head and (in Batalov's words) ''learning his method of handling the students, which had an enormous influence on my interpretation of the role.''

Ekk steers his simple down-to-earth story of good and evil daringly close to, but (despite the tear-jerking presence of his band of boys) always clear of sentimentality, always remembering that the boys are wicked as well as innocent. He is never afraid of shock sequences—mutiny in the commune, smashing up the thieves' den, Mustafa's death on the railroad—for they seem to arise logically from the realistic documentary course of the story and fit smoothly into the somewhat spiky but deeply expressive rhythm of his editing technique. A talented but sensitive and retiring man, Ekk was never again to equal the success of *Road to Life*, which had so great an influence on filmmakers both at home and abroad.

—Robert Dunbar

QIU JU DA GUANSI

(The Story of Qiu Ju)

Hong Kong-China, 1992

Director: Zhang Yimou

Production: Sil-Metropole Organisation, Youth Film Studio of Beijing Film Academy; colour, 35mm; running time: 100 minutes.

Producer: Feng Yiting; **screenplay:** Liu Heng, based on the story *Wanjia Susong* by Chen Yuanbin; **photography:** Chi Xiaoning, Yu Xiaoqun; **editor:** Du Yuan; **assistant directors:** Hu Xiaofeng, Zhang Zhenyan, Tian Weixi; **art director:** Cao Jiuping; **music:** Zhao Jiping; **sound recording:** Li Lanhua; **costume design:** Tong Huamiao.

Cast: Gong Li (*Qiu Ju*); Liu Peiqi (*Qinglai*); Yang Liuchun (*Meizi*); Lei Laosheng (*Wang*); Ge Zhijun (*Officer Li*).

Awards: Golden Lion, best actress, Venice International Film Festival, 1992; selection, New York Film Festival, 1992.

Publications

Articles:

Variety (New York), 14 September 1992.

Maslin, Janet, *The New York Times*, 2 October 1992.

Positif (Paris), November 1992.

Ciment, M., and others, *Positif* (Paris), December 1992.

Buck, Joan Juliet, *Vogue* (New York), April 1993.

Travers, Peter, *Rolling Stone* (New York), 15 April 1993.

Corliss, Richard, *Time* (New York), 26 April 1993.

Denby, David, *New York*, 26 April 1993.

Lane, Anthony, *The New Yorker*, 26 April 1993.

Cheng, Scarlet, *The World & I* (Washington, D.C.), May 1993.

Rayns, T., *Sight and Sound* (London), May 1993.

Klawans, Stuart, *The Nation*, 3 May 1993.

Kauffman, Stanley, *The New Republic*, 17 May 1993.

Spence, Jonathan, *The New York Review of Books*, 24 June 1993.

Sklar, R., *Cineaste* (New York), July 1993.

Cloutier, M., *Séquences* (Montreal), July-August 1993.

Kissin, E.H., *Films in Review* (New York), July-August 1993.

Sterritt, David, *The Christian Science Monitor* (Boston), 13 January 1994.

Rayns, T., ''Propositions and Questions,'' in *Cinemaya* (New Delhi), no. 30, Autumn 1995.

Feinstein, Howard, ''Losing a Muse and Moving On,'' in *The New York Times*, 6 February 2000.

* * *

After making his fame on period pieces in which the willful young woman (played inevitably by Gong Li) confronts the formidable power of feudalism, Chinese director Zhang Yimou turned to a more contemporary story line and humble cast of characters in his fifth feature, *The Story of Qiu Ju*. This time leading lady Gong Li plays Qiu Ju, the simple but most stubborn country wife who decides to get justice for her husband—and ultimately, for herself.

At the start of the movie, her husband, Qinglai, has been beaten up by the ill-tempered village head, Wang Shantang, during an altercation, and Qiu Ju and relatives rush Qinglai in a litter to the nearest town doctor. When they arrive, Qiu Ju proves herself a pragmatic skeptic, wondering if the fellow is a real doctor (''He looks more like a veterinarian . . . '') and making sure he washes his hand before treatment. Our heroine is especially upset because Wang has kicked her mate in the groin. As she says, ''But how could he kick you *there* where it affects future generations?''

At first Qiu Ju takes up the matter with the local policeman, who mediates a settlement which includes a cash payment. However, when the very pregnant woman goes to collect her due, Wang arrogantly scatters the money to the ground saying, ''And each time you pick up a bill, you'll bow to me.'' Naturally, proud Qiu Ju walks off, with nary a cent—and seeks other remedy.

Soon she is going off to towns, accompanied by her sister, and it is comic watching this very determined and very pregnant woman waddling in and out of wagons and buses and in and out of various offices seeking redress. Meanwhile, the trips are financed by sales of great bunches of the red chilies the family grows.

As Qiu Ju climbs higher and higher up the levels of justice, she moves into more modern and more foreign environments. In the big city, she and her sister stare in wonder about them as cars and motorcycles whiz by, when they find street upon street of shops and food stalls. Qiu Ju indulges herself by buying a ''high fashion'' jacket that is garish and serves only to emphasize her bulge.

Finally, she has to hire a lawyer to bring suit against Wang. In the end, in a kind of O. Henry twist, justice comes in a cold, swift way Qiu Ju did not intend. Gong Li here is unexpectedly unglamorous, with freckles on her ruddy cheeks, and waddling about in a heavily padded jacket. Her low-keyed and completely convincing performance won her rave reviews, as well as a best actress prize in at the Venice International Film Festival.

The Story of Qiu Ju is an intriguing experiment in filmmaking. Zhang actually enlisted the acting talents of a whole village, caught ordinary people unaware in their daily activities, sometimes shooting situations with a hidden camera using Super 16 film. There were only four professional actors used—for the characters of Qiu Ju, her husband, the village head, and the local policeman. As such, it has a languid feel, with far less tension than his usually tightly constructed films. Perhaps because of the deliberately down-played tone of *Qiu Ju*, the cinematography is pedestrian. It is competent but certainly not outstanding—something which we have come to expect in the films of one who was first trained as a cinematographer.

Some Western critics were enraptured by the film, sensing the truth of a kind of Neo-Social Realism in it. And indeed, here was a feature that showed the craggy humdrum aspect of Chinese life few Westerners had seen up close. Janet Maslin of the *New York Times* wrote that the film ''reaffirms Zhang Yimou's stature as storyteller and sociologist extraordinaire, and as a visual artist of exceptional delicacy and insight.''

However, others, who have been to China, know that village life and the government bureaucracy are much more gritty and harsh than Zhang has let on. Indeed, some have accused the director of deliberately trying to please the cadres with his portrayal of decent and upstanding functionaries, especially when in reality indifference and corruption are rampant.

Still, as China's best-known director, perhaps Zhang is held to account for more than his share of responsibilities. After all, his ambitions in this film were modest. Zhang has said, ''I strived for realism because I felt this was the best way to convey the true spirit and simplicity of the people of China's countryside, who for me are the heart and soul of China itself.'' In 1992 the film won the top prize of the Golden Lion and the best actress award for Gong Li at the Venice International Film Festival. It was also a selection of the New York Film Festival.

—Scarlet Cheng

LE QUAI DES BRUMES

France, 1938

Director: Marcel Carné

Production: Ciné-Alliance (some sources state Sigma-Frogerais); black and white, 35mm; running time: 91 minutes. Released 18 May 1938, Paris. Filmed January-February 1938 in the Pathé-Nathan studios, exteriors shot in Le Havre.

Producer: Grégor Rabinovitch (some sources list Simon Schiffrin); **screenplay:** Jacques Prévert, from the novel by Pierre MacOrlan; **photography:** Eugene Schufftan; **editor:** René Le Hénaff; **sound:** Antoine Archaimbaud; **production designers:** Alexandre Trauner with Paul Bertrand; **music:** Maurice Jaubert.

Cast: Jean Gabin (*Jean*); Michèle Morgan (*Nelly*); Michel Simon (*Zabel*); Aimos (*Quart-Vittel*); René Génin (*Doctor*); Pierre Brasseur (*Lucien*); Edouard Delmont (*Panama*); Robert Le Vigan (*Michel Krauss*); Marcel Perès (*Chauffeur*); Kiki (*the dog*).

Awards: Prix Louis Delluc, 1938; Académie du Film, Prix Méliès, 1938; Grand Prix National du Cinéma Français, 1939.

Le Quai des Brumes

Publications

Script:

Prévert, Jacques, *Le Quai des brumes*, in *Avant-Scène du Cinéma* (Paris), 15 October 1979.

Books:

Beranger, Jean-Louis, *Marcel Carné*, Paris, 1945.
Sadoul, Georges, *French Film*, Paris, 1947.
Landry, Bernard, *Marcel Carné: Sa vie, ses films*, Paris, 1952.
Quéval, Jean, *Marcel Carné*, Paris, 1952.
Whitaker, Rodney W., *The Content Analysis of Film: An Exhaustive Study of ''Le Quai des brumes,''* Ann Arbor, Michigan, 1966.
Armes, Roy, *French Film since 1946: The Great Tradition*, New York, 1970.
Gauteur, Claude, and Andre Bernard, *Gabin; ou, Les Avatars d'un mythe*, Paris, 1976.
Missiaen, Jean-Claude, and Jacques Siclier, *Jean Gabin*, Paris, 1977.
Ellis, Jack C., *A History of Film*, Englewood Cliffs, New Jersey, 1979.
Milhaud, Sylvie, *Jean Gabin*, Paris, 1981.
Pérez, Michel, *Les Films de Carné*, Paris, 1986.
Brunelin, André, *Jean Gabin*, Paris, 1987.
Turk, Edward Baron, *Child of Paradise: Marcel Carné and the Golden Age of French Cinema*, Cambridge, 1989, 1992.
Carné, Marcel, *Ma vie à belles dents: mémoires,* Paris, 1996.

Articles:

Variety (New York), 15 June 1938.
Cinematographie Française (Paris), 12 August 1938.
Monthly Film Bulletin (London), no. 62, 1939.
Spectator (London), 27 January 1939.
Sight and Sound (London), Spring 1939.
New York Times, 30 October 1939.
Manvell, Roger, ''Marcel Carné,'' in *Sight and Sound* (London), Spring 1946.
Lodge, J. F., ''The Cinema of Marcel Carné,'' in *Sequence* (London), December 1946.
Lambert, Gavin, ''Marcel Carné,'' in *Sequence* (London), Spring 1948.
Duvillars, Pierre, ''Jean Gabin's Instinctual Man,'' in *Films in Review* (New York), March 1951.
Daquin, Louis, ''Les 20 Ans de cinéma de Marcel Carné,'' in *Lettres Françaises* (Paris), 1 March 1956.
Sadoul, Georges, ''Les Films de Marcel Carné, expression de notre époque,'' in *Lettres Françaises* (Paris), 1 March 1956.
Stanbrook, Alan, ''The Carné Bubble,'' in *Film* (London), November-December 1959.
Nolan, Jack E., ''Jean Gabin,'' in *Films in Review* (New York), April 1963.
Cowie, Peter, ''Jean Gabin,'' in *Films and Filming* (London), February 1964.
Kael, Pauline, in *Kiss Kiss Bang Bang*, Boston, 1968.
''Carné Issue'' of *Cahiers de la Cinémathèque* (Perpignan), Winter 1972.
Carné, Marcel, ''Comment est né *Le Quai des brumes*,'' in *Avant-Scène du Cinéma* (Paris), 15 October 1979.
Magill's Survey of Cinema: Foreign Language Films, Englewood Cliffs, New Jersey, 1985.
Revue du Cinéma (Paris), no. 466, December 1990.
Leahy, James, in *Monthly Film Bulletin* (London), vol. 58, no. 687, April 1991.
Faulkner, C., ''Affective Identities: French National Cinema and the 1930s,'' in *Canadian Journal of Film Studies* (Ottawa), vol. 3, no. 2, 1994.
Bates, Robin, ''Audiences on the Verge of a Fascist Breakdown: Male Anxieties and Late 1930s French Film,'' in *Cinema Journal* (Austin), vol. 36, no. 3, Spring 1997.

* * *

Marcel Carné's *Le quai des brumes* and *Le jour se lève* are examples of ''poetic realism,'' a filmic style and narration often found in the French cinema of the 1930s. The term is, however, an unreliable critical rubric since the generalities and imprecisions associated with ''poetry'' and ''realism'' mask the specific elements of the texts it presumes to characterize.

In the case of Carné, many of those specific elements can be traced to his collaborators. Assistant to Jacques Feyder, Carné was clearly influenced by the world-weariness of the older director's *Le grand jeu* and by the fascination of marginal lives in *Pension Mimosas*. Carné's first film, *Jenny*, stars Feyder's wife, Françoise Rosay. Other consistencies in Carné's films are provided by Jacques Prévert, who was responsible for all of Carné's scripts until the 1950s, as well as by the sets of Alexandre Trauner and the music of Maurice Jaubert. Jean Gabin, the hero of *Le quai des brumes* and *Le jour se lève*, is the actor whose persona most insistently dominates Carné's pre-war films.

One of Gabin's mid-1930s' successes was in Duvivier's *La bandéra*, based upon a novel of Pierre MacOrlan, who was also the author of *Le quai des brumes*. The most apparent changes wrought by Carné and Prévert in MacOrlan's novel were the transpositions of time (from the turn-of-the-century to sometime vaguely contemporary) and place (from Paris to Le Havre). Carné, who would prove himself so expert in the rendition of period detail in *Les enfants du paradis*, opts here for a non-specific temporality, for an epoch that is both removed from and familiar to viewers. The port city is exploited for the degree to which it suggests the edge of the world, a jumping-off place (enacted in the suicide of one of the film's characters), the place for final decisions, the place for taking the last chance. Whatever might have been specific to the real city of Le Havre (location shooting was begun there on January 2, 1938) is sacrificed to the evocation of *port* per se, the port of all ports, and to the allegorization of place appropriate to the film's schematics of plot and character. The ''realism'' of Carné's ''poetry'' is shrouded in the dark shadows and fog that enhance the elusiveness of the fiction. Plot is the skeleton required to sustain the trajectory of Jean, the hero, the deserter, from arrival (he materializes out of nearly pitch darkness on a deserted road) to departure (his death) through his encounter with the other desperate men and his love for a mysterious woman. The script provides little in terms of background or motivation beyond the basic tensions of its good/evil, outsider/bourgeois society oppositions. If lines such as ''C'est difficile de vivre'' (living is difficult) and ''Oui on est seul'' (Yes, you're alone) suggest a proto-existentialism, the incorporeal nature of the film's texture is distant from the tangibilities of existential art.

But *Le quai des brumes* does generate a specific density through its enactments and stagings. Gabin may appear from nowhere, but he bears with him the weight of a highly identifiable presence, that of the most bankable star in French cinema. (In fact, it was Gabin's faith in the project that kept it from foundering when, just a few days before shooting was about to begin, the head of the production company financing the film, Gregor Rabinovitch, read the script and tried to dissuade the star from doing such a downbeat subject. Gabin persisted. He undoubtedly saw in the role of Jean a rich variation of the type of doomed hero that had brought him such success in Duvivier's *Pépé-le-Moko*, Grémillon's *Gueule d'amour*, and Renoir's *Les bas-fonds*.) The very young Michèle Morgan matched enigma to Gabin's mixture of strength and tenderness. Their first meeting takes place in a café that seems to be in the middle of nowhere. Shots ring out. A deserter and a woman wearing a beret and a transparent raincoat exchange names and fall in love. This configuration defines French film noir, its style and milieu, its challenge to bourgeois aesthetics and ethics. Here, far from the light of the natural world (in this darkness a patch of light is a privilege), far from families and social contexts, even far from conventional plots with their careful, ''logical'' identifications of situation and character, there flourish these emblems of gallantry and beauty.

Gabin and Morgan retain something of their emblematic status for the duration of a fiction that so sharply designates good and evil. The lovers are tormented by the petty criminal (Pierre Brasseur, who figures so importantly in *Les enfants du paradis*) and by the girl's guardian, the prototypical dirty old man. Played by Michel Simon (if Gabin is the most popular leading man in French cinema, Simon is its most popular character actor), Zebel, the character no one can bear to be with or see, locates the film's moral conflict in a contrast of surfaces, of beauty and ugliness.

It is the very notion of surface, however, that distinguishes the film, that makes *Le quai des brumes* an examination of the concept of image. Near the beginning, Jean meets a painter who soon after commits suicide. He jumps off this ''edge of the world'' and provides Jean, the deserter, with the clothes and identity that take him through the rest of the film. The painter is tormented by the acuity of his own vision. He sees behind things, through things. He sees to the core of images, to their decay. He would paint Jean with his hands in his pockets, at night, in fog. This is a project for a portrait filled with signs of concealment. And in the space between the hidden and the revealed lies the truth. The painter is a surrogate for Carné and Prévert. What he says clearly defines the relationship between image (both visual and verbal) and meaning in the film. It is from this expression of style that character, narrative, and film are generated.

—Charles Affron

LES QUATRES CENTS COUPS

(The 400 Blows)

France, 1959

Director: François Truffaut

Production: Les Films du Carrosse and SEDIF; black and white, 35mm, Dyaliscope; running time: 94 minutes. Released 3 June 1959, dedicated to André Bazin.

Producer: Georges Charlot; **screenplay:** Marcel Moussy, from an original story by François Truffaut; **photography:** Henri Decaë; **editor:** Marie-Joseph Yoyotte; **sound:** Jean-Claude Marchetti; **art director:** Bernard Evein; **music:** Jean Constantin.

Cast: Jean-Pierre Léaud (*Antoine Doinel*); Claire Maurier (*Gilberte Doinel*); Albert Rémy (*Julien Doinel*); Guy Decomble (*''Little Quiz''*); Georges Flamant (*Monsieur Bicey, René's Father*); Patrick Auffray (*René*); Daniel Couturier, François Nocher, Richard Kanayan, Michel Girard, Henri Moati, Bernard Abbou, Michael Lesignor, Jean-François Bergouignan (*the children*); special guest appearances by Jeanne Moreau and Jean-Claude Brialy.

Awards: New York Film Critics' Award, Best Foreign Film, 1959; Best Director and Catholic Film Office Awards, Cannes Film Festival, 1959.

Publications

Scripts:

Truffaut, François, and Marcel Moussy, *Les quatre cents coups*, Paris, 1959; as *The 400 Blows*, edited by David Denby, New York, 1969; in *The Adventures of Antoine Doinel: 4 Screenplays by François Truffaut*, New York, 1971.

Books:

Taylor, John Russell, *Cinema Eye, Cinema Ear*, New York, 1964.
Graham, Peter, *The New Wave*, New York, 1968.
Petrie, Graham, *The Cinema of François Truffaut*, New York, 1970.
Crisp, C. G., *François Truffaut*, New York, 1972.
Fanne, Dominique, *L'Univers de François Truffaut*, Paris, 1972.
Allen, Don, *Finally Truffaut*, London, 1973; revised edition, 1985.
Monaco, James, *The New Wave*, New York, 1976.
Collet, Jean, *Le Cinéma de François Truffaut*, Paris, 1977.
Insdorf, Annette, *François Truffaut*, Boston, 1978.
Thiher, Allen, *The Cinematic Muse: Critical Studies in the History of French Cinema*, Columbia, Missouri, 1979.
Walz, Eugene P., *François Truffaut: A Guide to Reference and Resources*, Boston, 1982.
Winkler, Willi, *Die Filme von François Truffaut*, Munich, 1984.
Bergala, Alain, and others, *Le Roman de François Truffaut*, Paris, 1985.
Collet, Jean, *François Truffaut*, Paris, 1985.
Truffaut, François, *Truffaut par Truffaut*, edited by Dominique Rabourdin, Paris, 1985.
De Fornari, Oreste, *I filme di François Truffaut*, Rome, 1986.
Dalmais, Hervé, *Truffaut*, Paris, 1987.
Gillian, Anne, *François Truffaut: le secret perdu*, Paris, 1991.
Holmes, Diana, and Robert Ingram, *François Truffaut*, Manchester, 1998.

Articles:

Rivette, Jacques, ''Du côté de chez Antoine,'' in *Cahiers du Cinéma* (Paris), May 1959.
Corbin, Louis, in *Films in Review* (New York), November 1959.
Mekas, Jonas, in *Village Voice* (New York), 25 November 1959.
Hartung, P. T., ''Screen,'' in *Commonweal* (New York), 27 November 1959.
Croce, Arlene, in *Film Quarterly* (Berkeley), no. 3, 1960.
Rhode, Eric, in *Sight and Sound* (London), Spring 1960.
New Yorker, 20 February 1960.
Rotha, Paul, in *Films and Filming* (London), April 1960.
Franci, R. M., and Marshall Lewis, ''A Conversation with François Truffaut,'' in *New York Film Bulletin*, nos. 12, 13 and 14, 1961.
Interview with L. Marcorelles, in *Sight and Sound* (London), Winter 1961–62.
Franci, R. M., and Marshall Lewis, ''Conversation with François Truffaut,'' in *New York Film Bulletin*, no. 3, 1962.
Shatnoff, Judith, ''François Truffaut—The Anarchist Imagination,'' in *Film Quarterly* (Berkeley), Spring 1963.
Ronder, Paul, ''François Truffaut—An Interview,'' in *Film Quarterly* (Berkeley), Fall 1963.
Klein, Michael, ''The Literary Sophistication of François Truffaut,'' in *Film Comment* (New York), Summer 1965.
Sawyer, Paul, in *Cineaste* (New York), Winter 1967–68.
Jacob, Gilles, in *Sight and Sound* (London), Autumn 1968.

Les Quatres Cents Coups

Helman, A., ''Czterysta batów,'' in *Kino* (Warsaw), November 1973.

''Dialogue on Film: Interview with Truffaut,'' in *American Film* (Washington, D.C.), May 1976.

Poague, Leland, ''On Time and Truffaut,'' in *Film Criticism* (Edinboro, Pennsylvania), Summer 1976.

Mast, Gerald, ''From *400 Blows* to *Small Change*,'' in *New Republic* (New York), 2 April 1977.

Thiher, Allen, ''The Existential Play in Truffaut's Early Films,'' in *Literature/Film Quarterly* (Salisbury, Maryland), Summer 1977.

Carreño, J. M., in *Casablanca* (Madrid), February 1984.

Turner, D., ''Made in the USA: The American Child in Truffaut's *400 Blows*,'' in *Literature/Film Quarterly* (Salisbury, Maryland), April 1984.

Schmidt, N., ''Cinéma et télévision,'' *CinémAction* (Conde-sur-Noireau, France), no. 2, June 1992.

Neupert, R., ''The Musical Score as Closure Device in *The 400 Blows*,'' in *Film Criticism* (Meadville, Pennsylvania), no. 1, 1989.

Lucas, Tim, ''The 400 Blows / Jules et Jim,'' in *Video Watchdog* (Cincinnati, Ohio), no. 19, September/October, 1993.

Bjorkman, S., ''En stillbild i en stillbild . . . still,'' *Chaplin* (Stockholm), vol. 36, 1994.

Colville, G.M.M., ''Pere perdus, peres retrouves dans l'oeuvre de François Truffaut,'' *French Review*, vol. 68, no. 2, 1994.

Söderbergh Widding, Astrid, ''En stillbild ur François Truffaut's *De 400 slagen*,'' *Chaplin* (Stockholm), vol. 38, no. 1, 1996.

Raskin, R. ''A Note on Closure in Truffaut's *Les quatre cents coups*,'' *P.O.V.* (Denmark), no. 2, December 1996.

Mandolini, C., ''Les quatre cents coups,'' *Sequences* (Quebec), no. 189–190, March/June 1997.

* * *

The film career of François Truffaut is marked by paradox. As the ''enfant terrible'' of French film criticism he was barred from attending the Cannes Film Festival of 1958. But in 1959 his first feature-length film, *Les quatre cents coups*, earned him honors as Best Director. Similarly, Truffaut's role as champion of the ''politique des auteurs'' also involved a species of paradox, in his attacking the French ''tradition of quality'' while praising American film noir in traditional aesthetic terms, in his praising of individual self-expression while creating a ''counter tradition'' of filmic reference points from sources as diverse as neorealism and Hollywood. Especially important in Truffaut—given the tensions implicit in his critical stance—is the fact of language, at once a social institution *and* a means of personal expression. Repeatedly it is through language that Truffaut's central characters—most of them loners of one sort or another—attempt to reconcile themselves to society, as Truffaut himself, perhaps, has used language, especially the language of cinema, to establish his position as the most consistently successful of the *Cahiers du cinéma* group of New Wave directors that included not only Truffaut but also Jean-Luc Godard, Claude Chabrol, and Jacques Rivette.

To see *Les quatre cents coups* against the background of the European cinema is to become especially conscious of Truffaut's indebtedness to Vigo, Rossellini, and Renoir. Vigo's short documentary *A propos de Nice* is a study of a city, with particular emphasis on the contrast between rich and poor. *Les quatre cents coups* is similarly concerned with Paris as a city, and again there is a contrast between affluence (the many shop windows against which Truffaut frames his action) and poverty (the cramped Doinel apartment; various acts of theft). Equally resonant are the oft-noted parallels between *Les quatre cents coups* and Jean Vigo's *Zéro de conduite*. Though the action in *Les quatre cents coups* is not limited to interiors—the exterior shots of Paris connote a sense of almost lyrical freedom (partly the result of Jean Constantin's gently energetic score)—the film's action is effectively ''framed'' by two ''institution'' sequences, the first in the school where Antoine Doinel (Jean-Pierre Léaud) is constantly at odds with his teacher, the second in the ''Observation Center for Delinquent Minors'' to which Antoine is sent after stealing a typewriter. Both settings recall the boys' boarding school in Vigo's *Zéro de conduite*, as Antoine's revolt against his social and familial circumstances recalls that of Vigo's quartet of young rebels.

Truffaut's debts to Rossellini and Renoir are as much stylistic as thematic—in both cases it is a matter of camera mobility and take duration, as well as the use of real-world rather than studio sets. But the theme of rebellion against rigid social authority is common both to Rossellini's and Renoir's modes of ''film realism.'' In this regard *Les quatre cents coups* recalls Renoir's *Boudu sauvé des eaux* especially, in setting (Paris) and in its tone of affection for the innocent self-assertiveness of its central character; Boudu polishes his shoes with a fancy bedspread, while Antoine wipes his dirty hands on the dining room drapery. It is also worth remarking that water is an important image in both films—for Boudu, who is ''saved'' from drowning, only to escape his bourgeois rescuers by eventually returning to the river, and also for Antoine Doinel, who speaks longingly of the sea throughout *Les quatre cents coups*, and who finds himself (ambiguously) at the seashore at the film's end.

Equally important to the texture and tone of *Les quatre cents coups* are Truffaut's references to the American cinema, especially to Hitchcock and Welles. The entire sequence of Antoine's arrest and detention, for instance, recalls in spirit and detail (right down to Antoine's hat) a similar sequence in Hitchcock's *The Wrong Man*; questions are asked, fingerprints or mug shots are taken, and the prisoner is eventually led to his cell. And the sense of shock in both cases follows from the disproportion or dissonance of the accused (Manny is innocent; Antoine was *returning* the typewriter) and the accusation.

Far more central to *Les quatre cents coups* are its submerged (almost retroactive) relations to the Wellesian cinema. In *La nuit américaine* the childhood figure of the director played by Truffaut dreams of stealing stills of *Citizen Kane* through the grill work protecting the front of a local cinema (in *Les quatre cents coups* Antoine and René filch a still from Bergman's *Sommaren med Monika*); in several respects the basic situation in *Les quatre cents coups* recalls that in Welles's *Citizen Kane* and *The Magnificent Ambersons*. In all three films a young boy endeavors to reconcile himself to his mother, and in each instance the father figure is weak to the point of desertion: Kane's father quickly gives in to the scheme that sends Charlie east with Thatcher, Georgie Amberson's father dies midway through the narrative, and Antoine Doinel's stepfather has neither the courage nor the insight to understand the basic honesty and earnestness of Antoine's attempts to please or to be independent.

All of which is especially important given the stylistic and thematic affinity of Truffaut to Welles. That stylistic energy of both Truffaut and Welles is evidenced by the range of their filmic devices; both are masters equally of montage and of long take. And yet in each case the energy evident in film style is set thematically against a lack of energy in the depicted world of the film. The danger is one of denial (as Antoine is eventually denied by his mother) or exhaustion (as Antoine reaches the verge of exhaustion in his long run to the seashore).

The alternative—at least for Truffaut—is to find a way of life that allows for repetition, as children ''repeat'' and hence ''replace'' their parents, without falling prey to mechanical regimentation or cynical bitterness. It is Madame Doinel's bitterness toward her own past, toward her son, which is most directly responsible for Antoine's delinquency and exile. By contrast, Truffaut always works in his films to incorporate the past creatively into the present, to sustain the past by revising and reviewing it. Hence, in *Les quatre cents coups* he pays homage to the history of cinema (and also literature) in the very process of renewing it, of using it again. And *Les quatre cents coups* is itself subsequently revised and thereby sustained in a series of films about the further adventures of Antoine Doinel, a series that culminates in *L'amour en fuite* in which footage from all of the earlier films in the Doinel saga (*Les quatre cents coups*, *Antoine et Collete*, *Baisers volés*, and *Domicile conjugal*), as well as from *Les deux anglais et le continent* and *La nuit américaine*, is recombined with new footage to demonstrate with remarkable clarity and feeling the possibilities for human renewal.

—Leland Poague

THE QUEEN OF SIN AND THE SPECTACLE OF SODOM AND GOMORRAH

See **SODOM UND GOMORRHA**

RAGING BULL

USA, 1980

Director: Martin Scorsese

Production: United Artists; part in color, prints by Technicolor; running time: 129 minutes; length: 11,588 feet. Released November 1980.

Producers: Irwin Winkler and Robert Chartoff, in association with Peter Savage; **screenplay:** Paul Schrader and Mardik Martin, from the book by Jake La Motta with Peter Savage; **photography:** Michael Chapman; **editor:** Thelma Schoonmaker; **sound recordists:** Les Lazarowitz, Michael Evje, Walter Gest, and Gary Ritchie; **sound re-recordists:** Donald O. Mitchell, Bill Nicholson, and David J. Kimball; **sound effects supervising editor:** Frank Warner; **production designer:** Gene Rudolf; **art directors:** Alan Manser, Kirk Axtell, and Sheldon Haber; **consultant:** Jake La Motta; **technical advisers:** Frank Topham and Al Silvani.

Raging Bull

Cast: Robert De Niro (*Jake La Motta*); Cathy Moriarty (*Vickie La Motta*); Joe Pesci (*Joey La Motta*); Frank Vincent (*Salvy*); Nicholas Colasanto (*Tommy Como*); Theresa Saldana (*Lenore*); Mario Gallo (*Mario*); Frank Adonis (*Patsy*); Joseph Bono (*Guido*); Frank Topham (*Toppy*); Lori Anne Flax (*Irma*); Charles Scorsese (*Charlie, Man with Como*); Don Dunphy (*Himself*); Bill Hanrahan (*Eddie Eagen*); Rita Bennett (*Emma, Miss 48's*); James V. Christy (*Dr. Pinto*); Bernie Allen (*Comedian*); Michael Badalucco (*Soda Fountain clerk*); Thomas Beansy Lobasso (*Beansy*); Paul Forrest (*Monsignor*); Peter Petrella (*Johnny*); Geraldine Smith (*Janet*); Mardik Martin (*Copa waiter*); Peter Savage (*Jackie Curtie*); Daniel P. Conte (*Detroit Promoter*); Joe Malanga (*Bodyguard*); Allan Malamud (*Reporter at Jake's House*); D. J. Blair (*State Attorney Bronson*); Laura James (*Mrs. Bronson*); Richard McMurray (*J.R.*); Mary Albee (*Underage ID Girl*); Candy Moore (*Linda*); Nick Trisko (*Bartender Carlo*); Lou Tiano (*Ricky*); Allan Joseph (*Jeweller*); Martin Scorsese (*Barbizon Stagehand*); Floyd Anderson (*Jimmy Reeves*); Johnny Barnes (*''Sugar'' Ray Robinson*); Kevin Mahon (*Tony Janiro*); Eddie Mustafa Muhammad (*Billy Fox*); Louis Raftis (*Marcel Cerdan*); Coley Wallis (*Joe Louis*); Fritzie Higgins (*Woman with Vickie*); Johnny Turner (*Laurent Dauthuille*).

Awards: Oscars for Best Actor (De Niro) and Best Editing, 1981; BAFTA Award for Best Editing, 1982.

Publications

Books:

Kolker, Robert Phillip, *A Cinema of Loneliness: Penn, Kubrick, Coppola, Scorsese, Altman*, Oxford, 1980; revised edition, 1988.

Arnold, Frank, and others, *Martin Scorsese*, Munich, 1986.

Bliss, Michael, *Martin Scorsese and Michael Cimino*, Metuchen, New Jersey, 1986.

Cameron-Wilson, James, *The Cinema of Robert De Niro*, London, 1986.

Cietat, Michel, *Martin Scorsese*, Paris, 1986.

Domecq, Jean-Philippe, *Martin Scorsese: Un Rève italo-américain*, Renens, Switzerland, 1986.

McKay, Keith, *Robert De Niro: The Hero Behind the Masks*, New York, 1986.

Weiss, Ulli, *Das neue Hollywood: Francis Ford Coppola, Steven Spielberg, Martin Scorsese*, Munich, 1986.

Wood, Robin, *Hollywood from Vietnam to Reagan*, New York, 1986.

Weiss, Marian, *Martin Scorsese: A Guide to References and Resources*, Boston, 1987.

Lourdeaux, Lee, *Italian and Irish Filmmakers in America: Ford, Capra, Coppola, and Scorsese*, Philadelphia, 1990.

Connelly, Marie Katheryn, *Martin Scorsese: An Analysis of His Feature Films, With a Filmography of His Entire Directorial Career*, Jefferson, North Carolina, 1993.

Kellman, Steven G., editor, *Perspectives on Raging Bull*, New York, 1994.

Bliss, Michael, *The Word Made Flesh: Catholicism and Conflict in the Films of Martin Scorsese*, Lanham, Maryland, 1995, 1998.

Friedman, Lawrence S., *The Cinema of Martin Scorsese*, New York, 1997.

Kelly, Mary P., *Martin Scorsese: A Journey*, New York, 1997.

Dougan, Andy, *Martin Scorsese—Close Up: The Making of His Movies*, New York, 1998.

Brunette, Peter, editor, *Martin Scorsese: Interviews*, Jackson, Mississippi, 1999.

Articles:

Wiener, Thomas, ''Martin Scorsese Fights Back,'' in *American Film* (Washington, D.C.), November 1980.

Variety (New York), 12 November 1980.

Georgakas, Dan, in *Cineaste* (New York), Winter 1980–81.

Thomson, David, ''The Director as Raging Bull,'' in *Film Comment* (New York), January-February 1981.

Gentry, R., ''Michael Chapman Captures *Raging Bull* in Black and White,'' in *Millimeter* (New York), February 1981.

Jenkins, Steve, in *Monthly Film Bulletin* (London), February 1981.

Millar, Gavin, in *Listener* (London), 26 February 1981.

''Dialogue on Film: Robert De Niro,'' in *American Film* (Washington, D.C.), March 1981.

''*Raging Bull* Section'' of *Cahiers du Cinéma* (Paris), March 1981.

''*Raging Bull* Section'' of *Positif* (Paris), April 1981.

Rinaldi, G., in *Cineforum* (Bergamo), April 1981.

Combs, Richard, in *Sight and Sound* (London), Spring 1981.

Sinyard, Neil, in *Films Illustrated* (London), May 1981.

Williams, A. L., in *American Cinematographer* (Los Angeles), May 1981.

Henry, M., in *Casablanca* (Madrid), June 1981.

Cook, Pam, ''*Raging Bull:* Masculinity in Crisis,'' in *Screen* (London), September-October 1982.

Wood, Robin, ''The Homosexual Subtext: *Raging Bull,*'' in *Australian Journal of Screen Theory* (Kensington, New South Wales), no. 15–16, 1983.

Hemmeter, G. C. and T., ''The Word Made Flesh: Language in *Raging Bull,*'' in *Literature/Film Quarterly* (Salisbury, Maryland), April 1986.

Bruce, Bryan, ''Martin Scorsese: Five Films,'' in *Movie* (London), Winter 1986.

Lane, J., ''Martin Scorsese and the Documentary Impulse,'' in *Framework* (London), no. 1, 1991.

Sitney, P. A., ''Cinematic Election and Theological Vanity,'' in *Raritan* (New Brunswick, New Jersey), no. 2, 1991.

Librach, R. S., ''The Last Temptation in *Mean Streets* and *Raging Bull*,'' in *Literature/Film Quarterly* (Salisbury, Maryland), no. 1, 1992.

Clements, Marcelle, ''Martin Scorsese's Mortal Sins,'' in *Esquire*, vol. 120, no. 5, November 1993.

O'Neill, E.R., '''Poison'-ous Queers: Violence and Social Order,'' in *Spectator* (Los Angeles), vol. 15, no. 1, 1994.

Combs, Richard, ''Hell Up in the Bronx,'' in *Sight & Sound* (London), vol. 5, no. 2, February 1995.

Borden, L., ''Blood and Redemption,'' in *Sight & Sound* (London), vol. 5, February 1995.

Scorsese, Martin, ''De Nero & Moi,'' in *Cahiers du Cinéma* (Paris), no. 500, March 1996.

Mortimer, B., ''Portraits of the Postmodern Person in *Taxi Driver*, *Raging Bull*, and *The King of Comedy*,'' in *Journal of Film and Video* (Los Angeles), vol. 49, no. 1/2, 1997.

Thompson, David, ''The Director as Raging Bull: Why Can't a Woman Be More Like a Photograph?'' in *Film Comment* (New York), vol. 34, no. 3, May-June 1998.

* * *

Martin Scorsese's telling of the story of Jake La Motta has given rise to a number of different, often conflicting, readings. For Scorsese himself, La Motta's trajectory from promising boxer to middleweight champion of the world to night-club performer is the story of ''a guy attaining something and losing everything, and then redeeming himself.'' Such a reading is clearly reinforced by the quotation from St. John's gospel preceding the final credits, which tells of a man whose sight has been restored by Christ rebuking the Pharisees: ''Whether or not he is a sinner, I do not know,'' the man replied. ''All I know is this: once I was blind and now I can see.'' On this level, La Motta's life becomes a kind of spiritual odyssey of the kind encountered before in the work of Schrader and Scorsese, both separately and in collaboration one with another. As Scorsese describes La Motta: ''He works on an almost primitive level, almost an animal level. And therefore he must think in a different way, he must be aware of certain things spiritually that we aren't, because our minds are too cluttered with intellectual ideas, and too much emotionalism. And because he's on that animalistic level, he may be closer to pure spirit.''

Others have rejected such an approach as spurious, self-justificatory, high-flown theorizing and have condemned the film as endorsing macho values. On the other hand, there are those who completely invert this argument and, like Neil Sinyard, read *Raging Bull* as ''a militantly feminist film'' in that it ''presents men at their most pointlessly repulsive and destructive. The effect of the film is to aim a pulverizing blow at male values.''

Such contradictory readings and responses become more comprehensible if one considers the film's extraordinary style, however, in which it is frequently very difficult to locate any kind of authorial voice or attitude. Scorsese's presence is clearly there in the film's frequently stunning visuals, but what does he want us to think of La Motta? As Richard Combs puts it in the course of a long analysis of the film in *Sight and Sound*, *Raging Bull* ''seems to have been made out of an impatience with all the usual trappings of cinema, with plot, psychology and an explanatory approach to character.'' Conversations, though intense in the extreme, are elliptical, muffled, barely heard. There are few ''period'' traces, and even fewer familiar faces. In spite of the opportunity offered by the trajectory of the real La Motta's life, Scorsese largely refuses to let the film arrange itself into a conventional rise-and-fall pattern, concentrating instead on simple, often highly elliptical chronological units, with some of La Motta's fights communicated solely by a still and a title. In all of these details the film differs markedly from the boxer's autobiography on which it is loosely based and which supplies ''interpretation'' and background detail in large amounts. What Scorsese has done, however, is to throw out all this ''excess baggage,'' and to reveal La Motta's interior drama by means of a rigorous concentration on externals. In this respect, *Raging Bull* may be his most Bressonian film, in which, as Combs puts it, ''the spirit is only evident in its absence.''

Several critics, notable among them Robin Wood, have read a homosexual subtext in *Raging Bull* (and other Scorsese films for that matter). This is at its clearest in the scenes around the Janiro fight. Janiro's good looks have attracted the attention of La Motta's wife Vickie, and La Motta is determined to ruin them, although he jokes that he doesn't know whether to ''fuck him or fight him.'' Sexual doubts also hover over a scene in which La Motta worries that he has ''girl's hands,'' and inform much of the film's floridly sexual language. According to Wood, traces of repressed homosexuality in *Raging Bull* ''exist threateningly close to the surface—to the film's conscious level of articulation—accounting for its relentless and near-hysterical intensity.''

In the end, it has to be admitted that *Raging Bull* is a profoundly ambivalent film which refuses to fit easily into Scorsese's schema or into any straightforwardly feminist analysis either. But neither is it an unproblematic celebration of machismo. One of the few critics sensitive to the film's ambivalence is Pam Cook who argues that while it does indeed put masculinity in crisis it does not, for all its profoundly disturbing qualities, offer a radical critique of either masculinity or violence: ''The film's attitude to violence is ambiguous. On one hand, it is validated as an essential component of masculinity, making possible resistance to a corrupt and repressive social system. On this level violence is seen as inseparable from desire, and is celebrated. On the other, the tragic scenario of *Raging Bull* demands that the hero be shown to be the guilty victim of his transgressive desires: his violence is so excessive, so self-destructive that it has to be condemned. . . .The tragic structure of *Raging Bull* has consequences for its view of masculinity: masculinity is put into crisis so that we can mourn its loss.'' In this reading La Motta's ''fall'' is not the result of some kind of innate guilt or ''original sin'' but intimately tied up with his social position as a member of the Italian-American immigrant community, a victim-hero desperate to improve the conditions of his existence by becoming a champion boxer but limited by a culture which at one and the same time offered power and success but insisted on the inferior status of Italian immigrants. According to Cook the film thus looks back to a time when the values of the Italian-American community were still current.

—Julian Petley

RAIDERS OF THE LOST ARK

USA, 1981

Director: Steven Spielberg

Production: Lucasfilm Productions; color, 35mm, Panavision; running time: 115 minutes. Released summer 1981 by Paramount Pictures. Filmed 1980 in France, Tunisia, and Hawaii, and in Elstree Studios, England. Cost: about $20 million.

Producer: Frank Marshall; **executive producers:** George Lucas and Howard Kazanjian; **screenplay:** Lawrence Kasdan; **story:** George Lucas and Philip Kaufman; **photography:** Douglas Slocombe; **editor:** Michael Kahn; **sound effects supervisor:** Richard L. Anderson; **sound effects editors:** Steve H. Flick and Mark Mangini; **production designer:** Norman Reynolds; **art director:** Leslie Dilley; **music:** John Williams; **special effects supervisor:** Richard Edlund; **costume designer:** Deborah Nadoolman; **stunt co-ordinator:** Glenn Randall.

Cast: Harrison Ford (*Indiana Jones*); Karen Allen (*Marion Ravenswood*); Paul Freeman (*Belloq*); John Rhys-Davies (*Sallah*); Wolf Kahler (*Dietrich*); Ronald Lacey (*Toht*); Denholm Elliot (*Marcus Brody*).

Awards: Oscars for Sound, Visual Effects, Art Direction, and Editing, 1981.

Publications

Books:

Taylor, Derek, *The Making of Raiders of the Lost Ark*, New York, 1981.
Crawley, Tony, *The Steven Spielberg Story*, London, 1983.
Miller, Bob, *The Raiders Guide*, Sherman, 1983.
Goldau, Antje, and Hans Helmut Prinzler, *Spielberg: Filme als Spielzeug*, Berlin, 1985.
Honeyford, Paul, *Harrison Ford: A Biography*, London, 1986.
Mott, Donald R., and Cheryl McAllister Saunders, *Steven Spielberg*, Boston, 1986.
Smith, Thomas G., *Industrial Light and Magic: The Art of Special Effects*, London, 1986.
Weiss, Ulli, *Das Neue Hollywood: Francis Ford Coppola, Steven Spielberg, Martin Scorsese*, Munich, 1986.
Clinch, Minty, *Harrison Ford: A Biography*, London, 1987.
Godard, Jean-Pierre, *Spielberg*, Paris, 1987.
Sinyard, Neil, *The Films of Steven Spielberg*, London, 1987.
Von Gunden, Kenneth, *Postmodern Auteurs: Coppola, Lucas, De Palma, Spielberg & Scorsese*, Jefferson, North Carolina, 1991.
Taylor, Philip M., *Steven Spielberg: The Man, His Movies, and Their Meaning*, New York, 1992, 1998.
Sanello, Frank, *Spielberg: The Man, the Movies, the Mythology*, Dallas, 1996.
Brode, Douglas, *The Films of Steven Spielberg,* Secaucus, New Jersey, 1997.
Yule, Andrew, *Steven Spielberg*, New York, 1997.
Knight, Bertram, *Steven Spielberg: Master of Movie Magic*, Parsippany, New Jersey, 1998.
Perry, George, *Steven Spielberg-Close Up: The Making of His Movies*, New York, 1998.
McBride, Joseph, *Steven Spielberg: A Biography*, New York, 1999.
Friedman, Lester D., and Brent Notbohm, editors, *Steven Spielberg: Interviews*, Jackson, Mississippi, 2000.

Raiders of the Lost Ark

Articles:

Hollywood Reporter, 5 June 1981.
Variety (New York), 5 June 1981.
New York Times, 12 June 1981.
Newsweek (New York), 15 June 1981.
New Yorker, 15 June 1981.
Time (New York), 15 June 1981.
New Republic (New York), 4–11 July 1981.
Reiss, D., interview with Steven Spielberg, in *Filmmakers Monthly* (Ward Hill, Massachusetts), July-August 1981.
Combs, Richard, in *Monthly Film Bulletin* (London), August 1981.
Films (London), August 1981.
Furtak, G., in *Films in Review* (New York), September-August 1981.
Benayoun, Robert, ''Le Retour au plaisir,'' in *Positif* (Paris), September 1981.
Mérigeau, P., in *Image et Son* (Paris), September 1981.
Païni, D., in *Cinéma* (Paris), September 1981.
Tonnerre, J., in *Cinématographe* (Paris), September 1981.
Assayas, O., in *Cahiers du Cinéma* (Paris), October 1981.
Martini, E., in *Cineforum* (Bergamo), October 1981.
Shay, D., ''The Wrath of God and Other Illusions,'' in *Cinefex* (Riverside, California), October 1981.
''*Raiders of the Lost Ark* Section'' of *American Cinematographer* (Los Angeles), November 1981.
Filme (Paris), November-December 1981.
Ecran Fantastique (Paris), nos. 21 and 22, 1981–82.
Neale, Stephen, ''Hollywood Corner,'' in *Framework* (Norwich), 1982.
Wilson, John, in *Magill's Cinema Annual*, Englewood Cliffs, New Jersey, 1982.
Orto, N., in *Cinema Nuovo* (Turin), February 1982.
Auty, Chris, ''The Complete Spielberg?,'' in *Sight and Sound* (London), Autumn 1982.
Tomasulo, F. P., ''Mr. Jones Goes to Washington: Myth and Religion in *Raiders of the Lost Ark*,'' in *Quarterly Review of Film Studies* (New York), Fall 1982.
Dorminsky, M., in *Cinema Novo* (Porto), September-October 1982.
Zimmerman, Patricia R., ''Soldiers of Fortune: Lucas, Spielberg, Indiana Jones and *Raiders of the Lost Ark*,'' in *Wide Angle* (Athens, Ohio), vol. 6, no. 2, 1984.
Rissik, A., ''Steven Spielberg: Indiana Jones and the 007 Myth,'' in *Films and Filming* (London), November 1984.

Cinéfantastique (Paris), May 1985.
Noel, J., ''Steven Spielberg (Suite No. 4),'' in *Grand Angle* (Mariembourg, Belgium), September 1990.
Sheehan, H., ''The Panning of Steven Spielberg,'' in *Film Comment* (New York), May-June 1992.
Deemer, Charles, ''The Rhetoric of Action: Five Classic Action Scenes,'' in *Creative Screenwriting* (Washington, D.C.), vol. 2, no. 4, Winter 1995.
Aronstein, S., '''Not Exactly a Knight:' Arthurian Narrative and Recuperative Politics in the 'Indiana Jones' Trilogy,'' in *Cinema Journal* (Austin), vol. 34, no. 4, 1995.
Bond, J., in *Film Score Monthly* (Los Angeles), no. 62, October 1995.
Larson, R.D., in *Soundtrack!: The Collector's Quarterly* (Mechelen), vol. 15, June 1996.
Score (Lelystad), no. 99, June 1996.

* * *

Raiders of the Lost Ark is historically important because it marks the first collaboration between George Lucas and Steven Spielberg, the two most financially successful of American filmmakers. Released in the summer of 1981, the film garnered some of the best critical accolades in either man's career; it also continued their phenomenal success: it is now one of the top ten money-makers of all time.

An homage to old movie serials in much the same way as are George Lucas's *Star Wars* films, *Raiders* is also derivative of westerns, horror films, war films and James Bond films. In fact, Lucas reportedly mentioned his *Raiders* story to Spielberg in 1977 after Spielberg said that he had always wanted to make a James Bond film. *Raiders* even opens with an initial adventure scene unrelated to the main story of the film, a device used in the James Bond films.

Relying on Spielberg's TV experience and extensive ''storyboarding,'' the elaborate action film was shot in 73 days in France, Tunisia, Hawaii, and the famed Elstree Studios in England, which Lucas also used for his *Star Wars* films. Special effects for the film were made at Industrial Light and Magic, Lucasfilms' own facility in northern California. Spielberg used English cinematographer Douglas Slocombe, who worked on his *Close Encounters*, and editor Michael Kahn, who edited *Close Encounters* and *1941*. Spielberg also brought screenwriter Lawrence Kasdan to Lucas's attention.

The primary distinction of *Raiders*, in addition to its constant high level of thrills and chills, is the vivid portrayal of its hero, Indiana Jones, played by Harrison Ford. As Spielberg himself has said, Ford in this film is a combination of Errol Flynn in *The Adventures of Don Juan* and Humphrey Bogart in *The Treasure of the Sierra Madre*. A vulnerable but heroic figure, Ford's Indiana Jones also has a shadowy side. Indiana's search for the Ark which contains the original Ten Commandments becomes a dark obsession, a passion that causes him twice to abandon the film's heroine, Marion Ravenswood, played by Karen Allen.

Around this larger than life hero, Lucas and Spielberg weave a tale of intrigue and adventure, full of Nazi villains, a nasty but engaging Frenchman who is Indy's rival and shadowy double, and numerous references to Biblical and Egyptian mythology. There is an atmosphere of evil and mysterious power, and a demonic transformation of many of the film's settings and props. Thus, the ancient city of Tanis in *Raiders* has become deserted wasteland, an Egyptian temple becomes the prison full of snakes for Indy and Marion, and the mysterious Ark of the Covenant brings fiery destruction to the Nazis.

In the end, the Ark eludes Indy's grasp and is tucked away in an immense warehouse, a scene reminiscent of the last shot in *Citizen Kane*. Through the course of the film, Indy discovers that he is both free and bound—although he loses the Ark, he does get Marion. In this respect the film seems to be saying, True love or friendship is its own reward.

—Thomas Snyder

RAISE THE RED LANTERN

See **DAHONG DENGLONG GAOGAO GUA**

RAN

France-Japan, 1985

Director: Akira Kurosawa

Production: Greenwich Film Productions (Paris)/Herald Ace/Nippon Herald Films (Tokyo); in color, Dolby Stereo; running time: 160 minutes; length: 14,435 feet. Released 1985.

Executive producer: Katsumi Furukawa; **producers:** Serge Silberman, Masato Hara; **screenplay:** Akira Kurosawa, Hideo Oguni, Masato Ide; **photography:** Takao Saito, Masaharu Ueda, Asakazu Nakai; **sound recordists:** Fumio Yanoguchi, Shotaro Yoshida; **sound re-recordist:** Claude Villand; **production designers:** Yoshiro Muraki, Shinobu Muraki; **costume designer:** Emi Wada; **music:** Toru Takemitsu; **musical director:** Hiroyuki Iwaki.

Cast: Tatsuya Nakadai (*Hidetora Ichimonji*); Akira Terao (*Taro Takatora Ichimonji*); Jinpachi Nezu (*Jiro Masatora Ichimonji*); Daisuke Ryu (*Saburo Naotora Ichimonji*); Mieko Harada (*Lady Kaede*); Yoshiko Miyazaki (*Lady Sue*); Kazuo Kato (*Kageyu Ikoma*); Shinnosuke Ikehata (*Kyoami*); Hitoshi Ueki (*Nobuhiro Fujimaki*); Jun Tazaki (*Seiji Ayabe*); Norio Matsui (*Shumenosuke Ogura*); Hisashi Igawa (*Shuri Kurogane*); Kenji Kodama (*Samon Shirane*); Toshiya Ito (*Mondo Naganuma*); Takeshi Kato (*Koyata Hatakeyama*); Takeshi Nomura (*Tsurumaru*); Masayuki Yui (*Tango Hirayama*); Heihachiro Suzuki (*Fujimaki's General*); Haruko Togo (*Kaede's Old Lady*).

Awards: Oscar for Best Costume Design, 1985. BAFTA Award for Best Foreign Language Film, 1986.

Publications

Script:

Kurosawa, Akira, Hideo Oguni, and Masato Ide, *Ran*, Boston, 1986.

Books:

Raisom, Bertrand, with Serge Toubiana, *Le Livre de Ran*, Paris, 1985.
Davies, Anthony, *Filming Shakespeare's Plays*, New York,1988.

Ran

Chang, Kevin K.W., editor, *Kurosawa: Perceptions on Life: An Anthology of Essays*, Honolulu, 1991.

Prince, Stephen, *The Warrior's Camera: The Cinema of Akira Kurosawa*, Princeton, New Jersey, 1991; revised and expanded edition, 1999.

Goodwin, James, *Akira Kurosawa and Intertextual Cinema*, Baltimore, 1994.

Goodwin, James, editor, *Perspectives on Akira Kurosawa*, New York, 1994.

Richie, Donald, *The Films of Akira Kurosawa*, with Joan Mellen, Berkeley, 1996.

Yoshimoto, Mitsuhiro, *Kurosawa: Film Studies and Japanese Cinema*, Durham, North Carolina, 2000.

Articles:

Bock, Audie, in *American Film* (Washington, D.C.), December 1984.

Variety (New York), 5 June 1985.

''*Ran* Issue'' of *Revue du Cinéma* (Paris), September 1985.

Kehr, Dave, ''Samurai Lear,'' in *American Film* (Washington, D.C.), September 1985.

Grilli, Peter, ''Production Diary,'' in *Film Comment* (New York), September-October 1985.

''*Ran* Issue'' of *Positif* (Paris), October 1985.

Larsen, J. Kornum, ''Interview med Akira Kurosawa,'' in *Kosmorama* (Copenhagen), October 1985.

Nave, B., in *Jeune Cinéma* (Paris), November-December 1985.

Silberman, Rob, in *Cineaste* (New York), vol. 14, no. 4, 1986.

Roth-Lindberg, O., in *Chaplin* (Stockholm), vol. 28, no. 1, 1986.

Ross, T. J., in *Post Script* (Jacksonville, Florida), Winter 1986.

Simons, J., in *Skrien* (Amsterdam), February-March 1986.

Sigal, Clancy, in *Listener* (London), 13 March 1986.

Shakespeare on Film Newsletter, April 1986, December 1987, and December 1988.

Fisher, B., in *American Cinematographer* (Los Angeles), April and July 1986.

Rayns, Tony, in *Monthly Film Bulletin* (London), April 1986.

Milne, Tom, in *Sight and Sound* (London), Spring 1986.

Filmfaust (Frankfurt), June-August 1986.

Roddick, Nick, in *Cinema Papers* (Melbourne), September 1986.

Thompson, A., ''Kurosawa's *Ran*: Reception and Interpretation,'' in *East-West Film Journal* (Honolulu), vol. 3, no. 2, 1989.

Forgach, A., ''A kaosz gyemanttengelye,'' in *Filmvilag* (Budapest), no. 7, 1990.

Bannon, C. J., ''Man and Nature in *Ran* and *King Lear*,'' in *New Orleans Review*, no. 4, 1991.

Avant Scène du Cinéma (Paris), June-July 1991.

Geist, K., ''Late Kurosawa: *Kagemusha* and *Ran*,'' in *Post Script* (Commerce, Texas), no. 1, 1992.

Revesz, A., ''Bolondok roppant szinpadan,'' in *Filmkultura* (Budapest), no. 5, 1992.

Vidal Estevez, M., ''William Akira Shakespeare Kurosawa,'' in *Nosferatu* (San Sebastian), no. 8, February 1992.

Crowl, S., ''The Bow is Bent and Drawn: Kurosawa's *Ran* and the Shakespearean Arrow of Desire,'' in *Literature/Film Quarterly* (Salisbury, Maryland), vol. 22, no. 2, April 1994.

Manheim, M., ''The Function of Battle Imagery in Kurosawa's Histories and the *Henry V* films,'' in *Literature/Film Quarterly* (Salisbury, Maryland), vol. 22, no. 2, April 1994.

Howlett, Kathy, ''Are You Trying to Make Me Commit Suicide?: Gender Identity, and Spacial Arrangement in Kurosawa's *Ran*,'' in *Literature/Film Quarterly* (Salisbury, Maryland), vol. 24, no. 4, October 1996.

Kane, Julie, ''From the Baroque to Wabi: Translating Animal Imagery from Shakespeare's *King Lear* to Kurosawa's *Ran*,'' in *Literature/Film Quarterly* (Salisbury, Maryland), vol. 25, no. 2, April 1997.

* * *

Akira Kurosawa's *Ran* is not so much an homage to Shakespeare's *King Lear* as it is a re-examination and deepening of its main themes and ideas. Shakespeare's story is built on all the elemental themes which have characteristically interested Kurosawa: greed, betrayal, and disloyalty to codes of personal honor. In Kurosawa's hands these themes become contemporary and expansive despite the fact that the film is set in feudal Japan. Ultimately, Kurosawa achieves this universality because *Ran* is an almost complete marriage of content and style.

Kurosawa turns to many of the stylistic techniques that have come to be associated with his career. Sweeping panoramas, rich and powerful shot composition, and dramatic depth within the frame accomplished by combinations of back and foreground action and layers of synchronously recorded sound are the building blocks out of which *Ran* grows. For example, Kurosawa creates conflict and dynamism within the frame with contrapuntal movement. When troops are laying siege to the aging warlord's castle, regiments of samurai pass in front of the camera, some running horizontally, others directly away from or directly toward the camera. There is a sense of chaos that is heightened by the red and yellow banners each soldier wears according to his allegiance. Visually the battle is a melee of red and yellow banners blowing freely, falling out of sight as troops fall, and finally the yellow are simply engulfed by the red.

Shot composition has also been one of the earmarks of Kurosawa's career. While many modern filmmakers have gone to the moving camera as a staple of their visual style, Kurosawa has remained loyal to the still frame and stationary camera. *Ran* is little different in this regard, since essentially it is constructed from a series of still frames, each one a painting come to life. During the battle at the warlord's castle, for example, the shots of troops rushing to do battle are juxtaposed with still shots of bodies heaped on top of each other and battlements burning in silent agony. Each of these shots is composed with an eye to detail and maximizing its power while it is on the screen.

The true technical virtuosity of *Ran*, though, lies in the post-production stage. The power inherent in the visuals is given depth and dimension when the externals—elements such as sound effects and music—are added. As the captain of the warlord's army dies, for example, he calls out to his master, ''We are truly in hell.'' As he does, the sounds of battle are replaced by a tranquil, orchestral theme which plays point-counterpoint with the ongoing images of death and destruction. It is as if we are truly standing back watching hell rise up until that moment when we are brought back to the film's present by screams from within it.

It has been said that Akira Kurosawa's work in the work of images, and is therefore concerned not with things but with ideas and metaphors. This being the case, in *Ran* the still frame is the world that has grown stagnant and is being destroyed from within by the visual turmoil. The film ends with a shot of the warlord's greedy, traitorous daughter-in-law standing on a mountain peak watching the return of troops that have slaughtered her allies. At the moment when the camera holds her in long shot, eclipsing a blood-red sunset, we too are standing on the precipice, a *footfall away* from falling into the abyss.

—Rob Winning

RASHOMON

Japan, 1950

Director: Akira Kurosawa

Production: Daiei Productions; black and white, 35mm; running time: 88 minutes; length: 2406 meters. Released 25 August 1950, Tokyo. Filmed at Daiei Studios on outdoor sets.

Producers: Jingo Minuro, later titles list Masaichi Nagata; **screenplay:** Shinobu Hashimoto and Akira Kurosawa, from two short stories by Ryunosuke Akutagawa; **photography:** Kazuo Miyagawa; **art directors:** So Matsuyama (some sources list Takashi Matsuyama); **music:** Fumio Hayasaka.

Cast: Toshiro Mifune (*Tajomaru, the bandit*); Masayuki Mori (*Takehiro, the samurai*); Machiko Kyo (*Masago, his wife*); Takashi Shimura (*Woodcutter*); Minoru Chiaki (*Priest*); Kichijiro Ueda (*The commoner*); Daisuke Kato (*Police agent*); Fumiko Homma (*The medium*).

Awards: Venice Film Festival, Best Film: Lion of St. Mark, 1951; Honorary Oscar as most outstanding foreign film, 1951.

Publications

Script:

Hashimoto, Shinobu, and Akira Kurosawa, *Rashomon: A Film by Akira Kurosawa*, edited by Donald Richie, New York, 1969; also published as *Rashomon*, New Brunswick, New Jersey, 1987.

Rashomon

Books:

Hashimoto, Shinobu, and Marcel Giuglaris, *Le Cinéma japonais (1896–1955)*, Paris, 1956.

Tyler, Parker, *The Three Faces of Film*, New York, 1960.

Richie, Donald, *The Films of Akira Kurosawa*, Los Angeles, 1965; revised edition, with Joan Mellen, Berkeley, 1984, 1996.

Richie, Donald, *Focus on Kurosawa*, New York, 1972.

Tucker, Richard, *Japan: Film Image*, London, 1973.

Bock, Audie, *Japanese Film Directors*, New York, 1978; revised edition, Tokyo, 1985.

Erens, Patricia, *Akira Kurosawa: A Guide to References and Resources*, Boston, 1979.

Bazin, André, *The Cinema of Cruelty: From Buñuel to Hitchcock*, New York, 1982.

Kurosawa, Akira, *Something Like an Autobiography*, New York, 1982.

Sato, Tadao, *Currents in Japanese Cinema*, Tokyo, 1982.

Desser, David, *The Samurai Films of Akira Kurosawa*, Ann Arbor, Michigan, 1983.

Tassone, Aldo, *Akira Kurosawa*, Paris, 1983.

Jarvie, Ian, *Philosophy of the Film: Epistemology, Ontology, Aesthetics*, London, 1987.

Richie, Donald, editor, *Rashomon: Akira Kurosawa, Director*, New Brunswick, New Jersey, 1987.

Chang, Kevin K.W., editor, *Kurosawa: Perceptions on Life: An Anthology of Essays*, Honolulu, 1991.

Prince, Stephen, *The Warrior's Camera: The Cinema of Akira Kurosawa*, Princeton, New Jersey, 1991; revised and expanded edition, 1999.

Goodwin, James, *Akira Kurosawa and Intertextual Cinema*, Baltimore, 1994.

Goodwin, James, editor, *Perspectives on Akira Kurosawa*, New York, 1994.

Yoshimoto, Mitsuhiro, *Kurosawa: Film Studies and Japanese Cinema*, Durham, North Carolina, 2000.

Articles:

Jacchia, Paolo, ''Drama and Lesson of the Defeated,'' in *Bianco e Nero* (Rome), October 1951.

Crowther, Bosley, in *New York Times*, 27 December 1951.

McCarten, John, in *New Yorker*, 29 December 1951.

Farber, Manny, in *Nation* (New York), 19 January 1952.

Griffith, Richard, in *Saturday Review* (New York), 19 January 1952.

Life (New York), 21 January 1952.

Ghelli, Nino, in *Bianco e Nero* (Rome), March 1952.

Whitebait, William, in *New Statesman* (London), 15 March 1952.

Harrington, Curtis, ''*Rashomon* et le cinéma japonais,'' in *Cahiers du Cinéma* (Paris), May 1952.

Barbarow, George, in *Hudson Review* (New York), Autumn 1952.

Crowther, Bosley, in *New York Times*, 6 January 1962. (R. 1952?)

Harcourt-Smith, Simon, in *Sight and Sound* (London), July-September 1952.

Mercier, Pierre, ''*Rashomon* et le pédantisme,'' in *Cahiers du Cinéma* (Paris), June 1953.

Sadoul, Georges, ''Existe-t-il un néorealisme japonais?,'' in *Cahiers du Cinéma* (Paris), November 1953.

Davidson, James F., ''Memory of Defeat in Japan: A Reappraisal of *Rashomon*,'' in *Antioch Review* (Yellow Springs, Ohio), December 1954.

Rieupeyrout, Jean-Louis, in *Cinéma* (Paris), June-July 1955.

Leyda, Jay, in *Film Culture* (New York), no. 10, 1956.

Iida, Shinbi, ''Kurosawa,'' in *Cinema* (Los Angeles), August-September 1963.

''Akira Kurosawa,'' in *Etudes Cinématographiques* (Paris), Spring 1964.

Richie, Donald, ''Kurosawa on Kurosawa,'' in *Sight and Sound* (London), Summer and Autumn 1964.

Sarris, Andrew, in *Village Voice* (New York), 15 October 1964.

Iwasaki, Akira, ''Kurosawa and His Work,'' in *Japan Quarterly*, January-March 1965.

Pinto, Alfonso, ''Akira Kurosawa,'' in *Films in Review* (New York), April 1967.

Tyler, Parker, ''*Rashomon* as Modern Art,'' in *Renaissance of the Film*, edited by Julius Bellone, London, 1970.

Mellen, Joan, ''The Epic Cinema of Kurosawa,'' in *Take One* (Montreal), June 1971.

Almendarez, Valentin, in *Cinema Texas Program Notes* (Austin), 19 March 1974.

Kauffmann, Stanley, in *Horizon* (Los Angeles), Spring 1974.

Poppelaars, G., in *Skoop* (Amsterdam), August 1980.

McDonald, K. I., ''Light and Darkness in *Rashomon*,'' in *Literature/Film Quarterly* (Salisbury, Maryland), vol. 10, no. 2, 1982.

Tucker, G. M., in *Soundtrack* (Los Angeles), June 1985.

Jones, Elizabeth, ''Locating Truth in Film 1940–80,'' in *Post Script* (Jacksonville, Florida), Autumn 1986.

Boyd, D., ''*Rashomon*: From Akutagawa to Kurosawa,'' in *Literature/Film Quarterly* (Salisbury, Maryland), vol. 15, no. 3, 1987.
Guneratne, A., ''Cinehistory and the Puzzling Case of Martin Guerre,'' in *Film & History* (Coral Gables, Florida), no. 1, 1991.
Medine, D., ''Law and Kurosawa's *Rashomon*,'' in *Literature/Film Quarterly* (Salisbury, Maryland), no. 1, 1992.
Séquences (Haute-Ville), no. 179, July-August 1995.
Corliss, Richard, ''From Asia's Film Factories: 10 Golden Greats,'' in *Time International*, vol. 154, no. 7/8, 23 August 1999.

* * *

When *Rashomon* won the Grand Prix at the Venice International Film Festival in 1951, the event represented the opening of the Japanese cinema to the West, and the film itself was regarded as a revelation. Ironically, it has never been very highly thought of in Japan. This does not necessarily mean that the West was wrong (consider the number of major Hollywood films that had to wait to be discovered by the French). It should, however, make us pause to question the grounds for its acclamation.

The film's exotic appeal is very obvious, and in some respects inseparable from its genuine qualities—the originality of its structure, the bravura virtuosity of its camera work, the strength and force of the performances—its success at Venice (and subsequently throughout the western world) was doubtless due to its fortuitous knack of combining the exotic with the appearance of precisely the kind of spurious profundity that western intellectuals have tended to see as necessary for the validation of cinema as an art form. The film was (mis-)taken for a vast metaphysical statement (or, at least, question) along the lines of ''What is truth?'' Little wonder that there has been a considerable backlash. The initial mis-recognition of *Rashomon* no doubt played its part in the subsequent rejection of Kurosawa by numerous critics in the process of discovering Ozu and Mizoguchi. Re-seeing the film now, one is apt to challenge both extremes.

The ''What is truth?'' school of *Rashomon* admirers always (quite understandably) felt some embarrassment at the film's ending: the film's ''great subject'' seemed suddenly displaced and evaded, the film collapsing in ''sentimentality'': certainly a poor woodcutter deciding to adopt an abandoned baby seems to have little relevance to a philosophical inquiry into the nature of truth and reality. It is, however, open to question whether a demonstration that different people will tell the same story in different ways to suit their own convenience really amounts to such philosophical inquiry in the first place. There is no evidence anywhere in Kurosawa's work to suggest that he is a profound ''thinker.'' That is not at all to belittle him as an artist, philosophy and art (though capable of intimate inter-relationships) being quite distinct human activities with quite distinct functions. To demand that a work of art be philosophically profound is merely a crass form of intellectual snobbery. (This is not of course to deny that all art has philosophical *implications*, which is another matter altogether.)

One must, as always, ''Never trust the artist—trust the tale''; yet Kurosawa's own far more modest and earthly account of *Rashomon*'s subject (from his splendid and delightful *Something Like an Autobiography*) seems to me to tally more satisfactorily with the actual film:

> Human beings are unable to be honest with themselves about themselves. They cannot talk about themselves without embellishing. This script portrays such human beings—the kind who cannot survive without lies to make them feel they are better people than they really are. Egoism is a sin the human being carries with him from birth; it is the most difficult to redeem . . . .

This account has a number of advantages. For one thing, it ties the film in closely with Kurosawa's other work, as the ''relativity of truth'' account does not. For one example, the last third of *Ikiru* is singlemindedly concerned with the gradual revelation of an unquestioned and authentic ''truth'' that the self-serving bureaucrats are bent on concealing. For another, it accords much more readily with the general tone and attitude of Kurosawa's films—what one might describe as a bitter humanism, a tenacious belief in the human spirit and in human goodness juxtaposed with a caustic and often savage view of human egoism, duplicity and pettiness. Thirdly, it is much more compatible than philosophical abstractions with one of *Rashomon*'s most immediately striking qualities, its intense physicality, the direct visual communication of sensory experience. It also makes perfect sense of the ending, which becomes, indeed, the logical and very moving culmination of the whole film.

Rashomon is adapted from two very short stories by Akutagawa. The first, ''In a Grove,'' provides the basis for the main body of the film; the second, ''Rashomon'' (the name of the ruined stone gate), is the framing story; the two are brilliantly tied together by the woodcutter's narration of the final version of the story. What many westerners fail to recognize is how *funny* the film is—at least in part. The use of its premise by the Hollywood cinema is well-known: there are Martin Ritt's painstakingly literal (and somewhat labored) translation of it to the American southwest (*The Outrage*), and George Cukor's marvelous transformation of its premise into the basis for a musical comedy (*Les Girls*). But the Hollywood movie that seems closest to *Rashomon* in structure actually antedates it: *Unfaithfully Yours*. Sturges's comedy gives us three quasi-serious episodes (Rex Harrison's fantasies) which prove to be but the necessary build-up to the final, comic, episode, in which the protagonist attempts to put his fantasies into action. *Rashomon* follows the same pattern: the first three ''full'' versions of the story (the bandit's, the wife's, the nobleman's)—which certainly contain their longeurs—are best read as the equally necessary preliminary to the explosion of savage farce in the woodcutter's version. The function of the farce in both films is strikingly similar: the deflation of presumption and pretension. We are not invited to read the woodcutter's story as ''the truth,'' yet its status is clearly different from that of the other three: its purpose is not that of bolstering his own ego. It is especially important that his version uses the woman as its central figure to make the two men look ridiculous: the proletarian and the woman fuse for the purpose of puncturing class pretension and male egoism.

The woodcutter is the real hero of the film and a fully characteristic Kurosawa hero, a point underlined by the casting, since Takashi Shimura also plays the heros of *Ikiru* and *The Seven Samurai*. His adopting the baby (although he and his family are near starvation-level) follows logically from the scathing denunciation of self-serving egoism that is the central impulse of his version of the story: rising above the moral squalor of his time and the physical squalor of his environment, he performs the action that at once establishes his heroic status and redeems the film's almost desperate, almost nihilist view of humanity.

—Robin Wood

THE RAT TRAP

See **ELIPPATHAYAM**

REAR WINDOW

USA, 1954

Director: Alfred Hitchcock

Production: Paramount Pictures; Technicolor, 35mm; running time: 112 minutes. Released 1954. Filmed 1954 in Paramount studios and backlots.

Producer: Alfred Hitchcock; **screenplay:** John MichaelHayes, from the novel by Cornell Woolrich; **photography:** Robert Burks; **editor:** George Tomasini; **sound:** Harry Lindgren and John Cope; **production designers:** Hal Pereira, Ray Mayer, Sam Comer, and MacMillan Johnson; **music:** Franz Waxman; **special effects:** John P. Fulton; **costume designer:** Edith Head.

Cast: James Stewart (*L. B. Jeffries*); Grace Kelly (*Lisa Fremont*); Wendell Corey (*Detective Thomas J. Doyle*); Thelma Ritter (*Stella*); Raymond Burr (*Lars Thorwald*); Judith Evelyn (*Miss Lonely Hearts*); Ross Bagdasarian (*The Composer*); Georgine Darcy (*Miss Torso, the dancer*); Jesslyn Fax (*Sculptress*); Rand Harper (*Honeymooner*); Irene Winston (*Mrs. Thorwald*).

Awards: New York Film Critics' Award, Best Actress to Grace Kelly for *The Country Girl*, *Rear Window*, and *Dial M for Murder*, 1954.

Publications

Books:

Rohmer, Eric, and Claude Chabrol, *Hitchcock*, Paris, 1957.
Amengual, Barthélemy, *Hitchcock*, Paris, 1960.
Bogdanovitch, Peter, *The Cinema of Alfred Hitchcock*, New York, 1962.
Manz, Hans-Peter, *Alfred Hitchcock*, Zurich, 1962.
Perry, George, *The Films of Alfred Hitchcock*, London, 1965.
Wood, Robin, *Hitchcock's Films*, London, 1965.
Truffaut, François, *Le Cinéma selon Hitchcock*, Paris, 1966; as *Hitchcock*, New York, 1985.
Kittredge, William, and Steven M. Krauzer, editors, *Stories into Film*, New York, 1979.
Douchet, Jean, *Alfred Hitchcock*, Paris, 1967.
Simsolo, Noel, *Alfred Hitchcock*, Paris, 1969.
Russell Taylor, John, *Hitch*, New York, 1978.
Bellour, Raymond, *L'Analyse du film*, Paris, 1979.
Hemmeter, Thomas M., *Hitchcock the Stylist*, Ann Arbor, Michigan, 1981.
Narboni, Jean, editor, *Alfred Hitchcock*, Paris, 1982.
Rothman, William, *Hitchcock—The Murderous Gaze*, Cambridge, Massachusetts, 1982.
Villien, Bruno, *Hitchcock*, Paris, 1982.
Weis, Elisabeth, *The Silent Scream: Alfred Hitchcock's Sound Track*, Rutherford, New Jersey, 1982.
Spoto, Donald, *The Life of Alfred Hitchcock: The Dark Side of Genius*, New York, 1982; London, 1983.
Phillips, Gene D., *Alfred Hitchcock*, Boston, 1984.
Barbier, Philippe, and Jacques Moreau, *Alfred Hitchcock*, Paris, 1985.
Deutelbaum, Marshall, and Leland Poague, *A Hitchcock Reader*, Ames, Iowa, 1986.
Humphries, Patrick, *The Films of Alfred Hitchcock*, Greenwich, Connecticut, 1986.
Kloppenburg, Josef, *Die Dramaturgische Funktion der Musik in Filmen Alfred Hitchcocks*, Munich, 1986.
Sinyard, Neil, *The Films of Alfred Hitchcock*, London, 1986.
Modleski, Tania, *The Women Who Knew Too Much: Hitchcock and Feminist Theory*, New York, 1988.
Thomas, Tony, *A Wonderful Life: The Films and Career of James Stewart*, Secaucus, New Jersey, 1988.
Finler, Joel W., *Hitchcock in Hollywood*, New York, 1992.
Sterritt, David, *The Films of Alfred Hitchcock*, New York, 1993.
Arginteanu, Judy, *The Movies of Alfred Hitchcock*, Minneapolis, 1994.
Boyd, David, editor, *Perspectives on Alfred Hitchcock*, New York, 1995.
Auiler, Dan, *Hitchcock's Notebooks: An Authorized and Illustrated Look Inside the Creative Mind of Alfred Hitchcock*, New York, 1999.
Freedman, Jonathan, and Richard Millington, editors, *Hitchcock's America*, New York, 1999.
Harris, Robert A., *Complete Films of Alfred Hitchcock*, Secaucus, New Jersey, 1999.

Articles:

Sondheim, Steve, in *Films in Review* (New York), October 1954.
May, Derwent, in *Sight and Sound* (London), October-December 1954.
Borneman, Ernest, in *Films and Filming* (London), November 1954.
Arland, R. M., in *Arts* (Paris), 6 April 1955.
Garson, G., in *Cahiers du Cinéma* (Paris), April 1955.
Chabrol, Claude, in *Télécíné* (Paris), May-June 1955.
Positif (Paris), November 1955.
''Hitchcock Issue'' of *Cahiers du Cinéma* (Paris), August-September 1956.
Pett, John, in *Films and Filming* (London), November and December 1959.
Douchet, Jean, ''Hitch and His Public,'' in *New York Film Bulletin*, no. 7, 1961.
Agel, Alfred, ''Alfred Hitchcock,'' in *New York Film Bulletin*, no. 15, 1961.
Higham, Charles, ''Hitchcock's World,'' in *Film Quarterly* (Berkeley), December 1962-January 1963.
Sweigert, William R., ''James Stewart,'' in *Films in Review* (New York), December 1964.
Sonbert, Warren, ''Alfred Hitchcock: Master of Morality,'' in *Film Culture* (New York), Summer 1966.
Hitchcock, Alfred, in *Take One* (Montreal), December 1968.
Scarrone, C., in *Filmcritica* (Florence), January 1981.
Delpeut, P., and E. Kuyper, in *Skrien* (Amsterdam), September 1981.
''Hitchcock Issue'' of *Camera/Stylo* (Paris), November 1981.
Stam, R., and R. Pearson, ''Hitchcock's *Rear Window*: Reflexivity and the Critique of Voyeurism,'' in *Enclitic* (Minneapolis), Spring 1983.
Strick, Philip, in *Films and Filming* (London), November 1983.

Wood, Robin, ''Fear of Spying,'' in *American Film* (Washington, D.C.), November 1983.

Chion, M., ''Le Quatrième Côte,'' in *Cahiers du Cinéma* (Paris), February 1984.

Jenkins, Steve, ''Hitchcock [x] 2: Refocusing the Spectator,'' in *Monthly Film Bulletin* (London), February 1984.

Magny, Joel, in *Cinéma* (Paris), February 1984.

Kehr, Dave, ''Hitch's Riddle,'' in *Film Comment* (New York), June 1984.

Aubenas, J., in *Revue Belge du Cinéma* (Brussels), Autumn 1984.

Duval, B., and R. Lefèvre, ''Hitchcock Dossier,'' in *Revue du Cinéma* (Paris), January 1985.

Perlmutter, Ruth, ''*Rear Window*: A 'Construction-Story,''' in *Journal of Film and Video* (River Forest, Illinois), Spring 1985.

Palmer, R. Barton, ''The Metafictional Hitchcock: The Experience of Viewing and the Viewing of Experience in *Rear Window* and *Psycho*,'' in *Cinema Journal* (Champaign, Illinois), Winter 1986.

Miller, G., ''Beyond the Frame: Hitchcock, Art and the Ideal,'' in *Post Script* (Jacksonville, Florida), Winter 1986.

Allen, Jeanne T., and R. Barton Palmer, ''Dialogue on Spectatorship,'' in *Cinema Journal* (Champaign, Illinois), Summer 1986.

Harris, Thomas, ''*Rear Window* and *Blow Up*: Hitchcock's Straightforwardness vs Antonioni's Ambiguity,'' in *Literature/Film Quarterly* (Salisbury, Maryland), vol. 15, no. 1, 1987.

Atkinson, D., ''Hitchcock's Techniques Tell *Rear Window* Story,'' in *American Cinematographer* (Hollywood), January 1990.

Weinstock, J., ''5 Minutes to Alexanderplatz,'' in *Camera Obscura* (Bloomington, Indiana), September 1991.

Smith, J., ''The Strange Case of Lars Thorwald: Rounding Up the Usual Suspect in *Rear Window*,'' in *New Orleans Review*, no. 2, 1992.

Leconte, B., ''Fenetre sur film,'' in *Review du Cinéma* (Paris), July-August 1992.

Odabashian, B., ''The Unspeakable Crime in Hitchcock's *Rear Window:* Hero as Lay Detective, Spectator as Lay Analyst,'' in *Hitchcock Annual* (Gambier, Ohio), Fall 1993.

Reid's Film Index (Wyong), no. 13, 1994.

Mooney, J., ''Grace Kelly in *Rear Window*,'' in *Movieline* (Escondido), vol. 7, January/February 1996.

Garmon, Ronald Dale, ''Stalking the Blue-Chip Nightmare: The Two Legacies of Cornell Woolrich,'' in *Scarlet Street* (Glen Rock, New Jersey), no. 21, Winter 1996.

Valley, Richard, ''The Hayes Office: John Michael Hayes,'' in *Scarlet Street* (Glen Rock, New Jersey), no. 21, Winter 1996.

Stempel, Tom, ''*Rear Window*: A John Michael Hayes Film,'' in *Creative Screenwriting* (Washington, D.C.), vol. 4, no. 4, 1997.

Ehrlich, L.C., ''Courtyards of Shadow and Light,'' in *Cinemaya* (New Delhi), no. 37, Summer 1997.

Mogg, K., ''*Rear Window* in the News,'' in *Macguffin* (East Melbourne), no. 23, November 1997.

Care, Ross, ''Rear Window: The Music of Sound,'' in *Scarlet Street* (Glen Rock, New Jersey), no. 37, 2000.

* * *

In his article on ''Film Production'' for the 1968 *Encyclopaedia Britannica* Alfred Hitchcock gave the following example of ''pure cinema:'' ''Show a man looking at something, say a baby. Then show him smiling. By placing these shots in sequence—man looking, object seen, reaction to object—the director characterizes the man as a kindly person. Retain shot one (the look) and shot three (the smile) and substitute for the baby a girl in a bathing costume, and the director has changed the characterization of the man.'' In these terms, his 1954 film, *Rear Window*, would be a sustained exercise in pure cinema. It is a film about the power, the pleasure, and the moral (and even physical) danger inherent in the shot/countershot alternation Hitchcock takes to be at the heart of cinematic representation. His protagonist, the news photographer L. B. Jeffries (James Stewart), confined to a wheelchair with a broken leg, experiences alternately the thrills and fears of a filmmaker and a moviegoer as he unravels a murder story from the fragmentary evidence he manages to glimpse from the rear window of his second storey apartment.

Hitchcock had an unusually large set constructed to represent the interior courtyard of a New York City apartment complex in a lower middle-class neighborhood. The array of characters visible to the peeping Jeffries exteriorize the tensions and dynamics of his sexual fantasies. They are known to us by the names he assigns them: Miss Torso, a scantily dressed dancer attracts his prurient interest as she exercises or entertains her many suitors; the Newlyweds carry on behind a drawn shade, but when the husband appears at the window for a respite his insatiable wife calls him back for more activity; a middle-aged Miss Lonelyhearts comes to the verge of suicide in her failure to find a suitable companion; an older couple sleep on the fire escape hot summer nights, head to foot; a father is briefly seen dressing his very young daughter. At opposite ends of the courtyard are two artists, of image and sound, corresponding to the two tracks of a film. A middle-aged woman at one side makes modernist sculpture: her annular creation, *Hunger*, suggests sexual as well as gastronomic need. Her opposite is a young male composer of songs, who drinks too much until his music brings him together with Miss Lonelyhearts.

In the center of this psychic microcosm, a row of windows like a strip of cinematic frames looks in on the apartment of the unhappily married Lars Thorwald (Raymond Burr) and his bedridden wife. When Mrs. Thorwald disappears, Jeffries convinces himself, his doting girlfriend, Lisa (Grace Kelly), and eventually his visiting nurse, Stella (Thelma Ritter), that Thorwald has murdered her, dismembered her body in the bath-tub, buried some of her limbs in the courtyard, and mailed the rest in a trunk.

Most of the drama is concentrated in the confines of Jeffries's small apartment. Lisa, an affluent fashion designer, is so eager to get a permanent commitment from the reluctant Jeffries that she has his meals catered from the Stork Club, and ignores his discouragement when she comes to spend the night in the apartment. Stella, a voice of earthy common sense, insists that there must be something wrong with Jeffries to reject the attention of someone like Lisa. Although she puts up a formidable resistance to his ''ghoulish'' fascination with the Thorwalds, she too enters his fantasy and joins Lisa in a hunt for limbs under flower beds in the yard.

Behind the witty comedy of Lisa's seductions and Stella's homely analogies, Hitchcock explores the sexual trauma at the core of Jeffries's fear of marriage as if it were linked to the scopophiliac pleasure involved in film-viewing. As Jeffries becomes engrossed with the evidence of his murder story, he uses his large telephoto lens to get close-up views of Thorwald's rooms. The changes of lenses indicates an optical erection. Lisa instinctually recognizes that the way to Jeffries's heart is through his eyes. She calls her overnight lingerie a ''preview of coming attractions.'' She threatens to rent a back apartment and do Salome's dance of the seven veils unless he pays more attention to her. When threats and enticements fail, she actually enters his fantasy, first digging with Stella in the yard, then climbing into Thorwald's apartment, when he is out, to find incriminating evidence: his wife's ring. Thorwald catches her in the act, but Jeffries saves her by telephoning the police.

Significantly, it is when she signals to Jeffries that she has found the ring—by putting it on her finger and waving it behind her back toward his window—that Thorwald triangulates the view and thus spots Jeffries as a mortal threat. This is the moment when Lisa's fantasy, symbolized by the wearing of the ring, coincides with Jeffries's masochistic excitement at seeing her gravely threatened. Thorwald then breaks the cinematic analogy by looking directly at Jeffries, as if an actor could see a spectator.

Within the psychodynamics of the film as well as the rules of the genre, this is the beginning of the inevitable denouement. Once the immobile Jeffries becomes the potential victim his identification with Mrs. Thorwald is complete. His latent fantasy of being the victim of male aggression comes to the fore, and the Oedipal nature of his erotic confusion is underlined by his last minute efforts to blind temporarily the attacking Thorwald with flashes of his camera lights.

Jeffries survives the attacks with another broken leg, whereby Hitchcock suggests that his fantasy is doomed to repetition. A series of black jokes about the limb the police have recovered culminates in a Freudian topos: they have it in a hatbox. This body part which we never see, but seek through the second half of the film, is both Mrs. Thorwald's head and imaginatively her castrated phallus; for the latter fantasy is central to Jeffries's voyeurism and his fear of women.

—P. Adams Sitney

REBEL WITHOUT A CAUSE

USA, 1955

Director: Nicholas Ray

Production: Warner Bros. Pictures, Inc.; Warnercolor, 35mm, Cinemascope; running time: 111 minutes. Released 1955. Filmed in 9 weeks in 1955.

Producer: David Weisbart; **screenplay:** Stewart Stern, from an adaptation by Irving Shulman of a storyline by Nicholas Ray inspired from the story ''The Blind Run''; **title:** from a book by Dr. Robert M. Lindner (1944); **photography:** Ernest Haller; **editor:** William Ziegler; **production designer:** William Wallace; **music:** Leonard Rosenman.

Cast: James Dean (*Jim Stark*); Natalie Wood (*Judy*); Jim Backus (*Jim's father*); Ann Doran (*Jim's mother*); Rochelle Hudson (*Judy's mother*); William Hopper (*Judy's father*); Sal Mineo (*Plato*); Corey Allen (*Buzz*); Dennis Hopper (*Goon*); Ed Platt (*Ray*); Steffi Sydney (*Mil*); Marietta Canty (*Plato's nursemaid*); Virginia Brissac (*Jim's grandmother*); Beverly Long (*Helen*); Frank Mazzola (*Crunch*); Robert Foulk (*Gene*); Jack Simmons (*Cookie*); Nick Adams (*Moose*).

Publications

Script:

Stern, Stewart, *Rebel Without a Cause*, in *Best American Screenplays*, edited by Sam Thomas, New York, 1986.

Books:

Bast, William, *James Dean: A Biography*, New York, 1956.
Thomas, T. T., *I, James Dean*, New York, 1957.
Backus, Jim, *Rocks on the Roof*, New York, 1958.
Whittman, Mark, *The Films of James Dean*, London, 1974.
Dalton, David, *James Dean—The Mutant King*, San Francisco, 1974.
Herndon, Venable, *James Dean—A Short Life*, New York, 1974.
Kreidl, John, *Nicholas Ray*, Boston, 1977.
McGee, Mark Thomas, and R.J. Robertson, *The JD Films: Juvenile Delinquency in the Movies*, Jefferson, North Carolina, 1982.
Masi, Stefano, *Nicholas Ray*, Florence, 1983.
Morrissey, Steven, *James Dean Is Not Dead*, Manchester, 1983.
Blaine, Allan, *Nicholas Ray: A Guide to References and Resources*, Boston, 1984.
Dalton, David, and Ron Cayen, *James Dean: American Icon*, London, 1984.
Hillier, Jim, editor, *Cahiers du Cinéma 1: Neo-Realism, Hollywood, New Wave*, London, 1985.
Beath, Warren Newton, *The Death of James Dean*, London, 1986.
Erice, Victor, and Jos Oliver, *Nicholas Ray y su tiempo*, Madrid, 1986.
Wilson, George M., *Narration in Light: Studies in Cinematic Point-of-View*, Baltimore, Maryland, 1986.
Giuliani, Pierre, *Nicholas Ray*, Paris, 1987.
Wagner, Jean, *Nicholas Ray*, Paris, 1987.
Grob, Norbert, and Manuela Reichart, *Ray*, Berlin, 1989.
Parker, John, *Five for Hollywood*, Secaucus, New Jersey, 1991.
Eisenschitz, Bernard, *Nicholas Ray: An American Journey*, translated by Tom Milne, London, 1993.
McCann, Graham, *Rebel Males: Clift, Brando, and Dean*, New Brunswick, New Jersey, 1993.
Alexander, Paul, *Boulevard of Broken Dreams: The Life, Times, and Legend of James Dean*, New York, 1994.
Hofstede, David, *James Dean: A Bio-Bibliography*, Westport, Connecticut, 1996.
Spoto, Donald, *Rebel*, New York, 1997.
Tanitch, R., *James Dean the Actor*, London, 1999.

Articles:

Archer, Eugene, ''Generation Without a Cause,'' in *Film Culture* (New York), no. 7, 1956.
''Portrait de l'acteur en jeune homme,'' in *Cahiers du Cinéma* (Paris), no. 66, 1956.
Houston, Penelope, ''Rebels Without Causes,'' in *Sight and Sound* (London), Spring 1956.
Ray, Nicholas, ''Story into Script,'' in *Sight and Sound* (London), Autumn 1956.
Cole, Clayton, ''The Dean Myth,'' in *Films and Filming* (London), January 1957.
Houston, Penelope, and John Gillett, ''Conversations with Nicholas Ray and Joseph Losey,'' in *Sight and Sound* (London), Autumn 1961.

Rebel Without a Cause

Kempton, Murray, ''Mother, Men and the Muse,'' in *Show* (Hollywood), March 1962.
Walters, R., ''Enhancement of Punitive Behavior by Audio-Visual Displays,'' in *Science*, 8 June 1962.
Bean, Robin, ''Dean—10 Years After,'' in *Films and Filming* (London), October 1965.
''*La Fureur de vivre*,'' in *Arts et Spectacles* (Paris), 15 May 1967.
Godfrey, Lionel, ''Because They're Young—Parts I and II,'' in *Films and Filming* (London), October and November 1967.
Kael, Pauline, in *New Yorker*, 3 October 1970.
Perkins, Victor, ''The Cinema of Nicholas Ray,'' in *Movie Reader*, edited by Ian Cameron, New York, 1972.
Rosenbaum, Jonathan, ''Circle of Pain: The Cinema of Nicholas Ray,'' in *Sight and Sound* (London), Autumn 1973.
Biskind, Peter, ''Rebel without a Cause: Nicholas Ray in the Fifties,'' in *Film Quarterly* (Berkeley), Fall 1974.
Lardinois, J. M., in *Apec-Revue Belge du Cinéma* (Brussels), no. 1, 1975.
McVay, D., in *Films and Filming* (London), August 1977.
Pedersen, B. T., ''Nicholas Ray, nattens diktare,'' in *Chaplin* (Stockholm), vol. 21, no. 6, 1979.
Thomson, D., in *Take One* (Montreal), no. 4, 1979.
Cinema (Bucharest), March 1979.
Fox, Terry, ''Nicholas Ray, Without a Cause,'' in *Village Voice* (New York), 9 July 1979.
Boyero, C., in *Casablanca* (Madrid), May 1981.
Bíró, G., in *Filmkultura* (Budapest), January-February 1982.
Nielsen, Ray, ''Corey Allen in *Rebel Without a Cause*,'' in *Classic Images* (Muscatine), no. 216, June 1993.
Smith, J., ''The Sound Track,'' in *Films in Review* (New York), vol. 45, March/April 1994.
Beller, J.L., ''The Radical Imagination in American Film,'' in *Creative Screenwriting* (Washington, D.C.), vol. 1, no. 4, Winter 1994.
Village Voice (New York), 2 May 1995.
Simmons, Jerrold, ''The Censoring of *Rebel Without a Cause*,'' in *Journal of Popular Film and Television* (Washington, D.C.), vol. 23, no. 2, Summer 1995.
Glatzer, Richard, ''Daddy Cool,'' in *Sight & Sound* (London), vol. 5, no. 8, August 1995.
Valley, Richard, ''Character Actress: Ann Doran,'' in *Scarlet Street* (Glen Rock, New Jersey), no. 17, Winter 1995.
Lilley, Jessie, ''Night Rebel: Jack Grinnage,'' in *Scarlet Street* (Glen Rock, New Jersey), no. 17, Winter 1995.

Braudy, L, "'No Body's Perfect': Method Acting and 50s Culture," in *Michigan Quarterly Review*, vol. 35, no. 1, 1996.

Thomson, D., "Ten Films That Showed Hollywood How to Live," in *Movieline* (Escondido), vol. 8, July 1997.

Paulin, S.D., "Unheard Sexualities? Queer Theory and the Soundtrack," in *Spectator* (Los Angeles), vol. 17, no. 2, 1997.

* * *

In an overheated moment part-way through Laslo Benedek's 1953 film *The Wild One*, Johnny (Marlon Brando) responds to the question "What are you rebelling against?" with "Watcha got?" That film detailed the restless rebellion of two motorcycle gangs, one bent on havoc, the other on less violent forms of social rebellion, and in Johnny lay the seed of many a Hollywood rebel, the pose of many an aspiring Hollywood actor, and the essence of a new breed of teenager. The following year, two films were released that immediately secured a position for their star as spokesperson for and icon of America's frustrated youth. In both *East of Eden* and *Rebel Without a Cause* James Dean embodied a restless youngster unable to cope with his future because of the insecurity of the present and the failings of his parents. Unlike Johnny, his anger was still internalized, waiting for the moment of explosion. As director Nicolas Ray said: "When you first see Jimmy in his red jacket against his black Merc, it's not just a pose. It's a warning. It's a sign."

Ever in sympathy with the outsider, Ray fashioned a modern Romeo and Juliet story, a romance set among teenagers seeking satisfaction outside the traditional systems, misunderstood by their parents, misunderstanding and mistrusting of their parents' values. Soon America would explode with the sound of rock 'n roll, and teens would find a form of social rebellion that was non-violent but nonetheless highly charged. Ray caught both the immediate and timeless qualities of frustrated adolescence.

A plea for understanding of the day's younger generation, *Rebel Without a Cause* focused on three youngsters: Plato, whose divorced parents had abandoned him; Judy, who felt her father had withdrawn his love; and Jim, the offspring of a domineering mother and henpecked father. Disenchanted with their own families, these three alienated individuals sought a new sense of family, Plato and Judy looking to Jim as the head of the new unit. Unlike many of the teen rebel films which followed, *Rebel* placed a blame on the parents rather than the teens; teens were unbalanced by parents rather than the reverse.

The main action of the film is compressed into one day, a day in which Jim moves from confusion to a possible sense of clarity, from wanting to be a man to the beginning stages of becoming one. After going through the various initiation rights into manhood—knife fight, chicken run, girlfriend, homosexual advance, drinking, etc.—Jim begins to realize that perhaps responsibility for his life rests within himself. The end of the film, in which he asserts independence and self-determination rings slightly optimistic and therefore false, making the spectator wonder whether Jim has been liberated or tamed. If Jim-as-a-rebel refers to his status at the beginning of the film, what is his status after Plato's death?

In this, his first film in Cinemascope, Nicholas Ray signalled his reputation as the American master in the format. Having studied on a Frank Lloyd Wright scholarship, Ray had a clearly defined sense of spatial relations, an ability which made much of his film noir work especially charged. In his Cinemascope features he developed an aesthetic of the horizontal which, particularly in *Rebel Without a Cause*, lent a sensuality to the images of alienation. If this feeling pervaded exteriors, a sense of claustrophobia permeated the spatial tensions of the cluttered interiors.

Ray is also just beginning his metaphorical use of color in this film. Originally begun in black and white, *Rebel* was changed to color while in production, and Ray began to code his characters through changes in costume. Among the obvious examples are Plato's wearing of one black and one red sock, signalling his confusion, Jim's move from neutral browns to his bright red jacket, Judy's move from red to soft pink.

Ray's ability to elicit strong performances is a key to the successes of his best films. Having trained as an actor and having come to film through a friendship and apprenticeship with Elia Kazan, he was particularly attuned to the problems and the practices of performance. Previously he had worked in close collaboration with Humphrey Bogart for the actor's production company (Santana Films) on both *Knock on Any Door* and *In a Lonely Place*, and on *Rebel Without a Cause* he included Dean in the decisions of production. As actor Jim Backus wrote in his autobiography, Dean was practically the co-director of *Rebel*. Ray and Dean were so compatible that they had planned to collaborate on a second project on which Dean would serve as both actor and producer while Ray continued to direct (a project that was never realized because of Dean's death). Ray was later to establish that relationship with James Mason on *Bigger Than Life*.

Like Nick Romano in *Knock on Any Door* and Bowie in *They Live By Night*, Jim Stark is a misunderstood teenager seeking a better deal before it is too late. His gestures are those of alienation and pressurized anxiety, his overheated condition and need to cool down or explode best visualized by the scene in which he sensually presses a cold bottle of milk to his cheek. As much as any, that image became both a warning and a prediction.

—Doug Tomlinson

THE RED AND THE WHITE

See **CSILLAGOSAK, KATONAK**

RED PSALM

See **MEG KER A NEP**

RED RIVER

USA, 1948

Director: Howard Hawks

Production: Monterey Productions; black and white, 35mm; running time: 125 minutes, some sources list 133 minutes. Released 1948.

Red River

Filmed in 85 days. An extract of the film is featured in *The Last Picture Show* directed by Peter Bogdanovich.

Producers: Charles K. Feldman with Howard Hawks; **screenplay:** Borden Chase and Charles Schnee, from the story ''The Chisholm Trail'' by Borden Chase; **photography:** Russell Harlan; **editor:** Christian Nyby; **sound:** Richard de Weese and Vinton Vernon; **art director:** John Datu Arensma; **musical director:** Dimitri Tiomkin; **special effects:** Donald Stewart and Allan Thompson.

Cast: John Wayne (*Thomas Dunson*); Montgomery Clift (*Matthew Garth*); Joanne Dru (*Tess Millay*); Walter Brennan (*Groot Nadine*); Coleen Gray (*Fen*); John Ireland (*Cherry Valence*); Noah Beery, Jr. (*Buster*); Harry Carey, Jr. (*Dan Latimer*); Mickey Kuhn (*Matt as an infant*); Paul Fix (*Teeler*); Hank Worden (*Slim*); Ivan Parry (*Bunk Kenneally*); Hal Taliaferro (*Old Leather*); Paul Fierro (*Fernandez*); Billie Self (*Cowboy*); Ray Hyke (*Walt Jergens*); Dan White (*Laredo*); Tom Tyler (*Cowboy*); Glenn Strange (*Naylor*); Lane Chandler (*Colonel*); Joe Dominguez (*Mexican guard*); Shelley Winters (*Girl in wagon train*).

Publications

Books:

Bogdanovitch, Peter, *The Cinema of Howard Hawks*, New York, 1962.
Missiaen, Jean-Claude, *Howard Hawks*, Paris, 1966.
Wood, Robin, *Howard Hawks*, New York, 1968; revised edition, 1981.
Ricci, Mark, Boris Zmijewsky, and Steve Zmijewsky, *The Films of John Wayne*, New York, 1970; revised edition, as *The Complete Films of John Wayne*, Secaucus, New Jersey, 1983.
Bazin, André, *What Is Cinema 2*, Berkeley, 1971.
Gili, Jean A., *Howard Hawks*, Paris, 1971.
Cameron, Ian, editor, *Movie Reader*, London, 1972.
McBride, Joseph, editor, *Focus on Howard Hawks*, Englewood Cliffs, New Jersey, 1975.
Willis, D. C., *The Films of Howard Hawks*, Metuchen, New Jersey, 1975.
Parish, James Robert, and Michael Pitts, *The Great Western Pictures*, Metuchen, New Jersey, 1976.
LaGuardia, Robert, *Monty: A Biography of Montgomery Clift*, New York, 1977.

Bosworth, Patricia, *Montgomery Clift: A Biography*, New York, 1978.
Murphy, Kathleen A., *Howard Hawks: An American Auteur in the Hemingway Tradition*, Ann Arbor, Michigan, 1978.
Eyles, Allen, *John Wayne*, South Brunswick, New Jersey, 1979.
O'Connor, John E., and Martin A. Jackson, *American History/ American Film: Interpreting the Hollywood Image*, New York, 1979.
Ciment, Michael, *Les Conquérants d'un nouveau monde: Essais sur le cinéma américain*, Paris, 1981.
Giannetti, Louis, *Masters of the American Cinema*, Englewood Cliffs, New Jersey, 1981.
Kass, Judith, *The Films of Montgomery Clift*, Secaucus, New Jersey, 1981.
McBridge, Joseph, *Hawks on Hawks*, Berkeley, 1982.
Mast, Gerald, *Howard Hawks, Storyteller*, New York, 1982.
Poague, Leland, *Howard Hawks*, Boston, 1982.
Simsolo, Noël, *Howard Hawks*, Paris, 1984.
Kieskalt, Charles John, *The Official John Wayne Reference Book*, Secaucus, New Jersey, 1985.
Shepherd, Donald, and others, *Duke: The Life and Times of John Wayne*, London, 1985.
Branson, Clark, *Howard Hawks: A Jungian Study*, Los Angeles, 1987.
Lepper, David, *John Wayne*, London, 1987.
Buscombe, Ed, editor, *BFI Companion to the Western*, London, 1988.
Levy, Emanuel, *John Wayne: Prophet of the American Way of Life*, Metuchen, New Jersey, 1988.
Riggin, Judith M., *John Wayne: A Bio-Bibliography*, New York, 1992.
Fagen, Herb, *Duke, We're Glad We Knew You: John Wayne's Friends and Colleagues Remember His Remarkable Life*, New York, 1996.
Hillier, Jim, *Howard Hawks: American Artist*, Champaign, Illinois, 1997.
McCarthy, Todd, *Howard Hawks: The Grey Fox of Hollywood*, New York, 1997.
Roberts, Randy, *John Wayne: American*, Lincoln, Nebraska, 1997.

Articles:

Variety (New York), 14 July 1948.
New York Times, 1 October 1948
New Yorker, 9 October 1948.
Perez, Michel, ''Howard Hawks et le western,'' in *Présence du Cinéma* (Paris), July-September 1959.
Sarris, Andrew, ''The World of Howard Hawks,'' in *Films and Filming* (London), July and August 1962.
''Hawks Issue'' of *Cahiers du Cinéma* (Paris), January 1963.
Roman, Robert, ''Montgomery Clift,'' in *Films in Review* (New York), November 1966.
Austen, David, ''Gunplay and Horses,'' in *Films and Filming* (London), October 1968.
Brode, Douglas, in *Cineaste* (New York), Fall 1968.
Hall, Dennis John, ''Tall in the Saddle,'' in *Films and Filming* (London), October 1969.
Goodwin, Michael, and Naomi Wise, ''An Interview with Howard Hawks,'' in *Take One* (Montreal), November-December 1971.
''Hawks Issue'' of *Filmkritik* (Munich), May-June 1973.
McBridge, Jim,''Hawks Talks: New Anecdotes from the Old Master,'' in *Film Comment* (New York), May-June 1974.
Tiroiu, A., in *Cinema* (Bucharest), September 1974.
Belton, J., in *Movietone News* (Seattle), 11 October 1976.
Bourget, Jean-Loup, ''Hawks et le mythe de l'ouest américain,'' in *Positif* (Paris), July-August 1977.
Thomson, D., ''All Along the River,'' in *Sight and Sound* (London), Winter 1976–77.
Sklar, Robert, ''*Red River*: Empire to the West,'' in *Cineaste* (New York), Fall 1978.
Ramirez Berg, Charles, in *Cinema Texas Program Notes* (Austin), 14 February 1979.
Reeder, R., *et al.*, ''Conflict of Interpretations: A Special Section on *Red River* by Howard Hawks,'' in Ciné-Tracts (Montreal), Spring 1980.
Marias, M., in *Casablanca* (Madrid), July-August 1981.
Lippe, R., ''Montgomery Clift: A Critical Disturbance,'' in *Cineaction* (Toronto), Summer 1989.
Cahiers du Cinéma (Paris), no. 494, September 1995.
O'Brien, Stella Ruzycki, ''Leaving Behind *The Chisholm Trail* for *Red River*: Or Refiguring the Female in the Western Film Epic,'' in *Literature/Film Quarterly* (Salisbury, Maryland), vol. 24, no. 2, April 1996.
Aachen, G., in *Reid's Film Index* (Wyong), no. 23, 1996.
Premiere (Boulder, Colorado), vol. 11, no. 5, January 1998.

* * *

Red River is a film about a cattle drive. To depict this story of Texas cattlemen driving thousands of cattle across thousands of miles northward to Kansas, Howard Hawks, the film's director, in effect recreated that original task to make the film. In both 1865, when the narrative was set, and 1946, when the film was shot, the epic task confronting a group of men was that of moving all those animals across all that space. The epic task is mirrored by the film's vast, epic shots of men, cattle, sky, and space.

The epic story is both a view of American history and a view of the American civilization as a successor to those of the past. Set just after the Civil War, the film's journey reaffirms and re-establishes the oneness of the American nation and the oneness of the American continent. The journey to bring Texas beef to the north reveals the conquest of space and distance to produce one whole nation. But this journey has a relation to Homeric epic as well as to American history, for, like the *Odyssey*, the film chronicles a vast and epic task in which the threatened dangers are external (in *Red River*, the threat is from Indian attack and cattle rustlers) but the real dangers are internal (in the will, the judgment, and the dedication of the travellers themselves, and in the tension between the leader and his followers).

In converting a sprawling serialized story by Borden Chase into his own taut film, Hawks chose a metaphoric title, *Red River*, which has little specific meaning in the story (crossing the Red River signifies the departure from the familiar homeland and the journey into the unknown) but which has obvious Biblical parallels to the epic journey of the Israelites in ''Exodus.'' Hawks anchors these epic and metaphoric suggestions with a sensitive psychological study of the journey's two leaders, Thomas Dunson, the older man who founded the cattle spread in 1851, and Matthew Garth, his adopted son. In the role of Dunson, Hawks cast John Wayne, giving Wayne the kind of role that became indistinguishable from his own persona for three decades—tough, hard, absolutely committed to accomplishing the task before him no matter what the cost, old but not too old to get a tough job done, bull-headed but bound by personal codes of duty, honor, and morality. Opposite Wayne, Hawks cast the young Montgomery Clift in his first film role. The contrast between the sensitive ''soft,'' almost beautifully handsome Clift and the hard, determined, indomitable Wayne not only provides the essential psychological contrast required for the film's narrative but also provides two brilliant and brilliantly contrasted acting styles for the film's dramatic tension.

In the film's narrative, the more supple leader, Garth, replaces the unbending Dunson when the inflexible older man's decisions threaten the success of the enterprise. Dunson vows to take revenge on Garth for this ouster, and the climax of the film, after Garth has successfully delivered the cattle to market, promises a gun battle between the vengeful Dunson and his own spiritual son. In what has become the most controversial issue about the film, that gun battle never takes place. While some see Hawks's avoidance of the climactic duel as some kind of pandering to Hollywood taste. Hawks has carefully built into his narrative pattern the terms that guarantee that a man with Dunson's sense of honor and morality could never kill a man who does not intend to kill him first. Matthew Garth demonstrates he could never kill his ''father,'' and Dunson, despite his previous verbal threats and his unswerving commitment to his word, could never kill the ''son'' who loves him. As is typical of a Hawks film, beneath the superficial talk the two men love one another, and they demonstrate that love by what they do rather than what they say.

—Gerald Mast

THE RED SHOES

UK, 1948

Directors: Michael Powell and Emeric Pressburger

Production: The Archers; Technicolor; running time: 136 minutes; length: 12,209 feet. Released July 1948.

Producers: Michael Powell and Emeric Pressburger; **screenplay:** Emeric Pressburger; **photography:** Jack Cardiff; **editor:** Reginald Mills; **production designer:** Hein Heckroth; **art director:** Arthur Lawson; **choreography:** Robert Helpmann; **music:** Brian Easdale, performed by Royal Philharmonic Orchestra conducted by Sir Thomas Beecham.

Cast: Marius Goring (*Julian Craster*); Jean Short (*Terry*); Gordon Littman (*Ike*); Julia Lang (*A Balletomane*); Bill Shine (*Her Mate*); Leonide Massine (*Ljubov*); Anton Walbrook (*Boris Lermontov*); Austin Trevor (*Professor Palmer*); Eric Berry (*Dimitri*); Irene Browne (*Lady Neston*); Moira Shearer (*Victoria Page*); Ludmilla Tcherina (*Boronskaja*); Robert Helpmann (*Ivan Boleslawsky*); Albert Basserman (*Ratov*).

Awards: Oscars for Best Color Art Direction and Best Drama Music Score, 1948.

Publications

Books:

Franks, A. H., *Ballet for Film and Television*, London, 1950.

Durgnat, Raymond, *A Mirror for England: British Movies from Austerity to Affluence*, London, 1970.

Armes, Roy, *A Critical History of the British Cinema*, London, 1978.

Christie, Ian, editor, *Powell, Pressburger, and Others*, London, 1978.

Cosandey, Roland, editor, *Retrospective: Powell and Pressburger*, Locarno, 1982.

Gottler, Fritz, and others, *Living Cinema: Powell and Pressburger*, Munich, 1982.

Christie, Ian *Arrows of Desire: The Films of Michael Powell and Emeric Pressburger*, London, 1985, 1994.

Martini, Emanuela, editor, *Powell and Pressburger*, Bergamo, 1986.

Powell, Michael, *A Life in Movies: An Autobiography*, London, 1986.

Murphy, Robert, *Realism and Tinsel: British Cinema and Society 1939–48*, London, 1989.

Cintra Ferreira, Manuel, *Michael Powell*, Lisbon, 1992.

MacDonald, Kevin, *Emeric Pressburger: The Life and Death of a Screenwriter*, London, 1994.

Howard, James, *Michael Powell*, London, 1996.

Salwolke, Scott, *Films of Michael Powell and the Archers*, Lanham, Maryland, 1997.

Articles:

Williamson, Andrew, ''Filming *Red Shoes*,'' in *The Dancing Times* (London), January 1948.

Kine Weekly (London), 22 July 1948.

Lejeune, C. A., in *Observer* (London), 25 July 1948.

Monthly Film Bulletin (London), August 1948.

Variety (New York), 4 August 1948.

Sight and Sound (London), Autumn 1948.

New York Times, 23 October 1948.

Lightman, Herb, in *American Cinematographer* (Los Angeles), March 1949.

Taylor, John Russell, ''Michael Powell: Myths and Supermen,'' in *Sight and Sound* (London), Autumn 1978.

Everson, William K., ''Michael Powell,'' in *Films in Review* (New York), August-September 1980.

Thomson, David, ''The Films of Michael Powell: A Romantic Sensibility,'' in *American Film* (Washington, D.C.), November 1980.

Everson, William K., in *MOMA Program Notes* (New York), 29 November 1980.

McVay, Douglas, ''Cinema of Enchantment: The Films of Michael Powell,'' in *Films and Filming* (London), December 1981.

Percival, John, in *The Times* (London), 21 July 1982.

Anderson, Jack, in *New York Times*, 27 September 1984.

Blanchet, C., in *Cinema* (Paris), November 1984.

Tobin, Yann, in *Positif* (Paris), March 1985.

Fraser, Peter, ''The Musical Movie: Putting on the Red Shoes,'' in *Cinema Journal* (Champaign, Illinois), Spring 1987.

The Red Shoes

Benson, Sheila, in *Film Comment* (New York), May-June 1990.

Holthof, M., ''*The Red Shoes*,'' in *Sinema*, no. 102, March/April 1991.

Harris, W., ''Revamp *The Red Shoes*?'' in *New York Times*, vol. 143, section 2, 31 October 1993.

Kelly, D., ''Filling *The Red Shoes*,'' *Dance Magazine*, vol. 67, November 1993.

Ostlere, H., ''Pursued by *The Red Shoes*,'' in *Dance Magazine*, vol. 67, November 1993.

Jacobs, Laura, ''*The Red Shoes* Revisited: An Appreciation of the Balletomane's Classic Film,'' in *Atlantic Monthly* (Boston), December 1993.

Cohn, E., in *Village Voice* (New York), vol. 39, 4 January 1994.

Backstein, K., ''A Second Look: *The Red Shoes*,'' in *Cineaste* (New York), vol. 20, no. 4, 1994.

Kass, Sarah A., ''Their Movies Were 'Beautiful Fantasies,''' in *The New York Times*, vol. 144, section 2, H25, 16 April 1995.

Elrick, Ted, ''The Day the Earth Freeze-Framed,'' in *DGA Magazine* (Los Angeles), vol. 20, no. 4, September-October 1995.

Erens, Patricia, ''A Childhood at the Cinema: Latency Fantasies, the Family Romance, and Juvenile Spectatorship,'' in *Wide Angle* (Baltimore), vol. 16, no. 4, October 1995.

Reid, J.H., in *Reid's Film Index* (Wyong), no. 31, 1997.

Turner, G., ''*The Red Shoes*: A Ballet for Camera,'' in *American Cinematographer* (Hollywood), vol. 79, February 1998.

* * *

The success of their previous collaborations, most notably *A Matter of Life and Death* and *Black Narcissus*, permitted Powell and Pressburger to make *The Red Shoes*, a ''ballet'' film, an ''art'' film whose commercial prospects were dim indeed. Powell describes the reaction of executives at an early screening: ''They . . . left the theatre without a word because they thought they had lost their shirts. They couldn't understand one word of it.'' *The Red Shoes* went on to critical acclaim and, less predictably, to sustained popularity with the public. The lushness of its colour-drenched images and its passion-drenched depiction of the characters were not, in themselves, the factors that determined the initial appeal. It was the dancing, the very thing that had made those executives so leery of the film's viability with something approaching mass audience.

As so often happens to films that are deliriously received, *The Red Shoes* later fell subject to revisionist readings that dismissed its plot as excessively melodramatic, its characters as absurdly overdrawn, even its depiction of the world of ballet as false. Although Powell and Pressburger have been canonized as filmmakers, and a number of their works subjected to the kind of analysis that is the warrant of seriousness, *The Red Shoes* has continued to be neglected, in the main, as an object of critical concern. *The Red Shoes* has suffered for its glamour and for its apparently simplistic, reductive tale of the beautiful ballerina torn between art and love. Yet it has been frequently revived and continues to exert its allure.

One of the primary keys to the persistent audience appeal of *The Red Shoes* is precisely the persistence (and the complexity) with which the film depicts audience appeal. From the opening sequence—the rush for seats to an evening of ballet at Covent Garden, the detailed reactions of the music students, the balletomanes, the aspiring ballerina, the snobbish impresario—to the climax—a performance of the ballet *The Red Shoes* in which the dead ballerina is represented by a spotlight, the film dramatizes a variety of responses to art, of connections to the performance of art. We find the range of our own experience as spectators echoed on the screen by the actors who play an array of dancers, musicians, and other creative members of a ballet troupe. Caught in the shifting points of view, we are given access to the expertise and the knowledge of those ''inside'' the world of ballet. The fervour of spectatorship, manifested by all the principal characters, is summed up in the obsessive gaze of the impresario, for whom art is a matter of life and death, a level of vision the film challenges us to meet. As we watch the ballet of *The Red Shoes*, staged with the illusionistic freedom afforded only by techniques of cinema, we are reminded of our privileged point-of-view as moviegoers.

We also come to believe the phrase reiterated throughout the course of the film: ''The music is all that matters. Nothing but the music.'' It is music that goes beyond the banalities of plot and character, that liberates the film from its dramatic conventions. It is music as wordless, storyless sensation that finds its analogy is the film's memorable images—the redhead in the long green dress climbing on interminable staircase on a hillside in the south of France, her precipitous descent down other staircases just before leaping to her death, the repeated gestures of the ballet in rehearsal and performance, the images of eyes watching in ecstatic concentration. These hyperboles of gesture and attitude, sometimes condemned, are the best proof of its success in finding a place in the sound film for the close affinities of the mimetic discourses of ballet and of silent cinema.

—Charles Affron

RED SORGHUM

(Hong gao liang)

People's Republic of China, 1988

Director: Zhang Yimou

Production: Xi An Film Studio; color, 35mm; running time: 91 minutes. Filmed 1987; released 1988.

Producer: Li Changqing; **screenplay:** Chen Jianyu, Zhu Wei, Mo Yen; **photography:** Gu Changwei; **editor:** Du Yuan; **art director:** Yang Gang; **music director:** Zhao Jiping.

Cast: Gong Li (*My Grandma*); Jing Wen (*My Grandpa*); Liu Ji (*Father, as child*); Teng Rijun (*Uncle Luohan*); Ji Chunhua (*Bandit*); Qian Ming; Zhai Chunhua.

Awards: Golden Bear Award, Berlin Film Festival, 1988; New York Film Festival Best Film Award, 1988.

Publications

Articles:

Kauffmann, Stanley, ''*Red Sorghum*'' (review), in *New Republic*, 17 October 1988.

Klawans, Stuart, ''Zhang Yimou: Local Hero,'' in *Film Comment*, September-October 1995.

Ye, Tan, ''From the Fifth to the Sixth Generation'' (interview), in *Film Quarterly*, Winter 1999.

* * *

When *Red Sorghum* was released in 1988, it attained immediate fame and success, both in its Chinese homeland and around the world. To the outside world, the film promised a rare view into a China just emerging from the protective isolationism that surrounded the Cultural Revolution of the 1960s and 1970s. To moviegoers inside the People's Republic, *Red Sorghum* marked a new kind of cinema and the beginning of a new generation of filmmakers.

Zhang Yimou, who directed *Red Sorghum*, was born in 1950, in the thick of the revolution. Like many others born into privileged families at that time, his higher education was factory labor, and his cultural entertainment consisted of government sponsored films and theatrical productions, which were usually simplistic, moralistic, and patriotic. Though Zhang was fascinated by film, and managed to buy his first camera while working in factories, he would be forever influenced by his disgust with the overtly propagandistic films of his youth. Later he would recall, ''When we were in film school, we swore to each other we would never make films like that.''

By 1982, the Beijing Film Academy, which had been closed during the Cultural Revolution, was reopened, and Zhang was part of the first post-Mao graduating class. It was the fifth class to ever graduate the Academy, giving Zhang and his classmates their sobriquet, the ''fifth generation'' of Chinese filmmakers. The fifth generation were not establishment filmmakers, but they gained international notice because of the moral complexity and gritty realism of their films.

Adapted from a novel by Mo Yan, *Red Sorghum* was one of the first of this new breed of Chinese film. Set mostly in the 1920s, the film is told in flashbacks from the point of view of a man recalling his grandparents' lives as they try, and finally fail, to protect their village winery from Japanese invaders. It is a lyrical film, which seems at times almost like an epic or folk tale, as it challenges repressive traditions such as the subjugation of women. Zhang, who was trained to be a cinematographer, has a sharp eye for the visual elements of his film and the color red—of the sorghum crop, the wine, the Chinese bridal dress, and blood—permeates the film. The red, red setting sun that ends the film might represent the flag of the Japanese conquerors, or simply the inevitable shortness of every human life.

Red Sorghum

Red Sorghum is a film of contradictions. Containing darkly comic elements, it is also a violent film; the villagers treat each other violently and the men treat women violently, but their violence pales compared to their treatment at the hands of the Japanese army. The reception of the film was itself contradictory. Director Zhang received ten thousand letters accusing him of treason when *Red Sorghum* was released, yet the movie houses showing the film in China were packed. A new generation of Chinese audiences were hungry for a film that expressed the moral ambiguity and the sense of chafing under authority that they themselves were beginning to feel.

After the release of *Red Sorghum*, Chinese leader Den Xiaoping increased the repression of Chinese intellectuals. Where *Red Sorghum* had been an accepted film that brought international awards home to China, Zhang's next films (*Ju Dou* and *Raise the Red Lantern*, for example) were banned in his own country, though they were popular around the world. In 1994, Zhang was forbidden to make films for five years.

Red Sorghum was a breakthrough to a new kind of filmmaking in China. It was also a bridge between China and the world outside it, from which it had been largely cut off during the years of the Cultural Revolution. Later, as the government cracked down, and the fifth generation filmmakers outgrew their youthful rebelliousness, Chinese film stepped back under a more comfortable umbrella of popular propaganda. But, thanks to films like *Red Sorghum*, the world outside China would never be shut out in the same way again.

—Tina Gianoulis

LOS REDES

(The Wave)

Mexico, 1936

Directors: Fred Zinnemann and Emilio Gómez Muriel

Production: Secretaria de Educación Púlica, Mexico; black and white, 35mm; running time: 65 minutes. Released 1936. Filmed beginning 9 April 1934, in natural settings in Alvarado, Tlacotalpan, and the mouth of the Papaloapan River. Cost: 55,000 pesos.

Producers: Carlos Chávez and Narciso Bassols; **scenario:** Agustín Velázquez Chávez and Paul Strand, adapted by Emilio Gómez Muriel, Fred Zinnemann, and Henwar Rodakiewicz; **photography:** Paul Strand; **editors:** Emilio Gómez Muriel with Gunther von Fritsch; **sound:** Roberto and Joselito Rodriguez; **music:** Silvestre Revueltas.

Cast: Silvio Hernández (*Miro*); David Valle González (*The packer*); Rafael Hinojosa (*The politician*); Antonio Lara (*El Zurdo*); Miguel Figueroa; and native fishermen.

Publications

Books:

Griffith, Richard, *Fred Zinnemann*, New York, 1958.

Garcia Riera, Emilio, *Historia documental del cine mexicano*, Mexico City, 1969.

Paul Strand: A Retrospective Monograph, The Years 1915–1946, and *The Years 1950–1968*, New York, 1971.

Barsam, Richard, *Nonfiction Film: A Critical History*, New York, 1971.

Mora, Carl J., *Mexican Cinema: Reflections of a Society, 1896–1980*, Berkeley, 1982.

Rausa, Giuseppe, *Fred Zinnemann*, Florence, 1985.

Goldau, Antje, and others, *Zinnemann*, Munich, 1986.

Zinnemann, Fred, *A Life in the Movies: An Autobiography*, New York, 1992.

Nolletti Jr., Arthur, editor, *The Films of Fred Zinnemann: Critical Perspectives*, Albany, New York, 1999.

Articles:

New York Times, 21 April 1937.

New Yorker, 24 April 1937.

Variety (New York), 28 April 1937.

Belitt, B., ''Camera Reconnoiters,'' in *Nation* (New York), 20 November 1937.

Chavez, Carlos, ''Films by American Government: Mexico,'' in *Films*, Summer 1940.

Cine (Mexico City), November 1978.

Gutierrez Heras, J., ''La musica de Silvestre Revueltas en el cine,'' in *Dicine*, no. 43, January 1992.

Zinnemann, F., ''Letter From Fred Zinnemann,'' in *Film Criticism* (Meadville), vol. 19, no. 2, 1994/1995.

Roud, R., ''Iz rezhisserskogo arkhiva,'' in *Iskusstvo Kino* (Moscow), no. 12, 1996.

Horton, Robert, ''Day of the Craftsman: Fred Zinnemann,'' in *Film Comment* (New York), vol. 33, no. 5, September-October 1997.

Neve, Brian, ''A Past Master of His Craft: An Interview with Fred Zinnemann,'' in *Cineaste* (New York), vol. 23, no. 1, Winter 1997.

* * *

A progenitor of the classical Mexican visual style, *Los Redes* is also one of the very few instances of genuine social criticism in the history of Mexican cinema. The fact that *Los Redes* was directed and photographed by foreigners is ironic as well as illustrative of a neocolonial tendency in Mexican films. *Los Redes* was born out the collaboration of Paul Strand, a photographer from New York who had come to Mexico to do a book of photos on the country, and two Mexicans: Carlos Chávez, the noted composer who occupied a government post at the time, and Narciso Bassols, a Marxist who was then the Secretary of Public Education. 1930–40 was the decade in which the social ideals of the Mexican Revolution (1910–17) achieved their greatest artistic and political expression. Many of the important murals were painted during this period, which was also the time of the expropriation of foreign oil companies and extensive land distribution by President Lazaro Cardenas. Bassols and Chávez desired to participate in this revolutionary process by financing films, which were to be ''with the people for the people,'' with government funds. In addition to Paul Strand, they hired a young Austrian, Fred Zinnemann (who later went on to a long distinguished career in Hollywood), to direct the film which was to portray life and struggle in a fishing village.

Los Redes combines many of the elements which were afterward to make up the classical Mexican film style. The excellent photography focuses on the beauty of natural and famous forms: rolling masses of luminous clouds, swirling eddies of water, fishermen's nets draped out on lines to dry, palm fronds against thatched huts, stoic native faces set off by white shirts or dark *rebozos*, their sinuous arms entwined with ropes. Both the images and the dialectical montage of the editing appear to be influenced by the work of Sergei Eisenstein, who had filmed the never-released *Que Viva Mexico* several years earlier. Equally important, however, must have been Paul Strand's background in the National Film and Photo League, many of whose photographers went on to produce the extraordinary documentation of the depression in the United States under the auspices of the Farm Security Administration.

These radical influences from abroad fused with the evolutionary experience of Mexico to produce a work of penetrating social criticism. Incredibly exploited by the packer's monopoly, the fishermen attempt to form a union under the leadership of Miro, whose young son has died for lack of medicine. Miro is killed by the politician who has been paid by the packer, but the other fishermen continue the struggle. The film not only lays bare a situation of exploitation, it also criticizes religion, reformist politics, and anarchism by indicating that none of these provide as effective an answer as does organized resistance. The use of non-professional actors adds to the film's realism, and the intelligent employment of montage and music keeps the actors from being overwhelmed by the demands made upon them.

Although the film was an economic failure, critics both inside and outside Mexico have since perceived it to be an important work. Within Mexico, *Los Redes* and *Que Viva Mexico* are seen as the precursors of the style later made internationally known in the films of Emilio Fernández and the cinematographer Gabriel Figueroa. Outside Mexico, several writers have stated that it may well have been a major influence on Italian neo-realism. Whatever its effects, *Los Redes* is an interesting example of socially committed art and a key film in the history of Mexican cinema.

—John Mraz

RÈGLE DU JEU

(Rules of the Game)

France, 1939

Director: Jean Renoir

Production: La Nouvelle Edition Française; black and white, 35mm; running time: 85 minutes, restored version is 110 minutes; length: restored version is 10,080 feet. Released 7 July 1939, Paris. Re-released 1949 in Great Britain, and 1950 in New York. Restored to original form and released at 1959 Venice Film Festival. Filmed February through the Spring of 1939, in the Chateau de le Ferté-Saint-Aubin and at La Motte-Beuvron, Aubigny; interiors shot at the Billancourt Studios, Joinville. Cost: 5,000,000 F.

Producer: Claude Renoir; **screenplay:** Jean Renoir with Camille François and Carl Koch; **assistant directors:** André Zwobada and Henri Cartier-Bresson; **photography:** Jean Bachelet; **editor:** Marguerite Houlet-Renoir; **sound engineer:** Joseph de Bretagne; **production designer:** Eugène Lourié; **assistant designer:** Max Douy; **music director:** Roger Desormières; **costume designer:** Coco Chanel.

Cast: Marcel Dalio (*Robert de la Chesnaye*); Nora Grégor (*Christine de la Chesnaye*); Roland Toutain (*André Jurieu*); Jean Renoir (*Octave*); Mila Parély (*Geneviève de Marrast*); Paulette Dubost (*Lisette*); Gaston Modot (*Schumacher*); Julien Carette (*Marceau*); Anne Mayen (*Jackie*); Pierre Nay (*Saint-Auben*); Pierre Magnier (*The General*); Odette Talazac (*Charlotte*); Roger Forster (*The homosexual*); Richard Francouer (*La Bruyère*); Claire Gérard (*Madame de la Bruyère*); Tony Corteggiani (*Berthelin*); Nicolas Amato (*The South American*); Eddy Debray (*Corneille*); Lisa Elina (*Radio announcer*); André Zwobada (*Engineer*); Léon Larive (*Chef*); Célestin (*Kitchen servant*); Jenny Helia (*Serving girl*); Henri Cartier-Bresson (*English servant*); Lise Elina (*Female radio announcer*); André Zwobada (*Engineer at the Caudron*); Camille François (*Radio announcer*); friends of Jean Renoir as guests in the shooting party; local villagers as the beaters.

Publications

Script:

Renoir, Jean, Camille François, and Carl Koch, *La Règle du jeu*, in *Avant-Scène du Cinéma* (Paris), October 1965; as *The Rules of the Game*, New York, 1969.

Books:

Sadoul, Georges, *French Film*, London, 1953.
Cauliez, Armand-Jean, *Jean Renoir*, Paris, 1962.
Chadere, Bernard, *Jean Renoir*, Lyons, 1962.
Analyses des films de Jean Renoir, Paris, 1966.
Simon, John, *Private Screenings*, New York, 1967.
Sarris, Andrew, *The American Cinema*, New York, 1968.
Cowie, Peter, *70 Years of Cinema*, New York, 1969.
Poulle, François, *Renoir 1938*, Paris, 1969.
Leprohon, Pierre, *Jean Renoir*, New York, 1971.
Braudy, Leo, *Jean Renoir: The World of his Films*, New York 1972.
Bazin, André, *Jean Renoir*, edited by François Truffaut, Paris, 1973, 1992.
Burch, Noël, *Theory of Film Practice*, New York, 1973.
Mast, Gerald, *Filmguide to The Rules of the Game*, Bloomington, Indiana, 1973.
Solomon, Stanley, *The Classic Cinema*, New York, 1973.
Durgnat, Raymond, *Jean Renoir*, Berkeley, 1974.
Renoir, Jean, *My Life and My Films*, New York, 1974, 1991.
Gilliatt, Penelope, *Jean Renoir: Essays, Conversations, Reviews*, New York, 1975.
Faulkner, Christopher, *Jean Renoir: A Guide to References and Resources*, Boston, 1979.
Sesonske, Alexander, *Jean Renoir: The French Films, 1924–1939*, Cambridge Massachusetts, 1980.
Gauteur, Claude, *Jean Renoir: Oeuvres de cinéma inédites*, Paris, 1981.
Ropars-Wuilleumier, Marie-Claire, *Le Texte divisé: Essai sur l'écriture filmique*, Paris, 1981.
McBride, Joseph, editor, *Filmmakers on Filmmaking: The American Film Institute Seminars on Motion Pictures and Television, volume 2*, Los Angeles, 1983.
Renoir, Jean, *Lettres d'Amérique*, edited by Dido Renoir and Alexander Sesonske, Paris, 1984.
Serceau, Daniel, *Jean Renoir*, Paris, 1985.
Weis, Elisabeth, and John Belton, editors, *Film Sound: Theory and Practice*, New York, 1985.
Bertin, Celia, *Jean Renoir*, Paris, 1986.
Faulkner, Christopher, *The Social Cinema of Jean Renoir*, Princeton, 1986.
Vincendeau, Ginette, and Keith Reader, *La Vie est à nous: French Cinema of the Popular Front 1935–1938*, London, 1986.
Viry-Babel, Roger, *Jean Renoir: Le Jeu et la règle*, Paris, 1986.
Guislain, Pierre, *La règle du jeu, Jean Renoir*, Paris, 1990.
Bergan, Ronald, *Jean Renoir: Projections of Paradise*, Woodstock, 1994.
Cavagnac, Guy, *Jean Renoir: le désir du monde*, Paris, 1994.
O'Shaughnessy, Martin, *Jean Renoir*, New York, 2000.

Articles:

Lo Duca, Giuseppe, ''Il cinema e lo Stato: inter-vista con Françoise Rosay e Jean Renoir,'' in *Cinema* (Rome), 25 March 1939.
Plant, Richard, ''Jean Renoir,'' in *Theatre Arts* (New York), June 1939.
Variety (New York), 30 August 1939.
Lambert, Gavin, ''French Cinema: The New Pessismism,'' in *Sequence* (London), Summer 1948.
Menard, Louis, in *Temps Modernes* (Paris), no. 43, 1949.
Lambert, Gavin, ''A Last Look Round,'' in Sequence (London), no.14, 1952.
''Renoir Issue'' of *Cahiers du Cinéma* (Paris), January 1952.
Renoir, Jean, ''Personal Note,'' in *Sight and Sound* (London), April-June 1952.
Sadoul, Georges, ''The Renaissance of the French Cinema—Feyder, Renoir, Duvivier, Carné,'' in *Film: An Anthology*, edited by Daniel Talbot, New York, 1959.
Brunelin, André G., ''Histoire d'une malédiction,'' in *Cinéma* (Paris), February 1960.
Dyer, Peter John, ''Renoir and Realism,'' in *Sight and Sound* (London), Summer 1960.

Règle du jeu

Corbin, Louise, in *Films in Review* (New York), 26 January 1951.
New York Times, 19 January 1961.
Mekas, Jonas, in *Village Voice* (New York), 26 January 1961.
Whitehall, Richard, in *Films and Filming* (London), November 1961 and November 1962.
Marcorelles, Louis, ''Conversation with Jean Renoir,'' in *Sight and Sound* (London), Spring 1962.
Russell, Lee, and Peter Wollen, ''Jean Renoir,'' in *New Left Review* (London), May-June 1964.
Esnault, Philippe, ''Le Jeu de la verité,'' in *Avant-Scène du Cinéma* (Paris), October 1965.
''Renoir, cinéaste de notre temps, à coeur ouvert,'' in *Cinéma* (Paris), May 1967 and June 1967.
Joly, J., ''Between Theatre and Life: Jean Renoir and *The Rules of the Game*,'' in *Film Quarterly* (Berkeley), Winter 1967–68.
Grelier, Robert, ''Dialogue avec une salle, in *Cinéma* (Paris), March 1968.
Budgen, Suzanne, ''Some Notes on the Sources of *La règle du jeu*,'' in *Take One* (Montreal), July-August 1968.
Gilliatt, Penelope, in *New Yorker*, 23 August 1969 and 20 September 1969.
Fofi, Goffredo, ''The Cinema of the Popular Front in France, (1934–38),'' in *Screen* (London), Winter 1972–73.
Mary, A., ''L'Analyse du film,'' in *Image et Son* (Paris), December 1972.
Roud, Richard, in *Favorite Movies: Critics' Choice*, edited by Philip Nobile, New York, 1973.
Litle, Michael, ''Sound Track: *Rules of the Game*,'' in *Cinema Journal* (Evanston, Illinois), Fall 1973.
Wood Jr, George A., ''Game Theory and *The Rules of the Game*," in *Cinema Journal* (Evanston, Illinois), Fall 1973.
Gauteur, Claude, ''*La règle du jeu* et la critique en 1939,'' in *Image et Son* (Paris), March 1974.
Sarris, Andrew, ''Renoir: Impressions at Twilight,'' in *Village Voice* (New York), 6 and 12 September 1974.
Sitney, P. Adams, ''Bergman et Renoir: A propos des *Sourires d'une noit d'été*,'' in *Cinema* (New York), 1975.
Jehle, W., in *Cinema* (Zurich), no. 4, 1975.
Lewis, Marshall, ''A Masterpiece on 8th Street,'' in *The Essential Cinema*, edited by P. Adams Sitney, New York, 1975.
Boost, C., ''*La règle du jeu:* Renoir's spelregel: de leugen,'' in *Skoop* (Wageningen), March 1976.

Haakman, A., ''Hoe moet een acteur geregisseerd worden?. . . ,'' in *Skoop* (Wageningen), March 1976.

Lesage, Julia, ''*S/Z* and *Rules of the Game*,'' in *Jump Cut* (Chicago) 30 December 1976.

Perebinossoff, P. R., ''Theatricals in Jean Renoir's *Rules of the Game* and *Grand Illusion*,'' in *Literature/Film Quarterly* (Salisbury, Maryland), Winter 1977.

Roy, J., in *Cinéma* (Paris), June 1978.

Strebel, Elizabeth Grottle, ''Jean Renoir and the Popular Front,'' in *Feature Films as History*, edited by K. R. M. Short, London, 1981.

Renoir, Jean, ''Presentacion de *La regla del juego*,'' in *Contracampo* (Madrid), March 1982.

Marias, M., in *Casablanca* (Madrid), April 1982.

''*Règle du jeu* Issue'' of *Quarterly Review of Film Studies* (New York), Summer 1982.

Snyder, J., ''Film and Classical Genre . . . : Rules for Interpreting *Rules of the Game*,'' in *Literature/Film Quarterley* (Salisbury, Maryland), July 1982.

Gauteur, Claude in *Positif* (Paris), July-August 1982.

Rafferty, T., ''The Essence of the Landscape,'' in *New Yorker*, 25 June 1990.

Tifft, S., ''Drole de Guerre: Renoir, Farce, and the Fall of France,'' in *Representations* (Berkeley), Spring 1992.

Bramkamp, R., and H.-J. Kapp, ''Dialog ueber *La règle du jeu* von Jean Renoir,'' in *Filmwaerts* (Hannover), June 1993.

Brisseau, Jean-Claude, in *Cahiers du Cinéma* (Paris), no. 482, July-August 1994.

Legrand, Gérard, and Alain Masson, and B. Asscher, ''Homage à Jean Renoir,'' in *Positif* (Paris), no. 401–402, July-August 1994.

Smith, Gavin, ''A Man of Excess: Paul Schrader on Jean Renoir,'' in *Sight and Sound* (London), vol. 5, no. 1, January 1995.

Buchsbaum, Jonathan, '''My Nationality is Cinematography': Renoir and the National Question,'' in *Persistence of Vision* (Maspeth), no. 12–13, 1996.

Bergstrom, J., ''Jean Renoir's Return to France,'' in *Poetics Today*, vol. 17, no. 3, 1996.

Reader, K., in *Sight and Sound* (London), vol. 6, September 1996.

Bates, Robin, ''Audiences on the Verge of a Fascist Breakdown: Male Anxieties and Late 1930s French Film,'' in *Cinema Journal* (Austin), vol. 36, no. 3, Spring 1997.

Mayer, H., ''Figaro 1939,'' in *Trafic* (Paris), no. 24, Winter 1997.

* * *

Detested when it first appeared (for satirizing the French ruling class on the brink of World War II), almost destroyed by brutal cutting, restored in 1959 to virtually its original form, *La règle du jeu* is now universally acknowledged as a masterpiece and perhaps Renoir's supreme achievement. In the four international critics polls organized every ten years (since 1952) by *Sight and Sound*, only two films have been constant: one is *Battleship Potemkin*, and the other is *La règle du jeu*. And in the 1982 poll *La règle du jeu* had climbed to second place. Its extreme complexity (it seems, after more than 20 viewings, one of the cinema's few truly inexhaustible films) makes it peculiarly difficult to write about briefly; the following attempt will indicate major lines of interest:

Sources. The richness of the film is partly attributable to the multiplicity of its sources and influences (all, be it said, totally assimilated: there is no question here of an undigested eclecticism). It seems very consciously (though never pretentiously) the product of the vast and complex cultural tradition, with close affinities with the other arts, especially painting, theatre and music. If it evokes impressionist painting less directly than certain other Renoir films (for example *Partie de campagne* or *French Can-Can*), it is strikingly faithful to the *spirit* of impressionism, the desire to portray life-as-flux rather than as a collection of discrete objects or figures. The influence of theatre is much more obvious, since it directly affects the acting style, which relates to a tradition of French boulevard comedy. Renoir specifically refers to Musset's *Les Caprices de Marianne* as a source (indeed, it was to be the title of the film at an early stage of its evolution) and to Beaumarchais (the film is prefaced by a quotation from *The Marriage of Figaro*). This last points us directly to music, and especially to Mozart, whose music opens and closes the film, the ''overture'' (in fact the first of the ''3 German Dances'' K.605) accompanying the Beaumarchais quotation. This is perhaps the most Mozartian of all films: it constantly evokes Bruno Walter's remark (in a celebrated rehearsal record of a Mozart symphony), ''The expression changes in every bar.''

Method. Every frame of *La règle du jeu* seems dominated by Renoir's personality; yet the most appealing facets of that personality are generosity, openness, responsiveness. As a result, *La règle* is at once the *auteur* film *par excellence* and a work of co-operation and active participation. In Renoir's words, ''of all the films I have made, this one is probably the most improvised. We worked out the script and decided on the places we were going to shoot as we went along. . . .'' It is clear that much of the film's complexity derives from its improvisatory, co-operative nature. Renoir cast himself as Octave (a role originally intended for his older brother Pierre), and developed Octave's relationship with Christine, because of his own pleasure in the company of Nora Grégor; the role of Geneviève was greatly extended (originally, she was to have left the château after the hunt) because of Renoir's appreciation of the talent of Mila Parély; the entire sub-plot involving the servants was similarly elaborated during shooting, partly because of Renoir's delight in Carette's characterization.

Stylistics. The film marks the furthest elaboration of certain stylistic traits developed by Renoir since his silent films: the use of off-screen space (see Nöel Burch's seminal account of *Nana* in *Theory of Film Practice*); the mobile camera, always at the service of the action and the actors yet unusually free in its movements, continuously tracking, panning, re-framing; the fondness for the group shot, in which several characters (sometimes several diverse but simultaneous actions) are linked; depth of field, enabling the staging of simultaneous foreground and background actions, which often operate like counterpoint in music; the re-thinking of ''composition'' in terms of time and movement (of the camera, of the actors) rather than static images; the constant transgressing of the boundaries of the frame, which actors enter and exit from during shots. There are various consequences of this practice: 1) Renoir's ''realism'' (a word we should use very carefully in reference to so stylized a film)—the sense of life continuing beyond the borders of the frame, as if the camera were selecting, more or less arbitrarily, a mere portion of a continuous ''real'' world. 2) A drastic modification of the habits of identification generally encouraged by mainstream cinema. Close-ups and point-of-view shots are rare (though Renoir does not hesitate to use them when he feels them to be dramatically appropriate—interestingly, such usages are almost always linked to Christine). The continual reframings and entrances/exits ensure that the spectator's gaze is constantly being transferred from character to character, action to action. If Christine is gradually defined as the film's central figure, this is never at the expense of other characters, and she never becomes our sole object of identification. 3) The style of the film also assumes a metaphysical dimension, the apprehension of life-as-flux. The quotation from Lavoisier that Renoir applied to his father is apt for him too: "In nature nothing is created, nothing is lost, everything is transformed. . . ."

Thematics. La règle du jeu defies reduction to any single statement of "meaning." As with any great work of art, its thematic dimension is inextricably involved with its stylistics. Renoir's own statements about the film indicate the complexity of attitude it embodies: on the one hand, "the story attacks the very structure of our society"; on the other, "I wish I could live in such a society—that would be wonderful." People repeatedly quote Octave's line. "Everyone has his reasons," as if it summed up the film (and Renoir), reducing its attitude to a simple, all-embracing generosity; they ignore the words that introduce it: ". . . *there's one thing that is terrible*, and that is that everyone has his reasons." As to the "rules" of the title, the attitude is again highly complex. On the one hand, the film clearly recognizes the need for order, for some form of "regulation"; on the other, the culminating catastrophe is precipitated by the application of opposed sets of rules by two characters (who happen to be husband and wife): Schumacher, who believes in punishing promiscuity with death, and Lisette, who believes in sexual game-playing but has rigid notions of propriety in questions of age and income. Not surprisingly, the film plays on unresolved (perhaps, within our culture, unresolvable) tensions and paradoxes: the Marquis "doesn't want fences" (restrictions), but also "doesn't want rabbits" (total freedom). Few films have treated the issue of sexual morality (fidelity, monogamy, freedom) with such openness: a film about people who go too far, or a film about people who don't go far enough?

—Robin Wood

REISE DER HOFFNUNG

See **JOURNEY OF HOPE**

REPENTANCE

See **POKAIANIE**

A REPORT ON THE PARTY AND THE GUESTS

See **O SLAVNOSTI A HOSTECH**

REPULSION

UK, 1965

Director: Roman Polanski

Production: Compton-Tekli; black and white; running time: 104 minutes; length: 9,360 feet. Released June 1965.

Producer: Gene Gutowski; **associate producers:** Robert Sterne, Sam Wayneberg; **screenplay:** Roman Polanski, Gerard Brach; **assistant director:** Ted Sturgis; **photography:** Gilbert Taylor; **editor:** Alistair McIntyre; **sound:** Stephen Dalby; **art director:** Seamus Flannery; **music:** Chico Hamilton.

Cast: Catherine Deneuve (*Carol*); Yvonne Furneaux (*Helen*); John Fraser (*Colin*); Ian Hendry (*Michael*); Patrick Wymark (*The Landlord*); Valerie Taylor (*Mme Denise*); Helen Fraser (*Bridget*); Renee Houston (*Miss Balch*); James Villiers (*John*); Hugh Futcher (*Reggie*); Mike Pratt (*Workman*); Monica Merlin (*Mrs. Rendlesham*); Imogen Graham (*Manicurist*).

Publications

Script:

Polanski, Roman, and Gerard Brach, *Repulsion*, in *Three Films by Roman Polanski*, London, 1975.

Books:

Butler, Ivan, *The Cinema of Roman Polanski*, New York, 1970.
Kane, Pascal, *Roman Polanski*, Paris, 1970.
Belmans, Jacques, *Roman Polanski*, Paris, 1971.
Durgnat, Raymond, *Sexual Alienation in the Cinema*, London, 1974.
Bisplinghoff, Gretchen, and Virginia Wexman, *Roman Polanski: A Guide to References and Resources*, Boston, 1979.
Kiernan, Thomas, *The Roman Polanski Story*, New York, 1980.
Leaming, Barbara, *Polanski: The Filmmaker as Voyeur: A Biography*, New York, 1981; as *Polanski: His Life and Films*, London, 1982.
Tuska, Jon, editor, *Close-up: The Contemporary Director*, Metuchen, New Jersey, 1981.
Fisher, Jens Malte, *Filmwissenschaft—Filmgeschichte: Studien zu Welles, Hitchcock, Polanski, Pasolini, and Max Steiner*, Tübingen, 1983.
Polanski, Roman, *Roman*, London, 1984.
Dokumentation: Polanski und Skolimowski; Das Absurde im Film, Zurich, 1985.
Wexman, Virginia Wright, *Roman Polanski*, Boston, 1985.
Jacobsen, Wolfgang, and others, *Roman Polanski*, Munich, 1986.

Repulsion

Avron, Dominique, *Roman Polanski*, Paris, 1987.
Bruno, Edoardo, *Roman Polanski*, Rome, 1993.
Parker, John, *Polanski*, London, 1993.
Stachówna, Grazyna, *Roman Pola'nski I jego filmy*, Warsaw, 1994.
Cappabianca, Alessandro, *Roman Polanski*, Recco, 1997.

Articles:

Brach, Gerard, in *Cinéma* (Paris), February 1965.
Dyer, Peter John, in *Sight and Sound* (London), Summer 1965.
Variety (New York), 16 June 1965.
Milne, Tom, in *Monthly Film Bulletin* (London), July 1965.
Barr, Charles, and Peter von Bagh, in *Movie* (London), Autumn 1965.
Delahaye, Michael, and J. A. Fieschi, ''Paysage d'un cerveau: Entretien avec Roman Polanski,'' in *Cahiers du Cinéma* (Paris), February 1966.
Caen, Michel, in *Cahiers du Cinéma* (Paris), March 1966.
Johnson, Albert, in *Film Quarterly* (Berkeley), Spring 1966.
McArthur, Colin, ''Polanski,'' in *Sight and Sound* (London), Winter 1968–69.
Ross, T. J., ''Roman Polanski, *Repulsion*, and the New Mythology,'' in *Film Heritage* (Dayton, Ohio), Winter 1968–69.
Reisner, Joel, and Bruce Kane, ''An Interview with Roman Polanski,'' in *Cinema* (Los Angeles), no. 2, 1969.
Ciment, Michel, and others ''Entretien avec Roman Polanski,'' in *Positif* (Paris), February 1969.
Leach, J., ''Notes on Polanski's Cinema of Cruelty,'' in *Wide Angle* (Athens, Ohio), vol. 2, no. 1, 1978.
Amiel, M., and others, ''L'Univers de Roman Polanski,'' in *Cinéma* (Paris), February 1980.
Film Reader (Evanston, Illinois), no. 5, 1982.
Corfman, S., ''Polanski's *Repulsion* and the Subject of Self,'' in *Spectator* (Los Angeles), vol. 10, no. 1, 1989.
Lucas, Tim, in *Video Watchdog* (Cincinnati), no. 33, 1996.
Taubin, A., ''Sex on the Brain,'' in *Village Voice* (New York), vol. 42, 23 September 1997.
Biodrowski, S., ''Reissues, Revivals, and Restorations: *Repulsion* and *Dracula*,'' in *Cinefantastique* (Forest Park), vol. 29, no. 11, 1998.

* * *

In the early 1960s Roman Polanski's producer, seeking financial backing for what was to be that director's second feature film and his first in the English language, approached Hammer Films. That the company promptly turned down the project which would eventually become Polanski's third film, *Cul de Sac*, is perhaps not surprising: the robust Manichaeism of Hammer horror at this time stands in stark contrast to Polanski's distinctly surrealist sensibility.

Repulsion, the film that Polanski made before *Cul de Sac*, bears only a tangential relationship to the country in which it was produced. While the director very convincingly captures the London of the mid-1960s, he also works to universalise this setting, so that it becomes as much a representation of an existential situation as it is a specific geographical location. The tension between the particular and the general thereby generated is the source of much of the film's uncanny qualities. It also enables Polanski to pursue a theme which runs through several of his films (for example, *The Tenant* and *Frantic*), and that is the reactions of an outsider or foreigner to an alienating, Kafkaesque urban landscape. *Repulsion*'s restless camera becomes in this sense a correlative of Polanski's and his central character Carol's unease in their surroundings.

The film is also one of cinema's finest and most uncompromising treatments of madness. Through a brilliant manipulation of space, time, and sound, Polanski vividly recreates a schizophrenic experience. The essential physicality of his approach is most apparent in his visual treatment of Carol's flat. As Carol gradually loses her tentative hold on reality, walls are torn asunder, and what initially were small rooms become cavernous, menacing lairs. Significantly, psychoanalysts and other mental health specialists (staple ingredients in most films dealing with madness) are absent throughout. The film offers us *an experience of madness* rather than an intellectual—and inevitably distancing and reassuring—understanding of that condition.

However, it does not follow from this that no explanation is offered for what happens to Carol. Avoiding the case-history approach which could so easily have become reductive and facile, Polanski instead subtly shades her condition into the world through which she moves. Madness is seen to lie not in an individual's psychology but as emerging from an apparently immutable social reality. In the world of *Repulsion* the possibilities of meaningful communication between the sexes are limited by the stereotypical roles assigned to male and female: the morgue-like beauty parlour where Carol works stands rigorously opposed to the pub where Colin, her prospective boyfriend, meets his male friends and where the conversation seems rooted in depressingly humourless dirty jokes. The film's most disturbing moment in this respect is the one where a hopelessly insane Carol applies heavy make-up to her face and lies in bed smiling, a mocking representation of the woman as object around which both the beauty parlour and the dirty jokes are structured.

Within this context both Carol and Colin are presented sympathetically. There is a delicate poignancy in their early scenes together as they make awkward and increasingly desperate conversation. Their sensitivity renders them uncomfortable in their respective roles but they are incapable of finding other ways of behaving and relating to each other. It appears that only the crass insensitivity embodied in Michael, the lover of Carol's sister, enables people to survive (although even this character is allowed to exhibit tenderness at the film's conclusion when he gently carries Carol away from the flat).

Polanski seems throughout the film to be suggesting that Carol's actions merely represent an understandable reaction to a world that, when viewed clearly, is unbearable. It is the bleakest of outlooks, and it is a credit both to Polanski's enormous technical skill and his humanism that he succeeds so completely in drawing his audience into it.

—Peter Hutchings

RESERVOIR DOGS

USA, 1992

Director: Quentin Tarantino

Production: Live America Inc., A Dog Eat Dog production; color, 35mm; running time: 99 minutes.

Producer: Lawrence Bender; **co-producer:** Harvey Keitel; **executive producers:** Monte Hellman, Richard N. Gladstein, Ronna B. Wallace; **screenplay:** Quentin Tarantino; **photography:** Anrzej Sekula; **editor:** Sally Menks; **assistant directors:** Jamie Beardsley, Francis R. Mahoney III; **production design:** David Wasco; **sound editors:** Curt Schulkey, Chuck Smith, Dave Stone; **sound recordists:** Ken Segal, Dave Moreno, Matthew C. Belleville, Mark Coffey.

Cast: Harvey Keitel (*Mr. White/Larry*); Tim Roth (*Mr. Orange/ Freddy Newendyke*); Michael Madsen (*Mr. Blonde/'Toothpick'' Vic Vega*); Steve Buscemi (*Mr. Pink*); Chris Penn (*Nice Guy Eddie*); Lawrence Tierney (*Joe Cabot*); Randy Brooks (*Holdaway*); Kirk Baltz (*Marvin Nash*); Eddie Bunker (*Mr. Blue*); Quentin Tarantino (*Mr. Brown*); Steven Wright (*K-Billy DJ*).

Publications

Script:

Tarantino, Quentin, *Reservoir Dogs*, London, 1994.

Books:

Fuller, Graham, ''Answers first, questions later,'' in *Projections 3*, edited by John Boorman and Walter Donohue, London, 1994.

Dawson, Jeff, *Quentin Tarantino: The Cinema of Cool*, New York, 1995.

Barnes, Alan, and Marcus Hearn, *Tarantino: A to Z*, North Pomfret, 1996; revised edition, 1999.

Woods, Paul A., *King Pulp: The Wild World of Quentin Tarantino*, London, 1996, 1998.

Nagel, Uwe, *Der rote Faden aus Blut: Erzählstrukturen bei Quentin Tarantino*, Marburg, 1997.

Peary, Gerald, *Quentin Tarantino: Interviews*, Jackson, 1998.

Woods, Paul A., *Quentin Tarantino: The Film Greek Files*, Austin, 1999.

Reservoir Dogs

Articles:

McCarthy, T., *Variety* (New York), 27 January 1992.

Nevers, C., ''Rencontre avec Quentin Tarantino,'' in *Cahiers du Cinéma* (Paris), June 1992.

Ciment, M., and others, ''Quentin Tarantino,'' in *Positif* (Paris), September 1992.

Lyons, D., ''Scumbags,'' in *Film Comment* (New York), November-December 1992.

Taubin, A., ''The men's room,'' in *Sight and Sound* (London), December 1992.

Case, B., and N. Floyd, ''Dog Days,'' in *Time Out* (London), 30 December 1992.

Dubeau, A., *Séquences* (Montreal), January 1993.

Newman, Kim, *Sight and Sound* (London), January 1993.

Horguelin, T., ''Noirs et blancs en couleurs,'' in *24 Images* (Montreal), February-March 1993.

Charlton, S., *Cinema Papers* (Melbourne), May 1993.

Tsalamandris, Con., ''Warehouse of Games,'' in *Cineaste* (New York), 1993/94.

Willis, S., ''The Fathers Watch the Boys' Room,'' in *Camera Obscura* (Bloomington), no. 32, September/January 1993/1994.

Dalton, Mary, M., and Steve Jarrett, in *Creative Screenwriting* (Washington, D.C.), vol. 1, no. 4, Winter 1994.

Deemer, Charles, and Ira Nayman, ''The Screenplays of Quentin Tarantino: Pop Go the Weasles,'' in *Creative Screenwriting* (Washington, D.C.), vol. 1, no. 4, Winter 1994.

Smith, Gavin, ''When You Know You're in Good Hands: Quentin Tarantino,'' in *Film Comment* (New York), vol. 30, no. 4, July-August 1994.

Williams, D.E., ''Gone to the Dogs,'' in *Film Threat* (Beverly Hills), no. 17, August 1994.

Pace, William R., ''Writing for Low-Budget Feature Films,'' in *Creative Screenwriting* (Washington, D.C.), vol. 2, no. 1, Spring 1995.

Bush, L., ''Doing Brando,'' in *Film Comment* (New York), vol. 32, January/February 1996.

Telotte, J.P., ''Fatal Capers: Strategy and Enigma in Film Noir,'' in *Journal of Popular Film and Television* (Washington, D.C.), vol. 23, no. 4, Winter 1996.

Douglas, Torin, ''Does This Film Go Too Far?'' in *Radio Times* (London), vol. 194, no. 3826, 31 May 1997.

Mank, G.W., and others, ''Our Favorite Psychos,'' in *Midnight Marquee* (Baltimore), no. 55, Fall 1997.

* * *

With *Pulp Fiction*, his second film as writer/director, Quentin Tarantino has clearly ''arrived,'' though how long he will stay is another matter. In the present (anti-)critical climate, where reviewers seem motivated primarily by the desire to demonstrate how much they are ''with it'' rather than by any vestigial sense of the need for responsible evaluation, the latest idols pass by like comets, a brief blaze followed by a swift fizzle: the Coens (*Barton Fink*) seem already on the way down, and David Lynch (*Blue Velvet*) has already sunk below the horizon. *Pulp Fiction*, a work of phenomenal cleverness and very little intelligence, does not strike me as the realization of the promise of *Reservoir Dogs*, the embodiment of the kind of creativity that endures and develops. But creativity is scarcely nourished by the values of contemporary critical ''taste'': cynicism, nihilism, the irresponsibilities of postmodernism, ''sick'' humour. *Pulp Fiction* gives the critics exactly what they appear to want.

Reservoir Dogs (although discernibly the work of the same artist) is another matter. The essential difference between the two films is epitomized in the two torture scenes: that in *Reservoir Dogs* is genuinely appalling, while that in *Pulp Fiction* is clearly offered as funny. The earlier film's relative modesty, combined with its force, tautness and precision, suggests an underlying seriousness of purpose that its successor fritters away in adolescent self-indulgence; it is a far more impressive debut than the first films of Lynch or the Coens. Its distinction lies not only in its formal perfection (the intricately non-chronological narrative structure) and the single-minded rigour with which its thesis (''reservoir dogs'' end up eating each other) is worked out, but in its very particular relation to the contemporary crisis of ''masculinity.'' The threat to masculinity represented by feminism—the growing emancipation, independence, and activeness of women—has evoked a range of responses in the culture which are mirrored in the Hollywood cinema. There has been the attempt (almost invariably compromised and recuperative) to depict strong and ''liberated'' women, and the corresponding attempt to define a new version of ''Mr. Nice Guy,'' the sensitive and caring male. The alternative response is the hysterical overvaluation and exaggeration of masculinity represented by Schwarzennegger, Stallone, and Norris (often spilling over, at least in the case of the first two, into knowing but uneasy parody that allows us sophisticates to indulge ourselves while not taking it all too seriously). *Reservoir Dogs* carries this almost to the point of a kind of mass psychosis, the characters (not one of whom remains alive at the end) are destroyed by the very drives that make them so destructive.

Women scarcely appear in the film: one is brutally dragged from her car (required for a getaway) and hurled to the ground, the other is shot dead on the rebound by the gang-member she gut-wounds (who turns out to be an undercover cop). The references to women in the dialogue define them exclusively as sex-objects (there are no marriages or families). The men's total and apparently unanimous inability to relate to women on any other level has two inevitable consequences: the repression of their own femininity, and the constantly lurking threat of homosexuality. (Tarantino's films, and for that matter his interviews, are shot through by homoerotic reference, and less frequently by its converse, homophobia. See especially his account of *Top Gun* in his cameo appearance as an actor in *Sleep With Me*). Unable to love women, the men are evaluated in terms of their ability (or in most cases inability) to love each other. The poles are represented by the characters played by Michael Madsen and Harvey Keitel. The former is the film's explicitly psychotic character, incapable of relating to anyone except by violence. When, during the notorious torture scene, he slices off the cop's ear with a razor, his immediate taunt defines the act's essentially sexual nature: ''Was that as good for you as it was for me?'' This is answered at the end of the film by the erotic tenderness with which Keitel cradles and embraces the gut-wounded undercover man (Tim Roth), who responds to this sudden intimacy by confessing his identity—whereupon Keitel shoots him.

—Robin Wood

RETRATO DE TERESA

(Portrait of Teresa)

Cuba, 1979

Director: Pastor Vega

Production: Instituto Cubano del Arte e Industria Cinematográficos (ICAIC); color, 35mm. Released 1979. Filmed in Cuba.

Screenplay: Ambrosio Fornet.

Cast: Adolfo Llauradó (*Ramón*); Daisy Granados (*Teresa*).

Publications

Books:

Chanan, Michael, *The Cuban Image*, London, 1985.
Burton, Julianne, editor, *Cinema and Social Change in Latin America: Conversations with Filmmakers*, Austin, Texas, 1986.

Articles:

Ranvaud, Don, ''Pastor Vega: An Interview,'' in *Framework* (London), Spring 1979.
Moskowitz, G., in *Variety* (New York), 5 September 1979.
Segers, F., in *Variety* (New York), 7 November 1979.
Peyton, P., and C. Broullon, ''*Portrait of Teresa*: An Interview with Pastor Vega and Daisy Granados,'' in *Cineaste* (New York), no. 1, 1979–80.
Randall, M., ''*Portrait of Teresa*: A Letter from Havana,'' in *Cineaste* (New York), no. 1, 1979–80.
Gonzalea Acosta, A., ''Con Teresa, punto y seguido . . . ,'' in *Cine Cubano* (Havana), no. 97, 1980.
Rich, B., ''*Portrait of Teresa*: Double Day, Double Standard,'' in *Jump Cut* (Chicago), May 1980.
Allen, Tom, in *Film Comment* (New York), vol. 17, May-June 1981.
Coleman, John, ''*Portrait of Teresa*,'' in *New Statesman*, vol. 101, 5 June 1981.
Prieto, L., ''*Retrato de Teresa*: De la realidad a la ficcion,'' in *Cine Cubano* (Havana), no. 98, 1981.
Burton, Julianne, in *Film Quarterly* (Berkeley), Spring 1981.
Imeson, J., in *Monthly Film Bulletin* (London), August 1981.
Ahlander, R. Centenari, interview with Daisy Granados, in *Chaplin* (Stockholm), vol. 24, no. 5, 1982.

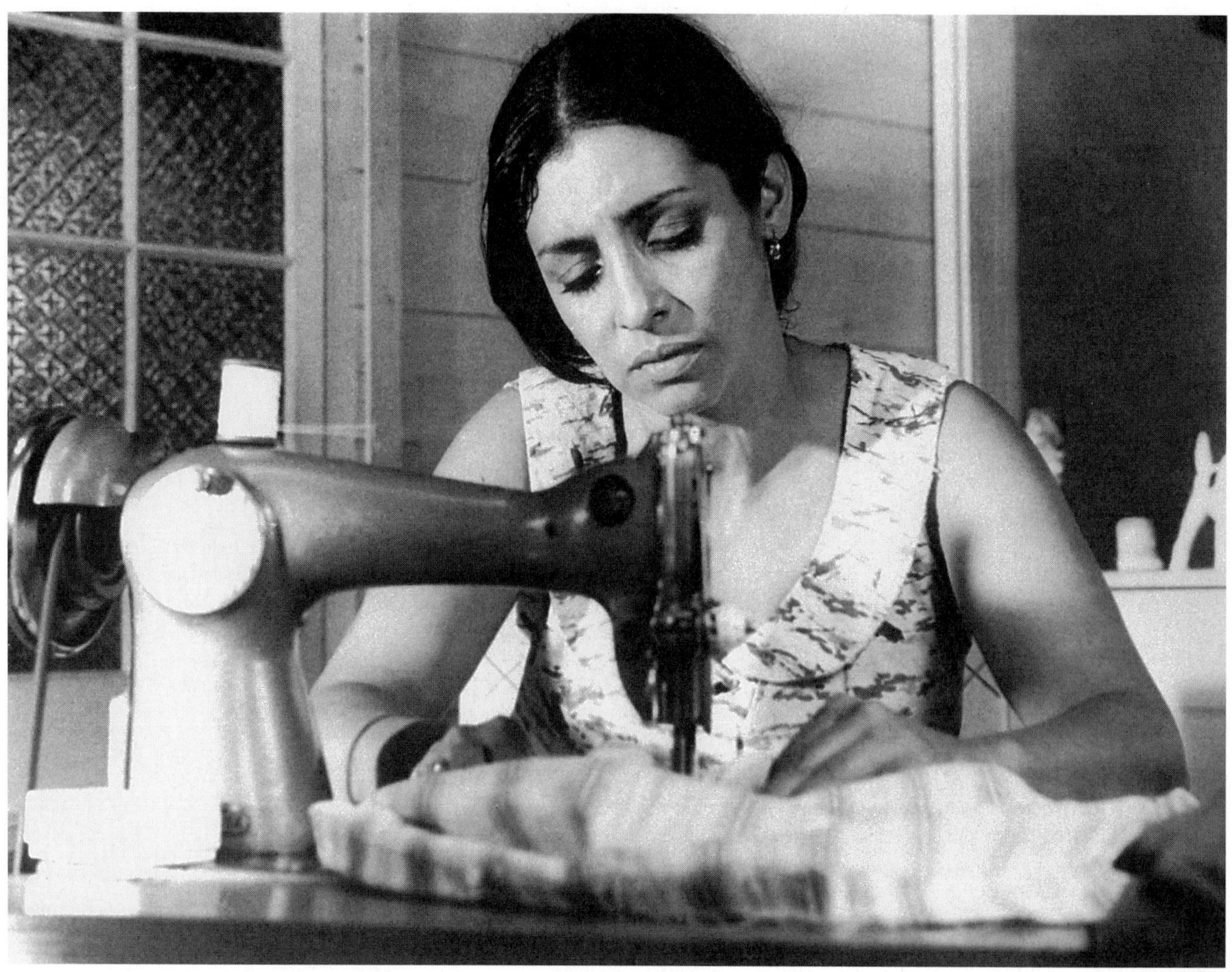

Retrato de Teresa

Interview with Pastor Vega, in *Casablanca* (Madrid), October 1982.
Film Library Quarterly (New York), vol. 16, no. 4, 1983.
Gonzalez, J. A., "Retrato de Daisy Granados," in *Cine Cubano* (Havana), no. 104, 1983.
Cine Cubano (Havana), no. 198, 1984.

* * *

The most polemical film in the history of Cuban cinema, *Portrait of Teresa* was seen by 500,000 spectators in less than two months and has been the focus of more than two dozen articles and the subject of innumerable marital discussions on the island. The reason for such controversy lies not in the form utilized by the film (it resembles an undistinguished "made-for-TV" movie), but in its content: a critique of *machismo* and its double standard for men and women. Ramón objects to Teresa's growing involvement in her work and politico-cultural activities, accusing her of neglecting her household duties. Despite the fact that they both work full-time, Teresa has to labour the familiar "double-day" of women, doing the domestic chores before and after her shift in a textile factory. Her attempts to incorporate herself into some of the cultural activities offered by the revolution are met by Ramón's increasingly intransigent defense of his male privileges, and they separate.

The film is a criticism to the "Law of the Funnel" ("Ley del embudo"), under which a different set of rules apply for men than for women. Impelled by its female integrants, the Cuban revolution has made great efforts to overcome the traditional subservience of women, insisting on a coherence of theory and practice and the integration of political principles into daily life. In the film's pivotal scene, Teresa confronts Ramón's assertion that he has changed (and thus wants her to return to him) by asking him how he would feel if she had had a relationship with someone else, as he did. His answer, "It's not the same," confirms her suspicion that he continues to maintain a double standard, and determines her decision to remain separated from him.

The leading actors spent much time and effort familiarizing themselves with the lives of the workers they were to represent, and were caught up in the controversy that swept Cuba after the release of the film. Daisy Granados (Teresa) saw it as an issue of the Cuban revolution: "I think that we women still make too many concessions to men. However, Teresa is no feminist symbol, but the conclusive proof that a new type of human being is arising among us. The revolution needs Teresa, because she is a symbol to all of us who believe that the revolution is a constant and permanent advance toward a superior and more complex person.'' Adolfo Llauradó (Ramón) saw it somewhat differently: ''I've grown, and I think that intellectually I'm totally in agreement with women's equality. I understand Teresa's necessities and aspirations, but when they clash with patterns and customs established throughout millenniums, I can't deny that, like Ramón, it disturbs me.''

The Cuban revolution has consistently struggled against *machismo* and its repressive patters, among other things, by explicitly legislating against a double sexual morality and by requiring men to share in the housework. However, the profundity of male-dominance is perhaps nowhere expressed more ironically than in the fact that, although both the director and scriptwriter see themselves as battling against ''paternalism,'' no women were included at decision-making levels in the film. *Portrait of Teresa* is a useful film, though hardly a radical one. The fact that it provoked such controversy in Cuba is indicative of how far we all have to go.

—John Mraz

THE RETURN OF THE JEDI

See **THE STAR WARS SAGA**

RIDE THE HIGH COUNTRY

(Guns in the Afternoon)

USA, 1962

Director: Sam Peckinpah

Production: MGM; CinemaScope, Metrocolor; running time: 93 minutes; length: 8,391 feet. Released May 1962.

Producer: Richard E. Lyons; **screenplay:** N. B. Stone, Jr.; **assistant director:** Hal Polaire; **photography:** Lucien Ballard; **editor:** Frank Santillo; **sound:** Franklin Milton; **art directors:** George W. Davis, Leroy Coleman; **music:** George Bassman.

Cast: Randolph Scott (*Gil Westrum*); Joel McCrea (*Steve Judd*); Ronald Starr (*Heck Longtree*); Mariette Hartley (*Elsa Knudsen*); James Drury (*Billy Hammond*); R. G. Armstrong (*Joshua Knudsen*); Edgar Buchanan (*Judge Tolliver*); Jenie Jackson (*Kate*); John Anderson (*Elder Hammon*); L. Q. Jones (*Sylvus Hammond*); Warren Oates (*Henry Hammond*); John Davis Chandler (*Jimmy Hammond*); Carmen Phillips (*Saloon Girl*).

Publications

Books:

Kitses, Jim, *Horizons West*, London 1969.
Evans, Max, *Sam Peckinpah: Master of Violence*, Vermillion, South Dakota, 1972.
Wright, Will, *Sixguns and Society: A Structural Study of the Western*, Berkeley, 1975.
Caprara, Valerio, *Peckinpah*, Bologna, 1976.
McKinney, Doug, *Sam Peckinpah*, Boston, 1979.
Butler, T., *Crucified Heroes: The Films of Sam Peckinpah*, London, 1979.
Seydor, Paul, *Peckinpah: The Western Films*, Urbana, Illinois, 1980.
Tuska, Jon, editor, *Close-Up: The Contemporary Director*, Metuchen, New Jersey, 1981.
Simmons, Garner, *Peckinpah: A Portrait in Montage*, Austin, Texas, 1982.
Arnold, Frank, and Ulrich von Berg, *Sam Peckinpah: Eine Outlaw in Hollywood*, Frankfurt, 1987.
Buscombe, Ed, editor, *BFI Companion to the Western*, London, 1988.
Fine, Marshall, *Bloody Sam: The Life and Films of Sam Peckinpah*, New York, 1992.
Bliss, Michael, *Justified Lives: Morality and Narrative in the Films of Sam Peckinpah*, Carbondale, 1993.
Weddle, David, *If They Move, Kill 'Em: The Life and Times of Sam Peckinpah*, New York, 1994.
Prince, Stephen, *Savage Cinema: Sam Peckinpah and the Rise of Ultraviolent Movies*, Austin, 1998.
Seydor, Paul, *Peckinpah: The Western Films: A Reconsideration*, Champaign, 1999.

Articles:

Films in Review (New York), April 1962.
Variety (New York), 9 May 1962.
Motion Picture Herald (New York), 16 May 1962.
Monthly Film Bulletin (London), June 1962.
Jones, DuPre, in *Sight and Sound* (London), Summer 1962.
Scott, Darrin, ''Photographing *Ride the High Country*,'' in *American Cinematographer* (Los Angeles), July 1962.
Positif (Paris), June 1963.
McArthur, Colin, ''Sam Peckinpah's West,'' in *Sight and Sound* (London), Autumn 1967.
Reisner, Joel, and Bruce Kane, ''Sam Peckinpah,'' in *Action* (Los Angeles), June 1970.
''Peckinpah Issue'' of *Film Heritage* (New York), Winter 1974–75.
Pettit, Arthur, ''Nightmare and Nostalgia: The Cinema West of Sam Peckinpah,'' in *Western Humanities Review* (Salt Lake City), Spring 1975.
Kael, Pauline, ''Notes on the Nihilist Poetry of Sam Peckinpah,'' in *New Yorker*, 12 January 1976.
Lumière du Cinéma (Paris), October 1977.
''Sam Peckinpah Section'' of *Film Comment* (New York), February 1981.
Sanchez Valdés, J., in *Casablanca* (Madrid), October 1981.
Skerry, P. J., ''The Western Film: A Sense of an Ending,'' in *New Orleans Review*, no. 3. 1990.
Nielsen, R., ''Ray's Way: James Drury,'' in *Classic Images* (Muscatine), no. 193, July 1991.
Roth-Bettoni, Didier, ''Coups de feu dans la Sierra: l'ouest du crépuscule,'' in *Mensuel du Cinéma*, no. 12, December 1993.
Humphreys, J., ''L.Q. Jones,'' in *Psychotronic Video* (Narrowsburg), no. 21, 1995.
''I primi film,'' in *Castoro Cinema* (Milan), no. 22, 2nd ed., March 1997.

* * *

Ride the High Country

Apart from his first feature, the rarely screened *The Deadly Companions*, few of Sam Peckinpah's films have escaped controversy. The obvious exception is *Ride the High Country*, acclaimed a classic within months of its release—and which still remains the Peckinpah movie that people who hate Peckinpah movies can like. It's clear enough why this should be so. Such violence as occurs is relatively muted; the film exudes a melancholy, autumnal gentleness, enhanced by the presence of two much-loved veterans of the genre, Randolph Scott and Joel McCrea, in what are evidently conceived as farewell performances. The characters—the upright lawman, the bad guy who becomes good in the end, the brash youngster who learns wisdom, and so on—are all comfortingly familiar types, and the plot itself springs few surprises. With *Ride*, Peckinpah openly staked his claim to the mantle of Great Western Director, heir to Ford, Mann, and Boetticher—before striking out, in *Major Dundee* and *The Wild Bunch*, on the maverick trail to a more equivocal position as (in Jim Kitses's phrase) ''John Ford's bastard son.''

Yet, beneath all the conventional elements—which are handled, it should be said, with a vigour and assurance which prevent them ever seeming merely routine—the thematic preoccupations of the later films are already in place. If Peckinpah didn't invent the elegiac, passing-of-the-west western (Ford, for one, could stake a claim with *Liberty Valance*), he made more telling use of it than any other director, and *Ride* locates us there from the start. From the majestic wildness of the ''high country'' we cut, as the credits end, to the bustling vulgarity of a California township where the shabby old lawman, Steve Judd (McCrea), is nearly run down by an automobile (anticipating the fate of another Peckinpah hero, Cable Hogue). Meanwhile his former colleague, Gil Westrum (Scott) has been reduced to running a carnival side-show, got up in a phony Buffalo Bill outfit as ''The Oregon Kid.''

These two, creaky and rheumatic, rehashing ancient exploits, bedding down in baggy long-johns, clearly enough embody the old, heroic, outmoded west. But they also foreshadow, in their contrasted attitudes, such later opposed pairs as Bishop and Thornton (*Wild Bunch*), Steiner and Stransky (*Cross of Iron*), Billy and Pat Garrett. *Ride*, like most of Peckinpah's work, explores the tensions of relative morality. Judd professes absolute values (''He was right. I was wrong,'' he says of his one-time mentor. ''That's something you just know''), and can trade biblical texts with Knudsen, the grimly puritanical rancher. But after Westrum's treachery, doubts creep in. ''My father says there's only right and wrong, good and evil,'' says

Elsa, Knudsen's daughter. ''It isn't that simple, is it?'' ''No, it isn't,'' Judd responds. ''It should be—but it isn't.'' The old, clear-cut frontier code—the code of a Ford movie—no longer holds up; and maybe it never really did.

Having set up his stock types, Peckinpah slyly subverts them. Judge Tolliver, the venal old drunk performing Elsa's wedding ceremony in a brothel, comes out with a wistful speech about marriage: ''A good marriage—there's a kind of simple glory about it.'' Even the squalid Hammond clan can be goaded into an open showdown through their ''sense of family honor''—which, of course, promptly gets them killed. By all the conventions of the genre, Westrum should die in the final shootout, atoning for his earlier misdeeds. But it's Judd who dies, gazing up at the austere purity of the mountains, granted his wish ''to enter my house justified'' (a phrase Peckinpah borrowed from his own father). Westrum can adapt and compromise; he survives.

The casting of Scott, icon of integrity, as the devious Westrum, is a master stroke; and while Peckinpah didn't originate the idea (McCrea and Scott, initially cast the other way round, spontaneously suggested a swap) he makes shrewd use of it, bringing out a foxiness which, we can recognize, was always latent in the actor's persona. That Westrum should survive, though, *was* the director's idea, part of his extensive—and uncredited—rewrite of Stone's script. *Ride* also marks Peckinpah's first cinematic collaboration with the veteran Lucien Ballard, whose lyrical widescreen cinematography makes it one of the most beautiful of all westerns.

Not for the last time, a Peckinpah movie hit studio problems. *Ride*, victim of a front-office feud, was taken away from him in post-production and released as a second feature. Critical enthusiasm and prizes at European festivals embarrassed MGM into giving it a re-release; and its reputation remained unaffected by the hostility aroused by Peckinpah's subsequent work. If not, as some have claimed, his best film, it's surely his most perfect.

—Philip Kemp

RIEN QUE LES HEURES

(Only the Hours)

France, 1926

Director: Alberto Cavalcanti

Production: Néofilm (Paris); black and white, 35mm, silent; running time: 45 minutes. Released 1926. Filmed in Paris.

Photography: Jimmy Rogers; **editor:** Alberto Cavalcanti; **art director:** M. Mirovitch.

Publications

Books:

Klaue, Wolfgang, and others, *Cavalcanti*, Berlin, 1962.

Barsam, Richard, *Nonfiction Film: A Critical History*, New York, 1973.

Barnouw, Erik, *Documentary: A History of the Non-Fiction Film*, New York, 1974.

Ellis, Jack C., *The Documentary Idea*, Englewood Cliffs, New Jersey, 1989.

Articles:

Grierson, John, ''Documentary,'' in *Cinema Quarterly* (London), Winter 1932.

''Cavalcanti: His Film Works,'' in *Quarterly of Film, Radio, and Television* (Berkeley), Summer 1955.

Rodriquez Monegal, Emir, ''Albert Cavalcanti,'' in *Quarterly of Film, Radio, and Televisions* (Berkeley), Summer 1955.

Minish, Geoffrey, ''Cavalcanti in Paris,'' in *Sight and Sound* (London), Summer 1970.

Beylie, Claude, and others, ''Alberto Cavalcanti,'' in *Ecran* (Paris), November 1974.

Rodriguez Monegal, Emil, ''Alberto Cavalcanti,'' in *Nonfiction Film Theory and Criticism*, edited by Richard Barsam, New York, 1976.

Jacobs, Lewis, ''Two Aspects of the City: Cavalcanti and Ruttmann,'' in *The Documentary Tradition*, New York, 1979.

Buache, F., in *Travelling*, no. 56/57, Spring 1980.

Nave, B., ''Alberto Cavalcanti: portrait d'un explorateur du cinema,'' in *Jeune Cinéma* (Paris), no. 195, June/July 1989.

Cosandey, R., ''Alberto Cavalcanti,'' in *Plateau*, vol. 10, no. 2, 1989.

Rodrigues, A., and A. Marchand, ''Alberto Cavalcanti: An 'Extraordinary Ordinary Man,''' in *Griffithiana*, no. 60/61, October 1997.

* * *

Rien que les heures was the first of the ''city symphony'' films. It was followed by *Berlin: Die Sinfonie der Grossstadt (Berlin: Symphony of a Great City)* (1927, Walter Ruttmann), *Chelovek s kinoapparatom (The Man with a Movie Camera)* (Moscow, 1929, Dziga Vertov), and *Regen (Rain)* (Amsterdam, 1929, Joris Ivens). This genre grew out of the interest of 1920s avant-garde filmmakers in the interrelationship between space and time. It is related to the method of the earlier French impressionist painters in their attempts to capture quick views and concentration on surfaces and light. The genre is also related to novels of the time which offer a cross-section of city life during a limited period, e.g. Joyce's *Ulysses* (1922) and Dos Passos's *Manhattan Transfer* (1925). The city symphony films were one of the strands that led into the documentary; Cavalcanti, Ruttmann, Vertov, and Ivens all subsequently became identified with documentaries. Paul Rotha, of British documentary, called these filmmakers ''continental realists.'' Cavalcanti moved from the avant-garde of France in the 1920s to the documentary of Britain in the 1930s.

Rien que les heures is a curious and fascinating mixture of the aesthetic and the social. It deals with Paris from pre-dawn to well into the following night—roughly 24 hours. The opening titles promise that we will not be looking at the elegant life but rather at that of the lower classes. Thus the social viewpoint is established. A philosophical thesis about time and space is also introduced and returned to. At the end we are asked, after we have seen what the filmmaker can show us of Paris, to consider Paris in relation to Peking. The titles assert that we can fix a point in space, immobilize a moment in time, but that space and time both escape our possession. Life is ongoing and interrelated. Without their monuments you can't tell cities apart.

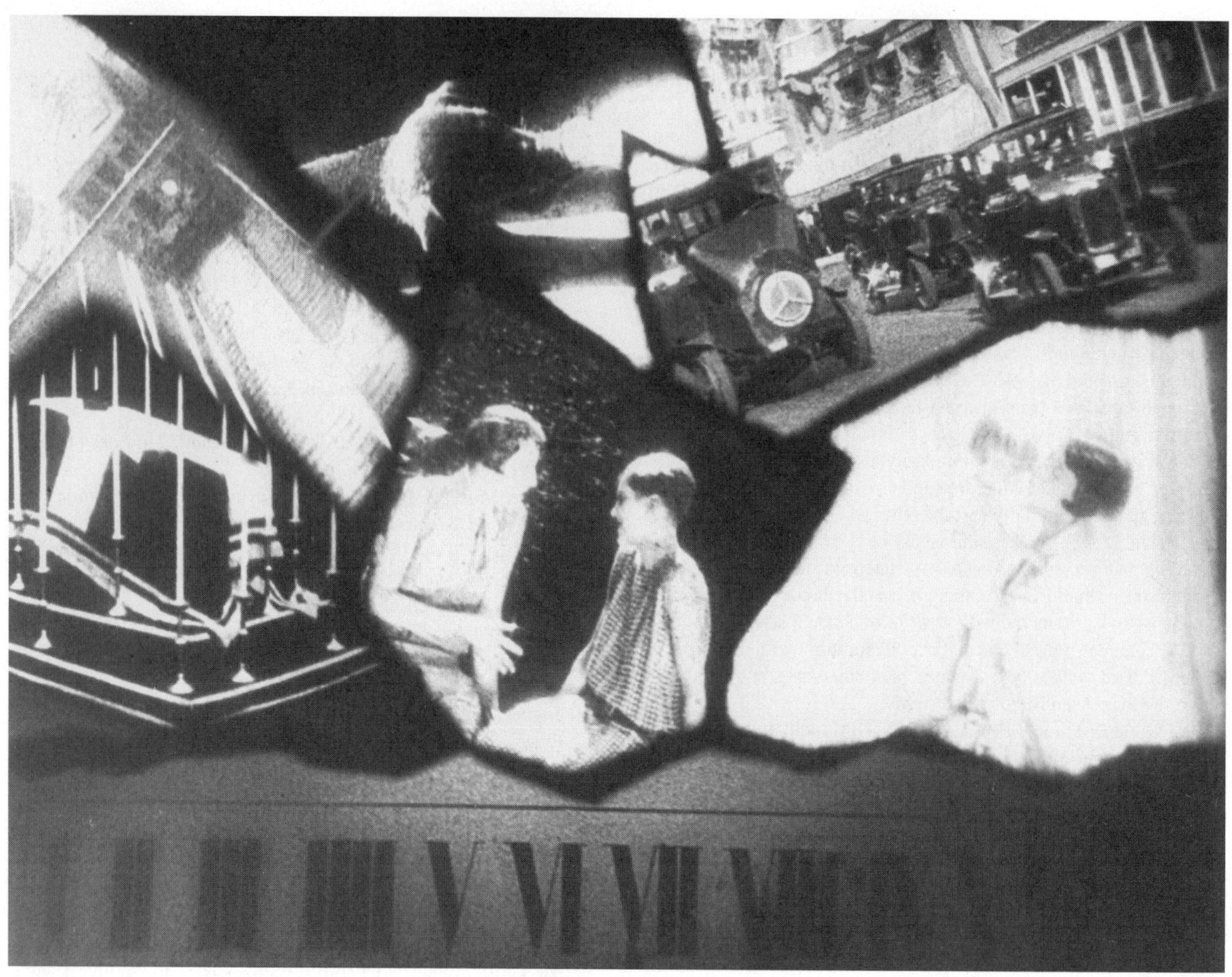

Rien que les heures

Mainly the film is devoted to contrasting scenes and changing activities of Paris during the passing hours: early morning revellers, deserted streets, the first workers appear; then there are workers at work; then lunchtime; some people are swimming in the afternoon; work ceases, rest and recreation occupy the evening. But among these views of unstaged actuality are inserted three brief, staged, fragmented narratives. The subjects of all three are female—an old derelict (drunken or ill), a prostitute, a newspaper vendor—all of them pathetic figures. The overall mood of the film is a bit downbeat; there is a sweet sadness, a sentimental toughness about it that looks ahead to the poetic realism of the 1930s and the films of Jacques Prévert and Marcel Carné.

Still, Cavalcanti's viewpoint about all of this seems to be one of detachment: ''c'est la vie,'' he seems to be saying. Though some concern with social matters is evident, the considerable number and variety of highly stylized special effects—wipes, multiple exposures, fast motion, spinning images, split screen, freeze frames—seem to confirm that Calvalcanti's greatest interest was in the artistic experimentation.

—Jack C. Ellis

RIFIFI

See **DU RIFIFI CHEZ LES HOMMES**

RIO BRAVO

USA, 1959

Director: Howard Hawks

Production: Armada Productions; Technicolor, 35mm; running time: 141 minutes. Released 1959. Filmed in Old Tucson, Arizona.

Producer: Howard Hawks; **screenplay:** Jules Furthman and Leigh Brackett, from a novelette by B. H. McCampbell; **photography:** Russell Harlan; **editor:** Folmar Blangsted; **sound:** Robert B. Lee; **art director:** Leo K. Kuter; **music director:** Dimitri Tiomkin; **songs:** Dimitri Tiomkin and Francis Webster; **costume designer:** Marjorie Best; **makeup:** Gordan Bau.

Cast: John Wayne (*John T. Chance*); Dean Martin (*Dude*); Ricky Nelson (*Colorado Ryan*); Angie Dickinson (*Feathers*); Walter Brennan (*Stumpy*); Ward Bond (*Pat Wheeler*); John Russell (*Nathan Burdette*); Pedro Gonzalez-Gonzalez (*Carlos*); Estelita Rodriguez (*Consuelo*); Claude Akins (*Joe Burdett*); Malcolm Atterbury (*Jake*); Harry Carey, Jr. (*Harold*); Bob Steele (*Matt Harris*); Myron Healey (*Barfly*); Fred Graham and Tom Monroe (*Hired hands*); Riley Hill (*Messenger*).

Publications

Books:

Bogdanovich, Peter, *The Cinema of Howard Hawks*, New York, 1962.
Fenin, George N., *The Western: From Silents to Cinerama*, New York, 1962.
Agel, Henri, *Romance américaine*, Paris, 1963.
Rieupevrout, Jean-Louis, *La Grande Aventure du Western*, Paris, 1964.
Missiaen, Jean-Claude, *Howard Hawks*, Paris, 1966.
Wood, Robin, *Howard Hawks*, New York, 1968; revised edition, 1981.
Ricci, Mark, Boris Zmijewsky, and Steven Zmijewsky, *The Films of John Wayne*, New York, 1970; revised edition, as *The Complete Films of John Wayne*, Secaucus, New Jersey, 1983.
Gigli, Jean A., *Howard Hawks*, Paris, 1971.
McBride, Joseph, editor, *Focus on Howard Hawks*, Englewood Cliffs, New Jersey, 1972.
French, Philip, *Westerns—Aspects of a Movie Genre*, New York, 1973.
Willis, D. C., *The Films of Howard Hawks*, Metuchen, New Jersey, 1975.
Parish, James Robert, and Michael Pitts, *The Great Western Pictures*, Metuchen, New Jersey, 1976.
Murphy, Kathleen A., *Howard Hawks: An American Auteur in the Hemingway Tradition*, Ann Arbor, Michigan, 1978.
Ciment, Michael, *Les Conquérants d'un nouveau monde: Essais sur le cinéma américain*, Paris, 1981.
Giannetti, Louis, *Masters of the American Cinema*, Englewood Cliffs, New Jersey, 1981.
McBride, Joseph, *Hawks on Hawks*, Berkeley, 1982.
Mast, Gerald, *Howard Hawks, Storyteller*, New York, 1982.
Poague, Leland, *Howard Hawks*, Boston, 1982.
Simsolo, Noël, *Howard Hawks*, Paris, 1984.
Kieskalt, Charles John, *The Official John Wayne Reference Book*, Secaucus, New Jersey, 1985.
Shepherd, Donald, and others, *Duke: The Life and Times of John Wayne*, London, 1985.
Branson, Clark, *Howard Hawks: A Jungian Study*, Los Angeles, 1987.
Lepper, David, *John Wayne*, London, 1987.
Buscombe, Ed, editor, *BFI Companion to the Western*, London, 1988.
Levy, Emanuel, *John Wayne: Prophet of the American Way of Life*, Metuchen, New Jersey, 1988.
Riggin, Judith M., *John Wayne: A Bio-Bibliography*, New York, 1992.
Fagen, Herb, *Duke, We're Glad We Knew You: John Wayne's Friends and Colleagues Remember His Remarkable Life*, New York, 1996.
Hillier, Jim, *Howard Hawks: American Artist*, Champaign, 1997.
McCarthy, Todd, *Howard Hawks: The Grey Fox of Hollywood*, New York, 1997.
Roberts, Randy, *John Wayne: American*, Lincoln, 1997.

Rio Bravo

Articles:

Films and Filming (London), 1959.
Perez, Michel, ''Howard Hawks et le western,'' in *Présence du Cinéma* (Paris), July-September 1959.
Sarris, Andrew, ''The World of Howard Hawks,'' in *Films and Filming* (London), July 1962 and August 1962.
''Howard Hawks,'' in *Movie* (London), December 1962.
Wood, Robin, in *Movie* (London), December 1962.
''Hawks Issue'' of *Cahiers du Cinéma* (Paris), January 1963.
Austen, David, ''Gunplay and Horses,'' in *Films and Filming* (London), October 1968.
Hall, Dennis John, ''Tall in the Saddle,'' in *Films and Filming* (London), October 1969.
Renaud, T., in *Cinéma* (Paris), January 1973.
Bourget, J. L., ''Hawks et le mythe de l'ouest américain,'' in *Positif* (Paris), July-August 1977.
Masson, A., ''Organiser le sensible,'' in *Positif* (Paris), July-August 1977.
Boyero, C., in *Casablanca* (Madrid), July-August 1981.
Daney, S., ''Un art adulte,'' in *Cahiers du Cinéma* (Paris), July-August 1992.
Sijan, S., ''Une image de *Rio Bravo*,'' in *Positif* (Paris), no. 400, June 1994.
Cabrera Infante, G., ''Infante,'' in *Filmihullu* (Helsinki), no. 5, 1994.

* * *

Rio Bravo is one of the supreme achievements (hence justifications) of ''classical Hollywood,'' that complex network of determinants that includes the star system, the studio system, the system of genres and conventions, a highly developed grammar and syntax of shooting and editing, the interaction of which made possible an art at once personal and collaborative, one nourished by a rich and vital tradition: it is an art that belongs now to the past; the period of *Rio Bravo* was its last flowering.

The film at once is one of the greatest westerns and the most complete statements of the themes of director Howard Hawks. One can distinguish two main currents within the western genre, the ''historical'' and the ''conventional'': the western that is concerned with the American past (albeit with its mythology as much as its reality), and the western that plays with and develops a set of conventions, archetypes, ''stock'' figures. Ford's westerns are the finest examples of the former impulse, and in the westerns of Anthony Mann (for example, *Man of the West*) the two achieve perfect fusion. *Rio Bravo* is among the purest of all ''conventional'' westerns. Here, history and the American past are of no concern, a point amply demonstrated by the fact that the film is a virtual remake (in its thematic pattern, its characters and character relationships, even down to sketches of dialogue) of Hawks's earlier *Only Angels Have Wings* (set in the Andes mountains) and *To Have and Have Not* (set on Martinique). Hawks's stylized and anonymous western town is not a microcosm of American civilization at a certain point in its development but an abstract setting within which his recurrent concerns and relationships can be played out. All the characters are on one level ''western'' archetypes: the infallible sheriff, the fallible friend, the ''travelling lady,'' the garrulous sidekick, the comic Mexican, the evil land-baron. On another level, however, they are Hawksian archetypes: the overlay makes possible the richness of characterization, the detail of the acting, so that here the archetypes (western and Hawksian) achieve their ultimate elaboration. With this goes the remarkable and varied use Hawks makes of actors' personas: Martin, Dickinson, and Brennan have never surpassed (perhaps never equalled) their performances here, and the use of Wayne is etremely subtle and idiosyncratic, at once drawing on his ''heroic'' status and satirizing its limitations.

The film represents Hawks's most successful transcendence of the chief ''binary opposition'' of his work, its division into adventure films and comedies. Here the thematic concerns of the action pictures—self-respect, personal integrity, loyalty, stoicism, the interplay of mutual respect and affection—combines with the sexual tensions of the comedies (Wayne's vulnerability to women permitting a fuller development of this than is possible with, for example, Bogart in *To Have and Have Not*). The ambiguous relationship of Hawks's work to dominant American ideological assumptions (on the one hand the endorsement of individualism and personal initiative, on the other the rejection of established society in favour of the ''primitive'' male group, the total lack of interest in such central American ideals as marriage, home and family) permeates the whole film. The ''gay subtext'' that many critics have sensed in Hawks's films—their tendency to become (in his own words) ''love stories between men''—surfaces quite clearly in the Dean Martin-Ricky Nelson relationship, though it is never allowed expression beyond the exchange of looks and is swiftly ''contained'' within the group (a progression beautifully enacted in the famous song-sequence). Within a system necessarily committed, at least on surface level, to reinforcing the status quo, Hawks's cinema continuously suggests the possibility of alternative forms of social and sexual organization.

—Robin Wood

THE RIVER

See **He Liu**

THE RIVER

USA, 1937

Director: Pare Lorentz

Production: Farm Security Administration, United States Government; black and white, 35mm; running time: 32 minutes. Released 20 October 1937, premiering in New Orleans. Filmed October 1936–1 March 1937 along the Mississippi River Valley, beginning in West Virginia and concluding in New Orleans. Cost: budgeted at $50,000, plus additional funds for shooting flood sequences.

Screenplay: Pare Lorentz; **photography:** Floyd Crosby, Stacy Woodward, and Willard Van Dyke; **editors:** Pare Lorentz with Lloyd Nosler; **music:** Virgil Thomson; **conductor:** Alexander Smallens.

Cast: Thomas Chalmers (*Narrator*).

Awards: Venice International Film Festival, Best Documentary, 1938.

Publications

Script:

Lorentz, Pare, *The River: A Scenario*, New York, 1938.

Books:

Snyder, Robert L., *Pare Lorentz and the Documentary Film*, Norman, Oklahoma 1968, 1993.
Barsam, Richard, *Nonfiction Film: A Critical History*, New York, 1973.
Dyer MacCann, Richard, *The People's Films: A Political History of U.S. Government Motion Pictures*, New York, 1973.
Barnouw, Erik, *Documentary: A History of the Non-Fiction Film*, New York, 1974.
Alexander, William, *Film on the Left: American Documentary Film from 1931–1942*, Princeton, New Jersey, 1981.
Ellis, Jack C., *The Documentary Idea*, Englewood Cliffs, New Jersey, 1989.
Lorentz, Pare, *FDR's Moviemaker: Memoirs and Scripts*, Reno, 1992.

Articles:

Time (New York), 8 November 1937.
Ferguson, Otis, in *New Republic* (New York), 10 November 1937.

Seldes, Gilbert, in *Scribner's* (New York), January 1938.
Barnes, Harold, in *Herald-Tribune* (New York), 5 February 1938.
Nugent, Frank, in *New York Times*, 5 and 6 February 1938.
Saturday Review of Literature (New York), April 1938.
''Award to Pare Lorentz.'' in *Magazine of Art* (New York), July 1938.
Goodman, Ezra, ''The American Documentary,'' in *Sight and Sound* (London), Autumn 1938.
White, W. L., ''Pare Lorentz,'' in *Scribner's* (New York), January 1939.
''Pare Lorentz,'' in *Current Biography Yearbook*, New York, 1940.
Lorentz, Pare, ''The Narration of *The River*,'' in *Film Comment* (New York), Spring 1965.
Van Dyke, Willard, ''Letters from *The River*,'' in *Film Comment* (New York), March-April 1965.
''Conscience of the 30s,'' in *Newsweek* (New York), 5 August 1968.
Engle, Harrison, ''30 Years of Social Inquiry: An Interview with Willard Van Dyke,'' in *Nonfiction Film: Theory and Criticism*, edited by Richard Barsam, New York, 1976.
Rollins, P. C., ''Ideology and Film Rhetoric: Three Documentaries of the New Deal Era,'' in *Journal of Popular Film* (Washington, D.C.), no. 2, 1976.
Miller, C. A., ''A Note of Pare Lorentz's *The River*,'' in *Film and History* (Newark, New Jersey), December 1980.
Georgakas, D., ''Cinema of the New Deal,'' in *Cineaste* (New York), vol. 21, no. 4, 1995.

* * *

Persuasive and poetic, *The River* is probably the best film ever made about conservation of natural resources. Produced by the U.S. government during 1936, released in theatres in 1937 to extraordinary critical acclaim, it competed with 70 other films to win the prize for documentary at the Venice Film Festival in 1938. For many years, *The River* was a popular rental item for 16mm libraries for classroom use, and it is still used to evoke the spirit of the 1930s in history courses. Brilliant and beautiful today, especially when projected in an auditorium from a recent print, it is a prime example of art bearing a message.

The River is usually thought of in connection with *The Plow That Broke the Plains* (1935–36), also produced for the special New Deal relief agency called the Resettlement Administration (later the Farm Security Administration) and also written and directed by Pare Lorentz. The first film had been about the overplowing of midwestern land, resulting in the devastating dust storms of the 1930s. The second film was about the erratic and widespread cutting of trees and destruction of grass cover which resulted in repeated floods on the Mississippi.

Lorentz was a young maverick liberal from West Virginia who used to hear his father and friends sound off on the dangers to the land when timber was cut from the ridges and chemicals were dumped in the rivers. He left the state university to go to work as a writer in New York City, working for the General Electric house organ, for *Newsweek* (where he did a long piece on the dust storms), and for ten years as movie editor for *Judge* magazine. Friends of his wife in Washington brought him together with Rex Tugwell, one of the Franklin Roosevelt ''brain trusters'' who had plans for publicizing widely the need for conservation and for government action.

Although as a critic he was something of an expert on movies, Lorentz had never in his life been responsible for making any part of a motion picture. He learned how on *The Plow That Broke the Plains*, which was originally proposed as a training film for RA staff people helping farmers to be ''resettled'' on good land and use it more effectively. It developed into a highly controversial documentary shown in theatres, reviewed by critics, and used in the 1936 campaign by Democratic candidates for Congress. In style and approach, it came out as strong negative propaganda, ending with dust and displaced people, leaving audiences with a sense of guilt and hopelessness,

The River became a different kind of persuasive statement. It ended with an extended coda, starting with a map of the valley, from the Missouri down to the gulf, then closing in on the Tennessee River, where the Tennessee Valley Authority had begun the taming of the floods, the control of navigation, and the kind of planning for power distribution which would bring safety and prosperity to that valley. It was a positive and heartening conclusion, an affirmation of man's political ability to plan.

The River was also a unique attempt to offer a kind of American frontier style of poetry in its narration. Twice a list of the major rivers in the Mississippi system is given a rhythmic reading, once to suggest how the waters come down every spring, again to show how they come down disastrously at time of flood. This risky kind of monologue occurred to Lorentz as an ideal way to write an article in *McCall's* magazine. It received such a big response of reader mail that he decided to adapt it for his film.

The communicative virtues of the creative imagination are nicely illustrated in this U.S. government film, which was in large part based upon an official document. The Mississippi Valley Committee had written about forest and grass cover: ''When this protective cover is disturbed by forest destruction, tillage, or overgrazing of livestock, erosion is accelerated.'' Lorentz the artist put it this way: ''Year in, year out, the water comes down, down from a thousand hillsides, washing the top off the Valley.''

The trusting, powerful narration, combined with the compelling use of U.S. themes in Virgil Thomson's musical track and the aesthetic values of the black-and-white photography—evoking beauty in the early scenes, stark tragedy later—made *The River* a striking achievement from almost every critical standpoint. Frank Nugent in the *New York Times*, called it ''poetic, stirring, and majestic,'' Gilbert Seldes in *Scribner's* gave the film a special write-up, and Howard Barnes in the *New York Herald-Tribune* praised its ''brooding beauty and impact,'' its unity and economy, making ''social history vital, understandable, and dramatic.'' As for popular response, theatre managers reported to Paramount, which had agreed to release it, that *The River* drew audience ''applause at every showing.''

Lorentz went on to make and to supervise other films for an agency Roosevelt and his advisers called the U.S. Film Service. He hired Robert Flaherty to do a film called *The Land* for the Agricultural Adjustment Administration, and Joris Ivens to dramatize the services to one family by the Rural Electrification Administration in *Power and the Land.* But his own melodramatic feature-length story about a local maternity centre, *The Fight for Life*, was objected to by Congressional committees and by Senator Robert Taft on the floor of the Senate. The threat of World War II and a history of conflict between the Congress and Pare Lorentz's various sponsors overshadowed any possibilities for good in centralized U.S. government film making comparable to such agencies in England and Canada. Appropriations for the Film Service were finally denied in 1940.

—Richard Dyer MacCann

THE ROAD

See **STRADA, LA**

THE ROAD TO LIFE

See **PUTYOVKA V ZHIZN**

ROCCO E I SUOI FRATELLI

(Rocco and His Brothers)

Italy-France, 1960

Director: Luchino Visconti

Production: Titanus and Les Films Marceau; black and white, 35mm; running time: 182 minutes; length: 4,973 meters originally, usually distributed in versions of 3,600 meters. Released 15 October 1960, premiered at Venice Film Festival on 6 September 1960.

Producer: Goffredo Lombardo; **subject:** Luchino Visconti, Vasco Pratolini, and Suco Cecchi D'Amico; **screenplay:** Luchino Visconti, Suso Cocchi d'Amico, Pasquale Festa Campanile, Massimo Franciosa, and Enrico Medioli, from the book *Il ponte della ghisolfa* by Giovanni Testori; **assistant directors:** Jerry Macc and Lucio Orlandini; **photography:** Giuseppe Rotunno; **editor:** Mario Serandrei; **sound:** Giovanni Rossi; **art director:** Mario Garbuglia; **music:** Nino Rota; **costume designer:** Piero Tosi.

Cast: Alain Delon (*Rocco*); Renato Salvatori (*Simone*); Annie Girardot (*Nadia*); Katina Paxinou (*Rosaria*); Roger Hanin (*Morini*); Paolo Stoppa (*Impresario*); Suzy Delair (*Luisa*); Claudia Cardinale (*Ginetta*); Spiros Focas (*Vincenzo*); Rocco Vidolazzi (*Luca*); Corrado Pani (*Ivo*); Max Cartier (*Ciro*); Alessandra Panaro (*Ciro's fiancée*); Claudia Mori (*Laundry worker*); Becker Masocro (*Nadia's mother*).

Awards: David di Donatello prize for best production, 1960; Venice Film Festival, Special Jury Prize and International Film Critics Award, 1960; Festival of Workers (Czechoslovakia), First Prize, 1961.

Publications

Script:

Visconti, Luchino, Vasco Pratolini, and Suso Cecchi D'Amico, *Rocco e i suoi fratelli*, edited by Guido Aristarco and G. Carancini, Milan, 1960; also published Bologna, 1978; as *Rocco and His Brothers*, in *Luchino Visconti: Three Screenplays*, New York, 1970.

Books:

Elizondon, Salvador, *Luchino Visconti*, Mexico, 1963.
Baldelli, Pio, *I film di Luchino Visconti*, Manduria, 1965.
Sitova, V., *Luchino Visconti*, Moscow, 1965.
Guillaume, Yves, *Visconti*, Paris, 1966.
Nowell-Smith, Geoffrey, *Luchino Visconti*, New York, 1968; revised edition, 1983.
Buache, Freddy, *Le cinema italien, d'Antonioni a Rosi*, Yverdon, 1969.
Speranzi, M., editor, *L'Opera di Luchino Visconti*, Florence, 1969.
Ferrara, Guiseppe, *Visconti*, Paris, 2nd edition, 1970.
La crisi dell'uomo e della societe nei film di Visconti e di Antonioni, Alba, 1972.
Luchino Visconti, Munich, 1975.
Callegari, G., and N. Lodato, editors, *Leggere Visconti*, Pavia, 1976.
Ferrara, Adelio, editor, *Visconti: il cinema*, Milan, 1977.
Tornabuoni, Lietta, editor, *Album Visconti*, Milan, 1978.
Stirling, Monica, *A Screen of Time*, New York, 1979.
Visconti, Luchino, *Il mio teatro*, Bologna, 1979.
Servadio, Gaia, *Luchino Visconti*, Milan, 1980; translated as *Luchino Visconti*, New York, 1983.
Rondolino, Gianni, *Luchino Visconti*, Turin, 1981.
Bencivenni, Alessandro, *Luchino Visconti*, Florence, 1982.
Tonetti, Claretta, *Luchino Visconti*, Boston, 1983.
Ishaghpour, Youssef, *Luchino Visconti: Le sens et l'image*, Paris, 1984.
Sanzio, Alain, and Paul-Louis Thirard, *Luchino Visconti: Cinéaste*, Paris, 1984.
De Guisti, Luciano, *I film di Luchino Visconti*, Rome, 1985.
Geitel, Klaus, and others, *Luchino Visconti*, 4th edition, Munich, 1985.
Mancini, Elaine, *Luchino Visconti: A Guide to References and Resources*, Boston, 1986.
Villien, Bruno, *Visconti*, Paris, 1986.
Schifano, Laurence, *Luchino Visconti: Les feux de la passion*, Paris, 1987.
Rohdie, Sam, *Rocco and His Brothers*, London, 1992.
Renzi, Renzo, *Visconti segreto*, Rome, 1994.
Bacon, Henry, *Visconti: Explorations of Beauty and Decay*, New York, 1998.
Bacon, Henry, *Visconti: His Life, His Films*, New York, 1998.
Tonetti, *Luchino Visconti*, New York, 1998.

Articles:

Moravia, Alberto, in *Espresso*, 6 March 1960.
''Visconti Interview,'' in *Cinema Nuovo* (Turin), September-October 1970.
Dal Sasso, Rino, in *Filmcritica* (Rome), October 1960.
Visconti, Luchino, ''Oltre il fato dei Malavoglia,'' in *Vie nuove*, October 1960.
Prouse, Derek, in *Sight and Sound* (London), Winter 1960–61.
Pandolfi, Vito, in *Film* (Milan), 1961.
Aristarco, Guido, ''The Earth Still Trembles.'' in *Films and Filming* (London), January 1961.
Visconti, Luchino, ''The Miracle That Gave Man Crumbs,'' in *Films and Filming* (London), January 1961.
Sadoul, Georges, in *Lettres Françaises* (Paris), 9 March 1961.
''Visconti Issue'' of *Premier Plan* (Lyons), May 1961.
Crowther, Bosley, in *New York Times*, 28 June 1961.
Benayoun, Robert, in *Positif* (Paris), July 1961.
Young, Vernon, in *Film Quarterly* (Berkeley), Fall 1961.
Manvell, Roger, in *Films and Filming* (London), October 1961.
Armitage, P., ''Visconti and Rocco,'' in *Film* (London), Winter 1961.

Rocco e i suoi fratelli

Minoff, L., ''New Old Master,'' in *Saturday Review* (New York), 29 December 1962.

''Visconti Issue'' of *Etudes Cinématographiques* (Paris), no. 26–27, 1963.

Cinéma (Paris), September-October 1963.

Buschkowsky, Madina, in *Jahrbuch des Film 1962*, Berlin, 1964.

Koppel, Helga, in *Film in Italien, Italien in Film*, Berlin, 1970.

Elsaesser, Thomas, ''Luchino Visconti,'' in *Brighton Film Review*, February 1970.

Korte, Walter, ''Marxism and Formalism in the Films of Luchino Visconti,'' in *Cinema Journal* (Evanston, Illinois), Fall 1971.

Zolotuski, I., ''Treska i sintez,'' in *Kinoizkustvo* (Sofia), January 1972.

Verstappen, W., ''Visconti laat zich niet bij pilsje navertellen: *Rocco* op de montagetafel,'' in *Skoop* (Amsterdam), August-September 1978.

New York Times, 7 January 1979.

Verhage, G., in *Skrien* (Amsterdam), May 1979.

Shivas, Mark, in *Film* (London), November 1979.

Filmfaust (Frankfurt), February-March 1983.

Meyer, M. P., in *Skrien* (Amsterdam), April-May 1984.

Listener, vol. 124, no. 3188, 25 October 1990.

Nowell-Smith, Geoffrey, in *Monthly Film Bulletin* (London), vol. 57, no. 683, December 1990.

Canby, V., ''Review/Film: Vintage Visconti, At Full Length,'' in *New York Times*, vol. 141, C8, 24 January 1992.

Brown, G., ''Family Plots,'' in *Village Voice* (New York), vol. 37, 4 February 1992.

Ehrenstein, David, ''*Rocco* Is One Of the Key Works of Luchino Visconti's Career,'' in *The Advocate*, no. 604, 2 June 1992.

* * *

Rocco e i suoi fratelli appeared in the same year as Fellini's *La dolce vita*, and together they indicated, in opposite ways, the major possibilities for the Italian cinema of that decade. As artistically successful as director Visconti's earlier *La terra trema* (1948) and *Senso* (1954), *Rocco* is, however, even more rigorous and has its roots in a larger and richer cultural base. Although not an adaption of any particular literary piece, it draws from works as diverse as Dostoevski's *The Idiot* (Myshkin inspiring the character of Rocco, Rogosin inspiring that of Simone), Giovanni Testori's stories of Milan (especially *Il ponte della Ghisolfa*), and Thomas Mann's *Joseph and His Brothers*. The film also displays the interests and the realistic style of most of Visconti's theatre work from 1945, which included studies of emigrants and the social community to which they belong, as in his staging of Arthur Miller's *A View from a Bridge* (1958). Most Italian critics saw this film as the finest example of the critical realism called for in the writings of Lukacs. Visconti himself saw it as a further examination of Verga's characterizations and Gramsci's analysis of the Southern social and political condition. In fact, Visconti considered *Rocco* a sequel to *La terra trema*.

Visconti's critical realism takes the form of a study of each member of a Sicilian family of five sons and a mother (some characters receiving more emphasis than others) who have emigrated to the industrial Northern city of Milan. Each character responds to his or her situation in utterly different ways. Visconti thus achieved a complex structure that was to be attempted again by Bertolucci, one of his greatest admirers, in *1900*. Originally Visconti conceived of the film as built around the mother, but the final film analysed more closely the two middle sons, Rocco and Simone, both of whom become boxers but have entirely opposite personalities. Simone is fierce and instinctual; Rocco is passive and thoughtful. Rocco sacrifices himself, his love (Annie Girardot's portrayal of Nadia was universally praised), and his dreams, for his brother and his family. The last scene is devoted to Ciro, the son who reaches political awareness, the only member of the family to become truly a part of the urban community. Ciro's final speech to his younger brother reveals Visconti's intention to "arrive at social and political conclusions, having taken during the film the road of psychological investigation and faithful reconstruction of a drama."

Visconti often had problems with the censors, and *Rocco* was no exception. During production he was forced to change a location because it was felt that to film Nadia's death scene there would harm the tourist trade. At its world premiere in Venice, the film was projected with scenes cut and run with the soundtrack only. Many cuts were required before general release, and later the city of Milan refused to have it distributed there. The prints circulated in Italy run 45 minutes shorter than the original version. Nevertheless, *Rocco* was the first Visconti film to achieve enormous commercial success in its national market, and it convinced the film community that Visconti was indeed a major film director. For the most part, the film earned praise throughout the world, though a few critics abhorred the portrayal of violence and considered the film morally questionable.

—Elaine Mancini

THE ROCKY HORROR PICTURE SHOW

USA, 1975

Director: Jim Sharman

Production: Twentieth Century-Fox; Eastmancolor, 35mm; running time: 100 minutes. Released 1975.

The Rocky Horror Picture Show

Producers: Michael White with John Goldstone; **executive producer:** Lou Adler; **screenplay:** Jim Sharman and Richard O'Brien, from the play by O'Brien; **photography:** Peter Suschitzky; **editors:** Graeme Clifford; **art director:** Terry Ackland Snow; **design consultant:** Brian Thomson; **songs:** Richard O'Brien; **music director:** Richard Hartley; **special effects:** Wally Veevers; **costume designers:** Richard Pointing and Gillian Dods; **costume consultant:** Sue Blane.

Cast: Tim Curry (*Dr. Frank N. Furter*); Barry Bostwick (*Brad Majors*); Susan Sarandon (*Janet Weiss*); Richard O'Brien (*Riff Raff*); Jonathan Adams (*Dr. Everett Scott*); Nell Campbell (*Columbia*); Peter Hinwood (*Rocky*); Meat Loaf (*Eddie*); Patricia Quinn (*Magenta*); Charles Gray (*Narrator*); Hilary Labow (*Betty Munroe*); Jeremy Newson (*Ralph Hapschatt*); Frank Lester (*Wedding Dad*); Mark Johnson (*Wedding guest*); Koo Stark, Petra Leah, and Gina Barrie (*Bridesmaids*); John Marquand (*Father*).

Publications

Books:

Henkin, Bill, *The Rocky Horror Picture Show Book*, New York, 1979.
Hoberman, J., and Jonathan Rosenbaum, *Midnight Movies*, New York, 1983.
Samuels, Stuart, *Midnight Movies*, New York, 1983.

Articles:

Hollywood Reporter, 26 October 1974.
Rayns, Tony, in *Monthly Film Bulletin* (London), August 1975.
Listener (London), 28 August 1975.
Stuart, A., in *Films and Filming* (London), September 1975.
Pitman, J., in *Variety* (New York), 24 September 1975.
Care, R., in *Cinefantastique* (Oak Park, Illinois), no. 2, 1976.
Monthly Film Bulletin (London), March 1976.
Behar, H., in *Revue du Cinéma* (Paris), October 1976.
''South Africa Bans *Rocky Horror* Pic,'' in *Variety* (New York), 13 October 1976.
Time Out (London), April 1979.
Segell, M., ''*Rocky Horror*: The Case of the Rampant Audience,'' in *Rolling Stone* (New York), 5 April 1979.
Baer, W., in *Film und Ton* (Munich), July 1979.
Von Gunden, K., ''The RH Factor,'' in *Film Comment* (New York), September-October 1979.
Bold, R., in *Christian Century* (Chicago), 12 September 1979.
Rosenbaum, Jonathan, ''The Rocky Horror Picture Cult,'' in *Sight and Sound* (London), Spring 1980.
Starburst (London), no. 36, 1981.
Austin, B. A., ''Portrait of a Cult Film Audience: *The Rocky Horror Picture Show*,'' in *Journal of Communication* (Philadelphia), Spring 1981.
Screen International (London), July 1982.
Schaefer, S., ''*Rocky X*, Penny, and the Mylons,'' in *Film Comment* (New York), January-February 1986.
Studlar, G., ''Midnight S/excess: Cult Configurations of 'Femininity' and the Perverse,'' in *Journal of Popular Film and Television* (Washington, D.C.), vol. 17, no. 1 1989.
Hoberman, J., and Jonathan Rosenbaum, ''Curse of the Cult People,'' in *Film Comment* (New York), January-February 1991.
Aviram, A. F., ''Postmodern Gay Dionysus: Dr. Frank N. Furter,'' in *Journal of Popular Culture* (Bowling Green, Ohio), no. 3, 1992.
Aknin, Laurent, '''I Was a Regular Frankie Fan': *Rocky Horror Picture Show*, mode d'emploi,'' in *Vertigo* (Paris), no. 10, 1993.
Webb, C.H., ''(Twenty) 20 Years Late to See *The Rocky Horror Picture Show*,'' in *Michigan Quarterly Review*, vol. 34, no. 4, 1995.
''In a Time Warp,'' in *Newsweek*, vol. 133, no. 3, 18 January 1999.

* * *

Less interesting as cinema than as a social phenomenon, *The Rocky Horror Picture Show* began as a hit British fringe musical. Richard O'Brien's *The Rocky Horror Show* was first staged in 1973 at the Theatre Upstairs, with Tim Curry and O'Brien creating the roles of Frank N. Furter, bisexual transvestite mad scientist from another world, and Riff-Raff, Furter's hunchbacked assistant. *The Rocky Horror Picture Show* arrived on screens in 1975 just after *The Rocky Horror Show* closed disastrously on Broadway, prompting 20th Century Fox to throw it away. Nevertheless, the film made a comeback as a midnight attraction across America, gaining an increasingly devoted following. The fancy-dress fanatics who patronize the film indulge in an unprecedented interaction with the on-screen events, interpolating new lines as footnotes to the dialogue (yelling ''No Neck'' every time Charles Gray appears, for instance), and challenging the passive nature of the cinema-going experience. A write-off on its straight release, this midnight movie has been playing continuously for nearly 20 years, a rare cult movie whose cumulative earnings rank it financially with a mainstream first-run hit.

Informed by O'Brien's love for the arcana of 1950s American pop culture (rock 'n' roll, monster movies, Charles Atlas ads, rebel bikers), the show is filtered through a staid British sensibility (Americans can hardly be expected to recognize Gray's criminologist as a parody of Edgar Lustgarten), unleashed by the rock opera conventions of *Hair* (which O'Brien and Curry had been in) and the early 1970s craze for androgynous glitter rock. Borrowing an archetypal plot (perhaps from Edgar G. Ulmer's *The Black Cat*, 1934; or Don Sharp's disguised remake *Kiss of the Vampire*, 1964), the story opens with staunch hero Brad (Barry Bostwick) and virginal heroine Janet (Susan Sarandon) forced by a flat tire and a rainstorm to spend the night in a Middle American castle. They encounter a troupe of dancing aliens from the Planet Transylvania, and the fun-loving Dr. Frank N. Furter, who minces around in a basque and fishnet stockings belting out a torch song (''I'm a Sweet Transvestite From Transsexual, Transylvania''), creates a new-born beefcake monster Rocky Horror (Peter Hinwood) for sexual purposes, and takes time to seduce both Janet and Brad. The liberated Janet has a fling with Rocky which, in a surprisingly conservative touch for such an abandoned production, brings disaster down as Frank goes out of control and has to be repressed by his puritanical servant Riff Raff.

O'Brien's catchy score is outstanding (the lyrics are especially clever) and the cast all have real attack (only Sarandon attempts subtlety), but the film is a less satisfying blend of horror pastiche and rock 'n' roll than Brian DePalma's *The Phantom of the Paradise* (1974). DePalma uses a classical horror story to get inside the equivalent myths of rock as an industry and a cultural force, but Sharman and O'Brien just scatter train-spotterish references to *Famous Monsters of Filmland* trivia (the first line, sung by a disembodied set of lips, is ''Michael Rennie was ill the Day the Earth Stood Still. . . .'') and scorchin' rock numbers through a panto-level plot. While its audience might take *The Rocky Horror Picture Show* as an endorsement of polysexual liberation, with an enthusiastic if joky depiction of transvestism and homosexuality, the theme has mainly been included to make jokes at the expense of Alice Cooper and David Bowie's Ziggy Stardust phase. Curry energetically makes a case for Frank, a camp icon over-the-top enough to be unthreatening, as a sympathetic libertarian, but the script has him as a Frankensteinian father who has created a child solely to molest him and, in a peevish moment, the casual murderer of a cast-off lover (Meat Loaf). The most honest emotional moment comes after the servant's slaying of his master, as Riff Raff's sister Magenta (Patricia Quinn) puzzles, ''I thought you liked him . . . he liked you'' only to have the hunchback, played by the real creator of *Rocky Horror*, howl ''*He never liked me*!''

The straining necessary to restage an intimate musical in a studio makes the film ragged at the edges: the camera doesn't know where it should be in the dances, characters run about to little purpose, the action never strays from the old dark house, numbers end on awkward pauses for applause and feeble jokes (''Do any of you know how to Madison?'' Brad asks after ''The Time Warp''). These pauses invite the catcalls of the cultists, but they show up as dead spots when the film is seen on video or television or in a ''straight'' venue. The freakish nature of the film's success is underlined by its creators' inability, in the semi-sequel *Shock Treatment* (1981), to do it again.

—Kim Newman

THE ROLE

See **BHUMIKA**

ROMA, CITTÀ APERTA

(Rome, Open City)

Italy, 1945

Director: Roberto Rossellini

Production: Excelsa Film; black and white, 35mm; running time: 100 minutes; length 9,586 feet. Released September 1945, Rome. Filmed in part during the liberation of Rome by the Allies, the remainder shot during early 1944. Filmed in and around Rome, and in improvised studios at the ''via degli Avignonesi'' (Liborio Capitani) and at the home of Sergio Amidei.

Screenplay: Sergio Amidei with Federico Fellini and Roberto Rossellini, from an original story by Sergio Amidei in collaboration with Alberto Consiglio and Roberto Rossellini; **photography:** Ubaldo Arata; **editor:** Eralda da Roma; **production designer:** R. Megna; music: Renzo Rossellini.

Cast: Anna Magnani (*Pina*); Aldo Fabrizi (*Don Pietro Pellegrini*); Marcello Pagliero (*Giorgio Manfredi, alias Luigi Ferraris*); Harry Feist (*Major Bergmann*); Maria Michi (*Marina Mari*); Francesco Grandjaquet (*Francesco, the typist*); Giovanna Galletti (*Ingrid*); Vito Annichiarico (*Marcello, son of Pina*); Carla Revere (*Lauretta*); Nando Bruno (*Agostino*); Carlo Sindici (*Treasurer from Rome*); Joop van Hulzen (*Hartmann*); Akos Tolnay (*Austrian deserter*); Eduardo Passarelli (*Police sergeant*); Amalia Pelegrini (*Landlady*).

Award: Cannes Film Festival, Best Film, 1946.

Publications

Script:

Amidei, Sergio, Federico Fellini, and Roberto Rossellini, *Open City*, in *Roberto Rossellino: The War Trilogy*, edited by Stefano Roncoroni, New York, 1973; first published in Bologna, 1972.

Books:

Hovald, Patrice, *Roberto Rossellini*, Paris, 1958.
Mida, Massimo, *Roberto Rossellini*, Parma, 1961.
Verdone, Mario, *Roberto Rossellini*, Paris, 1963.
Sarris, Andrew, *Interviews with Film Directors*, New York, 1967.
Ivaldi, Nedo, *La Resitenza nel cinema italiano del dopoguerra*, Rome, 1970.
Guarner, Jose Luis, *Roberto Rossellini* New York, 1970.
Armes, Roy, *Patterns of Realism: A Study of Italian Neo-Realist Cinema*, Cranbury, New Jersey, 1971.
Wlaschin, Ken, *Italian Cinema Since the War*, Cranbury, New Jersey, 1971.
Baldelli, Pio, *Roberto Rossellini*, Rome, 1972.
Leprohon, Pierre, *The Italian Cinema*, New York, 1972.
Rondolino, Gianni, *Roberto Rossellini*, Florence, 1974.
Klinowski, Jacek, and Adam Garbicz, editors, *Cinema, The Magic Vehicle: A Guide to Its Achievement: Journey One: The Cinema Through 1949*, Metuchen, New Jersey, 1975.
Rossi, Philip C., *A Rhetorical Analysis of Italian Neo-Realism in Roberto Rossellini's ''Rome, Open City,''* Ann Arbor, Michigan, 1977.
Ranvaud, Don, *Roberto Rossellini*, London 1981.
Rossellini, Roberto, *Le Cinéma Révélé*, edited by Alain Bergala, Paris 1984.
Hillier, Jim, editor, *Cahiers du Cinéma 1: The 1950s: NeoRealism, Hollywood, New Wave*, London, 1985.
Serceau, Michel, *Roberto Rossellini*, Paris, 1986.
Brunette, Peter, *Roberto Rossellini*, Oxford, 1987.
Gansera, Rainer, and others, *Roberto Rossellini*, Munich, 1987.
Rossellini, Roberto, *Il mio metodo: Scritti e intervisti*, edited by Adriano Apra, Venice, 1987.
Rossi, P., *Roberto Rossellini: A Guide to References and Resources*, Boston, 1988.
Bondanella, Peter, *Films of Roberto Rossellini*, Cambridge, 1993.
Rossellini, Roberto, *My Method: Writings and Interviews*, New York, 1995.
Gallagher, Tag, *The Adventures of Roberto Rossellini*, Cambridge, 1998.

Articles:

Desternes, Jean, ''Poesie et réalité,'' in *Revue du Cinéma* (Paris), December 1946.
Martin, Roland, in *Bulletin de l'Idhec* (Paris), March-May 1947.
Ordway, Peter, ''Prophet with Honor: Roberto Rossellini,'' in *Theatre Arts* (New York), January 1949.
''Rossellini,'' in *New Yorker*, 19 February 1949.
Venturi, Lauro, ''Roberto Rossellini,'' in *Hollywood Quarterly*, Fall 1949.
Parri, Ferruccio, ''Lo stil nuovo,'' in *Cinema Nuovo* (Turin), April 1955.
Gow, Gordon, ''The Quest for Realism,'' in *Films and Filming* (London), December 1957.
Bazin, André, ''Une Esthetique de la réalité: le Néo-Réalisme,'' in *Ou'estce que le cinéma*, 2nd edition, Paris, 1962.
Debreczeni, Francois, ''Le Néo-Réalisme italien, bilan de la critique,'' in *Etudes Cinématographique* (Paris), nos. 32–35, 1964.
Sarris, Andrew, ''Rossellini Rediscovered,'' in *Film Culture* (New York), no. 32, 1964.
Casty, Alan, ''The Achievement of Roberto Rossellini,'' in *Film Comment* New York, Fall 1964.
''Roberto Rossellini,'' in *Cinema* (Beverly Hills), Fall 1971.
MacBean, J. R., ''Rossellini's Materialist Mise-en-Scène,'' in *Film Quarterly* (Berkeley), Winter 1971–72.
Walsh, M., ''*Rome, Open City*: The Rise to Power of Louis XIV,'' in *Jump Cut* (Chicago), no. 15, 1977.
Heijs, J., in *Skrien* (Amsterdam), October 1977.
Lawton, B., ''Italian Neorealism: A Mirror Construction of Reality,'' in *Film Criticism* (Edinboro, Pennsylvania), no. 2, 1979.

Roma, città aperta

Burgoyne, Robert, ''The Imaginary and the Neo-Real,'' in *Enclitic* (Minneapolis), Spring 1979.

Veillon, O. R., in *Cinématographe* (Paris), June 1980.

''Le Neo-Réalisme Issue'' of *Cahiers Lumières* (Paris), November 1980.

Mitchell, T., ''The Construction and Reception of Anna Magnani in Italy and the English-Speaking World, 1945–1988,'' in *Film Criticism* (Meadville, Pennsylvania), no. 1, 1989.

Kramer, R., ''Pouvoir des images, mission du cinema,'' in *Cahiers du Cinéma* (Paris), no. 443/444, May sup 1991.

Wagstaff, Chris, ''True Stories,'' in *Sight and Sound* (London), vol. 3, no. 8, August 1993.

Chase, D., ''Anna Magnani: Miracle Worker,'' in *Film Comment* (New York), November-December 1993.

Denby, David, ''Naples, Open City,'' in *Premiere* (Boulder), no. 1, September 1994.

Séquences (Haute-Ville), no. 179, July-August 1995.

Simels, Steve, ''*Open City*,'' in *Entertainment Weekly*, no. 295, 6 October 1995.

Brunette, P., ''The Neo Bible,'' in *Village Voice* (New York), vol. 40, 17 October 1995.

Orr, C., ''Pasolini's *Accattone*, or Naturalism and Its Discontents,'' in *Film Criticism* (Meadville), vol. 19, no. 3, 1995.

Fisher, J., ''Deleuze in a Ruinous Context: German Rubble-Film and Italian Neorealism,'' in *Iris* (Iowa City), no. 23, Spring 1997.

* * *

Roberto Rossellini's *Roma, città aperta* emerged from the ashes of World War II to become Europe's first post-war masterpiece, and in doing so demonstrated once again an increasingly accepted axiom of filmmaking: cinema is perhaps the only one of the major art forms in which scarcity and deprivation periodically unite with genius to produce technical innovations that drastically influence the course of the art form for generations to follow. For example, the filmless experiments (caused by scarcities of film stock) of the Soviet Union's Kuleshow workshop, between 1922 and 1924, produced the concept of montage and led to the great works of Vsevolod Pudovkin and Sergei Eisenstein. Somewhat earlier, in Germany, director Robert Wiene utilized painted backdrops and shadowy lighting induced by a power failure to create *The Cabinet of Dr. Caligari* and popularize the film style known as Expressionism. Similarly, Rossellini, trying to produce a film in 1945 with fragments left from an industry decimated by war, pioneered a style that became known as neo-realism, the influence of which can still be seen in films as diverse as Ermanno Olmi's *Tree of Wooden Clogs* (1978) and Michael Cimino's *Heaven's Gate* (1980).

Roma, città aperta, which was begun within two months of the Allied liberation of Rome, was actually conceived and planned several months earlier when Rossellini and some colleagues were dodging Nazi patrols to avoid being conscripted for military service on the side of the Fascists. In a purely professional sense, the attempt to make the film itself should have been doomed: Rossellini could obtain a permit from the allied administrators to make a documentary film only, and the prohibitive cost of the sound film on the black market virtually mandated the use of cheaper stock normally reserved for silent films. In addition, all of the performers with the exception of Anna Magnani, a sometime music hall performer, were non-professionals.

The resulting film, unlike anything produced before, turned these seeming drawbacks into tenets of a major new mode of expression—neo-realism—which shook the Italian film industry from its doldrums and returned it to the forefront of cinematic innovation. But, *Roma, città aperta's* employment of this mode of representation was not the end product of the application of conscious artistic principle in the manner of the less influential *Ossessione* (1943), which many feel was the real harbinger of neo-realism. Rossellini's version of the form placed heavy emphasis on the re-creation of incidents in, whenever possible, the exact locales in which such events had taken place and accordingly spotlighted the everyday occurrences of Italian life. It also featured real people in the actors' roles which served to convey a sense of the immediacy of the post-war Italian experience.

Yet, several features of *Roma, città aperta* make it difficult to classify its director as simply or purely a neo-realist, particularly given the way that the form was subsequently defined by such filmmakers as Luchino Visconti, Vittorio De Sica, and others who took up the style in the late 1940s. Its plot is highly melodramatic in the worst sense of the word. Characters are clearly defined as either good or evil according to the strength of their commitment to a better tomorrow for Italy or, conversely, by their lack of faith in themselves and their cynicism in adhering to an obviously corrupt ideology.

Rossellini makes little pretence at objectivity in rendering even the surface appearance of things which characterized later neo-realistic works. His employment of his brother Renzo's music is emotionally manipulative in a number of scenes, while, in other instances, certain images represent a definite intrusion of the director's personal feelings. His use of babies and children, for example, as an embodiment of Italy's hopes for the future not only shapes our anguish in a scene such as the one in which pregnant Anna Magnani is murdered but it also reaffirms the validity of the sacrifice and the Italian cause in the final scene when the children are neatly juxtaposed with a shot of the dome of St. Peter's as they leave the execution of the priest Don Pietro.

Although these overly dramatic inconsistencies make if difficult to classify *Roma, città aperta* as a textbook example of the mode of expression it popularized, such contradictions actually heighten its powerful depiction of the conflicting realities inherent in the struggle against fascism. Rossellini's shifting perspectives alternating between comedy and pathos when focused upon a select number of crucial episodes in the lives of some real people effectively isolates a specific historical reality that exerted a profound effect upon filmgoers of the late 1940s.

Though the grainy, black-and-white images of *Roma, città aperta* are at least one step removed from actuality, conforming instead to a verity appropriate to documentary films, they promulgate a very real social humanism that pervades the entire body of Rossellini's work and transcends the narrow boundaries of specific modes of expression. The film is ultimately a hopeful vision of the future of Italy and indeed of mankind in general, and while it establishes techniques that would subsequently evolve into filmmaking codes, it reflects more the personality of its director and his belief in innate goodness than it does a rigid ideology of realistic representation.

—Stephen L. Hanson

LA RONDE

France, 1950

Director: Max Ophüls

Production: Saint-Maurice; black and white, 35mm; running time: 97 minutes; length: 2,600 meters. Released 17 June 1950, Paris. Filmed 23 January 1950–18 March 1950 in Saint-Maurice studios.

Producer: Sacha Gordine; **screenplay:** Jacques Natanson and Max Ophüls, from the play *Reigen* by Arthur Schnitzler; **photography:**

La Ronde

Christian Matras; **editor:** Leonide Azar; **sound operator:** Pierre Calvet; **production designer:** Jean d'Eaubonne; **music:** Oscar Straus; **costume designer:** Georges Annenkov.

Cast: Anton Walbrook (*Master of Ceremonies*); Simone Signoret (*Léocardie, the prostitute*); Serge Reggiani (*Franz, the soldier*); Simone Simon (*Marie, the chambermaid*); Jean Clarieux (*Sergeant*); Daniel Gélin (*Alfred, the young man*); Robert Vattier (*Professor Schuller*); Danielle Darrieaux (*Emma Breitkopf*); Fernand Gravey (*Charles*); Odette Joyeux (*Working girl*); Marcel Merovee (*Toni*); Jean-Louis Barrault (*Robert Kühlenkampf*); Isa Miranda (*Charlotte, the comedienne*); Charles Vissiere (*Theatre manager*); Gerard Philipe (*Count*); Jean Ozenne, Jean Landier, Rene Marjac, and Jacques Vertan (*Silhouettes*).

Publications

Script:

Ophüls, Max, and Jacques Natanson, *La Ronde*, in *Avant-Scène du Cinéma* (Paris), 15 April 1963; in *Masterworks of the French Cinema*, London, 1974.

Books:

Roud, Richard, *Max Ophüls: An Index*, London, 1958.
Annekov, Georges, *Max Ophüls*, Paris, 1962.
Ophüls, Max, *Max Ophüls par Max Ophüls*, Paris, 1963.
Beylie, Claude, *Max Ophüls*. Paris, 1963.
Armes, Roy, *French Cinema Since 1946: The Great Tradition*, New York, 1976.
Willemen, Paul, editor, *Ophüls*, London, 1978.
Klinowski, Jacek, and Adam Garbicz, *Cinema, The Magic Vehicle: A Guide to Its Achievement: Journey Two*, Metuchen, New Jersey, 1979.
Williams, Alan, *Max Ophüls and the Cinema of Desire*, New York, 1980.
Horton, Andrew, and Jan Magretta, editors, *Modern European Filmmakers and the Art of Adaptation*, New York, 1981.
Beylie, Claude, *Max Ophüls*, Paris, 1984.
Tassone, Aldo, *Max Ophüls, l'enchanteur*, Torino, 1994.
White, Susan M., *The Cinema of Max Ophüls: Magisterial Vision and the Figure of a Woman*, New York, 1995.

Articles:

Koval, Francis, ''Interview with Ophüls,'' in *Sight and Sound* (London) July 1950.
Archer, Eugene, ''Ophüls and the Romantic Tradition,'' in *Yale French Studies* (New Haven), no. 17, 1956.
''Ophüls Issue'' of *Cahiers du Cinéma* (Paris), March 1958.
Beylie, Claude, ''De l'amour de l'art à l'art de l'amour,'' in *Avant Scène du Cinéma* (Paris), 15 April 1963.
Beylie, Claude, ''Max Ophüls,'' in *Anthologie du Cinéma* (Paris), June 1965.
''Ophüls Issue'' of *Film Comment* (New York), Summer 1971.
Sarris, Andrew, ''Max Ophüls,'' in *Film Comment* (New York), Summer 1971.
Williams, A., ''The Circles of Desire: Narration and Representation in *La Ronde*,'' in *Film Quarterly* (Berkeley), Fall 1973.
Camper, Fred, ''Distance and Style: The Visual Rhetoric of Max Ophüls,'' in *Monogram* (London), no. 5, 1974.
Koval, Francis, ''Interview with Ophüls (1950),'' in *Masterworks of the French Cinema*, edited by John Weightman, New York, 1974.
''Ophüls Issues'' of *Filmkritik* (Munich), November and December 1977.
Wyndham, F., in *Sight and Sound* (London), Spring 1982.
Shipman, David, in *Films and Filming* (London), May 1982.
Thomas, D., in *Movie* (London), Summer 1982.
Revue du Cinéma (Paris), no. 456, January 1990.
Ophuls, Marcel, ''*La Ronde* et le droit d'auteur,'' in *Positif* (Paris), no. 347, January 1990.
Piazzo, Philippe, in *Jeune Cinéma* (Paris), no. 200, March-April 1990.
Amiel, Vincent, ''La scène, primitive,'' in *Positif* (Paris), no. 350, April 1990.
Alter, Maria P., ''From *Der Reigen* to *La Ronde*: Transposition of a Stageplay to the Cinema,'' in *Literature/Film Quarterly* (Salisbury), vol. 24, no.1, January 1996.

* * *

With *La Ronde*, Max Ophüls returned home—to France, his adopted country, and in subject matter to Vienna, his spiritual home. After nine years of uneasy exile in America, the film marks the opening of the last, finest phase of his peripatetic career. Its mood of consummate artifice is established in the very first shot. In one long, unbroken take Anton Walbrook, dressed as an elegant man-about-town, strolls on to a sound stage, past lighting equipment, backdrops, and other paraphernalia, chatting urbanely to camera the while; hangs up hat, scarf and cape, wanders into the set of a small lamplit square, in which stands a carousel; steps on to it and—as Simone Signoret's prostitute emerges from the shadows—starts the mechanism. The merry-go-round of love is under way.

''Passion without love, pleasure without love, love without reciprocation''—these, according to Truffaut and Rivette, are the themes that engaged Ophüls, and certainly they sum up *La Ronde*. Each of his chain of characters pursues or is pursued, exploits or is exploited, loves or is not loved, as the carousel turns; and each encounter centres around the act, or the acting, of love. Schnitzler's play *Reigen* furnished the basis of the film, but his bleak cynicism is transmuted by Ophüls into a bitter-sweet irony, viewed through a haze of poetic nostalgia. Schnitzler intended his play as a metaphor for the transmission of venereal disease; the film scarcely lends itself to any such reading.

The film, like the play, is set in the Vienna of 1900: present actuality for Schnitzler (though the play's first public performance was not until 1921), but for Ophüls a romantic, fairy-tale city, stylised and charmingly unreal. To the tune of Oscar Straus's insidious waltz, the infinitely fluid camera which Ophüls made his own leads through an opulent world of boudoirs, cafés, misty streets and *chambres privées*, as each puppet-character repeats the same words, the same gestures, with different partners, at once deceiving and self-deceived. Only the master of ceremonies, the director's alter ego, is granted freedom, able to range through time and identity, proteanly appearing as waiter or coachman to nudge the action on its way, or share an epigram with the audience. Walbrook's subtle, delicate performance, gracefully avoiding the least hint of pretentiousness, holds the centre of the film, while around him circles a dazzling array of the finest acting talent of the period: Signoret, Serge Reggiani, Simone Simon, Danielle Darrieux, Jean-Louis Barrault, Gérard Philipe (the latter two, admittedly, not quite at their best).

La Ronde was Ophüls's most successful, and most widely distributed, film. To audiences everywhere, especially in Britain and North America, it represented the epitome of everything witty, sophisticated and elegant: quintessentially French and Viennese at once. The Oscar Straus waltz became a popular hit. For some years the film was unavailable, due to legal complications, and Vadim's meretricious remake of 1964 offered a distinctly poor substitute. The Ophüls version resurfaced early in the 1980s, its reputation enhanced by its long absence, and proved as stylish and compelling as ever in its exposition of the director's perennial theme: the gulf between the ideal of love and its imperfect, transient reality.

—Philip Kemp

ROOM AT THE TOP

UK, 1958

Director: Jack Clayton

Production: Romulus Films, Ltd.; black and white, 35mm; running time: 115 minutes. Released 1958, Britain.

Room at the Top

Producers: John and James Woolf; **screenplay:** Neil Paterson, from the novel by John Braine; **photography:** Freddie Francis; **editor:** Ralph Kemplen; **art director:** Ralph Brinton; music: Mario Nascimbene.

Cast: Laurence Harvey (*Joe Lampton*); Simone Signoret (*Alice Aisgill*); Heather Sears (*Susan Brown*); Donald Houston (*Charles Soames*); Donald Wolfit (*Mr. Brown*); Hermione Baddeley (*Elspeth*); John Westbrook (*Jack Wales*).

Awards: British Academy Awards for Best Film, Best British Film, and Best Foreign Actress (Signoret), 1958; Cannes Film Festival, Best Actress (Signoret), 1959; Oscars for Best Actress (Signoret) and Best Screenplay Based on Material from Another Medium, 1959.

Publications

Books:

Manvell, Roger, *New Cinema in Britain*, New York, 1969.
Durgnat, Raymond, *A Mirror for England: British Movies from Austerity to Affluence*, New York, 1971.
Betts, Ernest, *The Film Business—A History of British Cinema: 1896–1972*, New York, 1973.
Perry, George, *The Great British Picture Show*, New York, 1974.
Walker, Alexander, *Hollywood U.K.*, New York, 1974.
Hickey, Des, and Gus Smith, *The Prince . . . Laurence Harvey*, London, 1975.
Gaston, Georg, *Jack Clayton: A Guide to References and Resources*, Boston, 1981.
Sandre, Didier, *Simone Signoret*, Paris, 1981.
Hill, John, *Sex, Class, and Realism: British Cinema 1956–63*, London, 1986.

Articles:

Dyer, Peter John, in *Films and Filming* (London), February 1959.
Houston, Penelope, in *Sight and Sound* (London), Spring 1959.
Mekas, Jonas, in *Village Voice* (New York), 29 April 1959.
Fitzpatrick, Ellen, in *Films in Review* (New York), May 1959.
Alexander, A. J., in *Film Culture* (New York), Summer 1961.
Kael, Paulin, ''Commitment and Strait Jacket,'' in *Film Quarterly* (Berkeley) Fall 1961.
''Laurence Harvey: Following My Actor's Instinct,'' in *Films and Filming* (London), October 1961.
Cowie, Peter, ''Clayton's Progress,'' in *Motion* (London), Spring 1962.
Signoret, Simone, ''On Being under a Director's Spell,'' in *Films and Filming* (London), June 1962.
Cowie, Peter, ''The Face of 63: Britain,'' in *Films and Filming* (London), February 1963.
Stanbrook, Alan, ''Laurence Harvey.'' in *Films and Filming* (London), May 1964.
Gregory, C. T., ''There'll Always Be Room at the Top for Nothing But the Best,'' in *Journal of Popular Film* (Washington, D.C.), Winter 1973.
Donaldson, Leslie, in *Magill's Survey of Cinema 3*, Englewood Cliffs, New Jersey, 1980.

Philbert, B., in *Cinématographe* (Paris), September 1982.
Cluny, C. M., in *Cinéma* (Paris), October 1982.
Lefèvre, Raymond, in *Image et Son*, November 1982.
Combs, Richard, ''Upward Mobility,'' in *Listener*, vol. 114, no. 2931, 17 October 1985.
Palmer, R.B., ''What Was New in the British New Wave?: Reviewing *Room at the Top*,'' in *Journal of Popular Film and Television* (Washington, D.C.), vol. 14, no. 3, Fall 1986.
Ward, L.E., ''The Great Films: *Some Came Running* and *Room at the Top*,'' in *Classic Images* (Muscatine), no. 168, June 1989.

* * *

From post-war Britain emerged the syndrome of the angry young man, one apparently intent on overthrowing established social conventions and codes of behavior. In the theatre, John Osborne's *Look Back in Anger* set the pace; in fiction, John Braine's *Room at the Top*. With Jack Clayton's film of the Braine novel, the syndrome became known internationally to film audiences, its central character, Joe Lampton, becoming the epitome of the restless young Englishman fed up with social traditions that made life forever one situated in the lower or middle class.

In this his feature film debut, Clayton displayed a feeling for atmosphere and character delineation that made this study of social, political and sexual behavior one of the most significant and successful British films of the 1950s. Its failure to receive Code approval in the United States only increased its popularity, confirming the notion that the film-going public was ready for more mature films, films that involved a more realistic portrait of current social and sexual realities.

Having spent three years as a prisoner of war, Joe Lampton decides that he is owed more than slavery for his wartime duties and thus he seeks to break through the rigid provincial social structure of the industrial town of Warnley. Convinced that ability is not the key to advancement, he sets his sights on marriage to Susan Brown, the daughter of a local industrialist and community leader. The more his status-seeking is discouraged, the more actively he pursues his goals, bribery, public embarrassment, and removal of the object of affection all failing to curtail Joe's activities. Almost from the beginning it is clear that Joe's love is not for Susan but for the status she will provide.

Ever the opportunist, Joe takes advantage of the disastrous marital situation of Alice Aisgill, the leading lady of the village theatre group, and before long they are lovers. Alice falls in love; Joe continues to place his priorities on money and status. When Susan returns from her father-induced exile, Joe seduces her, subsequently realizing that while he desires what Susan can provide, his love is for Alice. Joe, however, must pay for his crime. When Susan becomes pregnant, her father attempts to bribe Joe, offering to set him up in business if he agrees never to see Susan again, and, when that fails, forcing him to marry Susan and agree never to see Alice again. Joe now finds himself caught in the web he has constructed, realizing too late that his freedom from social structures is not a function of money and status but of self, that before he can be outwardly free he must be inwardly free. His room at the top may be lined with gold, but the achievement of that position ensures not happiness but misery. The ending of this film is a bitter parody of the conventional happy ending: a two-shot situates the wedding couple, she in her joy, he in his misery, the tightness of the frame depicting the restrictiveness of Joe's new social position.

The success of *Room at the Top* set in motion a new genre of British cinema, the ''kitchen sink drama'' with its emphasis on social realism. Over the next five years such strong examples as *Saturday Night and Sunday Morning* and *This Sporting Life* won international acclaim.

—Doug Tomlinson

A ROOM WITH A VIEW

UK, 1986

Director: James Ivory

Production: A Room with a View Productions; Technicolor, Dolby Stereo; running time: 117 minutes; length: 10,501 feet. Released January 1986. Cost: £2,000,000.

Producer: Ismail Merchant; **screenplay:** Ruth Prawer Jhabvala, from the novel by E. M. Forster; **photography:** Tony-Pierce Roberts; **second unit photography:** Sergio Melaranci; **editor:** Humphrey Dixon; **sound editors:** Tony Lenny, Peter Compton, Alan Killick; **sound recordists:** Ray Beckett, Brian Masterson; **sound re-recordist:** Richard King; **production designers:** Gianni Quaranta, Brian Ackland-Snow; **art directors:** Brian Savegar, Elio Altamura; **costume design:** Jenny Beavan, John Bright; **music:** Richard Robbins; **musical directors:** Francis Shaw, Barrie Guard.

Cast: Maggie Smith (*Charlotte Bartlett*); Helena Bonham-Carter (*Lucy Honeychurch*); Denholm Elliot (*Mr. Emerson*); Julian Sands (*George Emerson*); Daniel Day-Lewis (*Cecil Vyse*); Simon Callow (*Reverend Arthur Beebe*); Judi Dench (*Miss Eleanor Lavish*); Rosemary Leach (*Mrs. Honeychurch*); Rupert Graves (*Freddy Honeychurch*); Patrick Godfrey (*Mr. Eager*); Fabia Drake (*Catherine Alan*); Joan Henley (*Teresa Alan*); Maria Britneva (*Mrs. Vyse*); Amanda Walker (*The Cockney Signora*); Peter Cellier (*Sir Harry Otway*); Mia Fothergill (*Minnie Beebe*); Patricia Lawrence (*Mrs. Butterworth*); Mirio Guidelli (*Santa Croce Guide*); Matyelock Gibbs and Kitty Aldridge (*The New Charlotte and Lucy*); Freddy Korner (*Mr. Floyd*); Elizabeth Marangoni (*Miss Pole*); Lucca Rossi (*Phaeton*); Isabella Celani (*Persephone*); Luigi Di Fiori (*Murdered Youth*).

Awards: Oscars for Best Adapted Screenplay, Best Art Direction, Best Costume Design, 1986. BAFTA Awards for Best Film, Best Actress (Smith), Best Supporting Actress (Dench), 1986.

Publications

Books:

Pym, John, *The Wandering Company: Twenty-One Years of Merchant Ivory Films*, London, 1983.
Long, Robert Emmet, *The Films of Merchant Ivory*, New York, 1991, 1997.
Pym, John, *Merchant Ivory's English Landscape: Rooms, Views, and Anglo-Saxon Attitudes*, New York, 1995.

A Room with a View

Articles:

Hollywood Reporter, 29 January 1986.
Variety (New York), 29 January 1986.
Johnston, Sheila, in *Stills* (London), April 1986.
Strick, Philip, in *Monthly Film Bulletin* (London), April 1986.
Sigal, Clancy, in *Listener* (London), 17 April 1986.
Mayne, R., in *Sight and Sound* (London), Spring 1986.
Anderson, P., in *Films in Review* (New York), June-July 1986.
McFarlane, Brian, in *Cinema Papers* (Melbourne), July 1986.
Magny, Joel, in *Cahiers du Cinéma* (Paris), November 1986.
Pierce-Roberts, Tony, in *American Cinematographer* (Los Angeles), April 1987.
Monthly Film Bulletin (London), November 1987.
Levine, J. P., ''Two Rooms with a View: An Inquiry into Film Adaptation,'' in *Mosaic* (Washington, D.C.), no. 3, 1989.
LeMahieu, D. L., ''Imagined Contemporaries: Cinematic and Televised Dramas about the Edwardians in Great Britain and the United States, 1967–1985,'' in *Historical Journal of Film, Radio and Television* (Abingdon, Oxfordshire), no. 3, 1990.
Kaaber, L., ''Forster pa film,'' in *Kosmorama* (Copenhagen), Fall 1992.
Hipsky, M., ''Anglophil(m)ia: Why Does America Watch Merchant-Ivory Movies?,'' in *Journal of Popular Film and Television* (Washington, D.C.), vol. 22, no. 3, 1994.
Chambers, L, ''Fade In,'' in *The Journal: Writers Guild of America, West* (Los Angeles), vol. 8, December/January 1995.

* * *

During a visit to Florence in 1907 with her cousin Charlotte Bartlett, Lucy Honeychurch meets the bohemian Mr. Emerson and his son George. During the course of a country outing George makes a pass at Lucy, who rebuffs him. The incident is seen by Charlotte, and both women return to England before the allotted end of their stay. Back home in the village of Summer Street with her mother and brother Lucy becomes engaged to Cecil Vyse. At the same time the Emersons rent a cottage in the area and, through becoming friendly with Lucy's brother, George is soon a regular guest at the Honeychurch home. He again attempts to seduce Lucy, who tells him to leave. However, she begins to realise that she is attracted to George, breaks off her engagement with Cecil, and she and George return to Florence on their honeymoon.

The theme of Forster's second novel—the counterpoint between uncomplicated Mediterranean passions and the stultifying, hypocritical restrictions of Edwardian social order—fits in particularly comfortably with one of the favourite subjects of the remarkably unified and consistent Merchant/Ivory/Jhabvala oeuvre, namely the clash of conflicting cultures, be they based on race, class, or generational differences—witness *Shakespeare Wallah*, *The Europeans*, *The Bostonians*, and *Heat and Dust*. But, above all else, *A Room with a View* stands out as a re-creation of the Indian summer of Edwardian England—quite an achievement considering the diverse origins of producer, director, and screenplay writer. Significantly (and courageously) even the Florentine scenes are not milked for all their considerable visual worth; rather, the film concentrates on the relations between the English visitors to Florence and the various goings-on at the Pensione Bertolini, faithfully reflecting its characters' blinkered, insular sensibilities.

On the other hand, it has to be admitted that, as a reflection on ''Englishness,'' the film, like the novel, does not stray beyond the bounds of lightly critical satire and affectionately observed comedy of manners. Like so many of its ilk on both film and television *A Room with a View* is decidedly ambivalent about the England which it portrays—one eye cocked at the oppressive effeteness of the Edwardian upper and middle classes, the other captivated by all those ravishing country walks and languorous games of tennis. It is almost certainly these latter elements which have made the film such a commercial success (not least outside Britain) along, of course, with a particularly impressive display of acting skills. Again, one might be critical of the British cinema's over-reliance on essentially theatrical performers and performances but on the other hand it would miss half the point of the film to ignore Maggie Smith's Charlotte, Lucy's spinster chaperon who has clearly got enough ''nous'' to realise, and regret, what she has missed in life, and who eventually connives at Lucy's affair with George; or Daniel Day-Lewis's Cecil, a prissy wimp who is as different to the actor's earlier incarnation as a punk in *My Beautiful Laundrette* as it is possible to imagine.

In the last analysis, however, it's hard not to apply Forster's comment on his novel—''clear and bright and well constructed but so thin''—to this beautifully made but ultimately rather gossamer-like film.

—Julian Petley

ROSEMARY'S BABY

USA, 1968

Director: Roman Polanski

Production: William Castle Enterprises for Paramount Pictures; Technicolor, 35mm; running time: 137 minutes. Released 12 June 1968, New York. Filmed on location in New York City and Playa del Rey, California.

Producers: William Castle with Dona Holloway; **screenplay:** Roman Polanski, from the novel by Ira Levin; **photography:** William Fraker; **editors:** Sam O'Steen and Robert Wyman; **sound recordists:** Harold Lewis and John Wilkinson; **production designer:** Richard Sylbert; **art director:** Joel Schiller; **music:** Krzysztof Komeda; **costume designer:** Anthea Sylbert; **makeup:** Allan Snyder.

Rosemary's Baby

Cast: Mia Farrow (*Rosemary Woodhouse*); John Cassavetes (*Guy Woodhouse*); Ruth Gordon (*Minnie Castevet*); Sidney Blackmere (*Roman Castevet*); Maurice Evans (*Hutch*); Ralph Bellamy (*Dr. Sapirstein*); Angela Dorian (*Terry*); Patsy Kelly (*Laura-Louise*); Elisha Cook (*Mr. Nicklas*); Emmaline Henry (*Elsie Dunstan*); Marianne Gordon (*Joan Jellico*); Philip Leeds (*Doctor Shand*); Charles Grodin (*Dr. Hill*); Hanna Landy (*Grace Cardiff*); Hope Summers (*Mrs. Gordon*); Wende Wagner (*Tiger*); Gordon Connell (*Guy's agent*); Janet Garland (*Nurse*); Joan Reilly (*Pregnant woman*); Tony Curtis (*Voice of Donald Baumgart*); William Castle (*Man at telephone booth*).

Award: Oscar for Best Supporting Actress (Gordon), 1968.

Publications

Books:

Butler, Ivan, *The Cinema of Roman Polanski*, New York, 1970.
Kane, Pascal, *Roman Polanski*, Paris, 1970.
Belmans, Jacques, *Roman Polanski*, Paris, 1971.
Kaminsky, Stuart, *American Film Genres*, Dayton, Ohio, 1974.

Crouch, William P., *Satanism and Possession in Selected Contemporary Novels and their Cinematic Adaptations*, Ann Arbor, Michigan, 1977.
Bisplinghoff, Gretchen, and Virginia Wexman, *Roman Polanski: A Guide to References and Resources*, Boston, 1979.
Kiernan, Thomas, *The Roman Polanski Story*, New York, 1980.
Leaming, Barbara, *Polanski: The Filmmaker as Voyeur: A Biography*, New York 1981, as *Polanski: His Life and Films*, London, 1982.
Tuska, Jon, editor, *Close-up: The Contemporary Director*, Metuchen, New Jersey, 1981.
Fischer, Jens Malte, *Filmwissenschaft—Filmgeschichte: Studien zu Welles, Hitchcock, Polanski, Pasolini, and Max Steiner*, Tübingen, 1983.
Polanski, Roman, *Roman*, London, 1984.
Dokumentation: Polanski und Skolimowski; Das Absurde im Film, Zurich, 1985.
Wexman, Virginia Wright, *Roman Polanski*, Boston, 1985.
Jacobsen, Wolfgang, and others, *Roman Polanski*, Munich, 1986.
Avron, Dominique, *Roman Polanski*, Paris, 1987.
Bruno, Edoardo, *Roman Polanski*, Rome, 1993.
Parker, John, *Polanski*, London, 1993.
Stachówna, Grazyna, *Roman Pola'nski I jego filmy*, Warsaw, 1994.
Cappabianca, Alessandro, *Roman Polanski*, Recco, 1997.

Articles:

Gilliatt, Penelope, in *New Yorker*, 15 June 1968.
Hamilton, Jack, in *Look* (Des Moines), 25 June 1968.
Sarris, Andrew, in *Village Voice* (New York), 25 July 1968.
Hart, Henry, in *Films in Review* (New York), August-September 1968.
Ellison, Harlan, in *Cinema* (Beverly Hills), Fall 1968.
Engle, Harrison, in *Film Comment* (New York), Fall 1968.
Kinder, Marsha, and Beverle Houston, in *Sight and Sound* (London), Winter 1968–69.
McArthur, Colin, ''Polanski,'' in *Sight and Sound* (London), Winter 1968–69.
Ross, T. J., ''Roman Polanski, *Repulsion*, and the New Mythology,'' in *Film Heritage* (Dayton, Ohio), Winter 1968–69.
Reisner, Joel, and Bruce Kane, ''An Interview with Roman Polanski,'' in *Cinema* (Los Angeles), no. 2, 1969.
Ciment, Michel, and others ''Entretien avec Roman Polanski,'' in *Positif* (Paris), February 1969.
Gow, Gordon, in *Films and Filming* (London), March 1969.
Chappetta, Robert, in *Film Quarterly* (Berkeley), Spring 1969.
Gow, Gordon, ''Satisfaction: A Most Unpleasant Feeling,'' in *Films and Filming* (London), April 1969.
Corliss, Richard, ''Still Legion, Still Decent,'' in *Commonweal* (New York), 23 May 1969.
McCarty, John Alan, ''The Polanski Puzzle,'' in *Take One* (Montreal), May-June 1969.
Bradbury, Ray, ''A New Ending to *Rosemary's Baby*,'' in *Films and Filming* (London), August 1969.
Leach, J., ''Notes on Polanski's Cinema of Cruelty,'' in *Wide Angle* (Athens, Ohio), vol. 2, no.1, 1978.
Amiel, M., and others, ''L'Univers de Roman Polanski,'' in *Cinéma* (Paris), February 1980.
Jankun, M., in *Kino* (Warsaw), April 1985.
Bergendy, P., ''Az orvos valaszol,'' in *Filmkultura* (Budapest), no. 4, 1989.
Razlogov, K., and I. Levin, ''Rebenok Rozmari,'' in *Iskusstvo Kino* (Moscow), no. 11, 1989.
Berenstein, R., ''Mommie Dearest: *Aliens, Rosemary's Baby* and Mothering,'' in *Journal of Popular Culture* (Bowling Green, Ohio), no. 2, 1990.
Alion, Y., in *Revue du Cinéma* (Paris), no. 476, November 1991.
Fischer, L., ''Birth Traumas: Parturition and Horror in *Rosemary's Baby*,'' in *Cinema Journal* (Austin, Texas), no. 3, 1992.
Marcus, S., ''Placing *Rosemary's Baby*,'' in *Differences*, vol. 5, no. 3, 1993.
Landrot, Marine, ''La beauté du diable,'' in *Télérama* (Paris), no. 2295, 5 January 1994.
Joly, Martine, ''Architecture et cinéma: une recontre parfois magique,'' in *CinémAction* (Conde-sur-Noireau, France), no. 75, April 1995.
Diski, Jenny, ''Sitting Inside,'' in *Sight and Sound* (London), vol. 5, no. 4, April 1995.
Indiana, G., ''Bedeviled,'' in *Village Voice* (New York), vol. 40, 29 August 1995.

* * *

Based on Ira Levin's 1967 best-selling novel of the same name, *Rosemary's Baby*, in Roman Polanski's hands becomes a multi-layered, seminal horror film that exposes collective subconscious fears and cultural anxieties. Satanism and motherhood are only the obvious starting points of inquiry for Polanski, whose body of work includes complex psychological studies such as *Knife In The Water* (1962), *Repulsion* (1965), *Cul De Sac* (1966), *Chinatown* (1974), and *The Tenant* (1976).

Polanski's penchant for inverting and subverting clichés serves him particularly well in telling this story of modern city living juxtaposed against ancient rites of witchcraft and devil worship. The paradoxes, dualities, and contrasts are immediately apparent from the film's title sequence as the camera moves slowly across a bright, contemporary New York city skyline, finally coming to rest on an ominous and dark building of old-world style and construction. The ancient looking apartment building, so out of time and place, is called the Bramford, and is every bit as much a character in the story as Rosemary's baby itself. Though working from his own screenplay, Polanski has commented that *Rosemary's Baby* was ''less personal'' than other films because it didn't begin as his own project. Yet he managed to integrate his themes of paranoia, alienation, identity confusion, and ''otherness'' so effectively as to make *Rosemary's Baby* an important work in his oeuvre. The unexpected success of his film adaptation of Levin's book initiated an entire genre of similarly themed ''devil/child'' horror films, including *The Exorcist* and *The Omen. Rosemary's Baby* started a trend in popular movies which succeeded in tapping into a collective subconscious fear of all things Satanic.

A newly wed, self-described ''country girl at heart'' from America's heartland is drawn unsuspecting, into a possibly occult web of conspiracies when she and her husband move into the Bramford and become entangled in its dark history. Mia Farrow, as first-time mother, Rosemary Woodhouse, gives the character a remarkable childlike frailty coupled with surprising strength, making it easy for the audience to identify with her predicament. Unlike Levin's book, in which the religiosity is clear-cut, Polanski depicts Rosemary's plight as an ongoing balancing act between fearful fantasy and stark reality. In his autobiography, *Roman*, Polanski explains:

> The (Levin) book was an outstandingly well-constructed thriller, and I admired it as such. Being an agnostic, however, I no more believed in Satan as evil incarnate than I believed in a personal God; the whole idea conflicted with my rational view of the world. For credibility's sake, I decided that there would have to be a loophole: the possibility that Rosemary's supernatural experiences were figments of her imagination. The entire story, as seen through her eyes could have been a chain of only superficially sinister coincidences, a product of her feverish fancies.

Using pregnancy as a device—a hormonal, physical change that alters both the mind and the body—Polanski provokes his audience with situations that question the mind/body dichotomy, the nature of good and evil (God and Devil), the instinct for survival, and the ultimate essence of motherhood. These questions give Polanski's treatment of the material an ambiguous, open-ended and surreal edge which he masterfully exploits. The audience is forced to ask, "How can something ancient and unholy exist in this peppy and bright young couple's world?" Rosemary continuously sinks into a nightmare of shadows, symbols, and whispers that keep her—and the audience—questioning her sanity. Did she dream or hallucinate a demonic rape? Could there really be a coven of witches living in the Bramford?

Rosemary's main motivation from the beginning of the film is the desire to have a child, and this propels her into the diabolical plot that seems to be taking shape around her. She even unwittingly offers that she is of "fertile stock" when describing her family to her nosy, elderly, and suspiciously friendly neighbor, Minnie Castevet. Before long, Minnie and her husband—named Roman—have insinuated themselves into the Woodhouse's lives, and especially Rosemary's pregnancy. As the joy of her pregnancy slowly turns to fear, we begin to understand what an outsider Rosemary has been all along. In a sense, she is a double outsider and this provides Polanski with the essentials for a protagonist with which he can readily identify. Transplanted from Omaha, Nebraska, Rosemary is not nearly as worldly or cosmopolitan as her new husband. Guy, a struggling actor from Baltimore, is completely at home in the big city, while Rosemary merely attempts to adapt. Secondly, Rosemary is an outsider in the mysterious Bramford. She is naive and open, while the Bramford is sly and full of secrets. She is unlike anyone else in the apartment building, whose tenants all seem to be over fifty. The one woman her age, that she meets in the basement laundry, soon winds up a suicide on the sidewalk.

The feelings of aloneness and alienation that Rosemary is experiencing only escalate with her pregnancy. She is an "Alice" gone "Through the Looking Glass" of her own body. As her body grows, so does her paranoia and her separation from the world she once knew. Rosemary works frantically to put the pieces together and solve the mystery that threatens her life and the life inside her. Polanski wants us to feel her victimization at the hands of everyone she trusts. As viewers, men and women alike are unsettled by the dilemma of this soon-to-be mother. Her peril resonates strongly the mother-child bond that lies deep within us all. After giving birth, Rosemary is told that the baby has died, despite the sounds of an infant crying in the distance. By solidly identifying with Rosemary's manipulation, whether real or imagined, the audience expects a resolution. But, in the end, instead of typical Hollywood cathartic vengeance, we are left with more questions. Did Rosemary have a complete mental breakdown, or did the Devil actually take human form and impregnate an unsuspecting, drugged, Manhattan housewife? The final shot in the film is of Rosemary surrounded by the coven as she feels herself drawn to her crying child. Will she follow an impulse to comfort, or kill the infant? By reintroducing the opening lullaby over a close-up of Rosemary's smiling face, Polanski slyly suggests that only motherhood is real, and a more powerful magic than evil. With the lullaby taking over the scene, the close-up dissolves into an exterior shot of the Bramford and we are back, full circle, where we began.

—Ralph Anthony Valdez

ROUGE

See **YANZHI KOU**

RULES OF THE GAME

See **RÈGLE DU JEU**

THE RUNNER

See **DAWANDEH**

THE SACRIFICE

See **OFFRET**

SAIKAKA ICHIDAI ONNA

(The Life of Oharu)

Japan, 1952

Director: Kenji Mizoguchi

Production: Shintoho; black and white, 35mm; running time: 148 minutes originally, cut to 133 minutes; length: 13,339 feet originally, cut to 11,970 feet. Released 1952.

Producers: Hideo Koi, Yoshikata Yoda, and Kenji Mizoguchi; **screenplay:** Yoshikata Yoda and Kenji Mizoguchi, from the novel *Koshuku ichidai onna* by Saikaku Ihara; **photography:** Yoshimi Hirano; **editor:** Toshio Goto; **art director:** Hiroshi Mizutani; **music:** Ichiro Saito; **historical consultant:** Isamu Yoshi.

Saikaku Ichidai Onna

Cast: Kinuyo Tanaka (*Oharu*); Toshiro Mifune (*Katsunosuke*); Hisako Yamane (*Lady Matsudaira*); Yuriko Hamada (*Yoshioka*); Tsukie Matsura (*Tomo, Oharu's mother*); Ichiro Sugai (*Shinzaemon, Oharu's father*); Toshiaki Konoe (*Lord Tokitaka Matsudaira*); Jukichi Uno (*Yakichi Senya*); Eitaro Shindo (*Kohei Sasaya*); Akira Oizumi (*Fumikichi, Sasaya's friend*); Masao Shimizu (*Kikuno Koji*); Daisuke Kato (*Tasaburo Hishiya*); Toranosuke Ogawa (*Yataemon Isobei*); Eijiro Yanagi (*Daimo Enaka*); Hiroshi Oizumi (*Manager Bunkichi*); Haruo Ichikawa (*Iwabashi*); Kikue Mori (*Myokai, the old nun*); Chieko Hagashiyama; Sadako Sawamura.

Awards: Venice Film Festival, International Prize, 1952.

Publications

Books:

Anderson, Joseph, and Donald Richie, *The Japanese Film: Art and Industry*, Rutland, Vermont, 1960; revised edition, Princeton, 1982.
Ve-Ho, *Kenji Mizoguchi*, Paris, 1963.
Connaissance de Mizoguchi, Paris, 1965.
Mesnil, Michel, *Kenji Mizoguchi*, Paris, 1965.
Tessier, Max, *Kenji Mizoguchi*, Paris, 1971.
Mellen, Joan, *Voices from the Japanese Cinema*, New York, 1975.
Mellen, Joan, *The Waves at Kenji's Door: Japan Through Its Cinema*, New York, 1976.
Bock, Audie, *Japanese Film Directors*, New York 1978; revised edition, Tokyo, 1985.
Garbicz, Adam, and Jacek Klinowski, editors, *Cinema, The Magic Vehicle: A Guide to Its Achievement: Journey Two*, Metuchen, New Jersey, 1979.
Il cinema di Kenji Mizoguchi, Venice, 1980.
Freiberg, Freda, *Women in Mizoguchi Films*, Melbourne, 1981.
Sato, Tadao, *Currents in Japanese Cinema*, Tokyo, 1982.
Serceau, Daniel, *Mizoguchi: De la revolte aux songes*, Paris, 1983.
Andrew, Dudley, *Film in the Aura of Art*, Princeton, 1984.
McDonald, Keiko, *Mizoguchi*, Boston, 1984.
O'Grady, Gerald, editor, *Mizoguchi the Master*, Ontario, 1996.
Tomasi, Dario, *Kenji Mizoguchi*, Milano, 1998.

Articles:

Bazin, André, in *France Observateur* (Paris), February 1954.
Sadoul, Georges, in *Lettres Françaises* (Paris), 11 February 1954.
Demonsablon, Philippe, "Qui naquit à Newgate. . . ," in *Cahiers du Cinéma* (Paris), March 1954.

Richie, Donald, and Joseph Anderson, ''Kenji Mizoguchi,'' in *Sight and Sound* (London), Autumn 1955.
Marcorelles, Louis, ''Retrospective Mizoguchi,'' in *Cahiers du Cinéma* (Paris), March 1958.
Mizoguchi, Kenji, ''Mes Films,'' in *Cahiers du Cinéma* (Paris), May 1959.
''Mizoguchi Kenji,'' in *Cinéma d'aujord'hui* (Paris), no. 31, 1965.
Yoda, Yoshikata, ''Souvenirs sur Mizoguchi,'' in *Cahiers du Cinéma* (Paris), January 1967.
Yoda, Yoshikata, ''The Density of Mizoguchi's Scripts,'' in *Cinema* (Los Angeles), Spring 1971.
Rosenbaum, Jonathan, in *Monthly Film Bulletin* (London), March 1975.
Cohen, R., ''Mizoguchi and Modernism,'' in *Sight and Sound* (London), Spring 1978.
Masson, A., in *Positif* (Paris), November 1978.
Richie, Donald, ''Kenji Mizoguchi,'' in *Cinema: A Critical Dictionary*, edited by Richard Roud, London, 1980.
Andrew, Dudley, and Tadao Sato, ''On Kenji Mizoguchi,'' in *Film Criticism* (Edinboro, Pennsylvania), Spring 1980.
Monty, Ib, in *Kosmorama* (Copenhagen), June 1983.
Revue du Cinéma (Paris), no. 481, April 1992.

* * *

The Life of Oharu is surely Kenji Mizoguchi's most important film. Artistically it ended a series of critical failures and indicates the half-dozen masterpieces that close his career. Financially it ultimately made enough money to land Mizoguchi a carte blanche contract with Daiei films, resulting in the artistic freedom he enjoyed at the end. Critically, *Oharu* marks the recognition of Mizoguchi by the West for the film captured top prize at the Venice Film Festival and made him a cult hero of *Cahiers du Cinéma*. Mizoguchi may have made more perfect films (Westerners prefer *Ugetsu monogatari*; the Japanese choose *Crucified Lovers*), but seldom has a film meant so much to a director and his future.

Beyond these practical considerations, *Oharu* was, of all his films, the one he struggled the longest to get on the screen. The idea of adapting Saikaku's 17th-century picaresque classic came to him at the beginning of the war, and he actively sought to produce it once the war had ended. But American restrictions against historical subjects and the evident expense this film would entail frightened all the studios he approached.

When the Americans pulled out of Japan in 1950, Mizoguchi could count eight films made during the occupation, not one of which satisfied him or pleased the critics. He needed a big success more than ever. While shooting the last of these films, he was galled to learn that Akira Kurosawa had received the top prize at Venice for *Rashomon*. How could a young director with only a handful of films and little personal experience win such a prize? In a rare interview Mizoguchi claimed that he had cut down his drinking to extend his life so that he could make at least one great film. No artist, he felt, achieved anything truly great until after he was 50. Mizoguchi was 52 when he said this, and it was clear that from then on he would waste no more time. He wanted greatness. His ambition was matched by that of his longtime leading actress, Kinuyo Tanaka, whose trip to the United States had halted a skid in her artistic reputation. Mizoguchi had been appalled at the gaudy welcome she received at the airport on her return. He shamed her into working with him, and together they agreed to risk their careers on this film.

Mizoguchi was able to subcontract the film from a newly established company through Shin Toho, assuring it some distribution, though he would have no studio at his disposal for its production. Filming took place in a bombed-out park midway between Kyoto and Osaka. Every 15 minutes a train between these cities passed nearby, the noise allowing for no more than one of Mizoguchi's invariably long takes at a time; to Mizoguchi the idea of dubbing was unacceptable. Planning went on for days, since he refused to begin until his crane arrived from Kyoto, and until his assistants returned from museums, where they were trying to secure authentic props to replace the copies which had already been prepared. The concentration on the set was legendary. When his chief assistant argued with him over a problem in which Mizoguchi was clearly being unreasonable, he fired the assistant. After an unexpected snowfall he had 30 men spend an exhausting 3 hours clearing it away, only to scrap the proposed site when he noticed a snowcapped peak in the background.

The film took months to complete and cost 46 million yen. Japan had never seen a film to match its scope and rigor; it was perhaps too taxing a film for Japanese audiences. The intellectuals complained that Mizoguchi had lost Saikaku's irony and humor in his realistic and sympathetic treatment of Oharu. The populace was no doubt frustrated by its length, tempo, and inevitability. The film virtually sank Shintoho, but the critics continued to discuss it. While it placed only 9th on the annual list of Japan's 10 best films, it was selected to represent the country at Venice, where it stunned the jury who awarded it the grand prize.

What made the film so exceptional was the camera perspective which was omniscient yet sympathetic. As Oharu descends from a privileged life at court down the ladder to the untouchable, nameless, mendicant nun at the end, she achieves nobility and wisdom. Where Saikaku had parodied her erotic exploits and used her to satirize all levels of Tokugawa culture, Mizoguchi finds her odyssey painful and sacred. She is the purest of all his sacrificing women who suffer at the hands of a male world not worthy of them.

This hagiographic tone is felt in the incredible camera flourishes that terminate so many sequences. The falling of the camera away from the beheading of Toshiro is the most hysterical fall; indeed, its point of rest is a perfect composition, including the sword still glistening from its bloody work. When the family flees in exile from the court, the camera coolly watches them cross the bridge, only to dip under the bridge at the last moment and catch a final glimpse of them passing a single tree far away. The graceful movement here serves to keep the subject in view, but more importantly, it is the melancholy reaction of an observer to a woeful tale. In the final shot Oharu, bowing to the temple, passes out of the frame, allowing the camera to hold on to that temple in a sacramental finale that comprehends a life gone so low it is now forever out of view. Long and solemn, *The Life of Oharu* is an immensely mature work of art.

—Dudley Andrew

SALAAM BOMBAY!

India-France-Great Britain, 1988

Director: Mira Nair

Production: National Films Development Corporation (New Delhi)-Cadrage (Paris)-Channel 4 (London). A Mirabi Films production; in color; running time: 113 minutes; length: 10,271 feet. Released 1988. Filmed in Hindi, with English subtitles.

Executive producers: Anil Tejani, Michael Nozik, Gabriel Auer; **producer:** Mira Nair; **co-producer:** Mitch Epstein; **screenplay:** Sooni Taraporevala; **Hindi dialogue:** Hriday Lani; **photography:** Sandi Sissel; **editor:** Barry Alexander Brown; **supervising sound editor:** Margie Crimmins; **production designer:** Mitch Epstein; **art directors:** Nitish Roy, Nitin Desai; **costume designers:** Deepa Kakkar, Nilita Vachani, Dinaz Stafford; **music:** L. Subramaniam; **children's workshop director:** Barry John; **film extract:** *Mr. India* (1987).

Cast: Shafiq Syed (*Krishna, ''Chaipau''*); Raghubir Yadav (*Chillum*); Aneeta Kanwar (*Rekha*); Nana Patekar (*Baba*); Hansa Vithal (*Manju*); Mohnaraj Babu (*Salim*); Chandrashekhar Naidu (*Chungal*); Chanda Sharma (*Solasaal, ''Sweet Sixteen''*); Shaukat Kaifi (*Madame*); Sarfuddin Quarrassi (*Koyla*); Raju Barnad (*Keera*); Dinshaw Daji (*Parsi Bawaji*); Alfred Anthony (*Lalua Chor*); Ramesh Deshavani (*Murtaza*); Anjan Srivastava (*Superintendent*); Irshad Hashmi (*Chacha*); Yunus Parvez (*Hashimbhai*); Ameer Bhai (*Ravi, Rekha's Rich Cousin*); Sulbha Deshpande (*Hemlata Joshi*); Mohan Tanturu (*Chillum II*); Amrit Patel (*Circus Boss*); Murari Sharma (*Ticket Seller*); Ram Moorti (*Mad Man*); Kishan Thapa (*Nepali Middleman*); Haneef Zahoor (*Bouncer*); Ramesh Rai (*Barber*); Shaukut H. Inamdar (*Crawford Market Shopkeeper*); Irfan Khan (*Scribe*); Neil Gettinger (*American Big Dog*); Double Battery Stafford (*Sexy Woman in Movie Theatre*); Rana Singh (*Sleazy Man in Movie Theatre*); Ali Bhai (*Butcher at Crawford Market*); Jayant Joshi (*Tailor*); Prashant Jaiswal (*Crooner at Wedding*); Joyce Barneto (*Bride*); Hassan Kutty (*Bridegroom*).

Publications

Articles:

Variety (New York), 8 June 1988.
Nair, Mira, in *Première* (Paris), August 1988.
Revue du Cinéma (Paris), September 1988.
Dieckmann, Katherine, in *Village Voice* (New York), 11 October 1988.
Nair, Mira, in *Film Comment* (New York), September-October 1988.
Malcolm, Derek, ''Street Credibility,'' in *Guardian* (London), 20 January 1989.
Interview with Mira Nair, in *City Limits* (London), 26 January 1989.
Parmar, Prathiba, ''Mira Nair: Filmmaking in the Streets of Bombay,'' in *Spare Rib* (London), February 1989.
Pym, John, in *Monthly Film Bulletin* (London), February 1989.
Moore, Suzanne, in *New Statesman and Society* (London), 3 February 1989.
Ehrlich, L. C., ''The Name of the Child: Cinema as Social Critique,'' in *Film Criticism* (Meadville, Pennsylvania), no. 2, 1990.
Arora, P., and K. Irving, ''Culturally Specific Texts, Culturally Bound Audiences: Ethnography in the Place of its Reception,'' in *Journal of Film and Video* (Los Angeles), no. 1–2, 1991.
Orenstein, Peggy, ''Salaam America!: An Interview with Director Mira Nair,'' in *Mother Jones*, vol. 17, no. 1, January-February 1992.
Simpson, Janice C., ''Focusing on the Margins,'' in *Time*, vol. 139, no. 9, 2 March 1992.
Virdi, J., ''(Mis)representing Child Labor,'' in *Jump Cut* (Berkeley), July 1992.
Cinema in India, vol. 4, no. 1, 1993.
''The 'Tough' Sister,'' in *UNESCO Courier*, November 1998.

* * *

It is difficult to distinguish Mira Nair's film about Bombay's street children, *Salaam Bombay!*, from its existence as a media event. In India, radio shows, newspaper advertising, and *Salaam Bombay!* t-shirts have been harnessed to ''sell'' the film in ways similar to the marketing of the usual western film industry product. This might account for the rather cool response of domestic reviewers; in addition, the expatriate status of the director and even certain inflections of the narrative have been cited as indices of the film's tainted, inauthentic ''foreignness.''

Nair's objective is evidently to promote the film, and she is prepared to use whatever means are at hand. However, this unabashed approach to the promotion of what would ordinarily rank as a social problem film in the tradition of India's state-supported ''middle'' cinema does present problems.

To redress this uncertainty about the zone between strategy and message, it is important to acknowledge that *Salaam Bombay!* does exist at the level of a reforming social project. The seriousness of the filmmakers' engagement with their subject has been fully indicated. Nair and her colleagues undertook detailed research into the lives of the street children. They set up a *Salaam Bombay!* trust for them and a school for their education. Concern for the children has extended beyond the film in the monitoring of each child's development and the attempt to ensure that the children are given the opportunity of improving their situation.

There is, however, a complex relationship between this activity—one predicated on knowledge, commitment, and thereby trust—and the re-ordering of the performative and existential attributes of the film's subject. Nair has remarked that it was observing the facility of the street children performing for their living that set her thinking about the film. Workshops were used to channel the children's skills into realist conventions of acting; their urge to perform in terms of the Hindi popular cinema's excesses of gesture and ''theatrically'' articulated dialogue was discouraged. The film allows such ''artificiality'' only in strictly regulated contexts, notably those used to dramatize the humiliation of the individual by the group and the delineation of a kind of daydream make-believe. Otherwise there is an underplaying of performance in the representation of the individual, a stress on the imperative of ''capturing'' intimate psychological states rather than essaying broad melodramatic flourishes. This re-education of the children's performative skills extended to the way in which even camera performance was registered; Nair has noted that lead child actor Shafiq Syed reprimanded another actor for disturbing spatial continuity between shots.

Salaam Bombay!

How relevant is the question of "true" representation to the attributes of the street children? Which was the "normal" mode of relating to their world—the melodramatic one which they first presented, or the realist one into which they were educated? What is interesting is the way in which the film re-orders the children's perception of the way they should relate to the world. Nair's ability to bring this about is probably related to earlier documentary work in which she drew a responsive interaction from the people she was dealing with. She has used interview and *cinéma vérité* techniques *(So Far from India*, 1982, *India Cabaret*, 1985), but in ways which suggest a complicity of the subjects in the construction of their image. In *Salaam Bombay!* it is the induction of the *cinéma vérité* subject into an active fictionalization of his/her experience which leads not only to representation but, in a sense, reconstitution.

None of this is intended to suggest that the film is "inauthentic"; realist narration is certainly not an alien phenomenon in India, though it may be a minority one. Further, the rapport Nair and her crew struck up not only with individuals but with crowds is indicated by the vivid portrait the film presents of Bombay; in this context it may be placed alongside such documentary essays on the city as *Bombay, Our City* (Anand Patwardhan, 1985), about the struggle of street dwellers to protect their habitation.

As for the film's "foreignness," one may speculate that it is precisely the multiplicity of cultural positions that the director occupies that enables her to regard her characters with a peculiar, resonating effect. On the one hand the film draws upon the need of the children to find some kind of stability and affection. On the other, it shows this drive as frustrated and leading to violence. The duality here re-enacts the recurrent, indeed obsessive concerns of the Hindi commercial cinema of the 1970s, though on very different representational terms. It also, interestingly, has another possible point of reference. The leading child character is obsessed with a teenage girl who is being inducted into prostitution by a pimp. The relationship between the girl and the man is ambiguous. The analogy with Scorsese's *Taxi Driver* is too striking to be missed. Perhaps the relationship lies within certain modern male obsessions and anxieties. Whatever the reason, it is likely that only an Indian living in New York could have drawn out these subterranean links between American modernism and Hindi "kitsch."

—Ravi Vasudevan

LE SALAIRE DE LA PEUR

(The Wages of Fear)

France-Italy, 1953

Director: Henri-Georges Clouzot

Production: Filmsonor-C.I.C.C.-FonoRoma-Vera Film; black and white; running time: 140 minutes, some sources list 150 minutes; length: 12,600 feet, some sources list 13,000. Released 1953.

Screenplay: Henri-Georges Clouzot, from the novel by Georges Arnaud; **photography:** Armand Thirard; **editors:** Madeleine Gug, Henri Rust; **art director:** René Renoux; **music:** Georges Auric.

Cast: Yves Montand (*Mario*); Charles Vanel (*Jo*); Vera Clouzot (*Linda*); Folco Lulli (*Luigi*); Peter van Eyck (*Bimba*); William Tubbs (*O'Brien*); Centa (*Chief of ''Boss'' Camp*); Mario Moreno (*Hernandez*); Jo Dest (*Smerloff*).

Awards: British Film Academy Award for Best Film from any Source, 1954.

Publications

Script:

Clouzot, Henri-Georges, *Le Salaire de la peur*, in *Avant-Scène du Cinéma* (Paris), no. 17, 1962; as *The Wages of Fear*, in *Masterworks of the French Cinema*, London and New York, 1974.

Books:

Cournot, Michel, *Le Premier Spectateur*, Paris, 1957.
Lacassin, Francis, and others, *Le Procès Clouzot*, Paris, 1964.
Pilard, Philippe, *H. G. Clouzot*, Paris, 1969.
Armes, Roy, *French Cinema Since 1946: The Great Tradition*, New York, 1970.
Remond, Alain, *Yves Montand*, Paris, 1977.
Rouchy, Marie-Elisabeth, *Yves Montand*, Paris, 1980.
Monserrat, Joëlle, *Montand*, Paris, 1983.

Articles:

Variety (New York), 29 April 1953.
Cahiers du Cinéma (Paris), May 1953.
Bianco e Nero (Rome), June 1953.
Cineaste (New York), nos. 7–8, 1954.
Mauriac, Claude, in *L'Amour du cinéma*, Paris, 1954.
Houston, Penelope, in *Monthly Film Bulletin* (London), April 1954.
Sight and Sound (London), April-June 1954.
Brulé, Claude, ''Clouzot est-il vraiment diable,'' in *Ciné-Revue* (Paris), 2 May 1955.
Film Culture (New York), May-June 1955.
Tennant, Sylvia, ''Henri-Georges Clouzot,'' in *Film* (London), March-April 1956.
Bianchi, Pietro, ''Henri-Georges Clouzot,'' in *Yale French Studies* (New Haven, Connecticut), Summer 1956.
Fontaine, A., ''Clouzot sort de sa legende,'' in *Lettres Françaises* (Paris), July 1960.
Schrader, Paul, ''An Interview with Henri-Georges Clouzot,'' in *Cinema* (Beverly Hills), no. 4, 1969.
Prédal, René, ''Une Carrière exemplaire: Charles Vanel,'' in *Cinéma Aujourd'hui* (Paris), no. 10, 1976.
Lacourbe, R., ''Henri-Georges Clouzot, 1907–1977,'' in *Avant-Scène du Cinéma* (Paris), 15 April 1977.
Le Peron, S., ''Charles Vanel par Charles Vanel,'' in *Avant-Scène du Cinéma* (Paris), 15 November 1981.
Yakir, D., ''Clouzot: The Wages of Film,'' in *Film Comment* (New York), November-December 1981.
Films and Filming (London), January 1986.
Thomajan, Dale, ''Clouzot's Wild Bunch,'' in *Film Comment* (New York), no. 376, January 1986.
Hoberman, J., ''Being and Nitroglycerin,'' in *Village Voice* (New York), vol. 36, 22 October 1991.
Van Gelder, L., ''At the Movies,'' in *New York Times*, vol. 141, C10, 11 October 1991.
Canby, V., ''Review/Film: Clouzot's *Wages of Fear*: Version Complete,'' in *New York Times*, vol. 141, C8, 18 October, 1991.
Pitman, Randy, in *Library Journal*, vol. 117, no. 7, 15 April 1992.
Porton, Richard, ''A Second Look,'' in *Cineaste* (New York), vol. 19, no. 1, 1992.
The New York Times, 11 June 1992.
Andrew, Geoff, ''Hell on Wheels,'' in *Time Out* (London), no. 1319, 29 November 1995.
Howard, T., in *Reid's Film Index*, no. 16, 1995.
Elia, M., in *Séquences* (Haute-Ville), no. 189/190, March/June 1997.

* * *

The international acclaim accorded the French New Wave has tended to shroud the pre-New Wave French cinema in desultory neglect. Henri-Georges Clouzot has particularly been underappreciated, his films decreasingly programmed. With *The Wages of Fear* this is particularly surprising, given the huge initial success of the film, both critically and commercially. A suspense thriller with clear philosophical overtones, *The Wages of Fear* deals with a group of international losers who end up down-and-out in a poor, underdeveloped section of Venezuela, with few prospects for escaping the torpor and petty tensions of their lives. The texture of the film, with its multiplicity of spoken languages, is strikingly dense and in keeping with Clouzot's theme of universal alienation. Although the set-up is quite slow by contemporary narrative standards, Clouzot's visual design is masterful: the first hour is dominated by constant and oppressive imprisoning shadows cast over the main characters and by costumes overwhelmed with vertical or horizontal stripes. Indeed, when Yves Montand's Mario says, ''It's like prison here,'' the sentiment seems almost redundant, so pervasive is Clouzot's visual expression of the entrapment by life itself.

When, midway through the film the down-and-outs are given the opportunity to escape their lot by undertaking an incredibly dangerous task, the fact that hundreds are willing to risk their lives is just more evidence that lives are worth little indeed. This opportunity is created by an oil-well fire, an ecological disaster, but, more to the point, a financial catastrophe for the American Oil Company. It must transport one ton of highly explosive nitroglycerine to the site in order

Le salaire de la peur

to extinguish the fire. Ultimately, four disparate men are chosen to drive the two explosive-laden trucks across the dangerous terrain. The core of *The Wages of Fear* is this trip itself, which functions as metaphor for the existential horror that comprises Clouzot's world view. Clouzot presents at least four striking images of existential nothingness, one for each of the natural elements. Perhaps the strongest, conceptually, is the explosion that literally blows up two of the men into thin air—leaving no trace of their having ever existed, save for a solitary cigarette holder, soon forgotten. The second metaphor is a liquid, black pit, into which one of the adventurers—Charles Vanel's Jo, Clouzot's archetypal man: non-heroic, petty, venal, and, above all, human—is sucked and crushed. It is not until Mario sees the third metaphor, however—the all-engulfing, destructive fire itself, that his own search for escape climaxes in Jo's death. The final image of nothingness has Mario, apparently saved from the nitroglycerine, nevertheless destroyed as he is smashed into the earth and rock of the destructive terrain, which imposes its monolithic destiny. Air, liquid, fire, earth: all are revealed as horrific and naturally violent, like men's souls.

What particularly impresses today about *The Wages of Fear* is its striking influence on a variety of other films and filmmakers. Its metaphorical opening shots, for instance—children being entertained by bugs in the earth—suggest the similar opening of *The Wild Bunch*, directed by Sam Peckinpah, a filmmaker with a similar brutal world view. As an exemplary thriller of the navigated space, dealing with psychological concepts that relate human beings to objects and to empty spaces and with philosophical notions concerning the human condition, *The Wages of Fear* provides a model for John Boorman's *Deliverance*, Andrei Konchalovsky's equally existential *Runaway Train* (written in part by Akira Kurosawa), and William Friedkin's rather incongruously entitled remake *Sorcerer*. In its representation of Third-World poverty and local color, *The Wages of Fear* suggests the Peter Weir of *The Year of Living Dangerously* and *The Mosquito Coast;* and in its indictment of capitalist imperialism in the context of suspense, it suggests Costa-Gavras, if filtered through the surreal acceptance of Luis Buñuel. As action adventure genre, it has inspired films like Robert Aldrich's *The Flight of the Phoenix;* as a rather cynical male-bonding film, it has anticipated films as disparate as Franklin J. Schaffner's *Papillon*, Don Siegel's *Escape from Alcatraz*, and Dino Risi's *The Easy Life*. And finally, in one of its penultimate scenes, when Jo—rotting on the inside from a gangrenous leg and covered on the outside with black oil as he is driven by Mario along a clearly metaphorical road of like in the dead of night—announces, after ''What a long street it is'' that ''there is nothing. . . ,'' and then dies, the imagery, dialogue, and psychological insights are surprisingly similar to the climactic scene of Claude Chabrol's *Le boucher*, a thriller of the New Wave period which rather unfairly made Clouzot seem old-fashioned.

—Charles Derry

SALT OF THE EARTH

USA, 1954

Director: Herbert J. Biberman

Production: Independent Productions Corporation and the International Union of Mine, Mill, and Smelter Workers; black and white, 35mm; running time 92 minutes. Released 1954, New York City. Filmed 1953 in the Bayard Region of New Mexico.

Producers: Paul Jarrico with Sonja Dahl Biberman and Adolfo Barela; **screenplay:** Michael Wilson with Herbert J. Biberman; **photography:** Leonard Stark and Stanley Meredith, some sources list director of photography as Simon Lazarus; **editors:** Ed Spiegel and Joan Laird; **sound:** Dick Staunton and Harry Smith; **production design:** Sonja Dahl and Adolfo Bardela; **music:** Sol Kaplan.

Cast: Professional actors—Rosaura Revueltas (*Esperanza Quintero*); Will Geer (*Sheriff*); David Wolfe (*Barton*); Melvin Williams (*Hartwell*); David Sarvis (*Alexander*); non-professional actors—Juan Chacón (*Ramón Quintero*); Henrietta Williams (*Teresa Vidal*); Ernest Velásquez (*Charley Vidal*); Angela Sánchez (*Consuelo Ruíz*); Joe T. Morales (*Sal Ruíz*); Clorinda Alderette (*Luz Morales*); Charles Coleman (*Antonio Morales*); Virginia Jencks (*Ruth Barnes*); Clinton Jencks (*Frank Barnes*); E. A. Rockwell (*Vance*); William Rockwell (*Kimbrough*); Frank Talavera (*Luís Quintero*); Mary Lou Castillo (*Estella Quintero*); Floyd Bostick (*Jenkins*); Victor Torres (*Sebastian Prieto*); E. S. Conerly (*Kalinsky*); Elvira Molano (*Mrs. Salazar*); Adolfo Barela and Albert Muñoz (*Miners*); and the men and women of Local 890, International Union of Mine, Mill, and Smelter Workers, Bayard, New Mexico.

Publications

Script:

Wilson, Michael, *Salt of the Earth*, compiled by Deborah Silverton Rosenfelt, New York, 1978.

Books:

Cogley, John, *Report on Blacklisting I: Movies*, New York, 1956.
Biberman, Herbert, *Salt of the Earth: The Story of a Film*, Boston, 1965.
Lorence, James J., *Suppression of Salt of the Earth: How Hollywood, Big Labor, and Politicians Blacklisted a Movie in Cold War America*, Albuquerque, 1999.

Articles:

''Hollywood Film Writers,'' in *Nation* (New York), 15 January 1949.
''Interview with Herbert Biberman,'' in *Jeune Cinéma* (Paris), November 1950.
''I.U.M.M.S.W. with Love,'' in *Time* (New York), 23 February 1953.
''Silver City Troubles,'' in *Newsweek* (New York), 16 March 1953.
Bloom, H., ''Vigilantism Plays the Villain, Silver City, N. Mex.,'' in *Nation* (New York), 9 May 1953.
Biberman, Herbert, and Paul Jarrico, in *Cinéma* (Paris), March 1955.
McFadden, Patrick, ''Blacklisted,'' in *Take One* (Montreal), no. 5, 1967.
''Interview with Herbert Biberman,'' in *Positif* (Paris), Summer 1969.
Avant-Scène du Cinéma (Paris), June 1971.
McCormick, R., in *Cineaste* (New York), no. 4, 1973.
Debacker, J., ''Dossier: *Le Sel de la terre,*'' in *Apec—Revue Belge du Cinéma* (Brussels), no. 4, 1974–75.
Fausing, B., in *Kosmorama* (Copenhagen), Autumn 1975.
Borde, Raymond in *Filmihullu* (Helsinki), no. 5, 1976.
''Special Issue'' of *Film und Fernsehen* (Berlin), July 1977.
Hoen, P. R., in *Filmavisa* (Oslo), no. 4, 1978.
Haudiquet, P., ''Le Sel de la terre à la liste noire,'' in *Image et Son* (Paris), June 1978.
Turroni, G., in *Filmcritica* (Rome), May 1979.
Heredero, C. F., in *Cinema 2002* (Madrid), November 1979.
Rosenfelt, D., ''Ideology and Structure in *Salt of the Earth,*'' in *Jump Cut* (Chicago), 30 December 1979.
Peary, Danny, in *Cult Movies 2*, New York, 1983.
Miller, Tom, ''Class Reunion: *Salt of the Earth* Revisited,'' in *Cineaste* (New York), vol. 13, no. 3, 1984.
Crowdus, Gary, in *Cineaste* (New York), vol. 15, no. 1, 1986.
Bosshard, A., ''Which Side Are You On?'' in *Illusions* (Wellington), no. 8, June 1988.
Jarrico, P., ''Letters: *Salt of the Earth*,'' in *Cineaste* (New York), vol. 17, no. 1, 1989.
Riambau, Esteve, and C. Torreiro, ''This Film is Going to Make History: An Interview with Rosaura Revueltas,'' in *Cineaste* (New York), vol. 19, no. 2–3, 1992.
Jerslev, A., ''*Salt of the Earth* Revisited,'' in *Kosmorama* (Copenhagen), vol. 42, no. 218, Winter 1996.
Hoberman, J., ''West Side Story,'' in *Village Voice* (New York), vol. 43, 13 January 1998.

* * *

Salt of the Earth was produced as a self-consciously radical film during one of the most repressive periods in American political history. Started by a number of Hollywood's blacklisted, it soon attained the status of a truly collective film enterprise, employing the talent and experience of many of those involved in the real events the film portrays as well as the original group of ousted Hollywood professionals. Because it was conceived as a politically radical statement on working conditions, union organizing, and relations between the races and sexes, *Salt of the Earth* faced official and unofficial harassment from political and industrial leaders whose thinking characterized the McCarthy era.

Salt of the Earth began as a film project when blacklisted producer Paul Jarrico and his family visited a miners' strike in Grant County, New Mexico. Previously, a number of blacklisted Hollywood professionals, including some of the recently released Hollywood Ten, had

Salt of the Earth

formed Independent Productions Corporation in 1951 with $10,000 from theater operator Simon Lazarus, and another $25,000 from an array of sympathetic businessmen. The group was unable to decide on a project until Jarrico returned with his suggestion to film a story based on the miners' real experiences in the strike he had just witnessed. Screenwriter Michael Wilson then ventured to Grant County three months prior to the end of the almost one and a half year strike. Wilson made several trips between Los Angeles and Grant County, each time preparing a new script incorporating the input of the miners and their families. In its final form, the film tells a fictionalised story of New Mexico's Union of Mine, Mill, and Smelter Workers strike against Empire Zinc, lasting from October 1950 to January 1952. The strike was characterized by an especially tense and violent atmosphere between Anglos and Chicanos. Ultimately, the miners' wives took over the picket line to avoid a court injunction against the all male union workers, an event which profoundly affected the Chicano community's attitudes about women's rights. The emotional tensions generated by the strike—between Chicano and Anglo, and when the women walked the picket line, between husbands and wives—are portrayed in their impact on a fictional married couple, Ramon and Esperanza Quintero.

Collective decision-making distinguished not only the script's preparation but all aspects of the film's production, marking an abrupt change in the hierarchical collaboration that characterized Hollywood filmmaking. Most of the roles were filled by the miners themselves and local Anglos, including the male lead Ramon, played by unionist Juan Chacon. The heroine was originally to be played by Gale Sondergaard, already involved in the project, but was finally cast with Rosaura Revueltas, a highly successful Mexican film star. Her participation in the film led to her deportation from the United States, and ultimately to the end of her film career.

The production and post-production of *Salt* was hampered by constant harassment from industrial and political leaders. Hiring a union crew proved impossible as Roy Brewer, red-baiter and head of the I.A.T.S.F., refused to allow union personnel to participate. During the film's shooting, the project and all those involved were denounced by union representatives in Hollywood, the trade press, and Congressman Donald Jackson in the House of Representatives, all leading to increasing tension in Grant County which hindered the film's completion.

Post-production was impeded not only by Hollywood union recalcitrance but also by Howard Hughes's attempts to organize an industry-wide boycott of the film by post-production facilities throughout the country. The film's exhibition encountered such strong resistance from I.A.T.S.E. projectionists, who under Brewer's orders refused to project the finished film, that it was and still is seen most widely at union activities and outside the United States.

The film is marred aesthetically by these outside pressures, since the tension and violence that marked the final shooting days and Revueltas's deportation necessitated the inclusion of some poor sound footage and mismatched edits. Nevertheless, even today the film presents in its fictionalized account of the strike a powerful statement on workers' conditions, union organizing, and changing relations between women and men and Chicanos and Anglos.

—Michael Selig

SALVATORE GIULIANO

Italy, 1961

Director: Francesco Rosi

Production: Lux Film and Vides-Galatea (Italy); black and white, 35mm; running time: 125 minutes, some sources list 135 minutes. Released 1961. Filmed in Sicily.

Producer: Franco Cristaldi; **screenplay:** Francesco Rosi, Suso Cecchi D'Amico, Enzo Provenzale, and Franco Solinas, based on official court records and journalistic reports on the career of Salvatore Giuliano; **photography:** Gianni Di Venanzo; **editor:** Mario Serandrei; **sound:** Claudio Maielli; **art directors:** Sergio Canevari and Carlo Egidi; **music:** Piero Piccioni; **costume designer:** Marilù Carteny.

Cast: Frank Wolff (*Gaspare Pisciotta*); Salvo Randone (*President of Viterbo Assize Court*); Federico Zard (*Pisciotta's defense counsel*); Pietro Camarata (*Salvatore Giuliano*); Fernando Cicero (*Bandit*); Sennuccio Benelli (*Reporter*); Bruno Ekmar (*Spy*); Max Cartier (*Francesco*); Giuseppe Calandra (*Minor official*); Cosimo Torino (*Frank Mannino*); Giuseppe Teti (*Priest of Montelepre*); Ugo Torrente.

Awards: Berlin Film Festival, Best Direction, 1962.

Publications

Books:

Rondi, Gian Luigi, *The Italian Cinema Today 1952–1965*, New York, 1966.

Wlaschin, Ken, *Italian Cinema Since the War*, Cranbury, New Jersey, 1971.

Bolzoni, Francesco, *I film di Francesco Rosi*, Rome, 1986.

Ciment, Michel, *Le Dossier Rosi: Cinéma et politique*, Paris, 1976; revised edition, 1987.

Kezich, Tullio, *Salvatore Giuliano*, Acicatena, Italy, 1991.

Testa, Carlo, editor, *Poet of Civic Courage: The Films of Francesco Rosi*, Westport, 1996.

Articles:

Films and Filming (London), December 1962.

Bean, Robin, in *Films and Filming* (London), June 1963.

Lane, John, in *Films and Filming* (London), August 1963.

''Francesco Rosi: Interview,'' in *Film* (London), Spring 1964.

Thomas, John, in *Film Society Review* (New York), September 1966.

Ravage, Maria-Teresa, in *Film Society Review* (New York), October 1971.

Crowdus, Gary, and D. Georgakas, ''The Audience Should Not Be Just Passive Spectators,'' in *Cinearte* (New York), no. 1, 1975.

Netzeband, G., ''Eisenstein, Rosi, Kieslowski und andere,'' in *Film und Fernsehen* (Berlin), no. 12, 1979.

Baker, F. D., ''Solo lo psicologo del film e non del personaggio: Colloquio con Francesco Rosi,'' in *Cinema Nuovo* (Turin), October 1979.

''Rosi Issue'' of *Cinema* (Zurich), vol. 28, no. 2, 1982.

Elbert, L., in *Cinemateca Revista* (Montevideo), November 1983.

Domecq, J.-P., in *Positif* (Paris), April 1984.

Ciment, Michel, ''Rosi in a New Key,'' in *American Film*, vol. 9, September 1984.

Rosi, Francesco, in *Filmkultura* (Budapest), January 1986.

Dibilio, P., ''Quand Rosi filmait Giuliano,'' in *Cinéma* (Paris), no. 424, 13 January 1988.

''Spéciale première,'' in *Revue du Cinéma* (Paris), no. 435, February 1988.

Crowdus, G., ''Francesco Rosi: Italy's Postmodern Neorealist,'' in *Cineaste* (New York), vol. 20, no. 4, 1994.

Klawans, Stuart, and Howard Feinstein, ''Illustrious Rosi,'' in *Film Comment* (New York), vol. 31, no. 1, January-February 1995.

Restivo, Angelo, ''The Economic Miracle and Its Discontents: Bandit Films in Spain and Italy,'' in *Film Quarterly* (Berkeley), vol. 49, no. 2, Winter 1995–1996.

''La Sicilia al presente storico: *Salvatore Giuliano*,'' in *Castoro Cinema* (Milan), no. 31/32, 2nd edition, March 1998.

* * *

Salvatore Giuliano, a Sicilian bandit who became a force in that island's violent political affairs from the end of World War II until his violent death in 1950, is the subject of the third feature film by Francesco Rosi, former assistant director to Luchino Visconti. But in a real sense it is Sicily—the texture of its land and the interwoven social and political forces which shaped the career of this bandit—that is the true subject of the film.

In many ways *Salvatore Giuliano* produces the effect of documentary. The scenario is based on extensive research into official court records as well as historical and journalistic reports surrounding the

Salvatore Giuliano

career of Giuliano. The confusion of these reports and records is preserved by the fractured structure of the film's narrative.

The non-fictional subject is the basis of a complex structure which relies more on selection of events and reconstruction than on invention. The major structuring device is a voice-over narration, spoken by Rosi himself in the Italian version. This device, along with a few printed titles, accounts for much of the film's documentary impact and serves to specify space and time in the major narrative sections.

The structure alternates events following the bandit's death in 1950 with flashbacks chronicling his career from the end of World War II. Within both the present and the flashback segments, the development is chronological but sharply elliptical. Within the flashbacks, events are selected around certain themes in Sicilian politics and Giuliano's career—the Separatist movement, kidnapping, the attack on a leftist peasant gathering.

The voice-over, with its verbal overload of information may contribute as much as the temporal structure to the film's ambiguity. The various sources of power in Sicily—government, Separatists, police, army—are all eventually linked with the mafia, a connection more often implied by juxtaposition of image and voice-over than by direct statement.

Salvatore Giuliano is concerned with Sicily not only in terms of its politics. The film was shot on location, using Sicilian non-professionals as actors. Sweeping camera movements describe the uneven terrain that concealed and protected the bandits from their opponents.

Rosi systematically withholds critical information. The bandit himself is on view as a corpse in the first sequence and then appears briefly several times in the flashbacks, his identity often obscured. And yet Rosi took pains to select an actor who resembled the real bandit. Giuliano's murderer is the closest approximation to a developed character, although he emerges from the background very late in the film.

The lack of emphasis on characters is one clear distinction between this 1961 film and Italian neorealism. There is also, despite the location shooting and the careful research that contributed to the film, a new scepticism regarding the status of photographic reality. In the opening scene, a city official reads a fastidiously detailed description of the death scene, its precision revealing absolutely nothing. In the course of the film, the viewer is shown that these apparent circumstances mask a complicated system of deception.

—Ann Harris

SAMMA NO AJI

(An Autumn Afternoon)

Japan, 1962

Director: Yasujiro Ozu

Production: Shochiku Co.; Agfacolor, 35mm; running time: 113 minutes. Released November 1962, Japan.

Producer: Shizuo Yamanouchi; **screenplay:** Yasujiro Ozu and Kogo Noda; **photography:** Yushun (or, Yuharu) Atsuta; **editor:** Yoshiyasu Manamura; **sound:** Yoshisaburo Senoo; **art director:** Tatsuo Hamada; **music:** Takanobu Saito.

Cast: Chisu Ryu (*Shuhei Hirayama*); Shima Iwashita (*Michiko Hirayama*); Shin-ichiro Mikami (*Kazuo Hirayama*); Keiji Sada (*Koichi Hirayama*); Mariko Okada (*Akiko Hirayama*); Nobuo Nakamura (*Shuzo Kawai*); Kuniko Miyake (*Nobuko Kawai*); Ryuji Kita (*Susumu Horie*); Eijiro Tono (*Sakuma*); Teruo Yoshida (*Miura*).

Publications

Books:

Richie, Donald, *Japanese Cinema: Film Style and National Character*, New York, 1971.

Sato, Tadao, *Ozu Yasujiro no Geijutsu* (The Art of Yasujiro Ozu), Tokyo, 1971.

Satomi, Jun, and others, *Ozu Yasujiro—Hito to Shigoto* (Yasujiro Ozu—The Man and His Work), Tokyo, 1972.

Schrader, Paul, *Transcendental Style in Film: Ozu, Bresson, Dreyer*, Berkeley, 1972.

Richie, Donald, *Ozu*, Berkeley, 1974.

Schrader, Leonard, and Haruji Nakumara, editors, *Masters of Japanese Film*, Tokyo, 1975.

Bock, Audie, *Japanese Film Directors*, New York, 1978; revised edition, Tokyo, 1985.

Burch, Noël, *To the Distant Observer*, Berkeley, 1979.

Tessier, Max, editor, *Le Cinéma japonais au prèsent: 1959–1979*, Paris, 1980.

Sato, Tadao, *Currents in Japanese Cinema*, Tokyo, 1982.

Bordwell, David, *Ozu and the Poetics of Cinema*, Princeton, 1988.

Articles:

Richie, Donald, ''The Face of '63—Japan,'' in *Films and Filming* (London), July 1963.

Milne, Tom, ''Flavour of Green Tea over Rice,'' in *Sight and Sound* (London), Autumn 1963.

Richie, Donald, ''Yasujiro Ozu: Syntax of His Films,'' in *Film Quarterly* (Berkeley), Winter 1963–64.

''Ozu Issue'' of *Kinema Jumpo* (Tokyo), February 1964.

Ryu, Chisu, ''Yasujiro Ozu,'' in *Sight and Sound* (London), Spring 1964.

Iwasaki, Akira, ''Ozu,'' in *Film* (London), Summer 1965.

Tung, in *Film Quarterly* (Berkeley), Winter 1965–66.

Haruji, and Leonard Schrader, ''Ozu Spectrum,'' in *Cinema* (Beverly Hills), no. 1, 1970.

Farber, Manny, ''Ozu,'' in *Artforum* (New York), June 1970.

Phillipe, Jean-Claude, ''Yasujiro Ozu,'' in *Dossiers du cinéma: Cinéastes*, no. 1, Paris, 1971.

Rosenbaum, Jonathan, ''Ozu,'' in *Film Comment* (New York), Summer 1972.

Zeman, Marvin, ''The Zen Artistry of Yasujiro Ozu,'' in *Film Journal* (New York), Fall-Winter 1972.

Tessier, Max, in *Anthologie du Cinema 7*, Paris, 1973.

Thompson, Kristin, and David Bordwell, ''Space and Narrative in the Films of Ozu,'' in *Screen* (London), Summer 1976.

Bezombes, R., in *Cinématographe* (Paris), November 1978.

Magny, Joel, in *Cinéma* (Paris), December 1978.

Tessier, Max, in *Ecran* (Paris), December 1978.

Delmas, J., in *Jeune Cinéma* (Paris), December-January 1979.

Colpart, G., in *Revue du Cinéma* (Paris), series 23, 1979.

Biette, J. C., in *Cahiers du Cinéma* (Paris), January 1979.

Masson, A., in *Positif* (Paris), January 1979.

Richie, Donald, ''Ozu,'' in *Cinema: A Critical Dictionary*, edited by Richard Roud, London, 1980.

Piccardi, A., ''La tarda primavera di Yasujiro Ozu,'' in *Cineforum* (Bergamo), July-August 1982.

Geist, Kathe, ''Yasujiro Ozu: Notes on a Retrospective,'' in *Film Quarterly* (Berkeley), Fall 1983.

Backer, F., and others, ''Ozu: Meester in de beperking,'' in *Skrien* (Amsterdam), Winter 1983–84.

Berta, R., ''A la recherche du regard,'' in *Cahiers du Cinéma* (Paris), December 1985.

Tomczak, R., ''*Samma No Aji*,'' in *Filmfaust*, vol. 12, no. 64, February-March 1988.

Ortiz, A., ''El sabor de pescado de otono,'' in *Nosferatu* (San Sebastian, Spain), no. 25/26, December 1997.

* * *

The title of Yasujiro Ozu's last film, *Samma no aji* (*An Autumn Afternoon*), literally ''taste of autumn swordfish,'' symbolizes the ordinary in life, and represents another contemplative study of the serenity of Japanese middle-class family life.

Ozu's characteristic stylistic techniques are evident here. The film begins with a series of shots of chimneys from different angles, and proceeds to the corridor of an office building preparing our introduction to a company executive, Mr. Hirayama—an editing pattern common in Ozu's work. Another characteristic Ozu device is the use of a number of shots of restaurant and bar signs appearing for several seconds before the story inside the restaurant develops. We soon lose track of how often we witness the character enjoying a conversation over food and drink. All of these scenes are very deliberately

Samma no aji

composed, including the placement of food, dishes and beer bottles. The movements of the characters seem carefully choreographed throughout these scenes. We are shown in detail a high-school reunion, casual gossip between intimate friends, and discussions of household topics among couples and family members.

The film's central plot is the arrangement of the marriage of Hirayama's daughter, Michiko, further developed by other marriage-related subplots. For example, Hirayama's old high school teacher and his old maid daughter make Hirayama realize his duty to arrange Michiko's marriage despite his own loneliness which will surely continue. We also see Michiko's older brother's trifling marriage problems; Michiko's unsuccessful love for her brother's friend; Hirayama's friend's happy remarriage to a younger wife; Hirayama's secretary's marriage; and Hirayama's encounter with a barmaid who reminds him of his deceased wife.

Subplots such as these are developed in lengthy, carefully edited conversation scenes. Ozu frequently uses frontal, close-up shot-reverse shots of characters' faces (occasionally including unmatching eyelines). Indeed, the film's narrative is developed more in these conversations and less by direct actions. Each dialogue is extremely concise, often omitting subjects and objects in the sentences, making it impossible to translate directly in the English subtitles.

Ozu is obsessed with showing the empty space after any action takes place. After Michiko leaves her house on the wedding day, a series of shots showing her empty room during the day and at night are used to accentuate the emptiness after her departure. Particularly, the close-up shots of the big mirror and the vacated stool force us to realize that she, sitting there in her wedding gown just moments before, is now gone. The pathos is suggested by the systematic arrangement of shots of inanimate objects.

Through the depiction of the non-dramatic atmosphere of peaceful human relationships between good-willed people, the film conveys the feeling of the quiet realization of the loneliness in life. It is deftly symbolized by the sequences at the bar where Hirayama drinks, listening nostalgically to the Japanese Navy march and then, at home, drinks water silently in the kitchen at the end of the corridor.

The audience and critics appreciated the distinctive loneliness of Ozu's world all the more for the light and even humorous nature of many of *An Autumn Afternoon*'s individual scenes.

—Kyoko Hirano

SAMO JEDNOM SE LJUBI

(You Only Love Once/Melody Haunts My Memory)

Yugoslavia, 1981

Director: Rajko Grlic

Production: Jadran Film; Eastmancolour, 35mm; running time: 104 minutes.

Screenplay: Rajko Grlic, Branko Somen, and Srdan Karanovic; **photography:** Tomislav Pinter; **editor:** Zivka Toplak; **art director:** Stanislav Dobrina; **music:** Branislav Zivkovic.

Cast: Predrag Manojlovic (*Tomislav*); Vladica Milosovljenic (*Beba*); Mladen Budiscak (*Vule*); Zijah Sokolovic (*Mirko*); Erland Josephson (*Father*).

Publications

Articles:

Variety (New York), 27 May 1981.
Kolsek, P., *Ekran* (Ljubljana), no. 6–7, 1981.
Dolmark, J.-M. Z., *Ekran* (Ljubljana), no. 8–9, 1981.
White, Armond, and Marcia Pally, ''The 16th New Directors: New Films Series,'' in *Film Comment* (New York), vol. 23, no. 3, May-June 1987.

* * *

Samo Jednom Se Ljubi, or *You Only Love Once*, refers to a popular song of the early 1950s. But the viewer shouldn't be fooled by the romantic implications of the title. Once more, as in Grlic's earlier *Bravo Maestro* (1978), the theme of the film is political. Although the figures are all fictional, the screenplay itself was inspired by a young ballerina's diary which was expanded to fit the atmosphere of the times. Grlic has described the scope of the film's narrative as follows:

> My film, *You Only Love Once*, is based upon an authentic event that happened a few years after the war. Turning the pages of private memoirs and official documents of that time, I was struck by the harness of behaviour and relations, by that ''social realism'' which seems to get reincarnated—although with a step backward and without sentiments—and form a sort of an ''image'' of today's kids.

It is also important to recognize the collaboration on the script between Grlic and Srdjan Karanovic, Grlic's classmate at the Prague Film School and a Belgrade director. They have, throughout the years, reciprocated on each other's screenplays repeatedly. This collaboration was essential to the process of creating the film, which Grlic described as such: ''In researching my project, I had the feeling of discovery of origins of certain current states of mind, which seem born in that transition period from war to peace.''

The film tells the story of a small village in Croatia shortly after the war where there is a feeling of hope and promise between three ex-partisans who are now companions: the mayor, the chief of police, and the cultural head of the town (who is also a member of the secret police). But when an entertainment group arrives in town, Tomislav, the cultural wing of the trio, falls in love with Beba, a dancer from a bourgeois background who is attracted by Tomislav's crude, bluffing manners. Violating the spirit of this trust, Tomislav persuades Beba to marry him—whereupon his new wife's aristocratic family moves in seeking to better their lot in a new society, or at least find a way to emigrate out of their old one. The couple's love survives even when the times change and Tomislav is imprisoned. Tomislav eventually tracks her down in a sleazy nightclub in what is perhaps one of the strongest endings of all Yugoslav films.

The films succeeds in working on two levels. First, as an examination of postwar Yugoslavia trying to find its identity. Secondly, as a study of the destructiveness of human relationships, and the strength of love.

—Mike Downey

LE SAMOURAI

France, 1967

Director: Jean-Pierre Melville

Production: Filmel, C.I.C.C., Fida Cinematografica; colour, 35mm; running time: 105 minutes. Filmed in Paris, 1966.

Producer: Raymond Borderie, Eugène Lepicier; **screenplay:** Jean-Pierre Melville, from the novel *The Ronin* by Joan McLeod; **photography:** Henri Decae; **editors:** Monique Bonnot, Yolande Maurette; **assistant director:** Georges Pellegrin; **art director:** Francois de Lamothe; **music:** Francois de Roubaix; **sound editors:** Alex Pront, Robert Pouret; **sound recordist:** René Longuet.

Cast: Alain Delon (*Jeff Costello*); Francois Perier (*The Inspector*); Nathalie Delon (*Jane Lagrange*); Cathy Rosier (*Valérie*); Jacques Leroy (*The Gunman*); Jean-Pierre Posier (*Olivier Rey*); Catherine Jourdan (*Hat-check girl*); Michel Boisrond (*Wiener*); Robert Favart (*Barman*); André Salgues (*Garage Man*).

Publications

Books:

Nogueira, Rui, *Melville on Melville*, London, 1971.
McArthur, Colin, *Underworld U.S.A*, London, 1972.
Nogueira, Rui, *Le Cinéma selon Melville*, Paris, 1973.
Zimmer, Jacques, and Chantal de Béchaude, *Jean-Pierre Melville*, Paris, 1983.
Armes, Roy, *French Cinema*, London, 1985.
Bantcheva, Denitza, *Jean-Pierre Melville: de l'oeuvre à l'homme*, Troyes, 1996.

Le Samourai

Articles:

Variety (New York), 8 November 1967.
Image et Son (Paris), December 1967.
Cahiers du Cinéma (Paris), December 1967.
Truffaut, François, and Rui Nogueira, ''A Samurai in Paris,'' in *Sight and Sound* (London), Summer 1968.
Focus on Film (London), September-October 1970.
Milne, Tom, *Monthly Film Bulletin* (London), June 1971.
Gow, G., *Films and Filming* (London), July 1971.
Milne, Tom, ''*Le Samourai*,'' in *Focus on Film*, No. 7, 1971.
Filmfacts (London), no.16, 1972.
Koebner, Thomas, ''Aus dem Leben der Automaten,'' in *Film-Dienst* (Cologne), vol. 46, no. 11, 25 May 1993.
Reader, Keith, *Sight and Sound* (London), September 1993.
Rouyer, Philippe, ''Le petit théâtre de Jean-Pierre Melville,'' in *Positif* (Paris), no. 418, December 1995.
Hogue, Peter, ''Melville,'' in *Film Comment* (New York), vol. 32, no. 6, November-December 1996.
Hoberman, J., ''Portrait of a Hit Man,'' in *Village Voice* (New York), vol. 42, 4 March 1997.
Canby, Vincent, in *The New York Times*, 26 December 1997.
Peachment, Chris, ''A Man Apart,'' in *New Statesman*, vol. 127, no. 4405, 2 October 1998.

* * *

Jean-Pierre Melville had made his first, highly distinctive contribution to the ''policier'' in 1956 with *Bob le flambeur*, returning to it in 1963 with *Le Doulos* which, with *Le Deuxième souffle* (1963) and *Le Samourai* (1967), comprises a loose trilogy that represents one of the very summits of the genre.

The French crime film is less well-known than the American variety (with the possible exception of *Du Rififi chez les hommes)*, but its relative neglect is unjust, and Melville is one of its finest exponents. As Roy Armes has noted, he has adapted the mythology and iconography of the gangster film to his own distinct ends: ''His criminals are idealised figures, their appearance stylised (with raincoat, hat and gun predominant) and their behaviour oddly blending violence with ritualised politeness. The director has no interest in the realistic portrayal of life as it is and disregards both psychological depth and accuracy of location and costume. He uses his stars to portray timeless, tragic figures caught up in ambiguous conflicts and patterns of deceit, relying on the actor's personality and certainty of gesture to fill the intentional void.''

Le Samourai opens with a quote (though largely made up by Melville) from the ''Book of Bushido'' to the effect that ''there is no greater solitude than that of the Samurai, unless it be that of the tiger in the jungle.'' Solitude is a particularly Melvillian theme, explored in different ways in *Bob le flambeur, Le Silence de la Mer, Leon Morin, pretre, Les Enfants terribles* and *L'Ainé des Ferchaux.* Indeed, in his own life Melville was a fiercely independent filmmaker. In *Le Samourai* this theme of solitude is embodied in the hired killer Jeff Costello, depicted while on a series of increasingly mysterious and dangerous contracts, with the police gradually closing in on him and a beautiful nightclub pianist, Valérie, mesmerising him.

From the opening shot, with Jeff lying stretched out and silent on his bed in a darkened room (as if ''laid out'' in death, as Melville himself put it), it is as if we are witnesses to a long, drawn-out, ritualistic process of *harakiri.* The mood of doom and fatefulness is as tangible as in a Fritz Lang film, and Melville heightens the feeling of strangeness and unease by zooming in and simultaneously tracking back—not an unusual technique by this time, but Melville considerably refines it by stopping the track occasionally as he continues the zoom, producing the effect that ''everything moves, but at the same time everything stays where it is.''

From here, the film progresses both as a classic American gangster film *a la francaise* and a wonderful exercise in mythology that quite specifically recalls *Orphée* (Melville had directed the film of Cocteau's novel *Les Enfants terribles* at Cocteau's own request). On the gangster level, as Tom Milne has evocatively described the film, *Le Samourai* is ''redolent of night, of gleaming city streets, of fast cars and guns weighed down by silencers as the lone wolf killer lopes steadily and disdainfully through a battery of police line-ups and interrogations, of encounters with syndicate hoods on lonely railway bridges and in the silence of his own room, never moving an inch from his chosen trail.'' Quite outstanding in this respect is the elaborate pursuit of Jeff by the police through the Paris metro (according to Melville, one of the officers on the Paris crime squad remarked enviously to him: ''If we were given the resources to set up tailing jobs like that, our task would be a lot easier''). Almost equally striking, however, are the scenes in which Melville simply observes the mechanics of Jeff going about his business, such as the complex setting-up of an alibi that occupies the first two, virtually dialogueless, reels of the film. As Milne notes, scenes such as these hinge entirely on ''Melville's meticulous observation of the precise, self-absorbed gestures and movements of a man alone and sufficient unto himself, whether he is hunter or hunted.''

As a myth, on the other hand, *Le Samourai* is a variation on the theme of Orpheus being called to the underworld. If, in *Orphée*, it was the otherworldly Princess who becomes susceptible to human feelings and returns Orpheus's love, here it is the icy, solitary Jeff whose feelings are awakened and who, thus shorn of his strength, deliberately accepts death and destiny. And just to underline the parallel with *Orphée*, the Princess is a white woman dressed in black, while Valérie is a black woman dressed in white.

Le Samourai presents us with an utterly compelling, totally self-contained universe. Accordingly, nothing, but nothing, has been left to chance in the mise-en-scène. This is a film of almost Bressonian rigour and austerity, as elliptical as Jeff is abstract. So muted and atonal are the colours that at first one has the impression of watching a black-and-white film, or a bleached-out print. But gradually one realises that what we are witnessing is, as Milne has it, ''a visual equivalent to Jeff's steely, passionless mind. In him and around him, cold and toneless, Paris becomes a city of shadows, as silent and mysterious as Cocteau's 'zone de la mort:' a place, in fact, where one is not in the least surprised to find Death herself waiting, beckoning the lonely samurai into her arms with her alluring promise of peace and companionship.'' A word of warning, however. The dubbed version of this film is hideously duped and is also missing nine minutes of footage. To appreciate the true beauties of *Le Samourai* it is absolutely vital to see the original, or subtitled, version.

—Julian Petley

LE SANG DES BÊTES

(Blood of the Beasts)

France, 1949

Director: Georges Franju

Production: Forces et Voix de France; black and white, 35mm; running time about 20 minutes; length: 600 meters. Released 1949. Filmed 1949 in a slaughterhouse outside Paris.

Producer: Paul Legros; **screenplay:** Georges Franju; **commentary:** Jean Painlevé; **assistant directors:** André Joseph and Julien Bonardier; **photography:** Marcel Fradetal assisted by Henri Champion; **editor:** Andre Joseph; **sound engineer:** Raymond Vachere; **music:** Joseph Kosma.

Cast: Nicole Ladmiral and Georges Hubert (*spoken parts*).

Publications

Script:

Franju, Georges, and Jean Painlevé, *Le Sang des bêtes*, in *Avant-Scène du Cinéma* (Paris), October 1964.

Books:

Lovell, Alan, *Anarchist Cinema*, London, 1962.
Armes, Roy, *French Cinema Since 1946: The Personal Style*, New York, 1966.
Durgnat, Raymond, *Franju*, Berkeley, 1968.
Vialle, Gabriel, *Georges Franju*, Paris, 1968.

Articles:

Goretta, Claude, ''Aspects of French Documentaries,'' in *Sight and Sound* (London), Winter 1956–57.
Grenier, Cynthia, ''Franju,'' in *Sight and Sound* (London), Spring 1957.
Godard, Jean-Luc, ''Georges Franju,'' in *Cahiers du Cinéma* (Paris), December 1958.

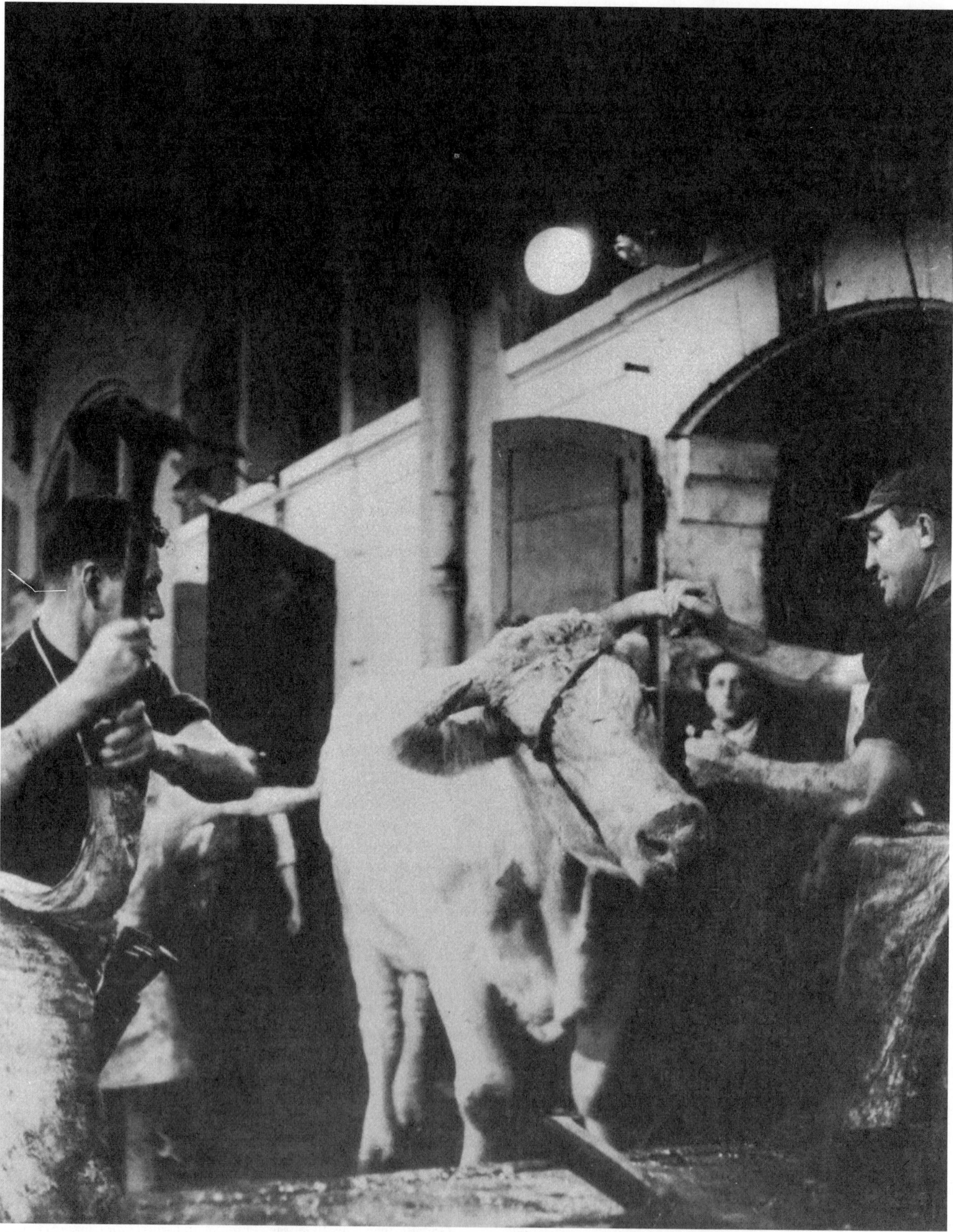

Le sang des bêtes

''Franju Issue'' of *Image et Son* (Paris), March 1966.
MacLochlainn, A., ''The Films of Luis Buñuel and Georges Franju,'' in *Film Journal* (New York), Summer 1971.
Gow, Gordon, ''Franju,'' in *Films and Filming* (London), August 1971.
Wood, Robin, ''Terrible Buildings: The World of Georges Franju,'' in *Film Comment* (New York), November-December 1973.
''Le Sang des bêtes de Franju,'' in *Avant-Scène du Cinéma* (Paris), 15 October 1976.
Barbaro, Nick, in *Cinema Texas Program Notes* (Austin), 27 April 1978.
Boost, C., in *Skoop* (Amsterdam), August 1981.

* * *

The unique tone of Georges Franju's best work—which includes *Le sang des bêtes*—arises from its combination of hypersensitivity to pain (inseparable from an obsession with it) with an extraordinary poise. The peculiar distinction of his work goes inextricably with its very limited range: he is one of the cinema's authentic minor poets.

Although *Hôtel des Invalides* (Franju's masterpiece) is more complex, and although one would not wish to be without the other documentaries and many characteristic, privileged moments in the features, *Le sang des bêtes* already contains, in a form at once concentrated and comprehensive, all the major components of the Franju *oeuvre*. It is a film totally at odds with the Grierson school of documentary filmmaking (i.e., the task of documentary is to explain the world to us so that we can all understand each other): ''understanding,'' to Franju, is the realization that civilization is constructed upon pain and horror and cannot be extricated from them.

The opening of the film—typically casual and disarming—establishes the location of the slaughterhouse. It is carefully set apart from the city that depends upon its activities, so that those who devour its products may be spared awareness of its existence, and of the physical realities of its interior. Separating it from Paris is a no-man's land where a young worker kisses his girlfriend goodbye, and where the debris of civilization—a heterogeneous, quasi-Surrealist assortment of junk objects divorced from their domestic contexts and deposited on the wasteland grass—is offered for sale, secondhand. The sequence (before we are introduced to any of the film's horrors) establishes with gentle irony and tenderness, a sense of the absurd and the arbitrary, of a world that never confronts the oddity of what it terms ''reality.''

The slaughterhouse itself is the first in the long succession of ''terrible buildings'' that provide Franju's work with one of its dominant recurrent motifs. It is a building at once thoroughly familiar, as everyone knows that slaughterhouses exist, but also hidden away because no one wants to confront or know about them. We are briefly shown the tools of slaughter. Then a white horse is led in through the gate. No one who has seen the film ever forgets the moment when a so-called humane killer is casually applied to its head and fired. From that moment on, the film spares us nothing of the details of slaughter, disembowellment, dismemberment. What is remarkable about the film is the way in which it scrupulously avoids, on the one hand, sadistic relish, and, on the other, the note of protest. Everything is shown calmly, dispassionately, generally at a distance. If a close-up is used, it is to clarify a detail of method or procedure. If the film converts some spectators to vegetarianism, this is purely incidental, a by-product of the audience's exposure to material they would prefer not to know about. The film is at once far more ambitious and far less presumptuous: it wishes to make us confront, with neither hysteria nor coercion, an aspect of the material reality on which our civilization is based.

—Robin Wood

LE SANG D'UN POETE

(The Blood of a Poet)

France, 1930

Director: Jean Cocteau

Production: Black and white, 35mm; running time: 58 minutes. Released 1930.

Producer: Vicomte de Noailles; **screenplay:** Jean Cocteau; **photography:** Georges Périnal; **sound:** Henri Labrély; **production design:** Jean Gabriel d'Aubonne; **music:** Georges Auric.

Cast: Lee Miller (*The Statue*); Enrico Rivero (*The Poet*); Jean Desbordes (*The Louis XV Friend*); Féral Benga (*The Black Angel*); Pauline Carton; Odette Thalazac; Fernand Duchamps; Lucien Jager; Barbette; Jean Cocteau (*Narrator*).

Publications

Script:

Cocteau, Jean, *Le sang d'un poète*, Paris, 1948; as *The Blood of a Poet*, New York, 1949; also included in ''*Le sang d'un poète* Issue'' of *Avant-Scène du Cinéma* (Paris), 1–15 May 1983.

Books:

Crosland, Margaret, *Jean Cocteau*, London, 1955.
Dauven, Jean, *Jean Cocteau chez les sirènes*, Paris, 1956.
Kihm, Jean-Jacques, *Cocteau*, Paris, 1960.
Pillaudin, Roger, *Jean Cocteau tourne son dernier film*, Paris, 1960.
Fraigneau, Andre, *Cocteau*, New York, 1961.
Fowlie, Wallace, *Jean Cocteau: The History of a Poet's Age*, Bloomington, Indiana, 1968.
Lannes, Roger, *Jean Cocteau*, Paris, 1968.
Sprigge, Elizabeth, and Jean-Jacques Kihm, *Jean Cocteau: The Man and the Mirror*, New York, 1968.
Gilson, Rene, *Cocteau*, New York, 1969.
Armes, Roy, *French Cinema Since 1946: The Great Tradition*, New York, 1970.
Phelps, R., editor, *Professional Secrets: an Autobiography of Jean Cocteau Drawn from His Lifetime Writings*, New York, 1970.
Steegmuller, Francis, *Cocteau*, Boston, 1970.
Cocteau on the Film, New York, 1972.
Evans, Arthur, *Jean Cocteau and His Films of Orphic Identity*, Philadelphia, 1977.
Thiher, Allen, *The Cinematic Muse: Critical Studies in the History of French Cinema*, Columbia and London, 1979.

Le sang d'un poete

Anderson, Alexandra and Carol Saltus, editors, *Jean Cocteau and the French Scene*, New York, 1984.
de Miomandre, Philippe, *Moi, Jean Cocteau*, Paris, 1985.
Keller, Marjorie, *The Untutored Eye: Childhood in the Films of Cocteau, Cornell, and Brakhage*, Cranbury, New Jersey, 1986.
Peters, Arthur King, *Jean Cocteau and His World: An Illustrated Biography*, London, 1987.

Articles:

New Statesman and Nation (London), 8 April 1933.
New York Times, 3 November 1933.
Variety (New York), 7 November 1933.
Wallis, C. G., in *Kenyon Review* (Gambier, Ohio), Winter 1944.
Yale French Studies (New Haven, Connecticut), Summer 1956.
Oxendandler, Neal, "On Cocteau," in *Film Quarterly* (Berkeley), Fall 1964.
Image et Son (Paris), March 1972.
Gauteur, C., "Jean Cocteau et le Cinéma Issue" of *Image et Son* (Paris), June-July 1972.
Campigli, M., in *Bianco e Nero* (Rome), March-April 1973.
Renaud, T., "Retrospective. Jean Cocteau. Un Cinéaste? Peut-être. Un Auteur? Certainement," in *Cinéma* (Paris), December 1973.
Rayns, Tony, in *Monthly Film Bulletin* (London), May 1977.
Gow, Gordon, "The Mirrors of Life," in *Films and Filming* (London), February 1978.
Milani, R., "Cocteau dell'immaginario," in *Filmcritica* (Florence), June 1984.
Paech, J., "Orpheus hinter den Spiegeln," in *EPD Film* (Frankfurt), July 1989.
Lalanne, Jean-Marc, "Profession: Phenixologe," *Mensuel du Cinema* (Paris), no. 10, October 1993.

* * *

Though the 1920s are generally considered the most significant years of experiment with filmic forms in French cinema, two of the acknowledged masterpieces of the avant-garde, Jean Cocteau's *Le sang d'un poète* and Luis Buñuel's *L'age d'or*, both date from the beginning of the sound era in the early 1930s. The bitter opposition, feuds and mutual denunciations existing at this time between Cocteau and the Surrealists seem in retrospect of less importance than the common avant-garde impulse which unites them. Significantly, both *Le sang d'un poète* and Buñuel's film were funded in exactly the same way, through private commissions by the wealthy art lover and socialite, the Vicomte de Noailles. Despite their differences and incompatibilities both films have proved to be lasting works of cinematic imagination. They provide a common inspiration for later independent filmmakers throughout the world.

Jean Cocteau came to the cinema as an amateur who had already acquired a literary reputation, though he was never concerned with the application of literary ideas or practices to film. Instead he saw filmmaking as a manual craft and gave far greater weight to the qualities of the film image than to the demands of a conventional narrative development. As *Le sang d'un poète* shows so clearly, he was a filmmaker able to disregard the conventionalities of cinematic construction simply because he never learned them in the first place. His essentially amateur approach is reflected in his choice of non-professional players for most of the key roles of the film. This did not preclude him from calling upon highly talented collaborators with real professional skills—such as George Périnal or Georges Auric—to assist him with the photography and music for *Le sang d'un poète*.

Cocteau has often denied that *Le sang d'un poète* contains either symbols or allegorical meaning. It uses some of the mechanics of the dream, not to explore social or psychological realities, but as ends in themselves. His concern is less to analyze than simply to recreate a state of inner consciousness, a world preceding rational thought. To this end he applies a whole range of trick devices—animation, mirrors, reverse action, false perspectives—and deliberately blurs the boundaries between the live action and graphic work or sculpture. Though haunted, like so much of Cocteau's work, by the omnipresence of death, *Le sang d'un poète* is a lyrical, idyllic work without tension or conflict. In Cocteau's mythology, death is reversible, just one aspect of a constant play of transformation. It is the director's ability to present this in a totally personal manner—aided by the first-person narration spoken by Cocteau himself—which makes the film such a fascinating work.

Le sang d'un poète introduces a distinctive new voice to world cinema. It contains an initial statement of virtually all the guiding themes of Cocteau's film work, and since it was followed by a dozen or more years of silence, it has a hauntingly premonitory quality. The wealth of themes and obsessions it contains is brought out clearly by the rich series of films from *La belle et la bête* to *Le testament d'Orphée*, which Cocteau made when he returned to film directing after World War II. Both as a work in its own right and as a forerunner of the director's later feature work, *Le sang d'un poète* has lost nothing of its power to fascinate and intrigue.

—Roy Armes

SANS SOLEIL

(Sunless)

France, 1982

Director: Chris Marker

Production: Argos Films; colour; running time: 100 minutes.

Producer: Anatole Dauman; **screenplay:** Chris Marker; **photography:** Chris Marker, Sana na N'hada, Jean-Michel Humeau, Mario Marret, Eugenio Bentivoglio, Danièle Tessier, Haroun Tazieff; **editor:** Chris Marker; **assistant director:** Pierre Camus; **music (electronic sounds):** Michel Krasna.

Publications

Articles:

Gauthier, G., *Revue du Cinéma* (Paris), February 1983.

Jeancolas, J.P., ''Le monde à la lettre,'' in *Positif* (Paris), February 1983.

Amiel, M., *Cinéma* (Paris), March 1983.

Lardeau, Y., ''L'empire des mots,'' in *Cahiers du Cinéma* (Paris), March 1983.

Marker, Chris, ''Reécrire la mémoire,'' in *Jeune Cinéma* (Paris), March 1983.

Variety (New York), 13 April 1983.

Martineau, R., *Séquences* (Paris), April 1984.

Jenkins, Steve, *''Sans Soleil (Sunless),''* in *Monthly Film Bulletin* (London), July 1984.

Rafferty, Terrence, ''Marker Changes Trains,'' in *Sight and Sound*, Autumn 1984.

Biro, Yvette, ''In the Spiral of Time,'' in *Millennium Film Journal*, Autumn-Winter 1984–85.

Eisen, K., *Cineaste* (New York), 1985.

Casebier, A., ''A Deconstructive Documentary,'' in *Journal of Film and Video* (New York), Winter 1988.

Rouch, J., and others, ''Culture and Representation,'' in *Undercut*, no. 17, Spring 1988.

Michael Walsh, ''Around the World, Across All Frontiers: *Sans Soleil* as Depays,'' in *CineAction* (Toronto), Autumn 1989.

Wilmott, G., ''Implications for a Sartrean Radical Medium: From Theatre to Cinema,'' in *Discourse* (Detroit), no. 12.2, Spring-Summer 1990.

Bluemlinger, C., ''Futur anterieur,'' in *Iris*, no. 19, Autumn 1995.

Kohn, Olivier, ''Chris Marker,'' in *Positif* (Paris), no. 433, March 1997.

Kohn, O., ''Si loin, si proche,'' in *Positif* (Paris), no. 433, March 1997.

Jousse, Thierry, ''Trois vidéos et un CD-ROM autour de Chris Marker,'' in *Cahiers du Cinéma* (Paris), no. 515, July-August 1997.

* * *

Almost impossible to synopsise, *Sans Soleil* has been described by Michael Walsh as ''surely among the most physically beautiful, the most inventively edited, and the most texturally sophisticated of recent European films.'' Yvette Biro described the film as ''a sort of *Gesamtkunstwerk* which defies the conventional pose between the 'raw and the cooked,' that is: document and fiction, but also between word and image; unclassifiable as all his former films, *Sans Soleil* appears as a summary of Marker's long travellings.''

Put at its simplest, the film takes the form of a series of letters, from an imaginary cameraman (''Sandor Krasna'') to an equally

Sans Soleil

imaginary woman, which comment on the global array of images presented. At their most immediate level, the images present themselves as a meditation on present day Japan, and also on the phenomenon of globalization. Marker had already confronted the global subject in *Si j'avais quatre dromadaires* (1966), an assemblage of stills taken all over the world between 1955 and 1965 for which he invented a commentary for three separate voices. His fascination with Japan had first revealed itself in *Le mystère Koumiko* (1965), in which Marker meditates on his subject after he has returned to Paris, has something of the allusive richness of *Sans Soleil.* Underlying the subjects of Japan and globalization, however, are concerns with rather less tangible matters such as time and memory. And underpinning the whole complex edifice is a fascinating and highly suggestive enquiry into images—what they mean, what might link them, and also what separates them. *Sans Soleil* is an absolute tour-de-force of editing, but it is much more than just a flashy exercise. Marker is the inheritor of the great montage tradition established by Vertov, Kuleshov, Eisenstein, and Medvedkin—and he made two films about this last cinematic pioneer: *Le Train en marche* (1971) and *Le Tombeau d'Alexandre* (1993). Like these filmmakers (and his contemporary, Godard), Marker is an indefatigable anti-realist: what concerns him above all are images as images, how their meanings change across time, across space, and according to the other images with which they're placed. As Marker's Japanese friend says of the images we see him synthesising in *Sans Soleil*, they "at least proclaim themselves for what they are—images—not the portable and compact form of an already inaccessible reality." Marker is fascinated by the world of appearances ("I wonder how people remember things who don't film, don't photograph, don't tape"), and in this vision of things nothing is insignificant or worthless, indeed quite the opposite; as "Krasna" says: "I've been around the world a dozen times and now only banality interests me. On this trip I've pursued it with the relentlessness of a bounty hunter." Not surprisingly, the commentary contains a reference to Levi-Strauss' well-known remark about the "poignancy of things."

As Michael Walsh has noted, the elaborate montage patterns in *Sans Soleil* "proceed now by theme, now by association, now by disposition in the frame, now by camera angle, now by screen direction. Such matches leap audaciously across cuts from Japan to Iceland to Holland, from original to borrowed to found footage, from film to television to video." Perhaps the most impressive sequence in a film full of impressive sequences is the one in which "Krasna" imagines "a single film made of the dreams of people on trains," and sleeping passengers on the Tokyo underground are provided with a kaleidoscope of images from the previous night's television as their "dreams." Another theme that provides for a whole series of montage-based variations (*Sans Soleil*, with its title borrowed from Mussorgsky's song cycle of the same name, is nothing if not musical, and more specifically, fugal, in form) is that of commemoration. This unites footage both of historical events and images of the "mediating animals" (and especially of the "maniki neko" cat) that Marker finds all over Tokyo. As Terrence Rafferty has observed: "Japan seems one huge festival of commemoration, a precise reflection of the mood of the traveller who's left so many places, people, political movements behind, but kept bits of them on film, notes which have lost their immediacy, things which have stopped moving but inspire in him the desire to reanimate them at the editing table the only way available to him to commemorate the things that have quickened his heart."

The concern with memory is also at the heart of *Sans Soleil*'s fascination with *Vertigo* (the only film "capable of portraying impossible memory, insane memory"). Utilising a combination of stills and refilmed locations, the film itself seems to enter the famous spirals of Saul Bass's title sequence, giving us an impression of "time covering a field ever wider as it moved away, a cyclone whose present moment contains motionless—the eye." As Steve Jenkins has suggested, *Sans Soleil* is, in the end, a film about time travel and, like Marker's earlier *La Jetée* (1964), has elements of science fiction about it. However, Jenkins concludes: "Marker avoids the romantic pessimism which so often inflects both speculative fantasy and self-reflexivity. He attacks our present understanding of images, while at the same time exploring optimistic possibilities for the future. Whilst most filmmakers are crawling towards 2001, barely emerging from the nineteenth century, Marker is running on ahead."

—Julian Petley

Sansho Dayu

SANSHO DAYU

(Sansho the Bailiff)

Japan, 1954

Director: Kenji Mizoguchi

Production: Daiei (Kyoto); black and white, 35mm; running time: 119 minutes, some sources list 123 minutes; length: 11,070 feet. Released 1954.

Producer: Masaichi Nakata; **screenplay:** Yahiro Fuji and Yoshikata Yoda, from the novel by Ogai Mori; **photography:** Kazuo Miyagawa; **editor:** Mitsuji Miyata; **sound engineer:** Iwao Otani; **production designers:** Kisaku Ito with Uichiro Yamanoto and Nakajima Kozaburo; **music:** Tamekichi Mochizuki, Fumio Hayasaka, and Kanahichi Odera; **traditional music:** Shinichi; **costume designer:** Yoshio Ueno; **consultant on ancient architecture:** Giichi Fujiwara.

Cast: Kinuyo Tanaka (*Tamaki/Nakagimi*); Yoshiaki Hanayagi (*Zushio, his son*); Kyoko Kagawa (*Anju, his daughter*); Eitaro Shindo (*Sansho*); Ichiro Sugai (*Nio, Minister of Justice*); Bontaro Miyake (*Kichiji*); Yoko Kosono (*Kohagi*); Chieko Naniwa (*Ubatake*); Kikue Mori (*Miko*); Ken Mitsuda (*Morosane Fujiwara*); Masao Shimizu (*Masaji Taira, the father*); Ryosuke Kagawa (*Ritsushi Ummo*); Akitake Kono (*Tara, Sansho's son*); Kanji Koshiba (*Kudo*); Shinobu Araki (*Sadayu*); Masahiko Kato (*Zushio, a boy*); Keiko Enami (*Anju, young girl*); Naoki Fujima (*Zushio, as small boy*); Teruko Taigi (*The other Nakagimi*); Reiko Kongo (*Shiono*).

Awards: Venice Film Festival, Silver Prize, 1954.

Publications

Script:

Yoda, Yoshikata, and Yahiro Fuji, *L'Intendant Sansho*, in *Avant-Scène du Cinéma* (Paris), 1 May 1979.

Books:

Anderson, Joseph, and Donald Richie, *The Japanese Film: Art and Industry*, Rutland, Vermont, 1960; revised edition, Princeton, 1982.
Ve-Ho, *Kenji Mizoguchi*, Paris, 1963.
Mesnil, Michel, *Kenji Mizoguchi*, Paris, 1965.
Yoda, Yoshikata, *Mizoguchi Kenji no hito to geijutsu* (Kenji Mizoguchi: The Man and His Art), Tokyo, 1970.
Tessier, Max, *Kenji Mizoguchi*, Paris, 1971.
Mellen, Joan, *Voices from the Japanese Cinema*, New York, 1975.
Mellen, Joan, *The Waves at Kenji's Door: Japan Through Its Cinema*, New York, 1976.

Bock, Audie, *Japanese Film Directors*, New York, 1978; revised edition, Tokyo, 1985.
Garbicz, Adam, and Jacek Klinowski, editors, *Cinema, The Magic Vehicle: A Guide to Its Achievement: Journey Two*, Metuchen, New Jersey, 1979.
Freiberg, Freda, *Women in Mizoguchi Films*, Melbourne, 1981.
Sato, Tadao, *Currents in Japanese Cinema*, Tokyo, 1982.
Serceau, Daniel, *Mizoguchi: De la revolte aux songes*, Paris, 1983.
Andrew, Dudley, *Film in the Aura of Art*, Princeton, 1984.
McDonald, Keiko, *Mizoguchi*, Boston, 1984.
O'Grady, Gerald, editor, *Mizoguchi the Master*, Ontario, 1996.
Tomasi, Dario, *Kenji Mizoguchi*, Milan, 1998.

Articles:

''Mizoguchi Issue'' of *Cinéma* (Paris), no. 6, 1955.
Richie, Donald, and Joseph Anderson, ''Kenji Mizoguchi,'' in *Sight and Sound* (London), Autumn 1955.
Godard, Jean-Luc, ''L'Art de Kenji Mizoguchi,'' in *Arts* (Paris), no. 656, 1958.
''Mizoguchi Issue'' of *Cahiers du Cinéma* (Paris), March 1958.
''Mizoguchi Issue'' of *Ecran* (Paris), February-March 1958.
Mizoguchi, Kenji, ''Mes films,'' in *Cahiers du Cinéma* (Paris), May 1959.
''Dossier Mizoguchi'' in *Cahiers du Cinéma* (Paris), August-September 1964.
Yoda, Yoshikata, ''Souvenirs sur Mizoguchi,'' in *Cahiers du Cinéma* (Paris), January 1967.
Yoda, Yoshikata, ''The Density of Mizoguchi's Scripts,'' in *Cinema* (Los Angeles), Spring 1971.
Wood, Robin, ''The Ghost Princess and the Seaweed Gatherer,'' in *Film Comment* (New York), March-April 1973.
Coleman, John, in *New Statesman* (London), 20 February 1976.
Cohen, R., ''Mizoguchi and Modernism,'' in *Sight and Sound* (London), Spring 1978.
Bokanowski, H., ''L'Espace de Mizoguchi,'' in *Cinématographe* (Paris), November 1978.
Andrew, Dudley, and Tadao Sato, ''On Kenji Mizoguchi,'' in *Film Criticism* (Meadville, Pennsylvania), Spring 1980.
Gauthier, G., in *Image et Son* (Paris), April 1980.
Gourdon, G., in *Cinématographe* (Paris), April 1980.
Tobin, Yann, in *Positif* (Paris), November 1980.
Ehrlich, L. C., ''The Name of the Child: Cinema as Social Critique,'' in *Film Criticism* (Meadville, Pennsylvania), no. 2, 1990.
Santos, A., in *Nosferatu* (San Sebastian), no. 11, January 1993.
Burdeau, Emmanuel, and others, ''Mizoguchi Encore,'' in *Cahiers du Cinéma* (Paris), no. 504, July-August 1996.
Lopate, Philip, ''A Master Who Could Create Poems for the Eyes,'' in *The New York Times*, 15 September 1996.
Macnab, Geoffrey, in *Sight & Sound* (London), vol. 8, no. 12, December 1998.

* * *

Sansho dayu can be taken as representing the ultimate extension and one of the supreme achievements of a certain tendency in the world cinema, the tendency celebrated in the critical writings of André Bazin and associated with the term ''realism.'' The only way in which the term is useful, and not actively misleading, is if it is applied to specific stylistic options. (Clearly, Mizoguchi's late films are not ''realistic'' in the sense in which a newsreel is ''realistic.'') The following features are relevant.

1. *The Long Take*, tending to the sequence-shot. Mizoguchi developed a long-take technique quite early in his career; in Japan, he was frequently criticized as old-fashioned for not adopting the editing techniques of Western cinema. One must distinguish, however, between the sequence-shots of *Sisters of Gion* (1936), for example, and those of *Sansho dayu.* As Nöel Burch has convincingly argued in *To the Distant Observer*, the earlier type of long take, where the camera is held at a great distance from the characters, remaining static for long stretches of the action, with its occasional movements maintaining emotional and physical distance, is peculiarly Japanese, rooted in elements of a national aesthetic tradition. The sequence-shots of late Mizoguchi, on the contrary, are compatible with certain practices of Western cinema, for example, the works of Wyler, Welles and Ophüls. Whether one is content to say, with Burch, that Mizoguchi *succumbed* to the Western codes of illusionism, or whether one places the stress on his plastic realization of their full aesthetic and expressive potential, doubtless depends on one's attitude to the codes themselves.

2. *Camera Movement.* The clinical detachment with which the camera views the characters of *Sisters of Gion* is replaced in the late films by an extremely complex tension between contemplation and involvement. The camera moves in the great majority of shots in *Sansho dayu*, sometimes identifying us with the movements of the characters, sometimes (perhaps within a single shot) withdrawing us from them to a contemplative distance. The film's famous closing scene contains particularly beautiful examples in the two shots that frame it: in the first, the camera begins to move *with* Zushio at the moment he hears his mother's voice and is drawn towards it, then cranes up to watch the movements towards reunion, until the mother is also visible within the frame; in the last shot of film, the camera moves upward away from the reunited couple, to reveal the vast seascape and the solitary figure of the old seaweed-gatherer, his task now completed.

3. *Depth of field.* Again and again Mizoguchi makes marvellously expressive use of simultaneous foreground and background action. That something is amiss with the priestess's plan for the family travel by sea is subtly hinted by the presence, in distant long-shots, of a small hunched figure sinisterly scuttling away as the family walks to the water. The impact of the following sequence of the kidnapping and separation of mother and children is largely created by their being kept consistently within the frame as Mizoguchi cuts back and forth between the mother's struggles and the children's struggles, so that we are continuously aware of the widening distance between them.

It is true that this bringing to perfection of a certain kind of cinematic art in Mizoguchi's last period coincides with a shift to a more conservative ideological position. The rage against oppression and cruelty is still there, but it is now heavily qualified by resignation, by a commitment to notions of spiritual transcendence. However, the tradition that feeds the film is rich and complex, and one must honor—whatever one's own political position—an art that brings such a tradition to its fullest realization.

—Robin Wood

SATURDAY NIGHT AND SUNDAY MORNING

UK, 1960

Director: Karel Reisz

Production: Woodfall Film Productions; black and white, 35mm; running time: 89 minutes. Released October 1960, London.

Producer: Tony Richardson; **executive producer:** Harry Saltzman; **screenplay:** Alan Sillitoe; from his own novel; **photography:** Freddie Francis; **editor:** Seth Holt; **sound:** Peter Handford and Bob Jones; **sound editor:** Chris Greenham; **art director:** Ted Marshall; **music:** John Dankworth.

Cast: Albert Finney (*Arthur Seaton*); Shirley Ann Field (*Doreen Gretton*); Rachel Roberts (*Brenda*); Hylda Baker (*Aunt Ada*); Norman Rossington (*Bert*); Bryan Pringle (*Jack*); Robert Cawdron (*Robboe*); Edna Morris (*Mrs. Bull*); Elsie Wagstaff (*Mrs. Seaton*); Frank Pettitt (*Mr. Seaton*); Avis Bunnage (*Blowzy woman*); Colin Blakely (*Loudmouth*); Irene Richmond (*Doreen's mother*); Louise Dunn (*Betty*); Peter Madden (*Drunken man*); Cameron Hall (*Mr. Bull*); Alister Williamson (*Policeman*); Anne Blake (*Civil defence officer*).

Awards: British Academy Awards for Best British Film, Best British Actress (Roberts) and Most Promising Newcomer (Finney), 1960.

Publications

Script:

Sillitoe, Alan, *Saturday Night and Sunday Morning*, in *Masterworks of the British Cinema*, London and New York, 1974.

Books:

Manvell, Roger, *New Cinema in Britain*, London, 1969.
Durgnat, Raymond, *A Mirror for England: British Movies from Austerity to Affluence*, London, 1970.
Walker, Alexander, *Hollywood, England: The British Film Industry in the 60s*, London, 1974.
Armes, Roy, *A Critical History of the British Cinema*, London and New York, 1978.
Gaston, George, *Karel Reisz*, Boston, 1980.
Richards, Jeffrey, and Anthony Aldgate, editors, *Best of British: Cinema and Society 1930–1970*, Oxford, 1983.
Walker, Alexander, editor, *No Bells on Sunday: The Journal of Rachel Roberts*, London, 1984.
Cattini, Alberto, *Karel Reisz*, Firenze, 1985.
Barr, Charles, editor, *All Our Yesterdays: 90 Years of British Cinema*, London, 1986.
Hill, John, *Sex, Class and Realism: British Cinema 1956–63*, London, 1986.

Articles:

''From 'Free Cinema' to Feature Film: Interview,'' in *Times* (London), 19 May 1960.
Films and Filming (London), August 1960.
Barr, Charles, in *Granta* (Cambridge), 26 November 1960.
Gow, Gordon, in *Films and Filming* (London), December 1960.
Dyer, Peter John, in *Sight and Sound* (London), Winter 1960–61.
''Karel Reisz: Free Czech,'' in *Films and Filming* (London), February 1961.
Marcorelles, Louios, ''Talking about Acting: Albert Finney and Mary Ure,'' in *Sight and Sound* (London), Spring 1961.
Dunham, Harold, in *Films in Review* (New York), April 1961.
Sutherland, Elizabeth, in *Film Quarterly* (Berkeley), Summer 1961.
Kael, Pauline, in *Film Quarterly* (Berkeley), Fall 1961.
Nowell-Smith, Geoffrey, ''Movie and Myth,'' in *Sight and Sound* (London), Spring 1963.
Phillips, Gene, ''An Interview with Karel Reisz,'' in *Cinema* (Beverly Hills), Summer 1968.
Kennedy, H., ''Minute Reisz: 6 Earlier Films,'' in *Film Comment* (New York), September-October 1981.
''*Saturday Night and Sunday Morning* Issue'' of *Avant-Scène du Cinéma* (Paris), 15 October 1982.
Listener (London), 10 November 1983.
Higson, Andrew, ''Space, Place, Spectacle,'' in *Screen* (London), July-October 1984.
Macnab, Geoffrey, ''Northern Exposure,'' in *Sight & Sound* (London), vol. 7, no. 9, September 1997.

* * *

Saturday Night and Sunday Morning has a reputation as one of British cinema's finest achievements, a status very much dependent upon its accomplished mobilisation of qualities defined as realist by the majority of British film commentators. But the film can also be seen as a melodrama: its dramatic core, like that of romantic fiction, concerns desire and its vicissitudes and the conflict between individual desire and social responsibility, elements which are even occasionally plotted in terms of fate, chance, and coincidence (the unwanted pregnancy; the meeting at the fairground. . .); clearly, it is a *patriarchal* melodrama, since its central protagonist is a rampant male who must be ''domesticated'' by the end of the film—and there are only very occasional moments when patriarchy is resisted (for instance, in the scene when Aunt Ada and Brenda discuss abortion and men, while Arthur is cast outside, reduced to sneaking a look in through the window, an outsider confronted with this all-female world in the domestic space of the home). On the other hand, the film seems realistic precisely because it rejects the conventional devices of cinematic melodrama: the film is emotionally understated; there is no heavily scored orchestral music track or complex expressionist mise-en-scène; and the film's relatively loose narrative development, with little sense of a goal to be achieved, means that chance and coincidence are rarely experienced as such.

The film encapsulates in a particularly forthright way a number of the key social anxieties and fantasies of the period: there is both an angry, anarchic confrontation with the alienation of manual labour (most clearly stated in Arthur's opening soliloquy), and a nostalgic

Saturday Night and Sunday Morning

celebration of traditional working-class cultures and communities (the two different bars in the pub in which Arthur has his drinking match at the beginning of the film are very revealing: one contains mainly older people, some of whom are having a communal sing-song around the piano; the other contains the brash dynamism of a skiffle band and Arthur's irresponsible boozing, surrounded by much younger people). The film also struggles with middle-class fears about the increasing commodification of leisure, and the apparent growth of mass culture and Americanisation—with television as the major scapegoat, making clear the distinction between cultural enlightenment, or at least active participation, and cultural passivity (note Arthur's conversation with his father when the latter is watching television).

Along with numerous social problem films of the 1950s and 1960s, *Saturday Night and Sunday Morning* also feeds the moral panic surrounding the emergent youth cultures and the increasing legitimisation of individual self-expression (''What I'm out for is a good time; all the rest is propaganda!'' says Arthur at the start of the film), cultures articulated in terms of the generation gap, within both the family, and the wider community (Mrs. Bull, the nosey parker on the corner of the street, becomes the symbol of community as an oppressive institution, restricting Arthur's hedonism). While social mobility is less of an issue here than in other contemporary British films, *Saturday Night and Sunday Morning* still touches on fantasies of social betterment, the individualising of social issues, and the myth of classlessness (in the final scene of the film Doreen and Arthur look down on a new housing development, the product of 1950s affluence; for Doreen, this represents modernity, the way ahead, the possibility of a better social existence; for Arthur, however, it's a further extension of the city into the countryside where he used to go blackberrying as a child). Looking forward to the 1960s, the film also tentatively explores the discourses of sexual liberation (which are of course revealed as decidedly ambivalent for women).

Like so many of the films of Britain's new wave of the late 1950s and early 1960s, the film was an adaptation, this time from the successful novel of the same name by the working-class writer Alan Sillitoe. Much of the critical acclaim for the film has concerned its depictions of working-class characters as real, psychologically rounded characters. Clearly, by adopting the point-of-view of a factory worker and focussing on his milieu, the film is a powerful achievement in this respect. But the film also constructs another more problematic point-of-view, the sympathetic gaze of a class outside the city, looking from a safe distance at the working class who become heroic victims of the city, desiring to escape to the "better" culture and environment of the onlooker, who is thus placed in a position of superiority. Ironically, from this point-of-view, outside and above the city (sometimes literally, as in the scene where Arthur and Brenda meet to discuss her failed attempts at getting rid of the unwanted baby, or in the brief shots which precede Arthur's second soliloquy and the "Sunday morning" section of the film), the city becomes a beautiful aesthetic object, a spectacular visual image. As the reviewer in the top people's paper, *The Times*, unwittingly comments, "Mr. Reisz's direction for most of the time beautifully reflects working-class life in the back-streets of Nottingham." In the end, however, it is this conflict in points-of-view and social positions which makes this film such an interesting and important work.

—Andrew Higson

SAVAGE NIGHTS

See **NUITS FAUVES**

SAWDUST AND TINSEL

See **GYCKLARNOS AFTON**

SCARFACE: THE SHAME OF A NATION

USA, 1932

Director: Howard Hawks

Production: Atlantic Pictures; black and white, 35mm; running time: 99 minutes. Released April 1932, New York. Filmed during Spring and Summer 1931.

Producers: Howard Hughes and Howard Hawks; **screenplay:** Ben Hecht, Seton I. Miller, John Lee Mahin, and W. R. Burnett, with Fred Palsey, from the novel by Armitage Trail; **assistant director:** Richard Rosson; **photography:** Lee Garmes and L. W. O'Connell; **editor:** Edward Curtis; **sound:** William Snyder; **production designer:** Harry Olivier; **music:** Adolph Tandler and Gus Arnheim.

Cast: Paul Muni (*Tony Camonte*); Ann Dvorak (*Cesca Camonte*); Karen Morley (*Poppy*); Osgood Perkins (*Johnny Lovo*); Boris Karloff (*Gaffney*); George Raft (*Guido Rinaldo*); Vince Barnett (*Angelo*); C. Henry Gordon (*Inspector Guarino*); Ines Palance (*Tony's mother*); Edwin Maxwell (*Commissioner*); Tully Marshall (*Editor*); Harry J. Vejar (*Big Louis Costello*); Bert Starkey (*Epstein*); Henry Armetta (*Pietro*); Maurice Black (*Sullivan*); Purnell Pratt (*Publisher*); Charles Sullivan and Harry Tembrook (*Bootleggers*); Hank Mann (*Worker*); Paul Fix (*Gaffney hood*); Howard Hawks (*Man on bed*); Dennis O'Keefe (*Dance extra*).

Publications

Script:

Hecht, Ben, and others, *Scarface*, in *Avant-Scène du Cinéma* (Paris), January 1973.

Books:

Bogdanovitch, Peter, *The Cinema of Howard Hawks*, New York, 1962.
Missiaen, Jean-Claude, *Howard Hawks*, Paris, 1966.
Wood, Robin, *Howard Hawks*, London, 1968; revised edition, 1981.
Gerber, Albert B., *Bashful Billionaire*, New York, 1968.
Bergman, Andrew, *We're in the Money: Depression America and Its Films*, New York, 1971.
Gili, Jean A., *Howard Hawks*, Paris, 1971.
McArthur, Colin, *Underworld USA*, London, 1972.
Druxman, Michael B., *Paul Muni: His Life and Films*, New York, 1974.
Lawrence, Jerome, *Actor—The Life and Times of Paul Muni*, New York, 1974.
Parish, James Robert, and Steven Whitney, *The George Raft File: The Unauthorized Biography*, New York, 1974.
Yablonsky, Lewis, *George Raft*, New York, 1974.
Willis, D. C., *The Films of Howard Hawks*, Metuchen, New Jersey, 1975.
Clark, Norman H., *Deliver Us from Evil: An Interpretation of American Prohibition*, New York, 1976.
Parish, James Robert, and Michael Pitts, *The Great Gangster Pictures*, Metuchen, New Jersey, 1976.
Shadoian, Jack, *Dreams and Dead Ends: The American Gangster/Crime Film*, Cambridge, Massachusetts, 1977.
Murphy, Kathleen A., *Howard Hawks: An American Auteur in the Hemingway Tradition*, Ann Arbor, Michigan, 1978.
Clarens, Carlos, *Crime Movies: An Illustrated History*, New York, 1980.
Giannetti, Louis, *Masters of the American Cinema*, Englewood Cliffs, New Jersey, 1981.
Schatz, Thomas, *Hollywood Genres*, New York, 1981.
Jenkins, Steve, *The Death of a Gangster*, London, 1982.
McBride, Joseph, *Hawks on Hawks*, Berkeley, 1982.
Mast, Gerald, *Howard Hawks, Storyteller*, New York, 1982.
Poague, Leland, *Howard Hawks*, Boston, 1982.
Simsolo, Noël, *Howard Hawks*, Paris, 1984.
Martin, Jeffrey Brown, *Ben Hecht: Hollywood Screenwriter*, Ann Arbor, Michigan, 1985.
Branson, Clark, *Howard Hawks: A Jungian Study*, Los Angeles, 1987.
Hillier, Jim, *Howard Hawks: American Artist*, Champaign, 1997.
McCarthy, Todd, *Howard Hawks: The Grey Fox of Hollywood*, New York, 1997.
Gandini, Leonardo, *Howard Hawks: Scarface*, Torino, 1998.

Articles:

New York Times, 20 May 1932.
Variety (New York), 24 May 1932.

Wright, C. M., in *Christian Century* (Chicago), 3 August 1942.
Rivette, Jacques, and François Truffaut, ''Howard Hawks,'' in *Films in Review* (New York), November 1956.
Jacobs, Jack, ''Paul Muni,'' in *Films in Review* (New York), November 1961.
Agel, Henri, ''Howard Hawks,'' in *New York Film Bulletin*, no. 4, 1962.
Sarris, Andrew, ''The World of Howard Hawks,'' in *Films and Filming* (London), July and August 1962.
''Hawks Issue'' of *Cahiers du Cinéma* (Paris), January 1963.
Warshow, Robert, ''The Gangster as Tragic Hero,'' in *The Immediate Experience*, New York, 1970.
Velvet Light Trap (Madison, Wisconsin), June 1971.
''Hawks Issue'' of *Filmkritik* (Munich), May-June 1973.
Kjørup, S., in *Kosmorama* (Copenhagen), August 1973.
Frezza, G., in *Filmcritica* (Rome), May 1974.
Beylie, Claude, in *Ecran* (Paris), January 1975.
Cooney, K., ''Demonology,'' in *Movietone News* (Seattle), April 1975.
Sarris, Andrew, in *Village Voice* (New York), 15 October 1979.
Mank, Gregory William, in *Magill's Survey of Cinema 3*, Englewood Cliffs, New Jersey, 1980.
Pulleine, Tim, in *Monthly Film Bulletin* (London), August 1980.
Jourdat, A., in *Cinématographe* (Paris), December 1980.
Marinero, M., in *Casablanca* (Madrid), July-August 1981.
Dominicus, M., in *Skrien* (Amsterdam), Summer 1984.
Cinéma (Paris), no. 423, 6 January 1988.
Vergerio, F., in *Revista Del Cinematografo* (Rome), vol. 63, April supp. 1993.

* * *

Scarface was one of the three major films (along with *Little Caesar* and *Public Enemy*) that defined the American gangster genre in the early 1930s. Of the three, *Scarface* was simultaneously the most violent and most humorous; it was also the most controversial. Its gleeful depiction of the gangster's life as brutal fun lacked the mean, growing swagger of *Little Caesar* and the sociological analysis of *Public Enemy*. For two years, Howard Hughes, the film's producer, battled with the industry's censors, who only allowed the film's release with the deletion of some scripted material (for example, a scene showing an elected public official as a paid collaborator of the gangsters) and the addition of other material (a morally sententious scene in which the newspaper publisher implores a group of public-spirited citizens to stop the gangster menace by taking some sort of public action on election day). Even with the censorship and the changes, the film was cited as an example of what the industry would try to avoid when it implemented its Hollywood Production Code two years later. As a result of the controversy, the film has been seen far less often in America (especially on television) than the other two major gangster films, and for decades the film could only be shown legally in Europe. (Hughes's death allowed his estate to find an American distributor for it.)

Much of the power of *Scarface* derives from its director, Howard Hawks, and the choices he made. Rather than make a film of snarling gangsters, he decided to treat the gangsters as children playing games, having fun—since Hawks felt that the gangsters who talked to him about their adventures always sounded like children. Another Hawks decision was to turn the leading gangster's affection for his sister into a repressed, unexplored, and unarticulated form of incest so that the gangster himself does not understand the power and shape of his feelings for her. As Hawks told his chief writer for the film, Ben Hecht, the intention was to get the Borgia family into Chicago, and the script for the film made explicit references to incest and the Borgias (scenes either deleted by the censors or removed by Hawks himself, who preferred to give less away). The incest motif underlies the plot of the film, as the leading gangster, Tony Camonte, kills his best friend, Guido Rinaldo, because he believes Guido is sleeping with his sister.

In casting his film, Hawks found several minor or unknown players to fit the roles. Paul Muni, a noted actor from New York with roots in the Yiddish theater, played his first major film role as Tony Camonte. Hawks claimed that he found George Raft, who played Tony's best friend, at a prizefight. Raft's nervous, perpetual flipping of a coin occurs for the first time in this film; the action has since become a cultural icon of movie gangsterism, duplicated decades later in the ''Broadway Melody'' ballet of *Singin' in the Rain*, when two dancing thugs flip coins in unison, and by a minor thug in *Some Like It Hot*, an act which occasions George Raft himself to ask, ''Where'd you learn that cheap trick?'' For the role of Cesca Camonte, Tony's sister, Hawks found Ann Dvorak, a lithe, sharp-talking mixture of toughness and softness who would become the prototype for all Hawksian women in future films. And for the role of ''Dope,'' Tony's comic ''seckatary,'' Hawks found the quirky character actor Vince Barnett, who provides most of the film's comedy by being a secretary who cannot write and can never even remember who the caller is or what the message might be.

The overall shape of *Scarface* reveals the classic narrative of the gangster's rise and fall, roughly patterned on the same tragic model as Shakespeare's *Macbeth*: the gangster climbs to the top by taking action against his betters, then falls from that summit when he is deserted by his own allies and underlings. The first scene of the film is one of its most memorable, a very lengthy traveling shot, extended in both time and space, in which we watch a shadowy, whistling figure (only later identified as Tony) murder the gangster who then sits at the ''top of the world.'' At the end of the film Tony himself will be gunned down (by the police, not by one of his own), and as he dies in the gutter an electric sign above him ironically flashes, ''The World Is Yours—Cook's Tours.'' The shadowy irony of the film's opening shot and the cynical irony of its final image enclose a narrative full of other ironic, comic, or subtle touches that are clearly lacking from the other major films of this type. Tony's fall is precipitated not by the forces of law in the film (who are shown to be totally inept or unable to contain the gangster menace) but by Tony himself. The murder of his best friend (like Macbeth's murder of Banquo) and the death of his sister, whom he loved not wisely but well, lead to his emotional breakdown and collapse. His resolution to die ''with harness on his back,'' like Macbeth, shooting gleefully at the police from his heavily armored lair, collapses when his sister dies from a stray police bullet—turning Tony into a puling, weeping coward.

Among the other memorable scenes in the film is a violently comic sequence which juxtaposes the brutal crashing of machinegun bullets, spraying a restaurant with deadly destruction, with Dope's comic attempts to take a telephone message for Tony. Dope keeps complaining that he is unable to hear the message because of all the noise from the crashing glass around him. This method of deflection dominates the film to produce its wry, ironic, understated tone; deflecting a scene from a brutal gun battle to a comic telephone conversation, deflecting emotion from brutal words to a flipping coin, deflecting Tony's motivation to a smothered and incomprehensible love for his own sister, deflecting the gangster menace to a series of childhood games.

The irony and deflection not only make *Scarface* unique among gangster films but make it consistent with the other films of its director, Howard Hawks. Hawks enjoys depicting the lives of professionals who do their work well and love what they do. In this film, those professionals are gangster. Hawks also comments on a related group of professionals in the film—newspaper reporters and editors—who do not condemn the gangster menace but excitedly exploit the gangsters' activities—to sell more newspapers. Hawks would return to this theme—the conflict between morality and professionalism in the newspaper world—in *His Girl Friday*. Still another of the film's delights (equally true of *Public Enemy* and *Little Caesar*) was the pleasure of simply listening to the private lingo and argot of tough gangsters. The gangster film was born with the talkies, at least partially because listening to the slang was a major delight of the genre.

—Gerald Mast

THE SCARLET EMPRESS

USA, 1934

Director: Josef von Sternberg

Production: Paramount Pictures, Inc.; black and white, 35mm; running time: 109 minutes. Released 7 September 1934.

Screenplay: Josef von Sternberg, adapted from a diary of Catherine the Great by Manuel Komroff; **photography:** Bert Glennon; **production designers:** Hans Dreier, Peter Balbusch, and Richard Kollorsz; **music arrangers:** John Leipold and W. Frank Harling; **additional music:** Josef von Sternberg; **special effects:** Gordon Jennings; **costume designer:** Travis Banton.

Cast: Marlene Dietrich (*Sophia Fredericka*, or *Catherine II*); John Lodge (*Count Alexei*); Sam Jaffe (*Grand-Duke Pierre*); Louise Dresser (*Elizabeth*); Maria Sieber (*Catherine as a child*); C. Aubrey Smith (*Prince August*); Ruthelma Stevens (*Countess Elizabeth*); Olive Tell (*Princess Johanna*); Gavin Gordon (*Gregory Orloff*); Jameson Thomas (*Lieutenant Ovtsyn*); Hans Von Twardowski (*Ivan Shuvolov*); Erville Anderson (*Chancelor Bestuchef*); Marie Wells (*Marie*); Edward Van Sloan (*Herr Wagner*).

Publications

Books:

Harrington, Curtis, *An Index to the Films of Josef von Sternberg*, London, 1949.
Griffith, Richard, *Marlene Dietrich—Image and Legend*, New York, 1959.
von Sternberg, Josef, *Fun in a Chinese Laundry*, New York, 1965.
Sarris, Andrew, *The Films of Josef von Sternberg*, New York, 1966.
Josef von Sternberg: Dokumentation: Eine Darstellung, Mannheim, 1966.
Weinberg, Herman G., *Josef von Sternberg*, Paris, 1966; as *Josef von Sternberg: A Critical Study*, New York, 1967.
Baxter, John, *The Cinema of Josef von Sternberg*, New York, 1971.
Mérigeau, Pascal, *Josef von Sternberg*, Paris, 1983.
Navacelle, Thierry de, *Sublime Marlene*, London, 1984.
Seydel, Renate, *Marlene Dioetrich: Eine Chronik ihres Lebens in Bilden und Dokumenten*, East Berlin, 1984.
Walker, Alexander, *Dietrich*, London, 1984.
Spoto, Donald, *Falling in Love Again: Marlene Dietrich*, Boston, 1985.
Dietrich, Marlene, *Ich bin, Gott sei dank, Berlinerin*, Frankfurt, 1987.
Zucker, Carole, *The Idea of the Image: Josef Von Sterberg's Dietrich Films*, Cranbury, 1988.
Bowman, Barbara, *Master Space: Film Images of Capra, Lubitsch, Sternberg, and Wyler*, Westport, 1992.
Del Gaudio, Sybil, *Dressing the Part: Sternberg, Dietrich, and Costume*, Cranbury, 1993.
Studlar, Gaylyn, *In the Realm of Pleasure: Von Sternberg, Dietrich, and the Masochistic Aesthetic*, New York, 1993.
Baxter, Peter, *Just Watch!: Sternberg, Paramount and America in 1932*, London, 1994.
Hanut, Eryk, *I Wish You Love: Conversations with Marlene Dietrich*, translated by Anne-Pauline de Castries, Berkeley, 1996.
Bach, Steven, *Marlene Dietrich: Life and Legend*, New York, 2000.

Articles:

Sennwald, Andre, in *New York Times*, 15 September 1934.
Variety (New York), 18 September 1934.
Dekobra, Maurice, ''Comment Marlene Dietrich est devenue star,'' in *Cinémonde* (Paris), 16 April 1939.
Harrington, Curtis, ''Josef von Sternberg,'' in *Cahiers du Cinéma* (Paris), October-November 1951.
Knight, Arthur, ''Marlene Dietrich,'' in *Films in Review* (New York), December 1954.
Weinberg, Herman G., ''Josef von Sternberg,'' in *Film Heritage* (Dayton, Ohio), Winter 1965.
Green, O. O., ''Six Films of Josef von Sternberg,'' in *Movie* (London), Summer 1965.
Weinberg, Herman G., ''On Sternberg,'' in *Sight and Sound* (London), Summer 1967.
Martineau, Barbara, ''Thoughts on the Objectification of Women,'' in *Take One* (Montreal), November-December 1970.
Flinn, Tom, in *Velvet Light Trap* (Madison, Wisconsin), Fall 1972.
Gow, Gordon, ''Alchemy: Dietrich [+] Sternberg,'' in *Films and Filming* (London), June 1974.
Wood, Robin, ''Sternberg's *Empress:* The Play of Light and Shade,'' in *Film Comment* (New York), March-April 1975.
Cappabianca, A., in *Filmcritica* (Rome), April 1976.
Pulleine, Tim, in *Monthly Film Bulletin* (London), June 1978.
Zucker, C., ''Some Observations on Sternberg and Dietrich,'' in *Cinema Journal* (Evanston, Illinois), Spring 1980.
Peary, Danny, in *Cult Movies*, New York, 1981.
Luft, Herbert, ''Josef von Sternberg,'' in *Films in Review* (New York), January 1981.
Jacobs, L., and R. de Cordova, ''Spectacle and Narrative Theory,'' in *Quarterly Review of Film Studies* (New York), Fall 1982.
Viviani, C., ''Marlene Mélo: Splendeurs de l'artifice,'' in *Positif* (Paris), September 1984.
''Josef von Sternberg Section'' of *Skrien* (Amsterdam), April-May 1985.

Revue du Cinéma (Paris), no. 482, May 1992.
Murphy, K., "Portrait of a Lady Times 2," in *Film Comment* (New York), July-August 1993.

* * *

The Scarlet Empress was the penultimate work in the series of six films Josef von Sternberg made with Marlene Dietrich for Paramount—a series made possible by the international success of *The Blue Angel*. The series must stand, taken *in toto*, as one of the most remarkable achievements within the Hollywood cinema, and *The Scarlet Empress* as one of its peaks, yet its relationship to that cinema is highly ambiguous. Scarcely conceivable outside the studio/star/genre system, the films were progessively unsuccessful at the box office, and increasingly frowned upon by the studio bosses. The reasons for this are complex. First, von Sternberg (like Orson Welles after him) broke the fundamental rule of classical Hollywood cinema by attempting consistently to assert himself as an "artist" through elaboration of a highly idiosyncratic personal style; whereas Ford, Hawks and Lang, for example, were able to develop, quite unobtrusively, personal styles that did not conflict with the law of authorial invisibility. Secondly the tone of the films proved increasingly disconcerting. On a superficial level, they seemed frivolous and cavalier (and audiences perhaps suspected that, if there *was* a joke, they themselves were its ultimate butt); on a deeper level the films were disturbingly intense and obsessional.

Critics, committed to characteristically unsophisticated bourgeois notions of what is serious (*The Blue Angel*) and what isn't (*The Scarlet Empress*), missed the deeper level altogether, repudiating the films as decadent exercises in "style" with no "content," as though the two were logically separable. Von Sternberg's own pronouncements have unfortunately endorsed this view, describing the film's subjects as "fatuous" and declaring his own exclusive interest in "the play of light and shade." Sergei Eisenstein acknowledged the influence of *The Scarlet Empress* on his own *Ivan the Terrible* (leaving aside obvious similarities of imagery, they do have the same essential subject, the perversion of sexuality into the power drive). Generally, however, the two works have been assigned to quite distinct categories: *Ivan the Terrible* is a work of art, *The Scarlet Empress* an example of "camp." But in fact, a scrupulous analysis of the films will reveal that von Sternberg's is no less serious than Eisenstein's.

The matter of levels is important. *The Scarlet Empress* defines meticulously the level on which it is serious and the level on which it isn't. It is *not* serious about Russian history: the intermittent facetiousness (John Lodge ridiculing Catherine's old-fashioned notions of conjugal fidelity on the grounds that "this is the eighteenth century") is there to repudiate the meretricious solemnity of the Hollywood historical epic. It *is* serious about sexuality and gender roles. Dietrich's complex star persona involves the difficulties surrounding a woman's assertion of autonomy in a world created and dominated by men. *The Scarlet Empress* develops her persona to one of its extremes. The film's imagery is amazingly dense, suggestive and systematic: for example, the dissolve from the young Catherine innocently clutching her doll to the "adult" doll of the Iron Maiden; or the progression from the child's innocent question "Can I be a hangman some day?" through the intricate bell imagery that recurs throughout, to the moment when the adult Catherine rings the bell that is the sign for the assassination of her husband and her seizure of absolute power. The action of the film is dominated by women throughout, but by women who have accepted patriarchal roles and thereby become monstrous. Catherine herself, her natural desires frustrated and perverted, becomes the ultimate monster, cynically using her sexuality as a weapon. Her growing assumption of the male role is answered by the increasingly feminization of her husband (at the climax, she is in soldier's uniform, he in a flowing white nightgown). The culmination is one of Hollywood's most ambiguous and devastating happy endings: the heroine triumphs over all adversity—at the expense of her humanity, and perhaps her sanity.

—Robin Wood

THE SCENT OF GREEN PAPAYA

See **L'ODEUR DE LA PAPAYE VERTE**

SCHATTEN

Germany, 1923

Director: Arthur Robison

Production: Pan-Film for Dafu Film Verlieh; black and white, 35 mm, silent; running time: 62 minutes currently, but original version was longer. Released 1923.

Schatten

Screenplay: Arthur Robison and Rudolf Schneider, from an idea by Albin Grau; **photography:** Fritz Arno Wagner; **editor:** Arthur Robison; **production designer:** Albin Grau; **original accompanying score:** Ernst Riege; **costume designer:** Albin Grau.

Cast: Fritz Kortner (*Husband*); Alexander Granach (*Mesmerist*); Ruth Weyher (*Wife*); Gustav von Wangenheim (*Lover*); Max Gülstorff, Eugen Rex and Ferdinand von Alten (*Cavaliers*); Fritz Rasp (*Manservant*); Lilli Herder (*Maid*); Karl Platen.

Publications

Books:

Rotha, Paul, *The Film Till Now*, London, 1930.
Kracauer, Siegfried, *From Caligari to Hitler: A Psychological History of the German Film*, Princeton, 1947.
Eisner, Lotte, *The Haunted Screen*, Berkeley, 1969.
Fritz Kortner, Berlin, 1970.
Brand, Matthias, *Fritz Kortner in der Weimarer Republik: Annäherungsversuche an die Entwicklung eines jüdischen Schauspielers in Deutschland*, Rheinfelden, 1981.

Articles:

Bioscope (London), 20 November 1924.
Potamkin, Harry, ''The Rise and Fall of the German Cinema,'' in *Cinema* (New York), April 1930.
Wagner, Fritz Arno, in *Film Art*, no. 8, 1936.
Rayns, Tony, in *Monthly Film Bulletin* (London), June 1975.
Close Up (London), October 1975.
Bertetto, Paolo, ''*Schatten*: l'illusione del vedere,'' in *Cinema Nuovo* (Bari), vol. 37, no. 316, November-December 1988.
Cappabianca, A, ''Il corpo dell'ombra,'' in *Filmcritica* (Siena), vol. 47, no. 475, May 1997.

* * *

Schatten combines with great power and unity of purpose the talents of painter Albin Grau, the film's originator who also designed the sets and costumes, the cameraman Fritz Arno Wagner, and the director-scriptwriter Arthur Robison. The action of the film is compressed to one evening and, apart from an introductory title and an explanation in the middle, the story is told in entirely visual terms. The plot concerns a flirtatious wife, a jealous husband, an indiscreet lover, three philanderers and a sinister servant. Tragedy is impending; a travelling shadow theater showman hypnotizes the characters and lets them see the directions in which their follies will take them. The lesson is learned. The wife and husband are reconciled and the lover departs at dawn. The intensity of the action and the simplification of the characters is representative of Expressionism, as is the chiaroscuro lighting which heightens the mood. An air of unreality is deliberately sought and mirror reflections take us further from the concrete action. This makes it quite easy to accept the marvellous scene of the dinner table viewed slightly from above and from the side, when the shadows of the characters stretch away from them and the magic of the unreal begins.

The beautiful period settings and costumes carry a romantic air, consistent with the film's style and action. The performances of the actors are controlled, and the powerful and dynamic Fritz Kortner dominates the film, creating a tension which never falters. Alexander Granach gives an impish performance as the Mesmerist. Though his contribution to the German Cinema was considerable, he will best be remembered as the disgruntled Commissar Kowalsky in the Garbo-Lubitsch, *Ninotchka*.

A unity of space is preserved allowing the transactions from the dining room to hall and the corridors outside the bedroom to be effectively managed. Details impinge on our consciousness—the ropes that will bind the wife, the candelabra held by the husband, the swords that will be forced into the cavaliers' hands, all take on a new meaning and significance.

Expressionism was the simultaneous simplification and heightening of mood, atmosphere, and ''feeling'' to suggest the essence of an action or thought-process. As such it was a highly subjective style—both exaggerated and neurotic. Expressionism came at the time of national tension in Germany and found its exponents in the theater as well as in literature and painting. Many of the actors from the stage were trained in Expressionist theater, and that influence is very evident in *Schatten*.

The fact that this film was made for ordinary cinema distribution indicates how rich popular film culture was at the time. Films such as *Schatten*, today viewed as rare classics in cine-clubs and specialized cinemas, were in their day part and parcel of ordinary film-going entertainment.

Perfect films like this were not without their influence. Much of the innovative camera work and visual style has been absorbed into the accepted techniques of the cinema. But there is a special patina which the pioneer film has that can never be transmitted and that is the excitement generated by an original and creative spirit; *Schatten* is unique in the history of film, and unlike anything its creator, Arthur Robison, ever attempted again.

—Liam O'Leary

SCHINDLER'S LIST

USA, 1993

Director: Steven Spielberg

Production: Amblin Entertainment, Universal Pictures; black and white/color, 35mm; running time: 195 minutes. Released December 1993, USA.

Producer: Steven Spielberg, Gerard R. Molen; **executive producer:** Kathleen Kennedy; **screenplay:** Steven Zaillian, based on the novel *Schindler's Ark* by Thomas Keneally; **photography:** Janusz Kaminski; **editor:** Michael Kahn; **assistant directors:** Sergio Mimica-Gezzan, Michael Helfand, Marek Brodzki, Krzystof Zbieranek; **production design:** Allan Starski; **art directors:** Ewa Skoczkowska, Maciej Walczak; **music:** John Williams; **supervising sound editors:** Charles L. Campbell, Ronald Judkins, Robert Jackson; **costumes:** Anna Biedrzycka-Sheppard.

Cast: Liam Neeson (*Schindler*); Ralph Fiennes (*Amon Goeth*); Ben Kingsley (*Itzhak Stern*); Caroline Goodall (*Emilie Schindler*); Jonathan Sagalle (*Poldek Pfefferberg*); Embeth Davidtz (*Helen Hirsch*);

Schindler's List

Malgoscha Gebel (*Victoria Klonowska*); Shmulik Levy (*Wilek Chilowicz*); Mark Ivanir (*Marcel Goldberg*); Beatrice Macola (*Ingrid*); Andrzej Seweryn (*Julian Scherner*); Friedrich Von Thum (*Rolf Czurda*); Krzystof Luft (*Herman Toffel*).

Awards: Oscars for Best Picture, Best Director, Best Adapted Screenplay, Best Photography, Best Editing, Best Art Direction, and Best Score, 1993.

Publications

Book:

Mott, Donald R. and Saunders, Cheryl McAllister, *Steven Spielberg*, New York, 1986.

Fensch, Thomas, editor, *Oskar Schindler and His List: The Man, the Book, the Film, the Holocaust and its Survivors*, Forest Dale, 1995.

Sanello, Frank, *Spielberg: The Man, the Movies, the Mythology*, Dallas, 1996.

Brode, Douglas, *The Films of Steven Spielberg*, Secaucus, 1997.

Loshitzky, Yosefa, editor, *Spielberg's Holocaust: Critical Perspectives on Schindler's List*, Bloomington, 1997.

Yule, Andrew, *Steven Spielberg*, New York, 1997.

Knight, Bertram, *Steven Spielberg: Master of Movie Magic*, Parsippany, 1998.

Palowski, Franciszek, *The Making of Schindler's List: Behind the Scenes of an Epic Film*, translated by Anna Ware and Robert G. Ware, Secaucus, 1998.

Perry, George, *Steven Spielberg-Close Up: The Making of His Movies*, New York, 1998.

McBride, Joseph, *Steven Spielberg: A Biography*, New York, 1999.

Friedman, Lester D., and Brent Notbohm, editors, *Steven Spielberg: Interviews*, Jackson, 2000.

Articles:

Kauffmann, Stanley, ''Stanley Kauffmann on Films: A New Spielberg,'' in *The New Republic* (New York) 13 December 1993.

Corliss, Richard, ''Topping Spielberg's List,'' in *Time* (New York) 13 December 1993.

McCarthy, Todd, *Variety* (New York), 13 December 1993.

Alter, Jonathan, ''After the Survivors,'' in *Newsweek* (New York), 20 December 1993.
Johnson, Brian D., ''Saints and Sinners,'' in *MacLean's* (Toronto), 20 December 1993.
Louvish, S., ''Witness,'' in *Sight and Sound* (London), March 1994.
Strick, P., *Sight and Sound*, (London), March 1994.
Thomson, D., ''Presenting Enamelware,'' in *Film Comment* (New York), March-April 1994.
White, A., ''Towards a Theory of Spielberg History,'' in *Film Comment* (New York), March-April 1994.
Doherty, T., *Cineaste* (New York), no. 3, 1994.
Jacobowitz, F., ''Rethinking History Through Narrative Art,'' in *Cineaction* (Texas), no. 34, 1994.
White, Les, ''My Father Is a Schindler Jew,'' in *Jump Cut* (Berkeley), no. 39, 1994.
Slavin, J., ''Witnesses to the Endtime: The Holocaust as Art,'' in *Metro* (Victoria), no. 98, Winter 1994.
Slavin, J., ''The Butterflies in the Bonfire: The Holocaust as Art. Part Two,'' in *Metro* (Victoria), no. 99, Summer 1994.
Cardullo, B., ''Schindler's Miss,'' in *Hudson Review*, vol. 48, no. 1, 1995.
Weissman, G., ''A Fantasy of Witnessing,'' in *Media Culture and Society*, vol. 17, no. 2, April 1995.
Rosenfeld, A.H., ''The Americanization of the Holocaust,'' in *Commentary*, vol. 99, June 1995.
Hansen, M.B., ''*Schindler's List* is not *Shoah*: The Second Commandment, Popular Modernism, and Public Memory,'' in *Critical Inquiry*, vol. 22, no. 2, 1996.
Young, R.A., ''Films, Tangos and Cultural Practices,'' in *Cinemas* (Montreal), vol. 7, no. 1/2, 1996.
Jayadeva, M.U., ''Family Matters: The Good and the Bad in 'HAHK,''' in *Deep Focus*, vol. 6, 1996.
Skoller, J., ''The Shadows of Catastrophe: Towards an Ethics of Representation in Films by Antin, Eisenberg, and Spielberg,'' in *Discourse* (Detroit), no. 19.1, Fall 1996.
Peacock, John, ''*Schindler's List:* Not All Black and White,'' in *Creative Screenwriting* (Washington, D.C.), vol. 4, no. 4, Winter 1997.
Jones, Alan, ''Production on an Epic Scale,'' in *Radio Times* (London), vol. 295, no. 3846, 18 October 1997.
Gelley, O., ''Narration and the Embodiment of Power in *Schindler's List*,'' in *Film Criticism* (Meadville), vol. 22, no. 2, 1997/1998.
Goldstein, Warren, ''Bad History is Bad for a Culture,'' in *The Chronicle of Higher Education*, vol. 44, no. 31, 10 April 1998.
Manchel, Frank, ''Mishegoss: *Schindler's List*, Holocaust Representation and Film History,'' in *Historical Journal of Film, Radio and Television* (Abingdon), vol. 18, no. 3, August 1998.

* * *

The initial skepticism surrounding Steven Spielberg's directorial undertaking quickly dissipated when *Schindler's List*, an alarmingly powerful and affecting tale of an unlikely German-Czech industrialist who manages to save 1100 Jews from the Nazi death camps, hit theater screens late in 1993 during the holiday season. In March of the following year, Spielberg won an Academy Award for ''Best Director'' and *Schindler's List* went on to win ''Best Picture.'' But the climb to capture the Academy of Motion Picture Arts and Sciences' most prestigious award—Best Director—has been a long (twenty years) and arduous one for the ''wunderkind'' filmmaker, whose 15 films to date have grossed more than four billion dollars worldwide, making him the most successful filmmaker of all time.

It is not as though Spielberg hadn't tried to capture this top Oscar before, especially when he turned to directing serious dramas like *The Color Purple* (1984) and *Empire of the Sun* (1987), both of which were based on novels, or his remake of *A Guy Named Joe*, an old black & white love story that he updated and retitled *Always*. But it was clear from these films that Spielberg was trying to find his way with his new literary directions. Film critic Brian D. Johnson noted in *MacLean's* that ''Spielberg's attempt at serious drama. . . [has] been disappointing.'' And so the idea of a Holocaust story as told by ''Hollywood's emperor of escapism'' was, for that reviewer ''at first glance, alarming,'' since ''reality has never been [his] strong suit.''

The Schindler project actually began in 1982 when Sidney Sheinberg, MCA/Universal's president, bought the movie rights to Thomas Keneally's novel with Spielberg in mind. But he wasn't ready to make it, because ''in '82 I wasn't mature enough,'' Spielberg told *Newsweek* in 1993. ''I wasn't emotionally resolved with my life. I hadn't had children. I really hadn't seen God until my first child was born.''

Novelist Keneally was the first to create a screenplay based on his own book, but when he produced nothing shorter than a mini-series, the project was turned over to screen writer Kurt Luedtke, who penned *Out of Africa*. After three years of diligently working on *Schindler's List*, however, Luedtke gave up. At various times the project was considered by such notable directors as Syndey Pollack and Martin Scorsese, the latter of whom brought in writer-director Steven Zaillian, who made *Searching for Bobby Fischer*. It was Zaillian who successfully transformed Keneally's novel into a workable screenplay. By then, Spielberg had decided to direct *Schindler's List* after filming *Jurassic Park*. Spielberg was quoted in a *Newsweek* article by David Ansen as saying, ''[Making *Schindler's List*] was a combination of things: my interest in the Holocaust and my horror at the symptoms of the Shoah again happening in Bosnia. And again happening with Saddam Hussein's attempt to eradicate the Kurdish race. We were racing over these moments in world history that were exactly what happened in 1943.''

A number of critics, including Johnson, intimated in their reviews that Spielberg's choice in directing *Schindler's List* was highly unusual, considering his previous dramatic attempts. But Spielberg had consistently tried since 1983 to rid himself of his ''shark and truck'' director's image when he alluded to ''turning to the written word'' in his acceptance speech upon receiving the Irving G. Thalberg Award in the mid-1980s. But nothing could have been more ''non-Spielbergian'' than Alice Walker's novel, *The Color Purple*: a stark and brooding story of an abused black woman named Ceilie who finds love, and ultimately her self-worth, in a lesbian relationship. By contrast, *Schindler's List* was much less of a stretch for Spielberg, who by now realized that his previous cinematic style, noted by Donald R. Mott and Cheryl M. Saunders as ''Spielbergesque,'' was perhaps incompatible with most serious types of dramas. Spielberg had to discard his usual style of filmmaking in favor of something more congruent to the visual mood of the story, a style that would be dictated by the material itself. The end result in *Schindler's List*, therefore, is a much restrained and subdued film than any of Spielberg's previous works, something that was imposed partially by the black and white cinematography—noted by Johnson as ''both appropriate and haunting''—and the documentary style that Spielberg occasionally employed throughout the film, engendering critic Stanley

Kauffmann of *The New Republic* to comment, "To this end he often uses newsreel angles and newsreel cutting. Yet, he is not hand-held-nutty: where a panorama is needed—Jews in a long street assembling for deportation, Jews in a (seemingly) mile-wide file coming over a great field toward liberation—he understands how to present it and leave it alone."

If *Schindler's List* was considered unusual material for Spielberg, it was because he was making yet another film about the Holocaust after the stunning documentary *Shoah* and the TV mini-series "Holocaust." It seemed as though Spielberg was treading on familiar territory, and the big marketing question was whether audiences would be receptive to yet another film about the Nazi's extermination of the Jews. Kauffmann clearly supports Spielberg's choice of material when he wrote, "Presumably there are at least some people who have never seen a Holocaust film and may see this one because it's by Spielberg and [it] will have mainstream promotion." In *Newsweek*, Jonathan Alter defends Spielberg's subject by citing an interesting fact from film history: "For all the hundreds of movies employing World War II themes, the strange truth is that until now no major feature film has unflinchingly faced the horror of the Holocaust itself."

Schindler's List was also unusual in that the controversial hero was both a German Christian and Nazi sympathizer whose life before and after the war remained relatively uneventful, further complicating the real reasons why Schindler risked his life and newfound wealth for his doomed Jewish employees. Mark Miller reported in *Newsweek* that when Schindler was asked why he did what he did after the war, he tersely replied, "I had no choice." Sometime later, he told former prisoner Moshe Bejski, "If you saw a dog going to be crushed under a car, wouldn't you help him?" Liam Neeson, the actor chosen to play Oskar Schindler, is quoted in a *Time* article by Richard Corless as saying, "I still don't know what made him save all those lives. He was a man everybody liked. And he liked to be liked; he was a wonderful kisser of ass. Perhaps he was inspired to do some great piece of work. I like to think—and maybe it comes across in the film—that he needed to be needed."

Schindler's List ranks as one of Spielberg's greatest achievements in his growth and development as one of America's leading contemporary filmmakers. His choice of Irish actor Liam Neeson to play the lead "inhabits. . . Schindler with the authority of a round voiced, juggernaut con man," said Kauffmann. Ben Kingsley plays the role of Itzhak Stern (a character that was a compilation of several of Schindler's Jews), the Jewish accountant who Schindler saves from a condemned group of Jews to run his enamelware factory. Johnson described Kingsley's performance with the words, "Quietly brilliant," while Kauffmann offers an interesting aside: "Actors who want to study the basis of acting—concentration—should watch Kingsley." The only other major character in the film is Commandant Amon Goeth, played by English actor Ralph Fiennes, whom David Ansen of *Newsweek* observes, "finds fresh horrors that owe nothing to Hollywood clichés . . . the insecurity that Fiennes finds in the character makes him all the more frightening." And Johnson adds, "Fiennes gives the movie's most crucial performance, capturing the human psychology that permits genocide."

Spielberg's weaving of these three atypical characters together within the framework of the Nazi terror is nothing short of remarkable. *Schindler's List* begins at the start the Holocaust, at which point Oskar Schindler is introduced wining and dining the Nazi brass for favors. Eventually he moves to the center of the action when he sets up the enamelware factory with Stern, and later when he begins his so-called "friendship" with Commandant Goeth.

What unfolds on the screen for the next three and a quarter hours is a striking portrait of a most unusual man undertaking the most frightening risks imaginable amid the sheer terror, brutality and ugliness of the Nazi war machine. In Alter's article, he reprints what survivor Elie Wiesel had previously written: "How is one to tell a tale that cannot be—but must be—told? I don't know." Filmmaker Steven Spielberg knew exactly how.

—Donald R. Mott

SCIUSCIA

(Shoeshine)

Italy, 1946

Director: Vittorio De Sica

Production: Alfa Cinematografica (Italy); black and white, 35mm; running time: 93 minutes; length: 8,340 feet. Released 1946. Cost: less than 1 million lire.

Producer: P. W. Tamburella; **screenplay:** Cesare Zavattini, Sergio Amidei, A. Franci, Cesare Giulio Viola, and Vittoria De Sica, from a story by Zavattini; **photography:** Anchise Brizzi; **editor:** Nicolo Lazzari; **production designer:** Ivo Batteli; **music:** A. Cicognini.

Cast: Franco Interlenghi (*Pasquale*); Rinaldo Smordoni (*Giuseppe*); Amiello Mele (*Raffaele*); Bruno Otensi (*Archangeli*); Anna Pedoni (*Nannarella*); Enrico de Silva (*Giorgio*); Antonio Lo Nigro (*Righetto*); Emilio Cigoli (*Staffera*); Angelo D'Amico (*The Sicilian*); Antonio Carlino (*Inhabitant of the Abruzzes*); Francesco De Nicola (*Ciriola*); Pacifico Astrologo (*Vittorio*); Maria Campi (*Palmreader*); Leo Garavaglia (*Commissioner*); Giuseppe Spadare (*The Advocate*); Irene Smordoni (*Giuseppe's mother*).

Publications

Books:

Malerba, Luigi, editor, *Italian Cinema 1945–51*, Rome, 1951.
Castello, G. C., *Il cinema neorealistico italiano*, Turin, 1956.
Rondi, Brunello, *Il neorealismo italiano*, Parma, 1956.
Ferrara, Giuseppe, *Il nuovo cinema italiano*, Florence, 1957.
Hovald, Patrice G., *Le Néo-Realisme italien et ses createurs*, Paris, 1959.
Bazin, Andre, *Qu'est-ce que le cinéma?*, Paris, 1962; as *What is Cinema* (2 vols.), Berkeley, 1971.
Agel, Henri, *Vittorio De Sica*, Paris, 1964.

Sciuscia

Leprohon, Pierre, *Vittorio De Sica*, Paris, 1966.
Armes, Roy, *Patterns of Realism: A Study of Italian Neo-Realist Cinema*, New York, 1971.
Lawton, Benjamin Ray, *Literary and Socio-Political trends in Italian Cinema*, Los Angeles, 1971.
Wlaschin, Ken, *Italian Cinema Since the War*, Cranbury, New Jersey, 1971.
Garbicz, Adam, and Jacek Klinowski, *Cinema, The Magic Vehicle: A Guide to Its Achievement: Journey One: The Cinema Through 1949*, Metuchen, New Jersey, 1975.
Guaraldi-Rimini, Mario, editor, *Neorealismo e vita nazionale: Antologia di cinema nuovo*, Florence, 1975.
Mercader, Maria, *La mia vita con Vittorio De Sica*, Milan, 1978.
Anthologie du cinéma 10, Paris, 1979.
Bolzoni, Francesco, *Quando De Sica era Mister Brown*, Turin, 1984.
Darreta, John, *Vittorio De Sica: A Guide to References and Resources*, Boston, 1988.
Micciche, Lino, *Sciuscia di Vittorio De Sica: letture, documenti, testimonianze*, Turin, Italy, 1994.
Nuzzi, Paolo, and Ottavio Iemma, editors, *De Sica and Zavattini: parliamo tanto di noi*, Rome, 1997.

Articles:

Variety (New York), 22 May 1946 and 13 August 1947.
Doniol-Valcroze, J., in *Revue du Cinéma* (Paris), February 1947.
New York Times, 27 August 1947.
Koval, Francis, "Interview with De Sica," in *Sight and Sound* (London), April 1950.
Hawkins, R. F., "De Sica Dissected," in *Films in Review* (New York), May 1951.
De Sica, Vittorio, in *Films and Filming* (London), December 1955-January 1956.
Sargeant, Winthrop, "Bread, Love, and Neo-Realism," in *New Yorker*, 29 June and 6 July 1957.
Rhode, Eric, "Why Neo-Realism Failed," in *Sight and Sound (London)*, Winter 1960–61.
McVay, Douglas, "Poet of Poverty," in *Films and Filming* (London), October and November 1964.
Passek, J. L., "Le Cinéma du néo-réalisme italien est en berne: Vittorio De Sica," in *Cinéma* (Paris), January 1975.
"De Sica Issue" of *Bianco e Nero* (Rome), September-December 1975.

Barbaro, Nick, in *Cinema Texas Program Notes* (Austin), 22 November 1977.
"De Sica Issue" of *Avant-Scène du Cinéma* (Paris), 15 October 1978.
Lawton, B., "Italian Neo-Realism: A Mirror Construction of Reality," in *Film Criticism* (Edinboro, Pennsylvania), no. 2, 1979.
Carcassone, P., in *Cinématographe* (Paris), January 1979.
"De Sica Issue" of *Cahiers Lumière* (Paris), November 1980.
Ardanaz, S., "Sin mi Vittorio De Sica no habría pasado a las historia del cine," in *Cine Cubano* (Havana), 1984.
Horvilleur, G., in *Cinématographe* (Paris), September-October 1984.
Alix, Y., "*Sciuscia* et Le voleur de bicyclette: les enfants nous regardent," in *Positif* (Paris), February 1985.
James, Caryn, "De Sica's Reputation Gets a Shine," in *The New York Times*, 4 October 1991.

* * *

Vittoria De Sica's first major film, *I bambini ci guardano*, the account of a broken marriage as seen through the eyes of a child, was also his first significant attempt at the social realism which would characterize his pre-1960s films. From the beginning he explained that his films were a protest "against the absence of human solidarity, against the indifference of society towards suffering. They are a world in favour of the poor and the unhappy." *I bambini ci guardano* was De Sica's first collaboration with screenwriter Cesare Zavattini. Their fruitful partnership produced the most admired films of neorealism—*Sciuscia* and *Ladri di biciclette*. Each is an extraordinary indictment of the social circumstances which existed during post-Fascist Italy; *Sciuscia* is uncompromisingly tragic, while *Ladri di biciclette*, tempered by less cruelty, conveys a sense of tenderness.

Sciuscia is a neologism coined by the shoe-shine boys of Rome. These youngsters plied their trade to American soldiers who were among those few able to afford this minor luxury in a country filled with unemployment and poverty following the war. The embryo for the film was the result of De Sica's close observation of two shoe-shine boys in the streets of Rome. He studied their habits, their hand-to-mouth existence, and their dealing in black market contraband. Inevitably, he recalled, the two boys were arrested for stealing a gas mask and sent off to a reformatory. They were victims, he said, of "the legacy from war . . . the drama was not invented by me but staged by life instead, drawing to its fatal conclusion." He related his story to Zavattini, who fashioned it into a screenplay, resulting in a major neorealist film. *Sciuscia* emphasized the creators' commitment to showing, through actual incidents, "the indifference of humanity to the needs of others."

De Sica uses two non-professional actors and the streets of Rome to tell of the two boys, Pasquale and Giuseppe, who shine shoes and become involved in crime in order to raise money to buy a white horse. Their black market activities get them arrested and sent to reform school where, supposedly, they will be rehabilitated. Reformatory life turns out to be far more harsh and corrupt than life on the streets and in their struggle for survival they betray each other, resulting in the death of Giuseppe. The anguish of all suffering humanity is displayed in Pasquale's unforgettable cry of despair at the end of the film.

Though *Sciuscia* was universally hailed by critics as a work of art, it was by no means a financial success. The Academy of Motion Picture Arts and Sciences presented De Sica with a special Academy Award describing the film as "an Italian production of superlative quality made under adverse circumstances." *Sciuscia* was successful only in art houses and De Sica would later say, "*Shoeshine* was a disaster for the producer. It cost less than one million lire but in Italy few people saw it as it was released at a time when the first American films were reappearing . . . . "

At the time of its American release, James Agee's first response was, "*Shoeshine* is about as beautiful, moving, and heartening a film as you are ever likely to see." Soon after he recanted these remarks, describing it as "the raw, or at its best, the roughed-out materials of art" rather than the perfected work of art he had first thought. Such critical reassessment has diminished the reputation of most of De Sica's work and today he is often written off as a minor director. Yet for many, including Orson Welles, his films retain a poeticism and sincerity. In 1960, Welles said, "I ran his *Shoeshine* recently and the camera disappeared, the screen disappeared; it was just life . . . . "

—Ronald Bowers

SCORPIO RISING

USA, 1963

Director: Kenneth Anger

Production: Color, 16mm; running time: 29 minutes. Released 1963. Filmed in Brooklyn and Manhattan.

Screenplay: Kenneth Anger; **photography:** Kenneth Anger; **editor:** Kenneth Anger; **music:** Little Peggy March, The Angels, Bobby Vinton, Elvis Presley, Ray Charles, The Crystals, The Ron-dells, Kris Jensen, Claudine Clark, Gene McDaniels, and The Surfaris.

Cast: Bruce Bryon (*Scorpio*); Johnny Sapienza (*Taurus*); Frank Carifi (*Leo*); John Palone (*Pinstripe*); Ernie Allo (*Joker*); Barry Rubin (*Fall Guy*); Steve Crandall (*Blondie*); Bill Dorfman (*Back*); Johnny Dodds (*Kid*).

Publications

Books:

Anger, Kenneth, *Magick Lantern Cycle: A Special Presentation in Celebration of the Equinox Spring 1966*, New York, 1966.
Youngblood, Gene, *Expanded Cinema*, New York, 1970.
History of the American Avant-Garde Cinema, New York, 1976.
Sitney, P. Adams, *Visionary Film: The American Avant-Garde*, New York, 1979.
Landis, Bill, *Anger: The Unauthorized Biography of Kenneth Anger*, New York, 1995.
Suárez, Juan Antonio, *Bike Boys, Drag Queens, and Superstars: Avant-Garde, Mass Culture, and Gay Identities in the 1960s Underground Cinema*, Bloomington, 1996.

Articles:

"*Scorpio Rising* Issue" of *Film Culture* (New York), Winter 1963–64.
Schneeman, Carolee, in *Film Culture* (New York), Spring 1964.
Haines, Fred, in *Nation* (New York), 14 September 1964.

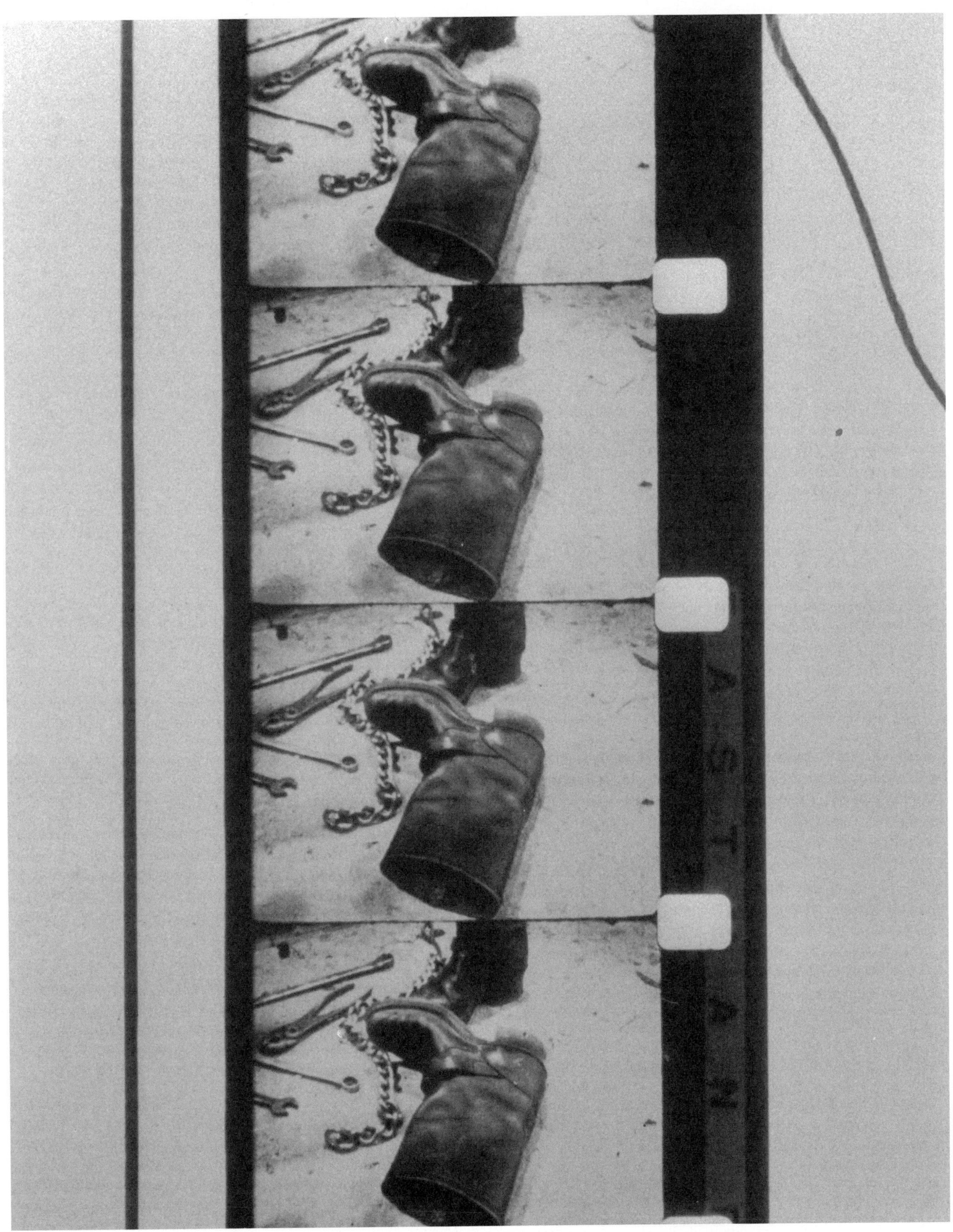

Scorpio Rising

Dietsfrey, Harris, in *Artforum* (New York), 1965.
"*Spider* Interviews Kenneth Anger," in *Spider* (New York), 15 April 1965.
Interview with Anger, in *Film Culture* (New York), Spring 1966.
Gill, Brendan, in *New Yorker*, 23 April 1966.
Alexander, Thomas Kent, "San Francisco's Hipster Cinema," in *Film Culture* (New York), no. 44, 1967.
Martin, Bruce, and Joe Medjuck, "Kenneth Anger," in *Take One* (Montreal), no. 6, 1967.
Cornwall, Regina, "On Kenneth Anger," in *December*, no. 1, 1968.
Rayns, Tony, "Lucifer: A Kenneth Anger Kompendium," in *Cinema* (Cambridge), October 1969.
Sitney, P. Adams, "The Avant-Garde: Kenneth Anger and George Landow," in *Afterimage* (Rochester, New York), no. 2, 1970.
"Kenneth Anger Issue" of *Body Politic*, April 1982.
Lowry, Ed, "The Appropriation of Signs in *Scorpio Rising*," in *Velvet Light Trap* (Madison, Wisconsin), Summer 1983.
Suarez, J., "Kenneth Anger's *Scorpio Rising:* Avant-Garde Textuality and Social Performance," in *Cinefocus* (Bloomington, Indiana), no. 2, 1992.
Gariazzo, G., in *Cineforum* (Bergamo), vol. 36, no. 355, June 1996.
Haug, Kate, "An Interview with Kenneth Anger," in *Wide Angle* (Baltimore), vol. 18, no. 4, October 1996.

* * *

Scorpio Rising, a landmark in the American underground film, confirmed Kenneth Anger's reputation as a major talent and, at the time of its release, created a stir which reached from the pages of New York's *Film Culture* to the courts of California, where it was judged obscene. It is testimony to the film's aesthetic power that 20 years later it continues to shock and dismay as many viewers as it amuses and exhilarates through its artfully subversive reinterpretation of the American mythos.

A product of the period which produced Andy Warhol's Brillo boxes and Roy Lichtenstein's comic-strip canvases, *Scorpio Rising* is a pop-art collage of found artifacts which submerges itself in the chrome-and-leather, skull-and-swastika iconography of the motorcycle cult that provides its subject. (Anger shot many scenes using an actual Brooklyn biker's club.) Yet, almost instantly, the film extends these symbols of machismo to include the entirety of American culture via the re-reading of its popular imagery. Structured around 13 "top forty" songs from the period in which it was made (1962–63), *Scorpio Rising* mounts a dialectical collision between images and music to reveal the strains of romanticized violence, morbidity and homoeroticism just beneath the surface of "Dondi" and "Li'l Abner," of Brando's and Dean's rebels, of hit tunes by Rick Nelson, Elvis Presley and Martha and the Vandellas. The juxtaposition of the Angel's "My Boyfriend's Back" with shots of a biker working on his machine, for example, not only suggests the violent eroticism and fetishization inherent to the cycle cult, but reveals the open brutality of the song's lyrics as well, implicating the whole civilization in its imagery of obsession. And when Anger plays Bobby Vinton's "Blue Velvet" over a loving tilt up a biker's jeans as he zips his fly, the effect is both erotic and a savage parody of eroticism as it is packaged by the culture industry.

Scorpio Rising's short-circuitry of traditional readings of familiar objects ultimately represents the joyous celebration of the dawning of the Age of Scorpio, the erratic astrological sign associated with chaos, and the concomitant downfall of the ascetic and repressed reign of Christianity. In the film's most notorious juxtaposition, Anger poses this cosmological convulsion by a clever intercutting of a black-and-white Sunday School movie of the last days of Christ (set, in part, to the Crystals' "He's a Rebel") with profanely contrasting scenes from a biker's "Walpurgisnacht." The multiple layering of subversive associations generated by Anger's various techniques of collision provides the basically non-narrative means by which *Scorpio Rising* drives toward its disturbing, yet cathartic conclusion. It is a method equally explicit in his punning description of the film as "A conjuration of the presiding Princes, Angels and Spirits of the Sphere of MARS, formed as a 'high' view of the American Motorcyclist. The Power Machine seen as tribal totem, from toy to terror. Thanatos in chrome and black leather and bursting jeans."

Clearly, *Scorpio Rising* has had its influence, from the found-footage collages of Bruce Conner to the pop-flash sound and color imagery of *American Graffiti*. Yet the film remains one of a kind in terms of the immediacy and savagery of its critique. Anger's manipulations of the culturally overloaded imagery of Nazism, sado-masochism, and the occult finally result in a film which refuses to conform to any dominant, edifying reading whatsoever—an almost unparalleled achievement which should earn *Scorpio Rising* an enduring place in the artistic annals of the 1960s, a decade remembered for the challenges it posed to ruling ideology.

—Ed Lowry

THE SEARCHERS

USA, 1956

Director: John Ford

Production: C. V. Whitney Pictures; Technicolor, 35mm, Vistavision; running time: 119 minutes. Released 1956. Filmed from February through the Summer of 1955 in Monument Valley, Utah and Colorado.

Producers: Merian C. Cooper and C. V. Whitney; **associate producer:** Patrick Ford; **screenplay:** Frank S. Nugent, from the novel by Alan LeMay; **photography:** Winton C. Hoch and Alfred Gilks; **editor:** Jack Murray; **sound:** Hugh McDowell and Howard Wilson; **art directors:** Frank Hotaling and James Basevi; **music:** Max Steiner; **special effects:** George Brown; **costume designers:** Frank Beetson and Ann Peck.

Cast: John Wayne (*Ethan Edwards*); Jeffrey Hunter (*Martin Pawley*); Vera Miles (*Laurie Jorgensen*); Ward Bond (*Capt. Rev. Samuel Clayton*); Natalie Wood (*Debbie Edwards*); John Qualen (*Lars Jorgensen*); Olive Carey (*Mrs. Jorgensen*); Henry Brandon (*Chief Scar*); Ken Curtis (*Charlie McCorry*); Harry Carey, Jr. (*Brad Jorgensen*); Antonio Moreno (*Emilio Figueroa*); Hank Worden (*Mose Harper*); Lana Wood (*Debbie as a child*); Walter Coy (*Aaron Edwards*); Dorothy Jordan (*Martha Edwards*); Pippa Scott (*Lucy*

The Searchers

Edwards); Pat Wayne (*Lt. Greenhill*); Beulah Archuletta (*Look*); Jack Pennick (*Private*); Peter Mamakos (*Futterman*); Away Luna, Billy Yellow, Bob Many Mules, Exactly Sonnie Betsuie, Feather Hat, Jr., Harry Black Horse, Jack Tin Horn, Many Mules Son, Percy Shooting Star, Pete Grey Eyes, Pipe Line Begishe, Smile White Sheep (*Comanches*); Mae Marsh; Dan Borzage.

Publications

Books:

Fenin, George, and William K. Everson, *The Western from Silents to Cinerama*, New York, 1962.

Haudiquet, Philippe, *John Ford*, Paris, 1964.

Bogdanovich, Peter, *John Ford*, Berkeley, 1968; revised edition, 1978.

Ricci, Mark, and Boris and Steve Zmijewsky, *The Films of John Wayne*, New York, 1970; revised edition, as *The Complete Films of John Wayne*, Secaucus, New Jersey, 1983.

Baxter, John, *The Cinema of John Ford*, New York, 1971.

Cawelti, John, *The Six-Gun Mystique*, Bowling Green, Ohio, 1971.

Place, J. A., *The Western Films of John Ford*, Secaucus, New Jersey, 1973.

Barbour, Alan, *John Wayne*, New York, 1974.

Kaminsky, Stuart, *American Film Genres*, Dayton, Ohio, 1974.

Maynard, Richard A., *The American West on Film: Myth and Reality*, Rochelle Park, New Jersey, 1974.

Nachbar, Jack, editor, *The Western*, Englewood Cliffs, New Jersey, 1974.

McBride, Joseph, and Michael Wilmington, *John Ford*, New York and London, 1975.

Sarris, Andrew, *The John Ford Movie Mystery*, London, 1976.

Eyles, Allen, *John Wayne*, South Brunswick, New Jersey, 1979.

Ford, Dan, *Pappy: The Life of John Ford*, Englewood Cliffs, New Jersey, 1979.

Sinclair, Andrew, *John Ford*, New York and London, 1979.

Anderson, Lindsay, *About John Ford*, London, 1981; New York, 1983.

Turvey, Sarah, *Barthes' S/Z and the Analysis of Film Narrative: The Searchers*, London, 1982.

Kieskalt, Charles John, *The Official John Wayne Reference Book*, Secaucus, New Jersey, 1985.

Shepherd, Donald, and others, *Duke: The Life and Times of John Wayne*, London, 1985.
Gallagher, Tag, *John Ford: The Man and His Films*, Berkeley, 1986.
Stowell, Peter, *John Ford*, Boston, 1986.
Lepper, David, *John Wayne*, London, 1987.
Buscombe, Ed, editor, *BFI Companion to the Western*, London, 1988.
Levy, Emanuel, *John Wayne: Prophet of the American Way of Life*, Metuchen, New Jersey, 1988.
Lourdeaux, Lee, *Italian & Irish Filmmakers in America: Ford, Capra, Coppola and Scorsese*, Springfield, 1990; 1993.
Darby, William, *John Ford's Westerns: A Thematic Analysis, with a Filmography*, Jefferson, 1996.
Davis, Ronald L., *John Ford: Hollywood's Old Master*, Norman, 1997.
Davis, Ronald L., *Duke: The Life and Image of John Wayne*, Norman, 1998.
Girus, Sam B., *Hollywood Renaissance: The Cinema of Democracy in the Era of Ford, Capra, and Kazan*, New York, 1998.
Levy, Bill, *John Ford: A Bio-Bibliography*, Westport, 1998.
Eyman, Scott, *Print the Legend: The Life and Times of John Ford*, New York, 1999.

Articles:

Cutts, John, ''Press Conference,'' in *Sight and Sound* (London), Spring 1956.
Reed, Allen C., in *Arizona Highways*, April 1956.
Phipps, Courtland, in *Films in Review* (New York), June-July 1956.
Anderson, Lindsay, in *Sight and Sound* (London), Autumn 1956.
Baker, Peter, in *Films and Filming* (London), September 1956.
American Cinematographer (Los Angeles), November 1956.
Barkun, Michael, ''Poet in an Iron Mask,'' in *Films and Filming* (London), February 1958.
Barkun, Michael, ''Notes on the Art of John Ford,'' in *Film Culture* (New York), Summer 1962.
McVay, Douglas, ''The Five Worlds of John Ford,'' in *Films and Filming* (London), June 1962.
Mitchell, George, ''The Films of John Ford,'' in *Films in Review* (New York), March 1963.
Bogdanovich, Peter, ''Autumn of John Ford,'' in *Esquire* (New York), April 1964.
''Ford on Ford,'' in *Cinema* (Beverly Hills), July 1964.
''John Ford Issue'' of *Présence du Cinéma* (Paris), March 1965.
''John Ford Issue'' of *Cahiers du Cinéma* (Paris), October 1966.
Mitry, Jean, in *Interviews with Film Directors*, edited by Andrew Sarris, New York, 1967.
Kennedy, Burt, ''Our Way West,'' in *Films and Filming* (London), October 1969.
Pechter, William, ''A Persistence of Vision,'' in *24 Times a Second: Films and Filmmakers*, New York, 1971.
''John Ford Issue'' of *Focus on Film* (London), Spring 1971.
Anderson, Lindsay, ''John Ford,'' in *Cinema* (Beverly Hills), Spring 1971.
Sarris, Andrew, in *Film Comment* (New York), Spring 1971.
''John Ford Issue'' of *Velvet Light Trap* (Madison, Wisconsin), August 1971.
McBride, Joseph, and Michael Wilmington, ''Prisoner of the Desert,'' in *Sight and Sound* (London), Autumn 1971.
Ford, D., ''The West of John Ford and How It Was Made,'' in *Action* (Los Angeles), September-October 1971.
Wollen, Peter, ''The Auteur Theory,'' in *Signs and Meanings in the Cinema*, London, 1972.
''John Ford's Stock Company Issue'' of *Filmkritik* (Munich), January 1972.
McInery, Joe, ''John Wayne Talks Tough,'' in *Film Comment* (New York), September 1972.
Jorgensen, U., in *Kosmorama* (Copenhagen), June 1974.
Dempsey, Michael, ''John Ford: A Reassessment,'' in *Film Quarterly* (Berkeley), Summer 1975.
''*The Searchers* Issue'' of *Screen Education* (London), Winter 1975–76.
Steinman, Clay, ''The Method of *The Searchers*,'' in *Journal of the University Film Association*, Summer 1976.
Boyd, D., ''Prisoner of the Night,'' in *Film Heritage* (Dayton, Ohio), Winter 1976–77.
''John Ford Issue'' of *Wide Angle* (Athens, Ohio), vol. 2, no. 4, 1978.
Lowry, Ed, in *Cinema Texas Program Notes* (Austin), 2 November 1978.
Byron, S., ''*The Searchers*: Cult Movie of the New Hollywood,'' in *New York*, 5 March 1979.
Henderson, B., ''*The Searchers:* An American Dilemma,'' in *Film Quarterly* (Berkeley), Winter 1980–81.
Peary, Danny, in *Cult Movies*, New York, 1981.
Lehman, Peter, ''Added Attraction: Looking at Look's Missing Reverse Shot: Style in John Ford's *The Searchers*,'' in *Wide Angle* (Athens, Ohio), vol. 4, no. 4, 1981.
Sineux, M., in *Positif* (Paris), May 1982.
Combs, Richard, in *Listener* (London), 3 July 1986.
Yoshimoto, M., ''Myth of Demystification in Structural Film Criticism,'' in *Quarterly Review of Film and Video* (New York), no. 4, 1990.
Russell, D., ''The American Trauma,'' in *Movie* (London), Winter 1990.
Skerry, P. J., ''What Makes a Man to Wander?: Ethan Edwards of John Ford's *The Searchers*,'' in New *Orleans Review*, vol. 18, no. 4, 1991.
Roth, M., '''Yes, My Darling Daughter': Gender, Miscegenation, and Generation in John Ford's *The Searchers*,'' in *New Orleans Review*, vol. 18, no. 4, 1991.
Winkler, M. M., ''Tragic Features in John Ford's *The Searchers*,'' in *Bucknell Review*, vol. 35, no. 1, 1991.
Walker, M., ''Melodramatic Narrative,'' in *Cineaction* (Toronto), Spring-Summer 1993.
Shively, J., ''Indianer gillar John Wayne,'' in *Filmhaftet* (Uppsala, Sweden), May 1993.
Brown, G., ''Ride Away,'' in *Village Voice* (New York), vol. 38, 18 May 1993.
Travers, P., ''*The Searchers* Ride Again,'' in *Rolling Stone*, no. 658, 10 June 1993.
Wall, J. M., ''Of Lawyers and Dinosaurs,'' in *Christian Century*, vol. 110, 28 July/4 August 1993.
Gallagher, T., ''John Ford's Indians,'' in *Film Comment* (New York), September-October 1993.
Legrand, Gérard, and others, ''John Ford,'' in *Positif* (Paris), no. 427, September 1996.
Humbert, M., ''Doorways,'' in *Vertigo* (Paris), no. 18, 1996.

Reid's Film Index, no. 20, 1996.

Whissel, K., ''Racialized Spectacle, Exchange Relations, and the Western in *Johanna d'Arc of Magnolia*,'' in *Screen* (Oxford), vol. 37, no. 1, 1996.

Oldmeadow, H., ''Tracking *The Searchers*: A Survey of the Film's Critical Reception,'' in *Continuum*, vol. 11, no. 1, 1997.

Thomson, David, ''Open and Shut: A Fresh Look at *The Searchers*,'' in *Film Comment* (New York), vol. 33, no. 4, July-August 1997.

O'Brien, Geoffrey, ''The Movie of the Century: It Looks Both Backward to Everything Hollywood Had Learned About Westerns and Forward to Things Films Hadn't Dared to Do,'' in *American Heritage*, vol. 49, no. 7, November 1998.

* * *

A popular though critically ignored Western at the time of its release, John Ford's *The Searchers* was canonized a decade later by auteur critics as the American masterpiece *par excellence* exerting its influence as a cinematic touchstone and ''cult film'' among such directors of the New Hollywood as Martin Scorsese, Paul Schrader, Steven Spielberg and George Lucas. Representing Ford's most emotionally complex and generically sophisticated work, *The Searchers* manages to be both a rousing adventure movie and a melancholy film poem exploring the American values at the heart of the Western genre.

At the center of the film is Ethan Edwards, a bitter, ruthless and frustrated crusader engaged in a five-year quest to retrieve a niece kidnapped by the Comanches. Edwards is perhaps John Wayne's most accomplished characterization, bringing to bear the iconography which has made Wayne synonymous with the Western. Isolated by the violent individualism which defines his heroic status, Edwards is torn by the neurotic split inherent in the archetype: he belongs neither to the civilized community of settlers nor with the savages he fights on their behalf. A crusty, intolerant misanthrope, he occasionally betrays a wellspring of emotion which again and again is sublimated in violent action and an insane hatred of the Indian.

Returning to his brother's Texas home after many years' absence, Edwards arrives just in time to be lured away by a Comanche trick while the homestead is burned, his brother, sister-in-law and nephew are slaughtered, and his two nieces are taken captive by the brutal chief Scar. Embarking with a posse to recover the kidnapped girls, Edwards is eventually left to pursue his search with a single companion, young Martin Pawley, an eighth-blood Cherokee who was the adopted son of Ethan's brother. Though Edwards begins by despising Pawley as a ''half-breed,'' their companionship eventually draws them together as father and son. Yet when they finally discover Debbie, the sole survivor of the raid, now grown and living as a Comanche squaw, Edwards is determined to kill her, and Pawley is forced to defy his wrath and his gun in order to save her.

For all his hatred of the Comanches, Edwards is clearly aligned with them psychologically. Not only can he speak their language, but on one occasion, he shoots the eyes of a dead warrior in tacit acknowledgement of an Indian belief that this will force the man's soul to ''wander forever between the winds.'' Further, there is a strongly sexual undercurrent to Edwards's search, manifested on one hand by his obsession with revenge for the violation of his sister-in-law Martha, and on the other by his insistence on killing Debbie for ''living with a Comanche buck.'' His ultimate decision to spare the girl and to temper his anger thus assumes the proportions of a kind of transcendental grace.

In one of the most poignant subtexts provided by any Western, *The Searchers* suggests a source for Edwards's anger by hinting at his unspoken and unfulfilled love for his brother's wife Martha. Ford subtly conveys this attachment through gesture and staging alone in the early scenes, yet extends its ramifications to inform Pawley's treatment of Laurie, the fiancée he leaves behind. After years of waiting, Laurie finally opts for a less attractive suitor, an action which threatens to cut Pawley off from the civilized community much like Edwards. Without stating it in so many words, the film suggests that the situation echoes a frustrated romance, prior to the beginning of the story, between Edwards and Martha, who finally chose to marry his brother instead of waiting indefinitely for the man she loved.

Within the auteurist context, *The Searchers* assumes an even greater significance. Never before in a Ford Western has the wilderness seemed so brutal or settlements so tenuous and threatened. There are no towns—only outposts and isolated homesteads, remote and exposed between the awesome buttes of Ford's mythic Monument Valley. And while the Comanches are depicted as utterly ruthless, Ford ascribes motivations for their actions, and lends them a dignity befitting a proud civilization. Never do we see the Indians commit atrocities more appalling than those perpetrated by the white man. Not only does Edwards perform the only scalping shown in the film, but Ford presents the bloody aftermath of a massacre of Indian women and children carried out by the same clean-cut cavalrymen he depicted so lovingly in films like *Fort Apache*.

The Searchers's status as a masterpiece of the genre may finally lie in its abundant poetic imagery: a massacre presaged by a startled covey of quail, a cloud of dust and an artificially reddened sunset; the echoing voices reverberating from the towering stones surrounding men who, 40 miles from home, realize they have been drawn away so that the Comanches can attack their families; the image of Debbie running down a distant dune, unseen by the searchers whom she approaches; the repetitive tossing of objects between Edwards and the garrulous preacher/Texas Ranger Captain Clayton, conveying the delicate balance between their mutual respect and enmity; the way in which Martha strokes Edwards's coat before their unplanned final farewell.

But the most significant visual motif in *The Searchers* is surely the doorway open onto the wilderness. It is the image which begins and ends the film. Ford introduces Edwards through the frame of an opening doorway in the first shot of the film, and repeats the image on several occasions: once to frame (and parallel) the introduction of Pawley, and twice again with the mouth of a cave as the framing doorway. It is an image which expresses both the subject and the conflict of the film: inside the door are the values cherished by civilization; outside, in the glaring sun, is the savage land which threatens them. *The Searchers*' final shot watches the reunited family walk in through the door, while Edwards remains behind, looking after them. He starts to enter, then hesitates. Realizing that he has served his purpose, that there is really no place for the western hero by the hearthside within, he turns and walks away, as the door closes behind him.

—Ed Lowry

THE SEASHELL AND THE CLERGYMAN

See **LA COQUILLE ET LE CLERGYMAN**

SECRETS AND LIES

UK, 1996

Director: Mike Leigh

Production: Film Four (UK), CiBy 2000 (France), Thin Man Films; color (Metrocolor), 35mm; running time: 141 minutes. Released 23 April 1996 (Cannes Film Festival), 24 May 1996, United Kingdom. Filmed on location in London, England. Budget: $4.5 million (US).

Producer: Simon Channing-Williams; **screenplay:** Mike Leigh; **photography:** Dick Pope; **editor:** Jon Gregory; **production design:** Alison Chitty; **original music:** Andrew Dickson.

Cast: Timothy Spall (*Maurice Purley*); Brenda Blethyn (*Cynthia Rose Purley*); Phyllis Logan (*Monica Purley*); Marianne Jean-Baptiste (*Hortense Cumberbatch*); Claire Rushbrook (*Roxanne Purley*); Elizabeth Berrington (*Jane*); Michele Austin (*Dionne*); Lee Ross (*Paul*).

Awards: Cannes Film Festival Palme d'Or (Mike Leigh) and Award for Best Actress (Brenda Blethyn), 1996; Cameraimage Golden Frog Award (Dick Pope), 1996; Los Angeles Film Critics' Association (LAFCA) Awards for Best Actress (Brenda Blethyn), Best Director (Mike Leigh), and Best Picture, 1996; Australian Film Institute Best Foreign Film Award (Simon Channing-Williams), 1997; British Academy Awards (BAFTA) Alexander Korda Award for Best British Film (Simon Channing-Williams), BAFTA Film Award for Best Performance by an Actress in a Leading Role (Brenda Blethyn), and Best Screenplay—Original (Mike Leigh), 1997; Golden Globe for Best Performance by an Actress in a Motion Picture—Drama (Brenda Blethyn), 1997; Golden Satellite Award for Best Director of a Motion Picture (Mike Leigh), Best Motion Picture—Drama (Simon Channing-Williams), and Best Performance by an Actress in a Motion Picture (Brenda Blethyn), 1997; Humanitas Prize (U.S.) in the Feature Film Category (Mike Leigh) 1997; Independent Spirit Award for Best Foreign Film (Mike Leigh), 1997; London Critics' Circle ALFS Awards for British Actress of the Year (Brenda Blethyn), British Director of the Year (Mike Leigh), and British Film of the Year, 1996–97.

Publications

Script:

Leigh, Mike, *Secrets and Lies*, London, 1997.

Articles:

Cavanagh, David, review in *Empire* (London), June 1996.
Jones, Alan, review in *Film Review* (London), June 1996.
Ansen, David, review in *Newsweek* (New York), 30 September 1996.
Corliss, Richard, ''Family Values,'' in *Time* (New York), 30 September 1996.
Quart, Leonard, ''Raising Questions and Positing Possibilities: an Interview with Mike Leigh,'' in *Cineaste* (New York), vol. 22, no. 4, 1997.

* * *

Best known for his bleak take on life in the suburbs, in *Secrets and Lies* Mike Leigh surprised many critics with a happy, perhaps rather sentimental ending. Besides its general point about our ability to hide our feelings even from those we love most, the film also confronts head-on an issue that remains pertinent in Britain; namely the extent to which British society is a multiethnic, multicultural one. It tells the story of Hortense, a young, black optometrist looking for her biological parents. To her surprise, her mother turns out to be a poorly educated white factory worker, living with her daughter from another relationship. Unmarried and pregnant at a young age, Cynthia was shamed into giving up her black baby at birth, and at first denies their relationship.

At their first meetings Brenda Blethyn (Cynthia) and Marianne Jean-Baptiste (Hortense) play the parts of damaged naif and young sophisticate with a rawness that has become a hallmark of Leigh's filmmaking. Constructing the script through extensive improvisation sessions with the cast, he manages to draw from his actors a level of commitment and realism in their roles that is seldom achieved by other directors. In the case of *Secrets and Lies*, the two female leads were kept apart until it was necessary to film their on-screen meeting, so that the first meeting of the characters was also the first meeting of the actors. Between them the two women produce the most extraordinary moments in the film, such as one awkward eight-minute scene, produced in a single take, in which the pair talk in a restaurant and the bond between them grows despite their different experiences of life.

Secrets and Lies, like Leigh's other films, champions people whose ambitions are simple and honest over those who pretend sophistication and social superiority. Leigh is well known for revealing in his films the dignity and extraordinary resilience of people whose lives seem mundane and uninteresting. Leigh's fascination with the difference between the way things are and the way they appear is embodied in *Secrets and Lies* in the professions of Cynthia's brother, Maurice, and her newly discovered daughter. As a professional portrait photographer, Maurice's skill with lenses involves creating illusions about his subjects. At one point, for example, he takes a photograph of a woman with a facial disfigurement, cleverly disguising her face to make her look conventionally beautiful. The art of illusion continues in his own life: Maurice and his unhappy, childless wife, Monica, live in a big house, hiding their misery behind expensive furnishings. In contrast, as an optometrist, Hortense is dedicated to improving the vision of her clients, enabling them to see the world more clearly. Through her relationship with Cynthia, Hortense helps the family to see the truth about themselves and each other.

Secrets and Lies is Leigh's fifth feature film, in a career going back to *Bleak Moments* in 1971, and it is arguably his lightest work for the big screen before *Topsy Turvy* (2000). The technique of scriptwriting by improvisation seems more accomplished here than in earlier films, and, unusually for a Leigh film, *Secrets and Lies* was successful at the box office and with critics outside the United Kingdom. While his

Secrets and Lies

other films are noted for their dark humour, *Secrets and Lies* alternates between moments of heart-rending sadness, flamboyant comedy, and situations that had cinema audiences, in Britain at least, squirming in their seats with recognition and embarrassment.

—Chris Routledge

SEPPUKU

(Harakiri)

Japan, 1962

Director: Masaki Kobayashi

Production: Shochiku Co. (Kyoto); black and white, 35 mm, Shochiku GrandScope; running time: 135 minutes; length: 3,686 meters. Released 1962, Japan.

Producers: Tatsuo Hosoya with Gin-ichi Kishimoto; **screenplay:** Shinobu Hashimoto, from the novel by Yasuhiko Tokigushi; **photography:** Yoshio Miyajima; **editor:** Hisashi Sagara; **sound:** Hideo Nishizaki; **art directors:** Jun-ichi Ozumi and Shigemasa Toda; **music:** Toru Takemitsu.

Cast: Tatsuya Nakadai (*Hanshiro Tsugumo*); Shima Iwashita (*Mihio Tsugumo*); Akira Ishihama (*Motome Chijiiwa*); Yoshio Inaba (*Jinai Chijiiwa*); Rentaro Mikuni (*Kageyu Saito*); Masao Mishima (*Tango Inaba*); Tetsuro Tamba (*Hikokuro Omodaka*); Ichiro Nakaya (*Hayato Yazaki*); Yoshio Aoki (*Umenosuke Kawabe*); Jo Azumi (*Ichiro Shimmen*); Hisashi Igawa, Shoji Kobayashi, Ryo Takeuchi (*Young samurai*); Shichisaburo Amatsu (*Page*); Kei Sato (*Masakazu Fukushima*).

Awards: Cannes Film Festival, Special Jury Prize, 1963.

Publications

Books:

Richie, Donald, *The Japanese Movie: An Illustrated History*, Tokyo, 1966.

Richie, Donald, *Japanese Film Style and National Character*, New York, 1971.

Mellen, Joan, *Voices from the Japanese Cinema*, New York, 1975.

Seppuku

Bock, Audie, *Japanese Film Directors*, New York, 1978; revised edition, Tokyo, 1985.
Blouin, Claude R., *Le Chemin détourné: Essai sur Kobayashi et let cinéma japonais*, Quebec, 1982.

Articles:

Iwabuchi, M., ''Kobayashi's Trilogy,'' in *Film Culture* (New York), Spring 1962.
Donaldson, Geoffrey, in *Films and Filming* (London), March 1963.
Sadoul, Georges, in *Lettres Françaises* (Paris), 23 May 1963.
Martin, Marcel, in *Lettres Françaises* (Paris), 30 May 1963.
Billard, Pierre, in *Cinéma* (Paris), June 1963.
Silke, James R., ''*Hakari*, Koboyashi, Humanism,'' in *Cinema* (Beverly Hills), June-July 1963.
Shivas, Mark, in *Movie* (London), July-August 1963.
Cinema (Beverly Hills), August-September 1963.
Labarthe, Andre S., in *Cahiers du Cinéma* (Paris), September 1963.
Phillipe, Pierre, in *Cinéma* (Paris), September-October 1963.
Ciment, Michel, in *Positif* (Paris), November 1963.
Arnault, Hubert, in *Image et Son* (Paris), January 1964.
Corman, Cid, in *Film Quarterly* (Berkeley), Spring 1964.
Films and Filming (London), March 1965.
Eyles, Allen, in *Films and Filming* (London), May 1965.
Esnault, Philippe, in *Image et son* (Paris), February 1969.
Blouin, Claude R., ''Kobayashi: L'Homme et l'oeuvre,'' and ''Kobayashi, à l'uquam: Anarchiste ou utopiste?,'' by G. Therien in *Cinéma Québec* (Montreal) February-March 1974.
Tessier, Max, in *Image et Son* (Paris), November 1981.
Sartor, F., ''*Harakiri:* de eer van de samoerai,'' in *Film en Televisie* (Brussels), February 1986.
Jackiewicz, Aleksander, ''Moje zycie w kinie,'' in *Kino* (Warsaw), vol. 21, no. 3, March 1987.

* * *

Seppuku marks Masaki Kobayashi's first venture into the genre of *jidai-geki* (costume drama). But his choice of a historical subject entails no lessening of the distinctive social and moral preoccupations which informed the contemporary subjects of his earlier films. Rather, those preoccupations are intensified by their placement in a historical perspective, their universal relevance underlined; while in the stylized conventions of the samurai ritual, Kobayashi found the ideal context for the slow, measured cadences of his cinematic language. The result was his finest film to date, a work of masterly narrative construction and outstanding visual beauty.

Through an intricate pattern of flashbacks, the story is revealed to us in reverse. The *ronin* (masterless, hence destitute, samurai) Tsugumo, who comes seeking to be allowed to commit ritual suicide in the house of Lord Iyi, is told a cautionary tale of the fate of another *ronin*, Chijiwa, who had made the same request. In his turn, Tsugumo relates his own story: he already knew of Chijiwa's brutal death, for the man was his son-in-law, and he has now come to take vengeance on the Iyi clan. The film culminates in a superbly choreographed explosion of violence.

As so often in his films, Kobayashi's concern is with the solitary, courageous individual who stands against a corrupt, inhuman and oppressive system. The vaunted samurai traditions of honor and nobility, as professed by the members of the Iyi clan, are shown to be a hollow sham, adhered to only in public view. In the film's opening shot, a huge suit of armor, surmounted by a horned battle helmet, looms out of the mist, to eerie and impressive effect. This armor, it transpires, embodies the ancestral spirits of the Iyi household, who pay it exaggerated deference. But in the final headlong combat, Tsugumo contemptuously knocks it out of his way, then uses it as a shield. The armor, like the samurai system, is an empty show.

The recurrent image in *Seppuku* is of Tsugumo in his black robes (having refused the white ones appropriate to the ritual suicide), seated cross-legged on the white harakiri mat in the center of the courtyard, surrounded by the massed spears of the Iyi warriors, and speaking in calm, unhurried tones. Around this image of charged stillness, the action of the film proceeds through visual compositions of intense lyrical beauty: most notably in the duel between Tsugumo and Omadaka, finest of the Iyi swordsmen, breathtakingly staged as a formal ballet of stylized, sweeping gestures amid long wind-tossed grass. Kobayashi's coolly reticent camera perfectly matches the rhythms of his studied narrative, supported by Toru Takemitsu's evocative score and, in the central role, a performance of epic stature from Tatsuya Nakadai.

Seppuku was awarded the Special Jury Prize at the 1963 Cannes Festival, the first of Kobayashi's films to become widely known in the west. It was to be equalled in visual beauty by *Kaidan* (*Kwaidan*). In his most famous film, *Joiuchi*, he once again made telling use of the samurai system as the epitome of an ossified, authoritarian tradition. *Seppuku*, though, combines both elements in unsurpassable fashion, and remains the most achieved expression of Kobayashi's central belief that all systems, even the most malignant and entrenched, can be resisted by the power of ''sheer human resilience.''

—Philip Kemp

THE SERVANT

UK, 1963

Director: Joseph Losey

Production: Springbok Films-Elstree; black and white; running time: 115 minutes; length: 10,382 feet. Released 1963.

The Servant

Producers: Joseph Losey, Norman Priggen; **assistant director:** Roy Stevens; **screenplay:** Harold Pinter, from the novel by Robin Maugham; **photography:** Douglas Slocombe; **editor:** Reginald Mills; **sound:** John Cox, Gerry Hambling; **sound recordist:** Buster Ambler; **art directors:** Richard Macdonald, Ted Clements; **music:** John Dankworth.

Cast: Dirk Bogarde (*Barrett*); James Fox (*Tony*); Wendy Craig (*Susan*); Sarah Miles (*Vera*); Catherine Lacey (*Lady Mounset*); Richard Vernon (*Lord Mounset*); Ann Firbank (*Society Woman*); Doris Knox (*Older Woman*); Patrick Magee (*Bishop*); Alun Owen (*Curate*); Jill Melford (*Young Woman*); Harold Pinter (*Society Man*); Derek Tansley (*Head Waiter*); Gerry Duggan (*Waiter*); Brian Phelan (*Irishman*); Hazel Terry (*Woman in Big Hat*); Philippa Hare (*Girl in Bedroom*); Dorothy Bromley (*Girl outside Phone-box*); Alison Seebohm (*Girl in Pub*); Chris Williams (*Coffee Bar Cashier*).

Awards: British Film Academy Awards for Best Black and White Cinematography, Best British Actor (Bogarde), Most Promising Newcomer Actor (Fox).

Publications

Script:

Pinter, Harold, *The Servant*, in *Five Screenplays*, London, 1971.

Books:

Leahy, James, *The Cinema of Joseph Losey*, New York, 1967.
Baker, William, and Stephen Ely Tabachnick, *Harold Pinter*, Edinburgh, 1973.
Durgnat, Raymond, *Sexual Alienation in the Cinema*, London, 1974.
Hinxman, Margaret, and Susan D'Arcy, *The Films of Dirk Bogarde*, London, 1974.
Bogarde, Dirk, *Snakes and Ladders*, London, 1978.
Ciment, Michel, *Conversations with Losey*, Paris, 1979; London, 1985.
Hirsch, Foster, *Joseph Losey*, Boston, 1980.
Klein, Joanne, *Making Pictures: The Pinter Screenplays*, Columbus, Ohio, 1985.
Carbone, Maria Teresa, *I luoghi della memoria: Harold Pinter sceneggiatore per il cinema di Losey*, Bari, 1986.
Tanitch, Robert, *Dirk Bogarde: The Complete Career Illustrated*, London, 1988.
Palmer, James, and Michael Riley, *The Films of Joseph Losey*, New York, 1993.
Caute, David, *Joseph Losey: A Revenge on Life*, New York, 1994.

Articles:

Variety (New York), 11 September 1963.
Baker, Peter, in *Films and Filming* (London), December 1963.
Dyer, Peter John, in *Monthly Film Bulletin* (London), December 1963.
Taylor, John Russell, in *Sight and Sound* (London), Winter 1963–64.
Losey, Joseph, in *Cahiers du Cinéma* (Paris), March 1964, and June 1964.
Losey, Joseph, in *Sight and Sound* (London), Spring 1964.
Callenbach, Ernest, in *Film Quarterly* (Berkeley), Autumn 1964.
Ross, T. J., ''*The Servant* as Sex-Thriller,'' in *Renaissance of the Film*, edited by Julius Bellone, New York and London, 1970.
Brighton Film Review, February 1970.
Image et Son (Paris), no. 274, 1973.
Finetta, U., ''Tra il vecchio e il nuovo una varieta di simbola morbosi,'' in *Cinema Nuovo* (Bari), August 1979.
Riley, Michael M., and James W. Palmer, ''An Extension of Reality: Setting as Theme in *The Servant*,'' in *Mise-en-Scène* (New York), Spring 1980.
Weiss, J., ''Screenwriters, Critics, and Ambiguity: An Interview with Joseph Losey,'' in *Cineaste* (New York), vol. 13, no. 1, 1983.
Tronowicz, H., ''W kregu sylogizmow moralnych Josepha Loseya,'' in *Kino* (Warsaw), March 1985.
''Losey Issue'' of *Positif* (Paris), July-August 1985.
Medhurst, Andy, ''Dirk Bogarde,'' in *All Our Yesterdays*, edited by Charles Barr, London, 1986.
Listener (London), 7 January 1988.
Amiel, Vincent, ''Le désir, et la subtilité des gris,'' in *Positif* (Paris), no. 370, December 1991.
Piazzo, Philippe, ''Une absurde simplicité,'' in *Télérama* (Paris), no. 2308, 6 April 1994.
Gardner, C., ''Naturalism, Immanence and the Primordiality of Class: Deleuze's 'Impulse-Image' and the Baroque Intriguer in Joseph Lousey's *The Servant*,'' in *Iris* (Iowa City), no. 23, Spring 1997.

* * *

The Servant marks the beginning of the extremely fruitful Losey-Pinter relationship, although in fact Pinter had originally scripted Robin Maugham's novel (in which Losey had always been interested) for Michael Anderson. When Pinter first took his script to Losey he wasn't exactly thrilled by the latter's reaction but, after this rocky start, the two produced one of the finest works in both their oeuvres. The film also launched Sarah Miles and James Fox, re-invigorated the career of cinematographer Douglas Slocombe, and marked Bogarde's final, decisive break with his matinee idol image (though Losey had also cast Bogarde rather against type some years earlier in *The Sleeping Tiger*).

Given Losey's abiding interest in relations of class and power it is hardly surprising that he should have been drawn to this story of a servant, Barrett, who is taken on by an effete young Englishman, Tony, and gradually takes over his master's life. Barrett is aided by his girlfriend Vera, who seduces Tony and eventually displaces his financée Susan, who eventually abandons this household in which master and servant have eventually achieved some kind of equality in degradation.

In many ways *The Servant* can be seen as a continuation of *Eve.* Both chart a process of degeneration, and the destruction of one character by another. More specifically, the destroyer in each case belongs to a traditionally exploited and downtrodden social group, has learned the hard way how the world works, and takes revenge through sex. In another respect, the film might be seen as a re-working of the Faust legend or even of *The Picture of Dorian Gray.* However, this would be to ignore a crucial aspect of the film, namely that by the end of the film *all* the major characters (with the possible exception of Susan) have been morally destroyed. Losey is not so simple-minded as to stage a simple victory of Barrett over Tony; rather he shows how the rigid English class system corrupts *all* human relationships by turning them into a form of warfare in which the roles of aggressor and victim seem constantly to be shifting. Thus Tony is weak and rather foolish but nonetheless in a powerful social situation because of his class position. Barrett, on the other hand, belongs to a subordinate class, but one which is needed by Tony and his ilk, and knows how to play on that need. The kernel of this relationship is beautifully conveyed in their very first meeting, Tony asleep after too much to drink at lunchtime discreetly woken by Barrett's deliberate, soft cough but probably unaware (unlike the viewer) of the faintly superior smile which flickers across Barrett's face. The film is haunted by triangular relationships (the most obvious one being between Barrett, Tony, and Susan) whose terms are constantly shifting but all of which are ultimately destructive of all concerned. Indeed, Losey seems to be suggesting that it is not just the rigidity of the class system which is at fault here, but human psychology itself. As James Leahy perceptively put it in *The Cinema of Joeph Losey*, ''the house in which the drama is acted out grows into a womb-like prison in which Tony and Barrett, master and servant, boss and worker, and, at times homosexual couple in a sado-masochistic relationship, husband and wife, son and mother even, are bound inseparably together by bonds of knowledge, hate, guilt and love from which they have not the strength of will to escape . . . . The ambiguity of Losey's symbolism here results from no confusion on his part: he is expressing the underlying identity of all relationships—sexual, marital, economic, political—which involve servility or exploitation rather than the co-operative and collaborative efforts of free individuals. Thus *The Servant* lends itself to both a socio-political and psychoanalytical interpretation.''

As in plays such as *The Birthday Party* and *The Caretaker* Pinter's spare, elliptical dialogue, with its pauses and silences, is the perfect vehicle for expressing the unspoken dynamics of human relationships and for establishing a pervasive sense of menace and unease. More important still, however, is Losey's masterly direction, elaborate yet tightly controlled and never merely decorative. Particularly impressive is Losey's consistent use of circular motifs which complement the film's triangular relationships and underline its essentially circular plot structure. Thus the house itself is circular, as are the opening and closing shots, and so on. At the same time Losey accentuates the changing nature of the relationship between Barrett and Tony by changes in the look, tempo, and structure of the film. In particular he works subtle alterations on the physical space of the house itself. As he put it, the house is the ''central icon, an index of the characters' taste, their place in society, and their relationship to each other. The house assumes different personalities during the course of the film, reflecting the evolution of the master-servant contract.''

—Julian Petley

THE SEVEN SAMURAI

See **SHICHININ NO SAMURAI**

THE SEVENTH SEAL

See **DET SJUNDE INSEGLET**

SHADOWS OF FORGOTTEN ANCESTORS

See **TENI ZABYTYKH PREDKOV**

SHAFT

USA, 1971

Director: Gordon Parks

Production: MGM, Shaft Productions Ltd.; distributed by MGM-UA; color, 35mm; running time: 98 minutes. Released July 1971, USA. Cost: $1.5 million.

Producers: Joel Freeman, David Golden (associate); **screenplay:** Ernest Tidyman, John D. F. Black; **cinematography:** Urs Furrer; **editor:** Hugh Robertson; **sound:** Lee Bost, Hal Watkins; **art director:** Emanuel Gerard; **costume designer:** Joseph Aulisi; **original music:** Isaac Hayes; **makeup:** Martin Bell; **casting:** Judith Lamb.

Cast: Richard Roundtree (*John Shaft*); Moses Gunn (*Bumpy Jonas*); Charles Cioffi (*Lieutenant Victor Androzzi*); Christopher St. John

Shaft

(*Ben Buford*); Gwenn Mitchell (*Ellie Moore*); Lawrence Pressman (*Sergeant Tom Hannon*); Victor Arnold (*Charlie*); Sherri Brewer (*Marcy Jonas*); Rex Robbins (*Rollie*); Camille Yarbrough (*Dina Greene*); Margaret Warncke (*Linda*); Joseph Leon (*Bryan Leibowitz*); Arnold Johnson (*Cul*); Dominic Barto (*Patsy*); George Strus (*Carmen*); Edmund Hashim (*Lee*); Drew Bundini Brown (*Willy*); Tommy Lane (*Leroy*); Al Kirk (*Sims*); Shimen Ruskin (*Dr. Sam*); Antonio Fargas (*Bunky*).

Awards: Oscar Award for Best Music, Song (Isaac Hayes), 1972; Golden Globe Award for Best Original Score (Isaac Hayes), 1972; Grammy Award for Best Original Score written for a Motion Picture (Isaac Hayes), 1972; MTV Movie Award for Lifetime Achievement (Richard Roundtree), 1994.

Publications

Books:

Tidyman, Ernest, *Shaft*, New York, 1971.

Parish, James, *Black Action Films*, Jefferson, North Carolina, 1989; revised, Secaucus, New Jersey, 1993.

Guerrero, Ed, *Framing Blackness: The African American Image in Film*, Philadelphia, 1993.

Belton, John, *American Cinema/American Culture*, New York, 1994.

James, Darius (a.k.a. Dr. Snakeskin), *That's Blaxploitation! Roots of the Baadasssss 'Tude (Rated X by an All-Whyte Jury)*, New York, 1995.

Martinez, Gerald, Diana Martinez, and Andres Chavez, *What It Is. . . What It Was! The Black Film Explosion of the 70s in Words and Pictures*, New York, 1998.

Articles:

Bannon, Barbara, ''What's Happening to Ernest Tidyman's '*Shaft*' On the Way to the Screen,'' in *Publishers Weekly*, April 1971.

Canby, Vincent, '''*Shaft*'—At Last, a Good Saturday Night Movie,'' in *New York Times*, 11 July 1971.

Oberbeck, S. K, ''Black Eye,'' in *Newsweek*, 19 July 1971.

Riley, Clayton, ''A Black Movie for White Audiences?'' in *New York Times*, 25 July 1971.

Elson, John T, ''Black Moses,'' in *Time*, 20 December 1971.

* * *

''He's cool and tough. He's a black private dick who's a sex machine with all the chicks. He doesn't take orders from anybody, black or white, but he'd risk his neck for his brother man. I'm talkin' about Shaft. Can you dig it?'' These lines, from Isaac Hayes' Oscar Award-winning ''Theme from *Shaft*,'' serves as a good introduction to Richard Roundtree's African American hero/rebel/icon John Shaft, eponymous star of the wildly successful 1971 feature film directed by Gordon Parks. One of the first entries to fall under the controversial heading of ''blaxploitation'' cinema, *Shaft* followed directly on the heels of Martin Van Peeble's *Sweet Sweetback's Baadassss Song* (1971), and is widely acknowledged as the film which initiated the black film explosion of the 1970s (along with *Superfly*, directed by Parks' son, and released one year later).

Shaft's screenplay was written by Ernest Tidyman, author of a series of popular detective novels featuring the film's protagonist. (Tidyman would go on to win an Oscar for Best Screenplay in 1972 for his work on William Friedkin's *The French Connection.*) After the success of *Sweetback*, MGM gave Parks the go-ahead—and a modest (even for the time) $1.5 million budget—for a project which would hopefully capitalize on the fast-emerging black market. Parks was already an extremely accomplished individual, having a reputation as one of America's preeminent still photographers of African descent (his work appeared in *Life* magazine from the 1940s through the late 1960s), as well as being an esteemed author, composer, and filmmaker. In 1969, Parks became the first African American to direct a major studio production, the autobiographical *The Learning Tree.* Parks wanted a fresh face to play the lead role in his new film, and found exactly what he was looking for in Roundtree, a former Ebony model and occasional theatre actor whose looks, ability, and physical presence provided just the right combination of machismo, virility, and confidence for the part.

Shaft's convoluted plot is actually fairly standard hard-boiled detective fare. After inadvertently causing the death of a gangster who showed up at his office for some unexplained reason, John Shaft is coerced by a pair of white police inspectors to help them gather information about a gang war rumored to be taking place in Harlem. Meanwhile, a drug-dealing black godfather, Bumpy Jonas (played wonderfully by Moses Gunn), hires Shaft to save his daughter from the people who have recently kidnapped her. This turns out to be the Italian mafia, so with the help of a former comrade (Ben Buford, played by Christopher St. John) and his cadre of black nationalist followers, Shaft undertakes a dangerous but ultimately successful rescue mission. All of this non-stop action is interrupted by dated romantic interludes (Shaft seems to have no qualms about cheating on his girlfriend, and proves himself an equal-opportunity lover), and opportunities for Shaft to make whitey look square, stupid, or worse.

If ever there existed a film in which the narrative is simply a vehicle for showcasing a particular character, *Shaft* is it. Together, Tidyman, Parks, and Roundtree created a strong black hero who—for the first time in Hollywood cinema—made his own rules, listened to no one, *gave* the orders instead of taking them, and was not in the least afraid of making jokes at the expense of white authority figures. It is worth comparing Roundtree's character with those so often portrayed by legendary African American thespian Sidney Poitier, figures who were polite, elegant, and generally acceptable to caucasian audiences. *Shaft*'s revolutionary implications are inadvertently revealed in the press booklet accompanying its release, which protests (too strongly) that the film ''has a black hero, but don't confuse that with a message—it's for fun!'' Despite its subversive protagonist and militant undertones, *Shaft* did remarkable business among both black *and* white audiences, eventually grossing over $23 million at U.S. box offices alone. Such broad-ranging success can only be explained by the fact that Shaft is perfectly comfortable in any situation, with people of every stripe (including a blatantly typecast homosexual bartender, who feels compelled to pinch his butt), and that his magnetism and coolness under fire transcend mere color boundaries.

None of this, however, is to say that Parks' film escaped all criticism. Like so many of its blaxploitation offspring, *Shaft* was accused of perpetuating negative stereotypes of African Americans, including promiscuity, immorality, and a propensity towards violence. In another vein, black cultural critics such as Darius James have argued that *Shaft*—which originally had a white man in the title role—is merely ''a conventional action film for general audiences, enlivened by its Black cast members.'' In interviews, Martin Van Peebles concurs with this assessment and goes even further, asserting that while John Shaft is allowed to be flamboyant and do little things, the film's subliminal message is actually counterrevolutionary—that a white authority figure (the police commissioner) is still there hovering over him, simply tolerating his excesses.

Whether *Shaft* is of any political or ideological value for African Americans remains a debatable issue. What cannot be denied is the impact the picture has had on later black (and white) filmmakers. *Boyz N The Hood* (1991) director John Singleton eloquently sums up this complex legacy when he writes, ''Mind you, it's not a perfect movie. But. . . you have a whole generation totally influenced by the image of a Black man walking down the street in a leather coat, walking through Harlem; the close-ups on his face.'' And it should not be forgotten that Hayes' score for the film was groundbreaking in that here, music effectively led the narrative. Following on the heels of *Shaft*'s success, Parks, Tidyman, and Roundtree collaborated on a sequel in 1972, *Shaft's Big Score!* John Guillermin's *Shaft In Africa* arrived in theatres the next year. And with a blaxploitation revival gaining steam in the late 1990s (*Original Gangstas*, *Jackie Brown*), Roundtree—who made only $13,000 for his work in the original—is slated to reprise his signature role in Singleton's *Shaft Returns* (2000).

—Steven Schneider

SHAKESPEARE IN LOVE

USA, 1998

Director: John Madden

Production: Bedford Falls Productions, Miramax Films, Universal Pictures; color, 35mm, Super 35; running time: 122 minutes. Filmed in London, Norfolk, Oxfordshire, and Buckinghamshire, England. Cost: $25 million.

Producer: Marc Norman, David Parfitt, Harvey Weinstein, Edward Zwick, Donna Gigliotti, Bob Weinstein (executive), Julie Goldstein (executive), Linda Bruce (associate); **screenplay:** Marc Norman, Tom Stoppard, with passages from the plays of William Shakespeare; **cinematographer:** Richard Greatrex; **editor:** David Gamble; **music:** Stephen Warbeck; **casting:** Michelle Guish; **production design:** Martin Childs; **art direction:** Steve Lawrence, Mark Raggett; **set decoration:** Jill Quertier; **costume design:** Humberto Cornejo, Sandy Powell; **makeup:** Veronica Brebner.

Cast: Joseph Fiennes (*William Shakespeare*); Gwyneth Paltrow (*Viola De Lesseps*); Geoffrey Rush (*Philip Henslowe*); Judi Dench (*Queen Elizabeth*); Simon Callow (*Tilney, Master of the Revels*); Colin Firth (*Lord Wessex*); Imelda Staunton (*Nurse*); Tom Wilkinson (*Hugh Fennyman*); Ben Affleck (*Ned Alleyn*); Martin Clunes (*Richard Burbage*); Jim Carter (*Ralph Bashford*); Rupert Everett (*Christopher Marlowe [uncredited]*); and others.

Awards: Academy Awards for Best Picture, Best Actress (Gwyneth Paltrow), Best Writing, Best Supporting Actress (Judi Dench), Best Art Direction/Set Direction (Martin Childs and Jill Quertier), Best Costume Design (Sandy Powell), Best Music, Original Musical or Comedy Score (Stephen Warbeck); Golden Globe Awards for Best Picture, Best Screenplay (Tom Stoppard and Marc Norman), Best Single Achievement (Stoppard and Norman, for screenplay), and Best Actress in a Musical or Comedy (Paltrow); British Academy Awards for Best Film and Best Editing; and others.

Publications

Script:

Norman, Marc, and Tom Stoppard, *Shakespeare in Love: A Screenplay*, New York, 1999.

Books:

Brode, Douglas, *Shakespeare in the Movies: From the Silent Era to Shakespeare in Love*, New York, 2000.

Articles:

Abramowitz, R., ''Long Cool Woman,'' in *Premiere* (Boulder), vol. 11, February 1998.

Dawtrey, A., and M. Roman, '''Love' Triangle Times 3,'' in *Variety* (New York), vol. 370, 23/29 March 1998.

Hirschberg, Lynn, ''A Dresser for the Ages: In Just One Short Season, Sandy Powell Has Managed to Design Movie Costumes Four Centuries Apart, Each With a Sublime Ratio of Grandeur to Grit,'' in *New York Times*, 20 December 1998.

Gussow, Mel, ''In Love, With Shakespeare,'' in *New York Times*, 12 January 1999.

Rothwell, Kenneth S., in *Cineaste* (New York), vol. 24, no. 2–3, 1999.

Elias, Justine, ''Joseph Fiennes,'' in *Interview*, vol. 29, no. 2, February 1999.

Kemp, Philip, in *Sight & Sound* (London), vol. 9, no. 2, February 1999.

McMahon, Michael, ''A Codpiece and LSD Experience: Influence of Films Such as *Shakespeare in Love* on the Young,'' in *New Statesman*, vol. 128, no. 4422, 5 February 1999.

''Firth and Foremost: *Shakespeare In Love's* Colin Firth Relishes a Good Role, His Son, and a Little Road Rage,'' in *People Weekly*, vol. 51, no. 5, 8 February 1999.

Goodale, Gloria, ''How they Imagined *Shakespeare in Love*,'' an interview with Marc Norman and Tom Stoppard, in *The Christian Science Monitor*, vol. 91, no. 68, 5 March 1999.

Calhoun, John, ''Tudor City: Production Design of *Elizabeth* and *Shakespeare in Love*,'' in *Interiors*, vol. 158, no. 3, March 1999.

Sterritt, David, ''A Director in Love with Shakespeare,'' an interview with John Madden, in *The Christian Science Monitor*, vol. 91, no. 73, 12 March 1999.

Harries, Martin, ''Hollywood in Love: Explaining the Popularity of *Shakespeare in Love*,'' in *The Chronicle of Higher Education*, vol. 45, no. 32, 16 April 1999.

Berthomieu, Pierre, ''*Shakespeare in Love*: Et je t'appellerai Viola,'' in *Positif* (Paris), no. 548, April 1999.

Kroll, Jack, ''Nothing Like the Dame,'' in *Newsweek*, vol. 133, no. 17, 26 April 1999.

Marks, Peter, ''Great Literature. Period Costumes. That is So Cool: On the Slick Heels of *Shakespeare in Love*, Another Entry in a Growing Genre: The Hip Theatrical Period Film,'' in *New York Times*, 20 June 1999.

Bemrose, John, ''In Love With Shakespeare: His Plays are More Popular Than Ever: To Be or Not to Be a Fan of the Bard is Not in Question,'' in *Maclean's*, 5 July 1999.

Caro, Jason, ''1999: The Best and the Worst of a Great Year in Cinema,'' in *Film Review Special* (London), no. 30, 1999/2000.

* * *

Around the mid-1990s that staple of British cinema, the period costume drama, began to mutate from its erstwhile Merchant-Ivory-esque good taste into something altogether fiercer, shaggier, and far less well-mannered. The change was signalled by Richard Loncraine's tour de force *Richard III*, set in an alternative-history 1930s fascist Britain, and further explored in two *realpolitik* takes on British monarchs, John Madden's subversive *Mrs. Brown* and Shekhar Kapur's dark, ruthless *Elizabeth.* At the same time the vogue for adapting and updating British literary classics, sparked by Amy Heckerling's *Clueless* (Jane Austen in Beverly Hills), gathered pace with such revisionist exercises as *Great Expectations* (Dickens in present-day New York), *10 Things I Hate About You* (high school *Taming of the Shrew*) and Baz Luhrmann's Latino-punk *Romeo + Juliet.* These two strands came together in Madden's next film after *Mrs. Brown*, *Shakespeare in Love*, in which the Bard himself gets

Shakespeare in Love

pushed off his exalted pedestal and thoroughly dusted down for present-day audiences. Taking advantage of the fact that almost nothing about Shakespeare's life is known for certain, Madden presents us not with the balding, pensive figure of the Droeshout portrait that adorns the flyleaf of most collected works, but with an ambitious, randy young hack writer struggling to make his way in the precarious world of Elizabethan London. Though the film is a comedy, the sense of a tough, dangerous era is never played down: the first image we're confronted with is of the hapless Henslowe, debt-ridden impresario, being tortured by his creditor's hired thugs.

But while it doesn't gloss over the crueller aspects of the period, the film makes no pretence at consistent historical authenticity—or consistent anything, come to that. *Shakespeare in Love* is frankly a hodgepodge—or as the Elizabethans might more pungently have put it, a gallimaufry and an ollapodrida, a dish into which any available ingredients might be tossed, the more the merrier. The main plot-line (well-born young woman named Viola dresses up as a boy, joins Shakespeare's troupe, and has an affair with the playwright) is pinched straight from Caryl Brahms and S. J. Simon's classic 1941 comic novel *No Bed for Bacon.* The stagestruck heavy is a blatant lift from Woody Allen's *Bullets Over Broadway*, and the scene-setting pays homage to the Monty Python school of scatological reconstruction: Henslowe, striding through the London streets, treads in a heap of dung and is narrowly missed by the contents of a pisspot. We get romance, slapstick, bedroom farce, satire, star-crossed tragedy, a shipwreck, a full-on swashbuckling swordfight, and enough sly literary allusions to sink a concordance.

Which is fine since this heterogeneous mixture, a rich but satisfying plum-pudding, works perfectly well on its own terms, absorbing its borrowings and negotiating its switches of mood with little sense of strain. (There's only one serious lapse, a jarring descent into Carry-On inanity when Will puts on a squeaky voice, holds a veil over his beard and pretends to be Viola's female cousin.) Besides, style and subject are ideally matched, since we're dealing with the greatest magpie genius of all time. Shakespeare was notoriously disinclined to devise his own plots, preferring to snaffle them from Plutarch, Holinshed, or whatever dog-eared chapbook came to hand; he cared nothing for unity of mood, tossing dirty jokes into high tragedy in a way that gave the Augustans the vapours; and several of his plays (*Richard II*, for one) contain whole scenes written by someone else, presumably borrowed when the harassed playwright ran out of time or inspiration. *Shakespeare in Love*, diverting though it is, hardly attains the Bard's own exalted standard, but it can be claimed as a film after his own heart.

Even the jocular anachronisms can quote good Shakespearean precedent; this was the dramatist, after all, who had his Cleopatra propose a game of billiards. The film is lavish with throwaway jokes: Will swigs ale from a mug inscribed ''A Present from Stratford'' and consults a ''Priest of Psyche'' over his writer's block. (''The proud tower of my genius is collapsed,'' he complains; the Priest, a Freudian avant la lettre, inquires after the state of Will's other proud tower.) Elsewhere a chatty ferryman boasts ''I 'ad that Christopher Marlowe in my boat once,'' and the school of Bardic conspiracy-theorists who insist that Marlowe wrote Shakespeare is spoofed when the elder playwright casually tosses Will the plot for Romeo and Juliet. These and other more literary gags that may bypass the groundlings (a bloodthirsty small boy, given to tormenting mice, proves to be John Webster, future writer of gore-spattered Jacobean dramas) can no doubt be credited to co-screenwriter Tom Stoppard, author of *Rosencrantz and Guildenstern Are Dead.*

Shakespeare in Love delighted the public, the critics, and the voters of the Academy, who awarded it a string of Oscars. The secret of its appeal, perhaps—along with its gamy exuberance and a peerless display of acting ability from all concerned—is the way it succeeds in being at once frivolous and serious about its subject. The central plot-device—that *Romeo and Juliet* started out as an absurd piece of fustian entitled *Romeo and Ethel the Pirate's Daughter*—is patently ludicrous, and the film abounds in backstage jokes about the vanities of writers, actors, producers, and so forth. Yet if the process of poetic creativity is sent up, the end result is wholeheartedly celebrated. The final triumphant staging of Shakespeare's first true masterpiece, while edging dangerously near luvvie-ish self-regard, conveys something of what Nabokov called *shamanstvo*—the ''enchanter-quality'' of great theatre. As Henslowe remarks, smiling beatifically as the whole shambles comes magically together, ''It's a mystery.''

—Philip Kemp

SHANE

USA, 1953

Director: George Stevens

Production: Paramount Pictures; Technicolor, 35mm; running time: 118 minutes. Released 1953. Oscar for Best Cinematography-Color, 1953.

Producer: George Stevens; **associate producer:** Ivan Moffat; **screenplay:** A. B. Guthrie, Jr. with additional dialogue by Jack Sher, from the novel by Jack Schaefer; **photography:** Loyal Griggs; **editors:** William Hornbeck and Tom McAdoo; **sound recordists:** Harry Lindgran and Gene Garwin; **art directors:** Hal Pereira and Walter Tyler; **music score:** Victor Young; **special effects:** Gordon Jennings; **costume designer:** Edith Head; **technical adviser:** Joe DeYong.

Cast: Alan Ladd (*Shane*); Jean Arthur (*Marion Starrett*); Van Heflin (*Joe Starrett*); Brandon de Wilde (*Joey*); Jack Palance (*Wilson*); Ben Johnson (*Chris*); Edgar Buchanan (*Lewis*); Emile Meyer (*Ryker*); Elisha Cook Jr. (*Torrey*); Douglas Spencer (*Shipstead*); John Dierkes (*Morgan*); Ellen Corby (*Mrs. Torrey*); Paul McVey (*Grafton*); John Miller (*Atkey*); Edith Evanson (*Mrs. Shipstead*); Leonard Strong (*Wright*); Ray Spiker (*Johnson*); Janice Carroll (*Susan Lewis*); Martin Mason (*Howell*); Helen Brown (*Mrs. Lewis*); Nancy Kulp (*Mrs. Howell*); Howard J. Negley (*Pete*); Beverly Washburn (*Ruth Lewis*); George Lewis (*Ryker man*); Charles Quirk (*Clerk*); Jack Sterling, Henry Wills, Rex Moore, and Ewing Brown (*Ryker men*).

Publications

Books:

Fenin, George N., and William K. Everson, *The Western: From Silents to Cinerama*, New York, 1962.

Babcock, David, *The Hero*, Waltham, Massachusetts, 1968.

Everson, William K., *A Pictoral History of the Western Film*, New York, 1969.

Richie, Donald, *George Stevens: An American Romantic*, New York, 1970, 1985.

Bazin, Andre, *What Is Cinema? 2*, edited by Hugh Gray, Berkeley, 1971.

Cawelti, John, *The Six-Gun Mystique*, Bowling Green, Ohio, 1971.

Fenin, George N., and William K. Everson, *The Western: From Silents to the 70s*, New York, 1973.

French, Philip, *Westerns—Aspects of a Movie Genre*, New York, 1973.

Phillips, Gene D., *The Movie Makers: Artists in the Industry*, Chicago, 1973.

Nachbar, Jack, editor, *Focus on the Western*, Englewood Cliffs, New Jersey, 1974.

Parish, James, and Michael Pitts, *The Great Western Pictures*, Metuchen, New Jersey, 1976.

Henry, Marilyn, and Ron De Sourdis, *The Films of Alan Ladd*, Secaucus, New Jersey, 1981.

Petri, Bruce, *A Theory of American Film: The Films and Techniques of George Stevens*, New York, 1987.

Articles:

Stern, Nina, in *Films in Review* (New York), April 1953.

Luft, H. G., ''George Stevens,'' in *Films in Review* (New York), April 1953.

Time (New York), 13 April 1953.

Martin, B., in *Saturday Evening Post* (Philadelphia), 8 August 1953.

Houston, Penelope, *''Shane* and George Stevens,'' in *Sight and Sound* (London), Fall 1953.

Archer, Eugene, ''George Stevens and the American Dream,'' in *Film Culture* (New York), no. 11, 1957.

Stang, Joanne, ''Hollywood Romantic—A Monograph of George Stevens,'' in *Films and Filming* (New York), July 1959.

Warshow, Robert, ''Movie Chronicle: The Westerner,'' in *The Immediate Experience*, New York, 1962.

Roman, Robert C., ''Alan Ladd,'' in *Films in Review* (New York), April 1964.

Shane

''Viewing Report of *Shane,*'' in *Screen Education* (London), September-October 1964.

McVay, Douglas, ''George Stevens—His Work,'' in *Films and Filming* (London), April 1965 and May 1965.

Silke, James R., in *Cinema* (Beverly Hills), December-January 1965,

Stanbrook, Alan, ''The Return of Shane,'' in *Films and Filming* (London), May 1966.

Vermilye, Jerry, ''Jean Arthur,'' in *Films in Review* (New York), June-July 1966.

''Stevens Issue'' of *Dialogue on Film* (Washington, D.C.), no. 1, 1972.

Albright Jr., Charles, in *Magill's Survey of Cinema 4*, Englewood Cliffs, New Jersey, 1980.

Miller, G., ''*Shane* Redux: *The Shootist* and the Western Dilemma,'' in *Journal of Popular Film and Television* (Washington, D.C.), Summer 1983.

Desser, D., ''Kurosawa's Easternd 'Western','' in *Film Criticism* (Meadville, Pennsylvania), Fall 1983.

Dominicus, M., and S. Daney, in *Skrien* (Amsterdam), November-December 1985.

Zizek, S., ''Looking Awry,'' in *October* (Cambridge, Massachusetts), Fall 1989.

Ronald, A., ''*Shane*'s Pale Ghost,'' in *New Orleans Review*, no. 3, 1990.

Holtsmark, E. B., ''The Katabasis Theme in Modern Cinema,'' in *Bucknell Review*, vol. 35, no. 1, 1991.

Reid's Film Index, no. 12, 1993.

Norman, Barry, in *Radio Times* (London), vol. 279, no. 3648, 4 December 1993.

Berthomieu, Pierre, ''L'homme des vallées perdues: Le passage du cavalier,'' in *Positif* (Paris), no. 397, March 1994.

Flora, J. M., ''*Shane* (Novel and Film) at Century's End,'' in *Journal of American Culture*, vol. 19, no. 1, 1996.

Cieutat, M., '''L'homme des vallees perdues' ou le western retrouve,'' in *Cinemaction* (Conde-sur-Noireau), vol. 86, no. 1, 1998.

Nichols, Peter M., ''Restoring What Time, and Editors, Took Away: Renovated Film Classics Find Their Way Back Onto Big Screens and Video, Often In Version Never Seen Before,'' in *The New York Times*, vol. 147, section 2, AR28, 17 May 1998.

* * *

Narrative films can be generally categorized into those that are motivated by plot and those that are motivated by character. Many

American films are often cited as belonging to the former category, particularly in comparison to some of the European films. *Shane* is pure plot and pure American. The characters, rather than autonomous individuals, are functions of the plot and move through their respective roles with the assurance of legend. They possess no depth or dimension beyond the surface; they are always and exactly what they seem to be. And, ironically, this is their strength and the strength of the film.

The plot of *Shane* is a masterpiece of simplicity. The Indian Wars have been fought and won. The homesteaders have settled in to farm the land, threatening the open range of the ranchers. The law is a three-day ride from the community, and the tenuous co-existence waits for eruption into ''gunsmoke.'' The ranchers, led by the Ryker brothers, try to intimidate the homesteaders in an effort to force them out of the valley, but the homesteaders are held together by the determination of a single man, Joe Starrett, who wants to build a life on the land for his wife Marion and young son Joey. Into this tension rides Shane, a stranger who is befriended by the Starretts. A gunfighter by profession, Shane tries to renounce his former trade and join the community of homesteaders. As the tension increases, another gunfighter is recruited to bait and kill the helpless homesteaders. When Starrett is left with no alternative but to meet the hired gunfighter, it is obvious that only Shane is a match for the final shootout. He overpowers Starrett and rides into town where he kills the gunman and the Rykers. Now that the valley is safe, Shane bids farewell to Joey and rides off into the distant mountains.

Of all American genres, the Western is arguably the most durable. The Western has tended to document not the history of the West but those cultural values that have become cherished foundations of our national identity. The Western certifies our ideals of individualism, initiative, independence, persistence and dignity. It also displays some of our less admirable traits of lawlessness, violence and racism. Possibly more than any previous American film, *Shane* tries to encapsulate the cultural ethos of the Western.

Rather than avoiding the clichés, platitudes and stereotypes of the genre, *Shane* pursues and embraces them. With the exception of a saloon girl and an Indian attack, all of the ingredients of the typical Western are present: the wide open spaces, the ranchers feuding with the farmers, the homesteading family trying to build a life, the rival gunman, the absence of law, the survival of the fastest gun, even the mandatory shoulder wound. Embodying as it does the look and feel of the Western, *Shane* becomes an essential rarity; it not only preserves but honors our belief in our heritage.

As myth, it is appropriate that *Shane* is seen through the eyes of a small boy. Joey is the first to see Shane ride into the community, more than the others he perceives the inner strength of the man, and he's the only one to bid Shane farewell as he leaves the valley. As both the child's idolization of an adult and the creative treatment of a myth, *Shane* is not a story of the West; it is, rather, *the* West as we believe it to have been.

Everything in the film favors its treatment of the myth. Alan Ladd—with his golden hair, his soft voice, his modest manner—is more the Olympian god than the rugged frontiersman or the outcast gunfighter. He rides down from the distant mountains and into lives of a settlement in need of his special talents. A stranger who doesn't belong and can never be accepted, he is a man without a past and without a future. He exists only for the moment of confrontation; and once that moment has passed, he has no place in the community. Even the way in which his movements are choreographed and photographed seem mythic—when riding into town for the final shootout, for example, the low angle tracking of the camera, the gait of his horse, the pulsing of the music with its heroic, lonely tones and the vast, panoramic landscapes all contribute to the classical dimensions of the film.

Shane is the generic loner who belongs to no one and no place. He possesses capability, integrity, restraint; yet there is a sense of despair and tragedy about him. Shane is that most characteristic of American anachronisms, the man who exists on the fringe of an advancing civilization. His background and profession place him on the periphery of law and society. The same skills as a warrior that make him essential to the survival of the community also make him suspect and even dangerous to that same community. In the tradition of William S. Hart, Tom Mix, John Wayne and Clint Eastwood, Shane is the embodiment of the Western hero.

Shane is a reluctant mediator. There is a moral guilt about his profession that he carries with him as clearly as his buckskins. He wants to lay aside the violence of his past, but like the Greek heroes, of which he is kin, fate will not allow him to alter what is destined for him. Although he conspicuously tries to avoid the kind of confrontations he is best prepared to face, he suffers humiliation in doing so which is mistaken for cowardice. Once again he must prove himself, as if serving as the defender of those weaker will atone for his past and his profession. Consequently, a paradox emerges; he is both necessary and a threat to the survival of the community. In the Starrett family, for example, he begins to be more important to Joey than his father and more attractive to Marion than her husband. If the community is to grow and prosper, it must do so without him. Once he has served his function, he has no place and must again move on.

Shane is a tapestry laced with contrasts. The gun and the ax, the horse and the land, the buckskins and the denims, the loner and the family. In the end, the ax (peace) replaces the gun (violence), the land (stability) replaces the horse (transience), the denims (work) replace the buckskins (wilderness), the family (future) replaces the loner (past).

The unheralded mythic god leaves and the community is safe. Good has triumphed over evil, the family has been preserved, all the guns have been silenced. And yet there is a sense of loss. We have admired and appreciated Shane, but he exists for a single purpose and a single moment. When he has departed, we know we're safer and better for his presence; but we also know that we are again vulnerable.

—Stephen E. Bowles

SHE DONE HIM WRONG

USA, 1933

Director: Lowell Sherman

Production: Paramount Pictures; black and white, 35mm; running time: 65 minutes. Released 1933. Filmed in Paramount studios.

Producer: William LeBaron; **screenplay:** Mae West with Harvey Thew and John Bright (some sources do not list West with script

She Done Him Wrong

credit), from the play *Diamond Lil* by Mae West; **photography:** Charles Lang; **music and lyrics:** Ralph Rainger.

Cast: Mae West (*Lady Lou*); Cary Grant (*Captain Cummings*); Gilbert Roland (*Serge Stanieff*); Noah Beery, Sr. (*Gus Jordan*); Rafaela Ottiano (*Russian Rita*); David Landau (*Dan Flynn*); Rochelle Hudson (*Sally*); Owen Moore (*Chick Clark*); Fuzzy Knight (*Rag-Time Kelly*); Tammany Young (*Chuck Connors*); Dewey Robinson (*Spider Kane*); Grace La Rue (*Frances*).

Publications

Books:

Baxter, John, *Hollywood in the Thirties*, Cranbury, New Jersey, 1968.
West, Mae, *Goodness Had Nothing to Do with It*, New York, 1970.
Deschner, Donald, *The Films of Cary Grant*, New York, 1971.
Moley, Raymond, *The Hays Office*, New York, 1971.
Mellen, Joan, *Women and Sexuality in the New Film*, New York, 1973.
Tuska, Jon, *The Films of Mae West*, Secaucus, New Jersey, 1973.
Vermilye, Jerry, *Cary Grant*, New York, 1973.
Cashin, Fergus, *Mae West: A Biography*, London, 1981.
Eells, George, and Stanley Musgrove, *Mae West*, New York, 1982.
Britton, Andrew, *Cary Grant: Comedy and Male Desire*, Newcastle upon Tyne, 1983.
Schickel, Richard, *Cary Grant: A Celebration*, London, 1983.
Chandler, Charlotte, *The Ultimate Seduction*, New York, 1984.
Dupuis, Jean-Jacques, *Cary Grant*, Paris, 1984.
Ashman, Chuck, and Pamela Trescott, *Cary Grant*, London, 1986.
Higham, Charles, and Ray Moseley, *Cary Grant: The Lonely Heart*, New York, 1989.
Buehrer, Beverley Bare, *Cary Grant: A Bio-Bibliography*, New York, 1990.
Wansell, Geoffrey, *Haunted Idol: The Story of the Real Cary Grant*, New York, 1992.
Hamilton, Marybeth, *When I'm Bad, I'm Better: Mae West, Sex, and American Entertainment*, Berkeley, 1995, 1997.
McCann, Graham, *Cary Grant: A Class Apart*, New York, 1996.
Wansell, Geoffrey, *Cary Grant: Dark Angel*, New York, 1996.

Articles:

New York Times, 10 February 1933.
Variety (New York), 14 February 1933.
New Yorker, 18 February 1933.
''Mae West'' in *Vanity Fair* (New York), March 1933.
Troy, William, ''Mae West and the Classic Tradition,'' in *Nation* (New York), 8 November 1933.
Roman, Robert, ''Cary Grant,'' in *Films in Review* (New York), December 1961.
Bowser, Eileen, and Richard Griffith, in *Film Notes*, edited by Eileen Bowser, New York, 1969.
Braun, Eric, ''Doing What Comes Naturally,'' in *Films and Filming* (London), October and November 1970.
Raines, Elaine, in *Magill's Survey of Cinema 4*, Englewood Cliffs, New Jersey, 1980.
Deffaa, Chip, in *Entertainment Weekly*, no. 183, 13 August 1993.

* * *

Given the variety and richness of Hollywood in the 1930s and 1940s—the decades now called the classical period of American film—it is difficult to claim that any stretch of time belonged to any star, director, or studio. Still, it is tempting to proclaim the years from 1932 to 1934 as the age of Mae West.

From her movie debut in *Night after Night* (in a small part: the studios were not sure how the movie public would take to the woman whose contempt for all proprieties and censors was so manifest), Mae West asserted her force as a screen presence. However, it was not until her second film, *She Done Him Wrong*, that the audience could appreciate the range of West's appeal. Based on one of West's most celebrated stage vehicles, *Diamond Lil*, the film showed us a woman of uncanny sensitivity to verbal sex-play (she was responsible for transcribing the lines she wrote for herself in *Diamond Lil* to the screen); a woman whose self-assurance was matched only by her capacity for self-caricature; a woman who would give ground to no mere male; a woman who calmly overturned all the principles of what we now call sexism; and a woman with a voice like none other heard in the movies.

There is no overestimating the last of these characteristics. With the death of silent film, individuality of vocal inflection assumed paramount importance; with the demise specifically of silent comedy, the human voice substituted for some of the comic uniqueness implicit in the bodies of Chaplin, Keaton and the others. (Significantly, when Chaplin at last gave in to speaking on the screen, a new visual presence had to be devised.) The stage, radio and vaudeville comedians, for a while at least, could provide what was needed, but no one with more dazzling public success than Mae West. There could be no separation of her dialogue from her voice. Her popularity was for a time so enormous that the movie censors waited to put her in her place, or rather the place the censors thought she ought to occupy. Eventually the censors had their way: with the advent of the Breen Office in 1934, Mae West was fated to become a rather bowdlerized memory of the star of *She Done him Wrong* and *I'm No Angel*.

The woman was indomitable; she continued making films through the 1930s and early 1940s. In the final years of her life, she made atrocities such as *Myra Breckinridge* and *Sextette*. Even in the later 1930s, however, few of the pleasures of *She Done Him Wrong* and *I'm No Angel* were to be duplicated.

Aside from West herself, *She Done Him Wrong* is notable for West's ''discovery'' of Cary Grant (he had actually appeared in several earlier movies). Grant manages to make himself noticed despite his relative inexperience, despite his function as a foil for Mae West, and despite the fact that he has to impersonate a policeman impersonating a Salvation Army officer. And in the course of its preposterous little plot, involving such unlikely comic topics as white slavery, the film somehow manages to come up with a villainess called ''Russian Rita.'' The real lure is, of course, Mae West, the woman who could make America howl by introducing herself as one of the finest women who ever walked the streets.

—Elliot Rubenstein

SHERLOCK, JR.

USA, 1924

Director: Buster Keaton

Production: Metro Pictures and Buster Keaton Productions; black and white, 35mm, silent; running time: about 45 minutes. Released April 1924.

Producer: Joseph M. Schenck; **scenario:** Clyde Bruckman, Jean Haves, and Joseph Mitchell; **photography:** Elgin Lessley and Bryon Houck; **editor:** Buster Keaton; **art director:** Fred Gabourie; **costumes:** Clare West.

Cast: Buster Keaton (*The Projectionist*); Kathryn McGuire (*The Girl*); Ward Crane (*The Rival*); Joseph Keaton (*The Father*).

Publications

Books:

Keaton, Buster, with Charles Samuels, *My Wonderful World of Slapstick*, New York, 1960.
Pantieri, José, *L'originalissimo Buster Keaton*, Milan, 1963.
Turconi, Davide, and Francesco Savio, *Buster Keaton*, Venice, 1963.
Oms, Marcel, *Buster Keaton*, Lyons, 1964.
Coursodon, Jean-Pierre, *Keaton et compagnie: Les Burlesques américaines du ''muet,''* Paris, 1964.
Blesh, Rudi, *Keaton*, New York, 1966.
Lebel, Jean-Pierre, *Buster Keaton*, New York, 1967.
McCaffrey, Donald, *Great Comedians*, New York, 1968.

Sherlock, Jr.

Robinson, David, *Buster Keaton*, London, 1968.

Anthologie du cinéma 7, Paris, 1971.

Mast, Gerald, *The Comic Mind*, New York, 1973; revised edition, Chicago, 1979.

Coursodon, Jean-Pierre, *Buster Keaton*, Paris, 1973; revised edition, 1986.

Kerr, Walter, *The Silent Clowns*, New York, 1975.

Anobile, Richard, editor, *The Best of Buster*, New York, 1976.

Wead, George, *Buster Keaton and the Dynamics of Visual Wit*, New York, 1976.

Moews, Daniel, *Keaton: The Silent Features Close Up*, Berkeley, 1977.

Wead, George, and George Ellis, *The Film Career of Buster Keaton*, Boston, 1977.

Dardis, Tom, *Keaton: The Man Who Wouldn't Lie Down*, New York, 1979.

Benayoun, Robert, *The Look of Buster Keaton*, Paris, 1982; London, 1984.

Eberwein, Robert T., *Film and the Dream Screen: A Sleep and a Forgetting*, Princeton, 1984.

Kline, Jim, *The Complete Films of Buster Keaton*, Secaucus, 1993.

Brunovska Karnick, Kristine, and Henry Jenkins, editors, *Classical Hollywood Comedy*, New York, 1995.

Mead, Marion, *Buster Keaton: Cut to the Chase*, New York, 1995.

Oldham, Gabriella, *Keaton's Silent Shorts: Beyond the Laughter*, Carbondale, 1996.

Knopf, Robert, *The Theater and Cinema of Buster Keaton*, Princeton, 1999.

Bengtson, John, *Silent Echoes: Discovering Early Hollywood through the Films of Buster Keaton*, Santa Monica, 2000.

Articles:

New York Times, 26 May 1924.

Variety (New York), 28 May 1924.

Life (New York), 19 June 1924.

Agee, James, ''Comedy's Greatest Era,'' in *Agee on Film*, New York, 1958.

''Keaton Issue'' of *Cahiers du Cinéma* (Paris), August 1958.

Bishop, Christopher, ''The Great Stone Face,'' in *Film Quarterly* (Berkeley), Fall 1958.

Baxter, Brian, ''Buster Keaton,'' in *Film* (London), November-December 1958.

Leuwen, Jean-Marc, ''Buster Keaton,'' in *Cinéma* (Paris), August-September 1960.

Blue, James, and John Gillett, ''Keaton at Venice,'' in *Sight and Sound* (London), Winter 1965–66.

Sadoul, Georges, ''Le Génie de Buster Keaton,'' in *Lettres Françaises* (Paris), 10 February 1966.

Benayoun, Robert, ''Le Regard de Buster Keaton,'' in *Positif* (Paris), Summer 1966.

Villelaur, Anne, ''Buster Keaton,'' in *Dossiers du Cinéma: Cinéastes 1* (Paris), 1971.

Lindberg, I., in *Kosmorama* (Copenhagen), March 1973.

Pasquier, Sylvain de, ''Buster Keaton's Gags,'' in *Journal of Modern Literature* (Philadelphia), April 1973.

Pratt, George, ''Anything Can Happen—And Generally Did! Buster Keaton on His Silent Film Career,'' in *Image* (Rochester), December 1974.

Lefèvre, Raymond, ''Sherlock Junior: Le Forcené de l'intelligence,'' in *Cinéma* (Paris), September-October 1975.

Beylie, Claude, in *Ecran* (Paris), October 1975.

Sauvaget, D., in *Revue du Cinéma* (Paris), October 1976.

Eberwein, Robert T., ''The Filmic Dream and Point of View,'' in *Literature/Film Quarterly* (Salisbury, Maryland), no. 3, 1980.

Valot, J., ''Discours sur le cinéma dans quelques films de Buster Keaton,'' in *Image et Son* (Paris), February 1980.

Magill's Survey of Cinema: Silent Films, Englewood Cliffs, New Jersey, 1982.

''Buster Keaton,'' in *Film Dope* (London), March 1984.

Cazals, Thierry, ''Un Monde à la démesure de l'homme,'' in *Cahiers du Cinéma* (Paris), March 1987.

Sweeney, K. W., ''The Dream of Disruption: Melodrama and Gag Structure in Keaton's *Sherlock Junior*,'' in *Wide Angle* (Baltimore), no. 1, 1991.

Pernod, P., ''L'odyssée des espaces Keatoniens,'' in *Positif* (Paris), September 1991.

Télérama (Paris), no. 2374, 12 July 1995.

D'Elia, Joseph, ''*Sherlock, Jr. / Our Hospitality*,'' in *Library Journal*, vol. 121, no. 13, August 1996.

Rommetveit, I., ''Buster Keaton's *Sherlock Jr.*,'' in *Z Filmtidsskrift* (Oslo), vol. 1, no. 55, 1996.

* * *

Although he had been popular with critics and the public for several years, Buster Keaton became a major star with *The Navigator*, released after *Sherlock, Jr.* Nevertheless, *Sherlock, Jr.* is a masterpiece. It contains a story within a story, through which Keaton deals with opposition central to Western culture: dream versus reality, and reality versus art.

The film starts routinely. Beginning the dream/reality opposition, we learn that Keaton yearns to be a detective, but works merely as a projectionist. The action of the story is instigated by the announcement of a missing object. The watch belonging to the father of Keaton's girlfriend has been stolen, and as Keaton is the prime suspect, the father expels him from the house. Developing a narrative around the absence (the watch) and an expulsion of the hero is much like nineteenth-century melodrama. Even in comedies, though, this structure is not extraordinary.

After Keaton's expulsion, the film takes on a less traditional structure. Keaton falls asleep on the job. In a dream, he looks out the projectionist's window, and sees his girlfriend, her father, and his rival as performers in a film. Though the dream mirrors ''real life,'' there are some significant changes. The setting is aristocratic, and instead of a watch, a necklace is missing. The biggest change is with Keaton himself. Awake he is only an aspiring investigator with little Holmesian ability, but once he enters the story of the film within the film, he becomes a master detective.

After the dream begins, *Sherlock, Jr.* takes on characteristics of an avant-garde film. The projectionist walks to the screen, and tries to become part of the film. Like a film spectator suspending disbelief, Keaton is fooled by the realistic effect of the cinema, so much so that he cannot separate life from the movies. However, unlike the ordinary spectator, Keaton is able to participate in the film he watches. This, however, has its hazards. As he is about to enter a house, the scene cuts to an African veldt where Keaton confronts a lion. Another cut places Keaton in a snowbank; with another he is transported to the ocean. Upon entering the film within the film, the projectionist believed he would be taking part in a narrative as neat and linear as his real life one. Instead, he is at the mercy of the most artificial of cinematic devices, the cut, which allows for instant changes of locale, or the ellision of large chunks of time.

A normal story eventually returns, and Keaton (the detective) solves the mystery. A normal visual style returns, too. During the quick-cutting sequence, the movie screen, the curtain around it, and the theater audience were visible in the frame. Once the detective story begins, however, the camera moves in, no longer showing any of the theater or the edges around the screen. The film within the film (Keaton's dream) comes to look just like the character's ''real life'' (the beginning, when Keaton works as a projectionist). Thus, art seems to imitate life.

When Keaton awakes, his girlfriend visits him in the projectionist's booth, and tells him he has been absolved of all guilt in the watch theft. Keaton looks at the film he has been showing, and sees a man and woman reconciling. He watches for instructions, doing everything the man does, kissing his girlfriend only after the man and woman have kissed on the screen. Here, in a final blurring of the two, life imitates art.

—Eric Smoodin

SHICHININ NO SAMURAI

(The Seven Samurai)

Japan, 1954

Director: Akira Kurosawa

Production: Toho Productions (Tokyo); black and white, 35mm; running time: original version: 203 minutes, international version:

Shichinin no samurai

160 minutes (no copies of longer print extant); length: original version: 5,480 meters, international version: 4,401 meters. Released 26 April 1954, Tokyo. Re-released 1982.

Producer: Shojiro Motoki; **screenplay:** Shinobu Hashimoto, Hideo Oguni, and Akira Kurosawa; **photography:** Asakasu Nakai; **sound engineer:** Fumio Yanoguchi; **art director:** So Matsuyama; **music:** Famio Hayasaka; **coordinator of wrestling and sword stunts:** Yoshio Sugino; **archery masters:** Ienori Kaneko and Shigeru Endo.

Cast: The Samurai: Takashi Shimura (*Kambei, the leader*); Toshiro Mifune (*Kikuchiyo*); Yoshio Inaba (*Gorobei*); Seiji Miyaguchi (*Kyuzo*); Minoru Chiaki (*Heihachi*); Daisuke Kato (*Shichiroji*); Isao (*Ko*) Kimura (*Katsuchiro*); The Peasants: Kuninori Kodo (*Gisaku, the old man*); Kamatari Fujiwara (*Manzo*); Yoshio Tsuchiya (*Rikichi*); Bokusen Hidari (*Yohei*); Yoshio Kosugi (*Mosuke*); Keiji Sakakida (*Gosaku*); Jiro Kumagai, Haruko Toyama, Tsuneo Katagiri, and Yasuhisa Tsutsumi (*Peasants and farmers*); Keiko Tsushima (*Shino, son of Manzo*); Toranosuke Ogawa (*Grandfather*); Noriko Sengoku (*Wife from burned house*); Yu Akitsu (*Husband from burned house*); Gen Shimizu (*Small master*); Jun Tasaki and Isao Yamagata (*Other samurais*); Jun Tatari (*Laborer*); Atsushi Watanabe (*Guardian of the stable*); Yukiko Shimazaki (*Rikichi's woman*); Sojin Kamiyama (*Singer*); Eijiro Igashino (*Bandit chief*).

Award: Venice Film Festival, Silver Prize, 1954.

Publications

Script:

Kurosawa, Akira, Shinobu Hashimoto, and Hideo Oguni, *The Seven Samurai*, New York, 1970.

Books:

Anderson, Joseph, and Donald Richie, *The Japanese Film: Art and Industry*, Rutland, Vermont, 1960; revised edition, Princeton, 1982.
Ezratti, Sacha, *Kurosawa*, Paris, 1964.

Sato, Tadao, *Kurosawa Akira no Sekai* (The World of Akira Kurosawa), Tokyo, 1968.
Richie, Donald, *The Films of Akira Kurosawa*, Berkeley, 1970; revised edition, 1996.
Richie, Donald, *Japanese Cinema: Film Style and National Character*, New York, 1971.
Mesnil, Michel, *Kurosawa*, Paris, 1973.
Mellen, Joan, *The Waves at Genji's Door: Japan Through Its Cinema*, New York, 1976.
Bock, Audie, *Japanese Film Directors*, New York, 1978; revised edition, Tokyo, 1985.
Erens, Patricia, *Akira Kurosawa: A Guide to References and Resources*, Boston, 1979.
Bazin, André, *The Cinema of Cruelty: From Bunuel to Hitchcock*, New York, 1982.
Kurosawa, Akira, *Something Like an Autobiography*, New York, 1982.
Sato, Tadao, *Currents in Japanese Cinema*, Tokyo, 1982.
Desser, David, *The Samurai Films of Akira Kurosawa*, Ann Arbor, Michigan, 1983.
Tassone, Aldo, *Akira Kurosawa*, Paris, 1983.
Chang, Kevin K.W., editor, *Kurosawa: Perceptions on Life: An Anthology of Essays*, Honolulu, 1991.
Prince, Stephen, *The Warrior's Camera: The Cinema of Akira Kurosawa*, Princeton, 1991; revised and expanded edition, 1999.
Goodwin, James, *Akira Kurosawa and Intertextual Cinema*, Baltimore, 1994.
Goodwin, James, editor, *Perspectives on Akira Kurosawa*, New York, 1994.
Yoshimoto, Mitsuhiro, *Kurosawa: Film Studies and Japanese Cinema*, Durham, 2000.

Articles:

Leyda, Jay, ''The Films of Kurosawa,'' in *Sight and Sound* (London), Fall 1954.
Richard, Tony, in *Sight and Sound* (London) Spring 1955.
Barnes, Peter, in *Films and Filming* (London), April 1955.
Leyda, Jay, in *Film Culture* (New York), no. 4, 1956.
Crowther, Bosley, in *New York Times*, 20 November 1956.
Hines, T. S., in *Films in Review* (New York), December 1956.
Knight, Arthur, in *Saturday Review* (New York), 1 December 1956.
McCarten, John, in *New Yorker*, 1 December 1956.
Hartung, Philip T., in *Commonweal* (New York), 14 December 1956.
Life (New York), 14 January 1957.
Gaffary, F., in *Positif* (Paris), March 1957.
McVay, Douglas, ''Samurai and Small Beer,'' in *Films and Filming* (London), August 1961.
Anderson, Joseph, ''When the Twain Meet: Hollywood's Remake of *Seven Samurai*,'' in *Film Quarterly* (Berkeley), Spring 1962.
Iwasaki, Akira, ''Kurosawa and His Work,'' in *Japan Quarterly* (Tokyo), 1965.
''*Les Sept Samourais* Issue'' of *Avant-Scène du Cinéma* (Paris), April 1971.
Kaminsky, Stuart, ''The Samurai Film and the Western,'' in *Journal of Popular Film* (Washington, DC), Fall 1972.
Tucker, Richard, ''Kurosawa and Ichikawa: Feudalist and Individualist,'' in *Japan, Film Image*, London, 1973.
Silver, Alain, in *Film Comment* (New York), September-October 1975.
Nolley, K., ''The Western as Jidai-geki,'' in *Western American Literature* (Logan, Utah), no. 3, 1976.
Kaplan, F., in *Cineaste* (New York), no. 1, 1979–80.
Hosman, H., in *Skoop* (Amsterdam), August 1980.
Carbonnier, A., in *Cinéma* (Paris), February 1981.
Ramasse, F., in *Positif* (Paris), February 1981.
Cardullo, B., ''The Circumstance of the East, the Fate of the West: Notes, Mostly on the Seven Samurai,'' in *Literature/Film Quarterly* (Salisbury, Maryland), April 1985.
Tucker, G. M., in *Soundtrack* (Los Angeles), June 1985.
Amengual, Barthélemy, in *Positif* (Paris), October 1985.
Parshall, P. F., ''East Meets West: *Casablanca* vs. *The Seven Samurai*,'' in *Literature/Film Quarterly* (Salisbury, Maryland), no. 4, 1989.
Moskowitz, G., ''Action Movie with Art,'' in *Variety* (New York), vol. 349, 9 November 1992.
Crowdus, Gary, ''*Seven Samurai*,'' in *Cineaste* (New York), vol. 19, no. 4, 1993.
Lord, S., in *Metro Magazine* (St. Kilda West), no. 113/114, 1998.
''Toshiro Mifune,'' in *Variety* (New York), vol. 369, no. 8, 5 January 1998.
Hogue, Peter, ''The Kurosawa Story,'' in *Film Comment* (New York), vol. 35, no. 1, January 1999.

* * *

From its opening shot of silhouetted horsemen galloping across a horizon line, *The Seven Samurai* announces its sources. The setting may be a 16th-century Japan convulsed by civil war, but those wide-open, lawless spaces are immediately recognizable as those of the Hollywood West.

Kurosawa has made no secret of his debt to the Western in general and John Ford in particular: the small farming village of *The Seven Samurai*, nestled between mountain and plain, might be the Tombstone of *My Darling Clementine*. The marauding brigands who wait in the woods could be the vicious Clantons of Ford's film, and the seven samurai hired by the villagers for their defense could be the band of deputies, saloon girls, and alcoholic hangers-on assembled by Henry Fonda's Wyatt Earp. There is, no doubt, a broad and general resemblance between the American Western and the Japanese samurai film—in terms of the themes both genres treat, and in the historical setting they choose for their work—but in *The Seven Samurai* the correspondences are strict and specific. We recognize the rules of the game that Kurosawa is playing in *The Seven Samurai*, where in a more arcanely Japanese samurai film such as Hideo Gosha's *Bandits vs. Samurai Squadron*, we do not.

Like Ford in his Westerns, Kurosawa organizes the action of *The Seven Samurai* around three different elements: the civilized (the villagers), the savage (the brigands), and those who live in between (Ford's soldiers and lawmen, Kurosawa's samurai), defending civilization by savage, violent means. (This three-point, triangular structure is something personal to Kurosawa; it pops up in different contexts throughout his work, most decisively in *Kagemusha*.) By placing his samurai in the same mediating position as Ford's lawmen, Kurosawa is self-consciously breaking with the traditions of the genre, in which the samurai represent civilization at its most refined, entrenched, and aristocratic. The heroes of Kurosawa's films are masterless samurai, no longer attached to a royal house (and hence no longer entitled to be called samurai—masterless samurai are called *ronin*). Both Ford's lawmen and Kurosawa's samurai are profoundly marginal figures, prevented from fully entering society by the possession of the same skills they must employ upholding it. But where Ford in his middle-period films searches constantly for the ways to reintegrate the lawmen in to society (before resolving, in his late work, that such a reconciliation is impossible), Kurosawa in *The Seven Samurai* emphasizes the unbridgeable differences between the villagers and their hired defenders. Though the townspeople and the samurai can fight in temporary alliance, they can never fight for the same goals: the villagers fight for home and family, the samurai for professional honor. The only society allowed to the samurai is their own; if civilization has no place for them, they must make a place of their own. The formation of the samurai's separate, self-enclosed society—the professional group—is the subject of some of the finest passages in Kurosawa's film: once a suitable father has been found, in the form of the veteran warrior Kambei, the other members of the family fall into place, down to a wifely companion for Kambei (Shichiroji, an old comrade-in-arms), a dutiful son (the apprentice Katsushiro), and a black sheep (Kikuchiyo). The remaining samurai are distributed like the Three Graces—Wisdom (Gorobei), Skill (Kyuzo), and Hope (Heihachi). As schematic as this arrangement may sound, Kurosawa never lets it solidify; there is no flat sense of allegory here, but rather an open vision of different talents and attributes brought into harmony. To distinguish between the members of the group, Kurosawa gives each a defining gesture, much as Walt Disney differentiated his seven dwarfs: Kambei's reflective rubbing of his scalp, Kikuchiyo's leaps and whoops, Katsushiro's imploring eyes, etc. This, too, is classic Hollywood shorthand technique, in which a ritual gesture completely subsumes a character's psychology. And there is a pleasure in its repetition: each time Kambei scratches his head, he is reassuring the strength and constancy of his character. The gesture never changes, and neither does he. He is permanent, and in this one movement we know him and trust him.

At least one-quarter of *The Seven Samurai* is devoted to the relations between the townspeople and the professional group. Kurosawa seems to be looking for a stable, workable relationship, but he rejects each possibility in turn; there is always a dissonance, a contradiction, between the two groups. The samurai take charge of fortifying the village and training the farmers to fight, yet because they are, in the end, mere employees of the villagers, they are never in a position of genuine authority. The samurai tell themselves that they are fighting on behalf of the poor and helpless, but the cozy paternalism of this relationship is undermined by the suggestion that the farmers have been holding out—that they have secret reserves of rice and sake they refuse to share with their protectors. Two of the samurai have ties to the villagers—Katsushiro, who falls in love with a village girl, and Kikuchiyo, who is revealed to be a farmer's son—yet neither of these bonds is allowed to endure. By insisting so strongly on the absolute separation of the groups, Kurosawa departs radically from the Western archetype: the lawmen can no longer derive their values from the community, as they did in Ford and Hawks, but must now define those values for themselves. This sense of moral isolation—fresh and startling in the genre context of 1954—eventually became Kurosawa's gift to the American Western, his way of giving back as much as he took. Even before *The Seven Samurai* was officially remade as a Western (John Sturges's 1960 *The Magnificent Seven*), Kurosawa's variation had been incorporated in the genre, giving rise to the series of ''professional'' Westerns that runs from Hawks's optimistic *Rio Bravo* to the final cynicism of Sergio Leone.

Separation is also the subject of Kurosawa's mise-en-scène. Using both foregound-background separation of deep-focus shots and the flattening, abstracting effect of telephoto lenses, Kurosawa puts a sense of unbridgeable space in nearly all of his shots. Even in what should be the most intimate and open scenes among the samurai themselves, Kurosawa arranges his compositions in distinct rigid planes, placing one or two figures in the extreme foreground, two or three more in a row in the middle, the balances lined up in the background (this will also be the design applied to the burial mound at the film's conclusion). The primary visual motif is one of boundaries: the natural ones formed around the village by the mountains, woods, and flooded rice fields, the manmade boundaries of fences, stockades, and doorways. The extreme formality of Kurosawa's compositions also emphasizes the boundaries of the frame; there is only occasionally a sense of off-screen space, as if nothing existed beyond the limits of the camera's eye. The world of *The Seven Samurai* is carefully delineated, compartmentalized; not only are the characters isolated in their separate groups, but in separate spaces.

The compartmentalization reflects Kurosawa's theme, but it also works (more originally, I think) in organizing the film emotionally—in building its suspense and narrative power. Three hours pass between the announcement of the brigands' attack and its arrival—an impossibly long time to keep the audience waiting for a single event. But where most filmmakers would try to fill the interval with minor flurries of action, Kurosawa gives us only two: Kambei's rescue of a child and the guerilla foray into the brigands' camp. These incidents are so widely spaced (misplaced, even, in terms of conventional rhythm) that they don't serve at all to support the structure of crest and valley, crest and valley that the long form usually depends on. Instead, Kurosawa sticks to a strict linearity: the narrative has been divided (compartmentalized?) into discrete acts (the posing of the threat, the recruitment of the samurai, the fortification of the village, the battle), separated not by strongly marked climaxes but by the slow and subtle transitions. The rigorous chopping, dividing, and underlining of space is the only constant factor through these transitions: no matter what the characters may be doing, the visual style is bearing down on them, forcing them further into immobility, isolation, entrapment. The suspense builds visually, subliminally, until we long for the final battle with its promise of release.

The battle in the rain is the most celebrated passage in Kurosawa's work, justly famous for its overwhelming physicality—the sense of force and texture, of sensual immersion, produced by staging the sequence in the mud and confusion of a fierce storm. But the rain also accomplishes something else—it fills in the spaces that Kurosawa has so carefully carved off, creating a continuity, an even density, from foreground to background. The rain begins the night before the battle, during the greatest moment of divisiveness between the townspeople and the samurai—the confrontation over Kikuchiyo's right to love a village girl. By forcing the two groups to fight more closely together, the rain closes this gap during the battle. And suddenly, all other boundaries are broken open: as part of their strategy, the samurai allow some of the brigands to cross the fortifications (cut off from support, they can be killed more easily in the village square) and the camera loses its fixity and formality, panning wildly to follow details of action within the struggle. It is an ineffable moment of freedom, and of course it cannot last.

For his epilogue, Kurosawa returns to divided space. The surviving samurai are seen in one shot, standing still before the graves of those who fell; the villagers are seen in another, singing and moving in unison as they plant the new rice crop. There probably isn't a more plangent moment in all Kurosawa's work than this juxtaposition of two different tempos, two different worlds. They are separated only by a cut, but they are separated forever.

—Dave Kehr

SHOAH

France, 1985

Director: Claude Lanzmann

Production: Les Films Aleph-Historia Films, with assistance from the Ministry of Culture; Fuji-color; in two parts; running time, part 1: 274 minutes, part 2: 292 minutes; length, part 1: 24,660 feet, part 2: 26,280 feet. Released May 1985.

Production administrator: Raymonde Bade-Mauffroy; **production managers:** Stella Gregorz-Quef, Severine Olivier-Lacamp; **photography:** Dominique Chapuis, Jimmy Glasberg, William Lubchansky; **assistant photographers:** Caroline Champetier de Ribes, Jean-Yves Escoffier, Slavek Olczyk, Andres Silvart; **editors:** Ziva Postec, Anna Ruiz; **sound editors:** Danielle Fillios, Ann-Marie L'Hote, Sabine Mamou; **sound recordists:** Bernard Aubouy, Michel Vionnet; **sound re-recordist:** Bernard Aubouy; **research assistants:** Corinna Coulmas, Irene Steinfeldt-Levi, Shalmi Bar Mor; **interpreters:** Barbara Janica, Francine Kaufman, Mrs. Apfelbaum; **subtitles:** A. Whitelaw, W. Byron.

Award: Recipient of the Robert Flaherty Documentary Award, BAFTA, 1986.

Publications

Books:

Lanzmann, Claude, *Shoah: An Oral History of the Holocaust*, New York, 1985.

David, Jonathan, Riva Krut, and Jeremy Schonfield, editors, *Film History, and the Jewish Experience: A Reader*, London, 1986.

Cuau, Bernard, *Au sujet de Shoah: le film de Claude Lanzmann*, Paris, 1990.

Hazan, Barbara, *Shoah: le film*, Paris, 1990.

Forges, Jean-François, *Eduquer contre Auschwitz*, Paris, 1997.

Articles:

Variety (New York), 15 May 1985.

Osmalin, P., in *Cinéma* (Paris), June 1985.

Chevrie, M., and Hervé Le Roux, in *Cahiers du Cinéma* (Paris), July-August 1985.

Kieffer, A., in *Jeune Cinéma* (Paris), July-August 1985.

Marienstras, E., in *Positif* (Paris), July-August 1985.

Ophuls, Marcel, ''Closely Watched Trains,'' in *American Film* (Washington, DC), November 1985.

Film (Frankfurt), February 1986.

Film (Warsaw), 16 February 1986.

Film Français (Paris), 21 February 1986.

Luft, H., in *Films in Review* (New York), May 1986.

Rubenstein, Lenny, in *Cineaste* (New York), vol. 14, no. 3, 1986.

Erens, Patricia, in *Film Quarterly* (Berkeley), Summer 1986.

Pym, John, in *Sight and Sound* (London), Summer 1986.

Interview with Lanzmann, in *Time Out* (London), 12 November 1986.

Interview with Lanzmann, in *City Limits* (London), 13 November 1986.

Sweet, Louise, in *Monthly Film Bulletin* (London), March 1987.

Listener (London), 15 and 22 October 1987.

Sandor, T., in *Filmkultura* (Budapest), no. 1, 1990.

Williams, L., ''Mirrors without Memories: Truth, History, and the New Documentary,'' in *Film Quarterly* (Berkeley), no. 3, 1993.

Suranyi, V. and F. Eros, ''A megsemmisites metaforai,'' in *Filmkultura* (Budapest), February 1993.

Louvish, Simon, and Philip Strick, ''*Witness/ Schindler's List*,'' in *Sight & Sound* (London), vol. 4, no. 3, March 1994.

Roy, L, ''L'infatigable image ou les horizons du temps au cinema,'' in *Cinemas*, vol. 5, no. 1/2, 1994.

Slaving, J., ''The Butterflies in the Bonfire: The Holocaust as Art, Part Two,'' in *Metro Magazine* (St. Kilda West), vol. 99, Summer 1994.

Hartman, G., ''The Cinema Animal: On Spielberg's *Schindler's List*,'' in *Salamagundi*, no. 106/107, Spring/Summer 1995.

Hansen, M.B., ''*Schindler's List* Is Not *Shoah*: The Second Commandment, Popular Modernism, and Public Memory,'' in *Critical Inquiry*, vol. 22, no. 2, 1996.

LaCapra, D., ''Lanzmann's *Shoah*: 'Here There Is No Why,''' in *Critical Inquiry*, vol. 23, no. 2, 1997.

Olin, M., ''Lanzmann's *Shoah* and the Topography of the Holocaust Film,'' in *Representations*, vol. 57, Winter 1997.

* * *

Shoah, Claude Lanzmann's 9½ hour-meditation on the Nazi extermination of Europe's Jews, is possibly the only documentary film that contains no imagery of its central subject. We see many interviews with survivors; we see the sites of the camps today; we see footage of the once-Nazi corporations of modern Germany. There are interviews with present-day Poles who lived through the Nazi occupation and who make no attempt to hide their past and present anti-Semitism; there are interviews with holocaust historians; there are interviews with ''former'' Nazis. But what Lanzmann excludes is the

Shoah

imagery that we've seen in every *other* film about the period: footage of the Jewish ghettoes, of the emaciated camp survivors, of the piles of corpses.

Lanzmann's film thus takes the form of a whirlpool swirling around a void, a hurricane with an empty center. The film's great length is not an accident, nor an act of directorial arrogance. It is necessitated in part by the many small facts that Lanzmann wished to accumulate, in imitation of the method of a historian in the film who speaks of starting with tiny facts and hoping thereby to reach the whole. But it is also a way of asserting the importance of the subject; the running time cannot be easily accommodated into a daily schedule, but rather cuts significantly into one's living time. Most of all, the almost endless accretion of details and witnesses over many hours serves to deepen one's sense of an awful and unseen void. With every passing minute the film's chasm becomes ever more yawning, its unimaginably inhuman heart ever more incomprehensible.

Lanzmann's exclusion of corpse and prisoner footage is partly a reaction to the overuse of such footage in previous films about the Nazi period. But there is a more important reason for this exclusion. The filmmaker understands the extent to which in any film an image of something inevitably advocates its subject. There is something about the intimacy between viewer and image that makes it very hard to imagine a film which unequivocally condemns its own imagery. Such condemnation may be a part of a film, conveyed through sound, intertitles, editing, or cinematography, but inevitably the primary intimacy that exists between viewer and screen renders any such condemnation ambiguous at best. To show footage of corpses is in some sense to traffic in murder.

Lanzmann further understands that the reality of the Nazi genocide for our present time cannot be conveyed through a corpse, which no longer holds the life that makes the human form meaningful to us. He has quoted Emil Fackenheim: ''The European Jews massacred are not just of the past, they are the presence of an absence.'' It is the lives unlived, the generations that can never be born, that represent the true meaning, for us, of the Nazi horror. But this unrealized and unrealizable possibility is an abstraction beyond all imagery, and it is out of a desire to be true not to the Nazi vision-corpses—but to the vision we might wish to have today—of the ineffable lost possibilities, of an eternal emptiness—that Lanzmann has constructed his film around a void.

The impossibility of ever representing what happened and its continuing consequences is a theme throughout the film. Lanzmann's first witness, a rare Treblinka survivor, begins the film by saying, ''This is an untellable story.'' He then proceeds to describe the indescribable: how as a young boy shot in the head but not killed, he hid amidst a pile of corpses. Near the film's end, the camera slowly zooms in on a greyish pond while a voice-over explains that the ashes of thousands of cremated Jews were dumped here. As we zoom closer and closer to the water, we see less and less detail, as the screen fills with grey. Lanzmann has found a perfect metaphor for the impossibility of forming a mental image of the cremated ashes of thousands, of the impossibility of ever taking measure, in cinema or in the mind, of genocide. Throughout the film Lanzmann repeats an image of the main entrance gate at Auschwitz, shot from a train car approaching on a railroad track, the camera thus assuming the position of an entering prisoner. In each view, we move closer, but finally Lanzmann takes us through the gates not on the tracks but via a zoom. By shifting from a movement through space to a mechanical, lens-created effect, Lanzmann acknowledges the impossibility of our ever retracing the prisoner's steps. Neither he, nor we, can ever relive what they went through, and so, in an act of the profoundest respect, he remains physically outside the gates, entering only in the mind's eye.

These poetic renderings of the unimaginable are countered by the film's careful accretion of facts. We hear former Nazis fail to acknowledge that they did anything wrong, even as one describes in great detail the many trains he routed. Lanzmann also includes his own subterfuges—we see him lie to a Nazi to get his testimony—and his own rage, as when he confronts a former SS man with his camera, trying to get him to talk.

The film thus achieves a remarkable balance. Lanzmann gives us many facts about the Nazi methods, as well as a haunting evocation of the result of those methods, a result that transcends all possible imagery. It wouldn't be correct to say he gives us the ''Nazi side'' (would anyone wish for that?), but he does let several Nazis speak—one even sings a song about the ''glories'' of Treblinka—and juxtaposes that with hints of his own rage. All possible ethical approaches to his subject are included; the excluded methods are those that would be false to the spirit of those who were killed.

—Fred Camper

SHOESHINE

See **SCIUSCIA**

SHONEN

(Boy)

Japan, 1969

Director: Nagisa Oshima

Production: Sozo-sha and A.T.G.; Eastmancolor with black and white sequences, 35mm, Cinemascope; running time: 97 minutes; length: 2,676 meters. Released 1969, Japan.

Producers: Masayuki Nakajima and Takuji Yamaguchi; **screenplay:** Tsutomu Tamura; **photography:** Yasuhiro Yoshioka and Seizo Sengen; **editor:** Sueko Shiraishi; **sound:** Hideo Nishizaki; **sound effects:** Akira Suzuki; **art director:** Jusho Toda; **music:** Hikaru Hayashi.

Cast: Tetsuo Abe (*Toshio*); Fumio Watanabe (*Father*); Akiko Koyama (*Stepmother*); Tsuyoshi Kinoshita (*Little brother*).

Publications

Books:

Cameron, Ian, *Second Wave*, New York, 1970.
Sato, Tadao, *Oshima Nagisa no sekai* (The World of Nagisa Oshima), Tokyo, 1973.
Bock, Audie, *Japanese Film Directors*, New York, 1978; revised edition, Tokyo, 1985.
Oshima, Nagisa, *Ecrits (1956–1978): Dissolution et jaillissement*, Paris, 1980.
Tessier, Max, editor, *Le Cinéma japonais au présent 1959–79*, Paris, 1980.
Sato, Tadao, *Currents in Japanese Cinema* (in English), Tokyo, 1982.
Magrelli, Enrico, and Emanuela Martini, *Il rito, il rivolta: Il cinema di Nagisa Oshima*, Rome, 1984.
Polan, Dana B., *The Political Language of Film and the Avant-Garde*, Ann Arbor, Michigan, 1985.
Danvers, Louis, and Charles Tatum, *Nagisa Oshima*, Paris, 1986.
Turim, Maureen Cheryn, *The Films of Oshima Nagisa: Images of a Japanese Iconoclast*, Berkeley, 1998.

Articles:

Cameron, Ian, ''Nagisa Oshima,'' in *Movie* (London), Winter 1969–70.
''Oshima,'' in *Film* (London), Spring 1970.
Strick, Philip, in *Sight and Sound* (London), Summer 1970.
Tarratt, Margaret, in *Films and Filming* (London), August 1970.
Delmas, J., in *Jeune Cinéma* (Paris), November 1972.
Burch, Noël, ''Nagisa Oshima and Japanese Cinema in the 60s,'' in *Cinema: A Critical Dictionary*, edited by Richard Roud, London, 1980.
''Nagisa Oshima Section'' of *Contracampo* (Madrid), July-August 1980.
Suga, S., ''Campaigner in the World of the Absurd: Nagisa Oshima,'' in *Framework* (Norwich), nos. 26–27, 1985.
Steinborn, B., and C. Göldenboog, ''Ein Gespräch mit Nagisa Oshima. Der Tod geschieht fortwährend,'' in *Filmfaust* (Frankfurt), August-September 1985.
Vinke, Hermann, ''Japan's 'World Citizen,''' in *World Press Review*, vol. 33, April 1986.
Casebier, A., ''Oshima in Contemporary Theoretical Perspective,'' in *Wide Angle* (Baltimore), vol. 9, no. 2, 1987.
''Nagisa Oshima,'' in *UNESCO Courier*, July-August 1995.

* * *

Based on a real event which shocked Japan in the mid 1960s, *Shonen* depicts a family that travels the country, collecting out-of-court settlement money in automobile accident scams. The film is clearly Nagisa Oshima's: thematically, it deals with crimes; it is based on a real event; and it develops many of his stylistic devices.

The character of the lazy and self-indulgent father, for example, represents the victim complex that Oshima sees as typical of the postwar Japanese mentality. The character serves as a microcosm of the problems of the patriarchal Japanese emperor state. Oshima's criticism is ultimately of a society where uneducated and unskilled parents can use and exploit their own children in illegal schemes. The cruelty of the authorities is shown by the arrest of the family after they have given up their life of crime and settled in the city. The omnipresence of state authority is conveyed by the Japanese national flags: in the street, in the hand of the baby, on the boat, and in the background.

Basically, the film follows a linear narrative, though it includes many experimental stylistic devices, such as the occasional insertion of black-and-white footage. The first insert, showing the family's flight to a new town, works like a fantasy scene. The second insert, a car accident, masks the colors of the blood and the victim's red boot. Later, when the film returns to color, the viewers are shocked by the red of the blood and the boot in the white snow (corresponding to the colors of the Japanese flag).

There are occasional suspensions of sound as well as the use of still photographs accompanied by the boy's narration reminiscent of a school composition, and newspaper clips accompanied by a newsreel-like narration. Other such techniques used to emphasize important points include: the slow-motion scene of the boy (never called by name throughout the film) destroying the snowman, one of the few scenes in which he displays strong emotion, and the theatrical setting where the father fights with the mother and the son beside what appears to be a funeral altar in front of a large national flag. In addition, Oshima often deliberately confuses the sense of time between shots.

Abstract music, often resembling actual sounds, is used disjointedly with the image, and the intentional decentralization of the Cinemascope composition is visually jarring as many actions take place on the far left or right side of the screen. Such stylistic techniques are intended to destroy our suspension of disbelief and therefore destroy our subconscious identification with (and sympathy for) the main characters. Oshima is careful not to trivialize his subject by sentimentalizing it. He avoids this all-too-easy trap by, for example, never using music to enhance the character's emotion.

Shonen does not make simplistic judgments on the characters or the situations. We simply see the boy's solitude, playing by himself and pretending to visit his grandmother. Only twice in the film do we see his tears, despite all the mental and physical exploitation he suffers. We are never told why the boy keeps silent after his family is arrested. Instead, on many levels and in many subtle ways, this film urges us to think. Perhaps for this reason, this film was more successful critically than commercially.

—Kyoko Hirano

SHOOT THE PIANO PLAYER

See **TIREZ SUR LE PIANISTE**

THE SHOP ON MAIN STREET

See **OBCHOD NA KORZE**

SIBERIADE

(The Siberiad)

USSR, 1979

Director: Andrei Mikhalkov-Konchalovsky

Production: Mosfilm Studios; Sovcolour and black and white, 35mm; running time: 206 minutes. Released in USSR in 1979; released in USA 1979, IFEX; US video release, Kino International, 1994. Filmed on location in Siberia and in Moscow.

Screenplay: Valentin Yezhov and Andrei Mikhalkov-Konchalovsky; **photography:** Levan Paatashvili; **editor:** Valentina Kulagina; **music:** Edouard Artemiev; **sound:** Valentin Bobrovsky; **production designer:** Nikolai Dvigubsky; **newsreel director:** Artur Peleshian.

Cast: Vladimir Smailov (*Afanassi Ustiuzhanin*); Vitaly Solomina (*Nikolai Ustiuzhanin*); Nathalia Andreitchenko (*Anastassia Solomina*); Erqueni Petrov (*Evofei*); Mikhail Knonov (*Radion*); Nikita Mikhalkov (*Alexei* Ustiuzhanin); Liudmila Gourtchenko (*Taya Solomina*); Sergei Shakourov (*Spiridou Solomin*); Pavel Kadochnikov (*Eternal Grandad*); Yelena Koreneva (*Young Taya*); Igor Okhlupin (*Filipp Solomin*); Ruslan Mikaberidze (*Tofik*); Vsevolod Larionov (*Fyodor Nikolayevich*).

Publications

Books:

Goulding, Daniel J., editor, *Post New Wave Cinema in the Soviet Union and Eastern Europe*, Bloomington, 1989.

Zorkaya, Neya, *The Illustrated History of the Soviet Cinema*, Hippocrene Books (New York), 1989.

Lawton, Anna, editor, *The Red Screen: Politics, Society, Art in Soviet Cinema*, Routledge (London and New York), 1992.

Thompson, Kristin, and David Bordwell, *Film History: An Introduction*, McGraw Hill (New York), 1994.

Articles:

Variety (New York), 6 June 1979.

Logette, L., *Jeune Cinéma* (Paris), September-October 1979.

Martin, M., *Ecran* (Paris), October 1979.

Haustrate, G., *Cinéma* (Paris), November 1979.

Bosseno, C., and others, *Image et Son* (Paris), December 1979.

Daney, S., *Cahiers du Cinéma* (Paris), December 1979.

Sterritt, David, ''*Siberiade*: A Provocative Glimpse of Russian History—Filmmaker Compares US and Soviet Attitudes,'' in *The Christian Science Monitor*, vol. 74, 23 September 1982.

Siberiade

Wise, Naomi, in *San Francisco*, vol. 24, December 1982.
Menashe, L., *Cineaste* (New York), 1983.
Menashe, L., ''Glasnost in the Soviet Cinema,'' *Cineaste* (New York), 1987–88.
Jaehue, Karen, ''Family Ties: An Interview with Nikita and Andrei Mikhalkov-Konchalovsky,'' *Cineaste* (New York), 1987–88.

* * *

An auteur with many styles, Andrei Mikhalkov-Konchalovsky is an extravert filmmaker whose imagination often needs a wake-up call from the outside. He has banked on the literary classics (Turgenev's *Nest of Gentry* and Chekhov's *Uncle Vanya*); genre stereotypes (*Romance of the Lovers*); other directors' concepts (Akira Kurosawa's script for *Runaway Train*); and his own past (his 1994 *Ryaba My Chicken* is a ''sequel'' to his 1967 *Asya's Happiness*). In 1979, three years after the release of *1900*, Konchalovsky made *Siberiade*, an epic as indebted to Bernardo Bertolucci's masterpiece as it was ambitious, beautiful, and uneven.

Like *1900*, *Siberiade* scans several decades, from the early days of the century to the 1960s. Like *1900*, it focuses on several generations of two families—one rich, one poor—which are the entire population of the village of Elan in the midst of the Siberian swamps. Like *1900*, it is a Tolstoyan novel of a movie, overpopulated with well- and not-so-well developed characters who appear and disappear like patterns in a kaleidoscope; broad and deliberately paced; keen on detail; determinist in its view of history; and in love with a landscape. Like *1900*, it is exhaustingly long—3.5 hours—(in Russia it was first shown as a 4-part television mini-series) and hard to embrace at one sitting. It also contains at least one direct reference to Bertolucci's film in the scene where a boy, armed with a rifle, guards a village ''capitalist'' whose time has passed.

Every historical epic, from *Quo Vadis* to *Gone With the Wind*, from *Intolerance* to *Apocalypse Now*, is driven by a secret desire to exhaust the subject and the genre. *Siberiade*, whose title suggests nothing less than that we see its creator as a Homer of moving images, succeeds unyieldingly in this. The film is confidently directed by Konchalovsky who remains unintimidated by the scope of the story, breathtakingly photographed by Levan Paatashvili, and perfectly cast, with a stand-out performance by Nikita Mikhalkov, Konchalovsky's half-brother and director of *Slave of Love*, *Dark Eyes*, and *Close to Eden*. But the true meaning and charm of *Siberiade* comes from the tension that sets it aside from other epics—the tension between the film's ambition and the historical circumstances under which this ambition had to be realized.

The oblivious 1970s were hardly the best time in Russia to probe history, but inability to tell the whole truth, strangely, works for and not against *Siberiade.* To offset the film's historical stance, unavoidably official, Konchalovsky plays out history as a grand melodrama that stretches and strives to be a tragedy.

Bertolucci opened with Verdi's death and closed at the end of World War II, because in the first forty-five years of this century he found the arena for a tragedy of global proportions: the death of aristocracy, rebirth of the proletariat, and ruthless march of the Fascist bourgeoisie. Konchalovsky's chronology is more arbitrary: he skips the 1950s and closes in the 1960s, but it says very little about his understanding of historical processes and logistics. While Bertolucci's drama served the history, Konchalovsky's history serves the drama.

In the heat of the decline of the communist empire, Soviet culture was made either by sell-outs, or by escapists. A totalitarian state gives its own interpretation to escapism—not from the hardships of life, but from tenets of ideology. Some artists, like Tarkovsky, escaped into cerebral esoterica of "auterism"; some, like Nikita Mikhalkov, into the stylized past; some, like the director of *Moscow Doesn't Believe in Tears*, Vladimir Menshov, into Hollywood-style melodrama; some, like Georgian filmmakers, into folklore. This may be why Russian intelligentsia adored Garcia Marquez, as a loophole into the world unconstrained by the laws of materialist dialectics.

Konchalovsky, in a rare attempt to materialize "magic realism," creates a world in which the truth comes not from the newspaper Pravda, but from a star, shining over the village of Elan as a reminder of a higher order, and from pine-trees that talk and weep. In this world, animals listen to people, and those who listen to animals don't age. That this world is a compromise between magic and dogma is an important part of what *Siberiade* is really about.

—Michael Brashinsky

SIEGFRIED

See **DIE NIBELUNGEN**

THE SILENCE

See **TYSTNADEN**

THE SILENCE OF THE LAMBS

USA, 1991

Director: Jonathan Demme

Production: Orion Pictures, A Strong Heart/Demme Production; Technicolour, Panavision; running time: 118 minutes.

Producer: Edward Saxon, Kenneth Utt, Ron Bozman; **screenplay:** Ted Tally, based on the novel by Thomas Harris; **photography:** Tak Fujimoto; **editor:** Craig McKay; **assistant directors:** Ron Bozman, Kyle McCarthy, Steve Rose, Gina Leonetti; **production design:** Kristi Zea; **art director:** Tim Galvin; **music:** Howard Shore; **sound editor:** Skip Lievsay; **sound recording:** Christopher Newman, John Fundus, Alan Snelling.

Cast: Jodie Foster (*Clarice Starling*); Anthony Hopkins (*Hannibal Lecter*); Scott Glenn (*Jack Crawford*); Ted Levine (*Jamie Gumm*); Anthony Heald (*Dr. Frederick Chilton*); Brooke Smith (*Catherine Martin*).

Awards: Oscars for Best Picture, Best Director, Best Actor (Hopkins), Best Actress (Foster), Best Adapted Screenplay, 1991.

Publications

Books:

Kael, Pauline, *Pauline Kael on Jonathan Demme: A Selection of Reviews Accompanying the Retrospective Jonathan Demme: An American Director*, Minneapolis, 1988.

Demme, Jonathan, "Demme on Demme," in *Projections*, edited by John Boorman and Walter Donohue, London, 1992.

Falk, Quentin, *Anthony Hopkins: The Authorized Biography*, New York, 1993.

Garber, Marjorie, and Jann Matlock, editors, *Media Spectacles*, New York, 1993.

Bliss, Michael, and Christiana Banks, *What Goes Around Comes Around: The Films of Jonathan Demme*, Carbondale,1996.

Smolen, Diane, *The Films of Jodie Foster*, Secaucus, 1996.

Articles:

Variety (New York), 11 February 1991.

Seidenberg, R., *American Film* (Washington D.C.), February 1991.

Katsahnias, I., "La puritaine," in *Cahiers du Cinéma* (Paris), April 1991.

Ross, P., "Papillon de mort," in *Revue du Cinéma* (Paris), April 1991.

Rouyer, P., "Le complexe du papillon," in *Positif* (Paris), April 1991.

Jean, M., "Le sang de l'agneau," in *24 Images* (Montreal), Spring 1991.

Bahiana, A.N., *Cinema Papers* (Melbourne), May 1991.

Taubin, A., "Killing Men," in *Sight and Sound* (London), May 1991.

Magil, M., *Films in Review* (New York), May-June 1991.

Francke, L., *Sight and Sound* (London), June 1991.

Caron, A., *Séquences* (Montreal), June 1991.

Garsault, A., "Du conte et du mythe," in *Positif* (Paris), June 1991.

Tharp, J., "The Transvestite as Monster" in *Journal of Popular Film and Television* (Maryland), Fall 1991.

Greenberg, H.R., "Psychotherapy at the Simplex," in *Journal of Popular Film and Television* (Maryland), Summer 1992.

Nevers, C., "A l'ombre des serial killers," in *Cahiers du Cinéma* (Paris), November 1992.

Sundelson, D., "The Demon Therapist and Other Dangers," in *Journal of Popular Film and Television* (Maryland), Spring 1993.

The Silence of the Lambs

Beller, J.L., ''The Radical Imagination in American Film,'' in *Creative Screenwriting* (Washington, D.C.), vol. 1, no. 4, Winter 1994.

Redman, Nick, Tri Fritz, and Ted Elrick, ''Lambs, Wolves and Carpenters,'' in *DGA Magazine* (Los Angeles), vol. 19, no. 6, December-January 1994–1995.

Reichman, R., ''I Second That Emotion,'' in *Creative Screenwriting* (Washington, D.C.), vol. 2, no. 1, Spring 1995.

Kennedy, A.L., ''He Knows About Crazy,'' in *Sight & Sound* (London), vol. 5, no. 6, June 1995.

Sihvonen, J., ''Technobody Metamorphoses,'' in *Lahikuva* (Truku), vol. 3, 1995.

Stewart, J.A., ''The Feminine Hero of *Silence of the Lambs*,'' in *San Francisco Jung Institute Library Journal*, vol. 14, no. 3, 1995.

Tally, Ted, in *Scenario* (Rockville), vol. 1, no. 1, Winter 1995.

Lippy, Tod, ''Adapting *The Silence of the Lambs*,'' in *Scenario* (Rockville), vol. 1, no. 1, Winter 1995.

Weis, E., ''Synch Tanks,'' in *Cineaste* (New York), vol. 21, no. 1/2, 1995.

Wolfe, C., and J. Elmer, ''Subject to Sacrifice: Ideology, Psychoanalysis, and the Discourse of Species in Jonathan Demme's *The Silence of the Lambs*,'' in *Boundary 2*, vol. 22, no. 3, 1995.

Negra, Diane, ''Coveting the Feminine: Victor Frankenstein, Norman Bates, and Buffalo Bill,'' in *Literature/Film Quarterly* (Salisbury), vol. 24, no. 2, April 1996.

Bishop, Ellen, ''Film Frames: Cinematic Literacy and Satiric Violence in Contemporary Movies,'' in *Post Script* (Commerce), vol. 16, no. 2, Winter-Spring 1997.

Fleck, Patrice, ''Looking in the Wrong Direction: Displacement and Literacy in the Hollywood Serial Killer Drama,'' in *Post Script* (Commerce), vol. 16, no. 2, 1997.

Hantke, Steffen, '''The Kingdom of the Unimaginable': The Construction of Social Space and the Fantasy of Privacy in Serial Killer Narratives,'' in *Literature/Film Quarterly* (Salisbury), vol. 26, no. 3, July 1998.

* * *

The Silence of the Lambs is the most authentically terrifying movie since *Psycho*, and it is appropriate that Hannibal Lecter (as incarnated in the superb performance of Anthony Hopkins) should have established a position within our culture's popular mythology comparable to that of Anthony Perkins' Norman Bates three decades earlier. By ''authentically'' I mean that the terror the film induces is not merely a matter of contrived ''shock'' moments (though, as in *Psycho*, those are not lacking). The film brings us into intimate and disturbing contact with the darkest potentialities of the human psyche and, by locating the existence of the serial killer within a context of ''normality,'' connects it to those manifestations of what one might call the ''normal psychosis'' of the human race which we read about daily in our newspapers: the practice of ''ethnic cleansing,'' the protracted torture and eventual murder of a teenager by ''peacemakers'' in Somalia, the horrors of child abuse (sexual, physical, psychological) that are the product of our concept of ''family'' and the guarantee of their own continuance into future generations.

The humanity of Hannibal Lecter is clearly a central issue: if we see Lecter as *only* a monster, quite distinct from ourselves, then the film fails, becomes ''just another horror movie''; as Jodie Foster says of Lecter in the laser disc commentary, ''he just wants to be accepted as a human being.'' Therefore the filmmakers' problem lies in persuading us to do just that without ever becoming complicit in his obsessions (killing and eating other human beings): a difficult and dangerous tightrope to walk. It is their degree of success that distinguishes the film from *The Texas Chainsaw Massacre*, in which the fascination exerted by the monstrous cannibal family is not countered by any adequate positive force, the undercharacterized victims mere objects for torment, the film (for all its undeniable power) degenerating into an exercise in sadism.

The success is not complete: it seems to me that Jonathan Demme made two unfortunate errors of judgment. The first is the excision of a crucial sequence that was shot and is included in the supplement to the Criterion laser disc. This sequence includes Lecter's ''psychological profile'' of the serial killer, accompanied by evocative tracking-shots around Jamie Gumm's living quarters, in which he explains to Clarice Starling that a serial killer was a severely abused child (a theory for which there is a great deal of factual support), and that Gumm grew up with no sense of identity whatever, so that his attempts to construct one are unreal fabrications. The scene would have partly answered the widespread complaint that Gumm is presented as gay, reinforcing a malicious popular stereotype; it would also have linked the phenomenon of the serial killer to familial practices we now know to be all too common. I find the decision to suppress it inexplicable.

The second error (for which the screenwriter Ted Tally must share responsibility) is the film's famous last line, Lecter's ''I'm having an old friend for dinner.'' Ironically, Tally complains at length (in the commentary on the laser disc's alternative audio track) about the appropriation of Lecter for ''camp'' purposes, that so many young people find him smart and seductive and even collect Lecter memorabilia: that last line precisely invites such a response, especially in view of the fact that Lecter's imminent victim Dr. Chilton/Anthony Heald is presented throughout as irredeemably despicable, enabling the audience to view his fate with equanimity and even satisfaction. The punch line is slick and funny: one can readily understand the temptation, but it is one that should have been resisted.

The film's distinction lies ultimately in its powerful and convincing embodiment of the force for life, in the character of Clarice Starling, Jodie Foster's performance matching that of Hopkins in its strength and vividness. There is another documented fact about serial killers too obvious for the film to have to state explicitly (it is enacted clearly enough): virtually all serial killers are male. Like the issue of child abuse, this reinforces the need to see the phenomenon not in terms of individual and inexplicable ''monsters'' but as intimately involved in the so-called ''normal'' actualities of the culture: the issue of gender-as-social-construction, of the cultural production of ''masculinity'' in terms of aggression and domination. The achievement of Demme and Foster is to create Starling both as a clearly defined and convincing character and as the embodiment of an ideal: the human being in whom the finest qualities traditionally associated with ''masculinity'' and ''femininity'' coexist in perfect balance. The film's title derives from Starling's definitive childhood memory: the young girl's unsuccessful attempt to save one lamb from those waiting to be slaughtered, whose frantic bleating distressed her. The ''silence'' of the lambs is brought about only by her rescue of Gumm's latest female victim, a feat of heroism requiring a fusion of ''masculine'' activeness, energy, reasoning and determination with the capacity for identification with the ''feminine'' vulnerability, sensitivity, empathy with the oppressed. If we recognize Lecter and Gumm as 'human beings' produced by the worst excesses of patriarchal culture, we simultaneously recognize Clarice as the *fully* human being of a possible future.

—Robin Wood

SINGIN' IN THE RAIN

USA, 1952

Directors: Gene Kelly and Stanley Donen

Production: Metro-Goldwyn-Mayer Pictures Corp.; Technicolor, 35mm; running time: 103 minutes; length: 9,228 feet, Released 1952. Filmed in MGM Studios and backlots.

Singin' in the Rain

Producer: Arthur Freed; **screenplay:** Betty Comden and Adolph Green, from the play by Betty Comden and Adolph Green; **photography:** Harold Rosson; **editor:** Adrienne Fazan; **sound recording supervisor:** Douglas Shearer; **set decoration:** Edwin B. Willis and Jacques Mapes; **art directors:** Cedric Gibbons and Randall Duell; **music director:** Lennie Hayton; **orchestrations:** Conrad Salinger, Wally Heglin, and Skip Martin; **songs:** Arthur Freed, Nacio Herb Brown, Betty Comden, and Roger Edens; **vocal arrangements:** Jeff Alexander; **special effects:** Warren Newcombe and Irving G. Ries.

Cast: Gene Kelly (*Don Lockwood*); Donald O'Connor (*Cosmo Brown*); Debbie Reynolds (*Kathy Selden*); Jean Hagen (*Lina Lamont*); Millard Mitchell (*R. F. Simpson*); Rita Moreno (*Zelda Zanders*); Douglas Fowley (*Roscoe Dexter*); Cyd Charisse (*Dancer*); Madge Blake (*Dora Bailey*); King Donovan (*Rod*); Kathleen Freeman (*Phoebe Dinsmore, diction coach*); Bobby Watson (*Diction coach*); Tommy Farrell (*Sid Phillips, ass't. director*); Jimmie Thompson (*Male lead in ''Beautiful Girls'' number*); Dan Foster (*Ass't. director*); Margaret Bert (*Wardrobe woman*); Mae Clark (*Hairdresser*); Judy Landon (*Olga Mara*); John Dodsworth (*Baron de la Bouvet de la Toulon*); Stuart Holmes (*J. C. Spendrill III*); Dennis Ross (*Don as a boy*); Bill Lewin (*Villain in Western, Bert*); Richard Emory (*Phil, cowboy hero*); Julius Tannen (*Man on screen*); Dawn Addams and Elaine Stewart (*Ladies in waiting*); Carl Milletaire (*Villain, ''Dueling Cavalier''* and *''Broadway Rhythm''*); Jac George (*Orchestra leader*); Wilson Wood (*Vallee impersonator*).

Publications

Script:

Comden, Betty, and Adolph Green, *Singin' in the Rain*, London and New York, 1972; revised edition 1986.

Books:

Griffith, Richard, *The Films of Gene Kelly*, New York, 1962.

Springer, John, *All Talking, All Singing, All Dancing*, New York, 1966.

Kobal, John, *Gotta Sing, Gotta Dance: A Pictorial History of Film Musicals*, New York, 1970.

Thomas, Lawrence B., *The MGM Years*, New York, 1972.

Stern, Lee Edward, *The Movie Musical*, New York, 1974.

Fordin, Hugh, *The World of Entertainment: Hollywood's Greatest Musicals*, New York, 1975.

Hirschhorn, Clive, *Gene Kelly*, Chicago, 1975; revised edition, London, 1984.

Charness, Casey, *Hollywood Cine-Dance: A Description of the Interrelationship of Camera Work and Choreography in the Films of Stanley Donen and Gene Kelly*, Ann Arbor, Michigan, 1978.

Altman, Rick, editor, *Genre: The Musical*, London, 1981.

Delameter, James, *Dance in the Hollywood Musical*, Ann Arbor, Michigan, 1981.

Feuer, Jane, *The Hollywood Musical*, London, 1982.

Casper, Joseph Andrew, *Stanley Donen*, Metuchen, New Jersey, 1985.

Altman, Rick, *The American Film Musical*, London, 1989.

Wollen, Peter, *Singin' in the Rain*, London, 1992.

Silverman, Stephen M., *Dancing on the Ceiling: Stanley Donen and His Movies*, New York, 1996.

La Polla, Franco, *Stanley Donen, Gene Kelly: Cantando sotto la pioggia*, Torino, 1997.

Yudkoff, Alvin, *Gene Kelly: A Life of Dance and Dreams*, New York, 1999.

Articles:

Jablonski, Edward, in *Films in Review* (New York), April 1952.

Morgan, James, in *Sight and Sound* (London), July-September 1952.

de Baroncelli, Jean, in *Le Monde* (Paris), 20 September 1953.

Knight, Arthur, ''From Dance to Film Director,'' in *Dance* (New York), August 1954.

Johnson, Albert, ''The 10th Muse in San Francisco,'' in *Sight and Sound* (London), Summer 1956.

''Musical Comedy Issue'' of *Cinéma* (Paris), August-September 1959.

Gilson, René, in *Cinéma* (Paris), May 1962.

Tavernier, Bertrand, and Daniel Pallas, ''Entretien avec Stanley Donen,'' in *Cahiers du Cinéma* (Paris), May 1963.

Behlmer, Rudy, ''Gene Kelly,'' in *Films in Review* (New York), January 1964.

Cutts, John, ''Dancer, Actor, Director,'' in *Films and Filming* (London), August and September 1964.

Kelly, Gene, ''Le Premier Film 'Camp': *Singin' in the Rain*,'' in *Cinéma* (Paris), July-August 1971.

Lefèvre, Raymond, in *Cinéma* (Paris), February 1973.

Pasche, F., in *Travelling* (Lausanne), January-February 1974.

Winer, Stephen, in *Velvet Light Trap* (Madison, Wisconsin), no. 11, 1974.

Dagneau, G., and A., in *Image et Son* (Paris), February 1977.

Day, B., in *Films and Filming* (London), April 1977.

Dyer, Richard, ''Entertainment and Utopia,'' in *Movie* (London), no. 24, 1977.

Giles, Dennis, ''Show-Making,'' in *Movie* (London), no. 24, 1977.

Mariani, J., ''Come on with the Rain,'' in *Film Comment* (New York), May-June 1978.

Wolf, W. R., ''Making *Singin' in the Rain*,'' in *Film en Televisie* (Brussels), March 1979.

Johnson, Julia, in *Magill's Survey of Cinema 4*, Englewood Cliffs, New Jersey, 1980.

Peary, Danny, in *Cult Movies*, New York, 1981.

Company, J. M., and J. Talens, in *Contracampo* (Madrid), September 1981.

Telotte, J. P., ''Ideology and the Kelly-Donen Musicals,'' in *Film Criticism* (Meadville, Pennsylvania), Spring 1984.

Card, J., '''More Than Meets the Eye' in *Singin' in the Rain* and *Day for Night*,'' in *Literature/Film Quarterly* (Salisbury, Maryland), April 1984.

Biesty, P., ''The Myth of the Playful Dancer,'' in *Studies in Popular Culture*, vol. 13, no. 1, 1990.

Roth, M., ''Pulling the Plug on Lina Lamont,'' in *Jump Cut* (Berkeley), April 1990.

Masson, A., ''An Architectural Promenade,'' in *Continuum*, vol. 5, no. 2, 1992.

Clover, C.J., ''Dancin' in the Rain,'' in *Critical Inquiry*, no. 21, no. 4, 1995.

Reid's Film Index (Wyong), no. 16, 1995.

Chumo, Peter N., ''Dance, Flexibility, and the Renewal of Genre in *Singin' in the Rain*,'' in *Cinema Journal* (Austin), vol. 36, no. 1, Fall 1996.

Svehla, S., ''Gene Kelly,'' in *Films of the Golden Age* (Muscatine), no. 10, Fall 1997.

* * *

Traditionally, the film musical is said to have reached its pinnacle in the 1950s at MGM studios. The creative personnel at MGM responsible for this perfection were Arthur Freed, Vincente Minnelli, Stanley Donen and Gene Kelly. The ''golden era'' began with *On the Town* (1949) and ended with *Gigi* (1958); between were *An American in Paris*, *Singin' in the Rain*, *The Bandwagon*, *Seven Brides for Seven Brothers*, *It's Always Fair Weather*, and *Funny Face*. With the exception of *On the Town*, all were originally conceived for the screen. They were, in a sense, the last of their kind, because the early 1950s began the great mass adaptions of Broadway musicals. As television began to effect box office returns, the studios were hesitant to produce big budget musicals unless they were proven hits.

All were developments on Arthur Freed's concept of organic integration. The production numbers would, ideally, grow directly out of the emotional needs of the characters or would serve as plot motivation. Song and dance would replace dialogue as a means of discourse. Whether or not this is the perfect structure for the musical is debatable. Richard Dyer feels that critical stances which champion this form recapitulate the dominant ideology. In ''Entertainment and Utopia,'' he states that entertainment is escapist/wish-fulfilling, a longing for something better—a literal Utopia. Musicals manage contradictions in the system (music/narrative, success/failure, love/hate, wealth/poverty, male/female) on all levels in such a way as to make them disappear. A film that offers no distinction between narrative (reality) and musical numbers (escapist fantasy) suggests that the narrative is also (already) Utopian. The films of the 1950s can be seen as the most ideologically repressive, because of the ease in which that ideology can be hidden.

Of the musicals of the 1950s, *Singin' in the Rain* is the best remembered. In 1977, the American Film Institute conducted a poll that listed *Singin' in the Rain* as one of the top ten American films. ''*Singin' in the Rain* is generally accepted as the apogee of screen musical art, a virtually faultless film by any standards'' says Arthur Jackson, in *The Best Musicals*. Clive Hirschorn notes that *Singin' in the Rain*, released ''. . . on the heels of *An American in Paris*, did not receive the glowing reviews of the Gershwin film . . . . Over the years, however, it has surpassed *An American in Paris* in popularity and is now recognized as one of the all time greats.'' Following so closely behind *An American in Paris*, *Singin' in the Rain* was not as generally well received. *Time* felt it was ''without much warmth or wit,'' and *Newsweek* called it ''sluggish.'' It was nominated for only two Oscars; Jean Hagen for supporting actress and musical score. Notwithstanding, it was listed as one of the best films of 1952 by the National Board of Review and *Films in Review*, was the number one money-making film in April 1952, and number ten money-making film of the same year. Written by Betty Comden and Adolph Green (who also wrote *On the Town*), the screenplay won the award for best writing in an American musical from the Writers Guild of America.

The work of Comden and Green usually ridiculed an industry (filmmaking in *Singin' in the Rain*, theater in *The Bandwagon*, and television in *It's Always Fair Weather*) but without bitterness; ''there was always wit, and so they were able to create musical movies full of joy that were still effective satire,'' says Stephen Winer in *Velvet Light Trap*. Based on a catalogue of songs written by Arthur Freed and Nacio Herb Brown during the late 1920s and early 1930s, the film spoofed the turmoils of the transition from silent to sound film. Originally planned for Howard Keel, who was extremely popular at that time, it eventually shifted to accommodate the persona of Gene Kelly, who also co-directed with Stanley Donen. Kelly's career is firmly rooted in film history not only for his solo routine to the title song, but also because of the ''Broadway Rhythm'' ballet. As expensive (in rehearsal/shooting time and overall cost) as the climactic ballet from *An American in Paris*, it was also as out of place. Gene Kelly commented on the ''Broadway Rhythm'' ballet at an American Film Institute symposium in 1979. Not being able to use Donald O'Connor or Debbie Reynolds, ''we got Cyd Charisse and just wrote a whole ballet and stuck it in. That's how it came about. We had to have a number there. We never meant it to be that long, but since we were introducing a new character into the show, we had to keep adding to it and adding to it. It went on for hours, it seems.'' Donald O'Connor is possibly best remembered for his song and dance solo ''Make Em Laugh,'' an athletic *tour-de-force* that helped him win the Golden Globe for Best Actor in 1952. *Singin' in the Rain* was Debbie Reynolds's third film for MGM and her first major role. Reportedly he age (she was only 19) and lack of professional experience was problematic. Playing the role of an understudy who dubs the voice of a silent star, she was dubbed by Betty Noyes for the singing and by Jean Hagen for the lines Debbie was supposedly dubbing for Jean Hagen's character, Lina Lamont.

Dennis Giles, offers a psycho-analytical reading of *The Bandwagon* and *Singin' in the Rain* that is particularly interesting. He sees the successful production of the show (in *Singin' in the Rain*, the revamping of *The Duelling Cavalier* into *The Singing Cavalier*) as a visually uncensored form of love-making. ''The private show of love is displayed through the vehicle of the public spectacle: the lovers sing and dance to each other as if they were alone, at the same time that they openly display this love to the on-screen (diegetic) audience and to ourselves, the off-screen spectators.'' A successful show guarantees a consummated relationship between the male and female leads. Needless to say, *The Singing Cavalier* is a hit and Gene Kelly and Debbie Reynolds embrace as *Singin' in the Rain* fades out.

—Greg S. Faller

SIR ARNE'S TREASURE

See **HERR ARNES PENGAR**

DET SJUNDE INSEGLET

(The Seventh Seal)

Sweden, 1957

Director: Ingmar Bergman

Production: Svensk Filmindustri; black and white, 35mm; running time: 96 minutes. Released 16 February 1957, Stockholm. Filmed in

Det sjunde inseglet

the Summer of 1956 in Svensk Filmindustri's studios, Råsunda, Sweden, and on location at Hovs Hallar, Sweden.

Producer: Allan Ekelund; **screenplay:** Ingmar Bergman, from his dramatic sketch *Wood Painting*; **photography:** Gunnar Fischer; **editor:** Lennart Wallin; **sound:** Aaby Wedin and Lennart Wallin; **special sound effects:** Evald Andersson; **sets:** P. A. Lundgren; **music:** Erik Nordgren; **costume designer:** Manne Lindholm.

Cast: Bengt Ekerot (*Death*); Nils Poppe (*Joff*); Max von Sydow (*The Knight, Antonius Blok*); Bibi Andersson (*Mia*); Inga Gill (*Lisa*); Maud Hansson (*Tyan, the witch*); Inga Landgré (*Knight's wife*); Gunnal Lindblom (*The girl*); Berto Anderberg (*Raval*); Anders Ek (*Monk*); Ake Fridell (*Plog, the smith*); Gunnar Olsson (*Church painter*); Erik Strandmark (*Skat*); Benkt-Åke Benktsson (*The merchant*); Gudrum Brost (*Woman at the inn*); Ulf Johansson (*Leader of the soldiers*); Lars Lind (*The young monk*); Gunnar Börnstrand (*Jöns, the squire*).

Awards: Cannes Film Festival, Special Prize, 1957.

Publications

Script:

Bergman, Ingmar, *The Seventh Seal*, in *Four Screenplays of Ingmar Bergman*, New York, 1960; also published separately, London and New York, 1963.

Books:

Béranger, Jean, *Ingmar Bergman et ses films*, Paris, 1959.
Höök, Marianne, *Ingmar Bergman*, Stockholm, 1962.
Chiaretti, Tommaso, *Ingmar Bergman*, Rome, 1964.
Donner, Jörn, *The Personal Vision of Ingmar Bergman*, Bloomington, Indiana, 1964.
Nelson, David, *Ingmar Bergman: The Search for God*, Boston, 1964.
Steene, Birgitta, *Ingmar Bergman*, New York, 1968.
Gibson, Arthur, *The Silence of God: Creative Response to the Films of Ingmar Bergman*, New York, 1969.
Wood, Robin, *Ingmar Bergman*, New York, 1969.
Sjögren, Henrik, *Regi: Ingmar Bergman*, Stockholm, 1970.

Young, Vernon, *Cinema Borealis: Ingmar Bergman and the Swedish Ethos*, New York, 1971.
Steene, Birgitta, *Focus on the Seventh Seal*, Englewood Cliffs, New Jersey, 1972.
Björkman, Stig, and others, editors, *Bergman on Bergman*, New York, 1973.
Ranieri, Tino, *Ingmar Bergman*, Florence, 1974.
Kaminsky, Stuart, editor, *Ingmar Bergman: Essays in Criticism*, New York, 1975.
Bergom-Larsson, Maria, *Ingmar Bergman and Society*, San Diego, 1978.
Kawin, Bruce, *Mindscreen: Bergman, Godard, and the First-Person Film*, Princeton, 1978.
Marion, Denis, *Ingmar Bergman*, Paris, 1979.
Manvell, Roger, *Ingmar Bergman: An Appreciation*, New York, 1980.
Mosley, Philip, *Ingmar Bergman: The Cinema as Mistress*, Boston, 1981.
Petric, Vlada, editor, *Film and Dreams: An Approach to Bergman*, South Salem, New York, 1981.
Cowie, Peter, *Ingmar Bergman: A Critical Biography*, New York, 1982.
Livingston, Paisley, *Ingmar Bergman and the Ritual of Art*, Ithaca, New York, 1982.
Steene, Birgitta, *Ingmar Bergman: A Guide to References and Resources*, Boston, 1982.
Jones, William G., editor, *Talking with Bergman*, Dallas, 1983.
Lefèvre, Raymond, *Ingmar Bergman*, Paris, 1983.
Slayton, Ralph Emil, *Ingmar Bergman's The Seventh Seal: A Criticism*, Ann Arbor, Michigan, 1983.
Dervin, Daniel, *Through a Freudian Lens Deeply: A Psychoanalysis of Cinema*, Hillsdale, New Jersey, 1985.
Gado, Frank, *The Passion of Ingmar Bergman*, Durham, North Carolina, 1986.
Bergman, Ingmar, *Laterna Magica*, Stockholm, 1987; as *The Magic Lantern: An Autobiography*, London, 1988.
Cohen, James, *Through a Lens Darkly*, New York, 1991.
Bjorkman, Stig, Torsten Maans, and Jonas Sima, *Bergman on Bergman: Interviews with Ingmar Bergman*, Cambridge, 1993.
Cohen, Hubert I., *Ingmar Bergman: The Art of Confession*, New York, 1993.
Long, Robert Emmet, *Ingmar Bergman: Film & Stage*, New York, 1994.
Tornqvist, Egil, *Between Stage and Screen: Ingmar Bergman Directs*, Amsterdam, 1995.
Blackwell, Marilyn J., *Gender and Representation in the Films of Ingmar Bergman*, Rochester, 1997.
Michaels, Lloyd, editor, *Ingmar Bergman's Persona*, New York, 1999; revised edition, Cambridge, 2000.

Articles:

Dyer, Peter John, in *Sight and Sound* (London), Spring 1958.
Whitebait, William, in *New Statesman* (London), 8 March 1958.
Powell, Dilys, in *Sunday Times* (London), 9 March 1958.
Rohmer, Eric, ''Avec *Le Septième Sceau* Bergman nous offre son Faust,'' in *Arts* (Paris), 23 April 1958.
Mambrino, Jean, ''Traduit du silence,'' in *Cahiers du Cinéma* (Paris), May 1958.
Hart, Henry, in *Films in Review* (New York), November 1958.
Allombert, Guy, in *Image et Son* (Paris), February 1959.
Young, Colin, in *Film Quarterly* (Berkeley), Spring 1959.
Archer, Eugene, ''The Rack of Life,'' in *Film Quarterly* (Berkeley), Summer 1959.
Holland, Norman, ''*The Seventh Seal:* The Film as Iconography,'' in *Hudson Review* (New York), Summer 1959.
Jarvie, Ian, ''Notes on the Films of Ingmar Bergman,'' in *Film Journal* (Melbourne), November 1959.
Sarris, Andrew, in *Film Culture* (New York), no.19, 1959.
Time (New York), 14 March 1960.
Simon, John, ''Ingmar, the Image-Maker,'' in *Mid-Century* (New York), December 1960.
Napolitano, Antonio, ''*Dal settimo sigillo* alle soglie della vita,'' in *Cinema Nuovo* (Turin), May-June 1961.
Furstenau, Theo, ''Apocalypse und Totentantz,'' in *Die Zeit*, 16 February 1962.
Cowie, Peter, in *Films and Filming* (London), January 1963.
Steene, Birgitta, ''The Isolated Hero of Ingmar Bergman,'' in *Film Comment* (New York), September 1965.
Scott, James F., ''The Achievement of Ingmar Bergman,'' in *Journal of Aesthetics and Arts* (Cleveland, Ohio), Winter 1965.
Bergman, Ingmar, in *Film Comment* (New York), Summer 1970.
Steene, Birgitta, ''The Milk and the Strawberry Sequence in *The Seventh Seal*,'' in *Film Heritage* (Dayton, Ohio), Summer 1973.
Helman, A., ''Ingmar Bergman albo parabola pytan odwiecznych,'' in *Kino* (Warsaw), August 1974.
Wimberly, Darryl, in *Cinema Texas Program Notes* (Austin), 15 September 1977.
Malmkjaer, P., in *Kosmorama* (Copenhagen), Spring 1978.
Peary, Danny, in *Cult Movies 2*, New York, 1983.
Pressler, M., ''The Idea Fused in the Fact: Bergman and *The Seventh Seal,'' in Literature/Film Quarterly* (Salisbury, Maryland), April 1985.
Winterson, J., ''Bloodied with Optimism,'' in *Sight & Sound* (London), vol. 1, May 1991.
Trasatti, S., ''Bergman, il paradosso di un 'Ateo cristiano,''' in *Castoro Cinema* (Florence), November-December 1991.
''*Det Sjunde inseglet* Section'' in *Avant Scène du Cinéma* (Paris), March 1992.
Lucas, Tim, in *Video Watchdog* (Cincinnati), vol. 33, 1996.
Merjui, Darius, ''The Shock of Revelation,'' in *Sight & Sound* (London), vol. 7, no. 6, June 1997.

* * *

The Seventh Seal is one of the films in Ingmar Bergman's mature, highly individualized style, coming after an initial period he considers merely an imitative apprenticeship, in which he made films in the style of other directors. It was derived from a dramatic sketch, *Wood Painting*, which Bergman had written in 1954 for his drama students in Malmö. *The Seventh Seal* was made on a very low budget in 35 days.

In his late thirties, Bergman was still struggling with religious doubts and problems after having been reared very strictly in the Protestant Lutheran tradition, his father having been a prominent Swedish pastor. *The Seventh Seal*, which Bergman has termed an oratorio, is the first of three films (the others being *The Face* and *The Virgin Spring*) made at this time in which he tried to purge the uglier aspects of religious practice and persecution, as well as confront the absence of any sign of response from God to human craving for help and reassurance. As the film makes clear at the beginning, the title refers to God's book of secrets sealed by seven seals; only after the breaking of the seventh seal will the secret of life, God's great secret, be revealed. In *Bergman on Bergman* he is quoted as saying, "For me, in those days, the great question was: Does God exist? or doesn't God exist?. . . If God doesn't exist, what do we do then? . . . What I believed in those days—and believed in for a long time—was the existence of a virulent evil, in no way dependent upon environmental or hereditary factors . . . an active evil, of which human beings, as opposed to animals, have a monopoly." He regards the 1950s as a period of personal convulsion, the remnants of his faith altering with a strengthening scepticism.

In *The Seventh Seal*, Antonius Blok, a 14th-century knight, returns home with his earthy, sensual squire, Jöns, after a decade of crusading in the Holy Land. He finds his native country plague-stricken and the people, haunted by a sense of guilt, given over to self-persecution, flagellation, and witch-hunting, a movement induced by a fantastic and sadistic monk, Raval. The Knight, God's servant-at-arms, finds that he has lost his faith and can no longer pray. In the midst of his spiritual turmoil, he is suddenly confronted by the personification of Death, a figure cloaked and implacable, who coldly informs him that his time has come. The Knight, unable to accept demise when in a state of doubt, wins a brief reprieve by challenging Death to a game of chess, the traditional ploy adopted by those seeking more time on earth, for Death is supposedly unable to resist such a challenge.

The film, Bergman has said, is "about the fear of death." Bergman had been steeped since childhood in the kind of imagery portrayed in this film, with its legendary concepts and simple pictorial forms; he had looked endlessly at the mural paintings that decorate the medieval Swedish churches. A painter of such images appears in the film, contriving studies of death to frighten the faithful. The stark but theatrical Christian imagery comes to life in *The Seventh Seal*. The Knight wins a brief reprieve, but Death still stalks his native land as the plague takes hold, and continues to haunt him with constant reappearances. The Knight demands:

> Is it so cruelly inconceivable to grasp God with the senses? Why should he hide himself in a midst of half-spoken promises and unseen miracles? . . . What is going to happen to those of us who want to believe but aren't able to? . . . Why can't I kill God within me? Why does he live on in this painful and humiliating way even though I curse him and want to tear him out of my heart? . . . I want knowledge, not faith. . . . I want God to stretch out his hand toward me, reveal himself to me. . . . In our fear, we make an image and that image we call God.

But death has no answers, and God is silent. As for Jöns, he is faithful to his master, but cynical about the horrors of the Crusades: "Our crusade," he says, "was such madness that only a genuine idealist could have thought it up . . . . This damned ranting about doom. Is that good for the minds of modern people?" He prefers the simplicity of drink and fornication. To him Christianity is just "ghost stories."

In total contrast to the Knight's fearful dilemmas concerning faith and self-persecution is the position of Joff, a poor travelling entertainer and his beautiful young wife Mia. Joff, in his simplicity of heart, has continual visions of the Virgin and Child. Although Mia laughs lovingly at his excitement following the vision, she is happy to share his unquestioning faith. Only with these unpretentious people does the Knight find solace, "Everything I have said seems meaningless and unreal while I sit here with you and your husband," he says. Mia gives him milk and wild strawberries to eat, the latter symbols of spring or rebirth. It is, as Brigitta Steene suggests in her book on Bergman, a kind of private Eucharist which momentarily redeems the Knight from his doubts. It is only to be expected that Joff is hunted and persecuted by the puritanical and guilt-ridden religious community he seeks innocently to amuse.

At the close, when the chain-dance of Death tops the horizon, it is Joff and Mia who are spared by the Knight's intervention when he distracts Death while they escape. The Knight and his Lady have to accept death, and the squire can do nothing but go along with them. In a program note released with the film, Bergman wrote: "In my film the crusader returns from the Crusades as the soldier returns from war today. In the Middle Ages men lived in terror of the plague. Today they live in fear of the atomic bomb. *The Seventh Seal* is an allegory with a theme that is quite simple: man, his eternal search for God, with death as his only certainty."

Bergman has turned against this group of films, especially *The Virgin Spring* whose motivations he now finds "bogus." With its sparse, stylized, thematic dialogue, its austere sound effects, and its dignified melancholy music, *The Seventh Seal* survives as a compelling, if obsessive film, visually beautiful but permeated by the lighter as well as the darkest aspects of religious experience. It remains a powerful study in the cruelty of the religious impulse once it has soured in the human consciousness and merged with the darker aspects of the psyche. Bergman, at this spiritually troubled time in his life, was concerned with, "the idea of the Christian God as something destructive and fantastically dangerous, something filled with risk for the human being and bringing out in him the dark destructive forces instead of the opposite." Later, by 1960, he had adopted a more humanist position, and "life became much easier to live."

—Roger Manvell

SKUPLIJACI PERJA

(I Even Met Happy Gypsies)

Yugoslavia, 1968

Director: Alexsandar Petrovic

Production: Avala, in association with Prominent; color; running time: 90 minutes.

Screenplay: Aleksandar Petrovic, based on the play by Dan Hampton; **photography:** Tomislav Pinter; **editor:** Milo Mica; **music:** Aleksandar Petrovic; **art designer:** Veljko Despotovic.

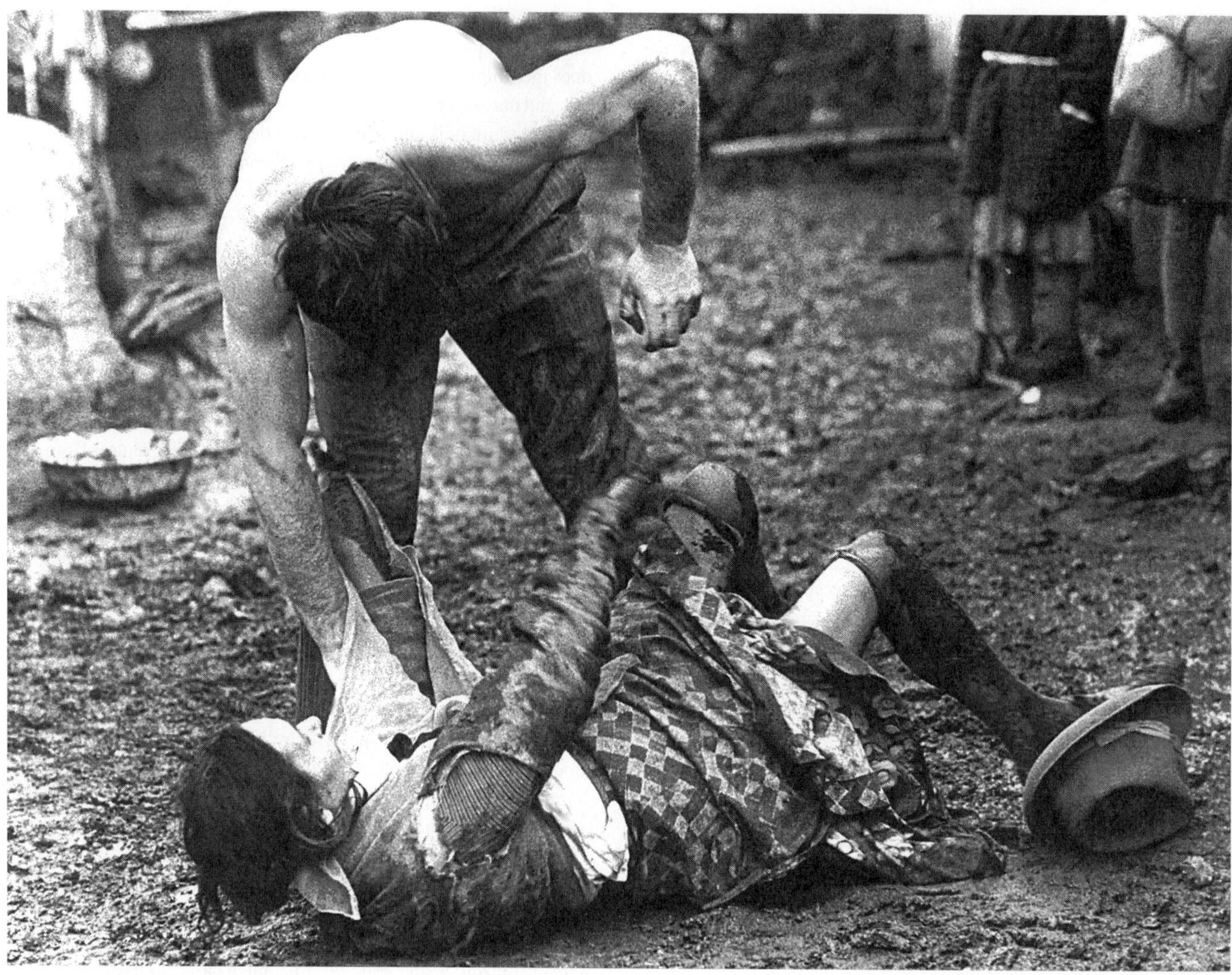

Skuplijaci Perja

Cast: Bekim Fehmiu (*Bora*); Gordana Jovanovic (*Tisa*); Bata Zivojinovic (*Mirta*); Olivera Vuco (*Lence*); Mija Aleksic (*Father Pavle*); Etelka Filipovski (*Bora's Wife*); Milorad Jovanovic (*Toni*); Milivoje Djordjevic (*Sandor*); Rahela Ferari (*Nun*); Severin Bijelic (*Religious peasant*).

* * *

I Even Met Happy Gypsies is the progenitor of all the Yugo-gypsy movies that came after it, most notably Emir Kusturica's *The Time of the Gypsies* and Goran Paskaljevic's *Guardian Angel*, neither of which even recapture the raw authenticity of Petrovic's acutely observed and *felt* picture.

Alexander Petrovic, one of the grand old men of the Yugoslav cinema who died shortly after completing his epic *Migrations*, enjoyed the only major international success of his career with *I Even Met Happy Gypsies*, which was nominated for Best Foreign Film Oscar in 1967, as was Petrovic's *Three* on the previous year. The film actually picked up the Special Jury Prize in Cannes in 1967.

In all of *Happy Gypsies*, there is not a single happy gypsy—the title is an ironic quote from a traditional *tzigane* tune. The actors who play the gypsies may be elated now, however, for this Yugoslav movie has been nominated for an Academy Award, and with good reason. Though it is full of flaws and inconsistencies of style, it depicts, with melancholy and muted colour, the odd, anachronistic ways of all-but-forgotten people.

On the Pannonian plain near Belgrade, a colony of gypsies dwell in a clot of squalor, surviving on what they earn from buying and selling goose feathers. Outstanding among them is an erotic, intemperate feather merchant named Bora, played by Bekim Fehmiu, a Yugoslav actor strongly reminiscent of Jean-Paul Belmondo. Endlessly indulging in wife-beating and mistress-bedding, Bora downs litres of wine and scatters his seed, his feathers, and his future. As the film's principal character, he meanders from confined hovels to expansive farm fields, from rural barrooms to the streets of Belgrade. Where ever he travels, he witnesses—and sometimes acts out—the gypsies' heritage of violence and tragedy, providing the viewer with astonishing glimpses of a rapidly vanishing life.

—Mike Downey

SMILES OF A SUMMER NIGHT

See **SOMMARNATTENS LEENDE**

SMOKE

USA, 1995

Director: Wayne Wang

Production: Miramax Film presents an NDF/Euro Space production in association with Peter Newman; color, Panavision; running time: 108 minutes; length: 3180 meters. Released 9 June 1995 in USA. Cost: $7 million.

Producers: Greg Johnson, Peter Newman, Hisami Kuriowa, Kenzo Horikoshi, Bob Weinstein (executive), Harvey Weinstein (executive), Satoru Iseki (executive); **screenplay:** Paul Auster, based on his short story ''Auggie Wren's Christmas Story''; **photography:** Adam Holender; **editor:** Maysie Hoy; **production design:** Kalina Ivanov; **music:** Rachel Portman.

Cast: Harvey Keitel (*Auggie Wren*); William Hurt (*Paul Benjamin*); Harold Perrineau (*Rashid Cole*); Forest Whitaker (*Cyrus Cole*); Stockard Channing (*Ruby*); Ashley Judd (*Felicity*); Michelle Hurst (*Aunte Em*); Malik Yoba (*The Creep*).

Awards: Silver Bear (Wayne Wang), Berlin International Filmfestival, 1995; Danish Film Critics Bodil Award for Best American Film, 1995; German Film Award for Best Foreign Film, 1995; Independent Spirit Award for Best First Screenplay (Paul Auster), 1995.

Publications

Scripts:

Auster, Paul, *Smoke and Blue in the Face: Two Films*, preface by Wayne Wang, New York, 1995.

Smoke

Articles:

Svendsen, Erik, ''Fortællingens nødvendighed,'' in *Kosmorama*, no. 213, Autumn 1995.

Felperin, Leslie, and Chris Darke, ''Smoke Opera,'' in *Sight and Sound* (London), April 1996.

Nichols, Hayden Bixby, review in *Film Quarterly* (Berkeley), Spring 1998.

* * *

As Auggie Wren (Harvey Keitel) finally tells Paul Benjamin (William Hurt) his Christmas story, we get the only ultra-close-ups of the film *Smoke*. We see Auggie's mouth in ultra-close-up, and the camera then cuts to a corresponding shot of Paul Benjamin's eyes. As it ends the film thus pays tribute to the spoken word and the moving image: next we see Paul Benjamin writing Auggie's story, followed by a visual version. Wayne Wang's film comes alive through its pictures and its many stories, cultivating digression with affection in its superabundance of successful attempts to capture something as volatile as smoke and as weightless as the human soul.

The fulcrum of the story is Auggie's tobacconist's store and in five chapters, named after the five characters of the story, a series of plots unfold that reflect on one another, interweave with one another, and together become the music of the happiest of chances. The characters all are more than meets the eye. The three men, Auggie, Paul, and Rashid (Harold Perrineau), are everyday people, but artists, too. Paul is an author, but with writer's block; Rashid sketches; and Auggie turns out to be an artistic soul with the unique photographic project of taking a picture of the same street corner every morning, every day of the year. Auggie has taken 4000 photographs so far, and although Paul thinks they look the same at first, closer examination reveals the rich variety of people, situations, and by no means least, light. This little corner of the universe is replete with stories if one listens properly, and Auggie does so, transforming everyday life into poetry by his almost meditative project. In his photographs people are captured at a specific moment in their own stories, which take place outside the photographs, just as vital parts of the narrative unfurl off-frame and beyond the plot we are following—in the pasts and futures of the characters, for example.

The three characters all have stories behind them, problematic pasts. Paul has lost his wife, the tragic victim of a robber's stray bullet that took her life just outside Auggie's tobacconist's store. If only she hadn't had the exact change, Auggie meditates, it would not have happened. The black lad Rashid, who saves Paul from being run over, has not only many identities but also many stories he uses to conceal his identity. Perhaps the vagueness of his identity is due to the loss of his mother in infancy and the disappearance of his father when he was young. The same may be true of Auggie, who is sought out by a former girlfriend, Ruby, who says he is the father of Felicity, now a pregnant junkie. Felicity's mother lacks an eye, Rashid's father an arm; both lack proper relationships with their children. Interwoven with this story is the tale of the $5000 Rashid hid in Paul's bookcase. The money changes hands several times in the film, ending in Ruby's possession and disappearing from the plot. We are not told how this story ends any more than we hear who begins to take an interest in Paul's health or what happens to Rashid and his newly-found father. In this way, too, important parts of the plot are played out after the film ends and the film assumes more and more the character of a cross-section of life than a story, narrated with a light-headed facility like the smoke that has given the film its title.

It is the long, inexplicable arm of coincidence that makes the world appear to hang together and which directs its characters towards a resolution of their traumatic pasts. Rashid chances upon the trail of his father, but must be forced by his friends to reveal himself to his father. Auggie has a daughter foisted on him, and Paul learns to reconcile himself to his loss and become a productive author again. Through the examples and support of the others each comes to terms with his thorny past and becomes more complete as a person.

Auggie dates and times his photographs, which he asks Paul to take the time to examine properly. We must take our time over the film, too, and watch it carefully: running across the chapter divisions, which may seem somewhat random, is a wealth of nuances and facets of technique so peculiar to screenplay author Paul Auster that *Smoke* urges itself upon us as actually being his film. Yet it is the director, Wayne Wang, who has imbued it with the pleasure and intangibility of smoke. *Smoke* is a tangible, intense narrative in words and pictures, perhaps a fairy tale played out in the same time frame as Auggie's Christmas story: from summer to Christmas. If so it is a fairy tale full of little stories from one corner of the universe, a film that opens our eyes to the wonderful variety of the world and the music of chance.

—Dan Nissen

SMULTRONSTÄLLET

(Wild Strawberries)

Sweden, 1957

Director: Ingmar Bergman

Production: Svensk Filmindustri; black and white, 35mm; running time: 90 minutes; length: 2,490 meters. Released 26 December 1957. Filmed summer 1957 in Svensk studios and backlots in Rosunda, some exteriors shot in and around Stockholm.

Producer: Allan Ekelund; **screenplay:** Ingmar Bergman; **photography:** Gunnar Fischer; **editor:** Oscar Rosander; **sound:** Aaby Wedin and Lennart Wallin; **art director:** Gittan Gustafsson; **music:** Erik Nordgren; **costume designer:** Millie Ström.

Cast: Victor Sjöström (*Professor Isak Borg*); Bibi Andersson (*Sara*); Ingrid Thulin (*Marianne*); Gunnar Björnstrand (*Evald*); Jullan Kindahl (*Agda*); Folke Sundquist (*Anders*); Björn Bjelvenstam (*Viktor*); Naima Wifstrand (*Isak's mother*); Gunnel Broström (*Mrs. Alman*); Gertrud Fridh (*Isak's wife*); Ake Fridell (*Her lover*); Sif Rund (*Aunt*); Max von Sydow (*Åkerman*); Yngve Nordwall (*Uncle Aron*); Per Sjöstrand (*Sigfrid*); Gio Petré (*Sigbritt*); Gunnel Lindblom (*Charlotta*); Maud Hansson (*Angelica*); Anne-Marie Wiman (*Mrs. Åkerman*); Eva Norée (*Anna*); Monica Ehrling (*The twins*).

Smultronstället

Publications

Script:

Bergman, Ingmar, *Wild Strawberries*, in *Four Screenplays of Ingmar Bergman*, New York, 1960; also published separately, London and New York, 1970.

Books:

Béranger, Jean, *Ingmar Bergman et ses films*, Paris, 1959.
Höök, Marianne, *Ingmar Bergman*, Stockholm, 1962.
Chiaretti, Tommaso, *Ingmar Bergman*, Rome, 1964.
Donner, Jörn, *The Personal Vision of Ingmar Bergman*, Bloomington, Indiana, 1964.
Nelson, David, *Ingmar Bergman: The Search for God*, Boston, 1964.
Steene, Birgitta, *Ingmar Bergman*, New York, 1968.
Gibson, Arthur, *The Silence of God: Creative Response to the Films of Ingmar Bergman*, New York, 1969.
Wood, Robin, *Ingmar Bergman*, New York, 1969.
Sjögren, Henrik, *Regi: Ingmar Bergman*, Stockholm, 1970.
Young, Vernon, *Cinema Borealis: Ingmar Bergman and the Swedish Ethos*, New York, 1971.
Björkman, Stig, and others, editors, *Bergman on Bergman*, New York, 1973.
Ranieri, Tino, *Ingmar Bergman*, Florence, 1974.
Kaminsky, Stuart, editor, *Ingmar Bergman: Essays in Criticism*, New York, 1975.
Bergom-Larsson, Maria, *Ingmar Bergman and Society*, San Diego, 1978.
Kawin, Bruce, *Mindscreen: Bergman, Godard, and the First-Person Film*, Princeton, 1978.
Marion, Denis, *Ingmar Bergman*, Paris, 1979.
Manvell, Roger, *Ingmar Bergman: An Appreciation*, New York, 1980.
Mosley, Philip, *Ingmar Bergman: The Cinema as Mistress*, Boston, 1981.
Petric, Vlada, editor, *Film and Dreams: An Approach to Bergman*, South Salem, New York, 1981.
Cowie, Peter, *Ingmar Bergman: A Critical Biography*, New York, 1982.
Livingston, Paisley, *Ingmar Bergman and the Ritual of Art*, Ithaca, New York, 1982.

Steene, Birgitta, *Ingmar Bergman: A Guide to References and Resources*, Boston, 1982.
Jones, William G., editor, *Talking with Bergman*, Dallas, 1983.
Lefèvre, Raymond, *Ingmar Bergman*, Paris, 1983.
Dervin, Daniel, *Through a Freudian Lens Deeply: A Psychoanalysis of Cinema*, Hillsdale, New Jersey, 1985.
Gado, Frank, *The Passion of Ingmar Bergman*, Durham, North Carolina, 1986.
Bergman, Ingmar, *Laterna Magica*, Stockholm, 1987; as *The Magic Lantern: An Autobiography*, London, 1988.
Cohen, James, *Through a Lens Darkly*, New York, 1991.
Bjorkman, Stig, and Torsten Maans, and Jonas Sima, *Bergman on Bergman: Interviews with Ingmar Bergman*, Cambridge, 1993.
Cohen, Hubert I., *Ingmar Bergman: The Art of Confession*, New York, 1993.
Long, Robert Emmet, *Ingmar Bergman: Film & Stage*, New York, 1994.
Tornqvist, Egil, *Between Stage and Screen: Ingmar Bergman Directs*, Amsterdam, 1995.
Blackwell, Marilyn J., *Gender and Representation in the Films of Ingmar Bergman*, Rochester, 1997.
Michaels, Lloyd, editor, *Ingmar Bergman's Persona*, New York, 1999; revised edition, Cambridge, 2000.

Articles:

Films and Filming (London), October 1958.
Dyer, Peter John, in *Films and Filming* (London), December 1958.
Cavender, Kenneth, in *Sight and Sound* (London), Winter 1958–59.
Stanbrook, Alan, ''An Aspect of Bergman,'' in *Film* (London), March-April 1959.
Hart, Henry, in *Films in Review* (New York), April 1959.
Mekas, Jonas, in *Village Voice* (New York), 1 July 1959.
Archer, Eugene, in *Film Quarterly* (Berkeley), Fall 1959.
McCann, Eleanor, ''The Rhetoric of *Wild Strawberries*,'' in *Sight and Sound* (London), Winter 1960–61.
Blackwood, Caroline, ''The Mystique of Ingmar Bergman,'' in *Encounter* (London), April 1961.
Durgnat, Raymond, and Ian Johnson, ''Puritans Anonymous,'' in *Motion* (London), Autumn 1963.
Steene, Birgitta, in *Film Comment* (New York), Spring 1965.
Scott, James, ''The Achievement of Ingmar Bergman,'' in *Journal of Aesthetics and Art Criticism* (Cleveland), Winter 1965.
Comstock, W. Richard, ''Ingmar Bergman: An Assessment at Mid-Point,'' in *Film Society Review* (New York), April 1966.
Greenberg, H. R., in *American Image*, Spring 1970.
Steene, Birgitta, ''Images and Words in Ingmar Bergman's Films,'' in *Cinema Journal* (Evanston, Illinois), Fall 1970.
Welsh, James, in *Cinema Journal* (Evanston, Illinois), Fall 1971.
Tulloch, J., ''Images of Dying and the Artistic Role: Ingmar Bergman's *Wild Strawberries*,'' in *Australian Journal of Screen Theory* (Kensington, New South Wales), March 1977.
Magny, Joel, in *Cinéma* (Paris), October 1978.
Eberwein, Robert T., ''The Filmic Dream and Point of View,'' in *Literature/Film Quarterly* (Salisbury, Maryland), no. 3, 1980.
Casebier, Allan, ''Reductionism without Discontent: The Case of *Wild Strawberries* and *Persona*,'' in *Film Psychology Review* (New York), Winter-Spring 1980.
''*Smultronstället* Issue'' of *Avant-Scène du Cinéma* (Paris), July-August 1984.
Andersson, L. G., ''*Smultronstället* och homo viator-motivet,'' in *Filmhaftet* (Uppsala, Sweden), May 1988.
Trasatti, S., ''Bergman, il paradosso di un 'Ateo cristiano,''' in *Castoro Cinema* (Florence), November-December 1991.
Clark, John, ''Ingmar Bergman,'' in *Premiere* (Boulder), vol. 6, no. 1, September 1992.
Lansing Smith, Evans, ''Framing the Underworld: Threshold Imagery in Murnau, Cocteau, and Bergman,'' in *Literature/Film Quarterly* (Salisbury), vol. 24, no. 3, 1996.
Lucas, Tim, in *Video Watchdog* (Cincinnati), no. 34, 1996.
Bouda, Marek, ''Film a sen,'' in *Film a Doba* (Prague), vol. 44, no. 4, Winter 1998.

* * *

Wild Strawberries is to Ingmar Bergman what *King Lear* was to Shakespeare—a study in old age and the need for an old man to discover the errors and inhumane deeds of his life and, as he cannot mend them, come to terms with his own fallibility. Lear (''four score and upward'') learns the truth about himself by passing through a violent period of deprivation and madness, occasioned by the cruelty of his two married daughters. Professor Isak Borg (played by Victor Sjöström in his late 70s) is an honored physician, and he learns his home-truths through a succession of dreams experienced during a drive by car to Lund, where he is to receive yet another academic honor. He is accompanied by his daughter-in-law, Marianne, who is estranged from her husband, Isak's son. She is quite unafraid of Isak, prompting in him the self-examination that the dreams, forming the principal action of the film, represent. Like Lear, Isak Borg emerges purged, if not wholly changed, from the subconscious confrontations with self-truth. Much of the film he narrates himself as part of the self-examination, as if under some form of analysis. The concept of the film was influenced by Strindberg's *Dream Play*, which Bergman had directed for the theater.

The title, *Wild Strawberries*, refers to the fruit that symbolizes for the Swedish the emergence of spring, the rebirth of life. The motif of wild strawberries frequently recurs in Bergman's films. Isak Borg is revealed as a cold-natured, egotistical, irascible and authoritarian old man, even though the journey should be a time of happiness for him in terms of academic recognition. The most macabre of the dreams comes before the journey has even begun; it is a dream Bergman claims frequently to have had himself, that of seeing a coffin fall free into the street from a driverless hearse and then breaking open. In the film a hand emerges from the coffin and grasps Isak; he finds the face of the corpse to be his own.

During the journey by car, Marianne is very blunt with her father-in-law, whose cold nature and lack of humanity match that of his son. The professor dozes as the car rides along the country highway. A succession of dreams reveals to him the shortcomings and losses of his youth. On the journey they pass the now empty house among the birchwoods where, in distant years, Isak had spent his youth. He dreams of the loss of the girl he had loved but was afraid to kiss, his cousin Sara, who picked wild strawberries for him to share with her during their failing courtship. He eventually loses her to his more ardent brother, Sigfrid. Another stop is made for the professor to see his 96-year-old mother. ''We imagined her,'' says Bergman, ''to be somewhere between 90 and 100—almost mythical.'' Marianne considers her to be ''ice-cold, in some ways more frightening than death itself''; Isak, then, is the product of a cold womb.

Sara is re-incarnated as a student who, hitchhiking with a couple of young men, is offered a lift by the professor and his daughter-in-law. The presence of this double excites Isak to dream of the youthful Sarah who shows him his now-aged face in a mirror, for in his dreams he remains his present age, while those from his past are seen as they were when they were young. When he begs her not leave him this time, he finds himself voiceless. She can no longer hear him. Though she leaves him for his brother, her seducer, in a later dream she takes him by the hand and shows him the joy of happy parenthood.

The professor's final dream is at once the most revealing and the most tormenting. Like a young student, he faces a humiliating oral examination which is somewhat like a trial. Those who have been most intimate with him are witnesses. He can make no sense of what is asked of him; even the female cadaver he is called upon to examine, rises and laughs in his face. He is forced to be the witness concerning his dead wife's unfaithfulness with her sensual, middle-aged lover, and to hear her bitter description of him as "completely cold and hypocritical." (There is a melancholy burlesque of this ill-fated marriage in the behavior of a bickering couple from an earlier scene.) At the conclusion of this trial-examination, Isak is condemned by the judge-examiner and sentenced to a punishment of loneliness. When he wakes, Marianne reveals she is pregnant and determined to go back to her husband, insisting on her right to have the child he, as the father, does not want her to have.

Wild Strawberries, for all the horror of certain moments, is a film full of compassionate understanding and the need for warmth and humanity. There is a compassion for this old man who cannot respond to people and who lacks the important quality of love and concern for others, particularly for women. Yet there is humor, even touches of light-heartedness, in the film, particularly in the scenes with the students and those between Isak and his aged housekeeper, who proves his match when it comes to mutual criticism. It is indeed this overall compassion that makes *Wild Strawberries* so memorable, crowned by the magisterial performance of Victor Sjöström, the pioneer Swedish film director.

—Roger Manvell

SNOW WHITE AND THE SEVEN DWARFS

USA, 1937

Supervising Director: David Hand

Production: Walt Disney Studios; Technicolor, 35mm, animation; running time: 83 minutes. Released 4 February 1938, but premiered in December 1937, released through RKO Radio Pictures Inc. Re-released 1943, 1952, 1958, 1967, 1975, 1983. Filmed in Walt Disney Studios. Cost: $1,500,000.

Producer: Walt Disney; **screenplay:** Ted Sears, Otto Englander, Earl Hurd, Dorothy Ann Blank, Richard Creedon, Dick Richard, Merrill de Maris and Webb Smith, from the fairy tale "Snow White" from *Grimm's Fairy Tales*; **sequence directors:** Perce Pearce, Larry Morey, William Cottrell, Wilfred Jackson, and Ben Sharpsteen; **art directors:** Charles Phillippi, Hugh Gennesy, Terrell Stapp, McLaren Stewart, Harold Miles, Tom Codrick, Gustaf Tenggren, Kenneth Anderson, Kendall O'Connor, and Hazel Sewell; **music:** Frank Churchill, Leigh Harline, Paul Smith, and Larry Morey; **character designers:** Albert Hunter and Jo Grant; **supervising animators:** Hamilton Luske, Vladamir Tytla, Fred Moore, and Norman Ferguson; **animators:** Frank Thomas, Dick Lundy, Arthur Babbitt, Eric Larson, Milton Kahl, Robert Stokes, James Algar, Al Eugster, Cy Young, Joshua Meador, Ugo D'Orsi, George Rowley, Les Clark, Fred Spencer, Bill Roberts, Bernard Garbutt, Grim Natwick, Jack Campbell, Marvin Woodward, James Culhane, Stan Quackenbush, Ward Kimball, Wolfgang Reitherman, and Robert Martsch; **backgrounds:** Samuel Armstrong, Mique Nelson, Merle Cox, Claude Coats, Phil Dike, Ray Lockrem, and Maurice Noble.

Snow White and the Seven Dwarfs

Cast: Voices: Adriana Caselotti (*Snow White*); Harry Stockwell (*Prince Charming*); Lucille LaVerne (*The Queen*); Moroni Olsen (*Magic Mirror*); Billy Gilbert (*Sneezy*); Pinto Colvig (*Sleepy and Grumpy*); Otis Harlan (*Happy*); Scotty Mattraw (*Bashful*); Roy Atwell (*Doc*); Stuart Buchanan (*Humbert, the Queen's huntsman*); Marion Darlington (*Bird sounds and warbling*); The Fraunfelder Family (*Yodeling*).

Awards: Oscar, Special Award to Walt Disney, 1938; Venice Film Festival, Great Art Trophy, 1938; New York Film Critics Award, Special Award, 1938.

Publications

Books:

Field, Robert D., *The Art of Walt Disney*, New York, 1942.
Eisenstein, Sergei, *Film Sense*, edited by Jay Leyda, New York, 1942.
Miller, Diane Disney, *The Story of Walt Disney*, edited by Pete Martin, New York, 1957.
Stephenson, Ralph, *Animation in the Cinema*, New York, 1967.
Schickel, Richard, *The Disney Version: The Life, Times, Art, and Commerce of Walt Disney*, New York, 1968; revised edition, London, 1986.
Bessy, Maurice, *Walt Disney*, Paris, 1970.
Kurland, Gerald, *Walt Disney, The Master of Animation*, Charlottesville, Virginia, 1971.
Finch, Christopher, *The Art of Walt Disney, from Mickey Mouse to the Magic Kingdoms*, New York, 1973; revised edition, 1999.
Maltin, Leonard, *The Disney Films*, New York, 1973; revised edition, 1984; 2000.
Thomas, Bob, *Walt Disney: An American Original*, New York, 1976.
Edera, Bruno, *Full Length Animated Features*, edited by John Halas, New York, 1977.
Leebron, Elizabeth, and Lynn Gartley, *Walt Disney: A Guide to References and Resources*, Boston, 1979.
Peary, Gerald and Danny, editors, *The American Animated Cartoon*, New York, 1980.
Thomas, Frank, and Ollie Johnston, *Disney Animation: The Illusion of Life*, New York, 1982; revised edition, 1999.
Bruno, Eduardo, and Enrico Ghezzi, *Walt Disney*, Venice, 1985.
Mosley, Leonard, *Disney's World: A Biography*, New York, 1985; as *The Real Walt Disney*, London, 1986.
Culhane, Shamus, *Talking Animals and Other People*, New York, 1986.
Grant, John, *Encyclopaedia of Walt Disney's Animated Characters*, New York, 1987; revised edition, 1998.
Holliss, Richard, and Brian Sibley, *Walt Disney's Snow White and the Seven Dwarfs: The Making of the Classic Film*, London, 1987; revised edition 1994.
Krause, Martin F., and Linda Witkowski, *Walt Disney's Snow White and the Seven Dwarfs: An Art in Its Making Featuring the Collection of Stephen H. Ison*, Indianapolis, Indiana, 1994.
Thomas, Bob, *Building a Company: Roy O. Disney and the Creation of an Entertainment Empire*, New York, 1998.
Smith, Dave, *Disney A to Z: The Updated Official Encyclopedia*, New York, 1999.
Solomon, Charles, *The Art of Disney*, New York, 2000.

Articles:

Ferguson, Otis, in *Life* (New York), 13 December 1937.
Variety (New York), 29 December 1937.
Boone, Andrew, in *Popular Science Monthly* (New York), January 1938.
New York Times, 14 January 1938.
Spectator (London), 4 March 1938.
Grauer, G. W., ''The *Snow White* Debate Continues,'' in *Christian Century* (Chicago), August 1938.
La Farge, Christopher, ''Walt Disney and the Art Form,'' in *Theatre Arts* (New York), September 1941.
MacGowan, Kenneth, in *Hollywood Quarterly*, no.1, 1945.
''A Wonderful World: Growing Impact of the Disney World,'' in *Newsweek* (New York), 18 April 1955.
Panofsky, Erwin, in *Film: An Anthology*, edited by Daniel Talbot, New York, 1959.
Sadoul, Georges, in *Cahiers du Cinéma* (Paris), June 1962.
Brewer, Roy, ''Walt Disney, R.I.P.,'' in *National Review* (New York), 10 January 1967.
Poncet, Marie-Therese, ''Walt Disney de Mickey à Disneyland,'' in *Anthologie du cinéma 2*, Paris, 1968.
Village Voice (New York), 2 August 1973.
Cassian, N., in *Cinema* (Bucharest), September 1973.
Sorel, S., in *Télécine* (Paris), December 1973-January 1974.
Brody, M., ''The Wonderful World of Disney: Its Psychological Appeal,'' in *American Image* (Detroit), no. 4, 1976.
Paul, William, ''Art, Music, Nature, and Walt Disney,'' in *Movie* (London), Spring 1977.
Culhane, John, ''The Last of the Old Nine Men,'' in *American Film* (Washington, DC), June 1977.
Canemaker, J., ''Disney Animation: History and Technique,'' in *Film News* (New York), January-February 1979.
Canemaker, J., ''Disney Design 1928–1979,'' in *Millimeter* (New York), February 1979.
Gomiscek, T., in *Ekran* (Ljubljana), nos. 5–6, 1979.
Kinney, Nancy S., in *Magill's Survey of Cinema 4*, Englewood Cliffs, New Jersey, 1980.
Hulsens, E., in *Film en Televisie* (Brussels), April 1984.
Reid's Film Index (Wyong), no. 3, 1989.
Hawkins, Harriet, ''The Wonderful World of Carl Jung,'' in *Modern Review*, vol. 1, no. 3, Spring 1992.
Holusha, J., ''*Snow White* Is Made Over Frame by Frame and Byte by Byte,'' in *New York Times*, vol. 142, D5, 30 June 1993.
Harmetz, Aljean, ''Disney's 'Old Men' Savor the Vintage Years,'' in *New York Times*, 4 July 1993.
Kennedy, L., in *Village Voice* (New York), vol. 38, 13 July 1993.
''*Snow White* Is Fairest of All, Thanks to Digital Makeover,'' in *Film Journal* (New York), vol. 96, August 1993.
Fisher, Bob, ''Off to Work We Go: The Digital Restoration of Snow White,'' in *American Cinematographer* (Hollywood), vol. 74, no. 9, September 1993.
Care, R., ''Record Track,'' in *Scarlet Street* (Glen Rock), no. 12, Fall 1993.
Care, Ross, and others, ''Walt Disney's *Snow White and the Seven Dwarfs / Pinocchio*,'' in *Cue Sheet* (Hollywood), vol. 10, no. 1–2, Spring 1993–1994.
Felperin Sharman, Leslie, in *Sight & Sound* (London), vol. 4, no. 8, August 1994.
Catsos, G., ''Disney's Folly!'' in *Filmfax* (Evanston), no. 48, January/February 1995.
Nesbet, Anne, ''Inanimations: *Snow White* and *Ivan the Terrible*,'' in *Film Quarterly* (Berkeley), vol. 50, no. 4, Summer 1997.
Wright, Terri Martin, ''Romancing the Tale: Walt Disney's Adaptation of the Grimm's *Snow White*,'' in *Journal of Popular Film and Television* (Washington, D.C.), vol. 25, no. 3, Fall 1997.

* * *

In his years as an animator, director, producer, and magnate, Walt Disney did more than any other individual to influence and shape the look of animated films. As a pioneer he was willing to take risks by experimenting with various technical inventions. In almost every case these experiments were successful. By searching for new and different ways to expand and advance the cartoon format, Walt Disney kept several steps ahead of his competitors. His animated films became the technological standard of the industry and no one came close to matching them.

Among Disney's most innovative films is *Snow White and the Seven Dwarfs*, one of the first feature-length animated cartoons. Part of his reason for venturing into the feature film market was economic. Although Disney's eight-minute cartoons were among the most popular of their day, these shorts had a limited earning potential. Cartoons were only a secondary attraction at the movie theaters and did not receive top billing or top dollar. With accelerating production costs, Disney realized that it would soon become more and more difficult to turn a profit. Looking ahead to the future, he saw feature film production as a way to keep his studio in the black.

The production of his first feature-length cartoon proved to be an enormous undertaking. Many of Disney's competitors felt that the task was impossible and news spread throughout the trade papers about ''Disney's Folly.'' By his own admission Disney was not totally aware of all the complexities that would accompany his new project. He viewed the film as a learning experience and tackled each obstacle with undaunted perseverance.

Disney soon discovered that the scope of a feature-length cartoon dictated some technical changes from the shorter length format. For example, the field size (the size of the painted cels) would have to be enlarged to make room for more detail. This not only required the manufacture of larger cels, but also new drawing boards. In addition, the animation cameras had to be adjusted to photograph the larger field size.

Another innovation used was the multi-plane camera. Actually, Disney's multi-plane camera was first used to a small extent in a short cartoon called *The Old Mill*. The ability of this tool to enhance a feeling of depth proved more useful in Disney's features. With conventional flat animation cels it is difficult to simulate a dolly or a pan. For example, when a camera dollys in on a flat animation cel, all the objects in the scene appear to grow larger at the same rate, whereas in reality the foreground would grow much quicker while the background objects would stay relatively the same size. Since the multi-plane camera holds the foreground and background cels on different planes, it is possible to manipulate the images on each cel at different speeds. Disney's first multi-plane camera was fourteen feet tall with seven different levels, all of which could be controlled independently of each other.

With the expansion of the screen time for *Snow White and the Seven Dwarfs*, Disney also had to expand the number of employees in his company. Approximately 750 artists worked on the two million drawings that made up the film. These artists worked in an assembly-line fashion, each group responsible for a specific task. Some artists worked on the layout, others on background, some worked as in-betweeners for the chief animators, and other artists were inkers and painters. One group worked in special effects animation. In the past, cartoon animators had paid little attention to special effects. However, *Snow White and the Seven Dwarfs* contains many examples of effects animation in the representation of lighting, smoke, rain, and other details.

Snow White was also different from other cartoons in that some of the characters were human. Most cartoons feature animals, and although they had anthropomorphic traits, they were all removed from the actual world. The characters of the Queen, Prince, Snow White, and the Huntsman presented a special problem in their ''realism.'' To help keep the animation natural, live-action reference footage was shot of actors as a rotoscope (where the animation is traced directly off the live-action film), but mainly as a guide for the animators to follow.

After three years in the making, *Snow White* was finally ready for a Christmas release in 1937. The film was an instant success and received nothing less than glowing reviews. During its initial release the film grossed over $8 million and it continues to be a financial success with each subsequent re-issue. ''Disney's Folly'' proved to be the way of the future and feature-length animated films continue to be made today, long after the eight-minute theatrical cartoon format has died out. Once again, Walt Disney was proven to be a most important innovator and promoter of the art of animation.

—Linda J. Obalil

SODOM UND GOMORRHA

(Die Legende von Sünde und Strafe; The Queen of Sin and the Spectacle of Sodom and Gomorrah)

Austria, 1922

Director: Michael Kertész (later Michael Curtiz)

Production: Sascha-Filmindustrie AG, Vienna; black and white, 35 mm, partly colored. Originally in two parts: Part I, 2,100 meters, prologue and four acts; Part II, 1800 meters, 6 acts. Reconstruction by Josef Gloger, Filmarchiv Austria, in 6 reels, length: 3,253.7 meters; running time: 150 minutes. Released 13 October 1922 (Part I: *Die Sünde*) and 20 October 1922 (Part II: *Die Strafe*) in Vienna; released in Berlin, Germany, 15 August 1923. Filmed 1921/22 in Laaerberg, Vienna, in the city of Vienna, at Schönbrunn, at Hermesvilla in Vienna, Laxenburg near Vienna, and Erzberg in Styria.

Producer: Count Alexander Kolowrat; **screenplay:** Ladislaus Vajda, Michael Kertész; **photography:** Gustav Ucicky; **art directors:** Julius von Borsody (chief architect), Hans Rouc, Stephan Wessely; **costume design:** Remigius Geyling; **music arrangement:** Giuseppe Becce.

Cast: Lucy Doraine (*Miss Mary Conway; Sarah, Lot's wife; Lia, Queen of Syria*); Erika Wagner (*Mrs. Agathe Conway*); Georg Reimers (*Mr. Jackson Harber, banker*); Walter Slezak (*Eduard Harber; student; gold smith in Galilea*); Michael Varkonyi (*Angel; priest*); Kurt Ehrle (*Harry Lighton*); thousands of extras (some sources say 3000, others 14,000), including Willi Forst, Paula Wessely, Hans Thimig, and Béla Balázs.

Publications

Books:

Gottlein, Arthur, *Der österreichische Film. Ein Bilderbuch*, Vienna, 1976.

Fritz, Walter, and Götz Lachmann, editors, *Sodom und Gomorrha—Die Legende von Sünde und Strafe*, Vienna, 1988.

Pluch, Barbara, *Der österreichische Monumentalstummfilm—Ein Beitrag zur Filmgeschichte der zwanziger Jahre*, Master's thesis, University of Vienna, 1989.

Fritz, Walter, *Im Kino erlebe ich die Welt. 100 Jahre Kino und Film in Österreich*, Vienna, 1997.

Articles:

Krenn, Günter, ''Sodom und Gomorrha 96—Die unendliche Geschichte einer Rekonstruktion,'' in *Österreichisches Filmarchiv Jahrbuch*, Vienna, 1996.

Büttner, Elisabeth, and Christian Dewald, ''Michael Kertész. Filmarbeit in Österreich bzw. bei der Sascha-Filmindustrie A.-G., Wien, 1919–1926,'' in *Elektrische Schatten. Beiträge zur österreichischen Stummfilmgeschichte*, edited by Francesco Bono, Paolo Caneppele, and Günter Krenn, Vienna, 1999.

* * *

Sodom und Gomorrha remained a near mythical film for many decades. Only a few fragments of the most grandiose film, not only of producer Sascha Kolowrat, but also of the Austrian silent film era, were available to film historians. The present copy, restored by the Filmarchiv Austria, presents a substantial portion of the original film with missing scenes replaced by intertextual commentaries to maintain the narrative flow.

The demise of the Austro-Hungarian Monarchy in 1918 forced the enterprising Kolowrat to look for new business strategies and markets for his Sascha-Film industrie, the largest film company in Austria. On a trip to New York in 1919/20, where he set up the Herz Film Corporation as an American distribution outlet, he was inspired by D.W. Griffiths's *Intolerance* (1916) to create his own spectaculars.

For the biggest project, *Sodom and Gomorrha*, he assigned the direction to Michael Kertész, a Hungarian director with great organizational skills who had fled to Vienna for political reasons, but also because Budapest had become too small for his aspirations. Eventually he also outgrew Vienna and responded to an offer from Hollywood, where he became famous as Michael Curtiz. He co-wrote the script with his fellow Hungarian Ladislaus Vajda. The director's then wife, Lucy Doraine, played the leading role; soon after the film was completed they were divorced. The son was played by Walter Slezak, who also moved to Hollywod.

Other members of the crew went on to fame. Julius von Borsody became a highly regarded set designer for many decades in Austrian film. The cameramen were Gustav Ucicky, who worked as a director in Germany in the 1930s and from 1938 to 1945 at Wien-Film, and Franz Planer, who became a highly successful cinematographer in Hollywood. In short, the film was a concentration of young talents who later made their mark in Hollywood or Austria; among the crowd of extras were also the future stars Paula Wessely and Willi Forst.

The film opens at the London stock exchange, showing Harber as a ruthless capitalist. He wants to marry Mary Conway, the daughter of his former lover. The young girl does not love him, but both she and her mother want the life of luxury he can provide. She rejects her true love, the sculptor, who tries to commit suicide. Mary's personality has changed: she flirts with Harber's son Eduard and tries to seduce his teacher, a priest. To present her altered character, the first of the symbolic acts shows Mary as the cruel Queen of Syria, capable of ordering the execution of a young jeweller (played by the same actor as Eduard), who has tried to help her. The action returns to the present with Eduard and his father planning to meet Mary in the garden pavillon. Before they arrive, Mary falls asleep and dreams that Eduard kills his father in a fight over her. She now suddenly finds herself in biblical Sodom as Lot's wife, who serves the love goddess Astarte. The film revels in lavish orgiastic scenes until God destroys the town in punishment. Mary, denounced by the priest, is being led out for execution, when the horror of the situation awakens her from her nightmare. Purified in spirit she recognizes that a loveless marriage for money and her flirtatious behaviour will end in disaster. She returns to the sculptor Harry and a moral life.

With its elaborate structure—a frame story with a plot within a plot—there is no doubt that *Sodom und Gomorrha* is confusing. Kolowrat and Kertész were clearly striving for sensationalism with the enormous cast, the daring (for their time) orgy scenes, and the cruel, shameless, seductive behavior of Mary. Today the mass scenes border at times on the unintendedly comic, showing as they do hundreds of people moving around aimlessly waving their arms or palm fronds. Remarkable are Lucy Doraine's extravagant contemporary gowns, sexy historical skimpy dresses, and bizarre head wear in the biblical flashback, all created by Remigius Geyling, head set designer at the Vienna Burgtheater. Lucy Doraine plays the roles of Mary Conway, Lot's wife and the Queen of Syria.

The imposing buildings in the film, with the temple of Sodom as the centerpiece, were erected in the south of Vienna on Laaerberg; the studio in Sievering was much too small for such grandiose sets. In this time of economic depression the film offered work for many of the area's unemployed, including technicians, painters, carpenters, hairdressers, sculptors, and extras. While the film cannot be considered a cinematic masterpiece, it commands admiration as the grandest monumental film of the Austrian silent film era and an important milestone in filmmaking.

—Gertraud Steiner Daviau

SOME LIKE IT HOT

USA, 1959

Director: Billy Wilder

Production: Ashton Productions and the Mirisch Company; black and white, 35mm; running time: 120 minutes. Released 1959 by United Artists.

Producers: Billy Wilder with Doane Harrison and I. A. L. Diamond; **screenplay:** Billy Wilder and I. A. L. Diamond, from an unpublished story by R. Thoeren and M. Logan; **photography:** Charles Lang; **editor:** Arthur Schmidt; **sound:** Fred Lau; **art director:** Ted Haworth; **music:** Adolph Deutsch; **costume designer:** Orry-Kelly.

Cast: Marilyn Monroe (*Sugar Kane*); Tony Curtis (*Joe/Josephine*); Jack Lemmon (*Jerry/Daphne*); George Raft (*Spats Colombo*); Pat

Some Like It Hot

O'Brien (*Mulligan*); Joe E. Brown (*Osgood Fielding III*); Nehemiah Persoff (*Little Bonaparte*); John Shawlee (*Sweet Sue*); Billy Gray (*Sig Poliakoff*); George Stone (*Toothpick*); Dave Barry (*Beinstock*); Mike Mazurki and Harry Wilson (*Spats's henchmen*); Beverly Wills (*Dolores*); Barbara Drew (*Nellie*); Edward G. Robinson Jr. (*Paradise*); Tom Kennedy (*Bouncer*); John Indrisano (*Walter*).

Award: Oscar for Costume Design-Black and White, 1959.

Publications

Script:

Wilder, Billy, and I. A. L. Diamond, *Some Like It Hot: A Screenplay*, New York, 1959.

Books:

Conway, Michael, and Mark Ricci, editors, *The Films of Marilyn Monroe*, New York, 1964.
Madsen, Axel, *Billy Wilder*, Bloomington, Indiana, 1969.
Wood, Tom, *The Bright Side of Billy Wilder, Primarily*, New York, 1970.
Kobal, John, *Marilyn Monroe: A Life on Film*, New York, 1974.
Widenen, Don, *Lemmon: A Biography*, New York, 1975.
Parish, James R., and Michael Pitts, *The Great Gangster Pictures*, Metuchen, New Jersey, 1976.
Baltake, Joe, *The Films of Jack Lemmon*, Secaucus, New Jersey, 1977; revised edition, 1987.
Seidman, Steve, *The Film Career of Billy Wilder*, Boston, 1977.
Zolotow, Maurice, *Billy Wilder in Hollywood*, New York, 1977; reprinted, 1988.
Dick, Bernard F., *Billy Wilder*, Boston, 1980; revised edition, Cambridge, 1996.
Giannetti, Louis, *Masters of the American Cinema*, Englewood Cliffs, New Jersey, 1981.
Freedland, Michael, *Jack Lemmon*, London, 1985.
Summers, Anthony, *Goddess: The Secret Lives of Marilyn Monroe*, London, 1985.
Rollyson, Carl E., *Marilyn Monroe: A Life of the Actress*, Ann Arbor, Michigan, 1986.
Dyer, Richard, *Heavenly Bodies: Film Stars and Society*, London, 1987.
Jacob, Jerome, *Billy Wilder*, Paris, 1988.
Seidl, Claudius, *Billy Wilder: Seine Filme, sein Leben*, Munich, 1988.
Lally, Kevin, *Wilder Times: The Life of Billy Wilder*, New York, 1996.
Sikov, Ed, *On Sunset Boulevard: The Life and Times of Billy Wilder*, New York, 1998.
Crowe, Cameron, *Conversations with Wilder*, New York, 1999.
Leaming, Barbara, *Marilyn Monroe*, New York, 2000.

Articles:

Life (New York), 20 April 1959.
McVay, Douglas, ''The Eye of a Cynic,'' in *Films and Filming* (London), January 1960.
Schumach, Murray, ''The Wilder—and Funnier—Touch,'' in *New York Times Magazine*, 24 January 1960.
Lemmon, Jack, ''Such Fun to Be Funny,'' in *Films and Filming* (London), November 1960.
Roman, Robert, ''Marilyn Monroe,'' in *Films in Review* (New York), October 1962.
Higham, Charles, ''Cast a Cold: The Films of Billy Wilder,'' in *Sight and Sound* (London), Spring 1963.
''The Films of Billy Wilder,'' in *Film Comment* (New York), Summer 1965.
Mundy, Robert, and Michael Wallington, ''Interview with I. A. L. Diamond,'' in *Cinema* (London), October 1969.
Baltake, Joe, ''Jack Lemmon,'' in *Films in Review* (New York), January 1970.
McBride, Joseph, and Michael Wilmington, ''The Private Life of Billy Wilder,'' in *Film Quarterly* (Berkeley), Summer 1970.
Farber, Stephen, ''The Films of Billy Wilder,'' in *Film Comment* (New York), Winter 1971.
Froug, William, ''Interview with I. A. L. Diamond,'' in *The Screenwriter Looks at the Screenwriter*, New York, 1972.
Kaufmann, Stanley, in *Horizon* (Los Angeles), Winter 1973.
''Dialogue on Film: Billy Wilder and I. A. L. Diamond,'' in *American Film* (Washington, DC), July-August 1976.
Broeske, Pat H., in *Magill's Survey of Cinema 4*, Englewood Cliffs, New Jersey, 1980.
''Billy Wilder Issue'' of *Filmcritica* (Rome), November-December 1982.

Frank, Sam, ''I. A. L. Diamond,'' in *American Screenwriters*, edited by Robert E. Morsberger, Stephen O. Lesser, and Randall Clark, Detroit, 1984.

Cinema Novo (Porto), May-August 1984.

Buckley, M., ''Jack Lemmon,'' in *Films in Review* (New York), December 1984 and January and February 1985.

Columbus, C., ''Wilder Times,'' in *American Film* (Washington, DC), March 1986.

Palmer, J., ''Enunciation and Comedy: *Kind Hearts and Coronets*,'' in *Screen* (Oxford), vol. 30, no. 1/2, 1989.

Hommel, Michel, ''Woman's Director,'' in *Skrien* (Amsterdam), no. 176, February-March 1991.

Cohan, S., ''Cary Grant in the Fifties: Indiscretions of the Bachelor's Masquerade,'' in *Screen* (Oxford), vol. 33, no. 4, 1992.

Straayer, C., ''Redressing the 'Natural': The Temporary Transvestite Film,'' in *Wide Angle* (Baltimore), no. 1, 1992.

Wilmington, Michael, ''Saint Jack,'' in *Film Comment* (New York), vol. 29, no. 2, March-April 1993.

Thomson, D., ''Ten Movies That Showed Hollywood How to Live,'' in *Movieline* (Escondido), vol. 8, July 1997.

Premiere (Boulder), vol. 11, February 1998.

Rothman, Cliff, ''A 40-Year-Old Comedy That Hasn't Grown Stale,'' in *The New York Times*, section 2, AR24, 1 August 1999.

* * *

If there is a candidate for the funniest closing line in cinema history, it must surely be Osgood's declaration ''Nobody's perfect!'' at the end of Billy Wilder's spoof on sexual role playing, *Some Like It Hot*. Utterly unshakeable in his love for Daphne and trusting of his passionate instincts, Osgood overlooks all, including gender.

Men masquerading as women have been the source of great comic scenes and characters throughout the history of entertainment, whether the sexual identity beneath the garments and makeup was straight or gay. Until recently, men in women's clothes have found acceptance on the screen only when their sexual identity was either ambiguous or categorically heterosexual: dressing up was only an extension of the act of performance. While sexual politics were not the focus of Wilder and Diamond's script, audiences were left with a closing line which was a non-resolution of the issue at hand. Of the two men whose lives were saved by dressing as women, one found love by maintaining that persona: Jerry's acceptance of Osgood's proposal was the best single example of *l'amour fou* since Buñuel. Many years later Hollywood is still putting straight men in dresses and then confirming their heterosexuality (albeit with a greater understanding of what it means to be a woman, as in *Tootsie*.)

While many of the comic scenes from *Some Like it Hot* revolve around a spoof of the gangster era (the film begins in Chicago in 1929 with Joe and Jerry witnessing a Valentine's Day-like massacre) and its screen incarnations (George Raft parodies his coin flip from *Scarface*), much of the best comedy results from an examination of sexual identity. In the beginning of the film, the all-girl band which Jerry and Joe have joined is bedding down for the night in their train berths. Having erased their masculinity to avoid being erased by gangsters, Joe and Jerry (now Josephine and Daphne) participate in an evening of ''berth rights.'' When Joe tries to assert his masculinity with Sugar, Jerry insists he maintain his female identity. Aware of their dilemma, our pleasure becomes dependent on the ramifications of gender identification and sexual exposure. In the course of the film Joe re-asserts his masculinity and finds love with Sugar while Jerry pursues his femininity and finds love with Osgood.

Legendary in Hollywood for the trouble Marilyn Monroe caused Wilder on the set, the film was a great commercial success and escalated Wilder's position in Hollywood. His esteem hit its peak with his next release, *The Apartment*. These two films signalled the beginning of one of the most successful director/actor teams in the history of American cinema. Until 1959 Jack Lemmon had been a talent in search of expansion; with Wilder he unleashed his neurotic mannerisms and became the director's favourite performer, appearing in seven Wilder films.

With *Some Like It Hot*, Billy Wilder and his writing partner, I. A. L. Diamond, combined the physicality of the Mack Sennett era with the wit and complications of 1930s screwball comedy to make the funniest American film of the 1950s and one of the greatest of the genre.

—Doug Tomlinson

SOMETHING IN BETWEEN

See **NESTO IZMEDJU**

SOMMARNATTENS LEENDE

(Smiles of a Summer Night)

Sweden, 1955

Director: Ingmar Bergman

Production: Svensk Filmindustri; black and white, 35mm, running time: 108 minutes; length: 2,975 meters. Released 26 December 1955. Filmed Summer 1955 in Svensk studios in Råsunda, exteriors shot in small towns such as Malmö and Ystad. Cost: Bergman states $75,000, other sources claim up to $150,000.

Producer: Allan Ekelund; **screenplay:** Ingmar Bergman; **photography:** Gunnar Fischer; **editor:** Oscar Rosander; **sound:** P. O. Petterson; **art director:** P. A. Lundgren; **music:** Erik Nordgren; **costume designer:** Mago.

Cast: Ulla Jacobsson (*Anne Egerman*); Eva Dahlbeck (*Desirée Armfeldt*); Margit Carlquist (*Charlotte Malcolm*); Harriet Andersson (*Petra, the maid*); Gunnar Björnstrand (*Fredrik Egerman*); Jarl Kulle (*Count Malcolm*); Ake Fridell (*Frid, the groom*); Björn Bjelvenstam (*Henrik Egerman*); Naima Wifstrand (*Mrs. Armfeldt*); Gull Natorp (*Malla, Desirée's maid*); Birgitta Valberg and Bibi Andersson (*Actresses*); Anders Wulff (*Desirée's son*); Gunnar Nielsen (*Niklas*); Gösta Prüzelius (*Footman*); Svea Holst (*Dresser*); Hans Straat (*Almgen,*

Sommarnattens leende

the photographer); Lisa Lundholm (*Mrs. Almgren*); Sigge Fürst (*Policeman*).

Award: Cannes Film Festival, Special Prize for Most Poetic Humor, 1956.

Publications

Script:

Bergman, Ingmar, *Smiles of a Summer Night*, in *Four Screenplays of Ingmar Bergman*, New York, 1960.

Books:

Béranger, Jean, *Ingmar Bergman et ses films*, Paris, 1959.
Höök, Marianne, *Ingmar Bergman*, Stockholm, 1962.
Chiaretti, Tommaso, *Ingmar Bergman*, Rome, 1964.
Donner, Jörn, *The Personal Vision of Ingmar Bergman*, Bloomington, Indiana, 1964.
Nelson, David, *Ingmar Bergman: The Search for God*, Boston, 1964.
Steene, Birgitta, *Ingmar Bergman*, New York, 1968.
Gibson, Arthur, *The Silence of God: Creative Response to the Films of Ingmar Bergman*, New York, 1969.
Wood, Robin, *Ingmar Bergman*, New York, 1969.
Sjögren, Henrik, *Regi: Ingmar Bergman*, Stockholm, 1970.
Young, Vernon, *Cinema Borealis: Ingmar Bergman and the Swedish Ethos*, New York, 1971.
Björkman, Stig, and others, editors, *Bergman on Bergman*, New York, 1973.
Ranieri, Tino, *Ingmar Bergman*, Florence, 1974.
Kaminsky, Stuart M., editor, *Ingmar Bergman: Essays in Criticism*, New York, 1975.
Bergom-Larsson, Maria, *Ingmar Bergman and Society*, San Diego, 1978.
Kawin, Bruce, *Mindscreen: Bergman, Godard, and the First-Person Film*, Princeton, 1978.
Marion, Denis, *Ingmar Bergman*, Paris, 1979.
Manvell, Roger, *Ingmar Bergman: An Appreciation*, New York, 1980.
Mosley, Philip, *Ingmar Bergman: The Cinema as Mistress*, Boston, 1981.

Petric, Vlada, editor, *Film and Dreams: An Approach to Bergman*, South Salem, New York, 1981.
Cowie, Peter, *Ingmar Bergman: A Critical Biography*, New York, 1982.
Livingston, Paisley, *Ingmar Bergman and the Ritual of Art*, Ithaca, New York, 1982.
Steene, Birgitta, *Ingmar Bergman: A Guide to References and Resources*, Boston, 1982.
Jones, William G., editor, *Talking with Bergman*, Dallas, 1983.
Lefèvre, Raymond, *Ingmar Bergman*, Paris, 1983.
Gado, Frank, *The Passion of Ingmar Bergman*, Durham, North Carolina, 1986.
Bergman, Ingmar, *Laterna Magica*, Stockholm, 1987; as *The Magic Lantern: An Autobiography*, London, 1988.
Cohen, James, *Through a Lens Darkly*, New York, 1991.
Bjorkman, Stig, and Torsten Maans, and Jonas Sima, *Bergman on Bergman: Interviews with Ingmar Bergman*, Cambridge, 1993.
Cohen, Hubert I., *Ingmar Bergman: The Art of Confession*, New York, 1993.
Long, Robert Emmet, *Ingmar Bergman: Film and Stage*, New York, 1994.
Tornqvist, Egil, *Between Stage and Screen: Ingmar Bergman Directs*, Amsterdam, 1995.
Blackwell, Marilyn J., *Gender and Representation in the Films of Ingmar Bergman*, Rochester, 1997.
Michaels, Lloyd, editor, *Ingmar Bergman's Persona*, New York, 1999; revised edition, Cambridge, 2000.

Articles:

''Dreams and Shadows,'' in *Films and Filming* (London), October 1956.
Gauteur, Claude, ''Ingmar Bergman,'' in *Cinéma* (Paris), July-August 1958.
Weightman, J. G., ''Bergman: An Uncertain Talent,'' in *20th Century*, December 1958.
Stanbrook, Alan, ''An Aspect of Bergman,'' in *Film* (London), March-April 1959.
Austin, Paul, ''Ingmar Bergman, Magician of Swedish Cinema,'' in *Anglo-Swedish Review* (London), April 1959.
Archer, Eugene, ''The Rack of Life,'' in *Film Quarterly* (Berkeley), Summer 1959.
Blackwood, Caroline, ''The Mystique of Ingmar Bergman,'' in *Encounter* (London), April 1961.
Scott, James F., ''The Achievement of Ingmar Bergman,'' in *Journal of Aesthetics and Art Criticism* (Cleveland), Winter 1965.
Lefèvre, Raymond, ''Ingmar Bergman,'' in *Image et Son* (Paris), March 1969.
Grabowski, Simon, ''Picture and Meaning in Bergman's *Smiles of a Summer Night*,'' in *Journal of Aesthetics and Art Criticism* (Cleveland), Winter 1970.
Young, Vernon, ''Cinema Borealis,'' in *Hudson Review* (New York), Summer 1970.
Pintilie, L., in *Cinema* (Bucharest), February 1972.
Haustrate, Gaston, in *Cinéma* (Paris), November 1973.
Monty, Ib, in *Kosmorama* (Copenhagen), Spring 1978.
Trasatti, S., ''Bergman, il paradosso di un 'Ateo cristiano,''' in *Castoro Cinema* (Florence), November-December 1991.
Clark, John, ''Ingmar Bergman,'' in *Premiere* (Boulder), vol. 6, no. 1, September 1992.
Charity, Tom, ''Swede Dreams,'' in *Time Out* (London), no. 1305, 23 August 1995.
''Special Issue: *Sourires d'une nuit d'été*,'' in *Avant-Scène du Cinéma* (Paris), no. 454, July 1996.
Visscher, J. de, ''Bergman op Video,'' in *Film en Televisie + Video* (Brussels), no. 463, July 1996.

* * *

Comedies have featured more frequently in Ingmar Bergman's output than in his popular image as a purveyor of Nordic gloom might suggest, but few of them have achieved wide success. The sole exception—and the first film to bring him international recognition when it was acclaimed at the 1956 Cannes Festival—is *Sommarnattens leende*. Not without reason; for though the relative neglect of, for example, *En Lektion i Kärlek* or *Djävulens Oga* seems undeserved, *Sommarnattens leende* is without doubt Bergman's most perfectly achieved comedy to date.

The tone of the comedy is formalized, openly theatrical in its pattern: four men and four women who circle around each other, constantly changing partners in an elaborate dance of love played out amid the baroque splendor of a country mansion at the turn of the century. Presiding over the spectacle is the aged chatelaine, the former courtesan Madame Armfeldt, a burnt-out relic of bygone loves. Parallels are irresistibly suggested with Mozartian opera, especially *The Marriage of Figaro* and *The Magic Flute* (which Bergman was later to film), as well as with *A Midsummer Night's Dream*; the Swedish cinema also offers a precedent in Stiller's sexual comedy *Erotikon*. Yet the film is very much Bergman's in the skillful juxtaposition of its contrasting moods and event, most notably in the scene of Henrik Egerman's attempted suicide. The script, witty and epigrammatic, plays teasingly with such archetypally Bergmanesque themes as the nature of love, the problem of identity, and the impossibility of lasting emotional satisfaction.

Within the intricate plot, Bergman explores diverse attitudes towards love using each character, each pairing, to comment on and illuminate the others. In their direct, earthy pleasure, the servants, Petra and Frid, expose the hollowness and pretensions of their supposed betters, yet they sense their own limitations beside the enchanted idealism of Henrik and Anne, the young lovers. Fredrik Egerman's futile infatuation with Anne, his virgin bride, weakened by the feline seductions of Countess Charlotte, finally crumbles before the sardonic maturity embodied in his ex-mistress, Desirée Armfeldt. Yet even Fredrik, an absurd and repeatedly humiliated figure, evinces in his perplexed strivings a humanity lacking in the poised and coldly brutal Count Malcolm. As so often in Bergman's films, the women come out of the whole affair distinctly better than the men.

Sommarnattens leende is all of a piece; the studied elegance of the subject matter complemented by the sinuously smooth camera technique, and by the seamless ensemble playing of a cast drawn largely from Bergman's regular ''rep company.'' The film marks the culmination of his early work, and also paved the way, in its rich complexity, for the tortured Gothicism of *Det sjunde inseglet* and the symbolic dream-landscape of *Smulstronstället*. In his subsequent output comedies became increasingly rare, and those that he produced—such as *Ansiktet* and *För att inte tala om alla dessa kvinnor*—tended to suffer distortion through the intensity of the director's personal preoccupations. But in *Sommarnattens leende* Bergman achieved the ideal balance between emotional involvement and ironic detachment to create a wholly satisfying comedy, and one which remains unsurpassed among his films.

—Philip Kemp

SONG OF CEYLON

UK, 1934

Director: Basil Wright

Production: GPO Film Unit for Ceylon Tea Marketing Board, begun as an Empire Marketing Board film; black and white, 35mm; running time: 40 minutes. Released 1934. Filmed in Ceylon.

Producer: John Grierson; **screenplay:** John Grierson, Basil Wright, and others, based, in part, on a book about Ceylon written by traveller Robert Knox in 1680; **photography:** Basil Wright; **editor:** Basil Wright; **sound supervisor:** Alberto Cavalcanti; **sound recordist:** E. A. Pawley; **music:** Walter Leigh; **the "voices of commerce" heard in the sound track montage:** John Grierson, Alberto Cavalcanti, Stuart Legg and Basil Wright.

Cast: Lionel Wendt (*Narrator*).

Publications

Books:

Grierson, John, *Grierson on Documentary*, edited by Forsyth Hardy, London, 1946; revised edition, 1979.

Wright, Basil, *The Use of Film*, London, 1948; reprinted 1972.

Lovell, Alan, and Jim Hillier, *Studies in Documentary*, London, 1972.

Barsam, Richard, *Nonfiction Film: A Critical History*, New York, 1973.

Barnouw, Erik, *Documentary: A History of the Non-Fiction Film*, New York, 1974.

Wright, Basil, *The Long View*, London, 1974.

Sussex, Elizabeth, *The Rise and Fall of British Documentary: The Story of the Film Movement Founded by John Grierson*, Berkeley, 1975.

Ellis, Jack C., *The Documentary Idea*, Englewood Cliffs, New Jersey, 1989.

Articles:

Wright, Basil, "Filming in Ceylon," in *Cinema Quarterly* (London), Summer 1934.

Greene, Graham, in *Spectator* (London), 4 October 1935.

McManus, John T., in *New York Times*, 16 August 1937.

Variety (New York), 18 August 1937.

Tallents, Stephen, "The Birth of British Documentary," in *Journal of University Film*, nos. 1, 2, and 3, 1968.

Sussex, Elizabeth, "Cavalcanti in England," in *Sight and Sound* (London), Autumn 1975.

Starr, Cecile, "Basil Wright and *Song of Ceylon*," in *Filmmakers Newsletter* (Ward Hill, Massachusetts), November 1975.

Cinema d'Aujourd'hui (Paris), February-March 1977.

Gerstein, Evelyn, "English Documentary Films," in *The Documentary Tradition*, edited by Lewis Jacobs, 2nd edition, New York, 1979.

Fredrickson, D., "Jung/Sign/Symbol/Film," in *Quarterly Review of Film Studies* (Pleasantville, New York), Fall 1980.

Jayamanne, L., "Image in the Heart," in *Framework* (London), no. 36, 1989.

Rodrigo, A., "Do You Think I Am a Woman, Ha! Do You?" in *Discourse* (Detroit), no. 11, Spring/Summer 1989.

* * *

One of the finest achievements of the British documentary movement was Basil Wright's *Song of Ceylon*, which has been called the world's finest example of lyrical documentary. The film's theme, as its producer John Grierson described it, is "Buddhism and the art of life it has to offer, set upon by a Western metropolitan civilization which, in spite of all our skills, has no art of life to offer."

Graham Greene, reviewing the film when it played as the second feature in a London art theatre, described it as having an "air of absolute certainty in its object and assurance in its method." He singled out shots of birds in flight as "one of the loveliest visual metaphors I have ever seen on any screen." Wright later said that he had seen the birds at the end of a day's shooting, when the light was practically gone; he made his assistant unpack the cameras and get out the telephoto lens, though at the time he had no idea how the shots would be used.

Wright had been sent to Ceylon to film four one-reel travelogues as publicity for the Ceylon Tea Propaganda Board, but that purpose soon gave way to an "inner impulse" that made him film other sites and themes. In practical terms, he did not realize he was filming *Song of Ceylon* until he was back in London and had the material on a cutting bench. There was no shooting script for the film, and Wright could not screen his rushes in Ceylon. Without air transportation, it took a month just to get reports on the footage he had shot.

Wright worked with one assistant, three cameras and two tripods, one of which had a finely balanced free-head which he found tricky to use but once mastered was capable of very delicate movement. This permitted some of the most remarkable panning shots ever made in film, an art he had learned from Robert Flaherty a few years earlier.

The editing and sound in *Song of Ceylon* were done in England. Composer Walter Leigh created and recorded every effect in the film as well as all the music. Combining as many as eight tracks was both difficult and costly on the primitive equipment available to documentary filmmakers in the mid-1930s; at that time, sound was developed and edited on film, not on tape.

The film's narration was taken from a book written by Robert Knox in 1680, which Wright had discovered by chance in a store

Song of Ceylon

window. At the last minute, Wright inserted four titles which prescribes the film's symphonic structure: ''The Buddha,'' ''The Virgin Island,'' ''Voices of commerce,'' and ''The Apparel of the Gods.'' The first section, extremely slow, follows pilgrims up a mountainside to pray. The second shows the daily life of the people. ''Voices of Commerce'' juxtaposes two systems of labor, with the sound track ironically quoting British stock market prices and the arrival and departure times for ships while Ceylonese natives gather coconuts and tea leaves by hand. The last section returns to the religious and cultural life as it had been lived by the Ceylonese people centuries before the arrival of the British.

Not everyone responded favorably to the film's poetry and beauty. *Variety*'s reviewer called *Song of Ceylon* ''a shade too arty,'' despite its ''splendid camera work.'' John T. McManus, in the *New York Times*, attributed the film entirely to John Grierson (without mentioning Basil Wright's name) and seemed bothered by what he called the film's ''basic aloofness.'' He objected not so much to the film (''beautiful job. . . striking in photographic values. . . painstaking in composition and montage'') as to its approach. ''It certainly deserves the prizes it has won, but there are prizes it could not win,'' McManus concluded. The same could be said, however, for any film which, like *Song of Ceylon*, is one of a kind.

Basil Wright summed up his feelings about the film in this way: ''I think *Song of Ceylon* is the work of a young man exposed for the first time to an oriental as opposed to occidental way of life, and to a very impressive and convincing oriental religion . . . . Without any question it's the only film I've ever made that I can bear to look at.'' Wright directed or co-directed some 25 other documentaries (including the celebrated *Night Mail*, with Harry Watt, and *World without End*, with Paul Rotha). He was also author of many film articles and reviews, as well as two books—*The Use of Film* and *The Long View*.

—Cecile Starr

THE SORROW AND THE PITY

See **LE CHAGRIN ET LA PITIE**

LE SOUFFLE AU COEUR

(Murmur of the Heart)

France, 1971

Director: Louis Malle

Production: NEF/Marianne Productions (Paris), Vides Cinematografica SAS (Rome), and Franz Seitz Productions (Munich); color, 35mm; running time: 118 minutes. Released 1971.

Producers: Vincent Malle and Claude Nedjar; **screenplay:** Louis Malle; **photography:** Ricardo Aronovich; **music:** Charlie Parker and Sidney Bechet.

Cast: Lea Massari (*Mother*); Benoit Ferreux (*Laurent*); Daniel Gelin (*Father*); Marc Winocourt (*Marc*); Michel Lonsdale (*Father Henry*); Fabien Ferreux (*Thomas*).

Publications

Script:

Malle, Louis, *Le Souffle au coeur*, Paris, 1971.

Books:

Malle, Louis, with S. Kant, *Louis Malle par Louis Malle*, Paris, 1978.
Arnold, Frank, *Louis Malle*, Munich, 1985.
Prédal, René, *Louis Malle*, Paris, 1989.
Malle, Louis, *Malle on Malle*, edited by Philip French, London, 1993.

Articles:

Greenspun, Roger, in *New York Times*, 17 October 1971.
Kael, Pauline, in *New Yorker*, 23 October 1971.
Newsweek (New York), 8 November 1971.
Kalmar, S., ''Louis Malle om den naturlige incest,'' in *Fant* (Oslo), no. 21, 1972.
Grenier, C., ''There's More to Malle Than Sex, Sex, Sex,'' in *New York Times*, 6 February 1972.
Brustellin, A., in *Filmkritik* (Munich), March 1972.
Pasquariello, N., ''Louis Malle: Murmuring from the Heart,'' in *InterView* (New York), July 1972.
Silverman, M., in *Take One* (Montreal), October 1972.
Muzić, N., in *Ekran* (Ljubijana), nos. 100–103, 1973.
McVay, Douglas, ''Louis Malle,'' in *Focus on Film* (London), Summer 1974.
''Louis Malle,'' in *Current Biography Yearbook*, New York, 1976.
''Verso una progressiva perdita di senso,'' in *Castoro Cinema* (Milan), no. 42, November 1977.
Yakir, D., ''From *The Lovers* to *Pretty Baby*,'' in *Film Quarterly* (Berkeley), Summer 1978.
Macksey, R., ''Malle on Malle: Part I,'' in *Post Script* (Commerce), vol. 2, no. 1, 1982.
Macksey, R., ''Malle on Malle: Part II,'' in *Post Script* (Commerce), vol. 2, no. 2, 1983.
Wechster, Maia, ''A Tale of Two Cultures: Conversation with French Film Maker Louis Malle,'' in *U.S. News & World Report*, vol. 104, no. 6, 15 February 1988.
Kramer, Jane, ''The French & Louis Malle,'' in *Vogue*, vol. 178, no. 3, March 1988.
Roud, Richard, ''Malle x 4: Louis Malle,'' in *Sight & Sound* (London), vol. 58, no. 2, Spring 1989.
''Louis Malle,'' an interview, in *American Film*, vol. 14, no. 6, April 1989.
Hickenlooper, G., ''My Discussion with Louis,'' in *Cineaste* (New York), vol. 18, no. 2, 1991.
Santamarina, A., and J. Angulo, in *Nosferatu* (San Sebastian), no. 21, April 1996.

* * *

For all the deliberate diversity and stylistic versatility of Louis Malle's films—qualities for which he has often been criticized—certain clear thematic preoccupations can readily be seen to recur in his work. One such favorite theme is adolescence, which he handles with consistent sympathy and sensitivity—albeit from widely different standpoints—in *Zazie dans le Métro, Lacombe Lucien, Black Moon, Pretty Baby* and, most successfully of all, in *Le Souffle au coeur.*

Malle has described *Souffle au coeur* as ''my first film.'' In fact it was his eighth feature; but it was the first which he had scripted entirely himself, and was also, he felt, ''my first happy, optimistic film.'' Loosely based on reminiscences of Malle's own childhood, the film represents a world seen entirely from the viewpoint of its 15-year-old hero, Laurent, who is present in every scene. Little in the episodic plot is unpredictable: the boy hates his father, loves his mother, veers uncontrollably between infancy and adulthood, and is fascinated, perplexed and disconcerted by his own rampant, unfocused sexuality. The film's freshness lies in the complexity and ironic affection with which Malle depicts Laurent's fumbling attempts at self-definition, and in the physical immediacy of the family which surrounds him—a rich, convincing mixture of jokes, rows, awkwardness, horseplay, feuds and alliances.

Le Souffle au coeur also evocatively re-creates *haut-bourgeois* provincial society of the early 1950s—the adults obsessed with the imminent fall of Dien-Bien-Phu, their children far more interested in Camus or the latest Charlie Parker album. Beneath the light-hearted charm and the period detail, Malle's concern, as so often in his films, is with the struggle of the individual to assert an independent existence in the face of society's demands (and especially those of the family). Laurent's illness (the ''heart murmur'' of the title) is shown as a response to the insistent pressures of the world about him—a tactical withdrawal which corresponds, in the more tragic context of *Le Feu follet* or *La Vie privée*, with the protagonist's suicide. His liberation from this impasse comes through the act of incest with his mother, a crucial moment treated by Malle with exceptional subtlety and discretion, and played with total conviction by Benoît Ferreux and Lea Massari.

At the time, this scene caused considerable scandal. The French government refused the film its sanction as the official French entry at Cannes, and also banned it from being shown on ORTF (thus automatically entailing the loss of a sizable subsidy). Malle's fault, apparently, was not in having depicted mother-son incest, but in having presented it as an event to be looked back on, in the mother's words, ''not with remorse, but with tenderness. . . as something beautiful.'' Had he shown the participants tormented by guilt, or driven to suicide, it would presumably have been found more acceptable.

Despite official disapproval, or possibly because of it—*Le Souffle au Coeur* was well received at Cannes, widely distributed in France and abroad, and nominated for an Academy Award for Best Script. With the controversy now long forgotten, the film can be taken on its own terms, and seen as one of Malle's most personal, engaging, and thoroughly accomplished works.

—Philip Kemp

THE SOUTHERNER

USA, 1945

Director: Jean Renoir

Production: United Artists; black and white, 35mm; running time: 91 minutes. Released 1945. Filmed in Hollywood.

Producers: David Loew and Robert Hakim; **screenplay:** Jean Renoir and Hugo Butler, uncredited assistance by William Faulkner, from the novel *Hold Autumn in Your Hand* by George Sessions Perry; **photography:** Lucien Andriot; **editor:** Gregg Tallas; **music:** Werner Janssen.

Cast: Zachary Scott (*Sam Tucker*); Betty Field (*Nona Tucker*); Beulah Bondi (*Granny Tucker*); Bunny Sunshine (*Daisy Tucker*); Jay Gilpin (*Jot Tucker*); Percy Kilbride (*Harmie*); Blanche Yurka (*Ma Tucker*); Charles Kemper (*Tim*); J. Carrol Naish (*Devers*); Norman Lloyd (*Finlay*); Nestor Paiva (*Bartender*); Paul Harvey (*Ruston*).

Award: Venice Film Festival, Best Film, 1946.

Publications

Script:

Renoir, Jean, and Hugo Butler, *The Southerner*, in *Best Film Plays of 1945*, edited by John Gassner and Dudley Nichols, New York, 1946.

Books:

Davay, Paul, *Jean Renoir*, Brussels, 1957.
Cauliez, Armand-Jean, *Jean Renoir*, Paris, 1962.
Analyses des films de Jean Renoir, Paris, 1966.
Gregor, Ulrich, editor, *Jean Renoir und seine Film: Eine Dokumentation*, Bad Ems, 1970.
Cuenca, Carlos, *Humanidad de Jean Renoir*, Mexico, 1971.
Leprohon, Pierre, *Jean Renoir*, New York, 1971.
Braudy, Leo, *Jean Renoir: The World of His Films*, New York, 1972.
Bazin, André, *Jean Renoir*, edited by François Truffaut, Paris, 1973.
Durgnat, Raymond, *Jean Renoir*, Berkeley, 1974.
Renoir, Jean, *My Life and My Films*, New York, 1974.
Beylie, Claude, *Jean Renoir: Le Spectacle, la vie*, Paris, 1975.
Gilliatt, Penelope, *Jean Renoir: Essays, Conversations, Reviews*, New York, 1975.
Faulkner, Christopher, *Jean Renoir: A Guide to References and Resources*, Boston, 1979.
McBride, Joseph, editor, *Filmmakers on Filmmaking: The American Film Institute Seminars on Motion Pictures and Television 2*, Los Angeles, 1983.
Renoir, Jean, *Lettres d'Amérique*, edited by Dido Renoir and Alexander Sesonske, Paris, 1984.
Serceau, Daniel, *Jean Renoir*, Paris, 1985.
Bertin, Celia, *Jean Renoir*, Paris, 1986.
Faulkner, Christopher, *The Social Cinema of Jean Renoir*, Princeton, 1986.
Viry-Babel, Roger, *Jean Renoir: Le Jeu et la règle*, Paris, 1986.
Guislain, Pierre, *La règle du jeu, Jean Renoir*, Paris, 1990.
Bergan, Ronald, *Jean Renoir: Projections of Paradise*, Woodstock, 1994.
Cavagnac, Guy, *Jean Renoir: le désir du monde*, Paris, 1994.
O'Shaughnessy, Martin, *Jean Renoir*, New York, 2000.

Articles:

Theatre Arts (New York), May 1945.
Variety (New York), 2 May 1945.
Gilson, Paul, ''Jean Renoir à Hollywood,'' *Ecran Française* (Paris), 15 August 1945.
New York Times, 27 August 1945.
The Times (London), 3 September 1945.
Schoenfield, Bernard, ''The Mistakes of David Loew,'' in *Screen Writer* (London), October 1945.
''Renoir Issue'' of *Cahiers du Cinéma* (Paris), January 1952.
Truffaut, François and Jacques Rivette, ''Renoir in America,'' in *Sight and Sound* (London), July-September 1954; reprinted in *Films in Review* (New York), November 1954.
''Renoir Issue'' of *Cahiers du Cinéma* (Paris), Christmas, 1957.
Agee, James, in *Agee on Film*, New York, 1958.
Béranger, Jean, ''Why Renoir Favors Multiple Camera, Long Sustained Take Technique,'' in *American Cinematographer* (Los Angeles), March 1960.
Springer, John, ''Beulah Bondi,'' in *Films in Review* (New York), May 1963.
Russell, Lee, ''Jean Renoir,'' in *New Left Review* (New York), May-June 1964.
Kass, Judith M., in *Magill's Survey of Cinema 4*, Englewood Cliffs, New Jersey, 1980.
Combs, Richard, in *Listener* (London), 12 June 1986.
Tutt, R., ''Realism and Artifice in Jean Renoir's *The Southerner*,'' in *Post Script* (Commerce, Texas), no. 2, 1989.
Viry-Babel, R., ''Jean Renoir à Hollywood ou la recherche américaine d'une image française,'' in *Cinémas* (Montreal), vol. 1, no. 1–2, Autumn 1990.
Ostria, Vincent, ''*L'homme du sud*,'' in *Cahiers du Cinéma* (Paris), no. 482, July-August 1994.
Magny, Joël, ''Renoir en quête d'un monde nouveau,'' in *Cahiers du Cinéma* (Paris), no. 489, March 1995.
Alcalde, J.A., and G. Lazaro, in *Nosferatu* (San Sebastian), no. 17/18, March 1995.

The Southerner

Aldarondo, R., ''America: mas que un parentesis,'' in *Nosferatu* (San Sebastian), no. 17/18, March 1995.

Reid's Film Index (Wyong), no. 16, 1995.

* * *

The Southerner was the third of Jean Renoir's American films (after *Swamp Water* and *This Land is Mine*), the first of his independent Hollywood productions, and the object of controversy from the start. The debates that surrounded the film upon its release and continued long thereafter, disparate as they are in origin and intent, bear one upon the other in defining the film's central critical issue.

The Southerner recounts the struggles of a family to live in independence on the land, if not their own, at least not belonging to another visible presence. The enemies are, as one expects, the extremities of weather, and unyielding soil, illness and—less conventionally—mean-spirited, even hostile neighbors. If ''the southerner'' is the courageous Sam Tucker, he is also the dour, stone-hearted Devers, as well as the tight-fisted Harmie. The film's very title, in its generality (suggesting ''the southerner'' as a type) proved, perhaps as much as the story, a provocation.

The first of the controversies was local. Considered a sordid depiction of life in the southern states, the film was banned in Tennessee and attacked throughout the South. The Ku Klux Klan announced a boycott. To these inhabitants, *The Southerner* presented in realistic terms a derogatory image of the people of that region. The second of the controversies was critical. James Agee, who knew the South well, objected that, on the contrary there was nothing realistic in Renoir's depiction of the region; Renoir had failed to convey not only the character of the southerner, but the speech, the gait, the facial expressions. To Agee, in spite of William Faulkner's well-publicized consultation on dialogue, the film rang false. Agee's was, as Raymond Durgnat points out, an objection based on the definition of authenticity borrowed from naturalism: from appearance to essence, from the outside in. Renoir had understood none of the codes of the region or its people.

Renoir's South was clearly not one of surface verisimilitude, but neither did his definition of realism depend on what André Bazin called ''the crust of realism which blinds us.'' The direction of realism is from the inside out. The camera work, particularly in the exterior locations often shot in deep focus, captures the desolate landscape of a southern winter. A foggy river bank; Beulah Bondi, alone, stubborn and miserable, atop a cart in the pouring rain; and a hut hardly fit for human shelter are a few of the quasi-surreal images that translate Renoir's vision of rural America as a land of loneliness and isolation, without the comfort of neighbor or faith, depressed materially and especially morally. It was on the spirit of the place and times, not on the accent or gesture, that Renoir based and defined his portrait of ''the southerner.''

—Mirella Jona Affron

SOY CUBA

(I Am Cuba; Ja Kuba)

USSR/Cuba, 1964

Director: Mikhail Kalatozov

Production: Mosfilm (USSR) and ICAIC (Instituto Cubano del Arte e Industrias Cinematográficos); black and white, 35 mm; running time: 141 minutes. Filmed in Cuba; released 1964; released in United States, 1995.

Cinematographer: Sergei Urusevsky; **screenplay:** Yevgeny Yevtushenko and Enrique Pineda Barnet; **editor:** Nina Glagoleva; **production design:** Yevgeny Svidetelev; **music:** Carlos Farinas; **costume design:** René Portocarrero; **makeup:** Luz M. Cáceres, Vera Rudina; **sound:** Vladimir Sharun, Rodolfo Plaza (assistant); **special effects:** Boris Travkin, A. Vinokurov.

Soy Cuba

Cast: Luz Maria Collazo (*Maria/Betty*); José Gallardo (*Pedro*); Sergio Corrieri (*Alberto*); Raúl Garcia (*Enrique*); Celia Rodriquez (*Gloria*); Jean Bouise (*Jim*); Roberto García York (*American activist*); Luisa María Jiménez (*Teresa*); Mario González Broche (*Pablo*); Raquel Revuelta (*The voice of Cuba*); Salvador Wood; Alberto Morgan; Fausto Mirabal; María de las Mercedes Díez; Bárbara Domínquez; Jesús del Monte; Tony López; Héctor Castañeda; Rosenda Lamadriz; Robert Villar; Roberto Cabrera; Alfredo Ávila; José Espinosa; Rafael Díaz; Pepe Ramírez; Isabel Moreno; Manuel J. Mora; Aramis Delgado.

Awards: National Society of Film Critics Archival Award, 1995.

Publications

Books:

Bogomolov, Iurij, *Mikhail Kalatozov: stranicy tvorcheskoj biografii*, Moscow, 1989.

Zorkaya, Neya, *The Illustrated History of the Soviet Cinema*, New York, 1989.

Articles:

Hill, Steven P., ''The Soviet Film Today,'' in *Film Quarterly* (Berkeley) vol. 20, no. 4, Summer 1967.

Thomajan, Dale, ''*I Am Cuba*: Handheld Heaven, Agitprop Purgatory,'' in *Film Comment* (New York), vol. 31, March-April 1995.

Iordanova, Dina, ''*I Am Cuba*,'' in *The Russian Review*, vol. 56, January 1997.

Hoberman, J., ''I Am Cuba,'' in *The Red Atlantis: Communist Culture in the Absence of Communism*, Philadelphia, 1998.

Morris, Gary, ''The Poetry of Revolution: *I Am Cuba*!,'' in *Bright Lights Film Journal*, no. 23, December 1998; http://www.brightlightsfilm.com/23/iamcuba.html.

Smith, Paul Julian, ''*I Am Cuba*,'' in *Sight & Sound* (London), no. 8, August 1999.

Films:

Turksib and *Salt for Svanetia* (videorecording), New York, Kino on Video, 1997.

* * *

I Am Cuba is a masterpiece from the USSR, co-produced with Cuba in a grand style with a large Communist Party budget by two of the greatest cinema artists from the Soviet Union, director Mikhail Kalatozov and cameraman Sergei Urusevsky. It was the success of Kalatozov and Urusevsky's 1957 classic, *Cranes Are Flying* (which won the Palme d'Or at Cannes in 1958), that landed them the film and a prolonged stay on the island that fascinated so many Soviets in the early 1960s.

Set in pre-Castro days, *I Am Cuba* presents four separate stories of poor and downtrodden victims of capitalist and imperialist exploitation who are brought, individually and personally, to revolution. In episode number one, a beautiful Cuban girl, dressed in white, meets with her fiancé (a handsome fruit dealer and a political activist) in front of a church, as he speaks of their upcoming wedding. She subsequently goes off to her night job—into the dark and decadent space of an exclusive jazz club catering to tourists, where she works as a prostitute. Her customer insists on spending the night in her home, where her fiancé happens upon the morning aftermath of this transaction. In episode number two, an old sugar cane farmer, a widower, loses his farm to local barons and the United Fruit Company, and torches all of his fields. Episode three features a young student revolutionary who rescues a local girl from a stalking group of inebriated, American sailors looking for prey and is later killed in a demonstration—proud, resisting martyr to an evil regime. Episode four moves to the Sierra Maestra mountains, where a peasant refuses to join the liberation forces until his hut and his family are hit by an aerial bombing attack by the Batista regime. While some Americans may object to the stereotypical depiction of the United States and U.S. citizens in the film, it should be noted that the film was labeled ''anti-revolutionary'' in Cuba and accused of ''idealizing the Yankees'' in Russia. Resisting a single reading, *I Am Cuba* is a moving testament to the Cold War and to some of the most dramatic moments of that war—the stand-off between the United States and the Soviet Union in relation to Cuba.

It is not the story line of the film that has caught the attention of cinema audiences world-wide, however, but its dramatic, passionate, and impulsive cinematic style. Accused of ''formalism'' or ''art for art's sake,'' and said to lack drama and personal interest, *I Am Cuba* received stern criticism in official Soviet publications and was a box-office failure in Russia in the 1960s. It was, however, the daring cinematic style and technical sophistication of the film that was responsible for its second birth in the 1980s in the West, where it has been hailed as ''the greatest Soviet film since the 1920s'' by Steven P. Hill, and ''a supreme masterpiece of the poetic documentary form'' by Gary Morris. Fascinating film-makers and professionals with its unbelievable angles and shots, *I Am Cuba* uses a bold, reckless, hand-held camera that rises and falls, tips and sways with a Latin beat to look at the world through a wide-angle, 9.8 mm lens, flattening and distorting many of the film's images. The infrared film stock chosen by the director further heightens the emotion of the film, bringing black and white into stark contrast. Penetrating into the life of the island, into the rhythm of a culture for sale, pursuing and following, the film presents the spectator with elaborate crane shots and extreme long takes ''that make Welles' *Touch of Evil* seem mild,'' according to one critic. The unusual tilts and unexpected camera angles recall early Soviet film, especially propaganda films, or agit-prop, but depart from traditional uses of those angles, hence undermining simple readings and challenging viewer expectations.

While much credit for the unusual camera work has been given to cameraman Urusevsky, many elements of the film style must be attributed to Kalatozov, who began his cinema career as a cameraman at the Georgian Film Studio in Tbilisi (Tiflis) in the 1920s. All of Kalatozov's films are marked by his signature style—striking, unexpected camera angles, the dramatic use of light and shade, a free-wheeling hand-held camera, perpetual motion shots, swish pans, and 360 degree horizontal pans. The dramatic sequence so often cited in descriptions of *I Am Cuba*—where the camera descends, slowly, from a bikini fashion show atop a Havana high-rise hotel, to the swimming pool at the base of the building, and dives under water, to gaze upon more girls in bikinis swimming with Urusevsky (who holds the camera?)—was a modernized, technically improved version of the trip up the side of an ancient tower and a rushing descent (like a rock, hurled at an invader), in Svanetia, high in the Caucasus Mountains, from Kalatozov's film of 1930, *Salt for Svanetia.* The script for *I Am Cuba* was written by Russian poet Yevgeny Yevtushenko, with Cuban poet Enrique Pineda Barnet, and is limited to the voice of Cuba herself, a first person narration intoning the sad fate of Cuba, invaded, exploited, raped, pillaged, and sold to the highest bidder. Some of the most unforgettable sequences in the film include the arrival in Cuba, by air and by water; the descent of the camera from the sky-scraper fashion show (mentioned above); the fire in the sugar cane field; and the escape of the American tourist from the neighborhood where he took his pleasure from a local girl.

—Julie Christensen

THE SPANISH EARTH

USA, 1937

Director: Joris Ivens

Production: Contemporary Historians, Inc. (New York); black and white, 35mm; running time: 53 minutes. Released 1937. Filmed March-May 1937 in the village of Fuentedueña and Madrid, Spain; also on the Jarama and Morata de Tajuña fighting fronts.

Screenplay (commentary): Ernest Hemingway; **narration** (English version): spoken by Ernest Hemingway; **narration** (French version): translated by E. Guibert and spoken by Joris Ivens; **narration** (original narration used in previews at the White House) spoken by Orson Welles; **photography:** John Ferno; **editor:** Helen Van Dongen; **sound supervisor:** Irving Reis; **music:** Marc Blitzstein; **arranger:** Virgil Thomson.

Award: National Board of Review of Motion Pictures, one of Top Ten of 1937.

Publications

Script:

Hemingway, Ernest, *The Spanish Earth*, Cleveland, Ohio, 1938.

Books:

Klaue, W., and others, *Joris Ivens*, Berlin, 1963.
Zalzman, Abraham, *Joris Ivens*, Paris, 1963.
Grelier, Robert, *Joris Ivens*, Paris, 1965.
Wegner, Hans, *Joris Ivens, Dokumentarist den Wahreit*, Berlin, 1965.
Ivens, Joris, *The Camera and I*, New York, 1969.
Barsam, Richard, *Nonfiction Film: A Critical History*, New York, 1973.
Barnouw, Erik, *Documentary: A History of the Non-Fiction Film*, New York, 1974.
Kremeier, Klaus, *Joris Ivens: Ein Filmer an den Fronten der Weltrevolution*, Berlin, 1976.
Jacobs, Lewis, editor, *The Documentary Tradition*, second edition, New York, 1979.

The Spanish Earth

Delmar, Rosalind, *Joris Ivens: 50 Years of Filmmaking*, London, 1979.
Devarrieux, Claire, *Entretiens avec Joris Ivens*, Paris, 1979.
Passek, Jean-Loup, editor, *Joris Ivens: 50 ans de cinéma*, Paris, 1979.
Phillips, Gene D., *Hemingway and Film*, New York, 1980.
Alexander, William, *Film on the Left: American Documentary Film from 1931 to 1942*, Princeton, 1981.
Ivens, Joris, and Robert Destanque, *Joris Ivens; ou, La Mémoire d'un régard*, Paris, 1982.
Brunel, Claude, *Joris Ivens*, Paris, 1983.
Waugh, Thomas, editor, *''Show Us Life'': Towards a History and Aesthetic of the Committed Documentary*, Metuchen, New Jersey, 1984.
Schoots, Hans, *Gevaarlijk leven: een biografie van Joris Ivens*, Amsterdam, 1995.
Bakker, Kees, editor, *Joris Ivens and the Documentary Context*, Amsterdam, 1999.

Articles:

Hemingway, Ernest, in *New York Times*, 10 April 1937.
Variety (New York), 21 July 1937.
New Yorker, 21 August 1937.
Time (New York), 23 August 1937.
Ferguson, Otis, in *New Republic* (New York), 1 September 1937.
Spectator (London), 12 November 1937.
Stebbins, R., and Jay Leyda, ''Joris Ivens: Artist in Documentary,'' in *Magazine of Art* (New York), July 1938.
Grenier, Cynthia, ''Joris Ivens: Social Realist vs. Lyric Poet,'' in *Sight and Sound* (London), Spring 1958.
Cobos, Juan, and others, ''Orson Welles,'' in *Cahiers du Cinéma* (Paris), no. 165, April 1965.
Giraud, T., in *Cahiers du Cinéma* (Paris), February 1976.
Cornaud, A., in *Revue du Cinéma* (Paris), October 1976.
Oms, Marcel, and Robert Grelier, in *Cahiers de la Cinemathèque* (Perpignan), January 1977.
Verstappen, W., ''Hemingway or Ivens: *Spaanse aarde,*'' in *Skoop* (Amsterdam), November 1978.
''*Spanish Earth* Issue'' of *Avant-Scène du Cinema* (Paris), 1 January 1981.
Waugh, Thomas, ''Men Cannot Act in Front of the Camera in the Presence of Death,'' in *Cineaste* (New York), vol. 12, nos. 2, 1982, and no. 3, 1983.

Trojan, Judith, in *Wilson Library Bulletin*, vol. 59, October 1984.
Biltereyst, Daniel, ''Temps et espace dans *Terre d'Espagne*,'' in *Revue Belge du Cinéma* (Brussels), no. 17, Autumn 1986.
Snoek, S., ''Orson Welles, Ernest Hemingway: le voci di *Spanish Earth*,'' in *Cinegrafie* (Ancona), vol. 5, no. 8, 1995.

* * *

When the Spanish Civil War broke out, in July 1936, Joris Ivens was in the USA at the invitation of the New York Film Alliance, and had already begun to involve himself in the cultural politics of the New Deal and the Popular Front. His first response to the outbreak of the war was to collaborate on a project with his editor Helen Van Dongen and the novelist John Dos Passos which, by means of re-edited newsreel footage of the conflict, would explain the issues and background to the American people. However, the original material's pro-Franco stance proved a problem and, as Ivens put it, ''I remarked that it would be cheaper and more satisfactory in every respect to make such a documentary film on the spot, instead of being at the mercy of newsreel costs and newsreel attitudes.'' *Spain in Flames* was thus rapidly completed, and, on the initiative of the editor of *Fortune*, Archibald MacLeish, a group of writers, including Lillian Hellman and Dorothy Parker, got together and formed a production company, Contemporary Historians Inc., which sent Ivens to Spain with the princely sum of $3,000 with which to make a film about the war. In Paris he teamed up with his cameraman John Ferno, who shot the bulk of the Spanish footage, and they were later joined in Spain by Dos Passos. When the latter left his place was taken by Ernest Hemingway, then war correspondent for the North American News Alliance, who both wrote and spoke the film's commentary.

Ivens's original idea was to illustrate the background to and causes of the Civil War by telling the story of a village's political growth, from the fall of the monarchy, the period of agricultural reform, the outbreak of war, the village's capture by Franco's forces, through to its recapture by the Republicans. Much of the action would focus on one particular peasant family, whose coming to political consciousness would symbolise the development of the peasantry as a whole, while the village itself would stand in as a cross section of Spanish society. Obviously, such a project would involve a great deal of dramatization and re-enactment, but Ivens had already experimented along these lines in the remarkable *Borinage*. Once in Spain, however, Ivens and Ferno realised that such a complex film would be impossible in the circumstances. As Ivens himself said: ''How could we ask people who had fought in the fields and in the trenches in and around Madrid to help reconstruct the atmosphere of King Alfonso's abdication? These people were too deeply involved in their fight to think how a typical village had behaved before the war. We felt shame at not having recognised this. One could not possibly ask people who were engaged in a life and death struggle to be interested in anything outside that struggle.'' They therefore set off for Madrid and the front, eager to film the conflict itself. However, something of the original plan remained in their development of ''an approach that would place equal accents on the defence of Madrid and on one of the small nearby villages linked to the defence because it produced Madrid's food.'' They finally settled on one particular village, Fuenteduena, which was on the vital Valencia-Madrid highway, in an area which had only recently been confiscated from landlords, and where an important irrigation project was under construction. The front and the village, each of which depends upon the other, are further linked by the figure of the young peasant from Fuenteduena who has become a soldier and is now fighting for the Republic in Madrid, thereby accentuating the main theme of the film: ''Working the earth and fighting for the earth,'' in Ivens's words.

In the end, with its mix of documentary and re-constructed elements, *Spanish Earth* is at once a less elaborate but more complex film than that first conceived by Ivens: one critic aptly describes it as ''an improvised hybrid of many filmic modes.'' This gives the film a curiously contemporary feel, but what really marks it out as a landmark of documentary filmmaking is its directness, its sense of immediacy, and its refusal to have any truck with spurious notions of ''objectivity.'' Ivens himself states that ''My unit had really become part of the fighting forces,'' and again, ''We never forgot that we were in a hurry. Our job was not to make the best of all films, but to make a good film for exhibition in the United States, in order to collect money to send ambulances to Spain. When we started shooting we didn't always wait for the best conditions to get the best shot. We just tried to get good, useful shots.'' When asked why he hadn't tried to be more ''objective'' Ivens retorted that ''a documentary film maker has to have an opinion on such vital issues as fascism or anti-fascism—he *has* to have feelings about these issues, if his work is to have any dramatic, emotional or art value,'' adding that ''after informing and moving audiences, a militant documentary film should agitate—mobilise them to become active in connection with the problems shown in the film.'' Not that *Spanish Earth* is in any sense strident—indeed, quite the reverse. Ivens understands fully the power of restraint and suggestion, quoting approvingly, à propos his film, John Steinbeck's observation of the London blitz that ''In all of the little stories it is the ordinary, the commonplace thing or incident against the background of the bombing that leaves the indelible picture.''

Ivens's visual restraint is matched by that of the commentary. Originally this was spoken by Orson Welles, but Ivens felt that ''There was something in the quality of his voice that separated it from the film, from Spain, from the actuality of the film.'' Hemingway's manner of speaking, however, perfectly matched the pared-down quality of his writing. Ivens saw the function of the commentary as being ''to provide sharp little guiding arrows to the key points of the film'' and as serving as ''a base on which the spectator was stimulated to form his own conclusions.'' He described Hemingway's mode of delivery as sounding like that of ''a sensitive reporter who has been on the spot and wants to tell you about it. The lack of a professional commentator's smoothness helped you to believe intensely in the experiences on the screen.''

The film's avoidance of overt propagandizing reflected not only Ivens's conception of the documentary aesthetic—it was also hoped that this might help *Spanish Earth* achieve a wide theatrical release. However, as in Britain, there was thought to be no cinema audience for documentary films, and the plan failed. Nor did it help the film to escape the watchful eye of the British Board of Film Censors (who had previously attacked Ivens's *New Earth)*, who insisted that all references to Italian and German intervention were cut from the commentary, those countries being regarded as ''friendly powers'' at the time.

—Julian Petley

THE SPIRIT BREATHES WHERE IT WILL

See **CONDAMNE A MORT S'EST ECHAPPE**

SPIRIT OF THE BEEHIVE

See **ESPIRITU DE LA COLMENA**

SPOORLOOS

(The Vanishing)

Netherlands-France, 1988

Director: George Sluizer

Production: Golden Egg Film, Ingrid Productions, for MGS Film; colour, 35mm; running time: 106 minutes.

Producers: Anne Lordon and George Sluizer; **screenplay:** Tim Krabbé, based on his novel *The Golden Egg;* **photography:** Toni Kuhn; **editor:** George Sluizer and Lin Friedman; **assistant directors:** Natasa Hanusova and Anouk Sluizer; **art directors:** Santiago Isidro Pin and Cor Spijk; **music:** Henny Vrienten; **sound editor:** Stefan Kamp; **sound recording:** Piotr Van Dijk.

Cast: Gene Bervoets (*Rex Hofman*); Johanna Ter Steege (*Saskia*); Bernard-Pierre Donnadieu (*Raymond Lemorne*); Tania Latarjet (*Denise*); Lucille Glen (*Gabrielle*).

Publications

Articles:

Variety (New York), 19 October 1988.

Stillwater, M., ''Donnadieu le dur au coeur tendre,'' in *Cinéma* (Paris), December 1989.

Cordaiy, H., '''I Hope I Disturb You,''' in *Metro Magazine* (St. Kilda West), no. 81, Summer 1989/1990.

Pernod, P., ''Savoir et pouvoir,'' in *Positif* (Paris), February 1990.

Newman, Kim, *Monthly Film Bulletin* (London), June 1990.

Desjardins, D., ''L'homme qui voulait savoir,'' in *Séquences* (Paris), September 1990.

Maslin, J., ''Review/Film: How Evil Can One Person Be?'' in *New York Times*, vol. 140, C8, 25 January 1991.

Rafferty, T., ''Full Stop,'' in *New Yorker*, vol. 66, 28 January 1991.

Dargis, M., ''National Obsessions,'' in *Village Voice* (New York), vol. 36, 29 January 1991.

Denby, D., ''Fatal Distraction,'' in *New York Magazine*, vol. 24, 4 February 1991.

Kauffmann, S., ''Three from Europe,'' in *New Republic*, vol. 204, 4 March 1991.

Nicastro, N., ''Passengers,'' in *Film Comment* (New York), March-April 1991.

Simon, J., ''Horror, Domestic and Imported,'' in *National Review*, vol. 43, 29 April 1991.

Anderson, P., *Films in Review* (New York), May-June 1991.

Avins, Mimi, ''From a Dutch Director: A Scary Twice-Told Tale,'' in *The New York Times*, vol. 142, section 2, H20, 14 February 1993.

Jones, A., in *Cinefantastique* (Forest Park), vol. 29, no. 11, 1998.

*　*　*

Spoorloos represents one of the most extraordinary realisations of the psychological thriller captured on film. The heartbreaking, yet horrific ending of the film leaves the spectator in no doubt of their own vulnerability in the battle of human nature against a society in which random acts of madness occur.

On many levels comparisons can be drawn by the obsessive nature of both protagonists. The obsessive curiosity of the boyfriend, Rex (Gene Bervoets), to reveal what has happened to his girlfriend, Saskia (Johanna Ter Steege), who was abducted from a service station on route to a holiday destination, is mirrored by the abductor's, Raymond Lemorne (Bernard-Pierre Donnadieu), own curiosity of human nature's darker side, and its ability to manifest itself through evil deeds. The abductor's approach and rationale are entirely scientific, thus allowing him to distance himself emotionally from the actual deed. This approach allows him the luxury of maintaining a seemingly happy marriage and family life, unlike the boyfriend, whose very ability to have insight and uncalculated emotions causes his ultimate demise.

The continuation of Raymond's exploration of his dark side, without any thought of redemption or forgiveness, amplifies the depth of his pathology. Over a period of years Rex's search for Saskia is brought to public attention by his poster and TV campaign through which he hopes to gain knowledge of her whereabouts. Raymond's very normalcy juxtaposed with his victim's anguish creates superb filmic tension.

The film's lulling pace and parallel plot line takes the audience on a terrifying journey as the eventual fate of Saskia is revealed in the final minute of the story. The ensuing shock is created when we realise that Rex, who has insisted that the madman tell him what has happened, drinks spiked coffee in exchange for this knowledge, awakens to discover he has been buried alive. The climax of the film is surely one of greatest shocking moments in cinema.

An intricate examination of the human condition, *Spoorloos* represents the emergence of a new wave of psychological thrillers. A thoroughly discomfiting film, *Spoorloos* succeeds through its expert storytelling and the absolutely jolting denouement. In the 1993 American remake—an insult to the original film version—director George Sluizer was unable to translate Tim Krabbe's vision from his novel *The Golden Egg*.

—Marion Pilowsky

THE SPRAYER SPRAYED

See **L'ARROSEUR ARROSE**

SPRING IN A SMALL CITY

See **XIAO CHENG ZHI CHUN**

Spoorloos

STACHKA

(Strike)

USSR, 1924

Director: Sergei Eisenstein

Production: Goskino; black and white, 35mm, silent; running time: 73 minutes; length: 1,969 meters. Released 1924.

Producer: Boris Mikhine; **screenplay:** V. Pletniev, I. Kravtchunovsky, Grigori Alexandrov, and Sergei Eisenstein (called the Proletkuit Collective); **photography:** Edouard Tisse with V. Popov and V. Khvatov; **production designer:** Vasili Rakhas; **assistant directors:** G. Alexandrov, A. Levshin, and I. Kravchinovski.

Cast: Maxim Straukh (*The Spy*); Grigori Alexandrov (*The Foreman*); Mikhail Gomorov (*The Worker*); I. Ivanov (*Chief of Police*); I. Klyukvine (*The Activist*); A. Antonov (*Member of the strike*); J. Glizer, B. Yourtzev, A. Kouznetzov, V. Ianoukova, V. Ouralsky, M. Mamine, and members of the Proletariat Troup.

Publications

Script:

Eisenstein, Sergei, and others, *Stachka*, in *Iskusstvo Kino* (Moscow), November 1981.

Books:

Eisenstein, Sergei, *Film Sense*, edited by Jay Leyda, New York, 1942.
Rotha, Paul, Ivor Montagu, and John Grierson, *Eisenstein, 1898–1948*, London, 1948.
Eisenstein, Sergei, *Film Form*, edited by Jay Leyda, New York, 1949.
Sergei Eisenstein—Kunstler der Revolution, Berlin, 1960.
Leyda, Jay, *Kino: A History of the Russian and Soviet Film*, London, 1960.
Mitry, Jean, *S. M. Eisenstein*, Paris, 1961.

Stachka

Moussinac, Léon, *Sergei Eisenstein*, New York, 1970.
Barna, Yon, *Eisenstein*, Bloomington, Indiana, 1973.
Fernandez, Dominique, *Eisenstein*, Paris, 1975.
Sudendorf, W., and others, *Sergei M. Eisenstein: Materialien zu Leben und Werk*, Munich, 1975.
Seton, Marie, *Sergei M. Eisenstein*, London, 1978.
Aumont, Jacques, *Montage Eisenstein*, Paris, 1979; London, 1987.
Leyda, Jay, and Zina Vignow, *Eisenstein at Work*, New York, 1982.
Eisenstein, Sergei M., *Immoral Memories: An Autobiography*, Boston, 1983.
Marshall, Herbert, *Masters of the Soviet Cinema: Crippled Creative Biographies*, London, 1983.
Bordwell, David, *Narration in the Fiction Film*, London, 1985.
Polan, Dana B., *The Political Language of Film and the Avant-Garde*, Ann Arbor, Michigan, 1985.
Eisenstein, Sergei M., *Selected Works, Volume 1: Writings 1922–1934*, edited by Richard Taylor, London, 1988.
Bordwell, David, *The Cinema of Eisenstein*, Cambridge, 1993.
Goodwin, James, *Eisenstein, Cinema, and History*, Champaign, 1993.
Lovgren, Hakan, editor, *Eisenstein's Labyrinth: Aspects of a Cinematic Synthesis of the Arts*, Philadelphia, 1996.
Taylor, Richard, editor, *The Eisenstein Reader*, Bloomington, 1998.
Bergan, Ronald, *Sergei Eisenstein: A Life in Conflict*, New York, 1999.

Articles:

Montague, Ivor, ''Sergei Eisenstein,'' in *Penguin Film Review* (London), September 1948.
Montagu, Ivor, ''Rediscovery: *Strike*,'' in *Sight and Sound* (London), Autumn 1956.
Knight, Arthur, ''Eisenstein and the Mass Epic,'' in *The Liveliest Art*, New York, 1957.
Cutts, John, in *Films and Filming* (London), March 1961.
Kuiper, John, ''Cinematic Expression: A Look at Eisenstein's Silent Montage,'' in *Art Journal*, Fall 1962.
Yourenev, Rostislav, ''Eisenstein,'' in *Anthologie du cinéma*, Paris, 1966.
''*La Greve* Issue'' of *Avant-Scène du Cinéma* (Paris), October 1967.
New York Times, 15 March 1968.
Siegler, R., ''Masquage: An Extrapolation of Eisenstein's Theory of Montage-as-Conflict to the Multi-Image Film,'' in *Film Quarterly* (Berkeley), Spring 1968.

McDonald, Dwight, ''Eisenstein, Pudovkin, and Others,'' in *The Emergence of Film Art*, edited by Lewis Jacobs, New York, 1969.

Kuleshov, Lev, ''Kuleshov on Eisenstein,'' in *Film Journal* (New York), Fall-Winter 1972.

Eisenstein, Sergei, in *Skrien* (Amsterdam), May-June 1973.

Sklovskij, V., in *Filmwissenschaftliche Beiträge* (East Berlin), no.15, 1974.

Crofts, Stephen, ''Eisenstein and Ideology,'' in *Framework* (Norwich), Spring 1978.

Perry, T., ''Sergei Eisenstein: A Career in Pictures,'' in *American Film* (Washington, DC), January-February 1983.

Amengual, Barthélemy, ''Ejzenstein-Faure: Rapporto senza dissonanze?'' in *Cinema Nuovo* (Bari), December 1984.

Doufour, D., ''!Revolutie? (2),'' in *Film en Televisie + Video* (Brussels), vol. 428, January 1993.

Doufour, D., ''!Revolutie? (3),'' in *Film en Televisie + Video* (Brussels), vol. 430, March 1993.

Beller, J., ''The Spectatorship of the Proletariat,'' in *Boundary 2*, vol. 22, no. 3, 1995.

Virmaux, A., and O. Virmaux, ''*La greve* (1924) d'Eisenstein,'' in *Jeune Cinéma* (Paris), vol. 239, September/October 1996.

Richardson, Paul E., ''The First Master of Russian Film,'' in *Russian Life*, vol. 41, no. 2, February 1998.

* * *

Envisioning a film which would both reflect and embody the essence of Russia's 1917 revolution, the 26-year-old Sergei Eisenstein directed his first feature film, *Strike*, in 1924. *Strike* was to have been one of eight projects in a state-sponsored series entitled *Towards Dictatorship*, with reference to the dictatorship of the proletariat. The focus of the series was intended to be the struggles of the working class which preceded and paved the way for the revolution. Eisenstein's *Strike* was the only film of this group to be realized.

At that time Eisenstein's central aesthetic concerns were the practice of montage and the concept of the mass hero. It is not his political or social intent but, rather, his methods which continue to be of interest. As propaganda the film cannot be termed an unqualified success; it does not arouse passion or provoke protest today as does Leni Riefenstahl's *Triumph of the Will*, for example. But the impact of *Strike*'s aesthetic boldness remains undiminished.

It is an impact which can be explained in terms of mechanical energy, on both formal and material levels. One function of art is to subordinate man's environment to man, to bring the technical landscape into the realm of human affairs rather than allow it to dominate or intimidate its creators.

Eisenstein, in accepting this challenge, depicts the environment of the workers in *Strike* as part of their lives. The film's opening shot of factory smokestacks sets the tone. Shots of written communications which urge, ''Workers of the world, unite,'' are intercut with shots of machinery in motion. The workers look healthy and at home in the factory amid shining, powerful machines and moving parts; and Edouard Tisse's camera embraces factory as readily as it embraces worker. The human is not oppressed by machinery. On the contrary, the workers enlist the machinery in their struggle against the representatives of capitalism. The machines become weapons. On another level, the machinery serves a musical function; the very conscious internal rhythm of the film is often determined by spinning flywheels or other moving mechanical parts.

This Constructivist approach is less notable in the long run than is the more personal aspect of Eisenstein's work in *Strike*—his use of montage. He described his conception of montage as collision, and it is important to note that the collision of elements in his work never results in a loss of energy. The film as a whole is something of a perpetual motion machine, with each action or movement yielding its force to a subsequent action or movement. One of the most pleasing examples of this principle is contained in the following sequence: a large crowd is seen in long shot making its way through the village; at the instant the crowd passes a liquor store, an explosion occurs and the crowd as a whole turns and veers slightly toward the explosion in a movement as graceful and precise as the movement of the arm of a conductor bringing an orchestra to a sudden halt. The pause is but momentary, and the movement continues in a new direction as the crowd flows toward the camera in the next shot.

Most of the forms of montage which Eisenstein elaborated in his books *Film Form* and *The Film Sense* can be found in *Strike*. For example, association montage compares a hand-operated citrus fruit crusher used by the dining businessmen to the rearing horses of the mounted police as they harass a peaceful crowd of strikers. Eisenstein believed that the meaning of a film should arise from the juxtaposition of its elements rather than be continued within those elements. Although the official purpose of his government-sponsored film was to inform the masses, Eisenstein believed that films should not merely carry information but impart sensation and impression.

For this reason *Strike* is meant to inspire action, not reflection. The film never bogs down in its theoretical base. It is perhaps for these reasons that *Strike* can be distinguished from so-called ''bourgeois'' films. Not even when a worker commits suicide after being falsely accused of theft does the film pause for any emotion to be displayed. Rather, the worker's suicide note—''Goodbye, remember, I am not guilty''—initiates the strike. It also anticipates the film's conclusion after the slaughter of the strikers—a close shot of a pair of staring, admonishing eyes and the caption ''Remember—Proletarians!''

—Barbara Salvage

A STAR IS BORN

USA, 1954

Director: George Cukor

Production: Transcona Enterprises; Technicolor, 35mm, CinemaScope; running time: 154 minutes, originally 182 minutes. Released 1954 by Warner Bros. Re-released 1983 with original 47 minutes restored.

Producers: Sidney Luft with Vern Alves; **screenplay:** Moss Hart, from the screenplay for the 1937 version (Wellman) based, in turn, on the film *What Price Hollywood?* (Cukor); **photography:** Sam Leavitt; **editor:** Folmar Blangsted; **production designer:** Gene Alen; **art**

A Star Is Born

director: Malcolm Bert; **music:** Harold Arlen and Ira Gershwin, and Leonard Gershe; **costume designers:** Jean Louis and Mary Ann Nyberg; **choreography:** Richard Barstow.

Cast: Judy Garland (*Esther Blodgett/Vicki Lester*); James Mason (*Norman Maine*); Jack Carson (*Matt Libby*); Charles Bickford (*Oliver Niles*); Tommy Noonan (*Danny McGuire*); Lucy Marlow (*Lola Lavery*); Amanda Blake (*Susan Ettinger*); Irving Bacon (*Graves*); Hazel Shermet (*Libby's secretary*); James Brown (*Glenn Williams*); Lotus Robb (*Miss Markham*); Joan Shawlee (*Announcer*); Dub Taylor (*Driver*); Louis Jean Heydt (*Director*); Bob Jellison (*Eddie*); Chick Chandler (*Man in car*); Leonard Penn (*Director*); Blythe Daly (*Miss Fusselow*); Mae Marsh (*Party guest*); Frank Ferguson (*Judge*); Nadene Ashdown (*Esther, age 6*); Heidi Meadows (*Esther, age 3*); Henry Kulky (*Cuddles*); Jack Harmon (*1st dancer*); Don McCabe (*2nd dancer*); Eric Wilton (*Valet*); Grady Sutton (*Carver*); Henry Russell (*Orchestra leader*); Robert Dumas (*Drummer*); Laurindo Almeida (*Guitarist*); Bobby Sailes (*Dancer*); Percy Helton (*Drunk*); Charles Watts (*Harrison*); Stuart Holmes (*Spectator*); Grandon Rhodes (*Producer*); Frank Puglia (*Bruno*); Wilton Graff (*Master of Ceremonies—last scene*).

Publications

Books:

Langlois, Henri, and others, *Hommage à George Cukor*, Paris, 1963.

Domarchi, Jean, *George Cukor*, Paris, 1965.

McVay, Douglas, *The Musical Film*, London, 1967.

Morella, Joe, and Edward Epstein, *Judy—The Films of Judy Garland*, New York, 1969.

Steiger, Brad, *Judy Garland*, New York, 1969.

Carey, Gary, *Cukor and Co.: The Films of George Cukor*, New York, 1971.

Lambert, Gavin, *On Cukor*, New York, 1972.

Clarens, Carlos, *George Cukor*, London, 1976.

Parish, James R., and Michael Pitts, *Hollywood on Hollywood*, Metuchen, New Jersey, 1978.

Mason, James, *Before I Forget: Autobiography and Drawings*, London, 1981.

Phillips, Gene D., *George Cukor*, Boston, 1982.

Bernadoni, James, *George Cukor: A Critical Study and Filmography*, Jefferson, North Carolina, 1985.

Dyer, Richard, *Heavenly Bodies: Film Stars and Society*, London, 1987.
Haver, Ronald, *A Star Is Born: The Making of the 1954 Movie and its 1983 Restoration*, New York, 1988; 1990.
Morley, Sheridan, *James Mason: Odd Man Out*, New York, 1989.
McGilligan, Patrick, *George Cukor: A Double Life—A Biography of the Gentleman Director*, New York, 1992.
Shipman, David, *Judy Garland: The Secret Life of an American Legend*, New York, 1993.
Levy, Emanuel, *George Cukor, Master of Elegance: Hollywood's Legendary Director and His Stars*, New York, 1994.
Sweeney, Kevin, *James Mason: A Bio-Bibliography*, Westport, 1999.
Clarke, Gerald, *Get Happy: The Life of Judy Garland*, New York, 2000.

Articles:

Brinson, Peter, in *Films and Filming* (London), December 1954.
Bitsch, Charles, ''Naissance du cinémascope,'' in *Cahiers du Cinéma* (Paris), June 1955.
Tozzi, Romano, ''George Cukor,'' in *Films in Review* (New York), February 1958.
Reid, John Howard, ''George Cukor,'' in *Films in Filming* (London), August and September 1960.
Jomy, Alain, ''Connaissance de George Cukor,'' in *Cinéma* (Paris), June 1963.
''Retrospective Cukor,'' in *Cahiers du Cinéma* (Paris), February 1964.
Overstreet, Richard, ''Interview with George Cukor,'' in *Film Culture* (New York), no. 34, 1964.
Nogeuira, Rui, ''James Mason Talks About His Career in the Cinema,'' in *Focus on Film* (London), March-April 1970.
Beylie, Claude, in *Ecran* (Paris), January 1974.
Legrand, M., in *Positif* (Paris), February 1974.
Sarris, Andrew, ''Cukor,'' in *Film Comment* (New York), March-April 1978.
Jennings, W., ''Nova: Garland in *A Star Is Born,*'' in *Quarterly Review of Film Studies* (Pleasantville, New York), no. 3, 1979.
Mitchell, Robert, in *Magill's Survey of Cinema 4*, Englewood Cliffs, New Jersey, 1980.
Bodeen, DeWitt, ''George Cukor,'' in *Films in Review* (New York), November 1981.
Phillips, Gene D., ''George Cukor: Fifty Years of Filmmaking,'' in *Films and Filming* (London), January 1982.
Villien, Bruno, and others, ''George Cukor,'' in *Cinématographe* (Paris), February 1982.
''Cukor Section'' of *Casablanca* (Madrid), March 1983.
Magny, Joel, ''George Cukor: Un Homme qui s'affiche,'' in *Cinéma* (Paris), March 1983.
New York Times, 15 April 1983.
Haver, R., ''*A Star Is Born* Again,'' in *American Film* (Washington, D.C.), July-August 1983.
Simons, J., in *Skrien* (Amsterdam), Winter 1983–84.
Roddick, Nick, in *Monthly Film Bulletin* (London), January 1984.
''*A Star Is Born* Issue'' of *American Cinematographer* (Los Angeles), February 1984.
Calum, P., in *Kosmorama* (Copenhagen), August 1984.
Magny, Joel, in *Cinéma* (Paris), September 1984.
Rabourdin, D., ''Deux rencontres avec James Mason,'' in *Cinéma* (Paris), September 1984.
Cieutat, M., ''James Mason, Bigger Than Stars,'' in *Positif* (Paris), November 1984.
Arts, A., in *Skrien* (Amsterdam), November-December 1984.
Eyquem, O., in *Positif* (Paris), April 1985.
Doyle, N., ''Letters,'' in *Films in Review* (New York), vol. 40, October 1989.
Stanbrook, A., ''As It Was in the Beginning,'' in *Sight and Sound* (London), no. 1, 1989–90.
Lassell, M., ''Mirror of the Mind,'' in *Movieline* (Escondido, California), March 1990.
Berthomé, Jean-Pierre, ''L'oeuvre insaisissable,'' in *Positif* (Paris), no. 424, June 1996.

* * *

The ''birth of a star'' has proved to be a durable cinematic conceit. The story of the fading, alcoholic male actor who discovers a talented young woman, fosters her career, marries her, and finally commits suicide was first made in 1937, directed by William Wellman, with Janet Gaynor and Fredric March. The 1954 George Cukor version represents the basic outline of the original scenario while transforming the woman into a singer. And in 1976, the situation served rock stardom as well, with Barbara Streisand and Kris Kristofferson. The germ for this theme and its variations is the 1932 *What Price Hollywood?*, also directed by George Cukor, starring Constance Bennett, Lowell Sherman and Neil Hamilton. There, the male figure is divided in two—a drunken director and a society husband—and the film reunites husband and wife in a happy ending. But it is the 1954 *Star* that is most often revived and best remembered.

Hollywood has made many reflexive films in which it examines its own procedures, manners, and mythology. The trenchant reflexivity of *Sunset Boulevard*, *The Bad and the Beautiful* and *A Star Is Born* (products of those difficult Hollywood years, 1950–54) is in the intimate exposure of the performer's craft, a particularly painful exposure when we learn that craft and life are so intimately connected. It is impossible to separate Gloria Swanson and Lana Turner from the fictions they incarnate. The connections are most troubling in the case of Judy Garland, the star who is presumably born, but who, in fact, is nearly at the end of her musical career. The only other film in which her singing is prominently featured is her last effort, made in England, *I Could Go on Singing*, with its sickeningly ironic title. *A Star Is Born* was meant to be the vehicle that re-established her as a viable movie star, after her humiliating dismissal from MGM in 1950. The public was aware of her personal problems, her fluctuating weight, and her suicide attempt. Now, with our knowledge of Judy Garland's difficulties in Hollywood, of her missed concert dates, her failed TV program and her tragic, drug-related death, it is impossible not to see the film's ultimate reflexivity in the way the figure of the unreliable star, the husband, is a surrogate for Garland herself. Each time Vicki Lester ''bails out'' Norman Maine and ''understands'' his problems, it is Garland looking at Garland, not James Mason—Garland exposing her own fears and weaknesses through the male character.

Made at great expense, over a long shooting schedule, the production of *A Star Is Born* was fraught with difficulties that seemed to echo those of Garland. After director George Cukor finished his work, it was decided the film wasn't musical enough. Cuts were made (and deplored by Cukor) to permit the inclusion of a long sequence, ''Born in a Trunk,'' a musical biography of a performer reminiscent of the ''Broadway Melody'' number in *Singin' in the Rain.* Still nervous about the film's length, the studio, several days after its release (to excellent reviews), cut it from 182 minutes to 154 minutes, hoping it would fit into a more conventional exhibition program. The film was further cut to 135 minutes.

The film's appeal survived its radical surgery. And that appeal is not limited to Garland. Rather, she is not put in relief by the elegant mise-en-scène that exploits with great care the compositional elements mandated by the CinemaScope format, by the lighting and set direction that keep in balance both the film's intimacy and its grand proportions, by the Harold Arlen score that provided Garland and all subsequent torch singers with the classic ''The Man That Got Away,'' and by the performance of James Mason, supportive yet stellar in its own right.

A Star Is Born is, in fact, a celebration of a dual register of performance—as a function of artifice, technique, audience and as the revelation of personal intimacy captured by the movie camera. The stage that opens and closes the film is the gigantic Shrine Auditorium. It first exposes Norman Maine's drunken disruption of a charity show. In the final shot, it is the frame for Vicki Lester's return to her public, performing self, when she receives an ovation for presenting herself as ''Mrs. Norman Maine.'' The performer's identity shifts through a series of qualifying frames. Norman falls in love with Vicki (still called Esther Blodgett) when he hears her sing ''The Man That Got Away'' with and for a small group of musicians. The song is sustained in a camera movement that accommodates her own position as well as her connection to the instrumentalists, the privileged witnesses/collaborators. Norman's witnessing is, like our own, full of wonder at the talent generated by personality and technique. Norman exhibits his talent at the end of the film, when he ''acts'' happy and cured just before going out to drown himself.

Vicki's progress to stardom is the occasion for satirical views of the movie industry, episodes familiar from other films but done here with exceptional care and wit. The starlet is literally given the runaround during her first day at the studio, as unceremoniously pushed through a series of departments and doors, only to exit where she entered. No one has really taken the time to find out who she is. That process of Hollywood de-identification is made graphic when the makeup artists examine Vicki's face, declare it is all wrong, and transform her into a caricatural idea of beauty. During her first screen appearance, the director wants only to see her arm, waving a handkerchief from a departing train. When she finally does become a star she performs her big production number all by herself in her living room, turning the furniture into the ''sets'' for exotic locales.

The varied scope of the star's identity is most emphatically emblemized in the scene where Vicki Lester receives an Academy Award. Norman drunkenly interrupts the ceremony and accidentaly slaps his wife. This private gesture is exposed before three audiences—the spectators within the fiction, those implied by the presence of the gigantic television screen within the shot, and ourselves. Yet another painful irony of this painful moment is the fact that Judy Garland, expected to win an Oscar for her performance in *A Star Is Born*, lost to Grace Kelly.

—Charles Affron

THE STAR WARS SAGA

STAR WARS

USA, 1977

Director: George Lucas

Production: Lucasfilm Productions; Technicolor, 35mm; running time: 121 minutes. Released Spring 1977 by 20th Century-Fox. Cost: $10 million.

Producer: Gary Kurtz; **screenplay:** George Lucas; **photography:** Gilbert Taylor; **editors:** Paul Hirsch, Marcia Lucas, and Richard Chew; **sound:** Derek Ball, Don MacDougall, Bob Minkler, and Ray West, sound effects editor: Benjamin Burtt, Jr.; **art directors:** John Barry, Norman Reynolds, and Leslie Dilley; **music:** John Williams; **special effects:** John Dykstra, John Stears, Richard Edlund, Grant McCune, and Robert Blalack; **costume designer:** John Mallo.

Cast: Mark Hamill (*Luke Skywalker*); Harrison Ford (*Han Solo*); Carrie Fisher (*Princess Leia Ograna*); Alec Guinness (*Ben ''Obi-wan'' Kenobi*); Peter Cushing (*Grand Moff Tarkin*); David Prowse (*Lord Darth Vader*, voice by James Earl Jones); Kenny Baker (*R2-D2*); Anthony Daniels (*C-3PO*); Peter Mayhew (*Chewbacca*).

Awards: Oscars for Art Direction/Set Direction, Sound, Best Original Score, Film Editing, Costume Design, and Visual Effects, 1977; Special Oscar to Ben Burtt, Jr. for sound effects, 1977.

Publications

Script:

Lucas, George, *Star Wars: A New Hope*, New York, 1999.

Books:

McConnell, Frank, *Storytelling and Mythmaking: Images in Film and Literature*, New York, 1979.
Hunter, Allan, *Alec Guinness on Screen*, London, 1982.
Short, Robert, *The Gospel from Outer Space*, San Francisco, 1983.
Velasco, Raymond L., *A Guide to the Star Wars Universe*, New York, 1984.
Austin, Bruce A., *Current Research in Film: Audiences, Economics and Law, Volume 1*, Norwood, New Jersey, 1985.
Von Gunden, Kenneth, *Alec Guinness: The Films*, Jefferson, North Carolina, 1987.

Articles:

Strick, Philip, in *Sight and Sound* (London), Summer 1976.
Filmfacts (Los Angeles), no. 5, 1977.
Zito, S., ''George Lucas Goes Far Out,'' in *American Film* (Washington, D.C.), April 1977.
Murphy, A. D., in *Variety* (New York), 25 May 1977.

The Star Wars Saga: Star Wars

Collins, Robert, ''*Star Wars:* The Pastiche of Myth and the Yearning for a Past Future,'' in *Journal of Popular Culture* (Bowling Green, Ohio), Summer 1977.

''*Star Wars* Issue'' of *American Cinematographer* (Los Angeles), July 1977.

Canemaker, J., ''*Star Wars* Special Effects,'' in *Millimeter* (New York), July-August 1977.

Fok, T. C., and A. Lubow, in *Film Comment* (New York), July-August 1977.

Morris, G., in *Take One* (Montreal), July-August 1977.

Lindberg, I., in *Kosmorama* (Copenhagen), Autumn 1977.

Rosenbaum, Jonathan, ''The Solitary Pleasures of *Star Wars*,'' in *Sight and Sound* (London), Autumn 1977.

Ciment, Michel, and Robert Benayoun, in *Positif* (Paris), September 1977.

Clouzot, C., ''Le Matin du magicien: George Lucas et *Star Wars,*'' in *Ecran* (Paris), September 1977.

Nicholson, D. W., ''Special Effects in *Star Wars*,'' in *Cinema Papers* (Melbourne), October 1977.

Gow, Gordon, in *Films and Filming* (London), December 1977.

Le Peron, S., in *Cahiers du Cinéma* (Paris), December 1977.

Wood, Denis, ''The Stars in Our Hearts—A Critical Commentary on George Lucas's *Star Wars,*'' in *Journal of Popular Film* (Washington, D.C.), no. 3, 1978.

Mathers, F., in *Cinema Papers* (Melbourne), January 1978.

Rubey, D., ''Not So Far Away,'' in *Jump Cut* (Berkeley), August 1978.

Ulbrich, P., in *Film und Fernsehen* (East Berlin), August 1978.

Tosi, V., in *Bianco e Nero* (Rome), January-February 1979.

Pye, Michael, and Lynda Miles, in *Atlantic* (Boston), March 1979.

Roth, L., ''Bergsonian Comedy and the Human Machine in *Star Wars*,'' in *Film Criticism* (Edinboro, Pennsylvania), Winter 1979.

Hirayama, Ruth L., in *Magill's Survey of Cinema 4*, Englewood Cliffs, New Jersey, 1980.

Wood, Denis, ''The Empire's New Clothes,'' in *Film Quarterly* (Berkeley), Spring 1981.

Edwards, Phil, in *Starburst* (London), March 1982.

Lafficier, Randy and Jean-Marc, ''Les Origines de *Star Wars*,'' in *Ecran Fantastique* (Paris), April 1983.

Harmetz, Aljean, ''Burden of Dreams: George Lucas,'' in *American Film* (Washington, D.C.), June 1983.

Chion, M., ''Cinema de rêve,'' in *Cahiers du Cinéma* (Paris), October 1983.

Lewis, J., ''A Situationist Perspective,'' in *Jump Cut* (Berkeley), March 1985.
Malmquist, Allen, ''Saga Time at the 01' Bijou,'' in *Cinefantastique* (Oak Park, Illinois), October 1985.
McMahon, D. F., ''The Psychological Significance of Science Fiction,'' in *Psychoanalytic Review* (New York), no. 2, 1989.
Meyer, D. S., ''Star Wars, *Star Wars*, and American Political Culture,'' in *Journal of Popular Culture* (Bowling Green, Ohio), no. 2, 1992.

THE EMPIRE STRIKES BACK

USA, 1980

Director: Irvin Kershner

Production: Lucasfilm; Rank Film Color, 35mm, Panavision, Dolby sound; visual effects shot in Panavision; running time: 124 minutes. Released 14 June 1980 by 20th Century-Fox. Filmed in Elstree Studios, England, and on location in Finse, Norway; special effects shot at Industrial Light and Magic, California.

Producer: Gary Kurtz; **executive producer:** George Lucas; **screenplay:** Leigh Brackett and Lawrence Kasdan, from an original story written for the screen by George Lucas; **photography:** Peter Suschitzy; **editor:** Paul Hirsch; **visual effects editor:** Conrad Buff; **sound:** Peter Sutton; **special sound effects:** Ben Burtt; **production designer:** Norman Reynolds; **art directors:** Leslie Dilley, Harry Lange, and Alan Tomkins; **visual effects art director:** Joe Johnston; **music:** John Williams; **special effects:** Brian Johnson and Richard Edlund; **effects photography:** Dennis Muren; **optical photography:** Bruce Nicholson; **stop motion animation:** Jon Berg and Phil Tippet; **costume designer:** John Mollo; **design consultant:** Ralph McQuarrie.

Cast: Mark Hamill (*Luke Skywalker*); Harrison Ford (*Han Solo*); Carrie Fisher (*Princess Leia*); David Prowse (*Lord Darth Vader*, voice by James Earl Jones); Anthony Daniels (*C-3PO*); Peter Mayhew (*Chewbacca*); Kenny Baker (*R2-D2*); Frank Oz (*Voice and mechanical workings of Yoda*); Billy Dee Williams (*Lando Calrissian*); Alec Guinness (*Ben ''Obi-wan'' Kenobi*).

Awards: Oscar for Sound, 1980; Special Achievement Oscar for Visual Effects, 1980.

Publications

Script:

Brackett, Leigh, Lawrence Kasdan, and George Lucas, *The Empire Strikes Back: Script Facsimile*, Los Angeles, 1998.

Books:

Arnold, Alan, *Once Upon a Galaxy: A Journal of the Making of ''The Empire Strikes Back,''* New York, 1980.
Smith, Thomas G., *Industrial Light and Magic: The Art of Special Effects*, New York, 1986.

Articles:

Brosnan, John, ''Interview with Brian Johnson,'' in *Starburst* (London), no. 26, 1980.
''*Empire Strikes Back* Dossier,'' in *Ecran Fantastique* (Paris), no. 13, 1980.
Films and Filming (London), April 1980.
McGee, R., in *American Film* (Washington, D.C.), May 1980.
Harwood, J., in *Variety* (New York), 14 May 1980.
''Special Issue'' of *American Cinematographer* (Los Angeles), June 1980.
Reiss, D., in *Filmmakers Newsletter* (Ward Hill, Massachusetts), June 1980.
Combs, Richard, in *Monthly Film Bulletin* (London), July 1980.
Vallerand, F., ''John Williams et *The Empire Strikes Back,*'' in *Séquences* (Montreal), July 1980.
Shay, D., ''Interview with Richard Edlund,'' in *Cinefex* (Riverside, California), August 1980.
Rogers, T., in *Films in Review* (New York), August-September 1980.
Clarke, Frederick S., in *Cinefantastique* (Oak Park, Illinois), Fall 1980.
Ciment, Michel, and A. Garsault, in *Positif* (Paris), September 1980.
Tessier, Max, in *Image et Son* (Paris), September 1980.
Gordon, Andrew, ''*The Empire Strikes Back:* Monsters from the Id,'' in *Science Fiction Studies*, November 1980.
Lierop, P., in *Skoop* (Amsterdam), November 1980.
Mandrell, P., ''Tauntauns, Walkers, and Probots,'' in *Cinefex* (Riverside, California), December 1980.
Tellez, J. L., in *Contracampo* (Madrid), December 1980.
Termine, L., in *Cinema Nuovo* (Bari), December 1980.
Shay, Don, in *Ecran Fantastique* (Paris), no. 16, 1981.
de Kuyper, E., in *Skrien* (Amsterdam), March 1981.
Lancashire, Anne, ''Complex Design in *The Empire Strikes Back,*'' in *Film Criticism* (Edinboro, Pennsylvania), Spring 1981.
Also see list of publications following *Star Wars* credits.

THE RETURN OF THE JEDI

USA, 1983

Director: Richard Marquand

Production: Lucasfilm Ltd.; color, 35mm, Dolby sound; running time: about 120 minutes. Released Spring 1983 by 20th Century-Fox. Filmed Elstree Studios, England, and on location in Yuma, Arizona and Crescent City, California; special effects shot at Industrial Light and Magic, California.

Producer: Howard Kazanjian; **executive producer:** George Lucas; **screenplay:** Lawrence Kasdan and George Lucas, from an original story for the screen by George Lucas; **photography:** Alan Hume; **editors:** Sean Barton, Marcia Lucas, and Duwayne Dunham; **sound designer:** Ben Burtt; **production designer:** Norman Reynolds; **music:** John Williams; **special effects:** Richard Edlund, Dennis Muren and Ken Ralston; **makeup and creature designers:** Stuart Freeborn and Phil Tippett; **costume designers:** Aggie Guerard Rodgers and Nilo Rodis-Jamero.

Cast: Mark Hamill (*Luke Skywalker*); Harrison Ford (*Han Solo*); Carrie Fisher (*Princess Leia*); Billy Dee Williams (*Lando Calrissian*); Anthony Daniels (*C-3PO*); Kenny Baker (*R2-D2 and Paploo*); Peter

Mayhew (*Chewbacca*); Ian McDiarmid (*The Emperor*); David Prowse (*Darth Vader*, voice by James Earl Jones); Sebastian Shaw (*Anakin Skywalker*); Warwick Davis (*Wicket*); Michael Carter (*Bib Fortuna*); Denis Lawson (*Wedge*); Alec Guinness (*Ben ''Obi-wan'' Kenobi*).

Publications

Script:

Kasdan, Lawrence, and George Lucas, in *The Art of ''The Return of the Jedi,''* New York, 1985.

Articles:

Variety (New York), 18 May 1983.
''Special Issue'' of *American Cinematographer* (Los Angeles), June 1983.
Callahan, J., ''Raiders of the *Jedi* Secret,'' and *''Jedi's* Extra Special Effects,'' by Adam Eisenberg, in *American Film* (Washington, D.C.), June 1983.
Murdoch, Alan, ''Interview with Richard Marquand,'' in *Starburst* (London), June 1983.
Solman, G., in *Films in Review* (New York), June-July 1983.
Cohen, P., in *Skoop* (Amsterdam), July 1983.
Crawley, Tony, ''The Making of *The Return of the Jedi,*'' in *Starburst* (London), July 1983.
Edlund, Richard, Dennis Muren, and Ken Ralston, *''Jedi* Journal,'' in *Cinefex* (Riverside, California), July 1983.
Kobal, J., in *Films and Filming* (London), July 1983.
Schupp, P., in *Séquences* (Montreal), July 1983.
Strick, Philip, in *Monthly Film Bulletin* (London), July 1983.
Hibbin, S., in *Stills* (London), July-August 1983.
''Special Issue'' of *Ecran Fantastique* (Paris), October 1983.
Dumont, P., in *Cinéma* (Paris), October 1983.
Philbert, B., in *Cinématographe* (Paris), October 1983.
Marinero, P., in *Casablanca* (Madrid), January 1984.
Film Criticism (Meadville, Pennsylvania), Winter 1984.
Lewis, Jon, in *Jump Cut* (Berkeley), March 1985.
Starburst (London), May 1986.
Also see list of publications following *Star Wars* credits.

THE PHANTOM MENACE

USA, 1999

Director: George Lucas

Production: Lucasfilm; 35mm, Arriscope, color (Deluxe), Dolby Sound; running time, 136 minutes. Released 19 May 1999, USA; filmed in Tozeur, Tunisia, Royal Palace, Caserta, Naples, Italy, and Elstree Studios, Leavesden, England; special effects created at Industrial Light and Magic, California. Cost: $115 million.

Producer: Rick McCallum; **executive producer:** George Lucas; **screenplay:** George Lucas; **photography:** David Tattershall; **editors:** Ben Burtt and Paul Martin Smith; **special effects:** Rob Coleman, John Knoll, Dennis Muren, Scott Squires; **original music and conductor:** John Williams; **production designer:** Gavin Bocquet; **costume design:** Trisha Biggar.

Cast: Liam Neeson (*Qui-Gon Jinn*); Ewan McGregor (*Obi-Wan Kenobi*); Natalie Portman (*Queen Amidala/Padmé Naberrie*); Jake Lloyd (*Anakin Skywalker*); Ian McDiarmid (*Naboo Senator Cos Palpatine/Darth Sidious*); Pernilla August (*Schmi Skywalker*); Oliver Ford Davies (*Governor Sio Bibble*); Hugh Quarshie (*Captain Panaka*); Ahmed Best (voice of *Jar Jar Binks/Senator*); Anthony Daniels (*C-3PO*); Kenny Baker (*R2-D2*); Frank Oz (voice of *Yoda*); Terence Stamp (*Chancellor Finis Valorum*); Brian Blessed (*Boss Nass*); Andrew Secombe (*Watto*); Ray Park (*Darth Maul*).

Awards: Las Vegas Film Critics Society Awards, Sierra Award for Best Costume Design (Trisha Biggar), 2000; Razzie Award for Worst Supporting Actor (Jar-Jar Binks), 2000; Young Artist Award for Best Performance by a Young Actor in a Drama Film (Jake Lloyd), 2000.

Publications:

Script:

Lucas, George, *Star Wars Episode I The Phantom Menace: Script Facsimile*, Los Angeles, 2000.

Books:

Pollock, Dale, *Skywalking: The Life and Films of George Lucas*, New York, 1999.
Cavelos, Jeanne, *The Science of Star Wars: An Astrophysicist's Independent Examination of Space Travel, Aliens, and Robots as Portrayed in the Star Wars Films*, New York, 1999.
Anderson, Kevin J., and Daniel Wallace, *Star Wars: The Essential Chronology*, Los Angeles, 2000.

Articles:

Blake, Larry, ''Finishing *The Phantom Menace*—The Complete Post-Production for *Star Wars Episode I*,'' in *Mix* (Berkeley), 1 May 1999.
French, Lawrence, ''Star Wars: The Phantom Menace,'' in *Cinefantastique* (New York), 1 May 1999.
McCarthy, Todd, ''Mighty Effects but Mini Magic,'' in *Variety* (New York), 17 May 1999.
Corliss, Richard, ''The Phantom Movie,'' in *Time* (New York), 17 May 1999.
Gleiberman, Owen, ''Force of Nature?'' in *Entertainment Weekly* (New York), 21 May 1999.
''The Second Coming,'' in *Maclean's* (Toronto), 24 May 1999.
''Star Wars: A New Hype,'' in *Film Review* (London), 1 June 1999.
Robertson, Barbara, ''Star Wars,'' in *Computer Graphics World* (San Francisco), 1 June 1999.
Travers, Peter, ''Star Wars, Episode I: The Phantom Menace,'' in *Rolling Stone* (New York), 10 June 1999.
Duncan, Jody, Kevin H. Martin, and Mark Cotta Vaz, ''Heroes' Journey,'' in *Cinefex* (Riverside), 1 July 1999.
Romney, Jonathan, ''Cause and Effects,'' in *New Statesman* (London), 12 July 1999.
Alleva, Richard, ''Star Wars: The Phantom Menace,'' in *Commonweal* (New York), 16 July 1999.
Steyn, Mark, ''Cinema: Star Wars Episode One: The Phantom Menace,'' in *The Spectator* (London), 17 July 1999.

Robertson, Barbara, ''Behind the Screens,'' in *Computer Graphics World* (San Francisco), 1 August 1999.
Freer, Ian, review in *Empire* (London), August 1999.
Doherty, Thomas, ''Star Wars: The Phantom Menace,'' in *Cinefantastique*, 1 October 1999.
Carson, Tom, ''The Screen,'' in *Esquire* (New York), 1 November 1999.

* * *

In terms of scope, the *Star Wars* films are a modern equivalent to *The Iliad* or *The Odyssey.* Not only do they depict a mythic history in the form of an epic narrative, they also tell a personal tale of courage and cowardice, adventure and romance. Supported by a dazzling display of special effects and cinematic technology, the films are set in a vivid fantasy world, ''a long time ago in a galaxy far, far away.'' The series is so popular that each new film has joined the ranks of the top moneymakers of all time. More importantly, the early films generated a demand for big-budget science fiction and fantasy films, a demand that has continued into the 1990s and beyond.

The Disneyesque creator behind the films is George Lucas, who used the success of *American Graffiti* as a springboard for the production of the first *Star Wars* film, subtitled *A New Hope.* Lucas retained the rights to future *Star Wars* films and produced two sequels in the 1980s, subtitled *The Empire Strikes Back* and *Return of the Jedi.* These three films are the middle trilogy of a tentatively planned nine film opus. The fourth film to be made, *The Phantom Menace*, which appeared in 1999, begins the sequence, and Lucas has plans to make its two sequels within ten years.

The middle trilogy relates the adventures of Luke Skywalker as he and his companions battle the evil Empire, led by Luke's archnemesis, Lord Darth Vader, who is actually the tool of the Emperor, a far more malevolent being. As they're now planned, the first trilogy will relate how the Emperor took power and will end with Luke as a young boy, while the third trilogy will begin years after Luke and his rebel allies have defeated the Emperor in *Return of the Jedi.* The first three films to be made are full of youthful energy, from the exuberance of the performers to the powerful but subtle strains of John Williams's Academy Award-winning score. Lucas may be the genius behind these films, but the contributions of others involved in the films should not be overlooked.

Although the series as a whole can be seen as a simple tale of good versus evil, this doesn't do justice to its moral complexity, which is particularly in evidence in the middle trilogy through the character of Luke. Luke's story is not only a fight against the evil Empire, it is also a fight against the evil within himself. His moral dilemma is complicated by the fact, as revealed in *The Empire Strikes Back*, that the villainous Darth Vader is Luke's father.

Luke's confrontation with his dark father is part of his initiation as a Jedi Knight, an initiation which involves training in the ways of ''the Force,'' the mysterious power that exists in everything and ''binds the universe together.'' An important theme in the films is how the Force can be used to control technology, for good or evil ends. Luke's initiation into this mysterious Force is a rite of passage. As such, aspects of his story conform to the classic structure of separation, transition and incorporation described by anthropologist Arnold van Gennep in his 1909 book *Rites of Passage.* For example, in *The Empire Strikes Back* Luke's right hand is cut off by his father during a fight and is later replaced with a mechanical hand. Despite this symbolic castration, Luke still sees goodness in his father, and in *Return of the Jedi* he spares his father's life when he sees that his father, who has become more machine than man, also has a mechanical hand. This device of the hands signifies a permanent separation that leads to a permanent incorporation—it is a symbol of union with the father and a mark of membership in the knighthood of the Jedi. As a result, Luke becomes a Jedi Knight and his father is again incorporated into the good side of the Force.

The duplication and inversion which exists in the confrontation between Luke and his father is reflected throughout the three early *Star Wars* films. For instance, the rebels must destroy two Death Stars, Luke has a twin sister, the two robots are a comical inversion of the courage and cowardice of the other main characters, and Obi-wan Kenobi is a benevolent double of the Emperor. Most importantly, the furry Ewoks of *Return of the Jedi* are an inverted duplication of the small, nasty Jawas of *A New Hope.* The primitive technology of the Ewoks is the crucial factor that defeats the more advanced technology of the Empire. The Ewoks thus demonstrate how the Emperor's inflated sense of power has caused him to minimize the powers of others resulting in the Emperor's own downfall.

In this respect, the communal celebration of all of the heroes at the forest home of the Ewoks in the final scene of *Return of the Jedi* represents an interesting development of the theme of duplication and inversion because it demonstrates the process whereby two can become one. Ultimately, the trilogy not only proclaims the unity of Luke with his father or Luke with his sister, it also proclaims the unity of the Many with the One. The spirit of togetherness at the end illustrates the essential oneness of the individual and the group.

The Emperor loses because he ignores the symbiotic nature of all such dualities; he fails to realize that the existence of the master depends on the existence of his servant. And the power of Luke as a mythic hero is his ability to transcend the distinctions between good and evil, to see the good within the bad and the human being behind the mechanical mask.

With their combination of fantastical settings, spectacular special effects and slick action sequences, it is little wonder that these three films captured the imagination of a generation of filmgoers. It was with intense anticipation, then, that early in 1999 fans awaited the release of *Episode I: The Phantom Menace*, Lucas's first directorial project since *A New Hope* in 1977.

So tense was the build-up that bootleg copies of the film, taken on camcorders at preview screenings, circulated on the internet months in advance, and when the release date became known, fans camped outside cinemas to buy advance tickets. Some cinemas even reported fans buying cinema tickets just to watch the *Phantom Menace* trailer.

Set thirty years before the original three-film sequence, in *The Phantom Menace* two Jedi knights set out to rescue Queen Amidala from the planet Naboo, and become involved in a battle with the Dark Side to prevent the Empire taking over the galaxy. *The Phantom Menace* did not disappoint in terms of its special effects, its battle scenes, or its action set pieces. Yet the film has been criticized on many fronts, including its lack of humor and clear story line, poor dialogue, and the apparent lack of directorial guidance in the performances of the actors.

It has been suggested that Lucas has become so involved with the saga that he is no longer able to judge where audiences need help working out the details of the plot. A less charitable view is that he no longer needs to make an effort in order to make money. Nevertheless, many critics look towards the next two films, due out in 2002 and 2005, to make sense of *The Phantom Menace.* Despite the failings of the latest film, it is inevitable that the next two episodes will be at least as successful at the box office as the others. While the overall concept may have the cultural weight of an *Iliad* or *Odyssey*, *The Phantom Menace* exposes serious narrative limitations in the execution of this modern saga.

—Thomas Snyder, updated by Chris Routledge

STARÉ POVESTI CESKÉ

(Old Czech Legends)

Czechoslovakia, 1953

Director: Jiří Trnka

Production: Puppet Film Prague; color, animated puppets, 35mm; length: 2,480 meters. Released September 1953, Prague. Filmed 1953.

Producers: Vladimír Janovský, Vojen Masník, and Jaroslav Možiš; **story:** Jiří Trnka and Milos Kratochvíl; **screenplay:** Jiří Trnka and Jiří Brdečka, from the book by Alois Jirásek; **photography:** Ludvík Hájek and Emanuel Franek; **editor:** Helena Lebdušková; **sound:** Emanuel Formánek, Emil Poledník and Josef Zavadil; **music:** Václav Trojan; **consultants:** Rudolf Turek and Albert Pek; **animation:** Břetislav Pojar, Bohuslav Srámek, Zdeněk Hrabě, Stanislav Látal, Jan Karpaš, Josef Kluge, and František Braun.

Cast: (*Voices*) Ružena Nasková; Václav Vydra, Sr.; Karel Höger; Zdeněk Stěpánek; Eduard Kohout.

Awards: Venice Film Festival, Silver Medal from the president of the Festival, Lion of St. Mark, and Honorable Mention for Short Films, 1953; Locarno Festival, Prize of the Swiss Film Press, 1953.

Publications

Books:

Boček, Jaroslav, *Jiří Trnka, Artist and Puppet Master*, Prague, 1963.
Benešová, Marie, *Jiří Trnka*, Prague, 1970.
Liehm, Mira and Antonin, *The Most Important Art: East European Film After 1945*, Berkeley, 1977.
Habova, Milada, and Jitka Vysekalova, editors, *Czechoslovak Cinema*, Prague, 1982.

Articles:

Brož, J., ''The Puppet Film as Art,'' in *Film Culture* (New York), no. 5–6, 1955.
Brož, J., ''An Interview with the Puppet-Film Director, Jiří Trnka,'' in *Film* (London), January-February 1956.
Orna, Bernard, ''Trnka's Little Men,'' in *Films and Filming* (London), November 1956.
Polt, Harriet, ''The Czechoslovak Animated Film'' in *Film Quarterly* (Berkeley), Spring 1964.
Boček, Jaroslav, in *Film a Doba* (Prague), no. 5, 1965.
''Trnkaland,'' in *Newsweek* (New York), March 1966.
Fiala, Miloš, in *Film a Doba* (Prague), no. 4, 1970.
Schepelern, P., in *Kosmorama* (Copenhagen), Summer 1978.

* * *

After exhausting work on a long puppet film, *Bajaja*, Trnka gathered his creative strength for another ambitious enterprise, to transpose into the form of a puppet movie the ''Legends of Old Bohemia,'' a collection of narratives about the oldest period of Czech history, in which history is mixed with mythology. It was not a simple task and doubts appeared from the very beginning. However, Trnka was convinced that puppets were most suitable for expressing the magic as well as the solemnity of old stories and myths. From the book by Alois Jirásek, who had shaped these legends according to old chronicles and records (the book was published in 1894), he selected six stories: the arrival of First Father (Patriarch) Czech in the territory of contemporary Bohemia; the legend about the strong Bivoj; the legend of Prłemysl the Ploughman, founder of the royal dynasty of Prłemyslites reigning in Bohemia until the 15th century; the story of the Young Women's War; about Horymír who stood up to defend the farmers' labor; and the legend of the Lucko War which is won by Cestmír, a hero of the people. Trnka did not restrict himself exclusively to Jirásek's conception; while planning the screenplay, he took into consideration the most recent archaeological research which helped him interpret the probable material and cultural conditions of life in those days. However, Jirásek's text, together with the archaeological research, was, for Trnka, merely a foundation on which he built a structure according to his own imagination and invention.

From the point of view of Trnka's creative career, *Old Czech Legends* represents a fundamental metamorphosis in his work. This change was manifested most expressively in the puppets themselves. In comparison with *Spalíclek*, *The Emperor's Nightingale*, and *Bajaja*, whose common trait was fragility and charm, the puppets in the *Legends* are monumentally dramatic and tragic, more individualized; their countenance expresses their character, the inner essence of the represented person. Another radical innovation was the breaking of unity between the music and the picture because, in this film, Trnka's puppets speak for the first time. Václav Trojan's music does not lose its importance but it is incorporated into the overall sound design including dialogue and sound effects.

The stories in *Old Czech Legends* combine to form a total composition. The majestic arrival of Patriarch Czech is followed by the struggle of Bivoj with a wild boar; the epic about Prłemysl has lyrical passages, the Young Women's War a capricious, almost erotic mood. The dramatic narrative about Horymír is remarkable for its crowd scenes and its conclusion in which Horymír jumps over the Moldau River. The most remarkable is probably the last episode of the Legends, the narrative about the cowardly Duke Neklan, who must be replaced in the war by a people's hero, Cestmír. The characterization of Neklan pushes the puppet movie to its farthest limits in expressing psychological attitudes. In his monograph about Trnka, Jaroslav Boček describes it as an extraordinary study of cowardice which we can only rarely find even in a movie with human actors. The second part of the story—Cestmír's battle with the Lukanians—is remarkable from another point of view. Trnka used from 70 to 100 puppets in battle scenes. Control of such a multitude of inanimate actors was, from the artistic and technical standpoint, an unusually demanding task, unthinkable in a puppet movie until then. Moreover, Trnka found, jointly with his animators, the precise shade of dramatic mood and rhythm, so that the movements of the crowd were harmonious.

The *Legends* occupy an important place in Trnka's extensive work. Trnka discovered here a new style of puppet movie, characterized by a transition from lyricism to drama and by the depiction of an individualized, psychologically conditioned hero. That this new style had the potential for further development was demonstrated by Trnka's subsequent puppet movies *The Good Soldier Svejk* and *The Dream of the Night of St. John*.

—B. Urgosíková

STEAMBOAT WILLIE

USA, 1928

Director: Walt Disney

Production: Walt Disney Productions; black and white, 35mm, animation; length: 500 feet. Released 18 November 1928 in New York. Filmed in California.

Producers: Roy Disney and Walt Disney; **scenario:** Walt Disney and Ub Iwerks; **sound recordist:** P. A. Powers; **music:** Carl Stalling; **animation supervisor:** Ub Iwerks; **animation:** Wilfred Jackson, Les Clark, and Johnny Cannon.

Cast: Character voices by Walt Disney.

Publications

Books:

Field, Robert D., *The Art of Walt Disney*, New York, 1942.
Manvell, Roger, and J. Huntley, *The Technique of Film Music*, New York, 1957.
Miller, Diane Disney, *The Story of Walt Disney*, edited by Pete Martin, New York, 1957.
Stephenson, Ralph, *Animation in the Cinema*, New York, 1967.
Schickel, Richard, *The Disney Version: The Life, Times, Art, and Commerce of Walt Disney*, New York, 1968; revised edition, London, 1986.
Bessy, Maurice, *Walt Disney*, Paris, 1970.
Kurland, Gerald, *Walt Disney: The Master of Animation*, Charlottesville, Virginia, 1971.
Finch, Christopher, *The Art of Walt Disney, from Mickey Mouse to the Magic Kingdoms*, New York, 1973.
Sklar, Robert, *Movie Made America: A Social History of American Movies*, New York, 1975.
Thomas, Bob, *Walt Disney: An American Original*, New York, 1976.
Leebron, Elizabeth, and Lynn Gartley, *Walt Disney: A Guide to References and Resources*, Boston, 1979.
Maltin, Leonard, *Of Mice and Magic*, New York, 1980.
Peary, Gerald and Danny, editors, *The American Animated Cartoon*, New York, 1980.
Crafton, Donald, *Before Mickey: The Animated Film 1898–1928*, Cambridge, Massachusetts, 1982.
Thomas, Frank, and Ollie Johnston, *Disney Animation: The Illusion of Life*, New York, 1982.
Bruno, Eduardo, and Enrico Ghezzi, *Walt Disney*, Venice, 1985.
Mosley, Leonard, *Disney's World: A Biography*, New York, 1985; as *The Real Walt Disney*, London, 1986.
Culhane, Shamus, *Talking Animals and Other People*, New York, 1986.
Grant, John, *Encyclopaedia of Walt Disney's Animated Characters*, New York, 1987; revised edition, 1998.
Abrams, Robert E., contributor, *Treasures of Disney Animation Art*, New York, 1992.
Thomas, Bob, *Building a Company: Roy O. Disney & the Creation of an Entertainment Empire*, New York, 1998.
Smith, Dave, *Disney A to Z: The Updated Official Encyclopedia*, New York, 1999.
Solomon, Charles, *The Art of Disney*, New York, 2000.

Articles:

Variety (New York), 21 November 1928.
''Making of a Sound Fable,'' in *Popular Mechanics*, Summer 1930.
''Mickey Mouse's Miraculous Movie Monkeyshines,'' in *Literary Digest* (New York), 9 August 1930.
Carr, Harry, ''The Only Unpaid Movie Star,'' in *American*, March 1931.
Mann, Arthur, ''Mickey Mouse's Financial Career,'' in *Harper's* (New York), March 1931.
Seldes, Gilbert, ''Walt Disney,'' in *New Yorker*, 19 December 1931.
''Profound Mouse,'' in *Time* (New York), 15 May 1933.
Hollister, P., ''Walt Disney: Genius at Work,'' in *Atlantic* (Boston), December 1940.
Ericsson, Peter, ''Walt Disney,'' in *Sequence* (London), no. 10, 1950.
''A Silver Anniversary for Walt and Mickey,'' in *Life* (New York), 2 November 1953.
Time (New York), 27 December 1954.
Manvell, Roger, ''Giving Life to the Fantastic: A History of the Cartoon Film,'' in *Films and Filming* (London), November 1956.
Poncet, Marie-Therese, ''Walt Disney de Mickey à Disneyland,'' in *Anthologie du cinéma 2*, Paris, 1968.
Armes, Roy, ''Disney and Animation,'' in *Film and Reality*, London, 1974.
Brody, M., ''The Wonderful World of Disney: Its Psychological Appeal,'' in *American Image* (Detroit), no. 4, 1976.
Canemaker, J., ''Disney Animation: History and Technique,'' in *Film News* (New York), January-February 1979.
Canemaker, J., ''Disney Design 1928–1979,'' in *Millimeter* (New York), February 1979.
Barrier, M., ''Building a Better Mouse! 50 Years of Disney Animation,'' in *Funnyworld* (New York), Summer 1979.

* * *

Steamboat Willie—starring the most famous of cartoon mice, Mickey—has the distinction of being the very first sound cartoon. While that feat may not seem so remarkable in the context of modern sound technology, by 1928 standards it was a bold and potentially disastrous step on the part of Walt Disney. Not only was early equipment difficult and cumbersome to use, but Disney had to decide what cartoons should sound like. Since cartoons are totally fabricated, it was feared that sound might bring too much reality into play and shatter the illusion of make-believe. Luckily, Disney took a very logical (and correct) approach by using silly and bizarre sounds to match the characters and situations in his cartoons.

Up to this point Walt Disney's career was fairly active, but not secure. His *Alice* series had not been a profitable venture, and he lost the rights to the Oswald Rabbit character to his former partner Charles Mintz. In 1928 Disney and his chief animator Ub Iwerks developed a new character named Mickey Mouse. They made two cartoons with Mickey, *Plane Crazy* and *Gallopin' Gaucho*, but Disney was unable to find a distributor for the films. At this point Disney knew he had to find something unique to make his films stand out from all the others. He decided to take a risk by adding a musical soundtrack to his cartoon.

The most difficult aspect of making *Steamboat Willie* was the synchronization of picture and sound. For this reason, dialogue was kept to a bare minimum (with Walt Disney himself supplying the voices of his characters). The music for the cartoon was planned, although not scored, before any of the animation was begun. Since music can be broken down mathematically, the animation was drawn to follow a musical pattern. For example, if the music had two beats per second, the animation would hit a beat every 12 frames (based on 24 frames per second).

The last half of *Steamboat Willie* contains several excellent examples of the synchronization of action to music. In this sequence Mickey and Minnie play a version of "Turkey in the Straw" using barnyard animals as instruments. The early Mickey Mouse was a bit more crude than the sweet and lovable creature he eventually became. In this cartoon he pulls on a cow's udders, stretches a cat's tail, throws a mother pig and her babies across the room, and plays a cow's teeth like a xylophone. All of these actions fit into the beat of the music.

Because the synchronization between picture and sound was so important, Disney knew that his recording should use the sound-on-film method rather than disc. In 1928 sound equipment was at a premium in Los Angeles, so Disney took his film to New York. The first attempt to record the soundtrack was not to his satisfaction, and Disney sold his car to finance a second attempt. His confidence in the project paid off. *Steamboat Willie* was a tremendous success and received terrific reviews. What started out as a novelty—the first sound-on-film cartoon—became the standard of cartoons to follow.

—Linda J. Obalil

STERNE

(Stars)

Bulgaria-East Germany, 1959

Director: Konrad Wolf

Production: DEFA (Berlin) and Studiya za igralni filmi (Sofia); black and white, 35mm; running time: 93 minutes; length: 2,513 meters. Released March 1959, Berlin and Sofia. Filmed 1958 in Bulgaria.

Screenplay: Anzhel Wagenstein; **co-director:** Rangel Vulchanov; **photography:** Werner Bergmann; **editor:** Christina Wernicke; **sound:** Erich Schmidt; **production designer:** Jose Sancha; **music:** Simeon Pironkov; **costume designer:** Albert Seidner.

Cast: Sasha Krusharska (*Ruth*); Jürgen Frohriep (*Walter*); Erik S. Klein (*Kurt*); Stefan Peichev (*Uncle Petko*); Georgi Naumov (*Blazhe*); Ivan Kondov (*Ruth's father*); Milka Tuikova (*Police officer*); Stiliyan Kanev (*The "Doctor"*); Naicho Petrov (*Police officer*); Elena Hranova (*Old Jewish woman*); Albert Zahn (*Soldier on duty*); Hannjo Hasse (*Captain*); Hans Fiebrandt (*Soldier*); Tsonka Miteva (*Mutsi*); Waltraut Kramm (*Mutsi's girlfriend*); Trifon Dzhonev (*Schmied*); Leo Konforti (*The nervous Jew*); Gani Staikov (*Feverish person*); Avram Pinkas (*Water carrier*); Luna Davidova (*Pregnant Jew*); Petar Vasilev (*Jewish merchant*); Milka Mandil (*Jewish merchant*); Marin Toshev (*Jew with cigarettes*); Bella Eschkenazy (*Jew with girl*); Kancho Boshnakov (*Greedy Jew*); Georgi Banchev (*Woodcutter*); Yuri Yakovlev (*Soldier at the station*).

Awards: Cannes Film Festival, Special Jury Prize, 1959; Edinburgh Film Festival, First Prize and Honorary Diploma, 1959.

Publications

Books:

Cervoni, Albert, *Les Ecrans de Sofia*, Paris, 1976.
Liehm, Mira and Antonin, *The Most Important Art: East European Film After 1945*, Berkeley, 1977.
Gregor, Ulrich, *Geschichte des Films ab 1960*, Frankfurt, 1978.
Wolf, Konrad, *Direkt in Kopf und Herz: Aufzeichnungen, Reden, Interviews*, Berlin, 1989.
Wolf, Markus, *Die Troika*, Düsseldorf, 1989.

Articles:

Tok, Hans-Dieter, "Konrad Wolf," in *Regiestuhle*, Berlin, 1972.
Gehler, Fred, in *Film und Fernsehen* (East Berlin), no. 4, 1986.
Schwalbe, K., "*Sterne*," in *Beiträge zur Film und Fernsehwissenschaft*, vol. 31, no. 39, 1990.
Hoberman, J., in *Village Voice* (New York), vol. 43, 13 January 1998.

* * *

The lights and shadows of the Nazi night understandably dominated the cinemas of the East European socialist countries for almost two decades after the end of World War II before melting away, slowly and painfully, from memory into history. *Sterne* was made at that particular point when the schematic black and white "bad German" mode of depiction had already been recognised as artistically insufficient, but the new perception of human conflicts and contradictions in a complicated world, sparked by the Italian neorealism, had yet to gain prominence.

Sterne

Though both Bulgaria and the German Democratic Republic had produced their own films on similar themes and of equal quality (*On The Little Island*—1958, *Lesson One*—1960, and *And We Were Young*—1961, in Bulgaria; and *Stronger Than the Night*—1954, *Betrayed Until the Last Day*—1957, *They Called Him Amigo*—1959 and *Naked Among Wolves*—1962, in the GDR), it was *Sterne* that introduced the cinemas of the two countries to the international film scene, where the Polish school and the Soviet ''thaw'' in the mid 1950s had already stirred the attention and dispersed the bias towards the cinema of the socialist countries. Much later Albert Cervoni in his *Les Ecrans de Sofia* (Paris, 1976) called the film ''a masterpiece or a little less than that, but certainly a moving work where—rather uncustomarily—the formula of the co-production was justified on all levels, political, esthetic and also that of the screenplay itself.'' He stated this in part to cast a passing remark at the Quai d'Orsay, the French ministry of external affairs, for which the GDR did not exist in 1959. For this reason *Sterne* was shown at Cannes only as a Bulgarian entry. There was a shared tragic national experience behind the co-production; the Kingdom of Bulgaria was an ally of the Third Reich from 1940 to 1944, yet managed through firm resistance to save its Jews from extermination. A personal friendship was also involved as screenwriter Anzhel Wagenstein, a Bulgarian Jew and a member of a resistance unit, and director Konrad Wolf, son of exiled Communist writer Friedrich Wolf and an officer in the Red army, studied together at Moscow's VGIK in the early fifties.

The story of the disillusioned Aryan *Unteroffizier* who falls in love with the girl from the doomed transport of Greek Jews and tries to save her could have easily turned into melodrama but for its authenticity and sharpness, imbued with elegiac overtones. Starting with its title (the stars are twinkling witnesses of the lovers, and also humiliating yellow signs of racial *Minderwertigkeit*), the film attempts to blend poetic dreams with grim reality. The poetic side is less successful partly because of the somewhat old-fashioned and artificial cinematographic means that are applied, but mostly because of the inherent intellectual approach seeking—unlike *Hiroshima, mon amour* which is structured as an emotional, unpredictable and uncontrollable response to war traumas—a rational explanation for what seems an absurd and inevitable one-way situation. Highly realistic in its sight and sound, the film's images remain in one's mind: the small and quiet Bulgarian town, the yard of the school turned temporarily into a camp, the people behind the barbed wire and their eyes that keep looking out. Eyes that bring to mind the final sequence of

Mikhail Romm's *Ordinary Fascism*; eyes that seem to have seen death at the end of the tunnel and are trying, hopelessly, to hide it.

—Dimitar Bardarsky

STORM OVER ASIA

See **POTOMOK CHINGIS-KHAN**

THE STORY OF ASIA KLIACHINA WHO LOVED BUT DIDN'T GET MARRIED

See **ISTORIA ASI KLIACHINOI KOTORAIA LUBILA DA NIE VYSHLA ZAMUZH**

THE STORY OF GÖSTA BERLINGS

See **GÖSTA BERLINGS SAGA**

THE STORY OF QIU JU

See **QIU JU DA GUANSI**

STORY OF THE LATE CHRYSANTHEMUMS

See **ZANGIKU MONOGATARI**

LA STRADA

(The Road)

Italy, 1954

Director: Federico Fellini

Production: Ponti-De Laurentiis (Rome); black and white, 35mm; running time: 102 minutes, some sources state 107 minutes or 94 minutes; length: about 2,800 meters. Released 1954, Venice Film Festival. Filmed December 1953-May 1954 in Ponti-De Laurentiis studios in Rome; also on location in Viterbo, Ovindoli, Bagnoregio, and in various small towns in Central and Southern Italy.

Producers: Carlo Ponti and Dino De Laurentiis; **screenplay:** Federico Fellini and Tullio Pinelli with Ennio Flaiano; **photography:** Otello Martelli; **editor:** Léo Catozzo; **sound engineer:** A. Calpini; **production designer:** M. Ravesco, with artistic collaboration by Brunello Rondi, assisted by: Paolo Nuzzi; **music:** Nino Rota; **special effects:** E. Trani; **costume designer:** M. Marinari.

Cast: Giulietta Masina (*Gelsomina*); Anthony Quinn (*Zampano*); Richard Basehart (*Il matto, ''the fool''*); Aldo Silvani (*Monsieur Giraffa*); Marcella Rovere (*The widow*); Lina Venturini (*The sister*).

Awards: Venice Film Festival, Silver Prize, 1954; New York Critics Award, Best Foreign Film, 1956; Oscar for Best Foreign Film, 1956.

Publications

Script:

Fellini, Federico, and Tullio Pinelli, *La strada*, in *Cinema Nuovo* (Turin), September-October 1954; also published in *Il primo Fellini*, Bologna, 1969; translated as *La Stada*, edited by Peter Bondanella and Manuela Gieri, New Brunswick, New Jersey, 1987.

Books:

Renzi, Renzo, *Federico Fellini*, Parma, 1956.
Budgen, Suzanne, *Fellini*, London, 1966.
Salachas, Gilbert, *Federico Fellini: An Investigation into His Films and Philosophy*, New York, 1969.
Silke, James R., *Federico Fellini: Discussion*, Beverly Hills, 1970.
Samuels, Charles Thomas, *Encountering Directors*, New York, 1972.
Pecori, Franco, *Federico Fellini*, Florence, 1974.
Betti, Liliana, *Fellini*, Zurich, 1976.
Ketcham, Charles B., *Federico Fellini: The Search for a New Mythology*, New York, 1976.
Murray, Edward, *Fellini the Artist*, New York, 1976; revised edition, 1985.
Rosenthal, Stuart, *The Cinema of Federico Fellini*, London, 1976.
Fellini, Federico, *Fellini on Fellini*, edited by Christian Strich, New York, 1976.
Stubbs, John C., *Federico Fellini: A Guide to References and Resources*, Boston, 1978.
Alpert, Hollis, *Fellini: A Life*, New York, 1981; 1998.
Costello, Donald P., *Fellini's Road*, Notre Dame, Indiana, 1983.
Grazzini, Giovanni, editor, *Federico Fellini: Intervista sul cinema*, Rome, 1983.
Burke, Frank, *Federico Fellini: Variety Lights to La Dolce Vita*, Boston, 1984.
Chandler, Charlotte, *The Ultimate Seduction*, New York, 1984.

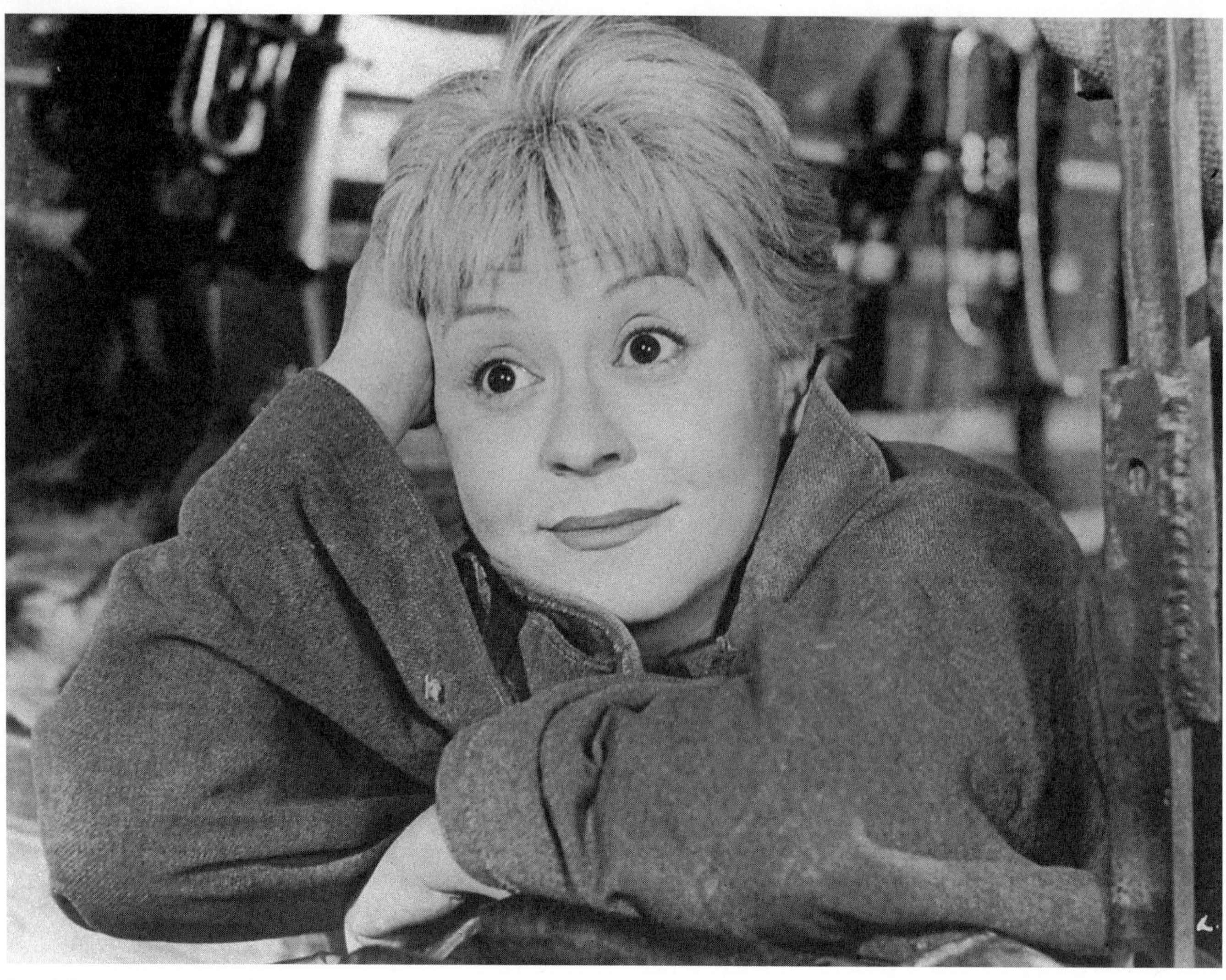

La strada

Fava, Claudio F., and Aldo Vigano, *The Films of Federico Fellini*, Secaucus, New Jersey, 1985.

Kezich, Tullio, *Fellini*, Milan, 1987.

Baxter, John, *Fellini*, New York, 1994.

Costantini, Costanzo, editor, *Fellini on Fellini*, translated by Sohrab Sorooshian, London, 1995.

Gieri, Manuela, *Contemporary Italian Filmmaking: Strategies of Subversion: Pirandello, Fellini, Scola, and the Directors of the New Generation*, Toronto, 1995.

Fellini, Federico, *Fellini on Fellini*, translated by Isabel Quigley, New York, 1996.

Articles:

Martini, Stelio, in *Cinema Nuovo* (Turin), 1 November 1953.

''*La Strada* Issue'' of *Cinema* (Rome), 10 August 1954.

Bruno, Eduardo, in *Filmcritica* (Rome), August-September 1954.

Koval, Francis, ''Venice 1954,'' in *Films in Review* (New York), October 1954.

Aristarco, Guido, in *Cinema Nuovo* (Turin), 10 November 1954.

Benayoun, Robert, in *Positif* (Paris), no. 1, 1955.

Mangini, Celia, in *Cinéma* (Paris), January 1955.

Lambert, Gavin, in *Sight and Sound* (London), January-March 1955.

Bazin, André, in *Esprit* (Paris), May 1955.

L'Her, Yves, in *Téléciné* (Paris), May-June 1955.

Aubier, Dominique, in *Cahiers du Cinéma* (Paris), July 1955.

Chardère, Bernard, in *Positif* (Paris), November 1955.

''New Names,'' in *Sight and Sound* (London), Winter 1955.

de Laurot, Edouard, ''*La Strada*—A Poem on Saintly Folly,'' in *Film Culture* (New York), no. 1, 1956.

Lefèvre, Raymond, ''Peut-on parler du néo-surréalisme de Fellini?'' in *Image et Son* (Paris), January 1956.

Newsweek (New York), 16 July 1956.

Weiler, A. H., in *New York Times*, 17 July 1956.

Young, Vernon, ''*La Strada:* Cinematic Intersections,'' in *Hudson Review* (Nutley, New Jersey), Autumn 1956.

Reichley, James, in *New Republic* (New York), 31 December 1956.

Del Fra, Lino, ''A proposito di Fellini,'' in *Bianco e Nero* (Rome), June 1957.

Bluestone, George, ''An Interview with Federico Fellini,'' in *Film Culture* (New York), October 1957.

Lane, John Francis, ''No Road Back,'' in *Films and Filming* (London), October 1957.
Aristarco, Guido, in *Cinema Nuovo* (Turin), December 1959.
Gauthier, Guy, in *Image et Son* (Paris), Summer 1962.
Taylor, John Russell, in *Cinema Eye, Cinema Ear*, New York, 1964.
Harcourt, Peter, ''The Secret Life of Federico Fellini,'' in *Film Quarterly* (Berkeley), Spring 1966.
Boffa, Franco, ''La splendida automaniera di Fellini,'' in *Cineforum* (Bergamo), April 1966.
Eason, Patricia, ''Notes on Double Structure and the Films of Fellini,'' in *Cinema* (London), March 1969.
Gow, Gordon, in *Films and Filming* (London), October 1969.
''*La Strada* Issue'' of *Avant-Scène du Cinéma* (Paris), April 1970.
Rizzo, Eugene, ''Fellini's Musical Alter Ego, Nino Rota: How They Work,'' in *Variety* (New York), 21 May 1975.
Gili, J. A., in *Image et Son* (Paris), January 1981.
Guajardo, J. M., in *Contracampo* (Madrid), February 1981.
Taconet, C., in *Cinéma* (Paris), February 1981.
Rjasanov, E., in *Film und Fernsehen* (East Berlin), March 1985.
''Fellini Section'' of *Cinématographe* (Paris), January 1986.
Reid's Film Index (Wyong), no. 6, 1991.
Pinkerton, R.N., ''*La Strada*: Look Down That Lonesome Road,'' in *Classic Images* (Muscatine), no. 203, May 1992.
Scorsese, Martin, ''Film View: Amid Clowns and Brutes, Fellini Found the Divine,'' in *New York Times*, 24 October 1993.
Landrot, Marine, ''*Gelsomina mia/La Strada*,'' in *Télérama* (Paris), no. 2348, 11 January 1995.
Amengual, Barthélemy, ''Propositions pour un portrait du jeune Fellini en néo-réaliste,'' in *Positif* (Paris), no. 413–414, July-August 1995.

* * *

La strada, one of the true masterpieces of modern cinema, is the film which brought international acclaim to director Federico Fellini. It is also an important transitional work in Italian cinema because its poetic and lyrical qualities set it apart from the literalness of the neo-realism school which had dominated post-World War II Italy.

Fellini is an exponent of neo-realism, having apprenticed with Roberto Rossellini as a writer and assistant director on *Open City* and *Paisan*. However, when he began directing on his own, preceding *La strada* with *The White Sheik* and *I vitelloni*, he opted for a subjectivity which, while evidencing the influences of neo-realism, resulted in an interior and personalized cinema second only to Buñuel.

One of the recurring motifs in Fellini's films is the circus. As a youth, Fellini had spent a number of years with an itinerant circus troup and came to admire their simplicity and their affinity with nature. Other motifs center on his Franciscan-like religious beliefs of which he stated: ''If one is to understand Christianity as an attitude of love towards another human being, then all my films revolve around it. I show a world without love inhabited by people who exploit other people, but there is always among them some significant person who wants to give love and to live for the sake of love.'' Both elements can be found in *La strada*, where a simple story involving the theme of redemption is set among itinerant circus folk.

Fellini wrote *La strada* (with Tullio Pinelli and Ennio Flaiano) for his actress-wife Giulietta Masina. When he presented the project to producers Dino De Laurentiis and Carlo Ponti, they rejected it as uncommercial, then suggested filming it with Silvano Mangano (Mrs. De Laurentiis) and Burt Lancaster as the stars. Fellini insisted that only his wife would play Gelsomina, and was finally able to convince Anthony Quinn, then in Italy making *Attila, the Hun*, to accept the role of Zampano. His producers acquiesced and the project was underway.

La strada is a serio-comic tragedy in which Fellini presents many levels of emotion and contrasting images. Its abiding message is that everyone has a purpose in life, a philosophy manifested through the lives of the three leading characters. Gelsomina is the self-sacrificing, doe-eyed simpleton (love) who becomes the chattel of Zampano, the animalistic circus strong-man (brutality). The catalyst in their fatal relationship is Il Matto, the Fool, whose prescience helps the ignorant Gelsomina to see her own value as a human being (imagination). On one level the story is a fable, a variation on Beauty and the Beast, with Gelsomina, whose beauty is within, loving the beast. On another level it is a religious allegory in which the Fool, says Fellini, represents Christ. It is also an unprepossessing story of life's rejects, for whom Fellini has always shown compassion, struggling with their own solitude. This juxtaposition of realism, fantasy and spirituality makes Fellini's *La strada* unique.

As defined by the title, *La strada*, or *The Road*, is an episodic journey in the lives of these three outcasts. Zampano travels from village to village with his motorcycle and three-wheeled trailer performing a strongman's feat of breaking an iron chain by expanding his muscular chest. His act requires a helpmate so he purchases Gelsomina from her destitute mother for 10,000 lire. (Zampano's former helpmate had been Gelsomina's sister who had died on the road.) Gelsomina becomes Zampano's slave. With much difficulty she learns to beat a drum, announce his act—''Zam-pan-o is here''—, play the trumpet, and fulfill his sexual needs. Zampano lives in a world of physical appetites, while Gelsomina communicates with the sea, the birds, the flowers. For a while they join a travelling circus where Il Matto, the equilibrist, taunts the brutish Zampano, and counsels Gelsomina in the spiritual.

After leaving the circus, their paths once again cross with that of Il Matto. This time when the Fool derides the strongman, Zampano accidently kills him. The Fool's death sends Gelsomina into a state of depression and Zampano selfishly deserts her. Five years later he learns that she has died and only then, through her loss, is he able to recognize his remorse and the magnitude of his own solitude. Fellini closes his film with a chilling scene by the sea where Gelsomina had always felt at home.

The impact of the film is the result of Fellini's poetic imagery and not any cinematic tricks. The most apparent cinematic device is the moving camera and beautiful photography of Otello Martelli. Nino Rota's enchanting musical score has since become an international classic. Most important to the effectiveness of the film is the acting. Quinn's performance as Zampano is superb and brought him long overdue acclaim as an actor of stature, and Basehart is a commendable and mischievous Il Matto. Most outstanding of all is the wonderful face and pantomime of Giulietta Masina whose comedic abilities were compared to those of Chaplin and Harry Langdon.

The majority of reviews were overwhelmingly positive, with the Catholic press describing it as a ''parable of charity, love, grace, and salvation.'' There were, however, dissenting votes. The Italian leftists felt Fellini had betrayed neorealism, and some government factions protested the film's exportation to other countries, claiming it presented a sordid and immoral view of ordinary Italians.

The film is the first of what is often described as Fellini's trilogy of solitude—*Il bidone* and *The Nights of Cabiria* completing the trilogy. *La strada* won over 50 international awards, including the Grand Prize at the Venice Festival, The New York Film Critics Award, and the Academy Award as Best Foreign Language Film.

—Ronald Bowers

STRANGERS ON A TRAIN

USA, 1951

Director: Alfred Hitchcock

Production: Warner Bros. Pictures, Inc.; black and white, 35mm; running time: 101 minutes. Released June 1951. Filmed fall 1950 in New York City, Washington, D.C., and Darien, Connecticut, and at an amusement park constructed on Rowland V. Lee's ranch in Los Angeles.

Producer: Alfred Hitchcock; **screenplay:** Raymond Chandler and Czendi Ormonde, adapted by Whitfield Cook from the novel by Patricia Highsmith; **photography:** Robert Burks; **editor:** W. H. Ziegler; **sound:** Dolph Thomas; **production designers:** Ted Haworth and George James-Hopkins; **music:** Dimitri Tiomkin; **special effects:** H. F. Koenekamp; **costume designer:** Leah Rodes.

Cast: Farley Granger (*Guy Haines*); Ruth Roman (*Ann Morton*); Robert Walker (*Bruno Anthony*); Leo G. Carroll (*Senator Morton*); Patricia Hitchcock (*Barbara Morton*); Laura Elliot (*Miriam Haines*); Marion Lorne (*Mrs. Anthony*); Jonathan Hale (*Mr. Anthony*); Howard St. John (*Capt. Turley*); John Brown (*Professor Collins*); Norma Varden (*Mrs. Cunningham*); Robert Gist (*Hennessey*); John Doucette (*Hammond*); Charles Meredith (*Judge Dolan*); Murray Alper (*Boatman*).

Publications

Script:

Chandler, Raymond, and Czendi Ormonde, *L'Inconnu du nord-express (Strangers on a Train)*, in *Avant-Scène du Cinéma* (Paris), 1 December 1982.

Books:

Rohmer, Eric, and Claude Chabrol, *Hitchcock*, Paris, 1957.
Amengual, Barthélemy, *Hitchcock*, Paris, 1960.
Bogdanovitch, Peter, *The Cinema of Alfred Hitchcock*, New York, 1962.
Wood, Robin, *Hitchcock's Films*, London, 1965; revised edition, as *Hitchcock's Films Revisited*, New York, 1989.
Truffaut, François, *Le Cinema selon Hitchcock*, Paris, 1966; as *Hitchcock*, New York, 1985.
Simsolo, Noël, *Alfred Hitchcock*, Paris, 1969.
LaValley, Albert J., editor, *Focus on Hitchcock*, Englewood Cliffs, New Jersey, 1972.
Durgnat, Raymond, *The Strange Case of Alfred Hitchcock*, Cambridge, Massachusetts, 1974.
Spoto, Donald, *The Art of Alfred Hitchcock*, New York, 1976.
Taylor, John Russell, *Hitch*, London, 1978.
Silver, Alain, and Elizabeth Ward, editors, *Film Noir*, New York, 1979.
Hemmeter, Thomas M., *Hitchcock the Stylist*, Ann Arbor, Michigan, 1981.
Bazin, André, *The Cinema of Cruelty: From Buñuel to Hitchcock*, New York, 1982.
Narboni, Jean, editor, *Alfred Hitchcock*, Paris, 1982.
Rothman, William, *Hitchcock—The Murderous Gaze*, Cambridge, Massachusetts, 1982.
Spoto, Donald, *The Life of Alfred Hitchcock: The Dark Side of Genius*, New York, 1982; London, 1983.
Villien, Bruno, *Hitchcock*, Paris, 1982.
Weis, Elisabeth, *The Silent Scream: Alfred Hitchcock's Sound Track*, Rutherford, New Jersey, 1982.
Phillips, Gene D., *Alfred Hitchcock*, Boston, 1984.
Deutelbaum, Marshall, and Leland Poague, editors, *A Hitchcock Reader*, Ames, Iowa, 1986.
Humphries, Patrick, *The Films of Alfred Hitchcock*, Greenwich, Connecticut, 1986.
Kloppenburg, Josef, *Die dramaturgische Funktion der Musik in Filmen Alfred Hitchcock*, Munich, 1986.
Sinyard, Neil, *The Films of Alfred Hitchcock*, London, 1986.
Modleski, Tania, *The Women Who Knew Too Much: Hitchcock and Feminist Theory*, New York, 1988.
Finler, Joel W., *Hitchcock in Hollywood*, New York, 1992.
Sterritt, David, *The Films of Alfred Hitchcock*, New York, 1993.
Arginteanu, Judy, *The Movies of Alfred Hitchcock*, Minneapolis, 1994.
Boyd, David, editor, *Perspectives on Alfred Hitchcock*, New York, 1995.
Auiler, Dan, *Hitchcock's Notebooks: An Authorized and Illustrated Look Inside the Creative Mind of Alfred Hitchcock*, New York, 1999.
Freedman, Jonathan, and Richard Millington, editors, *Hitchcock's America*, New York, 1999.
Harris, Robert A., *Complete Films of Alfred Hitchcock*, Secaucus, 1999.

Articles:

Hart, Henry, in *Films in Review* (New York), June-July 1951.
Winnington, Richard, in *Sight and Sound* (London), August-September 1951.
''Hitchcock Issue'' of *Cahiers du Cinéma* (Paris), October 1953.
Feuga, Pierre, in *Arts* (Paris), May 1954.
Truffaut, François, and Claude Chabrol, ''Rencotre avec Hitchcock,'' in *Arts* (Paris), February 1955.
Seguin, Louis, in *Positif* (Paris), November 1955.
Chabrol, Claude, in *Arts* (Paris), 28 December 1955.
''Hitchcock Issue'' of *Cahiers du Cinéma* (Paris), August-September 1956.

Strangers on a Train

Higham, Charles, ''Hitchcock's World,'' in *Film Quarterly* (Berkeley), Winter 1962–63.

Sonbert, Warren, in *Film Culture* (New York), Summer 1966.

Zucker, Phyllis, ''Robert Walker,'' in *Films in Review* (New York), March 1970.

Humbert, M., and D. Delosne, in *Image et Son* (Paris), no. 286, 1974.

Laemmle, Ann, in *Cinema Texas Program Notes* (Austin), 14 September 1978.

Marty, A., ''*L'Inconnu du nord-express* et le Maccarthisme,'' in *Image et Son* (Paris), July-August 1980.

Douglas, J.Y., ''American Friends and Strangers on Trains,'' in Literature/*Film Quarterly* (Salisbury, Maryland), vol. 16, no. 3, 1988.

Sered, J., ''The Dark Side,'' in Armchair Detective, no. 22, no. 2, 1989.

Corber, R. J., ''Reconstructing Homosexuality: Hitchcock and the Homoerotics of Spectatorial Pleasure,'' in *Discourse* (Bloomington, Indiana), Spring-Summer 1991.

Matthews, J.J., in *Scarlet Street* (Glen Rock), no. 6, Spring 1992.

Reid's Film Index (Wyong), no. 8, 1992.

Desowitz, B., ''Strangers on Which Train?'' in *Film Comment* (New York), vol. 28, no. 3, May-June 1992.

Chin, Paula, ''Through a Mind, Darkly: Writing of Murder and Madness, Patricia Highsmith Heeds a Strange Muse,'' in *People Weekly*, vol. 39, no. 1, 11 January 1993.

Séquences (Haute-Ville), no. 179, July-August 1995.

Lilley, Jessie, ''Granger on a Train,'' in *Scarlet Street* (Glen Rock), no. 21, Winter 1996.

Valley, Richard, ''The Trouble with Hitchcock: *Stage Fright* and *Strangers on a Train* Investigated!'' in *Scarlet Street* (Glen Rock), no. 21, Winter 1996.

* * *

Alfred Hitchcock based *Strangers on a Train* (1951), one of his most suspenseful thrillers, on the novel by Patricia Highsmith. It begins with a railway journey, in the course of which Bruno Antony, a wealthy homosexual (Robert Walker, in an immaculate performance), ingratiates himself with Guy Haines, a handsome tennis champion (Farley Granger). The slightly effeminate Bruno has all the earmarks of a textbook case in abnormal psychology, since he combines a deep-seated, implacable hatred of his domineering father with a curious attachment to his eccentric mother. As the two lunch together on the train, it is evident that Guy, who is unhappily married to a conniving, promiscuous spouse, is fascinated by this fey, coyly ingratiating creature—so much so that from the start there is an unacknowledged homosexual undertone to their relationship.

Farley Granger is cited in Vito Russo's *The Celluloid Closet* (1987) as saying that "it was Robert Walker's idea to play Bruno Antony as a homosexual." On the contrary, it should be obvious from the foregoing remarks about Bruno's background and behaviour that his approach to Guy as a rather blatant homosexual courting a latent one is embedded in the subtle screenplay, and not something Walker, as brilliant as he is in the part, superimposed on the characterization.

Before they part company at journey's end, Bruno tries to manipulate Guy into agreeing to kill Bruno's father, in exchange for Bruno murdering Guy's wife, Miriam. Since neither of them has an ostensible motive for committing the other's crime, they would both, according to Bruno's logic, successfully elude detection. This proposal appeals to Guy more than he is prepared to admit, since he would like to be rid of his hateful wife. Consequently, he does not reject Bruno's plan immediately. Taking Guy's indecision for tacit approval, the deranged Bruno kills Miriam and demands that Guy keep his part of the bargain, which Guy, in a moment of panic, agrees to do, just to get rid of Bruno.

For novelist Patricia Highsmith, the way in which Bruno plays on the baser instincts of the fundamentally good-natured Guy signifies the duality that lies at the heart of human nature. Gordon Gow quotes her in *Hollywood: 1920–70* as saying, "I'm very much concerned" with the way that good and evil exist in everyone "to a greater or lesser degree." Raymond Chandler, the eminent crime novelist (*The Big Sleep*) and screenwriter, was very much preoccupied, as was Hitchcock, with bringing to light the dark corners of the human psyche; he accepted Hitchcock's offer to draft the screenplay for *Strangers.* One of the most tense scenes in the picture is that in which Bruno strangles Guy's estranged wife in a secluded corner of the amusement park. Ironically, the murder is accompanied by the distant music of the merry-go-round's calliope, as it grinds out its cheery rendition of "The Band Played On." Horrified, we watch the murder as it is reflected in Miriam's glasses, which have fallen onto the grass during her struggle with Bruno. Photographed in this grotesquely distorted fashion, the strangling looks as if it were being viewed in a fun-house mirror, another reminder of the grimly incongruous carnival setting of the crime.

Given the fact that Guy subconsciously wanted Miriam dead, he has, in effect, accomplished her death through the mediation of Bruno as his proxy. Guy has become, however unwittingly, allied with the perverse force of evil that Bruno represents; this is confirmed in the scene in which the two men stand on opposite sides of an iron fence, as Bruno informs Guy that he has taken Miriam's life. When a police squad car appears across the street, instinctively Guy joins Bruno on the same side of the barrier, and thus acknowledges implicitly his share of the guilt in Miriam's demise. Moreover, the image of Guy's troubled face barred by the sinister shadows of the gate grill signals his imprisonment by Bruno in an unholy alliance from which he finds himself, for the time being, powerless to escape.

Guy is suspected of killing his wife; but he is given the chance to redeem himself by pursuing Bruno back to the scene of Miriam's murder and forcing him to confess the truth about her death. As they wrestle with each other aboard the carousel, the mechanism suddenly goes berserk, changing from a harmless source of innocent fun into a whirling instrument of terror. Thus the carousel is a reflection of Hitchcock's dark vision of our chaotic, topsy-turvy planet. As the runaway merry-go-round continues to spin at top speed, its rendition of "The Band Played On" is also accelerated to a dizzying tempo and mingles with macabre persistence with the screams of the hysterical riders trapped on board. A mechanic at last manages to bring the carousel to a halt, but it stops so suddenly that the riders go sailing off in all directions, as the machinery collapses into a heap of smoldering wreckage. As the movie draws to a close, Bruno dies in the debris, unrepentant to the last.

—Gene D. Phillips

STRAWBERRY AND CHOCOLATE

See **FRESA Y CHOCOLATE**

STREET OF SHAME

See **AKASEN CHITAI**

A STREETCAR NAMED DESIRE

USA, 1951

Director: Elia Kazan

Production: Warner Bros. Pictures Inc.; black and white, 35mm; running time: 125 minutes. Released 1951.

Producer: Charles K. Feldman; **screenplay:** Tennessee Williams, from Oscar Saul's adaptation of the play by Williams; **photography:** Harry Stradling; **editor:** David Weisbart; **art director:** Richard Day; **music:** Alex North.

Cast: Vivien Leigh (*Blanche DuBois*); Marlon Brando (*Stanley Kowalski*); Kim Hunter (*Stella Kowalski*); Karl Malden (*Mitch*).

Awards: Oscars for Best Actress (Leigh), Best Supporting Actor (Malden), Best Supporting Actress (Hunter), and Art Direction/Set Direction—Black and White, 1951; Venice Film Festival, Best Actress (Leigh) and Special Jury Prize, 1951; New York Film Critics Awards for Best Motion Picture, Best Actress (Leigh), and Best Direction, 1951.

Publications

Script:

Williams, Tennessee, *A Streetcar Named Desire*, in *Film Scripts One*, edited by George P. Garrett and others, New York, 1971.

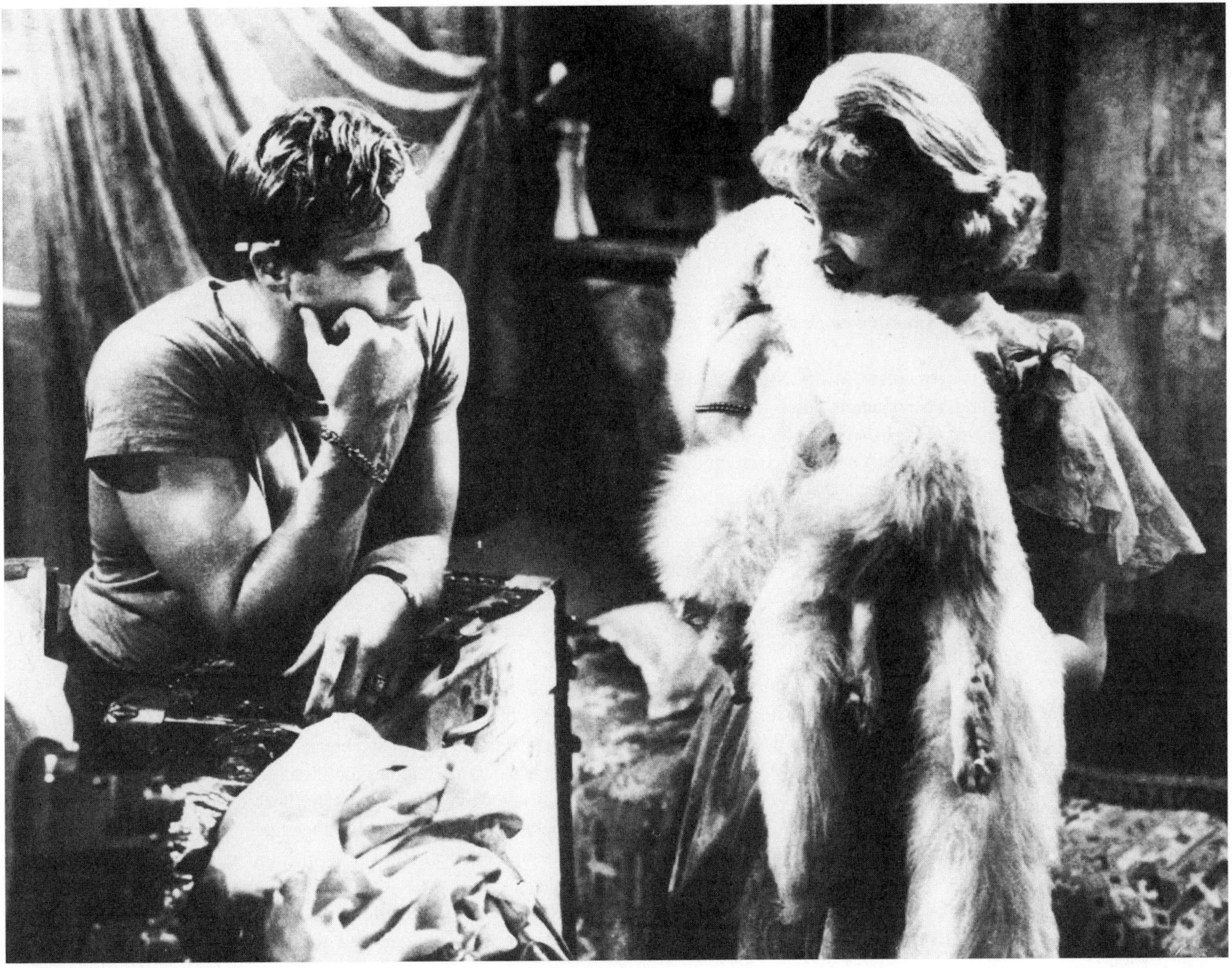

A Streetcar Named Desire

Books:

Lawson, John Howard, *Film in the Battle of Ideas*, New York, 1953.
Robyns, Gwen, *Light of a Star: The Career of Vivien Leigh*, New York, 1970.
Basinger, Jeanine, editor, *Working with Kazan*, Middletown, Connecticut, 1973.
Kazan, Elia, *Elia Kazan on What Makes a Director*, New York, 1973.
Thomas, Tony, *The Films of Marlon Brando*, Secaucus, New Jersey, 1973.
Ciment, Michel, *Kazan on Kazan*, New York, 1974.
Shipman, David, *Brando*, London, 1974.
Edwards, Anne, *Vivien Leigh: A Biography*, New York, 1977.
Yacowar, Maurice, *Tennessee Williams and Film*, New York, 1977.
Manvell, Roger, *Theatre and Film: A Comparative Study of the Two Forms of Dramatic Art, and of the Problems of Adaptation of Stage Plays into Films*, Rutherford, New Jersey, 1979.
Giannetti, Louis, *Masters of the American Cinema*, Englewood Cliffs, New Jersey, 1981.
Pauly, Thomas H., *An American Odyssey: Elia Kazan and American Culture*, Philadelphia, 1983.
Downing, David, *Marlon Brando*, London, 1984.
Carey, Gary, *Marlon Brando: The Only Contender*, London, 1985.
Michaels, Lloyd, *Elia Kazan: A Guide to References and Resources*, Boston, 1985.
Higham, Charles, *Brando: The Unauthorized Biography*, New York, 1987.
Kazan, Elia, *A Life*, New York, 1988.
Niemeier, Susanne, *Ein Fall im Medienvergleich: Film- und Fernsehversion von A Streetcar Named Desire*, Frankfurt, 1990.
Grobel, Lawrence, *Conversations with Brando*, Lanham, 1993, 1999.
Brando, Marlon, *Songs My Mother Taught Me*, with Robert Lindsey, New York, 1994.
Malden, Karl, and Carla Malden, *When Do I Start?: A Memoir*, New York, 1997.
Girgus, Sam B., *Hollywood Renaissance: The Cinema of Democracy in the Era of Ford, Capra and Kazan*, New York, 1998.
Lobrutto, *Elia Kazan*, Old Tappan, 1999.
Young, Jeff, editor, *Kazan—The Master Director Discusses His Films: Interviews with Elia Kazan*, New York, 1999.
Baer, William, editor, *Elia Kazan: Interviews*, Jackson, 2000.

Articles:

Lightman, Herb A., ''Uninhibited Camera,'' in *American Cinematographer* (Los Angeles), October 1951.

Isaacs, Hermine, Eleanor Nash, and Francis Patterson, in *Films in Review* (New York), December 1951.

Reisz, Karel, in *Sight and Sound* (London), Spring 1952.

Brinson, Peter, ''The Brooder,'' in *Films and Filming* (London), October 1954.

Archer, Eugene, ''Elia Kazan—The Genesis of a Style,'' in *Film Culture* (New York), vol. 2, no. 2, 1956.

Bowers, Ronald, ''Vivien Leigh,'' in *Films in Review* (New York), August-September 1956.

''A Quiz for Kazan,'' in *Theatre Arts* (New York), November 1956.

Delahaye, Michel, ''A Natural Phenomenon: Interview with Elia Kazan,'' in *Cahiers du Cinema in English* (New York), March 1967.

Corliss, Richard, in *Film Comment* (New York), Summer 1968.

''Kazan Issue'' of *Movie* (London), Winter 1971–72.

Kitses, Jim, ''Elia Kazan: A Structuralist Analysis,'' in *Cinema* (Beverly Hills), Winter 1972–73.

Burles, Kenneth T., in *Magill's Survey of Cinema 4*, Englewood Cliffs, New Jersey, 1980.

Dowling, E., ''The Derailment of *A Streetcar Named Desire*,'' in *Literature/Film Quarterly* (Salisbury, Maryland), vol. 9, no. 4, 1981.

Black, David Alan, ''Sexual Misdemeanor/Psychoanalytic Felony,'' in *Cinema Journal* (Champaign, Illinois), Winter 1987.

Weinraub, B., ''For a Less Restrained Era, a Restored *Streetcar*,'' in *New York Times*, vol. 142, C12, 16 September 1993.

Schickel, R., ''A '50s Masterpiece for the '90s,'' in *Time*, vol. 142, 1 November 1993.

Kauffmann, S., ''Back to Brando,'' in *New Republic*, vol. 209, 29 November 1993.

Cahir, Linda Costanzo, ''The Artful Rerouting of *A Streetcar Named Desire*,'' in *Literature/Film Quarterly* (Salisbury), vol. 22, no. 2, April 1994.

Manso, P., ''Brando's Way,'' in *Vanity Fair* (New York), vol. 57, September 1994.

Manso, P., ''Bringing Up Baby,'' in *Premiere* (Boulder), vol. 8, October 1994.

Care, Ross, ''Record Track,'' in *Scarlet Street* (Glen Rock), no. 19, Summer 1995.

Benedetto, Robert, ''*A Streetcar Named Desire:* Adapting the Play to Film,'' in *Creative Screenwriting* (Washington, D.C.), vol. 4, no. 4, Winter 1997.

*   *   *

Partisans of America's Broadway stage, the ''fabulous invalid'' of 1920s, when pessimists feared that talking pictures would lure new generations away from live theatre, were greatly heartened when after the early successes of Tennessee Williams' *The Glass Menagerie* (1945), and Arthur Miller's *All My Sons* (1947), the promising newcomers followed up their success with *A Streetcar Named Desire* (1947) and *Death of a Salesman* (1949). World War II over, a glorious new theatrical era appeared to be underway. However, the two dazzling Expressionist tragedies proved the climax of the period of psychodrama between the wars rather than the prologue to another era of greater accomplishment.

Both plays were directed in New York by the same socially conscious Greek immigrant, Elia Kazan, who had gained extensive experience, both acting and directing during the 1930s, and who, just as he turned 40, had begun moving between the stage and screen. After scoring impressive successes in the late 1940s with controversial films about social problems (*Pinky*, *Gentleman's Agreement*, and *Panic in the Streets*), he was engaged to direct the film version of *Streetcar*, but *Death of a Salesman* was assigned to Hollywood newcomer Laslo Benedek. Although the latter made headlines by being picketed by the American Legion, it proved unmemorable, but *A Streetcar Named Desire* was a smashing success, despite the problems of transferring the play to the screen.

The principal problem was censorship. Williams' play depicts the pathetic degeneration of Blanche DuBois, daughter of a once wealthy family of Mississippi planters, whose socially proper young husband killed himself after being discovered in bed with another man. Blanche watches her family squander its fortune on ''epic debaucheries'' until they lose their beautiful dream mansion, Belle Rêve. She is obliged to take a poorly paid job as a school-teacher and move into a squalid hotel, from which she is finally evicted because of her ''intimacies'' with travelling salesmen and high school boys. She is forced to take refuge in New Orleans with her unenthusiastic sister Stella, who has sought to escape the past by marrying a vulgar but virile Polish immigrant. Hostilities immediately flare up between pretentious Blanche and Stella's husband, Stanley Kowalski, who suspects that the sister is trying to cheat his wife out of an inheritance. He investigates her past and breaks up a budding romance with one of his poker-playing buddies and finally completes her degradation by raping her while Stella is in the hospital bearing their first child. Blanche's shift into probably congenital madness is completed by this traumatic violence, and she is institutionalized as Stella returns to Stanley.

Kazan wanted the film to be as true as possible to the play. Tennessee Williams refused to write the script, but insisted on approving any changes. When Kazan took Oscar Saul's script to Joseph Breen's office, which administered the Production Code, Thomas Pauly reports that he learned that to get the seal of approval that most exhibitors required, 68 changes, including major omissions of any references to homosexuality, nymphomania, or the rape—the principal causes of Blanche's downfall, would have to be made. The first two big no-nos were handled by awkwardly glossing over them with euphemistic references to ''nervous tendencies'' that many viewers already understood from widespread discussion of the play. Kazan insisted, however, that the rape was essential. Breen acquiesced, so long as there was no evidence of evil intention on Stanley's part, as leeringly suggested by the line in the play, ''We've had this date with each other for a long time,'' and by merely suggesting what will transpire as Stanley advances on the terrified Blanche, brandishing a beer bottle which he smashes into a mirror. Since the Code also demanded that crimes could not be exonerated, Breen insisted that Stella must make it clear that she will not return to Stanley, even though many viewers would realize that in the still patriarchal South a woman with a baby might have no alternative.

Other problems arose. Kazan had at first wanted to open up the film with scenes from Blanche's life in Mississippi; but he finally realized, as Pauly points out, that Williams' intentions could only be realized by confining the principal action to the Kowalski's claustrophobic apartment. Only the opening scene of Blanche's arrival walking down a street that is certainly not—as identified in the movie—the wide, tree-lined Elysian Fields, was shot on location.

As production began, the conflict in the storyline between the decadent tradition of a self-destructive, snobbish society, and the macho violence of a vigorous outsider seeking to take over its social position provided the opportunity of a subtext, probably unintended by the playwright or director, about another conflict between tradition and innovation. Kazan had brought most of his Broadway cast with him; but Vivien Leigh, playing Blanche, had developed her interpretation of the role in the London production under the direction of her husband, Laurence Olivier. Although Williams and Kazan agreed that the emphasis in the film, as in the play, must be on Blanche, Kazan and Leigh clashed over her demeanour in the early scenes, as she argued that Blanche should be played sympathetically throughout. One senses beyond the surface class and gender conflict about which Tennessee Williams had ambiguous feelings an even tougher though understated conflict between two acting traditions—the exacting standards of classically trained performers for an established society and the controversial new method acting of the New York Actors Studio, with which Kazan was associated, which emphasized improvization and reflected in its work the alienation of a rebellious generation at a time when social and artistic traditions were under attack.

The result, abetted by the Breen office's inflexibility, was an immediate victory for tradition. Vivien Leigh gives an almost incomparable performance, transcending medium limitations and, by invoking the ''suspension of disbelief'' that sublime art requires, getting in touch with the audience as Blanche DuBois, a woman they may suffer with or scorn, but cannot ignore. Leigh triumphs by reversing the memorable image of her related role as Scarlett O'Hara in *Gone with the Wind* or indomitable will, to become a symbol of the ever-suffering victims of maligned self-glorifiers with whom the world had become so familiar prior to and during World War II. She justly won her second Academy Award for best actress in a troublesome year when the bitter contest for best picture honours between *Streetcar* and *A Place in the Sun* (George Stevens' version of Theodore Dreiser's novel *An American Tragedy*), was settled by default with the award going to Vincente Minnelli's lightweight but uplifting *An American in Paris*. (Hollywood veteran Stevens was consoled with the Best Director's award, while Humphrey Bogart as Best Actor in *The African Queen* beat relative newcomer Brando.)

In the long run, however, while the sometimes fatal struggle continues between unreconciled extremist groups in the United States, Williams' vision of his ending for the tragedy seems prophetic as the ''natural'' behaviour of those struggling for survival and advancement grows, a stronger force than that defending artificialities of traditional culture—an American tendency that is increasingly exported abroad. Inevitably a flawed film because of the conditions imposed upon its creation, *A Streetcar Named Desire* remains an indispensable period piece that vividly projects an image of more aspects of its period than its creators may have realized.

—Warren French

STRIKE

See **STACHKA**

STROMBOLI

Italy, 1950

Director: Roberto Rossellini

Production: Berit Films, for RKO; black and white; running time: 81 minutes, originally 107 minutes; length: 7,300 feet. Released 1950.

Producer: Roberto Rossellini; **assistant director:** Marcello Caracciolo; **screenplay:** Roberto Rossellini, Art Cohn, Sergio Amidei, Gianpaolo Callegari, from a story by Rossellini, religious theme inspired by Father Felix Morlion; **photography:** Ottello Martelli; **editor:** Roland Gross; **sound:** Terry Kellum, E. Giordani; **music:** Renzo Rossellini.

Cast: Ingrid Bergman (*Karin*); Mario Vitale (*Antonio*); Renzo Cesana (*Priest*); Mario Sponza (*Lighthouse-keeper*); the people of Stromboli.

Publications

Books:

Hovald, Patrice, *Roberto Rossellini*, Paris, 1958.
Steele, Joseph Henry, *Ingrid Bergman*, London, 1960.
Mida, Massimo, *Roberto Rossellini*, Paris, 1961.
Verdone, Mario, *Roberto Rossellini*, Paris, 1963.
Sarris, Andrew, *Interviews with Film Directors*, New York, 1967.
Guarner, Jose Luis, *Roberto Rossellini*, New York, 1970.
Ivaldi, Nedo, *La Resitenza nel cinema italiano del dopoguerra*, Rome, 1970.
Quirk, Lawrence J., *The Films of Ingrid Bergman*, New York, 1970.
Armes, Roy, *Patterns of Realism: A Study of Italian Neo-Realist Cinema*, Cranbury, New Jersey, 1971.
Wlaschin, Ken, *Italian Cinema Since the War*, Cranbury, New Jersey, 1971.
Baldelli, Pierre, *Roberto Rossellini*, Rome, 1972.
Brown, Curtis F., *Ingrid Bergman*, New York, 1973.
Rosen, Marjorie, *Popcorn Venus*, New York, 1973.
Rondolini, Gianni, *Roberto Rossellini*, Florence, 1974.
Bergman, Ingrid, with Alan Burgess, *Ingrid Bergman: My Story*, New York, 1980.
Ranvaud, Don, *Roberto Rossellini*, London, 1981.
Taylor, John Russell, *Ingrid Bergman*, London, 1983.
Rossellini, Roberto, *Le Cinéma révélé*, edited by Alain Bergala, Paris, 1984.
Hillier, Jim, editor, *Cahiers du Cinéma 1: The 1950s: Neo-Realism, Hollywood, New Wave*, London, 1985.
Leamer, Laurence, *As Time Goes By: The Life of Ingrid Bergman*, New York, 1986.
Serceau, Michel, *Roberto Rossellini*, Paris, 1986.
Brunette, Peter, *Roberto Rossellini*, Oxford, 1987; reprinted, Berkeley, 1996.

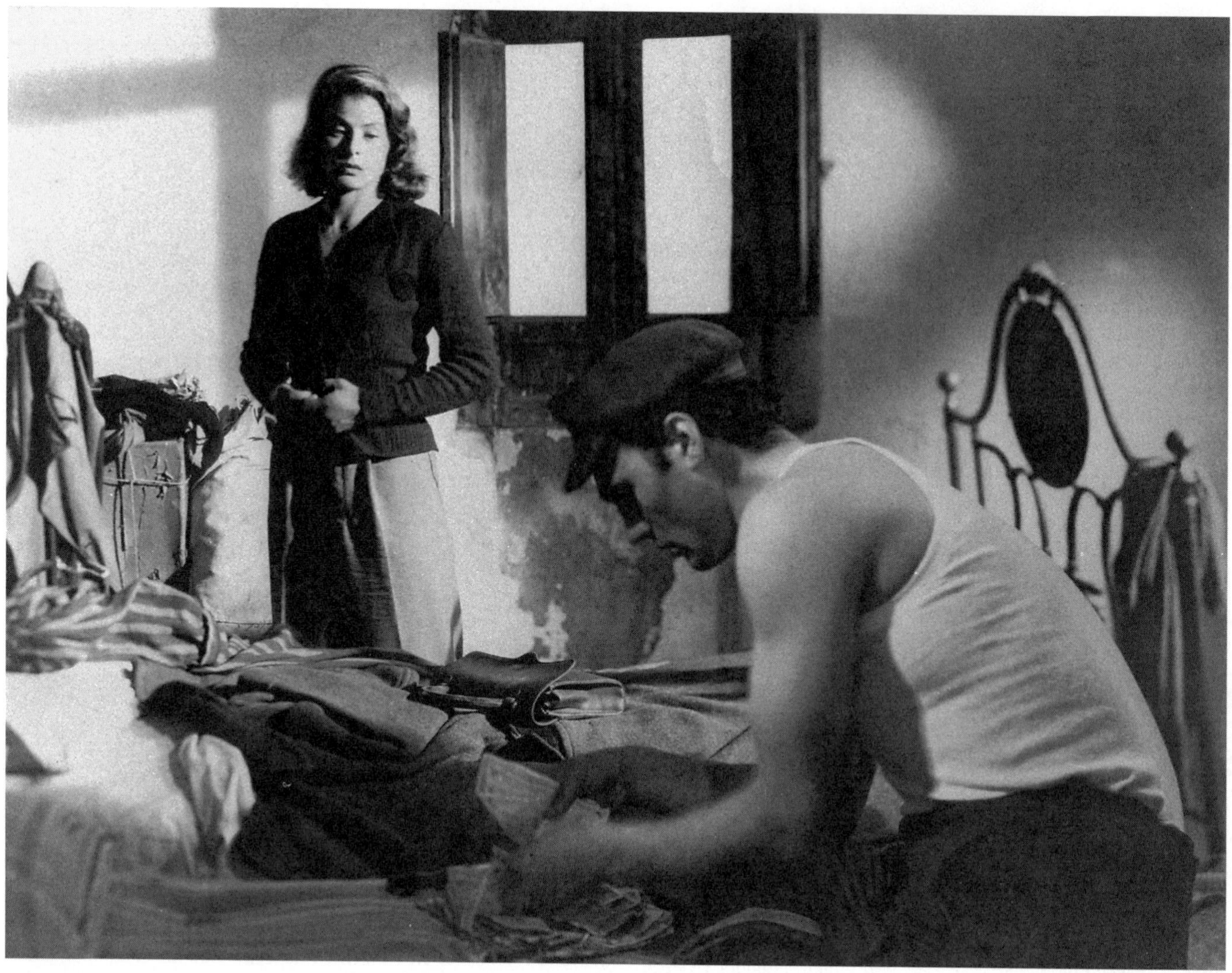

Stromboli

Gansera, Rainer, and others, *Roberto Rossellini*, Munich, 1987.

Rossellini, Roberto, *Il mio metodo: Scritti e intervisti*, edited by Adriano Apra, Venice, 1987.

Rossi, P., *Roberto Rossellini: A Guide to References and Resources*, Boston, 1988.

Bondanella, Peter, *Films of Roberto Rossellini*, Cambridge, 1993.

Rossellini, Roberto, *My Method: Writings and Interviews*, New York, 1995.

Gallagher, Tag, *The Adventures of Roberto Rossellini*, Cambridge, 1998.

Articles:

Motion Picture Herald (New York), 18 February 1950.

Harcourt-Smith, Simon, ''The Stature of Rossellini,'' in *Sight and Sound* (London), April 1950.

Houston, Penelope, in *Monthly Film Bulletin* (London), June 1950.

Cahiers du Cinéma (Paris), April 1951.

Schèrer, Maurice, and François Truffaut, ''Entretien avec Roberto Rossellini,'' in *Cahiers du Cinéma* (Paris), July 1954.

Truffaut, François, ''Rossellini,'' in *Arts* (Paris), January 1955.

Tynan, Kenneth, ''The Abundant Miss Bergman,'' in *Films and Filming* (London), December 1958.

Sarris, Andrew, ''Rossellini Rediscovered,'' in *Film Culture* (New York), no. 32, 1964.

Casty, Alan, ''The Achievement of Roberto Rossellini,'' in *Film Comment* (New York), Fall 1964.

Apra, Adriano, and Maurizio Ponzi, ''Intervista con Roberto Rossellini,'' in *Filmcritica* (Rome), April-May 1965.

Wood, Robin, in *Film Comment* (New York), July-August 1974.

Damico, J., ''Ingrid from Lorraine to Stromboli: Analyzing the Public's Perception of a Film Star,'' in *Journal of Popular Film* (Washington, D.C.), vol. 4, no. 1, 1975.

Beylie, Claude, and C. Clouzot, interview with Rossellini, in *Ecran* (Paris), July 1977.

Lawton, H., ''Rossellini's Didactic Cinema,'' in *Sight and Sound* (London), Autumn 1978.

''Rossellini's *Stromboli* and Ingrid Bergman's Face,'' in *Movietone News* (Seattle), December 1979.

Adair, Gilbert, in *Monthly Film Bulletin* (London), November 1980.

Ranvaud, Don, in *Monthly Film Bulletin* (London), February and March 1981.

Tesson, C., ''La Méprise, le mépris,'' in *Cahiers du Cinéma* (Paris), November 1981.

Cinématographe (Paris), November 1981.

Serceau, M., ''Rossellini—le prisme des idéologies,'' *Image et Son* (Paris), April 1982.

Amiel, M., ''Ingrid Bergman: Force, dignité, courage,'' in *Cinéma* (Paris), October 1982.

''Ingrid Bergman Section'' of *Casablanca* (Madrid), October 1982.

''Rossellini Issue'' of *Casablanca* (Madrid), March 1985.

Nieuwenweg, L., ''De liefdes van Roberto Rossellini: 'Ik haat actrices, het zijn ijdele wezens,''' in *Skoop* (Amsterdam), September-October 1985.

Zizek, S., ''Rossellini: Woman as Symptom of Man,'' in *October* (Cambridge, Massachusetts), Fall 1990.

Durançon, Jean, ''Stromboli, ou le réalisme n'existe pas,'' in *CinémAction* (Conde-sur-Noireau, France), no. 70, January 1994.

Philippon, A., ''*Stromboli*, c'est pas fini,'' in *Cahiers du Cinéma* (Paris), no. 481, June 1994.

Télérama (Paris), no. 2384, 23 September 1995.

McLean, A.L., ''The Cinderella Princess and the Instrument of Evil: Surveying the Limits of Female Transgression in Two Postwar Hollywood Scandals,'' in *Cinema Journal* (Austin), vol. 34, no. 3, 1995.

Jacobwitz, F., ''Rewriting Realism: Bergman and Rossellini in Europe 1949–1955,'' in *CineAction* (Toronto), no. 41, 1996.

Magny, J., ''Eric Rohmer: cineaste chretien?'' in *Cinemaction* (Conde-sur-Noireau), vol. 80, no. 3, 1996.

Azua, F. de, ''Mas que mala,'' in *Nosferatu* (San Sebastian), vol. 23, January 1997.

* * *

Stromboli was the first of five features which Rossellini made with Ingrid Bergman, the others being *Europa '51, Viaggio in Italia, Giovanna d'Arco al rogo* and *La paura.* He also directed her in an episode of the portmanteau film *Siamo donne.* The making of *Stromboli* was fraught with problems and difficulties. For one thing, the film coincided with the start of the much publicised and, in the United States at least, much frowned-upon affair between Bergman and Rossellini. After the failure of *Joan of Arc* and *Arch of Triumph*, Bergman, who was becoming increasingly unhappy in Hollywood and in her marriage, was looking for a way out of both. However, she was highly bankable, and both Samuel Goldwyn and RKO's Howard Hughes showed interest in her idea of doing a picture with Rossellini. In the event Goldwyn backed out after seeing *Germany, Year Zero* and it was RKO which financed *Stromboli.* In spite of her feelings for Rossellini, Bergman found the director's improvisatory methods somewhat alien (although she coped far better than George Sanders in *Viaggio)*, conditions on the island itself were primitive and arduous (indeed, during the final eruption sequence one of Rossellini's crew succumbed to the sulphurous fumes and died of a heart attack), the shoot was dogged by inquisitive paparazzi, and the picture went over schedule and over budget. It had always been agreed to release an Italian and an English language version of the film, both of which were to be edited by Rossellini. However, as a result of rows about the budget RKO edited the English version itself, which differs considerably from the Italian one (which Rossellini himself edited) and was disowned by the director.

The existence of two different versions makes it even more difficult to judge this particularly controversial film. With few exceptions (notably Robin Wood, Andrew Sarris, and Peter Brunette), the film has found no friends among Anglo-Saxon critics and, given the treatment meted out by them to *Viaggio*, it is doubtful that things would have been any different had they seen Rossellini's own version. In France, *Stromboli*, like the other Rossellini-Bergman collaborations, was championed by *Cahiers*, and especially by André Bazin, Jacques Rivette, and Maurice Schèrer (Eric Rohmer). Meanwhile, in Italy the situation was rather more complicated; those who disliked the film tended to accuse Rossellini of ''abandoning neorealism'' (often with the implicit suggestion that this was due to his infatuation with Ingrid Bergman), thus pushing the film's supporters into *defending* it as a neo-realist text, which is perhaps not the most productive or helpful way to look at *Stromboli.* The film is set in a Europe still suffering from the after effects of World War II. In order to get out of an internment camp, Karin, a Lithuanian refugee, marries Antonio, a young fisherman from the volcanic island of Stromboli, and goes to live with him there. However, she cannot adapt to life there and decides to escape. Crossing the island she becomes caught up in a volcanic eruption, and the enormity of the event brings her to reconsider her position. The ''story'' is the same in both versions, but the emphases, and the whole manner of telling, are quite different. In particular the English version comes complete with a portentous commentary which frequently forces a specific reading on scenes which the director preferred to remain ''open.'' This is particularly damaging in the film's climax, where the commentary insists that ''out of her terror and her suffering Karin had found a great need for God. And she knew that only in her return to the village could she hope for peace.'' In Rossellini's version it is by no means clear that Karin has decided to return to the village, nor are her experiences presented in such overtly religious terms, although it is made quite clear that she has undergone a momentous inner experience. As Rossellini himself put it, ''a woman has undergone the trials of war; she comes out of it bruised and hardened, no longer knowing what a human feeling is. The important thing was to find out if this woman could still cry, and the film stops there, when the first tears begin to flow.''

Equally as damaging as the addition of the commentary in the English version is the excision of all sorts of scenes in which nothing ''happens'' in a story sense, but a great deal is communicated about Karin and about her ambivalent relationship with the island and her husband. On the other hand, it has to be said that even RKO couldn't turn *Stromboli* into a conventional narrative film, and that enough of Rossellini's original conception remains for it to have been generally dismissed as simply ''badly made!'' Such epithets are usually employed à propos the film's *apparent* casualness, even roughness, of style and construction, but far more to the point is Bazin's remark that *Stromboli* and the other Bergman films ''make one think of a sketch; the stroke indicates but does not paint. But should one take this sureness of stroke for poverty or laziness? One might as well reproach Matisse.'' Unfortunately, however, while Rossellini's approach may well alienate those looking for the ''well-made film,'' it does not offer the kind of pleasures usually sought by art house audiences. As Robin Wood has pointed out, *Stromboli* will disappoint cinephiles looking for ''striking images, imaginative effects, a sense (whether justified or not) of intellectual profundity. Rossellini's art rests on a paradox. As the true heir (as well as one of the founders) of neorealism, he is committed to showing only the surfaces of physical reality, without distortion or intervention in the form of special effects, surrealist images, dramatic compositions or symbolic lighting (though the last two are not unknown in his work); yet no director is more single-mindedly concerned with the invisible, the spiritual. More than with any other director the essential meaning has to be read behind and between the images, in the implications of the film's movement which rise to the surface only in rare privileged moments whose significance is never overtly explained and which draw their intensity as much from the accumulation of context as from anything present in the image'' *(Film Comment*, July-August 1974).

Stromboli is very much ''about'' Karin and the development of her consciousness. (On another level it's also ''about'' Bergman too.) However, what seems to have confused and alienated most commentators is Rossellini's refusal to have anything to do with the conventional paraphernalia of ''subjective'' cinema. As in the films of Antonioni, only in a much more subtle, less self-conscious fashion, we come to understand the central character largely through the ways in which she is placed in and reacts to the landscape. However, the spectator looks *at* Karin rather than *with* her, and we come to *understand* rather than *empathise with* her. Such an approach to his central character is absolutely consistent with Rossellini's approach to his subject matter as a whole in the film, which, as befitting his neo-realist heritage, remains resolutely objective, and even distanced. As Peter Brunette has noted, one is frequently tempted in *Stromboli* to ask ''where is Rossellini in all of this?'' Equally, one wonders whether a good deal of the critical hostility towards this film stems from its refusal to yield any easy answers on this point. The truth is that, just as Rossellini *shows* rather than *explains*, so he refuses to come down on the side either of Karin or Antonio/the island, thus leaving spectators the space largely to make up their own minds. The film may focus largely on Karin and her developing consciousness but, as Wood points out, ''our sense of the alien-ness of the primitive community seen through Karin's eyes is everywhere counterpointed by our sense of the integrity of Stromboli's culture and its functional involvement with nature, against Karin's sophisticated needs and moral confusion.'' This, of course, is *not* the same thing as saying that the film takes Stromboli's side against Karin's (as some have indeed suggested that it does) but, rather, it is simply to be aware of the film's rich ambivalence and the director's openness towards both his material and the spectators of his film. How sad, then, that such admirable sentiments should have resulted in such ill-informed, shortsighted critical vilification.

—Julian Petley

DER STUDENT VON PRAG

(The Student of Prague)

Germany, 1913

Director: Stellan Rye

Production: Deutsche Bioscop GmbH (Berlin); black and white, 35mm, silent; length: 5 to 6 reels, 5,046 feet, later cut to 4,817 feet. Released 1913. Filmed at Belvedere Castle and on Alchemist Street in Prague and at Fürstenburg and Lobkowitz Palaces. Cost: 30,000 marks.

Screenplay: Hanns Heinz Ewers with Paul Wegener, epigraphs from Alfred de Musset's poem ''The December Night''; **photography:** Guido Seeber; **art director:** Klaus Richter and Robert A. Dietrich.

Cast: Paul Wegener (*Balduin*); Fritz Weidemann (*Baron Schwarzenberg*); John Gottowt (*Scapinelli*); Lida Salmonova (*Lyduschka, country girl*); Grete Berger (*Margit, Countess Waldis-Schwarzenberg*); Lothar Körner (*Count Waldis-Schwarzenberg*).

Publications

Script:

Ewers, Hanns Heinz, with Paul Wegener, *Der Student von Prag: Einführung und Protokoll*, edited by Helmut H. Diederichs, Stuttgart, 1985.

Books:

Ewers, Hanns Heinz, Langheinrich-Anthos, and Heinrich Noeren, *Der Student von Prag: Eine Idee von Hanns Heinz Ewers*, Berlin, 1930.
Sadoul, Georges, *Histoire générale du cinéma*, Paris, 1946.
Kracauer, Siegfried, *From Caligari to Hitler: A Psychological History of the German Film*, Princeton, 1947.
Bucher, Felix, *Germany*, London and New York, 1970.
Eisner, Lotte, *The Haunted Screen*, Berkeley, 1973.
Garbicz, Adam, and Jacek Klinowski, *Cinema, The Magic Vehicle: A Guide to Its Achievement: Journey One: The Cinema Through 1949*, Metuchen, New Jersey, 1975.

Articles:

Magill's Survey of Cinema: Silent Films, Englewood Cliffs, New Jersey, 1982.
Schlüpmann, Heide, ''Zum Doppelgängermotiv in *Der Student von Prag*,'' in *Frauen und Film* (Frankfurt), February 1984.
Thüna, Ulrich, ''Aus dem Reich der Toten,'' in *EPD Film* (Frankfurt), vol. 5, no. 11, November 1988.
Veress, J., ''A pragai diak,'' in *Filmkultura* (Budapest), no. 12, January 1993.
Holl, S., and F. Kittler, ''Kabbale et medias,'' in *Trafic* (Paris), no. 22, Summer 1997.

* * *

Stellan Rye's version of *The Student of Prague* has been unjustly neglected in the 70 years since its production. Seen today, the film's technical facility, though not innovative in illustrating the *Doppelgänger* motif, is nevertheless particularly adroit, serving its subject with taste, restraint and subdued visual elegance. As a tale of the fantastic, the film looks both backward to similar thematic treatments in the Germanic legend of Faust and the tales of E. T. A. Hoffman (as well as Poe's *William Wilson* and Wilde's *Dorian Gray*) and forward to the overtly Expressionist treatment of alter egos in the great films of the 1920s (Caligari and his somnambulist-slave Cesare, Maria and her robot double in *Metropolis*.) Expressionism as an art form was flourishing by 1910, but it had not yet taken hold in film by 1913

Der Student von Prag

because the cinema was still held in contempt by most "serious" artists. *The Student of Prague* is a story of the fantastic told in a naturalistic manner, photographed against picturesque backdrops of the castles and streets of Prague's old city.

The director Stellan Rye was a Danish expatriate who had staged plays and scripted films in Copenhagen. Screenwriter Hanns Heinz Ewers was already celebrated for his supernatural tales tinged with elements of eroticism and sadism; today most critics view his work in light of his subsequent notoriety as official chronicler in prose and film of Nazi hero Horst Wessel. Paul Wegener, already one of the most famous actors of Max Reinhardt's Deutsches Theater, had long been fascinated by the artistic potential of film, and he found the inspiration for his cinematic debut in a series of comic photographs of a man fencing and playing cards with himself. Together with Ewers, Wegener concocted the story of Balduin, a student who sells his mirror reflection to the gnomish eccentric Scapinelli in exchange for fortune and the woman of his dreams. The reflection begins to haunt Balduin, appearing with greater frequency until the desperate student shoots it, and in the process, kills himself.

To effect the multiple exposure technique necessary to make Wegener's dual roles convincing, Rye enlisted the talents of cinematographer Guido Seeber, who was already considered a master. From a photographic standpoint, Seeber's work is an unusual mixture of the archaic and the innovative. Interiors are shot in a flat, uninteresting manner, but the exteriors feature exquisitely composed vistas of Prague's castles and courtyards. The scenes in which Balduin flees from his double through the deserted streets of Prague only to encounter him at every juncture are worthy of the nightmare images of films to follow in the wake of *The Cabinet of Dr. Caligari.* Though no stylization is evident in the set design, Seeber's lighting technique becomes quite striking—indeed almost expressionist—in the gambling scene. Perhaps inspired by Reinhardt's productions, a simple overhead light illuminates Balduin's gaming table as, one by one, his card-playing adversaries lose, disappearing into darkness. Balduin remains alone for a few seconds until he is joined by his double who asks "Dare you to play with me?"

The Student of Prague was the most expensive film produced in Germany up to that time, and it was an enormous success both with the critics and audiences. Although Rye and Wegener were to work together on several more projects, the collaboration was cut short by Rye's untimely death in a French war hospital in 1914. The two remakes of the film have their individual merits: Henrik Galeen's

1926 version reteams Conrad Veidt and Werner Krauss (Cesare and Caligari) and is extolled by Paul Rotha for its exceptional pictorial qualities; the 1936 Arthur Robison version with Anton Walbrook gives human motivation to the demonic pact by making Scapinelli (Theodor Loos) a jealous rival of Balduin's. The original, however, remains most important to film history. *The Student of Prague*'s marriage of naturalism to the first glimmers of Expressionism in German film provides an eloquent signpost to the dark visions to come.

—Lee Tsiantis

SULLIVAN'S TRAVELS

USA, 1941

Director: Preston Sturges

Production: Paramount Pictures; black and white, 35mm; running time: 90 minutes. Released 1941.

Producer: Paul Jones; **original story and screenplay:** Preston Sturges; **photography:** John Seitz; **editor:** Stuart Gilmore; **art directors:** Hans Dreier and Earl Hedrick; **music:** Leo Shuken and Charles Bradshaw; **special effects:** Farciot Edouart.

Cast: Joel McCrea (*John L. Sullivan*); Veronica Lake (*The Girl*); Robert Warwick (*Mr. Le Brand*); William Demarest (*Mr. Jones*); Franklin Pangborn (*Mr. Casalsis*); Porter Hall (*Mr. Hadrian*); Byron Foulger (*Mr. Vadelle*); Margaret Hayes (*Secretary*); Torben Meyer (*Doctor*); Robert Greig (*Sullivan's butler*); Eric Blore (*Sullivan's valet*); Al Bridge (*Sheriff*); Esther Howard (*Miz Zeffie*); Almira Sessions (*Ursula*); Frank Moran (*Chauffeur*); George Renavent (*Old tramp*); Victor Potel (*Cameraman*); Richard Webb (*Radio man*); Harry Rosenthal (*The trombenick*); Jimmy Conlin (*The trusty*); Jan Buckingham (*Mrs. Sullivan*); Robert Winkler (*Bud*); Chick Collins (*Capital*); Jimmie Dundee (*Labor*); Charles Moore (*Black chef*); Al Bridge (*The mister*); Harry Hayden (*Mr. Carson*); Willard Robertson (*Judge*); Pat West (*Counterman—roadside lunch wagon*); J. Farrell MacDonald (*Desk sergeant*); Edward Hearn (*Cop—Beverly Hills station*); Roscoe Ates (*Counterman—Owl Wagon*); Paul Newlan (*Truck driver*); Arthur Hoyt (*Preacher*); Gus Reed (*Mission cook*); Robert Dudley (*One-legged man*); George Anderson (*Sullivan's ex-manager*); Monte Blue (*Cop in slums*); Harry Tyler (*R.R. information clerk*); Dewey Robinson (*Sheriff*); Madame Sul-te-wan (*Harmonium player*); Jess Lee Brooks (*Black preacher*); Perc Launders (*Yard Man*); Emory Parnell (*Man at R.R. shack*); Julius Tannen (*Public defender*); Edgar Dearing (*Cop—Mud Gag*); Howard Mitchell (*Railroad clerk*); Harry Seymour (*Entertainer in air-raid shelter*); Bill Bletcher (*Entertainer in hospital*); Chester Conklin (*Old man*); Frank Mills (*Drunk in theater*).

Publications

Script:

Sturges, Preston, *Sullivan's Travels*, in *Five Screenplays*, edited by Brian Henderson, Berkeley, 1985.

Books:

Sarris, Andrew, *Interviews with Film Directors*, New York, 1967.
Lake, Veronica, with Donald Bain, *Veronica: The Autobiography of Veronica Lake*, London, 1969.
Mast, Gerald, *The Comic Mind*, New York, 1973; revised edition, Chicago, 1979.
Ursini, James, *The Fabulous Life and Times of Preston Sturges, An American Dreamer*, New York, 1973.
Byron, Stuart, editor, *Movie Comedy*, New York, 1977.
Parish, James Robert, and Michael Pitts, *Hollywood on Hollywood*, Metuchen, New Jersey, 1978.
Cywinski, Ray, *Satires and Sideshows: The Films and Career of Preston Sturges*, Ann Arbor, Michigan, 1981.
Gordon, James R., *Comic Structures in the Films of Preston Sturges*, Ann Arbor, Michigan, 1981.
Curtis, James, *Between Flops: A Biography of Preston Sturges*, New York, 1982.
Cywinski, Ray, *Preston Sturges: A Guide to References and Resources*, Boston, 1984.
Dickos, Andrew, *Intrepid Laughter: Preston Sturges and the Movies*, Metuchen, New Jersey, 1985.
Spoto, Donald, *Madcap: The Life of Preston Sturges*, Boston, 1990.
Sturges, Preston, *Preston Sturges*, adapted and edited by Sandy Sturges, New York, 1990.
Jacobs, Diane, *Christmas in July: The Life and Art of Preston Sturges*, Berkeley, 1992.
Rozgonyi, Jay, *Preston Sturges's Vision of America: Critical Analyses of Fourteen Films*, Jefferson, 1995.
Harvey, James, *Romantic Comedy: In Hollywood, From Lubitsch to Sturges*, Cambridge, 1998.

Articles:

''Preston Sturges,'' in *Current Biography Yearbook*, New York, 1941.
Variety (New York), 10 December 1941.
Times (London), 1 January 1942.
Ferguson, Otis, in *New Republic* (New York), 26 January 1942.
New York Times, 29 January 1942.
Crowther, Bosley, ''Where Satire and Slapstick Meet,'' in *New York Times Magazine*, 27 August 1944.
Ericsson, Peter, ''Preston Sturges,'' in *Sequence* (London), Summer 1948.
Kracauer, Siegfried, ''Preston Sturges; or, Laughter Betrayed,'' in *Films in Review* (New York), February 1950.
King, Nel, and G. W. Stonier, ''Preston Sturges,'' in *Sight and Sound* (London), Summer-Autumn 1959.
Farber, Manny, and W. S. Poster, ''Preston Sturges: Success in the Movies,'' in *Film Culture* (New York), no. 26, 1962.
Houston, Penelope, ''Preston Sturges,'' in *Sight and Sound* (London), Summer 1965.
Budd, Michael, ''Notes on Preston Sturges and America,'' in *Film Society Review* (New York), January 1968.
Bowser, Eileen, in *Film Notes*, New York, 1969.
Corliss, Richard, ''Preston Sturges,'' in *Cinema* (Beverly Hills), Spring 1972.
Cluny, C. M., in Cinéma (Paris), February 1973.
Dupuich, J. J., in *Image et Son* (Paris), March 1973.

Sullivan's Travels

Beylie, Claude, in *Ecran* (Paris), April 1973.

Chacona, Hollis, in *Cinema Texas Program Notes* (Austin), Fall 1976.

Rubinstein, R., ''Hollywood Travels: Sturges and Sullivan,'' in *Sight and Sound* (London), Winter 1977–78.

Bodeen, DeWitt, ''Joel McCrea and Francis Dee,'' in *Films in Review* (New York), December 1978.

Ursini, James, in *Magill's Survey of Cinema 4*, Englewood Cliffs, New Jersey, 1980.

Wineapple, B., ''Finding an Audience: *Sullivan's Travels,*'' in *Journal of Popular Film and Television* (Washington, D.C.), Winter 1984.

Shokoff, J., ''A Kockenlocker by Any Other Word: The Democratic Comedy of Preston Sturges,'' in *Post Script* (Commerce), vol. 8, no. 1, 1988.

Magny, Joël, and others, ''Preston 'Dynamite' Sturges,'' in *Cahiers du Cinéma* (Paris), no. 426, December 1989.

Kieffer, Anne, and Andrée Tournés, ''Locarno: Preston Sturges redécouvert,'' in *Jeune Cinéma* (Paris), no. 199, February-March 1990.

Amiel, Vincent, and others, ''Preston Sturges: Hollywood et Lilliput,'' in *Positif* (Paris), no. 349, March 1990.

Levine, L.W., ''The Folklore of Industrial Society: Popular Culture and its Audience,'' in *American Historical Review*, vol. 97, no. 5, 1992.

Morris, R., ''Role Models,'' in *Movieline* (Escondido), vol. 4, October 1992.

* * *

Sullivan's Travels is writer-director Preston Sturges's version of ''the clown who wants to pay Hamlet'' in which he proves that the world needs a clown more than it needs a Hamlet. Sturges was a director of such skill and cunning that he could both destroy and elevate an institution simultaneously. *Sullivan's Travels*, one of his best films and certainly one of his most personal (as it is about a Hollywood director), both attacks and celebrates Hollywood with such balance and panache that fans and detractors are equally satisfied with the results. This ambivalence characterizes the work of Sturges, whose career has undergone a recent critical re-evaluation. One of the most successful and respected writer-directors of the 1940s, his career fell apart after a decade of critical and commercial success. He died an out-of-fashion, nearly forgotten man in 1959. Throughout the 1960s and into the 1970s, his work was largely unknown. Now that his career is being favourably re-assessed, his comedies of American life, manners and mores are being restored to their rightful position as first-rate examples of Hollywood filmmaking and humor.

Sullivan's Travels undertakes a bold assignment. Its narrative shifts from comedy to tragedy and back to comedy, something seldom successfully accomplished in film. Those who criticize the film do so on the basis of its serious scenes when the hero, Joel McCrea, is arrested and sent to a prison chain gang, where the only thing the convicts have to look forward to is the cartoon they share with a black church group on special occasions. The film's structure, however, is skillfully executed, and the hero's descent into a social hell uncushioned by money and power is presented largely through an effective montage, followed by the prison sequence. The ultimate return to comedy is indeed abrupt, but it demonstrates the theme of the film. The structure is attuned to the basic universe of the Sturges world, which is a schizophrenic one, part sophistication and part slapstick, a world of contradiction and conflict. Sturges's technical presentation carries out this confusion and chaos, by frequently disintegrating into rapid montage. Although he was a master of writing witty repartee, Sturges also loved visual gags and the sort of pratfalls associated with silent film comedy. He wove these two seemingly contradictory traditions—dialogue comedy and physical comedy—together into films like *Sullivan's Travels* which fans call ''free-wheeling'' and critics call ''frenzied.'' The slambang quality of the Sturges films, coupled with the basic violence of his comedy, contributed to the eventual disfavor of his work.

Today Sturges may be seen as a great American satirist, and *Sullivan's Travels* is often called ''Swiftian.'' It ably demonstrates the Sturges brand of comedy. The script is dense with hilarious dialogue, and the characterizations demonstrate his incredible attention to detail that makes a real human being out of the smallest, most outrageous part. The most successful portions of the film are those in which he satirizes Hollywood with an insider's advantage. As always, Sturges was adept at pointing out the absurdity and essential phonies of a world which, rotten to the core and corrupted by the desires for money and success, maintains an outward sheen of respectability and good manners.

—Jeanine Basinger

SULT

(Hunger)

Denmark-Norway-Sweden, 1966

Director: Henning Carlsen

Production: Henning Carlsen (Denmark), ABC Film, Sandrews (Norway), and Svensk Filmindustri (Sweden); black and white, 35mm, widescreen; running time: 111 minutes; length: 3,055 meters. Released 19 August 1966, Oslo, Copenhagen, and Stockholm.

Producer: Bertil Ohlsson; **screenplay:** Henning Carlsen and Peter Seeberg, from the book by Knut Hamsun; **photography:** Henning Kristiansen; **editor:** Henning Carlsen; **sound:** Erik Jensen; **art directors:** Erik Aaes and Walther Dannerford; **music:** Krzysztof Komeda; **costume designer:** Ada Skolmen.

Cast: Per Oscarsson (*The Writer*); Gunnel Lindblom (*Ylajali*); Sigrid Horne-Rasmussen (*Landlady*); Osvald Helmuth (*Pawnbroker*); Birgitte Federspiel (*Ylajali's sister*); Henki Kolstad (*Editor*); Sverre Hansen (*Beggar*); Egil Hjort Jensen (*Man in the park*); Per Theodor Haugen (*Shop assistant*); Lars Nordrum (*The Count*); Roy Björnstad (*Painter*).

Publications

Books:

Kauffmann, Stanley, *Figures of Light*, New York, 1971.
Wagner, Geoffrey, *The Novel and the Cinema*, Rutherford, New Jersey, 1975.

Articles:

Sussex, Elizabeth, in *Sight and Sound* (London), Winter 1967–68.
''Biographical Note on Henning Carlsen,'' in *International Film Guide*, London, 1968.
Duperley, Denis, in *Films and Filming* (London), May 1968.
Hart, Henry, in *Films in Review* (New York), October 1968.
Canham, Kingsley, in *Films and Filming* (London), February 1969.
Decaux, E., ''Entretien avec Henning Carlsen,'' and ''Le Cinéma danois,'' in *Cinématographe* (Paris), January 1980.
Devaux, F., in *Cinéma* (Paris), January 1980.

* * *

All through his career Henning Carlsen has been concerned about the relationship between literature and film. Many of his films are based on important novels, but Carlsen has never been satisfied when his films were characterized as adaptations. He wanted to use literary sources as inspirations for works in another medium, works in their own right. Maybe the greatest challenge of his career was his film based on Knut Hamsun's famous, semi-autobiographical novel *Hunger*, published in 1890. The novel is about a young man, coming from the country to Kristiania, the capital of Norway. He wants to be a writer, but he is suffering from both physical and mental hunger in a hostile city. His sufferings and humiliations lead to hallucinations, and his permanent condition of starvation brings him to the brink of insanity. But his urge to express himself also results in moments of euphoria. The novel is primarily a study about the state of mind of an artistic genius. The transformation of this story, told by the main character in many inner monologues, into film presented intricate problems, which eventually were solved by Carlsen and Peter Seeberg, a highly original Danish author.

The two main characters of the book and film are the starving young man and the city. Carlsen, his cameraman Henning Kristiansen, and the set designer Erik Aaes have authentically recreated the cityscape of Kristiania of the 1890s. The establishment of the surroundings, where the young man faces his humiliations, shows Carlsen's experience as a documentary filmmaker. It is a very

Sult

impressive presentation of the place and the time. Less satisfying is the manner in which the young man is integrated into the surroundings. Part of the problem concerns the character's view of the city as a prison. The sense of claustrophobia in the film is communicated to us by the use of many close-ups of medium shots, but only results in a confusing orientation of the city.

Sult, of course, is Per Oscarsson's film. His portrait of the budding artist, split between moments of lucidity and moments of darkest despair, is film acting of the highest order. Oscarsson has occupied the mind and the body of his character to such a degree that there is an absolute congruence between the actor and the role, in the physical manifestations and in the inner mental state. It is to Carlsen's credit that he has coached Oscarsson's unique talent and Carlsen also shows his ability as an actors' director in the way he has handled the other actors in the film. As a director he hides behind his actors, though still maintaining control. For example, one of the most magic moments in the film, the love scene between the young man and the girl Ylajali, is a complex mixture of the tragic and the comic, which could only be created by a true artist.

—Ib Monty

SUNA NO ONNA

(Woman in the Dunes)

Japan, 1963

Director: Hiroshi Teshigahara

Production: Teshigahara Production; black and white, 35mm; running time: 127 minutes, some versions are 115 minutes; length: 4,021 meters. Released 1963.

Producers: Kiichi Ichikawa and Tadashi Ohno; **screenplay:** Kobo Abe, from a novel by Kobo Abe; **photography:** Hiroshi Segawa; **editor:** Masako Shuzui; **art directors:** Totetsu Hirakawa and Masao Yamazaki; **music:** Toru Takemitsu.

Cast: Eiji Okada (*Jumpei Niki*); Kyoko Kishida (*Widow*); Koji Mitsui; Sen Yano; Hiroko Ito.

Award: Cannes Film Festival, Special Jury Prize, 1964.

Suna no onna

Publications

Script:

Abe, Kobo, *Woman in the Dunes*, New York, 1966.

Books:

Mellen, Joan, *Voices from the Japanese Cinema*, New York, 1975.
Tessier, Max, editor, *Le Cinéma japonais au présent 1959–1979*, Paris, 1980.
Jones, Alan, *Hiroshi Teshigahara*, New York, 1990.

Articles:

Borde, Raymond, ''Cannes 1964,'' in *Positif* (Paris), no. 64–65, 1964.
Sadoul, Georges, in *Lettres Françaises* (Paris), 7 May 1964.
Flacon, Michel, in *Cinéma* (Paris), June 1964.
Bory, Jean-Louis, in *Arts* (Paris), 18 November 1964.
Benayoun, Robert, in *Nouvel Observateur* (Paris), 19 November 1964.
Sadoul, Georges, in *Lettres Françaises* (Paris), 19 November 1964.
Avant-Scène du Cinéma (Paris), January 1965.
Jacob, Gilles, ''Un Beckett nippon,'' in *Cinéma* (Paris), January 1965.
Cousin, Fabienne, ''Introducing Teshigahara,'' in *Cinéma* (Paris), February 1965.
Narboni, Jean, in *Cahiers du Cinéma* (Paris), February 1965.
Gauthier, Guy, in *Image et Son* (Paris), March 1965.
''A Conversation with Two Japanese Film Stars,'' in *Film Comment* (New York), Winter 1965.
Mancia, Adrienne, in *Film Comment* (New York), Winter 1965.
Giles, Dennis, ''The Tao in *Woman in the Dunes*,'' in *Film Heritage* (New York), Spring 1966.
Bucher, Felix, ''Akira Kurosawa—Hiroshi Teshigahara,'' in *Camera*, September 1966.
van Oers, F., in *Skrien* (Amsterdam), May-June 1982.
Jackiewicz, Aleksander, ''Moje zycie w kinie,'' in *Kino* (Warsaw), vol. 21, no. 2, February 1987.
Ahearn, Charlie, ''Teshigahara Zen and Now,'' in *Interview*, vol. 20, no. 8, August 1990.
Vidal, N., ''*La mujer en la arena*,'' in *Nosferatu* (San Sebastian), no. 11, January 1993.

Atkinson, M., ''Against the Grain,'' in *Village Voice* (New York), vol. 42, 15 April 1997.

Holden, Stephen, in *The New York Times*, vol. 146, B8 and C8, 11 April 1997.

Lucas, Tim, ''*Woman in the Dunes*,'' in *Video Watchdog* (Cincinnati), no. 48, 1998.

* * *

Hiroshi Teshigahara, born in 1927 in Tokyo, is a graduate of the Tokyo Art Institute. The formal beauty of *Woman in the Dunes* reflects this artistic background. In 1961 he organized his own production company and produced his first feature film, *Pitfall*, which established him as an avant-garde director. Based on a novel by Kobo Abe, one of Japan's most respected novelists, *Pitfall* is a documentary fantasy, according to Teshigahara. *Woman in the Dunes*, also based on an Abe novel and scripted by him, was Teshigahara's second feature. The film received much attention outside of Japan. It was awarded the Special Jury Award at Cannes in 1964 and was nominated for an Academy Award.

The story of *Woman in the Dunes* is simple. While on a scientific exploration in the dessert, Jumpei Niki, an entomologist from Tokyo, misses the last bus back to the city. He is given accommodation for the night at the home of a widow at the bottom of a sand pit. Next morning when he is prepared to leave, he discovers that the rope ladder, which is the only means of exit, has been removed by the villagers up above who intend to keep him in the sand pit. The remainder of the film involves Niki's struggle for freedom, his evolving relationships with the widow, and his final resolution concerning his destiny.

As in other films with similar plot situations (Jean Paul Sartre's *No Exit* and Luis Buñuel's *Exterminating Angel*), *Woman in the Dunes* is an allegory. Basically the film deals with man's confrontation with life and the nature of freedom. Coming out of the tradition of Oriental philosophy, the film is more affirmative than either of the works by Sartre or Buñuel.

Although Niki is representative of all men in general and modern man in particular, he also serves as a specific representative of Japan who has adopted the ways of the Occident. The conflict between Eastern and Western traditions is a recurrent theme in modern Japanese literature. Niki is not only dressed in modern European clothing, but he is infused with the spirit of the West. The opening scenes reveal his obsession with material possessions, with documents and schedules, with the value of a scientific approach to life, and with ambitious desires to get ahead—all antithetical to the notions found in traditional Japanese philosophy and religion. Devoid of any human involvement, Niki exists in a spiritual wasteland as dry and arid as the desert of the opening scenes.

Although we are never shown the city, modern man's environment, Teshigahara skillfully evokes its presence. The opening credits are accompanied by the sounds and noises of the city while images of official stamp marks and fingerprints, an everpresent factor in modern life, are seen on the screen.

Niki's examination of the sand and insects through his magnifying glass typify his distance from an emotional involvement with life itself. He is little more than a microscopic organism, living out his existence as one of the millions who inhabit cities like Tokyo. Yet his arrogance belies his understanding of the true nature of his existence.

During the long months which Niki spends in the sand pit, he moves from rebellion against his fate, to accommodation, and ultimately to active affirmation. His progress can be gauged by what he gives up—his flask, his camera, his watch, his insect collection, his western clothing, and finally his desire to leave. His gains are emotional involvement, social commitment, and spiritual freedom—for true freedom is an internal state not determined by physical limitations. In order to move forward, it was necessary for Niki to have first taken several steps backward—backward to a more primitive state of existence, backward to the values of an earlier era. In order to reach salvation, he has had to return to nature, to find a means to live in harmony with nature, and lastly to accept his position in the true order of the universe.

Niki's acceptance of life in the sand pit is not to be seen as resignation, but rather as a form of enlightenment. Dennis Giles explains in his article on the influence of Taoist philosophy on *Woman in the Dunes* how the film demonstrates Niki's acceptance of the Tao:

> The Tao can be called the path of least resistance. To be in harmony with, not in rebellion against, the fundamental laws of the universe is the first step on the road to Tao. Tao, like water, takes the low-ground. Water has become, perhaps, the most popular taoist symbol. The symbolic value of water is also one of the most striking elements in *Woman in the Dunes* . . . . Only by remaining passive, receptive, and yielding can the Tao assert itself in the mind.

Giles further points out that ''the yielding nature of water is a feminine characteristic, and concave surfaces are also female in nature. Thus the valley, the pit, and the Tao are all feminine.''

Teshigahara's camera style is perfectly suited to the allegorical nature of the film. His propensity for close-ups reflects his documentary interests and serves to distance the viewer from the characters and to allow the audience to objectively contemplate the universal meanings implicit in the story. At the same time Teshigahara creates images of rare abstract beauty which reflect the serenity and harmony implied by the Tao.

—Patricia Erens

SUNLESS

See **SANS SOLEIL**

SUNRISE

USA, 1927

Director: F. W. Murnau

Production: Fox Film Corporation; black and white, 35mm, silent; running time: 117 minutes; length: 2,792 meters. Released 29 November 1927, with music by Carli Elinor. Filmed in Fox studios and backlots.

Sunrise

Scenario: Carl Mayer, from the novel *The Journey to Tilsit* by Hermann Sudermann; **sub-titles:** Katherine Hilliker and H. H. Caldwell; **photography:** Charles Rosher and Karl Struss; **production designers:** Rochus Gliese, assisted by Edgar Ulmer and Alfred Metscher; **music:** Dr. Hugo Riesenfeld.

Cast: George O'Brien (*The Man—Ansass*); Janet Gaynor (*The Woman—Indre*); Bodil Rosing (*The Maid*); Margaret Livingstone (*The Vamp*); J. Farrell Macdonald (*The Photographer*); Ralph Sipperly (*The Hairdresser*); Jane Winton (*The Manicurist*); Arthur Houseman (*The Rude Gentleman*); Eddie Boland (*The Kind Gentleman*); Gina Corrado; Barry Norton; Sally Eilers.

Awards: Oscars for Best Actress (Gaynor, in conjunction with her roles in *7th Heaven* and *Street Angel*). Cinematography, and Artistic Quality of Production, 1927–28.

Publications

Script:

Mayer, Carl, *Sonnenaufgang: Ein Drehbuch mit handschriftlichen Bemerkungen von F. W. Murnau*, Wiesbaden, 1971; English-language version included in *F. W. Murnau's Sunrise: A Critical Study*, by Elliot M. Desilets, Ann Arbor, Michigan, 1979.

Books:

Huff, Theodore, *An Index to the Films of F. W. Murnau*, London, 1948.

Jacobs, Lewis, editor, *Introduction to the Art of the Movies: An Anthology of Ideas on the Nature of Movie Art*, New York, 1960.

Jameux, Charles, *Murnau*, Paris, 1965.

Anthologie du cinéma 1, Paris, 1966.

Brownlow, Kevin, *The Parade's Gone By. . . .* London and New York, 1969.

Eisner, Lotte, *Murnau*, Berkeley, 1973.

Garbicz, Adam, and Jacek Klinowski, *Cinema, The Magic Vehicle: A Guide to Its Achievement: Journey One: The Cinema Through 1949*, Metuchen, New Jersey, 1975.

Harvith, Susan and John, *Karl Struss: Man with a Camera*, Ann Arbor, Michigan, 1976.

Andrew, Dudley, *Film in the Aura of Art*, Princeton, 1984.

Collier, Jo Leslie, *From Wagner to Murnau: The Transposition of Romanticism from Stage to Screen*, Ann Arbor, 1988.

Murnau, Lisbon, 1989.

Gehler, Fred, and Ullrich Kasten, *Friedrich Wilhelm Murnau*, Augsburg, 1990.

Fischer, Lucy, *Sunrise: A Song of Two Humans*, London, 1998.

Articles:

New York Times, 24 September 1927.

Variety (New York), 28 September 1927.

Close Up (London), no. 2, 1928.

Murnau, F. W., ''The Ideal Picture Needs No Titles,'' in *Theatre Magazine* (New York), January 1928.

Blin, Roger, ''Murnau—ses films,'' in *Revue du Cinéma* (Paris), July 1931.

White, Kenneth, ''F. W. Murnau,'' in *Hound and Horn* (New York), July-September 1931.

Jones, Dorothy, in *Quarterly of Film, Radio, and Television* (Berkeley), Spring 1955.

Carr, Chauncey, ''Janet Gaynor,'' in *Films in Review* (New York), October 1959.

Durgnat, Raymond, in *Films and Filming* (London), May 1962.

Douchet, Jean, ''Venise 1962,'' in *Cahiers du Cinéma* (Paris), November 1962.

Martin, David, ''George O'Brien,'' in *Films in Review* (New York), November 1962.

Gilson, René, in *Cinéma* (Paris), May 1963.

Lefèvre, Raymond, in *Revue du Cinéma* (Paris), no. 233, 1969.

Haskell, Molly, in *Film Comment* (New York), Summer 1971.

Wood, Robin, in *Film Comment* (New York), Summer 1971.

''*L'Aurore (Sunrise)* Issue'' of *Avant-Scène du Cinéma* (Paris), June 1974.

Bruno, E., in *Filmcritica* (Rome), July 1974.

Rayns, Tony, in *Monthly Film Bulletin* (London), April 1975.

Struss, Karl, ''Karl Struss: Man with a Camera,'' in *American Cinematographer* (Los Angeles), March 1977.

Marías, M., in *Casablanca* (Madrid), October 1981.

Magill's Survey of Cinema: Silent Films, Englewood Cliffs, New Jersey, 1982.

Almendros, Nestor, in *American Cinematographer* (Los Angeles), April 1984.

Elsaesser, Thomas, ''Secret Affinities: F. W. Murnau,'' in *Sight and Sound* (London), Winter 1988–89.

Wood, R., ''*Sunrise:* A Reappraisal,'' in *Cineaction* (Toronto), Summer 1989.

Reid's Film Index (Wyong), no. 3, 1989.

Wolf, R., and others, ''De films van F. W. Murnau,'' in *Skrien* (Amsterdam), February-March 1990.

Pedler, G., ''Garth's Vintage Viewing: Murnau's *Sunrise* (1927),'' in *Classic Images* (Muscatine), vol. 194, August 1991.

Ramasse, François, and Aurélien Ferenczi, ''L'eclaireur allemand: *L'aurore*,'' in *Télérama* (Paris), no. 2346, 28 December 1994.

Magny, Joël, ''*Lumière de l'aurore*,'' in *Cahiers du Cinéma* (Paris), no. 487, January 1995.

Most, M., ''Restoration Film,'' in *Eyepiece* (Greenford), vol. 16, no. 6, 1995/1996.

Darke, Chris, ''Inside the Light,'' in *Sight & Sound* (London), vol. 6, no. 4, April 1996.

Klepper, R.K., ''Video Tape Reviews,'' in *Classic Images* (Muscatine), vol. 270, December 1997.

Amiel, Vincent, ''Murnau: La chair des images,'' in *Positif* (Paris), no. 457, March 1999.

* * *

The plot of *Sunrise* was adapted to Hollywood conventions from a naturalistic novella by Hermann Sudermann. It is wrong, however, to assume the changes were all for the bad, as so many critics have done. The film's plot is neither hopelessly sentimental nor melodramatic. It is true that Carl Mayer and F. W. Murnau, with a free hand from the studio, changed the tragic ending of the novella to a happy one for the film. This change can be viewed as an improvement upon Sudermann's gratuitously ironic ending of having the young husband's death occur after the couple's reconciliation. If not viewed as an improvement, the popular-art convention of the happy ending is certainly no worse than the naturalistic one of culminating a work with a tragic twist whether it is apt or not. Also the third party of the love triangle was, in the novella, a servant girl and, in the film, is a vamp from the city. On the basis of this change, all too many critics have accused Mayer and Murnau of setting up a simplistic ''good-country'' and ''evil-city'' polarity; however, they forget that the couple's experiences in the city, with all its modern delights, bring the husband and wife back together—or perhaps together for the first time. The plot allowed Murnau to draw upon his background in art history and literature, and above all it offered the basis for a cinematic narrative *par excellence*. This plot was made for the camera, especially in motion, and for the radical oscillations of lighting and mood that are so conducive to a temporal art like film. In such fertile soil, the talents of cameramen Rosher and Struss flourished.

Human characters, in *Sunrise*, are secondary to the true protagonist—the camera. The scenes in this film are neither conceived as a staged work, like so many silent films, nor as slices of actuality on which the camera allows us to spy. The premise of the film is that the camera will move; and that it will have any excuse to move. Plots and characters seem pretenses for movement and light; boats, dance halls, trolley cars, and other city traffic—not intrigue and love—are the true forces of motion in *Sunrise*. Akin to the ballets created by the avant-garde in the Paris of the 1910s and 1920s, patterns of movement seek their *raison d'être* in the slimmest threat of plot. In addition, the camera (and the cameramen) have been allowed so much freedom that the camera soon takes on a life of its own. Even when the camera is at rest or pauses within a shot, the effect is electric.

According to the testimony of Rosher, Murnau was obsessed with capturing the play of light, especially as it occurred on the surface of the lake—either in nature or in the studio. Water, boats, moonlight, and reeds are pretenses for capturing the fleeting effects of light, much in the same way that clouds and waterlilies are used in Claude Monet's last paintings. Indeed, the film's frequent use of mist, dim lighting, and blurred exposures reminds one of Monet's work. This impressionistic concentration on light is not just limited to the scenes of the lake; in the city, glass replaces water. In the famous restaurant scene, lighted figures are seen dancing behind a glass window; people move in front of the window and are reflected in it; and the camera moves to catch the reflected light from different angles. The effect is shimmering.

A frequent complaint concerning *Sunrise* is that the film is divided into disjointed parts and stylized scenes often clash with more naturalistic ones. Murnau compared his own narrative structure to that used by James Joyce. Just as in *Ulysses*, there is a radical shift of style to match the spirit of different episodes; so too, in *Sunrise*, is there a fluctuation between the actual and the artificial. Murnau may have had another source for his scene-structuring in the German Expressionist theatre—especially in the works of Ernst Toller, where naturalistic scenes alternate with expressionistic ones. There are few films that depict such an astute sense of the spirit of place and the events that occur there, as, for example, where the husband secretly meets the vamp, and passes through a studio-set marsh with a broodingly low horizon lit by a moon shining through the haze. Also, the trolley ride taken by the husband and wife gives the sense of a location shot made in daylight; the joyful effect is complete down to the bouncing of the trolley car. The trolley soon moves into the city, actually a studio backlot construction, that is scaled larger than life in order to convey the awe of the country couple who are seeing the city for the first time. The actual only seems to be so. Acting, like the lighting and the sets, is conceived of scene by scene. Murnau took great pains in making the actors' gestures and facial expressions fit the moment; therefore, the styles of acting fluctuate between the naturalistic and the expressionistic. And over all there is the evermoving mercurial camera. In every way, each scene is contrived to have its own particular mood, and each fits with another like pieces of Byzantine mosaic.

Hollywood fell under the spell of *Sunrise*, and under its influence the camera took wings, only to have them clipped by the limitations of primitive sound equipment. In the long run, however, the lessons of *Sunrise* resurfaced in such films as John Ford's *The Informer* and Orson Welles's *Citizen Kane*. The camera searching through the night and fog for a reflected gleam of light was a thematic and formalistic motif in these films. On the one hand, *Sunrise* culminated film's silent experience; but, on the other, it foreshadowed the first maturity of sound.

—Rodney Farnsworth

SUNSET BOULEVARD

USA, 1950

Director: Billy Wilder

Production: Paramount Pictures; black and white, 35mm; running time: 110 minutes. Released 1950. Filming completed 18 June 1949 on location in Los Angeles.

Producer: Charles Brackett; **associate producer:** Maurice Schorr, though uncredited; **screenplay:** Charles Brackett, Billy Wilder, and D. M. Marshman, Jr., from the story ''A Can of Beans'' by Brackett and Wilder; **photography:** John F. Seitz; **editor:** Arthur Schmidt; **editing supervisor:** Doane Harrison; **sound:** Harry Lindgren and John Cope; **art directors:** Hans Dreier and John Meehan; **music:** Franz Waxman; **songs:** Jay Livingston and Ray Evans; **special effects:** Gordon Jennings; **process photography:** Farciot Edouart; **costume designer:** Edith Head.

Cast: William Holden (*Joe Gillis*); Gloria Swanson (*Norma Desmond*); Erich von Stroheim (*Max von Mayerling*); Nancy Olson (*Betty Schaefer*); Fred Clark (*Sheldrake*); Lloyd Gough (*Morino*); Jack Webb (*Artie Green*); Franklyn Barnum (*Undertaker*); Larry Blake (*1st finance man*); Charles Dayton (*2nd finance man*); Cecil B. De Mille, Hedda Hopper, Buster Keaton, Anna Q. Nilsson, H. B. Warner, Ray Evans, Sidney Skolsky, and Jay Livingston play themselves.

Awards: Oscars for Best Screenplay and Best Score for a Dramatic or Comedy Picture, 1950.

Publications

Script:

Brackett, Charles, Billy Wilder, and D. M. Marshman, Jr., *Sunset Boulevard*, in *Bianco e Nero* (Rome), November-December 1951.

Books:

del Buono, Oreste, *Billy Wilder*, Parma, 1958.
Madsen, Axel, *Billy Wilder*, Bloomington, Indiana, 1969.
Wood, Tom, *The Bright Side of Billy Wilder, Primarily*, New York, 1970.
Seidman, Steve, *The Film Career of Billy Wilder*, Boston, 1977.
Zolotow, Maurice, *Billy Wilder in Hollywood*, New York, 1977.
Parish, James Robert, and Michael Pitts, *Hollywood on Hollywood*, Metuchen, New Jersey, 1978.
Silver, Alain, and Elizabeth Ward, editors, *Film Noir*, New York, 1979.
Dick, Bernard F., *Billy Wilder*, Boston, 1980.
Giannetti, Louis, *Masters of the American Cinema*, Englewood Cliffs, New Jersey, 1981.
Thomson, David, *Overexposures: The Crisis in American Filmmaking*, New York, 1981.
Koszarski, Richard, *The Man You Loved to Hate: Erich von Stroheim and Hollywood*, New York, 1983.
Bessy, Maurice, *Erich von Stroheim*, Paris, 1984.
Quirk, Lawrence J., *The Films of Gloria Swanson*, Secaucus, New Jersey, 1984.
Jacob, Jerome, *Billy Wilder*, Paris, 1988.
Seidle, Claudius, *Billy Wilder: Seine Filme, sein Leben*, Munich, 1988.
Lally, Kevin, *Wilder Times: The Life of Billy Wilder*, New York, 1996.
Sikov, Ed, *On Sunset Boulevard: The Life and Times of Billy Wilder*, New York, 1998.
Crowe, Cameron, *Conversations with Wilder*, New York, 1999.

Articles:

Agee, James, in *Films in Review* (New York), May-June 1950.
''Forever Gloria,'' in *Life* (New York), 5 June 1950.
Newsweek (New York), 26 June 1950.
Lightman, Herb A., ''Old Master, New Tricks,'' in *American Cinematographer* (Los Angeles), September 1950.
Agee, James, in *Sight and Sound* (London), November 1950.
Houston, Penelope, in *Sight and Sound* (London), January 1951.
Sarris, Andrew, in *Village Voice* (New York), 18 August 1960.
Higham, Charles, ''Cast a Cold Eye: The Films of Billy Wilder,'' in *Sight and Sound* (London), Spring 1963.
Bodeen, DeWitt, ''Gloria Swanson,'' in *Films in Review* (New York), April 1965.
''The Films of Billy Wilder,'' in *Film Comment* (New York), Summer 1965.
Higham, Charles, ''Meet Whiplash Wilder,'' in *Sight and Sound* (London), Winter 1967–68.
Nogueira, Rui, in *Sight and Sound* (London), Winter 1967–68.
Bradbury, Ray, ''The Tiger (poem),'' in *Producers Guild of America Journal* (Los Angeles), no. 3, 1976.
Colpart, G., in *Téléciné* (Paris), December 1976.
Merigeau, P., in *Image et Son* (Paris), December 1980.
Peary, Danny, in *Cult Movies*, New York, 1981.
Guibert, Hervé, in *Cahiers du Cinéma* (Paris), January 1981.
''Wilder Issue'' of *Filmcritica* (Rome), November-December 1982.
Hersant, Y., ''Portrait de la star en singe mort,'' in *Positif* (Paris), September 1983.
Vrdlovec, Z., ''Filmska naratologija,'' in *Ekran* (Ljubljana, Yugoslavia), no. 5–6, 1989.
Pichler, O.H., ''Some Like It Black,'' in *Blimp* (Graz), no. 18, Fall 1991.
Reid's Film Index (Wyong), no. 6, 1991.
Kartseva, E., in *Iskusstvo Kino* (Moscow), no. 3, 1993.
Freeman, D., ''*Sunset Boulevard* Revisited,'' in *New Yorker*, 21 June 1993.
Elley, D., ''Movie Was Almost Left in Dark,'' in *Variety* (New York), vol. 351, 19 July 1993.
Gerard, J., ''*Sunset Boulevard*: Still Bumpy,'' in *Variety* (New York), vol. 353, 20 December 1993.
Clarke, Gerald, ''Billy Wilder: *Sunset Boulevard*'s Creator Talks of the Town,'' in *Architectural Digest* (Los Angeles), vol. 51, no. 4, April 1994.
Girard, Martin, ''Hollywood Gothique: *Sunset Blvd.*,'' in *Séquences* (Haute-Ville), no. 171, April 1994.

Sunset Boulevard

Grob, N., ''Days of the Living Dead,'' in *Filmbulletin* (Winterthur), vol. 36, no. 3, 1994.
Sandla, R., ''*Sunset* Dawns on Broadway,'' in *Dance Magazine*, vol. 69, February 1995.
Premiere (Boulder), vol. 9, February 1996.

* * *

Between 1950 and 1952, Hollywood produced a cycle of classic films that looked at the business of making movies: *Singin' in the Rain*, *The Bad and the Beautiful*, and *Sunset Boulevard*. Of the three, the latter gives the darkest view of the motion picture industry.

The first two films chronicle success and failure, while *Sunset Boulevard* deals only with decline. It is, in fact, a sort of mirror image of *Singin' in the Rain*, a film which was concerned with the problems caused by the coming of sound to the movies. In *Singin'* one star deservedly falls from grace with the public, another has his career transformed for the better, while a sweetfaced ingenue becomes a box-office sensation because of her singing. *Sunset Boulevard*, however, which takes place 25 years after the coming of sound, shows us a silent film star scorned by the changes brought on by the new technology, and a modern day screenwriter whose dialogue is not good enough to get him work.

One cannot ignore the film's autobiographical aspects. Gloria Swanson plays Norma Desmond, the aging silent film star, and like Norma, Swanson's career declined shortly after the advent of sound. Also, Max, Norma's chauffeur, had been one of her greatest directors. Erich von Stroheim plays the role and, like Max, he had been one of the more talented directors of the 1920s whose career ended abruptly during the next decade. Completing the mixture of film history and fiction, Norma watches one of her films from 30 years previous; it is *Queen Kelly*, one of Swanson's movies that had been directed by von Stroheim.

Aside from holding a reflecting glass to the industry, the film itself has something of a mirror construction. After Joe, the screenwriter, meets Norma, she convinces him to work on her comeback project, a ponderous *Salome* screenplay. Joe agrees because times are hard, and as an added convenience he becomes Norma's lover. During the second half of the film, Joe meets Betty, and they too begin working on a script as the conventional counterpart to Joe's involvement with Norma. While Joe knows that Norma's script is unfilmable, both he and Betty are excited about the script they write together, and shape it to the demands of the industry. Joe and Betty also form the normal, attractive movie couple, but Joe and Norma's relationship stands out as anomalous, at least for films of the period. Norma is much older than Joe, who plays the role of a ''kept man,'' accepting money, gifts, and a place to live from a woman protector.

In the end, jealous of Betty, Norma kills Joe. However, this is known from the beginning, for *Sunset Boulevard* is a tale told by a dead man. After the opening credits, we see Joe lying face down in Norma's swimming pool, with detectives trying to fish him out of the water. Joe then begins to narrate the events that led up to the murder. But neither this posthumous narration, nor its baroque *film noir* style, nor the bitterness with which the film examines Hollywood, made the movie unpalatable to critics of the period. At its release, it was considered a major work, and today *Sunset Boulevard* remains one of the most highly respected films from the post-World War II period.

—Eric Smoodin

THE SWEET LIFE

See **DOLCE VITA**

THE SWEET SMELL OF SUCCESS

USA, 1957

Director: Alexander Mackendrick

Production: Norma-Curtleigh Production; black and white, 35mm; running time: 96 minutes, press screening was 103 minutes. Released 27 June 1957 by United Artists. Filmed Spring 1957 in New York City.

Producer: James Hill, a Hecht-Hill-Lancaster presentation; **screenplay:** Clifford Odets, adapted by Ernest Lehman, from the short story ''Tell Me About It Tomorrow'' by Ernest Lehman; **photography:** James Wong Howe; **editor:** Alan Crosland, Jr.; **sound:** Jack Solomon; **art director:** Edward Carrere; **music:** Elmer Bernstein.

Cast: Burt Lancaster (*J. J. Hunsecker*); Tony Curtis (*Sidney Falco*); Susan Harrison (*Susan Hunsecker*); Sam Levene (*Frank D'Angelo*); Barbara Nicholls (*Rita*); Martin Milner (*Steve Dallas*); Jeff Donnell (*Sally*); Joseph Leon (*Robard*); Edith Atwater (*Mary*); Emile Meyer (*Harry Kello*); Joe Frisco (*Herbie Temple*); David White (*Otis Elwell*); Lawrence Dobkin (*Leo Bartha*); Lurene Tuttle (*Mrs. Bartha*); Queenie Smith (*Mildred Tam*); Autumn Russell (*Linda*); Jay Adler (*Manny Davis*); Lewis Charles (*Al Evans*).

Publications

Books:

Silver, Alain, and Elizabeth Ward, editors, *Film Noir*, New York, 1979.

Hunter, Allan, *Burt Lancaster: The Man and His Movies*, Edinburgh, 1984.

Lacourbe, Roland, *Burt Lancaster*, Paris, 1987.

Kemp, Philip, *Alexander Mackendrick*, London, 1989.

Kemp, Philip, *Lethal Innocence: The Cinema of Alexander Mackendrick*, London, 1991.

Articles:

Cutts, John, in *Films and Filming* (London), June 1957.

Weiler, A. H., in *New York Times*, 27 June 1957.

Tallmer, Jerry, in *Village Voice* (New York), 28 August 1957.

Films in Review (New York) August-September 1957.

Prouse, Derek, in *Sight and Sound* (London), Autumn 1957.

Rittgers, Carol, in *Film Culture* (New York), October 1957.

''Alexander Mackendrick,'' in *Films and Filming* (London), January 1963.

Sarris, Andrew, ''Oddities and One-Shots,'' in *Film Culture* (New York), Spring 1963.

Schuster, Mel, ''Burt Lancaster,'' in *Films in Review* (New York), August-September 1969.

''Mackendrick Issue'' of *Dialogue on Film* (Washington, D.C.), no. 2, 1972.

Blackburn, Richard, ''Bullies of Broadway,'' in *American Film* (Washington, D.C.), December 1983.

Denby, D., ''The Best Movie,'' in *New York Magazine*, vol. 18, 23/30 December 1985.

Kemp, Philip, ''Mackendrick Land,'' in *Sight and Sound* (London), vol. 58, no. 1, Winter 1988–89.

Denby, D., ''The Lullaby of Broadway,'' in *Premiere* (Boulder), vol. 4, April 1991.

Lane, Anthony, ''No Illusions: Movie Director Alexander Mackendrick,'' in *New Yorker*, vol. 69, no. 48, 31 January 1994.

Buford, K., ''Do Make Waves: Sandy,'' in *Film Comment* (New York), vol. 30, no. 3, May-June 1994.

Hoberman, J., ''Once Upon a Time in Times Square,'' in *Village Voice* (New York), vol. 39, 22 November 1994.

Reid's Film Index (Wyong), no. 30, 1997.

Roddam, Franc, ''Power, Corruption and Lies,'' in *Sight and Sound* (London), vol. 7, no. 1, January 1997.

Dzenis, A., in *Metro Magazine* (St. Kilda West), no. 113/114, 1998.

* * *

One of the most original and off-beat films to be labelled a *film noir*, *The Sweet Smell of Success* takes a cynical bite at the underbelly of the New York publicity game. As Sidney Falco, a thoroughly ruthless and utterly amoral press agent scrambling for his place in the sun, Tony Curtis gives the performance of his career—charming yet sleazy, ingratiating yet duplicitous. Falco aspires to a position of influence in the orbit of J. J. Hunsecker, king of the gossip pen. As impeccably played by Burt Lancaster, Hunsecker is a smooth, cold-blooded mudslinger; crewcut, single and implicitly gay; more ruthless than Falco, yet completely unsullied. The bittersweet irony of the film is that, for all of Falco's slimy dealings, it is he (and his type) who ends up doing Hunsecker's dirty work.

To curry Hunsecker's favor, Falco sets out to break up the relationship between the columnist's sister (to whom Hunsecker has more than a brotherly attachment) and a young jazz musician by circulating accusations that the musician is a Communist and a drug

The Sweet Smell of Success

addict. It is a premise which provides screenwriter Clifford Odets the perfect opportunity to mount a scathing exposé of the lying, blackmailing, pimping and full-fledged witchhunting involved in the daily abuse of media power. It also provides the material from which British director Alexander Mackendrick is able to render a taut, suspenseful film in which the violence is more psychological than physical; and to create the ambience of a glamorous nocturnal world which is rotting at the core. These elements alone are enough to make *The Sweet Smell of Success* one of the most cynical *film noirs* of the 1950s; but it is the superb black-and-white cinematography of James Wong Howe which earns the film its place among the classics of the genre. Shooting much of the film at night on the streets of New York, Howe manages to combine expressive lighting with a kind of vérité realism, anticipating by several years the crystalline location cinematography of Henri Decae and Raoul Coutard in the early films of the French New Wave. If the subject of *The Sweet Smell of Success* seems unusual for a *film noir*, its biting tone and duplicitous characters represent the form at its most scathing, and its visual style points ahead from 1940s expressionism toward the direction of *Alphaville*.

—Ed Lowry

SWEET SWEETBACK'S BAADASSSSS SONG

USA, 1971

Director: Melvin Van Peebles

Production: Yeah; color, 35mm; running time: 97 minutes. Released January 1971, USA. Cost: $500,000. Distributed by Image Entertainment (laserdisc), Xenon Entertainment Group, Direct Cinema Limited (video), and Cinemation Industries.

Producers: Jerry Gross, Melvin Van Peebles; **screenplay:** Melvin Van Peebles; **cinematography:** Bob Maxwell; **assistant director:** Clyde Houston; **editor:** Melvin Van Peebles; **sound editors:** John Newman, Luke Wolfram; **musical score:** Melvin Van Peebles; **production manager:** Clyde Houston; **original music:** Earth Wind and Fire; **special effects:** Cliff Wenger; **makeup supervisor:** Nora Maxwell.

Sweet Sweetback's Baadasssss Song

Cast: Melvin Van Peebles (*Sweetback*); Simon Chuckster (*Beetle*); Hubert Scales (*Moo Moo*); John Dullaghan (*Commissioner*); Rhetta Hughes (*Old Girl Friend*); Mario Van Peebles (*Young Sweetback*); West Gale; Niva Rochelle; Nick Ferrari; Ed Rue; Johnny Amos; Lavelle Roby; Ted Hayden; Sonja Dunson; Michael Agustus; Peter Russell; Norman Fields; Ron Prince; Steve Cole; Megan Van Peebles; Joe Tornatore; Mike Angel; Jeff Goodman; Curt Matson; Marria Evonee; Jon Jacobs; Bill Kirschner; Vincent Barbi; Chet Norris; Joni Watkins; Jerry Days; John Allen; Bruce Adams; Brer Soul.

Publications

Books:

Van Peebles, Melvin, *Sweet Sweetback's Baadasssss Song*, New York, 1971.

Leab, Daniel, *From Sambo to Superspade*, Boston, 1976.

Guerrero, Ed, *Framing Blackness: The African American Image in Film*, Philadelphia, 1993.

James, Darius (a.k.a. Dr. Snakeskin), *That's Blaxploitation! Roots of the Baadasssss 'Tude (Rated X by an All-Whyte Jury)*, New York, 1995.

Martinez, Gerald, Diana Martinez, and Andres Chavez, *What It Is . . . What It Was! The Black Film Explosion of the 70s in Words and Pictures*, New York, 1998.

Articles:

Newton, Huey, ''He Won't Bleed Me: A Revolutionary Analysis of 'Sweet Sweetback's Baadasssss Song',' ' in *Black Panther*, no. 6, 19 January 1971.

Riley, Clayton, ''What Makes Sweetback Run?'' in *New York Times*, May 9, 1971.

Riley, Clayton, ''A Black Movie for White Audiences?'' in *New York Times*, July 29, 1971.

Bennett, Jr., Lerone, ''The Emancipation Orgasm: Sweetback in Wonderland,'' in *Ebony*, no. 26, September 1971.

Lee, Don, ''The Bittersweet of Sweetback, or, Shake Yo Money Maker,'' in *Black World*, November 1971.

Broun, Hale, ''Is It Better to Be Shaft Than Uncle Tom?'' in *New York Times*, 26 August 1973.

Peavy, Charles, ''Black Consciousness and the Contemporary Cinema,'' in *Popular Culture and the Expanding Consciousness*, edited by Ray Browne, New York, 1973.

* * *

In 1970, Melvin Van Peebles—along with Gordon Parks and Ossie Davis, one of the first African-American filmmakers to find work in Hollywood—directed a moderately successful serio-comedy entitled *Watermelon Man*, about a white bigot who suddenly finds himself in the body of a black man. With the $70,000 he earned from that film, plus additional funds from a number of independent sources (including a $50,000 emergency loan from Bill Cosby), Van Peebles was able to finance his new project, *Sweet Sweetback's Baadasssss Song*—so named in order to solicit at least a modicum of coverage from the mainstream media. Desperate to keep production costs to a minimum, he signed a deal with Cinemation Industries, a small distributor specializing in low-budget exploitation fare, and pretended to be making a porno flick, a move which enabled him to hire black and nonunion crewmen. In addition, Van Peebles wrote, directed, scored, and starred in the film, which was not only a sound decision economically, but one which ensured his creative control over every facet of production. Early in 1971, *Sweetback* opened in the only two theaters (in Detroit and Atlanta) that would agree to show it on a first-run basis. By the end of the year, the film had become the most profitable independent production in history to that point; a sleeper hit across the nation, it would wind up grossing over $15 million.

On the one hand, *Sweetback* is a film so original in both conception and realization that it managed to defy all traditional genre expectations, thereby satisfying the desire (at least temporarily) for a popular alternative to the dominant Hollywood paradigm. On the other hand, *Sweetback* is a film that borrows narrative threads and conventions from an assortment of different genres (including the chase film, the biker film, and soft-core porno), thereby proving itself a forerunner of those ''postmodern'' hybrids so prevalent in theaters today. Finally, *Sweetback* is a film whose staggering and completely unexpected commercial success ensured its place at the head of an explosion in black-marketed, black-cast, and/or black-directed productions, an explosion that soon went by the ambivalent name of ''Blaxploitation cinema.''

Sweetback makes manifest its revolutionary pretensions with the following words, which appear at the bottom of the screen before the opening credits role: ''This film is dedicated to all the Brothers and Sisters who have had enough of the Man.'' The shocking first scene finds a pre-teen Sweetback (played by Melvin's son, Mario Van Peebles) working in a whorehouse, where a grateful call-girl screams out his nickname during orgasm. Though some viewers found symbolic beauty here (Black Panther leader Huey Newton went so far as to claim that the woman ''in fact baptizes [Sweetback] into his true manhood''), others in the African-American community, such as *Ebony* reviewer Lerone Bennett, Jr., felt that Sweetback's initiation is not so much an ''act of love'' as ''the rape of a child by a 40-year-old prostitute.'' We next observe (the now grown-up) Sweetback performing as a stud in a black-run sex show in South-Central Los Angeles. On his way to a police station, where he is scheduled to stand in temporarily as a suspect in a widely-publicized murder case, his two guards stop to detain a black activist (Moo Moo, played by Hubert Scales) and proceed to beat the young man senseless. Having seen enough/too much, Sweetback jumps the officers, and nearly kills them with his handcuffs. The rest of the movie tracks our hero's progress as he rides, runs, and hitches his way through decaying cityscapes in a desperate effort at avoiding capture. At one point, Sweetback has his life threatened by a motorcycle gang, and only manages to survive by winning a public sex duel with the female leader. And that is just the beginning; as Ed Guerrero describes it, Sweetback ''evades the police by raping a Black woman at knifepoint at a rock concert, spears a cop with a pool cue, kills a number of dogs tracking him, heals himself with his own urine, and bites off the head of a lizard before escaping across the Mexicn border into the desert.'' The film concludes on an ominous note for white audiences, as the words ''A Baadasssss nigger is coming to collect some dues'' flash across the screen.

Although neither the popularity of *Sweetback* at the time of its release, nor its influence on future black filmmakers, can possibly be denied, its legacy—as well as that of Blaxploitation cinema generally—remains a matter of controversy to this day. In interviews, as well as in the promotional book accompanying its theatrical release, Van Peebles called the film ''revolutionary,'' as it tells the story of a ''bad nigger'' who mounts a successful challenge against the oppressive white power system. This view was supported by Newton, who devoted an entire issue of the Black Panther party newspaper to *Sweetback.* Bill Cosby has reportedly called the film a work of genius. And a number of African-American intellectuals sought to add Sweetback's name to the roll call of black folkloric heroes in virtue of his prodigious virility. On the negative side, Bennett argued in a scathing review that the film serves to romanticize the poverty and wretchedness of the ghetto, that Sweetback is a self-serving, apolitical individualist rather than a revolutionary, and that the protagonist's sexploitative construction actually reinforces negative African-American male stereotypes. These criticisms were seconded by, among others, Black nationalist author and poet Haki R. Madhubuti.

Unfortunately, what tends to get lost in the heated debates surrounding *Sweetback*'s socio-political ''message'' is an acknowledgment and consideration of Van Peeble's innovative directorial style. By making creative use of such techniques as montage, superimposition, freeze frames, jump cuts, zoom-ins, split-screen editing, stylized dialogue, multiply-exposed scenes, and a soulful musical score by the black rock group Earth Wind and Fire, Van Peebles broke new ground and challenged viewers' expectations. All of this should make obvious the point that *Sweet Sweetback's Baadasssss Song* is not just a statement, protest, or historical oddity, but a unique cinematic experience for people of all colors to reflect upon, appreciate, and enjoy.

—Steven Schneider

DAS TAGEBUCH EINER VERLORENEN

(Diary of a Lost Girl)

Germany, 1929

Director: G. W. Pabst

Production: Hom-Film; black and white, silent; running time: 130 minutes.

Producer: G. W. Pabst; **screenplay:** Rudolf Leonhardt, based on the novel by Margarethe Boehme; **photography:** Sepp Algeier; **assistant directors:** Marc Sorkin and Paul Falknberg; **art directors:** Erno Metzner and Emil Hasler.

Cast: Louise Brooks (*Thymiane Henning*); Josef Rovensky (*Robert Henning*); Fritz Rasp (*Meinert*); Edith Meinhard (*Erika*); Vera Pawlowa (*Aunt Frieda*); Franziska Kinz (*Meta*); Andre Roanne (*Count Osdorff*); Arnold Korff (*Elder Count Osdorff*); Andrews Engelmann (*Director of the reform school*).

Publications

Books:

Borde, Raymond, and others, *Le cinema realiste allemand*, Lausanne, 1965.
Amengual, Barthelemy, *Georg Wilhelm Pabst*, Paris, 1966.
Atwell, Lee, *G. W. Pabst*, Boston, 1977.
Brooks, Louise, *Lulu in Hollywood*, New York, 1977.
Groppali, Enrico, *Georg W. Pabst*, Firenze, 1983.
Rentschler, Eric, editor, *The Films of G.W. Pabst*, Piscataway, 1990.
Jacobsen, Wolfgang, *G.W. Pabst*, Berlin, 1997.

Articles:

Interim, L., ''La fille perdue et retrouvée,'' in *Cahiers du Cinéma* (Paris), January 1982.
Lefèvre, R., *Image et Son* (Paris), January 1982.
Petat, J., *Cinéma* (Paris), January 1982.
Kral, P., ''Par-dela le bien et le mal,'' in *Positif* (Paris), February 1982.
Milne, T., *Monthly Film Bulletin* (London), December 1982.
Petley, J., *Films and Filming* (London), December 1982.
Schlüpmann, Heide, ''Das Bordell als arkadischer Ort?: *Tagebuch einer Verlorenen* von G.W. Pabst,'' in *Frauen und Film* (Frankfurt am Main), no. 43, December 1987.
Sarris, Andrew, in *Video Review*, vol. 11, no. 11, February 1991.
Clark, Jeff, in *Library Journal*, vol. 116, no. 4, 1 March 1991.
Cox, T., ''Diary of a Lost Spectator: Carving a Space for Female Desire in Patriarchal Cinema,'' in *Spectator* (Los Angeles), vol. 16, no. 1, 1996.
Schluepmann, H., ''Spending Money on Laughter,'' in *Cinegrafie* (Ancona), vol. 6, no. 10, 1997.
Knop, M., ''The Brothel as a Convalescent Home,'' in *Cinegrafie* (Ancona), vol. 6, no. 10, 1997.

*   *   *

American actress Louise Brooks achieved stardom after abandoning Hollywood, where she was most frequently cast as a flapper in an unvaried array of cinematic concoctions. Brooks opted for the artistically richer pastures of Europe—where she teamed with the great German director G. W. Pabst for a pair of scandalous films, *Pandora's Box* and *Diary of a Lost Girl*, that packed movie houses and outraged the censors on several continents in the waning days of the silent cinema.

Based on Frank Wedekind's play of the same name, *Pandora's Box*, the movie highlights Brooks as the alluring Lulu, who uses her considerable beauty and sexual charms to get ahead, destroying the lives of several men in the process. Lulu gets her comeuppance at the hands of Jack the Ripper when her wanton ways reduce her to a life of prostitution on the streets of London.

The film caused a sensation for its remarkable frankness and potent images of an amoral society swamped in sin and perversity. But it was but a harbinger of things to come from the Brooks-Pabst team. Their follow-up collaboration, *Diary of a Lost Girl*, caused even more a furor. Pabst cast Brooks not as a sexual predator this time around but as a waif whose repeated victimization by men leads her into a life of prostitution. She triumphs in the end—at least in the sense that she suffers no retribution for the sinful life she, however involuntarily, has been forced to pursue.

Diary of a Lost Girl pushed the envelope of sexual frankness on the screen even further than *Pandora's Box* with its earthy look inside the daily, not just nightly, workings of a brothel and the candor of its seduction scenes.

These scenes were presented symbolically rather than graphically, but their content was no less clear. For example, when Brooks's character, Thymiane, is carried to bed by her first seducer (Fritz Rasp), her swaying legs knock a glass of red wine off a nightstand, splashing the dark liquid across the sheets—an unmistakable visual metaphor for the subsequent taking of her virginity. Such a hue and cry arose among contemporary watchdog groups on both sides of the Atlantic that this scene was cut. Other equally potent scenes were altered so that the film could be released. The film's original sins-go-unpunished ending was also changed. By simply chopping the ending off and letting the film conclude, albeit somewhat abruptly, at a low

Das Tagebuch einer Verlorenen

point in Thymiane's travails, it suggests if not outright penance, at least a pattern of continued woe in the character's life. Fortunately, the print of *Diary of a Lost Girl* that is in circulation and available for appraisal today is, for the most part, Pabst's original cut and not the butchered version.

Had Louise Brooks and G. W. Pabst continued working together, they might have enjoyed the ongoing success of that later actress-director duo, Marlene Dietrich and Josef von Sternberg, whose pairing on a number of steamy extravaganzas the Brooks-Pabst team-up somewhat anticipated. But after making one more film in France for another director, Brooks returned to her native country to resume the stalled Hollywood career which had spurred her to seek fame, fortune—and better roles in better films—in Europe. By then the talkies had arrived to finish off the careers of many a silent screen superstar. Brooks was not one of them. It was not the advent of sound that drove her from the screen, but her unwillingness to pick up her career where it left off. She demanded the kinds of roles in the kinds of arty films that made her a name in Europe. What she was offered instead was froth, and she retired from the screen permanently in 1933.

G. W. Pabst fared little better. Although he continued directing movies until 1956, his work never again achieved the acclaim or the notoriety *Pandora's Box* and, especially, *Diary of a Lost Girl* had brought him.

—John McCarty

TA'M E GUILASS

(Taste of Cherry)

Iran, 1997

Director: Abbas Kiarostami

Production: Abbas Kiarostami Productions, CiBy 2000 (France); color, 35mm; running time: 99 minutes in UK, 96 minutes in Argentina, and 95 minutes in Iran and USA. First released 10 October 1997, Italy; 20 March 1998, USA. Language: Farsi with English subtitles. Filmed in Tehran and its outskirts.

Producer: Abbas Kiarostami; **screenplay:** Abbas Kiarostami; **photography:** Homayoon Payvar; **assistant directors:** Hassan Yekta Panah, Bahman Kiarostami; **editor:** Abbas Kiarostami; **sound:** Jahangir Mirshekari; **art director:** Hassan Yekta Panah; **special effects:** Asadollah Majidi; **title design:** Mehdi Samakar; **assistant cameraman:** Farshad Bashir Zadeh; **sound assistant:** Sassan Bagherpour; **cameraman:** Alireza Ansarian; **mixer:** Mohamadreza Delpak.

Cast: Homayoun Ershadi (*Mr. Badii*); Abdolhosein Bagheri (*Mr. Bagheri, taxidermist in Natural History Museum*); Afshin Khorshid Bakhtari (*soldier*); Safar Ali Moradi (*soldier from Kurdistan*); Mir Hossein Noori (*seminarian*); Ahmad Ansari (*guard in the tower*); Hamid Masoumi (*man in telephone booth*); Elham Imani (*woman near the museum*); Ahmad Jahangiri (*blacksmith*); Nasrolah Amini (*gravel pit worker*); Sepideh Askari, Davood Forouzanfar (*passengers in VW car*); Iraj Alidoost, Rahman Rezai, Hojatolah Sarkeshi (*museum ticket personnel*); Ali Noornajafi (*soldier from Ilam*); Kianoosh Zahedi Panah, Gholam Reza Farahani, Morteza Yazdani, Moghadam, Ali Reza Abdollah Nejad, Akbar Khorasani, Hossain Mehdikhah, Ghorban Cheraghi, Ali Akbar Torabi, Seyed Mehdi Mirhashemi, Amir Reza Zendeh Ali, Abootaleb Moradi (*soldiers from Tehran*); Mehdi Bastami (*soldier from Shahrood*); Mohamad Aziz Ghasaei (*soldier from Hast-par*); Karim Rostami (*soldier from Khalkhal*); Kambiz Baradaran, Valliolah Halzaei (*soldiers from Kermanshah*); Ali Ghanbari, Jalal Ghafari, Ahmad Jozie, Ali Asghar Seyedi (*soldiers from Hamedan*); Ali Reza Bayat (*soldier from Toysarkaran*); Klanoosh Yooshan-Lou (*soldier from Bandar Anzali*); Ali Tabee Ahamadi (*soldier from Ahwaz*); Jamshid Torabi, Gholam Reza Fattahi (*soldiers from Karaj*); Ali Akbar Abbasi (*soldier from Qom*); Rahim Imanie (*soldier from Ardabil*); Ali Mohammad Moravati (*soldier from Takab*); Ali Mohammad Rezaei, Mahmood Reza Edalati (*soldiers from Malayer*); Seyyed Javad Navabi (*soldier from Arak*).

Awards: Palme d'Or (shared with Shohei Imamura's *Unagi* [*The Eel*]), Cannes Film Festival, 1997; Best Foreign Language Film, Boston Society of Film Critics, 1998; nominated for Best Foreign Language Film, Chicago Film Critics Association, 1999.

Publications

Articles:

Cheshire, Godfrey, ''Abbas Kiarostami: A Cinema of Questions,'' in *Film Comment* (New York), vol. 32, no. 4, July-August 1996.

Lopate, Phillip, ''Kiarostami Close Up,'' in *Film Comment* (New York), vol. 32, no. 4, July-August 1996.

Hamid, Nassia, ''Near and Far: Director Abbas Kiarostami Talks about Images from 'Through the Olive Trees' and His Career,'' in *Sight and Sound* (London), vol. 7, no. 2, February 1997.

Ditmars, Hadani, ''Talking Too Much With Men: From Angels in Paris to Martyrs in Tehran, Hadani Ditmars on Iranian Directors and the Fajr Film Festival,'' in *Sight and Sound* (London), vol. 7, no. 4, April 1997.

Roddick, Nick, ''Cannes Notes,'' in *Sight and Sound* (London), vol. 7, no. 7, July 1997.

Corliss, Mary, ''Cannes at 50,'' in *Film Comment* (New York), vol. 33, no. 4, July-August 1997.

Lopate, Phillip, ''New York,'' in *Film Comment* (New York), vol. 33, no. 6, November-December 1997.

Graffy, Julian, ''A Taste of Cherry/Ta'ame-gilas,'' in *Sight and Sound* (London), vol. 8, no. 6, June 1998.

Mulvey, Laura, ''Kiarostami's Uncertainty Principle,'' in *Sight and Sound* (London), vol. 8, no. 6, June 1998.

Films:

Interview with Abbas Kiarostami, in *Friendly Persuasion*, directed by Jamsheed Akrami, forthcoming.

* * *

Jean-Luc Godard reportedly said, ''Cinema starts with Griffith and ends with Kiarostami.'' His admiration for the Iranian director, expressed when Abbas Kiarostami accepted the Palme d'Or for *Taste of Cherry* at the 1997 Cannes Film Festival, is shared by many within the international film community. When *Taste of Cherry* gained world-wide attention by becoming the first Iranian film to win the top prize at Cannes, Kiarostami was introduced to a wider audience as one of the most original, thought-provoking artists of contemporary cinema. *Taste of Cherry*, Kiarostami's eloquent meditation on life and death, is a sublime masterpiece.

Like other Kiarostami films, the simple parable focuses on a journey. A seemingly affluent middle-aged man, Mr. Badii (Homayoun Ershadi), drives a white Range Rover around the hilly outskirts of Tehran in search of someone who will accept his job offer. He wants to hire a man for 200,000 tomans, the amount of money a soldier would receive for six months work. That person would accompany him to a predetermined grave site and return there the next morning to bury his dead body, if he succeeds in committing suicide, or to help him to his feet if he is still alive. His anguish is never explained. As Mr. Badii's car repeatedly loops along the narrow road, one wonders if he will choose the route to death or turn left and take the ''longer but better and more beautiful'' road towards the spirited city of Tehran. Is this the road to life?

The narrative piques the spectator's curiosity. Who is this brooding man and what does he want? The enigmatic protagonist approaches an assortment of ordinary people and invites each to take a ride with him: Afghans, Kurds, Turks, a young soldier, a security guard, an Islamic seminarian, and a museum employee. Mr. Badii very gradually reveals his suicidal intent—a taboo subject in the Islamic republic—to his passengers and to his audience. The impoverished Kurdish soldier bolts from the vehicle, the seminary student lectures on Muslim strictures against suicide, and the elderly museum taxidermist formulates a persuasive philosophical argument before agreeing to help him. Their reactions keep the arguments about life and death in perfect balance. To be or not to be? *Taste of Cherry* respectfully explores different points of view, raising questions rather than providing answers.

Despite its metaphysical concerns, the film is persistently earthbound. When Mr. Badii is in transit, the camera is largely confined to the car and close-ups of the driver and his passengers. Each has his own space, and the one-shots emphasize individual isolation. At other times the camera pulls back for long shots of soldiers marching through the parched countryside or of workers moving piles of red dirt with heavy equipment. Often taken from Mr. Badii's point of view, these shots connect him to the environment and the teeming vitality of earthly life. The powerful visual imagery, accompanied by the howling wind or punctuated by the wail of animals, presents the bleak but beautiful landscape as a place of social meaning, and, perhaps, a metaphor for the human condition.

Taste of Cherry is at once consistent with Kiarostami's previous work and a risky departure. Similar to *And Life Goes On* . . . (1992) and *Through the Olive Trees* (1994), a mythic quest leads to personal transformation. A minimal storyline, the use of structural repetition, and poetic images are Kiarostami trademarks. Working with a modest budget and under government control, the Iranian director managed to reinvent neorealism in the context of the art film. In the tradition of postwar Italian filmmakers, he coaxed strikingly natural performances from nonactors and shot on-location in and around Tehran. But Kiarostami's realist sensibilities, which foster comparisons between his work and Vittorio De Sica's humanist cinema, intersect with the grand themes, intellectual complexity, and formalist concerns associated with art cinema. The simplicity and spiritual intensity of *Taste of Cherry* recall the films of Ozu, Dreyer, and Bresson.

Kiarostami's cinema is highly self-reflexive, making excellent use of distanciation devices to remind viewers that they are ''only'' watching a film. In *Where Is My Friend's House* (1987) and *Close-Up* (1989), Kiarostami addresses the filmmaking process itself, making a distinction between the real world and the reconstructed reality of cinema. At the beginning of *Through the Olive Trees*, Kiarostami has an actor turn to the camera and say, ''I am the man who is playing the director of this film'' and in *And Life Goes On* . . . , the script girl interrupts a scene to hand an actor a glass of water. So the film crew's appearance at the end of *Taste of Cherry* is more than the director's whim. This reminder about the movie's artifice encourages audiences to think about the film's open ending and to confront the intellectual issues on their terms. As Kiarostami stated in a February 1997 *Sight and Sound* interview, ''The filmmaker can only raise questions, and it is the audience who should seek the answer, should have the opportunity for reflection . . . to complete the unfinished part of a work. So there are as many different versions of the same film as there are members of a given audience.''

Only one interpretation, however, can be inferred from the tossed-off remark that provides the film's title. Before the taxidermist of the Natural History Museum agrees to assist Mr. Badii, he tells of his own suicide attempt. Years ago he had thrown a rope over a mulberry tree with the intent of hanging himself. Suddenly he noticed the rising sun, the beauty of his surroundings, and the cries of children begging him to shake the tree so that they could eat the fallen mulberries. Simple pleasures—including the succulent berries—reclaimed his zest for life. Although the older man credits a mulberry for saving him, he asks Mr. Badii, ''You want to give up the taste of cherries?'' By refusing to reveal the answer, Abbas Kiarostami allows us to savor the sensuous and intellectual pleasures of his film.

—Susan Tavernetti

TAMPOPO

Japan, 1986

Director: Juzo Itami

Production: Itami Productions, New Century Producers; colour, 35mm; running time: 114 minutes.

Producer: Juzo Itami, Yasushi Tamaoki, Seigo Hosogoe; **screenplay:** Juzo Itami; **photography:** Masaki Tamura; **editor:** Akira Suzuki; **assistant directors:** Kazuki Skiroyama, Kubota Nobuhiro, Suzuki Kenji; **art director:** Takeo Kimura; **music**: Kunihiko Murai; **sound:** Fumio Hashimoto; **food design:** Izumi Ishimori; **cooking stylist:** Seiko Ogawa.

Cast: Tsutomu Yamazaki (*Goro*); Nobuko Miyamoto (*Tampopo*); Koji Yakusho (*Gangster*); Ken Watanabe (*Gun*); Rikiya Yasuoka (*Pisken*); Kinzo Sakura (*Shohei*); Manpei Ikeuchi (*Tabo*); Yoshi Kato (*Sensei*).

Publications

Articles:

Variety (New York), 3 September 1986.

Magny, J., ''A la recherche de la nouille absolue,'' in *Cahiers du Cinema* (Paris), December 1987.

Freiberg, F., *Cinema Papers* (Melbourne), March 1988.

Rayns, T., *Monthly Film Bulletin* (London), April 1988.

Stanbrook, A., ''Ronin with a Roguish Grin,'' in *Films and Filming* (London), April 1988.

Niel, P., ''De la substantifique molle des nouilles nippones,'' in *Positif* (Paris), May 1988.

O'Conner, Patricia T., in *The New York Times*, vol. 137, H30, 17 July 1988.

Lavigne, N., *Sequences* (Montreal), September 1988.

Seesslen, Georg, ''Tampopo,'' in *EPD Film* (Frankfurt), vol. 6, no. 6, June 1989.

* * *

Japanese writer-director Juzo Itami combines slapstick with light-as-a-feather whimsy of the Bill Forsyth school in this decidedly unusual blend of genres.

The plot centers on the quest of a young widow named Tampopo (Nobuko Miyamoto) to master the art of cooking the perfect noodle dish. She is guided, spiritually and otherwise, in her quest by a helpful truck driver (Tsutomu Yamazaki), a Clint Eastwood type who is strong, but not silent in his persistent tutelage.

In addition to Eastwood, Yamazaki's character is modeled on and a parody of the energetic samurai warriors in Akira Kurosawa's epics and every gunslinger who came to the rescue of the widow woman in every American western ever made.

He first meets Miyamoto when he stops at her restaurant for a bite and is turned off by the unsavoriness of her noodle recipe (due mostly to lack of proper boiling) and the rough, undiscriminating trade that frequents her restaurant. These goons beat him to a pulp in an offscreen rumble outside her place.

Taken with his strength and courage, she nurses his wounds and he stays on to improve her culinary skills and bring her more upscale business by putting her through a rigorous training program that parodies the classic Oriental quest for enlightenment through suffering.

Itami shifts back and forth between this framing story and a series of vignettes involving gangsters, a class in the proper etiquette of eating spaghetti, the techniques of professional noodle tasting and other odds and ends. The subject that links these disparate set pieces is food, and sometimes sex—occasionally both at once, as in an

Tampopo

amusingly kinky scene where an amorous couple gets it on in a hotel room over an elegantly prepared evening meal, using the various courses as sex aids.

The film's opening scene set in a movie theatre before the lights go down where an irate member of the audience admonishes his fellow patrons for always crinkling their snack wrappers and chewing their potato chips and popcorn too loudly during the show is also quite funny. It's a situation with which anyone who has ever gone to a movie can easily identify.

As one might expect from a film about the fine art of food preparation, the screen is awash in mouthwatering images that rival the alluring color photos in an average issue of *Bon Appetit.* Tampopo is clearly not meant for viewers on diets, for it is guaranteed to make you hungry.

The humor is simultaneously zany and yet so slyly understated that you're not always sure whether Itami is trying to tickle your ribs or pull your leg. Most American critics felt him to be aiming at the former and *Tampopo* wound up on the annual Top Ten Film lists of 23 of them, including the reviewers of the *New York Times*, the *Los Angeles Times* and *Time* magazine. Siskel and Ebert gave it a thumbs up, calling it ''brilliant and wacky.'' But the *New York Daily News* reviewer said it best, calling the film a ''one-of-a-kind, true original.'' For that it definitely is.

—John McCarty

TASTE OF CHERRY

See **TA'M E GUILASS**

TAXI DRIVER

USA, 1976

Director: Martin Scorsese

Production: Bill/Phillips Production, an Italo-Judeo Production; Metrocolor, 35mm; running time: 113 minutes. Released 1976 by Columbia Pictures. Filmed 1975 in New York City.

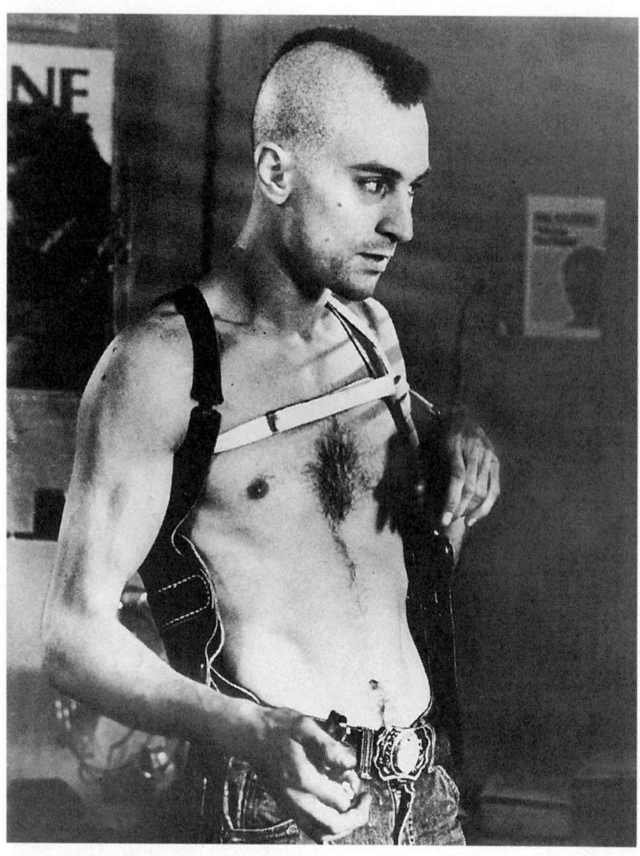
Taxi Driver

Producers: Michael Phillips and Julia Phillips with Phillip M. Goldfarb; **screenplay:** Paul Schrader; **photography:** Michael Chapman; **editors:** Tom Rolf and Melvin Shapiro; **editing supervisor:** Marcia Lucas; **sound:** Roger Pietschman and Tex Rudloff; **art director:** Charles Rosen; **music:** Bernard Herrmann; **costume designer:** Ruth Morley; **visual consultant:** David Nichols; creative consultant: Sandra Weintraub.

Cast: Robert De Niro (*Travis Bickle*); Cybill Shepherd (*Betsy*); Jodie Foster (*Iris*); Harvey Keitel (*Sport*); Leonard Harris (*Charles Palantine*); Peter Boyle (*Wizard*); Albert Brooks (*Tom*); Murray Mosten (*Timekeeper*); Richard Higgs (*Secret Service Agent*); Vic Aro (*Melio, deli owner*); Steven Prince (*Gun salesman*); Martin Scorsese (*Taxi passenger*); Dianne Abbot (*Concession girl*).

Awards: New York Film Critics Award, Best Actor (De Niro), 1976; Palme d'Or, Cannes Film Festival, 1976.

Publications

Books:

Silver, Alain, and Elizabeth Ward, editors, *Film Noir*, New York, 1979.
Ray, Robert B., *A Certain Tendency of the Hollywood Cinema 1930–1980*, Princeton, 1985.
Arnold, Frank, and others, *Martin Scorsese*, Munich, 1986.
Bliss, Michael, *Martin Scorsese and Michael Cimino*, Metuchen, New Jersey, 1986.
Cameron-Wilson, James, *The Cinema of Robert De Niro*, London, 1986.
Cietat, Michel, *Martin Scorsese*, Paris, 1986.
Domecq, Jean-Philippe, *Martin Scorsese: Un Rêve Italo-Américain*, Renens, Switzerland, 1986.
McKay, Keith, *Robert De Niro: The Hero Behind the Masks*, New York, 1986.
Weiss, Ulli, *Das Neue Hollywood: Francis Ford Coppola, Steven Spielberg, Martin Scorsese*, Munich, 1986.
Wood, Robin, *Hollywood from Vietnam to Reagan*, New York, 1986.
Weiss, Marian, *Martin Scorsese: a Guide to References and Resources*, Boston, 1987.
Lourdeaux, Lee, *Italian and Irish Filmmakers in America: Ford, Capra, Coppola, and Scorsese*, Philadelphia, 1990.
Schrader, Paul, *Schrader on Schrader*, edited by Kevin Jackson, New York, 1992.
Connelly, Marie Katheryn, *Martin Scorsese: An Analysis of His Feature Films, With a Filmography of His Entire Directorial Career*, Jefferson, 1993.
Bliss, Michael, *The Word Made Flesh: Catholicism and Conflict in the Films of Martin Scorsese*, Lanham, 1995, 1998.
Friedman, Lawrence S., *The Cinema of Martin Scorsese*, New York, 1997.
Kelly, Mary P., *Martin Scorsese: A Journey*, New York, 1997.
Pezzotta, Alberto, *Martin Scorsese: Taxi Driver*, Torino, 1997.
Dougan, Andy, *Martin Scorsese - Close Up: The Making of His Movies*, New York, 1998.
Brunette, Peter, editor, *Martin Scorsese: Interviews*, Jackson, 1999.

Articles:

Filmfacts (Los Angeles), no. 1, 1976.
Rice, J. C., ''Transcendental Pornography and *Taxi Driver*,'' in *Journal of Popular Film* (Bowling Green, Ohio), no. 2, 1976.
Golchan, F., ''Paul Schrader,'' in *Cinematographe* (Paris), June 1976.
Rubinstein, L., in *Cineaste* (New York), Fall 1976.
Eder, K., ''Rebel Heroes der 70er Jahre: Kontaklos und gewalttaetig: zu zwei Filmen von Martin Scorsese,'' in *Medium* (Frankfurt), July 1976.
Racheva, M., and K. Eder, ''*Taxi Driver*: Gespraecch mit Drehbuchator Paul Schrader,'' in *Medium* (Frankfurt), July 1976.
Renaud, T., in *Cinéma* (Paris), July 1976.
Chavardes, B., in *Téléciné* (Paris), July-August 1976.
Renaud, T., in *Cinéma* (Paris), July 1976.
Kane, P., in *Cahiers du Cinéma* (Paris), July-August 1976.
Amata, C., ''Scorsese on *Taxi Driver*,'' in *Focus on Film* (London), Summer-Autumn 1976.
Cowie, Peter, in *Focus on Film* (London), Summer-Autumn 1976.
Coleman, John, in *New Statesman* (London), 20 August 1976.
Beard, D., ''Mindless Audience Reaction,'' in *Cinema Canada* (Montreal), October 1976.
Desrues, H., in *Revue du Cinéma* (Paris), October 1976.
Thompson, R., ''Screenwriter: *Taxi Driver*'s Paul Schrader,'' in *Fernseh-und-kino-Technik* (Berlin), October 1976.
Giuricin, G., in *Cinema Nuovo* (Turin), November-December 1976.
Hosman, H., ''Een eindeloos verhaal zonder punten en komma's: de films van Martin Scorsese,'' in *Skoop* (Amsterdam), February-March 1977.

Rule, P., ''The Italian Connection in the American Film: Coppola, Cimino, Scorsese,'' in *America* (New York), 17 November 1979.

Mitchell, Robert, in *Magill's Survey of Cinema 4*, Englewood Cliffs, New Jersey, 1980.

Wood, Robin, ''The Incoherent Text: Narrative Texts in the 70s,'' in *Movie* (London), Winter-Spring 1980–81.

Sharrett, C., ''The American Apocalypse: Scorsese's *Taxi Driver*,'' in *Persistence of Vision* (Maspeth, New York), Summer 1984.

Bruce, Bryan, ''Martin Scorsese: Five Films,'' in *Movie* (London), Winter 1986.

Lane, J., ''Martin Scorsese and the Documentary Impulse,'' in *Framework* (London), no. 1, 1991.

Vickers, N. J., ''Lyric in the Video Decade,'' in *Discourse* (Bloomington, Indiana), Fall 1993.

Norman, Barry, in *Radio Times* (London), vol. 266, no. 3736, 26 August 1995.

Quart, L., ''A Slice of Delirium: Scorsese's *Taxi Driver* Revisited,'' in *Film Criticism* (Meadville), vol. 19, no. 3, 1995.

Maslin, Janet, in *The New York Times*, vol. 145, C12, 16 February 1996.

Taubin, Amy, ''A Checkered Past,'' in *Village Voice* (New York), vol. 41, 20 February 1996.

Scorsese, Martin, ''De Nero & Moi,'' in *Cahiers du Cinéma* (Paris), no. 500, March 1996.

Everschor, Franz, ''20 Jahre nach Travis Bickle,'' in *Film-Dienst* (Cologne), vol. 49, no. 7, 26 March 1996.

Mortimer, B., ''Portraits of the Postmodern Person in *Taxi Driver*, *Raging Bull*, and *The King of Comedy*,'' in *Journal of Film and Video* (Atlanta), vol. 49, no. 1/2, 1997.

Patterson, Patricia, and Manny Farber, ''The Power and the Gory,'' in *Film Comment* (New York), vol. 34, no. 3, May-June 1998.

Wilmington, Michael, ''The Wild Heart,'' in *Film Comment* (New York), vol. 34, no. 3, May-June 1998.

Taubin, Amy, ''God's Lonely Man,'' in *Sight & Sound* (London), vol. 9, no. 4, April 1999.

* * *

It was during the 1970s—the period of Vietnam and Watergate—that American society appeared in imminent danger of collapse, the crisis in ideological confidence being (quite logically) complemented by the growth of the major radical movements of contemporary culture: feminism, black militancy, gay activism. The confusions and hysteria of the social climate (the historical moment when the dominant ideology of bourgeois patriarchal capitalism and reinforcement under Carter and Reagan) were reflected in the products of Hollywood: one might say that the most interesting and distinguished films of the period were also the most incoherent, centered in the experience of contradiction, disillusionment and desperation. Their failure to develop beyond confusion and contradiction must be attributed to the continuing prohibition (within the American cultural establishment) on imagining any alternative form of cultural organization to patriarchal capitalism.

Taxi Driver is an outstanding product of this cultural situation. Its rich and fascinating incoherence has a number of sources. The collaboration of Scorsese and Schrader involved its own immediate problems. Scorsese's ideological/political position is very difficult to define (perhaps an example of the ability of art to transcend such definitions): he has consistently refused to commit himself to any definable radical position, yet, in their systematic analysis of the untenability of all our social institutions, his films clearly earn the term ''radical.'' Schrader, on the other hand, seems plainly (and quite unashamedly) neo-Fascist: his films (as writer and director) amount to a systematic repudiation of all minority groups and any possible social alternative, in order to re-assert a quasi-mystical sense of male supremacy, heterosexual superiority, and a total spurious ''transcendence'' (which amounts to little more than one person's right to slaughter other people, on the basis of some supposed achievement of spiritual transfiguration, with no foundation in material reality). One must see the curious paralysis of the film's closing sequence—clearly, on some level, ironic, but with the irony quite unfocused—as the result of this collaboration of partial incompatibles, a view confirmed by Scorsese's *King of Comedy* (made without Schrader), with its closely parallel but precisely focused ending.

A more profitable tension arises from the film's fascinating fusion of genres: film noir, the western, the horror film. Travis Bickle (Robert De Niro)—who has swiftly become established as a significant figure in American cultural mythology—is on one level the western hero transplanted into the modern urban wilderness: he derives particularly from Ethan Edwards (John Wayne) of *The Searchers*, and Scorsese and Schrader have made it clear that Ford's film was a conscious influence. But he is also the psychopath/monster of the contemporary horror film: it is perhaps the chief distinction of *Taxi Driver* to suggest the relationship between these two apparent opposed archetypes and its significance in relation to American ideology. In fact, the film's interest is inseparable from its sense of confusion, its failure to define a coherent attitude towards its protagonist. That confusion must be seen, not merely as the result of a clash of artistic personalities, but as the reflection of a national ideological dilemma.

—Robin Wood

TEN DAYS THAT SHOOK THE WORLD

See **OKTIABR**

TENI ZABYTYKH PREDKOV

(Shadows of Forgotten Ancestors)

USSR, 1964

Director: Sergei Paradzhanov

Production: Dovzhenko Studios (Kiev); Magicolor, 35mm; running time: variously noted as 100 minutes, 98 minutes and 95 minutes. Released 1964, USSR. Filmed on location among the Gutsuls in the Carpathians.

Screenplay: Sergei Paradzhanov and Ivan Chendei, inspired by the novelette *Wild Horses of Fire* by M. Kotsiubinsky, and by western Ukrainian folklore; **photography:** Yuri Ilyenko; **editor:** M. Ponomarenko; **sound:** S. Sergienko; **art directors:** M. Rakovsky and G. Yakutovich; **music:** M. Skorik.

Cast: Ivan Nikolaichuk (*Ivan*); Larissa Kadochnikova (*Marichka*); Tatiana Bestaeva (*Palagna*); Spartak Bagashvili (*Yurko the Sorcerer*); several Gutsul natives.

Publications

Books:

Gaby, H., and others, *Serge Paradjanov*, Lausanne, 1977.

Liehm, Mira, and Antonin Liehm, *The Most Important Art: East European Film After 1945*, Berkeley, 1977.

Cazals, Patrick, *Serguei Paradjanov*, Paris, 1993.

Korohods'skyi, R.M., *Serhii Paradzhanov: zlet, trahediia, vichnist'*, Kyïv, 1994.

Articles:

Seeyle, John, in *Film Quarterly* (Berkeley), Summer 1966.

Filmfacts (New York), no. 10, 1967.

International Film Guide (London), 1967.

Paradjanov, S., in *Film Comment* (New York), Fall 1968.

Gow, Gordon, in *Films and Filming* (London), June 1969.

Nemes, K., in *Filmkultura* (Budapest), September-October 1974.

Delmas, J., in *Jeune Cinéma* (Paris), September-October 1975.

Marshall, Herbert, ''The Case of Sergei Paradjanov,'' in *Sight and Sound* (London), no. 1, 1975.

Liehm, Antonin, ''A Certain Cowardice,'' in *Film Comment* (New York), July-August 1975.

Delmas, J., in *Jeune Cinéma* (Paris), September-October 1975.

Treilhou, M. C., in *Cinéma* (Paris), September-October 1975.

Potrel-Dorget, M. L., in *Image et Son* (Paris), May 1978.

Cook, D. A., ''*Shadows of Forgotten Ancestors*: Film as Religious Art,'' in *Post Script* (Jacksonville, Florida), Spring-Summer 1984.

Barsky, V., ''Uber Sergej Paradschanow und seine Filme: Im Schatten von vergessenen Ahnen,'' in *Filmfaust* (Frankfurt), October-November 1985.

Kroll, Jack, ''The Pas De Perestroika: A New Generation of Soviet Artists Try to Undo the Damage of Half Century of Stalinist Repression and Socialist Realism,'' in *Newsweek*, vol. 110, no. 24, 14 December 1987.

Iskusstvo Kino (Moscow), no. 11, 1989.

Payne, R., ''The Storm of the Eye: Culture, Spectacle, Paradzhanov,'' in *Spectator* (Los Angeles), vol. 10, no. 1, 1989.

Cook, D.A., ''Making Sense,'' in *Film Criticism* (Meadville), vol. 17, no. 2–3, Winter-Spring 1993.

Nebesio, Bohdan Y., ''Shadows of Forgotten Ancestors: Storytelling in the Novel and the Film,'' in *Literature/Film Quarterly* (Salisbury), vol. 22, no. 1, January 1994.

Holden, Stephen, in *The New York Times*, vol. 145, C8, 10 November 1995.

* * *

Sergei Paradzhanov's *Shadows of Forgotten Ancestors* first appeared in the West in 1965; it won 16 foreign festival awards and was released in the United States and Europe to critical acclaim. Not since the triumph of *Potemkin*, in fact, had a Soviet motion picture enjoyed such international esteem. At home, *Shadows of Forgotten Ancestors* was variously accused of ''formalism'' and ''Ukrainian nationalism,'' and it was deliberately underbooked in domestic theaters by Sovkino officials. Paradzhanov found himself personally attacked by the Party Secretary for Ideological Problems, and he was consistently denied permission to travel abroad. During the next ten years, Paradzhanov went on to write ten complete scenarios based on classical Russian literature and folk epics, all of which were refused by Soviet authorities, and to make one more film—*Sayat Nova (The Color of Pomegranates)*—which was banned on its release in 1969 and finally given limited distribution in a version ''re-edited'' by Sergei Yutkevitch in the early 1970s. In January 1974, Paradzhanov was arrested and charged with a variety of offences, including homosexual rape, the spreading of venereal disease, and the illegal sale of icons. Although only the charges of trafficking in art objects stuck, Paradzhanov was sentenced to six years hard labor in Gulag. An international petition campaign forced the Soviets to release him in late 1977, but he has not been allowed to work in the film industry since then. Recently, Paradzhanov told a friend: ''I am already a dead man. I can no longer live without creating. In prison my life had direction; there was a reality to surmount. My present life is worse than death.'' The question poses itself: What was *Shadows of Forgotten Ancestors* to have provoked such admiration, controversy and, finally, misery for its maker? How coul the unique sensibility mirrored in this richly poetic film have been perceived by the Soviet bureaucracy as a political threat at all?

Adapted by Paradzhanov and Ivan Chendei from a pre-Revolutionary novelette by the distinguished Ukrainian writer M. Kotsiubinsky to celebrate the centennial of his birth, *Shadows of Forgotten Ancestors* retells an ancient Carpathian folk legend of universal resonance.

Deep in the Carpathian mountains, at the farthest western reach of the Ukraine, live the Gutsuls, a proud peasant race cut off from the rest of the world by natural boundaries. They are impulsive, fierce, and—though nominally Christian—deeply superstitious and tied to pagan ways. The story begins in the childhood of the two future lovers, when the boy Ivan's father is killed in a fit of anger by the girl Marichka's father, initiating a blood-feud between the two families. But even as children Ivan and Marichka are drawn to each other by strong spiritual attraction. Later, when they are youths, the attraction becomes physical as well, and Ivan impregnates Marichka shortly before he must leave to work as a bondsman for a group of shepherds on the opposite mountain. (Ivan is the sole support of his aged and impoverished mother; Marichka's family is relatively wealthy—the source of the original dispute between the fathers.) As they part, the two lovers agree that every night before Ivan returns they will gaze at the north star to commemorate their love. One night Marichka is drawn out by the star, through the woods, to a bluff above the river. There, attempting to rescue a lost lamb (which is symbolically linked to her love for Ivan), she plunges into the river and drowns. Instinctively realizing that something is wrong, Ivan rushes to the river gorge and floats downstream on a logging barge to discover her body washed up on the shore.

After Marichka's death, Ivan goes through a long period of numbing grief and desolate wandering. Finally, however, he is able to experience love for another woman, Palagna, who eventually becomes his wife. But their marriage proves joyless and barren, for Ivan finds Palagna's carnality degrading compared to the purity of his lost love. More and more, he can think only of the dead Marichka, and finally he begins to look toward death himself. Palagna, scorned, contracts an affair with the local sorcerer who promises to make her fertile with his magic. One night, the sorcerer goads Ivan into a fight in the local tavern and cleaves his skull with an ax (the same mode of death as Ivan's father). Ivan stumbles deliriously through the woods to the river where Marichka drowned, and in a vision she appears to him. They embrace and Ivan dies. Then, like his father before him, his corpse is laid out, and the men, women, and children of the village observe their ancient ritual of death.

At the level of plot, then, *Shadows of Forgotten Ancestors* offers a relatively familiar tale of undying love which has variants in cultures all over the world. But in the telling of that tale, Paradzhanov has created a vision of human experience so radical and unique as to subvert all authority. To say that *Shadows of Forgotten Ancestors* violates every narrative code and representational system known to the cinema is an understatement—at times, in fact, the film seems intent upon deconstructing the very process of representation itself. The relationship between narrative logic and cinematic space—between point of view inside and outside the frame—is so consistently undermined that most critics on first viewing literally cannot describe what they've seen. Adjectives frequently used to characterize *Shadows of Forgotten Ancestors* are ''hallucinatory,'' ''intoxicating,'' and ''delirious''—terms that imply, however positively, confusion and incoherence. But the camera and editing techniques which elicit such comments are all part of Paradzhanov's deliberate aesthetic strategy to interrogate a whole set of historically evolved assumptions about the nature of cinematic space and the relationship which exists between the spectator and the screen.

Paradzhanov proceeds by means of perceptual dislocation, so that it becomes impossible at any given moment to imagine a stable time-space continuum for the dramatic action. Often, for example, the viewer will be invited by conventional stylistic means to share a point of view which is suddenly ruptured by camera movement or some other disjunction in spatial logic; spaces which appear to be contiguous in one shot sequence are revealed to be miles apart in the next; at other times, the camera assumes perspectives and executes manoeuvres which appear to be *physically*, as well as dramatically, impossible: the camera looks down from the top of a falling tree perhaps 100 feet tall; it looks up through a pool, with no optical distortion, as Ivan drinks from its surface; it whirls 360 degrees on its axis for nearly a full minute, dissolving focus and colour to abstraction; it turns corners and swoops down embankments with inhuman celerity. Finally, Paradzhanov and his cinematographer, Yuri Ilyenko, use a variety of lenses, including telephoto zoom and 180-degree wide-angle, or ''fish-eye,'' to wrap the film's scenographic space to the outer limits of narrative comprehension. The point of these techniques is not to confuse the spectator but to prevent him from constructing in his head the kind of comfortable, familiar, and logically continuous representational space associated with traditional narrative form. The reason is simply that the film posits a world which is neither comfortable, familiar, nor logically continuous, for *Shadows of Forgotten Ancestors* exists most fully not in the realm of narrative but of myth and the unconscious.

It is above all else a deeply psychological film, rich in both Freudian and Jungian imagery. Ivan's yearning after the dead Marichka is imaged in many ways as a positive desire to merge with the anima and become psychologically whole. But it is also imaged darkly as a plunging descent into a Hades-like chasm containing the river where Marichka drowned, as a terrible, desperate craving to return to womb of the mother with whom Ivan has lived in a figurally Oedipal relationship since his father's death as a child—that mother who disappears from the film inexplicably and without comment at the very moment that Marichka drowns.

Shadows of Forgotten Ancestors's psychological subtlety extends to its use of sound and color. It has been frequently noted that the film has an operatic, pageant-like quality; and Paradzhanov uses a complex variety of music—from atonal electronics, to lush orchestral romanticism, to hieratic religious chants, to vocal and instrumental folk music—to create leitmotifs for the various psychological elements in his film. For example, the dark side of the Ivan-Marichka union is first announced at their moment of sexual awakening as children (after they have just bathed in the river where Marichka will drown) by a disturbingly atonal violin piece which rises to a crescendo as the intensity of their longing mounts. This theme re-appears on the soundtrack whenever Paradzhanov wishes to summon forth the psychologically disruptive linkage between sex and death which underlies their relationship (as it underlied the human psyche). Similarly, the bright, innocent, psychologically integral side of their love is celebrated by a joyful folk song, sung both by and about them, not only while Marichka lives, but also, for example, at that moment later in the film when Ivan casts down his grief and becomes for a while at least, reconciled to her death. For the most part, however, Paradzhanov's use of sound is as anti-traditional as his use of the cinematography and editing. Characteristically, Ivan's grief-stricken wanderings after Marichka's death are accompanied not by music but by the off-screen gossip of neighbors commenting on his decline. And Paradzhanov manipulates his sound track in other ways, creating certain effects for symbolic purposes (such as the sound of the ''invisible ax'' hacking away off-screen which appears at fateful cruxes in Ivan's life).

Paradzhanov spoke of having created for *Shadows of Forgotten Ancestors* a ''dramaturgy of color,'' and this element of film composition too is used in a psychologically provocative way. When Ivan and Marichka are first drawn together by their fathers'' violence, the prevailing color of the film is the white of the snow, corresponding to their innocence (although its opposite is prefigured by the blood of Ivan's father running down the lens at the moment of his death); the green of spring dominates their young love; monochrome and sepia tones are used to drain the world of color during the period of Ivan's grieving; but color returns riotously, if briefly, after he meets Palagna; as that relationship turns barren, the film is dominated by autumnal hues; monochrome returns during Ivan's death delirium; and at the moment of his death the natural universe is painted in surreal shades of red and blue. Less noticed are the nearly subliminal fades to white and red which connect all the major sequences and the use of fades generally to isolate symbolic detail or create symbolic association.

The effect of both the soundtrack and the color system, like that of the film's optical distortions and dislocations, is to destabilize the spectator perceptually, and therefore psychologically, in order to present a tale that operates not at the level of narrative but of myth: youth passes from innocence to experience to solitude and death in a recurring cycle, eons upon eons. This is the ''shadow'' of ''forgotten ancestors,'' the archetypal pattern that outlasts and transcends all individual identity. Now the disconcerting violations of point of view through dizzying camera movement and impossible camera angles acquire new significance. For to annihilate individual point of view is to suggest a collective one, and the ''impossible'' perspectives of the film are only so to humans. From the beginning of *Shadows of Forgotten Ancestors* through its final frames, Paradzhanov has forced the viewer to ask himself at every turn a single question: Through whose eyes do I see? From the top of a tree, from the bottom of a pond, from the center of a violent 360-degree rotation—through whose eyes? There can only be one answer: We see this film through the eyes of something that is greater and older than all of humankind, that is everywhere at once, that discerns what things are and simultaneously what they are not. Paradzhanov may have dabbled in political dissent and been too outspoken in his criticism of officialdom, but the Soviet bureaucrats silenced him because *Shadows of Forgotten Ancestors* is an extraordinary testament to the powers of film as religious art, and its maker was a poet of God.

—David Cook

LA TERRA TREMA

Italy, 1947

Director: Luchino Visconti

Production: Universalia; black and white, 35mm; running time: about 160 minutes. Released 1947. Filmed 1947 in Aci Trezza, a small fishing village in Sicily.

Producer: Salvo d'Angelo; **screenplay:** Luchino Visconti, from the 19th century novel *I Malavoglia* by Giovanni Verga; **assistant directors:** Francesco Rosi and Franco Zeffirelli; **photography:** G. R. Aldo; **editor:** Mario Serandrei; **sound:** Vittorio Trentino; **music:** Willi Ferrero with Luchino Visconti.

La Terra Trema

Cast: The cast is composed of the people of Aci Trezza in Sicily.

Publications

Script:

Visconti, Luchino, *La terra trema*, in *Two Screenplays*, New York, 1970; as *La terra trema*, Bologna, 1977.

Books:

Gromo, Mario, *Cinema Italiano*, Milan, 1954.
Pellezzari, Lorenzo, *Luchino Visconti*, Milan, 1960.
Baldelli, Pio, *I film di Luchino Visconti*, Manduria, 1965.
Guillaume, Yves, *Visconti*, Paris, 1966.
Nowell-Smith, Geoffrey, *Luchino Visconti*, New York, 1968; 2nd edition, 1973.
Leprohon, Pierre, *The Italian Cinema*, New York, 1972.
Armes, Roy, *Patterns of Realism*, New York, 1972.
Ferrera, Adelio, editor, *Visconti: Il cinema*, Milan, 1977.
Tornabuoni, Lietta, editor, *Album Visconti*, Milan, 1978.
Stirling, Monica, *A Screen of Time*, New York, 1979.
Visconti, Luchino, *Il meo teatro* (2 volumes), Bologna, 1979.
Rondolini, Gianni, *Luchino Visconti*, Turin, 1981.
Servadio, Gaia, *Luchino Visconti: A Biography*, London, 1981.
Bencivenni, Alessandro, *Luchino Visconti*, Florence, 1982.
Tonetti, Claretta, *Luchino Visconti*, Boston, 1983.
Ishaghpour, Youssef, *Luchino Visconti: Le Sens et l'image*, Paris, 1984.
Sanzio, Alain, and Paul-Louis Thirard, *Luchino Visconti: Cinéaste*, Paris, 1984.
De Guisti, Luciano, *I film di Luchino Visconti*, Rome, 1985.
Mancini, Elaine, *Luchino Visconti: A Guide to References and Resources*, Boston, 1986.
Villien, Bruno, *Visconti*, Paris, 1986.
Schifano, Laurence, *Luchino Visconti: Les Feux de la passion*, Paris, 1987.
Micciché, Lino, *Visconti e il neorealismo: Ossessione, La terra trema, Bellissima*, Venice, 1990.
Renzi, Renzo, *Visconti segreto*, Rome, 1994.
Micciché, Lino, *Luchino Visconti: un profilo critico*, Venice, 1996.
Bacon, Henry, *Visconti: Explorations of Beauty and Decay*, Cambridge, 1998.

Articles:

Renzi, Renzo, ''Mitologia e contemplasione in Visconti, Ford, e Eisenstein,'' in *Bianco e Nero* (Rome), February 1949.
Bianco e Nero (Rome), March 1951.
Ecran Français (Paris), January 1952.
Speri, Pietro, ''Verismo litterario e neorealismo,'' in *Cinema* (Rome), 15 March 1954.
Castello, G. C., ''Luchino Visconti,'' in *Sight and Sound* (London), Spring 1956.
Sarris, Andrew, in *Village Voice* (New York), 14 October 1956.
Dyer, Peter, ''The Vision of Visconti,'' in *Film* (London), March-April 1957.
Domarchi, Jean, and Doniol Valcroze, interview with Visconti, in *Sight and Sound* (London), Summer-Autumn 1959.

Poggin, G., in *Film Quarterly* (Berkeley), Spring 1960.
Rhode, Eric, in *Sight and Sound* (London), Winter 1960–61.
Aristarco, Guido, ''The Earth Still Trembles,'' in *Films and Filming* (London), January 1961.
''Visconti Issue'' of *Premier Plan* (Paris), May 1961.
''Visconti Issue'' of *Etudes Cinématographique* (Paris), nos. 26–27, 1963.
Cinéma (Paris), September-October 1963.
Elsaesser, Thomas, in *Brighton Film Review*, February 1970.
''Visconti Issue'' of *Cinema* (Rome), April 1970.
Bazin, André, in *What is Cinema? 2*, edited by Hugh Gray, Berkeley, 1971.
Korte, Walter, in *Cinema Journal* (Evanston, Illinois), Fall 1971.
New York Times, 7 January 1979.
Rosi, Francesco, ''En travaillant avec Visconti: Sur le tournage de *La terra trema*,'' in *Positif* (Paris), February 1979.
Lyons, D., ''Visconti's Magnificent Obsessions,'' in *Film Comment* (New York), March-April 1979.
Prudente, R., ''I proverbi di Verga nelle variazioni di Visconti,'' in *Cinema Nuovo* (Bari), October 1980.
''Le Néo-Réalisme Issue'' of *Cahiers Lumières* (Besançon), November 1980.
Decaux, Emmanuel, in *Cinématographe* (Paris), May 1981.
Aristarco, Guido, ''La vera storia di Visconti a Venezia,'' in *Cinema Nuovo* (Bari), vol. 43, no. 347, January-February 1994.
Rosi, Francesco, ''Entre *Le kid* et *La terre tremble*,'' in *Positif* (Paris), no. 400, June 1994.
Nagel, Josef, ''Der Rhytmus der Pferde,'' in *Film-Dienst* (Cologne), vol. 49, no. 7, 26 March 1996.
Lopate, Phillip, ''A Master Who Confounded the Categorizers: Luchino Visconti Was an Aristocrat Whose Politics Were Progressive, a Neo-Realist Who Delighted in Melodrama and Decadence,'' in *The New York Times*, 16 November 1997.

* * *

1948, the year of *La terra trema*, is also the year of the crucial postwar Italian elections. As neo-realism often has it, political history and film history coincide. Italians went to the polls for the vote that was to determine the course of Italian political life for many decades: the election of a Christian Democrat legislative majority. *La terra trema* owes its genesis in part to that coincidence.

In 1947 the director Luchino Visconti went to Sicily with two young and promising assistant directors—Francesco Rosi and Franco Zeffirelli—and two reported intentions: to record in a short documentary the historic moment of political and social renewal that was expected to result from the collective action of the workers and peasants and to realize the old ambition of adapting Verga (here specifically *I Malavoglia*) to the screen. Visconti stayed for seven months. During that time the original projects underwent radical transformation: the film that finally resulted reflects an amalgam of the stylistic and ideological directions of the two. Confronted by the structures and spirit of Aci Trezza (the village on the eastern coast of Sicily that had served as setting for Verga's novel), Visconti fashioned a film honest to the reality he found rather than to the dictates of current political theory interpreted by Northern political logic. The conditions for revolution were not present; the Sicilian proletariat was in no sense prepared to rise against exploitation and oppression. Whatever few attempts there might be were doomed to failure. Nor could a version faithful to Verga bear witness to the struggle of contemporary fishermen. A powerful, essentially hostile universe, against which man is locked in the eternal drama of hopeless battle, would no longer satisfy the exigencies of the new *verismo*. The enemy needed to be identified unmistakably as capitalism—its closed system, its greed.

The developing narrative intention demanded a form consonant with its ambition. The epic portrait of the fishermen of the Sicilian village would, it was projected, be followed by two other films of equal scope to complete a trilogy on the ''southern question''—the first on the struggles of Sicilian mine workers, the second on that of peasants. But finances determined that only ''the episode of the sea,'' the story of the Valastros, be told.

Young 'Ntoni, enraged by the crooked dealings of the fish wholesalers, exhilarated by a first expression of revolt, in love and eager to marry, realizes that as long as he, his grandfather and brothers fish from a boat that belongs to others, they will remain in the relative poverty they have always known, cheated of the just rewards of their labor. Counter to the ways of generations of his family and neighbors, 'Ntoni mortgages the family home in order to buy a boat. After an initial moment of promise, the family fortunes begin to decline. The boat is lost in a storm, and then, because of the hostility of the wholesalers and boat owners, the family falls into debt and then abject poverty. The bank appropriates the house, the grandfather dies, one brother flees with a shadowy stranger, a sister is disgraced, another loses her chance of happiness. In the end, 'Ntoni and his younger brothers return to the sea as hired hands on another's boat. 'Ntoni realizes that individual action can only lead to failure, that in collective action alone is there any hope for success.

Like the story, the actors of *La terra trema* were found in the place of the action. The Valastros, their friends and neighbors, are played by fishermen, bricklayers, wives and daughters of Aci Trezza. The language they speak is the dialect of their village, hardly more comprehensible to the speaker of standard Italian than to any other foreigner. A narrator advances the plot through voiceover comments, and above all through translations from the dialect of Aci Trezza into the national tongue of that part of Italy the Sicilian calls ''the continent.''

In the approximately 160 minutes of *La terra trema*, the camera remains confined to Aci Trezza, to the horizon accessible to it from the fixed position of the church square. The world of the camera is enclosed towards the sea by the two rocks that form a gate for the harbor, and towards land by the fields beyond the cluster of houses that constitute the village. This is the world of the inhabitants of Aci Trezza. Beyond it lie danger and death. Within the space, Aldo, Visconti's cinematographer (for whom *La terra trema* represented a remarkable first experience with moving pictures), integrated characters, decor and landscape into a startling cogent whole. Through a mise-en-scène which, as Bazin points out, for the first time demonstrated the possibilities of depth of field to exterior as well as interior locations, Aldo achieved that which Visconti had perceived as necessary to an understanding of the Valastros: their integrity with the village and the sea, their dependency on both.

—Mirella Jona Affron

DAS TESTAMENT DES DOKTOR MABUSE

See **DOKTOR MABUSE, DER SPIELER**

THE TEXAS CHAINSAW MASSACRE

USA, 1974

Director: Tobe Hooper

Production: Vortex. A Henkel-Hooper production; CFI Color; running time: 87 minutes (British version is 81 minutes); length: 7,290 feet. Released November 1974.

Executive producer: Jay Parsley; **producer:** Tobe Hooper; **screenplay:** Kim Henkel and Tobe Hooper, from their own story; **photography:** Daniel Pearl; **additional photography:** Tobe Hooper; **editors:** Sallye Richardson, Larry Carroll; **sound recordists:** Ted Nicolau, Buzz Knudson, Jay Harding; **sound re-recordist:** Paul Harrison; **art director:** Robert A. Burns; **make-up:** Dorothy Pearl and Dr. W. E. Barnes; **music:** Tobe Hooper, Wayne Bell; **narrator:** John Larroquette.

Cast: Marilyn Burns (*Sally Hardesty*); Allen Danziger (*Jerry*); Paul A. Partain (*Franklin Hardesty*); William Vail (*Kirk*); Teri McMinn (*Pam*); Edwin Neal (*Hitch-hiker*); Jim Siedow (*Old Man*); Gunnar Hansen (*Leatherface*); John Dugan (*Grandfather*); Perry Lorenz (*Pickup Driver*); Joe Bill Hogan (*Drunk*); Robert Courten (*Window Washer*); William Creamer (*Bearded Man*); John Henry Faulk (*Storyteller*); Jerry Green (*Cowboy*); Ed Guinn (*Cattle Truck Driver*).

Publications

Books:

McCarty, John, *Splatter Movies*, New York, 1984.

Newman, Kim, *Nightmare Movies: A Critical History of the Horror Movie from 1968*, London, 1988.

Articles:

Variety (New York), 6 November 1974.

Journal of Popular Film (Washington, D.C.), vol. 5, no. 2, 1976.

Phelps, Guy, in *Sight and Sound* (London), Spring 1976.

Pym, John, in *Monthly Film Bulletin* (London), December 1976.

Gow, Gordon, in *Films and Filming* (London), January 1977.

Greenspun, Roger, ''Carrie and Sally and Leatherface Among the Film Buffs,'' in *Film Comment* (New York), January-February 1977.

Jump Cut (Berkeley), March 1977.

Williams, Tony, in *Movie* (London), Winter 1977–78.

Alion, Y., ''Massacre a la tronconneuse,'' in *Image et Son* (Paris), June 1982.

Philbert, B., ''Le Syndrome Black et Decker,'' in *Cinématographe* (Paris), July-August 1982.

''Tobe Hooper,'' in *Film Dope* (London), November 1982.

Bedoya, R., ''Otros dos nombres de cine fantastico: Romero y Hooper,'' in *Hablemos de Cine* (Lima), March 1984.

Carson, Kit, '''Saw' Thru: Choice Cuts,'' in *Film Comment* (New York), July-August 1986.

Clover, C.J., ''Her Body, Himself: Gender in the Slasher Film,'' in *Representations*, vol. 20, Fall 1987.

O'Brien, Geoffrey, in *The New York Review of Books*, vol. 40, no. 8, 22 April 1993.

Olszewski, Mike, ''Those Little Ol' Cannibals From Texas,'' in *Filmfax* (Evanston), no. 52, September-October 1995.

Brottman, M., ''Stories of Childhood and Chainsaws,'' in *Cinefantastique* (Forest Park), vol. 27, no. 6, 1996.

Svehla, S., in *Midnight Marquee* (Baltimore), no. 53, Spring 1997.

Williams, D.E., ''Bringing Back *Texas Chainsaw*'s Buzz,'' in *American Cinematographer* (Hollywood), vol. 78, April 1997.

Charles, John, in *Video Watchdog* (Cincinnati), no. 38, 1997.

* * *

The sensationalist brilliance of Tobe Hooper's independently made, regional horror masterwork begins with its eye-grabbing, unforgettable title. It takes guts to be so blatant up-front. More guts, in fact, than are spilled in the movie. Nothing could possibly be as bloody and atrocious as the title and the poster (''who will survive, and what will be left of them?'') suggest *The Texas Chainsaw Massacre* is going to be. Hooper goes completely the other way: there are no close-ups of open wounds (the gore film trademark), and all the limb-lopping happens out of shot. This restraint could as easily be due to dissatisfaction with the obvious fakery of low budget gore as to innate good taste and humanity. Restraint is exhibited in no other aspect of Hooper's direction. Instead of the single mummy of *Psycho*, which was based on the same real-life murder case, there is a whole houseful of human and animal remains. Rather than Hitchcock's delicate, suspenseful manipulation, Hooper follows the lead of fellow independent George A. Romero and feeds the audience through a mangle of unrelieved horror and violence.

Deep in the heart of Texas—a country of dead armadilloes, violated corpses and disused slaughterhouses—a group of vapid teenagers unwisely enter an old, dark house. The apparent leading man wanders down a filthy corridor towards a red room walled with animal trophies. Suddenly, without any Hitchcockian overhead shot to pre-empt the shattering shock, Leatherface, a squealing, obese killer, appears from nowhere and smashes his head with a sledgehammer. Before the audience has had time really to register what has happened, Leatherface slams an unexpected, grating steel shutter across the corridor and finishes off the still-twitching boy out of sight. After the film has been blooded by its first kill, Leatherface rapidly slaughters three more of the teenagers, using a meathook, the sledge, and a buzzing chainsaw. Fleeing from Leatherface, Sally, the heroine by virtue of her survival, is repeatedly caught in brambles and bushes that the killer easily saws his way through. This physically exhausting chase sequence tops the opening of *Night of the Living*

The Texas Chainsaw Massacre

Dead as a filming of the universal nightmare. The girl winds up at the mercy of the Leatherface clan, a family whose proud boast is that they have ''always been in meat.''

Following Romero, Larry Cohen and Wes Craven and *pace* Robin Wood's critical writings on the genre, Hooper sees the American family as the true locus of the horror film. His degenerates are a parody of the typical sit com family, with the bread-winning, long-suffering Gas Man as Pop, the preening, bewigged, apron-wearing Leatherface as Mom, and the rebellious, long-haired Hitch as the teenage son. Their house is a similarly overdone, degraded mirror of the ideal home. Impaled clocks hang from the eaves, an armchair has human arms, and a hen is cooped up in a canary cage. With an unlikely burst of superhuman strength that drags the film momentarily back into the sloppy contrivances of a typical ''B'' picture, Sally breaks free and crashes through a window. On the main road, Hitch is messily run over and Sally clambers into the back of a speeding pickup truck. She survives, but as a blood-covered, shrieking, probably insane grotesque. The film fades on a long shot of the enraged Leatherface whirling his chainsaw in the air.

Chainsaw is only defensible as a nightmare. It bristles with socio-psychological sub-texts, but is so visceral there is barely time for an audience to breathe, let alone ponder what it's all about. We sympathise with the victims not because they are particularly pleasant but because the only other choice Hooper gives us is walking out. The killers are unknowable, barely characterised monsters who resist the insight Hitchcock and Anthony Perkins make us have into Norman Bates. Hooper's achievement is that he brings back to the movies an awareness of violent death lost through the slow motion sentimentalisation of *Bonnie and Clyde* and the contemptible distortion of TV cop shows. Unlike the notorious and comparable *I Spit On Your Grave, Chainsaw* is not a complete turn-off. If Hooper and his collaborators do not make their subject palatable, at least they succeed in justifying the film with its own panache. With its surprising amount of intentional comedy, the film is an important precursor of the horror comic style of Wes Craven's *The Hills Have Eyes*, Sam Raimi's *The Evil Dead* and Stuart Gordon's *Re-Animator*.

The film is also remarkable for its technical proficiency, especially by comparison with such inept precedents as Herschell Gordon Lewis's ''gore'' movies, with particularly outstanding sound editing, art direction and editing, and a clutch of effective, if necessarily one-note, performances. Sadly, despite the promise demonstrated in this, his first mainstream film, Hooper's subsequent career has not been distinguished: his work on *Poltergeist* was eclipsed by the input of co-executive-producer/screenwriter Steven Spielberg, his big-budget science fiction efforts *Lifeforce* and *Invaders From Mars* proved disastrous and his attempts to recreate the mood of *Chainsaw* in *Death Trap*, *The Funhouse* and *The Texas Chainsaw Massacre, Part 2* have been variably unfortunate.

—Kim Newman

THELMA AND LOUISE

USA, 1991

Director: Ridley Scott

Production: Pathe Entertainment; color, 35mm; running time: 123 minutes.

Producer: Mimi Polk; **executive producers:** Dean O'Brien and Callie Khouri; **screenplay:** Callie Khouri; **photography:** Adrian Biddle; **editor:** Thom Noble; **production designer:** Norris Spencer; **music:** Hans Zimmer; **costume design:** Elizabeth McBride.

Cast: Susan Sarandon (*Louise*); Geena Davis (*Thelma*); Harvey Keitel (*Hal*); Michael Madsen (*Darryl*); Brad Pitt (*hitchhiker*).

Awards: Oscar for Best Original Screenplay, 1992

Publications

Books:

Griggers, Cathy, ''Thelma and Louise and the Cultural Generation of the New Butch-Femme,'' *Film Theory Goes to the Movies*, edited by Jim Collins, Hilary Radner, Ava Preacher Collins, New York, 1993.

Horton, Andrew, ''Thelma and Louise,'' *Writing the Character Centered Screenplay*, Berkeley, 1994.

Sammon, Paul, *Ridley Scott: Close Up*, New York, 1999.

Articles:

''Should We Go Along for the Ride?'' in ''A Critical Symposium on *Thelma and Louise*,'' in *Cineaste*, Vol. XVIII, No. 4 (1991): responses from Pat Dowell, Elayne Rapping, Alice Cross, Sarah Schulman & Roy Grundmann.

Royal, Susan, ''An Interview with Geena Davis,'' in *American Premiere*, May/June 1991.

Denby, David, ''Road Warriors,'' in *New York*, 10 June 1991.

Carlson, Margaret, ''Is This What Feminism is All About?'' in *Time*, 24 June 1991.

Schickel, Richard, ''Gender Bender,'' in *Time*, 24 June 1991.

Dargis, Manshia, ''Roads to Freedom,'' in *Sight & Sound*, 1 July 1991.

Kauffman, Stanley, ''Two for the Road'' in *New Republic*, 1 July 1991.

Amory, Mark, ''Two Birds in the Bush,'' in *Spectator*, 13 July 1991.

Krupp, Charles, ''Why Thelma and Louise Scares the Devil Out of Some Men and Women,'' in *Glamour*, August 1991.

Bruning, Fred, ''A Lousy Deal for Woman and Man,'' in *Mclean's*, 12 August 1991.

Granier, Richard, ''Killer Bimbos,'' in *Commentary*, September 1991.

Baber, Asa, ''Guerrilla Feminism,'' in *Playboy*, October 1991.

Mais, Kathi, ''Women Who Murder Men,'' in *Ms*, November 1991.

Sharrett, Christopher, ''Phony Feminism Fails on the Silver Screen,'' in *USA TODAY*, November 1991.

Greenburg, Harvey, ''The Many Faces of Thelma and Louise,'' in *Film Quarterly*, Winter 1991.

Taylor, John, ''Men on Trial,'' in *New York*, 16 December 1991.

Knode, Helen, ''Against All Odds,'' in *Movieline*, June 1992.

Nadeau, Chantal, ''Are You Talking to Me?: Les enjeux du women's cinema pour un regard féministe,'' in *Cinémas* (Montreal), vol. 2, no. 2–3, Spring 1992.

Tasker, Yvonne, ''Criminelles: *Thelma et Louise* et autres délinquantes,'' in *Cinemaction* (Conde-sur-Noireau), no. 67, March 1993.

Feaster, Felicia, ''Montage,'' in *Jump Cut* (Berkeley), no. 38, June 1993.

Man, G., ''Gender, Genre, and Myth in *Thelma and Louise*,'' in *Film Criticism* (Meadville), vol. 18, no. 1, Fall 1993.

Chumo, Peter N., II: ''At the Generic Crossroads with *Thelma and Louise*,'' in *Post Script* (Commerce), vol. 13, no. 2, Winter-Spring 1994.

Briggs, J.B., ''Mantrack,'' in *Playboy*, vol. 41, February 1994.

Boozer, Jack, ''Seduction and Betrayal in the Heartland: *Thelma and Louise*,'' in *Literature/Film Quarterly* (Salisbury), vol. 23, no. 3, July 1995.

Katz, S.B., ''A Conversation with Callie Khouri,'' in *The Journal: Writer's Guild of America, West* (Los Angeles), vol. 8, September 1995.

Bundtzen, L.K., ''*Thelma and Louise*: A Story Not to Be Believed,'' in *The Communication Review*, vol. 1, no. 2, 1995.

Laderman, D., ''What a Trip: The Road Film and American Culture,'' in *Journal of Film and Video* (Atlanta), vol. 48, no. 1/2, 1996.

Premiere (Boulder), vol. 11, October 1997.

Willman, Chris, ''Ridley's Believe It or Not,'' in *Entertainment Weekly*, no. 409, 12 December 1997.

* * *

''Two women go on a crime spree'' was, as first time screenwriter Callie Khouri has explained, the original inspiration behind the script that became a film and then something of a legend around the world, *Thelma and Louise*.

Khouri walked off with an Oscar for Best Original Screenplay for her efforts, but more importantly, the film became a ''must see'' and ''must discuss'' event that thrilled, angered, empowered, and frightened various audiences. The long list of articles listed above is testimony itself to the interest this female outlaw buddy road film evoked at the time it came out (they even made it to the cover of *Time*) and since.

Why such attention? First, the story is a fascinating reworking of two male dominated genres: the American road film including

Thelma and Louise

everything from *Easy Rider* and *Badlands* to *Smokey and the Bandit* and *Two Lane Blacktop*, together with the outlaw buddy Western as especially embodied in *Butch Cassidy and the Sundance Kid.* The twist is that this time the buddies are women and instead of horses, we're dealing with the open highway through the Western landscape (breathtakingly shot by cinematographer Adrian Biddle).

Furthermore, Khouri's script pushes these genres beyond what we had come to expect of these formula films. What appears to be a simple light-hearted Southwestern working class female adventure suddenly turns dark, dangerous, and absolutely engrossing the moment Louise kills Thelma's would-be rapist in the country bar parking lot. What follows is their flight from the law and their men until they finally take hold of their own lives and make one strong assertive statement: their death as they drive off the rim of the Grand Canyon rather than face surrender and capture by the "men with guns" packed around them, much like the hundreds of Bolivian troops surrounding Butch and Sundance at the end of their tale.

The ending, however, points a telling difference with and from *Butch Cassidy* and other road movies. While it's never quite clear how aware Butch and Sundance are that they are about to die (and they certainly do not express this thought in their dialogue), Thelma and Louise absolutely agree on "Let's not get caught," sealed with soulful and joyful glances at each other. Ironically they embrace each other as friends and life itself, free and pure, before plunging to their chosen death.

The film is also memorable for the strong performances by Susan Sarandon as Louise and Geena Davis as Thelma. Rather than busty Hollywood pre-twenty sex kittens, Sarandon and Davis give full bodied character to these thirty and forty-something women who come to enjoy the role-reversing situations they find themselves in. Audiences screamed with delight along with this dynamic duo when, for instance, Thelma blows up the oil tanker truck in the desert.

That said, the men in the film also play their less than flattering roles with brio. Newcomer Brad Pitt is sexy and devilishly dangerous as the hitchhiker who gives Thelma her first orgasm and steals all their money. Harvey Keitel plays the exasperated and sympathetic cop well, while Michael Madsen is "the guy you love to hate" as Thelma's redneck husband, Darryl.

Ridley Scott would seem the most unlikely director for the project, since his *Blade Runner* and *Aliens* are futuristic and expressionistic high tech nightmares. But Scott, who told Khouri when he met her for the first time, "We will never change the ending!" succeeded in reaching into the story and highlighting the mythic dimensions of it. As director he is responsible for the overall exhilaration the film provides of the wide open spaces, the open road, movement and wonder as well as for directing ''non dialogue'' moments between Thelma and Louise which have an almost improvisational feel to them.

As cultural phenomenon, *Thelma and Louise* touched a number of important cords. As a straightforward film about relationships, it thumbed its nose at ever-escalating budget heavy special effects films in which character seemed unimportant. As a film about women written by a woman and co-produced by a woman (Mimi Polk), this work became a text that many women felt empowered them while threatening many men who felt the film was somehow too ''feminist.'' Khouri denies she is a card-carrying feminist and prefers simply to talk about the characterization of strong women—certainly Thelma and Louise as characters are not portrayed as women conscious of the women's movement. As a narrative that ends in death instead of the ''happy ending'' usually championed by Hollywood, the film forces us all to rethink certain American myths and the ideology underpinning them.

—Andrew Horton

THÉRÈSE DESQUEYROUX

France, 1962

Director: Georges Franju

Production: Filmel; black and white, 35mm; running time: 109 minutes, English version is 107 minutes. Released September 1962, Paris. Filmed at Franstudio, Paris Studio Cinéma, and in Bazas, Villandraut, and Uzeste.

Producer: Eugène Lépicier; **screenplay:** François Mauriac, Claude Mauriac, and Georges Franju; **dialogue:** François Mauriac, from his book; **photography:** Christian Matras; **editor:** Gilbert Natot; **sound:** Jean Labussière; **art director:** Jacques Chalvet; **music:** Maurice Jarre; **costume designer:** Lola Prussac.

Cast: Emmanuele Riva (*Thérèse*); Philippe Noiret (*Bernard*); Edith Scob (*Anne de la Trave*); Sami Frey (*Jean Azévédo*); Jeanne Perez (*Baslionte*); Renée Devillers (*Madame Victor de la Trave*); Richard Saint-Bris (*Hector de la Trave*); Lucien Nat (*Jérôme Larroque*); Hélène Dieudonné (*Aunt Clara*); Jacques Monod (*Duros*); Jean-Jacques Rémy (*Specialist*).

Awards: Venice Film Festival, Best Actress (Riva), 1962.

Publications

Books:

Lovell, Alan, *Anarchist Cinema*, London, 1962; reprinted, New York, 1975.

Armes, Roy, *French Cinema Since 1946: The Personal Style*, New York, 1966.

Durgnat, Raymond, *Franju*, Berkeley, 1968.

Vialle, Gabriel, *Georges Franju*, Paris, 1968.

Georges Franju: ciclo organizado pela Cinemateca Portuguesa com a alto patrocíno da Embaixada de França, em Lisboa, Lisbon, 1982.

Articles:

Beylie, Claude, ''Les Paradoxes de la fidelité,'' in *Cahiers du Cinéma* (Paris), January 1963.

Fieschi, Jean-Louis, and Andre Labarthe, ''Nouvel entretien avec Georges Franju,'' in *Cahiers du Cinéma* (Paris), November 1963.

Sarris, Andrew, in *Village Voice* (New York), 28 November 1963.

Gow, Gordon, in *Films and Filming* (London), March 1965.

Price, James, ''Undertones,'' in *London Magazine*, April 1965.

Milne, Tom, in *Sight and Sound* (London), Spring 1965.

Leahy, James, in *Movie* (London), Summer 1965.

Desch, Bernard, in *Film Society Review* (New York), February 1966.

''Franju Issue'' of *Image et Son* (Paris), March 1966.

MacLochlainn, A., in *Film Journal* (New York), Summer 1971.

Gow, Gordon, ''Franju,'' in *Films and Filming* (London), August 1971.

Barbaro, Nick, in *Cinema Texas Program Notes* (Austin), 27 April 1978.

Conrad, R., ''Mystery and Melodrama: A Conversation with Georges Franju,'' in *Film Quarterly* (Berkeley), Winter 1981–82.

Conrad, Randall, ''Mystery and Melodrama: A Conversation with Georges Franju,'' in *Film Quarterly* (Berkeley), vol. 35, 10 March 1982.

Brown, R., ''Georges Franju: Behind Closed Windows,'' in *Sight and Sound* (London), Autumn 1983.

''Franju Issue'' of *Avant-Scène du Cinéma* (Paris), April 1984.

* * *

The fiercely anarchic and irreligious Georges Franju might seem an improbable choice to film a novel of sin and expiation by France's leading Catholic novelist—unless in a spirit of mocking parody. Yet *Thérèse Desqueyroux* succeeds in being both an exceptionally faithful version of François Mauriac's novel and at the same time fully consistent with Franju's own attitudes and beliefs. Mauriac himself (who co-scripted together with Franju and Mauriac's son Claude, film critic of *Le Figaro littéraire*) was delighted with the final film. With good reason: *Thérèse Desqueyroux* can be well considered one of the most successful fusions of cinema and literature ever produced.

Aided by Christian Matras's sombrely beautiful monochrome photography, Franju superbly captures the stifling claustrophobia that permeates the novel. Even before she is literally imprisoned by her relatives, Thérèse is trapped: by the narrow confines of her class and provincial society, by the oppressive monotony of the pine forests of the Landes, and by her own inability to communicate the confused, passionate emotions that torment her. Her only release lies in destruction. She disrupts the relationship between her sister-in-law Anne and a young Jewish intellectual, spurred by the ambiguous jealousy which she feels for each of them. And she tries to poison Bernard, her husband (a masterly portrayal of bovine complacency from Philippe Noiret), simply in order ''to see in his eyes a momentary flicker of uncertainty.''

Events are presented entirely through Thérèse's eyes; it is her interior monologue we hear on the soundtrack during the complex sequence of flashbacks that occupies the greater part of the film. Yet Franju, despite evident sympathy for his heroine, never palliates her stubborn self-absorption, the source of much of her suffering. As

Thérèse, Emmanuele Riva gives a flawless performance as a woman destroyed by her own agonised sensibility, pacing restlessly about her house, snatching at the umpteenth cigarette, or glaring in mute fury at the back of Bernard's impassive head. Images of fire pervade the film: the conflagrations that threaten Bernard's beloved pines, the basis of his wealth; the fire that burns constantly, an ironic symbol of cosy domesticity, in the hearth of the Desqueyroux household; Thérèse's endless succession of cigarettes with which, in her captivity, she leaves burns on her bed-sheets.

Where Franju diverges from Mauriac is in the implications he draws from the events of the story—a subtle, but crucial difference. Mauriac's Thérèse must work out, through imprisonment and suffering, expiation for her sin—which is not so much attempted murder as spiritual pride. For Franju, though, Thérèse is a victim, one of the outsiders whom society cannot accommodate and therefore persecutes or destroys—the fate of many of his protagonists, from *La tête contre les Murs* to *La faute de l'Abbé Mouret*. Building on Mauriac's austere parable, Franju constructs his own humane vision: a lucid, grave and compassionate study of isolation, rich in visual metaphor, which vividly conveys the emotional turbulence beneath its cool surface. In Franju's intense, idiosyncratic, and often uneven output, *Thérèse Desqueyroux* stands as perhaps his finest, most fully achieved film.

—Philip Kemp

They Live by Night

THEY LIVE BY NIGHT

(The Twisted Road)

USA, 1948

Director: Nicholas Ray

Production: RKO Radio; black and white; running time: 96 minutes; length: 8,597 feet. Released in UK as *The Twisted Road*, 1948; US Release, 1949.

Executive producer: Dore Schary; **producer:** John Houseman; **screenplay:** Charles Schnee, from the novel *Thieves Like Us* by Edward Anderson; **photography:** George E. Diskant; **editor:** Sherman Todd; **art directors:** Albert S. D'Agostino, Al Herman; **music:** Leigh Harline.

Cast: Cathy O'Donnell (*Keechie*); Farley Granger (*Bowie*); Howard da Silva (*Chicamaw*); Jay C. Flippen (*T-Dub*); Helen Craig (*Mattie*); Will Wright (*Mobley*); Ian Wolfe (*Hawkins*); Harry Harvey (*Hagenheimer*).

Publications

Books:

McArthur, Colin, *Underworld USA*, London, 1972.
Kreidl, John, *Nicholas Ray*, Boston, 1977.
Silver, Alain, and Elizabeth Ward, editors, *Film Noir*, New York, 1979.
Roffman, Peter, and Jim Purdy, *The Hollywood Social Problem Films*, Bloomington, Indiana, 1981.
Masi, Stefano, *Nicholas Ray*, Florence, 1983.
Allen, Blaine, *Nicholas Ray: A Guide to References and Resources*, Boston, 1984.
Hillier, Jim, editor, *Cahiers du Cinéma 1: Neo-Realism, Hollywood, New Wave*, London, 1985.
Erice, Victor, and Jos Oliver, *Nicholas Ray y su tiempo*, Madrid, 1986.
Giuliani, Pierre, *Nicholas Ray*, Paris, 1987.
Wagner, Jean, *Nicholas Ray*, Paris, 1987.
Grob, Norbert, and Manuela Reichart, *Ray*, Berlin, 1989.
Eisenschitz, Bernard, *Nicholas Ray: An American Journey*, translated by Tom Milne, London, 1993.

Articles:

Monthly Film Bulletin (London), January 1949.
Winnington, Richard, in *News Chronicle* (London), 14 March and 4 June 1949.
Powell, Dilys, in *Sunday Times* (London), 5 June 1949.
Graham, Virginia, in *Spectator* (London), 10 June 1949.
Whitebait, William, in *New Statesman* (London), 11 June 1949.
Crowther, Bosley, in *New York Times*, 4 November 1949.
Sight and Sound (London), January 1950.
Cahiers du Cinéma (Paris), September 1951.
Ray, Nicholas, ''Story into Script,'' in *Sight and Sound* (London), Autumn 1956.

Bitsch, Charles, ''Entretien avec Nick Ray,'' in *Cahiers du Cinéma* (Paris), November 1958.

Agel, Henri, ''Nicholas Ray,'' in *New York Film Bulletin*, no. 11, 1961.

Bastid, Jean-Pierre, ''Nicholas Ray en Amerique,'' in *Etudes Cinématographiques* (Paris), Spring 1961.

Houston, Penelope, and John Gillett, ''Conversations with Nicholas Ray and Joseph Losey,'' in *Sight and Sound* (London), Autumn 1961.

Pül, Morten, in *Vises i Ugen* (Copenhagen), nos. 15–19, 1962.

Douchet, Jean, and Jacques Joly, ''Entretien avec Nick Ray,'' in *Cahiers du Cinéma* (Paris), January 1962.

Apra, Adriano, and others, ''Interview with Nicholas Ray,'' in *Movie* (London), May 1963.

Ray, Nicholas, in *Interviews with Film Directors*, edited by Andrew Sarris, New York, 1967.

Perkins, Victor, ''The Cinema of Nicholas Ray,'' in *Movie Reader*, edited by Ian Cameron, New York, 1972.

Gomery, Douglas, in *Velvet Light Trap* (Madison, Wisconsin), Summer 1972.

Wilmington, Michael, ''Nicholas Ray: The Years at RKO (Part One),'' in *Velvet Light Trap* (Madison, Wisconsin), no. 10, 1973.

Rosenbaum, Jonathan, ''Circle of Pain: The Cinema of Nicholas Ray,'' in *Sight and Sound* (London), Autumn 1973.

Biskind, Peter, ''Rebel Without a Cause: Nicholas Ray in the Fifties,'' in *Film Quarterly* (Berkeley), Fall 1974.

Kolker, Robert P., ''Night to Day,'' in *Sight and Sound* (London), Autumn 1974.

Cagle, Anthony, in *Cinema Texas Program Notes* (Austin), 2 April 1975.

Biskind, Peter, ''*They Live by Night* by Daylight,'' in *Sight and Sound* (London), Autumn 1976.

Renaud, Tristan, ''Nicholas Ray,'' in *Cinéma* (Paris), July-August 1979.

Langlois, G., ''Nicholas Ray (1911–1979),'' in *Avant-Scène du Cinéma* (Paris), 1 May 1981.

Cinema Texas Program Notes (Austin), 6 March 1985.

Listener (London), 22 January 1987.

Dominicus, Mar, ''Nicholas Ray,'' in *Skrien* (Amsterdam), no. 176, February-March 1991.

Kennedy, Harlan, ''The Melodramatists,'' in *American Film*, vol. 17, no. 1, January-February 1992.

De Bruyn, Olivier, ''*Les amants de la nuit*: Géométrie d'un regard,'' in *Positif* (Paris), no. 382, December 1992.

Anger, Cédric, ''Un poème de l'espace,'' in *Cahiers du Cinéma* (Paris), no. 505, September 1996.

* * *

Jean-Luc Godard once declared that ''the cinema is Nicholas Ray.'' In a like part-for-whole spirit we might well declare that *They Live By Night* is Nicholas Ray. Both director and film achieved cult status quickly, yet both remain elusive ''strangers'' to the critical traditions which do them honor.

They Live By Night was produced by John Houseman at RKO in 1947, was held back from distribution when the studio was purchased by Howard Hughes, was twice retitled, was first released in Britain in 1948, and was finally marketed to American audiences in 1949 as a film about ''Hot-rod teenagers living on the razor edge of danger.'' Perhaps because of its baroque production and marketing history, *They Live By Night* was included for showing (as François Truffaut reports) in the ''Festival du Film Maudit'' put on by André Bazin and the *Objectif 49* ciné-club at Biarritz in the late summer of 1949, effectively granting the film cult status. Likewise, though Ray had just begun his career as a Hollywood director—by contrast with *Cahiers du Cinéma* favorites like Hawks and Hitchcock—he was already an auteurist cult figure, especially so because Ray and the *Cahiers* critics (Rohmer, Truffaut, Godard, Rivette) were 1950s cultural contemporaries. As a result, Ray's films were less ''reviewed'' than ''previewed'' in the pages of *Cahiers*; and because Ray was not explicitly ''neglected,'' he has not yet inspired the full measure of scholarly attention devoted to more obvious ''reclamation'' projects. In that sense he remains a stranger to film criticism.

The odd point to make against this ''Ray as auteur cult figure'' background, then, is that *They Live By Night* is perhaps Ray's *least* neglected, most written-about film. Yet even here a note of ''strangeness'' intrudes because the attention paid to Ray's first feature often has less to do with the Nick Ray cult than with the *film noir* cult or the Robert Altman cult, the latter occasioned by Altman's *Thieves Like Us* (1974), derived from Edward Anderson's 1937 novel of the same title which Ray had adapted in making *They Live By Night*. Moreover, the aura of ''strangeness'' which lingers about *They Live by Night* is only heightened on these accounts because both it and *Thieves Like Us* are typically taken as members of a ''limit case'' subgenre of *film noir*. Where ''primary'' instances of the genre focus on ''haunted or brutal or stupid'' male characters (gangsters and/or detectives) at hazard in an equally haunted or brutal urban shadow-scape, the ''country thieves'' sub-genre shifts focus to an ''outlaw couple'' (Bowie and Keechie in Ray's film), typically presented more as victims than as denizens of the underworld, who seek to escape their *film noir* destiny by automotive flight to the countryside. (In *They Live By Night* ''nature'' is the Capra-esque auto-camp where the honeymooning Bowie and Keechie hide out to avoid the law, and to avoid Bowie's bank-robber cohorts, Chicamaw and T-Dub, who need Bowie to pull off another job.)

That *They Live By Night* fits so neatly under the *film noir* rubric has occasioned some interpretive neglect. John Francis Kreidl's *Nicholas Ray* (1977), for example, barely mentions the film. Given the fact that much of Ray's critical reputation rests on his innovative use of color and of the wide CinemaScope screen, this makes some sense. Yet the consensus is fairly clear that *They Live By Night*, despite being shot in black and white and in the standard Academy aspect-ratio, remains a strong example of Ray's elusive yet forceful mise-en-scène, which we might describe, in the light of Robin Wood's analysis of Ray's *Bigger Than Life*, as a unique combination of the ''ethnographic'' and the ''architectural.''

The ''ethnographic'' element of *They Live By Night* evokes Ray's typically sympathetic concern for ''sub-cultural'' groups set within or against a larger (usually American, usually contemporary) society. The ''persecution of the innocents'' narrative of *They Live By Night* certainly accords with this description, though so too does Ray's transcendent, Griffith-inspired close-up treatment of Bowie and Keechie. Yet the romanticism implicit in this graphic valorization of Bowie and Keechie's innocence is set in thematic place by a narration strategy, both visual and temporal, which asserts a broader, more abstract (in that sense ''architectural'') perspective on their plight.

Ray repeatedly, for example, frames Bowie and Keechie within or against box-like or bar-like architectural enclosures—car windows, a teller's cage, the frame of the "altar" at Hawkin's "marriage parlor," etc.—all of them suggesting a degree of entrapment to which Ray's naive characters remain blind. And Ray's narration also posits a gap between the viewer and his characters by anticipating the film's outcome; we know in advance that T-Dub's sister-in-law Mattie, in the hope of freeing her husband from prison, has informed the police that Bowie and Keechie are holed up in the auto-camp she bought with money from the gang's first holdup.

The question of this difference in knowledge or perspective, and the difference it finally makes, is the substance of the only sustained controversy regarding *They Live By Night*. *Film noir* readings of *They Live By Night* typically assume that the victimization visited upon Bowie and Keechie amounts to an indictment of those who victimize them, just as Lang's depiction of the doomed Eddie and Jo Taylor in *You Only Live Once* amounts to an indictment of the society whose agents hunt them down, at which point Ray's perspective is taken to reinforce or validate the lovers'. Peter Biskind, by contrast, while agreeing that Ray shares the vantage point of his characters, denies that their perspective is an effective critique of their (and our) society. Especially by contrast with the Anderson novel, Biskind contends, Ray's film downplays social criticism by assigning blame exactly to the naivete of the central characters, a naivete resulting in part from their view that the "normal" life of the culture, touchingly epitomized by the honeymoon utopia of the first auto-camp, is utopia enough.

If *They Live By Night* is viewed primarily in economic terms, Biskind's case is plausible. A number of the film's secondary characters *are* sympathetic capitalists sympathetically portrayed (e.g., the Zelton jeweler who sells Bowie the fateful watch). Soon from a more sustainedly feminist perspective, however, *They Live By Night* can be read as a fairly thorough critique of the alliance between masculine brutality and capitalist alienation, each a cause and a result of the other.

The film's chief figure of this patriarchal symptomology is Keechie's one-eyed uncle, Chicamaw, who is repeatedly associated with money and spending (the flashy clothes, the hot cars), with unnecessary brutality (the farmer he clubs in the opening sequence), and with incestuous sexual aggression (his come-on to Keechie, his brutal and unwelcomed attentions to Mattie). But two moments are crucial to our understanding of this element of *They Live By Night*. The first is when T-Dub, hitherto the more avuncular of Bowie's two elder partners, confirms the brutality of Chicamaw (Keechie's real uncle). When Bowie tries to beg off the last bank job, T-Dub turns suddenly hostile, tells Bowie he's "an investment" who's "gonna pay off," and then proceeds to slap Bowie about while Chicamaw holds Bowie by the shoulders. The second moment echoes the masculine brutality of the first. Against the background of a pin-up calender with the word "sales" prominent in the shot, a desperate Bowie grabs Mattie roughly by the shoulders, tells her she's "a thief" like him, and that the ailing Keechie is going to stay at Mattie's auto-camp whether Mattie likes it or not ("if you or anybody else don't like it, it's just too bad").

The film's first shot, to the accompaniment of a folk tune (its title and unsung first lines are equally apt and ironic: "I know where I'm going, and I know who's going with me"), is a romantic two-shot close-up of Bowie and Keechie, described in a series of on-screen titles as a boy and a girl "never properly introduced to the world we live in." A last title appears: "To tell their story"; it is followed by a surge of music. Bowie and Keechie both look suddenly up and off-frame, as if startled by some intrusion into the off-screen space of their world. Cut, then, to the credit sequence of *They Live By Night*, a powerful and aggressive helicopter shot of the car bearing Bowie, T-Rub, and Chicamaw, over which we see inscribed a variety of "commercial" markers ("RKO Radio Pictures A Dore Shary Presentation"). To propose the film as an "introduction" implies an epistemic gap, a known and an unknown. And to mark the unknown as a commercial product, to mark its introduction as and by a violent sonic and visual intrusion, is to accept a kind of social responsibility barely hinted at by (if finally consistent with) Bowie's eventual apology to Mattie. Though a pregnant Keechie does survive the ambush which kills Bowie, to live on in a perpetual night, the *couple* of Bowie and Keechie does not survive the "proper" knowledge they are threatened by in the film's first moments. On Biskind's reading this knowledge is not deadly, or nearly deadly enough. In *They Live By Night*, Ray shows that it is, and shows why. Whether it will continue to be deadly is ours to determine.

—Leland Poague

O THIASOS

(The Travelling Players)

Greece, 1975

Director: Theodoros Angelopoulos

Production: Giorgos Papalios; colour, 35mm; running time: 230 minutes. Distribution in the USA: New Yorker Films.

Producer: Giorgos Papalios; **screenplay:** Theodorous Antgelopoulos; **photography:** Giorgos Arvanitis; **editors:** Takis Davlopoulos and Giorgos Trantafiliou; **production design:** Mikes Karapiperis; **music:** Lukianos Kiliadonis with Fotos Lambrinos, Nena Mejdi, Dimitri Kamberidis, and Kostas Messaris.

Cast: Eva Kotamanidou (*Electra*); Aliki Georgoulis (*Mother*); Stratos Pachis (*Agamemnon*); Maris Vassiliou (*Clytemnestra*); Vangelis Kazan (*Aegisthos*); Petros Zarkadis (*Orestes*); Kiriakos Katrivanos (*Piladis*); Grigoris Evangelatos (*Poet*).

Awards: FIPRESCI Prize, Best Film Award, Cannes Film Festival, 1975; Best Film in "Forum," Berlin Film Festival, 1975; Salonika Festival, Greek Critics' Association, Best Film, Best Director, Best Screenplay, Best Actor, and Best Actress, 1975; Italian Critics Association, Best Film in the World for 1970–80, 1979.

Publications

Script:

Angelopoulos, Theodoros, *O Thiasos*, Themelio, 1975.

Books:

Arecco, Sergio, *Anghelopoulos*, La Nuova Italia, Florence, 1978.
Estève, Michel, *Theo Angelopoulos*, Paris, 1985.

O Thiasos

Ciment, Michel, and Héléne Tierchant, *Theo Angelopoulos*, Paris, 1989.
Kolovos, Nikos, *Theodoros Angelopoulos*, Athens, 1990.
Jacobsen, Wolfgang, *Theo Angelopoulos*, Munich, 1992.
Horton, Andrew, *Films of Theo Angelopoulos: A Cinema of Contemplation*, Princeton, 1997.
Horton, Andrew, editor, *Late Modernist: The Films of Theo Angelopoulos*, Westport, 1997.

Articles:

Tarr, Susan, and Hans Proppe, ''*The Travelling Players*: A Modern Greek Masterpiece,'' in *Jump Cut* (Berkeley), Summer 1975.
Pappas, P., ''Culture, History and Cinema: A Review of *The Travelling Players*,'' in *Cineaste* (New York), Winter 1976–77.
Horton, Andrew, ''*O Thiasos:* The Most Original and Important Film of 1975,'' *Pilgrimage*, April 1976.
Horton, Andrew, ''*O Thiasos:* Not So Much a Film as an Experience,'' *Athenian*, October 1977.
Horton, Andrew, ''Theodoros Angelopoulos and the New Greek Cinema,'' *Film Criticism* (Meadville, Pennsylvania), Fall 1981.
Wilmington, M., ''Angelopoulos: The Power and The Glory,'' in *Film Comment* (New York), Winter 1990.
Angelopoulous, Theo, and Sylvie Rollet, ''En guise de prologue: *Les voyage des comédiens*,'' in *Positif* (Paris), no. 383, January 1993.
Pigoullie, J. -F., ''*Le voyage des comédiens*,'' in *Télérama* (Paris), no. 2244, 13 January 1993.
Alberto, P., and others, in *Nosferatu* (San Sebastian), vol. 24, May 1997.

* * *

A young man in a uniform walks onto a stage during a performance and murders an older woman and man. The two actually die on stage. The curtain closes as the audience applauds wildly.

The moment takes place more than half way through Angelopoulos's third feature, *O Thiasos*, and in this one tightening of a narrative strand which until then had seemed quite loose and desperate, we see drama, history, myth, and personal destinies cross paths. For the young man is Orestes, an actor and young communist in northern Greece during World War II, and the woman and man he has killed are his mother, Clytemnestra, and her lover, Aegisthos, who betrayed his father, Agamemnon, to the Nazis who executed him.

At almost four hours in length and as a non-chronological investigation of Greek history during the troubled period 1939 to 1952, *O Thiasos* (*The Travelling Players*) might seem an unlikely film to be considered by many as the most important Greek film ever made, and one of the most significant films shot anywhere in the first 100 years of cinema's appearance.

When it appeared in Greece in 1975, Angelopoulos's poetic historical epic was seen by more Greeks than any other Greek film before it. Angelopoulos has his own distinctive cinematic style, but the immediate appeal to Greeks was the content: he dared to present a Marxist left-wing vision of modern Greek history, including the very painful Civil War of 1945–49 in which almost one million Greeks died. No filmmaker before him had dared to do so. Immediately his film became part of a national discourse in a way in which few films have. ''The reason that *O Thiasos* has had a tremendous impact in Greece,'' wrote an editor of *Athenian* at the time of its release, ''is its presentation of a view of events which has been stifled, rarely discussed in polite company, and ignored in official accounts of history.'' In short, the film suggests what historians such as Dominique Eudes and others have detailed, that many Greeks who were not necessarily communist, worked with the Partisans to help liberate Greece from the Germans and then continued to side with the communists because they were even more disenchanted by right wing monarchists who catered more often to foreign interests than to the needs of the people.

With the release of the film in Europe shortly after, *O Thiasos* swiftly became a cult film for cineastes from London to Rome and around Eastern Europe as well as a favourite for left-wing filmmakers concerned with how to represent ''history'' on screen successfully without become either too didactic or over simplified. (The appreciation of Angelopoulos's work was much slower in developing, but with the Museum of Modern Art Retrospective of his films in 1992, critical and public interest began to grow.) Bertolucci in Italy, for instance, claimed that his study of Italian history in *1900* (1977) was directly influenced by Angelopoulos's epic. And at the end of the decade of the 1970s, Italian critics went as far as to vote *O Thiasos* the most important film in the world for the whole decade.

Angelopoulos appeared in the late 1960s as the most talented among a new generation of Greek filmmakers who ironically came of age cinematically under the difficult restrictions of the military Junta's rule (1967–74). Having studied film in Paris, Angelopoulos was, like many of his generation, influenced by a variety of ''foreign'' sources including Japanese cinema, East European models, the French New Wave, and Italian neo-realism. And yet Angelopoulos set out clearly to explore what he has called ''the Other Greece'' that Greece itself and the outside world had never seen. This ''Other'' Greece Angelopoulos observes is clearly much more ''Balkan'' than Mediterranean, full of towns and villages becoming depopulated by the changes in modern history, neither fully living in the 20th century or in the past, heavily influenced by a legacy of 400 years under Turkish rule and not sure that any future exists. Angelopoulos's characters are most often shot as stationary figures in grey winter landscapes rather than as passionate lovers, dancers, and warriors seen in Michael Cacoyannis's *Zorba the Greek.* Angelopoulos intertwines Greek myth and history in provocative ways. The travelling players are a troupe of actors wandering the small towns and villages of northern Greece performing a simple melodrama about a shepherd girl, ''Golfo.'' But their drama is constantly interrupted by ''history'' as the Italians invade in 1939, followed shortly after by the Nazis, and, after the war, by the Civil War itself. The final ''invasion'' is seen to be that of the American influence on Greece. Yet the actions and characters are reflected off an ancient mythical heritage as we learn the individual troupe members are named Electra, Orestes, and Aegisthos as we have already seen. We are thus invited to consider the parallels and differences between these modern representatives of the *Oresteia* trilogy of Aeschylus.

Angelopoulos offers no simplistic ''update'' or direct one-on-one correspondence between ancient myths and modern realities. In fact, he forces us to consider how different modern history has become from the reality of ancient drama and myth. No gods enter the scene in *O Thiasos.* Instead we see a family and a troupe torn apart by political divisions as some choose to join partisan communist forces both during World War II and during the Civil War that followed, while others, especially, Aegisthos, the ''traitor,'' become collaborators with the Germans and with right wing forces after the war.

Beyond the content, however, is Angelopoulos's striking visual style.

He champions the long take shot in long distance. At a time when film, video, and television have converged to offer audiences faster and faster editing as seen especially on music videos and television commercials, Angelopoulos has turned to a more poetic and meditative cinema through the haunting camera work of Giorgos Arvanitis, with whom he has worked his entire career. One tracking shot, for instance, in *O Thiasos* follows a group of left-wing protesters down the street of a Greek town. But in that single shot lasting over six minutes, three different time periods are captured, suggesting visually, therefore, the link of ''protest'' which bridges time.

His framing in long shots also helps to de-dramatize each scene. In many ways, Angelopoulos's art is that of what he leaves out: extreme violence, passion, conflict. He also breaks up any possibility of smooth Hollywood styled linear narrative or character development by having the characters turn from time to time to the camera and deliver long monologues as if they have known us well some other time, some other place. When Agamemnon is betrayed (as in the myth and drama), he is taken before a Nazi firing squad. But before he dies, he faces the camera in close up and explains who he is, ending with the simple question, ''And who are you?'' We then cut to an extreme long shot on a grey winter morning as he is shot dead and crumples to the ground. As in the whole epic, this moment asks us to consider a life rather than observe a bloodbath using the conventions of cinematic war violence.

Finally, Angelopoulos's epic is a cyclical one. We begin and end with the travelling players, travelling. They are standing, suitcases in hand, at the same train station in the opening and in the closing of the film, yet the difference in years is significant: the opening shot is in 1952, after the war and the Civil War, while the closing shot is 1939, poised just before these momentous changes take place.

We have ended at the beginning and must leave the cinema asking ourselves if history merely repeats itself or if such an inverted circle suggests any possibility of advancement. Twenty years after the release of this landmark film, we still respond to the beauty and warnings enclosed in Angelopoulos's haunting text.

—Andrew Horton

THE THIN MAN

USA, 1934

Director: W. S. Van Dyke

Production: Metro-Goldwyn-Mayer Picture Corp.; black and white, 35mm; running time: 91 minutes. Released June 1934. Filmed during 12 days (some sources list 16 days) of 1934 in MGM studios.

Producer: Hunt Stromberg; **screenplay:** Albert Hackett and Francis Goodrich, from the novel by Dashiell Hammett; **photography:** James Wong Howe; **editor:** Robert J. Kern; **sound recordist:** Douglas Shearer; **art director:** Cedric Gibbons; **music:** Dr. William Axt; **costume designer:** Dolly Tree.

Cast: William Powell (*Nick Charles*); Myrna Loy (*Nora Charles*); Maureen O'Sullivan (*Dorothy Wynant*); Nat Pendleton (*John Guild*); Minna Gombell (*Mira Wynant Jorgensen*); Porter Hall (*MacCauley*); Cesar Romero (*Chris Jorgensen*); Henry Wadsworth (*Tommy*); William Henry (*Gilbert*); Harold Huber (*Nunheim*); Natalie Moorhead (*Julia*); Edward Brophy (*Morelli*); Edward Ellis (*Clyde Wynant*); Cyril Thornton (*Tanner*); Thomas Jackson (*Reporter*); Ruth Channing (*Mrs. Jorgensen*); Gertrude Short (*Gloria*); Walter Long (*Study Burke*); Clay Clement (*Quinn*); Rolfe Sedan (*Kellner*); Bert Roach (*Foster*); Creighton Hale (*Reporter*).

Publications

Books:

Cannom, Robert, *Van Dyke and the Mythical City of Hollywood*, Culver City, California, 1948.
Baxter, John, *Hollywood in the Thirties*, New York, 1968.
Nolan, William, *Dashiell Hammett: A Casebook*, Santa Barbara, 1969.
Higham, Charles, *Hollywood Cameramen*, Bloomington, Indiana, 1970.
Everson, William K., *The Detective in Film*, Secaucus, New Jersey, 1972.
Cawelti, John, *Adventure, Mystery, Romance*, Chicago, 1976.
Quirk, Lawrence J., *The Films of Myrna Loy*, Secaucus, New Jersey, 1980.
Francisco, Charles, *Gentleman: The William Powell Story*, New York, 1985.
Kotsilibas-Davis, James, and Myrna Loy, *Myrna Loy: Being and Becoming*, New York, 1987.
Van Dyke, W.S., *W.S. Van Dyke's Journal: White Shadows in the South Seas, 1927–1928: and Other Van Dyke on Van Dyke*, Lanham, 1996.

Articles:

New York Times, 30 June 1934.
Variety (New York), 3 July 1934.
New Republic (New York), 25 November 1934.
Stage (New York), January 1937.
Jacobs, Jack, ''William Powell,'' in *Films in Review* (New York), November 1958.
Ringgold, Gene, ''Myrna Loy,'' in *Films in Review* (New York), February 1963.
Braun, E., ''Myrna Loy on Comedy,'' in *Films and Filming* (London), March 1968.
Dumont, Hervé, ''Woody S. Van Dyke et l'age d'or d'Hollywood,'' in *Travelling* (Lausanne), no. 37, 1973.
Sanders, Gregory, in *Cinema Texas Program Notes* (Austin), no. 1, 1975.
Dumont, Hervé, ''W. S. Van Dyke (1889–1943),'' in *Anthologie du cinéma*, Paris, 1975.
Black, Louis, in *Cinema Texas Program Notes* (Austin), 18 January 1978.
Roddick, Nick, in *Magill's Survey of Cinema 4*, Englewood Cliffs, New Jersey, 1980.
''James Wong Howe,'' in *Film Dope* (London), November 1982.
Tessier, Max, in *Image et Son* (Paris), November 1982.
Buckley, M., ''A Tribute to Myrna Loy,'' in *Films in Review* (New York), May 1985.
Reid's Film Index (Wyong), no. 5, 1990.
Szebin, Frederick C., ''Hammett Rewritten,'' in *Films in Review* (New York), vol. 45, no. 7–8, July-August 1994.
Drees, R., ''*The Thin Man*: Dashiell Hammett and Hollywood,'' in *Films in Review* (New York), vol. 46, September/October 1995.

* * *

The Thin Man is one of the brightest and most sophisticated comedy/mysteries of the 1930s. Based on Dashiell Hammett's novel of the same name, the film combines the elements of a classic detective story with overtones of the screwball comedies that had their heyday during the Depression. The result is a lighthearted murder mystery featuring perhaps the most engaging married couple in Hollywood's history: Nick and Nora Charles.

Screenwriters Frances Goodrich and Albert Hackett capture both the wit and the style of Hammett's original story. As is true of all good mysteries, strong character development is central to *The Thin Man*'s success. In the wealthy, fun-loving Charleses, film-going audiences

The Thin Man

soon discovered something that was quite new by Hollywood standards—a husband and wife who thoroughly enjoyed their marriage. The reverent tones with which the film industry had previously addressed the institution of matrimony had left little room for the playfulness and high spirits that mark Nick and Nora's relationship. For them, marriage is clearly an extended love affair, and the film conveys the enviable combination of companionship and romance that sets the pair apart from their staid counterparts in other films.

Dashiell Hammett is said to have modeled the Charleses on his own long-standing relationship with playwright Lillian Hellman, but for film enthusiasts the characters have become inextricably tied to the performers who brought them life. For both William Powell and Myrna Loy, *The Thin Man* represented a critical career milestone. Each had worked extensively in silent films, Powell playing dapper villains and Loy finding herself cast repeatedly as exotic vamps. The film's popular success, however, established Powell as a wisecracking, debonair leading man, while Loy's delightful portrayal of Nora was the beginning of her reign as Hollywood's "ideal wife." Over the next decade, the two would recreate their roles in five "Thin Man" sequels, and although none of the subsequent films ever quite equalled the effortless charm of the original, Powell and Loy remained perfectly paired throughout the series.

Goodrich and Hackett's script must share credit for *The Thin Man*'s breezy style and rapid pacing with the direction of W. W. "Woody" Van Dyke. Although Van Dyke's work has not won him a place alongside the John Fords and Howard Hawkses of the American cinema, he enjoyed a reputation during the 1930s as a highly professional director whose films generally proved popular at the box office. His efficient, no-nonsense working earned him the nickname "One-Take Woody," and he completed *The Thin Man* in a remarkable 12 days. Given its tight shooting schedule, it is no surprise that the finished film reflects a heady sense of energy and élan.

In the years since its release, *The Thin Man* has spawned a number of imitators, including several successful television series. Connoisseurs of the genre, however, return again and again to Nick and Nora—and their faithful Airedale, Asta—drawn by the appeal of a film that remains fresh and original after 50 years.

—Janet E. Lorenz

THINGS TO COME

UK, 1936

Director: William Cameron Menzies

Production: London Film Productions; black and white, 35mm; running time: 130 minutes, a shorter version of 96 minutes also exists. Released 1936 by United Artists.

Producer: Alexander Korda; **screenplay:** H. G. Wells and Lajos Biro, from Wells's novel *The Shape of Things to Come*; **photography:** Georges Perinal; **editor:** Charles Crichton; **art director:** Vincent Korda; **music:** Arthur Bliss; **special effects:** Ned Mann; **special camera effects:** Edward Cohen and Harry Zech; **costume designers:** John Armstrong, René Hubert and the Marchioness of Queensbery.

Cast: Raymond Massey (*John Cabal/Oswald Cabal*); Ralph Richardson (*The Boss*); Edward Chapman (*Pippa Passworthy/Raymond Passworthy*); Margaretta Scott (*Roxana Black*); Sir Cedric Hardwicke (*Theotocopulos*); Maurice Bardell (*Dr. Harding*); Sophie Stewart (*Mrs. Cabal*); Derrick de Marney (*Richard Gordon*); Ann Todd (*Mary Gordon*); Pearl Argyle (*Katherine Cabal*); Kenneth Villiers (*Maurice Passworthy*); Ivan Brandt (*Mitani*); Anthony Holles (*Simon Burton*); Allan Jeayes (*Mr. Cabal*); John Clements (*Airman*); Pickles Livingston (*Horrie Passworthy*); Patricia Hilliard (*Janet Gordon*); George Sanders (*Pilot*).

Publications

Script:

Wells, H. G., and Lajos Biro, in *The Prophetic Soul: A Reading of H. G. Wells's Things to Come together with his Film Treatment, Whither Mankind? and the Post Production Script*, by Leon Stover, Jefferson, North Carolina, 1987.

Books:

Balcon, Michael, and others, *20 Years of British Films, 1925–45*, London, 1947.

Tabori, Paul, *Alexander Korda*, New York, 1966.

Johnson, William, editor, *Focus on Science Fiction*, Englewood Cliffs, New Jersey, 1972.

Kulik, Karol, *Alexander Korda: The Man Who Could Work Miracles*, London, 1975.

Barsacq, Leon, *Caligari's Cabinet and other Grand Illusions: A History of Film Design*, New York, 1976.

Parish, James Robert, *The Science Fiction Pictures*, Metuchen, New Jersey, 1977.

Korda, Michael, *Charmed Lives*, London, 1979.

Stover, Leon E., *The Prophetic Soul: A Reading of H.G. Wells's Things to Come, Together with His Film Treatment, Whither Mankind? and the Postproduction Script*, Jefferson, 1987.

Frayling, Christopher, *Things to Come*, London, 1995.

O'Connor, Garry, *Ralph Richardson: An Actor's Life*, New York, 1999.

Articles:

Greene, Graham, in *Spectator* (London), 28 February 1936.

New Statesman and Nation (London), 29 February 1936.

Variety (New York), 4 March 1936.

Time (New York), 6 April 1936.

New York Times, 18 April 1936.

Campbell, Colin, "The Producer: Sir Alexander Korda," in *Sight and Sound* (London), Summer 1951.

Gilliat, Sidney, Graham Greene, and Ralph Richardson, "Sir Alexander Korda," in *Sight and Sound* (London), Spring 1956.

Stein, Jeanne, "Raymond Massey," in *Films in Review* (New York), August-September 1963.

Cowie, Peter, "Korda," in *Anthologie du cinéma 6*, Paris, 1965.

Roman, Robert, "Cedric Hardwicke," in *Films in Review* (New York), January 1965.

Coulson, Alan, "Ralph Richardson," in *Films in Review* (New York), October 1969.

McFeeley, Connie, in *Magill's Survey of Cinema 4*, Englewood Cliffs, New Jersey, 1980.

American Cinemeditor (Los Angeles), Summer-Fall 1983.

Reid's Film Index (Wyong), no. 15, 1995.

Burr, Ty, in *Entertainment Weekly*, no. 335, 12 July 1996.

* * *

One of the most characteristic aspects of science fiction in the 1930s is its being influenced by another fantastic genre—horror—so intensively that in many cases it is hardly possible to establish a dividing line between these two categories of fantastic creation. There are very few movies which are exclusively devoted to considering scientific and societal evolution in terms of an extrapolation into the future. An exception is the English film of 1936, *Things to Come*. The book on which the film is based, *The Shape of Things to Come*, is a speculative continuation of H. G. Wells's *The Outline of History* and is, according to the author, "basically an imaginative discussion about social and political forces and possibilities." The story of the movie covers a period of 100 years of civilization. It begins in 1940, in a time permeated by fear of an imminent war which finally explodes and lasts 25 years. During that period, the entire globe is devastated and almost all of mankind exterminated. However, the human will and spirit remain active, and so at the end of the book, in 2040, a completely different world is depicted, in which human hardships have been eliminated and man is assured of all his material as well as mental needs. Progress is unrelenting as mankind plans to leave Mother Earth and take over the universe.

Wells's work fascinated and still fascinates readers by its original images of the future. Wells himself, however, valued more highly his

Things to Come

scientific studies than his fiction, and so the speculative aspect of *Things to Come* receives more attention than the story. The plot of the film proceeds from Wells's assumption that a war will mean the end of the Western civilization. The structure of the story is based on a conflict of two forces always present in humanity's evolution. One of them represents chaos and regression and encourages man's barbaric nature; and the other represents order, healthy reasoning, scientific progress. When these forces collide, science and intellect win although this victory will always be threatened by other pressures, due to our imperfect understanding of how best to invest our human resources.

Wells, who wrote the screenplay, was not able to transfer his ideas, opinions, or doubts into a form which would utilize all the components of the psychic process involved during the perception of a movie. Only the spectator's intellect and reason are called upon, his emotions remain untouched. In the film, the characters are not people of flesh and blood; they are merely symbols of various ideological convictions. They do not furnish the spectator with an opportunity to penetrate into the soul and mind in order to identify with them. Director William Cameron Menzies, who was working with actors for the first time, was unable, because of his lack of experience, to influence the movie's screenplay as much as the production design. He concentrates fully on the visual aspect of the movie, its structuralizations, sets, and special effects. From this point of view, the film attracted well-merited attention and, till the present time, has kept its place in film history precisely for its remarkable formal design. Cameron Menzies thoughtfully composed the movie's space; his plastic fantasy triumphs especially in his presentation of a city of the future where he exhibits a sense of balance and visual contrast. The sets dominate the action as well as the characters who, deprived of their psychological hinterland, become the compositions's style-creating element. The refined sophistication of Ned Mann's special effects and his extraordinary miniature models and buildings give the impression of a ''life size'' dimension, and create a sense of unity of space and man. Some objects look real and concrete although they are a product of more fantasy, such as the machine by which the new city is built, or the attack of delta-winged airplanes which he used despite the protests of contemporary experts. Wells in his screenplay revealed a spirit of vision not only in details but also in basic principle—he announced the coming of the Second World War. The English public received the idea of an air attack on London with laughter; after a few years, however, this fiction became reality.

The filming of this ambitious movie devoured a significant sum of money. The producer never recovered his investment, but *Things to Come* remains a testament to its creator's thoughtful examination of mankind's path into the future, and it occupies an important place in the history of the science fiction genre.

—B. Urgošíkova

THE THIRD MAN

UK, 1949

Director: Carol Reed

Production: British Lion Films; black and white, 35mm; running time: 93 minutes, another version exists at 104 minutes. Released 1949. Filmed on location in Vienna.

Producers: Carol Reed with Hugh Perceval; **screenplay:** Graham Greene; **photography:** Robert Krasker; **editor:** Oswald Hafenrichter; **art director:** Vincent Korda; **music:** Anton Karas.

Cast: Joseph Cotten (*Holly Martins*); Alida Valli (*Anna Schmidt*); Trevor Howard (*Major Calloway*); Orson Welles (*Harry Lime*); Bernard Lee (*Sergeant Paine*); Ernst Deutsch (*Baron Kurtz*); Erich Ponto (*Dr. Winkel*); Wilfrid Hyde-White (*Crabbin*); Siegfried Breuer (*Popesco*); Paul Hoerbiger (*Harry's porter*); Hedwig Bleibtreu (*Anna's old woman*); Frederick Schreicker (*Hansel's father*); Herbert Halbik (*Hansel*); Jenny Werner (*Winkel's maid*); Nelly Arno (*Kurtz's mother*); Alexis Chesnakov (*Brodsky*); Leo Bieber (*Barman*); Paul Smith (*M.P.*).

Awards: Best Film, Cannes Film Festival, 1949; Oscar for Best Cinematography (black and white), 1950.

Publications

Script:

Greene, Graham, *The Third Man*, London and New York, 1968; as *The Third Man: A Film by Graham Greene and Carol Reed*, New York, 1984.

Books:

Higham, Charles, *The Films of Orson Welles*, Berkeley, 1971.

Phillips, Gene D., *Graham Greene: The Films of His Fiction*, New York, 1974.

Parish, James Robert, and Michael Pitts, *The Great Gangster Pictures*, Metuchen, New Jersey, 1976.

McBride, J., *Orson Welles: Actor and Director*, New York, 1977.

Bergala, Alain, and Jean Narboni, editors, *Orson Welles*, Paris, 1982.

Leaming, Barbara, *Orson Welles: A Biography*, New York, 1985.

Knight, Vivienne, *Trevor Howard: A Gentleman and a Player*, London, 1986.

Taylor, John Russell, *Orson Welles: A Celebration*, London, 1986.

Moss, Robert F., *Films of Carol Reed*, New York, 1987.

Wapshott, Nicholas, *The Man Between: A Biography of Carol Reed*, London, 1990.

Wapshott, Nicholas, *Carol Reed: A Biography*, New York, 1994.

Drazin, Charles, *In Search of the Third Man*, New York, 2000.

Articles:

Variety (New York), 7 September 1950.

Wright, Basil, ''A Study of Carol Reed,'' in *The Year's Work in the Film*, edited by Roger Manvell, London, 1950.

Sequence (London), New York, 1950.

Time (New York), 6 February 1950.

Life (New York), 13 March 1950.

De La Roche, Catherine, ''A Man with No Message,'' in *Films and Filming* (London), December 1954.

Manvell, Roger, in *The Film and the Public* (London), 1955.

Sarris, Andrew, ''Carol Reed in the Context of His Time,'' in *Film Culture* (New York), no. 10, 1956.

Sarris, Andrew, in *Films and Filming* (London), September and October 1957.

Fawcett, Marion, ''Sir Carol Reed,'' in *Films in Review* (New York), March 1959.

Denby, David, in *Favorite Movies: Critics' Choice*, edited by Philip Nobile, New York, 1973.

Voight, Michael, ''Pictures of Innocence: Sir Carol Reed,'' in *Focus on Film* (London), Spring 1974.

Gomez, J. A., ''*The Third Man*: Capturing the Visual Essence of Literary Conception,'' and ''Narrative Structure in *The Third Man*,'' by W. F. Van Wert, in *Literature/Film Quarterly* (Salisbury, Maryland), Fall 1974.

Carpenter, Lynette, ''I Never Knew the Old Vienna: Cold War Politics and *The Third Man*,'' in *Film Criticism* (Edinboro, Pennsylvania), 1978.

Classic Film Collector (Indiana, Pennsylvania), July 1979.

Fineman, Daniel D., in *Magill's Survey of Cinema 4*, Englewood Cliffs, New Jersey, 1980.

Palmer, J. W., and M. M. Riley, ''The Lone Rider in Vienna: Myth and Meaning in *The Third Man*,'' in *Literature/Film Quarterly* (Salisbury, Maryland), no. 1, 1980.

Weemaes, G., in *Film en Televisie* (Brussels), November 1982.

Listener (London), 18 December 1986.

Driver, P., ''A Third Man Cento,'' in *Sight and Sound* (London), no. 1, 1989–90.

Chatman, S., ''Who is the Best Narrator? The Case of *The Third Man*,'' in *Style* (Toronto), no. 2, 1989.

McFarlane, B., in *Metro Magazine* (St. Kilda West), no. 92, Summer 1993.

Man, G. K. S., ''*The Third Man:* Pulp Fiction and Art Film,'' in *Literature/Film Quarterly* (Salisbury, Maryland), no. 3, 1993.

Kemp, Philip, in *Sight & Sound* (London), vol. 4, no. 4, April 1994.

Thompson, D., ''Reeds and Trees,'' in *Film Comment* (New York), vol. 30, July/August 1994.

Reid's Film Index (Wyong), no. 16, 1995.

Naremore, J., ''High Modernism and Blood Melodrama: The Case of Graham Greene,'' in *Iris*, no. 21, Spring 1996.

The Third Man

Raskin, R., ''Closure in *The Third Man*: On the Dynamics of an Unhappy Ending,'' in *P.O.V.*, vol. 2, December 1996.

Mandolini, C., in *Séquences* (Haute-Ville), no. 189/190, March/June 1997.

Premiere (Boulder), vol. 10, June 1997.

Gribble, Jim, ''*The Third Man*: Graham Green [sic] and Carol Reed,'' in *Literature/Film Quarterly* (Salisbury), vol. 26, no. 3, July 1998.

Wollen, Peter, ''The Vienna Project,'' in *Sight & Sound* (London), vol. 9, no. 7, July 1999.

* * *

Carol Reed's *The Third Man* is a remarkably enigmatic film in many respects, drawing on a range of talents and traditions so broad as to raise the question of authorship in a particularly acute form. The film owes debts to the Grierson/Rotha tradition of British documentary film, as well as to the post-war neo-realism of Rossellini's *Roma Città Aperta* and DeSica's *Ladri di Biciclette*; like its Italian predecessors, *The Third Man* studies the effects of post-war economic and social corruption within the context of a once grand though now rubble-strewn European capital (Rome for the neo-realists, Vienna for Reed). And debts are also owed to the moralistic detective fiction of Graham Greene (who wrote the original screenplay), as well as to the similarly Catholic tradition of Hitchcock's pre-war British thrillers (e.g., *The 39 Steps*). But overshadowing all of these influences is the presence of Orson Welles in the role of Harry Lime. Welles wrote much of his own dialogue; as in *Citizen Kane* he is once again paired with Joseph Cotten, who plays his boyhood friend Holly Martins; even the film's overtly stylized use of camera angles, of expressionist lighting, of stairways, owes much to the Wellesian style. Indeed, *The Third Man* is very much a film *about* authorship, or about art more generally, and the issue raised is very much one of artistic ethics. Thus the film's three major characters are all artists of one sort or another—and the range of their actions and motives helps to define our sense of the film's theme.

Holly Martins, for instance, is a Western novelist (when asked about artistic influences he cites Zane Grey) whose initial interest in the investigation of the ''death'' of Harry Lime involves his conviction that Harry was a victim of ''the sheriff'' (i.e., the British military police) whose death Holly (''the lone rider'') must avenge. Later he even says he is planning a new novel, based on fact, to be called ''The Third Man.'' Likewise Anna—Harry's girlfriend (whom he betrays to the Russians)—is an actress; and her willingness to betray Harry involves both ignorance (she doesn't know he betrayed her) and a melodramatic sense of her role as the doomed man's mistress (she even sleeps in Harry's pajamas).

But clearly the film's central figure, its central artist, is Harry Lime himself. The complex relationship of money and art is a primary theme of the Wellesian cinema—and in *The Third Man* it finds vivid expression in the *use* Lime makes of art, to throw the occupation authorities off his trail and to further his traffic in black market drugs (diluted penicillin especially). Hence Lime plans and stage-manages his own death, even playing a part as ''the third man'' who helps to carry the body (actually, that of an implicated associate) from the street where it was run down by a truck; and he calls his boyhood friend, Holly Martins, to Vienna to serve as his stand in. The connection of art and corruption is confirmed in Harry's famous ''cuckoo clock'' speech wherein the political intrigues of the Borgias are correlated with the aesthetic triumphs of Michelangelo and da Vinci. There is something remarkably childish and self-indulgent about Lime's perspective—as evidenced by the fact that he utters the line at an amusement park. But Holly gets another view of childhood, when Major Calloway (Trevor Howard) takes him to the hospital ward populated by Lime's victims, all children; and ''The Third Man,'' as Holly eventually ''rewrites'' the story, becomes a parable of social responsibility. It is Holly who finally pulls the trigger and puts the wounded Lime out of his cynical misery.

—Leland Poague

38 - AUCH DAS WAR WIEN

(38 - Vienna Before the Fall)

Austria, 1986

Director: Wolfgang Glück

Production: SATEL-Fernseh-und Filmproduktionsges.m.b.H, Vienna/ Almaro Film Munich; color, 35 mm, running time: 97 minutes. Released 4 September 1986 in Venice (''Venezia speciali'').

Producers: Michael Wolkenstein, Boris Otto Dworak; **screenplay:** Wolfgang Glück, Lida Winiewicz (collaboration on dialogues), based on the novel by Friedrich Torberg, *Auch das war Wien;* **photography:** Gerhard Vandenberg; **editor:** Heidi Handorf; **art director:** Herwig Libowitzky; **music arranger:** Bert Grund; **sound:** Werner Böhm.

Cast: Tobias Engel (*Martin Hofmann*); Sunnyi Melles (*Carola Hell*); Heinz Trixner (*Toni Drechsler*); Romuald Pekny (*Sovary*); Ingrid Burkhard (*Frau Schostal*); Lukas Resetarits (*cab driver*); Lotte Ledl (*Carola's mother*).

Awards: Academy Award nomination for best foreign language film, 1986; Austrian Film Prize, 1987.

Publications

Books:

Ernst, Gustav, and Gerhard Schedl, editors, *Nahaufnahmen: Zur Situation des österreichischen Kinofilms*, Vienna and Zurich, 1992.

Articles:

Austrian Film Commission, *Austrian Films 1981–1986 and Ten Selected Films 1976–80*, Vienna, 1988.

* * *

The Austrian director Wolfgang Glück (born 1929) created *38* at a time when it was not yet common in film or literature for Austrians to address the Nazi past. Except for Peter Turrini's six-part television series *Alpensaga* (1976–1980), the topic was generally avoided since Austria had been deemed the first victim of Hitler, obviating any need to discuss the issue of war guilt. In this sense the film, released in 1986, served as prelude to the widespread media coverage and the many books, articles, and international conferences that appeared in 1988, on the occasion of the fiftieth anniversary of the Anschluss (the political unification of Nazi Germany and Austria).

Glück's filmscript, written with Lida Winiewiecz, is based on the novel *Auch das war Wien* by Friedrich Torberg (1908–1979). (Glück had made a very successful television film from Torberg's most famous novel, *Der Schüler Gerber* in 1981.) Torberg had emigrated to the United States during World War II and returned to become one of the most influential personalities in Austrian cultural life. A fervent anti-Communist, he joined with Hans Weigel during the Cold War to mount the infamous ''Brecht Boykott.'' Later it was found that his magazine *Forum* was secretly financed by the United States. Torberg had written *Auch das war Wien* before he left Austria, but he decided against publishing this book, which was critical of Vienna, because he planned to return and work in Austria. His widow discovered the manuscript after his death and published it.

The film presents the political events surrounding the Anschluss in March of 1938 through the lives of Carola Hell, a popular young actress at the prestigious Theater in der Josefstadt, and Martin Hofmann, the Jewish journalist she plans to marry. When we encounter the couple in the lovely springtime weather their future is full of promise. They are determined to stay clear of politics. Yet in the climate of the time, nobody of her prominence or his religion can remain apolitical. Although Martin's journalist friend, Drechsler, calls to inform them that the Nazis plan to take over Austria soon, they concentrate on their work and their private happiness and dismiss the warnings.

As they did with many writers, artists, and film people, the Nazis try to win Carola over to their cause by showing her the benefits of cooperation. They invite her to make a film and to perform in Berlin, and, despite her misgivings, she feels she must oblige them in the interest of her career, for the Nazis control the theaters in Austria. She is treated royally in Berlin and yet knows she is constantly under surveillance. She gets a taste of Nazi power when she openly criticizes the harassment of Jews and is detained for an educational ''briefing,'' which includes the suggestion that it is not advisable for her to have a Jewish friend.

The film shows Chancellor Schuschnigg's efforts to forestall Hitler by calling for a national referendum on the question of the Anschluss on March 13. Despite his efforts, the occupation begins on March 11. Carola, who has disclosed that she is pregnant, and Martin are attending a cabaret with friends when the news comes, and they discover the Nazis taking over the city. The film reaches its dramatic climax in scenes showing the panicked and frenetic attempts of Austrians to flee the country before the borders are closed. Glück excellently conveys the incredible rapidity of the takeover, thanks to the lengthy preparation and cooperation of Austrian National Socialists, who now no longer have to hide their affiliation. Carola and Martin head for the train station to travel to Prague, still a free city. She is allowed to board the train, but he is prevented from accompanying her. Guards haul him away and beat him. He seeks refuge with friends, but while all are sympathetic, they are too afraid to help him. Martin accepts his fate and walks along the streets until he is arrested.

1938 effectively dramatizes the events leading up to the German annexation of Austria, showing how the Nazis infiltrated the country's organizations, bribed the writers and artists, undermined the government, and intimidated the populace to prepare the way for the takeover. It also shows how the public tried to ignore the Nazi threat, and the way many Jews overlooked the increasingly anti-Semitic atmosphere and actions, until it was too late to stop the German occupation.

—Gertraud Steiner Daviau

THE 39 STEPS

UK, 1935

Director: Alfred Hitchcock

Production: Gaumont-British; black and white, 35mm; running time: 81 minutes. Released June 1935. Filmed in Lime Grove studios.

Producers: Michael Balcon with Ivor Montagu; **screenplay:** Charles Bennett and Alma Reville, additional dialogue by Ian Hay, from the novel by John Buchan; **photography:** Bernard Knowles; **editor:** Derek Twist; **sound:** A. Birch; **production designers:** Otto Wendorff and Albert Jullion; **music:** Louis Levy; **costume designer:** J. Strassner.

Cast: Madeleine Carroll (*Pamela*); Robert Donat (*Richard Hannay*); Lucie Mannheim (*Miss Smith/Annabella*); Godfrey Tearle (*Professor Jordan*); Peggy Ashcroft (*Margaret*); John Laurie (*John*); Helen Haye (*Mrs. Jordan*); Wylie Watson (*Mister Memory*); Frank Cellier (*Sheriff Watson*); Peggy Simpson (*Young girl*); Gus McNaughton and Jerry Vernon (*2 Voyagers*); Miles Malleson (*Director of the Palladium*).

Publications

Script:

Bennett, Charles, and Alma Reville, *Les 39 Marches*, in *Avant-Scène du Cinéma* (Paris), 1 June 1980.

Books:

Rohmer, Eric, and Claude Chabrol, *Hitchcock*, Paris, 1957.
Wood, Robin, *Hitchcock's Films*, London, 1965; revised edition, as *Hitchcock's Films Revisited*, New York, 1989.
Truffaut, François, *Le Cinema selon Hitchcock*, Paris, 1966; as *Hitchcock*, New York, 1985.
Trewin, J. C., *Robert Donat: A Biography*, London, 1968.
LaValley, Albert J., editor, *Focus on Hitchcock*, Englewood Cliffs, New Jersey, 1972.
Durgnat, Raymond, *The Strange Case of Alfred Hitchcock*, Cambridge, Massachusetts, 1974.
Parish, James Robert, and Michael Pitts, *The Great Spy Pictures*, Metuchen, New Jersey, 1974.
Spoto, Donald, *The Art of Alfred Hitchcock*, New York, 1976.
Armes, Roy, *A Critical History of the British Cinema*, London, 1978.
Taylor, John Russell, *Hitch*, London, 1978.
Fieschi, J. -A., and others, *Hitchcock*, Paris, 1981.
Mast, Gerald, *A Short History of the Movies*, New York, 1981.
Browne, Nick, *The Rhetoric of Film Narration*, Ann Arbor, Michigan, 1982.
Cook, David, *A Narrative History of Film*, New York, 1982.
Norboni, Jean, editor, *Alfred Hitchcock*, Paris, 1982.
Rothman, William, *Hitchcock—The Murderous Gaze*, Cambridge, Massachusetts, 1982.
Spoto, Donald, *The Dark Side of Genius: The Life of Alfred Hitchcock*, New York, 1982.
Villien, Bruno, *Hitchcock*, Paris, 1982.
Weis, Elisabeth, *The Silent Scream: Alfred Hitchcock's Sound Track*, Rutherford, New Jersey, 1982.
Phillips, Gene D., *Alfred Hitchcock*, Boston, 1984.
Douchet, Jean, *Alfred Hitchcock*, Paris, 1985.
Deutelbaum, Marshall, and Leland Poague, *A Hitchcock Reader*, Ames, Iowa, 1986.
Humphries, Patrick, *The Films of Alfred Hitchcock*, Greenwich, Connecticut, 1986.
Ryall, Tom, *Alfred Hitchcock and the British Cinema*, London, 1986.
Sinyard, Neil, *The Films of Alfred Hitchcock*, London, 1986.
Brill, Lesley, *The Hitchcock Romance: Love and Irony in Hitchcock's Films*, Princeton, 1988.
Modleski, Tania, *The Women Who Knew Too Much: Hitchcock and Feminist Theory*, New York, 1988.
Arginteanu, Judy, *The Movies of Alfred Hitchcock*, Minneapolis, 1994.
Condon, Pauline, *Complete Hitchcock*, London, 1999.
Mogg, Ken, *Alfred Hitchcock Story*, Dallas, 1999.

Articles:

Spectator (London), 14 June 1935.
New Statesman and Nation (London), 22 June 1935.
New York Times, 14 September 1935.
Variety (New York), 18 September 1935.
Hitchcock, Alfred, "My Own Methods," in *Sight and Sound* (London), Summer 1937.
Anderson, Lindsay, "Alfred Hitchcock," in *Sequence* (London), Autumn 1949.

The 39 Steps

Harcourt-Smith, Simon, in *Sight and Sound* (London), July 1950.
''Hitchcock Anglais,'' in *Cahiers du Cinéma* (Paris), September 1956.
Pett, John, in *Films and Filming* (London), November and December 1959.
Higham, Charles, ''Hitchcock's World,'' in *Film Quarterly* (Berkeley), Winter 1962–63.
Kael, Pauline, in *Kiss Kiss Bang Bang*, Boston, 1970.
Richards, Jeffrey, ''A Star Without Armour: Robert Donat,'' in *Focus on Film* (London), no. 8, 1971.
Beylie, Claude, in *Ecran* (Paris), September-October 1973.
Roud, Richard, ''In Broad Daylight,'' in *Film Comment* (New York), July-August 1974.
McDougal, S. Y., ''Mirth, Sexuality, and Suspense: Alfred Hitchcock's Adaptation of *The 39 Steps*,'' in *Literature/Film Quarterly* (Salisbury, Maryland), Summer 1975.
Goldstein, R. M., in *Film News* (New York), January-February 1979.
Graham, Olive, in *Cinema Texas Program Notes* (Austin), 5 February 1979.
Slide, Anthony, in *Magill's Survey of Cinema 4*, Englewood Cliffs, New Jersey, 1980.
Scarrone, C., in *Filmcritica* (Florence), January 1981.
Jameux, D., ''The 'Secret' in Hitchcock's *The Thirty-Nine Steps*,'' in *On Film* (Los Angeles), Summer 1983.
Thomas, F., in *Positif* (Paris), July-August 1984.
Hark, I. R., ''Keeping Your Amateur Standing: Audience Participation and Good Citizenship in Hitchcock's Political Films,'' in *Cinema Journal* (Austin, Texas), no. 2, 1990.
Cohen, T., ''Graphics, Letters, and Hitchcock's *Steps*,'' in *Hitchcock Annual* (Gambier, Ohio), no. 1, 1992.
Phillips, Louis, ''The Hitchcock Universe: Thirty-nine Steps and Then Some,'' in *Films in Review* (New York), March-April 1995.
''*Le grande stagione inglese*,'' in *Castoro Cinema*, July/August 1996.
Worden, J., ''Thirty-nine Steps to Immortality,'' in *Armchair Detective*, vol. 29, no. 4, 1996.

* * *

When he completed *The 39 Steps*, director Alfred Hitchcock explained his reasons for doing the film: ''I am out to give the public good, healthy, mental shake-ups. Civilization has become so screening and sheltering that we cannot experience sufficient thrills at firsthand. Therefore, to prevent our becoming sluggish and jellified, we have to experience them artificially.'' The film first brought Hitchcock to the attention of United States film-goers and initiated reference to the director as ''the master'' in his native England. The pairing of Robert Donat and Madeleine Carroll—the suave, clever, attractive man and the cool, intelligent blonde—helped to reinforce the pattern of Hitchcockian protagonists that would recur in many of his later films.

Many critics and viewers alike feel the *The 39 Steps* is one of Hitchcock's finest films; in fact, viewer response to the film today is often as enthusiastic as during the time of its release. Adapted from a novel by John Buchan, the movie gave Hitchcock the opportunity to display his finest non-stop action sequences. Most notably, it combines what would become Hitchcock's most often-treated themes with imaginative sound and visual techniques.

Numerous scenes in *The 39 Steps* have become cinema classics, particularly those merging suspense with surprise, humor with anxiety: the murdered, mysterious spy who, after warning him that ''they'll get you too,'' slumps over Donat's bed revealing the knife in her back; the surprise when master-spy Geoffrey Tearle shows Donat his ''half-pinkie,'' the top-joint of his finger missing; the funny and ironic sexual implications of adversaries Carroll and Donat handcuffed together, pretending to be newlyweds, ''forced'' to spend the night together. (As she removes her stockings, his hand must coast along with hers down her legs—''May I be of assistance?'' he asks.)

And Hitchcock's technical virtuosity highlights what is perhaps his most famous scene transition, used first in *Blackmail*: the chambermaid finds the spy's body and shrieks, her cries blended to the screaming whistle of a train as the plot ''relentlessly moves forward.'' Hitchcock's use of sound and careful lighting heighten the suspense—and humor—of the film. Throughout the melée in the music hall during the first sequence, persistent members of the audience ask, ''What causes Pip in poultry?'' and ''How old is Mae West?'' as the crowded mise-en-scène and the fast-paced editing reinforce the confusion. *The 39 Steps* also featured one of Hitchcock's favorite themes: the innocent caught in bizarre circumstances that he or she doesn't understand. The plot and its loopholes, however, provide the forum for the hero to do his or her ''stuff,'' to demonstrate a charm and cleverness in getting out of tight spots. As the confusing plot plays itself out, however, audiences are far more interested in the characters' relationships than in the overall impetus for the narrative. In fact, the original point of the title was forgotten, and a line had to be added to the script at the end by way of explanation. *The 39 Steps* then also illustrates the celebrated Hitchcockian ''McGuffin''—''what everybody on the screen is looking for, but the audience don't care.''

Particularly effective in the film are rapid changes of situation and Hitchcock's obvious contention that nothing is sacred, especially if a location or situation can be used to demonstrate the cleverness of his protagonist. Even patriotic parades and political lectures aren't safe from the thrilling chase: Donat escapes from a police station, ducks into a public hall where he is mistaken for a guest speaker, then gives an impromptu, rousing political address to a responsive audience. All of these events foreshadow Cary Grant's escape from killers at an auction and his flight from the same murderers around the Mount Rushmore National Monument in *North by Northwest* (1959); with Hitchcock, traditional connotations of safety and danger often reverse.

Visually, *The 39 Steps* enabled Hitchcock to transfer some of his skills as a director of silent films: the camera at long-shot lingers on an open window, curtains blowing in and around its frame on a stormy London night. This effective bit of ''mood-setting'' precedes revelation of the woman spy's murder. Later on in the film, we look through the window of a crofter's cottage from his point of view; within that tight frame, we witness the conspiritual, silent ''dialogue'' between Donat and Peggy Ashcroft, the crofter's kind wife. As with his use of sound, these sequences illustrate Hitchcock's mastery of a medium in which absence of dialogue or music can be strikingly effective. Sydney Carroll, writing in the London *Sunday Times*, said: ''In *The 39 Steps* the identity and mind of Alfred Hitchcock are continuously discernible, in fact supreme. There is no doubt that Hitchcock is a genius. He is the real star of the film.'' And interestingly, two ''modern'' remakes of the film pale miserably in comparison with the original.

—Deborah Holdstein

THREE COLORS: BLUE, WHITE, RED

See **TROIS COULEURS: BLEU, BLANC, ROUGE**

THE THREEPENNY OPERA

See **DIE DREIGROSCHENOPER**

TIEFLAND

Germany/Austria, 1945/1954

Director: Leni Riefenstahl

Production: Leni Riefenstahl Produktion; black and white; running time: 98 minutes. Filmed in Spain, the Austrian Alps, the Dolomites, and Barrandov Studios in Prague between 1942 and 1945. Footage confiscated by French occupation forces and returned incomplete to Riefenstahl, who then edited it for a February 1954 Austrian and West German release by Tobis.

Producer: Leni Riefenstahl; **screenplay:** Leni Riefenstahl; based on the opera *Tiefland* by Eugene d'Albert; **photography:** Albert Benitz; Trude Lechle; **assistant director:** G. W. Pabst; **editor:** Leni Riefenstahl; **sound:** Rudolf Kaiser and Herbert Janeczka; **production designers:** Erich Grave and Isabella Ploberger; **music:** Eugene d'Albert, with new compositions by Herbert Windt; performed by the Vienna Symphony Orchestra; **production managers:** Walter Traut and Max Hüske; **consultant:** Harald Reinl.

Cast: Leni Riefenstahl (*Martha*); Franz Eichberger (*Pedro*); Bernhard Minetti (*Marquez Don Sebastian*); Aribert Wäscher (*Camillo*); Maria Koppenhöfer (*Donna Amelia*); Luis Rainer (*Old Shepherd*); Frieda Richard (*Josefa*); Karl Skraup (*Mayor*); Max Holzboer (*The Miller*); Mena Main (*Miller's Wife*).

Tiefland

Publications

Books:

Hinton, David, *The Films of Leni Riefenstahl*, Metuchen, New Jersey, 1978.

Berg-Pan, Renata, *Leni Riefenstahl*, Boston, 1980.

Riefenstahl, Leni, *Memoiren*, Munich, 1987.

Riefenstahl, Leni, *A Memoir*, New York, 1993.

Articles:

Gunston, David, ''Leni Riefenstahl,'' in *Film Quarterly* (Berkeley), vol. 14, no. 1, Fall 1960.

Brownlow, Kevin, ''Leni Riefenstahl,'' in *Film* (London), Winter 1966.

Delahaye, Michael, ''Leni Riefenstahl,'' in *Interviews with Film Directors*, Indianapolis, 1968.

Rich, B. Ruby, ''Leni Riefenstahl: The Deceptive Myth,'' in *Sexual Stratagems: The World of Women in Film*, New York, 1979.

Rentschler, Eric, ''Fatal Attractions: Leni Riefenstahl's *The Blue Light*,'' in *October*, no. 48, Spring 1989.

Schulte-Sasse, Linda, ''Leni Riefenstahl's Feature Films and the Question of a Fascist Aesthetic,'' in *Framing the Past: The Historiography of German Cinema and Television*, Carbondale, 1992.

Sanders-Brahms, Helma, ''Tyrannenmord: *Tiefland* von Leni Riefenstahl,'' in *Das Dunkle zwischen den Bildern: Essays, Porträts, Kritiken*, Frankfurt 1992.

Von Dassanowsky, Robert, '''Wherever You May Run, You Cannot Escape Him': Leni Riefenstahl's Self-Reflection and Romantic Transcendence of Nazism in *Tiefland*,'' in *Camera Obscura* (Bloomington, Indiana), no. 35, May 1995.

* * *

Considering the ongoing interest in Leni Riefenstahl and the most recent attempts by academics to find something in her work that would satisfy her critics or release her from cinematic exile, it is inexplicable that Riefenstahl's final dramatic film, *Tiefland*, has received so little attention. German filmmaker Helma Sanders-Brahms asks: ''How is it possible that after fifty years the fear of dealing with this film is still so great that just the refusal to view it is considered a correct attitude for German intellectuals?'' The answer might be that the film would threaten much of the static image scholarship has dealt Riefenstahl and her work.

Riefenstahl originally considered *Tiefland* a likely follow-up to her first directorial effort, *Das blaue Licht* (1932), but *Sieg des Glaubens* (1933), *Triumph des Willens* (1935), and *Olympia* (1938) delayed this possible project. The film adaptation of the Eugene d'Albert (1864–1932) opera, *Tiefland*, with libretto by Rudolph Lothar (based on the 1896 Spanish play *Terra Baixa* by Angel Guimera) was reconsidered in 1939. Since *Tiefland* was not considered valuable for propaganda purposes it was given none of the financial support Riefenstahl requested from the government. *Tiefland* became Riefenstahl's ''inner emigration'' from the hostility of the Nazi inner circle, the shock of the war, and her slow disillusionment with Hitler. The footage was subsequently confiscated by the French government and returned incomplete to Riefenstahl after her several years in detention camps and her final clearance by French courts. Due to the lost material (shot early in the production in Spain), she has never been satisfied with the final edit. In 1949, a West German magazine claimed that Riefenstahl used Gypsy inmates from concentration camps as extras and mistreated them during the filming. A Munich court found Riefenstahl innocent of the charges that same year, but she has had to repeatedly defend herself against renewed charges based on the original libelous assertion.

Tiefland opens with a visual/musical poem on the beauty of nature and the tranquility of the mountains. The long shots emphasize space and freedom, a nature-worship more reminiscent of Arnold Fanck's early *Bergfilme* than of the mountain images in *Das blaue Licht*, where filtered daylight suggests a haunted twilight setting. Here, the view is clear and bright, offered without sophisticated technical manipulation. The isolated human inhabitant of *Tiefland*'s mountains is Pedro the shepherd (Franz Eichberger), whose hut we enter. Pedro is awakened by his dog, which warns him of a wolf threatening the sheep. Berg-Pan has commented on this symbolism of innocence in the confrontation between sheep and wolf: ''One wonders how the director and the Nazi authorities reconciled such action with Germany's own attacks on largely defenseless neighbors.'' The emphasis is unambiguous and it foreshadows the climax of the film. Pedro fights the wolf with his bare hands as they roll down the hill in mortal struggle. Having strangled the wolf, Pedro washes his wounds in the river and gently bathes the injured paw of his dog.

Like Junta in *Das blaue Licht* and the torchbearer from Mount Olympus in the prologue to *Olympia*, Pedro descends the mountain as the pure, nature-bound, and mystically empowered force. He passes through arid fields where tired peasants beg the Marquez's representative to let the river, undammed by the Marquez, flow back to their drought-stricken land. The overseer rejects their plea and informs them that the Marquez needs the water for his bulls. In the village, Pedro passes a covered gypsy wagon in which Martha (Riefenstahl) ties her shoes in preparation for her dance. The erotic tension between the Marquez and Martha is undeniable, but Martha is attracted to him because she misunderstands him to be both powerful and kind; when he discovers her gypsy companion has beaten her, he promises no one will hurt her again. Martha accepts this as Riefenstahl accepted Hitler, naively avoiding the obvious or wishing only to see self-serving aspects—a powerful man who will give her an important and protected existence. Indeed, Riefenstahl's opportunism on behalf of her art and fame governed her early life. As Martha dances for the Marquez (and his guitar accompaniment) to become his pampered mistress, so Riefenstahl filmed for Hitler (and his ideology) to become a renowned artist.

A number of elements in the film enforce Riefenstahl's use of the relationship between Martha and the Marquez to represent her Nazi experience. As she accepts her position in the castle and gives herself to the Marquez, Martha's gypsy dresses, the costume of (other) ethnicity and her art, are replaced by those of a noblewoman. These elitist outfits are uniforms that connect her to the ruling order and label her a possession of the Marquez. In her most masculine dress of the film, which in military-like regimentation mimics the Marquez's suit, Martha implores the Marquez to communicate with the drought-stricken peasants. His preceding ride through the town with Martha, who witnesses his reception as Riefenstahl witnessed Hitler's for the camera, and his arrogant consideration of the peasant's requests, quote Hitler's tour of Nuremberg in the early segments of *Triumph des Willens*. Unlike those moments, however, the poor crowds of *Tiefland* do not welcome or cheer their ''Führer'' but curse him in anger and misery. Martha, like Riefenstahl, who has admitted as much, is possessed by a leader she agreed to serve and whose sudden cruelty contradicts his generous behavior to her. One must also consider that Bernhard Minetti's Marquez bears a strong physical resemblance to Goebbels. Like the Propaganda Minister, the Marquez is known for his sexual dalliances and his abuse of Martha mimics Goebbels' alleged verbal assaults on Riefenstahl.

The capitalist support of authoritarian rule is introduced in the figure of Donna Amelia (Maria Koppenhöffer), the daughter of the Mayor (Karl Skraup), who is goaded on by her father to become the wife of the Marquez for a sizeable amount of money. The Marquez requires her finances to resolve his debts and Donna Amelia is therefore treated as a possession to be bartered by her father and as an object of financial desire by the Marquez. She readily accepts subservience to a man she hates for the sake of a title and to please her father. Riefenstahl, who celebrated the patriarchy in *Triumph*, creates powerful allegories of male domination and abuse in *Tiefland*. The class differences between Martha, Donna Amelia, and the servant women are revealed as irrelevant under male oppression. The Marquez's attempt to (re)possess Martha after the wedding is met with physical defense from Pedro. Having lost the duel with knives, the Marquez is blocked from escape by the peasants and Pedro strangles him as he did the wolf. Leaving the dead leader and the now free peasants behind, Martha and Pedro walk into the mountains and a new life together.

Riefenstahl's Martha rises blissfully into the happy ending because the director/writer/actress who previously assembled visions of Hitler's Germany to serve as a script for the regime's self-image has, with *Tiefland*, scripted her own escape from a pact with evil and a prominence gone sour. Through Martha, she does not relinquish her equality with men but leaves behind a leader and a society she previously celebrated. Gone is the self-sacrificing, fascist-friendly mysticism of *Das blaue Licht* and the grandiose celebration of the documentary films. What surfaces is parody and criticism of such previous notions. Servitude imprisons Martha and the peasantry, who come to hate their ''Führer.'' Egomania and grandiosity offer these people nothing and ultimately destroy the elite. The very center of the story, the heroine, is a non-Aryan, a gypsy. What remains, even in the naive romantic finale, reaches beyond most postwar dominant film: a strong, independent female at odds with patriarchal roles and images, and a male devoid of machismo beyond his desire to defend.

Perhaps because Riefenstahl's Martha seems somewhat older than Pedro, he is also conscious of her dominant quality. *Tiefland* is Riefenstahl's most personal cinematic statement, the result of a film oeuvre tied to the rise and fall of the Third Reich. It implies a perception that Riefenstahl's critics have failed to elicit from the filmmaker herself: namely that the warrior order she celebrated at Nuremberg would ultimately condemn her and those who would consider her post-*Triumph* films as a model.

—Robert von Dassanowsky

TIME OF THE GYPSIES

See **DOM ZA VESANJE**

THE TIN DRUM

See **BLECHTROMMEL**

TIRE DIÉ

(Toss Me a Dime)

Argentina, 1960

Director: Fernando Birri

Production: Instituto de Cinematografia de la Universidad Nacional del Litoral; black and white, 16mm blown up to 35mm; running time: 33 minutes. Filmed 1958–1960 in Santa Fe, Argentina. Released 1960.

Screenplay and photography: Fernando Birri and the students at the Instituto de Cinematografia of the Universidad Nacional de Litoral, Santa Fe, Argentina; **editor:** Antonio Ripoll; **sound:** Mario Fezia; **assistant director:** Manuel Horacio Gimenez.

Cast: Guillermo Cervantes Luro (*Narrator*); Voices of Francisco Petrone and Maria Rosa Gallo.

Publications

Books:

Mahieu, Jose Agustin, *Breve Historia del Cine Argentino*, Buenos Aires, 1966.

Micciche, Lino, editor, *Fernando Birri e la Escuela Documental de Santa Fe*, Pesaro, Italy, 1981.

King, John, and Nissa Torrents, *The Garden of Forking Paths: Argentine Cinema*, London, 1988.

Sendrós, Paraná, *Fernando Birri*, Buenos Aires, 1994.

Articles:

Pussi, Dolly, ''Breve historia del documental en la Argentina,'' in *Cine Cubano* (Havana), October 1973.

Couselo, Jorge Miguel, ''The Connection: 3 Essays on the Treatment of History in the Early Argentine Cinema,'' in *Journal of Latin American Lore*, volume 1, no. 2, 1975.

Burton, Julianne, interview with Fernando Birri in *Fernando Birri e la Escuela Documental de Santa Fe*, edited by Lino Micciche, Pesaro, Italy, 1981.

Pereira, Manuel, ''Carta a Fernando Birri,'' and ''Pequena critica agradecida a *Tire die*,'' by Rigoberto Lopez, in *Cinema Cubano* (Havana), no. 100, 1981.

Lombardi, Francisco, ''Fernando Birri y las Raíces del Nuevo Cine Latino-americano,'' in *Hablemos de Cine* (Lima), March 1984.

Acker, Alison, ''Pictures of the Other Americas: From Protest to Celebration,'' in *The Canadian Forum*, vol. 66, December 1986.

* * *

Though seldom seen, even in Latin America, *Tire dié*, a 33-minute documentary, is the most revered and influential of the hundreds of documentary shorts produced throughout the continent during the quarter century of the New Latin American Cinema movement. Most viewers know only the fragment presented in Fernando Solanas' and Octavio Getino's three-part feature documentary on Argentine politics, *The Hour of the Furnaces* (1969), but the example of director Fernando Birri's approach and philosophy can be detected in dozens of other films. In its genesis, mode of production and distribution, in its style and subject matter, in its successes and in its shortcomings, *Tire dié* blazed a trail that the entire New Latin American Cinema movement would continue to explore.

The film begins with an aerial shot of the provincial city of Santa Fe, Argentina. A voice-of-God narrator (anonymous, omniscient) intones over these perspective-of-God images in a style reminiscent of traditional, authoritarian documentary. As conventional descriptive data (founding dates, population) give way to the less conventional (statistics concerning the number of streetlamps and hairdressers), the parodistic intent becomes clear. The neat grid of organized neighborhoods gives way to random shanties, as the narrator declares, ''Upon reaching the edge of the city, statistics become uncertain. This is where, between four and five in the afternoon during 1956, 1957, and 1958, the first Latin American social survey film was shot.''

The railroad bridge which the aerial camera surveys just prior to the credits is the site of the first post-credit sequence. From God's vantage point, the camera has descended to the eye-level of the children who congregate there every afternoon. A little boy in a close-up stares directly at the camera, then turns and runs out of the frame. Other children appear in close-up, looking and speaking at the camera in direct address. Their barely audible voices are overlaid with the studied dramatic diction of two adult narrators, male and female, who repeat what the children are saying. This initial sequence ends as the camera follows one of the boys home and ''introduces'' his mother and then other members of the community.

The primary expectation deferred and eventually fulfilled by the film's intricate structuration is the arrival of the long and anxiously awaited train to Buenos Aires. The interviews in which local residents discuss their economic plight are repeatedly intercut with shots back to the tracks and the growing number of children keeping their restless vigil there. The eventual climax of expectation (subjects' and viewers') has the bravest and fleetest of the children running alongside the passing train. As they balance precariously on the narrow, elevated bridge, their hands straining upward to catch any coin the passengers might toss in their direction, children's voices on the soundtrack chant hoarsely, "Tire dié! Tire dié!" ("Toss me a dime!"). The final shot holds on the solemn, soulful face of the three-year-old, protected by his mother's embrace and her assertion that "he is too young to participate in the *tire dié*."

The first product of the first Latin American documentary film school, the Escuela Documental de Santa Fe founded by Birri in 1956, *Tire dié* was a collaborative effort the evolution and ethos of which recall the Italian neo-realism of the post-war years and anticipate certain aspects of the direct cinema of the 1960s. After selecting theme and locale from preliminary photo-reportages, Birri divided 60 students into various groups, each of which was to concentrate on a particular inhabitant of the riverside squatters' community under study. With their single camera and cumbersome tape recorder, the group made daily visits during a two-year period to the marginal community where the film was set. All the residents of the riverside squatters' camp attended the film's premiere along with municipal and university dignitaries. In response to consultations with the film's subjects and general audience questionnaires, the original 59-minute version was edited down to 33. A primitive mobile cinema kept the film circulating throughout the region.

Tire dié exemplifies the attempt to democratize the documentary form by giving voice and image to sectors of a culture which had previously been ignored and suppressed. Given the film's obvious commitment to direct visual and verbal address, the intervention of the anonymous male and female mediator/narrators is unexpected and disconcerting. Investigation into the film's mode of production reveals that this expedient derives not from prior design but from deficiencies in the original sound recording. *Tire dié* sought to give the effect of synchronous sound without the technical facilities to do so. The over-dubbing of social actors by professional actors is the central—but not the sole—contradiction of this social document: it brands a seminal attempt to democratize documentary discourse with the unwanted but unavoidable stamp of residual authoritarian anonymity, just as the intricate patterns of editing call assumptions of transparent realism into question. In its contradictions, as well as in its achievements, *Tire dié* stands as a landmark of Latin American social documentary.

—Julianne Burton

TIREZ SUR LE PIANISTE

(Shoot the Piano Player)

France, 1960

Director: François Truffaut

Production: Films de la Pléïade; black and white, 35mm, in Dyaliscope; running time: 80 minutes, English versions variously noted at 84 and 92 minutes. Released 22 August 1960, Paris. Filmed 1 December 1959–15 January 1960, additional shooting in March 1960. Filmed in Paris at a café and at Rue Mussard, also in Levallois and Le Sappey, France.

Producer: Pierre Braunberger; **screenplay:** François Truffaut and Marcel Moussy, from the novel *Down There* by David Goodis; **photography:** Raoul Coutard; **editors:** Claudine Bouché and Cécile Decugis; **sound:** Jacques Gallois; **art director:** Jacques Mely; **music:** Georges Delerue.

Cast: Charles Aznavour (*Charlie Kohler/Edouard Saroyan*); Marie Dubois (*Lèna*); Nicole Berger (*Michèle Mercier*); Serge Devri (*Plyne*); Claude Mansard (*Momo*); Richard Kanayan (*Fido*); Albert Rémy (*Chico*); Jacques Aslanian (*Richard*); Daniel Boulanger (*Ernest*); Claude Heymann (*Lars Schmeel*); Alex Joffé (*Passerby who helps Chico*); Bobby Lapointe (*Singer in café*); Catherine Lutz (*Mammy*).

Publications

Script:

Truffaut, François, and Marcel Moussy, *Tirez sur le pianiste*, in *Avant-Scène du Cinéma* (Paris), July-August 1987.

Books:

Taylor, John Russell, *Cinema Eye, Cinema Ear*, New York, 1964.
Armes, Roy, *French Cinema Since 1946: The Personal Style*, New York, 1966.
Petrie, Graham, *The Cinema of François Truffaut*, Cranbury, New Jersey, 1970.
Crisp, C. G., and Michael Walker, *François Truffaut*, New York, 1971.
Braudy, Leo, editor, *Focus on Shoot the Piano Player*, Englewood Cliffs, New Jersey, 1972.
Crisp, C. G., *François Truffaut*, London, 1972.
Fanne, Dominique, *L'Univers de François Truffaut*, Paris, 1972.
Allen, Don, *Truffaut*, London, 1973; as *Finally Truffaut*, 1985.
Monaco, James, *The New Wave*, New York, 1976.
Collet, Jean, *Le Cinéma de François Truffaut*, Paris, 1977.
Insdorf, Annette, *François Truffaut*, Boston, 1978.
Walz, Eugene P., *François Truffaut: A Guide to References and Resources*, Boston, 1982.
Winkler, Willi, *Die Filme von François Truffaut*, Munich, 1984.
Bergala, Alain, and others, *Le Roman de François Truffaut*, Paris, 1985.
Collet, Jean, *François Truffaut*, Paris, 1985.
Truffaut, François, *Truffaut par Truffaut*, edited by Dominique Rabourdin, Paris, 1985.
De Fornari, Oreste, *I Filme di François Truffaut*, Rome, 1986.
Dalmais, Hervé, *Truffaut*, Paris, 1987.
Brunette, Peter, editor, *Shoot the Piano Player: François Truffaut*, New Brunswick, New Jersey, 1993.
Insdorf, Annette, *François Truffaut*, New York, 1995.
Holmes, *François Truffaut*, New York, 1998.
Toubiana, Serge, and Antoine De Baecque, *Truffaut*, New York, 1999.
Jacob, Gilles, *François Truffaut: Correspondence 1945–1984*, Lanham, 2000.

Tirez sur le pianiste

Articles:

Baby, Yvonne, in *Le Monde* (Paris), 24 November 1960.
Kas, Pierre, in *Cahiers du Cinéma* (Paris), January 1961.
Martin, Marcel, in *Cinéma* (Paris), January 1961.
Durgnat, Raymond, in *Films and Filming* (London), February 1961.
Torok, Jean-Paul, ''The Point Sensible,'' in *Positif* (Paris), March 1961.
Houston, Penelope, ''Uncommitted Artist?,'' in *Sight and Sound* (London), Spring 1961.
Rhode, Gabriel and Eric, ''Cinema of Appearance,'' in *Sight and Sound* (London), Autumn 1961.
Kauffmann, Stanley, in *New Republic* (New York), 9 July 1962.
Crowther, Bosley, in *New York Times*, 24 July 1962.
Sarris, Andrew, in *Village Voice* (New York), 26 July 1962.
Cukier, Dan A., and Jo Gryn, ''Entretien avec François Truffaut,'' in *Script* (Paris), April 1962.
Kael, Pauline, in *Film Culture* (New York), Winter 1962–63.
Collet, Jean, and others, ''Entretien Avec François Truffaut,'' in *Cahiers du Cinéma* (Paris), December 1962.
Shatnoff, Judith, ''François Truffaut: The Anarchist Imagination,'' in *Film Quarterly* (Berkeley), Spring 1963.
Klein, Michael, ''The Literary Sophistication of François Truffaut,'' in *Film Comment* (New York), Summer 1965.
''Hommage à Truffaut à Annency,'' in *Cinéma* (Paris), January 1967.
Comolli, Jean-Louis, ''Au Coeur des paradoxes,'' in *Cahiers du Cinéma* (Paris), May 1967.
Comolli, Jean-Louis, and Jean Narboni, ''Entretien avec François Truffaut,'' in *Cahiers du Cinéma* (Paris), May 1967.
Wood, Robin, ''Chabrol and Truffaut,'' in *Movie* (London), Winter 1969–70.
Bordwell, David, ''A Man Can Serve Two Masters,'' in *Film Comment* (New York), Spring 1971.
Simsolo, Noël, in *Image et Son* (Paris), March 1972.
Thiher, A., ''The Existential Play in Truffaut's Early Films,'' in *Literature/Film Quarterly* (Salisbury, Maryland), Summer 1977.
Dudley, Don, in *Cinema Texas Program Notes* (Austin), 2 March 1978.
Chion, M., ''Un Film meteore,'' in *Cahiers du Cinéma* (Paris), March 1982.
Latil le Dantix, M., in *Cinématographe* (Paris), March 1982.
Blanchet, C., ''*Tirez sur le pianiste*: Le Second degré du cinéma,'' in *Cinema* (Paris), May 1982.
Marias, M., in *Casablanca* (Madrid), February 1984.

Gillain, A., ''La scène de l'audition,'' in *Avant-Scène du Cinéma* (Paris), no. 362–363, July-August 1987.

Guérif, François, ''François Truffaut et la série noire,'' in *Avant-Scène du Cinéma* (Paris), no. 362–363, July-August 1987.

Crowdus, Gary, in *Cineaste* (New York), vol. 18, no. 1, 1990.

Davis, H.L., ''Reminiscing About *Shoot the Piano Player,*'' in *Cineaste* (New York), vol. 19, no. 4, 1993.

Kehr, Dave, ''A Poet of Darkness, Who Longs for the Light,'' in *The New York Times*, 16 May 1999.

* * *

François Truffaut's astonishing success in his debut, *The 400 Blows*, was unpredictable, but that film does follow in the tradition of autobiographical first works by young and terribly sincere artists. As Truffaut himself recognized, the second work is the real test, and for his test he chose a subject and a style utterly opposed to that of *400 Blows*. *Shoot the Piano Player* is distant from Truffaut's personal life, distant some would say from life in general; it is as much as possible a filmmaker's film. Drawn from a standard detective novel called *Down There* by David Goodis, the film played with the conventions of the genre and with the stylistic possibilities of the medium. Thought to be too recherché, it received no American distribution until after the success of *Jules and Jim* (1961), but since then it has become prized by many people as Truffaut's most inventive work.

It was Truffaut's plan to inject life into contemporary French cinema first by emulating the American cinema (hence, the gangster genre) and then by gleefully upsetting the conventions and good taste that in his view had rigidified the movies in his country.

He began with casting, purposefully giving the central role to the timid and introspective Charles Aznavour. Aznavour, already a successful singer, was not without screen experience: Truffaut had admired him in Franju's *Tête contre les murs*. No one would have suspected that he could play Charlie Kohler, alias Edouard Saroyan, a concert pianist turned honky-tonk loser, especially when cast alongside typical tough guy characters. Truffaut exploited the contradictions by making the subject of timidity central to the film and treating it as it had never been treated in the movies before.

His chief gangsters came right out of the cartoon strips. Their tight-lipped argot is interrupted by long disquisitions about female sexuality and the unforgettable throwaway anecdote about a steel-fabric necktie. Truffaut embedded countless jokes and citations within his tale. Lars Schmeel, the lecherous impresario, is named for Lars Schimdt, the man who took Ingrid Bergman away from Rossellini, one of Truffaut's friends and heroes. Chico, Charlie's older brother, is named after Chico Marx. But far more than placing disruptive elements within a conventional story, Truffaut went out of his way to find a new way to tell such a story, to tell in fact a new kind of story.

In its first sequence *Shoot the Piano Player* announces the indirection of its method. Chico, chased down a dark street by an unseen car, runs into a lightpost and is knocked out. The first incongruity (crashing into the only bright object around) is replaced by a second as he is helped to his feet by a passerby. The chase is forgotten in a lengthy conversation about sexual fidelity and the joys of marriage. We will never see this ''extra'' again, but he has set the film on its way, interrupting its suspense with a tale about tenderness and love. The film as a whole proceeds in just this way: overly serious speeches (and even voice-overs) are cut short by ridiculous sub-actions (Clarisse tempting a client; the poor mug who owns the bar getting chummy with Charlie as he tries to choke him to death).

Visually, as Roger Greenspun has noted, the film alternates blacks and whites like the keyboard, which is its central image. Gangsters are funny, the heroine tells dirty jokes, milk poured on the car obscures the vision of the driver, snow on the windshield is alternately black or white depending on the sun's position.

The changes of mood that punctuate the story are actually central to its structure, for in the middle of this comic melodrama, an interior flashback gives us the tragic tale of Edouard's rise to fame and the suicide of his wife. Life itself is shown to be full of impossible shifts in fortune and feeling. It is all one big joke.

By the film's end Truffaut succeeds in bringing poignancy to the most trite of love stories through the incongruous juxtapositions of his style. Fame, obscurity, suicide, love, murder, robbery, and a whole family saga are woven together in 85 minutes under the routine theme song Charlie plays in the bar. Life is seen to be bigger than any of its events, bigger than the bitter end to which it leads all of us. Truffaut doesn't believe in his tale, but he does believe in the emotions it brings up and in the powers of cinema to evoke those emotions. In mixing genres and moods and in vigorously exploring powers of elliptical editing, fluid cinemascope, and lyrical music, *Shoot the Piano Player* exalts such power and remains a delight to watch. Beyond parody, its sincerity is the love Truffaut feels for the movies. That sincerity is infectious.

—Dudley Andrew

TITANIC

USA, 1997

Director: James Cameron

Production: 20th Century Fox, Paramount Pictures, and Lightstorm Entertainment; Color (DeLuxe), 70mm; running time: 194 minutes; length: 5,426 m (10 reels). Released 19 December 1997. Filmed July 1996—March 1997 at Rosarito, Baja California, Mexico; Vancouver, British Columbia, Canada; Halifax, Nova Scotia, Canada; Belmont Olympic Pool, Long Beach, California; and *Titanic* wreck, sea bed, North Atlantic. Cost: $200 million.

Producers: James Cameron and Jon Landau; **co-producers:** Al Giddings, Grant Hill, and Sharon Mann; **executive producer:** Rae Sanchini; **associate producer:** Pamela Easley; **screenplay:** James Cameron; **cinematography:** Russell Carpenter; **editors:** Conrad Buff IV, James Cameron, and Richard A. Harris; **sound:** Tom Johnson, Gary Rydstrom, Gary Summers, and Mark Ulano; **production designer:** Peter Lamont; **art direction:** Martin Laing and Bill Rea; **set decoration:** Michael Ford; **original musical score:** James Horner; **special effects:** Digital Domain; **makeup:** Greg Cannom, Tina Earnshaw, and Simon Thompson; **costume designer:** Deborah Lynn Scott; **casting:** Suzanne Crowley, Mali Finn, and Gilly Poole.

Cast: Leonardo DiCaprio (*Jack Dawson*); Kate Winslet (*Rose DeWitt Bukater*); Billy Zane (*Caledon ''Cal'' Hockley*); Kathy Bates (*Molly Brown*); Frances Fisher (*Ruth DeWitt Bukater*); Gloria Stuart (*Rose Dawson Calvert*); Bill Paxton (*Brock Lovett*); Bernard Hill (*Captain Edward John Smith*); David Warner (*Spicer Lovejoy*); Victor Garber

Titanic

(*Thomas Andrews*); Jonathan Hyde (*J. Bruce Ismay*); Suzy Amis (*Lizzy Calvert*); Lewis Abernathy (*Lewis Bodine*); Nicholas Cascone (*Bobby Buell*); Dr. Anatoly M. Sagalevitch (*Anatoly Milkailavich*); Danny Nucci (*Fabrizio De Rossi*); Jason Barry (*Tommy Ryan*); Ewan Stewart (*First Officer William Murdoch*); Ioan Gruffudd (*First Officer Harold Lowe*); Jonathan Phillips (*Second Officer Charles Lightoller*); Mark Lindsay Chapman (*Chief Officer Henry Wilde*); Richard Graham (*Quartermaster George Rowe*); Paul Brightwell (*Quartermaster Robert Hichens*); Ron Donachie (*Master at Arms*); Eric Braeden (*John Jacob Astor*); Charlotte Chatton (*Madeleine Astor*); Bernard Fox (*Col. Archibald Gracie*); Michael Ensign (*Benjamin Guggenheim*); Fannie Brett (*Madame Aubert, Mr. Guggenheim's mistress*); Jenette Goldstein (*Irish Mommy*); Camilla Overbye Roos (*Helga Dahl*); Linda Kerns (*3rd Class Woman*); Amy Gaipa (*Trudy Bolt, Rose's chambermaid*); Jonathan Evans-Jones (*Band Leader Wallace Henry Hartley*); Mike Butters (*Musician/Baker, uncredited*); James Cameron (*Brief cameo in steerage dance scene, uncredited*).

Awards: Los Angeles Film Critics Association Award for Best Production Design, 1997; Oscars for Best Picture, Best Director, Best Cinematography, Best Art Direction, Best Costume Design, Best Sound Effects Editing, Best Visual Effects, Best Film Editing, Best Original Dramatic Score, Best Song, Best Sound, 1998; American Society of Cinematographers award for Outstanding Achievement in Cinematography in Theatrical Releases, 1998; Chicago Film Critics Association Award for Best Cinematography, 1998; Directors Guild of America Awards for Outstanding Directorial Achievement in Motion Pictures, 1998; Golden Globes for Best Director-Motion Picture, Best Motion Picture-Drama, Best Original Score-Motion Picture, Best Original Song-Motion Picture, 1998; PGA Golden Laurel Award for Motion Picture Producer of the Year, 1998; Screen Actors Guild Awards for Outstanding Performance by a Female Actor in a Supporting Role (Stuart), Outstanding Performance by a Cast, 1998; Writers Guild of America Award for Best Screenplay Written Directly for the Screen, 1998; Grammy Award for Best Song Written Specifically for a Motion Picture or for Television, 1999; People's Choice Awards for Favorite Dramatic Motion Picture and Favorite Motion Picture, 1999.

Publications

Scripts:

Cameron, James. *Titanic: A Film Treatment.* Los Angeles, 25 March 1995.

Cameron, James. *Titanic: James Cameron's Illustrated Screenplay*, New York, 1999.

Books:

Cameron, James, Ed W. Marsh, et. al., photography by Douglas Kirkland. *James Cameron's Titanic*, New York, 1997.

Cameron, James and Joseph Montebello. *James Cameron's Titanic Poster Book*, New York, 1998.

Parisi, Paula. *Titanic and the Making of James Cameron: The Inside Story of the Three-Year Adventure that Rewrote Motion Picture History*, Newmarket Press, 1998.

Fritscher, Jack. *Titanic: Forbidden Stories Hollywood Forgot.* Palm Drive Publishing, 1999.

Sandler, Kevin S. and Gaylyn Studlar, editors. *Titanic: Anatomy of a Blockbuster*, Rutgers University Press, 1999.

Articles:

McCarthy, Todd, ''*Titanic*'' (rev.), in *Variety* (New York), 3 November 1997.

Parisi, Paula, ''*Titanic*: Man Overboard,'' in *Entertainment Weekly* (New York), 7 November 1997.

Corliss, Richard, ''*Titanic*'' (rev.), in *Time* (New York), 8 December 1997.

Masters, Kim. ''Trying to Stay Afloat,'' in *Time* (New York), 8 December 1997.

Brown, Corie and David Ansen, ''Rough Waters: The Filming of *Titanic*,'' in *Newsweek* (New York), 15 December, 1997.

Glieberman, Owen, ''*Titanic*'' (rev.), in *Entertainment Weekly* (New York), 19 December 1997.

Calhoun, James, ''That Sinking Feeling,'' in *Theater Crafts International*, January 1998.

Robertson, Barbara, ''The Grand Illusion,'' in *Computer Graphics World*, January 1998.

Kehr, Dave, ''Titanic Earns Its Sea Legs,'' in *New York Daily News*, 6 February 1998.

Gehring, Wes D., ''*Titanic*: The Ultimate Epic,'' in *USA Today Magazine* (New York), March 1998.

Klady, Leonard, ''Epics *Titanic* and *Wind* Crush Formulas,'' in *Variety* (New York), 2 March 1998.

Ansen, David, ''The Court of King Jim,'' in *Newsweek* (New York), 13 April 1998.

LoPiccolo, Phil, ''The Secret of *Titanic*'s Success,'' in *Computer Graphics World*, May 1998.

Chagollan, Steve, ''Reversal of Fortune,'' in *Variety* (New York), 14 December 1998.

Pence, Mike, ''Explaining the Appeal of *Titanic*,'' in *Saturday Evening Post*, May 1999.

Chumo, Peter N., II, ''Learning to Make Each Day Count: Time in James Cameron's *Titanic*,'' in *Journal of Popular Film and Television*, Winter 1999.

* * *

That James Cameron would make *Titanic* was inevitable, since the director of such blockbusters as *Aliens*, *Terminator 2*, and *True Lies* once likened filmmaking to creating ''spectacles,'' and what spectacle has proven costlier, grander, or more popular than *Titanic*? It is also appropriate that the current stage of Cameron's career has been capped by the biggest cinematic spectacle he (or anyone else for that matter) has yet created. Indeed, the film (as of late 1998) has brought in an overwhelming worldwide box office of $1.8 billion (a total that grows exponentially when added with a $30 million television sale, $400 million for the over 25 million copies of the soundtrack that have been sold; and an expected $700 million in global video sales when all is said and done). The unequaled box-office success this film has enjoyed in addition to the critical praise that has been heaped upon it (it tied *All About Eve* with a record 14 Academy Award nominations and consequently went on to win a record 11 including Best Picture and Best Director—tying *Ben-Hur*) has transformed *Titanic* into something more than a mere movie, it has become a cultural phenomenon.

The production story of *Titanic* (an epic on par with the film itself) began when Robert Ballard discovered the wreckage of the ship in 1985 on the ocean floor 400 miles off the coast of Newfoundland. Upon seeing the *National Geographic* documentary on the discovery, Cameron developed the following story idea: ''Do story with bookends of present-day [wreckage] scene…intercut with memory of a survivor…needs a mystery or driving plot element.'' Then, in early 1995, Cameron made the initial pitch to studio executives. A pitch which was reluctantly accepted based on the director's track record of profitability as well as the fact that he was maintaining that the film could be made for less than $100 million. In late 1995, as a precursor to the start of formal production, Cameron made 12 two-and-a-half mile descents to the *Titanic* wreckage site where he used a specifically designed 35mm camera to obtain footage for the bookend sections of the film. Armed with this footage, Cameron next had to convince the studio to back the film wholeheartedly. After the project was officially greenlighted in May 1996, ground was broken on a studio in Rosarito Beach in Baja California, since it had been determined some months prior that no one studio in the world could provide the facilities needed for the mammoth project. This custom-built studio featured a 17-million gallon exterior shooting tank (the largest in the world) which housed the 775 foot-long, 90% to scale replica of the *Titanic*; a five-million gallon interior tank housed on a 32,000 sq. ft. soundstage; three other stages; production offices; set/prop storage; a grip/electric building; welding/fabrication workshops; dressing rooms; and support structures. During this time, Fox was seeking a partnership with other studios to alleviate the film's already considerable financial risk. After pitching the deal to a few studios, Paramount agreed to co-finance the film (but they would ultimately limit their contribution to $65 million). Production on the film finally began in September 1996. Soon after the start of production, rumors were circulating regarding the expensive production, which would eventually jump from 138 to 160 days; the less-than-stellar working conditions some crew members likened to sweatshops (some even complained of having to work as long as two weeks without a break); unconfirmed accidents on the set; an infamous food-poisoning incident when the cast and crew were accidentally served food laced with PCP; as well as the usual screaming tirades from the compulsive director. Cameron and company also went to great lengths to ensure the historical authenticity of the film. It is through these technical aspects (i.e. the set decoration, costumes, etc.) that the film excels on an epic scale. When production finally wrapped in March 1997, over 12 days (288 hours) of footage had been shot. As Cameron secluded himself in the editing room, 18 special effects houses went to work on the more than 500 visual effects shots that the film would eventually require (a process that would take them the next several months to complete). Originally slated to open on 2 July, *Titanic* was pushed to December when it became clear that Cameron was nowhere near being done with the arduous editing process. When all was said and done, *Titanic* was released on 19 December in an attempt to maximize it's Oscar chances. The total shooting cost for the film was estimated at just over $200 million.

Titanic tells the fictional story of two class-crossed lovers who meet aboard the disaster-bound ship, fall in love, and then struggle to survive the grizzly sinking all within the context of a true-to-detail retelling of the actual disaster. This story within the film is launched from the present-day via a subplot that revolves around a missing diamond (the completely made-up ''Heart of the Ocean''). After treasure-hunter-for-hire Brock Lovett (Bill Paxton) finds a drawing of a naked young woman wearing the elusive diamond and features it in a television program on which he is appearing, an elderly woman (Gloria Stuart as a 101-year-old Rose) comes forward claiming to be the woman in the picture. After being whisked to the *Titanic* wreck site, Rose proceeds to recount the story of *Titanic*'s fateful voyage. It is here that a slew of stock characters are introduced: Jack Dawson (DiCaprio) is the American, free-spirit archetype from the wrong side of the tracks; Rose DeWitt Bukater (Winslet) a beautiful Philadelphia socialite who has no control over the course of her life; ''Cal'' Hockley (Zane), Rose's oppressive husband-to-be who sees her as nothing more than a possession; and Rose's domineering mother Ruth DeWitt Bukater (Fisher) who views Rose's marriage to Cal as vital to the family's survival and Rose's burgeoning romance with Jack as a threat to her current way of life. The romance between Jack and Rose begins when he thwarts her attempted suicide and infiltrates her first-class lifestyle. Slowly, Jack entices Rose to let go and to, as the film ensures we remember, ''make it count.'' Their relationship culminates in the creation of the aforementioned drawing and a torrid bit of lovemaking. *Titanic* then hits the iceberg and the film shifts from romance to an action-adventure. The final act of the film concentrates on the sinking of the ship and Rose and Jack's quest for survival. After some of the greatest special effects ever put on film, *Titanic* sinks and Rose is left atop a piece of wood while Jack floats nearby slowly freezing to death. While they wait for rescue, Jack makes Rose promise that she ''won't give up, no matter what happens, no matter how hopeless.'' After being rescued and reaching America, Rose takes the name of Dawson and lives the life that she promised the deceased Jack she would. The film then bounces back to the present day salvage ship to deliver the film's coda, wherein Lovett declares that although he's been searching for *Titanic* he never ''got it.'' Later that evening, Rose makes her way to the deck of the ship and drops the ''Heart of the Ocean'' necklace into the sea. Rose dies peacefully in her sleep (''an old lady warm in her bed,'' as Jack had predicted) later that night surrounded by the photographic memories of the life she had thanks to Jack. Upon her death, she is transported back to *Titanic* (presumably her entrance to the afterlife) and reunited with Jack, as well as all of those who died aboard the ship, at the grand staircase (where the clock reads 2:20-the time of *Titanic*'s sinking). She appears in this sequence as her 17-year-old self, thus suggesting that this is, as Dave Kehr suggests in the *New York Daily News*, ''the time it will always be: [both] the beginning of her life and its end.''

Before addressing the critical worth of *Titanic*, it is important to discuss the nature of its immense popularity. Perhaps the weakest explanation for *Titanic*'s popularity would lie in an offhand comment by Cameron himself wherein he referred to the film as nothing more than a ''$190 million chick flick.'' Although it is true that scores of women (mostly teenage girls) flocked to see this movie less for the special effects or sensational movie making than for the charismatic DiCaprio and the way he swept Winslet off her feet, to categorize the entire film as a so-called ''chick-flick'' does it a disservice. Instead, the appeal of *Titanic* exists in the relationship the audience has with the story of the film itself. That is, the film functions almost as a parable for the American Dream and the American way of life.

The core of the film is an epic romance. Cameron has long said that this was the ''great love story'' he thought *The Abyss* should have been. While the love story appears to be the heart of the film it is, however, the anachronistic characters of Jack and Rose that make the film so appealing to today's audiences. These two characters serve, as Peter N. Chum has noted, as the ''audience's surrogates.'' That is, neither character is really correct for the time period of the film, they are more like modern interpretations of a princess and a young rogue. Yet they are more than mere stereotypes. Both characters are archetypes of the American consciousness: Rose being the enlightened woman of the 20th century and Jack being the adventurous American. The way these modern characters function within the time-frame of the film is what endears them to the audience and is also what makes the film more a lesson in morality that a retelling of history. It is for this reason, as Mike Pence has pointed out, that ''what draws us to this film is an undeniable sense that we are seeing America of the late 20th century in metaphor before our eyes.''

The critical reception *Titanic* received was for the most part positive, but there was a faction that detested the film and it is this that causes the film's critical worth to be in question even today after all of its success and accolades. Much of the post-Oscar lambasting of *Titanic* can be traced to the backlash over the snub of *L.A. Confidential* in favor of *Titanic* in the categories of Best Picture and Director. The general opinion was that Oscars voters felt that if they didn't go along with the popular opinion then they would be subject to profound criticism. So, when the big box-office winner also won the two biggest awards, the assumption was that the Academy had been taken in by the hype and had been pathetically swayed by public sentiment. But, this is a very close-minded argument when one considers for a moment that *Titanic* was actually a good movie. Curtis Hanson (the director of *L.A. Confidential*) elaborated on this very point when he stated, ''As Frank Capra said, don't make your best movie the year somebody else makes *Gone With the Wind*.'' Does this mean that *Gone With the Wind* shouldn't have won Best Picture because Capra's *Mr. Smith Goes to Washington* (released that same year) had a better story, better characters, or even better acting, yet was considerably less popular than it's competitor? Each film exists on it's own terms and each is a fine piece of cinema in its own right. The inability to come to terms with this undeniable fact is the cause of division among critics and film scholars on the subject of *Titanic*. This does not mean that *Titanic* is free of flaws. One thing that stands out as sub par is the crude often inelegant dialogue of the script. (A problem that has plagued Cameron in all of his films, but has gone relatively unnoticed until he decided to do a period specific romantic epic in which his writing style is not a comfortable fit). As Brown and Ansen suggest in Newsweek, ''Cameron should have lavished more of his perfectionist's zeal on his dialogue.'' Logically speaking, several script problems exist within *Titanic* besides dialogue. For example, if the story is being related to us by Rose, how can she know anything about Jack before having met him during her attempted suicide (are his actions embellished by her to befit her memory of him?). Also of note are other instances wherein Rose recounts dialogue and actions she could have had no knowledge of (i.e. the framing of Jack by Cal or the decision by J. Bruce Ismay to push the engines as hard as they could go).

Although it can be argued that the acting throughout the film is at times wooden and merely meant to bring life to what amounts to simply stock characters (DiCaprio's Jack, throughout the first half of the film, stands out in this regard) none of these characters become, as Richard Corliss has accused them of being, ''caricatures...designed only to illustrate a predictable prejudice: that the first-class passengers are third-class people, and vice versa.'' These so-called caricatures never work against the audience forcing a dislike of the film on the grounds of insulting their intelligence. Consider this: *Titanic* achieved the level of popularity it did without the help of a single international box-office star (although it certainly created one in DiCaprio). Certainly this must attest to the entertaining value of the film. One thing that cannot be disputed is that once *Titanic* hits the iceberg 100 or so minutes into the film, the next 80 minutes are as thrilling as any action adventure film to date (and is definitely where Cameron shines). When combined with the romantic epic nature of the film, *Titanic*, as Owen Glieberman has stated, ''floods you with elemental passion in a way that invites comparison with the original movie spectacles of D.W. Griffith.''

All this is not to say that *Titanic* is a work of art, it has its problems. It is poorly written (please note that it was not nominated for an Oscar for Best Screenplay) and is at times rather shabbily acted (but hasn't somebody made that same argument about *Gone With the Wind* at some point in history?). (Certainly Cameron didn't help his own critical standing when he blasted Kenneth Turan of the *Los Angeles Times* in print for writing an unflattering review of *Titanic*.) But, where the film does succeed is in being a flat out good movie. It is enjoyable, pure and simple. Surely, nobody can doubt that *Titanic* is the most successful film in history, and no one can dispute that the film boasts some of the most spectacular effects ever put on film (in fact, apart from Best Picture and Director, all of the Oscars that *Titanic* won had something to do with the film's technical accomplishments). But, does all of this mean that it deserved to win Best Picture and Director over *L.A. Confidential*? That's a matter of opinion and endless debate. Perhaps 60 years down the road we will have a completely different consensus regarding *Titanic* than the argumentative one we have today.

—Michael J. Tyrkus

TO LIVE

See **IKIRU**

TODO SOBRE MI MADRE

(All About My Mother)

Spain/France, 1999

Director: Pedro Almodóvar

Production: El Deseo S.A., France 2 Cinéma, Renn Productions, Via Digital; color, 35mm, Panavision; sound: Dolby Digital; running time: 105 minutes. Released 8 April 1999 in Spain; filmed in Barcelona, Madrid, and A Coruña, Spain.

Producer: Agustín Almodóvar; **screenplay:** Pedro Almodóvar; **cinematographer:** Affonso Beato; **editor:** José; Salcedo; **music:** Alberto Iglesias; **production design:** Antxón Gómez; **art direction:** Antxón Gómez; **costume design:** Sabine Daigeler; José María De Cossio.

Cast: Cecilia Roth (*Manuela*); Marisa Parédes (*Huma Rojo*); Penélope Cruz (*Sister Rosa*); Candela Peña (*Nina*); Antonia San Juan (*Agrado*); Eloy Azorín (*Esteban*); Rosa María Sardà (*Rosa's Mother*); Toni Cantó (*Lola*); Fernando Fernán Gómez (*Rosa's Father*); Carlos Lozano (*Mario*); Fernando Guillén (*Doctor in ''Streetcar Named Desire''*); Juan José Otegui (*Ginecólogo*); Manuel Morón; José Luis Torrijo.

Publications:

Books:

Bouza Vidal, Nuria, *The Films of Pedro Almodovar*, translated by Linda Moore and Victoria Hughes, Madrid, 1988.

Smith, Paul Julian, *García Lorca/Almodóvar: Gender, Nationality, and the Limits of the Visible*, Cambridge, 1995.

Vernon, Kathleen M., and Barbara Morris, editors, *Post-Franco, Postmodern: The Films of Pedro Almodovar*, Westport, 1995.

Allinson, Mark, *A Spanish Labyrinth: The Films of Pedro Almodovar*, London, 2000.

Smith, Paul J., *Desire Unlimited: The Cinema of Pedro Almodovar*, New York, 2000.

Articles:

Menard, Valerie, ''El Conquistador Del Cine: Provocative Filmmaker Pedro Almódovar Explores the Human Experience,'' in *Hispanic*, vol. 11, no. 5, May 1998.

Holland, Jonathan, in *Variety* (New York), vol. 354, no. 9, 19 April 1999.

Smith, Paul Julian, and José Arroyo, ''Silicone and Sentiment: *All About My Mother*,'' in *Sight & Sound* (London), vol. 9, no. 9, September 1999.

''A Man of Many Women,'' an interview with Jonathan Van Meter, in *New York Times Magazine*, 12 September 1999.

Lemon, Brendan, ''A Man Fascinated by Women, as Actresses,'' in *New York Times*, 19 September 1999.

Ressner, Jeffrey, ''Loving Pedro: Almódovar, the Naughty Boy of Spanish Cinema, Pays Warm Tribute to Strong Women and Produces the Most Satisfying Work of His Career with *All About My Mother*,'' in *Time* (New York), vol. 154, no. 20, 15 November 1999.

Cortina, Betty, ''On the Verge: Pedro Almódovar Gets Big Raves with *All About My Mother:* And He May Just Go Hollywood,'' in *Entertainment Weekly*, no. 513, 19 November 1999.

''The Best of Cinema of 1999,'' in *Time* (New York), vol. 154, no. 25, 20 December 1999.

* * *

Women have almost always been at the center of the Almodóvar universe, and that is more than ever true in *Todo sobre mi madre* (*All About My Mother*). His 1999 film is explicitly dedicated to women and actresses, and particularly to actresses who have played actresses in such great films as *All About Eve*. That film, and Tennessee

William's *A Streetcar Named Desire*, are the primary influences on the director's latest work, but his story transcends even its influences.

Cecilia Roth plays Manuela, who once was an actress but now supports herself and her seventeen-year-old son with her work as a nurse in an agency that facilitates the donation and transplantation of human organs. We actually first meet her as she is playing the part in a training film for her organization of a woman who must decide amidst the grief of the sudden death of a family member whether or not to allow the transplantation of heart and liver to someone in need.

Manuela's son Esteban (Eloy Azorín) will be celebrating his birthday in a day or two, and would like nothing better from his mother than for her to tell him all about his father. Manuela recognizes that Esteban has nearly grown up, and that she can not rightly withhold this information from him any longer. But first they are going to see a performance of *Streetcar*, with the central role of Blanche played by a great actress named Huma Rojos. Marisa Parédes, who brought both *Tacones lejanos* (*High Heels*) and *La flor de mi secreto* (*The Flower of My Secret*) to vibrant life, seems the only possible choice for the role of Huma (which means "smoke").

After the performance, Manuela and Esteban wait in the rain to get an autograph from Huma, but she is engrossed in an argument with Nina, her heroin-addicted lover who plays Stella in the same production, and they disregard the boy who bangs on their window as they continue fighting. He runs after their car in the rain, and the chance of a moment transforms his mother from a nurse into a grieving parent who must make the same choices she has helped so many others to make.

All this takes place in the first ten minutes of the film, and the plot and characterizations develop ever more richly as the story progresses. After disposing of her son's heart, Manuela takes a train from Madrid to Barcelona, reversing a trip she had made eighteen years earlier, running away from the Esteban who was the father of her unborn child, and who was in the process of becoming Lola. This marks Almodóvar's first significant foray out of Madrid, which has been the location of his twelve previous feature films.

In Barcelona, Manuela comes again into the orbit of Huma and Nina, and also becomes reacquainted with an old friend, Agrado, another male-to-female transsexual who has not quite completed all the surgery of her transformation. At the same time she meets a young nun, Sister Rosa, who tries to be a nurse to people like Agrado who support their tangential existences with prostitution and drug dealing, but will soon be in need of nursing. No matter where Manuela runs to, she cannot run away from her work. Richard Corliss in his lovely, perceptive *Time* review says that "[Manuela] . . . is the ultimate organ donor. Now that her heart has been broken, she gives pieces of it to everyone."

These characters revolve around each other in ways that are sometimes mutually supportive, sometimes antagonistic, and mostly have the archetypal importance of characters from a story by Garcia Lorca. They deal with all of the issues of birth and life and death, sometimes as actresses, sometimes as working women, and sometimes in a blend of these roles that cannot be separated out.

Penélope Cruz and Candela Peña deliver wonderfully affecting performances as Sister Rosa and Nina. Nevertheless, with both of these wonderful performances, not to mention those of Parédes and of Antonia San Juan as Agrado, it is Cecilia Roth in the central role of Manuela who truly astonishes us with her mastery. She establishes her love of her son so compellingly that you cannot imagine how she can live after he dies. And then she shows you how she can live, and help other people to live as they deal with their own tragedies.

As tragic as some elements of *Todo sobre mi madre* can be, and as much as death and AIDS play a central part in the development of the plot, this is not a movie that overwhelms its audience in sadness. Many glints of the old Almodóvar humor shine through, particularly in a spur-of-the-moment monologue delivered by Agrado when Huma and Nina cannot go on in "Streetcar" one evening. Agrado regales the remaining audience with the story of her life, climaxing with the affirmation that "it cost me a lot to be authentic. . . Because a woman is more authentic the more she looks like what she has dreamed for herself."

This comic affirmation reinforces the more serious affirmation of the story—that life goes on even when faced with the inevitability of death, and that life is enriched more by helping each other in the living than in trying to go it alone. Almodóvar's community of women and actresses and children of all ages do just that, and have to be granted some kind of cinematic immortality for the beautifully simple way that they imprint themselves on our hearts.

While many critics agree with Corliss that *Todo sobre mi madre* is "the most satisfying work in a glittering, consistently surprising career," others cannot seem to adjust to an Almodóvar who does not continue to crank out the no-holds-barred satire with which he first introduced himself to international audiences. Roger Ebert foregrounds the elements of this old Almodóvar in his reliably mainstream, middle-brow review, but acknowledges that the "characters have taken on a weight and reality, as if Almodóvar has finally taken pity on them. . . "

Stanley Kauffmann starts off his review praising the old Almodóvar ("When he began his career . . . he seemed to burst forth, with satire ablaze, to revenge himself . . . on the oppressive stupidities and hypocrisies of society.") But in *Todo sobre mi madre*, Kauffmann finds ". . . no discernable theme: its purpose is to surprise us with non-soap incidents in a soap opera about women."

B. W. Ife, however, writing in the *Times Literary Supplement*, demonstrates that critics can break out of the mold of prior expectations. While he found Almodóvar's two previous films, *La flor de mi secreto* and *Carne tremulo* (*Live Flesh*) to possess ". . . a sense of compromise, of maturity achieved at the cost of a slight dulling of the edge," he can still see that with his latest feature the director has "found his true voice and written an intricate, insightful screenplay which allows it to be heard to full advantage."

—Stephen Brophy

TOKYO MONOGATARI

(Tokyo Story)

Japan, 1953

Director: Yasujiro Ozu

Production: Shochiku/Ofuna; color, 35mm; running time: 136 minutes; length: 12,509 feet. Released 3 November 1953, Tokyo.

Producer: Takeshi Yamamoto; **screenplay:** Yasujiro Ozu and Kogo Nada; **photography:** Yuhara Atsuta; **editor:** Yoshiyasu Hamamura; **sound:** Yoshisaburo Sueo; **production designers:** Tatsuo Hamada

Tokyo monogatari

with Itsuo Takahashi; **music:** Takanobu Saito; **costume designer:** Taizo Saito.

Cast: Chishu Ryu (*Father*); Chieko Higashiyama (*Mother*); So Yamamura (*Koichi*); Haruko Sugimura (*Shige Kaneko*); Setsuko Hara (*Noriko*); Kyoko Kagawa (*Kyoko*); Shiro Osaka (*Keizo*); Eijiro Tono (*Sanpei Numata*); Kuniko Miyake (*Fumiko*); Nobuo Nakamura (*Kurazo Kaneko*); Teruko Nagaoka (*Yone Hattori*); Zen Murase (*Minoru*); Mitsuhiro Mori (*Isamu*); Hisao Toake (*Osamu Hattori*); Toyoko Takahashi (*Shukichi Hirayama's neighbor*); Mutsuko Sakura (*Patron of the Oden restaurant*); Toru Abe (*Railroad employee*); Sachiko Mitani (*Noriko's neighbor*).

Publications

Script:

Ozu, Yasujiro, and Kogo Nada, *Tokyo Story*, edited by Donald Richie and Eric Klestadt, in *Contemporary Japanese Literature*, edited by Howard Hibbett, New York, 1977.

Books:

Richie, Donald, and Joseph Anderson, *The Japanese Film: Art and Industry*, Rutland, Vermont, 1960; revised edition, Princeton, 1982.
Richie, Donald, *Five Pictures of Yasujiro Ozu*, Tokyo, 1962.
Richie, Donald, *Japanese Cinema: Film Style and National Character*, New York, 1971.
Satomi, Jun, Tomo Shimogawara, and Shizo Yamauchi, editors, *Ozu—Hito to Shigoto* (Ozu—The Man and His Work), Tokyo, 1972.
Schrader, Paul, *Transcendental Style in Film*, Berkeley, 1972, 1988.
Burch, Noël, *Theory of Film Practice*, New York, 1973.
Richie, Donald, *Ozu*, Berkeley, 1974.
Schrader, Leonard, and Haruji Nakamura, editors, *Masters of Japanese Cinema*, New York, 1974.
Bock, Audie, *Japanese Film Directors*, New York, 1978; revised edition, Tokyo, 1985.
Burch, Noël, *To the Distant Observer*, Berkeley, 1979.
Klinowski, Jacek, and Adam Garbicz, editors, *Cinema, The Magic Vehicle: A Guide to Its Achievement: Journey Two*, Metuchen, New Jersey, 1979.
Sato, Tadao, *Currents in Japanese Cinema*, Tokyo, 1982.

Bordwell, David, *Ozu and the Poetics of Cinema*, Princeton and London, 1988.

Desser, David, editor, *Ozu's Tokyo Story*, Cambridge, 1997.

Articles:

Miner, Earl, in *Quarterly of Film, Radio, and Television* (Berkeley), Summer 1956.

Anderson, Lindsay, in *Sight and Sound* (London), Winter 1957–58.

Ryu, Chishu, ''Yasujiro Ozu,'' in *Sight and Sound* (London), Spring 1964.

Hatch, Robert, ''The Family of Ozu,'' in *Nation* (New York), 22 June 1964.

Wood, Robin, in *Movie* (London), Summer 1965.

Gow, Gordon, in *Films and Filming* (London), July 1965.

Farber, Manny, ''Ozu,'' in *Artforum* (New York), June 1970.

''Ozu on Ozu,'' in *Cinéma* (Paris), Summer 1970.

Richie, Donald, ''Yasujiro Ozu: A Biographical Filmography,'' in *Film Comment* (New York), Spring 1971.

Menon, N. S., in *Take One* (Montreal), May-June 1971.

Tessier, Max, ''Yasujiro Ozu,'' in *Anthologie du Cinéma* (Paris), July-October 1971.

Kauffman, Stanley, in *New Republic* (New York), 18 March 1972.

Menon, N. S., in *Take One* (Montreal), July 1972.

''Ozu on Ozu,'' in *Cinéma* (Paris), Winter 1972–73.

Coleman, Francis X.J., in *Favorite Movies: Critics' Choice*, edited by Philip Nobile, New York, 1973.

Bonnet, J., ''A la decouverte d'Ozu,'' in *Cinématographe* (Paris), February 1978.

Martin, M., in *Ecran* (Paris), February 1978.

Wood, Robin, in *Positif* (Paris), February 1978.

''*Tokyo Story* Issue'' of *Avant-Scène du Cinéma* (Paris), 15 March 1978.

Gauthier, G., in *Image et Son* (Paris), April 1978.

Richie, Donald, ''Yasujiro Ozu,'' in *Cinema, a Critical Dictionary*, London, 1980.

Konshak, D. J., ''Space and Narrative in *Tokyo Story*,'' in *Film Criticism* (Edinboro, Pennsylvania), Spring 1980.

Hosman, H., in *Skoop* (Amsterdam), September 1980.

Shipman, David, in *Films and Filming* (London), November 1983.

''*Tokyo Story* Section'' of *Skrien* (Amsterdam), Winter 1983–84.

Berta, R., Interview with Yahara Atsuta, in *Cahiers du Cinéma* (Paris), December 1985.

''Ozu, la vita e la geometria dei film,'' in *Castoro Cinema* (Florence), no. 151, 1991.

Wood, R., ''The 'Noriko' Trilogy,'' in *Cineaction* (Toronto), Winter 1992.

Zunzunegui, S., ''El perfume del Zen,'' in *Nosferatu* (San Sebastian), vol. 11, January 1993.

Modern Review, vol. 1, no. 12, December-January 1993–1994.

Berkes, Ildikó, ''Tokiói történet,'' in *Filmkultura* (Budapest), vol. 30, no. 12, January 1994.

Rayns, Tony, in *Sight & Sound* (London), vol. 4, no. 2, February 1994.

Aloff, Mindy, ''How American Intellectuals Learned to Love Ozu,'' in *The New York Times*, 3 April 1994.

Télérama (Paris), no. 2370, 14 June 1995.

Nicholas, Gregor, ''Slipper Shots,'' in *Sight & Sound* (London), vol. 7, no. 8, August 1997.

* * *

Film historians have long singled out three major directorial talents from Japan: Akira Kurosawa, Kenji Mizoguchi, and Yasujiro Ozu. And, at least in the West, and to almost as great a degree in his own nation, *Tokyo Story* stands for the best in Ozu's nearly forty-year career, a superior example of a filmmaker at the height of his powers.

The narrative of *Tokyo Story* seems straightforward and simple enough. An elderly couple, living by the sea in Onomichi in the south of Japan, go to visit their grown up children in Tokyo, but find they do not fit in. Their children (and grandchildren) have become mean and selfish, negatively effected by city living. The grandparents are only treated nicely by their widowed daughter-in-law, who despite having to live in poverty, has retained traditional values. The grandparents eventually return home, and the grandmother dies, leaving the grandfather to face the future alone.

Tokyo Story hardly has a happy ending. By closing the drama with the daughter-in-law going off, leaving the grandfather by the now familiar port, we confront the often sad reality of everyday existence. *Tokyo Story* presents an all too common situation, a tale of real life which happens more often than we like to consider. The point is that while the Hollywood system would not permit such a tragic tale to make it to the screen the Japanese industry would.

Most critics find *Tokyo Story* central to Ozu's final period of filmmaking, the last great excursions of a virtuoso in a lengthy career in the Japanese cinema. During the 1950s, after Japan had emerged from the war, Ozu often dealt with traditional values. The ''Tokyo'' in the title was central to the life of the nation after 1880, presenting to the world how Meiji Japan could succeed in western arenas. By the 1920s Tokyo stood as one of the more populous cities in the world. Of Ozu's fifty-four films, some forty-nine take place in Tokyo and five mention the city in their title. This city, more than any, symbolized the modern world, with its mass culture, including the ever growing obsession with motion pictures.

In certain respects *Tokyo Story* is a typical work, but in many it is not. Although not all of Ozu's films are about the family, certainly he was vitally interested in that part of Japanese life. He was, after the war, particularly intrigued with the changes his nation was undergoing. Although Ozu is most often seen as a traditionalist, he was always concerned with the events of everyday life. *Tokyo Story* is typical of late Ozu in that it arose from immediate concerns of the early 1950s, in particular Tokyo being rebuilt and families becoming more ''urbanized.''

Tokyo Story illustrates the structural rigor and richness of the later Ozu films. This is true for editing, camerawork, mise-en-scène, and sound. For example, three recurring sounds define the acoustic texture of the film: chugging boats, the noises of trains, and the sounds of cicadas. All three are established in the film's initial scene when the grandparents prepare to leave Onomichi. Their stay in Tokyo is then constantly punctuated by train whistles. Later when the grandmother is about to die the scene opens with train sounds and closes with the noises of harbor boats.

In the West Ozu is celebrated as an artist. But in the Japanese film industry he was seen as a steady worker. He created, on schedule, one film a year for the massive Shochiku studio. He was that studio's most famous director, and films such as *Tokyo Story* kept profits flowing in the years before television would become a rival for the mass entertainment audience. And he was honored in industry polls. *Tokyo Story* won the ''Kinema Jumpo'' first place for the best film of the year in Japan.

Although *Tokyo Story* was released in Japan in November, 1953, and was a popular success there, it did not make its impact in the West until nearly two decades later upon its release in the United States in 1972. But today critics around the world list it among the greatest films ever to be created in the nearly one hundred years of world cinema.

—Douglas Gomery

TOM JONES

UK, 1963

Director: Tony Richardson

Production: Woodfall; Eastmancolor; running time: 128 minutes; length: 11,565 feet. Released 1963.

Producer: Tony Richardson; **screenplay:** John Osborne, from the novel by Henry Fielding; **screenplay editor:** Sewell Stokes; **photography:** Walter Lassally; 2nd unit photography: Manny Wynn; **editor:** Antony Gibbs; **sound:** Don Challis; **production designer:** Ralph Brinton; **art director:** Ted Marshall; **music:** John Addison; **narrator:** Michael MacLiammoir.

Cast: Albert Finney (*Tom Jones*); Susannah York (*Sophie Western*); Hugh Griffith (*Squire Western*); Edith Evans (*Miss Western*); Joan Greenwood (*Lady Bellaston*); Diane Cilento (*Molly Seagrim*); George Devine (*Squire Allworthy*); Joyce Redman (*Jenny Jones*); David Warner (*Blifil*); David Tomlinson (*Lord Fellamar*); Rosalind Knight (*Mrs. Fitzpatrick*); Peter Bull (*Thwackum*); John Moffatt (*Square*); Patsy Rowlands (*Honour*); Wilfrid Lawson (*Black George*); Jack MacGowran (*Partridge*); Freda Jackson (*Mrs. Seagrim*); Julian Glover (*Lt. Northerton*); Rachel Kempson (*Bridget Allworthy*); George A. Cooper (*Fitzpatrick*); Angela Baddeley (*Mrs. Wilkins*); Avis Bunnage (*Landlady at George Inn*); Rosalind Atkinson (*Mrs. Miller*); James Cairncross (*Parson Supple*); Redmond Phillips (*Lawyer Dowling*); Mark Dignam (*Lieutenant*); Lynn Redgrave (*Susan*); Jack Stewart (*MacLachlan*); Michael Brennan (*Jailer*).

Awards: Oscars for Best Picture, Best Director, Best Score, and Best Screenplay. British Film Academy Awards for Best British Film, Best Film from any source, and Best Screenplay.

Publications

Script:

Osborne, John, *Tom Jones: A Film Script*, London, 1964.

Books:

Bull, Peter, *I Say, Look Here*, London, 1965.

Manvell, Roger, *New Cinema in Britain*, London, 1969.

Walker, Alexander, *Hollywood, England: The British Film Industry in the 60s*, London, 1975.

Klein, Michael, and Gillian Parker, editors, *The English Novel and the Movies*, New York, 1981.

Barr, Charles, editor, *All Our Yesterdays: 90 Years of British Cinema*, London, 1986.

Hill, John, *Sex, Class, and Realism: British Cinema 1956–63*, London, 1986.

Richardson, Tony, *Long-Distance Runner: An Autobiography*, New York, 1993.

Radovich, Don, *Tony Richardson: A Bio-Bibliography*, Westport, 1995.

Welsh, James M., and John C. Tibbetts, *The Cinema of Tony Richardson: Essays and Interviews*, Albany, 2000.

Articles:

Cowie, Peter, ''The Face of '63—Britain,'' in *Films and Filming* (London), February 1963.

Richardson, Tony, in *Kine Weekly* (London), 27 June 1963.

Variety (New York), 31 July 1963.

Baker, Peter, in *Films and Filming* (London), August 1963.

Milne, Tom, in *Monthly Film Bulletin* (London), August 1963.

New Yorker, 12 October 1963.

Cine Française (Paris), 21 December 1963.

Moller, David, ''Britain's Busiest Angry Young Man,'' in *Film Comment* (New York), Winter 1964.

Battestin, Martin C., ''Osborne's *Tom Jones*: Adapting a Classic,'' in *Man and the Movies*, edited by W.R. Robinson, Baton Rouge, Louisiana, 1967.

Villelaur, Anne, ''Tony Richardson,'' in *Dossiers du cinéma 1*, Paris, 1971.

City Limits (London), 11 February 1983.

''Albert Finney,'' in *Ciné Revue* (Paris), 30 August 1984.

Van Gelder, L., ''At the Movies,'' in *New York Times*, vol. 138, C6, 15 September 1989.

Revue du Cinéma (Paris), no. 475, October 1991.

Walker, A., ''Letters: *Tom Jones* at Home,'' in *Sight & Sound* (London), vol. 3, December 1993.

Holden, Stephen, ''An Angry Man Found Himself in *Tom Jones*,'' in *The New York Times*, 21 August 1994.

* * *

Tom Jones is one of those films of ambiguous national status, registered as British, and made by a British cast and crew, but funded entirely by the London office of United Artists. As such, it is one of the films on which is negotiated the shift from the ''committed social realism'' of the early 1960s British cinema to the mainly American-funded ''swinging sixties'' films of the middle years of the decade. At first sight, being a costume melodrama (and an adaptation of a classic novel) set in the eighteenth century, *Tom Jones* would seem to be aberrant in relation to both the earlier films, and the different contemporaneity of time, place and energy of the glamorous and eccentric pop culture fantasies of the mid 1960s. But the film was a huge success, accruing four Oscars, garnering much critical acclaim, and doing record business at the box-office. To some extent, the success of this film paved the way for subsequent films to work in the same free-wheeling, light-hearted and sexually ''permissive'' mode.

Richardson was quoted at the time as saying ''This is our holiday film. We thought it was time we made a really uncommitted film. No social significance for once. No contemporary problems to lay bare, just a lot of colourful, sexy fun'' (*Daily Mail*, 2.7.62). Even so, realism was still a key term in the publicity and critical reviews surrounding the film. As the *Daily Mail*'s reviewer put it, ''a holiday

Tom Jones

film it may be, but the master of screen realism is not letting glamour run amok on that account.'' Authenticity was assumed to be guaranteed by shooting entirely on location, and by seeking out ''correct'' period details in setting, props and costumes. Thus much of the power of the film depends upon the elaboration of such narratively redundant detail, fleshing out a richly detailed space within which the drama can unfold.

The reputation of the production team was important too. Richardson himself was a founder of and a prolific producer and director for Woodfall, one of the key companies in the film style and independent mode of production that characterised Britain's new wave. Osborne, who adapted Fielding's novel for the screen, was another of Woodfall's founders, and author of two of the plays that the company had adapted earlier, *Look Back In Anger* and *The Entertainer*. Finney, who played the lead role, had done the same in *Saturday Night and Sunday Morning*. And Lassally, the cameraman who had produced the gritty look of *A Taste of Honey* and *The Loneliness of the Long Distance Runner*, now used similar techniques for this period recreation: having attempted to achieve a realistic effect at one level through the authenticity of period detail, Lassally and Richardson pushed for a different kind of realism at another level by using contemporary documentary camera techniques wherever possible, including shooting on location, using light-weight hand-held cameras, comparatively fast film-stock, and natural light.

Without this veneer of surface realism and the cultural status of Fielding's novel, it seems unlikely that this spectacular and excessive period costume piece, with few of the moral or social commitments of earlier Woodfall films, could have been so easily accommodated by the British critics of the period. And, in fact, some of the reviewers of the film suggested that *Tom Jones* was far more socially relevant (because of its satire and its plea for tolerance) than the ''superficially contemporary'' films that had preceded it.

It is perhaps the question of style which enables the critic in retrospect to establish as strong a degree of repetition as of differentiation between the pre- and post-*Tom Jones* films. As with Richardson's previous two films, both canonised as realist films, *Tom Jones* displays an eclectic use of non-classical devices, many of them derived from the French *nouvelle vague*. Alongside relatively classical camera set-ups and scene construction, we find heavily stylised devices for shot- or scene-transitions; an obtrusive foregrounding of non-diegetic music; occasional use of under-cranked camera to speed up action; a particularly self-conscious use of montage sequences;

and so on. But perhaps the most famous of *Tom Jones*'s stylistic touches is the frequent use of direct address to camera and other means of establishing a subjective rapport between spectator and film (justified as a means of reproducing the narrative voice of the novel). There is much debate amongst critics as to whether this style is ''organic'' to the film, or whether the film has been invaded by merely disconcerting camera trickery (which was the view of the more ''serious'' British critics). Either way, it was this type of pop-art modernism that characterised many of the subsequent British films of the mid 1960s.

—Andrew Higson

TOP HAT

USA, 1935

Director: Mark Sandrich

Production: RKO Radio Pictures, Inc.; black and white, 35mm; running time: 105 minutes. Released 6 September 1935. Filmed in RKO studios.

Producer: Pandro Berman; **screenplay:** Dwight Taylor and Allan Scott, adapted by Karl Noti, from a play by Alexander Farago and Laszlo Aladar; **photography:** David Abel and Vernon Walker; **editor:** William Hamilton; **art director:** Van Nest Polglase; **set designer:** Carrol Clark; **music and lyrics:** Irving Berlin; **costume designer:** Bernard Newman; **choreographers:** Fred Astaire with Hermes Pan.

Cast: Fred Astaire (*Jerry Travers*); Ginger Rogers (*Dale Tremont*); Edward Everett Horton (*Horace Hardwick*); Helen Broderick (*Madge Hardwick*); Erik Rhodes (*Alberto*); Eric Blore (*Bates*); Donald Meek (*Curate*); Florence Roberts (*Curate's wife*); Gino Corrado (*Hotel manager*); Peter Hobbs (*Call boy*).

Top Hat

Publications

Books:

Astaire, Fred, *Steps in Time*, New York, 1959.
Springer, John, *All Talking! All Singing! All Dancing! A Pictorial History of the Movie Musical*, New York, 1966.
Baxter, John, *Hollywood in the Thirties*, New York, 1968.
Hackl, Alfons, *Fred Astaire and His Work*, Vienna, 1970.
Thompson, Howard, *Fred Astaire: A Pictorial Treasury of His Films*, New York, 1970.
Bergman, Andrew, *We're in the Money: Depression America and Its Films*, New York, 1971.
Taylor, John Russell, and Arthur Jackson, *The Hollywood Musical*, New York, 1971.
Croce, Arlene, *The Fred Astaire and Ginger Rogers Book*, New York, 1972.
Green, Stanley and Burt Goldblatt, *Starring Fred Astaire*, New York, 1973.
Green, Benny, *Fred Astaire*, London, 1979.
Neale, Stephen, *Genre*, London, 1980.
Altman, Rick, editor, *Genre: The Musical*, London, 1981.
Cebe, Gilles, *Fred Astaire*, Paris, 1981.
Delameter, James, *Dance in the Hollywood Musical*, Ann Arbor, Michigan, 1981.
Feuer, Jane, *The Hollywood Musical*, London, 1982.
Mueller, John, *Astaire Dancing: The Musical Films*, New York, 1985.
Thomas, Bob, *Astaire: The Man, the Dancer*, London, 1985.
Drouin, Frederique, *Fred Astaire*, Paris, 1986.
Satchell, Tim, *Astaire: The Biography*, London, 1987.
Altman, Rick, *The American Film Musical*, London and Bloomington, Indiana, 1989.
Rogers, Ginger, *Ginger: My Story*, New York, 1991, 1992.
Faris, Jocelyn, *Ginger Rogers: A Bio-Bibliography*, Westport, 1994.
Sheridan, Morley, *Shall We Dance: The Life of Ginger Rogers*, New York, 1995.
Billman, Larry, *Fred Astaire: A Bio-Bibliography*, Westport, 1997.

Articles:

Sennwald, Andre, in *New York Times*, 30 August 1935.
Variety (New York), 4 September 1935.
Time (New York), 9 September 1935.
Greene, Graham, in *Spectator* (London), 25 October 1935.
Eustis, M., ''Actor-Dancer Attacks His Part: Fred Astaire,'' in *Theatre Arts* (New York), May 1937.
Pratley, Gerald, ''Fred Astaire's Film Career,'' in *Films in Review* (New York), January 1957.

Conrad, Derek, ''Two Feet in the Air,'' in *Films and Filming* (London), December 1959.
Grieves, Jefferson, in *Films and Filming* (London), October 1962.
Dickens, Homer, ''Ginger Rogers,'' in *Films in Review* (New York), March 1966.
Thousand Eyes Magazine (New York), September 1976.
Dyer, Richard, ''Entertainment and Utopia,'' in *Movie* (London), no. 24, 1977.
Johnson, Julia, in *Magill's Survey of Cinema 4*, Englewood Cliffs, New Jersey, 1980.
Mueller, J., ''The Filmed Dances of Fred Astaire,'' in *Quarterly Review of Film Studies*, Spring 1981.
Medhurst, Andy, ''The Musical,'' in *The Cinema Book*, edited by Pam Cook, London, 1985.
Biesty, P., ''The Myth of the Playful Dancer,'' in *Studies in Popular Culture*, vol. 13, no. 1, 1990.
''Nabisco Faces the Music,'' in *Time*, vol. 17, 25 February 1991.
Silverman, S., ''In '35 Fred and Ginger Trip the Light Fantastic,'' in *Variety* (New York), vol. 349, 2 November 1992.
Reid's Film Index (Wyong), no. 16, 1995.

* * *

Top Hat was the fourth film made by Fred Astaire and Ginger Rogers for RKO/Radio and the first film written especially to showcase their own unique talents on the screen. In *Flying Down to Rio* (1933), their first film together, Astaire and Rogers were the second leads to Dolores Del Rio and Gene Raymond, but the screen chemistry created when they danced together made them the ultimate ''stars'' of that film. Their next two films, *The Gay Divorcee* (1934) and *Roberta* (1935), were adapted from successful stage plays with some alteration to suit the Astaire-Rogers combination. By 1935, when *Top Hat* was released, they were such established stars that RKO hired no less a figure than Irving Berlin to write a new score to accompany the Dwight Taylor and Allan Scott screenplay. Although the plot is run of the mill and displays the usual ''boy meets girl'' twists of most of the Astaire-Rogers films, the score is one of the best they ever worked with. It includes such now standard songs as ''Isn't It a Lovely Day (To Be Caught in the Rain)?'' ''Cheek to Cheek,'' and the title song, ''Top Hat,'' which has become synonymous with the image of Fred Astaire.

As with all of their films together, *Top Hat* is both musical and a story with music. A pure musical has only musical numbers that somehow advance or explicate the plot; the story with music has songs that may be interpolated to entertain the audience yet do not affect the story at all. The title number for *Top Hat* is an interpolation: Astaire, as Jerry Travers, is a musical star, so that audience sees him performing on stage, and although it is a magnificent example of the inimitable Astaire style, the ''Top Hat'' number does not give any information about the character or the plot. As Astaire and/or Rogers frequently played characters who are entertainers, their audience was given ample opportunity to see the stars dancing without the necessity of tying the number to the storyline.

In *Top Hat* the most memorable of the musical numbers that advances the plot is ''Cheek to Cheek,'' perhaps the single most beautiful popular dance for two performers ever filmed. Astaire and Rogers were always cool, perfectly groomed and the essence of 1930s sophistication. The grace and symmetry of their bodies, set against the sleek black-and-white Art Deco set created by Carrol Clark (under the titular direction of Van Nest Polglase), were perfect expressions of the music. In the sequence Travers entices Dale Tremont (Ginger Rogers) into the dance to win her love. Dale, who thinks that Jerry is married to her best friend Madge Hardwick (Helen Broderick), is at first reluctant. Eventually, though, the romance of the dance and her attraction to Jerry cannot be overcome, and by the midpoint she participates fully. The refrain of the song, ''Heaven, I'm in Heaven'' is illuminated not only by the dance and the set, but also by the graceful beauty of Rogers' ostrich feather dress. Although there have been many published reports of fights on the set over the unwieldiness of the dress, it is definitely an asset.

There are other important dances in the film, the most memorable of which is the casual, yet sophisticated, tap dance ''Isn't It a Lovely Day (To Be Caught in the Rain).'' The style of this dance is happy, flippant, and fun—the complete opposite of the more involved ''Cheek to Cheek'' dance in which the principals are troubled by their love. In this number, even the rain is a joke, and the stars are all smiles after a brief hesitancy on the part of Rogers. In ''Cheek to Cheek'' even the beauty of the dance cannot make Rogers smile, and the conclusion seems bittersweet.

Fred Astaire and Ginger Rogers went on to make five more successful films for RKO in the late 1930s and one more, less successful, film in 1948, *The Barkleys of Broadway*, for MGM. (Ironically, although their last film was the only one to be produced in color, in terms of style it is the most colorless.) Their popularity was a mainstay for RKO in the 1930s, and their reception by both critics and the public alike have barely diminished over the decades.

—Patricia King Hanson

TOSS ME A DIME

See **TIRE DIÉ**

TOUCH OF EVIL

USA, 1958

Director: Orson Welles

Production: Universal-International; black and white, 35mm; running time: 95 minutes, also variously noted at 105 and 115 minutes. Released 21 May 1958. Filmed spring 1957 in Venice, California.

Producer: Albert Zugsmith; **screenplay:** Orson Welles, from the novel *Badge of Evil* by Whit Masterson; **additional director:** Harry Keller; **photography:** Russell Metty; **editors:** Virgil M. Vogel and Aaron Stell; **sound:** Leslie I. Carey and Frank Wilkinson; **art directors:** Alexander Golitzen and Robert Clatworthy; **music:** Henry Mancini; **music director:** Joseph Gershenson; **costume designer:** Bill Thomas.

Cast: Charlton Heston (*Ramon Miguel ''Mike'' Vargas*); Janet Leigh (*Susan Vargas*); Orson Welles (*Hank Quinlan*); Joseph Calleia (*Pete Menzies*); Akim Tamiroff (*Uncle Joe Grandi*); Joanna Moore (*Marcia Linnekar*); Marlene Dietrich (*Tanya*); Ray Collins (*Adair*); Dennis Weaver (*Motel manager*); Victor Millan (*Manolo Sanchez*); Lalo Rios (*Rio*); Valentin de Vargas (*Pancho*); Mort Mills (*Schwartz*);

Touch of Evil

Mercedes McCambridge (*Hoodlum*); Wayne Taylor, Ken Miller, Raymond Rodriguez (*Gang members*); Michael Sargent (*Pretty Boy*); Zsa Zsa Gabor (*Owner of nightclub*); Keenan Wynn (*Man*); Joseph Cotten (*Detective*); Phil Harvey (*Blaine*); Joi Lansing (*Blonde*); Harry Shannon (*Gould*); Rusty Wescoatt (*Casey*); Arlene McQuade (*Ginnie*); Domenick Delgarde (*Lackey*); Joe Basulto (*Hoodlum*); Jennie Dias (*Jackie*); Yolanda Bojorquez (*Bobbie*); Eleanor Corado (*Lia*).

Publications

Script:

Welles, Orson, *Touch of Evil*, edited by Terry Comito, New Brunswick, New Jersey, 1985.

Books:

Bogdanovich, Peter, *The Cinema of Orson Welles*, New York, 1961.
Bessy, Maurice, *Orson Welles*, Paris, 1963.
Cowie, Peter, *The Cinema of Orson Welles*, London, 1965.
Bessy, Maurice, *Orson Welles*, New York, 1971.
Higham, Charles, *The Films of Orson Welles*, Berkeley, 1971.
Sarris, Andrew, editor, *Interviews with Film Directors*, New York, 1971.
McBride, Joseph, *Orson Welles*, London, 1972.
Cowie, Peter, *A Ribbon of Dreams*, New York, 1973.
Kaminskly, Stuart, *American Film Genres*, Dayton, Ohio, 1974.
McCarthy, Tod, and Charles Flynn, editors, *Kings of the Bs: Working Within the Hollywood System*, New York, 1975.
McBride, Joseph, *Orson Welles: Actor and Director*, New York, 1977.
Bazin, Andre, *Orson Welles: A Critical View*, New York, 1978.
Silver, Alain, and Elizabeth Ward, editors, *Film Noir*, Woodstock, New York, 1979.
Heath, Stephen, *Questions of Cinema*, Bloomington, Indiana, 1981.
Valentinetti, Claudio M., *Orson Welles*, Florence, 1981.
Bergala, Alain, and Jean Narboni, editors, *Orson Welles*, Paris, 1982.
Andrew, Dudley, *Film in the Aura of Art*, Princeton, New Jersey, 1984.
Leigh, Janet, *There Really Was a Hollywood*, South Yarmouth, 1984, 1985.
Higham, Charles, *Orson Welles: The Rise and Fall of an American Genius*, New York, 1985.

Leaming, Barbara, *Orson Welles: A Biography*, New York, 1985.
Parra, Daniele, and Jacques Zimmer, *Orson Welles*, Paris, 1985.
Weis, Elisabeth, and John Belton, editors, *Film Sound: Theory and Practice*, New York, 1985.
Crowther, Bruce, *Charlton Heston: The Epic Presence*, London, 1986.
Taylor, John Russell, *Orson Welles: A Celebration*, London, 1986.
Cotten, Joseph, *Vanity Will Get You Somewhere*, New York, 1987.
Wood, Bret, *Orson Welles: A Bio-Bibliography*, Westport, 1990.
Howard, James, *The Complete Films of Orson Welles*, Secaucus, 1991.
Beja, Morris, *Perspective on Orson Welles*, New York, 1995.
Heston, Charlton, *In The Arena: An Autobiography*, New York, 1995.
Callow, Simon, *Orson Welles: The Road to Xanadu*, New York, 1997.
Heston, Charlton, and Jean-Pierre Isbouts, *Charlton Heston's Hollywood: 50 Years in American Film*, New York, 1998.
Welles, Orson, *This Is Orson Welles*, New York, 1998.
Munby, Jonathan, *Public Enemies, Public Heroes: Screening the Gangster from Little Caesar to Touch of Evil*, Chicago, 1999.
Taylor, John Russell, *Orson Welles*, New York, 2000.

Articles:

Interview with Welles in *Lettres Françaises* (Paris), 20 May 1958.
Interview with Welles in *Cahiers du Cinéma* (Paris), June 1958.
Truffaut, François, in *Arts* (Paris), 4 June 1958.
Knight, Arthur, in *Saturday Review* (New York), 7 June 1958.
Sadoul, Georges, in *Lettres Françaises* (Paris), 12 June 1958.
Domarchi, Jean, in *Cahiers du Cinéma* (Paris), July 1958.
''L'Oeuvre d'Orson Welles,'' in *Cahiers du Cinéma* (Paris), September 1958.
Stanbrook, Alan, ''The Heroes of Welles,'' in *Film* (London), no. 28, 1961.
Allais, Jean-Claude, in *Premier Plan* (Lyons), March 1961.
Johnson, William, ''Orson Welles: Of Time and Loss,'' in *Film Quarterly* (Berkeley), Fall 1967.
Comito, Terry, in *Film Comment* (New York), Summer 1971.
Prokosch, Mike, ''Orson Welles: An Introduction,'' in *Film Comment* (New York), Summer 1971.
Delson, James, ''Heston on Welles,'' in *Take One* (Montreal), July-August 1971.
Schrader, Paul, ''Notes on Film Noir,'' in *Film Comment* (New York), Spring 1972.
Ecran (Paris), July 1972.
Krueger, E. M., ''*Touch of Evil*: Style Expressing Content,'' in *Cinema Journal* (Iowa City), Fall 1972.
Hale, N., ''Welles and the Logic of Death,'' in *Film Heritage* (Dayton, Ohio), Fall 1974.
Lacombe, A., in *Ecran* (Paris), January 1975.
Heath, Stephen, ''Film and System: Terms of an Analysis,'' in *Screen* (London), Spring 1975.
Rosenbaum, Jonathan, in *Sight and Sound* (London), Autumn 1975.
Wood, Robin, ''Welles, Shakespeare, and Webster,'' in *Personal Views: Explorations in Film* (London), 1976.
Norharrd, P., in *Kosmorama* (Copenhagen), Summer 1977.
Henley, John, in *Cinema Texas Program Notes* (Austin), 19 April 1978.
Bywater, W., ''Subject Position,'' in *Film Criticism* (Edinboro, Pennsylvania), no. 1, 1979.
Cremonini, G., in *Cineforum* (Bergamo), May 1982.
Stubbs, John, ''The Evolution of Orson Welles's *Touch of Evil* from Novel to Film,'' in *Cinema Journal* (Champaign, Illinois), Winter 1985.
Stubbs, John, and Terry Comito, ''Dialogue,'' in *Cinema Journal* (Champaign, Illinois), Spring 1985.
''*Touch of Evil* Issue'' of *Avant-Scène du Cinéma* (Paris), January-February 1986.
Nielsen, N. A., ''Et allerhelvedes perspektiv,'' in *Kosmorama* (Copenhagen), Fall 1989.
Bywater, W., ''The Visual Pleasure of Patriarchal Cinema: Welles' *Touch of Evil*,'' in *Film Criticism* (Meadville, Pennsylvania), no. 3, 1990.
Heston, C., ''Touch of Genius,'' in *National Review*, vol. 44, 3 February 1992.
Rosenbaum, J., ''Orson Welles' Memo to Universal: *Touch of Evil*,'' in *Film Quarterly* (Berkeley), no. 1, 1992.
Vaughan, Don, ''Confessions of a Teenage Heartthrob,'' in *Filmfax* (Evanston), no. 37, February-March 1993.
Wolthuis, J.J.C., in *Score* (Lelystad), vol. 89, December 1993.
Schmidt, N., ''Montage et scenario,'' in *Cinemaction* (Conde-sur-Noireau), vol. 72, no. 3, 1994.
Hall, John W., ''Touch of *Psycho?*: Hitchcock's Debt to Welles,'' in *Bright Lights* (Cincinnati), no. 14, 1995.
Wollen, Peter, ''Foreign Relations: Welles and *Touch of Evil*,'' in *Sight & Sound* (London), vol. 6, no. 10, October 1996.
Kau, E., ''Great Beginnings—and Endings: Made by Orson Welles,'' in *P.O.V.*, vol. 2, December 1996.
McCarthy, Todd, ''Restored *Evil* Approximates Welles' Editing-Room Touch,'' in *Variety* (New York), vol. 352, no. 4, 7 September 1998.
Weinraub, Bernard, ''Touch of Memory,'' in *The New York Times*, 18 September 1998.
Thomas, François, ''Henry Mancini et *La Soif du mal*,'' in *Positif* (Paris), no. 452, October 1998.
Bowman, James, ''Self-Ignorance: Nowadays, Self-Deception Passes for Self-Knowledge,'' in *The American Spectator*, vol. 31, no. 11, November 1998.

* * *

Touch of Evil shows how Orson Welles refashions the Baroque style, inaugurated in *Citizen Kane*, in terms of the post-war film anticipating the experiment of New Wave cinema. If Welles's oeuvre can be mapped according to Henri Focillon's concept of the ''life of forms in art,'' it can be said that *Citizen Kane* marks a classic, if not ''experimental'' phase in a cycle that *Touch of Evil* completes in its self-reflective and expressly decadent mode. Inspired by Whit Masterson's pulpy *Badge of Evil*, the film tells of an erstwhile narcotic agent's attempt to foil a crime committed on the Mexican border just as he prepares to celebrate his honeymoon with his shining new wife (Janet Leigh). Multiple frame-ups abound. The agent, Vargas (Charlton Heston), finds himself amidst a band of tawdry outlaws under the control of the local chief of police—the obese Hank Quinlan (Welles). The plot leads through the sleaze of Tijuana (set in Venice, California) over dusty vistas of dirt roads, into a decrepit motel filled with sexed-up punks reeking of booze and dope, and through a labyrinth of oil derricks by a river flowing with trash.

The film revives *film noir* at a time when the genre is spent. It brings into view questions of framing, editing, and desire at the basis of spectatorship in general. Because it alludes to former moments in Welles's oeuvre, it is both a filmic autobiography, like *The Lady from Shanghai*, and a collage of transfilmic obsessions. The plot hinges on a rebus. After strangling his wig-wearing henchman (Akim Tamiroff),

Quinlan forgets his *cane*—or former name in *Citizen Kane*—such that the play on the word and object returns, like the repressed, to convict him of his many former crimes. Shakespeare seems to inspire the scenario. The film essays decadence in ways that make Welles something of the Jack Falstaff of the second part of *Henry the Fourth*. Dennis Weaver plays the role of a fool clearly drawn from the comic character in *Macbeth*.

Welles's grotesque body occupies the center of the film. A wide-angle lens records from numerous angles its immensity in baroque caricature. The camera usually pans quickly or crabs to draw the spectator's eyes to spherical aberrations distorting the edges of the shots. A highly mannered perspective results, with curvilinear views extending the rotundity of Welles's body *all over* the frame. Elsewhere the wide angle lens accelerates the narrative by accentuating movement, compressing characters in the foreground and background alike, and turning with velocity such that no stable visual order results. The opening crane shot of over two minutes' duration registers the credits, engages the narrative, and breaks with the crack of an explosion behind the newlyweds' first kiss. The camera exploits the optical range of the shorter focal length of the lens by simulating high speed driving in matte shots projected behind a car to create the effect of Welles and Heston whizzing down the streets of Tijuana. They speak calmly on as the car goes at a breakneck clip through a landscape of poverty.

Welles amplifies the soundtrack. Voice and clatter are reported percussively and cacaphonously. ''Reported'' events resound in a remarkable final sequence: Vargas follows Quinlan through a maze of iron girders and under a bridge that echoes the speech on the sound track. Because Vargas has planted a microphone in Quinlan's pocket, the viewer hears the heave and slur of the antagonist's breathing and mutterings against a recording that plays back the immediate past of the film, inscribing the memory of episodes in the film on a register coextensive with the present. In the finale, blood drips from Quinlan's last victim, the body sprawled on the bridge above the murderer who is at the edge of the river below. Droplets fall onto Quinlan's chubby hand, thus bringing the play of sounds and visuals back into a context resembling Elizabethan tragedy. Quinlan is marked by the bloodstains, soon cornered and shot, his great body falling into a pool of flotsam. ''Too bad. He was a great detective but a lousy cop,'' eulogizes Menzies (Joseph Calleia); to which Tanya (Marlene Dietrich) responds in a thick German accent, topping the entire film, ''He was some kind of a man.''

Despite having no narrative role in the story, Dietrich's presence is manifold. One of Quinlan's former lovers, now a wizened fortune teller overlaid with heavy makeup, she smokes cigarettes in poses reminiscent of the aging beauty Fritz Lang created for *Rancho Notorious* six years before. By facing the camera frontally, she pulls into the present a filmic legacy that reaches back both to Lang and to von Sternberg of the 1930s. Her remark that Quinlan's time is ''all played out'' is doubly ironic in view of the portable television set, seen in the background of her cluttered quarters, presaging the end of the studio tradition. Their banter is laced with allusion to Quinlan's passion for candy bars: his obesity becomes a sign, on another allegorical level, of the director's career being one of excess, genius, and waste. Her Tarot reading seals the anti-hero's fate and forces him to return to the narrative.

Touch of Evil stages sexual violence in a sequence set at the ''Mirador'' motel. Having consigned his wife in a room while he chases his suspects, Vargas retrieves her after making repeated telephone calls. Supine, heaving, in the bondage of her corset, Suzy (Leigh, whose name is again a reminder of the Suzy of *Citizen Kane*) is framed in a pose epitomizing Hollywood's model of desire, but only before the camera tears it to shreds, in a style that combines the rhetoric of torture that Rossellini had inaugurated in *Open City* with oblique allusion to *Reefer Madness*. Time and again the effects suggest that violence is a matter of optics, and that it owes its force to conventions that Hollywood had produced in its representation of women in the tradition of *film noir*.

In *Touch of Evil* the studio style is distorted to comic excess. Here are located the virtual politics of Welles's work, in the mix of lenticular experiment and the essay of a Shakespearean type of narrative. In the last decade the film has been subject of a dazzling reading by Stephen Heath in *Questions of Cinema*. The renascence of Welles's feature owes much to the complexities Heath unravels through an alert and detailed reading inspired by a blend of psychoanalysis and politics. The film is of a force and heritage going far beyond its period.

—Tom Conley

TRAIN WITHOUT A TIMETABLE

See **VLAK BEZ VOZNOG REDA**

TRAINSPOTTING

UK, 1996

Director: Danny Boyle

Production: Channel Four Films, Figment Films, PolyGram Filmed Entertainment (U.S.), and Noel Gay Motion Picture Company; color, 35mm; running time: 93 minutes (94 in United States); length: 2650 meters. Released 23 February 1996. Filmed in Edinburgh, Glasgow, and Corrour Station, Scotland, and London, England. Cost: $3.5 million (U.S.).

Producer: Christopher Figg, Andrew Macdonald; **screenplay:** John Hodge; from the novel by Irvine Welsh; **cinematographer:** Brian Tufano; **editor:** Masahiro Hirakubo; **casting:** Andy Pryor, Gail Stevens; **production design:** Kave Quinn; **art direction:** Tracey Gallacher; **costume design:** Rachael Fleming; **makeup:** Robert McCann; **special effects:** Grant Mason, Tony Steers.

Cast: Ewan McGregor (*Mark ''Rent-boy'' Renton*); Ewen Bremner (*Daniel ''Spud'' Murphy*); Jonny Lee Miller (*Simon David ''Sick Boy'' Williamson*); Kevin McKidd (*Tommy MacKenzie*); Robert Carlyle (*Francis (Franco) Begbie*); Kelly MacDonald (*Diane*); Peter Mullan (*Swanney*); James Cosmo (*Mr. Renton*); Eileen Nicholas (*Mrs. Renton*); Susan Vidler (*Allison*); Pauline Lynch (*Lizzy*); Shirley Henderson (*Gail*); Stuart McQuarrie (*Gavin/US Tourist*); Irvine Welsh (*Mikey Forrester*); Dale Winton (*Game Show Host*).

Awards: British Academy Award for Best Screenplay (Adapted) (John Hodge), 1996; Seattle International Film Festival Golden Space Needle Awards for Best Director (Danny Boyle) and Best Film, 1996; Boston Society of Film Critics Award for Best Film, 1996; *Evening*

Trainspotting

Standard British Film Award for Best Screenplay (Hodge), 1997; London Critics Circle ALFS Awards for British Screenwriter of the Year (Hodge) and British Actor of the Year (McGregor), 1997; Bodil Festival Award for Best European Film (Boyle), 1997; Brit Award for Best Soundtrack, 1997.

Publications

Script:

Hodge, John, *Trainspotting*, London, 1996.

Articles:

Charity, Tom, ''The Other Side of the Tracks,'' interview with Danny Boyle in *Time Out* (London), no. 1328, 31 January 1996.

O'Hagan, Andrew, and Geoffrey Macnab, ''The Boys Are Back in Town,'' in *Sight and Sound* (London), vol. 6, no. 2, February 1996.

Kemp, Philip, review in *Sight and Sound* (London), vol. 6, no. 3, March 1996.

Kermode, Mark, ''End Notes,'' *Sight and Sound* (London), vol. 6, no. 3, March 1996.

Review in *Positif* (Paris), no. 425–426, July-August 1996.

Kennedy, Harlan, ''Kiltspotting: Highland Reels,'' in *Film Comment* (New York), vol. 32, no. 4, July-August 1996.

Thompson, Andrew, ''Trains, Veins and Heroin Deals,'' in *American Cinematographer* (Hollywood), vol. 77, no. 8, August 1996.

McCarthy, Todd, ''Highland Fling,'' in *Premiere* (London), August 1996.

Kauffman, S., ''On Films: Scotland Now, England Then,'' in *New Republic*, 19–26 August 1996.

Rall, Veronika, ''*Trainspotting*,'' in *EPD Film* (Frankfurt), vol. 13, no. 8, August 1996.

Gelman-Waxner, Libby, ''Swill Decor,'' in *Premiere* (Boulder), November 1996.

Carroll, Tomm, ''Criterion scores uncut heroin heroes,'' in *DGA* (Los Angeles), vol. 22, no. 2, May-June 1997.

Cardullo, Bert, ''Fiction into Film, or Bringing Welsh to a Boyle,'' in *Literature/Film Quarterly* (Salisbury, Maryland), vol. 25, no. 3, July 1997.

* * *

Until the mid-1990s, those British films that achieved any kind of overseas success were generally well-behaved affairs. There were sensitive literary adaptations from the school of Merchant-Ivory;

innocuous comedies about the twitteries of the idle rich; or, for more rarified audiences, the wry, politically-charged work of Ken Loach and Mike Leigh. The idea of a British movie that was fast, rude, energetic, scabrously funny, and fizzing with switched-on youth appeal would have seemed outlandish. Then came *Trainspotting*. The team of director Danny Boyle, screenwriter John Hodge, and producer Andrew Macdonald had already signaled the arrival of a new dynamic force in British cinema with their first film, the stylish, pitch-black comedy *Shallow Grave* (1994). *Trainspotting* shares its predecessor's headlong trajectory, while replacing its visual elegance and poised cruel humour with a mass of relentlessly shitty detail and a manic cackle of wrecked mirth—elements drawn from its source material, Irvine Welsh's cult novel of Edinburgh junkiedom. Like Welsh's prose, *Trainspotting* moves with the rhythm and energy of the fractured, street-level culture it portrays—and even celebrates. At once exhilarating and despairing, lurching from exuberance to inertia, from frenetic humour to gut-wrenching squalor, it enters into the lives of its deadbeat heroin-addicts on their own terms, without patronising or pitying. When the characters are hyped—whether on sex, drugs, booze, or violence—the film shares their mood, the camera scurrying, swooping, gliding or, as during one lad's speed-fueled monologue to a gobsmacked interview panel, pogo-ing back and forth before him in irrepressible delight.

Boyle's signature visual tropes—frenetic camera, skewed framing, overheated colours—are constantly in evidence. Scenes are often mockingly stylised: the mugging of a hapless American tourist in a pub toilet is choreographed into a deliberate, formalised ballet. Brian Tufano's lighting and Kave Quinn's production design move easily from heightened realism to near-surrealism. Scenes featuring the pusher Swanney, known as "Mother Superior" (from the length of his habit), are bathed in saturated reds and blues, in ironic simulation of light through stained glass. And when after the cot-death of a baby the agonised young mother's smackhead friends stand helplessly around, unable to drag themselves out of a state of numbed non-reaction, all colour seems drained from the scene, grey faces in a grey gloom.

Boyle draws superb ensemble acting from his cast—especially from Robert Carlyle as Begbie, a scarifying psychotic so high on mindless violence he doesn't even need drugs. As Mark Renton, the narrator through whose frequently zonked-out consciousness events are refracted, Ewan McGregor gives a fine weaselly performance, at once spiky and vulnerable. Rich in local colour—it was largely filmed around the mean streets of some of Edinburgh's less salubrious districts—*Trainspotting* is thoroughly Scottish in its caustic tone and gallows humour. Not that there's the least hint of tartan nationalism; on the contrary. Dragged off by a friend to appreciate the glories of the Scots countryside, Renton launches into a bitingly contemptuous riff on his fellow-countrymen. "I don't hate the English. They're just wankers. We're colonised by wankers. We can't even pick a decent, healthy culture to be colonised by. No—we're ruled by effete arseholes! What does that make us?"

The film's pace and insolent, scatological humour, set to a pulsing Britpop score, appealed strongly to younger audiences, as did its unpreachy attitude to drugs. As Renton reflects, in the script's most notorious line, heroin may screw you up but it can also give you a high a thousand times better "than the best orgasm you ever had." Though never discounting the ravages of heroin addiction, the film-makers rejected any simplistic just-say-no attitude. "The whole reason we wanted to do this film," Boyle remarked at the time, "is to say people do drugs because you actually have a good time. That's the bit that's always left out. . . . In the end the film conforms like every other film about heroin, it shows you how in fact it will destroy you. But there are people, like Irvine Welsh, who go through it and come out the other side. You have to tell the truth about that, even though you're accused of encouraging drug use."

Accused, of course, they were. The ensuing controversy did the film nothing but good at the box-office, and *Trainspotting*—along with its distinctive orange-toned publicity material—became one of the most influential films of the decade, headbutting audiences the world over into a lastingly new perception of what British films could look like. Boyle found himself compared to Scorsese, Kubrick, Tarantino, and other masters of guerilla cinema—influences he readily acknowledges, along with Dick Lester and Kathryn Bigelow. "I feed off other stuff deliberately. That's not unhealthy. . . . I love looting people and ideas." Since then, inevitably, *Trainspotting* has itself been looted, giving rise to a rash of often mediocre British crime 'n drugs youth-culture movies. Boyle, Hodge, and Macdonald, meanwhile, have yet to equal—let alone surpass—the impact of their seminal second movie.

—Philip Kemp

TRAUM VOM GLÜCK

See **Märchen vom Glück**

THE TRAVELLING PLAYERS

See **O THIASOS**

THE TREASURE OF THE SIERRA MADRE

USA, 1948

Director: John Huston

Production: Warner Bros. Pictures, Inc.; black and white, 35mm; running time: 126 minutes. Released January 1948. Filmed Spring through Summer 1947 in Tampico, Mexico and in the mountains near San José de Purua, Mexico. Cost: $3,000,000.

Producer: Henry Blanke; **screenplay:** John Huston, from the novel by B. Traven; **photography:** Ted McCord; **editor:** Owen Marks; **sound recordist:** Robert B. Lee; **art director:** John Hughes; **music:** Max Steiner; **special effects:** William McGann and H. F. Koenekamp; **technical advisers:** Ernesto A. Romero and Antonio Arriaga.

Cast: Humphrey Bogart (*Fred C. Dobbs*); Walter Huston (*Howard*); Tim Holt (*Curtin*); Bruce Bennett (*Cody*); Alfonso Bedoya (*Gold Hat*); Barton MacLane (*McCormick*); A. Soto Rangel (*Presidente*); Manuel Donde (*El Jefe*); José Torvay (*Pablo*); Margarito Luna (*Pancho*); Jacqueline Dalya (*Flashy girl*); Robert (Bobby) Blake (*Mexican boy*); John Huston (*Man in white suit*); Jack Holt (*Flophouse bum*); Ann Sheridan (*Streetwalker*).

The Treasure of the Sierra Madre

Awards: New York Film Critics Awards for Best Picture and Best Direction, 1948; Oscars for Best Direction and Best Supporting Actor (Walter Huston), 1948; Venice Film Festival, Best Music (Steiner), 1948.

Publications

Script:

Huston, John, *The Treasure of the Sierra Madre*, edited by James Naremore, Madison, Wisconsin, 1979.

Books:

Davay, Paul, *John Huston*, Paris, 1957.
Allais, Jean-Claude, *John Huston*, Paris, 1960.
McCarty, Clifford, *Bogey: The Films of Humphrey Bogart*, New York, 1965.
Michael, Paul, *Humphrey Bogart: The Man and His Films*, Indianapolis, Indiana, 1965.
Nolan, William, *John Huston, King Rebel*, New York, 1965.
Benayoun, Robert, *John Huston*, Paris, 1966; as *John Huston: La Grande Ombre de l'aventure*, Paris, 1985.
Cecchini, Riccardo, *John Huston*, 1969.
Parish, James Robert, and Michael Pitts, *The Great Western Pictures*, Metuchen, New Jersey, 1971.
Tozzi, Romano, *John Huston, A Picture Treasury of His Films*, New York, 1971.
Kaminsky, Stuart M., *American Film Genres*, Dayton, Ohio, 1974; revised edition, Chicago, 1985.
Pratley, Gerald, *The Cinema of John Huston*, New York, 1977.
Kaminsky, Stuart M., *John Huston: Maker of Magic*, London, 1978.
Madsen, Axel, *John Huston*, New York, 1978.
Huston, John, *An Open Book*, New York, 1980.
Miller, Gabriel, *Screening the Novel: Rediscovered American Fiction in Film*, New York, 1980.
Giannetti, Louis, *Masters of the American Cinema*, Englewood Cliffs, New Jersey, 1981.
Pettigrew, Terence, *Bogart: A Definitive Study of His Film Career*, London, 1981.
Hammen, Scott, *John Huston*, Boston, 1985.

McCarty, John, *The Films of John Huston*, Secaucus, New Jersey, 1987.
Studlar, Gaylyn, editor, and David Desser, *Reflections in a Male Eye: John Huston & the American Experience*, Washington, D.C., 1993.
Cooper, Stephen, editor, *Perspectives on John Huston*, New York, 1994.
Brill, Lesley, *John Huston's Filmmaking*, New York, 1997.
Cohen, Allen, *John Huston: A Guide to References and Resources*, London, 1997.
Myers, Jeffrey C., *Bogart: A Life in Hollywood*, Boston, 1997.
Cunningham, Ernest W., *Ultimate Bogie*, Los Angeles, 1999.
Duchovnay, Gerald, *Humphrey Bogart: A Bio-Bibilography*, Westport, 1999.

Articles:

Allen, L., ''On the Set with John Huston,'' in *Cinema* (Los Angeles), July 1947.
Variety (New York), 7 January 1948.
New York Times, 24 January 1948.
Time (New York), 2 February 1948.
Morton, Lawrence, in *Hollywood Quarterly*, Spring 1948.
Sequence (London), Spring 1949.
Fowler, Dan, ''Walter Huston's Bad Boy John,'' in *Look* (New York), 10 May 1949.
Desternes, Jean, in *Revue du Cinéma* (Paris), no. 8, 1950.
Subiela, Michel, in *Positif* (Paris), no. 3, 1950.
Pilati, Robert, in *Ecran Français* (Paris), 15 February 1950.
McCarty, Clifford, ''Humphrey Bogart,'' in *Films in Review* (New York), May 1957.
Archer, Eugene, in *Film Culture* (New York), no. 19, 1959.
''John Huston,'' in *Films and Filming* (London), September and October 1959.
Vermilye, Jerry, in *Films in Review* (New York), February 1960.
Majdalany, Fred, ''Viewing Report: *Treasure on Sierra Madre*,'' in *Screen Education* (London), March-April 1965.
Bachman, Gideon, ''How I Make Films: An Interview with John Huston,'' in *Film Quarterly* (Berkeley), Fall 1965.
Jones, Dupre, ''Beating the Devil: 30 Years of John Huston,'' in *Films and Filming* (London), January 1973.
Graham, Olive, in *Cinema Texas Program Notes* (Austin), 3 May 1979.
''John Huston,'' and ''Walter Huston,'' in *Film Dope* (London), January 1983.
Buckley, M., ''John Huston,'' in *Films in Review* (New York), April 1985.
Combs, Richard, ''The Man Who Would be Ahab: The Myths and Masks of John Huston,'' in *Monthly Film Bulletin* (London), December 1985.
Schickel, Richard, ''Bogart,'' in *Film Comment* (New York), May-June 1986.
Engell, J., ''*The Treasure of the Sierra Madre:* B. Traven, John Huston and Ideology in Film Adaptation,'' in *Literature/Film Quarterly* (Salisbury, Maryland), vol. 17, no. 4, October 1989.
Reid's Film Index (Wyong), no. 5, 1990.
Souder, William, ''High Adventure: The Art of Making a Film Epic,'' in *Minneapolis-St. Paul Magazine*, vol. 25, no. 2, February 1997.

* * *

The Treasure of the Sierra Madre has become the archetypal John Huston film. One reason is that it is a clear examination of the exploration or the quest. As in many of his films to come (and *The Maltese Falcon*, to some extent, before it), Huston here examines a small group of people on a quest for wealth. Generally, in his films with this theme the members of the group accomplish their initial goal: they obtain the money or the treasure. Once having attained it, however, they often find the potential power it brings too much to handle. Human greed, weakness, or obsession destroy their victory.

This is remarkably true of *Treasure, The Asphalt Jungle, Beat the Devil, The Kremlin Letter*, and *The Man Who Would Be King*. In all these films, however, Huston does not simply examine greed and present a moral statement about it. He examines the disintegration or change within the individual who has to learn to cope with the specter of wealth of power and the erosion of the fragile group or couple when chance, greed, envy, or obsession intrude on their existence. *Treasure* is not a moral statement by Huston but an examination of characters under pressure, who fall apart when least expected to and rise to noble reactions when no reason is given to believe they will.

In order to make *The Treasure of the Sierra Madre*, Huston convinced Warner Brothers to let him shoot on location for ten weeks in Mexico. In documentaries in the army, he had grown accustomed to location work and now felt comfortable with it. ''Locationing? Nothing to it,'' he said. ''The only time it's tough to make pictures on location is when someone is shooting at you.'' In his search for the concrete in making the film, Huston went to the extreme of shooting exteriors in San Jose de Purua, an isolated village 140 miles north of Mexico city. Humphrey Bogart, who played Dobbs, recalled: ''John wanted everything perfect. If he saw a nearby mountain that would serve for photographic purposes, that mountain was not good; too easy to reach. If we could go to a location site without fording a couple of streams and walking through snake-infested areas in the scorching sun, then it wasn't quite right.''

Huston's other stars included his father, Walter Huston, as Howard, and cowboy actor Tim Holt as Curtin. Dobbs is frequently described as a moral brute and a madman, but clearly he is a highly contradictory character until his crack-up. He is initially generous and willing to share his cash, and he rather nobly throws away the gold that Curtin offers him to pay back the extra money he has put to finance the trip. Later, it is Dobbs who agrees to help Howard rebuild the ''wounded'' mountain. Howard, the doctor/father, constantly warns that gold is a potential disease. He is aware of the danger and protects himself, and Curtin also learns to do so, but even Curtin has a moment of hesitation when he almost leaves Dobbs in the mine after a collapse. It is Dobbs who succumbs to the disease, but he is not viewed as evil by Huston or, for that matter, by Howard.

Time called the film ''one of the best things Hollywood has done since it learned to talk . Walter Huston's performance is his best job in a lifetime of acting.'' Bosley Crowther in the *New York Times* wrote that ''Huston has shaped a searching drama of the collision of civilization's vicious greeds with the instinct for self-preservation in an environment where all the barriers are down.'' James Agee and *Newsweek* also praised the film, but there was some antagonism. John McCarten in *The New Yorker* said the film could be reduced to the idea that greed does not pay. He went on to say that ''even if the premise is granted, the film's methods of elaborating on it are certainly something less than beguiling.''

While the mixed reviews filtered in, Huston plunged into his next project, but his work was disrupted when the Academy Awards for

1948 were announced. For the first time, a father-and-son team won the awards, John as best director, Walter as best supporting actor.

—Stuart M. Kaminsky

THE TREE OF THE WOODEN CLOGS.

See **L'ALBERO DEGLI ZOCCOLI**

TRETIA MESHCHANSKAIA

(Liubov v Troem; Bed and Sofa)

USSR, 1927

Director: Abram Room

Production: Sovkino; silent with Russian intertitles; black and white, 16 mm; running time: 75 minutes. Released 15 March 1927. Filmed in 1927 on location in Moscow.

Producer: Sovkino studio; **screenplay:** Viktor Shklovskii, Abram Room; **photography:** Grigorii Giber; **assistant directors:** Sergei Iutkevich, E. Kuzis; **art directors:** V. Rakhals, Sergei Iutkevich.

Cast: Nikolai Batalov (*Kolia*); Liudmila Semenova (*Liuda*); Vladimir Fogel (*Volodia*); L. Iurenev (*doorman*).

Publications

Articles:

''*Bed and Sofa*,'' in *Close Up*, December 1927.
A.W., ''*Bed and Sofa* at the Film Society,'' in *Close Up*, May 1929.
H.C., ''Note on *Bed and Sofa*,'' in *Close Up*, May 1929.
Hill, Steven P., ''*Bed and Sofa*,'' in *Film Heritage*, Fall 1971.
Burns, Paul E., ''An NEP Moscow Address: Abram Room's *Third Meshchanskaia* (*Bed and Sofa*) in Historical Context,'' in *Film and History*, December 1982.
Mayne, Judith, ''*Bed and Sofa* and the Edge of Domesticity,'' in Mayne, *Kino and the Woman Question: Feminism and Soviet Silent Film*, Columbus, Ohio, 1989.
Youngblood, Denise J., ''The Fiction Film as a Source for Soviet Social History: The *Third Meshchanskaia Street* Affair,'' in *Film and History*, September 1989.

* * *

Tretia Meshchanskaia, Abram Room's celebrated 1927 melodrama about a *menage a trois*, made its way West under a variety of titles, among them *Bed and Sofa*, *Three in a Cellar*, *Old Dovecots*, and *Cellars of Moscow*. The film enjoys the distinction of having been banned (as well as praised) on two continents. *Bed and Sofa*, as the film is best known in the United States, was Room's fourth film. Like many early Soviet directors, Room (1894–1976) had come to the cinema along a circuitous path. A physician specializing in psychiatry and neurology, he served as a medical officer with the Red Army during the Russian civil war that followed the revolutions of 1917. Originally from Lithuania, Room decided to stay in Moscow after demobilization and began to work in the Theater of the Revolution.

None of Room's three previous pictures—two short comedies from 1924 that are no longer extant and the action adventure *Death Bay* (*Bukhta smerti*, 1926)—prepared critics or audiences for *Bed and Sofa*, a brilliant psychological chamber drama that lay bare the dysfunctions and contradiction of early Soviet society. From the opening shot, we know that we are not going to see a schematic narrative about enthusiastic revolutionaries.

Liuda, a bored housewife who could not be more unlike the prototypical Bolshevik ''New Woman,'' lives in a one-room basement apartment on Third Meshchanskaia Street (the literal translation of the film's original title), a petty-bourgeois neighborhood in Moscow. She spends her days idly, mainly reading magazines, notably the popular movie fan magazine *Soviet Screen* (*Sovetskii ekran*). Her husband, Kolia, is a charming and good-natured but dictatorial and egocentric stonemason. The couple is soon joined by Kolia's old war buddy, Volodia, a printer who cannot find an apartment in Moscow due to the severe housing shortage that was still a major social problem ten years after the revolution.

Liuda is quite understandably annoyed by the addition of yet another person to their cramped apartment; of course she has not been consulted. Yet Volodia, ingratiating and helpful, quickly wins her over by proving the perfect lodger. The sexual tension between Liuda and Volodia is palpable from the beginning, so when Kolia is called to a job out of town, it is scarcely surprising that Volodia takes advantage of the opportunity to woo Liuda openly. In the movie's most famous and exhilarating scene, Volodia invites Liuda to take a plane ride with him as part of Aviation Day celebrations. This is the first time she has been outside the apartment since the movie began; what joy! (And what stunning aerial shots of a Moscow that is no more.) When Kolia returns home, he finds himself banished to the sofa.

But now that Volodia is the ''husband,'' he quickly begins acting like one. If anything, he is more boorish and tyrannical than Kolia ever was. The two men resume their friendship, joking and playing checkers while Liuda sulks. She attempts, fruitlessly, to regain control over her life by sleeping with her husband again. When Kolia and Volodia learn she is pregnant, they are outraged and demand that she have an abortion, since paternity definitely cannot be established. Sad and nervous, Liuda is packed off to a private clinic, where other clients are a prostitute and a young girl. Standing at a window, awaiting her turn, she spies (whether in reality or in her mind's eye) a baby in a carriage on the sidewalk below. She has a feminist epiphany. For the first time, Liuda decides to take control of her own life, to have the baby and leave the corruption of the big city. In the movie's closing scene, we see a confident, smiling Liuda leaning out the train window, cross cut with shots of her two husbands' annoyance, and then relief, that she has gone. They resume their immature, carefree, bachelor life in their dingy basement room on Third Meshchanskaia Street.

Bed and Sofa is beautifully shot, acted, and edited. It was quickly recognized as a masterpiece of silent film art and remains fresh and appealing three-quarters of a century after its release. The film's producer, the state-run studio Sovkino, eagerly offered this well-made film for international distribution, but it was banned in Western Europe and the United States for its sexual content and ambiguous moral message. Yet, though the film was not commercially exhibited in the West, it was widely seen through the film society circuits, which could avoid censorship since they were ''private'' clubs.

Bed and Sofa's reception in the USSR was controversial for reasons that sound the same as those in the West but were in fact quite different. Room had intended not only to make a picture exploring the social problems of urban life during the last years of the New Economic Policy (1921–28), but specifically to support the state's campaign against the sexual freedom of the revolutionary years and against abortion on demand. What went wrong? The Association of Revolutionary Cinematography (ARK) quickly and unequivocally praised the film in its journal *Cinema Front* (*Kino-front*) as ''one of the most successful pictures of Soviet production,'' which dealt with thorny problems in a ''soft [meaning non-didactic], artistic, and consistently Soviet way.''

Yet despite ARK's strong support, the film was excoriated for the six weeks *before* its release in a carefully orchestrated campaign carried out in the pages of the trade newspaper *Cinema* (*Kino*), the fan magazine *Soviet Screen* (which apparently did not appreciate Liuda's patronage), and the conservative *Soviet Cinema* (*Sovetskoe kino*, organ of the Commissariat of Enlightenment, which had oversight over the film industry). Room's movie was variously labelled ''psycho-pathological,'' a ''Western European adulterous romance,'' and an ''apology for adultery.'' Given the large number of European and American entertainment films that dominated Soviet screens in the late 1920s, along with the frankly Westernized products of the semi-private Mezhrabpom studio, the level of vilification *Bed and Sofa* was subjected to was suspiciously excessive. Indeed, the film was successfully released, although with a new title, *Menage a trois* (*Liubov v troem*), that would not connect it to the ''*Third Meshchanskaia Street* scandal.''

In 1927, although few Soviet citizens were aware of it, the stage was being set for the Cultural Revolution of 1928–32. By the early 1930s, Soviet arts and entertainments would be stripped of any remaining creative autonomy to serve the interests of the state. This period of social and cultural upheaval was followed by the formal adoption of the aesthetic credo of ''Socialist Realism'' at the Soviet Writers' Congress of 1934. Abram Room and his film were unwittingly swept up into the whirlwind of change, criticized for lack of foresight more than anything else.

Although Socialist Realism would not be canonized for another seven years, its attributes were central to the cultural debates of the late 1920s. *Bed and Sofa* fit many of Socialist Realism's main criteria: it was plotted, contemporary, realistic, and tendentious. But it had three major ideological failings—none of which were related to sex. The first was the lack of the positive hero, and worse, the fact that the film is dominated by three *negative* characters. While Liuda is indeed transformed from a passive and amoral social ''parasite'' to, presumably, a mother and a contributing member of society, this is only because of her desire to actualize her ''petty-bourgeois'' individualism. Kolia may be a worker, but he refuses to attend political meetings because they are boring. As for Volodia—he even *looks* neurotic (actor Vladimir Fogel's struggle with mental illness was well-known in film circles; he committed suicide in 1929). Second, Socialist Realism is supposed to show life as it should be; the path to the new world. Reform in *Bed and Sofa* is partial at best. Third, the film fails to include a true proletarian as counterexample to Kolia the stonemason and Volodia the printer, petty-bourgeois craftsmen. The cultural revolution about to be unleashed would be in large part an attack to eradicate *meshchanstvo* (petty-bourgeois philistinism). This film embodies it, especially in its original Russian title *Third Meshchanskaia Street*, which comes from the same root word. No wonder the studio decided to release it as *Menage a trois*. As a work of art, *Bed and Sofa* remains a superb example of European silent film. Given its context and subtext, it must also be considered one of the most important films in early Soviet cinema history.

—Denise J. Youngblood

THE TRIAL

See **LE PROCES**

A TRIP TO THE MOON

See **LE VOYAGE DANS LA LUNE**

TRIUMPH DES WILLENS

(Triumph of the Will)

Germany, 1935

Director: Leni Riefenstahl

Production: Universum Film Aktiengesellschaft (Ufa); black and white, 35mm; running time: 120 minutes. Released March 1935. Filmed 4–10 September 1934 in Nuremburg at the Nazi Party Congress.

Producer: Leni Riefenstahl; **editor:** Leni Riefenstahl; **subtitles:** Walter Ruttmann; **photography:** Sepp Allgeier, Karl Attenberger, and Werner Bohne, plus several assistants; **architectural designs:** Albert Speer; **music:** Herbert Windt.

Awards: National Film Prize of Germany, 1935; Venice Biennale, Gold Medal, 1936 (most sources do not list this award for *Triumph*, though David Gunston in *Current Biography* states that *Triumph* did receive this award); Exposition Internationale des Arts et des Techniques (Paris), Grand Prize, 1937.

Publications

Books:

Kracauer, Siegfried, *From Caligari to Hitler*, Princeton, New Jersey, 1947.

Hull, David Stewart, *Film in the Third Reich*, Berkeley, 1969.

Cadard, Pierre, and Francis Courtade, *Histoire du Cinema Nazi*, Paris, 1972.

Barsam, Richard, *Nonfiction Film: A Critical History*, New York, 1973.

Barnouw, Erik, *Documentary: A History of the Non-Fiction Film*, New York, 1974.

Barsam, Richard, *Filmguide to Triumph of the Will*, Bloomington, Indiana, 1975.

Triumph des Willens

Infield, Glenn, *Leni Riefenstahl: Fallen Film Goddess*, New York, 1976.

Phillips, Baxter, *Swastika: The Cinema of Oppression*, New York, 1976.

Rhodes, Anthony, *Propaganda, the Art of Persuasion: World War II*, New York, 1976.

Ford, Charles, *Leni Riefenstahl*, Paris, 1978.

Hinton, David, *The Films of Leni Riefenstahl*, Metuchen, New Jersey, 1978, 1991, 2000.

Infield, Glenn, *Leni Riefenstahl et le 3e Reich*, Paris, 1978.

Berg-Pan, Renada, *Leni Riefenstahl*, edited by Warren French, Boston, 1980.

Nowotny, Peter, *Leni Riefenstahl's Triumph des Willens: Zur kritik Dokumentarischer Filmarbeit im NS-Farchismus*, Dortmund, 1981.

Welch, David, *Propaganda and the German Cinema, 1933–1945*, Oxford, 1983; revised edition, 1987.

Heck-Rabi, Louise, *Women Filmmakers: A Critical Reception*, Metuchen, New Jersey, 1984.

Loiperdinger, Martin, *Der Parteitagsfilm Triumph des Willens von Leni Riefenstahl: Rituale der Mobilmachung*, Opladen, 1987.

Riefenstahl, Leni, *Memoiren*, Munich, 1987.

Deutschmann, Linda, *Triumph of the Will: The Image of the Third Reich*, Wakefield, New Hampshire, 1991.

Leeflang, Thomas, *Leni Riefenstahl*, Baarn, 1991.

Riefenstahl, Leni, *The Sieve of Time: The Memoirs of Leni Riefenstahl*, London, 1992.

Riefenstahl, Leni, *A Memoir*, New York, 1993, 1995.

Salkeld, Audrey, *A Portrait of Leni Riefenstahl*, London, 1997.

Articles:

Lewis, Marshall, in *New York Film Bulletin*, nos. 12–14, 1960.

Gunston, D., ''Leni Riefenstahl,'' in *Film Quarterly* (Berkeley), Fall 1960.

Muller, Robert, ''Romantic Miss Riefenstahl,'' in *Spectator* (London), 10 February 1961.

Berson, Arnold, ''The Truth About Leni,'' in *Films and Filming* (London), April 1965.

''Issue on Riefenstahl,'' of *Film Comment* (New York), Winter 1965.

Delahaye, Michel, ''Leni and the Wolf: Interview with Leni Riefenstahl,'' in *Cahiers du Cinéma in English* (New York), June 1966.

Corliss, Richard, ''Leni Riefenstahl: A Bibliography,'' in *Film Heritage* (Dayton, Ohio), Fall 1969.

Richards, Jeffrey, ''Leni Riefenstahl: Style and Structure,'' in *Silent Picture* (London), Autumn 1970.
Kelman, K., ''Propaganda as Vision—*Triumph of the Will*,'' in *Film Culture* (New York), Spring 1973.
Barsam, Richard, ''Leni Riefenstahl: Artifice and Truth in a World Apart,'' in *Film Comment* (New York), November-December 1973.
Gunston, David, ''Leni Riefenstahl,'' in *Current Biography* (New York), May 1975.
Hinton, Davie, ''*Triumph of the Will*: Document or Artifice?,'' in *Cinema Journal* (Evanston, Illinois), Fall 1975.
O'Donnell-Stupp, Vicki, ''Myth, Meaning, and Message in *The Triumph of the Will*,'' in *Film Criticism* (Edinboro, Pennsylvania), Winter-Spring 1978.
Neale, Steve, ''*Triumph of the Will*: Notes on Documentary and Spectacle,'' in *Screen* (London), no. 1, 1979.
Everson, William K., in *The Documentary Tradition*, edited by Lewis Jacobs, 2nd edition, New York, 1979.
Winston, B., ''Was Hitler There? Reconsidering *Triumph des Willens*,'' in *Sight and Sound* (London), Spring 1981.
''Cinema et Propaganda Issue'' of *Revue Belge du Cinema* (Brussels), Summer 1984.
Gyurey, V., ''A Harmadik Birodalom es a Fuehrer ket nezopontbol,'' in *Filmkultura* (Budapest), no. 6, 1989.
McCormack, T., ''The 1988 Southam Lecture: The Texts of War and the Discourse of Peace,'' in *Canadian Journal of Communication*, vol. 14, no. 1, 1989.
Wood, R., ''Fascism/Cinema,'' in *Cineaction* (Toronto), Fall 1989.
Szilagyi, A., ''Hitler Adolf szupersztar,'' in *Filmvilag* (Budapest), no. 1, 1990.
Foldenyi, F. L., ''A birodalmi szepseg buvoleteben,'' in *Filmvilag* (Budapest), no. 12, 1991.
Doherty, Thomas, ''The Filmmaker as Fascist,'' in *Boston Globe*, 13 December 1992.
Elsaesser, T., ''Portrait of the Artist as a Young Woman,'' in *Sight and Sound* (London), February 1993.
Schwartzman, R.J., ''Racial Theory and Propaganda in *Triumph of the Will*,'' in *Florida State University Conference on Literature and Film*, vol. 18, 1993.
Soussloff, C.M., and B. Nichols, ''Leni Riefenstahl: The Power of the Image,'' in *Discourse* (Detroit), vol. 18.3, Spring 1996.
Hitchens, Gordon, ''Recent Riefenstahl Activities and a Commentary on Nazi Propaganda Filmmaking,'' in *Film Culture* (New York), no. 79, Winter 1996.
Riefenstahl, Leni, ''After a Half-Century, Leni Riefenstahl Confronts the U.S.,'' in *Film Culture* (New York), no. 79, Winter 1996.
Winston, Brian, in *History Today*, vol. 47, no. 1, January 1997.

* * *

Triumph des Willens (Triumph of the Will) is one of the greatest examples of film propaganda ever made. Commissioned by Hitler, Leni Riefenstahl recorded the 1934 Nuremberg National Socialist Party rally, transforming it through innovative editing, montage, and lighting into a frighteningly impressive work of indoctrination.

Riefenstahl maintains that the film is an accurate record of a historical event. In the French periodical *Cahiers du Cinéma*, the director commented that:

> In those days one believed in something beautiful. . . . How could I know better than Winston Churchill, who even in 1935–36 was saying that he envied Germany its Fuhrer? . . . you will notice if you see the film today that it doesn't contain a single reconstructed scene. Everything is real. . . . It is history. A purely ''historical'' film.What is surprising is that Riefenstahl was approached at all to create the film. Given the Nazi attitude's chauvinistic attitude towards women—that they should act as wives and mothers before anything else—the fact that Hitler retained a female director to make such an important work is very interesting. Josef Goebbels, Hitler's Minister of Propaganda, hated Riefenstahl, and according to the director made filming *Triumph des Willens* as difficult as possible.

The film was viewed as an essential and important propaganda tool. The recent Rohm Purge which had resulted in the assassination of Ernst Rohm, head of the Sturmabteilung (S.A. or brownshirts), and his top men, on 30 June 1930 had effected Nazi morale. The S.A. was responsible for maintaining order at rallies, and controlling political opposition. Hitler had a major distrust of the S.A. leaders and of the German military, whom he felt was dominated by the aristocracy. Rohm's murder divided the Nazi Party, who were unsure about Hitler's political direction. The film thus served as an important way of conveying to the world the Party's unity, and strength in the light of recent disruptions.

Out of the 96 propaganda films produced during 1933–45 by Goebbels's ministry, Riefenstahl's two films *Triumph des Willens* and the very beautiful *Olympiad* have proved the most interesting examples and the most influential works on post-war cinema. The importance of this period to the Nazi Party is shown from the opening statement of the film:

> September 4, 1934. 20 years after the outbreak of World War I, 16 years after German woe and sorrow began, 19 months after the beginning of Germany's rebirth, Adolf Hitler flew again to Nuremberg to review the columns of his faithful admirers.

The aerial shot which tracks Hitler's arrival in his plane, and pans over the cheering crowds, military columns, and houses, focusing on a few happy, almost brainwashed looking people, creates the feeling that Hitler is a god descending from the heavens. This is emphasized by the shooting of scenes featuring Hitler from below using a low camera, which establishes the impression that the Fuhrer is an Olympian creature, larger than life. In contrast the cheering masses are shot from above, signifying that they are Hitler's minions—and are inferior to the Fuhrer.

The film's recurrent use of symbols: the swastika; the eagle; and flags, among them, help to control the audience by making it feel that it is participating in the action occurring on screen. The eagle, the symbol of the Party is most often seen silhouetted against the sky—again showing that the force and strength of the Party is divine.

Riefenstahl continuously intercuts images, alleviating the tediousness of the Party officials' speeches; emphasizing important words and phrases with relevant images. This technique is gleaned from Soviet propaganda films, particularly from the work of Eisenstein and

Pudovkin, and is effective in retaining the audience's interest. The use of montage is also important because what the viewer sees on screen is a carefully created image rather than a natural reality.

The film emphasizes the god-like status of the Fuhrer; the importance of the Volk and folk history; and the military strength of the Nazis. Long sweeping shots of the Hitler Youth, the military, and the Labour Movement, symbolically carrying spades instead of rifles, show the support that the Party enjoys.

Lutze, Rohm's successor, is also promoted by the film. William L. Shirer in *Berlin Diary* commented that Lutze was an unpopular successor to Rohm, but in *Triumph des Willens*, the S.A. leader is seen being mobbed by his men. Only the Fuhrer receives the same kind of treatment in the film.

To shoot the film, Riefenstahl used a team of 16 cameramen with a further 16 assistants, using a total of 30 cameras. The two-hour film is a perfectly edited document of Nazi fantacism. Accompanied by an impressively stirring soundtrack, which includes music by Wagner, *Triumph des Willens* is an example of how film can be used to manipulate and indoctrinate the masses.

Its influence on post-war cinema has been long-lasting, and the contemporary advertising industry uses many of the techniques used to such great effect in the film to capture the minds and thoughts of the audience: the repetition of motifs, montage, and a use of emotive and stirring music to manipulate the audience.

Triumph des Willens won a state award, and the Gold Medal at the Venice Biennale of 1935, and the French Grand Prix at the film festival held in Paris.

—A. Pillai

TROIS COULEURS: BLEU, BLANC, ROUGE

(Three Colours: Blue, White, Red)

Director: Krysztof Kieslowski

TROIS COULEURS: BLEU

France, 1993

Production: MK2 Productions SA, CED Productions, France 3 Cinema, CAB Productions, TOR Production, Canal Plus, Centre Nationale de la Cinématographie; colour, 35mm; running time: 98 minutes. Filmed in Paris, 1993.

Producer: Marin Karmitz; **screenplay:** Krzysztof Pisiewicz and Krzysztof Kieslowski; **photography:** Slawomir Idziak; **editor:** Jacques Witta; **assistant director:** Emmanuel Finkiel; **set design:** Claude Lenoir; **music:** Zbigniew Preisner; **sound editor:** Claire Bez, Bertrand Lanclos, and Jean-Claude Laureux; **sound recording:** Jean-Claude Laureux, Brigitte Taillandier, and Pascal Colomb; **costumes:** Virginie Viard and Naima Lagrange.

Cast: Juliette Binoche (*Julie*); Benoit Régent (*Olivier*); Florence Pernel (*Sandrine*); Charlotte Véry (*Lucille*); Hélène Vincent (*Journalist*); Emanuelle Riva (*Julie's Mother*); Claude Duneton (*Doctor*).

Award: Golden Lion, Venice 1993.

Publications

Script:

Kieslowski, Krzystof, *Three Colors Trilogy: Blue, White and Red*, New York, 1998.

Books:

Campan, Véronique, *Dix brèves histoires d'image: le Décalogue de Krzysztof Kieslowski*, Paris, 1993.
Amiel, Vincent, *Kieslowski*, Paris, 1995.
Lubelskiego, Tadeusza, *Kino Krzysztofa Kie'slowskiego*, Kraków, 1997.
Attolini, Vito, *Krzystof Kieslowski*, Manduria, 1998.
Insdorf, Annette, *Double Lives, Second Chances: The Cinema of Krzysztof Kieslowski*, New York, 1999.

Articles:

Nesselson, L., *Variety* (New York), 20 September 1993.
Ostria, V., ''Le hasard et l'indifférence,'' in *Cahiers du Cinéma* (Paris), September 1993.
Peck, A., and others, *Positif* (Paris), September 1993.
Andrew, Geoff, ''True *Blue*,'' in *Time Out* (London), no. 1207, 6 October 1993.
Macnab, G., *Sight and Sound* (London), November 1993.
Mensonge, S., ''*Three Colors Blue, White and Red*: Krzysztof Kieslowski and Friends,'' in *Cinema Papers* (Fitzroy), no. 99, June 1994.
Kehr, Dave, ''To Save the World: Kieslowski's *Three Colors* Trilogy,'' in *Film Comment* (New York), vol. 30, no. 6, November-December 1994.
Wall, J.M., ''No Sense of the Sacred,'' in *Christian Century*, vol. 112, 15 March 1995.
Jean, Marcel, ''Voir Rouge,'' in *24 Images* (Montreal), no. 76, Spring 1995.
Toh, H.L., ''Krzysztof Kieslowski's *Trois couleurs* Trilogy: The Auteur's Preoccupation with (Missed) Chances and (Missed) Connections,'' in *Kinema*, vol. 5, Spring 1996.
Pope, Angela, ''In Memory,'' in *Sight & Sound* (London), vol. 6, no. 8, August 1996.
Coates, Paul, ''The Sense of an Ending: Reflections on Kieslowski's Trilogy,'' in *Film Quarterly* (Berkeley), vol. 50, no. 2, Winter 1996–1997.
Portnoy, S., ''Unmasking Sound: Music and Representation in *The Shout* and *Blue*,'' in *Spectator* (Los Angeles), vol. 17, no. 2, 1997.
Wilson, Emma, ''*Three Colours: Blue*: Kieslowski, Colour and the Postmodern Subject,'' in *Screen* (Oxford), vol. 39, no. 4, Winter 1998.

Trois Couleurs: Bleu

TROIS COULEURS: BLANC

France-Poland, 1994

Production: MK2 Productions SA, France 3 Cinema, Cab Productions SA, TOR Production, with the participation of Canal Plus; colour, 35mm; running time: 92 minutes.

Producer: Marin Karmitz; **executive producer:** Yvon Crenn; **screenplay:** Krzystof Piesiewicz and Krzysztof Kieslowski; **photography:** Edward Klosinski; **editor:** Urszula Lesiak; **assistant directors:** Teresa Violetta Buhl and Emmanuel Finkiel; **art directors:** Halina Dobrowolska and Claude Lenoir; **music:** Zbigniew Preisner; **sound editors:** Piotr Zawadzki, Jean-Claude Laureux, and Francine Lemaitre; **sound recording:** Brigitte Taillandier and Pascal Colomb; **costumes:** Elzbieta Radke, Teresa Wardzala, Jolanta Luczak, and Virginie Viard.

Cast: Zbigniew Zamachowski (*Karol Karol*); Julette Delpy (*Dominique*); Janusz Gajos (*Mikolaj*); Jerzy Stuhr (*Jurek*); Grzegorz Warchol (*Elegant man*); Jerzy Nowak (*Old Farmer*); Aleksander Bardini (*Lawyer*); Cezary Harasimowicz (*Inspector*); Jerzy Trela (*Monsieur Bronek*).

Award: Golden Bear, Berlin 1994.

Publications

Articles:

Nesselson, L., *Variety* (New York), 31 January 1994.
Amiel, V., ''Le milieu, les origines,'' in *Positif* (Paris), February 1994.
Jousse, T., ''Marché noir,'' in *Cahiers du Cinéma* (Paris), February 1994.
Rayns, T., ''Glowing in the Dark,'' in *Sight and Sound* (London), June 1994.
Strick, P., *Sight and Sound* (London), June 1994.
Johnston, Trevor, interview with Julie Delpy, in *Time Out* (London), no. 1242, 8 June 1994.

Pawelczak, A., *Films in Review* (New York), July/August 1994.
Positif (Paris), September 1994.
Williams, D.E., ''*White*,'' in *Film Threat* (Beverly Hills), vol. 18, October 1994.
Jean, Marcel, ''Voir Rouge,'' in *24 Images* (Montreal), no. 76, Spring 1995.
Pope, Angela, ''In Memory,'' in *Sight & Sound* (London), vol. 6, no. 8, August 1996.
Coates, Paul, ''The Sense of an Ending: Reflections on Kieslowski's Trilogy,'' in *Film Quarterly* (Berkeley), vol. 50, no. 2, Winter 1996–1997.
Insdorf, A., ''*White*,'' in *Film Comment* (New York), vol. 33, March/April 1997.

TROIS COULEURS: ROUGE

France-Switzerland-Poland, 1994

Production: MK2 Productions SA, France 3 Cinema, CAB Productions SA, TOR Production, in association with Canal Plus; colour, 35mm; running time: 99 minutes.

Producer: Marin Karmitz; **screenplay:** Krzystof Kieslowski and Krzystof Piesiewicz; **photography:** Piotr Sobocinski; **editor:** Jacques Witta; **assistant director:** Emmanuel Finkiel; **set design:** Claude Lenoir; **music:** Zbigniew Preisner and Van Den Budenmayer; **sound editors:** Piotr Zawadski, Francine Lemaitre, Jean-Claude Laureux, and Nicolas Naegelen; **costumes:** Nadia Cuenoid and Véronique Michel.

Cast: Irène Jacob (*Valentine Dussaut*); Jean-Louis Trintignant (*Judge Joseph Kern*); Frédérique Feder (*Karin*); Jean-Pierre Lorit (*Auguste Bruner*); Samuel Lebihan (*Photographer*); Marion Stalens (*Veterinary Surgeon*); Teco Celio (*Barman*); Juliette Binoche, Julie Delpy, Benoit Régent, Zbigniew Zamachowski.

Publications

Articles:

Variety (New York), 24 May 1994.
Rayns, T., ''Glowing in the Dark,'' in *Sight and Sound* (London), June 1994.
Masson, A., ''La naiveté du manipulateur,'' in *Positif* (Paris), September 1994.
Strauss, F. ''Tu ne jouiras point,'' in *Cahiers du Cinéma* (Paris), September 1994.
Pawelczak, Andy, ''*Red*,'' in *Films in Review* (New York), vol. 46, no. 3–4, March-April 1995.
Jean, Marcel, ''Voir Rouge,'' in *24 Images* (Montreal), no. 76, Spring 1995.
Séquences (Haute-Ville), no. 181, November/December 1995.
Pope, Angela, ''In Memory,'' in *Sight & Sound* (London), vol. 6, no. 8, August 1996.
Rudolph, E., ''*Ransom* Ups the Ante,'' in *American Cinematographer* (Hollywood), vol. 77, November 1996.
Coates, Paul, ''The Sense of an Ending: Reflections on Kieslowski's Trilogy,'' in *Film Quarterly* (Berkeley), vol. 50, no. 2, Winter 1996–1997.

* * *

The thematics of Krysztof Kieslowski's trilogy, *Trois Couleurs (Three Colours)*, it seems, could hardly be more explicit—the colours of the French flag and the three cardinal principles of the French state: *liberté, égalité, fraternité.* However, when asked in an interview whether the trilogy's structure was not simply a pretext, in the same way that the Ten Commandments provided an overall grid for his *Dekalog*, Kieslowski replied: ''Yes, exclusively that.'' There may be a degree of provocation to this reply, but it also pinpoints an important aspect of the trilogy. The tripartite structure is indeed a little too schematic to ring true, but it serves an important purpose in inviting the viewer to read the work for continuities and substantive thematic content that might not otherwise be apparent either in each episode or in the trilogy as a whole.

Certain recurring themes suggest themselves more immediately than others in the trilogy. All three films are about people separated from those they love, or from the world; all are about communication, about language, and about transactions of various kinds. All three invoke the presence of the law in various forms: civic law, as well as moral and spiritual principles. The *tricolor* motif might lead us to identify this as the trilogy's key theme, implying a comparative analysis of the three principles in secular and transcendental terms. Yet there is no *a priori* reason to assume that these meanings are more important than any other ones, and nothing precludes us finding other tripartite structures: the films could, for example, be seen as essays on the three senses that dominate each film: sight (*Blue*), touch (in the sense of possession, in *White*), and hearing (*Red*).

If the trilogy encourages such varied speculation, it is because it operates more by discontinuity than by the self-enclosed unity that the title suggests. Kieslowski has characterised it as less a triptych and more a set of three individual stories assembled in one volume. The stories, and the ways they are told, are very different, making the trilogy more open to varied readings than the *Dekalog*, with its single location and recurring characters. Each story bears a slightly different narrative relation to its main theme. In the unremittingly sombre *Blue*, a young woman seeks freedom from the world after the death of her husband and child, but is recalled to it by contact with other people, and by the echoes of her husband's music. In *Blanc*—universally received by critics as a comedy—a Polish hairdresser divorced by his French wife returns home and revenges himself on her by becoming a successful black marketeer, thereby ''getting even'' as a cynical illustration of equality. More obscurely, *Red*'s story of fraternity concerns a young woman's chance encounter with an embittered judge; in an inversion of *Blue*, she restores him to society, from which he had distanced himself by adopting the god-like position of a cynical, omniscient observer. Fraternity here seems to be the interconnectedness of mortals, unknowingly caught in the machinations of a supercilious deity.

The threads of narrative continuity between episodes are ostentatiously tenuous and artificial. In *Blue*, Julie walks into a courtroom; in

White, it turns out that she has walked in on the divorce of Karol and Dominique. In the flourish of closure that ends *Red*, the trilogy's otherwise unrelated central couples are united as survivors of a cross-channel ferry disaster. In addition, the music of an apocryphal Dutch composer, van den Budenmayer, refers us to the universe of *La Double Vie de Véronique* (there is no reason why we shouldn't imagine Irène Jacob's character Valentine to be a third incarnation of that film's parallel heroines).

Other unifying threads suggest that it is futile to look for coherence of a realist variety, and that the trilogy's narrative unity is purely an effect of imagery. In all three episodes, and in different cities, an old woman struggles with a bottle bank; Valentine, the embodiment of spontaneous *caritas*, closes this circle by helping her. In *Red*, such parallelism verges on the supernatural, with Kern's life story mirrored by the younger judge Auguste. Again, this uncanny aspect is simply the effect of an arbitrary narrative manipulation; rather than staging a flashback to Kern's youth, Kieslowski has that past happen to another character, in what he calls a ''contemporary flashback.''

Such narrative flaunting of parallelism fulfills a classic function of coincidence that at once satisfies our desire for closure, and at the same time unsettles us by presenting us with a universe that is more implausibly coherent than any universe could be. Depending on our willingness, or otherwise, to see through such artifice, we can read the films' structure of coincidence either as a providential order in which everything—that is to say, nothing—is accidental, or as bare-faced string-pulling by a cavalier author. *Red* dramatises this very opposition in the figure of Kern, who moves from the position of an omniscient but distanced god, eavesdropping on the world from his Geneva eyrie, to that of a manipulative ''director'' who apparently orchestrates the film's final *coup de théâtre* on the ferry. Extrapolated onto the level of a world view, such ambivalent coincidence leaves us free to decide whether the trilogy posits a hopelessly contingent fictional universe or one in which all loose ends reassuringly join up.

The look of the films also militates against a too-obvious sense of unity. All three are shot by different cinematographers, are visually unlike each other, and each uses its dominant colour in a different way. Blue permeates the first film's lighting as well as appearing in discrete objects, while in the third, red objects stand out against a neutral framework, without the uncanny stridency of the blue ones; red is simply a thread of colour holding this world together, just as the film's tracking shots unite diverse characters. *White*, on the other hand, is dominated by a prosaic drabness, with white appearing as an absence of colour; white flashes appear on screen, suggesting the brief ecstasy of orgasm and marriage, but largely the neutrality of white means that we are free to look for it anywhere on screen—in snow, cars, paper, the sky—without being directed to see it, and without having its significance imposed on us.

The trilogy's immensely seductive quality does result in part from its over-stimulation of our visual attention. Kieslowski encourages us to constantly look for the significance of the objects he shows us, but his gauzy, decorative way of shooting a lampshade or a disordered table-top do not reveal them with the matter-of-fact analytic scrutiny of a Bresson. Rather, he overloads them with visual aura, so that we cannot help being aware that their function is to signify; Zbigniew Preisner's often portentous music tends to overstress the point. Rarely are films so prodigal with their epiphanies. In *Blue* especially, the camera constantly invests its, and our, attention in movements and in proximity, as when Julie trails her hand along a wall and the camera trails along with her at wall-level, or in the close-up that reveals a minuscule feather (*Blue* takes such poetic miniaturisation to unprecedented extremes). Even while the narrative encourages us to maintain an Olympian detachment, the camera rarely allows us to remain outside things. The result of such heavily signposted attention to the external world is to make us anxious that we might be missing the meaning of an object—or, in a more abstract sense, its *presence*—and therefore missing a piece of the puzzle. This treatment precludes the possibility that a lampshade may be just a lampshade. Alternatively, an image's meaning can be too brutally transparent, like the television footage of a bungee-jumper in *Blue*—at once free-falling and attached, too transparent a figure of Julie's own ambivalent suspension.

The trilogy is as much struck with the ''glamour'' of objects as it is with that of its leading actresses, who are very much objectified as complementary incarnations of some sort of feminine mystique. They are all curiously impassive, even when active: Julie a cool blue madonna of wounded isolation; Dominique a brutal example of the chilly attractions of the West; and Valentine quite explicitly the embodiment of warmth, alertness to the moment and—as it says on the chewing-gum billboard she poses for—''fraîcheur de vivre'' (''a breath of life,'' says the sub-title). They are there less to be empathised with than to be marvelled at and then contemplated as inimitable presences.

For the viewer, there is a somewhat factitious appeal to the act of visual contemplation in these films. Kieslowski always allows us to know something that the characters don't, thereby giving us at least the illusion of privileged distance. At the start of *Blue*, a close-up under the family's car gives us a warning that it will crash a moment later. By constantly granting us such flashes of insight, Kieslowski leads us to infer an overall scheme in which even the most apparently random image finds its place. From there it is a short step to inferring a metaphysical order. This perhaps is the secret of the trilogy's appeal—what we might call its theological fallacy. ''Something important is happening around me,'' says Valentine, and we too are inclined to believe that something important is happening before our eyes. These films shamelessly flatter our sensitivity to cosmic significance.

Much of their popularity may be due to the way that they encourage us to make our own associations and inferences; yet this apparent freedom is very much determined by the presence of so many heavily charged signposts. Everything in the trilogy signifies so unceasingly that we never feel as invigoratingly adrift as we do in the world of Antonioni, say, where things signify in the first instance because they so intransigently refuse to yield their meaning. Kieslowski's objects are never autonomous, but always significant, magical—which is to say, tied to human significance. The apparently sapient look to camera of the wounded dog in *Red* is an extreme example of this, where the camera's investment in the non-human world verges on anthropomorphism. None of this is meant to deny the trilogy's fascination, and indeed originality, only to acknowledge how problematic it is. It might seem churlish and paradoxical to attack the films on the grounds that they are over-stimulating, but Kieslowski seems unwilling to provide the viewer with any gaps that are not already orchestrated. In this sense, the visually blank *White*, the only episode not imbued with some sense of the uncanny, is also the only one that allows us to form our own position towards the drama.

Three Colours has been received by critics and audiences alike as a statement of faith in the regenerative possibilities of a traditional strain of European art-house cinema; but it is perhaps only the contingent circumstances of their international funding that truly makes them a statement about the current condition of Europe. (*White*, indeed, could be seen as a sort of picaresque allegory of a Polish film-maker's attempt to find the right country in which to make good.) And the portentous fanfare for a unified Europe, written by Julie and her husband in *Blue*, invokes the spiritual importance of high culture in a way that verges on kitsch. It is in their evocation of banal daily hustling—not quite pop culture perhaps, but a more prosaic real—that the films are most affecting.

Time will tell whether Kieslowski will continue to be regarded on the ''art cinema'' circuit with the spurious reverence due to an austere metaphysician, or whether he will be given proper credit as the consummate manipulator and sleight-of-hand artist that *Three Colours* reveals him to be—a filmmaker who could make remarkably complex and evocative capital out of the contingent facts of his chosen ''pretext.''

—Jonathan Romney

TROUBLE IN PARADISE

USA, 1932

Director: Ernst Lubitsch

Production: Paramount; black and white; running time: 80 minutes (some sources list 86 minutes); length: 7,200 feet. Released 1932.

Producer: Ernst Lubitsch; **screenplay:** Samson Raphaelson, adapted by Grover Jones from the play, *The Honest Finder* by Laszlo Aladar; **photography:** Victor Milner; **sets:** Hans Dreier; **music:** W. Franke Harling.

Cast: Herbert Marshall (*Gaston Monescu/Gaston Laval/The Baron*); Miriam Hopkins (*Lily, alias the Countess*); Kay Francis (*Mariette Colet*); Edward Everett Horton (*François*); Charlie Ruggles (*The Major*); C. Aubrey Smith (*Adolf J. Giron*); Robert Craig (*Jacques, the Manservant*); Leonid Kinskey (*A Russian*).

Publications

Script:

Trouble in Paradise in *Three Screen Comedies by Samson Raphaelson*, Madison, Wisconsin, 1983.

Books:

Jacobs, Lewis, *The Rise of the American Film*, New York, 1939.
Huff, Theodore, *An Index to the Films of Ernst Lubitsch*, London, 1947.
Verdone, Mario, *Ernst Lubitsch*, Lyons, 1964.
Weinberg, Herman, *The Lubitsch Touch: A Critical Study*, London and New York, 1968; 3rd edition, 1977.
Mast, Gerald, *The Comic Mind*, New York, 1973; revised edition, Chicago, 1979.
Baxter, John, *The Hollywood Exiles*, New York, 1976.
Poague, Leland, *The Cinema of Ernst Lubitsch: The Hollywood Films*, London, 1977.
Carringer, R., and B. Sabath, *Ernst Lubitsch: A Guide to References and Resources*, Boston, 1978.
Paul, William, *Ernst Lubitsch's American Comedy*, New York, 1983.
Prinzler, Hans Helmut, and Enno Patalas, editors, *Lubitsch*, Munich, 1984.
Bourget, Eithne and Jean-Loup, *Lubitsch; ou, La Satire romanesque*, Paris, 1987.
Harvey, James, *Romantic Comedy in Hollywood from Lubitsch to Sturges*, New York, 1987, 1998.
Nacache, Jacqueline, *Lubitsch*, Paris, 1987.
Bowman, Barbara, *Master Space: Film Images of Capra, Lubitsch, Sternberg, and Wyler*, New York, 1992.
Hake, Sabine, *Passions and Deceptions: The Early Films of Ernst Lubitsch*, Princeton, 1992.
Spaich, Herbert, *Ernst Lubitsch und seine Filme*, Munich, 1992.
Eyman, Scott, *Ernst Lubitsch: Laughter in Paradise*, New York, 1993, 2000.
Salotti, Marco, *Ernst Lubitsch*, Recco, 1997.
Henry, Nora, *Ethics and Social Criticism in the Hollywood Films of Erich von Stroheim, Ernst Lubitsch, and Billy Wilder*, Westport, 2000.

Articles:

New York Times, 9 November 1932.
Variety (New York), 15 November 1932.
New Statesman (London), 24 December 1932.
Wollenberg, H. H., ''2 Masters: Ernst Lubitsch and Sergei Eisenstein,'' in *Sight and Sound* (London), Spring 1948.
''A Tribute to Lubitsch, with a Letter in Which Lubitsch Appraises His Own Career,'' in *Films in Review* (New York), August-September 1951.
Cockshott, Gerald, in *Newsreel* (London), February 1952.
''A Tribute to Lubitsch,'' in *Action!* (Los Angeles), November-December 1967.
''Lubitsch Section'' of *Cahiers du Cinéma* (Paris), February 1968.
Weinberg, Herman, ''Ernst Lubitsch: A Parallel to George Feydeau,'' in *Film Comment* (New York), Spring 1970.
Sarris, Andrew, ''Lubitsch in the '30s,'' in *Film Comment* (New York), Winter 1971–72 and Summer 1972.
Gilliatt, Penelope, in *New Yorker*, 22 July 1972.
Literature/Film Quarterly (Salisbury, Maryland), Fall 1975.
Bond, Kirk, ''Ernst Lubitsch,'' in *Film Culture* (New York), no. 63–64, 1977.
Devillers, M., in *Cinématographe* (Paris), September-October 1983.
Ostria, V., in *Cahiers du Cinéma* (Paris), October 1983.
Rabourdin, D., in *Cinéma* (Paris), November 1983.
Tobin, Yann, in *Positif* (Paris), January 1984.
Hosman, H., in *Skoop* (Amsterdam), November 1984.

Trouble in Paradise

Truffaut, François, in *Jeune Cinéma* (Paris), March 1985.

Huie, W.O., ''Style and Technology in *Trouble in Paradise:* Evidence of a Technician's Lobby?'' in Journal *of Film and Video* (River Forest, Illinois), Spring 1987.

Sartor, F., in *Film en Televisie + Video* (Brussels), no. 384/385, May/June 1989.

Revue du Cinéma (Paris), no. 453, October 1989.

* * *

It's no coincidence that *Trouble in Paradise*, Lubitsch's own favourite among his films, should also be his most elegantly amoral. Lubitsch always took delight in subverting Hollywood's publicly professed standards of morality, and in *Trouble*, which sneaked through just ahead of the Hays Code, he wittily thumbed his nose at every moral precept in the book. Its characters make love without any intention—and scarcely even a mention—of marriage. No uplifting sentiments are expressed, save in situations of blatant hypocrisy; nobody is redeemed by love or suffering, nor wants to be. Crime not only pays, handsomely, but is presented as a sexy and stylish activity—and in any case hurts no one but the rich, who are either fools, or crooks themselves.

''Beginnings are always difficult,'' muses Gaston Monescu (Herbert Marshall), preparing for an intimate supper with an attractive fellow thief. Not in this film, they're not; from beginning to end, *Trouble* proceeds with seemingly effortless momentum. In the opening sequence a gondolier, giving a heartfelt rendition of *O Sole Mio*, glides along a nocturnal canal—collecting garbage; a robbery is affected in a darkened hotel room; and moments later Gaston leans pensively on his balcony, immaculate save only for a tiny leaf adhering to his sleeve. In the erotic sparring-match which follows, Lily (Miriam Hopkins) is visibly aroused by the knowledge that Gaston has just pulled off a crime, and their encounter becomes a seduction by mutual theft, each removing valuables from the other's person like intimate articles of clothing.

Throughout the film—crisply scripted by Samson Raphaelson, Lubitsch's favourite screenwriter of the sound period—sex and money are equated; wealth is erotic, illicitly acquired wealth doubly so, and larceny the finest aphrodisiac. ''As far as I'm concerned,'' says Gaston of Mme. Colet (Kay Francis), ''her whole sex appeal is in that safe,'' and Lily defines his attraction purely in terms of his criminality: "I want you as a crook. I love you as a crook. I worship you as a crook." With the lightest of satirical touches, Lubitsch portrays a society fuelled by luxury and greed. Barring only Hopkins, a touch too shrill in her later scenes, the casting is near impeccable; Marshall and Francis, never better, are supported by some of Hollywood's finest light comedians: Edward Everett Horton, Charlie Ruggles, C. Aubrey Smith and, buttling imperturbably, Robert Greig.

Claude Chabrol once described Fritz Lang's films as "based on a metaphysic of architecture." The same, in many ways, could be said of Lubitsch, for whom decor and props often assume hardly less importance than the actors. In *Trouble* doors, windows, landings, staircases are choreographed into the service of the plot; the course of an evening's emotional intrigue can be conveyed by a succession of clock faces and off-screen dialogue. Words are often downgraded or dispensed with—scenes are played entirely in Italian, or in dumbshow behind glass—and at other times mockingly multiplied far beyond dramatic need. The wretched M. Filiba (Horton), explaining how he was robbed by a fake doctor, has his every word translated by the hotel manager for a chorus of excitable Italian policemen. Manager: "What did you talk about, M. Filiba?" Filiba: "About tonsils." Manager (to police): "Tonsille!" Police (variously): "Tonsille!" The effect, like a verbal hall of mirrors, is to heighten the absurdity of the incident to a near-surrealist level.

The film scored a triumphant success with public and critics alike. "Never again," according to Andrew Sarris, "was Lubitsch to experience such rapport with his audience and his medium." With censorship poised to clamp down, *Trouble* can be seen as the culmination of his string of erotic comedies that had begun with *The Marriage Circle*. Yet it also, through its influence on such directors as Cukor, McCarey, Leisen and La Cava, ushered in the golden age of Hollywood comedy. The American moviegoing public, Lubitsch had remarked on first visiting the USA in 1922, "has the mind of a twelve-year-old child; it must have life as it isn't." Nobody—and certainly not its director—would be likely to claim *Trouble in Paradise* as a faithful record of "life as it is." But if, in the intervening ten years, the moviegoing public—or at any rate a sizeable sector of it—had matured enough to relish a somewhat more sophisticated brand of unreality, Lubitsch himself can claim a major share of the credit.

—Philip Kemp

TURKSIB

USSR, 1929

Director: Victor Turin

Production: Vostok Film (USSR); black and white; 35mm; running time: 85 minutes. Released 1929. Filmed in Turkestan and Siberia.

Producer: Victor Turin; **screenplay:** Victor Turin with Alexander Macheret, Victor Shklovsky, and Efim Aron; **English titles:** John Grierson; **assistant director:** Efim Aron; **photography:** Yevgeni Slavinski and Boris Frantzisson; **editor of English version:** John Grierson.

Publications

Books:

Leyda, Jay, *Kino: A History of Russian and Soviet Film*, London, 1960.

Barsam, Richard, *Nonfiction Film: A Critical History*, New York, 1973.

Barnouw, Erik, *Documentary: A History of the Non-Fiction Film*, New York, 1974.

Article:

Coldicutt, K. J., "*Turksib*: Building a Railroad," in *The Documentary Tradition*, edited by Lewis Jacobs, 2nd edition, New York, 1979.

"A aldeia do pecado: *Turksib*," in *Celuloide*, no. 303–305, November 1980.

Film (London), no. 105, April/May 1982.

* * *

Turksib is a world-famous documentary that depicts the building of a railway linking Turkestan with Siberia, to carry cotton from the former in exchange for cereals and vegetables from the latter: one of its very first large-scale construction projects in the Soviet Union. Victor Turin, its director, had spent his formative years in the United States—from 1912 when he was 17 until he returned to Russia in 1922—having attended Massachusetts Institute of Technology and worked as an actor and scenarist at the Vitagraph Studios in Hollywood. He had also, of course, missed both the First World War and the Russian Revolution, which, together with his rich, middle-class background, may have adversely affected his later career.

Before *Turksib*, Turin had already made three Soviet films, one of which was a feature about the class struggle in the capitalist world—*Borba Gigantov* (Battle of Giants). It was considered too "abstract" (i.e., bad). It was all the more surprising, therefore, that Turin broke away from the very romantic style then becoming popular, full of dingleberry (an old Hollywood term for foliage introduced into the top of the frame), diffusion, back-lighting, noble close-ups and a general obsession with beautiful photography. In stark contrast, *Turksib* was a clear, direct and realistic statement, which was also gripping, touched with humor and humanity and edited with verve and a sure sense of rhythm. It was also said by Soviet critics to be "lyrical" (i.e., good). Perhaps (as frequently happens in cinema history) it was even helped by a relatively small budget and tight schedule to achieve its clarity, economy and unity—and to escape too much interference from "above." But it was Turin himself who had carefully and deliberately planned the style and content of his film. It was received abroad with even more acclaim than it won at home, and it certainly helped to put the documentary tradition back on the rails of realism.

Turksib is still enjoyable to watch and deserves the permanent place it has won in the canon of Russian classical movies, along with the works of Pudovkin, Eisenstein, Dovzhenko and Dziga Vertov. Why did its director fail to make further masterpieces? It is difficult to determine whether Turin was rewarded—or merely "kicked upstairs"—by being given an executive post at the very moment he seemed to have "arrived." He was not to direct another film until 1938—*Bakintsy*, a feature about the 1905 revolution, made at the Azerbaijani studios in Baku. *Turksib* undoubtedly proved Turin's abilities as an organizer, but it seems tragic that his other, rarer talents

Turksib

were not given a chance for further documentaries in his fresh, purposeful style.

—Robert Dunbar

TWELVE ANGRY MEN

USA, 1957

Director: Sidney Lumet

Production: Orion-Nova (Fonda-Rose); black and white; running time: 96 minutes; length: 8,648 feet. Released February 1957.

Producers: Henry Fonda, Reginald Rose; **associate producer:** George Justin; **screenplay:** Reginald Rose; **photography:** Boris Kaufman; **editor:** Carl Lerner; **sound:** James A. Gleason; **art director:** Robert Markell; **music:** Kenyon Hopkins.

Cast: Henry Fonda (*Juror no. 8*); Lee J. Cobb (*Juror no. 3*); Ed Begley (*Juror no. 10*); E. G. Marshall (*Juror no. 4*); Jack Warden (*Juror no. 7*); Martin Balsam (*Juror no. 1*); John Fielder (*Juror no. 2*); Jack Klugman (*Juror no. 5*); Rudy Bond (*Judge*); James A. Kelly (*Guard*); Bill Nelson (*Court Clerk*); John Savoca (*Defendant*).

Publications

Script:

Rose, Reginald, *Twelve Angry Men*, in *Film Scripts 2*, edited by George P. Garrett and others, New York, 1971.

Books:

Perkins, W. H., *Learning the Liveliest Art*, Hobart, 1968.

Springer, John, *The Fondas: The Films and Careers of Henry, Jane, and Peter Fonda*, New York, 1970.

Kerbel, Michael, *Henry Fonda*, New York, 1975.

Twelve Angry Men

Bowles, Stephen, *Sidney Lumet: A Guide to References and Resources*, Boston, 1979.

Fonda, Henry, and Howard Teichmann, *Fonda: My Life*, New York, 1981.

Goldstein, Norm, *Henry Fonda: His Life and Work*, London, 1982.

Thomas, Tony, *The Films of Henry Fonda*, Secaucus, New Jersey, 1983.

Roberts, Allen, and Max Goldstein, *Henry Fonda: A Biography*, Jefferson, North Carolina, 1984.

Cunningham, Frank R., *Sidney Lumet: Film and Literary Vision,* Lexington, 1991.

Sweeney, Kevin, *Henry Fonda: A Bio-Bibliography*, New York, 1992.

Boyer, Jan, *Sidney Lumet*, Old Tappan, 1993.

Articles:

Film Culture (New York), no. 2, 1957.

Variety (New York), 27 February 1957.

Kine Weekly (London), 25 April 1957.

Monthly Film Bulletin (London), June 1957.

Hill, D., ''Press Conference,'' in *Sight and Sound* (London), Summer 1957.

Truffaut, François, in *Cahiers du Cinéma* (Paris), December 1957.

Positif (Paris), February 1958.

''Le Point de vue du metteur en scène,'' in *Cahiers du Cinéma* (Paris), April 1959.

Bogdanovich, Peter, ''An Interview with Sidney Lumet,'' in *Film Quarterly* (Berkeley), Winter 1960.

Springer, John, ''Henry Fonda,'' in *Films in Review* (New York), November 1960.

Cowie, Peter, ''Fonda,'' in *Films and Filming* (London), April 1962.

''Fonda on Fonda,'' in *Films and Filming* (London), February 1963.

Hagen, R., ''Fonda: Without a Method,'' in *Films and Filming* (London), June 1966.

Petrie, Graham, ''The Films of Sidney Lumet: Adaptation as Art,'' in *Film Quarterly* (Berkeley), Winter 1967–68.

''Dialogue on Film: Henry Fonda,'' in *American Film* (Washington, D.C.), May 1977.

''Sidney Lumet Issue'' of *Cinématographe* (Paris), January 1982.

American Film (Washington, D.C.), January-February 1982.

Cunningham, F., "Sidney Lumet's Humanism: The Return to the Father in *Twelve Angry Men*," in *Literature/Film Quarterly* (Salisbury, Maryland), vol. 14, no. 2, 1986.

Elia, Maurice, in *Séquences* (Haute-Ville), no. 188, January-February 1997.

* * *

Bought and produced by Henry Fonda as a vehicle for himself (from an earlier TV study of a jury by Reginald Rose), *Twelve Angry Men* can be characterized as a classic liberal response to the McCarthyist assault on American pluralism and tolerance which had scarred the country in the previous decade. In taking up issues of the defence of individual rights and ideals of justice, *Twelve Angry Men* shares common ground with other films of the period, such as Sturges' *Bad Day at Black Rock* (1954) and Kazan's *On the Waterfront* (1954). Though all studies of the roots and effects of victimization in American society, their expositions differ in their perspective. Spencer Tracy's Macreedy in *Black Rock* arrives as a lone avenger after the event, intent on laying bare and punishing, while Brando's Terry Malloy in *On the Waterfront* marks the victim himself fighting back. Fonda's juror 8 in *Twelve Angry Men* is neither. Where Macreedy is akin to a surgeon resorting to the knife in cutting out a cancerous tumour and Brando is a struggling fighter battering a way forward, Fonda is almost passive. He is a healer undermining the cancer before it can take effect. Where Brando and Tracy take centre stage in action, Fonda assumes the role of catalyst, persuading others into action in an almost "de-starred" role, effectively unnoticed by the camera until the moment he raises his hand as the sole "Not Guilty" voter.

Yet *Twelve Angry Men* is not so much a film about individual character—it is rather a probing of ideals in a country built upon the idea of active citizenship. The jurors function precisely as representatives of the American people in the pursuit of Justice (here added to Life, Liberty and the Pursuit of Happiness), a multi-bodied American Everyman: the sports-fanatic, the former slum-kid, the Swiss-German immigrant, the educated doctor, the advertising man, the self-made businessmen, the bigot. As symbolic representatives, even names are unnecessary.

The film's subject is made explicit in the opening pan up the pillars of the courts to show the proclamation engraved above the entrance: the subject is the practice of Justice as a foundation of America-as-concept. Yet these ideals are offered precisely as they are *not* abstract concepts. Fonda's function in the film is almost Socratic, testing his fellow citizens in their practice of the duties which uphold democracy. The trial of an accused is simply a broader trial of the functioning of America as democracy.

The film peels the jury apart in search of a common bedrock, and the revelation of threats to true democracy. From an over-concern with leisure (the sports fan's tickets for the game), empty images (the advertising man with no point of view), to outright bigotry (juror 10's McCarthyist "these people are dangerous" outburst near the end functioning as a revelation of naked prejudice that is pointedly ignored by a jury finally refinding its democratic soul), the threats are revealed and overcome. And it is important that is it those arguably closest to the *spirit* of the American ideal—the "poor, tired and homeless"—who first take juror 8's cue to defend it. In particular, it is the immigrant juror 11 who makes the link between the jury and democracy, the practice and the ideal, reminding America of its promise.

A beautifully precise construction in narrative terms, *Twelve Angry Men* handles a potentially clichéd situation with superb assurance. From a full set of excellent performances, Fonda as the quiet architect achieves a humbling serenity, while Lee J. Cobb's acid juror 3 echoes his role in *On the Waterfront*. The film also blends both a formal visual control—as in the framing of groups to emphasize sways of power within the jury process with a certain cinematic "looseness" that moves towards Naturalism, with actors wandering in and out of frame, speech from off-camera and overlapping dialogue.

Yet, arguably, it is a film of ideas and emotions more than style, an idealist film in a cynical world. It reaches toward a less tainted humanity, either on the grand scale of a Nation (to which the jurors go out at the end, recharged) or the smaller—but not lesser—scale of juror 3's rediscovery of the quality of mercy which culminates the jury's reaching a verdict.

Kazan's opening to *On the Waterfront* appeals to "right-thinking people in a vital democracy." *Twelve Angry Men* echoes this appeal as a foundation of the vision of America.

—Norman Miller

THE TWISTED ROAD

See **THEY LIVE BY NIGHT**

TWO ACRES OF LAND

See **DO BIGHA ZAMIN**

TWO ROADS

See **DUVIDHA**

TWO STAGE SISTERS

See **WUTAI JIEMEI**

2001: A SPACE ODYSSEY

USA-UK, 1968

Director: Stanley Kubrick

Production: Metro-Goldwyn-Mayer Pictures Corp.; Technicolor and Metrocolor, 35mm, Super Panavision; running time: 141 minutes, premiere versions were 160 minutes. Released 3 April 1968,

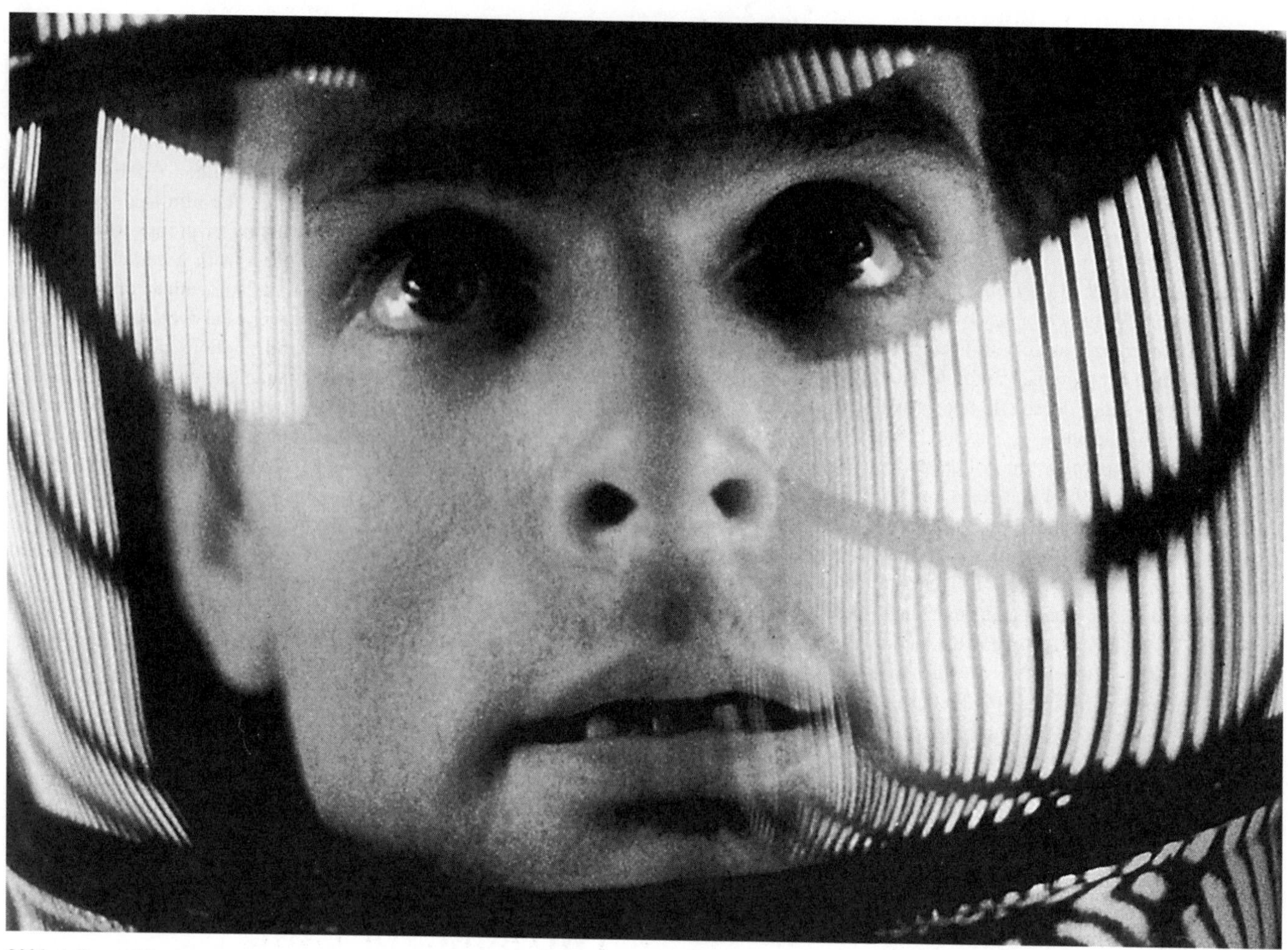

2001: A Space Odyssey

New York. Filmed beginning 29 December 1965 in MGM's Shepperton and Borehamwood Studios, England. Cost: $10,500,000.

Producers: Stanley Kubrick with Victor Lyndon; **screenplay:** Stanley Kubrick and Arthur C. Clarke, from "The Sentinel" in *Expedition to Earth* by Clarke; **photography:** Geoffrey Unsworth; **additional photography:** John Alcott; **editor:** Ray Lovejoy; **sound supervisor:** A. W. Watkins; **sound mixer:** H. J. Bird, sound editor: Winston Ryder; **production designers:** Tony Masters, Harry Lange, and Ernest Archer; **art director:** John Hoesli; **music:** from works by Khatchaturian, Ligeti, Johann Strauss and Richard Strauss; **special effects director:** Stanley Kubrick; **supervisors:** Wally Veevers, Douglas Trumbull, Con Pederson and Tom Howard; **costume designer:** Hardy Amies; **scientific consultant:** Frederick Ordway III.

Cast: Keir Dullea (*Dave Bowman*); Gary Lockwood (*Frank Poole*); William Sylvester (*Dr. Heywood Floyd*); Daniel Richter (*Moon-Watcher*); Leonard Rossiter (*Smyslov*); Margaret Tyzack (*Elena*); Robert Beatty (*Halvorsen*); Sean Sullivan (*Michaels*); Douglas Rain (*HAL's voice*); Frank Miller (*Mission Control*); Penny Brahms (*Stewardess*); Alan Gifford (*Poole's Father*).

Awards: Oscar for Special Visual Effects, 1968; American Film Institute's "100 Years, 100 Movies," 1998.

Publications

Script:

Clarke, Arthur C., *2001: A Space Odyssey*, New York, 1968.

Books:

Agel, Jerome, editor, *The Making of Kubrick's 2001*, New York, 1970.
Dumont, Jean-Paul, and Jean Monod, *La Foetus astral*, Paris, 1970.
Predal, Rene, *Le Cinéma fantastique*, Paris, 1970.
Walker, Alexander, *Stanley Kubrick Directs*, London, 1971.
Clarke, Arthur C., *The Lost Worlds of 2001*, New York, 1972.
Clarke, Arthur C., *Report on Planet 3: And Other Speculations*, New York, 1972.
De Vries, Daniel, *The Films of Stanley Kubrick*, Grand Rapids, Michigan, 1973.
Geduld, Carolyn, *Filmguide to 2001: A Space Odyssey*, Bloomington, Indiana, 1973.
Phillips, Gene D., *Stanley Kubrick: A Film Odyssey*, New York, 1975.
Ciment, Michel, *Kubrick*, Paris, 1980; revised edition, 1987; English edition, London, 1983.
Kolker, Robert Phillip, *A Cinema of Loneliness: Penn, Kubrick, Coppola, Scorsese, Altman*, Oxford, 1980; revised edition, 1988.

Short, Robert, *The Gospel from Outer Space*, San Francisco, 1983.
Dettmering, P., *Literatur, Psychoanalyse, Film: Aufsätze 1978 bis 1983*, Stuttgart, 1984.
Hummel, Christoph, editor, *Stanley Kubrick*, Munich, 1984.
Brunetta, Gian Piero, *Stanley Kubrick: Tempo, spazio, storia, e mondi possibili*, Parma, 1985.
Cagin, Seth, *Born to Be Wild: Hollywood & the Sixties Generation*, Boca Raton, 1994.

Articles:

Clarke, Arthur C., "The Sentinel," in *Expedition to Earth* (New York), 1953.
Crist, Judith, "Stanley Kubrick, Please Come Down," in *New York*, 22 April 1962.
Robinson, David, "Two for the Sci-Fi," in *Sight and Sound* (London), Spring 1966.
"Kubrick, Farther Out," in *Newsweek* (New York), 12 September 1966.
Spinrad, Norman, "Stanley Kubrick in the 21st Century," in *Cinema* (Beverley Hills), December 1966.
Sarris, Andrew, "Stanley Kubrick," in *The American Cinema* (New York), 1968.
Adler, Renata, in *New York Times*, 4 April 1968.
Shuldiner, Herbert, "How They Filmed *2001*," in *Popular Science* (New York), June 1968.
Trumbull, Douglas, "Creating Special Effects for *2001*," in *American Cinematographer* (Los Angeles), June 1968.
Barker, Cliff, and Mark Gasser, in *Cineaste* (New York), Summer 1968.
Hunter, Tim, and others, in *Film Heritage* (Dayton, Ohio), Summer 1968.
Austen David, in *Films and Filming* (London), July 1968.
Tavernier, Bertrand, "Londres a l'heure de Stanley Kubrick," in *Lettres Françaises* (Paris), 21 August 1968.
Capdenac, Michel, in *Lettres Françaises* (Paris), October 1968.
Ciment, Michel, in *Positif* (Paris), October 1968.
Walter, Renaud, "Entretien avec Stanley Kubrick," in *Positif* (Paris), December 1968.
Alpert, Hollis, in *Film 68–69*, edited by Hollis Alpert and Andrew Sarris, New York, 1969.
Rapf, Maurice, "A Talk with Stanley Kubrick," in *Action!* (Los Angeles), January-February 1969.
Eisenschitz, Bernard, in *Cahiers du Cinéma* (Paris), February 1969.
Michelson, Annette, "Bodies in Space: Film as Carnal Knowledge," in *Artforum* (New York), February 1969.
James, Clive, "Kubrick Versus Clarke," in *Cinema* (London), March 1969.
Sineux, Michel, in *Positif* (Paris), April 1969.
McKee, Mel, "*2001*: Out of the Silent Planet," in *Sight and Sound* (London), Autumn 1969.
Gelmis, Joseph, "Stanley Kubrick," in *The Film Director as Superstar* (New York), 1970.
Kael, Pauline, "Trash, Art, and the Movies," in *Going Steady*, Boston, 1970.
Youngblood, Gene, "The New Nostalgia," in *Expanded Cinema* (New York), 1970.
Sargow, Michael, in *Film Society Review* (New York), January 1970.
Pohl, Frederick, in *Film Society Review* (New York), February 1970.
Canby, Vincent, in *New York Times*, 3 May 1970.
Daniels, Don, in *Sight and Sound* (London), Winter 1970–71.
Kozloff, Max, in *Film Culture* (New York), Winter-Spring 1970.
Kauffman, Stanley, in *Figure of Light* (New York), 1971.
Phillips, Gene, "Kubrick," in *Film Comment* (New York), Winter 1971–72.
"Issue on *2001*" of *Cahiers du Cinéma* (Paris), Summer 1972.
Fisher, J., "Too Bad Lois Lane: The End of Sex in *2001*," in *Film Journal* (New York), September 1972.
Boyd, D., "Mode and Meaning in *2001*," in *Journal of Popular Film* (Washington D.C.), no. 3, 1978.
Kuckza, P., in *Filmkultura* (Budapest), March-April 1979.
"Le Dossier: *2001*, Stanley Kubrick," in *Avant-Scène du Cinéma* (Paris), 15 July 1979.
Hibbin, N., in *Chaplin* (Stockholm), no. 6, 1981.
Burgoyne, Robert, "Narrative Overture and Closure in *2001: A Space Odyssey*," in *Enclitic* (Minneapolis), Fall 1981-Spring 1982.
Rood, J., in *Skoop* (Amsterdam), November 1983.
Strick, Philip, "Ring Round the Moons," in *Monthly Film Bulletin* (London), March 1985.
Shelton, R., "Rendezvous with HAL: *2001/2010*," in *Extrapolation* (Kent, Ohio), no. 3, 1987.
Carter, S., "Avatars of the Turtles," in *Journal of Popular Film and Television* (Washington, DC), no. 3, 1990.
Fantauzzi, S., in *Quaderni di Cinema* (Florence), July-September 1992.
Hanson, E., "Technology, Paranoia and the Queer Voice," in *Screen* (Oxford), no. 2, 1993.
Debellis, J., "'The Awful Power': John Updike's Use of Kubrick's *2001: A Space Odyssey* in Rabbit Redux," in *Literature/Film Quarterly* (Salisbury, Maryland), no. 3, 1993.
Vallerand, François, "L'odyssée de la musique de *2001*," in *Séquences* (Haute-Ville), January 1994.
Miller, Mark Crispin, "*2001*: a Cold Descent," in *Sight & Sound* (London), January 1994.
Henderson, K., "Alex North's *2001* and Beyond," in *Soundtrack* (Mechelen), March 1994.
Jacquet-Françillon, Vincent, "An Interview with Jerry Goldsmith," in *Cue Sheet* (Hollywood), vol. 10, no. 3–4, 1993–1994.
Saada, Nicolas, "Caro Diario," in *Cahiers du Cinéma* (Paris), December 1994.
Sinema, Andere, "*2001: A Space Odyssey*," in *Andere Sinema* (Antwerp), May-June 1997.
Chion, M., "(Deux) *2001: l'Odyssee de l'espace*," in *Positif* (Paris), September 1997.
Scheurer, Timothy E., "Kubrick vs. North. The Score for *2001: A Space Odyssey*," in *Journal of Popular Film and Television* (Washington, D.C.), vol. 25, no. 4, Winter 1998.

* * *

In *2001: A Space Odyssey*, Stanley Kubrick further explored his dark vision of man in a materialistic, mechanistic age depicted in *Dr. Strangelove* four years earlier. In explaining how the original idea for this landmark science-fiction film came to him, he says, "Most astronomers and other scientists interested in the whole question are strongly convinced that the universe is crawling with life; much of it, since the numbers are so staggering, (is) equal to us in intelligence, or superior, simply because human intelligence has existed for so relatively short a period." He approached Arthur C. Clarke, whose science fiction short story, "The Sentinel," would eventually become the basis for the film. They first expanded the short story into a novel, in order to completely develop the story's potential, and then turned that into a screenplay.

MGM bought their package and financed the film for six million dollars, a budget that after four years of work on the film eventually rose to ten million. Though *2001* opened to indifferent and even hostile reviews, subsequent critical opinion has completely reversed itself. As the film is often revived, it has earned back its original cost several times over.

2001 begins with the dawn of civilization in which an ape-man learns to use a bone as a weapon in order to destroy a rival, ironically taking a step further toward humanity. As the victorious ape-man throws his weapon spiralling into the air, there is a dissolve to a spaceship from the year 2001. ''It's simply an observable fact,'' Kubrick comments, ''that all of man's technology grew out of the discovery of the tool-weapon. There's no doubt that there's a deep emotional relationship between man and his machine-weapons, which are his children. The machine is beginning to assert itself in a very profound way, even attracting affection and obsession.''

This concept is dramatized in the film when astronauts Dave Bowman and Frank Poole find themselves at the mercy of the computer HAL 9000, which controls their spaceship. (There are repeated juxtapositions of man with his human failings and fallibility immersed in machines: beautiful, functional, but cold and heartless.) When HAL the computer makes a mistake, he refuses to admit the evidence of his own capacity for error, and proceeds to destroy the occupants of the space ship to cover it up. Kubrick indicates here, as in *Dr. Strangelove*, that human fallibility is less likely to destroy man than the abdication of his moral responsibilities to presumably infallible machines.

Kubrick believes man must also strive to gain mastery over himself and not just over his machines, ''Somebody said man is the missing link between primitive apes and civilized human beings. You might say that that is inherent in the story of *2001* too. We are semi-civilized, capable of cooperation and affection, but needing some sort of transfiguration into a higher form of life. Since the means to obliterate life on earth exists, it will take more than just careful planning and reasonable cooperation to avoid some eventual catastrophic event. The problem exists as long as the potential exists; and the problem is essentially a moral one and a spiritual one.''

These sentiments are very close to those which Charlie Chaplin expressed in his closing speech in *The Great Dictator*: ''We think too much and feel too little. More than machinery we need humanity. More than cleverness we need kindness and gentleness. Without these qualities, life will be violent and all will be lost.''

The overall implications of the film suggest a more optimistic aspect to Kubrick's view of life than had been previously detected in his work. Here he presents man's creative encounters with the universe and his unfathomed potential for the future in more hopeful terms than he did, for example, in *Dr. Strangelove*.

The film ends with Bowman, the only survivor of the mission, being reborn as ''an enhanced being, a star child, an angel, a superman, if you like,'' Kubrick explains, ''returning to earth prepared for the next leap forward of man's evolutionary destiny.''

Kubrick feels that ''the God concept is at the heart of the film'' since, if any extraterrestrial superior being were to manifest itself to man, the latter would immediately assume it was God or an emissary of God. When an artifact of these beings does appear in the film, it is represented as a black monolithic slab. Kubrick thought it better not to try to be too specific in depicting these beings, ''You have to leave something to the audience's imagination,'' he concludes.

In summary, *2001* by neither showing nor explaining too much, enables the viewer to experience the film as a whole. As Kubrick comments, ''The feel of the experience is the important thing, not the ability to verbalize it. I tried to create a visual experience which directly penetrates the subconscious content of the material.'' The movie consequently becomes for the viewer an intensely subjective experience which reaches his inner consciousness in the same manner that music does, leaving him free to speculate about thematic content. As one critic put it, *2001* successfully brings the techniques and appeal of the experimental film into the studio feature-length film, ''making it the world's most expensive underground movie.'' It is this phenomenon, in the final analysis, which has made *2001: A Space Odyssey* so perennially popular with audiences. It is significant that Kubrick set the film in the year 2001, because Fritz Lang's groundbreaking silent film *Metropolis* takes place in the year 2000. This reference to Lang's film is a homage to the earlier master's accomplishment in science fiction—an achievement which Kubrick's film has successfully built on and surpassed.

—Gene D. Phillips

TYSTNADEN

(The Silence)

Sweden, 1963

Director: Ingmar Bergman

Production: Svensk Filmindustri; black and white, 35mm; running time: 95 minutes; length: 2623 meters. Released 23 September 1963, Stockholm. Filmed sporadically from Summer 1962-Summer 1963 in Sweden.

Producer: Allan Ekelund; **screenplay:** Ingmar Bergman; **photography:** Sven Nykvist; **editor:** Ulla Ryghe; **sound engineer:** Stig Flodin; **production designer:** P. A. Lundgren; **music:** Bach; **special effects:** Evald Anderson; **costume designer:** Marik Vos.

Cast: Gunnel Lindblom (*Anna*); Ingrid Thulin (*Ester*); Jörgen Lindström (*Johan*); Haakan Jahnberg (*Hotel manager*); Lissi Alandh (*Woman in the cinema*); Leif Forstenberg (*Man in the cinema*); Nils Waldt (*Cashier at the cinema*); Birgir Lesander; Eduardo Gutierrez.

Publications

Script:

Bergman, Ingmar, *Le Silence*, in *Avant-Scène du Cinéma* (Paris), May 1964; as *The Silence*, in *A Film Trilogy*, New York and London, 1967; revised edition, London, 1989.

Books:

Béranger, Jean, and François Guyon, *Ingmar Bergman*, Lyons, 1964.
Chiaretti, Tommaso, *Ingmar Bergman*, Rome, 1964.

Donner, Jorn, *The Personal Vision of Ingmar Bergman*, Bloomington, Indiana, 1964.
Nelson, David, *Ingmar Bergman: The Search for God*, Boston, 1964.
Steene, Birgitta, *Ingmar Bergman*, New York, 1968.
Gibson, Arthur, *The Silence of God: Creative Response to the Films of Ingmar Bergman*, New York, 1969.
Wood, Robin, *Ingmar Bergman*, New York, 1969.
Sjögren, Henrik, *Regi: Ingmar Bergman*, Stockholm, 1970.
Young, Vernon, *Cinema Borealis: Ingmar Bergman and the Swedish Ethos*, New York, 1971.
Björkman, Stig, and others, editors, *Bergman on Bergman*, New York, 1973.
Ranieri, Tino, *Ingmar Bergman*, Florence, 1974.
Kaminsky, Stuart, editor, *Ingmar Bergman: Essays in Criticism*, New York, 1975.
Bergom-Larsson, Maria, *Ingmar Bergman and Society*, San Diego, 1978.
Kawin, Bruce, *Mindscreen: Bergman, Godard and the First-Person Film*, Princeton, 1978.
Marion, Denis, *Ingmar Bergman*, Paris, 1979.
Manvell, Roger, *Ingmar Bergman: An Appreciation*, New York, 1980.
Mosley, Philip, *Ingmar Bergman: The Cinema as Mistress*, Boston, 1981.
Petric, Vlada, editor, *Film and Dreams: An Approach to Bergman*, South Salem, New York, 1981.
Cowie, Peter, *Ingmar Bergman: A Critical Biography*, New York, 1982.
Livingston, Paisley, *Ingmar Bergman and the Ritual of Art*, Ithaca, New York, 1982.
Steene, Birgitta, *Ingmar Bergman: A Guide to References and Resources*, Boston, 1982.
Jones, William G., editor, *Talking with Bergman*, Dallas, 1983.
Lefèvre, Raymond, *Ingmar Bergman*, Paris, 1983.
Dervin, Daniel, *Through a Freudian Lens Deeply: A Psychoanalysis of Cinema*, Hillsdale, New Jersey, 1985.
Gado, Frank, *The Passion of Ingmar Bergman*, Durham, North Carolina, 1986.
Bergman, Ingmar, *Laterna Magica*, Stockholm, 1987; as *The Magic Lantern: An Autobiography*, London, 1988.
Cohen, James, *Through a Lens Darkly*, New York, 1991.
Bjorkman, Stig, and Torsten Maans, and Jonas Sima, *Bergman on Bergman: Interviews with Ingmar Bergman*, Cambridge, 1993.
Cohen, Hubert I., *Ingmar Bergman: The Art of Confession*, New York, 1993.
Long, Robert Emmet, *Ingmar Bergman: Film and Stage*, New York, 1994.
Tornqvist, Egil, *Between Stage and Screen: Ingmar Bergman Directs*, Amsterdam, 1995.
Blackwell, Marilyn J., *Gender and Representation in the Films of Ingmar Bergman*, Rochester, 1997.
Michaels, Lloyd, editor, *Ingmar Bergman's Persona*, New York, 1999; revised edition, Cambridge, 2000.

Articles:

Bory, Jean-Louis, in *Arts* (Paris), March 1964.
Interview with Bergman in *Sunday Times* (London), 15 March 1964.
Collet, Jean, in *Télérama* (Paris), 18 March 1964.
Sadoul, Georges, in *Lettres Françaises* (Paris), 26 March 1964.
Billard, Pierre, in *Cinéma* (Paris), April 1964.
Kyrou, Ado, in *Positif* (Paris), Summer 1964.
Scott, James, ''The Achievement of Ingmar Bergman,'' in *Journal of Aesthetics and Art Criticism* (Cleveland), Winter 1965.
Hamilton, William, ''Ingmar Bergman on the Silence of God,'' in *Motive*, November 1966.
Lefèvre, Raymond, ''Ingmar Bergman,'' in *Image et Son* (Paris), March 1969.
Young, Vernon, ''Cinema Borealis,'' in *Hudson Review* (Nutley, New Jersey), Summer 1970.
Steene, Birgitta, ''Images and Words in Bergman's Films,'' in *Cinema Journal* (Evanston, Illinois), Fall 1970.
Alexander, W., ''Devils in the Cathedral: Bergman's Trilogy,'' in *Cinema Journal* (Evanston, Illinois), Spring 1974.
Amis du Film et de la Télévision (Brussels), February 1976.
Troelsen, A., in *Kosmorama* (Copenhagen), Spring 1978.
Holloway, R., ''Tystnaden som tema,'' in *Filmrutan* (Stockholm), vol. 28, no. 1, 1985.
Listener (London), 23 June 1988.
Trasatti, S., ''Bergman, il paradosso di un 'Ateo cristiano,''' in *Castoro Cinema* (Florence), November-December 1991.
Bergman, I., ''Kepek 2,'' in *Filmvilag* (Budapest), no. 10, 1992.
Sitney, P. A., ''Bergman's *The Silence* and the Primal Scene,'' in *Film Culture* (New York), June 1992.
Kieslowski, Krzysztof, ''Kan Kieslowski lösa Tystnadens gåta?'' in *Chaplin* (Stockholm), vol. 36, no. 5, 1994.
Visscher, J. De, ''Gods zwijgen?'' in *Film en Televisie + Video* (Brussels), no. 462, May 1996.
Kieslowski, Krzysztof, ''Peut-on résoudre l'énigme du 'silence?''' in *Positif* (Paris), no. 457, March 1999.
Lahr, John, ''The Demon-Lover: After Six Decades in Film and Theatre, Ingmar Bergman Talks About His Family and the Invention of Psychological Cinema,'' in *The New Yorker*, vol. 75, no. 13, 31 May 1999.

* * *

The Silence: there are alternative or multiple significances to that title by Ingmar Bergman. The most commonly understood is an allusion (yet again: as in *The Seventh Seal, Winter Light*, and *Through a Glass Darkly*) to the utter unresponsiveness of God to the tribulations of humankind, but another potential implication is the silence that follows upon non-communication, misunderstanding, and the lack of sympathy between human beings. The protagonists in this film are two sisters in their thirties—Anna, the younger (Gunnel Lindblom), with her small son Johan (Jörgen Lindström), and Ester (Ingrid Thulin), who are travelling by train (the published script emphasizing its stench) to an unspecified central European country where the language is utterly unknown to them and is, indeed, an invention by Bergman. They end up in what is to be the main setting for the film—a suite of two rooms in a vast, almost unoccupied hotel in a city full of people with whom they cannot communicate and which is strangely, eerily silent. As in *Persona* (Bergman's film to be released some three years later) the two women are involved in a form of love/hate intimacy which some have tried to interpret as lesbian. While Anna is full of a lust for life and sex (which she seeks out promiscuously in this strange city), Ester (forever jealous of her younger sister) is suffering from what appears to be a terminal sickness, her only faithful attendant being an elderly and cadaverous floor waiter who seems to resemble Death himself.

The essence of this film lies in the failing relationship of the two sisters, who represent a polarity of opposites in temperament. Ingrid

Thulin once told the writer that Bergman had considered inviting her to play both parts, thus emphasizing this polarity as dual aspects of a single person, but that the logistics of production with a single actress proved too daunting. Anna is sensual in all her contacts, even with her small son. The scenes between her and her eager lover (a man she picks up during an evening's solitary outing) caused the censors of the early 1960s some considerable concern, though they would cause little stir today. Anna's carnality contrasts with Ester's lonely austerity, and her demanding rationality. She is, according to the script, a translator, and she shows throughout the film her curiosity about certain words in the country's language, as conveyed to her by the waiter. As the elder, she attempts to dominate her sister (who is deeply resentful) and to adopt a guardian-like attitude to the boy, which makes Anna jealous. The boy himself wanders off to explore the hotel, large and empty like a mausoleum, and finds a kind of momentary, sick companionship with a party of dwarfs, creatures of his own size who are evidently a company of entertainers and virtually the only other inhabitants in the hotel. The effect of this perverse contact is somehow surreal. As for the country itself, Bergman says (*Bergman on Bergman*), ''It's a country preparing for war, where war can break out any day, all the time one feels it is something perverse and terrifying.'' Every so often tanks roll through the city streets, and the sinister wail of air-raid sirens can be heard.

Bergman has said much from time to time about this daunting film. In a press interview for the London *Sunday Times* (March 15, 1964), he said, ''Ester loves her sister; she finds her beautiful and feels a tremendous responsibility for her, but she would be the first to be horrified if it were pointed out that her feelings were incestuous. Her mistake lies in the fact that she wants to control her sister—as her father had controlled her by his love. Love must be open. Otherwise Love is the beginning of Death. That is what I am trying to say.'' Some years later in *Bergman on Bergman*, he added, ''The crux of the matter is that Ester—even though she is ill and inwardly decaying—is struggling against the decay within her. She feels a sort of disgust for Anna's corporeality . But Anna is uninhibitedly physical. She holds her little boy within the magic circle of her own animality, controls him.''

There is, however, at least the suggestion of hope at the close of the film. Anna leaves her sister to return home, taking the child with her. But the boy carries a secret message with him from his aunt in a strange language which has excited her curiosity. Ester entertains maternal feelings towards him; the message excites him as he struggles to spell it out. As Bergman puts it (*Bergman on Bergman*), ''To me Ester in all her misery represents a distillation of something indestructibly human, which the boy inherits from her. Out of all man's misery and conflicts and his insufferable condition is crystalized this clear little drop of something different—this sudden impulse to understand a few words in another language.'' The boy acts as a catalyst between the two sisters; both women, adds Bergman ''turn their best sides towards the kid. He escapes from the film almost unscathed.'' Nevertheless, he carries a toy gun and has a childlike vision of flight and the space age.

On its release, the film excited much hostile criticism—as anti-woman, anti-sex, as near-pornographic (partly because of Ester's moment of masturbation). The explosive, sometimes sick erotic suggestions and action in the film are thematic, not in any way pornographic. Bergman claims to have received after the film's release threatening or otherwise vicious letters and phonecalls, but in *Bergman on Bergman* he categorically rejects any of these hostile implications. The film, he says, ''tells its story by simple means, not by symbols or such antics. The people in my films are exactly like myself—creatures of instinct, of rather poor intellectual capacity, who at best only think while they're talking. My films draw on my own experience, however inadequately based logically and intellectually.''

—Roger Manvell

UDJU AZUL DI YONTA

(The Blue Eyes of Yonta)

Guinea-Bissau, 1992

Director: Flora Gomes

Production: Vermedia (Lisbon), Cooperativa Arco-Íris (Bissau), Eurocréation Production (Paris), and Rádiotelevisão Portuguesa (Lisbon); color, 35mm; running time: 90 minutes. Released 1992.

Producer: Paulo de Sousa; **screenplay:** Flora Gomes, Ina Césair, David Lang, and Manuel Rambout Barcelos; **assistant directors:** Manuel João Ěcuas, Odete Somedo, and Gildo Mendes; **photography:** Dominique Gentil; **editor:** Dominique Páris; **sound:** Pierre Donnadieu; **sound mixer:** Anita Fernandez; **costumes:** Seco Faye and Teresa Campos; **music:** Adriano G. Ferreira-Atchutchi; **set design:** Miguel Mendes.

Cast: Maysa Marta (*Yonta*); Pedro Dias (*Zé*); António Simã Mendes (*Vicente*); Mohamed Lamine Seidi (*Amílcar*); Bia Gomes (*Belante*); Dina Vaz (*Mana*).

Awards: Audience Award, Würzburg International Filmweekend, 1994.

Publications

Articles:

Deffontaines, Thérèse-Marie, ''Les Yeux bleus de Yonta,'' in *Ecrans d'Afrique*, vol. 1, 1992.

Libiot, Eric, review in *Première* (Paris), June 1993.

D'Yvoire, Christophe, review in *Studio* (Paris), June 1993.

Ukadike, N. Frank, ''In Guinea-Bissau, Cinema Trickles Down: An Interview with Flora Gomes,'' in *Research in African Literatures*, vol. 26, no. 3, 1995.

* * *

The African Party for the Independence of Guinea and Cape Verde (PAIGC) that liberated Guinea-Bissau was more successful than any other guerrilla movement in Africa. In *Those Whom Death Refused* Flora Gomes had contrasted guerrilla warfare and nonchalant bureaucrats. Four years later he created a beautiful film that reminds us of the sacrifices made during the war but focuses on the present in Bissau. *The Blue Eyes of Yonta* shows that the socialist transformation promised at independence failed to materialize and that the shift to economic liberalization in the late 1980s created new hardships. The film graphically conveys the run-down poverty of Bissau, the nation's capital: it may not look it, but all the action but one short scene takes place in the city. The contrast with an extravagant wedding reception at the local Sheraton Hotel illustrates the deep inequality that characterizes Guinea-Bissau less than a generation after independence was achieved at the cost of great sacrifices.

The Blue Eyes of Yonta takes a critical look at the infatuation with things Western. Zé copies his letter to Yonta out of a European brochure of love letters meant to be addressed to beauties with blue eyes, to be written while the snow falls. The poet wallows in his longing for the Swedish girl with the blue eyes. And a war hero returns with presents from Portugal that follow European fashion and taste rather than African needs. At the same time we see a comfortable amalgamation of tradition and Western import. We hear a few references to God, but we also see tradition observed with a libation of wine at a wedding ceremony that strikingly combines traditional marriage transactions between the spouses's families and a civil marriage. The bride's white gown and her African hairdo beautifully demonstrate the felicitous integration of old and new.

The various characters present different responses to the state of Guinea-Bissau nearly two decades after independence. Yonta stands at the center of this comedy of misplaced affections. Yonta's frivolity reflects the city and its superficiality. She admires Vicente but does not share his dreams: ''If your ideals have been spoiled, it's not my fault. We respect the past, but we can't live in it.'' In the end Yonta is rejected by both Vicente and Zé, but she remains secure in the affection of her parents and her younger brother, however much he may tease her.

Vicente is a war hero. But he has not been able to stick to the ideals he fought for. ''[M]oney is the weapon now,'' he tells Amilcar, ''The war is over.'' He drives a Volvo and brings the gifts from Europe, however inappropriate, that people will enjoy. When he is finally reunited with Nando, his comrade-in-arms, he observes resignedly: ''In the jungle we thought it would be for everyone. But it's not. What can I do?'' The fruits of independence have come to some, here in the capital, and Vicente asks Nando to join him to get his share. But Nando has been marked even more profoundly by the struggle. He wants no part of Bissau and returns to Catio, once at the center of the war for liberation. His quiet departure confronts Vicente with the failure of their struggle. As he talks to the sculpture he cradles and dances to circling vultures, we wonder whether he has gone out of his mind.

Zé is moonstruck by Yonta but comes to realize that they live in different worlds. Though her radiance bewitches him, he eventually rejects the conspicuous, Western-oriented consumption of Bissau she represents. He does not share the dream of the young who want to emigrate to Europe; he affirms that the place he came from—Bolama, the war-time capital, symbol of the struggle for independence—is as good as Bissau, and he is prepared to return there. If Yonta's glamor recalls the glittering promises that came with independence nearly two decades before, then his disappointment stands for all those whose aspirations have been frustrated.

Flora Gomes named his youngest protagonist for Amilcar Cabral, the distinguished guerrilla leader and intellectual. Young Amilcar is quick and witty, boisterous and ingenious, full of initiative, mischief, and energy. And he shows signs of following in the steps of his famous namesake. He is afraid of no one: his older sister, a truck driver, government authority. He leads the children in putting an evicted widow back into her house. If this rebellion against the callous disregard of people's needs suggests the prospect of a better future, Gomes does not tell us what it might look like: ''I do not suggest alternatives. As a 'contester,' I am someone who, above all, makes observations and remarks on issues.'' But with Nando and Zé he has firmly established that the country at large rejects the compromises that mark the capital.

Gomes created a beautiful and funny film. We follow the entanglements of our protagonists, relish their grace, enjoy the music, and discover Bissau. Through most of the film we revel in the caring among the adults and the prospect of romance among the young. Then, in the last fifteen minutes, the idyll unravels: Nando confronts Vincente with the betrayal of the ideals for which they fought, Vicente denounces Yonta and the consumer culture she represents, and Zé rejects Yonta in turn. Only at the very end do the children reassure us that all is not lost.

The actors Gomes chose and trained are key to the success of his film. Bia Gomes, who appears in the role of Yonta's mother Belante, had played a lead role in *Those Whom Death Refused*, but most of the actors in *The Blue Eyes of Yonta* were amateurs. Soon after he had completed *Those Whom Death Refused*, Gomes set out to search for actors amongst his friends, in the women associations, at the exit of schools, in poor neighborhoods, and also in some government ministries. He then spent nine months with the actors in regular work sessions. In the film they use the local Portuguese creole they are comfortable with. Gomes complimented the beauty of his actors by using soft colors to good advantage.

—Josef Gugler

UGETSU MONOGATARI

Japan, 1953

Director: Kenji Mizoguchi

Production: Daiei studios; black and white, 35mm; running time: 96 minutes; length: 8622 feet. Released 1953. Filmed 26 January-13 March 1953.

Producer: Masaichi Nagata; **screenplay:** Matsutaro Kawaguchi, from Yoshikata Yoda's adaptation of two stories, ''Asaji ga yado'' (''The Inn at Asaji'') and ''Jasei-no in'' (''Serpent of Desire''), from the collection of stories *Ugetsu monogatari* by Akinari Ueda (1768); **photography:** Kazuo Miyagawa; **editor:** Mitsuji Miyata; **sound:** Iwao Otani; **production designer:** Kisaku Ito; **music:** Fumio Hayasaka and Ichiro Saito.

Cast: Machiko Kyo (*Wakasa*); Kinuyo Tanaka (*Miyagi*); Mitsuki Mito (*Ohama*); Masayuki Mori (*Genjuro*); Sakae Ozawa (*Tobei*); Sugisaku Aoyama (*Old priest*); Kikue Nori (*Ukon*); Mitsusaburo Ramon (*Commander of the clan NIWA*); Ryosuke Kagawa (*Village chief*); Kichijiro Tsuchida (*Silk merchant*); Syozo Nanbu (*Shinto priest*); Ichiisaburo Sawamura (*Genichi*).

Ugetsu monogatari

Awards: Venice Film Festival, Silver Prize Winner and Italian Critics Award, 1953; Edinburgh Film Festival, Gold Medal Winner, 1955.

Publications

Script:

Kawaguchi, Matsutaro, *Les Contes de la lune vague après la pluie*, in *Avant-Scène du Cinéma* (Paris), 1 January 1977.

Books:

Tsumura, Hideo, *A Certain Mizoguchi Kenji* (in Japanese), Japan, 1958.
Anderson, Joseph, and Donald Richie, *The Japanese Film: Art and Industry*, Rutland, Vermont, 1960; revised edition, Princeton, 1982.
Ve-Ho, *Mizoguchi*, Paris, 1964.
Mesnil, Michel, *Kenji Mizoguchi*, Paris, 1965; revised edition, 1971.
Yoda, Yoshikata, *Mizoguchi Kenji no hito to geijutsu* (Kenji Mizoguchi: The Man and His Art), Tokyo, 1970.

Tessier, Max, *Kenji Mizoguchi*, Paris, 1971.
Mellen, Joan, *Voices from the Japanese Cinema*, New York, 1975.
Mellen, Joan, *The Waves at Kenji's Door: Japan Through Its Cinema*, New York, 1976.
Bock, Audie, *Japanese Film Directors*, New York, 1978; revised edition, Tokyo, 1985.
Burch, Noël, *To the Distant Observer: Form and Meaning in the Japanese Cinema*, Berkeley, 1979.
Garbicz, Adam, and Jacek Klinowski, editors, *Cinema, The Magic Vehicle: A Guide to Its Achievements: Journey Two*, Metuchen, New Jersey, 1979.
Freiberg, Freda, *Women in Mizoguchi Films*, Melbourne, 1981.
Sato, Tadao, *Currents in Japanese Cinema*, Tokyo, 1982.
Serceau, Daniel, *Mizoguchi: De la revolte aux songes*, Paris, 1983.
Andrew, Dudley, *Film in the Aura of Art*, Princeton, 1984.
McDonald, Keiko, *Mizoguchi*, Boston, 1984.
McDonald, Keiko, editor, *Ugetsu: Kenji Mizoguchi, Director*, New Brunswick, New Jersey, 1993.
O'Grady, Gerald, editor, *Mizoguchi the Master*, Ontario, 1996.
Tomasi, Dario, *Kenji Mizoguchi*, Milano, 1998.

Articles:

Richie, Donald, and Joseph I. Anderson, ''Kenji Mizoguchi,'' in *Sight and Sound* (London), Autumn 1955.
Godard, Jean-Luc, in *Arts* (Paris), February 1958.
Rohmer, Eric, in *Cahiers du Cinéma* (Paris), March 1958.
Sadoul, Georges, ''Diableries et miseres de la guerre,'' in *Lettres Françaises* (Paris), 26 April 1959.
''Mizoguchi Issue'' of *Cahiers du Cinéma* (Paris), May 1959.
Gilson, René, in *Cinéma* (Paris), May 1959.
Astruc, Alexandre, in *Films and Filming* (London), Summer 1961.
Rotha, Paul, in *Films and Filming* (London), May 1962.
''Mizoguchi Issue'' of *Cahiers du Cinéma* (Paris), August-September 1964.
Yoda, Yoshikata, ''Souvenirs sur Mizoguchi,'' in *Cahiers du Cinéma* (Paris), no. 174, 1966.
Iwasaki, Akira, ''Kenji Mizoguchi,'' in *Anthologie du Cinéma* (Paris), November 1967.
Yoda, Yoshikata, ''The Density of Mizoguchi's Scripts,'' in *Cinema* (Los Angeles), Spring 1971.
Wood, Robin, ''Mizoguchi: The Ghost Princess and the Seaweed Gatherer,'' in *Film Comment* (New York), March-April 1973.
Cohen, R., ''Mizoguchi and Modernism,'' in *Sight and Sound* (London), Spring 1978.
Godefroy, J. C., in *Cinématographe* (Paris), November 1978.
Masson, A., ''Revers de la quietude,'' in *Positif* (Paris), November 1978.
Richie, Donald, ''Kenji Mizoguchi,'' in *Cinema, A Critical Dictionary*, edited by Richard Roud, London, 1980.
Sato, Tadao, and Dudley Andrew, ''On Kenji Mizoguchi,'' in *Film Criticism* (Edinboro, Pennsylvania), Spring 1980.
Niogret, H., ''Mizoguchi: Un art sans artifice,'' in *Positif* (Paris), December 1980.
Martin, Marcel, ''Rencontre avec Yoshikata Yoda,'' in *Image et Son* (Paris), October 1982.
Millar, Gavin, ''The Climate of Beauty,'' in *Listener* (London), 5 May 1983.
Gaelen, H., in *Film en Televisie* (Brussels), March 1985.
Alion, Y., ''Les contes de la lune vague apres la pluie,'' in *Revue du Cinéma* (Paris), no. 459, April 1990.
Burdeau, Emmanuel, and others, ''Mizoguchi Encore,'' in *Cahiers du Cinéma* (Paris), no. 504, July-August 1996.
Lopate, Philip, ''A Master Who Could Create Poems for the Eye,'' in *The New York Times*, 15 September 1996.
MacNab, Geoffrey, in *Sight & Sound* (London), vol. 8, no. 12, December 1998.

* * *

Ugetsu monogatari was not the first Kenji Mizoguchi film to be shown in the West, but it was the first to reveal him to the West as a major artist. Swiftly establishing itself (especially in France) on many critics' ''Ten Best'' lists, the film opened the way for the acclamation of the work of Mizoguchi's final period. For some, he became the supreme filmmaker, the cinematic Shakespeare, realizing to the fullest the potential of film as an art form. That was at the time when the ''potential of film'' was generally felt to have been identified and adequately expounded by André Bazin; and assessment which can still be accepted if we add the proviso that Bazin accounted for only one of film's many potentials.

However, the supremacy of his ''late'' period and the *kind* of achievement that it represents, has been increasingly challenged since the 1960s. Two factors help account for this: one is the discovery of Mizoguchi's earlier films, previously almost unknown; the other is the politicization of film criticism and the growth, within it, of an ideological awareness. In recent years, Noël Burch's *To the Distant Observer*, Joan Mellen's *The Waves at Genji's Door*, and Frieda Frieberg's useful pamphlet *Women in Mizoguchi's Films*—three books written from quite distinct critical positions, with quite distinct estimates of Mizoguchi's work—have agreed on one point, the application (in a derogatory sense) of the term ''aestheticism'' to Mizoguchi's late work. Films previously hailed as the greatest ever made—*Ugetsu*, *Sansho dayu*, *The Life of Oharu*—are suddenly perceived as evidence of Mizoguchi's withdrawal from the radicalism of his work in the 1930s and 1940s, and a retreat from a social/political viewpoint into the realm of aesthetic contemplation.

The relationship between aesthetics and politics is incredibly complex: the critical problems it generates have never been successfully resolved. It is true that *Ugetsu monogatari* is ideologically more conservative than, say, *Sisters of Gion* or *My Love Has Been Burning*. The crux lies in the treatment of women. From the radical feminist protest of his earlier films to the celebration of woman as self-sacrificer, redeemer, and mother in *Ugetsu* is certainly a large and disconcerting jump. (Mizoguchi's conversion to Buddhism in the early 1950s is doubtlessly a related factor.) Further, *Ugetsu* can be read as advocating the resignation to and the acceptance of one's lot. This withdrawal from the active struggle in favor of a spiritual transcendence makes the hardships of the material world not so much endurable as irrelevant. The film encourages such a reading, yet cannot be reduced to it.

Ugetsu contains within itself an answer to the charge of aestheticism. The story of Genjuro the potter can be taken as Mizoguchi's artistic testament. At the beginning of the film Genjuro is a materialistic artisan, mass-producing pots as a commodity. His encounter with the Lady Wakasa introduces him to the world of the aesthetic. She shows him fragile and exquisite vessels that she presents, and he accepts, as his creations, but that are totally unlike the crude, functional wares we have seen him almost brutally shape earlier. The complexity of response that this whole central segment evokes is sufficient in itself to call into question the reduction of the film to a single clear-cut statement. The Lady Wakasa is both evil spirit and a pathetic, victimized woman; the world of the aesthetic (which is also the world of the erotic) has a fascination and authentic beauty that make it far from easily dismissible. That alluring world, however, has three negative connotations. First, it is presented as a possible option only if one turns one's back on reality. It is a world of fantasy and illusion where the suffering of human beings in a material world of oppression, cruelty, greed, and human exploitation cannot be permitted to intrude. (One of the most expressive cuts in the history of the cinema is that from the exquisite scene of love-making on the cultivated lawn beside the lake to Miyagi, fearfully peering out from her hiding-place, a woman vulnerable to attack from all sides of a society created by men.) Second, Wakasa herself is not presented as an autonomous character, even in her appreciation of beauty. Everything she knows, her father had taught her. Her father (long since dead) appears in the film as a hideous, emaciated skull-like mask speaking in a disturbingly strange subterranean voice. The aesthetic, whatever else it may be, is clearly defined as a patriarchal imposition: ''taste'' is what women are taught by men. Finally, the father is linked to war, domnation, and imperialism. Wakasa's father had the misfortune to lose, and have his clan exterminated, but the film makes clear that he would have inflicted precisely the same fate on his enemies, had the outcome been reversed.

The overall effect of the film is to suggest, not that the aesthetic is invalid in itself, but that it cannot validly exist in this world. (The film's contemporary relevance is by no means compromised by its setting in the sixteenth century.) The pot Genjuro is making at the end of the film, under Miyagi's spiritual supervision, is significantly different from the two previous kinds of work: it is made with loving care, but also the product of experience; it is a work of art yet made to be used by Genjuro's peers rather than admired by a cultivated elite. The great beauty of the film is of an order altogether different from the aestheticism of the Wakasa world. Mizoguchi never aestheticizes pain and suffering (in the manner of, say, David Lean in *Dr. Zhivago*). The extraordinary sequence-shot showing the mortal wounding of Miyagi is a case in point: the aesthetic strategies (long take, distance, complex camera movement, depth of field showing simultaneous actions in foreground and background) serve to sustain the characteristic Mizoguchian tension between involvement and contemplation, but do not in any way mitigate the horror of the scene.

If on one level *Ugetsu* tends to reinforce traditional myths of woman, on another it remains true to the radical spirit of Mizoguchi's earlier Marxist-feminist principles. The actions of both Genjuro and Tobei are motivated by the values forced upon them by patriarchal capitalism. They both seek success (Genjuro through the acquisition of wealth, Tobei through the prestige of becoming a Samurai) in order to impress their wives, neither of whom shows the smallest interest in such ambitions. The film is a systematic critique of the kind of male egoism (expressing itself in greed and violence and the destruction of human relationships, always at the expense of women) that a patriarchal capitalist civilization promotes.

—Robin Wood

L'ULTIMO TANGO A PARIGI

See **THE LAST TANGO IN PARIS**

ULYSSES' GAZE

See **TO VLEMMA TOU ODYSSEA**

UMBERTO D

Italy, 1952

Director: Vittorio De Sica

Production: Rizzoli-De Sica-Amato and Dear Films; black and white, 35mm; running time: 90 minutes, some sources state 80 minutes. Filmed 1951 in Cinecittà studios, and in and around Rome. Cost: about 140 million lire. Released 1952.

Director of production: Nino Misiano; **screenplay:** Cesare Zavattini with Vittorio De Sica; **photography:** Aldo Graziati (a.k.a. G. R. Aldo); **editor:** Eraldo di Roma; **sound engineer:** Ennio Sensi; **production designer:** Virgilio Marchi; **music:** Alessandro Cigognini.

Cast: Carlo Battisti (*Umberto*); Maria-Pia Casilio (*Maria*); Lina Gennari (*Landlord*); Alberto Albani Barbieri (*The Fiancé*); Elena Rea (*Sister at the hospital*); Memo Carotenuto (*Voice of light for Umberto in the hospital*); Ileana Simova (*Surprised woman in the bedroom*); plus many non-professional actors.

Awards: New York Film Critics Award, Best Foreign Film (shared with *Diabolique*), 1955.

Publications

Script:

Zavattini, Cesare, and Vittorio De Sica, *Umberto D*, Milan, 1953; published in ''*Umberto D* Issue'' of *Avant-Scène du Cinéma* (Paris), 15 April 1980.

Books:

Castello, G. C., *Il Cinema Neorealistico Italiano*, Turin, 1956.
Rondi, Brunello, *Il Neorealismo Italiano*, Parma, 1956.
Hawald, Patrice, *Le Neo-realisme Italien et ses createurs*, Paris, 1959.
Agel, Henri, *Vittorio De Sica*, 2nd edition, Paris, 1964.
Leprohon, Pierre, *Vittorio De Sica*, Paris, 1966.
Bazin, André, *What Is Cinema? 1 and 2*, Berkeley, 1967.
Armes, Roy, *Patterns of Realism*, New York, 1972.
Samuels, Charles Thomas, *Encountering Directors*, New York, 1972.

Umberto D

Mercader, Maria, *La mia vita con Vittorio De Sica*, Milan, 1978.
Darreta, John, *Vittorio De Sica: A Guide to References and Resources*, Boston, 1983.
Bolzoni, Francesco, *Quando De Sica era Mister Brown*, Turin, 1984.
Darreta, John, *Vittorio De Sica: A Guide to References and Resources*, Boston, 1988.
Micciche, Lino, *Sciuscia di Vittorio De Sica: letture, documenti, testimonianze*, Turin, Italy, 1994.
Nuzzi, Paolo, and Ottavio Iemma, editors, *De Sica and Zavattini: parliamo tanto di noi*, Rome, 1997.

Articles:

Sadoul, Georges, in *Lettres Françaises* (Paris), October 1952.
Films in Review (New York), November 1952.
Reisz, Karel, in *Sight and Sound* (London), October-November 1953.
De la Roche, Catherine, in *Films and Filming* (London), December 1954.
Lambert, Gavin, ''Italian Notes,'' in *Sight and Sound* (London), 1 January 1955.
Fenin, George, in *Film Culture* (New York), Winter 1955.
De Sica, Vittorio, ''Money, the Public, and *Umberto D*,'' in *Films and Filming* (London), January 1956.
Village Voice (New York), 8 February 1956.
Sargeant, W., ''Bread, Love, and Neo-Realism,'' in *New Yorker*, 29 June and 6 July 1957.
Rhode, Eric, ''Why Neo-Realism Failed,'' in *Sight and Sound* (London), Winter 1960–61.
McVay, D., ''Poet of Poverty,'' in *Films and Filming* (London), October-November 1964.
''Entire Issue of Articles by De Sica'' in *Bianco e Nero* (Rome), Fall 1975.
La Polla, F., ''La citta e lo spazio,'' in *Bianco e Nero* (Rome), September-December 1976.
Passalacqua, J., ''Vittorio De Sica,'' in *Films in Review* (New York), April 1978.
Agel, Henri, ''Vittorio De Sica 1902–1974,'' special issue of *Avant-Scène du Cinéma* (Paris), 15 October 1978.
Agel, Henri, ''Vittorio De Sica,'' in *Anthologie du cinéma 10*, Paris, 1979.
Goodman, Walter, in *The New York Times*, vol. 136, section 2, H22, 30 August 1987.

Kinder, M., ''The Subversive Potential of the Pseudo-Iterative,'' in *Film Quarterly* (Berkeley), no. 2, 1989–90.

Langkjoer, B., ''Det indre melodrama,'' in *Kosmorama* (Copenhagen), vol. 139, no. 205, Fall 1993.

Bailey, Paul, ''Looking Up For Rain,'' in *Sight & Sound* (London), vol. 3, no. 12, December 1993.

Bonadella, Peter, ''Three Neorealist Classics by Vittorio De Sica,'' in *Cineaste* (New York), vol. 23, no. 1, 1997.

* * *

Umberto D is often considered Vittorio De Sica's masterpiece, the purest example of Cesare Zavattini's aesthetic, and most highly developed expression of this historic collaboration of director and screenwriter. It may also be the most relentlessly bleak of the great works of neo-realism.

De Sica was aware from the start that *Umberto D* might be susceptible to the same charge of subversion that had greeted *Miracle in Milan.* On the other hand, he had hoped, as he pointed out in a later comment, that ''the story of that old retired office worker, his tragic solitude, his boundless sadness and his pathetic, awkward attempts at warming his heart (would have) a kind of universality that would be understood by everyone.'' This was not to be the case. De Sica was accused by many, including the then junior minister Giulio Andreotti, of washing Italy's dirty laundry in public, of irresponsibility in projecting a negative view of the country. Against *Umberto D* were mobilized forces strongly opposed to exporting images of an Italy depressed and without justice; following *Umberto D*, the foreign distribution of films that were declared unflattering to Italian society was banned. The authorities feared, and with good reason, what the critic Georges Sadoul and a few others most admired. At the time of its first showing, Sadoul noted that *Umberto D* (along with *Sciuscia*, *Bicycle Thief*, and *Miracle in Milan*) constituted an extraordinary ''act of accusation'' against contemporary Italy. Official hostility was followed by critical indifference, and to complete the disastrous reception, *Umberto D* failed miserably at the box office. The story of old age, loneliness, and spiritual and material poverty was not likely to appeal to audiences who, in 1952, were eager to forget the past and to embrace the economic miracle that they thought—correctly as it turned out—was just around the corner.

Critical debate since the release of the film has focused on what is generally understood to be its central aesthetic question, the question of duration. Jean Collet was among the first to underscore that through the restitution to film of real time, De Sica had succeeded in giving the most banal of situations remarkable depth. But it is André Bazin's essay, ''De Sica: Metteur en Scène,'' that most completely delimits and defines the issue. Bazin is specifically interested in those privileged moments in *Umberto D* that afford a glimpse of what ''a truly realist cinema of the time could be, a cinema of 'duration.''' Two scenes particularly—Umberto going to bed and the awakening of the servant girl—exemplify those perfect instances in which duration determined by character creates a mise-en-scène that replaces drama with gesture, narrative with act. For Bazin, in these sequences ''it is a matter of making 'life time'—the continuing to be a person to whom nothing in particular happens—(that) takes on the quality of spectacle.'' Zavattini's lengthy descriptions of the most minute though absolutely necessary movements and expressions, scrupulously performed under De Sica's direction and photographed in revealing long takes by G.R. Aldo, exhibit, for Bazin, ''complete fidelity to the aesthetic of neo-realism.'' A conflicting position is taken some years later by Jean Mitry whose objection is not to the concept of duration, but to what is, in his view, a duration without significance. Duration in *Umberto D*, according to Mitry, ''is nothing more than banality and is charged very simply with prolonging, beyond the tolerable, events whose sense is clear from the very first images.''

These events are as follows: Umberto D., a retired civil servant is among the aging demonstrators at a rally in support of increased pensions. (Umberto is played by a Carlo Battisti, a university professor De Sica pressed into service after a chance meeting on the streets of Rome.) Impoverished but genteel, about to be dispossessed, completely alone except for the company of his dog, Flike, and the occasional companionship of a young servant girl, Umberto determines to take his own life. His only concern is for Flike, for whom he attempts to find a home before doing away with himself. Failing in the first attempt, Umberto determines to kill himself *and* Flike, and failing again, has no recourse but to take up once more an entirely hopeless existence. Were it not for his indifference to hostility, Umberto's confrontation with cold, often hostile persons and institutions would earn him the sympathy of the viewers, and the viewers the pleasure of the well-earned sentimental response. But De Sica, Zavattini, and Aldo take the necessary measures of script, direction, and camera that distance the viewer and deny easy sympathy. The cruelty of society's neglect of Umberto (which so offended the authorities), and lack of compassion of peers and institutions (which no doubt offended the charitable), and Umberto's grievous self-centeredness finally elicit, through the manipulations of style, the detachment of the viewer (and his or her attendant dissatisfaction) from Umberto's despair. The rigor of *Umberto D* explains both its initial failure and its subsequent reputation. Bazin's prediction was borne out; *Umberto D* would prove ''a masterpiece to which film history is certainly going to grant a place of honor .''

—Mirella Jona Affron

UMUD'A YOLCULUK

See **JOURNEY OF HOPE**

UNDERGROUND

France-Germany-Hungary-Yugoslavia, 1995

Director: Emir Kusturica

Production: CiBY 2000 (France), Pandora Film (Germany), Novo Film (Hungary), with the participation of Radio-TV-Serbia, Komuna-Belgrade and Chaplain Films (Bulgaria); color; 35 mm; running time: 167 minutes (some prints are 192 minutes). Released 19 June 1995 in Belgrade, Yugoslavia, and 20 June 1997 in the United States;

Underground

distributed in the U.S. by New Yorker Films; filmed 1994 on location in Belgrade and Plovdiv, Bulgaria, and at the Barrandov studios in Prague, Czech Republic.

Producers: Pierre Spengler (executive), Maksa Catovic, Karl Baumgartner; **screenplay:** Dusan Kovacevic with Emir Kusturica; **photography:** Vilko Filac; **editor:** Branka Ceperac; **production design:** Miljen Kreka Kljakovic; **art directors:** Branimir Babic, Vladislav Lasic; **set design:** Aleksandar Denic; **costumes:** Nebojsa Lipanovic; **original music:** Goran Bregovic.

Cast: Miki (Predrag) Manojlovic (*Marko*); Lazar Ristovski (*Petar Popara Crni — Blacky*); Mirjana Jokovic (*Natalija*); Slavko Stimac (*Ivan*); Ernst Stötzner (*Franz*); Srdjan Todorovic (*Jovan*); Mirjana Karanovic (*Vera*); Milena Pavlovic (*Jelena*); Danilo ''Bata'' Stojkovic (*Deda*); Davor Dujmovic-Perhan (*Bata*); Dr. Nele Karajlic (*Falling Gypsy*); Dragan Nikolic (*Film Director*); Emir Kusturica (*Arms Dealer*); and others.

Awards: Palme d'Or, Cannes International Film Festival, 1995; Best Foreign Language Film, Boston Society of Film Critics Awards, 1997.

Publications

Books:

Handke, Peter, *A Journey to the Rivers: Justice for Serbia*, New York, 1997.

Norris, David, *In the Wake of the Balkan Myth*, London, 1999.

BFI Companion to Eastern European and Russian Cinema, London, 2000.

Articles:

Levy, Emmanuel, ''Underground,'' in *Variety* (New York), 29 May-4 June 1995.

Finkielkraut, Alain, ''L'imposture Kusturica,'' in *Le Monde* (Paris), 2 June 1995.

Malcolm, Derek, ''The Surreal Sarajevan Dreamer,'' in *Guardian* (London), 29 June 1995.

''Propos de Emir Kusturica,'' in *Cahiers du Cinéma* (Paris), no. 492, June 1995.

Zizek, Slavoj, ''Multiculturalism, or the Cultural Logic of Multinational Capitalism,'' in *New Left Review*, no. 225, September-October 1995.

Kusturica, Emir, ''Mon imposture,'' in *Le Monde* (Paris), 26 October 1995.

Gopnik, Adam, ''Cinéma Disputé,'' in *The New Yorker*, 5 February 1996.

Hedges, Chris, ''Belgrade Journal: Scathing 'Conscience' of Balkans Spares no One. An interview with Dusan Kovacevic,'' in *The New York Times*, 8 February 1996.

Robinson, David, ''A Tunnel Vision of War: An Interview with Emir Kusturica,'' in *The Times* (London), 5 March 1996.

Yates, Robert, ''Gone Underground,'' in *The Guardian* (London), 7 March 1996.

Maslin, Janet, ''From Former Yugoslavia, Revelry with Allegory,'' in *New York Times*, 12 October 1996.

Dieckmann, Katherine, ''When Kusturica Was Away on Business,'' in *Film Comment* (New York), vol. 33, no. 5, 19 September 1997.

Turan, Kenneth, ''Sarajevan's Journey from Cinema Hero to 'Traitor,''' in *Los Angeles Times*, 6 October 1997.

Iordanova, Dina, ''Kusturica's *Underground* (1995): Historical Allegory or Propaganda,'' in *Historical Journal of Film, Radio and TV* (Hants), vol. 19, no. 1, 1999.

* * *

Underground is a historical film exploring the violent state of affairs in Yugoslavia. The film's narrative spans over five decades, highlighting episodes taking place in 1941, 1961, and 1993. Real events are combined with fictional historical encounters and occurrences. Documentary footage of selected moments of Yugoslav history is used as a background against which the fictional protagonists mingle with real historical personalities à la *Forrest Gump*. The film is characterized by elaborate scenes, ornate props, and a haunting musical score. Visually, the film is very dark, shot mostly in various shades of brown. There is even a shot taken from an unborn baby's point of view, watching out of the darkness of the womb. The film leaves a lasting and unsettling impression.

Underground is screenwriter Dusan Kovacevic's and director Emir Kusturica's personal take on Yugoslav history. In the film they follow closely the lives of three protagonists—Marko, a cunning cynic; Blacky, an artless dunce; and Natalia, an opportunistic blonde—who are shown at various stages of their lives that largely coincide with the highlighted moments of Yugoslav history. Marko and Blacky both have a crush on Natalia, and many of their actions are determined by this romantic rivalry. The somber backdrop to these sensual affairs, however, is a war with no end.

In the first part, called ''War,'' which opens with the Nazi bombing of Belgrade in 1941, Marko, an energetic black marketeer, takes a group of friends and relatives to a cellar which he has equipped as an air-raid shelter. It soon turns out that he has planned the whole rescue operation with the intention of enslaving the people in the cellar. Above ground, Marko and Blacky complete a series of reckless burglaries that they present as motivated by anti-Fascist zeal. After performing a daring anti-Nazi stunt which is nothing else but another manifestation of a philanderer's showmanship, Marko gets rid of Blacky by sending him to ''hide'' in the cellar. He can finally claim Natalia exclusively for himself.

The events of the second part, ''The Cold War,'' take place in 1961. In postwar communist Yugoslavia, Marko has become a celebrated poet, close to president Tito. He has married Natalia, and together they have created a mythology of themselves as brave anti-Fascists. A film is to be shot about their heroic experiences in the struggle. Simultaneously, Marko and Natalia still keep a large number of people, Blacky included, in the cellar. They trick them into thinking that the war goes on by playing soundtracks of Nazi bombings and Hitler's speeches. They use them as slave labor to manufacture arms that Marko trades internationally. One day Marko and Natalia descend to the cellar to attend the wedding of Blacky's son. Sweaty drunkenness reigns over this claustrophobic celebration and the wedding guests, all intoxicated, end up fighting over unsettled accounts. In the turmoil, the walls of the cellar crumble. The members of the wedding disperse in disarray and most of the enslaved inhabitants of the underground run away. Blacky and his son climb above ground and end up at the shooting site of a film which is supposed to glorify the heroic past. Mistaking the set for reality and believing that World War II is still going on, they kill all the extras wearing German uniforms. The son drowns in the Danube, and Blacky is captured by the police. Marko and Natalia escape the coming trouble, blowing up the house and the cellar.

The third part, again called ''War,'' is set in the 1990s at an unidentified battlefield, presumably Bosnia, where the protagonists cross paths one last time. Marko and Natalia have continued in international arms sales, and are wanted by Interpol. Blacky, still mourning the loss of his son thirty-five years earlier, is now in command of the paramilitary forces shelling a nearby city. In a final showdown Marko is killed by his own brother, Ivan, one of the people formerly confined in the underground. The paratroopers shoot Natalia. Blacky passes by without recognizing his former friends.

The film's epilogue offers a sharp contrast to this apocalyptic ending. In a utopian wedding scene all the protagonists come back to life and gather together for a wedding feast on the Danube's sunny shores. As they cheerfully celebrate, the piece of land on which they stand breaks apart from the mainland and quietly floats away. The wedding guests are too busy dancing and singing to notice that they are being carried away into an unknown destination.

This final scene is the defining image that screenwriter Kovacevic and director Kusturica had in mind for this project. They were determined to use it as a metaphor for the Yugoslav people, who, as Kusturica explained in a 1996 interview with David Robinson: ''go away never really knowing what has happened to them. That is the way of the Balkan people. They never rationalize their past. Somehow the passion that leads them forward is not changed. I hope some day people may find better ways to use the passion they have so far persistently used to kill one another.''

Underground was awarded the Golden Palm at the 1995 Cannes International Film Festival, adding to the previous Golden Palm for Kusturica's *When Father Was Away on Business* (1985) and his Best Director award for *Time of the Gypsies* (1989), and enhancing the director's reputation as a ''Balkan Fellini.'' The award carried weight with international critics, most of whom saw the film as an esoteric piece of elitist cinema preoccupied with the messy state of Balkan affairs but nonetheless endorsed it. *Underground*, however, came under critical fire for the historical and political propositions upon which the story was built. The main accusation was that the film was a well-masked version of Serbian propaganda, presented at a time when Serbia was largely believed to be the aggressive force in the Yugoslav break-up war. Others charged that by making a film in

Belgrade at the time when Serbia was at war with his own native land, a Sarajevan director like Kusturica was committing an act of betrayal. Many in his native Bosnia denounced him as an intellectual traitor who had taken the side of the aggressor. The media noise was significant, but the debate remained quite cryptic for larger audiences. The director was so upset by the controversy that he declared a withdrawal from filmmaking—a promise which he did not keep. He returned to cinema soon thereafter and continued shooting in Serbia and internationally.

—Dina Iordanova

THE UNFAITHFUL WIFE

See **LA FEMME INFIDELE**

UNFORGIVEN

USA, 1992

Director: Clint Eastwood

Production: Warner Bros.; Technicolour, Panavision; running time: 131 minutes. Filmed on location in Alberta, Canada.

Producer: Clint Eastwood; **executive producer:** David Valdes; **screenplay:** David Webb Peoples; **photography:** Jack N. Green; **editor:** Joel Cox; **assistant directors:** Scott Maitland, Bill Bannerman, Grant Lucibello, and Tom Rooker; **production design:** Henry Bumstead; **art director:** Rick Roberts and Adrian Gorton; **music:** Lennie Niehaus; **sound editors:** Neil Burrow, Gordon Davidson, Marshall Winn, Butch Wolf, Cindy Marty, James Isaacs, and Karen G. Wilson; **sound recording:** Rob Young, Michael Evje, and Bobby Fernandez; **costumes:** Valerie O'Brien.

Cast: Clint Eastwood (*William Munny*); Gene Hackman (*Little Bill*); Morgan Freeman (*Ned Logan*); Richard Harris (*English Bob*); Jaimz Woolvett (*Schofield Kid*); Saul Rubinek (*W. W. Beauchamp*); Frances Fisher (*Strawberry Alice*); Anna Thompson (*Delilah Fitzgerald*); David Mucci (*Quick Mike*).

Awards: Oscars for Best Picture, Best Director, Best Supporting Actor (Hackman), Best Cinematography, and Best Editing, 1992.

Publications

Books:

Smith, Gus, *Richard Harris: Actor by Accident*, 1990, 1999.
Zmijewsky, Boris, and Lee Pfeiffer, *The Films of Clint Eastwood*, New York, 1993.
Bingham, Dennis, *Acting Male: Masculinities in the Films of James Stuart, Jack Nicholson, and Clint Eastwood*, Piscataway, 1994.
Gallafent, Edward, *Clint Eastwood: Filmmaker and Star*, New York, 1994.
Knapp, Laurence F., *Directed by Clint Eastwood: Eighteen Films Analyzed*, Jefferson, 1996.
Munn, Michael, *Gene Hackman*, London, 1997.
O'Brien, Daniel, *Clint Eastwood: Film-Maker*, North Pomfret, 1997.

Articles:

McCarthy, Todd, *Variety* (New York), 3 August 1992.
Merrick, H., and P. Ortoli, ''Le survivant d'un monde englouti,'' in *Revue du Cinéma* (Paris), September 1992.
Jameson, R. T., and H. Sheehan, ''Deserve's got nothin' to do with it,'' in *Film Comment* (New York), September-October 1992.
Combs, R., and others, ''Shadowing the Hero,'' in *Sight and Sound* (London), October 1992.
Coursodon, J. P., and M. Henry, *Positif* (Paris), October 1992.
Jousse, T., and C. Nevers, *Cahiers du Cinéma* (Paris), October 1992.
Boutroy, P., *Séquences* (Montreal), November 1992.
Pawelczak, A., *Films in Review* (New York), November-December 1992.
Tesson, C., ''L'aventure intérieure,'' in *Cahiers du Cinéma* (Paris), December 1992.
Dowell, P., *Cineaste* (New York), 1992.
Horguelin, T., ''L'étérnel retour,'' in *24 Images* (Montreal), December-January 1993.
Tibbets, J. C., ''Clint Eastwood and the Machinery of Violence,'' in *Literature/Film Quarterly* (Salisbury, Maryland), January 1993.
Wilson, M. H., ''The Perfect Subject for the Final Western,'' in *Cinema Papers* (Melbourne), January 1993.
Greenberg, H. R., *Film Quarterly* (Berkeley), Spring 1993.
Witteman, Paul, ''Go Ahead, Make My Career,'' in *Time* (New York), 5 August 1993.
Grenier, Richard, ''Clint Eastwood Goes PC,'' in *Commentary*, vol. 97, no. 3, March 1994.
Beard, William, ''*Unforgiven* and the Uncertainties of the Heroic,'' in *Canadian Journal of Film Studies* (Ottawa), vol. 3, no. 2, Autumn 1994.
Engel, L., ''Rewriting Western Myths in Clint Eastwood's New 'Old Western,''' in *Western American Literature*, vol. 29, no. 3, 1994.
Kelley, Susan M., and Armando J. Prats, ''Giggles and Guns: The Phallic Myth in *Unforgiven*/Back from the Sunset: The Western, the Eastwood Hero, and *Unforgiven*,'' in *Journal of Film and Video* (Atlanta), vol. 47, no. 1–3, Spring-Fall 1995.
Deloria, P. J., ''Title: America,'' in *American Historical Review*, vol. 11, no. 5, 1995.
Premiere (Boulder), vol. 9, July 1996.
Ingrassia, Catherine, '''I'm Not Kicking, I'm Talking': Discursive Economies in the Western,'' in *Film Criticism* (Meadville), vol. 20, no. 3, Spring 1996.
McCarthy, T., in *Premiere* (Boulder), vol. 11, October 1997.
Ingrassia, Catherine, ''Writing the West: Iconic and Literal Truth in *Unforgiven*,'' in *Literature/Film Quarterly* (Salisbury), vol. 26, no. 1, January 1998.

Unforgiven

McReynolds, Douglas J., ''Alive and Well: Western Myth in Western Movies,'' in *Literature/Film Quarterly* (Salisbury), vol. 26, no. 1, January 1998.

Plantinga, Carl, ''Spectacles of Death: Clint Eastwood and Violence in *Unforgiven*,'' in *Cinema Journal* (Austin), vol. 37, no. 2, Winter 1998.

* * *

Like its predecessor *Tightrope*, *Unforgiven*—a film critic Pat Dowell calls ''droll, dry and deadpan''—marks a turning point in the career of Clint Eastwood. Just as the almost cartoonish, ultra-violent Dirty Harry image changes in *Tightrope* to a single father nearly overcome by his human frailty and seeking redemption through family values, so *Unforgiven* challenges earlier film stereotypes, not just of Eastwood's own spaghetti-western type but also of what has become of the Western genre itself. The classic American morality story has fallen on sad days, exhausted by overexposure and made decadent by the gimmickry of special effects exaggerating form over substance. Producer and director Eastwood returns the form to its moral roots, especially in the precise calculation of the effects of violence, its running commentary on honourable behaviour, and its consciousness of the power of falsity of reputation.

At a time of increasing violence in society, a return to a classic genre permits a distanced examination of issues of revenge, guns, and respect. The story stems from an incident wherein a drunken cowboy slices up the face of a prostitute in Big Whiskey, Wyoming, in 1880. Gene Hackman, as Little Bill Doggett, in a wonderfully written and performed part that reveals unexpected depths in the hackneyed role of small town sheriff, decrees financial reimbursement as punishment for the cowboy, choosing economic stability for the whoremaster over a harsher justice, and thereby enraging Strawberry Alice, who leads the other prostitutes to put up a $1,000 reward for the lives of the two cowboys involved. This incentive draws a collection of misfit bounty hunters, including English Bob (Richard Harris), a British dandy, accompanied by his own dime-novel journalist/flack; the ''Schofield Kid,'' a self-promoting would-be Billy-the-Kid, whose extreme myopia makes him potentially lethal to his comrades; and Eastwood himself, as Bill Munny, a long-retired gunfighter turned marginal pig farmer, who is a widower with two children and friendless, except for an old colleague—Ned Logan (Morgan Freeman).

The film is replete with unexpected reversals and new takes on old clichés, beginning with the feminist/activist roles of the prostitutes in revenging the injury to one of their own: they are not simple pawns or victims. By standing against the powerful and devious Little Bill, they create their own justice. Harris's English Bob is introduced as a fearsome shooter and a dominating personality, only to be humiliated and pummelled fatally in front of his newspaperman-cum-promoter (Saul Rubinek), by Little Bill, who has banned guns in his town. The deflation of English Bob is completed when we learn that his victims have been unarmed Chinese, and that his hagiography as a gunfighter, enhanced by pulp fiction, conceals cowardly and incompetent behaviour.

The distance between myth and reality is best exemplified by Eastwood's Bill Munny. The director portrays himself unshaven and dissolute, wrestling with pigs in a muddy sty and losing—no dialogue is needed to comment on this iconography of western hero passed his prime and tragically domesticated. The scene is all the more affecting given the opening long shot of Eastwood burying his wife on the loneliest prairie imaginable. The decision to pursue the bounty is wonderfully fuzzy and vague, that of a man who has battled with the bottle and is trying hard to be a responsible father. To all appearances Jaimz Woolvett's Schofield Kid is the ''true'' gunfighter, a brittle, barely controlled youngster bristling with hostile machismo, dangerous, unpredictable, and insecure. However, his physical myopia extends to his inability to recognize Eastwood as what he might become if he survives. Only after ignominiously killing an unarmed man in an outhouse does he give up his desire to be a gunfighter.

As the film, with an admirably ambling pace, proceeds to show the inevitable working out of the algebra of revenge and violence, we learn from varying sources and demonstrations that most bullets miss their mark and that, contrary to what tenderfoot Eastern journalists and shoot-em-up movies suggest, killing men is not easy, especially when they are shooting back. Even the battered face of the slimy English Bob evokes sympathy. The evidence mounts that a chain of violence has terrible consequences, from the scarred face of the prostitute to the illness that affects Eastwood at the prospect of resuming his killing career to the beating of Eastwood by Little Bill. There will be no dramatic shootout on Main Street at high noon; rather, violence is messy, bloody, and usually indulged under cover of night with unfair odds. When Eastwood finally returns to wreak his own revenge for Ned's murder, the action is brutal and the characters unforgiving: wounded, helpless men are killed where they lie on the floor, and being a successful gunfighter is shown as a terrible and inhuman instinct for effective violence, not as a romantic and heroic figure.

A box office success, winner of five Academy Awards and the Cahiers du Cinema best film of the year, *Unforgiven* returns the Western to its moral and thematic roots, but with a late 20th-century sensibility of cynicism, irony, and worldweariness. The cliché that violence begets violence is confirmed, as is its appeal: violence actually does resolve problems, though at an enormous cost even to its survivors. Not an easy tool, violence can turn unpredictably against its long-term practitioners. Revenge and honour prove complex questions, and apparently simple situations have a logic of their own that complicates and entraps. Reputation, a commodity often created and abused, leads to unwelcome pressures to conform to the expectations of others. This sometimes sad, sometimes comic, melancholic look back at the past speaks eloquently to our present and future. In doing so, Eastwood has given this old genre potential new life for the next century.

—Andrew and Gina Macdonald

UNSERE AFRIKAREISE

(Our Trip to Africa)

Austria, 1966

Director: Peter Kubelka

Production: Color, 16mm; running time: 12½ minutes. Released 1966. Filmed 1961 in Africa.

Photography: Peter Kubelka; **editor:** Peter Kubelka; **sound recordist and editor:** Peter Kubelka.

Publications

Books:

Sitney, P. Adams, *Visionary Film: The American Avant-Garde*, New York, 1979.

Jutz, Gabriele, and Peter Tscherkassky, *Peter Kubelka*, Wien, 1995.

Articles:

Sitney, P. Adams, ''Kubelka Concrete (Our Trip to Vienna),'' in *Film Culture* (New York), Fall 1964.

Mekas, Jonas, in *Village Voice* (New York), 13 October 1966.

Bodien, Earl, ''The Films of Peter Kubelka,'' in *Film Quarterly* (Berkeley), Winter 1966–67.

Mekas, Jonas, Interview with Kubelka, in *Film Culture* (New York), Spring 1967.

Sitney, P. Adams, in *New Cinema Bulletin* (New York), May 1967.

Téléciné (Paris), June 1973.

Wide Angle (Athens, Ohio), vol. 2, no. 3, 1978.

Masi, Stefano, ''Peter Kubelka, scultore del tempo,'' in *Bianco e Nero* (Rome), January-March 1984.

Sterritt, David, ''Kubelka Makes 'Music for the Eye,''' in *The Christian Science Monitor*, vol. 81, no. 115, 10 May 1989.

* * *

In 1961 Peter Kubelka was asked to make a documentary about a group of Europeans on an African hunting trip. He accompanied them, recorded many hours of film and sound, and then spent five years editing this material into a most unconventional film. The result, *Unsere Afrikareise*, is one of the most densely packed 12½ minutes in film history, and makes truly extraordinary use of the creative possibilities of sound.

Kubelka bases his use of sound on the notion that accompanying an image with its own synchronous sound adds little, and merely imitates nature; rather, he weds an image to a sound recorded elsewhere. These combinations, which he calls "sync events," are often matched quite precisely in timing and rhythm, as when a gunshot appears to shoot a hat off a man's head; or when white and black men shake hands to the sound of thunder. By combining disparate elements, Kubelka makes "articulations" (his words), which fuse separate pieces both rhythmically and thematically in a manner possible only in film.

Kubelka's juxtaposition of images in *Unsere Afrikareise* follows similar lines. Images taken at different times and places are cut together, often on matched movements, to create momentary illusions of continuity. The images are disparate enough, however, so that the viewer is never fooled. A hunter shakes an African's hand and we cut to a zebra's leg, shaking similarly, as if the hunter were shaking *it*, but the hunter is nowhere in the shot. When the next shot reveals that the zebra is being skinned, we understand that while the hunter was not literally causing the zebra's leg to move, there was a deeper causal connection between the two shakes. Kubelka's juxtapositions are anything but arbitrary; they reveal truths inherent in his material.

The intensely concentrated quality of *Unsere Afrikareise* stems in part from the multitude of connections between image and image, sound and sound, and image and sound that Kubelka orchestrated into a unified whole. There is often a temptation to read direct thematic statements in many of the film's articulations. Editing connections are continually made on the white hunters' gazes, hand gestures, and gun-pointing, linking those actions to suggest the Europeans' aggression toward their surroundings. Kubelka's cuts often suggest that a European has just "shot" an African, or the forest itself. The Africans, by contrast, appear as part of nature, rather than separate from it.

It would be a serious mistake, however, to limit one's perception of the film to such themes. What is most extraordinary about Kubelka's achievement is not the specific connections he establishes between elements, but rather the system that the entire network of connections form. Repeated viewings of the film reveal it as too multiple in its implications to be resolvable into a single interpretation. Thematic results of specific articulations are merely a few aspects of many in the film. Kubelka's almost musical form establishes a grand relation between virtually every image and sound and every other across the entire film. The resulting multitude of connections is expressive of many, rather than a few, possibilities. The viewer is ultimately led out of time, to contemplate these connections in memory, and to regard the film as if it were a monument erected as a record of civilization, not as a statement on it but as a kind of totem for it.

—Fred Camper

THE UNVANQUISHED

See **THE APU TRILOGY**

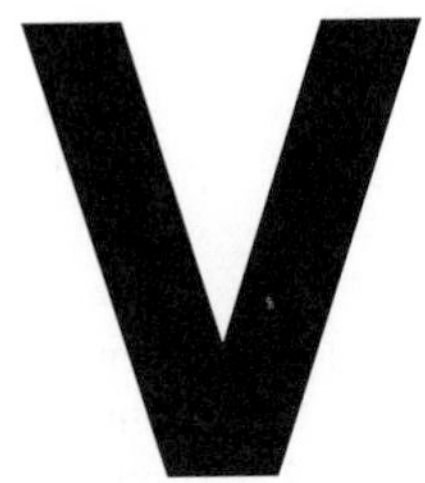

LES VACANCES DE MONSIEUR HULOT

(Mr. Hulot's Holiday)

France, 1951

Director: Jacques Tati

Production: Cady Films/Discina; black and white, 35mm; running time: 93 minutes. Released 1951.

Screenplay: Jacques Tati and Henri Marquet; **photography:** J. Mercanton and J. Mouselle; **production designer:** Henri Schmitt; **music:** Alain Romans.

Les Vacances de Monsieur Hulot

Cast: Jacques Tati (*M. Hulot*); Nathalie Pascaud (*Martine*); Michele Rolla (*Aunt*); Valentine Camay (*Old maid*); Louis Perrault (*Boatman*); André Dubois (*Colonel*); Lucien Frégis (*Hotel proprietor*); Raymond Carl (*Waiter*).

Publications

Books:

Carriere, Jean-Claude, *Monsieur Hulot's Holiday*, New York 1959.
Cauliez, Armans, *Jacques Tati*, Paris, 1968.
Armes, Roy, *French Cinema Since 1946*, Cranbury, New Jersey, 1970.
Mast, Gerald, *The Comic Mind*, New York, 1973; revised edition, Chicago, 1979.
Gilliatt, Penelope, *Jacques Tati*, London, 1976.
Maddock, Brent, *The Films of Jacques Tati*, Metuchen, New Jersey, 1977.
Fischer, Lucy, *''Homo Ludens'': An Analysis of Four Films by Jacques Tati*, Ann Arbor, Michigan, 1978.
Fischer, Lucy, *Jacques Tati: A Guide to References and Resources*, Boston, 1983.
Harding, James, *Jacques Tati: Frame by Frame*, London, 1984.
Chion, Michel, *Jacques Tati*, Paris, 1987; English translation by Monique Viñas, Patrick Williamson, and Antonio D'Alfonso, Toronto, 1997.
Haberer, Peter, *Aspekte der Komik in den Filmen von Jacques Tati*, Alfeld/Leine, 1996.
Bellos, David, *Jacques Tati: His Life and Art*, London, 1999.

Articles:

Weiler, A. H., in *New York Times*, 20 February 1952.
Time (New York), 31 March 1952.
''Mr. Hulot,'' in *New Yorker*, 17 July 1954.
Mayer, A. C., ''The Art of Jacques Tati,'' in *Quarterly of Film, Radio, and Television* (Berkeley), Fall 1955.
''Jacques Tati,'' in *Film* (London), September-October 1958.
Simon, John, ''Hulot; or, The Common Man as Observer and Critic,'' in *Yale French Review* (New Haven), no. 23, 1959.
Armes, Roy, ''The Comic Art of Jacques Tati,'' in *Screen* (London), February 1970.
Thompson, Kristin, ''Parameters of the Open Film: *Les Vacances de Monsieur Hulot,*'' in *Wide Angle* (Athens, Ohio), no. 4, 1977.
Chevassu, F., in *Image et Son* (Paris), May 1977.
Decaux, E., in *Cinématographe* (Paris), May 1977.
Tuominen, T., in *Filmihullu* (Helsinki), no. 5, 1978.
Prochnow, C., in *Film und Fernsehen* (East Berlin), vol. 7, no. 9, 1979.
''Tati Issue,'' in *Cahiers du Cinéma* (Paris), September 1979.

Codelli, L., in *Positif* (Paris), May 1982.
Magny, Joel, and others, in *Cinema* (Paris), January 1983.
Benson, Sheila, ''*Mr. Hulot's Holiday*,'' in *CoEvolution Quarterly*, vol. 38, Summer 1983.
Carriere, Jean-Claude, in *American Film* (Washington, D.C.), December 1985.
Hemming, Roy, in *Video Review*, vol. 11, no. 4, July 1990.
Rimbau, E., in *Nosferatu* (San Sebastian), no. 10, October 1992.
Jullier, Laurent, ''L'art des bruits chez Jacques Tati,'' in *Focales*, no. 2, 1993.
Maquestieau, K., ''Exit,'' in *Sinema*, no. 116, July/August 1993.
Segers, J., in *Film en Televisie + Video* (Brussels), no. 434, September 1993.
Sopeña Balordi, A. Emma, and Marie-France Lorente, ''Les (autres) vacances de Monsieur Hulot,'' in *Humoresques*, no. 6, February 1995.
Salonen, A., ''Hullunkurinen Herra Hulot,'' in *Filmihullu* (Helsinki), no. 4/5, 1997.

* * *

Les vacances de M. Hulot is one of the most radical films ever made—the *Sacre du printemps* of the movies. If its radicalism has never been fully perceived—it has entertained audiences around the world, rather than scandalize them—it is because *Les vacances* is a comedy, and everyone knows that comedies aren't to be taken seriously. But without *Les vacances*, there would be no Jean-Luc Godard, no Jean-Marie Straub, no Marguerite Duras—no modern cinema. With his 1953 film, Jacques Tati drove the first decisive wedge between cinema and classical narration. To do so, Tati had to return to the prehistory of movies—the age of Lumière, Méliès, Porter, and their anonymous predecessors, before the story-telling priority was firmly encoded in the way films were shot and edited—in order to find a non-narrative way of seeing. The gaze of Tati's camera is, as in the earliest films, almost entirely innocent: it does not make the value judgements, the selections of one element over another, that force a story out of an undifferentiated world. Tati shoots without prejudice, without priorities; he sees (or attempts to see, within the limits of the frame) everything.

Tati pretends that D. W. Griffith never existed. He holds his shots where the classical, story-telling grammar would demand that he cut away to another; he prefers long shots over close-ups, the embracing overview to the significant detail. One of the opening gags in *Les vacances* involves a group of passengers running back and forth from one train platform to another, misled by the unintelligible announcements on the P.A. system as to which track their train will arrive on. Griffith would film the scene with insert shots of passengers' panicked faces, and perhaps cut back and forth between the two tracks to emphasize the suspense—will the passengers make their train or not? But Tati simply mounts his camera on the roof of the station, where he has a clear, downward overview of the whole scene, and films the action in a single, continuous shot. As the group of travellers dashes from the far track to the near, from background to foreground, the shot becomes a kind of warm-up exercise for the film that is to follow: the viewer is led to explore the entire field of the shot, from near to far and from side to side, top to bottom. The viewer learns to direct his attentions for himself; Tati will not make the choice for him.

The English version of *Les vacances* is preceded by a warning: ''Don't look for a plot, for a holiday is meant purely for fun.'' The disingenuous wording disguises a serious challenge to the audience—what regular filmgoer would agree that ''plot'' and ''fun'' were contradictory terms? For Tati, the renunciation of narrative is a liberating act; M. Hulot's holiday will also be a vacation for the viewer, 93 minutes in which we are free to follow our own impulses, and not submit to the boss's orders. The story-teller is no longer in charge; there's no one hurrying us from one event to another, telling us where to look, when to laugh, what to feel. Tati's film is the exact opposite of ''escapist'' entertainment, in the sense that it doesn't relieve us of our own emotions and perceptions. It offers another kind of escape, perhaps a more profound one—an escape from domination, from regimentation—a cinematic flight to freedom.

Les vacances has no plot, but it does have a structure. The film begins and ends with images of waves washing onto an empty beach—images of permanence, steadiness, rhythmic motion. The steady, natural rhythm embodied by the waves is echoed in the film's pronounced alteration of day and night; the film thus acquires a powerful and unique sense of real time marked by natural events. This rhythm is never monotonous—there is also a strong sense of an ebb and flow of energy, of movement giving way to inertia and then regenerating itself. The day belongs to the outdoors—the open spaces of the beach, the sea, the countryside. Morning is announced by the beautiful blonde girl, Martine, standing on her balcony and looking down at the world below. She confers a sort of blessing, and the world comes into motion, energized by the lovely saxophone line of Alain Romans' theme music. Night belongs to the hotel, with the guests crowded into the tiny lobby, silently reading, playing cards, or listening to the radio. Overlaid on this natural rhythm is the human rhythm of habit—exemplified by the ringing of the noontime dinner bell, but reflected in a dozen specific ways in the behavior of the minor characters—the businessman continually called away to the phone, the English couple out for their promenade, the student lecturing on radical politics. Repetition is a traditional comic device, but in *Les vacances*, it acquires a transcendent, poetic quality; Tati seems to have captured the heartbeat of the world.

The film's other structuring principle is psychological. The early sequences are concentrated on the beach and the hotel, but as these locations lose their novelty for the guests, they wander further and further afield—to the tennis courts, to a picnic, even (accidently) to a funeral. Sheer boredom—the chief danger that a plotless film invites—is thus incorporated into the film; it becomes a kind of ally, pointing the movie in new directions. Both of these forward impulses—repetition and boredom—are exceedingly subtle; because they operate both on the level of subject (the repetition and possible boredom of a resort vacation) and of style (traditional comic techniques, the need to move to a new situation when the first has become exhausted), they are almost imperceptible.

Tati's own character, the tall, angular, perpetually astonished M. Hulot, is as often a straight-man to the other characters as he is a comedian. Tati doesn't want to foreground himself as a star or as the center of the humor, because doing so would mean intruding too much on the spectator's freedom of choice (by the time of the 1967 *Playtime*, Hulot has almost disappeared). Hulot does not embody the freedom of perception that the film strives for as much as he points the way to it, through his own spectacular failures of perception. Hulot does not see (or hear—many of the film's most imaginative gags involve sound) the same way the other characters do; his curse is to constantly perceive either too little (as when he lights a match in a storeroom full of fireworks) or too much (as when he's paralyzed by the fear that a wad of taffy will drop too low on its pulling hook). Hulot is unable to control this attention—to focus his look. But in this context, where the other characters have learned to focus their attentions so tightly and narrowly that they are no longer able to see and enjoy the world around them, Hulot's handicap is a privileged gift; in the land of the one-eyed, Tati suggests the blind man is king. Hulot's under- and over-perceptions pose a threat to the established social order, which depends on a cramped restricted way of seeing. His misadventures attract those few among the guests—a young boy, an elderly gentleman, and briefly, the blonde girl—who aren't part of that order, who haven't yet lost their innocence of vision or who have been able to regain it. With *Les vacances de M. Hulot*, Tati tells us how we can join them.

—Dave Kehr

THE VAGABOND

See **AWARA**

VALAHOL EUROPABAN

Hungary, 1947

Director: Géza Radványi

Production: Mafirt, Radványi produkió; black and white, 35mm; length: 2812 meters. Released 1947, Hungary.

Screenplay: Béla Belázs, Géza Radványi, Judit Fejér, and Felix Mariássy; **photography:** Barnabás Hegyi; **music:** Dénes Buday.

Cast: Arthur Somlay (*Péter Simon*); Miklós Gábor (*Boy*); Zsuzsa Bánki (*Girl*); Györgi Bárdi; László Kemény; Leci Horváth.

Publications

Books:

Paimann's Filmlisten, Vienna, 1949.

Gregor, W., and Patalas, E., *Geschicht des modernen Films*, Gutersloh, 1965.

Waldenkranz, R., and V. Arpe, *Das Buch vom Film*, Berlin, 1967.

Articles:

Eorsi, I., in *Filmkultura*, (Budapest), January-February 1977.

Dura, M., in *Jeune Cinéma* (Paris), December 1979-January 1980.

Gillisen, Olivier, in *Image et Son* (Paris), November 1979.

Trosin, A., in *Iskusstvo Kino* (Moscow), July 1983.

''Hungarian Cinema Section'' of *Filmfaust* (Frankfurt), March-April 1984.

Filmkultura (Budapest), February and March 1985.

''Geza von Radvanyi,'' in *Variety* (New York), vol. 325, 3 December 1986.

de la Breteque, F., ''Une 'logistique de la perception': guerre et representation cinematographique de l'espace,'' in *Cahiers de la Cinémathèque* (Perpgnan, France), December 1991.

* * *

Somewhere in the remote region, the war ends. In the midst of ruined cities and houses in the streets, in rural hamlets, everywhere where people still live, are children who have lost their homes and parents. Abandoned, hungry, and in rags, defenseless and humiliated, they wander through the world. Hunger drives them. Little streams of orphans merge into a river which rushes forward and submerges everything in its path. The children do not know any feeling; they know only the world of their enemies. They fight, steal, struggle for a mouthful of food, and violence is merely a means to get it. A gang led by Cahoun finds a refuge in an abandoned castle and encounters an old composer who has voluntarily retired into solitude from a world of hatred, treason, and crime. How can they find a common ground, how can they become mutual friends? The castle becomes their hiding place but possibly it will also be their first home which they may organize and must defend. But even for this, the price will be very high.

To this simple story, the journalist, writer, poet, scriptwriter, movie director, and film theoretician Béla Balázs applied many years of experience. He and the director Géza Radványi created a work which opened a new postwar chapter in Hungarian film. Surprisingly, this film has not lost any of its impact over the years, especially on a profound philosophical level. That is to say, it is not merely a movie about war; it is not important in what location and in what period of time it takes place. It is a story outside of time about the joyless fate of children who pay dearly for the cruel war games of adults.

At the time it was premiered, the movie was enthusiastically received by the critics. The main roles were taken by streetwise boys of a children's group who created their roles improvisationally in close contact with a few professional actors, and in the children's acting their own fresh experience of war's turmoil appears to be reflected. At the same time, their performance fits admirably into the mosaic of a very complex movie language. Balázs's influence revealed itself, above all, in the introductory sequences: an air raid on an amusement park, seen in a montage of dramatic situations evoking the last spasms of war, where, undoubtedly, we discern the influence of classical Soviet cinematography. Shooting, the boy's escape, the locomotive's wheels, the shadows of soldiers with submachine guns, the sound of a whistle—the images are linked together in abrupt sequences in which varying shots and expressive sharp sounds are emphasized. A perfectly planned screenplay avoided all elements of sentimentality, time-worn stereotypes of wronged children, romanticism and cheap simplification. The authors succeeded in bridging the

Valahol Europaban

perilous dramatic abyss of the metamorphosis of a children's community. Their telling of the story (the scene of pillaging, the assault on the castle, etc) independently introduced some neorealist elements which, at that time, were being propagated in Italy by De Sica, Rossellini, and other film artists. The rebukes of contemporary critics, who called attention to ''formalism for its own sake'' have been forgotten. The masterly art of cameraman Barnabás Hegyi gives vitality to the poetic images. His angle shots of the children, his composition of scenes in the castle interior, are a living document of the times, and underline the atmosphere and the characters of the protagonists. The success of the picture was also enhanced by the musical art of composer Dénes Buday who, in tense situations, inserted the theme of the Marseilaise into the movie's structure, as a motive of community unification, as an expression of friendship and the possibility of understanding.

Valahol Europaban is the first significant postwar Hungarian film. It originated in a relaxed atmosphere, replete with joy and euphoria, and it includes these elements in order to demonstrate the strength of humanism, tolerance, and friendship. It represents a general condemnation of war anywhere in the world, in any form.

—V. Merhaut

LES VAMPIRES

France, 1915–16

Director: Louis Feuillade

1. La tête coupée; 2. La bacque qui tue; 3. Le cryptogramme rouge; 4. Le spectre; 5. L'evasion du mort; 6. Les yeux qui fascinent; 7. Satanas; 8. Le maître de la foudre; 9. L'homme des poisons; 10. Les noces sanglantes

Production: Film Gaumont (Paris); black and white, 35mm, silent; running time: each part is approximately 40 minutes. Released November 1915 through June 1916.

Screenplay: Louis Feuillade; **photography:** Manichoux.

Cast: Edouard Mathé (*Philippe Guerande, reporter*); Delphine Renot (*His mother*); Louise Lagrange (*Jane Bremontier, his fiancée*); Jeanne-Marie Laurent (*Jane's mother*); Marcel Levesque (*Oscar Mazamette*); Jean Ayme (*The First Grand Vampire, alias Doctor Nox/Count of Noirmoutier/Big Jules/Monsieur Treps/Baron de Mortesaigues/Colonel Count de Derlor*); Musidora(*Irma Vep/Anne Marie Le Goff/Juliette Bertaux/Mlle. de Mortesaigues/The Viscount Guy de Kerlor/Marie Boissier/Aurelia Plateau*); Stacia Naperkowska (*Marfa Koutiloff, the dancer*); Bout de Zan (*Himself*); Renee Carl (*The Andalusian lady*); Fernand Hermann (*Juan-Jose Moreno the burgler, alias Brichonnet/ Manuel Arriga*); Louis Leubas (*Satanas, the Second Grand Vampire, alias The Bishop*).

Publications

Script:

Feuillade, Louis, and Georges Meirs, *Les Vampires*, Paris, 1916.

Books:

Vedres, Nicole, *Image du cinéma français*, Paris, 1945.
Sadoul, Georges, *French Film*, Paris, 1953; revised edition, New York, 1972.
Lacassin, Francis, *Louis Feuillade*, Paris, 1964.
Armes, Roy, *French Film*, New York, 1970.
Bastide, Régis, *Louis Feuillade*, Perpignan, 1987.
Lacassin, Francis, *Maître des lions et des vampires, Louis Feuillade*, Paris, 1995.

Articles:

Leprohon, Pierre, ''Louis Feuillade,'' in *Radio-Cinéma-Télévision* (Paris), 27 July 1958.
Beylie, Claude, ''Louis Feuillade,'' in *Ecrans de France* (Paris), 15 May 1959.
Fieschi, Jean-Andre, ''Feuillade (l'homme aimante),'' in *Cahiers du Cinéma* (Paris), November 1964.
Lacassin, Francis, ''Louis Feuillade,'' in *Sight and Sound* (London), Winter 1964–65.

Les Vampires

''Feuillade,'' in *Anthologie du cinéma 2*, Paris, 1967.

Roud, Richard, ''Memories of Resnais,'' in *Sight and Sound* (London), Summer 1969.

Champreux, J., ''Louis Feuillade, poète de la realité,'' in *Avant-Scène du Cinéma* (Paris), 1 July 1981.

Arnaud, P., ''Les Apparences transitoires,'' in *Cahiers du Cinéma* (Paris), 18 June 1986.

Niogret, Hubert, in *Positif* (Paris), February 1987.

Oms, Marcel, ''Entretien avec Jacques Champreux,'' in *Cahiers de la Cinémathèque* (Perpignan), no. 48, 1987.

Beylie, Claude, ''*Judex* et *Les Vampires*,'' in *Cinéma* (Paris), no. 482, November 1991.

Leplongeon, N., ''*Les Vampres* de Louis Feuillade: une strategie de cooperation spectatorielle,'' in *Iris*, no. 17, 1994.

Mansoz, Mathilde, ''La face cachée des Vampires,'' in *Cinéma* (Paris), no. 547, 1 February 1995.

Johnson, William, ''A Short Take on Long Films,'' in *Film Comment* (New York), vol. 31, no. 5, September-October 1995.

Thompson, Frank, in *Film Comment* (New York), vol. 34, no. 5, September-October 1998.

O'Brien, G., ''Silent Screams,'' in *New York Review of Books*, vol. 45, no. 20, 17 December 1998.

Callahan, Vicki, ''Detailing the Impossible,'' in *Sight & Sound* (London), vol. 9, no. 4, April 1999.

* * *

For French cinema, the years 1915–1922 constituted a period of renewal. A considerable number of young filmmakers emerged with their first works, and the basis of a highly important avant garde movement was created. But the bulk of commercial production continued in a solid and unadventurous way, as if France were still the world's leading film nation. This time of transition is symbolized by the situation at the Gaumont studios in Paris in 1919, where 46-year-old veteran director and head of production, Louis Feuillade, dressed in his grey ''chemist's overalls,'' directed alongside a 29-year-old beginner, the ex-*littérateur* Marcel L'Herbier, resplendent in his monocle and white gloves. Within this temporary co-habitation of opposites there was, of course, only one direction in which the cinema was moving. But if the early 1920s are aptly represented by L'Herbier's *L'homme du large* or Able Gance's *La roue*, Feuillade's *Les vampires* can stand for much that was the best in French cinema from 1915 to 1916.

Feuillade had resumed his role as artistic director at Gaumont after his release from army service in 1915. In addition to making the obligatory patriotic films and the occasional meditation on the horrors of war, Feuillade plunged his energies into the crime series, echoing the success of his own *Fantômas* and facing up to the new United States competition, spear-headed by *The Perils of Pauline* and *The Exploits of Elaine*, which was on the brink of dominating the French market. The years 1915 to 1920 saw the appearance of five successive series, of which the first and greatest was *Les vampires*, which appeared at irregular intervals in ten parts, each constituting a self-contained story, between 13th November 1915 and 30th June 1916.

Les vampires is strongly conditioned by the circumstances of its shooting. Forced to work quickly and without a smoothly operating studio machine behind him, and confronted with such strong American competition, Feuillade had no time to polish his scenarios or even establish a conventional script. The stories pitted an intrepid reporter and his comic side-kick against ever more bizarre and audacious exploits perpetrated by a gang of criminals led by the ruthless killer who was a master of disguise. In contrast to the American serials, *Les vampires* had a dark-haired villainess, Irma Vep (an anagram of ''vampire'') played with great relish by Musidora, in place of the innocent blonde heroine. Many of the stories, increasingly improvised on the streets around the studio, give the impression of having been started without any clear idea of how they will end. In addition, the pressures brought on by the changing cast of players meant that occasionally even the seemingly indestructible villain had to be suddenly and inexplicably killed off.

It is the improvisation and incoherence which give *Les vampires* its power. Continually we are confronted with moments of total incongruity—a huge cannon is wheeled from nowhere, a whole party of socialites is gassed, an actress killed on stage, and a character is kidnapped by being lured to the window and lassoed from below. Unexpected deaths and resurrections, sudden car chases or rooftop pursuits, secret panels and spooky catacombs follow in a vivid pattern which has clearly been orchestrated by a director who, in continuing in the traditional style, still organizes his action in depth, with the players facing the audience in theatrical style. It is the anarchistic view of society, the supreme disregard of logic—so appropriate when the old social order of Europe was crumbling under the impact of World War I—which led André Breton and Louis Aragon to see in *Les vampires* ''the reality of this century. Beyond fashion. Beyond taste.''

—Roy Armes

VAMPYR, OU L'ETRANGE AVENTURE DE DAVID GRAY

France, 1932

Director: Carl Theodor Dreyer

Production: Carl Th. Dreyer Filmproduktion Paris-Berlin; black and white, 35mm; running time: originally 83 minutes, currently 70 minutes, also some copies exist at 65 minutes 11 seconds; length: 2271 meters originally. Released 6 May 1932 in Berlin, also released in French and English versions. Filmed Summer 1930 in Senlis, Montargis, and surrounding areas.

Producer: Baron Nicolas de Gunzberg; **screenplay:** Carl Theodor Dreyer in collaboration with Christen Jul, from the novel *In a Glass Darkly* by Joseph Sheridan Le Fanu; **photography:** Rudolph Maté and Louis Née; **sound:** Dr. Hans Bittmann, synchronized by Paul Falkenberg; **art director:** Hermann Warm; **music:** Wolfgang Zeller; **dialogue director:** Paul Falkenberg.

Cast: Julian West, or Baron Nicolas de Gunzburg (*David Gray*); Henriette Gérard (*Marguerite Chopin*); Jan Hieronimko (*Doctor*); Maurice Schutz (*Lord of the Manor*); Rena Mandel (*His daughter Gisèle*); Sibylle Schmitz (*His daughter Léone*); Albert Bras (*Servant*); N. Babanini (*The girl*); Jane Mora (*The religious woman*).

Vampyr, Ou L'Etrange Aventure de David Gray

Publications

Script:

Dreyer, Carl Theodor, and Christen Jul, *Vampyr*, in *Four Screenplays*, London, 1970.

Books:

Neergaard, Ebbe, *Carl Theodor Dreyer: A Film Director's Work*, London, 1950.

Trolle, Børge, *The Art of Carl Dreyer: An Analysis*, Copenhagen, 1955.

Bowser, Eileen, *The Films of Carl Dreyer*, New York, 1964.

Dreyer, Carl Theodor, *Om Filmen*, Copenhagen, 1964.

Monty, Ib, *Portrait of Carl Th. Dreyer*, Copenhagen, 1965.

Dyssegaard, Soren, editor, *Dreyer, Danish Film Director*, Copenhagen, 1968.

Perrin, Claude, *Carl Th. Dreyer*, Paris, 1969.

Sémolué, Jean, *Carl Th. Dreyer*, Paris, 1970.

Milne, Tom, *The Cinema of Carl Dreyer*, New York, 1971.

Ernst, Helge, *Dreyer: Carl Th. Dreyer—en Dansk Filmskaber*, Copenhagen, 1972.

Schrader, Paul, *Transcendental Style in Film: Ozu, Bresson, Dreyer*, Los Angeles, 1972.

Skoller, Donald, editor, *Dreyer in Double Reflection*, New York, 1973.

Nash, Mark, editor, *Dreyer*, London, 1977.

Tone, Pier Giorgio, *Carl Theodor Dreyer*, Florence, 1978.

Bordwell, David, *The Films of Carl Theodor Dreyer*, Berkeley, 1981.

Drouzy, Martin, *Carl Th. Dreyer født Nilson*, Copenhagen, 1982.

Carney, Raymond, *Speaking the Language of Desire: The Films of Carl Dreyer*, New York, 1989.

Jensen, Jytte, editor, *The Films of Carl Theodor Dreyer*, New York, 1989.

Dreyer, Carl Theodor, *Dreyer in Double Reflection: Carl Dreyer's Writings on Film*, Cambridge, 1991.

Drum, Jean, and Dale D. Drum, *My Only Great Passion: The Life and Films of Carl Theodor Dreyer*, Lanham, 2000.

Articles:

Close-Up (London), no. 1, 1931.
New York Times, 31 July 1932.
Viazzi, Glauco, in *Bianco e Nero* (Rome), no. 10, 1940.
''Special Issue'' of *Ecran Français* (Paris), 11 November 1947.
Quarterly of Film, Radio, and Television (Berkeley), Winter 1952.
Harrington, Curtis, ''Ghosties and Ghoulies,'' in *Sight and Sound* (London), no. 4, 1952.
Everson, William K., in *Cinemages* (New York), no. 4, 1955.
Neergaard, Ebbe, in *Cinemages* (New York), no. 4, 1955.
Trolle, Børge, ''The World of Carl Dreyer,'' in *Sight and Sound* (London), Winter 1955–56.
Longatti, Alberto, in *Bianco e Nero* (Rome), no. 5, 1958.
Cutts, John, in *Films and Filming* (London), no. 3, 1960.
Weinberg, Herman and Gretchen, ''*Vampyr*—an Interview with Baron de Gunzburg,'' in *Film Culture* (New York), no. 32, 1964.
Kelman, Ken, ''Dreyer,'' in *Film Culture* (New York), no. 35, 1965.
Bond, Kirk, ''The World of Carl Dreyer,'' in *Film Quarterly* (Berkeley), Fall 1965.
Milne, Tom, ''Darkness and Light: Carl Theodor Dreyer,'' in *Sight and Sound* (London), Autumn 1965.
Chevallier, Jacques, in *Image et Son* (Paris), no. 221, 1968.
''Special Issue'' of *Kosmorama* (Copenhagen), June 1968.
''Dreyer Issue'' of *Cahiers du Cinéma* (Paris), December 1968.
Malmkjaar, Poul, in *Kosmorama* (Copehagen), no. 102, 1971.
Vaughan, Dai, ''Carl Dreyer and the Theme of Choice,'' in *Sight and Sound* (London), Summer 1974.
Petric, Vlada, ''Dreyer's Concept of Abstraction,'' in *Sight and Sound* (London), Spring 1975.
Nash, Mark, ''*Vampyr* and the Fantastic,'' in *Screen* (London) no. 3, 1976.
Vampyr Issue of *Avant-Scène du Cinéma* (Paris), May 1979.
Prawer, S. S., ''Book into Film—Dreyer's *Vampyr*,'' in *Caligari's Children: The Film as Tale of Terror*, New York and Oxford, 1980.
Carroll, N., ''Notes on Dreyer's *Vampyr*,'' in *Persistence of Vision* (Maspeth, New York), no. 8, 1990.
Thompson, Frank, in *American Film*, vol. 15, no. 6, March 1990.
Arecco, S., ''La piega barocca del vampiro,'' in *Filmcritica* (Rome), May 1993.
Megahey, L., ''The Wonderful Face,'' in *Sight & Sound* (London), vol. 3, no. 7, July 1993.
Larsen, Paul, ''I Dreyers væv,'' in *Kosmorama* (Copenhagen), vol. 41, no. 212, Summer 1995.
Senn, B., ''The Enigma of *Vampyr*,'' in *Midnight Marquee* (Baltimore), no. 49, Summer 1995.

* * *

There is a small handful of films that can only be accepted on their own terms, redefining as they do audience, even formalist expectation. The boundaries between subjective and objective camera, the chronological link inherent in editing, such as cross-cutting, assumptions made in relation to point of view or even a single shot, the logic of straight narrative—all are blurred. That a film made in 1932, especially, creates such an approach, maintained with aesthetic discipline and without a hint of self-indulgence, results in an event.

Carl Dreyer was master of such works. *Vampyr* is one of his finest examples, owing its unusual structure, in part, to the fact that the film was the first he produced independently. The plot has the illusion of simplicity. A young man, David, in one nightmarish evening, stumbles upon a series of unearthly events. The focus is on a young girl whose life is slowly being drained by a vampire, aided by a sinister village doctor. An early image of a reaper with his scythe, silhouetted, graphically establishes the film's preoccupation: death, its illusiveness, its mystery, its threat. Another scene encapsulates its theme, the idea of innocence in struggle, transformed and transforming back, with the curious sensuality beyond simple lust of the forbidden. Leone, wasting away through the vampire's continued attacks, observes her sister Gisele, first smiles with real affection, then, as the possession begins to take, with the calculated craving for her, another victim-to-be. Her face contorts, her lips pull back to reveal sharp teeth—then it passes. She falls back, a pitiable, vulnerable girl, bled not only by the monster, but by the impotence of those around her.

The scene is pivotal to the languorous rhythm; now the pace sharpens. With David's nightmare (his point of view), he is enclosed in a coffin, and we, too, learn the terror of helplessly watching our own imprisonment, the lid screwed on tightly over us, the vampire's face peering in with candlewax dripping on the glass lid, then the stake in her heart (which is dismissed in only five brief shots), the havoc created by her earthly release . . . climax. All has been constructed almost mathematically, yet the result is curiously poetic—Dreyer's gift. The final retribution—David and Gisele walking together in the sunlight—is kept from cliche with cuts to the doctor's horrific death, being trapped in the flour mill, the gear wheels jamming, the gasping, the smothering. (The idea was ''borrowed,'' incidentally, for the Harrison Ford film *Witness*, more than 50 years later.) All is well, yet the shadowy mist remains.

One strength of *Vampyr* is the unfolding of what Ken Kelman described in *Film Culture* (Winter 1964) as ''emotional images without adequate reason.'' The plot provides necessary foundation, but the events wrapped around the discovery are as elusive in logical application as those events in our own dreams. Dreyer has filmed an essential dream structure. There is a touch of Victor Sjöström's influence here, a director Dreyer has paid homage to. Both the pervading otherworldliness and his use, in his only film, of superimposition, which creates shadows and presences, is reminiscent of Sjöström's *Körkarlen* (Phantom Chariot), 1920, a film that affected Dreyer profoundly.

Everything here underlines atmosphere; *Vampyr* is a calculated, sensual nightmare. The air is misted greys and whites (black gauze over the lens), the gait of the characters is a glide, a floating. Night and day are confused. The dialogue is minimal, voices often muffled, odd snatches of conversation are barely understandable, at times, dislocated and difficult to recall—the way it is in dreams. Cries are mingled with an animal's growl, something disembodied calling, or a strain of music. Photographer Rudolph Mate's camera has become almost a force on its own, not just a recorder, moving before a character, after a noise. If a sound is heard off-screen, Dreyer allows a moment of suspense before showing its source, so awareness is seemingly predestined. His famed, delicately honed sensibility and his self-critical aesthetic nature paid off in exceptional visual intuition; each shot has the stamp of unusual deliberation, with long, slow pans, even simple reaction shots, and tracking shots.

There were no specially built sets—the film was shot in a derelict ice-factory, a deserted chateau, and a plasterworks—and, with two exceptions, no professional actors. The characters are ''ordinary'' people and could be any of us, which makes the identification with the emotional turmoil that much more effective. The vampire is an elderly, rather dignified Frenchwoman (interestingly, her dress echoes that of a Lutheran pastor), the young David (under the pseudonym Julian West) is Baron von Gunzburg, the film's backer, who couldn't act but could wander, perfect for the impersonal, impassive dreamer, vacant, to be impressed upon. Only the sister, Gisele, and her father are professionals.

With an essentially passive hero who experiences events—acting as manifestations of the unconscious—*Vampyr* has something in common with *The Cabinet of Dr. Caligari* (1919) with it's framing story, but there the similarity ends. While Herman Warm was the art designer of both films, and several scenes in the Danish film are reminiscent of the earlier German one, *Caligari's* expressionism was proper: exaggerated acting, stylised movement and distorted sets, photographed theatre. In his book *Transcendental Style*, Paul Schrader refers to *Vampyr* as "an exclusively expressionistic film," without a trace of *kammerspiel* ("chamber play"). I don't agree. The Nordic sober-mindedness and "weighty psychological intent" lent itself effectively to several of the latter's ingredients: intimate, slow-paced drama, with a deliberate symbolism and rhythm—the four walls of *kammerspiel* is certainly extended, but there is at times a suffocating intimacy nonetheless. *Caligari* was theatre, in shards of black and white, but *Vampyr* is filmic in its purest sense, its phenomenal lighting accentuating the otherworldliness, the myriad vague greys, mirroring the dream-states within, blurred, shaded. *Vampyr* combines elements of both expressionism and *kammerspiel*; Dreyer was no rigid formalist, but experimented successfully with different styles in all of his major works.

With the last scene combining the doctor stifled by cascades of flour with the wandering of the two now-less-innocent figures still in mist, out of the nightmare, Jonathan Rosenbaum writes that Dreyer has created "an exalted realm where the natural and supernatural, the physical and the metaphysical, can breathe the same enlightened air."

—Jane Ehrlich

IL VANGELO SECONDO MATTEO

(The Gospel According to St. Matthew)

Italy-France, 1964

Director: Pier Paolo Pasolini

Production: Arco Film (Italy) and C.C.F. Lux (Paris); black and white, 35mm; running time: 142 minutes; English version is 136 minutes and French version is 130 minutes. Released 1964, Italy. Filmed in Calabria, Lucania, and Puglia (southern Italy). (Note: the word "Saint" was used in English version against Pasolini's wishes.)

Producer: Alfredo Bini; **executive producer:** Manolo Bolognini; **screenplay:** Pier Paolo Pasolini, from "The Gospel According to St. Matthew" in the *New Testament*; **photography:** Tonino Delli Colli; **editor:** Nino Baragli; **sound:** Mario Del Pezzo; **art director:** Luigi Scaccianoce; **music:** Luis Enriquez Bacalov; **other music:** selections by Johann Sebastian Bach, Sergei Sergeevich Prokofiev, Wolfgang Mozart, and Anton Webern; **special effects director:** Ettore Catallucci; **costume designer:** Danilo Donati.

Il Vangelo secondo Matteo

Cast: Enrique Irazoqui (*Jesus Christ*); Margherita Caruso (*Mary, as a girl*); Susanna Pasolini (*Mary, as a woman*); Marcello Morante (*Joseph*); Mario Socrate (*John the Baptist*); Settimo Di Porto (*Peter*); Otello Sestili (*Judas*); Ferruccio Nuzzo (*Matthew*); Giacomo Morante (*John*); Alfonso Gatto (*Andrew*); Enzo Siciliano (*Simon*); Giorgio Agamben (*Philip*); Guido Cerretani (*Bartholomew*); Luigi Barbini (*James, son of Alpheus*); Marcello Galdini (*James, son of Zebedec*); Elio Spaziani (*Thaddeus*); Rosario Migale (*Thomas*); Rodolfo Wilcock (*Caiaphas*); Alessandro Tasca (*Pontius Pilate*); Amerigo Becilacqua (*Herod*); Francesco Leonetti (*Herod Antipas*); Franca Cupane (*Herodias*); Paola Tedesco (*Salome*); Rossana Di Rocco (*Angel*); Eliseo Boschi (*Joseph of Arimathea*); Natalia Ginzburg (*Mary of Bethany*); Renato Terra (*A Pharisee*); Enrio Maria Salerno (*Voice of Jesus*).

Awards: Venice Film Festival, Special Jury Prize; Catholic Film Office award, 1964.

Publications

Script:

Pasolini, Pier Paolo, *Il Vangelo secondo Matteo*, Milan, 1964.

Books:

Stack, Oswald, editor, *Pasolini on Pasolini*, London, 1969.
Gervais, Marc, *Pier Paolo Pasolini*, Paris, 1973.
Siciliano, Enzo, *Vito di Pasolini*, Milan, 1978; as *Pasolini: A Biography*, New York, 1982.
Bertini, Antonio, *Teoria e tecnica del film in Pasolini*, Rome, 1979.
Snyder, Stephen, *Pier Paolo Pasolini*, Boston, 1980.
Bergala, Alain, and Jean Narboni, editors, *Pasolini cinéaste*, Paris, 1981.
Gerard, Fabien S., *Pasolini; ou, Le Mythe de la barbarie*, Brussels, 1981.
Boarini, Vittorio, and others, *Da Accatone a Salo: 120 scritti sul cinema di Pier Paolo Pasolini*, Bologna, 1982.
De Giusti, Luciano, *I film di Pier Paolo Pasolini*, Rome, 1983.
Carotenuto, Aldo, *L'autunno della coscienza: Ricerche psicologiche su Pier Paolo Pasolini*, Turin, 1985.
Schweitzer, Otto, *Pier Paolo Pasolini: Mit Selbstzeugnissen und Bilddokumenten*, Hamburg, 1986.
Klimke, Cristoph, *Kraft der Vergangenheit: Zu Motiven der Filme von Pier Paolo Pasolini*, Frankfurt, 1988.
Greene, Naomi, *Pier Paolo Pasolini: Cinema as Heresy*, Princeton, 1990.
Jewell, Keala, *The Poiesis of History: Experimenting with Genre in Postwar Italy*, Ithaca, 1992.
Viano, Maurizio, *Certain Realism: Making Use of Pasolini's Film Theory and Practice*, Berkeley, 1993.
Rumble, Patrick, and Bart Testa, *Pier Paolo Pasolini: Contemporary Perspectives*, Toronto, 1994.
Rohdie, Sam, *Passion of Pier Paolo Pasolini*, Bloomington, 1995.
Ward, David, *A Poetics of Resistance: Narrative and the Writings of Pier Paolo Pasolini*, Madison, 1995.
Gordon, Robert S.C., *Pasolini: Forms of Subjectivity*, Oxford, 1996.
Bara'nski, Zygmunt G., *Pasolini Old and New: Surveys and Studies*, Dublin, 1999.

Articles:

Sussex, Elizabeth, in *Sight and Sound* (London), Winter 1964–65.
''Pier Paolo Pasolini: An Epical-Religious View of the World,'' in *Film Quarterly* (Berkeley), Summer 1965.
Kumlien, G. D., in *Commonweal* (New York), 2 July 1965.
Blue, James, ''Pier Paolo Pasolini,'' in *Film Comment* (New York), Fall 1965.
Butcher, Maryanne, ''Greatest Story Ever Told . . . By a Communist,'' in *Film Comment* (New York), Fall 1965.
Hitchens, Gordon, ''Pier Paolo Pasolini and the Art of Directing,'' in *Film Comment* (New York), Fall 1965.
Jordan, Rene, in *Films in Review* (New York), January 1966.
Walsh, M., in *America* (New York), 26 February 1966.
Kauffmann, Stanley, in *New Republic* (New York), 22 March 1966.
Whitehall, Richard, in *Cinema* (London), July 1966.
Bragin, J., ''A Conversation in Rome,'' in *Film Culture* (New York), Fall 1966.
Thomas, John, in *Film Society Review* (New York), December 1966.
Maakaroun, E., in *Etudes Cinématographiques* (Paris), no. 109–111, 1976.
Feringer, F. R., in *Film Society Review* (New York), April 1967.
Durgnat, Raymond, in *Films and Filming* (London), June 1967.
Orto, N., ''Il rapporto mito-realta nell'itinerario di Pasolini,'' in *Cinema Nuovo* (Bari), November-December 1977.
Hahn, I., in *Filmkultura* (Budapest), November-December 1979.
Escobar, R., ''Pasolini e la dialettica dell'irrealizzabile,'' in *Bianco e Nero* (Rome), July-September 1983.
''*Il Vangelo secondo Matteo* Section'' of *Filmkultura* (Budapest), March 1986.
Pezzotta, A., ''Io sono una forza del passato,'' in *Filmcritica* (Rome), October-November 1988.
Pescatore, G., ''La grana del cinema,'' in *Cinema & Cinema* (Bologna), January-August 1989.
Jorgensen, L.N., ''Jesus pa film: en balancegang mellem afmagt og overmod,'' in *Kosmorama* (Copenhagen), vol. 35, no. 187, Spring 1989.
Douin, Jean-Luc, ''Pasolini, touché par la grâce/ L'évangile selon saint Matthieu,'' in *Télérama* (Paris), no. 2255, 31 March 1993.
Beylot, Pierre, ''Pasolini, du réalisme au mythe,'' in *Cinemaction* (Conde-sur-Noireau), no. 70, January 1994.
Castoro Cinema (Milan), no. 166, July/August 1994.
Sitney, P. Adams, ''Three Filmmakers as Culture Heroes,'' in *Yale Review*, vol. 82, no. 4, October 1994.
Beylie, C., ''Trois visages du Christ,'' in *Cinemaction* (Conde-sur-Noireau), vol. 80, no. 3, 1996.
Warren, P., ''Le Christ n'est pas a son aise au cinema,'' in *Cinemaction* (Conde-sur-Noireau), vol. 80, no. 3, 1996.

* * *

Pier Paolo Pasolini was one of the most controversial and fascinating of modern Italian filmmakers, and his films covered a wide variety of subjects and cinematic styles. He once described himself appropriately as a *pasticheur*, one who selected ''items, objects and even styles from here and there.'' A writer, poet, critic, and filmmaker, as well as an avowed Marxist, atheist, and homosexual, it is ironic that Pasolini made what many hailed as ''the best life of Jesus Christ ever placed on film.'' *The Gospel According to St. Matthew* is the exact antithesis of Hollywood-produced biblical spectacles: a stark, austere, realistic, almost documentary re-enactment of the story of Christ.

Pasolini was drawn to St. Matthew's Gospel because he found it ''rigorous, demanding and absolute'' as opposed to Mark's version, which was ''too obviously written for people of little education''; or Luke who was ''too literary and mellifluous''; or John who was ''too much a mystic to be transmitted visually.'' Pasolini chose to use the dialogue intact from Matthew, using a ''standard Catholic translation to avoid polemics,'' with two exceptions from Isaiah: one where Christ is walking with the Apostles in Calabria prior to the investiture of Peter, and the other where Christ dies. Pasolini was quick to point out that ''the whole of Matthew is full of quotes from Isaiah, so I felt that was fair enough.''

This is not to say that Pasolini simply presented a literal translation of Matthew's text. His interpretation is a molding of that narrative with changes in chronology, some omissions, and some inventions, such as his version of Salome's dance. When he first began to shoot the film, Pasolini used the same ''reverential'' camera technique he had used with *Accatone*, but suddenly realized that approach was ''gilding the lily.'' After just two days, he thought of abandoning the project, then opted for a technique comparable to *cinéma vérité*, using a hand-held camera and zoom shots to create a documentary-like realism.

For the physical background of the film, Pasolini used the impoverished landscape and villages of southern Italy, which he found to be analogous to those of Palestine where he had visited prior to making the film. For the background music, he chose an electric combination that complimented his unorthodox approach to the film as a whole.

The major contribution to the successful sense of realism was his use of non-professionals as actors. On many occasions Pasolini had said, "I choose actors because of what they are as human beings, not because of what they can do . . . I steal from them; I use their reality." He particularly wanted no recognizable stars doing cameo turns in this interpretation of Christ's story, so his actors came from various walks of life. "Judas is a Roman truck driver," he said. "The Virgin Mary is my mother. Joseph is a lawyer and John the Baptist is a poet. I pick them for what they are; I ask them to play themselves." Likewise, for the pivotal role of Jesus Christ, Pasolini selected Enrique Irazoqui, a student from Barcelona who was visiting Rome. His voice was then dubbed in Italian by Enrico Maria Salerno.

Pasolini set out to create a "purely poetical and natural, non-denominational" version of the life of Christ and, despite his reputation as a Marxist and atheist, the critical reception was highly favorable, with some claiming it to be the finest biblical film ever made. Especially cited were the wonderful faces of the non-actors and Pasolini's pictorial recreation of tableaux inspired by the works of such painters as Botticelli, Rouault, Masaccio, and Piero della Francesca.

As a self-proclaimed non-believer, Pasolini had castigated the dying Pope Pius XII, and stated later that had Pius lived three or four more years he would never have been allowed to make this film. In gratitude for the new climate brought about by the new pope, *The Gospel According to St. Matthew* is dedicated to "the dear, familiar memory of John XXIII."

—Ronald Bowers

THE VANISHING

See **SPOORLOOS**

VARIETE

(Variety)

Germany, 1925

Director: E. A. Dupont

Production: Universum-Film-Aktiengesellschaft (Ufa); black and white, 35mm, silent; length: 2844 meters.

Producer: Erich Pommer; **screenplay:** Leo Birinski and E. A. Dupont, from the novel *Der Eid des Stefan Huller* by Felix Holländer; **photography:** Karl Freund; **production designer:** Oscar F. Werndorff; **music:** Ernö Rappdée.

Cast: Emil Jannings (*Boss Huller*); Lya de Putti (*Berthe-Marie*); Warwick Ward (*Artinelli*); Maly Delschaft (*Boss's wife*); Georg John (*Sailor*); Kurt Gerron (*Docker*); Paul Rehkopf; Charles Lincoln (*Actor*).

Publications

Books:

Mitry, Jean, *Emil Jannings*, Paris, 1927.
Moussinac, Leon, *Panoramique du Cinéma*, Paris, 1929.
Jacobs, Lewis, *The Rise of the American Film*, New York, 1939.
Kracauer, Siegfried, *From Caligari to Hitler: A Psychological History of the German Film*, Princeton, 1947.
Arnheim Rudolf, *Film as Art*, Berkeley, 1957.
Eisner, Lotte, *The Haunted Screen*, Berkeley, 1969.
Manvell, Roger, and Heinrich Fraenkel, *The German Cinema*, New York, 1971.
Klinowski, Jacek, and Adam Garbicz, editors, *Cinema, The Magic Vehicle: A Guide to Its Achievement: Journey One: The Cinema Through 1949*, Metuchen, New Jersey, 1975.
Monaco, Paul, *Cinema and Society: France and Germany during the Twenties*, New York, 1976.
Bretschneider, Jürgen, *Ewald André Dupont: Autor und Regisseur*, Munich, 1992.

Articles:

New York Times, 28 June 1926.
Variety (New York), 30 June 1926.
New Republic (New York), 28 July 1926.
Leprohon, Pierre, "Le Cinéma allemand," in *Rouge et le Noir* (Paris), July 1928.
Potamkin, Harry, "The Rise and Fall of the German Film," in *Cinema*, April 1930.
Crisler, B. C., "The Friendly Mr. Freund," in *New York Times*, 21 November 1937.
Luft, Herbert, "Karl Freund," in *Films in Review* (New York), February 1963.
Deschner, Donald, "Karl Freund," in *Cinema* (Beverley Hills), no. 4, 1969.
Truscott, Harold, "Emil Jannings—A Personal View," in *Silent Picture* (London), Autumn 1970.
Luft, Herbert, "E. A. Dupont, 1891–1956," in *Anthologie du Cinéma 6*, Paris, 1971.
Combs, Richard, in *Monthly Film Bulletin* (London), July 1979.
Magill's Survey of Cinema: Silent Films, Englewood Cliffs, New Jersey, 1982.

* * *

Variety is one of the most significant films of the silent era, a work of technical expertise that liberated the stationary camera. It is

Variete

a stunning example of montage, with overlapping dissolves perfectly executed—prior to the invention of the optical printing process.

The storyline of *Variety* is standard: on one level, the film is just a predictable melodrama, with characters who are more types than three-dimensional personalities. Middle-aged trapeze artist Emil Jannings leaves wife and child for a younger woman. He is cuckolded and later jailed for murdering her lover. The scenario unravels in flashback, as Jannings tells the warden his tragedy. (This character is a sexual victim, a fate shared by Professor Unrath in *The Blue Angel* and August Schiller in *The Way of All Flesh*—roles also played by Jannings.)

In *Variety*, the ordinary becomes the extraordinary in that the film is a technical tour de force, highlighted by exceptional editing and unusually striking camera movements and angles. Cinematographer Karl Freund's camera is flexible. He even sets it on a trapeze, photographing from a swinging position the actors' expressions of feelings. The camera becomes the conscience of the characters, who exist in a world of phoney glamor, two-bit circuses and decadent music halls, and, finally, in the case of Jannings, a cheerless prison. As the scenario unravels, the cutting from shot to shot suggests the changes in their points of view.

There is also a superior use of subjective camera, allowing the audience to be involved in the action. As an acrobat plunges to his death, the camera drops from a high wire directly into the faces of the collectively frightened members of the audience. Dramatic tension is enhanced by low-angle shots, and multiple exposures.

While directing a season of vaudeville in Mannheim, E. A. Dupont was summoned by Erich Pommer to the UFA studio to direct *Variety*. Originally, F. W. Murnau was set to make the film but, according to Freund, Pommer felt he lacked the appropriate passion for the project. Dupont had originally wanted to shoot the film utilizing mostly compositional shots; it was Freund's input that convinced the filmmaker to perfect the method that made *Variety* so extraordinary. In this regard, *Variety* is as much a work of art by Karl Freund as E. A. Dupont. The cinematographer was a master of lighting and movement: he had also shot *The Last Laugh* for Murnau (also starring Jannings), *Metropolis* for Fritz Lang, and later such Hollywood classics as *Dracula, Camille, The Good Earth, Pride and Prejudice*, and *Key Largo*. *Variety* breaks away from the Expressionist cinema then popular in Germany, and can be seen as the official starting point of an era that became increasingly characterized by realism. But the characters still exist in a quite unreal environment. The film is a psychological drama, with action based not on externals but thoughts and feelings.

Variety was an international hit; particularly in the United States, the film was both a critical and commercial smash. Most significant of all, it served as a model for an entire generation of filmmakers.

—Rob Edelman

VENGEANCE IS MINE

See **FUKUSHU SURU WA WARE NI ARI**

EL VERDUGO

(Not on Your Life)

Italy-Spain, 1964

Director: Luis García Berlanga

Production: Naga Films (Italy) and Zebra Films (Spain); black and white, 35mm; running time: 110 minutes, English version is 90 minutes. Released February 1964, Madrid.

Screenplay: Luis García Berlanga, Rafael Azcona, and Ennio Flaiano; **photography:** Tonino Delli Conti; **editor:** Alfonso Santacana; **art director:** José Antonio de la Guerra; **music:** Miguel Asins-Arbo.

Cast: Nino Manfredi (*José Luis*); Emma Penella (*Carmen*); José Luis López Vásquez (*Antonio*); Angel Alvarez (*Alvarez*); José Isbert (*Amedeo*); María Luisa Ponte (*Stefania*); Guido Alberti (*Governor of Prison*); Maruja Isbert (*Ignazia*); Félix Fernández (*1st Sacristan*); Alfredo Landa (*2nd Sacristan*); José Luis Coll (*Organist*).

Publications

Books:

Galan, Diego, *Carta abierta a Berlanga*, Huelva, 1978.
Santolaya, Ernesto, *Luis G. Berlanga*, Victoria, 1979.
Pérez Perucha, Julio, *Sobre Luis G. Berlanga*, Valencia 1980.
Hopewell, John, *Out of the Past: Spanish Cinema after Franco*, London, 1987.

Articles:

Cobos, J., ''The Face of '63—Spain,'' in *Films and Filming* (London), October 1963.
Durgnat, Raymond, in *Films and Filming* (London), November 1965.

El Verdugo

Deneroff, Harvey, in *Film Society Review* (New York), April 1966.
Hernandez, J., ''Luis Berlanga aujourd'hui et hier,'' in *Jeune Cinéma* (Paris), April-May 1979.
Guarnier, José Luis, ''Luis G. Berlanga,'' in *International Film Guide 1981*, London, 1982.
Kovacs, K. S., ''Berlanga Life Size,'' in *Quarterly Review of Film Studies* (New York), Spring 1983.
Riambau, Esteve, ''Une Chronique noir sur le franquisme: *El Verdugo*,'' in *Cahiers de la Cinémathèque* (Perpignan), Winter 1984.
Bagh, P. von, ''Pyoveli,'' in *Filmihullu* (Helsinki), no. 6, 1995.
''*Le bourreau (El verdugo)*,'' in a special issue of *Avant-Scène du Cinéma* (Paris), no. 465, October 1997.

* * *

El verdugo was the eighth feature film written and directed by Luis García Berlanga in collaboration with his longtime associate, Rafael Azcona. The story pivots upon the fate of a pleasant, if somewhat timid, young undertaker whose dream is to go to Germany and become a mechanic. This dream is thwarted when he happens to meet the executioner in a prison where both of them are plying their trade. In spite of the aversion that the young man (and everyone else) feels for the executioner, he not only ends up marrying the executioner's daughter, but even takes over his father-in-law's business.

El verdugo is a farce or domestic comedy filled with macabre touches and scenes of black humor in which the taboos associated with death are transgressed. Even the actual mode of execution is the subject of morbid jokes as the executioner, who garrots his victims, measures the neck size of his future son-in-law. The film is punctuated with these bits of gallows humor as well as with comic reversals that take the audience by surprise. A particularly fine example occurs at the end of the movie when the young executioner is carried kicking and screaming like the victim into the prison where he will perform his first execution. *El verdugo* shows that the biting black humor that we have come to associate with Buñuel is, in more general terms, a Spanish characteristic.

Berlanga's irreverent treatment of death is symptomatic of a tendency found in all of his movies—to poke fun at pomposity and pretensions, and to deflate generally accepted values and beliefs. At the same time that *El verdugo* is highly entertaining, it also has a message that was vaguely subversive in Franco's Spain in the early 1960s. In one sense, the movie is about two outcasts, the undertaker and the executioner's daughter, both of whom are avoided by everyone. When they join together, it is with the hope of having a better life. But as Berlanga demonstrates, these hopes cannot be realized. Like other Berlanga protagonists, the undertaker becomes caught up in a destiny which he did not choose. He is a victim of innocent concessions made along the way that ultimately lead him to be sentenced to his fate of becoming the executioner. He is the true victim, the one who is strangled in a web of circumstances beyond his control, caught up in the system of justice and retribution that is all encompassing. In the context of Franco's Spain, the ideological dimensions of this message are clear. As the executioner tells his son-in-law, where there's a law, someone has to enforce it; someone has to do the dirty work. Perhaps that was Berlanga's way of saying that in a dictatorial regime, whether they are willing or not, men are coerced into aiding and abetting the *status quo*.

—Katherine Singer Kóvacs

VERTIGO

USA, 1958

Director: Alfred Hitchcock

Production: Paramount Pictures; Technicolor, 35mm; running time: 127 minutes. Released May 1958. Re-released 1983. Filmed in part in San Francisco.

Producer: Alfred Hitchcock; **screenplay:** Alec Coppel and Samuel Taylor, from the novel *D'entre les morts* by Pierre Boileau and Thomas Narcejac; **photography:** Robert Burks; **editor:** George Tomasini; **art director:** Hal Pereira and Henry Bumstead; **music:** Bernard Herrmann.

Cast: James Stewart (*John Ferguson*); Kim Novak (*Madeline/Judy*); Barbara Bel Geddes (*Midge*); Tom Helmore (*Gavin Eister*); Henry Jones.

Vertigo

Publications

Books:

Amengual, Barthélemy, *Hitchcock*, Paris, 1960.
Bogdanovitch, Peter, *The Cinema of Alfred Hitchcock*, New York, 1962.
Manz, Hans Peter, *Alfred Hitchcock*, Zurich, 1962.
Wood, Robin, *Hitchcock's Films*, London, 1965; revised edition, as *Hitchcock's Films Revisited*, New York, 1989.
Truffaut, François, *Le Cinéma selon Hitchcock*, Paris, 1966; as *Hitchcock*, New York, 1985.
Douchet, Jean, *Alfred Hitchcock*, Paris, 1967.
Simsolo, Noël, *Alfred Hitchcock*, Paris, 1969.
Jones, Ken D., *The Films of James Stewart*, New York, 1970.
La Valley, Albert J., editor, *Focus on Hitchcock*, Englewood Cliffs, New Jersey, 1972.
Durgnat, Raymond, *The Strange Case of Alfred Hitchcock*, Cambridge, Massachusetts, 1974.
Spoto, Donald, *The Art of Alfred Hitchcock*, New York, 1976.
Taylor, John Russell, *Hitch*, London, 1978.
Fieschi, J. A., and others, *Hitchcock*, Paris, 1981.
Narboni, Jean, editor, *Alfred Hitchcock*, Paris, 1982.
Rothman, William, *Hitchcock—The Murderous Gaze*, Cambridge, Massachusetts, 1982.
Spoto, Donald, *The Dark Side of Genius: The Life of Alfred Hitchcock*, New York, 1982.
Villien, Bruno, *Hitchcock*, Paris, 1982.

Weis, Elisabeth, *The Silent Scream: Alfred Hitchcock's Sound Track*, Rutherford, New Jersey, 1982.
Eyles, Allen, *James Stewart*, London, 1984.
Phillips, Gene D., *Alfred Hitchcock*, Boston, 1984.
Bruce, Graham, *Bernard Herrmann: Film Music and Narrative*, Ann Arbor, Michigan, 1985.
Robbins, Jhan, *Everybody's Man: A Biography of Jimmy Stewart*, New York, 1985.
Burgin, Victor, and others, *Formations of Fantasy*, London, 1986.
Deutelbaum, Marshall, and Leland Poague, *A Hitchcock Reader*, Ames, Iowa, 1986.
Humphries, Patrick, *The Films of Alfred Hitchcock*, Greenwich, Connecticut, 1986.
Kloppenburg, Josef, *Die dramaturgische Funktion der Musik in Filmen Alfred Hitchcocks*, Munich, 1986.
Brill, Lesley, *The Hitchcock Romance: Love and Irony in Hitchcock's Films*, Princeton, 1988.
Modleski, Tania, *The Women Who Knew Too Much: Hitchcock and Feminist Theory*, New York, 1988.
Finler, Joel W., *Hitchcock in Hollywood*, New York, 1992.
Sterritt, David, *The Films of Alfred Hitchcock*, New York, 1993.
Arginteanu, Judy, *The Movies of Alfred Hitchcock*, Minneapolis, 1994.
Boyd, David, editor, *Perspectives on Alfred Hitchcock*, New York, 1995.
Pickard, Roy, *James Stewart: The Hollywood Years*, London, 1997.
Auiler, Dan, *Vertigo: The Making of a Hitchcock Classic*, New York, 1998.
Auiler, Dan, *Hitchcock's Notebooks: An Authorized and Illustrated Look Inside the Creative Mind of Alfred Hitchcock*, New York, 1999.
Trías, Eugenio, *Vértigo y pasión: un ensayo sobre la película ''Vertigo'' de Alfred Hitchcock*, Madrid, 1998.
Condon, Pauline, *Complete Hitchcock*, London, 1999.
Freedman, Jonathan, and Richard Millington, editors, *Hitchcock's America*, New York, 1999.
Harris, Robert A., *Complete Films of Alfred Hitchcock*, Secaucus, 1999.
Bellour, Raymond, *The Analysis of Film*, Bloomington, 2000.
McGilligan, Patrick, *Alfred Hitchcock*, New York, 2001.

Articles:

Crowther, Bosley, in *New York Times*, 29 May 1958.
Pett, John, in *Films and Filming* (London), November and December 1959.
Agel, Henri, ''Alfred Hitchcock,'' in *New York Film Bulletin*, no. 15, 1961.
Higham, Charles, ''Hitchcock's World,'' in *Film Quarterly* (Berkeley), December 1962-January 1963.
Sweigert, William R., ''James Stewart,'' in *Films in Review* (New York), December 1964.
Sonbert, Warren, ''Alfred Hitchcock: Master of Morality,'' in *Film Culture* (New York), Summer 1966.
Cook, Page, ''Bernard Herrmann,'' in *Films in Review* (New York), August-September 1967.
Nevins, Francis M., Jr., in *Journal of Popular Culture* (Bowling Green, Ohio), Fall 1968.
Samuels, Charles T., ''Hitchcock,'' in *American Scholar* (Washington, D.C.), Spring 1970.
Skoller, D., ''Aspects of Cinematic Consciousness,'' in *Film Comment* (New York), September-October 1972.
Silver, A. J., ''Fragments of a Mirror: Uses of Landscape in Hitchcock,'' in *Wide Angle* (Athens, Ohio), no. 3, 1976.
Joyce, P., ''25 Years of *Film* Interviews: Hitchcock and the Dying Art,'' in *Film* (London), November 1979.
Bitomsky, Herbert, and others, ''*Vertigo*—aus dem Reich der Toten,'' in *Filmkritik* (Munich), June 1980.
Ebert, J., ''*Vertigo*—The Secret of the Tower,'' in *Framework* (Norwich), Autumn, 1980.
Peary, Danny, in *Cult Movies*, New York, 1981.
Giacci, V., in *Filmcritica* (Florence), January 1981.
''Hitchcock Issue'' of *Camero/Stylo* (Paris), November 1981.
Wood, Robin, ''Fear of Spying,'' in *American Film* (Washington, D.C.), November 1983.
Andrew, Geoff, in *Time Out* (London), 1 December 1983.
Villien, Bruno, and G. Gourdon, in *Cinématographe* (Paris), March 1984.
Kehr, Dave, ''Hitch's Riddle,'' in *Film Comment* (New York), May-June 1984.
Tobin, Y., in *Positif* (Paris), July-August 1984.
''*Vertigo* Section'' of *Revue Belge du Cinéma* (Brussels), Autumn 1984.
Malberg, C. J., in *Chaplin* (Stockholm), vol. 27, no. 4, 1985.
''Hitchcock Dossier'' in *Revue du Cinéma* (Paris), January 1985.
Barten, E., in *Skoop* (Amsterdam), March-April 1985.
Frauen und Film (Frankfurt), May 1985.
Open, M., ''Fear of Falling,'' in *Film Directions* (Belfast), Summer 1985.
Gal, P. Molnar, in *Filmkultura* (Budapest), December 1985.
Brown, R. S., ''*Vertigo* as Orphic Tragedy,'' in *Literature/Film Quarterly* (Salisbury, Maryland), January 1986.
Serenellini, M., in *Cinema Nuovo* (Bari), January-February 1986.
Wright Wexman, Virginia, ''The Critic as Consumer: Film Study in the University, *Vertigo*, and the Film Canon,'' in *Film Quarterly* (Berkeley), Spring 1986.
Miller, G., ''Beyond the Frame: Hitchcock, Art, and the Ideal,'' in *Post Script* (Jacksonville, Florida), Winter 1986.
Johnson, W., ''Sound and Image,'' in *Film Quarterly* (Berkeley), no. 1, 1989.
Maxfield, J. F., ''A Dreamer and His Dream: Another Way of Looking at Hitchcock's *Vertigo*,'' in *Film Criticism* (Meadville, Pennsylvania), no. 3, 1990.
Braad Thomsen, C., ''Dodens engel,'' in *Kosmorama* (Copenhagen), Spring 1990.
Leonard, Garry M., ''A Fall from Grace: The Fragmentation of Masculine Subjectivity and the Impossibility of Femininity in Hitchcock's *Vertigo*,'' in *American Imago* (Highland Park, New Jersey), Fall-Winter 1990.
Linderman, D., ''The mise-en-abime in Hitchcock's *Vertigo*,'' in *Cinema Journal* (Austin, Texas), no. 4, 1991.
Groh, F., ''*Vertigo*'s Three Towers,'' in *Hitchcock Annual* (Gambier, Ohio), [no. 1], 1992.
Paini, D., ''Au commencement etait le portrait,'' in *Iris* (Iowa City), Autumn 1992.
Modleski, T., and G. Vincendeau, '''Les femmes qui en savaient trop': un nouveau regard sur Hitchcock,'' in *Cinemaction* (Conde-sur-Noireau, France), no. 2, 1993.
Reid's Film Index (Wyong), no. 10, 1993.
Chankin, D. O., ''Delusions and Dreams in Hitchcock's *Vertigo*,'' in *Hitchcock Annual* (Gambier, Ohio), Fall 1993.
Poague, Leland, ''Engendering *Vertigo*,'' in *Hitchcock Annual* (Gambier), 1994.

Hinton, L., ''A 'Woman's' View: The *Vertigo* Frame-Up,'' in *Film Criticism*, vol. 19, no. 2, Winter 1994–1995.

Street, S., ''Hitchcockian Haberdashery,'' in *Hitchcock Annual* (Gambier), Fall 1995/1996.

Bond, J., in *Film Score Monthly* (Los Angeles), no. 69, May 1996.

Doherty, J., in *Soundtrack!* (Mechelen), vol. 15, September 1996.

Hoberman, J., ''Lost in Space,'' in *Village Voice* (New York), vol. 41, 15 October 1996.

Perry, Dennis R., ''The Imps of the Perverse: Discovering the Poe/ Hitchcock Connection,'' in *Literature/Film Quarterly* (Salisbury), vol. 24, no. 4, October 1996.

Turner, George, ''Hitchcock's Acrophobic Vision,'' in *American Cinematographer* (Hollywood), vol. 57, no. 11, November 1996.

Lyons, Donald, ''Notes When Falling,'' in *Film Comment* (New York), vol. 32, no. 6, November-December 1996.

Morris, Christopher D., ''Feminism, Deconstruction and the Pursuit of the Tenable in *Vertigo*,'' in *Hitchcock Annual* (Gambier, Ohio), Autumn 1996–1997.

Brown, Royal S., ''Back From Among the Dead: The Restoration of Alfred Hitchcock's *Vertigo*,'' in *Cineaste* (New York), vol. 23, no. 1, 1997.

DeRosa, Steven L., ''A Very Different 'Slice of Cake': Restoring Alfred Hitchcock's *Vertigo*,'' in *Macguffin* (East Melbourne), no. 21, February 1997.

Charity, Tom, and Brian Case, ''Dizzy Heights/ The National Alf,'' in *Time Out* (London), no. 1391, 16 April 1997.

Nochimson, Martha P., ''Amnesia 'R' Us: The Retold Melodrama, Soap Opera, and the Representation of Reality,'' in *Film Quarterly* (Berkeley), vol. 50, no. 3, Spring 1997.

Ruedel, Ulrich, in *Macguffin* (East Melbourne), no. 22, May-August 1997.

Redman, Nick, in *DGA Magazine* (Los Angeles), vol. 22, no. 3, July-August 1997.

Johnson, William, ''Enigma Variations,'' in *Film Comment* (New York), vol. 33, no. 6, November-December 1997.

Lucas, Tim, ''*Vertigo*: *Vertigo* Before Hitchcock,'' in *Video Watchdog* (Cincinnati), no. 40, 1997.

Ames, Deborah Lee, ''*Vertigo*: The Nomenclature of Despair,'' in *Hitchcock Annual* (Gambier), 1997–1998.

* * *

Not particularly successful at the time of its release, *Vertigo* has come to be recognized as one of Alfred Hitchcock's greatest films, where his profounder obsessions are reinforced by his technical inventiveness. It can be argued that Hitchcock's ''greatness'' comes only from the accident that his recurring obsession with voyeurism is the topic that best meshes with the ontology of the filmgoing experience. In any case, the longstanding argument over the superiority of his British vs. American periods looks to have been settled in favor of the latter. The less savory aspects of Hitchcock's life revealed since his death come as little surprise if *Rear Window, Vertigo*, and *Psycho* are seen as a supreme voyeuristic trilogy.

The Peeping Toms in these films progress through ever-greater distress—from the ostensibly healthy (if significantly broken-legged) James Stewart with his telephoto lens in *Rear Window* through the psychotic Anthony Perkins with his motel peephole in *Psycho.* If Stewart's Scotty Ferguson, the private eye in *Vertigo*, is more fascinating than either, it's because he's so precariously balanced between their psychic states. A former police detective who's developed a pathological fear of heights since being responsible for the fatal fall of a fellow officer, Scotty is institutionalized for a year in the middle of the film after assuming (wrongly) that his ''weakness'' (as the coroner puts it) prevented him from stopping the suicidal leap of the woman he was hired to protect and with whom he's fallen in love. The film ends at the moment of her ''second'' death. It's as bleak a conclusion as in any American film of its decade; *Psycho* is a rich comedy in comparison.

The voyeuristic impulse behind Hitchcock's style is most immediately evident in the tourist sensibility that pervades his American films—a tourist will keep his careful distance from the grit of the world. Here, the Golden Gate Bridge, the Palace of the Legion of Honor, Podesta's flowershop, Ernie's restaurant, Coit Tower, Fort Point, the Palace of Fine Arts make up San Francisco's slick surface through Robert Burks's sharp-edged Technicolor. Hitchcock's silent film mastery pays off in the scenes involving Scotty's extended tailing of Madeleine, accompanied by Bernard Herrmann's haunting score.

Vertigo extends this passive, tourist's world into more intimate levels. The film's plotline is the hokiest of ghost stories (''Do you believe that someone out of the past, someone dead, can take possession of a living being?''), but it soon moves into tragedy through flaws wrought by sexual obsession. The highly charged, pivotal scene comes quite late: Scotty has met a woman who reminds him of his dead love (in fact, she is the same woman—her fabricated ''death'' having been the cover for a man's murder of his wife). They return to his bachelor apartment after an increasingly uncomfortable afternoon of buying clothes to make the woman resemble her previous incarnation. Judy's plea, spoken almost to herself, is: ''Couldn't you like *me*, just me, the way I am?'' What looks for an instant like Scotty's gaze of reciprocated love is instead his revelation of the key for her complete transformation: ''The color of your hair!'' The scene lurches forward into an ultimate degradation, as Judy agrees to remake her brunette-shopgirl self into the (Hitchcockian) blonde ice-goddess, with tailored grey suit and tightly bound hair. The scene, and the whole film, is the essence of the Hitchcockian sexuality—that is, sexuality only exists as obsession, one that degrades women and literally deranges men. In *Vertigo*, Hitchcock does manage to be pointed about the ironies of this quest: Scotty looks longingly at other blondes in harsh grey suits even while dining with a vibrant incarnation of the woman he ''loves.'' In a sense, he gets just what he deserves.

The film's genius is depicting such perversity as merely circumstance-crossed love. In other words, its genius is in revealing the perversity behind accepted ''normal'' practices. What's so odd about men redressing their women? Or in women remaking themselves in the adored image? Judy's plea puts it embarrassingly straight: ''If I let you change me, will that do it? Will you love me?'' Traditional sexual politics swells into a grand grotesque, a Chinese-box melodrama of tricks and betrayals. The scenario itself is complicated and inconsistent, but the repeated motifs in the dialogue (''Please try!'' ''It's too late.'') tie the disconnected love-pairings into the tightest of nets. Hitchcock is typically cruel to plain Midge, with her patient, enduring love for Scotty. Her explanation of cantilevered brassieres is a woman's anti-mystery, pathetically commonplace next to Madeleine's apparent possession by the dead. Madeleine's feigned obsession presages Scotty's genuine necrophilia. (And, as in *Psycho*, the psychiatrist can't strip away the necessary layers—the problem is more than the ''acute melancholia, complicated by a guilt complex'' offered as a diagnosis or explanation of the problem.)

It's easy enough to appreciate the best of Hitchcock's films, and to be jolted by them, but *Vertigo* stands alone in its ability to move audiences emotionally. Perhaps the events are uncharacteristically heartbreaking because both Scotty and Madeline/Judy are caught in another, grander (and almost unseen) male power-play: Gavin's murder of his wife, his betrayal of his friend Scotty, and his abandonment of his accomplice Judy. A bookseller, echoing Gavin's words (and his actions), tells the tale of the original Carlotta being ''thrown away'' by her husband: ''A man could do that in those days. He had the power and the freedom.'' On its visceral level, *Vertigo* succeeds because of James Stewart's explosive fury in the climax in the belltower, a betrayed idealist's fury practiced in his Frank Capra films and mastered through his Anthony Mann westerns.

It's remarkable that, considering all its plot twists, *Vertigo* should work even better after a first viewing. Once the secret's out, it's a completely different film, and a better one; no longer a harrowing ghost story, it is a profound study of sexual obsession, tied together by the city that best displays the essential acrophobic metaphor.

—Scott Simmon

VIAGGIO IN ITALIA

(Journey to Italy; Voyage to Italy)

Italy-France, 1953

Director: Roberto Rossellini

Production: Italiafilm/Junior (Rome), Sveva Films/Ariane/Francinex/SGC (Paris); black and white; running time: 106 minutes, English version 84 minutes, some sources list 70 minutes. Released 1953.

Producer: Roberto Rossellini; **screenplay:** Vitaliano Brancati, Roberto Rossellini; **photography:** Enzo Serafin; **camera operator:** Aldo Scavarida; **editor:** Jolanda Benvenuti; **sound recordist:** Eraldo Giordani; **art director:** Piero Filippone; **costumes:** Fernanda Gattinoni; **music:** Renzo Rossellini.

Cast: Ingrid Bergman (*Katherine Joyce*); George Sanders (*Alexander Joyce*); Maria Mauban (*Marie*); Paul Muller (*Paul Dupont*); Leslie Daniels (*Tony Burton*); Natalia Ray (*Natalia Burton*); Anna Proclemer (*Prostitute*); Jackie Frost (*Judy*); Lyla Rocco (*Miss Sinibaldi, Judy's friend*); Bianca Maria Cesaroli (*Judy's other friend*).

Publications

Script:

Rossellini, Roberto, and others, *Voyage to Italy* (in English and French), in *Avant-Scène du Cinéma* (Paris), June 1987.

Books:

Hovald, Patrice, *Roberto Rossellini*, Paris, 1958.
Steele, Joseph Henry, *Ingrid Bergman*, London, 1960.
Mida, Massimo, *Roberto Rossellini*, Paris, 1961.
Verdone, Mario, *Roberto Rossellini*, Paris, 1963.
Sarris, Andrew, *Interviews with Film Directors*, New York, 1967.
Guarner, José Luis, *Roberto Rossellini*, New York, 1970.
Ivaldi, Nedo, *La resitenza nel cinema italiano del dopoguerra*, Rome, 1970.
Quirk, Lawrence J., *The Films of Ingrid Bergman*, New York, 1970.
Armes, Roy, *Patterns of Realism: A Study of Italian Neo-Realist Cinema*, Cranbury, New Jersey, 1971.
Wlaschin, Ken, *Italian Cinema Since the War*, Cranbury, New Jersey, 1971.
Baldelli, Pierre, *Roberto Rossellini*, Rome, 1972.
Brown, Curtis F., *Ingrid Bergman*, New York, 1973.
Rondolini, Gianni, *Roberto Rossellini*, Florence, 1974.
Bergman, Ingrid, with Alan Burgess, *Ingrid Bergman: My Story*, New York, 1980.
Ranvaud, Don, *Roberto Rossellini*, London, 1981.
Taylor, John Russell, *Ingrid Bergman*, London, 1983.
Rossellini, Roberto, *Le Cinéma révélé*, edited by Alain Bergala, Paris, 1984.
Hillier, Jim, editor, *Cahiers du Cinéma 1: The 1950s: Neo-Realism, Hollywood, New Wave*, London, 1985.
Leamer, Laurence, *As Time Goes By: The Life of Ingrid Bergman*, New York, 1986.
Serceau, Michel, *Roberto Rossellini*, Paris, 1986.
Brunette, Peter, *Roberto Rossellini*, Oxford, 1987.
Gansera, Rainer, and others, *Roberto Rossellini*, Munich, 1987.
Rossellini, Roberto, *Il mio metodo: Scritti e intervisti*, edited by Adriano Apra, Venice, 1987.
Rossi, P., *Roberto Rossellini: A Guide to References and Resources*, Boston, 1988.
Bondanella, Peter, *Films of Roberto Rossellini*, Cambridge, 1993.
Rossellini, Roberto, *My Method: Writings and Interviews*, New York, 1995.
Gallagher, Tag, *The Adventures of Roberto Rossellini*, Cambridge, 1998.

Articles:

Schèrer, Maurice, and François Truffaut, ''Entretien avec Roberto Rossellini,'' in *Cahiers du Cinéma* (Paris), July 1954.
Variety (New York), 3 November 1954.
Truffaut, François, ''Rossellini,'' in *Arts* (Paris), April 1955.
Rivette, Jacques, in *Cahiers du Cinéma* (Paris), April 1955.
Monthly Film Bulletin (London), March 1958.

Viaggio in Italia

Tynan, Kenneth, ''The Abundant Miss Bergman,'' in *Films and Filming* (London), December 1958.

Sarris, Andrew, ''Rossellini Rediscovered,'' in *Film Culture* (New York), no. 32, 1964.

Casty, Alan, ''The Achievement of Roberto Rossellini,'' in *Film Comment* (New York), Fall 1964.

Apra, Adriano, and Maurizio Ponzi, ''Intervista con Roberto Rossellini,'' in *Filmcritica* (Rome), April-May 1965.

Cinema (London), Summer 1971.

Wood, Robin, in *Film Comment* (New York), Fall 1974.

Damico, J., ''Ingrid from Lorraine to Stromboli: Analyzing the Public's Perception of a Film Star,'' in *Journal of Popular Film* (Washington, D.C.), vol. 4, no.1, 1975.

Beylie, Claude, and C. Clouzot, interview with Rossellini, in *Ecran* (Paris), July 1977.

Lawton, H., ''Rossellini's Didactic Cinema,'' in *Sight and Sound* (London), Autumn 1978.

Bohne, Luciana, ''Rossellini's *Viaggio in Italia:* A Variation on a Theme by Joyce,'' in *Film Criticism* (Meadville, Pennsylvania), Winter 1979.

Ranvaud, Don, in *Monthly Film Bulletin* (London), February 1981.

Serceau, M., ''Rossellini—le prisme des idéologies,'' in *Image et Son* (Paris), April 1982.

Amiel, M., ''Ingrid Bergman: Force, dignité, courage,'' in *Cinéma* (Paris), October 1982.

''Ingrid Bergman Section'' of *Casablanca* (Madrid), October 1982.

''Rossellini Issue'' of *Casablanca* (Madrid), March 1985.

Nieuwenweg, L., ''De liefdes van Roberto Rossellini: 'Ik haat actrices, het zijn ijdele wezens,''' in *Skoop* (Amsterdam), September-October 1985.

Bergala, Alain, ''La vacance du cinéaste,'' in *Avant-Scène du Cinéma* (Paris), no. 361, June 1987.

Faux, A.-M., ''Mises en scènes de la confrontation,'' in *Avant-Scène du Cinéma* (Paris), no. 361, June 1987.

Marie, Michel, ''Un pélerinage esthétique,'' in *Avant-Scène du Cinéma* (Paris), no. 361, June 1987.

Roncoroni, S., ''Pour Rossellini,'' in *Avant-Scène du Cinéma* (Paris), vol. 361, June 1987.

Ostria, Vincent, ''Archéologie de l'amour,'' in *Cahiers du Cinéma* (Paris), no. 410, July-August 1988.

Truffaut, François, ''Roberto Rossellini par François Truffaut,'' in *Cahiers du Cinéma* (Paris), no. 410, July-August 1988.

Wagstaff, Chris, ''True Stories,'' in *Sight & Sound* (London), vol. 3, no. 8, August 1993.
Nosei, E., ''Invito al viaggio,'' in *Filmcritica* (Siena), vol. 45, no. 445, May 1994.
Denby, David, ''*Naples, Open City*,'' in *Premiere* (Boulder), vol. 8, no. 1, September 1994.

* * *

The five films that Rossellini made with Ingrid Bergman between 1950 and 1955 have still to receive their due recognition in the Anglo-Saxon world. The ridicule that was heaped on *Stromboli* can be largely attributed to the ''scandal'' of their personal relationship: more specifically, to the shock of the American public (and the critical establishment) on discovering that Bergman, who had become a national icon of female ''niceness,'' was actually a woman with autonomous sexual desires and professional aspirations. The continuing neglect of the films outside circumscribed academic circles must be attributed to the overwhelming dominance of expectations of the ''realistic'' (something quite distinct from ''realism''): most obviously, the use of post-synchronization is likely always to remain a problem, with Rossellini's indifference to the nationality of his actors ensuring that in every version of every film some performers will be *patently* dubbed. Beyond that (but not unconnected with it) is the uncertainty (a crucial manifestation of the films' distinction) as to what exactly they are really *about*. The aim of neo-realism in its early phase was the ''truthful'' depiction of contemporary social realities in as immediate and unmediated a way as possible. Yet the early neo-realist films *(Rome, Open City, Bicycle Thieves*, etc.), for all the quasi-documentary ambitions and the frequent use of non-professionals, are always patently *acted* and are always patently *fictions*: the ''reality'' we are invited to scrutinize is a constructed one. *Rome, Open City* can be seen to draw on a whole array of cinematic conventions, schemata, and stereotypes (one extended sequence even evokes Hitchcock). As he developed, Rossellini seems to have found such a method and aesthetic increasingly suspect, and the notion of ''filming the reality in front of the camera'' acquires a new dimension. That ''reality'' (or a significant aspect of it) consists, after all, of a group of actors speaking constructed dialogue. Is *Viaggio in Italia* a film about a woman called Katherine Joyce (British upper-middle-class, with an undisguised and unexplained Swedish accent) or an actress called Ingrid Bergman? While never directly autobiographical, Bergman's roles in the Rossellini films invariably make oblique reference to aspects of her life, and Rossellini's demand for spontaneity (handing the actors their lines—or simply a rough indication of what they were to talk about—immediately before the take, allowing no time for rehearsal, refusing to permit more than an absolute minimum of retakes) was clearly motivated by the desire that she reveal herself rather than act a character.

This clearly troubles our relationship to the character on the screen. On one level, Bergman's characters are always our primary identification-figures: in *Viaggio*, we discover Italy as Bergman discovers it, sharing her experiences. Yet identification is constantly disturbed. Scene after scene returns us from what Katherine sees to Katherine seeing it: are we studying ''Italy'' with her, or studying her with ''Italy'' as catalyst? Then there is the question of our relationship to the film's Italy (a very selective Italy). On one level, Katherine's journey is as banal as possible: she is offered all the obvious sightseeing attractions (famous sculptures, catacombs, Pompeii), and the banality is emphasized by the recurrent use of tour guides monotonously reciting their standard commentaries. Yet through (and beyond) the banality Katherine reaches a transcendent experience that transforms her perception of reality—an experience that remains unarticulated in any explicit manner, but which we are invited both to share and to understand.

Early neo-realist theory and practice suggest that the movement was strongly committed to the depiction of the material world, of contemporary social/political actuality. What came to obsess Rossellini, however, was the possibility of revealing the spiritual through the strict presentation of the material and physical. The cinema has constructed a whole panoply of signifiers of ''spiritual experience'': a rhetoric of acting, music, lighting, focus, big close-ups, special effects. Rossellini, knowing that the spiritual can only be implied, never shown, rigorously eschews all such rhetoric, employing the simplest, seemingly transparent methodology. Katherine/Bergman is brought into contact with all those fundamentals of existence from which in our daily lives we try to insulate ourselves: the terrifying power and mysteriousness of nature; otherness; time, transcience, eternity; death. Her experience is conveyed to us obliquely, through the structuring of sequence upon sequence, culminating in her climactic utterance at Pompeii (on paper, a line of staggering banality, in its context one of the cinema's supreme moments), ''Life is so short.'' The context (which is that of the entire film) transforms a cliché into a felt and lived essential truth.

The perfunctoriness of the ending (an apparent religious miracle, paralleled by the ''miracle'' of the couple's reconciliation) is often found problematic. It is helpful to recall that Rossellini and Bergman went on to make *La paura (Fear)*, for which Rossellini shot two quite different (and contradictory) endings. As there, the ending of *Viaggio* is an admission of uncertainty as to what may happen: no guarantee is offered that the couple's problems have been resolved, or that the reconciliation is more than momentary. One might say that the film doesn't really *end*: it just stops.

—Robin Wood

VICTIM

UK, 1961

Director: Basil Dearden

Production: Allied Film Makers/Parkway. A Michael Relph and Basil Dearden Production; black and white; running time: 100 minutes; length: 9,000 feet. Released 1961.

Producer: Michael Relph; **screenplay:** Janet Green, John McCormick; **photography:** Otto Heller; **editor:** John Guthridge; **sound:** Leslie Wiggins; **sound recordists:** C. C. Stevens, Gordon K. McCallum; **art director:** Alex Vetchinsky; **music:** Philip Green.

Cast: Dirk Bogarde (*Melville Farr*); Sylvia Syms (*Laura*); John Barrie (*Det. Inspector Harris*); John Cairney (*Bridie*); Norman Bird (*Harold Doe*); Peter McEnery (*Barrett*); Anthony Nicholls (*Lord*

Victim

Fulbrook); Dennis Price (*Calloway*); Peter Copley (*Paul Mandrake*); Donald Churchill (*Eddy Stone*); Derren Nesbitt (*Sandy Youth*); Alan MacNaughton (*Scott Hankin*); Nigel Stock (*Phip*); Charles Lloyd Pack (*Henry*); Mavis Villiers (*Madge*); Noel Howlett (*Patterson*); Hilton Edwards (*P. H.*); David Evans (*Mickey*); Margaret Diamond (*Miss Benham*); Frank Pettitt (*Barman*).

Publications

Books:

Hinxman, Margaret, and Susan d'Arcy, *The Films of Dirk Bogarde*, London, 1974.

Hill, John, *Sex, Class, and Realism: British Cinema 1956–63*, London, 1986.

Tanitch, Robert, *Dirk Bogarde: The Complete Career Illustrated*, London, 1988, 1990.

Articles:

Wilson, Cecil, ''Bogarde's First 'X,''' in *Daily Mail* (London), 19 August 1961.

Times (London), 30 August 1961.

Dyer, Peter John, in *Monthly Film Bulletin* (London), September 1961.

Dehn, Paul, in *Daily Herald* (London), 1 September 1961.

Powell, Dilys, in *Sunday Times* (London), 3 September 1961.

Variety (New York), 6 September 1961.

Whitebait, William, in *New Statesman* (London), 8 September 1961.

Cinématographe Française (Paris), 9 September 1961.

Partridge, Bruno, ''Some Chances Taken, and Some Not,'' in *Time and Tide* (London), 14 September 1961.

Films and Filming (London), October 1961.

''A Plea for Perversion?,'' in *Time* (New York), 23 February 1962.

Kael, Pauline, in *I Lost It at the Movies*, Boston, 1965.

Film Form (London), autumn 1977.

Medhurst, Andy, ''*Victim*: Text as Context,'' in *Screen* (London), July-October 1984.

Medhurst, Andy, "Dirk Bogarde," in *All Our Yesterdays*, edited by Charles Barr, London, 1986.
Stuart, Jan, in *The Advocate*, no. 744, 14 October 1997.
Lugowski, David M., in *Cineaste* (New York), vol. 23, no. 3, April 1998.
Umland, Rebecca, and Sam Umland, "*The Night Porter / Victim*," in *Video Watchdog* (Cincinnati), no. 45, 1998.

* * *

Victim is one of an impressive series of social problem films that Basil Dearden directed and Michael Relph produced between 1944 and 1963. Stylistically (and morally) they change very little, and to the radical young critics of the early 1960s Dearden and Relph epitomised everything that was wrong with British cinema. According to Victor Perkins, "Their method is to devise a number of stereotypes to represent every possible attitude to the matter in hand. . . . Thus in *Sapphire* and *Victim*, Basil Dearden and his scriptwriter Janet Green have produced thriller-problem films that work neither as thrillers nor as examinations of a problem, and particularly not as films." It is hardly a recommendation that Dearden and Relph were smiled on by the industry and liked by the more conservative critics, but now that the heat of battle has died down it is possible to see considerable virtues in their work—a civilised tolerance, a shrewd ability to combine exciting narrative stories with a less than superficial analysis of serious social problems, and a particular ability to probe and prod at English sexual repression.

Victim was the second of Dearden's and Relph's three collaborations with the talented scriptwriter Janet Green and the first British film to deal seriously and openly with homosexuality. The film takes its cue from the 1957 Wolfendon Report, which recommended the decriminalisation of homosexuality between consenting adults—proposals that were not enacted by Parliament until 1968. In its efforts not to be exploitative and sensational, *Victim* makes the lives of homosexuals seem sad, drab, pathetic. As one of the despairing victims puts it, "nature played me a dirty trick . . . tell them there's no magic cure for how we are." Gay writers like Richard Dyer and Andy Medhurst, while acutely aware of the film's limitations, have also seen good things in it—particularly Dirk Bogarde's portrayal of a man whose love, however deeply repressed, is reserved for other men.

Stylistically the film is much more distinguished than it has been given credit for. Dearden and Relph—and the veteran art director Alex Vetchinsky—make good use of the opportunity to break out of the studio and explore a hitherto unseen London. The Salisbury, a glittering Edwardian pub in St. Martin's Lane, well known even then as a gay meeting-place, is used effectively as the focal point of the film's homosexual community; and Otto Heller's lighting is superbly effective in creating a world that is always precarious and vaguely threatening. Perkins is right in the sense that all the characters—with the notable exception of Bogarde's sexually ambivalent hero—are stereotypes, but they are stereotypes who are cleverly deployed to get across the film's message that homosexuals are ordinary people from all walks of life rather than sub-criminal freaks.

Finally, though, it is the relationship between Bogarde and Sylvia Syms that now seems to give the film a dark resonance entirely missing from, for example, the Warner Brothers social problem films of the 1930s. In earlier British films like *Brief Encounter, The Passionate Friends*, and *Mandy*, it is women's sexuality that is the problem, as repressed but passionate women become discontented with their dull, drab husbands. In *Victim* it is Bogarde who is unable to adjust, tempted away from his dutiful, attractive wife by a passion that is all the more real because it is inappropriate to his career, his status, and his peace of mind.

—Robert Murphy

VIDAS SECAS

(Barren Lives)

Brazil, 1963

Director: Nelson Pereira dos Santos

Production: Produções Cinematográficas L. C. Barreto, Herbert Richers and Nelson Pereira dos Santos; 35mm; running time: 103 minutes. Released August 1963 in Rio de Janeiro. Filmed in Alagoas.

Producer: Luiz Carlos Barreto, Herbert Richers, and Nelson Pereira dos Santos; **screenplay:** Nelson Pereiras dos Santos, from the book by Gracialano Ramos; **photography:** José Rosa and Luis Carlos Barreto; **editor:** Nello Melli; **sound:** Geraldo José; **music:** Leonard Alencar.

Cast: Átila Iório (*Fabiano*), Maria Ribeiro (*Sinhá Vitória*), Orlando Macedo (*Soldado Amarelo*), Jofre Soares (*Coronel*); Gilvan Lima e Genivaldo Lima (*The boys*), and the dog Baleia.

Publications:

Books:

Rocha, Glauber, *Revisão Critica do Cinema Brasileiro*, Editora Civilização Brasileira, Rio de Janeiro, Brazil, 1963.
Ramos, Graciliano, *Vidas secas*, Livraria Martins Editora, 32 edition, São Paulo, Brazil, 1974.
Bernadet, Jean-Claude, *Brasil em Tempo de Cinema*, Editora Paz e Terra, Rio de Janeiro, Brasil, 1977.
Rocha, Glauber, *Revolução do Cinema Novo*, Alhambra/Embrafilme, Rio de Janeiro, Brazil, 1981.
Johnson, Randal, and Robert Stam, "The Cinema of Hunger" and "Nelson Pereira dos Santos Vidas Secas," *Brazilian Cinema*, Associated University Presses, Inc., 1982
Johnson, Randal, *Cinema Novo X5, Masters of Contemporary Brazilian Film* , University of Texas Press, Austin, 1984.
Salem, Helena, *Nelson Pereira dos Santos, o Sonho Possível do Cinema Brasileiro*, Editora Nova Fronteira, 1987.

Articles:

Vianna, A. Moniz, *Correio da Manhã* (Rio de Janeiro), 22 August 1963.
Azeredo, Ely, *Correio da Manhã* (Rio de Janeiro), 27/28 August 1963.

Mello e Souza, Cláudio, *Estado de Minas* (Minas Gerais), 20 October 1963.

Variety (New York), 25 Decemeber 1963.

Azeredo, Ely, *Tribuna da Imprensa* (Rio de Janeiro), 6 April 1964.

Estado de São Paulo, 9 May 1964.

Lefèvre, R., *Cinéma* (Paris), November 1965.

Petris, M., *Cahiers du Cinéma* (Paris), November 1965.

Viany, Alex, *Publicação do Departamento de Divulgação da Federação de Cineclubes do Rio de Janeiro*, March 1967.

Canby, Vincent, *New York Times*, 6 June 1969.

Conrad, R., *Film Quarterly* (Berkeley), no. 3, 1971.

Johnson, Randal, ''Vidas Secas and the Politics of Filmic Adaptation,'' in *Ideologies and Literature III*, number 15, January-March 1981.

Schild, Susana, ''A Arte de Recriar,'' *Revista IBM* (Rio de Janeiro), September 1984.

Augusto, Sérgio, *Folha de São Paulo* (São Paulo), Nelson Pereira, o pai do Cinema Novo, 22 June 1987.

Schild, Susana, *Jornal do Brasil* (Rio de Janeiro), Nelson por Nelson, 22 June 1987.

* * *

Nelson Pereira dos Santos is rightly considered the father of Brazil's Cinema Novo movement. With his first two films, *Rio 40 graus* (1956) and *Rio Zona Norte* (1957) influenced by Italian neo-realism, he started to sow the seeds of a film industry with a social conscience, resolving to portray the lifestyles of the country's most disadvantaged populations. His fifth film, *Vidas Secas (Barren Lives)*, acclaimed at Cannes in 1964, together with *Deus e O Diabo na Terra do Sol (Black God, White Devil)*, by Glauber Rocha, firmly established the Cinema Novo as an innovative trend in cinematography.

That said, the relevance and eloquence of *Vidas Secas* transcend the limits of the Cinema Novo movement. Notwithstanding its distinctly regional placement in the dry lands of Northeastern Brazil and its setting in the 1940s, it shares the timeless universal drama of poverty-stricken landless people who are obliged to move to the big cities in the hopes of a better life. For its piercingly realistic portrayal of this universal problem, *Vidas Secas* takes its place of honour not only as a masterpiece of Brazilian filmmaking, but on the international scene as well.

The film opens with an extreme long shot showing a stretch of desolate and arid countryside under a beating sun. From the distance a couple, their two children, and their dog slowly approach, heralded by the grating noise of the wheel of an ox-drawn wagon. There is nothing in this scene—the countryside, the light, the obvious poverty of the protagonists, the exasperatingly grating noise of the wagon wheel—to soothe the eyes or ears of the viewer. Its raw realism is transmitted quite naturally and without apology. The economy of the opening shot of *Vidas Secas*—which will persist throughout the narrative—reflects the perfect harmony between the style of the production and what it sought to portray. It is, in all senses, a frugal film and therein lies its strength.

Although the intention with *Vidas Secas* was to join the national debate on the subject of agrarian reform, Nelson Pereira dos Santos had no need of didacticisms or political language in order to get his message across and, likewise, discarded any sentimentality in the film's approach to the problem. He based the film on the Graciliano Ramos novel by the same name, which although written in 1938 remained topical in 1964—as it does, in dramatic terms, thirty years on. Among the film's merits is its fidelity to the spirit of Graciliano Ramos's text, with its concise style and literary qualities. (A return to the writings of Graciliano Ramos would yield another great moment in the career of Nelson Pereira dos Santos with *Memórias do Cárcere*, in 1983.)

Vidas Secas follows two years in the life of a family whose poverty and limitations are extreme, both in terms of their ability to express themselves and even in terms of their ability to survive. The family consists of Sinhá Vitória (Maria Ribeiro) and Fabiano (Átila Iório), two children (acted by the juveniles Gilvan and Genivaldo), and Baleia (whale), the dog. All they possess they carry on their backs, as they search for a little patch of land on which to settle. They come upon an abandoned farm, where Fabiano will work as a cow hand for just over a year. In this time, the family will experience some small advances and many humiliating set-backs, mainly due to Fabiano. Due to his ingenuousness and lack of understanding, Fabiano will be exploited by the owner of the farm, and forbidden by the ''authorities'' to sell his pathetic produce. Goaded by a soldier, Fabiano loses his money at gambling, and ends up in prison, where he is beaten. His only way out would be to join a band of outlaws, at the invitation of a cell mate. This he refuses to do: he is a good man, and wants only to live in peace with his family.

Surrender to social rules that are unfair or nonexistent is allied to impotence in the face of the ceaselessly blazing sun, drying up the land and the rivers, producing hunger and thirst, killing people and animals. To portray this desolate scenario, Nelson Pereira dos Santos sought to catch ''the true light of the Northeast.'' Filming took place under the most natural conditions possible, with no filters, using, as the director explained, ''God's light.'' The resulting over-exposure creates a suffocating atmosphere, which on several occasions seems to blind not only the protagonists but the viewer as well.

With authenticity and frugality as its touchstones, the camera—often hand held and subjective—reveals the daily existence of a family that can never be inserted into a ''normal'' social context, seen, most of the time, through the eyes of its members—including the dog. In its admirable austerity, *Vidas Secas* is a pungent treatise on aridity. The aridity is in the landscapes, in the hopelessness of the family's prospects, and in the relationships between the members of the family. It is present also in cruel details, such as in the scene in which Sinhá Vitória strangles the family parrot before cooking it for food, remarking, ''he couldn't even talk.''

Ironically, the lack of dialogue is one of the features of the film, true to Graciliano Ramos's novel. On several occasions, Sinhá Vitória and Fabiano say that they don't live as ''real people'' do. The woman dreams of exchanging her bed of dried twigs for one of leather, a bed such as ''real people'' might have. In a rare attempt at dialogue as they sit by the campfire, Sinhá Vitória and Fabiano actually talk to themselves more than to each other. They rarely touch each other, and their smiles and expressions of affection are directed not at each other but at the dog, which in a further irony, is treated in a ''human'' way in such an inhuman setting. (The very lifelike scene in which the dog dies inflamed the animal protection societies during the Cannes Festival of 1964. To prove that no murder had taken place, Baleia—a bitch, in fact—was taken to the Festival and accorded star treatment.)

The children are also largely silent, except for one of the boys who repeatedly asks ''what is hell?'' ''It is a hot place, where people go when they are condemned,'' replies his mother. With extreme sobriety and maturity, Nelson Pereira dos Santos showed that hell was in the dry lands of the Northeast, and is inhabited by thousands of Fabianos and Sinhás Vitória, who make for the big cities in order to become ''real people.'' They continue to do so to this day.

—Susana Schild

VIRIDIANA

Spain-Mexico, 1961

Director: Luis Buñuel

Production: Uninci S.A. and Films 59 (Spain) and Gustavo Alatriste (Mexico); black and white, 35mm; running time: 90 minutes. Released 17 May 1961, Cannes Film Festival. Filmed in Spain, near Madrid and Toledo. Cannes Film Festival, Best Film, 1961.

Producer: R. Muñoz Suay; **screenplay:** Luis Buñuel and Julio Alejandro, from a story by Buñuel; **photography:** José F. Aguayo; **editor:** Pedro del Rey; **art director:** Francisco Canet; **music:** Handel and Mozart; **arranger:** Gustavo Pittaluga.

Cast: Silvia Pinal (*Viridiana*); Francisco Rabal (*Jorge*); Fernando Rey (*Don Jaime*); Margarita Lozano (*Ramona*); Victoria Zinny (*Lucia*); Teresa Rabal (*Rita*).

Viridiana

Publications

Script:

Buñuel, Luis, and Julio Alejandro, *Viridiana*, Mexico City, 1963; in *Luis Buñuel: Three Screenplays*, New York, 1960.

Buñuel, Luis, *Viridiana: Scénario et dialogues—variantes—dossier historique et critique*, Paris, 1984.

Books:

Kyrou, Ado, *Le Surréalisme au cinéma*, Paris, 1963.

Durgnat, Raymond, *Luis Buñuel*, Berkeley, 1968.

Aranda, José Francisco, *Luis Buñuel: Biografia Critica*, Barcelona, 1969; as *Luis Buñuel: A Critical Biography*, New York, 1975.

Alcala, Manuel, *Buñuel*, Madrid, 1973.

Buache, Freddy, *The Cinema of Luis Buñuel*, New York, 1973.

Bazin, André, *Le Cinéma de la cruauté: De Buñuel à Hitchcock*, Paris, 1975; as *The Cinema of Cruelty: From Buñuel to Hitchcock*, New York, 1982.

Cesarman, Fernando, *El ojo de Buñuel*, Barcelona, 1976.

Mellen, Joan, editor, *The World of Luis Buñuel: Essays in Criticism*, New York, 1978.

Higginbotham, Virginia, *Luis Buñuel*, Boston, 1979.

Williams, Linda, *Figures of Desire: A Theory and Analysis of Surrealist Film*, Urbana, 1981, 1992.

Edwards, Gwynne, *The Discreet Art of Luis Buñuel: A Reading of His Films*, London, 1982.

Buñuel, Luis, *My Last Breath*, London and New York, 1983.

Rees, Margaret A., editor, *Luis Buñuel: A Symposium*, Leeds, 1983.

Lefévre, Raymond, *Luis Buñuel*, Paris, 1984.

Vidal, Agustin Sanchez, *Luis Buñuel: Obra Cinematografica*, Madrid, 1984.

Aub, Max, *Conversaciones con Buñuel: Seguidas de 45 entrevistas con familiares, amigos y colaboradores del cineasta aragones*, Madrid, 1985.

Bertelli, Pino, *Buñuel: L'arma dello scandalo: L'anarchia nel cinema di Luis Buñuel*, Turin, 1985.

Oms, Marcel, *Don Luis Buñuel*, Paris, 1985.

De la Colina, José, and Tomás Pérez Turrent, *Luis Buñuel: Prohibido asomarse al interior*, Mexico City, 1986.

Sandro, Paul, *Diversions of Pleasure: Luis Buñuel and the Crises of Desire*, Columbus, Ohio, 1987.

Baxter, John, *Buñuel*, London, 1994, 1998.

Evans, Peter William, *Films of Luis Buñuel: Subjectivity and Desire*, Oxford, 1995.

Tesson, Charles, *Luis Buñuel*, Paris, 1995.

Articles:

Hull, Davied, in *Film Quarterly* (Berkeley), Winter 1961–62.

Douchet, Jean, in *Cahiers du Cinéma* (Paris), January 1962.

Rothschild, Elaine, in *Films in Review* (New York), February 1962.

Buñuel, Luis, in *Film Culture* (New York), Spring 1962.

Riera, Emilio, in *Film Culture* (New York), Spring 1962.

Benayoun, Robert, in *Positif* (Paris), March 1962.

Seguin, Louis, ''*Viridiana* et les Critiques,'' in *Positif* (Paris), March 1962.

Sarris, Andrew, in *Village Voice* (New York), 22 March 1962.

Martin, Marcel, in *Cinéma* (Paris), April 1962.
Lefévre, Raymond, ''*Viridiana*; ou, Les Infortunes de la Charité,'' in *Image et Son* (Paris), Summer 1962.
Robinson, David, in *Sight and Sound* (London), Summer 1962.
Rotha, Paul, in *Films and Filming* (London), June 1962.
Sarris, Andrew, in *Movie* (London), June 1962.
Vas, Robert, in *Monthly Film Bulletin* (London), October 1963.
Milne, Tom, ''The Mexican Buñuel,'' in *Sight and Sound* (London), Winter 1965–66.
Mardore, Michel, in *Cahiers du Cinéma* (Paris), March 1966.
Rowe, Ian, in *Screen Education Yearbook*, London, 1968.
Sarris, Andrew, ''The Devil and the Nun: *Viridiana,*'' in *Renaissance of the Film*, edited by Julius Bellone, London 1970.
''Buñuel Issue'' of *Image et Son* (Paris), May 1971.
''Buñuel Issue'' of *Cine Cubano*, no. 78–80, 1973.
Hogue, P., in *Movietone News* (Seattle), February 1975.
''Buñuel Issue'' of *Contracampo* (Madrid), October-November 1980.
''Spanish Directors' Issue'' of *Cahiers de la Cinémathèque* (Perpignan), Winter 1984.
Steinborn, B., in *Filmfaust* (Frankfurt), April-May 1985.
Roger, A., ''*Viridiana* ou le *Tableau vivant*,'' in *Iris* (Iowa City), Autumn 1992.
Aub, M., ''Gustavo Alatriste parle de *Viridiana*,'' in *Positif* (Paris), no. 391, September 1993.
Special Issue of *Avant-Scène du Cinéma* (Paris), no. 428, January 1994.
Poulet, J., ''Espace mental et filmique dans le cinema espagnol,'' in *Cinemaction* (Conde-sur-Noireau), vol. 75, no. 2, 1995.
Castoro Cinema (Milan), no. 59, 2nd edition, January 1996.
Larraz, E., ''La vision ironique de don Luis,'' in *Cinemaction* (Conde-sur-Noireau), vol. 80, no. 3, 1996.
Moine, R., ''Mises en cene,'' in *Cinemaction* (Conde-sur-Noireau), vol. 80, no. 3, 1996.
Moine, R., ''*Je suis athee grace a Dieu*: la rhetorique chretienne d'un iconoclaste,'' in *Cinemaction* (Conde-sur-Noireau), vol. 80, no. 3, 1996.
Elia, M., in *Séquences* (Haute-Ville), no. 189/190, March/June 1997.

* * *

Viridiana is the most atypical of Luis Buñuel's films. If he had set out deliberately to antagonize and shock a whole school of faith, he certainly did it in this film, which, while it was his undoubted masterpiece, concealed a bomb that made it impossible for him ever to return to his native land, Spain.

Not that he wanted to. *Viridiana* was a film he had to make in order to free himself, to let the world know that he was not in idle jest when he broke away from his Roman Catholic faith. The score he had to settle with the Church must have been building for a long, long time. It took over 60 years for him to declare himself utterly free. He was always regarded as the great iconoclast of his time; no director was as unpredictable; but few would have guessed how deep was his hatred for Roman Catholicism.

When the Spanish Civil War was concluded and Spain had settled down to a forgiving and let-it-be-forgotten peace, he, as Spain's greatest film director, was invited by Franco's minister of culture to return to his native country and make whatever film he chose with the blessing of Franco. Nobody, even his co-workers, knew that he was planning so defiantly an anti-Catholic film as *Viridiana.* He always worked rapidly once he had begun and, in no time, he had finished shooting his picture and was safely across the Pyrenees, with the whole of his film smuggled out ahead of him. Franco raged, destroying the out-take films deliberately and tantalizingly left behind; he dismissed his minister of culture, and cursed the day he had ever trusted a faithless Spaniard who knew too much for Franco's good. It was not long before Spain acknowledged that it had been betrayed by its priesthood during the Civil War, and put its trust in its young, who had not seen their country go to the devil in the name of God and Franco.

Viridiana is basically the story of innocence betrayed and lost. The heroine, Viridiana, has completed her novitiate and is about to enter the Church forever, when her Mother Superior persuades her to pay a farewell visit to Don Jaime, her uncle, who had paid for her education and entry into the service of God. Although Viridiana consents to the visit, she has always loathed her uncle because he has never shown her the slightest affection. He is very rich, however, and she is persuaded that she must see him one last time before she takes her farewell of the world and its ways.

Don Jaime, to her surprise, is affectionate and charming, and lets her know that she is the very image of his dead wife, for whom he still maintains a kind of necrophiliac passion. He has a handsome illegitimate son named Jorge, who is attracted to the young and innocent Viridiana, but is willing to bide his time. Besides, he has brought a mistress of his own to his uncle's estate.

Don Jaime is able to drug Viridiana's wine, and later steals into her bedroom to look upon her as she lies happily unconscious. She is so devoted to Jesus that she wears a crown of thorns and a huge wooden crucifix. She is clothed only in a simple shift. Don Jaime, in a trance, utters his wife's name, removes the crown and crucifix that the girl wears, and brutally rapes her while she lies senseless before him. Consumed by guilt, he then hangs himself.

Viridiana, recovering consciousness, realizes sadly that she is not without guilt herself, for she has blinded herself to the realities of the world; she formally rejects the vows she had made, and returns to the estate she has inherited with Jorge, hoping to make her peace with God. Still imbued with a crippled kind of faith, she takes it upon herself to rescue a band of castaway and diseased gypsy beggars, inviting them to become workers on the land she inherited with Jorge.

They work the land lazily, and at night they indulge themselves in one of the most defiant orgies ever filmed. It is sacrilegious if one is a Christian, which Buñuel was pleased to say he was not. The drunken, diseased beggars stage a supper scene that is a deliberate parody of the grouping in Da Vinci's painting of ''The Last Supper.'' They dance grotesquely, entertaining themselves lewdly to the thunder of the ''Hallelujah Chorus.''

The picture Buñuel made of his country's plight is replete with symbolism of what Spain had become, a warning of what it might be in a world gone mad. The only moral salvation the film hints at is a hope that in a reformed Viridiana and a wiser, less destructive Jorge there may be the seed for a new generation of Spain, cut clean away from the ancient hypocrisies bred in the Church. His heroine comes of age, and realizing the falseness of her onetime faith, pledges herself to a new life that may embrace complete freedom.

Viridiana may be a compelling shocker, but it is also a beautifully made picture with wonderful visuals, and the shock it gives may be virtually necessary to its meaning. Buñuel himself expressed it well when he said, ''The sense of film is this: that we do not live in the best of all possible worlds.'' He was never afraid to show people how vicious and contemptible they are. When it is all over, Viridiana sits playing cards, listening to rock-and-roll music with her uncle's aggressive illegitimate son. But after the cardplaying and the record has come to an end, what then?

—DeWitt Bodeen

VISKNINGAR OCH ROP

(Cries and Whispers)

Sweden, 1972

Director: Ingmar Bergman

Production: Cinematograph, in cooperation with Svenska Filminstitutet; Eastmancolor; running time: 91 minutes; length: 8,190 feet. Released 1972. Oscar for Best Cinematography, 1973.

Producer: Ingmar Bergman; **production manager:** Lars-Owe Carlsberg; **screenplay:** Ingmar Bergman; **photography:** Sven Nykvist; **editor:** Siv Lundgren; **sound:** Owe Svennson; **art director:** Marik Vos.

Cast: Harriet Andersson (*Agnes*); Kari Sylwan (*Anna*); Ingrid Thulin (*Karin*); Liv Ullmann (*Maria*); Erland Josephson (*Doctor*); Henning Moritzen (*Joakim*); Georg Arlin (*Fredrik*); Anders Ek (*Isak*); Inga Gill (*Aunt Olga*).

Publications

Script:

Bergman, Ingmar, *Viskningar och rop*, in *Avant-Scène du Cinéma* (Paris), December 1973.

Books:

Björkman, Stig, and others, editors, *Bergman on Bergman*, New York, 1973.
Ranieri, Tino, *Ingmar Bergman*, Florence, 1974.
Ho, Thi Nhu Quynh, *La femme dans l'univers Bergmanien: Analyse de quatre films d'Ingmar Bergman*, Fribourg, 1975.
Kaminsky, Stuart, editor, *Ingmar Bergman: Essays in Criticism*, New York, 1975.
Hope, Kenneth Weaver, *Film and Meta-Narrative*, Ann Arbor, Michigan, 1976.
Bergom-Larsson, Maria, *Ingmar Bergman and Society*, San Diego, 1978.
Kawin, Bruce, *Mindscreen: Bergman, Godard, and the First-Person Film*, Princeton, 1978.
Marion, Denis, *Ingmar Bergman*, Paris, 1979.
Manvell, Roger, *Ingmar Bergman: An Appreciation*, New York, 1980.
Mosley, Philip, *Ingmar Bergman: The Cinema as Mistress*, Boston, 1981.
Petric, Vlada, editor, *Film and Dreams: An Approach to Bergman*, South Salem, New York, 1981.
Cowie, Peter, *Ingmar Bergman: A Critical Biography*, New York, 1982.
Livingston, Paisley, *Ingmar Bergman and the Ritual of Art*, Ithaca, New York, 1982.
Steene, Birgitta, *Ingmar Bergman: A Guide to References and Resources*, Boston, 1982.
Jones, William G., editor, *Talking with Bergman*, Dallas, 1983.
Lefévre, Raymond, *Ingmar Bergman*, Paris, 1983.
Dervin, Daniel, *Through a Freudian Lens Deeply: A Psychoanalysis of Cinema*, Hillsdale, New Jersey, 1985.
Gado, Frank, *The Passion of Ingmar Bergman*, Durham, North Carolina, 1986.
Bergman, Ingmar, *Laterna Magica*, Stockholm, 1987; as *The Magic Lantern: An Autobiography*, London, 1988.
Smith, Joseph H., and William Kerrigan editors, *Images in Our Souls: Cavell, Psychoanalysis and Cinema*, Baltimore, 1987.

Articles:

Chaplin (Stockholm), vol.14, no. 3, 1972.
Film in Sweden (Stockholm), no. 2, 1972.
Bergman, Ingmar, extract from diary, in *Cinéma* (Paris), December 1972.
Variety (New York), 20 December 1972.
Milne, Tom, in *Monthly Film Bulletin* (London), March 1973.
Strick, Philip, in *Sight and Sound* (London), Spring 1973.
Mellen, Joan, "Bergman and Women," in *Film Quarterly* (Berkeley), Fall 1973.
Positif (Paris), September 1973.
Le Fanu, Mark, "Bergman: The Politics of Melodrama," in *Monogram* (London), no. 5, 1974.
Gallerani, M., "L'anima e le forme nella scrittura di Bergman," in *Cinema Nuovo* (Bari), September-October 1978.
Lundell, T., and A. Mulac, "Husbands and Wives in Bergman Films: A Close Analysis Based on Empirical Data," in *Journal of University Film Association* (Carbondale, Illinois), Winter 1981.
Koskinen, M., "Det typiskt Svenska hos Ingmar Bergman," in *Chaplin* (Stockholm), vol. 26, nos. 5–6, 1984.
"Dialogue on Film: Sven Nykvist," in *American Film* (Washington, D.C.), March 1984.
Sitney, P. A., "Color and Myth in *Cries and Whispers*," in *Film Criticism* (Meadville, Pennsylvania), no. 3, 1989.
Sitney, P. A., "Liksom en saga av Broderna Grimm," in *Chaplin* (Stockholm), no. 3, 1989.
"Bergman, il paradosso di un 'Ateo cristiano,'" in *Castoro Cinema* (Florence), November-December 1991.

* * *

In the rare company of such films as *Marnie* and *Il deserto rosso, Cries and Whispers* fuses its meaning to its controlled use of color. Brilliantly simple, it is a film of reds, even punctuated with red-outs rather than darkening fades. Opening with crepuscular light in the sculpture garden of a 19th-century mansion, the film moves quickly indoors where it settles, with a single exterior flashback, until its epilogue. The house is remarkable for its red upholstery: richly saturated red walls and furnishings set off the white gowns in which three sisters, Agnes, Karin, and Maria, and their servant Anna, dress themselves following the model of their dead mother who appears in a flashback. Agnes lies dying, apparently of a cancer of the womb or stomach. After her death the white motif shifts to black. Perhaps the most brilliant and simple act of color organization comes from the dramatic placement of a final flashback motivated by Anna's reading in Agnes's diary (after her death) of an ecstatic afternoon of lush

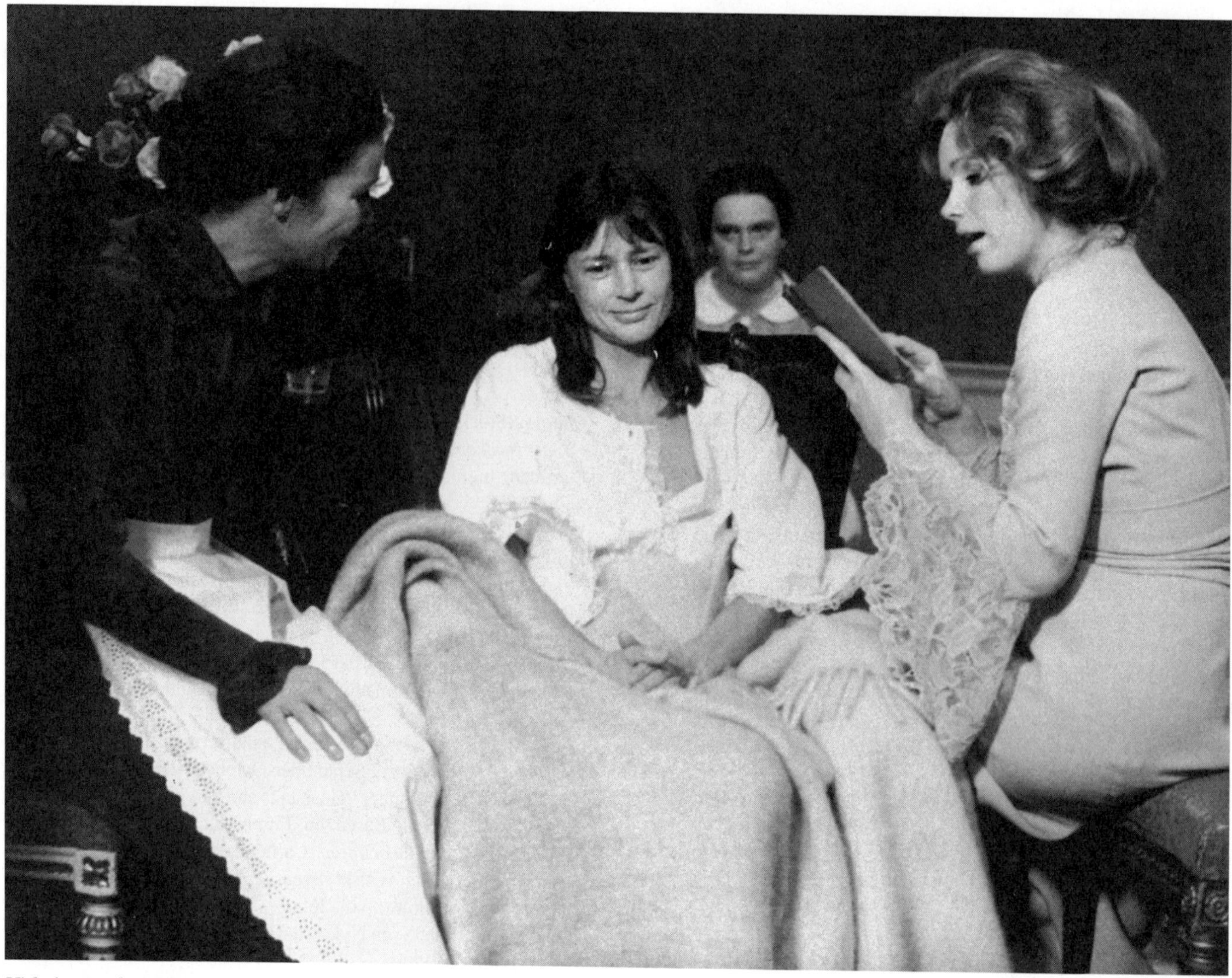

Viskningar och rop

autumnal colors. The natural effulgence is all the more striking for being reserved and isolated at the end of the film.

In the film's dramatic center, where the logic of dreams holds sway, the corpse of Agnes elicits comfort from the three surviving women. Anna alone cradles the dead body in an image that suggests a Pietà, but shows as well a full breast beside the "dead" face incapable of earthly nurture. As Mater Dolorosa, the servant has a religious faith in the liminality of death itself. This is consistent with the very first sight we get of her early in the film, waking and praying beside the fetishes of her dead daughter.

An elaborate linkage of gestures, both rhyming and reversing, throughout the film suggests that the different characters are vectors of a single fantasy system that generates its narrative complexity by scattering and redistributing its aspects among imagined persons who are in essence a single haunting presence. Anna is as much the absent mother as is Maria (Liv Ullmann plays both her and the mother); even the miserable Karin (named after the filmmaker's own mother) is her most threatening face.

The men of the film are all shadowy figures for the dead, radically absent father. Alternately fierce and weak, they underline the missing male presence in Agnes's life. The doctor, Maria's sometime lover, and Karin's husband, Frederick, represent the punishing power of musculinity, while Maria's suicidal husband and a minister illustrate male weakness as self-absorption.

Within the visual and color economy of the film the wound of Maria's husband (who stabs himself in the stomach reacting to her hint that she has slept with the doctor) is part of a covert symbolical equation with broken glass Karin inserts in her vagina (apparently to deny her husband sex) and their ultimate visual echo: a red book held against the mother's dress (in a memory flashback) as a displaced menstrual stain. In this dreamlike, liminal world of the metamorphic woman, fusing fantasies of defloration, menstruation, and castration, the four men are versions of masculine self-hatred in sadistic and masochistic registers.

We know from Bergman's autobiography the fetishistic importance he gives to the magic lantern. In the flashback of the mother there is a magic lantern version of *Hansel and Gretel.* Here the magic lantern represents simultaneously the gift of fairy tales, and thereby the psychic-defense machinery for exteriorizing infantile and oedipal terrors, and the gift of cinema for the incipient filmmaker. The oral gratification and oral aggression at the core of the fairy tale are prominent components of Bergman's film, whose very title brackets speech with labial (whispers) and dental (cries) suggestions. Maria's seduction of the doctor involves a sensual and somewhat greedy scene of eating; in direct contrast, the silent meal of Karin and Frederick, in which she spills wine and denies him sexual pleasure, precedes the horrific mutilation of her genitals, and that too ends with her rubbing the blood on her mouth and laughing; Agnes vomits, and Anna goes through the motions of breast-feeding her. Maria fulfills the role of the fairy-tale mother who fails to care for her children and abandons them to the forest. But in Anna we have the all-giving mother who has lost her daughter.

The lesson of *Hansel and Gretel*, according to Bruno Bettleheim, is that the child must learn to curb his infantile desires and win self-sufficiency through his own ingenuity. The ingenuity of *Cries and Whispers* is the Orphic transformation of terror into art, of the loss of the mother into the musical richness of autumnal color and the self-sufficiency of memory.

—P. Adams Sitney

I VITELLONI

(The Young and the Passionate)

Italy-France, 1953

Director: Federico Fellini

Production: Peg Films (Paris) and Cité Films (Rome); black and white, 35mm; running time: 104 minutes. Released 1953, Venice Film Festival. Filmed December 1952-Spring 1953 in Viterbo, Ostia, and Florence.

Producer: Lorenzo Pegoraro; **screenplay:** Federico Fellini, Tullio Pinelli, and Ennio Flaiano, from their screen story; **photography:** Otello Martelli, Luciano Trasatti, and Carlo Carlini; **editor:** Rolando Benedetti; **art director:** Mario Chiari; **music:** Nino Rota.

Cast: Franco Interlenghi (*Moraldo*); Alberto Sordi (*Alberto*); Franco Fabrizi (*Fausto*); Leopoldo Trieste (*Leopoldo*); Riccardo Fellini (*Riccardo*); Elenora Ruffo (*Sandra*); Jean Brochard (*Fausto's father*); Claude Farell (*Alberto's sister*); Carlo Romano (*Michele*); Enrico Viarisio (*Sandra's father*); Paolo Borboni (*Sandra's mother*); Lida Baarova (*Michele's wife*); Arlette Sauvage (*Lady in the movie theater*); Vira Silenti (*Chinese maiden*); Maja Nipora (*Chanteuse*).

Publications

Script:

Fellini, Federico, Tullio Pinelli, and Ennio Flaiano, *I vitelloni*, in *Il primo Fellini: Lo sceicco bianco, I vitelloni, La strada, Il bidone*, edited by Renzo Renzi, Bologna, 1969; translated as *I Vitelloni*, in *Fellini: Three Screenplays*, New York, 1970; also published in *Quattro film*, Turin, 1974.

Books:

Renzi, Renzo, *Federico Fellini*, Parma, 1956.
Taylor, John Russell, *Cinema Eye, Cinema Ear*, New York, 1964.
Rondi, Gian Luigi, *Italian Cinema Today*, New York, 1965.
Budgen, Suzanne, *Fellini*, London, 1966.
Salachas, Gilbert, *Federico Fellini*, New York, 1969.
Betti, Liliana, *Fellini*, Zurich, 1976.
Fellini on Fellini, New York, 1976.
Ketcham, Charles B., *Federico Fellini: The Search for a New Mythology*, New York, 1976.
Murray, Edward, *Fellini the Artist*, New York, 1976; revised edition, 1985.
Rosenthal, Stuart, *The Cinema of Federico Fellini*, Cranbury, New Jersey, 1976.
Stubbs, John C., *Federico Fellini: A Guide to References and Resources*, Boston, 1978.
Alpert, Hollis, *Fellini: A Life*, New York, 1981, 1998.
Fruttero, Carlo, and Franco Lucentini, *Je te trouve un peu pâle: Récit d'été avec trente fantasmes féminins de Federico Fellini*, Paris, 1982.
Costello, Donald P., *Fellini's Road*, Notre Dame, Indiana, 1983.
Grazzini, Giovanni, editor, *Federico Fellini: Intervista sul cinema*, Rome, 1983.
Burke, Frank, *Federico Fellini: Variety Lights to La Dolce Vita*, Boston, 1984.
Fava, Claudie F., and Aldo Vigano, *The Films of Federico Fellini*, Secaucus, New Jersey, 1985.
Kezich, Tullio, *Fellini*, Milan, 1987.
Baxter, John, *Fellini*, New York, 1994.
Costantini, Costanzo, editor, *Fellini on Fellini*, translated by Sohrab Sorooshian, London, 1995.
Gieri, Manuela, *Contemporary Italian Filmmaking: Strategies of Subversion: Pirandello, Fellini, Scola, and the Directors of the New Generation*, Toronto, 1995.
Fellini, Federico, *Fellini on Fellini*, translated by Isabel Quigley, New York, 1996.

Articles:

Fellini, Federico, in *Cinema Nuovo* (Turin), 1 January 1963.
Castello, Giulio Cesare, in *Cinema* (Rome), 31 August 1953.
Berger, Rudi, in *Filmcritica* (Rome), September 1953.
Ghelli, Nino, in *Bianco e Nero* (Rome), October 1953.
Koval, Francis, in *Films in Review* (New York), October 1953.
Martin, André, in *Cahiers du Cinéma* (Paris), May 1954.
Benedetti, B., in *Cinema Nuovo* (Rome), 15 August 1954.
Tailleur, Roger, and Bernard Chardère, in *Positif* (Paris), September-October 1954.
Mangini, Cecilia, ''Le Cas Fellini,'' in *Cinéma* (Paris), January 1955.
Lambert, Gavin, ''The Signs of Predicament,'' in *Sight and Sound* (London), January-March 1955.
Salachas, Gilbert, in *Télécinė* (Paris), October-November 1955.
Archer, Eugene, in *Film Culture* (New York), no. 4, 1956.
Young, Vernon, in *Hudson Review* (New York), Autumn 1956.
Crowther, Bosley, in *New York Times*, 24 October 1956.
''*Marty*—Italian Style,'' in *Newsweek* (New York), 12 November 1956.
Philippe, Pierre, in *Cinéma* (Paris), February 1958.
Bennett, Joseph, ''Italian Film: Failure and Emergence,'' in *Kenyon Review* (Gambier, Ohio), autumn 1964.

I Vitelloni

Sufrin, Mark, in *Film Society Review* (New York), May 1970.

Lefèvre, Raymond, ''Fellini,'' in *Image et Son* (Paris), January 1971.

Burke, F. M., ''Reason and Unreason in Federico Fellini's *I Vitelloni*,'' in *Literature/Film Quarterly* (Salisbury, Maryland), no. 2, 1980.

Italianist (Reading, Berkshire), no. 1, 1981.

Martin, Marcel, ''Federico Fellini,'' in *Revue du Cinéma* (Paris), January 1984.

Sragow, Michael, in *American Film*, vol. 14, no. 7, May 1989.

Prédal, René, ''Les vitelloni, du néoréalisme au cinéma moderne,'' in *Cinemaction* (Conde-sur-Noireau), no. 70, January 1994.

Schickel, R., ''Send in the Clowns: An Aspect of Fellini,'' in *Film Comment* (New York), vol. 30, September/October 1994.

Séquences (Haute-Ville), no. 179, July-August 1995.

Amengual, Barthélemy, ''Propositions pour un portrait du jeune Fellini en néo-réaliste,'' in *Positif* (Paris), no. 413/414, July-August 1995.

* * *

After *Lo sceicco bianco*, which despite its formal brilliance was a critical and financial failure, Fellini found himself unable to obtain backing for *La strada*, already in scenario form. Together with scenarists Ennio Flaiano and Tullio Pinelli, he devised the story of the prankish middle-class youths—or *vitelloni* (meaning literally ''big slabs of veal'')—that he remembered from his Romagnan boyhood. Having high opinions of their limited talents, these aging provincial good-for-nothings prefer banding together to amuse themselves at the expense of their neighbors in lieu of settling down into responsible lifestyles and the work they consider demeaning.

The film focuses on the lives of five buddies, drawn with the profound social observation of a great satirist. Each must come to terms with the inevitable alienation that they face when confronted with their worthlessness and with the bleakness of their futures. Alberto, the saddest of the group, lives with his mother and is supported by his sister. He tries desperately to remain an adolescent for everyone except his sister to whom he acts the commanding brother and man of the family. Against his will, his sister elopes, leaving him to become the breadwinner. Fausto, the handsome Don Juan of the group, is coerced into marrying Moraldo's sister whom he has gotten pregnant; however, he doesn't hesitate to abandon his new wife at the movies to pursue the woman in the seat next to him. Fausto loses his job in a religious statuary shop (a typical Fellini touch of uncommon satirical depth) after trying to seduce the owner's wife. Through Alberto and Fausto, Fellini comments on the predatory nature of that society, and of the middle-class in particular. Leopoldo, a romantic dreamer, plays the tortured dramatist to the maid across the courtyard. His hopes shatter when he petitions a fustian travelling actor for help. Pretending to be interested in Leopoldo's play, the actor makes homosexual advances toward him. Riccardo is the least clearly characterized of the group, perhaps only used to make the group a more convenient size. Moraldo represents an ethical center in the film; while he contributes to the group's sport, he clearly does not have the avocation. In moments signalled by camera placement, editing, and music, Moraldo merges with the subjective authorial consciousness that will become more direct and forceful in the later Fellini films. He is the only one with any curiosity about life and any courage to break away for good. Moraldo is undoubtedly Fellini. His story was to have been continued in the scripted, but never filmed, *Moraldo in città*. A similar character gets off the train at the beginning of *Roma*. Much of the wistfully tragic cadence of the film is derived from a despair behind the merry masks of the *vitelloni*, a rhetorical figuration actualized in the town's frenzied carnival celebration. This Dionysian event is the perfect visual and rhythmic representation of misdirected energy, leading to a critique of the grotesque, inebriated alienation and neurotic sexual frustration at the base of the Italian society in the 1950s. The mask motif points to the director's skill in utilizing Pirandellian themes with pointedness and originality. Alberto's drag costume and enormous mask, with its features set into a grotesque, scream-like demeanor, are indications that farcical anarchy and psychological anguish are never too distant from each other.

Like Gramsci, Fellini attributes Italian fascism to these inseparable adolescent qualities, and continues to explore this problem in different contexts in his later work. Specifically, *Il bidone*, a work of less technical polish, stands out as a transmutation of these provincial *vitelloni* from harmless, middle-class parasites into hostile, ruthless con-men and thieves.

I vitelloni was enormously successful, even among critics of the left, and became the director's first film distributed internationally.

—Joel Kanoff

VIVRE SA VIE

(My Life to Live)

France, 1962

Director: Jean-Luc Godard

Production: Films de la Pléiade; black and white, 35mm; running time: 85 minutes. Released September 1962, Paris. Filmed 1960 in Paris.

Producer: Pierre Braumberger; **screenplay:** Jean-Luc Godard with additional narrative from Judge Marcel Sacotte's *Où en est la prostitution* and Edgar Allen Poe's "The Oval Portrait"; **photography:** Raoul Coutard; **editors:** Agnès Guillemot and Lila Lakshmanan; **sound:** Guy Vilette and Jacques Maumont; **sound editor:** Lila Lakshmanan; **music:** Michel Legrand; **costume designer:** Christiane Fage.

Cast: Anna Karina (*Nana*); Sady Rebbot (*Raoul*); André S. Labarthe (*Paul*); Guylaine Schlumberger (*Yvette*); Gérard Hoffmann (*The cook*); Monique Messine (*Elizabeth*); Paul Pavel (*Journalist*); Dimitri Dineff (*Dimitri*); Peter Kassowitz (*Young man*); Eric Schlumberger (*Luigi*); Brice Parain (*The philosopher*); Henri Attal (*Arthur*); Gilles Quéant (*A man*); Odile Geoffrey (*Barmaid*); Marcel Charton (*Policeman*); Jack Florency (*Bystander*); Gisèle Hauchecorne (*Concierge*); Jean-Luc Godard (*Voice*).

Awards: Venice Film Festival, Special Jury Prize, and the Italian Critics Prize, 1962.

Publications

Script:

Godard, Jean-Luc, *Vivre sa vie*, in *Avant-Scène du Cinéma* (Paris), October 1962; "Scenario" in *Film Culture* (New York), Winter 1962.

Books:

Collet, Jean, *Jean-Luc Godard*, Paris, 1963; New York, 1970.

Taylor, John Russell, *Cinema Eye, Cinema Ear: Some Key Filmmakers of the 60s*, New York, 1964.

Roud, Richard, *Jean-Luc Godard*, New York, 1967.

Mussman, Toby, editor, *Jean-Luc Godard: A Critical Anthology*, New York, 1968.

Cameron, Ian, editor, *The Films of Jean-Luc Godard*, London, 1969.

Mancini, Michele, *Godard*, Rome, 1969.

Brown, Royal, editor, *Focus on Godard*, Englewood Cliffs, New Jersey, 1972.

Godard on Godard, edited by Tom Milne, London, 1972; as *Godard on Godard: Critical Writings*, edited by Milne and Jean Narboni, New York, 1986.

Farassino, Alberto, *Jean-Luc Godard*, Florence, 1974.

Monaco, James, *The New Wave*, New York, 1976.

MacCabe, Colin, *Godard: Images, Sounds, Politics*, London, 1980.

Walsh, Martin, *The Brechtian Aspect of Radical Cinema*, London, 1981.

Lefèvre, Raymond, *Jean-Luc Godard*, Paris, 1983.

Bordwell, David, *Narration in the Fiction Film*, London, 1985.

Weis, Elisabeth, and John Belton, *Film Sound: Theory and Practice*, New York, 1985.

Cerisuelo, Marc, *Jean-Luc Godard*, Paris, 1989.

Loshitzky, Yosefa, *Radical Faces of Godard and Bertolucci*, Detroit, 1995.

Dixon, Wheeler Winston, *The Films of Jean-Luc Godard*, Albany, 1997.

Silverman, Kaja, and Harun Farocki, *Speaking About Godard*, New York, 1998.

Sterritt, David, *The Films of Jean-Luc Godard: Seeing the Invisible*, Cambridge, 1999.

Articles:

Sontag, Susan, in *Against Interpretation*, New York, 1961.
Sarris, Andrew, ''A Movie Is a Movie Is a Movie Is a. . . ,'' in *New York Film Bulletin*, no. 5, 1962.
Truffaut, François, in *Avant-Scène du Cinéma* (Paris), October 1962.
Shivas, Mark, in *Movie* (London), October 1962.
Milne, Tom, in *Sight and Sound* (London), Winter 1962.
Films and Filming (London), December 1962.
Collet, Jean, and others, ''Entretien avec Jean-Luc Godard,'' in *Cahiers du Cinéma* (Paris), December 1962.
Baker, Peter, in *Films and Filming* (London), January 1983.
Fieschi, Jean-André, ''Godard: Cut-Sequence: *Vivre sa Vie,*'' in *Movie* (London), January 1963.
''Anna et les paradoxes,'' in *Cinéma* (Paris), July-August 1963.
Young, Colin, ''Conventional/Unconventional,'' in *Film Quarterly* (Berkeley), Fall 1963.
Sarris, Andrew, in *Village Voice* (New York), 26 September 1963.
Carey, Gary, and Marilyn Goldin, ''*My Life to Live:* Portrait of a Lady,'' in *Seventh Art* (New York), Winter 1963.
Sontag, Susan, ''Godard,'' in *Partisan Review* (New Brunswick, New Jersey), Spring 1968.
Crofts, Stephen, ''The Films of Jean-Luc Godard,'' in *Cinema* (London), June 1969.
Beh, Siew Hwa, in *Women and Film*, no. 1, 1972.
Campbell, M., ''Life Itself: *Vivre sa Vie* and the Language of Film,'' in *Wide Angle* (Athens, Ohio), no. 3, 1976.
Baumgarten, Marjorie, in *Cinema Texas Program Notes* (Austin), 20 November 1977.
Conley, Tom, ''Portrayals of Painting: Translations of *Vivre sa Vie*'' in *Film Reader* (Evanston, Illinois), no. 3, 1978.
de Graaff, T., in *Skrien* (Amsterdam), Winter 1978–79.
Brown, R. S., ''Music and *Vivre sa Vie*,'' in *Quarterly Review of Film Studies* (Pleasantville, New York), Summer 1980.
Ropars, Marie-Claire, ''The Erratic Alphabet,'' in *Enclitic* (Minneapolis), no. 10–11, 1981.
''Godard Issue'' of *Camera Obscura* (Berkeley), Fall 1982.
''Godard Issue'' of *Revue Belge du Cinéma* (Brussels), Summer 1986.
van der Kooij, F., ''Wo unter den Bildern sind die Klaenge daheim?,'' in *Cinema (Switzerland)* (Basel), no. 37, 1991.
Landry, G., in *24 Images* (Montreal), no. 77, Summer 1995.
Castoro Cinema (Milan), no. 176, part 1, March/April 1996.
La Rochelle, R., ''Les petites revolutions,'' in *24 Images* (Montreal), no. 83/84, Autumn 1996.
Elia, Maurice, ''*Vivre sa vie* de Jean-Luc Godard,'' in *Séquences* (Haute-Ville), no. 192, September-October 1997.
Sterritt, David, in *The Christian Science Monitor*, vol. 89, no. 226, 17 October 1997.

* * *

Jean-Luc Godard's fourth feature-length film, *Vivre sa vie*, forms the second shutter of a diptych with *A bout de souffle* (1959). The latter had rewritten the American studio tradition through the filter of French literature and philosophy. *Vivre sa vie* goes in the same direction but with sharper visual impact and keen filmic control. Its composition externalizes to an extreme degree many obsessions found in all of Godard's work. A Brechtian experiment in aesthetic and political distance, it uses the theme of prostitution to bind a number of formal experiments that touch on a variety of problems, including the relation of art and lithography to cinema, the depressing squalor of an all-encompassing zone of tastelessness comprising modern life (hence the film's allegiance to Baudelaire and to Apollinaire), the breakdown of intimacy and experience as valid measures of morality, the interfilmic mix of allusions saturating single shots and entire sequences, and the break-up of the illusion of perspective, by which words and image form an immensely ambiguous hieroglyph of contemporary life, taken from cinema, the backdrop of advertising, billboards, and newspapers.

Few of Godard's films attain the same rigor of rhythm in their play of sound and image, or their formal camera movement, as *Vivre sa vie*. Raoul Coutard, Godard's cameraman, insists on keeping a medium distance between the lens and Anna Karina, who plays the role of an exemplary, almost sacred—but very common—female who, because of economic circumstances, is forced into prostitution. She becomes a martyr in her own film. In the first sequence, he shoots the backsides of Karina and her husband as they sit apart on barstools in a café and face a mirror on the wall in front of them. The camera pans indifferently to the left and right as the futile expression of their speech shows no ostensible explanation for the dilemma. The failed meeting is conveyed by a camera that cannot reach an intimate rapport with the characters' faces. Ensuing tableaux have the camera standing fixed for long periods of time (following Nana's pen, in extreme close-up, as she writes a marginally literate letter of application for employment), or tracing a dolly of 180 degrees from profile to the front of Nana's face as she stares at her pimp who is indentified with the sightlines of the viewer. She sits in front of a wallpapered vista of Paris, copied from a painting in the Impressionist style, that flattens the heritage of art prevailing throughout the film. *Tableaux vivants* are seen in Nana's mimicry of Degas's absinthe lady seated in a café, Manet's bar at the Folies-Bergère, Van Gogh's taverns by night, and Monet's cityscapes.

Like *A bout de souffle, Vivre sa vie* is filmed in silence (in Parisian streets), with on-location noise (in record shops or in the clatter of cafés), with ruptures of music and silence (melodies being started and stopped without any cues from the image track), with speech detached from the image-track (a voice describing prostitution in a flat documentary style *off camera* while the shots register hands fumbling for pocket money or latching onto doorknobs), or with uncanny matches (the jukebox plays vivacious notes when Nana presses her body against it in the famous mating dance in the pool hall). The film makes a plastic collage of musical and filmed fragments.

Citing Montaigne on the urgency of experience (that is, of the need to draw life from death) at the outset, Godard cuts the story of Nana's life into 12 stations of sainthood. Nana's death, shot in front of a ''Café des Studios'' in a suburban zone, casually depicts the heroine falling to the asphalt between two cars; it also tells of metaphysical stress that sustains all of Godard's work, from *A bout de souffle* to *Je vous salue, Marie*, 25 years later. *Vivre sa vie* underscores an obsession with mimesis, defined in strict accord with the roots of prostitution, in the ways the film works through the etymology of *prostatuere*. In its theology of visibility, it makes of prostitution a matter of ''standing forward'': to reveal oneself to others, to ''come into view'' from anonymity, in a sort of cinematic *ecce homo*, entails the heroine's demise. An interview with a philosopher stages Nana as an everywoman who queries Brice Parain (who plays himself) on the relations of words, things, and existence to action. A comic and pathetic register is attained. Godard reaches religious and Marxian undertones as well, confirmed in a remarkable sequence, just prior to the last tableau, when Nana's new lover, a young man (banal as all the men who figure in his work), reads excerpts from Baudelaire's translation of Poe's ''The Oval Portrait.'' The passage treats of the stakes of doubling (and dubbing) a picture with words, and of the dialectic of the two, by which a narrative is finished at the price of the death of the woman portrayed. ''The Oval Portrait'' becomes *Vivre sa vie en abyme.* Godard's voice actually reads Poe by way of Baudelaire; the young man's face, covered to eye level by the book, affords no lip-synch: Godard, the male character, Baudelaire, and Poe are all part of the same travesty. Because the quotation is doubled with English subtitles that bear the ''original'' of Poe, the film reveals its own essence of ventriloquism. The relation of words to image is complicated by the same subtitles that offset the illusion of a ''true'' image or voice.

The film is a venturous mix of allusions. Godard cites Dreyer's close-ups of the martyrdom of Falconetti in shots taken from *The Passion of Joan of Arc.* Nana sees Dreyer's film in a Left Bank theater and cries in apparent sympathy for Joan/Falconetti. Already in *A bout de souffle* Jean Seberg had been aligned with the saint of Dreyer's film. That after the sequence-filming of *The Passion of Joan of Arc* Falconetti suffered a nervous breakdown and became a prostitute is well known; that Godard uses the reference to ''script'' the end of his own marriage to Karina, through allusion to Catherine Hessling in Renoir's *Nana* (of 1925), effectively complicates the quotation. It makes the sensuous close-ups of Anna (the anagram of Nana) all the more powerful in the ambivalent rapport of allusion, self-consciousness, and film history in Godard's long autobiography of cinema.

—Tom Conley

VLAK BEZ VOZNOG REDA

(Train without a Timetable)

Yugoslavia, 1959

Director: Veljko Bulajic

Production: Jadran Film; Totalscope, colour; running time: 120 minutes.

Producer: Stjepan Gurudulic; **screenplay:** Veljko Bulajic, Ivo Braut, Stjepan Perovic, and Elio Petri, based on an idea by Veljko Bulajic; **photography:** Kreso Grcevic; **editor:** Blazenka Jenci; **art director:** Dusko Jericevic; **music:** Vladimir Kraus-Rajteric.

Cast: Olivera Markovic (*Ika*); Lia-Rho Barberi (*Venka*); Inge Ilin (*Dana*); Liljana Vajler (*Zeka*); Ivica Pajer (*Nikolica*); Milan Milosevic (*Perisa*); Stole Arandjelovic (*Lovre*); Jan Sid (*Jole*).

Publications

Articles:

Variety (New York), 13 May 1959.
Kostelofsky, J., *Film Quarterly* (Berkeley), Spring 1960.

*   *   *

During the 1950s foreign directors came to Yugoslavia to make films that they were not able to make in their own countries for cultural or political reasons.

In 1959 Veljko Bulajic (one of De Sica's assistants) made *Vlak bez voznog reda* (*Train without a Timetable*), a neo-realistic epic about the transferral of whole villages from the poverty-stricken coastal regions of Dalmatia to the fertile plains of Vojvodina. By far his best film to date, *Vlak bez voznog reda* was made in the days before Bulajic embarked on a career making big budget international co-productions (usually glorifying the major battles of the Partisan war and the exploits of Comrade Tito).

The participants in this great migration travelled in freight cars with their few possessions. These trains travelled very slowly and their frequent stops allowed them to meet new people and undergo hitherto unknown experiences. Thus, the film becomes a picture about the possibilities of a better life for the travelling peasants, and about their desires and aspirations for their new land.

A film that explores human dignity, at times harshly realistic and bursting with the bitter mirth and acrid coarseness of the rough, volatile, and high-spirited people of Dalmatia, *Vlak bez voznog reda* is one of the best films of its time.

—Mike Downey

TO VLEMMA TOU ODYSSEA

(Ulysses' Gaze)

Greece-France-Italy, 1995

Director: Theo Angelopoulos

Production: Istitua Lice (Italy), La generale d'images, La Sept Cinéma, and Paradis Films (France), Basic Cinematografica, and Greek National Film Center; color; 35 mm; running time: 177 minutes; language: Greek, Albanian, Macedonian, Romanian, Bulgarian, English, and French. Released in Greece, June 1995, and in the United States, November 1997. Filmed during the Fall of 1994 and the Winter of 1994/95 in an improvised studio near the Belgrade airport; some scenes shot on location in Florina and Thessaloniki, Greece, Mostar, Bosnia, Vukovar, Croatia, Bucharest and Constanca, Romania, and Belgrade, Serbia.

Producer: Phoebe Economopoulos (executive), Eric Heumann, Giorgio Silvagni; **screenplay:** Theo Angelopoulos and Tonino Guerra with Petros Markaris; **photography:** Yorgos Arvanitis with Andreas Sinanos; **editor:** Yannis Tsitsopoulos; **production designer:** Miodrag Mile Nikolic, Giorgos Patsas, Yorgos Patsas; **sound:** Thanassis Arvanitis; Bernard Leroux; **costumes:** Giorgos Ziakas; **original music:** Eleni Karaindrou.

Cast: Harvey Keitel (*A.*); Maia Morgenstern (*Ulysses' wife and other female roles*); Erland Josephson (*Ivo Levi*); Thanassis Vengos (*taxi driver*); Yorgos Michalakopoulos (*friend in Belgrade*); Dora Volanaki (*old woman*); and others.

Awards: Grand Jury Prize and FIPRESCI Award, Cannes International Film Festival, 1995; FIPRESCI Award, European Film Awards, 1995.

Publications

Books:

Horton, Andrew, *The Films of Theo Angelopoulos: A Cinema of Contemplation.* Princeton, New Jersey, 1997.

Horton, Andrew, editor, *The Last Modernist: The Films of Theo Angelopoulos.* Westport, Connecticut, 1997.

Articles:

Maslin, Janet, "Two Films on Strife in Balkans Win Top Prizes at Cannes," in *New York Times*, 29 May 1995.

Stevens, Julie, "*Ulysses' Gaze*," in *Empire* (London), March 1996.

Rosenbaum, Jonathan, "*Ulysses' Gaze*," in *Chicago Reader* (Chicago), 18 October 1996.

Portuges, Catherine, "*Ulysses' Gaze*," in *American Historical Review* (Washington, D.C.), vol. 101, no. 4, October 1996.

Maslin, Janet, "*Ulysses' Gaze*," in *New York Times*, 17 January 1997.

* * *

Greek director Theo Angelopoulos, best known for his 1979 *The Traveling Players* (*O Thiassos*), has always been preoccupied with the complex issues of Greek history and politics. In the 1990s, he widened his interest and became interested in Balkan-wide issues, which found expressions in his films of the decade—*The Suspended Step of the Stork* (1991), *Ulysses' Gaze* (1995), and the Cannes-winner *Eternity and a Day* (1998). The characters in these films are all involved in painful, introspective journeys and confront issues of distorted harmony, irrecoverable identities, and fin-de-siècle sadness. The director's characteristic atmosphere—lonely wandering through a misty landscape—prevails throughout. Angelopoulos daringly claims that universal identity problems lurk within his peculiar Balkan universe, and raises issues of displacement and lost homelands. He endows the idiosyncratic Balkan problems with a universal humanistic dimension, far beyond the geopolitical intricacies that dominate the approaches of other Balkan filmmakers. *Ulysses' Gaze* is exclusively preoccupied with the problems of historical reconstruction and personal remembrance. The film, co-scripted by the legendary European screenwriter Tonino Guerra, carries out a nostalgic reconstruction of peaceful and colorful ethnic cohabitation at the Balkan crossroads between Orient and Occident. The narrative of the film breaks away from the linear not only time-wise, but also spatially, providing an ultimately subjective account of a personal experience of history and regionality.

The protagonist, a successful American film director named "A." (Harvey Keitel), has returned to visit his native Greece after 35 years of exile. During his brief sojourn, he hears of several film reels, now missing, shot early in the century by the legendary brothers Miltos and Yannis Manaki, who are considered patriarchs of filmmaking in the Balkan region and who lived all around the Balkans in the first half of the century, mostly in Macedonia, Bulgaria, and Greece, and made films about the region.

The memory of happy multicultural co-existence is presumably recorded on the Manaki's missing reels. A. sets off to search for the footage, and gradually grows obsessed with the belief that tracking it down and restoring it is the key to overcoming the confrontations in the Balkans. In a pensive and melancholy journey, he travels across the bleak Balkans winter, searching not only for the footage but for his own roots as well. The journey takes him on a winding road—from Greece to Albania, Macedonia, Bulgaria, Romania, Serbia, and, finally, to Sarajevo in today's Bosnia. While some of these places are explored in their present-day dimensions, others figure in the film only as memory sites of distant times and events, now called back into the mind of the protagonist.

As well as travel in space, there is travel in time. A.'s personal memories define an episode that develops in his childhood home and spans several years, starting in 1945 and running to the mid-1950s, within a sequence that lasts only a few minutes. Each minute of screen time seems to equal a year, an approach which Angelopoulos used before in his famous *Traveling Players.*

All historical explorations of the mind are referenced to the present, however. The ending point of the journey is besieged Sarajevo, where, among the shelling, A. finally finds the lost footage and the man who is able to give him access to the cherished image—Ivo Levi, the old Jewish film curator who has revealed the secret of the reels (Erland Josephson). The two men have finally found each other in this kingdom of war, and are both relaxed because now, it seems, they have all the time on Earth. They go out for a walk in the foggy but peaceful day, not suspecting that only minutes later Levi will be taken away and shot, without A. being able to react. He cries helplessly. So soon after the ultimate moment of tranquillity with Ivo Levi, he is once again alone and helpless, confronted with the absurdity of death.

By the end of the film, A. has found and seen the revered footage. But it does not matter any longer. Whatever may have been on these tapes cannot compensate for the feeling of profound dejection. The film has been about the desire to, and the impossibility of, recognizing one's own true self. By the time A. reaches what he is searching for, so much has happened and so many illusions are destroyed, that he no longer believes that the secrets of the past hold the key to harmony. *Ulysses' Gaze* is a deconstruction of self-perceptions and identity believed to be firmly rooted in space and time. Nothing can be certain anymore. Even if one is willing to adopt a conditional identity, the choice is easily invalidated. The nostalgia for lost roots is meaningless, and all that remains is the longing for something that cannot be attained. In the context of this existential pessimism, the Balkan troubles are seen as the problems of the world, as a part of the tiresome recognition of its deterioration.

Angelopoulos always preferred to discuss history as lived in personal destinies, and by the time he matured to make *Ulysses' Gaze*, he had created the prefect cinematic language that allowed him to talk of an individual experience of history as superseding time and space. The remarkable use of elaborately manipulated long shots enables the narrative to include complex and magnificent subtleties. The mostly hand-held camera of cameraman Yorgos Arvanitis moves very slowly and is often positioned in such a way that it reveals actions taking place in different semantic layers of the screen space. The events lose their objectivity and are constructed through the gaze of the onlooking protagonist. Older historical interpretations intersect with the perceived significance of newer ones.

Angelopoulos was disappointed when the Golden Palm at Cannes in 1995 went to Emir Kusturica's *Underground* rather than to his *Ulysses' Gaze*. Nonetheless, he received the Golden Palm for his next film, *Eternity and a Day* (1998). This later film, however, is nothing more than a compendium of Angelopoulos's image inventory, and can hardly be considered superior to *Ulysses' Gaze*.

—Dina Iordanova

VOINA I MIR

(War and Peace)

USSR, 1967

Director: Sergei Bondarchuk

Production: Mosfilm; Sovcolor, 35mm, scope; running time: originally 373 minutes (some sources list 507 minutes), and released in two parts, later cut to 170 minutes. Released 1967. Cost: rumored to have been anywhere between 40 and 100 million dollars.

Voina i mir

Screenplay: Sergei Bondarchuk and Vasily Solovyov; **photography:** Anatoly Petritsky, Dmitri Korzhikin and A. Zenyan; **production designer:** Mikhail Bogdanov and Gennady Myasnikov; **music:** Vyacheslav Ovchinnikov.

Cast: Ludmilla Savelyeva (*Natasha*); Sergei Bondarchuk (*Pierre*); Vyacheslav Tikhonov (*Andrei*); Anastasia Vertinskaya (*Princess Liza*); Vasily Lanovoi (*Kuragin*); Irina Skobotseva (*Hélène*); Boris Zakhava (*Kutuzov*); Vladislav Strzhelchik (*Napoleon*).

Awards: Academy award for Best Foreign Film, 1968; New York Film Critics Award, Best Foreign Film, 1968.

Publications

Books:

Khaniutin, Iurii Mironovich, *Sergei Bondarchuk*, Moscow, 1962.
Adler, Renata, *A Year in the Dark: Journal of a Film Critic 1968–1969*, New York, 1969.
Podvig, V.P., *Masterskaia Sergeia Bondarchuka*, Moscow, 1985.
Tiurin, Iurii Petrovich, *Serguéi Bondartchouk*, Moscow, 1988.

Articles:

Miller, Edwin, ''A Budding Ballet Dancer Becomes the Greatest Heroine of All Russia,'' in *Seventeen*, August 1968.
''Director of the Year,'' in *International Film Guide*, London, 1969.
Napier, Alan, ''Tolstoy Betrayed,'' in *Film Heritage* (Dayton, Ohio), Spring 1969.
Zolutossky, Igor, ''*War and Peace:* A Soviet View,'' in *London Magazine*, March 1969.
Gillett, John, ''Thinking Big,'' in *Sight and Sound* (London), Summer 1970.
Lind, John, ''The Road to *Waterloo*,'' in *Focus on Film* (London), September-October 1970.
''The Coming of the Russians,'' in *Action* (Los Angeles), June 1971.
Iskusstvo Kino (Moscow), August 1973.
Tschertok, S., in *Film und Fernsehen* (Berlin), April 1975.
Gerasimov, S., ''Soviet Cinema: Films, Personalities, Problems,'' in *Soviet Film* (Moscow), no. 271, 1979.
Kryukov, V., ''Sergei Bondarchuk,'' in *Soviet Film* (Moscow), March 1983.
Gonzalez Abreu, T., ''Crear es sufrir,'' in *Cine Cubano* (Havana), no. 107, 1984.
Houdek, J., in *Film a Doba* (Prague), July 1985.
Evtushenko, E., ''Sergei Bondarchuk,'' in *Soviet Film* (Moscow), May 1986.
''Serguei Bondartchouk,'' in *Revue du Cinéma* (Paris), no. 464, October 1991.
Birchenough, T., ''Sergei Bondarchuk,'' in *Variety* (New York), vol. 357, 7/13 November 1994.
''Never To Be Forgotten,'' in *Psychotronic Video* (Narrowsburg), no. 20, 1995.

* * *

Sergei Bondarchuk's *War and Peace*, budgeted at over $100 million, is easily the definitive version of Tolstoy's masterpiece. In *War and Peace*, the world's greatest historical novel, Tolstoy created a panorama of vivid characters who are so realistic they breathe life before the reader's eyes. ''We strove,'' Bondarchuk explained, ''with the aid of modern cinematic means, to reproduce Tolstoy's thoughts, emotions, philosophy, and ideals.'' As Penelope Gilliatt wrote in the *New Yorker*, ''Not the smallest blunder of style or proportion was made . . . . ''

Bondarchuk was not the first filmmaker to attempt to translate Tolstoy's narrative to the screen. In 1915, Vladimir Gardin and Yakov Protazanov directed a ten-reel *War and Peace*; 41 years later King Vidor made a static, overly simplified Italian-American version with Henry Fonda, Audrey Hepburn, and Mel Ferrer. Bondarchuk's film is easily the most ambitious. It is uncannily faithful to Tolstoy's characterizations, and the most spectacular feature ever made in Russia—perhaps also the most successful at the box office. The filmmaker labored on the project for over half a decade. His original cut, released in Russia in four parts, features battle scenes as grand as any ever put on the screen. Cannons were reproduced exactly as they were at the time of the story; paintings and props were borrowed from museums; 158 separate scenes were filmed, utilizing a similar number of locations all over the USSR. There were 272 sets, 6,000 military costumes, 2,000 civilian costumes, 30 starring roles, and 120,000 soldier-extras. Not unexpectedly, the most memorable sequences are the spectacles: the ball at which Natasha and Andrei are introduced; the burning of Moscow; and specifically, the Battle of Borodino. Ballerina Ludmila Savelyeva is ravishing as Natasha; Bondarchuk himself appears as Pierre.

An hour was cut for the American print, which runs 373 minutes. It was also dubbed (unnecessarily) and released in two parts—one would be presented in the afternoon, the other in the evening. Later, it was further cut to 170 minutes. Still *War and Peace* is enormous in scope. Bondarchuk, a postwar Russian actor whose career behind the camera began during the late 1950s, specialized in epic productions. *Waterloo*, the follow-up to *War and Peace*, could almost be considered a sequel.

—Rob Edelman

LE VOYAGE DANS LA LUNE

(A Trip to the Moon)

France, 1902

Director: Georges Méliès

Production: Star Film Studios (Montreuil, France); black and white, 35mm, silent; running time: 14 minutes, but varying lengths exist; length: about 825 feet. Released 1902, at Méliès's Théâtre Robert Houdin in Paris. Filmed in 1902 in Méliès's Star Film Studios at Montreuil. Cost: 10,000 francs.

Scenario: Georges Méliès; **photography:** possibly by one or more of Méliès' regular cameramen who included Leclerc, Michaut, Lallemand, and Astaix.

Le voyage dans la lune

Cast: Georges Méliès (*Barbenfouillis, President of the Astronomer's Club*); Bluette Bernon (*Phoebe on the crescent moon*); acrobats from the Folies-Bergère (*Members of the Selenite Army*).

Publications

Script:

Méliès, Georges, *Le Voyage dans la lune*, in *Avant-Scène du Cinéma* (Paris), November 1984.

Books:

Sadoul, Georges, *An Index to the Creative Work of Georges Méliès*, London 1947.
Sadoul, Georges, *French Film*, Paris, 1953.
Ford, Charles, *Georges Méliès*, Brussels, 1959.
Bessy, Maurice, and Lo Duca, *Georges Méliès, Mage*, Paris, 1961.
Sadoul, Georges, *Georges Méliès*, Paris, 1961.
Deslandes, Jacques, *Le Boulevard du cinéma à l'epoque de Georges Méliès*, Paris, 1963.
Kyrou, Ado, *De Méliès à l'expressionisme: Le Surréalisme au Cinéma*, Paris 1963.
Ceram, C. W., *Archaeology of the Cinema*, New York, 1965.
Jeanne, Rene, *Cinéma 1900*, Paris, 1965.
Malthête-Méliès, Madeleine, *Méliès, l'enchanteur*, Paris, 1973
North, Joseph, *Early Development of the Motion Picture*, New York, 1973.
Hammond, Paul, *Marvellous Méliès*, New York, 1975.
Frazer, John, *Artificially Arranged Scenes: The Films of Georges Méliès*, Boston, 1979.
Ellis, Jack C., *A History of Film*, Englewood Cliffs, New Jersey, 1979.
Usai, Paolo Cherci, *Georges Méliès*, Florence, 1983.
Jenn, Pierre, *Georges Méliès cinéaste: La Montage cinématographique chez Georges Méliès*, Paris, 1984.
Malthête-Méliès, Madeleine, *Méliès et la naissance du spectacle cinématographique*, Paris, 1984.
Sadoul, Georges, *Lumière et Méliès*, Paris, 1984.
Langlois, Henri, and others, *Méliès: Un Homme d'illusions*, Paris, 1986.

Redi, Riccardo, editor, *Verso il centenario: Méliès*, Rome, 1987.
Malthête, Jacques, *Méliès: images et illusions*, Paris, 1996.
Thompson, Frank T., *The Star Film Ranch: Texas' First Picture Show*, Plano, 1996.

Articles:

Lapierre, Marcel, ''Histoire d'un film: *Le Voyage dans la lune,*'' in *Ce Soir* (Paris), December 1937.
Cavalcanti, Alberto, ''Father of the Fantasy Film,'' in *Listener* (London), 2 June 1938.
''Méliès, pére du Cinéma, fils de Jules Verne,'' in *Cahiers du Cinéma* (Paris) no. 10, 1952.
Bessy, Maurice, ''Méliès,'' in *Anthologie du cinéma 2*, Paris, 1967.
Brakhage, Stan, ''George Méliès,'' in *Caterpillar* (New York), Spring 1970.
Langlois, Henri, ''Georges Méliès, magicien du cinéma,'' in *Cinéma* (Paris), January 1971.
Helmani, A., in *Kino* (Warsaw), January 1974.
Barnouw, Erik, ''The Magician and the Movies,'' in *American Film* (Washington D.C.), April and May 1978.
Courant, G., ''Point d'histoire: Méliès: La Fin d'un mythe?,'' in *Cinéma* (Paris), May 1979.
Quevrain, Anne Marie, ''L'Ideologie de Méliès et son époque,'' in *Cinéma* (Paris), September 1979.
Veillon, O.-R., in *Cinématographe* (Paris), January 1981.
Quevrain, Anne Marie, ''A la rédecouverte de Méliès: *Le Voyage dans la lune*,'' in *Cahiers de la Cinémathèque* (Perpignan), Autumn 1982.
Beylie, Claude, ''Actualité de Georges Méliès,'' in *Avant-Scène du Cinéma* (Paris), April 1984.
Waldekranz, R., in *Chaplin* (Stockholm), vol. 27, no. 3, 1985.
Masson, A., ''Le Cinéma incomparables: Sur Georges Méliès,'' in *Positif* (Paris), April 1985.
Miller, Ron, ''Silent Space,'' in *Filmfax* (Evanston), no. 49, March-April 1995.
Ede, François, ''De la terre à la lune,'' in *Cahiers du Cinéma* (Paris), no. 503, June 1996.
Jefferson, Margo, ''Moonstruck Magic by the Grandfather of Film Fantasies,'' in *New York Times*, vol. 147, A13 and B7, 15 November 1997.

* * *

Partly inspired by Jules Verne's early work of science fiction *De la terre à la lune* (1865) and by H. G. Wells's prophetic novel *The First Men in the Moon* (1901), Georges Méliès's *Le voyage dans la lune* (1902) is remarkable for its imaginative, and continually diverting, narrative development. The serious, didactic purpose of the literary antecedents is ignored to provide an engaging entertainment. By the turn of the century lunar episodes featured regularly in fairground shows and theatrical spectacles, and as early as 1898 Méliès had followed the fashion with short fairy-tale sequences such as *La lune à un métre.* However, with *Le voyage dans la lune*—his account of the pioneering journey to the moon undertaken by the intrepid Professor Barbenfouillis and his companions, and of their adventures with the Selenites—he surpassed all previous lunar spectacles, creating new standards in film entertainment, and in so doing accelerated the trend towards more sophisticated studio-based productions. Comprising 30 tableaux using 18 decors, the film is about 14 minutes long, and for its period was both ambitious in conception and lavish in its production values. Méliès was director, producer, set-designer, and leading actor.

In his exuberant narrative Méliès successfully mixes traditional stage-craft with his extensive repertory of special effects. The painted backdrops for the Astronomers Club, the industrial landscape with smoke rising from a host of chimneys, and the opulent Palace of the Moon King are magnificent examples of theatrical *trompe l'oeil.* Although fixed cameras are used throughout, Méliès films from different angles on the same set to create changes of perspective and viewpoint. Transitions between successive tableaux are achieved by overprinting frames, a technique borrowed from magic-lantern shows and already used extensively by the filmmaker in his version of *Cendrillon* in 1899. Several episodes, such as the launching of the spaceship and the hectic chase across the lunar landscape, have rightly become anthology pieces. Méliès's growing mastery of special effects is witnessed in the depiction of the spaceship drawing closer to the moon and landing in the moon's eye. The simulated forward travelling shot, in which a model of the moon is brought closer to a static camera, had already been exploited in *L'homme à la tête de caoutchouc* (1902). After this visual joke about the Man in the Moon, the spaceship is seen to land again in a more realistic mode, and in this double presentation Méliès extended traditional narrative conventions. Stop-camera techniques are used to change the passing stars and planets into pretty maidens, and the same trick is used to convert umbrellas into gigantic mushrooms, or to remove Selenites in a puff of smoke. For the return of the spaceship to Earth a series of different scale models was used in a rapid montage sequence, while the scenes of the craft dropping to the ocean floor and the subsequent rescue exploited the resources of an aquarium. As Pierre Jenn's analysis has shown, Georges Sadoul's long-acceptd direct equation between tableau and decor does not hold for *Le voyage dans la lune.* A given tableau may exploit more than one decor, and on occasions one decor may give rise to several tableaux.

Made in May 1902 and marketed in August of that year, the film was an immediate success. As with so many of Méliès's productions, counterfeit copies were soon circulating in America and this finally prompted Méliès to open up a transatlantic office to protect his rights. Capitalising on his success, Méliès extended the space travel genre with *Voyage à travers l'impossible* (1904), this time recounting a trip to the sun.

With its evocative sets *Le voyage dans la lune* has been frequently cited as seminal to the development of the German expressionist movement, while for its spontaneity and fantasy the film became a reference point for avant-garde filmmakers and surrealists. Buñuel, for one, acknowledged *Le voyage dans la lune* as a formative influence, while the films of René Clair and Jacques Prévert owe much to their pioneering compatriot. In *Shoot the Moon* (1962) the underground director Rudy Burckhardt paid explicit homage to Méliès, while in his film tribute *Le grand Méliès* (1952), Franju uses footage from *Le voyage dans la lune* to illustrate the director's innovative approach to filmmaking and his technical brilliance.

—R. F. Cousins

VOYAGE TO ITALY

See **VIAGGIO IN ITALIA**

VOZVRASHCHENIYE MAXIMA

See **THE MAXIM TRILOGY**

VREDENS DAG

(Day of Wrath)

Denmark, 1943

Director: Carl Theodor Dreyer

Production: Palladium Copenhagen-Tage Nielson; black and white, 35mm; running time: 92 minutes, some sources state 98 minutes; length: about 2675 meters, some sources state 2790 meters. Released 13 November 1943, Copenhagen.

Screenplay: Carl Theodor Dreyer, Mogens Skot-Hansen, and Poul Knudsen, from the play *Anne Pedersdotter* by Hans Wiers-Jenssen; **photography:** Karl Andersson; **editors:** Edith Schlüssel and Anne Marie Petersen; **sound:** Erik Rasmussen; **art director:** Erik Aaes; **music:** Poul Schierbeck; **costume designers:** K. Sandt Jensen and Olga Thomsen, from designs by Lis Fribert; **historical consultant:** Kaj Uldall.

Cast: Thorkild Roose (*Absalon*); Lisbeth Movin (*Anne, his wife*); Sigrid Neiiendam (*Merete, his mother*); Preben Lerdorff Rye (*Martin, his son*); Anne Svierkier (*Herlof's Marte*); Olaf Ussing (*Laurentius*); Albert Høeber (*The Bishop*).

Publications

Script:

Dreyer, Carl Theodor, Mogens Skot-Hansen, and Poul Knudsen, *Vredens Dag*, in *Five Films of Carl Theodor Dreyer*, Copenhagen, 1964; as *Day of Wrath*, in *Four Screenplays*, London, 1970.

Books:

Neergaard, Ebbe, *Carl Theodor Dreyer: A Film Director's Work*, London, 1950.

Trolle, Børge, *The Art of Carl Dreyer: An Analysis*, Copenhagen, 1955.

Bowser, Eileen, *The Films of Carl Dreyer*, New York, 1964.

Dreyer, Carl Theodor, *Om Filmen*, Copenhagen, 1964.

Monty, Ib, *Portrait of Carl Th. Dreyer*, Copenhagen, 1965.

Dyssegaard, Soren, editor, *Carl Th. Dreyer, Danish Film Director*, Copenhagen, 1968.

Perrin, Claude, *Carl Th. Dreyer*, Paris, 1969.

Sémolué, Jean, *Carl Th. Dreyer*, Paris, 1970.

Milne, Tom, *The Cinema of Carl Dreyer*, New York, 1971.

Ernst, Helge, *Dreyer: Carl Th. Dreyer—en Dansk Filmskaber*, Copenhagen, 1972.

Schrader, Paul, *Transcendental Style in Film: Ozu, Bresson, Dreyer*, Los Angeles, 1972.

Skoller, Donald, editor, *Dreyer in Double Reflection*, New York, 1973.

Nash, Mark, editor, *Dreyer*, London, 1977.

Tone, Pier Giorgio, *Carl Theodor Dreyer*, Florence, 1978.

Bordwell, David, *The Films of Carl Theodor Dreyer*, Berkeley, 1981.

Drouzy, Martin, *Carl Th. Dreyer født Nilson*, Copenhagen, 1982.

Carney, Raymond, *Speaking the Language of Desire: The Films of Carl Dreyer*, New York, 1989.

Jensen, Jytte, editor, *The Films of Carl Theodor Dreyer*, New York, 1989.

Dreyer, Carl Theodor, *Dreyer in Double Reflection: Carl Dreyer's Writings on Film*, Cambridge, 1991.

Drum, Jean, and Dale D. Drum, *My Only Great Passion: The Life and Films of Carl Theodor Dreyer*, Lanham, 2000.

Articles:

Duca, Lo, ''Dreyer à son sommet,'' in *Revue du Cinéma* (Paris), no. 4, 1946–47.

Manvell, Roger, in *Sight and Sound* (London), no. 60, 1947.

''Special Issue'' of *Ecran Français* (Paris), 11 November 1947.

New York Times, 26 April 1948.

Variety (New York), 28 April 1948.

Rowland, Richard, ''Carl Dreyer's World,'' in *Hollywood Quarterly*, Fall 1950.

Dreyer, Carl Theodor, ''Film Style,'' in *Films in Review* (New York), January 1952.

Laurent, Frédéric, in *Image et Son* (Paris), no. 67, 1953.

Trolle, Børge, ''The World of Carl Dreyer,'' in *Sight and Sound* (London), Winter 1955–56.

Cinéma (Paris), no. 32, 1958.

Luft, Herbert, ''Dreyer,'' in *Films and Filming* (London), June 1961.

Image et Son (Paris), no. 65, 1963.

Filmkritik (Munich), no. 2, 1963.

Bond, Kirk, ''The World of Carl Dreyer,'' in *Film Quarterly* (Berkeley), Fall 1965.

''Special Issue'' of *Kosmorama* (Copenhagen), June 1968.

''Dreyer Issue'' of *Cahiers du Cinéma* (Paris), December 1968.

''*Dies Irae* (Day of Wrath) Issue'' of *Avant-Scène du Cinéma* (Paris), February 1970.

Vaughan, Dai, ''Carl Dreyer and the Theme of Choice,'' in *Sight and Sound* (London), Summer 1974.

Petric, Vlada, ''Dreyer's Concept of Abstraction,'' in *Sight and Sound* (London), Spring 1975.

Gow, Gordon, in *Films and Filming* (London), no. 8, 1977.

De Benedictis, M., ''Dreyer: La regola de pendolo,'' in *Bianco e Nero* (Rome), January-February 1979.

Devilliers, M., ''Dreyer: La Chair et l'ombre,'' in *Cinématographe* (Paris), November 1983.

Lardeau, Y., and C. Tesson, ''Dreyer en images,'' in *Cahiers du Cinéma* (Paris), December 1983.

Coiner, M., ''Dramaturgy and Theme: A Comparison of *Day of Wrath* and Anne Pedersdotter,'' in *Literature/Film Quarterly* (Salisbury), vol. 17, no. 2, 1989.

Vredens dag

Pipolo, Tony, ''Historical Consciousness in Carl Dreyer's *Day of Wrath,*'' in *Persistence of Vision* (Maspeth, New York), no. 8, 1990.

Aparicio, J., ''*Dies Irae*,'' in *Nosferatu* (San Sebastian), no. 5, January 1991.

Masoni, T., ''Carl Theodor Dreyer: l'assoluto e il dubbio,'' in *Cineforum* (Bergamo), vol. 34, no. 339, November 1994.

Purtell, Tim, in *Entertainment Weekly*, no. 305, 15 December 1995.

* * *

Eleven years passed between Carl Th. Dreyer's first sound film, *Vampyr*, and his second, *Vredens dag*, his first Danish film in 18 years. Dreyer saw *Anne Pedersdotter*, the Norwegian play by Hans Wiers-Jenssen on which the film was based, in Copenhagen in 1909, and had always wanted to film this story of a young woman burned as a witch. However, he altered the original drama in various ways.

The film takes place in a pastor's house in the country in 1623. The 21-year-old Anne, the second wife of the elderly vicar, is suffocating in the stern atmosphere of the house and suffering from the tyranny of her mother-in-law. When the pastor's young son returns, Anne falls in love with him, finally setting free her suppressed feelings. But society strikes back. Anne, whose mother was accused of being a witch, begins to fear that she too is a witch after the pastor dies. Typical of a Dreyer film, *Vredens dag* is also about the struggle between good and evil. Anne is not only a victim of a hostile and intolerant society, she must also endure the struggle within herself.

Vredens dag is an erotic drama about a love triangle played against a background of superstition and Christian mercilessness. In the characters Dreyer has mixed the individual with the universal, showing the strong impact of society on the formation of the individual. Whether the reactions of the main characters are based on individual, personal and egotistical motives or are the results of ideas and prejudices of the time is deliberately difficult to ascertain.

In this way, *Vredens dag* is an historical film, trying to capture the spirit of the past. But it is also obvious now what was not clear at the time of the film's release; the film was also commenting on another dark period of Danish history—the German occupation, the time in which *Vredens dag* was produced. In addition, the film can also be considered a timeless drama about a human being fighting for her right to self-realization.

The film is remarkable for its intense, but quiet acting and its austere visual style, which grew out of the theme. The slow camera movements, the long travelling shots, the close-ups and medium close-ups, and the beautiful compositions, inspired by 17th-century paintings, serve as a means for Dreyer to recreate the slow pulse of the time. The formal beauty, the contrasts between black and white, the use of horizontal and vertical camera movements, and particularly the rhythm caused the Danish critics to call it formalistic. The film was negatively received in 1943, although there were those who defended it. Similarly, when the film was shown in New York in 1948, it got very mixed reviews. In England, however, where it was shown in 1946, it was praised by the press. Since then, *Vredens dag* has grown in critical reputation and is now considered one of Dreyer's masterpieces.

—Ib Monty

VYBORGSKAYA STORONA

See **THE MAXIM TRILOGY**

THE WAGES OF FEAR

See **LE SALAIRE DE LA PEUR**

WALKABOUT

Australia, 1971

Director: Nicolas Roeg

Production: Twentieth Century-Fox; Eastmancolor, 35mm; running time: 95 mins. Released 1 July 1971, New York. Filmed in Australia.

Producer: Si Litvinoff; **executive producer:** Max L. Raab; **screenplay:** Edward Bond, from the novel by James Vance Marshall; **photography:** Nicolas Roeg; **editors:** Anthony Gibbs and Alan Patillo; **production designer:** Brian Eatwell; **music:** John Barry.

Cast: Jenny Agutter (*Girl*); Lucien John (*Brother*); David Gumpilil (*Aborigine*); John Mellon (*Father*); Peter Carver (*No Hoper*); John Ilingsworth (*Husband*).

Publications

Books:

Feineman, Neil, *Nicolas Roeg*, Boston, 1978.

Houston, Beverle, and Marsha Kinder, *Self and Cinema: A Transformalist Perspective*, New York, 1980.

McFarlane, Brian, *Australian Cinema 1970–85*, London, 1987.

Lanza, Joseph, *Fragile Geometry: The Films, Philosophy and Misadventures of Nicolas Roeg*, New York, 1989.

Izod, John, *Films of Nicolas Roeg: Myth and Mind*, New York, 1992.

Salwolke, Scott, *Nicolas Roeg: Film by Film*, Jefferson, 1993.

Articles:

Filmfacts (New York), no. 14, 1971.

Variety (New York), 19 May 1971.

Canby, Vincent, in *New York Times*, 2 July 1971.

McGregor, Craig, ''*Walkabout:* Beautiful But Fake?,'' in *New York Times*, 18 July 1971.

Nichols, Bill, in *Cinema 7*, Fall 1971.

Millar, Gavin, in *Sight and Sound* (London), Winter 1971–72.

Cowie, Peter, in *International Film Guide* (London), 1972.

Gow, Gordon, ''Identity: An Interview with Nicolas Roeg,'' in *Films and Filming* (London), January 1972.

Film Quarterly (Berkeley), Summer 1973.

Milne, Tom, and Penelope Houston, ''Interview with Nicolas Roeg,'' in *Sight and Sound* (London), Winter 1973–74.

Kleinhans, Chuck, ''*Performance, Walkabout, Don't Look Now*, Nicolas Roeg—Permutations without Profundity,'' in *Jump Cut* (Chicago), September-October 1974.

Greenway, J., ''Film: No Sex, No Bushman,'' in *National Review* (New York), October 1975.

Waller, N., ''Nicolas Roeg—A Sense of Wonder,'' in *Film Criticism* (Edinboro, Pennsylvania), no. 1, 1976.

Kolker, Robert Phillip, ''The Open Texts of Nicolas Roeg,'' in *Sight and Sound* (London), Spring 1977.

Boyle, A., ''Two Images of the Aboriginal: *Walkabout*, the Novel and Film,'' in *Literature/Film Quarterly* (Salisbury, Maryland), vol.7, no. 1, 1979.

Allen, T., in *Village Voice* (New York), 10 December 1979.

Izod J., ''*Walkabout:* Wasted Journey,'' in *Sight and Sound* (London), Spring 1980.

Gomez, Joseph, ''Another Look at Nicolas Roeg,'' in *Film Criticism* (Edinboro, Pennsylvania), no. 6, 1981.

Johnson, Timothy, in *Magill's Survey of Cinema 6*, (Englewood Cliffs, New Jersey), 1981.

Lochen, K., in *Filmtidsskrift*, vol. 3, no. 4, 1985.

Held, L., ''Myth and Archetype in Nicolas Roeg's *Walkabout*,'' in *Post Script* (Jacksonville, Florida), Spring-Summer 1986.

Hickling-Hudson, A., ''White Construction of Black Identity in Australian Films about Aborigines,'' in *Literature/Film Quarterly* (Salisbury, Maryland), no. 4, 1990.

Matloff, J., ''The Video Monitor,'' in *Premiere* (Boulder), vol. 10, March 1997.

Neumaier, Joe, in *Entertainment Weekly*, no. 373, 4 April 1997.

Parsons, D., ''*Lost Highway, Walkabout*,'' in *Cinefantastique* (Forest Park), vol. 28, no. 12, 1997.

Smith, Margaret, in *Cinema Papers* (Fitzroy), no. 125, June 1998.

Macnab, Geoffrey, ''Going Walkabout,'' in *Sight & Sound* (London), vol. 9, no. 3, March 1999.

* * *

Whilst exploring the cultural clash between black and white Australia embodied in three children, Nicolas Roeg, in his first solo directorial film, inadvertently perpetuates 1960s Western thought about the death of Aboriginal culture. It was only two years prior to the making of *Walkabout* that the 1967 Referendum (necessary to make any Constitutional changes) empowered the Australian federal government to legislate on Aboriginal affairs. Suffrage was granted to Aboriginals in 1962, and whilst it is undoubtedly true that they had suffered through the imposition of an imported white culture, it is not true that Aboriginal culture is dying. David Gulpilil, a tribal man from Arnhem Land in the Northern Territory, at 16 years old, was chosen by Roeg to play the lead role in *Walkabout.* He went on to appear in

Walkabout

numerous films, television programmes, and dance performances around the world, was awarded the Australia Medal in 1987, yet continues to live in Arnhem Land.

As a white Englishman, Roeg cannot escape a European viewpoint when looking at Australia. Linear reason is eschewed for the qualities embodied by Romanticism, a movement in European art, music, and literature in the late-18th and early-19th centuries, current in England at the time of colonizing Australia. Romanticism was characterized by ''an emphasis on feeling and content rather than order and form, on the sublime, supernatural, and exotic.'' These things, along with Roeg's interest in colour, emotion, adventure, and fantasy, reflect the Romantic qualities found in this beautifully photographed film. Roeg's extensive experience behind the camera is evident here.

The film starts with a premise ''explaining'' what a walkabout is:

> In Australia when an Aborigine man-child reaches 16, he is sent out into the land. For months he must live from it. Sleep on it. Eat of its fruit and flesh. Stay alive. Even if it means killing his fellow creatures. The Aborigines call it the Walkabout.

The construction is reminiscent of an opera plot—inspired by real countries or situations, but actually a total fantasy. I long for an Ed McBain-like disclaimer at the beginning of his novels: Any similarity to real people and places is entirely unintentional. Yet the statement places the audience firmly in a real country. Where is this Australia?

The erroneous statement which suggests that walkabout is only done by boys undergoing initiation, reflects the impossibility of white culture being able to really understand Aboriginal culture. *An Illustrated Encyclopedia of Aboriginal Life* describes walkabout as being:

> The English equivalent of an expressive word which describes the nomadic habits of the large number of tribes inhabiting the drier parts of Australia. It was not a compulsive urge but dire necessity which forced them to spend the dry season wandering from one waterhole to another in search of game, vegetable, food, and water. They sometimes established scores of camps and travelled hundreds of miles; and it must be remembered that each group included elderly people, pregnant mothers, young children, and babies born on the journey, as well

as young men and women and full-grown hunters, and
that they had to carry all their possessions with them.

However, we must accept that film is a construction, and not a document of place. If a statement is presented as fact though, it should be correct. The desire for verisimilitude cannot be satisfied here, in this complex and fantastic film.

Three children, the unnamed protagonists, are thrown together as a result of far away colonising history. England needed a solution to overcrowded prisons. In 1788, the first British invaded Australia. British prisoners were deported to the unimaginable other side of the world, peopled by hundreds of distinct Aboriginal nations. Less than 200 years later, an Englishman makes an exploration on film of the friction and interchange between the indigenous and imported cultures. It is an account of their long walk together: the white siblings, near victims of a murderous father, are abandoned like the prisoners of the Crown, in a land that they do not understand and that almost kills them. They are saved by an Aboriginal boy who is undergoing his initiation into manhood. He must survive alone in the bush, as one of the conditions of his initiation. Just by being with him, they destroy him. By helping the white children, he breaks tribal law. However grateful they are to their black saviour, they cannot help but kill him, just through contact, just by misunderstanding.

The great beauty and indifference of the land unfolds as the children escape from their father. Roeg repeats the motif of animals throughout this film (predating Peter Greenaway) and capitalizes on the brilliant colour and light of the country they travel through. The young brother and older sister's school clothes are put away, and the vestiges of their culture diminish the further they walk. Eventually their guide paints them in ochres, yet he begins to turn on the transistor radio they have with them. His indigenous knowledge is contrasted with the commanding male radio voice which interrogates the audience with mathematical problems. The white boy responds with enthusiasm. He wants to take his shirt off, as his new friend has no shirt. He wants to give him his, but his sister comments that it would not fit him, and that he should keep it. She cannot help but admire the Aboriginal boy's ''nakedness,'' and an adolescent awareness of their bodies grows. The further they walk together, the more influenced by each other they become. Their friendship develops outside white society, and outside tribal culture.

The use of freeze frame, montage, almost subliminal imagery, combined with the soundtrack and music by John Barry, present a sequence of remembered fragments, like trying to recall a dream. This hauntingly moving film, despite flaws that fix it in the era of its production, allows the audience to ''complete'' it themselves. Like any successful work of art, the audience participates, freeing themselves of passivity.

The pessimism of the conclusion may be inappropriate to Australia, and particularly to Aboriginal life today, but perhaps we can see *Walkabout* as a memorial representation of all those indigenous peoples who have died in the colonising process.

The sigh of regret we hear in A. E. Housman's *A Shropshire Lad* is spoken over the memory the girl has of the three children swimming in an exquisite waterhole. It looks like Eden before awareness.

Into my heart an air that kills
From yon far country blows:
What are those blue remembered hills,
What spires, what farms are those?
That is the land of lost content,
I see it shining plain,
The happy highways where I went
And cannot come home again.

Finally, we are reminded that we can never go back: change is irreversible, *rien ne va plus.*

—Iris Wakulenko

WANDAFURU RAIFU

(After Life)

Japan, 1999

Director: Hirokazu Kore-eda

Production: Engine Film Inc. and TV Man Union; color, 35mm; running time: 118 minutes. Filmed 1998, released 1999.

Producers: Yutaka Shigenobu, Masayuki Akieda, and Shiho Sato; **screenplay:** Hirokazu Kore-eda; **photography:** Masayoshi Sukita and Yutaka Yamazaki; **editor:** Hirokazu Kore-eda; **art directors:** Toshihiro Isomi and Hideo Gunji; **music director:** Yasuhiro Kasamatsu; **sound designer:** Osamu Takizawa.

Cast: Arata (*Takashi Mochizuki*); Erika Oda (*Shiori Satonaka*); Susumu Terajima (*Satoru Kawashima*); Taketoshi Naitô (*Ichiro Watanabe*); Tanitakashi Naitô (*Takuro Sugie*); Hisako Hara (*Kiyo Nishimura*); Kyôko Kagawakei; Sadao Abe; Kisuke Shoda; Kazuko Shirakawa; Yusuke Iseya; Sayaka Yoshino; Kotaro Shiga; Natsuo Ishido; Akio Yokoyama; Tomomi Hiraiwa; Yasuhiro Kasamatsu.

Awards: Montgolfiere d'Or, Festival des Trois Continents, 1999, FIPRESCI Prize, San Sebastian International Film Festival, Holden Award for Best Script, Torino International Festival of Young Cinema, and Best Film, Buenos Aires International Festival of Independent Cinema, 1999.

Publications

Articles:

Holden, Stephen, ''In Death, a Fond Remembrance of Things Past,'' in *The New York Times*, 12 May 1999.

Klawans, Stuart, ''Memory Hotel (It's Haunted),'' in *The Nation*, 24 May 1999.

Johnson, William, ''Hirokazu Kore-eda: A Japanese Filmmaker and His Use of Memory,'' in *Film Comment* (New York), July 1999.

* * *

There are few topics so near to a filmmaker's heart and soul as that of artistic creation and of the creation of films in particular. *After Life*, part parable, part fantasy, is a film about the choices and dilemmas that face filmmakers, who must sift through the human experience to choose which images contain the power to inspire and endure.

After Life is the story of a week in the death of a group of twenty-two newly deceased souls. After their various demises, they arrive at a sort of halfway house between the living world and the afterlife, where they are interviewed by ghostly counselors who brief them on the next stage of their journey. To their surprise, they learn that they will spend this week selecting one joyful memory of the life they just left. This memory will be filmed by the crew of counselors and they will be allowed to take only the film of that one memory with them into the afterlife.

This motley group contains diverse souls: a teenage girl, a shy old woman, a punked out rebel, a staid war veteran. Each member reacts to this unexpected after-death routine in a different way, and the unfolding of their search for the perfect memory provides the dramatic thrust of the movie. The tone of *After Life* is both melancholy and comic. Though its premise is fanciful, director Kore-eda anchors the film firmly in the pedestrian, setting his post-life limbo in what appears to be (and, in fact, is) an abandoned school, with institutional beige walls and dilapidated furniture. Kore-eda's vision of the afterlife is neither mystical nor sentimental, but simply a probing search for the essence of experience.

The director of *After Life* has been obsessed throughout his career with the subject of memory, placing it again and again at the center of his films. Trained as a documentarian, he approached *After Life* by first conducting hundreds of interviews, putting the film's central question to his subjects: what memory would you choose from all your life to keep forever? Along with the dramatic story line of the film, Kore-eda intersperses these interviews, giving *After Life* the feel of an other-worldly documentary.

The film, whose title literally translates as ''Wonderful Life,'' was named for Frank Capra's 1946 film *It's a Wonderful Life*, which also relies on the device of a protagonist revisiting his memories to gain meaning from his life. Unlike most other memory films, however, Kore-eda refuses to use flashbacks to show us the memories of his characters. ''I've made it a rule never to show what someone is remembering,'' he has said ''because you begin to participate in the atrophying of the viewer's imagination.''

Instead, Kore-eda uses the film-within-a-film to emphasize the mutable nature of memory. Even our most vivid memories may be limited or embellished by time, desire, and imagination, just as the most faithful film must necessarily alter events by the act of reproducing them.

After Life, therefore, acts on many different levels. It is a gently humorous look at the tragedy of unfulfilled life. It is a modern history of Japan seen through the memories of those who lived it. It is a quizzical look at the predicament of the artist who seeks to preserve and illuminate the human condition. In a subtly ironic twist, those who refuse or are unable to choose a memory to film remain on as the filmmakers in the blandly institutional limbo, counseling the newly arrived dead about how to sort through their lives.

—Tina Gianoulis

WAR AND PEACE

See **VOINA I MIR**

THE WAVE

See **LOS REDES**

WAVELENGTH

USA, 1968

Director: Michael Snow

Production: Color, 16mm; running time: 45 minutes. Released January 1968. Filmed during one week of December 1966 in a loft in New York City.

Producer: Michael Snow; **screenplay and photography:** Michael Snow; **editor and sound recordist:** Michael Snow; **music:** Tom Wolff.

Cast: Hollis Frampton (*Man who dies*); Joyce Weiland (*Woman with bookcase/Woman listening to radio*); Amy Taubin (*Woman on telephone/Woman listening to radio*).

Awards: 4th International Experimental Film Competition (Knokke, Belgium), Grand Prize, 1968.

Publications

Books:

Youngblood, Gene, *Expanded Cinema*, New York, 1970.

Curtis, David, *Experimental Cinema*, London, 1971.

History of the American Avant-Garde Cinema, New York, 1976.

Kubelka, Peter, and others, *Une Histoire du cinéma*, Paris, 1976.

Le Grice, Malcolm, *Abstract Film and Beyond*, Cambridge, Massachusetts, 1977.

Sitney, P. Adams, *Visionary Film: The American Avant-Garde*, New York, 1979.

Dompierre, Louise, *Collected Writings of Michael Snow*, Waterloo, 1994.

Shedden, Jim, editor, *Presence and Absence: The Films of Michael Snow, 1956–1991*, Toronto, 1995.

Articles:

''Letter from Michael Snow,'' in *Film Culture* (New York), no. 46, 1967.

Mekas, Jonas, and P. Adams Sitney, ''Conversation with Michael Snow,'' in *Film Culture* (New York), Autumn 1967.

Stoller, James, in *Village Voice* (New York), 11 January and 11 April 1968.

Yalkut, Jud, in *Film Quarterly* (Berkeley), Summer 1968.

Lamberton, Bob, in *Film Culture* (New York), October 1968.

Snow, Michael, ''Letter,'' in *Film Culture* (New York), October 1968.

Sitney, P. Adams, ''Avant-Garde Film,'' in *Afterimage* (Rochester, New York), Autumn 1970.

Medjuck, Joe, "The Life and Times by Michael Snow," in *Take One* (Montreal) January-February 1971.
Michelson, Annette, "Toward Snow," in *Artforum* (New York), June 1971.
Skoller, Donald, "Aspects of Cinematic Consciousness: Suspense and Presence/Disillusion/Unified Perceptual Response," in *Film Comment* (New York), September-October 1972.
Rosenbaum, J., in *Monthly Film Bulletin* (London), February 1975.
Heath, Stephen, "Narrative Space," in *Screen* (London), no. 3, 1976.
Michelson, Annette, "About Snow," in *October* (Cambridge, Massachusetts), Spring 1979.
Goldsmith, Catherine, "The Complete Films of Michael Snow," in *The Gallery* (Toronto), March 1981.
Wees, W. C., "Prophesy, Memory, and the Zoom: Michael Snow's *Wavelength* Reviewed," in *Ciné-Tracts* (Montreal), Summer-Fall 1981.
Hamlyn, N., "Seeing Is Believing: *Wavelength* Reconsidered," in *Afterimage* (London), Winter 1982–83.
Dunovicova, N., "Focus on Plot: Michael Snow's *Wavelength*," in *On Film* (Los Angeles), Spring 1984.
Rabaté, François, "Image, récit énonciation: A propos de *Wavelength*," in *Revue d'Esthetique*, no. 6, 1984.
Sterritt, David, "Savoring the Art of Experimental Cinema," in *The Christian Science Monitor*, vol. 83, no. 163, 18 July 1991.
Johnson, K., "Being and Seeing: Michael Snow," in *Art in America*, vol. 82, July 1994.

* * *

Michael Snow's *Wavelength* established his reputation as a filmmaker and, with the prestige of the winning prize at the 4th International Experimental Film Competition, it quickly became the showpiece of a movement toward monomorphic, minimalist films (often called "structural films"). The decisiveness with which Snow staked out a territory for investigation, the simplicity and clarity of the film's overall gesture, and the intricacy of its details, were factors in the immediate and continuing attention this film has claimed.

Wavelength describes a single zoom movement for three quarters of an hour across an almost empty New York loft, resting eventually with the frame of a black-and-white photograph of waves pinned to the wall of the room. Within this pseudo-continuity there are innumerable changes of color filters, sudden shifts into negative, changes from day to night, occasional super-impositions, and a series of human events of increasing dramatic significance. The events include moving in a bookcase, listening to a song on the radio, a tramp breaking in and collapsing on the floor, and finally a woman entering and upon seeing the body, telephoning for help because she thinks he is dead.

The human events are filmed with the direct sound which interrupts the steadily increasing sine wave of piercing electronic sound which contributes largely to the uncanniness of the film. The filmmaker dissects the illusion of continuity imposed by zoom, evoking an impressive series of metaphors for memory and death in the process. The opening installation of the bookcase, with its live, unmuffled sound of footsteps mingled with the noises of the street and its commercial traffic, sets the tone of a casual documentary. As we wait for something to happen, that casualness is cancelled by the non-realistic visual and auditory events arranged to emphasize the autonomy of the camera and sound recorder of the audio-visual stimuli. Gradually we come to realize that even such conventional tools as the radio and the telephone are machines for translating sound waves into electronic traces and back into audible sound.

The zoom is a particularly appropriate tool for Snow's critique, because its movement is virtual, in actuality a relationship between two lenses, the image of an image. In the film's temporal scheme, that inner mechanism of the lens is echoed by the frame-to-frame relationship that suggests either movement or stasis depending upon the nature of the still images. The end of the film dramatizes this when Snow dissolves from one image of the photograph of the wave framed on the wall to a closer shot wholly within the photograph. The dissolve cannot be distinguished from the act of zooming. Finally, he declares the fragility of the image itself by simply changing focus on the photograph so radically that the screen goes white: the very threshold of visibility is inscribed within the lens.

Other avant-garde films have dwelled upon the uniqueness of the cinematic images, but none so systematically as *Wavelength*.

—P. Adams Sitney

LE WEEKEND

(Weekend)

France-Italy 1967

Director: Jean-Luc Godard

Production: Films Copernic, Comacico, and Lira Films (France) and Ascot-Cineraïd (Rome); Eastmancolor, 35mm; running time: 95 minutes, English version is 103 minutes. Released September 1967, Venice Film Festival. Filmed September-October 1967 around Paris.

Screenplay: Jean-Luc Godard; **assistant director:** Claude Miller; **photography:** Raoul Coutard; **editor:** Agnès Guillemot; **sound:** René Lavert; **music:** Antoine Duhamel, from Mozart, Piano Sonata, K. 576.

Cast: Mireille Darc (*Corinne*); Jean Yanne (*Roland*); Jean-Pierre Kalfon (*F.L.S.O. Leader*); Valérie Lagrange (*His companion*); Jean-Pierre Léaud (*Saint-Just/Man in phone booth*); Yves Beneyton (*F.L.S.O. member*); Paul Gégauff (*Pianist*); Daniel Pommereulle (*Joseph Balsamo*); Virginie Vignon (*Marie-Madeleine*); Yves Alfonso (*Tom Thumb*); Blandine Jeanson (*Emily Brontë/Young woman in farmyard*); Ernest Menzer (*Cook*); Georges Staquet (*Tractor driver*); Juliet Berto (*Woman in car crash/F.L.S.O. member*); Anne Wiazemsky (*Woman in farmyard/F.L.S.O. member*); Jean Eustache (*Hitchhiker*); J. C. Guilbert (*Tramp*).

Publications

Script:

Godard, Jean-Luc, *Weekend*, Paris, 1968; in *Weekend and Wind from the East: Two Films by Jean-Luc Godard*, London and New York, 1972.

Books:

Mussman, Toby, editor, *Jean-Luc Godard: A Critical Anthology*, New York, 1968.

Cameron, Ian, editor, *The Films of Jean-Luc Godard*, London, 1969.

Mancini, Michele, *Godard*, Rome, 1969.

Roud, Richard, *Jean-Luc Godard*, 2nd edition, New York, 1970.

Goldmann, Annie, *Cinéma et societé moderne: Le cinéma de 1968 à 1968: Godard, Antonioni, Resnais, Robbe-Grillet*, Paris, 1971.

Brown, Royal, editor, *Focus on Godard*, Englewood Cliffs, New Jersey, 1972.

Godard on Godard, edited by Tom Milne, London, 1972; as *Godard on Godard: Critical Writings*, edited by Milne and Jean Narboni, New York, 1986.

Farassino, Alberto, *Jean-Luc Godard*, Florence, 1974.

MacBean, James Roy, *Film and Revolution*, Bloomington, Indiana, 1975.

Monaco, James, *The New Wave*, New York, 1976.

Braudy, Leo, *The World in a Frame*, New York, 1977.

Houston, Beverle, and Marsha Kinder, *Self and Cinema: A Transformalist Perspective*, New York, 1980.

MacCabe, Colin, *Godard: Images, Sounds, Politics*, London, 1980.

Walsh, Martin, *The Brechtian Aspect of Radical Cinema*, London, 1981.

Lefèvre, Raymond, *Jean-Luc Godard*, Paris, 1983.

Bordwell, David, *Narration in the Fiction Film*, London, 1985.

Weis, Elisabeth, and John Belton, *Film Sound: Theory and Practice*, New York, 1985.

Cerisuelo, Marc, *Jean-Luc Godard*, Paris, 1989.

Loshitzky, Yosefa, *Radical Faces of Godard and Bertolucci*, Detroit, 1995.

Dixon, Wheeler Winston, *The Films of Jean-Luc Godard*, Albany, 1997.

Silverman, Kaja, and Harun Farocki, *Speaking About Godard*, New York, 1998.

Sterritt, David, *The Films of Jean-Luc Godard: Seeing the Invisible*, Cambridge, 1999.

Articles:

Capdenac, Michel, in *Lettres Françaises* (Paris), 9 January 1968.

Moskowitz, Gene, in *Variety* (New York), 10 January 1968.

Lefèvre, Raymond, in *Image et Son* (Paris), February 1968.

Salachas, Gilbert, in *Télériné* (Paris), February 1968.

Collet, Jean, and Jacques Aumont, ''Le Dur Silence des galaxies—*Weekend*,'' in *Cahiers du Cinéma*, (Paris), March 1968.

Delmas, Jean, ''*Le Weekend*: Un Utile Exercise qui s'appelle: Chine,'' in *Cinéma* (Paris), May 1968.

Taddei, Nazereno, in *Bianco e Nero* (Rome), May-June 1968.

Dawson, Jan, in *Sight and Sound* (London), Summer 1968.

Powell, Dilys, ''The Manic Side of Godard,'' in *Sunday Times* (London), 7 July 1968.

Hobson, Harold, in *Christian Science Monitor* (Boston), 29 July 1968.

Millar, Gavin, in *Monthly Film Bulletin* (London), August 1968.

Kael, Pauline, in *New Yorker*, 5 October 1968.

Adler, Renata, in *New York Times*, 27 October 1968.

Medjuck, Joe, in *Take One* (Montreal), no. 11, 1968.

Time (New York), November 1968.

MacBean, James Roy, ''Godard's *Weekend*; or, The Self-Critical Cinema of Cruelty,'' in *Film Quarterly* (Berkeley), Winter 1968.

Wood, Robin, in *Movie* (London), Winter 1968.

Whitehead, Peter, in *Films and Filming* (London), February 1969.

Henderson, Brian, ''Toward a Non-Bourgeois Camera Style,'' in *Movies and Methods*, edited by Bill Nichols, Berkeley, 1976.

Dolfi, Glen, in *Cinema Texas Program Notes* (Austin), 2 May 1978.

Fisher, R., ''*Weekend* Cinematographer Discusses His Style,'' in *Millimeter* (New York), April 1979.

Nicholls, D., ''Godard's *Weekend*: Totem, Taboo, and the Fifth Republic,'' in *Sight and Sound* (London), Winter 1979–80.

''Godard Issue'' of *Camera Obscura* (Berkeley), Fall 1982.

Lovell, Alan, ''Epic Theater and Counter Cinema,'' in *Jump Cut* (Berkeley), April 1983.

Goldschmidt, D., and P. Le Guay, interview with Agnes Guillemot, in *Cinématographe* (Paris), March 1985.

Durgnat, Raymond, ''Jean-Luc Godard: His Crucifixion and Resurrection,'' in *Monthly Film Bulletin* (London), September 1985.

''Godard Issue'' of *Revue Belge du Cinéma* (Brussels), Summer 1986.

Cahiers du Cinéma (Paris), no. 437 (supp.), November 1990.

Romney, Jonathan, ''Militant Tendency,'' in *Time Out* (London), vol. 1099, 11 September 1991.

''Lontano dal Vietnam,'' in *Castoro Cinema* (Milan), part 1, no. 176, March/April, 1996.

Rosenbaum, Jonathan, ''Godard in the Nineties: An Interview, Argument and Scrapbook,'' in *Film Comment* (New York), vol. 34, no. 5, September-October 1998.

* * *

Weekend is perhaps the most problematic film of the modern cinema's most problematic (if arguably most important) filmmaker. The problem lies partly in the complexity of the issues involved. There are the difficulties of the film itself, difficulties of obscurity in meaning, but also those arising from the nature of its radicalism, plus the wider difficulties concerning the whole 20th-century political and aesthetic debate centered on ''realism'' vs. ''modernism.''

The dominant tradition of cinema, since its inception (the Lumière films of 1895), has been ''realist'' (a better word might be ''illusionist''), based on deceiving the audience into believing they are seeing reality instead of an artificial construct. Even documentary and the newsreel are based on principles of selection and juxtaposition; reality in art can never be unmediated. This illusion of reality can easily become (and without awareness, inevitably becomes) a disguise under cover of which the dominant ideology (i.e. bourgeois, patriarchal capitalism) reproduces and reinforces itself: the representation of physical reality becomes the guarantee of a ''truth'' that is in fact ideological. Hence the first duty of the radical filmmaker is to shatter the dominant modes of representation—to destroy the illusion, to overthrow the tyranny of narrative. In our century, the cinema (with ''reality'' apparently guaranteed by the camera—''the truth 24 times a second,'' as Godard remarked in his earlier days, or ''lies 24 times a second,'' as he subsequently reformulated it) has been the last stronghold of traditional realist art, a tradition long since challenged in literature and painting. Godard's work has been central to the emergence and development of a modernist cinema, and *Weekend* is one of the key texts in that development.

The fundamental rule of a classical cinema is that everything serves the narrative: settings, characterization, realistic detail, style, presentation, etc. The narrative of *Weekend* might be linked to a clothesline: it is a necessity for hanging the wash, but what is interesting and important are the garments, linens, etc., that it sustains. The rejection of realism/illusionism and narrative dominance is at once achieved by and makes possible (it is difficult here to distinguish cause and effect) a number of strategies. For example: there are references to the film as a film (introductory captions tell us it is "a film found on the scrap-heap" and "film astray in the cosmos," and the male protagonist complains about the craziness of the movie he's in); references to other films (Buñuel's *The Exterminating Angel, Johnny Guitar, Saga of Gosta Berling*, and *Battleship Potemkin—The Searchers* are code names on the walkie-talkies while the Renoir and Truffaut references are telescoped in the caption "Arizona Jules"); printed captions throughout the film are used as interruptions which are frequently more enigmatic than explanatory; and, finally, *Weekend* is largely composed of digressions, its plot being capable of summation in a couple of sentences. Other strategies include: the use of direct address to the camera, monologue, and interview (*Weekend* contains an interesting—and exceptionally distancing—variation on this in the "Third World" section where the black African and Algerian garbage-collectors speak for each other, one staring insolently into the camera while the other, off-screen, speaks his thoughts); the foregrounding of camera-technique, as in the celebrated tracking shot along the seemingly interminable traffic jam where the camera moves steadily, imperturbably, refusing to privilege any incident or detail by linering, as well as the three 360-degree circular tracks around the farmyard during the lecture on a Mozart piano sonata; and, finally, the intrusion into the film of a number of characters superfluous to the narrative, some historical, some fictitious, and in certain cases played by the same actor (St. Just and the young man in the phone-booth, Emily Brontë—dressed as Alice-in-Wonderland—and the pianist/lecturer's assistant.)

Instead of the closed text of classical narrative, in which an omniscient author (the connection of the term to "authority" is important) leads the reader/viewer step by step towards a position of "knowledge" (which corresponds to the imposition of a value-system), we have the open text of modernism. The author ("enunciator" has become the preferred term) foregrounds himself, and in a sense discredits himself. The lack of coherent narrative frees the viewer, making him the active explorer of an open-ended network of data, references, statements, and positions. The voices that speak within the film are not structured or "placed" in relation to a dominant discourse; we are not told how we must listen to them. So, at least, runs the argument. One can accept it up to a point; certainly, as a challenge to dominant forms and dominant norms, Godard has been salutary and indispensable.

Nevertheless, *Weekend* is a film towards which, as time passes, one feels increasingly less indulgent. When it appeared (after the events of May '68, but made before them), it seemed uncannily prescient, its formal, aesthetic, and political anarchism exhilarating and liberating. Yet there were always doubts—an uneasiness, a *squeamishness*, which the film itself seemed to define as "bourgeois," and scoffed at one for feeling. Clearly in intention it is a film about the brutalization of contemporary capitalist society, but it is also in effect a brutalizing film. This becomes explicit in one of its final statements, where we are told that the horror of the bourgeoisie must be countered with even greater horror. In practice, the results of the theoretical argument outlined here became increasingly ambiguous. The abdication from "authority" can be read as Godard's somewhat disingenuous denial of responsibility, ("*I* am not making these statements, voices in the film are making them"—voices which Godard has chosen and permitted to speak). The overthrow of "realism" (the blood is obviously red paint, the film is a film) becomes a means of allowing us to find degradation (especially of women), slaughter and cannibalism *funny*. One cannot resist the suggestion that Godard is using revolutionary politics as an excuse for indulging a number of very unpleasant fantasies of sexuality and violence.

The film constructs a position for the viewer just as surely as any classical narrative (true, that position contains a certain ambivalence, but that is a phenomenon scarcely alien to classical cinema). The presentation, in the final third of the film, of the band of revolutionary guerillas is crucial to this. Godard is careful not to endorse them in any obvious, unequivocal way. Their activities are made to appear largely ridiculous and pointless, unsupported by any coherent body of revolutionary theory. Yet he is plainly fascinated by them; their very emptiness and dehumanization provide the necessary conditions for the fantasies of violence that a *constructive* radical position could only impede. The attitude found in the later *Vent d'Est* that could explicitly encourage the placing of bombs in supermarkets and label "bourgeois" any scruples we might feel about this is already fully present in *Weekend*. Foregrounding the mechanics of cinema and the process of narration by no means guarantees ideological awareness (on the part of either the filmmaker or the spectator): that is just as pernicious a myth as its corollary, that all realist art necessarily reinforces the dominant ideology.

—Robin Wood

WEST SIDE STORY

USA, 1961

Directors: Robert Wise and Jerome Robbins

Production: Mirisch Pictures, Seven Arts Productions, Beta Productions; Technicolor, Panavision, 70mm; running time: 152 minutes.

Producer: Robert Wise; **screenplay:** Ernest Lehman; **photography:** Linwood G. Dunn; **editors:** Thomas Stanford and Marshall M. Borden; **assistant directors:** Robert E. Relyea and Jerome M. Siegel; **production design:** Boris Leven; **music:** Leonard Bernstein; **sound:** Gilbert D. Merchant; **sound recording:** Murray Spivak; **choreography:** Jerome Robbins.

Cast: Natalie Wood (*Maria*); Richard Beymer (*Tony*); George Chakiris (*Bernardo*); Russ Tamblyn (*Riff*); Rita Moreno (*Anita*); Tony Mordente (*Action*); Tucker Smith (*Ice*); Simon Oakland (*Lieutenant Shrank*);

West Side Story

William Bramley (*Officer Krupkey*); Ned Glass (*Doc*); Jose De Vega (*Chino*); Sue Oaks (*Anybody's*); John Astin (*Glad Hand*); Penny Santon (*Madam Lucia*); Jay Norman (*Pepe*); Gus Trikonis (*Indio*); Robert Trompson (*Luis*); Eliot Field (*Baby John*); Larry Roquemore (*Rocco*); David Winters (*A-Rab*).

Awards: Oscars for Best Picture, Best Director, Best Supporting Actor (George Chakiris), Best Supporting Actress (Rita Moreno), Best Cinematography, Best Score, Best Editing, Best Art Direction, Best Costume Design, and Best Sound, 1961.

Publications

Books:

Kael, Pauline, *I Lost It at the Movies*, Boston, 1965.
McDonald, Dwight, *On Movies*, New Jersey, 1969.
Brode, Douglas, *The Films of the Sixties*, New Jersey, 1980.
Prouty, Howard J., in *Magill's Survey of Cinema-Volume 4*, edited by Frank Magill, Englewood, New Jersey, 1980.
Staskowski, Andrea, *Movie Musicals*, Minneapolis, 1992.
Garebian, Keith, *The Making of West Side Story*, Toronto, 1995.
Leemann, Sergio, *Robert Wise On His Films: From Editing Room to Director's Chair*, Los Angeles, 1995.
Thompson, Frank T., *Robert Wise: A Bio-Bibliography*, Westport, 1995.

Articles:

Gussow, Mel, ''*West Side Story*: The Beginnings of Something Great,'' in *The New York Times*, vol. 140, H5, 21 October 1990.
Kutner, C.J., ''Robert Wise: Part Two: Life at the Top,'' in *Bright Lights* (Cincinnati), no. 11, Fall 1993.
Sanchez, A.S., ''A Puerto Rican Reading of America,'' in *Jump Cut* (Berkeley), no. 39, June 1994.

* * *

The film *West Side Story* is based on the 1950s Broadway stage play, from an idea inspired by Shakespeare's *Romeo and Juliet*. The idea of taking one of the most famous and tragic love stories of all time and translating it to modern America, focusing it around the racial and inner city problems arising at that time (and which still exist today) was a radical one.

The Capulet and Montague families are transformed into two street gangs whose members live in the urban ghettos. The Jets (the poor, white local youth) are led by Riff (Russ Tamblyn) who centres his hatred on the local Puerto Ricans who have moved into the area to make a new beginning. The immigrant gang, the Sharks, are led by the charismatic Bernardo (George Chakiris), who still believes in the customs and patriarchy of his old world.

Conflict arises not just between the two groups that struggle to live together in this emerging new society, but also within the factions when the conventions and beliefs of the older society are put to the test and are questioned. Thus, Tony (Richard Beymer) is torn between his old solidarity with the Jets, his wish to escape from the ghetto and move on, and his instantaneous love for Maria, a girl from a different culture and race. Similarly, Maria (Natalie Wood) must face the conflict that arises between her loyalty to her family, as epitomized by her brother Bernardo, and her love for Tony. Both Tony and Maria must pay the price for breaking the existing rules of the dominant society—and both Tony and Bernardo are sacrificed in order to establish rules for the new order.

Garnering ten Academy Awards, *West Side Story* is today regarded as a classic musical. The film boasts an impressive cast, a musical score composed by Leonard Bernstein, and Jerome Robbins's choreography, which introduced a new kind of dance in musicals. Robert Wise's clever and often shocking direction brought an immediacy and pace rarely seen in musicals. The audience is immediately immersed in the plot from the opening credits when the camera zooms in at great speed on the first shot. However, critic Pauline Kael commented that the use of stereophonic music in the opening sequence left her ''clutching'' her head.

The racial tension is evident from the beginning when gang members chase a Puerto Rican down the street only to be pursued in turn. Brilliantly choreographed, the energetic routines illustrate the violence and intensity of living on the streets through dance and movement. Most impressive is the fact that Maria is played by Natalie Wood who could neither sing nor dance. Most of the routines in which she is featured compensate for these deficiencies through skillful choreography and a clever use of camera.

Rita Moreno is excellent as Anita, Bernardo's voluptuous and sexy girlfriend, who manages and manipulates her lover very well. The innocent gossipy antics of the Puerto Rican girls, who are alternately excited by and frightened of their new country, are contrasted with the ''political games'' of their male counterparts.

Although for the most part the encounters between the gangs are part of a game to keep them all amused, the fun quickly spirals out of control when the Sharks and Jets plan a final confrontation, which results in Riff's accidental stabbing by Bernardo, and Bernardo's subsequent death at Tony's hands.

Tony is the least credible character in the film. He believes that he can leave the Jets and his past behind without any problems. He sees Maria at a dance and instantly falls in love with her, ignoring all of the obvious problems arising from an interracial love match. He seems too soft to belong to a street gang; yet Tony's loyalty to his friend Riff leads him to kill Bernardo, despite the impact this will have on Maria. Even after this tragic episode Tony croons ''There's a Place for Us'' to Maria, a future for them somewhere—but there is nowhere to run. He is killed by Chico, a Shark gang member who is in love with Maria. Only after Tony's death, when the police arrive and Maria has condemned both gangs for the senseless deaths of Riff, Bernardo, and Tony, do the two gangs finally join together and carry Tony away. The confusion and fear on all of their faces makes children of them once more.

In spite of its sadness *West Side Story* ends on a positive note—with the idea that out of the violence and hatred a better society can be created in which different groups can live together.

—A. Pillai

WHEN FATHER WAS AWAY ON BUSINESS

See **OTAC NA SLUZBENOM PUTU**

WHERE CHIMNEYS ARE SEEN

See **ENTOTSU NO MIERO BASHO**

WHITE HEAT

USA, 1949

Director: Raoul Walsh

Production: Warner Bros. Pictures, Inc.; black and white: 35mm, running time: 114 minutes. Released 2 September 1949. Filmed in Warner Bros. studios; final episode filmed in Torrence, California.

Producer: Louis F. Edelman; **screenplay:** Ivan Goff and Ben Roberts, from a story by Virginia Kellogg; **photography:** Sid Hickox; **editor:** Owen Marks; **sound:** Leslie G. Hewitt; **art director:** Edward Carrere; **music:** Max Steiner; **special effects:** Roy Davidson and H. F. Koenekamp; **costume designer:** Leah Rhodes.

Cast: James Cagney (*Cody Jarrett*); Virginia Mayo (*Verna Jarrett*); Edmond O'Brien (*Hank Fallon/Vic Pardo*); Margaret Wycherly (*Ma Jarrett*); Steve Cochran (*Big Ed Somers*); John Archer (*Phillip Evans*); Wally Cassell (*Cotton Valetti*); Fred Clark (*Trader*); Ford Rainey (*Zuckie Hommell*); Fred Coby (*Happy Taylor*); G. Pat Collins (*Reader*); Mickey Knox (*Het Kohler*); Paul Guilfoyle (*Roy Parker*); Robert Osterloh (*Tommy Ryley*); Ian MacDonald (*Bo Creel*); Ray Montgomery (*Trent*); Marshall Bradford (*Chief of Police*).

White Heat

Publications

Script:

Goff, Ivan, and Ben Roberts, *White Heat*, edited by Patrick McGilligan, Madison, Wisconsin, 1984.

Books:

Marmin, Michel, *Raoul Walsh*, Paris, 1970.
Dickens, Homer, *The Films of James Cagney*, Secaucus, New Jersey, 1972.
Bergman, Andrew, *James Cagney*, New York, 1973.
Canham, Kingsley, *The Hollywood Professionals*, London and New York, 1973.
Hardy, Phil, editor, *Raoul Walsh*, Colchester, Essex, 1974.
Walsh, Raoul, *Each Man in His Time*, New York, 1974.
Higham, Charles, *Warner Brothers*, New York, 1975.
Cagney, James, *Cagney on Cagney*, New York, 1976.
Shadoian, Jack, *Dreams and Dead Ends: The American Gangster/Crime Film*, Cambridge, Massachusetts, 1977.
Silver, Alain, and Elizabeth Ward, editors, *Film Noir*, New York, 1979.
Clinch, Minty, *Cagney: The Story of His Film Career*, London, 1982.
Jenkins, Steve, *The Death of a Gangster*, London, 1982.
McGilligan, Patrick, *Cagney: The Actor as Auteur*, San Diego, 1982.
Warren, Doug, *James Cagney: The Authorised Biography*, London, 1983; revised edition, 1986.
Bookbinder, Robert, *Classics of the Gangster Film*, Secaucus, New Jersey, 1985.
Schickel, Richard, *James Cagney: A Celebration*, London, 1985; New York, 1999.
Giuliani, Pierre, *Raoul Walsh*, Paris, 1986.
Dickens, Homer, *The Complete Films of James Cagney*, Secaucus, 1989.
McCabe, John, *Cagney*, New York, 1997.

Articles:

Warshow, Robert, ''The Gangster as Tragic Hero,'' in *Partisan Review* (New York), February 1948.
Variety (New York), 31 August 1949.
New York Times, 3 September 1949.

New Yorker, 10 September 1949.

Tynan, Kenneth, ''Cagney and the Mob,'' in *Sight and Sound* (London), May 1951.

Miller, Don, ''James Cagney,'' in *Films in Review* (New York), August-September 1958.

''Walsh Issue'' of *Présence du Cinéma* (Paris), May 1962.

''Walsh Issue'' of *Cahiers du Cinéma* (Paris), April 1964.

Lloyd, R., ''Raoul Walsh,'' in *Brighton Film Review*, November and December 1969 and January 1970.

Bleys, J. P., ''William Keighley, Raoul Walsh, et le style Warner,'' in *Cahiers de la Cinémathéque* (Perpignan), Spring-Summer 1978.

Clark, T., ''*White Heat*: The Old and the New,'' in *Wide Angle* (Athens, Ohio), no. 1, 1979.

Benayoun, Robert, in *Avant-Scène du Cinéma* (Paris), 1 October 1979.

Mank, Gregory William, in *Magill's Survey of Cinema 4*, Englewood Cliffs, New Jersey, 1980.

Conley, Tom, ''Apocalypse Yesterday,'' in *Enclitic* (Minneapolis), Fall 1981-Spring 1982.

Sklar, Robert, ''L'Acteur en lutte: James Cagney contre Warner Bros.,'' in *Filméchange* (Paris), Summer 1983.

Peary, Gerald, in *American Film*, vol. 9, March 1984.

Listener (London), 17 May 1984.

Villadsen, E., ''Raoul Walsh—en gudbenådet fortaeller,'' in *Kosmorama* (Copenhagen), May 1985.

Osteen, M., ''The Big Secret: Film Noir and Nuclear Fear,'' in *Journal of Popular Film and Television* (Washington, D.C.), vol. 22, no. 2, 1994.

Cahiers du Cinéma (Paris), no. 500, March 1996.

Reid's Film Index (Wyong), no. 23, 1996.

Grob, N., ''Die Schwaerze des Schwarz,'' in *Filmbulletin* (Winterthur), vol. 39, no. 4, 1997.

* * *

One of the toughest, most hard-bitten crime films of the 1940s, *White Heat* stands at the crux between the 1930s gangster movie and the post-war *film noir*. At the center of the film is gang leader Cody Jarrett, a cold-blooded killer who runs his gang of thieves with an iron fist and a blazing pistol. As Jarrett, James Cagney gives one of the most maniacal, yet complex performances of his masterful career, harking back to the tragically ambitious mobster he played in *Public Enemy*, but adding the *noir*-ish twist of psychopathy to the character. The white heat of the title refers in part to the debilitating headaches Cody suffers; he describes them as feeling like a buzzsaw in his brain. Jarrett's migraine attacks and insane rages clearly equate his mental condition and his sociopathic profession; yet the film plays out Cody's psychosis quite astutely in the determinant relationship of the film—his perversely oedipal attachment to his mother. Although accompanied by his voluptuous (and ultimately duplicitous) bride, Cody ignores her in favour of Ma Jarrett, a hard-nosed old woman who is mentor, advisor and comforter to her only son, and who never leaves his side until he is taken to prison. Significantly, only she seems capable of seeing Cody's migraines.

Ostensibly, it is Edmond O'Brien, as police agent Hank Fallon, who plays the hero of the film, going undercover in prison to gain Jarrett's confidence and lead him to the gas chamber. Exploiting Jarrett's psychological weaknesses, Fallon manages to partially fill the emotional void left when Cody finds out his mother has been killed (the scene that provides the film's emotional peak—upon hearing the news, Jarrett wreaks havoc in a tour-de-force mad rage in the prison mess hall). Curiously, the vulnerability displayed by Jarrett—psychopathic and cold-blooded as he may be—makes the betrayal of his friendship by the bland, emotionless Fallon seem utterly reprehensible, no matter what side of the law he represents.

As directed by Raoul Walsh, the most accomplished craftsman working at Warner Brothers, *White Heat* never succumbs to heavy psychologism, but remains a lean and powerful, unrelentingly fast-paced film—the epitome of classical Hollywood filmmaking. Characteristic of Walsh, the film's mise-en-scène is filled with flourishes of camera movement, cutting and composition seamlessly constructed so as to avoid the ''artiness'' of more expressionistic *films noir*. Such classicism at the service of metaphor is nowhere better demonstrated than in the intercutting of the churning machinery of the prison workshop with close-ups of Jarrett suffering one of his disabling headaches. The sense of locale evoked by Walsh, as atmospheric in this film as in his renowned *High Sierra*, is impeccable and quite contemporary, making imaginative use of such settings as tourist courts and drive-in movie theaters. The signs of modernity are everywhere (most obviously in the ''scientific'' surveillance techniques used by the police to track Jarrett in his final caper) and add to the sense that the tragic figure of the gangster has outlived his day.

It is this sense of a modern world no longer concerned with the individual that finally lends *White Heat* its most biting, *film noir* edge, adding a thoroughly chilling level to Jarrett's self-immolation in the film's final moments. Perched atop a refinery oil drum, engaged in a hopeless gun battle with the police, and realizing his betrayal by Fallon, Jarrett fires his pistol into the drum, shouting, ''Top of the world, Ma!'' The white-hot explosion that follows not only marks Jarrett's ascension to the tragic, but equates his madness with the end of the world, announcing the definitive entry of the crime film into the atomic age.

—Ed Lowry

WHY WE FIGHT

USA, 1943–45

Directors: Frank Capra, Anatole Litvak, and Anthony Veiller

Production: Signal Services, US Army (Parts 1–4), Signal Corps Army Pictorial Service (Parts 5–7); black and white, 35mm; running time: Part 1—53 mins.; Part 2—42 mins.; Part 3—58 mins.; Part 4—54 mins.; Part 5—80 mins.; Part 6—64 mins.; Part 7—70 mins. Part 1 compiled in the 834th Signal Service Photograph Detachment, Dept. of the Interior Building, Washington, D.C.; Parts 2–7 compiled in 20th-Century studio facilities, Hollywood. Parts 1–4 released in 1943, Parts 5 and 6 released in 1944, Part 7 released in 1945.

1. PRELUDE TO WAR

Producer: Frank Capra; **screenplay:** Anthony Veiller and Eric Knight; **director:** Frank Capra; **editor:** William Hornbeck; **music:** Alfred Newman.

Why We Fight

Cast: Walter Huston (*Narrator*).

2. THE NAZIS STRIKE

Producer: Frank Capra; **screenplay:** Eric Knight, Anthony Veiller, and Robert Heller; **directors:** Frank Capra and Anatole Litvak; **editor:** William Hornbeck; **music:** Dimitri Tiomkin.

Cast: Walter Huston and Anthony Veiller (*Narrators*).

3. DIVIDE AND CONQUER

Producer: Frank Capra; **screenplay:** Anthony Veiller and Robert Heller; **directors:** Frank Capra and Anatole Litvak; **editor:** William Hornbeck; **music:** Dimitri Tiomkin.

4. THE BATTLE OF BRITAIN

Producer: Frank Capra; **screenplay:** Anthony Veiller; **director:** Anthony Veiller; **editor:** William Hornbeck; **music:** Dimitri Tiomkin.

Cast: Walter Huston and Anthony Veiller (*Narrators*).

5. THE BATTLE OF RUSSIA

Producer: Frank Capra; **screenplay:** Anatole Litvak, Anthony Veiller, and Robert Heller; **director:** Anatole Litvak; **editor:** William Hornbeck; **music:** arranged by Dimitri Tiomkin and selected from Tchaikovsky, Stravinsky, Prokofiev, Shostakovich, Rachmaninoff, and Rimsky Korsakov.

Cast: Walter Huston and Anthony Veiller (*Narrators*).

6. THE BATTLE OF CHINA

Producer: Frank Capra; **screenplay:** Anthony Veiller and Robert Heller; **directors:** Frank Capra and Anatole Litvak; **editor:** William Hornbeck; **music:** Dimitri Tiomkin.

Cast: Walter Huston and Anthony Veiller (*Narrators*).

7. WAR COMES TO AMERICA

Producer: Frank Capra; **screenplay:** Anatole Litvak and Anthony Veiller; **director:** Anatole Litvak; **editor:** William Hornbeck; **music:** Dimitri Tiomkin.

Cast: Walter Huston and Anthony Veiller (*Narrators*).

Publications

Books:

Thompson, George Raynor, and others, *The Signal Corps: The Test*, Washington, D.C., 1957.
Leyda, Jay, *Films Beget Films*, New York, 1964.
Thompson, George Raynor, Frank Capra, and others, *The Signal Corps: The Outcome*, Washington, D.C., 1966.
Capra, Frank, *Name above the Title*, New York, 1971.
Barsam, Richard, *Nonfiction Film*, New York, 1973.
Barnouw, Erik, *Documentary: A History of the Non-Fiction Film*, New York, 1974.
Willis, Donald, *The Films of Frank Capra*, Metuchen, New Jersey, 1974.
Glatzer, Richard, and John Raeburn, editors, *Frank Capra: The Man and His Films*, Ann Arbor, Michigan, 1975.
Poague, Leland, *The Cinema of Frank Capra*, New York, 1975.
Bohn, Thomas, *An Historical and Descriptive Analysis of the Why We Fight Series*, New York, 1977.
McCann, Richard Dyer, *The People's Art*, New York, 1977.
Bohnenkamp, Dennis, and Sam Grogg, editors, *Frank Capra Study Guide*, Washington, D.C., 1979.
Maland, Charles, *Frank Capra*, Boston 1980.
Zagarrio, Vito, *Frank Capra*, Florence 1985.
Carney, Raymond, *American Vision: The Films of Frank Capra*, Cambridge, 1986.
Wolfe, Charles, *Frank Capra: A Guide to References and Resources*, Boston, 1987.
Ellis, Jack C., *The Documentary Idea*, Englewood Cliffs, New Jersey, 1989.
McBride, Joseph, *American Madness: The Life of Frank Capra*, New York, 1990.
Lourdeaux, Lee, *Italian and Irish Filmmakers in America: Ford, Capra, Coppola and Scorsese*, Springfield, 1993.
Gehring, Wes D., *Populism and the Capra Legacy*, Westport, 1995.
Girgus, Sam B., *Hollywood Renaissance: The Cinema of Democracy in the Era of Ford, Capra, and Kazan*, New York, 1998.
Sklar, Robert, and Vito Zagarrio, *Frank Capra: Authorship and the Studio System*, Philadelphia, 1998.
McBride, Joseph, *Frank Capra: The Catastrophe of Success*, New York, 2000.

Articles:

Farber, Manny, ''Memorandum to the Makers of Documentary War Movies,'' in *New Republic* (New York), 5 October 1942.
Nicholson, Harold, ''*Battle of Britain*,'' in *Spectator* (London), 8 October 1943.
Agee, James, ''Newsreels and War-Record Films,'' in *Nation* (New York), 24 June 1944.
Isaacs, Hermine, ''War and Love,'' in *Theatre Arts* (New York), May 1945.
Jones, Dorothy B., ''Hollywood War Films,'' in *Hollywood Quarterly*, October 1945.
Katz, Robert and Nancy, ''Documentary in Transition, Part 1: The United States,'' in *Hollywood Quarterly*, Summer 1948.
Gallaz, Douglas W., ''Patterns in Wartime Documentaries,'' in *Quarterly of Films, Radio, and Television* (Berkeley), Winter 1955.
Nolan, Jack Edmund, ''Anatole Litvak,'' in *Films in Review* (New York), November 1967.
Murphy, William, ''The Method of *Why We Fight*,'' in *Journal of Popular Culture* (Bowling Green, Ohio), Summer 1972.
Bailey, G., ''Why We (Should Not) Fight,'' in *Take One* (Montreal), September 1975.
''Capra Issue'' of *Film Criticism* (Edinboro, Pennsylvania), Winter 1981.
Basinger, Jeanine, ''America's Love Affair with Frank Capra,'' in *American Film* (Washington, D.C.), March 1982.
Springer, C., ''Military Propaganda: Defense Department Films from World War II and Vietnam,'' in *Cultural Critique*, no. 3, Spring 1986.
Cieutat, Michel, and others, ''The Name Above the Title,'' in *Positif* (Paris), no. 317–318, July-August 1987.
Denby, David, ''It's a Wonderful War,'' in *Premiere* (Boulder), vol. 3, no. 5, January 1990.
American Heritage, vol. 45, no. 8, December 1994.
Kock, I. de., ''Frank Capra: *Why We Fight*,'' in *Film en Televisie + Video* (Brussels), no. 456, November 1995.

* * *

The *Why We Fight* series was a massive effort on the part of the United States government to indoctrinate the millions of young men and women inducted into military service following the American entry into World War II. The making of this series and other large-scale information and education films, as they were called, was planned and supervised by Frank Capra. One of the most popular Hollywood filmmakers of the late 1930s, he had no prior documentary experience.

Why We Fight was based on the assumption that servicemen would be more willing and able fighters if they knew the events that led up to, and the reasons for our participation in the war. It had to counteract the spirit of isolationism still strong in this country up to the Japanese attack on Pearl Harbor. In this attempt it offered a gigantic historical treatise from a particular, ''liberal'' point of view—that is to say the New Deal viewpoint of the Democratic administration, prevalent in the country at the time. (There is an irony here in that Capra's personal politics have always seemed to be conservative Republican, but they rested on a kind of populism that united him with the common effort led by President Franklin Roosevelt.) The historical approach was a frequent one in American documentaries, going back to *The Plow that Broke the Plains* (1936) and *The River* (1937). It was scarcely used by the wartime filmmakers of other governments, such as Great Britain or Canada, Germany or the Soviet Union.

The series is perhaps most impressive in the scale of its conception and in the skill of its execution. Almost entirely compiled from existing footage including newsreels, Allied and captured enemy records of battle, bits from Hollywood features, and Nazi propaganda films—it presents a vast and coherent panorama through editing and commentary.

The first three films—*Prelude to War, The Nazis Strike*, and *Divide and Conquer*—cover the period 1918 to 1940. They document Japanese aggression in the Orient, the growing menace of Hitler in Europe, and—above all—the changing American foreign policy and public opinion throughout these years. *The Battle of Britain, The Battle of Russia*, and *The Battle of China* cover the efforts of the allies, who were in the war before the Americans and continued to fight alongside them. *War Comes to America* offered a recapitulation and an even more detailed examination of the tremendous changes in American opinions and attitudes, as well as the conflicting impulses and ideologies that shaped them. Picking up and consolidating the themes of the first three films, it was the last one made but was intended to be shown first. Though the seven films were designed for military personnel, their excellence and dramatic power were recognized by the War Department, and some of them were made available for civilian audiences through theatrical exhibition. They were shown to all servicemen; viewing all seven was compulsory before embarkation for overseas duty.

The chief artistic problem for the makers of the films was one of giving structure to vast amounts of unstructured history. In this respect their work was like the work of Shakespeare in his chronicle plays. Dramatic form was given to each of the seven films, with exposition, mounting action, climax, denouement. They can be broken down into acts, in fact. *Divide and Conquer*, for example, has five acts, like the classical tragedy. Act I contains exposition: Germany has overrun Poland; Britain was now the goal; German strategy is outlined, and the theme of Hitler's lying treachery sounded. The content of Act II is the successful German campaign against Denmark and Norway. Act III deals with the position of France, the Maginot Line, and French weakness. Act IV comprises the German conquest of Holland and Belgium. Act V is the fall of France. The various participant countries are given character; they become characters, like dramatic personae. In this respect, rather than the Shakespearian histories, this film bears a curious resemblance to *Hamlet*, with Germany as Claudius, the murderous villain, France as Hamlet, DeGaulle and French North Africa as Horatio, and England as Fortinbras. Here, as in *Hamlet*, things are not what they seem, with the villain protesting friendship and the tragic hero constricted by an incapacity for action.

A considerable variety of visual and audio resources are used in these compiled documentaries—very nearly the full range conceivable. Visuals in *The Nazis Strike*, for instance, include, in addition to newsreel footage, excerpts from the Nazi's *Triumph of the Will, Hitlerjunge Quex*, and *Baptism of Fire;* bits of staged action (the victims of firing squads); still photos, drawings and maps; animated diagrams (animation by the Walt Disney Studio); and printed titles (Hitler's pronouncements). The sound track includes two narrators (Veiller for the factual, Huston for the emotional), quoted dialogue (Churchill, and an impersonation of Hitler), music (by one of Hollywood's best), and sound effects.

Dramatic conflict is obtained by painstaking manipulation of the combat footage. The editing conventions of matched action and screen direction are observed. The German attackers always move from right to left. A synthetic assemblage of diverse material is edited into a cause-effect order: German bombers in formation, bombs dropping from planes, explosions in villages, rubble. The result is as if all of this footage had been shot for these films—under Capra's direction.

The maps and animated diagrams give scope to the live-action sequences, clarify and relate random material for formalized patterns consistent with the actual movement involved. In *Divide and Conquer* the sequence of refugees on the roads being strafed is especially striking; one reads into the actual what has just been seen in animated representation. In another instance from the same film, the animated arrows representing the armoured Panzer divisions thrust into an outlined Ardennes forest with speed and power. The animation by itself takes on symbolic and rhetorical meaning; again in *Divide and Conquer*, swastika termites infest the base of a castle, and python-like arrows lock around the British Isles.

It must be admitted that, though the *Why We Fight* series may be greatly admired on technical and aesthetic grounds, there is some convincing evidence that it was not as effective an indoctrination as was hoped for and even thought to be. The problem, the social scientists inferred from their testings, was with the historical approach. It seemed to have the desired effects only on those with the equivalent of some college education; it seemed to be too intellectual for a majority of soldiers tested. As films, though, *Why We Fight* offer incontrovertible evidence of very great filmmaking skill and a remarkably full and varied use of film technique.

—Jack C. Ellis

THE WILD BUNCH

USA, 1969

Director: Sam Peckinpah

Production: Warner Bros. and Seven Arts, Inc.; Technicolor, 33mm, Panavision 70 (US), 70mm, CinemaScope (Europe); running time: 143 minutes (after release, the studio cut 4 scenes reducing running time to 135 minutes). Released 18 June 1969, Los Angeles. Filmed in Torréan, El Rincon del Montero, and El Romeral, Mexico.

Producers: Phil Feldman with Roy N. Sickner; **screenplay:** Walon Green and Sam Peckinpah, from an original story by Walon Green and Roy N. Sickner; **photography:** Lucien Ballard; **editor:** Louis Lombardo; **sound:** Robert Miller; **art director:** Edward Carrere; **music:** Jerry Fielding; **music supervisor:** Sonny Burke; **special effects:** Bud Hulburd; **costume designer:** Gordon Dawson.

Cast: William Holden (*Pike Bishop*); Ernest Borgnine (*Dutch Engstrom*); Robert Ryan (*Deke Thornton*); Edmond O'Brien (*Sykes*); Warren Oates (*Lyle Gorch*); Jaime Sanchez (*Angel*); Ben Johnson (*Tector Gorch*); Emilio Fernandez (*Mapache*); Strother Martin (*Coffer*); L. Q. Jones (*T. C.*); Albert Dekker (*Pat Harrigan*); Bo Hopkins (*Crazy Lee*); Dub Taylor (*Major Wainscoat*); Jorge Russek (*Lieutenant Zamorra*); Alfonso Arau (*Herrera*); Chano Urueta (*Don José*); Sonia Amelio (*Teresa*); Aurora Clavel (*Aurora*); Elsa Cardenas (*Elsa*); Fernando Wagner (*German army officer*).

The Wild Bunch

Publications

Books:

Kitses, Jim, *Horizons West*, Bloomington, Indiana, 1970.
Evans, Max, *Sam Peckinpah: Master of Violence*, Vermillion, South Dakota, 1972.
Caprara, Valerio, *Peckinpah*, Bologna, 1976.
Parish, James Robert, and Michael Pitts, *The Great Western Pictures*, Metuchen, New Jersey, 1976.
McKinney, Dough, *Sam Peckinpah*, Boston, 1979.
Seydoe, Paul, *Peckinpah: The Western Films*, Urban, Illinois, 1980.
Tuska, Jon, editor, *Close-Up: The Contemporary Director*, Metuchen, New Jersey, 1981.
Simmons, Garner, *Peckinpah: A Portrait in Montage*, Austin, 1982.
Thomas, Bob, *Golden Boy: The Untold Story of William Holden*, New York, 1983.
Arnold, Frank, and Ulrich von Berg, *Sam Peckinpah: Eine Outlaw in Hollywood*, Frankfurt, 1987.
Buscombe, Ed, editor, *The BFI Companion to the Western*, London, 1988.
Fine, Marshall, *Bloody Sam: The Life and Films of Sam Peckinpah*, New York, 1992.
Bliss, Michael, *Justified Lives: Morality and Narrative in the Films of Sam Peckinpah*, Carbondale, 1993.
Bliss, Michael, editor, *Doing It Right: The Best Criticism on Sam Peckinpah's The Wild Bunch*, Carbondale, Illinois, 1994.
Weddle, David, *If They Move, Kill 'Em: The Life and Times of Sam Peckinpah*, New York, 1994.
Prince, Stephen, *Savage Cinema: Sam Peckinpah and the Rise of Ultraviolent Movies*, Austin, 1998.
Prince, Stephen, editor, *Sam Peckinpah's The Wild Bunch*, Cambridge, 1999.

Articles:

Schrader, Paul, ''Sam Peckinpah Goes to Mexico,'' in *Cinema* (Beverly Hills), no. 3, 1969.
''Sam Peckinpah Lets It All Hang Out,'' in *Take One* (Montreal), January-February 1969.
''Man and Myth,'' in *Time* (New York), 20 June 1969.
Gilliatt, Penelope, in *New Yorker*, 5 July 1969.

Kauffmann, Stanley, in *New Republic* (New York), 19 July 1969.
Sarris, Andrew, in *Village Voice* (New York), 31 July 1969.
Clark, Arthur, in *Films in Review* (New York), August-September 1969.
Farber, Stephen, ''Peckinpah's Return: An Interview,'' in *Film Quarterly* (Berkeley), Fall 1969.
Milne, Tom, in *Sight and Sound* (London), Autumn 1969.
Whitehall, Richard, ''Talking with Peckinpah,'' in *Sight and Sound* (London), Autumn 1969.
''What the Directors Are Saying,'' in *Action* (Los Angeles), September-October 1969.
Austen, David, in *Films and Filming* (London), October 1969.
Cutts, John, ''Shoot: An Interview with Sam Peckinpah,'' in *Films and Filming* (London), October 1969.
Sragow, Michael, in *Film Society Review* (New York), November 1969.
Brown, Kenneth, in *Cineaste* (New York), Winter 1969–70.
McCarty, John, ''Sam Peckinpah and *The Wild Bunch*,'' in *Film Heritage* (Dayton, Ohio), Winter 1969–70.
Simon, John, ''Violent Idyll,'' in *Film 1969/70*, edited by Hollis Alpert and Andrew Sarris, New York, 1970.
Avant-Scène du Cinéma (Paris), May 1970.
Blum William, ''Towards a Cinema of Cruelty,'' in *Cinema Journal* (Evanston, Illinois), Spring 1972.
Shaffer, Lawrence, ''*The Wild Bunch* versus *Straw Dogs*,'' in *Sight and Sound* (London), Summer 1972.
''Peckinpah Issue'' of *Film Heritage* (Dayton, Ohio), Winter 1974–75.
Pettit, Arthur, ''Nightmare and Nostalgia: The Cinema West of Sam Peckinpah,'' in *Western Humanities Review* (Salt Lake City, Utah), Spring 1975.
Barbaro, Nick, in *Cinema Texas Program Notes* (Austin), 8 September 1975.
Pearson, M., in *Jump Cut* (Berkeley), August 1978.
Meyerson, Harold, in *Magill's Survey of Cinema 4*, Englewood Cliffs, New Jersey, 1980.
Simmon, Scott, ''Return of the Badmen,'' in *Journal of Popular Film* (Washington, D.C.), Fall 1981.
Boyero, C., in *Casablanca* (Madrid), December 1981.
Camy, G., ''Sur le sentier de l'oubli: Sam Peckinpah,'' in *Jeune Cinéma* (Paris), April-May 1982.
Rentero, J. C., ''Sam Peckinpah: El largo adios,'' in *Casablanca* (Madrid), March 1985.
Engel, L., ''Space and Enclosure in Cooper and Peckinpah: Regeneration in the Open Spaces,'' in *Journal of American Culture* (Bowling Green, Ohio), no. 2, 1991.
Holtsmark, E.B., ''The Katabasis Theme in Modern Cinema,'' in *Bucknell Review*, vol. 35, no. 1, 1991.
Triggs, J. A., ''*The Wild Bunch:* Scourges or Ministers?'' in *New Orleans Review*, no. 3, 1991.
Segaloff, N., ''Greenland,'' in *Film Comment* (New York), January-February 1993.
Torry, R., ''Therapeutic Narrative: *The Wild Bunch, Jaws*, and Vietnam,'' in *Velvet Light Trap* (Madison, Wisconsin), Spring 1993.
Weddle, David, ''Dead Man's Clothes: The Making of *The Wild Bunch*,'' in *Film Comment* (New York), May-June 1994.
Sragow, Michael, ''The Homeric Power of Peckinpah's Violence,'' in *Atlantic Monthly* (Boston), June 1994.
Redman, Nick, ''Peckinpah's Bunch,'' in *DGA Magazine* (Los Angeles), vol. 19, no. 4, August-September 1994.
Gaydos, Steven, ''Peckinpah's *Wild* Vision Restored After 26 Years,'' in *Variety* (New York), vol. 358, no. 4, 27 February 1995.
Rafferty, T., ''Artist of Death,'' in *New Yorker*, vol. 71, 6 March 1995.
Brown, G., ''Once Were Westerns,'' in *Village Voice* (New York), vol 40, 7 March 1995.
Travers, P., in *Rolling Stone*, no. 703, 9 March 1995.
Ansen, D., ''The Return of a Bloody Great Classic,'' in *Newsweek*, vol. 125, 13 March 1995.
Girard, Martin, in *Séquences* (Haute-Ville), no. 177, March-April 1995.
Simon, J., ''Wilder and Wilder,'' in *National Review*, vol. 47, 3 April 1995.
Alleva, R., ''Nihilism on Horseback,'' in *Commonweal*, vol. 122, 21 April 1995.
Higson, Charlie, ''The Shock of the Old,'' in *Sight & Sound* (London), vol. 5, no. 8, August 1995.
Seydor, Paul, David Weddle, and Edward Buscombe, ''Sam Peckinpah: Wild Things,'' in *Sight & Sound* (London), vol. 5, no. 10, October 1995.
Seydor, Paul, ''Facts about Sam,'' in *Sight & Sound* (London), vol. 6, no. 9, September 1996.
Seydor, Paul, ''*Bunch* Continued,'' in *Sight & Sound* (London), vol. 6, no. 11, November 1996.

* * *

When it was first released, *The Wild Bunch* became the subject of heated controversy among critics and the public alike due to its extraordinary level of violence. Following close on the heels of *Bonnie and Clyde*, *The Wild Bunch* surpassed the slow-motion death balletics of that film by quantum leaps, shocking and/or revolting large numbers of viewers. (At the Kansas City test screening of the 190-minute rough cut, over 30 members of the audience walked out in disgust, some reportedly throwing up in the alley behind the theater.) Twenty years later, in an age inured to graphic screen violence and gore, the violence of *The Wild Bunch* is still remarkably provocative and disturbing. This is partially because the violence is *not* gratuitous, as some have claimed, but central to the film's vision of human experience: it posits a world in which degrees of violence provide the only standards, and violent death the only liberation. If it is a world not predicated entirely on human evil, it is one at least in which there is very little good or hope for change. It seems clear today that what many people object to in Peckinpah's extravagant depiction of violence in *The Wild Bunch* is actually his dark view of human nature.

Another reason the film's violence still shocks and scintillates is its rendition by Peckinpah's stylized, optically jolting montage. Not since Eisenstein has a filmmaker so radically explored the conventions of traditional editing form. Much of the action in *The Wild Bunch* was filmed by as many as six Panavision, Mitchell, and Arriflex cameras running simultaneously at different speeds, each equipped with different lenses, including wide-angle, telephoto, and zoom. Peckinpah and his editor, Louis Lombardo, then created elaborate montage sequences by cutting footage shot in ''real time'' together with footage shot at varying decelerated speeds—all shot through a variety of lenses, some of which created a unique optical tension by zooming in and out nervously (and, amazingly, without calling attention to themselves) at appropriate moments. The perceptual impact of rapidly intercutting violent action shot at standard speed with slow-motion footage and a variety of telephoto zooms, in sequences that last as long as seven minutes, is both exhilarating and exhausting. *The Wild Bunch* is the most *optically* violent film ever made, one which relentlessly assaults the senses of its audience with a torrent of violent images to rival and finally exceed Eisenstein's achievement in ''The Odessa Steps'' sequence of *Potemkin.* (In fact, *The Wild Bunch* contains more individualized cuts than any color film ever made—3,642, in a decade when 600 was standard for the average dramatic feature.)

It seems ironic and not a little crazy today that a film so clearly focussed on themes of loyalty, honor, integrity, and heroism could have been reviled in its time for what one major critic called, ''moral idiocy.'' But that was the late 1960s, when the issues of violence in American society and American foreign policy had become central to virtually every national forum of public opinion. We stood at the end of a decade of political assassinations whose magnitude was unprecedented in our history, and we were deeply mired in a genocidal war in Vietnam. The My Lai massacre was revealed less than a year after the release of *The Wild Bunch*, but many Americans already knew what that revelation confirmed: that to fight a war against a popular insurrection is to fight a war against the populace. For many critics *The Wild Bunch* seemed to be an allegory of our involvement in Vietnam, where outlaws, mercenaries, and federal troops fought to produce the largest civilian ''body count'' since World War II. Others saw the film more generally as a comment on the level and nature of violence in American life. But nearly everyone saw that it bore some relationship to the major social issues of the times, and, depending on how one felt about *those*, one's reaction to the film was enthusiastically positive or vehemently negative—both mistaken responses to a work whose prevailing tenor is moral ambiguity from start to finish. Today it is possible to find a middle ground; for whatever else *The Wild Bunch* may be (as it is, for example, the greatest western ever made), it is clearly a major work of American art which changed forever the way in which violence would be depicted in American films, as well as permanently restructuring the conventions of its genre. That Peckinpah was unable to equal it later—as with Welles and *Citizen Kane*—is not testimony to his insufficiency a a film artist but to the extraordinary achievement of *The Wild Bunch* itself. It is, as Robert Culp remarked on its release, a film ''more quintessentially and bitterly American than any since World War II.'' Like *Kane*, *The Wild Bunch* will remain an enduring work of American art—vast and explosive, vital and violent, with something both very dark and very noble at its soul.

—David Cook

WILD STRAWBERRIES

See **SMULTRONSTÄLLET**

THE WIND

USA, 1928

Director: Victor Sjöström

Production: Metro-Goldwyn-Mayer; black and white: 35mm, silent; running time: 73 minutes; length: 6721 feet. Released 23 November 1928.

The Wind

Screenplay: Francis Marion, from the novel by Dorothy Scarborough; **titles:** John Colton; **photography:** John Arnold; **editor:** Conrad Nevrig; **production designers:** Cedric Gibbons and Edward Withers; **costume designer:** Andre-ani; **assistant director:** Harold S. Bucquet.

Cast: Lillian Gish (*Letty*); Lars Hanson (*Lige*); Montagu Love (*Roddy*); Dorothy Cummings (*Cora*); Edward Earle (*Beverly*); William Orlamond (*Sourdough*); Laon Ramon (*Leon Janney*); Carmencita Johnson and Billy Kent Schaefer (*Cora's children*).

Publications

Script:

Marion, Francis, *The Wind*, in *Avant-Scène du Cinéma* (Paris), July-August 1984.

Books:

Paine, Albert Bigelow, *Life and Lillian Gish*, New York, 1932.
Penser, Hans, *Seastrom and Stiller in Hollywood*, New York, 1969.
Gish, Lillian, *Dorothy and Lillian Gish*, New York, 1973.
Parish, James Robert, and Michael Pitts, *The Great Western Pictures*, Metuchen, New Jersey, 1976.

Petrie, Graham, *Hollywood Destinies: European Directors in Hollywood 1922–31*, London, 1985.

Forslund, Bengt, *Victor Sjöström: His Life and His Work*, translated by Peter Cowie with the assistance of Anna-Maija Marttinen and Christer Frunck, New York, 1988.

Articles:

Photoplay (New York), November 1928.

New York Times, 5 November 1928.

Film Spectator, 1 June 1929.

Vaughan, Dai, ''Victor Sjöström and D. W. Griffith,'' in *Film* (London), January-February 1958.

Turner, Charles L., ''Victor Seastrom,'' in *Films in Review* (New York), May-June 1960.

Tozzi, Romano, ''Lillian Gish,'' in *Films in Review* (New York), December 1962.

''Victor Sjöström (Seastrom),'' in *Anthologie du cinéma 1*, Paris, 1966.

Tibbetts, J. C., ''Vital Geography: Victor Seastrom's *The Wind*,'' in *Literature/Film Quarterly* (Salisbury, Maryland), Summer 1973.

Beylie, Claude, and Marcel Martin, ''Sjöström, Stiller, et l'Amérique,'' in *Ecran* (Paris), September 1978.

''Victor Sjöström,'' in *Films and Filming* (London), September 1979.

Weinberg, Herman, ''Seastrom: The Hollywood Years,'' in *American Classic Screen* (Shawnee Mission, Kansas), Fall 1979.

Jacob, L., in *Cinema Novo* (Porto), January-February 1981.

Listener (London), 20 September 1984.

Everson, William K., in *Video Review*, vol. 12, no. 8, November 1991.

DeCroix, Rick, and James L. Limbacher, ''In Memory of Lillian Gish (1893–1993),'' in *Journal of Popular Film and Television* (Washington, D.C.), vol. 22, no. 2, Summer 1994.

Brown, G., ''Deliverance,'' in *Village Voice* (New York), vol. 40, 20 June 1995.

Tumbleson, Ray, ''Potboiler Emancipation and the Prison of Pure Art: *Clarissa*, *The Wind*, and Surviving Rape,'' in *Literature/Film Quarterly* (Salisbury), vol. 25, no. 3, July 1997.

* * *

The Wind represents a turning point in two of the most important careers in film history, those of Victor Seastrom (the anglicized version of Sjöström that appeared in the credits of his American films) and Lillian Gish. *The Wind* was the last silent film either of them made, and it virtually marked the end of their star status in Hollywood. Seastrom directed one talkie before returning to Sweden; Gish's first leading lady vehicle of the sound era, *One Romantic Night*, was also her last.

The Wind belongs to that moment of precious finality when the stylistics and the techniques of cinema, developed to serve narrative without speech, were being discarded because of the exigencies of sound recording. After the success of Warner Brothers, in the late 1920s the major studios rushed to integrate the new technology. *The Wind* suffered the fate of many of the most important non-sound films made during the period of transition. It was released without the care required by a film of such unusual qualities. It is perhaps a miracle that the film survives at all when we remember that two other MGM films made by Gish at this period and the single film directed by Seastrom, *The Divine Woman*, are lost.

Gish and Seastrom had already collaborated with success on *The Scarlet Letter*. *The Wind* is another story of a woman at odds with the community in which she lives. Letty, the genteel Easterner, is alien to the rough manners of a prairie village and a prairie husband. The film expresses this directly, in the dramatization of her disgust when her sister-in-law butchers a side of beef, when her husband tries to kiss her, and when she tries in vain, to prettify their cabin. *The Wind* also depicts the disintegration of Letty's mind and spirit in this hostile world. Letty not only acts; she is acted upon by the elements, in particular the sand incessantly blown in the wind. It comes in through the cracks in the door, and she is as helpless to stop its invasion of the physical space as she is helpless to prevent it from driving her mad. *The Wind* repeatedly tests the body of the actress against the presence of nature. Even in the tacked-on happy ending mandated by the studio—Gish stretching in the doorway, defying the wind and embracing her husband—the cinematic body becomes a measure of nature.

Left alone during a particularly severe storm, Letty's anxiety mounts. She is raped by a travelling man and then manages to shoot him. After burying him, she stares through the window, in mounting hysteria, as the sand uncovers his body. This sequence is suggestive of the degree to which director and actress conspire in the creation of images that contain both the exterior world and the interpretation of those images. The camera records nature (abetted, it must be admitted, by wind machines). It also frames Gish and her eyes in the window, an interior frame. These framings, without and within, hold characters and place in precise narrative equilibrium.

—Charles Affron

WINGS OF DESIRE

See **DER HIMMEL ÜBER BERLIN**

THE WIZARD OF OZ

USA, 1939

Director: Victor Fleming

Production: Metro-Goldwyn-Mayer Pictures Corp.; Technicolor (opening and closing sequences in black and white), 35mm; running time: 101 minutes. Released 25 August 1939; re-released 1948. Filmed 1938–39 in MGM studios, Culver City, California.

Producer: Mervyn LeRoy; **screenplay:** Noel Langley, Florence Ryerson, and Edgar Allen Woolf, from the novel by L. Frank Baum; **uncredited director:** King Vidor; **photography:** Harold Rosson; **editor:** Blanche Sewell; **sound recording director:** Douglas Shearer; **production designer:** Edwin B. Willis; **art director:** Cedric Gibbons; **music:** Harold Arlen; **lyrics:** E. Y. Harburg; **special effects:** Arnold Gillespie; **costume designer:** Adrian; **assistant to Mervyn LeRoy:** Arthur Freed; **makeup:** Jack Dawn.

Cast: Judy Garland (*Dorothy*); Ray Bolger (*Hunk; the Scarecrow*); Bert Lahr (*Zeke; the Cowardly Lion*); Jack Haley (*Hickory; the Tin Woodsman*); Billie Burke (*Glinda*); Margaret Hamilton (*Miss Gulch;*

The Wizard of Oz

the Wicked Witch); Charles Grapewin (*Uncle Henry*); Clara Blandick (*Auntie Em*); Pat Walsh (*Nikko*); Frank Morgan (*Professor Marvel; the Wizard*); the Singer Midgets (*Munchkins*).

Awards: Oscars for Best Song (''Over the Rainbow''), Best Original Score, and Special Award for Judy Garland for her ''outstanding performance as a screen juvenile,'' 1939.

Publications

Books:

Zierold, Norman, *The Child Stars*, New York, 1965.
Baxter, John, *Hollywood in the Thirties*, New York, 1968.
Morella, Joe, and Edward Epstein, *Judy: The Films and Career of Judy Garland*, New York, 1969.
Taylor, John Russell, and Arthur Jackson, *The Hollywood Musical*, New York, 1971.
Juneau, James, *Judy Garland*, New York, 1974.
Finch, Christopher, *The Stormy Life of Judy Garland*, New York, 1975.
Peary, Gerald, and Roger Shatzkin, *The Classic American Novel and the Movies*, New York, 1977.
Hirschhorn, Clive, *The Hollywood Musical*, New York, 1981.
Dyer, Richard, *Heavenly Bodies: Film Stars and Society*, London, 1987.
Altman, Rick, *The American Film Musical*, London, 1989.
Cox, Stephen, *Munchkins Remember ''The Wizard of Oz'' and Beyond*, New York, 1989.
Fricke, John, and Jay Scarfone, and William Stillman, *The Wizard of Oz: The Official 50th Anniversary Pictorial History*, New York, 1989.
Harmetz, Aljean, *The Making of The Wizard of Oz*, London, 1989.
Nathanson, Paul, *Over the Rainbow: The Wizard of Oz as a Secular Myth of America*, Albany, New York, 1991.
Rushdie, Salman, *The Wizard of Oz*, London, 1992.
Cox, Stephen, *The Munchkins of Oz*, Nashville, 1996.
Harmetz, Aljean, *The Making of the Wizard of Oz: Movie Magic and Studio Power in the Prime of MGM—and the Miracle of Production #1060*, New York, 1998.
Morley, Sheridan, and Ruth Leon, *Judy Garland: Beyond the Rainbow*, New York, 1999.
Clarke, Gerald, *Get Happy: The Life of Judy Garland*, Thorndike, 2000.

Articles:

Variety (New York), 16 August 1939.
Nugent, Frank S., in *New York Times*, 18 August 1939.

New Yorker, 19 August 1939.
Green, Ward H., and others, in *Photoplay Studies* (New York), no. 12, 1939.
Greene, Graham, in *Spectator* (London), 9 February 1940.
Rosterman, Robert, ''Judy Garland,'' in *Films in Review* (New York), April 1952.
McVay, Douglas, ''Judy Garland,'' in *Films and Filming* (London), October 1961.
Sarris, Andrew, ''Likable but Elusive,'' in *Film Culture* (New York), Spring 1963.
Reid, John Howard, ''The Man Who Made *G.W.T.W.*,'' in *Films and Filming* (London), March 1967.
Reid, John Howard, ''Fleming: The Apprentice Years,'' in *Films and Filming* (London), January 1968.
Lefèvre, Raymond, in *Cinéma* (Paris), February 1972.
Tessier, Max, in *Ecran* (Paris), February 1972.
Bolger, Ray, ''*The Wizard of Oz* and the Golden Era of the American Musical Film,'' in *American Cinematographer* (Los Angeles), February 1978.
''Following the Yellow Brick Road from the Wonderful *Wizard of Oz* to *The Wiz*,'' in *American Cinematographer* (Los Angeles), November 1978.
De Fornari, O., in *Filmcritica* (Rome), February 1979.
Kahn Atkins, Irene, in *Magill's Survey of Cinema 4*, Englewood Cliffs, New Jersey, 1980.
Billman, C., ''I've Seen the Movie: Oz Revisited,'' in *Literature/Film Quarterly* (Salisbury, Maryland), vol. 9, no. 4, 1981.
Cinema Novo (Porto), January-February 1981.
Hollywood Studio, vol. 17, no. 3, 1984.
Soundings, vol. 67, no. 1, 1984.
New York Times, 16 March 1984.
Carpenter L., ''There's No Place Like Home: *The Wizard of Oz* and American Isolationism,'' in *Film and History* (Newark, New Jersey), May 1985.
Hagen, M., interview with Ray Bolger, in *Films and Filming* (London), July 1985.
Reid's Film Index (Wyong), no. 3, 1989.
Selcer, R. F., ''Home Sweet Movies,'' in *Journal of Popular Film and Television* (Washington, D.C.), no. 2, 1990.
Conlon, J., ''Kansas, Oz, and the Function of Art,'' in *Journal of Aesthetic Education* (Champaign, Illinois), no. 3, 1990.
Lindroth, J., ''Down the Yellow Brick Road: Two Dorothys and the Journey of Initiation in Dream and Nightmare,'' in *Literature/Film Quarterly* (Salisbury, Maryland), no. 3, 1990.
MacDonnell, F., ''*The Emerald City Was the New Deal:* E. Y. Harburg and the Wonderful Wizard of Oz,'' in *Journal of American Culture* (Bowling Green, Ohio), no. 4, 1990.
Rushdie, S., ''Out of Kansas,'' in *New Yorker*, 11 May 1992.
Catsos, G. J. M., ''That Wonderful Witch,'' in *Filmfax* (Evanston, Illinois), October-November 1993.
Norman, Barry, in *Radio Times* (London), vol. 280, no. 3655, 29 January 1994.
Brantley, Ben, ''Why Oz Is a State of Mind in Gay Life and Drag Shows,'' in *New York Times*, 28 June 1994.
Duncan, Jody, '''They Keep Going and Going','' in *Cinefex* (Riverside), no. 59, September 1994.
Caron, André, '''The Definitive Collector's Edition of *The Wizard of Oz*,''' in *Séquences* (Haute-Ville), no. 177, March-April 1995.
Roberts, T., in *Film Score Monthly* (Los Angeles), no. 59/60, July/August 1995.
Parla, P., ''Interview with Harry Monty,'' in *Classic Images* (Muscatine), no. 248, February 1996.
Flynn, R., ''Imitation Oz: The Sequel as Commodity,'' in *The Lion and the Unicorn*, vol. 20, no. 1, 1996.
Friedman, B., ''Relinquishing Oz: Every Girl's Anti-Adventure Story,'' in *Michigan Quarterly Review*, vol. 35, no. 1, 1996.
Page, Linda Rohrer, ''Wearing the Red Shoes: Dorothy and the Power of the Female Imagination in *The Wizard of Oz*,'' in *Journal of Popular Film and Television* (Washington, D.C.), vol. 23, no. 4, Winter 1996.
Rees, R.R., ''Munchkin Memories: Margaret Pellegrini,'' in *Classic Images* (Muscatine), no. 266, August 1997.
Sullivan, D., in *Scarlet Street* (Glen Rock), no. 25, 1997.
Celeste, R., ''*Lost Highway:* Unveiling Cinema's Yellow Brick Road,'' in *CineAction* (Toronto), no. 43, 1997.
McCarthy, Todd, ''Enhanced Reissue Proves *Wizard* Still Works Like Magic,'' in *Variety* (New York), no. 372, no. 13, 9 November 1998.
Sragow, Michael, ''A Forgotten Maker of the Unforgettable: A Name Deserving of Credit: Victor Fleming, Creator of Great Films, Favorite of Great Actors,'' in the *New York Times*, 15 November 1998.

* * *

''By courtesy of the wizards of Hollywood *The Wizard of Oz* reached the screen yesterday as a delightful piece of wonderworking which had the youngsters' eyes shining and brought a quietly amused gleam to the wiser ones,'' begins Frank Nugent's review of *The Wizard of Oz* in *The New York Times*. Produced and distributed by MGM at a cost of $2.5 million, the film is a tribute to the Hollywood style and system of filmmaking. It was a bit of ''wonderworking'' indeed, as this fantasy film would forever alter the course of the Hollywood film musical.

Begun in 1938, *The Wizard of Oz* was produced at the apex of the classic Hollywood era, when MGM had at its disposal the foremost technical experts available in Hollywood at that time. It was this standby of talent that made the production of a film like *Wizard* feasible. To mount such a project today would cost at least $50 million. Ray Bolger (the Scarecrow), then a contract player at MGM, explains: ''Working at MGM during that period was the ultimate in motion picture making, musical or otherwise.''

Wizard was photographed in a little-used three-strip technicolor process. In this process, three separate strips of black-and-white film were exposed through a prism which segregated the three primary colors. It was an extremely intricate process to handle and required enormous amounts of light to properly expose. While it was the most expensive process available to Hollywood at the time, it yielded an unequaled color quality. The studio chose the three-strip process because it worked out well with black-and-white stock. The framing of Dorothy's fantasy was processed in black-and-white, heightening the effect of the technicolor journey to Oz. The fact that the three-strip process originated in a black-and-white stock made this easier.

For these reasons the production of *Wizard* occurred entirely indoors on the sound stages of MGM. Because the film was studio-bound, a lot of responsibility fell on the special effects department. Mattes were used extensively to give depth to the Kansas landscape, and a sense of distance to the Land of Oz. Intricate trick photography was employed to allow a bicyclist and a man rowing a boat to float helplessly in a tornado.

No less important was the MGM art department. It was headed at the time by Cedric Gibbons whose career garnered 11 Academy Awards while at MGM. Elaborate sets were conceived and constructed in full scale to create Oz, the Wicked Witch's sanctuary, and the throne room of the Wizard of Oz. Working with the limitations imposed by the tri-color film process, Gibbon's department had to create a color scheme that the film stock could exploit. The result was a beautiful, color-conscious mise-en-scène.

Perhaps most miraculous was the role played by Jack Dawn and the MGM makeup department. It was Dawn's task to take three non-humans—a scarecrow, a tin man, and a lion—and bring them to life. He had to give them personalities and human characteristics that would evoke an humanity amidst the costumes dictated by their roles. This was done convincingly, resulting in three of the most elaborate makeup/costume designs to date in Hollywood: the costumes did pose certain critical problems for production, however. Bert Lahr's costume for the Cowardly Lion, for instance, weighed nearly 100 pounds. This, coupled with the intense heat caused by the lighting needed to shoot, made filming for long durations impossible, and the film had to be shot in segments with a day's shooting often ending before a scene was complete. As a result, before the next day's shooting could begin, makeup had to be meticulously matched and perfectly recreated to retain consistency. Daily rushes were used to aid this process. While this precision slowed down the production, the commitment to perfection became a trademark of MGM.

For their efforts both Jack Dawn and Cedric Gibbons received Academy Award nominations (though Gibbon's contract insured that his name would appear in the credits of *all* MGM films regardless of his involvement). This recognition, while falling on individuals, was no less a tribute to the system. It was a recognition of the elaborate collaborative nature of Hollywood filmmaking.

Though *Wizard* remains an elaborate technical achievement for its time, the technology involved has since become obsolete. Perhaps the longterm contribution of the film is the precedent it set for the type of Hollywood musical identified with MGM. *Wizard* was perhaps the earliest example of what came to be called the "integrated musical." Traditionally, music in films had been incorporated in a performance setting, establishing logical moments in which to include musical numbers, such as the review films of the thirties, including *Golddiggers* and *Forty-Second Street*. In *The Wizard of Oz* the music became another dimension of the characters' language, an extension of their personalities and feelings. There is no intrinsic logic in Dorothy's singing "Somewhere Over The Rainbow," but it is understood as a viable expression of some inner longing. The film narrative is advanced by musical numbers. Songs often replace dialogue as when the Munchkins pay tribute to Dorothy for killing their nemesis, the Wicked Witch of the East. In *Wizard*, music isn't a digression, but instead a fundamental part of the narrative structure.

The Wizard of Oz has witnessed more than 20 years of revival on both television and in theaters, remaining widely popular. Internationally, the film has enjoyed wider distribution than any other American film in history—fantasy, musical or otherwise. It would seem that the directness of the film's message—"There's no place like home"—and the sincerity of its presentation is the key. However, beneath the fantasy is one of the most polished and elaborate productions ever mounted in Hollywood. The film remains a reminder of that as well.

—Robert Winning

WOMAN IN THE DUNES

See **SUNA NO ONNA**

THE WOMEN

USA, 1939

Director: George Cukor

Production: Metro-Goldwyn-Mayer; black and white and colour; running time: 132 minutes.

Producer: Hunt Stromberg; **screenplay:** Anita Loos, Jane Murfin, from the original play by Clare Booth Luce; **photography:** Oliver T. Marsh; **editor:** Robert J. Kern; **art director:** Cedric Gibbons; **music:** Edward Ward, David Snell; **sound:** Douglas Shearer.

Cast: Norma Shearer (*Mrs. Mary S. Haines*); Joan Crawford (*Crystal Allen*); Rosalind Russell (*Mrs. Sylvia Howard Fowler*); Mary Boland (*Countess Flora Delave*); Paulette Goddard (*Miriam Aarons*); Joan Fontaine (*Mrs. Peggy John Day*); Lucille Watson (*Mrs. Moorehead*); Phyllis Poovah (*Mrs. Edith Philip Potter*); Florence Nash (*Nancy Blake*); Virginia Weidler (*Little Mary*); Ruth Hussey (*Miss Watts*); Muriel Hutchinson (*Jane*); Dennie Moore (*Olga*); Mary Cecil (*Maggie*); Marjorie Main (*Lucy*); Esther Dale (*Ingrid*); Hedda Hopper (*Dolly Dupuyster*); Mildred Shay (*Hélène*).

Publications

Books:

Carey, Gary, *Cukor and Company: The Films of George Cukor and His Collaborators*, New York, 1971.

Bernadoni, James, *George Cukor: A Critical Study and Filmography*, Jefferson, North Carolina, 1985.

Todd, Janet, *Women and Film*, New York, 1988.

Lambert, Gavin, *Norma Shearer: A Life*, New York, 1990.

McGilligan, Patrick, *George Cukor: A Double Life: A Biography of the Gentleman Director*, New York, 1992.

Levy, Emanuel, *George Cukor: Master of Elegance: Hollywood's Legendary Director and His Stars*, New York, 1994.

Guiles, Fred Lawrence, *Joan Crawford: The Last Word*, Thorndike, 1995.

Articles:

Monthly Film Bulletin (London), December 1939.

Finkle, David, and others, *Filmograph* (London), no. 4, 1973.

Bourget, Eithne, "Couleurs de Femmes de George Cukor," in *Positif* (Paris), no. 275, January 1984.

Rosterman, R. E., in *Hollywood Studio Magazine* (Studio City), vol. 22, no. 5, 1989.

Bibby, Bruce, in *Premiere* (Boulder), vol. 3, no. 11, July 1990.

Arnold, Frank, in *EPD Film* (Frankfurt), vol. 8, no. 9, September 1991.

The Women

Gretton, V., ''Talk '39: Re-Reading George Cukor's *The Women*,'' in *CineAction* (Toronto), no. 29, Fall 1992.
Reid's Film Index, no. 27, 1996.
Pierson, Melissa, in *Entertainment Weekly*, no. 312, 2 February 1996.
Télérama (Paris), no. 2440, 16 October 1996.

* * *

George Cukor's *The Women*, a comedy with an unabashedly misogynist premise, occupies a curious position in the work of a Hollywood artist celebrated for directing sympathetic, women-centred narratives. *The Women*, promoted and critically received as a sophisticated bitch-fest, capitalized as much on the well-publicized professional rivalry between MGM's leading stars—Joan Crawford, Norma Shearer, and Rosalind Russell—as upon Cukor's perceived ability to ''handle'' them.

Mary (Shearer), an upper-middle-class beauty, discovers her husband's affair with a streetsmart shopgirl (Crawford). Mary's marital troubles are publicly monitored by the women in her life who alternately gossip, scheme, and offer advice, all the while embroiled in their own less-than-successful relationships.

Initially *The Women* seems little more than an annoying, woman-against-woman film. From its notorious opening ''menagerie'' sequence to the final shot of a repentant Shearer rushing to surrender herself to domestic bliss, the film vigorously sustains the notion that a ''natural'' enmity exists between women. Nevertheless, despite the film's decidedly pre-feminist consciousness, *The Women* provides moments of pleasure and strong identifications with such powerful, glamorous, and uncompromising star presences as Crawford, Shearer, and Russell, each equal combatants in a dazzling war of words.

Paradoxically, the all-female cast of *The Women* results in the predominance of a masculine ''presence'' that serves to organize the narrative; absent men are the sole and unquestioned objects of feminine desire in the film's chaotically comic universe. Yet a subtle tension exists between this silent, monolithic male ''voice'' and the multitude of feminine voices that appear to have internalized all of its demands. Women offer advice that seems to wholly endorse a system of patriarchal values; yet, while the voice of feminine experience prescribes submissive behaviour, silence, and compromise, the women themselves rarely exhibit any of these ''qualities.'' In fact, submissive behaviour is revealed as little more than a fabulously calculated performance, silence only signals a retreat before a relentless barrage of feminine wit, and compromise becomes an aggressive tactic deployed to ensure survival.

Despite the unseen male that divides the women from one another, each woman discovers strength and wields power in an ever-shifting series of strictly female alliances; such power is further exercised and regulated as a relentless discourse that operates and intersects at all levels of class, age, and experience. Further, the film's ''blissful'' resolution is complicated when romantic love and bourgeois domesticity are comically exposed as cynical constructions that afford women their only hope for economic security or social status. Mary rushes to stand by her man, but only after she has shed all of her notions about the ''naturalness'' of marriage. Peggy's (Fontaine) ecstatic telephone reconciliation with her controlling husband comes only after she reviews the grim options open to her as a single, pregnant woman.

Crystal, the film's nominal ''bad'' woman, has much in common with Miriam (Goddard), the tough chorus girl who counsels Mary on sexual tactics and survival. Both Crystal (the leopard) and Miriam (the fox) exist outside the domesticated menagerie associated with the other women. The showdown between the ''good'' and the ''bad'' women is evenly matched, with Mary's patrician superiority losing the first round to Crystal's streetwise cool. Mary eventually triumphs, yet Crystal's defeat is temporary at best, and she delivers the final, cutting word.

While voices in *The Women* may be pitched to suggest the incoherent chattering of animals, words are, in fact, wielded with deadly efficiency and precision. Anita Loos, who completed the final version of the screenplay with Jane Murfin, claimed: ''It's always been men who find *The Women* offensive'' (see Gary Carey's *Anita Loos: A Biography*). Loos' comment underscores the way in which women's ability to master and deploy language can provoke fear and resentment in men, a theme in other Cukor films such as *Born Yesterday* (1950) and *My Fair Lady* (1964).

The Women ''naturalizes'' the inequities of the power struggle that exists between men and women, yet it also recognizes the economic powerplay that exists between women. *The Women* reflects a sympathy for the shopgirls, servants, and beauticians who are as actively engaged in the exchange of information as are their privileged, female employers. Further, the working-class women that populate the film's upper-middle-class setting include black women who are not only subject to the whims of the rich but who are also engaged in economic struggles with other white working-class women.

Women's experiences become dramas that the characters literally perform for one another; women re-enact seduction scenes, quarrels, and private conversations in loving detail to rapt audiences. Women recount their life stories, exchange confidences, and inspect each other to the point of obsessiveness. While the absent male is often invoked, each woman remains entirely focused on other women. In fact, *The Women*'s dark and horrific inverse can be found in Cukor's later film, *Gaslight* (1944), which dramatizes the deterioration of a woman kept in isolation. If the explicit project of *The Women* is to present the ''truth'' about women's relationships with one another, the film indirectly dramatizes the potential power of feminine alliances (even if, in the end, the enmity between these articulate, tough, and glamorous women diffuses any threat they might pose to male power).

Far from being passive receptacles or glamorous, fetishized objects that simply reflect male desire or anxiety, these women are continually at work shoring up, reinscribing, or controlling their positions as objects of desire. Mary's mother explains to her daughter that women have the ability to reinvent themselves while men can only see a new self ''reflected in some woman's eyes.'' Indeed, women exercise power using the options available to them, reinventing themselves through fantasy or fashion. Even if the issues of feminine desire and sexuality remain themselves buried, they nonetheless invariably re-emerge in a torrential flood of language.

Sidney's Beauty Salon becomes a site not only for women to talk, but to watch other women. The ''Jungle Red'' nail polish that circulates within this enclosed female community acquires meaning and significance, not merely as a violent and fetishized image, but as a glamorous extension that empowers women to move further away from the domestic enclosure inhabited by Mary and Peggy, and closer to the dangerous, untamed sexuality of Crystal, whose gaze, when trained upon the masculine subject, is reported to have the illuminating power of a ''searchlight.''

Indeed, women scrutinize each other, eye to eye, under the magnifying glasses at the beauty salon, and Sylvia (Russell) actually wears a suit emblazoned with applique eyes. In the end, Crystal turns her ''searchlight'' eyes upon Mary, in a gesture of defiance that threatens, if only momentarily, the passivity which defines the domestic concerns of the narrative. While Cukor's film remains disappointing for its overt endorsement of patriarchal values, pleasure is nonetheless generated by powerful women who are as obsessed with looking as they are with speaking.

—Viveca Gretton

WOMEN ON THE VERGE OF A NERVOUS BREAKDOWN

See **MUJERES AL BORDE DE UN ATAQUE DE NERVIOS**

THE WORD

See **ORDET**

THE WORLD OF APU

See **THE APU TRILOGY**

W.R.: MYSTERIJE ORGANIZMA

(W.R.: Mysteries of the Organism)

Yugoslavia, 1971

Director: Dusan Makavejev

Production: Neoplanta Film and Telepool; color, 35mm. Released 1971.

Screenplay: Dusan Makavejev; **photography:** Pega Popovic and Aleksander Perkovíc.

W.R.: Mysterije Organizma

Cast: Milena Dravíc (*Milena*); Jagoder Kaloper (*Jagoder*); Zoran Radmilovíc (*Radmilovíc*); Vica Vidovic (*Vladimir Ilyich*); Miodrag Andríc (*Soldier*); Tuli Kupferberg (*Guerilla soldier in New York City*); Jackie Curtis; Betty Dodson; Nancy Godfrey.

Awards: Luis Buñuel Prize, Cannes Film Festival, 1971.

Publications

Script:

Makavejev, Dusan, *W.R.: Mysteries of the Organism. A Cinematic Testament to the Life and Teachings of Wilhelm Reich*, New York, 1972.

Books:

Taylor, John, *Directors and Directions*, New York, 1975.
Callow, Simon, *Shooting the Actor, Or, The Choreography of Confusion*, with Dusan Makavejev, London, 1990, 1991.

Articles:

Bienstock, David, ''Why Did He Do That to Wm. Reich?,'' in *New York Times*, 7 November 1971.
Sarris, Andrew, *Village Voice* (New York), 11 November 1971.
MacBean, J. R., and E. Callenbach, ''Fight Power with Spontaneity and Humor: An Interview with Dusan Makavejev,'' in *Film Quarterly* (Berkeley), Winter 1971–72.
Mellen, Joan, in *Cineaste* (New York), Winter 1971–72.
Tirnanic, B., in *Ekran* (Ljubljana), no. 92–93, 1972.
Weightman, J., in *Ekran* (Ljubljana), no. 94–95, 1972.
MacBean, J. R., ''Sex Politics: Wilhelm Reich, World Revolution, and Makavejev's *WR*,'' in *Film Quarterly*, (Berkeley), Spring 1972.
Gow, Gordon, in *Films and Filming* (London), May 1972.
Weiner, B., in *Take One* (Montreal), June 1972.
Bonitzer, P., in *Cahiers du Cinéma* (Paris), July-August 1972.
Becker, L., in *Film Journal* (New York), September 1972.
Braucourt, G., ''Entretien avec Dusan Makavejev,'' in *Ecran* (Paris), September-October 1972.
Cervoni, A., ''Entretien avec Dusan Makavejev,'' in *Cinéma* (Paris), September-October 1972.

Lefèvre, Raymond, ''Une Affaire du coeur,'' in *Cinéma* (Paris), September-October 1972.

Tournes, A., ''Deux cinéastes yougoslaves,'' in *Jeune Cinéma* (Paris), September-October 1972.

Schiller, H., in *Filmrutan* (Stockholm), no. 3, 1973.

Webster, O., ''The Success and Failure of *WR*,'' in *Lumière* (Melbourne), May 1973.

Thomsen, C. B., ''Let's Put Life Back in Political Life: An Interview with Dusan Makavejev,'' in *Cineaste* (New York), no. 2, 1974.

Walsh, M., in *Monogram* (London), no. 5, 1974.

Santamaria, J. V. G., in *Contracampo* (Madrid), June-July 1981.

''Yugoslavia's Makavejev: Distilling Entertainment from Politics,'' in *World Press Review*, vol. 29, June 1982.

Young, Deborah, ''Yugoslavian Director Makavejev Says His Pix 'American in Feel,''' in *Variety* (New York), vol. 332, no. 13, 19 October 1988.

''*W.R.: Misterije Organizma* Section'' in *Filmkultura* (Budapest), no. 2, 1990.

Pitman, Randy, in *Library Journal*, vol. 115, no. 7, 15 April 1990.

Kenny, Glenn, in *Video Review*, vol. 11, no. 1, April 1990.

Hoberman, J., ''Socialist Realism: From Stalin to Sots,'' in *Artforum*, vol. 32, November 1993.

Cernenko, Miron, ''*Big Mak*: ili tragedija s celoveceskin licom,'' in *Iskusstvo Kino* (Moscow), no. 1, January 1994.

Hoberman, J., ''Big Mak Attack,'' in *Village Voice* (New York), vol. 40, 4 April 1995.

* * *

Dusan Makavejev's *W.R.: Mysteries of the Organism* opens with the statement; ''This film is in part a personal response to the life and teachings of Dr. Wilhelm Reich (1897–1957).'' Part documentary, part narrative fiction, part examination of contemporary American sexual mores, and part condemnation of the legacy of Stalin in the Eastern Block, *W.R.* uses the career of Wilhelm Reich as a springboard from which to tackle the still burning issue of the relationship of political oppression to sexual repression.

Both a colleague of Sigmund Freud and a member of the German Communist Party in the 1920s, Reich was one of the first psychoanalysts to attempt to show the importance of the relationship between the individual psyche and the material relations of production. For Reich, sexual repression was one of the by-products of class oppression, sexual liberation one of the goals of a revolutionary struggle. After organizing a group called SEXPOL to further develop his ideas of radical psychotherapy, Reich was thrown out of the Communist Party for advocating the ideas of Freud and kicked out of German psychoanalytic circles for being a Marxist. Fleeing Hitler, Reich immigrated to the United States in 1934; he set up a clinic in a small town in Maine. In 1956, he was arrested for quackery, his books burned; he died in a federal prison in 1957.

After moving to the United States, Reich renounced his earlier Marxist theories and often boasted of voting for Eisenhower. Interestingly, in *W.R.*, Makavejev focuses on this Reich—the later, American Reich—and on the development of his therapy techniques in the United States and Britain (outside a socialist context). Most of the first part of the film examines this Reich—through interviews with his relatives, his American neighbours, his students, even his barber—and the state of American sexual mores after Reich, but before the Sexual Revolution. An editor of *Screw* magazine conducts business in the buff and then has his penis plastercasted. Jackie Curtis discusses her sex change and the romantic difficulties it created as Pepsi ads blare over the radio. Tuli Kupferberg engages in guerilla street theater, roaming New York and fondling his toy M-16 like a giant phallus. New York shows signs of sexual emancipation, but it is commercialized. It supports rather than contradicts American capitalism and militarism; it bears no resemblance to Reich's notion of ''worker democracy.''

The last half of *W.R.*, a fictional allegory, takes place in Yugoslavia—a country which is presented as a land caught between Stalin and the U.S. dollar, where ''Marx Factor'' rules. A young worker, Milena, calls for the end of sexual repression in post-revolutionary Yugoslav society. However, after breaking off her relationship with the worker next door, Milena can only make up sermons on the value of free love, while her roommate puts the theory into practice by exuberantly screwing a member of the army home on leave. At a performance of the Soviet Ice Capades, Milena sees and falls in love with Vladimir Ilyich, a handsome young skating star. (Of course, this is a self-conscious reference to Lenin, whose real name was Vladimir Ilyich Ulyanov. In the film, Vladimir Ilyich even recites a number of Lenin's more famous sayings verbatim.) Milena seduces Vladimir Ilyich, but unable to deal with the liberating force of his orgasm, Vladimir Ilyich goes mad and decapitates Milena with his iceskate. In the morgue, Milena's severed head analyzes the problem: ''Vladimir is a man of noble impetuousness, a man of high ambition, of immense energy. He's romantic, ascetic, a genuine Red Fascist Comrades! Even now I'm not ashamed of my Communist past!'' The film ends with a photograph of Reich's smiling face.

W.R. was the last film Makavejev made in Yugoslavia. After it was banned there, Makavejev was effectively excluded from the Yugoslav film industry. Also, although *W.R.* won the Luis Buñuel prize at Cannes in 1971, the film never received a large theatrical release in the United States, its distribution limited in some areas to pornography cinemas where it was billed as a ''sex film.''

—Gina Marchetti

WRITTEN ON THE WIND

USA, 1956

Director: Douglas Sirk

Production: Universal Pictures; Technicolor, 35mm; running time: 99 minutes. Released 1956. Filmed November 1955-January 1956.

Producer: Albert Zugsmith; **screenplay:** George Zuckerman, from the novel by Robert Wilder; **photography:** Russell Metty; **editor:** Russell Schoengarth; **art directors:** Alexander Golitzen, Robert Clatworthy, Russell A. Gausman, and Julia Heron; **music:** Frank Skinner and Joseph Gershenson; **special effects:** Clifford Stine; **costume designer:** Bill Thomas.

Cast: Rock Hudson (*Mitch Wayne*); Lauren Bacall (*Lucy Moore Hadley*); Robert Stack (*Kyle Hadley*); Dorothy Malone (*Marylee Hadley*); Robert Keith (*Jasper Hadley*); Grant Williams (*Biff Miley*); Harry Shannon (*Hoak Wayne*); Robert J. Wilke (*Dan Willis*); Edward Platt (*Dr. Cochran*); John Latch (*Roy Carter*); Joseph Cranby (*R. J. Courtney*); Roy Glenn (*Sam*); Maide Norman (*Bertha*).

Written on the Wind

Awards: Oscar for Best Supporting Actress (Malone), 1956.

Publications

Books:

Halliday, Jon, *Sirk on Sirk*, London, 1971; New York, 1972.
Bourget, Jean-Loup, *Douglas Sirk*, Paris, 1984.
Althen, Michael, *Rock Hudson: Seine Filme, sein leben*, Munich, 1986.
Hudson, Rock and Sara Davidson, *Rock Hudson: His Story*, London, 1986.
Quirk, Lawrence J., *Lauren Bacall: Her Films and Career*, Secaucus, New Jersey, 1986.
Gledhill, Christine, editor, *Home Is Where the Heart Is: Studies in Melodrama and the Woman's Film*, London, 1987.
Läufer, Elisabeth, *Skeptiker des Lichts: Douglas Sirk und seine Filme*, Frankfurt, 1987.
Fischer, Lucy, editor, *Imitation of Life: Douglas Sirk, Director*, New Brunswick, 1991.
Parker, John, *Five for Hollywood*, Secaucus, 1991.
Scott Royce, Brenda, *Lauren Bacall: A Bio-Bibliography*, Westport, 1992.
Scott Royce, Brenda, *Rock Hudson: A Bio-Bibliography*, Westport, 1995.

Articles:

Marcorelles, Louis, ''Le Film gratuit,'' in *Cahiers du Cinéma* (Paris), March 1957.
Hagen, Ray, ''Lauren Bacall,'' in *Films in Review* (New York), April 1964.
Brion, Patrick, and Dominique Rabourdin, ''Biofilmographie de Douglas Sirk,'' in *Cahiers du Cinéma* (Paris), April 1967.
Comolli, Jean-Louis, ''L'Aveugle et le miroir; ou, L'Impossible Cinéma de Douglas Sirk,'' in *Cahiers du Cinéma* (Paris), April 1967.
Daney, Serge, and Jean Louis Noames, ''Entretien avec Douglas Sirk,'' in *Cahiers du Cinéma* (Paris), April 1967.
Halliday, Jon, ''Sirk on Sirk,'' in *Cinema One* (London), no. 18, 1971.
''Sirk Issue'' of *Screen* (London), Summer 1971.
Bourget, E., and J. L. Bourget, ''Sur Douglas Sirk,'' in *Positif* (Paris), April and September 1972.

Willemen, Paul, ''Towards an Analysis of the Sirkian System,'' in *Screen* (London), Winter 1972–73.

Stern, M., ''Patterns of Power and Potency, Repression and Violence,'' in *Velvet Light Trap* (Madison, Wisconsin), Fall 1976.

Mulvey, Laura, ''Douglas Sirk and Melodrama,'' in *Australian Journal of Screen Theory* (Kensington, New South Wales), no. 3, 1977.

Mulvey, Laura, ''Notes on Sirk and Melodrama,'' in *Movie* (London), Winter 1977–78.

Honickel, T., ''Idol der Münchner Filmstudenten: Douglas Sirk weider in der HFF,'' in *Film und Ton* (Munich), February 1979.

Place, Janey, in *Magill's Survey of Cinema 4*, Englewood Cliffs, New Jersey, 1980.

Orr, Christopher, ''Closure and Containment: Marylee Hadley in *Written on the Wind*,'' in *Wide Angle* (Athens, Ohio), vol. 4, no. 2, 1980.

Interim, L., in *Cahiers du Cinéma* (Paris), November 1981.

Schmittze, A., in *Cinématographe* (Paris), December 1981.

Courant, G., in *Cinéma* (Paris), January 1982.

Wegner, H., ''Melodrama as Tragic Rondo: Douglas Sirk's *Written on the Wind*,'' in *Literature/Film Quarterly* (Salisbury, Maryland), July 1982.

Tobin, Yann, in *Positif* (Paris), September 1982.

Orr, Christopher, ''*Written on the Wind* and the Ideology of Adaptation,'' in *Film Criticism* (Meadville, Pennsylvania), Spring 1985.

Klinger, B., ''Much Ado about Excess: Genre, Mise-en-Scène and the Woman in *Written on the Wind*,'' in *Wide Angle* (Baltimore), no. 4, 1989.

Bibby, Bruce, in *Premiere* (Boulder), vol. 3, no. 11, July 1990.

Babington, B., and P. Evans, ''All That Heaven Allowed,'' in *Movie* (London), Winter 1990.

Reid's Film Index, no. 7, 1991.

Graham, Don, in *Texas Monthly*, vol. 19, no. 7, 1991.

Kennedy, Harlan, in *American Film*, vol. 17, no. 1, January-February 1992.

Walker, M., ''*While the City Sleeps*,'' in *Cineaction* (Toronto), Fall 1992.

Mulvey, Laura, in *Sight & Sound* (London), vol. 8, no. 2, February 1998.

* * *

The story of the oil-wealthy Hadley children can be seen as the archetype for decades of melodrama to follow: The abject alcoholic Kyle and his trampy bleach-blonde sister Marylee are beautiful, filled with implacable longing and despair, and drive great cars. The stage is set for a sordid wedding of *eros* and *thanatos* by Universal's ''Stairway of the Stars,'' which sits grandly in the centre of the Hadley mansion. (The ''stairway'' is alleged to have a 30-year screen history and is seen later in Hitchcock's *Marnie*, 1964.) The story of Kyle's doomed-to-fail marriage to sensible Lucy Moore is complicated by much gun-waving, bar-brawling and, clothing-changing, as well as Marylee's lusty passion for her brother's best friend, nature-boy Mitch Wayne (who experiences feelings of a purer sort for Lucy).

Written on the Wind opened to a *New York Times* (1957) review that characterized the actors' performances as ''absurd'' and criticized the plot, where ''nothing really happens'' and the central character as ''sloppy, self-pitying, and a bore.'' But in the years that have elapsed since its premier, it is precisely these characteristics that have transformed the film into a critical darling. The rise of director Sirk's reputation as an *author*, the influence on film theory of German dramatist Bertolt Brecht's ideas, and the appropriation of psychoanalysis by film scholars have made *Written on the Wind* a central text for feminist and genre critics. There is no firm consensus on the film's status as a powerful critique of patriarchal capitalism, but few would dispute its canonization as an enduring camp classic that solicits both laughter and tears—often in the same moments.

Hard-working city girl Lucy marries Kyle after he reveals his troubled lineage and self-loathing on an airplane ride above ''the big poker table.'' (''Down there I'm a guy with too many chips. Throw'em up in the air and a few end up on my shoulders.'') But the gun that Lucy finds under his pillow on their honeymoon is much smaller than the double-barrel shotgun Mitch totes around. ''Let's call it a weakness,'' suggests Doctor Cochran when Kyle inquires about his lack of success in producing a Hadley heir, and his sense of his failed masculinity increases exponentially.

Meanwhile, Marylee engages in various stunts to capture Mitch's attention (among other things), all of them unsuccessful but highly entertaining to watch (especially in the light of queer readings of Rock Hudson's performance). Marylee gives her long-suffering father a heart attack when police find her in a motel room tryst with a gas station attendant and, in perhaps the most cinematic patricide Hollywood ever produced, she dances wildly in her room as he plummets down 48 stairs to his death.

These two plot trajectories converge when Lucy becomes pregnant and Kyle, thick in the drunken haze into which he descends after learning of his ''weakness,'' suspects that it is Mitch's baby. Kyle hits Lucy and causes her to miscarry. This incurs the wrath of Mitch, whose shoulders seem even wider than Joan Crawford's when he bellows her line from *Mildred Pierce* (1945), ''Get out before I kill you!'' Unfortunately for Mitch, this crack in his otherwise stoic veneer is key to implicating him in Kyle's subsequent death. Marylee's first and final act of ''goodness,'' revealing Mitch's innocence at his murder trial, leaves Mitch free to go away with Lucy and leaves Marylee alone, sitting behind her father's desk in a drab grey suit, caressing a miniature oil derrick.

Early critical interest in Douglas Sirk focused on his expressive *mis-en-scène:* the affective use of decor and costuming, dramatic framing and lightning, and links to painting and music. These are all clearly significant elements in *Written on the Wind*, where a highly authentic recreation of the ''21 Club'' is juxtaposed with ridiculous rear-projections and back-drops, and characters are surrounded by eerily coloured walls and mirrored surfaces. But discussion beyond these arenas was minimal until almost ten years after Sirk's last Hollywood film (*Imitation of Life*, 1959). An increased enthusiasm for his films (particularly the Universal melodramas, c. 1954–59) was fuelled by new ideas about understanding contradiction-riddled Hollywood films as ripping themselves apart at the seams: blatantly artificial acting, garish stylization and implausible plot lines became the hallmark of a self-conscious, subversive cinema. Such a reading of *Written on the Wind* was encouraged by Sirk himself, who worked with Brecht in the German theatre and believed in his principles (hinging on the idea of audience distanciation which results in detached intellectual analysis rather than emotional catharsis). An eloquent expositor of the theories behind his films, discussing his intentions in an age where authorship mattered, Sirk drew a meticulous road map by which the convoluted paths of his films could be followed and understood in a politically progressive way.

But regardless of Sirk's intellectual predilections, the man who is reported to have once said, ''Cinema is blood, tears, violence, hate, death, and love'' was never one to make an academic film. At the end of *Written on the Wind*, we are left with the memory of Kyle's voice as he wraps his arms around his knees and cries, ''I don't even love myself,'' and the images of amber liquor thrown against a mirror, the black bow of a funeral wreath as it blows across an empty driveway, and Marylee's diaphanous pink negligee swirling about her suntanned legs.

German filmmaker Rainer Werner Fassbinder writes, ''For Douglas Sirk, madness is a sign of hope, I think.'' If Fassbinder was right, then the true tragedy of *Written on the Wind* lies not in its characters' excesses, but in their apparent ''normalization.'' Mitch and Lucy may ''escape'' from the Hadley household, but it is at the expense of the only people who ever really knew what was wrong with it.

—Stephanie Savage

WUTAI JIEMEI

(Two Stage Sisters)

China, 1964

Director: Xie Jin

Production: Tianma Film Studio, Shanghai; color; running time: 114 minutes; length: 10,223 feet. Released 1964.

Production manager: Ding Li; **screenplay:** Lin Gu, Xu Jin, and Xie Jin; **photography:** Zhou Daming; **editor:** Zhang Liqun; **sound recordist:** Zhu Weigang; **art director:** Ge Schicheng; **stage scenery:** Xu Yunlong; **music:** Huang Zhun; **music director:** Chen Chuanxi.

Cast: Xie Fang (*Chunhua*); Cao Yindi (*Yuehong*); Feng Ji (*Xing*); Gao Yuansheng (*Jiang Bo*); Shen Fengjuan (*Xino Xiang*); Xu Caigen (*Jin Shui*); Shangguan Yunzhu (*Shang Shuihua*); Ma Ji (*Qian Dukui*); Luo Zhengyi (*Yu Guiqing*); Wu Baifang (*Little Chunhua*); Li Wei (*Manager Tang*); Deng Nan (*A'xin*); Shen Hao (*Mrs. Shen*); Dong Lin (*Ni*); Ding Ran (*Pan*).

Publications

Books:

Leyda, Jay, *Dianying: An Account of Films and the Film Audience in China*, Cambridge, Massachusetts, 1972.

Lösel, Jörg, *Die politische Funktion des Spielfilms in der Volksrepublic China zwischen 1949 und 1965*, Munich, 1980.

Rayns, Tony, and Scott Meek, *Electric Shadows: 45 Years of Chinese Cinema*, London, 1980.

Bergeron, Regis, *Le Cinéma chinois 1949–1983*, 3 vols., Paris, 1983–84.

Jenkins, Alan, and Cathy Grant, *A Teaching Guide to the Films of the People's Republic of China*, Oxford, 1984.

Berry, Chris, editor, *Perspectives on Chinese Cinema*, Ithaca, New York, 1985.

Quiquemelle, Marie-Claire, and Jean-Loup Passek, editors, *Le Cinéma chinois*, Paris, 1985.

Armes, Roy, *Third World Filmmaking and the West*, Berkeley, 1987.

Clark, Paul, *Chinese Cinema: Culture and Politics since 1949*, Cambridge, 1987.

Semsel, George Stephen, editor, *Chinese Film: The State of the Art in the People's Republic*, New York, 1987.

Articles:

China's Screen, no. 2, 1981.

Variety (New York), 22 April 1981.

Wiley, Derek, in *Films and Filming* (London), November 1981.

Jenkins, Steve, in *Monthly Film Bulletin* (London), November 1981.

Blanchet, C., in *Cinéma* (Paris), January 1985.

Ostria, V., in *Cahiers du Cinéma* (Paris), January 1985.

Tessier, Max, in *Revue du Cinéma* (Paris), February 1985.

Marchetti, Gina, ''The Blossoming of a Revolutionary Aesthetic,'' in *Jump Cut* (Berkeley), no. 34, March 1989.

* * *

When Xie Jin made *Two Stage Sisters* in 1964, it marked the culmination of a certain aesthetic thrust within post-1949 Chinese cinema. At this time, Xie Jin already had a reputation for making films with strong female protagonists and clearly revolutionary themes, including *Woman Basketball Player #5* (1957) and *The Women's Red Army Detachment* (1961). As a part of the first generation of filmmakers to come of age after the Revolution, Xie embarked on his career at a time when the new People's Republic of China was searching for its own identity outside as well as within the cinematic world. Blending elements of Hollywood melodrama, Soviet socialist realism, pre-war Chinese critical realism, and folk opera traditions, *Two Stage Sisters* can be looked at as an answer (particularly after the Sino-Soviet split in the late 1950s) to what a peculiarly Chinese socialist film should look like. Using the lives of women in an all-female Shaoxing opera troupe to represent the changes the Revolution brought, Xie Jin, working from an original script (unusual in an industry which still bases most of its productions on well-known literary works), also used the setting as a way of exploring the tremendous aesthetic, cultural, and social changes that gripped modern China.

Covering the years 1935 through 1950, *Two Stage Sisters* focuses on the lives of two very different women. One, Chunhua (Xie Fang), is a young widow who runs away from her in-laws and finds sanctuary in the world of Shaoxing opera. The other, Yuehong (Cao Tindi), is born into that world. Both suffer the hardships of the life of itinerant performers. However, when they find themselves in Shanghai, Chunhua throws herself into her career and eventually into revolutionary politics, while Yuehong chooses a romance with their prosperous and ruthless theatrical manager. After 1949, both return to the countryside—Chunhua with a travelling Communist theatrical troupe and Yuehong to eke out a living after being abandoned by her husband. The film ends with the sisters' reunion; however, the fate of Yuehong remains somewhat uncertain despite the films generally optimistic resolution.

In spite of the extremely positive view of revolutionary change the film puts forward, *Two Stage Sisters* was suppressed during the Cultural Revolution and only really came to the screen in the late 1970s. The reasons behind this range from the personal displeasure of Jiang Qing (Madame Mao—then in power as head of ''The Gang of Four'') with one of the advisors on the film to its condemnation as

Wutai jiemei

''bourgeois'' for incorporating characters which were neither ''good'' nor ''bad'' vis-à-vis the Revolution (e.g., Yuehong) and thus opening the text to ambiguous readings. Unfortunately, looking at *Two Stage Sisters* as some sort of veiled statement against either Mao or the Revolution misses the point. The film really must be taken as a contribution to the construction of socialist film aesthetics in China, even though it represents a very different path than that taken by Madame Mao in her support for the highly stylized ''model opera.''

Two Stage Sisters represents an eclectic aesthetic that blends the critical vigor of the ''golden era'' of left-wing filmmaking of 1930s Shanghai with the ''revolutionary romanticism'' of the arts that developed in Yenan, where the Chinese Communist Party had a stronghold during World War II. Like many earlier Shanghai films, *Two Stage Sisters* has a Hollywood flavor. After all, it deals with the occasionally glamorous world of the opera stage and the lives of its charismatic stars. Also, like its Shanghai predecessors, the film has a critical realist's eye for the gritty details of urban life. From Yenan, however, *Two Stage Sisters* takes its heroic elevation of ordinary people through the revolutionary process, its interest in folk life and folk aesthetics, and an often ethereal, fairytale-like quality which comes from a blend of these folk roots with political idealism. To all this, the sobriety of the historical moment, an interest in looking at the nature of class oppression, feudal gender relations, nationalism, and the Japanese occupation within a dialectical framework grounds *Two Stage Sisters* within the tradition of its better known Soviet cinematic cousins. Its sweep from the poor villages of Zhejiang province to the grandeur of the Shanghai opera stage puts it within a tradition of epic socialist dramas made in other post-revolutionary societies.

However, *Two Stage Sisters* seems to add up to more than the sum of its aesthetic parts. Perhaps this is due to the elaborate mirror structure of the film which uses the world of the stage as an aesthetic reflection of the changes taking place in the lives of the film's characters. The Shaoxing opera stage, for example, represents an inverse reflection of the feudal world of the countryside. Whereas the stage features stories of warrior heroines and romances between beautiful ladies and young scholars, the actual conditions the actresses live in show a world of poverty, oppression, and constant humiliation at the hands of men.

In Shanghai, *Two Stage Sisters* shows a different kind of opera emerging. Based on the work of the radical author Lu Xun, this new opera goes outside the realm of highly stylized heroines and the fantasy of romance to deal with the poor and the homeless. Decidedly anti-romantic, it features the gritty, everyday world of contemporary Chinese life.

Lastly, *Two Stage Sisters* features opera after the Revolution with a snippet from *The White-Haired Girl*, perhaps the best-known revolutionary play to emerge from Yenan. It has the folkloric roots of Shaoxing and the critical sensibilities of Lu Xun blended together within a fantasy which features an everyday woman who becomes a revolutionary heroine.

All three of these aesthetic traditions are self-consciously represented in *Two Stage Sisters*. They serve as markers of historical change. They also allow the viewer a certain ironic distance from the drama to stand back and place the film's fiction within a broader political and cultural context. However, more than simply documenting aesthetic and social changes by incorporating these opera allusions, *Two Stage Sisters* chronicles its own roots, giving the viewer a rare glimpse of the history behind Chinese film aesthetics of the mid-1960s. It is as a document of this unique Chinese socialist cinematic sensibility that *Two Stage Sisters* is particularly important to an understanding of Chinese film culture as well as socialist cinema aesthetics in general.

—Gina Marchetti

XALA

Senegal, 1975

Director: Ousmane Sembène

Production: Domirev; 35mm; running time: 90 minutes. Released 1975. Filmed in Africa.

Director of production: Paulin Soumanou Vieyra; **screenplay:** Ousmane Sembène; **photography:** Georges Caristan; **editor:** Florence Eymon; **sound:** El Hadji Mbow; **music:** El Hadji Mbow.

Cast: Tierno Seye; Donta Seck; Younouss Seye; Senn Samb; Fatim Diange; Myriam Niang; Markhouredia Seck; Babou Faye.

Publications

Script:

Sembène, Ousmane, *Xala*, Paris, 1973; Westport, Connecticut, 1976.

Books:

Martin, Angela, editor, *African Films: The Context of Production*, London, 1982.
Moore, Carrie Dailey, *Evolution of an African Artist: Social Realism in the Works of Ousmane Sembène*, Ann Arbor, Michigan, 1984.
Pfaff, Françoise, *The Cinema of Ousmane Sembène*, Westport, Connecticut, 1984.
Armes, Roy, *Third World Filmmaking and the West*, Berkeley, 1987.
Peters, Jonathan A., *Ousmane Sembène: Contemporary Griot*, Boulder, 1987.
Pines, Jim, and Paul Willemen, editors, *Questions of Third Cinema*, London, 1989.
Gadjigo, Samba, and others, editors, *Ousmane Sembène: Dialogues with Critics and Writers*, Amherst, 1993.
Petty, Sheila, editor, *A Call to Action: The Films of Ousmane Sembène*, Westport, 1996.

Articles:

Cheriaa, T., ''Problématique du cinéaste africain: L'Artist et la révolution,'' in *Cinéma Quebec* (Montreal), August 1974.
Dagneau, G., in *Image et Son* (Paris), April 1976.
Ghali, N., ''Ousmane Sembène,'' in *Cinéma* (Paris), April 1976, and *Cinématographe* (Paris), April 1976.
Jouvet, P., in *Cinématographe* (Paris), April-May 1976.
Mruklik, B., in *Kino* (Warsaw), February 1976.
Dubroux, D., in *Cahiers du Cinéma* (Paris), May 1976.
Bosseno, C., in *Revue du Cinéma* (Paris), October 1976.
Coleman, J., in *New Statesman* (London), 5 November 1976.
Dewey, L., in *Film* (London), December 1976.
Forbes, Jill, in *Monthly Film Bulletin* (London), December 1976.
Csala, K., in *Filmkultura* (Budapest), July-August 1977.
Van Wert, William, ''Ideology in the Third World Cinema: A Study of Ousmane Sembène and Glauber Rocha,'' in *Quarterly Review of Film Studies* (Pleasantville, New York), Spring 1979.
''Ousmane Sembène,'' in *Avant-Scène du Cinéma* (Paris), 1 June 1979.
Bosseno, C., interview with Ousmane Sembène, in *Image et Son* (Paris), September 1979.
Fischer, Lucy, ''*Xala*: A Study in Black Humor,'' in *Millenium* (New York), Fall-Winter 1980–81.
Landy, M., and others, ''Ousmane Sembène's Films,'' in *Jump Cut* (Berkeley), July 1982.
Film Library Quarterly (New York), vol. 6, no. 4, 1983.
Landy, M., ''Political Allegory and 'Engaged Cinema': Sembène's *Xala*,'' in *Cinema Journal* (Champaign, Illinois), Spring 1984.
Pfaff, Françoise, and others, in *Jump Cut: Hollywood, Politics, and Counter-Cinema*, edited by Peter Steven, Toronto, Ontario, 1985.
Turvey, G., ''*Xala* and the Curse of Neocolonialism,'' in *Screen* (London), May-August 1985.
Listener (London), 25 February 1988.
''Sembène Ousmane: Poet of the African Cinema,'' in *UNESCO Courier*, January 1990.
Atkinson, M., ''Ousmane Sembène,'' in *Film Comment* (New York), July-August 1993.
Mowitt, John, ''Sembène Ousmane's *Xala*: Postcoloniality and Foreign Film,'' in *Camera Obscura* (Bloomington), no. 31, January-May 1993.
Mulvey, Laura, ''Ousmane Sembène (1974): The Carapace that Failed,'' in *Camera Obscura* (Bloomington), no. 31, January-May 1993.
Atkinson, Michael, ''Ousmane Sembène: 'We Are No Longer in the Era of Prophets,''' in *Film Comment* (New York), vol. 29, July/August 1993.

* * *

Ousmane Sembène's *Xala* is the fourth major film by one of black Africa's most important directors. Based on Sembène's novel of the same title, *Xala* demonstrates his ongoing social, political, and cultural concerns. Sembène had previously attacked the relatively easy targets of European racism (*Black Girl*), African bureaucracy (*The Money Order*), and past colonialism (*Lords of the Sky*), but here he denounces the neo-colonial deformities resulting from the collaboration of European businessmen and African elite.

Sembène structures his film around the concept of *xala*—in Wolof, a state of temporary sexual impotence. The protagonist, El

Xala

Hadji, is a polygamous Senegalese businessman who becomes afflicted with *xala* on the occasion of taking his third wife. In search of a cure, he visits various witchdoctors, who take his money but fail to cure him. At the same time, he suffers reverses in business, is accused of embezzlement, and ejected from the Chamber of Commerce. In the end, he discovers that the *xala* resulted from a curse sent by a Dakar beggar whose land El Hadji had expropriated. The protagonist finally recovers his manhood by submitting to the beggar's demands that he strip and be spat upon; the film ends with a freeze-frame of his spittle-covered body.

On a psychological level, *xala* functions as a truth-teller. El Hadji has taken a third wife purely for reasons of sexism and conspicuous consumption. "Every polygamous man," his daughter tells him, "is a liar," and although his mouth can lie, his penis cannot. The *xala*, on one level, constitutes the revenge of the women in the film; on another, it is the revenge of the oppressed classes of Senegal, represented by the beggars who have been defrauded by the new African bourgeoisie. On still another level, the *xala* symbolizes the political and economic impotence of the many newly established independent countries. El Hadji, with his Europeanized habits and tastes, encapsulates the conditions of neo-colonialism, in which an African elite takes over the positions formerly occupied by the colonizers.

Sembène portrays this elite as a kind of caricature of the European bourgeoisie. In the pre-credit sequence, we see them throw out the Europeans and take over the Chamber of Commerce. While their public speeches are in Wolof and their dress African, they speak French among themselves and reveal European suits underneath their African garb. (Continuing indirect European domination is underlined by the immediate return of the same Europeans as "advisors.") The Senegalese businessmen slavishly adore all that is European. They pour imported mineral water into the radiators of the Mercedes, and one complains that he no longer visits Spain because there are "too many blacks." The elite, in other words, have absorbed European racism and paradoxically turned it against themselves. At the same time, the film reminds us of the presence of the uncorrupted poor who look in on the ostentatious wedding celebration, and linger in the streets outside El Hadji's office. By spitting on El Hadji, they express the anger of the oppressed against the leaders who have betrayed their hopes. Yet the symbolic purging of the spittle will lead, it is implied, to the end of impotence and a kind of rebirth, for El Hadji and for his country.

Sembène masterfully deploys a diversity of narrative and aesthetic strategies in *Xala*. At times, his approach is allegorical, as in the satirical scene involving the African take-over of the Chamber of Commerce, a moment clearly evoking the historical juncture of formal independence. Each of the key women in the film has an allegorical dimension in that each represents a different stage of African history. Awa, with her traditional clothes and manners, represents the pre-colonial African woman. Omui, with her wigs, sunglasses, and low-cut dress, represents the colonized woman who imitates European fashions. El Hadji's daughter Rama, finally, represents an ideal synthesis of Africa and Europe. She speaks Wolof but studies French; she rides a moped, practical and inexpensive. She is culturally proud and politically aware, but she can also appreciate Charlie Chaplin, whose poster decorates her wall.

Sembène's achievement is that he has made an accessible political film, which speaks honestly to the problems of post-independent Africa, while skillfully orchestrating realism, humor, satire, and allegory.

—Ella Shochat

XIAO CHENG ZHI CHUN

(Spring in a Small City)

China, 1948

Director: Fei Mu

Production: Wenhua Film Company, Shanghai, 35mm; running time: 85 minutes. Released September, 1948.

Producer: none credited; **screenplay:** Li Tianji; **photography:** Li Shengwei; **music:** Huang Yijun; **set designer:** Chi Ning; **editors:** Xu Ming and Wei Shunbao.

Cast: Wei Wei (*Zhou Yuwen*); Shi Yu (*Dai Liyan*); Li Wei (*Zhang Zhichen*); Zhang Hongmei (*Dai Xiu*); Cui Chaoming (*Old Huang*).

Publications

Book:

Clark, Paul, *Chinese Cinema, Culture and Politics Since 1949*, New York, 1987.

Articles:

Sek Kei, ''The Journey of Desires,'' in *Hong Kong International Film Festival Catalogue: A Study of Hong Kong Cinema in the Seventies* (Hong Kong), 1984.

Variety (New York), 9 April 1986.

* * *

Like most Chinese films regarded in the West as art-house successes, *Spring in a Small City* is grounded in a popular genre—in this case, the *wenyi* movie. ''Wenyi'' is the term Chinese critics use to refer to the melodrama, and is abbreviated from the Chinese words for literature (wenxue) and art (yishu), the nearest Chinese equivalents to signify *melos* and drama. ''Wenyi'' therefore denotes a genre that is more ''cultured'' and cerebral (as opposed to a genre that is martial and action-oriented), biased towards women, and hosting a cast of highly literate characters. Films roughly classified as family soap operas or, more usually, love stories, fall within the realm of *wenyi* melodramas. Perhaps the prime characteristic of the *wenyi* melodrama in the love story category is the romantic triangle—the classic situation of a woman caught between her husband and lover.

In *Spring in a Small City*, Zhou Yuwen (Wei Wei) is the married female protagonist who has been nursing a sick husband, Dai Liyan (Shi Yu), for most of their marriage. One day, Dai's best friend, Zhang Zhichen (Li Wei) turns up in their dilapidated mansion, bombed during the war. Coincidentally, Zhichen happens to be Yuwen's former lover. During Zhichen's stay, Yuwen attempts to rekindle their affair. An extraordinary seduction scene takes place in which Yuwen wavers between libertarian abandonment and conscientious adherence to her personal obligations to custom and duty. As she seduces Zhichen, Yuwen intermittently covers her face with a silk scarf—an action that reveals her moral dilemma: should she leave her husband or see through her duties as a wife? The silk scarf seems to imply a tone of light-hearted coquetry but is in fact, a fitting symbol for the psychological fragility of Yuwen and the delicate caution with which she approaches her dilemma.

Spring in a Small City can be seen as the acme of the *wenyi* movie because its high artistic and stylistic achievement has elevated the theme of the romantic triangle into classic heights. It offers a lasting model of *wenyi* movies that has as its centre a woman of repressed desires poised to make certain choices—whether to take the plunge (to fulfill her desires) or to pull back from the brink. The aesthetic and psychological momentum of the film makes clear that Yuwen's choice is not a simple one. The choice is between instinct (love) and institution (marriage), personal motivation and tradition. Should she leave her husband, she discards all that is implied by tradition (repression and mental agony along with the sense of duty, loyalty, and security). Although her choice in the end to stay with her husband is determined by events (the husband attempts suicide and is saved by Zhichen, who is a doctor), it is as if tradition has proven to be too innate a factor to be easily discarded—it is something, in fact, that could have pre-determined the outcome.

Tradition, in the form of an ethical conservatism, is the lynchpin of the movie. All the characters are bound by such a tradition. Director Fei Mu works on the Confucian maxim of ''desire bound by ethics'' (*fahu qing, zhihu li:* literally, to express emotion or desire, to stop at the point of ethics). His style is completely refined by this maxim. He punctuates his scenes with subtle reminders of musical and poetic rhythm; his sets are spare but filled with reminders of a once opulently endowed manor-house; and Yuwen's narrative, which carries the psychological weight of the whole film, is never overloaded—it complements the poetic intensity of her desires and illustrates the ethical limits of her role as a Chinese woman and wife.

The inherent conservatism of the tradition theme, with its humanitarian, moral-ethical considerations, has never come out so succinctly in the *wenyi* genre or even tackled with such aesthetic conviction in the history of Chinese cinema (one film that comes close is Fei Mu's own earlier classic *Filial Piety/Tian Lun*, made in 1935—a *wenyi* film of another order, dealing with the family as the highest of Confucian institutions). It is perhaps this factor that has put the film in cold storage in Mainland China all these years. Fei Mu's aesthetic style was dismissed in Cheng Jihua's standard *History of the Development of Chinese Cinema* as ''playing up the decadent emotions of a declining bourgeois class'' (translation is author's own).

In addition, the tone and mood of the film (exacerbated by its post-war setting amidst ruins and featuring a sick husband whose bleak outlook on life leads his wife to contemplate an affair with his friend, her ex-lover) was seen as too negative for the period just when the Communist Party was on the verge of victory in the Civil War. The film's critical fortunes revived slightly with the opening up of China in the late '70s; it was shown for the first time outside of China in Hong Kong in 1983 and exerted an influence on films such as Stanley Kwan's *Rouge/Yanzhi Kou* (1989). But it is only now in the 1990s that this masterpiece is beginning to be exposed to the world beyond China and Hong Kong.

—Stephen Teo

YAABA

Burkina Faso, 1989

Director: Idrissa Ouedraogo

Production: Arcadia Films (Paris), Les Films de l'Avenir (Ouagadougou), and Thelma Film (Zürich); color, 35mm; running time: 90 minutes; length: 2465 meters (Sweden). Released 1989; filmed in Tougouzagué Village, Burkina Faso.

Producers: Freddy Denaës, Michael David, Pierre-Alain Meier, and Idrissa Ouedraogo; **screenplay:** Idrissa Ouedraogo; **assistant directors:** Paul Zoumbara and Ismaël Ouedraogo; **photography:** Matthias Kälin; **editor:** Loredana Cristelli; **music:** Francis Bebey; **sound:** Jean-Paul Mugel; **sound mixer:** Dominique Dalmasso; **costumes:** Marian Sidibé.

Cast: Fatimata Sanga (*Yaaba*); Noufou Ouedraogo (*Bila*); Roukietou Barry (*Nopoko*); Adama Ouedraogo (*Kougri*); Amadé Touré (*Tibo*); Sibidou Ouedraogo (*Poko*); Adamé Sidibé (*Razougou*); Rasmane Ouedraogo (*Noaga*); Kinda Moumouni (*Finse*); Assita Ouedraogo (*Koudi*); Zenabou Ouedraogo (*Pegda*); Ousmane Sawadogo (*Tibo*).

Awards: FIPRESCI Award, Cannes Film Festival, 1989; Gold Award, Tokyo International Film Festival, 1989.

Publications

Books:

Diawara, Manthia, *African Cinema: Politics & Culture*, Bloomington, Indiana, 1992.

Barlet, Olivier, *Les cinémas d'Afrique noire: Le regard en question*, Paris, 1996.

Articles:

Bernard, Jean-Jacques, review in *Première* (Paris), August 1989.

Vartanian, Isabelle, review in *Studio* (Paris), August 1989.

Cardullo, Bert, ''Rites of Passage,'' in *The Hudson Review* (New York), vol. 44, 1991.

* * *

Yaaba first brought international recognition to Idrissa Ouedraogo, winning the International Critics Prize at the Cannes Film Festival, the Special Jury Prize at FESPACO, and the Sakura Gold Prize at the Tokyo International Film Festival. *Yaaba* is indeed one of the finest African films. A beautifully filmed morality tale of superstition and intelligence, it touchingly conveys the humanity of its characters and offers a message of tolerance. And it is one of the few African films to have achieved a measure of commercial distribution: in France it sold close to 300,000 seats.

Yaaba distinguishes itself from Western films set in Africa by a whole set of characteristics that make it a distinctly African film: characters, setting, pacing, language, music, and last, but certainly not least, finance. *Yaaba* takes us to an all-African context where we come to know a wide range of distinctly drawn characters. The film focuses on people and their interactions rather than the setting. The camera allows us to see the beauty in their faces. *Yaaba* is set in the Sahel, which holds no particular attractions or excitement: the fauna is limited; we never get to see any game; the desert does not threaten rapid death, even if droughts are a recurring calamity; nor are there any dangers lurking in the dark. In stark contrast to Western films, *Yaaba* follows a slow peasant mode: Ouedraogo takes his time with long scenes, the camera leisurely pans the wide open landscape, following the slow progress of characters dwarfed by the vast expanse, e.g. Sana on her way to the healer. In this respect *Yaaba* follows a pattern established by Gaston Kaboré in *Wend Kuuni*, the pioneering attempt to ''Africanize'' film language by unfolding at a measured pace consonant with the time-honored customs and seasonal rhythms of African village life. All speech in *Yaaba* is in Moré, the language of the Mossi villagers it portrays. Indeed, if viewers are so inclined, they can learn some Moré as they keep counting with Bila and Nopoko, the two children, playing their games; they can pick up a greeting, and perhaps a couple of insults too; they will certainly remember that *yaaba* means grandmother. The music in *Yaaba* is credited to Francis Bebey, a well-known writer, poet, and composer-performer from Cameroon. It is used sparingly. Gentle music accompanies the inteludes when long shots take in the countryside. A faster rhythm conveys drama as in the prelude to the fight of the boys and during the burial of Sana.

Like all African films, *Yaaba* is a low-budget production: it cost 6 million francs, about one million dollars. Though many African films suffer from shortcomings that can be traced to financial constraints, Idrissa Ouedraogo managed to produce a first rate film. He accomplished this feat by taking on the roles of both writer and director, by shooting the film in Tougouzagué, a village a few miles from his birth place, and by recruiting villagers and his relatives to act—and getting them to act naturally.

Yaaba was a low-budget production, but it nevertheless required financing from overseas sponsors—like most African films produced outside Nigeria and South Africa. In this case financial support came from France, Switzerland, and Germany. Whatever Ouedraogo's preferred audience, this sponsorship presumably determined that the film should aim to reach a Western audience. Anybody familiar with village life in Africa wonders whether presenting Bila and Nopoko as single children is intended to obviate the difficulty for Western viewers of distinguishing them from their siblings; whether it is all that common for Mossi peasant women to have the final say like Bila's mother; whether the drunkard-wife-lover triangle is more the classic French film scenario than Mossi village reality. The close-ups of the lovers may be seen to play to Western expectations, the parsimonious dialogue complemented by body language—gestures, laughter, raspberries—serving to limit tiresome sub-titles.

Ouedraogo has explained that "*Yaaba* is based on tales of my childhood and on that kind of bedtime story-telling we hear just before falling asleep." And indeed, the film portrays a village out of history. Nothing takes the viewer to pre-colonial times, nor is there any indication of a colonial presence. But if the action is contemporary, the village appears altogether isolated. There is no trace of government, taxes, schools, or clinics. Market relations do not reach beyond a big tree within walking distance where a few people gather with local products, even though coins are common: the diviner demands them, the beggar collects them, the children wager them. And in Burkina Faso, where at any one time about ten percent of the population work outside the country on a temporary basis, there is no indication that any migrant ever returned to this village, no trace of anything he might have sent, or brought, or be using now, no transistor radio, not even a single t-shirt. *Yaaba* portrays a village such as would be hard to find in Africa today—or anywhere else for that matter.

An ordinary village that time forgot is unlikely to hold much interest for African audiences. Rather, a film of an African village supposedly isolated since times immemorial seeks to reach a Western audience that is interested in such a different culture, but wants to be diverted rather than be reminded of the West's role in slavery and colonialism, of the West's continued dominance in the contemporary world, of the manifold problems plaguing contemporary Africa. Western viewers may appreciate their good luck of not living in village poverty, but in *Yaaba* that poverty is taken for granted, its causes not at issue. We see the barren landscape of the Sahel, but people have food reserves to share when a family's granary burns down. Sana is destitute because she has been marginalized, not because of a general state of poverty. The only incident of illness is the consequence of a fight among children. Nopoko, Bila, and Sana are beautifully drawn—and their very status, two children and an old destitute woman, invite the patronizing Western gaze: Western viewers are encouraged to strike, once again, a posture of patronizing benevolence vis-à-vis Africans.

The parallels between *Yaaba* and *Pather Panchali*, Satyajit Ray's classic portrayal of village life in India, are striking. Both films share a sense of serenity as they linger at length on natural scenery. And both avoid the trap of romanticizing village life. Instead they contrast the quarrels of adults with the complicity between a marginalized old woman and two children. In each film the link between old and young is broken when a child touches the seated woman and discovers that she is dead. Unlike *Yaaba*, *Pather Panchali* does situate its story historically, but the conflicts of the day, land ownership and taxation, are barely alluded to, caste never at issue.

The isolation of the village in *Yaaba* leaves aside complex social, political, and historical issues. Instead the plot turns on superstition and human foibles. Western audiences are unlikely to connect Sana's marginal position to her status as an orphan. Rather, they are encouraged, once again, to assign superstition to the Other while taking their own supposed rationality for granted and forgetting how ready we are to blame others for our misfortunes. There is barely a hint that the village in a way killed Sana: we saw her exposed to the rain, and we know that, with her hut burned down, she had no place to dry herself. The constancy of the two friendships—between the two children, and between Bila and Sana—assures us that we are witnessing a society in harmony but for superstition and personal failings. The occasional quarrels between Bila and Nopoko dissipate quickly with a joke and a smile: they make us anticipate their lovers' quarrels to come in just a few years' time. And the tension created between Bila's parents by his mother's affirmative role is contained by her humor and his father's acquiescence.

If *Yaaba* fails to convey the full reality of contemporary African villages, it shares with most African films a realism in plot that distinguishes it from much Western film production. This realism is particularly striking in the ending, which gives us neither happy end nor great drama: the lovers elope, Sana dies quietly in her sleep, and Ouedraogo keeps us at a distance as he compresses much of her burial in a long shot. The woman who saved Nopoko's life has remained an outcast, Noaga has been abandoned by his wife, and the camera lingers on the children who run into the distance and, we may presume, a better future. *Yaaba* is an African production, altogether different from Western films situated in Africa, even as it reaches out to Western audiences.

Ouedraogo went on to become the most important African filmmaker since Ousmane Sembène in terms of the quantity of his production—he has directed seven feature films to date—as well as the appeal of his films. Two years after *Yaaba*, Kini and Nopoko appear as lovers in Ouedraogo's *A Karim na Sala* (1991). *Tilaï*, released in 1990, dramatizes a legend explicitly set in the precolonial past. Ouedraogo's film, *Kini and Adams*, released in 1997, once again tells a story of friendship. But it is a very different story. From the constancy of the friendship between two children and an old woman in a village that time forgot, Ouedraogo takes us to two men struggling to realize their aspirations in a world that is constantly changing—even out in the "bush." Now the endurance of friendship, however profound, is no longer assured.

—Josef Gugler

YANZHI KOU

(Rouge)

Hong Kong, 1987

Director: Stanley Kwan

Production: Golden Way Films, A Golden Harvest presentation; colour, 35mm; running time: 96 minutes. Released January 1988.

Executive producer: Leonard Ho; **producer:** Jackie Chan; **screenplay:** Li Bihua, Qiu-Dai Anping, based on the novel by Li Bihua; **photography:** Bill Wong; **editor:** Peter Cheung; **lighting:** Lin

Yanzhi kou

Shaorong; **assistant directors:** Paul Cheung, Cub Chin; **art director:** Piao Ruomo, Horace Ma; **music:** Michael Lai; **sound editing:** Deng Shaolin; **sound recording:** Zhou Shaolong; **costumes:** Wen Fenglan.

Cast: Anita Mui (*Fleur*); Leslie Cheung (*Chan Chen Pang*); Alex Man (*Yuen*); Emily Chu (*Ah Chor*); Irene Wan (*Suk-Yin*); Patrick Tse (*Fleur's rich customer*); Wang Fu (*Seventh Master*); Tan Qianhong (*Chan's father*); Zhu Ruitang (*Chan's mother*).

Publications

Articles:

Variety (New York), 24 February 1988.

Jousse, T., ''L'obscure objet du désir,'' in *Cahiers du Cinéma* (Paris), December 1989.

Rayns, T., ''Love unto Waste,'' in *Monthly Film Bulletin* (London), February 1990.

Stanbrook, A., in *Films and Filming* (London), no. 420, October 1989.

Kwan, Stanley, ''Carrying the Past Lightly,'' in *Cinemaya* (New Delhi), Spring 1993.

Chow, R., ''Un souvernir d'amour,'' in *Cinemas* (Paris), Spring 1993.

Eng, D.L., ''Love at Last Site: Waiting for Oedipus in Stanley Kwan's *Rouge*,'' in *Camera Obscura* (Bloomington), no. 32, September/January 1993/1994.

Abbas, A., ''The New Hong Kong Cinema and the Deja Disparu,'' in *Discourse* (Detroit), vol. 16, no. 3, Spring 1994.

Atkinson, M., ''Songs of Crushed Love,'' in *Film Comment* (New York), vol. 32, May/June 1996.

Stringer, J., '''Centre Stage': Reconstructing the Bio-pic,'' in *CineAction* (Toronto), no. 42, 1997.

* * *

There are seemingly mutually contradictory strands that run through *Rouge*. It is a deep, serious romance with a somewhat frivolous veneer (the romance being set in a gaudy, high-class brothel). It is also a ghost story, set in the modern environment of

Hong Kong, that evokes virtually none of the gothic suspense or special effects that are associated with the genre since it is, at the same time, a love story of the *wenyi* melodrama genre. It is eerily nostalgic, recreating the rich textures and atmosphere of a 1930s Hong Kong brothel and contrasting these with scenes of modern Hong Kong, vastly changed and still in transition. That the movie comes across as an atypical Hong Kong production is a comment in itself. It differs from the normal run of Hong Kong movies that stress action and an easy facility with modern gadgets, fashions, and values.

The film brings out the starkness of these contradictions and pinpoints an irony, by deliberately placing its narrative in the past and the present. In present Hong Kong, a thoroughly modern city, there is little or no trace of the past. Yet *Rouge* evokes a past through its tale of the ghost Fleur (Anita Mui), a high-class prostitute of the old world who reappears in modern Hong Kong to search for her lover, the dilettantish Twelfth Master Chan (Leslie Cheung). Fleur hardly recognises the city, and it is only with the help of a reporter and his girlfriend that she is able finally to locate Twelfth Master, who was supposed to have died with her in a suicide pact (having waited a day in the nether world—a cycle of fifty years on earth—Fleur decides to return to earth to look for him).

Through Fleur's links with the past and a lifestyle that is now lost, the modern couple realises that Hong Kong has a history and tradition to call its own. But that history and tradition is marked by loss and betrayal, signified by Twelfth Master's failure to die with Fleur. Twelfth Master has become a lonely old man, subsisting on work as an extra in a film studio, thus reinforcing the suggestion that he is living in a private world of make-believe. The modern city of Hong Kong is of no relevance to Twelfth Master. At the same time, the couple that helps Fleur begin to question their contemporary values and the changes which have overcome their city. Thus, *Rouge* transcends its contradictory strands by signalling the desire of modern Hong Kong citizens for self-reflection and the sight of things beyond their preoccupation with hi-tech modernity and all things glossy and new. On this basis, *Rouge* is a rare achievement.

Stanley Kwan's direction adds a graceful, stylish dimension. His third film, *Rouge* represents the director's breakthrough movie not only in the assured handling of generic elements (not to mention the various contradictory strands of the narrative), but also in the depiction of his central character, Fleur. Kwan had acquired a reputation as a woman's director, but his characterisation of Fleur as the cultured artist-prostitute puts him in a special group of filmmakers who combine social grace with impressionistic creations of memorable female characters. One thinks of Renoir, Truffaut, and Von Sternberg, but perhaps the most important aesthetic influence is Fei Mu (with a particular reference to Fei's masterpiece, *Spring in a Small City*), whose mastery of the *wenyi* genre is invoked by Kwan not only through the stylish use of the camera and the mise-en-scéne, but also through use of a female character as the beguiling epicentre of the plot.

In addition, Fleur is a character stemming from the *fenghua xueyue* vein of popular Chinese culture. *Fenghua xueyue* (literally, wind, flower, snow, moon: the term is usually abbreviated to *fengyue*) denotes a literary genre of light, frivolous subject matter. In cinema, it usually denotes a genre of soft-core entertainment. *Rouge* inherits the legacy of *fengyue* literature (and movies) depicting the brothels of old China and, in particular, Shanghai during its development as a treaty port in the 19th and early 20th centuries. Fleur is the Hong Kong Cantonese variation of the classic Shanghai sing-song girl: the exquisite details of behaviour and mannerisms of these old-world prostitutes are captured by Stanley Kwan. He wins the hearts of his audience with Fleur's highly refined style and melancholy as she searches for her lost lover—and longs for the old world in the concrete background of a hopelessly urbanized Hong Kong.

—Stephen Teo

YAWAR MALLKU

(Blood of the Condor)

Bolivia, 1969

Director: Jorge Sanjinés

Production: Grupo Ukamau (Bolivia); black and white, 35mm; running time: 74 minutes. Released 1969.

Producer: Ricardo Rada; **screenplay:** Oscar Soria and Jorge Sanjinés; **photography:** Antonio Eguino; **music:** Alberto Villalpando, Alfredo Dominquez, Gregorio Yana, and Ignacio Quispo.

Cast: Marcelino Yanahuaya (*Ignacio*); Benedicta Mendoza Huanca (*Paulina*); Vicente Salinas (*Sixto*); also featuring the people of the Kanta rural community.

Yawar Mallku

Publications

Book:

Mesa, Carlos D., and others, *Cine Boliviano: Del realizador al critico*, La Paz, 1979.

Articles:

''A Talk with Jorge Sanjinés,'' in *Cineaste* (New York), Winter 1970–71.
''*Ukamau* and *Yawar Mallku*: An Interview with Jorge Sanjinés,'' in *Afterimage* (London), Summer 1971.
Wilson, David, ''Aspects of Latin American Political Cinema,'' in *Sight and Sound* (London), Summer 1972.
Apon, A., in *Skrien* (Amsterdam), November 1972.
Tarratt, Margaret, in *Films and Filming* (London), June 1973.
Ferrero, A., in *Cineforum* (Bergamo, Italy), December 1973.
Alemanno, R., in *Cinema Nuovo* (Turin), May-August 1975.
Cardenas, F., and F. J. Lombardi, ''Breve encuentro con Antonio Eguino,'' in *Hablemos de Cine* (Lima), vol. 13, no. 69, 1977–78.
Campbell, Leon G., and Carlos Cortes, ''Film as Revolutionary Weapon: A Jorge Sanjinés Retrospective,'' in *History Teacher*, May 1979.
Ledgard, M., ''Jorge Sanjinés: El cine urgente,'' in *Hablemos de Cine* (Lima), June 1981.
Gervais, G., ''Faire du cinéma un instrument de liberation,'' in *Jeune Cinéma* (Paris), March 1982.
Sanjinés, Jorge, ''Nuestro principal destinatario,'' in *Cine Cubano* (Havana), no. 105, 1983.
Hess, John, ''Neo-Realism and New Latin American Cinema: *Bicycle Thieves* and *Blood of the Condor*,'' in John King, Ana M. Lopez, and Manuel Alvarado, editors, *Mediating Two Worlds: Cinematic Encounters in the Americas*, London, 1993.

* * *

The Bolivian fiction feature *Yawar Mallku* is one of the most famous examples of Latin American militant cinema. Like most of these American militant films, this one was made on a modest budget in spite of major obstacles. Bolivia has no significant filmmaking traditions or facilities. Mules had to be used to transport the filmmakers and their equipment to a high and remote Indian community where parts of the film were shot. The Quechua-speaking Indians of this Andean community were initially hostile to the filmmakers until a coca-leaf divination ritual confirmed the filmmakers' good intentions.

It is in cultural and ideological terms that *Yawar Mallku* is most important. This controversial film is a powerful and thorough attack on United States imperialism. In the film, members of a Progress Corps (read Peace Corps) working, ironically, in an obstetric clinic, surgically sterilize unsuspecting Indian women. Jorge Sanjinés, aware of Bolivia's historic underpopulation and high infant mortality rate, had been deeply disturbed by media reports that the U.S. Peace Corps operated in such a fashion in his country. Though U.S. officials denied such activities, the film created a furore and, in the opinion of Sanjinés, was a major factor in the expulsion of the Peace Corps from Bolivia in 1971.

In *Yawar Mallku*, U.S. imperialism is not depicted solely as an attempt to biologically eliminate an ''inferior'' race, but also as a more subtle yet all-pervasive force. The theme of cultural imperialism is amply illustrated: the rock music played in the clinic (in contrast to the indigenous flute music), the American-style clothes donated to the Indians (in contrast to the traditional, hand-woven garb), the pin-ups in the house of the Indian who has migrated to La Paz. Linguistic imperialism is exemplified in a sequence in which an upper-class Bolivian mother addresses her children in English, a language commonly used by the upper classes but generally not available for study by the Indians. Sanjinés emphasizes the ties of Bolivia's ruling classes to U.S. imperialism in a banquet sequence where leading Bolivian doctors and their U.S. counterparts fail to supply the blood that a wounded Indian needs to survive. For Sanjinés, U.S. imperialism is literally and figuratively robbing Bolivian Indians of their blood—their right to life according to their own traditions and customs.

Yawar Mallku also paints an unforgettable portrait of a common figure in modern Bolivia—the rural Indian migrant (Sixto) who seeks his fortune in the metropolis of La Paz. Sixto attempts to change his cultural identity by speaking Spanish, wearing Western-style clothes, and denying his Indian roots. Nevertheless, he remains a member of a subordinant class and as such he is ''kept in his place''—begging for blood for his brother, waiting outside the club, riding in the back of the truck. At the end of the film, Sixto has adopted Indian clothing and is returning to his rural community. The final freeze-frame of upraised rifles suggests that the Indians of the traditional rural communities must unite in the armed defense of their lives and culture.

The Bolivian government, allegedly at the insistence of U.S. officials, initially banned *Yawar Mallku*. After 24 hours, however, the ban was lifted due to public pressure generated by widespread protests and demonstrations. Because of its socially significant national themes and its controversial nature, *Yawar Mallku* became immensely popular with Bolivians. Critics continue to regard the film as a leading example of Latin American militant cinema.

—Dennis West

YEELEN

(The Light)

Mali, 1987

Director: Souleymane Cissé

Production: Les Films Cissé, in association with Atriascop and Midas, with assistance from the government of Mali, the Burkino Faso Ministry of Information and Culture, the French Ministry of Culture, CNC, UTA, WDR Television; in color; running time: 106 minutes, English version 104 minutes; length: 9,401 feet. Released 1987.

Producer: Souleymane Cissé; **screenplay:** Souleymane Cissé; **photography:** Jean-Noël Ferragut; **editors:** Dounamba Conulibaly, Andree Davanture, Marie-Catherine Miqueau, Jenny Frenck, Seipati N'Xumalo; **sound:** Daniel Olivier, Michel Mellier; **art director:** Kossa Mody Keita; **music:** Michel Portal, Salif Keita.

Cast: Issiaka Kane (*Nianankoro*); Aoua Sangare (*Attu*); Niamanto Sanogo (*Soma*); Balla Moussa Keita (*Peul King*); Soumba Traore

Yeelen

(*Nianankoro's Mother*); Ismaila Sarr (*Djigui*); Youssouf Tenin Cissé (*Attu's Son*); Koke Sangare (*Komo Chief*).

Publications

Book:

Pines, Jim, and Paul Willemen, editors, *Questions of Third Cinema*, London, 1989.

Articles:

Braunschweig, Stéphane, and Antoine de Baecque, ''Pionnier en son pays: Entretien avec Souleymane Cissé,'' in *Cahiers du Cinéma* (Paris), March 1986.
Variety (New York), 13 May 1987.
Roud, Richard, in *Guardian* (London), 21 May 1987.
Tesson, Charles, in *Cahiers du Cinéma* (Paris), June 1987.
James, Caryn, in *The New York Times*, vol. 137, C37, 8 October 1987.
Positif (Paris), December 1987.
Adair, Gilbert, in *Sight and Sound* (London), Autumn 1988.
Walters, Margaret, in *Listener* (London), 20 October 1988.
French, Philip, in *Observer* (London), 23 October 1988.
Solanka, Adeola, ''Sands of the Time,'' in *Guardian* (London), 27 October 1988.
Leahy, James, in *Monthly Film Bulletin* (London), November 1988.
Johnston, Sheila, ''Tales of a Painful Initiation,'' in *Independent* (London), 25 November 1988.
Witte, K., ''Blickvermeidung und Blickschaerfung,'' in *Filmbulletin* (Winterthur, Switzerland), no. 5, 1989.
Diawara, M., ''African Cinema Today,'' in *Framework* (London), no. 37, 1989.
Stein, Elliot, ''The Bloody and the Brightest,'' in *Village Voice* (New York), 18 April 1989.
Chiacchiari, F., in *Cineforum* (Bergamo), June 1989.
Gadjigo, S., ''Africa through African Eyes,'' in *Research in African Literatures* (Columbus, Ohio), no. 4, 1992.
Cunneen, Joseph, in *National Catholic Reporter*, vol. 29, no. 29, 21 May 1993.
Gentile, P., ''In the Midst of Secrets: Souleymane Cisse's *Yeelen*,'' in *Iris* (Iowa City), no. 18, Spring 1995.

Lalanne, Jean-Marc, and Frédéric Strauss, ''Terre et mère: Entretien avec Souleymane Cissé,'' in *Cahiers du Cinéma* (Paris), no. 492, June 1995.

MacRae, S.H., ''*Yeelen*: A Political Fable of the Komo Blacksmith/ Sorcerers,'' in *Research in African Literatures* (Columbus, Ohio), vol. 26, no. 3, 1995.

''Special Issue on *Yeelen*,'' in *Avant-Scène du Cinéma* (Paris), no. 476, November 1998.

* * *

Yeelen has provided the West with one of its all too rare glimpses of African cinema. Made in Mali, it is the fourth full-length feature to have been directed by Souleymane Cissé, who studied at the VGIK film school in Moscow under Mark Donskoi. *Den Muso* (1975) was the first feature to be shot in Mali in the Bambara tongue and concerned the plight of child-mothers; *Baara* (1978) looked at the problems of the peasantry and the growing working class; *Finye* (1982) focussed on student unrest.

After making *Finye* Cissé said, ''I hope in the future to be able to make films in which the ancient depths of African culture will surge up again. To this end, I spend my time visiting old men who tell me stories of the past, true or mythical. A cinema imitating that of America or Europe will be in vain. We must immerse ourselves in our own sources.'' In *Yeelen* Cissé has drawn on just such traditional sources in creating a narrative which describes in stark and elemental detail (images of light, water, earth, and fire abound in the film) Nianankoro's epic quest. He is a young African from Bambara pursued by his vengeful father, Somo, who has devastating magic powers that he often uses for evil purposes. Aided by his mother, Nianankoro sets out both to avoid his father and to seek help elsewhere. On his journey, dogged by his father, he manages to come to the aid of a rival tribe which is being attacked. Using magic powers of his own, Nianankoro repels the would-be invaders and the grateful king allows him to ''acquire'' the king's own wife, Attu, as a gift for his labours. She subsequently becomes pregnant, and the young couple finally reach the home of Nianankoro's uncle, Djigui. Nianankoro explains to Djigui that his father turned against him because he wanted to use his magic powers for the common good. The film ends with a confrontation between father and son in which they are both destroyed by a blinding light. Attu arrives with her young son, gathers two fetish objects left behind by the men in their deadly struggle, then walks away with the child.

For many Western critics the film was perceived in classic psychoanalytic terms as an Oedipal drama, a conflict between father and son for control over power and knowledge (indeed Nianankoro's ''marriage'' to the king's wife draws a parallel with Oedipus's marriage to his own mother). This appraisal, comforting and familiar though it is, has not met with the approval of the Africans themselves who regard psychoanalysis as incompatible with their own cultures, nor does it do any justice to what, after all, is the major quality of the film—its extraordinary mythic dimension. As Cissé himself says, ''For every individual imagination is personal, intuitive. For me imagination is planetary, cosmic.'' The cosmic is effortlessly represented by many different aspects of the film: the grandeur of the landscape, an immensity of sky, a searing relentless sun, the Great Tree in each village scene under which counsel is taken, a sense of timelessness in the unfolding of the narrative, and the characters themselves, who have a universal resonance in the dignity and ardour of their endeavours. The symbology, too, apparent in the use of a magic eye which is to be found both in the wing of Kôré, sceptre of the initiates, and in Somo's magic pestle, seizes the imagination in a direct and compelling manner.

Yeelen is a profound evocation of a belief system which is founded on magic. As Cissé says, ''In Africa we are all believers in magic. But for Africans, this magic is a part of the everyday experience. What is thrown into relief is not magic; it is knowledge and the power of knowledge. People who ignore this will not be able to understand the film.''

—Sylvia Paskin

YELLOW EARTH

See **HUANG TUDI**

LES YEUX SANS VISAGE

(Eyes Without a Face)

France-Italy, 1959

Director: Georges Franju

Production: Champs-Elysées/Lux; black and white; running time: 90 minutes, some sources say 88 minutes; length: 7,885 feet. Released 1959.

Producer: Jules Borkon; **screenplay:** Georges Franju, Jean Redon, Claude Sautet, Boileau and Narcejac, from the novel by Redon; **photography:** Eugen Schüfftan; **editor:** Gilbert Natot; **sound:** Antoine Archimbaud; **art director:** Auguste Capelier; **special effects:** Assola, Georges Klein; **music:** Maurice Jarre.

Cast: Pierre Brasseur (*Professor Génessier*); Alida Valli (*Louise*); Edith Scob (*Christiane*); François Guérin (*Jacques*); Juliette Mayniel (*Edna Gruber*); Béatrice Altariba (*Paulette*); Alexandre Rignault (*Inspector Parot*); René Genin (*Bereaved father*).

Publications

Script:

Franju, Georges, and others, *Les Yeux sans visages*, in *Avant-Scène du Cinéma* (Paris), June 1977.

Books:

Durgnat, Raymond, *Franju*, Berkeley, 1968.

Vialle, Gabriel, *Georges Franju*, Paris, 1968.

Benichou, P. J. B., *Horreur et epouvante*, Paris, 1977.

Grant, Barry Keith, editor, *Planks of Reason: Essays on the Horror Film*, Metuchen, New Jersey, 1984.

Les yeux sans visage

Articles:

La Technique Cinématographique (Paris), no. 196, 1959.
Lebovits, Jean-Marc, and Francis Tranchant, ''Entretien avec Georges Franju,'' in *Cinéma* (Paris), March 1959.
Vérité, J. M., in *Cinéma* (Paris), July 1959.
Variety (New York), 26 August 1959.
Truffaut, François, ''Entretien avec Georges Franju,'' in *Cahiers du Cinéma* (Paris), November 1959.
Dyer, Peter John, in *Monthly Film Bulletin* (London), March 1960.
Delahaye, Michel, in *Cahiers du Cinéma* (Paris), April 1960.
Vas, Robert, in *Sight and Sound* (London), Spring 1960.
Oms, Marcel, in *Positif* (Paris), May 1960.
Tailleur, Roger, ''Pour un portrait,'' in *Prèsence du Cinéma* (Paris), June 1960.
Callenbach, Ernest, in *Film Quarterly* (Berkeley), Summer 1962.
Ajame, Pierre, ''Georges Franju; ou, La Terreur comme un des beaux-arts,'' in *Nouvelles Littéraires* (Paris), 30 January 1964.
MacLochlainn, A., ''The Films of Luis Buñuel and Georges Franju,'' in *Film Journal* (New York), Summer 1971.
Gow, Gordon, ''Franju,'' in *Films and Filming* (London), August 1971.
Wood, Robin, ''Terrible Buildings: The World of Georges Franju,'' in *Film Comment* (New York), November-December 1973.
Milne, Tom, ''Georges Franju: The Haunted Void,'' in *Sight and Sound* (London), Spring 1975.
Badder, D. J., ''Georges Franju,'' in *Film Dope* (London), April 1979.
Conrad, Randall, ''Mystery and Melodrama: A Conversation with Georges Franju,'' in *Film Quarterly* (Berkeley), vol. 35, 10 March 1982.
Revault d'Allonnes, Fabrice, in *Cinéma* (Paris), 24 September 1986.
Chevrie, Marc, in *Cahiers du Cinéma* (Paris), November 1986.
Klein, Andy, in *Los Angeles Magazine*, vol. 33, no. 9, September 1988.
Svehla, G.J., ''Revisiting *The Horror Chamber of Dr. Faustus*,''' in *Midnight Marquee* (Baltimore), no. 38, Spring 1989.
Peyras, P., ''Si tes yeux t'offensent, arrache-less!'' in *Focales*, no. 1, 1992.
Peyras, P., ''Que cache le cadre de Bazin?'' in *Focales*, no. 2, 1993.
Brownlie, T., ''*Eyes Without a Face* (*Les yeux sans visage*),'' in *Film* (London), vol. 4, no. 3, 1995.
Sinclair, Iain, ''Homeopathic Horror,'' in *Sight & Sound* (London), vol. 5, no. 4, April 1995.

Télérama (Paris), no. 2371, 21 June 1995.
Brown, G., ''The Looking Glass,'' in *Village Voice* (New York), vol. 40, 21 November 1995.
''Franju Classic Gets New Facelift,'' in *Video Watchdog* (Cincinnati), no. 31, 1996.

* * *

''When I shot *Les Yeux sans visage*,'' Georges Franju recalled, ''I was told: 'No sacrilege because of the Spanish market, no nudes because of the Italian market, no blood because of the French market and no martyrised animals because of the English market.' And I was supposed to be making a horror film!'' Coming to the horror genre after co-founding the Cinémathèque Française, a varied career as a documentarist (*Le Sang des bêtes*, *Le Grand Méliès*), and the production of a single feature (*La Tête contre les murs*), Franju was bringing an unusually high-toned sensibility to a field at that time being revitalized by the new blood poured into old myths by Hammer Films in Britain and Roger Corman in the United States. However, for all his poetic approach, *Les Yeux san visage* is a triumphantly disreputable movie, closely allied to the Sadeian strain exemplified in Britain by *Circus of Horrors* (with which it shares a fascination with disfigurement and plastic surgery) and the misanthropic gimmickry of William Castle, whose *The Tingler* and *The House on Haunted Hill* are still undervalued for their lunatic originality.

The storyline is deliberately rooted in the pulp tradition: a mad scientist, Dr. Génessier, kidnaps runaway girls for use in his diabolical experiments. Guilt-ridden because he is responsible for the disfigurement of his daughter Christiane, Génessier peels the faces of his victims and tries to graft their beautiful faces onto the girl's ruined features. And Franju is not above the usual flaws of the genre: he is very obviously not interested in the scenes of police investigation required to keep the plot moving, and he hurries through the mundane side of the story to get back to the bizarre ménage of the Génessier household, where Christiane prowls the dark corridors in a long raincoat and an eerily blank mask, her active eyes the only sign of life. Pierre Brasseur's smug scientist is a memorable monster, more plumply self-satisfied than Bela Lugosi or Boris Karloff, mistreating the vicious dogs who finally tear him to pieces, or presiding imperiously over surgical flayings which are depicted with all the dispassionate bloodiness of an unflinching documentary. But the most radical departure from the generic norm is the role assigned to Alida Valli—perhaps a development of the Simone Signoret character in *Les Diaboliques*, also written by the Boileau-Narcejac team—who plays the scientist's devoted assistant. No hunchbacked Igor figure, Louise is an ambiguously sexual predator who prowls the streets of Paris in a 2CV—the car's appearance given a sinister significance by Maurice Jarre's impertinent waltz—searching for the young girls her master needs for his doomed attempts at redemption.

Les Yeux is a cruel but tender film, with Edith Scob's extraordinarily delicate performance as Christiane constantly reminding us that Génessier, however deranged, is sincerely acting out of love. The gothic trappings of the mystery-plotted first half, during which Génessier's house is lent an almost Cocteau-like life of its own by Eugen Schüfftan's outstanding photography, give way to a surgical cool as we follow the apparent success and ultimate disintegration of Christiane's latest facial graft. Here, the poignancy of the inevitable regression to monstrosity is as powerfully expressed as it is in such related science-fictional narratives as *Frankenstein*, *The Island of Lost Souls*, and *Charly*. *Les Yeux* was to remain Franju's best film, the one instance of harmony found between pulp poetry and art cinema. Although derivative of many earlier horrors, in particular Riccardo Freda's *I vampiri*, it even crystallized a certain sub-genre that became the province of maverick European horror filmmakers, as can be seen by the echoes in Jesus Franco's *Gritos en la noche* and Robert Hartford-Davis's *Corruption*. Franju takes a scalpel to genre cinema, piercing the conventionality of too many horror movies, and produces a personal, evocative nightmare fully worthy of comparison with its equally disturbing, equally Sadeian contemporary, Michael Powell's *Peeping Tom*.

—Kim Newman

YOJIMBO

Japan, 1961

Director: Akira Kurosawa

Production: Toho, in association with Kurosawa Films; black and white, Tohoscope; running time: 110 minutes.

Executive producers: Tomoyuki Tanaka, Ryuzo Kikushima; **screenplay:** Ryuzo Kikushima, Akira Kurosawa; **photography:** Kazuo Miyagawa; **art director:** Yoshiro Mikami; **lighting:** Choshiro Ishii; **music:** Masaru Sato; **sound:** Hisashi Shimonaga.

Cast: Toshiro Mifune (*Sanjuro Kuwabatake*); Eijiro Tono (*Gonji*); Seizaburo Kawazu (*Seibei*); Isuzu Yamada (*Orin*); Hiroshi Tachikawa (*Yoichiro*); Susumu Fukita (*Honma*); Kyu Sazanka (*Ushitora*); Daisuke Kato (*Inokichi*); Tatsuya Nakadai (*Unosuke*); Kamatari Fujiwara (*Tazaemon*); Takashi Shimura (*Tokuemon*); Atushi Watanabe (*Coffin maker*).

Publications:

Books:

Kael, Pauline, *I Lost it at the Movies*, New York, 1965.
Richie, Donald, *The Films of Akira Kurosawa*, Berkeley, 1970.
Richie, Donald, *Japanese Cinema*, New York, 1971, 1996.
Burch, N., *To the Distant Observer: Form and Meaning in the Japanese Cinema*, 1979.
Desser, D., *The Samourai Films of Akira Kurosawa*, 1983.
Buehrer, Beverly Bare, *Japanese Films*, London 1990.
Chang, Kevin K.W., editor, *Kurosawa: Perceptions on Life: An Anthology of Essays*, Honolulu, 1991.
Prince, Stephen, *The Warrior's Camera: The Cinema of Akira Kurosawa*, Princeton, 1991; revised and expanded edition, 1999.
Goodwin, James, *Akira Kurosawa and Intertextual Cinema*, Baltimore, 1994.

Yojimbo

Goodwin, James, editor, *Perspectives on Akira Kurosawa*, New York, 1994.

Yoshimoto, Mitsuhiro, *Kurosawa: Film Studies and Japanese Cinema*, Durham, 2000.

Articles:

Variety (New York), 30 August 1961.

Gillett, J., *Monthly Film Bulletin* (London), July 1970.

Gow, G., *Films and Filming* (London), August 1970.

McDonald, Keiko I., ''Swordsmanship and Gamesmanship: Kurosawa's historical milieu in *Yojimbo*,'' in *Literature/Film Quarterly* (Salisbury, Maryland), no. 3, 1980.

Peary, Gerald, in *American Film*, vol. 14, no. 6, April 1989.

Tesson, C., ''L'homme enrage,'' in *Cahiers du Cinéma* (Paris), no. 440, February 1991.

Carty, Brad, in *Wilson Library Bulletin*, vol. 67, no. 4, December 1992.

Felperin, Leslie, ''John Sayles Walking Alone,'' in *Sight & Sound* (London), vol. 6, no. 9, September 1996.

Charity, Tom, ''Hill's Angel,'' in *Time Out* (London), no. 1362, 24 September 1996.

Boxoffice (Chicago), vol. 132, September 1996.

Filipski, Kevin, ''Return of the Samurai: Two Akira Kurosawa Originals,'' in *The New York Times*, AR30, 24 October 1999.

* * *

Yojimbo is possibly Akira Kurosawa's best-known film in the West, a samurai sword-fighting movie that, though entirely Japanese, still resonates nicely for Americans used to their own period gunfighting film genre, the western, the ''grammar'' of which Kurosawa learned from John Ford, just as Sergio Leone and Clint Eastwood in turn learned from *Yojimbo*. As is typical of much of Kurosawa's canon, Yojimbo involves ironies and tensions in its use of its genre, a mark of this great filmmaker's innovative approach to conventional materials. Here, the central figure of the samurai, involved with the town and yet distant from it, becomes a metaphor for anyone torn between active opposition to evil and the far safer course of staying on the sidelines.

According to Donald Ritchie in *The Films of Akira Kurosawa* (1970), Kurosawa consciously set out to deal with the problem of choice when ''both sides are equally bad.'' Toshiro Mifune plays Sanjuro Kawabatake, a *ronin*, a masterless samurai who happens on a dreary small town evenly divided between a silk merchant and a sake merchant, Tazaemon and Tokuemon. As their echoing names suggest, there is little from which to choose between these two worthies, the feud having reached the point at which hope for sensible compromise has been overwhelmed by mindless hatred. It is 1860, and in his wanderings as an unattached *ronin* Sanjuro has seen this pattern repeated all too often as the old social order of the Tokugawa Shogunate has broken down and the feuding upstarts of the merchant class have taken over. He plays the two sides against each other, first hiring out as *yojimbo* or bodyguard to the silk merchant, then switching sides when the sake merchant's younger brother Urosuke appears with the only firearm in the district, a revolver.

However, Sanjuro's bedrock sympathy is for the few beleaguered innocent citizens caught up in the chaos of conflict. Gonji (Eijiro Tono), a humble saki seller with whom Sanjuro stays, reflects the basic decency and outrage of the city's ordinary citizenry, who have helplessly watched their town being taken over by ruffians and their neighbours greedily seeking to profit from it (like the busy coffin maker next door), but who bravely dare to further Sanjuro's efforts. Sanjuro, competent, sure, cynical and worldwise, is set against Unosuke, a ruthless, cruel, and ambitious sadist who places his trust in a weapon from the West, a technological trump card; ultimately Sanjuro brings him down with a humble villager's knife.

Sanjuro's involvement with one side and the other is both whimsical and practical: it is a way of passing time while amusing himself and earning a bowl of rice. Throughout, there is a comic counterpoint between Mifune's patented samurai swagger and the small humanizing touches he brings to the role: his shrugs, scratches, chin-rubs, and grunts, his chewed-on toothpick. For the two camps in the village, only total victory will serve; for Sanjuro, victory is surviving another day and moving on in his journey. He cleverly manipulates the hatreds and hopes of both sides but is almost undone by a simple act of human kindness. After he slaughters the jailers of a poor farmer's enslaved wife, who was abducted by the sake dealer's party, Sanjuro threatens to kill his protégés if they are too grateful (''Shut up—I hate grateful people''), and, ironically, their intercepted letter of thanks brings Sanjuro an horrific beating. Ultimately, however, he overcomes near impossible adversity and odds to kill all the combatants; arms and innards fly when with masterful swordsmanship Sanjuro demonstrates the difference between skilled samurai and hired thug. At the end, like Shane, Yojimbo leaves the town to its own devices, peaceful but decimated, its silk burned, its sake spilled: ''Now it will be quiet in this town.''

Several elements raise this story above its tawdry characters and plot into a profound commentary on human passion, greed, and folly. Mifune's Sanjuro is a brilliant character, a supremely confident samurai *übermensch* who figuratively and literally looks down on the grovelling and bickering villagers. He is above them morally because, in ways that encompass both Zen and existential thought, he understands the meaninglessness of material gain and the total folly of their grasping for temporal advantage. Two early scenes establish the vanity of human wishes and Sanjuro's submission to the unseen forces that rule us: in one, a dog trots happily down the village street, a human hand in his mouth; in another, Sanjuro chooses his direction by throwing a stick in the air at a crossroads. In a dog-eat-man world, only fools squabble over who owns the gutters.

Also, *Yojimbo* is a model of efficient cinematic storytelling. The filmic exposition captures visually the claustrophobic closeness of village life and the local reign of terror as Sanjuro eats rice and observes the plotting of the sake lord out of one window and that of the silk lord out of another. Later, the camera-eye is that of the battered Sanjuro, inside a coffin, watching with approval the bloodletting his shifting allegiance has precipitated. Miyagawa's telephoto lenses visually compact and intensify the sword-fighting scenes: the disorganized bloodlust of cowardly bullies versus the cool efficiency of the samurai. Symmetrical framing, shots at right angles, carefully orchestrated ballet-like action, and inspired synchronizing of music and movement make for an artistically stylized whole, not quite Kabuki, but mythic in resonance. As Ritchie points out, the combination of a ''cheerfully anarchistic philosophy . . . presented with a stylistic unity'' results in a satisfying whole.

Ultimately, Yojimbo glorifies the individual who is willing to take on organized monopolies. Its black humour, bleak realism, and brutal violence are offset by the image of a lone individual, competent, aloof, who sympathizes with the ordinary townsfolk, restores order and rights wrong at heavy cost, and then moves on.

—Andrew and Gina Macdonald

YOU ONLY LOVE ONCE

See **SAMO JEDNOM SE LJUBI**

THE YOUNG AND THE DAMNED

See **LOS OLVIDADOS**

THE YOUNG AND THE PASSIONATE

See **I VITELLONI**

YOUNG MR. LINCOLN

USA, 1939

Director: John Ford

Production: Twentieth Century-Fox; black and white, 35mm; running time: 100 minutes. Released 1939. Filmed in Fox studios.

Producers: Darryl F. Zanuck with Kenneth MacGowan; **screenplay:** Lamar Trotti; **photography:** Arthur Miller; **editor:** Walter Thompson; **sound:** Eugene Grossman and Roger Heman; **art directors:** Richard Day and Mark-Lee Kirk; **music:** Alfred Newman; **costume designer:** Royer.

Cast: Henry Fonda (*Abraham Lincoln*); Alice Brady (*Abagail Clay*); Marjorie Weaver (*Mary Todd*); Arleen Whelan (*Hannah Clay*); Eddie Collins (*Efe*); Pauline Moore (*Ann Rutledge*); Richard Cromwell (*Matt Clay*); Donald Meek (*John Felder*); Judith Dickens (*Carrie*

Young Mr. Lincoln

Sue); Eddie Quillan (*Adam Clay*); Spencer Charters (*Judge Herbert A. Bell*); Ward Bond (*Palmer Cass*); Milburn Stone (*Stephen A. Douglas*); Cliff Clark (*Sheriff Billings*); Steven Randall (*Juror*); Charles Tanner (*Ninian Edwards*); Francis Ford (*Frank Ford*); Fred Kohler Jr. (*Scrub White*); Kay Linaker (*Mrs. Edwards*); Russell Simpson (*Woolridge*); Clarence Hummel Wilson (*Dr. Mason*); Edwin Maxwell (*John T. Stuart*); Robert Homans (*Mr. Clay*); Charles Halton (*Hawthorne*); Jack Kelly (*Matt Clay, as a boy*); Dickie Jones (*Adam Clay, as a boy*); Harry Tyler (*Barber*).

Publications

Books:

Wooten, W. P., *An Index to the Films of John Ford*, London, 1948.
Mitry, Jean, *John Ford*, Paris, 1954.
Haudiquet, Philippe, *John Ford*, Paris, 1966.
Bogdanovich, Peter, *John Ford*, Berkeley, 1968; revised edition, 1978.
Springer, John, *The Fondas: The Films and Careers of Henry, Jane, and Peter Fonda*, New York, 1970.
Baxter, John, *The Cinema of John Ford*, New York, 1971.
McBride, Joseph, and Michael Wilmington, *John Ford*, London, 1975.
Sarris, Andrew, *The John Ford Movie Mystery*, London, 1976.
Ford, Dan, *Pappy: The Life of John Ford*, Englewood Cliffs, New Jersey, 1979.
Sinclair, Andrew, *John Ford*, New York, 1979.
Fonda, Henry, and Howard Teichmann, *Fonda: My Life*, New York, 1981.
Anderson, Lindsay, *About John Ford*, London, 1981.
Caughie, John, editor, *Theories of Authorship: A Reader*, London, 1981.
Schatz, Thomas, *Hollywood Genres: Formulas, Filmmaking, and the Studio System*, New York, 1981.
Eisenstein, Sergei, *Film Essay and a Lecture*, edited by Jay Leyda, Princeton, 1982.
Goldstein, Norm, *Henry Fonda: His Life and Work*, London, 1982.
Thomas, Tony, *The Films of Henry Fonda*, Secaucus, New Jersey, 1983.
Cole, Gerald, and Wes Farrell, *The Fondas*, London, 1984.
Roberts, Allen, and Max Goldstein, *Henry Fonda: A Biography*, Jefferson, North Carolina, 1984.

Reed, Joseph W., *Three American Originals: John Ford, William Faulkner, Charles Ives*, Middletown, Connecticut, 1984.
Norman, Barry, *The Film Greats*, London, 1985.
Gallagher, Tag, *John Ford: The Man and His Films*, Berkeley, 1986.
Stowell, Peter, *John Ford*, Boston, 1986.
Buscombe, Ed, editor, *BFI Companion to the Western*, London, 1988.
Lourdeaux, Lee, *Italian and Irish Filmmakers in America: Ford, Capra, Coppola and Scorsese*, Springfield, 1990; 1993.
Sweeney, Kevin, *Henry Fonda: A Bio-Bibliography*, New York, 1992.
Davis, Ronald L., *John Ford: Hollywood's Old Master*, Norman, 1997.
Girus, Sam B., *Hollywood Renaissance: The Cinema of Democracy in the Era of Ford, Capra, and Kazan*, New York, 1998.
Levy, Bill, *John Ford: A Bio-Bibliography*, Westport, 1998.
Eyman, Scott, *Print the Legend: The Life and Times of John Ford*, New York, 1999.

Articles:

Herzberg, Max J., ''A Guide to the Study of the Historical Photoplay *Young Mr. Lincoln*,'' in *Photoplay Studies* (New York), no. 9, 1939.
New York Times, 31 May 1939.
Variety (New York), 7 June 1939.
New Yorker, 10 June 1939.
Greene, Graham, in *Spectator* (London), 22 September 1939.
Johnson, Albert, ''The 10th Muse in San Francisco,'' in *Sight and Sound* (London), Spring 1955.
Hill, Derek, ''Press Conference,'' in *Sight and Sound* (London), Summer 1957.
Smith, Maynard T., ''Lamar Trotti,'' in *Films in Review* (New York), August-September 1958.
Springer, John, ''Henry Fonda,'' in *Films in Review* (New York), November 1960.
McVay, Douglas, ''The Five Worlds of John Ford,'' in *Films and Filming* (London), June 1962.
McBride, Joseph, and Michael Wilmington, in *Film Heritage* (Dayton, Ohio), Summer 1971.
''Ford Special Issue'' of *Velvet Light Trap* (Madison, Wisconsin), August 1971.
''Ford's Stock Company Issue'' of *Filmkritik* (Munich), January 1972.
Gieure, R., ''Une 'Reprise' ciné-club: *Young Mr. Lincoln* de John Ford,'' in *Cinéma* (Paris), March 1972.
''John Ford's *Young Mr. Lincoln*: A Collective Text by the Editors of *Cahiers du Cinéma*,'' in *Screen* (London), Autumn 1972.
Wollen, Peter, ''Afterword,'' in *Screen* (London), Autumn 1972.
Mairal, J. C., ''Notes sur deux films Hollywoodiens,'' in *Image et Son* (Paris), no. 269, 1973.
Mate, Ken, ''How Green Was Your Valley Then, John Ford,'' in *Velvet Light Trap* (Madison, Wisconsin), vol. 8, 1973.
Brewster, Ben, ''Notes on the Text: 'John Ford's Young Mr. Lincoln by the Editors of Cahiers du Cinéma,''' in *Screen* (London), Autumn 1973.
Henderson, Brian, ''Critique of Cine-Structuralism,'' in *Film Quarterly* (Berkeley), Winter 1973–74.
''*Young Mr. Lincoln* Issue'' of *Filmkritik* (Munich), February 1974.
Abel, R., ''Paradigmatic Structures in *Young Mr. Lincoln*,'' in *Wide Angle* (Athens, Ohio), no. 4, 1978.
Place, J. A., in *Wide Angle* (Athens, Ohio), no. 4, 1978.
Abramson, R., and R. Thompson, ''*Young Mr. Lincoln* Reconsidered: An Essay on the Theory and Practice of Film Criticism,'' in *Ciné-Tracts* (Montreal), Fall 1978.
''*Young Mr. Lincoln* de John Ford,'' in *Skrien* (Amsterdam), Winter 1978–79.
Browne, Nick, ''The Spectator of American Symbolic Forms: Re-Reading John Ford's *Young Mr. Lincoln*,'' in *Film Reader* (Evanston, Illinois), no. 4, 1979.
Place, Janey, in *Magill's Survey of Cinema, 4*, Englewood Cliffs, New Jersey, 1980.
Kinder, Marsha, ''The Image of Patriarchal Power in *Young Mr. Lincoln* and *Ivan the Terrible Part 1*,'' in *Film Quarterly* (Berkeley), Winter 1985–86.
Oms, Marcel, ''Lincoln et Guillaume Tell sur l'autel de la patrie,'' in *Cahiers de la Cinémathèque* (Perpignan), no. 45, 1986.
Goodman, Walter, in *The New York Times*, vol. 138, H32, 18 September 1988.
Andrew, D., ''Revolution and the Ordinary: Renoir's *La Marseillaise*,'' in *Yale Journal of Critcism*, vol. 4, no. 1, 1990.
Carty, Brad, in *Wilson Library Bulletin*, vol. 64, no. 9, May 1990.
Darby, W., ''Musical Links to *Young Mr. Lincoln*, *My Darling Clementine*, and *The Man Who Shot Liberty Valence*,'' in *Cinema Journal* (Austin), vol. 31, no. 1, Fall 1991.
Rother, R., ''Sentiment und Kalkuel—John Ford,'' in *Filmwaerts* (Hannover), Summer 1991.

* * *

Young Mr. Lincoln was one of three John Ford films, all among his finest, to be released in 1939. Each was noteworthy for a number of reasons, and each introduced to the director's work a particular aspect that would become identified with the thematic concerns of the rest of his career. *Stagecoach*, for example, was his first film with John Wayne and his first use of Arizona's spectacular Monument Valley as a locale. Both would become Ford institutions in succeeding years. *Drums Along the Mohawk*, the earliest of his histories, in terms of its internal chronology, also marked the beginning of an examination of the American past that would occupy much of the rest of his life.

Young Mr. Lincoln was Ford's first film with Henry Fonda, another actor with a very definite function within the director's films. Through careful crafting of Fonda's character and the script, Ford created for the actor a persona that embodied the traditional qualities of American idealism and a liberal attitude toward the development of the absolutes of civilization. Though this persona was continued in other Ford-Fonda collaborations until 1948 when the actor returned to the New York stage, it was initially employed to elevate the story of Lincoln's early years to the level of a national myth, a myth consistent with the director's own philosophy.

In *Drums Across the Mohawk*, the Fonda persona's aspirations toward civilization are inherent in his yearning for land and a home. When he loses his home, much of his personal stability and self-reliance vanishes with it, and the structure of his family life hovers near fragmentation. In *Young Mr. Lincoln*, however, the idea of civilization is represented by the broadest concept of the law—one that is indicated by Lincoln's statement in the trial scene. His profession that ''I may not know much about the law, but I know what is right!'' has less to do with a court of justice than it does with Ford's idea of a higher law. The future president is presented by the film as a proponent of God's law, which Ford relates through a number of scenes, as being intertwined with concepts of family, the future and nature itself. One scene, in which Lincoln is sitting by a river studying Blackstone's *Commentaries* and is interrupted by Ann Rutledge who wants to talk about the future, ties all of these ideas together as does his monologue at her grave when he invokes her memory (as well as that of his deceased mother) to aid in his decision to become a lawyer. The entire trial sequence, in fact, casts Lincoln in the role of a defender of the American family, attempting to keep it intact.

The use of the poem, ''Nancy Hanks,'' at the beginning of the film establishes for the viewer a consciousness of the historical Lincoln while, at the same time, serving notice that the function of art is not simply a retelling of history but a rewriting as well. Therefore, the story that follows utilizes the audience's already mythical assumptions concerning the historical personage as one element in Ford's creation of the new myth. The character is removed from its historical context, its useful qualities extracted and merged with those of the carefully constructed Fonda persona to be employed for Ford's own purposes. So striking was the merger of the Fonda and Lincoln qualities that, for many years, the film was heralded solely for the youthful exuberance of Fonda's performance. Now, however, the film is appreciated for its classic craftsmanship and as an exposition of the mythmaking process in America.

—Stephen L. Hanson

YUNOST MAXIMA

See **THE MAXIM TRILOGY**

Z

France-Algeria, 1968

Director: Constantin Costa-Gavras

Production: Reggane Films (Algeria) and O.N.C.I.C. (France); EastmanColor (print by Technicolor), 35mm; running time: 123 minutes, American version: 127 minutes, Canadian version: 152 minutes, West German version: 145 minutes; length: 3472 meters. Released February 1969, Paris. Filmed in Algiers.

Producers: Jacques Perrin and Hamed Rachedi with Eric Schlumberger and Philippe d'Argila; **screenplay:** Constantin Costa-Gavras and Jorge Semprun, from the novel by Vassilis Vassilikos; **photography:** Raoul Coutard; **editor:** François Bonnot; **sound:** Michèle Boehm; **art director:** Jacques d'Ovidio; **music:** Mikis Theodorakis.

Cast: Yves Montand (*The Deputy Z*); Jean-Louis Trintignant (*The Magistrate*); Jacques Perrin (*The Journalist*); François Pértier (*The Public Prosecutor*); Irene Papas (*Hélène*); Georges Géret (*Nick*); Charles Denner (*Manuel*); Bernard Fresson (*Matt*); Jean Bouise (*Pirou*); Jean-Pierre Miquel (*Pierre*); Renato Salvatori (*Yago*); Marcel Bozzufi (*Vago*); Julien Guiomar (*Colonel*); Pierre Dux (*General*); Guy Mairess (*Dumas*); Magail Noël (*Nick's sister*); Clotilde Joano (*Shoula*); Maurice Baquet (*Bald man*); Jean Dasté (*Coste*); Gérard Darrieu (*Baron*); José Artur (*Newspaper editor*); Van Doude (*Hospital director*); Eva Simonet (*Niki*); Hassan Hassani (*General's chauffeur*); Gabriel Jabbour (*Bozzini*); Jean-François Gobbi (*Jimmy the boxer*); Andrée Tainsy (*Nick's other*); Steve Gadler (*English photographer*); Bob de Bragelonne (*Undersecretary of State*).

Awards: Cannes Film Festival, Best Actor (Trintignant), 1969; Oscars for Best Foreign Film and Film Editing, 1969; New York Film Critics Awards, Best Motion Picture and Best Direction, 1969.

Publications

Script:

Costa-Gavras, Constantin, and Jorge Semprun, *Z; ou, L'Anatomie d'un assassinal politique*, in *Avant-Scène du Cinéma* (Paris), October 1969.

Book:

Michalczyk, John, *Costa-Gavras: The Political Fiction Film*, Philadelphia, 1984.

Articles:

Kostolefsky, Joseph, in *Take One* (Montreal), March-April 1969.

Georgakas, Dan, and Gary Crowdus, ''Costa-Gavras Talks,'' in *Take One* (Montreal), July-August 1969.

Esnault, Philippe, ''Cinéma et politique,'' in *Avant-Scène du Cinéma* (Paris), October 1969.

Georgakas, Dan, and Gary Crowdus, ''Costa-Gavras Talks about Z,'' in *Cineaste* (New York), Winter 1969–70.

Loewinger, Lawrence, in *Film Quarterly* (Berkeley), Winter 1969–70.

Georgakas, Dan, in *Film Society Review* (New York), December 1969.

Gow, Gordon, in *Films and Filming* (London), December 1969.

Sarris, Andrew, in *Village Voice* (New York), 11 December 1969.

Kael, Pauline, in *New Yorker*, 13 December 1969.

Derain, Aline, in *Films in Review* (New York), January 1970.

Costa-Gavras, Constantin, ''Pointing Out the Problems,'' in *Films and Filming* (London), June 1970.

Haskell, Molly, ''Jean-Louis Trintignant,'' in *Show* (Los Angeles), 20 August 1970.

''An Interview with Costa-Gavras and Jorge Semprun,'' in *Film Society Review* (New York), January 1971.

Mellen, Joan, ''Fascism in the Contemporary Cinema,'' in *Film Quarterly* (Berkeley), Summer 1971.

Hennebelle, G., ''Z Movies; or, What Hath Costa-Gavras Wrought,'' in *Cineaste* (New York), no. 2, 1974.

Marty, A., ''In contresens idéologique sur l'oeuvre de Costa-Gavras,'' in *Image et Son* (Paris), December 1977.

Camy, G., ''Costa-Gavras: Un certain cinéma politique,'' in *Jeune Cinéma* (Paris), November 1983.

Johnston, Sheila, ''Costa-Gavras,'' in *Sight and Sound* (London), Summer 1984.

Poulle, F., ''Le cinéma politique de grande audience, autopsie d'un prototype: Z,'' in *Cinemaction* (Conde-sur-Noireau), no. 35, November 1985.

Serceau, Daniel, ''La trilogie,'' in *Cinemaction* (Conde-sur-Noireau), no. 35, November 1985.

Dreifus, Claudia, ''Constantin Costa-Gavras: Politics at the Box Office,'' in *The Progressive*, vol. 52, no. 9, September 1988.

Castiel, E., in *Séquences* (Haute-Ville), no. 189/190, March/June 1997.

* * *

On 22 May 1963, after speaking at an anti-nuclear rally in Salonika, the charismatic Greek deputy Grigoris Lambrakis was clubbed to death in the street. The conservative government described the event as ''an unfortunate traffic accident,'' but following protests from the opposition leader, George Papandreou, a young examining magistrate was appointed to investigate the incident. Contrary to

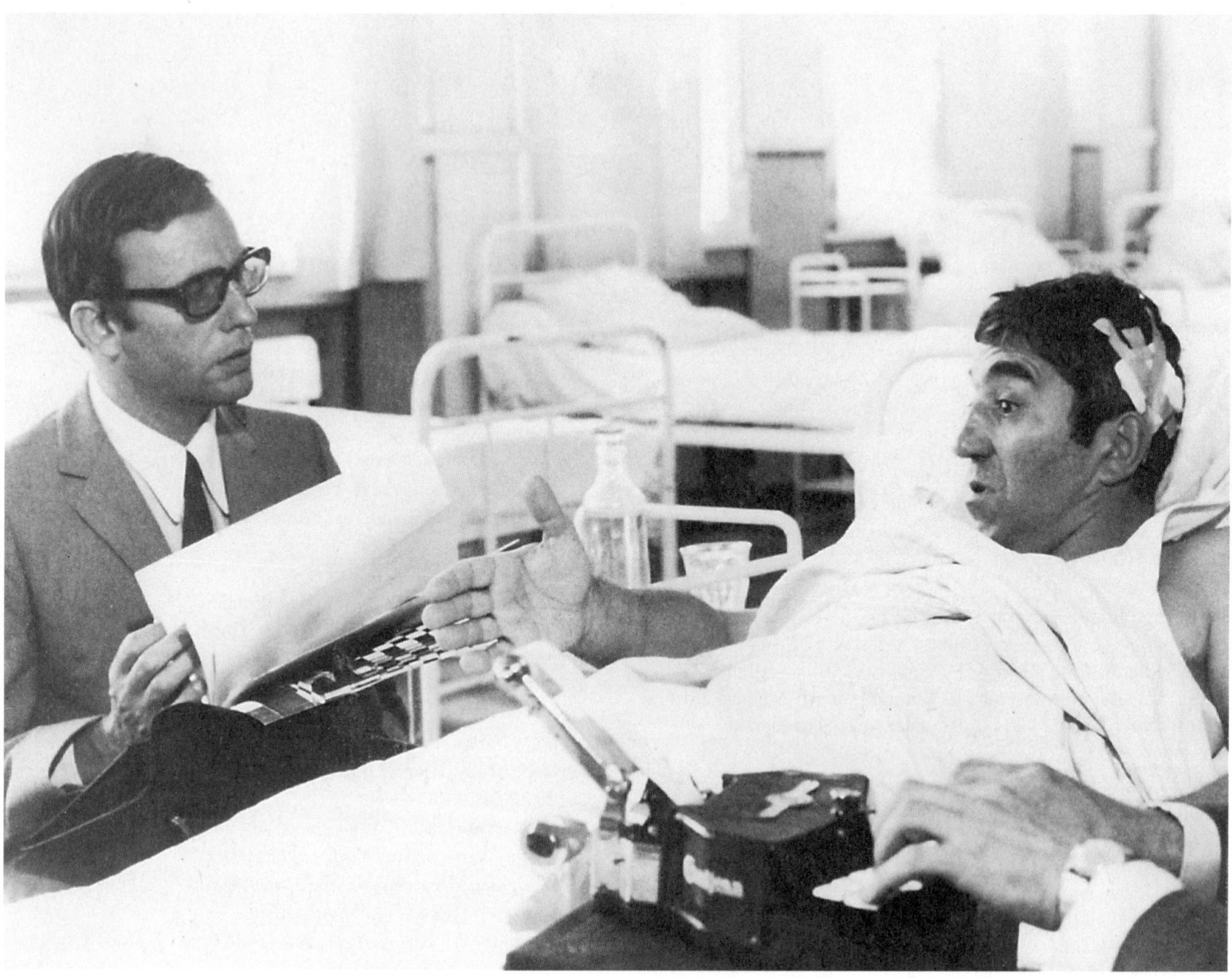

Z

government expectations the magistrate refused to be manipulated and the intended cover-up became an embarrassing revelation: Lambrakis had been murdered by an extreme right-wing organization sanctioned by the authorities. Key witnesses began to disappear, and the deepening scandal eventually brought down the Karamanlis government. The Centre Left under George Papandreou came to office, but the king discharged his government, and on 21 April 1967 the military seized power. The examining magistrate was relieved of his responsibilities and strict censorship imposed.

These chilling facts form the basis for Costa-Gavras's gripping political thriller *Z*. His narrative came not directly from the investigation, but from the novel by Vassilis Vassilikos, a Lambrakis follower, who had been given access to the evidence during the brief period of Centre Left rule. Published in 1966, the novel ends with the trial of the conspirators, but Costa-Gavras, benefiting from historical hindsight, extends his version to include the military coup.

For his adaptation, Costa-Gavras sought the collaboration of Jorge Semprun who had previously worked with Resnais on *La guerre est finie*. The flashbacks providing background to the protagonists or exposing government manipulation, are characteristic of Semprun's organizing strategies. To produce a taut, fast-moving film narrative, the filmmaker discarded the novel's philosophical and reflective passages and reduced the range of characters, so that the journalist/photographer, for example, is a composite of several reporters. The dialogue has also been pared down, though some contemporary allusions to the May 1968 events in Paris have been added.

Casting posed few problems since left-wing activists like Yves Montand were more than keen to participate. His engaging performance as *Z* is matched by that of Irene Papas as his tearful Hélène; Jean-Louis Trintignant lends a steely authority to the magistrate's role. Financing the production, however, proved difficult: United Artists, for one, fearing retaliation, declined to back the project. Eventually the Algerian authorities, eager to add stature to their embryonic film industry, provided both finance and locations.

Although the film contains no explicit topographical references, visual clues such as barely disguised portraits of the Greek royal family, the insignia of Olympian airways, and the *Fix* brand of beer indicate Greece as the setting, while the distinctive music of Mikis Theodorakis seals this identification. A challenging screen statement invites the viewer to associate the film's action with contemporary events: ''Any similarity to actual events or persons living or dead is not coincidental. It is intentional.''

With the subtitle ''Anatomy of a Political Assassination,'' the film exploits the investigative thriller format with more than a hint of melodrama. The characters, starkly differentiated, border on caricatures. The fascist elements have few physical or moral virtues: they are fat, ugly, or bald, and count pederasts amongst their numbers. Members of the humanitarian left, epitomized in Yves Montand, are attractive, warm-hearted, sensitive, and dignified to the point that Lawrence Loewinger termed them ''cardboard saints.'' Political arguments are equally simplified and the foregrounding of dramatic situations leaves little room for objectivity. If derisive music accompanies the grotesque comic-opera officials as they parade before the magistrate, for the idolized Z the theme is resonant and emotionally charged, while tragic tones prepare the arrival of his widow Hélène. Camerawork, too, points up the message with telescopic close-ups for the long-awaited arrival of the deputy's plane, while blurred subjective shots after the clubbing reinforce the emotional participation. Similarly close-ups, alternating with all-embracing longshots, draw the viewer into the physical violence of the mob behaviour, and satirically emphatic zoom shots pick out the medal-bedecked chests of the corrupt generals. Such rhetorical devices effectively preclude a reflective approach: the persuasive presentation carries the viewer forward eager to unravel the web of deceit and obfuscation.

Central to the film's narrative strategy is the editing process. Each witness will give a subjective account of events, set against a narrative flashback, to provide a further piece in the jigsaw. As false witnesses parrot their prepared statements, betraying themselves by the too-often repeated phrase ''supple and ferocious like a tiger,'' there is a revealing disjuncture between speaker and image. Again, parallel editing juxtaposes the sentiments of the peace rally with the mob violence outside. Finally, repeated flashbacks of the murdered deputy create a sense of his immanence, thus providing a visual metaphor for the meaning of the Greek word ''Z'': ''he still lives.''

—R. F. Cousins

ZANGIKU MONOGATARI

(Story of the Late Chrysanthemums)

Japan, 1939

Director: Kenji Mizoguchi

Production: Shochiku; black and white, 35mm; running time: 143 minutes.

Producer: Nobutaro Shirai; **screenplay:** Yoshikata Yoda and Matsutaro Kawaguchi, from the original theatrical adaptation by Sanichi Iwaya of an original story by Shofu Muramatsu; **photography:** Shigeto Miki and Yozo Fuji; **editor:** Koshi Kawahigashi; **art director:** Hiroshi Mizutani; **music:** Senji Ito and Shiro Fukai; **choreography:** Otowa; **costumes:** Seizo Yamaguchi and Yoshizaburo Okumura; **sound:** Ryuichi Shikita and Fumizo Sugimoto.

Cast: Shotaro Hanayagi (*Kikonosuke Onoe*); Kakuko Mori (*Otoku*); Kokichi Takada (*Fukusuke Nakamura*); Gonjuro Kawararaki (*Kikugoro Onoe V*); Yoko Umemura (*Osato*); Tokusaburo Arashi (*Shikan Nakamura*); Kinnosuke Takamatsu (*Matsusuke Onoe*); Benkei Shiganoya (*Genshun Motosuke*); Ryotaro Kawanami (*Dayu Eijyu*).

Zangiku monogatari

Publications

Books:

Mesnil, Michel, *Mizoguchi Kenji*, Paris, 1965.

Serceau, Daniel, *Mizoguchi: De la revolte aux songes*, Paris, 1983.

McDonald, Keiko, *Mizoguchi*, Boston, 1984.

Kirihara, Donald, *Patterns of Time: Mizoguchi and the 1930s*, Madison, Wisconsin, 1992.

O'Grady, Gerald, editor, *Mizoguchi the Master*, Ontario, 1996.

Tomasi, Dario, *Kenji Mizoguchi*, Milan, 1998.

Articles:

Pym, J., *Monthly Film Bulletin* (London), April 1981.

Mellen, Joan, ''Japanese Film's 'Truest Creator,''' in *The New York Times*, vol. 130, section 2, D23, 17 May 1981.

Tessier, M., ''Contes des chrysanthemes,'' in *Image et Son* (Paris), June 1981.

Cuel, F., *Cinematographe* (Paris), July 1981.

Bergala, A., ''Japon, tour, decor,'' in *Cahiers du Cinema* (Paris), September 1981.

Carbonnier, A., *Cinema* (Paris), September 1981.

Legrand, G., ''Lumiere, rituel, l'amour,'' in *Positif* (Paris), February 1982.
Bullot, E., ''La gifle et le sanglot,'' in *Vertigo* (Paris), no. 14, 1996.
Burdeau, Emmanuel, and others, ''Mizoguchi Encore,'' in *Cahiers du Cinéma* (Paris), no. 504, July-August 1996.
Lopate, Philip, ''A Master Who Could Create Poems for the Eye,'' in *The New York Times*, 15 September 1996.

* * *

Although *Zangiku monogatari* is one of the greatest achievements of its director Mizoguchi Kenji (to follow the Japanese custom of placing family name first) non-Japanese audiences, and even many contemporary Japanese, may be puzzled and alienated by its very title, let alone by its theme of the triumph of family duty over personal love and its loving recreations of a vanished period in Japanese history and a decreasingly popular traditional art form. (The film is rendered even less accessible by the fact that many prints of it are defective or incomplete.) Yet making the intellectual and emotional effort to understand and enjoy it is rewarding, for what seems at first to be a stiff and formal drama is really a subtle and unforgettable exercise in subverting traditional values.

Zangiku may be variously translated as ''late/last/remaining chrysanthemum(s)''; *monogatari* means ''tale'' or ''story.'' Onoe Kikunosuke, whose personal name contains the word for ''chrysanthemum'' and whose family *mon* (badge) is that flower, is the adopted son of a Kabuki star. He is first seen on stage—in Tokyo in 1885—giving what aficionados would see was a bad performance; he prefers not to study his parts, until the maid Otoku tells him to. She is fired by his mother, but Kiku announces his wish to marry her and leaves home when his father, who now has a natural son to succeed him anyway, refuses to permit their union. The lovers reunite in Osaka, where Kiku has joined a relative's theatre company. They then travel with yet another group until 1890, when it falls apart and Otoku visits Nagoya to plead with Kiku's father, who is performing there. Kiku is invited back into the family but Otoku agrees to stay away (without his knowledge). Many years later, when the family theatre group is performing in Osaka, Kiku is permitted to visit Otoku there, finding her on her deathbed. The film closes with her death and his appearance in a parade on the Yodo river, scenes which are intercut to maximise the contrast between her failure and isolation and his success and acceptance.

Summarised in this way *Zangiku monogatari* may seem to be a fairly routine melodrama, in which issues are raised in order to be neatly resolved. Perhaps the stage play from which it was derived fitted such a description. If so, Mizoguchi transforms it, using all the cinematic resources at his disposal in the endeavour to bring the story to life, to make Kiku, Otoku, and the others plausible as human beings rather than symbols or puppets—and to insert his own characteristically understated but powerful sense of the fragility and ambiguity of human feelings into the narrative.

The principal technical means that Mizoguchi uses to intensify the varying moods of the film is to shoot the ''real'' scenes and the three Kabuki excerpts in contrasting ways. The former are shot in long takes, with speakers' faces often in shadow or turned away while the camera pans and tracks to show different perspectives and the presence of third parties, as when Kiku's father remains in the room (offscreen) as a silent but intimidating witness to a discussion of Otoku between Kiku and his mother. The latter are presented in short takes that concentrate on Kiku to the exclusion of other actors and also disregard the convention of filming stage action as if from a realistic audience perspective. The cumulative effect of this contrast is to emphasise the artificiality of the stage performance, its distance from the confusions and complications of real life, and therefore to heighten the illusion that we are overhearing conversations among real people, about real concerns, in the offstage scenes.

These real concerns, as in several other films directed by Mizoguchi, include the question of the position of women in society. Although *Zangiku monogatari* is unusual among his films for having a male central character, its dramatic and moral weight is actually placed upon the fate of Otoku. In doing so Mizoguchi indicates a respect for the audience's ability to work things out for themselves, implicit in the distinctive camera technique described above. Unlike conventional melodramas, *Zangiku monogatari* never forces a single ethical message on its viewers. Because it seemed to endorse the subordination of women proclaimed by the official ideology of the Japanese government of the day, the film received a prize from the Ministry of Education in 1940. Yet the film also contains, in Otoku's character, a portrait of a strong and independent woman making her own choices; in Kiku's, a depiction of good intentions stifled and diverted by family pressure; and, in their respective fates, an implicit protest against the distorting effects of systematic subordination on women and men alike.

Aside from its story, its initially unfamiliar but eventually impressive visual style, and its ambiguous and thought-provoking moral concerns, *Zangiku monogatari* offers other pleasures, which grow with each year that passes since its initial release, and with Japan's steady development away from the society that it represents and now commemorates. Otoku and Kiku's first long conversation is punctuated by the traditional cries of street vendors, few of whom remain in contemporary Japan; the details of the family home and the attic room in which Otoku dies are as evocative as (say) shots of prewar New York, London or Berlin can be for anyone who knows those cities today; and such scenes as the Kabuki excerpts and the closing procession have become valuable records of a rich cultural tradition. In thus functioning on several levels at once—as an absorbing drama, a classic demonstration of film technique, a provocation to serious thought and complex feeling, and a record of a receding past—*Zangiku monogatari* transcends its origins as a filmed play, and its status as a specifically Japanese film, to stand as a classic of world cinema.

—Patrick Heenan

ZASEDA

(The Ambush)

Yugoslavia, 1969

Director: Zivojin Pavlovic

Production: Filmska Raedna Zajednica; running time: 78 minutes.

Screenplay: Zivojin Pavlovic, from his short story ''Pavolvic's Legends'' and another, ''Po Treci Put,'' by Antonije Isakovic; **photography:** Milorad Jaksic-Fando; **editor:** Olga Skirigin; **art director:** Dragolub Ivkov; **music:** Archival.

Cast: Ivica Vivodic (*Ivo*); Milena Dravic (*Milica*); Severin Bijelic (*Bunny*); Slobodan Aligrudic (*Jetic*).

Awards: Golden Lion, Venice, 1969.

Publications

Article:

Variety (New York), 1969.

* * *

The Ambush is the fifth feature film by Zivojin Pavlovic. When it appeared in 1969 it became one of the most controversial films of the Yugoslav Black Cinema. Pavlovic, who is also well known in Yugoslavia for his tightly written neo-realistic prose, based this film, which focuses on the gap between the ideals of the Socialist revolution at the end of World War II and the often brutal reality of the Stalinist period, on one of his own stories and another by Antonije Isakovic. It is a harsh view of the political and social climate in Yugoslavia after the war. The hero participates in a killing during the Revolution—but is then killed himself.

Pavlovic has forged his subject matter from raw material supplied by the first Yugoslav writer to call attention to the darker side of Tito's Partisan movement. Released but never distributed at home until very recently, the film was highly praised from the very beginning by those few Yugo-critics who managed to see it for both the purity of Pavlovic's style and the honesty of his subject matter. The film won the Golden Lion in Venice in 1969.

Pavlovic's influence on Yugoslav cinema has been profound. In a 1983 survey of ninety Yugoslav film critics, for instance, Pavlovic and Aleksander Petrovic were the only directors with three films listed among the top twenty Yugoslav films ever made. A graduate of the Academy of Applied Arts and Sciences in Belgrade in 1959, Pavlovic began his career as an amateur filmmaker. He made his feature debut in 1962, scripting and directing one part of a three part omnibus film *Kapi, Vode, Ratnici* (*Raindrops Water Warriors*). His story of an ex-con who returns home to find no one wishes to help him, foreshadowed Pavlovic's unswerving interest in outsiders living on the margins of society.

—Mike Downey

ZEMLYA

(Earth)

USSR, 1930

Director: Alexander Dovzhenko

Production: VUFKU (Kiev); black and white, 35mm, silent; length: 1704 meters, 6 reels. Released 8 April 1930, Kiev. Filmed April-November 1929 in Poltava.

Screenplay: Alexander Dovzhenko; **photography:** Danilo Demutsky; **art director:** Vasily Krichevsky; **music for performance:** Leonid Revutsky; **assistant directors:** Julia (Ioulya) Solntseva and Lazar Bodyk.

Cast: Stepon Shkurat (*Opanas Trubenko*); Semen Svashenko (*Vasilly, the son*); Nikola Nademsky (*Grandfather Semen*); Yelena Maximova (*Natalka, Vasilly's fiancée*); I. Franko (*Arkhip Belokon, a Kulak*); P. Masokha (*Khoma*); V. Mikhailov (*Father Gerasim, the priest*); P. Petrik (*Kravchina-Chuprina, the Komsomol Secretary*); Julia Solntseva (*Vasilly's sister*).

Publications

Script:

Dovzhenko, Alexander, *La Terre* (in Russian, English, and French), Moscow, 1965; also published in *Mother: A Film by V. I. Pudovkin and Earth: A Film by Alexander Dovzhenko*, New York, 1973.

Books:

Rotha, Paul, *Celluloid: The Film Today*, London, 1931.
Leyda, Jay, *Kino: A History of the Russian and Soviet Film*, New York, 1942; revised edition, London, 1960.
Leyda, Jay, *An Index to the Creative Work of Alexander Dovjenko*, London, 1947.
Martin, Marcel, *Panorama du cinéma sovietique*, Paris, 1960.
Rachuk, Igor, *Poetika Dovzhenko*, Moscow, 1964.
Schnitzer, Luda and Jean Schnitzer, *Dovjenko*, Paris, 1966.
Mariamov, Alexander, *Alexandre Dovzhenko*, Moscow, 1968.
Oms, Marcel, *Alexandre Dovjenko*, Lyons, 1968.
Yourenev, R., *Alexander Dovzhenko*, Moscow, 1968.
Amengual, Barthélemy, *Alexander Dovzjenko*, Paris, 1970.
Carynnyk, Marco, editor, *Alexander Dovzhenko: The Poet as Filmmaker*, Cambridge, Massachusetts, 1973.
Garbicz, Adam, and Jacek Klinowski, editors, *Cinema, The Magic Vehicle: A Guide to Its Achievement: Journey One: The Cinema Through 1949*, Metuchen, New Jersey, 1975.
Marshall, Herbert, *Masters of the Soviet Cinema: Crippled Creative Biographies*, London, 1983.
Kepley, Vance, *In the Service of the State: The Cinema of Alexander Dovzhenko*, Madison, Wisconsin, 1986.

Articles:

''Interview with Dovjenko,'' in *Close-Up* (London), no. 4, 1930.
Sadoul, Georges, ''Interview de A. Dovjenko,'' in *Lettres Françaises* (Paris), 1956.
Montagu, Ivor, ''Dovzhenko—Poet of Eternal Life,'' in *Sight and Sound* (London), 1957.
''Special Issue'' of *Film* (Venice), August 1957.
Dovzhenko, Alexander, ''Autobiography,'' in *Iskusstvo Kino* (Moscow), no. 5, 1958.

Zemlya

Shibuk, Charles, ''The Films of Alexander Dovzhenko,'' in *New York Film Bulletin*, no. 11–14, 1961.
Capdenac, Michel, ''Julia Solntseva et la terre ukrainienne,'' in *Lettres Françaises* (Paris), 25 May 1961.
Kelman, Ken, in *Film Culture* (New York), Winter 1963–64.
''Alexander Dovzhenko,'' in *Anthologie du cinéma 1*, Paris, 1966.
Kael, Pauline, in *Kiss Kiss Bang Bang*, Boston, 1968.
Frejlih, S., ''Ein Epos unserer Epoche,'' in *Film und Fernsehen* (Berlin), August 1974.
''Dovzhenko Issue'' of *Iskusstvo Kino* (Moscow), September 1974.
Pym, John, in *Monthly Film Bulletin* (London), February 1980.
Burns, P. E., ''Cultural Revolution, Collectivization, and Soviet Cinema,'' in *Film and History* (Newark, New Jersey), December 1981.
Mayne, J., ''Soviet Film Montage and the Woman Question,'' in *Camera Obscura* (Bloomington), no. 19, January 1989.
Margolit, E., ''*Zemlja*, SSSR (1930),'' in *Iskusstvo Kino* (Moscow), no. 12, December 1990.
Kepley, V., Jr., ''Dovzhenko and Montage: Issues of Style and Narration in the Silent Films,'' in *Journal of Ukrainian Studies*, vol. 19, no. 1, 1994.
Williams, B., ''A Mirror of the Cinema: Poetic Discourse and Autotelic Aesthetics in Dovzhenko's *Earth*,'' in *Journal of Ukrainian Studies*, vol. 19, no. 1, 1994.
Trimbac, S., ''Pocva I sud'ba,'' in *Iskusstvo Kino* (Moscow), no. 12, December 1994.

* * *

Earth is a tribute to life in the Ukraine, the birthplace of its creator, Alexander Dovzhenko. The film's star is essentially the Ukrainian village in which the story is set: it is not necessarily a tale of Russian farmers and kulaks but a visual poem about life and the calm acceptance of death.

Earth's scenario is virtually lacking in plot: in fact, one of its themes—the triumph of modern farm equipment over a primitive methodology—is similar to that of Sergei Eisenstein's *Old and New*. Youthful peasants in the community join together to purchase a tractor, to efficiently operate their farms. Vasilly, head of the village committee, reaps corn with the assistance of the machine, women fasten together the stalks cut from the earth, a threshing machine toils in the fields, and the peasants produce an abundant harvest. The town's kulaks (or, well-to-do landowners who profited from the sweat of the poorer farmers; as a class they opposed Soviet politics and collectivization of the land) are intimidated by this show of unity. At the end of a workday, young lovers stare at the sunset, and animals peacefully graze in the meadows. Vasilly, who had earlier plowed beyond the boundaries of a kulak's farm, strolls home in the moonlight and is shot by a kulak. His father grieves over the corpse, but will not allow a traditional Christian burial. Instead, the villagers carry Vasilly in an open bier, through the fields. His murderer runs into the cemetery, blurts out that he is the peasant's killer, and dances amid the graves in a weak imitation of Vasilly's movements before the moment of his death. But the killer is ignored. A rain—tears from the sky—falls and shines on the crops. The clouds disappear, and the sun glistens and dries the earth.

This short synopsis does not effectively describe the film's content and impact on the viewer. Dovzhenko lyrically captures what the earth—the soil and the life-sustaining crops it produces—means to human beings. The earth must be lovingly nurtured so that corn and wheat may be reaped and mouths may be fed. (Dovzhenko shot the film on the rich terrain of his beloved Ukraine.) Most significantly, the film is at once a celebration of life and an acknowledgement of the inevitability of life's end. Dovzhenko's images, all in meticulously composed shots, are unforgettable: in the film's prologue a dying man (the grandfather of Vasilly, a character patterned after the filmmaker's grandfather), serene as he approaches his end, happily pierces an apple with his teeth; Vasilly ecstatically dances in the summer moonlight, kicking up dust and feeling every moment of his life before it is abruptly ended by a bullet; apple tree branches brush over the face of Vasilly's corpse in the funeral caravan. In sequence after sequence, Dovzhenko brings together the two ultimate but contrasting realities: life and death. Death is not a gloomy, depressing finality, but a necessary and logical occurrence. If babies are to be born and the world replenished with the hopes, desires and energy of youth, some must vacate the earth and allow them time and space. Similarly, the earth must yield its crops so that it may again commence the cycle necessary to feed and nourish the hungry.

Earth is clearly not apolitical. Lewis Jacobs described it as a "rhapsody of victory for a new society." Dovzhenko himself explained, "I conceived *Earth* as a film that would herald the beginning of a new life in the villages." But, in its day, the film was quite controversial. Some Soviet critics were quick to condemn it as politically incorrect because the lyricism overrides the storyline. In addition, it focuses on a universal, philosophical theme; it does not just merely detail specific events and struggles relating to the Revolution. A particularly pointed article in *Izvestia* entitled "The Philosophers," by Demyan Bedny (the pseudonym for Yefim Pridvorov, considered a major proletarian poet of the 1920s), resulted in the editing of several sequences, including the scene where the tractor's radiator boils over and is cooled by the collective urine of the peasants, and another depicting Vasilly's betrothed, naked and crazed with grief, mourning his death. "I was so stunned by (Bedny's) attack," Dovzhenko wrote, "so ashamed to be seen in public, that I literally aged and turned gray overnight. It was a real emotional trauma for me. At first I wanted to die."

After *Earth* premiered in Russia, Dovzhenko brought the film to Paris and Berlin, and under the title *Soil*, it opened in New York during the fall of 1930. The negative of *Earth* was destroyed by the Germans during World War II, but a copy of the original release print fortunately survived.

Earth created a sensation outside the Soviet Union. Its simple imagery influenced other directors, particularly documentary filmmakers in England and the United States. Today, it is Dovzhenko's most famous film, and one of the great achievements of world cinema.

—Rob Edelman

ZENDEGI EDAME DARAD

See **And Life Goes On**

ZERKALO

(Mirror)

USSR, 1974

Director: Andrei Tarkovsky

Production: Mosfilm; color, 35mm; running time: 106 minutes.

Producer: E. Waisberg; **screenplay:** Andrei Tarkovsky, Aleksandr Misharin; **photography:** Georgi Rerberg; **editor:** L. Feiginova; **assistant directors:** L. Tarkovskaya, V. Karchenko, M. Chugunova; **music:** Eduard Artemiev, J. S. Bach, Giovanni Battista Pergolese, Henry Purcell; **costumes:** N. Fomina; **sound:** Semyon Litvinov.

Cast: Margarita Terekhova (*Alexei's mother/Natalia*); Philip Yankovsky (*Alexei, aged 15*); Ignat Daniltsev (*Ignat/Alexei, aged 12*); Oleg Yankovsky (*Father*); Nikolai Grinko (*Man at printing shop*); Alla Demidova (*Lisa*); Yuri Nazarov (*Military instructor*).

Publications

Books:

Le Fanu, Mark, *The Cinema of Andrej Tarkovsky*, London 1987.
Gauthier, Guy, *Andrej Tarkovsky*, Paris, 1988.
Turovskaya, Maya, *Tarkovsky: Cinema as Poetry*, London 1989.
Turovskaya, Maya, *About Andrei Tarkovsky*, Moscow, 1990.
Tarkovsky, Andrei, *Time within Time: The Diaries 1970–1986*, Calcutta, 1991.
Green, Peter, *Andrei Tarkovsky: The Winding Quest*, Hampshire, 1993.
Johnson, Vida T., and Graham Petrie, *Films of Andrei Tarkovsky: A Visual Fugue*, Bloomington, 1994.

Articles:

Marshall, H., *Sight and Sound* (London), Spring 1976.
Variety (New York), 2 February 1977.

Edelmann, F., *Lumiere du Cinema* (Paris), January-February 1978.
Fieschi, J., and D. Maillet, *Cinematographe* (Paris), February 1978.
Cros, J., *Image et Son* (Paris), March 1978.
Delmas, J., "Tarkovsky declavelise," in *Jeune Cinema* (Paris), March 1978.
Grant, J., *Cinema* (Paris), March 1978.
Jweancolas, J. P., *Positif* (Paris), May 1978.
Adair, G., *Monthly Film Bulletin* (London), March 1980.
Strick P., *Sight and Sound* (London), Spring 1980.
Ward, M., "The Idea that Torments and Exhausts," in *Stills* (London), Spring 1981.
Dempsey, M., "Lost Harmony: Tarkovsky's *The Mirror* and *The Stalker*," in *Film Quarterly* (Berkeley), vol. 35, no. 1, Fall 1981.
Amiel, Vincent, "Mon fils, ou l'avenir de ma mémoire," in *Positif* (Paris), no. 324, February 1988.
Petric, Vlada, "Tarkovsky's Dream Imagery," in *Film Quarterly* (Berkeley), vol. 43, no. 2, Winter 1989–90.
Wiese, I., "Andrej Tarkovskij," in *Z Filmtidsskrift* (Oslo), no. 1, 1996.
Wright, Alan, "A Wrinkle in Time: The Child, Memory, and *The Mirror*," in *Wide Angle* (Baltimore), vol. 18, no. 1, January 1996.
Graffy, Julian, Layla Alexander Garrett, and Bérénice Reynaud, "Tarkovsky," in *Sight & Sound* (London), vol. 7, no. 1, January 1997.
Reynaud, B., "Tarkovsky: Seeing is Believing," in *Sight & Sound* (London), vol. 7, January 1997.

* * *

At a press conference in 1975, Andrei Tarkovsky asserted that *Mirror* "is no more than a straightforward, simple story" which "doesn't have to be made any more understandable"; yet it has acquired an intimidating reputation for inaccessibility and self-indulgence. All the incidents are taken from his own or his relatives' lives, three members of his family can be seen or heard in it and there are several dream sequences; but why should anyone who is not a Tarkovsky be interested in them? As for the occasional extracts from documentary footage, notably of Soviet troops in the Second World War, are they anything more than disconnected bits of history, especially now that the Soviet Union is as dead and gone as the Holy Roman Empire? Yet *Mirror* does go on impressing those who see it through and can resonate in the mind long afterwards, whether through specific images or as an atmosphere, a sense of dream and memory coming together. Perhaps the best way into it is through another of Tarkovsky's remarks at that press conference, his invitation to "look, learn, use the life shown here as an example." Looking and learning do not require a Ph.D. in Tarkovsky Studies. Even a child can do all three—which is another clue to Tarkovsky, for whom children seem to have represented idealism (as in *Ivan's Childhood*), inventiveness (as in *Andrei Rublev*), and other qualities which adult life may distort or erode.

Mirror begins with a boy in a city apartment watching a television demonstration of hypnosis; a young woman stands in a field at twilight, smoking a cigarette and waiting for someone, though not for the soldier who passes by; her son plays with a cat while a voice reads a poem which refers to a "domain . . . beyond the mirror" (in Kitty Hunter-Blair's translation). These first few minutes suggest that two separate periods of time are being depicted and that the "mirror" of the title—as in Lewis Carroll's story *Through the Looking Glass* or Jean Cocteau's film *Orphée*—is a gateway between two worlds. The suggestion (not so much mysticism as truism) is confirmed later on, when the same woman is reflected in a real mirror that shows her to be much older.

This is in fact Tarkovsky's mother, the boy in what we learn is the 1930s represents Tarkovsky, the voice on the soundtrack is that of his father (the poet Arseny Tarkovsky) and the 1970s boy is his son. But these purely personal facts actually matter much less than they would in a more mainstream, linear narrative, precisely because of the intercutting between story (private memories) and newsreel (public memories), reality and dreams, children and adults. The connections among these elements are made clearer rather than more obscure by Tarkovsky's careful alternation of colour, sepia tinting and black and white, as well as by the slow pace of every scene. Thus the almost always absent father (in the 1930s), seen returning at last in soldier's uniform, is linked to footage of the Soviet army slogging through marshland and to a comic scene of military training disrupted by the instructor's incompetence and the boys' distractedness. The almost always present mother is recalled by her resemblance to a woman in a painting by Leonardo da Vinci, seen in the 1970s. Both of these lonely people are reflected by shots of Spanish refugees living in Moscow and, perhaps, by contrast with the crowds hailing Mao Tse-tung in shots of China. Again, the early log cabin, isolated between fields and woods, is paralleled by the later Moscow apartment, another refuge from human and climatic coldness.

The dissolving of the everyday barriers among these phenomena culminates in the dream sequences, each grounded by being shown to be inside the mind of the boy in the 1930s. He sees water cascading through the room and down the walls after watching his mother wash her hair; the house burns in dreams after burning in reality; he imagines his mother floating away from her bed while he is waiting anxiously for her to emerge from a doctor's surgery; the wind moves across the meadow as his father would if he were to come back.

Tarkovsky's meditative approach, his presentation of a broad range of loosely connected images and events in a variety of cinematic formats, actually frees audiences from the need for too many footnotes or translations. *Mirror* tells us something of what it was like to live in the Soviet Union in Stalin's 1930s and Brezhnev's 1970s but it also evokes as much recognition as surprise, for even viewers who know nothing of Tarkovsky's life, Soviet history or, for that matter, the paintings which he "quotes" in some scenes, know as much as he did about nostalgia, dreaming and other forms of longing, and about comparing and contrasting what is, and what was, with what might have been.

In *Mirror* Tarkovsky opens up his world—arguably more successfully than in his later films, which are less autobiographical but also more tightly bound to an increasingly explicit and unsubtle religiosity—just as, in the film, his son opens a book of Leonardo's paintings, inviting readings that will differ from viewer to viewer, and indeed (given the film's main themes) at different times in any viewer's life. Orson Welles, whom Tarkovsky greatly admired, once said that a film is "a ribbon of dreams." *Mirror* is an example of the many ways in which filmmakers and audiences together can transform private dreams into shared visions.

—Patrick Heenan

ZÉRO DE CONDUITE

(Zero for Conduct)

France, 1933

Director: Jean Vigo

Production: Argui-Film; black and white, 35mm; running time: 44 minutes, some sources list 47 minutes; length: 1200 meters. Filmed 24 December 1932 to 22 January 1933 in Gaumont studios. Released 1946 (banned by the censors in August 1933 until 15 February 1946).

Production supervisor: Henri Storck; **screenplay:** Jean Vigo; **assistant directors:** Albert Riera, Henri Storck, and Pierre Merle; **photography:** Boris Kaufman; **editor:** Jean Vigo; **sound engineers:** Royne and Bocquel; **music:** Maurice Jaubert.

Cast: Jean Daste (*Superintendent Huguet*); Robert Le Flon (*Superintendent Parrain, called ''Pète-Sec''*); Delphin (*Principal*); Blanchar (*Superintendent Général, called ''Bec de gaz''*); Larive (*Chemistry professor*); Mme. Emile (*Madame Colin, called ''Mère Haricot''*); Louis de Gonzague-Frick (*Le Préfet*); Rafa (Raphael) Diligent (*Fireman*); Felix Labisse (*Fireman*); Georges Vakalo (*Fireman*); Georges Patin (*Fireman*); Henri Storck (*Le Curé*); Michele Fayard (*Correspondent's girl*); Georges Berger (*Correspondent*); Louis Lefebvre (*Caussat*); Gilbert Pruchon (*Colin*); Coco Golstein (*Bruel*); Gerard de Bedarieux (*Tabard*).

Publications

Script:

Vigo, Jean, *Zéro de conduite*, in *Avant-Scène du Cinéma* (Paris), 15 December 1962; in *The Complete Jean Vigo*, edited by Andrew Sinclair, New York, 1983; in *Oeuvre de cinéma: Films, scénarios, projets de films, texts sur le cinéma*, edited by Pierre Lherminier, Paris, 1985.

Books:

Feldman, Joseph and Harry Feldman, *Jean Vigo*, London, 1951.
Kyrou, Ado, *Le surréalisme au cinéma*, Paris, 1953; revised edition, 1963.
Sallès-Gomès, P. E., *Jean Vigo*, Paris, 1957; revised edition, Los Angeles, 1971; New York, 1999.
Buache, Freddy, and others, *Hommage à Jean Vigo*, Lausanne, 1962.
Esteve, Michele, *Jean Vigo*, Paris, 1966.
Lherminier, Pierre, *Jean Vigo*, Paris, 1967.
Lovell, Alan, *Anarchist Cinema*, London, 1967.
Smith, John M., *Jean Vigo*, London, 1967.
Mast, Gerald, *The Comic Mind*, New York, 1973; revised edition, Chicago, 1979.
Simon, William G., *The Films of Jean Vigo*, Ann Arbor, Michigan, 1981.
Gorbman, Claudia, *Unheard Melodies: Narrative Film Music*, London, 1988.

Articles:

Cinémonde (Paris), 2 February 1933.
Cavalcanti, Alberto, ''Jean Vigo,'' in *Cinema Quarterly* (Edinburgh), Winter 1935.
Spectator (London), 13 September 1946.
Kracauer, Siegfried, ''Jean Vigo,'' in *Hollywood Quarterly*, April 1947.
Weinberg, Herman G., ''The Films of Jean Vigo,'' in *Cinema* (Beverly Hills), July 1947.
Agee, James, in *Nation* (New York), 12 July 1947.
Barbarow, George, ''The Work of Jean Vigo,'' in *Politics*, Winter 1948.
''Vigo Issue'' of *Ciné-Club* (Paris), February 1949.
Positif (Paris), no. 7, 1953.
Sight and Sound (London), July-September 1953.
Manvell, Roger, in *The Film and the Public*, London, 1955.
Mekas, Jonas, ''An Interview with Boris Kaufman,'' in *Film Culture* (New York), Summer 1955.
Chardère, Bernard, ''Jean Vigo et ses films,'' in *Cinéma* (Paris), March 1955.
Ashton, Dudley Shaw, ''Portrait of Vigo,'' in *Film* (London), December 1955.
''Vigo Issue'' of *Premier Plan* (Lyons), no. 19, 1961.
Mills, B., ''Anarchy, Surrealism and Optimism in *Zéro de Conduite*,'' in *Cinema* (London), no. 8, 1971.
Velvet Light Trap (Madison, Wisconsin), Summer 1973.
Teush, B., ''The Playground for Jean Vigo,'' in *Film Heritage* (Dayton, Ohio), Fall 1973.
Gorbman, Claudia, ''Vigo/Laubert,'' in *Ciné-Tracts* (Montreal), Summer 1977.
Henrikson, H. W., in *Chaplin* (Stockholm), vol. 26, no. 5–6, 1984.
Agee, James, in *Cahiers du Cinéma* (Paris), no. 448, October 1991.
Sidler, V., ''Traeumer des kinos, Rimbaud des films,'' in *Filmbulletin* (Winterthur, Switzerland), no. 4, 1992.
Steiff, D., ''A Cutting Art,'' in *Sight & Sound* (London), vol. 3, no. 4, April 1993.

* * *

Zéro de conduite is one of only four films made by Jean Vigo during his brief but notable career in film. (He died in 1934 at the age of 29 just before the release of his final film, *L'atalante*.) *Zéro de conduite* is a short feature concerning life in a boys' boarding school, focusing on four of the students. The title refers to the frequent ''zeroes'' they receive when they fail to conform to the standards of behavior imposed on them by their teachers. The film culminates with a student rebellion launched during a school assembly in the presence of local dignitaries.

Before it received general distribution, the film was banned by the French Board of Censorship, presumably for its harsh, derogatory portrayal of French bourgeois institutions, and was not commercially released in France until after World War II. (In his biography of Vigo, P. E. Sallès-Gomès claims there is reason to believe the order to ban the film originated from a higher government ministry.) *Zéro de conduite* is often cited as the precursor of François Truffaut's *Les 400 coups* and Lindsay Anderson's *If.* The comparisons are based on the film's sympathetic attitude towards the position of the children, culminating in the rallying cry for liberty, and its corresponding condemnation of the rigid policies and hypocritical posture adopted

Zéro de conduite

by the adults who control the children's lives. But in other ways the film is very different from its so-called successors.

Vigo's films are admired for, among other things, their blend of realistic detail and a poetic-surrealist sensibility. This quality pervades *Zéro de conduite*. The opening sequence of the film is exemplary in this respect. As the film begins, two of the schoolboys share a train compartment on the way back to school after vacation. They play with various toys they have recently acquired, transforming them in the process: balloons become breasts, a small flute is played through the nose, and, using feathers, they dress themselves as chickens. Finally they light cigars, filling the compartment with smoke, creating a hazy dream-like image. In this atmosphere, the one adult in the compartment, who is sleeping and limp, is declared dead. If the scene opens with ''realistic,'' concrete details (of decor and costume), it shifts in the course of the children's play, effecting an alteration in the tone and perception of the space. Similar transformations occur throughout the film. In the middle class a new teacher, and the only sympathetic one, performs balancing tricks on his desk and sketches a cartoon figure which suddenly becomes animated. In the world of childhood and imagination, magical metamorphosis can occur at any time.

The behavior and appearance of the authority figures are held up for ridicule. The school principal is a midget who sports a large top hat; in his office he keeps the hat like a relic under a glass dome on the mantlepiece which he can barely reach. The science teacher is an obese, overbearing man who almost walks into a skeleton dangling in the classroom. During the commemoration day ceremony, the public audience is comprised of dignitaries in full-dress uniforms and life-size, costumed dummies. (If this was in part due to financial restraints on the production, it is fully in line with the film's representation of adults and ceremonious activity.) These characterizing details not only condemn the adult world to absurdity, but also contribute to the bizarre visual texture of the film and its partially dreamlike world.

The most extreme excursion into fantasy occurs the night before the commemoration day assembly. In the dormitory, the rebellion is launched: all of the objects in the room are thrown around as the children express their disdain for authority. Part way through the scene there is a shift to slow motion as pillows and feathers fly, and the children parade through the room. The teacher in charge is unable to constrain them and falls asleep. In the morning he is tied to his bed and set upright in a gesture of mock crucifixion. The four leaders of the rebellion carry their flag to the roof and hurl various objects at the dignitaries assembled in the courtyard. The film concludes with the four boys marching up the rooftops towards the sky.

Vigo's depiction of school life in *Zéro de conduite* is often described in biographical terms. In particular it is seen as expressing the misery he experienced as a child in boarding school and the subversive tendencies of his father, a militant anarchist who died (reportedly murdered) in prison when Vigo was 12 years old. While his personal circumstances certainly influenced his attitudes and ideas, the emphasis on the film as an autobiography obscures the degree to which the film transforms the world. In this regard it should be recalled that Vigo's career was closely affiliated with French avant-garde film activity in the late 1920s.

Vigo did experience difficulties in the production of the film, notably in the area of finance. But he was aided by a group of committed assistants. Foremost among those was Boris Kaufman, director of photography on all Vigo's films. They had worked closely on *A propos de Nice*, Vigo's first film, establishing the basis for future collaboration. This film revealed Vigo's interest in combining an avant-garde use of the medium with aggressive social critique. The music for *Zéro de conduite* was composed by Maurice Jaubert, and contributes to the overall tone of the film. He worked particularly hard on the music for the night-time revolt in order to achieve a dream-like effect; after writing the basic score it was rescored and recorded in reverse, and then re-recorded backwards to restore the original.

—M. B. White

PICTURE ACKNOWLEDGMENTS

The editors wish to thank the copyright holders of the photographs included in this volume and the permissions managers of many book and magazine publishing companies for assisting us in securing reproduction rights. We are also grateful to the staffs of the Detroit Public Library, the Library of Congress, the University of Detroit Mercy Library, Wayne State University Purdy/Kresge Library Complex, and the University of Michigan Libraries for making their resources available to us. Every effort has been made to trace copyright, but if omissions have been made, please bring them to the attention of the editors. The following is a list of the copyright holders who have granted us permission to reproduce material in the *International Dictionary of Films and Filmmakers* as well as from where said resources were received;

AP/Wide World Photos. *Blade Runner*; *Casablanca*; *Chinatown*; *City Lights*/Associated Press/United Artists; *Double Indemnity*; *Dr. Strangelove or: How I Learned To Stop Worrying And Love The Bomb*; *Modern Times*; *A Streetcar Named Desire*.

Archive Photos, Inc. *Apocalypse Now*; *Blue Velvet*; *Close Encounters of the Third Kind*/Fotos International; *Easy Rider*/Fotos International; *GoodFellas*; *High Noon*; *Midnight Cowboy*; *Psycho*; *Public Enemy*/Warner Bros.; *Rear Window*; *The Silence of the Lambs*/Ken Regan/Fotos International.

CORBIS. *Great Expectations*/Springer/Bettmann; *Lolita*; *The Maltese Falcon*/Bettmann.

All remaining images were provided courtesy of the Kobal Collection.

NOTES ON ADVISERS AND CONTRIBUTORS

AFFRON, Charles. Essayist. Professor of French, New York University, since 1965. Author of *Star Acting: Gish, Garbo, Davis,* 1977; *Cinema and Sentiment,* 1982; *Divine Garbo,* 1985; and *Fellini's 8½,* 1987. General editor of Rutgers Films in Print Series. **Essays:** *The Best Years of Our Lives; It's a Wonderful Life; The Little Foxes; Ninotchka; Le Quai des brumes; The Red Shoes; A Star Is Born; The Wind.*

AFFRON, Mirella Jona. Essayist. Professor, Program in Cinema Studies, since 1985, and dean of Humanities and Social Sciences, since 1987 at College of Staten Island, City University of New York. Former member of the executive council, Society for Cinema Studies. **Essays:** *The Southerner; La Terra trema; Umberto D.*

AMBROGIO, Anthony. Essayist. Procedures analyst, Maccabees Life Insurance. Film and composition instructor, Wayne State University, Detroit, 1975–85. Contributor to *Film Criticism* and *Pukka Afflatus,* and to *Erotic Universe* (ed. D. Palumbo, 1986). **Essays:** *Dracula* (1931); *Paths of Glory.*

ANDREW, Dudley. Adviser and Essayist. Angelo Bertocci Professor of Critical Studies and director of the Institute for Cinema and Culture at the University of Iowa (joined faculty in 1969). Author of *Major Film Theories,* 1976; *André Bazin,* 1978; *Kenji Mizoguchi: A Guide to References and Resources* (co-author), 1981; *Concepts in Film Theory,* 1984; and *Film in the Aura of Art,* 1984. **Essays:** *A propos de Nice; La Bataille du rail; Les Dames du Bois de Boulogne; Le Diable au corps; Les Jeux interdits; Journal d'un curé de campagne; Jules et Jim; Le Million; Pépé le Moko; Saikaku ichidai onna; Tirez sur le pianiste.*

ARMES, Roy. Essayist. Reader in film and television at the Middlesex Polytechnic, London. Author of *French Cinema since 1946,* 1966, 1970; *The Cinema of Alain Resnais,* 1968; *French Film,* 1970; *Patterns of Realism,* 1972, 1983; *Film and Reality,* 1974; *The Ambiguous Image,* 1976; *A Critical History of British Cinema,* 1978; *The Films of Alain Robbe-Grillet,* 1981; *French Cinema,* 1985; *Third World Filmmaking and the West,* 1987; *On Video,* 1988; and *Studies in Arab and African Film,* 1991. **Essays:** *L'Argent; La Belle et la bête; Le Chagrin et la pitié; Charulata; Chronique des années de braise; Les Diaboliques; Farrebique; La Femme du boulanger; Feu Mathias Pascal; Napoléon; Le Sang d'un poète; Les Vampires.*

BARDARSKY, Dimitar. Essayist. With the Short Films Department, Bulgarian Cinematography, Sofia, since 1982. With the Programming and Publications Department, Bulgarian National Film Archive Sofia, 1978–81. Contributor to and editor of the biographical section, *In the World of Cinema,* 3 volumes, 1982–83. **Essays:** *Koziyat rog; Sterne.*

BARNOUW, Erik. Adviser and essayist. Professor emeritus of dramatic arts, Columbia University. Author of *Indian Film,* 1963; *A History of Broadcasting in the United States,* 1966; *Documentary: A History of the Nonfiction Film,* 1974; *Tube of Plenty: The Evolution of American Television,* 1975; *The Sponsor: Notes on a Modern Potentate,* 1978; *The Magician and the Cinema,* 1981; *House with a Past,* 1992; and *Media Marathon: A Twentieth Century Memoir,* 1996. Editor in chief, *International Encyclopedia of Communications,* 1989. Writer, director, and producer of films. **Essay:** *Kino-pravda.*

BASINGER, Jeanine. Adviser and essayist. Professor of film, Wesleyan University, Middletown, Connecticut, since 1969. Trustee, American Film Institute, National Center for Film and Video Preservation. Member of advisory board, Foundation for Independent Video and Film. Author of *Working with Kazan,* 1973; *Shirley Temple,* 1975; *Gene Kelly,* 1976; *Lana Turner,* 1977; *Anthony Mann: A Critical Analysis,* 1979; *The World War II Combat Book: Anatomy of a Genre,* 1986; *The ''It's a Wonderful Life'' Book,* 1986; and numerous articles. **Essays:** *An American in Paris; The Devil is a Woman; Sullivan's Travels.*

BAXTER, John. Essayist. Novelist, screenwriter, television producer, and film historian. Visiting lecturer, Hollins College, Virginia, 1974–75; broadcaster with BBC Radio and Television, 1976–91. Editor of two anthologies of science fiction; author of six novels, various screenplays for documentary films and features, and works of film criticism: *Hollywood in the Thirties,* 1968; *The Australian Cinema,* 1970; *The Gangster Film,* 1970; *Science Fiction in the Cinema,* 1970; *The Cinema of John Ford,* 1971; *The Cinema of Josef von Sternberg,* 1971; *Hollywood in the Sixties,* 1972; *An Appalling Talent: Ken Russell,* 1973; *Sixty Years of Hollywood,* 1973; *Stunt,* 1974; *The Hollywood Exiles,* 1976; *King Vidor,* 1976; *The Video Handbook* (with Brian Norris), 1982; *Filmstruck,* 1989; *Fellini,* 1993; and *Buñuel,* 1994. **Essays:** *Accattone; Balada o soldate; Der blaue Engel; Casablanca; Chronique d'un été; The Crowd; Dirty Harry; Et . . . Dieu créa la femme; The Grapes of Wrath; The Last Wave.*

BECK, Sandra L. Essayist. Technical assistant, Museum of Modern Art Film Study Center and Film Circulation Department, New York City. **Essays:** *Fröken Julie; Körkalen; Pickpocket.*

BERGAN, Ronald. Adviser. Regular contributor, *The Guardian* (London); consultant and writer for several TV documentaries; lectured on literature, theatre, and film during ten years in France; author of numerous books on the cinema, including biographies of the Coen Brothers, Sergei Eisenstein, Jean Renoir, Anthony Perkins, and Dustin Hoffman, as well as *The United Artists Story* and *The Great Theatres of London.*

BOCK, Audie. Essayist. Freelance author and lecturer; visiting lecturer posts held at Harvard, Yale, University of California, and other institutions, 1975–83; assistant producer of the international version of Kurosawa's *Kagemusha,* 1980. Author of *Japanese Film Directors,* 1978 and *Mikio Naruse: un maitre du cinema japonais,* 1983; translator of *Something Like an Autobiography,* by Kurosawa, 1982. **Essay:** *Ai no corrida.*

BODEEN, DeWitt. Essayist. Screenwriter and film critic. Author of screenplays, *Cat People,* 1942; *Seventh Victim,* 1943; *Curse of the Cat People,* 1944; *The Yellow Canary,* 1944; *The Enchanted Cottage,* 1945; *Night Song,* 1947; *I Remember Mama,* 1948; *Mrs. Mike,* 1949; and *Billy Budd,* 1962; author of also numerous teleplays, 1950–68. Author of film criticism/history, *Ladies of the Footlights; The Films of Cecil B.DeMille; Chevalier; From Hollywood;* and *More From Hollywood;* novel, *13 Castle Walk*; editor of *Who Wrote the Movie and What Else Did He Write?.* Died 1988. **Essays:** *Camille; City Lights; Les Enfants du paradis; Greed; Henry V* (1944); *Viridiana.*

BOWERS, Ronald. Essayist. Financial editor, E. F. Hutton and Company, since 1982. Editor, *Films in Review,* 1979–81. Author of *The MGM Stock Company,* with James Robert Parish, 1973; and *The Selznick Players,* 1976. **Essays:** *Le Carrosse d'or; Le Crime de Monsieur Lange; Gösta Berlings Saga; Lola; The Magnificent*

Ambersons; Miracolo a Milano; Los Olvidados; Orphée; Sciuscia; La Strada; Il Vangelo secondo Matteo.

BOWLES, Stephen E. Essayist. Associate professor of film, University of Miami, since 1976. Author of *An Approach to Film Study,* 1974; *Index to Critical Film Reviews British and American Film Periodicals 1930–1971,* 3 volumes, 1974–75; *Sidney Lumet: References and Resources,* 1979; and *Index to Critical Film Reviews: Supplement 1, 1971–1976,* 1983; associate editor of *The Film Book Bibliography 1940–1975,* 1979. **Essays:** *Blow-Up; On the Waterfront; Shane.*

BRASHINSKY, Michael. Essayist. Instructor in film studies at the School of Visual Arts, New York City; author of film column for *The Westsider.* Author of *The Zero Hour: Glasnost and Soviet Cinema in Transition;* and editor of *Russian Critics on the Cinema of Glasnost* (both with Andrew Horton). **Essays:** *Dekalog; Igla; Last Tango in Paris; Siberiade.*

BROPHY, Stephen. Essayist. Freelance writer and film critic, Boston, Massachusetts. **Essay:** *Todo Sobre Mi Madre.*

BURTON, Julianne. Essayist. Associate professor, Merrill College and member of the Board of Studies in Literature, University of California at Santa Cruz, since 1982 (assistant professor, 1974–82). Author of more than 40 publications on the Latin American cinema. **Essay:** *Tire dié.*

CAMPBELL, John. Adviser. Publisher, *Moving Pictures International*; managing director, *Pilgrim Films.*

CAMPER, Fred. Essayist. Independent filmmaker and writer and lecturer on film since 1965. Has taught at various American colleges and universities. **Essays:** *Kiss Me Deadly; Shoah; Unsere Afrikareise.*

CHENG, Scarlet. Essayist. Senior contributing editor of *Asian Art News* magazine. Organizer, film series and seminar ''The Fifth Generation of Chinese Filmmakers,'' Freer Gallery of Art, Washington D.C. Contributor many articles on film, visual arts, and books to *Washington Post, International Herald Tribune, Asian Wall Street Journal, The World and I, Belles Lettres Review of Books*, and many others. **Essays:** *Ahfei zheng zhuan; Ba wang bie ji; Daoma zei; Odeur de la papaye verte; Qiu Ju da Guansi.*

CHRISTENSEN, Julie A. Essayist. Associate Professor, Department of Modern and Classical Languages, George Mason University; specializes in Russian and Georgian cinema, literature, and language. **Essay:** *Soy Cuba.*

CIMENT, Michel. Essayist. Associate professor in American Studies, University of Paris. Member of the editorial board, *Positif,* Paris. Author of *Erich von Stroheim,* 1967; *Kazan by Kazan,* 1973; *Le Dossier Rosi,* 1976; *Le Livre de Losey,* 1979; *Kubrick,* 1980; *Les Conquérants d'un nouveau monde* (collected essays), 1981; *Schatzberg, de la photo au cinema* (co-author), 1982; *Portrait of a 60% Perfect Man: Billy Wilder* (co-author), 1980; *Elia Kazan: An Outsider,* 1982; *All about Mankiewicz,* 1983; *Boorman,* 1985; *Francesco Rosi: Chronique d'un film annoncé,* 1987; and *Passport pour Hollywood* (collected interviews), 1987. **Essays:** *Foolish Wives; Lolita.*

COLE, Lewis. Adviser. Professor of Screenwriting, Columbia University, co-founder Meditteranean Film Institute, Chair of Film Division, Columbia University, 1996–2000. Television critic, *Nation Magazine,* 1994–1997. Author of *A Loose Game,* 1978; *Dream Team,* 1982; *Never Too Young to Die,* 1990; *This Side of Glory,* 1996. Also author of numerous screenplays and articles.

CONLEY, Tom. Essayist. Professor of French and comparative literature, Harvard University; former professor, University of Minnesota. Former editor, *Enclitic.* Author of *Su realismo: lectura de Bunuel, Las Hurdas,* 1988; and *The Writing of Film,* 1990. Contributor to *Theater Journal, MLN, Hors Cadre, Revue des Lettres Modernes,* and *Litterature.* **Essays:** *High Sierra; The Killers; The Lady from Shanghai; Touch of Evil; Vivre sa vie.*

COOK, David A. Essayist. Professor and director of film studies, Emory University, since 1985. Author of *A History of Narrative Film,* 1981, 2nd ed., 1990. **Essays:** *Teni zabytykh predkov; The Wild Bunch.*

COOK, Samantha. Essayist. Freelance editor and researcher, London. Editor of *1989 Women's Film List;* and contributor to *Neglected Audiences,* 1990. **Essay:** *Dance, Girl, Dance.*

COUSINS, R. F. Essayist. Lecturer in French, University of Birmingham. Author of *Zola's Therese Raquin,* 1990; and contributor to *University Vision* and *Literature/Film Quarterly.* Executive member of British Universities Film and Video Council. **Essays:** *L'Arroseur arrosé; La Bête humaine; Le Boucher; Le Voyage dans la lune; Z.*

CRIPPS, Thomas. Essayist. Professor of history and coordinator of the graduate program in popular culture, Morgan State University, Baltimore, since 1961. Producer-writer, Westinghouse Broadcasting, 1968–72. Author of *Slow Fade to Black: The Negro in American Film 1900–1942,* 1977, and *Black Film as Genre,* 1978; editor of *The Green Pastures,* 1979. **Essay:** *Der Ewige Jude.*

CROWDUS, Gary. Adviser. Founder and Editor-in-Chief, *Cineaste* magazine; editor of *A Political Companion to American Film,* Lake View Press.

DASSANOWSKY, Robert von. Adviser and essayist. Associate Professor of Languages and Cultures, Director, Film Studies, and Head of German Studies, University of Colorado, Colorado Springs; Vice President, Austrian American Film Association; actor, television writer and independent film producer; author of *Phantom Empires: The Novels of Alexander Lernet-Holenia,* 1996; and *Cinema: From Vienna to Hollywood and Back,* forthcoming; contributing editor, ''Austria's Hollywood/Hollywood's Austria,'' special issue of *Filmkunst,* 1997; contributing editor, *Gale Encyclopedia of Multicultural America,* 2000. **Essays:** *Casino Royale, Märchen vom Glück, Tiefland.*

DAVIAU, Gertraud Steiner. Essayist. Lecturer at the Universities of Vienna and Klagenfurt, Austria; visiting scholar, University of California, Riverside, and University of California, Los Angeles; civil servant, Austrian Federal Chancellery/ Federal Press Service, Austria; working on a research project and screenplay for the documentary *Austria's Hollywood—Hollywood's Austria*; author of *Die Heimat-Macher. Kino in Österreich 1946–1966,* 1987; *Filmbook Austria,* 2nd edition, 1997; and *Traumfabrik Rosenhügel (The Dream Factory of Rosenhügel),* 1997. **Essays:** *38, Der Engel mit der Posaune, Sodom und Gomorrha.*

DEANE, Pamala S. Essayist. Independent writer and media historian; M.A. in Radio/TV/Film, University of Maryland, College Park; author of fiction and screenplays for documentary programming. **Essay:** *Fresa y Chocolate.*

DE ROMERO, Sara Corben. Essayist. Assistant press officer and production manager for British television. Instructor at private university. Worked for BBC news crews in Mexico. Produced charity viedos. **Essays:** *Alsino y el Condor; El Chacal de Nahueltoro.*

DERRY, Charles. Essayist. Ph.D. in Film, Northwestern University. Coordinator of Film Studies, Wright State University, Dayton, Ohio, from 1978. Author of *Dark Dreams: A Psychological History of the Modern Horror Film,* 1977. Co-author, with Jack Ellis and Sharon Kern, of the reference work *The Film Book Bibliography: 1940–1975,* 1979. Director of the short films *Cerebral Accident* and *Joan Crawford Died for Your Sins.* Fiction has appeared in *Reclaiming the Heartland: Gay and Lesbian Voices from the Midwest,* 1996. **Essays:** *The Birds; La Femme infidèle; Le Salaire de la peur.*

DIXON, Wheeler Winston. Essayist. Director, film studies program, University of Nebraska, Lincoln. Filmmaker and author of *The "B" Directors: A Biographical Directory,* 1985; *The Cinematic Vision of F. Scott Fitzgerald,* 1986; and *Terence Fisher: The Critical Reception,* 1990. Contributor to *Films in Review, Literature/Film Quarterly,* and *Post Script.* **Essay:** *Dracula* (1958).

DORAISWAMY, Rashmi. Essayist. Freelance writer. **Essay:** *Meghe dhaka tara.*

DOWNEY, Mike. Adviser and essayist. Director and associate publisher, *Moving Pictures International,* London; film critic and producer. **Essays:** *Budjenje pacova; Nesto izmedju; Samo jednom se ljubi; Skuplijaci perja; Vlak bez voznog reda; Zaseda.*

DUNAGAN, Clyde Kelly. Essayist. Instructor in mathematics, University of Wisconsin Center, Sheboygan. **Essays:** *Bronenosets Potemkin; Gone With the Wind; M*A*S*H.*

DUNBAR, Robert. Essayist. Freelance film critic and historian; held various visiting professorships and lectureships, since 1975. Worked for Gainsborough and Gaumont-British Studios, 1933–38, 1948–49; director of public and cultural relations, British Embassy, Moscow, 1944–47; general manager, Imperadio Pictures, 1949–51; independent producer of feature films and documentaries, 1952–63; chairman, London School of Film Technique, 1963–74. Died 1988. **Essays:** *Maxim Trilogy; Putyovka v zhizn; Turksib.*

DURGNAT, Raymond. Essayist. Visiting professor of film, Wright State University, Dayton, Ohio. Author of numerous publications on film, including *Durgnat on Film,* 1975; co-author, *King Vidor-American,* 1988; and *Michael Powell and the English Genius,* 1990. **Essays:** *Cléo de cinq à sept; Nieuwe Gronden.*

DURIE, John. Adviser. Managing director, *Strategic Film Marketing.*

EDELMAN, Rob. Essayist. Author of *Great Baseball Films,* 1994; and *Baseball on the Web,* 1998. Co-author of *Angela Lansbury: A Life on Stage and Screen,* 1996; *The John Travolta Scrapbook,* 1997; and *Meet the Mertzes,* 1999. Contributing editor of *Leonard Maltin's Movie & Video Guide*; *Leonard Maltin's Movie Encyclopedia*; and *Leonard Maltin's Family Film Guide.* Director of programming of Home Film Festival. Contributor to *The Political Companion to American Film, Women Filmmakers & Their Films, Total Baseball, The Total Baseball Catalog, International Film Guide,* and *The Whole Film Sourcebook.* Film critic/commentator, WAMC (Northeast) Public Radio. Lecturer, University at Albany. Former film critic/columnist, New Haven Register and Gazette Newspapers. Former adjunct instructor, The School of Visual Arts, Iona College, Sacred Heart University. **Essays:** *L'America; Un Coeur en hiver; Die Dreigroschenoper; La Haine; Hana-Bi; Hoop Dreams; J'accuse; Jana Aranya; Ju Dou; Lan fengzheng; Mat; The Naked City; On the Town; Once Upon a Time in America; One Flew Over the Cuckoo's Nest; Outomlionnye solntsem; Variété Voina i mir; Zemlya.*

EHRLICH, Jane. Essayist. Instructor in German and Scandinavian film at Washington University, 1972–74, and University of California, Los Angeles, 1976–77. Author of columns published in *Arts Editor, Knave, Forum, Ludus, Active Life, Everywoman,* and *London Traveletter.* Contributor to numerous periodicals, including *Harpers & Queen, She Movie Scene, Spare Rib, Irish Post, Good Housekeeping, Period Living, Relax,* and *For Him.* Founder of freelance company, The Editorial Board. Contributor to *Annual Obituary.* **Essays:** *Mr. Smith Goes to Washington; Olympia; Ordet; Vampyr.*

ELLIS, Jack C. Adviser and essayist. Professor of film and former chair of the Department of Radio/Television/Film at Northwestern University, Evanston, Illinois. Also taught at UCLA, New York University, and the University of Texas at Austin. Author of *A History of Film,* 1979; *John Grierson: A Guide to References and Resources,* 1986; and *The Documentary Idea,* 1989. Founding member and past president of Society for Cinema Studies, editor of its journal, *Cinema Journal,* 1976–1982. **Essays:** *Drifters; Fires Were Started; Man of Aran; The March of Time; Rien que les heures; Why We Fight.*

ELSNER-SOMMER, Gretchen. Essayist. Film critic and director of Foreign Images distribution company. Formerly associate editor of *Jump Cut.* **Essays:** *Die Ehe der Maria Braun; Mädchen in Uniform.*

ERENS, Patricia. Essayist. Professor, Rosary College, River Forest, Illinois, since 1977. Author of *Akira Kurosawa A Guide to References and Resources,* 1979; and *The Jew in American Cinema,* 1984; editor of *Sexual Stratagems: The World of Women in Film,* 1979. **Essays:** *Biruma no tategoto; Film d'amore e d'anarchia; Hadaka no shima; O slavnosti a hostech; Suna no onna.*

ERSKINE, Thomas L. Essayist. Professor of English, Salisbury State University, Maryland. Co-founding editor of *Literature/Film Quarterly.* Chairman, film division, Modern Language Association. **Essays:** *Five Easy Pieces; Klute.*

ESTRIN, Mark W. Essayist. Professor of English and film studies, Rhode Island College, Providence, since 1966. Has published widely on film, dramatic literature, and theatre. Author of books including *Conversations with Eugene O'Neill,* 1990, and *Critical Essays on Lillian Hellman,* 1989. **Essay:** *Notorious.*

FALICOV, Tamara L. Essayist. Assistant Professor, Department of Theatre and Film and Latin American Studies, University of Kansas; teaches courses in Latin American film; author of articles in academic journals such as *Studies in Latin American Popular Culture* and *Media, Culture, and Society.* **Essay:** *Central do Brasil.*

FALLER, Greg S. Essayist. Professor, Department of Electronic Media & Film, Towson University, Towson, Maryland, since 1986; Assistant/Associate editor of *The International Dictionary of Films & Filmmakers,* first edition, vols. 3, 4, and 5, and *Journal of Film & Video,* 1985–87; advisor, *The International Dictionary of Films & Filmmakers,* second and third editions. **Essays:** *Anticipation of the Night; 42nd Street; If. . . ; Little Caesar; Singin' in the Rain.*

FARNSWORTH, Rodney. Essayist. Ph.D., Indiana University, 1980. Associate professor of comparative studies, Indiana University-Purdue University, Fort Wayne. Has published internationally in scholarly publications, including *Literature/Film Quarterly.* **Essays:** *India Song; Ivan Grozny; Sunrise.*

FEINSTEIN, Howard. Essayist. Film editor, *The Village Voice,* New York. **Essay:** *Konyets Sankt-Peterburga.*

FELLEMAN, Susan. Adviser and essayist. Assistant Professor of Cinema Studies, Southern Illinois University, Carbondale; author of *Botticelli in Hollywood: The Films of Albert Lewin* (1997) and many articles on art and film. **Essay:** *The Picture of Dorian Gray.*

FERN, Annette. Essayist. Librarian, freelance arts critic, and researcher. **Essays:** *Duck Soup; A Night at the Opera.*

FRENCH, Warren. Essayist. Freelance writer. **Essays:** *The Birth of a Nation; Philadelphia; A Streetcar Named Desire.*

FULKS, Barry A. Essayist. Assistant professor of history, University of Pittsburgh, since 1983. Author of various articles on the German cinema. **Essay:** *Berlin: Die Sinfonie der Grossstadt.*

GEORGAKAS, Dan. Essayist. Instructor in film courses at New York University and Queens College of the City University of New York. Organizer of film programs for community groups. Co-author of *In Focus: A Guide to Using Filmsy*; and *Solidarity Forevery* (based on the documentary *The Wobbliesy*). Co-editor of *The Cineaste Interviews.* Member of editorial board of *Cineaste,* since 1969. Contributor of film criticism to numerous publications. **Essay:** *Malcolm X.*

GIANOULIS, Tina. Essayist. Freelance writer; contributor to *St. James Encyclopedia of Popular Culture,* 1999; *Gay and Lesbian Literature,* 1997; www. mystories.com, daytime drama website, 1997–98; *Common Lives, Lesbian Lives, Sinister Wisdom,* and others. **Essays:** *Red Sorghum, Wandafuru Raifu.*

GIBSON, Ben. Adviser. Head of production, British Film Institute, since 1990. Partner in Metro Pictures (formerly The Other Cinema), 1981–87. Writer on cinema for numerous magazines. Co-editor of *Framework* film magazine. Co-founder of the London International Festival of Theatre. Member of executive committee, European Film Distribution Office. Member of advisory board, Merseyside Film Fund. Producer or executive producer of features, including *Out of Order,* 1987; *Silent Scream,* 1990; *Young Soul Rebels,* 1991; *The Long Day Closes,* 1992; *Anchoress,* 1992; *Wittgenstein,* 1993; *London,* 1994; *Don't Get Me Started,* 1994; *Loaded,* 1994; *Three Steps to Heaven,* 1995; and *Madagascar Skin,* 1995.

GILLESPIE, Jill. Essayist. Doctoral candidate, Department of German Studies, Cornell University. **Essays:** *Deutschland im Herbst; Marat/Sade.*

GLAESSNER, Verina. Essayist. Freelance critic and lecturer, London. Contributor to *Sight and Sound.* **Essay:** *Huang tudi.*

GLANCY, H. M. Essayist. Graduate student in film studies, University of East Anglia. **Essay:** *Mrs. Miniver.*

GLUR, Beat. Adviser. Freelance film and music critic for newspapers and magazines in Switzerland and Germany. Festival adviser for Locarno Film Festival and Cinemusic in Gstaad. Swiss correspondent for *Moving Pictures and Blickpunkt: Film.* Member of Cultural Commission of Suissimage; member of board of Swiss filmcritics organisation, Fipresci.

GOLOVSKOY, Val. Essayist. Graduated from the Institute of Cinematography in Moscow; editor and film critic in the Publishing House *Iskusstvo* (*Art*), *Iskusstvo kino* (*Cinema Art*), and *Sovetskij Ekran* (*Soviet Screen*) magazine; has taught in several U.S. universities since 1981; author of *Behind the Soviet Screen,* 1986. **Essay:** *Istoria Asi Kliachinoi kotoraia lubila da nie vyshla zamuzh.*

GOMERY, Douglas. Essayist. Professor, Department of Radio/Television/Film, University of Maryland, and senior researcher, Media Studies Project, Woodrow Wilson Center for International Scholars, Washington, D.C. Author of *High Sierra: Screenplay and Analysis,* 1979; co-author, *Film History: Theory and Practice*, 1985; *The Hollywood Studio System,* 1986; *The Will Hays Papers,* 1987; co-author, *American Media,* 1989; and *Movie History: A Survey,* 1991. **Essays:** *L'Age d'or; Apocalypse Now; The Band Wagon; Jaws; Johnny Guitar; The Man Who Shot Liberty Valance; My Darling Clementine; Tokyo monogatari.*

GOMEZ, Joseph A. Essayist. Lecturer in film studies, North Carolina State University. Contributor to *Literature/Film Quarterly.* **Essay:** *Meg ker a nep.*

GRETTON, Viveca. Essayist. Screenwriter in Toronto. Regular contributor to *CineAction.* M.A. in film studies, York University. **Essay:** *The Women.*

GRLIC, Rajko. Adviser. Eminent scholar, School of Film, Ohio University, Athens, Ohio, since 1993; visiting professor, Tisch School of the Arts, New York University, 1992–93; professor of film directing, The Academy of Dramatic Arts, Zagreb, Croatia, 1972–74, 1989–91. Director and screenwriter of numerous films, including: *Pass* (short), 1966; *If It Kills Me,* 1974; *Bravo Maestro,* 1978; *You Love Only Once,* 1981; *In the Jaws of Life,* 1985; *Three for Happiness,* 1987; *That Summer of White Roses,* 1989; and *Charuga,* 1991. Producer of films, including: *Consecration* (short), 1990; and *Virdzina,* 1991.

GUGLER, Josef. Essayist. Professor of Sociology, University of Connecticut; author of several books, including *Cities, Poverty, and Development: Urbanization in the Third World,* 1992; editor, *Cities in the Developing World: Issues, Theory, and Policy,* 1997; contributor of essays on film to *African Studies Review* and other periodicals. **Essays:** *Kongi's Harvest; Udju Azul di Yonta; Yaaba.*

HANSON, Patricia King. Essayist. Executive editor, American Film Institute, Los Angeles, since 1983. Film critic, *Screen International,* since 1986. Associate editor, Salem Press, 1978–83. Editor, *American Film Institute Catalog of Feature Films 1911–1920* and *1931–1940.* Co-editor of *Film Review Index,* vols. I and II, 1986–87; and *Sourcebook for the Performing Arts,* 1988; executive editor of *Meet Frank Capra,* 1990. **Essays:** *All the King's Men; Kaos; A Matter of Life and Death; Top Hat.*

HANSON, Stephen L. Essayist. Humanities bibliographer, University of Southern California, Los Angeles, since 1969. Associate editor, Salem film critic, *Screen International,* since 1986. Associate editor, Salem Press, 1978–83. Co-editor of *Film Review Index,* vols. I and II, 1986–87, and co-editor of *Sourcebook for the Performing Arts,* 1988. **Essays:** *Arsenal; East of Eden; Freaks; Madame de . . . ; Neobychanye priklyucheniya Mistera Vesta v strane bolshevikov;*

Novyi Vavilon; 8½; Potomok Chingis-Khan; Public Enemy; Roma, città aperta; Young Mr. Lincoln.

HARRIS, Ann. Essayist. Doctoral student in cinema studies, New York University. **Essays:** *Im Lauf der Zeit; Die Mörder sind unter uns; Salvatore Giuliano.*

HECK-RABI, Louise. Essayist. Freelance writer. Public and special librarian, 1955–70. Author of *Women Filmmakers: A Critical Reception,* 1983. Died 1995. **Essay:** *La Coquille et le clergyman.*

HEENAN, Patrick. Essayist. Lecturer in European history and politics at Kobe Institute; English teacher and adviser at schools in Osaka, Marugame, Kagawa-ken, and Tokyo, 1981–85. Researcher and writer for *International Directory of Company Histories,* 1990–91; *The International Dictionary of Historic Places,* since 1993; *Encarta,* since 1994; and *Great Illustrated Encyclopedia,* since 1995. **Essays:** *Bab el hadid; Narayama bushi-ko; Zangiku monogatari; Zerkalo.*

HENRY, Catherine. Essayist. Director of college publications, University of Chicago, since 1980. **Essays:** *The African Queen; M; Orfeu Negro.*

HIGSON, Andrew. Essayist. Lecturer in film studies, University of East Anglia. On the editorial board of *Screen.* Author of *Cinema,* 1988; and numerous articles on British Cinema. **Essays:** *The Blue Lamp; Gregory's Girl; Saturday Night and Sunday Morning; Tom Jones.*

HILL, John. Essayist. Senior lecturer in media studies, University of Ulster. Author of *Sex, Class and Realism: British Cinema 1956–63,* 1986; and co-author, *Cinema and Ireland,* 1987. **Essays:** *A Hard Day's Night; Odd Man Out.*

HIRANO, Kyoko. Essayist. Film program coordinator, Japan Society, New York, since 1986. Editor, *Cinéma Gras,* Tokyo, 1977–79; and contributor to *Cineaste* and *Theater Craft.* **Essays:** *Entotsu no mieru basho; Jujiro; Koshikei; Samma no aji; Shonen.*

HOLDSTEIN, Deborah H. Essayist. Assistant professor of English, Illinois Institute of Technology, Chicago, since 1980. **Essays:** *Blackmail; Easy Rider; The 39 Steps.*

HOPEWELL, John. Adviser. Film critic; bureau chief in Spain, *Moving Pictures International.*

HORTON, Andrew. Adviser and essayist. Professor of film, screenwriting, and literature at Loyola University in New Orleans. Author of numerous books, including *The Zero Hour: Glasnost and Soviet Cinema in Transition* (with Michael Brashinsky); *Comedy/Cinema/Theory, Writing the Character Centered Screenplay;* and *The Films of George Roy Hill.* Screenwriter of *Something in Between,* 1985; and *Virgina,* 1991. Member of editorial board of numerous film journals; series editor for ''Film Handbooks'' series, for Cambridge University Press. **Essays:** *Dom za vesanje; Thelma and Louise; O Thiasos.*

HUTCHINGS, Peter. Essayist. Lecturer in film studies, Department of Historical and Critical Studies, Newcastle Polytechnic. **Essays:** *Dead of Night; The Masque of the Red Death; Repulsion.*

IORDANOVA, Dina. Essayist. Contributing editor, BFI's Companion to Eastern European and Russian Cinema; works in the field of Balkan cinema and transnational film. **Essays:** *Angi Vera; Journey of Hope; Underground; To Vlemma Tou Odyssea.*

JAMES, Nick. Essayist. Freelance writer. **Essay:** *Guling jie shaonian sha ren shijian.*

JOHNSON, Timothy. Essayist. Freelance writer, Los Angeles, since 1978. Editor and co-compiler, *Crime Fiction Criticism: An Annotated Bibliography,* 1981; author of *Celluloid Egghead: Hollywood's Portrayal of the Intellectual,* 1984. **Essay:** *Jigokumon.*

KAMINSKY, Stuart M. Essayist. Professor of film, Northwestern University, Evanston, Illinois. Author of *Don Siegel, Director,* 1973; *Clint Eastwood,* 1974; *American Film Genres,* 1977; *John Huston, Maker of Magic,* 1978; *Coop: The Life and Legend of Gary Cooper,* 1980; co-author, *Basic Filmmaking,* 1981; and *American Television Genres,* 1985; co-author (with Mark Walker) of *Writing for Television,* 1988. Editor of *Ingmar Bergman: Essays in Criticism,* 1975. Also a novelist: works include *Murder on the Yellow Brick Road,* 1978; *He Done Her Wrong,* 1983; *A Cold Red Sunrise,* 1988; *Buried Caesars,* 1989; and *Blood and Rubles,* 1996. **Essays:** *Il Buono, il brutto, il cattivo; High Noon; Invasion of the Body Snatchers; The Maltese Falcon; The Treasure of the Sierra Madre.*

KANOFF, Joel E. Essayist. Lecturer in the visual arts, Princeton University, New Jersey, since 1983. **Essays:** *Ladri di biciclette; Ossessione; I Vitelloni.*

KARANOVIĆ, Srdjan. Adviser. Professor of film, Wesleyan University, Middletown, Connecticut.

KARNEY, Robyn. Adviser. London-based freelance writer, critic, and editor specializing in film subjects; editor-in-chief of *The Chronicle of the Cinema,* 1995, 1998; co-author, *The Faber Foreign Film Guide,* 1993; author of *A Star Danced: The Life of Audrey Hepburn,* 1995; *A Singular Man: Burt Lancaster,* 1998; and numerous other publications.

KEHR, Dave. Essayist. Film critic, *Chicago Tribune,* since 1986. **Essays:** *Playtime; Shichinin no samurai; Les Vacances de Monsieur Hulot.*

KEMP, Philip. Adviser and essayist. London-based freelance reviewer and film historian; contributor to *Sight and Sound, Variety,* and *Film Comment.* Author of *Lethal Innocence: The Cinema of Alexander Mackendrick,* 1991; and of a forthcoming biography of Michael Balcon. **Essays:** *Aranyer din Ratri; The Asphalt Jungle; Casque d'or; The Conversation; The Dead; Du Rififi chez les hommes; Fargo; He Liu; Le Jour se lève; Kind Hearts and Coronets; Korol Lir; Kwaidan; The Lavender Hill Mob; The Life and Death of Colonel Blimp; Lone Star; Ningen no joken; Ride the High Country; La Ronde; Seppuku; Shakespeare in Love; Sommarnattens leende; Souffle au coeur; Thérèse Desqueyroux; Trainspotting; Trouble in Paradise.*

KHANNA, Satti. Adviser and essayist. Research associate, Center for South and Southeast Asia Studies, University of California, Berkeley, since 1976. Author of *Indian Cinema* and *Indian Life,* 1980. **Essays:** *The Apu Trilogy; Do bigha zamin.*

KINSEY, Tammy. Essayist. Assistant Professor of Film, University of Toledo, Ohio, since 1997; made her first film at the age of eight; M.F.A. in Filmmaking, Virginia Commonwealth University, 1996. **Essay:** *Garam Hawa.*

KOVÁCS, Katherine Singer. Essayist. Assistant professor, Department of comparative literature, University of Southern California, Los Angeles. Editor, *Humanities in Society*; member of the executive committee, *The Quarterly Review of Film Studies*. Author of *Le Reve et la Vie: A Theatrical Experiment* by Gustave Flaubert, 1981. Died 1989. **Essays:** *Muerte de un ciclista*; *El Verdugo*.

KUPFERBERG, Audrey E. Essayist. Film historian, appraiser, and archivist. Co-author of *Angela Lansbury: A Life on Stage and Screen,* 1996; *The John Travolta Scrapbook,* 1997; and *Meet the Mertzes,* 1999. Lecturer, University at Albany. Contributing editor of *Leonard Maltin's Family Film Guide*. Contributor to *Women Filmmakers & Their Films* and *The Whole Film Sourcebook*. Film consultant to the Peary-MacMillan Arctic Museum at Bowdoin College. Former director, Yale University Film Study Center. Former assistant director, the National Center for Film and Video Preservation at the American Film Institute. Former project director, the American Film Institute Catalog. **Essays:** *Cyrano de Bergerac; Flaming Creatures; Once Upon a Time in America.*

LAMONTAGNE, Monique. Essayist. Research and writer for *International Directory of Company Histories,* 1990–91; *International Dictionary of Historic Places,* since 1993; *Encarta,* since 1994. Part-time researcher and language adviser for publications on international economics. **Essays:** *1900 (Novecento); Otac na sluzbenom putu.*

LANZA, Joseph. Essayist. Freelance writer. Author of *Fragile Geometry: The Films Philosophy and Misadventures of Nicolas Roeg,* 1989. Contributor to *Christopher Street, ReSearch,* and *High Times*. **Essays:** *The Bride of Frankenstein; Frankenstein.*

LARSEN, Susan K. Adviser. Assistant Professor of Russian Literature, University of California, San Diego. Author of *Reading and Writing Girlhood in Late Imperial Russia,* forthcoming; and many articles on Russian film and popular culture. Former chair of the Working Group on Cinema and Television in Eastern Europe and the Former Soviet Union.

LEAB, Daniel. Essayist. Film critic and historian, New York City. **Essays:** *Crossfire; I Am a Fugitive from a Chain Gang.*

LEE, Sharon. Essayist. Formerly public information director, Wisconsin Arts Board, Madison. **Essays:** *Chelovek s kinoapparatom; Le Joli Mai.*

LIMBACHER, James L. Essayist. Audio-visual librarian, Dearborn, Michigan Department of Libraries, 1955–83; national president, American Federation of Film Societies, 1962–65; and Educational Film Library Association, 1966–70; host of television series *Shadows on the Wall* and *The Screening Room*. Author of *Four Aspects of the Film,* 1968; *Film Music: From Violins to Video,* 1974; *Haven't I Seen You Somewhere Before,* 1979; *Sexuality in World Cinema,* 1983; and *Feature Films on 8mm, 16mm, and Video,* 7 editions. **Essay:** *The Informer.*

LIPPE, Richard. Essayist. Lecturer in film at Atkinson College, York University, Ontario. On the editorial board of *CineAction* and contributor to *Movie*. **Essays:** *All That Heaven Allows; The Apartment; Breakfast at Tiffany's; The Misfits.*

LOCKHART, Kimball. Essayist. Member of the faculty, Department of Romance Studies, Cornell University, Ithaca, New York. Founding editor, *Enclitic,* 1977–80. Member editorial board, *Diacritics,* Cornell University, since 1978. **Essay:** *Professione: Reporter.*

LORENZ, Janet E. Essayist. Associate editor and film critic *Z Channel magazine,* since 1984. Assistant supervisor, University of Southern California Cinema Research Library, Los Angeles, 1979–82; and film critic, *SelecTV Magazine,* 1980–84. **Essays:** *La Battaglia di Algeri; The Last Picture Show; Morte a Venezia; The Thin Man.*

LOVELL, Glenn. Essayist. Recent National Arts Journalism Fellow; film critic, *San Jose Mercury News* and Knight-Ridder Newspapers; teaches film history and esthetics at universities throughout the Bay Area, and does weekly film commentary for KGO-radio in San Francisco; contributed articles on film to the *Los Angeles Times, Variety, Washington Post,* and other papers; contributor to *Tender Comrades: A Backstory of the Hollywood Blacklist,* 1997. **Essay:** *Detour.*

LOWRY, Ed. Essayist. Formerly assistant professor of film studies, Southern Illinois University, Carbondale. Contributor to various film periodicals. Died 1987. **Essays:** *Angst essen Seele auf; Chelsea Girls; Scorpio Rising; The Searchers; The Sweet Smell of Success; White Heat.*

MacCANN, Richard Dyer. Essayist. Professor of film, University of Iowa, Iowa City, 1970–1986, emeritus professor, since 1986. Editor, *Cinema Journal,* 1967–76. Author of *Hollywood in Transition,* 1962; *The People's Films: A Political History of U.S. Government Motion Pictures,* 1973; *The First Tycoons,* 1987; and *The First Film Makers,* 1989. Editor of *Film and Society,* 1964; *Film: A Montage of Theories,* 1966; *The New Film Index,* 1975; and *Cinema Examined,* 1982. **Essay:** *The River.*

MACDONALD, Andrew. Essayist. Associate professor of English at Loyola University, New Orleans. Ph.D. in English from the University of Texas at Austin. Co-author of text for bi-lingual writing students, *Mastering Writing Essentials;* has written on popular culture concerns. Author of book on Howard Fast. **Essays:** *Das Boot; Moskva slezam ne verit; Mujeres al borde de un ataque de nervios; Picnic at Hanging Rock; Unforgiven; Yojimbo.*

MACDONALD, Gina. Essayist. Ph.D. in English from the University of Texas at Austin. Co-author of text for bi-lingual writing students, *Mastering Writing Essentials;* contributor of numerous articles and dictionary/encyclopedia entries about detective fiction, popular fiction, popular culture, and film to various presses. Has written two books for Greenwood Press on James Clavell and on Robert Ludlum. **Essays:** *Das Boot; Moskva slezam ne verit; Mujeres al borde de un ataque de nervios; Picnic at Hanging Rock; Unforgiven; Yojimbo.*

MACNAB, G. C. Essayist. Freelance writer, researcher, and filmmaker, London. Author of *J. Arthur Rank and the British Film Industry,* 1993. **Essays:** *Andrei Rublev; Distant Voices, Still Lives; Offret.*

MANCINI, Elaine. Essayist. Has taught film at the College of Staten Island, and at St. John's University, New York. Author of *The Free Years of the Italian Film Industry, 1930–1935,* 1981; *Struggles of the Italian Film Industry during Fascism, 1930–1935,* 1985; and *Luchino Visconti: A Guide to References and Resources,* 1986. **Essays:** *L'Albero degli zoccoli; I Pugni in tasca; Rocco e i suoi fratelli.*

MANVELL, Roger. Essayist. University professor and professor of film, Boston University. Director, British Film Academy, London, 1947–59, and a governor and head of the Department of Film History, London Film School, until 1974; Bingham Professor of the Humanities, University of Louisville, 1973. Editor, *Penguin Film Review,* 1946–49, and the Pelican annual *The Cinema,* 1950–52; associate editor, *New Humanist,* 1968–75; and member of the board of directors, Rationalist Press, London, since 1966; editor-in-chief, *International Encyclopedia of Film,* 1972. Vice-chairman, National Panel of Film Festivals, British Council, London, 1976–78. Author of *Film,* 1944; *The Animated Film,* 1954; *The Film and the Public,* 1955; *On the Air,* 1955; *The Technique of Film Music,* 1957, 1976; *The Technique of Film Animation,* with John Halas, 1959; *The Living Screen,* 1961; *Design in Motion,* with John Halas, 1962; *What Is a Film?,* 1965; *New Cinema in Europe,* 1966; *This Age of Communication,* 1967; *New Cinema in U.S.A.,* 1968; *New Cinema in Britain,* 1969; *Art Movement,* 1970; *The German Cinema,* with Heinrich Fraenkel, 1971; *Shakespeare and the Film,* 1971; *Films and the Second World War,* 1975; *Love Goddesses of the Movies,* 1975; *Theatre and Film,* 1979; *Art and Animation: Halas and Batchelor, 1940–1980*; *Ingmar Bergman,* 1980; also author of novels, biographies of theatrical personalities, and of personalities of the Third Reich. Died 1987. **Essays:** *Doktor Mabuse der Spieler; Das Testament des Dr. Mabuse; Det Sjunde inseglet; Smultronstället; Tystnaden.*

MARCHETTI, Gina. Essayist. Associate professor, University of Maryland, College Park. Author of *Romance and the ''Yellow Peril'': Race, Sex, and Discursive Strategies in Hollywood Fiction,* 1993. Staff editor of *Jump Cut.* **Essays:** *W.R.: Mysterije Organizma; Wutai jiemei.*

MAST, Gerald. Essayist. Formerly professor of English and general studies in the humanities, University of Chicago. Member of the faculty, Richmond College, New York, 1967–78. Author of *A Short History of the Movies,* 1971, 3rd edition 1981; *The Comic Mind: Comedy and the Movies,* 1974, 1979; *Film/Cinema/Movie: A Theory of Experience,* 1977, 1982; and *Howard Hawks, Storyteller,* 1982; editor, with Marshall Cohen, of *Film Theory and Criticism: Introductory Readings,* 1974, 1979; editor of *The Movies in Our Midst: Documents in the Cultural History of Film in America,* 1982. Died 1987. **Essays:** *The Gold Rush; The Great Dictator; The Kid; Red River; Scarface: The Shame of a Nation.*

McCAFFREY, Donald W. Essayist. Professor of English, University of North Dakota, Grand Forks, since 1960. Author of *Four Great Comedians: Chaplin, Lloyd, Keaton, and Langdon,* 1968; *The Golden Age of Sound Comedy: Comic Films and Comedians of the Thirties,* 1973; and *Three Classic Silent Film Comedies of Harold Lloyd,* 1976. Editor of *Focus on Chaplin,* 1971. **Essay:** *The Music Box.*

McCARTY, John. Essayist. Supervising writer and co-director of *The Fearmakers: Screen Masters of Suspense and Terror,* a video documentary series based on his 1994 book of the same name; author of numerous books on film, including *Splatter Movies: Breaking the Last Taboo of the Screen,* 1984; *The Modern Horror Film: 50 Contemporary Classics,* 1990; *John McCarty's Official Splatter Movie Guide, Vols. 1 and 2,* 1989, 1992; and *Hollywood Gangland,* 1993. **Essays:** *The Big Parade; Blade Runner; Chinatown; Double Indemnity; Faces; The Godfather Trilogy; Heavenly Creatures; Howards End; Lawrence of Arabia; The Night of the Hunter; North by Northwest; The Player; Pulp Fiction; Das Tagebuch einer Verlorenen; Tampopo.*

McCLUSKEY, Audrey T. Adviser. Director of the Black Film Center/Archive and associate professor of Afro-American Studies, Indiana University-Bloomington; specializes in education, gender, and cultural studies; co-editor, with Elaine M. Smith, *Mary McLeod Bethune: Building a Better World,* 2000.

McELHANEY, Joe. Essayist. Freelance film critic, New York. **Essay:** *Mean Streets.*

MERHAUT, Vacláv. Essayist. Film historian and member of staff, Film Archives of Czechoslovakia, Prague. Author of *Actors and Actresses of the Italian Cinema;* co-author (with Karel Caslavsky) of *Hvezdy Ceskeho Filmu,* 1995. **Essays:** *Noz w wodzie; Valahol Europaban.*

MERRITT, Russell. Essayist. Professor, University of Wisconsin, Madison. **Essays:** *Broken Blossoms; Intolerance.*

MICHAELS, Lloyd. Essayist. Professor of English and chairman of the English Department, Allegheny College, Meadville, Pennsylvania. Editor, *Film Criticism,* since 1977. Author of *Elia Kazan: A Guide to References and Resources,* 1985. **Essay:** *La Dentellière.*

MILICIA, Joseph. Essayist. Professor of English, University of Wisconsin, Sheboygan; writes about film and literature for such periodicals as *Multicultural Review* and *The New York Review of Science Fiction.* **Essays:** *L'Année dernière à Marienbad; Babettes Gaestebud; Der Himmel Uber Berlin; Diva; The General; Le Mépris.*

MILLER, Norman. Essayist. Library administrator and freelance writer, London. Author of *Toontown: A Study of the Hollywood Cartoon;* and contributor to *FSM* and *Marxism Today.* **Essay:** *Twelve Angry Men.*

MONTY, Ib. Adviser and essayist. Director of Det Danske Film museum, Copenhagen, since 1960. Literary and film critic for the newspaper *Morgenavisen Jyllands-Posten,* since 1958. Editor-in-chief of the film periodical *Kosmorama,* 1960–67; member, Danish Film Council, 1965–69. Author of *Leonardo da Vinci,* 1953; editor, with Morten Piil, *Se-det er film I-iii* (anthology of articles on film), 1964–66; and *TV-Broadcasts on Films and Filmmakers,* 1972. **Essays:** *Der var engang en krig; Gertrud; La Passion de Jeanne d'Arc; Sult; Vredens dag.*

MORRIS, Gary. Adviser. Editor and publisher, *Bright Lights* film journal, formerly print, now online as *brightlightsfilm.com.* Author of *Roger Corman,* 1985. Regular film critic for *Bay Area Reporter* and *San Francisco Weekly* and author of numerous articles for various American and Italian newspapers, magazines, film festival catalogs, and online journals.

MOTT, Donald R. Essayist. Professor, academic dean, and coordinator of communications/public relations, Huron Yniversity Tokyo, Tokyo, since 1994. Associate professor at colleges and universities, including Western Kentucky University, Xavier University of New Orleans, and Butler University. Author of *Steven Spielberg,* 1986. Film and video review editor, *Southern Quarterly,* 1987–94. Contributor of articles and reviews to numerous publications. Publisher and co-editor of *Metairie* magazine. **Essays:** *Midnight Express; Schindler's List.*

MRAZ, John. Essayist. Researcher in graphic history, Center for Historical Research on the Labor Movement, University of Puebla, Mexico, since 1984. Visiting professor of history, University of California, Santa Cruz, 1988. Coordinator of graphic history, Center for the Historical Study of the Mexican Labor Movement, 1982–83. Contributor to *Jump Cut*. **Essays:** *De cierta manera; La Hora de los hornos; Memorias del subdesarrollo; La Primera carga al machete; Los Redes; Retrato de Teresa.*

MURPHY, Robert. Essayist. Lecturer in film studies at Sheffield City Polytechnic. Author of *Realism and Tinsel,* 1989; and *Sixties British Cinema,* 1992. **Essays:** *Great Expectations; Victim.*

MURPHY, William T. Essayist. Chief, Motion Picture, Sound and Video Branch, National Archives, Washington, D.C., since 1976. Author of *Robert Flaherty: A Guide to References and Resources,* 1978. **Essays:** *Louisiana Story; Nanook of the North.*

NARDUCY, Ray. Essayist. Film critic and historian, Chicago. **Essays:** *The Adventures of Robin Hood; From Here to Eternity.*

NASTAV, Dennis. Essayist. Critic and documentary filmmaker. **Essay:** *Lola Montès.*

NEWMAN, Kim. Essayist. Freelance writer and broadcaster. Author of *Nightmare Movies,* 1988. Contributor to *Monthly Film Bulletin, Sight and Sound,* and *City Limits;* and film critic for *Box Office* on Channel 4, London. Also a writer of fiction. **Essays:** *The Big Heat; Blue Velvet; Eraserhead; Espiritu de la colmena; Gilda; Mildred Pierce; The Rocky Horror Picture Show; The Texas Chainsaw Massacre; Les Yeux sans visage.*

NISSEN, Dan. Adviser and essayist. Deputy Curator, 1988–1998; Head of Department Archive & Cinematheque, since 1998; Danish Film Institute. Teacher of film and literature, 1978–88; film critic for the daily newspaper *Information,* since 1976; editor of the film periodical *Kosmorama,* since 1988; contributor to several books and dictionaries on film. **Essays:** *Breaking the Waves; Festen; Idioterne; My Name is Joe; Smoke.*

OBALIL, Linda J. Essayist. Assistant, Special Effects Unit, Dreamscape, Bruce Cohn Curtis Productions/Bella Productions, since 1983. **Essays:** *Gycklarnas afton; King Kong; Snow White and the Seven Dwarfs; Steamboat Willie.*

O'LEARY, Liam. Essayist. Film viewer, Radio Telefis Eireann, Dublin, 1966–86. Director, Liam O'Leary Film Archives, Dublin, since 1976. Producer, Abbey Theatre, 1944. Director of the Film History Cycle at the National Film Theatre, London, and Acquisitions Officer, National Film Archive, London, 1953–66; co-founder, 1936, and honorary secretary, 1936–44, Irish Film Society. Director of the films, *Our Country,* 1948; *Mr. Careless,* 1950; and *Portrait of Dublin,* 1951. Author of *Invitation to the Film,* 1945; *The Silent Cinema,* 1965; *Rex Ingram, Master of the Silent Cinema,* 1980; and *Cinema Ireland, 1896–1950,* 1990. Died 1992. **Essays:** *A nous la liberté; Brief Encounter; Cabiria; Un Chapeau de paille d'Italie; Erotikon; Fièvre; The Four Horsemen of the Apocalypse; Herr Arnes Pengar; Kameradschaft; La Kermesse héroique; Die Nibelungen; Proshchanie; Schatten.*

ORMAN, Tom. Essayist. Instructor in Department of English, University of Toronto. Regular contributor to *CineAction.* **Essay:** *GoodFellas.*

OTTER, Kelly. Essayist. Teacher and administrator, New York University. Doctoral candidate in arts and humanities. **Essays:** *Chapayev; Kommisar; Malenkaya Vera.*

PALMER, R. Barton. Essayist. Calhoun Lemon Professor of Literature and Director of the South Carolina Film Institute, Clemson University; books include *Hollywood's Dark Cinema, Perspectives on Film Noir,* and *Joseph Mankiewicz: A Bibliographical and Critical Study.* **Essays:** *Black Sunday; The Deer Hunter; Gojira; Der Letze Mann.*

PASKIN, Sylvia. Essayist. Freelance film critic, London. Contributor to *Monthly Film Bulletin.* **Essays:** *Cria cuervos . . . ; The Draughtsman's Contract; Judex; My Brilliant Career; Yeelen.*

PATTERSON, Hannah. Essayist. Freelance film critic; part-time Research and Editorial Assistant, Wallflower Press. **Essay:** *Funny Games.*

PEÑA, Richard. Essayist. Director, New York Film Festival. Formerly director, Film Centre at the School of the Art Institute of Chicago. **Essay:** *Fukushu suru wa ware ni ari.*

PERCIVAL, Kris. Essayist. Freelance writer. **Essays:** *Letyat zhuravli; Les Nuits fauves.*

PETLEY, Julian. Adviser and essayist. Freelance writer and critic, London. Contributor to *Monthly Film Bulletin* and *Sight and Sound,* and to *All Our Yesterdays: 90 Years of British Cinema,* 1986; and *The BFI Companion to the Western,* 1988. **Essays:** *Der Amerikanische freund; Belle de jour; Die Bleierne Zeit; La Caduta degli dei; C'est arrivé près de chez vous; Cristo si e fermato a Eboli; Csillagosok, katonák; Il Gattopardo; Heimat; Die Zweite Heimat; Idi i smotri; The Lost Weekend; Mona Lisa; Raging Bull; A Room with a View; Le Samourai; Sans Soleil; The Servant; The Spanish Earth; Stromboli.*

PETRIE, Duncan. Essaysist. Research officer at the British Film Institute, London. Author of *Creativity and Constraint in the British Film Industry,* 1991. **Essays:** *Black Narcissus; The Douglas Trilogy.*

PHILLIPS, Gene D., S.J. Essayist. Professor of English, Loyola University, Chicago, since 1970. Contributing editor, *Literature/Film Quarterly,* since 1977. Author of several books, including *Hemingway and Film,* 1980; *George Cukor,* 1982; *Alfred Hitchcock,* 1984; *Fiction, Film, and F. Scott Fitzgerald,* 1986; *Fiction, Film, and Faulkner,* 1988; *Major Film Directors of the American and British Cinema,* 1990; and *Conrad and Cinema,* 1995. **Essays:** *Dr. Strangelove; or, How I Learned to Stop Worrying and Love the Bomb; Midnight Cowboy; Strangers on a Train; 2001: A Space Odyssey.*

PICKARD, Christopher. Adviser. Latin American bureau chief, Moving Pictures International. Author of *Rio: The Insider's Guide* and *Sao Paolo: The Insider's Guide.* Editor of *Riohfe, Brazil Travel Update.*

PILLAI, A. Essayist. Screenwriter and journalist. **Essays:** *All about Eve; Cabaret; Laura; The Piano; A Place in the Sun; Triumph des Willens; West Side Story.*

PILOWSKY, Marion. Essayist. Head of acquisitions for cable movie channels, Showtime and Encore. Head of programme planning for Bravo Television, London. Currently completing M.A. in film and television studies at the University of Westminster. **Essays:** *Badlands; Spoorloos.*

POAGUE, Leland. Essayist. Professor of English, Iowa State University, Ames, since 1978. Author of *The Cinema of Frank Capra: An Approach to Film Comedy,* 1975; *The Cinema of Ernst Lubitsch: The Hollywood Films,* 1978; *Howard Hawks,* 1982; and co-author, *Film Criticism: A Counter Theory,* 1982. Co-editor of *A Hitchcock Reader,* 1986. **Essays:** *Bonnie and Clyde; Chimes at Midnight; Citizen Kane; Fury; Out of the Past; Psycho; Les Quatre cents coups; They Live By Night; The Third Man.*

POLAN, Dana B. Adviser. Professor of Critical Studies, School of Cinema-TV, University of Southern California. Author of *Pulp Fiction* (BFI Modern Classics), *In a Lonely Place* (BFI Film Classics), two other books, and numerous essays on film and cultural studies; former president of the Society for Cinema Studies. **Essay:** *Cat People.*

PORTON, Richard. Essayist. Graduate student in film studies, New York University. **Essays:** *Jonah qui aura 25 ans en l'an 2000; Lucia.*

RABINOVITZ, Lauren. Essayist. Associate professor of American studies and communication studies, University of Iowa, since 1986. **Essays:** *Adam's Rib; Bringing Up Baby; Gertie the Dinosaur; His Girl Friday; It Happened One Night; Meshes of the Afternoon; Nashville; Now Voyager; The Philadelphia Story.*

RACHEVA, Maria. Essayist. Selector of films for the International Film Festival, Munich, since 1983. Teacher of film history, High School for Cinema, Sofia, Bulgaria, 1974–81; editor of the cultural review, *Westermanns Monatschefte,* Munich, 1981–82. Author of *Presentday Bulgarian Cinema,* 1970; *Nowa fala i nowa powiesc,* 1974; *Der bulgarische Film,* with Klaus Eder, 1977; *Andrzej Wajda,* with Klaus Eder, 1980; *Neostariavashti filmi,* 1981; and *Kino: For and Against,* 1986. **Essays:** *Czlowiek z marmuru; Jeder für sich und Gott gegen alle; Matka Joanna od aniolow.*

RAJADHYAKSHA, Ashish. Essayist. Freelance writer. **Essays:** *Akaler sandhane; Bhumika; Duvidha; Elippathayam; Kaagaz ke phool.*

RANVAUD, Don. Adviser. Producer of films.

RAYNS, Tony. Adviser. Film critic for Chinese and Japanese cinema.

REYNOLDS, Herbert. Essayist. Historian and project coordinator, Museum of Modern Art Department of Art, New York City, since 1981; Consultant, American Federation of Arts Film Program, since 1982. Member, Curatorial Staff of Film Archive, George Eastman House, Rochester, New York, 1976–81. **Essay:** *Mephisto.*

ROBSON, Arthur G. Essayist. Professor and chairman, Department of Classics, and professor of comparative literature, Beloit College, Wisconsin, since 1966. Editor of *Latin: Our Living Heritage, Book III,* 1964; author of *Euripides' ''Electra'': An Interpretive Commentary,* forthcoming; and author, with Rodney Farnsworth, of *Alexandre Alexeieff and Claire Parker: The Artistry of Animation,* forthcoming. **Essay:** *Une Nuit sur le Mont Chauve.*

ROMNEY, Jonathan. Essayist. Deputy film critic, *The Guardian;* and regular contributor to *New Statesman and Society,* and *Sight and Sound.* Co-editor of *Celluloid Jukebox: Popular Music and the Movies since the 1950s.* **Essays:** *Celine et Julie vont en bateau: Phantom Ladies Over Paris; Trois Couleurs.*

ROUTLEDGE, Chris. Essayist. Freelance writer and lecturer in literature and film; published essays on detective fiction, popular culture, and poetics; eo-editor of *Mystery in Children's Literature,* forthcoming. **Essays:** *Becky Sharp; C'era una volta il west; Gun Crazy; JFK; Secrets and Lies; The Star Wars Saga.*

RUBINSTEIN, Elliot. Essayist. Coordinator of the Program in Cinema Studies, College of Staten Island, City University of New York, since 1968. Author of *Filmguide to ''The General,''* 1973. Died 1988. **Essay:** *She Done Him Wrong.*

SAELI, Marie. Essayist. Adjunct faculty in English and the Humanities, Triton Community College, River Grove, Illinois, since 1983. Free-lance film reviewer. **Essays:** *Alexander Nevsky; Oktiabr.*

SALVAGE, Barbara. Essayist. Researcher, Circulating Film Catalogue Project, Museum of Modern Art, New York, since 1982. **Essays:** *Die Büchse der Pandora; Stachka.*

SAVAGE, Stephanie. Essayist. Instructor at University of Iowa. Ph.D. candidate at University of Iowa. Awarded 1996 Seashore Fellowship in the Humanities. Contributor to *Film History* and *No Angels: Women Who Commit Violence.* **Essay:** *Written on the Wind.*

SCHADE, Curtis. Essayist. Director of Admissions, Westover School, Connecticut. **Essay:** *La Noire de. . . .*

SCHILD, Susana. Essayist. Journalist specializing in movies; film critic for *Jornal do Brasil,* Rio de Janeiro, for twenty years. Director of Cinemateca of the Museum of Modern Art of Rio de Janeiro, since 1993. **Essays:** *Bye Bye Brasil; O Cangaceiro; Deus e o diabo na terra do sol; Dona Flor e seus dois maridos; Limite; Pixote a lei do mais fraco; Vidas secas.*

SCHNEIDER, Steven. Essayist. Ph.D. student in Philosophy at Harvard University, and in Cinema Studies at New York University; has written on horror films for *Post Script, CineAction, Paradoxa,* and *Other Voices;* contributed to *Drive-In Horrors, Violated Bodies: Extreme Film, Horror Film Reader,* and *Autogedden*; editing a collection of essays on psychoanalysis and the horror film, entitled *Freud's Worst Nightmares.* **Essays:** *The Blair Witch Project; The Matrix; Shaft; Sweet Sweetback's Baadasssss Song.*

SCHUTH, H. Wayne. Essayist. Professor of drama and communications, University of New Orleans. Author of *Mike Nichols,* 1978. Editor of ''Louisiana and Film'' issue, *Southern Quarterly,* Fall 1984. Member of the board of trustees of the University Film and Video Foundation. **Essays:** *Giant; The Graduate.*

SELIG, Michael. Essayist. Assistant professor, University of Vermont, since 1983. Contributor to *Film Reader, Jump-Cut,* and *Journal of Popular Film and Television.* **Essay:** *Salt of the Earth.*

SELLARS, Lee. Essayist. Worked with technical department of the National Film Theatre and Museum of the Moving Image, London. President of the Australian Theatrical and Amusement Employees Association, 1986–89. **Essays:** *Die Blechtrommel; Dawandeh.*

SHIELDS, Paul. Adviser. Director of The Box Office, a London-based film and TV consultancy with clients including *Bravo.*

SHOCHAT, Ella. Essayist. Freelance writer, New York. **Essay:** *Xala.*

SICKELS, Robert. Essayist. Assistant Professor of Film, English Department, Whitman College, Washington; teaches a wide variety of film courses; has published articles and reviews in *Film & History, Popular Culture Review, Journal of Popular Culture,* and on H-NET; Film and Television Review Editor, *Film & History.* **Essays:** *American Beauty; Do the Right Thing; L.A. Confidential.*

SIEGLOHR, Ulrike. Essayist. Film lecturer and writer, London. **Essay:** *Hitler: Ein Film aus Deutschland.*

SILET, Charles L. P. Essayist. Professor of English, Iowa State University, Ames, since 1979. Author of *Lindsay Anderson: A Guide to References and Resources,* 1979. Contributor to *Quarterly Review of Film, Film Heritage,* and *Magill's Cinema Annual.* **Essays:** *The Lady Vanishes; Letter from an Unknown Woman; Paisà; Une Partie de campagne; Le Procès.*

SIMMON, Scott. Essayist. Film programmer, Mary Pickford Theatre, Library of Congress, Washington, D.C., since 1983. Contributor to *Film Comment, Journal of Popular Film and Video,* and *Literature/Film Quarterly;* and co-author of *King Vidor—American,* 1989. **Essays:** *Hallelujah; Vertigo.*

SITNEY, P. Adams. Essayist. Lecturer, Princeton University. Formerly Director of Library and Publications, Anthology Film Archives. Author of *Film Culture Reader,* 1970; *Visionary Film,* 1974; *The Avant-Garde Film,* 1978; *Modernist Montage: The Obscurity of Vision in Cinema and Literature,* 1990; and *Visual Crises in Italian Cinema,* 1995. **Essays:** *Amor de perdicão; La dolce vita; L'Eclisse; Fanny och Alexander; Jeanne Dielman, 23 Quai du Commerce, 1080 Bruxelles; Menilmontant; La Notte; Persona; Rear Window; Viskningar och rop; Wavelength.*

ŠKVORECKÝ, Josef. Essayist. Professor of English and film, University of Toronto, Canada, since 1969. Author of *All the Bright Young Men and Women: A Personal History of the Czech Cinema,* 1972; and *Jiri Menzel and the History of ''Closely Watched Trains,''* 1982. Works as novelist include *Miss Silver's Past,* 1975; *The Bass Saxophone,* 1977; *The Engineer of Human Souls,* 1984; and *The Miracle Game,* 1990. **Essay:** *Jud Süss.*

SLIDE, Anthony. Essayist. Freelance writer. Associate film archivist, American Film Institute, 1972–75; resident film historian, Academy of Motion Picture Arts and Sciences, 1975–80. Author and editor of more than 50 books on the history of popular entertainment, including *The Films of D. W. Griffith,* 1975; *The American Film Industry: A Historical Dictionary,* 1986; *Nitrate Won't Wait: A History of Film Preservation in the United States,* 1992; and *The Encyclopedia of Vaudeville,* 1994. Also editor of the Scarecrow Press ''Filmmakers Series,'' and a documentary filmmaker. **Essays:** *All Quiet on the Western Front; The Jazz Singer; The Phantom of the Opera; The Private Life of Henry VIII.*

SMALL, Edward S. Essayist. Director of film studies, University of Missouri, Columbia, since 1983. Executive vice president, University Film and Video Association, 1983–86. Author of *Direct Theory: Experimental Film/Video as Major Genre,* 1994. **Essay:** *Le Ballet mécanique.*

SMOODIN Eric. Essayist. Doctoral candidate, film studies, University of California at Los Angeles. Contributor to *Film Studies Annual* and *Journal of the University Film and Video Association.* **Essays:** *Sherlock, Jr.; Sunset Boulevard.*

SNYDER, Thomas. Essayist. Freelance writer, Chicago. Reviewer for *Video Movie Magazine,* Chicago. **Essays:** *Close Encounters of the Third Kind; Raiders of the Lost Ark; The Star Wars Saga.*

STARR, Cecile. Essayist. Freelance writer, lecturer, and filmmaker. Film reviewer, *The Saturday Review,* New York, 1949–59. Author of *Discovering the Movies,* 1977; and, with Robert Russett, *Experimental Animation,* 1976. **Essays:** *The Land; Song of Ceylon.*

STRICK, Philip. Essayist. Freelance critic and lecturer, London, and deputy chairman, FIPRESCI. Formerly head of film distribution, British Film Institute. Author of *Science Fiction Movies* and *Great Movie Actresses.* Contributor to *Films and Filming, Monthly Film Bulletin,* and *Film Review.* **Essays:** *Brazil; A Clockwork Orange.*

SULLIVAN, Bob. Essayist. Writer; received a Bachelor of Arts in Creative Writing from Purdue University and attended the University of Southern California graduate film school; postgraduate work at The Actors and Directors Lab under Jack Garfein; formerly film reviewer for the *Los Angeles Free Press*; author of the B-movie sci-fi classic *Clonus*; contributor, *St. James Encyclopedia of Popular Culture.* **Essay:** *Exotica.*

TAVERNETTI, Susan. Essayist. Instructor of Film, De Anza College, Cupertino, California; film reviewer and writer, *Palo Alto Weekly,* since 1988; co-author, with Margo Kasdan, of *The Critical Eye: An Introduction to Looking at Movies,* 1998; author of ''Native Americans in a Revisionist Western: *Little Big Man*'' in *Hollywood's Indian: The Portrayal of the Native American in Film,* 1997. **Essay:** *Ta'm e Guilass.*

TEO, Stephen. Essayist. Film critic, journalist, and writer. Programmer for Yamagata International Documentary Film Festival, 1989, 1991. Author of *Hong Kong Cinema.* English editor of annual catalogues specialising in studies on Hong Kong cinema, Hong Kong International Film Festival. Contributor, editor, and translator of articles to numerous periodicals. **Essays:** *Dahong denglong gaogao gua; Haizi wang; Xiao cheng zhi chun; Yanzhi kou.*

THOMAS, Nicholas. Adviser. Editor of second editon, *Films, Directors, Actors and Actresses* volumes of *International Dictionary of Film and Filmmakers.* Publications officer, British Film Institute, London.

TOMASULO, Frank P. Adviser. Professor of Film, Georgia State University; editor, *Journal of Film and Video,* 1992–97; and *Cinema Journal,* 1998–2003; author of over 50 scholarly articles and 100 conference papers.

TOMLINSON, Doug. Essayist. Associate professor of film studies, Montclair State College, New Jersey. Principal researcher for *Voices of Film Experience,* edited by Jay Leyda, 1977; editor of *Actors on Acting for the Screen,* 1994. Died 1992. **Essays:** *American Graffiti; Annie Hall; The Big Sleep; Un Condamné à mort s'est échappé; Entr'acte; In a Lonely Place; Manhattan; Modern Times; Rebel Without a Cause; Room at the Top; Some Like It Hot.*

TSAO, Leonardo Garcia. Adviser. Editor of *Dicine,* the longest-running film magazine in Mexico; film critic for Mexico City newspapers, including *Unomásuno, La Jornada,* and *El Nacional,* since 1977; contributor of articles to *Film Comment, Sight and Sound, Variety, Moving Pictures, Cine,* and *Imágenes,* among other periodicals. Author of books on Orson Welles, François Truffaut, Andrei

Tarkovski, and Sam Peckinpah, as well as a book of interviews with Mexican director Felipe Cazals; author of screenplay for feature film *Intimidad (Intimacy),* directed by Dana Rotberg. Member of FIPRESCI jury. Teacher of film courses at the Centro de Capacitación Cinematográfica and the Universidad Iberoamericana. Creator of TV programs of film criticism in Mexico City.

TSIANTIS, Lee. Essayist. Publicist, Twentieth Century Fox, Atlanta, Georgia. Taught film history at University of South Carolina, 1976–78. Research assistant, PBS series *Cinematic Eye.* **Essay:** *Der Student von Prag.*

TUDOR, Andrew. Essayist. Head of the Department of Sociology, University of York. Author of *Theories of Film: Image and Influence* and *Monsters and Mad Scientists.* **Essays:** *L'Avventura; Deliverance; Hustler; Peeping Tom.*

TYRKUS, Michael J. Essayist. Independent filmmaker, author, and editor. Co-writer and director of over a dozen short films. Writer and editor specializing in biographical and critical reference sources in literature and the cinema. Contributor to numerous references, including *Twentieth-Century Young Adult Writers.* Editor of *Gay & Lesbian Biography* and co-editor of *Outstanding Lives: Profiles of Lesbians and Gay Men.* In-house project editor and contributor to the *St. James Film Directors Encyclopedia,* edited by Andrew Sarris; in-house project editor of the *St. James Women Filmmakers Encyclopedia.* Co-founder of Lamb-Kiss Productions and founder of CityScene Films. **Essays:** *Dead Ringers; Titanic.*

URGOSIKOVÁ, B. Essayist. Film historian. Head of Department of Film History and Cataloguing, Národní filmovýarchiv Praha. Author of *A Famous Era of the Swedish Cinema,* 1969; *Rudolph Valentino,* 1970; *History of Science Fiction Films,* 1973, 1982; *Remakes,* 1977; and *Czech Fiction Films,* 1995. **Essays:** *Alphaville; Eroica; Kanal; Lásky jedné plavovlásky; Metropolis; Obchod na korze; Ostre sledované vlaky; Popiol i diament; Staré pověsti české; Things to Come.*

VALDEZ, Ralph Anthony. Essayist. Freelance film, music, and art critic for periodicals, including *Metro Times,* and *Orbit.* Host of film, music, and art discussion and interview radio program, WDET, Detroit, Michigan. **Essay:** *Rosemary's Baby.*

VASUDEVAN, Aruna. Adviser. Editor of *Cinemaya: The Asian Film Quarterly.* Head of FIPRESCI, India.

VASUDEVAN, Ravi. Essayist. Free-lance film critic. Former film critic of *The Sunday Observer,* Delhi. **Essays:** *Awara; Bharat Mata; Salaam Bombay!.*

VINCENDEAU, Ginette. Essayist. Lecturer in film studies at the University of Warwick. Co-editor of *French Film: Texts and Contexts,* 1989. **Essay:** *The Marius Trilogy.*

WAKULENKO, Iris. Essayist. Freelance writer. Received Bachelor of Visual Arts from Sydney College of the Arts. **Essay:** *Walkabout.*

WEES, William C. Essayist. Professor Emeritus, McGill University, Montreal. Editor, *Canadian Journal of Film Studies.* Author of *Light Moving in Time: Studies in the Visual Aesthetics of Avant-Garde Film,* 1992; and *Recycled Images: The Art and Politics of Found Footage Films,* 1993. **Essay:** *Dog Star Man.*

WELLS, Paul. Essayist. Freelance writer. **Essays:** *Baron Prasil; Life Is Sweet; Passport to Pimlico.*

WELSH, James Michael. Essayist. Associate professor of English, Salisbury State University. Editor, *Literature/Film Quarterly.* Author of *His Majesty the American: The Films of Douglas Fairbanks, Sr.,* 1977; *Abel Gance,* 1978; and *Peter Watkins: A Guide to References and Resources,* 1986. **Essay:** *Fantasia.*

WEST, Dennis. Essayist. Associate professor, University of Idaho, Moscow, since 1981. Director, Indiana University Film Studies Program, 1976–77. Contributor on Latin American and Spanish cinema to such journals as *Latin American Research Review, Cineaste, New Scholar,* and others. **Essays:** *Antônio das Mortes; La Batalla de Chile: la lucha de un pueblo sin armas; Os Fuzis; El Otro Francisco; Yawar Mallku.*

WHITE, M. B. Essayist. Assistant professor, Department of Radio-TV-Film, Northwestern University, Evanston, Illinois, since 1982. Contributor to *Enclitic, Purdue Film Studies Annual,* and other periodicals. **Essays:** *A bout de souffle; Aguirre, der Zorn Gottes; Un Chien andalou; Chronik der Anna Magdalena Bach; Hiroshima mon amour; Das Kabinett des Dr. Caligari; Pirosmani; Zéro de conduite.*

WILLIAMS, Daniel. Essayist. Film critic and lecturer, London. **Essays:** *My Beautiful Laundrette; Paris, Texas.*

WINNING, Robert. Essayist. Author and film scholar, Pittsburgh. **Essays:** *Dr. Jekyll and Mr. Hyde; Ran; The Wizard of Oz.*

WOOD, Robin. Essayist. Retired; taught Film Studies at Queen's University, Kingston, Canada, University of Warwick, England, and York University, Toronto, Canada; author of twelve books on film, most recently *Hollywood from Vietnam to Reagan, Hitchcock's Films Revisited,* and *Sexual Politics and Narrative Film,* all published by Columbia University Press, and a monograph on *The Wings of the Dove* for the British Film Institute; editor of, and regular contributor to, *CineAction* magazine. **Essays:** *Akasen chitai; And Life Goes On; L'Atalante; Banshun; Boudu sauvé des eaux; Le Charme discrèt de la bourgeoisie; City of Sadness; Il Conformista; Days of Heaven; E.T.—The Extraterrestrial; Il Fiore delle mille e una notte; La Grande illusion; Higanbana; Ikiru; The Lady Eve; Meet Me in St. Louis; Naniwa ereji; Nosferatu (1922); Nuit et brouillard; Rashomon; Règle du jeu; Reservoir Dogs; Rio Bravo; Le Sang des bêtes; Sansho dayu; The Scarlet Empress; The Silence of the Lambs; Taxi Driver; Ugetsu monogatari; Viaggio in Italia; Le Weekend.*

YOUNGBLOOD, Denise J. Essayist. Professor of History, University of Vermont; specialist in Russian silent cinema and the Soviet historical film; has published extensively on these subjects, including *The Magic Mirror: Moviemaking in Russia, 1908-1918,* 1999; *Movies for the Masses: Popular Cinema and Soviet Society in the 1920s,* 1992; and *Soviet Cinema in the Silent Era, 1918-1935,* 1985, 1991. **Essays:** *Pokaianie; Tretia Meshchanskaia.*

LIST OF FILMS BY DIRECTOR

Tengiz Abuladze
Pokaianie

Chantal Akerman
Jeanne Dielman, 23 Quai du Commerce, 1080 Bruxelles

Robert Aldrich
Kiss Me Deadly

Alexander Alexeieff
Nuit sur le Mont Chauve

Marc Allégret
Marius Trilogy

Woody Allen
Annie Hall
Manhattan

Pedro Almodóvar
Mujeres al borde de un ataque de nervios
Todo Sobre Mi Madre

Robert Altman
M*A*S*H
Nashville
The Player

Gianni Amelio
L'America

Lindsay Anderson
If. . .

Métodi Andonov
Koziyat rog

Theodoros Angelopoulos
O Thiasos
Vlemma Tou Odyssea

Kenneth Anger
Scorpio Rising

Michelangelo Antonioni
L'Avventura
Blow-Up
L'Eclisse
La Notte
Professione: Reporter

Gillian Armstrong
My Brilliant Career

Dorothy Arzner
Dance, Girl, Dance

Alexander Askoldov
Kommisar

Claude Autant-Lara
Le Diable au corps

Gabriel Axel
Babettes Gaestebud

Hector Babenco
Pixote a lei do mais fraco

Lloyd Bacon
42nd Street

Juan Antonio Bardem
Muerte de un Ciclista

Bruno Barreto
Dona Flor e seus dois maridos

Jacques Becker
Casque d'or

Jean-Jacques Beineix
Diva

Marco Bellocchio
I Pugni in tasca

Rémy Belvaux
C'est arrivé près de chez vous

Shyam Benegal
Bhumika

Ingmar Bergman
Fanny och Alexander
Gycklarnas afton
Persona
Sjunde inseglet
Smultronstället
Sommarnattens leende
Tystnaden
Viskningar och rop

Bernardo Bertolucci
1900 (Novecento)
Il Conformista
Last Tango in Paris

Herbert J. Biberman
Salt of the Earth

Fernando Birri
Tire dié

Peter Bogdanovich
The Last Picture Show

Sergei Bondarchuk
Voina i mir

André Bonzel
C'est arrivé près de chez vous

John Boorman
Deliverance

Danny Boyle
Trainspotting

Stan Brakhage
Anticipation of the Night
Dog Star Man

Robert Bresson
Un Condamné à mort s'est échappé
Les Dames du Bois de Boulogne
Journal d'un curé de campagne
Pickpocket

Peter Brook
Marat/Sade

Tod Browning
Dracula (1931)
Freaks

Clyde Bruckman
The General

Alf Brustellin
Deutschland im Herbst

Veljko Bulajic
Vlak bez voznog reda

Luis Buñuel
L'Age d'or
Belle de jour
Le Charme discrèt de la bourgeoisie
Un Chien andalou
Los Olvidados
Viridiana

James Cameron
Titanic

Jane Campion
The Piano

Marcel Camus
Orfeu Negro

Frank Capra
It Happened One Night
It's a Wonderful Life
Mr. Smith Goes to Washington
Why We Fight

Henning Carlsen
Sult

Marcel Carné
Les Enfants du paradis
Le Jour se lève
Quai des brumes

John Cassavetes
Faces

Alberto Cavalcanti
Dead of Night
Rien que les heures

Claude Chabrol
Boucher
La Femme infidèle

Youssef Chahine
Bab el hadid

Charles Chaplin
City Lights
The Gold Rush
The Great Dictator
The Kid
Modern Times

Chen Kaige
Ba wang bie ji
Haizi wang
Huang tudi

Grigori Chukhrai
Balada o soldate

Michael Cimino
The Deer Hunter

Souleymane Cissé
Yeelen

René Clair
A nous la liberté
Un Chapeau de paille d'Italie
Entr'acte
Le Million

Jack Clayton
Room at the Top

René Clément
La Bataille du rail
Jeux interdits

Hans Peter Cloos
Deutschland im Herbst

Henri-Georges Clouzot
Les Diaboliques
Le Salaire de la peur

Jean Cocteau
La Belle et la bête
Orphée
Le Sang d'un poete

Joel Coen
Fargo

Cyril Collard
Les Nuits fauves

Merian C. Cooper
King Kong

Francis Ford Coppola
Apocalypse Now
The Conversation
The Godfather Trilogy

Roger Corman
The Masque of the Red Death

Henry Cornelius
Passport to Pimlico

Constantin Costa-Gavras
Z

Charles Crichton
Dead of Night
The Lavender Hill Mob

David Cronenberg
Dead Ringers

Alan Crosland
The Jazz Singer

George Cukor
Adam's Rib
Camille
The Philadelphia Story
A Star Is Born
The Women

Michael Curtiz
The Adventures of Robin Hood
Casablanca
Mildred Pierce
Sodom und Gomorrha

Jules Dassin
Du Rififi chez les hommes
The Naked City

Terence Davies
Distant Voices, Still Lives

Ossie Davis
Kongi's Harvest

Basil Dearden
The Blue Lamp
Dead of Night
Victim

Arthur de Glahs
Märchen vom Glück

Louis Delluc
Fièvre

Jonathan Demme
Philadelphia
The Silence of the Lambs

Manoel de Oliveira
Amor de perdicão

Maya Deren
Meshes of the Afternoon

Louis de Rochemont
The March of Time

Vittorio de Sica
Ladri di biciclette
Miracolo a Milano
Sciuscia
Umberto D

Carlos Diegues
Bye Bye Brasil

Walt Disney
Steamboat Willie

Edward Dmytryk
Crossfire

Stanley Donen
On the Town
Singin' in the Rain

Nelson Pereira dos Santos
Vidas secas

Bill Douglas
The Douglas Trilogy

Alexander Dovzhenko
Arsenal
Zemlya

Carl Theodor Dreyer
Gertrud
La Passion de Jeanne d'Arc
Ordet
Vampyr
Vredens dag

Germaine Dulac
La Coquille et le clergyman

E. A. Dupont
Variété

Marguerite Duras
India Song

Guru Dutt
Kaagaz ke phool

Julien Duvivier
Pépé le Moko

Clint Eastwood
Unforgiven

Blake Edwards
Breakfast at Tiffany's

Atom Egoyan
Exotica

Sergei Eisenstein
Alexander Nevsky
Bronenosets Potemkin
Ivan Grozny
Oktiabr
Stachka

Nikolai Ekk
Putyovka v zhizn

Victor Erice
Espiritu de la colmena

Rainer Werner Fassbinder
Angst essen Seele auf
Deutschland im Herbst
Ehe der Maria Braun
Lola

Federico Fellini
8½
La dolce vita
La strada
I Vitelloni

Louis Feuillade
Judex
Les Vampires

Jacques Feyder
La Kermesse héroique

Terence Fisher
Dracula (1958)

Frances H. Flaherty
The Land

Robert Flaherty
The Land
Louisiana Story
Man of Aran
Nanook of the North

Victor Fleming
Gone with the Wind
The Wizard of Oz

John Ford
The Grapes of Wrath
The Informer
The Man Who Shot Liberty Valance
My Darling Clementine
The Searchers
Young Mr. Lincoln

Miloš Forman
Lásky jedné plavovlásky
One Flew Over the Cuckoo's Nest

Bill Forsyth
Gregory's Girl

Piero Fosco
Cabiria

Bob Fosse
Cabaret

Georges Franju
Le Sang des bêtes
Thérèse Desqueyroux
Les Yeux sans visage

John Frankenheimer
Black Sunday

Stephen Frears
My Beautiful Laundrette

Carl Froelich
Mädchen in Uniform

Pál Gábor
Angi Vera

Abel Gance
J'accuse
Napoléon

Luis García Berlanga
El Verdugo

Ritwik Ghatak
Meghe dhaka tara

Terry Gilliam
Brazil

Sergio Giral
Otro Francisco

Wolfgang Glück
38 - Auch das war Wien

Jean-Luc Godard
A bout de souffle
Alphaville
Le Mépris
Vivre sa vie
Le Weekend

Flora Gomes
Udju Azul di Yonta

Manuel Octavio Gómez
La Primera carga al machete

Sara Gómez
De cierta manera

Emilio Gómez Muriel
Los Redes

Adoor Gopalakrishnan
Elippathayam

Claude Goretta
La Dentellière

Heinosuke Gosho
Entotsu no mieru basho

Joe Grant
Fantasia

Peter Greenaway
The Draughtsman's Contract

John Grierson
Drifters

D. W. Griffith
The Birth of a Nation
Broken Blossoms
Intolerance

Rajko Grlic
Samo jednom se ljubi

Ruy Guerra
Os Fuzis

Val Guest
Casino Royale

Tomás Gutiérrez Alea
Fresa y Chocolate
Memorias del subdesarrollo

Patricio Guzmán
La Batalla de Chile: la lucha de un pueblo sin armas

Robert Hamer
Dead of Night
Kind Hearts and Coronets

David Hand
Snow White

Michael Haneke
Funny Games

Curtis Hanson
L.A. Confidential

Karl Hartl
Der Engel mit der Posaune

Howard Hawks
The Big Sleep
Bringing Up Baby
His Girl Friday
Red River
Rio Bravo
Scarface: The Shame of a Nation

Werner Herzog
Aguirre, der Zorn Gottes
Jeder für sich und Gott gegen alle

Fritz Hippler
Der Ewige Jude

Alfred Hitchcock
The 39 Steps
The Birds
Blackmail
The Lady Vanishes
North by Northwest
Notorious
Psycho
Rear Window
Strangers on a Train
Vertigo

Ishirô Honda
Gojira

Tobe Hooper
The Texas Chainsaw Massacre

Dennis Hopper
Easy Rider

Hou Hsiao-Hsien
City of Sadness

Ken Hughes
Casino Royale

John Huston
The African Queen
The Asphalt Jungle
Casino Royale
The Dead
The Maltese Falcon
The Misfits
The Treasure of the Sierra Madre

Kon Ichikawa
Biruma no tategoto

Shohei Imamura
Fukushu suru wa ware ni ari
Narayama bushi-ko

Rex Ingram
The Four Horsemen of the Apocalypse

Juzo Itami
Tampopo

Joris Ivens
Nieuwe Gronden
The Spanish Earth

James Ivory
Howards End
A Room with a View

Peter Jackson
Heavenly Creatures

Steve James
Hoop Dreams

Miklós Jancsó
Csillagosok, katonák
Meg ker a nep

Humphrey Jennings
Fires Were Started

Neil Jordan
Mona Lisa

Rupert Julian
The Phantom of the Opera

Ján Kadár
Obchod na korze

Mikhail Kalatozov
Letyat zhuravli
Soy Cuba

Raj Kapoor
Awara

Srdjan Karanovic
Nesto izmedju

Mathieu Kassovitz
Haine

Mani Kaul
Duvidha

Jerzy Kawalerowicz
Matka Joanna od aniolow

Elia Kazan
East of Eden
On the Waterfront
A Streetcar Named Desire

Buster Keaton
The General
Sherlock, Jr.

William Keighley
The Adventures of Robin Hood

Gene Kelly
On the Town
Singin' in the Rain

Irvin Kershner
Star Wars

Michael Kertész
Sodom und Gomorrha

Mehboob Khan
Bharat Mata

Abbas Kiarostami
And Life Goes On
Ta'm E Guilass

Krzysztof Kieślowski
Dekalog
Trois Couleurs

Teinosuke Kinugasa
Jigokumon
Jujiro

Dimitri Kirsanoff
Menilmontant

Takeshi Kitano
Hana-Bi

Palle Kjaerulff-Schmidt
Der var engang en krig

Elem Klimov
Idi i smotri
Proshchanie

Elmar Klos
Obchod na korze

Alexander Kluge
Deutschland im Herbst

Masaki Kobayashi
Kwaidan
Ningen no joken
Seppuku

Xavier Koller
Journey of Hope

Andrei Konchalovsky
Istoria Asi Kliachinoi kotoraia lubila da nie vyshla zamuzh

Alexander Korda
The Marius Trilogy
The Private Life of Henry VIII

Hirokazu Kore-eda
Wandafuru Raifu

Grigori Kozintsev
Korol Lir
The Maxim Trilogy
Novyi Vavilon

Peter Kubelka
Unsere Afrikareise

Stanley Kubrick
A Clockwork Orange
Dr. Strangelove; or, How I Learned to Stop Worrying and Love the Bomb
Lolita
Paths of Glory
2001: A Space Odyssey

Lev Kuleshov
Neobychanye priklyucheniya Mistera Vesta v strane bolshevikov

Akira Kurosawa
Ikiru
Ran
Rashomon
Shichinin no samurai
Yojimbo

Emir Kusturica
Dom za vesanje
Otac na sluzbenom putu
Underground

Stanley Kwan
Yanzhi kou

Mohammed Lakhdar Hamina
Chronique des années de braise

Fritz Lang
The Big Heat
Doktor Mabuse der Spieler; Das Testament des Dr. Mabuse
Fury
M
Metropolis
Die Nibelungen

Claude Lanzmann
Shoah

Charles Laughton
The Night of the Hunter

David Lean
Brief Encounter
Great Expectations
Lawrence of Arabia

Spike Lee
Do the Right Thing
Malcolm X

Fernand Léger
Le Ballet mécanique

Mike Leigh
Life Is Sweet
Secrets and Lies

Sergio Leone
Il Buono, il brutto, il cattivo
C'era una volta il west
Once Upon a Time in America

Mervyn LeRoy
I Am a Fugitive from a Chain Gang
Little Caesar

Richard Lester
A Hard Day's Night

Albert Lewin
The Picture of Dorian Gray

Joseph H. Lewis
Gun Crazy

Marcel L'Herbier
L' Argent
Feu Mathias Pascal

Victor Lima Barreto
Cangaceiro

Miguel Littin
Alsino y el Condor
Chacal de Nahueltoro

Anatole Litvak
Why We Fight

Ken Loach
My Name Is Joe

Pare Lorentz
The River

Joseph Losey
The Servant

Ernst Lubitsch
Ninotchka
Trouble in Paradise

George Lucas
American Graffiti
Star Wars

Sidney Lumet
Twelve Angry Men

Louis Lumière
L'Arroseur arrosé

David Lynch
Blue Velvet
Eraserhead

Alexander Mackendrick
The Sweet Smell of Success

John Madden
Shakespeare in Love

Maximiliana Mainka
Deutschland im Herbst

Beate Mainka-Jellinghaus
Deutschland im Herbst

Dusan Makavejev
W.R.: Mysterije Organizma

Terrence Malick
Badlands
Days of Heaven

Louis Malle
Souffle au coeur

Rouben Mamoulian
Becky Sharp
Dr. Jekyll and Mr. Hyde

Joseph L. Mankiewicz
All about Eve

Chris Marker
Le Joli Mai
Sans Soleil

Richard Marquand
Star Wars

Leo McCarey
Duck Soup

Winsor McCay
Gertie the Dinosaur

Joseph McGrath
Casino Royale

Georges Méliès
Le Voyage dans la lune

Jean-Pierre Melville
Le Samourai

Sam Mendes
American Beauty

Vladimir Menshov
Moskva slezam ne verit

Jiří Menzel
Ostre sledované vlaky

William Cameron Menzies
Things to Come

Nikita Mikhalkov
Outomlionnye solntsem

Andrei Mikhalkov-Konchalovsky
Siberiade

Lewis Milestone
All Quiet on the Western Front

Vincente Minnelli
An American in Paris
The Band Wagon
Meet Me in St. Louis

Kenji Mizoguchi
Akasen chitai
Naniwa ereji
Saikaku ichidai onna
Sansho dayu
Ugetsu monogatari
Zangiku monogatari

Edgar Morin
Chronique d'un été

Terrell O. Morse
Gojira

Fei Mu
Xiao cheng zhi chun

Andrzej Munk
Eroica

F. W. Murnau
Der Letze Mann
Nosferatu (1922)
Sunrise

Daniel Myrick
The Blair Witch Project

Amir Naderi
Dawandeh

Mira Nair
Salaam Bombay

Jan Němec
O slavnosti a hostech

Mike Nichols
The Graduate

Rashid Nugmanov
Igla

Laurence Olivier
Henry V

Ermanno Olmi
Albero degli zoccoli

Marcel Ophüls
La Chagrin et la pitié

Max Ophüls
Letter from an Unknown Woman
Lola Montès
Madame de . . .
La Ronde

Nagisa Oshima
Ai no corrida
Koshikei
Shonen

Idrissa Ouedraogo
Yaaba

Yasujiro Ozu
Banshun
Higanbana
Samma no aji
Tokyo monogatari

G. W. Pabst
Die Büchse der Pandora
Die Dreigroschenoper
Kameradschaft
Das Tagebuch einer Verlorenen

Marcel Pagnol
La Femme du boulanger
The Marius Trilogy

Alan J. Pakula
Klute

Sergei Paradzhanov
Teni zabytykh predkov

Alan Parker
Midnight Express

Claire Parker
Nuit sur le Mont Chauve

Gordon Parks
Shaft

Robert Parrish
Casino Royale

James Parrott
The Music Box

Pier Paolo Pasolini
Accattone
Il Fiore delle mille e una notte
Il Vangelo secondo Matteo

Giovanni Pastrone
Cabiria

Zivojin Pavlovic
Budjenje pacova
Zaseda

Sam Peckinpah
Ride the High Country

The Wild Bunch

Mario Peixoto
Limite

Arthur Penn
Bonnie and Clyde

Wolfgang Petersen
Das Boot

Alexsandar Petrovic
Skuplijaci perja

Vasili Pichul
Malenkaya Vera

Benoît Poelvoorde
C'est arrivé près de chez vous

Roman Polanski
Chinatown
Noz w wodzie
Repulsion
Rosemary's Baby

Gillo Pontecorvo
Battaglia di Algeri

Michael Powell
Black Narcissus
The Life and Death of Colonel Blimp
A Matter of Life and Death
Peeping Tom
The Red Shoes

Otto Preminger
Laura

Emeric Pressburger
Black Narcissus
The Life and Death of Colonel Blimp
A Matter of Life and Death
The Red Shoes

Vsevolod Pudovkin
Konyets Sankt-Peterburga
Mat
Potomok Chingis-Khan

Géza Radványi
Valahol Europaban

Bob Rafelson
Five Easy Pieces

Jean-Paul Rappeneau
Cyrano de Bergerac

Irving Rapper
Now Voyager

Nicholas Ray
In a Lonely Place
Johnny Guitar
Rebel without a Cause
They Live by Night

Satyajit Ray
The Apu Trilogy
Aranyer din Ratri
Charulata
Jana Aranya

Carol Reed
Odd Man Out
The Third Man

Karel Reisz
Saturday Night and Sunday Morning

Edgar Reitz
Deutschland im Herbst
Die Heimat; Zweite Heimat

Jean Renoir
La Bête humaine
Boudu sauvé des eaux
Le Carrosse d'or
Le Crime de Monsieur Lange
La Grande illusion
Une Partie de campagne
Règle du jeu
The Southerner

Alain Resnais
L'Année dernière à Marienbad
Hiroshima mon amour
Nuit et brouillard

Tony Richardson
Tom Jones

Leni Riefenstahl
Olympia
Tiefland
Triumph des Willens

Jacques Rivette
Celine et Julie vont en bateau: Phantom Ladies Over Paris

Jerome Robbins
West Side Story

Arthur Robison
Schatten

Glauber Rocha
Antônio das Mortes
Deus e o diabo na terra do sol

Nicolas Roeg
Walkabout

Abram Room
Tretia Meshchanskaia

Francesco Rosi
Cristo si e fermato a Eboli
Salvatore Giuliano

Roberto Rossellini
Paisà
Roma, città aperta
Stromboli
Viaggio in Italia

Robert Rossen
All the King's Men
The Hustler

Jean Rouch
Chronique d'un été

Georges Rouquier
Farrebique

Bimal Roy
Do bigha zamin

Katja Rupé
Deutschland im Herbst

Walter Ruttmann
Berlin: Die Sinfonie der Grossstadt

Stellan Rye
Der Student von Prag

Leontine Sagan
Mädchen in Uniform

Walter Salles
Central do Brasil

Eduardo Sánchez
The Blair Witch Project

Mark Sandrich
Top Hat

Jorge Sanjinés
Yawar Mallku

M.S. Sathyu
Garam Hawa

Carlos Saura
Cria Cuervos . . .

Claude Sautet
Un Coeur en hiver

John Sayles
Lone Star

John Schlesinger
Midnight Cowboy

Volker Schlöndorff
Die Blechtrommel
Deutschland im Herbst

Ernest B. Schoedsack
King Kong

Peter Schubert
Deutschland im Herbst

Martin Scorsese
GoodFellas
Mean Streets
Raging Bull
Taxi Driver

Ridley Scott
Blade Runner
Thelma and Louise

Ousmane Sembène
Noire de . . .
Xala

Mrinal Sen
Akaler sandhane

Jim Sharman
Rocky Horror Picture Show

Ben Sharpsteen
Fantasia

Georgy Shengelaya
Pirosmani

Lowell Sherman
She Done Him Wrong

Kaneto Shindo
Hadaka no shima

Don Siegel
Dirty Harry
Invasion of the Body Snatchers

Bernhard Sinkel
Deutschland im Herbst

Robert Siodmak
The Killers

Douglas Sirk
All That Heaven Allows
Written on the Wind

Alf Sjöberg
Fröken Julie

Victor Sjöström
Körkalen
The Wind

George Sluizer
Spoorloos

Jack Smith
Flaming Creatures

Michael Snow
Wavelength

Fernando E. Solanas
Hora de los hornos

Humberto Solás
Lucia

Steven Spielberg
Close Encounters of the Third Kind
E.T.--The Extraterrestrial
Jaws
Raiders of the Lost Ark
Schindler's List

Wolfgang Staudte
Die Mörder sind unter uns

George Stevens
Giant
A Place in the Sun
Shane

Mauritz Stiller
Erotikon
Gösta Berlings Saga
Herr Arnes Pengar

Oliver Stone
JFK

Jean-Marie Straub
Chronik der Anna Magdalena Bach

Preston Sturges
The Lady Eve
Sullivan's Travels

Hans-Jürgen Syberberg
Hitler: Ein Film aus Deutschland

István Szabó
Mephisto

Juan Carlos Tabio
Fresa y Chocolate

Alain Tanner
Jonah qui aura 25 ans en l'an 2000

Quentin Tarantino
Pulp Fiction
Reservoir Dogs

Andrei Tarkovsky
Andrei Rublev
Offret
Zerkalo

Jacques Tati
Playtime
Les Vacances de Monsieur Hulot

Paolo Taviani
Kaos

Vittorio Taviani
Kaos

Hiroshi Teshigahara
Suna no onna

Tian Zhuangzhuang
Daoma zei
Lan fengzheng

Jacques Tourneur
Cat People
Out of the Past

Tran Anh Hung
L'Odeur de la papaye verte

Leonid Trauberg
The Maxim Trilogy
Novyi Vavilon

Jiří Trnka
Staré povesti ceské

François Truffaut
Jules et Jim
Quatre cents coups
Tirez sur le pianiste

Tsai Ming-liang
He Liu

Victor Turin
Turksib

Edgar G. Ulmer
Detour

Roger Vadim
Et . . . Dieu créa la femme

W. S. Van Dyke
The Thin Man

Melvin Van Peebles
Sweet Sweetback's Baadasssss Song

Agnès Varda
Cléo de cinq à sept

Georgi Vasiliev
Chapayev

Sergei Vasiliev
Chapayev

Pastor Vega
Retrato de Teresa

Anthony Veiller
Why We Fight

Harlan Veit
Jud Süss

Dziga Vertov
Chelovek s kinoapparatom
Kino-Pravda

Charles Vidor
Gilda

King Vidor
The Big Parade
The Crowd
Hallelujah

Jean Vigo
A propos de Nice
Atalante
Zéro de conduite

Thomas Vinterberg
Festen

Luchino Visconti
La Caduta degli dei
Il Gattopardo
Morte a Venezia
Ossessione
Rocco e i suoi fratelli
La Terra trema

Josef von Sternberg
Der Blaue Engel
The Devil Is a Woman
The Scarlet Empress

Erich von Stroheim
Foolish Wives
Greed

Lars von Trier
Breaking the Waves
Idioterne

Margarethe von Trotta
Die Bleierne Zeit

Andy Wachowski
The Matrix

Larry Wachowski
The Matrix

Andrzej Wajda
Czlowiek z marmuru
Kanal
Popiol i diament

Raoul Walsh
High Sierra
White Heat

Wayne Wang
Smoke

Andy Warhol
Chelsea Girls

Peter Weir
The Last Wave
Picnic at Hanging Rock

Orson Welles
Chimes at Midnight
Citizen Kane
The Lady from Shanghai
The Magnificent Ambersons
Le Procès
A Touch of Evil

William Wellman
The Public Enemy

Wim Wenders
Der Amerikanische freund
Der Himmel Uber Berlin
Im Lauf der Zeit
Paris, Texas

Lina Wertmüller
Film d'amore e d'anarchia

James Whale
The Bride of Frankenstein
Frankenstein

Robert Wiene
Das Kabinett des Dr. Caligari

Billy Wilder
The Apartment
Double Indemnity
The Lost Weekend
Some Like It Hot
Sunset Boulevard

Robert Wise
West Side Story

Konrad Wolf
Sterne

Wong Kai-Wai
Ahfei zheng zhuan

Sam Wood
A Night at the Opera

Basil Wright
Song of Ceylon

William Wyler
The Best Years of Our Lives
The Little Foxes
Mrs. Miniver

Xie Jin
Wutai jiemei

Edward Yang
Guling jie shaonian sha ren shijian

Yang Fengliang
Ju Dou

Karel Zeman
Baron Prasil

Zhang Yimou
Dahong denglong gaogao gua
Ju Dou
Qiu Ju da Guansi
Red Sorghum

Fred Zinnemann
From Here to Eternity
High Noon
Los Redes

GEOGRAPHIC INDEX

Algeria
- Chronique des années de braise
- Z

Argentina
- Hora de los hornos
- Tire dié

Australia
- The Last Wave
- My Brilliant Career
- The Piano
- Picnic at Hanging Rock
- Walkabout

Austria
- 38 - Auch das war Wien
- Engel mit der Posaune
- Funny Games
- Märchen vom Glück
- Sodom und Gomorrha
- Tiefland
- Unsere Afrikareise

Belgium
- C'est arrivé près de chez vous
- Jeanne Dielman, 23 Quai du Commerce, 1080 Bruxelles

Bolivia
- Yawar Mallku

Brazil
- Antônio das Mortes
- Bye Bye Brasil
- O Cangaceiro
- Central do Brasil
- Deus e o diabo na terra do sol
- Dona Flor e seus dois maridos
- Os Fuzis
- Limite
- Orfeu Negro
- Pixote a lei do mais fraco
- Vidas secas

Bulgaria
- Koziyat rog
- Sterne

Burkina Faso
- Yaaba

Canada
- Dead Ringers
- Exotica
- Nanook of the North

Chile
- La Batalla de Chile: la lucha de un pueblo sin armas
- Chacal de Nahueltoro

China
- Ba wang bie ji
- Dahong denglong gaogao gua
- Daoma zei
- Haizi wang
- Huang tudi
- Ju Dou
- Lan fengzheng
- Qiu Ju da Guansi
- Red Sorghum
- Wutai jiemei
- Xiao cheng zhi chun

Cuba
- De cierta manera
- Fresa y Chocolate
- Lucia
- Memorias del subdesarrollo
- El Otro Francisco
- La Primera carga al machete
- Retrato de Teresa
- Soy Cuba

Czechoslovakia
- Baron Prasil
- Lásky jedné plavovlásky
- O slavnosti a hostech
- Obchod na korze
- Ostre sledované vlaky
- Staré povesti ceské

Denmark
- Babettes Gaestebud
- Breaking the Waves
- Cristo si e fermato a Eboli
- Festen
- Gertrud
- Idioterne
- Ordet
- Sult
- Vredens dag

Egypt
- Bab el hadid

France
- A bout de souffle
- A nous la liberté
- A propos de Nice
- L'Age d'or
- Alphaville
- L'Année dernière à Marienbad
- L'Argent
- L'Arroseur arrosé
- Atalante
- Le Ballet mécanique
- La Bataille du rail
- Belle de jour
- La Belle et la bête
- La Bête humaine
- Die Blechtrommel
- Le Boucher
- Boudu sauvé des eaux
- Le Carrosse d'or
- Casque d'or
- Celine et Julie vont en bateau: Phantom Ladies Over Paris
- Le Chagrin et la pitié
- Un Chapeau de paille d'Italie
- Le Charme discrèt de la bourgeoisie
- Un Chien andalou
- Chronique d'un été
- Un Coeur en hiver
- Un Condamné à mort s'est échappé
- La Coquille et le clergyman
- Le Crime de Monsieur Lange
- Cyrano de Bergerac
- Les Dames du Bois de Boulogne
- La Dentellière
- Le Diable au corps
- Les Diaboliques
- Diva
- La dolce vita
- Du Rififi chez les hommes
- L'Eclisse
- Les Enfants du paradis
- Entr'acte
- Et . . . Dieu créa la femme
- Farrebique
- La Femme du boulanger
- La Femme infidèle
- Feu Mathias Pascal
- Fièvre
- IlFiore delle mille e una notte
- IlGattopardo
- La Grande illusion
- Haine
- Hiroshima mon amour
- India Song
- Jeanne Dielman, 23 Quai du Commerce, 1080 Bruxelles
- Jeux interdits
- Le Joli Mai
- Jonah qui aura 25 ans en l'an 2000
- Le Jour se lève
- Journal d'un curé de campagne
- J'accuse
- Judex
- Jules et Jim
- La Kermesse héroique
- Last Tango in Paris
- Lola Montès
- Mépris
- Madame de . . .
- The Marius Trilogy
- Menilmontant
- Le Million
- Napoléon
- Noire de . . .
- La Notte
- Nuit et brouillard
- Nuit sur le Mont Chauve
- Les Nuits fauves
- L'Odeur de la papaye verte
- Offret
- Orphée
- 8½

Une Partie de campagne
La Passion de Jeanne d'Arc
Pépé le Moko
Pickpocket
Playtime
Le Procès
Professione: Reporter
Quai des brumes
Les Quatre cents coups
Règle du jeu
Rien que les heures
Rocco e i suoi fratelli
La Ronde
Salaam Bombay
Le Salaire de la peur
Le Samourai
Le Sang des bêtes
Le Sang d'un poete
Sans Soleil
Shoah
Souffle au coeur
Spoorloos
Thérèse Desqueyroux
Tirez sur le pianiste
Todo Sobre Mi Madre
Trois Couleurs
Les Vacances de Monsieur Hulot
Les Vampires
Vampyr
Il Vangelo secondo Matteo
Viaggio in Italia
I Vitelloni
Vivre sa vie
Le Voyage dans la lune
Le Weekend
Yeux sans visage
Z
Zéro de conduite

Germany

Aguirre, der Zorn Gottes
Der Amerikanische freund
Angst essen Seele auf
Berlin: Die Sinfonie der Grossstadt
Der Blaue Engel
Die Blechtrommel
Die Bleierne Zeit
Das Boot
Die Büchse der Pandora
Chronik der Anna Magdalena Bach
Il Conformista
The Dead
La Dentellière
Deutschland im Herbst
Doktor Mabuse der Spieler; Das Testament des Dr. Mabuse
Die Dreigroschenoper
Ehe der Maria Braun
Der Ewige Jude
Die Heimat; Zweite Heimat
Der Himmel Uber Berlin
Hitler: Ein Film aus Deutschland
Im Lauf der Zeit
Jeder für sich und Gott gegen alle
Jud Süss
Das Kabinett des Dr. Caligari
Kameradschaft
Der Letze Mann
Lola
Lola Montès
M
Mädchen in Uniform
Mephisto
Metropolis
Die Mörder sind unter uns
Die Nibelungen
Nosferatu (1922)
Olympia
Paris, Texas
Schatten
Der Student von Prag
Das Tagebuch einer Verlorenen
Tiefland
Triumph des Willens
Variété

Greece

O Thiasos
Vlemma Tou Odyssea

Guinea-Bissau

Udju Azul di Yonta

Hong Kong

Ahfei zheng zhuan
Ba wang bie ji
Dahong denglong gaogao gua
Lan fengzheng
Qiu Ju da Guansi
Yanzhi kou

Hungary

Angi Vera
Csillagosok, katonák
Meg ker a nep
Mephisto
Valahol Europaban

India

Akaler sandhane
Apu Trilogy
Aranyer din Ratri
Awara
Bharat Mata
Bhumika
Charulata
Do bigha zamin
Duvidha
Elippathayam
Garam Hawa
Jana Aranya
Kaagaz ke phool
Meghe dhaka tara
Salaam Bombay

Iran

And Life Goes On
Dawandeh
Ta'm E Guilass

Italy

Accattone
L'Albero degli zoccoli
L'America
L'Avventura
La Battaglia di Algeri
Il Buono, il brutto, il cattivo
Cabiria
La Caduta degli dei
C'era una volta il west
Chronik der Anna Magdalena Bach
Il Conformista
Cristo si e fermato a Eboli
La dolce vita
L'Eclisse
Film d'amore e d'anarchia
IlFiore delle mille e una notte
IlGattopardo
Kaos
Ladri di biciclette
Last Tango in Paris
Miracolo a Milano
Morte a Venezia
La Notte
1900 (Novecento)
Ossessione
8½
Paisà
Professione: Reporter
I Pugni in tasca
Rocco e i suoi fratelli
Roma, città aperta
Salvatore Giuliano
Sciuscia
La strada
Stromboli
La terra trema
Umberto D
Il Vangelo secondo Matteo
El Verdugo
Viaggio in Italia
I Vitelloni

Japan

Ai no corrida
Akasen chitai
Banshun
Biruma no tategoto
Entotsu no mieru basho
Fukushu suru wa ware ni ari
Gojira
Hadaka no shima
Hana-Bi
Higanbana
Ikiru
Jigokumon

NAME INDEX

The following list of names cites all individuals listed in the *Films* volume of this series. The film title(s) in parentheses following the name refer the reader to the appropriate entry or entries where full information is given.

Peebles, Melvin Van (Sweet Sweetback's Baadasssss Song)
Peel, Dave (Nashville)
Peet, Bill (Fantasia)
Pegoraro, Lorenzo (Vitelloni, I)
Pei Xiaonan (Ba wang bie ji)
Peichev, Stefan (Sterne)
Peil, Edward (Broken Blossoms)
Peiqi, Liu (Qiu Ju da Guansi)
Peirse, Sara (Heavenly Creatures)
Peixoto, Mario (Limite)
Pejškova, Helena (O slavnosti a hostech)
Pek, Albert (Staré povesti ceské)
Pekny, Romuald (38 - Auch das war Wien)
Pelegri, Jean (Pickpocket)
Pelegri, Pierre (Fuzis)
Pelegrini, Amalia (Roma, città aperta)
Peleshian, Artur (Siberiade)
Pellegrin, Georges (Samourai)
Pellegrini, Ines (Fiore delle mille e una notte)
Pellerani, Franco (Conformista)
Pellow, Clifford (Hustler)
Pema, Sefer (America, L')
Pempeit, Lila (Deutschland im Herbst)
Peña, Candela (Todo Sobre Mi Madre)
Peña, Elizabeth (Lone Star)
Peña, Julio (Chimes at Midnight)
Pendleton, Gaylord (Informer)
Pendleton, Nat (Thin Man)
Penella, Emma (Verdugo)
Pénev, Milèn (Koziyat rog)
Penn, Arthur (Bonnie and Clyde)
Penn, Chris (Reservoir Dogs)
Penn, Leonard (Star Is Born)
Penna, Rosa Maria (Antônio das Mortes)
Pennasilico, Amato (Avventura)
Pennell, Peter (Blade Runner)
Penner, Erdman (Fantasia)
Pennick, Jack (Man Who Shot Liberty Valance; My Darling Clementine; Searchers)
Pennington-Richards, C. (Fires Were Started)
Penrose, John (Kind Hearts and Coronets)
Pens Rode, Nina (Gertrud)
Peoples, David (Blade Runner; Unforgiven)
Peploe, Mark (Professione: Reporter)
Peppard, George (Breakfast at Tiffany's)
Pérè, Marcel (Jour se lève)
Pêra, Marilia (Central do Brasil)
Pera, Marilia (Pixote a lei do mais fraco)
Perakis, Nikos (Blechtrommel)
Perceval, Hugh (Third Man)
Percy, Esme (Dead of Night)
Pereira, Gilbert (Celine et Julie vont en bateau: Phantom Ladies Over Paris)
Pereira, Hal (Double Indemnity; Man Who Shot Liberty Valance; Rear Window; Shane; Vertigo)
Perès, Marcel (Quai des brumes)
Pereverzeva, Valentina (Malenkaya Vera)
Perez, Aricle (Pixote a lei do mais fraco)
Pérez, Conchita (Cria Cuervos . . .)
Perez, Elba (Memorias del subdesarrollo)
Perez, Jeanne (Thérèse Desqueyroux)
Perez, Jorge (Olvidados)
Perez, Jose Ramon (Alsino y el Condor)
Perez, Juan (Carrosse d'or)
Perez, Marta Lorena (Alsino y el Condor)
Perez, Rosie (Do the Right Thing)
Perez, Vincent (Cyrano de Bergerac)
Perfort, Holger (Der var engang en krig)
Pergolese, Giovanni Battista (Zerkalo)
Périer, François (Orphée; Samourai)
Périnal, Georges (A nous la liberté; Life and Death of Colonel Blimp; Million; Private Life of Henry VIII; Sang d'un poete)
Perinal, Georges (Things to Come)
Perkins, Anthony (Procès; Psycho)
Perkins, Curtiss D. (Fantasia)
Perkins, Osgood (Scarface: The Shame of a Nation)
Perkovíc, Aleksander (W.R.: Mysterije Organizma)
Perl, Arnold (Malcolm X)
Pernel, Florence (Trois Couleurs)
Peroni, Geraldine (Player)
Peronne, Denise (Jeux interdits)
Perovic, Slobodan (Budjenje pacova)
Perovic, Stjepan (Vlak bez voznog reda)
Perpignani, Roberto (Kaos)
Perrault, Louis (Vacances de Monsieur Hulot)
Perri, Dan (Nashville)
Perrin, Jacques (Z)
Perrin, Nat (Duck Soup)
Perrineau, Harold (Smoke)
Perrot, Irma (Feu Mathias Pascal)
Perry, George Sessions (Southerner)
Persaud, Stephen (Mona Lisa)
Persoff, Nehemiah (Some Like It Hot)
Persson, Bo (Fanny och Alexander; Offret)
Pértier, François (Z)
Perugorria, Jorge (Fresa y Chocolate)
Pesci, Joe (GoodFellas; JFK; Once Upon a Time in America)
Pesovár, Ferenc (Meg ker a nep)
Pessin, Leo B. (Letter from an Unknown Woman)
Pester, Jan (Gregory's Girl)
Petakovic, Gordana (Dom za vesanje)
Petek, Ljubomir (Otac na sluzbenom putu)
Peterman, Melissa (Fargo)
Peters, Clarke (Mona Lisa)
Peters, Hans (Picture of Dorian Gray)
Peters, Karsten (Lola)
Peters, Walter (Chronik der Anna Magdalena Bach)
Petersen, Anne Marie (Vredens dag)
Petersen, Else (Babettes Gaestebud)
Petersen, Erik (Babettes Gaestebud)
Petersen, Jan (Babettes Gaestebud)
Petersen, Maria-Antoinette (Das Boot)
Petersen, Wolfgang (Das Boot)
Peterson, Robert (Big Heat; In a Lonely Place)
Peterson-Berger, Wikee (Offret)
Peticca, Sandro (Professione: Reporter)
Petigk, Helmut (Lola)
Petit, Jean-Claude (Cyrano de Bergerac)
Petitgand, Laurent (Der Himmel Uber Berlin)
Petitjean, Antoine (Casque d'or; Lola Montès)
Petitjean, Arman (Jour se lève)
Petito, Enzo (Buono, il brutto, il cattivo)
Petitot, Georges (Et . . . Dieu créa la femme)
Petré, Gio (Smultronstället)
Petrenko, Alexei (Korol Lir; Proshchanie)
Petri (Hiroshima mon amour)
Petri, Elio (Vlak bez voznog reda)
Petrie, Hay (Great Expectations)
Petrik, P. (Zemlya)
Petritsky, Anatoly (Voina i mir)
Petrone, Francisco (Tire dié)
Petrov, Erqueni (Siberiade)